TREASURY OF QUOTATIONS
ON RELIGIOUS SUBJECTS

TREASURY OF QUOTATIONS
ON RELIGIOUS SUBJECTS

From The Great Writers And Preachers Of All Ages

By F.B. Proctor

KREGEL PUBLICATIONS

GRAND RAPIDS, MICHIGAN 49501

Library of Congress Catalog Card Number 76-15741
ISBN 0-8284-3500-5

Printed in the United States of America

CONTENTS

PREFACE

The funny old volume, too tall for the ordinary shelf, snorted a cloud of dust when I hauled it out of its bin at a used bookstore. I opened the treasure chest of centuries and sniffed the air of immortality. F. B. Proctor's *Classified Gems of Thought* had come to live at my house. That was a half-century ago. My library has been culled several times since then, but this outsize mine of the thoughts of brilliant minds and sparkling spirits has been kept as a permanent possession.

Henry Wace of King's College, London, wrote in the original preface to this volume: "A book may be properly replaced by another on the whole, and yet there may be thoughts and sayings in it which well deserve preservation. It is, indeed, strange to think of the mass of living experience which passes away with each generation and is lost to the successors; and there is the more reason for gleaning from time to time some printed records of that experience, partial as they must needs be, and storing some if its treasures."

It is to stem some of that inevitable, but indecent, erosion of great thought and experience that this volume was put together. The publishers who now *renew its lease* deserve our thanks.

It's new name realistically expresses it's contents. *Treasury of Quotations on Religious Subjects* is a treasury of thoughts old and new on 3,000 subjects — the product of wise men and able expositors of the Word of God.

What will this book do for you?

(1) It is a masterpiece of the classification of material. Dialogue, as practiced by the contemporary religious and non-religious, is a drifter: it moves restlessly from subject to subject, it repairs no broken conviction, it corrects no impoverished philosophy, and it accepts too many authorities, as though the willingness to speak were a toga of truth. Open discussion may start with God's sovereignty and wind up with potty training or begin with the subject of marriage and end with tax write-offs.

Not so with Proctor's parley. The conversationalists demand that you listen and think, weigh and conclude. There is no changing of their opinions. The material has been classified and stays within the boundaries. It does not wander from room to room as though looking for a place to lie down for a nap.

Those of us who speak about serious subjects as being deep-as-eternity and as-terrible-as-destiny need to learn the severity of style of these speakers. No one can cover all subjects in ten minutes. The torment of counseling is the expectation that one hour of consulting can cure forty years of problems and that the only acceptable authority is today's experience.

(2) The power and beauty of language come glistening from these pages. Proctor has kept the stars shining. In today's culture which neglects spelling, manhandles punctuation, and nibbles away at sensitivity with vulgarity and

blasphemy, it is refreshing to company with the masters of words. A spiritual man recognizes that the power is of God, but God uses the polished instrument as well as the unlettered clod. To rummage through Proctor's old trunks is to get a whiff of Christmas Evans, Lange, Samuel Rutherford, Bishop Hall, Milton, Shakespeare, and a covey of rare birds who know how to turn words into plumage and flight.

(3) These quotations are gems of thought which can run, walk, creep, and sit down, as well as soar. They have practical application to life. Thoroughly Christ-centered, this volume renews the contention that "Christ is all and in all." It does not apologize for exalting Him nor quibble about where He fits into life: He fits in everywhere. If He doesn't fit in, the life is out of place.

Proctor's Introduction to this collection described the then current "Mystery of Iniquity" as *infidelity* — "the infidelity which is sure to increase with the spread of education — the people have 'come to believe a lie.' " It is improbable that infidelity is the number one scourge today. God has been given a little standing place in our culture. He receives some notice from scientists, politicians, and intellectuals. Their definition of God does not rival Revelation, but God is acceptable in polite society.

The current plague may be *laxity:* a casualness about Truth, as though to know the Truth obviated the necessity to obey it by application to daily life. Rotherham[1], awkwardly but accurately, translates II Timothy 3:7 as those who are "ever learning and never unto a personal knowledge of truth able to come." Personal knowledge involves personal experience. Learning to put snow chains on automobile tires by viewing a diagram or a filmstrip is not to be equated with lying on your back on the side of a hill some snowy night and putting chains on your car tires while truck traffic dances around you in a choreography of sleet and commerce.

Bishop Moule comments on the same passage with an incident: " 'What are the great non-Christian religions?' said a friend of mine in my hearing long ago. And he answered his own question — 'Judaism, Mahometanism, Brahmanism, Buddhism, and *unspiritual Christianity.' "[2]

One should read this book of quotations as though he were spreading jam on bread. It's too rich to be gulped down in great gobs, but a little on your fingers will do no harm. "Those who never quote, in return are seldom quoted," quotes Proctor.

Obviously these are the choice passages of all ages, the loveliest phrases, the most potent paragraphs of many authors. It would take a lifetime to sift through the common clay for these gems. "The true university of these days is a collection of books," said Carlyle. Many of the books of Carlyle's University are mildewed and worm-eaten, but much that was in them comes shouting forth, fresh and vibrant, in this contribution to our Christian thought.

There are not many shallows in this volume. It is deep water most of the way. As you wade in, be prepared for the big wave that may send you sprawling on the sands; but when you stand again on both your feet, you will recognize you have toyed with an ocean.

Louis Paul Lehman

---

[1](The Emphasized Bible, Rotherham. Kregel Publications, 1959)

[2]The Second Epistle to Timothy, H.C.G. Moule. Religious Tract Society, London. N.D.
Reprinted by Kregel Publications, 1977

INTRODUCTION

1. The Contents and Object of this Book

THIS book contains a readable collection of THOUGHTS, gathered from a wide range of Authors, on Religious Subjects. It is not a Cyclopœdia, neither does it make any pretensions to be exhaustive. It is simply what it claims to be, a Treasury of things New and Old: Illustrations, Readings, Papers, Sermons, Notes, Suggestions, Condensed Narratives, Adaptations, Analogies, Analyses, and Digests of Topics from many a learned volume. And the attempt has been to make it as readable and as attractive to the general reader as a Magazine. There are in it about Three Thousand Subjects, more or less fully treated of, drawn from Ancient and Modern, English and Foreign sources. For the most part the quotations have been made direct from the Authorities whose names are attached. In the case of Foreign Authors the translations of Messrs. T. and T. Clark, of Edinburgh, have been relied on. Where the abbreviation " Cf " is used, it denotes, not responsibility, but that the statement is corroborated by the writer whose name is added. Several Sermons, either ver-batim or condensed, of some of the leading preachers of the day, have been in-serted; but the popularity of the Preacher has influenced the choice less than his power of edification. Many skeletons and outlines, with accompanying suitable illustrations, will be found, which, it is hoped, will often be found useful to the weary preacher and the busy parish worker in his preparation for the pulpit. The prophet's axe was borrowed (2 Kings vi. 5); and a certain preacher, when accused of preaching Howe's sermons, excused himself by replying: " I often go to Mr. Howe's shop for tallow, but I make my own candles." A distinguished living Bishop, and no less distinguished scholar, said to the writer, some years since, " I always keep it at my elbow when writing a sermon "—alluding to a book of " Re-mains," not much read now, and the product of but one mind. This Book of Thoughts and pregnant sayings, the product of wise and good men of all ages, able expositors of the oracles of God, asks for a like place, as a book of reference, which may be opened anywhere and at any time, and which may furnish a train of thought, and help to elucidate and interpret that Word which is able to make us wise unto salvation.

2. Arrangement of the Contents

Everything in the volume, whether learned or unlearned, critical, homiletical, or expository; whether appropriate to age or to childhood and youth—Sermons, Outlines, Essays, Papers, Notes, Thoughts, Suggestions—has, in the first instance, been arranged ALPHABETICALLY, under some prominent title or otherwise familiar heading. But, to facilitate reference, a GENERAL INDEX OF SUBJECTS, with references to other parts of the book, where additional information may be found on them, is given at the end. An INDEX OF TEXTS follows, and a list of all AUTHORITIES quoted completes the arrangement, in which simplicity throughout has been aimed at more than system; and the simplest form of arranging so numerous and diverse a collection of Thoughts as this seemed to be that of a

" DICTIONARY OF RELIGIOUS SUBJECTS "

3. On the Use of Quotation, and the " Raison d'être "

To say anything on this head in a book which is mainly one of Quotation, must of necessity remind one of the man in the old Attic jest, who, having a house to sell, took a brick to the market as a specimen of the premises. We venture however to try the experiment, by showing what has been said on the use of Quotation. "The true University of these days is a collection of books" (*Carlyle*). But a collection of books, to be of much use to a man, requires leisure to read them. Life is short; time is precious; and men are busy, and for the most part have no time for research. Whereas a book of this kind has, to a great extent, done the work for him: it has dug the precious ore from the mine, and brought it to him for use. The well is deep, and he may have nothing to draw with, but here is the sparkling water presented to his lips.

If, as has been said, "Reading makes a full man, Writing an exact man, and Conversation a ready man," both the Writer and the Talker will be indebted to the Reader for his stores of apt Quotations. Happy the speaker who has his quiver full of them, and the pen of the ready writer that knows how to use them.

"Those who never quote, in return are seldom quoted." "The wisdom of the wise, and the experience of age, may be preserved by Quotation."

"Cicero is as little sparing of Quotations as Plutarch. Old Montaigne is so stuffed with them, that he owns, if they were taken out of him, little of himself would remain."

"I suspect that Addison hardly ever composed a 'Spectator' which was not founded on some quotation; and Addison *lasts*, while Steele, who always wrote from first impressions, has passed away."

"Every transplantation has, however, always altered the fruit of the tree." "A well-read writer, with good taste, is one who has the command of the wit of other men; he searches where knowledge is to be found. Epicurus is said to have borrowed from no writer in his 300 volumes. Plutarch, Seneca, and Pliny made free use of their libraries. Epicurus, with his unsubstantial nothingness, has 'melted into thin air,' while the solid treasures of the others have outlasted the wrecks of nations."

"The name of *Samuel Clark*, the great compiler of books in 1680, was ana-grammatized to "*suck all cream*," in allusion to his indefatigable labours in sucking all the cream of every other author" (*Disraeli: Curiosities of Literature*).

This book is little more than an attempt at the same thing. It aims at giving the cream skimmed off, during the reading of a quarter of a century, from a fairly good number of Authors, in a form that experience has shown to be a requirement in these busy days. But the armour here supplied will be found largely to be of a very serious kind, and for a very special need. Christianity in our day has not to struggle against either Paganism or the Papacy, as in the past, but with a far subtler form of the Mystery of Iniquity, viz., INFIDELITY—the Infidelity which is sure to increase with the spread of education—the people have come to "believe a lie." And every antidote or corrective—whether in the form of writing or preaching—must be with the object of relaxing the grip of the old serpent which is coiling and tightening around the Church of Christ, perhaps for a final persecution. "Nothing is more clearly proved than that the modern infidel hates, not this or that Church, not this or that expression of religion, but Christianity itself. In France it is easy to see that the hostility which is now directed against 'le cléricalisme' would soon be turned against Christianity itself were the ecclesiastical outposts once removed. On every bookstall in Paris there are traces of a furious attack on all that every Christian, whether Catholic or Protestant, holds sacred; not more than three years ago, a hymn to Satan was publicly sung in Turin; and now we have in Bern men declaring that they would gladly crucify Christ afresh. These things ought not to surprise us" (*The Guardian, Sept.* 19, 1884).

4. This leads us to

THE THEME

"What is your Creed?"—"JESUS CHRIST" (*Geo. Macdonald*)

"JESUS CHRIST, or Despair" (*Lavater*).

"That in all things HE might have the Pre-eminence" (Col. i. 18).

As in the Bible "The Testimony of Jesus is the Spirit of Prophecy." So here, where we quote many authorities, His Name is to be above every name.

"In Him are hid all the treasures of wisdom and knowledge." All that man needs to know, all that man seeks to know, are hid in Him. A man may be learned in every department of knowledge, and yet, apart from JESUS CHRIST, he will know nothing as he ought to know. HE must be Pre-eminent here as in everything.

I. Pre-eminent as the Revealer of the Father

This is a point of the utmost consequence, to be noted in these days of Agnosticism. Philosophy aims at knowing God by abstract reasoning. It wants to get at the bottom of things, and know the Why? and the Wherefore? of them in its own way. It has all along tried to find out God by its own light; and all along the line it has signally failed. And in these last days it has honestly given the result of the past centuries of abstract speculation and thought in the now familiar Agnostic declaration: "Touching the Almighty, we cannot find Him out." This confession of failure is perhaps the beginning of their wisdom. Certainly it is the exact position accorded them in the Scriptures:—

(i.) "*God is unknowable*"—Yes: "No one knoweth the Son save the Father; neither doth any know the Father, save the Son, and he to whomsoever the Son willeth to reveal Him" (Mat. xi. 27).

(ii.) "*God is invisible*"—Yes: And when the disciples, with similar longing and incapacity, asked, "Lord, show us the Father and it sufficeth us"—"Let us have a Theophany." Jesus answered, "Have I been so long time with you, and dost thou not know Me, Philip? He that hath seen Me, *hath seen the Father*" (John xiv. 9). "I am the Theophany;" "I am the invisible God made visible;" your hands can handle Me; your eyes can see Me; your ears can hear Me—*I am the Image of the Invisible God*—God manifest in the flesh, so that mortal men,—men whose capacities are limited by earthly conditions,—may have a knowledge

of God. In this way JESUS CHRIST is Pre-eminent as the Revealer of the Father.
And no man will ever know God apart from Him. Philosophy may, as it has done,
teach man his blindness and incapacity, but it can do no more. It may take him
to the shore of the great ocean of the Unknown, but it cannot carry him over.

II. Pre-eminent in Creation.

Natural Science also aims at getting to the bottom of things, and of explaining everything in the Physical World. It has become the fashion to talk
about "Cosmic gas," as if that were the "Beginning" from which everything has
sprung, and which contained the potency of all else. It goes on investigating,
analyzing, weighing, comparing, classifying, and arranging, hoping eventually to
have everything correctly ticketed, labelled, and assigned to its right place, so that a
scientific explanation may be arrived at concerning everything that appeals to our
senses. In other words, it wants to know by indisputable scientific proof and
precision, what things are, and how they came to be. Here, again, the inspired
Scriptures are in advance of Science. They tell us that JESUS CHRIST, and not
"cosmic gas," is at the beginning of things: He "is the Firstborn of all Creation;
for in Him were all things created, in the heavens and upon the earth, things
visible and things invisible; . . . all things have been created through Him,
and unto Him; and He is *before* all things, and in Him all things consist" (Col. i.
15–17).

"All things were made by Him; and without Him was not anything made that
hath been made" (John i. 3).

That is: "in Him" all Creation is, and apart from Him, it is not at all.

All Creation is included in JESUS CHRIST—Himself the Firstborn of all Creation
—Creation came into being in Him. Just as, afterwards, it is said that the Church
of Christ is included in Him, and without Him is not at all; so Creation is included
in Him, and without Him is not at all. Or, as the invisible God became visible
in Jesus Christ, so the invisible universe became a visible creation in Him. (See
p. 711*f*.)

III. Pre-eminent as Redeemer

"And He is the Head of the body, the Church: who is the Beginning, the
Firstborn from the dead" (Col. i. 18).

Before, we noticed that He was described as "the Firstborn of Creation."
Now He is described as "the Firstborn from the dead;" and, as such, the Head of
the Church, the Beginning of it. A New Beginning. Death had hitherto claimed
everything and every one. It is the inevitable law of Nature, that everything
succumbs to Death. In other words, Nature, though so beautiful and strong, is
tyrannized over by Death. This tyrant is the marplot of every earthly happiness.
Who hath resisted him? Who hath been down into the regions of this tyrant,
and plucked the poisoned arrow from his hand? Who shall deliver us from this
remorseless Conqueror, Death—the hideous birth of Sin?

> "Death!
> Hell trembled at the hideous name, and sighed
> From all his caves, and back resounded, DEATH " (*Milton*).

His captives have been the entire human race. The Prison-house is barred and
locked, so that none can return to tell its awful secrets. "Death and Despair,"

might be an appropriate epitaph over the whole human family, so hopeless seems their lot. Is there, we ask, no Saviour, no Redemption from this tyranny? For more than four thousand years this question was asked and answered in silence. And then One, pre-eminent here, as elsewhere, visited those captives in their prison; One who had the " Keys of Hades and of Death." He released the captives, and led captivity captive. He vanquished the tyrant in his own territory; He abolished death, and brought life and immortality to light, drove away Despair, and gave men Hope. In His own right He came back from the grave, because it was "not possible that He should be holden of it." And in Him was included His Church, which is His Body—the blessed company of all faithful people. These are they who come back from death, and whom the grave cannot keep: it is now no more possible that they should be "holden of it" than that the "First-born from the dead" should. He included them. The Body follows the Head in due order, and in its own time. This is Redemption; and in this He is pre-eminent.

There is, however, a condition to be noticed.

He gives a pledge to the participants in this great victory. There is no com-fortable assurance of Redemption from Death without it. The pledge is called the " earnest of the Spirit." We must be born members of His Church now, by the New Birth of the Spirit; for without that we have no title to the inheritance. In other words, the present possession of that " earnest " is the evidence of our being *included* in Him who is the Firstborn from the dead.

IV. He must be Pre-eminent at our Death-bed

If He be not, the King of Terrors will be master of the situation, claiming us for his prey.

If He be not, Giant Despair will be there with his Anti-Gospel of Hopelessness, saying, " It is too late for Repentance."

If we are to die in peace, in hope, in comfortable assurance of Salvation, Jesus Christ must be pre-eminent at our death-bed. His Omnipotent arm alone can bring us salvation. His hand alone can pluck the sting from death. His voice alone can silence Despair, and say, " To-day thou shalt be with Me in paradise." None other can: " For it hath pleased the Father that in Him should all fulness dwell;" and though, in life and in death, we may go to other fountains and to other sources for living waters and for consolation, we shall get nothing, for they have nothing.

Jesus Christ is made unto us wisdom, and righteousness, and sanctification, and redemption—everything!

JESUS CHRIST, then, in Life and in Death, or DESPAIR!

Our science is JESUS CHRIST—Jesus and Him Crucified; the best of all sciences.

Our theme is JESUS CHRIST, the theme of the Holy Scriptures: " To Him give all the prophets witness." The Name we invoke is that of JESUS. That Name is the rod in the prophet's hand, which, when uplifted, will work miracles, " Neither is there salvation in any other: for there is none other name under heaven given among men, whereby we must be saved " (Acts iv. 12).

5. Christian Evidences

To a spiritual Christian, Christianity is no guess. He has no need of " evi-dences " beyond those he already possesses. His faith rests upon no broken reed of human support, but upon the power of God. He knows that he has to do with a kingdom which cannot be moved. Things which are *unknowable* by means of the ordinary senses and faculties—which eye hath not seen nor ear heard, and which it hath not entered into the heart to conceive—God hath revealed unto him by His Spirit; and he knows them with a certainty which cannot be argued out of him any more than, formerly, it could be argued into him, and which no adverse criticism can shake. The Christian to whom this demonstration of the Spirit and of power has come, has no more fear for his religion than a mathematician has for a demonstrated problem.

6. The Demand of the Times

Our times demand a Reason for this Hope, a reason that is reasonable—an apology that can meet the destructive scientific and other arguments now so rampant, and which are tauntingly asking, "What is this confidence wherein thou trustest?" There have been moments during late years when a boastful confederacy against the Church of Christ has all but been heard to repeat the old cry, "Come and let us cut them off from being a people;" and, as of old, "out of the eater came forth meat." Both Pagan and Papal persecutions produced their champions and apologists for the Faith. As "the doctrine of our Lord's Divinity, always the faith of the Church, was reasserted and brought into full light in the course of the Arian controversy; and the doctrine of Grace was explained and justified in opposition to the Pelagian heresy; and as, in a similar manner, the principle of Faith was brought out into fuller consciousness and distinctness during the struggles of the Reformation" (*Dr. Wace*); so, in a scientific age like ours, may we confidently look for a prophet to arise who shall be able to pluck the sword out of the hand of an adverse science, and wield it with redoubled force wholly on the side of Christianity. And in the apologetic literature of recent years, in the excellent papers read at our great Church Congresses; and, not least, the remarkable analogies between the Natural and Spiritual Laws, of *Prof. Drummond*—all able scientifically-religious apologists, alive to the need of the time—the Church of Christ does seem to be labouring at some such birth. In any case, let the Christian speak out the thing that is in him—let him produce what he can—if it be nothing more than the bare reiteration of what "is written," of what is "according to the Scriptures," or the mere echo of other men's beliefs, it shall at least help to stem the tide and stop the way of that Materialism which now threatens to loosen all moral restraints. He will be doing what he can "to save some;" and though the waters around rage horribly, and the shore be strewn with the wrecks of those who have broken loose from their moorings—who, through an evil heart of unbelief, have departed from the living God, yet the Foundation of God standeth sure—the Lord knoweth them that are His. Their hope maketh not ashamed—is not delusive—though it cannot be established on scientific evidence, such as is demanded. St. Paul's own statements could not have been scientifically demonstrated. *The mystery was made known unto him by revelation—hence his knowledge and assured conviction.*

7. Religion and Science

The attitude of Religion towards Science, in the present stage of its development, should undoubtedly be that of a "suspended judgment," and of a calm dignified waiting in the assured strength of superiority and truth. Faith allies itself not only with Omnipotence, but with Omniscience; and to cry out in every moment of danger, "Master, Master, we perish!" is to lay ourselves open to the rebuke, "Where is your faith?" You have lost your shield when most you needed to entrench yourself behind it. And perhaps, after all, the strain is not greater now than in former periods. The Church must not be slow to take advantage of the increase of light on all sides. The past victories of science have been victories for the Church too. All that has been lost and surrendered has been the imperfect interpretations of men, for which Revelation is in no wise responsible. Perhaps one of the strongest evidences of the inspiration of the Bible, is its power of keeping itself abreast with every fresh advance on the part of Natural Science. The uninitiated may not perceive this, but others do. In Bacon's time, "the mass of men shrank in fear, as some are still apt to shrink, from the blaze of the new knowledge, which was bursting on them." . . . But "from that moment . . . have they made advances in all departments of life greater than were ever achieved before" (p. 690 *f*). Modern Science is the child of true Religion; and though it is sad to see Science now turning her hand on that which liberated it in the Reformation of the 15th century, yet we are persuaded that both need only to be better understood in order to their agreement. "In using to the utmost the resources of science; in watching for light, from whatever quarter; in sifting and searching all that comes before us to the very bottom, we are fulfilling one of the chief calls of our religion, we are accomplishing the very will of our Founder. Whatever is good science is good theology; whatever is high morality and pure civilization is high and pure religion" (*Dean Stanley*). (See also the remarks of *Bishop Lightfoot*, pp. 495, 596, on "*He hath made both one.*")

8. The Bible and the Triumphs of Science

"Impossible," said Sir Walter Scott, when it was proposed to light our towns with gas. "It can't be done—it is only the dream of a lunatic!" So said the bystanders when Fulton proposed to ascend the Hudson River with his first steamboat: "It can't be done!" And the thing was talked of as "Fulton's folly." So said Dr. Lardner, when it was proposed to navigate the Atlantic by steamers; *and he demonstrated that it was impossible.* And the zeal to defend the Bible from false attacks, and to prop up the ark of God to keep it from falling, no doubt proceeds from a noble and a worthy motive; but "the history of the past is a continuous lesson of the supreme importance" of suspending our judgment. Every great discovery in science has, in turn, been viewed with suspicion (*Geikie*). Even *errors* in physical science have been vindicated by what was held to be the voice of Scripture. Augustine denounced the idea of there being "Antipodes," "as on no account to be believed," since it would contradict Scripture. The roundness of the earth was held to be disproved by Ps. civ. 2, which spoke of the heavens being "stretched out like a curtain." Galileo was forced to sign a statement denying both that the sun was the centre of the universe, and that the earth went round the sun, as "absurd, philosophically false, and formally heretical, because it is expressly contrary to Scripture. . . . Did not the Bible say that the world was established that it should not be moved (Ps. xciii. 1)?" Columbus was assailed with quotations from the Book of Genesis, the Psalms, Prophets, Gospels, and Epistles, to prove the impiety of his belief in the existence of a Western Hemisphere. The mistakes of all were, that they had read their own preconceived notions into the Bible (*Geikie*). After that, it was easy to get any meaning they wanted out of it.

"A Brahmin crushed with a stone the microscope that first showed him living things among the vegetables of his daily food. The prophets of Israel were persecuted and killed, because they placed purity of heart higher than ceremonial worship. Socrates was ridiculed in the 'Clouds' of Aristophanes, because he was favourable to an explanation of thunder and storms by natural causes; he was compelled to empty the poisonous cup, because he declared the gods of Homer to be the offspring of imagination. Huss suffered death by fire, merely on account of the same doctrines which, a century later, made Luther the founder of a new era in the history of mankind. Robespierre was, in the early part of his life, persecuted for his exertions to introduce Franklin's lightning conductor into France, as it was considered an audacious attempt to avert the decrees of Providence.

"The Book of Nature is no longer a sealed secret; it is no longer the exclusive privilege of the initiated. The study of Nature belongs to the very elements of education.

"Are the Expositors of Scripture prepared to stem this torrent? Will they oppose this universal movement towards the knowledge of the physical sciences? Will they once more proclaim open war against academies and observatories? Will they brand with the odious names of heretic, infidel, and atheist, those whom God has gifted with the subtle intellect to penetrate into the abstrusest laws of nature? (The 'High Priests of Science.') 'Shall men curse where God has blessed?' Fatal error! demented fanaticism!

"The natural sciences have a right to ascend to the first causes of Creation. This is no arrogance, no ungodly assumption on their part. Only let 'the axe not boast itself against him who wields it.'

"The mission of the Bible is the diffusion of *truth*. Truth can never be aided by falsehood; zeal preserves, but blind zeal destroys.

"The Bible was not intended to supersede Science, but to control it; Faith should not awe Reason, but guide it, and protect its daring flight from degrading aberrations" (*Kalisch*).

Everything goes to show that Religion must become comprehensive, and take in Science as a grand ally in the cause of Truth. In other words, in a scientific age, Religion must assert her claim to be the true Science.

It is a pleasant reflection, after this, to notice the indebtedness of the British and Foreign Bible Society (for instance) to scientific inventions and discovery. That Society has turned to good account the progress in science and art, in multiplying copies of the Bible, and in spreading them abroad.

These statements should be compared with Voltaire's (pp. 37 *f*, 38 *d*),—who said, "We were living in the twilight of Christianity:" he ought to have said, The twilight before the dawn,—and may be taken as indications of the immense part that Science in all its departments may be destined to take in the spread of the kingdom of God. But the limits of scientific knowledge, apart from Christ—"in whom are hid all the treasures of wisdom and knowledge"—are clearly defined by an inspired Apostle—"**If any man thinketh that he knoweth anything, he knoweth not yet as he ought to know**" (1 Cor. viii. 2; *cf.* p. 392*a*).

F. B. P.

ALPHABETICAL ARRANGEMENT

A

ABSTRACT AND CONCRETE

It is a great mistake to think anything too profound or rich for a popular audience. No train of thought is too deep, or subtle, or grand; but the manner of presenting it to their untutored minds should be peculiar. It should be presented in anecdote, or sparkling truism, or telling illustration, or stinging epithet; always in some concrete form, never in a logical, abstract, syllogistic shape.

(a)   *Choate*

ACCESS into the standing of grace (Rom. v. 1, 2)

1. Our Lord commenced His ministry by a *proclamation:* "the kingdom of heaven is at hand" (Mark i. 14, 15).
2. Conditions of entering are *repentance* and *faith*.
3. The admitted have a new *standing* before God—that of *grace*.
Observe then,
(i.) **We live in a time of GRACE:** *i.e.* we can come to God without being dealt with as sinners; confirmed by succeeding joy and hope. There was a time when this was all *mystery*, and in our ignorance we attempted to propitiate God.
The practical question is: On which side of the threshold am I?—There is no middle position: either *within* or *without*.
(ii.) **We live not only in a time of grace, but grace is SOVEREIGN:** greater, stronger than the sin which opposes it.
(*a*) Suppose the voice of sin is heard the *loudest*, declaring its wages is *death;* and we conclude that *sin* is paramount, it aboundeth, hath dominion over us; and is therefore *sovereign*.
Grace is opposed to this: "I will be merciful to their unrighteousness, and their sins . . . I will remember no more." This breaks the reign of sin.
Again, "Where sin aboundeth . . . grace super-aboundeth." Hence grace, not sin, is *sovereign*.
(*b*) **Allow that the Law is SUPREME:** "Thou shalt not," etc., speaks with a terrible voice, as of Sinai. Remember you come to God on the footing of *grace* and *mercy*. Now the Law and Grace mutually exclude each other; Christ died in vain, if your salvation is through the law: "Ye are not under the law, but under grace."—Hence grace is *sovereign* in the matter of salvation.
(*c*) **Grace excludes our own works:** The law demands works as means of salvation. But by grace *all the doing is done:* "By grace ye are saved—not by works: if by grace, then it is no more of works;" etc. Grace will have no aid, God saves; His grace is *sovereign*.
(*d*) **Grace excludes merit, is diametrically opposed to it.** The law demands works, and works possess *merit*, being either *good* or bad. To this Scripture is no less emphatic; *grace and merit* are totally opposed to each other; grace is God's GIFT —*undeserved*. "We are justified freely by His grace," etc. Therefore in the matter of salvation, *grace is sovereign*, we stand on it alone.
If God is not gracious, and does not freely give us salvation, then our salvation is an impossibility. Sin reigns; the law is against us; our own works worthless; as for merit, we have none.
4. But our *access* into such a privileged standing is all owing to Christ.
Through *Him* we have it.
Through His death we, once enemies are reconciled.
Through Him we have peace.
Through Him we have salvation full and free.
Through Him comes resurrection of the dead.
Through Him the final victory: "Thanks be to God," etc.
Through Him comes the love of God, from which nothing can separate us.
Through Him we have eternal life.
Through Him we have an interest in the exceeding great and precious promises of God.
Everything through Him; and on this INFINITE GRACE let us draw every day of our lives.
His *grace is sufficient for us*.

(b)   *Adapted from Weiss*

ACCUSER OF THE BRETHREN, THE (Rev. xii. 10, 11)

Two persons interested about us before God, the **Accuser** and the **Advocate**.
1. The **Accuser** is the Devil, the Calumniator: his business is mischief; the destroyer of character (Milton's description is misleading; he makes Satan a hero).
(i.) He calumniates us before God—"Doth Job fear God for nought?"—insists that his portrait of us is true.
(ii.) **God to us:** represents Him as terrible, hard master, hasty to strike, etc.
2. The **Accused:** are the "Brethren" of Christ; those who do the Father's will "my *brother* and sister," etc.; "He is not ashamed to call them *brethren*." (Christians are called *saints* to indicate holiness: *brethren* to indicate their *love*.)
These harmless people are an eyesore to Satan;

(c)

1

he watches them night and day, and seeks to ruin both their character and their comfort.

3. **The Accusation is threefold**: As a disease is inferred from the remedy, so the accusation may be inferred from the means taken to clear their characters:

(i.) "**They overcame him by the Blood of the Lamb.**" Hence they were accused of *sin*. The enemy aims to keep us away from *the blood of Christ*, which cleanseth, etc. See him opposing Joshua, the High Priest—"the sin is too great for cleansing": and is rebuked by the Advocate with the Father—"Is not this a brand plucked from the burning?" Satan's endeavour is to keep the sinner from that blood: so Bunyan's pilgrim and the *lions ;* so with all who set out to Zion with faces thitherward; and he has no more effectual method than *delay* (see *Blood, Delay, Neglect*).

(ii.) **By the word of their testimony**: "The sword of the Spirit." Hence they were accused of *unfaithfulness*, of falls, backslidings, relapses—for we fall on that side to which we lean: we are no stronger than our weakest point. He will have us down on that side. Peter is venturesome, he will attack there, and when down he harasses and taunts, "*No wheat*," "Fallen from grace," "Unpardonable sin." Quotes Scripture, and tells us God has given us up, "When ye call I will not hear," etc. But these answer, "It is written," "I will in no wise cast out." "He that walketh in darkness . . . Stay upon his God." Thus *armed* they overcome.

(iii.) **Accused of selfishness**: And they overcame by loving not "*their lives unto the death.*" "Ye cannot die for Christ," "Skin for skin, yea all that man hath will he give for his life." But God gives a martyr's grace for a martyr's crown. These overcame the accusation by becoming martyrs for Jesus.

Think when all is over, and the accuser cast out of earth, as he is out of heaven, what a shout of victory there will be. "Now is come salvation, for," etc. But till then we shall be exposed to his accusations; let us therefore be armed with the whole panoply of God, lest he prevail over us.

(a)

ACHAN : the Troubler (Josh. vii. 10)

"Get up ; wherefore liest thou thus upon thy face?"
The cause is in thee, not in me.

(b)　　　　　　　　　　　　*Hengstenberg*

ADAM AND CHRIST (1 Cor. xv. ; Rom. vi.)

The whole human race is, as it were, two men, Adam and Christ, Death and Life.

(c)　　　　　　　　　　　*Bishop Wordsworth*

ADAM, FIRST AND SECOND, THE.

The last Adam is the Messiah; He will be higher than Moses, higher than the angels who serve Him, and the old sin by which death has been introduced will be abolished by Him, for in His days the dead will rise. This was the Divine intention at the creation of man, that he should be eternal; But sin occasioned death: *now the Divine intention is fulfilled by the second Adam, who is the antitype of the first.*

(d)　　　　*N. S. R. Abraham Ben Isaac* (1593), quoted by *Tholuck*

"ADD TO YOUR FAITH," etc. (2 Pet. i. 5–8)

1 Pet. = dangers from without mainly.
2 Pet. = dangers from within (iii. 17). "Beware lest," etc.

1. God's part in our salvation (1–4) is-
(i.) Faith as His gift.
(ii.) All things pertaining thereto.
(iii.) The means of our partaking in the Divine nature.

2. Our part (5–7) is-
(i.) To put out God's gift to usury; to "occupy."
(ii.) Working out our salvation.
(iii.) Making our salvation and election sure.

EXPOSITION: "Give Diligence:" Luther ; "Ye have a good inheritance, a fair field : take care that no thistles grow therein."

"**Add to your faith**,"—which has been given—the seven following graces. A tree bearing seven fruits of the Spirit. The idea is that these are not gained easily :

(i.) "**Virtue**": Manliness—decided Christian conduct, which instinctively recoils from evil. It has no palliatives for vice : "I will not know a wicked person." Cf. Phil. iv. 8: "Whatsoever things are *true*, honest, just, pure, lovely, of good report," etc. This first and best of the seven fruits.

(ii.) "**Knowledge :**" Not learning, but prudent and sagacious conduct, a wise demeanour; distinguishes between the *harmful* and the *useful ;* what to do and what not to do; zeal according to knowledge. Even virtues become faults and exaggerations if not directed by knowledge. Cf. Phil. i. 9: "I pray that your love may abound . . . in *knowledge*, and judgment."

(iii.) "**Temperance**": Self-control, soberness, and chastity. Not limited to natural passions : refers to whole person, body, soul, and spirit. The *ego* to be kept under : "I die daily," and not only "I keep under my body."

(iv.) "**Patience**," endurance of trial, perseverance under abuse, want, danger. After self-control patience can endure hardness, and have its perfect work, not otherwise.

(v.) "**Godliness**," the disposition in which "God is in all our thoughts"; the whole life centres in Him, refers all to Him. Eli="It is the Lord, let Him . . . good." Cowper="Happy the man that sees a God in all the good and ill that chequer life"; everything done with a reference to God's glory, "whether ye eat or drink," etc.

(vi.) "**Brotherly kindness**," the Christian brotherhood, brethren in faith ; "especially the household of faith"; Cf. (1 Thess. iv. 9) "As touching brotherly love ye need not that I write," etc. This first, then—

(vii.) "**Charity**," the bond of perfectness, the universal love, likest to God's.

Faith then, is evidenced by *works*, which result in a sevenfold chain, the links grow out of one another: *manly conduct, wise conduct, bodily and mental self-control, patience under wrongs, a godly disposition, a large-hearted charity towards all men*, especially towards the "household of faith."

(e)

These are seven, the number of perfection and completion. Cf. "sevenfold gifts of the Spirit," and being "filled with the Spirit." And if these be *in us* and *abound*, we cannot be barren Christians, nor stumble to our ruin; but are working out our salvation with diligence.

These, too = the order of **Temptation** (cf. *Temptation of Christ*).

Cf. (*a*) "He that overcometh shall inherit all things," with (*b*) "an abundant entrance" = a ship arriving in port in full sail, not *just saved*.

(*a*)

ADVENT

It is the peculiar computation of the Church to begin her years, and to revive the annual course of her services, with this time of Advent. For she neither follows the sun nor moon, to number her days and measure her seasons according to their revolution; but JESUS CHRIST being to her as the only Sun and Light whereby she is guided, following His course alone, she begins, and counts on her year with HIM. When this Sun of Righteousness, therefore, doth arise—that is, when His coming and incarnation are first propounded to us—then begins the year of the Church, and from thence are all her other days and times computed.

(*b*) *Hook*

ADVENT, SCEPTICAL THOUGHTS CONCERNING

"*Every vision faileth*"; "*a time very far off*"— (Ezek. xii. 22–28).

Cf. Heaven and earth pass away, but God's word never.

The words have a history: The last of three remarkable passages; three distinguished prophets sent to the people successively and at different stages in their career of sin :

1. Isaiah, the prophet of hope: "The ox knoweth . . . but my people doth not consider"—still the case not hopeless. "Wash you, make you clean," etc. "Come, let us reason together," etc. Isaiah, at this stage of their career, and his own ministry, is full of *hope* for the people, and the success of his ministry among them; but later on he seems to despair of success—" *Who hath believed our report ?* " etc. This failing, God next sends

2. Jeremiah, the tearful prophet, full of lamentations, almost of despair. To him there is little *hope*—sin has become *habit*, and he knows habit is second nature. The people are being hardened. Notice how differently he speaks: "In vain have I smitten you," etc.; "They have made their faces harder than a flint"; "They have refused to return"; "Can the Ethiopian change his skin, or the leopard his spots? Then shall this people, who are habituated to do evil, learn to do well." This is the language not of hope, but of despair— yet the *uttermost* is not reached.

[N.B.—Habitual sin destroys freewill. The tide of inclination rolls on, the floodgates are carried before it, the sinner is a slave to his sin-

Then angels weep over us—as a contrast to the joy in Heaven over one, etc. ;

Good men weep over us—to see to what we are blindly rushing;

Jesus weeps over us—"How often would I have . . . now hid," etc.

God, who gives no man over, says—"Have I any pleasure at all in the death of him that dieth? I have no pleasure."]

3. Then comes an Ezekiel—stern in voice and manner—a sign of the impending evil—the inevitable. He brings no invitations, promises, but utters his note of warning: The hour for judgment is come: "*Because I will do this, prepare to meet thy God, O Israel.*"

Cf. Sin, when it is finished brings forth *death*. Men may despise, mock, etc., but the hour cometh—the inevitable cometh naturally and morally, a necessity.

So Christ will come the second time—sudden to the unprepared, yet like the history above, in the true order of things. Whilst there is time there is hope. . . . There is a *Refuge*. "Flee from the wrath to come."

(*c*) *A. P. Stanley (adapted)*

ADVENT. FOUR ADVENT SERMONS

John Baptist, the great Advent preacher :

1. **The Birth of John Baptist.** "And thou, child" (Luke i. 76).

2. **The Ministry of John Baptist.** "What shall we do" (Luke iii. 11, etc.).

3. **The Stumble of John Baptist.** "Blessed is he that shall not be offended in me" (Luke vii. 23).

N.B.—John Baptist knew nothing of the Second Advent. Hence his stumble.

4. **The Greatness and the Littleness of John Baptist.** "There hath not risen a greater. . . . He that is least in the kingdom of heaven is greater" (Luke vii. 28).

(*d*) *See Godet, in loc*

ADVENT, THE SECOND

"As it was in the days of Noah and Lot (Luke xvii. 26, etc.), they ate, they drank, they married and were given in marriage." Thus Jesus does not once upbraid them with the scandalous crimes which they committed, but with that very thing in their way of life which was commendable, but which becomes hideous when nothing higher can be told of an age ; when its whole life is a worldly life, in which God is no longer taken into account. A great increase of outward power and culture, reliance on science, industry, the conquest of the external world, lead to an arrogance that no longer admits its dependence on God.

(*e*) *Lange*

ADVENT, THE SECOND, ASPECTS OF (2 Pet. iii. 4)

1. "**Slow.**"—The Lord delayeth His coming; no hurry. God laughs at the impotence of man ; waits to be gracious. Not slack, however, concerning His promise. He will come.

The work meanwhile is of great magnitude. The Church is growing up inside the scaffolding, increasing according to the increase of God. Nations come and go; great men, heathenism and Christianity, all help to bring on the end, which *will* come in due time.

2. "**Sudden**"—as a thief in the night; when men say *peace* and *safety;* as in days of Noah and Lot. No gross sin mentioned by our Lord; simply every-day employments and pleasures, in

(*f*)

which the mass of people are engaged; so when He comes again will it be with our cities.

No pre-intimation. "The sun was risen upon the earth when Lot entered into Zoar." The day promised well, like others before it; yet in one hour judgment came *suddenly*.

"*They shall not escape*." Think of escaping the Flood; and of some great shipwrecks.

"*So shall ye likewise perish*," etc., *i.e.* just as suddenly; lesser calamities are all warnings. God strikes a blow here and there; it falls on a definite locality, produces a sensation; we call it an "accident." Sent to people who are not sinners above others, but *as* others, to warn them to repent and prepare to meet Him.

3. No hope that the world will become a Paradise before Christ returns. Cf. Distress of nations, perplexities of statesmen; "perilous times"; "evil men wax worse and worse." The love of the elect shall wax cold. A grand struggle is intimated between powers of light and darkness, of which we see germs now.

The tares must first ripen; the mystery of iniquity must fully unfold itself; Satan will seem to be winning; the anti-Christian kingdom apparently paramount, ready to take the last step of dominion.

Then at the opportune moment Christ comes to undertake the cause of his "*little flock*." The Church up to the last will be at work: "Ye shall not have gone over the cities of Israel until the Son of Man be come" = a double prophecy (i.) of destruction of Jerusalem, (ii.) of the end of the age.

N.B.—Some of the more prominent signs of the day:

A wide-spread and aggressive unbelief, fostered by vast strides made in science and art—intended handmaids, yet used as enemies.

A gathering hatred of all that is Divine and holy; a deep-rooted scepticism; the worship of genius; the creature exalted above the Creator.

German infidelity taking root, even among the Hindoos, who reject alike their own idols and Christianity, and take to the study of modern infidelity, the seeds of which are fermenting in the depths of the society of the whole world. We have discussions about the *efficacy of prayer*, whether *the Bible shall be read in our schools*.

Strauss has asked, "Whether, considering our advanced culture, religious worship is necessary in any form whatever? . . . We must reply that we are Christians no longer. . . . There is no personal God—no future state. All religious worship ought to be abolished."

Does not such teaching indicate that *the mystery of iniquity* is making vast strides; that the spirit of anti-Christ is verily amongst us, challenging and denying our most holy faith to a combat of life and death—the great battle of Armageddon of the Apocalypse? These at least = *a promise of His coming*, and are leading up to it.

(*a*)

ADVENT, THE SECOND, "THE LORD HIMSELF" (1 Thess. v. 16)

Not a mere amelioration, gradual or sudden, of the condition of the Church or the world; not a mere displacement of evil and triumph of good; not a mere crisis of human affairs, issuing in times of universal blessing and happiness; it shall be a *personal coming*.

(*b*)   *Vaughan*

ADVENT, THE SECOND, "SURELY I COME QUICKLY," etc. (Rev. xxii. 20).

A dialogue most sublime and brief. Notice,-

1. The certainty that *Jesus will return* : "Surely I come."

2. The certainty that He will come *quickly* : "Surely I come *quickly*."

3. The certainty that we cannot welcome Him then, by responding as St. John did, "*Yea, come Lord Jesus*," except upon certain conditions :

(i.) We must first *come* to Jesus, before we can desire *His coming; i.e.* we must accept the Gospel invitation, "*Come*."

(ii.) We must be at peace with Him.

(iii.) We must be in sympathy with Him and His work.

(*c*)   *Lange (adapted)*

In the first ages it would have been deemed a kind of apostasy not to have sighed after the day of the Lord.

(*d*)   *Massillon*

ADVICE

Advice, like snow, the softer it falls the longer it dwells upon, and the deeper it sinks into the heart.

(*e*)   *Coleridge*

ADVICE, GOOD

"*Look up*," thundered the captain of a vessel, as his boy grew giddy while gazing from the topmast. "*Look up!*" The boy looked up and returned in safety. Young man, look up, look up, and you will succeed. Never look down and despair. Leave dangers uncared for, and push on. If you falter, you fall. *Look up*. Do right, and trust in God.

(*f*)

ADVOCATE (1 John ii. 1)

The office of an advocate is to appear for his client in a court of justice, and to plead his cause, where an accuser also appears against him on the other side. This office Jesus executes for His people.

The Holy Spirit also is our Advocate; but the Holy Spirit intercedes *in* us at the throne of grace.

But Jesus intercedes *for* us at the throne of glory and power. The Holy Spirit "helps us to pray," but Jesus presents our prayers and prays for us.

(*g*)   *Simeon*

My sins plead against me, but my Saviour is my Advocate. It is much that my rebellions have deserved, but it is more that my Redeemer hath merited; so that though my flesh hath provoked Thee to vengeance, yet the flesh of Christ can move Thee to mercy.

(*h*)   *Anselm*

[Zech. iii. 1-6

Joshua the High Priest stood before the Angel, clothed, not with righteousness, but with

(*i*)

filthy rags. Sin upon him, and Satan by him. And this before the Angel! What must he do? Go away? No, there he must stand. Can he speak for himself? Not a word; guilt had made him dumb! Had he nothing clean? No! But his lot was to stand before Jesus Christ, that maketh intercession for transgressors; and the Lord said, The Lord rebuke thee, Satan! But is Joshua now quit? No; he standeth yet, nor can he clear himself. How then? Why, the Lord clothes him with change of raiment. The iniquity was his own; the raiment was the Lord's.

(a)   *Bunyan*

ÆSTHETICISM AND JESUS

" *Sir, we would see Jesus* " (John xii. 21).

Time: close of our Lord's earthly ministry; last week.

Question: inquiry after Jesus; not salvation, yet not idle curiosity.

The people: "certain Greeks" (Gentiles *inquiring*) ask Philip to procure them an interview with Jesus. Philip, cautious, consults Andrew, and they two tell Jesus.

The effect on our Lord. This is something of world-important significance: " *The hour is come.*" The hand of the clock of Time is now significantly pointing to that time when salvation shall be brought to the Gentiles. But their *thought* is of another kind, and Jesus answers their *thought*.

These men were the representatives of art, taste, and culture—*æsthetes*. To whom *life* was everything—pleasure and happiness, and to whom *death* was a destroyer and spoiler, and therefore a thought ever to be avoided.

These thought Jesus was throwing Himself away amongst those unappreciative Jews. Such matchless beauty, worth, wisdom, etc., could only be appreciated by the cultured Greeks. They regarded Him as the "Desire of all nations, the unparalleled One."

Jesus replies to this thought (perhaps unexpressed, but He knew men). He tells them He is going to DIE, to be buried as a grain of corn in the ground, that in the end He may reap a plentiful harvest of saved souls. His words=that death is no spoiler, no destroyer; but that only through the grave and gate of death will man attain unto his best estate and fullest development in glory. Happiness is unattainable in any other way. " I am not throwing My life away, I am gaining it; through death I shall be glorified, and through death I shall draw all men unto Me."

Think of the rebuke this conveys to modern culture and æsthetic homes and costly furniture as a means of satisfying the soul's need for blessedness. We=the Greeks in our view of death; and in nothing are we so unchristian as in that.

There are those who run off to paradises on earth to avoid gloomy thoughts, they are unwilling to *see Jesus* as He was on earth.

(b)

The peculiar essence of Hellenism consists in a fleeing from death and the cross in the embellishof the present life. The Greek's aim is levelled at beauty of appearance.

(c)   *Lange*

They remind us of the rich oratories of some court ladies, where everything is beautiful and costly, but where a classic statue of Apollo stands by the side of a crucifix, a Venus with Our Lady, a Cupid near St. Michael, and a pair of beads hanging on Mercury's Caduceus.

Paul did not desire spiritual insight; he wanted Jesus.

(d)   *Shorthouse*

If you adored a god crowned with roses and with pearls, it were a matter nothing strange; but to prostrate yourselves daily before a crucifix charged with nails and thorns,—you living in such excess and superfluity in the flesh, dissolved in softness,—how can that be cruel? Think of that crucifix as you lie warm in silken curtains, perfumed with *eau de naffe*, as you sit at dainty feasts, as you ride forth in the sunshine in gallantry. He is cold and naked; He is alone; behind Him the sky is dreary and streaked with darkening clouds, for the night cometh, the night of God. His locks are wet with the driving rain; His hair is frozen with the sleet; His beauty is departed from Him; all men have left Him—all men, and God also, and the holy angels hide their faces. He is crowned with thorns, but you with garlands. He wears nothing in His hands but piercing nails; you have rubies and diamonds on yours. Will you tell me you can still be faithful though in brave array? I give that answer which Tertullian gave, " I fear this neck snared with wreaths and ropes of pearls and emeralds. I fear the sword of persecution can find no entrance there." No! hear you not the voice of the crucifix? Follow Me? We are engaged to suffer by His sufferings, as we look on Him. Suffering is our vow and profession. Love which cannot suffer is unworthy of the name of love.

(e)   *Shorthouse (John Inglesant)*

AFFLICTION (Exod. iii. 7, 8)

1. " I have seen "—What?

" The affliction of *My* people which are in Egypt;

2. " And have heard "—What?

" Their cry, by reason of their task-masters ";

3. " I know "—What?

" Their sorrows "

[The grief that does not speak, whispers the o'erwrought heart, and bids it break] ;

4. " And I am come down "—Why?

" To deliver them out of the hand of the Egyptians " (worldly bondage);

5. " And to bring them "—Where?

" Unto a good land and a large, unto a land flowing with milk and honey" (to make them a free people).

N.B.—"He that formed the eye, shall He not see? He that formed the ear, shall He not hear? or He that formed man's heart, shall He not know?"

Cf. "Speak ye comfortably to Jerusalem, and cry unto her that her warfare is accomplished, that her iniquity is pardoned; for she hath received of the Lord's hand double for all her sins."

(f)

AFFLICTION, CAUSES OF

We fancy that all our afflictions are sent us directly from above; sometimes we think it in piety and contrition, but oftener in moroseness and discontent. It would be well, however, if we attempted to trace the causes of them; we should probably find their origin in some region of the heart which we never had well explored, or in which we had secretly deposited our worst indulgences. The clouds that intercept the heavens from us come not from the heavens, but from the earth.

(a)   *Landor*

AFFLICTION, USES OF

Luther used to say there were many of the Psalms he could never understand till he had been afflicted. Rutherford declared he had got a new Bible through the furnace.

(b)

AFFLICTION, NEEDFUL

A friend was asked, concerning a beautiful horse of his feeding on the pasture with a clog on its foot: "Why do you clog such a noble animal?" The reply was: "I would a great deal sooner clog him than lose him; he is given to leap hedges." That is why God clogs His people. He would rather clog them than lose them; for if He did not, they would leap and be gone.

(c)   *C. H. Spurgeon*

AFFLICTIONS

Hard weather tries what health we have; afflictions try what sap we have, what grace we have. Withered leaves soon fall off in windy weather; rotten boughs quickly break with heavy weights.

(d)   *Thomas Brooks*

AFFLICTIONS, APPOINTED US (1 Thess. iii. 3, 4)

To find one's bearings by the word of prophecy—this was a great consolation for the Lord Jesus in His career of suffering (Luke xviii. 31; John xvii. 12; Matt. xxvi. 54); to say nothing of ourselves. For us, when in tribulation, it is indispensable that we know that so it must be—it was told us before.

(e)   *Starke*

The Christian is appointed to suffer affliction. It is, therefore, just when we are appointed to a time of refreshing that a strange thing happens to us (1 Pet. iv. 12). According to worldly sentiment, it is to our discredit when things go troublesome and hard with us; we almost suspect that everything is wrong with us. According to the Word of God that is rather a badge of Christians, a badge of honour.

(f)   *Chrysostom*

AFTERWARD, [cf. Heb. xii. 11, and xii. 17]

Examples of the first text are,
1. Abraham—leaving all—a stranger here, but *afterwards* the friend of God; the father of the faithful; and His bosom = heaven, the city which hath foundations.
2. Moses, who in this life accounted reproach of Christ greater riches than the treasures of Egypt, having respect unto the recompense of the reward —"*afterward*."
3. Lazarus, a beggar *here*, but "afterwards" comforted.

These all counted that the suffering of this present time is not worthy to be compared with the glory that shall be revealed in us.

Examples of the second text are,

Esau and Dives. They had all in the present. But "*afterwards*," when they would have inherited a blessing, *what?*

So all would *afterward* inherit a blessing—would wish to die the death of the righteous. But "if we suffer with Christ here, we shall reign with Him hereafter."

(g)

AGES

It is through a series of *ages*, or æons, that St. Paul considers the work of redemption to be progressively carried on, all separated by certain great crises. The "present age" is that dating from the Fall, is to last until the second coming of Christ. At this point the "future age" will begin to date, and this will be the age of redemption completed, the age of the Messiah's kingdom and glory.

(h)   *Lange*

AGNOSTICISM (Acts xvii. 23)

The following letter from Charles Darwin appears in a work just issued:—It seems to me absurd to doubt that a man can be an ardent Theist and an Evolutionist. You are right about Kingsley. Asa Gray, the eminent botanist, is another case in point. What my own views may be is a question of no consequence to any one but myself. But, as you ask, I may state that my judgment often fluctuates. Moreover, whether a man deserves to be called a Theist depends on the definition of the term, which is much too large a subject for a note. In my own extreme fluctuations I have never been an atheist in the sense of denying the existence of a God. I think that generally (and more and more as I grow older), but not always, that an Agnostic would be the more correct description of my state of mind.

(i)

What is Agnosticism? The Agnostic is very careful to distinguish his philosophical (even his religious) creed from all the isms of the past or the present. The insinuation that Agnosticism is only a disguised form of atheism he denounces. Pantheism he rejects. While holding much in common with Positivism, he repudiates several of its most important positions. While he denounces every form of Theism which has been held by mankind during the past and the present as involving contradictions in thought, and as no better than Anthropomorphism, yet by the mouths of its two great prophets, Mr. H. Spencer in England, and Mr. Fiske in America, Agnosticism proclaims itself to be not only theistic, but the only rational Theism. Both of these writers affirm

(j)

that a belief in the existence of a First Cause of the universe, which we may if we please designate God, is a necessity of thought. But while they make this concession to Theism, they lay it down as a fundamental truth, that owing to the nature of our faculties, this First Cause must for ever remain unknowable and inscrutable by man; to affirm that God is a being Who unites in Himself the conceptions of the infinite, the absolute, and the first cause involves us in hopeless logical contradictions; that He has created the finite is simply unthinkable, and to affirm an attribute respecting Him is nothing else than to deify a number of finite human conceptions.

From these premises a number of consequences follow, the importance of which it is hardly possible to exaggerate. We cannot predicate of Him either personality, or consciousness, or intelligence, for these are merely human conceptions, and not objective realities We cannot, therefore, affirm that He is holy, or just, or benevolent, or the moral Governor of the Universe, or the rewarder of virtue, or the punisher of vice. In a word, the God of the Agnostic is an infinite algebraic X, the value of which is insoluble in any known quantities of human thought, to whom if worship is rendered it must not be a service of which reason can take cognisance, but it must be of the silent sort offered through the imagination to the unknowable and the inscrutable. Its philosophy, which for the sake of brevity may be designated the Agnostic theory of evolution, is one of the most portentous dimensions, being nothing short of an attempt to propound a philosophy which shall embrace the whole universe of phenomena, past, present, and to come, including man intellectually, morally, and socially, under the reign of one necessary law —the law of evolution.

(a)   *Preb. Row*

"AGONIZE (strive) to enter in " (Luke xiii. 24)

Note, when "*many* believed," a certain man asked, "Are there *few* that be saved?"

= There are *many* who are called Christians; but *few* who have agonized to enter the kingdom, which the violent take by force.

Numbers are no criterion of success. The kingdom cometh not with observation—the seed grows *secretly*. His people are *hidden*, rarely among the prominent ones. But a day will come when they will come from the uttermost parts of the earth, and take their proper places amongst the nobility of heaven.

Specimens of the few are given: Abraham, Isaac, Jacob, and all the prophets; not all accounted the grandest in their day, but often as the offscouring of the earth. Not the *first* but the *last*.

Characteristics of the many = *external* religion—attended by no spiritual struggles and revolutions; fallow ground never broken up; all goes merrily as a marriage bell; no cross to bear; a striking ministry attracts them; parochial opportunities for prominence interest them. But of things in their deeper significance they have no acquaintance —*superficiality* is the keynote to their whole religion—alike without a true foundation and a true after-building. Content to be *as* others, " comparing themselves with themselves," in their unwisdom. (See also " *Superficiality*.")

(b)

ALL (Gen. xli. 56, 57)

The famine was over *all* the land.
Joseph opened *all* the granaries.
All countries came unto him.
Suggestive of man's universal need—" all your need "; of Christ's fulness—" in Him all fulness dwells," unsearchable riches; and of *all coming* to Him—of His fulness have *all we received*, etc.

(c)   *Bathurst*

" ALL " occurs four times (Col. i. 9–11)

Observe: 1. Things have their instinct (or properties): *Stones* fall downward—as low as they *can*—to the centre; *Sparks* fly upward—as high as they *can*; *Eagles* fly high—to get as near the sun as they can.

GRACE likewise is ambitious. It ascends as high as it can; it would be as much like Christ as possible; it would shine more in the dark world. A Christian would be *all* of that of which he is so little. . . . And so he prays for " ALL " Christian graces.

2. Things have their sense: Senses are greedy, never satisfied; " Give, give." The eye not satisfied with seeing; the ear with hearing; the mouth with tasting.

GRACE has its SENSE, which is always craving more *grace*—" grace upon grace." It has tasted, it must taste again. The Christian has come upon a stream, he *pants* for the waterbrooks. Hence he prays that this *craving* may be satisfied. " Fill me with *all* wisdom and spiritual understanding; to walk worthy . . . *all* pleasing . . . strengthened with ALL might . . . all patience."

3. Things have their reason: Man acts upon judgment. He sees a worth and value in things. Pearls are not lumber, gold and silver are treasures; they represent a value and a power. He has found this out, and so desires to have *more* of such treasures.

So the " *new man* " is of a better reason. He has made out the worth of spiritual things. Pearls, gold, silver are seen to be contemptible things. He possesses the true jewel of " *grace*." The more he has of this, the more he has of God. Here is something of supreme worth and value; hence he desires all he can get of it, and prays for " *all* " wisdom, understanding, faithfulness, might, patience, joy.

4. Things have their rule and measure: And so must be sought after. Earthly things are bounded, heavenly things not.

If we pray for earthly things = " Neither poverty nor riches," or " No poverty, only riches." But when we pray for heavenly things = Not some but " ALL." This is the measure, " *all*." The measure is no measure—no *stint ;* give me " ALL," etc., otherwise we should aim too low.

(d)   *Lockyer*

ALL GONE ASTRAY (Isa. liii 6)

1. The indictment: " All," without exception; not the openly wicked only, but the whole race of men, have strayed from God, like so many prodigals.

2. " Like sheep," stupidly, following a leader; unthinkingly or foolishly, without meaning to lost one's self—lost, like sheep out of the field, before aware of our danger. So God's Word speaks of our wanderings.

(e)

3. This first; but not all,

"*We have turned every one to his own way.*"

This denotes personal guilt; every one has acted the part of Adam, sinned in the face of light and warning: voices have said, "Go not in that path," yet we have gone; "Touch not, taste not, handle not," yet we have disobeyed and become familiar with sins that we never need have known. We have listened to the Siren's voice, and have transgressed, and are now *wilful* sinners, with all our guilt resting at our own door. We have done our own will, not God's, *every one*.

4. The next statement is of a different nature

"The Lord hath laid on *Him* the iniquity of us all."

We have had indications of what the iniquity is. We know, too, who is meant by "HIM." But though we believe in our guilt, *do we believe* what the text states here? Few do. In Old Testament times "*city of refuge*"; "shadow of great rock in a weary land;" "the Ark," Zoar; "the rock that followed them," were all realities, remedies for pressing needs, no guess-work about them; each knew what benefit they were to him. So here Christ is to the sinner what they were to the needy one. God knew you would be in need, and He provided accordingly.

5 Do you believe it?

(i.) Believe that you have gone astray? Yes; can't deny it.

(ii.) Believe that you have wilfully gone astray; turned your own way, not God's? Yes, can't deny it; that is the very guilt which oppresses me.

(iii.) Do you believe the third statement, "The Lord hath laid on Him . . . of all"?

Now you hesitate—you believe nothing of the kind. For if you did you would feel benefited, just as the people of old did when they fled for refuge, etc. "*You would know it and rejoice.*" Heaven would be begun. It is no guess-work, but a reality, just as much as your guilt.

"Dr. Martin," said an old monk to Luther, "you don't believe in *the forgiveness of sins.*" Neither did he up to that time. We, too, like him repeat that article of the Creed, but few believe it. Yet as a statement of God's Word it is to be believed, and when we believe it we experience sensible relief and comfort—even "peace and joy in the Holy Ghost."

(*a*)

ALL MEN, SALVATION BROUGHT UNTO (Tit. ii. 11.)

Not, "Grace hath appeared to all men"; but "Salvation is brought to all men."

1. The extent of Salvation = *universal*.

(i.) This is one of the N. T. passages which show that the length, breadth, height, and depth of God's salvation *passeth knowledge*.

We are limited by our creeds; like a beetle crawling on a cabbage leaf and thinking it is the whole world.

(ii.) "God so loved the *world*," etc., not the *Jews*, not a sect, a clique, etc.

(iii.) "Jesus is the propitiation . . . for the sin of *the whole world.*"

Caution: What is stated is that this universal salvation is enough for all—brought to all, but not that all will avail themselves of it. There is no limit to its efficacy, but it may be refused, rendered useless by neglect, and made light of. God offers salvation, but does not compel it. The Saviour *draws* men, not drives.

2. That salvation is universal, is not merely an *opinion*, but proved by Holy Scripture.

(i.) Rom. x. 12. God is "*rich* unto all that call upon Him." His grace is an unsparing, unlimited supply. He gives much where much is wanted. It is not *all* the truth to say,

"Thou art coming to a *king*,
   Large petitions with thee bring."

He is God, and not man, and gives only as God can; and that not to selected recipients, but to *all who call upon Him.* . . . His *riches in Christ are unsearchable.*

(ii.) James v. 11 = "He is *very pitiful*": not simply gracious, forgiving, merciful, or even pitiful, but *very*, VERY, VERY pitiful. Could this be true if *less* than a universal salvation were provided? No. Infinite *pity* goes hand in hand here with infinite resources and infinite need.

(iii.) Rom. v. 20 = "Where sin abounded, *grace super-abounded.*"

Sin reached a certain height and enormity—cup of iniquity full and overflowing. The world lay in God's sight like a sickening mass of putrefaction, and the remedy for this was not simply enough to hide it—as much grace as sin, and no more—but it overtopped it, a surplus over and above what was wanted remained. So, too (1 Tim. i. 4), The grace of God not simply *abundant*, but "*exceeding abundant*"—if sin flowed like a bottomless pit, an abyss never satisfied, then grace = a stronger and a fuller current, exceeding it in measure—prevailing like the waters of the Flood until the very tops of the highest mountains were covered; it fills a greater sea than the sea of iniquity; more than enough to pardon the sins of the world or of other worlds. This is the salvation which God's free grace hath *brought unto* ALL *men*.

(*b*)

"ALL THINGS ARE YOURS" (1 Cor. iii. 21-23)

All things belong to the Christian: this is the assertion of the Apostle—Christians are slow to perceive their rights.

1. Ministers are yours: The world says "Yes, *they* are yours; they are in your line, pander to your tastes and views of life." But,

2. "The world is yours": The world with its beauties, riches, treasures, art, science, music. "But," says the world, "*we have got them*, they are ours by right of possession." "Nay," replies St. Paul, "ye are usurpers, ye have no title to your possessions, *ye* shall be turned out,—they are all ours." The Christian is the heir *to all things*.

3. "Life is yours": Such pleasures as life and health bring, and they are not few. The world = "Ye are dull, soul-less, inanimate; ye have no enjoyment of life, ye think it sinful to be glad." "Not so; we think it sad to see those whose souls are in jeopardy leading the life of a butterfly, making life a perpetual holiday, as if this brief sunshine were all. *Life is ours*, ours to enjoy; we have the fullest right to do so, as *reconciled to God*, and under *no condemnation.*"

4. "Death is yours": Your servant, your friend, the gate of *life*. "You are welcome to that," says the world.

5. "Things present are yours": "Nay, that is a lie," says the world. "What about *theatres* and so forth? They at least are ours." Reply:

(*c*)

"What right has the world, as such, with them, soiling all such with polluted fingers."

6. "**Things to come are ours**": The heavenly Jerusalem, and the new heavens and earth. Which the world disdains as mere visionary mists and uncertainties.

ALL, ALL ARE YOURS "

The claim is based on this :

1. Because *all things* are God's, and Christ is God s, and *we* are Christ's.

2. And because God has committed *all things* unto His Son, by whom He made the worlds.

3. And He says, "All things that the Father hath are *mine*" and "*ye are Christ's.*"

The greater includes the less. There will come a day when this world will become the kingdom of God and His Christ; the *usurpers* will be dispossessed; the rightful heirs to *all things*, who have waited for this, will enter into their inheritance. Cf. The dispossession of the Canaanites, and the division of the land among the ten tribes.

(*a*)

Christians who, by virtue of their union with Christ and God, are precluded from dependence on men, have a direct claim on everything which belongs to God and Christ; all things serve them, and promote their destiny (Rom. viii. 28).

(*b*)   *Lange*

The sovereignty over the world was indeed conferred on man in his original state; lost through sin, was restored by redemption. The spirit which is bestowed on Christians, carries in itself a principle which everything must eventually obey, and which will subjugate the world, until the promise is fulfilled "The meek shall inherit the earth." . . . Christians (heirs) have even now a claim upon the world (Rom. iv. 38). The universe is upheld for their sake. The course of Providence is ordered for their welfare. The greatest men of the world, kings, statesmen, heroes, ministers, individual believers and unbelievers, live and die, just as best subserves the interest of Christ's kingdom.

(*c*)   *Hodge and Lange*

If you were but willing to hearken to Christ you might then draw near to God with boldness, and call Him your Father, and comfortably trust Him with your souls and bodies. If you look upon the promises, you may say, They are all mine. If upon the curse, you may say, From this I am delivered. When you read the law, you may see what you are saved from; when you read the gospel, you may see Him that redeemed you, and trace Him in His temptations, tears and blood, in the work of your salvation. You may see death conquered and heaven opened, and your resurrection and glorification provided for.

(*d*)   *Baxter*

ALL THINGS FREELY GIVEN US (Rom. viii. 32)

We see the hurricane tearing up by the roots the largest trees in the forest, and do not doubt for a moment that the same power can destroy a few saplings.

Or we see a beautiful ship laden with passengers and goods, carrying a heavy cargo, borne by the waters of the ocean. Do we ever doubt that the same waters can bear a little skiff with but a couple of oarsmen?

Doubt in either case would be absurd. No less is it so to limit the power and love of God, who hath given us the greater blessing of His Son; *how shall He not also freely give us all things in Him ?*

(*e*)

We have *all* things in Christ, and Christ is all things in us. If we are sick, He is a physician; if we fear death, He is life; if in darkness, He is light; if in want, He is abundance; if hungry, He is food; if thirsty, He is drink, if miserable, He is mercy; if covetous of Heaven, He is the way.

(*f*)   *Ambrose*

ALL THINGS WORK FOR GOOD (Rom. viii. 28)

"Don't you know, my dear brother," said the Rev. C. Simeon, when trying to explain how God can make all things plain which to us seem contrary, "Don't you know that the wheels of your watch move in opposite directions; yet they are all tending to one result?"

(*g*)

1. **Some** things. "Yes, I acknowledge that. It's very easy to see, and believe."

2. **Most** things. "Little comfort in that; because *the* thing, or things, which trouble me most may not be included."

3. **All** things makes the matter quite different. . . . It comprehends "all things,"good or bad, even sin—the whole course of one's life and experiences, and nothing less—as working together for good.

(*h*)

It is very remarkable how every opposition they met with wrought for their good in the end.

(*i*)   *Nicholl's Help to Reading the Bible*

1. "**We know.**" Why such supreme certainty? Because the apostle had been assured of it by God, and had it verified in his experience.

2. "**All things**"—all facts, forces, laws of the universe; a measureless compass!

3. "**Work:**" nothing inactive, all things, beings under God's ordination, doing His work.

4. "**Work together :**" in harmony, as all proceeding from one mind, and developing one supreme plan.

5. "**For good :**" the beneficence of the final result; such as must be anticipated from a *good* God, who cannot do otherwise than manifest His character in the ends to which the universe tends.

6. But it is for good "**to them that love Him :**" to those in union, by moral sympathy, with the Head of Creation, having been inspired by His inviting and quickening grace.

(*j*)   *Storrs*

ALMSGIVING (1 Cor. xvi.)

Ought to be made a part of our Sunday worship, as a tribute, not so much of kindness to the needy

(*k*)

and destitute, as of thanksgiving and honour unto the God of our salvation.

(a)   *Lange*

ALMSGIVING: CHARITY BLESSES THE GIVER

Two statements of Our Lord with regard to almsgiving, which in this view demand serious consideration.

1. " Make to yourselves friends of the mammon of unrighteousness " (authentic).

2 " Show yourselves tried money-changers " (apocryphal), (*Westcott : Introd. Gosp.* pp. 425–6).

Both call on us to look on charity in a business light, and in business we consider ourselves first.

We are to look on charity, not merely as the gratification of an impulse, not even as the discharge of a duty requiring only the expenditure of money : the money is to be so laid out as to produce a return (see parable of the Unjust Steward, R. V.). Almsgiving is to be an investment as well as a gift.

The first text points out the results in the benefit to the giver; the second, the care which he is to use in the administration of his charity.

(i.) We are kings and priests *here*, and as such called upon to exercise those gifts, which develop in us the powers which we shall one day use in the judgment of angelic beings. . . . Our Lord, regarding us as the future judges of the world, lays stress on the fact that the unjust in the least, is unjust also in much, and that only those who have been faithful in the unrighteous mammon can have the distribution of the eternal riches committed to their care. It is in this view that almsgiving forms so important a discipline.

(ii.) " Be ye good business men : "

The very first lesson a business man learns, is the risk of an unwise investment. Be sure he was no beginner who sold his all to buy the pearl of great price. Smaller men make their gains in smaller ways. He was neither niggard, nor rash speculator, but a man who could wait, and do a bold thing when experience justified it. . . . In charity how few think of investing their money, of waiting till a really good object comes before them, and helping it adequately. As a rule, we spend our money in doles on any harrowing case, and then, like children, see something on which we would have liked to spend the money which is gone.

THREE things seem specially to be wanting in almsgiving. *First*, the setting apart a regular sum for charity; putting it on one side as a man puts by his money for rent and taxes, etc., considering it a claim on his resources, not allowing the amount spent to depend on the accident of appeals. The principle of laying by in store as God has blessed us is little observed. We give according to the fervour of the appeal, the obstinacy of the beggar, the fascination of a bazaar, or the social rank of the concert giver. If not so, what mean the advertisements which differ not in style and taste, but only in the object for which money is asked, from the appeals to join a company—appeals of which a French writer said, in speaking of an untruthful man—" he lied—he lied like a prospectus ! " The appeal to unworthy motives is killing out the spirit of charity.

Secondly, we want wise management of charity as an investment. We want not merely to spend the money we have, but to watch where it goes. (In undeserving cases we may do positive harm :

we may pour in vitriol and caustic, instead of oil and wine, into the wounds of the pauper.) . .

The business parallel is pretty exact. A man who knows of a good thing does not invest only in shillings. He puts in all he has saved by wise management.

The *third* thing we want is a business way of doing matters. The Charity Organization Society is only a pioneer. Each parish should have a Charity Board, such as exists under the Vicar of St. Mary's, Marylebone. . . .

The case stands thus. He who " was rich, yet for our sakes became poor that we through His poverty might be rich," found the work, hard work It cost Him thirty-three years' work, and a death for which we have no epithet. The disciple is not above his master : is it likely that we can with ease vicariously relieve the misery of the work ? No ; we must have something of His spirit, work with somewhat of His method. Some thirty years since, the engineers at Dover built a sea-wall ; they built it strong and thick in a line at right angles to the swell. The waves dashed against it, and their force was increased by the resistance it offered. They broke over the softer ground behind, till, the support being washed away, the wall became an easy prey to their violence. Then the engineers, wise by experience, built the wall in a semicircle ; the waves dashed along it, and finding no resistance, were diverted at the end of the wall into the sea, and harmlessly expended themselves on an unresisting medium. Our charity has hitherto lacked this element of thought. It has met evil by opposing money bags to misery. The money-bags have been dissipated, but the misery has not abated.

To meet the misery of man, human thought, human exertion, the lack of which has caused the misery, must be called into activity. The evil thus met will not overpower the agencies created to resist it. It will melt away before the agencies called into existence by the example of our Divine Master.

(b)   *Brooke Lambert*

ALMSGIVING : " I CAN'T AFFORD IT."

Christ may say the same to you when you ask something of Him.

It is said that a certain man dreamed that the Saviour appeared to him and upbraided him with giving so little for His cause.

" The man replied " I can't afford it."

" Very well," said the Saviour ; " let it be so. But do you remember that when that business panic happened, how you prayed to Me to keep you out of difficulties ? And I heard your prayer and tided you over the trouble. And do you remember also, when your little child was sick, How you prayed that her life might be spared, and again I heard your prayer, and restored her.

" But now let it be an understanding between us, that henceforth when you are in trouble—I do nothing for you, seeing you can't afford to help Me."

The man's conscience was touched, and he exclaimed, " Lord take what I have, it is Thine."

(c)

ALMSGIVING, AND ILL-GOTTEN WEALTH

To steal a sheep, and give away the trotters for God's sake.

(d)   *Cervantes (Proverb of)*

ALONE.

I have often said that the universal cause of man's misfortunes, was their not being able to stay quietly in a room . . . But, upon stricter examination I found, that this aversion to home, this restless disposition, proceeded from a cause no less powerful than universal; from the native unhappiness of our frail and mortal state, which is so wretched as to be incapable of all comfort, if we have nothing to divert our thoughts, and are forced to contemplate ourselves.

(a) *Blaise Pascal*

ALONE. "LET HIM ALONE."

God is most angry when He shows no anger. God keep us from this kind of mercy. This kind of mercy is worse than all other kinds of mercy.

(b) *Thomas Brooks*

"ALPHA AND OMEGA, I AM " (Rev. i. 8)

The testimony of Jesus is the spirit of prophecy; accordingly He is preached from Genesis to Revelation as the *Alpha* (the seed of the woman) and *Omega*, the first and the last.

" To Him give all the prophets witness."
He is the beginning of the Church's history, and He pilots it safe to the end.

He is the Author and Finisher of our faith; He has sown the seed, and will reap His harvest. He is not only the A and Z of our faith, but also *all* the intervening letters. Without Him we can do nothing—no life, no growth, no fruit, no perseverance; we absolutely depend on Him.

Observe,
1. The Christian life has its beginning and ending, its Alpha and Omega (A and Z).
(i.) Its beginning is taught: " Born not of blood, . . . but of God."
" Except a man be born again . . . cannot see the kingdom of God."
" Old things passed away, *all* become new."
(ii.) Its close is taught :
" I am ready to be offered up."
" I have kept the faith, . . . fought the fight," etc.
" Forgetting things behind, . . . *I press toward the mark*," etc.
These indicate the *Alpha* and the *Omega* of the life in Jesus.
Caution: The danger here is to mistake the *Beginning* of this life for the end. The child just born into a family has a long life of various *stages* before it, and before the end comes. There are many letters between A and Z.
2. The earlier stages of Christian experience differ from the latter:
Christian life is not a dead level; the road is strait and precipitous; the traveller is " oft in danger, oft in woe."
An oak tree lies hid in an acorn, *in posse*, not *in esse*.
The new born babe is a man, in like manner; but what a wide difference between the beginning and maturity—the child learning its A B C at its mother's knee and the abstruse mathematician or the ripened scholar ! Yet in this wide difference there is a unity and a continuousness, which find analogy in the spirtual life. Stages exist,

though undefined, like the seven stages of man. And Jesus is with us all through; not starting us at A, and meeting us again at Z, but with us, as our life, throughout.
3. Though a life of stages, yet not of fatalism or destiny—so many and no more—but of *continuous developments*. It is a life of faith.
Spiritual life in Christ is a fact, though, like all life, a mystery. And where there is a true beginning the life will ripen and develop unto a proper ending.

(c)

AMBITION

" *Seekest thou great things ?* " (Jer. xlv.)
Ambition is generally proportioned to men's capacities. Providence seldom sends any into the world with an inclination to attempt great things, who have not abilities likewise to perform them.

(d) *Dr. Johnson*

Great offices will have great talents, etc.
(e) *Cowper*

AMBITION (CARELESS OF MEANS)

Napoleon knew distinctly the price which he must pay for the eminence which he coveted. He knew that the path to it lay over wounded and slaughtered millions, over putrifying heaps of his fellow creatures, over ravaged fields, smoking ruins, pillaged cities. He knew that his steps would be followed by the groans of widowed mothers and famished orphans, of bereaved friendship and despairing love; and that, in addition to this amount of misery, he would create an equal amount of crime, by multiplying indefinitely the instruments and participators of his rapine and fraud. . . . His system was a repetition of old means, when the state of the world was new. The sword and the police, which had sufficed him for enslaving France, were not the only powers required for his designs against the human race. Other resources were to be discovered or created; and the genius for calling them forth did not, we conceive, belong to Napoleon.

(f) *Channing*

Napoleon was affectionate, we are told, to his brothers and mother; but his brothers, the moment they ceased to be his tools, were disgraced, and his mother, it is said, was not allowed to sit in the presence of her imperial son. He was sometimes softened, we are told, by the sight of the field of battle strewn with the wounded and dead. But if the Moloch of his ambition claimed new heaps of slain to-morrow, it was never denied.

(g) *Channing*

AMEN AND EPHPHATHA

Ephphatha is not so good a word as *Amen*. . . . It is better to acquiesce in a doctrine than to see it clearly. Better say, " *Be as it is*," than " *Let it be opened* to me."

(h) *R. S. Hawker*

AMEN (BLESSING AND CURSING)

"*Amen*" under the law was answered to the *curses*, but not to the *blessings* (Deut. xxvii. 15-26). Every particular curse must have an Amen. But in the next chapter, where the blessings follow, there is no *Amen* affixed to them (xxviii. 2-1ᵔ). But it is otherwise in the gospel. To the *blessings* there is an *Amen*, but not to the *curses*. *If any man love not the Lord Jesus Christ, let him be anathema*, saith the apostle (1 Cor. xvi. 22); a fearful curse, but there is no *Amen* to that. *Grace be with all them that love the Lord Jesus Christ in sincerity* (Eph. vi. 24), there is an *Amen* to that.

(a)   *N. Rogers*, 1659

AMUSEMENTS

The apostle lays down no rule respecting worldly amusements. He does not say, You must avoid this or that, but he lays down broad principles. People often come to ministers, and ask them to draw a boundary line, within which they may safely walk. There is none. It is at our peril that we attempt to define where God has not defined. . . . We have to live out principles rather than maxims; and the principle here is *Be unworldly*.

(b)   *F. W. Robertson*

ANARCHY

Our fervent desire is social, absolute, and complete levelling. Anarchy is our only formula. Everything for everybody, from government to women. The black flag is hoisted: war against families—war against property—war against God.

(c)   *The Shirtless (Descamisados)*

ANATHEMA, MARANATHA (1 Cor. xvi. 22)

The language of cursing and excommunication, or such as in the imprecatory psalms, is alien to the spirit of Christianity. "Blessing, not cursing," rules now; though their prophetic strains were right, as will be seen in the long run.

The spirit of Christ seen in His rebuke to the disciples who would call down fire, after the manner of Elijah: He came not to destroy but to save men's lives.

Yet St. Paul seems to lapse into an Old Testament spirit: "If any man love not the Lord Jesus Christ, let him be," etc.

Note, however-

1. What he does not say: The Corinthian Christians were not a model Church. Sectarianism rampant; rent with schisms: "I of Paul," etc. Party badges, distinctions, and shibboleths showed their spirit: each struggling for the supremacy and popedom of his own sect, and anathematising all else. St. Paul has no sympathy for this; if a man *loves Christ* it is sufficient for him, though in many respects he be lacking in wisdom and discernment.

We unhappily too much resemble the Corinthians. The rancour of opposing sects and parties proves this.

Hearts however are better than heads: Hence we sing each other's hymns, use prayers in common, worship one God and Father of all, one Saviour, one spirit, and are animated by one hope.

Jew, Gentile, Roman Catholic and Protestant, Churchmen and Dissenters emulate in good works. Our hatreds then are not consistent. Madame Guyon, Fénelon, T. Moore, Baxter, Luther, Calvin, Whitefield, Wesley, John Knox, Chalmers, and that pope who on his death-bed exclaimed, "Call me not *holy father; I am a poor sinner*," were widely separated here, yet lovely and pleasant in their lives, and in death united.

"He that is not against us is on our part," said the Master; St. Paul likewise does not anathematise differences of opinion amongst Christians.

2. What the apostle does say: "If a man *love* not, . . . let *him* be anathema."

The man who sees no beauty in Christ, who has no affectionate love for Him, who cannot say with Peter, "Thou knowest that I *love* Thee "—if such a man continues impenitent, *let him be anathema*.

If there be such a monster among men who counts the blood of Jesus an unholy thing, a common thing, to be trampled under foot, and not sprinkled on his heart, *let him be anathema*.

If there be one among you who accepts not Jesus Christ as God's unspeakable *gift* to a lost world—its Bread of life, and Water of life, without participating in which whosoever liveth is counted dead—*let him, perhaps, be anathema*. So far only does he go; he does not condemn a man for "following not with us." The one crucial point, the point upon which all else turns, is *love*, a *personal* and an *individual love* for Jesus Christ. Here only does the apostle launch into invective and imprecation; here only he excommunicates, and shuts the door of hope. With such a one says St. John, we must not associate, neither eat nor drink with him, nor wish him "God speed," lest we become abettors and partakers with his denial of the Father and the Son.

3. But this is not all: The apostle adds the word *Maranatha, the Lord is coming; i.e.* coming to judge. His it is to take vengeance, not mine. As if he wished to indicate who amongst men—whether Paul or Peter or pope—shall dare to imprecate a solemn curse upon his fellow man, upon one for whom Christ died, be that man worthy or unworthy, heretic, infidel, or atheist? NO ONE. Leave him to be judged by the *one infallible Judge* when He comes: and here the apostle leaves such an extreme instance as this.

See the legend of Abraham (BRETHREN)

(d)

ANDREW, ST. (Matt. iv. 18–22)

The conquest of the world is begun by calling four *fishermen* to begin the task. Their work was typical. Andrew especially anxious for conversions, and is therefore the typical missionary.

Peter and Andrew found "*casting* their nets "; James and John found "*mending* their nets "; and when these become *fishers of men*, we find Peter and Andrew are the *preachers* of the gospel, whilst John especially is the *mender*, the writer and thinker. This is more than accident:= diversities of gifts in the Christian ministry. One has gift of *speech*, another gift of *thought;* one an eloquent tongue to persuade men (as Peter), another the pen of the ready writer to confound the sceptic (as John). The *active* man casts the net, the *contemplative* man mends it.

(e)

In fishing, whether in sea or among men, there is wanted:

1. **A net**: The gospel, "good news," "The old old, story," "God so loved the world," etc. This is the *power* of God unto salvation, and it catches men.

2. **Casting the net**: Andrew did this first when he caught Peter his brother; Peter did this most energetically afterwards with his splendid work of preaching. In doing this Christ directs *where*: "I have much people in *this* city"; we may toil all night *in vain* otherwise.

3. **Dragging the net to land**: After preaching the minister likes to know of his success. No fisherman would like to find his net empty. The so-called "inquiry room," confessional, etc., answers this purpose, for which the Church of England has no special provision. She confines her efforts to *casting* and *mending* the net, *general* rather than particular operations.

4. **Mending the nets**: Nets get broken; they gather of all kinds, bad and good: Simon Magus, Balaams, Gnostics, receive the truth, but afterwards become either heretics or schismatics, etc., unite against it, and so *break* the net. The inside foes are the worst—the dogfish and sharks of the gospel-net. Hence a mender is wanted.

5. **Counting the fish** (see John xxi. 11). They are *named* and *numbered*—153; the number has no significance, but the numbering has. The elect and chosen are many and great. These do not break the nets. These = "Bring with you the fish which you have now caught," and at that final feast the Master and the servant rejoice together.

(*a*)

ANGELS

T. Aquinas composed 358 articles on ANGELS. He treats of their substance, orders, offices, natures, habits, etc., as if he himself had been an old, experienced angel. Angels were not before the world! Angels might have been before the world!

Angels were created by God,—immediately by Him—in the empyrean sky—in grace—in imperfect beatitude. He shows that angels are incorporeal compared to us, but corporeal compared to God. An angel is composed of action and potentiality; the more superior he is, he has the less potentiality. Every angel differs from another in species. An angel is of the same species as a soul. Angels have not a body. They may assume bodies, but this they do for us only.

The bodies assumed by angels are of thick air. An angel may be the same with a body. This body possesses a soul performing natural functions, and the angel operating supernaturally.

Angels administer and govern every corporeal creature.

God, an angel, and the soul, are not contained in space, but contain it. Many angels cannot be in the same space, etc., etc.

(*b*)   *Vide Dis.*: " *Curiosities of Lit* "

ANGELS AND JESUS

No angel during the life of Jesus, ever in His presence spoke to man. It behoved the servants to be silent when the Master stood by.

(*c*)   *R. Stier*

The angelic apparitions at the birth, passion, resurrection, and ascension of the Lord mark these moments as the great epochs in the life of Jesus. For the angelic world does, in general, emerge into view in the grand epochs of the kingdom of God.

Cf. Abraham, Moses, etc.

(*d*)   *Lange*

ANGELS AND MAN

" The entire Old Testament is related to the New as the angels are related to the Son "—a reason for comparing the Son with angels. Note the mediation of angels as a feature of the Old Testament.

Man's superiority to angels lies in his capability of development, the loss of the latter = that of a diamond, once fallen, for ever lost; but fallen man resembles a rose-bush, which sends forth from its root *new life*, and develops new beauties. "Christ in us, the hope of glory," hence the greatness of that glory.

Angels resemble fixed stars revolving round fixed stars. Man resembles a planet dependent upon fixed stars, and yet between the sun and the moon —between an independent and the animal existence.

(*e*)   *Ebrard and Hengstenberg* (?)

ANGELS, MINISTRATION OF

Certainly there are many thousand events wherein common eyes see nothing but nature, which yet are effected by the ministration of angels.

(*f*)   *Bishop Hall*

ANGELS, EVIL

2 Pet. ii. 4 and Jude 6 are important texts bearing on the *present condition* and *future destiny* of *evil angels*, and consequently of those persons whom they influence (Matt. xxv. 4).

1. Some angels sinned, and for penalty were cast out of their *original* habitation.

2. They have been committed in *custody to chains of darkness;* and are *now* kept in them, and endure *some* punishment.

3. They *remain* there to the end of the world, and are *reserved* for the *judgment of the great day*.

This appears also from Matt. viii. 29, Luke viii. 31: "Art Thou come to judge us *before* the *season*" (καιροῦ, of judgment)?

The Lord pre-announces that He will then say unto them on the left hand, " Depart from Me, ye cursed, into everlasting fire, that *hath been prepared* for the devil and his angels." They are therefore *not yet* in it.

Rev. xx. 10 = The casting of the devil into the *lake of fire* has *not* taken place, but is yet *future*.

4. Compare also 1 Pet. v. 8, "*walking about*"; Rev. xx. 7, "loosed "; Eph. ii. 2, "the prince of the power of the air "; 2 Cor. iv. 4, "the god of this world"; and we must conclude that the *chains of darkness*, in which Satan and his angels are now confined, and in which they will be kept *till the day of judgment*, are such as restrain them from ever recovering their place in the *regions of light*; but *not* such as to prevent them from exercising great power over those persons in the lower world who *allow themselves* to be taken captive by them at their will.

(*g*)   *Wordsworth*

ANGELS, MINISTERING (Heb. i. 4)

The ministry of angels entered largely into the life of our Lord, and therefore deserves more than a passing notice. N.B.—At His (1) birth, (2) temptation, (3) passion, (4) resurrection, and (5) ascension.

1. They are numerous

Dan. vii. 10, "Thousands ministered unto Him." Ps. lxxviii. 17, " The chariots of God are twenty thousand."

2 Kings vi. 16, 17, " They with us *more*," etc.

Heb. xii. 22, " To an innumerable company of *angels.*"

Matt. xxvi. 53, " Twelve legions of angels," etc.

2. They are the guardians of the heirs of salvation, as of the Lord Jesus Himself. " The godly are the *protégés* of the angels."

(i.) Of the Lord

Matt. ii. 13, etc., " Flee into Egypt."

xix. 20, " When Herod was dead."

iv. 11, " Angels ministered unto Him."

John i. 51, "Hereafter . . . angels ascending," etc.

Luke xxii. 43, " An angel strengthening Him."

Matt. xxviii. 27, " Not here, He is risen."

Acts i. 10, " Two . . . in white apparel."

(ii.) Of individuals

Matt. xviii. 10, " Their angels do always," etc.

Gen. xxxii. 1, "The angels of God met him." Jacob said, " This is *God's host* " (500 armed men with Esau).

2 Kings vi. 17, "Elisha" (above).

Ps. xxxiv. 7, " The angel of the Lord encampeth," etc.

Acts xii. (7–15), Peter in prison.

(iii.) Of nations and kingdoms

Exod. xiv. 19, " The angel went before the camp."

Exod. xxiii. 20, " I send an angel before thee."

xxxiii. 2, " I will send an angel before thee to drive out," etc.

Num. xx. 16, " When we cried, . . . the Lord sent an angel," etc.

Num. xxii. (22–35), The angel that stood in Balaam's way.

Josh. v. 15, " Art thou for us, or for our adversaries ? "

Isa. lxiii. 9, " The angel of His presence saved them."

3. Active during the captivity to preserve the chosen nation

Dan. x. (5, 13), (20, 21). Daniel talks with angels as we with each other. " Michael *your* prince "=the patron angel of the Jewish nation. Zech. i. (8, 14), iii. (1, 2). The angel talked with the prophet.

We know not how far we are individually indebted to their beneficent ministry, as the agents of a heavenly Father.

They are the ministers of Christ's grace now, hereafter they will be the ministers of His vengeance and judgment.

(*a*)

The pious are *protégés* of heaven, and of the angels.

(*b*)   *Heubner*

The *means* which God employs for the protection and support of the pious in this wicked world are numerous in proportion as He is unfathomable in wisdom, unlimited in power, and inexhaustible in love. Besides the forces, creatures, and instrumentalities which belong to the sphere of *earth* and *human* action, He has equally at command, for the exigencies of even our temporal life, *heavenly and angelic agencie*, and that in unmeasured abundance and untold variety.

(*c*)   *J. Lange*

ANGELS, "EQUAL UNTO THE " (Luke xx. 36)

We wonder indeed, when we are told that one day we shall be as the angels of God. I apprehend that as great a wonder has been realized already on the earth. I apprehend that the distance between the mind of Newton and of a Hottentot may have been as great as between Newton and an angel. There is another view, still more striking. This Newton, who lifted his calm, sublime eye to the heavens, and read among the planets and stars the great law of the material universe, was, forty or fifty years before, an infant, without one clear perception, and unable to distinguish his nurse's arm from the pillow on which he slept. Howard too, who, under the strength of an all-sacrificing benevolence, explored the depths of human suffering, was, forty or fifty years before, an infant wholly absorbed in himself, grasping at all he saw, and almost breaking his little heart with fits of passion when the idlest toy was withheld. Has not man already traversed as wide a space as separates him from angels ?

(*d*)   *Channing*

ANIMAL LIFE

Take a purely instinctive world (animal) at its highest, and you cannot rate it higher than this : it is a mode of existence which has its enjoyments and its drawbacks, its beauties and its blots. But the worst blot, the ugliest drawback of all, is that it fails to image and pursue a life nobler and better than its own. The life of animality contains *in itself* its own beginning and its own end. There is no solemn *preluding* upon heart-strings, which vibrate with undertones of infinite depth ; and oft-times of infinite sweetness. . . . We desire then a world of moral being . . . because a world of stocks and stones, or of animal pleasure and pain, is, in our sense, no world at all.

(*e*)   *W. Jackson (Bampton Lect.)*

ANNIHILATION

Death is now at work, cutting down the barren professor, hewing both bark and heart asunder. The man groans, but Death hears him not. He looks ghastly, *care*-ful, dejectedly. He sighs, he sweats, he trembles. Death matters not ! And now, could the soul be *annihilated*, how happy it would count itself ! But it sees that this must not be. Stay in the body it may not. Go out of the body, it dares not. Life is going ; the blood settles in the flesh, the lungs being no more able to breathe through the nostrils. At last, *out* goes the trem-

(*f*)

bling soul, and is seized by the devils that lay lurking for it in the chamber ! Friends take care of the body, wrap it up in the sheet or coffin; but the soul is out of their reach.

(a) *John Bunyan*

ANTHROPOMORPHISM

Earnest piety at the present day will not dispute that God has eyes and ears, hands and feet, " an arm which is not shortened," and will never cease to seek for His finger in the great events of the world and in the lives of individuals. For although the figurative, the symbolical, is perceived and acknowledged in such descriptions, yet it must be maintained that to all this there must be something in God which really corresponds.

(b) *Martensen*

ANTICHRIST (mystery of iniquity, lawless one, etc.) 2 Thess. ii. 1–12

We should not be exercising that modesty which is the first requisite in a student of prophecy, if we positively asserted the prediction here to point to a person. I know not why it might not be so. I count him presumptuous who scoffs at it. Why should it be a thing incredible with you that the empire of unrule shall at last have a personal head, in whom the final discomfiture by the advent of the great Lord shall manifest itself, so that he who runs may read? But of this I am certain, that the revelation of the " *lawless one* " has not yet received its accomplishment, often as it may have seemed in the course of the world's history to be on the very point of doing so.

Suffer no man, my brethren, to divert the eye of perpetual expectancy from that forward gaze into the great future which is the proper attitude and occupation of the man whose faith and hope are in God. The *lawless one* has not his place or his home in the past, whether pagan, Moham-medan, or papal, if only for this reason, that upon his *revelation* follows, all but instantly, the advent of Jesus Christ; and that advent yet tarries, though we know not, and may not know, for how long.

But the profitable thought is this, that *lawless-ness* is the predicted characteristic of the last age, already working beneath the surface in the days of St. Paul—always working wheresoever is the spirit of the first fall (which indeed was itself actuated by the rebelliousness of the self-will), but as the time of the end draws on, to be stimulated and exasperated into a terrible virulence, as to which I shall turn suddenly and ask this congregation, Is it not now—is it not abroad on the continent of Europe? is it not abroad in one integral portion of what we still term " the United Kingdom "? Is it not abroad amongst ourselves in the family and the Church; in the workshop and in the study; in the literature of a " *science falsely so called* "; and in the lurking-places of political fanatics, who count not their lives dear to them if they can only but embitter an existence or topple down a throne?

Yes; the reign of *lawlessness* is begun, though a few years, or a few tens of years, may yet intervene before the actual unveiling of the *lawless one*.

(c) *Dr. Vaughan.*

ANTINOMIANISM

" Bind him hand and foot " (Matt. xxii. 13)

After the ingathering there must a *scrutiny* of the guests.

1. Bind the man who will not be bound by any law.

Bind him who is not under law to Christ.

Put fetters on him who would put none on him-self = not curb his sinful appetites, though calling himself a Christian.

Bind him, who though not a despiser, nor a mocker, nor a persecutor, nor a murderer, like others mentioned (see), yet is an antinomian. He *will* keep his sins; he will not put off the old man with his deeds, nor *put on* the new man = the wedding garment.

Bind him who useth his liberty as a cloak for sinning.

Bind him, as a *rebel*, and as a presumptuous man.

Bind him; who fears not God = " pass the time of your sojourning here in fear."

2. " Cast him out "—into outer darkness.

Cf. " *without* are dogs "—dogs of uncleanness, etc. (Rev. xxi.) There is an " OUT " and an " IN " —a place for dogs.

It *is* a place of misery and loss :
(i.) *Weeping* = hopeless.
(ii.) *Gnashing teeth* = despair.

3. Two horns of a dilemma : Take heed lest we be hoisted on one or the other :
(i.) Of neglecting and despising the offered gospel = the danger from *without;*
(ii.) Of antinomianism (*within*), to whom it is said, " Depart, ye workers of ἀνομία."

(d)

APOSTASY, Nature of

Those who forsake God to return to the world do it because they find more gratification in earthly pleasures than in those arising from communion with God; and because this overpowering charm, carrying them away, causes them to relinquish their first choice, and renders them, as Tertullian says, the penitents of the devil.

(e) *Blaise Pascal*

APOSTASY

" *Take heed lest there be,*" etc. (Heb. iii. 12)

1. Introduction = (i.) The occasion. (ii.) Two different things, " unbelief in the heart," and " an evil heart of unbelief in *departing*," etc.

2. Cases illustrating
(i.) Negative = *Job, Joseph,* Peter.
(ii.) Positive = *Cain, King Saul,* Nobleman of Israel (2 Kings vi. 7), *Judas Iscariot.*

3. Inquire why (i.) resisted and overcame the temptation to apostasy, and why (ii.) fell under its power.

See Heman's aim (Ps. lxxxviii. all, and 13 specially), also Jeremiah's (Lam. iii. 25), and our Lord's words to Peter, " I have prayed for thee, that thy faith fail not "; " In the hour of trial, Jesus, pray for me."

Therefore we see (i.) were held by a twofold cord, and the others, not having this cord, had no stay in their calamity, but carried away by its onward rush.

(f)

The two strands of the cord = $\begin{cases} \text{(i.) Man saying, "}God\ is\ good.\text{"} \\ \text{(ii.) Christ's intercession, and} \\ \qquad \text{helping hand.} \end{cases}$

4. Practical lessons

= Anchor upon Christ = "sure and steadfast"; no stay for a tempted man in life, or in death, apart from Christ. Intoxication, suicide, etc., are the rocks on which unstable souls may make shipwreck.

Cf. J. Owen, quoting Bacon = O. T. examples are N. T. doctrines. "They that know Thy name will put their trust in Thee,"—others not.

Apostasy is especially the sin warned against in Ep. to Heb.

(a)

APOSTASY

"For it is impossible," etc. (Heb. vi. 4)

If this and like passages in Hebrews *do* teach the possibility of falling from grace, they teach in like manner the impossibility of restoration to it. The saint who has once apostatized *has apostatized for ever*. Meantime, the case is only put hypothetically. There is not, so far as I am aware, a distinct declaration that such a falling away does actually occur; but only a declaration, if it should occur, what, in the nature of the case, must be the inevitable consequence. And I cannot forbear adding, that in my judgment the tenour of many passages of the New Testament is decidedly against the *actual possibility* of such apostasy, and that the admission of the doctrine would revolutionize the whole orthodox conception of the New Testament system of salvation.

(b)　　　　　　　　　*A. C. Kendrick (Lange)*

APOSTASY, SIN OF

The essence of righteousness (according to the Epistle to the Hebrews) consists in faith; there is therefore but one sin pre-eminently designated as sin simply, and that is a falling from faith (xii. 4; iii. 13). Even the first generation of the covenant people did not obtain the promise on account of their sin (iii. 16, 17), and this sin was their disobedience to the Divine requirement of faith (18), *i.e.* unbelief. Thus the cowardly shrinking from faith is now (x. 38, 39) a despising of God speaking from heaven (xii. 25); it is a falling away from the living God (iii. 12), and even a fornication in the sense of the Old Testament (xii. 16), inasmuch as one prefers the promise of the world to His service, and the service of His promise. But the falling of such as have gotten the knowledge of salvation in Christ (x. 26), and have experienced all His blessings (vi. 4-6), is therewith characterised as a sin, which is yet more terrible than that of frivolous disobedience, for which, under the old covenant, death was assigned (x. 28); it is a daring sin, a wilful sinning against better knowledge and conscience, for which there is no more sacrifice, but only the avenging judgment over the enemies of God (26, 27). There is therefore even in the new covenant, as in the old, a malignant sin for which its atoning institute is not available, and which can hence never be forgiven, like the sin against the Holy Ghost, of which Jesus speaks, because he who commits it *can* no more be renewed to repentance (iv. 4-6) as even Esau found no more room for repentance (xii. 17).

(c)　　　　　　　　　*Weiss, on Ep. to Heb*

APOSTLES' CREED.

The Apostles' Creed is the only document of the kind that ever served the purpose of unity, and this because "it is an avowal of belief in simple facts, and makes not the slightest effort to philosophise or refine."

(d)　　　　　　　　　*Dr. Lyman Abbott*

APOSTOLIC PERIODS

The three successive =

(i.) The Petrine. (ii.) The Pauline. (iii.) The Johannean.

John has the promise that he shall not die, but live till the Lord come, and doubtless come forth in some special way toward the end of the days, before the coming of the Lord.

(e)　　　　　　　　　*Cf. Schelling*

APPEARANCES of our Lord after His resurrection (1 Cor. xv. 3-8)

St. Paul enumerates six, in reality there were ten (see gospels).

1. The first three appearances have a peculiar beauty. Jesus reappears to downcast hearts to comfort and reanimate them.

(i.) To **Mary Magdalene.** In xx. (11-18) full of comfort to the disconsolate Mary—significant recognition: "He calleth His own by name"; "My sheep hear My voice."

(ii.) **To Peter**—the fallen disciple—bitterly repenting—"He ran to the sepulchre" (Luke xxiv. 12 and 34). Jesus first sends him a special message, lest Peter despair. "Go, tell . . . Peter." Then a private interview, and Peter is reinstated. Full of comfort to the backslider.

(iii.) The **two disciples** journeying to Emmaus (Luke xxiv.). Not two of the twelve. They "walk and are sad"; faith gone. "We trusted," etc.; Jesus draws them out, then instructs them. This is how Jesus reanimates drooping faith: He sends us to the Scriptures. See how to search the Scriptures, "beginning at Moses," etc.

2. The next three appearances are to His "witnesses."

(i.) To the ten apostles, Thomas absent (Luke xxiv. 36-46). To establish their faith in His resurrection: proofs given of a real *body*—"Handle Me,"—"hands and feet,"—"He ate with them." These the future preachers of Christ—*witnesses of these things.*"

(ii.) This repeated eight days later, Thomas being present (John xx. 26, 27).

(iii.) **At Sea of Tiberias** (John xxi. 1-6). He directs where the "*fishers*" are to throw the nets —so afterwards "they catch men."

3. The third set of appearances = **missionary:** the present work of the Church.

(i.) Matt. xxviii. (16-20). To the eleven apostles + 500 mentioned here = 500 torches alight in the dark world.

"All power," etc. Therefore, "go ye," etc. = their mission work would not fail, nor be unfruitful, for two reasons. Because

(1) He is at the seat of *power*, directing all things.

(2) He would be with them *always*, even to the end.

(f)

This is our hope now, as it was theirs then, otherwise *our preaching is in vain.*

(ii.) To **James** (probably the Lord's brother): "His brethren did not believe in Him," but after His resurrection Jesus appeared especially to James, who was then numbered with the apostles. James appears to have tarried in Jerusalem—Paul speaks of him as a *pillar*—afterwards he was the first bishop in Jerusalem, and eventually killed with the sword by Herod.

N.B.—Mission work is twofold:

(i.) To the *Jew first = James.*

(ii.) To the nations = *apostles.*

4. The concluding appearances were of a *special* nature:—

(i.) (Luke xxiv. 49). "Then of all the apostles." To wait for the promise of the Father. Not to hurry. Their witness useless without the Holy Ghost; at that time Jesus bids farewell also, and gives parting instructions.

(ii.) Lastly, to **St. Paul:** a chosen vessel for a definite work; a rebuke to those who think any-one will do, irrespective of gifts and qualifications.

(a) *Adapted from Godet, Maclear, etc.*

ARISTOCRACY, THE TRUE

Every government ought to be a true "aristocracy"; that is to say, a "government of the best"—of those who are best fitted to rule and to command the obedience of their fellow men. The highest state of human society is that in which leadership is not despotic or compulsory, but rests on the allegiance of conviction, and in which obedience is not mechanical or slavish, but free and loyal. But in any case there must always be certain powers which give leadership in human society. Let us consider, as a matter of fact, what these powers are. There is one power which belongs to rank, whether it be hereditary or official. No one who has studied history can have failed to see that the influence of rank has played a most important part in history, and must have some reality of strength. Yet no one who looks at the condition of England at the present day will doubt that the power of rank is diminished. Whether this be for evil or for good I do not now inquire; I am concerned only with the fact that this power of leadership is fading away in England, although less in England than in many other countries. Then there is another power—the power of money: money being a kind of dormant, concentrated power—not gold as mere gold, but gold for what it will buy; and this undoubtedly in England at the present time not merely maintains its influence, but, I fear, partly from the decay of rank and conventional distinctions, partly from other causes, is daily and rapidly increasing it. But, besides this aristocracy of rank and this aristocracy of wealth, there is a third aristocracy, which men call aristocracy of intellect; but as I believe the power of character to be far greater than the power of mere intellect, I will call it the aristocracy of mind, meaning by this the aristocracy of both intellect and character. Now it is in the dominion of this third element that the power of education is felt. I believe it to be increasing every day; and most desirable it is that it should increase, partly because it is good in itself, and partly because it tempers that which is the vulgarest of all aristocracies—the aristocracy of wealth.

(b) *Bishop Barry (Sydney)*

ARISTOCRACY AND MONEY

In the higher ranks a difference of income implies none in education or manners, and the poor "gentleman" is a fit companion for dukes or princes,—thanks to the old usages of Norman chivalry, which after all were a democratic protest against the sovereignty, if not of rank, at least of money. The knight, however penniless, was the prince's equal, even his superior, from whose hands he must receive knighthood. . . . But in the commercial classes money most truly and fearfully "makes the man."

(c) *Chas. Kingsley*

ARK

Some forty years ago, an American bishop preached in the parish church of Leeds these most impressive words: "Brethren, it is written in the older records of our faith that, when the ark of God was on its progress to the hill of Sion, it rested once for three months in the house of Obed-edom. And it was told King David, saying, 'The Lord hath blessed the house of Obed-edom, and all that pertaineth unto him, because of the ark of God.' And, as I have gone from scene to scene, of highest interest and rarest beauty, in this the most favoured land of all the world—contemplated its arts, its industry, its wealth, enjoyed its comforts and refinements, and shared with a full heart the peace and happiness of its dear Christian homes; as I have thought of its attainments in science and in letters; as I have recounted its feats of arms and fields of victory; as I have followed through every ocean and through every sea its cross-emblazoned flag, and seen that on the circuit of its empire the sun never sets: I have asked myself instinctively, whence, to so small a speck on the world's map, a sea-beleaguered island, sterile in soil and stern in climate, Britain, cut off in ancient judgment from the world, such wealth, such glory, and such power? And the answer has come spontaneous to my heart, 'The Lord hath blessed the house of Obed-edom, and all that pertaineth unto him because of the ark of God.' Yes; from my heart I say the strength of England is in the Church. Your wealth, your glory, and your power is but God's blessing upon your kingdom, as the home and shelter of His ark."

(d) *S. R. Hole*

"ARM OF THE LORD" (Isa. liii. 1)

This day two persons obtained relief and comfort, which appeared solid, rational, and scriptural. . . . I inquired what they wanted God to do more for them? They replied, "They wanted that Christ should wipe their hearts quite clean." I can say no less of this day, and no more than that "the arm of the Lord" was powerfully revealed." . . . The power of God seemed to descend upon the assembly "like a rushing mighty wind," and with an astonishing energy bore down all before it. . . . I stood amazed at the influence which seized the audience almost universally. . . . Persons of all ages were bowed down with concern, and scarcely one was able to withstand this surprising operation. . . . Stubborn hearts were now obliged to bow. . . . I

(e)

hearkened to the prayer of one, and perceived it to be, "Have mercy on me, and help me to give Thee my heart." . . . There was indeed a very "great mourning" among them, and yet every one seemed to "mourn apart," as if none had been near. "*Have mercy upon me*," was the common cry. . . . God's manner of working upon them appeared so entirely supernatural and above means, that I could scarcely believe He used me as an instrument, or what I spake as means of carrying on His work; for it seemed, as I thought, to have no connection with nor dependence upon means in any respect. And though I could not but continue to use the means I thought proper for the promotion of the work, yet God appeared to work entirely without them; so that I seemed to do nothing, and indeed to have nothing to do, but to stand still and see the salvation of God. . . .

(Again.) It was a season of great power among them; it seemed as if God had "bowed the heavens, and come down." So astonishingly prevalent was the operation upon old and young, that it seemed as if none could be left in a state of carnal security, but that God was now about to convert the world. And I was ready to think then that I should never again despair of the conversion of any man or woman living, be they who or what they would.

(*a*)   *David Brainerd*

ARMOUR, THE WHOLE, OF GOD (Eph. vi. 10–20)

But now, in this Valley of Humiliation, poor Christian was hard put to it; for he had gone but a little way before he espied a foul fiend coming over the field to meet him; his name Apollyon. Then did Christian begin to be afraid, and to cast in his mind whether to go back or to stand his ground. But he considered again that he had no armour for his back, and therefore thought that to turn the back to him might give him greater advantage with ease to pierce him with his darts: therefore he resolved to venture, and stand his ground; for, thought he, had I no more in my eye than the saving of my life, it would be the best way to stand.

So he went on, and Apollyon met him. Now the monster was hideous to behold: he was clothed with scales like a fish, and they are his pride; he had wings like a dragon, feet like a bear, and out of his belly came fire and smoke, and his mouth was as the mouth of a lion. When he was come up to Christian, he beheld him with a disdainful countenance, and thus began to question with him.

Apol. Whence come you? and whither are you bound?

Chr. I am come from the City of Destruction, which is the place of all evil, and am going to the City of Zion.

Apol. By this I perceive that thou art one of my subjects; for all that country is mine, and I am the prince and god of it. How is it then that thou hast run away from thy king? Were it not that I hope that thou mayest do me more service, I would strike thee now at one blow to the ground.

Chr. I was indeed born in your dominions, but your service was hard, and your wages such as a man could not live on; for the wages of sin is death (Rom. vi. 23); therefore, when I was come

to years, I did, as other considerate persons do, look out if perhaps I might mend myself.

Apol. There is no prince that will thus lightly lose his subjects, neither will I as yet lose thee; but since thou complainest of thy service and wages, be content to go back; and what our country will afford, I do here promise to give thee.

Chr. But I have let myself to another, even to the King of princes; and how can I with fairness go back with thee?

Apol. Thou hast done in this according to the proverb "changed a bad for a worse": but it is ordinary for those who have professed themselves His servants, after a while to give Him the slip, and return again to me. Do thou so too, and all shall be well.

Chr. I have given Him my faith, and sworn my allegiance to Him; how then can I go back from this, and not be hanged for a traitor?

Apol. Thou didst the same by me, and yet I am willing to pass by all, if now thou wilt yet turn and go back.

Chr. What I promised thee was in my nonage; and, besides, I count that the Prince under whose banner I now stand is able to absolve me; yea, and to pardon also what I did as to my compliance with thee. And, besides, O thou destroying Apollyon! to speak truth, I like His service, His wages, His servants, His government, His company and country, better than thine; therefore leave off to persuade me further: I am His servant, and I will follow Him.

Apol. Consider again, when thou art in cool blood, what thou art like to meet with in the way that thou goest. Thou knowest that, for the most part, His servants come to an ill end, because they are transgressors against me and my ways. How many of them have been put to shameful deaths! And besides, thou countest His service better than mine; whereas, He never came yet from the place where He is to deliver any that served Him out of their hands: but as for me, how many times, as all the world very well know, have I delivered, either by power or fraud, those that have faithfully served me, from Him and His, though taken by them! And so will I deliver thee.

Chr. His forbearing at present to deliver them is on purpose to try their love, whether they will cleave to Him to the end; and as for the ill end thou sayest they come to, that is most glorious in their account; for, for present deliverance, they do not much expect it; for they stay for their glory, and then they shall have it when their Prince comes in His, and the glory of the angels.

Apol. Thou hast already been unfaithful in thy service to Him; and how dost thou think to receive wages of Him?

Chr. Wherein, O Apollyon, have I been unfaithful to Him?

Apol. Thou didst faint at first setting out, when thou wast almost choked in the Gulf of Despond. Thou didst attempt wrong ways to be rid of thy burden, whereas thou shouldest have stayed until thy Prince had taken it off. Thou didst sinfully sleep, and lose thy choice thing. Thou wast almost persuaded to go back at the sight of the lions. And when thou talkest of thy journey, and of what thou hast seen and heard, thou art inwardly desirous of vain-glory in all that thou sayest or doest.

Chr. All this is true, and much more which thou hast left out; but the Prince whom I serve

(*b*)

and honour is merciful, and ready to forgive. But besides, these infirmities possessed me in thy country, for there I sucked them in; and I have groaned under them, being sorry for them, and have obtained pardon of my Prince.

Apol. Then Apollyon broke out into a grievous rage, saying, I am an enemy to this Prince; I hate His Person, laws, and people: I am come out on purpose to withstand thee.

Chr. Apollyon, beware what you do, for I am in the King's highway, the way of holiness; therefore take heed to yourself.

Apol. Then Apollyon straddled quite over the whole breadth of the way, and said: I am void of fear in this matter. Prepare thyself to die; for I swear by my infernal den that thou shalt go no farther: here will I spill thy soul. And with that he threw a flaming dart at his breast; but Christian had a shield in his hand, with which he caught it, and so prevented the danger of that.

Then did Christian draw, for he saw it was time to bestir himself; and Apollyon as fast made at him, throwing darts as thick as hail, by the which, notwithstanding all that Christian could do to avoid it, Apollyon wounded him in his head, his hand, and foot. This made Christian give a little back: Apollyon therefore followed his work a-main, and Christian again took courage, and resisted as manfully as he could. This sore combat lasted for above half a day, even till Christian was almost quite spent; for you must know that Christian, by reason of his wounds, must needs grow weaker and weaker.

Then Apollyon, espying his opportunity, began to gather up close to Christian, and, wrestling with him, gave him a dreadful fall; and with that Christian's sword flew out of his hand. Then said Apollyon, I am sure of thee now. And with that he had almost pressed him to death, so that Christian began to despair of life. But, as God would have it, while Apollyon was fetching his last blow, thereby to make a full end of this good man, Christian nimbly reached out his hand for his sword, and caught it, saying, Rejoice not against me, O mine enemy! when I fall, I shall arise (Mic. vii. 8); and with that gave him a deadly thrust, which made him give back, as one that had received his mortal wound. Christian, perceiving that, made at him again, saying, Nay, in all these things we are more than conquerors through Him that loved us (Rom. viii. 37-39). And with that (Jas. iv. 7) Apollyon spread forth his wings, and sped him away, so that Christian saw him no more.

In this combat no man can imagine, unless he had seen and heard, as I did, what yelling and hideous roaring Apollyon made all the time of the fight—he spake like a dragon; and on the other side, what sighs and groans burst forth from Christian's heart! I never saw him all the while give so much as one pleasant look, till he perceived that he had wounded Apollyon with his two-edged sword; and then, indeed, he did smile, and looked upward! But it was the dreadfullest sight that ever I saw.

So when the battle was over, Christian said, I will here give thanks to Him that hath delivered me out of the mouth of the lion, to Him that did help me against Apollyon. And so he did. . . . Then there came to him a hand, with some of the leaves of the tree of life, which Christian took and applied to his wounds that he had received in the battle, and was healed immediately.

He also sat down in that place to eat bread, and to drink of the bottle that was given him a little before: so, being refreshed, he addressed himself to his journey with his sword drawn in his hand; for he said, I know not but some other enemy may be at hand. But he met with no other affront from Apollyon quite through this valley.

Bunyan (Christian's Fight with Apollyon in the Valley of Humiliation). See "PANOPLY."

(a)

ASCENSION (Nature of). John xx. 17

The ascension of Christ = a change of state from earthly to heavenly [so heaven].

Progressive during the forty days—a gradual becoming "*invisible.*"

Final, when *the cloud received Him out of sight.*
Present, though *invisible.*

Expedient, because before only *locally* present, now as *spirit* = omnipresent.

These thoughts help in the interpretation of the text: wherein notice

1. The Rebuke: "Touch Me not, for I am not yet ascended" = "*Hold Me not*"—*Retain* Me not, or "*Retard* Me not."

Mary wished to retain our Lord, as she had known and seen Him—*bodily* and *visibly present with her.*

The rebuke =

There is a higher goal both for you and Me

"*I ascend unto My Father*" = I become now a spiritual being = I ascend to a higher state of being—throned! highly exalted! = crowned with many *crowns.*

Whilst as for you,

You are henceforth "*to live by faith, not by sight*" = a higher state of religion. "Blessed are they who have not seen, yet have believed." "He that cometh to God must believe *that He IS,*" though unseen.

But this is not all that the rebuke aims at. It is aimed at a

Religion of personal feeling wholly absorbed in self.

(i.) The contemplative *hermit* or *recluse,* spending his time in being wholly absorbed in holy meditation on *death* and *eternity,* and abstracted from the world, is *rebuked.*

(ii.) That "*adoring,*" "*seraphic*" state of ecstatic love of the Saviour, and of angelic beings, as seen in the pictures of mediæval saints, etc., is *rebuked* as (not wrong) incomplete.

(iii.) That almost unceasing occupation in religious services, holy rites and ceremonies, common now amongst us, as the highest acts of religion, is I think, *rebuked* in these words, "*Touch Me not.*" It is not the best and highest part of religion.

2. The Commission: "*Go and tell My brethren*" = activity = the best cure for these feelings, "*Go and do something for Me.*"

Religion, above all things, must be *practical.*

(i.) *Now,* in the form of stirring words:

(*a*) Go and tell My brethren that I am *risen,* and going to My *Father*—to glory—to be crowned.

Go and make proclamation of the good tidings that I have *conquered death,* and that they shall follow Me.

(*b*) Go into all the world and preach Christ.

(*c*) Go into highways and hedges, and save lost souls. "Compel them to come *in.*"

(*b*)

(ii.) *Anon* it is the time for practice:

Go, and do a Christlike deed.

Go, and feed the hungry and thirsty.

Go, and clothe the naked.

Go, and visit the sick, the fatherless, and widows in their affliction.

Go, and keep yourself unspotted from the world.

For such is pure and undefiled religion.

To such at the last is the welcome given,

" *Come, ye blessed of My Father*, etc.

There is work to be done.

Stand not all the day (of your short life) IDLE; say not, " *No man hath hired us :* but go and work for Christ. Soon the day will be ended, and the night cometh wherein no man can work.

3. The Message: "Go: . . . . I ascend to My Father and your Father, . . . My God and your God."

(i.) Go, and tell them *this* as the *very best news you can carry to them*, that My Father is their Father and My God their God.

(ii.) Go and tell them that through My death a NEW RELATIONSHIP has come about between them and God—that God is not simply the *Almighty God*, but their *Heavenly Father*.

(*a*)

ASCENSION OF CHRIST, THE   (Acts i. 2.)

So long as a lamp in a room is placed on a low level, its light may be intercepted by the bodies of persons around it, and so prevented from reaching others who are in the remoter corners. But let it be lifted up to the ceiling, and it sheds its beams down on all who are below. Our Lord, while on earth, was circumscribed by place and by earthly relationships ; but now since His ascension, His presence and influence are diffused abroad everywhere through the spiritual world as the rays of the sun are through the natural.

(*b*)   *H. Goulburn*

The foremost place is here assigned to the history of the ascension to heaven, in order that we may continually remember that all that occurred in the visible world and that is related in this book originates in the invisible world, whither the Lord Jesus is for us entered (Heb. vi. 20).

(*c*)   *C. H. Rieger*

ASCENSION OF CHRIST, THE   (Acts i. 9.)

The ascension of Christ as bearing on our ascension :

1. God's design in regard to us is that we should be :-

(i.) Believers; (ii.) holy; (iii.) a family of children like *one* perfected One (Rom. viii. 22–29).

2. This design is *realized* in our *salvation*, in two parts, or acts :

(i.) All is done in *one* Person, *first of all*, as the *Head* (Eph. ii. 6, i. 10; Heb. ii. 10).

(ii.) By *uniting* all believers with that one Person (Christ), as the *body*. (Cf. woman taken out of man ; " He made them a male and a female.")

Till then He and we are *units*.

3. This work of *assimilation* is done

(i.) By Pentecost = new birth = a moral change.

(ii.) By the second coming of Christ = an exter-

---

nal change: " He will come in like manner"; " We shall be caught up," etc.

This will be our *ascension, perfection*, and *glory*.

(*d*)   *Godet*

ASCETICISM

Our Christianity does not lead one to hide himself in deserts and convents, and thus to remain blameless, but in the midst of the perverted, degenerate world to guard himself from sin.

(*e*)   *Starke*

ASK

" *In that day . . . nothing* " (John xvi. 23).

Ye shall in that day ask—inquire of—Me nothing. That is, their immature disciplehood and pupilage—that condition in which they were continually becoming astonished or startled at something, and were consequently led into many questionings (xiv., xvi. 17), failing however to put the true and decisive question (xvi. 5)—shall come to an end, and be replaced by the higher condition of enlightenment. The condition of enlightenment is a condition of ever-living revelation—revelation suited to all the true needs of the intellectual spirit (1 John ii. 20).

(*f*)   *Lange*

ASSURANCE   (John xiii. 31–38)

The Divine assurance of Christ in view of the treason of Judas and the denial of Peter, an assurance of the absolute victory of Divine Providence over all the contradictions of evil ; of the triumph of truth and righteousness over wickedness ; of the triumph of love and grace over needy sinners.

(*g*)   *Lange*

ASSURANCE

" These things have I written unto you that believe in the name of the Son of God ; that ye may *know* that ye have eternal life, and that ye may believe on the name of the Son of God " (1 John v. 13).

That the believer is a *saved sinner* is clear and certain.

That such a one is already and really saved by *union* with Christ.

That he has, not a future only but a *present* interest in all the mercies and blessings of the covenant of peace will not, I presume, be for an instant called in question.

For this truth is written, as with a pen of light: " He that believeth on the Son of God *hath* everlasting life."

" There is therefore now no condemnation to them which are in Christ Jesus, who walk not after the flesh, but after the Spirit."

But it is one thing *to be saved*, and another thing to *know* it.

To have a claim, an indisputable claim, to eternal life, and to KNOW that claim are two distinct things.

The first in the case of the Christian is never doubted, but the latter is seldom grasped, and often doubted. But undoubtedly a clear understanding of both points is needful to our spiritual comfort and stability.

We will briefly consider the doctrine of assur-

(*h*)

ance, as (1) one *contained in the Gospel;* and (2) as a Christian's *privilege,* but not *necessary for his salvation.*

1. The Doctrine contained in the Gospel

Many think it a doctrine not contained there; others that it is a presumptuous doctrine, one which cannot possibly be found in the word of God.

Indications of it, glimpses of it, hopes of such a doctrine there may be possibly. But to expect more, to see more, to teach more, is looked upon by many as a *self-delusion.*

Now we turn *away* from the opinions of our fellow men, and we turn *to* the "law and the testimony," to find what it says; for I take it we shall all regard the word of God as authoritative and final upon a matter of doctrine.

We are in this position: we are told by many that the doctrine of assurance is a presumptuous doctrine, and not to be found either *directly* or *indirectly* in the word of God. Now WE are anxious to have the best authority upon it; and we are engaged on the present occasion in "searching the Scriptures" to ascertain the mind of the Spirit on this subject, to find, if possible, whether we have any warrant for believing and teaching this doctrine. And the search may be split up into three sections.

(i.) We shall *search* for *direct statements* of the doctrine.

(ii.) We will endeavour to ascertain whether the teaching of Scripture *requires it.*

(iii.) Whether the experiences of the saints recorded in Scripture give any indications of it.

(i.) As to direct statements. I point you first of all to our text, and indeed to the whole epistle. It is the epistle of *assurance.*

The apostle's design in writing it is, he tells us,— "That ye may *know* that ye have eternal life."

He is writing to believers, and through them to us, that we may individually KNOW ourselves to be saved.

Not *hope* it is so—not to rest it upon a *peradventure;* but he writes that we may be altogether persuaded, and assured of the matter.

And we may well believe that St. John would not teach perilous or presumptuous doctrine.

This one passage then, were there no others, would establish the doctrine.

But there are many others.

God promises "to show (His people) His covenant," to "manifest Himself to them," nay, to "take up His abode with them."

Now we ask ourselves (for we are anxious inquirers after the truth),—

How can God "show His people His covenant," or, "manifest Himself to them," or "take up His abode with them," and they not *know,* or be *conscious* of it? *Who can suppose it?*

It was because St. Paul *knew it* himself that he exhorts us to

"*Draw near unto God in full assurance of faith,*" and "*not to cast away our confidence, which hath great recompense of reward.*"

Or what was David's prayer?

"Remember me, O Lord, with the favour which thou bearest unto Thy people. Oh visit me with Thy salvation; that I may *see* the good of Thy chosen, that I may rejoice in the gladness of Thy nation, that I may glory with Thine inheritance."

Is not this a prayer for the *personal* assurance of the love of God?

But he goes further still, wrestling in prayer; and with a panting soul he exclaims—

"SAY *unto my soul, I am thy salvation*"; and when we discover this, we have to pause at the first stage of our inquiry, and ask whether this was *daring presumption,* or a *self-delusion,* or *fanatical enthusiasm on David's part?* or, whether on the other hand, it was not the groaning of the Spirit helping our infirmities, making intercession according to the will of God? *Which was it? It was one or the other.*

(ii.) We find Scripture REQUIRES this doctrine: because such demands are made upon the faithful as none but the *assured* believer could yield to—

For instance, the believer is bidden to "rejoice in the Lord always, and again I say rejoice."

The reiteration of the language shows the importance of spiritual joy, and the nature of that is shown from the words "*in the Lord.*"

Now we ask, Can the doubting, and the feeble, and the wavering Christian obey this injunction? *Can he rejoice at all,* much less *habitually?*

Can the awakened and trembling sinner rejoice, standing between light and darkness, trembling in his sin, because he knows nothing of forgiveness and pardon—conscious of his pollution, but not of the blood of cleansing; of his danger, but not of deliverance; of his ruin, but not of refuge and escape—can such a one rejoice?

Can the guilty and sentenced criminal rejoice? Must he not first know of the remission of his sentence, and see the royal signature affixed to the deed of his acquittal.

It were mockery to tell a man in such a condition to "rejoice," or to be *glad in the Lord* whilst oppressed by a load of doubts and misgivings and unpardoned sin; and yet Scripture does exhort us to "*rejoice in the Lord,*" "*to rejoice evermore.*" "Rejoice in the Lord, ye righteous, and sing for joy, all ye that are upright in heart"; and we pause again to ask whether such injunctions do not imply the doctrine of assurance, nay, whether their very nature does not REQUIRE it? for of none but those assured of their salvation can the "*joy be full.*"

(iii.) Experiences of saints

St. John, the beloved disciple, thus speaks: "That which was from the beginning, which we have heard, which we have seen with our eyes, and which we have looked upon, and our hands have handled of the word of life, declare we unto you, that ye also may have fellowship with us: *and truly our fellowship is with the Father and with His Son Jesus Christ.*" And all through this beautiful and touching epistle he writes in the same strain: as one who considered his salvation a certainty; as if a doubt of his personal interest in Jesus Christ had not entered his mind, since the time he had first found Him and followed Him." "*We* KNOW," is his favourite expression.

"We *know* that we have passed from death unto life."

"We *know* that we dwell in Him, and He in us." And he closes this letter of assurance as he began it by reiterating his confidence:—

"And we *know* that the Son of God is come, and hath given us an understanding that we may know Him that is true; *and we are in Him that is true,* even in His Son Jesus Christ. This is the true God, and eternal life.

Again, St. Peter says—and this, be it remem-

(a)

bered, is his experience and teaching after his grievous fall; mark his sense of *personal safety* even then,

"Blessed be the God and Father of our Lord Jesus Christ, which, according to His abundant mercy, hath begotten us again unto a lively hope by the resurrection of Jesus Christ from the dead; to an inheritance *incorruptible, and undefiled, and that fadeth not away*."

And he speaks of the assurance of others in a similar way:

"Whom having not seen, ye love, in whom though *now ye see Him not, yet believing, ye rejoice with joy unspeakable and full of glory*; RECEIVING the end of your faith, even the salvation of your souls."

Once more, what is the constant frame of St. Paul's mind?

It is expressed in few words:

"I know whom I have believed; and am persuaded that He is able to keep that which I have committed unto Him until that day." And in the hour of peril, temptation, and suffering he says:—"The Lord shall deliver me from every evil work, and WILL *preserve me* unto His heavenly kingdom."

The prospect of death does not shake His convictions:

"If our earthly house of this tabernacle were dissolved, we have a building of God, a house not made with hands, eternal in the heavens."

The hour of his departure draws nigh, but his assurance brightens.

"I have fought the good fight, I have finished my course, I have kept the faith: henceforth *there* is *laid up for me* a crown of righteousness, which the Lord the righteous Judge shall give me at that day."

And here we end our threefold search of the Scriptures concerning the doctrine of *assurance*.

It *is* there: *in direct statements*, in *Scriptural requirement;* and it IS shown us in *the experiences of the saints*.

2. Let us, if we feel we are strangers to this privilege—for such it is, and such only, for it is nowhere taught as necessary to our salvation; it is not said, "Be *assured, and be saved*," but, "*Believe, and be saved*,"—let us, if we have not the comfort, give the Saviour no rest unless we can say of Him HE IS BECOME MY SALVATION.

(a)   *Patterson*

ASSURANCE

"*The Spirit beareth witness* . . . *children of God*."—Rom. viii. 16.

There is no wonder that any setting forth of this doctrine is received with incredulity, because it is a doctrine taught of the Spirit; and vagueness and uncertainty will ever remain for those who can say, "We have not so much as heard whether there be any Holy Ghost."

The appeal in the text is not to outward facts, but to an inward experience. The Spirit witnesseth not *to*, but *with* our spirit, etc.

But of course there must be the concurrent testimony of the life.

Note.—There is a wide difference between the agitated feelings of early discipleship and those of maturity, similar to that between convalescence and perfectly restored physical health.

Reasons for expecting to find the doctrine of assurance in the Bible.

1. From the nature of the scheme of redemption:

All is done by Christ. "Ye are complete in Him."

"The blood of Jesus Christ cleanseth from all sin."

Were it otherwise assurance would be impossible; but being so, it is conceivable that the Holy Spirit (the Comforter) should make this known at the outset.

Yet if this be considered unlikely, we are justified in expecting that, at some period along the line of our spiritual history, the light should become brighter.

2. We expect to find it because it is consistent with the fatherly love of God towards us.

It is almost inconceivable that God should withhold the manifestation of Himself as *Father*; and yet if assurance is rare, this too is rare. It is necessary for Christian comfort that we should know that our sin is forgiven—whether a child or a reprobate.

Confirmation of the assurance:

"Thy sins be forgiven thee";

"Go in peace";

"Thy faith hath saved thee."

Are we, under the Spirit less favoured? Jesus said, "It is *expedient* for you that I go away," etc. The third revelation of God is the most perfect.

3. We expect to find it, on account of the nature of the Holy Spirit. He makes His presence felt. There is mystery, yet reality in it: "The wind bloweth . . . sometimes gently, sometimes as a hurricane; we hear, and see, and know its effects."

(b)

ASSURANCE. (1 Thess. i. 3–5)

1. "*Your work of faith*";
2. " . . . *labour of love*"; and
3. "*patience of hope*,"

were the fruit of *your* *election of God*. Because the gospel came to the Thessalonians in,

1. "*Power*";
2. "*Holy Ghost*"; and in
3. "*Much assurance.*"

Compare each pair:
1, 1. *Power to believe;*
2, 2. *Holy Spirit* = sonship—therefore labour of *love;*
3, 3. *Much assurance*—qualified for *endurance* unto the end, knowing that their *hope* was not delusive.

(c)

ASSURANCE AND PEACE

There is a great difference between peace and assurance. The former may be be obtained by the sincere search of truth; the latter only by truth itself.

(d)   *Blaise Pascal*

ATHANASIAN CREED

It is well to see what is intended by this clear, simple, logical formula of the fundamental principles of our faith. As in legal documents it is customary to adopt a phraseology that shall insure them from misrepresentation and fraud, so in this creed the undercurrent throughout is the Divine nature of our Lord, which even in the apostles' days had been denied.

(e)   *G. Calthrop*

ATHEISM

Ἄθεος, *without God* (Eph. ii. 12).
The essence of heathenism is atheism. (Rom.
i. 21, etc.).

(*a*) *Lange*

ATHEISM

How did the atheist get his idea of that God
whom he denies.

(*b*) *S. T. Coleridge*

ATHEISM, CAUSES OF

Theology has often precipitated minds into
atheism. . . .
A philosopher (Isaac Newton) has been given to
the world, who has discovered by what simple and
sublime laws all the celestial bodies move in the
abyss of space. Thus the work of the universe,
better known, shows a workman; and so many
laws, always constant, prove a legislator. Sound
philosophy has thus destroyed that *atheism* to
which an obscure theology lent weapons.

(*c*) *Voltaire*

ATHEISM, INCONSISTENCY OF

The tempter asks you to give up the idea of God
derived from the Scriptures. Well, *what then?*
Remember, you refuse to give up the humblest
cottage, until you know where you are to go; you
will not throw away the poorest garment in winter
until you have a better one; nor put out the dimmest
lantern until you have a better light in its place.
Will you then recklessly give up the idea of God at
the bidding of any man—the idea of the living,
loving, personal God, ruling over all—without
asking, "To whom shall I go?" You can put
away the mystery of God, and you get in return
the greater mystery of *godlessness*. Your account
of creation is then neither more nor less than a
fool's account. A *chair* could not have made
itself; but the *sun* is self-created. Your *coat* had
a maker, but your *soul* had none. The wax flower
on your table was made, but the roses in your
garden grew there by chance. The brass instrument was fashioned by a skilled hand, but the
voice of man, the grandest of all organs, was self-
created. The figure-head on the ship was carved,
but the face of the carver became a face by chance,
without design or without law!

(*d*) *J. Parker*

ATHEISM, INSIGNIFICANCE OF

Obliged as I am, even by my education, to pass
in review the races of men, I have sought for
atheism in the lowest and in the highest; but
nowhere have I met with it, except in an individual
or at most in some school of men, more or less
known, as we have seen in Europe in the last
century, and as we see at the present day. *Everywhere and always the masses of the people have
escaped it.*

(*e*) *M. Quatrefages*

ATHEISM, POPULAR.

Nothing draws more rapturous plaudits in an
atheistic lecture room than the plain assertion
that man is a machine; that he is driven by a

natural law, in the same sense that a splash of
mud is thrown by a carriage-wheel.

(*f*) *W. Jackson's Bampton Lectures*, 1875.

ATHEISM AND UNCERTAINTY

The philosopher who recognises a God has with
him a crowd of probabilities equivalent to certainty,
while the atheist has nothing but doubts.

Voltaire

[N.B. Christianity has certainty, not mere probability.]

(*g*)

ATONEMENT, THE

Holy Scripture uses three grand images to aid
in setting forth the inestimable benefits of Christ's
death and passion. The central truth is approached from different quarters, showing it on
all sides; each supplying the deficiencies of the
other:
  1. ἀπολύτρωσις, or *redemption;*
  2. καταλλαγή, or *reconciliation;*
  3. ἱλασμός, or *propitiation*
(denoting the original *bondage, enmity,* and *need
of sacrifice,* or *offering*) are the capital words summing up three such families of images; to one or
other of which almost every word bearing on this
work of our salvation through Christ may be most
or less referred.
  1. Is the form of the word invariably used by St.
Paul? Chrysostom, on Romans iii. 24, observes that
by this ἀπο the apostle expresses the *completeness*
of our redemption in Christ Jesus, a redemption
which no later bondage should follow.
  It is not recall from captivity merely, but recall
through the payment of a ransom (Origen: Rom.
iii. 24). The idea of deliverance through a λύτρον,
or price paid, is the central one of this family of
words. Keeping this in mind, we find a whole
group of significant words connecting themselves
with 1. See Matt. xx. 28; Mark x. 45; 1 Tim. ii.
6; Tit. ii. 14; 1 Pet. i. 18; Heb. ix. 12; 1 Cor.
vi. 20; Gal. iii. 13, iv. 5.
  Here is a point of contact with 3. Also 1. is
linked with all those statements of holy Scripture
which speak of sin as slavery, and sinners as
slaves (Rom. vi. 17, 20; John viii. 34; 2 Pet.
ii. 19); of deliverance from sin as freedom, from
bondage (John viii. 33, 36; Rom. viii. 21; Gal.
v. 1).
  2. Occurs four times in New Testament. It has
two sides: and =
  (i.) a **reconciliation**, "quâ Deus nos sibi recon-
ciliavit," laid aside His holy anger against our
sins, and received us into His favour—a reconciliation effected for us *once for all* by Christ upon His
cross (2 Cor. v. 18, 19; Rom. v. 10).
  (ii.) It is the reconciliation, "quâ nos Deo
reconciliamur," the daily deposition, under the
operation of the Holy Spirit, of the enmity of the
old man toward God (2 Cor. v. 20; 1 Cor. iii. 11).
The attempts to make *this* secondary the primary
meaning of the word rest on a prejudiced exegesis
and a foregone determination to get rid of the
reality of God's anger against sin.
  (iii.) All those passages in Holy Scripture which
speak of sin as a state of *enmity* with God
(Rom. iii. 7; Eph. ii. 15; Jas. iv. 4); sinners as

(*h*)

alienated from Him (Rom. v. 10; Col. i. 21); Christ on the Cross as the *peace* and *peacemaker* between God and man (Eph. ii. 14; Col. i. 20); and such invitations as this, "Be ye reconciled to God" (2 Cor. v. 20), connect themselves with this word.

(iv.) This word when our translation was made signified *atonement*, and is so rendered; all its uses = at-one-ment, but this is not its proper rendering. *Atonement* as we now use the word would be a fitter rendering of 3.

3. Is found twice in 1 John (ii. 2; iv. 10); nowhere else in New Testament.

(i.) The inherent idea is that the "*goodwill toward men*" has been gained by means of some offering or other *placamen*.

(ii.) Christ does not merely propitiate, but is also the propitiation. Ep. to Heb. = in the offering of Himself, He is both *priest and sacrifice*. The typical sacrifices of the law met and were united in Him, the sin-offering, by and through whom the just anger of God against our sins was appeased, and God, without compromising His righteousness, was able to show Himself propitious to us once more. All this the word used of Christ declares.

(iii.) A larger group of words connect themselves with 3. than either 1. or 2.—all those, viz., which set forth the benefits of Christ's death as a *propitiation* of God, as a *sacrifice*, an *offering* (Eph. v. 2; Heb. x. 14; 1 Cor. v. 7), as the Lamb of God (John i. 29, 36; 1 Pet. i. 19), as the Lamb slain (Rev. v. 6, 8), all those which speak of Him as washing us in His blood (Rev. i. 5).

(iv.) Compared with 1. ἱλασμός is the deeper word, and goes to the innermost heart of things. If we had 1. only and its group, these would = that we *were* enemies, and by His death made friends; but *how* it would not describe at all. It would not = satisfaction, propitiation, the Daysman, the Mediator, the High Priest; all which in 3. are involved.

(v.) Bengel's note on Romans iii. 24, ἱλασμός, *atonement* (expiation) or *propitiation*, and ἀπολύτρωσις, *redemption*, are fundamentally one single benefit and no more, viz. *the restoration of the lost sinner*. This is an exceedingly commensurate and pure idea, and adequately corresponds to the name of JESUS. *Redemption* has regard to *enemies*, and *reconciliation* refers to *God;* and here, again, there is a difference between ἱλασμός and καταλλαγή. ἱλασμός takes away the offence against God; the latter removes (i.) God's indignation against *us*, 2 Cor. v. 19; (ii.) and *our* alienation from *God*, 2 Cor. v. 20.

(a)   *From Abp. Trench*

ATONEMENT

You never heard me, and you never shall hear me, urge you to accept the atonement. I urge you to accept the Lord Jesus Christ. I never urged you to accept salvation through your belief in any doctrine of historical circumstances. Those historical circumstances opened to my mind such a conception of the nature of Christ as made me accept Him, but they did not prepare a way by which He might make a revelation of Himself to me. And the mode of handling this subject by *doctrinaires*, I aver, is an obstruction to men's acceptance of Christ. They, instead of bringing men face to face with a living Saviour, bring them face to face with an historical fact of two thousand

years ago. They take men back to Judaism, and substitute in their minds visible things for the living force and power of an invisible God.

(b)   *Beecher*

ATONEMENT, SUBSTITUTION

When the sea wrought and was tempestuous, and Jonah saw the storm, he said, "Cast me into the sea, and it shall be calm to you"; but the storm was raised for his own sake. Now Christ when he saw the misery of mankind, He said, "Let it come on Me." We raised the storm, but Christ would be cast in to allay it.

(c)   *J. Manton*

ATONEMENT, THE VICARIOUS

The objection to Christ's *vicarious* offering, to the assertion that He died, not merely for the good of, but in the room and in the stead of, others, tasted death for them, commonly assumes this form: Must not righteousness, it is asked, be the law of all God's dealings? Most of all, must we not expect to find consistent with highest righteousness that which is the most solemn and awful of all God's dealings with His creatures? But how is it agreeable with this, how can it be called just, nay, how can it be acquitted of extremest injustice, to lay on one Man the penalties of others, so that He pays the things which He never took, so that they sin and He is punished, on Him being laid the iniquities of them all? What have we here, an adversary will insist, but, in the awfullest sphere of all, and in matters the most tremendous, the same injustice which, even in least things, provokes our indignation? . . .

The question to be effectually answered, needs only to be more accurately stated : that the form which it ought to assume is this, How can it be righteous for one Man *to take upon Himself* the penalties of others? And none, who remember the "*Lo! I come*" of the Saviour, the willing sacrifice of our Isaac, prefigured by his who climbed so meekly in his father's company the hill of Moriah, will deny our right to make this change, while surely the whole aspect of the question is now by this little change altered altogether. It were unrighteous to force our sins on Christ, if He were reluctant; it would then cease to be self-sacrifice: but He has freely offered Himself thereunto. This is *not only righteous*, but more than righteous, because it moves in that higher region where law is no more known, *but only known no more because it has been transfigured into love*. . . .

Vicarious suffering! it is strange to hear the mighty uproar which is made about it; when indeed in lower forms—not low in themselves, but low as compared with the highest,—*it is everywhere, where love is at all*. For indeed is not this, of one freely taking on himself the consequences of others' faults, and thus averting from those others, at least in part, the penalties of the same, building what others have thrown down, gathering what others have scattered, bearing the burdens which others have wrapped together, healing the wounds which others have inflicted, paying the things which he never took, smarting for sins which he never committed: is not this, I say, the law and the condition of all highest nobleness in the world? is it not that which God is continually demanding of His elect, they approving themselves His elect, as they do not shrink from this demand,

(d)

as they freely own themselves the debtors of love to the last penny of the requirements which it makes?

And if these things be so, shall we question the right of God Himself to display this nobleness which He demands of His creatures? Shall we wish to rob Him of the opportunity, or think to honour Him who is highest love, by denying Him the right to display it?

(a) *Abp. Trench*

ATONEMENT, SATISFACTION

But the sufferings and death of Christ were *not merely vicarious, they were also satisfactory;* and thus atoning or setting *at one*, bringing together the holy and the unholy, who could not have been reconciled in any other way. When thus we speak we are sometimes taunted at the outset with the fact that the word "satisfaction," as applied to the death of Christ and its results, nowhere occurs in Scripture; so belongs to the later Latin theology (Anselm being the first to employ it), that the Greek theology does not so much as possess any Greek equivalent for the word. This is true; but though the *word* "satisfaction" is not in Scripture, the *thing* is everywhere there, and we are contending not about *words, but things;* the idea of it is inherent in *ransom*, in *redemption*, in *propitiation*, in scriptural words and phrases and images without number. . . . Careless whether the word be in Scripture or no, the Church has a perfect right to the term, seeing that it best expresses and sums up the truth which in this matter she holds.

(b) *Ibid*

ATONEMENT, WELL-PLEASING TO GOD

But how, it is further urged, could God be well pleased with the sufferings of the innocent and the holy? What "satisfaction" could He find in these? Here, as so often, the faith of the Church is first caricatured, that so it may be more easily brought into question. Could God have pleasure in the sufferings of the innocent and the holy, and that Innocent and Holy His own Son?

Assuredly not; but He could have pleasure, nay, according to the moral necessities of His own being, He must have pleasure, yea, the highest joy, satisfaction, and delight in the love, the patience, the obedience, which those sufferings gave Him the opportunity of displaying, which but for those He could never have displayed; above all, He must have rejoiced in these as manifested in His own Son.

For even we ourselves, when we read in story of those who for the love of their fellows have made their lives one long, patient martyrdom, or who, witnessing for the truth, have been borne from earth in the fire-chariot of some shorter but sharper agony, do we not feel that we have a right to rejoice in these martyrs of truth and love, yea, in the very pains and sufferings which they endured? that only as the nerves of our own moral being are weak and unstrung, only as we have become incapable, not merely of doing, but even of appreciating what is noble and great, do we grudge them those pains, do we wish for them, one of these to have been less; seeing that these were the conditions of their greatness, that without which it could never have been shown, without which it might never have existed?

Even the heathen moralist could say of God in His dealings with good men, "*fortiter amat.*"

There is no weakness in His love; it is love according to which He does not spare His own, but thrusts them forth to labour and difficulty and pains, in which alone they can be perfected; even as the same heathen could affirm that God had joy in nobly suffering men; not, of course, for the sufferings' sake, but for the virtues which were manifested therein.

And should not the God and Father of our Lord Jesus Christ have pleasure in the faith, the love, the obedience of His Son? Yea, it was a joy such as only the mind and heart of God could contain, that in His Son this perfect pattern of self-forgetting, self-offering love was displayed. We do not shrink from accepting in the simplest sense the assertion of the apostle, that Christ, giving Himself for us on the cross, became *therein* and *thereby* "a sacrifice of a sweet-smelling savour" unto God; that He was well-pleased therewith, and said at length what He would never else have said, "I have found a ransom."

Christ satisfied herein, not the *Divine anger*, but the Divine craving and yearning after a perfect holiness, righteousness, and obedience *in man*, God's chosen creature, the first-fruits of His creatures; which craving no man had satisfied, but all had disappointed, before. There had been a flaw in every other man's escutcheon; every other, instead of repairing the breach which Adam had made, had himself left that breach wider than he found it. But here at length was one, *a son of man*, yet fairer than all the children of men, one on whom the Father's love could rest with a perfect complacency, in regard of whom He could declare, "This is My beloved Son, in whom I am well pleased," in whom He had pleasure without stint and without drawback. And that life of His, the long self-offering of that life of love, was crowned, consummated, and perfected by the sacrifice of His death, wherein He satisfied to the uttermost every demand which God could make on Him, and satisfied for all the demands which God had made upon all the other children of men, and which they had not satisfied for themselves.

(c) *Ibid*

ATONEMENT, INFINITE VALUE OF

But if the question is here asked, How could one man satisfy for many? how by one man's obedience could many be made righteous? The answer is not far to seek. The transcendent worth of that obedience which Christ rendered, of that oblation which He offered, the power which it possessed of countervailing and more than counterbalancing a world's sin, lay in this, that He who offered these, while He bore a human nature, and wrought human acts, was a Divine Person; not indeed God alone, for as such He would never have been in the condition to offer or to die; nor man alone, for then the worth of His offering could never have reached so far; but He was God and man in one person indissolubly united, and in this person performing all those acts,—man that He might obey and suffer and die,—God that He might add to every act of His obedience, His suffering, His death, *an immeasurable worth*, steeping in the glory of His Divine personality all of human that He wrought. Christ was able so summarily to pay our debt, because He had *another and a higher coin* in which to pay it than that in which it was contracted. *It was contracted in the*

(d)

currency of earth; He paid it in the currency of heaven.

(a)   *Abp. Trench*

ATONEMENT, INHERENT VALUE OF

Nor was it, as some among the schoolmen of the middle ages taught, that God arbitrarily ascribed and imputed to Christ's obedience unto death a value which made it equal to the needs and sins of the world, such a value as it would not have had but for this imputation. We affirm rather, with the deeper theologians of those and of all times, who crave to deal with realities, not with ascriptions and imputations, that His offering had in it this intrinsic value, that there was no ascription to it, as of God's mere pleasure, of a value which it did not in itself possess; for then the same might have been imputed to the work of an angel or of a saint; the whole exclusive fitness of the Son of God undertaking the work would then pass away; and another might have made up the breach as well as He. We affirm rather that what the Son of God claimed in behalf of that race whereof He had become the representative and the head, He claimed as of *right*, although indeed that right was one which the Father as joyfully conceded as the Son demanded. Without a satisfaction such as this, the eternal interests of that righteousness whereof God is the upholder in His own moral universe would not have permitted Him to be, as He now is, the passer-by of transgression, the justifier and the accepter of the ungodly.

(b)   *Ibid*

ATONEMENT, RECONCILIATION

Such is the Church's faith in respect of the atonement. That atonement is not, as some would persuade us, a one-sided act; it looks not one way only, but two, having a face with which it looks toward God, as well as one with which it looks toward man. It is no mere reconciling of man to God, as though its object were to remove the distrust, to kill the emnity in man's heart, to persuade him to throw down his arms and yield himself the vanquished of eternal love. It is most truly this, but it is much more than this. It is a reconciling, not merely of man to God, but of God to man; whose love could not have gone forth upon the children of men in its highest forms, in those of forgiveness, acceptance, renewal, if this had not found place. Think not then, my brethren, of Christ the peace-*maker* as though He came only to *announce* peace, to say to the doubting and distrustful children of men, Why will ye remain at such a miserable and guilty distance from your heavenly Father, when His arms are stretched out to receive you, when He is only waiting to enfold you within them? No doubt Christ did come bringing this message, did proclaim that those arms were open, and that heavenly Father waiting to be gracious; but He only brought this message inasmuch as He *made* the peace which He announced. "Having *made* peace by the blood of His cross," "He entered into the holiest of all, having obtained eternal redemption for us." In Him and through Him, through the sacrifice of His death, the disturbed, and in part suspended, relations between God and His sinful creatures were re-constituted anew; *His blood being shed to cleanse men from their sins, and not to teach them that those sins needed no cleansing, and could be forgiven without one.*

(c)   *Ibid*

ATONEMENT, PRACTICAL CONSIDERATIONS

And will any faith which is short of this faith satisfy the deepest needs and cravings of your souls? You may struggle against it with your understandings, though, I think, very needlessly; for it seems to me to approve itself to the reason and the conscience, quite as much as to demand acceptance of our faith; but you will crave it with your inmost spirits. There are times when, perhaps nothing short of this will save you from the darkness of a hopeless despair. Let me imagine, for example, one, who with many capacities for a nobler and purer life, and many calls thereunto, has yet suffered himself to be entangled in youthful lusts, has stained himself with these; and then after awhile awakens, or is rather awakened by the good Spirit of God to ask himself, "What have I done?" How fares it with him at the retrospect then, when he, not wholly laid aside in spirit, is made to possess (oh, fearful possession!) the sins of his youth? Like a stricken deer, though none but himself may be conscious of his wound, he wanders away from his fellows; or if with them, he is alone among them, for he is brooding still and ever on the awful mystery of evil, which he now too nearly knows. And now too all purity, the fearful guilelessness of children, the holy love of sister and of mother, and the love which he had once dreamed of as better even than these, with all which is supremely fair in nature or in art, comes to him with a shock of pain, is fraught with an infinite sadness; for it wakens up in him by contrast a livelier sense of what he is, and what, as it seems, he must for ever be; it reminds him of a paradise for ever lost, the angel of God's anger guarding with a fiery sword its entrance against him. He tries by a thousand devices to still, or at least to deaden, the undying pain of his spirit. What is this word sin, that it should torment him so? He will tear away the conscience of it, this poisonous shirt of Nessus, eating into his soul, which in a heedless moment he has put on. But no; he can tear away his own flesh, but he cannot tear away that. Go where he may, he still carries with him the barbed shaft which has pierced him. The arrow which drinks up his spirit, there is no sovereign dittany which will cause it to drop from his side—none, that is, which grows on earth; but there is which grows in heaven, and in the Church of Christ, the heavenly inclosure here.

And you too—if such a one as I have pictured should be among us to-day—you too may find your peace; you will find it when you learn to look by faith on Him, "the Lamb of God, that taketh away the sin of the world." You will carry, it may be, the *scars* of those wounds which you have inflicted upon yourself, to your grave; but the wounds themselves, He can heal them, and heal them altogether. He can give you back the years which the cankerworm has eaten, the peace which your sin has chased away, and, as it seemed to you for ever. He can do so, and will. "Purge me with hyssop, and I shall be clean; wash me, and I shall be whiter than snow"; this will be then your prayer, and this your prayer will be fulfilled. The blood of sprinkling will purge, and you will feel yourself clean. Your sin will no longer be yourself; you will be able to look at it as separated from you, as laid upon another, upon One so strong that He did but for a moment stagger under the

(d)

the weight of a world's sin, and then so bore, that bearing he has borne it away for ever.

(a)   *Abp. Trench*

ATTIRE, Clerical

I, for one, do not believe in the value of clerical attire, although we are often obliged to submit to it, but I believe it helps to isolate the priest from the people. I can never believe that it is the "cowl that makes the monk," any more than I believe in the orthodoxy or the religion of a white tie, which seems to be a distinguishing mark of undertakers, waiters, and clergymen, although I am perfectly well aware that there are some whose only credential for the ministry is their clothes.

(b)   *E. Husband*

AUTHORITY (Acts vii. 30–35)

The Israelite to whom Moses appealed retorted: "Who made thee a ruler and a judge over us?" so too the sanhedrists asked Jesus: "Who gave Thee this authority?" (Matt. xxi. 23; Luke xx. 2). The *Divine* authorization is doubted when visible and tangible *human* credentials are not presented. The truth is, that men unconsciously conceive of God as if He were controlled in His acts by human forms and limitations, and they deny His absolute authority and sovereign power (v. 2).

(c)   *Lange*

AVENGE His own Elect, Shall not God?

Longfellow tells us in one of his poems that a brazen statue of justice, raised on a column, stood in the midst of an ancient city. It held the scales of justice in its left hand, and a sword in its right, to signify that justice presided over the laws of the land, and that the hearts and homes of the people were protected under a righteous rule. There the statue stood, year after year, a silent and beautiful symbol. Even the birds built their nests in the scales of the balances, having no fear of the sword flashing in the sunshine above them. But, in the course of time, the laws of that land were corrupted; might took the place of right, and the weaker were oppressed. During this period it happened that a necklace of pearls was lost in a nobleman's palace. Suspicion fell on an orphan girl, who lived there as maidservant, and after a formal trial she was condemned to die on the scaffold for her supposed theft. Patiently she met her doom at the foot of this very statue of justice; and as her innocent spirit ascended to her Father in heaven, the Father of the fatherless, and the righteous judge, lo! a tempest burst over the city, and a thunderbolt smote the bronze statue of justice, hurling the scales to the ground: and in the hollow of one of them was found the nest of a magpie, into which was woven this very necklace of pearls.

(d)

AUDI ALTERAM PARTEM

We have seen how Romish priests, and even English clergymen, can speak of Martin Luther. We will take other cases. Take Cicero. Many have represented him as a pure and lofty patriot, a great writer, and a good man; and others have held him up to uttermost scorn—as a mean, shifty,

dishonest timeserver. Or take a modern instance. Take Archbishop Laud. You will find him depicted by some as a holy martyr, as an all but perfect saint; turn to others, and you will find him described as a cold, narrow, foolish, cruel bigot. Take Cromwell, by one writer in the "Biographical Dictionary" he is set down with Judas Iscariot and the emperor Phocas as one of three of the worst men that ever lived. By Milton you will see him invoked as-

> "——our chief of men, who through a cloud
> Not of war only, but detractions rude,
> Guided by faith and matchless fortitude,
> To peace and truth thy glorious way hast ploughed,
> And on the neck of crownèd fortune proud
> Hast reared God's trophies, and His work pursued."

Take Milton himself. In the pages of Lord Macaulay he is described as the noblest man of his own and almost of any age. And the poet Wordsworth, appealing to him as a sort of modern regenerator, invokes him in that noble sonnet of his:

> "Milton! thou shouldst be living at this hour:
> England hath need of thee: she is a fen
> Of stagnant water: altar, sword, and pen,
> Fireside, and heroic wealth of hall and bower,
> Have forfeited their ancient English dower
> Of inward happiness. We are selfish men,
> Oh! raise us up, return to us again;
> And give us manners, virtue, freedom, power.
> Thy soul was like a star, and dwelt apart:
> Thou hadst a voice whose sound was like the sea:
> Pure as the naked heavens, majestic, free,
> So didst thou travel on life's common way,
> In cheerful godliness; and yet thy heart
> The lowliest duties on herself did lay."

Now, after reading this judgment, if you want the other side of him, read Bishop Hackett's description of him as "that serpent Milton, that blackmouthed Zoilus; he that wrote with all irreverence of the fathers, that showed as little duty to the father that begat him; he that wrote against Christ for not allowing divorce"; "Get thee behind me, Milton," says the bishop, "thou cankerworm, thou Shimei, a dead dog, thou savourest of pride, bitterness, and falsehood." Take even a more modern instance. In one of the gossiping note-books of posthumous reminiscences which disgrace our literature, Bishop Stanley, of Norwich, was characterized by one who had only known well of him, and to whom he had shown nothing but continual kindness, as being a man as vain as a girl, and as timid as a deer. "Vain as a girl, and as timid as a deer!" exclaimed his son, the late Dean of Westminster, indignantly, "He could not have been described in words more profoundly false. His simplicity was absolute, his courage was almost boyish; he was brave as a lion, and as affectionate as a child."

(e)   *Archdeacon Farrar*

"AWAKE, thou that sleepest" (Eph. v. 14)

Compare this command with that given by our Lord to the man with the withered hand, "Stretch it forth." The man might have objected and said, "Could I obey Thee in this, I would not have troubled Thee. Why mock me with my infirmity, and bid me do the very thing I cannot?" But the man did not perplex himself; and Christ, in exciting the desire to obey, imparted the power to obey. If every man would understand the philosophy of waking up before he gets up, what a world of sleepers we would have!

(f)   *Eadie*

B

BACKSLIDERS (2 Pet. ii. 20)

I can certainly testify, after sixteen years' ministry, that by far the most hopeless deathbeds I have attended have been those of backsliders. I have seen such persons go out of the world without hope, whose conscience appeared really dead, buried, and gone, and on whom every truth and doctrine and argument appeared alike thrown away. They seemed to have lost the power of feeling, and could only lie still and despair.

(a)   *Rev. J. C. Ryle*

If by any chance the vestal fires of Greece were allowed to go out, they could only be rekindled by the rays of the sun. So with grace in the soul of man; if it should expire, nothing but the rays of the Sun of righteousness can rekindle it.

(b)

[Ps. cxix. 176

True Christians may be suffered to go far astray, to show them their weakness, to check self-confidence, and to produce dependence on Jesus Christ, that they may be able to show how weak and feeble and rash they are.

(c)

BACKSLIDERS (INVITED)

" If thou wilt return, O Israel, return unto Me, saith the Lord" (Jer. iii. 12 ; iv. 1). The Bible is full of advertisements like those we so often see in the "agony column" of certain newspapers, praying anxiously for the return of runaway ones, and promising forgiveness and oblivion for the past.

(d)

BACKSLIDING

But it occurs, alas ! too often, that they who have escaped, as drowning mariners, to this rock, are enticed again to stray. They cease to watch and pray. Then the tempter finds an open door. They neglect the preserving means of grace. Then the foe creeps in. The Spirit is grieved and withdraws. Corruptions regain their power. Woe to backsliders! what wretchedness is theirs ! Consciousness of peril returns, and it is embittered by keen self-reproach. They see how basely they have deserted the Friend, who had said to them, while in their blood, "Live." Reader, perhaps this agony is yours. You once had rest in Jesus, but it is gone. The fault is wholly your own. He did not drive you from Him. You would depart. And now you sigh, Oh that it were with me, as in the days when the Sun of righteousness shone upon my path ! Be not tearless, for grievous is your fall. But be not hopeless, for Jesus is yet near. His voice still follows you, "Return, and I will not cause Mine anger to fall upon you " (Jer. iii. 12). In nothing is His tenderness more tender than in stilling the sobs of those who sob in penitence before Him. Return then. The Lord still extends the arms of His pitifulness. He is the balm in Gilead. He is the Physician there. He cannot be silent to the cry, "Restore to me the joy of Thy salvation."

(e)   *Dean Law*

BALAAM

" *Let me die the death of the righteous, and let my last end be like his* " (Num. xxiv. 10).

1. Characteristics

(i.) **Who said this?**—Saint? No. Hypocrite? No. Villain? No. Balaam, a false prophet.

(ii.) **An ambitious man** — hearing of Moses' miracles, and desirous of similar power—he allies himself with Jehovah—and so hopes for notoriety ; =an *anti-Moses.*

(iii.) **His character**—twofold : two conflicting principles—He wishes to die a saint, but not to live like one—self-denial expected of the Christian —He had a *besetting sin*—and it proved *master*— all his actions were to gratify it—hence wreck in the end.

2. Trace his downward career :

(i.) **The opportunity comes**—Balak's request— " Come, curse me . . . etc." : Balaam is WILLING —but he has a *scruple*—hence his actions—*He will go if he can.*—" *Thou shalt not go,*" etc. The messengers return — report — " *Raise your price.*"

(ii.) **The second embassy:** "Let nothing hinder thee." " I will promote thee." " Come curse, etc." The question is now—Can this man be bought? Money is said to be the *god* of this world—others say "filthy lucre," but all depends upon the use it is put to—*like oil on your dress*— *or on wheels of machinery* =either " filthy," or it makes all go right. Balaam's heart set on getting these rewards ; he gets half a permission to go— God recedes ; warnings useless—Passions strong =*brooklet and Cataract of Niagara*=He does not *curse*—though quite willing to do so.

(iii.) **The man's last stage :**

He now tempts—His curse=" nobody a bit the worse"; but he knew how to make God forsake His people—" Fleshly lusts war against the soul " —(Balaam perished). " He digged a pit, and is fallen into it himself."

3. Lessons

(i.) *Warning.* The man himself a fearful warning.

(ii.) We cannot be hurt from without but from *within-*

(iii.) One of *comfort :* " He hath given commandment to bless, and who shall reverse it ? "

(iv.) " I am persuaded that neither death, nor life, nor angels, nor principalities, nor powers, shall be able to separate us from the love of God which is in Christ Jesus our Lord."

(f)

BALAAM, SPIRITUAL STANDPOINT OF (Num. xxiv. 15, 16)

(i.) " **A hardened villain**," say some, " who carried on his profession of soothsayer and enchanter by the aid of evil spirits."

(ii.) Others regard him as presenting "**an awful example of apostasy.**" This is to give him more than he ever possessed.

(iii.) The more correct view is supplied by study of surrounding Scripture. It was the time of the

(g)

strange and eventful history of the departure of the Israelites from Egypt, and their passage through the Red Sea. This made a profound impression on the surrounding nations (Exod. xv. 14) = "The people shall hear and be afraid; sorrow shall take hold on the inhabitants of Palestina." Ch. ix. (of Pharaoh), "And in very deed for this cause have I raised thee up, for to show in thee My power : *and that My name should be declared throughout all the earth.*" This was fulfilled (Josh. v. 1) = "And it came to pass, when all the kings of the Amorites, which were on the side of Jordan westward, and all the kings of the Canaanites, which were by the sea, heard that the Lord had dried up the waters of the Jordan from before the children of Israel, until we were passed over, that their heart melted, neither was there spirit in them any more, because of the children of Israel."

Thus God's doings on behalf of Israel produced a great impression. The people everywhere were *astounded* with fear and wonder. It was God's voice waking them up; for the moment their spirit was paralysed, but the impression passed off ; they lapsed into their old habits. Still in a few the impression was deeper, and they investigated the matter; they wanted to have a knowledge of Jehovah, by whom such mighty works were done. Such was Jethro (Exod. xviii. 10, 11) :

"And Jethro said, Blessed be the Lord, who hath delivered you out of the hand of the Egyptians, and out of the hand of Pharaoh, and who hath delivered the people from under the hand of the Egyptians. *Now know I that the Lord is greater than all gods.*"

= no more than that Jehovah was *one of other gods. Rahab* = another such (Josh. ii. 9).

"I know that the Lord hath given you the land, and that your terror is fallen upon us, and that all the inhabitants of the land faint because of you. For we have heard how the Lord dried up the waters of the Red Sea for you, when ye came out of Egypt ; and what ye did unto the two kings of the Amorites, that were on the other side Jordan, Sihon and Og, whom ye utterly destroyed. And as soon as we had heard these things, our hearts did melt, neither did there remain any more courage in any man, because of you : *for the Lord your God, He is God in heaven above, and in earth beneath.*"

= a fuller confession than Jethro's, yet a remarkable omission in it : compare it with what Moses says of Jehovah (Deut. iv. 35) = "Unto thee it was showed that thou mightest know that the Lord He is God, *there is none else beside Him.*"

Again : "Know therefore this day, and consider it in thine heart, that the Lord He is God in heaven above, and upon the earth beneath (so far like Rahab's confession); *there is none else*" (marks the difference).

Now amongst this class of minds—the inquirers, who "knew the knowledge of the Most High," yet did not possess Israel's knowledge of Him, we must place Balaam : it is his standpoint at the time when he is sent for and tempted by the offers of Balak.

(*a*)   *Adapted from Hengstenberg*

BALAAM'S PLOT TO SEDUCE ISRAEL INTO SIN (Num. xxv)

The elect of God cannot be hurt from without, but from within : "so long as God had "not beheld iniquity in Jacob, nor seen perverseness in Israel," no harm could happen to them, no Balak

could injure them, no Balaam could curse them ; but once let iniquity and perverseness be seen in them, then the Lord's displeasure would be manifest. Balaam knew this, and hence the hellishness of his counsel : he could not curse, but he could seduce them into sin ; and then when they yielded their members servants unto uncleanness, God's anger would speedily be shown. So is it ever with God's elect. "Who is he that can harm you, if ye be followers of that which is good?"

(*b*)   *Ibid*

BALANCES, Weighed in the (Dan. v. 27)

A *king* = a *cunning man*, capable man, the man who *can.—Carlyle.*

The king = the example-setter—cannot be hid.

The king of Babylon = the god of millions ; moreover, he = the representative of the *world-power*, which was now matching its strength against God (Jehovah).

But a king is not in his place by accident. Daniel tells us that God "*appointeth as king whomsoever He will.*"

"Whom He will He setteth up, and whom He will He puts down." His alone is the absolute power ; though Belshazzar imagines himself autocrat of Assyria, God has put him there, and holds him responsible, and will *weigh his actions.*

Belshazzar was a young man for such a position. But he could have had the aid of wise counsellors. Belshazzar however allied himself with a profligate set ; we find him with the chief men of his kingdom indulging in unseemly debaucheries ; and when wine had taken away what little sense he had, he proceeds to *blaspheme* the God of heaven and earth. He orders the sacred vessels, brought from the Jewish temple, to be brought in, that he and his company might profane them by drinking wine out of them.

The deed was done, and the madman was exulting at the indignity he had heaped upon the God of the Jews. . . . "A God who cannot protect His people. . . . I use the vessels consecrated to His worship as I would use the drinking cups and goblets sacred to Bacchus !!"

Presently pallor spreads over his face ; he starts as if shot by an arrow, his knees knock together, his hand shakes, he drops the wine-cup ! Is he ill? In a fit—see his stare fixed to one object in the room? The amazed guests ask, What transfixes him? Something moving ; writing in the corner of the room ; on the ceiling : noiselessly tracing some characters there. It is but a man's hand, and yet it frightens them all. There is something supernatural about it. It is writing three or four mysterious words, which the king cannot read, and yet his conscience tells him that they are about himself. Conscience says, "*That is God, my Master, and that is how He SPEAKS to you.*" You have been speaking in a loud voice, blaspheming His name, showing off before your companions ; but HE has uttered no voice in reply : He might have commanded the thunder to shake your palace, the lightning to strike you dead ; He might have showed you His power in a thousand ways, but He has merely sent those fingers to trace a word or two on the wall opposite you ; and you, who bragged that you had conquered Him, and did not care about such a God, are completely crushed in a moment, there is neither speech nor courage left in you."

(*c*)

"Conscience makes cowards of us all."—
(*Shakespeare.*)

Learn how easily God can spoil the pleasures of the wicked.

Learn too that God is a God of judgment, and by Him actions are weighed.

These words =
"*Thou art weighed in the balances, and art found wanting.*"

Your actions, as king, in the station in which God has called you, are found wanting in moral worth.

You represented the King of kings and Lord of lords ; you were His ambassador, His minister ; it was your duty to glorify His name : instead of which you have glorified dumb idols, deified yourself, and have ended by blaspheming the name of the most high God ; who now deposes and degrades you, in order that He may put a better representative of the kingly office in your place.

(*a*)

BALL-ROOM, HEROD'S (Matt. xiv. 6)

1. Before the ball

The news of Christ's miracles had reached Herod. He was startled. Who is this Jesus ? John risen from the dead ? Why these fears ? John had reproved Herod, and Herod imprisoned John for eighteen months. The guilt of an unlawful marriage was on his conscience. He rushes into gaiety to drown his troubles. The pleasures of the feast and the ball-room "minister to a mind diseased."

Men fly to the ball, the theatre, the card-table, the tavern, not simply for pleasure's sake, and to "taste life's glad moments," but to drown care, to smother conscience, to laugh away the impressions of the last sermon, to soothe an uneasy mind, to relieve the burden, or to pluck out the sting of conscious guilt ! O slaughter-houses of souls ! O shambles, reeking with blood ! O "lasciviousness, lusts, excess of wine, revellings, banquetings, and abominable idolatries ! " How long shall men "run on in this excess of riot " ? O lust of the flesh, lust of the eye, and pride of life, when will ye cease to intoxicate, and lead men captive at your will ? O God-forgetting gaiety ! O dazzling worldliness ! O glittering balls of midnight, where

"Youth and pleasure meet
To chase the glowing hours with flying feet,"

when will ye cease to be resorted to by the sons of men to "heal the hurt" of the human soul, to still its throb and heartache, and to medicate the immedicable wound ? "

[Woe to thee, O *river of human custom !* Who resists thee ? When shalt thou be dried up ? How long wilt thou toss the sons of Eve upon a vast and terrible ocean, which even they who have gone up into the cross (as their vessel) can hardly navigate ?—*Augustine.*]

Would that these solemn words were sounded over our land, and through our churches, in these days of approved, and licensed, and *consecrated* worldliness.

2. During the ball

A gay scene. The lust of the flesh, the lust of the eye, and the pride of life are there. All that can minister to these are there. Herod is there, stupifying conscience. The fair daughter is there,

in all the splendour of gay wantonness. The vile mother is there, lascivious and revengeful, Courtiers are there in pomp and glitter. Music and mirth are there. The dance and the song.

But some are absent : John is not there ; his disciples are not there. Jesus is not there, nor His disciples. They were present at the marriage festival at Cana ; but this ball-room is not for them. It is not the place for a follower, either of Jesus or of John. The beauty of "this world" is one thing, and the beauty of the "world to come" another.

These scenes of vanity are instructive : they present the world in its most fascinating aspects. . . . These balls are the most seductive specimens of pure worldliness that can be found. Surely the god of this world knows how to enchant both eye and ear. Here the natural man is at home. It is a place where God is not ; where the cross is not. Where such things as sin and holiness must not be named. It is a ball where the knee is not bent except in the waltz ; where music in the praise of Jesus is not heard ; where the book of God and the name of God would be out of place ; where you might speak of Jupiter, Venus, Apollo, but not of Jesus. . . . It was during that ball that the murder of John was plotted and consummated ("Lust hard by hate."— *Milton*); that a drunken, lustful king, urged on by two women, perpetrated that foul deed. . . . Such are the masquerades of time. . . . Such was the *coarse worldliness* of old days ; but is the *refined worldliness* of modern times less fatal to the soul ? . . . "Ye adulterers and adulteresses, know ye not that the friendship of the world is enmity with God ? "

3. After the ball

Of the chief actors in this ball-room murder nothing more is said. They pass to the judgment seat. They have sent John before them to receive his reward. . . . His lips are silenced, and his disciples bury the body ; then they go and *tell Jesus.* Jesus hears of the murder, and is silent ! . . . This is the day of endurance and patient suffering. The day of recompense is coming.

O gaieties of earth ! Feasts and revellings and banquetings, how often have ye slain both body and soul ! Men call you innocent amusements, harmless pleasures ; but can ye be innocent, can ye be harmless,when ye steal away the soul from God, when ye nurse the worst lusts of humanity, when ye smother conscience, when ye shut out Jesus, when the floors on which your votaries dance off their immortal longings are red with the blood of souls !

(*b*)   *Horatius Bonar (condensed)*

Do you know what a ball is ? It is a queer thing, a mixture of angelic delight and devilish invention. One is carried along, floating, as it were, in the airy spaces between heaven and earth and hell.

(*c*)   *Letters from Hell*

BAPTISM (1 Cor. vii. 14)

The baptismal question is this :—Whether we are baptized because we *are* the children of God, or whether we are the children of God because we are baptized ; whether we are to understand thereby that we are made something which we

(*d*)

were not before—magically and mysteriously changed, or, that we are made the children of God by baptism in the same sense that a sovereign is made a sovereign by coronation? The apostle's argument is decisive and unanswerable: *These children were the children of God because the children of one Christian parent.*

(a)   *F. W. Robertson*

BAPTISM DOTH SAVE (1 Pet. iii. 21)

Christians, yet no Christians. Baptized, yet unbaptized. The prophet includes God's covenanted people with the nations outside. A Church within the Church. An Israel within Israel (Rom. ii. 28, 29; Jer. ix. 26). All baptized unto Moses, yet not all saved. It is clear they stopped short at the external rite.

(b)   *Leighton*

BAPTISM OF JOHN (Acts xviii. 25)

Apollos = " a learned man," eloquent, mighty in Scriptures; an oracle—an *expositor;*
Instructed = taught orally, " in the way of the Lord ";
Fervent in spirit = zeal for souls, *sympathetic* teaching;
Taught carefully = after due preparation, not fanatically;
Things concerning Jesus : yet something lacking; for when the Christians heard him preach, they soon perceived that, notwithstanding his gifts, they knew more of Jesus than he did.
Why? Because he knew " *only the baptism of John.*"
N.B.—Acts xix. = a similar instance of twelve professedly Christian men, who had not so much as heard whether there is a Holy Spirit.
Baptism is ONE, but it has different aspects.
1. As an ordinance of the Church : we can make *too much* and *too little* of this. *Too much*, if rested in as sufficient; *too little*, if undervalued as a means of grace.
All will admit that, at the very lowest estimate, baptism has as high a place among Christians as rite of circumcision had among the Jews, of which St. Paul says the advantage was "*much every way* " = a mark of the covenant-relationship; represents our profession; shows to whom we belong.
Ask : What advantage has a child in being born of English or of Hottentot parents; in a Christian land or in a heathen land? The answer is obvious : *Much every way.* So of infant baptism, both in its *privileges* and its *possibilities.*
2. The Baptism of John (*i.e.* of *repentance*).
John's baptism could not be *Christian* baptism, but it could be a preparatory rite, and that it was.
As John Baptist preceded Christ historically, so *repentance* precedes *Christian life.* And as repentance is only known by its *fruits*, so this is what John Baptist demanded :
(*Forgiveness* is no element of this baptism.)
Pharisees and Sadducees came to John's baptism = "*offspring of vipers.*"
He demands a changed life, fruits of which = laying aside *besetting sins*, deeds of charity to hungry and naked.
See also publicans, soldiers, etc. *All* must do right and cease to do wrong *before* he will admit them to his baptism. This was truly (and is now) preparing the way for Christ. But this is em-

phatically *no more* than that—it is not *admission*, but preparation for admission, into the kingdom of heaven. Christ alone, who baptizes with the Holy Ghost, admits into His kingdom; then men become new creatures in Christ. We must never stop short of that. This is the great mistake of so many to " muse in their hearts " whether the baptism of *repentance, ipso facto*, constitutes a Christian. It does not. The foot is on the threshold, but it has not access—is not inside.
3. The Baptism of the Spirit must succeed.
Such—
(i.) *Know* the forgiveness of sins;
(ii.) Have the *witness* of the Spirit;
(iii.) Have the spirit of *sonship;*
(iv.) Date from *Pentecost,* and ever since then those added to the Church have been baptized with this baptism. Then it was accompanied with gift of tongues, now we are *sealed* with the *earnest of the Spirit.*

(c)

BAPTISM AND REGENERATION (John iii. 5)

[With this compare chap. vi. for the *idea* of both sacraments—baptism and Lord's supper.]
The idea underlying all forms of baptism is the *forgiveness of sins* on condition of repentance. This is the *negative* part of regeneration, whilst the new life communicated by the Holy Spirit is the *positive* part, or regeneration proper. So Peter in his Pentecostal sermon represents the matter when he calls upon his hearers, " Repent, and be baptized...in the name of Jesus Christ for the remission of sins, and ye shall receive the gift of the Holy Ghost " (Acts ii. 38). The chief matter is the *positive* part, the gift of the Holy Ghost, who is the efficient cause, the creative and vivifying agent of regeneration, and who alone can make the word and the sacrament effective. Hence the Spirit alone is mentioned in 6 and 8. The omission of water here is as significant as the omission of baptism in the negative clause (Mark xvi. 16), where the condition of salvation and the reason of damnation are laid down. This is a sufficient hint that the necessity of water baptism to salvation is not absolute, but relative only. The penitent thief passed into paradise without water baptism. Cornelius was regenerated before he was baptized, and many martyrs in the early ages died for Christ before they had a chance to receive the sacrament. It is possible to have the substance without the form, the baptism of the Spirit without the baptism of water; as it is quite common, on the other hand, to be baptized with water and have the Christian name without the Christian spirit and life. We are bound to God's appointed means of grace, but God is free, and the Spirit " bloweth where It listeth."

(d)   *P. Schaff*

BAPTISM AND REGENERATION

There are three points of comparison between the wind and the Spirit in the work of regeneration :—
1. The freedom and independence: ὅπου θέλει πνεῖ;
2. The irresistible effect : τὴν φωνὴν αὐτοῦ ὁκούεις;
3. The incomprehensibility : οὐκ οἶδας, both as to origin (πόθεν) and termination (ποῦ ὑπάγει).
To these might be added a fourth analogy, which however is not stated in the text; viz. the different degrees of power. The Holy Spirit acts

(e)

now like the gentle breeze upon minds as tenderly constituted as John, Melanchthon, Zinzendorf; now like the sweeping storm or whirlwind upon characters as strong as Paul, Luther, Calvin, Knox. Hence the presumption and folly to make our own experiences the measure and rule for all others. We should rather adore the wisdom and goodness of God in the variety of His operation.

(a) *P. Schaff*

BAPTISM OF THE SPIRIT, THE, ILLUSTRATION (John iii.)

In a charity school sat a Jewish maiden, quick at learning. It was a Christian school, and the Scripture lesson was forbidden her. Whilst however working at geography lessons or sums instead, she listened to the words of the Christian teacher, who soon became aware of her eager attention. "Read your book, Sarah," said he. Again and again the dark eyes were on him— she heard and understood. The teacher went to her father, whose conditions for putting her there were that she should not become a Christian. Moreover, she had made a vow to her mother not to become a Christian. So she was removed from the school. . . . Years passed. In a small town, in a humble house, was a servant; her black hair and eyes marked her as a Jewess—it was Sarah: working, too, on *her* Sabbath—asking herself, "Does God reckon by days and hours?" She read the Old Testament on the Christian Sabbath; the New Testament was a sealed book, yet she knew a great deal of it. One evening she heard her master read a story book. A Christian knight was taken prisoner by a Turkish pasha, who, cruel of heart, yoked him to a plough and whipped him till the blood came. His wife at home sold jewels and land and castle to raise money to ransom her husband, and he came home. Soon again war was renewed, and the knight went forth to battle. This time he took the pasha prisoner, shut him up in a dungeon, and there visited him. "What," asked he, "do you suppose awaits you?" "*Retribution*," replied his captive. "Yes; the retribution of a Christian. Christianity teaches to forgive our enemies, love our neighbours; for God is love. Go home in peace. I give thee back thy liberty, but be merciful and humane." In pain, torment, and tears, the wretched man confessed that he had taken poison. "I must die; nothing can save me. But before I die explain this religion of love and mercy. Oh that I may die a Christian!" His prayer was granted. At the recital of this story Sarah's heart burst with excitement. Tears came, and old memories were revived. All her school recollections returned, and with them her mother's dying words, "Let not my child become a Christian"; together with the command, "Honour thy father and thy mother," etc. The words mocked her. She had felt the power of Christianity.

Years again passed. Her master died. Sarah would not leave the widow, who was an invalid, but worked for the support of both, and proved an angel of blessing. Her mistress thirsted for the word of God, and as her Bible lay on the table asked Sarah to read to her, and Sarah read the Christian's Bible. Tears came into her eyes and light shone *into her own heart* as she did so. She read of Christ, and of the fruits of repentance; she trembled as she spake the name. One evening, watching long over her mistress, she fainted

and fell; neighbours carried her to the hospital, where she died, and they buried her not among the Christians, because she was not *baptized*, but outside the walls in the Jews' burial ground. But what availed that to undo the work of the Spirit, for "in Christ Jesus neither circumcision *availeth* anything, nor uncircumcision, but a *new creature*"?

(b) *From Hans Andersen*

BAPTISM VERILY PROFITETH (2 Tim. ii. 19) if we obey the gospel; but if we walk contrary to the precepts of it, our baptism is no baptism, and our Christianity is heathenism.

(c) *Archbishop Tillotson*

BAPTISM, "YE ARE CLEAN" (John xxv. 3)

The living word of Christ received by faith into the heart and dwelling there is the principle of regeneration and purification (xvii. 17; Jas. i. 18; 1 Pet. i. 23; Eph. v. 26).

It is not said *by reason of baptism;* the apostles were not baptized (except with the preparatory baptism of John), and regeneration is possible still without water baptism, which receives its force and efficacy only from the word and power of the Spirit present with it and working through it.

(d) *P. Schaff*

"Why did He not say: "Ye are clean by baptism?" Because it is the word which cleanses in the water. Take away the word, and what is the water? Add the word to the element, and it becomes a sacrament. Whence is this power of the water that it touches the body and the heart is cleansed? Whence, but because the word operates not merely in being spoken, but in being believed."

(e) *Augustine*

BAPTIZED," UNTO WHAT WERE YE?"(Acts xix. 1–7).

1. Unto God the Father,—then ye have received the adoption of sons;
2. Unto God the Son,—then ye have redemption through His blood;
3. Unto God the Holy Ghost—then ye have become the temple of God.

(f) *Lange (Leonh. and Sp.)*

BARABBAS (Matt. xxvii. 21)

"Not this Man, but Barabbas." Anybody but Christ. It is possible to live with Barabbas, but not with Christ.

(g)

BARREN FIG TREE, THE

I observe that as there are trees wholly noble, so there are also their semblance; not right, but ignoble. There is the grape, and the wild grape; the rose, and the canker-rose; the apple, and the crab. Now, fruit from these wild trees, however it may please children to play with, yet the prudent and grave count it of little or no value. There are also in the world a generation of Professors, that bring forth nothing but wild-olive berries. Saints only before men; devils and vipers at home. Saints in world; but sinners in heart and life.

(h) *Bunyan*

Many are beguiled with this, that they are free of scandalous and crying abominations : but the tree that bringeth not forth good fruit is for the fire : the man that is not born again cannot enter into the kingdom of God ; common honesty will not take men to heaven.

(a)   S. Rutherford

BATH KOL

The Jewish writers hold, that there were three sorts of revelation anciently among them ; the first by Urim and Thummim ; the second by the spirit of prophecy ; and the third by Bath Kol. *Bath Kol* they say was a voice from heaven. That they called it *bath kol*, i.e. " The daughter voice," " the daughter of a voice " (for it may be interpreted both ways), seems to be with respect to the oracular voice delivered from the mercy seat, when God was there consulted by Urim and Thummim. That was the grand and primary voice of revelation, this of a secondary dignity, and inferior to it, as the daughter is to the mother ; and therefore in respect to it, and as succeeding in its stead, it is called the daughter voice. That it may be understood what kind of oracle this was, I shall here give one instance of it out of the Talmud : " Rabbi Jochanan and Rabbi Simeon Ben Lachish, desiring to see the face of Rabbi Samuel, Babylonish doctor, Let us follow, said they, the hearing of *Bath Kol*. Travelling therefore near a school, they heard the voice of a boy reading these words out of the First Book of Samuel xxv. 1 : ' And Samuel died ' ; from this they inferred that their friend Samuel was dead ; and so they found it had happened, for Samuel of Babylon was dead." This is enough to let the reader see that their *bath kol* as no such voice from heaven, as they pretend, but only a fantastical way of divination of their own invention, like the *sortes Virgilanæ* among the heathens : for as, with them, the words first dipped at in the book of that poet was the oracle whereby they prognosticated those future events which they desired to be informed of ; so with the Jews, when they appealed to *bath kol*, the next words which they should hear of any one's mouth were the same. And this they called a voice from heaven, because thereby they thought the judgment of Heaven to be declared as to any dubious point they desired to be informed of, and the decrees of Heaven to be revealed concerning the future success of any matter which they would be pre-informed of, whensoever, in either of these two cases, they this way consulted it.

(b)   Prideaux

BAZAARS

Millions are annually spent on deer forests and moors, and hunting, and yachting, and racing, and gambling, and balls, and theatres, and dressing, and pictures, and furniture, and recreation. Little comparatively, ridiculously little, is given or done for the cause of Christ. A miserable guinea subscription too often is the whole sum bestowed by some Crœsus on the bodies and souls of his fellow-men. The very first principles of giving seem lost and forgotten in many quarters. People must be bribed and tempted to contribute by bazaars, as children in badly managed families are bribed and tempted to be good by sugar-plums. They must not be expected to give unless they get something in return ? And all this goes on in a country where people call themselves Christians, and go to church, and glory in ornate ceremonials, and histrionic rituals, and what are called " hearty services," and profess to believe the parable of the Good Samaritan. I fear there will be a sad waking up at the last day.

(c)   Bishop Ryle.

BEAST, THE (Rev. xiii. 7, 8)

The universal power of the beast as seen in-
1. Formalism.
2. Spiritualism.
3. Evangelicism.
4. Nothingism.
5. Shibbolethism.

The devil is of no " party."

(d)   Hengstenberg

The 1st beast = antichrist ;
The 2nd ditto = the corrupt Church ;
But the woman (Rome) rides on ; *i.e.* directs the apostate Church.

(e)

BEATITUDE OF THE DEAD, THE

A peculiar solemnity associated with these words, *I heard a voice from heaven,* saying what the epitaph should be over the Christian dead :
" Write, *Blessed are the dead which die in the Lord.*"
And in the midst of our sorrow and bereavement the assurance is added—
" *Yea, saith the Spirit, for they rest from their labours.*"
Consider

1. The Beatitude itself :

(i.) " Blessed . . . which die *in the Lord* " —*in the Lord* = not as Balaam wished, " Let me die death of the righteous " ; nor, " Lord, have mercy upon me." But *in Christ,* as vine and branches are one ; as Noah in and one with the ark ; = a *new creature,* as that which alone availeth anything.

(ii.) Blessed from henceforth :
(a) From the proclamation of the Gospel. Christ altered the condition of the dead—He emptied Hades, led captivity captive.
(b) From the very moment of death, no purgatory—" *To-day* with Me in paradise " ; " To die and be *with Christ* " ; " To die *is gain* " ; " Absent from the body, *present with the Lord.*"

(iii.) This is a *faithful* (true) saying :
Therefore
(a) *Write* it ;
(b) Make it *emphatic*—" Yea, saith the Spirit." = This word of God is unquestionable. Therefore our common trappings of woe and funeral arrangements are heathenish and unchristian to the highest degree. Why such gloomy surroundings, in the face of such a faithful saying ? Why *seem* to sorrow as those without hope ? In nothing are we so unchristian as in our views of death.

2. In what the Beatitude consists :

(i.) *In rest :* From the struggle, toil, temptations, and all which imperilled ultimate salvation "—" For ever with the Lord."

(f)

(ii.) In that *their works do follow them :*
Throws light upon future life. Their *activities,* as
God's true servants, follow them, and they go to
continue them. Death is no *sleep,* nor *idleness* and
inactivity. Their work not done. On this side of
death = only apprenticeship—afterwards comes the
real work : "Servant of God, well done." "Enter
into the joy of thy Lord." "Have rule over," etc.

(iii.) In that there is a higher joy to follow
(chap. xx.). "Blessed . . . first resurrection."
(*a*)

BEGINNING

" *In the beginning* " (Gen. i. 1 and xxviii. 12)

The material universe, so the sages allege, is a
vast assemblage of atoms or molecules, "motes in
the sunbeam" of science,—which has existed for
myriads of ages under a perpetual system of evolution, restricture, and change, traversed by forces
electrical or magnetic : and these, by their incessant and indomitable action, are adequate to
account for all the phenomena of the world of
matter, and of man. The upheaval of a continent ;
the drainage of a sea ; the creation of a metal ;
nay, the origin of life, and the development of a
species in plant, or animal, or man : these are the
achievements of fixed and natural laws among the
atomic materials under the vibration of the forces
alone. Thus far the vaunted discoveries of science
have arrived. Let us indulge them with this
theory, that these results are accurate and real.
But a thoughtful mind will demand, Whence did
these atoms derive their existence ? and from
what, and from whom, do they inherit the propensities wherewithal they are imbued ? Tell me
what is the origin of these forces ? And with
whom resides the impulse of their action and the
guidance of their control ? *Nothing so difficult as
a beginning.*
Your philosopher is mute ! He has reached the
horizon of his domain, and to him all beyond is
doubt, uncertainty, and guess. We must lift the
veil. We must pass into the borderland between
two worlds, and there inquire at the oracles of
revelation, touching the unseen and spiritual
powers which thrill through the visible creation :

" Myriads of spiritual things that walk unseen,
   Both when we wake and when we sleep ! "

They mould the atom : they wield the force ; and,
as Newton rightly guessed, they rule the world of
matter beneath the silent omnipotence of God.
"And he dreamed a dream, and behold a ladder
set up on the earth, and the top of it reached to
heaven ; and behold the angels of God ascending
and descending on it. And behold the Lord stood
above it " (Gen. xxviii. 12). *Tolle, lege.*
(*b*)   *R. S. Hawker*

" BEGINNING AT JERUSALEM " (Luke xxiv. 47)

It would have been a sad thing for the world if
the Lord of it had not sought first the lost sheep
of the house of Israel : one awful consequence of
our making haste to pull out the mote out of our
heathen brother's eye, while yet the beam is in our
own, is, that wherever our missionaries go, they
are followed by a foul wave of our vices.
(*c*)   *G. MacDonald*

BEHOLD

The four " *beholds* " in Isaiah—" Behold, My
servants shall eat, but ye shall be hungry ; Behold,
My servants shall drink, but ye shall be thirsty ;
Behold, My servants shall rejoice, but ye shall be
ashamed ; Behold, My servants shall sing for joy
of heart, but ye shall cry for sorrow of heart, and
howl for vexation of spirit " (lxv. 13).
How many Beholds are here ! Every Behold is
not only a call to the careless to consider, but also
a declaration from heaven : that thus it shall be at
last with all impenitent sinners. That is, when
others sing in heaven, they shall sorrow and howl
in hell ! Wherefore let me advise that you be not
afraid of, but rather covet a broken heart and contrite spirit. I say, covet it now, now the white
flag is hung out, now the golden sceptre of grace
is held forth to you. And take this notice, that
this is not the *first* time that I have given you this
advice.
(*d*)   *John Bunyan*

BELIEF

There are some men who are capable of believing everything but the Bible.
(*e*)   *Napoleon*

BELIEF CONTAINS AN INTELLECTUAL ELEMENT :—
Association of *means* to an *end.*
(i.) The lamb running to its ewe mother for
milk and warmth.
(ii.) Every animal with a home, and able to leave
it and return, knows a little geography.
(*f*)   *Bain*

BELIEF HAS A MENTAL FOUNDATION

There is a spontaneous and voluntary belief ;
we believe whatever is not contradicted. Human
nature believes that its own experience is the
measure of all men's experience, and it takes a
long education to abate the feeling, which Bacon
calls " the anticipation of nature."
(*g*)   *Bain*

RELIGIOUS BELIEF is a belief in cheering circumstances, and is a tonic to the mind. Alternating
according to the strength of faith : if feeble, joy
will increase it, or sorrow depress it.
Its opposite is *doubt,* as when we are not able to
arrive at a conviction.
Hope is belief in its cheering aspect.
Its opposite is *despondency*—the belief in coming evil, as an over-matched enemy.
The extremity of despondency is *despair.*
N.B.—When we are able to give an answer for
our hope—*i.e.* base it on evidence—a well-balanced
mind ensues, which will not be affected by fits of
elation or depression.
(*h*)   *Bain*

BELIEF ; WHAT WE BELIEVE WE ACT UPON, as
in the case of good and bad coin. But there are
apparent exceptions.
1. Acting against our belief, as in taking strong
drink. The pleasure is a stronger motive than the
Belief. Belief is an inducement to act, but it may
be overpowered by a stronger motive. It has
(*i*)

different degrees of force; yet if it vanquishes the smallest resistance it *is belief*. So with a believer in a future life; he may not act in the face of a strong opposition, yet if he does anything at all he would not otherwise do, the smallest *present* sacrifice, his is *real*, though feeble, belief.

2. Believing where there is no occasion to act upon, as in past history. The facts of astronomy, geology, etc., we believe, though there is no intention of acting.

3. Belief determined by feeling, as in the emotional part of our nature.

4. Belief engendered by intellectual processes; doubt is changed into conviction; here belief follows argument or action.

(a) *Bain*

BELIEF AND DECISION

It is interesting to note who are the *decided characters* in life. *Men prompt in action on all occasions.* They are men distinguished for energy (not intelligence), a profuse spontaneity lending itself to *motives few and strong* (belief). Intelligence in excess paralyses action, and reduces it in quantity, though doubtless improving it in quality.

(b) *Bain*

BELIEVE, BY THIS WE (John xvi. 30-32)

Disciples indicate that their doubts and uncertainties henceforth had left them—now they *believe*. Jesus—incredulous—" Do ye now *Believe?*" —knowing them thoroughly, He adds, " Soon your faith will be tried, and then ye will forsake Me." Hence even genuine faith is at *first somewhat delusive.*

There is a flush of holy joy at conversion, a buoyant pulse of spiritual being, the thought that we are strong, that nothing could make us ashamed of Christ, or induce us to be faithless to Him. Like a ship we expand every sail; we walk with giddy head and unheeding steps : storms, rocks, traps, alike unheeded. Safe through the " slough of despond," we think we are safe from danger=" *Now we believe.*"

Presently the storm gathers, the hurricane, like a wild tornado, sweeps over us, the foundations are all but uprooted—we tremble, and in our terror we experience the truth of the poet's words :

> I asked the Lord that I might grow
> In faith and love and every grace,
> Might more of His salvation know,
> And seek more earnestly His face;
> Instead of this He made me feel
> The hidden evils of my heart,
> And let the angry powers of hell
> Assault my soul in every part.
> " Lord, what is this? " I trembling cried ;
> " Wilt Thou pursue Thy worm to death? "
> " 'Tis in this way," the Lord replied,
> " I answer prayer for grace and faith."

So the disciples had to experience—for that which we call faith is at first little more than a mixed, adulterated article, which requires testing and purifying by all the after vicissitudes of life.

An additional reason for such changes may be found in the fact that we oftentimes take our *feelings*, which at first are strongly excited, for *faith;* only the buffetings apparently of the after experiences enable us to " distinguish between things that differ." (*See* FEELINGS.)

(c)

BELIEVER

" *In that very day his thoughts perish* " (Ps. cxlvi. 4).

I had rather be the poorest believer than the greatest king on earth. . . . How can you affright him? Bring him word that his estate is ruined. " Yet my inheritance is safe," says he. " Your wife, or child, or dear friend, is dead." " Yet my Father lives." " You yourself must die." " Well, then, I go home to my Father, and to my inheritance."

(d) *Leighton*

BELIEVERS are made so pure by the full, free, and all-sufficient sacrifice of Christ, that we are accounted before God as if we had never committed any sin.

(e) *J. Reeve*

BELIEVING

There are three means of believing : by inspiration, by reason, and by habit.

(f) *Blaise Pascal*

" BELIEVING " = BE-LIVING.

(g) *Carlyle*

BELIEVING ONLY WHAT WE UNDERSTAND, ABSURDITY OF

S. T. Coleridge mentioned a rebuke of a clergyman to a young man who said that he would believe nothing which he could not understand :— " Then, young man, your creed will be the shortest of any man's that I know."

(h) *Table Talk*

We are compelled to believe in mysteries. Two travellers went to hear a sermon—and after they had returned to their hotel, they said the minister did not appeal to their *reason*, and they would not believe anything they could not *reason out.* An old man, sitting by, overheard them, and said —" You say you will not believe anything you can't reason out. Now as I was coming to this place in the train yesterday, I noticed some sheep and cattle and swine and geese, all eating grass in the same field. Now, can you tell me by what process that same grass is turned into feathers, hair, bristles, and wool ? "

" No, we can't tell that."

" Do you believe it is a fact ? "

" Oh, yes, it is a fact."

Then said he, " But I thought you said you would not believe anything you *could not reason out ?* "

(i)

BELIEVING, JOY AND PEACE IN (1 Pet. i. 8, 9; Rom. xv. 13 ; xiv. 17).

There is at stake peace and joy of conscience, except God alone, who holds out to us in His word of grace forgiveness of sins and justification for Christ's sake. That is " the sun which daily rises in the heavens, and not only chases away the past night, but ever pursues its course, and lights up the whole day. Although it comes into darkness and is enveloped in thick clouds—nay, although a

(j)

man may shut out its light from himself with closed doors and windows—yet does it remain the same sun, and breaks forth again, that we may continually look upon it again."

(a)   *Harless and Luther*

BELIEVING AND SALVATION

There is no way under heaven to be interested in Christ, but by believing. *He that believeth shall be saved*, let his sins be ever so great; and *He that believeth not shall be damned*, let his sins be ever so little.

(b)   *Thos. Brooks*

BELSHAZZAR

"In *that night* was Belshazzar slain" (Dan v. 30).

On what *night*?

1. The night of his impious *feast*—when he blasphemed the God of heaven and earth. On that night God shows the insensate king and his nobles that they are but dancing and revelling over hell, and that there is but a step between them and death.

The story runs that when Moscow was burning, a party was dancing in the palace over a gunpowder magazine. They did not know it was there. The flames came on, and one of the revellers said—"Let us have one dance more," and they all shouted through the palace—"*One dance more.*" The music played, the feet bounded, the laughter rang; but suddenly through the smoke and fire and thunder of the explosion, death and eternity broke in. So was it with Belshazzar that night—it was his last revel. Retribution sure and steady was awaiting him. Men die as they live—true of all, Christian or no Christian, "Whether we live, we live unto the Lord: living or dying we are the Lord's." As Belshazzar lived, so he died.

2. The night of the mysterious handwriting. Cf. guilty Paris: during the Commune, it was said, "In one hour is thy judgment come." The course of guilty pleasure may be sweet, but it is short. In a moment God steps in and spoils the sport. Those fingers writing silently on the wall are enough to sober Belshazzar. (See "Balances.")

3. On the night when he was weighed and found wanting—his minutes *numbered*, his conduct *weighed*, his kingdom *divided*.

(c)

BENEDICTION (1 Cor. i. 3)

The heathen commenced their letters with the salutation, "Health!" There is a life of the flesh, and there is a life of the spirit—a truer, more real, and higher life; above and beyond all the Apostle wished them this. He wished them neither "health" nor "happiness," but "grace and peace from God our Father, and from the Lord Jesus Christ."

(d)   *F. W. Robertson*

BETHEL = The House of God

The spot consecrated to God by Jacob. The stone which was his pillow during the night he anointed with oil, and set up as a memorial of the Divine manifestation.

From this fact arose the custom of anointing stones, which superstition soon, imagined, became animated with some Divine power. Hence their name βαιθύλια, βαιθύλιοι, Baithylia, or *consecrated stones*, which were false Bethels.

Bochartus = that the Phœnicians first worshipped *this* stone, and afterwards consecrated others, to which they gave the above names.

Other heathen writers attribute them to Saturn. Herodotus = that in the temple of Heliopolis, in Syria, there was a stone, said to be dropped from heaven, called *Baityli*.

Cf. 1 Pet. ii. 4: "As oil is the emblem of the gifts of the Holy Spirit, so those who receive this anointing are considered as being *alive* unto God, and are called by St. Peter *living stones*."

(e)   *Adam Clarke*

It is probable that the Apostle here refers to these βαιτύλια, or *living stones* of antiquity, as representing the true worshippers of God, who are consecrated to His service, and are made partakers of the Holy Ghost, and these alone are the true *living stones* of which the spiritual temple (or House of God) is raised.

Tradition says that Jacob's pillar was taken to Jerusalem, and put in the second temple; and after that was destroyed by Titus, it was removed to Spain, thence to Ireland, then to Scotland, and from times unknown the kings of Scotland had been crowned upon it. Edward I. brought it to Westminster, and there this stone (Jacob's pillar) now rests under the chair where the monarchs of England are crowned.

(f)   *Jones' Dictionary of Proper Names*

[Gen. xxxii

Jacob called the place, where he had slept and dreamed, *Bethel*. He made a vow, that if the Lord would be with him, and keep him, "*in this way that I go*," giving him also bread and raiment; and bring him back again to his *father's house* in peace, then the Lord should be his God. This, as the subsequent narrative shows, was fulfilled.

(i.) At Padan-Aram God blessed him, so that *the man increased*, etc. (xxx. 43).

(ii.) But being justly dissatisfied with Laban's treatment of him, he resolved upon making a change; and God in a dream said to him, "I AM THE GOD OF BETHEL, *where thou madest a vow; now arise, get thee from this land, and return unto the land of thy kindred.*" He immediately set out.

(iii.) But hearing that Esau was come out, with hostile intentions, to meet him, *Jacob was greatly afraid and distressed*, and resorted unto prayer, pleading God's promise to him, "Surely I will do thee good." Having made arrangements, and taken all necessary precautions, "there wrestled a man with him," to whom he said, "I will not let thee go, except thou bless me." Prevailing with God, he was comforted as to the future. Having met Esau amicably, he followed slowly behind; but instead of immediately going *to his father's house*, he settled down at Shalem (Shechem), where his daughter was defiled and his house polluted, and his son's violence caused his name "to stink among the people of the land." Again he had recourse to prayer, and God reminds him

(g)

of his error in settling at Shalem : "*Arise, go to Bethel, and dwell there.*" Cleansing his household, he obeyed ; fear fell on the people of the land, and they did not pursue him. At *Bethel*, God again blessed him. Finally we find (xxxv. 27) that Jacob "came unto Isaac his father . . . where Abraham and Isaac sojourned." Thus we learn that God keeps His people to the original terms. He had said to Jacob, " Go back to thy father's house "—on his way Jacob, from some unexplained cause, stayed at Shalem, where sin and consequent trouble befel him, till finally he was brought through Bethel home to his father, where he received a further blessing, and was "*anointed* with fresh oil." He "*renewed* his strength."

(*a*)

BETHEL, A HOUSE OF GOD

A barn, or a stable, hedge, or any other place, is truly desirable if God is there.

(*b*)   *D. Brainerd*

[Gen. xxviii. 17

BETHEL, the consecrated (Jacob at). Bethel, the desecrated (by dead men's bones).

(*c*)   *Stokoe*

BETHLEHEM, GOLGOTHA, AND EASTER

Though Christ were born a thousand times in Bethlehem, and *not in thee*, thou remainest, nevertheless, eternally lost. If the cross of Golgotha is not erected in thy heart, it cannot deliver thee from the evil one. Mark, that it is to thee of no avail that Christ has risen, if thou continuest lying in sin and the bonds of death.

(*d*)   *Angelus Silesius*

BIBLE, THE (John xxi. 24, 25)

This collection of books has been to the world what no other book has ever been to a nation. States have been founded on its principles. Kings rule by a compact based on it. Men hold the Bible in their hands when they prepare to give solemn evidence affecting life, death, or property ; the sick man is almost afraid to die unless the Book be within reach of his hands ; the battleship goes into action with one on board whose office is to expound it ; its prayers, its psalms are the language which we use when we speak to God ; eighteen centuries have found no holier, no diviner language. If ever there has been a prayer or a hymn enshrined in the heart of a nation, you are sure to find its basis in the Bible. There is no new religious idea given to the world, but it is merely the development of something given in the Bible. The very translation of it has fixed language and settled the idioms of speech. Germany and England speak as they speak because the Bible was translated. It has made the most illiterate peasant more familiar with the history, customs, and geography of ancient Palestine than with the localities of his own country. Men who know nothing of the Grampians, of Snowdon, or of Skiddaw, are at home in Zion, the lake of Gennesaret, or among the hills of Carmel. People who know little about London, know by heart the palaces in Jerusalem, where those blessed feet

trod which were nailed to the cross. Men who know nothing of the architecture of a Christian cathedral, can yet tell you all about the pattern of the Holy Temple. Even this shows us the influence of the Bible. The orator holds a thousand men for half an hour breathless—a thousand men as one, listening to his single word. But this Word of God has held a thousand nations for thrice a thousand years spell-bound ; held them by an abiding power, even the universality of its truth ; and we feel it to be no more a collection of books, but *the* Book.

(*e*)   *F. Robertson* (?)

And in that charter reads with sparkling eyes
Her title to a treasure in the skies.

(*f*)   *Cowper*

Within that awful volume lies
The mystery of mysteries !
Happiest they of human race,
To whom our God has granted grace
To read, to fear, to hope, to pray,
To lift the latch and force the way ;
And better had they ne'er been born,
Who read to doubt, or read to scorn.

(*g*)   *W. Scott*

Whence, but from heaven, could men unskilled in arts,
In several ages born, in several parts,
Weave such agreeing truths ? or how or why
Should they conspire to cheat us with a lie ?

(*h*)   *Dryden*

Begins with Genesis=the Book of the *First Things*.
1. In the kingdom of nature.
2. In the kingdom of sin.
3. In the kingdom of the world and culture.
4. In the kingdom of grace and redemption.
And closes with the Book of Revelation = the Book of the *Last Things*.
1. The last struggles between God's kingdom and the hostile world.
2. The last conclusion of peace on earth, the new heaven and the new earth.
Jesus is all through, " I am the *First and the Last*," for " the testimony of Jesus is the spirit of prophecy."

(*i*)   *Martensen.*

BIBLE, ASSAULTS ON

Voltaire said that the Bible would not be read in the 19th century.
Some appear to think that it argues great pluck for a man to assail the Bible and the Church. The fact is, it requires no courage at all to do so, for he is always sure of the favour and applause of a multitude who hate the Bible and would be glad to see it struck on any side, and to have Christianity crippled. But the Bible goes right on, and the Church of God goes right on, and Christianity goes right on, and the chief damage is done to the critics. There have never been so many live churches as to-day. More people believe the Gospel than ever before, and vaster multitudes are attempting to practise its precepts. The attempt to shatter the Bible for the last three

(*j*)

hundred years has not rent asunder or dislodged a single doctrine or sentiment. After its present assailants are all dead, their funeral sermons will be preached from the Book—not one verse omitted —from the first page of Genesis to the last page of Revelation. One would think the world would get tired of the bombardment of the Bible castle when, with all their concentrated fire of three hundred years, they have not been able to knock out a splinter large enough to make the most sensitive eyeball quiver.

(a)					*Bishop Temple*

BIBLE (A CASE-BOOK)

In Genesis, in the patriarchal times—of which Genesis tells the tale—I find the record of enough sin. (Yes, and I should not believe in my Bible if I did not, any more than I should believe in a medical book which professed to give an account of the human body, but omitted all mention of disease.)

(b)					*Gordon Calthrop*

BIBLE, DEFENCE OF

It has been for thirty years the deep conviction of my soul that no book can be written on behalf of the Bible like the Bible itself. Man's defences are man's word . . . the Bible is God's word, and by it the Holy Ghost, who first spoke it, still speaks to the soul that closeth itself not against it.

(c)					*Pusey*

BIBLE, DEMOLISHING THE

They overthrew the Bible a century ago, in Voltaire's time. "In less than a hundred years," said Voltaire, "Christianity will have been swept from existence, and will have passed into history." Infidelity ran riot through France, red-handed and impious. A century has passed away. Voltaire has "passed into history," but his old printing press, it is said, has been used to print the Word of God; and the very house where he lived is packed with Bibles, a depôt for the Geneva Bible Society.

Thomas Paine thought he had demolished the Bible; but after he had gone despairingly to a drunkard's grave in 1809, more than twenty times as many Bibles have been produced and scattered through the world than had been produced since the creation of man. Up to the year 1800, from four to six million copies of the Scriptures, in thirty different languages, was the total of production since the world began.

Eighty years later, in 1880, the statistics of the eighty different Bible Societies now in existence, give a total of 165,000,000 Bibles and Testaments and portions of Scripture, with 206 translations, distributed alone since 1804, to say nothing of the unknown millions circulated by private publishers throughout the world. For a book that has been demolished so many times, it still shows signs of considerable life.

(d)

BIBLE, "EAT THE BOOK" (Ezek. ii. 8)

The prophet is to "*eat*" the Book sent to him. So with us. The Book, by the help of the Spirit, is to become part of ourselves. We are to become,

as it were, "living Bibles," the words translated into the actions and feelings of human life.

(e)					*Gordon Calthrop*

BIBLE, EPOCHS OF EXEGESIS

There are *three* such.

1. The Patristic is, to a large extent, the result of a victorious conflict of ancient Christians with Ebionism, Gnosticism, Arianism, Pelagianism, and other radical heresies, which roused and stimulated the fathers to a vigorous investigation and defence of the truth as laid down in the Scriptures and believed by the Church.

2. The Reformatory bears on every page the modes of the gigantic war with Romanism and its traditions of men.

3. The Modern evangelical theology of Germany has grown up amidst the changing fortunes of a more than thirty years' war of Christianity with Rationalism and Pantheism.

The future historian will represent this intellectual and spiritual conflict, which is not yet concluded, as one of the most important and interesting chapters in history, and as one of the most brilliant victories of faith over unbelief, of Christian truth over anti-Christian error. . . . Never before has the Bible been assailed and defended with more learning, acumen, and perseverance. Never before has the critical apparatus been so ample, or so easy of access.

(f)					*Lange*

BIBLE FACTS

The Prince of Grenada, heir to the Spanish throne, imprisoned by order of the Crown, was kept in solitary confinement in the old prison of Skulls, Madrid. After thirty-three years in this living tomb, death came to his release, and the following amongst other remarkable researches taken from the Bible, and marked with an old nail on the rough walls of his cell, told how the brain sought employment through the weary years :—

Acts of Apostles xxvi. is the finest chapter to read.

Psalm xxiii. is the most beautiful chapter in the Bible.

John xiv. 2 ; vi. 37 ; Matt. xi. 28 ; and Ps. xxxvii. 4 are the four most inspiring promises in the Bible.

Isaiah lx. 1 is the verse for new converts to study.

All who flatter themselves should learn Matt. vi.

Every one should learn Luke vi. (20 to end).

(g)

THE BIBLE AND HOPE

The Bible is a precious storehouse, and the Magna Charta of a Christian. There he reads of his Heavenly Father's love, and of his dying Saviour's legacies. There he sees a map of his travels through the wilderness, and a landscape, too, of Canaan. And when he climbs on Pisgah's top, and views the promised land, his heart begins to burn, delighted with the blessed prospect, and amazed at the rich and free salvation. But a mere professor, though a decent one, looks on the Bible as a dull book, and peruseth it with such indifference as you would read the title-deeds belonging to another man's estate.

(h)					*Berridge*

BIBLE, THE ONE BOOK

It is said that on one occasion when a number of wits among the French Encyclopedists were conversing, the question having been proposed, what book each would choose to take with him into prison or exile, if his choice were restricted to one, all exclaimed, "The Bible." I do not know on what authority the story rests, though I have seen it recently quoted by a French writer.

(a) *Perowne.*

"Bring THE *Book*," said Sir Walter Scott, when dying. "What book?" asked his friend. "There is *only* ONE *Book*—the Bible," replied the dying man.

(b)

THE BIBLE, PAST AND FUTURE OF

A book that has had such a past as the Bible, will also have a future.

(c) *Tholuck*

BIBLE, POWER OF

Missionaries are frequently startled by discovering persons, and even communities, who have hardly ever seen or heard an ordained missionary, who have nevertheless made considerable progress in Christian knowledge, obtained by means of hap-hazard circulation of tracts and portions of Scripture.

In an instance, which I know was carefully investigated, all the inhabitants of a remote village in the Deccan had abjured idolatry and caste, removed from their temples the idols which had been worshipped there time out of mind, and agreed to profess a form of Christianity which they had deduced for themselves from a careful perusal of a single Gospel and a few tracts. These books had not been given by any missionary, but had been casually left with some clothes and other cast-off property by a merchant, whose name even had been forgotten, and who, as far as could be ascertained, had never spoken of Christianity to his servant, to whom he gave at parting these things with others of which he had then no further need.

(d) *Sir Bartle Frere on Indian Missions*

The more the Bible is spread, the more the Bible is studied, the deeper, the profounder the thought that is spent upon it, the more earnest the inquiry bestowed upon it, the more careful the criticism, the closer the examination, all the more shall it stand out conspicuous for the spiritual nature, the marvellous power which breathes through all its pages, and tell mankind of the truth. I fear not any examination to which it can be subjected. I fear not criticism of its history nor any investigation of its sources. I fear not any examination of the details of its meaning. I know that whatever else shall go, this will stand. This is, indeed, the message of God Almighty to man; and as long as man remains here on earth, still shall he find, in ever-increasing measure, the power which the Book has to uplift his soul. It is always for that reason a matter of joy to me that the Church of England, of which I am an unworthy minister, should put forward this Book so promi-

nently before all its sons, should provide that it be read publicly from end to end, should provide that so large a portion should be read in every service which she offers to God, should tell all her members to look there for the authority for everything that she teaches, and should rest the proof of her claim to be indeed commissioned by Almighty God on the evidence that she can collect from the pages of God's Holy Word.

(e) *Bishop Temple*

" *Thou hast been a strength to the needy in his distress* " (Isa. xxv. 4).

A few years since, in a fearful gale on Christmas-eve, an old man-of-war's man and his wife, who lived in a lighthouse constructed on wooden piles driven into the sand, were awoke by the violence of the storm. The whole place rocked and shook through and through, as if each wave would be its destruction. . . . There seemed scarcely a hope of safety. In the midst of the tempest these people *had one comfort*—the Bible! . . . The wife only could read; and putting her mouth close to her husband's ear, for the roaring of the storm, she read to him from God's Word, expecting every moment to be their last. . . . So they continued till morning broke and the storm ceased.

We have often thought how powerful this scene might be for the painter—or as the basis of a tract on the power of the Holy Scriptures.

(f) *(Authentic.) See the "Theologian" for* 1846

BIBLE, PROHIBITION OF

. . . The cardinal, finding a Bible on her table, immediately crossed himself, beat his breast, and otherwise so well acted his part, that, "having thrown the Bible down and condemned it, he' remonstrated with the fair penitent that it was a kind of reading not adapted for her sex, containing dangerous matters. If she was uneasy in her mind, she should hear two masses instead of one, and rest content with her Paternosters and her Primer, which were not only devotional but ornamented with a variety of elegant forms from the most exquisite pencils of France." . . . This story is drawn from a Huguenot letter, by which we infer that the reformed religion was making considerable progress in the French Court, had the Cardinal of Lorraine not interfered by persuading the mistress, and she the king, and the king his queen, at once to give up psalm-singing and reading the Bible!

(g) *Disraeli: Cur. Lit*

BIBLE-READING (*See* Bath-Kol)

Let me go to the Bible, dismissing my reason and taking the first impression which the words convey, and there is no absurdity, however gross, into which I shall not fall.

(h) *Channing*

BIBLE, SOURCE OF SUPERNATURAL TRUTH

H. Stilling "found the *source* of super-sensible truths in the revelation of God to man, *in the Bible;* and the *source* of all the truths which appertain to this earthly life, in *nature and reason.*"

(i)

BIBLE, THE WORLD'S (2 Cor. iii. 2)

The Christian is the world's Bible, "known and read of all men." It is said the worldly man does not read his Bible. This is not quite true. He does not read *your* Bible, but he reads *you*, and he reads this Bible of his very critically. So take heed to have a correct copy—*a revised edition.*
(a)

BIBLE STUDY

Intense study of the Bible will keep any writer from being *vulgar* in point of style.
(b)   *S. T. Coleridge*

A *Book in cipher*, which none but believers can decipher.
(c)

Look out in a wintry night : at first you see only a few glittering stars, but as you continue to gaze, thousands will burst upon your view. So with regard to the reading of the Bible : at first merely a superficial view of its beauties and comforts, but as you continue to read, thousands and thousands of before unknown gems will shine forth from the Word of Life.
(d)   *Anon*

Of all books in the world, the Bible is one which will not yield up its riches and its sweetness except to the diligent and faithful and earnest student. All great works demand long and patient and persevering study. The lesser mind cannot expect to grasp at once the purpose of the greater. Sir J. Reynolds tells us of the profound disappointment with which he first beheld Raphael's great picture of the Transfiguration at the Vatican. It was only as he came again and again, only as he lingered over it and dwelt upon it till the picture took possession of him, that he at last perceived its grandeur and its harmony.
(e)   *Perowne*

Proceeding from the Spirit of God, it is fully understood *only* by the Spirit, even as it can only be explained and applied by the Spirit. To those who are called and waiting, it opens its mysteries; while to the hardened and the sinner it proves a closed book, as it were with seven seals.
(f)   *Lange*

BIBLE SOCIETY, THE.

The Bible Society defends the Bible by circulating it. What a wondrous defence it is ! It found the world with five million Bibles; it has given to it more than ninety-five millions, nearer 100 million copies. It found the Bible in fifty languages; it sent it out in 250. How wonderful it is when we think that forty of these languages were specially reduced to writing for that purpose ! There are forty languages that eighty years ago were only spoken languages; and now men are reading in their own tongue wherein they were born the wonderful works of God ! I believe that when the Oriental Congress sat in this city some few years ago, and visited the Bible Society's House, in Queen Victoria Street, where they saw the various versions on the shelf, they did not fail to acknowledge that, though this is a Christian, not a literary society, it had done even more for the interests of philology than any literary society in the world. Then you have the number of the issues. How marvellous they are! Last year the number was three millions. It is difficult to comprehend. Put it in another form— five every minute of the day and night all through the year without intermission ! I ask every thoughtful Christian man to ponder well that wonderful fact ! A stream of Divine truth going out over this poor sinful world of ours at the rate of five copies every sixty seconds of the day and night all throughout the year without intermission !
(g)   *Bishop Temple*
[*Compare " Voltaire on the Bible."*]

BIGOTRY   "The Jews have no dealings with the Samaritans " (John iv. 9).

Jewish and Samaritan bigotry continued in the sectarian quarrels of Christendom, contrary to the spirit of Christ. Catholics "have no dealings " with Protestants, nor Episcopalians with Presbyterians, Lutherans with Calvinists, Baptists with Pædobaptists, High Churchmen with Low Churchmen, etc.
(h)   *P. Schaff*

BILLOWS

When the shore is won at last,
Who will count the billows past?
(i)   *Bishop Wordsworth*

BIRTH, THE NEW (John iii. 7)

1. To whom words spoken.
(i.) St. John's Gospel = our Lord's ministry to Jews at Jerusalem ; and He selects one—*best, learned, oldest,* for His first discourse—Nicodemus.
(ii.) He addresses our Lord as " Rabbi" = *Doctor.* Jesus intimates, in reply, that not *learning* but *life* is wanted for the Messiah's kingdom, and life begins with birth.
This Jesus teaches him.
(a) *Indirectly* (ver. 3) : " *Except a man . . . see*" —says nothing of entering and taking part therein.
(b) *Directly* (ver. 7) : " Ye *must be born again* " = you, yourself, Nicodemus.
Mark who this man was.
(a) As to *nationality*—a Jew, one of the chosen people.
(b) As to *religion*—a Pharisee of the better sort, like Paul, zealous for the law ; a circumcised, orthodox Jew, and a teacher of the law.
(c) As to his *social position*—he was a man of rank, a " ruler of the Jews"—a member of the supreme council.
(d) As to his *attitude towards Jesus*—favourable, ready to see Him as the Messiah.
Jesus astonishes this good, estimable old man, of unblemished name, by His words (ver. 7) = "You must *start* in life again, Nicodemus, begin afresh, for you are on the wrong tack." This is to Nicodemus as impossible as that an old man should naturally be born into this world over again.
2. New Birth—regeneration—the central thought of the chapter, the *locus classicus* for the doctrine.
It stands at beginning of John's Gospel, because
(j)

Christianity, according to St. John, is unintelligible without it.

N.B.—His first miracle is one of *transformation.* (water into wine).

First act of Jesus = *reformation* (cleansing the temple).

First *discourse* = *regeneration*, teaching that we must be transformed, reformed, and reborn spiritually and morally, or else we remain outside the Messiah's kingdom.

3. Features of the New Birth

(i.) It is a *new creation*—the agent of which is the Holy Spirit; the means are the ordinary "means of grace."

(ii.) It occurs but *once;* conversions and it are not identical. There may be *relapses* and recoveries = conversions, but the *life* is one throughout. See Peter's " *Once for all.*"

(iii.) It is a *mystery;* so is all life, but it is a manifest fact all the same. Cows, swine, geese, may be seen feeding on the same grass in the field. That grass becomes in one case hair, in another bristles, in a third feathers; but no man can explain the mystery—it is a secret belonging only to the "Lord and Giver of Life." New birth evidences itself in a man's life.

(iv.) It is *absolutely necessary* to salvation. "Ye MUST," not *ought, better,* or *proper.* It is the only appointed way of entering the Kingdom of God. There is a way by *water* into the visible Church, and a way by the *Spirit* into the invisible Church. Cf. *the Vine and its branches* = "*in Me.*"

(v.) It is necessary for *all*, whether good Jew like Nicodemus, heathen like Socrates, or outcast publican. To each and all alike, "Ye must be born again."

Hannibal with his army wanted to cross the Alps, but the towering masses of granite were impassable; yet by a silent work of months he succeeded. How? Did his engineers blast the rocks with huge charges of gunpowder or gun cotton? Not so. They knew nothing of those powerful and destructive agencies then. But by the simple method of pouring vinegar on the rocks and leaving the sun to do the rest. Under their united action the rocks softened, and Hannibal made his road and effected his passage. Man's heart is like the rock; but God's Word, when used by His Spirit, is as a hammer that breaketh the rock—it pierces even to the dividing asunder of the thoughts and intents of the heart. But we must put ourselves in the way of the means; the ship's sails must be unfurled if the wind is to waft the ship on her way. A man's conversion is not likely to happen if he sits at home over his fire, or reads his newspaper, when the Spirit is powerfully present with a neighbouring congregation met together in the name of Jesus.

(a)

BIRTH, NEW: BEGOTTEN AGAIN (1 Pet. i. 3; John iii. 3; Tit. iii. 5; Jas. i. 18; Col. iii. 1; Eph. ii. 10.)

He has kindled in us a new spiritual life by Holy Baptism and the influences of the Holy Spirit connected therewith (Eph. i. 19, 20). He has laid the foundation of re-creating us into His image. He has made us other men in a far more essential sense than it was once said to Saul, "Thou shalt be turned into another man" (1 Sam. x. 6).

What is the principal fruit and end of this new generation? A living hope. Its object is not only our future resurrection, but the whole plenitude of the salvation still to be revealed by Jesus Christ, even until the new heavens and the new earth shall appear (2 Pet. iii. 13, 14; Rev. xxi. 1).

Birth implies life; so it is with the hope of believers, which is the very opposite of the vain, lost, and powerless hope of the worldly-minded. It is powerful, and quickens the heart by comforting, strengthening, and encouraging it, by making it joyous and cheerful in God. Its quickening influence enters even into our physical life. Hope is not only the fulfilment of the new life created in regeneration, but also the innermost kernel of the same.

(b) *Weiss*

BLINDNESS (John ix. 5)

Simple-minded laymen have a sounder eye, a more correct judgment, than false proud scholars and theologians.

(c) *Heubner*

Christ has come into the intellectual world to transform the seeing into blind men, and to endow with sight those who are blind.

(d) *Lange*

On my bended knee
  I recognise Thy purpose clearly shown;
My vision Thou hast dimmed, that I may see
  Thyself, Thyself alone.

(e) *E. Lloyd, on Milton's blindness.*

I can no more believe old Homer blind,
Than those who say the sun hath never shined;
The age wherein he lived was dark; but he
Could not want sight who taught the world to see.

(f) *Denham*

In the blind beggar seated outside the walls of Jericho, the Bible gives us a living portraiture of our natural selves; *i.e.* of what you and I are, with all our excellences, if apart from Jesus Christ. Ay, a preacher may have an audience before him comprising some of the noblest specimens, for character and intellect, of the human race; and if he should happen to know them to be Christless, he is not exceeding the limits of his commission, and we are not to be surprised and offended at him, if we hear him exclaim to them, "You, in spite of your beauty and youth and purity; and you, for all your boundless wealth; and you, for all your gentleness of disposition and kindliness of heart; and you, who are respected for your rank, but far more for the grace with which you bear it; and you, whose name rings round the world, and on whose colossal intellect men are everywhere gazing with astonishment and wonder; yes! one and all of you, without any exception, if you want to know what you are like in the sight of God—look on that beggar there by the roadside at Jericho! Rolling his sightless eyeballs in the vain search after a ray of light from heaven, he reproduces to the very letter your spiritual blindness, your insensibility to the glory of Christ. Poor and helpless, he represents your utter destitution of those

(g)

spiritual possessions which alone can be carried with you into the eternal world. See yourselves depicted in that pitiable object! But see also that the advantage is on his side. For whilst he knows himself to be miserably poor and helplessly blind, you are perfectly satisfied with your condition and seek no cure.

(a)   *Gordon Calthrop*

To Newton and to Newton's dog Diamond, what a different pair of universes; while the painting on the optical retina of both was, most likely, the same!

(b)   *Carlyle*

When I consider the blindness and misery of man, and those amazing contrarieties which discover themselves in his nature; when I observe the whole creation silent, and man without light, abandoned to himself, and, as it were, strayed into this corner of the universe, neither knowing who placed him here, nor what is the end of his coming, nor what will befall him at his departure, I feel the same horror as a person who has been carried in his sleep into a desolate and savage island, and who awakes without knowing where he is, or by what way he may escape. And what is more, I am at a loss to conceive how so miserable a condition can produce anything but despair. I behold other persons near me, of a nature like my own: I ask if they are any better informed than myself; and they tell me they are not. And, what is more, these wretched wanderers, having looked about them, and espied certain pleasurable objects, are become attached and devoted to them. For my own part, I cannot rest here; I cannot repose in the society of these persons, whose condition is no better than my own, being equally wretched, equally helpless. I find they will be able to give me no assistance at my death. I shall die alone, and therefore I must proceed as if I lived, alone.

(c)   *Blaise Pascal*

Hence, reflecting how probable it seems, that there may be something besides what I see, I begin to examine whether that God, who is talked of by all the world, has not left some intimation of Himself. I look around and discover only general darkness; . . . and I have a thousand times wished that if nature have indeed a God, she would distinctly manifest Him; or, if the tokens which she offers are fallacious, she would entirely conceal them: that she would either say all or nothing, so as to determine which course I ought to adopt.

(d)   *Blaise Pascal*

It betrays unnatural blindness to live without inquiring what we are. It betrays far more terrible blindness to live wickedly while we believe in a God. Nearly the whole of mankind are in one or the other of these conditions.

(e)   *Blaise Pascal*

BLINDNESS, PHYSICAL

Saunderson, the optician, blind from his birth, yet, in spite of his terrible disadvantages, made discoveries in the science of light. He who had never seen the sun, nor the tiniest drop of dew, never in fact any external mirror of the Almighty,

cried out when dying, "*God of Newton and of Clarke, have mercy on me!*"

(f)   *J. Baggenson, quoted by Martensen*

BLOOD

When the destroying angel sees the blood of the spotless Lamb of God on the doorposts and lintel of our hearts (the City of My-soul), he will pass over without destroying.

Then Satan comes and says, God will by no means spare the guilty; and by fair words and subtle speeches endeavours to obtain a footing in the city. But he, too, sees the blood-marks, and is arrested; he cannot enter, and with a malignant scowl passes by.

Then Conscience assails the city, and harasses it by bringing to remembrance all the deep and dark sins of the past, and asks whether salvation is possible for such. It, too, is silenced by the blood, and remembers that "the blood of Jesus Christ . . . cleanseth from *all* sin."

(g)   *G. Calthrop*

[Exod. xii.

We must not put our faith in the place of the Saviour, but *in Him.* He said to the Israelites, "When *I* see the blood," not "When *you* see it." Lord, I can't see my assurance in Christ as I want to see it, but Thou canst. Forgive my sin and save my soul.

(h)   *S. Bridge*

No doubt many an anxious and weak-hearted Israelite feared and trembled lest the blood on the lintel should not be seen, nor be efficacious; but this did not alter his fate. When God saw the blood, it was sufficient—the destroyer passed over that house.

(i)   *Cumming.*

"*When I see the BLOOD I will pass over you*" (Exod. xii. 13).

Judgment was averted by the sprinkling of blood =type; but *we have the blood of Christ, as of a Lamb slain for us.* His is the blood of sprinkling which we must use, for there is salvation in no other.

Two simple truths are taught:
1. **The way of salvation is easy**
(i.) *For them.* The blood was shed, stood ready. The hyssop was a very common wayside thing, easily obtained outside any cottage. They had but to obey, sprinkle the blood, to be safe on that dreadful night.
(ii.) *For us,* too. *The blood* is shed; all is ready for our using. We have to exercise faith in it, and faith is a common every-day thing—we live by it. The sun sets, we *believe* it will rise again; we sow seed, we *believe* it will grow; we enter a boat, because we *believe* it will carry us across a stream, etc. Faith is an *easy* thing, and yet it is the way of salvation. "*Believe on the Lord Jesus Christ,*" etc.

2. **The great peril of neglect**
(i.) *Neglect then.* The blood was put into a basin; suppose they left it there, neglected, or *forgot what to do with it*—there would have been no escape.
(ii.) *Neglect now.* Treating the blood of Christ as a common thing—a theme for the preacher—no-

(j)

thing to us—of no value. Or worse, treading it under foot, putting it on the threshold instead of on the doorposts and lintel of our hearts, counting it an unholy thing, and so crucifying Christ afresh.

(iii.) *How shall we escape if we neglect such great salvation?* A man may neglect taking his medicine, or throw physic to the dogs, or out of the window, and so imperil his health; but in the matter of salvation he risks everything by *neglect.*

(*a*)

BLOOD

Illustration of the Danger of Delay and Neglect

On the night of the Passover in a Jewish family there lay ill in bed a little daughter. She knew of the instructions given by Moses for their safety; she understood their urgency and the importance of obedience. As night drew on she asked her father whether the blood had been sprinkled as commanded. "Hush, child," he replied; "I ordered it to be done." Waiting a while and not being satisfied, the child again asked the same question; and again the father answered as before. But as midnight drew near, and her anxiety could not be restrained, she raised herself and said, "Father, take me in your arms and carry me outside, that I may see whether the blood is sprinkled on the doorposts and lintel." He did so, but only to find that his order had not been executed. Then, the story relates, at the last moment he rushed into the house, seized the hyssop-brush, and with a swish dashed the blood on the posts and lintel, and thus made the household secure. It was all but *too late.* How narrow the escape! Those that *neglect* suffer equally with the *despisers* in the Day of Judgment.

(*b*)   *Jewish Legend*

BLOOD BE ON US, HIS (Matt. xxvii. 25)

The deed of blood was done. That last one of a long score. No immediate sad results followed. Forty years elapsed, and then the "eagles (of Rome) were gathered together." The "carcase" was there, and the avenger of blood was at the door. Josephus, an eye-witness of the tribulation such as never was, tells us how fearful was the *blood* reckoning which then ensued.

The Jews fought so desperately that, when captured, the Romans showed them no mercy.

The famine within the city was so severe that hundreds and thousands risked their lives by venturing outside the walls in search of food. Of these the Romans captured sometimes *more than five hundred* a day, and the captives were (i.) whipped, (ii.) horribly tortured, (iii.) crucified before the walls of the city, in order to intimidate those within.

The Roman soldiers, out of hatred to their Jewish foes, nailed their captives, as they caught them, one after another, to rude crosses of wood, one on this side and another on the other; and the number of such became so great, that room was wanting for the crosses, and crosses wanting for the bodies. Literally a living belt of writhing agony surrounded the doomed city.

"*His blood be on our children*" likewise found fulfilment. The sufferings of women and children, not immediately engaged in the defence of the city, but bound up in its doom, is likewise graphically pictured by Josephus.

The famine destroyed every proper feeling: children pulled away the morsels which their fathers were eating; mothers did the same to their children. If a house was shut up, the Jewish soldiers, concluding that food was therein, broke in and pulled the food out of the mouths of those who were eating. Old men were beaten, children lifted up and dashed down again to make them relax their grasp of a piece of bread. But, to crown all, the words of Moses found literal fulfilment: mothers, driven by dire extremity, did eat the flesh of their own children. Josephus gives the horrible details of one instance. The woman's name, her family, house, village, are mentioned in detail, bearing the stamp of truth. This woman —having retired from the city, to be free of the seditious Jews, who plundered every house, and were dreaded more than the Romans—when she could find no more food, caught up her infant son, and said, "Oh thou miserable infant, come, be thou my food, and a bye-word to the world." She then killed the child, roasted the body, and ate one part, and concealed the other. Then when the seditious Jews, discovering that she had food, rushed in, threatening to kill her unless she gave them food, she replied that she had saved a portion for them. Having uncovered it, she said, "This is my own son. Come, eat; for I have eaten myself." Seeing their horror, she continued, "Do you pretend to be more tender than a woman, or more compassionate than a mother?" The dreadful tale got abroad, and, adds the same authority, "Never did a city suffer such miseries, nor any age breed a generation more fruitful in wickedness than this, since the beginning of the world."

Portents alarmed the now terrified Jews. False prophets, maniacal deceivers, told them of deliverance never to come. A comet appeared over the city a whole year, with a tail like a sword. Chariots and troops of soldiers were seen in the clouds. Strange and supernatural voices were heard in the Temple. The priests, going by night into the inner court of the Temple, as was their custom, said they first felt a quaking of the ground, then heard a great noise, and after that a sound as of a great multitude saying, "Let us remove hence," "Let us remove hence"; and one is reminded of Ezekiel's description of the Spirit of God forsaking His temple—a people whose God had given them up.

(*c*)   *See "Josephus"*

BLOTTING OUT HANDWRITING (Col. ii. 13, 14)

We *pray,* "Forgive us our trespasses."
We *read,* "Having forgiven you all trespasses."
N.B.—Our position before God.

1. He is our creditor; we His debtor.
(i.) He is *omniscient.* . . . We cannot *hide* our debt; the thief thinks no eye can see him.
(ii.) He is *Almighty.* . . . He can *exact* payment by force . . . to the "uttermost farthing."
(iii.) He is *just* . . . He *will* and *must* be paid.
(iv.) He is *omnipresent.* . . . We cannot *escape* Him, as Jonah thought to do.
"Whither shall I flee from Thy presence?"

2. But we are taught in the text that our debt, great as it is, has been paid for us by Another (Christ): "And you being dead," etc. (ver. 13).
(i.) The bill has been sent in:
The handwriting opposite our names is against

(*d*)

us—contrary to us. Some have seen this account, and cried out, "Have mercy on me, and I will pay all."

(ii.) But the bill has been paid, "blotted out"; obliterated; cancelled; paid in blood. "Come, let us reason together" (Isa. i. 18).

(iii.) The bill, moreover, has been destroyed—invalid—"took it out of the way"—crumpled up and torn, thrown into fire—not *against you* now. It is out of sight, "behind His back ; " like a stone thrown into water, sunk.

(iv.) Nailed to His cross. That was the reckoning for *your* sin. That blood payeth, dischargeth, *cleanseth* you. " Who shall condemn when Christ hath died? " See the cancelled bill nailed to His cross, and go thy way a pardoned man, that can again hold up thy head and not be ashamed.

(*a*)

BODY

" *Keep under the body* " (1 Cor. ix. 27)

Be careful to give the precept its proper meaning, and to obey it in the right sense. Keep under the body, as a rider keeps his horse beneath him; as the sailor keeps the deck ; as the builder keeps ladder and scaffolding beneath. Keep it in constant subjection to the mind. Keep it under, that the whole intellectual force may securely rest and rise upon it; that it may not be an opponent of the spirit, but its continual support and minister.

(*b*)　　　　　　　　　　　　　　　　*Storrs*

BOLDNESS

" *Let us therefore come boldly* " (Heb. iv. 16)

For the *ground* of the exhortation, see context.

(i.) **Divine knowledge**=that we cannot hope to screen ourselves in any way ; not even our thoughts *hid* from the gaze of Him with whom we have to do.

(ii.) Notwithstanding this fact, we are reminded that the Divine Being *sympathizes* with us, as encompassed with infirmities : we have a *brother* on the throne.

(iii.) This sympathy is not merely passive, but active ; it leads Him to be gracious unto us, and merciful towards our sins.

= Divine *Knowledge, Sympathy, and Grace.*

1. **Divine Knowledge of us** (vers. 12, 13).

(i.) We live in a blaze of light—have to do with a *Heart-Searcher.*

(ii.) The Omniscient Author of our being, *in whom,* etc.

(iii.) *Whose word*=quick, powerful, sharper, piercing, dividing, discerning between body, soul, and spirit.

No creature, motive, thought, intention escapes ; everything naked and open to the eye of Him with whom we have to do.

(iv.) *N.B.*—*The Bible,* which we despise, is the *Word of God.* We have to do with Him, not with its writers. *Sermons* (=feebleness)=*God's Word,* not the preacher's—able to save souls.

(v.) Therefore, conscience-smitten, we are speechless in self-defence=like Peter and others : " Depart from me, for I am a sinful man, O Lord."

How can we come *boldly* ?

2. **Divine Sympathy.**

Note the advance from Old Testament conceptions of God :

Old Testament=(i.) " I *know,*" " I have *seen,*" " I have *heard* " their sorrows.

(ii.) The Lord God *merciful* and *gracious,* etc.

(iii.) " Merciful and *full* of compassion."

(iv.) " He *knoweth* our frame, *remembereth* that we are but dust."

A manifold gradation ; but all fall short of the *sympathy* here taught us. Before God can have experimental knowledge of human nature and its trials and sorrows, there must be an *incarnation.*

(v.) The text builds itself on this fact,·

" He is *touched* with a feeling of our infirmities."

" He took our infirmities "=He became *brotherly.*

N.B.—Not sympathy with *sin,* but with our infirmities. This=His qualification for helping us.

3. **Divine Grace,** based on the foregoing.

The throne of grace illustrated by Joseph's treatment of his brothers. Therefore COME BOLDLY :

(i.) **Because our case is desperate,** our sins and sorrows many. " There is no corn in the land."

" We perish if we do not come."

" We may, we must, draw near."

(ii.) Because we have a Joseph on the throne.

(iii.) Because it is a throne of *grace,* freely bestowed on condition of faith, and not merit.

(iv.) Because, as Jewish high priest came sprinkled with blood into the holy of holies without fear, so we, sprinkled with the blood of Jesus, may approach and stand before God without fear.

Wherefore let us hold fast our profession without wavering.

(*c*)

BOOK OF LIFE (Rev. xxi. 27)

The most lasting families have only their seasons, more or less, of a certain constitutional strength. They have their spring and summer sunshine glare, their wane, decline, and death. They flourish and shine, perhaps for ages; at last they sicken, their light grows pale, and at a crisis, when the offsets are withered, and the old stock is blasted, the whole tribe disappears. There are limits ordained to everything under the sun. Man will not abide in honour. Of all human vanities, family pride is one of the weakest. Reader, go thy way ; secure thy name in the Book of Life, where the page fades not, nor the title alters nor expires ; leave the rest to heralds and the parish register.

(*d*)　　　　　　　　　　　　　　　　*Borlasse*

BOOKS, THE APOCALYPTIC (Rev. v. 1–14, and vi. 1–17)

The Book with Seven Seals : or, the History of the World in Seven Volumes.

Three books mentioned in Revelation :

1. Book of World's History.

2. The Little Book ; or, the History of the End.

3. The Book of the Redeemed.

1. **This book** (v. 1–5).

(i.) *Written within* and without=full. *Seven seals*=a sealed book of dark problems and enigmas which perplex men ; such as reconciling the moral and physical phenomena of earth with the character of God.

(ii.) *Strong angel* with loud voice is not merely dramatic, but==importance of this book.

(iii.) No one in heaven, nor earth=no one in Hades could return and explain this book.

(*e*)

(iv.) Wept much (see ch. iv.), probably to indicate disappointment at the delay.

(v.) ONE only is worthy to open it, viz. Christ. In Him the gloom is turned into light, problems are solved, all is plain; and we learn that things as now existing are parts of a PROCESS working out the purposes of God; and the result will be a bright, happy, and glorious future for the human race.

(vi.) *Lamb . . . slain* = the death of Christ is the pivot upon which the whole turns—the central idea. The *key to the world's history*—otherwise unexplained.

The opening of the seals (or the explanation of the riddle of the world) (see ch. vi. 1–17) should be compared with Matt. xxiv.

2. The opening of the seven seals (vi. 1–4) = the human aspect of the world

(i.) *The rider on the white horse* = not Christ, but *human culture* = education or *science*, as "conquering and to conquer": says it can regenerate the world; but it has always failed, and ever will. Thus it is a FALSE Christ (not Antichrist). Antichrist denies Christ, but a *false* or a *mock* Christ = progress without Christ.

(ii.) *Red horse* = war. "Great sword"—battlefields and destruction through greed of conquest and ambition.

(iii.) *Black horse* = dearth and famine. See the balances: when there is plenty, food is not weighed.

(iv.) *Death and Hades on pale horse* = aggravated mortality: by pestilence, plagues, wild beasts, accidents, etc.

These four = human aspects of the world's course. Comp. Matt. xxiv. 5–7.

3. The spiritual aspect of the world; or, true religion

(v.) *Souls under the altar:* (*a*) in the world; (*b*) in heaven = Persecutions, and white robes, and waiting. Comp. Matt. xxiv. 9, 10.

4. Presages of the end

(vi.) *Earthquakes, sun,* etc. = portents in the world and in nature, rapidly increasing till the end: = political and physical lawlessness. Comp. Matt. xxiv. 29, 30.

5. The end

(vii.) The seventh seal = (after elect are *sealed*, ch. vii.; in ch. viii. the trumpets; Comp. Matt. xxiv. 30, 31) THE ADVENT ITSELF.

N.B.—Outside of Christ we do not understand the book of the world's history; we do not know what it is about. *To the unbeliever* the world is still a great unsolved puzzle, a dark enigma. And not till Christ unseals the book for him can he in the least understand it.

(*a*)   *Lange (adapted)*

BOOK, THE LITTLE (Rev. x. 8–10)

The Little Book; or, the History of the End of the World

1. See end of ch. ix. = God's judgments on the world fail to bring the unbelieving to repentance. Hence we learn three facts:

(i.) That not a development of the kingdom brings about *the end* of the world: in a *good* sense, the world will not be ripe for it;

(ii.) Nor because of the ungodliness of the world; but

(iii.) Because of the *conflict between the two.* It will be *in consequence* of an intensified struggle between Christianity and the worldly spirit; and at the moment in history when it becomes necessary for God to interfere for the preservation of His Church.

2. This chapter = "strong angel"—right foot on sea and left foot on earth: a symbol of Christ *in His power.*

Right foot on sea = nations—peoples—national life (not religious life), the region from which Antichrist, the last enemy, will rise = Christ has power over him.

Left foot on earth = religious life—the region from which another beast arises, but who is subservient to the former.

A loud cry awakes the seven thunders.

3. What signified by the seven thunders?

(i.) We ask what *thunder* does in NATURE Thunder purifies the atmosphere.

(ii.) It is the voice of God (Ps. xxix.)

Hence these seven thunders = seven voices of Christ, as thunders to purify the *atmosphere of His Church* when it has grown corrupt and needs purifying; *i.e.* the seven thunders are *reformations*—reformations that the Church has needed, such as that of the 16th century, and such as apparently we are going through now. There are rottennesses to be cut off, and many reforms needed. Such appears to be the key to the strifes of our unsettled days.

4. Seal up the things, etc. (ver. 4) = the greatest difficulty of the Book of Revelation. What God has shut, no one can open. But though the actual words are sealed, the RESULT of the seven thunders is given us (ver. 6, 7).

But perhaps we may suggest why apparently the words of the seven thunders were sealed:

The reformers must not recognise themselves nor their work.

If they did, how could they "walk by faith and not by sight"?

5. The result (ver. 6, 7) shows that the seven thunders

(i.) Gravitate towards the end;

(ii.) They become the preparation for the end: "*The bride adorning herself,*" making herself fit for the coming of her Lord. John the Baptist prepared for the first coming of Christ; so do *all reformers* prepare the way of the Lord. As the thunders sound, the result is that the end—the SEVENTH THUNDER—is imminent; each one brings the end nearer. (The last reformation will completely purify the Church.)

"There should be time no longer."

"The mystery of God should be finished" (see Mark xiii. 33)—on "*mystery of God.*"

6. The little book to be eaten (ver. 8–11)

(i.) *Little* book, in contrast to the seven-sealed one, written within and without.

That = history of the *world;*

This = history of the *end* of the world.

Much time was covered by the account in first, a short time only needed for the latter.

These events occur rapidly—in quick succession, as all *catastrophes* do; as the thief in the night, or any sudden catastrophe amongst ourselves. The readiness with which people believe the end to be near shows the nature of the second coming of Christ. Events occurring in rapid succession,

(*b*)

and which, being spread over a short space of time, may be described in a "LITTLE BOOK."

7. To eat the book = to appropriate it, to make *it his own*

How explain "*sweet*" and "*bitter*"?

(i.) God's promises are very sweet, "exceeding great and precious promises"; but it is a BITTER experience to have to need them, *e.g.* "When thou passest through the waters, they shall not overflow thee, and through the fire, they shall not harm thee." The promise is *sweet*, but the experience is BITTER. Again

(ii.) Our Christianity itself is precious, as the kingdom of God is "righteousness and peace and joy in the Holy Ghost."

This is the *sweetness*; but a Christian is a marked man, a target for arrows. Satan puts stumblingblocks in his way. Our Lord says, "I came not to give peace on earth, but a sword." This is the BITTER side of it.

This will explain this passage about the little book:

John, like any Christian, wished to know definitely of the END. That knowledge was given him. He took the *little book* "*open*" and read its contents. *He knew;* there was the pleasure and the sweetness. But the knowledge showed him that he must have no *romantic* or *idyllic* conceptions of the future of the Church; it would be a history of changes and chances, of darkness, persecutions, reformations, and sad apostasies; anything but pleasant to contemplate. Thus his knowledge would become *bitterness*.

(*a*)   *Adapted from Lange*

BOOKS AND CHRIST

Except a living man, there is nothing more wonderful than a book!—a message to us from the dead—from human souls whom we never saw, who lived, perhaps, thousands of miles away; and yet there, in those little sheets of paper, speak to us, amuse us, terrify us, teach us, comfort us, open their hearts to us as brothers. . . . I say we ought to reverence books, to look at them as useful and mighty things. If they are good and true, whether they are about religion or politics, farming, trade, or medicine, *they are the message of Christ*, the Maker of all things, the Teacher of all truth.

(*b*)   *Kingsley*

BOOKS, MAKING MANY

'Tis pleasant, sure, to see one's name in print; A book's a book, although there's nothing in't.

(*c*)   *Byron*

BOOKS AND PROGRESS

In the days when scholasticism, barren but pretentious, ruled the Universities of Europe, and a bigoted priesthood proclaimed that ignorance is the mother of devotion, only those men in whom the love of learning was strong enough to tempt to any sacrifice, could own, or cared to own, those precious treasures—books; precious, for the most part, rather because of scarcity than because of intrinsic worth To-day, when science orders the affairs of men, the boy who blacks the thinker's boots may, with the dime that is tossed him, buy the thinker's book. He has within his own reach and means, could he but appreciate and comprehend it, the best thoughts of the best minds of the world's best age; works for a single glance at which the intellectual pioneers who laid the foundations of our modern life would have given years of toil. What mightier progress can this epoch of progress show, what traditions of a golden age can equal it? "It doth win from the old imaginers their wit and novelty."

(*d*)   *Munro*

BONDAGE (Deut. viii. 2-5)

1. From the bondage of the *world;*
2. From the bondage of *sin;*
3. From the bondage of *earth.*

The ten plagues on Egyptians = God ten times striking them, saying, "Let My people go"; and then *judgment.*

The ten trials of His people = to humble and to prove them, to know what was in their heart; and then *rejection* of the hardened.

1. I will allure,
2. And draw thee into the wilderness,
3. And speak comfortably unto thee.

= Three stages of religious experience: (i.) Egypt; (ii.) The Wilderness; (iii.) Canaan.

(*e*)   *Hengstenberg*

BOND AND FREE, THE (Gal. iv. 31)

Two classes of godly people: the Bond and the Free = slaves and sons.

1. Characteristics of the Bond

(i.) They know not God as *Father*, but as hard master. "Wherewith shall I come before Thee," etc.

(ii.) Nor Jesus as *Emancipator*, Deliverer = "O wretched man that I am," "If the Son shall set you free," Hence they go in *fear* all their life, subject to bondage. Cf. "*Jesu mercy*."

(iii.) Nor the Holy Ghost as *Comforter*, dwelling in His temple, witnessing within. "For where the Spirit of the Lord is, there is liberty."

Hence they are *slaves*, and their proper home is Mount Sinai, which gendereth to bondage; and their religion is *Judaism*, not Christianity.

2. Characteristics of the Free.

Liberated, delivered, emancipated from bondage and fear, they are "*free* indeed." The *truth* has set them free. Their sins are forgiven; the Holy Spirit is the witness thereto. This they *know*. Their condition = "glorious liberty of sons." This they have to contend for: "Be not again entangled in yoke of bondage"; "Stand fast in the liberty wherewith Christ hath made us free"; "Ye have been called unto liberty." They have a *filial spirit:* "God hath not given spirit of fear, but of power and *love*, and of a sound mind"; "Christ hath delivered them . . . subject to bondage"; "He hath also blotted out the handwriting," (*see*) etc., and in so doing He hath abolished ritualism, legalism, and bondage.

Hence these *free* ones are sons, and their proper home is Jerusalem above.

3. St. Paul's illustration of both parties. The tent of Abraham held both. Cf. The characters of Hagar and Ishmael with Sarah and Isaac.

(i.) Hagar has a son in ordinary way of nature; Sarah has a son contrary to nature.

(*f*)

(ii.) Hagar is a slave in that household; her son, too, is such, and has no rights. Whilst Sarah is a free woman, and her son is a child having family rights.

A quarrel ensues; the same tent cannot hold them. History has all along proved the truth of this.

This quarrel in Abraham's tent is an Old Testament picture of a New Testament thing:—

(i.) Hagar = covenant of Sinai = the bondage state;

(ii.) Sarah = new covenant = state of liberty;

(iii.) Ishmael, birth being natural (*nature*), is no heir to kingdom of heaven;

(iv.) Isaac, birth being supernatural (and of promise), is a rightful heir, and teaches the necessity of a new birth.

These are types of *nature* and *grace*, the *flesh* and the *spirit*. There is no concord or common ground of hope between them. And what saith the Scripture? "*Cast out the bondwoman and her son,*" etc. They may live in the same tent, but no power on earth can make them agree.

4. But this is not all. Hagar was an Egyptian. She and her son settle in *Arabia*, which is neither Egypt nor Palestine. Arabia thenceforth becomes their home = type of *half-conversions* = neither the world nor Christ, but amid the terrors, the gloom, and the thunderings of Sinai. And like them we *must* be in bondage, dreaming of averting the anger of God by hours of painful kneeling, tears of penitence, etc., until Christ, the Emancipator, comes revealing two things:

(i.) The forgiveness of sins,

(ii.) The Holy Ghost.

Without which, *bondage;* with which, *free.*

(*a*)

"**BONES** . . . live" (Ezek. xxxvii. 3)

Think of the sublimity, I should rather say the profundity, of that passage in Ezekiel: "Son of man, can these bones live? And I answered, O Lord God, Thou knowest." I know nothing like it.

(*b*)   *S. T. Coleridge*

BOTTOMLESS PIT (Hell)

"It is an awful thought to you who are still in your sins, that you are hanging, as it were, by a thread over the bottomless pit."

(*c*)   *C. Clayton*

BRAZEN SERPENT (John iii.; Num. xxi. 8)

Here we have two kinds of serpents:

1. The living, poisonous serpent, whose bite is deadly: image of sin.

2. The dead, brazen serpent, without poison: a symbol of Christ and His salvation. He was made in the "likeness of sin," yet without sin. (Rom. viii. 3; 2 Cor. v. 21; 1 Pet. ii. 24.)

This furnishes the first point of comparison between the brazen serpent and Christ. The other two points are the elevation to the pole—to the Cross; and the healing effect, which in the Old Testament was physical and temporary, in the New Testament is spiritual and permanent. . . .

Moses took not a living serpent, but a dead image of it, which had the appearance but not the poison of a serpent, and acted as a healer instead of a destroyer.

(*d*)   *P. Schaff*

The serpent is in Scripture symbolism *the devil*, from the historical temptation (Gen. iii.) downwards. But *why* is the devil set forth by the *serpent?* How does the bite of the serpent operate? *It pervades with its poison the frame of the victims;* that frame *becomes poisoned*, and *death ensues.* So sin, *the poison of the devil*, being instilled into our nature, that nature has become σὰρξ ἁμαρτίας, a poisoned nature—a *flesh of sin.* Now the brazen serpent was made *in the likeness of the serpents* which had bitten them. It represented to them the poison which had gone through their frames, and it was hung up there on a banner staff as a trophy, to show them that *for the poison there was healing,*—that the plague had been overcome. In *it* there was *no poison*, only the *likeness* of it. Now, was not the Lord Jesus *made in the likeness of sinful flesh?* (Rom. viii. 3.) Was not He made "*sin for us, who knew no sin*"? (2 Cor. v. 21.) Did He not, on the Cross, make an open show of and triumph over the enemy, so that it was *as if the enemy himself had been nailed to that cross?* (Col. ii. 15.) Were not sin and death and Satan crucified when *He was* crucified?

(*e*)   *Alford*

BRAZEN SERPENT, THE (John iii. 14, 15)

1. The significance of the Type (Num. xxi. 8)

(i.) It represented *moral evil*—the devil, temptation, sin, and peril; hence it called up painful recollections.

(ii.) *Repulsive*, especially to a Jew, who consequently thought it strange that God should exhibit the remedy thus.

We find a parallel to this in:

"The offence of the Cross," which is "*foolishness*" to a Greek (the cultivated) and a *stumbling-block* to a Jew (the religious). "Foolish" to deify a man—a felon—as *the Son of God.* The self-righteous ever stumble at that stumbling-stone and rock of *offence.*

2. An illustration of the Atonement

(i.) The Cross of Christ represents *sin as a vanquished foe.*

Sin, the cause of all trouble, separates from God. Therefore we hide, as Adam did, and are afraid. Hence, for our comfort, we need the assurance that our sin is *harmless.* We want to see it dealt with as a venomous serpent is: caught, exposed, and crushed as a conquered foe, unable to harm us.

In the type this was what the dying people saw: their enemy exhibited as *dead* and harmless. Therefore the cross at Calvary represents sin as harmless, as far as our *condemnation* is concerned.

This = the "Good News" of the Gospel, which we are slow to believe.

(ii.) But further, it was not a serpent at all, *only the likeness of one.*

Christ was the sinner's *substitute*, not the poisonous serpent, though he looked like one: "*He was made in the likeness of sinful flesh*"; "*made sin for us*"; "*He became a curse for us*";

(*f*)

and was " *reckoned among transgressors* " as one of them.

This means that·

He bore our sins: the accumulated sins of all mankind—as a *burden.*

It was *laid on Him,* and He could only separate Himself from it by offering Himself as a sacrifice on the Cross.

In this way " He hath put away sin by the sacrifice of Himself."

3. The healing effect of Faith

(i.) " *That whosoever* " = Then a mere camp of Israelites; now it means the *whole world.*

(ii.) " *Believeth* " = Faith now takes the place of looking. The way of salvation is easy.

(iii.) *Not perish* = Peril of eternal death; consider *their* peril. Their physicians could do nothing for them; neither can our own works avail us; we are saved, not by works, but by *believing.* (*See.*)

N.B.—Think of the *cost* of our redemption, " *the precious blood of Christ* " ; of the foolhardiness of *neglecting it;* and the wickedness of " *counting it an unholy thing.*"

(*a*)

BREAD

" *Man doth not live by bread alone* " (Matt. iv. 4).

Our danger is to forget our double nature— body and soul; both require food. Consider our danger in-

1. Labouring only for the bread that perisheth

(i.) The temptation to this is *daily* in the common round of labour for *daily bread.* We think of *income, struggle for existence,* say we *must live,* and are not always scrupulous of the means. " Get money—honestly if you can." This is to live like a dog that steals to satisfy nature's hunger; or to have the means of *faring sumptuously every day* at the expense of something immeasurably higher.

But man is more than a *digesting machine;* man has a soul to be fed, and the food for that is " *every word which proceedeth out of the mouth of God.*" Man is religious, and must live by faith in God.

(ii.) To make us sensible of this, God often suffers us *to want, to fail,* to come into straits and difficulties. He closes up our way and we say, *We can't get on.*

How many cry out, " We shall perish in the wilderness for want of bread! " and murmur like the people when water failed and bread failed, and they ·kept going backwards and forwards in the wilderness forty years, forgetting " *The Lord is my Shepherd, I shall not want.*"

And how does God explain it? (Deut. viii. 3.) He suffered this to *prove* them, and to teach them that *man doth not live by bread alone,* etc. God suffers us to hunger, that He may feed us with *manna.*

(iii.) Our first parents tempted in like manner:

To take of prohibited food;

To put natural before spiritual wants;

To eat of the tree of death, instead of the tree of life.

(iv.) Our blessed Lord likewise-

Forty days in wilderness, hungry—and that moment was used for the temptation to put natural needs (bread) before spiritual (faith in God's providence). The temptation resisted. —Angels ministered unto Him.

2. Practical thoughts

The flesh and the spirit are rival spheres, in either of which we may *live* and forget the other. Tendency is either upwards or downwards, accordingly.

(i.) *Down—" If ye live after the flesh, ye shall die.*"

= Self-indulgence, worldliness, labouring for this life only. The body becomes master, and drags all down with it. Man deteriorates, the end is death, Gehenna, the abyss, " dogs " = bestialized lost souls, demons, just the opposite to what was possible.

(ii.) *Up—" If ye live after the spirit, ye shall live.*"

Through regeneration and holiness, to glory and honour and immortality. Thus living, you shall carry your *body* with you, and have it spiritualized, and become a glorious body, like Christ's. " We know not what we shall be," but we shall be at our *best.*

(*b*)

BREAD, BREAKING OF

Christ was the Word that spake it,
He took the bread and brake it;
And what that Word did make it,
That I believe, and take it.

(*c*) *Queen Elizabeth*

BROAD ROAD, THE

" *Broad is the way that leadeth to destruction* " (Matt. vii. 13).

Men find it a pleasant road; they go along dancing and singing, as it were, enjoying the moment, and never asking whether they give it to God or to the devil. They think of the future only as far as it may concern some pleasure they are anticipating, some ball or play perhaps, or even the new clothes they are going to wear. They call the hour of waiting an eternity, and know not the awful import of the word. Death holds them in his embrace. Holbein's well-known " Dance of Death," is more than a picture, I assure you. They dance, they make love, they chatter, they sit and sleep through life. A sudden wrench—and lo! they wake in hell.

(*d*) *Letters from Hell·*

BROKEN BONES (Ps. li. 8)

I was lately speaking to the chaplain of a London hospital about a case in which we were mutually interested. My friend said, " The surgeons will break his leg this afternoon." I replied, " Is this absolutely necessary ? " The answer was: " If they do not, he will be a cripple for life ! " The patient's " bones " were literally to be " broken," that he might afterwards rejoice.

(*e*)

BROTHERHOOD : All one in Christ (Eph. ii.)

The whole of mankind should be one man, one holy body, whose head is Christ. Humanity must be held together by one Head, else unity is impossible. The highest union of men is that of becoming one in Christ; then they make one family, one household. Since the establishment of Christianity, God no longer knows any distinc-

(*f*)

tion of natures; all have the same access to the Father, because Christianity gives one Spirit to all. . . . The Christian Church is the only edifice that will last. What the freemasons, for instance, boast of as their building amounts to nothing; it will perish.

(a) *Lange*

BROTHERHOOD: " MY BRETHREN " (Matt. xxviii.; Heb. ii. 12)

A designation dating from the resurrection. For the disciples it indicates something great and most consolatory. Joseph a type of this (Gen. xlv. 4).

(b) *Starke*

He first named them *disciples*, then *friends*, then *little children;* now, BRETHREN.

(c) *Braune*

BROTHERHOOD AND CHRIST

[The Name of Jesus Christ] has it not been in every age the watchword of self-conceit and bigotry, excommunication and persecution?

Yes; men have separated from each other, slandered each other, murdered each other in that Name, and blasphemed it by that very act. But when did they unite in any Name but that? Look all history through, from the early churches, unconscious and infantile ideas of God's kingdom, as Eden was of the human race, when love alone was law, and none said that aught that he possessed was his own, but they had all things in common.— Whose Name was the bond of unity for that Brotherhood such as the earth had never seen— when the Roman lady and the negro slave partook together at the table of the same bread and wine, and sat together at the feet of the Syrian tent-maker? "One is our master, even Christ, who sits at the right hand of God; and in Him we are all brothers." . . . Look, too, at the first followers of St. Bennet and St. Francis, at the Cameronians, or the little persecuted flock around Wesley. Look, too, at the great societies of our own days, which, however imperfectly, still lovingly and earnestly do their measure of God's work at home and abroad. And say, when was there ever real union, co-operation, philanthropy, equality, brotherhood, among men save in loyalty to Him—Jesus, who died upon the cross?

(d) *Charles Kingsley*

BROTHERHOOD OF CHRISTIANS

I hold that no one is a child of God merely because he belongs to this or that religion [Christian confession]; to him who receives Jesus Christ, power will be given to become a son of God. In Christ Jesus nothing avails save faith, which works by love. He in whom I find this faith is my brother. Is he of another religion? that makes no difference; he is still my brother, and nearer to me than my fellow-professors who have no faith. Indeed, because he is of another religion, in which the Gospel does not shine so brightly, he is to me a miracle of grace.

(e) *Spangenberg (Moravian)*

BROTHERHOOD AND THE CHURCH (1 Pet. i. 19)

When a Christian entered a foreign city, his first inquiry was for the Church (the Brotherhood); and here he was received as a brother, and supplied with whatever could contribute to his spiritual or bodily refreshment.

(f) *Eusebius*

BROTHERHOOD : BROTHERLY LOVE (John xiii. 35)

Mutual brotherly love the distinctive mark of Christians (1 John iii. 10). "The heathen were wont to exclaim with astonishment: 'Behold how these Christians love one another, and how they are ready to die for one another'" (*Tertullian*). "They love each other before knowing each other" (*Minucius Felix*). Lucian sneeringly remarks: "Their Law-giver has persuaded them that they are all brethren."

(g) *Tholuck*

Yea, verily this must strike them (the heathen); for they hate each other, and are rather ready to kill one another. And even that we call each other brethren seems to them suspicious, for no other reason than that among them all expressions of kindred are only feigned. We are even your brethren in virtue of the common nature which is the mother of us all; though ye, as evil brethren, deny your human nature. But how much more justly are those called and considered brethren who acknowledge the one God as their Father; who have received the one Spirit of holiness; who have awaked from the same darkness of uncertainty to the light of the same truth!

(h) *Tertullian*

BROTHERHOOD, NEED OF

The race of mankind would perish, did they cease to aid each other. From the time that the mother binds the child's head, till the moment that some kind assistant wipes the death-damp from the brow of the dying, we cannot exist without mutual help. All, therefore, that need aid, have a right to ask it from their fellow-mortals; no one who holds the power of granting, can refuse it without guilt.

(i) *Sir Walter Scott*

BROTHERHOOD AND RELIGION

When Abraham sat at his tent door, according to his custom, waiting to entertain strangers, he espied an old man, stooping and leaning upon his staff, weary with age and travel, coming towards him, and who was a hundred years old. He received him kindly, washed his feet, provided supper, caused him to sit down; but observing that the old man ate and prayed not, nor begged a blessing on his meat, asked him why he did not worship the God of the Hebrews?

The old man told him that he worshipped the fire only, and acknowledged no other God; at which answer Abraham grew so zealously angry that he thrust the old man out of his tent, and exposed him to all the evils of the night and an unguarded position. When the old man was gone, God called to him and asked him where the stranger was. He replied, "I thrust him away because he did not worship Thee." God answered, "I have suffered him these hundred years, though he has dishonoured Me; and couldest thou not endure him for one night, when he gave thee no trouble?"

Upon this, saith the story, Abraham fetched him back again, and gave him hospitable enter-

(j)

tainment and wise instruction. Go thou and do likewise, and thy charity will be rewarded by the God of Abraham.

"That ye may be the children of your Father which is in heaven; for He maketh His sun to rise on the evil and on the good, and sendeth rain on the just and on the unjust" (Matt. v. 45).

(a)   *Jewish Legend.*

BROTHERHOOD AND FRENCH REVOLUTION

(One) hastily flings down his coat, waistcoat, and two watches, and is rushing to the work (wheelbarrowing). "But your watches?" cries the general voice. "Does one distrust his *brothers*?" answers he. Nor were his watches stolen.

(b)   *Carlyle.*

BROTHERHOOD AND SCIENCE

A plan for uniting all sects and parties on the one broad, fundamental ground of the unity of God as revealed by science, is very like uniting men by just pulling off their clothes and telling them, "There, ye are all brothers now, on the one broad, fundamental principle of 'want o' breeks.'"

(c)   *Charles Kingsley.*

"SIRS, YE ARE BRETHREN" (Acts vii. 26)

1. Moses had himself striven with and slain an Egyptian the day before. He does not therefore object to strife and contention wholly—not when it is with an Egyptian enemy of God's people.

2. But he says, "Wherefore do YE strive?" Ye Israelites, ye, who are God's people; *ye* are brethren, and ought to live in harmony.

3. Apply to hostilities inside the Christian Church. We take sides. Moses' words are suggestive. There are enemies without the camp, *infidels, worldlings*, etc.; if *they* oppose us, and seek to flood the world with infidel teaching, we must oppose them, by contending for the Faith. But as to the differences within the camp, to strive about them would be to divide a house against itself, and so imperil its existence. "Ye are brethren," and your differences are of another kind; one brother is more advanced than another—has more light, deeper experiences, younger, older, etc.; and remember that the strife about Christ, even about the "body of Christ," is a very different thing to the strife *against* Christ. "Take heed, then, how ye bite and devour one another."

(d)

BRETHREN AND UNITY (Ps. cxxxiii. 1)

Psalm dates from return after exile.
The people met to celebrate a religious festival.
Now they met as *one* people—old-standing jealousies suspended. "Judah did not vex Ephraim, and Ephraim did not envy Judah."
The people assembled from the north and the south as *brethren*, to worship *one* God, in their *one* city, where God had commanded a blessing.

As to the brotherhood of men.
Ask, Is it a *name* or a *reality*?
The facts are-
(i.) God hath made all men of *one blood*.

(ii.) He fashioneth all their *hearts* alike.
(iii.) There is, then, a common relationship of blood and heart by nature.
Has this natural brotherhood been realized?
The facts in answer are—
(i.) Everywhere, and always, men have erected social barriers, caste, "upper classes" and "lower classes," to keep each other asunder.
(ii.) As in the temple at Jerusalem, a middle wall of partition has been put up—on this side the Jew, on that the Gentile; on this circumcised, on that the uncircumcised; on this the citizen, on that the barbarian; on this side the wise, on that the unlearned and ignorant.

Thus "brotherhood" of men exists only as a mere *name*; and the *explanation* is to be found in some *separating* power which has come between man and man, as between man and God, and that something is called SIN. For so long as jealousies, suspicions, distrust, and so forth, exist among men, so long will the true idea of brotherhood be lost sight of. "A man does not distrust his brother" (Carlyle, *Fr. Revol.*). Something thicker than blood even is wanted as cement, viz. LOVE.

At Babel men made the attempt to live in *unity;* but building without God, they built without love. Thus *sin*, the separating power, easily broke up the building, tore men asunder, and scattered the fragments over the face of the earth; and thenceforth men became *strangers, barbarians, aliens, Scythians, "bond* and *free,"* anything but brethren, and fought with each other like encarnalized demons.

Till the moment came when God poured out upon a little company of Christians at Jerusalem His *Holy Spirit of promise*, and baptized them with a baptism of *love*. Then men began to realize that they were brethren—*all one in Christ*—one family. Then they had all things in common, none lacked. Then the poor and the rich began to be cared for; and men were *no more strangers, aliens*, etc., *but fellow-citizens* with the *saints, and of the household of God*. The true building cement was found. The Holy Spirit had come to teach men that they were brethren; the children of one Father; the citizens of one Republic; the city of God; Jerusalem on high; the mother of us all.

(e)

BUDDHA, SOCRATES, AND CHRIST

Endeavours have been made to put Buddha, Socrates, and others in place of Christ.

1. Buddha

Buddha was born no one knows when: birth and life, ranging from B.C. 2000 to B.C. 543. Bohlen, *Ancient India*, vol. i. pp. 315-17, gives results of endeavours to get at date of Buddha's birth:—Four sections over 2000 B.C., four over 1200 B.C., eighteen between 1081 and 1000 B.C. The remaining thirteen between 959 and 543. Such uncertainty led Professor Wilson to declare Buddha a myth. For it seems that each of thirty-five countries has a Buddhism of its own, different from others.

Max Müller: "It was only after Buddha had left the world to enter Nirvana that his disciples attempted to recall the sayings and doings of their departed friend and master. At that time everything which seemed to redound to the glory of

(f)

Buddha, however, extraordinary and incredible, was eagerly welcomed; while witnesses who would have ventured to criticize, or reject unsupported statements, or detract in any way from the holy character of Buddha, had no chance of ever being listened to.". "The Buddhist legends teem with miserable miracles attributed to Buddha and his disciples." "Buddhism we know indeed very little of its origin or early growth."

Rhy. David's *Encl. Britt.* iv., p. 432: "It is to be regretted that the books we have to compare as yet are of a comparatively modern date."

Dr. Eitel, *Buddhism*, "The very earliest compilation of the Buddhists, that of Ceylon, was first compiled between the years 412 and 432 A.D. The Chinese canon was not completed till about 1410 A.D."

Mr. Hardy, *Manual of Buddhism*, declares the part translated from the Pujawalya was written between A.D. 1267 and 1301. Professor Beal's canon, translated, is admitted as not earlier than the sixth century A.D.

Bishop Bigandet, of Burmah, has a Burmese translation, the original of which is not earlier than 1773 A.D.

From these and such-like a certain class of scholars quote. We do not know what Buddha said or did, if he ever lived; but this we know, that wherever Buddhism has gone, it has degraded the civilization of the people accepting teaching of Buddha.

2. Socrates

Of Socrates we know more; we are treading on historic ground. We know from Plato and Xenophon, that Socrates was a God-fearing man, and, of all the ancient philosophers, the one whose teaching came nearest to Christ, and the only philosopher, as far as the writer knows, who put his trust in God. And if Socrates was great, that greatness was brought about, as Socrates declared again and again, by a supernatural power.

Xenophon—*Memoirs of Socrates:*

"He [Socrates] was persuaded the gods watched over the actions and affairs of men; every word, every action, nay, even our most retired deliberations, were open to their view; that they were everywhere present, and communicated to mankind all such knowledge as related to the conduct of human life."

"That the gods would give to him those things that were good" (when he prayed).

"But Socrates always reckoned upon it as a most indubitable truth that the services paid the Deity, by the pious and pure soul, was the most grateful sacrifice, and therefore it was he so much approved that precept of the poet which bids us offer to the gods according to our power."

"Socrates therefore esteemed all those as no other than madmen who, excluding the Deity, referred the success of their designs to nothing higher than human prudence."

"And that I [Socrates] lied not against God, I have this indisputable fact, that whereas I have often communicated to many of my friends, yet hath no one ever detected me speaking falsely."

"That it is the voice of God which giveth me significations of what is most expedient."

"And truly God foreknoweth the future and also showeth it to whomever He pleases," etc., a plain irrefutable answer to that class which claim Socrates as an atheist. Great as Socrates was, through a belief in God, to compare him as

above and beyond Christ in sublimity and teaching, we say with sceptical Rousseau, "What prejudice, what blindness must possess the mind of that man who dares to compare the son of Sophraniscus (Socrates) to the son of Mary (Christ). What a distance between the one and the other!"

Socrates, Plato, and the sages of ancient times looked for One to come who would teach mankind the true way, and deliver mankind from superstition. Of that Teacher we now proceed to speak:—

3. Christ

The world seemed to herald the appearance of Jesus of Nazareth: all seemed to be peace, war for the time was silent. The events of Syria were so ordinary and so peaceful that six years of history were unwritten, and there is a break of six years' Syrian history (Dion Cassius; Josephus is also very short). The angels heralded Christ's birth as "peace and goodwill to men"; truly it has been so in proportion to the adoption of His teaching.

Christ born as the Gospels date. No amount of critical scholarship has ever demonstrated to the contrary. The question of Cyrenius has been raised again and again, and it in a marvellous manner supports the date.

Josephus does not in any wise condemn the four Gospels, but rather in strange coincidences supports the birth and life of Christ.

Philo does not mention Christ. Scholars are agreed that Philo's theological works were compiled early—before the birth of Christ; at any rate, Philo was about middle age when Christ was born.

Josephus mentions Christ but twice; it has been said passage 18, *Antiquities*, is a forgery—no proof has ever been given. Renan accepts it, as do some of the most learned English scholars; recent investigations are coming to the truth of the passage. The oldest MSS. contain it. It is the writer's opinion no one could insert such a passage in a Jew's book, which the Jews held sacred, watched with extreme caution; to insert such a passage would be impossible, since the Jews had a decided bias to Christ that they have even gone so far as to erase twenty passages out of the Talmud where the name of Christ occurred.

Tacitus, first secular historian, xv. 44 (*Annals*), mentions Christ, confirms the Gospels. Pliny's letter to Trajan declares the Christians worshipped Christ as God. There is no classical historian that has written after Christ without mentioning Christ, Christians, or having some reference thereto. In fact, we have twenty-fold more evidence for Christ than we have for Socrates; we have a thousandfold more evidence for Christ as an historical character than we have for Buddha. We have certainty for Christ, we have uncertainty for Buddha. We have progress, civilization with Christianity; we have degradation and barbarism with Buddhism.

Buddhism, even if true, has had at least 2200 years, and what has it done? Christianity has had 1800 years: it has abolished slavery, introduced representative government, raised woman into her proper sphere, banished infanticide, Suttee, inhumanity, and protected the poor. "By their fruits ye shall know them." "Christianity," says Lecky, "has been the most powerful lever that has ever been applied to the affairs of men. (a)

Christianity transformed the character of the multitude, vivified the cool heart by a new enthusiasm ; redeemed, regenerated, and emancipated the most depraved of mankind."

(*a*)   *Mitchell*

BUILD

The man who builds, and wants wherewith to pay,
Provides a home from which to run away.

(*b*)   *Young*

BUILDING UP (Jude 20, 21)

" But ye, beloved,
1. Building up yourselves on your most holy faith,
 (By diligence and study.)
2. Praying in the Holy Ghost,
 (Always, " without ceasing ".)
3. Keep yourselves in the love of God,
 (By abiding in Christ, both by doctrine and practice.)
4. Looking for the mercy of our Lord Jesus Christ unto eternal life."
 (When He appears as Judge)

(*c*)

BURIED (Rom. vi. 4)

When Christ was buried, all His former life was over. Now read the 12th verse. Paul says that those who receive Christ are " buried with Him in baptism." Baptism was a rite administered by the Jews to all Gentile proselytes. It was a very significant rite. It meant that all their former life was forsaken, that they were as " dead " to it. So when the Baptist called Jews to his baptism, they understood that they were dead to their past. Now refer to Rom. vi. 4 : " Buried with Him by baptism into death." Such passages teach us that when we receive Christ, we part from all our past life—we turn our back upon it—we are as if " dead " to it.

(*d*)   *Gill*

THE BURNING BUSH (Exod. iii.)

The Burning Bush :

1. A *type of Christ*=Burned and yet preserved.
2. A *type of the Church*=Burned (persecuted) in the world, and yet preserved.
3. A *type of the Christian*=Burned by trials, and yet preserved.
=You *are* preserved,
 You *have been* preserved, and

You *shall be* preserved, according to a great many promises.

(*e*)   *Beveridge*

BUSINESS

"*I must be about my Father's business* " (Luke xxi. 49)
 =Manliness in struggling.
 1. Against wrong-doing and injustice ;
 2. Against cowardice ;
 3. Against uncleanness.
What else does our Baptism into His Name much more our conversion afterwards—commit us to ?

(*f*)

BUSYBODYISM

I am never forward to offer spiritual consolation to any one in distress or disease. I believe that such resources, to be of any service, must be self-evolved in the first instance. I am something of the Quaker's mind in this, and am inclined to *wait* for the Spirit. . . . The most common effect of this mock evangelical spirit, especially with young women, is self-inflation and busybodyism

(*g*)   *S. T. Coleridge*

BUT (Acts xii. 5)

"*Now Peter was indeed kept in prison : but prayer was made.*"
A most happy expression, " indeed—but." Herod, make thy preparations, if thou wilt, but they cannot be of avail; they are opposed by a powerful BUT, which thou canst not overcome. What is this *but ?* Apparently less than nothing —mere prayers ! And yet, a single word of believing prayer can overthrow all the power of hell. Why may it not then prevail against Herod and his sixteen soldiers ? (*Williger*.)
God can refuse nothing to a praying congregation (*Chrysostom*).
By the blood and prayers of Christians, Herod's arm was paralyzed and his sceptre broken, yea, the Roman empire destroyed.

         (Leonh. and Sp.)
(*h*)   *Lange*

Oh, now comes that bitter word—*but*,
Which makes all nothing that was said before.
That smooths and wounds, that strikes and dashes more
Than flat denial or a plain disgrace.

(*i*)   *Daniel*

C

CAIAPHAS (John xviii.)

"Caiaphas was high priest that same year."

(i.) When a *bad thing* was to be done by a high-priest, according to the foreknowledge of God, Providence so ordered it that a *bad man* should be in the chair to do it.

(ii.) When God would make it to appear what corruption there was in the heart of a *bad man*, He put him into a place of power; many a man's *advancement* has lost him his *reputation*.

(a)   M. Henry

CALCUTTA, BLACK HOLE OF, AND PRAYING

I used to think, in attempting to realize the story of the Black Hole of Calcutta, that terrible as every incident was, the climax of suffering must have been the moment when the victims of the despot's cruelty had prevailed upon one of the guards to go with the petition that they might be removed into a wider place of confinement, or at least might have water supplied to cool their tongues, and when the messenger returned to say that the sultan had laid down for his mid-day sleep, and they dared not disturb him. Pangs of hunger and thirst, the bitter conflict of brother with brother, must have been as nothing compared with that disappointment. This is an experience that the real petitioner to our God can never know.

(b)   J. A. Macfayden

CALL (Luke v. 32)

Jesus came to call by the proclamation, "The kingdom of heaven is at hand."

1. The call is to individuals:

(i.) To repentance = begin life again;
(ii.) To a feast: "Come," = invitation into the kingdom. To its joys (Luke xiv. 16; Matt. xxii. 2).

Thus *all* are called to Repentance, and invited to a feast.

2. This call will be successful if we desire it:

(i.) Having susceptible hearts—honest and good = the soil;
(ii.) If "poor in spirit" = repentant;
(iii.) If we, hunger after righteousness," = desire for the feast.

3. How the call is made of none effect:

(i.) The worldly heart—preoccupied—makes effectual calling impossible (Luke xiv. 16, 20).
(ii.) The "wise and prudent" do not like it (Matt. xi. 25).
(iii.) The stupid heart, wayside = no soil;
(iv.) By levity, "They made light of it."
(c)

CALL of Chosen Vessels, The

"It was in the bleeding heart of a father who buried four children in one month, that God planted a tree to give fruit and shadow to many hundred children of the land." He felt that that first fourfold sorrow was God's call. Years passed, and he and his wife sat in the darkened room; a son of nineteen had died but an hour before, and they sat in the shadow, silent. A hand tapped at the door, "Oh, my Edward," cried the mother, "would that it were thou!" It was a poor ragged lad of fourteen, and he struggled through his tears to say, "You have taken so many children from our place! Have pity upon me also! Since I was seven I have had neither father nor mother," and he could say no more. Then the mother lifted up her eyes to heaven and cried, "Lord, Lord, Thou sendest us strange children without pause, and oh, Thou takest away our own!" And the father prayed, "Thy will be done," and took poor Bennenitz to his heart. Two years, and again the room was darkened, Angelica had died at sixteen. "Pray for me," Falk had written, "for I must still be far from the Lord, when He needs to lay me again and again upon the anvil."

(d)   *Stevenson's Mem. of John Falk*

"Moses, Moses"; "Samuel, Samuel"; "Simon, Simon," "Saul, Saul." The name called twice marked those thus called as chosen vessels of the Lord.

(e)   Oosterzee

CALL, THE EFFECTUAL

When Christ calls, He also draws. "Come"! says the sea to the river. "Come!" says the magnet to the steel. "Come!" says the spring to the sleeping life of field and forest. And, like the obedience of the river to the sea, of the steel to the stone, of earth's charmed atoms to spring's effectual call, is the obedience of the soul to Christ's word and spirit.

(f)   C. Stanford

A CALL TO THE UNCONVERTED

"Say unto them," etc. (Ezek. xxxiii. 11)

1. It is the unchangeable law of God, that wicked men must turn or die.

If you will believe God, believe this. There is but one of two ways for every man, either conversion or damnation:

Proofs: Matt. xviii. 3; John iii. 3; Rom. viii. 9; Ps. ix. 17.

Objections: God is too merciful to damn us-

(i.) Must the Almighty stand at the bar of a worm?
(ii.) If sin be such an evil as to require the death of Christ for its expiation, no wonder if it deserve our everlasting misery.
(iii.) If the sin of devils deserve an endless torment, why not also the sin of man?
(iv.) We are not competent judges of the desert of sin. Few children but who think the father is unmerciful. The vilest wretch thinks the Church wrongs him if they excommunicate him; scarce a thief or murderer is punished, but would accuse the law of cruelty.

Who are wicked men:

(i.) To be a wicked man and to be an unconverted man, is all one.
(g)

As a lion has a fierce and cruel nature before it devours; and as an adder has a venomous nature before it stings; so in our very infancy we have those sinful natures and inclinations before we think, or speak, or do amiss. And hence spring all the sin of our lives. Every man in this state of completed nature, is a wicked man and in a state of death.

(ii.) A wicked man is one who makes it the principal business of his life to prosper in the world and attain his fleshly ends.

(iii.) The soul of a wicked man did never truly discern and relish the mystery of redemption, nor thankfully entertain an offered Saviour, nor is he taken up with the love of the Redeemer.

Conversion is another kind of work than most are aware of.

(a)

2. It is the promise of God, that the wicked shall live if they will but turn.

This is what God takes pleasure in. It is life, not death; that is the first part of our message. Our commission is to offer salvation; certain salvation to every one. Heaven is no fancy, but a true felicity.

Proofs :—Text and following verses: Ezek. xviii.; 2 Cor. v. 17–21; Mark xvi. 15, 16; Luke xxiv. 46, 47; Acts v. 30, 31; Acts xiii. 38, 39; Gal. vi. 15; Luke xiv. 17, 23, 24.

Here you may safely trust your souls. The love of God is the fountain of this offer (Mark iii. 16); the blood of the Son hath purchased it; the faithfulness and truth of God is engaged to make the promise good. Miracles have sealed it; preachers throughout the world proclaim it; the sacraments are instituted (as the outward and visible sign of it); and the Spirit is the earnest of full possession. The truth of it is past controversy. But alas! the majority believe the devil's lie, as at the first, " Ye shall not surely die."

(b)

3. God taketh pleasure in men's conversion and salvation, but not in their death or damnation; He had rather they would return and live, than go on and die.

Proofs: The gracious nature of God, Exod. xxxiv. 6, xx. 6; the promises and invitations of the Gospel; His commission to its ministers, and the appointment of ordinances; by the course of His Providence, and daily mercies to " lead you to repentance; " God has waited so long on thee to see whether thou wilt at last return and live; the cost of thy ransom. God hath thus proved that He takes no pleasure in the death of the wicked, etc.

(c)

4. This most certain truth God hath confirmed by an oath.

Dare not to question His oath. Christ has solemnly said that the unregenerate and unconverted cannot enter the kingdom of heaven, so God hath sworn that His pleasure is not in their death, but in their conversion and life. We study day and night what to say to you, that may convince and warn, and yet the work is undone. We lay before you God's word, chapter and verse, where it is written, that ye cannot be saved except ye be converted; and yet we leave most of you as we find you.

(d)

5. The Lord redoubles His commands and exhortations with vehemency : " Turn ye, turn ye." Earnest declaration of the *will* of God. Every leaf of the Bible adds " Turn ye, turn ye." It is the voice of every sermon. It is the secret voice of the Spirit, of conscience, of the godly, of the works of God—they also are His books; the heavens declare it; the rising sun calleth thee, " Awake, thou that sleepest," etc. (Eph. v. 14). " The night is far spent," etc. (Rom xiii. 11–14) = this text was the means of Augustine's conversion.

(e)

6. The Lord reasons with the unconverted, and asks, " Why " they will die?

No wonder men will not hear us, when they will not hear the Lord Himself (Ezek. iii. 7); Mal. ii. 17; i. 6, 7; Isa. xlv. 9.

Can there be a more dangerous madness, than to neglect your everlasting welfare?

(f)

7. If, after all this, men will not turn, it is not owing to God that they are condemned, but of themselves, even their own wilfulness. They die because they will die; that is, because they will not turn.

God here acquits Himself of your blood. Because a professor cuts his finger, you think you may boldly cut your throats.

In conclusion, my heart is troubled to think how I shall leave you; lest after this the flesh should still deceive you, and the world and the devil should keep you asleep, and I should leave you as I found you. If you will be converted and saved, read the word of God, which is the ordinary means, and constantly attend on the public preaching of the word. As God will lighten the world by the sun, and not by Himself alone, so will He convert and save men by His ministers, who are the lights of the world, Acts xxvi. 17, 18; Mat. v. 14. If you will turn and live, do it resolvedly, stand not deliberating. It is not a doubtful case. Don't waver. Before you sleep another night, before you stir from the place, before Satan have time to take you off, RESOLVE.

Baxter's " Call to the Unconverted " (condensed)

(g)

CALLING

No man's calling is a calling away from God or godliness. Our particular callings should never drive out our general calling of Christianity.

(h)   *Thos. Brooks*

CALUMNY

Be thou as chaste as ice, as pure as snow, thou shalt not escape calumny.

(i)   *Shakspeare*

CALVINISM

= " The foundation of the Lord standeth sure."
Arminianism-
= " Let every one that nameth the name of Christ depart from iniquity."
Both, when read aright, appear as arcs of the same circle.

(j)

CALVINISM.

The wonderful work, "The Pilgrim's Progress," is one of the few books which may be read over repeatedly at different times, and each time with a new and a different pleasure. I read it once as a theologian—and there is great theological acumen in the work; once with devotional feelings; and once as a poet. I could not have believed beforehand that Calvinism could be painted in such exquisitely delightful colours.

(a)   *S. T. Coleridge*

CANAANITES, The Destruction of the, by the Israelites

Was it right? Was it cruel? Consider the question-

1. In reference to the Canaanites.

(i.) Their destruction is always presented in Scripture as a judgment of God, sent on them because of their wickedness. They had not only fallen into total apostasy from God, but into forms of idolatry of the most degrading kind. Their false religion cannot be regarded as a mere error of judgment; cruelty the most atrocious, and unnatural crimes the most defiling, were part and parcel of its observances (cf. Lev. xviii. 21, sqq. ; Deut. xii. 30, sqq.).—*Cook.* Nor did they sin thus through ignorance. They were not a savage race, but among the more cultivated ones of the time. They had commerce, coined money, iron chariots, probably books.

(ii.) The Canaanites had received repeated warnings and instructions in the general Deluge, in the destruction of Sodom and Gomorrah, in the holy example of Abraham, Isaac, Jacob, and Melchizedek, and in the slow advance of Israel from Egypt to their borders, attended by miracles which caused them to tremble (Exod. xv. 14–16).

(iii.) God not only sent them these lessons, but He bore with them many centuries in patience, while they abused His grace.

(iv.) It is impossible to acknowledge God as the moral governor of the earth, and not to admit that it may be right, or even necessary on occasions, for Him to remove summarily from His dominions a mass of hopeless depravity, such as these nations had long been.

(v.) Nor is it any real objection to this view, that innocent children were indiscriminately slaughtered (Josh. vi. 17, 21). To say nothing of the practical difficulties which the sparing of infants would involve, when the parents generally were put to death, and to pass by the obvious parallel supplied by the wholesale destruction caused, for example, by an earthquake, it is evident that, since God's dealings with men do not terminate with this life, He can redress hereafter inequalities arising out of the acts of His providence here.

(vi.) It can make no difference to those who are thus destroyed, whether the agent of their destruction is a natural catastrophe, like an earthquake, or an army divinely commissioned for the purpose.

(b)

2 In relation to the Israelites

(i.) It is objected, that in commissioning the Israelites to exterminate the Canaanites, God sanctioned cruelty. But if it be sanctioning cruelty to direct a human agent to execute a lawful sentence against crime, then we are involved in the charge when we elect officers to perform the same duty towards criminals.

(ii.) The slaughter of enemies in moments of passion, without just cause and without due authority, may cultivate cruel instincts. But the solemn execution of the law, with no heat of passion, but with an awful sense of the crime to be avenged, and with a religious reference to the command of God, cannot produce such an evil effect.

(iii.) To employ the Israelites in the execution of the fearful sentence, was adapted to inspire them with horror of the crimes thus severely punished, and to prevent their intimacy with the surrounding heathen and the contamination which intimacy would have produced.

(iv.) Had not the Israelites been thus inspired with detestation of idolatry and its attendant immoralities, they would probably have sunk soon into the most degraded heathenism. Their sacred books would have been destroyed or corrupted.

(c)   *Johnson.*

If, on the one hand, the character of the religion of the Canaanites be remembered, and, on the other, the Divine purpose to develop among the Israelites a pure and lofty theocracy, through which, hereafter, the highest manifestation of the kingdom of God on earth was to be made known among men, the apparent difficulty in accepting the policy commanded to Joshua disappears. The heathenism of Palestine and Syria was so foul and degrading in every sense, that there is no State, even at this time, which would not put it down ; if necessary, by the severest penalties. Its spread to Rome was bewailed 1,500 years later by the satirists of the day as a calamity marking the utter decay of the times. It was imperative, therefore, that the land in which the Chosen People were to be educated in the true religion, so as to become the disseminators of its doctrines through the world, should be cleared of whatever would so certainly neutralize the gracious plans of the Almighty. Nor is it wonderful that no other means of securing this great end presented itself to the Hebrew legislater or reformer, in the presence of such hideous immorality and corruption, than the rooting it out with the edge of the sword.

(d)   *Geikie.*

3. In relation to mankind

If the Jews had failed, the world would have been lost. The true religion would have vanished, the mission of Christ would have been impossible. In these contests, on the fate of one of these nations of Palestine, the happiness of the human race depended. The Israelites fought not for themselves only, but for us. It has been well shown that the results of the discipline of the Jewish nation may be summed up in two points—a settled national belief and an acknowledgment of the paramount importance of purity as a part of morality ; and, further, that these two ideas were cardinal points in the education of the world. It was these two points especially which were endangered by the contact and contamination of the idolatry and sensuality of the Phœnician tribes.

(e)   *Stanley*

The Israelites' sword, in its bloodiest executions, wrought a work of mercy for all the countries of the earth, to the very end of the world.

(f)   *Dr. Thomas Arnold.*

CANT

Cant is the echoing of other persons' beliefs. It is frightful to live amongst echoes.

(a)   *T. Carlyle*

CARCASE

"*Wheresoever the carcase is,*" etc. (Matt. xxiv. 28)

It is commonly thought that *the carcase* = Jerusalem ; and the *eagles* = the Roman standards with the figure of an eagle upon them.

This, however, is very unlikely. Because our Lord never indicated so plainly who or what are the ministers of wrath. A man is told to prepare for death, but he is not told by what disease he will die.

The words indicate that where the *carrion* is, there the birds of prey will gather around it, as natural scavengers, to rid the earth of a nuisance.

The word rendered *eagles* = birds of prey = more probably *vultures*, as eagles do not prey on dead flesh or carrion ; whereas vultures do, and also follow armies for days, ready to pounce down upon the slain.

The *carcase* is twofold : There is-
1. The carcase of the Jewish world.
2. The carcase of the Gentile world.

A carcase is offensive ; and God has His birds of prey ready when a nation has arrived at such a stage as is indicated by that term.

1. The carcase of the Jewish World

How may a nation or a city arrive at such a condition ? *By Death.* The birds of prey do not settle down upon a *living*, but a *dead* nation. The Jewish nation, before such a judgment befell it, would be dead, *spiritually* and *politically*. And this was the condition of Jerusalem at the time of its destruction. It was both an irreligious and a lawless city. Neither life nor property was secure : bands of criminals trod its streets. Every man did what was right in his own eyes.

This = the *carcase*, which lay rotting under the face of Heaven, fit only to be swept away by the besom of destruction. Such was Jerusalem in its last days ; and around it the birds of prey gathered and did their work as scavengers.

2. There will be apparently another such sight

The Gentile world, now having its day of grace, will, because iniquity shall abound, ripen for judgment much in the same way. There will be another *carcase* : lifeless and unspiritual. Society will again be disorganized—confusion and anarchy will prevail. And when this iniquity is "fully ripe"—when the cup of the world's iniquity is full to overflowing, then God will bring in His executioners—the birds of prey as before—always ready to do His bidding. "*For wheresoever the carcase is, there will the eagles be gathered together.*"

3. But sin passes through stages before it comes to this point of flagrancy

As a fever passes through several stages before there is delirium and death, so does sin before it is *fully ripe.*

(i.) It may be *disobedience*, like Adam's sin.

(ii.) It may be a *coming short of the mark*, like an arrow that misses its object.

(iii.) It may be *transgression*, as when we overstep a landmark, and trespass on forbidden ground.

(iv.) It may be *unbelief*, for "whatsoever is not of faith is sin."

Sin may be all these, and yet stop short of being "fully ripe" iniquity. *There is a form of sin which always precedes judgment.* And our Lord indicates what that is.

"Because INIQUITY shall abound, the love of many shall wax cold."

The word *iniquity* = LAWLESSNESS : a form of sin which signifies that all moral and political barriers and restraints, which had hitherto dammed up the torrent of evil, are broken down, and carried away with its on-rush. Now, when sin has reached this height and enormity, it has also reached its last stage ; and the next step is *judgment*. When laws neither human nor Divine are regarded by a people, the nation is *dead* : it has become a *carcase*, over which are hovering the ministers of God's judgment.

Such a state of society evidently prevailed before

(i.) The Flood, in Noah's time.

(ii.) The destruction of the Cities of the Plain, in Lot's time.

(iii.) The destruction of Jerusalem.

[Compare also the destruction of Herculaneum ; the history of the French Revolution, and the Commune in Paris.]

(b)   *See Josephus, Godet, and others*

CARDS, FOLLY OF

It is very wonderful to see persons of the best sense passing away a dozen hours together in shuffling and dividing a pack of cards, with no other conversation but what is made up of a few game phrases, and no other ideas but those of black or red spots ranged together in different figures. Would not a man laugh to hear a man of his species complaining that life is short ?

(c)   *Addison*

CARE

"*Casting all your care upon Him, because He careth for you*" (1 Pet. v. 7)

Care is the great enemy of Christian peace. It is essential for our peace that we fall not a *prey* to care and anxiety.

The *future* is not ours ; why be anxious about it ?

The *past* is done with.

The *present* is provided for : "Give us this day our daily bread."

The ancient custom of *distracting* a criminal, by tying him to the wheels of two chariots, which were then driven in opposite directions, well illustrates how cares may be allowed to distract the mind. We put ourselves on the rack, when we ought to *cast our care on God ;* not in part, nor occasionally ; but "all" and always.

1. Why are we to cast our care upon God ?

(i.) Because He is our Father. A Father's office is to provide for his family. It is out of place for a *child* to be anxiously making provision for emergencies—asking where to-morrow's *food* and *clothing* are to come from ; and how the "bills" are to be paid ? We should rebuke such precocity, and send the child to school or to play, and leave all such matters to the ordained caretakers.

The birds of the air are taken care of ; so will the Christian be, though of little faith.

(d)

Objection:—" His hand is heavy upon me "—a *mighty hand.*

Answer :—There is a *" needs be."* He is pruning —cutting away some superfluous growth. Be sure that it is the hand of a *Father* that is at work on you.

(ii.) " Because He careth for you."

There is such a thing as a Divine Providence. Men of the world do not believe in it. Hence they take unworthy means to gain their ends : Their doctrine = " The end justifies the means." This controverts the doctrine that " God will provide." There is a *Divine directing* of a man's steps— guiding him to his *work* and *place,* as sure as if a man dropped into his niche from above. This is as true as that Joseph was not in an Egyptian prison by accident. The same directing hand which created us and redeemed us in Christ, provides for the minutest wants of body and soul, though we allow care to distract us.

His Promises =
" I will never leave thee," etc. ;
" As our day is, our strength shall be ";
" The hairs of our head all numbered."

Abraham, ascending the mountain and saying to Isaac " *The Lord will provide* "= a daily motto for the Christian. Afterwards = " *In the Mount of the Lord it shall be seen* "= " The hill from whence cometh our help."

There it shall be seen how rich is that provision God hath made for those who love Him. They that watch for Providences shall never lack a Providence to watch. Whoso is wise will ponder these things, they shall understand the loving-kindness of the Lord.

2. This Providence is caricatured. The Christian must be on his guard. He must remember that he is passing through an enemy's land, who never sleeps :

Your Adversary the Devil is watching you.

He seeks to lead you off the right road, dazzles your eyes with a false light; and when he has succeeded he makes you his *prey,* and tries to break down your faith in God's Providence. It is one of the wiles of the devil, one of the special features of his work, to destroy belief in *God's Providence.*

= " No one acts upon it ;" " Every one helps himself and pushes himself forward." " Only simple ones believe in an over-ruling providence —you read of such a thing in the Bible ; but when ever have you seen things happen so in daily life —such a belief is *exploded.*"

Many, even Christians, are made a *prey* of by these arguments, and filled with doubts, worried with cares. The adversary succeeds too well in indoctrinating them with his creed : " Yea, hath God said ? " He knows that distraction and doubt will spoil a Christian frame of mind.

Note that the two things are parallels·

God's providence = eyes that run over all the earth, beholding the evil and the good ; His ears are open to the prayers of the just.

But the adversary goes about everywhere—like an evil providence—seeking to counteract our belief in this ; and when he takes a Christian captive he makes him miserable.

Hence the necessity :
(i.) To cast our care upon God ;
(ii.) To be vigilant, because of the tactics of the adversary—whom resist steadfast in the faith.

(a)

CARPENTER'S SON, Is not this the ? (Matt. xiii. 55.)

1. A stumblingblock to His own countrymen and townspeople.

They knew Him in His youth, knew His friends, were at school with Him, etc. How, then, can He have superior wisdom and teach *us ?*

The offence was, that Jesus was of *plebeian birth* —of humble social position = *The Carpenter's Son.* A Jewish peasant, in the place of the *Royal Messiah* that men looked for.

2. The Christian is a follower of his Master in this respect.

(i.) From necessity—God calls " not many wise," " mighty," " noble," men ; but instead thereof the " weak," " base," and " despised." " Earthen vessels," chipped and cracked and flaws in them. And when one of such begins to teach his fellow-men—They ask again, " *Is not this the Carpenter's Son ? "* = an uneducated, an untrained man, one of ourselves, whose antecedents we know well. They are *offended* at him, and sometimes the enmity expresses itself with great bitterness . " *He hath a devil, and is mad.*"

3. In either case—They could not see the Divine in the veil of the Human.

This man, whom they despise, is *born from above, adopted* into God's family, a child of God, and a joint-heir with Christ.

Moreover, this man is an organ of the Spirit, and has *revelations* made to him—mysteries have been revealed.

The truth about him really is, that he is of true patrician birth and rank, a noble of the highest caste, a king and a priest unto God, already a citizen of the kingdom of heaven—Hence the answer to the question : " Whence hath this man these things, and how came he by this authority ? "

True, you may know all the earthly accidents of his appearance and position, but there is something immeasurably beyond this, viz. :
(i.) The mystery of the New Birth ;
(ii.) The being rooted in Christ ;
(iii.) The walking in the Light which places him outside the ordinary sphere of lives, and which can only be estimated by the spiritually minded.

(b)

CARPENTER AND FISHERMEN

The qualities which we observe in the Christian religion would have been extraordinary had the religion come from any person ; from the person from whom it did come, they are exceedingly so. What was Jesus in external appearance ? a Jewish peasant, the son of a carpenter, living with His father and mother in a remote province of Palestine, until the time that He produced Himself in His public character. He had no master to instruct Him ; He had no books, but the works of Moses and the prophets ; He had visited no polished cities ; He had received no lessons from Socrates or Plato,—nothing to form in him a taste or judgment different from that of the rest of his countrymen, and of persons of the same rank of life with himself. Supposing it to be true, which it is not, that all His points of morality might be picked out of Greek and Roman writings, they

(c)

were writings which *He* had never seen. Supposing them to be no more than what some one or other had taught in various times and places, He could not collect them together. . . . Who were His coadjutors in the undertaking,—the persons into whose hands the religion came after His death? A few fishermen upon the lake of Tiberias, persons just as uneducated, and, for the purpose of framing rules of morality, as unpromising as Himself. Suppose the mission to be real, all this is accounted for; the unsuitableness of the authors to the production, of the characters to the undertaking, no longer surprises us: but without *reality*, it is very difficult to explain how such a system should proceed from such persons. Christ was not like any other carpenter; the apostles were not like any other fishermen.

(*a*)   *Paley*

CATASTROPHES

There will be an *end of the world*—a winding up of its affairs—a *day of the Lord*. But how will it come about? Some say the world will freeze to death. The sun is losing its heat at the rate of one degree in 35,000 years; and that after a while the furnace of the sun will be exhausted, and our world will roll round a great orb of ice. The Bible says that *the earth and all things therein shall be burned up*. It will not be ice, but *fire*. Imagination has pictured *that day*. It is comparatively easy to sketch a burning city; but the conflagration of a burning world who shall paint? It is easy to comprehend an earthquake that destroys a town, but not that which shakes two hemispheres. All the mountains falling; all the seas boiling; all the stars dropping; the heavens rolling; the earth vanishing; the angels flying; the graves bursting; the dead rising; the thrones hoisting; and Christ, the Judge of quick and dead, coming? Who can picture this? Again, St. Peter says all this shall be accompanied with "*great noise*." The slide of an avalanche deafens the ear, but what is that compared to the crumbling of the mountains into dust; the thunderings; the sound of trumpets "exceeding loud"; the groans of the lost; the cries of wild beasts; the clangor and the vociferation, the echo and re-echo of heaven and earth—when "*the heavens and the earth shall pass away with a great noise, and the elements shall melt with fervent heat, the earth also and the works that are therein shall be burned up*." . . . When the ropes and pulleys and wheels of the universe shall shrivel up and crack, for "*the powers of heaven shall be shaken*," and the earth shall stagger like a drunken man, and reel to and fro in mid heaven.

(*b*)

CATHEDRALS, OUR

Etymologically, the cathedral is the *cathedra*, a chair or throne of a bishop; historically, it is an endowed mausoleum, originating generally as a provision for the refuge of the saints till the last great day of awakening—thus resembling in the object of its creation the magnificent Taj Mahal of India or the seemingly imperishable pyramids of Egypt; spiritually, it is a house dedicated to the worship of God, itself perpetually pointing heavenward with its generally multitudinous spires, and echoing twice every day in the year with the strains of sacred music and the murmured prayers of a hallowed liturgy; practically and politically, it is a great endowed educational establishment; æsthetically, it is a picture and a poem in stone, its walls the fitting frame of a series of historical memories which it keeps ever fresh, a royal binding of a series of romantic legends of a sainted and chivalric past. It is this last aspect of the cathedral which most attracts the attention of the traveller. His guide-book tells him the story; the verger puts emphasis upon it. He stands where the martyred Becket was slain, where the sainted Augustine taught, where the ashes of the Black Prince lie; he reads in successive forms of architecture the successive stories of a Saxon, a Norman, and an English Christianity; he walks the cloisters where the monks took their daily exercise, or lingers in the underground chapel where the Huguenots held their Calvinistic services under the same roof with the stately ceremonial of the English Episcopal Church; and he forgets the present and lives again in the past. It will be indeed strange if he does not come out of this sacred past into the bustle of modern activities, temporal and spiritual, with a new sense of the continuity of human life and a deeper realization of the reality of that faith which has survived all changes of creed and form, and has sung and prayed its praise and its penitence in Roman mass and Anglican liturgy through so many centuries under the same roof.

(*c*)

CATHOLICS

The adherents of the Church of Rome are not *Catholic* Christians. If they are, then it follows that we Protestants are heretics and schismatics, as, indeed, the Papists very logically, from their own premises, call us. And "*Roman* Catholics" makes no difference. . . . There can be but one body of Catholics, *ex vi termini*.

(*d*)   *S. T. Coleridge*

CENSURE: The tax paid by eminent men

Censure, says an ingenious author, is the tax a man pays to the public for being eminent. It is a folly for an eminent man to think of escaping it, and a weakness to be affected with it. All the illustrious persons of antiquity, and indeed of every age in the world, have passed through this fiery persecution. There is no defence against reproach but obscurity; it is a kind of concomitant to greatness, as satires and invectives were an essential part of a Roman triumph.

(*e*)   *Addison*

CERTAINTY OF FUTURE GLORY, THE (Rom. viii. 18, 39)

1. The Subjective Certainty: or, the three groanings-
   (i.) Of the Creature,
   (ii.) Of the New Creature,
   (iii.) Of the Spirit.
Believers are now subjectively *certain* of future glory.
Their present sufferings = birth-pangs of it . . . especially as manifested in the groanings, longings, and hopes of believers, and in the unutterable groaning of the Spirit who intercedes for them.
Though they have the spirit of adoption, it is because they have it that they still groan for its

(*f*)

consummation. Their principial salvation is not their finished salvation; but the latter is testified by their hope and confirmed by their patience. All point to the future objective certainty of glory.

2. The Objective Certainty
(i.) The Purpose of God,
(ii.) The Gift of His Son.
Because "God is for us," and because of the love and faithfulness of the Son.

(a) *From Lange*

[Rom. viii. 31–39

Meyer takes verses 31–39 as a conclusion from verses 29, 30: "The Christian has, then, nothing to fear that can be detrimental to his salvation; but he is, with the love of God in Christ, certain of this salvation." This whole passage is a commentary on verse 28; and what a commentary!

(b) *Lange*

CERTAINTY, PERSONAL

"We have heard Him ourselves." Theirs was the faith of experience. It had grown out of personal intercourse with Christ. These men had found the very way of faith. This is the way to get faith. Come to Jesus. Listen to Jesus. Open your mind and your heart to Jesus. This is a test nothing can break down. Give the incident of the infidel at a public meeting, challenged to call upon God, and the result. State the case of the scientist, "You test every hypothesis, have you tested this?" Tell of Vénhayye, of whom an account was given at the recent meeting of the Church Missionary Society, and of his "Great God, who art Thou, where art Thou? Show Thyself to me!" and of his conversion to Christ.

(c) *Gill*

After the death of Pascal there was found in the lining of his coat a parchment which he never parted from, in order to keep in his memory a certain epoch in his life. It contained these words: "Certainty—joy—the God of Jesus Christ, not of the philosophers and savants. Oh that I may never be separated from Him." The explanation of this is: That on one memorable night, during a holy watching, he had met not merely the machinist of the universe, the God who is but the substance of the law of the world, but the God who wills and creates the happiness of His children.

(d) *Prof. E. Naville*

A report of a report, says Manton, is a cold thing and of small value; but a report of what we have witnessed and experienced ourselves comes warmly upon men's hearts. So a mere formal description, observes Spurgeon, of faith and its blessings falls flat on the ear; but when a sincere believer tells of his own experience of the Lord's faithfulness, it has a great charm about it. We like to hear the narrative of a journey from the traveller himself. In a court of law they will have no hearsay evidence. "Tell us," says the judge, "not what your neighbour said, but what you saw yourself." Personal evidence of the power of grace has a wonderfully convincing force upon the conscience. "I sought the Lord, and He heard me," is better argument than all the Butler's Analogies that will ever be written, good as they are in their place.

(e)

CERTAINTY AND PROBABILITY

"*Now we believe, not because of thy saying: for we have heard Him ourselves, and* KNOW *that this is indeed the Christ, the Saviour of the world*" (John iv. 42).

There is a
1. Faith of hearing = probability = the woman's surmise, "Is not this the Christ?"
2. Faith of personal experience and certainty = The Samaritans = "We have *heard*, and KNOW."
Question: How is religious certainty to be attained to?"
We are told that religion is at most guesswork —no certainty about God or Christ. Before people *believe*, they ask to have it *proved*; and as proofs, such as science recognises, are not forthcoming, we are told that our religion cannot get above *probability*. To this it is asserted that there is such a thing as *religious* CERTAINTY. . . . We may *know* if we will; but we must begin at the *beginning*. America was but a *probability* till Columbus took ship and discovered it. That the earth went round the sun, and not *vice versâ*, was but a *probability* until Galileo made it certain. Each man arrived at certainty, but neither of them *began* with it.

1. Certainty is not to be arrived at
(i.) Through *external and visible* things—such as church membership and the ordinances of religious worship. These may be mere *tradition*, *superstition*, and *priestcraft*, and may increase doubt rather than remove it.
(ii.) Nor by mere *teaching* and *preaching*. These may be no more than "the wisdom of men." Neither the preaching of an Apollos nor of an angel from heaven can produce certainty in the minds of the hearers. "What will this babbler say?" will probably be the question of many after all is said and done by human instrumentality.
(iii.) Nor by the mere *study of the Bible*. All may agree that it is a wonderful old Book—that its theme is one, though written by different writers and at great distances of time from each other. "The testimony of Jesus" is the spirit throughout, and by whomsoever written. The Book, too, has had a wonderful history; has survived kingdoms, persecutions, fires; has been translated, revised; and nations with it and without it are in wonderful contrast. Students will grant all this, and yet rise from its study very little further advanced than before. They will admit that there is a mysterious something about this Book which others do not possess; but they can get no further than before in admitting the PROBABILITY of its record being true, and of the Book being a Divine revelation.
These are as might be expected; for these are not the roads to certainty—not how our Lord and His apostles began with men.
So far, and by these methods, you have been putting a book into a blind man's hand. Before he can read it, you must open his eyes. Or, you have asked a man to read a book before he has learned his A B C. First, you must begin at the beginning, and then all the rest will follow.
There is an A B C of religion, and until a man learns that he cannot have *certainty*.
See how our Lord began:
Matt. iv. "Repent, for the Kingdom of Heaven is at hand."

(f)

Matt. xviii. "Except ye be converted, and be-come as little children, ye shall in no wise enter the Kingdom of Heaven."

John iii. "Except a man be born again, he cannot see . . . enter the Kingdom of Heaven."

These = REPENTANCE and REGENERATION = the first steps—the A B C of religion; and religious certainty cannot be arrived at unless a man begin with them.

2. So Peter taught :-

"Repent and be baptized, and ye shall receive the gift of the Holy Ghost."

"Him hath God exalted to be a Prince and a Saviour, to grant repentance and the remission of sins."

3. So Paul taught :-

"Repentance towards God, and faith towards our Lord Jesus Christ."

[This has always been the beginning, the strait gate through which we must enter. Compare the teaching and experience of Augustine, Luther, Bun-yan, or any other of the great and decided workers in God's kingdom here.]

Upon this there follows a *new life;* every one who begins here receives the gift of the Holy Spirit, "the unction from the Holy One," and *knows* all things. Cf. 1 John v. "We know that the Son of God is come, and hath given us an understanding," etc.

This is the knowledge of the Samaritans in our text—the knowledge of experience and certainty, which is a part of our life; no guess, no opinion, and which cannot be talked *out* of us any more than it can be talked *into* us.

Such persons can give "a reason for the hope" that is within them. "The Kingdom of God is *within* you"; "The Kingdom of God is light," and peace, and joy in the Holy Ghost." It is sim-ply indestructible; survives everything—though heaven and earth pass away—this is the kingdom which cannot be moved, and against which the gates of hell cannot prevail.

Galileo once thought it *probable* that the earth went round the sun, but after a time he *knew* it did, and though they imprisoned him as a heretic, and made him recant, yet aside he said, "*It does go round all the same.*" You cannot burn a man's convictions out of him.

(a)

CERTAINTY AND PROBABILITY (THE OXFORD MOVE-MENT)

"When I entered at Oxford, John Henry New-man was beginning to be famous. The responsible authorities were watching him with anxiety; clever men were looking with interest and curiosity on the apparition among them of one of those per-sons of indisputable genius who was likely to make a mark upon his time. His appearance was striking. He was above the middle height, slight and spare. His head was large, his face remark-ably like that of Julius Cæsar. The forehead, the shape of the ears and nose, were almost the same. The lines of the mouth were very peculiar, and I should say exactly the same. I have often thought of the resemblance, and believed that it extended to the temperament. In both there was an original force of character which refused to be moulded by circumstances, which was to make its own way, and become a power in the world; a clearness of intellectual perception, a disdain for

conventionalities, a temper imperious and wilful, but along with it a most attaching gentleness, sweetness, singleness of heart and purpose. Both were formed by nature to command others, both had the faculty of attracting to themselves the passionate devotion of their friends and followers, and in both cases, too, perhaps the devotion was rather due to the personal ascendency of the leader than to the cause which he represented. When I first saw him he had written his book upon the Arians. An accidental application had set him upon it, at a time, I believe, when he had half resolved to give himself to science and mathe-matics, and had so determined him into a theo-logical career. He had published a volume or two of parochial sermons. A few short poems of his had also appeared in the "British Magazine" under the signature of "Delta," which were re-printed in the "Lyra Apostolica." They were unlike any other religious poetry which was then extant. It was hard to say why they were so fascinating. They had none of the musical grace of the "Christian Year." They were not har-monious; the metre halted, the rhymes were irregular, yet there was something in them which seized the attention, and would not let it go. Keble's verses flowed in soft cadence over the mind, delightful, as sweet sounds are delightful, but are forgotten as the vibrations die away. Newman's had pierced into the heart and mind, and there remained.

"Greatly as his poetry had struck me, he was himself all that the poetry was, and something far beyond. I had then never seen so impressive a person. I met him now and then in private; I at-tended his church, and heard him preach Sunday after Sunday; he is supposed to have been insidi-ous, to have led his disciples on to conclusions to which he designed to bring them, while his purpose was carefully veiled. He was, on the contrary, the most transparent of men. He told us what he believed to be true. He did not know where it would carry him. Newman's mind was world-wide. He was interested in everything which was going on in science, in politics, in literature. Nothing was too large for him, nothing too trivial, if it threw light upon the central question, what man really was, and what was his destiny. He was careless about his personal prospects. He had no ambition to make a career, or to rise to rank and power. Still less had pleasure any seductions for him. His natural temperament was bright and light; his senses, even the com-monest, were exceptionally delicate. Newman had read omnivorously; he had studied modern thought and modern life in all its forms, and with all its many-coloured passions. The soundest arguments, even the arguments of Bishop Butler himself, went no further than to establish a pro-bability. But religion with Newman was a personal thing between himself and his Maker, and it was not possible to feel love and devotion to a Being whose existence was merely probable. As Carlyle says of himself when in a similar condition; a religion which was not a certainty was a mockery and a horror; and unshaken and unshakable as his own convictions were, Newman evidently was early at a loss for the intellectual grounds on which the claims of Christianity to abstract belief could be based.

"With us undergraduates Newman, of course, did not enter on such important questions, although

(b)

they were in the air and we talked about them among ourselves. He, when we met him, spoke to us about subjects of the day, of literature, of public persons and incidents, of everything which was generally interesting. He seemed always to be better informed on common topics of conversation than any one else who was present. He was never condescending with us, never didactic or authoritative; but what he said carried conviction along with it. When we were wrong he knew why we were wrong, and excused our mistakes to ourselves while he set us right. Perhaps his supreme merit as a talker was, that he never tried to be witty or to say striking things. Ironical he could be, but not ill-natured. Not a malicious anecdote was ever heard from him. Prosy he could not be. He was lightness itself—the lightness of elastic strength—and he was interesting because he never talked for talking's sake, but because he had something real to say.

"Personal admiration, of course, inclined us to look to him as a guide in matters of religion. No one who heard his sermons in those days can ever forget them. They were seldom directly theological. We had theology enough and to spare from the select preachers before the University. Newman, taking some Scripture character for a text, spoke to us about ourselves, our temptations, our experiences. His illustrations were inexhaustible. He seemed to be addressing the most secret consciousness of each of us—as the eyes of a portrait appear to look at every person in a room. He never exaggerated; he was never unreal. A sermon from him was a poem, formed on a distinct idea, fascinating by its subtlety, welcome—how welcome!—from its sincerity, interesting from its originality, even to those who were careless of religion, and to others who wished to be religious, but had found religion dry and wearisome, it was like the springing of a fountain out of the rock."

(a) *Froude.*

CERTAINTY AND SPECULATION

The grand simplicity and clearness of the Prologue (of St. John's Gospel) shows with what truly apostolic *certainty* John *experienced* the influence of the speculations of his age, and yet remained *master* over them, modifying, correcting, and making them available for his ideas.

(b) *Meyer.*

CHANCE

Thou camest not to thy place by accident: It was the very place God meant for thee.

(c) *Cowper*

Was it mere *chance*, or a mere coincidence, that Ahasuerus could not sleep on a certain night?

(d) (*See* PRAYER, *answer to.*)

CHANGE

"I am the Lord, I *change* not" [Mal. iii. 6]. God may cast thee *down*, but He will not cast thee *off*.

The rock does not shake or *change*, though the sea may ebb and flow about it.

(e) *S. Rutherford*

"CHANGED, WE SHALL BE" (1 Cor. xv. 51, 52)

The *change* is a qualifying one : for " Flesh and Blood " cannot inherit the kingdom of God.
The *time* is that of the Second Advent.

1. "WE": Who?

The Quick, Believers, Regenerate:
(i.) Because the argument is concerning their Resurrection only;
(ii.) Because at the First Resurrection, when believers are raised, "WE who remain shall be caught up and be for ever with the Lord." As the magnet attracts iron-filings, so Christ attracts like-minded ones.
" The *dead* shall be raised, and *we* shall be changed." Cf. LAZARUS and MARY (a dead and a living saint), " The Master is come, and calleth for thee."
(iii.) Because " the change " is not the *moral* change of conversion, but the *physical* one of being clothed with an incorruptible body.
Hence those who will be *changed* = the elect, the wheat, gathered from the four winds, who are living looking *for* Jesus, as well as looking *unto* Him. Cf. Ps. l., " Gather My saints together unto Me, those who have made a covenant with Me by sacrifice."

2. Glimpses of these things in the Lord's teaching

(i.) From what He says about *the days of Noah and Lot*, which indicate that the world will be going on then as now. There will be no ill omens. —" The sun was risen upon the earth when Lot entered Zoar."—Men will be busy with their occupations, eating, drinking, marrying, buying and selling up to the last moment. There will be no hush; the world will not stand still; but ships will sail; trains will run; there will be wars and rumours of wars and political changes; the newspaper columns will be full of daily reports as usual —everything will go on as heretofore, till *suddenly* —as the lightning shineth out of heaven from the east unto the west, whilst the ship is sailing across the sea, and the train is running on land— the blow comes, the end is at hand.
(ii.) *The sudden and eternal separation:* " I tell you that two shall be in one bed, one shall be taken and the other left "—Two shall be working together in the field; or two women grinding together at the mill, with the like result. Relations will be separated; men associated in business will be separated; friendships will be severed—all bonds and ties will be snapped in a moment, except spiritual ties—men may have taken sweet counsel together as David and Ahithophel, but that moment will draw each to his own place.
From the same home, the same office and desk; from the same pew in church; or walking together in the street. Wherever they are, there they shall be changed—one taken to be with Christ, and the other left . . . left because " too late," or unready, or because, first of all as a preparation for this change into glory, there must be the *change of conversion.*

3. Old Testament Examples of this change

ELIJAH and ENOCH—the former, being more removed from the ordinary life of men, is perhaps less appropriate; but Enoch was a man of like passions with ourselves—the father of a family, the head of a household—he *walked with God*, till one day he was missed. He *was not* in the

(f)

.house ; he *was not* with his family ; he *was not* in the street ; he *was not* doing business, for GOD TOOK HIM—took him from toil, from being weary with earth's sin—one man was taken and another left. Taken, not by death, as Adam had been, but by being " CHANGED."

4. Wherefore " be ready "

(i.) Enoch was *ready*—because he *pleased God*, and without FAITH it is impossible to please Him ; —and at a moment when he thought not, God took him.

(ii.) Ready because he WALKED with God,—for " if we walk in the light, as He is in the light, we have fellowship one with another, and the blood of Jesus Christ cleanseth us from all sin."

Be ready, so that whether we *wake* or *sleep* we may be accepted with Him.

(a)

" *Who shall'* CHANGE *our vile body*, etc. (Phil. iii. 21)

The power = The Lord Jesus Christ ; *The time* alluded to is His second coming (see verse 20). *The work He will then do* = " Change our vile body," *i.e.*, not that the body as a construction is *vile*, for it is God's workmanship—His masterpiece ; not that man's body as such is vile—for Christ took part of the same—and has taken a man's body into heaven. But a body of humiliating tendencies, of grovelling and low affections, permeated with earthly-mindedness and carnal admixtures : this body, as such, is a clog to the spirit ; and will be changed at Christ's second coming into a body in harmony with man's destiny as a son of God. *The pattern*,—after which He will work,—will be His *own glorious body :* " we know not what we shall be, but we shall be *like Him*."

The power required will be " according to the working whereby He is able even to *subdue all* things unto Himself "—Almighty power.

Some things can no man tame, nor subdue = almightiness is required. Jesus has all *power* committed unto Him ; and working with this power— even the unruly wills and affections of sinful men— will be subdued unto Himself. Our body of humiliation will, under His power, be tamed and subdued ; its lusts conquered ; its innate selfishness destroyed ; that which now makes us groan within ourselves,—whilst waiting for the *redemption of the body*—because it is our weak part—subject to the tempter's temptations—liable to sin and disease and death—under which we cry, " *Good Lord, deliver us* " . . . " The spirit indeed is willing, but the flesh is weak."

Illustration :—A man of much natural ability but born in a humble sphere of society, by means of his natural abilities he rises superior to his lot and takes his place amongst the honourable of the earth. But the instincts of his lowly birth and breeding will cling to him—notwithstanding his abilities he will perhaps never possess the instincts of the true gentleman ; somewhere or other the coarser vein will show itself, and help to spoil his character. Daily life illustrates this frequently. The instincts of a gentleman are born in a man. Neither education nor great natural endowments will wholly and effectually make up for the deficiency of genteel birth and breeding ; and the man himself will be conscious of this as a real defect in his character, against which he will have to strive and watch continually.

So the Christian—born on earth, of the earth earthy, yet a citizen of heaven, a nobleman of the kingdom to come—will often have to mourn over his innate depravity. The instincts of his lowly origin lead him to do what he would not. " How to do that which I would I know not." Such a nature clings to him and spoils all his hopes, ambitions, and aims. He is of the dust,— literally a worm, and, as yet, no man,—no noble, no hero, no saint. The defects in his natural character constantly obtrude themselves into his spiritual character, and prove to those around him how little as yet the spirit of Christ and the instincts of heaven's nobility are really his. How little, indeed, his affections are set on things above.

To such a man, with a high aim, seeking to live as a citizen of heaven, comes the *assurance :*— " He shall change our vile body, that it may be like unto His glorious body."

Till then—we shall have to mourn over defeat, over spiritual loss, over the constant re-appearance of the old nature—proving too truly our old lineage.

But then, we shall be freed from it. It will be *changed*—and so changed as that we shall be secure from falls and relapses—we shall be at our best, " Like Christ," the sons of God. The instincts of earth will be exchanged for the instincts of heaven.

(b)

CHAPTER

Who read a chapter when they rise,
Shall ne'er be troubled with sore eyes.

(c)   *Geo. Herbert*

CHARACTER

The Devil, with respect to his *sinfulness*, not his existence, is his own creator.

(d)   *Daub, quoted by Sartorius*

On *a boy of bad character* admitted into a school :—

" Better for them if their gates had been open to the pestilence could but have killed the body, but this boy,—this fore-front fighter in the devil's battle—did much ruin to many an immortal soul. He systematically called evil good and good evil, put bitter for sweet and sweet for bitter. He openly threw aside the admission of any one moral obligation. Never did some of the boys forget to their dying day the deep, intolerable, the unfathomable flood of moral turpitude and iniquity which he bore with him ; a flood which seemed so irresistible, that the influence of good characters to stay its onrush seemed as futile as the weight of a feather to bar the fury of a mountain stream."

(e)   *Farrar's Eric*

CHARACTER, UNDEVELOPED

Every man has in himself a continent of undiscovered character. Happy is he who acts the Columbus to his own soul.

(f)   *Sir J. Stevens.*

CHARACTER, NATURAL EXCELLENCES

I do not doubt that there is a most appreciable value about the excellences of character not unfrequently displayed by the unconverted, unspiritual man—the man who is not born again of the Spirit, and who has not at any time been made a new creature in Jesus Christ. Are we, because we call ourselves religious, to treat with scorn the integrity which nothing can corrupt; the unsullied honour which shrinks from trickery and fraudulent dealing as it would from a stab; the kindliness which has an ear ready for every true tale of distress, and a hand open to relieve the son or daughter of sorrow that tells it; or the noble self-control and self-restraint which walks amongst a thousand temptations to passionate indulgence, and puts them all, resolutely and persistently, beneath its feet? Are we to despise these things, and count them as of no importance? Are we to speak slightingly of them, as being the virtues of the mere man of the world? God forbid that we should do such a thing! These excellences have their own appointed reward; and, independently of the advantage to society at large, a man is the better and the happier for being pure, instead of impure; honest instead of dishonest; liberal instead of grasping; kind and thoughtful for others, instead of having his every plan and his every calculation centered upon himself.

(a)   *Gordon Calthrop*

CHARITY

O poor Charity! Thou art seldom found in scarlet.
(b)   *Webster*

From all matter together, we are not able to extract one thought. This is impossible and quite of another sphere. Again, all matter and spirit together are unable to produce one spark of *charity*. This is likewise impossible, and of a sphere altogether above nature.
(c)   *Blaise Pascal*

CHARITY " THINKETH NO EVIL " (1 Cor. xiii.)

The sins we do, people behold with optics,
Which show them ten times more than common vices,
And often multiply them.
(d)   *Fletcher*

CHARITY AND GIFTS

Charity endures; prophecy, tongues, knowledge, "fail." What the Corinthians got by miracle, we obtain by the persevering use of our faculties. Prophecy means the power of interpreting Scripture. A precious gift, but valuable only as a means to an end; "A time will come when they shall not teach every man his neighbour, saying, Know ye the Lord, but all shall know Him from the least unto the greatest." All those qualifications which go to make an expounder of Scripture, such as eloquence, critical knowledge, biblical lore, are only designed for Time, and soon shall be obsolete.
Tongues, also, shall "fail,"—that is, pass away. Miraculous then: now acquired. This faculty gives more cause for vanity than any other. He who

knows two languages is able to express his thoughts to two persons; this is valuable, but not a double means of thought. Yet we see the expert linguist generally more proud of his gift, and more vain, than the deep thinker and knower, so with the Corinthians, this gift produced more vanity than the useful ones of prophecy and teaching. The knowledge of the physician and of the lawyer—all knowledge hived in centuries by the barrister and the judge will vanish away (as useless, when "they shall hunger no more, and thirst no more," when sickness and death shall cease, when men shall neither "hurt nor destroy") when Christianity reigns upon the earth.
(e)   *F. W. Robertson*

CHASTISEMENT

Heaven is not always angry when He strikes,
But most chastises those whom most He likes.
(f)   *Pomfret*

Beloved children: let the Master train you:
 Surely to you He meaneth nothing ill,
His love to you can never know decreasing,
 He knoweth what He does,—'tis wisdom still.
Patience in heavy days of dark distress
Works out for you the heavenly blessedness.
  Ulysses Van Salis.   Translated by H. Bonar
(g)

CHASTISEMENT, NEED OF

Our pride must have winter weather to rot it. So narrow is the entry to heaven, that our knots, our hunches, and lumps of pride, and self-love, and idol love, and world love, must be hammered off us, that we may squeeze in, stooping low, and creeping through that narrow and thorny entry.
(h)   *S. Rutherford*

CHASTITY

She that has that, is clad in complete steel.
(i)   *Milton*

CHILD JESUS IN THE TEMPLE, THE. (Luke ii. 41–52)

The only incident in the *childhood of our Lord*. Anecdotes of the childhood of great men foreshadow their destiny: so here—a glimpse of the spiritual greatness of the Lord Jesus Christ. Observe three features in this narrative.

1. Jesus doing His Father's business

(i.) At Jerusalem He had seven days of holy delight. His soul feasted. Every rite spoke a Divine language to Him. He had an intuitive knowledge of the meaning of the Temple service.
(ii.) He stays behind because He could not tear Himself away. To Him it was quite natural that He should be there. The Child was at home in His Father's house.
(iii.) "How is it that ye *sought* Me?" Did it not occur to you where to find Me? Where else should a child be but in His Father's house? It was a mistake to look for Me elsewhere: for where My Father's business is carried on, there you are sure to find Me.
(j)

In all this Jesus recognises the necessity of improving the world. He came into a world and found it full of unrealities; to improve it is to do His Father's work. Thus we, too, become "fellow workers with God."

If Jesus recognises this duty at TWELVE, how much more ought we of riper years! We are called upon to heal some of the world's sores—to reform abuses—to do our *work* well, knowing that "the gods will see it" (see Anecdote), "Life is real."

2. Jesus doing His Father's will

"*He went down to Nazareth*," etc. It was doubtless a real trouble to leave the Temple, where everything was in harmony with His spirit, and return to Nazareth, where no one understood Him. "He learned obedience by the things that He suffered." Having now, perhaps for the first time, realized His relation to the Father, it seems strange that He should not have been left to grow up (as in the case of Samuel) in the Temple, and when mature to issue forth as the Messiah.

(i.) *Why did not God permit this?* The answer is not difficult. The Saviour must develop in *obscurity*. At Jerusalem He would have been too soon in the strife. His original mind would have early provoked the hatred of the doctors. Like Moses in Midian, Joseph in prison, David in the wilderness, He must spend eighteen years in the vicinity of a village carpenter's shop at Nazareth. There was no halo (nimbus) round His head, as in pictures. There He was to be unknown from others, till His hour was come.

To this He submits. "Thy will, not Mine, be done." *We* chafe against this. To exchange the Temple for Nazareth, the Father's house for the carpenter's shop, to go back to distasteful duties, indicates a great step in spiritual obedience. We are not in our places by accident.

3. The shadow of the Future

He grew

(i.) In stature, as others.

(ii.) In wisdom, spiritually and intellectually (His teachers being many: the Old Testament, nature, the yearly visit to Jerusalem); so He learnt to *know men*, and was prepared for His conflicts with them afterwards. He would compare the long prayers, Temple services, phylacteries, etc., with the stern righteousness of the prophets. They thinking about *Theology*, He about *Religion*; they about *Rubrics*, He about His *Father's will*.

(iii.) "*In favour with God and men.*" = a Reconciler. Ask: Is He in favour with us? Do we *know* the Son? Do we see any beauty in Him?

"*The Father Himself loveth you, because ye have loved Me.*" . . The Father loveth those who love His Son.

(*a*)							*See Godet, in loc*

Good Christian people, here lies for you an inestimable loan;—take all heed thereof, in all carefulness employ it;—with high recompense, or else with heavy penalty will it one day be required back.

(*b*)								*Carlyle*

CHILDHOOD

The childhood shows the man, as morning shows the day.

(*c*)								*Milton*

CHILDREN

No child finds any difficulty in accepting the words of scripture; but polemical writers make meanings difficult.

(*d*)								*Mozley*

Happy the child who is suffered to be, and content to be, what God meant it to be—a child while childhood lasts! Happy the parent who does not dare force artificial manners, precocious feelings, premature religion!

(*e*)							*F. W. Robertson*

A CHILD'S FAITH

Birdie was only four years old, but she had already been taught that God loved her, and always took care of her. One day there was a very heavy thunderstorm, and Birdie's sisters and mamma even laid by their sewing, and drew their chairs into the middle of the room, pale and trembling with fear. But Birdie stood close by the window, watching the storm with bright eyes. "Oh, mamma! ain't that bu'fu!" she cried, clapping her hands with delight, as a vivid flash of lightning burst from the black clouds and the thunder pealed and rattled over their heads. "It is God's voice, Birdie," said mamma, and her own voice trembled. "He talks velly loud, don't He, mamma? S'pose it's so as deaf Betsey can hear, and the uver deaf folks." "Oh, Birdie, dear, come straight away from that window," said one of her sisters, whose cheeks were blanched with fear. "What for?" asked Birdie. "Oh! because the lightning is so sharp, and it thunders so loud." But Birdie shook her head, and looking over her shoulder with a happy smile on her face, lisped out: "If it funders, let it funder! 'Tis God makes it funder, and He'll take care of me. I ain't a bit afraid to hear God talk, Maizy." Was not Birdie's faith beautiful? Mamma and sisters did not soon forget the lesson.

(*f*)

CHILDREN'S CHAPTER, THE (Matt. xviii.)

1. The teaching of a child's life (ver. 3)

Its comparative innocence—freedom from craft and guile.

"*Become as a little child*" = repentance = ye must unravel your life, and begin again.

So to Nicodemus (John iii.).

2. The teaching about a child's salvation (ver. 11)

"For the Son of Man is come *to save* that which was lost." The parallel passage in St. Luke is, "The Son of Man is come *to seek* and to *save;*" and the connection there is the story of Zacchæus. The difference is apparent. Men like Zacchæus, having outlived the days of childhood, have each repeated Adam's sin: in the face of the "Thou shalt not" of God, they have plucked and eaten forbidden fruit, and so become transgressors; then, as a consequence, they have wandered astray, after whom the Good Shepherd, in His errand of mercy, goes in pursuit, "*to seek and to save.*" But these children, who have not sinned after the similitude of Adam's transgression, He comes to *save* only. He has simply to "*gather the lambs in His bosom.*" This is a point which will be found, it is hoped, of great beauty, force, and significance.

(*g*)

3. The teaching of a child's death (ver. 14)

(i.) *As to themselves.*—It is a *double salvation*—from contracting sin and sorrow.

"Give me back my child!" cried the anguished mother to Death. Instead of which she was shown what the earthly future of that child would have been. Then said she: "It is better as it is; grant not my prayer." [*Hans Andersen.*]

In Christ's nursery they grow and develop—like plants transferred from a chilly climate to a warm and tropical atmosphere—into what they could not otherwise become.

"She is not dead, the child of our affection,
    But gone unto that school
Where she no longer needs our poor protection,
    And Christ Himself doth rule.

Not as a child shall we again behold her;
    For when, with raptures wild,
In our embraces we again enfold her,
    She will not be a child."
                                                Longfellow

(ii.) *As to the parents.*—God takes a child when He wants the parents. It was when the nobleman's son was dying that the father came to Christ, and got a blessing himself.

A Scotch shepherd had folded a flock of ewes, with the exception of one. The gate stood wide open, but all suitable means failed to entice the sheep to enter. Evening was coming on, and a storm was brewing—the flock must be housed and left in safety for the night. At last the shepherd sprang out, seized the little lamb belonging to the obstinate ewe, gently carried it into the fold, and then quickly, without more ado, the poor mother ran in too.

(iii.) These deaths help to make heaven more of a reality. They link us to the shore beyond. A recent writer says:—" As a boy, I thought of heaven as a city with domes, spires, and beautiful streets, inhabited by angels. By-and-by my little brother died, and I thought of heaven much as before, but with one inhabitant that I knew. Then another died, and then some of my acquaintances, so that in time I began to think of heaven as containing several people that I knew. But it was not until *one of my own* little children died that I began to think that I had treasure in heaven myself. Afterwards another went, and yet another; at last a fourth; and by that time I had so many acquaintances and children in heaven, that I no more thought of it as a city of walls and towers and streets of jasper, but of its inhabitants; for now there are so many of us there that I sometimes think that I know more people in heaven than I do upon earth."
(a)

[Matt. xviii.]

1. Men must resemble children: be child-like, not childish.

2. The danger of offending them, *i.e.* both children and child-like people. They have a special guardian angel: "I, the Lord, do keep them." "He shall give His angels charge concerning thee," etc.

3. The Saviour came to save them, not "seek"; children have not strayed. They are included both in the loss entailed by the Fall and in the

atonement of Christ. They have not sinned after "the similitude of Adam's transgression."

4. The Father's will and the Saviour's work correspond, and are co-extensive.
(b)

CHILDREN, CHARGE OF

The great perhaps take as good charge of their posterity as the ants; the eggs once laid, the male and female ants fly about their business, and confide them to the trusty *working-ants.*
(c)   *J. P. F. Richter*

CHILDREN, CHRISTIANITY, AND INFANTICIDE.

The Poetry of Childhood.

"O tender gem, and full of heaven;
    Not in the twilight stars on high,
Nor in moist flowers at even,
    See we our God so nigh!"

Why is it that in ancient poetry and literature you find no allusion to childhood, no reminiscences of childhood; while modern literature and poetry are full of them? Why is it that modern soldiers, in the very heat and rage of battle, have been known to save, and cherish, and surround with kindness some little wandering child? Why has Christendom adopted the precious custom of infant baptism, signing even the infant with the sign of the cross, and receiving him into the ark of Christ's Church?
(d)   *Archdn. Farrar*

INFANTICIDE.

Contrast these feelings with those that prevailed in the world when Christ was born! Now infanticide is justly regarded with horror; it is justly punished as murder; *then* infanticide was not even looked upon as a disgrace. Greece and Rome were the most gifted and the grandest of ancient empires. Did their glory, did their grandeur, did their wisdom, save them from this infamy? In Greece, when a child was born, if there were any defect about it, it was instantly killed; but, if not, the father was only taken to see it on the ninth day, and if, on seeing it, he stooped down, and took it in his arms, it was then reared; but if he did *not* do this—and no Greek father ever did if he already had one or two children, or as many as he cared to support—what happened? Can you believe it that then, even in the very best days of Athens, the little Greek child was taken up and exposed in the open air upon some hill, and there left to perish by starvation, unless some one chose to save its life? Horrible to relate, there was even a class of women to whom this infanticide by exposure was a regular and recognised profession!

It was the same in Rome. Speaking in the Senate of Rome, speaking without a blush, a noble Roman once openly said that, of all the Senators whom he was addressing, there was probably not one who had not thus got rid of one or more of his children. He was speaking to Consuls and Censors and Prætors—the most powerful aristocrats, the lordliest rulers of the Imperial city, and yet not a voice was raised to deny with execration the hideous charge—a charge which here in Eng-
(e)

land, thanks to Christianity, would consign the meanest pauper to the gallows or the gaol.

And in China,—spite of all the polish and all the philosophy of the Chinese,—so common to this day is infanticide, that one main work of the Mission Sisters of Mercy is to save the life of infants flung out to die; and only a year or two ago a French nobleman found seven dead children in a short morning walk in the environs of Canton. Nay, what did even a modern philosopher do? Rousseau, the sentimental, the impassioned, the eloquent, deliberately had every one of his children left to be brought up by public and promiscuous charity. Think of unblushing infamies like these, and then may we not say with the poet, in answer to the question of what use Christianity has been—

> "Askest thou in exultation
>   What the Cross of Christ has done?
> Ask the splendours of creation
>   If they feel the noon-day sun.

> "Ask reviving vegetation,
>   Rushing forth on joyful wing,
> If it feels the inspiration
>   Of the soul-entrancing Spring!"

(a)   *Archdn. Farrar*

CHILDREN, POTENTIALITIES OF

"*Like as the arrows in the hand of the giant, even so are the young children.*" They may be arrows of the holy, aimed only at what is pestilent and deadly —they may be arrows of the evil one, ruinous as the missiles of the madman who scatters firebrands and death. Who can say how vast are the potentialities involved in the life of a young child? More than nineteen hundred years ago, in the civil wars of Rome, the life of a beautiful child was again and again saved from the extremest peril. That child grew up to be a heavy curse to himself, a heavy curse to others; he grew up to be one of the worst men who ever lived; the Emperor Tiberius, in whose reign Christ was crucified. Again, some hundred and fifty years ago, a house in an English village was found to be in flames. The clergyman and his family—for it was the vicarage—were roused, and when they had escaped, it was found that one little boy was still in the burning house. A ladder was placed to the window, he was rescued, and handed unhurt into his father's arms. What would the world have lost had that little boy perished? For his name was John Wesley, and by his piety and zeal he fanned into flame once more the dead white embers of Christian faith. Now, who can tell what a little child may be! He may grow up, as has been said, like Beethoven, to lift the soul by the magic of divine melody into the seventh heaven of ineffable vision and incommensurable hope; or like Newton, to weigh the far-off stars in the balance, and measure the heavings of the eternal flow; or like Luther, to scorch up what is cruel and false by a word, as by a flame; or like Milton and Burke, to awake men's hearts with the note of an organ trumpet; or like the great saints of the Churches and the great sages of the Schools, to add to those acquisitions of spiritual beauty and intellectual mastery which have, one by one, and little by little, raised men from being no higher than the brute to be only a little lower than the angels. You never know but what the child, in rags and pitiful squalor, that meets you in the streets, may have in him the germ of gifts that might add new treasure to the storehouse of beautiful things or noble acts. In that great storm

of terror which swept over France in 1793, a certain man who was every hour expecting to be led off to the guillotine uttered this memorable sentiment: "Even at this incomprehensible moment," he said, "when morality, enlightenment, love of country, all of them only make death at the prison door or on the scaffold more certain—yes, on the fatal tumbril itself, with nothing free but my voice, I could still cry 'Take care' to a child that should come too near the wheel. Perhaps I may save his life; perhaps he may one day save his country."

(b)   *Archdn. Farrar*

CHILDREN, DEATH OF

How pathetic, how heartrending, is the news which comes to us from Sunderland to-day; how in one deplorable accident, more than 190 little ones—little boys and little girls, and they only of ages from four or five to fourteen—have lost their lives. I know few things more deplorable in history. I know not that such a calamity has ever before occurred in an English city. Louder than at Bethlehem, when a voice was heard at Ramah, "*Lamentation, and weeping, and great mourning, Rachel weeping for her children, and would not be comforted, because they are not.*" Louder than at Ramah, in that massacre of the innocents, the voice comes from the banks of the Wear, of fathers and of mothers whose houses are in one moment left unto them desolate—who have, in one moment, ashes for joy, and for the garment of praise the spirit of heaviness. My brethren, whose heart is so hard as not to bleed when he thinks of those dead children, of those white faces as they lay side by side, of the parents breaking into wild cries, or, in the stupefaction of grief, carrying in their arms to desolate homes their dead or dying little ones? O God of mercy, have mercy on those poor parents! and as Thou hast sent Thine Angel of Death (ah! did no mercy stay the beating of his wings?) to turn the children's feast into a funeral—so send Thy white-winged Messengers of Mercy with balm and consolation to those wounded hearts.

But death may itself be mercy.

> "An innocent to die, what is it less
> Than to give angels to Heaven's blessedness!"

The dead are dead. The parents of those dead little ones must say with weeping David, "*We shall go to them, but they shall not return to us.*"

(c)   *Ibid.*

CHILDREN, DEATH OF

"*Rachel mourning for her children.*"

The Church of England shows us that as these children died *for Christ*, therefore they are among *His witnesses*—His *martyrs*; theirs is the blessedness of those who are *killed for His Name's sake.* Moreover, she seeks to comfort Rachel by these words, "These were redeemed from among men, being the *first-fruits* to God and the Lamb." Yes, the *first-fruits* of the Saviour's humiliation and travail He came to save; and the act of His coming is made an act of salvation, being the occasion of saving all the male children of two years old and under in His native town.

(d)

It is of responsible persons that in the Day of Judgment it is said, "*The books were opened;*"

(e)

i.e., the record of each individual's *choice*, whether he or she, looking at the life God had given and the instructions for its guidance, had deliberately chosen good for evil, whether each had taken the road marked out respectively as leading to life or death.

But, be it remarked, of the "small "—*i.e.*, children—who stand before God, nothing of the kind is stated. Rather, may we not conclude, the Judge of all the earth does right? He reaps not where He has not sown; He deals with these as He did with the irresponsible children of Nineveh of old: "Should not I spare Nineveh, that great city, wherein are more than six score thousand persons that cannot discern between their right hand and their left?"

(*a*)

When the Philistines took the ark of the covenant to Philistia, and were considering whether they should send it back to Israel, they, as a test, put a cow in the car, and placed the ark upon it, and said, "If it goes on, the calf being left behind, we will take it as a sign that it is the hand of the Lord that is guiding it"; and behold, although that blind creature with its brute nature loved its child as we love our children with our intelligent nature, it went on bearing the ark to its proper home, but lowing for its calf as it went on.

Many a man who is obliged to drag the car of the business of this life goes on, but goes alone, longing and crying out for that which is behind—only it is not behind. It has gone before; and it stands at the head of the shining road waiting for you.

(*b*)   *H. Ward Beecher*

" *Woman, why weepest thou ?*—John xx. 13

Why dost thou weep?—say, can it be,
Because for ever blest, and free
From sin, from sorrow, and from pain,
Thy child shall never weep again-
Shall never feel, shall never know
E'en half thy little load of woe?

What was thy prayer, when his first smile
Did thy fond mother-heart beguile ?
When his first cry was in thine ear,
And on thy cheek his first warm tear?
And to thy heart at first were pressed
The throbbings of his little breast ?

What was thy prayer? Canst thou not now
See in his bright cherubic brow-
Hear in his soft seraphic strain,
So full of joy, so free from pain-
An answer (as if God did speak)
To all thy love had dared to seek?

Why therefore weep, when all the cares,
The doubts, the troubles, and the snares-
The threatening clouds, the falling tears,
Childhood's wild hopes and manhood's fears,
That might have been for him—for thee,
Have passed away, and ne'er shall be ?

.   .   .   .

A child of thine, a child of bliss !
Why therefore weep for joy like this ?
(*c*)   *J. S. Monsell*

CHILDREN, DEATH OF :—THE GOOD SHEPHERD

In a cold howe, far among the hills, where the winter was a sad thing, there lived an honest couple, a man with a gey lot of sheep and his wife. They war fowk weel aff in respect of this world's gear, an luikit up til amang the neighbours, but no to be envyed, seein' they had lost one after the other of a bonny family, till there was left in the house, but just ae laddie, the bonniest and best o' them a', and as a matter of course, the verra apple o' their eye. "Weel this last ane o' a' began in his turn to dwine and dwindle like the rest; and wherever thae twa poor folk turnt themselves in their pangs there stude death, glowerin' at them out of his empty eyes. Pray they did, ye may be sure, an' greit when a' was mirk, but prayers nor tears made no differ; the bairn was sent for, and away the bairn maun gang. An' when at length he lay streekit in his last clean claes till the robe of righteousness that wants not washing was put on him, what cud they but think the world was dune for them !

But the world maun wag, though the heart may sag; an' whan the dead lies streekit, there's a house to be theekit. Sae freens an' neebours gathered from far and from near, and there was a heap of folk in the house, come to the buryin' o' the bonny bairn. An' though death be in a house, folk maun eat none the less, and so the night afore the burial their dinner when they came back from the kirkyard had to be fore-ordained. It was the spring time o' the year, unco late in those "heich" parts. The most of the lambs had come ; but storm and drift were loth to lift from the laps of the hills, and long after it had begun to be something like weather lower down, the sheep couldn't be let out to pick their bit meat for themselves, but had to be kept in the cot. So to the cot the gudeman would go to fetch hame a lamb for a dinner to his freens and neebours. And as it fell out, it was a fearsome night of wind and driving snaw. But the gudeman turned not aside for wind or for snaw, for little cared he, with such a hollow in his heart, what came to him or what came of him. The storm in fact was a veil to his grief, and behind it he fell to greitin' an' bewailin' and lamentin' lood oot, judgin', na doubt, if he judged at a', he might groan and sigh, wi' nobody nigh, as he daren't do among the folk, or even before his ain wife, for the heartbreak o't. To the sheepcot, as I say, he gaed, wailing and plaining and crying after his bonny bairn, the last of his flock, oontimeous ta'en.

Half blind wi' the night an' snow and his ain tears, he came at length to the sheep-cote, an' what sud he see there but a man stan'in'. afore the door—straight up and still in the mirk an' storm, as if neither wind nor snaw came nigh him. It was maist fearsome to see ony one there, so far from ony place, no to say upon sic a night. The stranger was rowed in some kin' o' plaid like the gudeman himsel', whether a lowlan' or a highlan' plaid he cudna tell. But the face of the man was not one to be forgotten—an' that for the vera freenliness o't ! An' when he spake it was as if all the voices o' them' at was hame afore war made up into one, for the sweetness and the power of the same.

"What mak ye here in sic a storm, man ?" he speirt. An' the soon' of his voice, was aye softer nor the words of his mooth.

"I come for a lamb," the gudeman he answered.

"What kin' of a lamb," asked the stranger.

"The best I can lay my han's upo' i' the cot," answered he, "for it's to set afore my freens 'an
(*d*)

neebours. Sir, ye'll come hame wi' me and share o't?"

"Du yer sheep mak' ony resistance whan ye tak' the lamb? or whan it's gone do they mak' ony ootcry?"

"No, sir," said the gudeman.

The stranger ga'e a kin' o' sigh, an' says he,

"That's no hoo mine treat me! Whan I gang to my sheepfold, an' tak' the best an' the fittest, —no to kill him an' ait him—but to tak' him hame, an' fess him up i' my father's ain hoose, my ears are deant, an' my hert torn wi' the clamours, the bleatin' an' the baain' o' my sheep—my ain sheep! compleenin' sair again' me! An' me feedin' them, and cleedin' them, an' haudin' the tod frae them, a' their lives, frae the first to the last! It's some sair to bide!"

By this time the man's head was hanging down; but when the voice ceased, he dared to look up. There was no man there! Like one in a dream, wherein he knew not joy from sorrow, nor pleasure from pain, he gaed into the cot, an' grat ower the heids o' the 'oo'y craturs that cam' croodin' aboot 'im, sought out the best lamb, and carried it hame. The next day they saw him come back from the funeral with a smile upon his face where had been nane for sae mony a lang; and the next Sunday they heard him singing i' the kirk as naebody had ever heard him sing afore. An' never from that night was moan or plaint to be heard from the lips o' aither o' the twa o' them. They had not a bairn to close their eyes when their turn came, but what o' that? Whaur nane's left ahin', there's the mair to fin'.

(a)   *George Macdonald*

CHILDREN, DEATH OF

Epitaph in Willesden Churchyard.

" WILLIAM ROBINSON, aged 2,
And
SALLY ROBINSON, aged 4,
Children of
WILLIAM ROBINSON, of the Inner Temple,
London, Gt.
And ANNE, his wife.
Anno Domini, 1750.

Fled from scenes of guilt and misery,
Without partaking of them;
And their bodies sleep in this monument,
United by mutual tenderness.
Their sympathizing souls, impatient
Of a separation,
And eager to rejoin their kindred angel
With a smile took leave of their
Weeping parents here,
And together ascended to their
Immortal Sire above,
To sit at His right hand,
To be cherished in His paternal bosom,
To enjoy ineffable happiness,
And part no more;
These reflections, inspired by heaven,
Have taught their otherwise
Inconsolable parents to dry up their tears,
And yield a perfect resignation to the
Divine will,
Insomuch that they congratulate the
Dear deceased
On their timely departure,
And mourn only for the living."

(b)

"Who gathered these lilies?" asked the gardener, as he came into the garden and found some of his fairest and loveliest lilies cut. "I did," replied the Master. Then the gardener held his peace.

(c)   *Inscription in an English Churchyard*

" CHILDREN OF YOUR FATHER, THAT YE MAY BE " (Matt. v. 45)

Steps:—
1. Do no wrong.
2. Return not evil for evil.
3. Revile not (Be silent: " I held my tongue ").
4. Rather *take* wrong.
5. Offer more than is demanded.
6. Hate not the offender.
7. Love him even.
8. Do him good.
9. Pray for him.

(d)   *Chrysostom*

CHILDREN, AND THE KINGDOM OF HEAVEN

Such are without guile, not without *sin*. Compare them with grown-up and crafty people— " Beware of men." The members of God's kingdom are to be guileless.

(e)

CHILDREN, AS LITTLE

" *Except ye be converted, and become as little children,*" etc. (Matt. xviii. 2, 3)

Occasion : When the disciples disputed who should be greatest in the kingdom of heaven.

Another occasion was, when Jesus was teaching His disciples, as a Jewish rabbi would instruct his class, some mothers brought their children to Him that He should touch them; but the disciples rebuked them as interrupting the teaching going on, being shocked at their presuming to break in upon the words of the great Teacher. But Jesus Himself was displeased with His disciples, and welcomed the children, uttering the same weighty words—" Verily I say unto you, Except," etc.

1. The idea of conversion, and of becoming as little children is one

It is evident that our Lord does not mean that we must become ignorant as children are, nor weak and helpless, nor anything whereby the imperfection of childhood is implied, before we can enter His kingdom.

In order to understand what is meant, we may take an average adult person, not young, say in mid-life, and who, in obedience to the invitation of Christ, " Come unto Me," does come, and seeks admission into His kingdom.

We are assured that Jesus will not reject him. He has said, " Him that cometh unto Me, I will in no wise cast out"; but He demands of this man, as the one indispensable, absolutely necessary condition of his becoming a subject in that kingdom, that he *become as a little child first :* otherwise he can in no wise enter therein.

In other words, the Lord's demand implies that this man has acquired something in his past life, which he cannot take with him into that kingdom. Something, like wearing apparel, has been *put on,*

(f)

which now he must *put off;* something has been *taken up,* which now must be *laid aside.* (This is CONVERSION.)

The things which this man has acquired and put on, and which have become a part of his life, but which he must now lay aside, are elsewhere enumerated as so many black threads which have been spun or woven into his life : they are *malice, guile, hypocrisies, envies,* and *evil-speakings.* His previous life has been a web into which these have been woven. The shuttle has been continually flying backwards and forwards, daily weaving in new threads, many of which are the wrong ones, and which have spoilt the whole; consequently the life is a wrong one, it is not like the perfect pattern—it is not " after Christ."

This is the common experience of life. Malignant passions, hatreds, jealousies, suspicions, revenges, cruelties, insincerities, hypocrisies, craft, and so forth, have more or less been woven into it; so that by the time mature manhood is reached, our minds have become distorted, biassed, full of prejudice, swayed right and left by predisposition : all as the result of our breeding and education, to such an extent that not a Christian, but a " man of the world," as might have been expected, is the result.

And the person, whose case we are supposing, and who comes to Christ for admission into His kingdom, is a product of such influences. His life has been woven with the wrong threads; the pattern is spoilt. We can therefore now understand why it is that our Lord should at the outset demand of him that he should unspin, or unravel, the whole of the web of his past life. " You must pull it all out and spin it over again." This is, in other words, to become as a little child. The life must be begun again with Christ, and have the right threads spun into it, so that the pattern may be " after Christ."

For Jesus wants living, guileless, genuine, honest men as the subjects of His kingdom ; and except a man be converted and begin again with Him, or become as a little child, he can in no wise enter that kingdom.

2. As little children

We inquire next how a little child's life can exactly teach us this great and fundamental truth.

Take the case of a little child whose life is as yet unspun ; or it is as a clean page to be written upon. There is, so far, no actual sin, no settled evil disposition, no acquired sinful habit; neither craft nor guile are there, save in germs which may soon develop, but with them now we have nothing to do.

As such does the little child come into our families, a life uninfluenced by any malignant bias, warped by no prejudice, fresh, guileless, artless ; totally free from all the insincerities, the crafts, and the hypocrisies of the world, against which we have to fence, and be continually on our guard. But as soon as the child comes amongst us, there is a world teeming full of ill examples for it to copy ; and soon it begins to receive its first impressions, and the threads of life have begun to be woven into it. Every one with whom that young life has to do is either consciously or unconsciously weaving a new thread into that life, or writing upon the clear page characters written as it were with a pen of adamant and which are destined to remain. . . . Whatever is said or done by others, by the nurse, servants, father, mother, brothers, and

sisters, all go to make up that life, till in time a copy of one of themselves is reproduced, either good or bad.

Observe that our Lord's demand is, that we come to Him, as the little child comes to us. He wants to write on the fresh page, to weave the web of that life. The result of that will be a *new life,* a Christian life.

3. But this work of unravelling the past life, and of beginning again is a hard matter. Hence Christ has His own methods of producing it. He puts us through a process of *tribulation:* "We must through much tribulation enter the kingdom of heaven"; and this process is effectual in humbling proud man, and bringing him down to a childlike spirit, and when that is reached the true life may be begun.

(*a*)

" CHILDREN, AS LITTLE "

The man of learning and research, of wide accomplishments and high culture, too often, like the self-righteous man, is prejudiced against Christ. He too has to begin again, and become *as a little child :* "Let him become a fool that he may be wise" (1 Cor. iii. 18).

(*b*)

CHILDREN, SALVATION OF (Rom. v.)

This belief and hope has strong support in the universal sufficiency of the Atonement, and especially in the words of our Saviour concerning little children, spoken without qualification or limitation (Matt. xix. 14 ; Mark x. 14). There can be no salvation without Christ, even for children ; but God is not bound to the use of His own appointed means, by which the benefits of Christ are ordinarily applied to men.

(*c*) *P. Schaff*

A child is born a member of a redeemed race, and early death secures it from future loss, and introduces it into the fold of the Good Shepherd, from which nothing can pluck it.

(*d*)

(1 John ii. 12, 13)

1. CHILDREN = Beginners, Forgiveness of sins

(i.) Characteristics of-

New birth, adoption, "*Abba,*" childlike disposition, lowly, obedient, sincere, joyful.

(ii.) Failings of-

Credulity, carelessness, inconstancy.

(iii.) Treatment of-

Nursing and oversight, guidance, milk diet until they grow, love tokens and caresses.

2. Young men = Warriors

(i.) Characteristics of-

Exposed to threefold temptations, to which they oppose something better, overcome by blood of the Lamb.

(ii.) Failings of-

Undue ardour (compare Moses with Christ when young), strength is to be still, unwatchfulness, undue depression.

(iii.) Treatment of-

Without Me *ye* can do nothing = bread for *strong* = need of Christian armour (Eph. vi.).

(*e*)

3. Fathers = Mature Christians—Spiritual adults

(i.) Characteristics of-

Subjective religion, forgiven long since, have withstood trials and temptations, lay up spiritual riches for children, power of begetting—more works than words.

(ii.) Failings of-

Usurp authority, require blind obedience, expect others to agree with them.

(iii.) Treatment of-

Christ calls them "*His friends*," ripening on the heavenly manna, the food for all, whether children, young men, or fathers.

(*a*)

CHOICE

Life, at first, seems abounding with resources, just as it did to the prodigal son in the parable. But a few years' experience convinces us, as it did him, that all motives for choice resolve themselves into an *alternative*. We must find our inducements, hopes, and happiness in this life only; *or* we must look beyond the grave. If we are able to do the latter, our choice may seem settled at once; for everything we enjoy in this life is perishable, and we ourselves have no continuing city here.

(*b*)   *Jackson's Bampton Lectures*

We have one and all of us to *choose* between two systems of life; and the choice is a serious, not to say an anxious, event for us all. Our time for deliberation is short, and the danger of drifting into the wrong path considerable. Cf. *Similitude* = .

"We stand on a mountain pass in the midst of whirling snow and blinding mist, through which we get glimpses now and then of paths which may be deceptive. If we stand still, we shall be frozen to death. If we take the wrong road, we shall be dashed to pieces."

(*c*)   *Fitz-James Stephen*

Weak Christians are very apt to choose their mercies, to choose their crosses, and to choose their employments.

(*d*)   *Thos. Brooks*

CHRIST AND CHRISTIANITY (Matt. xxii. 42)

A parallelism-

1. { (i.) *Christ* = the Son of God;
   { (ii.) Christianity = supernatural.

Of Christ it was said, "This man ought to die, because He made Himself the Son of God."

Christianity is now being tried for its life on the charge of being supernatural and Divine.

2. (i.) At His trial. *Many* false witnesses agreed not together.

(ii.) *Many* false witnesses are now speaking and writing against Christianity, but with precisely similar non-agreement.

3. (i.) The remarkable coalition: Herod and Pontius Pilate were on *that* day (of His trial) made friends. At daggers drawn on other points, but *one* on this matter. Significant: Herod, the Jew, and Pontius Pilate, the sceptic, making common cause over the death of Christ.

(ii.) Outside *infidelity* and inside *apostasy* are doing the same thing to-day; and between them

they will, to a certain extent, crush Christianity, as they succeeded in crucifying Christ. But-

4. (i.) Christ rose from the dead, and is enthroned in glory, whilst

(ii.) The Church of Christ will likewise rise from its ashes, and be the dominant kingdom.

These parallels are striking, and help to show that the hostile attitude which the world assumed against Christ repeats itself in the case of His Church.

The world does to it what it did to Him; light has come, and the world, which prefers darkness, puts the light out. Yet points have been enlightened. Twelve Galilæan peasants and fishermen, seven Churches in Asia, spread the light, which ere long reached to the west. Rome was lighted, Britain was lighted, and still farther westward has it spread. The people that sat in darkness have received great light. But the world, true to its preference, loves darkness better than light, and is as busy as ever in its efforts to put out the light of Christianity, as it was eager to get rid of Christ. It will *write* it down, *lecture* it down, *talk* it down, *ridicule* it down, *oppose* science to it; and will, apparently, so far succeed as to make it a laughing-stock and a derision to the ungodly and profane. Persecution will finish what has thus been begun: "Then shall be tribulation such as never was." *Then shall be the crucifixion of Christianity.* But the light, though obscured, shall not really be extinguished; Christianity will triumph as Christ did.

(*e*)

CHRISTIANITY AND NATURAL THEOLOGY

Christianity bears a definite relation to natural theology, partly complementary and partly supplementary. "It confirms the known, and reveals the unknown." Hence also it is at once natural and supernatural, but not in any wise preternatural. It builds on nature, adding to it, but not contradicting it. It demands faith, but does no violence to reason. And the fact that it meets those needs of humanity, which natural theology indicates but is unable to satisfy, creates a strong presumption in its favour—a presumption which experience strengthens into almost absolute assurance, by showing the power of the gospel to guide men through the perplexities and contradictions of life, and nerve them both to dare and to endure all things.

(*f*)   *Bp. Barry*

CHRISTIANITY AND REVELATION

It is as though, by various convergent paths, we had been brought to the threshold of the mystery of God. As we have moved along each towards that central mystery, there has been a light before us and a voice of solemn import in our ears. Now the everlasting doors of the shrine fly open, and One stands before us, claiming to be the manifestation of God. As we gaze on Him, we see that in His crown of light there shine, blended together in perfect harmony, all the various rays of light which have hitherto been our guides. As we listen to the music of His voice, we recognise the tones which have so long been sounding dimly in our ears. But yet in His face there is a glory beyond what we have ever conceived, and the story

(*g*)

which His voice tells unlocks to us mysteries beyond the highest thought. What can we do but fall down before Him and acknowledge that God, who in sundry times and divers manners spake to men from the beginning by His servants, has at last spoken to us once for all in His Son?

(a)   *Bp. Barry*

REVELATION, PROGRESSIVE

The " conception of covenant between man and God, running through all the Scripture history," is shown to correspond to the two great principles of natural theology, a personal God and a spiritual nature in man, and to found on them a supernatural but appropriate relation. For it not only brings out vividly the true personality of God, and the true spirituality of man, but represents the Divine and human natures as endowed with the power of a real communion with each other. We open the book of Genesis, and at once find God in creation, framing man in His own image; and God in history, dealing with man as His own child, weak indeed and fallen, yet destined to redemption. Passing on to the subsequent books of the Pentateuch, we discover God in law, training His chosen people in obedience, and educating them through the sense of their own sinfulness, as contrasted with His righteousness, for a future manifestation of His grace. When we reach the age of prophetic teaching, we enter on a more advanced stage of the communion between the living God and His people, and hear Him speaking directly to the soul, and the soul making answer to His voice, now by the intellect, and now by the conscience and the spiritual faculty. But prophecy does not stop here; it looks onward to the future with an inspired hope, and glows with a prevision of salvation and glory to be realized in God's anointed King. The Messianic expectation, pervading in different degrees the whole of the Old Testament, draws the bond still closer between God and man, and sustains the anticipation of a union as yet unimaginable, but mysteriously foreshadowed in the name Immanuel, God with us. Then in the fulness of time Christ manifests Himself, the end of the law, the fulfilment of prophecy; yet " infinitely greater, fuller of light and inspiration, than the Christ as painted even in the noblest prophetic utterances of the Old Testament." We watch Him " unfolding gradually, in the midst of His lonely lot and spirit, a unique power and dignity, a perfect sinlessness, a superiority to all material influences, to which no other child of man has ever shown even an approach," until the passion is crowned by His resurrection, which with irrefragable proof seals Him as the Son of God. Then the gospel of the resurrection goes forth with matchless energy, conquering and to conquer; for it is a gospel of mediation, assuring to man fellowship with God in spite of the mystery of sin; and it completes that manifestation of the Divine in and through man, for which the intellect, conscience, and spiritual aspiration of mankind had been yearning with inarticulate desire.

(b)   *Quarterly Review*

CHRISTIANITY AND FINAL REVELATION

In relation to Christian doctrine, Christian morality, Christian spiritual life, the cycle is completed in the proclamation of the eternal " Word of God." The contemplation of this ultimate truth is full of instruction, as throwing light at once on the unity and finality of the Scriptural revelation. However we may account for it, it is certainly true, that up to this, in fundamental unity and continuous development, all previous teaching had led, from the *Protevangelium* of Genesis, through all the various stages of the ancient knowledge of God, in history and law, in psalm and prophecy, and even through the earlier phases of the revelation of Christ Himself. At no previous stage could we vaguely stop; for nowhere else could we find any adequate completion of the great pervading ideas of covenant with God. But beyond this we cannot go. For it has to do, not with earth, but with heaven; not with time, but with eternity.

(c)   *Bp. Barry*

CHRISTIANITY, A REASON FOR OUR HOPE

If an ordinary believer were asked why he is a Christian, he would probably reply, " Because, having inherited Christianity, and having been taught to be a Christian, I have tried the truth and the grace of Christ for myself, and I have found in them the words of eternal life." Even if he were to enter in some degree on theological study, his object in most cases would be to make a survey of the beauty and variety of the domain which God has given us, rather than to scrutinize the title-deeds by which we possess it. And till the security of the possessor is invaded by the challenge of an enemy, this position is as sufficient as it is common. But when the challenge sounds sharp and shrill in the believer's ear, as it is sounding now with greater insistance than ever before, another kind of answer is needed. Christians who would bear the assault without flinching or damage must be able to say: " We are Christians, because, having been challenged to give a defence for the faith in us, we have looked into all the rich variety and complexity of that witness which leads men to Christ; we have convinced ourselves that it stands still, as it stood of old, unshaken by speculative or moral difficulty. Whatever points may still be dark, waiting for fuller light, still what we can see is sufficient, and more than sufficient, to teach us that ' He is the Christ, the Son of the living God.' "

(d)   *Ibid.*

CHRISTIANITY, A LIVING POWER

Miracles and the fulfilments of prophecy ought no longer to be put forward in the forefront of our plea for Christianity, but should be subordinated to the exhibition of the actual power of Christianity in the intellectual, moral, and spiritual spheres of our being. In the place of prophecy we have history—the history of eighteen centuries, during which the power of Christ's light and grace has been seen in actual operation, subduing to Him the human soul and human society, and thus evincing its unique and supernatural character. Instead of the miracles of the gospel, we have in present reality what may fairly be called a moral and spiritual miracle, in the transcendent influence which Christ, at this moment, is exercising over the world. We stand face-to-face with an actual Christianity, which is unquestionably the most marvellous spiritual phenomenon in the world's history; and it cannot be right for us to endeavour to learn Christ by proceeding as if we could obliterate eighteen centuries, and forget that there is such a thing as a living Christianity.

(e)   *Ibid.*

CHRISTIAN EVIDENCES

Christian evidence, of whatever kind it be, does not profess to demonstrate the doctrines of the gospel. Its work is done, if it produces on our mind the conviction that Jesus Christ is one in whose word and grace we may place an absolute confidence. . . . The function of Christian evidence is discharged when it has led us, with the apostles, to confess that He has the "words of eternal life," not only in the "earthly things" which we can understand and test, but in the "heavenly things"—the mysterious realities—which no man can know.

(a)   *Bp. Barry*

CHRISTIANITY AND HUMAN PROGRESS

The gospel leaves the freest possible scope to human reason and energy in all the three great spheres of thought and experience. In nature it bids the reason go on boldly, studying all forms of law, learning to discern the nature and correlation of all physical forces, tracing out the evolutions in a wonderful order of all forms of being, striving to go back from the organized *kosmos* to the first original condition, without form and void—now gazing on the vastness of the universe, now peering into the infinite minuteness of perfection in each separate thing. . . . In the contemplation of humanity it encourages the reason to study in each human being the secret of the bodily and spiritual life, to discern the subtle laws which rule the little world within, to mark the links of connection between man and other animate beings, to note the strange action and reaction ever going on between individual freedom and universal law, and between the bodily and the spiritual natures. Nor does it leave the reason less free for wide historical survey, going back by direct or indirect study to the dim ages of antiquity, tracing out from first beginnings the civilization, material, intellectual, moral, spiritual, which is the privilege of the present time, and watching here also the power of universal laws and forces, underlying the rich and turbulent play of individual energies. . . . So, also, in the search after God Himself, Christianity encourages the confident hope that, as the ages roll on, we may know more and more of Him as the Creator of all things and the Father of all men—outgrowing some superstitions, putting aside some forms of thought which satisfied earlier ages—perhaps learning, here as elsewhere, that lesson of greater simplicity which belongs to the more advanced stages of knowledge, and better distinguishing what we know from what we can only approach in speculation and hope.

(b)   *Ibid*

CHRISTIANITY AND AGNOSTICISM

Man, with his restless intellect and aspiring heart has not, assuredly, the making in him of a contented agnostic.

(c)   *Ibid*

CHRIST AND CREATION

He is the end of creation, containing the reason in Himself, why creation is at all, and why it is as it is.

(d)   *Alford*

CHRIST CRUCIFIED (1 Cor. i. 23, 24)

Introduction: WE PREACH-

1. A Christian minister's chief work—not *baptize* (14); not with *wisdom of words*—which hide Christ and are of none effect.

2. We preach *Christ:*
Not ourselves, Paul, Peter, etc. The temple must not be polluted with name of the sub-architect. Cf. churches, etc., built to the *glory of God*, whereas often for the glory of the founder.

3. We preach Christ *crucified*.
Not Christ the philosopher (Greeks).
Not Christ the conquering King (Jews).
But Christ, the crucified one—numbered with transgressors—as a felon, a criminal !
How contrary to all notions of things, *then* and *now !*
But-

4. This preaching of *Christ crucified* is a matter of life and death : "savour of life . . . death," etc.

Observe-

1. That this preaching of Christ crucified is to some people a stumbling-block.
These rest on self-merit, good works, righteousness, respectability, keeping the commandments of God, etc.
They ask : Whether life and character count for nothing ?
Answer : " You have your reward now—it is better to do right than to do wrong—to have a good name than a bad one." But this plea means generally—No repentance, no confession of sin needed on their part : consequently no need of forgiveness, nor of the teaching of the Holy Spirit.
The self-righteous Jew stumbled at this stumbling stone.
N.B.—The free grace of God is one thing, and human merit another ; and we are saved by grace, not by works.

2. That the preaching of Christ crucified is to other people foolishness.
We live in days of increased culture. Some want us to preach *that* (accounting the simple gospel *foolishness*). Clever preaching—talent, science, philosophy, listened to by these.
They say gospel of Christ crucified has "nothing in it," " a worn-out theme," "education has dispelled superstition," etc.
This is the old objection that Paul met when the polished Greeks thought his preaching "foolishness." Remember that Christ came into this world as a *working man*, not as a *scribe*, who had the key of knowledge. Remember too that *goodness* is one thing, and *talent* another, and that good men are wanted in God's kingdom, and the preaching of Christ crucified draws them unto Him.

3. That the preaching of Christ crucified is the wisdom of God, and the power of God unto believers.
(i.) It may be a strange subject, but for those who seek salvation, asking " What must I do to be saved ? " it *is everything*.
(ii.) It may be an old, old story, often told poorly ; but it is the *story of love*, love passing the love of women, love that never faileth.
(iii.) It is the story of how One died in our stead, as our substitute, the Just for the unjust, that He might bring us to God.
Not *duty*, but love paid the *ransom* for many.

(e)

(iv.) It is the story of One who died praying for His murderers. "Father, forgive them," etc., and we all of us had a hand in that murder.

See the story of the *Coster's Dog*. (MURDERERS.) The secret of its *power* and its wisdom is, that every man's *conscience* is on the side of the gospel.

A conscience of sin feels its power, and to it it is no stumbling-block nor foolish babblement, but the power of God unto salvation. To every one that believeth Christ is everything : *wisdom and righteousness and sanctification and redemption.*

(a)

CHRIST CRUCIFIED

1. **Divides men**—between two thieves—one believes, the other rejects. This goes on continually —of two persons in a pew on Sunday—one taken and another left. Christ is set for the rise and fall of many.

2. **Rejection, not the act of a few.**—Look at the crowd around His cross—not the rabble only—not the back streets, filthy alleys, and overcrowded courts and dens of the city have vomited forth their rude occupants to witness the deed of blood ; but all classes have their representatives at the cross.

Wealth is there, respectability is there, religion, so called, is there, magistrates, nobles, priests are there, drawn together by one magnet, the common hatred of Jesus of Nazareth, and to gloat their eyes on His crucifixion.

3. "**Yet He shall see of the travail of His soul, and be satisfied**" (Isa. lv. 11)

Redemption is as wide as creation (Rom. v.).

What can satisfy infinite love?

In a commercial sense, a great outlay warrants a corresponding return.

Whilst the price of redemption is being paid down, one soul, the penitent thief, is snatched from destruction.

When Jesus ascends to heaven, 3,000 souls are converted ; and ever on and on since, the number of the faithful has increased like eddying circles. From the north and south, east and west they come, an exceeding great army, which no man can number. The arithmetic of earth is altogether at fault to calculate the extent and the fruits of redeeming love.

(b)

It is the consciousness of sin which draws souls to Christ.

And even this does not prevent the preaching of the cross becoming foolishness to one person, and a stumbling block to another, and to many a savour of death unto death. The first try to remove the burden of sin by an atonement of their own ; the second explain it away ; the third account it an unholy thing ; whilst the fourth esteem it the gift of God.

(c)

CHRIST, DIVINITY OF

"*Ye have heard the blasphemy*" (Mark xiv. 63)

Consider just two points.

1. This, that on a certain most important occasion Christ Himself asserted His Godhead in a manner which could not possibly be misunderstood.

2. That a denial of the Godhead of Christ involves consequences from which we should most of us shrink, consequences which affect the nature and the character of Deity itself.

The first topic I connect with the words of our text. Those words belong to the narrative of the examination of the Saviour before the great ecclesiastical tribunal of His nation. It appears that Annas had sent Christ, bound, to the palace of Caiaphas, the high priest, where a committee of the Sanhedrim, consisting of at least three-and-twenty persons, and most of them of the sacerdotal order, awaited the Prisoner, their minds already made up—to bring Him in guilty of death. But the difficulty was, how to give a colour to their nefarious design. It was useless to lay against Jesus the accusation which prevailed with the Roman governor, that He had fomented seditious movements and plotted for the overthrow of the Roman authority. That plea would serve their purpose before long ; but under present circumstances it was necessary to convict the Prisoner of some offence which would place Him within the reach of Jewish ecclesiastical law. Accordingly they "sought for witness against Jesus to put Him to death." But although there is seldom any difficulty in an eastern country, and assuredly there was none then, in finding wretches ready to swear away a fellow-creature's life for the sake of gain, they were baffled in their search. They could find no instrument to serve their purpose. No one was willing to come forward and speak a word against the pure and spotless life of Jesus of Nazareth. At last however a gleam of hope appeared. Two men presented themselves to denounce Jesus for some statements they had heard Him make about the overthrow of the temple. But again the expectation of the sanhedrim was doomed to be disappointed. The witnesses could not agree. There was a semblance of truth in the charges they brought, for Christ had certainly spoken, in public, about the destruction of the temple ; but the charges were not consistent. One witness said one thing, the other said another. And the judges could not, out of respect for the law which they were professing to administer, condemn a man to death upon evidence so insufficient and contradictory as that which they had managed to secure. What then was to be done? After all, would their victim escape? The thought was intolerable. And His calm, majestic silence, whilst it cowed and perplexed them, exasperated them into a more frantic determination than ever to take away His life. But how was the thing to be done? How was Jesus of Nazareth, against whose character and teaching no witness could be found to offer a trustworthy testimony, how was He to be entangled in the meshes of a law which came from God, and which had no terrors, because it had no condemnation, for innocent men? Our narrative informs us.

(d)

In utter despair of success by legitimate means, the high priest rises up from his seat and advances towards the centre of the chamber, confronting the august Prisoner, who stood bound before him. With loud and threatening voice, as if he expects to intimidate Christ, he put the question : "Answerest Thou nothing? What is it that these witness against Thee?" Met with the same awful silence which he well knew how to interpret, and which was, in effect, the most

(e)

terrible of rebukes, Caiaphas resorts to his last expedient. "In the name of God, then," he says, "inform us who you are." "I adjure Thee by the living God that Thou tell us whether Thou be the Christ, the Son of God."

(a)

It is clear that an answer must come to this adjuration. But *what* answer? On several occasions the Saviour had been charged with blasphemy, had been, indeed, on the point of being stoned, because—as the Jews said—He had made Himself equal with God. Now, if this charge is a false one, and He be no more than a man—a mere prophet sent from God with a commission to instruct and enlighten mankind—what an opportunity is here presented to Him to remove misconception and to announce the truth! If He makes no pretensions whatever to be considered Divine, what an opening there is for a disclaimer, distinct and emphatic enough to set the matter at rest, and at rest for ever! He is in the presence of the chief ecclesiastics of the land. He stands before a tribunal, the authority of which He Himself is ready to recognise. He has been asked a solemn question in a most solemn manner; and life or death depends upon the reply which He gives. What more easy, what more natural, indeed, what more required by the circumstances, than to have said: "I am not the Son of God in the sense in which you now employ the term. I am a man, a man sent from the Father. And if I have ever used the words 'Son of God' of myself, or if my disciples have ever applied it to me, the expression referred, not to any claim that I have set up to be a partaker of the Divine nature, but simply to the supernatural gifts with which I have been endowed for the fulfilment of my mission. Understand, then, that—except in a loose, vague, inaccurate, metaphorical sense, I am not the Son of the living God?"

(b)

Why, when we come to think of it, Christ was bound, if He were no more than man, to seize this opportunity of explanation, in order to prevent misconception in the future, and to put a stop to the idolatrous homage which His followers were only too ready to render to Him. But now, mark His words! Here is the question: "Art Thou the Christ, the Son of the Blessed?" And here is the answer: "I AM. And ye shall see the Son of man sitting on the right hand of power, and coming in the clouds of heaven." "I am. I am the Son of the Blessed." This expression sealed the Saviour's condemnation. Immediately the high priest, in a paroxysm of well-simulated indignation, rent his linen robe, exclaiming, "Ye have heard the blasphemy; what think ye?" And the fatal words burst forth, in every direction, from the assembled judges. "He is guilty of death." The conclusion is inevitable. The Lord Jesus Christ allowed Himself to be condemned and put to death on a charge of blasphemy. At a most solemn juncture, and under the most solemn circumstances, He accepted a title, the acceptance of which, as He well knew, would be considered and treated as blasphemous. The conclusion is inevitable. If Christ be God, the whole procedure is in accordance with the facts of the case, and with the position He assumed.

(c)

Consider certain consequences that will follow, upon the denial of the true and essential Deity of the Lord Jesus Christ.

1. In the first place then, on the supposition that Christ was a mere man, or a created being, who allied Himself with human nature, the further supposition becomes inevitable—that in the bygone eternity God dwelt in a lonely and uncompanionable isolation. We believe in what is commonly called creation. Our minds travel up to a period at which no creatures existed; at which no stars swam in the ocean of space; at which no angel fanned the ether with his wings; at which, of course, there were no human creatures and no earth for them to inhabit; at which the only being was the one eternal Essence, the Lord God Almighty Himself. At this time, then, did the Lord God dwell alone? Inhabiting His own eternity, had He, whose name is Love, had He, literally, no object on which to expend the wealth of His infinite affection? The idea seems to be perfectly inconceivable. There are many things mysterious about the nature of God. We cannot, for instance, comprehend that He should be absolutely boundless; that He should be contained within no limits. And yet we know that it must be so. We cannot understand a Being who never began to be, who is self-derived and self-existent. And yet we know that such must be the Deity we worship. But difficult as these things are to conceive, I have far more difficulty in conceiving of such a God as our God dwelling in the eternity of the past—in a cold, cheerless, selfish isolation—contemplating His own perfection, and only quickened into love when the work of creation began. And yet this is the conclusion to which we are driven if we deny the Godhead of the Lord Jesus Christ. We escape the conclusion only by believing that the Father had always a Son in whom His soul delighted, and with whom the interchange of a Divine and ineffable affection was eternally possible. The Father, then, was never without the Son. The Son was never without the Father. They are co-equal and co-eternal. And to this the ancient Scriptures point, though after their manner somewhat obscurely, when they say: "The Lord possessed Me, in the beginning of His way, before His works of old. I was set up from everlasting, from the beginning, or ever the earth was. When there were no depths, I was brought forth. When there were no fountains abounding with water. Before the mountains were settled, before the hills, was I brought forth: while, as yet, He had not made the earth: nor the fields: nor the highest part of the dust of the world. Then I was by Him, as one brought up with Him: and I was daily His delight, rejoicing always before Him."

(d)

2. The denial of the Godhead of Christ limits and impairs the Divine capability of manifesting love to man. In what does the great power of the gospel consist? In this: that it exhibits in a most marvellous way the love of God. It is this which wins men's hearts. Threatenings may arouse them. They may be startled from the slumber of indifference and apathy by being told of the worm that never dieth, and of the fire that is not to be quenched. But what attracts and softens and changes is the love of God in Christ.

(e)

And in what way does love manifest itself? In self-sacrifice. Now consider, If Jesus Christ were just a perfect man, and not the eternal Son of the Father, what did it cost God to part with Him? Nothing, that I can see. Where then is the self-sacrifice? The gospel is ushered in, with great pomp and parade, as the highest manifestation of the character of Jehovah, and His choicest instrumentality for accomplishing the salvation of mankind. And it issues after all in the sending of a mere man—a remarkable teacher no doubt—to scatter seeds of spiritual truth over the human mind, and then, for some very abstruse and very unintelligible reason, to die upon a cross. But now change your hypothesis, and what an exhibition of Divine love you get at once! Jesus of Nazareth is God manifest in the flesh. Before the world was, He was from everlasting with the Father. When He came down to earth, and took upon Him our flesh, and bound Himself up with the fortunes of sinful man, God parted with Him. "God sent His Son into the world." More especially when He came forward as the sacrifice for sin; when He agonized in Gethsemane; when He stood a criminal before the bar of the Sanhedrim and of the Roman procurator; when He suffered and groaned and died on Calvary—more especially then God parted with Him. "God spared not His own Son: but gave Him up for us all." In dealing with such a subject we soon, of course, find ourselves out of our depth. The mystery of the Divine feelings is not for us to meddle with. Yet this we may say (for Scripture entitles us to say it), that it cost God something to part with His Son for us, and that it is this self-sacrifice of God which really gives the gospel its commanding power over the hearts of men.

(a)

3. *Comparison.* We have paced, in imagination, beside the patriarch as he took that terrible three-days journey to Moriah, with Isaac, the unconscious victim, by his side. We have pictured to ourselves the feelings of the man: his stern resolve, yet his utter misery; his faith that all would come right in the end, and yet his perplexed horror at the scene of bloodshed upon which he felt himself called so soon to pass through. From what did his trouble arise? Chiefly from this, that he had to sacrifice Isaac, his well-beloved son; Isaac, in whose life all the promises were involved. When, in place of Isaac, was substituted the ram, was that anything to him? It was nothing. *The self-sacrifice consisted in the surrender of his son.* And what would it be to God, to give up a creature, a man, an angel, an archangel, for the well-being of myriads of the human race? Why, it were nothing. It were no self-sacrifice at all. The mother, who sends her child out to the deadly missionary station; the father, who parts with his son so that the lad may lay down, if need be, his life for his country,—know more about love than God does—on this supposition. But when God gave up His Son, His own Son, His only begotten, His well-beloved, in order to accomplish the salvation of mankind, then indeed was exhibited to us that Divine love: the length and breadth and depth and height of which surpasseth all human knowledge.

(b)

4. Again, *another consequence.* If Christ be not God, I cannot avoid the inference, that God

has done everything in His power to transfer my affection from the Creator to the creature. I read in the Bible that God is a jealous God, and that the honour which is His own He will not permit to be given to another. And yet what has He done? In those Scriptures, which are the revelation of His mind and will, He has taken all the grand, incommunicable titles which belong to Himself, and has laid them upon Christ. In every way He has put Christ forward, to be the object of my adoration and love. Everything is done to make the tendrils of my human affection twine round Jesus Christ. It is Christ that I am to look to! It is Christ that I am to trust to! It is Christ that I am to follow! It is Christ that I am to imitate! What wonder then—take the Scriptures in your hand and tell me!—what wonder, if I pass by the Creator and give my homage, my adoration, my love to the creature? In fact, it is not at all too bold a thing to say that, if the worship of Christ be idolatrous, I may charge my idolatry on God Himself, and say that it is He who taught me to practise it.

Such seem to me to be some of the consequences which flow from a denial of the true Godhead of the Lord Jesus Christ. Minor consequences perhaps they are, and yet leading to important results. The heart must be chilled towards God which does not recognise in Jesus Christ the eternal Son of the eternal Father. To such a heart the life, the death, the resurrection, the ascension, the coming again, must be very different things from what they are to us. But the worst consequence seems to be this, that if a man deliberately refuses, when Christ is clearly presented to him, to see in Christ the Son of God, he shows himself to be in opposition to the Divine character and the Divine will. Christ is the test of the human race. "What think ye of Christ?" is the dividing question. "This is the record, that God hath given to us eternal life, and this life is in His Son. He that hath the Son hath life, but he that hath not the Son hath not life."

(c) *Gordon Calthrop.*

CHRIST, FIRST COMING OF

God had prepared for Christ's coming by three nations: two for temporal purposes, and one for spiritual.

The *Jew* was dispersed throughout the world to witness for God.

The *Greek* had shaped his wondrous language; and the *Roman* had by arms conquered the known world, and made it one empire.

Here were the means of Christ's drawing all men unto Himself, of setting up the kingdom of God. And it is remarkable that there was then a general expectation of all nations—"a general hush" (for the temple of Janus was shut), a looking towards Judæa for what was to be done.

Maclear

Cf. the threefold inscription on the cross, written in *Hebrew and Greek and Latin.*

(d)

CHRIST, THE GENEALOGY OF

These chronicles have a mission. As no star was useless in the heavens, and as every atom has been created for a purpose, so God would not

(e)

devote seventeen verses of His book to a pedigree without a purpose. Even the desert has a mission, and although the text might appear like a desert, at the end of it there was the holy Child Jesus. We learn from this genealogy:

1. God's fidelity to His promise. God had promised Abraham that in him should all the families of the earth be blessed, and here we read of its fulfilment.

2. The eternal God never works hurriedly. Scientists say that the earth existed ten millions of years before any life came into existence upon it. And God took two thousand years before He gave His Son to the world.

3. The human race is very closely inter-related. Between every verse we read: "God hath made of one blood all the nations of the earth. Mankind is one family, and every war that occurred was a family strife.

4. The universality of death. Forty-two generations pass before us, and sink into the grave.

5. The all-inclusiveness of Christ's mission. Christ touched all sorts of people in this pedigree in order that He might save all sorts of people. All the race may participate in the riches of His grace.

6. The marvellous way in which God overrules evil in order to give due prominence to Christ. Who but God could have produced a perfect Man out of such a pedigree? "All's well that ends well." The pedigree ends with Christ. Christ is the apex of this pyramid, and the crown and glory of the race.

(a) *J. Ossian Davies*

CHRIST, HUMAN NATURE OF (Rom. viii. 3).

God unmasked and judged sin in the flesh, and condemned it to be cast out as a foreign element, a ruinous pseudo-plasma in the flesh, by Christ's assuming a pure, consecrated σάρξ, and by His keeping His white robes spotless on the whole filthy road of His pilgrimage, and maintaining its holiness until it was illuminated in glorified splendour. Thus the question, whether Christ assumed human nature in its paradisiacal state before the fall, or the fallen nature of Adam, is a thoroughly incorrect one, for it rests on a misconception of biblical facts. *Christ assumed neither the unfallen nor the fallen human nature, but the nature raised from the fall and made holy.*

(b) *Lange*

" CHRIST, IN,"—" IN THE LORD " (Rev. xiv. 13)

A peculiar expression. The Old Testament makes much of Moses, who through Israel has influenced the fortunes of the human race. But although men may follow Moses, obey his precepts, etc., you never heard of any of them as being *in* Moses. . . . Again, the New Testament puts the Apostle Paul prominently forward as one of the greatest inspired teachers, yet nowhere do we meet with the expression, " in Paul," or any equivalent for it.

The words " in Christ," however, occur over and over again; the best and truest description of a disciple is this, that he is one who is *in* Christ. "There is no condemnation " for them that are in Christ Jesus. " If any man be *in* Christ, he is a new creature," and so on.

It is obvious, then, that the expression conveys more than the idea of imitation, or obedience. It implies a living personal union, real though mysterious, and shows its existence in certain unmistakable results produced upon heart and conduct. . . . The Christian becomes an instrument through which the Saviour acts. " I live; yet not I, but Christ liveth in me, and the life which I now live in the flesh, I live by the faith of the Son of God, who loved me, and gave Himself for me." The agency by which this mysterious incorporation is brought about is *God the Holy Ghost*. The immediate means employed is *faith*—faith given and maintained by God Himself. The time at which the living union takes place is when the soul, accepting the testimony of the Spirit, casts itself in full confidence upon the personal Christ;—makes a full surrender; recognises His ownership; accepts Him as Saviour, friend, guide, King, portion, both for this world and for that which is to come.

(c) *Gordon Calthrop*

CHRIST JESUS.

It is not without good reason that the name *Christ* is sometimes put before *Jesus*. From the Old Testament point of view, progress is made from the knowledge of Christ to the knowledge of Jesus; from the New Testament point of view, the progress is from the knowledge of Jesus to the knowledge of Christ. Cf. 1 Tim. i. 15.

(d) *Bengel*

CHRIST, POWER OF

"*What manner of man is this?* "—Luke viii. 25

Notice,

1. His power over the forces of Nature

Always a storm where Jesus was; so now. " I came not to send peace on earth, but a sword." Man is born to trouble; but the Christian has more storms than all.

The disciples are blamed for their *agitation*. Right to pray, " Master, Master "—to see safety in Him alone; but wrong to be so agitated, so troubled and alarmed. Faith, where it exists, calms. " In the world ye shall have tribulation,"—for the world = the sea, in which we meet with storms; but if we have faith in God, we ought never to be in *despair*—which shows the absence of faith. "With Christ in the vessel, I smile at the storm," wrote an old sailor and Christian, John Newton.

2. His power over the powers of Darkness, in the spirit world

The unseen tormentors of men (see this man's state).

Possession = Two tenants in one house. Here the usurper is the master—alternately attracted and repulsed. The presence of Jesus wakes up the sleeping demon, which cries in a loud voice:— " What have I to do with Thee?" "I know Thee"; "torment me not"; "let us alone": for "what concord hath Christ with Belial?" Such cases, not so rare, perhaps, as may be thought = *wrecked lives*, the mental balance is lost, and may be described as CONVERSIONS TO DEVILRY—and caricatures of the work of the Holy Spirit.

(e)

To all appearance such cases are hopeless, degraded, depraved, human wrecks, the worst forms of the FALL. Yet let us take heed how we pronounce upon them; see here the power of the Saviour, to whom *all power is committed.* HE COMMANDETH THE UNCLEAN SPIRITS, AND THEY COME OUT," and this very man is presently *sitting at the feet of Jesus, and in his right mind !* (35.)

3. His Power over Death.
Death is a universal conqueror—apparently the greatest power, and undisputed. Clovis cried out when dying :—" Wa, wa! What power is this which pulls down the strength of the strongest kings ? " . . . How hopeless it seems to think of conquering death, . . . to arrest that law, " Dust thou art," etc.; yet Jesus did this when he spoke the word of power, and death obeyed and yielded back *this* case, the widow's son at *Nain*, and *Lazarus.* Over Himself " death hath no dominion "; and He teaches us that " whosoever *liveth and believeth* in Him shall never die." . . . " I will raise him up at the last day." Hence He hath power over it too: death has met its conqueror.

4. The groundwork is Faith : *Where is our faith ?* We want it at hand like a sword in a soldier's hand. Are we meeting trouble in this world, encountering the powers of darkness, tasting death, without it ? It must be then that Giant Despair makes us his prey. " Jesus Christ, or Despair," cried Lavater. Without faith we cannot please God ; without faith Jesus will do no mighty works for us. But if we have faith in God, then nothing is impossible.—" All things are possible to him that believeth." The power that stilled the *storm*, that cast out the *demon*, and that raised the *dead* will be put forth for us. Consider WHAT MANNER OF MAN IS THIS ? whom nature obeys, the devils obey, and death even, when he hears His voice, returns his captives !
(*a*)

CHRIST, PRECIOUSNESS OF

" *Unto you which believe He is precious* "—1 Pet. ii. 7

We believe concerning the men of genius, the poets, the artists, the authors, the orators who have greatly influenced their fellow-men, that the circumstances of their lives were so ordered by Divine providence as to qualify them for the part they were destined to play in human affairs. Nothing, we know, happens by accident, and nothing happens suddenly, in the creation of God. Everything is the result of previously arranged and long-continued processes. And if so, we cannot allow ourselves to doubt that even the birth of such men as Milton, and Newton, and Shakespeare, and Raffaelle—their birth from particular parents, and with particular surroundings—was an item in the infallible calculations of Him who seeth the end from the beginning, and who ordereth all things according to the counsel of His own will. How much more then must we feel this to have been the case with respect to the incarnate Son of God? The importance of Him, not only to the race of man, but also to the whole universe, it were utterly impossible for language to describe. He is the centre to which everything converges, the pivot upon which everything turns, the nail, fastened in a sure place, upon which hangs the whole of the vast framework of the Divine administration. Had He gone wrong in any particular of His redeeming work (if such a supposition may be for the moment allowed)—had He failed to accomplish any one part of His appointed task —it would have been like removing the sun from the solar system ; nay, like removing that grand central sun round which, as some suppose, the other tributary suns, with their systems, perpetually revolve. Dislocation, confusion, ruin, would have been the inevitable result, and the whole beautiful order of the moral government of God would have been reduced to a hideous and almost unimaginable chaos.

What significance then gathers round the mysterious person of that Infant cradled in the manger of Bethlehem ; of that Child saying His prayers and learning His earliest lessons at His mother's knee; of that Boy listening to the discourse of the doctors in the temple, and astonishing them with His searching yet child-like questions; of that Man working in the carpenter's shop at Nazareth ; of that Preacher announcing to the multitude that the kingdom of heaven is nigh at hand ; of that solitary Combatant confronting in the wilderness the assaults of the tempter, or enduring in Jerusalem the contradiction of sinners against Himself ; of that pale Sufferer standing worn and drooping before His judges, and at last stretched, dying upon the cross, a spectacle to heaven and earth ! Every word that drops from such lips is fraught with heavenly wisdom. Every action of such a life tells upon the destiny of the human race. Yes; it is not competent for the heart of man to conceive, or for the tongue of man to utter, the importance of Jesus Christ. It were to be expected, then, that concerning this Jesus Christ—this incarnate Son of God—everything was most carefully, most sedulously appointed and prepared by the Father. And so we believe it to have been. All the surroundings of the Saviour's life, even the very prospect that met His view as He gazed from the heights of Nazareth upon the glories of His native land, all, we believe, contributed their share to the formation of that lovely character, to the expansion of that wonderful mind.
(*b*) *Gordon Calthrop*

The people of Christ are not at all fanatical. They take no extreme views of things. They prefer health to sickness, competence to poverty, pleasure to pain, honour and the respect of their fellow-men to obloquy and contempt. I find, too, that Christianity quickens the sensibilities and refines the feelings of him who is really influenced by it ; so that a Christian man, with his religion, is a better husband, father, brother, son, friend, master, than he could have been without it. But, for all that, he prefers Christ to everything else, and he cannot consent to give up " the pearl of great price," when once he has found it, for the sake of any other pearl of inferior value. It is too " precious " to be surrendered. And yet men have been placed in positions of cruel temptation to surrender Christ. Years ago, in the reign, I believe, of that fiendish woman who disgraced the name of Mary, and made the English throne drip with the blood of her best and truest subjects, a man was being led to the stake for his testimony to the truth of Christ. His influence was great, and strenuous efforts had been made, but made in vain, to induce him to recant. As a last resource, his wife and children (one of the
(*c*)

children an infant in arms) were placed in his path on the way to execution. The procession was made to halt in sight of them, and, once again, the man was urged, by his affection for his own flesh and blood, by his professed regard for those whom his death would cast upon the cold charity of an unfeeling world, to reconsider his determination, and retract his errors. The trial was a bitter one. The man was a loving husband and father, and his heart was torn at the sight of his wife and little ones, with a conflict of agonizing emotions. On the one side was Christ and his duty to Christ; on the other side those whom he loved better than life. But the trial, though sharp and bitter, was soon over. He could not be untrue to the Saviour. He would not give up Christ. "Lead on!" he said, "lead on! My wife and children are dear to me. God knows that I love them well; but in comparison with Christ I love them not."

(a)   *Gordon Calthrop*

Christ is more precious to His people the longer and the better they know Him. I have heard it said that the feeling of many persons, when they first see the far-famed Cathedral of St. Peter's at Rome, is one of disappointment. The building seems neither so large, nor so grand, nor so imposing, nor so beautiful, as they had expected it to be. But when they become better acquainted with it the feeling of disappointment passes away. The visitor walks again and again in these magnificent aisles, and his eyes become educated by degrees to appreciate the scene. The beauty, the glory, grows upon him. The marvel of the structure opens out to his perception more and more, and at every visit he discovers some grandeur, some loveliness, some exquisiteness of proportion, or some finish of detail, which he had not detected before. And is it not so with that grandest of all objects, with Jesus Christ, with Him who is "the chiefest among ten thousand, and altogether lovely." I do not mean, of course, to say that our first feeling about Christ, when we come to Him, is one of disappointment. Far from it! Christ at a distance, Christ unknown, Christ unsympathized with, may be, I grant you, an unattractive object. "He has no form nor comeliness," as the prophet says, that we should desire. But Christ, when we have accepted Him, answers all our expectations from the very first. He meets all our wishes. He satisfies all our desires. But this is what I mean, that what we knew and appreciated of Christ when we first put ourselves into His hands is as nothing when compared with what we know and appreciate of Him upon further acquaintance. He grows upon us day by day. Day by day we see more of the wonders of His person and of His work. Day by day fresh beauties, fresh grandeurs, fresh glories, unfold themselves. And the reason is that our inner spiritual eye is being educated by the Spirit of God, and that we are being enabled to "comprehend, with all saints, what is the breadth, and length, and depth, and height, and to know the love of Christ that passeth knowledge."

(b)   *Gordon Calthrop*

CHRIST, UNSPEAKABLE RICHES OF (Eph. iii.)

Many make Christianity something local, temporal, and thus degrade it. Christ is inexhaustible for mind and heart; we find all in Him. Let us never make of this rich Christ a poor one. What Christ has instituted must be something transcendent, and not so common that every intellect can discover it.

(c)   *Heubner*

" WHAT THINK YE OF CHRIST ? " (Matt. xxii. 4.)

There will be, until the consummation of all things, two distinct and by no means uncertain answers to this question. Ask the unregenerate man. His reply = that
" *He sees no beauty in Him that he should desire Him.*"
Ask the Christian : his reply =
" *Christ is the chief among ten thousand, and altogether lovely.*"
Ask the same question of Christianity, and the first will reply :
Christianity is a used-up, worn-out superstition ; whilst the second will say-
Christianity is a light which shall one day enlighten the whole world, as the leaven does the whole lump of meal.

(d)

As long as Christ sits at the right hand of God we shall be lords and masters over sin, death, devils, and all things.
The Lord's Prayer suffers more abuse and contumely than the greatest martyr on earth.
We should pray *in* the Church, *with* the Church, and *for* the Church. These things preserve the Church—faithful teaching, diligent prayer, and patient suffering.
The Bible is my mirror, in which I see what I was in Adam before the fall, what I became by the fall, what I am and should be in Christ now and what I shall be through eternity.
It cannot be otherwise than that where Christ is there must be a Judas, Pilate, Herod, Caiaphas, Annas, and also His cross, or there is not the right Christ.
That a man may lift up his head to heaven, he must find nothing on earth whereon to lean it.
All our doing is to suffer God to work in us ; He giveth the word, which, when we have received, by faith given from above, we are new born and made the sons of God.

(e)   *Luther*

Everything in Christ astonishes me. His spirit overawes me, and His will confounds me. His ideas and His sentiments, the truth which He announces, His manner of convincing, are not explained either by human observation or the nature of things. His birth, and the history of His life; the profundity of His doctrine, which grapples the mightiest difficulties and which is of those difficulties the most admirable solution; His gospel; His apparition; His empire; His march across the ages and the realms—everything is for me a prodigy, a mystery insoluble, which plunges me into a reverie from which I cannot escape— a mystery which is there before my eyes, a mystery which I can neither deny nor explain. Here I see nothing human. The nearer I approach, the more carefully I examine, everything is above me. Everything remains grand, of a grandeur which overpowers. His religion is a revelation from an Intelligence which certainly is not that of man.

(f)   *Napoleon I*

CHRIST, WHAT SHALL I DO WITH JESUS? (Matt. xxvii.)

"What shall I do then with Jesus, which is called the Christ?" The people were in the position of Pilate. They had got Christ in their hands, and they had to decide what they would do with Him. Some people had been very much offended, because he told them that they had to decide *for or against Christ that night.* They said, "Can you not decide it some other time?" Pilate tried to shirk the responsibility, and to shift it upon Herod; but even the bloodthirsty Herod refused to take the life of an innocent man, and sent him back to Pilate, and Pilate's wife said to him, "Have thou nothing to do with that just Man, for I have suffered much in a dream concerning Him." Pilate left it to the Jews to decide who should be released, and they said Barabbas. What made Pilate take that course? Public opinion. There were tens of thousands in this great city who were kept from the Cross of Christ by public opinion. As in the case of Pilate, public opinion was worth more to them than the kingdom of heaven. He believed thousands were trembling in the balance between Barabbas and Christ, between heaven and hell. Every one of them must decide the question for themselves. He asked worldly Christians, What they were going to do with Christ? What had they done for Christ during the last twenty years of their lives? The longer he lived the more thoroughly he was convinced that professing Christians retarded the salvation of souls more than either infidels or sceptics. What were they going to do with Jesus? Were they going to accept Him or deny Him by their life and daily conversation? He prayed that God might help them to trim their lamps, and give light to those that were walking in darkness. The moment they commenced to work for Jesus they would get rid of doubts and fears, and be brought into another atmosphere, and then they would know something about the joy of the Lord. A lighthouse-keeper once let his lights go out. A wreck ensued; and when he went to view the bodies cast up along the shore, he recognised the corpse of his son, who had gone on a whaling voyage three years before. How many fathers and mothers let their lights go out, and wrecked their children's lives! There were young men at the present day who did not believe in the reality of the Christian religion, and said it was all a sham and a myth. Why? Because their parents did not live as if they believed in what they professed. They went to church every Sunday, and said prayers, but they were not living in or for Christ. He called on them to live for Christ. If all did, how the dark waves of sin would be driven back! Another class was the backsliders. They had denied Christ by their lives, turned their backs on Him, and wounded Him afresh. Now they were scoffers, sceptics, infidels. Might God bring them back! The Shepherd was looking for them. They had wandered into the dark plains of sin, but the Shepherd was crying, "Come home; your father calls you!" "Come unto Me, all ye that labour and are heavy laden, and I will give you rest." They would find no rest in the world. What did the prodigal who wandered into the devil's territory lose? He had to take care of swine, which was contrary to the law of Moses. He lost his food, for he had to live on husks. He lost his home. He lost his testimony, for he could do nothing for God where he was. If he, a miserable, dirty, ragged wretch, said he was the son of a rich father, nobody would believe him. But there was one thing which he did not lose—his father's love. He never lost that. All the years that he was away his father loved him. Don't believe that God hated them because they had wandered away from Him.

Men of pleasure! what were they going to do with Christ? Were they going to join with the Jews who cried, "Crucify Him"? That was the cry of the world to-day. They said, "We don't want Christ; give us pleasure." Solomon, the wisest of men and kings, tried all the phases of earthly happiness, and said at the end, "All is vanity and vexation of spirit." Another class of people were the selfish. But the Lord Jesus was not selfish; and if they had His Spirit they would not be selfish. The selfish man loved himself, his wife, and children better than Christ; but they could do nothing for him in his dying hour. He would need Christ then. He had better take Him to-day. It would not do to say that he was "almost persuaded to be a Christian." A hair's breadth from heaven was just an inch from hell. Selfish women, who had lived for themselves and for the world—what were they going to do with Jesus? They could not do anything which would please God so much as to receive His Son that afternoon. Another class was the scoffers. They were scoffing and jeering there. If they saw any one going into the inquiry-room, they said, "Look at him," and laughed. What were they going to do with Jesus Christ? Were they going to scoff on down to hell? In hell there would be no scoffing, but crying for one drop of water. It was appointed to man once to die; but after death the judgment. Then they would have to stand before Christ as a consuming fire. What then would they do? Would they scoff at Jesus Christ? would they trample His blood under foot? He asked them, would they join with Jesus Christ, or would they cry, "Crucify Him," and scoff on down to hell? Their hell would be a terrible one. Then they would remember all that they had heard there—how he had feebly tried to tell them of a better world, and how they had scoffed and jeered and ridiculed. O scoffers! were they going to scoff on down to hell? Another class consisted of those who came and went, neither receiving nor rejecting Christ, but trifling. They had only to neglect salvation in order to go down into the pit; they need not even be scoffers. "How shall we escape if we *neglect* so great salvation?" The wheels of time were rolling on, and by-and-by that vast assembly would be landed on the shores of eternity. It was for them to choose now. Blasphemers! he had a word for them. They who had cursed the God that gave them existence, what were they going to do with Christ? Their only hope was to fly to Christ for refuge. Did the devil give them good wages for their service? Were they happy in blaspheming the name of Jesus Christ? Infidels! what were they going to do with Jesus Christ? If infidelity had done more for the world than Christianity, then let the sceptic and the infidel cling to their convictions, and don't give them up; but if the Lord Jesus could save them, let infidelity go to the four winds of heaven. Young ladies, what were they going to do with Jesus Christ? He prayed that his text might be so carried by the Spirit of God into every heart, that every man and

(a)

woman would be so troubled that night that they would not be able to sleep until they had decided the question. If Christ was the Saviour of the world, receive Him. If Christ was an impostor—and a young man told him the other night that He was a downright impostor—reject Him, lift up their hand and tongue against Him, and do all they could to overthrow Christianity. If he were of that opinion, he would throw his whole soul into it; but he believed from the depth of his heart that Christ was the Saviour of the world, and that the man that rejected Him was lost for all eternity, while the man that received Him was saved for all eternity. Young women should receive Christ just as they would receive an offer of marriage, as a bride received a bridegroom. Rebekah consented to take Isaac and to forsake her home and her kindred for him, although she had never seen him or he her. But Christ loved them beforehand, therefore they should accept Him. They should give up everything for Christ, just as a girl gave up everything for her husband that she loved, and was ready to go round the world with him. Now, at that last meeting he prayed that they would settle the question for all eternity. Nobody could help them but Christ. They need not look to that large army of ministers on the platform, for they could not help them. A man in a boat on the river Niagara fell overboard and was swept on a little islet close to the cataract. The news of this dreadful position spread by telegraph all round the country, and thousands arrived by train. The most intense excitement prevailed. They shouted to him, "Be of good cheer; we will save you." If he cried for help it could not be heard by reason of the roar of the cataract. They tried various experiments without success until the sun went down, and they lost sight of that little islet. During the night fires were lit on the banks, and thousands were there. When the cold, gray morning broke they looked, but the man was gone. They could not save him. But did ever any one come to Christ and fail to be saved? He would save them that night, He was their only hope. Might God bring thousands to a decision that night!

(a)   *Address by Mr. Moody*

CHRISTIAN, A

Four things necessary to constitute a Christian :

(i.) Faith *makes* a Christian;
(ii.) Life *proves* a Christian;
(iii.) Trials *confirm* a Christian;
(iv.) Death *crowns* a Christian.

(b)   *Höffner*

" *By their fruits ye shall know them* " (Matt. vii. 20)

For what is a man converted and made a new creature, but to help to turn the devil out of the world?

(c)

Fifty years ago, at a dinner party which was given in the West End of London, the conversation of the gentlemen turned on what was dishonouring to our Lord. One guest was silent, and presently he asked that the bell might be rung. On the appearance of the servant he ordered his carriage,

and, with polished courtesy, apologized to his host for his enforced departure, for he was still *a Christian*. Canon Liddon, in telling this anecdote in a recent sermon at St. Paul's Cathedral, proceeded : " All will think that he must have been a bishop, or at least a clergyman. He was not; he was then a rising member of Parliament, and became the popular prime minister of the early days of Queen Victoria's reign. He was the late Sir Robert Peel."

(d)

No man deserves the name of Christian, but he who adheres to his principles amidst the unbelieving, the intolerant, and the depraved.

(e)   *Channing*

There must be no mistake about a Christian. It must not be said, such a man *may be a Christian*, but he *is* a Christian, his life testifies it.

(f)   *Gordon Calthrop*, 1862

A CHRISTIAN IS THE WORLD'S BIBLE

Known and read of all men. (*See* BIBLE.)

It is well-known that the greatest obstruction to Christianity in heathen countries is the palpable and undeniable depravity of Christian nations. They abhor our religion, because we are such unhappy specimens of it. They are unable to read our books, but they can read our lives; and what wonder if they reject with scorn a system under which the vices seem to have flourished so luxuriantly. The Indian of both hemispheres has reason to set down the Christian as little better than himself. He associates with the name, perfidy, fraud, rapacity, and slaughter.

(g)   *Channing*

" Ah ! your man of religion is no better than others ; nay, he is sometimes *worse*." *The Indian chief to the missionary*: plumed and painted savage drawing himself up—indignation quivering on his lip, flashing in his eye, replied, " *Christian lie, Christian cheat, Christian steal, drink, murder ! Christian has robbed me of my lands, and slain my tribe*," adding as he turned away, " *The devil Christian; I will be no Christian.*"

(h)   *Guthrie*

" CHRISTIANUS SUM " :

In one of the persecutions for the faith in the second century, a man was brought before a heathen magistrate. The charge against him was that he was *a Christian*, but of his name and nationality they could make nothing.

" What is your name? " demanded the judge.
" I am a Christian," was the reply.
" What is your country? "
" I am a Christian."
" What is your business? "
" I am a Christian ? "
" How dare you refuse to swear by the emperor? "
" I am a Christian," once more was the reply ; and to every question, through torture unto death, he made the same reply.

(i)

WHY AM I NOT A CHRISTIAN?

1. Is it because I am afraid of ridicule?
"Whosoever shall be ashamed of Me and My words, of him shall the Son of man be ashamed."

2. Is it because of the inconsistencies of professing Christians?
"Every man shall give an account of himself to God."

3. Am I not willing to give up all to Christ?
"What shall it profit a man, if he gain the whole world and lose his own soul?"

4. Am I afraid I shall not be accepted?
"Him that cometh unto Me I will in no wise cast out."

5. Is it for fear I am too great a sinner?
"The blood of Jesus Christ His Son cleanseth us from all sin."

6. Is it because I fear I shall not "hold out"?
"He that hath begun a good work in you will perform it unto the day of Jesus Christ."

7. Am I thinking I will do as well as I can, and that God ought to be satisfied with that?
"Whosoever shall keep the whole law, and yet offend in one point, he is guilty of all."

8. Is it because I am postponing the matter without any definite reason?
"Boast not thyself of to-morrow, for thou knowest not what a day may bring forth."
(a)

CHRISTIANS, NOMINAL

Many there are who, while they bear the name of Christians, are totally unacquainted with the power of the Divine religion. But for their crimes the gospel is in no way answerable. Christianity is with them a geographical, not a descriptive appellation.
(b)   *Faber*

CHRISTIANITY

CHRISTIANITY AND THE BIBLE

There are those in this day who tell us that Christianity is falling back, and that in twenty-five years it will be extinct. These men found their opinion on the assumed fact that the Bible is not as much of a book as it used to be, and many chapters of it, they say, are repulsive to the people. I answer this by asking which one of the publishing houses of New York, Boston, Philadelphia is publishing the Bible with a single chapter or verse left out? Are not our publishers intelligent men? If they found that the Bible was an unpopular book, would they, against their own financial interests, continue to publish it as it is? When I find the fact that in Christendom there are hundreds of printing presses publishing the Bible from Genesis to Revelation, without one verse left out, I come to the conclusion that the Bible is still the most popular book on this planet. Suppose that Harper, or Appleton, or Ticknor, or Lippincott should publish a Bible with a chapter left out. They would not sell ten copies in ten years. The Bible unpopular! I will go through all the court rooms of this land, and wherever I find a judge's bench and a clerk's desk I find the Bible. What book is there apt to be on the table amid the bride's presents? The Bible. What book is almost sure to go in the young man's trunk when he starts for city life? The Bible? More Bibles published in this country in the last decade than in any decade since the world began. Voltaire wrote: "The Bible in the nineteenth century will be an obsolete book." Well, we are pretty well on through the century. Has the prophecy come true? Is there any prospect of its coming true? Are you aware of the fact, that in the very room where Voltaire wrote that prophecy in regard to the Bible, not long ago there was a great cargo of Bibles packed from floor to ceiling for Switzerland?
(c)   *Talmage*

CHRISTIANITY, CARICATURE OF

(Some persons) invent a caricature of Christianity, and pompously proclaim their quarrel with this as a quarrel against Christianity itself. They have no idea that Christianity is only humanism in its highest potency.
(d)   *Harless*

CHRISTIANITY—CAUSES OF FAILURE

It may be said without censoriousness, that the ordinary mode in which Christianity has been exhibited in past times does not suit the illumination of the present. That mode has been too narrow, technical, pedantic. Religion has been made a separate business—and a dull, unsocial, melancholy business too,—instead of being manifested as a truth which bears on and touches everything human. . . . And this narrow, forbidden mode of exhibiting Christianity is easily explained by its early history. Monks shut up in cells; a priesthood cut off by celibacy from the sympathies and most interesting relations of life; and universities enslaved to a scholastic logic, and taught to place wisdom in verbal subtleties and unintelligible definitions: these took Christianity into their keeping, and at their chilling touch this generous religion, so full of life and affection, became a dry, frigid, abstract system.
(e)   *Channing*

CHRISTIANITY AND THE CHURCH

The Church of God is losing its power. People caricature the Church, and talk about its being a great collection of hypocrites; but when their children are swept off with diphtheria, for whom do they send? For the postmaster, the attorney-general, the alderman; or for the pastors of the churches? And then, if the private house be too small for the obsequies, what building do they solicit? The Art Gallery, the Academy of Music, the hotel? No; the church. And if they want music on that sad occasion, do they select the "Marseilles Hymn," or "God save the Queen," or our national air? No. They want the hymn with which we hushed their old Christian mother into the last slumber, or they want the Sunday-school hymn that was sung by their little girl the last Sabbath afternoon she was out before she was seized with that awful sickness which broke father's heart and mother's heart. The Church of God to-day is the most popular institution in this country.
(f)   *Talmage*

CHRISTIANITY, THE EUCHARIST AN EVIDENCE OF

Philosophers might scoff at the first believers; politicians might suspect them; the populace might pursue them with ferocious yells; successive emperors might pour upon them the fury of their anger: but the new faith took its way. What at first had been the consolation of the slave or the fugitive in the catacombs, became the creed of the statesman and the magistrate; and from that day to this, a rite which, under its simplest and most obvious aspect, " sets forth" and commemorates the cruel and ignominious death of its Institutor, has been uninterruptedly celebrated, and regarded as the most solemn ordinance of their religion by all orders and degrees of men.

(a)   *Maclear*

CHRISTIANITY, EVIDENCE OF

The moment we begin to compare Christianity with any other religion, its difference and superiority stand out conspicuous in two respects. First, Christianity alone can point to anything which can properly be called evidence. Whatever else it is, Christianity is an historic religion. From the first hour of its rise to the present time, its origin and progress have been registered in contemporaneous and independent records, which the world is willing to accept. Tacitus, Suetonius, and Pliny are witnesses that are not to be silenced; and in the next age, the Christian faith, according to the promise of its Founder, has become a great tree, shooting forth branches in which the birds of the air have taken refuge. And so rich is the abundance of material from which to judge of this faith, that we can be in no doubt as to its nature; but what is more, its own native documents, which on this matter must be regarded as the best testimony, are earlier and more definite than any others.

(b)   *Stanley Leathes*

CHRISTIANITY, EVIDENCE OF

That suddenness with which this religion broke forth, that maturity of the system at the very moment of its birth, that absence of gradual development, seems to me a strong mark of its Divine original.

(c)   *Channing*

Nor can I easily believe that Christianity—the religion of unbounded love, a religion which broke down the barrier between Jew and Gentile, and the barriers between nations, which proclaimed one universal Father, which abolished forms, and substituted the worship of the soul, which condemned alike the false greatness of the Roman and the false holiness of the Jew, and which taught an elevation of virtue that the growing knowledge of succeeding ages has made more admirable,—I say, I cannot easily believe that such a religion was suddenly, immediately struck out by human ingenuity, among a people distinguished by bigotry and narrowness of spirit.

(d)   *Ibid*

CHRISTIANITY, EVIDENCE OF (NOT OF THIS WORLD)

Christianity was not the growth of the age in which it appeared. It had no sympathy with that age. It was the echo of no sect or people. It stood alone at the moment of its birth. It used not a word of conciliation. It stooped to no error or passion. It had its own tone—the tone of authority and superiority to the world. Such a religion had not its origin in this world.

(e)   *Ibid*

CHRISTIANITY, EVIDENCES OF

As to the Christian religion, besides the strong evidence we have for it, there is a balance in its favour from the number of great men who have been convinced of its truth after a serious consideration of the question. Grotius was an acute man, a lawyer, a man accustomed to examine evidence, and he was convinced. Grotius was not a recluse, but a man of the world, who certainly had no bias on the side of religion. Sir Isaac Newton set out as an infidel, and came to be a very firm believer.

(f)   *Dr. Johnson*

CHRISTIANITY, FIRST CONDITIONS OF

Christianity, though it may in certain persons reveal itself under a splendid aspect, so as to command the homage of the world, remains true to its first conditions, beginning at Bethlehem, and ending upon Calvary between the two thieves.

(g)   *Dora Greenwell*

CHRISTIANITY, FROM HEAVEN

There is no romance in a minister's proposing and hoping to forward a great moral revolution on the earth; for the religion which he is appointed to preach was intended and is adapted to work deeply and widely, and to change the face of society. Christianity was not ushered into the world with such a stupendous preparation, it was not foreshown through so many ages by enraptured prophets, it was not proclaimed so joyfully by the songs of angels, it was not preached by such holy lips, and sealed by such precious blood, to be only a pageant, a form, a sound, a show. Oh! no. It has come from heaven, with heaven's life and power—come to "make all things new," to make " the wilderness glad, and the desert blossom as the rose," to break the stony heart, to set free the guilt-burdened and earth-bound spirit, and to "present it faultless before God's glory with exceeding joy."

(h)   *Channing*

CHRISTIANITY, FROM HEAVEN.

I know not precisely what advances may be made by the intellect of an unassisted savage; but that a savage in the woods could not compose the " Principia " of Newton, is about as plain as that he could not create the world. I know not the point at which bodily strength must stop; but that a man cannot carry Atlas or Andes on his shoulders, is a safe position. The question, therefore, whether the principles of human nature, under the circumstances in which it was placed at Christ's birth, will explain His religion, is one to which we are competent, and is the great question on which the whole controversy turns.

Now we maintain that a great variety of facts belonging to this religion,—such as the character

(i)

of its Founder; its peculiar principles; the style and character of its records; its progress; the conduct, circumstances, and sufferings of its first propagators; the reception of it from the first on the ground of miraculous attestations; the prophecies which it fulfilled and which it contains; its influence on society, and other circumstances connected with it;—are utterly inexplicable by human powers and principles, but accord with, and are fully explained by, the power and perfections of God.

(a)   *Channing*

Christianity and Infidelity

Of course, an opposition to Christianity will make a great stir—just as one man jumping overboard from a Cunard steamer will make more sensation than the five hundred passengers who stay on the decks or in the cabins. But does that stop the ship? Does that wreck the five hundred sane passengers? It is an awful plunge for a man to make from off the lecturing platform or the pulpit into infidelity; but does the fact that he jumps overboard hinder this glorious Bible from taking its millions into the skies?

(b)   *Talmage*

Christianity and Infidelity

The clear, consistent, quickening truth which came from the lips of Jesus has been exchanged for a hoarse jargon and vain babblings. The stream, so pure at the fountain, has been polluted and poisoned through its whole course. Not only has Christianity been overshadowed by absurdities, but by impious doctrines, which have made the universal Father, now a weak and vain despot, to be propitiated by forms and flatteries, and now an almighty torturer, foreordaining multitudes of His creatures to guilt, and then glorifying His justice by their everlasting woe. When I think what Christianity has become in the hands of politicians and priests, how it has been shaped into a weapon of power, how it has crushed the human soul for ages, how it has struck the intellect with palsy and haunted the imagination with superstitious phantoms, how it has broken whole nations to the yoke, and frowned on every free thought; when I think how, under almost every form of this religion, its ministers have taken it into their own keeping, have hewn and compressed it into the shape of rigid creeds, and have then pursued by menaces of everlasting woe whoever should question the divinity of these works of their hands; when I consider, in a word, how, under such influences, Christianity has been, and still is, exhibited in forms which shock alike the reason, conscience, and heart, I feel deeply, painfully, what a different system it is from that which Jesus taught, and I dare not apply to unbelief the terms of condemnation which belonged to the infidelity of the primitive age.

(c)   *Channing*

Christianity and Modern Doubt

Christianity has now to contend with the whole accumulated forces of anti-christianity, philosophy, and science; and against this must be opposed an enlightened Christian philosophy and science. The old rose-water will not do any good, and empty churches are the result. Christianity is wisdom, is science, is philosophy, is in fact the highest and only *humanism*.

(d)

Christianity, Origin of

We have the plain testimonies of the greatest enemies of Christianity, that there was such a person as Christ, who suffered according to the Scripture story; for Tacitus not only mentions the Christians as suffering at Rome for their religion in the time of Nero, but saith that the Author of this religion was one Christ, who suffered under Pontius Pilate, procurator of Judæa, in the time of Tiberius, which is an irrefragable testimony of the truth of the story concerning Christ, in an age when, if it had been false, nothing could have been more easily detected than such a fiction by the number of Jews which was continually at Rome; and neither Julian, nor Celsus, nor Porphyry, nor Lucian did ever question the truth of the story itself, but only upbraided the Christians for attributing too much to Christ.

(e)   *Stillingfleet*

Talleyrand was anything but a Christian, yet he was shrewd, keen, and one of the wittiest of men. One of the disciples of Rousseau, a Mons. Lepaux, had invented a new religion, which he wished to see adopted in France. But somehow he made but little headway. He complained to Talleyrand of his slow progress. Talleyrand replied: "I am not surprised at the difficulty you experience. It is not easy to get a new religion accepted. But I will make a suggestion to you. I recommend you to be crucified, and to rise again on the third day." We commend this advice of the witty Frenchman to those in our day who propose a new religion in place of Christianity.

(f)

Christianity and Paganism

In the fifth century Christianity had conquered paganism, and paganism had infected Christianity. The Church was now victorious and corrupt. The rites of the Pantheon had passed into her worship, the subtleties of the Academy into her creed. In an evil day, though with great pomp and solemnity —we quote the language of Bacon—was the ill-starred alliance stricken between the old philosophy and the new faith. Questions widely different from those which had employed the ingenuity of Pyrrho and Carneades, but just as subtle, just as interminable, and just as unprofitable, exercised the minds of the lively and voluble Greeks. When learning began to revive in the West, similar trifles occupied the sharp and vigorous intellects of the schoolmen. There was another sowing of the wind, and another reaping of the whirlwind.

(g)   *Macaulay*

Christianity, Peculiarity of

Christianity throughout eighteen centuries has shown itself possessed of the peculiar power of recovering life when apparently almost defunct,— a peculiarity entirely absent in every mythology, which, when once dead, never can be restored, but

(h)

remains for ever in the realm of shadows; that Christianity has a phœnix-nature, and after every historic death arises anew from the grave; and that along with the resurrection which Christianity has had in our day, has also arisen from the grave the *true conception of humanity.*

(*a*) *Martensen*

Christianity and Preaching

Christianity is too much preached as a theology, too *little* as the religion of daily life; too much as a religion of feeling, too little as a religion of principles; too much as a religion only for individuals, too little as a religion for nations and the world.

(*b*) *F. W. Robertson*

Christianity and Science

But, say a great many, "Christianity is falling away from this country and from the world, in the fact that science, its chief antagonist, is triumphing over it." I reply: There is not a fact in science that may not be reconciled with Bible statement. So said Hugh Miller, so said Joseph Henry, so said Professor Hitchcock and Professor Mitchell, and so have said scores of the best scientists of the world. Beside that, have you not noticed that infidel scientists, instead of waging so hot a war against Christianity, are now beginning to fight among themselves? If infidel science came up with solid front, perhaps it might do some damage; but, as far as I can read the signs of the times, it is going to be telescope against telescope, Leyden jar against Leyden jar, chemical apparatus against chemical apparatus. Do you think there is any danger that ever the Bible account of the origin of life will be overthrown as long as the scientists differ about the origin of life, some adopting the theory of biogenesis, and others the theory of abiogenesis (I use that phrase because it sounds learned!), and while Agassiz comes out and puts both feet on the doctrine of evolution, and rebukes the young scientists of the day by saying: "I have noticed that many of the young naturalists are falling into the mistake of adopting for theories of science that which has never passed under observation." Agassiz discovered what we have discovered, that men talk wisely very often in proportion as they know little, and just as soon as these young scientists know the difference between the feelers of a wasp and the horns of a beetle, they begin to patronize the Lord Almighty, and to talk about culture as though it were spelled c-u-l-c-h-a-r, culchar. It makes me sick to see these literary fops coming down with Darwin under one arm and a case of transfixed grasshoppers and butterflies under the other arm, talking about Huxley's protoplasm, and "natural selection," and nebular hypothesis—lithping with an exquithit lithp, and calling all common men fools.

(*c*) *Talmage*

Christianity, True

I should be ashamed of it, did I not believe it true.

(*d*) *Channing*

Christianity, True

It is *true;* and I say this not lightly, but after deliberate examination. I am not repeating the accents of the nursery. I do not affirm the truth of Christianity because I was so taught before I could inquire, or because I was brought up in a community pledged to this belief.

(*e*) *Ibid*

Christianity and Zeal

It must be seen not only to correspond, and to be adapted to the intellect, but to furnish nutriment and appeals to the highest and profoundest sentiments of our nature. It must not be exhibited in the dry, pedantic divisions of a scholastic theology; nor must it be set forth and tricked out in the light drapery of an artificial rhetoric, in prettinesses of style, in measured sentences with an insipid floridness, and in the form of elegantly feeble essays. No; it must come from the soul in the language of earnest conviction and strong feeling.

(*f*) *Ibid*

CHRISTOPHER, ST., LEGEND OF

There was a giant in Canaan called Offero. He was prodigiously large and strong, and very proud because of this; but he was so poor that he was obliged to be somebody's servant. He made up his mind, however, that only the mightiest king should be his master, and he set out to find him. He journeyed many days, and at last reached the kingdom of one who was said to be the most powerful monarch on earth. Here he offered his services, and was accepted; for the king liked to have such followers as no one else could boast. For a time Offero served him faithfully; but it chanced one day that he was present when a minstrel sang a song before the king, in which he made frequent mention of Satan, and as often as the dreadful name occurred, the monarch trembled and crossed himself.

"Why doest thou that?" the giant asked.

But the king gave him no answer.

"If thou tellest me not, I must leave thee," he urged.

Then the king said: "I make the sign that Satan may have no power over me. He is both strong and wicked; therefore I fear him."

"Since thou fearest him, he must be more powerful than thou art; therefore he shall be my master," replied Offero; and he immediately set out to find him.

He travelled many days in vain, but at last he met a mighty and terrible being marching on the borders of a dreary desert at the head of a host of armed men. He did not seem to notice Offero's great size, but demanded who he was and whither he was going.

"I seek Satan, who is the mightiest king of whom I have yet heard," the giant replied; "I wish to be his servant."

At this the leader of the host was pleased.

"Thou hast found him; I am he; and I will make thy services both easy and pleasant," he said.

So Offero joined himself to this new master, until in their travels they came one day upon a wayside cross that stood where four roads met. When Satan saw it, he turned pale, and went a long way round to avoid it.

"What means this?" the giant asked.

But his master gave him no answer.

(*g*)

"Unless thou tellest me, I must leave thee," he said.

Then the devil spoke: "I fear the Cross, because on it Christ died. I fled lest He overcome me."

"Then will I leave thee, and search till I find Him. He is greater than thou art, else thou wouldst not tremble. My master must fear nothing."

Again Offero set out and wandered long in vain, till one day he came to the cell of a hermit.

"Tell me where I can find Christ," he said; "I would serve Him; for He is the most powerful King of whom I have yet heard."

"Thou hast well said," the hermit answered, "He is mighty in heaven and earth; but His service is no light matter. If thou wouldst serve Him, thou must pray often and fast much."

"That I will not do," answered the proud giant, "I know not how to pray; neither will I waste my strength by fasting."

"Then if thou wilt neither fast nor pray," the hermit replied, "perhaps thou canst serve Christ with that thou hast. Knowest thou that broad, deep river, that in time of rain is swollen and dangerous?"

"I know it well," Offero answered.

"Then go to it, and bear across on thy broad shoulders the weak and little ones; so shall thy great strength be useful in the saving of many lives. And if thy service be accepted of Christ He will give thee a sign."

Then Offero answered joyfully: "Thou hast now set me a task that I can perform, and I will do it."

So he went at once to the river, and built himself a hut upon its bank; and when he had pulled up in the forest a tall palm-tree, with which to steady his steps in the strong current that had swept many away, he began his work. For a long time he carried over all who wished to cross, so that not one life was lost where so many had perished. So our Lord looked down upon him out of heaven with pleasure, and said within Himself: "Behold this strong man who knoweth not yet how to worship Me, but hath found a way to serve Me."

At last, one night, when the giant rested in his hut of boughs, he heard a little child calling him: "Offero, wilt thou carry me over?" He went out quickly, but could find no one, and returned to the hut. Presently he heard the voice again, and, when it came a third time, he took his lantern and made a careful search. Then he found a tiny boy, who begged that he would carry him over. He set the child on his back, and, staff in hand, went down into the river; when suddenly a dreadful storm burst upon them. The wind swept down with terrible fury and the waters roared with a noise like thunder. The child grew heavier every moment, till he seemed like a mountain on the giant's shoulders, and he began to fear that he should be utterly overborne; but, nothing daunted, he struggled on till he reached the opposite shore. Putting down his burden in safety, he cried: "Who art thou that seemest so small, and yet art heavier than the world?"

"I am the Master thou servest," the child answered. "Thou hast proved thyself faithful, and I have accepted thee. If thou wouldst have a proof of My power and approval, plant thy staff in the earth, and it shall put forth leaves and bear fruit."

Offero obeyed, and instantly the bare branches were covered with foliage, amid which the dates hung in rich clusters. He turned to the wonderful child in amazement, but He was gone. So Offero knew that he had borne on his broad back Christ, the King of kings; and falling on his knees, he worshipped Him.

Then the giant went to Samos, where a terrible persecution against the Christians was raging, and he did much to encourage and strengthen them. One day a heathen struck him; but Offero did not return the blow. "I am a Christian, therefore I do not take vengeance on thee," he said. When the people heard this, they seized and bound him, for he would not use his great strength against them. They carried him before Dagnus the king of Syria; but when he saw Offero he fainted. On reviving he cried: "Who art thou, O most terrible giant?"

"My name was Offero, the bearer; but since I serve Christ and have borne Him on my shoulders, I am called Christ-Offero" (Christo-phero) the captive answered.

Then the king sent him to prison, and tried every means to seduce him from the Master he had chosen; but his soul was as strong as his body, and Dagnus had no power over it. He was very angry at this, and put the mighty Christian to the most cruel torture; but he remained unshaken in his allegiance to his Master. Finally he was led out to execution. Before he was beheaded, he kneeled down and prayed fervently, asking that all Christians who witnessed his martyrdom might henceforth be safe from fire, tempest, and earthquake.

In his painting, Albert Dürer represents the giant wading in the swollen, turbulent river, manfully struggling with the powerful current, and breasting the fearful storm that tosses his garments as if each gust of wind would strip them from his body. The mighty palm-tree is in his hand, and with its resistance he keeps his uncertain footing, and bears the mysterious weight of the seemingly small burden that grows so strangely heavier every moment. His countenance is brave, noble, determined, full of gentleness and good humour, in which there is an expression of wonder and perplexity very natural under the circumstances. Serene, calm, and smiling in the midst of warring elements, the Christ-child sits upon his shoulder, His lovely face just seen above the giant's bushy hair, on which His little hand rests. In the background, upon the shore, a hermit holds a lantern to light the way.

(a) *Christian Age*

CHURCH, AGGRESSIVENESS OF THE

Dr. Chalmers, who belonged to the Church of Scotland, said that the Established Church was aggressive, the other Churches only attractive; by which he meant that other religious bodies *drew* persons to them whom their services and teaching suited; but the Church *went out* into the highways, and took her message and machinery and organization to those whom she felt belonged to her.

(b) *Bishop Thorold*

CHURCH, ATTENDANCE AT

He who comes not willingly to church, shall one day go unwillingly to hell.

(c) *Bede*

M. went to church, because it was the right thing to do : God was one of the heads of society, and His drawing-rooms had to be attended.

(a)   *G. MacDonald*

CHURCH-BUILDING

Who builds a church to God, and not to fame,
Will never mark the marble with his name.

(b)   *Pope.*

CHURCH, CHARACTERISTICS OF THE

The Petrine characteristic is the trait of the Church as influenced by *law;* as the *confessing* Church.

The Pauline, is the trait of the Church as influenced by the freedom of faith ; as the *witnessing* Church.

The Johannean, the trait of the Church as filled with the ideality of faith, *working* and *keeping joyful holiday = the adorned Bride* (Rev. xix. 7, 8).

(c)   *Lange*

CHURCH (OF CHRIST), THE VISIBLE

The *abstract* conception of a river, is that of a stream of pure, unmixed water ; but the *actual* river is the Rhine, or the Rhone, or the Thames, muddy and discoloured, and charged with impurity ; and the conception of this or that river necessarily contains within it these peculiarities. So of the Church of Christ : abstractedly, and invisibly, it is a Kingdom of God, in which no evil is ; in the concrete, and actually, it is the Church of Corinth, of Rome, or of England, tainted with impurity. . . . . . . So far, in any age, the *visible* Church is *the* Church. But beyond the limits of the visible, is there no true Church ? Are Plato, Socrates, Marcus Antoninus, etc., to be reckoned by us as lost ? Surely not. The Church exists for the purpose of educating souls for heaven ; but it would be a perversion of this purpose to think goodness will not be received by God, because it has not been educated in the Church. Goodness is goodness, find it where we may. . . . The truth is, the Eternal Word has communicated Himself to man in the expressed thought of God (Christ). They to whom that Light has been manifested are Christians. But that Word has communicated Himself *silently* to human minds, on which the *manifested* Light has never shone. Such men *lived* with God, and were guided by His Spirit. They entered into the invisible ; they lived by Faith. They were beyond their generation.

(d)   *F. W. Robertson.*

CHURCH OF CHRIST.

This is the idea of the Church of Christ : men " washed, sanctified, justified in the name of the Lord Jesus, and by the Spirit of our God." But drunkards, revilers, extortioners, covetous men, gross sensualists, ought not to be in your society at all. Regenerate thieves ! regenerate libertines ! regenerate extortioners ! There is a horrible contradiction in the very thought ; there is something radically wrong, when such men, remaining in their vices, are imagined as belonging to the true kingdom of God. This is what you *were* as heathens, not what you *are* to be as Christians. . . . Here observe the great *Idea* of the Church

of God, . . . humanity as it exists in the Divine mind . . . the standard. . . . This you *are.* If you fall, you contradict your nature. . . . How opposite this to the common way of insisting on man's depravity. St. Paul insists on man's dignity ; he does not say to a man, You are fallen, you cannot think a good thought, you are half beast, half devil, sin alone is to be expected of you, it is your nature to sin. But he says rather, It is your nature not to sin ; you are not the child of the devil, but the child of God. . . . The Baptismal Service of the Church of England tells the child that he *is* a child of God—not that by faith or anything else he can make himself such. . . . There is a system common enough which begins by telling a child he is a child of the devil, to become *perhaps* the child of God. The foundation of Adam or of Christ. The one has on it nothing but what is debasing ; the other full of hope. . . . St. Paul says to all, " *Ye are redeemed.*" *This is the one foundation.*

(e)   *Ibid*

CHURCH OF CHRIST

" *I shall not die, but live, and declare the works of the Lord*" (Ps. cxviii. 17)

Now, in three ways the Church of Christ has been from time to time brought down to all appearance to the very chambers of the dead ; and from this deep depression she has risen again to newness of life. First, there has been the distress and suffering produced by outward persecution. For nearly 300 years the Imperial Government of Rome was engaged in an almost uninterrupted attempt to stamp out the Church by physical force. No forms of torture were unemployed in order to expel religious conviction from the souls of Christians ; and old men and maidens, and young men and children, gave their witness on scaffolds, in amphitheatres, in deserts, on mountain sides, to the sacred name of Jesus. One Emperor failed in the enterprise, but another was not wanting to take up the task. After Nero came Domitian, Marcus Aurelius, Diocletian, and Tiberius ; and at last the arms of the old empire became enfeebled by age, and the wild cries of the barbarians were heard more and more distinctly along the thousand miles of frontier ; and paganism, in its decay, could persecute no more. At first it seemed as if the faith might be killed out in its infancy among men. It was usual to take this view if the mind had no idea of the forces in conflict, organized physical force on one side, and a creed resting on unseen realities on the other. All through these dark and dreary years the secret leaven of the resurrection power of Jesus was working in the heart of Christendom. Never was the darkness so thick that no ray of light reached the soul of the suffering Church. Never was her case so desperate but that she could, not in scorn, but in broken accents of faith and hope, utter her unfailing conviction, " The empire will pass, but Jesus Christ lives." " I shall not die, but live, and declare the works of the Lord."

And next the Church has been exposed more than once to a more formidable danger—the decay of vital convictions within her fold. So it was in the early part of the thirteenth century, when the Arabian philosophers of Moorish Spain were so widely studied in all the universities of Europe, and

(f)

caused for some years a secret but profound unsettlement of faith in the central truths of Christianity. So it was at the revival of letters in the fifteenth and sixteenth centuries, especially in Italy. So it was conspicuously in the eighteenth century, throughout almost all Europe. The great anti-Christian campaign—for such it was—was opened in England by Bolingbroke, by Bentley, and by the English Deists. It was carried on in France by their pupil —for such he virtually was—Voltaire, and the Encyclopædic writers, who found a powerful patron in Frederick the Great; and it was acquiesced in in Germany by Lessing, who mistook criticism for faith, and to whom the search for truth seemed better than the possession; and it closed with Nicholi, and other writers of the period of enlightenment; while on the other banks of the Rhine the worship of the Goddess of Reason went hand-in-hand with the revolutionary tribunal and the reign of terror. "I am tired of hearing," said Voltaire, "that it took twelve men to set up Christianity in the world; I will show that it needs but *one* man to destroy it." There were Christians to whom it seemed that Christianity had had its day, that God must have withdrawn His protective survey of the world of human thought, and that the waves and storms of insurrection and blasphemy were bearing out of sight the Gospel of the Lord Jesus Christ. But that age was the age of not a few sincere Christians in England and elsewhere; and they were sure the Church of Christ had not forfeited the power of recovery which is lodged in her by Christ's resurrection. Years passed, and, without being religious, men came to see that, whatever were Voltaire's powers in other directions, his shallow, scornful treatment of the Bible was most like the act of the schoolboy, who earns the cheap laughter of his playmates by painting a moustache on a fine antique, and then running away. Years passed, and theories which were merely negative, and had no substantial truth whereby men's minds might be illuminated, human wills invigorated, and human souls refreshed, were seen in their real poverty and nakedness, and men turned their eyes back to the creed of their forefathers and to the mother who blessed them in infancy. But all through that dreary century, in the heart of the Church, was repeated the profound and unassailable conviction : "These writers may say what they will, 'I shall not die, but live, and declare the works of the Lord.'"

(a)   *Liddon*

"*The blessed company of all faithful people.*"

Take a mass of quicksilver, let it fall on the floor, and it will split into a vast number of distinct globules. Gather them up and put them together again, and they will coalesce into one body as before. Thus God's elect below are sometimes crumbled and distinguished into various parties, though they all are, in fact, members of one and the same mystic body. But when taken up from the world, and put together in heaven, they will constitute one glorious, undivided Church for ever and ever.

(b)   *Bowes*

The Church was for them divided, not into Roman and Anglican, Catholic and Protestant, but into the wrestlers and the victors, the combatants and the crowned, the faint and few,

struggling still through the waves of this troublesome world, and the glorious multitude innumerable, welcomed and welcoming on the other shore.
(c)

CHURCH, THE, AND DISSENT

I believe that the first seeds of Dissent were sown by the narrow intolerance of the Church in the days of the Stuarts. The wretched attempt to produce uniformity by fines and penalties and imprisonment " drove wise men almost mad," and made them say, " Can any good thing come out of a Church which sanctions such things ? " I believe that the utter deadness and apathy of the Church in the last century did even more to drive men and women out of our pale than the intolerance of the Stuarts. Bishops who scandalously neglected their dioceses, and were everything that bishops ought not to be ; parochial clergymen who did nothing for souls, preached no Gospel, performed hasty, cold, slovenly services in dirty churches full of high square pews like sheep-pens, and lived terribly worldly lives—these unhappy representatives of our Church filled the country : these were the real founders of Dissent, and caused half the chapels to be built in the land. I declare my own firm conviction, that if the Bishops and clergy of the last century had done their duty, and understood their times as well as many do now, an immense proportion of English Nonconformity would never have existed, and John Wesley and his companions would never have seceded from the Church of England. We reap what our forefathers sowed, and it is no use to complain. In short, Church apathy has created English Nonconformity ; and to speak angrily and contemptuously of those whom we ourselves have made Dissenters, is, to say the least, most unjust. That old saying is too much forgotten, " *Schismaticus est qui separationem causat, non qui separat.*"
(d)   *Bishop Ryle*

CHURCH OF ENGLAND, THE

(Vitality and comprehensiveness of) is the greatest bulwark against infidelity and anarchy now existing in the world.
(e)   *Dr. Döllinger*

CHURCH OF ENGLAND, THE

The Church of England occupies the glorious *Via Media*, and, in the grand words of Tennyson,

Turns to scorn, with lips divine,
The falsehood of extremes.

(f)   *Richard Glover*

CHURCH OF ENGLAND, THE TRUE

We often hear that the Church is in danger ; and truly so it is,—in a danger it seems not to know of ; for, with its tithes in the most perfect safety, its functions are becoming more and more superseded. The true Church of England, at this moment, lies in the *Editors of its Newspapers.* These preach to the people, daily, weekly, admonishing kings themselves ; advising peace or war with an authority which only the first reformers and a long-past class of Popes were possessed of ;
(g)

inflicting moral censure; imparting moral encouragement, consolation, edification; in all ways diligently "administering the discipline of the Church." It may be said too, that in private disposition the new preachers somewhat resemble the mendicant friars of old times; outwardly full of holy zeal; inwardly, not without stratagem, and hunger for terrestrial things.

(a)   *T. Carlyle*

Church of England

Mankind will do wrong if it allows it to drop out of existence, merely because the position on which it stands seems to be illogical, an agency by which the devotional instincts of human nature are enabled to exist side by side with the rational. The English Church offers the supernatural to all who choose to come. It is like the Divine Being Himself, whose sun shines alike on the evil and on the good. . . . The way is open; it is barred by no confession, no human priest, . . . won for us by the death and torture of men like ourselves. . . . Shall we throw thee aside? It is not a question of religious freedom only; it is a question of learning and culture in every form. . . . Standing between two extremes, there is a danger that its position will engender indifference and sloth; . . . nevertheless, as a Church it is unique: if suffered to drop out of existence, nothing like it can ever take its place.

(b)   *Shorthouse (J. Inglesant)*

Church of England

The ritual of England breathes a Divine calm. You think of people walking through ripening fields on a mild day to their church door. It is the work of a nation sitting in peace, possessing their land. It is the work of a wealthy nation, that, by dedicating a part of its wealth, consecrates the remainder, acknowledges the fountain from which it flows. The prayers are devout, humble, fervent, they are not impassioned. A wonderful temperance and sobriety of discretion, that which in worldly things would be called good sense, prevails in them; but you must name it better in things spiritual. The framers evidently bore in mind the continual consciousness of waiting for all. Nor must it be forgotten that the received version and the Book of Common Prayer,—observe the word "Common," expressing exactly what I affirm,—are beautiful by the words, that there is no other such English, simple, touching, apt, venerable, hued as the thoughts are, musical, the most English that is known, of a Hebraic strength and antiquity, yet lucid and gracious, as if of and for to-day.

(c)   *Carlyle*

Church of England, A Nonconformist on the

The Rev. Thomas Jones preaching at Walter-road Congregational Chapel, Swansea, . . . in the course of his remarks referred to the Church of England in the following eulogistic terms:—"The dear old Church, the repository of so much learning, so much wisdom, and so much piety; she has her grand old liturgy to fall back upon, while the Nonconforming pulpits are being filled by men, weak men, men of no intellectual attainments; and were it not that eight out of every ten of the hearers were unthinking and unreading listeners, such preachers would never venture to ascend the pulpit stairs."

(d)   *The Record*

Church, The Evangelical

In order to meet the necessities of the age, a Church must be thoroughly *evangelical*. Its mission is not to make men philosophers, although it teaches the best philosophy; nor to make scientific explorations, although it is the best friend of science; nor to organize Governments and write Constitutions, although its inculcations lead to the wisest political economy. But to balk profligacy, to dethrone superstition, to emancipate spiritual bondage, to break in twain the prison bolts, to soothe human pain, to turn the human race on to the pathway of heaven, this is the Church's mission; and whatever cross it may have on the church-top, and however beautiful an altar or pulpit or font, and however high-sounding and magnificent the service, failing in this, it fails in all. It may be a brazen candlestick, or a bronze candlestick, but not a golden candlestick.

(e)   *Talmage*

Church of England

[A commendation of the doctrine and practice of one body of Christians by a minister of another so unqualified and hearty, as to be without a parallel in the history of preaching.]
Of all Protestant Churches none has a Prayer Book containing lessons, gospels, psalms, collects, confessions, thanksgivings, which can for a moment stand comparison with that of the Episcopal Church, in the qualities of richness and age. . . . You rarely hear in *any* Church a prayer spoken in English which is not indebted to the Prayer Book for some of its choicest expressions. . . . I doubt whether life has in store for you an uplift so high, or a downfall so deep, but that you can find company for your soul and fitting words for your life among the treasures of this Book of Common Prayer. . . . Christians, because this Episcopal Church is a reformed Church, and not revolutionary; because her Book of Prayer is rich and venerable above all in the English tongue; because her ritual promotes decency, dignity, prosperity, and permanence; because her historic union through the apostles with Christ comforts and satisfies so many souls; because she adopts her infant children, and provides for them a Christian education, and because with a large hospitality she proffers her sacrament to all true believers of every name; therefore from her own Psalter let us take the words wherewith to bless her: "They shall prosper that love thee. Peace be within thy walls and plenteousness within thy palaces. For my brethren and companions' sakes I will wish thee prosperity. Yea, because of the house of the Lord our God I will seek to do thee good."

A Leading Nonconformist Minister in America
(f)

Church History, Facts of, Compared with the Characteristics of the Seven Churches of Asia

1. The first period, immediately succeeding the Apostolic, = one of falling from first love: false
(g)

apostles and teachers from the body of the Church itself, together with zeal and intolerance of error on the part of true Christians = *Ephesian* period.

2. Next came the period of Pagan persecution and of martyrdom. Remarkable that the Church endured exactly *ten* distinct outbursts of fury, the last which lasted ten years = the *Smyrna* period.

3. Christianity became the established religion of the Roman Empire; passed almost at a bound from being a persecuted Church to high prosperity and affluence, under Constantine. Worldliness and coveteousness crept in. . . . Grace of God was turned into lasciviousness = Christian liberty is liberty to sin—a period not unlike the Church in *Pergamos*.

4. The age of full-developed Popery followed, and of Papal supremacy. Yet there were a faithful few. No historical character so well typifies the Papacy as does that of the adulterous and idolatrous wife of Ahab, whose name (Jezebel) is here used to express the character and doctrine of the false prophetess in the Church at *Thyatira*.

5. The next period, following the Reformation, is attested to, beyond all doubt, as being characterized by a dead orthodoxy in the Protestant Churches. The Church was, from the end of the sixteenth century till the latter half of the eighteenth century, a very *Sardis*.

6. A great change took place towards the close of the last century, when a revival began; and ever since then a Christian brotherly love, manifesting itself in increased efforts for the welfare of others, has been the chief characteristic of the Church as a whole. Missionary societies for the heathen; Home Missions; Religious machinery = " I have set before you an open door " = the Church of *Philadelphia*.

7. But who sees not the characteristics of the last of the seven more and more evident amongst us? A religion splendidly formal; a Christianity of architecture and art, and eloquence and music, or of sensationalism and mere animal excitement. An intense antagonism between the world and true spirituality; a hatred of positive doctrine; a disposition to regard all religious teachings as mere opinions, equally right or wrong. And over all this, the boasted enlightenment of this nineteenth century. These are realities amongst us and = the characteristics of the *Laodicean* Church.

(a)   Cf. *T. Graham, Lange, and others*

CHURCH, IDEA OF

The true and grand idea of a Church, is a society for the purpose of making men like Christ, earth like heaven, the kingdoms of the world the kingdom of Christ.

(b)   *T. Arnold*

The kingdom of Christ, not being a kingdom of this world, is not limited by the restrictions which fetter other societies, political or religious. It is in the fullest sense free, comprehensive, universal. It accepts all comers, irrespective of race, or caste, or sex. It has no sacred days or seasons, no special sanctuaries, because every time and every place alike are holy—above all, it has no sacerdotal system. It interposes no sacrificial tribe or class between God and man, by whose intervention alone God is reconciled and man forgiven. Each individual member holds personal communion with the Divine Head. To Him immediately he is responsible, and from Him directly he obtains pardon and draws strength. This, then, is the Christian ideal; a holy season extending the whole year round—a temple confined only by the limits of the habitable world—a priesthood co-extensive with the human race.

(c)   *Bishop Lightfoot*

CHURCH AND INFIDELITY

Infidelity, and methods employed for extending it

We made idols of old armour and old weapons, which did good service in the past, but were worse than useless in the present. No one reverenced the Prayer Book more than he did; but for all that there were points which ministered to infidelity. The most salient of these was the retention of the Athanasian Creed. While ninety out of every hundred of an ordinary congregation did not know the scientific meaning of such words as " substance " and " person," it was notorious that they did understand the creed to affirm that damnation was a penalty declared by their Church to attach to inability to accept intellectually a series of abstruse propositions in metaphysics. In the same way the Church's attitude towards physical science and its professors seemed to him to be driving the cleverest of our children into infidelity. No doubt the provocation from many (though not the ablest or the best) of these professors was very great; but what could this matter to a Christian? Surely we believed that the physical and visible world was God's was created and ordered by Him, and therefore that everything these men were discovering which was really true about it was and must be a revelation of and from Him.

(d)   *T. Hughes*

CHURCH

" I the Lord do KEEP it " (Isa. xxvii. 3)

He will give His angels charge over thee. Oh, what reverence, what love, what confidence, deserveth so sweet a saying? For their presence, reverence; for their good-will, love; for their tuition, confidence.

(e)   *Bernard*

CHURCH

Let her be known to be Thy Ark, and let Dagon fall down before her.

(f)   *Prayer by F. Quarles*

CHURCH

He cannot have God to be his Father, who owns not the Church as his mother.

Cf. Jerusalem above = mother of us all.

(g)   *Cyprian*

CHURCH

Arise, run to the Church : there is the Father, there is the Son, there is the Holy Ghost.

(h)   *Ibid*

CHURCH, MISSION WORK OF THE

Whenever any Church has ceased to be missionary, it has ceased to be healthy; whenever any Church has begun to narrow its efforts, from " prudential " or other motives, it has come near

(i)

to the time when its candlestick shall be removed. Christianity tottering to its fall? Never! save by the indolence of her sons. Christianity defeated on the coast of Africa? Let the Church of God answer in the words that have come down through the ages: "The gates of hell shall not prevail against this Church," that is founded upon this eternal principle. It is always in the power of ourselves to make our Church that it shall never disgrace the cause of Christ, but that we shall everywhere overthrow the idea of being ornamental Christians, and bear ever upon our foreheads the mark of our high calling by carrying out the very law by which Christianity can find expression; believe me, it is in reality that Christianity shall exercise itself in the power of blessing others.

You *live* Christianity by the law of self-surrender. Jesus Christ tells us what the result will be: "Except it die it abideth alone; but if it die it bringeth forth much fruit." The curse of selfishness is solitude. It abides alone. Look at life! The man that accumulates wealth lives for himself. He gathers into his coffers, and he entertains his friends; old age creeps upon him. You know what he is; an isolation, a monument in the midst of a wilderness, a monument of miserliness, of selfishness, a monument that stands solitary.

(a) *Bishop Boyd Carpenter*

MY CHURCH, "*I will build my Church*" (Matt. xvi. 18)

I think it would have been well, if in all ages of the Church the emphasis of these words had been considered. "*I will build My Church*"—so saith the great Head and Architect of the building—so saith our Lord Jesus Christ. It is *His* Church, and *He* will build it: whether the building rests more upon *this* living stone, upon *this* Apostle, upon Peter, or upon John, or upon Paul,—all this is matter of detail: there are many stones in that great building; there are some beneath the earth (as it were) serving for foundation-stones, not seen or known by ordinary eyes, but nevertheless bearing a great weight upon them; and there are some in more conspicuous places, carved work (as it were) of God's beautiful Temple, which every one sees and to which there may be a temptation to assign exaggerated importance; but whatever the stones may be, and whatever their beauty or their importance, they have been placed where they are by the great Lord of all: and a devout mind will rise above the materials of the building to the thought of the builder, and the most prominent and the most comforting part of our Lord's promise to St. Peter will be that which is contained in the words of my text, "I will build My Church."

The Church which Christ promised to build was not an edifice which could be built in Apostolic times, and last in the condition in which it then was to all generations: it was not like the buildings which we call churches amongst ourselves, which we erect of wood and stone, and then use for centuries as temples for the worship of God: the Church of which Christ spoke was a thing which should increase and grow from year to year, and from generation to generation: if you compare it to a building, then it must be a building which is constantly being added to and increased, a building which is ever in the architect's hands, and which can never be regarded as finished, so long as there are men and women who have been redeemed by Christ, but who at present can find no room within it.

The Church of England at the time of the Reformation, more than any other reformed Church, preserved the continuity of her existence: she maintained the ancient order, the apostolical succession, the old order of service; she laid no claim to be called a new Church; she was not the Church of Cranmer, or of Luther, or of Calvin: she required no affix or suffix to describe her; she was the *Church of England*: this is what she had been before, and this is what she professed to remain.

(b) *Bishop Harvey Goodwin*

CHURCH OF ROME

Either the claims of the Church of Rome are just, or they are not. If they are,—she is *infallible* and *indefectible*. She is the mother and mistress of Churches. Her Pontiff is the universal pastor; the centre of unity; the father of the faithful; the supreme head and spiritual judge of Christendom; the infallible teacher of Divine truth; and (as he himself asserts) it is necessary for every one to be in communion with him and to be in subjection to him. Out of his communion there is no salvation.

Now, we hold in our hand the Apocalypse of St. John, *the Revelation of Jesus Christ, the voice of the Spirit to the Churches;* the prophetic history of the Church from the Apostolic age to the day of doom. In it St. John places us at *Rome;* he points to its *seven hills;* he shows us the city enthroned upon them; he detains us there, while he reveals unto us Rome's future history, even to its total extinction, which he describes.

(c) *Bishop Wordsworth*

CHURCH OF ROME.

The Papal Church has had three phases,—Anti-Cæsarean, extra-national, anti-Christian.

(d) *S. T. Coleridge.*

CHURCH OF ROME

Having, at his being in Rome, made acquaintance with a pleasant priest, who invited him one evening to hear their vesper music at church, the priest, seeing Sir Henry stand obscurely in a corner, sends him by a boy of the choir this question, writ in a small piece of paper—"Where was your religion to be found before Luther?" To which question Sir Henry presently under-writ—"My religion was to be found then, where yours is not to be found now—in the written word of God."

(e) *Isaak Walton's Life of Sir Henry Wotton*

CHURCH OF ROME

The course of Christianity and the Christian Church may not unaptly be likened to a mighty river, which filled a wide channel, and bore along with its waters mud, and gravel, and weeds, till it met a great rock in the middle of its stream. By some means or other, the water flows purely, and separated from the filth, in a deeper and narrower course on one side of the rock, and the refuse of the dirt and troubled water goes off on the other in a broader current, and then cries out, "*We are* the river."

(f) *S. T. Coleridge*

Church of Rome

The Church of Rome has traded upon the highest instincts of humanity, upon its faith and love, its passionate remorse, its self-abnegation and denial, its imagination and yearning after the unseen. It has based its system upon the profoundest truths; and upon this platform it has raised a power which has, whether foreseen by its authors or not, played the part of human tyranny, greed, and cruelty. To support this system it has habitually set itself to suppress knowledge and freedom of thought, before thought had taught itself to grapple with religious subjects, because it foresaw that this would follow. It has, therefore, for the sake of preserving intact its dogma, risked the growth and welfare of humanity; and has, in the eyes of all except those who value this dogma above all other things, constituted itself the enemy of the human race.

(a)   *Shorthouse (J. Inglesant)*

The Church and the Scriptures

The Papacy elevated the Church to the virtual exclusion or suppression of the Scriptures; the modern Church of England, since Chillingworth, has so raised up the Scriptures as to annul the Church. Both alike have quenched the Holy Spirit as the mesothesis of the two.

(b)   *Coleridge*

Church and State

I never believed that the Establishment, as such, was Christ's Church in England, or that the withdrawal of the favour of the State would be the putting out in our communion of the Divine Shechinah. It is not so much for the Church that I fear, for I firmly believe Christ's words, "Lo, I am with you alway," and doubt not that the old, the everlasting benediction is able to repeat itself in many new, many diverse forms. I do fear something for the State when it ceases to have a religion. I do fear something for the average tone of religion in our cottages and in our palaces.

(c)   *C. J. Vaughan*

Church, The

When will the clergy learn that their strength is in action, and not in argument? If they are to re-convert the masses, it must be by noble deeds, as Carlyle says, "not by noisy theoretic laudation of *a* Church, but by the silent practical demonstration of THE Church."

(d)   *Chas. Kingsley*

Church, The True

It is possible to have a great show of spiritual prosperity, without an inner reality corresponding to it. We may have eloquent preaching, crowded churches, magnificent music, and all the superficial appearance of a great religious movement, whilst yet the vaunted revival is only a poor galvanized thing; a corpse twitching with a strange mimicry of life, but possessed of none of its vital energy and power.

They tell us, that when a Russian Empress, in days gone by, wished to make a progress through her dominions for the purpose of inspecting them, those who were interested in keeping her blinded to the real state of the case, contrived to surround her with the tokens of prosperity, even in the most unprosperous regions. Sending their emissaries a day's march in advance of the Royal company, they extemporized scenes of rustic happiness. Villages, hastily erected, were surrounded by gardens, and these gardens filled with flowers and shrubs. The neighbouring peasantry, dressed and tutored for their part, were brought in. Flocks and herds were gathered together for the occasion. And when the Empress came, a smiling prospect of abundance and comfort everywhere met her view. The next day the monarch departed, well pleased with what she had seen. Then the flocks and herds were scattered; the flowers withered; the shrubs were removed; the cottages were pulled down; the peasantry, after their one day's masquerading, returned to their squalor and degradation; and the actors in the wretched farce hastened forward to repeat it at the next station at which their duped and deluded mistress intended to rest. I see in this the emblem of a religious movement grounded upon some human device, and not upon the truth and the blessing of God. "Except the *Lord* build the house, their labour is but lost that build it." And sooner or later, a time of testing comes, when all that is merely external and superficial, being tried, shall be pronounced wanting and shall pass away; and when that alone which is based on the Truth and upheld by the Spirit of God, shall be found to abide.

(e)   *Gordon Calthrop*

Church, True Unity of

Though the Church of Christ has failed to learn this, and though, by an attempt at forced uniformity, it has rent its own unity, we can see what may be called the breadth of view of the Great Head, in that He does not identify Himself with their narrowness, nor confine His reviving influences to any one portion where His truth remains. The showers of His grace come from too high a source to be limited by the walls they build against each other.

(f)   *Ker*

In England, in this nineteenth century, as a matter of fact, there exist more than one form of ecclesiastical organization, deeply rooted in the hearts and homes of the people, rich in historical memories, and strong with the force of early hereditary association, and in the activity of expansive Christian life.

(g)   *Schönberg Cotta Series*

An organ is composed of several instruments—the choir, the swell, the pedal, the great; and many stops—the diapason, the flute, the trumpet; and yet it is one. And the Church of Christ is one. One Spirit—one breath of wind, turned on by one living hand, makes all the organ vocal.

(h)   *J. Morse*

The Church, Unity of

It imports exceedingly the *Peace of the Church*, that the *League of Christians*, prescribed by our Saviour in those two clauses which seem to cross one the other, were well and clearly expounded: (i.) "*He that is not with us is against us*"; and, (i) (ii.) "*He that is not against us is with us.*" Whence it appears, that there are some Articles wherein whosoever dissenteth is to be held as not comprehended in the league; and there are other Articles, wherein a man may dissent, and yet the league be kept entire. For the bounds of Christian community are set down: *one Faith, one Baptism,* and not *one Rite, one Opinion.* . . . The coat of our Saviour *was entire without seam;* but the garment of the Church was of *divers colours.* The *chaff* must be severed from the corn in the ear; but the *tares* may not be presently pulled up from the corn in the field. When Moses saw an Egyptian fighting with an Israelite, he did not say, Why strive you? but drew his sword and slew the Egyptian; but when he saw two Israelites fight, though it could not be possible that both parties had a just cause; yet he thus speaks to them both, *You are brethren, why strive you?* . . . If these things be well observed, it will be found a matter of great moment and use to define what, and of what latitude, those points are which discorporate men from the body of the Church, and cast them out and quite cashier them from the communion and fellowship of the faithful. Meanwhile *Peace* is not the matter that many seek after, but *parties* and *siding:* "What hast thou to do with Peace? *turn and follow me.*"

(a)   *Lord Bacon*

CHURCHES

I don't believe in Churches, but in my Lord Jesus Christ, who is made unto me wisdom and righteousness and sanctification and redemption.

(b)   *R. W. Sibthorp (died Jan. 1879)*

Churches, Union of the, through the Head, not through the Members.

Converts, Instincts of

The appointment of converts brought up among the influences of Rational Protestantism to positions of authority in the Roman Church, has this remarkable effect: They cannot restrain their instincts of publishing, of appealing to the public through the press; and that Romanism should be brought into the light of day and its pretensions calmly examined by reasonable men, is all that Protestantism desires or hopes for.

In general, the prejudices of our congregations are so distinctly Protestant that it would be a mere stirring up of that wrath of man by which God's righteousness can never be advanced, to discuss such matters in the pulpit. But the appearance of such a book as Dr. Manning's "England and Christendom" was hailed with delight by all who give any serious attention to such questions, as the occasion of clearly and soberly examining what there is of good in the position of the writer.

(c)

Rome's Tactics

There will be no disposition to deny that a systematic organized attempt is being made to reduce this country to the faith of Rome. Dr. Manning says, (p. 113): "Every [Roman] Catholic must wish to see the Church of England give way under the intellectual and spiritual action of the Catholic Church, and must watch with satisfac-

tion every change, social and political, weakening the hold of the Anglican Church on the country, and would faithfully use all his power and influence for its complete and speedy removal." Now, as long as any reform is sought openly by fair constitutional means, we have no idea of crying down any attempt at reformation; but we must remember that the Reformation which Luther and the Jesuits accomplished, was not possible till the then establishment had lost all living power through the abounding of gross moral iniquity—that indulgences, and the sloth and sensuality of the professedly religious, and the worldliness of pontiffs and spiritual chiefs; had convinced the moral sense of mankind that the religion of the Church was a mockery and deceit. Rome abandoned all belief in religion long before Wittemberg abandoned Rome. But to shake the established form of religion in this country, is to remove a living agency whose influence is great, and zealously exerted to suppress the immorality and practical heathenism which the enemy has sown in the field of God; and it is necessary to feel very sure that the other system, which it is proposed to make way for, will really be an effectual living power in the hearts of Englishmen. It is no use to say that consequences are in God's hands, that we must not doubt that He can and will work good through His Church. No one is asked to doubt God's power to bring good at the last out of any evil which any man is permitted to work. What is doubted is, whether any of the Church systems which by human hands God has allowed to grow up in various lands is the exclusive channel by which God converts the hearts of men.

(d)

Rome's Demand

Dr. Manning describes the difference between the English and Roman Churches as "questions removed from the primary truths of conscience and Christianity." And it is much to be regretted that any working power that there is in our Church or in the Roman Church should be directed to such minor matters to the neglect of the great truths which we all hold in common.

The position he maintains is, that it is the duty of such members of the Church of England as have the leisure and intelligence which enables them to form any opinion on the subject, as they value their hope of peace in this world or of safety in the next, to accept as the revelation of God the teaching of the chair of Peter, and to find it a rule to which their reason and conscience should be submitted.

Now it would be idle to enter into any argument from Scripture or from antiquity, simply because he believes all such authorities are to be understood in such sense as the Church is pleased to put upon them; and an appeal to documents which one party reserves the right of interpreting in its own sense, would be mere beating of the air.

But if to "the unlearned in all classes," and to a great many of the poor and unlettered, it is often physically and very morally impossible to judge "which is the true revelation or Church of God:" there must be some marks by which learning and leisure may detect it.

If, as he says most truly, "Reason leads us to the feet of a Divine teacher, though the last act of reason is generically distinct from the first act

(e)

Churches, Union of the, etc.—*continued*

of faith," it is not an unfair demand to make, that some person of learning and leisure will kindly lead us with him up to the last act of reason, although " thenceforward his voice, and not the balancing of probabilities, will be the formal motive of our faith."

(*a*)

Our Demand

We, who grope with weak hands, ask them who have safely made this passage to aid our reason in making the same, and then, if we reject the manifest light (εν δε φαει και ολεσσον). But less than a page of the book is spent over this question. Though, surely, if this is common ground, it is here, and not in the Paradise of certainty in which he is landed, that Dr. Manning should lift his voice. Our rest will be long enough when we meet before the throne of God ; but now, whilst he can still make his voice heard over the jarring strifes which he has safely passed through, let him turn back and help us who cannot see our way through the thicket of reason which has to be fought through before we reach the light. His faith, indeed, may " terminate no longer in a cumulus of probabilities," but we are striving to mount among shifting blocks of such a talus ; and though he may have reached the firm brow of the cliff beyond, it is in vain to tell us how pleasant it is when the last step is made, but let him tell us how he trod to reach it ; though in truth my belief is, the Cardinal has no more reached the top than we have, though he may have ceased to climb ; but is merely sitting down in a place which he thinks safe and pleasant. But that the garden of God is far above us both, and that ceaseless struggling to the end will alone enable us to see and grasp the Divine hand which the Saviour reaches down to draw us up.

(*b*)

Rome's Assumption

But still let us make the most of the half page on this subject. "Historical criticism teaches us that Christianity has penetrated the nations of the world for eighteen hundred years, united them in one family, elevated the intellect and purified the heart of mankind, created the new Christian civilization, taught immutably one dogma, and reigned inflexibly by one divine law : that its unity and universality fulfil the prophecies, and that the multitude of its martyrs, saints, and penitents attest a supernatural power. The cumulus of evidence, and the ever growing weight of probabilities, determine the reason imperatively to believe that Christianity is a divine revelation, and the Church a divine kingdom upon earth." How true, how just this is. But is the one dogma taught only at Rome ? Surely it is that Jesus Christ is come in the flesh. Is the one divine law to follow the Pope ? Is it not that ye love one another as I have loved you ? The saints and penitents and martyrs, have they been found only among the adherents of the chair of Peter ?

It is, indeed, historically certain, that the glorious army of martyrs numbers multitudes of every age and creed, who have loved the Lord Jesus in sincerity ; and that the Roman communion has increased that army, but not by methods which

witness to its exclusive possession of truth. The Inquisition, and the slaughtered Piedmontese, the fires of Smithfield, and the safe conduct of Prague, and the eve of St. Bartholomew are unexpected witnesses for the Cardinal to call into court.

But these are matters beyond discussion, for the Church has pronounced its approval. Let us return to the argument from the Cardinal's own mouth.

Are the works done by Christianity for society surer witnesses to the Papal claims ? For, even if we were convinced that the work of God among our brethren was impossible in the established ministry, we should yet have to decide whether the fruits of Dissent or of Romanism were most certain evidence that God is working in them.

(*c*)

Rome's Admission

The Cardinal gives honourable testimony to the work of Methodists and Evangelicals. "Sensual immorality and spiritual death reigned widely over society in England when they rose. It is undeniable that the zeal and piety of these two movements brought multitudes back to the consciousness that they had souls to save, and that unless they turned from sin to God they would perish eternally. . . In thirty years they had won their position and so far changed the aspect of society that they were perhaps only too much followed and respected. . . To this deeper personal religion, founded on interior convictions and affections, and sustaining itself chiefly upon the writings of Puritans and the devotional use of the Holy Scripture, may be ascribed the change which has come over the Church of England." Then arose the movement of the Oxford men, "who hated the Puritan theology," who replaced the "heterodoxies" of the Evangelicals by "hierarchical and sacramental principles." With what result we read ; "They who can remember what was the public opinion of England thirty years ago in respect to Christianity, and know what it is now, will perceive that a flood has gone over it. By common consent, Christianity is banished from public life. It is a matter for individuals, not for society ; society is without faith." And this is when "there never was a moment since the Reformation when the Anglican body was more inclined to the Catholic Church," and when "there is a flow in the stream which has carried the minds of men onward for these thirty years nearer and nearer to the frontiers of the Catholic faith."

By their fruits ye shall know them, the question for all thinking, religious men is, Which is of God, the writings of the Puritans and the devotional use of the Holy Scripture which broke up the reign of sensual immorality, or the hierarchical, sacramental movement, which has led to a society without faith ?

(*d*)

The Press and the Pulpit

Since 1830 the "emancipation of Catholics revived the action of the Catholic Church upon the people of England." And what is this action worth. The great teaching power of the present day is not the Pulpit, but the Press ; by it a man may make his voice heard in every palace, (for even the

(*e*)

Churches, Union of the, etc.—*continued*

Pope learns from the public journals,) and in every cottage in Christendom; but in England, of the volumes and fly leaves which are so plentifully produced, "not one thousandth part is Catholic;" and when we study the published manifesto of the chief pastor of Rome in England, about the same fraction of a thousandth part is occupied with those grounds of human criticism and reason which are, he tells us, the means to lead into the serene security into which he has passed.

(*a*)

MUTUAL HOSTILITIES

Whilst the acknowledged work of Evangelicalism and Methodism has been to lead multitudes from sin to God, the strength of the Roman champion is spent on destroying the faith of men in the system which is the great practical *worker* in the education and civilization of England, though he knows that his own Church is not likely to fill its place; but "the state of England gives little promise of any diminished hostility to the Catholic Church. It is to be feared it is already far more estranged from the Catholic faith than it was in 1688. The insular pride, national Protestantism, Royal jealousy of any superior, the aristocratic independence, and insubordination to the Church, which descends from the sixteenth century, all these are at least as strong now as in 1688."

(*b*)

ROMISH TREASON

But surely, if a Pretender to a throne knew that his great-grandfather had been formally expelled with such solemn forms as can be expected in times of trouble and revolution; if he confessed that before he began to agitate, the *de facto* rule had been doing admirable work; if he allowed that nineteen-twentieths of the population would prefer all the horrors of anarchy to his return; surely his conduct in seeking to loosen the allegiance of men to the powers that be, would be high treason, such that no language could exaggerate the sin and mischief of such conduct; especially when the *de facto* ruler allows this Pretender to live side by side, to receive the aid and support of every human being who prefers her service, and only begs that she will not seek to weaken our power for good, but show her faith by her works and co-operate side by side in putting down the disorder and lawlessness which all regard as a common evil.

(*c*)

ANGLICAN TREASON

The seekers after formal external union play the part of the Jacobites, who said; "Box it about, it will come to my father;" meaning, that if only they could keep the country sufficiently unquiet, men would in sheer disgust recall the Stuarts. The Church is evil spoken of because, as Father Lockhart says, p. xv., "The leaders of the party are doing a work which, humanly speaking, could be done in no other way—teaching with all the prestige of their position nearly every Catholic doctrine, and celebrating what they believe to be the Mass; and multitudes are learning from them what, on account of early prejudice, they would not accept from avowed Romanists."

(*d*)

THE TRUE CHURCH AND CIVILIZATION

But to return to the crumb of advice to be found in the volume. The elevation of the intellect and purification of the heart of mankind, and especially the creation of the new Christian civilization, is a mark of the true Church. Is this work a characteristic distinction of the chair of Peter? The "congeries of heresies and schisms which make up the Evangelical Protestantism of Prussia," or the 999 parts which are not Catholic, of the literature of England, whose Church "is not the Catholic Church, nor any part of it, nor in any divine and true sense a Church at all," are these parts of that civilized world witnessing to the Church? Are Spain and Austria, or the Irish and Italian poor, compared with whose "vividness and intuitive quickness the intelligence of the English is so inert and tardy," are they the pioneers of progress. Or is Lord Macaulay's opinion true: "that the North owes its great civilization and prosperity chiefly to the moral effect of the Protestant Reformation; and that the decay of the southern countries of Europe is to be mainly ascribed to the great Catholic revival." Still it may be equally true that "no Catholic desires to see it swept away by an infidel revolution such as that of 1789 in France."

(*e*)

THE ROMISH CHURCH AND CIVILIZATION

Most surely we trust that no Protestant Church will ever neglect the condition and earn the hatred of the masses so as to run any risk of being swept away by such a wild stream of passion as can only be when every high and ennobling sentiment has been crushed in the heart of man, such as the unrivalled sway of Holy Church had let grow up in France. Such as that public opinion which glories in the assassination of feeble old men in Ireland, such as periodically steeps in blood the States which Roman Catholic nations have planted in America.

We trust that if we give up our stewardship, we shall have the gratitude and respect for real work done to which the Cardinal bears such hearty and eloquent tribute.

(*f*)

PROTESTANTISM AND REFORM

How a Protestant training disposes men to reform was seen in Scotland, when the dissatisfaction with the existing arrangements became so strong that they established a Free Church. They destroyed nothing, they took nothing from those who had any legal title. Without riot or clamours they reconstructed everything, and destroyed nothing. Compare this fruit of three centuries of Protestantism with the passions which marked the close of the period during which the Catholic priesthood had professed to teach the same nation, and measure the difference of the moral training. Is that the vine of God which was planted in the land for the centuries before that the passions of men swept away the Roman Church, and that the mere bramble which has borne such fruits of soberness and justice? The actors in the tumults of the Reformation were not those whose hearts the study of Scripture had touched, but the ambitious and covetous, whom the Church had totally failed to Christianize.

(*g*)

Churches, Union of the, etc.—*continued.*

Rome and Reform

Of course, when the appeal is made to the sword, the passions of men will ever work violence and evil. But in one country appeal is made to greater principles, and hope of reunion in peace and love as brothers united throughout the broad land ever held out to the vanquished; whilst in others men fight as wild beasts, knowing their sole hope of safety lies in the extermination of their rivals. Most true it is, that it is a mark of Christianity, that under it alone has civilization been possible, for that it has taught men to give freely from their abundance and their penury alike to succour the less fortunate, instead of reducing them to despair and violence; and even in the moment of victory to forbear to take full advantage of their strength, but exercise sentiments of mercy and pity to the fallen. But it is well that statesmen of all creeds and of no creed should remember that the chair of Peter has never spared an enemy, and that it is totally unfitted to civilize the masses; but that when the restraints of police or foreign bayonets are withdrawn, the living population, among whom the Church has celebrated its worship, and been supported for its ministry for the souls of the dead, have displayed the untouched and untamed nature of the savage.

(a)

The Rivalry in Good Works

The Catholic Church may be provoked into activity even in works of godliness, when, as in England, the public opinion which Protestantism has formed makes a rivalry in these, a rivalry for power; contact with Reformers led to a counter reformation within the Church, but of itself it is a law of ordinances which do not even appeal to, much less purify, the heart of man.

In quiet times and days of ignorance, before men wake to think of these things, the formal acts of worship may satisfy men; but if man is once freed from authority, and even God Himself will not constrain men to serve Him, a religion which its most zealous advocates admit to be corrupt,—such religion as this can do nothing in England. "A people's religion is ever a corrupt religion, in spite of the provisions of Holy Church." Our countrymen report from abroad "a high grand faith and worship which compels their admiration, and puerile absurdities among the people which excite their contempt."—*Newman to Pusey.*

(b)

The Anglican Church

The Cardinal sums up of the Anglican Church. "It is a human institution, sustained as it was founded by a human authority, without priesthood, without sacraments, without absolution, without the Real Presence of Jesus on its altars."

But in the sense in which he uses these hard words, I do not believe that any single one of them was intended by God to be in any visible society. All external systems are powers that be; as the House of Commons, or even the Crown in Council are ordained of God. God may use any system to do His work, but He has put no mark of exclusive approval on any.

(c)

Personal Religion

I believe in the personal work of God dealing individually with each human soul. Not that God has appointed a vicar or set up any self-acting machinery.

The growth of personal religion in the soul is a miracle, greater than any of the visible works which Christ showed, so far surpassing all means employed that we are compelled to recognise God's hand. But the growth of the temporal powers and visible Church has been the work of human agents and human passions over which the friendly historian would only too gladly draw the veil of a discreet silence; and it is sheer idolatry to exalt human persons and human systems into Divine honour sitting in the place of God. For it seems strictly true that Roman Catholics do find in Mary that large heart of love and human sympathy which is the glory of the Son, and in the voice of the earthly visible Church, that perpetual counsel and strength which we have through the indwelling of the Holy Spirit in each of us.

(d)

Mariolatry

Dr. Newman speaks clearly enough of Mary, and his words have not the fervour of a southern worshipper but the calm measured judgment of an educated Englishman. "He who charges us with making Mary a divinity, is thereby denying the divinity of Jesus. Such a man does not know what divinity is. Our Lord cannot pray for us as a creature, as Mary prays; He cannot inspire those feelings which a creature inspires. To her belongs, as being a creature, a natural claim on our sympathy and familiarity, in that she is nothing else than our fellow. She is our pride. In the poet's words, 'Our tainted nature's solitary boast.' We look to her without any fear, any remorse, any consciousness that she is able to read us, judge us, punish us."

Now, in the first place, since, according to the same writer, our every prayer must pass through the mind of God, and be by Him communicated to the saint who is to be our advocate, it is hard to see that fear can be cast out, any more than if we prayed to God alone. But surely this is the very picture of Jesus,—as strong only to strike, as knowing our thoughts only to judge, as gifted with all power only to exact penance,—which made Luther in his convent cell hate the thought of Jesus; but which a knowledge how He has suffered, and for us, constrains us to cast aside.

(e)

Mariolatry

We do not envy any man the privilege which we read springs from worship of Mary, that when he kneels in prayer he can put away from his consciousness that mind of God towards sin, that sense of the reality and justice of God's condemnation of it, which was the mind of Jesus when He felt for the sins of His brethren, which must be our mind, when we would, in sorrow for our own, share the fellowship of His sufferings. We do not wish that our prayers should be heard where that other larger mind does not look us through and through. Perfect love casts out the fear that there is any limit to the tender sympathy of God. Nor do we need to fall back on a human

(f)

Churches, Union of the, etc.—*continued*

heart, that image of His love that He Himself has made. We must not be told that He has entered into our flesh, and after all neither knows nor sympathizes with our infirmities. It seems that this new divinity is set up exactly in the centre of those loves which God Himself took flesh to meet; that this very difficulty of natural religion, which Dr. Newman feels, that no man had seen God at any time, and must necessarily feel that he is not quite at home with Him, is the precise *raison d'être* of revealed religion. That man should not fashion idols that his sense could touch, or new gods that his mind could grasp, whether Mary or Humanity. But the Son took flesh that He might declare God, that He might stamp upon human flesh that nearest image of the divine perfections that it was capable of bearing, that henceforth they who had seen our Lord's human life had seen the Father.

(*a*)

MARIOLATRY

It is a gross, carnal conception, to think of God and man meeting in Mary, or even in the flesh of our Lord through the temporal accidents of flesh and blood. It was by the human mind and affections which the Son took into Himself; and we are partakers of Him as our hearts are daily fashioned into His image. Mary is no doubt highly honoured in being the channel of bodily contact. But we no longer know Christ after the flesh. Dr. Newman represents it as the teaching of Athanasius, "That man is God and God is man, that in Mary they meet, and that in this sense ' Mary is the centre of all things.' Again he mentions that Irenæus bestows on her the special name and office proper to the Holy Ghost. Now this may or may not fairly represent these Fathers, but at all events it is the way in which we are invited to look upon her. Dr. Newman would have us meet the difficulty of natural religion,—that no man has seen, or can see God, that His infinite holiness may well make us shrink from coming before Him who is of purer eyes than to be satisfied with our works,—not by the scriptural doctrine, that God Himself tabernacling among us has shown the Father, and patterned in human life all it can follow or admire, and the recollection that the dear Son of His love felt every innocent human weakness and sorrowed for every human sin, is a reconciling of the world, so that God accepts the imperfect walk of those who seek to tread in the footsteps of the well-pleasing man; but by a doctrine which he professes to found on references to patristic authority —a shaping out by human fancy, without one shadow of historical reality, an idol of the imagination, clothed with some of the attributes of the Incarnate God, and calling her the Blessed Virgin Mary. He transfers to her that confidence in a sympathizing friend which is the very principal act of worship which Jesus calls for from us. And in place of the Divine Comforter whom the Saviour has sent forth to work in every heart,—so that every man should be taught of God, and He dwell even among His enemies,—Dr. Manning would have us blindly submit reason and conscience, the pleadings of the Spirit within us, to this voice of the present Church, whose kingdom is of this world.

(*b*)

ROME, HURTFUL

And thus, themselves being witnesses, the activity of the Romanist party has the most hurtful influence in religious matters. The legitimate work of the members of Christ in England, which seemed to be really overtaking the irreligion of the world, has been during the last thirty years arrested by earnest-minded men's thoughts being drawn off to a study of the claims of the chair of Peter. God gives no light, no further grace to men who are absorbed in questions so far removed from the primary truths of religion and conscience. By the Archbishop's confession, the result has been that religion has fallen into public contempt, and justly so; for while the clergy are seen frittering their energies and hindering each other for differences about postures and dresses, or strifes who shall sit on thrones, no one who standeth by can avoid the taunt, that there can be nothing in that which they profess to hold in common. No mind fully realizing those Catholic verities which have been held everywhere and always by the members of Christ, who are that true Church by which His glory is set in sight of men, would hinder those who did mighty works in the Saviour's name because they follow not Peter. He would rejoice with the Apostle that any way Christ was preached in the world; he would remember how St. Paul condemns the parties at Corinth, not because one looked to the chair of Cephas, another professed to hear Christ alone, but because they thought their special chiefs and special developments of doctrine a ground of separation, more important than their one common faith that Jesus was Messiah and Jehovah was a bond of charity, a common foundation upon which it was the responsibility of each for himself to look to it what he built. The Apostle could be without law at one time, and at another, a Jew to win the Jews. Respecting the sincere minds of those who took pleasure in the full rites of the old temple, his zeal was only moved when they tried to enforce the same bondage on others. He never would labour where another had planted a Church already, creeping in and sowing dissensions in an already christian land, and perverting their minds with unhealthy jangling on points not essential, for " the infallible authority of the Church does not of necessity enter into the essence of an act of faith." Whilst " the last article of the creed which enters, and that slowly, and for a long time painfully, into the English intelligence, is the nature and office of the Church." Then surely a rational man who was earnestly bent to bring Englishmen to the feet of Jesus, would not insist upon their first accepting, before every other, this unessential and to them most repulsive belief.

(*c*)

THE WORD " CHURCH "

And in truth it is the use or abuse of this word "Church," which is the root of every difference between us. It is a little word, but one which the Cardinal uses oftener in a page, than the New Testament in all the Gospels; and among the many various senses that have been attached to this word, it may mean a visible external organized society, united in observance of certain acts of worship, professing obedience to a recognised superior. But it may mean those who, with less

(*d*)

Churches, Union of the, etc.—*continued*

of visible external connection, are the called of God in every place and age. The belief that God specially organized an institution among men,—in a word, that Jesus came to set up a kingdom of this world, and perpetually teaches through its visible agency,—is sufficiently clear and precise. But it is an equally intelligible belief, that all the visible external forms are of human setting up, local attempts to realize before men the eternal fellowship and communion in which the saints are united before God. And how are we to decide between these two ideas of the Church of God? If we compare them with the Cardinal's own marks, we find that the Roman Church had no existence whilst the first great strides were being made, and the Gospel spread from Jerusalem through all lands. Refusing to be in communion with many nations who call on the same Lord, that it has endeavoured and is endeavouring to fetter intellect and progress, as destructive of its claims and incompatible with its existence. That nations most denounced by it are the most progressive leaders of civilization. That it is ever adding new developments to the faith. That Kings and worldly-minded Popes have by turns guided its policy, that it has been scandalously and notoriously divided by rival Popes. And it is a "mystery that the Church is not universal." That its martyrs probably fall short of those whom its tribunals have martyrized in single years. That wickedness and corruption have at times made its courts a hell upon earth. That the name of religion has been evil spoken of among men, because of the notorious worldliness and profligacy of its chief professors; and that the sure fruits of holy life are often conspicuous among those whom it denounces as its worst opposers. The leavening influence of Christianity has worked through it in countless instances to God's glory. But the creeds of Mahomet and M. Comte also owe all that is of good in them to the light which Christ brought into the world, and might as well claim to be the exclusive channels of God's grace. On the other hand, the civilized world is conterminous with those nations who unite to call one God their Father, trust in, and follow one Lord; are baptized with one Baptism, to the graces of one Spirit. Christ's teaching has so prevailed that the most cultivated men talk sometimes as if morality and benevolence were so recognised to be the law of life, that Christianity, which has worked this good, could now be discarded as having done its work. That we may kick away the ladder by which our present elevation has been gained, instead of helping the millions of our fellow-creatures who are still toiling up. That churches, hospitals, and schools cover every Christian land, and mercy to the vanquished, liberality to the distressed, make permanent and progressive civilization possible in Protestant countries also. And that among all who everywhere believe that Jesus is the Messiah come in the flesh, the one law of love has ever been the one service of all His saints, whose bond of union has been personal loyalty to the author and perfecter of our faith, in every confession of faith and every rival communion. I find no single mark of the Church of God limited to one single communion.

(*a*)

The Gospel and the Poor

When our Saviour recounted the signs of His mission, he added as the last, that His gospel was preached to the poor, for the Spirit would be on all flesh, on slaves and hand-maidens, that all from the least to the greatest, all might know the Lord; for that is not the gift of God which is not plain for the common labourer to read whilst he runs about his daily toil. But Dr. Newman himself witnesses that Holy Church can only provide a corrupt religion, loaded with puerile absurdities, for the masses; but if so, do let him pause before, merely to make room for the chance of a Roman Church, he labours to destroy a system which, by the Cardinal's testimony, in thirty years so far changed the face of society that they were perhaps only too much followed and respected, till the Oxford movement gave that new direction which has resulted in a society without faith.

(*b*)

Testimony of J. S. Mill

But that the home study of Scripture and the Puritan theology are living forces tending to practical godliness, let us hear Mr. J. S. Mill. "In those Protestant countries, accordingly, whose Churches were not, as the Church of England always was, principally political institutions,—in Scotland, for instance, and the New England States,—an amount of education was carried down to the poorest of the people, of which there is no other example. Every peasant expounded the Bible to his family (many to their neighbours). We cannot be blind to the sharpening and strengthening exercise which such great topics gave to the understanding. One of the consequences of which was, the privilege long enjoyed of supplying the greater part of Europe with professors for its universities, and educated and skilled workmen for its practical arts." (*Essay on Comte*, p. 113.)

(*c*)

Testimony of Macaulay

Such is the influence of the study of Scripture in education. Lord Macaulay (i. 154) points out the practical fruits of Puritan theology. "Fifty thousand men accustomed to the profession of arms, were at once thrown on the world; and experience would warrant the belief that the change would produce much misery and crime, that the discharged veterans would be seen begging in every street, or that they would be driven by hunger to pillage. But no such results followed. The Royalists themselves confessed, that in every department of honest industry, the discarded warriors prospered beyond other men. That none was charged with any theft or robbery, that none was heard to ask an alms, and that if a baker, a mason, or a waggoner attracted notice by his diligence and sobriety, he was in all probability one of Oliver's old soldiers."

(*d*)

The True Church

It must be something more than a thing of names and words which has attracted the notice of three such very different witnesses; and even those who have sworn allegiance to the chair of

(*e*)

Churches, Union of the, etc.—*continued*

Peter, may consider whether it would not be a sacrifice of pride and credit clearly required of them, to listen to those sharp twinges of conscience which it is their merit to stifle, and obey that clear light of reason which they profess to submit to the authority of the Church's organs, and hold their hands from weakening the hold upon the country of a faith, not of dogma, or of ritual, but where the poor and unlearned are taught to be rulers of themselves, priests offering the reasonable services of pure and holy bodies, in which no human mediator steps between God and the lowly and contrite souls of His brethren whom He has loved. The service of love and kindness in every thought and deed to all around, this alone is Christianity, or the following of the Incarnate God; but this the meanest peasant in his own household may present before God as readily as the greatest king or bishop; built up as lively stones on the one eternal rock; upon which St. Peter, who first confessed the Lord, was one stone, the first stone laid, of the temple which is the bodies of the Saints, which the Holy Ghost dwells in and daily builds up in every Christian land.

(*a*)

Terms of External Union

The terms on which external union with Rome is possible, or rather by which in God's providence such union has been made impossible, were laid down three hundred years ago. (p. 275.) "That they submit themselves, and will, and consent to submit to the decrees, determinations, and declarations of the said Council. But if they decline this, they ought in no wise to be heard on whatsoever point contending; . . . in that case they are to be dealt with as condemned schismatics and heretics, not as equals having equal rights with ourselves."

(*b*)

The Only Real Union

We may thank God, however, that neither things present nor things to come, neither Pope nor Council, can step between us and the love of God; the only real union is that by which every member, in every age or sect, is directly united with the only Head, whose Spirit flows down severally to each as He wills. It is a sad thing that men who profess to be members of the one Lord, praying to one Father, sanctified by one Baptism, should seek each to destroy what the other builds up. As an historian says, "It is amongst the mysteries of Divine providence, that holy men in this life have to suffer sometimes in a cause which, although by themselves accounted good, is by brethren equally honest, branded as evil; and thus there comes to be, in ecclesiastical conflicts, so much pain at once conscientiously inflicted and conscientiously endured. No calm thinker can fail to discern the anomaly, and no loving heart but must long for that blessed future when the fruits of such strange discipline will be reaped by souls now divided on earth, but who will then be united in heaven, amidst the purest charity and the humblest joy.

(*c*)

External Union Undesirable

But it is our sins, our ignorance, which defer our being led into the rest prepared by God. Now is the day of salvation; the kingdom of God is already in our reach. The uniting of the limbs of Christ by an outward connection, is no more desirable than possible, if we will learn the parable of the natural body, the last of created works, in which are clearly seen the glory of the invisible, the mystical body of members through which Christ lives and works among men. The unity of the hand is, that every finger separately acts to work out the designs of the head; each may wear its own dress so long as it is united in faithful obedience to the one source of life. It is through the apparent opposition of one that the five fingers are perfected.

If we will only believe, the great designs of the head are perfected by the faithful service and willing obedience of every part minding its own work, and trusting to the head to utilize the work and correct the mistakes of others; and the duty of each one is not to be anxious that all should be the same length, or move just in the same way, but to trust the head to profit by their diverse operations.

The desire for visible external unity and communion, instead of being satisfied that every servant of God is in direct union in the lifegiving Saviour, whose every working limb is directly filled with life flowing into it from the great Head, retards all real Christian work by devoting energy and thought to a mere minor point of Church organization.

(*d*)

Wasted Energies

The refusal to accept the Reformation and the Protestant Churches as accomplished facts in God's order, by which any way Christ is preached, causes that (to quote another Roman witness, Mr. Oxenham, p. 68), "The religious energies of Christendom are frittered away on the pitiful but pressing exigencies of internal struggle and defence; p. 69. Twice the energy has been exhausted in contending with Protestants that might have won the irreligious, and cut up the roots of unbelief. Closely connected is the temper and line of action it creates and fosters. p. 70. It controls our whole religious ἦθος, shapes our policy, colours our literature, regulates our charities, limits our sense of justice, rearranges our standard of veracity, almost articulates our prayers." English Churchmen fall into the same error when they will not be friends with Nonconformists.

(*e*)

Name of Jesus

The minor character of the questions in dispute is shown by Dr. Newman, who has published 500 pages of history of his religious opinions, without once mentioning the name of Jesus. The only explanation is, that all his changes have never affected the way in which he regards the Saviour. But if Rome hath nothing to teach us about Jesus, this is all I contend for, that a Protestant may be as true a follower of Jesus; men's minds forget the truth as it is in Jesus which alone can draw all men to Him, whilst blown about and jangling on minor matters. The words of this writer

(*f*)

Churches, Union of the, etc.—*continued*

which speak of our common faith are above praise from me; but all that he has of good he owes to early Anglican training, and is no whit the better for his Roman development.

(*a*)

LOVE AS BRETHREN

If we would only believe-

The final purpose of Revelation is Love

Not dogma, not ritual, not Church government; these things have no value of their own, they are means which may produce the desired end. If we would live and let live, leaving disputes on such points as mischief still for idle hands to do, and be assured that Christ did not die to win for us the privilege of eating of the fruit of the tree of knowledge and theological definition; but He sends all who love Him to be in the world as He was in the world when sent by the Father, caring only that we should manifest His character by practical action, by hands quick to do good and feet unwearied in doing His work, as He manifested the Father, caring only that those brethren whom each can see should love one another as they have Christ for an example. The union of all Christian hearts, which alone are God's kingdom among us, is accomplished by each being immediately united with the one only Head, the Shepherd and Bishop of souls, the Man Christ Jesus, who till the end of the world is ever really present in every loving heart.

(*b*)   *Brandreth*

CIRCUMCISION AND UNCIRCUMCISION

"*For in Christ Jesus neither circumcision availeth anything, nor uncircumcision; but a new creature* (Gal. vi. 15).

1. That which is NOTHING in Christianity.
= *Neither circumcision nor uncircumcision.*
= Jew and Gentile.
= Denominationalism.

Observe :
(i.) The Galatians had received the Gospel eagerly : impulsive and changeable people. When St. Paul had gone, new teachers, wolves came in, and scattered the flock. Those taught "*Ye must become Jews, legally ;* for *unless ye be circumcised Christ shall profit you nothing.*" = God's promises are made to the Jews. Therefore, if ye would be safe, ye must come into the Jewish fold.

(ii.) St. Paul's refutation of this *absurdity :*— His teaching hereon is of great moment at such times when, as now, *party spirit* runs strong, and we are asked to ally ourselves with this or that party as an *essential step.* He reminds them that as Christians they had become possessed of certain privileges.

(*a*) They had become the children of God : "*Because ye are sons, God hath sent forth,*" etc. How did they attain to this great privilege?
"Ye are all the children of God by FAITH IN JESUS CHRIST" (not by a legal rite).

(*b*) They had been justified, but how?
"A man is justified by the FAITH OF JESUS CHRIST, not by the works of the law."

(*c*) They had received the Gift of the Holy Ghost—*the* promise of the New Testament.

But how?
"Received ye the Spirit by the works of the law, or by the hearing of FAITH?
(*d*) God had removed the old barriers and distinctions between Jew and Gentile; such exist no longer; men are now *Believers* or *Unbelievers.*
But how was this done?
"In Christ Jesus there is neither Jew nor Greek ; neither circumcision, nor uncircumcision ; *ye are all* ONE *in Christ, who hath made* BOTH ONE."
Now, he asks, being in possession of such privileges—"*after ye have known God,*" will ye erect the old barriers of separation between man and man, and say, "Ye must come on this side if ye would be safe?" This is to go back to the days of your childhood, pupilage, and to your A, B, C, to the spirit of fear and bondage, and to your old ignorance of the love of God. PREPOSTEROUS! "I am afraid of you lest I have preached in vain."

2. But lest, on the other hand, the Gentile might rejoice over the Jew, and say, "Not so; *but ye must become uncircumcised.*"
The question is represented as having two sides. These are opposite poles, and both equally dangerous:
"*Circumcision is nothing*, and *uncircumcision is nothing.*"
Illustrate by Scylla and Charybdis; rocks on one hand, and a whirlpool on the other. The question is, how to steer past Scylla so as not to fall into Charybdis-.
In Reformations this danger has often occurred. In leaving a corrupt Church, some have fallen into opposite errors; and so, by going too far east, they have gone west.
Hence the Apostle's teaching is, that Denominationalism, religious sects and party distinctions in the Church are NOTHING, because *non-essential.* They may have their uses, but they do not touch the real thing.

3. That which is EVERYTHING—or that which *availeth*, is a NEW CREATURE. (*See.*)
This is the essential thing in Religion-
Your Nationality counts for nothing ;
Your Religious Party counts for nothing.
Your Sect or Denomination counts for nothing ;
Your Church Membership counts for nothing;
The facts of your having been baptized, or of being a communicant, though deeply significant, in themselves count for nothing-
But a NEW CREATURE is *everything.* And when, by God's grace, we get to heaven, we shall see men come from the east and from the west, from the north and from the south. From all Sects, Parties, Churches, and they shall sit down with Abraham, Isaac, and Jacob in the Kingdom of Heaven; whilst many, perhaps, who thought themselves legally secure may be thrust out.

(*c*)   *Vide a sermon by Dr. Maclaren*

CITIZENSHIP, our, is in Heaven (Phil. iii. 20)

Imagine a fellow-countryman of ours, a born-and-bred Englishman, possessing all the instincts of an English gentleman, settled for a time amongst some one of the tribes of Central Africa. He witnesses their revolting customs, gross immorality, drunken orgies, bloodshed, and cruelty ; the very atmosphere teems with the shrieks of the dying, and the soil is sodden with their blood, shed

(*d*)

like water by the tyrants who rule over them. He is asked by these people to partake in their customs, to live as they do, to make himself one with them—to form alliances, to associate, eat, drink, buy, and sell as they do. In fact, to erase his own nationality, and to identify himself with the people in whose country he finds himself. Imagine this; and what would be his indignant reply. It would be this: "I am an Englishman—a citizen of no mean city, a member of the dominant Anglo-Saxon race, whose mission it is to Christianize the world. I have pleasures that you know not of; cultivated tastes, habits, customs, and rules for the guidance of my life, as far removed from yours as the heaven is from the earth. There is a great gulf between us. I cannot degrade myself to your level; I cannot, being what I am, live as you live and do as you do. Such, in effect, would be his reply. So, too, the Christian, finding himself for a time living in this world, as in a dark place; where other gods are worshipped; where men sell themselves for gain; where he is tempted to do as others do, and is asked to coquette with the world; to do all, no matter what, not to the glory of God, but for other ends—to "mind earthly things"—to act unworthily of his vocation, would reply, "I cannot; I am a citizen of heaven; my affections are set on things above; I cannot come down to your level; I have come out from the world, and may not touch the unclean thing; I have formed other tastes, have other pleasures, other rules regulate my conduct; I cannot live as you live, nor do as you do."

(a)

CITIZENSHIP

It is quite a mistake to suppose that the Greeks or the Romans were ever *civilized*, in the full meaning of the phrase. They were only *polished*.

(b)   *Dr. Marsh*

"CLEANSE" . . . "PURIFY" (1 John i. 7; iii. 3)

Indicate Christian *privilege* and Christian *habit*. Note the antitheses: The spheres of light and darkness. The 1st passage-
=Christians are members of the Kingdom of Light, where the privileges are-
1. One family.
2. Who live in an atmosphere of forgiveness, for whom a Great High Priest appears in the presence of God, continually and actively engaged in their behalf (compare Col. i. 13, 14).
2nd passage.
=Beyond this, which is the privilege of all the family alike, we are what we make ourselves, by the proper use of the means of grace; and our unknown position and work in the future kingdom will be the result of *self-denial, hardness, faithfulness*, gifts *added to*; judged according to *works*, whether we shall be *vessels of honour*, etc., depends upon our *habit* of purifying ourselves now (*i.e.* living a holy life).
Compare St. Paul's "If by any means I might attain to the resurrection from the dead."
=The *prize* of the high calling of God in Christ Jesus is for them that *win* it.
(c)

CLERGY, THE

Who was to blame for it? (that the clergy had lost their hold of the people). The clergy of the 18th century, so many of whom were neither Christians nor gentlemen; and the clergy of the present century, because so many of them are nothing but gentlemen—men, ignorant of life, of human needs, of human temptations, yea of human aspiration. Because in the city-pulpits their voice is not uplifted against city vices—against speculation, falsehood, money-lending, dishonesty, selfishness. Because elsewhere their voices are not uplifted against the worship of money, rank, and equipage; against false shows in dress and scenery; against buying and not paying; against envy and emulation; against effeminacy and mannishness; against a morality which consists in discretion. . . . One half of Christendom is so intent upon saving souls, instead of doing its duty, that the other half think it all humbug.
(d)   *Geo. Macdonald*

CLERGY (1 Pet. v. 3)

It is erroneous to expound κλῆρος as denoting the clergy in orders.
(e)   *Lange.*

κλῆροι=the faithful people of Christ, distributed in regular order into various dioceses, parishes, churches, and congregations, like the companies to which our Lord distributed the loaves and fishes by the hands of the apostles.
(f)   *Wordsworth*

All believers are God's clergy
(g)   *Leighton*

The clergy are the class which God has appointed to unite all others; which, in as far as it fulfils its calling, and is indeed a priesthood, is above and below all rank, and knows no man after the flesh, but only on the ground of his spiritual work and his birthright in that kingdom which is the heritage of all.
(h)   *C. Kingsley*

CLERGYMEN

S. T. Coleridge said, that the state of religion, when he was in Germany, was really shocking. He had never met one clergyman a Christian; and he found professors in the Universities lecturing against the most material points in the Gospel (*e.g.* Paulus, whose lectures he attended). The object was to resolve the miracles into natural operations; and such a disposition evinced was the best road to preferment.
(i)   *Table Talk*

CLOKE (2 Tim. iv. 13)

"*The cloke that I left at Troas with Carpus, when thou comest, bring with thee, and the books, but especially the parchments.*" And who, as he reads this last message, can help remembering the touching letter written from the damp cells of his prison by our noble martyr, William Tyndale, one of the greatest of our translators of the English Bible: "I entreat your lordship," he writes, "and
(j)

that by the Lord Jesus, that, if I was to remain here for the winter, you would beg the Commissary to be so kind as to send me from the things of mine which he has, a warmer cap; I feel the cold painfully in my head; also a warmer cloke, for the one I have is very thin; also some cloth to patch my leggings. My overcoat is worn out, my shirts even are threadbare. The Commissary has a woollen shirt of mine, if he will be so kind as to send it. But most of all I entreat your kindness to do your best with the Commissary to be so good as to send me my Hebrew Bible, grammar, and vocabulary, that I may spend my time in that pursuit.—WILLIAM TYNDALE." The noble martyr was not thinking of St. Paul; but history repeats itself, and what is this fragment from the letter which he, too, wrote so soon before his death, but the same thing as, "*The cloke which I left at Troas with Carpus, bring with thee, and the books, but especially the parchments*"?

(*a*) *Archdn. Farrar*

CLOUD

Every cloud has a silver lining.
Believe, and fear not! in the blackest cloud
A sunbeam hides; and from the deepest pang
Some hidden mercy may a God declare.

(*b*) *R. Montgomery*

COCK-CROWING

Jesus shows that the cock, even, does not crow at hap-hazard, but that God is able, in His economy, to make use of his outcry as a good domestic medicine—as at this time, when He had to preach repentance to the first apostle.

(*c*) *Lange*

COLOSSIANS, EPISTLE TO THE

Compared with that to the Ephesians. Here *Christ's Person* is more prominent than Christ's Body.

In contrast with the Universalism of the Epistle to the Ephesians, there prevails here a *Monism*.

The Person of Christ, again and again, and this *exclusively*. Hence, instead of

"*The word of God*" (i. 25; Rom. ix. 6; 1 Cor. xiv. 36; 2 Cor. ii. 17; iv. 2), or,
"*Of the Lord*" (1 Thes. i. 18),
"*Of truth*" (i. 5),
"*Of wisdom*," "*of knowledge*" (1 Cor. xii. 8),
"*Of the cross*" (1 Cor. i. 18),
"*Of reconciliation*" (2 Cor. v. 19),
We find here alone (iii. 16),
"*The word of Christ*."

The epistle is thoroughly *Christological;* Christ's Person is the Lord of Eternity, ruling heaven and earth, the visible and invisible (i. 14–16, 19; ii. 9), who by entering into our race and the history of humanity (i. 18) has reconciled all things and all classes to God (i. 20, 21), has so spanned all centuries of development, that out of Him and before Him even the highest mental culture and noblest morality are but rudiments, elements of the world which pass away (ii. 8); in Him are given *peace* (i. 20), *life* (i. 18; ii. 13; iii. 1–3), *salvation* and *bliss* (i. 22; iii. 4), likewise all virtue (iii. 5–14) in all the moral relations of life (iii. 4; iv. 1); and this is done by the ethical

method of *faith* (i. 23; ii. 13), in obedience to His word (iii. 16), in vital fellowship with Him (ii. 11–15; iii. 1–4), and in prayer (iv. 2), so that Christ FOR us becomes Christ IN us (ii. 13–15; iii. 3, 4).

(*d*) *Lange*

"COME UNTO ME, all . . . rest," etc. (Matt. xi. 28–30)

Connection with preceding (20) reveals *failure* of our Lord's ministry: The wise and prudent rejected Christ.

Under similar circumstances in O. T. :
(i.) *Elijah*, despondingly said, "I have been very jealous . . . and they seek my life to take it away."
(ii.) *Isaiah* = "Who hath believed our report?"
The late veteran missionary, *Dr. Moffat*, spake to "hearts of granite."
(iii.) We all despair of success, and complain that the tide of worldliness and indifference is too strong for us. But-
(iv.) *Jesus* (25) *acquiesces*. "For at that time Jesus answered and said, I thank Thee, O Father, Lord of heaven and earth, because Thou hast hid these things from the wise and prudent, and hast revealed them unto babes. Even so, Father; for so it seemed good in Thy sight."

The worldly heart rejects; but the humble heart opens to Christ and His word, and receives His invitation with joy.

Then follows a hint (27) to the *wise* of this world as to the impossibility of knowing God without Christ.

For the peculiar mission of the Son, was to reveal *The Father*.

There are those, however, who are disposed to accept His message; these are the "babes," "the poor in spirit," whom He invites, "Come unto Me." "To them the porter openeth." Jesus has the *key* of knowledge, and will teach them the true wisdom. Consider-

1. The Invitation

To those who "*labour*" with heavy toil, and are *fatigued*, because their toil is fruitless. How many have thought *life not worth living*, because of this fruitlessness! Yet this sense of FAILURE is the very first step in the spiritual life :
(i.) You must *fail*, and be worn out with your own efforts towards your salvation—be humbled—before you will accept Christ's invitation.
(ii.) He is your last resort : you would not come to Him if you could do without Him.
(*a.*) *The Prodigal Son* did not return till necessity compelled him.
(*b.*) "*The whole need not a physician, but they that are sick.*"
So we have to wait until we have nothing else to turn to—till we are sick, perhaps dying—till we have found out that we cannot help ourselves, before we come to Jesus.
(i.) Broken with labour; wearied with burdens; wretched.
(ii.) Till the world has mocked us; and health is gone.
(iii.) Broken in fortune, deluded, humbled by sense of *failure* and of sinfulness, before we accept this invitation. It has ever been so.

2. The Promise : "Rest" = satisfaction—content.

The physician prescribes *rest* to the overworked

(*e*)

man. So Jesus goes straight to what we want; to the root of what is amiss, and promises relief.

He sees our fruitless toil—that we are unsatisfied in our many labours—weary of them, and says—

(i.) You have tried the world's husks, and found no "rest"—satisfaction in them.

(ii.) You have tried to find rest by your own works, and have found none; peace of conscience is as far off as ever. Now cease from your own works henceforth, and—

(iii.) TRY ME: I can satisfy your soul's need = "*I am the Bread* of life; of which if a man eat he shall never hunger."

3. The Secret of Rest

It is the opposite of *unrest*, which comes from dissatisfaction, and discontent with our lot in life. We think we should be more useful elsewhere, and in some other field of work. Now—

"*Learn of Me*" . . . "Let this mind be in you, which was in Christ Jesus"—I am always at *rest*, at peace, never troubled. [Yet I, the Son of God, am here in a humble condition—I am made of no reputation—a worm and no man; as a man, I take the lowest position, and become obedient unto a slave's—a criminal's death.] "*I am content to do it*," because it is My Father's appointment. I do not chafe against My yoke— I make it *easy* by submitting to it—therefore it does not hurt Me. Humility is never offended and disappointed, whilst pride is. Do the same. Learn of me, be content with your lot and sphere in life, (for you come not to it by accident; the cross in it was laid upon you by your Heavenly Father, it will do you good,) *and ye shall find rest unto your souls.*

(a)

"COME UNTO ME" (John vii. 37, 38)

"If any man thirst, let him *Come unto Me*." If any one wants living satisfying water, let him come unto ME.

No prophet or apostle ever took on himself to use such language as this. "Come with us," said Moses to Hobab (Num. x. 29); "Come to the waters," says Isaiah (Isa. lv. 1); "Behold the Lamb," says John the Baptist (John i. 29); "Believe on the Lord Jesus Christ," says St. Paul (Acts xvi. 31). But no one except Jesus of Nazareth ever said, "Come to Me." That fact is very significant.

(b)   *Bishop Ryle.*

[John vi. 37

Every one who *comes* to Him is *welcome*. The only criterion is the coming or the not coming; no matter what the previous condition or guiltiness.

(c)   *Lange*

"COME OUT OF HER, MY PEOPLE" (Rev. xviii. 4)

Babylon = a corrupt semi-religious worldly power. The lines of demarcation indistinct. The world and the Church overlap and intermingle. At such times notice three things:—

1. An Apostasy;
2. Approaching Judgment;
3. A calling out of the few for whom the world exists: "Come out;" "Be separate;" "Let there be a clearly defined line of demarcation between you and the world."

N.B.—The number *seven*, as used in the Bible, denotes *completion*:

Seven days of Genesis;
Seven circuits of Jericho;
Seven in book of Daniel;
Seven in book of Revelation;
Seven parables in Matt. xiii.

Now the judgment threatened in the text is the seventh of a series of similar ones, in each of which *Apostasy, Judgment,* and *Calling out* are main features.

There are seven great epochs of the Church:—

1. **The Antediluvian** (Gen. vi. 2–12).
   (i.) Apostasy of the race,
   (ii.) The Deluge threatened,
   (iii.) "Come out of her, my people" = Noah.

2. **The Noachic** (Josh. xxiv. 2).
   (i.) The apostasy into idolatry,
   (ii.) The rejection of the Canaanites.
   (iii.) "Come out" = the call of Abraham.

3. **The Patriarchial** (Ezek. xx. 8).
   (i.) Idolatry in Egypt,
   (ii.) Egyptian oppression,
   (iii.) "Come out" = The Exodus.

4. **The Mosaic** (1 Sam. ii. 3).
   (i.) Idolatry of Astoreth,
   (ii.) Ichabod,
   (iii.) Mizpeh (1 Sam. vii.) = "Come out," from Philistines.

5. **The Kingly.**
   (i.) Idolatry,
   (ii.) Babylonian captivity,
   (iii.) "Come out" (not to all) at the return.

6. **The Restoration.**
   (i.) Alliance between High Priest, Herod, and Pontius Pilate,
   (ii.) The destruction of Jerusalem,
   (iii.) "Come out" = Pella.
   N.B.—The new order is always based upon those who "come out."

7. **The Existing Epoch.**
   (i.) Does apostasy exist?
   (ii.) Judgment threatened when the Church and world overlap, and the former has lost lines of demarcation.
   (iii.) "Come out of her, my people" = a new order of things, "all things become new."

As it has been before, so will it be again: an apostate Church is threatened with judgment; but before that is inflicted, the servants of God are made safe.

(d)

COMFORT

"Knowing the terrors of the Lord, we persuade men; but knowing the *comforts* too, we importune men to this consideration, that as He has accepted us, . . . so He will bring us with comfort to that place so pathetically described by the tongue of Paul, moved by the Holy Ghost: "*Ye are come unto Mount Sion, and unto the city of the living God, the heavenly Jerusalem, and to an innumerable company of angels, to the general assembly and Church of the firstborn, which are written in heaven, and to God . . . and to Jesus.*"

(e)   *Donne*

COMFORTER, THE (John. xiv.)

Whom the devil tries to terrify and dispirit, Christ comforts ; but whom the devil lulls into security and emboldens, Christ terrifies (Jer. xvii. 9)

(a)   *Starke*

COMFORTER, THE (John xiv. 16)

A comforter is a *spiritual* helper. We have no single word co-extensive in signification.

(b)   *P. Schaff*

COMING TO CHRIST

"*In the last day, that great day of the feast, Jesus stood and cried, saying, If any man thirst, let him come unto Me, and drink. He that believeth on Me, as the Scripture hath said, out of his belly shall flow rivers of living water.*"—John vii. 37, 38.

I. One of those mighty sayings of Christ which deserve to be printed in letters of gold.

You have a case supposed. "If any man thirst." Bodily thirst is notoriously the most painful sensation to which the frame of mortal man is liable. Read the story of the miserable sufferers in the black hole at Calcutta.—Ask any one who has travelled over desert plains under a tropical sun.—Hear what any old soldier will tell you is the chief want of the wounded on a battle-field.—Remember what the survivors of the crews of ships lost in mid-ocean, like the Cospatrick, went through.—Mark the awful words of the rich man in the parable : " Send Lazarus that he may dip the tip of his finger in water to cool my tongue : for I am tormented in this flame" (Luke xvi. 24). The testimony is unvarying. There is nothing so terrible and hard to bear as thirst.

But if bodily thirst is so painful, how much more painful is thirst of soul ! To see the value of our souls, and find out they are in danger of eternal ruin,—to feel the burden of unforgiven sin, and not to know where to turn for relief,—to have a conscience sick and ill at ease, and to be ignorant of the remedy,—to discover that we are dying, and yet unprepared to meet God,—to have some clear view of our own guilt and wickedness, and yet be in utter darkness about absolution. This no doubt is the thirst of which our Lord is speaking. It is thirst after pardon, forgiveness, absolution, and peace with God.

This is the thirst the Jews felt, when Peter preached to them. "Men and brethren, what shall we do ? " (Acts ii. 37).

This is the thirst the Philippian jailor felt, when he " came trembling, and fell down before Paul and Silas, and saying, Sirs, what must I do to be saved ? " (Acts xvi. 31).

This is the thirst many of the greatest servants of God have felt, when light first broke in on their minds. Augustine seeking rest among the Manichean heretics and finding none.—Luther groping after truth among monks in Erfurt monastery,—John Bunyan agonizing amidst doubts and conflicts in his Elstow cottage,—George Whitefield groaning under self-imposed austerities, for want of clear teaching, when an undergraduate at Oxford,—all have left on record their experience. I believe they all knew what our Lord meant when he spoke of " thirst."

And surely all of us ought to know SOMETHING of this thirst. Living in a dying world,—knowing that there is a world beyond the grave, and that after death comes the judgment,—feeling what poor, weak, unstable, defective creatures we all are, and how unfit to meet God,—conscious that on our use of time depends our place in eternity, —we ought to feel and to realize something like " thirst" for a sense of peace with the living God. But alas, nothing proves so conclusively the fallen nature of man as the general want of spiritual appetite ! For money, for power, for pleasure, for rank, for honour, for distinction,—for all these the vast majority are now intensely thirsting. To lead forlorn hopes, to dig for gold, to storm a breach, to try to hew a way through thick-ribbed ice to the North Pole—for all these objects there is no lack of adventurers and volunteers. Fierce and unceasing is the competition for corruptible crowns. But few are those who thirst after eternal life. No wonder the natural man is called in Scripture " dead," and " sleeping," and blind, and deaf. There is no surer symptom of mortification in the body than insensibility. There is no more painful sign of an unhealthy state of soul than an utter absence of spiritual thirst. Woe to that man of whom the Saviour can say, " Thou knowest not that thou art wretched, and miserable, and poor, and blind, and naked " (Rev. iii. 17).

But who is there that feels the burden of sin, and longs for peace with God ? Who is there that really feels the words of our Prayer-book confession,—" I have erred and strayed like a lost sheep, —there is no health in me,—I am a miserable offender " ? Who is there that enters into the fulness of our Communion Service, and can say with truth, " The remembrance of my sins is grievous, and the burden of them is intolerable " ? You are the man that ought to thank God. A sense of sin is the first stone laid by the Holy Ghost, when He builds a spiritual temple. He convinces of sin. Light was the first thing called into being in the material creation (Gen. i. 3). Light about our own state is the first thing in the new creation. Thirsting soul, I say again, You are the person that ought to thank God. The kingdom of God is near you. It is not when we begin to feel *good*, but when we feel *bad*, that we take the first step towards heaven. Who taught thee that thou wast naked? Whence came this inward light ? Who opened thine eyes and made thee see and feel ? Know this day that flesh and blood hath not revealed these things unto thee, but our Father which is in heaven. Universities may confer degrees, and schools may impart knowledge of all mysteries, but they cannot make men feel sin. To realize our spiritual need, and feel true spiritual thirst, is the A, B, C, in saving Christianity.

(c)   *Bp. Ryle*

COMING TO CHRIST

II. *The remedy proposed.* "If any man thirst, let him come unto Me, and drink."

There is a grand simplicity about this little sentence which cannot be too much admired. Yet, simple as it appears, it is rich in meaning. Like the Koh-i-noor diamond, which you may carry between finger and thumb, it is of unspeakable value. It solves that mighty problem which all the philosophers of Greece and Rome could

(d)

never solve,—"How can man have peace with God?" Place it in your memory side by side with six other golden sayings of your Lord. "I am the bread of life, he that cometh unto Me shall never hunger; and he that believeth on Me shall never thirst."—"I am the light of the world: he that followeth Me shall not walk in darkness, but shall have the light of life."—"I am the door: by Me if any man enter in, he shall be saved."—"I am the Way, the Truth, and the Life: no man cometh unto the Father but by Me."—"Come unto Me, all ye that labour and are heavy laden, and I will give you rest."—"Him that cometh to Me I will in no wise cast out." Get the whole seven by heart. Rivet them down in your mind, and never let them go. When your feet touch the cold river, on the bed of sickness and in the hour of death, you will find these seven texts above all price. (John vi. 35; viii. 12; x. 9; xiv. 6; Matt. xi. 28; John vi. 37.)

For what is the sum and substance of these simple words? It is this. Christ is that fountain of living water which God has graciously provided for thirsting souls. From Him, as out of the rock smitten by Moses, there flows an abundant stream for all who travel through the wilderness of this world.

This rich provision Christ has bought for us at the price of His own precious blood. To open this wondrous fountain He suffered for sin, the just for the unjust, and bore our sins in His own body on the tree. He was made sin for us, who knew no sin, that we might be made the righteousness of God in Him (1 Pet. ii. 24; iii. 18; 2 Cor. v. 21.) And now He is sealed and appointed to be the Reliever of all who are labouring and heavy laden, and the Giver of living water to all who thirst. It is His office to receive sinners. It is His pleasure to give them pardon, life, and peace. And the words of the text are a proclamation He makes to all mankind,—"If any man thirst, let him come unto Me, and drink."

The efficacy of a medicine depends on the manner in which it is used. The best prescription of the best physician is useless if we refuse to follow the directions which accompany it. Suffer the word of exhortation.

He that thirsts and wants relief must come *to Christ Himself*. He must not be content with coming to church ordinances, the assemblies for prayer and praise. He must not stop short even at His holy table, or rest satisfied with privately opening his heart to His ordained ministers. He that is content with only drinking these waters "shall thirst again" (John iv. 13). He must go further than this. He must have personal dealings with Christ Himself. The King's palace, the servants, the banqueting house, the very banquet itself, all are nothing unless we speak with the King. His hand alone can take the burden off our backs and make us free. The hand of man may take the stone from the grave and show the dead; but none but Jesus can say to the dead, "Come forth and live" (John xi. 41–43).

He that thirsts and wants relief from Christ must actually *come to Him*. It is not enough to wish, and talk, and mean, and intend, and resolve, and hope. Hell is truly said to be paved with good intentions. Thousands perish just outside the harbour. Meaning and intending they live; meaning and intending they die. We must "arise and come!" If the prodigal son had been content with saying, "How many hired servants of my father have bread enough and to spare, and I perish with hunger! I *hope some day* to return home," he might have remained for ever among the swine. It was when he AROSE AND CAME to his father that his father ran to meet him, and said, "Bring forth the best robe and put it on him . . . Let us eat and be merry" (Luke xv. 20–23). Like him we must not only "come to our selves" and think, but we must actually come to the High Priest, to Christ. We must come to the Physician.

He that thirsts and wants to come to Christ must remember that SIMPLE FAITH IS THE ONE THING REQUIRED. By all means let him come with a penitent, broken, and contrite heart; but let him not rest on that. *Faith* is the only hand that can carry the living water to our lips. *Faith* is the hinge on which all turns in the matter of our justification. It is written again and again, that "whosoever believeth shall not perish, but have eternal life" (John iii. 15, 16). "To him that worketh not, but believeth on Him that justifieth the ungodly, his faith is counted for righteousness" (Rom. iv. 5). Happy is he that can lay hold on the principle laid down in that matchless hymn,

"Just as I am! without one plea,
    Save that Thy blood was shed for me,
    And that Thou bidd'st me come to Thee,
    O Lamb of God, I come!"

How simple this remedy for thirst appears! But how hard to persuade some persons to receive it! Tell them to do some great thing, to mortify their bodies, to go on pilgrimage, to give all their goods to feed the poor, and so to merit salvation, and they will try to do as they are bid. Tell them to throw overboard all idea of merit, working, or doing, and to come to Christ as empty sinners, with nothing in their hands, and, like Naaman, they are ready to turn away in disdain (2 Kings v. 12). Human nature is always the same in every age. There are still some people like the Jews, and some like the Greeks. To the Jews Christ crucified is a stumbling-block, and to the Greeks foolishness. Their succession, at any rate, has never ceased! Never did our Lord say a truer word than that which He spoke to the proud scribes in the Sanhedrim,—"Ye WILL NOT come unto Me that ye might have life" (John v. 40).

But, simple as this remedy for thirst appears, it is the only cure for man's spiritual disease. Kings and their subjects, preachers and hearers, masters and servants, high and low, rich and poor, learned and unlearned, all must alike drink of this water of life. For eighteen centuries men have laboured to find some other medicine for weary consciences; but they have laboured in vain. Thousands, after blistering their hands, and growing grey in hewing out "broken cisterns which can hold no water" (Jer. ii. 13), have been obliged to come back at last to the old Fountain.

And simple as the old remedy for thirst may appear, it is the root of the inward life of all God's greatest servants in all ages. What have the saints and martyrs been in every era of Church history, but men who came to Christ daily by faith, and found His flesh meat indeed and His blood drink indeed? (John vi. 55). What have they all been but men who lived the life of faith in the Son of God, and drank daily out of the fulness there is in Him? (Gal. ii. 20). Here, at all events, the truest and best Christians, who have made a

(a)

mark on the world, have been of one mind. Holy fathers and reformers, holy Anglican divines and Puritans, holy Episcopalians and Nonconformists, have all in their best moments borne uniform testimony to the value of the Fountain of life. Separated and contentious as they may sometimes have been in their lives, in their deaths they have not been divided.

We live in a land where the great remedy for spiritual thirst is known. We do not realize the value of our privileges. The very familiarity of the manna makes us think little of it, just as Israel loathed "the light bread" in the wilderness (Num. xxi. 5). But turn to the pages of a heathen philosopher like the incomparable Plato, and see how he groped after light like one blindfold, and wearied himself to find the door. The humblest peasant who grasps the four "comfortable words" of our beautiful Communion Service, in the Prayer-book, knows more of the way of peace with God than the Athenian sage. Turn to the accounts which trustworthy travellers and missionaries give of the state of the heathen who have never heard the Gospel. Read of the human sacrifices in Africa, and the ghastly self-imposed tortures of the devotees of Hindostan, and remember they are all the result of an unquenched "thirst." And then learn to be thankful that your lot is cast in a land like your own. Alas, I fear God has a controversy with us for our unthankfulness!

(a)   *Bp. Ryle*

COMING TO CHRIST

III. *The promise held out to all who come to Christ.* "He that believeth on Me, as the Scripture hath said, out of his belly shall flow rivers of living water."

The subject of Scripture promises is a vast and most interesting one. Few Christians realize the number, and length, and breadth, and depth, and height, and variety of the precious "shalls" and "wills" laid up in the Bible for the benefit of all who will use them.

Yet *promise* lies at the bottom of nearly all the transactions of man with man in the affairs of this life. The labourer on the land works hard from Monday morning to Saturday night, because he believes that at the end of the week he shall receive his promised wages. The soldier enlists in the army, the sailor enters his name on the ship's books in the navy, in the full confidence that those under whom they serve will at some future time give them their promised pay. The humblest maid-servant in a family works on from day to day at her appointed duties, in the belief that her mistress will give her the promised wages. In the business of great cities, among merchants, and bankers, and tradesmen, nothing could be done without incessant faith in promises. Every man of sense knows that cheques, and bills, and promissory notes, are the only means by which the immense majority of mercantile affairs can possibly be carried on. Men of business are compelled to act by faith and not by sight. They believe promises. In short, promises, and faith in promises, and actions springing from faith in promises, are the backbone of nine-tenths of all the dealings of man with his fellow-men.

Now in the Bible " There are given to us exceeding great and precious promises " (2 Pet. i. 4). He who has mercifully caused all Holy Scripture to be written for our learning, has shown His perfect knowledge of human nature, by spreading over the Book a perfect wealth of promises, suitable to every kind of experience and every condition of life.

But there is one difference between the promises of men and the promises of God. The promises of man are not sure to be fulfilled. With the best wishes and intentions, he cannot always keep his word. Disease and death may take away him that promises. War, or pestilence, or famine, or failure of crops, or hurricanes, may strip him of his property, and make it impossible for him to fulfil his engagements. The promises of God, on the contrary, are certain to be kept. He is almighty: nothing can prevent His doing what He has said. He never changes: He is always " of one mind ; " and with Him there is " no variableness or shadow of turning " (Job xxiii. 13 ; James i. 17). He will always keep His word. There is one thing which, as a little girl once told her teacher, to her surprise, God cannot do : " It is impossible for God to lie " (Heb. vi. 18). The most unlikely and improbable things, when God has once said He will do them, have always come to pass. The destruction of the old world by a flood, and the preservation of Noah in the ark, the birth of Isaac, the deliverance of Israel from Egypt, the raising of David to the throne of Saul, the miraculous birth of Christ, the resurrection of Christ, the scattering of the Jews all over the earth, and their continued preservation as a distinct people,—who could imagine events more unlikely and improbable than these? Yet God said they should be, and in due time they all came to pass. In short, with God it is just as easy to do a thing as to say it. Whatever He promises, He is certain to perform.

Concerning the variety and riches of Scripture promises, their name is legion. There is hardly a step in a man's life, hardly any position in which man can be placed, for which the Bible has not held out encouragement. There are " shalls " and " wills " in God's treasury for every condition. About God's infinite mercy and compassion,—about His readiness to receive all who repent and believe,—about His willingness to forgive, pardon, and absolve the chief of sinners,—about His power to change hearts and alter our corrupt nature,—about the encouragements to pray, and hear the gospel, and draw near to the throne of grace,—about strength for duty, comfort in trouble, guidance in perplexity, help in sickness, consolation in death, support under bereavement, happiness beyond the grave, reward in glory,—about all these things there is an abundant supply of promises in the Word. If any one doubts it, I can only say, " Come and see." Like the Queen of Sheba at Solomon's court, you will soon say, " The half was not told me " (1 Kings x. 7).

The promise of our Lord Jesus Christ, which heads this paper, is somewhat peculiar. It is singularly rich in encouragement to all who feel spiritual thirst and come to Him for relief, and deserves peculiar attention. The promise seems to refer to many others beside those to whom He spoke. For what says He?—" He that believeth on Me, as the Scripture hath said, out of his belly shall flow rivers of living water. But this spake He of the Spirit, which they that believe on Him should receive." Figurative undoubtedly are these words,—figurative, like the earlier words of the sentence,—figurative, like " thirst " and " drinking." But all the figures of Scripture contain

(b)

great truths; and what the figure before us was meant to convey I will now try to show.

1. I believe our Lord meant that he who comes to Him by faith shall receive an abundant supply of everything that he can desire *for the relief of his own soul's wants.* The Spirit shall convey to him such an abiding sense of pardon, peace, and hope, that it shall be in his inward man like a well-spring never dry. He shall feel so satisfied with "the things of Christ," which the Spirit shall show him (John xvi. 15), that he shall rest from spiritual anxiety about death, judgment, and eternity. He may have his seasons of darkness and doubt, through his own infirmities or the temptations of the devil. But, speaking generally, when he has once come to Christ by faith, he shall find in his heart of hearts an unfailing fountain of consolation. This is the first thing which the promise before us contains. "Only come to Me, poor anxious soul, and thy spiritual anxiety shall be relieved. I will place in thy heart, by the power of the Holy Spirit, such a sense of pardon and peace, through My atonement and intercession, that thou shalt never completely thirst again. Thou mayest have thy doubts, and fears, and conflicts whilst thou art in the body. But once having come to Me, and taken Me for thy Saviour, thou shalt never feel thyself entirely hopeless. The condition of thine inward man shall be so thoroughly changed, that thou shalt feel as if there was within thee an ever-flowing spring of water."

What shall we say to these things? I declare my own belief, that whenever a man or woman really comes to Christ by faith, he finds this promise fulfilled. He may possibly be weak in grace, and have many misgivings about his own condition. He may possibly not dare to say that he is converted, justified, sanctified, and meet for the inheritance of the saints in light. But for all that, I am bold to say, the humblest and feeblest believer in Christ has got something within him which he would not part with, though he may not yet fully understand it. And what is that "*something*"? It is just that "river of living water" which begins to run in the heart of every child of Adam as soon as he comes to Christ and drinks. In this sense this wonderful promise of Christ is always fulfilled.

2. But is this all that is contained in the promise? No. There is more to follow. I believe our Lord meant us to understand that he who comes to Him by faith shall not only have an abundant supply of everything which he needs for his own soul, but shall also become *a source of blessing to the souls of others.* The Spirit who dwells in him shall make him a fountain of good to his fellow-men, so that at the last day there shall be found to have flowed from him "rivers of living water."

This is a most important part of our Lord's promise, and opens up a subject which is seldom realized and grasped. It is one of deep interest. "No man liveth unto himself" (Rom. xiv. 7), so no man is converted only for himself. The conversion of one man or woman always leads on, in God's wonderful providence, to the conversion of others. I think it likely that many live and die in the faith, who are not aware that they have done good to any soul. But I believe the resurrection morn and the judgment day, when the secret history of all Christians is revealed, will prove that the full meaning of the promise before us has never failed. I doubt if there will be a believer who will not have been to some one or other a "river of living water,"—a channel through whom the Spirit has conveyed saving grace. Even the penitent thief, short as his time was after he repented, has been a source of blessing to thousands of souls!

(i.) Some believers are "rivers of living water" while they live. Their words, their conversation, their preaching, their teaching, are all means by which the water of life has flowed into the hearts of their fellow-men. Such, for example, were the apostles who wrote no Epistles and only preached the Word. Such were Luther, and Whitefield, and Wesley, and Berridge, and Rowlands, and thousands of others of whom I cannot now speak particularly.

(ii.) Some believers are "rivers of living water" when they die. Their courage in facing the king of terrors, their boldness in the most painful sufferings, their unswerving faithfulness to Christ's truth even at the stake, their manifest peace on the edge of the grave,—all this has set thousands thinking, and led hundreds to repent and believe. Such, for example, were the primitive martyrs, whom the Roman Emperors persecuted. Such were John Huss, and Jerome of Prague. Such were Cranmer, Ridley, Latimer, Hooper, and the noble army of Marian martyrs. The work that they did at their deaths, like Samson, was far greater than the work done in their lives.

(iii.) Some believers are "rivers of living water" long after they die. They do good by their books and writings in every part of the world, long after the hands which held the pen are mouldering in the dust. Such men were Bunyan, and Baxter, and Owen, and George Herbert, and Robert M'Cheyne. These blessed servants of God do more good probably by their books at this moment, than they did by their tongues when they were alive. "Being dead, they yet speak" (Heb. xi. 4).

(iv.) Finally, there are some believers who are "rivers of living water" by the beauty of their daily conduct and behaviour. There are many quiet, gentle, consistent Christians, who make no show and no noise in the world, and yet insensibly exercise a deep influence for good on all around them. They "win without the Word" (1 Peter iii. 1). Their love, their kindness, their sweet temper, their patience, their unselfishness, tell silently on a wide circle, and sow seeds of thought and self-inquiry in many minds. It was a fine testimony of an old lady who died in great peace, —saying that under God she owed her salvation to Mr. Whitefield:—"It was not any sermon that he preached; it was not anything he ever said to me. It was the beautiful consistency and kindness of his daily life, in the house where he was staying, when I was a little girl. I said to myself, if I ever have any religion, Mr. Whitefield's God shall be my God."

Reader, lay hold on this view of our Lord's promises. Think of the blessedness of being a "river of living water" to others. Who can tell that you may not be the means of bringing many others to Christ? I knew a family, consisting of a father, mother, and ten children, in which true religion began with one of the daughters; and when it began she stood alone, and all the rest of the family were in the world. And yet, before she died, she saw both her parents and all her brothers and sisters converted to God; and all this,

(a)

humanly speaking, began from her influence! Surely in the face of this, we need not doubt that a believer may be to others a " river of living water." Conversions may not be in your time, and you may die without seeing them. But never doubt that conversion generally leads to conversions, and that few go to heaven alone. When Grimshaw, of Haworth, the apostle of the north, died, he left his son graceless and godless. Afterwards the son was converted, never having forgotten his father's advice and example. And his last words were, " What will my old father say when he sees me in heaven?" Let us take courage and hope on believing Christ's promise.

(a) *Bp. Ryle*

COMING TO CHRIST

IV. *A plain question.* Do you know anything of spiritual thirst? Many know nothing about it. I have learned, by the painful experience of the third of a century, that people may go on for years attending God's house, and yet never feel their sins, or desire to be saved. The cares of this world, the love of pleasure, the "lust of other things" choke the good seed every Sunday, and make it unfruitful. They come to church with hearts as cold as the stone pavement on which they walk. They go away as thoughtless and unmoved as the old marble busts which look down on them from the monuments on the walls. Well, it may be so ; but I do not yet despair of any one, so long as he is alive. That grand old bell in St. Paul's Cathedral, London, which has struck the hours for so many years, is seldom heard by many during the business hours of the day. The roar and din of traffic in the streets have a strange power to deaden its sound and prevent men hearing it. But when the daily work is over, and desks are locked, and doors are closed, and books are put away, and quiet reigns in the great city, the case is altered. As the old bell strikes eleven, and twelve, and one, and two, and three at night, thousands hear it who never heard it during the day. And so I hope it will be with many an one in the matter of his soul. Now, in the plenitude of health and strength, in the hurry and whirl of business, I fear the voice of your conscience is often stifled, and you cannot hear it. But the day may come when the great bell of conscience will make itself heard, whether you like it or not. The time may come when, laid aside in quietness, and obliged by illness to sit still, you may be forced to look within, and consider your soul's concerns. And then may you come to Christ for relief !

(b) *Bp. Ryle*

COMMENTATORS

Some future strain, in which the muse shall tell
How *science* dwindles, and how *volumes* swell,
How Commentators each dark passage shun,
And hold their farthing candle to the sun.

(c) *Young*

COMMONWEALTH OF ISRAEL (Eph. ii. 12)

The Gentile lapsed from it, the Jew made it invalid (Matt. xv. 6) ; and they parted, only to unite again (ἔθνη καὶ λαοὶ Ἰσραήλ. Acts iv. 27), in one act of uttermost rebellion, and yet, through the mystery of redeeming love, to remain thereby (15, 16) united in Christ for ever.

(d) *Lange*

COMMUNION WITH GOD

Oh, it is not the pleasures of the world can comfort me. If God deny His presence, what are the pleasures of the city to me ; one hour of sweet retirement with God is better than the whole world.

(e) *D. Brainerd*

COMMUNION WITH GOD, ON

" *They saw God, and did eat and drink.*"—Exod. xxiv. 11.

Moses and his company = climbing the same hill as in ch. 19. = dark clouds, tempest thunders, voice of trembling, lightnings, and fire ; but not to see *these* suddenly disperse, and sunshine bathe the heights above and the plain below.

A Transfiguration Scene = Old Testament picture of a New Testament doctrine. *Then* Moses " exceedingly feared and quaked" ! *now* he and the elders go up into the mount in perfect serenity and delight. They see God, and eat and drink in His presence. How has the wonderful transfiguration come about? Give attention to the details. (See whole ch. 4–12.)

1. The blood of the sacrifice :

Altar of twelve pillars = twelve tribes, ALL : = not one individual excluded from the blessing.

The blood of the victims *collected* in basins for USE. (*N.B.*—How much in Old Testament is made to depend upon the USE of the Blood, which now we are content to neglect.)

Half was poured on the altar = *bathed in blood.* (Heb. ix. 19) = Book of the Covenant sprinkled with it,

= a roll, or scroll—seen by the people spotted with blood !

= an all-important truth : God cannot give blessings to us except through *Blood.* Not even those of the Covenant (the Bible), except through blood = *the spots on it.*

How vain, then, to expect Heaven, forgiveness, except through God's own appointed way !

2. Next, Moses was to sprinkle the people with blood.

He and those assisting him would *use* for this purpose the blood in the basins—go through the camp and sprinkle every man, woman, and child (ALL) = New Testament, " *God so loved the world,*" etc.

The immediate effect of the Blood sprinkled on the *altar,* on the *book,* and on the *people* = a grand type. The hill, with mass of clouds, smoke, darkness, NOW, when blood is sprinkled, is *changed.*

1. Not even *vapour,* but light, sunshine, peace
2. A pavement of blue sapphire = glory ;
3. A proclamation of the Gospel,—" I have blotted out as a thick cloud thy transgressions, and as a cloud thy sins.

= " *See,* I have blotted out thy transgressions, as I have broken up and melted away the clouds, and left a blue sky."

Then God could look upon these elders and they too *saw God.*—(How. = ?)

(f)

"*They saw God, and did eat and drink.*"

They were treated as "nobles," who had come to sit at the table with the king. They feasted; enjoyed intercourse; had conversation (see John xiv.). All the company (name them) were sinners: but see to what height of blessing they, as pardoned sinners, attained.

And through the *sprinkled Blood*, on the opened-way, we each may come into the presence of God, into blissful company with Him.

N.B.—The blessing comes at the *moment* we sprinkle with the blood.

1. The *natural heart* spurns the atonement: Because sin is not believed to be a tremendous evil, demanding such a *cost*.

2. Also the natural heart rejects anything that cannot be found out by the human intellect.

The effects: after the feast, invitation = "*Come up higher,*" to Moses.

On this and a later occasion.

He was invited, and was able to ascend to the top of the hill, and enter the cloud of glory.

In going up there, he needed nothing more than the *sprinkled blood*.

The same blood is his warrant to sit at the feast, and to go higher still.

N.B.—The Power of the Atoning Blood.

1. Some who are sprinkled, remain at the foot of the hill, and see the clear sky afar off ;

2. Some join the seventy elders ;

3. A *few* climb higher and higher with Moses.

But *N.B.* no more is required as warrant for going higher and higher, *than the blood*. Every one who is washed has the right to go higher ; and there are few who might not go higher and higher, Eph. iii. (14–20) shows how the Holy Spirit is willing to lead us upward, and how the Father waits to welcome us.

Because of this there are blood-sprinkled souls who never make full use of their privileges : who have not full assurance of faith ; they don't know the thoughts that God thinks concerning them; they do not use the "boldness" of Heb. x. 19, which rightly belongs to them.

Conclusion.

"Whosoever will . . . water freely" ;

"Look unto Me, and be saved, all the ends of the earth" ;

"Come unto Me" ;

= An open door to heaven *for all*—:

But "God will by no means clear the guilty ;

"He will not at all acquit the wicked ;

"The soul that sinneth, it shall die, is also *true*: the door shut against such.

But one word reconciles the two sets of statements.

i.e. "BLOOD."

"The precious blood of Christ cleanseth from all sin."

This is the key that unlocks heaven's door; every soul in glory sings a song of thanksgiving to Him who hath "redeemed us by *His Blood* out of every kindred, and tongue, and people, and nation."

(a)   *H. Bonar*

COMMUNION, the Holy

COMMUNION is a contraction for *common-union*. It implies a common union with each other in things spiritual, and also with the Lord.

It is in the ordinance of the Lord's Supper where believers enjoy the nearest and closest communion or fellowship with their Saviour. It was "in the breaking of bread" that He was "made known" unto His disciples, and "manifested Himself to them," during the forty days after His resurrection (Luke xxiv. 30, 31).

(b)   *Richard Glove*

COMMUNISM

The wealth of the Rothschild family is proverbial; but it will strike every reflecting mind that it must stand as the unmistakable sign of qualities of a very high order of mind—perhaps of no one quality more than the flexibility which adapts itself to circumstances. Republic or Monarchy, regular Government or a Revolutionary Convention, this great house can keep open and transact business with and under all. After the suppression of the Paris Commune, in 1871, an interesting story was related in print of the manner in which Baron Rothschild dealt with a mob which one morning found its way into his counting-house, the scene being somewhat as follows :

Rothschild.—Gentlemen, your business ?

First Communard.—Monsieur, you are a financial aristocrat—a millionaire !

R.—Well, what then ?

F. C.—It is unequal and unjust !

All.—It is shameful, intolerable.

R.—Pray tell me plainly what you want.

F. C.—The toiling people are stricken with poverty, and you are rolling in wealth.

R.—What people ?

F. C.—The 36,000,000 of France.

R.—And you would like to distribute my property among them. At how much do you reckon it ?

F. C.—125,000,000 francs.

R.—And that would be how much for each?

[A great fumbling for pencils and scraps of paper in Communistic blouses, and hurried performance of sums.]

F. C.—Three and a half francs, Monsieur.

R.—Good, I see there are thirty of you. Take this to my cashier (handing a cheque for 105 francs). Now, remember that you have received your share, and don't let me see your faces again.

[Exeunt Communists, surprised, pleased, ashamed.]

(c)

COMPANIONS

Evil companions first make us sad; afterwards they make us bad.

(d)   *Sunday at Home*

"COMPLETE IN CHRIST, YE ARE" (Col. ii. 10)

Observe—

1. The position of these people.

"*Ye have received Christ*" (6).

2. The signs of danger.

"*This I say lest any man delude you with persuasiveness of speech*" (4).

N.B.—The Christian is exposed to the same danger as our first parents,—when "the serpent

(e)

beguiled Eve ; " he may delude us, and none the less that we have been restored to God's favour, and are in communion with Him.

3. The consequent warning

Take heed lest ye fall a prey to his delusions (8). Ask-

1. *What was the* DANGER ?

As the tempter insinuated to Eve, " Yea, hath God said?" So now he insinuates that the Christian is *not complete in Christ; you have not got everything in Him*=ye are not yet made full in Christ. Hence, *Ye must do something of your own—mix with it an imposing* RITUAL—*ceremonialism—tradition—a little heresy—*" *The commandments of men.*" So anxious is the seducer to *make the Gospel of Christ of none effect.* He would destroy its simplicity. Dilute it, and it *is* spoilt. The enemy knows this ; therefore his beguiling speech.

Hence the Apostle's emphatic protest :
" YE ARE COMPLETE IN CHRIST " !
(i.) " He is the fulness of the Godhead bodily " —Can you add to that ? Can you have a thing more than full ? Can you add to the light of the sun ? Is your farthing taper needed when the noonday sun is shining in full blaze ?
(ii.) " And of His fulness have all we received." In receiving Christ, we have received EVERYTHING. Can you have more than everything ? " He, of God, is made unto us wisdom, and righteousness, and sanctification, and redemption "—What more than that is wanted to secure a man's salvation ! Take heed ! Take heed ! The unctuous serpent is about—about in the Churches—and will make *you* his prey, unless ye remain steadfast, rooted and built up in Christ.

2. Further, This completeness consists (i.) in an ADVANCE from the stage of rudimentary religion—
The Rudiments = the Beginning = the First-steps :
The O. T. Religion of the Jews = Rudiments compared with Christianity ;
= The A, B, C, of Religion, as the spelling-book and First-steps are to the child learning to read ;
= Type or pictures of Christ, the Anti-type and Reality ;
= The shadow of Christ, the Substance ;
= The bud and germ of Christ, the full-flower or Blossom.
All good, in their time and stage, and because they suited God's purpose in educating the world for Christ. When the world was young it had to be taught as we teach children. But *ye*—ye Christians—who have *received Christ,* have got beyond this stage, ye have developed as the rose-bud has = " *Ye are made full in Him.*" If so, why do I find you learning your A, B, C, again?

3. Again, This completeness consists (ii.) in our *Freedom from the Condemnation of the Law* (14).
There is a *hand-writing* = a bond = a bill of debts—*against us*—written with the *finger of God* in His book.
We have got to settle that account—say the account with Conscience ; and we have tried to settle it in various ways and have always failed. It still remains *against us.*—This we know from repeated experience. " In any kind of danger " we see this *hand-writing,* like the hand-writing on the wall before Belshazzar, and we know it is a writing *against* us. It is conscience at work ; and con-

science has the law on its side, written, like the Commandments, with the *finger of God.*

The question now is : *How can the law be made to relax its hold ?*
To which the answer is : " *By death.*" For death is the penalty of sin, and the law has dominion over a man only so long as he liveth.
Now, adds the apostle, *Ye have received Christ,* *i.e.,* By your repentance (= " *putting off* "), ye have *died,* and have been *buried* with Christ. Hence the answer to conscience and to the demands of the law. The man is dead and buried, and ye cannot get anything from a dead man; for ye have dominion only so long as he liveth.
Meanwhile this dead man has undergone a resurrection = " *risen with Christ,*" and as Christ, to a NEW LIFE (for no man comes from the grave as he went to it), where he is no longer bound by the old conditions of the *law of sin and death,* but he is under GRACE—completely set free from the condemnation of the law. Thus he is *made full —complete in Christ—*because we cannot get beyond the standing of grace ; there is nothing higher.
4. If so, if the Christian is in advance of a mere rudimentary religion, asks the apostle, *Why then are ye subject to ordinances ?* Why this hankering after something else ? Why ritual—imposing services and array of priests ? Why philosophy and vain deceits ? If ye are advanced and complete, why are ye at your A, B, C, again, like children ? "
" If ye have indeed received Christ, and are made full in Him, ye have received an inestimable, a priceless gift—by no means be talked out of your privilege. " *Let no man rob you of your prize.*" " BEWARE ! BEWARE ! BEWARE ! lest, as the serpent beguiled Eve, he beguile you too ; and ye *fall from your steadfastness.*"
Or, again,—
If our standing is that of *grace*—grace to help in time of need—if as our day is so our strength will be. Why this inconsistent and senseless hankering after *higher privileges,* a higher standing, according to the " tradition of men "? *There is no higher standing,* no higher life than this, for the Christian here below. Again, then, BEWARE ! BEWARE !—the serpent has crept into Eden again —and he is beguiling you Christians, and splitting you up into fanatical sects, unfitting you for your duties and work here on earth.
N.B.—The *danger* is most real, and on all sides ; but let us hold fast to what we have received in Christ, *in whom dwelleth all the fulness of the Godhead bodily ;* and *of whose fulness have all we received.*
(a)

COMPLETE IN CHRIST, YE ARE (Col. ii. 10)

= " Ye are made full in Christ."
He is fulness, and ye in Him are made full.

CAUTION : This completeness in Christ does not mean that the Christian has nothing more to learn, but it signifies that, as " ye have received Christ " Jesus, in whom the fulness of the Godhead dwells bodily (= the incarnation), and " of His fulness have all we received," therefore ye have received the full revelation of God in receiving Christ : Hence, " Ye are complete in Christ."
(b)

In other words: The whole of your religion is summed up in Jesus Christ. He is everything— "Wisdom, and righteousness, and sanctification, and redemption."

(a)

COMPLETE IN CHRIST

" Ye are complete in Him."
= Ye are made full.
= The bud has opened into the full flower.

N.B.:
1. The Jew had his religion ;
2. The heathen had his philosophy;

Both were elementary = "rudiments of this world."
3. The Christian has something better—he has the rudiments expanded into the full flower.

Question = Why, then, after this, go back to the elements again—Why go back to Judaism, in any form (as ritualism); Why go back to heathenism in any form (as philosophy)? Beware lest any man make a spoil of you through deceits! Beware of relapses into any form of rudimentary religion.

(b)

CONDEMNETH, WHO IS HE THAT?

" *Who is he that condemneth ? It is Christ that died, yea rather, that is risen again, who is even at the right hand of God, who also maketh intercession for us.*"—Rom. viii. 34.

" *Who is he that condemneth ?*" This is the second question that arises as to a possible adversary who may succeed in breaking the bond betwixt Christ and the Christian.

There is a day coming when the secrets of all hearts will be judged. May not the judge Himself on that occasion be against the Christian,—and so show the unsoundness of the Apostle's doctrine?

We proceed to examine his answer:

We have to suppose a case : It is a believing man who asks this question, but he is in some degree of uncertainty and doubt. How his doubts arose it is not necessary to inquire ; it may well be supposed that some inconsistency or waywardness in his christian walk has been the cause, and in consequence the Spirit has not been witnessing with his spirit that he is a child of God. However that may be, for it is little to the point, the man is now suffering from spiritual depression and despondency. He is, we say, in a state of uncertainty and doubt as to the verdict of the Judge at the last day. Will the Judge, on that occasion, acquit or condemn him?

This is our case supposed. This is the man troubled in conscience, through the disturbing effect of sin (and we admit that there is enough to disturb him), lest after all, after all that Christ has been to him, after his resting in Christ, he may yet be condemned at the last and dreadful Day of Judgment.

But the question is, " *Who is to condemn him.*"

There must of course be some one to act the part of a condemner ; and he must be one in authority, for the condemnation of an unauthorized person will count for nothing. When our conduct is to be put into the balances and weighed, when our actions are to be dragged into a court and subjected to the closest scrutiny, it is not the judgment which people generally may pass upon us that we have to fear so much ; but it is the opinion which the judge will form, and the verdict which he will give, that we have to fear, for he alone has power to punish.

And so in the case supposed. There must be a properly qualified and authorized person whose part it will be to judge, to condemn, or to acquit, as the case may be determined ; and whose fiat will be looked for with that awe which His dread office inspires, for He hath power to cast into hell.

(c)

1. " WHO IS HE THAT CONDEMNETH ? "

But who is He?

Will it be SATAN, the great adversary, who will sit as judge, and have the opportunity of condemning the man? For, undoubtedly, we may conclude his verdict would be an adverse one, seeing he has made himself personally acquainted with the man, and is cognisant of all his actions, and is not likely to take into account any extenuating circumstances whatever. But is he properly qualified, and has he authority to undertake the office of judge in this case ? abundant testimony answers decidedly, "No." For not only is the office delegated to another, but the adversary's own character disqualifies him for so important an office ; he is a biased person, and has a personal spite and dislike to the man who bears ever so slighty the image of Christ; moreover, he has been known to be a liar from the beginning, a quality which absolutely unfits him to be the judge of others. Therefore we confidently conclude that he cannot condemn the man, for he has no condemning power; it lies altogether outside the sphere of his operations, and he has nothing whatever to do with it.

(d)

2. " WHO IS HE THAT CONDEMNETH ? "

Will the man be condemned by his OWN HEART ?

Now, the heart *has* a condemning power, and justly so ; for that power has been planted within it by God Himself, and consequently it is to be expected that the man will be condemned by his own heart and conscience. Constituted as he is, there is no escape from such condemnation. And if it condemns now, is it likely to be altogether silent *then* ?

But here again it is to be observed, that the heart, though possessing a judging power, is not the supreme Judge in a case of so much importance. Even now an appeal can be made against its verdicts ; for St. John expressly says, " If our heart condemn us, God is *greater* than *our heart* and knoweth all things ; " and *knowledge* is an especial requisite in a judge. There is then a higher court to which this case will be carried, presided over by a Judge who " knoweth all things," and who has power to upset and annul the verdict of the heart in things spiritual.

Therefore we conclude again, that neither is the man's heart to be his judge on that day. That Judge must know " *all things,*" not only things in the man's history, but things which lie outside his

(e)

history also; such as may belong to the purpose of God, and which have their origin in the spirit-world. The Judge must have cognisance of all these things, and for such an office the heart is necessarily disqualified.

(a)

3. "Who is He that Condemneth?"

Will God Himself judge the man?

The great and dreadful God who inhabiteth eternity, who is of purer eyes than to behold iniquity, who chargeth the angels with folly, in whose sight the heavens are not clean. Will He, unto whom all hearts are open, all desires known, from whom no secrets are hid, who has searched us and known us, who spies out all our ways, to whose eye all things are naked and laid bare to their inmost recesses, will He, who dwelleth in the light that no man can approach unto, amid "everlasting burnings," condemn this poor, fearful, and troubled man?

His own word assures us that He will not. We are to be judged by One who is *One* of ourselves. "The Father judgeth no man, but hath committed all judgment unto the Son, *because He is the Son of man.*"

Likely then, as it might seem, that the great God Himself, from the very nature of the case, would condemn the man whose case is supposed, and banish the sinful being from His presence, or consume him with the splendour of His effulgence; yet for some special and beneficent reasons He has delegated that office to His Son, who is also "bone of our bone and flesh of our flesh," and so "*touched with a feeling of our infirmities.*"

(b)

4. "Who is He that Condemneth?"

We ask then next, will Jesus, as the Judge, condemn the man?

He alone is appointed to be "the Judge of quick and dead," and is in every way qualified for that great office. His relationship with the Father will lead Him to act in this, as in all other matters, according to the will of God; whilst His relationship to the man to be judged will incline Him to be merciful.

His authority and His qualifications for the office are alike indisputable. No man could ask for more: "Justice and mercy have kissed each other," and meet together in Him.

Here, then, rests the issue of this great unsettling question. It rests with Jesus. Will He condemn or acquit this man? He has power to do either, He can but do right. Will He say to this man, "Depart," "I know you not"; or, "Come, thou blessed of *my* Father"? Will He assign this man a place on His right hand with the saved, or, on His left hand amongst those who go away from His presence for evermore? What a question! Do we wonder that it should oppress the spirits and distress the conscience of any? The wonder is rather, *that it should not.*

Can we lighten this man's anxiety by giving him a satisfactory and a comforting assurance that "*it shall be well with him*"? May we say to him, as was said to Daniel, "Go thy way; thou shalt stand in thy lot at the last day"? Assuredly we can.

(c)

The Answer

For in such a case the question asked is also answered by the Apostle in such a way as to afford strong consolation. The degree of faith is not taken into the account, nor is the amount of alloy in the believer's character regarded as excluding him from the full benefit of what is here stated. His faith may be weaker or stronger, great or little. He may but just touch the hem of Christ's garment. The question is not, How much? but, Is there any faith? If only "a touch," the man is a believer, and is reckoned with at the Judgment as such. His grip of Christ may be slight, yet "as many as touched Him were made perfectly whole." The Divine life may not be more than as "smoking flax" or a smouldering flame. He may be a "bruised reed," fit only, as some might think, to be broken and thrown away as useless. Yet we read of no such qualifying condition beyond this: "Hast thou faith?"

It is then upon such strong evidence, and in the face of such exceeding great and precious promises, that we are enabled to quiet this uneasy conscience, by pointing out to him the answer St. Paul gives to the question. Certainly "the consolations of God are not small."

There is a *fourfold* answer to this question = "Who is he that condemneth?" And if a threefold cord be not quickly broken, surely a fourfold cord ought to afford strong consolation.

(d)

This is the Fourfold Cord

1. "It is Christ that died,
2. Yea, rather, that is risen again,
3. Who is even at the right hand of God,
4. Who also maketh intercession for us."

(e)

How full the Consolation!—

The Judge of this man *then* will be Jesus, the Saviour of the man *now*. And we say to this disconsolate man—"Call to mind what Jesus has been to thee, and what He has done for thee in the past, as "the Lamb of God." What is the force of thine own relationship by faith to Him who said, "Because I live, ye shall live also"? What is the significance of His being at the right hand of God? And what is the value of His continual intercession for thee as our great *High Priest?*

From the fact that *He died*, remember that "He was delivered up for us *all*," and "wounded for our transgressions," thou mayest see that His death has made an atonement for thy sin, and has removed thy condemnation. There is no condemnation for those who died in Him.

Also, from the fact that *He rose again*, thou hast the assurance that God has accepted Him in thy stead: thou too hast risen from the sense of condemnation into the confidence of a forgiven man. For "He was raised for our justification," and in Him thou art regarded as a just person.

And, again, from the fact that He is sitting at the right hand of God, thou hast the assurance of His protection against all accusing and condemning powers, and also the pledge that thou too wilt be on His right hand, and not on His left, in that

(f)

great day of which thou standest in dread. His position there is the pledge of thine own acquittal and position too.

And, lastly, seeing that He is actively engaged in making *intercession* for thee, thou hast the assurance that His blood cleanseth thee from all sin, that He will effect thy sanctification by effectually subduing and abolishing the remains of sin in thee; and that He will secure thee against relapses and apostasy. As thy great High Priest, appearing in the presence of God for thee, He prays that " thy faith fail not " in the gusts of great temptations, and when thou art assailed by the fiery darts of the wicked one. There is the same relationship between Christ's death for thee and His intercession, as there is between Creation and Providence. God did not make the world and put it in its place in the universe and then abandon it; but His Providence daily looks after it, even to the minutest things. And so does Christ continually intercede for those who come unto God by Him. As surely as He died for them, so surely will He look after their spiritual interests to the uttermost. His death for thee must not be considered apart from His daily intercession for thee. Since without the latter, even the Bible does not hold out a hope of perseverance unto the end.

Now look at the several strands in this fourfold cord:

He died, He rose, He appears, He prays—all in relation to you. If this is not enough to quiet your fears, what more can be said or done? The question about your condemnation is decided. *There is no one to do it.* The *Judge* is your *Saviour*, your Friend. You and He have entered into relationship with each other. You have met before. When you first came to Him, you put this matter of your salvation *into His hands* as a trust, " Lord, do Thou for me." Will He, think you, be false to His trust? Will He meet you as a stranger, as one whom He has never met before, as one for whom He has not died, and for whom He has not ever prayed, and say, "*Depart, I know you not.*" Think of it, and of the whole transaction. The fact is, *you are judged already.* For " He that believeth on the Son of God hath everlasting life, and shall not come into condemnation (judgment), but is passed from death unto life."

(*a*)

WHO IS HE THAT CONDEMNETH?

In all this the Apostle is but reminding us of the starting-point of his whole argument in the opening words of this chapter, " There is no condemnation."

The whole condemning power lies with Jesus, but He is our Saviour; and has given His word, " Him that cometh unto Me, I will in no wise cast out." That promise cannot fail. " Heaven and earth shall pass away, but My words shall never pass away." Is it not written of Him: " Behold I lay in Zion a stone, *a sure foundation*, and he that believeth in Him shall not be confounded "?

One concluding word: Let us see that we take Jesus as our Saviour now, and we shall not fear Him as our Judge then. He will remember all the past—how you fled to Him for refuge—how your repentance was continual and genuine—how, when overcome with fresh and unexpected sin, you came to Him again and again—how you fed upon His word—how you kept the faith, and did not sinfully desert His standard in evil days.

He will remember all, for His intercession has been concurrent with it; and when you appear before the great white throne He will present you faultless with exceeding joy."

But the pivot upon which this all turns, the starting point without which there cannot be this ending, the seed from which this magnificent harvest springs, is, " IN CHRIST." If we would escape condemnation then, we must begin by being " *in Christ* "—now. And whatever has been said on this subject that may savour of *boldness*, is only *bold* on this foundation, " *in Christ.*" To such as are truly in Him, and one with Him—nothing which has been said here will appear as an overstatement. To have an understanding of this thing we must first have our standing in it. As for outsiders, they are condemned already, because they have not believed in the Son of God.

(*b*)

CONDEMNETH, WHO? (Rom. viii.)

A Christian woman once, after a great conflict with Satan, said, " Reason not with me, I am but a weak woman; if thou hast anything to say, say it to my Christ; He is my Advocate, my Strength, and my Redeemer; and He shall plead for me."

(*c*)   *Thos. Brooks*

All the arrows that are shot at a Christian stick in his buckler; they never reach his conscience, his soul. The raging waves beat sorely against Noah's ark, but they touched not him.

(*d*)   *Ibid*

CONDEMNED ALREADY (John v.)

Not because you have sinned, but because you believe not. Not because you are a sinner, but because you are an unbeliever. Not because you have lived in darkness, but because you come not to the light.

(*e*)

CONDUCT, MAXIMS OF. " *Walk circumspectly redeeming the time* " (Eph. v. 15, 16)

Persevere against discouragements. Keep your temper. Employ leisure in study, and always have some work in hand. Be punctual and methodical in business, and never procrastinate. Never be in a hurry. Preserve self-possession, and do not be talked out of a conviction. Rise early, and be an economist of time. Maintain dignity without the appearance of pride. Manner is something with everybody, and everything with some. Be guarded in discourse: attentive, and slow to speak. Never acquiesce in immoral or pernicious opinions. Be not forward to assign reasons to those who have no right to ask. Think nothing in conduct unimportant or indifferent. Rather set than follow examples. Practise strict temperance, and in all your transactions remember the final account.

(*f*)   *Bp. Middleton*

CONFESSING CHRIST

Augustine relates, that when Victorinus, deeply moved by reading the Holy Scriptures, said confidently to Simplicianus in Rome:—" Know that

(*g*)

I am already a Christian," and Simplicianus answered, " I will not believe it, neither do I count thee among the Christians till I see thee in the church of Christ." Victorinus laughed, and said, "Do the walls then make a Christian?" But afterwards, fearing Christ might not confess him unless he confessed Christ, he suddenly came to Simplicianus and said, " *Eamus ad ecclesiam. Christianus volo fieri.*"

(a)

Swift held . . . his family worship with his servants in perfect secresy, merely to avoid suspicion of hypocrisy. Learn to rise above the judgment of the world ; be not ashamed of Christ.

(b) *Heubner*

[Matt. x. 33

It is not enough only to believe with the heart, for God will have us confess with our mouth. Every one that confesses that Christ is God, shall find Christ professing to the Father, " That man is a faithful servant " ; but those who deny Christ shall receive that fearful doom, " *I know you not.*"

(c) *Quarles*

CONFIDENCE (BOLDNESS)

Cast not away your (Heb. x. 35)

The temptation = *The surrender of faith.* There was real danger. The Hebrew Christians were being drawn into a vortex, against which the whole tenour of the epistle is a continual warning.

" Cast not away your confidence " as a cowardly soldier would cast away his weapon, and shirk the fight. The prize is for him that wins it. Eternal life is for him that overcometh.

To cast away your confidence is
(i.) To sin wilfully after having received the knowledge of the truth ;
(ii.) To crucify Christ afresh, to put Him to an open shame ;
(iii.) To tread under foot, and to count His blood (the blood of atonement), wherewith ye are sanctified, an unholy thing, and to do despite to the Spirit of grace ;
(iv.) To *apostatize* from the faith—to imperil the soul by drawing back unto perdition : " For if any man draw back, My soul shall have no pleasure in him."

1. There is a like temptation, and a most real danger now as then :
(i.) There is the ever-increasing cry, going up from thousands of printing presses, which may be heard all over the globe, and seen in current literature, asking tauntingly, "*What confidence is this wherein thou trustest ?*"
(ii.) Around the citadel of faith there is an anti-Christian host gathered, like the heathen that gathered around the walls of Jerusalem, shouting, " *Down with it, down with it, even to the ground.*"
(iii.) Again may be heard that curious intermingling of cultured and uncultured voices in one hoarse whisper, "Crucify Him, crucify Him." For of a truth against the Church of Christ are the people gathered together.
And their demand of us is THE SURRENDER OF FAITH.
(i.) " *Cast away your confidence* " in GOD, say

they, for there is no personal God but Nature, in whom we live, and move, and have our being.
(ii.) " *Cast away your confidence* " in the BIBLE, for it is no inspired Book. Natural Science has exploded all belief in its account of Creation, and men no longer believe in it.
(iii.) *Cast away your confidence* in HEAVEN and HELL and Judgment to come. These are the stock-in-trade of superstition, with which the conscience of the feeble is alarmed.
Notwithstanding this—though the enemies of Christianity were never more in number nor more bitter ; though it be everywhere spoken against ; though it professes to give no evidence which will satisfy the sceptic, yet it thrives—it goes on making conquests—it is spreading all over the globe. It is a real power. Thousands come from east and west, north and south,—diverse in nationality, station, learning ; sundered by oceans and by social barriers,—who are yet all agreed on this one thing, *the saving of the soul ;* who have *no confidence in the flesh,* but their confidence, amounting even to *boldness,* is in Jesus Christ, in whom whosoever believeth shall not be confounded.

2. The Secret of this confidence :
(i.) It is not an *opinion*—opinions change—nor a religion which may be exchanged for another ; but it is a *life.* Observe how it is put :
" *Ye have tasted the powers of the world to come* "= Christians are in advance of their age. They have by their experience been, as it were, projected into *the age to come*—Into the regenerated world wherein dwelleth righteousness.
Cf. the words of Galileo's recantation. On his knees he uttered, under compulsion : " With a sincere heart and unfeigned faith I abjure, curse, and detest the said errors " (viz., that the earth moves round the sun, etc.). . . . Rising from his knees, he whispered, "It moves, *for all that.*" He was in advance of his age. He might recant, and the Christian may draw back, but the *conviction* remains unaltered. Having once tasted of the powers of the world to come, the experience is no matter of opinion, it is a part of a man's LIFE. . . . From which, if a man draw back, it is to perdition, an act of apostasy,—" My soul shall have no pleasure in him."
(ii.) It is a *right of access* to God, a right of way, a new and living way. " I am the Way. . . . No man cometh unto the Father but by Me." This way to God has been opened up for us by Jesus Christ. Who that knows this way, and uses it, ever thinks of yielding it up, or of being talked out of it by the glibbest talker of the day? What wanderer is there who has found his way back again to his Heavenly Father's house and heart, and is restored to communion and fellowship with Him, does not know that he possesses the very ESSENCE OF RELIGION, and has nothing else to seek, none other to go to ? What can there be higher for him than the fulfilment of the promise, " If a man love Me, he will keep My Word : and My Father will love him, *and We will come unto him,* and make our abode *with him* " ?
(iii.) Learn also the greatness of the sin of apostasy. It = to be cut adrift again, exiled from home, without God, hopeless and homeless.

3. See context for the *reward.* " After having done the will of God," " Ye have need of patience," because the road is long and rough, and the reward is for the future.

(d)

CONFIDENCE

Calm *confidence* rests not in imagination, superstition, nor enthusiasm ; but God gives it.
(*a*)   *S. Bridge*

CONFIDENCE AND FEAR

A person coming from confession told me that he was full of joy and confidence ; another, that he was full of fear. Upon this, I thought within myself that these two men put together would make one good one ; and that each was defective in wanting the feelings of the other.
(*b*)   *Blaise Pascal*

CONFIRMATION

" *To everything there is a season* " (Eccl. iii. 1)

1. A time to be born (of parents) ;
2. A time to be baptised (by others) ;
3. A time to be confirmed (self) ;
4. A time for life's work and duties (in the station to which God's providence calls us) ;
5. A time to die (when our work is done).

Let us not think any of these accidental. God arranges all ; and the time of confirmation, fixed to take place before life's work begins, its most important.
1. Before business, when cares come, like thorns, to choke the seed of the word—now appearing as the blade.
2. Before married life, with more and more cares, when this work, if not done, will probably never be done.
To defer it to a future time, is like the attempt to alter one season for another,—to sow in autumn and reap in winter. The time for one of these duties cannot be put in the place of another. The result would be confusion and loss.
(*c*)

CONFIRMATION, TIME OF (Eccles. iii. 1)

" To everything there is a season, and a time for every purpose under the heaven."
1. Examples in verses 1–8. Nothing accidental in these.
2. The time for one thing must not be delayed till the time has come for another.
1. The time for *Confirmation*, wisely chosen at the age fixed ; let that time pass, and you introduce *confusion*, *difficulty*, and *hardening*.
2. Thereafter will ensue times for *Business*, *Marriage*, *Family Cares*, *Illness*, and *Death*.
3. Therefore it is of the first importance that the time for Confirmation be not delayed.
" Seek ye first the kingdom of God."
= Begin life well. Leave nothing undone that ought to be done.
(*d*)

CONFLICT

There is an intestine war in man, between reason and the passions. He might enjoy some repose, had he reason alone without passion, or passion alone without reason. But, having both, he must needs live in a state of warfare, since he cannot maintain peace with one, without being at war with the other. Hence he is always divided, and always at variance with himself.
(*e*)   *Blaise Pascal*

No sooner is peace with God, through Christ, settled, than war is proclaimed ; and the man involved in its arduous and lifelong struggles. . . *Conflict* begins with conversion. . . (the infant Hercules has to strangle serpents in his cradle). So soon as a man is new-born, and turns his face heavenward, he has hell to confront and fight with. And besides the devil and his angels, the world and its influences, the passions that he loved in his breast and fed by long indulgence into strength, it may be said that " his enemies are the men of his own house." And such in number and power are the temptations with which a good man has to contend, that no Christian will think the language of David extravagant : " They compassed me about ; they compassed me about like bees. My soul is among lions ; and I lie even among them that are set on fire."
Thos. Guthrie, D.D. (" *Good Words*," 1861)
(*f*)

Jacob does not become Israel without a wrestling through the night ; the woman of Canaan does not obtain the restoration of her daughter ere she strives in faith and prayer ; Peter does not become the rock on which the Church is built before sinking in deep waters.
(*g*)   *Oosterzee*

CONGREGATION

A congregation is always a microcosm. Little children, adults ; the aged, the young and strong : all classes of minds, in all sorts of relations, each with a different past behind it. Preach, then, to individuals.
(*h*)   *Storrs*

CONGREGATION

There are all sorts of minds in a congregation, and in all sorts of states. Here a sceptic, perhaps propagating his scepticism, who is to be answered, silenced, if possible, convinced. Here is a person teased with disturbing doubts. Here one indifferent, whom you must arouse and startle into attention to the truth ; another, inquiring, undecided, whom you must direct. There are sinners to be converted, sufferers to be soothed, the tempted to be warned, the imperfect who need teaching, the poor to be cheered, and the rich to be exhorted to generous liberality.
(*i*)   *Ibid*

CONGREGATION, MISCELLANEOUS NATURE OF A

A Divinity Professor is reported to have said of his opportunities as a teacher of theology :—
" There were three men in my class : one of them was a sceptic, one a dyspeptic, and the third a Swedenborgian."
(*j*)   *Ibid*

CONGREGATION AND PREACHER

" *Jesus of Nazareth passeth by.*"
Oftentimes, when we are wholly unaware, there are minds in the congregation approaching the fateful point of transition, like men riding side by side in a railway carriage till they reach the
(*k*)

point where their paths diverge. They have come from M—— to R——, perhaps, riding together all the way. There one of them steps to another seat. For a space their tracks run parallel still, but by degrees they diverge; further and further they go asunder; till, of the two so lately riding and talking together, one has reached Boston, Liverpool, Berlin, the other San Francisco, Yokohama, Hong Kong. Side by side, a few weeks since, and now the diameter of the earth between them! At any time minds approaching such critical points may be before you; the turning point of life in one direction or another—No circle of the centuries shall again bring them together. You know not when these moments come. But always preach as if some before you had reached them.

(a)   *Storrs*

CONQUERORS AND CONFLICT (Rev. xxi. 6, 7, 8)

If you look at the context, you will find, in close connection with the statement about "overcoming," another statement about "thirsting for the water of life." The juxtaposition is significant; and it seems to imply, that those who long for the knowledge of God, and for the enjoyment of God—those who consider God the highest good, to be obtained at all risks, and at any cost, will be, of necessity, involved in a conflict with the forces of the world. Their thirsting makes them warriors; their determination to find their way into their proper spiritual element—which is God—compels them to encounter, and to overcome, the intervening obstacles which lie between them and the object of their desire. So long as we are in the world, and of it, we know nothing of spiritual conflict. Why should we? The dead fish floats with the current, and has no opposition to encounter. It is the living creature which meets the force of the stream, and has to make its way against it. But when we become sons of God, through faith in Christ Jesus,—then it is that we become conscious of conflict, because we are left in an element which is in opposition to the mind of Christ. "Conflict with what?" you say. "Be explicit!" I will be explicit. Conflict with the selfishness of our own hearts. Self wishes to be Lord, and forbids Christ to be Lord. We have to resist self. Conflict with the outer world. The maxims of society are opposed to the maxims of Christ. Men don't think you a fool if you just veneer yourself with religion. Put on an outer coating, and they commend you; of course they can easily see the wolf under the sheepskin, and they recognise their own. But let religion get into your heart—be Christ's in grain, as well as on the surface, and you will soon find the difference. Your conflict, then, is with the society in which you move. You must be in the world, and yet not of it; and that is not always a comfortable position. Conflict with the devil. Yes, real conflict! I do not mean to say that Satan will appear to you in bodily shape, and that you will feel called upon to fling an inkstand at his head as Martin Luther did; but I say that, if you are a real Christian, you will have to contend with many a subtle suggestion; with many an evil impulse; with many a misgiving about God; with many a perverted thought about the Gospel; with many a dark surmising—all of which will have had their origination with the father of lies. "Conflict." Yes! plenty of real, spiritual conflict with self, with the world, with the devil; and this you would never have known had you not entered the region of sonship; had you not numbered yourselves amongst those who are athirst for God, for the living God.

(b)   *Gordon Calthrop*

CONQUERORS AND COWARDS (Rev. xxi. 7, 8)

Two Contrasts : Those who overcome, and those who shrink from the fight. = The saved and the lost.

1. **Christian life is a warfare.**

(i.) The Christian is a soldier by *profession* :

See Baptismal Formula, "We receive . . . good soldier of Jesus Christ "—whose duty it is to fight against the three-fold foe, the World, the Flesh, and the Devil.

(ii.) The Christian is also a soldier of *necessity* :

He has a new principle of life and activity within him. He is not content with things as they are: He wants to make the world better than it is. He is opposed to everything that is *unreal*, all *shams, hypocrisies, tricks* in trade, in fact to every kind of wrong-doing and abomination that is done under the sun. He *thirsts after righteousness;* and his aim is to do whatever is *good*, and *right*, and *true*.

He cannot help, nor avoid the struggle, because he has that within him, his whole new nature, which revolts against unrighteousness in any form; and whether he will or no, he is of necessity a warrior, fighting in the ranks of Jesus Christ, to overthrow the kingdom of darkness, and to establish a kingdom wherein dwelleth RIGHTEOUS-NESS.

(iii.) Hence the kingdom of heaven is said to *suffer violence; and the violent taketh it by force.*

Hence the injunction,
"Fight the good fight of faith, lay hold on eternal life."
Hence also, "Quit you like men; be *strong*."

And there comes a solemn moment in after life, the moment of personal decision, when each baptized person is awakened to the necessity of enlisting him or her self more decidedly on the side of Jesus Christ. Then is felt the need of the *whole armour of God* (Eph. vi.).—The helmet, the breast-plate, the girdle, the sword of the spirit, and the shield of faith.—There is no chance of success without it.

The Christian has to meet with giants = giant sins, giant errors, giant customs, giant heresies. The world will be against him as it was against Christ : "Of a truth, against Thy Holy Child Jesus have the princes of this world gathered together." And the Christian has to become a hero in the strife : An *overcomer*—a CONQUEROR; Yea, more than a CONQUEROR. Such warriors have a promise : "*They shall inherit all things*"—(they shall have at last what they thirsted for—a world wherein dwelleth righteousness) ; and "they shall be my sons, and I will be their God."

(iv.) *But how?* By faith in Jesus Christ :
"This is the victory that overcometh, even our faith";
(c)

" Thanks be to God, who giveth us the victory, through our Lord Jesus Christ " ;

" Without Me, ye can do nothing." Hence the overcomers are the FAITHFUL.

> " Once they were warring here below,
> And wet their couch with tears :
> They wrestled hard as we do now,
> With sins, and doubts, and fears."

2. The Cowards

= The fearful; the unbelieving, who shirked the fight, and had not the courage to do right ; therefore are they THE LOST.

We learn from the context where they failed :·

(i.) The irreligious or *unbelieving* found that a *religious life* required *hardness, restraint, restrictions ;* whereas it was easier for them to float with the tide of inclination than against it = *cowardice.*

(ii.) The *dishonest* man found it easier to be dishonest than honest : his gains were quicker ; he had not to wait and *struggle* with poverty as the honest man had. " He that maketh haste to be rich shall not be innocent " = *cowardice.*

(iii.) The liar had not the courage to tell the truth and face the consequences ; but shirked it = *cowardice.*

(iv.) The *sensualist* found it easier and pleasanter to live a life of unrestrained self-indulgence, than to keep his body under, and bring it into subjection, by reining in his unruly appetites.

ALL WERE COWARDS : They had not the courage to deny themselves anything ; nor to do what was right when it cost them a struggle ; they shirked every difficulty ; refused to bear the cross ; turned away, and fled from Jesus Christ, because it was pleasanter to live a life of easy self-gratification in all things.

These are THE LOST, moral wrecks, the cowards in life's hard battle, who had not the courage to do right.

For these there is no promise—they had no thirst after God — their *lot,* or portion, is the SECOND DEATH.

Whatever this may mean more, it is here placed in direct contrast, and as the opposite to the promise made to the conquerors. They are *within,* these are *without.* They are *the sons of God,* these are *dogs.* They inherit *heaven,* these drop into the *abyss.* They are fit company for God and the holy inhabitants of the heavenly city, these for that of devils.

But, as the Apostle says, " We are persuaded better things of you, things that accompany salvation."

Oh, to say, with one of these conquerors, " I have fought the good fight ; I have kept the faith ; henceforth there is laid up for me a crown of glory, which the Lord, the righteous Judge, shall give me at that day."

(a)

CONQUERORS AND COWARDS

" *Be Strong* " (2 Tim. ii. 1)

The meeting of *Elijah* and *Ahab* at the plot of Naboth supplies an illustration, observe that *weakness* and wickedness are nearly allied.

Weakness and *strength* are contrasted in these two men.

Compare also : The fate of *cowards* and the *overcomers* in Rev. xxi. 7, 8.

" The fearful and unbelieving shall have their part in the . . . second death, whilst—

" He that *overcometh* shall inherit these things ; and I will be his God, and he shall be my son."

(b)

" CONQUERORS, MORE THAN "

" *Who shall separate us from the love of Christ ? shall tribulation, or distress, or persecution, or famine, or nakedness, or peril, or sword ? As it is written, for Thy sake we are killed all the day long ; we are accounted as sheep for the slaughter. Nay, in all these things we are more than conquerors through Him that loved us* " (Rom. viii. 35–37).

Four times already the question " who " has been asked—" Who can be against us ? " " Who shall lay anything to the charge of God's elect ? " " Who is he that condemneth ? " And now the question is " Who shall separate us from the love of Christ ? " Implying, of course, that nothing can ; for the proper reference here of the question is, not to persons, but to *things,* though personal enemies may lurk beneath them. Such things as might well be supposed to have a separating effect, or which might imply that such a separation had been effected, are afterwards enumerated. It has already been shown that *no person* could be against those whom Almighty God was for ; and that *no person* could condemn them for whom Christ died, and rose, and intercedes. It is now stated that *nothing*—out of the whole round of afflictive and distressing circumstances can separate the Christian from the love of Christ. It has been remarked that *sin* only is excepted, possibly because that can effect from within what no enemy could do from without ; and in accordance with the teaching of the prophet—" Your sins and your iniquities *have separated* between you and your God." But we must not forget that the supposition here, is that of a *living faith*—the faith by which the Christian is justified, and in which he lives. This is the key to the whole argument of the Apostle—and, under a dispensation of grace, sins of infirmity do not break the bond betwixt Christ and the Christian, whilst those of a deeper dye, and of wilful departure from Christ, are not and of course cannot be contemplated in the passage under discussion.

(c)

The " *love of Christ.*" ·It is superfluous to ask what this is, whether the love of the Christian for Christ, or that of Christ for us. The context sufficiently indicates that it is not our love for Christ so much as His love towards us which is intended here.

The child's grasp of his Father's hand is comparatively weak and powerless. Many a stumble in the rough road of life would be sufficient to separate his grasp from his Father's, if that were all ; but it is the strong grip of Omnipotence which holds him up and keeps him safe. The roughness of the road and the darkness of the way, the turnings and windings and the steepnesses of the path make no difference to Him with whom the darkness and the light are both alike. His hand holds us and never lets us go. This is the confidence conveyed in the Apostle's question :—" *Who*

(d)

shall separate us from the love of Christ?" And in answering this question he proves that the love of Christ is *inseparable* from the Christian. It does not, as a mere human love might do, withdraw itself from the object once loved, and change its mood towards it; but it is simply unchangeable and inseparable from its object; and consequently the certainties of eternal life and glory are assured to the Christian along with it.

(*a*)

If sufferings intervene, they must be explained on some other supposition than that of a possible change in the love of Christ for us; once and for all, that cannot be. We might as soon admit that a flaw existed somewhere in the mechanism of the universe, and that in consequence planetary or other movements could not be depended upon, as to admit such a possibility into the Redemptive work of Christ. Sufferings are evidences of *love*, not of wrath.

And they have a two-fold aspect: one, which shows us our relationship to Christ—"If *children*, then heirs, heirs of God and joint-heirs with Christ; if so be that we *suffer* with Him, that we may be also glorified together." The other, to show us the aim intended by them—"We know that all things work together for *good* to them that love God"; *all things*, not merely *some things;* all things afflictive, as well as joyous, work together for our good, just as rain and sunshine, heat and cold, summer and winter, work together in producing a harvest of glory in the golden grain of the autumn.

(*b*)

MORE THAN CONQUERORS: THE POSSIBLE SEPARATING CAUSES:

There are *seven*, a regular gradation, intensifying as they go on, from *tribulation*, through *distress, persecution, famine, nakedness,* and *peril,* to death itself by the *sword ;* seven *strands* twisted into one strong rope with which to pull the Christian away from Christ; seven strong temptations operating as causes to bring about a relapse, and to produce apostasy.

Through life-long trouble, ending with a violent and a martyr's death, they work, in order, if possible, to separate the Christian from the love of Christ. Nothing more trying, perhaps nothing more terrifying, nor any greater test, could be imagined; and yet they fail; for the seventh test ends in glory, not in separation. The Christian comes forth from the ordeal *more than a conqueror.*

(*c*)

But let us pass each of the seven possible separating causes in review, and see wherein lay the power of each to produce the result supposed.

1. "SHALL TRIBULATION" which means simply *trouble*—chiefly external trouble—do it? The word may be explained to mean the *sifting* and winnowing process that corn undergoes in order to separate it from the chaff; but it also means a painful tearing, pressing, and squeezing process of humiliation, which seems needful for all those to undergo who would enter in by the *door*, and tread the *narrow* way which leadeth unto life. By nature we are too big, too proud, too self-important, and carry too much luggage, to go in by that door and tread in that path; therefore it is that "we *must* through *much tribulation* enter into the kingdom of heaven;" for only by tribulation can we be reduced to the child-like mind and disposition of all who go in thereat; and be fitted to become disciples of Him who was "*meek and lowly in heart.*" Now the question with the Christian, when he is called upon to pass through much tribulation, is, whether his troubles are a sign of love or of condemnation. He cannot at such seasons realize the love of Christ; his condition contradicts it; great opposing obstacles are between him and it. Therefore he argues that the love of Christ is withdrawn from him, and can no longer exist for him, nor he for it, and consequently *the separation is effected.* That such reasoning should be uppermost is no marvel when, as is frequently the case, troubles come fast and thick one after another, as in the case of Job; overtaking him without warning, in the midst of prosperity, happiness, and usefulness; hardly giving him time to realize the extent of one trouble before news comes that another, and another, and yet another had befallen him. For while the first messenger was telling of the loss of his oxen and asses, there came *also another*, to say that his herds of sheep were struck with lightning and consumed; and while he was yet speaking there came *also another*, to say that the Chaldeans had made a raid upon them and had carried off the camels; and again, while he was yet speaking there came *also another*, to tell the saddest news of all, that the sons and daughters of Job were suddenly buried beneath the ruins of a fallen house. Such is the description of the suddenness and swiftness with which troubles may come, to show us how soon a bright sky may be overcast with dark clouds, and our faith subjected to the severest test. Job's faith did not indeed fail him; but he was staggered by the force of the successive blows; and though he fell upon the ground and worshipped God, and said, "Naked came I out of my mother's womb, and naked shall I return thither: the Lord gave, and the Lord hath taken away; blessed be the name of the Lord," yet, as his troubles continued to thicken after this, he was puzzled and knew not how to account for it. But as we stand at a distance, and behold the process through which he passed, we see, that though tribulation looked like wrath, "and was so interpreted by his friends, yet this was really the way in which the love of God for him was manifesting itself, making all things work for his good. Something, indeed, he lost in the process, but it was that which the patriarch most wanted to lose. When precious metal is melted in a crucible, it loses its dross and alloy; and when wheat is winnowed, the wind carries away the chaff; so Job's character underwent a purifying process. His tribulation purged away much dross and alloy which had previously marred the workmanship of God. The mistake is, to think that the love of Christ should always express itself in smiles and earthly prosperity; whereas, indeed, the hand which in faithfulness, cuts, and often cuts deeply, is the hand of love, since it cuts away proud flesh, which, if left alone, would kill us. The rough hand which suddenly plucks us back from the edge of a precipice, is the hand of love, not of wrath. The Psalmist so understood it when he wrote, "In very faithfulness Thou hast afflicted me."

Tribulation, then, does not separate the Christian from the love of Christ, but is really an evidence of its existence.

(*d*)

2. "OR DISTRESS?" which is trouble of a mental kind, tending to despair. Tribulation may be described as the "fightings without," whilst *distress* may be described as the "*fears within*," the "*anguish*" of the wicked. That kind of trouble is indicated which comes upon a wrestler, when his antagonist has succeeded in throwing him after a long struggle, and has now got his foot on him, and is holding him down, and all seems to be up with him; before, when wrestling, he was troubled, now he is *distressed*. Thus we see that the afflictions contemplated by the terms *tribulation* and *distress* are no light ones; and it is little wonder that under the strain of such untoward circumstances of outward and inward trouble, the Christian should lose heart and fear the worst.

(*a*)

3. Next, in the gradation of powers which might effect a complete separation from the love of Christ, comes "PERSECUTION," which is sure to test the genuine amongst Christ's flock; then it is asked whether "FAMINE, or NAKEDNESS, or PERIL, or SWORD," could effect it? *Persecution* drove the early Christians into the wilderness, where they were exposed to all the hardships of *famine*, cold, hunger, and *nakedness;* they went in *peril* of death, till finally they were hunted down, and suffered *martyrdom* for Christ's sake. Now, if anything could effect the separation supposed, surely such fiery trials as these would do so. If anything could make a man apostatize from the faith, it would be, we think, when he was called upon to suffer for Christ. But do they succeed? Have they succeeded in the past? "*Nay*," answers the Apostle, "*in all these things we are*

(*b*)

"MORE THAN CONQUERORS"

The attitude of the world is ever the same towards the kingdom of God. They slaughtered the people of God in Old Testament times, because they were first "accounted as sheep for the slaughter." The *sword* has ever been at work amongst them. Long ago the Psalmist wrote, "For Thy sake we are killed all the day long." The Saviour, too, told His disciples, that in the world they should have tribulation. "If they have persecuted Me, they will also persecute you." Therefore the New Testament Church, being forewarned, is not surprised by seasons of bitter persecution, nor ought individual Christians to stumble because of their "*much tribulation*." So Stephen, who prayed for his murderers as they stoned him to death; and Paul and Silas, singing whilst fettered in a Roman prison; and James, whom Herod slew with the *sword*, were "MORE THAN CONQUERORS."

(*c*)

NEW TESTAMENT TEACHING generally is to the same effect; sufferings for Christ's sake end triumphantly, instead of separating the victims of the world's enmity from His love. It may be well to recall some of the passages bearing on the subject:—In the Lord's teaching (Matt. v. 10–12) He says, "Blessed are they who are *persecuted* for righteousness sake, for theirs is the kingdom of heaven."

"Blessed are ye when men shall revile you, and *persecute* you, and say all manner of evil against you falsely, for My sake; "

"Rejoice and be exceeding glad, for great is your reward in heaven; for so *persecuted* they the prophets which were before you."

This certainly does not look like loss, and separation from His love. Persecuted here, they have a kingdom there; reviled by men, but blessed by the Saviour; a great reward for a little loss and ill-usage; numbered with the prophets, who underwent like treatment before them, and partakers of the sufferings of Christ, they are bidden to rejoice and be exceeding glad. Truly in all these things they are MORE THAN CONQUERORS. Their "light affliction worketh for them a far more exceeding and eternal weight of glory."

(*d*)

See also what is said in different places in "The Acts of the Apostles" concerning the effect of persecution on the Church of Christ, "At that time there was a *great persecution* against the Church which was at Jerusalem, and they were scattered abroad." The consequence was, "Therefore they that were scattered abroad *went everywhere* preaching the word; " and when, on another occasion, Paul and Barnabas were *persecuted*, and expelled from Antioch, they "were filled with joy, and with the Holy Ghost."

(*e*)

Hear also St. Paul's personal record of the tribulation, he experienced (1 Cor. iv. 11–13): (i.) "Even unto this present hour we both *hunger and thirst*, and are *naked*, and are buffeted, and have *no certain dwellingplace;* and labour, working with our hands : being reviled, we bless ; being *persecuted* we suffer it ; being defamed, we intreat ; we are made as the filth of the world, and are the offscouring of all things unto this day. (ii.) (1 Cor. xv. 31, 32) : "I die daily. . . . I have fought with beasts at Ephesus." (iii.) (2 Cor. iv. 8–11), "Troubled on every side, yet not *distressed;* perplexed, but not in despair ; *persecuted*, but not forsaken ; *cast down*, but not destroyed ; always bearing about in the body the *dying* of the Lord Jesus, that the life also of Jesus might be made manifest in our body. For we which live are always delivered unto *death*, for Jesus' sake, that the life also of Jesus might be made manifest in our mortal flesh." (iv.) (2 Cor. ii. 23–27) : "In stripes above measure, in prisons more frequent, in *deaths* oft. Of the Jews five times received I forty stripes save one. Thrice was I beaten with rods, once was I stoned ; thrice I suffered shipwreck ; a night and a day I have been in the deep ; in journeyings often ; in *perils* of waters ; in *perils* of robbers ; in *perils* by mine own countrymen ; in *perils* by the heathen ; in *perils* in the city, in *perils* in the *wilderness;* in *perils* in the sea ; in *perils* among false brethren. In weariness and painfulness ; in watchings often ; in *hunger* and *thirst;* in fastings often ; in cold and *nakedness*."

(*f*)

MORE THAN CONQUERORS: THE SEVEN-STRANDED ROPE

Here we see the *seven-stranded* rope at work, doing its utmost to pull the stout-hearted Apostle from the rock and to separate him from the love of Christ. *Tribulation, distress, persecution, famine, nakedness, peril*, and the *sword* are all here, all in

(*g*)

force, and with what result? Why, when near the end of his life, we hear the grand Apostle uttering such words as these, "for me to live is Christ, to die is gain," "To depart and be with Christ is *far better;*" and when almost in view of *the sword,* he said, "I am ready to be offered, and the time of my departure is at hand. I have fought a good fight, I have finished my course, I have kept the faith; henceforth there is laid up for me a crown of glory which the Lord, the Righteous Judge shall give me at that day: *and not to me only,* but unto all them also that love His appearing." Therefore in his case, *and not in his case only,* the strain put upon faith and endurance had quite the contrary effect to that supposed. The gradation all along tended to "a crown of glory" and not to separation from the love of Christ.

The day came at last, when Paul, the prisoner of Jesus Christ, prematurely old, small of stature, was led forth from his prison, his chain clanking heavily along the pavement; presently the uplifted blade of the headsman gleamed brightly in the Italian sun, and the head of Paul the Christian rolled at the feet of the Roman executioner.

(*a*)

The *sword,* the last of the SEVEN terrible things to flesh and blood, had done its work; there was nothing more that it could do. Yes, but what work? Had it succeeded in separating the Christian from the love of Christ? for that was the object aimed at all through. Nay, on the contrary, it had sent him to be "*for ever with the Lord.*" The *disciple* had gone home to the beloved Master; the *apostle* had gone to be crowned; the *warrior,* to make his triumphal entry into the Holy City, escorted by a joyous convoy of holy angels, who had come out on swift pinions to meet his rapt spirit as it wings its flight to the arms of everlasting bliss. He who had fought so well was indeed MORE THAN CONQUEROR.

(*b*)

But, as he said, "*not to me only*" is there awaiting such a cavalcade of angels, such a triumphal entry into the city of our God, and such an eternal weight of glory; all those also who love the Lord's appearing will have their share as well, along with those of whom it is written, "They were stoned, they were sawn asunder, were tempted, were slain with the sword; they wandered about in sheepskins and goatskins; being destitute, afflicted, tormented (of whom the world was not worthy); they wandered in deserts, and in mountains, and in dens and caves of the earth." But who also were *more than conquerors* in the end, for of them elsewhere it is said :—"*And white robes were given unto* EVERY ONE *of them.*"

(*c*)

MORE THAN CONQUERORS : HOW DO THEY CONQUER?

"*Through* HIM *that loved us.*" There are just two thoughts here: and first we are taught that the overcoming power is *not of ourselves.* We conquer through Him that loved us. Nor are we to understand by this that overcoming power comes merely through the *assistance* of the Saviour; but it is ours through the power of His *death,* His *resurrection,* and His own *victory.* "Be of good cheer, *I have overcome the world.*"

Now, by virtue of our union with Him, His *death* is ours; His *resurrection* is ours; and His *victory,* too, is ours. This is what the same apostle terms "*The exceeding greatness of His power* to usward who believe." Our victory over the sufferings of this present time; our issuing from troubles with gain and not loss; our coming forth from the furnace,—though heated seven times hotter than at other times,—like silver tried in the furnace, the purer and the better, is all *assured to us in the victory of our Lord Jesus Christ.*

The other thought is that of the supreme importance of *faith.* Everything which the Apostle here speaks of, and which he proves is *assured* to and made a *certainty* for those to whom he writes, depends upon their *faith;* without faith we have neither part nor lot in this great matter. The whole of our victory, our hope of bliss, everything, is at stake, if we have not faith. "All things are possible *to him that believeth;*" but to the unbelieving nothing is assured, nothing can be done. "All the promises of God are yea and amen in Jesus Christ;" but if we sunder ourselves from Him by unbelief, if we reject Him, there is *no promise* for us—no promise of eternal life—no promise of being saved from condemnation, no promise of being kept by the power of God, no promise of victory over the troubles of this life. For "this is the victory that overcometh the world, even *our faith.*"

"Who is He that overcometh the world, but *he that believeth* that Jesus is the Son of God?"

Therefore it is that believers, and only they, can join in the triumphant language of the Apostle when he asks, "O death, where is thy sting? O grave, where is thy victory? The sting of death is sin;" (*but Jesus has died for our sins*) "and the strength of sin is the law" (*but we are not under the law, but under grace*). Therefore, "Thanks be to God, which giveth us the victory through our Lord Jesus Christ." Listen to the new song of these victors in heaven : "THOU hast made us unto our God kings and priests; and we shall reign on the earth."

(*d*)

CONSCIENCE

Trust that man in nothing, who has not a conscience in everything.

(*e*)   *Sterne*

CONSCIENCE

Conscience is that consciousness of man by virtue of which a feeling of approval of truth and sincerity is attributed to him. Conscience approves of that which is true.

I stand before myself as before a riddle, whose key is not to be found in human self-consciousness. . . . For this reason the spirit of man's life is called at the same time "the candle of the Lord" (Prov. xx. 27). This is "that light in us," which may become "darkness." (Cf. "Knowing God.")

(*f*)   *Harless*

CONSCIENCE

If conscience had the power, as it has the right, it would rule the world.

(*g*)   *Bp. Butler*

CONSCIENCE

How comes it that man by nature ($\phi\acute{v}\sigma\epsilon\iota$) should find within him a higher and directing power ruling over him?

" Man is so organized physiologically," is the answer of modern physiology.

But he who takes his stand on the physiology of the nervous system, and will not move from that position, would do better not to speak of conscience at all, nay, not even of morality. For that has not its origin in physiological processes which we can examine with the microscope or measure out by millimetres.

Conscience is the knowledge of a divine law which every man bears in his heart, . . . written in ineffaceable characters in the hearts of the heathen, as it stands for Israel on the tables of stone, and on the parchment of the Thora."

(a)   *Harless and Delitzsch*

CONSCIENCE

When the unhappy Charles I. pleaded that to pass the bill of attainder against the Earl of Stafford was against his *conscience*, that remarkable character of " boldness and impiety," Williams, Archbishop of York, demonstrated " that there are *two sorts of conscience*, public and private; and that his public conscience as a king might dispense with his private conscience as a man!"

(b)   *Disraeli: Cur. Eng. Lit*

Hurt not your conscience with any known sin.

(c)   *S. Rutherford*

CONSCIENCE

When the compass loses its proper polarity at sea, the whole course of the vessel is altered. And when the conscience loses its right direction—Godward—the heart is filled with fears, the prospects of life become uncertain, and all the dispensations of providence are suspected to be judgments. The man walks through society dreading and suspecting every man, because his own conscience is wrong.

(d)   *Cumming*

CONSCIENCE, ROOT AND ESSENCE OF

We name the spirit, in so far as it is moral and religious consciousness, *conscience*. The faculty of human knowledge is the spirit. He who wishes to understand the nature of conscience, must first have understood that of the spirit. Everything is understood, not in the light of its existence, but in that of its *origin*. Man, consisting of body and soul, is now originated by procreation, by which human nature is only so perpetuated, as in the beginning it came into being, not by human generation, but by Divine creative act. The corporeal nature now perpetuated never loses or falsifies its original source, as not created directly for Himself, but indirectly, by means of the earth which He had first made. And the spirit, perpetuated also by generation, never loses or falsifies its original source, created without intermediate means, directly from God Himself, and made it the vital factor of the body; and thus, by the union of the two,

made man a living soul. . . . This characteristic of the spirit implanted in the life of the human race, is that which is perpetuated in every individual, and never loses its peculiar essence, . . . *a creature most immediately from God.* . . . The traces of this origin may indeed be obscured, but not altogether blotted out. . . . God stands in so marked a relation of creative Fatherhood to the human spirit, that even to the most degenerate child—the spirit in its greatest estrangement—the presentiment must still belong, " we are His offspring." . . . This remains, and manifests itself even in the fierce hate in which man praises the body alone, mocks at the soul, denies and blasphemes the nobility of a divine race, and takes pleasure in placing himself on a level with the brutes.

The last and deepest root of the spirit is the root of conscience: if the spirit were not and did not continue to be a spirit derived from God, it could neither comprehend, feel, nor conceive of God. . . .

The last factor of the spirit that is cognisant of God or of conscience, *is really God*, not man.

(e)   *Harless*

" CONSCIENCE OF SIN, NO MORE " (Heb. x. 2)

We may define conscience as man's *intuitive knowledge of himself, of God, of eternity.*

1. Consider Conscience as Man's Intuitive Knowledge of Himself.

In the lower animal world there is a faculty called *instinct*. This faculty enables an animal to seek its own good, to choose that which is serviceable to its bodily comfort and existence, and to reject whatever has an opposite tendency.

But man belongs to two worlds: the *carnal* and the *spiritual*, a higher and a lower; and his great danger is, lest the lower nature may too much engross him, and his efforts to gratify it may swamp the needs and the feebler demands of the higher. It is then to enable him to pay due attention to his spiritual nature that man's Creator has implanted within him this faculty of *conscience*, to remind him continually of the great things concerning himself, concerning God, and concerning eternity.

Conscience is, therefore, the sentinel which God has placed within man, to watch over and protect from harm his moral and spiritual well-being. It does not act with the same power in all persons: nor, in the same person, does it always act in the same degree; it is capable of being *hardened*, *seared*, and *deadened;* and as such its admonitions will be comparatively slight, unless roused up and awakened. But, less or more in every one, it is man's universal and perpetual reminder that he has a spiritual nature which demands watchfulness and care, training and development; and which will in the last great day leave all men " without excuse," inasmuch as having it in them, as a law unto themselves, they heeded it not, and lived lives of carnal gratification only—whilst their souls were entirely neglected, gradually deteriorating through neglect, until they died an everlasting death—a death of moral and spiritual suicide.

" For when the Gentiles, which have not the law, do by nature the things contained in the law, these, having not the law, are a law unto them-

(f)

selves : which show the work of the law written in their hearts, their *conscience* also bearing witness, and their thoughts the meanwhile accusing or else excusing one another." When, then, we say—" in the voice of conscience man hears the voice of God "—we do not mean anything supernatural—nor any special voice of inspiration,—but we speak of that which is quite natural, quite as it should be—we allude to an *evidence*, which cannot be rejected. Man thereby perceives and knows for a certainty that he has within him a something—which we call *spirit*—or *soul*—something supernatural—superior to all that he can otherwise see and know, by sensible experience of himself. It is something within him which is like a light shining in darkness, and the darkness perceiveth it not, and it is this something—which he cannot properly define—which tells him that the laws of the Old Testament Scriptures are a counterpart to itself—and that both proceed from the same Creator ; and he knows himself to be dependent on and accountable to a Holy God. So then conscience in man is the earliest notion a man has of his accountability and dependence upon a Holy God; and this consciousness every now and then, in the midst of unbelief and infidelity—of worldliness and of worldly wisdom—and in the midst of pleasures—flashes with lightning rapidity upon his mind, and reminds him that when all that this world can give him is passed away, when all his relations with time and men are snapped asunder by death, then there will not be an end of him—for he will appear in the presence of a Holy God to give account at the bar of judgment. But conscience—though reminding us of the judgment to come—waits not for that judgment, but arraigns us now at the same bar. For when the voices and businesses of the day are passed, when in the quietude and muteness of sleep, and upon our beds, it comes to remind us of the real state of things.

It spoke to St. Paul when he said, " With me it is a very small matter to be judged of you, or of man's judgment "—for conscience told him he was doing right, and it was a small matter that his enemies said otherwise.

To the bar of conscience comes the man who is misjudged, and who is persecuted for righteousness sake—knowing that though human judgments are wronging him, yet at the bar of his conscience he shall be acquitted.

To the bar of conscience, likewise, comes the sinner, where he finds that the trespass which he committed a long series of years ago—stands *as fresh* in his memory as if only done yesterday.

(*a*)   *Martensen and others*

2. Conscience as Man's Intuitive Knowledge of God

As we progress in self-knowledge, we shall discover that conscience reminds us that when we do wrong, we do not offend it, but we offend a sacred authority—God. This is especially true of an evil conscience ; for after the most notorious crimes we may notice a reaction setting in, impelling the wrong-doer to despair. Conscience makes the hardened villain, or criminal, to be ever picturing his crime ; he flees when no one pursueth. In an evil conscience there is always an inward disquiet and anguish for the present; and, as regards the future, there is a ceaseless dread and anticipation of being found out.

The laws which have been broken, the misdeeds that have been done, weigh upon the evil conscience like an oppressive burden, and put the whole will of man into the same condition as one is who cannot get air to breathe.

But not only is there this oppressive sense of guilt ; an evil conscience is likewise an *inward scourge*, which chases the transgressor like a wild beast ; and as such heathen mythology represents conscience under the name of the Furies ;—" They were three in number, and were the ministers of the vengeance of the gods, always *stern* and *inexorable*, always employed in punishing the guilty upon earth, as well as in the infernal regions. They inflicted their vengeance upon individual men by the secret stings of conscience, and in hell by perpetual torments. They were always represented with a grim aspect—bloody garments, and serpents wreathing round their heads instead of hair. They held a burning torch in one hand and a whip of scorpions in the other, and were always attended with terror, rage, paleness, and death."

Such was the heathen notion of a guilty conscience—an avenging Nemesis, pursuing the guilty by torturing recollections. Such a conscience had Cain, when, a fugitive and a vagabond on the earth, he went out from the presence of God and from his kindred, vainly endeavouring to flee from himself and from the harsh accusations of his inward conscience. *But no;* the evil doer has always the avenging power within him, he cannot flee from it—it is himself ; where he goes it goes, it dogs his steps like a shadow. " 'Twere best not know myself," exclaimed Macbeth. And mark in that wretched criminal the workings of an evil conscience, that will not let him separate himself from the remembrance of his crime. Not only do we see in him an ever-accusing conscience, but we see it also picturing to his fevered brain the persons and the instruments connected with his crimes. Now it is a dagger, clouted with blood, that floats in his imagination before him ; anon it is the ghost of one of his murdered victims—which persistently occupies the chair at the feast reserved for him. King, and surrounded with royal pomp; but his conscience comes between him and enjoyment ; and though there is a full cup of outward prosperity, he exclaims, " My mind is a nest of scorpions."

See, too, the terrors of conscience in his wife—which forces her in her sleep to disclose the deed of darkness, and nightly to arise from her bed and seek the bloodstained chamber which no perfumes nor odours can sweeten, nor water cleanse. Hear the criminal ask the physician :—

"Can'st thou not minister to a mind diseased:
Pluck from the memory a rooted sorrow ;
Raze out the troubles of the brain ;
And, with some sweet oblivious antidote,
Cleanse the stuffed bosom of that perilous stuff
Which weighs upon the heart ? "

Hear, too, the phrenzied words of Richard III., on the eve before the battle of Bosworth field—one who had literally waded through blood to the crown, but whose own hour was now come. Vengeance suffereth not such to live. Conscience, busy with her whip, tortures him in uneasy sleep. He starts out of his dream, and gives vent to the current of his thoughts, as he exclaims :—

"Have mercy, Jesu ! Soft ; I did but dream.
O *Coward conscience*, how dost thou afflict me !
The lights burn blue.—It is now dead midnight.
Cold fearful drops stand on my trembling flesh.

(*b*)

What, do I fear myself?—there's none ELSE by :
Richard *loves* Richard ; that is, I am I.
Is there a murderer here? *No;*—YES ;—I AM :
Then fly,—*What,* from myself? Great reason : Why?
Lest I revenge. What? *Myself* revenge *myself?*
Alas, *I love myself.* Wherefore? for any good
That I myself have done unto myself?
Oh, NO : alas, I rather hate myself
For hateful deeds committed by myself.
I am a villain : . . .
My conscience hath a thousand several *tongues,*
And every tongue brings in a several *tale,*
And every tale condemns me for a villain.
Perjury, perjury, in the highest degree ;
Murder, stern *murder,* in the direst degree ;
All several sins, all used in each degree,
Throng to the bar, crying all,—Guilty! *Guilty!* . . .
Methought, the souls of all that I had murdered
Came to my tent : and every one did threat
To-morrow's vengeance on the head of Richard."

See an evil conscience working again in Herod, when he heard of Jesus, and said, " It is John the Baptist *risen from the dead,* and therefore mighty works do show forth themselves in Him "—for an evil conscience is ever superstitious. It can hear of no unusual occurrence but it instantly recalls the past—and thinks the time of the avenger is come. Hence it was that Herod desired of a long time to see Jesus, to satisfy his curiosity, or to allay the promptings of his conscience ; and when, at last, Jesus *was* brought before Herod—and the coward tongue of the tyrant asked him many questions—it is significant that the Redeemer answered none of his questions—and why? Because He knew that conscience was at work, and the tyrant had only to listen to that for an answer.

Thus, from various sources, have we sought to portray the workings of a guilty conscience. We have seen that the ancient heathen rightly understood it when they wrapped around the head of the Furies wreaths of serpents and placed in their hands a whip of scorpions. We have seen how the greatest depicter of human passions likewise understood the absolute unrest and terror of a guilty conscience. And lastly, but not least, we have seen from the Bible, the same terrors of conscience. We have in it, also, direct statements of this condition, when it says, " The wicked are like the troubled sea, which cannot rest." " The wicked fleeth when no man pursueth, but the righteous is bold as a lion." The rustling of a leaf—the shaking of a tree alarms them, one can put 10,000 to flight. Whatever elements of comfort there may be in their temporal affairs, yet the terrors of their minds keep them in perpetual suspense and dread of the consequences of their misdeeds.

And what is the cause of this?

The cause of their unrest is this :—They know that their *inward tormentor* is only an officer of an avenging God, who will bring every work into judgment, of what sort it is—a God who is a rewarder of those who diligently seek Him—one who, without respect of persons, will repay every one according to his deeds—" tribulation and anguish upon every soul of man that doeth evil." It is this conviction of God, as a God of Justice— the avenger of His law—the conviction that the torture of the conscience is only a part of, and a prelude to, the *retribution* of a most just and Holy God, which makes them afraid. In other words, it is the conviction that the sinner has got *Omnipotence,* on the side of justice and right, arrayed against him.

(a)   *Martensen, Shakspeare, and others*

3. Conscience as Man's Intuitive Knowledge of Eternity

It is a conscience of eternity, because it warns the sinner of a judgment to come, a judgment not in this world fully carried out—a judgment in the life beyond. The heathen knew of this—for there is a remarkable passage in Plato, where an old man, speaking of old age and of the life beyond it, says :—

" Thou must know, that when a man believes death to be near, there is awakened within him a fear and an anxiety to which hitherto he had been a stranger. He had heard of a place of punishment and a condition of torment, during his lifetime, for wrong committed whilst on earth, and which he used to consider absurd ; but he begins now to distress his soul, lest, after all, it may be true, and he casts now a deeper and a penetrating glance into that world to which he is going, and because he is close upon its borders. Full of fear and anxiety, he begins to reflect, and to examine if he has wronged any one ; and he who finds many trespasses in his life, is constantly frightened from sleep : like a child, he trembles, and passes his life in sorrowful forebodings." Now this terror is that of conscience, reminding man of a future state. But the same thing is a matter of ordinary experience. Some years ago, by the giving way of a suspension bridge over the River Yare in Norfolk, a great number of people were suddenly precipitated into the water. One was amongst them, who, at the last moment, was rescued, and who gave it as his experience, that at the moment when he was in danger of drowning, the whole of his past life instantly flashed before him. Conscience was ready with its account—and with lightning rapidity showed him what he had to account for. Thus conscience reminds man of a judgment to come. We have stood by the bedside of the dying, when conscience apparently has been aroused from its lethargy—and a life's sins are spread out before the dying, and life has only a breath left—that breath has been spent in the utterance of one piercing cry, " *God be merciful to me a sinner* "—and we ask why the settlement of accounts between God and the soul had been put off till then?

These are the three functions of conscience— what it can do and what it does do ; and seeing that every man has this faculty of an intuitive knowledge of *himself,* of *God,* and of *eternity,* it may be asserted that *no man living can be an atheist.* There may be practical atheists ; but to find a man who is an out-and-out atheist, you must first find a man who is without a conscience.

There is however something which conscience cannot do : It can tell you of God. It can tell you of an eternity. It can tell you of yourself. It can hold up the stained pages of your history, and say, " O man, look at these ; " *but it cannot tell you one word about the forgiveness of sin*—It can tell you of a *conscience of sin,* but it cannot tell you of a " NO MORE *conscience of sin* "—nothing of sins blotted out. It can show you its wounds, but it cannot point you to the physician ; it can show you its stains, but it cannot tell you how to get the stains removed. This is no part of its work. When you come to deal with your conscience about the forgiveness of your sins, it will answer you : " Holiness I know, and guilt I know ; but what pardon is, I don't know. I have nothing to

(b)

do with it, I was not put here for that, it is not my office. I was put here as a sort of turnstile to the mind; I had to register everything that was done contrary to the wish and authority of God, and this I have done faithfully—here is the list, a long one; I cannot help you in getting quit of the score." This is quite true, a man's conscience knows nothing of the *forgiveness of sins.* Could conscience have told him this, Adam would not have hidden himself in the garden and have been afraid. Here is the very *essence* of *conversion:* the Spirit of God has to come in, and what a work it has to do to quiet the tumultuous tossings and agony of the conscience! It has, with its "still small voice"—to be heard above the roar of the tempest within and the thunders of Sinai. It has to take the Bible and spread it open, and point to what is written about Christ, about Atonement for sin, about the Lamb that was slain—" Who was wounded for our transgressions, bruised for our iniquities: the chastisement of our peace was upon Him, and with His stripes we are healed." "All we like sheep have gone astray; we have turned every one to his own way; and the Lord hath laid on Him the iniquity of us all." It tells him that "the blood of Jesus Christ cleanseth from all sin." It reminds him that whosoever cometh unto Jesus shall in no wise be rejected. The past shall be blotted out and forgotten, and shall not come into remembrance—whatever that past may be; it may have crimson stains upon it, —the most difficult of all stains and dyes to remove,—but when the Spirit draws a man, troubled with a conscience of sin, to Christ, He causes him to see, to read, and to believe that " though his sins be as scarlet, they shall be as snow; though they be red like crimson, they shall be as wool." And before the Spirit has done with that man, conscience will have to speak in another key—Jesus has become the Lord of conscience, " He looseth and no man bindeth "—" He openeth and no man shutteth "—the soul learns to sing with holy Robert M'Cheyne:

"My terrors all vanished before the sweet name;
My guilty fears banished, with boldness I came
To drink at the fountain, life-giving and free,—
Jehovah Tsidkenu is all things to me."

The *conscience of sin* has given way to "*a no more conscience of sin.*"

(a)   *Martensen, John Owen, and others*

CONSECRATION (ENTIRE)

" *Let My people go, that they may serve Me* " (Exod. viii. 1).

" *Come ye out from among them, and be ye separate,*" etc. (2 Cor. vi. 17).

Pharaoh = the world, who replies at first—
  (i.) " I will not let you go ";
      Afterwards,
  (ii.) " Sacrifice *in the land* ";
      Then,
  (iii.) " Go only *a little way* ";
      Again,
  (iv.) " Go, but leave *your children behind you* ";
      And,
  (v.) " Go, but leave your *cattle* behind you ";
      Lastly,
  (vi.) " Go, get you gone."

There must be entire consecration.
Ye must be unworldly.

(b)

CONSIDER CHRIST JESUS

" *Consider the Apostle and High Priest of our profession, Christ Jesus* " (Heb. iii.)

1. Object of Exhortation

The Jewish Christians, to whom this epistle is addressed, were in danger of apostatizing from the faith. Their security depended upon the recognition of the spiritual status to which they had been advanced when they became believers; and this recognition, again, depended upon the entertaining of a settled and established conviction of the unapproachable greatness of Jesus Christ. Should their estimate of the Saviour suffer abatement, it was likely that their allegiance to Him would immediately falter, and they would be drawn into a condition of impenitence from which it would hardly be possible for them to make their escape. Accordingly the writer of the epistle endeavours to fill the minds of his readers full of the glories of Christ. Christ in the mystery of His person, Christ in the greatness of His sacrificial and intercessory work, is presented to their view; and to Him their attention is directed with such a singular persistency that, if they should unhappily determine to relapse into the Judaism which they had abandoned, it could only be by dint of a resolute closing of their eyes to the majesty of Him who is the brightness of the glory and the express image of the substance of the eternal Father.

The words of our text are in strictest agreement with this purpose of the sacred writer. They describe the Saviour as Apostle and High Priest—Apostle, because He is one who stands in God's name before man—High Priest because he is one who appears in man's name before God. Thus they cover the whole field of the Saviour's mediatorial office, and then proceed to enjoin the most attentive examination, the most earnest and searching and exhaustive scrutiny, of the person described. " Consider the Apostle and High Priest of our profession, Christ Jesus."

(c)

2. Its Practical Bearing

For us, as well as for them, spiritual security lies in thinking rightly about Jesus Christ; and in having brain and heart—in having convictions and sympathies and affections and practical life— thoroughly filled and pervaded with the image of His glorious perfections. Let us endeavour to obey the precept of the text. Consider Jesus Christ as the High Priest of our profession.

(d)

3. Consider the relation in which the Jewish High Priest stood to the rest of the people

When the Hebrews, recently escaped from Egypt, were gathered together in the wilderness to learn from God's own lips what were His purposes concerning their future, they were expressly informed of the priestly character which He intended them to bear. The announcement must have seemed a startling one to a people demoralized by centuries of servitude, and probably conscious in themselves of the depths of moral degradation into which they had descended; but, strange as it may have seemed, it was nevertheless, explicit and intelligible enough. " Ye

(e)

shall be a peculiar treasure to me above all people. Ye shall be to me a *kingdom of priests*, and an holy nation." The Hebrews, however, at that time were not ripe for the realization of so lofty a privilege ; and inasmuch as this was the case, and inasmuch as important educational purposes for the world, were to be served by the temporary establishment of the Jewish polity, a priestly order was taken out of the priestly nation, and in the members of that order were concentrated and exhibited what were actually the privileges and dignity of the whole body of the people. But there was yet to be another step in this process of concentration. The limited priestly order itself was drawn up into a single personal head ; and at the apex of the system stood the majestic figure of a man in whom everything belonging to the priesthood reached its culminating point. That man was the Jewish High Priest.

(*a*)

(i.) Observe, then, as the result of this arrangement, that the High Priest was one taken out of the people and bound to the people by ties of the closest and most intimate kind. It might have been otherwise. This important official might have been a stranger introduced into the nation from an alien source ; or he might have occupied a position of such complete independence and isolation as should have placed him almost in antagonism to the rest of the community. Such was the case with the priestly caste in other countries. But with the Jews the divine method of constructing the ecclesiastical system, secured the most perfect identification of the man who was at the head of it with the feelings and sympathies and interests of the rest of the people.

(*b*)

(ii.) Observe as another result of the Divine arrangement, that all the Israelites, drawn up as they were towards a single person, were reckoned before God as being *in* the High Priest. The man who stands there in the sanctuary arrayed in his gorgeous robes, is not to be regarded as a mere individual—is not to be looked upon as merely one out of many, though one above the many and distinguished from the many by superior dignity and higher privileges ; but he is the head in whom the whole nation is included and involved and gathered and summed up before God. To this idea of the spiritual position of the great official, emphatic witness is borne by many statements of the ancient Scriptures. It was, for instance, as including in himself the entire mass of the nation that the High Priest on the day of atonement had to enter into the most holy place with the blood of sprinkling, and afterwards to confess the sins and iniquity of the people over the head of a living goat. It was in the same capacity that he appeared before God with the breast-plate on his heart, resplendent with its glittering gems, and with the onyx stones upon his shoulders engraven with the names of the twelve tribes of the House of Israel. On both these occasions it is manifest that the High Priest drew near to God in the name and in the stead of all, and that his acts involved the highest interests of the people to whom he belonged.

But a more important testimony still is furnished by the well-known fact, that when the High Priest committed any heinous sin his guilt was imputed to the people at large, and the

sacrifice for his sin had to be offered as were the public sacrifices which were offered for sin attributable to the entire community. In Lev. iv. 3, is the following statement : " If the High Priest that is anointed sin *to the trespass of the people* "— for that is the right translation of the original, and in the case of such a sin, the blood of the victim was brought into the holy place, and the body of the victim was burned without the camp, and that these regulations are precisely the same as the regulations enjoined when the offence to be atoned for was, not the offence of an individual but the offence of a whole congregation. All these facts point in the same direction. They indicate the relation in which the High Priest stood to the rest of the community ; they show that when he came before God he came in the place and the stead of the entire nation ; they depict him as the *inclusive* man ; or, they inform us that in the estimate and purpose of Jehovah, the whole Jewish people was reckoned as being *in* the Jewish High Priest.

(*c*)

(iii.) THE TYPE.—In all this we have a lively and striking portraiture of the position which the Lord Jesus Christ, the great Antitype of the Jewish official, occupies with respect to " the blessed company of all faithful people." The Lord Jesus is the ideal man. If you turn to the Jewish High Priest you find that he was what every Jew was intended to be. In him the privileges, the position, the dignity, of the members of the priestly kingdom were exhibited in full development ; and when the Israelite looked upon the High Priest, he might have thought within himself, " There is a man who fills out to the full the character of which *I* am the barest and most imperfect and most beggarly sketch. I see in him what is my position, if I could only attain to it. From his holiness I learn what my holiness ought to be ; and in his nearness to the sanctuary and intimacy with God, I contemplate what might be mine in happier circumstances and under more prosperous conditions." In other words, the High Priest, and the High Priest alone of the whole Jewish community, embodied the idea which lay at the foundation of the spiritual status of God's chosen people.

(*d*)

4. The Antitype

(i.) The Lord Jesus Christ alone possesses complete perfection of human character. " Holy, harmless, undefiled, separate from evil " as He was and is—loving and gracious and kind and self-sacrificing, finding it His meat and His drink to do His Father's will—we contemplate in Him the full development of qualities which exist indeed, but exist only in the germ, and exist in the midst of manifold inconsistencies, in the members of His Church. He did perfectly, that which we do imperfectly : He was absolutely, that which God intends us to be ; and it is for this reason that we are called upon to follow His steps, to be made like unto Him, to be conformed to His image, to copy Him as our ideal of what a man ought to be—for if there were not the fulfilment of character in Christ, and the capability of ultimate fulfilment of character in us, compliance with the injunction to imitate Him would become absolutely impossible.

(*e*)

(ii.) But Jesus Christ is very much more to us than the pattern man. He is also *the inclusive man*. He is the great Head in whom His people are gathered and summed up and presented before God. We have pointed out with respect to the Jewish High Priest, that all the Israelites were regarded as being *in* him. You might compare the man, if you like, to the ambassador of some mighty nation who appears in a foreign court, and whose position there is such that any insult offered to him is an insult offered to his people, and any benefit bestowed upon him is a benefit bestowed upon his people. But the comparison, although to a certain extent just, would be far from being adequate. Rather would we compare the Jewish High Priest, in his relation to the people, to a seed which includes in itself all the capabilities of stem and branch and leaves,—all the beauty and the fragrance and the sweetness and the glory of the plant which is to spring from it. Even so did the High Priest gather up into himself the whole body of the community. He was identified with them. What he did was their act : their sin was his sin ; his righteousness was their righteousness. In his fall, if he fell, they would fall also ; and his excellences were attributed and imputed to them. We are reminded here of the relation in which the Lord Jesus Christ stands to His living Church. The whole scheme of the Gospel turns upon the incorporation of the Christian with Christ—turns upon the identification of Christ with the body of the people who believe in His Name. Call it a mystery if you will. It *is* a mystery, but it is a *fact* nevertheless. There is a living personal union between the Christian and Christ, by virtue of which the two become one—so truly and completely one that God Himself does not behold them apart. The Christian, then, if he is a Christian indeed and not merely in name, is *in Christ*. Bring in St. Paul to bear his testimony upon the subject ! for the idea of this inclusion runs like a golden thread throughout the whole of that Apostle's writings. "Runs like a golden thread," do I say ? Nay, the thought is more like the deep and solid foundation upon which the whole intellectual superstructure has been subsequently raised. In Christ the Christian, because he is incorporated with Christ by the power of the indwelling Spirit, because he is inseparably united with his Saviour, dies unto sin, dies to its penalty, dies to its pollution, dies to its curse? and sin, for its part, clings to the man no longer, but falls off from him as an exhausted and inoperative thing. In Christ the Christian has risen again, risen again through his Master's resurrection to newness of the spiritual life now, and to the certainty of the resurrection of the body in the great day that is coming. In Christ, the Christian is virtually seated at the right hand of God in heavenly places, and, as the result of the elevation, sets his affection on things above and has his citizenship amidst the brightness and the purity and love of the eternal kingdom. And in Christ, the Christian will receive the full perfection and the full manifestation of the grace which has been bestowed upon him, for "when Christ who is our life shall appear, then shall ye also appear with Him in glory." Such are the statements of the great Apostle of the Gentiles ; and if he teaches us anything by his writings he teaches us this,—that the entire spiritual community, the whole body of the faithful in Christ Jesus, are reckoned by God as being gathered and summed up, involved, included, represented in Christ before the throne of God. And this, in its Christian form, is precisely what, in its Jewish form, the Israelite was taught by the existence of such a personage in the State as the Jewish High Priest.

(*a*)

COMMUNION WITH GOD

(iii.) The ordinary Israelite would look with longing desire upon the unbroken communion which the High Priest, by virtue of his office, maintained with God. The High Priest was continually within the precincts of the Temple and busied about its services. He seemed to enjoy, as no one else could enjoy, an intimate friendship with Jehovah. There was a calm, even, unbroken flow about his spiritual life ; whilst to the ordinary Jew who sometimes visited the Temple and sometimes was absent from it ; who now was engaged in religious duties, and now was harassed and perplexed with the worries and vexations of his every day life—existence seemed to be simply an alternation of drawing nigh to God and then of withdrawing from God again. Can we not detect in the contrast something which reminds us of the Lord Jesus Christ and His Church? One of the features in the character of Jesus is the perfect balance and equipoise of His mind. In the most exciting scenes we find Him always composed and calm. We have heard indeed of the " agitation " which He manifested when He first became conscious of having a mission from heaven, and when He retired into the wilderness to meditate over and to mature His plans for the establishment of the kingdom ; but certainly no trace of this agitation, no trace whatever, is discoverable in the sacred narrative. I see Him placed upon the pinnacle of the Temple, the crowd of worshippers gazing up at Him from below, and asking themselves if they are to witness some strange manifestation of supernatural agency. As I look He is suddenly transported to a lonely mountain-top from whence He can behold the vast panorama of the kingdoms of the world, and where the pomp, and the glory, and the riches, and the power of them are gathered together in one mighty offering and laid at His feet, if only He will condescend to stoop and take it up ; but in both these situations I see that He is perfectly composed ; I see that He is perfectly master of Himself. I cast my glance down the stream of time, and I see Him again. He is asleep on the deck of a rough fishing-boat after the fatigues of a laborious and exhausting day. The wind rises : the thunders mutter in the distance ; the waves swell and dash over the side of the little vessel ; and then the terrified disciples, forgetting their respect in their alarm, hastily awaken their Master from His slumbers and implore Him to rescue them from impending danger. He rises and rebukes the winds and the sea ; but I cannot detect the slightest appearance of discomposure or of flurry about Him. I see Him again ; it is at a later period of His history. He is descending the slope of the Mount of Olives. The air is rent with unwonted Hosannahs : the multitude wave their palm-branches and strew their garments in His path ; and the whole City of Jerusalem is stirred to its very depths by His approach. It seems as if He were now upon the very point of receiving the due reward of His

(*b*)

toilsome life, and of being accepted by the people as their long-expected Messiah. But notice under these circumstances how unlike Jesus of Nazareth is to other men! His pulse does not beat one single stroke faster, nor is there the faintest trace of the flush of triumph upon that wan and wasted cheek. And yet, once more, I see Him; but now the scene is sadly changed. With scarred and bleeding figure He fronts the fury of the fanatical populace who are disowning Him as an impostor, and who are surging wildly and tumultuously backward and forward over the broad area of the open court. Taunts and execrations are heard in every direction; the finger of scorn is pointed at Him; and the uproar waxes louder and fiercer until at last it swells into the maddened outburst which shakes the very palace walls, "His blood be on us and on our children." But, pale, drooping, saddened as the Saviour is, He is as calm as ever. Now why is this? Because His Spirit maintained an unbroken communion with His Father in heaven. There was no oscillation about His spiritual life; He was never alone; He was always with the Father, and the Father was always with Him. And this characteristic of His life upon earth is of course more emphatically characteristic of that wondrous resurrection-life which He is now living in heaven, and in which He is in an especial manner "the High Priest of our profession."

(*a*)

APPLICATION :

(**iv.**) Here then is presented to us the true idea of the spiritual life. In the close and intimate fellowship which the Lord Jesus Christ ever maintained with God—in His calm equipoise of mind as that of one who always was dwelling with the Father—we see one of the high privileges of those who have been made, through grace, kings and priests unto God. How far we fall short of the greatness of that privilege it can hardly be necessary to remind ourselves. Yes, trifles upset us; business harasses us; vexations, disappointments, petty sannoyances, frequently throw us off our balance; and, what is worse still, sins come in and darken over our hearts and interpose a cloud between us and God; and thus our life seems to be not so much a constant dwelling in the Divine presence—not so much an abiding in the courts of the Lord's house—as a sort of spiritual oscillation, an alternation of drawing nigh to God, and then of withdrawing to a distance from God again. And yet we may take comfort in the thought that, as we grow in knowledge and in grace, we advance towards the spiritual condition of our great High Priest. Something we know of communion with God now; we shall know more hereafter. It is our privilege as believers to have "fellowship with the Father and with His Son Jesus Christ." The privilege in this life is imperfectly realized; but it will be realized in its fulness and in its perfection, in the life to come.

(*b*)

(**v.**) When God in His mercy undertook the task of accomplishing our salvation, He had a most important problem to solve,—*how to combine in the hearts of sinners reverence and godly fear on the one side, with confidence and love on the other.* To crush men with awe, if that alone were necessary, was easy enough. To encourage them by

kindness, into friendship and familiarity was easy enough also. But to combine the two things— to make the two things compatible with each other—to harmonize them—this was the difficulty. In Jewish times the problem was wonderfully solved by means of the high-priestly system. Distance was preserved; reverence was secured, because the Jew must not himself draw nigh to God. And yet in the person of another, and that other taken out of His nation, "bone of his bone and flesh of his flesh," he had a visible representation of his own near relationship to God, and of his own calling to intimate communion with Him. Into the holy of holies, the symbol of Jehovah's immediate presence, the Jew dared not enter. Death would have been the penalty of his intrusion. And yet in the recesses of that mysterious sanctuary there appeared on the great day of atonement a man who stood in his stead, who was to him, as it were, another self, and in whom he felt that he, even he, could hold fellowship with the awful purity and holiness of the invisible God. But more wonderfully still is the problem solved by the gospel-scheme of which the high-priestly system was the type and the shadow. The God-man, Christ Jesus, commands our reverence and attracts our love; and when we draw nigh to Jehovah by the blood of a crucified Christ—when we realize that we are represented in heaven by One who, being Himself Divine, still wears the robe of our humanity, and still carries upon His sacred person the marks of the Cross, we feel that all our stores of reverence and all our stores of love are demanded; and we feel that whilst distinctly remembering that the God with Whom we have to do is a consuming fire, we can yet approach Him with confidence and boldness and call Him "Abba, Father!"

(*c*)   *Gordon Calthrop*

CONTEXT

If, indeed, there is one golden rule for a preacher, it is this, *Always look at your context.* We have all heard the story of the young man beginning his theological studies at Oxford, who asked the venerable president of Magdalen, then in his ninetieth year. "Is there any special piece of advice you can give me; any one rule more than another by which I am to guide myself in my studies?" The well-known answer was, "Always verify your references." I am sure that for all preachers, for all theologians, a yet more important rule is, ALWAYS LOOK AT YOUR CONTEXT.

(*d*)   *Perowne*

CONTRASTS (Luke xvi. 19, 20)

1. Between two lives :

There was a certain rich man, and a certain beggar ;

Unbeliever,	believer ;
Magnificence,	rags and nakedness ;
Banquets every day,	desiring to be fed with crumbs ;
Attendants,	dogs ;
No name, only, *A certain rich man*,	Lazarus = *God is my help.*

2. Between two deaths :

It came to pass . . . beggar died . . . the rich man also died and was *buried.*

(*e*)

The tables now turned—the last is become first,
the first last.

The rich man is now the beggar :
Lazarus dies first because he is ready ;
The rich man is spared that he may repent, =
" Let it alone this year also."
Angels,   no angels ;
Abraham's bosom
= the Jew's Heaven,   Hades and torment.

3. Between two funerals :·

Look at this picture and on that :—A procession
through streets of the city, grand, stately, imposing, worldly—long train befitting a rich man's
funeral—troops of hired mourners—priests—undertakers—spices, etc., accompany him to his new
tomb, on which his name and his virtues will be
imposingly emblazoned.

This goes on in the streets of the city. Now,
the Lord tears aside the curtain betwixt this and
the spirit world, and reveals what is going on
there.

The rich man is in torments ; what a terrible
mockery is that procession—that pomp and vanity
of a magnificent funeral, when the spirit is damned
and made the sport of demons ! What an awakening for the unbeliever !

The other death is unnoticed : unknown, and
yet well-known. Died, perhaps in the night :
" Found dead " ; and the body perhaps buried
with the burial of an ass ; or hurled for convenience sake over the battlements of the city ; at best,
nothing but a pauper burial. But what of that ?
The spirit is at rest, at home, comforted, convoyed
by angels to Abraham's bosom.

(*a*)

CONTROVERSY

Controversy may be sometimes needful ; but the
love of disputation is a serious evil. Luther, who
contended earnestly for the truth, used to pray :
"From a vain-glorious doctor, a contentious pastor, and nice questions, the Lord deliver His
Church ! "

(*b*)   *Luther*

CONVERSATION (John xiii. 31, etc.)

Christ's *Table-talk* with His disciples ; teaching
us to make conversation at table serviceable to
religion.

Christ did not begin His discourse till Judas had
gone out (31) ; the presence of wicked people often
a hindrance to good discourse.

(*c*)   *M. Henry*

CONVERSION

Might we but see a miracle, say some, how
gladly would we become converts ! They would
not speak thus, did they understand what *conversion* means. They imagine that this work consists
in the bare acknowledgment of God ; and that His
worship is mere lip service, little different from
that which the heathen offered to their idols.
True conversion is to annihilate ourselves before
this Sovereign Being, whom we have so often
provoked, and who, at any time, may justly
destroy us ; it is to acknowledge that we can do
nothing without Him, and that we merit nothing

from Him but His wrath ; it is to know that there
is a natural opposition between God and ourselves,
and that, without a Mediator, there could be no
intercourse between us.

(*d*)   *Blaise Pascal*

CONVERSION

There is one palm whose bud-sheath opens
suddenly, with a report which resounds through
the forest ; but most buds open very gently, and
silently unfold their petals to the sun. Even so is
it with human souls. The conversion of one is a
very violent and sudden process ; that of others
takes place gently and slowly as the opening of a
rosebud to the sun. Cæsar Malan likens his own
conversion to a child being awakened by its
mother's kiss. So is it with many. They wake
up to a new life under the gentle kiss of the
Divine love."

(*e*)   *Landels*

CONVERSION

Having been endeavouring to pray for near half
an hour, unspeakable glory seemed to open to the
view and apprehension of my soul ; I do not mean
any external brightness, for I saw no such thing ;
nor do I intend any imagination of a body of light
somewhere away in the third heavens, or anything
of that nature ; but it was a new inward apprehension or view that I had of God, such as I never
had before, nor anything which had the least resemblance of it. . . . At this time the way of
salvation opened to me with such infinite wisdom,
suitableness, and excellency, that I wondered I
should ever think of any other way of salvation ;
was amazed that I had not dropped my own con-
trivances and complied with this lovely, blessed,
and excellent way before. If I could have been
saved by my own duties, or any other way that I
had formerly contrived, my whole soul would now
have refused. I wondered that all the world did
not see and comply with this way of salvation,
entirely by the righteousness of Christ. . . .

The Lord by His grace so shined into my heart,
that I enjoyed full assurance of His favour, for
that time ; and my soul was unspeakably refreshed
with divine and heavenly enjoyments.

(*f*)   *David Brainerd.*

CONVERSION AND AVERSION

What is the opposite of conversion ? It is a
terrible word, because God is our only Good, our
Hope, our All ; but it is, you know, *aversion*. If
we are not turned *to* God, we are turned *away*
from Him. It is a terrible word, because it is so
outspoken, so true, and God is so good. Yet God
tells us plainly what we are doing. But is it not
so true ? Is there any thought which men so try
to get rid of, unless they are obeying Him, as the
thought of God ? For it is the thought of a
Master who is disobeyed, a Father who is dishonoured, a Benefactor to whom we are ungrateful, an Almighty who is defied, an Indweller who
is chased away, a Judge who can punish. It
speaks of engagements broken, duties violated,
conscience silenced.

(*g*)   *E. B. Pusey, D.D*

CONVERSION (FEAR IS NOT)

Felix trembled while Paul reasoned; the Princes of Judah were afraid while Baruch read. Fear is not conversion.

(a)   *C. Clayton*

CONVERSION OF ST. PAUL

" *For a pattern* " (1 Tim. i. 16)

St. Paul's conversion was typical of what true conversion is at all times.

1. Indications of the state of his mind before conversion.

He persecuted Christians, hated Christ, sought to exterminate the heresy, as he thought it. But *why* ? What motive urged him on?

He did it to save his soul. He thought that thereby he was " doing God service "—doing a good work, making God his debtor; and that his zeal would be placed to his account hereafter as a set-off against his sins.

The Epistle to the Romans (ch. vii.) indicates his spiritual standpoint at this time.

There he tells us that his whole inner being was out of harmony, and in a state of chaos and tumult—evil was struggling with the good in him. He knew what was good, but " how to perform that which is good I find not."

" *The good that I would, that I do not; but the evil which I would not, that I do.*"

Do what he would to quiet conscience and save his soul, he never succeeded. He knew no peace, but was internally wretched and miserable. Till at last his misery culminated in the despairing cry :—

" *O wretched man that I am, who shall deliver me from this body of death ?* "

Who will save me from myself—captive as I am, bound hand and foot to my own misery?

Thus, it appears that what St. Paul did as a persecutor, was an extreme effort, on his part, to deliver his soul. To get out of the seventh chapter of Romans into the eighth chapter. Hitherto seeking his salvation by his own works, he now owns his complete failure.

Whether, then, at the death of Stephen, or as being " exceeding mad " against Christians, he was as miserable as an awakened conscience could make a man. "Come, see the man who has been in hell ! " exclaimed the people when Dante walked the streets; and truly he and Paul, as many others, had been in the hell of an awakened conscience.

2. Indications of the state of his mind at the time of his conversion.

" Lord, what wouldst Thou have me to do ? " asked the awe-stricken man. In obedience to the directions given him, he met Ananias, who *baptized* him; . . and *straightway he preached Christ, that He is the Son of God.*= The greater miracle !

If we could lay a hand upon the fly-wheel of the Scotch express, running fifty or sixty miles an hour, and stop it, we should perform an astounding miracle. But this is what God does in His miracles of conversion. He laid his "mighty hand" upon the fly-wheel of Paul's life, and not only stopped its mad career, but turned it right round in the opposite direction. The *persecutor* becomes a *preacher !*

The significance of his conversion the Apostle gives us in Rom. vi. :

He had believed and was *baptized;* and his baptism had this significance :—

" Know ye not that so many of us as were baptized into Jesus Christ *were baptized into His death ?* (3).

" Therefore we are *buried with Him* by baptism into death : that like as Christ was raised up from the dead by the glory of the Father, even so we also should walk in *newness of life* (4).

"Now, if we be *dead with Christ,* we believe that we shall also *live with Him* (8).

" Knowing that Christ, being *raised from the dead,* dieth no more, *death hath no more dominion over Him* (9).

" For in that He died, He died unto sin once, but in that He liveth, *He liveth unto God.*

" *Likewise reckon ye also yourselves to be dead indeed unto sin, but alive unto God through Jesus Christ our Lord.*"

The old life—the old wretchedness—that hell of a disquiet conscience—was over and done with; he was out of that;—and a *new life* was begun, wherein indeed *all things had become new.* The captive was free. And he began to live that new life at once. Such is the significance once for all of conversion and baptism.

3. Indications supplied of his state of mind ever afterwards.

The whole eighth chapter of Romans is a poem upon the Christian life. It begins with " *No condemnation* " in Christ ; and ends with " *No separation* " from Christ.

The old law of *sin and death* is replaced by the law of the *spirit of life* in Christ Jesus.

If death comes, he knows that he shall be raised from it as Christ was (11).

If trouble comes, he knows that " All things work together for good to them that love God."——

If anything is laid to his charge, he knows that it matters not ; for God hath justified him.

If any one condemns him, he knows that Christ will answer for him.

If any one is against him, he knows that God is *for* him.

If they persecute him with cold, nakedness, fire, peril, sword, he answers that " *we are more than conquerors* "—we shall come out of it with gain, not with loss.

Such are the indications of the Apostle's state of mind *before, at,* and *after* his conversion ; and they help to show how it was a *pattern* (though on a grand and magnificent scale) of what true conversion is for all who should hereafter believe on Jesus Christ to life everlasting.

(b)
                                        Cf. Godet

CONVERSION, INSTANCE OF

The Duke of Burgundy was born terrible, M. de St. Simon declares. He would indulge in such paroxysms of rage that those who were standing by would tremble for his very life. He was hardhearted, passionate, furious to the highest degree, even against inanimate objects; incapable of bearing the least opposition to his wishes ; fond of gambling, violent hunting, and the gratifications of the table ; abandoned to his pleasures; barbarous; born to cruelty. With this was united a genius of the most extraordinary kind : a quickness of humour, a depth and justice of thought, a versatility and acuteness of a really marvellous kind

(c)

distinguished him. " The prodigy was, that in a short space of time religion and the grace of God made him a new man, and changed those terrible qualities into all the opposite virtues. From the abyss which I have described there arose a prince affable, gentle, moderate, patient, modest, humble, austere only to himself, attentive to his duties, and sensible of their great extent. His only object appeared to be to perform all his actual duties of son and subject and to qualify himself for his future obligations."

The Duc de St. Simon, quoted in Charles Butler's works.

(a)

CONVERTS, YOUNG, COUNSELS FOR

" *Who art thou that judgest another man's servant ? To his own master he standeth or falleth. Yea, he shall be holden up ; for God is* ABLE *to make him stand* " (Rom. xiv. 4).

Some young converts feared that they would not be able to hold out. But God would keep them. He was able to keep the weakest of them, provided they kept their eyes upon Him. Let them know in the morning of their experience that God had got hold of them, and was able to make them stand. Young converts had three terrible enemies —the flesh, the world, and the devil. The flesh clung to them, and would never leave them, although, if they resisted the devil, he would flee from them. If their old temper came up, keep it under ; and if it did get the better of them, go and confess it. Put no confidence in the flesh ; they never could trust it. They should keep self in its right place. But if they had three great enemies they had three great Friends to stand by them— the Father, the Son, and the Holy Ghost. Think not that when they were converted all their trials were over. The Christian life was a warfare—a conflict—a battle, and the sooner they learn that the better. They never would be able to walk alone. They needed Christ to secure them. They did not want to be like hot-house plants that could not bear the storms of the world. No child of God could be in any difficulty that he could not be helped out of if he only came to the Throne of Grace. Some people asked of what persuasion they were ? If they wanted to know Paul's persuasion (2 Tim. i. 12), he was persuaded that Christ was able to keep that which he had committed unto Him. Young converts should commit their souls and their bodies to Christ, who would be able to keep them. They could not be too cautious about the world. Nearly everything that they saw tended to draw them away from Christ. If they got their eyes off Him, it would not be long before their hearts would be away from Him also. To him it was a sweet thought that he had not kept himself, but that his life was hid with Christ in God, and that Satan could not get at it. No devil in hell could get at his life if it was hid with Christ in God. Why ? Because Christ was able to keep him. Turn to Romans, chapter iv. verse 20, where it was written, " He staggered not at the promise of God through unbelief, but was strong in faith, giving glory to God ; and being fully persuaded that what He had promised He was able also to perform." God's people could not get into any condition or by-path out of which there was not a promise to lead them, if they searched their Bibles for it. There was no discount on God's promises. Every promise that He had made He was able to fulfil. The dying thief on the cross asked to be remembered in Christ's kingdom ; but the Lord took him right into His kingdom with Him, so that he got more than he asked for. " Now unto Him that is able to keep you from falling, and to present you faultless before the presence of His glory with exceeding joy." Some people had an idea that they had got to fall. But they did not get that from the Bible. God was able to keep every one of them from falling. Might God help them not to disgrace the name of Christ ! Every infidel would be looking at them and scoffing at them. Hundreds were watching them and him—watching their acts, the expression of their faces, and their daily walk and conversation. An excellent man in London kept up an institution near the Seven Dials at his own expense. He spent his nights in bringing the homeless boys from the streets into it. When they came in, he photographed them, and then they were washed, clothed, and educated. When he succeeded in sending one out, after having taught him a trade, he photographed him again. That man was about as near the Lord Jesus Christ as any one he ever met. The object in photographing the boys was, that they might take away with them something which would remind them of what they were when the institution found them, and when it left them. He asked the young converts not to forget where the Lord Jesus found them. He found them in a pit—he found them bound in the chains of Satan—and had placed them on the Rock of Ages, and put a new song in their mouths. If they should sin, if their old passions should come back upon them, and they should be tripped up by Satan, he begged of them not to run away from the Lord Jesus, and think that He had turned His back upon them, and would not have anything more to do with them. Treat the Lord Jesus as they would treat any earthly friend—as they would the warmest bosom friend—only He was a great deal better—that they had got on earth. Go into their closet and get down on their knees, and tell the Lord Jesus all about it, and then say that they bade Him good-bye, and were going to leave His fold for ever— but oh ! he never heard of any one being able to do that ! Might God keep these young converts— that was the prayer of his heart. Cling close to the rock. They might tremble, but it never would.

(b)   *Moody*

CONVERTS, FOR NEW (Isa. lx. 1)

1. " **Arise**" :—Because hitherto " dead in sin " ; " no life " ; and conversion = a spiritual and moral resurrection to " newness of life " : cf. John v. 25, " Now is," etc.

2 **Shine** :—The immediate duty ; " Ye are the light of the world. A city that is set on an hill cannot be hid."

3. " **Thy light is come**," = (i.) " Christ the light of the world," in whom " God hath shined " ; (ii.) Personal illumination by His spirit.

4. **The glory of the Lord hath risen upon thee** :— = The sunrise of the soul. Therefore go forth to thy day's work in the world, and whatever thy hand findeth to do in God's vineyard, do it with thy might ; for *the night cometh*, etc.

(c)

CONVICTION OF SIN

When God has begun a series of convictions in the heart, and the subject of them has endured terrors of conscience, let it be remembered that God's beginnings may be regarded as completed, since He is the Lord. The question "Why then these terrors?" may be answered by the case of the young man who had an evil spirit within him —before it was cast out, *it rent him.* Mark the sequel.

(*a*)   *Gordon Calthrop*

CORN OF WHEAT THAT DIES, THE

"*Verily, verily, I say unto you, Except a corn of wheat fall into the ground and die, it abideth alone: but if it die, it bringeth forth much fruit. He that loveth his life shall lose it; and he that hateth his life in this world shall keep it unto life eternal. If any man serve Me, let him follow Me; and where I am, there shall also My servant be; if any man serve Me, him will My Father honour*" (John xii. 24-26).

The Greeks

These words were spoken only a short time before the crucifixion of our Lord; and they bear direct reference to that stupendous and mysterious event. Some "Greeks," it appears—and we are to understand by the expression, not Hellenistic Jews, but persons who represented the great mass of the Gentile nations—had requested to be admitted to an interview with Christ. Their desire did not originate in mere curiosity; it had a deeper source. The emotion into which Jerusalem had been stirred by the triumphal entry of Christ within its walls, had extended its contagion to them, and they began to suspect that they had here in this prophet of Nazareth in Galilee, the satisfaction of the blind longings of the heathen world for the knowledge of the living God. . . . The appearance of these Greeks served to remind the Saviour of His decease, which He should accomplish at Jerusalem, and of the issues that were bound up with it.

(*b*)

Gentiles

It served also to administer consolation to His sorrowful spirit. Gentiles had come to His cradle. The eastern Magi, led by a star, had traversed the wide deserts which separated the lowly Bethlehem from their own majestic home, and had poured their rich gifts—gold and frankincense and myrrh —in lavish profusion before His infant feet. And now, at the close of His eventful career, *Gentiles* were again appearing upon the scene, and desiring access to His presence. But they were drawing near to the Cross. The others had bowed themselves before the brightness of the rising light, but these men had come to gaze upon the broad luminary just as it was surrounded by the gathering clouds of hatred and persecution, just as it was on the point of setting in a sea of blood. The vision of His approaching death rose up before the Saviour's view when He heard of the request of the Gentiles who had come to worship at the feast. But behind that vision, behind the humiliation of the judgment hall, and the agony of the Cross, and the darkness of the sepulchre, His mind, overpassing the immediate prospect, beheld the radiance of the future glory; looked down the long vista of the ages, and saw the streams of believing men and women flowing from north and south and east and west, and converging upon Calvary—and rejoiced in that dark hour of approaching trial, to think that He, if He should be lifted up from the earth, would draw all men unto Him.

(*c*)

Death and Glory

Under such circumstances the words were spoken. And if we keep them in view we shall find ourselves in a better position for understanding the Saviour's meaning. It seems probable that His rapturous reception by the populace, and the loud hosannas which rent air as He rode through the streets of the holy city, had filled the disciples with ambitious thoughts. As the cry rose, unchecked by Jesus Himself, "Blessed is the King of Israel that cometh in the name of the Lord," His half-understood predictions about suffering and death faded from their recollection, and gave place to the anticipation of temporal honour and success. Surely—they thought—He will now take to Himself His power and reign. He will abandon those gloomy methods by which He once intended to accomplish His purposes. Now that hostility is disarmed or silenced, and the tide of popular enthusiasm is rising fast in every direction, the Son of Man will take advantage of the opportunity and permit Himself to be glorified. The hour is come. He will not surely let it pass away unseized and unimproved. "Yes!" is the Saviour's reply in answer to their thoughts, "the hour *is* come that the Son of Man should be glorified. But His glorifying is something very different from that which ye seem to suppose. The mode of it is different; the character of it is different. Look at a corn of wheat. If that corn preserve its life, it remains, in cold, self-contained, cheerless isolation. It gladdens nobody. It profits nobody. But if it fall into the ground and die, it bringeth forth much fruit, to the comfort and refreshment of many. Even so is it with the Son of Man. Glorified He will be—but through the decease which He is about to accomplish on the Cross of Calvary."

(*d*)

The Law of Self-Sacrifice

The Saviour connects His death with His future glorification, representing the one as the indispensable condition of the other. He speaks, too, of His glorification as if it consisted, mainly at least, in the power to communicate Himself; to bear—as He says—much fruit. . . . The Saviour points out the bearing upon His disciples of that law of the heavenly kingdom which concerns Himself—"I," He implies, "sacrifice my life in order that I may become a blessing to the world, and a path, similar in its essential nature to the path in which I tread, must be trodden by those who would serve Me. Only in the way of self-abnegation can men expect to be blessed in themselves and to be blessings to others. "He that loveth his life shall lose it, and he that hateth his life in this world shall keep it unto life eternal."

(*e*)

Corn of Wheat that Dies—*continued*

THE ILLUSTRATION

I. We consider the illustration employed in the text. Now, although the verse speaks of a corn of wheat that falls into the ground and " *dies*," we are not to imagine that an entire dissolution and destruction of the substance of the wheat takes place, when it sinks into the earth. The fact would rather seem to be this,—that whilst the greater part of the seed-corn rots and perishes, there remains behind an almost imperceptible living germ, from which the new plant, with its stem, and leaves, and flowers, and fruit, takes its origination and comes into being. There is then, so to speak, a kind of double life in the corn ; or perhaps we may say that there are two lives in it, the one encasing and enclosing the other, but at the same time, by that very circumstance, preventing the expansion and development of that which it encloses. So long as the seed-corn remains above the ground, these two lives lie side by side, quiescent and inoperative—and the " corn abideth alone." It exists, but it exists only for itself. It is isolated and unproductive. But when the corn of wheat falls into the ground and dies— the outward life, the exterior integument rotting and dropping away—the inner or real life of the plant is left disengaged and free, to commence the work of self-communication. Death then—in this sense—is necessary to the increase and fruitfulness of the plant.

(*a*)

ITS IMPORT

By such an image as this, our Lord depicts the importance of His own decease. His meaning seems obvious enough. It would have been perfectly possible for Him, even after assuming our nature, to have refused to submit to the degradation and agony of the Cross. Expressly does He assert that, if He lay down His life, He does so of His own free will, and that no one taketh it from Him. He might then have remained standing, self-centred in His own life and energy ; the Being Whose name is wonderful—because He is truly Son of God, and truly Son of Man. But then had He done so He must have remained alone, He must have dwelt in magnificent but cheerless isolation, independent of and above the whole human race. This was far from being His intention. He came for the distinct purpose of bringing many sons to glory. He came, that He might see His seed and prolong His days. And therefore, He adoped the only means by which that purpose could be accomplished. He submitted to death in order that He might be enabled to communicate life, to communicate *Himself* to all of them who are given to Him of the Father.

(*b*)

THE CROSS OF CHRIST

We have then here a point of view from which we may contemplate with advantage the Cross of the Lord Jesus Christ. About that Cross there are many things mysterious and difficult to be understood ; and perhaps it is better for us not to go too far in the attempt to assign reasons for what we yet believe to be unquestionable facts. We know, for instance, we are sure, that, by the sacrifice once offered upon the Cross, a complete atonement for human transgression has been made, that the question of moral evil has been gone into, and settled for ever, that the burden has been lifted off the soul of the believer, and that he has been separated from the penalty and curse, from the power and tyranny and oppression of his sin. Christ hath put away sin by sacrifice of Himself. About this we entertain no doubt. The thing is certain. But how the fact comes to be a fact, who shall undertake to explain ? Theories, of course, there are. But it seems better and wiser for us to leave the theories alone, and to be contented with the simple truth, that, somehow or other, by the death of Christ upon the Cross, you and I (if members of His mystiçal body) are detached from our sins and saved from their consequences, and that our polluted souls are cleansed from their stains in the stream of the Saviour's atoning blood. We know, too, we are sure, that from the Cross all peace of conscience flows. A delusive peace you may find elsewhere. It comforts a man sometimes to, think that he intends to repent, or that his life has not been worse than that of others, or that he has committed no grievous and notorious wrong, or that, if he has been faulty in some respects, his excess and superabundance of goodness in other ways will compensate for the defect, and cause the balances of the sanctuary to incline in his favour. But such comfort is deceptive and transitory. Real peace can be found nowhere but at the foot of the Cross. Your spirit can never be truly at rest until you have accepted the persuasion that you have an interest in the atoning blood of Christ, and that He by His death has lifted off from your soul the crushing load of your offences against God. But how that peace comes about, what is the exact link of connection between the dying of Christ and the pacification of my conscience, how the questionings which arise in my mind about it are to be satisfactorily answered—I cannot undertake to say—I know the fact. On that point, I have no doubt, no manner of doubt. But the explanation of the fact lies far beyond my intellectual depth.

(*c*)

SPIRITUAL LIFE

The life of a Christian—his spiritual life—is a communicated thing. It is not inherent in himself. He derives it from an external source. It is by virtue of his personal union with Christ, and of the spiritual power which thereby flows into him, that he is able to perform the functions of spiritual life, to love, to serve, to adore. In other words, Christ, mysteriously but really, communicates Himself to him. But this power of Christ to communicate Himself, to impart His life to His people, depended upon His death. If He had not died, this power would not have been His. He tells us so Himself. He tells us that His death was the indispensable condition of the acquisition of this power. But if you say to me, " Show me the manner how. Bring to light the point of indispensable connection between the death of Christ and this wondrous capacity of self-communication," you ask me for far, far more than I am able to perform. I can only assert the fact, that except that corn of wheat had died, it would have abode alone ; but that, inasmuch as it died, it brought forth much fruit.

(*d*)

Corn of Wheat that Dies—*continued*

ETERNAL LIFE

This is the aspect of the Cross of Christ, to which our subject leads us. Not so much dealing with the question of sin and the overthrow of sin —it deals with the impartation of eternal life. For that life, it tells us, we are indebted to the Cross—nay, for the power to bestow that life Christ Himself is indebted to the Cross. And when, in the days to come, the Redeemer looks round on the vast host of the redeemed—on those who, in the strength which He bestowed, lived holy lives upon earth, having their conversation in heaven, and seeking those things which are above—and when He presents Himself before the throne, saying, " Behold I and the children whom Thou hast given Me," He will feel, as His people will feel, that all is owing to that mysterious death which He condescended to die upon the Cross of Calvary.

(*a*)

A MISTAKE CORRECTED

The persons who expected the speedy glorification of the Saviour were mistaken (as we have seen) as to the manner in which His glory was to be attained. That the way to exaltation should lie through the dark and humiliating passage of death, was to them a novel and a startling idea. But they were mistaken also as to the nature of the glory itself. They expected that Christ was about to be raised to some lofty throne, and surrounded there by all the accessories of majesty and power. And so far, no doubt, they were right. But here their expectations stopped. They seemed to have no conception that the highest glory of the Godhead was the manifestation of self-sacrificing love. This conception, however, the language of the Saviour seems to supply. He admits that the time is come for the Son of Man to be glorified ; but when He goes on to explain in what that "glorification" consists, we find Him speaking about the " bearing of much fruit." In other words, the mind of the Saviour, whilst recognising the external glory with all its concomitants, which was soon to be His, passed beyond these things and rested with supreme delight in the contemplation of that greatness which consists in the manifestation of love. God's highest name is that of "love." He is light. He is holiness. He is justice. He is power. But, more than all, He is "love." We celebrate His highest praises when we speak of Him as love. And Christ, when He thought of His own approaching glorification, thought not so much of any external and superadded magnificence as of that manifestation of self-sacrifice for His own in which His soul delights. The corn of wheat, when it had died, was to bring forth "much fruit." In this its chief glory would consist.

(*b*)

THE APPLICATION OF THE STATEMENT TO OUR-
SELVES

II. " He that loveth his life shall lose it ; and he that hateth his life in this world shall keep it unto life eternal." To understand these words we may turn, with advantage, again to the preceding illustration. We said that there seems to be a

kind of pair of lives in the corn of wheat, the one enfolding and encompassing the other and restricting its action, needing, therefore, to perish and be removed before the other can be liberated and come into play. Just such a two-fold life there seems to be in the human spirit. If we look into ourselves we shall see that we have that within us which holds intercourse with the external world. It is partly intellectual, partly sensitive, and partly emotional—but it is one life. It is that which brings us into contact with, makes us conscious of, makes us desire and lay hold of, the things of the world by which we are surrounded. But we have also another principle within us. We have something (it matters little what we call it now— call it " spirit " if you like) we have something within us which is intended to lay hold of and apprehend God. To this something God is what thought is to our intellect, what food is to our body, what air is to our lungs. God, the possession of God, the enjoyment of God, is a necessity to it. Withhold God from this part of our being and we perish with an utter destruction. Now, this principle is our other life, our true and real life ; and there—in us, as in the seed of corn, are the two lives. They lie side by side. The tendency of the one, of the natural life, is to neutralize and stifle the action of the other ; and if the other is to have free play and to come into action, it must be disengaged and disentangled from the influence of that which encompasses and envelopes it. We begin, then, I think, to catch a glimpse of our Saviour's meaning. In order that the higher life of the man—that part of him which holds communion with the Divine—may be preserved and do its work, that lower life of his, that life in the world by which he holds communion with external things, must be checked and controlled and kept in proper subordination. If you " love " that lower life so as to indulge and pamper it, you will "lose" your higher life, because that higher life will be stifled, or will wither away in inaction. If you " hate " that lower life, *i.e.*, systematically sacrifice it to the interests of the higher, you will keep the higher unto life eternal, and receive the benediction of a glorified and multiplied existence. . . . We have here in one of our Lord's short but pregnant statements the whole teaching of the New Testament upon the subject of self-denial and self-mortification. How often do we hear the Apostles crying—" Mortify the flesh. Mortify the deeds of the body. Deny yourselves. Take up your cross. Crucify the old man. Love not the world neither the things that are in the world." What do they mean by these statements or precepts ? Trace them far enough, all root themselves in the same thought. "Self-indulgence is ruinous." Let it take whatever form it may, however respectable, however specious it may appear, to yield to self-inclination is to yield up your soul. Only by sacrificing the higher to the lower, that part of you which commences with the seen with that which commences with the unseen, can you hope to enter into the Kingdom of Heaven.

(*c*)

PRACTICAL APPLICATION

The very first step in the spiritual career is one in which we " hate " our life, for it is a step in which we " die " to self : *i.e.*, sacrifice our natural self-trust and self-dependence, in order to cast

(*d*)

Corn of Wheat that Dies—*continued*

ourselves into the arms of Christ. And all along the line on which we advance, Self is ever struggling to resume the lost ascendency, and has in the power of God's Spirit to be kept down and mortified and crushed. In this consists the great struggle of the Christian life. But, struggle as it may be, we may be sure of this, that our happiness and our usefulness depend upon our resolutely subordinating the lower natural life to the higher spiritual one. The self-seeker is ever an unhappy man ; and most assuredly he is one who brings no blessing to his fellows. We must die to self if we would bring forth fruit to the praise of God and the advantage of our fellow-men. And perhaps we may be justified in saying that the thought about the glorification of Christ will apply to His followers also. The highest glory of the creature as well as the highest glory of God, is in the manifestation of love. Heaven is doubtless a place of great magnificence. Images of the most gorgeous kind, gates of pearl, walls of precious stones, streets of gold, are heaped together in the Apocalypse to describe it. It is a place in which there is no pain, no sorrow, no sin, no decay, but in which we shall enjoy perfect strength, unfailing faculties, unsullied holiness, unchangeable youth. It is a place, too, in which the followers of Christ will be clothed with the strange and mysterious magnificence of new, supernatural faculties and powers. Yes! undoubtedly all this is true. But, after all, the highest glory of heaven is not recounted until we have told that it is a place where selfishness has entirely disappeared, and where the supreme joy is found in the living for others in the unceasing ministrations of an eternal and unchanging love.

(a) *Gordon Calthrop*

CORNELIUS (Acts x. 34, 35)

If the language meant that a heathen, a Jew, and a Christian were altogether alike in the eyes of God, and that any one of them could as easily be saved as another, provided that he was honourable and upright in his conduct, then Peter should have simply allowed Cornelius to remain what he was—a heathen—without leading him to Christ.

(b) *Lange*

COSTUME

Under all costumes seek the *man*. . . . If they hold no man, freely trample on them. "*All costumes ought to hold men.*"

(c) *Carlyle*

"The laced suit and peruque which called themselves Louis XV., and which resemble nothing so much as Feathertop, who was put together, clothed, and inspired with a kind of vitality by the old witch in Hawthorne's tale.

(d) *Hamley*

COUNCIL OF TRENT

I think I could have conformed to the then dominant Church before the Reformation. The errors existed, but they had not been riveted into peremptory articles of faith before the Council of Trent. If a Romanist were to ask me when my religion began, I should content myself by answering, that I could not exactly say when my religion, as he was pleased to call it, began, but that it was certainly some sixty or seventy years before *his*, at all events, which began at the Council of Trent.

(e) *S. T. Coleridge*

COUNTERFEIT PROVES THE TRUE, THE

1. Did you ever see a counterfeit five pound note ?—Yes.
2. Why was it counterfeited ?—Because it was worth counterfeiting.
3. Was the five pound note to blame ?—No.
4. Did you ever see a scrap of brown paper counterfeited ?—No.
5. Why ?—Because it was not worth counterfeiting.
6. Did you ever see a counterfeit Christian ?—Yes ; lots of them.
7. Why were they counterfeited ?—Because they were worth counterfeiting.
8. Were they to blame ?—No.
9. Did you ever see a counterfeit infidel ?—No, never.
10. Why ?

(f)

COUNTRY AND TOWN

God made the country ; and man made the town.

(g) *Cowper*

COWARDS AND THE LAKE OF FIRE (Rev. xxi. 6-8)

Who are the denizens of the "Lake of Fire"? "Murderers," you say, "and persons sunk in atrocious and abominable sensuality. For such, if for any, it would be a fitting locality." You are right. Murderers are mentioned, and profligates ; and with them sorcerers, and idolaters, and all liars. But look for a moment at those who lead the van of the black company. In the fore-front we notice persons whom, perhaps, we should not have expected to find there—the "fearful" and "unbelieving." What is that? What does that mean? I can only explain the statement by contrasting it with what is said about those who "overcome." The saved are the men of courage. They have feared nothing but God, and displeasing God. The "fearful" are the moral cowards, who have shrunk from what is displeasing to flesh and blood, who have not been willing to take up the Cross to follow Christ. And the difference between the two classes is radical ; going down to the very foundations of spiritual being. The one were athirst for God, they longed for God, for the possession and enjoyment of God, and this strong, irrepressible longing led them into conflict with the forces of evil, and in the end brought them triumphantly through. But the others cared nothing about the possession of God. The world in some shape or other, was what they really were anxious to secure, and so they had no inner strength to sustain them in the controversy with evil. And hence, instead of overcoming, they were overcome ; instead of being courageous on the side of

(h)

good, they were fearful, and fell under the power of evil. And notice into what terrible companionship their moral cowardice has brought them. Only "fearful"! Only "unbelieving"! Yes! But they are linked with the blood-thirsty, and unclean, and impure, and false; and they are cast with them into the pool which burneth with fire and brimstone, which is the second death.

There are three theories about God's moral government of the world, and dealing with the wicked. There is the old, orthodox theory of eternal punishment. Some think that it is exploded. Well, it may be; but remember, neither men's wishes nor men's speculations alter facts. Then there is the theory of universal restitution, a theory which I must confess has wonderful fascination for me, if I only could bring myself to believe it. According to those who maintain this theory, all men, no matter what their lives have been in this world, will ultimately be brought to the bosom of the universal Father, and restored to a holy, and therefore a happy state of existence. Lastly, there is the theory of what is called "conditional immortality." Life, it is said—eternal life—is only in Christ, and, consequently, there will ultimately be an annihilation of the wicked. God will either destroy them by an act of His almighty power, or else they will be withdrawn, necessarily, into the darkness of non-existence, just as a lamp goes out when you take away the oil from it. You see clearly that, on either of these two last suppositions, moral evil will disappear entirely from the universe of God. In the one case, it will be absorbed in good—all having become good. In the other case, it will be expunged and obliterated—the impenitent having been totally wiped out of existence, annihilated, reduced to nothingness. Now, my question is this—How are these two theories consistent with the statements made in the closing chapters of the Book of Revelation? In these chapters we are introduced to circumstances which take place *after* the present dispensation, *after* the thousand years, *after* the great final judgment of the human race; to circumstances, therefore, which constitute the final condition of the world, when Redemption has run its course and accomplished its work. There is no condition beyond the condition described. Now, according to the two theories, we ought to find no trace of the existence of moral evil in this condition. It has been either absorbed or expunged. How, then, is it that two classes of human beings are so distinctly spoken of in this closing book of Divine inspiration? How is it that, in addition to the mention of those who "inherit eternal life," we find mention of those who "are without," of those who are cast into the lake that burneth with fire and brimstone? How is it that such words as these (and they are almost the last words in the Bible) have any place or meaning there:—"He that is unjust, let him be unjust still; and he that is filthy, let him be filthy still; and he that is righteous, let him be righteous still; and he that is holy, let him be holy still"?

(a)

CREATION

The Bible speaks of three creations—the first marks the beginning; the second, the central and turning point; the third, the end of the history of the world. The Old Testament opens with the natural creation; the New Testament, with the

moral creation, or incarnation; and the Revelation closes with a description of the new heavens and the new earth, where Nature and Grace, the first and the second creation, shall be completely harmonized.

(b)　　　　　　　　　　　　　　　　　*Lange*

CREATION

Shem, who lived in the time of Lamech, who lived in the time of Adam, must at any rate have seen Abraham. And Abraham saw Jacob, who saw those who lived in the time of Moses. Therefore the Creation and the Deluge are true. This argument must be conclusive with those who duly appreciate its force.

(c)　　　　　　　　　　　　　*Blaise Pascal*

God did not make us out of nothing, but out of Himself. As He is the root of spirit, so He is the root of matter.

(d)　　　　　　　　　　　　*Geo. Macdonald*

CREATION OR EVOLUTION

Just as, when we consider the seed of a tree, we may say that there are in the seed roots and branches, and fruit and leaves, not because they exist already, but because they are to come into existence from that seed; and so Moses wrote, "In the beginning God created the heaven and the earth," as if this were the seed of the heaven, although as yet all the material of heaven and earth was in confusion, but because it was certain that from the matter the heaven and the earth would come into being, therefore the matter is so called.

(e)　　　　　　　　　　　　　　*Augustine*

CREATION AND REDEMPTION (Rom. v. 14)

Creation and *Redemption* go hand-in-hand: they proceed from the same source. We can therefore thank God for our creation, because with it He has given us redemption. We can conceive of the two as co-extensive; it appears so in the passage from which we start: "Adam the figure (type) of Him who is to come." We are to think of no loss to the race incurred by the first Adam, which is not remedied by the second Adam. "By the offence of one, *many* were made sinners; so by the obedience of one, *many* are made righteous."

(f)

CREATURE, THE NEW

Is not merely a gentle, kindly disposition, or an affectionate manner towards children, etc. This is quite another thing, and belongs to the realm of *nature*. The lower animals have these qualities—which are as true of a dog as of a man, and have no foundation in grace. A "new creature" is something so distinct as to have no parallel in nature — nature cannot produce this product, which is not born of *blood*, nor of the will of man, *but of God* (John i. 13)

(g)

CREED

The Lord's Prayer and the Apostles' Creed, which do seal up our hearts unto the service of God, are daily to be repeated every morning.

(h)　　　　　　　　　　　　　　*Ambrose*

CREED

Sapping a solemn creed with solemn sneer.

(a)   *Byron*

CREED, THE CHRISTIAN

The lofty and comprehensive, but at the same time modest, creed of Anglican Christianity, is a legitimate product of the three essential constituent principles of human nature—faith, conscience, and reason—working in the sphere of experience.

(b)   *Quarterly Review*

CREED, BASIS OF

The great question, whether there is any sufficient basis on which religious belief can rest, may, we think, be most simply and intelligibly brought before the mind, by supposing the inquirer to begin with searching the universe of which he finds himself a denizen, to ascertain whether it can yield him any information respecting its origin and cause. Aiding his senses by the most powerful instruments of observation that human ingenuity has invented, and linking his discoveries together by the processes of his thought, he will gradually arrive at a general conception of the vastness and complexity of the scene. Looking out into the boundless fields of space, his gaze will travel on from orb to orb, from galaxy to galaxy, through heights and depths of measureless expanse and unimaginable splendour, till, before the numbers and distances thus disclosed, thought sinks faltering and overpowered, and the earth by comparison dwindles down into a mere atom, the solar system into a scarcely noticeable speck. Turning to our globe, he will find himself confronted by a world of Being, which, if it lacks the impressiveness of incomprehensible vastness, yet is no less amazing for its manifold varieties of life, both animal and vegetable, with their orderly progressions and mutual relations and adaptations. But he will not be able to rest satisfied with the contemplation of the universe as it lies outspread before his eyes; he will be irresistibly led on to speculate upon its history. For he cannot help seeing that all things are undergoing a change. As a future is growing out of the present, so the present must have grown out of a past. Watching, then, the sequences by which things change, and patiently inferring from them the rules or laws of development, he will be able to reason his way backwards, and to recede, step by step, towards earlier stages of existence. Pursuing this reconstruction of past epochs in his thought, he will grope his path back, not insecurely, to an almost incredible simplification of the condition of the universe. It will seem to him that the further he traces back the successive gradations of life upon the earth, the less complex and various become the organisms in which it was embodied, till at last an enormously remote beginning is reached in creatures destitute of organs, mere shapeless monads or particles of animated matter. Moreover, as with the development of life, so he will see reason to infer that it must have been, in all probability, with the formation of planets, suns, and stars. They too will appear to have a history, a sequence of graduated changes, in slow condensation, cooling down, and becoming solid; and the conviction will grow upon

him, that if he could track the universe back, through inconceivable stretches of duration, to its primeval and simplest form, there would be no pause till he had arrived at a uniform fiery vapour, of inexpressible tenuity, seething and whirling in the immensity of space, the raw material out of which every fixed, revolving, or wandering orb of the skies was by slow degrees compacted and shaped.

Such is the majestic procession of Being which would unfold itself before the mind of the scientific observer, revealing to him how, step by step, the existing Cosmos proceeded from the primordial chaos of vapour. But the inquiring mind even then will refuse to be satisfied. Not to seek further would be to be false to itself. So far it has been concerned with nothing but the phenomenal sequences of change and growth. To penetrate behind the phenomenal, to discover something beneath the order and stages of development, to reach the very causes and motive forces of the mighty evolution, must now present itself as an achievement worthy of the most earnest intellectual endeavour. As the youthful Epicurus, reading Hesiod's "Theogony" with his tutor, when he had arrived at the starting of all things from chaos, was unable to refrain from asking, "And whence chaos?"—so the inevitable question follows now, "Whence the primordial vapour?" Things have always been changing, but why? What is the cause that originated, what the force that sustains and impels? Are there, behind Nature, an Intellect which designs, a Will which proposes and executes? Such questions will come to the front, and it is clear that the possibility of an Intelligent religion depends on the answers that can be obtained to them. Were they unanswerable, and were all knowledge unattainable beyond that of the phenomenal facts of the universe, religion, in any real, practical sense, could have no existence. We might gaze with amazement and awe at the stupendous scene, and be oppressed with a sense of the impenetrable mystery which invests it; but for all that goes to the making up of the true idea of religion,—for worship, reverence, trust, communion, gratitude,—there could be no place; for these are emotions which require for their object the qualities that we sum up under the term Personality.

(c)   *Ibid*

CREED, INCOMPETENCY OF SCIENCE TO FORM A

There is no origin of the world according to Science. Science, that is Natural or Physical Science, treats of the laws which govern matter; it studies and arranges and explains material phenomena; it traces back the history of the material universe in the past, and it calculates not a little of that which will be in the future: but it never gets to the actual origin of anything; it works upon that which it finds ready-made to its hands; it is cognisant of no time when matter did not exist, and when the laws of nature were different to what they are now. Science means *knowledge;* and it may be safely asserted that the origin of things, lying as it does absolutely outside our experience, belongs to the region of the *unknowable. . . .* What Holy Scripture says of the world is, that God made it; and the assertion is a very important one; but it is not an assertion of the same kind as those which can be made

(d)

concerning the material universe upon the strength of scientific investigations: these investigations deal with what can be proved and known concerning the things which we see: they cannot by their very nature take any account of a Divine hand acting below the surface; the moment they do anything of this kind they cease to be scientific. And therefore a scientific man, so far as he is only a scientific man, may believe in God or not believe in Him; he may be a devout worshipper of Him who has revealed Himself to us in Jesus Christ, or he may be a blank atheist; but whatever may be his belief or unbelief, it does not properly come into contact with his scientific investigations.

(a)   *Bp. Goodwin*

CREED, A RELIGIOUS, PRACTICALLY UNIVERSAL

But now, over against the conclusion, that *no basis of religious belief can be furnished by science,* we have to place the remarkable fact that, from the earliest dawn of history, such belief, in some form and degree, has always been practically universal among mankind. It has indeed been affirmed that here and there, in newly explored lands, small tribes of men in the lowest depths of barbarism have been discovered, among whom no signs of religion or worship could be traced. The statement, however, has failed to stand the test of further investigation; and even were it correct, the exception would be too insignificant to impair the virtual universality of religious belief in some form or other. And this we may go on to say with certainty, that all tribes and nations which have been advanced enough to possess and exhibit any distinctively human development and culture, have professed some kind of theistic belief. Rude the belief has undoubtedly been where civilization was but dawning amidst the dense gloom of barbarism; and in some of its various polytheistic and idolatrous shapes it might seem scarcely entitled to claim even a remote kinship with the monotheism of the Hebrew race. Still, beneath all the incrustations and deformities caused by ignorance and barbarism, there lay the germ of belief in God; and with every upward step of intellectual and moral growth its advance in purity, clearness, and strength may be historically traced. So far from showing any signs of dying out, as an effete and exploded superstition, which could not live in the atmosphere of ripening knowledge and culture, theistic belief has ever been rooting itself more deeply in the mental constitution of the most progressive portions of the human family, the imperial races which lead the world; and among these it has not been limited to faith in an Almighty Ruler and Judge, but has acquired new elements of strength, by expanding into the Christian doctrine of a heavenly Father who has revealed Himself to His earthly children by His own incarnate Son. In this most highly developed form, religious belief has shown itself able to live through every political revolution and social transformation; it has allied itself with all that is purest and loveliest in human affection and aspiration; it has pervaded the world's life and moulded its growth, and been more fruitful of the heroisms of morality than any other belief which has ever prevailed among mankind.

(b)   *Quarterly Review*

CREED: JUSTIFICATION OF RELIGIOUS BELIEF

Here then we come at last in sight of the question to which we are directing attention. What account can be given of this mighty tide of religious belief? We know with certainty that it was not derived from any scientific or experimental examination of the phenomena of the universe; from whence then did it spring, and on what does it rest? Is there beneath it any reality, of which satisfactory assurance can be obtained; or must it be assigned exclusively to the region of sentiment and emotion, and be accounted a merely subjective product of the imagination which forms ideals, or of the affections which invent supernatural objects to fill their embrace? Let us briefly see what can be said on both sides of the controversy.

What is urged on the negative side amounts to this,—that the only avenues to real knowledge are the senses, and that we have no right to believe in the objective existence of anything, unless its being can be established by an experimental verification, of which the senses are the ultimate instruments and judges. Everything in human thought and belief which cannot thus be verified must be consigned to a different category, the category of the subjective and unreal. It may be beautiful, or it may be useful; it may be playing an important part in the development of human culture, or throwing a tender grace over human life; but it must not be confounded with truth or knowledge, nor regarded as having any ascertained counterpart in the world of reality. Granting, then, that there has been among mankind an almost universal conviction that spiritual beings exist of whom the senses can give no information, and that the ideas of God, of the soul, and of immortality have very largely influenced the course of human thought and conduct; still, as no scientific verification of these conceptions is possible, they have no just claim to be recognised as true, but must ever remain among the unpractical questions which lie outside the range of the human faculties. Such is the position assumed by modern Agnosticism; and it may be tersely expressed in Professor Huxley's statement, that " in respect of the existence and attributes of the soul, as of those of the Deity, logic is powerless and reason silent."

To establish against this position a justification of religious belief, it is plain that the only practicable course is to show that there is some other method of attaining reasonable and sufficient assurance, besides that of sensible, scientific verification. The apologist of Faith must point to that religious experience of the race which we have very briefly sketched, and contend that this of itself supplies the required proof or verification. The fundamental conceptions of God, the soul, revelation, and immortality, have proved themselves, by their wide prevalence and magnificent effects, to be in harmony with all that is highest and best in human nature; they have found in its reason, its moral sense, its spiritual desires, and aspirations, a soil in which they root themselves ineradicably, and become fruitful of the noblest virtues; and thus they attest themselves to be more than visionary speculations or subjective modes of thought, and establish their claim to be accepted as absolute realities, able to bear the strain of human life, and to adorn it with the

(c)

crown of immortal hope. Such is the only line of defence which can foil the attack of the agnostic philosophy on the whole fabric of supernatural truth, for it is the only one which takes up the challenge to show how any beliefs can be reasonably held of which no scientific verification is possible.

(a)   *Quarterly Review*

CREED, THE CHRISTIAN, APPEALS NOT TO A LOGICAL FACULTY

The appeal on behalf of faith is addressed, not to the bare logical faculty on which the student of science relies for constructing his theory of the phenomenal universe, but to a very different part of human nature—to its moral intuitions, its faculties of faith and trust, its capacity for realizing the unseen and aspiring to the spiritual and eternal. If there were no such constituents in the nature of man, the appeal would be useless, for there would be nothing in him which it could touch. One might as hopefully sing to the deaf, or paint for the blind, as urge religious belief on a being whose mental constitution was limited to a capacity for constructing syllogisms and classifying physical phenomena. Just, therefore, in proportion as those finer elements of the human constitution are stunted or depressed, whether through a disproportionate development of the scientific intellect, or through moral obliquity and vicious indulgence, so must the appeal on behalf of religion meet with indifference and be barren of fruit.

(b)   *Ibid*

CREED, THE CHRISTIAN, AND SCIENTIFIC THOUGHT

There can be no doubt of the fact, that the habits fostered by scientific thought have of late been acquiring a predominance which is destructive, not so much of particular doctrines of the Christian creed, as of the essential principles of faith. . . . A general discredit is quietly and deliberately cast upon the whole fabric of our creed, as something which, whatever may be said for it, has no adequate basis on which to rest. Much has of late years been heard of the conflict between faith and science; and, however that conflict may be appeased on particular points, there remains, it is to be feared, that cardinal opposition in point of principle to which the consideration now in view directs our attention.

(c)   *Dr. Wace*

"Science," to use a familiar expression, "is in the air"—science in the special and limited sense in which the word is now chiefly understood; and there is a tendency to judge of all things on purely scientific grounds. It is positively asserted, or tacitly assumed, that Faith, as we have contemplated it in the general course of human history, is unjustifiable as a principle of action, and that the welfare of mankind is to be pursued by rigidly restricting our beliefs within the limits of that which can be sensibly verified. . . . Experience shows, in fact, that such a principle, in proportion as it is rigidly applied, tends not so much to produce a direct conflict with our Christian faith, as to undermine the grounds on which we adhere to it. So far as our creed is beyond the reach of verification, so far as it rests on the mere word and assertions of its founder, so far as it is a

matter of trust, and not of sight, its hold upon men's minds is liable to be shaken by the undue predominance of these habits of scientific thought.

(d)   *Dr. Wace*

The contrast drawn by the Agnostic between the logical firmness of the basis on which science rests and the precariousness of the foundation which is claimed for religious beliefs, needs a great deal of qualification. It adroitly conceals the fact, that underneath the imposing temple of knowledge, raised by scientific methods, there lie certain assumptions of which no logical proof is forthcoming, but which are indispensable before a single stone of the towering structure can be laid If we demand of the physical theorist how he becomes sure of the existence of the external universe which is the object of his researches, or of the law of causation and the uniformity of Nature on which his deductions depend, or even of the trustworthiness of his senses to report, and of his memory to register, the phenomena which are the materials of his theories; and if we pertinaciously insist on a definite answer, and refuse to be put off with vague and contradictory assertions, we shall discover that he is compelled at last to fall back for his ultimate foundation on the general intuitions and convictions of mankind. *Even he has to begin with believing*, in formulating his proofs and building up his knowledge.

(e)   *Quarterly Review*

We frankly accept the impossibility of finding an adequate basis for belief in the discoveries and conclusions of the scientific intellect.

(f)   *Ibid*

CREED, THE CHRISTIAN, AND REALITY

Man possesses in his reason and his heart, in the world without and in the world within, arguments enough to afford him a substantial knowledge of God, and to lead him to worship and to trust. But they are not demonstrative. They are not even mere arguments of probability. In other words, they are not simply intellectual. They put a strain upon the moral nature; and the manner in which that strain is borne determines the moral condition alike of individuals and of races. Once let men take the broader and easier road of moral supineness, and they at once lose their hold upon God, and are in imminent danger of falling into an abyss of corruption such as that described in this chapter [Rom. i.]. But let them choose the narrower and severer path, and God becomes more and more a vivid reality to them, and they advance from strength to strength.

(g)   *Dr. Wace*

Those who sigh for the absolute demonstrative knowledge, which of any other being than ourselves is impossible, may turn from it [the teaching of revelation] in a proud despair, crying out, "God is unknown and unknowable."

(h)   *Bp. Barry*

CREED, THE CHRISTIAN, IN ANTAGONISM TO SCIENCE

At this point it is obvious that Christianity stands out in antagonism to the exclusive and

(i)

unbounded claims of science as the one sole guide to truth, even while it looks gladly and thankfully on its accumulation of knowledge along the various lines of thought. If science declares that it can find no proof of the universal Atonement and the universal Judgment, of the true nature of the Godhead and its relation to humanity in Jesus Christ, Christianity will feel neither surprise nor apprehension. For on these things it appeals to a power which every student of human nature will acknowledge to be one of the truest and greatest in the world—the power of faith. In the contemplation of the life of Jesus Christ it is content to find the grounds of an absolute faith in Him, crowning all the lesser developments of faith of which human history is full. When it surveys the actual effects which that faith has wrought, not for the few but for the many—teaching the mind to know what passes knowledge, inspiring the moral nature with a strength made perfect in weakness, raising the spirit to a communion with God which it feels to be a life eternal,—it is not ashamed of blazoning faith upon its banner, and doubts not to find it "the victory which overcomes the world."

(a)　　　　　　　　　　　　*Bp. Barry*

CREED, THE: FAITH, THE BASIS OF ALL RELIGIONS

All religions rest upon faith, and without it could never have existed for a moment. Of the spiritual life and national characteristics of Israel it was the animating principle; and by reason of it the invisible world was, to that wonderful nation, more real than any of the things around them, and the predicted future more certain than that sun and moon would fulfil their ordinary courses. With the Christian Church it has ever been the same; the entire life of apostles, martyrs, saints, has been sustained by faith; and it is on trust in the word of a few witnesses that the whole fabric of Christendom has been reared. Every other religion, too, has the same principle at its root, and exhibits a similar supremacy of the faculty of faith.

(b)　　　　　　　　　　　*Quarterly Review*

In a word, it has been by the invisible rather than by the visible, by the future rather than by the present, by authority rather than by reason, by faith rather than by sight, that, as a matter of fact, mankind, as a whole, has been governed, has been organized, and has advanced to its present condition. The part played by reason in this marvellous course of development has, indeed, been momentous, and has been second only to that of faith. But regarding history as a whole, the part of reason must be admitted to have been a secondary one. It is faith which has grasped whole nations and ages within its sway, and which has determined the main principles of their conduct and their destiny.

(c)　　　　　　　　　　　　　*Dr. Wace*

CREED, THE, AND DOCTRINE OF THE INCARNATION

It is precisely in the most mysterious doctrines of our creed, in those which make the strongest demands on faith, and are the most remote from any possibility of scientific verification, that Christian souls find their support and refuge under these burdens of the flesh and these torments of the spirit. The message that "God so loved the world that He gave His only begotten Son, that whosoever believeth in Him, should not perish, but have everlasting life,"—this is a message, simple as are its terms, which transcends all philosophy, all reason, all experience, nay, all capacity of comprehension; and yet it is in reliance on this message, and on other assurances of the same kind, that Christians are delivered from despair, and are enabled, under whatever distresses, to cling to their belief in the love of their Father in Heaven. . . . The message of the Cross, interpreted by the doctrine of the Incarnation, is thus, in moments of real trial, the support of the most elementary principle of faith. In fact, the minimizing theology now in question depends for its plausibility upon a simple evasion of the real problems of philosophy, and of the practical difficulties of life. The full and explicit faith of the creeds recognises those difficulties, and looks them in the face. It owns that they are insuperable upon any grounds of mere natural wisdom, and it offers supernatural realities and supernatural assurances to overcome them.

(d)　　　　　　　　　　　　　*Dr. Wace*

CREED, THE: POSITIVE REVELATION

The next great step is the belief, not merely that there is a God of all righteousness and power, with whom we have to do, but that He has given us a positive revelation. The man who has apprehended God through the conscience cannot but crave for some actual communication from Him for the confirmation of faith and the enlargement of knowledge. Amidst the pressure, the struggles, the disappointments in human life, he will strain the ear to catch some voice from God, the eye to behold some manifestation of His Person and Will. To this instinctive and irrepressible desire the answer is found in the declaration of prophets and apostles. They announce a message from God; they solemnly declare that they have received from Him specific revelations for the information and comfort of mankind.

(e)　　　　　　　　　　　*Quarterly Review*

CREED, THE: THEOLOGY AND MORALITY

We here approach another point in which the Sermon on the Mount, considered as a typical instance of our Lord's teaching, is at the present day most strangely and flagrantly misrepresented. It is the favourite contention of those who impugn the faith of the Church, that the teaching of that sermon is purely moral and independent of theology. "It is undeniable," says the author of "Supernatural Religion," with characteristic strength of assertion, "that the earliest teaching of Jesus recorded in the Gospel which can be regarded as in any degree historical, is pure morality, almost, if not quite, free from theological dogmas. Morality was the essence of His system; theology was an afterthought." Two pages afterwards this writer states with perfect correctness, but with complete unconsciousness of inconsistency, that Christ's system "confined itself to two fundamental principles, love to God and love to man." But is there no theology involved in teaching love to God?—no theology in the belief that God is, and

(f)

that He is the rewarder of them that diligently seek Him, and that, in spite of all the difficulties, perplexities, and cruelties of the world, He is worthy of the whole love and trust of our hearts? Why, this is the very theological problem which has racked the heart and brain of man from the dawn of religious thought to the present moment. On these two commandments,—to which, in the curious phrase just quoted, Christ's system is said to have "confined itself," as though they were slight and simple,—on these two commandments hang all the Law and the Prophets. They are the germ from which has sprung the whole theological thought of the Christian Church, and to which it returns; and no theologian can wish to do more than to deepen his own apprehension of them, and to strengthen their hold upon others.

(a)   Dr. Wace

CREED, THE MEDIÆVAL, DEPARTURES FROM

When bishops, priests, and monks were unable to say to the tempter, "Get thee hence, Satan, for it is written, Thou shalt worship the Lord thy God, and Him only shalt thou serve," they entered into possession of the kingdoms of the world and the glory of them, but they lost the kingdom of God. When power instead of truth became the object of the dominant hierarchy, faith had been falsified at its source. The vision of God to whom they had thus been faithless became eclipsed, and a huge and portentous system of error and superstition developed, as by a natural law, from the first original untruth. The "ages of faith" became transformed into the ages of superstition.

(b)   Ibid

CREED, THE, AND INFALLIBILITY

Though we cannot appeal to any visible and infallible Authority, we do possess an unerring Guidance; and we possess it, moreover, not merely in the ambiguous, distant, and tardy utterances of a human oracle, but in the voice of a Divine Spirit, ever present with us, and helping us in all our infirmities. . . . He works in the hearts of Christ's people to purify their conscience and their will; and, in proportion as they yield to this influence, are they qualified to "know of the doctrine," and to become united in the truth.

(c)   Ibid

CREEDS

This is the most important lesson that a man can learn—that all men are really alike; that all creeds and opinions are nothing but the mere result of chance and temperament; that no party is on the whole better than another; that no creed does more than shadow imperfectly forth some one side of truth; and it is only when you begin to see this, that you can feel that pity for mankind, that sympathy with its disappointments and follies, and its natural human hopes, which have such a little time of growth, and such a sure season of decay.

(d)   Shorthouse (John Inglesant)

CREMATION (Gen. iii. 19)

The great importance which Christianity attaches to the body, makes it a sacred duty for Christians to show respect to the corpse. In this body the dead has lived his earthly life, has done his day's work; and if he was a Christian, this body has been a temple of the Holy Ghost.

Interment is the most worthy kind of burial. Although Holy Scripture gives no express command, yet this emerges as a necessary consequence of Gen. iii. 19, "Dust thou art, and unto," etc. Burial is presupposed throughout (John xii. 24; 1 Cor. xv. 44).

Interment = the mean between two other mutually opposed ways of dealing with human corpses—*embalming* and *cremation*.

The first, contrary to God's order, aims to *preserve* the lifeless body, which He has appointed to dissolution; it seeks to snatch his prey from death.

The other will not preserve the body, but hasten its dissolution by artificial practice; yea, cause this to be done in haste, as soon as possible send the corpse out of the world, that phenomenon so uncomfortable to the natural man. Interment is the right mean between these two extremes. We practise no arts either to preserve or annihilate the body, but deliver it to the dissolving power of nature, and let nature in all quiet and secrecy perform the work of annihilation.

We know that death is something more than a mere natural process; it is *the wages of sin* (Rom. vi. 23). . . . We therefore attempt not voluntary experiments to evade the law of dissolution confirmed by the Divine Word, whereby certainly not a process of burning is indicated, but dissolution in the bosom of the earth. And on the grave we plant the cross which reminds us of sin, and death as the wages of sin, and also that the crucified Christ has taken away the sting of death, and by His resurrection has changed death into an entrance into the heavenly kingdom.

When in our days voices are heard urging that burial be exchanged for cremation, we can only recognise the utterances of a modern heathenism. The spokesmen of this agitation lack all religious presuppositions, regarding death as a mere process of nature, and relying exclusively upon "sanitary" grounds, about which there may be infinite disputations *pro* and *contra*. That the Christian Church will never accept it, may be predicted with confidence. The Christian Church cannot *burn* her dead, cannot break with her old venerable traditions, without likewise committing to the fire her *figurative speech* founded on the Scriptures, which throughout speaks of death and resurrection under the presupposition of the burial of the dead.

(e)   Martensen

CRITICISM

Remember what Sheridan said, when he came out from the House of Commons, after they had hissed him: "*It's in me, and it shall come out.*"

(f)

CRITICISM, "RATIONAL"

That the reader may have some adequate idea of what has been the historical and inevitable development of the fundamental principle of Rationalism and Infidelity (viz., SUBJECTIVITY, in opposition to the Objective authority of the written Record of the Revelation of God), the following Synopsis of German speculations regarding the

(g)

Criticism—*continued*

facts and doctrines of the New Testament may be commended to his thoughtful study. "By their fruits ye shall know them."

(*a*)

With Bahrdt, the angel that announced the birth of John the Baptist to Zacharias was only a flash of lightning, mistaken for a heavenly messenger, and the conversation but a waking dream. With Paulus, the smoke from the pan of incense, as it ascends to the roof and catches the glimmer of the evening lamps, becomes straightway the angelic visitant. Alarm excited by the apparition affects the aged priest with a shock like paralysis, and makes him dumb till the joy of paternity loosens afresh the strings of his tongue; or else he punishes himself for the entertainment of a momentary doubt by maintaining a voluntary silence, after the Jewish manner, for a certain period. With some (*Paulus, Heidenreich*), the narrative is a family record;—with others (*Schmidt*), the legend so prevails in it that it has no historical value whatever. With Eichhorn, Kaiser, Wegscheider, De Wette, Winer, Hase, Fritsche, Ammon, Strauss, Hoffmann, and others, the genealogies of St. Matthew and St. Luke cannot both be true. They were composed, according to others (*Schmidt Schleiermacher*, etc., etc.), in the belief that Joseph was the father of Jesus. Paulus hints that some young man, by concert with Elizabeth, obtained access to the Virgin Mary as the angel Gabriel, and thus became the father of Jesus. Schmidt (*Eck, Paulus*) thinks the account of the taxing in Luke ii. too contrary to fact to be worth attempting to clear from its difficulties. The annunciation of the birth of Jesus to the shepherds at Bethlehem is only the approach of a messenger bearing a light, accompanied by a party of youths singing and making merry, or the play of an aurora or some meteor in the midnight sky, interpreted into an angelic vision, when the shepherds have ascertained the birth of Jesus on their return from the field.

(*b*)

Jesus was born among shepherds, merely because the historian knew that several heroes had such an education, Cyrus,—Romulus, etc.,—and the gods too,—Apollo, Jupiter, etc. The standing of the star over the house of Christ's nativity is not to be taken, according to Olshausen, as more than a figure of speech, or as precluding the necessity of inquiry on the part of the magi. Their visit to the young child is settled thus (*Krug*):—Some Arabian merchants, happening to be at Jerusalem, visited Bethlehem in the course of their perambulations, and hearing of the distress of the strangers in the town, relieved them with money and other things, and wished their child good luck, and left them. All besides this is mere historical embellishment. If Luke's narrative of the presentation in the temple be true, Matthew's of the flight into Egypt must be false (*Schleiermacher*).

(*c*)

According to Strauss, the statement of Luke and Matthew, that Jesus was born in Bethlehem, is destitute of all valid historical evidence, nay, is contravened by positive historical facts. John the Baptist and Jesus play into each other's hands, by

pretending not to have known each other till they met in public during their ministry (*Wolfenbüttel Fragments*). Bauer treats the notion that God should have spoken at the baptism of Jesus, and on other occasions, in a national dialect, as absurd (*Hebra, Mythologie*); while the circumstance is variously explained by others, most resolving it into a thunder-clap—and the dove into a lambent flame or a flash of lightning. The idea of angels or devils is a mere assemblage of incongruities, the creation of ignorance and sloth (*Schleiermacher*). The temptation of Christ is only a dream or vision (*Paulus*); or it may have been some Pharisee, prompted by his sect to make offers to Jesus, which the Lord rejected—and straightway thereupon He happed upon a travelling caravan that gave Him food, or upon a pleasant breeze that refreshed Him (*Henke's Magazin: Naturalischen Geschichte*); or, again, the narrative may be only a parable (*Schmidt, Schleiermacher, Usteri, Theile*). Some represent the plan of the Messiah to have been a purely political one; that His hope was to revolutionize the Jewish nation, and re-establish the glory of the theocracy; others, that He had two plans at two distinct periods, the former a political one; and that only on the subversion of it He adopted the latter, which was spiritual (*Paulus, Venturini, Hase*).

(*d*)

Strauss believes that Jesus at first took the same position as John the Baptist, in relation to the kingdom of the Messiah, and that it was only by slow degrees He allowed Himself to be persuaded into the idea that He was the Messiah in His own person (*Strauss*). When Christ promised thrones on His right and left to His Apostles, He merely accommodated Himself to their Messianic prejudices, or else spoke in irony (*Kuinöl, in loco; Liebe, in Winer*), ridiculing the inordinateness of their pretensions. Although the Church of Christ soon did embrace Gentiles, this was clearly not a part of His plan (*Wolfenbüttel Fragments*): therefore the command of Christ to " Go and teach all nations " has no historical truth. Our Saviour's knowledge of the discreditable life of the woman of Samaria was obtained from some passer-by, who warned Him not to converse with so disreputable a person (*Paulus*). Others go further, and say that the story itself has no foundation in fact (*Strauss*). It is a legend, an idyll, a poetical representation. The call to the Apostles in the words, "Come after Me!" "Follow Me!" is merely an invitation to accompany Jesus in a walk (*Paulus*). Either John's or Matthew's account must be erroneous— both cannot be true (*Fritsche, in loco*). Jesus learned Nathanael's character when He went to the wedding at Cana, so that there was nothing supernatural in His knowledge of him (*Paulus*). Lücke thinks there was nothing unusual in Christ's seeing Nathanael under the fig-tree. To suppose anything miraculous in the incident is not a little extravagant (*Strauss*). The miraculous draught of fishes was a happy fortuity, united with accurate observation of where the fishes lay, on the part of Jesus (*Paulus*); impossible to imagine such a miracle out of the realm of Magic (*Strauss*); a legend, in fact, of the same class as Pythagoras's telling the number of fish taken at a draught which he had no natural means of knowing. Christ's call to Matthew meant no more than that Jesus was now ready to go home with the publican

(*e*)

Criticism—*continued*

to dinner, according to the invitation he had previously received (*Paulus*). That ever Jesus appointed the seventy Evangelists, is unworthy of credence on the authority of Luke alone (*Strauss*). Matthew and Luke directly contradict each other in the circumstances attendant on the Sermon on the Mount. The woes recorded by Luke are owing to the inventive fertility of that author (*Schleiermacher*).

(a)

The Lord's Prayer, given by Matthew, is an interpolation of the writer (*Schleiermacher, Sieffert*). Part of Christ's charge to His Apostles is pronounced unsuitable to their circumstances (*Sieffert, Schulz*). When Jesus propounded the question to the Pharisees, if David called the Messiah Lord, how was He also his son? He intended to show them that David was not the author of Psalm cx. (*Paulus*). The first Gospel was not written by Matthew, but by some one considerably more recent than any Apostle (*Schulz*). The relation between Jesus and Nicodemus was possibly no more than the fabrication of tradition, and adopted by John without having any basis in reality (*Strauss*); while the conversation between them is in some parts so improbable that it never could have been maintained by Jesus, but claims, in its greater part, John as its author (*Paulus*). The discourses of Jesus in the fourth Gospel are free inventions of John (*Bretschneider*). The author of Matthew's Gospel was not an eye-witness of the events he records (*Schulz, Sieffert, Schneckenburger*). The course of events described by John is partly fictitious (*Strauss*). The style of Mark is one of palpable exaggeration, which is natural to him (*Strauss*). Schleiermacher calls Luke's epithet of "sinner," applied to the woman who anointed our Saviour, a false inference of the narrator.

(b)

The casting out of devils is only a figure or a parable (*Fritsche, Olshausen*); and demoniacal possession was nothing more than some form of insanity or epilepsy. The lunatics have lucid intervals, when they go to synagogues, and there learn about the Messiah the particulars they blurt out in the course of their cure. The possession of the herd of swine at Gadara is on a par with the story of Balaam's ass: it means only that the maniacs rushed towards the herd, and drove them into the sea (*Paulus*); or that they fell into the sea by accident before Jesus landed (*Krug*); or that, during the absence of the herdsman, who went to meet Jesus, a few strayed over the precipice into the deep (*Schmidt*). The prayer and fasting necessary to the expulsion of demons, means that the patient should use spare diet to effect a radical cure (*Paulus*). The cure of demoniacs was the easiest kind of miracles, because all resolvable into psychical action. Sometimes they only fancied themselves cured, because the crisis of their affection was broken by the work of Jesus (*Venturini, Kaiser*). The Evangelist John was too enlightened to sanction the notion of such miracles by the record of them (*Eichhorn, Herder, Wegscheider, De Wette*). The cure of the leper is merely pronouncing a leprous person over whom the contagious stage of the disease has passed sufficiently recovered to be viewed as clean in the

eye of the ceremonial law (*Paulus*). Matthew's informant must have mistaken the blind man's guide at Jericho for a second blind man. The blind men were cured by the removal of the irritating dust from their eyes, by means of a lotion previously prepared (*Venturini*). Or, touching their eyes removes the film or scale that hindered clear vision; and inserting the finger into the ear of the deaf is to remove the indurated secretion that stopped up the orifice; and touching the tongue of the dumb is severing, by some mechanical means (a caustic powder for instance), the ligature that forbade its distinct articulation (*Paulus, Natural History of the Life of Christ*). The washing in the pool of Siloam may mean a protracted cure of blindness by means of the bath. The healing of the blind man in John ix. is an incredible narrative; perhaps it never occurred (*Strauss*). The cure effected in the woman with the issue of blood was through the emotion she experienced on touching Christ, which caused a contraction of the relaxed vessels, and ultimately a cure through attention to the prescriptions of our Lord (*Paulus, Venturini, Koster*). Christ's acquaintance with semeiology enabled Him to predict the time of improvement in the condition of the Centurion's servant; or He sent a disciple who effected the cure in His stead (*Paulus*). The man with the withered hand was simply a person who had suffered from a sprain or the extreme heat (*Venturini, Paulus*); and the cure was only the public attestation of it, the proper medicaments having been already applied in private by Jesus (*Koster, Paulus*). The cure of the paralytic, at the pool of Bethesda, was merely the conviction of a hypocrite. The resuscitation of the little damsel, was her recovery from a swoon by medical treatment. The restoration of the widow of Nain's son is to be regarded in the same light. The resurrection of Lazarus, was his reviving from a state of lethargy by means of the stream of warm air that entered his sepulchre on the rolling away of the stone (*Paulus, Gabler*).

(c)

Matthew, Mark, and Luke, by not recording Lazarus's resurrection, prove that those persons were no Apostles who drew up the narratives bearing their names. The resurrection of Lazarus is not only in the highest degree improbable, but totally destitute of external evidence (*Strauss*). The calming of the storm at sea is a myth, representing the protecting power of Jesus and the troubles of the Church (*Schneckenburger, Strauss*). The walking of Jesus on the sea merely means on the lofty ridge of the sea shore; and Peter's and his own meeting in the sea is swimming or wading in the shallows (*Paulus, Bolten, Henke's Magazine, Schneckenburger*). The fish caught by Peter with the stater in its mouth, represents a fish worth the required sum, caught and sold for so much; while Peter opens his own mouth, instead of the fish's, to recommend it for sale (*Paulus, Hase*). The feeding the multitude by a miraculous multiplication of bread, is Jesus and His disciples producing their spare stores to supply the indigent, and inducing those of the company who had provisions to distribute those also, so that all were fed (*Paulus, Weisse*); or a mere parable (*Paulus, Venturini, Kaiser*). The transformation of water into wine resolves itself into a present of wine, such being customary at wedding feasts; and the command to draw it from the water jars a pleasantry on the part of

(d)

Criticism—*continued*

Jesus, who had deposited it there; that John took it for a miracle because he was tipsy (*Paulus, Hase*). The cursing of the barren fig-tree is a mere prediction, grounded on certain appearances in the tree that it would speedily wither (*Herder, Gratz*). The transfiguration of Christ was not real, but an ecstatic vision on His part and that of the disciples (*Rau, Gabler, Kuinöl*); or it was a dream (*Kuinöl, Venturini*) of Peter, James, and John in their sleep on the mount, aided by a flash of lightning on their waking, the voice of thunder, and the apparition of two strange men; or it was a preconcerted interview with two secret adherents of Jesus, whose talk awakens the sleeping apostles; that these imagine Christ invested with super-human glory because, as He stood on the peak of the mountain, the rays of the morning sun fell upon Him with unwonted brilliancy, reflected perhaps from a sheet of snow; that a luminous cloud shut out the two men suddenly from view, and that one in departing used the form of address contained in the narrative; or it is a mythus suggested by the glory of Moses (*De Wette, Bertholdt, Credner, Schulz, Kuinöl, Gratz*); or, finally, a metaphor or allegory (*Weisse*).

(a)

Christ's predictions of the manner of His own death are so many *vaticinia post eventum* (*Paulus, Ammon, Bertholdt, Wegscheider*). In the record of predictions of His resurrection, the Evangelists give a definiteness to the discourses of Jesus which they did not possess when spoken (*Paulus, Hase*); Christ never could have explained His resurrection by the sign of the prophet Jonah (*Paulus, Schulz*); Judas the traitor was an honest man, misunderstood (*K. Ch. L. Schmidt*); or a deluded one, exhibiting even in his despair an apostolic greatness (*Hase*); or else seeking an object decidedly good by questionable means (*Paulus*); wounded self-love was the motive of Judas for betraying his master, not covetousness (*Kaiser, Klopstock*). We know nothing of the price at which Jesus was sold, Matthew's authority being insufficient to fix it, the sum being suggested by Zechariah's prophecy (*Strauss*). There was no miracle in our Lord sending the disciples to prepare the Passover chamber, and in their meeting the man bearing the pitcher of water, etc., etc. The gospel of John is in error in stating Christ to have eaten the paschal supper with His disciples (*Olshausen*). The institution of the Lord's supper is not mentioned by John, because it was unknown to him (*Bretschneider*). Jesus had no idea of instituting His memorial supper till it glanced upon His mind from the sight of the loaf and the wine on the table before Him (*Paulus, Kaiser*).

(b)

The agony in the garden was only some malady with which the body of Jesus was suddenly attacked, perhaps a cold, contracted from the damp clayey soil bordering on the Kedron (*Thies, Paulus, Heumann*); or it may have been severe regret at the prospect of parting with His friends (*Schuster*). The angel strengthening Him was a man (*Venturini*), or a parable (*Eichhorn, Schleiermacher, Gabler*), or a poetical embellishment. Even Neander seems willing to give up the angel and the bloody sweat as inexplicable; Strauss

regards them and the threefold prayer of Jesus as mythical additions to the narrative of the betrayal. John has transposed erroneously the agony in the garden into an interview with the Greeks (*Theile*). Our Saviour's last discourses and prayer, so far from being His, are peculiarly the composition of John, and speak a language that could not have been employed by Christ. The Lord's full prescience of His sufferings is explained by His having some friend in the Sanhedrim, who informed Him of the designs of His enemies; and the approach of His captors could be easily anticipated, as He saw them from a distance, lighted by their torches. Jesus did not heal the ear of the high priest's servant, cut off by Peter, but merely handled it to ascertain the extent of the wound, and then prescribed what would do it good (*Paulus*). Peter denied his Lord eight times. Only one of the accounts of Judas's death can be apostolic both cannot be true (*Schmidt*). The field of blood derived its name from a cause no longer to be discovered, but having no relation to Judas (*Strauss*). The potter's field was entirely suggested by the passage in the prophecy quoted by Peter. We do not know with certainty even that Judas came to a violent death.

(c)

The statement that Pilate washed his hands, and pronounced Jesus a just person, owes its origin to the Christians alone, who were concerned for the reputation of their Master, and is not a fact. Jesus must have been three times clothed with the purple robe; and five times drink must have been offered to Him, according to the Evangelists. Probably there is nothing historical in the narrative, but the whole tissue is spun out of the prophecies. The rending of the veil of the temple never took place at all (*Schleiermacher, Paulus, Strauss*). The same must be said of the resurrection of the dead saints on the death of Christ; the violent earthquake may have laid open some tombs, which being found empty from the decay of the bodies, suggested the idea that the dead had arisen and forsaken them (*Paulus*). The angels play at hide and seek with the several visitors of the sepulchre (*Strauss*). The angel that rolled away the stone was a flash of lightning which struck the stone, and threw the guards to the earth; or an earthquake accompanied by flames of fire bursting from the earth (*Schuster*); or it was an Oriental figure of speech, to ascribe the personal conviction of the women, that Jesus was risen, to the suggestion of an angel (*Faedrich*); or the women, peeping in the dusk of the morning, mistook the grave clothes for angels (*Bauer, Schmidt, Eichhorn*); or two men, secret colleagues of Jesus, the two that personated Moses and Elias at the transfiguration (*Paulus, Bahrdt, Venturini*). Mary took Jesus for the gardener, because He had borrowed the gardener's clothes (*Paulus*). The prohibition to touch Him, addressed by Jesus to Mary, was occasioned by the nervous and painful sensitiveness of His body just after crucifixion; after living several years beyond the period of His crucifixion, Jesus at last died (*Brenneke*); He died of natural maladies and fever (*Paulus*). Jesus did not die on the cross; His seeming death was a collapse or swoon; or it was a simulated death, confiding in medical skill to easily repair the injury inflicted on His frame by crucifixion; or the semblance of it was occasioned

(d)

Criticism—*continued*

by a potion administered to Jesus by His disciples without His connivance (*Bahrdt*). The revivification of Christ was brought about by the smell of the unguents wherewith He had been anointed, together with the air of the cave, and the salutary shock of the earthquake acting upon a young body not destitute of vital power (*Paulus, Schuster*). The disciples stole the body, according to the Wolfenbüttel Fragmentist, so that there was not even the semblance of a resurrection, but the whole story is a shameless fraud. The ascension was not real, but a vision produced in the disciples (*Steudel*); or it was His raising Himself up on tiptoe to bless His disciples, and His gradually withdrawing from them till a mist, and the olive-trees on the hill, hid Him from their sight, when His two secret colleagues again appear to affirm His ascension.

(*a*)

The angels that attended the ascension of Christ were thunder and lightning, that seemed to say what the Apostles already thought about the disappearance of their Master, viz., that He had gone up to heaven; or else the circumstance was only a vision of the imagination, or only the garniture of the narrative suggested by the genius of the age, for which we are indebted to the historian alone. Judas hanging himself is nothing more than disease induced by remorse of conscience; or, again, nothing more than that extreme remorse itself. Mr. Wakefield, in his *Sylva Critica*, observes that Judas may have died from dysentery occasioned by distress of mind. There were two distinct traditions, according to others, regarding the manner of Judas's death, that Matthew adopted the one, and that Luke followed the other. The cloven tongues of the Pentecost were flashes of lightning pervading the room where the disciples met, accompanied by a storm of wind and thunder, and to the excited minds of the Apostles bearing the appearance of the miracle (*Moschius, Heinrichs*). Heumann thinks it a vision or semblance presented to the eyes of the disciples in a state of ecstasy. Eichhorn allows that there was a crash and noise, but makes the tongues of fire an Oriental figure for enthusiasm and eloquence : they were electric sparks. The gift of tongues was fluency in prayer and preaching; or it was the utterance of unintelligible sounds (*Eichhorn*); or it was the foreign Jews speaking in languages they knew already (*Paulus*); or it was the occasional introduction of foreign words or phrases in their discourse; or it was interpreting the prophecies so sensibly that the inhabitants of Jerusalem were struck with wonder, who used to call the Galileans fools (*Herder*); or it was bursting away from the trammels of the old Hebrew, which Heinrichs says was spoken at Jerusalem at the feasts, and expressing themselves each in his vernacular tongue (*Kleinius*).

(*b*)

The lame man said to be healed by Peter and John (Acts iii.), was an old impostor, feigning congenital lameness, and stripped of his mask by the Apostles (*Thies*). The angel who liberated the Apostles (Acts v.) was lightning, or an earthquake, the angels' address being only the current of their own thoughts; or, more likely still, it was the jailer who let them out, but kept the secret to himself, and they ascribed it to a celestial messenger (*Eichhorn, Thies, Eckermann, Heinrichs*). To the same causes is attributed Peter's release in Acts xii. Stephen's seeing " the glory of God " at the time of his martyrdom, was a flash of lightning in the heavens (*Hengel*); and his vision of Christ was only the persuasion of ecstatic emotion. The angel that directed Philip to journey toward Gaza (Acts viii.) was a strong impulse, or instinct—or a dream of the night (*Eichhorn, Eckermann, Heinrichs*). Paul's vision of Christ on the road to Damascus was either a dream or a crash of thunder, accompanied by lightning; most likely the former, for Paul was a man given to visions and ecstasies. The raising of dead Dorcas to life was recalling her from a swoon. That Cornelius saw an angel, is denied; it was a dream of the gladness of his mind when he had determined to send for Peter, of whose fame he had heard. Paul's vision of the angel before his shipwreck was of the same kind, impressions of his waking hours renewed in sleep.

(*c*)

Christ uttered no prophecies; He renounced the power : many prophecies in the Bible are of doubtful character, obscure, and imperfect, and some made after the event (*Ammon*). They are a mere poetical dress given to affairs acted in the prophet's lifetime (*Eichhorn*). Jesus spoke with contempt of the Hebrew prophets (*Wegscheider*). Some were of doubtful character (*Ammon*); and some spoke in a state of delirium. The whole theory of prophecy savours of fatalism (*Wegscheider*). There are no clear prophecies in either Testament. Not one in the Old Testament clearly refers to Christ (*Eckermann, Bahrdt, Bauer, Ammon*). Christ did not foretell His own resurrection (*Paulus*). The whole body of prophets were impostors (*Scherer*). No evidence can prove inspiration—can prove a miracle (*Wegscheider*). Miracles are only startling natural events, designed to arrest the wonder of a barbarous age, but explicable without departure from the ordinary course of things (*Paulus, Anton, Eck, Bretschneider, Bauer, Kaiser*). The most extraordinary in the Bible are only myths or allegories—the creation, Paradise, the serpent, the fall, the flood, Babel, etc., etc. (*Bertholdt, Bauer and Dathe's Glasse, Meyer, Gabler, Wegscheider*, etc., etc.). Need we add after this, that Christ is not divine, that man is not depraved, that the Atonement is a theological figment, that the Bible is but a book of fables with a moral purpose, that reason is everything with us, and God is nothing? There are worse things than those we have given, but we have purposely withheld them."

(*d*) *Selected by Robt. Young, Edinburgh, 1878.*

CROOK IN THE LOT, THE

" *Consider the work of God : for who can make that straight which He hath made crooked ?* " (Eccles. vii. 13).

Introduction :
1. The remedy; 2. Its suitableness.

The text teaches three doctrines :
1. The " Crook " is of God's making.
2. We cannot *mend* it.
3. Its proper consideration brings about the right deportment under it.

(*e*)

Doct. I. The "Crook" is of God's making

1. The "Crook" itself: (Preliminaries):

(i.) *Events, cross events, none exempt*, crook came by *sin. It speaks:*

(ii.) (*a*) Adversity ; (*b*) continuance.

(iii.) *It is threefold:*

(*a*) A *cross* dispensation ; (*b*) a *train* of the same ; (*c*) *lasting effects.*

(iv.) *Its qualities :.*

(*a*) *Disagreeable* ; (*b*) *unsightly* ; (*c*) *unfitness* for motion ; (*d*) *fretful.*

(v.) *Where it falls:*

(*a*) In *any* part ; (*b*) in *many* parts ; (*c*) in the *tender* part ; more particularly (*d*) in the *natural* part ; (*e*) in the *honorary* part ; (*f*) in one's *vocation ;* (*g*) in *relations.*

2. God's making: (How and why?)

(i.) Three considerations :.

(*a*) "Can there be evil and the Lord hath not done it?"

(*b*) Evident from Scripture doctrine of Providence.

(*c*) An eternal decree (life-plan).

(ii.) How? Distinguish between

(*a*) Pure and sinless crooks ; (*b*) impure and sinful crooks.

The latter (*a*) *permitted* ; (*b*) *bounded* ; (*c*) overruled.

(iii.) Why? Discover the *seven-fold design:*

(*a*) Trial of one's *state* ; (*b*) duty ; (*c*) *conviction of sin* ; (*d*) correction for sin ; (*e*) prevention of sin ; (*f*) corruption ; (*g*) for the exercise of *grace.*

3. The Doctrine has a threefold use:

1. *Reproof* ; **2.** consolation ; **3.** *exhortation.*

(i.) Persons needing *reproof :.*

(*a*) The *carnal* and *earthly* ; (*b*) the *unsubmissive* ; (*c*) the *careless* and unfruitful.

(ii.) *Consolation*=for the children of God.

(iii.) *Exhortation*=It is God's doing. Be reconciled to it.

4. Objections answered:

1. My crook is of *man:* answered.

2. Might be quickly *evened:* answered.

(i.) *Consider* our duty to God ; (ii.) no one can be without ; (iii.) unsubmission ; (iv.) great loss of self-will.

(*a*)

Crook in the Lot, The

Doct. II., What God mars we cannot mend ; and what God makes crooked we cannot even.

1. Prove the doctrine that God *mars*, and

2. Show man's vain attempts to *mend it.*

3. How the doctrine is to be understood.

4. Reasons.

1. God mars a lot:

(i.) God is sovereign ; (ii.) He sees our *"bias"* ; (iii.) He *"bends"* the contrary way ; (iv.) He leaves it so.

2. Man's vain attempt to mend it:

The efforts show (i.) uneasiness ; (ii.) desire for relief ; (iii.) use of means.

3. Sense in which the doctrine is to be understood :.

Negatively :—" Is anything too hard for the Lord?"

Positively :—*We* shall never be able to mend it. (i.) Not *by force* ; (ii.) efforts *successless* without God ; (iii.) not in *our time.*

4. Reasons:

(i.) We are *dependent* upon God.

(ii.) His *will is irresistible.*

Inferences :—(*a*) We must yield ; (*b*) our *work* will not last ; (*c*) apply to God.

Exhortation :—Apply to God.

Motives :—(*a*) Our efforts *vain* and fruitless ; (*b*) make it *worse* ; (*c*) all can be remedied by God ; (*d*) He loves to do it ; (*e*) such help=a *double mercy ;* (*f*) *cases in point*—richest mercies follow ; (*g*) God's way the *shortest* and *surest.*

Objections :—(i.) The case seems "*hopeless*" (answered) ; (ii.) I have applied to God about it, etc., answered. Delays=*not denials.*

Some *directions* for right applications about it :— (i.) *Pray* for relief ; (ii.) *Humble* yourself ; (iii.) *Wait.*

1. Exhortation :—As some things, (viz.) indwelling sin, cannot wholly be removed here,

(i.) Take *God in Christ* instead of that thing desired ; (ii.) Look for the *running streams ;* (iii.) *spiritual fruits ;* (iv.) grace ; (v.) eternal rest— glory.

2. Exhortation :—(i.) Bear it *patiently ;* (ii.) with *Christian fortitude ;* (iii.) profitably (get honey out of it).

Motives :—Consider

(i.) No relief while God says, "No." "He is of *one* mind, who can turn Him." (ii.) Awkward carriage under it *galls* us ; (iii.) *It is the* special *trial for thee*, to measure thyself by (1 Pet. i. 6, 7).

Question :—(i.) *Submission*, not without a *struggle ;* (ii.) *Cross*-bearing ; (iii.) *conformity* to Christ ; (iv.) prove ourselves by it.

Motives :—(i.) It cannot last *long ;* (ii.) labour to bear it ; (iii.) right bearing it not lost labour ; (iv.) otherwise it is (v.) private " crooks " presage " public crooks."

(*b*)

Crook in the Lot, The

Doct. III., To consider the crook as God's work, enables us rightly to bear it.

1. What is it, " To consider the crook as God's work ? "

(i.) Its *spring*—where it comes from.

(ii.) A perceiving the *hand* of God in it.

(iii.) So representing it to *ourselves* as (*a*) God's *decree*, (*b*) His *providence.*

(iv.) To *think* of it as such : (*a*) *habitually ;* (*b*) *occasionally.*

(v.) To have the " *end* " in view.

2. How understand it as enabling us to bear it?

(i.) *Negatively* (not of itself).

(ii.) *Positively* (by faith). Consider—(*a*) Fallen man cannot start as Adam ; (*b*) the necessity of faith ; (*c*) think of its difficulty, *only saints* enabled to bear it.

3. The Doctrine confirmed:

(i.) It diverts the gaze *to God.*

(ii.) Its moral strength.

(iii.) Its Divine appointment.

(iv.) The Spirit helps.

Consider—(*a*) It is God's work *in Christ* ; (*b*) think of the Divine *relations* to you ; (*c*) *what* a work it is ; (*d*) look for the help of the Spirit.

(*c*)

CROOK IN THE LOT, THE

" Better is it to be of a humble spirit with the lowly, than to divide the spoil with the proud " (Prov. xvi. 19).

Introduction :—In which
(i.) A comparison between the (*a*) *lowly* and (*b*) the *proud*.
(ii.) Which is to be preferred? (*a*) to be of a *lowly* spirit—or (*b*) one who divides the spoil? *i.e.*, present *humiliation* or *exaltation*.
Doctrine :
There are people now corresponding to *both*—and the *former* are better than the *latter*.

1. The Lowly :
(i.) General considerations :—(*a*) There are such ; (*b*) otherwise Christ would have no followers ; (*c*) they are rare ; (*d*) they = the godly in numbers ; (*e*) All the godly belong, but some in *particular ;* (*f*) God loves humility.
(ii.) *Character of these.* (*a*) Afflicted ; (*b* lowly ; (*c*) spirit brought down to their lot.

2. The Proud :
Their character.
(i.) They, too, have crosses.
(ii.) Pride.
(iii.) They get their *will*.

3. The Doctrine confirmed :
(i.) (*a*) Humility better than pride (one of God, the other of devil) ; (*b*) humility qualifies for communion with God (pride makes God our enemy) ; (*c*) humility is pleasing to God.
(ii.) The lowly have (*a*) *quiet* of mind, opposed to *disquiet*.
(iii.) The lowly have *gained* considerably :— (*a*) a *better* man ; (*b*) masters of self ; (*c*) shall appear when judged.
Use of the doctrine :—(i.) Not best to get our will ; (ii.) The afflicted one is a gainer ; (iii.) By yielding to Providence.
Motive :—(i.) Needful ; (ii.) effect good on a crossed lot ; (iii.) danger.
In *due* time exaltation will come.
(*a*)   *Boston's " Crook in the Lot "*

CROSS

The cross now hangs as an ornament from the neck of beauty. It blazes on the flags of navies and the standards of armies. Millions bow before it in adoration, as if it were a shrine of the Divinity.
(*b*)   *Channing*

CROSS, THE ATTRACTION OF (John xii. 32)

This attraction of the Cross is one of the richest emes for effective evangelical sermons.
(*c*)   *P. Schaff*

CROSS, THE ATTRACTION OF (John xii. 32)

1. Mark the *kind* of power. Not destructive, repulsive, or punitive, it is *attractive*. It *draws*.
As the sun draws the vapours of the sea, and then paints a rainbow on them ; so Christ draws men, and then glorifies them. His attraction is like that of the sun. It is magnetic too, like that of the magnet to the pole. . . . It is not simply the Christ that is the magnet ; it is the *crucified*

Christ. It is crucifixion that has given Him His attractive power ; just as it is death that has given Him His life-giving power. It is not Christ without the cross ; nor the cross without Christ ; it is both of them together.

2. The *greatness* of the Power
It is sufficient to draw all men. It has *not* drawn all men. It is almighty influence, irresistible power. A power that could draw the myriads of stars and planets, and cluster them around itself, must be great ; but a power that can draw millions of human hearts must be far greater.
But wherein consists its *magnetic power?*
(i.) In the *love* which it embodies. Herein is love ; the love that passeth knowledge ! The love of God in Christ. Christ crucified, dead, buried, risen, is the great revelation of the grace of God. What so magnetic as love ?
(ii.) In the *righteousness* which it exhibits.
This is a "great sight." It is the cross of righteousness ; the resurrection of righteousness. It is for the unrighteous, and yet it is righteous. It is righteousness combining with love and taking the sinner's side against law and judgment and the eternal penalty. How attractive is righteousness like this !
(iii.) In the *truth* which it proclaims.
All God's revealed truth is connected with the cross. Divine wisdom is concentrated there. In Jesus, the crucified, there is the wisdom of God, and He is made unto us wisdom. In the cross we have the refutation of man's errors and Satan's lies ; the great embodiment of heavenly and everlasting truth. Here all truth and all wisdom are centred ! How can it but be magnetic ?
(iv.) In the *reconciliation* which it publishes.
It proposes peace to the sinner ; for it has made peace. Jesus has made peace by the blood of the cross. Here is the meeting-place between man and God. Here we stand and say, "Be reconciled."
(v.) In the *healing* which it brings.
There is healing in its shadow. He who touches is healed—healed in every part. The healing begins now in the soul, and is completed in the resurrection of the body. Jesus, the dead and risen One, is our healer. This healing includes deliverance from *sin*. The Cross purifies. The fulness of the Crucified One is the fountain of our holiness.
Thus the Cross, the Gospel, the Crucified One, all make up the "power of God" : the power which *attracts, quickens, saves, purifies !* It draws—draws irresistibly ; for in it is the strength of Omnipotence.
(*d*)   *Horatius Bonar*

CROSS OF CHRIST

As I shall be uplifted on a cross
In darkness of eclipse and anguish dread,
So shall I lift up in my piercèd hands,
Not into dark, but light—not unto death,
But life—beyond the reach of guilt and grief,
The whole creation.
(*e*)   *E. B. Browning*

CROSS OF CHRIST

To save, then, means something more than to call with a voice sweeter than that of Orpheus, or
(*f*)

even to follow with patient, unwearied steps, and bring them home on the tender heart. It meant—ah ! it meant—to die.

" *The good Shepherd layeth down His life for the sheep.*"

So, by nothing easier, He sought us ; so, by nothing less, He saved us. By a love as real as the passions He came to rescue us from, and divinely stronger.

By an anguish as terrible as the miseries to which those passions lead, I began to understand why the Church has adopted the cross as her central symbol, more central than even that of the Good Shepherd.

(a)   *Schönberg Cotta Series*

Cross and Shame of Christ (Phil. iii. 19)

If a man values and seeks sensual good, he is then an enemy of the *cross* of Christ. If he has earthly honour in view, and desires to distinguish himself before the world, he is then an enemy to the *shame* of Christ, which accompanied His sufferings.

(b)   *Schleiermacher*

Cross and Crown

Whatever be your cross, don't keep with downcast head, looking at it ; but raise your eyes to the cross that hangs yonder in heaven beyond the grave. . . . Thanks be to God who bestows the crown of life on those that love Him, and can say, " Though I have not honoured Thee, nor served Thee, nor followed Thee, nor fought for Thee, nor wrought for Thee, nor suffered, nor sacrificed for Thee, as I should have done, yet Lord, Thou that knowest all things, knowest that I love Thee."

(c)   *Guthrie*

Cross, The Offence of the

Among the pictures at an Exhibition in Berlin there was to be seen a beautiful painting of the Crucifixion. Next to it had been hung a painting of Venus. But when the Minister of Worship perceived this, he gave orders that the two pictures should be separated. Whereupon the freethinking class in that country raised an outcry, and complained loudly of the narrow-mindedness of the minister.

In consequence of this order, the picture of Venus became famous and soon found a wealthy purchaser, who placed it in a prominent position in his own house. There it hung ; and many a merry company gathered before the picture; and often did the relation of its earlier story give rise to scornful witticisms.

But at length there came a commercial crisis, and in the crash many a rich man, and amongst them the owner of this picture, became poor. One day he was missed : they searched for him throughout his princely house, and at last they came to the room where this celebrated picture was hung. And this is what they saw : The famous picture was cut, pierced, and mangled everywhere—scarcely an inch of the canvas had escaped mutilation. And beneath it was stretched the bleeding corpse of the rich man, who had formerly bought it at a high price to express his scorn for religion, but who now in a frenzy of

madness had mangled the picture before he took away his own life. This story is said to be authentic.

(d)   *Christian Age*

CRUCIFIED, CHRIST

"*I determined to know nothing among you, save Jesus Christ and Him crucified* " (1 Cor. i.).

Not the crucifixion of Christ; but Christ, and that Christ crucified. (St. Paul) preached Christ crucified, though the Greeks might mock and the Jews reject Him with scorn—Christ *as* Christianity, Christ His own evidence. We know the result : the Church of Corinth, the largest and noblest harvest ever given to ministerial toil.

(e)   *F. W. Robertson*

. . . That which is to be a temple to God must never have the marble polluted with the name of the architect or builder.

(f)   *Ibid*

We think the only way to make heathen people receive the Gospel, is to preach sermons, and to be perpetually arguing and speechifying. We are profoundly convinced that if you can only talk long enough you must win a man over to your way of thinking. In the days of Fursey and Felix—*i.e.*, more than twelve hundred years ago—the leaders of thought and opinion did not believe in *talking ;* they did believe in *being* and living ! Their view of the wants of the age was—" Ours at any rate,

is not the time
For stringing words with satisfaction ;
What's wanted now's the silent rhyme
'Twixt upright will and downright action."

So Felix said to Fursey's company :

" Go to Bedericsworth, and *show* people what the Gospel is. *Be* Christians. Win over the heathen to the Gospel by the lives you lead and the example you show."

This was Bedericsworth in those days; and here those men settled—men who were doers and livers, not talkers and preachers ; and they ran up half a dozen beggarly hovels, and they somehow built something like a church, rudely constructed of the trees that were growing hereabouts ; and they set to work to teach the heathen how to gain a livelihood by tilling the soil and using the streams to turn the mill which ground the corn ; and they cleared the scrub and stubbed up the old roots ; and whereas everybody else was hunting, and fishing, and quarrelling, and fighting, they were men of peace, and, strangest of all, men of prayer. " What's the meaning of it all ? " said the heathen people. " Let's try and find out the secret of; he strange men; hearken, you Fullan and Ultan, or whatever your odd names are. How do you manage it all ? How is it you don't seem to be afraid of us, and don't want to hurt us or cheat us ? Nay, are not such bad fellows neither. We can hardly resist the conviction that you are really *good* fellows, and don't want to make anything out of us—positively nothing. What's your secret—speak ? "

That little band had only one secret, it was an open secret—JESUS CHRIST, AND HIM CRUCIFIED.

(g)   *Jessopp*

CRUCIFIED, THE FLESH (Gal. v. 24)

This well expresses how sin must, little by little, be disabled and slain, for the crucified man did not die at once ; he was first made fast with nails to the cross and then kept there, till, through the loss of blood and through hunger and thirst, he became weaker and weaker and finally died.

(a)   *Starke*

CRUCIFIXION

" *And they crucified Him* " (Mark xv.)

Note :

1. The Death of Crucifixion.

(i.) = Numbered with transgressors, not an honourable death — a degrading execution of criminals.

= *Humility* of our Lord, who " became obedient unto such a death."

Hence " Let this mind be in you."

(ii.) = First in the *will* (Gethsemane). "Not as I will, but as Thou wilt."

So for us to be crucified with Christ = " *Thy will be done.*"

= " Being made conformable to His death."

2. The Place of Crucifixion.

" The place of a skull " = common execution ground, for felons and outlaws.

= Desolation and horror, in keeping with the despairing cry,

" *My God, my God, why,*" etc.

The Lesson = " Let us go forth with Him without the camp, bearing His reproach."

3. The Blindness of Hate (as of love).

" They crucified Him," = the full extent of their power.

They had killed the body, now there was no more that they could do.

= The God of this world has no power beyond.

But what followed ?

(i.) That was the salvation-hour for the whole world.

That act of self-surrender, even unto death = " Delivered for our offences." = The expiation for the sin of the world.

(ii.) Jesus went to the realm of the dead and revolutionized it. Death hitherto had reigned, an unbroken power — supreme. The prison-house of the dead was fast locked. None returned. Now One comes there who has " the keys of Hades and of Death." He opens the door and sets the captives free ; He took them with Him to heaven — " He led captivity captive."

(iii.) He hath changed the aspect of death — rolled away its sting.

" Delivered them who through fear of death . . . subject to bondage."

" He that liveth and believeth on Me shall *never die.*" . . . " Death hath no dominion over him."

N.B.—The power of faith :

= (i.) Crucifixion with Christ. . . . Conformed to His death.

= (ii.) Raises the Christian above the sphere of death proper = " never die."

= (iii.) If we suffer we shall also reign with Him.

Note the sequence : The victory over death and the grave is through *crucifixion.*

(b)

CRUCIFIXION, THE.

I asked the Heavens—" What foe to God hath done
This unexampled deed ? " The Heavens exclaim,
" 'Twas man ; and we in *horror* snatched the sun
From such a spectacle of guilt and shame."

I asked the *Sea ;* the sea in fury boiled,
And answered with his voice of storms, " 'Twas Man ;
My waves in panic at his crime recoiled,
Disclosed the abyss, and from the centre ran."

I asked the *Earth ;* the earth replied aghast,
" 'Twas man ; and such strange pangs my bosom rent,
That still I groan and shudder at the past."

To Man, *gay, smiling, thoughtless Man,* I went,
And asked *him* next :—HE turned a scornful eye,
Shook his proud head, and deigned me *no reply.*

(c)   *Montgomery*

CRUCIFIXION OF CHRIST, OUR PART IN

A traveller ascends a hill : having reached the summit and seen the view, he descends. As he descends he sees at the foot of the hill a little cottage from which cries of lamentation proceed. He enters. He sees the mangled form of a strong man surrounded by a weeping wife and children. He sympathizes, he pities. But when, on inquiry, he learns that a stone rolling down the hill put an end to his life, how different are his feelings — not sympathy, but shame ; not pity, but anguish : for he remembers that he wilfully (for there was a notice up warning him) hurled a boulder down the hill-side for his own gratification.

(d)   *Gordon Calthrop*

That alters the case : Our place at the crucifixion is not as spectators at a distance, but in the crowd.

> " 'Twere you my sins, my cruel sins,
>   His chief tormentors were ;
> Each of my sins became a nail
>   And unbelief the spear."

(e)

CRUCIFIXION : CHRIST CARRYING HIS CROSS

Now Thine insulting enemies are so much more imperiously cruel, as they are more sure of their success. Their merciless tormentings have made Thee half-dead already ; yet now, as if they had done nothing, they begin afresh ; and will force Thy weakened and fainting nature to new tasks of pain. The transverse of Thy cross, at least, is upon Thy shoulder : when Thou canst scarce go, Thou must carry. One kicks Thee with his foot, another strikes Thee with his staff, another drags Thee hastily by Thy cord, and more than one spurs on Thine unpitied weariness with angry commands of haste.

(f)   *Bishop Hall*

CRUCIFIXION: CHRIST CARRYING HIS CROSS

It was not so heavy to them, or to Simon, as it was to Thee : they felt nothing but the wood; Thou feltest it clogged with the load of the sins of the whole world. No marvel, if Thou faintedst under that sad burden : Thou, that bearest up the whole earth by Thy word, didst sweat, and pant, and groan, under this insupportable carriage.

(a)　　　　　　　　　　　　　*Bishop Hall*

CRUCIFIXION: CHRIST CARRYING HIS CROSS

It is not out of any compassion of Thy misery, or care of Thine ease, that Simon of Cyrene is forced to be the bearer of Thy cross ; it was out of their own eagerness of Thy despatch; Thy feeble paces were too slow for their purpose ; their thirst after Thy blood made them impatient of delay. If Thou have wearily struggled with the burden of Thy shame all along the streets of Jerusalem, when Thou comest once past the gates, a helper shall be deputed to Thee : the expedition of Thy death was more sweet to them than the pain of a lingering passage. What Thou saidst to Judas, they say to the executioner, *What thou doest, do quickly.* While Thou yet livest, they cannot be quiet, they cannot be safe : to hasten Thy end, they lighten Thy carriage.

(b)　　　　　　　　　　　　　　　*Ibid*

CRUCIFIXION: SIMON OF CYRENE

Hadst thou done this out of choice, which thou didst out of constraint, how I should have envied thee, O Simon of Cyrene ; as too happy in the honour to be the first man that bore that Cross of thy Saviour, wherein millions of blessed martyrs have, since that time, been ambitious to succeed thee ! Thus to bear Thy Cross for Thee, O Saviour, was more than to bear a crown from Thee. Could I be worthy to be thus graced by Thee, I should pity all other glories.

(c)　　　　　　　　　　　　　　　*Ibid*

CRUCIFIXION. HOSANNA

While Thou thus passest, O dear Jesu, the streets and ways resound not all with one note. If the malicious Jews and cruel soldiers insulted upon Thee, and either haled or railed Thee on with a bitter violence, Thy faithful followers were no less loud in their moans and ejaculations ; neither would they endure that the noise of their cries and lamentations should be drowned with the clamour of those reproaches : but especially Thy blessed mother, and those other zealous associates of her own sex, were most passionate in their wailings. And why should I think that all that devout multitude, which so lately cried Hosanna in the streets, did not also bear their part in these public condolings?

(d)　　　　　　　　　　　　　　　*Ibid*

CRUCIFIXION: THE MALEFACTORS

Jerusalem could not want malefactors, though Barabbas were dismissed. That all this execution might seem to be done out of the zeal of justice, two capital offenders, adjudged to their gibbet, shall accompany Thee, O Saviour, both to Thy death and in it. They are led manacled after Thee, as less criminal : no stripes had disabled them from bearing their own crosses. Long ago was this unmeet society foretold by Thine Evangelical Seer ; " He was taken from prison and from judgment : He was cut out of the land of the living : He made His grave with the wicked." O blessed Jesu, it had been disparagement enough to Thee, to be sorted with the best of men, since there is much sin in the perfectest, and there could be no sin in Thee ! but to be matched with the scum of mankind, whom vengeance would not let to live, is such an indignity as confounds my thoughts. Surely, there is no angel in heaven but would have been proud to attend Thee ; and what could the earth afford, worthy of Thy train? yet malice hath suited Thee with company next to hell ; that their viciousness might reflect upon Thee, and their sin might stain Thine innocence.

(e)　　　　　　　　　　　　　　　*Ibid*

CRUCIFIXION: THE MALEFACTOR

Ye are deceived, O ye fond judges ! this is the way to grace your dying Malefactor ; this is not the way to disgrace Him, whose guiltlessness and perfection triumphed over your injustice. His presence was able to make your thieves happy ; their presence could no more blemish Him than your own.

(f)　　　　　　　　　　　　　　　*Ibid*

CRUCIFIXION: THE BITTER CUP

There, while Thou art addressing Thyself for Thy last act, Thou art presented with that bitter and farewell potion, wherewith dying malefactors were wont to have their senses stupified, that they might not feel the torments of their execution. It was but the common mercy of men, to alleviate the death of offenders; since the intent of their last doom is not so much pain as dissolution. That draught, O Saviour, was not more welcome to the guilty than hateful unto Thee. In the vigour of all Thine inward and outward senses, Thou wouldst encounter the most violent assaults of death ; and scornedst to abate the least touch of Thy quickest apprehension.

Thou well knewest, that the work Thou wentest about would require the use of all Thy powers. It was not Thine ease that Thou soughtest, but our redemption ; neither meantest Thou to yield to Thy last enemy, but to resist and overcome him: which, that Thou mightest do the more gloriously, Thou challengedst him to do his worst ; and in the meantime wouldst not disfurnish Thyself of any of Thy powerful faculties. This greatest combat that ever was, shall be fought on even hand : neither wouldst Thou steal that victory which Thou now achievedst over death and hell.

(g)　　　　　　　　　　　　　　　*Ibid*

CRUCIFIXION: THE CUP OF MY HEAVENLY FATHER

Thou didst but touch at this cup; it is a far bitterer than this, that Thou art now drinking up to the dregs : Thou refusedst that which was offered Thee by men; but that which was mixed by Thine Eternal Father, though mere gall and wormwood, Thou didst drink up to the last drop. And therein, O blessed Jesu, lies all our health and salvation. I know not whether I do more suffer in Thy pain, or joy in the issue of Thy suffering.

(h)　　　　　　　　　　　　　　　*Ibid*

CRUCIFIXION: THEY STRIPPED HIM

A cruel expoliation begins that violence. Again do these grim and merciless soldiers lay their rude hands upon Thee, and strip Thee naked; again are those bleeding wales laid open to all eyes; again must Thy Sacred Body undergo the shame of an abhorred nakedness. Lo, Thou that clothest man with raiment, beasts with hides, fishes with scales and shells, earth with flowers, heaven with stars, art despoiled of clothing, and standest exposed to the scorn of all beholders. As the first Adam entered into his paradise, so dost Thou, the second Adam, into Thine—naked; and as the first Adam was clothed with innocence when he had no clothes, so wert Thou, the second, too: and more than so; Thy nakedness, O Saviour, clothes our souls, not with innocence only, but with beauty. Hadst not Thou been naked, we had been clothed with confusion. O happy nakedness, whereby we are covered from shame! O happy shame, whereby we are invested with glory! All the beholders stand wrapped with warm garments; Thou only art stripped to tread the wine-press alone. How did Thy blessed mother now wish her veil upon Thy shoulders! and that disciple, who lately ran from Thee naked, wished in vain that his loving pity might do that for Thee, which fear forced him to do for himself.

(a)   *Bishop Hall*

CRUCIFIXION: THIEF ON CROSS

The offender came to die; nothing was in his thoughts but his guilt and torment: *while he was yet in his blood,* Thou *saidst, This soul shall live.* Ere yet the intoxicating potion could have time to work upon his brain, Thy Spirit infuses faith into his heart. He, that before had nothing in his eye but present death and torture, is now lifted up above his cross in a blessed ambition; "*Lord, remember me, when Thou comest into Thy kingdom.*" Is this the voice of a thief, or of a disciple? Give me leave, O Saviour, to borrow Thine own words: "*Verily, I have not found so great faith, no, not in all Israel.*" He saw Thee hanging miserably by him, and yet styles Thee, *Lord;* he saw Thee dying, yet talks of Thy *kingdom;* he felt himself dying, yet talks of a future *Remembrance.* O faith stronger than death, that can look beyond the cross at a crown; beyond dissolution at a remembrance of life and glory! Which of Thine eleven were heard to speak so gracious a word to Thee, in these Thy last pangs? After Thy resurrection and knowledge of Thine impassable condition, it was not strange for them to talk of Thy kingdom; but, in the midst of Thy shameful death, for a dying malefactor to speak of Thy reigning, and to implore Thy remembrance of himself in Thy kingdom, it is such an improvement of faith as ravisheth my soul with admiration. O blessed thief, that hast thus happily stolen Heaven! How worthy hath thy Saviour made thee to be a partner of His sufferings, a pattern of undauntable belief, a spectacle of unspeakable mercy! "*This day shalt thou be with Me in Paradise.*" Before, I wondered at thy faith; now I envy at thy felicity. Thou cravedst a remembrance; thy Saviour speaks of a present possession, "*this day*": thou suedst for remembrance as a favour to the absent; thy Saviour speaks of thy presence with Him: thou spakest of a kingdom; thy Saviour, of Paradise. As no disciple could be more faithful, so no saint

could be happier. O Saviour, what a precedent is this of Thy free and powerful Grace! Where Thou wilt give, what unworthiness can bar us from mercy? When Thou wilt give, what time can prejudice our vocation? Who can despair of Thy goodness, when he that in the morning was posting towards Hell, is in the evening with Thee in Paradise? Lord, he could not have spoken this to Thee, but by Thee, and from Thee. What possibility was there for a thief to think of Thy kingdom without Thy Spirit? That good Spirit of Thine breathed upon this man, breathed not upon his fellow. Their trade was alike, their sin was alike, their state alike, their cross alike; only Thy mercy makes them unlike: one is taken; the other is refused. Blessed be Thy mercy, in taking one; blessed be Thy justice, in leaving the other. Who can despair of that mercy? Who cannot but tremble at that justice?

(b)   *Ibid*

CRUCIFIXION, THE MOCKING

Is not all this enough, without your taunts and scoffs and sports at so exquisite a misery? The people, the passengers, are taught to insult, where they should pity. Every man hath a scorn ready to cast at a Dying Innocent. A generous nature is more wounded with the tongue than with the hand. O Saviour, Thine ear was more painfully pierced than Thy brows, or hands, or feet. It could not but go deep into Thy soul, to hear those bitter and girding reproaches from them Thou camest to save.

(c)   *Ibid*

CRUCIFIXION, THE MOCKING

But, alas! what were these, in comparison of those inward torments which Thy soul felt in the sense and apprehension of Thy Father's wrath for the sins of the whole world, which now lay heavy upon Thee for satisfaction? This, oh, this was it, that pressed Thy soul, as it were, to the nethermost hell. While Thine eternal Father looked lovingly upon Thee, what didst Thou, what needest Thou to care for the frowns of men or devils? But when He once turned His face from Thee, or bent His brows upon Thee, this, this was worse than death.

(d)   *Ibid*

CRUCIFIXION: FORSAKEN OF GOD

Thou, the second Adam, stoodst for mankind upon this tree of the Cross, as the first Adam stood and fell for mankind under the tree of offence. Thou barest our sins: Thy Father saw us in Thee, and would punish us in Thee; Thee for us. How could He but withhold comfort, where He intended chastisement? Herein, therefore, He seems to forsake Thee for the present, in that He would not deliver Thee from that bitter passion, which Thou wouldst undergo for us. O Saviour, hadst Thou not been thus forsaken, we had perished! Thy dereliction is our safety; and however our narrow souls are not capable of the conceit of Thy pain and horror, yet we know there can be no danger in the forsaking, while Thou canst say, "*My God.*" He is so Thy God, as He cannot be ours: all our right is by adoption; Thine, by nature: Thou art one with Him in

(e)

eternal essence; we come in by grace and merciful election: yet, while Thou shalt enable me to say, " *My God,*" I shall hope never to sink under Thy desertions.

(*a*)   *Bishop Hall*

" Crucifixion, Forgive Them "

" *Father, forgive them, for they know not what they do.*" They blaspheme Thee; Thou prayest for them: they scorn; Thou pitiest: they sin against Thee; Thou prayest for their forgiveness: they profess their malice. Thou pleadest their ignorance. Oh, compassion without example, without measure, fit for the Son of God, the Saviour of men! Wicked and foolish Jews! ye would be miserable; He will not let you: ye would fain pull upon yourselves the guilt of His blood; He deprecates it: ye kill; He sues for you remission and life. His tongue cries louder than His blood, " *Father, forgive them.*" O Saviour, Thou couldst not but be heard. Those who out of ignorance and simplicity thus persecuted Thee, find the happy issue of Thine intercession. Now I see whence it was, that three thousand souls were converted soon after, at one sermon. It was not Peter's speech, it was Thy prayer, that was thus effectual. Now they have grace to know and confess whence they have both forgiveness and salvation; and can recompense their blasphemies with thanksgiving. What sin is there, Lord, whereof I can despair of the remission, or what offence can I be unwilling to remit, when Thou prayest for the forgiveness of Thy murderers and blasphemers?

(*b*)   *Ibid*

" Crucifixion, I Thirst "

Thou, that not long since proclaimedst in the temple, " *If any man thirst, let him come to Me and drink: he that believeth in Me, out of his belly shall flow rivers of living waters,*" now Thyself thirstest. Thou, in whom we believe, complainest to want some drops. Thou hadst the command of all the waters both above the firmament and below it, yet Thou wouldst thirst. Even so, Lord, Thou, that wouldst die for us, wouldst thirst for us. Oh, give me to thirst after those waters which Thou promisest; whatever become of those waters which Thou wouldst want. The time was, when, craving the water of the Samaritan, Thou gavest better than that Thou askedst. Oh, give me to thirst after that more precious water; and so do Thou give me of that water of life, that I may never thirst again.

(*c*)   *Ibid*

Crucifixion: The Mediator

Lo, Thou that art the Mediator betwixt God and man, the Reconciler of heaven and earth, art lift up betwixt earth and heaven, that Thou mightest accord both. Thou, that art the great Captain of our Salvation, the Conqueror of all the adverse powers of death and hell, art exalted upon this triumphal chariot of the Cross, that Thou mightest trample upon death, and drag all those infernal principalities manacled after Thee. Those arms, which Thine enemies meant violently to extend, are stretched forth for the embracing of all mankind, that shall come in for the benefit of Thy all-sufficient redemption.

(*d*)   *Ibid*

Crucifixion: The Word cannot be Broken

Foolish executioners! ye look up at that Crucified Body as if it were altogether in your power and mercy; nothing appears to you but impotence and death: little do you know what an irresistible guard there is upon that Sacred Corpse, such, as if all the powers of darkness shall band against, they shall find themselves confounded. In spite of all the gates of hell, that word shall stand. " *Not a bone of Him shall be broken.*"

(*e*)   *Ibid*

Crucifixion: The Son of God

" *Now, when the centurion and they that were with him that watched Jesus, saw the earthquake, and the things that were done, they feared greatly, and glorified God, and said, Truly, this was the Son of God.*" What a marvellous concurrence is here, of strong and irrefragable convictions! Meekness in suffering, prayer for His murderers, a faithful resignation of His soul into the hands of His Heavenly Father, the sun eclipsed, the heavens darkened, the earth trembling, the graves open, the rocks rent, the veil of the Temple torn: who could say less than this, " *Truly, this was the Son of God*"? He suffers patiently; this is through the power of grace; many good men have done so, through His enabling. The frame of nature suffers with Him; this is proper to the God of Nature, the Son of God.

(*f*)   *Ibid*

CULTURE

Culture makes whole lands, for instance Germany, Gaul, and others, physically warmer, but spiritually colder.

(*g*)   *J. P. F. Richter*

CUMBERERS OF THE GROUND

President van Buren is reported to have remarked, when he heard that his son, a lawyer, had married a lady of large wealth: " Well, he is ruined! She is very rich. Now he'll give up his profession, for which he has great ability, and become merely a rich man—the least useful of human things."

(*h*)   *Cuyler*

D

DANGERS, SPIRITUAL

Every believer knows and feels that the time of closest communion is also the time of greatest danger. It was when the Saviour had been baptized, and the Holy Ghost, like a dove, had descended upon Him, and a voice saying—" This is My beloved Son, in whom I am well pleased," it was then that He was driven into the wilderness to be tempted by the devil: and just so it is when the soul is receiving its highest privileges and comforts, that Satan and his ministers are nearest—the foxes, the little foxes, that spoil the vines. (1) Spiritual pride is near. When the soul is hiding in the wounds of the Saviour, and receiving great tokens of His love, then the heart begins to say, " Surely I am somebody—how far I am above the every-day run of believers ! " This is one of the little foxes that eat out the life of vital godliness. (2) There is making a Christ of your comforts—looking to them, and not to Christ—leaning upon them, and not upon your Beloved. This is another of the little foxes, the little foxes that spoil the vines. (3) There is the false notion, that now you must surely be above sinning, and above the power of temptation, now you can resist all enemies. This is the pride that goes before a fall—another of the foxes, the little foxes, that spoil the vines. " Be not highminded, but fear." Never forget, I beseech you, that fear is a sure mark of a believer.

But if cautious fear be a mark of a believer in such a season, still more is appropriating love. When Christ comes anew over mountains of provocation, and reveals Himself to the soul free and full as ever, in another way than He doth unto the world, then the soul can say, " My Beloved is mine, and I am His." I do not say that the believer can use these words at all seasons.

In times of darkness and in times of sinfulness, the reality of a believer's faith is to be measured rather by his sadness than by his confidence. But I do say that, in seasons when Christ reveals Himself afresh to the soul, shining out like the sun from behind a cloud, with the beams of sovereign, unmerited love—then no other words will satisfy the true believer but these, " My Beloved is mine, and I am His."

The soul sees Jesus to be so free a Saviour—so anxious that all should come to Him and have life —stretching out His hands all day—having no pleasure in the death of the wicked—pleading with men, " Turn ye," etc. The soul sees Jesus to be so pitying a Saviour—the very covering which his soul requires.

When first he hid himself in Jesus, he found Him suitable to all his need—the shadow of a great rock in a weary land. But now he finds out a new fitness in the Saviour, as Peter did when he girt his fisher's coat unto him, and cast himself into the sea. He finds that He is a fitting Saviour for the backsliding believer: that His blood can blot out even the stains of him who, having eaten bread with Him, has yet lifted up the heel against Him. The soul sees Jesus to be so full a Saviour —giving to the sinner not only pardons, but overflowing, immeasurable pardons—giving not only righteousness, but a righteousness that is more than mortal, for it is all Divine—giving not only His Spirit, but pouring water on him that is thirsty and floods upon the dry ground. The soul sees all this in Jesus, and cannot but choose Him and delight in Him with a new and appropriating love, saying, " My Beloved is mine." And, if any man ask, " How darest thou, sinful worm, to call that Divine Saviour thine ? " The answer is here, " For I am His." He chose me from all eternity, else I never would have chosen Him. He shed His blood for me, else I never would have shed a tear for Him. He cried after me, else I never would have breathed after Him. He sought me, else I never would have sought after Him. He hath loved me, therefore I love Him. He hath chosen me, therefore I evermore choose Him. " My Beloved is mine, and I am His."

But, if love be a mark of the true believer at such a season, so also is prayerful hope.

There have been seasons when the Saviour manifested Himself so clearly to the soul, that we have felt that " it is good to be here." But though it be good and very pleasant, like sunlight to the eyes, yet the Lord sees that it is not wisest and best always to be there.

(a)   *Robert McCheyne*

DANIEL, BOOK OF (Chap. ii. 28)

" **There is a God in Heaven that Revealeth Secrets,** *and maketh known to the king what shall be in the latter days.*"

There are things *known* (revealed), and others *unknown* (not revealed) in the sphere of the Christian Religion. Of the unknown we might know more than we do, were we to make diligent use of the word of God—*He maketh known . . . latter days.*

This is the key to Daniel's Prophecies. He wrote down for our guidance what the **Course of the World** would be as time unrolled itself, and the end approached. Of this many Christian people are ignorant, for though the *times and seasons* are not revealed, yet the *course* is.

In this chapter, note the **Persons**, the **Subject**, and the **Style**.

1. The Persons : Daniel & Nebuchadnezzar. These mutually require each other—correlatives. The Bible is full of such contrasts, and would be incomplete as a guide to our knowledge of men without them. These two men represent the *sacred* and the *profane*, each stands at the head of a class, and thus becomes its type.

2. The Subject :

The Book of Daniel is divided into two portions (chaps i. to vii. and viii. to xiii.). The first part is about the **Kingdom of the World**; the second about the **Kingdom of God**. These are described as rival powers.

3. The Style :

Part I. (The World) is written in *Chaldee*, the language of the world at that time, *i.e.* the language of the Ruling Nation.

(b)

Whilst Part II. (the Kingdom of God) is written in Hebrew, the language of the Chosen Nation.

Both these facts are deeply significant.

Again, this book contains revelations of God to men, but all the revelations in the First Part (*i.e.* relating to the World-Kingdoms) are made to the Rulers of the World, Nebuchadnezzar, Belshazzar, etc., as representatives of it.

Whilst all the revelations about the Kingdom of God are made to Daniel, the Representative of it.

In other Words

(i.) When God wishes to reveal something about the future of the world, He does it to a *worldly man*, representing it ; and the record of it is kept in the court language of the time.

(ii.) But when, on the other hand, God would reveal something about the future of His own Kingdom, He makes the revelation to one of His own people—Daniel—and the record of it is kept in the language of the Chosen Nation. Cf. " Unto them were committed the oracles of God " (Rom. iii. 2).

Thus a rivalry is established at the outset between the two Great Powers. A line of demarcation is thus drawn between the Church and the World. They touch, but they do not mingle. Both are among the "things present," and act and re-act on each other ; yet they are as really and effectually separate and distinct as they will be in that day when the tares will be gathered out from among the wheat, when the goats will be divided from the sheep—in the great and final Day of Account.

(*a*)   *Keil, adapted*

DANIEL, BOOK OF (Chap. ii.)

The Dream of Nebuchadnezzar

The king saw a great image, of human form, terrible to behold, both in splendour and in its manifest import = a portent. The image consisted of 4 or 5 portions :

(i.) The Head of Gold.
(ii.) The Breast and Arms of Silver.
(iii.) The Belly and Thighs of Brass.
(iv.) The Legs of Iron.
(v.) The Feet of part Iron and part Clay.

In the interpretation the legs and the feet = one part, both of iron, but terminating in a mixture of two substances.

A slight glance is sufficient to show that a Great Power, or a series of Powers of some kind, is indicated as terrible : having a glorious beginning (gold), but terminating ingloriously (clay). The Power gradually deteriorates until it is broken up by a want of cohesion.

1. What is this Power?

(i.) The image = the World.
(ii.) The world in its antagonism to God under different phases and rulers.
(iii.) The world in its chief kingdoms (Babylonian, Median, Persian, Grecian, Roman), Great and Glorious Babylon at its head, gradually lessening in splendour until the fashion of this world pass away.
(iv.) This great and terrible image—at all times such to the people of God—exists until God's time comes ; then her hour of peril draws near, and the image is crushed to powder. For so Nebuchadnezzar saw in his dream, "a stone," "without hands," broke all to pieces, and scattered it like chaff. Here was the collapse of this world's grandeur : "In one hour is thy judgment come "—and what has done it ?

2. What is this Stone?

It was not fire and sword, but something superhuman and silent. God's Kingdom come at last. That for which we daily pray ; and when it comes down falls the world's opposition, and " the kingdoms of this world become the kingdoms of God and of His Christ."

The Church of Christ, oppressed by the great image, sighs and cries out for deliverance, " How long, O Lord, how long ? " and things are set right in the end.

3. Note.

(i.) That the dream is *certain*, sure, not a peradventure.
(ii.) That a time of affliction (such as this exile of Daniel's) is ever productive of good to the Church of Christ. = The blood of martyrs is the seedtime of the Church.
(iii.) To whom "revelations" are made—to men of prayer and eminent purity = spiritually minded men, as Daniel and John.

(*b*)   *Ibid*

DANIEL, BOOK OF (Chap. iii.)

" *Who is that God that shall deliver you out of my hands ?* " (15.)

" . . . *There is no other God that can deliver after this sort* " (29).

1. Observe

(i.) *The Connection* of these words with ii. 47. The king had evidently forgotten Daniel's God.

(ii.) *The Standpoint*: —
Nebuchadnezzar was now at the pinnacle of his greatness, and thought no power equal to his own, and no national God so great and glorious as his own. He had conquered the Jews, and argued that his god was greater than the God of the Jews, and was inclined to taunt them, " Where is now thy God ? " This was the heathen king's standpoint at this time. Not a bad man in his way ; but his belief about the power of heathen gods induced him to act as related in this chapter.

(iii.) *The Difference between the heathen idolaters and the Jews :*
All the heathen in his dominions could observe this decree ; but not the Jews, without breaking the First Commandment. This was their reason for not being present at the dedication. The king could not understand this, and therefore construed their refusal as rebellion.

2. The Erection of the Image

(i.) *The Inauguration of the Image.*
Of human form, grotesque, as were all their images. This, however, was not *any* image, but was meant to symbolize the *god of the world* which had made Babylon great. So that falling down to do homage to this, was equivalent to placing Babylon and its heathen gods above all. Thus the act of homage demanded meant much. Or we may regard it as the zenith of Nebuchadnezzar's power, when all the great officers of state with him inaugurated the glory of the leading nation of the world. No tribe or subdued nation was exempted (= λαοί and γλῶσσαι) ; attended with magnificence and pomp, all kinds of music. A

(*c*)

great inaugural festival. The penalty of refusal to participate in it was *death*.

(ii.) *Religious Toleration :—*
The heathen were tolerant of other religions. It was long known that the Jews did not worship idols. Now they made use of this knowledge ; and envy against them was at the root of it. Not against their religion, but against their elevation in the State. The world tolerates only the world.

3. Their Accusation

(i.) "*Is this design on your part ?*" (14)
"Think of the alternative—no god can deliver you !"
(ii.) "*But if not.*"
Note their reply (17), "We are not careful, etc." = We require no time to think it over—our minds are made up. Either our God will or will not save us: anyhow we *will not* serve thy gods.

They are not audacious, nor do they expect a miracle to be worked on their behalf ; neither do they act fanatically, or superstitiously, contrary to faith and conscience. They are simply *faithful*.

4. Their Judgment and Deliverance

(i.) *Deliverance*.
The decree is carried out. The king sat watching the issue. The three walked in the furnace unhurt, accompanied by a fourth = "*a son of the gods*."

The king, astonished and terrified, called them out, saying, not "Ye servants of *the only true God*," but "THE MOST HIGH" = *the chief of the gods*.

(ii.) *Impression on the King.*
After inspection, neither injury nor smell of fire was found upon them. The impression made upon the king = "*There is no other god that can deliver after this sort*."

5. A New Decree

By which the penalty of death would be inflicted upon any one who dishonoured the God of the Jews.

The Chaldæans had watched the Jews in order to accuse them of disobedience. Now the Jews might bring before the tribunal those of the Chaldæans who blasphemed their God.

Thus the first benefit of the trial is a respite.

6. Lessons : Learn

(i.) That the kingdom of God may come under the dominion of the world, be in difficulties, peril of life, for duty to God and religion ; yet, if it continue faithful, wonderful protection will be afforded; the omnipotent arm will be revealed, and the heathen shall praise its God.

(ii.) That as these men fell down *bound* in the furnace—afterwards loosed and accompanied by the Son of God, so, though all life-time subject to bondage, will be the Christian's experience in the hour of death.

(iii.) "Ye are the light of the world ;" "ye are the salt of the earth;" "a city set upon a hill cannot be hid."

= These young Jews in Babylon, where, in the midst of darkness, they shone as lights in the world.

Thus, too, the Jews in Captivity were spreading the knowledge of the true God.

(iv.) We are shown where to look for the *best Jews* of that time.

During the Captivity some fled to Egypt, others remained in Jerusalem, whilst the remainder went into captivity.

It was amongst the captives that we find such men as these.

Hence we learn that the exile was a wholesome discipline. Sorrow made them a new people. "To him that hath shall be given." The sorrow in itself was an evil. But when it produced such men as Daniel and his three friends, we have examples of the improvement that sorrow worked in them.

They felt that they were a marked people. Eyes were upon them, God's honour was to be vindicated. Away from their fatherland, their temple, and their God, their sins had made them a mockery, a scorn. How then should they join in the music, the chorus, and the pageantry of the Chaldæans, and appear as if nothing were amiss?

(a)   *Keil, adapted*

DANIEL, BOOK OF (Chap. iv.)

1. Nebuchadnezzar's Dream and Madness

Chapter commences with a proclamation of a wonderful event in his life and experience, viz., a Dream, which only Daniel could interpret.

The Dream = a great tree, vast branches, much fruit, reached to heaven, beasts found lodging, shelter, and food beneath it.

Then a holy watcher came down from heaven, cut the tree down, the roots only to remain, bound with brass and iron till seven times pass over it.

Daniel showed that the dream related to the king himself ; his pride was to be humbled, and he was to be insane for a period.

After twelve months the dream and the interpretation came true ; and after the appointed time had elapsed the king's reason was restored, a brilliant reign followed, and honour was done to the King of heaven.

2. Points of Instruction

(i.) The preceding history shows that God takes care of His servants ; and here, how He can humble the proud rulers of the earth, who think that they rule by their own power and might. The narrative is not of a miracle, but of a judgment. (Cf. The history of Napoleon Buonaparte.)

(ii.) Nebuchadnezzar relates (4) the wonderful experience himself : says he was at *rest* and *peace*, *undisturbed* in his *prosperity* (after his victories, and during the building of Babylon), in a state of security when he was disturbed by a dream. Evidently sudden and made him think.

His heart (6) was to be changed from a man's to a beast's = he was to be *dehumanized ;* and this was to last for *seven times, i.e.,* a definite time.

(iii.) Daniel reminds him that his period of tranquillity may be lengthened by his conversion and reformation. Daniel only speaks of "fruit," (righteousness and *showing mercy*), he does not require a "creed," but good works, knowing that a corrupt tree cannot bring forth good fruit. Cf. "What doth the Lord thy God require of thee?" etc. (A Calvinist would have required Five Points of salvation ; but Daniel requires "good fruit."

(iv.) The warning was unheeded; it had made no impression, but was apparently forgotten, till about a year afterwards (29, 30, 31). At the moment of pride and egotism = "Great Babylon which I have builded," giving no honour to God ; then the judgment comes. When man's heart is inflated with pride, like a balloon, then God punctures it, and the collapse of greatness ensues. Suddenly, too, "while the word was in the king's mouth," a voice fell from heaven, "The kingdom is departed from

(b)

thee." He recognised the voice as a Divine judgment, and he became insane—afflicted with a peculiar kind of insanity wherein men think themselves to be animals—other instances are on record.

(v.) "Seven times" passed over him = a definite time—the appointed time required to do God's *whole* work on him. So it is with all afflictive periods = a "set time"—which comes and goes according to God's laws respecting it.

(vi.) Nebuchadnezzar was a good sort of heathen —an instance of a man not being left "alone," without warnings for his benefit.

(*a*) His dream of the great image reminds him that Daniel's God and his are different.

(*b*) The deliverance of the three heroes of faith, leads him to recognise God as "the Most High God," and that "no other God can deliver after this sort."

(*c*) Notwithstanding this, he went on for twenty or twenty-five years without perceptible benefit— still a heathen in his religion. God next alarms him by this dream, "a decree of the Most High God;" still he forgets (though a place of repentance is allowed him for a year more).

(*d*) God teaches him next by affliction, does not remove him by death (the stump of the tree left and bound to keep it from being hurt).

He recognises the hand of God in it, as having dealt with him for his pride.

Calvin's judgment here is harsh and uncharitable —better to think that God's discipline was not wasted on him; 34-37 seem to show that he became the servant of Jehovah, and here the Bible narrative dismisses him.

(*a*)   *Keil, adapted*

DANIEL, BOOK OF (Chap. v.)

(*See* "BELSHAZZAR," and "BALANCES.")

"*The God . . . hast thou not glorified.*"

1. Belshazzar had glorified idol-gods, but scoffed at Jehovah, knowing all the while the story of Nebuchadnezzar's humbling (18-22).

2. **The Narrative**

(1-4) The great feast—the guests—"Whiles he tasted wine" = in his drunkenness—he put forth his hand to an act of sacrilege = the madness of unbelief. His intention being to insult the God of the captive Jews, whilst doing honour to his own gods. It is not an act of hostility to the Jews themselves, but to show that his gods had subdued the Jews' God. The sign of the defeat being the capture of the consecrated vessels from the Temple at Jerusalem, and placing them in that of Bel (Cf. Dagon).

(5-12) *The Warning signs :*

In the midst of the revel, the King was struck with terror, and is filled with dark and terrible forebodings (*See* BELSHAZZAR).

(9) The King's terror increased, because no interpreter can be found : his countenance greatly changed.

(10) In the midst of the confusion, the Queen-mother comes in and refers to Daniel.

(13-28) DANIEL IS SUMMONED :

He immediately points out the greatness of the sin = "Thou, knowing of Nebuchadnezzar, yet hast not honoured God." . . . Then (not till then) the part of the mysterious hand was taken away, and the writing left exposed to view :—

MENE (numbered and finished) = You have had your opportunity. You might have done good, but you have missed your aim in life. The kingdom is taken from you. The cup of your iniquity is full, and sudden destruction comes upon you unawares.

TEKEL (weighed and found wanting) = Too light in moral worth. This weighing is by opportunities missed. The example is not for the *man* but for the *many*—as the court is, so is the country.

PERES (divided)

The kingdom was divided amongst the Medes and Persians. In that night was Belshazzar slain. As he had lived, so he died.

3. **The Lessons.**

(i.) Belshazzar, as the son of Nebuchadnezzar, ought to have profited by his father's experience. Instead of being better, he becomes worse.

(ii.) Learn how the world-power becomes hardened against God. The more God reveals Himself, the more does the worldly heart reject and close itself against Him, till ripe for judgment.

(iii.) Why Belshazzar is dealt with more summarily than Nebuchadnezzar. He had more light. Cf. "It shall be more tolerable for Sodom and Gomorrah in Day of Judgment than for that city." "He that knew his master's will and did it not shall be beaten with *many stripes.*"

(*b*)   *Ibid*

DANIEL, BOOK OF (Chap. vi.)

1. Darius wished to make Daniel chief officer over his realm—Satraps (1-3).

Envy at this, and endeavours at finding faults in his character—failure of this—save only on religious grounds (4, 5).

Edict issued, that for thirty days no prayer to any God except to the king, who was deified for the occasion (7).

Daniel goes on as aforetime (10)—is watched, accused, committed to the den of lions, and comes forth uninjured.

Then a second Edict, to reverence the God of Daniel who did such wonders.

After this Daniel prospered = a good time for the captive Jews.

2. **As to the Deification of the King, and the Law of the Medes and Persians which altereth not.**

(i.) The fundamental principle of Heathenism is, that their king is the representative of their national gods; and the *World-Ruler* consequently the representative of all the gods.

This is the idea in the thirty days' petition.

The people, of whatever nationality, must make their prayer through Darius, as a sign that he had conquered them. This a pious Jew could not do ; and Daniel, knowing the decree to be signed, did as aforetime.

(ii.) The king, seeing the drift of the decree (15) which had been extorted from him, laboured all day to save Daniel.

How was it that he could not ?

On this ground : The decree was legally drawn up, and signed by the king. If he annulled it, his act would signify that some other power was greater than his own ; he would be going contrary

(*c*)

to the fundamental law of his kingdom—viz : that he was the representative of supreme power. The king, as Deity, was unerring, and could not change.

3. The character of Darius

A weak man, swayed by stronger minds. (Nebuchadnezzar was a perfect autocrat = " I.") Such men as Darius do good or evil, just as they may happen to be biased by stronger minds either way; and thus it comes to be an axiom—that *weakness is allied to crime.* Darius in himself = an amiable man, especially appreciative of Daniel. But he does not see through, until too late, the crafty designs of his satraps. He has no insight into character, and so becomes the tool of these men to carry out their evil intentions. Such men are all very well when in obscure positions ; but, when, as here, they are placed in authority, they make the worst rulers and wielders of authority possible : they are never o be depended upon—always amiable, always swayed by the stronger will this way or that ; and under them the greatest evils are done.

There was also this difference between Nebuchadnezzar and Darius. Nebuchadnezzar did not wish to banish Jehovah from the world, but to subordinate Him to his gods.

Darius, by his officers, set Him aside altogether, by this degree forbidding prayer to be made to Him.

4. As to Daniel

This is the last of the events concerning him in the earlier part of this Book. It is therefore to be regarded as a part of his training.

Daniel is the most spiritually-minded man of the Old Testament, and to be compared only with St. John of the New Testament.

Both suffer persecution for their faith : Daniel (lions' den) ; John (Isle of Patmos). John is *in the spirit* on the Lord's Day ; Daniel arrives at a like stage. And to spiritual men the spiritual world is open and revealed, (to carnal men it is closed). After this, Daniel is shown a series of visions, pointing out the history of the world and the kingdom of God until the end. Which visions are taken up and completed by St. John.

Consequently the more difficult part of the book remains to be considered. The vision of the world's history *to the* END and of the END itself. (Ch. vii. should be studied in conjunction with Rev. xiii. and xvii.).

(*a*)   *Keil, adapted*

DANIEL, BOOK OF (Chap. vii.)

1. The Rise of the Four Beasts

(2, 3) WINDS = powers by which God sets nations in commotion. The number *Four* = all the earth. The SEA = nations and peoples of the earth.

(4–8) Beasts rising one after another, diverse = Four world-kingdoms, as in chap. ii.

  (i.) Assyria.
  (ii.) Medes and Persians.
  (iii.) Grecian.
  (iv.) Roman = diverse from all before it, 10 horns, another horn (little) with " eyes and mouth " = intelligence.

(9–14) Judgment on the Beast because of the enormity of the doings of the " little horn " = the climax—" The Books opened " = The record of men's actions.

2. The Interpretation of the Vision

(15–28) Daniel grieved on account of the calamities the people of God would have to endure before the completion of His kingdom.

(17–18) *A Summary of the Interpretation.*

The Four Beasts (= four kingdoms) rise and disappear ; but the saints of God shall *receive* (not *found*) a kingdom, which shall be everlasting and permanent. Cf. " My kingdom is not of this world." No further explanation of the first three Beasts because the same as in chap. ii.

(23) The fourth kingdom diverse from all, rapacious, breaks up into Ten, and the " little horn " = the fullest development of Anti-Christ, who,—

(25) " Shall wear out the saints of the Most High," until the judgment comes, when matters will be set right.

This tyranny shall last for *a time and times and the dividing of time* = a period measured and allotted by God, and which shall be shortened for the elect's sake = 1, 2, and 4, as doubles, but the last period is shortened (divided).

3. We may regard the whole as thus summarized:

There are four world-kingdoms succeeding each other :—

Assyria, Medes and Persians, Grecian, Roman.

The greatest and most terrible of these is the fourth (the Roman).

During this fourth world-kingdom, Christ comes and sets up the kingdom of God.

Parallel with the kingdom an anti-Christian kingdom is set up (arising as a *Horn* out of the ruins of the fourth), whose attitude towards the Church is terrible, and increases in emnity as the " time is short."

The history of the world thenceforth is the history of these two powers.

Daniel saw the general outline of this, and the prophetic view he had of the sufferings of the saints *amazed* and *troubled* him.

John saw this (period of tribulation) too, and prayed Christ to shorten it. For when Christ said to him, " I come quickly," he answered with emphasis, " Even so come, Lord Jesus,"—Come quickly, and stay the madness and the ravings of the powers of darkness against Thy people.

Daniel kept on looking until the judgment was set.

N.B. We are mixed up with all this. In the present-day changes we are taking our part in the unfolding of this scheme :—

(i.) God's kingdom, we know something of.

(ii.) The " Little Horn," the Beast (Rev. xiii.), is the Anti-Christian kingdom—a great intelligence, having all the means of modern civilization diverted to serve its purpose. This power existed in Old Testament times, there it = the *ungodly ;* in New Testament = *Anti-Christian. The Devil becomes religious in New Testament times.* Seen in—

(i.) The infidelity of modern culture in the world.

(ii.) The superstition in the false forms and modes of present-day Christianity in the Church. These combined are his method of working now ; and these will bring about the last Tribulation, as the fruits of the Tree of Knowledge.

In the Book of Revelation Satan gives his power and authority to the Beast, to harass and extirpate the Church of Christ, " to wear out the saints of the Most High." But Anti-Christ has his turn

(*b*)

first; after he has grown to his full age (time, times, and half) he is fully ripe, then the harvest time comes, the earth is reaped. The Judgment shall sit, and Christ's kingdom takes the place of all others (Dan. vii. 26, 27). The Bible offers us no hope that a time of Gospel sunlight will intervene before the end of the world.

(a)   *Keil, adapted*

DANIEL, BOOK OF, PART II

Summary

Chap. viii. contains an account of what will happen to the people of God during the second and third world-kingdoms (*i.e.* the Medes and Persians, and Grecian).

Chap. ix., of what will happen to them during the period between the Babylonian Captivity and the first coming of Christ.

Chap. x.-xii. contain special revelations of the *near* future, which typify the more *remote* future: Antiochus Epiphanes and Anti-Christ as respectively the last foes until the time of the end.

(b)

DANIEL, BOOK OF (Chap. viii.)

The Vision

(Verses 1, 2) The place—Susa—Daniel saw:

(3-7) 1. *A ram* with two horns = the Medes and Persians.

2. *A goat* coming afterwards, running over the earth, which destroyed with a *Great Horn* = Alexander.

Afterwards the great horn was broken, four horns came up towards the four winds, and out of one of them came a *Little Horn* (not same as before) who contended against true religion (11-12).

(13-14) How long this sacrilege continues.

(15-26) Interpretation.

(27) The effect on Daniel.

The prominence in this chapter is given to the "LITTLE HORN."

= one of the successors of Alexander the Great.

= ANTIOCHUS EPIPHANES: He occupies a very prominent place in Holy Scripture, both of the Old and New Testament. The chief type of Anti-Christ. St. Paul, doubtless, alludes to him in 2 Thess. ii.; as "that man of sin." To understand the latter, it is necessary to have a general knowledge of the former.

1. The time of Antiochus Epiphanes' activity

It was a time of national apostasy from the faith. The Church of God was in a minority, overlapped by the heathen culture of the day. People were becoming ashamed of the old faith, looked at it as possessing no elasticity, and as behind the age.

The number of apostates was increasing. Antiochus seized the spirit of the times, took the lead, became the mouthpiece of the party. The High Priest publicly renounced the law of Moses (think of its significance). The Jews were massacred, a pig was sacrificed on the altar in the Temple, and *its* blood sprinkled. Those who came to worship on the sabbath were killed. A garrison was placed to attack the worshippers. Public contempt for God and His worship was becoming general.

The duration of this signified as 2,300 *days*,

import of *days* = not a day longer than was permitted (14). Morning and evening sacrifices taken away—no vestige of public worship left.

Religion abandoned

Antiochus next decreed that every one was to abandon his old religion, and worship as he did. This of course was aimed at the Jews; and the object was to destroy their nationality. Religion makes a nation exclusive—the Jew is so to this day. The Christian is so of necessity. The king was jealous of their allegiance. They served *another* better than they did him. Chagrined and annoyed, and in his daring presumption, he determined to destroy this homage to another—his *will* should be paramount. Hence he stopped circumcision; the sabbath was not observed; copies of the law were destroyed; the Temple was consecrated to Jupiter, whose statue was erected in it, and sacrifices offered to him, at which the people were compelled to attend, and eat swine's flesh.

Everything was at stake. God was ousted from His world, true religion crushed. And God sends this prophecy to Daniel as a comfort, to remind him and his co-religionists that the persecution should only last an appointed time, *not a day longer than was decreed.*

It is this which St. Paul teaches us shall be reproduced under the short reign of Anti-Christ—only on a wider sphere.

Antiochus appears before Christ comes the first time, whilst *Anti-Christ* appears before Christ comes the second time.

The world, as its chiefest representative, will try to cast God out of His world. The saints will suffer; but the time will be shortened. There is great comfort in knowing beforehand that the time will not only come to an *end*, but the end is determined and fixed. We, as Daniel was, are advised beforehand, "Ye, brethren, are not in darkness."

These things concern us; Daniel was terror-struck, and fainted at the revelation of lawlessness. The end was further off than he thought, and before the end much affliction; but yet it was a comfort to know concerning this, that each affliction had its bounds and its fixed limits, which it could not overpass. God's people = stars although trodden underfoot of men.

(c)   *Ibid.*

DANIEL, BOOK OF, CHAP. IX. (20-27)

The Seventy Weeks

The time of Daniel's prayer = the nearness of the close of the seventy years' Captivity. But the people have not repented—apparently none the better for the affliction.

Daniel, in a meditative mood, is puzzled at the wickedness of the earth. God's people, of Israel, are the same, whilst the heathen around them seem one mass of idolatry and sin.

Daniel is really wanting to solve the dark problem of sin: "O Lord, *how long, how long?*" The angel Gabriel brings him an answer = "There shall be a great deliverance for the people of God: there shall be a riddance of sin." But it is God's will that it continues in the world for a lengthy period—here denoted by *seventy weeks:* a symbolical time, meaning a *measured* time, in which good and evil are mingled together in the world;

(d)

and the result of the turmoil and strife between Good and Evil will be seen at the end of seventy weeks.

Two sets of statements to describe this:

1. Negatively

(i.) " To finish the transgression," (= sin shall be taken away) in *two ways :*

(ii.) *For unbelievers,*

" To make an end of sins,"=it shall be sealed up, restrained—held under lock and key (Zech. v. 8 ; Rev. xx. 3).

(iii.) *For believers,*—

" To make reconciliation for iniquity ; " *i.e.,* There shall be an atonement for sin.

2. Positively

(i.) " To bring in everlasting righteousness." = The kingdom of God shall come and be set up— also in *two ways :*

(ii.) *For unbelievers,*

" To seal up the vision and the prophecy." When it shall not be necessary to say, " Know the Lord," etc. They will have outlived their opportunities.

(iii.) *For believers,*

" To anoint the Most Holy " = The tabernacle of God is with men (Rev. xxi. 1–3).

Rev. xii. 10, " *Now is come salvation.*"

(25–27) To work this out will require a period of seventy weeks. Divided into three periods, thus :

(i.) *Seven weeks* = from termination of the exile to first coming of Christ, and the setting up of the *kingdom of heaven.*

(ii.) *Sixty-two weeks* = From the Christ to the " cutting off " of His kingdom, so that nothing remains to Him. In this period the Church develops as much as God intended. (In this period we are living.)

(iii.) *One week* = The reign of Anti-Christ—the destroyer of the Church ; and the final victory over him by the coming of Christ the second time.

N.B.—This last period begins by a crucifying of Christ afresh (in His body = His Church) = a second Good Friday ; and it ends in a " flood " of wrath (27), in which Anti-Christ himself is destroyed. Note, also, that *this is a short period* compared with others.

The comfort of this Revelation to Daniel and God's people at all times (and especially of those who suffer tribulation in the world).

The Seventy weeks is shown as a limited period, and its subdivisions are known and determined by God. Strong consolation is afforded of knowing that the fortunes of God's people are in His hands, not in the hands of the hostile power of the world. God permits things for a time to go on so for two reasons :—

(i.) That iniquity may fully ripen (cf. the iniquity of the Canaanites was not yet full).

(ii.) To fit His people for the life beyond. The affliction would purify them, whilst it would ripen the others for their doom.

And thus we see that all events in the history of nations—*war* and *oppressions*, etc., are not only measured by God, but they are for the increasing and benefit of His Church: "*All things are yours.*"

The object of these revelations is, then, not to make us curious about "times and seasons" ("of that day and hour knoweth no man "), but to console and strengthen us when any of these things come upon us, lest we be unbelieving, and think that the darkness of the night will never give way to a morning of light.

(*a*)   *Keil, adapted*

DANIEL, BOOK OF (Chap. x.)

Chaps. x., xi., xii., contain but ONE vision, and the last in the Book.

Ch. x. = The THEOPHANY, or the Preparation for the vision ; xi. = the events of the near Future ; xii., those of the far Future.

Ch. x : (i.) Illustrates the " Ministry of Angels " (good and bad) ; they mingle in the history of nations.

(ii.) How the " prayer of a righteous man availeth much."

Verse 1. = The third year of Cyrus—Daniel had been in Babylon 72 years. Edict for the return of the Jews in Cyrus's first year ; but Daniel sees only a partial return and reformation, and the glories of the second Temple and city are not worthy of the first.

(2, 3) Therefore he prays to know more of the future of his people. (Three weeks of prayer and fasting.)

(4–6) The Theophany in answer to his prayer = not a vision, a celestial being = the Lord in glory, as to Ezekiel and John.

(Note the progress of Daniel from interesting dreams to visions in broad daylight. His state corresponds to St. Paul's—" Whether in the body or out of the body, I cannot tell."

(7, 8) The effect on Daniel and the people with him. Human nature cannot endure Heavenly majesty—(i.) no strength, fell down.—

(9, 10) Daniel heard the voice, an unseen hand strengthened him a little—(ii.) on his knees and palms of his hands.

(iii.) The encouraging words. Daniel " stood trembling," but he could not speak, "Dumb " (15–19). His lips touched=he could speak, but yet without strength ; (19) touched again = full strength.

(12) Connection between his prayer and this vision :—" I am come for thy words." Daniel prayed for the removal of hindrances (political hindrances) to the advancement of his people, now in Jerusalem, rebuilding in troublous times. God shows him that He has taken steps for their removal.

(13) Prince of the king of Persia = a spirit of a demon, who influenced the actions and councils of the nation. God sends an angel of His to counteract the adverse influence, and is opposed by the demon-spirit twenty days (the whole time that Daniel had been praying and fasting).

Hence the angel came to bring a comforting answer ; but before he could do so he must overcome the evil influence of the demon-spirit. Having conquered this demon-agency, " I remained there to influence the king of Persia favourably towards Israel."

In this spirit-war Michael (" your Prince ") assisted the angel, = one of the highest celestial persons, who conducts the cause of Israel. Daniel is comforted by knowing that his people are under very powerful protection. Israel's guardian angel is one of the foremost spirits—of the highest dignity.

(20) " Know then that I am come to tell thee

(*b*)

what thou wantedst to know." I will return to carry on my influence with the king of Persia; but after Persia, Grecia will oppose.

(21) Shows why Michael in particular came. He is the "Prince of Israel."

(a) *Keil, adapted*

DANIEL, BOOK OF (Chap. xi.)

Verse 32. A heathen king comes to the "Covenant Nation" with hostile intentions:

He finds there two parties.

1. **An apostate party,** or those "who do wickedly against the covenant"; these go over to him, and in heart "they become heathen."

2. **A faithful party,** "who do know their God"; these, by their confidence, become "strengthened in the Lord."

In this description we have, not the actual anti-Christ, but a typical picture of the time in which he will appear. There will be two parties.—

(i.) Those who partake of Christian privileges—of the covenant—those who in the Christian Church are yet really its enemies, and join the ranks of anti-Christ, as he gains the ascendency.

(ii.) There will be also the party who remain faithful (it may be a minority). These will do "exploits" for the cause of God: they will make a stand against the kingdom of sin as it advances.

N.B. **The Distinguishing Features of the two Classes:**

(i.) The first, though in the covenant, are heathen at heart; they do not *know* their God. There is a Religiosity, not Christianity.

(ii.) The second *know* their God; they are not in fear and doubt and uncertainty: God is to them a *Father,* Jesus a *Saviour,* the Holy Ghost a *Comforter.* Their "communion is with the Father and with His Son Jesus Christ." Hence they remain "steadfast" in the midst of apostasy.

Things appear to be pressing on to this—droppings and foreshadowings of such a state of things we seem to have in the "perversions" of our time, who go out from us, because they are not of us; and in the terrible struggle going on between Christianity and Materialism.

33. EXPLAINS THE "EXPLOITS" (OF 32):

They that understand,—not intellect, but insight is meant; the true understanding of spiritual things comes from having a standing in them. By remaining steadfast, "they shall instruct many"—it is a contest on their part; but eventually they will be overpowered and fall "many days." Then, too, will be the days of anti-Christ; as they are coming on, the faithful, who have *insight,* shall become aware of it, and warn others; but though successful in their attitude, they will be eventually oppressed: the tide of opposition will rush on in full strength. In our day we may be successful in making a stand against infidelity and apostasy; but the tide which ebbs will flow again. It is bound to come on again, and to bring about the great and final tribulation.

(34) "THE LITTLE HELP"—not contemptuous this, but "little" in comparison with the *help* God's people will experience in the great tribulation. (Here the oppression comes to a sudden end; there it shall be overthrown by Christ, at His coming.)

(35) THE REASON OF THE "FALL" of *many*—through imprisonments, plunders, etc.

(i.) *To try them.* Some were hyprocrites, and such would fall away, as was the case, by flatteries (34).

(ii.) *To purge them and make them white: i.e.* the faithful, that they might be pure and unsullied, and this to fit them for glory. This should continue unto the END, which would come (not in the time of the LITTLE HELP), but in the time appointed by the Father—far in the distant future. The opposition should continue to go on and on—now ebbing, now flowing—till one day the tide would be *full* in—then God's appointed time would be ripe.

(b) *Ibid*

DANIEL, BOOK OF (Chap. xii.)

(1-3) "At that time"=the time of the end=the events of Chap. xi.—(i.) Tribulation. (ii.) Deliverance. (iii.) The Resurrection of the just and unjust. (iv.) Glory.

(4) (i.) Daniel, having done his work, is dismissed from his prophetic office.

The *sealing,* securing, or guarding the Revelation=It is to be preserved by that means until the time of the end, when all the tribulations detailed in Chap. xi. ending with the Resurrection and Glory (xii. 2 and 3) have come to pass: = not to be added to or deducted from.

(ii.) Many "*run to and fro*"=

Many will search the Scriptures (concerning these revelations of the future) for consolation during the lengthened period of trouble and of waiting, and shall find their faith and hope strengthened by so doing. And thus "Knowledge" of such things will be "increased."

This, indeed, is the object of the Book being sealed (or secured) and not being tampered with, so as to be a Book of reliable instruction concerning the unfolding of God's plans as to the course of the world's history. If not secured from interpolations it could not be a means of comfort to any.

(5) Two other angels appear.

(6) One of which asks, "*How long . . . to the end of these wonders?*" (extraordinary things.)

(7) The angel held up both hands (usually one in taking an oath) to mark its solemnity, and asserted that it would be for a definite time: when the "end" of the oppression should be gained—viz., the purification of God's people and the destruction of the oppressor.

It would take three and a half times fully to unfold all this anti-Christian power; and when the strength of God's people would be completely broken, *then* these terrible things would have an end.

Cf. Jesus walking on the sea; at the moment of extremity, when the disciples have ceased *hoping,* ceased *believing,* ceased *praying* (=the 4th watch of the night). So, when the Son of Man cometh, shall He find faith on the earth? Though we have Daniel and John to tell us what to expect.

(8) Daniel hears this, but does not understand: he wants particulars; so he asks:

Which event will be the *uttermost* of this series of extraordinary things—viz., which one will stand immediately before the *end?*

A natural question: a question which our hearts are disposed to ask when in trouble—when wait-

(c)

ing and witnessing the revolutions, or any of the great disturbing events on the earth.

(9) The answer = " BE AT PEACE, DANIEL, AND LEAVE THIS MATTER ALONE."

There is much in this reply to quiet and console the prophet ; but it is a distinct refusal as to data ; and yet not wholly a refusal.

(i.) It is a *refusal*, so far as giving data by which men may fix with certainty the *End* beforehand. But the END is revealed.

(ii.) It is not *wholly* a refusal. For the revelation about the End is secured to the world (the Church) and as the End approaches the events will interpret it.

(10) The *wise* will study it—in their trials—and the effect will be to purify and make them white, and *they shall have understanding of the times* (" Ye, brethren, are not in darkness," etc.) ; but the *wicked* will not heed this prophecy, nor will they understand : to them the day of the Lord will come as a thief in the night.

There is consolation for Daniel in the fact that he had been instrumental in *instructing* the people of God from his time unto the End. The things revealed unto him were for us (1 Pet. i. 12).

N.B.—Observe that whilst a distinguished member of the Church of God is in trouble (captivity), he is often made a source of great blessings to others :—

Daniel, in exile, has the future revealed to the time of the End ;

Luther, in the castle at Wartburg, translates the Bible for his country ;

Bunyan, in Bedford Gaol, writes the " Pilgrim's Progress," etc.

(11) A more particular detailing of the times—" days " (and the significance) = not one day longer than God ordains.

(12) The blessing of "*waiting*," every day of the tribulation brings the end nearer.

(13) As for thee, Daniel, " *Go thy way, thou shalt stand in thy lot at the end.*" Think of the significance of this assurance : The earth has yet a long period of time before it. During that period many tribulations, great waves, will toss the Church of Christ, and seek to wreck it. The last worse than any ; it almost succeeds in crushing it altogether—hope gone. But by that time the End is nearing ; then comes the End ; the Resurrection, the separation of good and bad ; *but as for thee, Daniel, thy lot is secured, thou shalt enter into rest.*

(*a*)   *Keil, adapted*

Compare here the TWO WEAVERS

No. 1 says :—

In spite of all the Scripture teaches,
In spite of all the parson preaches,
This world (indeed I've thought so long)
Is ruled, methinks, extremely wrong.

No. 2 replies :—

See'st thou that carpet, not half done,
Which thou, dear Dick, hast well begun?
Behold the wild confusion there,
So rude the mass, it makes one stare.

A stranger ignorant of the trade,
Would say, No meaning's there conveyed ;
For where's the middle, where's the border ?
Thy carpet now is all disorder."

No. 1 reminds him that the carpet on which he is at work is unfinished, and " *inside out* " for the present.

The other replies, that the world is unfinished in like manner at present.

" As when we view these shreds and ends,
We know not what the whole intends ;
So when on earth things look but odd,
They're working still some scheme of God."

(*b*)   *Hannah More*

DARKNESS BEFORE LIGHT

The Lord oft-times makes everything as dark as it can become, just that presently the light may shine more brilliantly :—

Ishmael faints, before Hagar finds the well ;

Joseph left in prison and oblivion before being raised to his dignity ;

The Assyrian host surrounds Jerusalem ere they are smitten by the angel ;

Jeremiah sinks into the pit before he is placed on a rock ;

Violent persecution of the Christians preceded the triumph of the Gospel ;

Mediæval darkness preceded the dawn of the Reformation.

(*c*)   *Oosterzee*

DARKNESS, SPIRITUAL

Man is at a loss where to fix himself. He is unquestionably out of his way, and feels within himself the remains of a happy state which he cannot retrieve. He searches in every direction, with solicitude, but without success, encompassed with impenetrable darkness !

(*d*)   *Blaise Pascal*

DARKNESS, CAUSE OF SPIRITUAL

Frequently spiritual clouds are the result of backsliding, of falls from the narrow path to the darker way of sin.

Indulgence of known sins, and neglect of known duties, grieve the Holy Spirit, and His influence is withdrawn. The pilgrim ceases to regret the lost sunshine ; he sinks into fatal languor, and is soon lulled into a deadly slumber, a state of semi-existence, unfelt and undeplored.

Thus he might remain until death sealed his doom ; but the Good Shepherd has said, " I will both gather My flock, and search them out from all places where they have been scattered in the dark and cloudy day." Those who have been once folded in His arms by regeneration to everlasting life, can never perish. He seeks out the sleeping pilgrim, and probably arouses him by some salutary chastisement. Then the backslider is left to prove the error of his wanderings, the sinfulness of his slumber ; he finds, by painful experience, that his sins have cast a separating cloud between him and his God. He gropes his way in chilling shadows. But by the upholding influence of the Holy Spirit he is enabled to persevere, until, at length,—perhaps not till after a tedious and painful probation,—his reconciled Father addresses to him the joyful invitation, " I have blotted out as a cloud thine iniquities, and as a thick cloud thy sins ; return unto Me, for I have redeemed thee." How gladsome, then, is the return to the sunshine of joy and blessedness !

(*e*)   *Moore's Sacred Symbols*

DAVID, THE FALL OF

David was sitting on his palace roof. That place of retirement had often been hallowed by his better thoughts. From thence he had sung: "Oh that I had the wings of a dove! for then would I flee away, and be at rest." There, as he gazed on the starry midnight, he had broken forth in the immortal psalm: "The heavens declare the glory of God, and the firmament showeth His handiwork." Far different was his mood in this evil hour. He was secure and full-fed; and his thoughts were base and sensual and vile. Doubtless, the prayers which might have saved him had been forgotten, or but carelessly uttered. Doubtless, his service in the house of God had become but one of dead orthodoxy and self-satisfied form, no better than the hawk's shriek, or the lake's murmur in the summer eve. But that was why evil thoughts and impure desires had entered into the temple of his heart. Satan wakes, though man sleeps; and, seizing the opportunity given him by the undefended soul, Satan flung upon it a fiery arrow, which should rankle and agonize until the end.

(a) *Archdeacon Farrar*

DAVID, THE MAN AFTER GOD'S OWN HEART

Who is called the man after God's own heart? David, the Hebrew King, had fallen into sins enough: blackest crimes—there was no want of sin. And therefore the unbelievers sneer, and ask, Is *this* your man according to God's heart? The sneer, I must say, seems to me but a shallow one. What are faults, what are the outward details of a life, if the inner secret of it—the remorse, temptations, the often-baffled, never-ended struggle of it—be forgotten? David's life and history, as written for us in those Psalms of his, I consider to be the truest emblem ever given us of a man's moral progress and warfare here below. All earnest souls will ever discern in it the faithful struggle of an earnest human soul towards what is good and best. Struggle often baffled, sore baffled—driven as into entire wreck—yet a struggle never ended; ever with tears, repentance, true, unconquerable purpose, begun anew.

(b) *Carlyle*

DAVID, THE ROYAL PSALMIST

We ought to be deeply grateful to God for the inspired history of the life of His servant David. It was a great life, a vigorous life, a life spent in many positions and conditions. I almost rejoice that it was not a faultless life, for its failings and errors are instructive. It is the life of a man after God's own heart; but still, the life of one who went astray, like a lost sheep, and was recovered by the great Shepherd's grace. By this fact he comes all the nearer to us poor, faulty men and women. I would venture to apply to David the description which has been applied to the world's own poet—

"A man so various, that he seemed to be
Not one, but all mankind's epitome."

Each one may find something like himself in the long, eventful, and chequered life of the son of Jesse. Among other things we learn this, that where there is faith there is sure to be trial; for David, though he trusted God so heartily, had good

need of all the faith he possessed. In his early days he was hunted like a partridge upon the mountains by Saul, and was constantly in jeopardy of his life. He had so choice a treasure of faith about him, that Satan was for ever trying to plunder him of it. Still, the worst trials that David suffered arose, not out of his faith, but out of his want of it. That which he did to avoid trouble brought him into deeper distress than ordinary providences ever caused him. He left the country where he was so ill at ease, which was, nevertheless, Thy land, O Emmanuel; and he went away into the land of the Philistines, expecting there to escape from further turmoil. In so doing he transgressed, and fresh trials came upon him, trials of a worse kind than those which had happened to him from the hand of Saul. Brethren, the poet said-

"The path of sorrow, and that path alone,
Leads to the land where sorrow is unknown."

and he spake truly; for "in the world ye shall have tribulation." If you have faith, it must be tried; and should that faith fail, you must be tried still more. There is no discharge from this war; difficulties must be faced. This is the day of battle, and you must fight if you would reign. You are like men thrown into the sea, you must swim or drown. It is useless to expect ease where your Lord had none. If you adopt the paltry shifts suggested by unbelief, not even then shall you avoid affliction; the probabilities are that you will be taken among the thorns and scourged with the briars of the wilderness. However rough the king's highway may be, the by-paths are far worse; therefore keep the way of the commandment, and bravely face its trial.

(c) *Spurgeon*

DAY (THE CREATION)

The twenty-four hours "day" theory is upset by the fact, that God's *day of rest* (the seventh day) still continues, *i.e.*, it is a *long period*; hence the days preceding it also were long periods. Other confirmatory reasons also—as, "Or ever man was created, I was," infers a longer period than five or six days between the creation of the earth and man.

(d) *Gordon Calthrop*

DAY (SUFFICIENT UNTO THE, ETC.)

When Christ bade us limit our cares to the day that is passing over our heads, He consulted our natural quiet no less than our spiritual welfare; since the chief sources of most men's uneasiness are chagrin at what is past, and forebodings of what is to come.

Whereas what is past ought to give us no uneasiness (except repentance for our faults), and whatever is to come ought much less to affect us, because, with regard to us and our concerns, it is not, and perhaps never will be.

(e) *Bishop Horne*

DAYS

Enlarge my life with multitude of days,
In health and sickness, thus the suppliant prays;
Hides from himself his state, and shuns to know
That life protracted is protracted woe.

(f) *Dr. Johnson*

DEATH

DEATH OF ABUSES

They lived in a country that was grand for Conservatism. A man living in a certain village which was exceedingly healthy was met by another, who said to him, " Your village is very healthy; nobody ever dies here." " Well, sir," he replied, " they do die; but it is the last thing they do." England was a wonderfully healthy country for abuses. These lived very long; they did die, but they took a great deal of killing, and dying was the very last thing they did.

(a)   *Spurgeon*

DEATH, CERTAINTY OF

It is certain thou must die, and uncertain when, how, or where; seeing death is always at thy heels, thou must (if thou be wise), always be ready to die.

(b)   *Bernard*

DEATH, CHRIST'S CONFLICT WITH

He began to wage war with Death, as " He went about " in the land of Judæa. In the house of Jairus, where the victim had only just been slain; in the street of Nain, where Death, like a lion, was in the act of taking home his prey; and in Bethany, where for four days he had been in possession of his spoil. But he could not withstand the Son of Mary; at His word he yielded up his prey. The devils of Judæa could not stand before Him; they vanished from His presence. Thus, for the space of three years, He moved about like a terrible " man-of-war," rescuing the captives from the power of Death. The people, from Samaria to the borders of Tyre and Sidon, were filled with joy and amazement. But on a day ever to be remembered, He drew near the ramparts of Sinai. The fierce contest began; the batteries were opened; and He sweat, as it were, great drops of blood. Having taken up this position between His Church and the artillery that played upon it, He was kept under constant fire, through the whole of that night, from the old cannon of Eden, " Thou shalt die." But on the following day, at the third hour in the afternoon, wounded in the conflict, he cried aloud: " My God, my God, why hast Thou forsaken Me?" The " man-of-war " sank in the Gulf of Death, in the midst of signs and wonders; the earth shook, the rocks rent, the sun darkened, the graves opened, and all nature seemed to dissolve, as if its God were in strange sympathy with the One who now died. Then the tempest grew calm. But the " man-of-war " sank not like any other. It went down with hoisted sail, its register safe, and with unmistakable signs that it sank not overpowered into the deep, but, as it were, of its own accord, to rescue the multitudes that were perishing. Earth trembles, and the sea is agitated as if some vast living thing were emerging from its depths. The vessel floats upon the waters, freighted, as it were, with a world of God's elect, in full sail, and bearing the new name of " The Resurrection and the Life." A voice is heard crying aloud, " Peace," to the disciples—" I, who was once dead." " O blessed Lord, hast Thou lost nothing in the deep?" " No; I have with Me, still undamaged, the Book of Life. I have also the life of My people—the cable of Faith, the anchor of Hope, and the sails of Love have ascended, no more to sink for ever. I live for ever, and hold the keys of death and hell."

(c)   *Christmas Evans*

DEATH OF CHILDREN

" Is it well with the child? " and she answered
    " 'Tis well "—
But I gazed on the mother who spake,
For the tremulous tear, as it sprang from its cell,
    Bade a doubt in my bosom awake;
And I marked that the bloom from her features
        had fled,
    So late in their loveliness rare,
And the hue of the watcher that bends o'er the
        dead
    Was gathering all languidly there.
" Is it well with the child? " and she answered
    " 'Tis well "—
But I thought of its beauty and grace,
When the tones of its laughter would merrily
        swell
    At affection's delighted embrace:
And through their long fringe, as it rose from its
        sleep,
    Its eyes beamed a rapturous ray,
And I wondered that silence should settle so deep
    O'er the home of a being so gay.
" Is it well with the child? " and she answered
    " *'Tis well* "—
No more will it shudder with pain;
Of the pang and the groan and the gasp it might
        tell,—
    It never will suffer again.

(d)   *Mrs. Sigourney*

DEATH OF CHILDREN

Little ones who have died may be used of the Spirit to exercise an influence more mysterious than the lodestone, drawing us by a power, silent and invisible, but true. Oh, glad hope! to be reunited to our child—to be in the same place with it again! Oh, blessed land! bright with the presence of our Saviour, bright with the presence of our child—He, the Great Light to rule the heart's eternal day; it, a lesser light, bright in the glory which streams magnificently from Him.

(e)   *P. B. Power*

She was my idol! night and day to scan
The fine expression of her form, and mark
The unfolding mind like vernal rosebud start
To sudden beauty was my chief delight.
To find her fairy footsteps following mine,
Her hand upon my garments, or her lip
Long sealed to mine, and in the watch of night
The quiet breath of innocence to feel
Soft on my cheek, was such a full content
Of happiness as none but mothers know.
Her voice was like some tiny harp that yields
To the slight-fingered breeze, and as it held
Brief converse with her doll, or playful soothed
The moaning kitten, or with patient care
Conned o'er the alphabet; but most of all
Its tender cadence in her evening prayer,
Thrilled on the ear like some ethereal tone
Heard in sweet dreams.
                    But now alone I sit
Musing of her, and dew with mournful tears

(f)

Her little robes, that once with woman's pride
I wrought, as if there were a need to deck
What God had made so beautiful.
                                        I start,
Half fancying from her empty crib there comes
A restless sound, and breathe the accustomed
        words,
"Hush! hush thee, dearest!"   Then I bend
        and weep,
As though it were a sin to speak to ONE
WHOSE HOME IS WITH THE ANGELS.
                        Gone to God!
Be still, my heart? what could a mother's
        prayer,
In all the wildest ecstasies of hope,
Ask for its darling like the bliss of heaven?
(a)   *Mrs. Sigourney*

DEATH IN CHRIST

Let us then reflect on death in Jesus Christ,
not without Jesus Christ. Without Jesus Christ,
it is dreadful, it is detestable, it is the terror of
nature. In Jesus Christ, it is lovely, it is holy,
it is the joy of saints. All things are sweet in
Jesus Christ, death itself not excepted.
(b)   *Blaise Pascal*

DEATH OF DEATH, THE (Heb. ii. 15)

The devil, as he who had the power of death,
delighted in death; and that in which he delighted, the Lord held out to him. Thus His
cross became a snare for the devil.
(c)   *Augustine*

DEATH

"*I die daily*" (1 Cor. xv. 31)

It is with men as with trees, they are notched
long before felling, that their life-sap may exude.
(d)   *J. P. T. Richter*

DEATH AND DUTY (John xi. 1–16)

The certainty of life within the bounds of duty.
The servant of God does not die until his work
is done.
(e)   *Lange*

DEATH, DOOR OF

Death hath ten thousand several doors
For men to take their exits.
(f)   *John Webster*

DEATH, EQUALITY IN

Death comes equally to us all, and makes us all
equal when it does come. The ashes of an oak
in a chimney are no epitaph of that, to tell me
how high or how large that was; it tells me not
what flocks it sheltered while it stood, nor what
men it hurt when it fell. The dust of great persons'
graves is speechless too; it says nothing, it distinguishes nothing. As soon the dust of a wretch
whom thou wouldst not, as of a prince whom thou
couldst not look upon, will trouble thine eyes if
the wind blow it thither; and when a whirlwind
has blown the dust of a churchyard into a church,
and the man sweeps out the dust of the church

into the churchyard, who will undertake to sift
those dusts again, and to pronounce, "This is
the patrician, this the noble flour, and this the
yeoman, this the plebeian bran"?
(g)   *Donne*

DEATH, FEAR OF

"*When thou passest through the waters, I will be
with thee*" (Isa. xliii. 2).

    "But timorous mortals start and shrink
        To cross that narrow sea."

Why should they? They may go over Jordan
DRYSHOD!
(h)   *Dr. Marsh*

DEATH OF THE FAITHFUL

Let us not regard the faithful, who are departed
in the grace of God, as having ceased to live,
though nature suggests this; but as beginning to
live, which is what truth declares. Let us regard their souls, not as lost and annihilated, but
as animated, and united to the sovereign life.
(i)   *Blaise Pascal*

DEATH, FEAR OF

The weariest and most loathèd worldly life
That age, ache, penury, and imprisonment
Can lay on nature, is a paradise
To what we fear of death.
(j)   *Shakspeare*

DEATH, FEAR OF, BY INFIDELS

Death has ever been the terror of infidels and
blasphemers: if nothing else could take the brag
out of them, Death has done it effectually. One
such being at sea, and a thunderstorm overtaking
and imperilling the ship, was seen to fall on his
knees and pray as others did. The description of
Voltaire's death-bed is simply awful. The infidel
can neither meet death nor offer anything to the
dying. The daughter of one sent for him to come
to her death-bed. The messenger found him in
the act of reading his infidel writings to a friend.
His wife was a Christian, and had trained her
child in the principles of Christianity. "Father,"
said the dying girl, "I am about to die; shall I
believe in what *you*, or in what my mother has
taught me?" After a short struggle, he said,
"Believe in what your mother has taught you."
(k)

DEATH, FEAR OF, PECULIAR TO MAN

Death is no more than every being must suffer,
though the dread of it is peculiar to man.
(l)   *Dr. Johnson*

DEATH AND HALLELUJAH

The Scripture has announced this, viz., that one
death devoured the other (1 Cor. xv. 54); death
has been turned into derision. Hallelujah!
(m)   *Luther*

DEATH WITHOUT HOPE

"I am going down a terrible hill, and can't get
the brake on," said a dying and once blasphemous
driver of the Western States of America.
(n)

DEATH WATHOUT HOPE

Rabelais, when dying, said, "I go to seek a great *may be*."

(a)   *Carlyle*

DEATH: THE LAST DAYS OF AN INFIDEL

Mr. ——, a gentleman of good family and considerable property, had up to the age of 60 lived not only in forgetfulness of God, but also in direct opposition to all laws, human and Divine. He was a great reader, but his library consisted only of infidel and other works destructive of truth and morality, such as are generally to be found on the shelves of the Jesuit. Mr. —— was also addicted to drinking; there are few infidels who are not thus trying to cheat conscience. At last the day came when abused nature had its revenge. Mr. —— was attacked by an illness which ended in dropsy, the usual result of intemperance. For months previous to his death, he was obliged to have two nurses in constant attendance day and night, being quite unable to turn or move himself in the bed. One of the nurses, Mrs. ——, was a Christian woman in every sense of the word. She did all in her power to awaken him to a sense of his soul's danger. When she first spoke to him of God, he said, "Who is He? and what is He like?" "Why, sir, have you not read the Bible? Have you not got one amongst all those books?" He said, "A Bible! do you believe in it? I tell you, woman, there is no truth in it; nor is there a God." Day after day she reasoned with him, or as he said, preached to him, but with no effect. He said, "I am not going to die, and won't die. I have read my planet, and have yet 20 years to live. I shall go to Malta, and take you with me." "Sir," she said, "don't deceive yourself. You are dying; and, oh! I beseech you, ere it be too late, seek your God, and pray to Him to have mercy upon you." He said, "Well, I will try." After a short time of silence, he said, "Well, I have called to Him to come to me, and He won't; it's no use." She begged he would allow her to send for a clergyman. To please her, he consented. When the minister came, he tried to reason with him; and, with some members of his family, knelt down to pray for him; but, strange as it may appear, speech and prayer utterly failed the clergyman. This occurred on a Thursday, a week previous to that on which he died. On Saturday night, at 12 o'clock, he suddenly commenced howling in the most awful manner, and shrieked out, "Oh! he is pulling me, he is dragging me down!" His hair stood quite on end, and he was as if taken out of a bath. In a moment he was hurled out of the bed on to the floor. Mrs. ——, the nurse, rushed to the door and called loudly for assistance, when the other nurse and man-servant came, supposing Mr. —— had died suddenly. On the floor, the colour of a coal, lay the wretched infidel moaning and trembling. He refused to be put into bed again; they placed him in a chair, where he remained until Thursday afternoon, when he died. On Sunday he solemnly assured Mrs. —— he had seen the devil, who threw him out of the bed. A moment before the spirit of life fled, he took the nurse's hand, and said, "My soul is lost for ever!"

K

[The names and places are given by our correspondent, in whom we have entire confidence, but for obvious reasons we omit them.—*Ed.* "*The Rock.*"]

(b)

DEATH AND LAST DAYS OF TWO GREAT MEN, THE

Writing to a lady who was in fear of death, one says: "I am of opinion that one ought never to think of death. This thought is of no use whatever, save to embitter life. *Death is a mere nothing.* . . . Those people who solemnly proclaim it are enemies of the human race; one must try to keep them off. Death is as like to sleep as one drop of water is to another. It is merely the idea that we shall not wake up again which gives us pain." Now, those were BIG WORDS. Who, we ask, was the writer? It was VOLTAIRE; and when his turn came to die we ought to have found him putting them into practice—*despising death*, and treating it as a mere sleep, and nothing more. Was it so? His physician tells us how this man died. He says: "When I compare the death of a righteous man, which is like the close of a beautiful day, with that of Voltaire, I see the difference between bright, serene weather and a black thunder-storm. It was my lot that this man should die under my hands. Often I told him the truth; no one else, unhappily, did so. 'Yes, my friend,' he would say, 'you are the only person who has given me good advice. Had I followed it, I should not be in the horrible condition in which I am. I have swallowed *nothing but* SMOKE; I have intoxicated myself with the incense which turned my head. You can do nothing more for me; *send me a mad doctor.* Have compassion on me, I am mad.' I cannot think of it without shuddering." From this moment madness took possession of his soul —death was constantly before his eyes. Think of the ravings of Orestes. He died under the torments of the Furies." In this way died the apostle of UNBELIEF.

Look on that picture, and on this:

Another man, with whose writings and opinions of death we are all familiar, wrote these words: "Whether we live, we live unto the Lord, or whether we die, we die unto the Lord: so that living or dying we are the Lord's." Again, we say, those are brave words, bold words; and again we inquire, How did the man die who wrote them? Did the author of them put them into practice when death stared him in the face? Yes. Hear his last *written* words: "*I am* READY to be offered up, and the time of my departure is at hand. I have fought the good fight, I have finished my course, I have kept the faith; henceforth there is laid up for me a crown of righteousness." And in the strength of that faith he met his end. One day he was called forth from his prison; he marched to the scaffold; the headsman's axe fell flashing in the bright Italian sun; and the head of Paul, the apostle of Jesus Christ, rolled at the feet of the Roman executioner.

(c)

DEATH, THE LAST ENEMY (1 Cor. xv. 26)

Lastly, death, the enemy, shall be destroyed. This enemy is destroyed when the resurrection is complete. By this event the power of death is for ever annulled, and there is no such thing more as dying or being dead.

(d)   *Lange*

DEATH AND LIFE

" Verily, verily, I say unto you, He that heareth My word, and believeth on Him that sent Me, hath everlasting life, and shall not come into condemnation; but is passed from death unto life" (John v. 24).

"And this is life eternal, that they might know Thee the only true God, and Jesus Christ, whom Thou hast sent" (John xvii. 17).

"He that hath 'the Son hath life; and he that hath not the Son of God hath not life" (1 John v. 12).

"Whosoever liveth and believeth on Me hath eternal life" (John ix. 26).

Four thoughts suggested:

(i.) There is a spiritual condition in which we may be placed, which our Lord calls "death"; and there is also a spiritual condition in which we may be placed, which our Lord calls "life."

(ii.) This "life," according to the Saviour's description, consists in the knowledge of God.

(iii.) The transference from the first condition to the second, from "death" to "life," is effected by believing on Christ, and thus becoming possessed of Him. "He that hath the Son hath life."

(iv.) For him who thus believes in Christ, death, as it is commonly understood, has no real terrors. Death is no interruption to the continuity of the man's existence, it is merely a change for the better, an introduction into the blessedness of a higher development and of a nobler mode of life.

Let us take these four thoughts in succession.

(a)　　　　　　　　　*Gordon Calthrop*

DEATH NOT ANNIHILATION

1. Great stress has been laid by some present-day students of Holy Scripture upon the literal interpretation of such terms as death and destruction. "Death," they say, means death; "destruction" means destruction—the absolute annihilation and crushing out of existence of the thing, or person, described as being the subject of it. And, consequently, when the Bible speaks of the destroying or death of the finally impenitent, it teaches us to believe that, by the putting forth of Almighty Power, the impenitent will be made as though they had not been; and God's creation will be purged of evil by the sweeping away into nothingness of all those personages in whom evil inheres. "But," we ask, "if this be so, how are we to understand the language of our Lord before us?" Just look at it. Christ speaks of persons—persons actually existing upon earth—who are in a condition which He denominates "death," but who may, under certain circumstances, pass into another condition which He denominates "life." That is perfectly clear. "Death," then, according to Christ, is not annihilation but a mode of existence. A man may be alive in the ordinary sense of the word—may be in the enjoyment of sensitive, of intellectual, of social existence, may be occupied busily in worldly affairs, may go in and out amongst his fellows and be held in reputation amongst them, and yet, according to Christ, may be all the while in a condition of "death." What, then, can "death" mean? for clearly it cannot mean ceasing to exist. It means the state of a man who is destitute of spiritual life because he is separated from God—the great, the only source

and fountain-head of that inestimable blessing. In such a case as this, the nature of the man is perverted. His faculties are turned away from their right end. His affections are devoted to the wrong objects. He is becoming gradually worse and more unfit for the great purpose for which he was created—more and more antagonistic in heart to the purity and holiness and goodness of the Divine Being. That is what Christ means. The man lives in a state of "death"—incipient death if you like—death in its germ, but a death which will develop, if unchecked, into the miseries and horrors of eternal perdition.

(b)　　　　　　　　　　*Ibid*

ETERNAL LIFE AND ETERNAL DEATH

This view you will find enforced and corroborated by our second thought. Christ informs us of the nature of "eternal life." And what is it? Is it never-ending existence? No, the existence is pre-supposed—*it is a mode of existence.* Life eternal, He says, is to know God, the only true God, as manifested in Jesus Christ whom He hath sent. By knowing God, we do not, of course, understand the bare intellectual comprehension of His character, and acceptance of His claims, for that is perfectly compatible with a career of worldliness, or indifference, or sin. To "know God," is to have a personal acquaintance with Him which shall enter into the thoughts and colour the life; to be in sympathy and harmony with Him—standing on His side—hating what He hates, and approving what He approves; to make Him the supreme centre and object to which everything tends; and to find in Him a satisfaction and repose of soul which we cannot hope to find in any other quarter. Possessed of this "knowledge," we are in possession of eternal life. Now, does it not seem fair to conclude that if to know God be "eternal life," the opposite of the knowledge of God must be the opposite of eternal life? In other words—that the condition of "death" must be,—not a state of annihilation, but a state in which God is so misrepresented to the mind—so misunderstood—that He is recoiled from and hated, and the soul is filled with antipathy and antagonism to His nature. The conclusion seems inevitable. *Eternal life* is not, as we have seen, mere existence, it is existence under certain conditions. And similarly, *eternal death* is existence under certain other and opposite conditions. And if to "know God" be "eternal life," to be and to remain in ignorance of Him, and in alienation from His nature and His will—must be "eternal death."

(c)　　　　　　　　　　*Ibid*

THE MODE OF TRANSITION

We consider the transition and the mode of transition from the one spiritual condition to the other. "He that believeth on Me," says Christ, "hath everlasting life." "He that hath the Son hath life." In these statements—and they might be almost indefinitely multiplied—the bridge which carries us over from one state to the other, the power which translates us from death unto life—is said to be belief, simply belief. We have but to accept the testimony which God hath given us concerning His son, and then we pass at once into the light and blessedness of the eternal

(d)

kingdom and enter into fellowship with Christ and with those who belong to Him. We come by that act of transition to the " Heavenly Jerusalem, and to the innumerable company of angels, to the general assembly and Church of the first-born, which are written in Heaven, and to God the judge of all, and to the spirits of just men made perfect."

(a)   *Gordon Calthrop*

Yes, but consider what this simple belief involves. A man says to me—" I believe in Jesus Christ. I am no infidel. I am constantly reciting the clauses of the Apostles' Creed, and I heartily accept and endorse every one of them. Don't tell me that I don't believe !" " But," I reply, " what is the practical result and outcome of this belief of yours ? What influence does it exert on your daily life ? Are you consecrated to Christ ? Are you living by Him and for Him ? Is He the example you imitate, the Master you obey, the rule by which you guide yourself, the centre to which everything is referred ? Does Christ enter into your thoughts, your feelings, your practice, and permeate and pervade your whole being, so that you can say—well, in some feeble but real way, say it with a painful feeling of manifold inconsistencies, and *yet say it*—' To me to live is Christ' ?" The man stares at me. " I don't know what you mean," he says. " I am a Christian as other people are Christians. I believe in Christ, and should be ashamed not to believe in Him ; but what you have been talking about—this consecration to Christ, this living by Christ—is simply, as far as I can see, unintelligible nonsense. I suppose it is right for you to say such things—you are a clergyman ; but to me they have no meaning whatever. I believe in Christ as the greater part of people I meet with believe in Christ, but nothing more." Very well then. I do not say that such a belief is utterly valueless. It is better than nothing. It may lead on to something better and higher. But I do say that it is not the belief of which our Lord speaks as bringing a man over the chasm from darkness to light, from death unto life, from the power of Satan to the brightness and glory of the Kingdom of God. It fact, it is an incomplete, a one-sided belief. It touches the intellect, it does not touch the heart. It does not lay its hand upon the whole being of the man. The faith which saves, is the acceptance of the entire testimony of the Spirit concerning Jesus Christ, and that " entire testimony " comprises the statement which our friend seems to have ignored—that men are lost and ruined without Jesus Christ— that in Him and Him alone can they have restoration to the Divine image and the favour of God ; and that those who are partakers of His salvation are, by that very fact, so united, so attached, so interwoven—if I may so speak—with Jesus Christ, that Christ liveth in them ; and that they no longer live unto themselves, but unto Him who died for them and rose again. Add to this, that this faith in question is the gift of God—the result of the working of the Spirit of God in the soul ; and then you will be able to understand—in part at least—by what means the great transition is effected, and how we become possessed of eternal life, because we are possessed of the Son of God. " He that hath the Son hath life."

(b)   *Ibid*

DEATH ROBBED OF ITS TERRORS

We are told that for those who are true disciples of Christ, true believers in His name—death has no terrors. There may be—nay, there is—something terrible about dying. Say what you will, the act of dissolution is unspeakably distressing. For the young to be arrested by the chill grasp of death, and to be hurried away into the unseen, to be separated from the activities and affections of life, to be called upon to give up everything, to drop their work, to lay aside their ambitions, to unloose their hold upon legitimate occupations, to quit their friends and those they love, and to sink into the cold and cheerless grave, " saying to corruption, Thou art my father, and to the worm, Thou art my mother and my sister,"—all this is no trifle ! *But dying is one thing and the state of death is another ;* and this state of death is not formidable to the believer. Why not ? Because death for him is nothing more than the dark transit into another and a better world. The Christian who dies, passes from the realm of shadows into the Kingdom of light—from conflict to rest—from God, seen in type and emblem, to God, seen as He is in the splendour of His own essential beauty. In fact, the Christian's death is a birth into the fulness of life. " He that believeth on Me shall never die."

(c)   *Ibid*

DEATH, IN THE MIDST OF LIFE WE ARE IN

Death finds us 'mid our playthings—snatches us, as a cross nurse might do a wayward child, from all our toys and baubles. His rough call unlooses all our favourite ties on earth ; and well if they are such as may be answered in yonder world, where all is judged of truly.

(d)   *Old Play ; and see Seneca, Epi. xxiii.*

On this side and on that, men see their friends drop off like leaves in autumn.

(e)   *Blair*

DEATH, GOD'S FRIENDLY MESSENGER

Death did not strike Adam, the first sinful man, nor Cain, the first hypocrite, but Abel, the innocent and righteous. The first soul that met with death overcame death ; the first soul that parted from earth went to heaven. Death argues not displeasure, because he whom God loved best dies first, and the murderer is punished with living.

(f)   *Bishop Hall*

DEATH AND MORALITY

The times at Rome under the early Cæsars, were days, not to live in, but to die in. All sorts of people,—rich men, philosophers, nobles,—felt them so, and acted on the feeling. The cause needs little explanation ; it is clear that morality was (so far as human rulers could compass it) simply annihilated. The early Roman empire is one orgy of wine, wickedness, and blood. We see in it what orgies do for mankind. . . Will such times ever come again ? It would be rash to prophesy. Before Rome was ultimately demoralized, the Saviour of Mankind had dashed Himself against the world of wicked men, and they had cast Him out and

(g)

killed Him. Suppose religion,—not revealed religion only, but natural religion also,—should be hated and cast out of men: suppose the very thought of immortality and retribution denied and vilipended, would not this new putting truth to an open shame bring back the old tale of sensuality and of sin ? Then must all incense to God be extinguished ; then must man cease to be manlike, and become simply bestial. Then would death once more become man's solitary refuge.

   (*a*)   *W. Jackson's Bampton Lectures*

DEATH OF A YOUNG MOTHER.

        . . . She made a sign
To bring her babe; 'twas brought and by her
     placed.
She looked upon its face that neither smiled
Nor wept, nor knew who gazed upon't, and laid
Her hand upon its little breast, and sought
For it with look that seemed to penetrate
The heavens—unutterable blessings—such
As God to dying parents only granted,
For infants left behind them in the world :
"God help my child !" we heard her say, and
     heard
No more : the Angel of the Covenant
Had come, and faithful to his promise stood
Prepared to walk with her through death's dark
     vale.
And now her eyes grew bright, and brighter still,
Too bright for ours to look upon, suffused
With many tears and closed without a cloud
They set as sets the morning star, which goes
Not down behind the darkened west, nor hides
Obscured among the tempests of the sky,
But melts away into the light of heaven.

   (*b*)   *Pollock*

DEATH, NATURAL

It is as natural to die as to be born ; and to a little infant, perhaps, the one is as painful as the other.

   (*c*)   *Bacon*

DEATH AND NATURE

Death is the tyranny of nature over human nature. The destruction of death—the assertion of a victorious life—is the defeat of the physical world, and the triumph of humanity. And all real progress towards the final consummation of our race can only be effected by a gradual and growing realization of this transcendent principle of life.

A bird, after issuing from its shell, puts on an outgrowth of perfected plumage, and becomes winged for distant flights. So within the soul of man there may be (and probably are) *latent* powers and senses capable of what we should now call superhuman development.

   (*d*)   *W. Jackson's Bampton Lectures*

DEATH, NIHILISM, AND MORALITY (John xi. 26)

We are *Persons*, not automata,—*Beings*, not things. . . . The problem of Nihilism has its complete solution in the realism of *absolute* Morality. Were we less than beings—could we in any way divest ourselves of our personality, we should cease to be *responsible*. The Law of Retribution must become a dissolving view, a mirage, a

Fata Morgana. Life ceases to be real or earnest. Its stream = a current foaming and frothing in darkness, we ourselves even as shadows or bubbles on its surface. Who, then, could say to each of us, "Be strong and of good courage, thou bubble ! Walk in the light of immortality, thou shadow ! . . . Soon must the poet's words be true of thee—

     "Like the dew on the mountain,
         Like the foam on the river ;
        Like the bubble on the fountain,
          Thou art gone, and for ever ! "

Contrast with these dark enigmas the clear, strong answer of Morality. Man's true being is *real*, amidst a life of enduring realities. And he who truly lives shall never really die.

   (*e*)   *Ibid*

DEATH, PAIN OF

The sense of death is most in apprehension ;
And the poor beetle that we tread upon,
In corporal sufferance feels a pang as great
As when a giant dies.

   (*f*)   *Shakspeare*

DEATH AND PRAISE

Death of Sarah Martin, the Yarmouth Prison Visitor :—

A friend asked, "*What shall I read ?*"
Her answer was, "PRAISE."
The friend asked, "*Are there no clouds ?*"
"NONE," she replied ; "HE NEVER HIDES HIS FACE. *It is our sins which cause the cloud between Him and us*: HE IS ALL LOVE, ALL LIGHT."

   (*g*)

DEATH, AND THE PREACHER.

In a visit which I once made, when a young clergyman, to the churches of Belgium, so remarkable for the grandeur and elaborate carving of their pulpits, my attention was especially attracted by one well suited to enforce a solemn lesson on every one who might occupy it. There arose from the back of it a gigantic figure of death, stretching its gaunt skeleton form over the head of the preacher, and holding in one hand a scythe, and with the other presenting a scroll on which was inscribed, "Hasten thou to gather in thy harvest, for I must soon reap mine."

   (*h*)   *Bp. Bayley (Durham)*

DEATH AND PREACHING

Death does always stand at the preacher's elbow.

"I preach as if I ne'er should preach again ;
    And as a dying man to dying men."

   (*i*)   *Baxter*

DEATH, SEEMING REMOTENESS OF

The hour concealed, and so remote the fear,
Death still draws nearer, never seeming near.

   (*j*)   *Pope*

DEATH AND SALVATION, ILLUSTRATED BY THE PARABLE OF THE BRIDGE :

There was once a beautiful city which stood upon the slope of a hill ; it could be seen from a great distance, and the fame of it was such that many people came from far to admire it, as well as to talk with its inhabitants, who were said to be a very wise race of men, skilful in all the arts of life, and constantly making new and great inventions.

One evening, a long time ago, a stranger came to this city. He had travelled a long way, and seemed weary, but he had heard so much of the city and its wise inhabitants, that he allowed himself little time for rest before he set out to inspect the streets, and admire the large squares with their long lines of overshadowing trees, the fountains springing up and tumbling into their deep marble basins, the tall graceful spires, and the clear windows shadowed with sweeping curtains, and filled with flowering plants.

The more he saw, the more he was delighted. The city was as beautiful as he had expected, and the people were wise and kind. Some of them were rich, and had houses like palaces ; others were poor : but the rich were very good, and had built schools for their children, where they taught them the peculiar learning of the place, with various arts and trades, by which the boys soon learned to get their own living, and the girls to practise needlework and other useful arts, besides which they had them instructed in the laws which had been made by the King ; and so well were the children taught on this point, that many of them knew as much about the King and his laws as their richer neighbours who had founded these schools.

The stranger thought this such a pleasant city that he wished to remain in it for a while that he might observe the manners of the people, and how they employed themselves. So he went about from day to day, and observed how industrious the men were—how they built houses and wove cloth, dug wells and made bread—and how the women spun and knitted, and took care of their children and of their houses. He was pleased, too, to see the children going so regularly to their schools ; and when their tasks were over, he often followed them into the meadows to see how happy they were, gathering flowers and playing about in the long grass.

"This town of yours seems a very good place to live in ? " he said, one day, to a man who was weaving a basket.

"So it would be," said the man, looking up thoughtfully, " if it were not for the river."

"What river ? " asked the stranger. "I have not seen or heard of any river."

"Why, no," replied the man, "I dare say not, for it runs a little way out of the city, and we have planted some trees in that direction that we may not see it ; you will not often hear it mentioned, for in fact we do not consider it good breeding to allude to it."

"But what harm does it do to the town ? " asked the stranger.

"I don't wish to say much about it," replied the man, " it is a very painful subject : but the truth is, our King, whom you may have heard of, lives a long way off, on the other side of the river, and sooner or later he sends for all here to cross over. We shall certainly all have to cross before long. The King sends messengers for us ; there is scarcely a day in which some one is not sent for."

"But are they obliged to go ? " asked the stranger.

"Oh, yes ; they must go," replied the man, "for the King is very powerful. If he were to send for me to-day, I could not wait even to finish my work. Sometimes he sends for our wives or our children, and the messenger never waits till we are ready."

"What sort of a country is it on the other side of the river ? " asked the stranger. "Is it as pleasant as it is here ? "

"The river is so wide that we cannot see across it distinctly," said the man ; "and when our friends and relations are once gone over, they never come back to tell us how it fares with them there. But yet every one here is agreed, and the highest evidence confirms it, that the country across the river is a far better one than this. The air is so pure that it heals all their diseases : besides, there is no such thing as poverty or trouble, and the King is very good to them, and so is His Son."

"Well, then," said the stranger, "if the country be so fine, I do not see why you should think it such a misfortune to have to go to it, particularly as you are to see there all your parents, and children, and friends who have gone there before you. Why are you so much afraid to cross the river ? "

The man did not answer at first ; he seemed to be thinking of his work : at length he looked up and said—" When any of our friends are sent for, we always say they are gone over into that beautiful country ; but, to tell you the truth, this river is so extremely deep and wide, and it rushes along so swiftly——"

"Well ? " said the stranger.

"I don't mind telling you," replied the man, " as you do not know much of these parts, that I think it very doubtful whether many of those who have to plunge in can get to the opposite side at all. I am afraid the strong tide carries some of them down till they are lost. Besides, sometimes they are sent for in the dark, and, as I said before, the messenger never waits till we are ready."

"Indeed ! " said the stranger ; "in that case, so far from envying these people, I wonder to see them looking so happy and so unconcerned. I should have thought they would have been so anxious lest the messenger should come. Pray cannot your friends help you over ? "

The man shook his head. " We have made a great many rafts at different times," he said, in a doubtful tone, " but they all went whirling down the stream, and were wrecked. We began a bridge, too, and it cost us incredible labour, but we could never make it reach beyond the middle of the river."

"Then," said the stranger, " are there no ships to convey you over : must you needs plunge alone and unhelped into those dark, deep waters ? "

"I am not learned in these matters," said the man, evidently uneasy, " and I do not pretend to be wiser than my betters, who generally think this a disagreeable subject, and one that we should not trouble ourselves about more than we can help."

"But if you must all go ? " said the stranger.

"I am a working man," replied the basket-maker, interrupting him, " and I really have no time to talk to you any further. If you want to

(a)

know anything more about this, you had better go and speak to that man whom you see talking to that group of children. It is his business to teach people how to get over the river, but I have not time to attend to him. I dare say, when my time comes, I shall get across as well as my neighbours.''

So the stranger went up to this man who had been pointed out to him, and inquired whether he could tell him anything about the dreadful river.

"Certainly," said the man; "I shall be very glad to tell you anything you wish to know. It is my duty: I am one of the ambassadors of the King's Son. If you will come with me a little way out of the town, I will show you the river."

So he led him over several green hills, and down into a deep valley, till they came to the edge of a whirling, hurrying torrent, deep and swollen. It moved along with such a thundering noise, that the stranger shuddered and said—

"I hope, sir, it is not true that all the people in the city are obliged to cross this river?"

"Yes, it is quite true," answered the man.

"Poor people!" said the stranger, "none of them can strive against such a stream as this: no doubt they are all borne away by the force of the torrent. Do you think any man could swim over here in safety?"

"No," said the man, looking very sorrowful, "it is quite impossible, and we should all be lost if it were not for the Bridge."

"THE BRIDGE!" exclaimed the stranger, very much surprised. "No one told me there was a bridge."

"Oh, yes," replied the man; "there is a bridge a short distance higher up; it was built by the King's Son, and by means of it we can pass in perfect safety."

"What! may you all pass?" asked the stranger eagerly.

"Yes, all. The bridge is perfectly free, and is the only way of reaching the country beyond. All who try to swim over, or cross any other way, will certainly be lost for ever."

"Sir," said the stranger, "if this be the case, I must hasten back to the city, and tell the people, that no more of them be lost in these swelling waters."

"You may certainly do so if you please," replied the man, "but know first that all the people have been duly informed of the bridge. My brethren and myself spend nearly all our time in telling them of the goodness of the King's Son, and how neither He nor His Father is willing that any should perish; but their pride is very great."

"What! so great that they would rather die than use the bridge?" asked the stranger in astonishment.

"Some of them have built up works of their own," replied the man, "which they think are strong enough to bear them over into the King's country; others say they do not believe there is but one way of getting over; and some men throw themselves headlong into the flood, saying they do not believe there is such a provision, or at least that it was not meant for them. But, as I told you before, it is perfectly free, and the voice of the King's Son may sometimes be heard calling to the people over the flood, and inviting them to come to Him; for, strange as it may seem to you, He loves them, though they are so backward to believe that He means them well."

"What!" interrupted the stranger, "does not the King's Son repent of what He has done? is He not sorry that He built a bridge for such a thankless race?"

"No," said the man; "though they slight His offers of safety, He still sends ambassadors to call them to Him, even at the very brink of the river. Nay, He often Himself visits them, and by night, when all is still, He comes to their doors and knocks; if any man will open to Him, He will enter and sup with him. He will tell him how He has loved our nation, and what He has done for our sake; for indeed it cost Him very dear to build that bridge, but now it stands stronger than a rock."

Now, when the stranger heard this, he wondered greatly at the ingratitude and foolishness of these people; and, as he turned away, I went up to the ambassador, and ventured to ask him the name of that city, and the country it stood in.

But it startled me beyond measure when he told me the name of that country; for it had the same name as my own!

(a)   *Jean Ingelow*

DEATH A FEARFUL SIGHT

O God! it is a fearful thing
To see the human soul take wing.

(b)   *Byron*

DEAD IN SIN

These wretched ones, who *never were alive.*
(c)   *Dante's Inferno*

DEATH, SWIFTNESS OF

Oh that you could but see what haste death makes, though yet it have not overtaken you! No post so swift! No messenger more sure! As sure as the sun will be with you in the morning, though it hath many thousands and hundreds of thousands of miles to go in the night, so sure will death be quickly with you.

(d)   *Baxter*

DEATH, THE KING OF TERRORS

"Wa, Wa," as the wild Clotaire groaned out, when life was departing, "what great God is this, that pulls down the strength of the strongest kings?"

(e)   *Carlyle*

DEATH, UNPREPARED FOR

When I lived, I provided for everything but death; now I must die, and am unprepared.
(f)   *Cæsar Borgia*

DEATH, VICTIMS OF

I ne'er forsooth could have believed it true, that death had slain such myriads of mankind.
(g)   *Dante's Inferno*

DEATH-BED OF DAVID BRAINERD

"Oh, the glorious time is now coming! I have longed to serve God perfectly: now God will gratify those desires!"
(h)

"I am almost in eternity; I long to be there. My work is done; I have done with all my friends; all the world is nothing to me. I long to be in heaven, praising and glorifying God with the holy angels; all my desire is to glorify God." . . . He said, that "the consideration of the day of death, and the day of judgment, had a long time been peculiarly sweet to him." . . . "Come, Lord Jesus, come quickly. Oh, why is His chariot so long in coming?"

He found an inexpressible love to those whom he looked upon as belonging to Christ, "It seemed like a little piece of heaven to have one of them near him."

"Oh, that dear book (the Bible); that lovely book! I shall soon see it opened: the mysteries that are in it, and the mysteries of God's providence, will all be unfolded. . . . He will come, He will not tarry—I shall soon be in glory—I shall soon glorify God with the angels."

(a)   *Pres. Edward's Life of Brainerd*

Death-bed of Charles IX

The massacre of St. Bartholomew took place in his reign. His singular death has been regarded by the Huguenots as an interposition of Divine justice : he died bathed in his blood, which burst from his veins. Charles, however, was a mere instrument in the hands of his mother, the cruel Catherine of Medicis. . . . Two days before his death, the king asked his physician to relieve his pains, "for I am cruelly and horridly tormented." The doctor told him that whatever depended on them had been tried, but that God only could be the sovereign physician in such complaints. "I believe," said the king, "that what you say is true." Orders were given that all should withdraw except three, one of whom was his Huguenot nurse. She approached his bed softly, and the king, shedding tears plentifully, said, "Ah, my dear nurse, my beloved woman, what blood! what murders! Ah, I have followed wicked advice! O my God! pardon me and be merciful. I know not where I am, they have made me so perplexed and agitated. How will all this end? What shall I do? I am lost for ever! I know it." Then the nurse thus addressed him: —"Sire, be the murders on those who forced you to order them; your majesty could not help it; and since you never consented, and now regret them, believe God will never impute them to you, and will cover them with the mantle of justice of His Son, to whom alone you should look for aid. Ah! for the honour of God, let your majesty cease from this weeping." Charles, having taken a handkerchief from her, made a sign that she should retire and leave him to repose.

(b)   *Disraeli's Cur. of Lit*

Death-bed of a Christian

Is that a *death-bed* where a Christian dies?
Yes; *but not his*—"'tis Death itself that dies."

(c)   *Coleridge*

Death-bed Experience

An infidel, on his death-bed, felt himself adrift in the terrible surges of doubt and uncertainty. Some of his friends urged him to hold on to the end. He replied, "I have no objection to holding on; but will you tell me by what I am to hold on?"

(d)

Death-bed Experience, A Remarkable

"*If ye believe not that I am He, ye shall die in your sins*" (John viii. 24).

This truth was illustrated in a remarkable manner towards the beginning of this century. A nobleman and statesman in his last illness sent for a clergyman of his acquaintance, and said to him :—

"I feel very ill, and I fear I must make up my mind to die, and so I wish very much that you would talk with me on religious topics; but, to prevent unnecessary trouble, I may as well forewarn you that I will not listen to anything about Jesus Christ."

"It is well," replied the clergyman, "that you have made that declaration, as otherwise most assuredly *He* would have been the chief subject of my conversation with you: however there are various other edifying topics on which I can enlarge, and to begin, I beg to know if you will permit me to speak to you concerning God?"

"Oh, assuredly, yes," replied the sick nobleman, "I shall listen with great readiness to all you say about God, for I have ever looked up to the Supreme Being with the highest veneration."

"So far, then, we are at one," said the preacher, who at once began to dwell on the LOVE of God to man; and the subject was so agreeable to his patient that he desired an early repetition of his visit.

On the next occasion the clergyman was eagerly welcomed by the sick man, who asked with much interest what new theme was to be brought forward for his mental enjoyment, adding, "I assure you I have longed for your return."

The clergyman this time discoursed on the *wisdom*, the *omnipotence*, and the *omniscience* of God; and these perfections, though calculated to suggest feelings of *awe*, still did not produce any painful impression on the blunted conscience of his hearer.

On his third visit, the preacher enlarged on the *spotless* holiness of God, and, as its sequence, that so pure and holy a nature must necessarily debar all other than pure and holy beings from His presence.

Whilst on the fourth occasion he treated of God's *inflexible justice*. Under these the sick man began to wince; and at length, unable to refrain any longer, cried out—"*Hold, Sir! hold;*—THIS is more than I can bear: if the *Almighty* be *really so holy*, and *so just*, as you describe Him, why *I am lost*—I cannot hope to come into His presence."

His faithful visitor made him *no* reply, but by a *bow* of acquiescence took his departure.

Another and another day came and went, but no clergyman appeared at the bedside of the sick man; but on the third day, unable to wait any longer, the nobleman sent for him, and eagerly asked why he had stayed away so long. "My mind," said he, "is in a chaos of doubt and terror, it is as if I were already in hell—or a hell in me. For God's sake, say something to relieve me if you can, and restore the quietude of my mind of which your discourses have robbed me. Surely you can mitigate some of the harsh assertions you have made, or suggest some topic of consolation."

"Verily," replied the clergyman, "I dare not unsay one word that I have spoken to you; but I must continue solemnly to maintain that the Lord God

(e)

with whom we have to do, is, although a gracious and merciful, *likewise* a *wise*, a *holy*, and a *just* Being, who must of necessity both condemn and punish the wicked; and though I could, most assuredly, tell you several glorious and consoling truths, yet, *as you* are resolved *not* to hear them, I have no choice but to leave you to linger on in this most unhappy state of mind, until death shall introduce you to your fate on the other side of time. And so, though my heart bleeds for you, I can do nothing for you, since you yourself forbade my offering consolation."

" *Oh, no, no!* " exclaimed the dying man, in agony, " tell me whatever you think can possibly help me; tell me at least whether you know of any way of escape which yet remains open to me! "

"Most assuredly I do," was the reply, "but then you must suffer me to speak of Jesus Christ."

"Well then," said the sufferer, "speak what you will and of whom you will, but show me a door of escape from this damnation begun already."

Then gladly did the clergyman "*preach unto him Jesus.*" He told of the glad tidings of the Gospel—the atoning sacrifice of that Saviour whom the *now* trembling sinner had so long despised and rejected, but who nevertheless was his Redeemer, and to whom even now, at the eleventh hour, he might confidently turn.

Greedily the dying man drank in those words of hope. He sought and found comfort, through faith in Him who came not to call the righteous, but sinners to repentance. He learnt to know Jesus as the *Way*, the *Truth*, and the *Life*, that in Him God's justice and mercy have met together— and that through Him "God can be just and yet the justifier of him that believeth."

(*a*)   "*Sunday at Home*"

Death-bed, A Wonderful Reasoner

A death-bed is a wonderful reasoner , many a proud infidel hath it humbled and refuted without a word, who but a short time before would have defied all the ability of man to shake the foundation of his system. All is well as long as the curtain is up, and the puppet-show of life goes on; but when the rapid representation draws to a close, and every hope of longer respite is precluded, things will appear in a very different light. Would to God I could say that that great and awful moment were as often distinguished by the dawn of repentance as by the groan of despair!

(*b*)   *Robert Boyle*

Death-bed Repentance

The devil was sick, the devil a monk would be; The devil was well, the devil a monk was he.

(*c*)   *Rabelais*

Death-bed and Thoughtlessness

Every act is a foundation-stone of future conduct, and every imagination a fountain of life or death! Be thoughtless in any after years rather than in youth,—though indeed there is only one place where a man may be nobly thoughtless, —his death-bed. No thinking should ever be left to be done there.

(*d*)   *John Ruskin*

Death : He Died for Me

In the cemetery at Nashville, Tennessee, a stranger was seen planting a flower over a soldier's grave. When asked: "Was your son buried there? " "No." "A brother? " "No." "A relation? " "No." After a moment, the stranger laid down a small board which he held in his hand, and said: "Well, I will tell you. When the war broke out, I was a farmer in Illinois. I wanted to enlist, but I was poor. I had a wife and seven children. I was drafted I had no money to hire a substitute, and so I made up my mind that I must leave my poor, sickly wife and little children, and go and fight the enemy. After I was all ready to go, a young man, whom I knew, came to me and said: ' You have a large family, which your wife cannot take care of. I will go for you.' He did go in my place, and in the battle of Chickamauga he was wounded, and taken to Nashville Hospital ; but, after a long sickness, he died, and was buried here. Ever since, I have wanted to come to Nashville and see his grave, and so I saved up all the spare money I could, and yesterday I came on, and to-day found my dear friend's grave."

With tears of gratitude running down his cheeks he took up the small board and pressed it down into the ground, in the place of a tombstone. Under the soldier's name were written only these words : " He died for me."

Could there have been a more eloquent epitaph than that? Did it not tell the whole story? And can we ever think rightly of Christ, if we leave out of the account that crowning act of His love—His resisting unto blood for our sakes?

(*e*)

Death : Dying

God respects not so much after what manner we die, as what manner of death we die.

(*f*)   *Augustine*

Is this dying? How have I dreaded as an enemy this smiling friend !

(*g*)   *Dr. Goodwin*

I feed on manna. Oh for arms to embrace Him ! Oh for a well-tuned harp.

(*h*)   *S. Rutherford*

DEBTS

God is our Creditor, we His debtors.

(i.) He is omniscient, we cannot conceal a debt from Him ;

(ii.) He is Almighty, He can exact the debt by force ;

(iii.) He is just, He will and must be paid ;

(iv.) He is Omnipresent, none can escape Him.

(*i*)   *Starke*

DECISION, WANT OF

Men first make up their minds (and the smaller the mind the sooner made up), and then seek for the reasons ; and if they chance to stumble upon a good reason, of course they do not reject it. But though they are right, they are only right by chance.

(*j*)   *Whately*

DECLENSION

"All nations shall say, Wherefore hath the Lord done thus unto this land? what meaneth the heat of this great anger? Then men shall say, Because they have forsaken the covenant of the Lord God of their fathers, which He made with them when He brought them forth out of the land of Egypt," etc. (Deut. xxix. 24, 25).

The consequences which Moses here foretold, as the result of the religious defection of the people, were such as no human wisdom could foresee, or experience suggest. The practice of idolatry did not prevent the aggrandisement of ancient Rome; nor any mere statesman insure the accomplishment of a prophecy that military success should *always* attend the worship of the one true God, and that military discomfiture should *always* follow idolatry. It is evident that Moses derived his accurate knowledge of futurity from immediate inspiration of God.

(a) *Annotated Paragraph Bible*

DECREES, DIVINE

By the doctrine of Divine decrees we mean, that God from eternity purposed or determined so to constitute and govern the universe as to make it certain that all events would take place precisely as they do take place.

(b) *D. T. Fiske*

Decrees and Presence of God

I like better to think of God's presence than His decrees. Decrees make me think of dead parchments and a dim unknown past; His presence is that of a living, loving Father, and on that my heart can rest. To His decrees I must submit. His presence makes me pray. The thought of His immutable foreordaining closes my heart in silent reverence. The thought of His now to-day living and listening and caring for me, opens my heart in trustful communion and entreaty. I think of Him, not as immutable, irresistible will, but as unquenchable love. I think of His hand, not as engraving unchangeable decrees in some inconceivable past, but as feeding the ravens and binding up the broken heart to-day.

(c) *Schönberg Cotta Series*

Decrees and Purposes of God

I learn by inevitable inference from the distinctive articles of my creed, that as certainly as the dynasty of the fish was predetermined in the scheme of Providence to be succeeded by the higher dynasty of the reptile, and that again by the still higher dynasty of the mammal, so it was equally predetermined that the dynasty of responsible fallible man should be succeeded by the dynasty of glorified, immortal man. . . . I feel my grasp of a doctrine first taught me by our Calvinistic catechism at my mother's knee tightening instead of relaxing. "The decrees of God are His eternal purposes, according to the counsel of His will, whereby for His own glory He hath foreordained whatsoever comes to pass." And what I was told early I still believe. . . . The present state of things is simply one scene in a foreordained series, a scene intermediate in place between the age of the irresponsible mammal and of glorified man; and to provide for the upward passage to the ultimate state, we know that . . . He through whom the work of restoration has been effected was in reality what He is designated in the remarkable text, " The Lamb slain from the *foundations* of the world."

First, man in the *image of God*, next God in the *form of man*, have been equally from all eternity pre-determined actors in the same great scheme.

(d) *Hugh Miller*

DEISM AND SUPERSTITION

The last illness of Voltaire could not have excited wider interest than Victor Hugo's state. Every kind of social distinction continues to be represented in the visitors' book.

The Archbishop of Paris has written to express his sympathy, and to say that he invokes on behalf of the poet Saint Joseph, the patron of the dying. He also begged to say that if wished for he would gladly attend in his pastoral capacity, and offer the consolations of the Church.

At the beginning of his illness, Victor Hugo showed his short will to those around him. It ordained that he is to go to the grave in a pauper's hearse, that no priest is to officiate, and stated that he believes in God. This belief he has since verbally affirmed.

(e) *Daily News, Victor Hugo's last illness* (1885)

DEIST, A

Bolingbroke professed himself a Deist, believing in a general Providence, but doubting (though by no means rejecting) the immortality of the soul and future state.

Lord Chesterfield on Henry St. John, Earl of
(f) *Bolingbroke*

Sir, he was a scoundrel and a coward; a scoundrel for discharging a blunderbuss against religion and morality; a coward because he had not resolution to fire it off himself, but left half-a-crown to a beggarly Scotchman (Mallet) to draw the trigger after his death.

(g) *Dr. Johnson on the same*

Deist

Pope was a Deist, believing in a future state; this he has often owned to me; but when he died, he sacrificed a cock to Esculapius, and suffered the priests who got about him to perform all their absurd ceremonies on his body.

(h) *Lord Chesterfield on Pope*

DEGRADATION

That which renders men so unwilling to believe themselves capable of union with God, is but the sense of their own degradation. . . . I would gladly be informed, whence this creature, who acknowledges himself so weak, obtains the right to measure and limit the Divine mercy, as his own fancy suggests. Man understands so little the nature of God, that he understands not himself; and yet, troubled by the contemplation of his own conditio , he boldly pronounces, that it is beyond the power of God to qualify him for this connection.

(i) *Blaise Pascal*

DEGRADATION

Is it not wonderful that base desires should so extinguish in men the sense of their own excellency, as to make them willing that their souls should be like to the souls of beasts, mortal and corruptible with their bodies ?

(a)   *Hooker, Eccl. Pol*

DEJECTION AND DESPAIR

The more that sin and corruption grow, and the man becomes fully conscious of it, the more does *dejection* grow also ; and this changes at last into *despair*, which is a state of entire hopelessness, where all possibilities have vanished, all gates and ways are closed to a man. There is a despair for a hard fate ; and it not seldom happens, that a man, in consequence of a single severe stroke, makes a sudden leap from his natural state of security into a state of despair ; be it that he has lost a beloved human being, or his means, or in any other misfortune. Against this form of despair even heathenism had a remedy, viz., resignation, submission to the inevitable. But the deepest despair is when a man gives up hope, not merely for this or that which he called his own, but for *himself* as a moral being. There is one sustaining and saving power, viz., faith in God. Despair may, and should become the transition to salvation, if the man only despairs of himself, but does not give up his God. In the expression of entire inability, of deepest helplessness, " O wretched man that I am," etc., there is latent a hope of redemption—the hope that what is impossible with man is possible with God.

(b)   *Martensen*

DEJECTION AND LEVITY :

Dejection is a consequence of the arrested development of the good, of hindered freedom, as well as of the urgent requirement of the law, which weighs upon the soul like a burden ever growing heavier. As a fact, dejection is already present in a state of levity, and rests within like a background of care and anxiety, although the man is unconscious of it. In the midst of security it often asserts itself ; in the midst of light-hearted joy it breaks forth for a moment, and the man does not then himself know what makes him sad. He is sad and out of humour about—nothing ; that is, nothing definite. And this secret dejection does not proceed, as many think, from the state of the body, though this may contribute to it, but from *indwelling sin*, from the disturbance present in the deepest foundation of existence. And in this state the man experiences that dejection is the inseparable companion of sin.

(c)   *Ibid.*

DELAY, DANGER OF

There is danger in delay. The Prophet says, " Seek ye the Lord while He may be found, call ye upon Him while He is near." It is implied in this language that there is a time when the Lord cannot be found, and that perhaps when we want Him He may not be near, but far off, and out of our reach. I am suggesting to you an old thought, but kindly bear with it. There are spiritual opportunities which, if allowed to pass by unimproved, may never return. The promising young man in the Gospels had Christ offered to him, but

he turned away, and we never hear that the offer was made a second time. Sometimes (we believe) there comes a crisis in our lives upon which everything depends. Let it pass—well, we may live for years after it, but the heart is stiffened, the destiny is decided, the rejection is complete. There can be no repentance, no change, no conversion now. Do you not think it is so, brethren ? Do you not think that both Scripture and experience point to the fact ? And if so, how perilous, how terribly perilous it must be, to trifle with even one offer of salvation. Now, when preachers talk in this manner, I know what people often say. They say, " Ah ! there he is again, with his dismal prognostications. Can't he let us alone ? " Let me tell you an incident which occurred some years ago. In a fit of desperation a woman had taken a tremendous dose of laudanum. The thing being discovered in time, remedies were applied, and she was comparatively safe. But a fatal drowsiness came on ; and nothing could save her unless the tendency was resisted. Accordingly, two medical students, one of them a relation of my own, took her between them the whole night long, walked her up and down, backwards and forwards, through the corridors of the hospital. She pleaded, she expostulated, she entreated with tears to be let alone. She accused them of cruelty ; "Let me alone, let me sleep, oh, let me sleep." But they persisted, in spite of the appearance of unkindness, and she lived to thank them for their resolute perseverance and care. And just so the preacher persists in worrying those amongst us who are inclined to sink into the fatal torpor which leads to spiritual death. They say, " Don't worry me so ; let me alone." But he will not let them alone. He lifts up the prophet's warning, " Seek ye the Lord while He may be found, call ye upon Him while He is near." And if he succeeds, God helping him, in so arousing his hearers that they flee in earnest to Christ, I know that he will have their earnest thanks for the incessant alarms and the clamorous exhortations which he has sounded so importunately, so unfeelingly, as it seemed, in their ears.

(d)   *Gordon Calthrop*

DELAY, DANGER OF

A man asleep in a canoe on one of the North American rivers : they shout, fire guns—still he sleeps and is only awakened by the roar of the cataract—when it is too late ; and with a terrible shriek he is hurled down the awful cataract to destruction.

(e)

DELAY AND NATURE

Heb. ii. 3—How shall we escape, if we neglect so great salvation ? "

Nature teaches that neglect leads to deterioration, and that when God says, " *Let him alone,*" it is a most fearful judgment.

To " *neglect* " is to let things take their course.

Analogy.—Let a certain number of pigeons, of different colours and varieties, be collected, and carried to a desert island. Let them fly wild in the woods, and found a colony there. After the lapse of many years let the collector return to the island, when he will find the pigeons *all of one colour :* a black and white dun, or a dark slaty hue.

(f)

All the beautiful colours will have vanished. Why? Because they have been *neglected*. The variations and improvements had been the result of care, nurture, and domestication : neglect has simply had the effect of letting them drop into their original state. So with plants—a rose—a strawberry ; it is a natural law. So with man. By neglect, his body will lapse into a savage state ; his mind, to imbecility ; his conscience, to lawlessness and vice ; his soul, to atrophy, ruin, and decay. " Let him alone," and all the rest will follow.

(*a*) *From C. Darwin*

DELAY NOT

True Christian Charity will put on angels' wings, and will hasten with a seraph's step ; and will be like the heavenly messengers despatched by God to Lot in Sodom ; and will lay hold on the hands of those who linger, and will urge them forth from the door, and will chide their delay, and will exclaim,—" Arise ! what dost thou here ? Take all that thou hast, *lest thou be consumed* in the iniquity of this city."

(*b*) *Bishop Wordsworth*

DELAY NOT

" *Now is the accepted time* " (2 Cor. vi. 2)

A young man came to me and said, " I will delay no longer."

" I said, " That is a good determination. ' Behold, *now* is the accepted time,' " etc.

He replied, " Well, I don't know that that text is for me, because——"

" Yes, it IS for you."

" I was going to say, that I did not think I had got so far as that YET, as to think salvation is for me *now*."

" You TOLD me, that you were not going to *delay* any longer, and therefore I said, ' Now,' etc."

" But I don't wish to be in a HURRY."

" You *ought* to be in haste. David was. ' I made haste, and *delayed* not to keep Thy commandments.' "

" I don't think I am in a fit state of mind to come to Christ NOW."

" You said you were determined to put it off no longer."

" Why, I want to get READY."

" *Are you getting ready ?* "

" No."

" Then you don't believe that NOW is the accepted time."

" Yes, I do ; for the Bible says so."

" Then don't wait for *any other time*."

" I have not a sufficient sense of sin."

" Then it can't be the *accepted time*."

" I have not FAITH enough yet."

" Then it can't be the *accepted* time."

" Well, I am not READY."

" Then it can't be the accepted time."

" But it seems to me *too* quick."

" Then it can't be the accepted time, and the Bible has made a *mistake*."

" But my heart is not *prepared*."

" Then it is not the accepted time."

" What shall I do ? "

" Repent and believe now."

Then he confessed, " But it seems to me that I am not *prepared* to give up the world on so short a notice."

" That is your very *difficulty*. *You* are not prepared. You wish to put off repentance and conversion to *another time*. But the Bible says, ' Now is the accepted time,' so you and the Bible *disagree*."

" But it seems so hard to shut a man up to the *present time*."

" If you were a dying man, and had only an hour to live, you would not say so ; you would be glad to have the Bible telling you, *Now is the accepted time,*' instead of telling you to wait for a week or a month."

He went away to reflect, and saw the force of the simple argument ; and afterwards confessed that when he examined his heart on the matter, he found his reasons for *delay* sprang from an *unwillingness to be saved by Christ*. So we learn, that not only the *ungodly* and *careless delay*, but the *self-righteous* also. They want to do without Christ.

(*c*) *Spencer's Pastor's Sketches*

DELAY IN SEEKING GOD (Isa. lv. 6)

Seek God whilst thou canst not see Him ; for when thou seest Him, thou canst not find Him. Seek Him by hope, and thou shalt find Him by faith. In the day of grace He is invisible, but near ; in the Day of Judgment He is visible, but far off.

(*d*) *Gregory*

If we would not seek God in vain, let us seek Him in truth, often and constantly ; let us not seek another thing instead of Him, nor for any other thing leave Him.

(*e*) *Bernard*

God, that hath promised pardon to the penitent, hath not promised the respite of to-morrow to the impenitent.

(*f*) *Gregory*

" **DELIVERED** us *from the power of darkness* " (Col. i. 13)

The Father hath delivered us, *i.e.*, has *snatched* us out of danger (*Passow*). He does not say delivered, but *snatched*, showing our and their great misery and captivity.

(*g*) *Chrysostom*

DEMONIAC, THE (Luke viii. 26–40)

Jesus as the Prince of Peace.

(26) After the storm on the lake, a worse storm of demoniac rage.

(27) *There met Him a demoniac :*
Note (i.) " Long time " ;
    (ii.) " No clothes " ;   ⎫
    (iii.) No house (" tombs ") ; ⎬ (Luke)
    (iv.) Impassable for travellers (Matt.).

(28) Not wholly impenitent—*cried, fell down,* cut *himself*. The true devilish spirit thinks it an injury not to be allowed to torment others.

(29) Explains 28.

(30) The name, " Legion."
   (i.) Why Jesus asks ;
   (ii.) The man's misery.
Truth and error mingled.

(*h*)

(31) The demons' regret. The prayer of the wicked granted, to their own ruin.

(34–37) The comparative value of a man and the swine.

The trial, *which?*

Note the dread of Christ:

They *all* came to meet Him (Mark), and they ask Him to go away.

(i.) The *coming—all* came;

(ii.) The *seeing*—they saw Jesus and the man;

(iii.) The *request* (unanimous)—Go away; notwithstanding His having healed the sick, fed the hungry, quelled the storm, and healed this man. = "We desire not the knowledge of Thy ways." They felt that He would not spare their sins (swine).

(iv.) He went away (37). Jesus will not force salvation on us.

(v.) They were near salvation: "I would," and "ye would not."

They wronged Jesus ("fear"), and they wronged themselves; for when Jesus sails away, with Him go Heaven, Salvation, Life, Joy.

(a)   *Various*

Demoniac of Gadara, The

I imagine that this demoniac was not only an object of pity, but he was really a terror to the country; so terrible was his appearance, so dreadful and hideous his screams, so formidable, frightful, and horrid his wild career, that all the women in that region were so much alarmed that none of them durst go to market.

And what made him still more terrible was the place of his abode. It was not in the city, where some attention might be paid to order and decorum —though he would sometimes ramble into the city, as in this case. It was not in a town, or village, or any house whatever, where assistance might be obtained in case of necessity; but it was among the tombs and the wilderness, not far, however, from the turnpike road. No one could tell but that he might jump at them like a panther, and scare them to death. The gloominess of the place made it more awful and solemn. It was among the tombs, where, in the opinion of some, all witches, corpse-candles, and hobgoblins abide.

By this time the devil became offended the Gadarenes, and in a pout he took the demoniac away, and drove him into the wilderness. He thought the Gadarenes had no business to interfere and meddle with his property—for he had possession of the man; and he knew that "a bird in the hand is worth two in the bush." It is probable that he wanted to send him home; for there was no knowing what might happen now-a-days. But there was too much matter about him to send him away as he was; therefore he thought it the best plan to persuade him to commit suicide, by cutting his own throat. But here Satan was nonplussed—his rope was too short; he could not turn executioner himself, as that would not have answered the design he had in view, when he wants his people to commit suicide; for the act would have been his own sin, and not the man's. The poor demoniac, therefore, must go about to hunt up a sharp stone or anything he could get. He might have been in search of such an article when he returned from the wilderness into the city whence he came, when he met the Son of God.

Jesus commanded the unclean spirit to come out of the man. And when he saw Jesus, he cried out, and fell down before Him, and with a loud voice said: "What have I to do with Thee, Jesus, thou Son of God Most High? I beseech Thee, torment me not."

Here is the devil's confession of faith. The devils believe and tremble, while men make a mock of sin, and sport on the verge of dark damnation. To many of the human race, Christ appears as a root out of a dry ground. They see in Him neither form nor comeliness, and there is no beauty in Him that they should desire Him. Some said that He was the carpenter's son, and would not believe in Him: others said that He had a devil, and that it was through Beelzebub, the chief of the devils, that He cast out devils. Some cried out, "Crucify Him, crucify Him"; and others said, "Let His blood be upon us and our children." The Jews would not have Him to rule over them. Many who call themselves Christians, say that He is a mere man; as such, He has no right to rule over their consciences, and demand their obedience, adoration, and praise. But Diabolus knows better—Jesus is the Son of God Most High. Many of the children of the devil, whose works they do, differ very widely from their father in sentiments respecting the person of Christ.

Jesus commanded the legion of unclean spirits to come out of the man. They knew that out they must go; but they were very unwilling to return to their own country again. And He suffered them to go into the herd of swine.

Methinks that one of the men who fed the hogs kept a better look-out than the rest of them, and said :

"What ails all the hogs? Look sharp there, boys—keep them in—make good use of your whips. Why don't you run? Why, true as I am alive, one of them has gone headlong over the cliff! There! there, Morgan, yonder goes another! Drive them back, Tom."

Never was there such running, and whipping, and hallooing;—but down go the hogs, before they were aware of it. One of them said:

" They are all gone ! "

" No, sure, not all of them gone into the sea ? "

" Yes, every one of them ; and if ever the devil entered anything in this world, he has entered into those hogs."

" What," says Jack, "and is the noble black hog gone ? "

" Yes ! yes ! I saw him scampering down that hill as if the very devil himself was in him ; and I saw his tail take the last dip in the water below."

" What," says Tom to Morgan, " what shall we say to our masters ? "

" What can we say? We must tell the truth, that is all about it. We did our best—all that was in our power. What could any man do more ? "

So they went their way to the city to tell their masters what had happened.

" Jack, where are you going ? " exclaimed one of the masters.

" Sir, did you know the demoniac that was among the tombs ? "

" Where did you leave the hogs ? "

" That madman, sir,—— "

" Madman ! Why did you come home without the hogs ? "

" That wild and furious man, sir, that mistress was afraid of so much—— "

(b)

" Why, Jack, I ask you a plain question—why don't you answer me ? Where are the hogs ? "

" That man who was possessed with the devils, sir,——"

" Why, sure enough, you are crazy ! You look wild ! Tell your story, if you can, let it be what it may ! "

" Jesus Christ, sir, has cast the unclean spirits out of the demoniac. They are gone into the swine ; and they are drowned in the sea ; for I saw the tail of the last when it went out of sight ! Now, master, you may depend it is as I say."

The Gadarenes went out to see what was done ; and finding that it was even so, they were afraid, and besought Jesus to depart from them.

How awful must be the state and condition of those men who love the things of this world more than Jesus Christ !

The man out of whom the unclean spirits were cast, besought Jesus that he might be with Him. But He told him to return to his own house, and show how great things God had done for him. And he went his way, and published throughout the whole city of Decapolis how great things Jesus had done unto him.

The act of Jesus casting so many devils out of him, was sufficient to persuade him that Jesus was God as well as man.

I imagine I see him going through the city, crying : " O yes ! O yes ! Please to take notice of me, the demoniac among the tombs. I am the man who was a terror to the people of this place ; that wild man, who could wear no clothes, and that no man could bind. Here am I, now in my right mind. Jesus Christ, the friend of sinners, had compassion upon me, when I was in my low estate. When there was no eye to pity, and no hand to save, He cast out the devils, and redeemed my soul from destruction."

Most wonderful must have been the surprise of the people to hear such a proclamation. The ladies running to the windows ; the shoemakers throwing their lasts one way and their awls another ; running out to meet him, and to converse with him, that they might be positive there was no imposition ; they found it to be a fact that could not be contradicted. Oh the wonder of all wonders ! Never was there such a thing ! must, I think, have been the general conversation.

And while they were talking—and everybody having something to say—homewards goes the man. As soon as he came in sight of the house, I imagine I see one of the children running in, and crying : " O mother ! father is coming, and he will kill us all ! "

" Children, come all into the house," said the mother, " let us fasten the doors. I think there is no sorrow like my sorrow ! " said the broken-hearted woman.

" Are all the windows fastened, children ? "

" Yes, mother."

" Mary, my dear, come from the window ; don't be standing there."

" Why, mother, I can hardly believe that it is father ! that man is well dressed."

" Oh, yes, my dear children, it is your own father. I knew him by his walk, the moment I saw him."

Another child stepping to the window, said : " Why, mother, I never saw father come home as he comes to-day. He walks on the footpath, and turns round the corner of the fences. He used to come towards the house as straight as a line, over fences, ditches, and hedges ; and I never saw him walk as slowly as he does now."

In a few moments, however, he arrives at the door of the house, to the great terror and consternation of all the inmates. He gently tries the door, and finds no admittance. He pauses a moment, steps towards the window, and says, in a low, firm, and melodious voice : " My dear wife, if you will let me in, there is no danger. I will not hurt you ; I bring you glad tidings of great joy."

The door was reluctantly opened, as it were between joy and fear. Having deliberately seated himself, he said :—

" I am come to show you what great things God has done for me. He loved me with an everlasting love. He redeemed me from the curse of the law and the threatenings of vindictive justice. He saved me from the power and dominion of sin. He cast the devils out of my heart, and made that heart, which was a den of thieves, the temple of the Holy Spirit. I cannot tell you how much I love the Saviour. Jesus Christ is the foundation of my hope, the object of my faith, and the centre of my affections. I can venture my immortal soul upon Him. He is my best friend—He is altogether lovely—the chief among ten thousands. He is my wisdom, righteousness, sanctification, and redemption. There is enough in Him to make a poor sinner rich, and a miserable sinner happy. His flesh and blood are my food ; His righteousness is my wedding garment ; and His blood is efficacious to cleanse from all sin. Through Him I can obtain eternal life ; for He is the brightness of the Father's glory, and the express image of His person, in whom dwelleth all the fulness of the Godhead bodily. He deserves my highest esteem and my warmest gratitude. Unto Him who loved me with an eternal love, and washed me in His own blood—unto Him be glory, dominion, and power, for ever and ever. For He has rescued my soul from hell : He has plucked me as a brand out of the burning. He took me out of the miry clay, and out of the horrible pit. He set my feet upon a rock, and established my goings, and put in my mouth a new song of praise and glory to Him ! Glory to Him for ever ! Glory to God in the highest ! Glory to God for ever and ever ! Let the whole earth praise Him ! Yea, let the whole world praise Him ! Hallelujah ! The Lord God Omnipotent reigneth ! ' "

It is beyond the power of the strongest imagination to conceive the joy and gladness of this family. The joy of seafaring men delivered from being shipwrecked ; the joy of a man delivered from a burning house ; the joy of not being found guilty at a criminal bar ; the joy of receiving pardon by a condemned malefactor ; the joy of freedom to a prisoner of war, is nothing in comparison to the joy of him who is delivered from going down to the pit of eternal destruction. For it is joy unspeakable and full of glory."

(a)   *Christmas Evans*

DEMONIACS

The demoniac was in the power of the evil spirit who spoke by him, in the same way that the sweet singer of Israel was in the power of God's Spirit when inspired by Him (Mark xii. 36). The radical matter of fact was simply this, that the sinful condition had reached a height where the man no longer had the mastery of sin, but sin of

(b)

him; and when, sunk in this utter impotence, and possessing no will of his own, he yielded to the enslaving power of sin, this dominion is referred to a superhuman spiritual power which held sway over him, and deprived him of all volition.

(a)   *Weiss*

It is easily conceivable that Jesus appeared at a time when the ancient world seemed to a peculiarly large extent to have been abandoned by all the forces of health and vitality, and therefore to have fallen more deeply into sin and under the powers of darkness.

(b)   *Ibid*

DEMONIACAL POSSESSION (Luke iv. 33–37)

What is meant by it? Lunacy? Extraordinary display of diabolical power when the Son of God was on earth? But, *what saith the Scripture?*

(i.) In every case of Possession there was also physical or mental disorder; hence classed amongst "*the sick*," and thus incapable of moral resistance. They resembled houses infested by robbers, where the lawful tenant was chained in a cell, too weak to offer resistance.

(ii.) They were not the "wicked," to whom our Lord said, "Ye are of your father the devil"; for He then addressed responsible people.

(iii.) The Possessed were not merely "sick," but were incapable of distinguishing right and wrong, and had lost freedom of *will:* a foreign power located itself within and regulated their actions. Our Lord recognises this power as that of a *demon* = a spirit of the devil. He gives His disciples "power to cast out devils," and to "tread on all the power of the enemy." This *power* was not alike in all: "This kind goeth not out, but by prayer." In all such cases Jesus saw two tenants in one house; and the usurping tenant was an evil spirit from the abyss of darkness, hiding away and torturing an incapable human being. And their presence was made manifest when He appeared amongst men. His presence seems to have tormented them, as the light tortures a diseased eye; and they evinced their dislike by crying out. "What have we to do with Thee?" There are cases now-a-days which baffle both mental and medical science, and which this hypothesis alone adequately accounts for. Contact with personal goodness, now, as then, wakes up the sleeping demon to yell out, "What have I to do with Thee?" = "What concord is there between Christ and Belial?" . . . Probably sin, either in others of the past, or in the individual, has wrecked the life, which these find, enter, master, and torment = a conversion of the man to devilry: the very opposite of being filled with the Holy Spirit. *Possession, then, is a caricature, or a mockery, of the Inspiration of the Spirit of God.* Christ inspires us with the Holy Ghost; the devil, with an "unclean spirit." The one is the highest work of God, the other the highest work of the devil. In either case there is the incoming of another personality—a usurpation. See, for illustration, the instance before us. This man *was in the Synagogue*—an unlikely place. It may have been that the demon thought it as safe as any other place. No power of exorcism lay hid in the perfunctory service there,—he could slumber in the man there as well as elsewhere. But on this particular Sabbath-day matters came to a crisis. No mere Jewish Rabbi ministered there that day,

no preacher of ordinary platitudes, but *that Prophet Himself*, filled with the Spirit. Two opposing powers: hence the ensuing conflict. Danger threatens the demon's dominion; and under this influence the demon wakes up in terror, and cries out, like a suddenly arrested criminal, "I KNOW THEE." But Jesus calmly replies "SILENCE, COME OUT;" and the territory is at once abandoned. The demon disappears. In like manner two powers dispute the ownership of each of us. *Who shall have him?* seems to be the question asked. There is but one Deliverer, Rescuer, Saviour—and the issue need not be doubtful.

(c)

DENUNCIATIONS OF PHARISEES AND SADDUCEES (Matt. xxiii., xxiv.)

Our Lord, in His terrible condemnation, singles out the Pharisees, who for the last hundred and fifty years had enjoyed the highest respect of the people for their zeal and rigid observance of the Law. During His whole ministry He had been making pharisaic formalism the constant object of reproof, while almost ignoring the unbelief of the Sadducees.

(d)   *Dr. Nast*

It is remarkable that the severest language Christ ever used, was directed against the orthodox, priestly, sanctimonious, hypocritical Pharisees, the leaders of the hierarchy, and rulers of the people. Let ministers and dignitaries in the Church never forget this! . . . Yet the Pharisees with all their wickedness, and not the indifferent, worldly, and rationalistic Sadducees, could produce a convert like *St. Paul*.

(e)   *P. Schaff*

As Christ once commenced His Sermon on the Mount in Galilee with pronouncing eight beatitudes, so He closes His last public address with pronouncing eight woes on Mount Moriah.

(f)   *M. Baumgarten*

DEPENDENCE ON CHRIST

My faith looks up to Thee,
Thou Lamb of Calvary,
   Saviour Divine!
Now hear me while I pray;
Take all my guilt away;
Oh, let me from this day
   Be wholly Thine.

May Thy rich grace impart
Strength to my fainting heart,
   My zeal inspire:
As Thou hast died for me,
Oh, may my love to Thee
Pure, warm, and changeless be—
   A living fire.

While life's dark maze I tread,
And griefs around me spread,
   Be Thou my guide:
Bid darkness turn to day,
Wipe sorrow's tears away,
Nor let me ever stray
   From Thee aside.

(g)

DEPENDENCE, MUTUAL

We enter upon life weak, unconscious infants, dependent on other eyes to watch for us, and other hands to minister to us. Not less dependent are we on our fellow-creatures for our continuance in life from the cradle to the grave. Not a thread of clothing covers our body, not a luxury is placed on our table, not an article which supplies the means of labour, not one thing required by us as civilized beings, but involves the labours and the sacrifices of others in our behalf. The cotton which the artisan weaves or wears has been cultivated by brothers beneath a tropical sun. The tea he drinks has been gathered for him by brothers on the unknown hill-sides of distant China. A mother writes a letter to her son in some distant spot in India, and conveys it to the post-office, perhaps thinking only when she may receive a reply from her boy. But how much is done before that letter reaches its destination! The hands of unknown brethren will receive it and transmit it; rapid trains will convey it over leagues of railways; steamships will sail with it; and hundreds of hands will pass it from post to post, from hand to hand. It is watched day and night through calm and hurricane; and precious lives are risked to keep it safe, until, after months of travel, it is delivered into the hand of her child.

(a)

DEPRAVITY

The natural depravity of the human heart was fully developed at the Crucifixion of our Lord. He, the only perfect man, is crowned with thorns, scourged, buffeted, cursed, murdered. A great multitude look on exultingly, gloating over the horrors of the day. And this multitude is not the mere scum of the city—it is a representative crowd: There is the educated as well as the ignorant; the scribe, the Pharisee, the priest, the governor, the soldier, indeed all ranks and grades of life, assembled to feast their eyes on the sufferings of the Redeemer. Yet not one voice is raised against the cruelty they are perpetrating. After this, can any one think lightly of *human depravity*.

(b)   *Gordon Calthrop*

Men sometimes object to the doctrine of the depravity of mankind. But the strongest teachings of the Bible and of the pulpit are more than confirmed by their own actions—by the conduct of the world itself. Every bolt and bar, and lock and key, every receipt, and cheque, and note of hand, every law book and court of justice, every chain, and dungeon, and gallows, proclaim that the world is a fallen world, and that our race is a depraved and sinful race.

(c)

DE PROFUNDIS

"*He brought me up out of the horrible pit*" (Ps. xl. 2).

Cry for help and He will help thee out. Is thy step on the lowest rung—only just at the bottom, and does it seem hard to get up? Place thy hand on the hand-rail of Faith—thy right hand. Canst thou not read the promise? "Who-soever cometh unto Me, I will in no wise cast out!" Keep firm hold, and cry again for deliverance, for thou wilt need help all the way. Once more, set thy foot forward and cling again, a little higher, to the hand-rail. See the next promise, "Let the wicked forsake his way, and the unrighteous man his thoughts; and let him return unto the Lord, and He will have mercy on him; and to our God, for He will abundantly pardon him." Thou needest *abundant* pardon, for thy sins are many; and so the fiend behind thee is saying. Heed him not. Keep hold of the hand-rail. Cry again for Almighty help, set thy foot forward again, stretch out thy hand boldly, and lay hold again higher up, and read the words just above thee, "The blood of Jesus Christ, His Son, cleanseth from *all* sin." *Thou* art not to despair. Do not halt either, the Avenger of Blood is behind thee!— Yet another struggle, another step upward, another grasp higher up on the hand-rail! Fiends are raging behind thee, old associates are mocking thee; but listen not, turn not backward—keep thy gaze upward and onward. Behold that glorious writing above thee. The Saviour wrote it with His own finger, "God so loved the world as to give His only begotten Son, that whosoever believeth in Him should not perish, but have everlasting life." It is everlasting life that thou art seeking, and thou art escaping from everlasting death. Again forward, again cry for help, and still clinging to the hand-rail, reading the encouraging words above thee at every step, "Behold the Lamb of God, that taketh away the sin of the world." "This is a faithful saying, and worthy of all acceptation, that Christ Jesus came into the world to save sinners." And I can assure thee thou *shalt be brought out* of the horrible pit.

(d)   *Thos. Cooper*

DE PROFUNDIS

From depth of dole wherein my soul doth dwell,
    From heavy heart which harbours in my breast,
    From troubled spirit which seldom taketh rest,
From hope of heaven, from dread of darksome
        hell,
O gracious God, to Thee I cry and wail.
    My God, my Lord, my lovely Lord alone,
    To Thee I call, to Thee I make my moan.
And Thou, good God, vouchsafe in gree to take
        This woeful plaint,
        Wherein I faint,
Oh, hear me then for Thy great mercies' sake.

Oh, bend Thine ears attentively to hear,
    Oh, turn Thine eyes, behold me how I wail,
    Oh, hearken, Lord, give ear for mine avail,
Oh, mark in mind the burdens that I bear:
See how I sink in sorrows everywhere.
    Behold and see what dolors I endure,
    Give ear and mark what plaints I put in ure.
Bend willing ear: and pity therewithal
        My wailing voice,
        Which hath no choice,
But evermore upon Thy Name to call.

If Thou, good Lord, shouldst take Thy rod in
        hand,
    If Thou regard what sins are daily done,
    If Thou take hold where we our works begun,
(e)

If Thou decree in judgment for to stand,
And be extreme to see our scuses scanned,
If Thou take note of everything amiss,
And write in rowles how frail our nature is,
O glorious God, O King, O Prince of power,
      What mortal wight
      May then have light
To feel Thy frown, if Thou have list to lower ?

But Thou art good, and hast of mercy store,
    Thou not delight'st to see a sinner fall,
    Thou hearken'st first, before we come to call,
Thine ears are set wide open evermore ;
Before we knock Thou comest to the door.
    Thou art more pressed to hear a sinner cry,
    Than he is quick to climb to Thee on high.
Thy mighty Name be praisèd then alway,
      Let faith and fear
      True witness bear,
How fast they stand which on Thy mercy stay.

I look to Thee, my lovely Lord, therefore,
    For Thee I wait, for Thee I tarry still,
    Mine eyes do long to gaze on Thee my fill.
For Thee I watch, for Thee I pry and pore,
My soul for Thee attendeth evermore.
    My soul doth thirst to take of Thee a taste,
    My soul desires with Thee for to be placed.
And to Thy word, which can no man deceive,
      Mine only trust,
      My love and lust,
In confidence continually shall cleave.

Before the break or dawning of the day,
    Before the light be seen in lofty skies,
    Before the sun appear in pleasant wise,
Before the watch, before the watch, I say,
Before the ward that waits therefore alway ;
    My soul, my sense, my secret thought, my spirit,
    My will, my wish, my joy, and my delight :
Unto the Lord that sits in heaven on high,
      With hasty wing,
      From me doth fling,
And striveth still unto the Lord to fly.

O Israel, O household of the Lord,
    O Abraham's sons, O brood of blessèd seed,
    O chosen sheep that love the Lord indeed :
O hungry hearts, feed still upon His word,
And put your trust in Him with one accord.
    For He hath mercy evermore at hand ;
    His fountains flow, His springs do never stand.
And plenteously He loveth to redeem
      Such sinners all
      As on Him call,
And faithfully His mercies most esteem.

He will redeem our deadly drooping state ;
    He will bring home the sheep that goes astray.
He will help them that hope in Him alway ;
He will appease our discord and debate ;
He will soon save, though we repent us late.
    He will be ours, if we continue His ;
    He will bring bale to joy and perfect bliss.
He will redeem the flock of His elect
      From all that is
      Or was amiss,
Since Abraham's heirs did first His laws reject.
  (a)   *Gascoigne*

DEPTHS, OUT OF THE (Ps. cxxx. 1)

Gracious souls, after much communion with God, may be brought into inextricable DEPTHS and entanglements on the account of sin. For such the Psalmist here expresses his own condition to have been, and such he was.

1. Warnings against :
(Rom. xi. 20 ; 1 Cor. x. 12 ; 1 Pet. i. 17.)

2. Instances of :
Noah (Gen. vi. 9 and ix. 20-25).
David sometimes complains of broken bones, depths, waves, water-spouts, wounds, diseases, wrath, sorrows, hell—everywhere of his sins, the burden and trouble of them. Some of the occasions we know of. As no man had more grace than he, so none is a greater instance of the power of sin, and the effects of its guilt upon the conscience, than he.

3. What is intended by the " Depths "
(i.) Loss of the sense of God's love, which was formerly enjoyed through the operation of the Holy Ghost : the effect of which is called " joy unspeakable, and full of glory."

(ii.) Loss of the gospel persuasion, of acceptance with God in Christ. One step into these depths is, that the consolation of this is lost.

(iii.) A revived sense of justly deserved wrath. The opening of old wounds. When men have passed through a sense of wrath, and have obtained deliverance and rest through the blood of Christ, to come to their old thoughts again, to be trading afresh with hell, curse, law, and wrath, is a depth indeed (Ps. lxxxviii. 7).
The Lord, as it were, gives the Law a fresh commission to take such a one into its custody ; and the Law will never be wanting in its duty.

(iv.) Apprehensions of temporal judgments : Judgment begins at the house of God (Ps. xix. 120), scandal (Ps. xxix. 8) ; Jonah ; Joseph's brethren. The soul rolled from one deep to another.

(v.) Fear of utter rejection (Ps. lxxxviii. 4, 5. Heman). The soul deprived of comfort, peace, and rest, until it be a terror to itself, and ready to choose strangling rather than life.

(vi.) God's secret arrows wounding the soul (Ps. xxxviii. 2 ; xxxix. 11 ; Job vi. 4).

(vii.) Disability unto duty, doing or suffering (Ps. xl. 12) ; spiritual strength worn away, communion with God arrested ; no life and power in prayer ; the soul is weak, sick, feeble, and bowed down. These make up the *depths* of which the Psalmist complains.

4. How possible to fall into such " Depths "
Under the First Covenant no mercy or forgiveness was provided for any sin. A sufficiency of grace was therefore necessary to preserve from sin. It is not so in the Covenant of Grace : It provides pardon in the blood of Christ, but not a stock of grace preserving from sin.

(i.) Provision in it is made against all sin that would disannul the Covenant, and finally separate from God. This provision is absolute (Jer. xxxii. 40). This security depends not on anything in us, but absolutely on the faithfulness of God.
  (b)

(ii.) Provision is made for constant peace and consolation, notwithstanding the daily guilt of sins of infirmity and temptation. We do not fall into "depths" every day (Rom. vii. 24 and viii. 1; 1 John ii. 1; Heb. vi. 17, 18). Consider the condition of him who fled for "refuge" in the Old Testament.

(iii.) Provision is made of grace to prevent and preserve from great and enormous sins (John i. 16; Rom. vi. 6). But this provision is not absolute: our duty is to watch, pray, improve faith, stand on guard, mortify sin, fight. Steadfastness, diligence, constancy, are everywhere prescribed unto us. These are the conditions of that abundant grace (2 Pet. i. 3–10). "Not fall into sin"? No. "Not fall totally from God"? No; the preservation of the elect from total apostasy is not suspended on such conditions, especially not on any degree of them, such as their abounding imports. But it is, that they shall not fall into their old sins, from which they were purged, (9) such as they once lived in.

Here lies the latitude of the New Covenant; the exercise of renewed free-will. There are extremes: To be wholly perfect, is not provided for, nor promised. It is a covenant of mercy and pardon, which supposes a continuance of sin. To fall utterly and finally from God, is absolutely provided against. Between these two extremes lies the large field of the believer's walking with God. Many a sweet heavenly passage there is, and many a dangerous *depth* in this field. Some walk near to the one side or the other; yea, the same person may sometimes press hard after perfection, sometimes be cast to the very border of destruction. Between these two lie many a soul-plunging sin, against which no absolute provision is made, and which, for want of due diligence in the use of means, believers are often overtaken with.

(iv.) No provision is made of abiding consolation under the guilt of great sins, fallen into through neglect of the means of abiding in a state of grace. God, by an act of sovereign grace, speaks peace unto such (Isa. lvii. 18, 19). Great provocation needs special relief.

5. Consider, further, the power of indwelling sin

Though the strength of sin is weakened by grace, yet the root is left.

The Canaanites, after the conquest of their land, still dwelt in it (Judg. i. 27; Rom. vii. 18; Gal. v. 17).

Some sins are very difficult to subdue. The Canaanites had *iron* chariots.

The properties of indwelling sin are such, as it is no wonder that some believers are by them cast into depths.

God's sovereignty in dealing with sinning saints; some shall have all their bones broken, others only the gentle strokes of the rod.

6. What sins usually bring believers into the "Depths"

(i.) Sins against light and nature (1 Cor. vi. 9, 10); These cut the locks of men's spiritual strength.

(ii.) Sins against special signs of God's love. Solomon fell into such, after God had appeared unto him twice. Sins after special mercies meet with special rebukes.

(iii.) Sins of neglecting golden opportunities for usefulness. Gifts are given to trade with for God; opportunities are the market-days for that trade. To napkin up the one and let slip the other, will end in trouble.

(iv.) Sins after special warning: as when a word in preaching, peculiarly suitable to the soul's condition, enters the heart. The soul takes notice that God is nigh, dealing with him, calling on him. To neglect this, is to merit reproof.

(v.) Sins that result in scandal, seldom suffer the soul to escape *depths*.

7. Aggravations of these sins

(i.) Grace is continually operative. "It lusteth against the flesh." To fall into sin, therefore, is to fight against the God that is within us.

(ii.) Neglect of the treasures of relief laid up in Jesus Christ (Heb. iv. 6). "Let us come boldly," etc.

God may say, See these poor creatures; once they had a stock of grace in themselves: this they cast away. That they might not perish, their stock is now laid up with another, as their treasurer; in Him their lives and comforts are secured. But see their negligence: they venture all rather than apply to Him for succour—they neglect the relief provided.

John Owen

(See "De Profundis.")

(*a*)

From the lowest depth, there is a path to the loftiest height.

(*b*) *Carlyle*

DESCENSUS AD INFEROS (Eph. iv. 8, 9)

1. Christ Descended.

(i.) Into *Hades*, not "Hell," not "Heaven;" but an intermediate place:

"Thou wilt not leave my soul in Hades."

(ii.) Not a state of *Inaction:* for

(1) He "preached" (1 Pet. iii. 18);

(2) He, who has the *Key* of Hades, opened the door for the captives.

2. Christ Ascended.

(i.) To *Heaven*, at right hand of God, "exalted a Prince and a Saviour."

(ii.) *Not alone:* for "He led captivity captive;" the result of going to Hades and opening the prison door.

Cf. "The bodies of the saints which arose . . . *after His resurrection*."

(iii.) Now engaged in salvation-work, giving "gifts unto men:"

(1) Repentance and Forgiveness } Exalted for this;

(2) Holy Spirit ("poured out");

(3) Ministerial gifts ("He gave some Apostles," etc.).

(*c*)

DESIRE

Desires increase with acquisition; every step a man advances brings something within his view,

(*d*)

which he did not see before, and which, as soon as he sees it, he begins to want. Where necessity ends, curiosity begins; and no sooner are we supplied with everything that nature can demand, than we contrive artificial appetites.

(a)   *Dr. Johnson*

DESPAIR, DEATH, AND JUDGMENT

A great writer of fiction, describing the death of a young nobleman who had been killed in a duel after a life of silly dissipation, describes his agonizing reflection, which came too late, that he might have died happy with children's faces round his bed. The great mediæval poet, seeing in purgatory the soul of a friend, hears from him that dying on the field of battle his last cry for mercy was heard, and as the angel of God took him, the spirit of hell cried out, " Oh, thou from heaven ! Why dost thou rob me ? Dost thou carry away to the eternal shore him for one poor tear that delivers him from me ? " And perhaps some of you may remember a similar scene in a great modern work of genius, when a poor, fallen, deserted woman dies in prison, and the deep voice of the evil spirit as he stands by and sees the last fluttering breath, and utters beside her : " She is judged ! " Even then from the upper air thrills the cry of the angel, " She is saved ! " If it seem unjust to us that a soul should be saved as by one flash and spasm of repentance, our thought may be only due to our own gross envy and ignorance. It may be otherwise with the larger, other eyes of God, to whom time and eternity are but one great *Now*. To Him who on the cross, turning upon the dying malefactor His kingly eyes, which were beginning already to be filmed by death, said : " This day shalt thou be with Me in Paradise." Only remember how much more often death ends, not in contrition, not in awakenment, and therefore not in repentance, but in dull torpor or hard defiance.

"Lord Cardinal, if thou think'st on heaven's bliss,
 Hold up thy hand, make signal of thy hope!—
 He dies and makes no sign—O God, forgive him ! "

(b)

Despair, Utter

But even when the conviction of guilt comes before the death-bed, if in some it produces penitence, there are others in whom it produces only retchlessness, and in others only an unfathomable despair. Retchlessness : as of him who, in the blasphemy of unclean defiance, said : " Knowing that I am predestined to damnation, I will give diligence to make my election sure "; despair : as of him who shrieked : " I have sinned, in that I betrayed the innocent blood," and hearing the brutal taunt of his priestly abettors ; " What is that to us ? " departed, and went away and hanged himself. The history of the Reformation produced an awful example of such a man in Francis Spira. Converted to Protestantism, but morally unchanged, he turned the grace of God into licentiousness, and then in awful renunciation recanted, first privately and then publicly, the Gospel truths which he had preached. But no sooner had he got home than he was seized with fearful torments of conscience. He seemed to hear a voice which cried to him : " Wretch ! thou hast denied Me ! Depart from Me ! " No comfort could reach him. He ceased to believe in prayer. He died remorseful and yet hopeless. One who saw his end described it as *horrenda desperatio;* and one exclaimed : " If all the students of Padua do not forsake all their books to gaze at this tragedy, their sensibilities must be exceedingly obtuse."

(c)

The Awakening

But some there are to whom, as to Dives, there seems to come in this life no awakening. Happy therefore ? Happy how long ? Happy till when ? You can appreciate the trembling rapture of awakening in heaven, that bursting glory, that infinite exultation, that triumph of peace indescribable. What must be that other awakening, the awakening of those who willingly to the end have broken the law of God, the awakening when the gold must drop from the relaxing grasp, when no jewelled star can hide the base heart any longer, when pleasure, which has become as loathly as it is impossible, shrivels like a withered garland, when the gains of men look as mean as the rouge and tinsel of the stage under the dawn ? Shall it not be as the luxurious dream, when man awaketh to gnawing hunger and to scorching thirst ? You may have read of the young somnambulist of the French village, who, in her sleep, got out of her garret window upon the roof, and in the sight of a silent and trembling crowd, walked up and down the giddy parapet, and, dreaming of a coming village festival, sometimes approaching the steep edge, sometimes leaving it, sometimes, while they held their breath from very horror, leaning down towards the street below, she kept smiling and murmuring gay songs ; and they were all powerless to help her. On a sudden a little candle was lit in an opposite window ; it flashed upon her ; she woke, she screamed, she fell. Her awakening was death. It had killed her. " Alas ! " says he who tells the story, " ye who are without faith and without God, ye to whom at this moment the world is God, what are ye but sleepers, who in your slumber walk to the edge of an abyss ? and ye too, perhaps, singing and dreaming of festival days. For what else is a dream but to take shadows for realities, and realities for shadows ? When one ray of light, one clear, cold ray, out of God's eternity, smites upon your dreaming eyes, do you not fear that start, that tottering over the abyss, that death, that awakenment in the world to come ? Is not your godless life pregnant with suicide ? "

(d)

And, O God, that awakening ! Another, not I, the greatest, perhaps, of living writers and living theologians, shall describe what, in his opinion, it may be—that terrible moment when the Judge speaks and consigns the soul to the jailers till the debt is paid. " ' Impossible ! I a lost soul ! I separated from hope and from peace for ever ! It is not I of whom the Judge so spake ! There is a mistake somewhere ! Christ, Saviour, hold my hand one minute to explain it ! My name is Demas ; I am Demas, not Judas ! What ! Eternal pains for me ! Impossible ! It shall not be so ! ' And the poor soul struggles and wrestles in the grasp of the mighty demon which has hold of it, and whose every touch is torment. ' Stop, horrible

(e)

fiend! Give over. I am a man, and not such as thou. I have been taught religion; I have a cultivated mind; I am well versed in science and art. I am a philosopher, a poet, a hero; nay, I have received the grace of redemption. I have attended sacraments for years. Nothing, nothing which I have ever been, which I have ever seen, bears any resemblance to thee. So I defy and abjure thee, O enemy of man!' Alas! poor soul! while it thus fights with that destiny which it has brought upon itself, and those companions which it has chosen, the man's name perhaps has been solemnly chanted forth on earth, men appeal to his authority, quote his words, write his history as so comprehensive, so keen, so profound! Oh, vanity of vanities! What profiteth it? His soul is lost, O ye children of men!"

Remember, I do not endorse the particular imagery of this passage, which I have greatly softened. To me it seems mediæval rather than Scriptural. But yet the dreadful imagery may serve to remind you that there are unspeakable realities, that there is a shame of awakening when sinners call the mountains to fall on them, and on the hills to cover them. Souls which should have entered into the world of light clad in white robes, bright and rejoicing as with a drift of angels' wings, find as they go to their own place, that it is in an outer darkness into which they shiver forth as souls lost, degraded, stained, ruined, the victims and triumphs of the powers of evil.

(a)   *Archdeacon Farrar*

DESPAIR, HORRORS OF

Which way shall I fly
Infinite wrath, and infinite despair?
Which way I flee is Hell—myself am Hell;
And in the lowest deep, a lower deep,
Still threatening to devour me, opens wide,
To which the Hell I suffer seems a Heaven.
. . . Is there no place
Left for repentance, none for pardon left?
(b)   *Milton*

DESPAIR, INSTANCE OF

The termination of Swift's career; the retributive justice which, if we believed in spirits, poor Stella's ghost might have witnessed; the joyless close of an existence which no affectionate cares sought to cheer; the consignment of the wretched and violent lunatic to servants and keepers; the moody silence of the once eloquent and witty ornament of courtly saloons; the deep despair to which medicine could not minister, but which a moral influence might have alleviated, but which no son nor daughter's tender perseverance, with untaught but often perhaps effectual skill, sought to solace; these, with all other gloomy particulars of Swift's awful aberrations and death, on which not one light of consciousness was shown, must be by all remembered.

Life of the Duchess of Marlborough, On Swift.
(c)

DESPAIR

I remember, as I and others were taking with Swift an evening walk, about a mile out of Dublin, he stopped short. We passed on; but perceiving he did not follow us, I went back and found him fixed as a statue, and earnestly gazing upwards at a noble tree which, in its upper branches, was much withered and decayed. Pointing at it, he said, " I shall be like that tree; I shall die atop."
(d)   *Dr. Young, on Swift*

DESPAIR: "IS GOD DEAD?"

" The Lord liveth."

A woman, truly godly for the main, having buried a child, and sitting alone in sadness, did yet bear up her heart with the expression, " God lives; " and having parted with another, still she redoubled, " Comforts die, but God lives." At last her dear husband dies, and she sat oppressed and most overwhelmed with sorrow. A little child she had yet surviving, having observed what before she spoke to comfort herself, comes to her and saith, " Is God dead, mother? Is God dead?" This reached her heart, and, by God's blessing, recovered her former confidence in her God, who is a " living God." " The Lord liveth, and blessed be my Rock."
(e)

DESPAIR, NATURE AND ESSENCE OF

Despair is the last result of sin, except an escape from this hell can be gained by means of repentance. Despair is the essence and proper meaning of Hell, wherefore the Inferno in Dante bears that inscription: " All hope abandon, ye who enter here." That sin not repented of must lead to despair, is evident in those men who have made greater progress in the path of sin. The farther a man proceeds in this path, the more a secret despair moves within him. False hopes may be conjured up; but at the bottom of the soul there exists a secret hopelessness in regard to his own person and his future. And if the moment occurs when the consciousness of guilt emerges in full view, it becomes manifest (Judas, and Richard III.). . . Such sinners cannot believe in the article of the Forgiveness of Sins.
(f)   *Martensen*

DESPAIR, NO PENITENT NEED

Had the Saviour come to befriend the righteous, I could have no claim; but I read He came to save sinners, and that He is able to save them to the uttermost. His own Word and Spirit first invited and enabled me to venture my all upon Him. I know that I have committed myself to Him a thousand times, how then can He give me up? Thus I endeavour to reason against the enemy: he can easily prove that I am worthless, ungrateful, and unfaithful; but he cannot prove that Jesus did not die, or that He did not say, " Him that cometh unto Me I will *in no wise cast out* " (John vi. 37). I would not part with this text for all the world; it sometimes seems the only one I can lay hold of; but *" in no wise "* extends to all the complicated varieties of my case.
(g)   *John Newton*

DESPAIR REBUKED

Spend not time in heartless complaints.
Drawn from what God said to Joshua:—
" Get up; why lie you thus upon your face? "
(h)

Your condition will not be mended by your wishing it better.

In things of worldly interest you would not content yourself with wishing—but would use great *diligence*.

The Scriptures call for *industry* and *activity* of *spirit* in your condition.

The nature of the thing requires it.

Distress yet unconquered, calls for *industry* and *diligence* in the use of means for deliverance.

Our Saviour tells us that "the kingdom of Heaven suffereth violence—and the violent *taketh it by force*."

Signifies "pressing"—or using violence upon ourselves—self-mortification.

There is then a *violence*, a *restless activity* and *vigour* to be used and exercised for an interest in this *Kingdom*.

We must apply this doctrine.

Are you in *depths* and *doubts*, *staggering* and *uncertain*, not knowing what is your condition, nor whether you have an interest in God's forgiveness ?

Are you tossed up and down between *hopes* and *fears*, want *peace, consolation*, and establishment ?

"Why lie you upon your face ?" Get up—

Watch, pray, fast, meditate, do violence to lusts and corruption, fear not, startle not at their crying to be spared ; press unto the throne of grace by prayer, supplications, importunities, *restless requests :* this is the way to take the Kingdom of Heaven.

These things are not peace, they are not assurance ; but they are part of the means that God hath appointed for the attainment of them.

What then is the peculiar instruction of such in such a condition ?

Plainly that of the Apostle, "Give all *diligence* to make your calling and election sure" (2 Pet. i. 10).

Cautions against taking immediate comfort from those who have good words in readiness for all comers.

Great judgment is needed.

N.B.—If *counsel* and consolation be given, *distinct* from the preceding advice of *watchfulness, diligence, spiritual violence* in a way of duty, *it is exceeding dangerous*, and will assuredly *prove useless*.

For notice the counsel of the Holy Ghost, given for this condition—unto those who would make their calling and election sure, who would be freed from present fears and uncertainties—who complain of darkness and danger, He saith :

"Giving *all diligence*, add to your faith virtue ; and to virtue knowledge ; and to knowledge temperance ; and to temperance patience ; and to patience godliness ; and to godliness brotherly kindness ; and to brotherly kindness charity.

"For if these things *be in you* and *abound*, they make you that ye be neither barren nor unfruitful in the knowledge of our Lord Jesus Christ. . . . Wherefore the rather, give diligence to make your calling and election *sure :* for if ye do these things ye shall never fall :

"For *so* an entrance shall be ministered unto you abundantly into the everlasting kingdom of our Lord and Saviour Jesus Christ. . . ."

You who now are in the skirts of it, who are in doubt whether you belong to it or not, you shall have an entrance into the kingdom of Christ ; and all the joy, comfort, and glory of it shall be administered unto you.

This is the advice of the Holy Ghost, and this is the blessed promise annexed to it.

Neither must be separated.

Spiritual peace and sloth will never dwell together in the same soul.

(a)　　　　　　　　　　　*John Owen*

DESPOT, THE FIRST

O execrable son, so to aspire
Above his brethren, to himself assuming
Authority usurped, from God not given.
He gave us only over beast, fish, fowl,
Dominion absolute ; that right we hold
By His donation ;—but man over man
He made not lord, such to Himself
Preserving, human left from human free.

(b)　　　　　　　　　　　*Milton*

DESPOTISM

Despotism is the abuse of royalty, as anarchy of republics. A Sultan who, without justice or form of justice, imprisons or puts to death his subjects, is a highway robber who calls himself Your Highness.

(c)　　　　　　　　　　　*Voltaire*

DESPOTS, GOVERNMENT OF

Despots govern by terror. They know, that he who fears God, fears nothing else ; and therefore they eradicate from the mind, through their Voltaire, their Helvetius, and the rest of that infamous gang, that only sort of fear which generates true courage.

(d)　　　　　　　　　　　*Burke*

DESTROY BY COMING (2 Thess. ii. 8)

There is nothing needed for the destruction of Antichrist than that the Lord *show Himself* (Ps. xciv. 1). Cf., as an earnest of this, John xviii. 6.

(e)　　　　　　　　　　　*Lange*

DEVIL, THE (John xvi.)

Even the Holy Ghost, who was to do away with all accommodations and strip off all Jewish embellishments of the truth, does not put an end to the teaching concerning a *Devil*, but rather begins it anew. The great cause is lost by the enemy of God, the author of all sin and unrighteousness, the blinder of men's minds into unbelief of a Saviour ; and it is *won for the world*, in which he has no longer either power or right.

(f)　　　　　　　　　　　*Ibid*

DEVIL, CAPTIVES OF

He hath not faster hold of any, than those that have learnt to ridicule everything of this kind, and who have put so much Sadduceeism into their creed (consisting of so many negatives or things they believe not, that they scarce leave enough positive to admit that name) as to think there is no such creature. But how near is he to them that think him out of the universe.

(g)　　　　　　　　　　　*J. Howe*

DEVIL, CAPTIVES OF

There are occasions when we go to Satan, when we put ourselves within his power, when we unheedingly, sometimes precipitately, sometimes wilfully, *enter into temptation*, and become his captives. He nets us at once: all is game that comes to his bag—believer or *unbeliever*. There is a story to this effect, worthless in itself, but valuable as to its moral.

Satan, it is said, was called to account by one of the ministering angels because he had entrapped one of God's people. He was ordered to release him, and to let the man go; but the wary enemy knew how to excuse himself, and replied : " I went not after this man; *he came to me*. I found him on such and such a day and in company with such and such people in the alehouse (or theatre), and we have kept him ever since."

(*a*)

DEVIL, THE, AS PORTRAYED IN LITERATURE AND THE BIBLE

1. Christian Portraiture of the Devil

We obtain this principally from the writings of Luther and Milton. The conception that both these great men had of the character of the Devil was a most imperfect and one-sided one, coloured in each instance by the times and surroundings in which they lived. There is truth in both descriptions; but in neither case is it presented to us quite as it is in the Bible.

(i.) LUTHER presents the devil to us in a light more or less ridiculous, whilst in Milton's description he is represented as a hero of no mean proportions. The Reformer, surrounded, as he was, with a false and corrupt ecclesiastical system rotten to the very core,—and against which he struggled, as did the infant Hercules with serpents in his cradle,—sees in it the very embodiment of the devil. To him the mystery of iniquity, as he saw it around him, is the very devil incarnate; and this image oftentimes, in the excited state of his brain, shaped itself before him, straddling (as Bunyan makes Apollyon do) right athwart his path, in order to hinder the great work in which the Reformer was engaged, and to which God was leading him on. Now, this kind of thing,—bad as it was then in its rottenness, worse as it is now in its insidiousness,—was and is but a *manifestation* of the agency of the *devil;* he was hidden behind it all, pulling the strings. His policy lies in the very fact of his hiding himself; for if men saw him, and as he is, they would not (as Eve was) be beguiled with his plausible and seductive talk. If the young man saw *him* who was tempting him, he would forsake his guilty pleasures; if men saw who was behind a religion of refined and sensuous attractiveness, they would flee from its shelter as from a false security, a refuge of lies. This angler catches men; but he is too wise to show himself; he uses other agencies,—our companions and the things of time and sense,—as his baits, for he knows our bias, our haunts and inclinations; and these baits are oftentimes so like the truth of God, that the very elect themselves need to watch and pray lest they be deceived, and drawn away with the errors of the wicked. For the reasons, then, that Luther, whilst rightly believing in the personality of the wicked one, presents him as a *demon*, ugly and loathsome, we are led to regard his as a one-

sided and imperfect delineation, cramped by the peculiar circumstances of his time and position. For if the devil were to appear to men as Luther pictures him, his design in appearing would be defeated; terrified and affrighted, they would flee from him. No, the being whom we are to "resist," to whom we are not to "give place," comes to us now, as of old he did to Eve, in a seductive form, with fascination and charm about him, too subtle and too pleasant for mortal man to resist in his own strength. The exhortation to " resist the devil," would scarcely have been necessary if it were his habit to tempt us in his own shape. His iniquitous design is not to terrify, but to please—not to come to us as the devil, but as an angel.

(ii.) MILTON writes from the standpoint of a Puritan, with a mind embued from his childhood with the theme of his great work, and is not wholly free from Luther's idea of a demon-shape. He nevertheless, in drawing for us the portraiture of the great adversary, has fallen into the unconscious error of making him a hero. It is hardly possible to read the "Paradise Lost," and not come to the conclusion, that the grandest character there, the most finished, the most prominent figure on the artist's canvas, is not the Saviour, but Satan. In the magnificence of his hellish surroundings,—his majestic tone and bearing, the pride and the hatred of the swarthy demon,—the author has put before us a hero whom every reader of taste and judgment must admire. And without doubt he is the grandest picture in that grandest of all poems. But again the Christian delineator is at fault, according to the Bible description. The Bible deals with facts; and the facts about the devil, as stated in that inspired Book, are, that he is not a hero, but a *sneak*, a*'liar* a *murderer*, a *pest*, a *thief*, and a *robber*, the spoiler of God's work wherever it be, and the author of all the *sin* and misery that has filled this earth with sorrow and tears. Not, then, till there is anything lovely or of good report in *sin*, not till there is something noble in a murderer, not till there is honour among thieves, not till there is manliness in a sneak, and health is found in a pestilence, can Milton's portraiture of the devil be translated from the region of fancy and poetry to that of fact. Like Luther, he *is* right in representing him as a mischievous personality, but wrong and unbiblical in painting him as a hero.

(*b*)

2. Secular Descriptions of the Devil

It is curious to note how secular, *i.e.* not intentionally and professedly Christian, writers have given more accurate portraitures of the devil. One of these writers is Shakspeare. Though not directly depicting the character of the devil, he yet does so indirectly, and with much scriptural correctness of detail, in the character of Iago, whose envy, intrigues, duplicity, baseness, and meanness bring about the tragedy of Othello. But unquestionably the most finished of such descriptions in secular literature is that given by Goethe, in the character of Mephistopheles. In drawing this character he has not fallen into Luther's error of depicting a demon in shape, nor that of Milton in making a hero; but, far more in accordance with the teachings of Holy Scripture, has he put before his readers a picture of the secret and hidden enemy of the human race, the destroyer of

(*c*)

souls, the ruiner of earthly happiness. Not like Milton's hero, who floated grandly from star to star, this fiend finds his sphere of action on earth, chiefly delighting in great cities. We see him coming less into contact with heavenly things than with earthly. Mean and clever to an extreme, he is represented as the evil spirit of modern society; always bent upon devilry; intimate with every conceivable way by which crime can be committed. There is not a wrong thing which people are in the habit of doing, but he knows all about it. If there is a joint loose anywhere, depend upon it he knows of it, and has a finger in it. He is profoundly versed in every species of professional quackery. Whatever promises to cause misery, to lead people astray, to break up alliances, to lead into error, to make them blaspheme the name of God and religion, is thoroughly in his line. He could draw up a catalogue of social vices; he could point out accurately enough the causes of deterioration in any individual man, here drink, there lust, ambition, avarice, greed. But it is not in the spirit of a philanthropist that he would do this, but in the spirit of a devil. His character is best described as a combination of knowing evil, and the way of producing it. He sees the rottenness of society; but he would not mend it. He sees the evil which ought to be rooted out; but he sees it only to enjoy it. Everything going wrong, twaddle and quackery, shams and counterfeits abounding everywhere; nothing to be seen under the sun but hypocritical priests, sharking attorneys, unhappy homes, children crying for bread, men and women *cheating, robbing, murdering* each other. And what is the effect upon him? Why, he sees all this only to *gloat* over it, and show that it is only as his devil-like nature would have it to be. . . . It is fun to him. He, as it were, throws his cap up in the air, and says, "Evil, be thou my good." Now this writer, in describing such a character as this, whether consciously or unconsciously, has given to the world of literature a far truer and more scriptural portraiture of the enemy of mankind than either Milton or Luther. For it is in the combination of the knowledge and enjoyment of evil, and in the ceaseless vigilance, ever bringing it about, and producing the most deplorable and disastrous consequences, that we best understand the character of the fallen spirit.

(*a*)

3. Biblical Portraiture of the Devil

In one word, he is the direct opposite to the Lord Jesus Christ. We read of him as the "god of this world"; he is said to "blind the eyes of those who believe not." He allures into sin, and afterwards drives the unhappy victim to despair and suicide: thus he has been a murderer from the beginning, the "Accuser" of God's people, the calumniator of their characters, the make-bate and peace-destroyer of consciences. As the father of lies, as the quoter of Scripture, the Bible puts him before us as mean, despicable, ignoble, base, and shameless, the personification of everything that is infamous, allied to stupendous abilities and power, whose works the Lord Jesus Christ came to *destroy*. From whose power the Lord will deliver His own; for whom the comforting promise stands, "The God of peace shall bruise Satan under your feet shortly" (Rom. xvi. 20).
Adapted from a work entitled " The Three Devils."
(*b*)

DEVIL DESTROYED BY HIS OWN MACHINERY, THE

The Apostles of Judæa taught very differently from the philosophers of Greece: the latter reasoned with a few scholars; the apostles bore witness to facts, with the demonstration of the Spirit and with power. They invited, they threatened, they promised; but it was all, not by might of human reasoning, but with the authority of the name of Christ. The facts were few: that Jesus was the Messiah, that He was born in Bethlehem, that He died under Pontius Pilate, that He was buried, that He rose from the dead and ascended into heaven, from whence He would come to judge the quick and the dead. These facts took hold of the multitude. The philosopher lurked in the school, but the Gospel went forth to the high places of the city, and the strange story secured a hearing from the wise and the foolish. Upon these facts, they based a great truth which crowned the whole, namely, that the forgiveness of sins, the sanctification of men, and life everlasting, proceeded from the death of one person. One Mediator and one sacrifice, provided a royal and infallible remedy for all the evil of sin. When this proved a stumbling-block to the Jew, and foolishness to the Greek, they witnessed that the One Person was "God manifest in the flesh;" that the two natures were united in Him; that as a man, He could obey, suffer, and die; and that as a God, infinite virtue and merit streamed like a sea from His death, to win pardon for the sinner and the influence of the Spirit. They asserted that He had, as the Wisdom and Power of God, so counterworked the machinery of sin, which the devil had devised for the destruction of man, as to employ it for other purposes. Many an inventor has lost his life by his own machine; so the wisdom of God was able to work this machinery in such a manner that the devil's own head was crushed by it. When he set it in motion to destroy the second Adam, after it had been successfully at work through the ages, its wheels whirled so fearfully on Calvary that the earth trembled and the rocks rent; but, by-and-by, it was found that the devil himself had been caught by the fiery wheels, and was destroyed by his own invention. "That through death He might destroy him that had the power of death, that is, the devil."

(*c*)   *Christmas Evans*

DEVIL AND SCRIPTURE

The devil can cite Scripture for his purpose.
(*d*)   *Shakspeare*

DEVIL AND SCRIPTURE

And thus I clothed my naked villany
With odd old ends, stolen forth of holy writ;
And seem a saint, when most I play the devil.
(*e*)   *Shakspeare*

DEVIL, WILES OF

The devil hath power to assume a pleasing shape.
                                              Shakspeare
(*See also* SATAN, SERPENT, ACCUSER.)
(*f*)

DEVILISH EGOISM

The utmost development and the last form of egoism is *devilish*. The devil, in his pride, would make himself god; but he can only do this by raging in his hatred against the one true God, in order to destroy His kingdom and dominion.

The question may be asked, whether this *devilish egoism* can occur among men at all? In principle their last stage of evil may be occupied in this world in so far as men place themselves in the service of the devilish principle: the Holy Scriptures speak of men who are " children of the devil " (John viii. 44). And experience shows us the presence of the devilish principle among us also, shows us manifestations of wickedness in which a demoniac energy is expressed, that unmistakably testifies of a connection with the demoniac kingdom. There is in the world of men an enmity against good, shown in that " pleasure in unrighteousness " which is not rare (1 Cor. xiii. 6); shown also in the frequently occuring envy, malice, cruelty, that finds pleasure in torturing other men with the most exquisite pains, bodily or mental; shown in a pleasure in destruction and annihilation, which may appear as frantic mania, as in the Roman Emperors, in a Nero or a Caligula, who wished that all the heads of the Roman people had but one neck, that he might at one stroke cut them off together.

(*a*)   *Martensen*

DEVILRY

On one occasion, so the story runs, the devils were met together in hell, to relate their experiences on earth. One had upset a train by putting an iron rail on the road. Another had roused the wind into a storm and so brought about the wreck of a noble ship. Another had caused a quarrel between kings, war had ensued, and thousands of hearts were wrung in anguish for the fallen. At the recital of each, the response from the Prince of Darkness was " *Well done !* " But when one said he had entangled the feet of a servant of God in an intrigue, and the man had fallen into gross sin, the answer was, " *Thou hast done best of all.*" Then were there hand-shakings and congratulations in hell, because a deed had been done which would give occasion for the enemy to blaspheme.

(*b*)

DEVILRY

" The teeth-grinding, glass-eyed, lone Caloyer " [Byron].

(*c*)   *Carlyle*

Of the work that I have done, it becomes me not to speak, save only as relates to the Satanic school, and its Coryphæus, the author of " Don Juan." I have held up that school to public detestation, as enemies to the religion, the institutions, and the domestic morals of the country. I have given them a designation *to which their founder and leader answers;* I have sent a stone from my sling which has smitten their Goliath in the forehead. I have fastened his name upon the gibbet, for reproach and ignominy as long as it shall endure.

(*d*)   *Southey*

His [Byron's] voice was such a voice as the devil tempted Eve with; you feared its fascination the moment you heard it.

(*e*)   *Mrs. Opie*

DEVILRY

He [Byron] makes virtue serve as a foil to vice. . . . He hallows in order to desecrate ; takes a pleasure in defacing the images of beauty his hands have wrought; and raises our hopes and our belief in goodness to heaven, only to dash them to the earth again.

(*f*)   *Hazlitt*

Byron's countenance is a thing to dream of. A certain lady, whose name has been too often mentioned in connection with his, told a friend of mine, that when she first saw Byron, it was in a crowded room, and she did not know who it was; but her eyes were instantly nailed, and she said to herself, *that pale face is my fate.* And, poor soul, if a godlike face and godlike powers could have made any excuse for devilry, to be sure she had one.

(*g*)   *Lockhart*

DIES IRÆ

[Author supposed to be *Thomas of Celano*, a small town near Lake Fucino.]

> Day of anger, day of wonder,
> When the world shall roll asunder,
> Quenched in fire, and smoke, and thunder.
>
> Oh, vast terror, wild heart rending,
> Of that hour when earth is ending
> And her Judge descending—
>
> When the trumpet's voice astoundeth,
> Through earth's sepulchres reboundeth,
> Summons universal soundeth !
>
> Death astonied, nature shaken,
> Sees all creatures as they waken,
> To that dire tribunal taken.
>
> Lo ! the Book, where all is hoarded,
> Not a secret unrecorded,
> Every doom is thence awarded.
>
> Lo the Judge, when He arraigneth,
> Every hidden thing explaineth,
> Nothing unavenged remaineth.
>
> In that fiery revelation
> Where shall I make supplication,
> When the just hath scarce salvation ?
>
> Fount of love, dread King supernal,
> Freely giving life eternal—
> Save me from the pains infernal !
>
> This forget not, sweet Life-giver,
> Me thou camest to deliver ;
> Cast me not away for ever !
>
> Seeking me Thy sad life lasted,
> On the cross death's pains were tasted,
> Let not toil like this be wasted !
>
> God of righteous retribution,
> Grant my sins full absolution
> Ere Thy wrath's last execution !

(*h*)

Lo ! I stand with face suffusèd,
Groaning, in my guilt accusèd,
Spare my soul, with sorrow bruisèd !

By the Magdalene forgiven,
By the dying robber shriven,
I too cherish hope of heaven.

Though my prayers are full of failing,
Save me, of Thy grace availing,
From the pit of endless wailing.

On Thy right a place provide me,
With Thy chosen sheep beside me ;
From the goats, good Lord, divide me !

When to penal fire are driven
Those who would not be forgiven,
Call me with Thy saints to heaven !

Kneeling, crushed in heart, before Thee,
Sad and suppliant, I adore Thee ;
Hear me, save me, I implore Thee !

Translated from the Latin by *P. S. Worsley*
(Blackwood's Magazine, March, 1860).

(a)

DIFFERENCES IN SIN

Sins are distinguished from each other, not only according as they are sins of omission or transgression, but by the *different degrees* of energy in the sinful will. The good will must overcome the temptations to evil ; and the evil will must overcome the hindrances that conscience places in its way. . . . It belongs to paradoxes to deny the *difference* of sins, to maintain that he who steals a penny and he who kills his mother are both in equal measure guilty. The Stoics, who set up this paradox, appeal no doubt to this, that he who is only a yard deep under water drowns just as much as he who is 500 fathoms deep ; that in both cases one is bad, or the opposite of what he ought to be ; wherefore Draco, the first lawgiver of Athens, imposed the penalty of death for every crime. They lean also on the argument that it is indifferent whether one is only one mile or a hundred miles distant from the city ; for in both cases he is outside the city (morality), while the point is to be inside. The truth in this paradox is the absolute difference of essence between good and evil, virtue and vice. . . . Stoicism holds fast to *quality*, and places quantity entirely out of view.

(b)   *Martensen*

DIFFERENCES IN SIN : ANSWERS TO STOICAL PARADOXES

If one steals an apple from the garden of a wealthy man, cuts a twig from another man's wood, and commits several actions of this sort about the same time, he yet sins less than he who murders a single innocent man, if one would not make, say, the arm or head of a man equal to an apple or twig.

(c)   *Holberg*

THE STOICAL PARADOX ANNULS THE DIFFERENCE BETWEEN NEARER AND FARTHER

What lies a mile distant from a place, is divided from it indeed, as well as what lies a hundred miles from it ; but it does not follow that both things lie equally distant from the place. All that deviates from the truth is a lie, but not equally great ; for one lie may approach the truth more nearly than another, as one wrong way may conduct the wanderer farther from the highway than another, although both are wrong ways. He goes most astray who wanders in the way that leads farthest from the goal ; as the mariner most misses his way who sails before a wind blowing directly from the harbour. For though the north-west is not the same as the north wind, yet the difference is not so great as between north and south. . . . If one earnestly considers the thing, it appears that the Stoic doctrine on this point is not only false and unfounded, but also foolish and childish ; and one may wonder that so many eminent men have zealously defended it.

(d)   *Holberg*

DIFFERENCES IN SIN : TEACHING OF COMMON SENSE AND OF HOLY SCRIPTURE

(i.) Common sense and moral feeling, as expressed in ordinary life, will also ever oppose the proposition that there is no difference between sinners.

(ii.) Holy Scripture unites both points of view, the *essence* (Stoicism) as well as *reality*.

The Essence :

" Whosoever shall keep the whole law, and yet offend in one point, he is guilty of all " (Jas. ii. 10).

The Reality :

"He that delivered me unto thee hath the greater sin " (John xix. 11). It shall be more tolerable for Tyre and Sidon at the Day of Judgment than for those cities where Christ Himself had preached the Gospel of Grace (Matt. xi. 24).

Some are mentioned as " not far from the kingdom of God " (Mark xii. 34).

Some are "nigh " and others are " far off" (Eph. ii. 17 ; Acts ii. 39).

Whence it clearly appears that the Lord and His apostles do not teach that it is indifferent whether one be one mile distant from the city or a hundred.

The difference in degree between sins is expressed in the distinction between sins of ignorance (1 Tim. i. 13) and deliberate sins (1 Tim. iv. 2) ; between sins of weakness (like Peter's denial) and sins of wickedness (Judas, the mockers, 2 Pet. iii. 3), flagitious sins (Jas. v. 4, of the rich who withhold their wages from the labourers), between human, bestial, and devilish sins.

As a special class may be mentioned the so-called "infinite sins," the greatness of which is undefinable and immeasurable, when a single sin is followed by an infinite, immense host. Thus an unjust and unconscientious declaration of war involves an immense and quite innumerable host of injustices against the life, health, property, of men, peaceful family and civil life, trade and industry, and so on. A false bankruptcy, or an unprincipled joint-stock swindle, which at last breaks out in a crisis or a crash, which produces an incomputable destruction of the well-being of innocent and guileless individuals and families, likewise belongs to the immeasurable sins, with an illimitable tail. There is a distinction also made between remissible sins, and sins unto death (1 John v. 16).

(e)   *Martensen*

DINNER

For his platter of meat, for his dinner of herbs, he could never give thanks enough. . . . It may truly be a subject of wonder how a man who has not, like the King of France, four hundred and forty-eight persons (the hundred and sixty-one *Garçons de la Maison-bouche* I do not reckon) in his kitchen, nor a *Fruiterie* of thirty-one human bipeds, nor a pastry-cookery of three-and-twenty, nor a daily expenditure of 387 livres 21 sous,—how such a man, I say, can eat with any satisfaction. Nevertheless, to me, a cooking mother is as dear as a whole royal cooking household, given rather to feed upon me than to feed me.

(*a*)   *J. P. F. Richter*

DINNER-BELL, INFLUENCE OF

Of all appeals—although
I grant the power of pathos and of gold,
Of beauty, flattery, threats, a shilling—no
Method's more sure at moments to take hold
Of the best feelings of mankind, which grow
More tender, as we every day behold,
Than that all-softening, overpowering knell,
The tocsin of the soul, the dinner-bell.

(*b*)   *Byron*

"DISCIPLE, HE CANNOT BE MY" (Luke xiv. 26, 27, 33)

Occasion

Our Lord surrounded with great multitudes of people. "They went with Him." Probably intending to journey with Him to Jerusalem, and there make Him their King. But, like all multitudes and great gatherings of masses of people, who flock around one central figure, they knew next to nothing about Him and His cause, nor why they were there at all. It was enough that the movement was popular, that it grew daily, and that adherents of their own class identified themselves with the movement. He was the popular hero ; and the people, glad to be led, glad to have an opportunity of ventilating their grievances and of vindicating their rights, rallied around Him. Thus the movement took the form of an opposition to the then existing ruling classes.

But they miscalculated. It was no such sympathy as this that Jesus wanted. Though they easily succeeded in deceiving themselves, they did not deceive Him. And it was to undeceive them, to give them an opportunity of withdrawing from His company before they had committed themselves too far, that He told them plainly the only conditions of discipleship ; warning them that, if they could not fulfil those conditions, they could not be His disciples, and had better retire from a false position.

The words, "*he cannot be My disciple*," occur here three times, and are the words of the Heart Searcher, who knows what is in man, searching the hearts of His followers, and of His Church, in all ages ; of congregations and ministers alike, that they may consider how the matter stands, when they hear from His own infallible lips what His sole conditions of discipleship are. How necessary, with David, to pray, " Search me, O God, and know my heart ; try me, and know my thoughts ; and see if there be any way of wickedness in me, and lead me in the way everlasting "

(Psa. cxxxix. 23). And when the heart-searching reveals that abyss of deceitfulness within us—the human heart—then, with the Church of England, add : " Cleanse, O Lord, the thoughts of our hearts by the inspiration of Thy Holy Spirit, that we may perfectly love Thee, and worthily magnify Thy Holy Name, through Jesus Christ our Lord."

(*c*)

" DISCIPLE, HE CANNOT BE MY "

1. Misconception of the Nature of Discipleship

This is the first error of the multitude. That there was something radically wrong with this people whom our Lord was addressing, was soon made painfully evident. When Jesus seemed to be successful and carrying all before Him, these people shouted, " Hosanna ! blessed is He who cometh in the name of the Lord." But as soon as the tide turned the other way, and nothing, as they think, is to be gained by siding with a man who has failed, they raise their voices, and shout amongst those of His murderers, " Crucify Him ! crucify Him ! "

It is proverbial that opinions easily adopted are as easily let go. And our Lord's teaching on this point is to the same effect ; " *He cannot be My disciple* " who has easily and lightly joined himself to the ranks of My followers. He has taken a position without knowing its nature, and what it may entail upon him. He has treated discipleship as a matter unworthy of the commonest calculation, such as he would bestow upon the minor matters of every-day life. Whereas, in fact, this is a matter of life and death ; it involves eternal issues ; it is a Rubicon which, once crossed, allows of no return, save that of ignominy and disgrace. Would a man undertake an affair of *great cost*, such as the building of a tower, a palace, or a house, without previously calculating the cost, and going minutely into all the details ? He would have the plan of it before him ; he would estimate quantities, and consider the ways and means of completing his design. Before beginning, he would take every means and precaution of ensuring success. For failure, after having once begun and made public his big idea, would bring upon him insufferable and life-long ridicule. Now *discipleship* is an affair of *great cost*. It may cost a man his life ; it may cost him life-long separation from his nearest relatives ; it may set him at variance with them ; it may take him, for My sake, before cruel magistrates and rulers ; it may require him to pack up and go wherever I may send him ; it will require of him the sacrifice of ease and self-indulgence ; it will make demands upon his time, his money, and his talents. In fact, My disciple has, in the first place, to give Me his heart, and the disposal of himself and all that is his will naturally follow.

But is this an easy affair ? Is this a little thing that I ask ? Is this something likely to cost less deliberate thinking about than any one of the businesses of life in which you may be engaged, and which demand your toil, watchfulness, and unceasing energy, if you would command success ?

If, then, you cannot get together and conduct a business in any happy-go-lucky or slipshod style, no more can ye be My disciples without first of all seriously counting the cost, and seeing what is involved in the very nature of discipleship.

(*d*)

MOREOVER, DISCIPLESHIP IS AN AFFAIR OF DANGER

It is a *warfare*, and you will have to fight. Not an individual amongst My followers can escape this. He will have to fight against self, against the world, and against a watchful, unscrupulous, malignant, crafty, spiritual foe, who has made conquest his study ever since men began to live on this earth. Will it do to let you enroll yourselves on My side without a moment's thought of the *dangers* you thereby incur? Will you, in your weakness and unpreparedness, go to meet a skilful general, with a host of veterans skilled in the art, and already on the march against you? You have not so much as a sling and a stone, and yet ye would join Me and go to war with the Prince of Darkness, against principalities and powers, against spiritual wickedness in high places; and who have allies even in your own camp, and the whole world on their side.

Ye cannot be My disciples without being prepared for this, without having contemplated this, and without buckling on the complete armour of a Christian soldier. You would forsake Me as soon as distress and persecution arose for My sake and the Gospel's. Ye cannot be My disciples unless, then, ye have counted the *cost*, and prepared yourselves for *danger*.

(*a*)

"HE CANNOT BE MY DISCIPLE"

2. The next stage in our Lord's teaching shows us the **INABILITY** of those persons **TO FULFIL THE CONDITIONS OF DISCIPLESHIP**

They would, it appears, meet with something unpleasant in His society from the very first. They would not have a Paradise to live in. They would not have all sunshine in their life. They might possibly find that they would scarcely have enough to eat and drink. They might have to go scantily clothed. In fact, they would have to bear what our Lord calls a CROSS. *Bearing His Cross:* What a misconception there seems to be about it! The CROSS is

(i.) *An Ornament*, dangling around the neck, on watch-chains with other trinkets. It enters largely into every architectural device of the church architect. On church furniture and fittings, tortured into gas brackets, picture frames, and on carpets, we find this symbol freely used. As such, however, it has no meaning, beyond being an æsthetical decoration befitting the surrounding associations.

(ii.) *It is a Symbol of our Profession*, the baptismal sign of a soldier of Jesus Christ.

(iii.) *It is a Symbol of our Faith*, and, as such, used as an external mark, or sign, upon our churches, to distinguish them from Jewish synagogues or Mahometan mosques. And thus it bears a silent witness that *Here Jesus Christ is worshipped and preached.*

(iv.) *It is a symbol, in its length and breadth, of the Love of God*, as was said by the martyred Archbishop of Paris, in the late Commune.

(v.) *It is a symbol of Hope*, and, as such, appropriately placed over the grave of a Christian, instead of the hideous and Pagan monstrosities which formerly disfigured our graveyards and cemeteries.

(vi.) *It is a symbol of the Triumph won by Christ over Death*, and appropriate as an Easter symbol, following the gloom of Good Friday, and triumphantly asking with the Apostle—

"O grave, where is thy victory?
O death, where is thy sting?"

All these are well, and more or less beautiful in their way, but they are all *dispensable:* we are not the better for their use, nor the worse for leaving them unused and undone.

But the CROSS-BEARING of which the Lord speaks is *indispensable:* He cannot be My disciple without it. This is the guinea-stamp upon the gold; without which none is genuine.

Let us examine it.

"His Cross" = the Christian's, not Christ's. Christ was crucified upon one; you will be crucified upon another. Yours, probably, will not be a material cross of wood or metal; but each has *his* or *her* cross.

THE CROSS IS THE SYMBOL OF THE CHRISTIAN LIFE.

It is Christ's yoke laid upon you, to denote that you are His.

A cross consists of two pieces of material—one longer than the other. These are laid transversely. The longer piece signifies the Christian life—straight, smooth, pleasant, all on a level, with no hitch, nor pain, nor trouble. Life, according to this, is Arcadian, brimful of sunshine and happiness. This is the *long piece.*

By-and-by another piece is laid athwart it—right straight across; now life ceases to be Arcadian; it is no longer a Paradise; it is almost tragical. *It is crucifixion*—that is your cross, O Christian! Something comes to you which does not fit in with your previously pleasant and smoothly flowing life: it goes right athwart your likings, your proclivities; it hurts you—you say it will kill you! Oh, how you worry and chafe against this cross; how you pray to be free of it! But no; it is *yours*, and you have to be crucified on it. "Thrice" did Paul beseech the Lord to remove his—but the answer was, "My grace is sufficient for thee." It is the best thing for thee; probably you would not be so useful, or you could not get to heaven at all, without that cross of yours. David said, "I know that in very faithfulness Thou hast afflicted me;" another asked, "What do I not owe to the cross?"

It is in this sense that we are to understand our Lord's teaching about the necessity of *cross-bearing.*

And when looked into more particularly, we find that a *living man* was nailed, or bound, hand and foot, to a rough and rude cross-tree. Crucifixion has no meaning for a corpse. The victim must be a living man; it is intended to *kill*. The Christian is *alive unto God;* hence the meaning of the Cross for him. He finds that crucifixion is as real a thing for him as it was for Christ. There he is a living man—spitted on his cross, and though struggling, unable to detach himself from it. The nails go through his likings, his desires, his hopes, his prospects, his flesh, his will: he cannot escape. He suffers because he is alive. In fact, crucifixion is a living death, designed to crucify the whole body of sin. And this, the Lord assures us, is an imperative condition of discipleship.

(*b*)

He cannot be My Disciple

3. The WORTHLESSNESS of this kind of Discipleship :

"*Ye are the salt of the earth.*" Your business is to preserve and to benefit the world. But if, like salt which has lost its properties, ye have no salt in you, and ye cease to be useful and beneficial, then, like it, are ye *worthless*, fit only to be cast away as useless—neither fit for the land, nor yet for the dunghill, but men cast it out. " He that hath ears to hear, let him hear."

(a)

Discipleship, Christian

"*Abide in Me, and I in you. As the branch cannot bear fruit of itself, except it abide in the vine ; no more can ye, except ye abide in Me* " (John xv. 4).

1. Peculiarities of :

"*Abide in Me, and I in you.*" These words indicate the peculiar relationship between Christ and His disciples. The relationship must never cease. The pupil, or the disciple, will never be independent of the Master. In point of fact, if the disciple becomes independent, and strikes out a course of action of his own, the relationship at once ceases—neither Master nor disciple "*abide* " in each other. Now, contrast this with the relationship existing between any *human* teacher and his disciples. The relationship in such cases is constantly changing : the instructions of the teacher render the disciple ever more and more independent of him ; and there comes a time when the teacher has imparted all that he can, and the disciple stands in no further need of his instructions. Nor can a human teacher demand that his disciples shall always remain, in personal association with him, as necessary to life and the right conduct of life. Yet, when Christ describes Himself as the Vine, and His disciples as the branches, He does demand all this. He teaches us that the relationship between Him and them is a *permanent* one, that they must ever be drawing out of His fulness,— and can never do anything in their future life without Him. They can never exhaust Him. Discipleship, then, becomes, in the deepest and truest sense, one of uninterrupted and incessant *reception* and *appropriation* of Christ : " I in you, and ye in Me."

(b) *Martensen*

Discipleship

2. Another Peculiarity :

When Christ spake these words, about the vine and its branches, He was still with His disciples. The fact that His disciples could *abide* in Him after He was taken away from them, and that we too can *abide* in Him, though centuries have elapsed since He sojourned on earth, rests on His being a living Christ, who, as Lord and Head of the Church, carries on and perfects the Communion betwixt Himself and His people by all the various means of grace or channels through which the grace of life flows to us, and by the agency of the Holy Spirit. And we do well to remember that He taught His disciples that, for the purpose of their truly abiding in Him, *it was expedient for them that He went away ;* "for," says He, " if I go not away, the Comforter will not come unto you." So long as in an outward and a material sense they could be His followers, so long was real discipleship imperfect. True discipleship began when He was taken away from them, and the Holy Spirit poured out upon them on the day of Pentecost. Then for the first time they realized the inner and real communion with Him. Then Christ's history was understood by them, then they understood the Scriptures, and *then* Christ began to be formed *within* them ; and then they, depending upon His gifts of Grace, began to reflect His image in the world. And, saving that they beheld the Saviour with their bodily eye, our position *as disciples* is the same as was theirs. For it is the constant work of the exalted Saviour, by means of His Spirit, to *collect* His disciples, to train them by His providential leadings, to fill them with His mind and His spirit, and thus, *He in them,* to be Himself perpetually in the presence of men and in the world. So that Christ here teaches us that, though He has ascended into the Heavens, yet He has not left this earth, for He is in it—in it, because He is in His people. We hear Him speak, when we listen to them ; we see Him, when we see them ; we see His actions, when we witness theirs. The sin only, which still clings to them and defiles them, is theirs—the graces which *shine* in them are all His ; and thus He is personally ever present in the world.

(c) *Ibid*

Discipleship, Stages of

1. Discipleship and Baptism

Baptism is the initiatory rite of Christianity : admission to Discipleship takes place by *Baptism.* God's saving grace, or " the grace which bringeth salvation," is for all men ; and not for a single people or a small section of people who may choose to call themselves " the elect of God." Christianity is no secret Society, but it is the people's religion—it is " for all men." Consequently it desires to make itself the public religion, the religion of the world, according to our Lord's own command : " Go ye therefore, and teach all nations, baptizing them in the name of the Father, and of the Son, and of the Holy Ghost." Now, it is just because the Church of Christ is the Universal Church, or the Church of the *Nations,* that it is the National Church ; and in the National Church Baptism must be the baptism of infants, otherwise it is not the National Church ; for if infants be excluded, it becomes the Church of a sect. And, again, the child who is brought up under Christian surroundings and influences, even from the commencement of its natural life, ought unquestionably to be initiated into Christian discipleship.

But does this publicity of doctrine and worship in the Christian Church, this free and open reception of infants into discipleship, this preaching of the Gospel to the masses, this instruction in holy things and in the mysteries of the kingdom of Heaven, seem to some to be *profanity,* and a casting pearls before swine ? Seemeth it so to any one ? Know then that this publicity in teaching and in practice is the consequence of " the grace which bringeth salvation having appeared unto all men ; likewise it is the consequence of Christ's command, " Teach whole nations, and baptize them."

(d)

Mark also how by this the Gospel invitation is scattered abroad, how fully and how plentifully the seed is sown by the sower, with no niggard hand nor stinted supply. Freely and thickly it falls over the whole field, which is "the world." God's unspeakable gift,—the gift of Salvation,—is a universal gift ; and the fulness of Divine love so orders it, that much of the precious seed falls on the "wayside," where it will speedily be trodden under foot of men, or devoured by the fowls of the air. And this He does, that in the last great day every one may be without excuse.

But though this deep and rich treasure of Grace and of life is thus open to all, and laid at the feet of all, yet it is like the treasure hid in the field, which must be found and bought at any price ; it is like the *pearl* which must be sought, and for which a man must give all that he hath.

(a)   *Martensen*

Discipleship and Awakening

The preparatory process,—which a man must undergo before he can "receive the things of the Spirit,"—is called "An Awakening :"—

Faith is a man's own act : we are responsible for our individual *belief* or *unbelief;* but yet, in its first cause, it is a work of Divine grace. And this preparatory work is like the preaching of John the Baptist "*to make ready* a *people prepared for the Lord.*" We call this influence of the Spirit an "Awakening," because the man is aroused from a state of sleep, awakened out of a dream. The Spirit uses the well-known words, "Awake, thou that sleepest, and arise from the dead, and Christ shall give thee light." It is not that these words apply only to the ungodly and the profane ; they apply to the baptized Christian, who from his childhood has kept the faith, and has never wandered into courses of open sin ; he or she, too, requires an *awakening,* so that he or she may perceive seriously and personally his or her responsibility before God, seriously examine in what his or her Christianity consists— what it gives to him, what it demands of him, and what mutual relationship exists between Christ and his or her soul. And if we ask the means by which this awakening is effected? It is by the Word of God, in conjunction with the *guidings of God's Providence.* Go back to the experience of the first disciples. They were first awakened by the preaching of John the Baptist, combined with the signs of the times and the study of the Old Testament Scriptures. They were then young men who felt within them a craving after the hope of Israel, and there was nothing in the religion of the period to satisfy that craving ; but gradually God led them (as He will lead all anxious souls) to Christ. Others are awakened during the judgments of God on nations and cities, in times of *war* and *pestilence.* Others by personal sufferings, a bed of sickness, the near approach of death, or by any other adversity. Others, as Luther, by a sudden flash of lightning at his side ; or, as John Newton, in danger of shipwreck, are awakened to the thought of *death* and *judgment to come.* Another, again, may be allowed to fall unthinkingly into such sin as may open his eyes to the weakness of his nature, to the peril in which he stood : thinking, it may be, that he stood too firmly and too securely to stumble and to fall, suddenly the abyss opens before him, he stumbles,

and is awakened to his peril. The Prodigal Son was awakened when, through want and degradation and distress, he came to himself. Mary Magdalen, whose soul was imperilled by seven devils, was awakened at the word of Jesus. Saul, "breathing out threatenings and curses against the saints," is awakened by the blinding flash of lightning on his way to Damascus. Others, again, are awakened by a gentler method : we meet a man who can tell us things that we wanted to know, who can explain our difficulties. Such was the awakening of the Ethiopian Eunuch, to whom, at the opportune moment, Philip came, as the messenger of God. Yes, and others by more ordinary methods still, in the ordinary associations of life. In the daily round of duties, how often has it been that we have been thrown into juxtaposition with a disciple of Christ whose personality has borne testimony to the Master. And how many more have been won to Christ by their home relations—by their wives. Won, as the Apostle says, "without the word, merely by their holy conversation." All these, however, are the outward leadings of Providence. There are yet other means which God uses for man's awakening, and they are *internal.* In many a man there is an inward disquietude and unrest, a heaviness of heart which will not allow him to find rest and happiness and consolation in anything created. From this inward melancholy there comes a craving after Christ, and a search after Him.

In the midst of so many religions, so many conflicting opinions, one man will ask,—not as Pilate, sceptically, but from the inward depths of his own being,—"What is truth?" Another wants the blessing of salvation, the forgiveness of his sins ; nothing profits him, nothing benefits him, no preaching nor teaching, until you can show him this, "*How can man be just before God?*" It is to no purpose that you tell such a man that Christianity is the true religion, unless you can first make him see that he himself is accepted by God. A man has for long years perhaps been oppressed with a sense of sin, with a burden of guilt ; he has striven to be pure and upright, but has constantly experienced the power of indwelling sin. He has been cast down by the stern rigour of the Law, and his own endeavours after holiness have shown him that the Law cannot give a new heart nor new desires. Enjoyment of existence is impossible in such a case. It were better not to live, if this be life, and all that life has to offer a man. It was in such a frame of mind that the old monk met Luther in the cloister of the monastery, and pointed out to him the article of the Creed which expresses belief in the forgiveness of sins, saying to him, "Dr. Martin, thou dost not believe in the forgiveness of sins."

There are others, again, whose hearts are as a desolate wilderness ; they crave for something to love and to cling to. Nothing on earth is sufficient to fill this void, or to be the proper companion of this loneliness. The heart must first meet an object worthy of its hopes and aspirations, before its disquietude can be allayed ; and this it does when spiritually it sits under the shadow of the Most High, and dwells in His tabernacle. These are they whom Christ invites, "Come unto Me, all ye who labour and are heavy laden, and I will give you rest." Thousands have not got this craving, consequently they can do without Christ ; their "*hour is not yet come.*"

(b)   *Martensen*

DISCIPLESHIP, EXAMPLES OF

Let such as desire to know more of this matter study the memoirs and histories of eminent men who have made their mark in the Christian world; and if such records be studied with the intention of ascertaining how the *inward and outward dealings* of Providence have at last resulted in Christian discipleship, they will possess the highest interest. Inquirers will thus see that all the paths, manifold as they may be, in which the inquirer after salvation has been led, have at last converged and met at one point—*all end at Christ*. Among such memoirs the " Confessions of Augustine " are the most remarkable. Looking at the man as he pictures his own life previous to his becoming a Christian, you see a chaos of the greatest confusion, the man at war with himself; now this passion swaying him one way, now that swaying him in another. A perfect network and labyrinth of entanglement. But through all this you may see, at the same time, the path of the soul towards God. Though the life be dark, its tendency is all one way; the soul travels along its appointed path, and finds God at the end. Most instructive is it to witness in Augustine's life, how the *inward* struggle within him and the *outward* dealings of Providence work together to bring about the same result. Mark his unquenchable desire after truth; see him, in order to find out what is truth, sifting one dogma of human teaching and learning after another, and getting to the bottom of it, then casting it aside for another. The restless and hungry soul could not stay itself upon these—there was no satisfaction in any of them. Mark, too, his career of sin, his unbridled licentiousness, and his vainly seeking to stay its strong impulses by his own power; and which at last brought him to feel his own helplessness and misery and condemnation. Mark also, on the other side, the exhortations and prayers of his pious mother, Monica; the preaching of Ambrosius, the reading of the Holy Scriptures, the examples of perdition around him: a great worldly life sinking into ruins. It was not one of these things merely, but all these things working together, which at last brought him to Christ, where, as a brand plucked from the burning, he became the greatest teacher of *sin* and *free grace* of his own and succeeding times. We may see the same thing, in a different phase of life and society, in Bunyan's " *Grace Abounding to the Chief of Sinners*," wherein he describes his life, and the way in which he was led to Christ, and in the lives of John Newton, Robert McCheyne of Scotland, James Smith of Cheltenham, etc., where-

" Determined to save, He watched over my path,
  When, Satan's blind slave, I sported with death."

(a)   *Martensen and others*

DISCIPLESHIP AND CONVERSION

But disciples of Christ must know something beyond an *awakening*: great and important as that is, we must not stop at it. Awakening must ripen into CONVERSION, and pass over into *regeneration*. The prodigal must not only " come to himself," but he must arise and go to his Father. Not till then do we become *new creatures*, and make a fresh start. Hitherto we have been without life, without hope, dead as pertaining to God: now life is communicated, and our history commences. We begin here, now our names are

inscribed in the *Baptismal Register in heaven;* and God adopts us as His children, puts us into His training school, in order in the end to bring us out, purified from the peculiar defilements each brought with him when he came to Christ. For it is quite true that Christ takes us *just as we are*, without our making ourselves fit for Him; but it must not for a moment be thought that He keeps us and leaves us as we are, or as He finds us. His work of subduing, disciplining, training, and purifying then begins; and well be it for us if we do not prove reprobate under the process. Only by abiding in Him, as we started so to continue, shall we be fruitful branches, which the husbandman will not cut off and reject. After *conversion*, not after *awakening*, all this ensues: for the awakened man, as such only, has no consistency; he has arrived at no steadfastness; as yet his soul is not anchored upon Christ. The formation of character can only start from our New Birth. And the sure mark that regeneration has taken place, is the attitude of the soul towards Jesus Christ, it *cannot do without Him*. He is necessary to it— its Manna, Bread and Water of Life. Justified by faith in Jesus Christ, the soul appropriates Him as its own possession; and a new development of life and character succeeds.

(b)   *Martensen (adapted)*

DISCIPLINE

Discipline is ever productive of the " peaceable fruit of righteousness." A sky never clouded would cause a barren earth.

(c)   *Good Words*, 1861

DISCIPLINE

I believe that one of the causes why men murmur so much against God's discipline, is because they do not understand it. Whenever something comes upon us that is hard to bear, and we do not see the meaning of it, the tendency of our hearts is to rebel against it; but if we understand it, if we see what God means, that it is His wisdom and His love which are dealing with us, then it is far easier to submit and to receive it with resignation. And thus we shall use it rightly; we shall make use of it for our sanctification, and the perfecting the work of God in the soul. Now, for these reasons it must be very important that the tried Christian should at the very outset of the trial pray to the Lord for wisdom to understand, to receive, and so to use profitably the discipline under which God has placed him.

(d)   *E. Bayley*

DISCONTENT

The discontented man is a watch over-wound wrested out of tune, and goes false.

(e)   *Owen Feltham*

DISHONESTY

" Tell me," said the king, " how to find a treasurer who will not rob me." " I know an infallible mode," replied Zadig, " of giving you a man who will keep his hands clean. You have only to cause all those who present themselves for

(f)

the dignity of treasurer to dance ; he who dances the lightest will be infallibly the most honest man." " You jest," said the king." " Do you pretend that he who cuts the neatest caper will be the most upright and skilful financier ? " " I will not answer for his being the most skilful," replied Zadig, " but I assure you that he will be the most honest. . . . " Do as you think proper," said the king. The same day Zadig made public, in the king's name, that all candidates for the post of receiver-in-chief of the king's moneys, must present themselves in habits of light silk, on the first day of the month of the crocodile, in the king's ante-chamber. They came, accordingly, to the number of sixty-four. Musicians had been placed in a neighbouring saloon. All was prepared for the ball ; but the door of this saloon was closed, and it was necessary, in order to enter it, to pass through a small gallery which was somewhat dark. An usher went to meet and introduce each candidate in succession by this passage, in which each was left alone for some minutes. The king, aware of the plan, had spread out all his treasures in this gallery. When all were assembled in the saloon, the king ordered the dance to begin. Never had any dancers performed more heavily or with less grace ; all held their heads down, their backs bent, their hands glued to their sides. " Rascals ! " murmured Zadig. One alone made his steps with agility, his head up, his look assured, his body straight, his arms extended, his thighs firm. " The honest man," cried Zadig. The king embraced this upright dancer, declaring him treasurer ; for every one of the others, in the time spent in the gallery, had filled his pockets till he could hardly walk. The king was distressed for human nature, that out of sixty-four men there should be sixty-three thieves.

(a)   *Voltaire*

DISQUIETUDE (Care)

How often we have disquieted ourselves with the apprehension of evils which, after all, may never have befallen us ! How often we have indulged in vain hopes and ambitious speculations which, if they have apparently been realized, have peradventure brought with them none of the happiness that we had anticipated as their result.

(b)   " *English Churchman*," 1859

DISTANCE AND APPEARANCE

In youth, like a blind man just couched (and what is birth but a couching of the sight ?), you take the Distant for the Near, the starry heaven for tangible room-furniture, pictures for objects ; and, to the young man, the whole world is sitting on his very nose, till repeated bandaging and unbandaging have at last taught him, like the blind patient, to estimate *Distance* and *Appearance*.

(c)   *J. P. F. Richter*

DIVERSIONS

Diversions beguile us, amuse us, and conduct us, unprepared, to our graves.

Mankind, having no remedy against death, misery, and ignorance, in order to secure happiness, contrive not to think of them. This is the only comfort they have been able to invent under their numerous calamities.

(d)   *Blaise Pascal*

DIVINE HONOURS, GOD'S (Acts xiv.)

" Sirs, we are *men*,"—nothing else, nothing more—" men of like passions with you "—of like susceptibilities to suffering, men of like destiny. Why are we here ? Why have we come ? To receive Divine honours ? Nay, but for the express purpose of turning you from these vanities ; to tell you that they are falsities, nothing less ; and to reveal to you the living and true God. . . . I wonder what these men who, when on earth were really the depositories, or, at least, the channels, of supernatural powers, but who rejected with horror anything like worship—I wonder what they think now of pretended bits of their bones, or shreds and patches of their old clothes, being had in reverence, or their supposed visible figures, in painting or marble, being bowed to and worshipped, with lights and candles burning before them, as a sort of perpetual sacrifice ! I wonder what they think of that.

(e)   *T. Binney*

DIVINE NATURE, PARTAKERS OF (2 Pet. i. 4)

(i.) There is such a thing as the glorification of the flesh (lower nature) through living in the spirit.

(ii.) There is such a thing also as materializing the spirit through living after the flesh (Rom. viii.).

(f)

DIVINITY

There's a divinity that shapes our ends,
Rough-hew them how we will.

(g)   *Shakspeare*

DIVINITY

One of the most sagacious men in this age, who continues, I hope, to improve and adorn it, Samuel Johnson, remarked in my hearing, that if Newton had flourished in ancient Greece, he would have been worshipped as a divinity.

(h)   *Sir William Jones*

DIVINITY OF CHRIST, THE

JOHN i.

(i.) " The WORD was God."

(ii.) " There was a *man* sent from God."

The key to St. John's Gospel, and the difference between Christ and John the Baptist.

(i)

DIVINITY, PRACTICAL

I wish there was not a polemic divine, said Yorick, in the kingdom. One ounce of practical divinity is worth a painted shipload of all their reverences have imported these fifty years.

(j)   *Sterne*

DIVINITY OF CHRIST

What is the value of a Socinian Saviour ? What is such a being ? A superior kind of Socrates, or Plato, or Confucius.

But a Socrates could not save you and me. Socrates never saved half-a-dozen Greeks in his life ; and he cannot save any now he is dead. Con-

(k)

fucius never saved half-a-dozen Chinese in the whole of his life; and he cannot save any now he is dead. I want a Saviour who can save me from the guilt and penalty and *power* of sin; and ONLY in the person of my Divine Lord do I find the Saviour that I need.

(*a*) *Thos. Cooper*

DIVISIONS

Discord and division become no Christian. For wolves to worry the lambs is no wonder; but for one lamb to worry another, is unnatural and monstrous.

(*b*) *Thos. Brooks*

DIVISIONS IN THE CHURCH

The Church of England astonished him by its singular conjunctions of contrarieties. He heard of a madman who was asked by a person visiting an asylum, "Who are you?" He replied, "I am Lucifer." "No; you were Gabriel last week." "Yes, that is quite right; but it is by different mothers." Mr. Spurgeon said he sat in a church not long ago, where he heard the Gospel most faithfully preached, to his intense delight. He went into the church a few days ago, and saw some of the prettiest artificial flowers on the altar that he had seen for a considerable time, and a respectable-looking brass cross set with jewels, and all kinds of things belonging to the Church of Rome. He said to himself, "But it is the same church—it was the angel Gabriel when I met it last week; now it is Lucifer. It must be by different mothers."

(*c*) *Spurgeon* (report)

DIVISIONS, HINDRANCES OF

Bishop Selwyn used to quote the answer of a New Zealand chief to his question, Why he refused to become a Christian? The chief stretched out three fingers, and said, "I have come to a cross road, and I see three ways—the English, the Wesleyan, and the Roman. Each teacher says his own way is the best. I am sitting down, and doubting which guide I shall follow."

(*d*)

DOGMATISTS

Most men of vigorous intellect, of iron resolve, and painstaking conscientiousness, are likely enough to be dogmatists in some shape or other.

(*e*) *Sunday at Home*, 1864

DOLE

"*Dole out all my Goods*" (1 Cor. xiii. 3)

"Though I dole away in mouthfuls all my property, or estates." Who that has witnessed the almsgiving in a Catholic monastery, or the court of a Spanish or Sicilian bishop's or archbishop's palace, where immense revenues are syringed away in farthings to herds of beggars, but must feel the force of the Apostle's half-satirical Ψωμίσω.

(*f*) *Coleridge*

DONE

"*Ye have done it unto Me*" (Matt. xxv.).

It is a lie to say that thou wouldst have done much good to Christ, if thou art not doing it to these, the wretched.

(*g*) *Luther*

DONNE

I have lived to be useful and comfortable to my good father-in-law, Sir George Moore, whose patience God hath been pleased to exercise with many temporal crosses. I have maintained my own mother, whom it hath pleased God after a plentiful fortune in her younger days to bring to a great decay in her very old age. I have quieted the consciences of many who have groaned under the burden of a wounded spirit, whose prayers I hope are available for me. I cannot plead innocency of life, especially of my youth; but I am to be judged by a merciful God, who is not willing to see what I have done amiss.

(*h*) *Donne*

DOOR

"*The Judge standeth at the door*" (Jas. v. 9).

O sinner, how many iniquities dost thou commit behind the door, in secret.
But behold, the Judge standeth at the door (Isa. xxix. 15).

(*i*) *Quesnel*

DOUBT AND CERTAINTIES

In contemplation, if a man begin with certainties, he shall end in doubts; but if he will be content to begin with doubts, he shall end in certainties.

(*j*) *Bacon*

DOUBT AS SCEPTICISM

The doubt by which a man seeks to escape from the truth, because he would gain a security against conscience and against the fulfilment of duty. . . . He finds a solace in the thought that it is by no means decided whether there is a super-natural and super-sensual world—not decided whether there is a moral order of the world, and whether duty and conscience are real powers; whether they may not possibly be mere imaginations, originating through habit, convenience, custom, tradition, and education; possibly have only arisen in ignorant ages, when right views had not yet been attained. In consequence, however, of the inner connection which in fact exists between religion and morality, this scepticism is also applied to Christianity; and this man is consoled to find that it is by no means sure that there is a living God. Possibly there is no other God than nature, possibly man is only a "product of nature," the history of the world only "a physico-chemical process." He who wishes to deceive himself by this mode of thought, gets in our days the help of a very extensive literature, not only God-denying, but spirit-denying and purely naturalistic, in which he will find abundant sup-

(*k*)

port. . . . This kind of scepticism at last passes over into dogmatism, into a body of definite dogmas that deny the *moral order of the world.* The man is now convinced that what stands fast is not the ethical and religious, but the *physical,* the world of senses, of which he is a member. His morality is that of instinct and natural impulse; his object in life is the greatest possible sum of earthly enjoyments; the opposition between good and evil is replaced by that between the agreeable and the disagreeable, the useful and the hurtful, what is prudent and what is stupid. His highest moral principle is—" Thou shalt love thyself above all, and all others and all else for thine own sake, or so far as it is of use to thee." In this merely physical view of life the man is secured against God, against Christianity, against a moral order of the world. . . . This kind of self-deception is designated in the Holy Scriptures as πλάνη—a wandering, founded in the will of man, which deliberately puts phantasms in the place of truth (Gal. vi. 7).

(a)   *Martensen*

DOUBTS

Hume was no propagandist; and, indeed, seems ever to have felt that a firm faith in Christianity, unshaken by our *doubts,* was an invaluable privilege.

(b)   *Burton*

Thus, when deeply moved by his mother's death, he explained to his friend that, notwithstanding his metaphysical speculations, he did not in other things think so differently from the rest of the world as was imagined. Of him and others, who have *nevertheless* argued out and printed unmoral or irreligious speculations instead of their own best convictions, it may be said emphatically

" The evil that men do lives after them,
   The good is oft interred with their bones."

Could we confidently say that Hume and others are with *Christ now?*

(c)   *Jackson's Bampton Lectures*

It is a device of our great adversary, the devil, to rob us of our precious privilege, by raising doubts and fears in our minds.

(d)   *Anon*

Doubts.

But now I am cabin'd, cribb'd, confined, bound in To saucy doubts and fears.

(e)   *Shakspeare*

DREAM AND A COVENANT, A

I found myself at the gate of hell, and, standing at the threshold, I saw an opening, beneath which there was a vast sea of fire in wave-like motion. Looking at it, I said: " What infinite virtue there must have been in the blood of Christ to have quenched for His people these awful flames!" Overcome with the feeling, I knelt down by the walls of hell, saying, " Thanks be unto Thee, O Great and Blessed Saviour, that Thou hast dried up this terrible sea of fire!" Whereupon Christ addressed me: " Come this way, and I will show thee how it was done." Looking back, I beheld that the whole sea had disappeared. Jesus passed over the place, and said: " Come, follow Me." By this time I was within what I thought were the gates of hell, where there were many cells, out of which it was impossible to escape. I found myself within one of these, and anxious to make my way out. Still I felt wonderfully calm, as I had only just been conversing with Jesus, and because He had gone before me, although I had now lost sight of Him. I got hold of something, with which I struck the corner of the place in which I stood, saying, " In the name of Jesus, open!" and it instantly gave way; so I did with all the enclosures, until I made my way out into the open field. Whom should I see there but brethren, none of whom, however, I knew, except a good old deacon; and their work was to attend to a nursery of trees. I joined them, and laid hold of a tree, saying, " In the name of Jesus, be thou plucked up by the root!" And it came up as if it had been a rush. Thence I went forth, as I fancied, to work miracles, saying, " Now I know how the apostles wrought miracles in the name of Christ."

(f)   *Christmas Evans*

" COVENANT," THE

1. I yield myself, body and soul, to Thee, Jesus, the true God and Eternal Life, to deliver me from sin and from eternal death, and to bring me into life everlasting.

2. I call the day, the sun, the earth, the trees, the rocks, my bed, table, and library, to witness that I come unto Thee, Saviour of sinners, to have rest for my soul from the thunders of guilt and the dread of eternity.

3. Trusting in Thy power, I earnestly beseech Thee, Thyself, to give me a circumcised heart to love Thee, and to create a right spirit within me, that I may seek Thy glory. Plant within me such principles as Thou wilt approve in the Day of Judgment, that I may not then stand speechless before Thee, seeing myself a hypocrite. Grant me this, for the sake of Thy most precious blood.

4. I implore Thee, Jesus, the Son of God, with power, to grant me, for the sake of Thine agonizing death, a covenant interest in Thy blood, which cleanses, Thy righteousness, which justifies, and Thy redemption, which delivers. I entreat an interest in Thy blood, for the sake of Thy blood; an interest in Thee, for the sake of Thy name, which Thou hast given among men.

5. O Jesus Christ, the Son of the living God! for the sake of Thy precious death, accept of my time and strength, and the gifts and talents I possess, which, with full purpose of heart I consecrate for Thy glory, to the building up of Thy Church in the world, for Thou art worthy of the hearts and talents of all.

6. I would have Thee, my Great Highpriest, to grant, by the authority of Thy Supreme Court, that my usefulness as a preacher, and my piety as a Christian, may be secured, like two adjoining gardens, that sin may not have dominion over me, to cloud my confidence in Thy righteousness; and that I may not commit any foolish act that would blight my talents and render me useless before the end of my days. Keep upon me Thy gracious eye, and watch over me, O my Lord and God, for ever!

(g)

7. I especially surrender myself to Thee, O Jesus Christ the Saviour, to keep me from those evil ways in which many stumble and fall, that Thy name, among Thy people, may not be blasphemed and dishonoured, that my peace and confidence may not be destroyed, that Thy people may not be grieved, and Thine enemies hardened.

8. I come unto Thee, beseeching Thee to be in covenant with me in my ministry : as Thou didst prosper Harris, Rowlands, Whitfield, Bunyan, and Vavasor Powell, O prosper Thou me ! Whatsoever hinders my success, do Thou remove ; work in me, in order to this, whatsoever is approved of God. Give me a heart sick of love, to Thyself and to the souls of men. May I experience the power of Thy word before I deliver it, as Moses did that of his rod, before he saw its power on the sea and on the land of Egypt. Grant this, for the sake of Thine infinitely precious blood, O Jesus, my hope and my all in all !

9. Search me now, and lead me in the midst of the paths of judgment. May I know, while here, what I am in Thy sight, that I may not otherwise appear when made known in the light of immortality. Wash me in Thy redeeming blood !

10. Grant me strength to depend upon Thee for food and raiment, and to make known my requests. Oh, let Thy care over me be as the peculiar favour of a covenant betwixt Thyself and me, and not as a general care, which feeds the ravens that perish, and clothes the lily that is cast into the oven ; but care Thou for me as one of Thy family, as one of Thine unworthy brethren.

11. Be pleased, O Jesus, to prepare me for death, for Thou art God, and needest only to speak the word. If it be possible—Thy will be done—let me not be afflicted long, nor die suddenly, without bidding farewell to my brethren, in whose presence, after brief suffering, may I die. Grant that all my affairs may be set in order for the day of my removal, so that there may be no confusion or bewilderment, but a departure in peace. Oh, grant me this, for the sake of Thine agony in the garden.

12. Grant, O blessed Lord, that nothing may spring up and be cherished within me, to cause Thee to cut me off from the service of the sanctuary, like the house of Eli ; and for the sake of Thy boundless merit, vouchsafe that I may not outlive my usefulness. Oh, suffer me not to become, towards the end of my days, as lumber in the way of others.

13. I beseech Thee, O Saviour, to present these my supplications before the Father. Oh, write them with Thine immortal pen in Thy book, while I, with mortal hand, write them down in mine upon the earth. According to the depths of Thy merit, Thine exhaustless grace and compassion, and Thy wont towards Thy people, oh, sign Thy name in Thy Court above to these unworthy petitions, and set to them Thine Amen, as I herewith do, on my part, to this covenant. Amen.

(a) *Christmas Evans*

" After this covenant, I felt a peaceful calm and happiness, like a poor man who had been taken into royal favour, with an annual settlement made upon him for life, and from whose home the harassing fear of poverty had been for ever banished. This is surely what the Psalmist must have meant when he said, ' My soul trusteth in Thee ; yea, in the shadow of Thy wings will I make my refuge, until these calamities be overpast.' "

(b) *Ibid*

DRESS, EVILS OF

It is for *you* (ladies) all this damnation ensues. Yes ! yes ! you must have rich satins, and girdles of gold out of this accursed money. When any one has anything to receive from the husband, he must make a present to the wife of some fine gown, or girdle, or ring. If you, ladies and gentlemen, who are battening on your pleasures, and wear scarlet clothes, I believe if you were closely put in a good press, we should see the blood of the poor gush out, with which your scarlet is dyed.

(c) *Oliver Maillard*, 1502

DRESS, ADVICE ON

If you are a young lady, and employ a certain number of semptresses for a given time, in making a given number of simple and serviceable dresses —suppose seven, of which you can wear one yourself for half the winter, and give six away to poor girls who have none, you are spending your money unselfishly. But if you employ the same number of semptresses for the same number of days in making four, or five, or six, beautiful flounces for your own ball-dress—flounces which will clothe no one but yourself, and which you yourself will be unable to wear at more than one ball—you are employing your money selfishly. . . . I say further, that as long as there are cold and nakedness in the land around you, so long can there be no question at all but that the splendour of dress is a crime. In due time, when we have nothing better to set people to work at, it may be right to let them make lace and cut jewels ; but, as long as there are any who have no blankets for their beds and no rags for their bodies, so long it is blanket-making and tailoring we must set people to work at, not lace.

(d) *Ruskin*

Dress.—Clothes.—Dandyism

Touching dandies, let us consider, with scientific strictness, what a dandy specially is. A dandy is a clothes-wearing man, a man whose trade, office, and existence consist in the wearing of clothes. Every faculty of his soul, spirit, purse, and person is heroically consecrated to this one object,—the wearing of clothes wisely and well ; so that, as others dress to live, he lives to dress. The all-importance of clothes has sprung up in the intellect of the dandy, without effort, like an instinct of genius : he is inspired with cloth, a poet of cloth.

(e) *Carlyle*

DRINK

Many a one becomes a free-spoken Diogenes, not when he dwells in the cask, but when the cask dwells in him.

(f) *J. P. F. Richter*

Drink

Drink not the *third glass*, which thou canst not tame
When once it is within thee, but before
Mayst rule it as thou list ; and pour the shame
Which it would pour on thee, upon the floor.

(g)

It is most just to throw that on the ground
Which would throw me there, if I keep the
round.

(a)   *George Herbert*

DRINK, STRONG

Oh, that men should put an enemy in their
mouths to steal away their brains.

(b)   *Shakspeare*

DROP OF WATER REFUSED, THE

Perhaps Dives, when he asked that he might dip
the tip of his finger in water to extinguish a world
of fire, imagined that if he could have obtained
this favour from the treasury of mercy, it would
have rendered the gulf passable, and proved the
beginning of a commerce between heaven and hell;
because He who could give a " drop of water,"
could as easily give an ocean; and He who could
permit a drop of water to be given, would have
called forth the hope that thousands of the chariots
of salvation might pass over the gulf to the land
of woe. The drop of water was refused, to discourage the slightest hope for mercy.

(c)   *Christmas Evans*

DRUNKENNESS

" *And he stood between the dead and the living* "
(Num. xvi. 48)

ENGLAND'S NATIONAL SIN

If ever England be ruined, what will be her
ruin? *Her national sin.* And what is the national
sin of England? Alas! there are many sins in
England, but ask the unbiassed opinion of those
who know; ask the unsuspected testimony of the
English judges; ask the exceptional experience of
the English clergy; ask the unguarded admissions
of the English press; and their unanimous answer
would be, I think, as would be the unanimous
answer of every thoughtful man—the national sin
of England is *drunkenness;* the national curse of
England is *drink.*

(d)   *Archdeacon Farrar*

DRUNKENNESS IN ANCIENT AND MODERN TIMES

" Woe to the drunkards of Ephraim, whose
glorious beauty is a fading flower," says Jeremiah.
The allusions to drunkenness in Scripture and in
classical literature are not unfrequent. Yet
drunkenness was not the prevalent sin of ancient
times; and an ancient Spartan, an ancient Roman,
or an ancient Hebrew would have stared with
contemptuous disgust at the sights in which Christian England are familiar as a jest. It was not
that they were less prone to sin, but they were less
petted with temptation. Southern and eastern
nations have never been so drunken as northern;
and ancient nations were ignorant of that deadly
spirit [derived from the fermentation of saccharine
matters which, as a distinct compound, was first
discovered about 1300] which has wrought a havoc
so frightful among us. The simple wines of
antiquity were incomparably less deadly than
the stupefying and ardent beverages on which
£150,000,000 are yearly spent in this suffering
land. The wines of antiquity were more like

syrups; many of them were not intoxicant, many
more intoxicant in but a small degree, and all of
them, as a rule, only taken when largely diluted
with water. The sale of these comparatively
harmless vinous fluids did not bear the remotest
resemblance to the drink trade among us, nor did
the same ghastly retinue of evils follow in its
train. They contained, even when undiluted, but
four or five per cent. of alcohol, whereas some of
our common wines contain seventeen per cent.,
and the maddening intoxicants of Scotch and
English cities contain the horrible amount of fifty-
four per cent. of alcohol. Take but one illustration of the difference of ancient and modern days.
Our blessed Lord, when He lived on earth, traversed
Palestine from end to end. He saw many a sinner
and many a sufferer; He saw the lepers, and
healed them; He saw weeping penitent women
and restored them to honour and holiness again;
there is not the slightest trace that He ever once
witnessed that spectacle of miserable degradation,
a drunken man, or that yet more pitiable spectacle
of yet deadlier degradation, a drunken woman.
He who scattered the obstinate formalism of the
Pharisee; He who flung into the sea with a millstone round his neck the corrupter of youthful
innocence, what would He have said, what would
He have felt, had He heard the shrieks of women
beaten by drunken husbands; had He seen little
children carried into the hospital stricken down
by their drunken mothers' senseless or infuriated
hands? Ah! estimate these things as He would
have estimated them, and then will you dare to
sneer at those who for very shame, for very pity,
for the mere love of their kind and country, cannot let these things be so?

(e)   *Ibid*

DRUNKENNESS, A RECENT VICE

And alas! but for these spirits England need
not be a drunken nation; for the day was when
she was not a drunken nation. Listen to a page
of your own history. In the reign of that great
king, King Henry V., who enlarged this Abbey, in
his army of heroic victors, the army of Agincourt,
drunkenness was deemed an utter disgrace; and
king Henry was so impressed with the curse of
it that he wanted to cut down all the vines in
France.
The great antiquary, Camden, who lies buried
there, says that in his day drunkenness was a
recent vice; and other writers say that " We
brought the foul vice of drunkenness from the
wars in the Netherlands, as we had brought back
the foul disease of leprosy from the Crusades."
In the bad reaction which followed the Restoration,
when the people broke loose from the stern but
noble bonds of Puritan restriction to plunge into
abominable licence, the evil habit was enormously
increased, and many a great statesman and great
writer of the subsequent epoch—a Pitt, an Addison,
a Bolingbroke, a Walpole, a Carteret, a Pulteney
—shattered his nerves and shortened his life by
drink. But it was about the year 1724, as we are
told by the last historian of the eighteenth century,
that " gin drinking " began to affect the masses,
and it spread with the rapidity and violence of an
epidemic. " Small," he says, " as is the place
which this fact occupies in English history, it was
probably—if we consider all the consequences that
have flowed from it—the most momentous in that

(f)

eighteenth century," because from that time "the fatal passion for drink was at once and irrevocably planted in the nation." Yes, it was only some 150 years ago that there began the disastrous era of the dram-shop and the gin-palace; from that epoch ardent spirits began to madden the brain, to poison the blood, to brutalize the habits of the lowest classes. Distillation replaced the comparatively harmless wines of our forefathers by those poisonous draughts of liquid fire which are at this moment the scathing, blighting, and degrading curse of myriads—the fellest and the foulest temptation with which our working-classes have to struggle. The Jewish rabbis have a legend that, when the first vineyard was planted, Satan rejoiced, and said to Noah that he should have his account in the results; and in truth the wine-cup, which poets so extol, is the cause, as Solomon has told us, of woes enough; but if ever the spirits of evil hailed a potent ally with shouts of triumph, it must have been when that thing was discovered, which, regarded as a harmless luxury by the virtuous, acts as a subtle and soul-destroying ruin of the unsuspecting—that thing in the use of which "intemperance, the great murderer of millions, doth creep for shelter into houses of moderation."

(a)   *Archdeacon Farrar*

Drunkenness, its History

Ardent spirits had not long been introduced when the Grand Jury of Middlesex, in a powerful presentment, declared that much the greatest part of the poverty, the robberies, the murders of London might be traced to this single cause. (Painted boards informed the poor that for 1*d*. they might purchase drunken stupefaction, and as though the adjuncts of the sty were necessary to complete the accessories of truly swinish degradation, the straw in the cellars was gratuitously supplied.) Even the morals of the eighteenth century—bad as they were—did not so acquiesce in this public demoralization as we, with our consciences seared with the hot iron of customs, are content with acquiescing. In 1736 a strenuous attempt was made to stem the rising tide of shame and ruin. (By placing prohibitive duties on all spirituous liquors. In 1743 those duties were enormously diminished—partly on the futile plea of stopping illicit distillation, but mainly to replenish the Exchequer for the German wars of George II.)

(b)   *Ibid*

The Gin Act

Against the Gin Act, as it was called, Lord Chesterfield, the most polished and brilliant peer of his day, flung his whole influence, alas, in vain! When I quote his words to you, remember that you are listening to a professed man of the world, perfectly cool-headed, the mirror of fashion, the idol of society, yet speaking simply as a patriot from ordinary observation of the notorious effect of what he calls "the new liquor." Had he used such language now, he would have been called an intemperate Pharisee; but he spoke to an age not yet hardened by familiarity with the horrors of dram-drinking. "Vice, my lords," he said, "is not properly to be taxed, but to be suppressed; and heavy taxes are sometimes the only means by which that suppression can be attained. Luxury, my lords, may very properly be taxed. But the use of these things which are simply hurtful—

hurtful in their own nature, and in every degree—is to be prohibited. If these liquors are so delicious that the people are tempted to their own destruction, let us at length, my lords, secure them from these fatal draughts by bursting the vials that contain them. Let us check these artists in human slaughter, which have reconciled their countrymen to sickness and to ruin, and spread over the pitfalls of debauchery such baits as cannot be resisted. When I consider, my lords, the tendency of this bill, I find it calculated only for the propagation of disease, the suppression of industry, and the destruction of mankind. For the purpose, my lords, what could have been invented more efficacious than shops at which poison may be vended, poison so prepared as to please the palate, while it wastes the strength and kills only by intoxication?" So spoke, so thought, Lord Chesterfield, about the ardent spirits which are now sold on every day in the week at 140 licensed houses within a small radius of the Abbey, into most of which hundreds of men, of women, and of children, will enter this very day. And he did not stand alone. If you would know what your fathers thought of these things, look at Hogarth's ghastliest pictures of Rum-lane and Gin-alley. If you doubt Art, take the testimony of Science. In 1750 the London physicians drew up a memorial to the effect that there were then 14,000 cases of fatal illness attributable to gin alone; and Benson, Bishop of Gloucester, wrote, "Our people have become what they never were before, cruel and inhuman. These accursed liquors, which, to the shame of our Government are so easily to be had, have changed their very nature;" and about the same time the entire bench of bishops protested against the Gin Act, as founded on the indulgence of debauchery, the encouragement of crime, and the destruction of the human race.

(c)   *Ibid*

Drunkenness, its Extent

It was amid these protests of men and these warnings of God, that in England the shameful and miserable tale began. You know, or you may know, and you ought to know, how it has gone on. The extent, indeed, of the calamity you do not and cannot know. That can be fully known to Him only who hears, and not in vain, the sighs and moans that lade the air with their quivering misery; to Him alone who can estimate the area of wreck and ruin, of human agony and human degradation, which is represented by the fact that this country spends £150,000,000 a year on drink, and that in this country there are, amongst the many who drink, 600,000 drunkards. No, you cannot estimate it; you have not even one fraction of such knowledge about it as we have who have seen it; but need you ignore it? Can you live in the very midst of facts so ugly and yet not lift a finger to make them better? Read for yourselves. Judge for yourselves. Refute these facts if you can; would to God that you could, but alas! you cannot. Convince yourselves, first, that alcohol, however much you may like it, is needless, seeing that the lives of four million total abstainers who never touch it are better in any insurance-office than those of other men; and that among our 20,000 prisoners—most of them brought there by it—there is, because they are not allowed to touch it, a better average healthiness than among any

(d)

other class. Convince yourselves, then, that it is absolutely needless, and then judge yourselves of its effects. Do not take our testimony, but inquire. Go and catch with your own eyes a glimpse here and there of the black waves of this subterranean stream.

(a)   *Archdeacon Farrar*

DRUNKENNESS, ITS EFFECTS

Health is the most priceless boon of life. Go to our London hospitals, and ask how many are brought there by the awful diseases, the appalling accidents, the brutal violence of drink. Pauperism is the curse of cities. Ask Poor-law guardians how paupers are made; ask any economist worth the name how pauperism can possibly be avoided when so much idleness is due to the waste in drink. Lunacy is one of the worst inflictions of humanity; ask at any public asylum the percentage of it due to drink. Idiocy is one of the saddest phenomena of life. Ask any doctor how many idiots are born of drunken parents. Visit our camps and barracks, and there is not an officer who will not tell you that drink is the deadliest curse of our army. Visit our ships and seaports, and there is not a captain who will not tell you that drink is the worst ruin of our sailors. Go to any parish or town or county all over the United Kingdom, where there are many public-houses and many poor, any clergyman will tell you that drink is the most overwhelming curse of our working classes. Philanthropists sigh for the dirt, the squalor, the misery, of our lowest classes. How can it be remedied so long as there is the maxium of temptation, where there is the minimum of wages to waste and the minimum of power to resist? Here, almost under the very shadows of the great towers of our Houses of Legislature, and within bowshot of this great Abbey, are streets in which house after house, family after family, is ruined or rendered miserable by this one cause; and, oh! how long will our Legislature still refuse to interfere? Oh that we could show them the misery of the innocent, the imbruting of the guilty; women broken-hearted, children degraded, men lowered beneath the level of the beasts; holidays changed into a bane, high wages wasted into a curse, the day of God turned into a day of Satan, our gaols filled, our criminal classes recruited, our workhouses rendered inevitable. This it was which made the late Mr. C. Buxton say that the struggle of the school, the library, and the Church were united, and united in vain, against the beershop and the gin-palace, and that this struggle was "one development of the war between heaven and hell." Have we not a right to expect, have we not a right to demand, that in this struggle the Legislature should take their part?

(b)   *Ibid*

DRUNKENNESS, ITS CRIMINALITY

Look at the statue of that glorious statesman who there "with eagle face and outstretched hand, still seems to bid England to be of good cheer, and hurl defiance at her foes." Speaking of the proposal to use Indians against our American colonists he burst into that memorable storm of words which you all have read:—"I call upon that Right Reverend Bench. I conjure them to join in the holy work and vindicate the religion of their God,

I call upon the bishops," he said, "to interpose the unsullied sanctity of their lawn; upon the learned judges to interpose the purity of their ermine to save us from this pollution. I call upon your lordships to stamp upon it an indelible stigma of the public abhorrence. And I again implore those holy prelates of our religion to do away these iniquities from amongst us. Let them perform a lustration. Let them purify this House and this country from this sin." In his burning wrath, so stormed, so thundered the mighty Earl of Chatham, when it was proposed to let loose on our revolted colonists "the hell-hounds of savage war." But against this hell-hound of savage intoxication the bishops did then and the judges do now their very best to interpose. They, at least, can estimate, if any can, the connection of drink and crime. Have they failed to estimate it? There is scarcely a judge on the bench who has not spoken of it, till it has become a commonplace of the Courts of Justice. "It is not from men that are drunk," said one judge; "but from men who have been drinking, that most of the crime proceeds." "The worst is," said another, "that men enter the public-house sober, and leave it felons." But for drink, others have said again and again, "not one of these cases would have been brought before me." "Do away with drink," say others, "and we may shut up two-thirds of our prisons." So they have said—well-nigh every one of them—and still the maddening wave of alcohol flows on, and sweeps legislators into Parliament upon its crest. And are these judges fanatics? are they Pharisees? Or is it that they are forced to see what every one of us might see if we chose—a fearful and intolerable fact? The New Year dawned upon us five months ago with all its cheerful prophecies and jubilant hopes, and when it began I thought I would make a record of a few out of the thousands of awful crimes with which drink would blight and desecrate its history. Very soon I paused, sickened, horror-stricken. The crimes were too awful, too inhuman, sometimes too grotesque in their pitiable horror. Other crimes are human crimes, but the crimes done in drink are as the crimes of demoniacs, the crimes of men who for the time have ceased to be men, and have become fiends. Oh that these walls should hear them! Oh that the angel of the nation might blot them out of his record with such tears as angels weep, to think that Christ, daily re-crucified in the midst of us, should from His throne in heaven-

> See only this
> After the passion of a thousand years!

I have some of them written here, but they are too black to tell you. Now it was a boy stabbing his father in a cellar at Liverpool; now a wife killing her husband with one savage blow; now a woman's suicide; now a little infant overlaid; now a drunken carman driving over a child, a woman, and a boy; now a man—I dare not go on. I dare not describe the least bad, much less tell the worst.

(c)   *Ibid*

DRUNKENNESS, THE INDIFFERENCE TOWARDS

These things—these daily incidents of the year of grace 1878—Christian men and Christian women, are they unfit for your fastidious ears? Ah! but things are as they are, and it is not your

(d)

fastidiousness that can undo them. And is it not an hypocrisy to shrink with delicate sensibility from hearing of crimes which are going on about you from day to day, and from week to week, and from year to year, while you do not shrink from the fact that they should be done, from the fact that they should be borne, by Englishmen like yourselves; done and borne by English women who might once have worn the rose of womanhood; done and borne by boys and girls who were once little bright-eyed children in our schools, and who but for drink might have grown up as happy and as sweet as yours. And if you are ashamed that these things should be, why do many of you not lift one finger to prevent this mingled stream of crime and pauperism from pouring its deluge through our streets? For where are these things being done? In savage islands? among Pacific cannibals? among ancient Pagans, such as St. Paul describes? No, I declare to you that I find no records of such chronic horrors among them as I find, normally, daily, as incidents of ordinary life, as items of common news, happening now; happening to-day; happening in Christian England; happening in Liverpool, in Dublin, in Glasgow, in Manchester; happening here under your minster towers. Here, even in these streets hard by—oh, what a tale I could tell!—the husband imprisoned for assaulting his wife; the son in gaol for striking his aged miserable mother; the father deserting his family of little children; the son dishonouring his home; the man once rich now ruined; the woman barely snatched from agonizing suicide. And, Christian men and Christian women, you wonder that our hearts are stirred within us when we see whole classes of a city—whole classes which should have been its marrow and its strength—thus given to drink! When will this indifference cease? When will a nation, half ruined by her vice, demand what the Legislature will not then withhold? Sooner or later it must be so, or England must perish. Weigh the gain and loss—strike the balance. On the one scale place whole tons of intoxicating and adulterated liquor—put alcohol, at the very best a needless luxury; on the other side put £150,000,000 a year, and grain enough to feed a nation, and grapes that might have been the innocent delight of millions; and load the scale—for you must, if you would be fair—load it with disease, and pauperism, and murder, and madness, and horrors such as no heart can conceive and no tongue tell; and wet it with rivers of widows' and orphans' tears; and if you will not strike the balance, God will one day strike it for you. But will you, as Christian men and Christian women—will you, as lovers of your country and lovers of your kind—stand up before high God, and say that the one is worth the other? Will you lay your hand upon your heart, and say that these things ought so to be?

(a)   *Archdeacon Farrar*

DRUNKENNESS AND BANDS OF HOPE

If we cannot and will not save ourselves, let us save our children. If the wealth and peace of this generation is to be a holocaust to drink, let the next be an offering to God. Let us do what Wellington said at Waterloo; let us have young soldiers. Let every young man in his strength, every maiden in her innocence and beauty, join the ranks of the abstainers. Let the manliness of the nation spring to its own defence, so that by a

sense of shame and a love of virtue, if this evil cannot be suppressed by law, it may perish of inanition. If so, I see no end to the greatness of England, no limit to the prolongation of her power. If not, in all history, as in all individual experience, I see but this one lesson—no nation, no individual, can thrive so long as it be under the dominion of a besetting sin. It must conquer or be conquered. It must destroy it or be destroyed by it. It must strike at the sources of it or be stricken down by it into the dust.

From a Sermon in Westminster Abbey by Archdeacon Farrar, May, 26, 1878.

(b)

" DRY PLACES "

I see the unclean spirit rise like a winged dragon, circling in the air, and seeking for a resting-place. Casting his fiery glances towards a certain neighbourhood, he spies a young man, in the bloom of life and rejoicing in his strength, seated on the front of his cart, going for lime.

" There he is," said the old dragon; " his veins are full of blood, and his bones of marrow; I will throw into his bosom sparks from hell; I will set all his passions on fire; I will lead him from bad to worse, until he shall perpetrate every sin; I will make him a murderer, and his soul shall sink, never again to rise, in the lake of fire."

By this time I see it descend with a fell swoop towards the earth, but nearing the youth, the dragon heard him sing :—

> " Guide me, O Thou Great Jehovah,
> Pilgrim through this barren land;
> I am weak, but Thou art mighty,
> Hold me with Thy powerful hand.
> Strong Deliverer,
> Be Thou still my strength and shield."

" A dry, dry place, this," says the dragon, and away he goes. But I see him again hovering about in the air, and casting about for a suitable resting-place. Beneath his eye there is a flowery meadow, watered by a crystal stream, and he descries, among the kine, a maiden about eighteen years of age, picking up, here and there, a beautiful flower. " There she is," says Apollyon, intent upon her soul; " I will poison her thoughts; she shall stray from the paths of virtue; she shall think evil thoughts and become impure; she shall become a lost creature in the great city, and at last I will cast her down from the precipice into everlasting burnings." Again he took his downward flight; but he no sooner came near the maiden, than he heard her sing the following words, with a voice that might have melted the rocks :—

> " Other refuge have I none,
> Hangs my helpless soul on Thee;
> Leave, ah, leave me not alone,
> Still support and comfort me."

" This place is too dry for me," says the dragon, and off he flies. Now he ascends from the meadow, like some great balloon, but very much enraged, and breathing forth " smoke and fire," and threatening ruin and damnation to all created things.

" I will have a place to dwell in," he says, " in spite of Decree, Covenant, or Grace." As he was thus speaking, he beheld a woman, " stricken in years," busy with her spinning-wheel at her cottage door. " Ah, I see," says the dragon, " she is

(c)

ripe for destruction: she shall know the bitterness of the wail which ascends from the burning marl of hell! He forthwith alights on the roof of the cot, when he forthwith hears the old woman repeat, with trembling voice, but with heavenly feeling, the words: "For the mountains shall depart, and the hills be removed; but My kindness shall not depart from thee." "This place is too dry for me," says the dragon, and away he goes again.

One might have imagined that the unclean spirit would have lost all hope and courage, with so many disappointments; but it was not so: he was determined to find a resting-place. So he arose again, to look out some other spot where he might have a better welcome. An inn, in a small village, attracted his notice: "There I will dwell," he said; "whoever crosses the threshold, I will lead into captivity, and hold him in everlasting bondage." He descends like lightning, enters the house, and goes into the parlour. But there he sees a number of ministers of the New Testament, talking about the great victory "once obtained on Calvary," discussing "resolutions," and making appointments. The unclean spirit could not remain long in an atmosphere like this, so again he hastened away, howling "This place is too dry for me. But in yonder cottage lies old Williams, slowly wasting away. He has borne the heat and the burden, and altogether has had a hard life of it; he has very little reason to be thankful for the mercies he has received, and has not found serving God a very profitable business. I know I can get him to 'curse God and die.'" Thus musing, away

he flew to the sick man's bedside; but, as he listened, he heard the words: "Though I walk through the valley of the shadow of death, I will fear no evil, for Thou art with me; Thy rod and Thy staff, they comfort me." Mortified and enraged, the dragon took his flight, saying: "I will return to the place from whence I came."

(a)   *Christmas Evans*

DUST

Dust thou art, etc. (Gen. ii. 19).

Imperial Cæsar, dead, and turned to clay,
Might stop a hole to keep the wind away;
Oh, that that earth, which kept the world in awe,
Should patch a wall, to expel the winter's flaw!

(b)   *Shakspeare*

DUTY

Wellington, standing in the battle of Waterloo when the bullets were buzzing around his head, saw a civilian on the field. He said to him, "Sir, what are you doing here? Be off." "Why," replied the civilian, "there is no more danger here for me than there is for you." Then Wellington flushed up, and said, "God and my country demand that I be here, but you have no such duty."

(c)

E

EARLY RISING

When Abraham and others had a great work on hand, they "rose up early in the morning."

Our foremost men have generally acted on the same plan. Bishop Burnett used to rise at four a.m., so did Jewel and Sir Thomas More. Gibbon the historian, began work at five, and Paley, the theologian, was only an hour later. This would be easy for all of us if we only had the power which Napoleon I. and Lord Brougham, amongst others, are said to have possessed, of feeling quite rested after four hours' sleep. But for most of us the secret of rising early consists in going to bed early, and that is usually within reach of all the young.

(*a*)

EARNEST

"*The earnest of our inheritance*" (Eph. i. 14)

"Earnest-money," the beginning of the payment which should take place in full afterwards. . . . Believers obtain the certainty that they are heirs and have an inheritance in eternity, not through an assurance from without, but chiefly through *the reality of the possession*, not at once in its entire extent, but in an *earnest*.

(*b*)   *Harless*

Earnest of Heaven, The

Sure I am that, if you knew what was before you, or if you saw but some glances of it, you would, with gladness, swim through the present floods of sorrow, spreading forth your arms, out of desire to be at land. If God have given you the earnest of the Spirit, as part of payment of God's principal sum, you have to rejoice; for our Lord will not lose His earnest, neither will He go back, nor repent Him of the bargain.

(*c*)   *Samuel Rutherford*

EARNESTNESS

O God, let me not fall from earnestness. Grant me to "hate every false way."

(*d*)   *Thomas Chalmers*

EARTH, A VESTIBULE

I believe this earth on which we stand
Is but the vestibule to glorious mansions
Through which a moving crowd for ever press.

(*e*)   *Joanna Baillie*

EARTHEN VESSELS, THE TREASURE IS IN

But why different schools, when the truth admits no difference? Schools are one-sided and partial; schools imply extravagance. The answer is, that we hold this treasure—the truth—not only in coarse, fragile, earthen vessels, but *in vessels of limited capacity also*. But the truth—the truth of the Gospel—is wide, is manifold. You or I, this or that school, cannot contain it all. If, perchance, we are mentally so constituted as to take comprehensive views, this comprehensiveness is only purchased, in our case, at the cost of some firmness of grasp. We do wisely, therefore, to tolerate divers types of thought and opinion within the pale, though by so doing we should tolerate some extravagance, and even some error. The price is trifling compared with the gain. The lessons are more direct, and the extravagances are tempered, so long as they come from within. By casting them out we magnify the evil and we minimize the good. But it will be said, " By your consecration vow you pledge yourself with all faithful diligence to banish and drive away all erroneous and strange doctrine contrary to God's Word." I do not forget this. But experience has shown that to expel the teacher is not always the best way to expel the doctrine. Experience has shown that the erroneous doctrine often springs up with greater luxuriance where the ground has been cleared by the removal of the erroneous teacher. Experience proclaims that a patient forbearance, a discriminating toleration, a sympathetic effort to appreciate the good and moderate the evil, is often a far more effective instrument of expulsion than the anathema or the excommunication.

So, then, after eighteen centuries we return once more to the old lessons which, taught then by the highest authority, have been confirmed now by the longest experience—"Let both grow together until the harvest." "The eye cannot say to the hand, I have no need of thee; nor, again, the head to the feet, I have no need of you."

(*f*)   *Bishop Lightfoot on Schools of Thought.*

Earthen Vessels

I was dining in a parliamentary party with Lord Castlereagh, and he produced for our amusement in the evening some volumes of original letters, curiously preserved by Lady C. My curiosity was immediately fixed by that of Dr. Young. I professed my enthusiastic admiration of his " Night Thoughts," and begged to see and admire as a relic the original letter of such a man. My request was immediately granted with a significant smile; and what had I the mortification to read. *Horresco referens!* It was the most fawning, servile, mendicant letter, perhaps, that ever was penned by a clergyman, imploring the mistress of George II. to exert her interest for his preferment.

(*g*)   *Hannah More*

EASE IN ZION

"Woe to them that are at ease in Zion" (Amos vi. 1).

1. Ease = sleepers = spiritually asleep. Woe to them.

2. Names of the sleepers gathered from the chapter =

    (i.) Presumptuous.
    (ii.) Procrastination.
    (iii.) Love-self.
    (iv.) Careless.
    (v.) Crossless.

(*h*)

3. Let us try to find a means of awaking those sleepers.

(i.) To let a *light* fall on them = useless as to try to put out a great fire by water brought in the hollow of the hand from a pool in the way. For mark, they are asleep in *Zion*, the city of God which is all light, and no darkness at all. . . . Asleep in Zion! Oh, dreadful state!

(ii.) By sounding a trumpet in their ears. The trumpet-sound = Woe, Woe, Woe! None ever yet fully understood the meaning of this word. Lost souls as yet know but the beginning of it. Of the whole none can ever know—for where there will be everlasting duration there will be an infinitude of suffering. Therefore, "Awake, awake, thou that sleepest," etc.

(a)　　　　　　　　　　　　　*Spurgeon*

Mark the opening of the 11th chapter of 2 Sam. "And it came to pass, after the year was expired, at the time when kings go forth to battle, that David sent Joab, and his servants with him, and all Israel; and they destroyed the children of Ammon, and besieged Rabbah. But—but David tarried still at Jerusalem." Tarried still at Jerusalem! thought he would be a gentleman-king for a while. Why should David keep a dog and always bark himself? Let Joab go with the armies! David, hitherto so energetic, so ever-active, so devoted to his kingly duties, would take his ease; he would be a gentleman king for a while.

"And it came to pass in an eveningtide," in the sweet cool of the evening, "that David arose from off his bed," from his *siesta*, as the Spaniards call it; or snooze, as we say, during the heat of the day—"and walked upon the roof,"—according to the custom in the East—"the roof of the king's house: and from the roof,"—I need not recite the rest—he saw Bathsheba.

(b)　　　　　　　　　　　　　*Thos. Cooper*

Ease and Christ (Song of Sol. v. 3–6)

Why it is *hard* to let in Christ.

Our light is corrupt and looks awry, and with a gleed [squinted] eye upon Christ; and it looks with many eyes to the world. Hence, when Christ knocketh, it says: (i.) He cannot come here. (ii.) I doubt if it be Christ that knocketh, because I wish it were not He. (iii.) I must live. (iv.) I dow [can] not suffer. (v.) This and this will befall me if I do it. (vi.) If I would let Him in, then my lusts would get no quarters with Him. My will, my affections, and He would never give one jot. They would flee upon each other. Nay, men's lusts are up where eyes should be, and their eyes down at their feet. . . .

"How can I? How can I, spouse?" thou askest, "how can I arise? how can I put on my coat?" I will tell thee how thou canst. Stir thy legs and arms, raise thy frozen fingers. It is strange to make a question how a whole strong man not bound can rise out of his bed! Stir ye, and cast the covering and bedclothes off, and come to the floor. If men would suffer their light to play fair play, and think judiciously and spiritually on the world and the delights of it, which is their soft bed, they might open to Christ. Men are but sleeping on a bed of ice. It will melt with the heat of God's anger, and they, and their night sheets, and the bed will swim, nay, men have reason to tire of this bed, both short and narrow.

Luke xii. 20: "Thou fool, this night thy soul shall be taken from you"; 1 Cor. vii. 31: "The fashion of this world passeth away." Is not this a short bed? Fools cannot get down their feet.

(c)　　　　　　　　　　　*Samuel Rutherford*

EASTWARD

Europeans and Orientalists may be well represented by two figures standing back to back: the latter looking to the east, *i.e.*, backwards; the former looking westward, or forwards.

(d)　　　　　　　　　　　*S. T. Coleridge*

"EAT, NOTHING TO"

"*The multitude . . . have nothing to eat*" (Matt. xv. 32).

Man is dependent upon others for daily food.

He hungers—others prepare and bring him bread to eat; He thirsts—others prepare and bring him drink.

Thus man learns and knows his dependence upon others. If he were dependent upon himself alone—it might soon be said of him in the language of the text:—"*He has nothing to eat.*"

But man has other and deeper needs than these.

He has a soul constantly developing within him—an unmaterial part, which also hungers and thirsts; for this food, too, is necessary.

And for the proper supply he again is dependent upon others-

Therefore he prays:

"*Give us this day our daily bread.*"

The words before us have something to say to us about the source of this supply:

"The multitude have nothing to eat."

1. Observe of whom the Saviour says this:

Not "*The disciples have nothing to eat*"

(i.) For Christ was daily feeding them—and as spiritual wants arose they were constantly being supplied—almost unconsciously they fed upon Christ—and got from Him that which satisfied them.

(ii.) Not "*Christians have nothing to eat*"

There were others—who believed in Him—and yet were not numbered amongst His disciples. But then they all constituted His body—and so were nourished in every part.

(iii.) Nor was it "*Worldly people have nothing to eat*"

For so long as the world is hunting after some good and satisfying thing, asking, "Who will shew us any good"? and are engaged in making experiments of what will stay the hunger of their souls, so long it cannot truly be said:—"They have nothing to eat." For they have, though the food indeed is nothing but *husks*.

(iv.) But the Saviour says: "The (This) multitude have nothing to eat."

Now these people followed Him from mixed motives. They were not Christians—nor were they worldlings; but halfway between the two.

They have tried the world, but finding no stay for their souls in it. They are still hungry and have come to know it. Now they are going to try what Christ can do for them.

"*They* (whom the world has cheated, deluded, and used badly) *have nothing to eat.*"

(e)

It might be said of a congregation, if a minister gave them not "*the Bread of Life*."

2. Learn

(i.) *That the world cannot satisfy us.*

The world offers us all something to eat; and after having tasted to the utmost, retire with the conviction that they have been following a delusion —and have spent their time in search of that which satisfieth not.

Listen to one who has the fullest right to speak to us and to warn us, for it was a man who had tried everything the world can offer.

He has been called "the Prince of Pleasure-seekers." He pursued the phantom over mountain, in the valley, during the light of day, and away into the softer radiance of night.

And at last, wearied out with the chase, he wrote these words,—

"I have made me great works; I have builded me houses; I planted me vineyards, I made gardens and orchards, and I planted trees in them of all kinds; I made me pools of water, to water therewith the wood that bringeth forth trees; I got me servants and maidens, and had servants born in my house; also, I had great possessions of great and small cattle above all that were in Jerusalem before me; I gathered me also silver and gold, and the peculiar pleasure of kings and of the provinces; I got me men-singers and women-singers and the delights of the sons of men . . . and whatsoever mine eyes desired I kept not from them, I withheld not my heart from any joy. . . .

"Then I looked on all the works that my hands had wrought, and on all the labour that I had laboured to do; and behold all was vanity and vexation of spirit, and there was no profit under the sun."

Having tried all the husks that this world can offer, he was still hungry, and still yearned for the bread of life.

(ii.) God purposely suffers us to hunger.

By our trying other things as sufficient for the needs of the soul.

As with the *Prodigal*, who, after trying the world's offers, at last finds himself further off than ever from satisfaction.

(iii.) Then, when we are ready, He reveals unto us Christ as the "*Bread of Life*."

(*a*) As multiplying a morsel into a quantity sufficient for all (see the context).

(*b*) They who eat are satisfied, and get eternal life.

(*c*) Whilst they who reject, go away unfed, unsatisfied, and without life.

(*a*) *Parker, adapted*

ECCLESIA

The great Church of the redeemed nourishes in its bosom and throws off from its central stem new forms of life, in each of which its own life reappears. Each of these is a true form of the Church, and partakes of the character of that from which it springs. The parts are miniatures of the whole. There are some plants which constantly produce new living plants like themselves. The trees send up suckers from their roots which bear the character of the parent stock. The most recent theories of biology assert that in each living organism there are circulating thousands of minute cellules, each of which under favouring circumstances is capable of reproducing the form of the original from which it springs. And just so it is that within the bosom of the universal Church of Christ grow up a great variety of societies, each of them instinct with the Divine power, in which God manifests Himself as the binding, drawing power, which unites men in loving relations. None of these gatherings of souls is itself the Church. But each of them may rightly be called a Church, inasmuch as it is instinct with the Divine love which is the formative principle of the Church.

The principal of these undoubtedly is the gathering of Christians for worship. It is this indeed which gave the Church its first name, *ecclesia*, or the congregation. Worship is not, it is true, the whole business of the Church, for the Church in its widest sense comprehends the whole life; but it is the highest and most heavenly function. The mistake which has identified the Church itself with the organization for public worship has had many evil results; and the chief of them is, that it has made men forbid or dishonour all other modes of worship except their own. It is said that there can be but one Church; and this is quite true, for the universal company of the redeemed in all the wide range of its common life can only be one. But then, it is argued, there can only be one form of worship, whereas in reality there are within the wide compass of the universal Church many forms of worship, through which the aspirations of the parts of the great whole are expressed. On this day, which directs our thoughts to the vastness and diversity of the Divine modes of existence, we should delight to trace out and recognise the many forms in which men make their approach to God. Those who unite together to pray, in however small a number and in however simple and informal a manner, are truly a Church of Christ; for where two or three are gathered in His name, He is there in the midst of them. Those who kneel together at family prayer form a Church; those who hold a prayer-meeting, those who have stated Sunday worship in whatsoever form and in whatsoever numbers, are a Church. What has been wrong in so many of these is, that they have each tried to assume the position of the Church itself, and hence have mutually excluded each other. If they would be more humble, and content themselves with being what they really are, organizations for the conduct of Christian worship and instruction, they would, instead of draining off the Church's vitality by their conflicts and their assumptions, enrich its life by their life in its ever fresh and varying experiences.

(*b*) *W. H. Freemantle*

ECHO, THE CHRISTIAN AND HIS

True faith produces love to God and man,
Say, Echo, is not this the Gospel plan?
— The Gospel plan.

Must I my faith and love to Jesus show,
By doing good to all, both friend and foe?
— Both friend and foe.

But if a brother hates and treats me ill,
Must I return him good, and love him still?
— Love him still.

If he my failings watches to reveal,
Must I his faults as carefully conceal?
— As carefully conceal.

(*c*)

But if my name and character he blast,
And cruel malice, too, a long time last;
And if I sorrow and affliction know,
He loves to add unto my cup of woe;
In this uncommon, this peculiar case,
Sweet Echo, say, must I still love and bless?
    —Still love and bless.

Whatever usage ill I may receive,
Must I be patient still, and still forgive?
    —Be patient still, and still forgive.

Why, Echo, how is this? thou 'rt sure a dove,
Thy voice shall teach me nothing else but love!
    —Nothing else but love.

Amen, with all my heart, then be it so,
'Tis all delightful, just and good, I know,
And now to practise I'll directly go.
    —Directly go.

Things being so, whoever me reject,
My gracious God me surely will protect.
    —Surely will protect.

Henceforth I'll roll on Him my every care,
And then both friend and foe embrace in prayer.
    —Embrace in prayer.

But after all the duties I have done,
Must I, in point of merit, them disown,
And trust for Heaven through Jesu's blood alone?
    —Through Jesu's blood alone.

Echo, enough! thy counsels to mine ear
Are sweeter than to flowers the dew-drop tear;
Thy wise, instructive lessons please me well:
I'll go and practise them. Farewell, farewell.
    —Practise them. Farewell, farewell.
    (a)   *Anonymous*

EDUCATION OF CHILDREN

Thelwall thought it very unfair to influence a child's mind by inculcating any opinions before it should have come to years of discretion, and be able to choose for itself. I showed him my garden, and told him it was my botanical garden. "How so?" said he, "it is covered with weeds." —"Oh," I replied, *"that* is only because it has not yet come to its age of discretion and choice. The weeds, you see, have taken the liberty to grow, and I thought it unfair in me to prejudice the soil towards roses and strawberries."
    (b)   *S. T. Coleridge*

EDUCATION, ECONOMY IN

There should be no economy in education. Money should never be weighed against the soul of a child. It should be poured out like water for the child's intellectual and moral life.
    (c)   *Channing*

EDUCATION IN HANDICRAFT

I should like to see the hammer and the saw, the spade and the scythe, the implements of trade and the implements of handicraft, as familiar in boys' hands as the cricket-bat or the fishing-rod. It was an old custom among the Jews, that every boy should learn a trade, as (you remember) one student in the University of Tarsus became a tent-maker. It is customary to praise this as a prudent provision against poverty. This it is, but it is a part of education too. No mistake can be greater than to think that skilled manual work is no head-work; the intelligence of our higher artisans proves the error in a moment. Surely the qualities of dexterity, quickness, attention, ingenuity, which it cultivates, the delight in visible production, and the habits of industry to which this delight is an incentive, are a part of educational training. The use of bicycles may break heads, but the manufacture of them in our workshops here certainly improved them.
    (d)   *Bishop Barry (Sydney)*

EDUCATION, INCAPACITY FOR

I have, indeed, known instances of a hopeless incapacity, which is like the want of one of the senses. There are those who really see no reason why, if it were properly managed, two and two should not make five, who never can conceive why the angle A B C is not the same as the angle A C B. I remember a friend of mine, and a very able man, who once asked me whether all chants were not the same, and another who did not know God Save the Queen from the Hundredth Psalm. These must be given up and allowed to develop as they can, just as you would treat a blind man or a deaf one. But these are rare and exceptional cases, scarcely one or two per cent. of the whole.
    (e)   *Bishop Barry (Sydney)*

EDUCATION, MORAL

The children that Falk gathered into his "Reformatory" were depraved. His principle was, that the root of the evil was not *ignorance*, but *sin;* that it was not enough, therefore, to teach writing and arithmetic; that that was the least part of education; that it was more important to impart the secret of a righteous life. "What in all the world," he said once boldly before the Estates, "does it profit the State to have thieves who can write and thieves who can cipher? They are only so much the more dangerous. Ay, and what profit is it though your thieves should speak Latin and Greek and French?"
    (f)   *Stevenson's Memoir of Falk.*

EDUCATION OF THE PEOPLE

To apprehend danger from the education of the people, is like fearing lest the thunderbolt strike into the house because it has *windows;* whereas the lightning never comes through these, but through their *lead* framing, or down by the *smoke* of the chimney.
    (g)   *J. P. F. Richter*

EDUCATION, SHALLOW

It is sometimes urged by those who consider the multitude as not intended to think, that at best they can learn but little, and that this is likely to harm rather than to do them good. "A little learning," we are told, "is a dangerous thing." "Shallow draughts" of knowledge are worse than ignorance. The mass of the people, it is said, can go to the bottom of nothing; and the result of stimulating them to thought will be the formation of a dangerous set of half-thinkers.
    (h)   *Channing*

Solver of problems, whether hard or easy,
Architect of verses, in arts a dabbler,
    Scribbler of essays,
Paddler in painting, pat in evolution,
Languages, music, chymical solutions,
Scorner of grammar, clever on the platform,
    Dribbler in Hebrew—

Then comes something with a Tennysonian ring about "smatterer" and "chatterer." The following stanza, contains the moral,

Surely 'tis better to be thought a perfect
Master of one thing than a dabbler and a
    Babbler in all things.
(a)   *The Modern Omniscient*

EGYPT: "OUT OF EGYPT HAVE I CALLED MY SON" (Matt. ii. 15)

An expression which pervades the whole course of history. But this calling implies not only the Son's residence in Egypt, but also His departure from it.

Cf. (i.) Israelites; (ii.) Christ; (iii.) The Christian.
(b)   *Lange*

" *When Israel was a child, then I loved him, and called My son out of* EGYPT " (Hos. xi. 1).

The words have had three fulfilments:

I. That under Moses: God's people might be in Egypt; but as it could not be their home, only a place of exile, or a sojourn, at the best—nothing more—they must be called out of it. Others might be allowed to remain there; but they whom God *loved* might not. For *them* there were Canaan and Jerusalem, and the land flowing with milk and honey. *Egypt was for others.*

This = first fulfilment: "When Israel was a child, then I loved him, and called My son out of Egypt."
(c)

II. After this another fulfilment—that of the only begotten Son of God. Israel's history was, as it were, the rehearsal of His. He trod in their steps: went over their history in Himself.

And this, perhaps, is to teach us the oneness and closeness of the connection between Him and them. They went down into Egypt. He, too, went down into Egypt. But Egypt was not to be their home. Neither was Egypt to be His home. Both had fled there for shelter. But both had work to do, and a mission to fulfil elsewhere.

The Israelites, many of whom were born in Egypt, were heirs of another heritage. Canaan was for them, and there they had to fulfil their mission.

The Son of God, too, could not do His work in the land of Egypt: for He was sent to the lost sheep of the house of Israel.

Whatever attractions Egypt might possess, neither He nor they could stop in it.

And so, when the Word of the Lord came, Joseph and Mary and the child Jesus returned to their own country. And thus brought about the second fulfilment of the words

" *Out of Egypt have I called My Son.*"
(d)

III. The Last Fulfilment. The Church of Christ —the Israel of the Spirit—like ancient Israel—and Clike hrist Himself—is called out of Egypt.

Each chosen one—each saint, each son, each child of God—is indeed CALLED out of the Egypt of this world. The *call*, when looked at in the light of the past, is·

(i.) A *call* out of Egypt;
(ii.) A *call* into the wilderness; and
(iii.) A *call* for us to arise and set out on our journey home.

(i.) Consider it as a *call for us to come out of Egypt.*
Egypt is a type of this present evil world. Evil it is, because the world as such is without God. It has its own things, pleasures, gaieties, riches, glories, pomps, magnificence, and gorgeousness. In this Egypt was one of the best types of the world, for in it were gathered all the world's *wealth*, *art*, *science*, and *philosophy* of that time. It was a fascinating country: every object in it magnetic to the natural man, and intoxicating to the unregenerate heart.

Everything was there but the true God. The world's *religion* was there, decked out in splendid temples, pictures, statues, and images of every kind.

The world's *wisdom* was there: for its astronomy, its natural sciences, its mechanical arts, its architecture, its skill in ornament, gave it the foremost place of the time. All had fascinations for the unregenerate heart—stimulants for the lust of the flesh, the lust of the eye, and the pride of life.

Everything worldly was there: knowledge, beauty, progress, intellect, power, greatness, pomp, splendour. Man in *intellect* at his highest, but man in *religion* at his lowest. Such was Egypt, and such is the world. But Egypt, notwithstanding all its wisdom, could not arrive at the knowledge of God. And the world, in like manner, by wisdom knows not God. Egypt, nevertheless, held within it the people of God. So, too, the world, "which lieth in wickedness," holds within it the Church of Christ. In it we all had our conversation in time past—the children of wrath even as others. But God called us out. "Come ye *out* from among them, and be ye separate: and I will be a Father unto you, and ye shall be My sons and daughters, saith the Lord Almighty."

Called out, because we should never have come if left to ourselves.

People tarry in the places they love best; and it is our nature to love our Egypt, and to take pleasure in its vanities. It is the home of our hearts, and the mistress of our affections.

But God, "who is rich in mercy," *called us* out. By some means or other He let us understand that to stay there would be at our peril.

He spake in some mysterious way to our inmost souls, that our further stay and delight in Egypt were made exceedingly uncomfortable.

He called us, as He did Abraham, to leave home, leave everything, and go out, not knowing where.

He called us, as He did the fisherman by the lake of Galilee, to leave fishing-boat and all else, and to follow Him.

The voice rung in our ears, meeting us at every hour of the day—in our homes, in hours of quiet, in business, in the crowd, in the church, everywhere—we heard it saying—

"Arise ye, and depart, for *this* is not your rest."
But for a while we resisted the voice of God, we tried not to hear, we tried to deaden the voice by louder voices.

We entered into larger enterprises—we left our-
(e)

selves no time for obtrusive thoughts. Still God pursued us.

He tried other means : pain came, trials came, disappointments came, vexations, bereavements—a thousand voices spake, and sometimes all of them together.

We felt that we were pursued, that we must hearken and yield.

The voice was an Almighty voice—irresistible.

God spake the effectual word and made us willing in the day of His power.

We were bidden to relax our hold and to detach ourselves from the world (the Goshen that we loved so well), and to gird our loins and set out on a life-long pilgrimage.

To put the Red Sea between us and Egypt, and to commit ourselves to a new order of things altogether-

For " Out of Egypt God Calls His Sons."

(a)   *Horatius Bonar and others, adapted*

Egypt and the Wilderness

The calling out of Egypt also a call into the Wilderness.

The people called out of Egypt; thenceforth have no home.

" Here we have no continuing city." The children of a king have as yet no kingdom, and are obliged to confess that they are " strangers and pilgrims on the earth."

Egypt, at any rate, offered them something like a home ; and there, too, they could reckon upon supplies of some sort from day to day—they might be coarse, but they were sure.

But as soon as the Red Sea lies between them and their former home, they are in a desert—a " waste howling wilderness "—a land of barrenness, of heat, thirst, hunger, and weariness. " Hungry and thirsty, their soul fainted in them ; they found no city to dwell in."

It is clear, then, that the wilderness life is not intended to be one of a fixed character. The newly converted man is soon taught that " man liveth not by bread alone, but by every word that proceedeth out of the mouth of God."

Whilst in the world he thought only of living, and getting a living, and of getting more than a living, and he was consistent in so doing; for if the world represented to him the chief and only good thing, then the more he could get of it the happier it was likely to make him. But as soon as we are come out of Egypt and are on the other side of the Red Sea, things are put before us in a new light.

God is *now* our chief good, and to become possessed of Him is our happiness ; and now begins that process of weaning the affections from its old idols ; now man is taught that he must live by faith, and that for him to do the *will* of God, and to live by every *word* that proceedeth from the mouth of God, is the real and the true life; and everything that God does to and for him now, is in reference to this new principle of his being— " *Old things are passed away, and all things are become new.*"

That this path of the pilgrims is the right one, we do not doubt, because God Himself is our leader.

It is safe ; for He is our Keeper.

It is a *blessed path*, for God is our companion ; He has promised to be with us.

But, for all this, it is a rough, dark, and a dreary road. And we may well believe that there is some great end in view, or else God would spare His people all the suffering that it entails upon them, and Himself the provocations of a stiffnecked people, whose manners He suffered in the wilderness " forty years."

But though this was undoubtedly the object of God in leading them into the *wilderness*, yet such a result was not contemplated by the Israelites themselves, nor do we expect to encounter such difficulties when we obey God's call, and separate ourselves in spirit from the world around us. An ancient writer says truly, " If thou comest to seek the Lord, prepare thyself for adversity."

That the Israelites did not expect such a train of events as came upon them in the wilderness, is plain from their behaviour at the very outset. They were hardly out of Egypt before they provoked God and rebelled against His appointments ten times.

Their conduct is but a rehearsal of our own. During their course from Egypt to Canaan, the forty years' wanderings in the wilderness is the Bible Version of the Pilgrim's Progress.

It is the most significant portion of Israelitish history for the *individual Christian*, who has left the Egypt of this world, and set his face Zionward.

There may be some exaggeration—all of us may not *murmur*, and *fall*, and rebel so grossly as they did ; but after all the allowances and abatements that can be made, it remains that the history of that people at that time is virtually the history of God's people from the time of their conversion to the end of their earthly life.

In their murmurings about the hardships and privations to which they were exposed, we may see what are our own *thoughts* about God's appointments concerning our lot in this life.

In their repeated unbelief we may see our own *unbelief* when new and untried difficulties beset us.

In their frequent falls into sin—old sins—sins of their old unrenewed life in Egypt—we may see our own backslidings and lapses into worldliness.

Now, this yielding up of His own personal will was the most distinguishing feature of our Lord's life on earth as a man amongst men. And it was this, which God had never found in man before, with which He was " *well pleased.*"

This, when arrived at, is the highest mark of sonship. We are reminded of it constantly by our Lord. " Not every one that saith unto Me, Lord, Lord, shall enter into heaven, but he that doeth the *will* of My Father which is in heaven "; and again, " Whosoever shall do the *will* of My Father, the same is My brother and sister and mother."

To make this rough material into sons and daughters of the Lord God Almighty, is the reason why, when God calls His people out of Egypt, He next leads them through so many trying circumstances, up and down for long years in the wilderness.

For such is His own explanation of the matter. In Deuteronomy viii. 2, He says, " Thou shalt remember all the way by which the Lord thy God led thee these forty years in the wilderness, to *humble* thee and to *prove* thee, and to *know* what
(b)

was in thine heart, whether thou wouldst keep His commandments or no. And He *humbled* thee and suffered thee to *hunger*, and fed thee with manna . . . that He might make thee know that man doth not live by bread only, but by every word that proceedeth out of the mouth of the Lord doth man live."

(a)   *Horatius Bonar and others, adapted*

EGYPT, THE WILDERNESS, AND CANAAN

The wilderness is not an end in itself, no more a stopping-place than was Egypt. Hence—

The calling out of Egypt into the Wilderness, is a call to set out on our journey home.

There may be some who think Religion's ways are ways of pleasantness and all her paths peace in some other sense than the Bible teaches; and hence it has been misrepresented as a religion of tears, and mildness, and fastidiousness, afraid of crossing people's prejudices, and with silken gloves lifting the people up from the church pew into glory, as if they were Bohemian glass, so very delicate, which one rough touch might destroy for ever. Heaven made easy! "We have not so learned Christ."

Men speak of religion as though it were a refined insensibility, or a sort of spiritual chloroform for people to take until the sharp cutting of life is over.

The Bible, so far from this, represents our religion as robust and brawny, ransacking and upsetting ten thousand things that now seem to stand on firm foundations.

Where is the mildness, or the weakness, or the fastidiousness of God's method of transforming worldlings into Christians, as taught us in the pilgrimage of the Israelites from Egypt to Canaan? Some one says, I thought religion *was* "peace," and "happiness," and "quietness," and "assurance for ever." The Israelites thought that they were going straight and easily to Canaan. *So it will be when the work is done.* But what "peace" can there be whilst we need so much *humbling*, and *proving*, and *heart-searching*? If a man's arm is out of joint, men come and with great effort put it back into its socket. It goes back with great pain. Then it gets well. Our whole being is disorganized. We must come under an omnipotent surgery, beneath which there will be pain and anguish before there can come perfect health and quiet. And the wilderness is the place where God reduces dislocation and puts that right which now is wrong. But heaven, the home to which all this preparatory work tends, is the place of quietness and assurance for ever. There it will be seen how necessary was the wilderness.

That people who thought they were ready for Canaan as soon as they had left Egypt, will be the first to exclaim: "Just and true are Thy ways, thou King of saints."

(b)   *Bonar, Talmage, and others, adapted*

ELECT, THE

The elect are whosoever will, says Beecher; and the non-elect are whosoever won't.

(c)

ELECT

As to God's Predestination of the Elect, "*What is that to thee? Follow thou Me.*" We have no more to do with that than with the government of China. It is not with God as *unsearchable*, that we have to do. We have no right to intrude into the Mysteries of the Royal Presence, we should count it enough if we are included in the Royal Proclamation of Mercy.

(d)   *See Chalmers' Works,* vol. iii. p. 198

ELECT, GOD'S

"*Who shall lay anything to the charge of* GOD'S ELECT? *It is God that justifieth*" (Rom. viii. 33).

I

After the Apostle's triumphant challenge, "If God be for us, who can be against us?" he imagines at least three possible accusing, condemning, and separating powers, that can be against the Christian.

The first of which is God Himself:—He alone might be against us; but the fact is, that He is "for us." The fifth chapter of this epistle had made it most unlikely, nay a contradiction, that God would lay anything to the charge of His ELECT; for, "Being justified by faith, we have peace with God through our Lord Jesus Christ." If "*at peace*" with Him, then we may banish the fear of an adverse verdict hereafter.

(e)

II

GOD HAS AN ELECT PEOPLE

The most obvious meaning of this and similar passages is, that God has an elect people. This is proved, if anywhere, in the previous argument, wherein the *predestination*, the *calling*, the *justification*, and the *glorification* of such are shown to be the several links in a long chain—one end of which is in eternity past, the other in that to come, whilst the middle portion only touches upon things temporal.

Similar passages are John x. and Eph. i.

(f)

III

PRECEPT AND PURPOSE

Whatever in this respect be our belief, practically we need not press the thought to any hard conclusion, as if the sphere of our duty lay in our properly knowing what is the purpose of God concerning us. With that we have nothing to do. Our duty is to be inferred from what is plainly revealed to us of His *will:* "And this is the will of the Father, that ye believe on His Son Jesus Christ." His *precept*, and not His *purpose*, should be the light unto our path and the guide for our feet. Great mistakes have been made as to this, notably in the case of Jacob, who, by acting upon what he believed to be the Purpose of God concerning the Birthright, took unfair means of securing what was to be his own in the ordinary Providence of God. He erred from the simple rule which tells us to "trust in the Lord and do right." God will see to the fulfilment of His purpose, whilst it is

(g)

our part to obey His precepts. God wants no help from Jacob, nor from the "sons of Jacob"; "His Purposes do ripen fast, . . . unfolding every hour," without their intervention. We cannot indeed look into the Book of His Eternal Decrees and read our names there, and so satisfy ourselves that we are of the elect, and then act accordingly; but we can, and ought to, look into the Book of His revealed will—the Bible—and read our names as included amongst those for whom God has a compassionate love; for it is written, "God so loved the *world*"; amongst those too for whom Christ died, since it offers the benefits of His atonement to "*all*" and to "*whosoever believeth.*" And by shaping our conduct accordingly we can make our "*calling and election sure.*" The only true evidence that the elect can give, which will satisfy observers, is that of the fruit tree, "By their fruits ye shall know them."

Having obeyed the call of God, of Christ, of the Spirit, and of the Church, which said "*Come*"—and where a holy life has ensued, the best and only reliable evidence of their election of God is given. St. Paul had no other evidence of the elect than this:

He inferred it from what he knew and saw of the people so designated, where he says, "Knowing, brethren, your election of God, for our Gospel came not unto you in word only, but also in *power* and in the Holy Ghost, and with much assurance, as ye know what manner of men we were among you for your sakes, and ye became followers of us and were examples to all." The Apostle, we see, drew his conclusions, not from inspiration, not because he could read their names in the Book of God's Decrees, but from his own observance of their ordinary behaviour.

(*a*)　　　　　　　*See Thomas Chalmers and others*

IV

Observe, that they are "God's Elect"

It is Him whom they have offended; against Him they, as all, have rebelled; and we are too apt to think that in consequence all the saving love is on the part of Christ our Redeemer—and not on the part of the Father. We are too ready to lend an ear to the calumniator of the character of God, and to think that He has no great desire to save those who have been rebellious—as if Salvation emanated solely from the Mediator, and was not equally the desire of the Father, "who Himself loveth us." By so thinking, we wrong the Parental heart of the Father, of whom we read that God so loved the world that He gave His dearest and His best for its salvation.

The Scriptures reveal God to us as a Parent bereaved of His family. "I have nourished and brought up children, and they have rebelled against Me." He devises means to bring these back unto Himself. And these "Elect," here spoken of, are the members of His family whom His love has succeeded in bringing back, by "making them willing in the day of His power." He has found a means by which He can be just and yet the justifier of them that believe—which justification means that He is reconciled to them—brings no accusation against them—and that they are "at peace" with Him who before were at enmity. The family feeling and filial relationship, which had been ruptured by disobedience and sin, are thereby restored.

But that this justification, which ensues upon their repentance and faith, is a first or even a second step in their spiritual history, is not in accordance with the teaching of this chapter, which assuredly teaches that a long antecedent train of causes, known only to God, preceded and led up to what is termed their *justification*.

This is intended for the comfort of any of those "sheep of His pasture," who during their earthly discipline—where the family are at school—get astray from the fold, and go into pastures and places where they forfeit His protection, and are pounced down upon and run off with by some wolf, ever lurking around for such opportunities. Then loss and peril ensues. Such cases too often happen.

What then are such to conclude when they find themselves again in deep waters, and through the blinding mists and darkness they cannot see their guiding star as before? Are they suffered to lapse altogether? Shall we call them "reprobate silver"? In answer to this, let us observe the argument of the Apostle here on this point. If the believer had attained to *perfection* and sinned not, but continued steadfastly to do his Master's will, where would accusations to trouble him come from, seeing nothing in his conduct gave occasion for such to arise? But hosts of accusers will ever be on the watch, and lose no opportunity of bearing their ill report as soon as the slightest occasion does arise.

The question here is, Will such charges alter the fundamental facts of the case? Will God go off from His covenant? or change His Purpose concerning them? If these foundations are destroyed, what will the righteous do? "If any man sin," we have the blood of Christ; but, "if any man love the world, the love of the Father is not in him." Not the former, but the latter imperils the soul.

And in this case, the Apostle seems to invite accusations, in order to show how each can be disposed of. "The fiery darts of the wicked one" fall harmlessly to the ground, being met by the shield of faith.

Compare Godet, Philippi, Lange, Moses Stuart, and others in loc.

(*b*)

V

The Accusers of the Elect

1. Let Conscience come and open the Book of Memory

Among things human nothing can be more damaging than the record on its pages.

It comes with a true bill, and a long list of sins and backslidings—records of mis-spent time and wasted opportunities. Let the man's own heart have the first word to say against him, and tell its worst; for no one except God can more justly condemn a man than his own heart and secret bosom. And when it has told its tale, what is there to be said in the man's defence? Can any one gainsay the condemnation of the heart, when it speaks of sins against light and knowledge, of things that it knows, of things that were written down indelibly at the time of commission? when all this is exposed to view, can such testimony fail to condemn? Or can the man after this lay claim to one iota of spiritual comfort? *Yes*, he can; for it in no wise alters the state of the case. God

(*c*)

knows all this. *" God is greater than the heart, and knoweth all things.* Notwithstanding this, " IT IS GOD THAT JUSTIFIETH."

(a)   *Compare as before*

VI

2. Let the great Adversary, the Accuser, come

He who has made it his special business to study the characters of the people spoken of. None others apparently cause him so much anxiety. He makes himself acquainted with their weaknesses. He studies the natural bent and inclination of their characters—their peculiar and besetting sins. He knows well what he is witnessing about when he comes forward with accusations and charges against them. His manifold victories give him confidence. Day and night, we read, he accuseth them before God. Let him come next and say what he has to say against one of God's elect. Let him tell of his many successes, when he or his emissaries have laid snares for their unwitting and too often heedless and almost presumptuous feet. Let him give his version of their religiousness—their profession and their practice. Let him assign unworthy motives for certain ostensibly Christian acts. Let him tell of his successes with Adam, with Noah, with David, with Peter, with all the disciples, and more or less with every one of these elect of God. Let him give his reasons for claiming particular cases as certainly his own. And when all is said that he can say,—when every truth has been perverted, and every lie has been told, and his case as the prosecutor as well as the accuser has been made out,—what rebutting evidence can be adduced on the other side? Just this :

"The Lord rebuke thee, Satan : thou hast nothing to do with it. It is God, not thou, who has been sinned against." " Is not this a brand plucked from the burning?" Let him alone. " IT IS GOD THAT JUSTIFIETH."

(b)   *Compare as before*

VII

3. Next let his Fellow-men come

Those with whom he has lived, and too often, alas ! with whom he has sinned. Let all who will come, and say everything that malice or spite can say against one who has come out from the world, and joined himself unto the Lord with a perpetual covenant. Let conduct and motives be equally inquired into. Let the companions of youth and of riper years, of unconverted as well as of converted days come, and witness against him ; for they too have keen eyes and cannot but sometimes have found flaws in his character. He is of like passions with themselves—encompassed with infirmity, and oftentimes off his watch-tower, often unfortified with prayer, often looking away from Christ—seemingly independent of Him, often on slippery ground.

Let Laban say all he can against the peccable Jacob, let Shimei curse David, and Pharaoh reprove Abraham. We excuse not their sins—trouble enough to themselves will ensue thereon ; but let the scandal fly abroad like a firebrand. And what then? Has it established a case? Does the earth open and swallow up the accused?

Does Heaven confirm the judgment on earth ? Does it shut where man shuts, and excommunicate where man excommunicates? *Nothing of the kind.* For when all its anathemas have been hurled, and its judgments pronounced,.

" IT IS GOD THAT JUSTIFIETH."

(c)

VIII

What Saith the Scripture ?

God, who knows all things, Who knows equally well what others know against these persons, knows also that some things which might have been said have not been said. No record has been given of their repentance, their faith, their prayer, and the general current of their lives. As repentant persons, they have put the conduct of their case into the hands of the Great Advocate, Jesus Christ the Righteous ; and through His intercessions they find mercy, and come off victorious.

God, Who is of tender mercy, more willing to save than to destroy, has accepted them into His family as His adopted children. Children, not yet adults ; and as folly is bound up in the heart of a child, consequently they need the chastening rod. But the chastening rod is rather an argument for than against their election. If Satan is more solicitous about these elect than he is of others, God, too, has His hand often upon them ; and because they are His children therefore He punishes them for their misdeeds. Witness the experiences of all the saints of old. Did Jacob get free of this fatherly discipline ? Did David ? Did Peter ? Do any ? Would they wish it ? Do not one and all of them say and feel that God in very faithfulness has afflicted them ; and that they oftentimes find a greater evidence of their adoption in their sufferings, than in the times when the " candle of the Lord shone upon them, when their corn and wine were increased " ?

God sees and knows all ; more than others who have given in their one-sided and biased evidence. Their repentance and faith have been overlooked and forgotten. But it is these which God makes so much of, because they show what these people are. Their " faith is counted unto them for righteousness." And if He, the SOVEREIGN, the supreme Being in Heaven and earth, be satisfied with them—who then, in all His universe, shall lay anything to the charge of God's elect ? If God gives peace, who can give trouble ? Rather than listen to these accusers one by one, it would shorten the whole matter by reducing it to the smallest compass, and ask,

What saith the offended person ? Who alone has power to cast into hell ? How readest thou the Scriptures ? This He saith—and thus " it is written,"

" IT IS GOD THAT JUSTIFIETH "

For, " being justified by faith, we have peace with God through our Lord Jesus Christ."—Rom. v. 5.

Compare the critical authorities as above ; also Samuel Rutherford's Letters, and John Owen on Ps. cxxx.

(d)

ELECTION

Calvinism teaches, that, by the decree of God, some men are fore-ordained to everlasting death; Paul teaches, that it is the will of God "that all men should be saved and come to the knowledge of the truth." Calvinism teaches, that "neither are any other redeemed by Christ, ... but the elect only;" Paul teaches, that "Christ gave Himself a ransom for all." Calvinism teaches, that God's choice falls on men when they are not "in Christ," and brings them into union with Him that they may receive the forgiveness of sins and eternal life; Paul teaches, that the elect are those who are "in Christ," and that being in Him, they enter into the possession of those eternal blessings which before the foundation of the world it was God's purpose, His decree, to confer upon all Christians. According to the Calvinistic conception, some men, who are still "children of wrath, even as the rest," to use a phrase which occurs later in this epistle, are among the "elect," and will therefore some day become children of God. That is a mode of speech foreign to Paul's thought. According to Paul, no man is elect except he is "in Christ." We are all among the non-elect until we are in Him. But once in Christ we are caught in the currents of the eternal purposes of the Divine love; we belong to the elect race; all things are ours; we are the children of God and the heirs of His glory. God has "blessed us with every spiritual blessing . . . . *in Christ.*" God "chose us *in Him* before the foundation of the world, that we should be holy and without blame before Him in love."

(a)   *R. W. Dale*

ELECTION

The true significance of God's gracious election is, not that the elect may be drawn out of the mass and multitude of perishing mankind, and so saved, but that they are chosen to become instruments of blessing, and distributors of salvation to the world. And this idea needs to be more generally recognised than it seems to be. It becomes more and more necessary to get rid of a selfish type of piety. They have the healthiest souls who care most for other souls.

(b)   *Anonymous*

"ELECTION SURE"

A senator related to his son the account of the book containing the names of illustrious members of the commonwealth. The son desired to see the outside. It was glorious to look upon. "Oh! let me open it," said the son. "Nay," said the father; "it's known only to the Council." "Then," said the son, "tell me if my name is there?" "And that," said the father, "is a secret known only to the Council, and it cannot be divulged." Then he desired to know for what achievements the names were inscribed in that book. So the father told him; and related to him the achievements and noble deeds by which they had eternalized their names. "Such," said he, "are written, and none but such are written in the book." "And will my name be there?" said the son. "I cannot tell thee," said the father: "If thy deeds are like theirs, thou shalt be written in the book; if not, thou shalt not be written." And then the son consulted with himself; and he found

that his whole deeds were playing, and singing, and drinking, and amusing himself; and he found this was not noble, nor temperate, nor valiant. And as he could not read, as yet, his name, he determined to "make his calling and election sure." And thus, by patient continuance in well-doing, the end is crowned with glory, honour, immortality, and eternal life."

(c)   *Hood*

ELECTION, DOCTRINE OF

It is not by the rapture of feelings, and by the luxuriance of thought, and by the warmth of those desires which descriptions of heaven may stir up within us, that I can prove myself predestined to a glorious inheritance. If I would find out what is hidden, I must follow what is revealed. The way to heaven is disclosed, am I walking in that way? It would be a poor proof that I were on my voyage to India; that, with glowing eloquence and thrilling poetry, I could discourse on the palm-groves and spice isles of the East. Am I on the waters? Is the sail hoisted to the wind? And does the land of my birth look blue and faint in the distance? The doctrine of election may have done harm to many, but only because they have fancied themselves elected to the end, and have forgotten that those whom Scripture calls elected are elected to the means. The Bible never speaks of men as elected to be saved from the shipwreck, but only as elected to tighten the ropes, and hoist the sails, and stand to the rudder. Let a man search faithfully; let him see that when Scripture describes Christians as elected, it is as elected to faith, as elected to sanctification, as elected to obedience; and the doctrine of election will be nothing but a stimulus to effort. It cannot act as a soporific. I shall cut away the boat, and let drive all human devices, and gird myself, amid the fierceness of the tempest, to steer the shattered vessel into port.

(d)   *Melvill*

There is an eternal election to life, but no eternal fore-ordination to perdition (except as a *secondary* or *conditional* and *prospective* decree); there is a book of life, but no book of death. But "they who would serve the devil must share with him in the end."

(e)   *P. Schaff*

ELECTION AND PREDESTINATION, DOCTRINES OF

Neither you nor I know how Paul *preached;* but his writings are designed to be a standing rule of faith and doctrine to the Church. If he and his brethren had said nothing in their epistles about election and predestination, we should not have so well understood those points, nor had the same authority for maintaining them. Though I think they may be fairly inferred from other parts of Scripture, perhaps we could not have made them so well out. But Paul says expressly, that he fed babes, not with *strong meat*, but with *milk*. I think I hardly said, that I never mention the words in preaching. When they lie in my text, they make part of my subject and sermon, but seldom otherwise. I think these doctrines should be in a sermon like sugar in a dish of tea, which sweetens every drop, but is nowhere to be found in a lump.

(a)   *John Newton*

ELIJAH AND CHRIST, SPIRIT OF

" Lord, wilt Thou that we command fire to come down from heaven, and consume them, even as Elias did? But He turned and rebuked them, and said, Ye know not what manner of spirit ye are of. For the Son of man is not come to destroy men's lives, but to save them " (Luke ix. 54–56)

1. Elijah and Jesus

Our Lord, on the occasion when these words were uttered, was journeying towards Jerusalem, and His route was through certain villages of the Samaritans. The inhabitants of one of these refused to receive Him. Thereupon two of His disciples, James and John, indignant at this incivility, wished for a revelation of His power " who maketh the winds His messengers, and a flame of lightning His minister of wrath "—and asked, in mistaken zeal, for a repetition of a terrible scene in the history of the great prophet Elijah. Such was the spirit which at that time animated these " sons of thunder "—fitting name for those who betrayed such intolerant zeal—a zeal, however, which (subsequent ages of the Church has proved) has not burnt itself out, notwithstanding the rebuke of our Lord, " Ye know not what manner of spirit ye are of,"—ye know not that the spirit of Elijah and the spirit of Christ are inharmonious,—" For the Son of man is not come to destroy men's lives but to save them."

This reply suggests the difference between the spirit of Elijah and the spirit of Christ. Elijah the Prophet, who, with all his transcendent grandeur, was in spirit the farthest of all removed from the spirit of Christ—a prophet who, if he had lived in our day, would have preached to men, as John the Baptist, his representative, did—denouncing the vices and the follies of men with no mean, no polished, no measured utterances. Sternly and severely he would have laid his axe at the root of the tree, and hewed down every system, every custom, and every institution wherein iniquity had enshrined itself, whilst with a voice of thunder he would have called on men everywhere to repent.

Had he been a preacher of our times, he would not have toned down the fearful doctrine of eternal punishment; rather would he have emphasized it as a means of alarming and terrifying the consciences of those whom he believed to be dead in sin.

We might picture him as preaching from such texts as:—" Ye generation of vipers, who hath warned you to flee from the wrath to come? " or, " How can ye escape the damnation of hell ? " He would have " reasoned of righteousness and of judgment to come," till every Felix trembled, as the words of righteous and indignant zeal rolled in burning torrents from the lips of the wondrous preacher.

But this, though in its place necessary and preparatory, is not the spirit of Jesus. Jesus quiets the storm. His speech droppeth as the gentle dew. He came, not to destroy, but to save. Not to take men's lives, but to give His own " a ransom for many." Not to look upon men as enemies, but to regard all as the possible servants of Christ and of God. The language of Christ in this respect strikingly reminds us of the pathetic words of David—" Deal gently with the young man, Absalom, *for my sake*." Such is the spirit of Christ and of Christianity, as distinguished from that of Elijah.

On one occasion Luther, when a monk, was assisting at the celebration of the mass; and as he carried the box containing the wafer—he trembled and was afraid—trembled because he, a sinful man, should be in such near contact with what he then believed to be the actual body of Christ. The thought of his unworthiness, and of his near contact with a Holy God, oppressed him. His friend Staupitz, the vicar-general, inquiring the cause of his distress, and being told, said, " *Luther, it was not Jesus—Jesus never terrifies.*" That was a true witness. He may send an Elijah before him to prepare His way, or a John the Baptist, as a porter, to open the door to the Shepherd when He comes. But He Himself never comes to us in that shape. When we hear His voice, it is the voice of One who has got the secrets of our hearts. We do not commonly associate with the characters of a " Friend," a " Brother," the " Bridegroom," the " Good Shepherd,"—anything but gentleness, tenderness, and love ; and in the passage before us He designates Himself as " *the Son of man*," so as to exclude the idea of judging and condemning.

(*a*)

2. Elijah and Jezebel

A weak king at that time occupied the throne. The old adage, that " weakness is allied to crime," perhaps nowhere finds stricter fulfilment than in his case.

His wife,—a descendant of the Canaanite stock,—is virtually at the helm; and he but a tool in her hands. Her religion,—the worship of Baal,—is introduced into the kingdom, where it is not only tolerated and protected, but soon becomes the court and fashionable religion ; for it tolerates worldliness, and any religion that does that may soon count upon a large following. Ultimately, under the queen's fostering care, it permeated the whole nation and became the dominant religion.

There was a wild licence and a fascination of manner and character about Jezebel, which strongly impressed the nation. She becomes the centre of the religious persecution in the reign of Ahab. This religious persecution is the first, on a large scale, of the persecutions the Church has encountered ; and all the bitter intolerance of modern times must therefore look back to Jezebel as its legitimate ancestress. In her time the altars of the one true God were destroyed. The prophets of Jehovah were hunted down as the chief enemies of the religion of the queen. Now first began those hidings " in dens and in caves of the earth " which afterwards found so prominent a place in the annals of early Christianity. The faithful Obadiah hid two companies of fifty in caves. Things arrived at a crisis. The great question was, whether true religion was or was not to be the religion of the country. It was at this crisis that the very chief of the prophets appeared. Elijah thinks himself the only faithful man left—" Alone, alone, alone," he says on three

(*b*)

occasions, "I only am left." He, the loftiest and sternest spirit of the true faith, was a Reformer, raised up face to face with the fierce spirit of Jezebel, to wrest the religious supremacy from Baal and to give it back to Jehovah. A marvellous character. Amongst all the wonders with which he and his times were surrounded, the prophet, it has been well remarked, was the "greatest wonder." An iron will, a lightning glance, a voice of thunder, the kingdom and the cause of God his only thought, God's name and God's honour his only passion—such a character defies all natural explanation. He stood alone against Jezebel. He stands alone amongst the Prophets. He is one of the three, Moses, Samuel, and Elijah, who have left the most permanent and abiding impress upon the people of Israel. Like Luther of later times, and in a similar period of apostasy and decay of true religion, he was a *Reformer*. He wrote, predicted, taught, almost nothing. His personality and his marvellous activity take the place of these things in others. He is to be valued for what he *did*, not for what he *said*—not for what he created, but for what he *destroyed*.

(a)

3. Elijah and John the Baptist

His sternness is afterwards reproduced in John the Baptist, who is himself a contrast to Christ. Elijah and the Baptist came "neither eating nor drinking." Elijah, like the disciples of John, "fasted oft." He was the original type of the hermit, the monk, and the Puritan. But not the type of ordinary Christians. "Among them that were born of woman," there were none greater than he and his representative; yet, notwithstanding this, the least in the Kingdom of Heaven is greater than either. For when the two Apostles, James and John, after the example of Elijah, would have called down fire from heaven, Jesus "rebuked them," "*Ye know not what spirit ye are of*"—ye know not that the times and the dispensation are changed—ye know not the "spirit of the age," "*Mercy rejoiceth against judgment.*"

(b)

4. Elijah and Ahab

The apostate nation was visited with a drought, as a judgment from God for their declension, in accordance with the word of Moses in Deut. xi. (16, 17), "Take heed to yourselves, that your heart be not deceived, and ye turn aside, and serve other gods, and worship them; and the Lord's wrath be kindled against you, and He shut up the heaven, that there be no rain, and the land yield not her fruit." In eastern countries, where life and water go always together, such a visitation is indeed a calamity. The springs are dried up, the brooks and rivers become beds of stone, the trees wither, the grass vanishes, the heaven overhead becomes brass, and the earth that is underneath as iron. In such a visitation God will make His power to be known; and such is an opportunity for a true prophet's voice to be heard. The prophet denounces the judgment, gives no indication of the duration of it, flees from the face of the king, is sustained in a miraculous way at the brook Cherith. Three years pass over, the dearth continues, when lo, as suddenly as before, the Prophet (whom Ahab had vainly sought)

stands again before him. "Art thou that *my lord* Elijah?" asks reverentially the faithful Obadiah. "Art thou *the troubler* of Israel?" asks, in anger, the recreant king. But Elijah, with reckless language, casts back the words in his teeth, "Thou and thy house are the troublers of Israel." And to prove it, he desires that the king would collect the prophets of Baal on Mount Carmel, the peculiar haunt of Elijah. There, ranged on one side were the king, the people, and the 450 prophets of Baal, dressed in their splendid vestments. On the other side stood the solitary figure of the Prophet, in his rough sheepskin cloak. Below them lay the city and the idol temple of Jezebel.

(c)

5. Elijah at Carmel

Elijah wants to gain the people back again to Jehovah. He therefore addresses them, and not the king. "How long (he cries) halt ye between two opinions? If the Lord be God, follow Him: but if Baal, then follow him." The people saw the force of the alternative. Of the amalgamated religion of Jehovah and Baal there was nothing to be said. They saw plainly enough that it must either be Baal or Jehovah, but for which of the two to decide, they did not know. They held their peace. Is it to be Jehovah, the exclusive God, who wrought such wonders for them in the land of Egypt,—the God of Abraham, of Isaac, and of Jacob; or is it to be *Baal*, the god of the world? —God after the notions, and according to the ideas of the world—for the world always has its own idea of God. The question now is, Is it to be the God of the Bible, or the god which the natural heart of man loves to fashion for itself, and such as it worships after its own fashion? The same question, in another shape, appears in our own day— whether religious worship is to be that of an enlightened Christian age, or that of the Middle Ages; whether that of the glorious liberty of the children of God, or of superstition. The question is, Which of the two will we have? not whether we will have both; but to make a choice of one or the other, Jehovah or Baal, and stand by it. At such a crisis God has His man ready. His people are turned, as the heart of one man, back again to Himself. As it was then, so it will be now: expect great things of God, and you will get them; "Ask of Me great things, and I will do them."

(d)

6. Elijah and the Prophets of Baal

The prophets of Baal have their turn first. The people will be with them if they can make good their position. The God who answers prayer by fire, he is to be God. They have accepted the challenge. The wild heathen dances begin. From morn till noon they cry, "O Baal, hear us; O Baal, hear us." They think they will be heard for their much speaking. But no answer. Then, being goaded on by the mocking taunts and bitter sarcasms of Elijah, first at their grotesque dances, then at the delay on the part of their god to answer their cry. He ridicules them—scarcely restraining himself from laughter—cheering them on with the words, "Cry with a loud voice, louder and louder yet, for he *is* a god; he has his head full, and is too busy to hear your prayer; or per-

(e)

chance he has his stomach full, and has gone into retirement; or perhaps, in the heat of the day, he is asleep, and must be awakened." They take Elijah at his word. They leap upon the altar, like the modern Dervishes in their frenzy; they lash themselves with knotty scourges, and cut themselves with knives and with swords, till they are smeared with blood. The hour of evening sacrifice draws near. Baal's prophets have failed.

(a)

7. Elijah's Prayer

Elijah's turn has come. Mark the contrast. The old altar of Jehovah is repaired roughly. With no frantic gesticulations, no vestments, no vain reiterations, no many-worded prayer, Elijah lays on the sacrifice and sends up a few words of prayer to the one true God: " Hear me, O Lord, hear me; that this people may know that Thou art the Lord God, and Thou hast turned their hearts back again "— Words, that only took a few seconds to utter, brought the answer which had been denied to the many hours of prayer of the false prophets. " There fell fire from heaven and consumed the sacrifice." A flash of lightning from a cloudless sky was the answer to Elijah's prayer. There was all the difference between the fanatical and unmeaning prayer of the superstitious, which availeth nothing, and " the effectual fervent prayer of a righteous man, which availeth much."

The flash of fire was the token that God had heard the prayer and turned the hearts of the people back again. The shout arose from the assembled multitudes: " The Lord He is God, the Lord He is God." The wheel came full cycle round. The prophets of Baal were seized and swept away by the wild multitude. Elijah himself led them down the mountain gorge to the river-side, and himself, in his righteous zeal, became the executioner. Sword in hand, the grand prophet, the vindicator of the Name and honour of Jehovah, with a swift and terrible slaughter, disposed of Jezebel's brood of ecclesiastical vermin—the prophets of Baal.

Again Elijah prays, and the signs of rain appear. The king,—ever the tool of the stronger mind,—is now hastened towards home. Elijah, still in the heat of the same zeal, twists his mantle around his loins, and runs before the royal chariot, and outstrides the speed of the horses.

(b)

8. Elijah's trial of faith

Jezebel is told the news: and now, notice the reaction on the part of the prophet. He had done much. God's servant had bearded the king and destroyed the prophets of Baal; he stood alone against the whole world, and now, lest he should be tempted to think of himself above that which he ought to think, his faith is tried and breaks down; he who stood before thousands on the top of Carmel now trembles and flees at the impotent threat of a woman. Because Jezebel sends a messenger to say, " As surely as thou art Elijah, and I am Jezebel, so may God do to me, and more also, if I make not thy life as one of them." Elijah expected great things, an almost momentary reformation, to succeed his great work; and now he thinks he has done all in vain; the evil is still dominant; God's authority is still set at nought. It is easy to trace the cause of this despondency;

the whole thing is so thoroughly human that unconsciously the impress of truth is on it. Look at the man's extraordinary exertions; mark the strain put on his physical strength; the mind and the will stretched beyond their wonted capacity; *hungry* and *fatigued,* his despondency is explained, for the body acts on the spirit. One half of our spiritual disquietudes and discomforts are to be traced to like causes. When the body is out of tune and racked with pain, or tired, or hungry, it is no easy thing to find within us evidences of our trust and faith in God. The faith of John Baptist gives way under a similar strain. In this frame of mind the weary and over-worked Elijah could stand out no longer in the great battle he was waging with idolatry; and in a pet of ill-humour with everything he flees and casts himself down at length under a tree, and says, " It is enough. Now, O Lord, take away my life; for I am not *better than my fathers."* These words reveal Elijah's weakness. He had done a great thing—a thing which would live in history—and he *knew* it, for a man cannot be wholly unconscious of his greatness; and now his temptation was to think himself " greater than his fathers." Overcome at last, with sorrow of spirit and increasing weariness of body, with nothing to allay the cravings of hunger in the wilderness, he " wishes to die." Mark how God deals with him. He is not reasoned with. " As one whom his mother comforteth," the body is first put into tune, and then the spirit. First, God sends " His beloved sleep "; the weary body finds needful rest; then *food* is miraculously supplied him.

(c)

9. Elijah in the Wilderness

And then, when the body has been restored, God sends him farther into the wilderness, where during forty days he receives a higher spiritual training. Into the very wilderness where Israel of old was trained, he is now sent to be trained. It takes them forty years; but Elijah in forty days learns his lesson. On one of the spurs of Sinai he has a revelation of the Divine nature, which hitherto, in his marvellous zeal, he had missed. In all probability in the same cave where Moses learnt the character of God (when God made all His GOODNESS to pass before him) there too, in the identical place, in order to deepen the impression, Elijah learns that God is " The Lord, the Lord God, merciful and gracious, longsuffering, and abundant in goodness and truth, keeping mercy for thousands, forgiving iniquity, transgression, and sin." For the word of the Lord came to him there in the cave—" What doest thou here, Elijah? " God wishes to draw from Elijah an expression of his mind. Elijah answers, " I have been very jealous for the Lord God of hosts: for the children of Israel have forsaken Thy covenant, thrown down Thine altars, and slain Thy prophets with the sword; and I, I only am left; and they seek my life to take it away."

Elijah here seems to reproach God, that He has not vindicated His Name and His honour by taking revenge. He cannot understand delay and waiting. He says that he *alone* is left, and soon they will *kill* him, for Jezebel has threatened his life, and there will not be one servant of God left in the land. Elijah wants swift vengeance—swift intervention on God's part, or else His cause will be

(d)

lost. Mark how he is brought to a different way of thinking and a new spirit. *It is a marked crisis in his life.* He is bidden to go forth and stand upon the mountain whilst the Lord passed by. First, a great and a strong wind rent the mountain, huge masses of granite were torn from the mountain sides and rolled down amongst other fragments of rock around him; but "the Lord was not in the wind." He still stood expecting something more, and presently the solid mountain heaved and shook with the shock of a mighty earthquake; but God was not in the earthquake. Again he looked forth into the darkness of the night, and the air flamed with flashes of lightning and fire such as at Sinai of old, at the giving of the Law; but the Lord was not in the fire. And then again, in the deep stillness of the midnight air, came the whisper of "*a still small voice*," a voice so gentle, it was like the breath 'of air which only just moves the leaves —a voice so low !that it was almost like silence. Then Elijah knew that the moment had come. He drew, as was his custom, his rough mantle over his head; he wrapped his face in its folds; he came out to hear the Divine communication, and the voice said again, with marked emphasis, "What doest thou here, Elijah? What doest thou, a prophet in Israel, here in the desert of Arabia?" And then he learns that God's ways are not as man's ways. In the still, small voice he was taught the main lesson of Christianity: "That God desires not the death of the wicked." "That God so loved the world that He gave His only begotten Son to redeem it."

And as for Elijah's mistake of thinking himself the only one of His servants left, God reminds him of a fact the prophet did not know, that at its worst—even in apostate Israel—His cause was not lost; His cause did not depend upon Elijah's life, for deep down in the caves and dens of Mount Carmel were 7000 of His people who had never bowed the knee to Baal. This was what Elijah wanted; it was humiliating, but at the same time consolatory; it showed even an Elijah his want of faith, and it also showed how, in the particular Providence of God, He knoweth His own, both by name and by number. Elijah, having learnt this lesson, and become a partaker of a better spirit, even the spirit of Christianity, is sent back to continue his work, to anoint kings and a successor to himself, as a proof that God's work and kingdom would go on even after he was taken away. Thus Elijah was taught that God was not so much manifested in his own mission, grand and gigantic as it was; not in the strong east wind which parted the Red Sea and afterwards rolled back upon his enemies; not in the fire and lightnings that swept over the heights of Sinai in the time of Moses and the giving of the Law; not in the earthquake that shook down the walls of Jericho and destroyed the Canaanites; but in the still, small voice of the Child of Bethlehem, and in the awful stillness of the Cross at Calvary was God best to be known and understood.

(a)   *Cf. Hengstenberg and Dean Stanley*

"Elijah? *What doest thou here*" (1 Kings xix. 13)

Elijah's great energy in the destruction of the priests of Baal was succeeded by a reaction; the prophet broke down, his faith failed, and he fled at Jezebel's threat.

1. **Interpretation**: "Here" (the place)—He had deserted his post = a rebuke:

(i.) *Where was he?* "Horeb, the mount of God" = Sinai. It was a backward movement. It reminded him of the past—he had gone back in spirit to the time of the giving of the *Law* (Moses), when the rocks were rent; the lightning and the thunder, = death to whosoever touched the mountain. But now he was reminded that the Lord was not in these, but in the *still small voice* of mercy. Hence the significant question—"What doest thou here?"—here, in the dead past, instead of being occupied in thy work of the present —the work I have given thee to do?

His work was a work of *Reformation*, and his time was one of *progress*. Hence the justice of the rebuke.

(ii.) *Application:* In this Elijah = a type of those who long for and speak of "*the good old times.*" Ask, when were they—since the Fall, and the incoming of sin and disease and death? "The good old times," in another sense, reminds us of horn windows instead of glass; pestilential odours in our streets, causing plagues; and when our forefathers made their wills before proceeding on a journey (now of a few hours), fearing highwaymen; and when gibbets stood at the roadside, etc., etc. The cry surely = standing still, to-day as yesterday, no progress in anything. No holier from day to day, no nearer God, no advance in spiritual things. The Christian at his A, B, C, all his life long, and not *growing in grace and in knowledge.* The *good time* is to come (Rev. xxi. 3, 4).

(b)

2 **Elijah's presence at Sinai showed the harshness of his own spirit**

(i.) It was a *protest* against God's merciful dealings at that time, as too gentle kind, and forbearing. Elijah thirsted for vengeance = the wrath of man working the vengeance of God. He would have no dilly-dallying, and so he had fled to Sinai to refresh his spirit—it reminded him of the times he loved to dwell on. Choose either Jehovah or Baal.

But now he was to learn a lesson: the old scene at Sinai was re-enacted. There was a wind, an earthquake, etc., as before, such as to strike terror to the beholder. *But the Lord was not in them.* Presently there came a *still, small voice,* and Elijah recognised the new manifestation of God. Now he learnt something about God which he did not know before.

(ii.) Nor was he *alone*, as he said three times, "*I only am left.*" God's kingdom did not depend on him; there were 7,000 in the nation who remained faithful. Hence, again, "*What doest thou here?*" away from thy work? Go back and finish thy work; anoint a new prophet in thy room, and a new king in Israel.

(iii.) *Application.* Many are constantly looking back to past times and workers—to the "Fathers," for a purer doctrine, forgetting that it = A, B, C; or to the "Middle Ages," for practice, forgetting that we are ahead (or ought to be) of that now in the nineteenth century. The question certainly applies to such longings, and asks, "What doest thou here?" in the first, second, and third century, or in the Middle Ages, instead of working on the higher level and in the spirit of your own time,

(c)

with all its immense advantages and increased light? The "Fathers," indeed, did nobly; but they built the first courses, and ye are entered into their labours and carry on the higher courses; ye stand on a higher scaffolding and are nearing the topstone, which will complete the fabric. Push on. "Be no more children." Grow in grace. Don't go back to the past; but forget the things which are behind, and reach forth unto the things which are before, press toward the mark of the prize of the high calling of God in Christ Jesus.

(a)

ELOQUENCE

Apollos met with two candid people in the Church. They neither ran away because he was *legal*, nor were carried away because he was *eloquent*.

(b) *John Newton*

EMMAUS, THE JOURNEY TO

"*And, behold, two of them went that same day to a village called Emmaus, which was from Jerusalem about threescore furlongs. And they talked together of all these things which had happened. . . . And Jesus Himself drew near, and went with them*" (Luke xxiv. 13–15)

A unique passage. The experience of two disciples on the evening of Easter Day. Many a time since then have the disciples of Jesus been puzzled and saddened at things that happen. Many a time, too, has He drawn near them in such moments, and they have not known Him.

Brief review of the whole narrative; and some of the lessons which lie on the very surface of it.

These two men—one of whom is named Cleopas, the other, we are left to conjecture, was probably Luke, the author of this passage—were walking from Jerusalem to Emmaus, on the evening of the day on which the Lord arose; and they were engaged in earnest conversation on the more recent phases of the great events which had happened during the last few days. . . . They "thought this had been He who should have redeemed Israel." This, together with the story of the Resurrection, was the theme of their conversation. The narrative furnishes at least three doctrines, which may help us in moments of similar perplexity, when it seeems to us, as it did to these men, that the providence of God belies His promises.

(c)

1. The first doctrine is this :—**We must unburden our hearts to Christ**

These men had to do so, and so must we, if we would experience His comfort. This doctrine lies at the very threshold of this unique passage. God will not comfort us unless we tell Him our trouble, and pour out our hearts before Him. Mark the course of the conversation between Jesus and these two men; how He draws them out, and gets to know all that is in their hearts:—"It came to pass that, while they communed and reasoned, Jesus Himself drew near, and went with them. But their eyes were holden that they should not know Him." At first Jesus listens—notices their troubled demeanour; next, He begins to ask them

questions. "What manner of communications are these that ye have one to another, as ye walk and are sad?" And they, naturally enough, think it very strange that any one could have been in the neighbourhood of Jerusalem for the last few days and not know what had taken place there— events not only deeply important to them, but which had disturbed the whole of society in the capital—the betrayal, the crucifixion, the darkened heavens, the earthquake, the affrighted soldiers, and now the story of the resurrection. These things were not done in a corner, nor confined to the knowledge of a few. Hence their astonished question in return, "Art Thou only a stranger in Jerusalem, and hast not known the things which have come to pass there in these days?" But Jesus, though questioning them, does not confess to being a "stranger." He merely asks, "What things?" as if He said, "Let Me have your version of these things; perhaps, when I have heard it, I can set you right about what seems to you wrong. Come, what are they? Tell me the things that have happened." Then, in the language of the Psalmist, "they showed unto the Lord their trouble." They kept nothing back from Him. They said, "Our trouble is about Jesus of Nazareth, a prophet mighty in deed and in word. But our rulers,—our Sanhedrim, who exercise the power of excommunication,—believed not on Him, and handed Him over to the Gentile authorities, who condemned Him to death, as one who ought not to live, and they have crucified Him. But we, who knew Him, loved Him, and believed in Him, trusted that it had been He who should have redeemed Israel. Our hope is perished; for this is the third day since these things were done. Yea, and certain women also of our company made us astonished, who were early at the sepulchre; and when they found not His body, they came saying that they had seen a vision of angels, which said that He was alive. Then certain of them which were with us went to the sepulchre, and found it even so as the women had said; but Him they saw not." So they unburdened their hearts.

(d)

We must do the same

Some adversity has happened to us in the course of our lives; it has made us sad; it has taken the gladness and the sunshine out of our life, and destroyed our hopes. Well, whatever it is, we must tell Jesus. It may be a tale of sorrow, or of injustice and cruel wrong. It may be a tale of some stain left upon us from some sin in the past. It may be a tale we cannot unfold to our fellowmen—something hidden away in the recesses of the past; a great sorrow, a corroding care, a festering sore, a peace-destroying thorn in the flesh. Whatever it is, this is the first step in the remedy—we must tell Jesus. If we keep it to ourselves, it will become a weight, crushing the very spirit out of our life—it will shorten our days. "The grief that does not speak, whispers the o'erwrought heart, and bids it break." But tell a friend—tell Jesus, who invites our confidence, and we shall be able to bear it. "Ah," some one says, "why need I tell God? What need is there for me to pray to Him? Does He not know my sorrows? Is He a STRANGER to my needs and distresses?" This, observe, is exactly what these

(e)

Emmaus, The Journey to—*continued*

disciples said to Jesus, "*Art Thou a stranger?*" "Do you not know what has happened? how our hopes are perished, and our hearts are desolate?" Of course Jesus did know all. And of course God does know our sorrows; He says so; He is no stranger to them. For the very "hairs of our head are all numbered." He who telleth the number of the stars, and calleth them by name, has a most intimate knowledge of us, who are the objects of His particular providence. "Then, if so, why tell Him?" Perhaps for the same reason that earthly parents like to have their children's confidence—for this is a matter of God's dealing with His children. Our children are never out of the range of our eye, or ear, or help; we are certainly no strangers to their needs. And yet do we not like to hear their voices? we invite their confidences, and expect them to trust in our sympathy and aid. So God deals with His children; He likes to hear their voices; He says to His redeemed, "Let Me hear thy voice, for thy speech is comely." He has unloosed our tongues, taught us to pray, made us what we are. He loved us first, or we had never loved Him; He, as we do, likes to hear the voices of those He loves. For these reasons:—Because it is better to tell our griefs to another; because God likes to hear our voices; and because we shall not get His comfort and help unless we do, we must unburden our hearts to God.

(*a*)

2. The next doctrine is this:—Oftentimes we copmlain of the very things that ought to be

It was so with these men. Their trouble was a crucified Christ; their preconceived notions about Him were thus upset altogether; they did not see that this act of rejection was in reality the carrying out of the determinate counsel and foreknowledge of God. The programme of the Old Testament Scriptures was being faithfully carried out, only they had not read it aright, as Jesus now tells them. He has heard their version of these things. His answer is, "O fools, and slow of heart to believe all that the prophets have spoken! Ought not Christ to have suffered these things, and to enter into His glory? And, beginning at Moses and all the prophets, He expounded unto them in all the Scriptures the things concerning Himself." Observe here exactly what Jesus in effect says to these men. He tells them that matters are all right—"These things ought to be." The world has not broken loose out of God's hands; He holds the reins, and His purpose is being done. He calls them "fools" as to their understanding: for they ought to have known this much. "Why," He says, "you don't understand your Bible, which you have been reading all your lives. You have either put a meaning into it which is not there, or you have got a meaning out of it which it does not teach. Nor is this all: you have not understood, because you did not want to understand, some things you found written there. You have read your Bible without believing it. You were slow of heart to believe all that the prophets had spoken." For a want of faith is worse than a want of knowledge. They had read of a suffering Christ.

(i.) David, in Psalm xxii., wrote of a Christ who cried out, "My God, My God, why hast Thou for-

saken Me? All they that see me laugh me to scorn: they shoot out the lip, they shake the head, saying, He trusted on the Lord, that He would deliver Him; let Him deliver Him seeing He delighted in Him. The assembly of the wicked have enclosed Me; they pierced My hands and My feet. They part My garments among them, and cast lots upon my vesture.

(ii.) Isaiah wrote of a suffering Christ: "His visage was so marred more than any man, and His form more than the sons of men." . . . "Despised and rejected of men, a Man of sorrows, and acquainted with grief." . . . "Smitten of God, and afflicted." . . . "Wounded for our transgressions;" "bruised for our iniquities;" . . . "cut off out of the land of the living," . . . . "making His grave with the wicked, and with the rich in His death."

(iii.) Zechariah wrote of a suffering Christ: "They shall look on Him whom they have pierced."

(iv.) The types of Isaac and the Paschal lamb testified that Christ should suffer.

And this Jesus now tells these men: "You have read these things often enough, but you did not understand them because you did not want to believe such things concerning your Christ. Ye were slow of heart to believe all the things predicted of Him, until now they have been forced upon you by their fulfilment." This is how Jesus corrects the mistakes both of the knowledge and faith of these disciples. He shows them that there has been no mistake. God has been working upon a plan sketched out in the Old Testament Scriptures, as a programme; and if they had been less prejudiced, they would now be less troubled. For the things which have happened are the things which God ordained and appointed, and therefore which "ought" to be.

This way of explaining difficulties has an important application. Nothing unforeseen, nothing which was not mapped out for him in the Old Testament, happened to Jesus. Therefore nothing which did happen was accidental. God's purpose was not defeated, nor was the exigency of the occasion an afterthought. And we believe much the same thing concerning ourselves. We believe that our life's journey is mapped out for us, that "the steps of a good man are ordered by the Lord." (Mistakes may be made by self-will; like horse and mule, we may have no understanding, and require bit and bridle to keep us in the right path.) The time of our life, the nature of our work, our friends and companions, who influence our lives and mould our characters, are all ordered by the Lord; otherwise we believe in "chance" and "accident," and our religion is heathenism or fatalism, not Christianity. And starting with this assurance, which every child of God has in some degree, we say, "Yes, it is a comfort to know that God overrules and governs, and arranges everything for us;" and when we read in the Bible such words as these, "All things work together for good to them that love God," we not only *believe* the statement, but we regard it as a most comforting assurance, "an anchor of the soul, sure and steadfast." So it is. Despair alone is left, if we did not think so. But wait till trouble comes, as it does come to all, and as it comes now and then to the Christian, sweeping over him like a wild tornado; when all the vials

(*b*)

Emmaus, The Journey to—*continued*

of wrath, as it seems, are poured out upon his head, and he is hurled to the ground by its force; when wave after wave of trouble comes rolling in over us—thud after thud of the tempest comes rattling over our heads in awful peals, and we are shaken out of our lap of ease—the light goes out of our life, and we are left in darkness. Then, amid this apparent displeasure of Heaven, and the awfulness of our peril, the old and natural unbelief of our hearts crops out, and we exclaim, as did Jacob of old, "All these things are against me"; we ask, "O God, what is this? wilt Thou pursue Thy child to wrath?" Wait till some such experience comes into our lives, and then we see that our faith about "all things working together for good" has broken down altogether at the very moment when we wanted all the comfort our faith could give us. *Then we, too, walk along life's road and are sad;* we say, "We don't know what these things mean"; our hearts are full of murmurings, full of dismay and uncertainty, born of unbelief. And it is, too, in such a time that Jesus draws nigh to us, as He did to these two men on that first Easter evening; and, after listening to our version of our woes, He just gently, and in His own matchless way, calls us "fools, and slow of heart to believe all that we had read in God's Word." He tells us that these things which have happened to us are indeed amongst the "all things which work together for our good," and were therefore things that "ought to be." Then it is that He makes our hearts "burn within us" as He points out such passages as these in His Word : " Whom the Lord loveth He chasteneth, and scourgeth every son whom He receiveth," and "If any man will come after Me, let him deny himself, and take up his cross and follow Me." And yet, notwithstanding this, when the time came for us to undergo chastisement, we rebelled against it; like a bullock unaccustomed to the yoke, we chafed against it. When the cross was laid upon our shoulder to bear it after Christ, we refused to carry it, because, though we had read our Bible, and thought we had faith in what we found there, yet when affliction came to try us and to purify us, then we were offended; we shrank from the cross, we could not endure it; we rebelled against it, and showed indeed that we were slow of heart to believe—really to believe—all the things written in God's Word concerning the way in which He trains His people. So we, too, like these two disciples, oftentimes complain of the things which ought to be.

(*a*)

3. Having received one blessing from Christ, it rests with ourselves whether we get another

By the time Jesus had expounded the Scriptures concerning Himself, and opened their understanding, and had made their hearts burn within them at the way in which He explained Scripture, they had arrived at the end of their journey, and were come to the house where they lived. Then we read, Jesus "made as though He would have gone farther." Now this was no pretence. He would have gone on if those disciples had shown no interest in Him. Jesus will not force Himself upon us. He shows Himself, He teaches, and kindles our heart; but if we do not want Him, if we show no interest in Him, and let Him go easily; if we part and say, " Good night, stranger,"

He will most assuredly pass on, and leave us without a second blessing. But these disciples did want Him. They had had a spiritual feast. Perhaps never before had they had such a treat in their whole life as on that night. Certainly, they never met with any one who could explain Scripture like that. Why, He had got the whole Bible at His fingers' ends—He knew it all by heart from Genesis to Malachi. It was new life to them to listen to His explanations; it was almost as good as having their beloved Master back again with them. They cannot let this man go; He must come in and sup with them. They must sit up till midnight to hear more of this; and so " they constrained Him, saying, Abide with us, for it is toward evening, and the day is far spent."

(*b*)

Is there not something most precious for us here? Cannot we, each of us, just for the same reason, pray this prayer: "Abide with us?" Has not Jesus met us somewhere in the past years our life, and given us some deep and priceless blessing? Cannot we urge this plea : " Lord, since Thou didst overtake us on our life's journey, we have known such blessedness, that Heaven seems to have come into our hearts; we have found such blessedness in Thy company that we dare not think of parting. We cannot do without Thee. Oh! abide with us—leave us not to our old darkness, to our old unbelief; open the Scriptures to us more and more, and may we see there the things concerning Thyself. Lord, we have tasted that Thou art gracious, and that taste has made us hungry; we want more, we must have more.

Are there not, beyond this, deep reasons why we should constrain Christ to abide with us? What is life, what is the present world, without Christ? If this were all, and there were no Christ, we should be like the disciples on the stormy sea, when Jesus had not come to them. This world without the sun, night without moon or stars, would be nothing compared to the present life, in its various vicissitudes, without Christ. But if the present would be dark, what of the unexplored future which lies beyond us? What should we know of our eternal destiny? We know the past and the present, but the future, whither we go, is wholly unknown; and for that future, with all its uncertainties, we want a Guide who will go before us, and throw a light upon the path—one who will be our companion and friend in the hour of trial, of sickness and death, which the future is sure to bring. The night, too, is coming—our night, when we cannot work. Childhood and youth are left behind us—the day is far gone—grey hairs are sprinkled on our heads. The night, too, of the world is coming. The shadows of its evening are lengthening, the sun is going down behind the western hills, the end of all things is at hand. Satan, as an angel of light, is abroad, deceiving men to their ruin. The landmarks of faith are being removed. Oh, let us then constrain Christ to abide with us—to see us safely through the worst. We cannot do without Him in life or in death.

> " Abide with me from morn till eve,
> For without Thee I cannot live;
> Abide with me when night is nigh,
> For without Thee I dare not die."

For surely, if we so constrain Christ to abide

(*c*)

Emmaus, The Journey to—*continued*

with us, we too shall have our reward. In answer to the prayer of these two disciples, "He went in to tarry with them." "Ah, but," some one says, "He did not tarry with them, He left them ; for when their eyes were opened, so that they recognised their guest, He vanished out of their sight." Notwithstanding this, we reply, *Jesus did tarry with them ;* He only became invisible to teach them that they (as Christians) must live by faith and not by sight. They got more than they asked, for ; instead of one night, He abides with them for ever. "Lo, I am with you always, even unto the end of the world." In this way He satisfieth the hungry soul. In this way, too, He answers every constraining prayer, "Lord, abide with me," with the assurance, " I will never leave thee nor forsake thee."

(*a*)

EMOTIONAL RELIGION

I do not think that God requires us to put ourselves on the strain ; to be always at full stretch ; indeed, such a thing, from the very constitution of our nature, can hardly be practicable. And I very much doubt whether those impulsive, emotional people, who are hot to-day and cold to-morrow ; whose religion is a thing of fits and starts ; who, under some new excitement, are roused into a frenzy of religious activity, only to sink back into torpor and inaction when the excitement is passed—I very much doubt whether such people as these are very much to be depended upon for real and substantial progress in the Divine life. But what I think God *does* demand of us in spiritual things, is a regular, systematic, steady, sturdy, course of procedure ; an undeviating pursuit of one great object ; a constant and unfailing vigilance ; a determination, by His help, not to be turned aside—in fact, a pressing onward toward the mark for the prize of the high calling of God in Christ Jesus.

(*b*)   *Gordon Calthrop*

END, THE, WHAT WILL IT BE

Like many fellows of most "excellent fancy," "wont to set the table in a roar," Hook—the humorist, all mirth and jocularity abroad—at home was subject to violent revulsion of feelings, to gusts of sadness and fits of dejection of spirits, which temporary excitement, produced by stimulants, did not much tend to remedy or remove. . . . He ended his miserable career worried to death by creditors, attorneys, and bailiffs.

"*Memoirs of Lady Blessington*" (*Theodore Edwd. Hook*).

(*c*)

END OF THE WORLD, THE (1 Thess. iv. 15–17)

With Christ began the world's last hour, and there comes none later, to establish another and higher relation between God and humanity.

A denial of the world's end would require the assertion that humanity has never had a beginning ; and this would imply that life has no aim.

There are things that must precede the end ;

not the conversion of the nations, but the preaching of the Gospel among all nations (Matt. xxiv. 14) ; along with this, the universal security of those who believe in no Advent, and by means of their unbelief are witnesses for the Truth (1 Thess. v. 3) ; the apostasy of Christendom (2 Thess. ii.). All these signs are growing.

(*d*)   *Lange*

"*Then shall the* END *come*" (Matt. xxiv. 14)

" End " = end of the *Age*, not world. As the age before the flood ended with it ; and end of Old Testament period ended with destruction of Jerusalem ; so the *end* of our age (Gentile), the present order of things, intended here (verse 3).

1. When ?
(i.) When the Gospel has been preached to all the world.
(*a*) As a witness unto it.
(*b*) As a witness against it : a savour of life or death.
(ii.) When the fulness of the Gentiles is come in.
2. Why ?
Because it *must :*
(i.) God's faithfulness demands it, in aid of His Church, endangered by worldliness, " cold."
(ii.) Iniquity demands it : " lawlessness " shall abound ; and " Where the carcase is," etc.
3. How ?
(i.) *Suddenly*, as a thief in the night.
(ii.) By *cosmic* irregularities, powers of nature shaken = act irregularly, not to be depended on.
= *Signs* or symptoms of *Christ's coming ;* " When ye see these, etc. . . . know that . . . Redemption draweth nigh."

(*e*)

[2 Pet. iii. 10, 11]

The leaf quivers on the branch which supports it. It lies at the mercy of the slightest accident. A breath of wind tears it from its stem, and it lights on the stream of water which passes underneath. In a moment of time, the life, which we know by the microscope it teems with, is extinguished ; and an occurrence so insignificant in the eye of man carries in it an event as terrible and as decisive as the destruction of a world. Now, on the grand scale of the universe, we, the occupiers of this ball, may feel the same littleness and the same insecurity. We differ from the leaf only in this circumstance, that it would require the operation of greater elements to destroy us. But these elements exist. The fire within may transform our planet into one wide and wasting volcano. The sudden formation of elastic matter in the bowels of the earth—and it lies within the agency of known substances to accomplish this—may explode it into fragments. . . . A blazing comet may cross our path and realize all the terrors which superstition has conceived of it. We cannot anticipate with precision the consequences of an event which every astronomer must know to lie within the limits of chance and probability. It may hurry our globe into the sun—or drag it to the outer regions of the planetary system—or give it a new axis of revolution ; and the effect would be to change the place of the ocean, and to bring another mighty flood upon our islands and continents. These are changes which might

(*f*)

happen in a moment of time, and against which nothing known in the present system of things provides us with any security. They might not annihilate the earth, but they would unpeople it; and we who tread its surface with such firm and assured steps, are at the mercy of devouring elements, which, if let loose upon us by the hand of the Almighty, would spread solitude and silence and death over the dominions of the world.

(a)   *Thomas Chalmers*

END, SIGNS OF THE (Matt. xxiv. 14)

The universal promulgation of the Gospel is the true sign of the end, both in the narrow and restricted sense in which the disciples put the question, and in the wider and universal sense, which in the Saviour's mind it really involved.

(b)   *Judge Jones*

The preaching of the Gospel throughout the Roman world preceded the end of the Jewish State; the promulgation of the Gospel throughout the *whole* world will be the sign of the end of the αἰὼν οὗτος.

(c)   *Schaff*

The gigantic missionary operations of our days have brought us considerably nearer to the fulfilment of this word of our Lord.

(d)   *Gerlach*

The apostasy of the latter days, and the universal dispersion of missions, are the two great signs of the end drawing near.

(e)   *Alford*

ENEMIES, BEHAVIOUR TO

If this storm were over, you must prepare for a new wound, for, five thousand years ago, our Lord proclaimed deadly war betwixt the seed of the woman and the serpent; and marvel not that one town cannot keep the children of God and the children of the devil; for one house could not keep peaceably together Isaac the son of the promise, and Ishmael the son of the handmaid. Be you upon Christ's side of it, and care not what flesh can do. . . .

Keep God's covenant in your trials; hold you by His blessed Word, and sin not; flee anger, wrath, grudging, envying, fretting; forgive a hundred pence to your fellow-servant, because your Lord hath forgiven you ten thousand talents. For I assure you by the Lord, your adversaries shall get no advantage against you, except you sin, and offend your Lord in your sufferings. . . .

When the sea is full, it will ebb again; and so soon as the wicked are come to the top of their pride, and are waxed high and mighty, then is their change approaching. They that believe make not haste.

(f)   *Samuel Rutherford*

ENEMIES, PRAYING FOR

" *Father, forgive them,*" etc. (Luke xxiii. 34)

" Memorandum to be given, after my death, with an affectionate letter, if it be possible, to the grenadier (D'Elsass, as I think) who shot at me, Sept. 26th, 1799; but care must be taken that his name be concealed. May God pardon thee, as I from my heart pardon thee! Oh, may you never

suffer what I suffer through you! I embrace you, my friend; you have done me a kindness, without knowing it. If you see these lines, may they be a seal to you of the grace of the Lord, who forgives penitent sinners; who delivers them and makes them happy! May God enable me earnestly to pray for you, so that I may never doubt that we may one day embrace each other before the presence of the Lord ! "

(g)   *Lavater*

ENEMIES RECONCILED, AND THE RECONCILED SAVED

" *For if, when we were enemies, we were reconciled to God by the death of His Son, much more, being reconciled, we shall be saved by His life*" (Rom. v. 10).

Three spiritual conditions, or relations towards God.

1. " ENEMIES," 2. " RECONCILED," 3. " SAVED."

We are taught that Divine love, which brought us from 1 to 2, will yet more certainly bring us from 2 to 3.

(i.) *Because it is the easier work.*

From 1 to 2 = the greater. And from 2 to 3 = the less : and the argument is from the greater to the less.

(ii.) Because, if God did not spare His Son the whole scene at Calvary (" *the death of His Son*"), in which is seen the immensity of the sacrifice made for sinners—if God did not shrink from this, but freely gave Him up for us all,—

How should He refuse to beings received into His favour, the communication, and preservation of life, which involves nothing but what is ineffably sweet and pleasant to Him ?

(iii.) Rom. viii. 2 declares that " the law of the spirit of life in Christ Jesus hath *made us free* from the law of sin and death." The spiritual man has escaped from the domination of nature.

Therefore God's treatment of His friends may be inferred from His treatment of His enemies.

= If enemies are reconciled, the reconciled will be saved.

(h)

1. ENEMIES

Enmity exists in the natural heart against God. Known by the force and tide of our natural inclinations, which go right against His laws.

Nor is this enmity on our side alone : God must be angry with sin. We are under His wrath (by nature) i.e. *apart from Christ*. Take away Christ and His redemption, and there is nothing but wrath.

Adam felt this in all its depths of despair, when he sinned against God and knew nothing of a remedy for his sin.

The awakened sinner knows this, too, when his conscience is awakened, and before he knows anything of Christ and forgiveness.

And, apart from Christ, there remaineth nothing more than a *condition of the wrath* of God against men, and of enmity in man's heart against God.

See " ENMITY "

(i)

2. ENEMIES RECONCILED

Now from such a condition there would have been (could have been) no remedy, if God on His side had not come towards us with overtures of peace.

And this He has done:

"*When we were enemies we were reconciled to God by the death of His Son.*"

God sent His Son; gave His Son; freely offered up His Son (=Calvary=expiation) in order that we might be brought into a condition of Reconciliation = *the taking away of His wrath.*

And when a sinful man believes that,—believes that God is reconciled to him,—he too lays aside his enmity and becomes reconciled to God.

He becomes a *justified man* = a man against whom God reckons no sin. The man is converted from being an enemy to a friend.

But true conversion is a step more. It is not merely exalted feeling, or an excited imagination, it is the time when God *imparts Himself to us* (see John xiv. 21, 23); and the reconciliation is thereby sealed.

But we are frail, and the question now is,

Will this condition of reconciliation hold good in the future?

Much lies before the man. He is not yet at the goal—a career of trials awaits him. How will he come through them? Will his present condition of reconciliation ripen into final salvation and glory?

This is an anxious question. Because even at his best state there lurks in the depths of a man's heart an apprehension of Divine wrath; and a single trespass will awaken it, and set the conscience on fire, and the whole experience has to be gone over again.

This is the very question which is here answered:

God loved us when we were enemies; and, if He did so much for His enemies, can He do less for His friends?

Oh, no-

"**Much more being reconciled we shall be saved.**"

(*a*)

3. THE RECONCILED SAVED WITH AN EVERLASTING SALVATION

A sick man not only needs *pardon*, but a *cure*.

An enemy not only needs pardon, but to have the cause of his enmity (sin) destroyed. "*Without holiness no man shall see the Lord.*" Now, observe that provision was made for this beforehand:—

Just as a sick man, before he is recovered, may often think that his relapses may result in death, so the reconciled man often thinks that he may not ultimately be saved.

There is, we are told, more than mere *expiation* for sin to be found in Christ. There is His mediation—as a living person—our High Priest within the veil, carrying on the work to completion.

"*ALIVE FOR EVERMORE.*"

Highly *exalted*—having *all authority and power committed unto Him* (and He the Saviour of His own).

Think, then, with what marvellous ways,—new ways,—He is able to interpose in behalf of His people, and bring to a successful end the work He has already begun in them!

Cf. Rom. viii. 34, "Who shall condemn?"

It is Christ that "DIED," "ROSE," "AT RIGHT HAND OF GOD." . . . "**MAKETH INTERCESSION.**"

And Heb. vii. 25, "Wherefore" (because He ever liveth). "**He is able to save to the "**UTTERMOST.**"**

His own can hardly get out of the reach of Christ's "UTTERMOST."

He lives to make "all things work together for their good," and *to ensure holiness;*

For we have a *faithful* Saviour, who, having loved once, loveth unto the end.

(*b*)

4. PRACTICAL

1. Are their passions strong?

He lives to subdue their iniquities.

2. Are they rebellious, self-willed, like horse and mule without understanding, knowing not that the Lord leads them?

He lives to *guide* them with curb and bit and bridle, that His will may be done.

3. Are they passing through tribulation?

He lives to make all things work together for their good.

4. Are they in greater distress than ever His people were in before?

He lives to open new ways for their feet, so that they shall see the lovingkindness of the Lord.

5. Have they strayed from the fold?

He lives, who hath promised *to search them out, and not forsake them.*

6. Finally, are they, through sin—through unfaithfulness to Him—come to the very uttermost of peril?

He ever liveth to make intercession for all who came unto God by Him—and therefore He is able to save to the uttermost, beyond which they cannot get.

(*c*)　　　　　　*See Godet, in loc*

ENGLAND AND THE BIBLE

Why was it, for instance, when the tempest of Revolution swept and tore through the rest of Europe, overthrowing thrones and kingdoms and ancient dynasties in its mad career, and bearing down with it a deluge of blood; when there seemed to be nothing on earth but distress of nations with perplexity, the sea and the waves roaring and men's hearts failing them for fear, why was it that our own little island stood fast and firm, while the storm howled fruitlessly round it, and the floods came but would not lay it desolate? Shall we say that it was by our own might, and by the strength of our own arm that this security was obtained? Shall we look to ourselves, to our well-balanced Constitution and to our sober, earnest character to account for it? Look to these things if you like. But if we look not beyond these things to something higher and greater than all, we shall rob God of His glory and deny the lofty calling wherewith we were called. It was not because we were a powerful people merely; it was not because the rights for which other nations were clamouring, and the theories which other nations were proclaiming as

(*d*)

recent discoveries, were no new or unknown thing to us, but had been already possessed and enjoyed for centuries, bound up with our every-day life, interwoven with everything which was near and dear to us; it was not because we inherited from our forefathers a grave and earnest disposition, a law-reverencing, and right-respecting character, not easily blown about by every breath of vain clamour, nor prone to give up certain and assured good for a wild chase after imaginary advantages, at the bidding of every specious propounder of theories, or every enthusiastic declaimer,—it was not because of these things that the waves of revolution swept past and left us uninjured. It was because, in spite of our manifold national sins, —and they are neither few nor slight—we were still, in the main, a religious, a God-fearing people. We had a character moulded by Bible precepts; we had a law and a government modified by Bible principles. The Gospel was the rock on which we stood; and when the rains descended and the floods came and the winds blew and beat upon our house, it fell not, because it was founded upon a Rock. "Not unto us, O Lord, not unto us, but unto Thy Name be the praise."

(a)   *Gordon Calthrop*

ENGLAND, CHURCH OF

And here I do profess that as I have lived, so I desire and (by the grace of God) resolve to die in the Communion of the Catholic Church of Christ, and a true son of the Church of England; which, as it stands by law established to be both in doctrine and in worship agreeable to the Word of God, and in the most, and most material points of both, conformable to the faith and practice of the godly Churches of Christ in the primitive and purer times. I do firmly believe: led so to do, not so much from the force of custom and education (to which the greatest part of mankind owe their different persuasions in points of religion) as upon the clear evidence of truth and reason, after a serious and impartial examination of the grounds as well of Popery as Puritanism, according to that measure of understanding and those opportunities which God had afforded me.

(b)   *Sanderson*

ENGLAND, A TEXT FOR

There is not a chapter in all the book we profess to believe, more specially and directly written for England than the second of Habakkuk; and I never in all my life heard one of its practical texts preached from. I suppose the clergymen are all afraid, and know that their flocks, while they will sit quite politely to hear syllogisms out of the Epistle to the Romans, would get restive directly if they ever pressed a practical text home to them. But we should have no mercantile catastrophes, and no distressful pauperism, if we only read often, and took to heart those plain words :—" Yea also because he is a proud man, neither keepeth at home, who enlargeth his desire as hell, and cannot be satisfied, shall not all these take up a parable against him, and a taunting proverb against him, and say, Woe to him that increaseth that which is not his, and to him that ladeth himself with thick clay : woe to him that coveteth an evil coveteousness that he may set his nest on high; woe to him that buildeth a town with blood."

(c)   *Ruskin*

ENMITY

1. Its Passive Side

Is the state in which receptivity for the good is extinguished—" Having eyes, they see not, and having ears they hear not, neither do they understand with their heart" (Isa. vi. 10); a full insusceptibility in which, void of all moral feeling (Eph. iv. 19), they are dead to every higher and nobler care, to every better motion, and so become like a corpse.

(d)

2. Its Active Side

Is to make evil and the kingdom of evil dominant, and to destroy good and the kingdom of good. It cannot, like good, rest in itself; it can make and fashion nothing. It is a never-satisfied hunger, which seeks its satisfaction in hatred and enmity of good, in the overthrow and destruction of that which is good. This utmost development of enmity is *devilish.*

(e)

3. Can this occur among men at all

In a certain sense this is imaginary; because, so long as we are in this age, and the opposition between good and evil is not ripened, so long can perfect wickedness be only sporadically and approximately realized among men. . . . Wickedness can only be fully unfolded when such men (as " the children of the devil," John viii. 44) have passed from this world of sense into the proper world of spirits. Experience, however, abundantly shows us the presence of the devilish principle amongst us also, shows us manifestations of wickedness in which a demoniac energy is expressed, that unmistakably testifies of a connection with the demoniac kingdom. That there is in the world of men an actual hatred, an enmity against good, as shown in that " pleasure in unrighteousness " (1 Cor. xiii. 6) which is not rare, is shown in the envy, malice, cruelty, that finds pleasure in torturing other men with the most exquisite pains, bodily or mental ; is shown in a pleasure in destruction and annihilation which may appear as frantic mania, as in the Roman Emperors, in a Nero or a Caligula, who wished that all the heads of the Roman people had but one neck, that he might at one stroke cut them all off together.

(f)

4. Enmity against good is enmity against GOD

Like love, hatred applies itself to persons. Who can deny that there is a hatred, an enmity against God, in which man would tear asunder the bonds that bind him to God (Ps. ii. 3), would make himself independent, and now mocks at the thought of God as a foolish imagination ; now, feeling the reality of it, utters blasphemies against Him, from whose holiness and omnipotence he cannot escape. As " the devils believe and tremble," so there are men who believe indeed, but only in this sense, and seek by blasphemies to allay this trembling. In our days such blasphemies have often been heard in democratic assemblies, at revolutionary congresses, and they may also be read in writings that are intended to stir up the multitude.

(g)

Enmity—*continued*

5. Hatred of God is combined with hatred of men

Especially is this so in the case of those who believe on Him, and would serve Him, and who have declared war with unbelief. Especially we may recall the hatred of the clergy, the ministers of religion, as it finds expression on certain occasions. True, one must guard—as need hardly be mentioned—against indiscriminately confounding hatred of priests and preachers with hatred of religion itself. On the other hand, it is by no means superfluous to remark, that hatred of priests in very many cases is the simple outflow of enmity to religion. Statements like this: that the last king must be hanged with the entrails of the last priest, testify of a hatred that indicates far more than a mere hatred of a certain class of men.

(*a*)

6. Enmity to Christ

To Christ, as the central point of the revelation of God's love, and is thereforet *he central enmity to God*.

Christ came into the world with this testimony—"He that hath seen Me hath seen the Father" (John xiv. 9). He, therefore, stands as the living witness of the holiness and love of God, of the God-consciousness, of the reality of sin and of grace. His appearance is the practical proof of the being and government of the living God among us men, and speaks more loudly and powerfully than all reasonings. If one, then, would get rid of God, one must first of all get rid of Christ. He is the One with whom the worldly mind especially takes offence. Hence, too, the men who believe on and confess Christ must be banished from the world, as they are the living personal witnesses of communion with God. The persecution of Christians is inseparable from the hatred of Christ, whether it be executed with fire and sword, or with words, the arrows of mockery and scorn.

(*b*)

7. Religious Enmity to Christ

This is a peculiarity to the enmity against Christ. It is developed from a certain standpoint of human virtue and righteousness. The Apostle Paul, before his conversion, as Saul of Tarsus, hated Christ and persecuted the Christians, and yet with all this was still leading a pious and righteous life according to the Law. Hatred of Christ is always developed from the offence that is taken at the appearance of Christ. But that offence springs from man's natural heart, and does not by any means merely occur in such as are " sinners before others," but also, and that with a peculiar colouring, in such as pursue their own ideals of virtue, and in secure repose of soul depend on their own virtue and righteousness. And herein consists the danger of this offence, that by it in itself, a man may, by a few steps, fall into regions of evil closely connected with the demoniac kingdom ; nay, may fall into a sin which, if consistently carried through, must at last end as *the* sin for which there is no forgiveness. For, by entering into a relation with Christ, we are brought into the central and direct relation to God, which may become not only "for our rising again," but also " for our fall " and destruction (Luke ii. 34). . . . Sooner or later a turning-point must occur in every

man's life, when he is placed face to face with Christ, and must make his choice. And here is confirmed the truth, that as sin in the history of our race has originated within the religious sphere, it must also end in the same sphere, as well for the race as for the individual.

(*c*)

8. The Offence of Christ

Offence is the umbrage of the unconverted heart at the appearance of Christ, and at the requirement that He makes of men (through His disciples), and which amounts to conversion, faith, holiness. By nature the heart finds all this in contradiction to its own conceptions of God and man, and is thereby provoked. The understanding is offended ; but it is essentially *the will* to which it is offensive. . . . Human pride is humbled by the appearance and entire revelation of Christ, and will not have this humiliation. . . . One wishes to rid the world of this form, a form which constantly crosses the path of human virtue and righteousness to disturb it, and condemns so much of what one would insist upon and maintain. One becomes more and more conscious of this, that if He is the truth, then there is an end of all *our* wisdom, and we are walking in ways from which we must turn, which we must leave. Thus one is set fast in this temper : we *will* not have it so ; we will not have this Man to reign over us. It is then sought to bring it about that Christ is anew accused and crucified. All arts are sought to invalidate His own testimony, to tear the crown of divinity from His head, to deny His sinlessness and holiness ; His royal dignity is mocked, His utterance is scorned, that all power is given to Him in heaven and on earth. In this respect it is interesting to hear, in our days, from the mouths of His enemies, the assurance that Christ has long since ceased to be a power in history and in life ; faith in Christ is given over to forgetfulness. According to this, one would expect them to speak of this dead thing with all quietness and indifference ; nay, that they would hardly find it worth while to speak of it at all. But their anger and passionate heat, and their unwearying repetition of the same assurances, clearly betrays that He who forms the object of their hatred is no dead One, but a living One ; hatred of Christ is inseparably connected with *fear of Christ*, the secret fear of the risen, living Christ, truly present in the midst of us.

(*d*)　　　　　　　　　　　　　　　*Martensen*

Enmity and the Serpent

" *I will put* ENMITY *between thee and the woman, and between thy seed and her seed ; it shall bruise thy head, and thou shalt bruise his heel* " (Gen. iii. 15).

In this passage some persons can see only a prophecy to the effect that

Serpents and men shall continually prey upon each other.

Undoubtedly this was the first and undisguised significance of the word. But to allege that it was all, is to belie the whole after Scriptures. For behind the apparent meaning of the passage, a deep and underlying truth is concealed, viz.,

(*e*)

The revenge of the woman on her deceiver

By the *woman* he gained access to man, and from the *woman* (without the man) will come forth the Great Deliverer. Satanic desire is to make others as unhappy as itself. This the tempter hoped would follow; whereas, on the other hand, the evil itself is made to rebound and crush the serpent himself.

The passage indicates a struggle between good and evil—between the kingdom of light and the kingdom of darkness.

It is a passage, not so much concerning the woman and the serpent, as it is

Concerning Christ and His Church

For behind the woman is the Church of Christ, and behind the serpent is the devil.

Mankind would split up from the very outset into two streams, running side by side all through succeeding ages. These were—

1. The seed of the woman, afterwards called the "sons of God" = or later, the Church of Christ.

2. *The seed of the serpent* = the sons of men—afterwards "the world."

Between these two there would be an undying enmity, and a conflict as between rival kingdoms.

The Rival Kingdoms

Trace the stream a little way.

Cain and Abel; Noah and the world; Isaac and Ishmael; Jacob and Esau; Israelites and Egyptians, Canaanites, Philistines, etc.; Christ and His enemies; the Church of Christ and the World; Nero burning the Christians as torches in his gardens; the early persecutions; the Marian martyrs, etc., etc., till the close of the Great Tribulation.

The world's antipathy is unaltered—nay, it cannot be altered, it may take new forms, such as physical force at one time; an *apostate religion* at another; philosophy and science as at the *present* time; but the enmity remains all the same, unaltered, because God has put it there.

" *I will put enmity between thee* and the woman, between thy seed and her seed," *i.e.* between the *Church* and the *World*.

(a) Cf. *Horatius Bonar, Oehler, Keil, and others.*

Even after the death and resurrection of Christ, Satan still wars against the Church, or the woman (the *enmity* in Genesis iii. 15, is concerning Christ and His Church).

(b)   Cf. *Oehler and Philippi*

ENTER INTO THE HOLIEST

" *Having, therefore, brethren, boldness to enter into the holiest by the blood of Jesus,* . . . *Let us draw near with a true heart, in full assurance of faith, having our hearts sprinkled from an evil conscience, and our bodies washed with pure water* " (Heb. x. 19–22).

1. " *Boldness.*"—The High Priest entered into the Holy of Holies and moved about in the (ναὸς), where God Himself was especially present, and yet did not die.

Because he was sprinkled with blood; and he sprinkled everything with blood.

2. *Note.*—The connection of this fact with the text. We, too, may enter into the holiest with confidence, not in fear; we may draw near with a true heart, not hesitatingly and doubting—but " in full assurance of faith " (not presumption).

Because-

(i.) Sprinkled with the blood of Jesus, which cleanseth from an evil conscience = " no more conscience of sin."

(ii.) And baptized in the Name of the Father, and of the Son, and of the Holy Ghost.

See " BOLDNESS."

(c)

ENTHUSIASM = " God within us."

(d)

EPHESIANS, EPISTLE TO THE

In this, the divinest composition of man, is every doctrine of Christianity: first, those doctrines peculiar to Christianity; and secondly, those precepts common to it with natural religion.

(e)   *Coleridge*

EPHESUS, CHURCH OF

" *I have somewhat against thee, because thou hast left thy first love. Remember therefore from whence thou art fallen, and repent, and do the first works; or else I will come unto thee quickly, and will remove thy candlestick out of his place, except thou repent* " (Rev. ii. 4, 5).

1. A vision of the Lord Jesus Christ "in the midst of seven golden candlesticks."

The seven candlesticks = seven Churches = seven light-givers.

Christ walking in the midst of the Churches = " Lo, I am with you always," seeing whether they were fulfilling their true office of shedding light on the world; and to trim the lamps as they burnt low.

He finds in these Churches some things to *praise* and some things to blame; and warns them, recommending *watchfulness* and *repentance*.

2. The text is addressed to the Church of Ephesus. That Church, to which St. Paul wrote his most profound epistle, had " *left its first love,*" —it had waned and fallen—its light was fast going out.

Christ sees this, He is active in their midst, " the star in His hand " = the Bishop of the Church, or the chief pastor, him He could remove; and unless the Church there did its proper work, He would remove that too. " The candlestick should be removed out of its place."

The words have a twofold *application*—(i.) to Churches, (ii.) to individuals. " He that hath ears to hear, let him hear." And are-

(f)

1. **Historically true**

(i.) *True of Ephesus.* The Church of Ephesus, having disregarded the warning, is perfectly desolate. Her candlestick has long ago been removed out of its place.

(ii.) True of the Jewish Church, which left its first love, and, not repenting, its candlestick has been removed.

" Thus saith the Lord; I remember thee, the kindness of thy youth, the love of thine espousals, when thou wentest after Me in the wilderness, in a land that was not sown."

(g)

"Israel was holiness unto the Lord" then (Jer. ii. 2, 3).

This was the bright beginning; but by the time of Jeremiah they had fallen from their first love—beyond compare. 2 Chron. xxxvi. 15, 16, "till there was no remedy." "Hath a nation changed their gods which are yet no gods: but My people have changed their glory for that which doth not profit.

"Be astonished, O ye heavens, at this, and be horribly afraid. For My people have committed two evils; they have forsaken Me, the fountain of living waters, and hewed them out cisterns, broken cisterns, which can hold no water" (Jer. ii. 11).

So they fell, deeper and deeper, and repented not.

Hence their candlestick has been removed out of its place.

(a)

2. Possibly true of the Church of England

"I have somewhat against thee."

There are some who predict that her candlestick will be removed out of its place.

If so, it is because there is something against her; she is ceasing perhaps to give light—ceasing to fulfil the end for which her candle was lighted at the first and again replenished at the time of the Reformation.

At any rate this much is certain. We live in days of great religious agitation, and we naturally ask at such a crisis :—

Is the Church of England doing her work faithfully and well? Has she ministered to all the nation's needs? The question is not, "Can she do this?"—but, "Does she do it?" Has the Church of England left her first love or not?

If she has not, she is shining with a glorious light, and her works and results are manifold.

But if she has left her first love, she is cautioned to repent, to do the first works, or else she will be judged. He who walketh in the midst of the Churches now, as He did then, to trim the lamps, will come to her quickly and remove her candlestick out of its place, because it is a useless and profitless ornament and nothing better. Christ does not want ornamental Churches, any more than He wants ornamental Christians. But He wants working Churches and working Christians.

(i.) *Let events answer our question :* Has the Church of England fallen from her first love? *We will briefly review them :—*

We are accustomed to speak of a certain period of our national history as " the Glorious Reformation."

We know what a terrible price was paid for freeing ourselves from the yoke of bondage, " which our fathers were not able to bear."

We know what a sea of blood our forefathers, "who bore the burden and heat of the day," waded through, in order that we, their descendants, might be free.

We know, too,—Can we ever forget it? Could ingratitude go further?—that our privilege of an open Bible, our freedom from priestcraft and all its evils,—evils which have blighted other nations,—came to us, as our inheritance, through the fires and the faggots and the stake at Smithfield, and because our forefathers "loved not their lives unto the death."

A noble army of martyrs laboured, and strove, and fought, and prayed, and died; and we are entered into their labours.

This is our inheritance. We gat it not by the works of our own hands. How then are we building on this foundation? Why, we are asked to ignore this foundation, to repudiate *their* building, and to regard *the Reformation as a great mistake after all, a great blot in our history,* and not a blessing AT ALL.

Therefore, seeing these things are so, it may be fearlessly asserted that the Church of England has fallen from her first love; and consequently she is in danger of having her candlestick removed out of its place.

(ii.) *Is the Church of England doing her work faithfully and well?* We do not deny her working power—but is her work *faithful work?* We do not deny her *energy*, but is it in the right *direction?*

Again we will let events answer the question.

Though we term the Reformation " glorious," yet it was not a perfect Reformation. Events have only too clearly shown this. The change was *radical* in the hearts of the people. But not so in the *formulas* of the Church.

It was not a root and branch, tooth and nail doing away with the evil that had so deeply rooted itself in the Church system.

For, like the tree in Nebuchadnezzar's dream, "*the stump and the roots*" of that pernicious system were left in the ground; and under the fostering care of *Archbishop Laud* (of historical renown) it once more began to bud and to grow; and we have lived to see it a tree again of no mean dimensions, and one which we cannot despise.

That this is so, who will deny?

Who can deny that Tractarianism and Ritualism have sprouted from this old stump of Sacerdotalism, whose roots were left in the ground at the time of the *Reformation?*

Who can shut his eyes to the painful facts, that we, as a Church, are flowing with the tide back again to the old apostasy? that important and influential organizations exist in the Church of England to undo all that our forefathers did?

For years past, almost silently though with much vitality, has this movement been progressing—till recently we were startled with a demand of a most audacious character, when over four hundred so-called Priests of the Church of England asked for a revival of the Confessional (1872-3), which means the unadulterated doctrines of Rome, pure and simple, over again—the surrender of our *open Bibles*, and the yielding of our consciences into the power of a domineering and an intolerant priesthood.

Yield but this point (as others have been yielded), and the foundations are sapped and destroyed; the Church of England will be a Reformed Church no longer.

Rome's own boast is, that, not France, Spain, Italy, but *Protestant England* is her stronghold; that from ritualistic centres and congregations and sisterhoods there is a continuous stream and flow of perverts back to the Romish communion.

Thus the Church of our land, of our hearts, our baptism, our families, of all our blessings, our " holy and beautiful place," where our fathers have loved to worship, is being regarded as a *feeder* and a tributary of the Church of Rome. And we, as it appears, are going as fast as we can back again to the thraldom of that system.

Our second question is thus answered. The Church of England is not doing her work *faith-*

(b)

fully and well—the energy and zeal is not in the right direction.

She has "fallen from her first love;" and He who walks in the midst of the candlesticks has seen that we suffer the doings of that woman Jezebel, which He hates.

That judgment will ensue, and the candlestick be removed, is unquestionable, except we repent and do the first works.

There may be a lengthening of our tranquillity; the judgment may not come in our day; repentance will avert it; but to secure that, we must do the first works; we must return to our first love.

That love is the love of Christ, who first loved us—a Christian first, a Churchman second.

And the works are evangelistic works—the Mission work of the Church.

(*a*)

EPICUREANS (Acts xvii. 18)

The Epicurean philosophy was antagonistic to the Gospel, as—
1. Holding the atomic theory, in opposition to the creation of matter.
2. The disconnection of the Divinity from the world and its affairs, in opposition to the idea of a ruling Providence.
3. And the indissoluble union and annihilation together of soul and body, as opposed to the hope of eternal life, and indeed to all spiritual religion whatever.

The Epicureans were the materialists of the ancient world.

(*b*)   *Alford*

EPISCOPATE

The Episcopate is a title, not of honour but of work; and in that spirit I trust to be enabled to exercise my office. . . . No earthly dignity, either in Church or State, can equal the moral grandeur of the leathern girdle and the raiment of camel's hair, or the going forth without purse or scrip and yet lacking nothing.

(*c*)   *Late Bishop Selwyn*

EPITAPH

Sardanapalus, the last Assyrian king, who died 820 B.C., surpassed his predecessors in effeminacy, luxury, and cowardice. He never went out of his palace, but lived among a company of women, dressed like him, and worked at the distaff. To him, happiness consisted of huge treasures, feasting and rioting. He ordered two verses to be put upon his tomb, which imported "that he carried away with him all that he had eaten, and all the pleasures he had enjoyed, but left all the rest behind him." "An epitaph," says Aristotle, "fit for a hog."

After his death, a statue was erected to him, representing him in the posture of a dancer, with an inscription upon it, "Eat, drink, and be merry; everything else is nothing:" an inscription very suitable to the above epitaph he himself had ordered to be put upon his monument.

(*d*)

EPITAPH

" Never believe . . . . an epitaph."

(*e*)   *Byron*

ERROR

" Do not err, my beloved brethren (Jas. i. 16)

The context, before and after, supplies the subject of the Apostle's argument, viz. :

The origin of moral evil

In all ages this has been the *one* question which has puzzled all philosophers. They have seen the effects, but have been unable to trace them back to the cause.

There is disorder, nay, more than disorder, daring opposition, in God's dominions. Things go wrong, contrary to His laws, contrary to His mind and wishes. Wrong is everywhere—we call it *sin*—who is the author of the wrong? What is the origin of sin? Is its genesis *in* man, or outside him? In the creature, or in the Creator? Is it positive ill, or merely a radical defect in man's nature?

These questions have been asked, and answered in various ways.

Examine the subject with the light thrown upon it by St. James.

(*f*)

1. Do we find man (naturally) admitting his guilt

(i.) *The heathen*, with their fatalist notions of life, said that they were *impelled* to act as they did by the indwelling of a demon, who over-mastered their own will.

(ii.) *The Jew*, similarly,—believing that God is sovereign, and hath mercy on whom He will have mercy, and whom He will He hardeneth,—asked, " *Why doth He yet find fault ?* "

(iii.) The *Rationalist*, who studies things only in the light of human reason, tells us that sin is a *defect* in man's nature—a sort of disease, of which he must learn to cure himself.

(*g*)

2. Leaving theories such as these, and which

perhaps do not interest us much, how do we find this question answered *practically* around us every day, and almost by every one?

Do we not find that personal guilt is denied?

(i.) Even infants, just able to talk, find it hard to admit guilt.

(ii.) The dullest tongues, amongst adult men, are eloquent in *excuses* for sin. The fault lies " *in others*," undue influence; or it is the fault of " *circumstances*," and being placed where they easily fell into wrong courses.

Another tells us that he has a peculiar "*temperament*"—easily excited into excesses beyond his control—in fact, his sin is his *infirmity* : he " can't help it."

(iii.) Even the Christian tries to lessen the guilt of his falls and backslidings by saying, "God let go my hand for a moment, and I fell; He hid Himself; and I was left in darkness and lost my path; then *sin* mastered me."

These excuses are all *self-deceptions*—lies told to self.

Every one of these rolls the responsibility of his actions off himself, and lays it upon God his Maker, saying :

" *I am as God made me* "—practically making God *the Author of sin.*

(*h*)

3. We test this deep-rooted tendency with Holy Scripture:

Is God the Author of sin?

(i.) Hear St. Paul: "Is there unrighteousness with God? GOD FOR-BID."

He condemns it *in toto.*

(ii.) Hear St. James: "Let no man say when he is tempted, I am tempted of God."

He disowns it emphatically.

It is clear, then, that neither of these two great Apostles' teaching sanctions such a phrase as, "*I am as God made me.*"

A man cannot charge God his Maker with the responsibility of his guilt.

He cannot argue, as some do:—God made me a *man*, not an angel, and my actions are therefore those of a man, not of an angel; and I am no more responsible for my actions than I am for not having *wings* as well as feet and hands.

It is here St. James comes to our aid, and puts us right. "Be not deceived," he says, with such specious and plausible arguments. *You are not as God made you.*

God did indeed make you after His image; but— *You yourselves are the makers of your own characters*—man helps to make himself. God has left you free to do that; and if you do your part badly, clumsily, and imperfectly, by copying bad models and following evil examples, don't lay it upon God, and say it is His workmanship—*it is your own.* What God made was *very good*, you have taken the rest of the work out of His hands into your own, and have marred and spoilt the whole, and now basely disown your own work. Having built up a bad character, or bad traits of character, you say, "*God made me so.*"

(*a*)

4. St. James does not merely disown the imputation that God is the Author of evil, but he shows how impossible it is that He could be.

He does this by instituting a striking contrast between the genesis of sin and the genesis of a new creature in Christ Jesus.

"*Do not err,*" he says, in thinking,

(i.) *The Father of Lights* is the Father of *Darkness as well*—it is impossible.

(ii.) *The Giver of every good and perfect gift* cannot be the Author of *the detestable sin which He punishes.* How could *He* be righteous and punish?

(iii.) *The Giver of the Holy Spirit*,—the highest and best of the *good things* that He gives,—cannot be the Giver, at the same time, of an *unclean spirit*—to travesty and caricature His own work.

(iv.) But above all, look how St. James opposes *the Birth* (origin) *of sin* to the *New Birth*, from above, of Christians.

How can the Author of *Regeneration* be also the Author of man's *degeneration?*

How can He who hath begotten us again by the Word of truth, be the Begetter also of our sin which ruins us?

Did He who sowed the good seed in the field, sow the tares also?

Can He who gives grace and glory, and withholds no good thing, be also the Author of that *sin* which brings forth Death; whose wages are Death; and which is *Death?*

He reduces the whole flimsy argument, if such we may term it, to an *absurdity.*

He brushes away all our self-deceptions, and warns us not to err on such an important point.

God is not the Author of evil—HE CANNOT BE

Evil is not a radical defect in man's nature— God made him upright and good.

Neither is man impelled to evil by any other power; but evil originates in himself, is born of his lust, and, unless arrested, develops its downward tendency unto death.

(*b*)   *Compare Lange, in loc*

ERROR

The mind that is always open to search into error, is itself in error, or at least, unstable.

(*c*)   *S. Bridge*

ERROR

It is a fact well known in the history of science and philosophy, that men, gifted by nature with singular intelligence, have broached the grossest errors, and even sought to undermine the grand primitive truths on which human virtue, dignity, and hope depend.

(*d*)   *Channing*

ESCAPE

"*Escape for thy life*" (Gen. xix. 17)

1. The necessity illustrated:

(i.) *A house on fire*—inmates in danger. "Escape for thy life"—the means = a FIRE-ESCAPE.

(ii.) *A ship on fire*—crew and passengers in danger. "Escape for thy life"—the means = a life boat.

(iii.) *Sodom about to be destroyed*—Lot and his family in danger. "Escape for thy life"—to the mountain, or Zoar.

(iv.) *The world is to be destroyed*—or, as Bunyan calls it, "The City of Destruction." "Escape for thy life"—the means provided = Christ our Refuge—"a very present help in time of trouble."

2. The lessons inculcated:

(i.) The *World* at large will be saying, up till the last minute, "Peace and safety."

(ii.) The *Church*, "a little flock," represented by Lot and his family, will be almost engulfed in the general mass of ungodliness.

3. Lot's family full of solemn warnings:

(i.) *Lot himself*—"scarcely saved." While he lingered, the angel had to thrust him out.

(ii.) *His wife*—though a relation of Abraham, and the wife of a righteous man, and with many privileges, likewise "*thrust out*," yet lost, = "one taken and another left."

(iii.) *His sons-in-law*—to whom he seemed as one that mocked, showing the evil of ungodly connections—"Come ye out"—"be separate"—"be not unequally yoked"—also lost.

4. Ask:

(i.) *Have you escaped* from the City of Destruction which is to be burned up? Have you done as Bunyan's Pilgrim did—fled from "condem-

(*e*)

nation" to "no condemnation?" If so, you would know it. "We *know* that we have passed," etc. Did not Lot know when he was out of Sodom?

(ii.) What means that *knocking* at the door? It is Jesus saying, "Escape for thy life."

(iii.) What means that long illness? It is God saying, "Escape for thy life."

(iv.) What means the Bible, "Flee from wrath to come?" It is the Spirit saying, "Escape for thy life."

(v.) What means our Lenten services? It is the Bride saying, "Escape for thy life."

(vi.) What means this anxiety of others at seeing you wholly given up to worldliness? It is "He that heareth," saying, "*Escape for thy life.*"

(*a*)

ESTABLISHED CHURCH

My confession of faith is very simple and explicit, and is at the service of anybody who asks for it. I do not agree with the High Churchmen in thinking that the State is always bound to teach religious faith to the people. I do not agree with the Voluntaries in thinking that it is always wrong in a State to support a religious establishment. I think the question a question of expediency, to be decided on a comparison of good and evil effects. I do not think it necessary to inquire whether, if there were no established Kirk in Scotland, it would be fit to set one up. I find a Kirk established. I am not prepared to pull it down: I will leave it what it has, but I will arm it with no new powers. I will impose no new burdens on the people for its support. I will make no distinction as to civil matters between the Churchman and the Dissenter. There are some questions which relate purely to the internal constitution of the Church. Those questions ought, in my opinion, to be decided with a view to the efficiency and respectability of the Church.

(*b*) *Macaulay*

ETERNITY, BELIEVED IN BY GREAT MINDS

There is, I know not how, in the minds of men, a certain presage, as it were, of a future existence; and this takes the deepest root and is most discoverable in the greatest geniuses and most exalted souls.

(*c*) *Cicero*

ETERNITY

Eternity stands always fronting God;
A stern Colossal image with blind eyes,
And grand, dim lips, that murmur evermore
"God, God, God!"

(*d*) *Elizabeth Barrett Browning*

EUCHARIST

No doubt Chrysostom and the other rhetorical Fathers contributed a good deal, by their rash use of figurative language, to advance the superstitious notion of the Eucharist; but the beginning had been much earlier. Clement treats it as did St. John and St. Paul; but in Hermas we see the seeds of the error, and more clearly in Irenæus; and so it went on till the *idea* was changed into an *Idol*.

S. T. Coleridge

Transubstantiation was nothing but rhetoric turned into logic.

(*f*) *Selden*

A rapid glance is sufficient to detect some prominent features which distinguished this meal from the Paschal sacrifice. The lamb was slain in the Temple; this feast was celebrated in the house. The blood was sprinkled by a priest; this supper had as its "proclaimer," or president, the master of a household. The sacrifice must be made before sunset; this supper was eaten after sunset. The lamb preached atonement for sin; this feast expressed joyful reception of "that inestimable benefit." The feast was a Eucharistic effect, consequent on its antecedent sacrificial cause.
The Lord's Supper in relation to the Paschal Meal.

(*g*) *G. H. Stanton*

EUREKA

The day of finding Christ (John i. 41–45).

Christ *finds* disciples, they *find* their friends, and report how they *have been found* by Christ, and *have found* Him.

[*Trench* calls this the chapter of the EUREKAS.]

(*h*) *Lange*

"*We have found the Messiah.*"

A great and a joyful εὕρηκα, and expected by the world for about forty centuries.

(*i*) *Bengel*

EUREKA

Two young ministers one day call at his cottage; and after Catherine has admitted them with a very few quiet words, they see, sitting at a little round table set out for tea, an evidently abstracted man, withdrawn from every object around him, Bible in hand, and in agonizing thought. He takes no more notice of the strangers than if they had been familiar pieces of household furniture. He moves to and fro in his chair, performing the "pumping" process of which John Foster has told us. But with little result; still he *cannot* abandon the endeavour. He closes and opens his eyes, but upon other scenes, and his face looks dark and clouded. His first cup has been drunk long ago, and his wife nudges him and asks him to forward the cup to be replenished: all unconscious of her meaning, he hands her the little Bible which he holds in his hand. Still the vision does not brighten. He becomes restless, gets up from his seat, and turns over page after page of Dr. Owen's volumes; tries another Puritan divine, and another, but in vain. What can he do? the result does not come; still he cannot let go the process. One resource remains: he there and then, undistracted by earthly presence, bends his knee in fervent prayer, and pours forth the most ardent supplications to Him who can "open the eyes of the understanding." Again he resumes his work, and his face grows calmer and brighter, his expression of agony wears away, and, in a short time, he has succeeded; he now emerges from the struggle, cordially addresses his visitors, and becomes playful and genial as a child.

(*j*) *Memoir of Christmas Evans*

EUREKA.

Can you doubt the ecstatic state of Archimedes when he jumped from the bath and ran home, oblivious of his nudity, crying *Eureka*? Or is it to be doubted that Franklin felt something of the same kind when he identified lightning with electricity, and when his friends had to force him away from his experiment lest the fluid should strike its devotee to the ground? And must we not say that Kepler was thrilled with joy and with awe when, establishing the truth of his conceptions, his celebrated laws, by rigid mathematical demonstration, he exclaimed, "O God, I think Thy thoughts after Thee."

(a)　　　　　　　　　　　*John Gill*

Evangelistic Weapons *are not carnal.* The Christian Faith once heard of the formidable incursions of her foes; so she determined to muster her preachers and teachers to review their weapons. She found beyond all her expectations everything prepared. There was a vast host of armed men; strong threatening forms, weapons which they used admirably, brightly flashing from afar. But as she came nearer she sank almost into a swoon; what she had thought iron and steel were toys; the swords were made of the mere lead of words; the breastplate of the soft linen of pleasure; the helmet of the wax of plumed vanity; the shields of papyrus scrolled over with opinions; the spears of thin reeds of weak conjecture; the colours, spiders' webs of philosophical systems; the cannon, Indian reed; the powder, poppy seeds; the balls of glass! Through the indolent neglect of their leaders, they had sold her true weapons, and had introduced these; nay, they had even made her former warriors,—whose armour, faithfulness, and strength were proved—contemptible; bitterly did Religion weep, but the whole assembly bid her be of good cheer; they would show their faith to the last breath. "What avails me," she cried, "your faith, since your actions are worthless? Of old, when I led naked, unarmed combatants to the field, one martyr, one warrior faithful to death, was worth more to me than a hundred of you in your gilded and silvered panoplies."—*E. B. Pusey.*

(b)

EVERLASTING LIFE AND DEATH

In ζωὴ αἰώνιος unlimited *intensity* is the first point, unlimited *extension* the second, and hence the opposite conception also must be understood in the religious and dynamic sense.

(c)　　　　　　　　　　　*Lange*

EVERLASTING PUNISHMENT (Matt. xxv. 46).

Observe the *same epithet* is used, κόλασις and ζωή, which are here *contraries*; for the ζωή here spoken of is not bare *existence*, which would have *annihilation* for its opposite; but *blessedness* and *reward*, to which *punishment* and *misery* are antagonistic terms.

(d)　　　　　　　　　　　*Alford*

The great facts of the Divine retribution, the eternal bliss of the righteous, the eternal woe of the wicked, are indisputable; and the images of uplifting or appalling grandeur in which they are enveloped cannot act too powerfully on the heart of man. But the particulars, the blissful or terrible details, are wisely withheld from our mind, which in its present state of knowledge could not comprehend them, and would only be confounded or misled by any description of them in human language.

(e)　　　　　　　　　　　*Morrison*

EVIDENCE, THE TRUE

This is the evidence which sustains the faith of thousands who never read and cannot understand the learned books of Christian apologists, who want, perhaps, words to explain the ground of their belief, but whose faith is of adamantine firmness, who hold the Gospel with a conviction more intimate and unwavering than mere argument ever produced.

(f)　　　　　　　　　　　*Channing*

If you would have a clear evidence that that little love, that little faith, that little zeal you have is true, then live up to that love, live up to that faith, live up to that zeal that you have; and this will evidence beyond all contradiction.

(g)　　　　　　　　　　　*Thos. Brooks*

EVIDENCES, CHRISTIAN (2 Pet. i. 16-21)

The evidence of

1. The eye :—" For we have not followed cunningly devised fables, when we made known unto you the power and coming of our Lord Jesus Christ, but were *eye witnesses of His majesty*."

2. The ear :—"For He received from God the Father honour and glory, when there came such a voice to Him from the excellent glory, This is My beloved Son, in whom I am well pleased. And this voice which came from heaven *we heard*, when we were with Him in the holy mount."

3. The Holy Ghost :—" We have also *a more sure word of prophecy*; whereunto ye do well that ye take heed, as unto a light that shineth in a dark place, until the day dawn, and the day star arise in your hearts.

" Knowing this first, that no prophecy of the Scripture is of any private interpretation.

" For prophecy came not in old time by the will of man : but holy men of God spake as they were moved by the HOLY GHOST."

= The Apostle's credentials :

We are *sure* about what we preach, because we have *seen*, and *heard* ourselves, and have also the testimony of the *Holy Ghost.*

(h)

" *We have not followed cunningly devised fables, when we made known unto you the power and coming of our Lord Jesus Christ, but were eye-witnesses of His majesty,*" etc. (2 Pet. i. 16-21)

Christian evidences rest on

1. Eye-witness of eleven persons, more especially of THREE in the mount of transfiguration, who *saw* His majesty.

2. Ear-witness . . . God's attesting voice " *This is my*," etc., " And this voice . . . we heard."

3. The written word: " We have *also, a more sure word of prophecy.*"

Peter accounts the " *word* " better evidence than his *eyes* and his *ears*—to which we do well to take heed, because

(i.) The word of God = a *light shining in a dark place.*

(ii.) Shining *until the day dawn* (when, though we may have it, we shall want it less).

(iii.) " SURE "—because the word is inspired by the Holy Ghost.

" Holy men of God spake as they were moved by the Holy Ghost."

(i)

EVIDENCES, EXTERNAL

I may be wrong in my opinion, but it is one of deep conviction, gained long ago, that no amount of external evidence in the way of proof of the truth of Christianity is worth anything in the way of saving a human soul.

(a)   *F. W. Robertson*

EVIDENCES OF FORGIVENESS (Ps. cxxx. 4)

I. The things that are spoken, or to be known of God, are of two sorts—natural and necessary, such as are His essential properties, or the attributes of His nature—His goodness, holiness, righteousness, omnipotence, eternity, and the like; these are called, "that which may be known of God" (Rom. i. 19). And there are two ways, as the Apostle there declares, whereby that which he there intimates of God may be known :

1. By the inbred light of nature ; "it is manifest in themselves" (ver. 19), in their own hearts; they are taught it by the common conceptions and presumptions which they have of God by the light of nature. From hence do all mankind know concerning God, that He is, that He is eternal, infinitely powerful, good, righteous, holy, omnipotent. There needs no special revelation of these things, that men may know them ; that, indeed, they may be known savingly, there is ; and therefore those who know these things by nature, do also believe them on revelation : "He that cometh to God must BELIEVE that He is, and that He is a rewarder" (Heb. xi. 6). Though men KNOW God by the light of nature, yet they cannot COME to God by that knowledge.

(b)

2. These essential properties of the nature of God are revealed by His works. So the Apostle in the same place, "The invisible things of God from the creation of the world are clearly seen, being understood by the things that are made, even His eternal power and Godhead" (Rom. i. 20). See also Ps. xix. 1–3. And this is the first sort of things that may be known of God.

Again, there are the free acts of His will and power, or His free eternal purposes, with the temporal dispensations that flow from them. Now of this sort is the forgiveness that we are inquiring after; it is not a property of the nature of God, but an act of His will, and a work of His grace. Although it hath its rise and spring in the infinite goodness of His nature, yet it proceeds from Him, and is not exercised but by an absolutely free and sovereign act of His will. Now, there is nothing of God, or with Him, of this sort, that can be any ways known, but only by special revelation. For,

(c)

1. There is no inbred notion of the acts of God's will in the heart of man, which is the first way whereby we come to the knowledge of anything of God. Forgiveness is not revealed by the light of nature ; flesh and blood, which nature is, declares it not. By that means, "No man hath seen God at any time" (John i. 18), that is, as a God of mercy and pardon, as the Son reveals Him. Adam had acquaintance, according to the limited capacity of a creature, with the properties and excellences of the nature of God. It was implanted in his heart, as indispensably necessary to that natural worship, which, by the law of his creation, he was to perform ; but, when he had sinned, it is evident that he had not the least apprehension that there was forgiveness with God. Such a thought would have laid a foundation of some further treaty with God, about his condition. But he had no other design but of "flying and hiding himself" (Gen. iii. 10), so declaring, that he was utterly ignorant of any such thing as pardoning mercy. Such, and no other, are all the first or purely natural conceptions of sinners: namely, that it is "the judgment of God" (Rom. i. 32), that sin is to be punished with death. It is true these conceptions in many are stifled by rumours, reports, traditions, that it may be otherwise; but all these are far enough from that revelation of forgiveness which we are inquiring after.

(d)

2. The consideration of the works of God's creation will not help a man to this knowledge, that there is forgiveness with God. The Apostle tells us (Rom. i. 20) what it is of God that His works reveal— even His eternal power and Godhead, or the essential properties of His nature; but no more, not any of the purposes of His grace ; nor any of the free acts of His will; not pardon and forgiveness. Besides, God made all things in such an estate and condition, namely, of rectitude, integrity, and uprightness (Eccl. vii. 29), that it was impossible they should have any respect to sin, which is the corruption of all, or to the pardon of it, which is their restitution, whereof they stood in no need. There being no such thing in the world as sin, nor any such thing supposed to be, when all things were made of nothing, how could anything declare or reveal the forgiveness of it?

(e)

3. No works of God's providence can make this discovery. God hath indeed borne testimony to Himself and His goodness in all ages, from the foundation of the world, in the works of His providence. Lo (Acts xiv. 15–17), "we preach unto you, that you should turn from these vanities, unto the living God, who made heaven and earth, and the sea, and all things that are therein : who, in times past, suffered all nations to walk in their own way. Nevertheless, He left not Himself without witness, in that He did good, and gave us rain from heaven, and fruitful seasons, filling our hearts with food and gladness."—" He left not Himself without witness ; " that is by the works of His providence there recounted, He thus far bare testimony to Himself, that He is, and is good, and doth good, and ruleth the world, so that they were utterly inexcusable, who,—taking no notice of these works of His, nor the fruits of His goodness, which they lived upon,—turned away after "vain things," as the Apostle there calls the idols of the Gentiles. But these things did not discover pardon and forgiveness; for still God suffered them to go on in their own ways, and winked at their ignorance. So again (Acts xvii. 23–27), "Whom ye ignorantly worship, Him declare I unto you. God that made the world, and all things therein, seeing that He is the Lord of heaven and earth, dwelleth not in temples made with hands, neither is worshipped with men's hands, as though He needed anything, seeing He

(f)

giveth unto all life, and breath, and all things, and hath made of one blood all nations of men, for to dwell on all the face of the earth; " (where, by the way, there is an allusion to Gen. xi. 8, " The Lord scattered them abroad upon the face of the earth,") " and hath determined the times before appointed, and the bounds of their habitation, that they should seek the Lord, if haply they might feel after Him and find Him, though He be not far from every one of us." By arguments taken from the works of God, both of creation and providence, the Apostle proves the being and properties of God; yea, he lets them know with whom he had to do, that God designed by His works, so far to reveal Himself to them as the true and living God, the maker and governor of all things, as that they ought to have inquired more diligently after Him, and not to look upon Him alone as the unknown God, who alone might be known; all their idols being vain and nothing. But of the discovery of pardon and forgiveness in God, by these ways and means, he speaks not; yea, he plainly shows that this was not done thereby. For the great call to saving repentance, is by the revelation of forgiveness. But now, by these works of His providence, God called not the Gentiles to saving repentance: " No," saith he, He " suffered them to walk still in their own ways " (Acts xiv. 16), " and winked at the times of their ignorance," but "now," that is, by the word of the Gospel, " commandeth them to repent " (chap. xvii. 30).

(a)　　　　　　　　　　　　　　*John Owen*

Evidences of Forgiveness

II. Whereas there had been one signal act of God's providence about sin, when man first fell into the snares of it, it was so far from revealing forgiveness in God, that it rather secretly intimated the contrary. This was God's dealing with sinning angels. The angels were the first sinners; and God dealt first with them about sin. And what was God's dealing with them? The Holy Ghost tells us, " He spared not the sinning angels " (2 Pet. ii. 4). He spared them not; it is the same word which He useth, where He speaks of laying all our iniquities on Christ, He undergoing the punishment due to them, " He spared Him not " (Rom. viii. 32), that is, He laid on Him the full punishment, that, by the curse and sanction of the law, was due to sin. So He dealt with the angels that sinned; He spared them not, but inflicted on them the punishment due to sin, shutting them up under chains of darkness for the judgment of the Great Day. Hitherto, then, God keeps all thoughts of forgiveness in His own eternal bosom; there is not so much as the least dawning of it upon the world. And this was at first no small prejudice against any thoughts of forgiveness. The world is made, sin enters by the most glorious part of the creation, whose recovery by pardon might seem to be most desirable; but not the least appearance of it is discovered. Thus it was hid in God from the foundation of the world (Eph. iii. 9).

(b)　　　　　　　　　　　　　　*John Owen*

Evidences of Forgiveness

III. God gave to man a law of obedience immediately upon his creation. Yea, for the main of it, He implanted it in him, by and in his creation. This law it was supposed that man might trans-

gress. The very nature of a law prescribed to free agents, attended with threatenings and promises of reward, requires that supposition. Now, there was not annexed to this law, or revealed with it, the least intimation of pardon to be obtained, if transgression should ensue. In Gen. ii. 17, we have this law, " In the day thou eatest, thou shalt surely die." Dying, thou shalt die; or bring upon thyself assuredly the guilt of death, temporal and eternal.

There God leaves the sinner under the power of that commination. Of forgiveness, or pardoning mercy, there is not the least intimation. To this very day, that law, which was then the whole rule of life and acceptance with God, knows no such thing. Dying, thou shalt die, O sinner, is the precise and final voice of it. From these previous considerations, added to what was formerly spoken, some things preparatory to the ensuing discourse may be inferred: As,

(c)

1. That it is a great and rare thing to have forgiveness in God discovered to a sinful soul. A thing it is, that, as hath been showed, conscience and law, with the inbred notions that are in the heart of man about God's holiness and vindictive justice do lie against: a matter whereof we have no natural presumption, whereof there is no common notion in the mind of man; a thing which no consideration of the works of God, either of creation or providence, will reveal, and which the great instance of God's dealing with sinning angels renders deep, admirable, and mysterious. Men who have common and slight thoughts of God, of themselves, of sin, of obedience, of the judgment to come, of eternity, that feed upon the ashes of rumours, reports, hearsays, traditions, without looking into the reality of things, may, and do take this to be an ordinary and acknowledged truth, easy to be entertained, which no man disbelieves. But convinced sinners, who make a trial of these things, as running into eternity, have other thoughts of them. And, as to that which it is pretended every one believes, we have great cause to cry out, " Lord, who hath believed our report? to whom hath this arm of the Lord been revealed? "

(d)

2. That the discovery of forgiveness in God, being a matter of such great difficulty, is a thing precious and excellent, as being the foundation of all communion with God here and of all undeceiving expectation of our enjoyment of Him hereafter. It is a pure Gospel truth, that hath neither shadow, footstep, nor intimation elsewhere; the whole creation hath not the least obscure impression of it left thereon: so that,

(e)

3. It is undoubtedly greatly incumbent on us to inquire diligently, as the prophets did of old, into this salvation; to consider what sure evidences faith hath of it, such as will not, as cannot fail us. To be slight and common in this matter, to take it up at random, is an argument of an unsound and rotten heart. He that is not serious in his inquiry into the revelation of this matter, is serious in nothing wherein God or his soul is concerned. The Holy Ghost knows what our frame of heart is, and how slow we are to receive this

(f)

blessed truth in a gracious saving manner. Therefore doth He confirm it to us with such weighty considerations as (Heb. vi. 17, 18), " God, willing more abundantly to show unto the heirs of promise the immutability of His counsel, confirmed it by an oath, that by two immutable things, in which it was impossible for God to lie, we might have strong consolation." It is of forgiveness of sin that the Apostle treats, as hath been made evident by the description of it before given. Now, to give evidence hereunto, and to beget a belief of it in us, he first engages a property of God's nature in that business. He with whom we deal, is the God that cannot lie, that cannot deceive, or be deceived (Tit. i. 2). It is impossible it should be so with Him. Now, as this extends itself in general to all the words and works of God, so there is peculiarly in this, whereof He treats, " an especial immutability of His counsel." Men may think, that although there be words spoken about forgiveness, yet it is possible it may be otherwise. No, saith the Apostle, it is spoken by God ; and it is impossible He should lie. Yea, but upon the manifold provocations of sinners, He may change His mind and thoughts therein : No, saith the Apostle, there is a peculiar immutability in His counsel concerning the execution of this thing ; there can be no change in it. But how doth this appear, that indeed this is the counsel of His will ? Why, saith he, He hath declared it by His word, and that given in a way of promise ; which, as in its own nature it is suited to raise an expectation in him or them to whom it is made or given, so it requires exact faithfulness in the discharge and performance of it, which God, on His part, will assuredly answer. But neither is this all ; but that no place might be left for any cavilling in this matter, " He interposeth Himself by an oath." Thus we have this truth deduced from the veracity of God's nature, one of His essential excellences, established in the immutable purpose of His will, brought forth by a word of promise, and confirmed by God's interposing Himself against all occasions of exception, (so as to put an end to all strife about it,) by an oath, swearing by Himself that so it should be. I have mentioned this only to show what weight the Holy Ghost lays upon the delivery of this great truth, and thence how deeply it concerns us to inquire diligently into it, and after the grounds and evidences which may be tendered of it ; which among others are these that follow.

(a)   *John Owen*

(*See* FORGIVENESS OF SINS.)

EVIL

I do not know why it is, that, by the constitution of the universe, evil has so much more power than good to produce its effect, and to propagate its nature. One drop of foul will pollute a whole cup of fair water ; but one drop of fair water has no power to appreciably improve a cup of foul.

(b)   *Bond*

EVIL, ORIGIN OF

Many have puzzled themselves about the origin of evil. I observe there *is* evil, and that there is a way to escape it ; and with this I begin and end.

(c)   *John Newton*

EVOLUTION

Herbert Spencer starts with *Cosmic gas*, or nebula.

J. Martineau asks, If *it* contains in it all that is afterwards evolved ; if all is potentially there, and inherent in it : Plato, and Shakspeare, and all the productions of the wisest men who have ever lived ; then there is nothing very wonderful in the evolution.

(d)

" I would sooner believe that the Iliad was formed by the fortuitous concourse of letters, than believe that the world was formed by a fortuitous concourse of atoms.

(e)   *Cicero*

Darwin has never committed himself to materialistic evolution. He has always asserted that the first living germs were brought into existence by the Creator of all things. But now if you put into these first germs a constitution that will develop on one line into vertebrates, on another into radiates, on another into articulates, and on another into mollusks, you have four fundamental forms of life, as Agassiz taught.

(f)

EVOLUTION

When the " Origin of Species " and the " Descent of Man " first appeared, they were largely regarded by religious men as containing a theory necessarily hostile to fundamental truths of religion. A closer study has greatly modified any such impression. It is seen that, whether the creative activity of God is manifested through catastrophes, as the phrase goes, or in progressive evolution, it is still His creative activity, and the really great questions beyond remain untouched. The evolutionary process, supposing it to exist, must have had a beginning : Who began it ? It must have had material to work with : Who furnished it ? It is itself a law or system of laws : Who enacted them ? Even supposing that the theory represents absolute truth, and is not merely a provisional way of looking at things incidental to the present stage of knowledge, these great questions are just as little to be decided by physical science now as they were when Moses began the Pentateuch ; but there are apparently three important gaps in the evolutionary sequence which it is well to bear in mind. There is the great gap between the highest animal instinct and the reflective, self-measuring self-analysing thought of man. There is the greater gap between life and the most highly organized matter. There is the greatest gap of all between matter and nothing. At these three points, as far as we can see, the Creative Will must have intervened otherwise than by way of evolution out of existing materials—to create mind, to create life, to create matter. But, beyond all question, it is our business to respect in science, as in other things, every clearly ascertained report of the senses ; for every such report represents a fact, and a fact is sacred as having its place in the temple of universal truth. But a fact is one thing, while theories, hypotheses, doctrines—like that of evolution itself—framed by men of genius so as to include or account for facts, are quite another.

(g)

These theories may or may not be true, even if they are brilliant and imposing; they may for a generation or for a century carry everything before them in the world of thought; but science knows no finality, and while theories pass and are forgotten, facts—like God's revelation of Himself in Christ—remain.

(a)   *Canon Liddon*

EXAMINE YOURSELVES

Examine yourself if you be in good earnest in Christ, for some " are partakers of the Holy Ghost, and taste of the good word of God, and of the powers of the world to come," and yet have no part in Christ at all. Many think they believe, but never tremble ; the devils are further on than these (James ii. 19).

(b)   *Samuel Rutherford*

EXAMPLES OF FORGIVENESS

We are encompassed about with a cloud of witnesses. For,

1. It is most certain that they were all sinners ; they were all so by nature ; for therein there is no difference between any of the children of men. And personally they were sinners also : they confessed so of themselves, and some of the sins of all of them stand upon record : yea, some of them were great sinners, or guilty of great and signal miscarriages. Some before their conversion, as Abraham, who was an idolater (Josh. xxiv. 2, 3), and Paul, who was a persecutor and a blasphemer. Some after their conversion ; some in sins of the flesh, against their obedience, as David ; and some in sins of profession, against faith, as Peter. Nothing, then, is more evident, than that no one of them came to rest with God but by forgiveness. Had they never been guilty of any one sin, but only what is left upon record concerning them in holy writ, yet they could be saved no other way ; for he that transgresseth the law in any one point, is guilty of the breach of the whole (James ii. 10).

(c)

What shall we now say ?

Do we think that God hath forgiveness only for this or that individual person ? No man questions but that all these were pardoned. Was it by virtue of any special privilege that was peculiar to them ? Whence should any such privilege arise, seeing by nature, they were no better than others, nor would have been so personally had not they been delivered from sin and prepared for obedience by grace, mercy, and pardon ? Wherefore, they all obtained forgiveness which is with God. And this is equally ready for others, who come to God the same way that they did ; that is, by faith and repentance.

(d)

2. Many of those, concerning whom we have the assurance mentioned, were not only sinners, but great sinners, which must be insisted on to obviate another objection.

For some may say, that although they were sinners, yet they were not such sinners as we are. And, although they obtained forgiveness, yet this is no argument that we shall do so also, who are guilty of other sins than they were, and those attended with other aggravations than theirs were. To which I say, that I delight not in aggravating, no, nor yet in repeating, the sins and faults of the

saints of God of old. Not only the grace of God, but the sins of men, have by some been turned into lasciviousness, or been made a cloak for their lusts. But yet, for the ends and purposes for which they are recorded by the Holy Ghost, we may make mention of them. That they may warn us of our duty ; that we take heed lest we also fall : that they may yield us a relief under our surprisals, are they written. So then, where the mention of them tends to the advancement of sovereign grace and mercy, which is the case in hand, we may insist on them. I think, then, that, without mention of particulars, I may safely say, that there is no sin, no degree of sin, no aggravating circumstance of sin, no kind of continuance in sin (one sin only excepted), but that there are those in heaven who have been guilty of them.

(e)

It may be yet, some one will say, that they have considered the sins and falls of Lot, David, Peter, Paul, and the thief himself on the cross, and yet they find not their own condition exemplified, so as to conclude that they shall have the same success with them.

(f)

Answer, 1. I am not showing that this or that man shall be pardoned, but only demonstrating that there is forgiveness with God, and that for all sorts of sins and sinners ; which these instances do assuredly confirm. And, moreover, they manifest, that if other men are not pardoned, it is merely because they make not that application for forgiveness which they did.

(g)

2. Yet, by the way, to take off this objection also, consider what the Apostle says in particular, concerning the several sorts of sinners that obtained mercy. " Be not deceived : neither fornicators, nor idolaters, nor adulterers, nor effeminate, nor abusers of themselves with mankind, nor thieves, nor covetous, nor drunkards, nor revilers, nor extortioners, shall inherit the kingdom of God. And such were some of you ; but ye are washed, but ye are sanctified, but ye are justified " (1 Cor. vi. 9, 10, 11). Hell can scarce, in mere words, yield us a sadder catalogue. Yet "some" of all these sorts were justified and pardoned.

(h)

3. Suppose this enumeration of sins doth not reach the condition of the soul, because of some especial aggravation of its sin, not expressed, let such an one add that of our Saviour. "I say unto you, All manner of sin and blasphemy shall be forgiven unto men, but the blasphemy against the Holy Ghost " (Matt. xii. 31). They are not, they shall not be, all actually remitted and pardoned, to all men ; but they are all pardonable to those that seek to obtain pardon for them according to the Gospel. There is with God forgiveness for them all. Now, certainly there is no sin, but only that excepted, but it comes within the compass of " all manner of sin and blasphemy ; " and so, consequently, some who have been guilty of it are in heaven.

(i)

We take it for a good token and evidence of a virtuous healing water, when, without fraud or pretence, we see the crutches of cured cripples and impotent persons hung about as a memorial of its

(j)

efficacy. And it is a great demonstration of the skill and ability of a physician, when many come to a sick person, and tell him that we had the same distemper with you, it had the same symptoms, the same effects, and by his skill and care we are cured. Oh! saith the sick man, bring him to me, I will venture my life in his hand. Now, all the saints of heaven stand about a sin-sick soul ; for, in this matter we are encompassed with a cloud of witnesses (Heb. xii. 1). And what do they bear witness to? What say they to a poor guilty sinner? As thou art, so were we ; so guilty, so perplexed, so obnoxious to wrath, so fearing destruction from God! And what way did you steer, what course did you take, to obtain the blessed condition wherein you now are? Say they, we went all to God, through Christ, for forgiveness, and found plenty of grace, mercy, and pardon in Him for us all! The rich man in the parable thought it would be a great means of conversion, if one should rise from the dead and preach ; but here we see, that all the saints departed and now in glory do jointly preach this fundamental truth, that there is forgiveness with God.

(a) *John Owen*

(*See* FORGIVENESS OF SINS.)

EXCEPTION

In an age in which Christianity was exerting some power, there was certainly a degree of deference due to the moral convictions of society. But Napoleon thought himself more than a match for the moral instincts and sentiments of our nature. He thought himself able to cover the most atrocious deeds by the splendour of his name, and even to extort applause for crimes by the brilliancy of his success. He took no pains to conciliate esteem. In his own eyes he was mightier than conscience ; and thus he turned against himself the power and resentment of virtue in every breast where that divine principle found a home.

(b) *Channing*

EXCEPTION

There is a man, usurping lordly sway,
Aiming alone to hold a world at bay ;
Who, mean as daring, arrogant as vain,
Like chaff, regards opinion as disdain,
As if the privilege with him were found
The laws to spurn by which mankind are bound ;
As if the arm which drags a despot down
Must palsied fall before a Byron's frown !

(c) *Joseph Cottle, on Lord Byron*

EXCOMMUNICATION

= Cut off from the " communion of saints," and from the " fellowship with the Father, and with His Son Jesus Christ " (1 John i.). This power the Popes once pretended to exercise over the consciences of men ; and in the past, terrible evils have arisen in consequence. We have passed beyond fear of that ; but the greater evil of-

SELF-EXCOMMUNICATION is still in force, and whereby people practically cut themselves off from fellowship and communion with the Lord Jesus Christ and His Church.

(d)

Observe,

1. **The Legitimate inference to be drawn from the habits of modern congregations.**

(i.) In the early Church, Christian congregations assembled for prayers, preaching, and *the breaking of bread*—all the congregation stayed.
(ii.) Our modern habits show a vast apostasy. Now many baptized persons, confirmed Church members, join in the prayers and praises, listen to the preaching, but who habitually leave the Church when the Holy Communion is administered. This act = an act of *self-excommunication*, and is deeply significant.

(e)

2. **The Facts are these :**

(i.) The Lord said,—
" Do this." You do not do it, but turn your back on it.
(ii.) " In remembrance of Me." Church Catechism,—" *For a continual remembrance.*"
St. Paul,—"*As oft as ye do this, ye do show the Lord's death till He come.*"
You do all that you can to forget it.
(iii.) The ordinance is regularly put before you.
="*Keep Jesus Christ in memory,*" and you obey not.
(iv.) The Church repeats the Gospel invitation,—
" *Come, for all things are now ready.*"
You reply by making *excuses*.
If you habitually leave a room when a certain person enters it = that you do not want to make his acquaintance. So your action in this matter has this significance, that you do not wish to remember Jesus Christ, nor to have communion with Him.

(f)

3. **Observe the connection between the Lord's Supper, and His Promises :**

The promises of,
(i.) The forgiveness of sins,
(ii.) The resurrection of the body,
(iii.) Eternal life, are made to those who " do this in remembrance " of Him.
And your act of self-excommunication = that you have no part nor interest in these promises ; you judge yourself " unworthy of eternal life."

(g)

4. **Observe the connection between the Lord's Supper and Heaven ; and the significance of your act in relation to the " last things."**

(i.) The custom among all nations of eating in common of the same meal = close relation, friendship, intimacy, brotherhood.
(ii.) This is what believers do here.
They eat of a common meal together, to show the same truth. " All partakers of the same bread " = one loaf—all have physically something in common. And Christ, the " Bread of Life," the staff of spiritual life = common to us all.
(iii.) And this meal is an *anticipation of Heaven* —of the close relation and friendship, and communion of Heaven = an act-prophecy of *the Marriage Supper of the Lamb.* See Matt. xxvi. 29, " I will not drink henceforth of this fruit of the vine, *until that day* when I drink it new with you in My Father's kingdom."

(h)

And, once more, the significant act of self-excommunication is not merely the cutting yourself off from communion with this or that local Church and its members, but from part and communion with Christ and His Church, which is the blessed company of all faithful people, His guests both here and at the Heavenly Feast.

(a)

EXCUSES

I find a common objection in the mouths of the ungodly : they say, We can do nothing without God. . . . If He have not predestinated us, and will not turn us, how can we turn ourselves, or be saved ? Thus they think they are excused.

I answer: (1) Though you cannot cure yourselves, you can hurt and poison yourselves. Will you wilfully do that ? (2) Though you cannot be converted without the special grace of God, yet know that God giveth His grace in the use of His holy means which He hath appointed to that end.

Are you not able to make use of them ?

You cannot say that you have done what you are able. (3) You can therefore forfeit the grace and help of God by wilful sinning or negligence, though you cannot without grace turn to God. (4) And for God's decrees : know that they separate not the end from the means, but tie them together. God never decreed to save any but the sanctified, nor to condemn any but the unsanctified. God doth as truly decree from everlasting whether your land this year shall be barren or fruitful, and just how long you shall live in the world, as He hath decreed whether you shall be saved or not. And yet you would think that man but a fool that would forbear ploughing and sowing, and say, if God have decreed that my ground shall bear corn, it will bear, whether I plough and sow or not. If God have decreed that I shall live, I shall live, whether I eat or not ; but if He have not, it is not eating that will keep me alive. If you know how to answer such a man, you know too how to answer yourselves ; for the case is alike. If you do not, then try these conclusions upon your bodies before you venture to try them on your souls. See first whether God will keep you alive without food or raiment, and give you corn without tillage and labour ; and whether He will bring you to your journey's end without travel or carriage ; and if you speed well in this, then try whether He can bring you to heaven without your diligent use of means.

(b)   *Baxter*

EXEGESIS

E. P. Whipple, who sometimes boils the maple sap of verbosity down to the maple sugar of an enduring proverb, says, The trouble in most of our theological schools is, that exegesis too often means, "Exit Jesus."

(c)

EXHORTATION TO BELIEVE IN FORGIVE-NESS

The poor convinced wretch, thinking of dealing with God (Micah vi. 6, 7), rolls in his mind what terms he is likely to meet with ; and fixes on the most dreadful, difficult, and impossible terms that can be imagined. If, saith he, anything be done with this great and most high God, it must be by rivers, thousands and ten-thousands, children, first-born ; whatever is dreadful and terrible to nature, whatever is impossible for me to perform, that is it which He looks for. But the matter is quite otherwise ; the terms are wholly of another nature ; it is a way of mere mercy, a way of free forgiveness. The Apostle lays it down (Rom. iii. 23–25), it is a way of propitiation, of pardon, of forgiveness in the blood of Christ ; the terms are the acceptance of the forgiveness that we have described. Who would not think now, that the whole world would run in to be made partakers of these terms, willingly accepting of them ? But it proves for the most part quite otherwise. Men like not this way of all others. "It had been something," says Naaman, "if the prophet had come and done so-and-so ; but this, ' Go, wash, and be clean,' I do not like it ; I am but deluded." Men think within themselves, that had it been some great thing that was required of them, that they might be saved, they would with all speed address themselves thereunto ; but to come to God by Christ, to be freely forgiven without more ado, they like it not. Some rigid, austere penances, some compensatory obedience, some satisfactory mortification, or purgatory, had been a more likely way ; this of mere pardon, in and by the Cross, is but folly (1 Cor. i. 18, 20). I had rather, saith the Jew, have it as it were by the works of the Law (Rom. ix. 32, and chap. x. 3), this way of grace and forgiveness I like not. So say others also : so practise others every day. Either this way is wholly rejected, or it is mended by some additions, which, with God, is all one with the rejection of it.

Here multitudes of souls deceive themselves, and perish. I know not whether it be more difficult to persuade an unconvinced person to think of any terms, or a convinced person to accept of these. Let men say what they will, and pretend what they please ; yet, practically, they like not this way of forgiveness.

(d)

1. *Positively.* "He that believeth not shall be DAMNED" (Mark xvi. 16). That is a hard word ; many men cannot endure to hear it. They would not have it named by their good wills, and are ready to fly in the face of him from whose mouth it proceeds. But let not men deceive themselves. This is the softest word that mercy and love itself, that Christ, that the Gospel speaks to despisers of forgiveness. It is Christ who is this legal, terrifying preacher ; it is He who cries out, "If you believe not, you shall be damned ; " and will come Himself, in flaming fire, to take vengeance of them "that obey not the Gospel" (2 Thess. i. 8). This is the end of the disobedient, if God, if Christ, if the Gospel may be believed.

(e)

2. *Comparatively*, in reference to the vengeance due to the breach of the law. We are, in the preaching of forgiveness by Christ to them that perish, "a savour of death unto death" (2 Cor. ii. 16) ; a deep death, a sore condemnation ; so (Heb. x. 29), "of how much sorer punishment, suppose ye, shall he be thought worthy ? " Sorer than ever was threatened by the Law, or inflicted for the breach of it ; not as to the kind of punishment, but as to the degrees of it. Hence arises the addition of many stripes.

(f)

Gospel pardon is a thing of another nature. It hath its spring in the gracious heart of the Father; is made out by a sovereign act of His will; rendered consistent with the glory of His justice and holiness by the blood of Christ; by which it is purchased in a covenant of grace, as hath been showed. If you shall say, Yea, this is the forgiveness we rely upon, it is that which you have described; then I desire further, that you would examine your own hearts.

(a)

If you shall say, Nay, but we will seek the Lord whilst He may be found, we will draw nigh to Him before He cause darkness; then consider, I pray,

1. What Joshua told the children of Israel, when they put themselves upon such a resolution, and cried out, "We will serve the Lord our God" (Josh. xxiv. 18, 19). "Ye cannot serve the Lord, for He is an holy God, a jealous God; He will not forgive your transgressions nor your sins." Go to Him upon your own account, and in your own strength, with your own best endeavours and duties; you will find Him too great and too holy for you to deal with. You will obtain neither acceptance of your persons nor pardon of your sins. But you will say, "These are heavy tidings. If we sit still, we perish; and if we rise to be doing, it will not be better. Is there no hope left for our souls? Must we pine away under our sins and the wrath of God for ever?" God forbid. There are yet other directions remaining to guide you out of these entanglements. Wherefore,

(b)

2. Ponder seriously on what hath been spoken of this way of approaching to God. Consider it in its own nature, as to all the ends and purposes for which it is proposed of God. Consider whether you approve of it or not. Do you judge it a way suited and fitted to bring glory to God? Doth it answer all the wants and distresses of your souls? Do you think it excellent, safe, and glorious to those who are entered into it. Or, have you anything to object against it? Return your answer to Him in whose name, and by whose appointment, these words are spoken to you. If you shall say, We are convinced that this way of forgiveness is the only way for the relief and deliverance of our souls; then·

(c)

3. Abhor yourselves for all your blindness and obstinacy, whereby you have hitherto despised the love of God, the blood of Christ, and the tenders of pardon in the Gospel. Be abashed and humbled to the dust, in a sense of your vileness, pollutions, and abominations; which things are every day spoken to, and need not here be repeated. And,

(d)

4. Labour to exercise your hearts greatly with thoughts of that abundant grace which; is manifested in this way of sinners coming to God; as also, of the excellency of the Gospel wherein it is unfolded. Consider the eternal love of the Father, which is the fountain and spring of this whole dispensation; the inexpressible love of the Son, in establishing and confirming it, in removing all hindrances and obstructions by His own blood, bringing forth to beauty and glory this redemption or forgiveness of sin, as the price of it. And let the

glory of the Gospel, which alone makes this discovery of forgiveness in God, dwell in your hearts. Let your minds be exercised about these things. You will find effects from them above all that hath as yet been brought forth in your souls. What, for the most part, have you hitherto been conversant about? When you have risen above the turmoiling of lusts and corruptions in your hearts, the entanglements of your callings, business, and affairs, what have you been able to raise your hearts to? Perplexing fears about your condition, general hopes, without savour or relish, yielding you no refreshment; legal commands, bondage duties, distracted consciences, broken purposes and promises, which you have been tossed up and down with, without any certain rest. And what effects have these thoughts produced? Have they made you more holy and more humble? Have they given you delight in God and strength to new obedience? Not at all. Where you were, there you still are, without the least progress. But now, bring your souls to these springs, and try the Lord, if, from that day, you be not blessed with spiritual stores.

(e)

5. If the Lord be pleased to carry on your souls thus far, then stir up yourselves to choose and close with the way of forgiveness that hath been revealed. Choose it only, choose it in comparison with and opposition to all others. Say, you will be for Christ, and not for another; and be so accordingly. Here venture, here repose, here rest your souls. It is a way of peace, safety, holiness, beauty, strength, power, liberty, and glory; you have the nature, the name, the love, the purposes, the promises, the covenant, the oath of God; the love, life, death or blood, the mediation, or oblation and intercession, of Jesus Christ; the power and efficacy of the Spirit, and Gospel grace by Him administered, to give you assurance of the excellency, the oneness, the safety of the way whereunto you are engaging.

(f)   *John Owen*

(*See* FORGIVENESS OF SINS.)

EXPEDIENCY

It is an eternal rule, from which we must in no case depart, that men must do nothing contrary to the rules and precepts of religion—no, not for the sake of religion itself.

(g)   *Nelson*

EXPERIENCE

Experience is like the stern-light of a ship at sea; it enlightens only the track which has been passed over.

(h)   *Coleridge*

EXPERIENCE, CHRISTIAN

"*More than others*" (Song of Sol. v. 7–10)

That the companions of the Church ask this question, "What the Kirk's beloved is more than others?" shows they are not so well acquainted with Christ, nor with the fits of spiritual ague and fevers for absent Christ. The Lord has bairns in His house, and Christ's bairns must creep ere they

(i)

gang. All within the Church have not a like experience of Christ. 1 John ii. 13 makes some fathers, some young men, and some little children. There may be two sons of one and the same father, and the one be thirteen years of age, and the other a sucking child that can neither speak, stand, nor walk as yet.

(a)   *Samuel Rutherford*

I have no remarkable experience to talk of; I never was, like Paul, at any difficulty to tell whether I was in the body or out of the body; I am burdened with a body of sin and death. But I have a little book, which I am enabled to believe is the sure Word of God. The doctrines and promises I meet with in it, which we call the Gospel, exactly suit my wants, and the temper and conduct it is designed to form, agrees with my leading desire.

I believe the most lively grace and the most solid comfort are known among the Lord's poor and undistinguished people. Every outward advantage has a tendency to nourish the pride of the human heart, and requires a proportionable knowledge of the deceitful self, and the evil of sin to counterbalance them. It is no less difficult to have great abilities than great riches, without trusting in them. And believers who are remarkably sensible and clever, are frequently teased with whims and vagaries of thought, which do not trouble plain people. If I was qualified to search out the best Christian in the kingdom, I should not expect to find him either in a professor's chair, or in a pulpit. I should give the palm to that person who had the lowest thoughts of himself, and the most admiring and cordial thoughts of the Saviour. And perhaps this person may be some bed-ridden old man or woman, or a pauper in a parish workhouse. But our regard to the Lord is not to be measured by our sensible feelings, by what we can say or write, but rather by the simplicity of our dependence, and the uniform tenour of our obedience to His will.

(b)   *John Newton*

EXPERIENCE OF FORGIVENESS

There must needs be great assurance of those truths which are thus received and believed

For hereby are "the senses exercised to discern good and evil" (Heb. v. 14). Where there is a spiritual sense of truth, of the good and evil that is in doctrines, from an inward experience of what is so good, and from thence an aversion to the contrary, and this obtained by reason of a habit, or an habitual frame of heart, there is strength, there is steadfastness and assurance. This is the teaching of the unction, which will not, which cannot deceive. Hence many of old and of late, that could not dispute, could yet die for truth. He who came to another, and went about to prove, by sophistical reasons, that there was no such thing as motion, had only this return from him who either was not able to answer his cavilling or unwilling to put himself to trouble about it; he arose, and walking up and down, gave him a real confutation of his sophistry. It is so in this case: when a soul hath a real experience of the grace of God, of the pardon of sins, of the virtue and efficacy of the death of Christ, of justification by His blood, and peace

with God by believing; let men or devils, or angels from heaven, oppose these things, if it cannot answer their sophisms, yet he can rise up and walk; he can, with all holy confidence and assurance, oppose his own satisfying appearance to all their arguings and suggestions. A man will not be disputed out of what he sees and feels; and a believer will abide as firmly by his spiritual sense as any man can by his natural sense.

(c)   *John Owen*

I went to Him, by Jesus Christ, against whom I have sinned, and have found Him better to me than I could expect, or ever should have believed, had not He overpowered my heart by His Spirit. Instead of wrath, which I feared, and that justly, because I had deserved it, He said to me in Christ, "Fury is not in Me." For a long time I could not believe it; I thought it impossible that there should be mercy and pardon for me, or such a one as I. But He still supported me, sometimes by one means, sometimes by another; until, taking my soul near to Himself, He caused me to see the folly of my unbelieving heart and the vileness of the hard thoughts I had of Him, and that indeed there is with Him forgiveness and plenteous redemption. This hath taken away all my sorrows, and given me quietness, with rest and assurance.

(d)   *John Owen*

(*See* FORGIVENESS OF SINS.)

EXPERIENCE, PAST

It will not do to live on past experience; it will not assist me. I must live by the day, by the hour, by the minute, on God. Recollecting I had a good meal this day week, will not feed me to-day. I must have new food, or I shall starve.

(e)   *John Newton*

EXPERIENCES

"William, your ale is not so good as it used to be, and what do you think is the reason of it? Some time ago there was an old woman living in the parish of Ystradfellte, in a cottage by the roadside, where she sold home-brewed ale, which became so famous that the neighbours, when they wished to praise anything, used to say: 'It is as good as Betty's ale.' By and by, the old dame thought it would be less troublesome to buy the ale in casks. The farmers' lads called as usual, tasted, made wry faces, and said: 'Bah! this is not your own brewing, Betty; good by.'" Then, turning to William, he said: "Brother, brew your own ale."

(f)   *Shenkyn*

On his frequent journeys from home he was greatly tried with the little hypocrisies of religious people. The horse which he rode was by no means a splendid specimen of its race, and required at least tolerable accommodation to be able to carry its master. But as this could not always be calculated upon, the preacher had to look pretty sharply after the welfare of his horse, at the same time shrewdly regarding its treatment as one of the "evidences" of the spiritual condition of his host. At one place he was received with cordial smiles and greetings by an individual so "respectable" in appearance, that Shenkyn hesitated for a

(g)

while whether he would, according to his custom, go into the stable to ascertain for himself how his animal was likely to fare. Still, he had not much faith in the smiling "steward;" so he lingered behind, allowing the friend who accompanied him, and the host, to precede him to the service which was about to commence. While the friend was reading and praying, Shenkyn proceeded to the stable, and, to his horror, found the hay in such a condition that the poor horse would have nothing to do with it. His soul was filled with righteous indignation; what to do he knew not; the more he mused, the more the fire burned. At last the inspiration came: he would fill his pockets with the mouldy hay, and take it with him to the meeting. He went, and preached as well as he could in the circumstances, biding his time for the "society" meeting, when he should probably hear the "experience" of the proprietor of the hay. The time came; the deacon-host announced that a meeting was to be held, which, after a few minutes' silence, he also commenced with an unctuous reference to the excellent service which they had just enjoyed, and then proceeded to call upon some of the brethren present to say a word or two on their spiritual condition. There was no response; and during the silence the preacher's prophetic contortions were so terrible, that those who knew him expected some extraordinary outbreak. Starting on his feet, he addressed his host: "Suppose you, sir, give us a little of *your* experience; you may have something to say on this occasion." The deacon began, and talked about his doubts and fears in such a strain that Shenkyn's patience could hold out no longer; he put his hands in his pockets, and brought out the mouldy hay, which he deliberately shook all over and about the deacon, powdering him from head to foot, exclaiming, at the same time, with tremendous energy: "Your religion, sir, is as musty as this hay which you have put before my horse."

(*a*)　　　　　　　　　　　　　　　　*Shenkyn*

"EXTREMITY, MAN'S, IS GOD'S OPPORTUNITY"

It is a current saying, "That the darkest cloud precedes the dawn;" and that "every dark cloud has a silver lining." Early risers tell us that the lowest temperature immediately precedes the sunrising. These things serve to illustrate God's kingdom of grace, "Before honour is humility." "Thou hast lift me up and cast me down." "How long, O Lord, how long?"

(*b*)

EYE

"*He that formed the eye, shall He not see?*" (Ps. xciv. 9.)

Some years ago an American astronomer, wanting to gaze at some object low down in the sky, lowered his telescope so as to sweep the horizon: a peculiar sight then appeared on the disc of the instrument, when he put his eye to it. The telescope was just in a line with an orchard of fruit trees, six miles distant; and, from his point of observation, he saw certain men robbing this orchard. Their features and actions were all seen: none could escape detection; for identification was complete. Little did they think of the big eye of that telescope being upon them—covered, too, as they might think, by the darkness of the night. Less did they think perhaps of that Omniscient Eye which beholds the evil and the good, and to which the darkness and the light are both alike.

(*c*)

EYE

"*If thine eye be single*" (Matt. vi. 22)

The eye which is sharp for self-interest is dimmed for moral insight. A *complexity* of motives betrays the sincere heart, and corrupts living Truth in its fountain. We all of us have felt the undeniable charm of singleness of purpose: it is simplicity, not complexity of character, which constitutes the talisman of influence over good and earnest spirits

　　"In wit a man, simplicity a child."

(*d*)　　　　　　*Jackson's Bampton Lectures*

EYES, OPENING OF

"*Ye shall be as gods, knowing good and evil*" (Gen. iii. 5).

It is the misery of man, that he arrives at understanding through the loss of innocence.

(*e*)　　　　　　　　　　　　*Ludwig Tieck*

EYES, THE SEVEN.

1. The Bible is the Book of books; the inspiration of Heaven. When John saw the Lamb with seven horns and seven eyes, in the midst of the Throne, he would at once conclude it was Divine. In the whole creation there was nothing like it. And the stone with seven eyes that Zerubbabel saw, could have been hewn from no earthly quarry. The scroll of the starry firmament has evidently been written by the Eternal Power, the traces of whose figures may be discerned in sun, moon, and stars. But in this Book we have something more. I thank God for human composition; but the Book of God lights up the whole with the dawn of everlasting life. I see that it has *seven eyes* ever looking out upon me.

(*f*)　　　　　　　　　　　*Christmas Evans*

2. I cannot often read, hear, or meditate upon it, without perceiving that the Great Eye of eternity, like a flame of fire, looks forth, as it were from another world. It lights up the mysteries of the immortal state, of the creation of the world and its invisible support. It leads me to the beginning of things; their fountain and cause. I feel placed, as it were, immediately under the eye of the eternal God, which is like a flame of fire. In its presence, I die, and yet live; I feel oppressed to the dust, and yet something at the same moment whispers: "Fear not; it is I, who was once dead, and behold I live." My heart melts in penitence, yet rejoices in faith; I am filled with fear and joy; I seek to hide myself, yet wish to abide in the light for ever!

(*g*)　　　　　　　　　　　　　　　*Ibid*

3. The Divine eye of Omniscience looks out upon me from every chapter and verse, doctrine and ordinance, of the Gospel. It searcheth me and knoweth me altogether, and vain is the attempt to conceal. The darkness and the light are

(*h*)

alike unto it. My darkest secrets are not hid from its gaze. Here, my character at every stage, before and after, my passing " from death unto life," is perfectly drawn. Even the future is fully known to it. We have here, centuries beforehand, prophecies which have been literally fulfilled. The gall mingled with the drink of Christ, and the lots cast for His vesture, were foretold. In the presence of this eye, I confess against myself my sins unto the Lord, and I am compelled to cry out for a clean heart and an upright spirit, and that I may be washed whiter than snow.

(a)   *Christmas Evans*

4. When, overwhelmed with a sense of corruption, I see before me " dark mountains " of trouble, and the terrors of the grave, the eye of infinite goodness, brighter than the Shekinah of old, glances upon me from the depths of eternity. It is the smile of the King Immortal from the throne of grace. I see in it free love, the infinite merits of Christ, riches of mercy and of grace, which compel me to look with amaze. I am made to listen to the still small voice that follows—a voice such as Elijah heard. It announces to me the mysteries of the Holy of Holies. " Lo, I come, in the volume of the Book it is written of me." " I came to seek and to save that which is lost." I rise from the depths of despair, and no longer " stumble upon the dark mountains."

(b)   *Ibid*

5. The infinite purity of God, like a consuming flame, looks out upon me from the doctrines of this Book, as it did to Israel from the midst of Sinai's fires, or as the great " I AM " appeared in the burning bush. " I exceedingly fear and quake." At the same time, I desire to behold the burning glory, because attempered with mercy. I take off my shoes, and draw near in all humility to the sight. Feeling that this eye is upon me, I cannot live in sin; yet it does not slay me. The Eternal Power with one hand hides me in the cleft of the Rock of Ages, and with the other points out the glory of a just God, who justifies through faith in Christ Jesus.

(c)   *Ibid*

6. In this Book I recognise an Eternal Power, which, like the eye of God Himself, penetrates everywhere. It is sharper than a two-edged sword.

Without my permission, it divides asunder soul and spirit, the joints and marrow. It searches my very bones; it unlocks the secrets of my heart; it sits as infallible judge upon all my actions and intents, making my whole being amenable to its law. Of this we have a striking example in the history of the Earl of Rochester, who, although a notorious sceptic, when he read the words : " He was wounded for our transgressions; He was bruised for our iniquities; the chastisement of our peace was upon Him, and with His stripes we are healed," was so wrought upon by their Divine power, that they agitated him body and soul, silenced every doubt and cavil, and inspired him in a minute with faith and love in Christ. So with many others. The dead who rose when Christ died, had no time to inquire how their inspiration came; the tide of life flowed in so mightily into the old channels of the grave, that they only rose upon the wave that bore them along. In like manner has the Gospel, which is mighty through God, wrought. So was Matthew, at the custom-house, called. The woman of Samaria at Jacob's well; the thief on the cross; the three thousand on the day of Pentecost; Saul of Tarsus, when he was met on the way; and the Philippian jailor ;—all obeyed the same power. It could be no more withstood than the great fiat : " Let there be " of the first creation !

(d)   *Ibid*

7. When I am sad and downcast, and unbroken silence reigns around me, I tread my lonely way; there is no one to hear my complaint, nor to whom I may open my bosom : none to give me comfort and counsel. Then, in the living words of the gospel, I feel that God is present, and that the Infinite Wisdom shines upon me through the clefts of my prison-house. I feel that He stands near me, and hears my sighing. He who notes the sparrow's fall, who clothes the lily of the field, and numbers the very hairs of my head, in all the richness of His grace and power is able to say to the comfortless, at the very gate of hell : " To-day shalt thou be with me in paradise." The fear of whatever hindrances there may be in the way from Calvary to the Heaven of heavens, is removed, —a long and perilous way, but as a single step to the " God made manifest in the flesh," " who leaps upon the mountains and skips upon the hills."

(e)   *Ibid*

F

FACE, THE HUMAN

There is in every human countenance either a history or a prophecy, which must sadden, or at least soften, every reflecting observer.

(a) *Coleridge*

That same face of yours looks like the title-page to a whole volume of roguery.

(b) *Colley Cibber*

Who cannot read that book?

(c) *Crabbe*

No more can you distinguish of a man
Than of his outward show: which God He knows,
Seldom or never jumpeth with the heart.

(d) *Shakspeare*

Oh, that deceit should dwell in such a gorgeous palace !

(e) *Ibid*

Oh, what a goodly outside falsehood hath !

(f) *Ibid*

A face without a heart.

(g) *Ibid*

FAIR

He loved her foul, that He might make her fair.
Augustine.—On Christ's love to His Church.

(h)

FAIRY QUEEN

I

The first book of Spenser's FAIRY QUEEN is deeply profound and allegorical. There is nothing in the language more worth reading. Spenser's letter to Raleigh explains it. Spenser, with Coleridge, says, " Nothing but religion will make a man a Christian."
The Armed Knight is not represented as a good man. He has to work out his own salvation. Many great failures : many dints on his armour.
Una = the Truth.
The wasted country = man's need, as despoiled by the Dragon of Evil.
The most imperfect teacher of the Truth, if in earnest, will do good. Notice this Knight, so untaught, is sent forth as the champion of Truth.
Una veiled, and only unveiled when about to be married, to signify that Truth is not easily to be got at.
The Dwarf, following directly after Truth, is Intellect.
Duessa = the double-faced, though she calls herself *Fida*, the faithful.
It is the beauty in evil that attracts us.

(i) *Geo. Macdonald*

II.

The Witch and her Daughter

Superstition and Abessa = the Clergy who are abettors (Monks and Nuns), who live by means of Kirk-rabin = church robbers. Una comes in, and is the cause of their being destroyed. = The power of Truth.
Truth uses no violence—it is the lion that destroys ; many of Truth's supporters must work violently.
Archimago deceiving Una fault in the allegory.
Sansloy and Archimago's fight = two false views clashing.

(j) *Ibid*

III

Canto IV

House of Pride—exquisite. Falsehood leads to the House of Pride.
We think most of ourselves when we have least to be proud of. Ignorance feeds Pride.
Gluttony has a long neck, to taste his food going down.
Duessa enclouds Sansloy, so that the Knight cannot slay him. Also she goes to his grandmother, Night, that she may help her child.
The Dwarf goes with the Knight, not with Una = the heart not right, therefore the head errs.

(k) *Ibid*

IV

" The Truth never forsakes a man."
The Lion and Una = The powers and the violences of Nature as the servants of Truth. Adverse sciences and so forth all help. Even the clever worldling is often apparently more the servant of Truth than her own children. Wordsworth's " Peter Bell " is a good commentary on this.

(l) *Ibid*

V

The Dwarf goes. Una is joined by Prince Arthur = a perfect man—finished. The Red Cross Knight was only a beginner.
See the description of the Prince's armour and helmet. (Canto 7.)

(m) *Ibid*

FAIRY QUEEN

Spenser, though assuredly one of the greatest poets that ever lived, could not succeed in the attempt to make allegory interesting. It was in vain that he lavished the riches of his mind on the House of Pride and the House of Temperance. One unpardonable fault, the fault of tediousness, pervades the whole of the " Fairy Queen." We become sick of cardinal virtues and deadly sins, and long for the society of plain men and women. Of the persons who read the first canto, not one in ten reaches the end of the first book, and not one in a hundred perseveres to the end of the poem. Very few, and very weary are those who are in at the death of the Blatant Beast.

(n) *Macaulay*

FAITH'S ANSWER

Will the Lord cast off for ever?	God forbid (Rom. xi. 1).

No; the Lord will not cast off His people (Ps. xciv. 14).

Will He be favourable any more?

Yes, He will; for though He cause grief, yet will He have compassion (Lam. iii. 32).

Is His mercy clean gone for ever?

No; His mercy endures for ever, as it *is from everlasting*, it *is to everlasting* (Ps. ciii. 17).

Does His promise fail for evermore?

No; it is impossible for God to lie (Heb. vi. 18).

Has God forgotten to be gracious?

No; He cannot deny Himself and His own name, which He hath proclaimed gracious and merciful (Exod. xxxiv. 6).

Has He in anger shut up His tender mercies?

No; they are new every morning (Lam. iii. 23). And therefore-

How shall I give thee up, Ephraim? (Hos. xi. 8, 9).

(a)					*Henry & Scott*

FAITH, THE COMMON

The common faith and country holiness, and week-day zeal, that are among people, will never bring men to heaven.

(b)					*Samuel Rutherford*

FAITH, EARNESTLY CONTEND FOR THE

A dog barks when any one seizes his master, and should I be silent when the truth of God is assailed?

(c)						*Calvin*

FAITH, DEFINITION OF

Faith is that strange faculty by which man feels the presence of the Invisible; exactly as some animals have the power of seeing in the dark. That is the difference between the Christian and the world.

(d)					*F. W. Robertson*

FAITH, GRACE, AND THE PROMISE

An inseparable connection, an absolutely necessary mutual relation, binds together πίστις, χάρις, καὶ ἐπαγγελία. Διὰ τοῦτο ἐκ πίστεως, ἵνα κατὰ χάριν, εἰς τὸ εἶναι βεβαίαν τὴν ἐπαγγελίαν (Rom. iv. 16). When, in any one point of this kind, anything is put out of place, the whole falls to the ground. To be found in Christ, means, not to have a self-righteousness springing out of the Law, but that which comes from faith in Christ. . . . The rock on which Israel split, and on which all pseudo-Christianity also splits, is the establishing a righteousness of their own, derived from the Law, in opposition to Rom. x. 3, 4: τέλος γὰρ νόμου Χριστὸς εἰς δικαιοσύνην παντὶ τῷ πιστεύοντι. If a man will have a righteousness, *not of faith, but of works*, then he will be dashed in pieces on the stone of stumbling, which is meant for the rock of salvation (Rom. ix. 32, 33).

(e)						*Harless*

FAITH AND FEELING

The ethical power of faith consists in this, that I pass out of myself, and beyond myself, and, contrary to all feeling and experience of life, hold fast to what is declared and promised me in the Word. There is much unnecessary talk about feelings of faith and experiences of faith. But whatever may be true therein, still that faith would be utterly unsound which should have no other guarantee of its certainty than the feelings and experiences of man, instead of that Word which cannot deceive. "Feeling is against faith, faith against feeling." "Faith is *not* experience, although we often experience that which we believe; but yet faith must always be put *before* experience." "Faith looks merely to the word or to the promise, *i.e.* to the truth."

(f)					*Luther and Harless*

FAITH AND FEELING

In feeling we take in; in faith we give out; and sense ofttimes makes us idle. While the bairn eateth an apple the book is laid by. But whether the spouse had feeling while Christ spake and knocked or not, yet the doctrine holdeth when Christ leaveth off to speak in His Word; and when to our feeling He is absent, we are often very humble in doing and seeking Him. When Christ is either not answering or giving rough answers, the woman of Canaan is then busiest, crying and again crying to Christ, following on, worshipping on her knees, disputing the matter hotly with Christ by force of reason to carry away her desires. So His Kirk (Cant. iii.), having lost Him, rises, seeks, and, better seeks in the streets, in the open gates, and about the walls: "Watchman, good watchman, saw ye Him whom my soul loveth?" And so was Mary Magdalene when her Lord was lost. What a din she made with watery eyes. She saith, "Angels, saw ye Him?" "Gardener, sir, have ye carried Him away?" "Grave, hast thou Him?" We, like fools, can complain, "He is away." Fye! "Now all is gone." Fye! Now say ye, "He is away. What will I do?" and ye cry black hunger. But if ye be carefully seeking Him, you are fatter now nor when ye were doated and feasted with His presence.

(g)					*Samuel Rutherford*

FAITH AND HOPE

Faith comes by hearing; hope by experience. Faith believeth the *truth* of the Word; hope waits for its fulfilment. Faith lays hold of that end of the promise that is *next* to us, viz., as it is in the Bible; hope lays hold of that end of the promise that is fastened to the mercy-seat. Thus faith and hope get hold of both ends of the promise, and carry ALL away! Faith fights for doctrine; hope, for a reward. Faith, for what is in the Bible; hope, for what is in heaven. Faith purifies the heart from bad principles; hope, from bad manners. Faith sets hope to work; hope sets patience to work." In a word, Bunyan might well close this discourse by saying to the reader, "Doth not all this make thy heart *twitter* after the mercy that is in God?"

(h)					*John Bunyan*

FAITH AND HOPE

A swallow in the spring
	Came to our granary, and 'neath the eaves
Essayed to make her nest, and there did bring
	Wet earth and straw and leaves.

(i)

Day after day she toiled
  With patient art; but, ere her work was crowned,
Some sad mishap the tiny fabric spoiled,
  And dashed it to the ground.

She found the ruin wrought;
  Yet, not cast down, forth from her place she
    flew,
And with her mate fresh earth and grasses brought,
  And built her nest anew.

But scarcely had she placed
  The last soft feather on its ample floor,
When wicked hands or chance again laid waste,
  And wrought the ruin o'er.

But still her heart she kept,
  And toiled again; and last night, hearing calls,
I looked, and lo! three little swallows slept
  Within the earth-made walls.

What trust is here, O man!
  Hath hope been smitten in its early dawn?
Have clouds o'ercast thy purpose, trust, or plan?
  Have faith, and struggle on.

(a) *Southey*

FAITH, HOPE, CHARITY

You may have strong, eagle-eyed faith: well, you will probably be enabled to do great things in life, to work wonders, to trample on impossibilities. You may have sanguine hope: well, your life will pass brightly, not gloomily. But the vision of God as He is, to see the King in His beauty, is vouchsafed not to science, nor to talent, but only to purity and love. "Blessed are the pure in heart, for they shall see God." "If we love one another, God dwelleth in us, and His love is perfected in us."

(b) *F. W. Robertson*

FAITH, HOPE, AND PATIENCE COMPARED

1. *Patience* comes with a broad back: It can bear anything—contumely, lies, defamations, etc. It is of grim aspect, marked with lines of endurance—*it can wait* and *bear*: says, "I can do all things through Christ who strengtheneth me." Job and Lazarus = examples. When it began to bear burdens it tottered; now the back is stronger, it has been bearing its burden for years, and as the burden got heavier the back grew stronger. Thus patience does not come to God empty-handed, but it brings something—a broad strong back.

2. *Hope* comes next, and with great *expectations:* "*Hope* on, hope ever"; "*Hope* maketh not ashamed"; "remember Thy word unto Thy servant upon which Thou hast caused me to *hope*"; Joseph, Jonah, the Jews sustained by hope. And

"Hope springs eternal in the human breast."

In the soul's "Via dolorosa"; in its "De Profundis," it says "In Thy word do I *hope*."
  Therefore hope likewise does not come empty-handed; but—
3. *Faith* comes with nothing: simple faith is empty-handed—no broad back; no great expectations; it is the substance of things hoped for. "Nothing in my hand I bring."
  Abraham staggered not through unbelief. God said, "Go," and he went, not knowing whither; "Offer Isaac," and he proceeded to do it.

Habakkuk also *believed*, when there was literally no external sign of the promise being fulfilled.
  The *Psalmist* said, "Over Philistia have I cast my shoe," meaning conquest; and proceeded to apportion out the land, as if really conquered.
  Thus, while *patience* can endure anything, and *hope* sustains us, yet *faith* is more wonderful still. And this is what we want, and what we lack. It is the coin of the Kingdom of Heaven. Pay down faith, and God will give you a suitable return. "All things are possible to him that believeth;" but "without faith it is impossible to please God." As to its degree, it is like earthly coin: a little money will not do for large transactions in the city, neither will "*little faith*" go far with the transactions between you and God.

(c)

FAITH, JUSTIFYING

2. *Faith, Justifying*, is a confidence in that which one hopes for, an evidence of things not seen (Heb. xi. 1). Our faith should never lean upon the present and visible, but on the comfortable promise alone, which lifts us above the present and makes us confident of the future. The nature of Justifying Faith is this (Rom. v. 10, 11). Not belief of the facts of salvation merely, is Justifying Faith; but to believe that, not for the sake of my faith, but for the sake of these acts, God in Christ is gracious to me, and forgives my sins. Justifying Faith is the answer to the Saviour's question, πιστεύετε ὅτι δύναμαι τοῦτο ποιῆσαι; and commits itself to the gracious promise of the Lord. "Faith is, and means, not a mere abstract idea of God, that He was born of the Virgin, suffered, was crucified, rose again, ascended into heaven; but such a heart as comprehends in itself and embraces the Son of God, according to the tenour of these words, and holds for a certainty that God has given up His only-begotten Son *for us*, and has so loved us that we, for His sake shall not be lost, but have everlasting life." Believing in Christ is not believing that Christ is a Person who is God and man, *for that would help no man in any way;* but that this very person is Christ—i.e., that He *for our sakes* has come forth from God, etc.

(d) *Harless and Luther*

FAITH, JUSTIFYING, AND CONSCIENCE

The preaching of faith is a preaching to the "*alarmed conscience*." Hence an inseparable connection between repentance and faith, turning *from* sin and turning *to* holiness, Mark i. 15; Acts iii. 19; xx. 21; xxvi. 20; 2 Cor. vii. 10. The drawing of the Father, who strikes the conscience by the Law, prepares the soul for faith in the Son. Thus true faith is not arrived at without the most definite moral self-knowledge (Rom. iii. 20). Hence Christ and His work appertain only to those who are in a state of alarm; the Law, the threatenings, terrors, and so forth, only to those who fancy themselves secure."

(e) *Luther and Harless*

FAITH AND KNOWLEDGE

Faith is the fruit of clear and definite knowledge. . . . "It is nothing else than wisdom and prudence; it dictates, distinguishes, teaches, and is

(f)

science and knowledge," the γνῶσις Ἰησοῦ Χριστοῦ, "In whom are hid all the treasures of wisdom and knowledge (Col. ii. 3). But this knowledge, which is of faith, has nothing in common with that which puffeth up (1 Cor. viii. 1, 2). Nothing with those learned discourses of human wisdom (1 Cor. ii. 13); earthly, sensual, devilish (Jas. iii. 15); a wisdom not born of the Spirit of God, which shuns nothing more than, "if any man among you seemeth to himself to be wise in this world, let him become a fool, that he may be wise: for the wisdom of this world is foolishness with God" (1 Cor. iii. 18, 19). To all this, the knowledge which comes by faith is *the very opposite,*—it comes through Jesus Christ (Phil i. 9–11), not knowledge for the sake of knowledge.

(*a*)   *Harless and Luther*

FAITH AND KNOWLEDGE

Those who are Christians, without the knowledge of prophecies or evidence, do yet form as good a judgment of their religion as those who possess this knowledge. They judge of it by the heart, as others judge by the understanding. It is God Himself who inclines them to believe; and hence their faith is of the most effectual kind.

(*b*)   *Blaise Pascal*

FAITH AND LIFE

For modes of faith let graceless zealots fight,
His can't be wrong whose life is in the right.
(*c*)   *Pope*

FAITH, THE LINK BETWEEN GOD AND MAN

Religion is the true philosophy,
Faith is the last great link 'twixt God and man.
There is more wisdom in a whispered prayer
Than in the ancient lore of all the schools:
The soul upon its knees holds God by the hand,
Worship is wisdom as it is in heaven;
"I do believe! Help thou mine unbelief!"
Is the last greatest utterance of the soul.
(*d*)   *Bigg*

FAITH, NECESSITY OF

Faith's necessity is never in a fair day known aright; but now I miss nothing so much as faith. Hunger in me runneth to fair and sweet promises; but when I come, I am like a hungry man that wanteth teeth, or a weak stomach having a sharp appetite, that is filled with the very sight of meat; or like one stupified with cold under the water, that would fain come to land, but cannot grip anything cast to him: I can let Christ grip me; but I cannot grip Him; I love to sit on Christ's knee; but I cannot set my feet to the ground, for afflictions bring the cramp upon my faith. All I now do, is, to hold out a lame faith to Christ, like a beggar holding out a stump, instead of an arm or leg; and cry, Lord Jesus, work a miracle. Oh, what would I give to have hands and arms, to grip strongly, and fold heartsomely about Christ's neck, and to have my claim made good with real possession. I think my love to Christ hath feet in abundance, and runneth swiftly to be at Him, but it wanteth hands and fingers to apprehend Him.

(*e*)   *Samuel Rutherford*

FAITH, OVERCOMING (1 John v. 4; 1 Cor. xiii.)

"This is the victory that overcometh the world, even our faith."

No man can conquer the world except by faith: no man can resemble God, except by love. It was by faith that St. Paul removed mountains of impossibility; it was by love that he became like God.

(*f*)   *F. W. Robertson*

FAITH, POSSIBILITIES OF

In prayer, it is faith that must make us successful; in obedience, it is faith that must make us cheerful; in afflictions, it is faith that must make us patient; in trials, it is faith that must make us resolute; in desertions, it is faith that must make us comfortable; in life, it is faith which must make us fruitful; and in death, it is faith which must make us victorious.

(*g*)   *Clarke*, 1642

FAITH, POWER OF

"Have faith in God."

The Psalmist =
"The Lord of Hosts is with us, the God of Jacob is our refuge."
"The Lord is on my side; I will not fear what man doeth unto me."

St. Paul = "If God be for us, who can be against us?"

It has been the Christian martyrs' talisman ever since.

Lord Bacon = "Man, when he resteth and assureth himself upon Divine protection and favour, gathereth a force and faith which human nature in itself could not obtain." And concerning the want of this faith he says, "As Atheism is in all respects hateful, so in this—that it depriveth human nature of the means to exalt itself above frailty."

(*h*)   *W. Jackson's Bampton Lectures*

Bishop Hall has only overstated a fundamental fact when he says, "There is *no* faith where there is either means or hope." Means and hopes may be "mixed with faith," but undoubtedly the mightiest deliverances ever wrought have been by faith alone. Difficulties and apparent impossibilities are the food on which faith feeds. *Abraham believed God.*

(*i*)

FAITH, POWER OF (Luke xvii.)

Faith is a miracle-worker. God's will is supreme, and the only factor in what is done in earth and heaven.

Faith allies itself to God's will—lays hold of the omnipotent arm of God; hence faith itself becomes omnipotent: it doeth wonders. "All things are possible" to it. It says to *this mountain*, etc. It is not the omnipotence of faith, but the *omnipotence* of God.

(*j*)   *Cf. Harless and Godet*

FAITH AND REASON

Nothing is so consistent with reason as the disclaiming of reason in matters of faith : and nothing so repugnant to reason as the disclaiming of reason in things which belong not to the province of faith.

Faith says many things on which the senses are silent ; but nothing which the senses deny. It is above them, but never contradicts them.

(a) *Blaise Pascal*

FAITH, THE RIGHTEOUSNESS OF

" *The righteousness of faith* " (Rom. iv. 13).

" *The righteousness of God which is by faith of Jesus Christ unto all and upon all them that believe : for there is no difference* " (Rom. iii. 22).

Doctrine : = Justification by faith

Importance of this doctrine : Abraham, David, Paul, as examples.

The Reformation in the 16th century rested upon this doctrine.

It is the doctrine of a standing or falling Church. And at the present time part of the great struggles in the Church arises from a departure from this teaching.

It may have been abused in the past. It used to be preached as if it were the whole of Christian teaching, whereas it is only the *beginning*, foundation ; but its importance will never lessen. For as often as a man comes asking the way of salvation, this is the answer : " Believe," etc.

(b)

FAITH, WHAT IS JUSTIFYING

1. A Faith in God's Word which is followed by obedience

Faith cometh by hearing ; but not by hearing only shall we be justified.

Obedience is necessary = subjection of our *will* to God's in the matter of Salvation. Perhaps we have some other way of Salvation.

(i.) *Our Lord* = " This is the work of God. *believe* on Him . . . . sent."

(ii.) *He also tells* us that where the Gospel does no good, it is because—

1. " Ye would not."

2. " We will not have this Man to reign over us."

3. " Ye will not come to Me that ye might have life."

Stephen.—" Ye do always resist the Spirit of the Holy One."

St. Paul.—1. " All have not *obeyed* the Gospel."

2. " All day long have I stretched out My hands to a disobedient and gainsaying people."

Clearly, then, *faith*, which is followed by *obedience*, is the first element in justifying faith.

(c)

2. True, justifying faith is not of ourselves

It is through grace that we believe in the *grace* of God.

Eph. ii. 8.—" By grace ye are saved, through faith, and that not of yourselves, *it is the gift of God.*

God's grace and love = the source ; faith the instrument ; both His gift.

Hence the meaning of the prayer :—

" *Lord, I believe, help Thou mine unbelief.*"

Jesus.—" No one can come to Me, except the Father, who hath sent Me, draw him.

= The origin of our coming to Christ is of God.

Paul.—" Faith cometh by hearing, and hearing by the word of God " = not the outward occasion, but when the word preached is made effectual through the operation of the Spirit of God.

Luther.—Justifying faith = not *human assent*, but a powerful, *vivifying* thing, which immediately works a change in the man, and makes him a new creature, and leads him to an entirely new and altered mode of life and conduct.

Acts xv.—" *Purifying their hearts by faith.*"

Hence justifying faith is a Divine work.

(d)

3. Justifying faith is an act of appropriation

On God's side, *Grace*.

On our side, *Faith*.

(i.) *It must be so.*

The *Gospel* = a *promise* of acquittal for the sinner, pronounced by God's own Word ; not a *demand*, and a duty to be performed—that is LAW.

The two things are wholly different. " The Law is not of faith," and the Gospel is not of doing.

" To him that worketh not, but believeth on Him who justifieth the ungodly, his faith is reckoned for righteousness."

(ii.) *Note the inseparable connection, and the absolutely necessary relation* between—

FAITH, GRACE, AND PROMISE (in the 16th verse).

The promise of forgiveness could not be *sure* on any other ground but that of *faith* resulting from the *Grace* of God.

N.B.—This righteousness of faith = the Rock of stumbling for *self-righteous people*, who go about to establish a righteousness of their own, which, if a man will have, he will be dashed to pieces on the Rock meant only for his salvation = " *a savour of life or of death.*"

(e)

4. Justifying faith is a faith of knowledge

But not common knowledge = *inspiration* = more than knowledge.

(i.) The Gospel is for an *alarmed conscience—The Law, for the secure.* (Turning *from* and turning *to*.)

Saving faith is only arrived at through definite self-knowledge.

The late gifted authoress, Geo. Elliot, said,—

" There is nothing against Christianity but its want of *evidence*."

= The spirit of our day = God unknowable.

(ii.) *N.B. The New Testament Teaching* : = that *faith and knowledge are inseparable*.

1. The disciples = " We believe and are *sure* that Thou art," etc.

2. Paul = " I *know* whom I have trusted."

3. John = " We have known and believed."

4. Luther = FAITH = wisdom — it dictates, distinguishes, teaches, and is science and knowledge.

Paul calls it " the knowledge of Christ."

Peter bids us " grow in grace and in the knowledge of Christ."

Paul again says, Christians " are enriched by Him in all knowledge."

(f)

" For in Him are hid all the treasures of wisdom and knowledge."

Christ is made unto us "wisdom, and righteousness, and sanctification, and redemption."

But it is not the *wisdom* of *Books*, *Schools*, and *Colleges* and Teachers of human wisdom. For in regard to that He says :—

" If any man among you seemeth to be wise in this world, let him become a fool, that he may be wise, for the wisdom of this world is foolishness with God."

(iii.) *But though real knowledge*, it is not an exhaustive knowledge. It is knowledge in part. There are depths " past finding out."

" The unsearchable riches of Christ."

To know the love of Christ which " passeth knowledge."

Yet faith is a confidence in things hoped for, an evidence of things not seen.

Luther.—*Faith* makes Christ ours, and His love makes us His ; and this when rightly apprehended is real knowledge, and carries its own evidence.

(a)

5. Justifying faith puts man into a new relation to God

Once he thought to deserve and to earn God's favour ; now he accepts it as a gift.

And more than this :

It is not merely a treasure given at the first, which he might hope to keep and retain by good conduct.

It acts in a twofold way :

(i.) *Confirms* the Law (conduct will never deserve it).

(ii.) Repels assaults of conscience, drives away despair. Since it requires us daily to comfort ourselves that this alone is the ground of our justification.

And God knows how much we stand in need of this comfort.

Only he who = " O wretched man," etc., knows what the comfort of the Gospel is. And throughout life this sun rises daily ; disperses clouds, chases away night and darkness, and lights up the whole day.

(b)   *Cf. Godet*

FAITH AND SALVATION

Faith hath made thee whole.—A man once dreamed that he was in a deep pit, sinking fast in the mire—feet, knees, body, neck, gone down beneath the surface—when he heard a voice, " *Look up.*" Looking up, he saw a star ; and, while gazing at it, he began to rise. Then, congratulating himself on his escape, he turned his eyes from the star to himself ; and immediately he began to sink again. All efforts of his own to rise but sank him deeper ; and when almost gone he again heard the voice, " *Look up.*" Then, once more gazing at the heavenly star, he began to rise higher and higher, till he was almost free ; then, turning to help himself, and to remove the mire clinging to him, he forgot to look up, and again he sank. Once more the voice came, " *Look up ; for only while you look, you rise.*" And looking steadfastly, he rose from the mire, and was saved.

(c)

FAITH, SAVING.

The faith which saves is summed up in the words of St. Paul : "Who loved me, and gave Himself for me."

(d)

Faith builds a bridge from this world to the next.

(e)   *Dr. Young*

FAITH, THE SHIELD OF (Eph. vi. 16)

The concern is, that the whole person be covered as indeed faith entirely covers and defends the Christian : as God's gift effecting salvation (ii. 8) [MEYER : *fides salvifica*], bringing about forgiveness of sins in the past (i. 7), affording for every moment access to God (iii. 12), assuring in advance of eternal life, by securing to us the gift of the Holy Ghost (i. 13, 14), rendering holy and without blame (i. 4). Cf. Rom. viii. 14–16, 31–39. Man's own holiness is not a shield for him, as in Wisdom, v. 20 ; God's holiness is his shield ; God Himself is our shield (Gen. xv. 1 ; Ps. xviii. 31 ; Prov. xxx. 5 ; 1 Pet. v. 9 ; 1 John v. 4).

(f)   *Schenkel*

FAITH, THREE KINDS OF (John iv. 46, etc.)

1. Three kinds of Belief

(i.) Credo Deum = " I believe that God is " ;

(ii.) Credo Deo = " I believe God is true " ;

(iii.) Credo in Deum = " I believe in God," *i.e.*, put my *trust* in Him.

For the (a) St. James " The devils *believe* and tremble." Cf. also Simon Magnus.

(b) = the Faith of *conviction*, as when multitudes believed in Jesus when they saw His miracles.

(c) = The *Faith of Job* : " Though He slay me, yet will I put my trust in Him." This = faith of love, " which many waters cannot quench."

2. All three kinds of Faith illustrated in this Miracle

(i.) The nobleman's faith in coming to Christ ;

(ii.) His faith in obeying the word of Christ ;

(iii.) His faith absolute and unshaken.

Learn from this, that there is a

(i.) Faith which *draws* men to Christ as Mediator = " He is " ;

(ii.) Faith in His *gracious* character : from report, or the Word ;

(iii.) Faith which is *saving* and joy-producing, arising from heartfelt experience.

Again :

(i.) Faith taught by the light of nature = " Have not all heard ? " (Rom. i.).

(ii.) Faith which cometh from hearing = " The hearing of faith " ;

(iii.) Faith inwrought by the Holy Ghost, which is not of ourselves, " It is the gift of God."

Further :

(i.) The faith of childhood, at the mother's knee = simple :

(ii.) The faith of riper years, proceeding from inquiry ;

(iii.) The faith of experience = the result of testing, and found solid, perhaps by means of

(g)

trouble, in which God = a sure Refuge = " approved in Christ," like Apelles.

Once more :

(i.) Faith = a seed sown = a day of small things = His coming to Christ ;

(ii.) Faith = as a blade of grass = growing = His obedience ;

(iii.) Faith = the fruit = His family believed.

3. (i.) It is not enough to believe there is a God, as the Deist does ;

(ii.) It is not enough to believe that God saves other people, and has saved *some*, such as Paul, David, Abraham, and other saints ;

(iii.) But faith must be personal, real, and an actual thing. Conviction carried on to appropriation, that says with Thomas : " *My* Lord, and *my* God."

4. Note the Priestly Character of the head of a Family

(i.) " And his whole house," so of Cornelius.

(ii.) God reckons the children as part of the parent : " Else were your children unclean, but now are they holy " (1 Cor.).

See also NOAH and his family.

JOB : " Thus did Job continually."

LOT might have saved all his family—" Hast thou any here," etc.

(a)

[John iv. 46–54]

1. Capernaum as the centre of interest.

2. Cana as the centre of interest.

3. Result = a *double miracle* :

(i.) The *son* was cured of his sickness.

(ii.) The *father* was cured of his unbelief.

4. Lessons from this miracle :

(i.) *Three kinds of faith :* Coming, obeying, absolute trust.

(ii.) How some people are brought to Christ : By a dying child.

(iii.) *Special application* to Christians at all times =

(a) *Capernaum* = earth the scene of our trouble.

(b) CANA = Heaven, where Jesus is.

(c) Our business is to establish a connection between the two = a Jacob's ladder.

(b)

FAITH OF UNBELIEVERS

O women, O men, great is your infidel faith !

(c) Carlyle

FAITH THE WORK OF GOD

Question = Τί ποιῶμεν, ἵνα ἐργαζώμεθα τὰ ἔργα τοῦ Θεοῦ ;

Answer = Τοῦτό ἐστι τὸ ἔργον τοῦ Θεοῦ, ἵνα πιστεύσητε εἰς ὃν ἀπέστειλεν ἐκεῖνος (John vi. 28, 29).

" Here God will so have it, that this shall be called His work, and true service—that thou shouldest believe on Christ. He speaks consequently of *the work that we are to perform,* viz., to believe. For this is to be the right *conduct, work, life,* and *merit,* wherewith God will be honoured and served. Without faith God accepts nothing as a service done to Him.

(d) Luther

FAITHFUL

Among the faithless, faithful only he.

(e) Milton

FAITHFUL IN COMMON DUTIES

Philip Henry one day, calling upon a tanner, found him so busy tanning a hide that he was not aware of his approach until he tapped him on the back : " Sir, I am ashamed you should find me thus." Philip Henry replied, " Let Christ, when He comes, find me equally faithful in the duties of my calling."

(f)

By the translation of Enoch and Elijah God showed how men should have left the world if they had not sinned—not by death, but by a glorious translation.

(g) Matthew Henry

FAITHFUL UNTO DEATH

The last will and testament of Dr. Rowland Taylor, parson of Hadleigh (burned at Hadleigh, Suffolk, Feb. 9th, 1555). " I say to my wife and to my children, The Lord gave you unto me ; and the Lord hath taken me from you and you from me : blessed be the name of the Lord. I believe that they are blessed which die in the Lord. God careth for sparrows, and for the hairs of our heads. I have ever found Him more faithful and favourable than is any father or husband. Trust ye, therefore, in him, by the means of our dear Saviour Christ's merits : believe, love, fear, and obey him, pray to Him, for He hath promised to help. Count me not dead, for I shall certainly live, and never die. I go before and you shall follow after, to our long home. I go to the rest of my children, Susan, George, Ellen, Robert, and Zachary. I have bequeathed you to the only Omnipotent. I say to my dear friends of Hadleigh, and to all others which have heard me preach, that I depart hence with a quiet conscience, as touching my doctrine, for the which, I pray you, thank God with me. For I have, after my little talent, declared to others those lessons that I gathered out of God's book, the blessed Bible. Therefore, if I, or an angel from heaven, should preach to you any other Gospel than that ye have received, God's great curse be upon that preacher. Beware for God's sake, that ye deny not God ; neither decline from the word of faith, lest God decline from you, and so do ye everlastingly perish. For God's sake beware of Popery ; for, though it appear to have in it unity, yet the same is vanity and anti-Christianity, and not in Christ's faith and unity. Beware of the sin against the Holy Ghost, now, after such a light opened so plainly and simply, truly, thoroughly, and generally to all England. The Lord grant all men His good and Holy Spirit, increase of His wisdom, contemning the wicked world, hearty desire to be with God and the heavenly company, through Jesus Christ, our only Mediator, Advocate, righteousness, life, sanctification, and hope. Amen, amen. Pray, pray." (Signed), ROWLAND TAYLOR, departing hence in sure hope, without all doubting, of eternal salvation, I thank God, my Heavenly Father, through Jesus Christ, my certain Saviour. Amen. The 5th of Febry, Anno 1555.

(h)

Faithful unto Death

A shepherd had driven part of his flock to a neighbouring fair, leaving his dog to watch the remainder during that day and the next night, expecting to revisit them the next morning. Circumstances prevented his returning home till the morning of the third day. His first inquiry was whether the dog had been visited. The answer was, "No." "Then he must be dead!" replied the shepherd, with a tone and gesture of anguish, "for I know he was too faithful to desert his charge." He instantly repaired to the heath. The dog had just sufficient strength remaining to crawl to his master's feet and express his joy at his return, and almost immediately after expired. "Be *thou* faithful unto death."

(a)

Faithful Saying, A

Once upon a time the devil came to me and said, "Luther, you are a great sinner, and you will be damned." "Stop," said I, "one thing at a time, I am a great sinner; that is true, though you have no right to tell me of it. I confess it. What next? 'Therefore you will be damned.' That is not good reasoning. It is true I am a great sinner, but it is written: 'Jesus Christ came to save sinners,' therefore I shall be saved." So I cut the devil off with his own sword; and he went away mourning because he could not cast me down by calling me a sinner.

(b) *Luther*

FAITHFULNESS

"*Whatsoever ye do, do it heartily, as to the Lord, and not unto men. . . . For ye serve the Lord Christ*" (Col. iii. 23, 24).

"It is related that when Phidias, the great sculptor, who carved statues for one of the great temples of antiquity, was labouring with minute fidelity upon the hair on the back of the head of one of the historic figures which was to be elevated from the pavement to the very apex of the building, or placed among the frieze, some one expostulated with him, saying, "Why do you take such pains with the hair? It will never be seen." His simple reply was, "*The gods will see it.*"

So he laboured thoroughly in the minutest things, not for the eye of man, but for the eyes of the gods.

(c) *H. W. Beecher*

Faithfulness of God

"*Faithful is He that calleth you*" (1 Thess. v. 24). In-
1. *Calling ;* 2. *Keeping.*
So in
1. *Creation ;* 2. *Providence.*

Cf. Ps. xxxvii. 5, "Commit thy way unto the Lord; trust also in Him; and He shall bring it to pass" with Ps. xxii. 31, "*He hath done this.*"

(d)

"*God is faithful*" (1 Cor. i. 8, 9)

Is the promise of verse 8 absolute or conditional? . . . If this promise be of any value, it is the fact that it furnishes a guarantee against that greatest of dangers, the fickleness of the human will (hence its special reference to the Corinthians). It were better therefore to take the promise *absolutely.* "Those to whom God gives the renewing influences of the Spirit, He thereby pledges Himself to save; for the "first-fruits of the Spirit" are of the nature of a pledge (*Hodge*). . . . God will not drop the work He has begun, after the fashion of weak inconstant men; but, persevering in love, He will carry out that which was commenced in love, even unto its goal (Phil. i. 6; 1 Thess. v. 24; 2 Thess. iii. 3; Rom. xi. 29).

Here, on this fidelity of God, and not on the strength of the believer's purpose to persevere, nor on any assumption that the principles of religion in their hearts was indestructible, was the confidence of the Apostle grounded (*Hodge*). This faithfulness of God is pledged in three directions:
1. To Himself, in the purpose formed.
2. To Christ, in the covenant made with Him (Isa. liii.).
3. To believers.

(e) *Lange*

Faithfulness of God, The

You may be faint and weary, but my God cannot. I may fluctuate and alter as to my frames and feelings; but my Redeemer is unchangeably the same always. I might utterly fail and come to nothing, if left to myself. But I cannot be so left to myself; for the Spirit of truth has said, "I will never leave thee nor forsake thee." He will renew my strength, either by changing my weakness into strength or by enduing me with His own power. He is wise to foresee and provide for all my dangers. He is rich to relieve and succour me in all my wants. He is faithful to perfect and perform all His promises. He is blessed and immortal, to enrich my poor desponding soul with blessedness and immortality. Oh, what a great and glorious Saviour for such a mean and worthless sinner! Oh, what a bountiful and indulgent friend for such a base and insignificant rebel! What, what am I, when I compare myself and all I am of myself, with what I can conceive of my God, and of what He hath kindly promised to me? What a mystery I am to myself, and to men! a denizen of earth to become a star of heaven; a corruptible sinner made an incorruptible saint; a rebel made a child; an outlaw an heir; a deserver of hell made an inheritor of heaven; a stronghold of the devil changed into a temple of the living God; an enemy and a beggar exalted to a throne, united in friendship with God, made one with Christ, a possessor of His Spirit, and a sharer of all this honour, happiness, and glory for evermore; oh, what manner, what matter of love is this! Lord, take my heart, my soul, my all! I can render Thee no more: I could render Thee no less. It is, indeed, a poor return! my body and my soul are but as two mites; and yet, glory to Thy great Name! Thou who didst esteem those of the poor widow, wilt not despise these of mine."

(f) *Ambrose Serle*

FAITHFULNESS OF GOD AND FINAL PERSEVERANCE

" Faithful is He that calleth you, who also will do it " (1 Thess. v. 24)

Note 1. *The apostle's concluding prayer :*—"And may your whole spirit and soul and body be kept blameless unto the coming of our Lord Jesus Christ."

2. *His conviction that they will be so kept.* "Faithful is He that calleth you, who also will do it."

In which words we note that—

(i.) These Christians had received a call into the Christian status and position of "No condemnation in Jesus Christ ; " and that their obeying that " call " constituted the beginning, so far as they personally were concerned, of their spiritual life.

(ii.) That this beginning would eventually attain to glorification hereafter through the successive stages of justification and sanctification.

(iii.) But that their **final perseverance** did not depend upon any inherent grace received in conversion (at least he does not assert this), but on the **faithfulness of God.**

1. Notice that our ground of confidence, in being kept unto the end, is not in any **decree of God** that we should be so kept, and whereby He elected us in eternity past, called us in time, and will finally glorify us hereafter. Which decree can in no wise be resisted and rendered of no effect by us.

This idea, though, perhaps, not quite so plainly expressed, preposterous as it may seem, is nevertheless one which some persons seem to hug to themselves, as their great sheet-anchor of comfort ; and are in no-wise disposed to let go of it, seeing that, as they say, it is the teaching of more than one passage of Scripture.

But wherever it may be found, we do not find such teaching here, and this certainly is not the ground of the Apostle's conviction that these Christians would be *preserved unto the end.*

2. Nor is the ground of confidence to be found in any supposed **inherent grace of regeneration** (there may be such, but it is not insisted upon here).

(i.) Nature is against it. All seeds that are sown do not come up, nor do all that come up eventually come to maturity. Many blossoms that appear in the spring drop off and leave no sign of fruit behind them ; whilst again, of those that are fruitful, only a few comparatively survive the rigours of the climate and ripen.

(ii.) In the field of grace there are indications of the operation of the same law. The barren fig-tree stood in the vineyard, and yet was cut down because it cumbered the ground.

St. Paul exhorteth the Corinthians not to " receive the grace of God in vain." Evidently then grace can be received in vain ; and all experience shows us that many do fall away and bring no fruit to perfection, showing that the final perseverance of the Christian rests upon some other ground than that of an inherent grace.

3. In the text which we have more immediately to deal with, it is made to rest upon the **faithfulness of God.**

(i.) *Faithful to His promise :* God's word to the Christian cannot be broken—" He is faithful that promised " and His promise stands—" I will never leave thee nor forsake thee ; " " Heaven and earth shall pass away, but My word shall never pass away." Therefore, we conclude that where God has begun a good work, and given His promise, there we have the assurance that He will carry it on unto a successful end.

" Commit thy way unto Him " (adds the Psalmist), thy way in life—thy way unto everlasting life—thy whole life, " *and He shall bring it to pass.*"

(ii.) Again, the final perseverance of the Christian rests upon the **unchangeableness of God and the Saviour.**

Old Testament = " I am the Lord, I change not, therefore ye sons of Jacob are not consumed."

New Testament = " Jesus Christ, the same yesterday, and to-day, and for ever."

His love is not a capricious thing, it is not given and withdrawn, but it is pledged to the Christian. " Having loved His own, He loved them unto the end."

(iii.) Further, **the ultimate salvation of the Christian is in the hands of his Saviour ; and work in His hands cannot be thwarted by counter agencies.**

He is the Good Shepherd who leaveth not His sheep in peril. For the Christian's salvation He died ; and for the tempted Christian's safety He interposes Himself—ever on the watch against our peril—He " prays for us that our faith fail not ; " " I pray for them ; " " Father, keep them whom Thou hast given Me," and such prayer is all-prevailing.

In addition to this, we have the fact of His **ever living** to make intercession for all who come unto God by Him.

Who shall condemn ? Who shall separate us from His love ? asks the great apostle.

1. It is Christ that died,
2. Yea, that is risen again,
3. And who is even at the right hand of God,
4. Who also maketh intercession for us.

Here is a four-fold cord, which no created power can break, and which guarantees the Christian a safe passage through the waves of this troublesome world unto glory. Therefore, because we have set our love upon Him, and because we come to Him in prayer, saying, " Deliver us from evil," from the peril unseen by us, and which may wreck our ship, He has pledged Himself to deliver us, and to save us to the very uttermost.

But this strong assurance rests not upon anything *in* us, nor upon any inherent grace of conversion, nor upon any decree of God, but upon the **faithfulness of our God and Saviour Jesus Christ.**

" Janet," said a Scotch minister to a Christian woman of great faith, whom he was visiting, " suppose, after all, God were to let you drop into hell ! "

" Even as He likes," was her reply ; " but if He does, He will lose mair than I'll do."

This was a true witness. God cannot break His word. She relied upon the **faithfulness of God.**

The Final Perseverance of the Christian—a subject which has ever caused bitter controversies amongst Christian people—is, in our text at least, taken out of the region of controversy, and made a practical fact, for it depends on the **perseverance of the Saviour and on the faithfulness of God.** Not my perseverance but His perseverance ; not my faithfulness but His faithfulness. If we had no ever-living Saviour to pilot our ship, no promise on which to rely, we *might* have cause for fear ; but " His faithfulness and truth shall be thy

(a)

shield and buckler." Wherefore, let all who are distressed on this account commit their souls unto Him, as unto a **Faithful Creator and Saviour.** Our salvation depends not upon what we are, but upon what He is.

(a)

FALL, THE

The Fall was not the apex of all sin, but the root of all sins. The sentence pronounced was not, "Thou shalt be put to death," but "Thou shalt die," not an arbitrary punishment, but the necessary consequence of the transgression.

(b) *Delitzsch*

There are two maxims of faith, equally unalterable; the one, that man, in his state of creation or of grace, is raised above all nature, made like unto God, and a partaker of the Divinity; the other, that man, in his state of corruption and sin, is fallen from this elevation to a level with the beasts.

(c) *Blaise Pascal*

The chasm between the sinful creature and the Holy One recognised, guarded; hollowed deeper and deeper through the centuries by man's sin, by deeper revealings of the Divine holiness; yet always, on the other side of that chasm, infinite pity. Man choosing to be "as gods," instead of to be like God, and with God; and losing God and the likeness to Him together; choosing to be the centre of the universe, and by that choice becoming a mere atom in the midst of a chaos; falling and dying inwardly with the loss of God. Love changing into selfish passion; aspiration into ambition. Still God seeking, speaking; pronouncing the sentence, yet promising, recalling; closing the spoiled Paradise, yet opening a Tabernacle in the wilderness, a Temple and Holy Place among thorns and thistles.

(d) *Anon*

Fall into Sin

The best of us may fall into the worst sin, without God's grace, and with it the worst of us may be made holy and happy.

(e) *Sunday at Home*

But as nothing will prevent the ruin of impenitent sinners, so believers will surely smart for and by their own inventions, when they commit iniquity, though the Saviour's intercession prevents their final condemnation.

(f) *Henry and Scott*

Fall, Effects of the

Good princes easily obtain good subjects; not so easily good subjects good princes. Thus Adam, in the state of innocence, ruled over animals, all tame and gentle, till, simply through his means, they fell and grew savage.

(g) *J. P. F. Richter*

Fall Down and Worship Me (Matt. iv.; Luke iv.).

If at great things thou would'st arrive,
Get riches first, get health, and treasure heap,
Not difficult, if thou hearken to me;
Riches are mine, fortune is in my hand,
They whom I favour thrive in wealth amain,
While virtue, valour, wisdom, sit in want.

(h) *Milton*

FALSE CHRISTS

The popular idea of the Messiah receives illustration from the writings of Josephus, and is realized in such men as the Sorcerer, who, during the procuratorship of Fadus, persuaded the great mass of the people to take up their property and follow him to the river Jordan, saying that he would divide the river by his command, and give them an easy passage, and thereby deceiving many. Or the Egyptian, who likewise persuaded the people that he was a prophet, and led thirty thousand from the wilderness to the Mount of Olives, promising to show them the walls of Jerusalem falling prostrate at his command. Such, Josephus tells us, were but a few out of many who persuaded the people to indulge rash hopes, and led them forth into the wilderness under the idea that they should witness signs and prodigies, the precursors of their deliverance and restoration to independence. "Some of these men," remarks Paley, "it is probable might be impostors who thought that an advantage was to be taken of the state of public opinion. Others, perhaps, were enthusiasts, whose imagination had been drawn to this particular object by the language and sentiments which prevailed around them. But, whether impostors or enthusiasts, they concurred in producing themselves in the character which their countrymen looked for, that is to say, as the restorers and deliverers of the nation, in that sense in which restoration and deliverance were expected by the Jews."

(i) *Maclear*

False Doctrine

False doctrine is a symptom of an unhealthy religious life.

True faith and piety, sound doctrine and godliness, go hand-in-hand. The mystery of godliness is no other than *the truth*. The doctrinal errors of the time are symptoms of an unhealthy corruption of the religious life. The loss of truth, like inability to believe, is traced back by St. Paul (pastoral epistles) to an unhealthy corruption of the νοῦς, *i.e.*, the organ for the consciousness of God and of sin; but this corruption is caused by oneself. The turning away from sound doctrine goes hand-in-hand with a predilection for such teachers as tickle the ear, while they teach only such things as correspond to the sinful inclinations of the hearers.

(j) *Weiss, on the Pastoral Epistles*

False Doctrine, The Hardening Nature of

Whoever gets hardened is to be regarded as an incorrigible transgressor, who has pronounced his own condemnation. The great danger of unsound doctrine lies even in this, that, like a cancer, it rankles, because it finds in the diseased condition of the religious life ever fresh nourishment.

(k) *Weiss*

FALSE WITNESS FOR GOD

St. Paul always took this ground:—"I will not have it said that I am very sincere, very earnest; that I believe what I say myself, but that I am mistaken. No; I will not have that. I am not mad; I speak the words of truth and soberness. I am not expressing an opinion. In that I might be innocently mistaken. A man's opinions may be false, his convictions baseless; but, if he honestly holds them, he himself may be morally upright and true. I do not talk about *opinions;* I TESTIFY TO A FACT. I tell you what I saw and what I heard. If the testimony is false, *I* am false; I am a living lie; I am a false witness for God."

T. Binney

[Cf. "We speak that we do know, and testify that we have seen" (John iii. 11).

(*a*)

FALSEHOOD, CULPABILITY OF

A lie should be trampled upon and extinguished wherever found. I am for fumigating the atmosphere, when I suspect that falsehood, like a pestilence, breathes around me.

(*b*) *Carlyle*

FAME

Fame is swiftest still when she goes laden
With news of mischief.
Thus are we Fortune's pastimes; one day live
Advanced to heaven by the people's breath,
The next, hurled down into th' abyss of death.

(*c*) *May*

FAMILY AND PARADISE

Even on earth, the most perfect government is that of a family where parents employ no tone but that of affectionate counsel.

(*d*) *Channing*

FANATICISM

Some one spreads a rumour in the world that there is a giant in existence seventy feet high. Very soon all the doctors discuss the questions, what colour his hair must be, what is the size of his thumb, what the dimensions of his nails; there is an outcry, caballing, fighting. Those who maintain that the giant's little finger is only an inch and a half in diameter, bring those to the stake who affirm that the little finger is a foot thick. "But, gentlemen, does your giant exist?" says a bystander, modestly. "What horrible doubt!" cry all the disputants; "what blasphemy! what absurdity!" Then they all make a little truce to stone the bystander; and after having assassinated him in due form, in a manner the most edifying, they fight among themselves, as before, on the subject of the little finger and the nails.

(*e*) *Voltaire*

FANATICISM, DEFINITION OF

Fanaticism is such an overwhelming impression of the ideas relating to the future world, as disqualifies for the duties of life.

(*f*) *Robert Hall*

FANATICISM IN THE SIXTEENTH CENTURY

In Paris, the close of Lent was a stimulus to the prevailing excitement. A series of processions took place, which were begun innocently enough, by children, girls and boys, who walked two by two, with tapers, chanting hymns and litanies prepared for them by the priests. . . . Then came the parish processions, in which all the parishioners, of whatever age, sex, or quality, joined; some of the most devout walking to do penance, as though in their shifts. Still a new impetus was wanting. It was necessary to warm the popular heart by a great theatrical display. A priest came forward and declared that in these processions over the hard pavements of Paris, nothing could be more meritorious, nothing more agreeable to God, than that the women should walk with their delicate little feet bare, however it might cause them to suffer. Immediately many an enthusiastic young girl devoted herself to this new mortification, and appeared, not with bare feet only, but almost naked, wearing only a slight linen drapery, not too carefully covering her form. These weeping and dishevelled Magdalenes produced more laughter than edification. At length, the Duchess of Montpensier, the Judith of the League, decided to act her part without hesitation. She abandoned robes and petticoats, and dispensed with the light drapery of the penitents, even over her bosom, with the exception of a simple veil of lace. The people rushed to see her. Crowded and pressed, the heroine was by no means disconcerted. She had set the fashion. Matrons and maidens followed it.

(*g*) *Michelet*

FAREWELL

So farewell hope, and with hope farewell fear,
Farewell remorse; all good to me is lost.

(*h*) *Milton (Paradise Lost).*

FAREWELL

Farewell! "But not for ever."
Cowper (Monumental Inscription to Northcote).

(*i*)

FASTING AND ALMSGIVING, CONNECTION BETWEEN

Is this a fast—to keep
 The larder lean,
  And clear
From fat of veals and sheep?

Is it to quit the dish
 Of flesh, yet still
  To fill
The platter high with fish?

Is it to fast an hour,
 Or ragged to go,
  Or show
A downcast look and sour?

No! 'tis a fast to dole
 Thy sheaf of wheat
  And meat
Unto the hungry soul.

(*j*)

It is to fast from strife,
    From old debate,
    And hate ;
To circumcise thy life ;

To show a heart grief-rent,
    To starve thy sin,
    Not bin,
And that's to keep true Lent.

(a)   *Robert Herrick*

FASTING AND THE BODY

In this journey take the Bridegroom, as you may have Him, and be greedy of His smallest crumbs ; but, buy none of Christ's delicates spiritual with sin, or fasting against your weak body : remember, you are in the body, and it is the lodging-house ; and you may not, without offending the Lord, suffer the old walls of that house to fall down through want of necessary food ; your body is the dwelling-house of the Spirit, and therefore, for the love you carry to the sweet guest, give a due regard to His house of clay ; when He looseth the wall, why not welcome, Lord Jesus ? but it is a fearful sin in us, by hurting the body by fasting, to loose one stone, or the least piece of timber in it ; for the house is not our own, the bridegroom is with you yet ; so fast, as that also you may feast, and rejoice in Him.

(b)   *Samuel Rutherford*

FASTING AND COMMON SENSE

Who can believe with common sense,
A bacon slice gives God offence ;
Or, how a herring hath a charm
Almighty vengeance to disarm ?
Wrapt up in majesty Divine,
Does He regard on what we dine ?

(c)   *Swift (Epigram from the French).*

FASTING AND RELIGION (Isa. lviii. 6, 7, etc.)

1. **The Commission** to the prophet : "Cry aloud," "Lift up voice " : = "prophesy not smooth things " —be direct, incisive—Tell the people what is amiss —Though you give offence.

(i.) *To whom ?*
To a *religious* people, who complain God takes no notice of their "*services.*" For they diligently attend the house of God ; praying and singing in public—we *fast*, "afflict ourselves," and " *Thou hearest not.*"
Speak to them faithfully.

(ii.) *The Proclamation :*
= What you call "*service*" is none at all. If you would do Me SERVICE,
Help My poor.
= Co-workers with God.
= Pure and undefiled religion.
I could do all Myself, but I have left you a share in it. Mere *fasting* and self-infliction in themselves do not commend you to Me.
So long as you are *unmerciful, unjust, worldly*, and *selfish*, it is in vain that ye call Me Lord, Lord, or attend public worship, and bow at the name of Jesus. *It is all mockery.*
But this is the fast I have chosen :
(i.) Go without food, in order that you may give *it* to a hungry brother or sister.

(ii.) You who live in every comfort, should give accommodation, blankets, coals, etc., to those who are homeless, houseless, friendless, and are often found sleeping in the open air, under railway arches, or in markets.

(iii.) You, who are well-clad, should give raiment to those who have none.

(iv.) Ye, who have superior notions of your own excellences—and stand aloof from your fellow-man, and say, *Rabbi, Rabbi !* Be more ready to say *Brother ! Brother !* and honour all men created in the image of God. Hide not thyself from thine own flesh.

2. **The Promises** to such a practical religion as this :—
(i.) Then I will regard your worship as real "*service.*"
(ii.) *Light* shall dawn upon thy hitherto dark spiritual condition.
(iii.) Health, joy, and peace shall it bring forth in thee.
(iv.) Thou shalt be a blessing to others ; they will speak well of thee ; and I will protect thee, behind and before, bless thee in thy going out and coming in.
(v.) Thou shalt call, and I will answer, "*Here am I.*"

(d)   *Cf. Delitzsch*

FASTING, TIME OF (Mark ii. 18–22)

" There is a time to every purpose under heaven : a time to weep, and a time to laugh ; a time to mourn, and a time to dance." The former was the season in which the Baptist's lot had been cast ; the latter, that which Christ came to inaugurate. Such was the broad distinction which our Lord drew when appealed to for a vindication of His conduct. He illustrated the principle by the use of a figure that was singularly appropriate to His hearers. They had heard their own Master say that "the friend of the Bridegroom, which standeth and heareth Him, rejoiceth greatly because of the Bridegroom's voice."

The friends of the bridegroom, or " the children of the bridechamber," as they are elsewhere called, were especially appointed to make preparation for the advent of the bride, to bear the bridal canopy for her reception, and to arrange generally for the wedding-feast. All their thoughts were of joy and happiness. For seven days there were prolonged festivities ; fatlings were killed, costly dresses were worn, torchlight processions were held, and there was every possible demonstration of gladness ; indeed, such was the festive character of the marriage week, that exemption was granted to the bride even from certain obligations of the great fast of "the Day of Atonement," if it fell within that period.

" The present," our Lord seems to say to those who questioned Him, " is such a time as that. What more incongruous than for My friends to seek to mar their enjoyment by introducing an air of sadness into such a scene ? The time will come when the Bridegroom will be taken away ; but do not anticipate the separation ; it will be here all too soon. The darkness of Calvary will spread a gloom over the disciples' hearts ; then there will be an end to rejoicing : " then shall they fast in those days."

(e)   *Luckock.*

FATHER

The little word "father" (saith Luther), lisped forth in prayer by a child of God, exceeds the eloquence of Demosthenes, Cicero, and all the famed orators of the world.

(a) *Thos. Brooks*

FATHERHOOD OF GOD

Look at the strong limbs of a father, look at his huge strength in comparison and contrast with that of his infant child ; and yet why is that child without fear when held within those powerful arms, which could as easily drop and injure as protect the child ? In the case of a stranger, of a giant, the child would cry in alarm and terror— why not now ? Because the strong arms are those of its *father*, whose heart the child knows is knit with his heart, so that, literally, he that toucheth it toucheth the apple of his eye.

God must be conceived of by us not only as the Almighty God, but as our Father ; for only then can our hearts rest in His love, only then can we truly *stay* ourselves upon our God.

And yet, notwithstanding this great revelation of God which Jesus has given us, God has cause to make the same complaint now as of His people of old : "If I be a father, where is My honour ? Why do ye not trust Me as a Father ? Why not make the relation more real ? Why call Me Father, and yet act as if I were not, and ye not My children ? Honour Me not merely with your lips, but give Me your heart, make the relationship real, and I will be a Father unto you, and ye shall be My sons and daughters, saith the Lord God Almighty."

(b)

Consider the position of one who says, "*Our Father.*" The moment you are able to say that, you have a right to say, " I am not a hired servant " —still less am I a slave—I am an heir of God, and a joint heir with Christ, I am a son, God has accepted me as His son. And how ought a child to *feel* towards such a parent? surely not less confident than towards a weak earthly parent. God knows our imperfections better than we know those of our children. But is there not a power of love which covers down all those imperfections? Note, too, the effect of this filial spirit on prayer, which ought to be that of *communion*, not of begging— that of *confidence*, and not that of constantly bringing up the *forgiven* past. What should we think of a child or a friend who did this ?

(c) *Beecher*

The one thing which separates the heart of man from God, is the sense of sin. It may be distinctly felt, or it may be vaguely and almost unconsciously felt ; but it is the one thing which produces distrust, which engenders suspicion, which promotes dislike, which prohibits, at least on my side, all confidence between me, the offender, and the Great Being against whom I have sinned. You may tell me that I ought to regard God as my Father ; and perhaps you are right. Perhaps I ought to do so. But there is an instinct in me, far stronger than your words, which refuses to allow me to find comfort in the alleged Fatherhood, until the preliminary question of my sin has been entered into and done with. Do what I will, a feeling of insecurity haunts me. I cannot get out of my ears a voice which floats round me,

and seems to say that, though God is a Father, yet God is also a Judge : that God is angry with the wicked : that God is a consuming fire to those who violate His laws and oppose themselves to His will. He may be unchangeable, I think. Yes, He *is* unchangeable. His name is unvarying, unalterable, eternal Love. But still my relations to this unchangeable Being may be of such a perverted kind, as that that which should have been a blessing, may prove to be to me a crushing and agonizing curse. At all events, I can feel no confidence ; and this repeating to myself that God is my Father, and this being assured by others that God is my Father, seems to bring to me, so long as the matter of my sin is not disposed of, an exceedingly small amount of comfort and peace. But then, how is the sin to be dealt with ? How is it to be put away, so that it shall no longer be a cold shadow between our souls and God : prohibiting confidence and rendering love impossible ? I cannot tell you, if Jesus Christ be not the Son of God. Then, so far as I can see, the sin which clings to us, must cling to us for ever. It must remain, throughout eternity, part of ourselves. But I can tell you on the hypothesis of the true Godhead of Christ. Then, the death of the Cross, which before was so unintelligible, becomes instinct with glorious meaning. It becomes a sacrifice. By that sacrifice of Himself, the God-man put away our sin. In His mysterious death, we, if we are one with Him, died unto sin. Our transgressions are forgiven. Our burden is lifted off. Our impurity is cleansed. Our conscience is satisfied. The barrier is removed. And now we are free to spring as loving children to the loving bosom of our Father and our God.

(d) *Gordon Calthrop*

FATHERS, THE (Ps. cxix. 99, 100)

1. "We are the fathers." They, babes ; we, adults. Christianity was to them in its germ ; to us it is a grown and expanding tree. The leaven then had but just been put into the meal ; now, it has leavened the world nearly all over. *They* stood on the first rung of the ladder ; we stand higher up, and have a wider survey and comprehension of things.

2. The desire for Patristic knowledge corresponds to a request to be fed with the spoon-meat we were fed with as infants, or invalids. Can a man who reads and thinks, and having years of personal Christian experience behind him, be satisfied with such spiritual food? And yet, some of us can testify that oftentimes we have gone to the House of God hungry, and came hungry away. We have been offered something out of the old stock of years ago—we have sat at the feet of preacher and teacher, and listened to the veriest A B C of spiritual things. We have not been refreshed, edified, guided. There has been no voice of living man's experience, saying, " Lo, this have we seen, we have searched it out." We asked for bread, and were given a stone.

(e)

FATHERS, SPIRITUAL (Phil. x.)

Towards no creature have we higher obligations than toward those to whom, next to God, we owe the life of our souls. Even Alexander could say that he owed more to Aristotle, that taught him, than to Philip, that begat him.

(f) *J. Trapp, and H. B. Hacket*

FAULTS

" They say, best men are moulded out of faults,
And, for the most, become much more the better
For being a little bad."

(a)   *Measure for Measure*

Oh, wad some power the giftie gie us,
To see oursels as ithers see us !
It wad frae monie a blunder free us,
          And foolish notion.

(b)   *Burns*

Bad men excuse their faults, good men will leave them.

(c)   *Ben Jonson*

A friend should not be hated for little faults.

(d)   *Pythagoras*

FEAR

" *And they were in the way going up to Jerusalem; and Jesus went before them : and they were amazed; and as they followed, they were afraid. And He took again the twelve, and began to tell them what things should happen unto Him,*

" *Saying, Behold, we go up to Jerusalem; and the Son of man shall be delivered unto the chief priests, and unto the scribes; and they shall condemn Him to death, and shall deliver Him to the Gentiles :*

" *And they shall mock Him, and shall kill Him : and the third day He shall rise again."*—Mark x. 32–34.

1st Parallel :
Here is a journey—a company of men going up to Jerusalem ; = Here are we, a company of Christians, going along life's journey on to the Heavenly Jerusalem.

2nd Parallel :
Their *Leader*—" Jesus went before them." We have a *Forerunner* = " The *Captain* of our Salvation." " When He putteth forth His own sheep He goeth before them." He has experience of the road. He astonished the disciples by the way He led them—a dangerous road.

3rd Parallel :
" And as they followed, they were afraid."
If they were afraid when Jesus was with them, as He led them, and at what He told them—is there not cause that we fear also ? " Lead, kindly light." " All night He led them by a pillar of fire."
If Peter was afraid, and John, is it not to be expected that we too should be afraid sometimes, as Jesus leads us along life's rough road ; though we believe " He led them by a right way unto a city of habitation."

4th Parallel :
Jesus took the twelve, and told them what was happen to Him.
He tells us—
" If thou comest to seek the Lord, prepare thyself for affliction."
To count the cost of discipleship.
See " DISCIPLESHIP."
(e)

FEAR

A pardoned sinner has only *one* fear left—the fear of defiling the white garment, of losing the ring, of being excluded from the marriage feast.

(f)   *Lange.*

FEAR OF GOD

" *He honoureth them that fear the Lord* " (Ps. xv. 4)

Look into the world, and you shall see men, most part esteemed according to their means. " The rich is had in reputation, because of his goods " (Ecc. x. 31). " Riches gather many friends " (Prov. xix. 4) : all happiness ebbs and flows with his money. He shall be accounted a gracious lord, a man of generous spirit, etc.
Tulley said of Octavianus, while he was adopted Cæsar, and an heir apparent of a great monarchy, he was a *golden child*. All honours, offices, applause, grand titles, are put upon him. All men's eyes are upon him : " God bless his worship ! his honour ! " . . . Every man riseth to him, as to Themistocles in the Olympics ; if he speak (as of Herod), it is the voice of God, not of man. . . . All the world labours for him, thousands of artificers are his slaves, to drudge for him, run, ride, and post for him ; divines, lawyers, physicians, philosophers, scholars, are wholly devote to his service. Every man scales his acquaintance, his kindred to match with him : though he be a ninny, a monster, etc., he is an excellent match for my son, my daughter, my niece, etc. Trumpets sound, bells ring, wherever he goes. Every man is ready to entertain him, etc.

(g)   *Burton (Anatomy of Melancholy)*

FEAR, INFLUENCE OF

There is a virtuous fear, which is the effect of faith ; and there is a vicious fear, which is the product of doubt. The former leads to hope as relying on God, in Whom we believe : the latter inclines to despair, as not relying on God, in Whom we do not believe. Persons of the one character fear to lose God ; persons of the other character fear to find Him.

(h)   *Pascal*

FEAR AND LOVE

When a man is awakened to a sense of sin, he is brought under the power of *fear*, and slavery ; but when he is regenerated, he is brought under the power of *love*, and then he enjoys " the glorious liberty of the children of God." The ungodly neither fear nor love, for they are " dead in trespasses and sins."

(i)   *Olshausen*

FEAR NOT

" *Fear not :* " " *Be not afraid.*"
When brought into unusual nearness to the manifestation of God.
  (i.) *Abram*—Gen. xv. 1 ;
  (ii.) *Gideon*—Judg. vi. 23 ;
  (iii.) *The Angels*—Matt. xxviii. 5 ;
  (iv.) *The Shepherds*—Luke ii. 10 ;
  (v.) *John*—Rev. i. 17.
= The first and the last word of the Gospel.
(j)

FEARS

Well, poor Christian, how much dost thou think, is there of God—of His Spirit, of His Word—in thy fears (lest thou shouldest be in a *delusion*), from fancy or the devil? Just *none* at all, for it cannot be that such fears are the natural and true workings of the Spirit of God; no, not even as a Spirit of bondage. These are not His doings. Dost thou not see the very paw of the devil in them? For they tend to the hardening of thy heart.

(*a*) *John Bunyan*

FEEDING THE FIVE THOUSAND (Luke ix.)

Noticed by all the Evangelists.

It was a "desert place," to which

(i.) *Matthew* = Jesus withdrew, after hearing of John the Baptist's death, seeking solitude, and to reflect on His own approaching end.

(ii.) *Mark* = "Come and *rest* awhile" to the disciples after their "Mission"—there were so many coming and going, that they had no leisure.

(iii.) *Luke* = That our Lord wished for private conversation with His disciples after their return from the Mission, and the desert was the more suitable place.

(iv.) *John* = It was the time of the Passover. Jesus could not visit Jerusalem because of the growing hatred; therefore they would have a *Passover* here in the "desert place"—for there was a hungry multitude.

N.B.—All this is designed to teach us that "*Christ is our Passover; . . .* therefore let us keep the Feast:"—in which, notice—

(i.) The Preparation.

(ii.) The Repast.

(*b*) *Cf. Godet*

FEELING

FEELING IN THE WRONG PLACE

A good-hearted man, who understood that a poor woman and her family were in distress by the loss of their principal support, generously went round among his neighbours to solicit aid he was unable to give himself. He told a plain, simple, and pathetic tale, and received from each a very liberal donation of regret, sorrow, sympathy, etc. But, thought he, this will not buy a cow. So he doubled his exertions, but to the same effect. He now lost all patience; and being answered as usual by a son of Midas, with a plentiful shower of feeling: "Yes, I don't doubt your feeling, but you don't feel in the right place." "Oh," said he, "I feel with all my heart." "Yes, yes," replied the solicitor, "I don't doubt that either; but I want you to feel in your *pocket*."

(*c*)

FEELINGS, EXCITED

The direction of the needle of the compass can only be accurately discovered in a calm sea.

(*d*)

FELLOWSHIP WITH GOD (1 John i. 5)

"This then is the message which we have heard of Him, and declare unto you, that God is light, and in Him is no darkness at all." God, then, with whom we are privileged to have fellowship, is absolute perfection. He is light—everything that really shines in the firmament of being. He is righteousness, and wisdom, and power, and goodness, and truth, and sweetness, and love; and all we see of such like qualities in other beings is of Him, and of Him only. There is not, and there never can be, any stain, flaw, speck, or shadow in His brightness. He is always the same, and always infinitely full of blessedness. He is light, and must glorify all who are brought near Him, gilding them with rays of His own glory. Was it not thus visibly, and I had almost said physically, with Moses? "And it came to pass, when Moses came down from Mount Sinai, with the two tables of testimony in Moses' hands, that Moses wist not that the skin of his face shone while He talked with him. And when Aaron and all the children of Israel saw Moses, behold, the skin of his face shone; and they were afraid to come nigh him." Was it not thus morally and spiritually, and I had almost said intellectually, with the Apostles, to whom this witness was borne by the Jewish Council (as the result of the Master's promise—"I will give you a mouth and wisdom, which all your adversaries shall not be able to gainsay nor resist"), "They marvelled, and they took knowledge of them, that they had been with Jesus"? Nay, in our own experience is it not much the same? Do not saintly men and women oftentimes testify to their fellowship with God by look, and voice, and manner, and tone? And have we not caught from them rays of reflected light ourselves, as we journeyed on side by side in happy Christian communing about many spiritual things? Nay, have they not sometimes brought into our midst our very Master Himself? and have we not thereby attained to a sensibly closer fellowship with Him through fellowship with them, and gone forth to our work thenceforward strengthened in a marvellous manner to trample down besetting sins, to present more costly sacrifices of service, to strive after a more inward and entire purity, and to be bolder in our prayers and ventures of faith, more certain than ever before that our Father's ways are ways of pleasantness here, and not only at the end? True, we have never yet seen a brother Christian in whom "is no darkness at all." True, in the holiest souls we have found large tracts of darkness which have disappointed us bitterly. True, our worthiest idols have been shattered again and again, even when we have loved them in the Lord, and for the Lord's sake. But could we expect it otherwise when the light was hid in earthen vessels? And shall we make no allowance for others, when we need so much for ourselves? "This is the message we have heard of Him." "We all with open face beholding as in a glass the glory of the Lord, are changed into the same image from glory to glory, even as by the Spirit of the Lord."

. . . Burnet bore this testimony to Leighton: "I never heard him say a word in conversation that was not to edification. I never met him in his house but there was something in his look which did me good."

(*e*) *J. Clements*

FESTUS THE ROMAN, PAUL THE CHRISTIAN, AND AGRIPPA THE JEW (Acts xxvi. 28)

(i.) This chapter places before us three representative men—Festus the Roman, Paul the Christian, and Agrippa the Jew.

(ii.) Christianity in the person of St. Paul stands to be judged before the Roman and the Jew—before a practical, worldly intellect, taught by the philosophy of the day, and before a mind educated amidst the traditions of a covenant people, and influenced—at least to some extent—by an acquaintance with the oracles of God. Earnest, living faith comes into contact with scepticism on the one hand, and with dead, inoperative belief on the other.

(iii.) As the Apostle proceeds with his address, we observe that the astonishment of the Roman governor deepens. A worldling himself, believing most firmly in the reality of the things of which his senses informed him, and as firmly disbelieving in the existence of an invisible kingdom, and of supernatural agencies, it was utterly incredible to Festus that any man whose reason was not impaired should entertain the views which he hears propounded by St. Paul. A vision seen on the road to Damascus! a voice heard speaking from heaven, a Divine commission given and accepted! a confident persuasion that Jesus Christ died for the sins of mankind, and that He rose again from the dead—what were these things? Why, what could they be, but the ravings of a man whose mind was unhinged, the delusions and frenzies of a fine intellect, disordered by long brooding over the subject of religion? And this was the honest conviction of Festus; and this conviction, becoming stronger and stronger as the Apostle proceeded, forced Festus at last into the blunt and uncourteous interruption, " Paul, thou art beside thyself; much learning doth make thee mad."

(iv.) Turn now to the other auditor, the Jew. Here the effect produced by St. Paul's address was very different from that produced upon the Roman. Agrippa was as thoroughly a man of the world as Festus was, nor was he at all likely, considering his antecedents, to make any sacrifice whatever for the sake of obeying conviction; but for all that, he could not put himself into the place which his companion occupied. He could not feel as Festus did. He was unable to shake off entirely the influence of his early education and of his acquaintance with the Jewish Scripture. Miracles, visions, voices from heaven, might seem to the Roman ridiculous and incredible, but they could not seem so to one of the covenant people; and, accordingly, we notice that an impression is being made upon the Jewish prince. He sits upon his throne, uneasily listening to the arguments of St. Paul. He is disturbed, and unsettled, and perplexed for the moment; and the Apostle, perceiving his discomposure, adroitly follows up the advantage by the personal appeal, " King Agrippa, believest thou the prophets? I know that thou believest." And the result of the appeal is the exclamation of Agrippa, " Almost thou persuadest me to be a Christian." Now, some think that Agrippa was sincere in this declaration. Others say that he is simply sneering at the attempt of Paul to win him over to the faith of Christ. It matters not; either way the man's condition is the same.

(a)

Festus the Roman, Paul the Christian, and Agrippa the Jew.

Three Representative Men

1. The Apostle Paul is the representative of those persons who have carried the problems of human existence to the foot of the Cross and solved them there; who believe in an invisible kingdom of truth and righteousness established now, and waiting to be manifested hereafter; who have accepted Jesus Christ into their hearts; who rest upon Him as the one sole foundation of their hope, and look up to Him as the one unquestioned Lord of their being; and who can say—or who at least earnestly desire to be able to say—" The life which I now live in the flesh is a life of faith in the Son of God, who loved me, and gave Himself for me."
(b)

2. Of a second group, Festus, the Roman governor, may be taken as the type. In this we have the men who find in this world little or nothing that is supernatural. In their estimation, a life of faith is a life of fanaticism; prayer is a weak instinct, to be repressed in yourself, and to be ridiculed in others. The Bible, if not an exploded imposture, is a congeries of fact and falsehood, interesting as an historical or pyschological study, but totally without any pretension or right to be considered as the revealer of truth or the guide of life; the future state is probably a dream; the judgment-seat of Christ is certainly the invention of priestcraft; this present world is all that an enlightened man will admit into his account; and the things which may be ascertained by his reason, or the things which may be brought under the cognisance of his senses—these, and these only, will he accept as being reliable or real.
(c)

3. But between the two there is a third group, occupying an apparently intermediate position. Of what class of persons this group is composed, we shall be better able to judge if we once more contemplate our three representative men. Observe, then, that whilst we have on the one side simple, open, avowed unbelief in Festus, and on the other side, earnest, devoted belief in St. Paul, we have in the Jewish prince Agrippa, a character which seems to stand half-way between the two, and to partake, for the moment, of the characteristics of both. Agrippa does not, like Festus, entirely reject, and he does not, like Paul, entirely accept, the claims of the crucified Saviour. He has too much knowledge to allow him to join the one; he has too much worldliness to allow him to cast in his lot with the other. Inwardly persuaded of the truth of Christianity, his heart is untouched. Knowing what was the right step for him to take, he has not the courage, or the self-denial, or the faith to take it. And so he inclines to steer a middle course. He would make it his aim to avoid, if he could, both the grossness of unbelief and the inconvenience of a profession of faith. Convinced, but not converted; influenced, but not changed; understanding, but not loving, he feels himself to be, and he confesses himself to be, almost, but not altogether, a Christian.
(d)

Of whom does Agrippa remind us? He reminds us of that numerous class, whom early education,
(e)

or traditional prejudice, or lingering convictions of conscience, prohibit from joining the open opponents of Christianity, but who as distinctly avoid committing themselves to the cause of the kingdom of Christ. Halting between two opinions, these persons cannot be induced to take that last great step of entire self-surrender, which places them within the border of the spiritual kingdom, and unites them with the fortunes of the people of God. They know the truth, but do not submit themselves to the truth. They believe in the existence of the Lord Jesus Christ, and they are even ready to admit the justice of the claim which He makes upon them; but still they hold their hearts back from Him, and the belief which they entertain exercises no practical, determinining, directing influence upon heart and life.

(a) *Gordon Calthrop*

FEW

Our Lord delighteth Himself in those FEW that are His jewels, and in the little flock that shall receive the kingdom, when the most shall reap the misery which they sowed. In nature, excellent things are few; the world hath not many suns or moons; it is but little of the earth that is gold or silver. Princes and nobles are but a small part of the sons of men; and it is no great number that are learned, judicious, or wise, here in the world. And, therefore, if, the gate being strait and the way narrow, there be few that find salvation, yet God will have His glory and pleasure in those few (2 Thess. i. 7–10).

(b) *Baxter*

FINDING CHRIST (John i.)

Coming to Christ is here illustrated in every way. Prophetic testimony, office, work, points to Him. Then brother brings brother, friend brings friend, townsman brings townsman. One comes with another, and one after another.

(c) *Lange*

See "EUREKA."

FIRE

"*And they burn,*" etc. (John xv. 6).

Emphatic. . . . Indicative of the conspicuous, rapid, and shocking ruin of apostates, or, in general, of dead members of Christ.

(d) *Lange*

All that is here expressed or implied of " the fire " (Matt. iii. 10), " the flame " (Luke xvi. 24), " the flaming fire " (2 Thess. i. 8), " the furnace of fire " (Matt. xiii. 42, 50), " the gehenna of fire " (Matt. v. 22; Mark ix. 43), " the lake of fire " (Rev. xx. 15; xxi. 8), " the everlasting fire " (Matt. xxv. 41; Jude vii.), with all the secrets of anguish which words like these, if there be any in words, *must* involve, demands rather to be trembled at than needs to be expounded.

(e) *Trench*

FIRST CAUSE

No created being is the first cause of those occurrences which the world calls evil. Since, therefore, they are all to be referred to God as their real Author and Sovereign Disposer, it is unquestionably our duty to go direct to the fountain head, and to expect thence the only solid comfort.

(f) *Blaise Pascal*

FIRST AND LAST

In the different degrees of life, there will be often found much *meanness* among the great, and much *greatness* among the mean.

(g) *Dr. Johnson*

FIRST LOVE

Geo. Mogridge (Old Humphrey), writing to his daughter, says:

" Like you, in my youthful days, did I withdraw myself from every eye save that of the Eternal, and many an aspiration has been poured in at the mercy-seat. . . . But these aspirations, ardent and sincere as they were, could not always be sustained. Few and far between were those sunny seasons of the soul's rejoicing; and so will it be with you. These fresh, fervent feelings of yours will pass away; and though they will come again, again they will retire. Moses was forty days in the Mount three times, but he was forty years in the wilderness."

" So long as we are what we are, the perishing bits and drops of this temporal being will, at times, take precedence of the Bread of Heaven, and things that are eternal. But this is no proof that we do not believe in eternal things."

(h)

FIRST LOVE

Red-hot religion has its place and value, but white-hot religion, the silent, intense force which acts without sparks or noise, is a diviner thing. Is it thus with our love to God? Has that passion simply changed from red to white? Has sentiment become principle, the ecstasy a habit, the passion a law? If so, the former days were not better than these.

(i) *W. L. Watkinson*

FISHERS

"*In that night they caught nothing*" (John xxi. 3).

The night season is the most favourable time for catching fish (Luke v. 5). Yet there were unsuccessful nights; such an one was this. A symbol of the utter failure of the fishers of men without Christ, as verse 6 illustrates their abundant success with Christ.

(j) *Lange and Schaff*

FIVE PRECIOUS THINGS

1. The trial of your faith is *precious*;
2. The *precious* blood of Christ (by some accounted an unholy thing);
3. The Corner-stone, elect, *precious*;
4. To you He (Christ) is *precious*;
5. Like *precious* faith.

(k)

FIXED CENTRE

What advance would a man make in the study of geometry if he consented to consider his axioms, his fundamental principles, his primary truths, as open questions? " None," you say, " none whatever." Some of you understand astronomy; what progress would you make in that science should you consider it doubtful whether the theory of gravitation was true or not, and could not make up your mind about it? Again, none whatever. In other words, you must have a starting-point, a fixed centre, a fulcrum on which to rest your lever; and then you can go on, and then you can work. And it is just so in spiritual things. You must start from a *fixed centre*. And what is that fixed centre?—the truths of the Gospel, the facts of the relation between God and man. These must not be open questions; you must be certain of them, if you want to have firm ground beneath your feet. Ay, and more than this: these facts must be facts *for you;* you must be able to realize your own personal concern in them; you must be able to say, God helping you, "I know in whom I have believed."

(a) *Gordon Calthrop*

FLEE YOUTHFUL LUSTS

Delicate and tender members become not a head stuck with thorns.

(b) *St. Bernard*

The pleasure of sin vanishes, the guilt remains, and the punishment is eternal.

(c) *Anon*

Let not the language of Delilah enchant thee, lest the hands of the Philistines surprise thee.

(d) *Quarles*

If with Esau thou hast sold thy birthright for broth, then with Jacob wrestle by prayer till thou get a blessing.

(e) *Ibid*

FLEECE

Once when he was baptizing in a river, a clergyman passing along, rudely addressed him, and in words, the exact resilient force of which he could not, we suspect, have anticipated: "You may wash, and I will shear them." The instant reply was: "If you must have the fleece, Christ must have the sheep."

(f) *Anecdote of Timothy Thomas, Welsh pastor*

FLEETING BLESSINGS

BLESSINGS, THEIR DUE RECOGNITION

When Daguerre was working at his sun-pictures, his great difficulty was to fix them. The light came and imprinted the image; but when the tablet was drawn from the camera, the image had vanished. Our lamentation is like his, our want the same—a fixing solution that shall arrest and detain the blessings. He discovered the chemical power which turned the evanescent into the durable. There is a Divine agency at hand that can fix the truth upon the heart of man—God's Holy Spirit.

(g) *J. Stoughton*

FLESH AND THE SPIRIT, THE

" *This I say then, Walk in the Spirit, and ye shall not fulfil the lusts of the flesh* " (Gal. v. 16).

1. The "*Flesh*" and the "*Spirit*" are rivals.
2. How the strong man is dispossessed by " the stronger than he"—*i.e., by living in the Spirit.* The master must rule the slave. "*I keep under*," etc. The life of a Christian is lived in a higher sphere. St. Paul's reply = Be a man, not a brute: not " Do as few fleshly things as you can,"=that is *repression*, but do as many spiritual things as you can = (negative and positive).

All prohibitions are *negative:* you can't kill an appetite by starvation. What is it keeps rich people from the disgusting and degrading vices os the lower classes? Not prohibition, but they have other and higher sources of social enjoyment; of is it in spiritual things—kill the flesh by living in the higher region of the Spirit, not merely ceasing to live in sin, *but loving Christ.* The more we live the new life, the more sin becomes impossible. This is the difference between *Law* and *Grace.*

(h) *H. W. Beecher and others*

The contest between the flesh and the spirit exists *alone* in the regenerate. *Lange*

See Müller, "*Christian Doctrine of Sin,*" 323–327

(i)

FLESH, THE STRONGHOLD OF NATURE

It is impossible a man can take his lusts to heaven with him; such wares as these will not be welcome there. Oh, how loth are we to forego our burdens, that hinder us in running our race with patience! It is no small work to displease and anger nature, that we may please God. Oh, if it be hard to go one foot or half an inch out of our own will, our own wit, out of our own ease and worldly lusts; and so to deny ourself and to say, " It is not I, but Christ; not I, but grace; not I, but God's glory; not I, but God's love constraining me; not I, but the Lord's word; not I, but Christ's commanding power, as King in me ": oh, what pains, and what a death is it to nature, to turn me, myself, my lust, my ease, my credit, over into my Lord, my Saviour, my King, and my God, my Lord's will, my Lord's grace! But, alas! that idol, *myself*, is the idol we all bow down to.

What made Eve fall, and hurried her headlong upon the forbidden fruit, but that wretched thing, *herself?* What drew that brother-murderer to kill Abel? What drove the old world on to corrupt their ways? Who but themselves and their own pleasures? What was the cause of Solomon's falling into idolatry, and multiplying strange wives? What but himself, whom he would rather please than God? What was the hook that took David, and snared him first in adultery, but his self-lust; and then in murder, but his self-credit, and self honour? What led Peter on to deny his Lord? Was it not a piece of himself, and self-love to a whole skin? What made Judas sell his Master for thirty pieces of money, but a piece of self-love, idolizing avaricious self? What made Demas go off the way of the Gospel to embrace this present world? Even self-love and love of gain for himself. Every man blameth the devil for his

(j)

sins; but the great devil, the house devil of every man, that eateth and lieth in every man's bosom, is that idol which killeth all—himself.

(a) *S. Rutherford*

FLESHLY LUSTS WAR AGAINST THE SOUL

The society of people who sleep soft, who eat too well, and who have very little to do, has always been loose and luxurious.

(b) *Daily News*

It has pleased the All-wise Disposer to encompass us from our birth by difficulty and allurement, to place us in a world where wrong-doing is often gainful, and duty rough and perilous, where many vices oppose the dictates of the inward monitor, where the body presses as a weight on the mind, and matter, by its perpetual agency on the senses, becomes a barrier between us and the spiritual world. We are in the midst of influences which menace the intellect and heart; and to be free is to withstand and conquer these.

(c) *Channing*

Flesh to the Spirit, How to Subdue the

There are, says a well-known writer, three methods of relieving the spirit (by which he means the nobler part of man) from the flesh (I should say he uses the word "flesh" in the more restricted sense, making it refer to the body and the bodily appetite). However, I might better phrase his meaning thus. "There are three recognised methods of relieving the higher and nobler part of man from the tyranny of its lower, baser, bodily desires.

1. "Sow your wild oats." Let the flesh have its fling. In due time sensualism will have exhausted its resources. The worn-out flesh will give up the ghost: and the nobler soul, relieved from her base partner, will be free to pursue her own nobler life.

2. Give the flesh no quarter; starve it, pinch it, punish it, mortify it—indulgence only feeds its strength.

3. Walk in the Spirit, and ye shall not fulfil the lusts of the flesh.

The *first* prescription (says the writer) has very great authority on its side; viz., that of the devil. It has a truth in it; but more of falsehood. It is quite true that the indulgence of the flesh will weaken, and, in the end, destroy it; but it is also true that the nature which yields to the government of the flesh will be an earthly, fleshly nature, when the flesh is dead.

The *second* prescription is better. It is that of the ascetics. But it is merely human, and it is altogether inadequate. Force may suppress, but it does not convert. A living power suppressed, secretly accumulates energy.

The *third* prescription says nothing about either indulging or restraining the flesh, but proposes a new life, a new sphere, for the spirit. Find (it says) occupation for yourself in a world that is above the flesh. You are a *citizen* of that world—assert your position there: enter into it, walk in the streets of the city. Familiarize yourself with its habits, associate with its inhabitants, strive to sympathize more and more with its pursuits. Another class of affections will be powerfully awakened in you—a higher class; and inferior

desires will abate. Ay! and the flesh itself, under the calm subduing influence of your purer spirit, will become a dignified servant in waiting on its superior. Good gardeners know a better way of conquering the wild thorn than by uprooting and destroying it. They set it in their garden. They graft it on some queenly rose. Then the wild thorn expends its energy not upon itself, but upon that which is above itself; and as a reward is crowned with a glory which itself could not possibly produce.

(d) *Gordon Calthrop*

FLOODS

" *The Lord sitteth upon the flood; yea,*
The Lord sitteth King for ever.
The Lord will give strength unto His people;
The Lord will bless His people with peace."
—(Ps. xxix. 10, 11)

This Psalm describes the course of a thunderstorm, and is called the Psalm of the Seven Thunders, because the thunder is seven times termed "The voice of the Lord."

The storm which the Psalmist witnessed, led him to reflect upon the past.

If the elements were uncontrolled, where was feeble man?

If the floods continued to deluge the plains, how could feeble man help himself?

What guarantee had he of safety—what promise as an anchor could he hold to?

To satisfy himself on this point, he looks back over the past history of man—to the greatest storm—the great deluge in the time of Noah, and he says,—

" The Lord sitteth upon the flood; yea,
The Lord sitteth King for ever.
The Lord will give strength unto His people;
The Lord will bless His people with peace."

(e)

Notice here two statements and two promises.

1. The first statement is that,
" **The Lord sitteth upon the flood**," or rather, " The Lord sat at the Flood "=sat upon His throne at the time of the deluge, directing and controlling the elements to the carrying out of His own purposes.

Notice that,

(i.) " *The Lord did it.*"

It did not occur by blind *chance*, nor by any freak or caprice of " Nature."

It did not come about because the elements had broken loose from her laws, and had got beyond all control—running away with the earth, as horses might run away with a chariot.

But the Lord did it.

The Lord Himself let loose the water floods. It was done at His command. The Lord sat upon His throne at the flood judging right.

(f)

Moreover, the Lord had a purpose in bringing about that flood.

(ii.) *He did it as an act of judgment.*

The people of that time had broken away from God.

He was not in their thoughts.

They had, so to speak, turned Him out of His own world, and in His place they had substituted

(g)

their heroes as gods, men of prowess and mark with whom might and physical force was right.

These " mighty ones " did " mighty things," and performed " exploits," and the people rendered them their homage.

Gradually men became atheists—ceased to believe in the God who had so recently brought them into being.

To repeat His authority on earth, and to show that He alone was the " Mighty One," God brought the flood upon the ungodly world, and took them all away with that sore destruction.

Let things come to the same pass again—let men dethrone God, and put in His place a god of their own invention, and they will find that, though He will not again bring upon earth a flood of waters to destroy it, yet the other elements are in His hand. And whensoever He will, He may give the word of command, and the very elements shall melt with fervent heat, whilst the earth and all works therein shall be burned up.

(a)

(iii.) *The Lord brought about that flood as an act of* " MERCY."

Judgment upon the ungodly, but " mercy " for His own " little flock."

God had a " little flock " of eight persons to think of and to look after.

" It could not be that the righteous perish with the wicked."

These eight persons (one family) constituted the Church of God.

Had God waited a little longer, in all probability this " little flock " would have degenerated too.

It was Noah's faith that saved them all. We do not notice much piety in his sons, so that the probability is that if God had waited till Noah was dead before He brought the flood, He would scarcely have *found faith on the earth.*

To save this little remnant just before a flood of ungodliness swept away His own Church from the earth, God intervened and saved Noah and his family from the fate which, at no distant date, seemed to await them.

(b)

2. The next statement is

" The Lord sitteth as King for ever."

The same Lord, who ruled at the flood, is still sitting as King.

(i.) And when other storms and floods came, such as the Psalmist was then witnessing,—when we are in danger and feel our peril, and know how helpless is man at such a time—the Psalmist reminds us that this thunder is God's voice.

These floods are His doing—He hath a controversy with the inhabitants of the earth again.

For—

We have learned to talk about " NATURE " as if it were the master, and by so doing, we have again ousted God from His throne, and we have put a rival in His place—a *mighty one*, forgetting that God is *Mightier*.

The Psalmist would have us learn from the flood of old, that the same God, who controlled that, sits on His throne still, a KING for ever—(Nature is not king).

(c)

3. The Two Promises

" The Lord will give strength to His people ;
    The Lord will bless His people with peace."

We are again reminded of the flood. After all storms there is a calm; after the great deluge there was a PROMISE.

And after this thunderstorm which the Psalmist witnessed, and which led him into this train of thought, there was " PEACE."

The storm was for His enemies.

The peace is for " His people."

(i.) After the flood, the heavens were spanned with a *rainbow*, and the promise of " *peace* " was made to mankind once more.

After the storm, which this Psalm describes ; after the seven thunders,

The blackened clouds,
The flames of fire,
The torn cedars of Lebanon,

The devastated country, and the snapping of trees in the forests ; after the peril that man and beast alike had been in, and during the raging of the storm ; after all this, we see the " BOW *in the cloud.*"

For these two closing verses span the whole Psalm like a rainbow.

They tell God's people that His eye is on them ; that He holds them, as well as the storm and the waters, in His hand, and they are safe.

" *The Lord will give strength unto His people ;*
    The Lord will bless His people with peace."

He will give them STRENGTH in the hour of weakness and peril.

" In the time of dearth, they shall have enough."

He will be their arm every morning, and their SALVATION in every time of need.

" *Strength* " most of all, when they need it most of all.

They shall be IN the " Ark " when His enemies are exposed to the storm outside.

" STRENGTH " according to their day. " As their day is their strength shall be "—" a very present help in time of trouble."

It is not then without the deepest meaning that the Psalmist assures us that " The Lord will give STRENGTH unto His *people.*"

(d)

(ii.) But He will do more than this, because we want more.

God promises more, and He will give more, " The Lord will bless His people with *peace.*"

That is the rainbow in the cloud spanning this stormy. Psalm.

It touches earth and heaven.

" PEACE " after a stormy voyage, after a stormy life, in the midst of peril, when conscience accuses of sin.

" PEACE "—such as pass man's understanding, such as this world cannot give nor take away.

" PEACE " such as keeps the mind in an even and a heavenly frame, as a sentinel that guards a door, lest foes should get in and make havoc where God hath commanded peace.

All this is in this promise, " The Lord will bless His people with peace."

(iii.) The Lord " WILL " do this.

He did it for Noah ; He *has* done it for *others* ; He will do it for us.

What a moment of weakness was it when the flood came. What could Noah do against it ? but

(e)

God was his strength. What a moment of trouble and doubt and uncertainty was it too, when the storm was raging without and beating in wild fury on the frail wooden ark; but the Lord blessed Him with "peace," the peace of God.

(a) *Cf. Delitzsch*

FOES, OUR SPIRITUAL (Eph. vi. 10-20)

The apostle brings out into bold relief the terrible foes which they are summoned to encounter.

As to their—

(i.) **Position**: They are no subalterns, but foes of mighty rank, the nobility and chieftains of the spirit-world.

(ii.) **Office**: Their domain is this darkness in which they exercise imperial sway.

(iii.) **Essence**: they are not encumbered with an animal frame, but are " spirits "; and as to their—

(iv.) **Character**: they are " evil "—their appetite for evil only exceeds their capacity for producing it.

(b) *Eadie*

" FOLLOW ME "

A reason from gold would not be a golden one to Paul, seeing for Christ all were loss and dirt and dung to Him. The disciples' nets and their lines and their fish-hooks were not worth a straw when Christ said, " Follow Me." Thou who art tethered to thy delights, when Christ comes by and cries, "Follow Me," if then thou canst break thy tether like a rotten straw rope, and gallop after Him, thou hast clear eyes and seest well.

(c) *Samuel Rutherford*

FOLLOWING CHRIST (John viii.)

He who follows Christ never misses the right way; always with will-o'-the wisps!

(d) *Starke*

FOLLY

Whether the charmer sinner it or saint it,
If folly grow romantic, I must paint it.

(e) *Pope*

Is folly then so old? Why, let me see
About what time of life may folly be?
Oh! she was born, by nicest calculation,
One moment after woman's first creation.

(f) *W. Spencer*

FOOL

No creature smarts so little as a fool.

(g) *Pope*

FOOLS

Where men of judgment creep and feel their way,
The positive pronounce without dismay.

(h) *Cowper*

Young men *think* old men are fools; but old men *know* young men are fools.

(i) *Chapman*

No place so sacred from such fops is barred,
Nor is Paul's church more safe than Paul's church yard;
Nay, fly to altars; there'll they talk you dead,
For fools rush in where angels fear to tread.

(j) *Pope*

FORETOLD

The prophets foretold, but never were foretold. The saints, who followed, were foretold; but had not the power of foretelling; Jesus Christ foretold, and was foretold.

(k) *Blaise Pascal*

FORGET

Men are men: the best sometimes forget.

(l) *Shakspeare*

FORGETTING THINGS BEHIND (Phil. iii. 13)

Paul forgets three things which were behind:
1. Those objects of pride which he formerly regarded as gain and glory.
2. The sins of his past life in general, and especially the many and great sins he had committed as a persecutor and blasphemer of the Church.
3. His progress hitherto in the spiritual life.

(m) *Passavant*

FORGIVENESS OF SINS, THE

" *There is* FORGIVENESS *with Thee*" (Ps. cxxx. 4)

There is not the least encouragement for the soul of a sinner to entertain any thoughts of approaching to God, without this discovery. All the rest of the world is covered with a deluge of wrath; this is the only ark whereunto the soul may repair and find rest; all without it is darkness, curse, and terror.

We have an instance and example of it, beyond all exception, in Adam. When he knew himself to be a sinner, and it was impossible for him, as we shall show afterwards, to make a discovery of any such thing as forgiveness with God, he laid aside all thoughts of treating with Him; the best of his foolish contrivance was for an escape. " I heard Thy voice (saith he to God) in the garden, and was AFRAID, because I was naked; and I HID myself " (Gen. iii. 10). Nothing but " Thou shalt die the death " sounded in his ears. In the morning of that day, he was made by the hand of God; a few hours before, he had converse and communion with Him, with boldness and peace; why, then, doth nothing now but FEAR, flying, HIDING, possess him? Adam had sinned; the promise was not yet given; no revelation made of forgiveness in God; and what other course, than that vain and foolish one, to fix upon, he knew not. No more can any of his prosperity, without this revelation. What else any of them hath fixed on in this case, hath been no less foolish than his hiding; and, in most, more pernicious. When Cain had received his sentence from God, it is said, " He went *out* from the presence, or face, of the Lord " (Gen. iv. 16). From His providential presence he could never withdraw himself; so the Psalmist informs us at large, Psalm cxxix. 7-9.

(n)

Forgiveness of Sins—*continued*

The very heathen knew, by the light of nature, that guilt could never drive men out of the reach of God. They knew that the vengeance of God would not spare sinners, nor could be avoided (Acts xxviii. 4); from God's gracious presence, which Cain never enjoyed, he could not depart. It was, then, God's presence as to his worship, and all outward acts of communion, that he forsook and departed from. He had no discovery by faith of forgiveness, and therefore resolved to have no more to do with God, nor those who cleaved to Him; for it respects his course, and not any one particular action.

(a)

This also is stated, " The sinners in Zion are afraid; fearfulness hath surprised the hypocrites. Who among us shall dwell with devouring fire ? who among us shall dwell with everlasting burnings ? " (Isa. xxxiii. 14.) The persons spoken of are sinners, great sinners, and hypocrites; conviction of sin, and the desert of it, was fallen upon them; **a light to discern forgiveness they had not; they apprehend God as devouring fire and everlasting burnings only.** One that would not spare, but assuredly inflict punishment according to the desert of sin; and thence is their conclusion couched in their interrogation, that there can be no intercourse of peace between Him and them; there is no abiding, no enduring of His presence. And what condition this consideration brings the souls of sinners into, when conviction grows strong upon them, the Holy Ghost declares, Micah vi. 6, 7, " Wherewith shall I come before the Lord, and bow myself before the High God ? shall I come before Him with burnt offerings, with calves of a year old ? Will the Lord be pleased with thousands of rams, or with ten thousands of rivers of oil ? shall I give my first-born for my transgression, the fruit of my body for the sin of my soul ? " Sense of sin presseth, forgiveness is not discovered, (like the Philistines on Saul, Samuel not coming to his direction), and how doth the poor creature perplex itself in vain to find out a way of dealing with God! Will a sedulous and diligent observation of His own ordinances and institutions relieve me ? " Shall I come before Him with burnt offerings, and calves of a year old ? " Alas! thou art a sinner, and these sacrifices cannot make thee perfect, or acquit thee. (Heb. x. 1): " Shall I do more than ever He required of any of the sons of men ? " " Oh that I had thousands of rams, and ten thousands of rivers of oil, to offer to Him ! " Alas! if thou hadst all the bulls and goats in the world, it is not possible that their blood should take away sin (ver. 4). But I have heard of them who have snatched away their own children from their mothers' breasts, and cast them into the fire until they were consumed, so to pacify their conscience in expiating the guilt of their iniquities; shall I take this course ? will it relieve me ? I am ready to part with my first-born into the fire, so that I may have deliverance from my transgressions. Alas! this never came into the heart of God to accept of ! And as it was then, whilst that kind of worship was in force, so is it still as to any duties really to be performed, or imaginarily. Where there is no discovery of forgiveness, they will yield the soul no relief, no support; God is not to be treated with upon such terms.

(b)　　　　　　　　　　　　*John Owen*

The constant voice of conscience lies against it. Conscience, if not seared, inexorably condemns, and pronounces wrath and anger upon the soul that hath the least guilt cleaving to it. Now, it hath this advantage, it lieth close to the soul, and by importunity and loud speaking it will be heard in what it hath to say. It will make the whole soul attend, or it will speak like thunder. And its constant voice is, that where there is guilt there must be judgment (Rom. ii. 14, 15).

(c)

Conscience naturally knows nothing of forgiveness; yea, it is against its very trust, work, and office, to hear anything of it. If a man of courage and honesty be entrusted to keep a garrison against an enemy, let one come and tell him that there is peace between those whom he serves and their enemies, so that he may leave his guard, and set open the gates, and cease his watchfulness; how worthy will he be, lest, under this pretence, he be betrayed! No, saith he, I will keep my hold, until I have express orders from my superiors. Conscience is intrusted with the power of God in the soul of a sinner, with command to keep all in subjection, with reference to the judgment to come; it will not betray its trust in believing every report of peace. No; but this it says, and it speaks in the name of God, " Guilt and punishment are inseparable twins; " if the soul sin, God will judge. What tell you me of forgiveness ? I know what my commission is, and that I will abide by; you shall not bring in a superior commander, a cross principle, into my trust; for if this be so, it seems I must let go my throne—another lord must come in—not knowing as yet how this whole business is compounded in the blood of Christ. Now, whom should a man believe, if not his own conscience ? which, as it will not flatter him, so it intends not to affright him; but to speak the truth as the matter requireth. Conscience hath two works in reference to sin: one to condemn the acts of sin, another to judge the person of the sinner; both with reference to the judgment of God. When forgiveness comes, it would sever and part these employments, and take one of them out of the hand of conscience; it would divide the spoil with this strong one. It shall condemn the fact, or every sin; but it shall no more condemn the sinner, the person of the sinner, that shall be freed from its sentence. Here conscience labours with all its might to keep its whole dominion, and to keep out the power of forgiveness from being enthroned in the soul. It will allow men to talk of forgiveness, to hear it preached, though they abuse it every day; but to receive it in its power, that stands up in direct opposition to its dominion; in the kingdom, saith conscience, I will be greater than thou; and in many, in the most, it keeps its possession, and will not be deposed.

Nor, indeed, is it an easy work so to deal with it. The Apostle tells us that all the sacrifices of the law could not do it (Heb. x. 2); they could not bring a man into that estate wherein he could have **no more conscience of sin**; that is, conscience condemning the person; for conscience, in a sense of sin, and condemnation of it, is never to be taken away. And this can be no otherwise done but by the blood of Christ, as the Apostle at large there declares.

(d)

Forgiveness of Sins—*continued*

It is no easy thing, then, to make a discovery of forgiveness to a soul, when the work and employment which conscience, upon unquestionable grounds, challengeth to itself, lies in opposition to it. Hence is the soul's great desire to establish its own righteousness, whereby its natural principles may be preserved in their power. Let self-righteousness be enthroned, and natural conscience desires no more; it is satisfied and pacified. The law it knows, and righteousness it knows; but as for forgiveness, it says, Whence is it? Unto the utmost, until Christ perfects His conquest, there are, on this account, secret strugglings in the heart against free pardon in the Gospel, and fluctuations of mind and spirit about it. Yea, hence are the doubts and fears of believers themselves; they are nothing but the strivings of conscience to keep its whole dominion, to condemn the sinner as well as the sin. More or less, it keeps up its pretensions against the Gospel whilst we live in this world. It is a great work that the blood of Christ hath to do upon the conscience of a sinner; for whereas, as it hath been declared, it hath a power, and claims a right, to condemn both sin and sinner, the one part of this its power is to be cleared, strengthened, made more active, vigorous, and watchful; the other to be taken quite away. It shall now see more sins than formerly; more of the vileness of all sins than formerly, and condemn them with more abhorrence than ever, upon more and more glorious accounts than formerly; but it is also made to see an interposition between these sins and the person of the sinner who hath committed them, which is no small or ordinary work.

(a)   *John Ower*

Forgiveness and the Law

The law lies against this discovery of forgiveness. The law is a beam of the holiness of God Himself; what it speaks to us, it speaks in the name and authority of God; and I shall briefly show, concerning it, these two things:—

1. That this is the voice of the law; namely, that there is no forgiveness for a sinner.

2. That a sinner hath great reason to give credit to the law in this assertion.

1. It is certain that the law knows neither mercy nor forgiveness. The very sanction of it lies wholly against it: "The soul that sinneth shall die." "Cursed is he that continueth not in all things written in the book of the law to do them" (Ezek. xviii. 4; Deut. xxvii. 26). Hence the Apostle pronounces universally, without exception, that they who are "under the law are under the curse" (Gal. iii. 10), and, saith he (ver. 12), "The law is not of faith." There is an inconsistency between the law and believing; they cannot have their abode in power together. Do this, and live; fail, and die; is the constant immutable voice of the law. This it speaks in general to all, and this, in particular, to every one.

(b)

2. The sinner seems to have manifold and weighty reasons to attend to the voice of this law, and to acquiesce in its sentence, for—

(i.) The law is connatural to him; his domestic, his old acquaintance; it came into the world with him, and hath grown up with him from his in-

fancy; it was implanted in his heart by nature; is his own reason; he can never shake it off, or part with it. It is his familiar, his friend, that cleaves to him as the flesh to the bone; so that they who have not the law written cannot but show "forth the work of the law" (Rom. ii. 14, 15); and that because the law itself is inbred to them, and all the faculties of the soul are at peace with it, in subjection to it. It is the bond and ligament of their union, harmony, and correspondence among themselves, in all their moral actings; it gives life, order, motion, to them all. Now, the Gospel, which comes to control this sentence of the law, and to relieve the sinner from it, is foreign to his nature, a strange thing to him, a thing he hath no acquaintance or familiarity with; it hath not been bred up with him; nor is there anything in him to side with it, to make a party for it, or to plead in its behalf.

Now, shall not a man believe a domestic, a friend, indeed himself, rather than a foreigner, a stranger, that comes with uncouth principles, and such as suit not his reason at all?

(c)

(ii.) The law speaks nothing to a sinner but what his conscience assures him to be true. There is a constant concurrence in the testimony of the law and conscience. When the law says this or that is a sin worthy of death, conscience says it is even so; and where the law of itself, as being a general rule, rests, conscience helps it on, and says, this and that sin, so worthy of death, is the soul guilty of; then die, saith the law, as thou hast deserved. Now, this must needs have a mighty efficacy to prevail with the soul to give credit to the report and testimony of the law; it speaks not one word but what he hath a witness within himself to the truth of it. These witnesses always agree; and so it seems to be established for a truth that there is no forgiveness.

(d)

(iii.) The law, though it speaks against the soul's interest, yet it speaks nothing but what is so just, righteous, and equal, that it even forceth the soul's consent. So Paul tells us, that men "Know this voice of the law to be the judgment of God" (Rom. i. 32). They know it, and cannot but consent unto it, that it is the judgment of God, that it is good, righteous, equal, not to be controlled. And, indeed, what can be more righteous than its sentence? It commands obedience to the God of life and death, promises a reward, and declares, that for non-performance of duty, death will be inflicted. On these terms the sinner cometh into the world; they are good, righteous, holy; the soul accepts of them, and knows not what it can desire better or more just. This the Apostle insists upon, Rom. vii. 12, 13: "Wherefore the law is holy, and the commandment holy, and just, and good; was then that which is good made death unto me? God forbid; but sin, that it might appear sin, working death in me by that which is good, that sin by the commandment might become exceeding sinful." Wherever the blame fall, the soul cannot but acquit the law, and confess that what it says is righteous and uncontrollably just; and it is meet things should be so. Now, though the authority and credit of a witness may go very far in a doubtful matter, when there is a concurrence of

(e)

Forgiveness of Sins—*continued*

more witnesses, it strengthens the testimony ; but nothing is so prevalent to beget belief, as when the things themselves that are spoken are just and good, not liable to any reasonable exception. And so it is in this case ; unto the authority of the law, and concurrence of conscience, this also is added, the reasonableness and equity of the thing itself proposed, even in the judgment of the sinner, namely, that every sin shall be punished, and every transgression receive a meet recompense of reward.

(a)

(iv.) But yet further : what the law says, it speaks in the name and authority of God. What it says, then, must be believed, or we make God a liar. It comes not in its own name, but in the name of Him who appointed it. You will say, then, Is it so, indeed ? Is there no forgiveness with God ? for this is the constant voice of the law, which you say speaks in the name and authority of God, and is therefore to be believed. I answer briefly, with the Apostle, " What the law speaks, it speaks to them that are under the law ; " it doth not speak to them that are in Christ, whom the " law of the Spirit of life hath set free from the law of sin and death." But to them that are under the law it speaks, and it speaks the very truth ; and it speaks in the name of God, and its testimony is to be received. It says there is no forgiveness in God—namely, to them that are under the Law—and they that shall flatter themselves with a contrary persuasion will find themselves woefully mistaken at the great day.

(b)   *John Owen*

Forgiveness, Ingrafted Notions of

The ingrafted notions that are in the minds of men, concerning the nature and justice of God, lie against this discovery also. There are in all men, by nature, indelible characters of the holiness and purity of God, of His justice and hatred of sin, of His invariable righteousness in the government of the world, that they can neither depose nor lay aside. For notions of God, whatever they are, will bear sway and rule in the heart, when things are put to the trial ; they were in the heathens of old ; they abode with them in all their darkness, as might be manifested by innumerable instances. But so it is in all men by nature ; their inward thought is, that God is an avenger of sin ; that it belongs to His rule and government of the world, His holiness and righteousness, to take care that every sin be punished. This is His judgment, which all men know, as was observed before (Rom. i. 32). They know that it is a righteous thing with God to render tribulation to sinners. From thence is that dread and fear which surprises men at an apprehension of the presence of God, or of anything under Him, above them, that may seem to come on His errand. This notion of God's avenging all sin exerts itself secretly but effectually ; so Adam trembled and hid himself ; and it was the saying of old, " 1 have seen God, and shall die." When men are under any dreadful Providence—thunderings, lightnings, tempests, in darkness—they tremble, not so much at what they see, or hear, or feel, as from their secret thoughts that God is nigh, and that He is a consuming fire.

(c)

Now, these inbred notions lie universally against all apprehensions of forgiveness, which must be brought into the soul from without-doors, having no principle of nature to promote them.

It is true men, by nature, have presumptions, and common ingrafted notions of other properties of God, besides His holiness and justice ; as of His goodness, benignity, love of His creatures, and the like. But all these have this supposition inlaid with them in the souls of men ; namely, that all things stand, between God and His creatures, as they did at their first creation ; as they have no natural notion of forgiveness, so the interposition of sin weakens, disturbs, darkens them, as to any improvement of those apprehensions of goodness and benignity which they have. If they have any notion of forgiveness, it is from some corrupt tradition, and not at all from any universal principle that is inbred in nature, such as are those which they have of God's holiness and vindictive justice.

And this is the first ground, from whence it appears that a real, solid discovery of forgiveness is indeed a great work. Many differences and hindrances lie in the way of its accomplishment.

(d)   *Ibid*

Forgiveness, Presumptions of

The common notion of forgiveness that men have in this world is twofold : an atheistical presumption on God that He is not so just and holy, or not just and holy in such a manner as He is by some represented, is the ground of their presumption of forgiveness. Men think that some declarations of God are fitted only to make them mad ; that He takes little notice of these things, and that what He doth, He will easily pass by, as they suppose better becomes Him. Come, " let us eat and drink, for to-morrow we shall die." This is their inward thought, " The Lord will not do good, neither will He do evil," which, says the Psalmist, is men's " thinking that God is such a one as themselves " (Ps. l. 21). They have no deep nor serious thoughts of His greatness, holiness, purity, severity, but think He is like themselves, so far as not to be much moved with what they do. What thoughts they have of sin, the same they think God hath. If, with them, a slight ejaculation be enough to expiate sin, that their consciences be no more troubled, they think it is enough with God that it be not punished. The generality of men make light work of sin, and yet in nothing doth it appear what thoughts they have of God. He that hath slight thoughts of sin had never great thoughts of God. Indeed, men's undervaluing of sin arises merely from their contempt of God. All sin's concernments flow from its relation to God ; and, as men's apprehensions are of God, so will they be of sin, which is an opposition to Him. This is the frame of the most of men ; they know little of God, and are little troubled about anything that relates to Him. God is not reverenced, sin is but a trifle, forgiveness is a matter of nothing ; whoso will may have it for asking ! But shall this atheistical wickedness of the heart of man be a discovery of forgiveness ? Is not this to make God an idol ? **He who is not acquainted with God's holiness and purity, who knows not sin's desert and sinfulness, knows nothing of forgiveness.**

(e)   *Ibid*

Forgiveness of Sins—*continued*

FORGIVENESS, PRESUMPTIONS OF

From the doctrines of the Gospel commonly preached and made known, there is a general notion begotten in the minds of men, that God is ready to forgive. Men, I say, from hence have a doctrinal apprehension of this truth, without any real satisfactory foundation of that apprehension as to themselves. This they have heard, this they have been often told; so they think, and so they are resolved to do. A general persuasion hereof spreads itself over all to whom the sound of the Gospel doth come. It is not fiducially resolved into the Gospel, but is an opinion growing out of the report of it.

(*a*)

1. **That which we reject is loose and general—not fixed, ingrafted, or planted in the mind.** So is it always where the minds of men receive things only in their notion, and not in their power. It wants fixedness and foundation, which defects accompany all notions of the minds that are only retained in the memory, not implanted in the judgment. They have general thoughts of it, which they use as occasion serves. They hear that God is a merciful God, and as such they intend to deal with Him. For the true rise and foundation of it, whence, or on what account, the pure and holy God, who will do no iniquity; the righteous God, whose judgment it is that they who commit sin are worthy of death, should yet pardon iniquity, transgression, and sin; they weigh it not, they consider it not; or, if they do, it is in a slight and notional way, as they consider the thing itself. They take it for granted that so it is, and are never put seriously upon the inquiry how it comes to be so; and that because indeed they have no real concern in it. How many thousands may we meet with, who take it for granted that forgiveness is to be had with God, who never yet had any serious exercise in their souls about the ground of it, and its consistency with His holiness and justice! But those who know it by faith have a sense of it fixed particularly and distinctly on their minds. They have been put upon an inquiry into the rise and grounds of it in Christ; so that, on a good and unquestionable foundation, they can go to God, and say, "There is forgiveness with Thee." They see how, and by what means, more glory comes to God by forgiveness than by punishing of sin, which is a matter that the other sort of men are not at all solicitous about. If they may escape punishment, whether God have any glory or not, for the most part they are indifferent.

(*b*)   *John Owen*

FORGIVENESS, PRESUMPTIONS OF

2. **The first apprehension ariseth, without any trial, upon inquiry in the consciences of those in whom it is.** They have not, by the power of their convictions, and distresses of conscience, been put to make inquiry, whether this thing be so or not. It is not a persuasion that they have arrived at in a way of seeking satisfaction to their own souls; it is not the result of a deep inquiry after peace and rest; it is antecedent unto trial and experience; and so is not faith, but opinion. For although faith be not experience, it is inseparable from it, as is every practicable habit. Distresses in their consciences have been prevented by this

opinion, not removed. The reason why the most of men are not troubled about their sins to any purpose, is from a persuasion that God is merciful, and will pardon; when, indeed, none can really, on a Gospel account, ordinarily, have that persuasion, but those who have been troubled for sin, and that to purpose. So is it with those who make this discovery by faith: they have had conflicts in their own spirits, and being deprived of their peace, have accomplished a diligent search, whether forgiveness were to be obtained or not. The persuasion they have of it, be it more or less, is the issue of a trial they have had in their own souls, of an inquiry how things stood between God and them, as to peace, and the acceptation of their persons. This is a vast difference: the one sort might possibly have had trouble in their consciences about sin, had it not been for their opinion of forgiveness. This had prevented or stifled their convictions—not healed their wounds, which is the work of the Gospel; but kept them from being wounded, which is the work of security. Yea, here lies the ruin of the most of those who perish under the preaching of the Gospel: they have received the general notion of pardon; it floats in their minds, and promptly presents itself to their relief on all occasions. Doth God at any time, in the dispensation of the word, under an affliction, upon some great sin against their ruling light, begin to deal with their consciences; before their conviction can ripen, or come to any perfection, before it draw nigh to its perfect work, they choke it, and heal their consciences with this notion of pardon. Many a man, between the assembly and his dwelling-house, is thus cured. You may see them go away shaking their heads, and striking on their breasts, and, before they come home, be as whole as ever: "Well! God is merciful—there is pardon," hath wrought the cure. The other sort have obtained their persuasion as a result of the discovery of Christ in the Gospel, upon a full conviction. Trials they have had, and this is the issue.

(*c*)   *Ibid*

FORGIVENESS, PRESUMPTIONS OF

3. **The one (which we reject) worketh no love to God, no delight in Him, no reverence of Him, but rather a contempt and commonness of spirit in dealing with Him.** There are none in the world that deal worse with God than those who have an ungrounded persuasion of forgiveness; and if they do fear Him, or love Him, or obey Him in anything, more or less, it is on other motives and considerations, which will not render anything they do acceptable, and not at all on this. As He is good to the creation, they may love; as He is great and powerful, they may fear Him; but sense of pardon, as to any such ends or purposes, hath no power upon them. Carnal boldness, formality, and despising of God, are the common issues of such a notion and persuasion. Indeed, this is the generation of great sinners in the world; men who have a general apprehension, but not a sense of the special power of pardon, openly or secretly, in fleshly or spiritual sins, are the great sinners among men. Where faith makes a discovery of forgiveness, all things are otherwise; great love. fear, and reverence of God, are its attendants. Mary Magdalene loved much, because much was forgiven. Great love will spring out of great for-

(*d*)

Forgiveness of Sins—*continued*

giveness. "There is forgiveness with Thee (saith the Psalmist), that Thou mayest be feared." No unbeliever doth truly and experimentally know the truth of this inference. But so it is, when men "fear the Lord and His goodness" (Hos. iii. 5). I say, then, where pardoning mercy is truly apprehended, where faith makes a discovery of it to the soul, it is endeared to God, and possessed of the great springs of love, delight, fear, and reverence (Ps. cxvi. 1–7).

(*a*)   *John Owen*

FORGIVENESS, PRESUMPTIONS OF

4. This notional apprehension of the pardon of sin, begets no serious thorough hatred and detestation of sin, nor is prevalent to a relinquishment of it: nay, it rather secretly insinuates into the soul encouragements to a continuance in it. It is the nature of it to lessen and extenuate sin, and to support the soul against its convictions. So Jude tells us, that some "turn the grace of God into lasciviousness," ver. 4; and, says he, "they are ungodly men;" let them profess what they will, they are ungodly men. But how can they turn the grace of our God into lasciviousness? Is grace capable of a conversion into lust or sin? Will what was once grace ever become wantonness? It is the doctrine, not the real substance of grace, that is intended. The doctrine of forgiveness is this grace of God, which may be thus abused. From hence do men, who have only a general notion of ·it, habitually draw secret encouragements to sin and folly. Paul also lets us know that carnal men, coming to a doctrinal acquaintance with Gospel grace, are very apt to make such conclusions (Rom. vi. 1). And it will appear, at the last day, how unspeakably this glorious grace hath been perverted in the world. It would be well for many if they had never heard the name of forgiveness. It is otherwise where this revelation is received indeed in the soul by believing (Rom. vi. 14). Our being under grace, under the power of the belief of forgiveness, is our great preservative from being under the power of sin. Faith of forgiveness is the principle of Gospel obedience (Tit. ii. 11, 12).

(*b*)   *Ibid*

FORGIVENESS, PRESUMPTIONS OF

5. The general notion of forgiveness brings with it no sweetness, no rest to the soul. Flashes of joy it may, abiding rest it doth not. The truth of the doctrine fluctuates to and fro in the minds of those that have it, but their wills and affections have no solid delight nor rest by it. Hence, notwithstanding all that profession which is made in the world, of forgiveness, most men, ultimately, resolve their peace and comfort into themselves. As their apprehensions are of their own doing, good or evil, according to their ruling light, whatever it be ; so, as to peace and rest, they are secretly tossed up and down. Every one, in his several ways, pleaseth himself with what he doth in answer to his own convictions, and is disquieted as to his state and condition according as he seems to himself to come short thereof. To make a full life of content upon pardon, they know not how to do it. One duty yields them more true repose than many thoughts of forgiveness. But faith finds sweetness and rest in it. Being thereby apprehended, it is

the only harbour of the soul : it leads a man to God, as good, to Christ as rest. Fading, vanishing joys do ofttimes attend the one ; but solid delight, with constant obedience, are the fruits only of the other.

(*c*)   *Ibid*

FORGIVENESS, PRESUMPTIONS OF

6. Those who have the former only, take up their persuasion on false grounds, though the thing itself be true; and they cannot but use it to false ends and purposes, besides its natural and genuine tendency. For their grounds, they will be discovered, when I come to treat of the true nature of Gospel forgiveness : for the end, it is used generally only to fill up what is wanting. Self-righteousness is their dependence, and when that is too short or too narrow to cover them, they piece it out by forgiveness. Where conscience accuses, this must supply the defect. Faith lays it on its proper foundation, of which afterwards also, and it useth it to its proper end, namely, to be the sole and only ground of our acceptance with God. That is the proper use of forgiveness, that all may be of grace ; for when the foundation is pardon, the whole superstructure must needs be grace. From what hath been spoken, it is evident that, notwithstanding the pretences to the contrary, insinuated in the objection now removed, it is a great thing to have Gospel-forgiveness discovered to a soul in a saving manner.

(*d*)   *Ibid*

FORGIVENESS, THE TRUE NATURE OF GOSPEL

The forgiveness inquired after hath relation to the gracious heart of the Father :

1. The infinite goodness and graciousness of His nature.

2. The sovereign purpose of His will and grace.

There is considerable in it, the infinite goodness of His nature. Sin stands in a contrariety to God ; it is a rebellion against His sovereignty, an opposition to His holiness, a provocation to His justice, a rejection of His yoke, a casting off what lies in the sinner of that dependence which a creature hath on its Creator. That God, then, should have pity and compassion on sinners, in every one of whose sins there is all this evil, and inconceivably more than we can comprehend, it argues an infinitely gracious, good, and loving heart and nature in Him ; for God doth nothing but suitably to the profit of His nature ; and from them all the acts of His will are the effects of His nature.

(*e*)

Forgiveness : its relation to the NAME of God

Now, whatever God proposes as an encouragement for sinners to come to Him, it is of, or hath a special influence unto, the forgiveness that is with Him ; for nothing can encourage a sinner, as such, but under this consideration, that it is, or it respects, forgiveness. That this graciousness of God's nature lies at the head, or spring, and is the root from whence forgiveness grows, is manifest from that solemn proclamation which He made of old of His name, and the revelation of His nature therein (for God is assuredly what by Himself He is called), "The Lord, the Lord God, merciful and gracious, long-suffering, and abundant in goodness and truth, keeping mercy for thousands, forgiving

(*f*)

Forgiveness of Sins—*continued*

iniquity, and transgression, and sin (Exod. xxxiv. 6, 7). His forgiving iniquity flows from hence, that in His nature He is merciful, gracious, long-suffering, abundant in goodness. Were He not so infinite in all these, it were vain to look for forgiveness from Him. Having made this known to be His name, and thereby declared His nature, He in many places proposes it as a relief, a refuge for sinners, an encouragement to come unto Him, and to wait for mercy from Him. "They that know Thy name will put their trust in Thee" (Ps. ix. 10). It will encourage them so to do. Others have no foundation of their confidence; but if this name of God be indeed made known to us by the Holy Ghost, what can hinder, why we should not repair to Him, and rest upon Him? So Isaiah l. 10: "Who is among you that feareth the Lord, that obeyeth the voice of His servant, that walketh in darkness and hath no light? let him trust in the name of the Lord, and stay upon His God." Not only sinners, but sinners in great distress, are here spoken to. Darkness of state and condition, in the Scripture, denotes everything of disconsolation and trouble. To be then in darkness, where yet there is some light, some relief, though darkness be predominating, is sad and disconsolate; but now, not only to be, but also to walk—that is, to continue a course in darkness, and that with no light, no discovery of help or relief—this seems to be an overwhelming condition; yet sinners in this estate are called "to trust in the name of the Lord." I have showed before, that nothing but forgiveness, or that which influences it, and encourages to an expectation of it, is of any use to a sinner, much more one in such great distress on account of sin; yet is such an one here sent only to the NAME of the Lord, wherein His gracious heart and nature is revealed. That, then, is the very fountain and spring of forgiveness; and this is that which John would work a sense of upon our souls where he tells us that "God is love" (1 John iv. 8), or one of an infinitely gracious, tender, good, compassionate, loving nature. Infinite goodness and grace is the soil wherein forgiveness grows. It is impossible that this flower should spring from any other root; unless this be revealed to the soul, forgiveness is not revealed. To consider pardon merely as it is terminated upon ourselves, not as it flows from God, will bring neither profit to us nor glory to God.

(*a*)

And this also will make it appear that this discovery of forgiveness, whereof we speak, is indeed no common thing, but a GREAT DISCOVERY. Let men come, with a sense of the guilt of sin, to have deep and serious thoughts of God; they will find it no such easy and light matter to have their hearts truly and thoroughly apprehensive of this loving and gracious nature of God in reference to pardon. It is an easy matter to say so in common, but the soul will not find it so easy to believe it for itself. What hath been spoken before, concerning the ingrafted notions that are in the minds of men about the justice, holiness, and severity of God, will here take place. Though men profess that God is gracious, yet that aversion which they have to Him and communion with Him, abundantly manifests that they do not believe what they say and profess. If they did, they could not but delight and trust in Him, which they do not; for "they that know His name will put their trust in Him." So the slothful

servant in the gospel said, "I knew that Thou wast austere," and not for me to deal with; it may be he professed otherwise before, but that lay in his heart when it came to the trial. But this, I say, is necessary to those to whom this discovery is to be made; even a spiritual apprehension of the gracious, loving heart and nature of God. This is the spring of all that follows; and the fountain must needs be infinitely sweet from whence such streams do flow. He that considers the glorious fabric of heaven and earth, with the things contained in them, must needs conclude that they were the product of "infinite wisdom and power"; nothing less or under them could have brought forth such an effect. And he that really considers forgiveness, and looks on it with a spiritual eye, must conclude that it comes from infinite goodness and grace. And this is that which the hearts of sinners are exercised about, when they come to deal for pardon: "Thou, Lord, art good, and ready to forgive" (Ps. lxxxvi. 5); "Thou art a God ready to pardon, gracious and merciful, slow to anger, and of great kindness" (Neh. ix. 17); and "Who is God like unto thee, that pardoneth iniquity? because He delighteth in mercy" (Micah vii. 18) And God encourageth them hereunto, wherever he says that He forgives sins and blots out iniquities for His own sake, or His name's sake; that is, He will deal with sinners according to the goodness of His own gracious nature. So, Hosea xi. 9: "I will not execute the fierceness of Mine anger; I will not return to destroy Ephraim, for I am God, and not man." Were there no more mercy, grace, compassion to be showed in this case than it is possible should be treasured up in the heart of man, it would be impossible that Ephraim should be spared; but, saith He, "I am God, and not man." Consider the infinite largeness, bounty, and goodness of the heart of God, and there is yet hope. When a sinner is in good earnest seeking after forgiveness, there is nothing he is more solicitous about than the heart of God towards him, nothing that he more labours to have a discovery of; there is nothing that sin and Satan labour more to hide from him; this he rolls in his mind, and exercises his thoughts about; and if ever that voice of God, "Fury is not in Me" (Isa. xxvii. 4), sound in his heart, he is relieved from his great distresses. And the fear of our hearts in this matter, our Saviour seems to intend the prevention, or a removal of, John xvi. 26: "I say not that I will pray the Father for you, for the Father Himself loveth you." The disciples had good thoughts of the tender heart and care of Christ Himself, the Mediator, towards them; but what is the heart of the Father? What acceptance shall they find with Him? Will Christ pray that they may find favour with Him? Why, saith He, as to the love of His heart, there is no need of it; "For the Father Himself loveth you." If this then belongeth to forgiveness, as whoever hath sought for it knoweth that it doth, it is certainly no common discovery to have it revealed to us.

To have all the clouds and darkness that are raised by sin, between us and the throne of God, dispelled; to have the fire, and storms, and tempests that are kindled and stirred up about him by the law, removed; to have His glorious face unveiled, and His holy heart laid open, and a view given of those infinite treasures and stores of goodness, mercy, love, and kindness which have had an unchangeable habitation therein from all

(*b*)

Forgiveness of Sins—*continued*

eternity; to have a discovery of these eternal springs of forbearance and forgiveness, is that which none but Christ can accomplish and bring about (John xvii. 6).

(a)　　　　　　　　　　　　*John Owen*

Forgiveness, True Nature of Gospel

II. This is not all. This eternal ocean, that is infinitely satisfied with its own fulness and perfection, doth not naturally yield forth streams for our refreshment. Mercy and pardon do not come forth from God as light doth from the sun, or water from the sea, by a necessary consequence of their natures, whether they will or not. It doth not necessarily follow, that any one must be made partakers of forgiveness, because God is infinitely gracious; for, may He not do what He will with His own? "Who hath given first unto Him, that it should be recompensed unto him again?" (Rom. xi. 35). All the fruits of God's goodness and grace are in the sole keeping of His own sovereign will and pleasure. This is His great glory (Exod. xxxiii. 18, 19): "Shew me Thy glory," saith Moses. "And He said, I will make all My goodness to pass before thee, and I will proclaim the name of the Lord before Thee; and I will be gracious to whom I will be gracious." Upon that proclamation of the name of God, that He is "merciful, gracious, long-suffering, abundant in goodness," some might conclude, that it could not but be well with all; He is such a one, as that men need scarce be beholden to Him for mercy; nay, saith He, but this is My great glory, that "I will be gracious to whom I will be gracious." There must be an interposition of a free act of the will of God, to deal with us according to this His abundant goodness, or we can have no interest therein. This I call the purpose of His grace, or the "good pleasure that He hath purposed in Himself" (Eph. i. 9); or, as it is termed, verse 5, 6, "the good pleasure of His will, that He hath purposed, to the praise of His glorious grace." This free and gracious pleasure of God, or purpose of His will to act towards sinners according to His own abundant goodness, is another thing that influences the forgiveness of which we treat. Pardon flows immediately from a sovereign act of free grace. This free purpose of God's will and grace, for the pardoning of sinners, is indeed that which is principally intended when we say, "There is forgiveness with Him;" that is, He is pleased to forgive, and so to do is agreeable to His nature. Now, the mystery of this grace is deep; it is eternal, and therefore incomprehensible. Few there are whose hearts are raised to a contemplation of it. Men rest and are content themselves in a general notion of mercy, which will not be advantageous to their souls. Freed they would be from punishment, but what it is to be forgiven they inquire not. So, what they know of it they come easily by, but will find in the issue it will stand them in little stead. But these fountains of God's actings are revealed, that they may be the fountains of our comforts.

(b)　　　　　　　　　　　　*Ibid*

Forgiveness, The True Nature of Gospel

1. There is His purpose of sending His Son to be the great means of procuring, of purchasing, forgiveness. Though God be infinitely and incomprehensibly gracious, though He purpose to exert His grace and goodness towards sinners, yet He will so do it, do it in such a way as shall not be prejudicial

to His own holiness and righteousness. His justice must be satisfied, and His holy indignation against sin made known; wherefore, He purposeth to send His Son, and hath sent Him to make way for the exercise of mercy, so as no way to eclipse the glory of His justice, holiness, and hatred of sin. Better we should all eternally come short of forgiveness, than that God should lose anything of His glory. This we have, Rom. iii. 25: "God set Him forth to be a propitiation through faith in His blood, to declare His righteousness for the remission of sins that are past." The remission of sins is the thing aimed at; but this must be so brought about, as that therein not only the mercy, but the righteousness of God, may be declared, and therefore it must be brought forth by a propitiation, or making of an atonement, in the blood of Christ. So, John iii. 16; 1 John iv. 9; Rom. v. 8. This, I say, also lies in the mystery of that forgiveness that is administered in the Gospel; it comes forth from this eternal purpose of making way by the blood of Christ to the dispensation of pardon; and this greatly heightens the excellency of this discovery.

(c)

Men who have slight thoughts of God, whose hearts were never awed with His dread or greatness, who never seriously considered His purity and holiness, may think it no great matter that God should pardon sin. But do they consider the way whereby it was to be brought about, even by the sending of His only Son, and that to die, as we shall see afterwards. Neither was there any other way whereby it might be done. Let us now lay aside common thoughts, assent upon reports and traditions, and rightly weigh this matter; doubtless we shall find it to be a great thing, that forgiveness should be so with God, as to be made out unto us (we know somewhat what we are), by sending His only Son to die. Oh, how little is this really believed, even by those who make a profession of it! and what mean thoughts are entertained about it when men seek for pardon! Immunity from punishment is the utmost that lies in the aims and desires of most, and is all that they are exercised in the consideration of when they deal with God about sin. Such men think, and will do so, that we have an easy task in hand, namely, to prove that there is forgiveness in God; but this ease lies in their own ignorance and darkness. If ever they come to search after it indeed, to inquire into the nature, reasons, causes, fountain and spring of it, they will be able to give another account of these things. Christ is the centre of the mystery of the Gospel, and forgiveness is laid up in the heart of Christ, from the love of the Father; in Him are all the treasures of it hid. And surely it is no small thing to have the heart of Christ revealed unto us. When believers deal about pardon, their faith exercises itself about this, that God, with whom the soul hath to do, hath sent the Lord Christ to die for this end, that it may freely be given out. General notions of impunity they dwell not on, they pass not for; they have a closer converse with God than to be satisfied with such thoughts. They inquire into the graciousness of His nature, and the good pleasure of His will, the purpose of His grace; they ponder, and look into the mystery of His wisdom and love in sending His Son. If these springs be not clear unto them, the streams will yield them but little refreshment. It is not enough that we seek after

(d)

Forgiveness of Sins—*continued*

salvation, but we are to inquire and search diligently into the nature and manner of it. These are the things that the "angels desire to bow down and look into" (1 Pet. i. 11–13). And some think if they have got a form of words about them, they have obtained a sufficient comprehension of them. It is doubtless one reason why many, who truly believe, do yet so fluctuate about forgiveness all their days, that they never exercised faith to look into the springs of it, its eternal fountains, but have merely dwelt on actual pardon. However, I say, these things lie utterly out of the consideration of the common pretenders to an acquaintance with the truth we have in hand.

(*a*)

2. There is another sovereign act of God's will to be considered in this matter, and that is, **His eternal designation of the persons who shall be made partakers of this mercy.** He hath not left this thing to hazard and uncertainties, that it should, as it were, be unknown to Him who should be pardoned and who not. Nay, none ever are made partakers of His forgiveness but those whom He hath eternally and graciously designed thereunto. So the Apostle declares it (Eph. i. 5–7). The rise is His eternal predestination; the end, the glory of His grace; the means, redemption in the blood of Christ; the thing itself, forgiveness of sins. None ever are or can be made partakers thereof but by virtue of this act of God's will and grace, which thereupon hath a peculiar influence into it, and is to be respected in the consideration of it. I know this may be abused by pride, profaneness, and unbelief; and so may the whole work of God's grace; and so it is, even the blood of Christ, in an especial manner; but in its proper place and use, it hath a signal influence as to the glory of God and the consolation of the souls of men.

(*b*) *John Owen*

Forgiveness, True Nature of Gospel

3. **Forgiveness hath respect to the propitiation made in and by the blood of Christ the Son.** Indeed, here lies the knot and centre of gospel forgiveness: it flows from the cross, and springs out of the grave of Christ.

(i.) Pardon is purchased and procured by it. Our redemption is our forgiveness, as the cause contains the effect. No soul is pardoned, but with respect to the blood of Christ, as the procuring cause of that pardon. Hence, He is said to " have washed us in His blood " (Rev. i. 5); "in Himself to have purged our sins " (Heb. i. 3); by " one offering to have taken away sin, and for ever to have perfected them that are sanctified " (Heb. x. 14); to be the " ransom and propitiation " of our sins (1 John ii. 2); to have made " an end of sin" (Dan. ix. 24), and to have "made reconciliation for the sins of His people" (Heb. ii. 17). God hath enclosed His rich stores of pardon and mercy in the blood of Jesus Christ.

(*c*)

(ii.) Because, **in His blood, the promise of pardon is ratified and confirmed,** so that nothing is wanting to our complete forgiveness but our pleading the promise by faith in Him. " All the promises of God are in Him yea, in Him Amen " (2 Cor. i. 20); that is, faithfully and irrecoverably and immutably established. And, therefore, the Apostle having told us that this is the covenant of God, that He " would be merciful to our sins and iniquities " (Heb. viii. 12), he informs us that, in the undertaking of Christ, this covenant is become a testament (chap. ix. 15, 16, 17), so ratified in His blood, that mercy and forgiveness of sin is irrevocably confirmed to us therein.

(*d*)

(iii.) Because He hath in His own Person, as the Head of the Church, received an equipment for the whole body. His personal discharge upon the accomplishment of His work was a pledge of the discharge which was in due time to be given to His whole mystical body. Peter tells us (Acts ii. 24) that it was impossible He should be detained by death: and why so? Because, death being penally inflicted on Him, when He had paid the debt, He was legally to be acquitted. Now, for whom, and in whose name and stead He suffered, for them, and in their name and stead, He received His acquitment.

(*e*)

(iv.) Because, upon His death, God the Father hath committed to Him the whole management of the business of forgiveness, " He (now) gives repentance and forgiveness of sins " (Acts v. 31). It is Christ that forgives us (Col. iii. 13). All forgiveness is now at His disposal, and He pardoneth whom He will, even all that are given to Him of the Father, not casting out any that come to God by Him. He is intrusted with all stores of His Father's purpose, and His own purchase; and thence tells us that " all things that the Father hath are His " (John xvi. 15).

In all these respects doth forgiveness relate to the blood of Christ. Mercy, pardon, and grace, could find no other way to issue forth from the heart of the Father, but by the heart's blood of the Son, and so do they stream to the heart of the sinner.

(*f*) *Ibid*

Forgiveness: Its Relation to the Blood of Christ.

Two things are principally to be considered in the respect that forgiveness hath to the blood of Christ.

1. **The way of its procurement;**
2. **The way of its administration by Him.**

The first is deep, mysterious, dreadful. It was by His blood, the blood of the cross, the travail of His soul; His undergoing wrath and curses. The other is gracious, merciful, and tender; whence so many things are spoken of His mercifulness and faithfulness, to encourage us to expect forgiveness from Him.

This also adds to the mysterious depths of forgiveness, and makes its discovery a great matter. The soul that looks after it in earnest must consider what it cost. How light do most men make of pardon! What an easy thing is it to be acquainted with it! And no very hard matter to obtain it. But to hold communion with God in the blood of His Son is a thing of another nature than is once dreamed of by many, who think they know well enough what it is to be pardoned. " God be merciful " is a common saying; and as common to desire He would be so " for Christ's sake." Poor creatures are cast into the mould of such expressions, who know neither

(*g*)

Forgiveness of Sins—*continued*

God, nor mercy, nor Christ, nor anything of the mystery of the Gospel. Others look on the outside of the cross, to see into the mystery of the love of the Father, working in the blood of the Mediator ; to consider, by faith, the great transaction of Divine wisdom, justice, and mercy therein, how few attain to it ! To come to God, by Christ, for forgiveness, and therein to behold the law issuing all its threats-and curses in His blood, and losing its sting, putting an end to its obligation to punishment ; in the cross to see all sins gathered up in the hands of God's justice, and made to meet on the Mediator ; and eternal love springing forth triumphantly from His blood, flourishing into pardon, grace, mercy, forgiveness—this the heart of a sinner can be enlarged to only by the Spirit of God.

(*a*)   *John Owen*

Forgiveness, The Promise of

There is in forgiveness free discharge or pardon according to the tenour of the Gospel ; and this may be considered two ways.

1. As it lies in *the promise* itself ; and so it is God's gracious declaration of pardon to sinners, by the blood of Christ ; His covenant to that end and purpose, which is variously proposed, according as He knew was needful for all the ends and purposes of ingenerating faith, and communicating that consolation which He intends therein. This is the law of His grace, the declaration of the mystery of His love, before insisted on.

2. There is the bringing home and application of all this mercy to the soul of a sinner by the Holy Ghost ; wherein we are "freely forgiven all our trespasses " (Col. ii. 13).

(*b*)   *Ibid*

Forgiveness : Faith's View of it

1. **Sometimes faith fixes upon the name and infinite goodness of the nature of God, and draws out forgiveness from thence.** So doth the Psalmist : " Thou, Lord, art good, and ready to forgive " (Ps. lxxxvi. 5). He rolls himself, in the pursuit and expectation of pardon, on the infinite goodness of the nature of God. So Nehemiah ix. 17, " Thou art a God of pardons, or ready to forgive ; of an infinite, gracious, loving nature ; not severe and wrathful :" and this is that which we are encouraged to, " to stay on the name of God " (Isa. l. 10), as in innumerable other places.

And thus faith oftentimes finds a peculiar sweetness and encouragement in and from the consideration of God's gracious nature. Sometimes this is the first thing it fixes on, and sometimes the last it rests in ; and oftentimes it makes a stay here, when it is driven from all other holds. Faith can say, However it be, yet God is gracious ; and at least make that conclusion which we have from it, " God is gracious and merciful. Who knoweth but He will return ? " (Joel ii. 13, 14). And when faith hath well laid hold of this consideration, it will not easily be driven from its expectation of relief and forgiveness, even from hence.

(*c*)

2. **Sometimes the soul by faith addresses itself in a peculiar manner to the sovereignty of God's will ;** whereby He is gracious to whom He will be gracious and merciful to whom He will be merciful,

which, as was showed, is another considerable spring or principle of forgiveness. This way David's faith steered him in his great strait and perplexity, " If I shall find favour in the eyes of the Lord, He will bring me again ; but if He thus say, I have no delight in thee ; behold here am I, let Him do unto me as seemeth good unto Him " (2 Sam. xv. 25, 26). That which he hath in consideration is, whether God hath any delight in him or not ? That is, whether God would graciously remit and pardon the great sin, against which at that time He manifested His indignation. Here he lays himself down before the sovereign grace of God, and waits patiently the discovery of the free act of His will concerning him ; and at this door, as it were, enters into the consideration of those other springs of pardon, which faith inquires after, and closes with. This, sometimes, is all the cloud that appears to a distressed soul, which after a while fills the heavens, by the addition of the other considerations mentioned, and yields plentifully refreshing showers. And this condition is a sin-entangled soul ofttimes reduced to, in looking out for relief it can discover nothing but this, that God is able, and can, if He graciously pleases, relieve and acquit him. All other support, or springs of relief, are shut up or hid from him. The springs indeed may be nigh, as that was to Hagar ; but their eyes are withheld, that they cannot see them. Wherefore they cast themselves on God's sovereign pleasure, and say with Job, " Though He slay us, we will put our trust in Him " ; we will not let Him go. In ourselves we are lost—that is unquestionable ; how the Lord will deal with us, we know not ; we see not our signs and tokens any more ; evidences of God's grace in us, or of His love and favour to us, are all out of sight. To a present special interest in Christ, we are strangers ; and we lie every moment at the door of eternity. What course shall we take ? what way shall we proceed ? If we abide at a distance from God, we shall assuredly perish. Whoever hardened Himself against Him and prospered ? Nor is there the least relief to be had but from and by Him ; for who can forgive sins but God ? We will then bring our guilty souls into His presence, and attend the pleasure of His grace ; what He speaks concerning us we will willingly submit to. And this sometimes proves an anchor to a tossed soul ; which, though it gives it not rest and peace, yet it saves it from the rock of despair. Here it abides, until light more and more breaks forth upon it.

(*d*)

3. **Faith, dealing about forgiveness, doth commonly eye, in a peculiar manner, its relation to the mediation and blood of Christ.** So the Apostle directs, (1 John ii. 2) : " If any man sin, we have an Advocate with the Father, Jesus Christ, the righteous ; and He is the propitiation for our sins." If any one hath sinned, and is in depths and entanglements about it, what course shall he take ? How shall he proceed to obtain deliverance ? Why, he must apply unto God for pardon. But what shall he rely upon to encourage him in so doing ? Saith the apostle, " Consider by faith the atonement and propitiation made for sin by the blood of Christ ; and that He is still pursuing the work of love, to the suing out of pardon for us, and rest thy soul thereon. This I say most commonly is that which faith, in the first place, immediately fixes on.

(*e*)

Forgiveness of Sins—*continued*

4. Faith eyes actual pardon. So God proposes it as a motive to further believing (Isa. xliv. 22): "I have blotted out as a thick cloud thy transgressions, and as a cloud thy sins; return unto me, for I have redeemed thee." Actual pardon of sin is proposed to faith, as an encouragement unto a full returning to God in all things (2 Sam. xxiii. 5). And the like may be said of all the other particulars which we have insisted on. There is not any of them but will yield peculiar relief to a soul dealing with God about forgiveness, as having some one special concern or other of forgiveness inwrapped in them.

(*a*)   *John Owen*

Forgiveness Discovered, or Revealed only to Faith. Reasons thereof

"That this discovery of forgiveness is, and can be made to faith alone." The nature of it is such, as that nothing else can discover it, or receive it. No reasonings, no inquiries of the heart of man, can reach into it. That guess or glimpse which the heathens had of old of somewhat so called, and which false worshippers have at present, is not the forgiveness we insist upon, but a mere imagination of their own hearts.

This the Apostle informs us (Rom. i. 17): the "righteousness of God is," in the Gospel, "revealed from faith to faith." Nothing but faith hath anything to do with it. It is that "righteousness of God" whereof he speaks, that consists in the forgiveness of sins by the blood of Christ, declared in the Gospel. And this is revealed from the faith of God in the promise, to the faith of the believer; to him that mixes the promise with faith. And again, more fully, "Eye hath not seen, nor ear heard, neither have entered into the heart of man, the things which God hath prepared for them that love Him" (1 Cor. ii. 9). The ways whereby we may come to the knowledge of anything, are by the seeing of the eye, or the hearing of the ear, or the reasonings and meditations of the heart; but now, none of these will reach to the matter in hand; by none of these ways can we come to an acquaintance with the things of the Gospel, that are prepared for us in Christ. How then shall we obtain the knowledge of them? This he declares (ver. 10), "God hath revealed them unto us by the Spirit." Now it is faith only that receives the revelations of the Spirit; nothing else hath to do with them.

To give evidence hereunto, we may consider, that this great mystery-

1. Is too deep;
2. Is too great for anything else to discover;
3. That nothing else but faith is suited to the making of this discovery.

(*b*)

1. It is too deep and too mysterious to be fathomed and reached by anything else. Reason's line is too short to fathom the depths of the Father's love, of the blood of the Son, and the promises of the Gospel built thereon, wherein forgiveness dwells. Men cannot, by their rational considerations, launch out into these deeps, nor draw water by them from these wells of salvation. Reason stands by amazed, and cries, How can these things be? It can but gather cockle-shells, like him of old, at the shore of this ocean: a few criticisms upon the outward letter, and so bring

an evil report upon the land, as did the spies. All it can do is but to hinder faith from venturing upon it; crying, "Spare thyself: this attempt is vain, these things are impossible. It is among the things that faith puts off, and lays aside, when it engages the soul in this great work. This, then, that it may come to a discovery of forgiveness, causes the soul to deny itself, and all its own reasonings, and to give up itself to an infinite fulness of goodness and truth. Though it cannot go to the bottom of these depths, yet it enters into them, and finds rest in them. Nothing but faith is suited to rest, to satiate, and content itself, in mysterious, bottomless, unsearchable depths. Being a soul-emptying, a reason-denying grace, the more it meets with beyond its search and reach, the more satisfaction it finds. This is that which I looked for, saith faith, even for that which is infinite and unsearchable; for I know that there is abundantly more beyond me, that I do not comprehend, than what I have attained unto; I know that nothing else will do good to the soul. . . . Now this is that which really puzzles and overwhelms reason, rendering it useless. What it cannot compass, it will neglect or despise. It is either amazed and confounded, and dazzled, like weak eyes at too great a light; or, fortifying itself by inbred pride and obstinacy, it concludes, that this preaching of the cross, of forgiveness from the love of God, by the blood of Christ, is plain folly, a thing not for a wise man to take notice of, or to trouble himself about; so it appeared to the wise Greeks of old (1 Cor. i. 23). Hence when a soul is brought under the power of a real conviction of sin, so as that he would anxiously be freed from the galling entanglements of it, it is then the hardest thing in the world to persuade such a soul of this forgiveness. Anything appears more rational to it; any self-righteousness in this world, any purgatory hereafter.

(*c*)

The greatest part of the world of convinced persons have forsaken forgiveness on this account; masses, penances, merits, have appeared more eligible; yea, men who have no other desire but to be forgiven, do choose to close with anything rather than forgiveness. If men escape these rocks, and resolve that nothing but pardon will relieve them, yet it is impossible for them to receive it in the truth and power of it, if not enabled by faith thereunto. I speak not of men who take it up by hearsay, as a common report, but of those souls who find themselves really concerned to look after it; when they know it is their sole concern, all their hope and relief; when they know that they must perish everlastingly without it; and when it is declared to them in the words of truth and soberness, yet they cannot receive it. What is the reason of it? What staves off these hungry creatures from their proper food? Why, they have nothing to lead them into the mysterious depths of eternal love, of the blood of Christ, and promises of the Gospel. How may we see poor diseased souls standing every day at the side of the pool, and yet not once venture themselves into it all their days.

(*d*)

2. It is too great for anything else to discover. Forgiveness is a thing chosen out of God for all eternity, to exalt and magnify the glory of His

(*e*)

Forgiveness of Sins—*continued*

grace; and it will be made appear to all the world, at the day of judgment, to have been a great thing. When the soul comes in any measure to be made sensible of it, it finds it so great, so excellent and astonishing, that it sinks under the thoughts of it. It hath dimensions—a length, breadth, depth, and height, that no line of the rational soul can take or measure. There is exceeding greatness in it (Eph. i. 19). That is a great work which we have prescribed (Eph. iii. 19). Even "to know the love of Christ that passeth knowledge." Here, I suppose, reason will confess itself at a stand, and an issue; to know that which passeth knowledge is none of its works. It cannot be known, saith reason, and so ends the matter.

(*a*)

3. But this is faith's proper work, even to know that which passeth knowledge. To know that in its power, virtue, sweetness, and efficacy, which cannot be thoroughly known in its nature and excellency; to have, by believing, all the ends of a full comprehension of that which cannot fully be comprehended. Hence (Heb. xi. 1), it is said to be the substance of "things not seen;" though in themselves absent, yet faith gives them a present subsistence in the soul. So it knows things that pass knowledge, by mixing itself with them, it draws out, and communicates their benefit to the soul. From all which is evident, what in the third place was proposed, of faith's being only suited to be the means of this discovery, so that I shall not need further to insist thereon.

(*b*)   *John Owen*

FORGIVENESS, ASSURANCE OF

It is the duty of every believer to labour after an assurance of a personal interest in forgiveness, and to be diligent in the cherishing and preservation of it when it is attained. The Apostle exhorts us all to it: "Let us draw near, in full assurance of faith" (Heb. x. 22); that is, of our acceptance with God, through forgiveness in the blood of Jesus. This he plainly discourses of. And this principle of our faith and confidence, he would have us to hold fast unto the end (chap. iii. 14). It is no small evil in believers not to be pressing after perfection in believing and obedience. Ofttimes some sinful indulgence to self, or the world, or sloth, is the cause of it. Hence few come up to Gospel assurance. But yet most of our privileges, and all our comforts, depend on this one thing. A little, by the way, to encourage to this duty, I shall desire you to consider, both whence this assurance is produced, and what it doth produce; what it is the fruit of, and what fruit it bears.

(*c*)

(i.) It is in general the product of a more plentiful communication of the Spirit than ordinary, as to a sense and participation of the choice fruits of the death of Christ, procured for those who are justified by their acceptance of the atonement.

It flourished not without His sealing, witnessing, establishing, and shedding abroad the love of God in our hearts. See Rom. v. 2–5. And what believer ought not to long for, and press after, the enjoyment of these things? Nay, to read of these things in the Gospel, not experiencing them in our own hearts, and yet to sit down quietly on this side of them, without continual pressing after them is

to despise the blood of Christ, the Spirit of Grace, and the whole work of God's love. If there are no such things, the Gospel is not true; if there are, and we press not after them, we are despisers of the Gospel. Surely he hath not the Spirit who would not have more of Him, all of Him that is promised by Christ. These things are the hundred-fold that Christ hath left us in the world, to counterpoise our sorrows, troubles, and losses; and shall we be so foolish as to neglect our only abiding riches and treasures? In particular, it is the product of an exercised, vigorous, active faith; that our faith should be such, always in every state and condition, I suppose it our duty to endeavour. Not only our comforts, but our obedience also, depends upon it. The more faith that is true and of the right kind, the more obedience; for all our obedience is the obedience of faith.

The fruits of this assurance are the choicest actings of our souls towards God: as love, delight, rejoicing in the Lord, peace, joy, and consolation in ourselves, readiness to do or suffer, cheerfulness in so doing. If they grow not from this root, yet their flourishing wholly depends upon it. So that surely it is the duty of every believer to break through all difficulties in pressing after this particular assurance. The objections that persons raise against themselves, in this case, may be afterwards considered.

(*d*)

(ii.) In ordinary dispensations of God towards us, and dealings with us, it is mostly by our own negligence and sloth that we come short of this assurance. It is true, it depends in a peculiar manner on the sovereignty of God; He is as absolute in giving peace to believers, as in giving grace to sinners. This takes place, and may be proposed as a relief; in times of trial and distress He createth light, and causeth darkness as He pleaseth. But yet, considering what promises are made to us, what encouragements are given us, what love and tenderness there is in God to receive us, I cannot but conclude, that ordinarily the cause of our coming short of this assurance is where I have fixed it. And this is the first thing that is supposed in the foregoing assertion.

(*e*)   *Ibid*

FORGIVENESS, ASSURANCE OF

The soul is enabled thereby to resign itself to the disposal of sovereign grace, in self-abhorrence, and a renunciation of all other ways of relief: "He putteth his mouth in the dust, if so be there may be no hope" (Lam. iii. 29). What God will, is his language. Here he lies at His disposal, humble, broken, but abiding His pleasure. "Though He slay me," saith Job, "yet will I trust in Him" (chap. iii. 15). "It is all one how He deals with me; whatever be the event, I will abide cleaving unto Him. I will not think of any other way of extricating myself from my distress. I will neither fly, like Jonah, nor hide, like Adam, nor take any other course for deliverance." Saith the soul, God is a God that hideth Himself from me (Isa. xlv. 15). "I walk in darkness, and have no light" (chap. l. 10). "My flesh faileth, and my heart faileth" (Ps. lxxiii. 26), "so that I am overwhelmed with trouble." "Mine iniquities have taken such hold on me, that I cannot look up" (Ps. xl. 12). "The Lord hath forsaken

(*f*)

Forgiveness of Sins—*continued*

me, and my God hath forgotten me " (Isa. xlix. 14). " Every day am I in dread terror, and am ready utterly to faint, and no relief can I obtain. What then shall I do?" Shall I curse God and die? or cry, " This evil is of the Lord: why should I wait for Him any longer?" Shall I take the course of the world, and, seeing it will be no better, be wholly regardless of my latter end? No; I know, whatever my lot and portion be, that there is forgiveness with God. This and that poor man trusted in Him; they cried unto Him, and were delivered. So did David in his greatest distress: "he encouraged his heart in the Lord his God" (2 Sam. xv. 25, 26). It is good for me to cast myself into His arms; it may be He will frown; it may be He is wroth still; but all is one, this way I will go; as it seems good to Him to deal with me, so let it be. And unspeakable are the advantages which a soul obtains by this self-resignation, which the faith treated of will infallibly produce.

(*a*)   *John Owen*

FORGIVENESS, ASSURANCE OF

In particular, it removes the overwhelming consideration of the unspeakable greatness of sin; this presses the soul to death when once the heart is possessed with it. Were not the sins so great, such as no heart can imagine, or tongue declare, it might possibly be well with them, say distressed sinners. They are not so troubled that they are sinners, as that they are great sinners; not that these and those sins they are guilty of, but that they are great sins, attended with fearful aggravations; otherwise they could deal well enough with them. Now, though this discovery free not men from the entanglement of their sins, as theirs, yet it doth from the whole entanglement of their sins as great and many. This consideration may be abstracted. The soul sees enough in God to forgive great sins, though it doth not, as yet, to forgive his sins. That great sins shall be pardoned, this discovery puts out of question; whether his sins shall be pardoned, is now all the inquiry. Whatever any faith can do, that this faith will do, unless it be the making of particular application of the things believed unto itself. The soul then can no longer justly be troubled about the greatness of sin; the infiniteness of forgiveness that he sees in God will relieve him against it. All that remains is, that it is his own sin about which he hath to deal. These, and the like difficulties are removed by it.

(*b*)   *Ibid*

FORGIVENESS, ASSURANCE OF

Some inferences concerning the true notion of believing

1. These effects ascribed to this faith of forgiveness in God, and always produced by it, make it evident that the most of those who pretend to it, who pretend to believe that there is forgiveness with God, do indeed believe no such thing. Although I shall on set purpose afterwards evince this, yet I cannot here utterly pass it by. I shall then only demand of those who are so forward in the profession of this faith as to think it almost impossible that any one should not believe it, what effects it hath produced in them, and whether they have been enabled to the performance of the duties before mentioned? I fear, with many, things on the account of their pretended

faith are quite otherwise. They love sin the more for it, and God never the better; supposing that a few barren words will issue the controversy about their sins, they become insensibly to have slight thoughts of sin, and of God also. This persuasion is not of Him that calls us. Poor souls! your faith is the devil's greatest engine for your ruin; the highest contempt of God and Christ, and forgiveness also, that you can be guilty of; a means to let you down quietly into hell; the Pharisees trusted in Moses, and will condemn you. As none is saved but by faith, so you, if it were not for your faith, as you call it, might possibly be saved. If a man's gold prove counterfeit, his jewels painted glass, his silver lead or dross, he will not only be found poor when he comes to be tried, and want the benefit of riches, but will also have a fearful aggravation of his poverty, by his disappointment and surprisal. If a man's faith, which should be more precious than gold, be found rotten and corrupt, if his light be darkness; how vile is that faith, how great is that darkness! Such, it is evident, will the faith of too many be found in this business.

(*c*)

2. The work we are carrying on is the raising of a sin-entangled soul out of its depths; and this we have spoken to is that which must give him his first relief. Commonly, when souls are in distress, that which they look after is consolation. What is it then which they intend thereby? That they may have assurance that their sins are forgiven them, and so be freed from their present perplexities. What is the issue? Some of them continue complaining all their days, and never come to rest or peace; so far do they fall short of consolation and joy. And some are utterly discouraged from attempting any progress in the ways of God. What is the reason hereof? Is it not, that they would fain be finishing their building, when they have not laid the foundation? They have not yet made thorough work in believing forgiveness with God, and they would immediately be at assurance in themselves. Now, God delights not in such a frame of spirit. For,

(*d*)

(i.) **It is selfish.** The great design of faith is to " give glory unto God " (Rom. iv. 20). The end of God's giving out forgiveness, is the praise of His " glorious grace " (Eph. i. 6). But let a soul in this frame have peace in itself, it is very little solicitous about giving glory to God. He cries, like Rachel, " Give me children, or I die;" give me peace, or I perish. That God may be honoured, and the forgiveness he seeks after be rendered glorious, it is cared for in the second place, if at all. This selfish earnestness, at first to be thrusting our hand into the side of Christ, is that which He will pardon in many, but accepts in none.

(*e*)

(ii.) **It is impatient.** Men act thus, because they will not wait. They do not care for standing afar off, for any season, with the publican. They love not to submit their souls to lie at the foot of God, to give Him the glory of His goodness, mercy, wisdom, and love, in the disposal of them and their concerns. This waiting comprises the universal subjection of the soul to God, with a resolved

(*f*)

Forgiveness of Sins—*continued*

judgment, that it is meet and right that we, and all we desire and aim at, should be at His sovereign disposal. This gives glory to God; a duty which the impatience of these poor souls will not admit them to the performance of; and both these arise,

(a)

(iii.) From weakness. It is weak; it is weakness in any condition that makes men restless and weary. The state of adherence is as safe a condition as the state of assurance, only it hath more combats and wrestling attending it. It is not, then, fear of the event, but weakness and weariness of the combat, that makes men anxiously solicitous about a deliverance from that state, before they are well entered into it.

(b)

Let, then, the sin-entangled soul remember always this way, method, and order of the Gospel, that we have under consideration. *First*, exercise faith on forgiveness in God; and when the soul is fixed therein, it will have a ground and foundation whereon it may stand securely, in making application of it to itself. Drive this principle, in the first place, to a stable issue, upon Gospel evidences; answer the objections that lie against it, and then you may proceed. In believing, the soul makes a conquest upon Satan's territories. Do, then, as they do who are entering on an enemy's country—secure the passages, fortify the strongholds as you go on, that you be not cut off in your progress. Be not as a ship at sea, which passeth on, and is no more possessed of, or master of, the water it hath gone through, than of that whereunto it has not yet arrived. But so it is with a soul that fixeth not on these foundation principles: he presses forwards, and the ground crumbles away under his feet, and so he wilders away all his days in uncertainties. Would men but lay this principle well in their souls, and secure it against assaults, they might proceed, though not with so much speed as some do, yet with more safety. Some pretend at once to fall into assurance. I wish it prove not a broad presumption in the most. It is to no purpose for him to strive to fly who cannot yet go; to labour to come to assurance in himself who never well believed forgiveness in God.

(c)   *Ibid*

FORGIVENESS, AND THE GIFT OF THE SON

We proceed to that evidence which is the centre wherein all the lines of those foregoing do meet and rest; the fountain of all those streams of refreshment that are in them, that which animates and gives life and efficacy unto them. This lies in *God's sending of His Son*. The consideration thereof will leave no pretence or excuse to unbelief in this matter.

To make this evidence more clear and legible as to what is intended in it, we must consider,—

1. What was the rise of this sending we speak of;
2. Who it was that was sent;
3. How or in what manner He was sent;
4. Unto what end and purpose.

(d)

1. The rise and spring of it is to be considered.

It came forth from the eternal mutual consent and counsel of the Father and the Son, " the

counsel of peace shall be between them both" (Zech. vi. 13). It is of Christ, the Branch, of whom he speaks. " He shall build the temple of the Lord; and He shall bear the glory, and shall sit and rule upon His throne; and shall be a Priest upon His throne; and the counsel of peace shall be between them both;" that is, between God the Father, who sends Him, and Himself; there lay the counsel of peace-making between God and man, in due time accomplished by Him who " is our peace" (Eph. ii. 14). So He speaks • " Then I was by Him, as one brought up with Him, and I was daily His delight, rejoicing always before Him; rejoicing in the habitable parts of the earth; and My delights were with the sons of men" (Prov. viii. 30, 31). They are the words of Wisdom; that is, of the Son of God. When was this done? " Then I was with Him." Why, before the mountains were settled, " whilst as yet He had not made the earth nor the fields;" that is, before the creation of the world, or from eternity (ver. 25, 26). But how then could He rejoice in the habitable parts of the earth? and how could His delight be with the sons of men, seeing as yet they were not? I answer, it was the counsel of peace towards them before mentioned, in the pursuit whereof He was to be sent to converse amongst them on the earth. He rejoiced in the forethoughts of His being sent to them, and the work He had to do for them. Then, with His own consent and delight, was He fore-ordained to His work, even before the " foundation of the world" (1 Pet. i. 20), and received of the Father " the promise of eternal life, even before the world began" (Tit. i. 2); that is, to be given to sinners, by way of forgiveness through His blood. So is this whole counsel expressed (Ps. xl. 7, 8); whence it is made use of by the Apostle, " Then said I, Lo, I come : in the volume of the book it is written of me, I delight to do Thy will, O God. " Thy law is in the midst of my heart" (Heb. x. 5, 6, 7). There is the will of the Father in this matter, and the law of its performance; and there is the will of the Son in answer thereunto, and His delight in fulfilling that law which was prescribed to Him.

(e)

Consider to what purpose was this eternal counsel of peace, this agreement of the Father and Son from eternity, about the state and condition of mankind. If God would have left them all to perish under the guilt of their sins, there had been no need at all of any such thoughts, designs, or counsel. God had given to them a law, righteous and holy, which, if they transgressed, He had threatened them with eternal destruction. Under the rule, disposal, and power of this law, He might have righteously left them to stand or fall, according to the verdict and sentence thereof. But now He assures us, He reveals to us, that He had other thoughts in this matter; that there were other counsels between the Father and the Son concerning us; and these such as the Son was delighted in the prospect of His accomplishment of them. What can these thoughts and counsels be, but about a way for their deliverance, which could no otherwise be, but by the forgiveness of sins? For whatever else be done, yet if God mark iniquities, there is none can stand. Hearken, therefore, poor sinner, and have hope. God is consulting about thy deliverance and freedom; and what cannot the wisdom and grace of

(f)

Forgiveness of Sins—*continued*

the Father and Son effect and accomplish? For to this end was the Son sent into the world, which is the second thing proposed to consideration.

(*a*)

2. Whom did God send about this business? The Scripture lays great weight and emphasis on this consideration; faith must do so also: "God so loved the world that He gave His only begotten Son" (John iii. 16); so 1 John iv. 9: "In this was manifested the love of God towards us, because that God sent His only-begotten Son into the world, that we might live through Him." And again, ver. 10, "Herein is love, not that we loved God, but that He loved us, and sent His Son to be the propitiation for our sins." And who is this that is thus sent, and called "the only begotten Son of God"? Take a double description of Him—one out of the Old Testament, and another from the New. The first from Isaiah ix. 6, "To us a child is born, to us a Son is given: and the government shall be upon His shoulder: and His name shall be called Wonderful, Counsellor, The mighty God, The everlasting Father, The Prince of Peace." The other from Hebrews i. 2, 3, "God hath spoken unto us by His Son, whom He hath appointed Heir of all things, by whom also He made the worlds; who being the brightness of His glory, and the express image of His person, and upholding all things by the word of His power, when He had by Himself purged our sins, sat down on the right hand of the Majesty on high." This is He who was sent. In nature He was glorious, even God over all, blessed for ever. In answerableness to the Father, the brightness of His glory, and the express image of His person, possessed of all the same essential properties with Him; so that, what we find in Him, we may be assured is in the Father also; for he that hath seen Him hath seen the Father, who is in Him. In power, omnipotent; for He hath made all things, and upholdeth all things, with an unspeakable facility, by the word of His power: in office, exalted over all; sitting at the right hand of the Majesty on high; in name, the mighty God, the everlasting Father; so that whatever He came about, He will assuredly accomplish and fulfil, for what should hinder this mighty One from perfecting His design?

(*b*)

Now, this consideration raises our evidence to that height, as to give us an unquestionable assurance in this matter. Here is a near and a particular object for faith to be exercised about, and to rest in. Wherefore did this glorious Son of God come and tabernacle amongst poor sinners? We beheld the glory of the eternal Word, the glory of the only-begotten of the Father; and He was made flesh, and pitched His tabernacle amongst us (John i. 14). To what end? It was no other but to work out and accomplish the eternal counsel of peace towards sinners before mentioned, to procure for them, and to declare to them, the forgiveness of sin. And what greater evidence, what greater assurance, can we have, that there is forgiveness with God for us? He Himself hath given it as a rule, that what is done by giving an only begotten, or an only beloved son, gives assured testimony of reality and sincerity in the thing that is confirmed by it. So He says to Abraham, "Now I know that thou fearest God, seeing that thou hast not withheld thy son, thine only son, from Me" (Gen xxii. 12). This way it may be known,

or no way. And there is a blessed conclusion that faith may make from this consideration: Now I know that there is forgiveness with God, seeing He hath not withheld His Son, His only Son, that He might accomplish it. To this purpose the Apostle teaches us to reason, "He that spared not His own Son, but delivered Him up for us all, how shall He not with Him also freely give us all things?" (Rom. viii. 32).

(*c*)

What further can any soul desire? What ground remains for unbelief to stand upon in this matter? Is there anything more to be done herein? It was to manifest that there is forgiveness with Him, and to make way for the exercise of it, that God sent His Son; that the Son of God came into the world, as will afterwards more fully appear.

(*d*)

3. To this sending of the Son of God for this purpose, there is evidence and security added from the manner wherein He was sent. How was this? Not in glory, not in power, not in an open discovery of His eternal power and Godhead. Had it been so, we might have thought that He had come merely to manifest and glorify Himself in the world. And this He might have done, without thoughts of mercy or pardon towards us. But He came quite in another manner; He was seen in the "likeness of sinful flesh" (Rom. viii. 3), "in the form of a servant" (Phil. ii. 7), "being made of a woman, being made under the law" (Gal. iv. 4). What He endured, suffered, underwent, in that state and condition, is in some measure known to us all. All this could not be merely, and firstly, for Himself. All that He expected at the close of it, was "to be glorified with that glory which He had with the Father before the world was" (John xvii. 5). It must then be for our sakes; and for what? To save and deliver us from that condition of wrath at present, and future expectation of vengeance, which we had cast ourselves into by sin; that is, to procure for us the forgiveness of sins. Had not God designed pardon for sin, He would never have sent His Son in this manner, to testify it; and He did it, because it could no other way be brought about, as hath been declared. Do we doubt whether there be forgiveness with God or not? or whether we shall obtain it, if we address ourselves to Him to be made partakers of it? Consider the condition of His Son in the world; review His afflictions, poverty, temptation, sorrows, sufferings; then ask our souls, To what end was all this? And if we can find any other design in it, any other reason, cause, or necessity of it, but only and merely to testify and declare that there is forgiveness with God, and to purchase and procure the communication of it to us, let us abide in and perish under our fears. But if it be so, we have a sufficient warrant to assure our souls in the expectation of it.

(*e*)   *John Owen*

FORGIVENESS, AND THE DEATH OF THE SON

Besides all this, there ensues that great and wonderful issue, the death of the Son of God. This thing was great and marvellous, and we may a little inquire what was designed therein. And hereof the Scripture gives us a full account. As,

(*f*)

Forgiveness of Sins—continued

1. That He died to make atonement for sin, or reconciliation for iniquity (Dan. ix. 24). He gave His life a ransom for the sins of many (Matt. xx. 28 ; 1 Tim. ii. 6). He was in it made sin, that others might become the righteousness of God in Him (2 Cor. v. 21; Rom. viii. 3). Therein He bare our "sins in His own body on the tree" (1 Pet. ii. 24). This was the state of the matter. Notwithstanding all the love, grace, and condescension before mentioned, yet our sins were of that nature, and so directly opposite to the justness and holiness of God, that unless atonement were made, and a price of redemption paid, there could be no pardon, no forgiveness obtained. This, therefore, He undertook to do, and that by the sacrifice of Himself ; answering all that was prefigured by, and represented in, the sacrifices of old, as the Apostle largely declares (Heb. x. 5–9). And herein is the forgiveness that is in God copied out and exemplified so clearly and evidently, that he who cannot read it will be cursed unto eternity : yea, and let him be accursed ; for what can be more required to justify God in his eternal destruction? He that will not believe His grace, as testified and exemplified in the blood of His Son, let him perish without remedy.

(a)

2. The curse and sentence of the law lies on record against sinners ; it puts in its demands against our acquittance, and lays an obligation upon us unto punishment : and God will not reject nor destroy His law ; unless it be answered, there is no acceptance for sinners. This, therefore, in the next place, His death was designed unto : as He satisfied and made atonement by it unto justice (which was the fountain, spring, and cause of the law), so He fulfilled and answered the demands of the law, as it was an effect of the justice of God : so Rom. viii. 3. He suffered in the likeness of sinful flesh, that the righteousness of the law might be fulfilled and answered. He answered the curse of the law, when He was "made a curse for us" (Gal. iii. 13), and so became, as to the obedience of the law, "the end of the law for righteousness unto them that do believe" (Rom. x. 3, 4). And as to the penalty that it threatened, He bore it, removed it, and took it out of the way. So hath He made way for forgiveness through the very heart of the law : it hath not one word to speak against the pardon of those who do believe. But,

(b)

3. Sinners are under the power of Satan ; he lays a claim to them, and by what means shall they be rescued from his interest and dominion ? This also His death was designed to accomplish : for as He was "manifested to destroy the works of the devil" (1 John iii 8), so by "death He destroyed him that had the power of death" (Heb. ii. 14), that is, to despoil him of his power, to destroy his dominion, to take away his claim to sinners that believe, as we have at large elsewhere declared.

(c)

And by all these things, with many other concerns of His death, that might be instanced, we are abundantly secured of the forgiveness that is with God, and of His willingness that we should be made partakers thereof.

(d)

4. Is this all? did His work cease in His death? did He no more for the securing of the forgiveness of sins unto us, but only that He died for them? Yes, He lives also after death for the same end and purpose. The Son of God, in that nature which He assumed to expiate sin by death, lives again after death, to secure unto us, and to complete the forgiveness of sins. And this He doth two ways : (1) Being raised from that death which He underwent, to make atonement for sin by the power and goodwill of God, He evinces and testifies unto us that He hath fully performed the work He undertook ; and that in our behalf, and for us, He hath received a discharge. Had He not answered the guilt of sin by His death, He had never been raised from it. (2) He lives after death a mediatory life, to make intercession for us, that we may receive the forgiveness of sin, as also Himself to give it unto us ; which things are frequently made use of, to encourage the souls of men to believe, and therefore shall not at present be further insisted on.

(e)   John Owen

FORGIVENESS, AND THE DEATH OF THE SON

To confirm our faith from hence, let us make a little search into these things, in some particular inquiries.

Question 1. Seeing the Son of God died in that way and manner that He did, according to the determinate counsel and will of God, wherefore did He do so, and what aimed He at therein?

Answer. It is plain that He died for our sins (Rom. iv. 25), that is, to make reconciliation for the sins of His people (Heb. ii. 17, 18). This Moses and the prophets, this the whole Scripture testifies unto, and without a supposal of it, not one word of it can be aright believed : nor can we yield any due obedience to God without it.

(f)

Qu. 2. What then did God do unto Him? What was in transaction between God as the judge of all, and Him that was the Mediator of the Church?

Ans. God indeed "laid on Him the iniquities of us all" (Isa. liii. 6), all the sins of all the elect ; yea, He made Him "a curse for us" (Gal. iii. 13). And making Him a sin-offering, or an offering for sin, He condemned sin in the flesh (Rom. viii. 3 ; 2 Cor. v. 21). So that all that which the justice or law of God had to require about the punishment due unto sin, was all laid and executed on Him.

(g)

Qu. 3. What then did Christ do in His death? What did He aim at and design? What was His intention in submitting unto and undergoing the will of God in these things?

Ans. "He bare our sins in His own body upon the tree" (1 Pet. ii. 24). He took our sins upon Him, undertook to answer for them, to pay our debts, to make an end of the difference about them, between God and sinners (Dan. ix. 24). His aim undoubtedly was, by all that He underwent and suffered, so to make atonement for sin, as that no more could on that account be expected.

(h)

Qu. 4. Had God any more to require of sinners on the account of sin, that His justice might be satisfied, His holiness vindicated, His glory exalted,

(i)

Forgiveness of Sins—*continued*

His honour be repaired, than what He charged on Christ? Did He lay somewhat of the penalty due to sin on Him, execute some part of the curse of the law against Him, and yet reserve some wrath for sinners themselves?

Ans. No, doubtless. He came to do the whole will of God (Heb. x. 7, 8). And God spared Him not anything that in His holy will He had appointed to be done unto sin (Rom. viii. 32). He would never have so dealt with His Son, to have made a half-work of it; nor is the work of making satisfaction for sin such, as that any, the least part of it, should ever be undertaken by another. Nothing is more injurious or more blasphemous against God and Christ, than the foolish imagination among the papists, of works satisfactory for the punishment due to sin, or any part of it; as also is their purgatory pains to expiate any remaining guilt after this life. This work, of making satisfaction for sin, is such as no creature in heaven or earth can put forth a hand unto. It was wholly committed to the Son of God, who alone was able to undertake it, and who hath perfectly accomplished it. So that God now says, "Fury is not in Me" (Isa. xxvii. 4); he that will lay hold on My strength, that he may have peace, he shall have peace.

(a)

Qu. 5. What then became of the Lord Christ in His undertaking? Did He go through with it? or did He faint under it? Did He only testify His love, and show His good-will for our deliverance? Or did He also effectually pursue it, and not faint until He had made a way for the exercise of forgiveness?

Ans. It was not possible that He should be detained by the pains of death (Acts ii. 24). He knew beforehand, that He should be carried through His work, that He should not be forsaken in it, nor faint under it (Isa. l. 6–8). And God hath given this unquestionable evidence of His discharge of the debt of sin to the utmost, in that He was acquitted from the whole account, when He was raised from the dead. For he that is given up to prison upon the sentence of the law for the debt of sin, shall not be freed until he have paid the utmost farthing. This, therefore, He manifested Himself to have done, by His resurrection from the dead.

(b)

Qu. 6. What then is now become of Him? Where is He, and what doth He? Hath He so done His work, and laid it aside? or doth He still continue to carry it on, until it be brought unto its perfection?

Ans. It is true, He was dead, but is alive, and lives for ever; and hath told us, that because He liveth we shall live also; and that, because this is the end of His mediatory life in heaven, He lives "for ever to make intercession for us" (Heb. vii. 25–27). And to this end, that the forgiveness of sin, which He hath procured for us, may be communicated unto us, that we might be made partakers of it, and live for ever.

(c)

What ground is left of questioning the truth in hand? What link of this chain can unbelief break in upon? If men resolve, notwithstanding all this evidence and assurance that is tendered to them thereof, that they will not yet believe there is

forgiveness with God, or will not be encouraged to attempt the securing of it unto themselves, or else despise it as a thing not worth the looking after; it is enough for them that declare it, that preach these things, that they are a sweet savour unto God in them that perish, as well as in them that are saved. And I bless God that I have had this opportunity to bear testimony to the grace of God in Christ, which, if it be not received, it is because "the god of this world hath blinded the eyes of men, that the light of the Gospel of the glory of God should not shine into their minds." But Christ will be glorified in them that believe on these principles and foundations.

(d)   *John Owen*

Forgiveness and Believing

1. **This is Gospel truth**; yea, the great, fundamental, and most important truth of the Gospel. It is the turning point of the two covenants, as God Himself declares (Heb. viii. 7–13). Now, a very easy consideration of the ways and walkings of men will satisfy us as to this inquiry, whether they do indeed believe the Gospel, the covenant of grace, and the fundamental principles of it. Certainly their ignorance, darkness, blindness, their corrupt affections, and worldly conversations, their earthly-mindedness, and open disavowing of the Spirit, ways, and yoke of Christ, speak no such language. Shall we think that proud, heady, worldly self-seekers, haters of the people of God and His ways, despisers of the Spirit of grace and His work, sacrificers to their own lusts, and such-like, do believe the covenant of grace, or remission of sins? God forbid we should entertain any one thought of so great dishonour to the Gospel. Wherever that is received or believed, it produces other effects (Tit. ii. 11, 12; Isa. xi. 6–9). It teaches men to deny all ungodliness and worldly lusts. It changes their hearts, natures, and ways. It is not such a barren, impotent, and fruitless thing as such an apprehension would represent it.

(e)

2. **They that really believe forgiveness in God, do thereby obtain forgiveness.** Believing gives an interest in it; it brings it home to the soul concerned. This is the inviolable law of the Gospel. Believing and forgiveness are inseparably conjoined. Among the evidences that we may have of any one being interested in forgiveness, I shall only name one; they prize and value it above all the world. Let us inquire what esteem and valuation many of those have of forgiveness, who put it out of all question that they do believe. Do they look upon it as their treasure, their jewel, their pearl of price? Are they solicitous about it? Do they often look and examine whether it continues safe in their possession or not? Suppose a man have a precious jewel, laid up in some place in his house; suppose it to be unto him as the poor widow's two mites, all her living; will he not carefully ponder on it? Will he not frequently satisfy himself that it is safe? We may know that such a house, such fields or lands, do not belong unto a man, when he passeth by them daily, and taketh little or no notice of them. Now, how do most men look upon forgiveness? What is their common behaviour in reference to it? Are their hearts continually filled with thoughts about it? Are they solicitous concerning their

(f)

Forgiveness of Sins—*continued*

interest in it? Do they reckon, that whilst that is safe, all is safe with them? When it is, as it were, laid out of the way by sin and unbelief, do they give themselves no rest until it be afresh discovered unto them? Is this the frame of the most of men? The Lord knows it is not. They talk of forgiveness, but esteem it not, prize it not, make no particular inquiries after it. They put it to an ungrounded venture, whether ever they be partakers of it or not; for a relief against some pangs of conscience, it is called upon, or else scarcely thought of at all. Let not any so minded flatter themselves that they have any acquaintance with the mystery of Gospel forgiveness.

(a)

3. Inquire of those who pretend to this persuasion, how they came by it, that we may know whether it be of Him who calleth us or not; that we may try whether they have broken through the difficulties in the entertaining of it, which we have manifested abundantly to lie in the way of it.

(b)

When Peter confessed our Saviour to be the Christ, the Son of the living God, He told him that "flesh and blood did not reveal that unto him, but His Father who is in heaven" (Matt. xvi. 17). It is so with those who indeed believe forgiveness in God: flesh and blood hath not revealed it unto them. It hath not been furthered by anything within them, or without them; but all lies in opposition unto it. "This is the work of God, that we believe" (John vi. 29). A great work, the greatest work that God requireth of us. It is not only a great thing in itself (the grace of believing is a great thing), but it is great in respect of its object, or what we have to believe, or forgiveness itself. The great honour of Abraham's faith lay in this, that deaths and difficulties lay in the way of it (Rom. iv. 18–20). But what is a dead body and a dead womb to an accusing conscience, a killing law, and apprehensions of a God terrible as a consuming fire? All which, as was showed, oppose themselves to a soul called to believe forgiveness.

(c)

What now have the most of men, who are confident in the profession of this faith, to say to this thing? Let them speak clearly, and they must say, that indeed they never found the least difficulty in this matter; they never doubted of it; they never questioned it, nor do know any reason why they should do so. It is a thing which they had so taken for granted, that it never cost them an hour's labour, prayer, meditation, about it. Have they had secret reasonings and contendings in their hearts about it? No. Have they considered how the objections that lie against it may be removed? Not at all. But is it so indeed, that this persuasion is thus produced in you, you know not how? Are the corrupted natures of men, and the Gospel, so suited, so complying? Is the new covenant grown so congenial to flesh and blood? Is the greatest secret that ever was revealed from the bosom of the Father become so familiar and easy to the wisdom of the flesh? Is that which was folly to the wise Greeks, and a stumbling-block to the wonder-gazing Jews, become, on a sudden, wisdom, and a plain path, to the same principles that were in them? But the

truth of this matter is, that such men have a general, useless, barren notion of pardon, which Satan, presumption, tradition, common report, and the customary hearing of the word, have furnished them with; but for that Gospel discovery of forgiveness, whereof we have been speaking, they are utterly ignorant of it, and unacquainted with it. To convince such poor creatures of the folly of their presumption, I would but desire them to go to some real believers, who are or may be known unto them: let them be asked, whether they came so easily by their faith and apprehensions of forgiveness or not? Alas! saith one, these twenty years have I been following after God, and yet I have not arrived to an abiding, cheering persuasion of it. I know what it cost me, what trials, difficulties, temptations, I wrestled with, and went through withal, before I obtained it, saith another. What I have attained to, hath been of unspeakable mercy, and it is my daily prayer that I may be preserved in it by the exceeding greatness of the power of God; for I continually wrestle with storms that are ready to drive me from my anchor. A little of this discourse may be sufficient to convince poor, dark, carnal creatures of the folly and vanity of their confidence.

(d)

4. There are certain means whereby the revelation and discovery of this mystery is made unto the souls of men. By these they do obtain it, or they obtain it not. The mystery itself was a secret, hidden in the counsel of God from eternity; nor was there any way whereby it might be revealed, but by the Son of God; and that is done in the word of the Gospel. If, then, you say you know it, let us inquire how you came so to do; and by what means it hath been declared unto you? Hath this been done by the word of truth; by the promise of the Gospel? Was it by preaching the word unto you, or by reading it, or meditating upon it? Or did you receive it from and by some reasonable word, of or from the Scriptures spoken unto you? Or hath it insensibly gotten ground upon your hearts and minds, upon the strivings and conflicts of your soul about sin, from the truth wherein you had been instructed in general? Or by what other ways or means have you come to that acquaintance with it whereof you boast? You can tell how you came by your wealth, your gold and silver; you know how you became learned, or obtained the knowledge of the mystery of your trade, who taught you it, and how you came by it; there is not anything wherein you are concerned, but you can answer these inquiries in reference unto it. Think it then no great matter if you are put to answer this question also, By what way or means came you to the knowledge of forgiveness, which you boast of? Was it by any of those before mentioned, or some other? If you cannot answer distinctly to these things, only you say you have heard it, and believed it ever since you can remember; so those said that went before you; so they say with whom you do converse; you never met with any one who called it in question, nor heard of any, unless it were one or two despairing wretches; it will be justly questioned, whether you have any portion in this matter or not. If uncertain rumours, reports, general notions, lie at the bottom of your persuasion, do not suppose that you have any communion with Christ therein.

(e)

Forgiveness of Sins—*continued*

5. Of those who profess to believe forgiveness, how few are there who indeed know what it is. They believe, they say; but, as the Samaritans, worship they know not what. With some a bold presumption, and crying, Peace, peace, goes for the belief of forgiveness. A general apprehension of impunity from God, and that, though they are sinners, yet they shall not be punished, passeth with others at the same rate. Some think they shall prevail with God by their prayers and desires to let them alone, and not cast them into hell. One way or other, to escape the vengeance of hell, not to be punished in another world, is that which men fix their minds upon. But is this that forgiveness which is revealed in the Gospel, that which we have been treating about? The rise and spring of our forgiveness is in the heart and gracious nature of God, declared by His name; have you inquired seriously into this? Have you stood at the shore of that infinite ocean of goodness and love? Have your souls found support and relief from that consideration? And have your hearts leaped within you with the thoughts of it? Or, if you have never been affected in an especial manner herewith, have you bowed down your souls under the consideration of that sovereign act of the will of God, that is the next spring of forgiveness, that glorious acting of free grace, that when all might justly have perished, all having sinned and come short of His glory, God would yet have mercy to some? Have you given up yourselves to this grace? Is this anything of what you do believe? Suppose you are strangers to this also, what communion with God have you had about it in the blood of Christ? We have showed how forgiveness relates thereunto; how a way is made thereby for the exercise of mercy, in a consistency with the glory and honour of the justice of God, and of His law; how pardon is procured and purchased thereby; with the mysterious reconciliation of love and law; and the new disposal of conscience in its work and duty by it. What have you to say to these things? Have you seen pardon flowing from the heart of the Father, through the blood of the Son? Have you looked upon it as the price of His life, and the purchase of His blood? Or, have you general thoughts that Christ died for sinners, and that on one account or other forgiveness relates to Him, but are strangers to the mystery of this great work? Suppose this also, let us go a little further, and inquire, whether you know anything that yet remains of the like importance in this matter? Forgiveness, as we have showed, is manifested, tendered, exhibited, in the covenant of graces and promises of the Gospel. The rule of the efficacy of these is, that they be mixed with faith (Heb. iv. 2). It is well if you are grown up hereunto; but you that are strangers to the things before mentioned are no less to this also. Upon the matter, you know not then what forgiveness is, nor wherein it consists, nor whence it comes, nor how it is procured, nor by what means given out unto sinners. It is to no purpose for such persons to pretend that they believe that whereunto, either notionally or practically, or both, they are such utter strangers.

(a) *John Owen*

6. Another inquiry into this matter regards the state and condition wherein souls must be, before it be possible for them to believe forgiveness. If there be such a state, and it can be evinced that very many of the pretenders, concerning whom we deal, were never brought into it, it is then evident that they neither do nor can believe forgiveness, however they do and may delude their own souls.

(b)

It hath been shown, that the first discovery that was made of pardoning grace, was unto Adam, presently after the fall. What was then his state and condition? How was he prepared for the reception of this great mystery in its first discovery? That seems to be a considerable rule of proceeding in the same matter. That which is first in any kind, is a rule to all that follows. Now, what was Adam's condition when the revelation of forgiveness was first made unto him? It is known from the story: convinced of sin, afraid of punishment, he lay trembling at the foot of God. Then was forgiveness revealed unto him; so the Psalmist states it, "If Thou, Lord, shouldest mark mine iniquity, O Lord, who shall stand?" (Ps. cxxx. 3). Full of thoughts he is of the desert of sin, and of inevitable and eternal ruin, in case God should deal with him according to the exigence of the law. In that state is the great support of forgiveness with God suggested unto him by the Holy Ghost. We know what work our Saviour had with the Pharisees on this account. " Are we," says they, " blind also?" No, saith he, " Ye say, we see; therefore your sin remaineth " (John ix. 40, 41). It is to no purpose to talk of forgiveness to such persons as you are, you must of necessity abide in your sins: I come not to call such righteous persons as you are, but sinners, to repentance; who not only are so, as you are also, and that to the purpose, but are sensible of their being so, and of their undone condition thereby. " The whole have no need of the physician, but the sick." Whilst you are seeming righteous and whole, it is to no end to tell you of forgiveness; you cannot understand it, nor receive it. It is impossible, then, that any one should, in a due manner, believe forgiveness in God, unless in a due manner he be convinced of sin in himself. If the fallow ground be not broken up, it is to no purpose to sow the seed of the Gospel. There is neither life, power, nor sweetness, in this truth, unless a door be opened for its entrance by conviction of sin.

(c)

Let us then, on this ground also, continue our inquiry upon the ordinary boasters of their skill in this mystery. You believe there is forgiveness with God: yes; but have you been convinced of sin? yes; you know well enough that you are sinners. Answer then but once more as to the nature of this conviction which you say you have: is it not made up of these two ingredients? 1. A general notion that you are sinners, as all men also are. 2. Particular troublesome reflections upon yourselves, when, on any eruption of sin, conscience accuses, rebukes, condemns. You will say, Yes, what would you require more? This is not the conviction we are inquiring after; that is a work of the Spirit by the word: this you speak of, a mere natural work, which you can no more be without than you can cease to be men. This will give no assistance until the receiving of forgiveness: but it may be you will say, you have proceeded farther than so; and these things have had an improvement in you. Let us then a little

(d)

Forgiveness of Sins—*continued*

try whether your process has been according to the mind of God; and so, whether this invincible bar in your way be removed or not: for although every convinced person do not believe forgiveness, yet no one who is not convinced doth so: have you then been made sensible of your condition by nature, what it is to be alienated from the life of God, and to be obnoxious to His wrath? Have you been convinced of the universal enmity that is in your hearts to the mind of God, and what it is to be at enmity against God? Has the unspeakable multitude of the sins of your lives been set in order by the law before you? And have you considered what it is for sinners, such sinners as you are, to have to deal with a righteous and a holy God? Hath the Holy Ghost wrought a serious recognition in your hearts of all these things, and caused them to abide with you, and upon you? If you will answer truly, you must say, many of you, that indeed you have not been so exercised. You have heard of these things many times, but to say that you have gone through with this work, and have had experience of them, that you cannot do. Then, I say, you are strangers to forgiveness, because you are strangers to sin. But if you shall say, that you have had thoughts to this purpose, and are persuaded that you have been thoroughly convinced of sin, I shall yet ask you one question more, What effects hath your conviction produced in your hearts and lives? Have you been filled with perplexities and consternation of spirit thereupon? Have you had fears, dreads, or terrors, to wrestle with? It may be you will say, No; nor will I insist upon that inquiry; but this I deal with you in. Has it filled you with self-loathing and abhorrence, with self-condemnation and abasement? If it will do anything, this it will do. If you come short here, it is justly to be feared that all your other pretences are of no value. Now, where there is no work of conviction, there is no faith of forgiveness, whatever is pretended. And how many vain boasters this sword will cut off, is evident.

(*a*)

7. **We have yet a greater evidence than all these.** Men live in sin, and therefore they do not believe forgiveness of sin. Faith in general purifies the heart (Acts xv. 9). Our souls are purified in obeying the truth (1 Pet. i. 22), and the life is made fruitful by it. Faith worketh by works, and makes itself perfect by them (Jas. ii. 22), and the doctrine concerning forgiveness hath a special influence unto all holiness. "The grace of God, which bringeth salvation, teacheth us to deny all unrighteousness and worldly lusts, and to live soberly, righteously, and godly, in this present world" (Tit. ii. 11, 12), and this is the grace whereof we speak. No man can then believe forgiveness of sin, without a detestation and relinquishment of it. The ground of this might be farther manifested, and the way of the efficacy of faith of forgiveness unto a forsaking of sin, if need were. But all that own the Gospel must acknowledge this principle. The real belief of the pardon of sin is prevalent with men not to live longer in sin.

(*b*)

But now, what are the greatest number of those who pretend to receive this truth? Are their hearts purified by it? Are their consciences purged?

Are their lives changed? Do they deny all ungodliness and worldly lusts? Does forgiveness teach them so to do? Have they found it effectual to these purposes? Whence is it, then, that there is such a bleating and bellowing to the contrary amongst them? Some of you are drunkards, some of you swearers, some of you unclean persons, some of you liars, some of you worldly, some of you haters of all the ways of Christ, and all His concerns upon the earth; proud, covetous, boasters, self-seekers, envious, wrathful, backbiters, malicious praters, slanderers, and the like: and shall we think that such as these believe forgiveness of sin? God forbid. Again, some of you are dark, ignorant, blind, utterly unacquainted with the mystery of the Gospel, nor do at all make it your business to inquire into it. Either you hear it not at all, or negligently, slothfully, customarily, to no purpose. Let not such persons deceive their own souls: to live in sin, and yet to believe the forgiveness of sin, is utterly impossible. Christ will not be a minister of sin, nor give His Gospel to be a doctrine of licentiousness for your sakes; nor shall you be forgiven, that you may be delivered to do more abominations, God forbid.

(*c*)

If any shall say, that they thank God they are no such publicans as those mentioned; they are no drunkards, no swearers, no unclean persons, nor the like; so that they are not concerned in this consideration; their lives and their duties give another account of them. Then yet consider further, that the Pharisees were all that you say of yourselves, and yet the greatest despisers of forgiveness that ever were in the world, and that because they hated the light, on this account, that their deeds were evil. And for your duties you mention, what, I pray, is the root and spring of them? Are they influenced from this faith of forgiveness you boast of, or not? May it not be feared that it is utterly otherwise? You do not perform them because you love the Gospel, but because you fear the Law. If the truth were known, I fear it would appear, that you get nothing by your believing of pardon, but an encouragement to sin. Your goodness, such as it is, springs from another root. It may be also, that you ward yourselves by it against the strokes of conscience, or the guilt of particular sins; this is as bad as the other. It is as good be encouraged to sin, to commit it, as be encouraged under sin, so as to be kept from humiliation for it. None under heaven are more remote from the belief of grace and pardon than such persons: all their righteousness is from the Law, and their sin in a great measure from the Gospel.

(*d*)

8. **They that believe forgiveness in a due manner, believe it for the ends and purposes for which it is revealed of God.** This will further improve and carry on the former consideration. If God reveals anything for one end and purpose, and men use it quite to another, they do not receive the word of God, nor believe the thing revealed; but steal the word, and delude their own souls.

Let us, then, weigh to what ends and purposes this forgiveness was first revealed by God; for which also its manifestation is still continued in the Gospel. We have showed before who it was

(*e*)

Forgiveness of Sins—*continued*

to whom this revelation was first made, and what condition he was in when it was so made to him. A lost, wretched creature, without hope or help he was ; how he should come to obtain acceptance with God, he knew not. God reveals forgiveness to him by Christ, to be his all. The intention of God in it was, that a sinner's all should be of grace (Rom. xi. 6). If anything be added to it for the same end and purpose, then grace is no more grace. Again, God intended it as a new foundation of obedience, of love and thankfulness. That men should love because forgiven, and be holy because pardoned, as I have showed before, that it might be the righteousness of a sinner, and a spring of new obedience in him, all to the praise of grace, were God's ends in its revelation.

(a) *John Owen*

FORGIVENESS OF SINS, THE

"*In whom we have redemption through His blood, even the forgiveness of sins*" (Col. i. 14).

Consciousness of sin in every man : of omission, if not wrong-doing ; of defect in virtue, if not depraved. Hence the inevitable need of forgiveness. Is there any answer, on the part of God, to this need ?

Current answers
1. *He never forgives :* He cannot, in the nature of the case. Moral forces are as irresistible, moral laws as inexorable as physical laws. The man who breaks law must take the consequences. This is the answer of the Positivist and the Deist. A terrible response to our keen need.
2. *He forgives capriciously :* Those born of good parents, who have lived in Christian society, who have a fortunate mental constitution, who have done nothing flagrantly bad ; such are forgiven. This answer is still more terrible than the other ; *it shows favour* to those who have had better opportunities. It *cannot* be admitted.
3. *He forgives universally :* without reference to circumstances, or distinction of character, because He is kind. This is the worst answer of all. By it moral law is annulled, and chaos comes into the spiritual universe. God ceases to have regard to His holiness. Mary Magdalene sits in heaven beside Herodias ; the two thieves enter its gates together ; even Judas Iscariot appearing there long before John. It is incredible that this should be the answer to man's need of forgiveness.
4. *The answer of the Gospel* in the text : God does forgive, yet not capriciously, but with wise, definite, Divine pre-arrangement ; forgives universally on the ground of the Atonement, on the condition of repentance and faith.

This answer suits God's character and man's need. It makes forgiveness attainable, and upholds moral order.

It shows the preciousness of the Bible, argues its Divine origin, the privilege of accepting God's offer, and the infinite hazard of neglecting or refusing it.

(b) *Storrs*

FORGIVENESS OF SINS

"*Through this Man is preached the forgiveness of sins*" (Acts xiii. 38). William Dawson, the Yorkshire local preacher, was the greatest of all preachers in my humble opinion. He had often a peculiar way of opening his discourse. "*Through*

this Man is preached unto you the forgiveness of sin," was his text one day ; and when he had announced where it was to be found, he sank down out of sight in the pulpit, and pronounced the words, keeping one hand on the Bible, and emphatically pressing it with his hand, "Through *this* Man," the Man in the Book, the Man Christ Jesus he meant. *Not* through William Dawson, *not* through the preacher, but through Him of whom the Book testifies.

(c) *Thomas Cooper*

FORGIVENESS OF SINS

Is not indeed deliverance from sin, but it is the sure pledge and earnest of future complete deliverance, and is necessary, and must form the beginning.

(d) *Menken*

FORGIVENESS OF SINS

If the forgiveness of my sins rests on my sanctification, then I must be in continual uncertainty. My best actions require forgiveness. With me moral effort is an alternation of rising and sinking, of advancing and retreating. I am, in the most favourable case, only in an approximation towards reconciliation. But my certainty of reconciliation requires an immovable foundation. This is Christ : . . . "Good deeds do not make a man pious, but a pious man does good deeds" (Luther).

(e) *Martensen*

FORGIVENESS OF SINS

"*To Him give all the prophets witness, that through His Name whosoever believeth in Him shall receive remission of sins*" (Acts x. 43).

This concluding sentence conveys a threefold truth. It refers to the *human race*, to the *Mediator*, and to the *Way of Salvation :*
1. It bears witness indirectly that *all* men are sinners, since it offers forgiveness to all, and thus declares that all need forgiveness.
2. It distinctly announces, in the next place, that Jesus Christ is the only Mediator and Reconciler, and that no one can obtain forgiveness and the grace of God except through Him.
3. It shows clearly and unmistakably, in the last place, that faith in Christ, or a confiding acceptance of the Redeemer, is the direct, and, indeed, the only way to forgiveness or to salvation in general, of which forgiveness is the central point.

Thus the whole Christian system of faith lies in this one sentence *in nuce*.

(f) *Lange*

FORMALISM

Formalism does for the present time. It satisfies the man's conscience; it satisfies his neighbours if he comes to church, if he lives creditably, if he has family prayer, if he attends the Holy Communion ; if, in fact, he has the outside of a Christian. It satisfies his pastor, too, very often. Who are we, that we should judge another man's servant? to his own master he standeth or falleth. It does very well for this world ; yes, but only for

(g)

this world. The lamp is an expiring lamp—it will go out; nay, it is going out fast now. The mere professor always deteriorates.

(a)

Notice the form of the Saviour's *rejection*—"I know you not." To whom is this said? To people who have worshipped in church; who have listened to sermons; who have attended prayer-meetings; who have knelt down at the Lord's table. "I know you not." But they are the words of Christ, and they must be true. "I know you not;" *i.e.*, "I do not acknowledge you as belonging to Me; there has been no personal acquaintance, no real communication between you and Me; you have never really drawn nigh to Me; you have always held back your hearts, and given them to another; your lip-service, your outward homage, your bowing of the knee, your singing My praises, I do not recognise. Heart, life, have been wanting in all that you have done. This vitiates the whole. And inasmuch as ye have virtually rejected My advances, and refused to enter into personal communication with Me, I, on My side, refuse to own and acknowledge you. I tell you, you are not Mine. Depart from Me; there is no sympathy between us. Verily, I say unto you, I know you not."

(b)   *Gordon Calthrop*

FORTUNE

Fortune in men has some small difference made,
One flaunts in rags, one flutters in brocade.

(c)   *Pope*

FOUNDATION OF THE WORLD, BEFORE THE
(Eph. 1. 4)

Matthew traces Christ's lineage back to Abraham, Luke to Adam, but Paul traces the Christian's lineage back to God *before the foundation of the world,*—before Abraham, before Adam, and before creation. Who then can thwart the eternal purpose of God concerning His elect?

(d)

FOUR GREAT WORDS

FOUR GREAT WORDS ON EATING THE FLESH AND DRINKING THE BLOOD OF THE SON OF MAN (John vi. 53–56).

1. Introduction :

(i.) These words = the summary of teaching on the *Bread of life;* based on the miracle of feeding the multitude in the wilderness. There it was, "the meat which perisheth;" here it is the meat "which endureth unto eternal life."

(ii.) Note the emphatic "*Verily, verily,*" marking this utterance of our Lord as one which it is perilous to neglect. It marks the difference between being *saved* and *unsaved;* of *having Christ,* or being *without Christ,* as few other passages do.

(iii.) *Flesh and Blood* denotes the human nature of Christ, given as food for the life of the world.

(iv.) *Eating and Drinking* denotes the act of personal appropriation; "The strengthening and refreshing of our souls," etc.

(v.) Words to be understood spiritually (63), not literally, grossly, and carnally: not the remotest basis for doctrine of Transubstantiation.

(vi.) Their relation to the *Lord's Supper* explained by (40):

(a) These words = *eating and drinking* as absolutely necessary to eternal life; but

(b) Verse 40 = that eternal life depends on *seeing,* and *believing in,* the Son of Man; therefore it is undeniable that—

(c) Whatever is taught so emphatically by our Lord in these words, and whatever is taught by visible signs in the Lord's Supper, are one and the same thing as *believing* in Him; and that thing, denoted sometimes as *seeing* Him, *believing, coming,* etc., is a *personal appropriation of His Death and Resurrection Life as necessary to our salvation.* It is not easy, then, to overstate the importance of these Four Great Words.

(e)

2. Exposition :

(i.) "*No life*" (53) = no spiritual or supernatural life. There is *natural life*—the life of Adam—of the race, but nothing superadded. But what is natural life?

(a) A *Tree* lives fifty, sixty, or a hundred years, then decays, dies, = Death has conquered *that* life.

(b) An *Animal* comes into existence, lives its time, does its work, waxes old and dies: again Death, not life, has conquered.

(c) *Man,* in like manner, subject to *the law of sin and death,* is natural; and though he may have living potency strong enough to attain the age of Methuselah, yet, in the end, Death is the conqueror: Death has dominion over everything in nature.

Now our Lord is careful not to call that *life* (absolutely and properly) which can be conquered by Death—it has proved itself worsted in the conflict with sin, temptations of world, flesh, and devil, and where such cannot be resisted, Death cannot. It is not a *Life* like His that has conquered all along the line, and therefore capable of overcoming Death. Hence the summary dismissal of this verse: where there is "no life," there is no birthday, no new name recorded, no biography or history, no *promise, no hope.*

(f)

(ii.) "*Life*" (54). "Hath" it *now,* a present possession, the very opposite to (53), and over which Death hath no dominion = "He that liveth and believeth in Me shall never die."

Objection: Death has power over the believer, he dies—all die, whether spiritual or not.

True, but mark the force of the *promise* made here. Death *has* got a partial hold of the Christian, but he shall be made to relax his hold, and give all, and more than all, back again. He takes the body in infirmity and dishonour, but shall be made to yield it in power and glory. It is only of these that this promise is given. See—

(39) Those "*Given to Me*". . . = to save;

(40) ,, "*Believe on Me*" . . = *trust;*

(44) ,, "*Come to Me*" . . . = *as Refuge;*

(54) He that "*eateth and drinketh*" Me . . . as *Bread of Life,* "*I will raise up at the last day.*"

It is a fallacy, wholly unsupported by Holy Scripture, to think that others will participate in this great promise (see *Resurrection:* comp. Luke xx. 35, 36; 1 Cor. xv.).

N.B.—To participate in this promise, we must be partakers of Christ, "the Life," now.

(g)

(iii.) Two reasons are next given why this life is *real, abiding, eternal,* and does not come under the *dominion of death:*

(h)

(a) " *Meat indeed,*" and " *drink indeed* " (55) ; =real food ; the true and only staff of life— satisfying the deepest need and craving of the human heart. We fear death is annihilation, and this fear is met by Christ Himself : " I am the Bread of Life " (48) ; daily bread, which all *labour* for, and in one shape or other, for which all are ready to sell their souls, is not the satisfying bread. " You will eat *that* and die," as the Jews did the manna in the wilderness. Death, the remorseless conqueror, conquers all such, and will do so (50, 51). There is but one true Bread, . . . eat and not die ; and *I am that* . . . the Bread is My Flesh . . . etc.

Hence, one reason why this life is eternal : Christians have become partakers of the *True Manna,* the Bread from Heaven, and this gives an overcoming life. . . . " They shall never perish," etc.

(b) *The other reason* is supplied in verse 56. Such partakers " *dwell in Me, and I in them :* " = Union with Christ ; partakers both of His *Death,* and *Life,* and *Inheritance.* His and theirs is thenceforth one life, as the slip grafted into the tree is. Without this union we can do nothing, and are nothing. From this is our fruit found ; and Christ in us is our only hope of glory.

(a)

FOUR GREAT FACTS, OR EPOCHS, IN THE LIFE OF OUR LORD

I

(1) Incarnation   (3) Resurrection
(2) Crucifixion   (4) Ascension

(i.) The first and fourth, second and third, are opposites, and mutually undo each other.

(ii.) These facts were stamped as " *Great* " by the manifestation of angels at each. The angelic world, and the Kingdom of God touch each other at certain epochs (Abraham and Moses) ; though this intercourse is stopped now, it will reappear at the end of the world.

(iii.) A sign of spirituality (Mary saw two). The reason is, that at such moments we are brought into proximity to the spiritual world.

(b)

II

The New Testament consists of two portions, or halves :
(1) The Gospels.
(2) The Acts and the Epistles.

In the Gospels the FOUR FACTS occur in the above order ; but in the second part of the New Testament they occur in an inverted order : Thus, in the

Gospels :	Acts and Epistles :
(i.) Incarnation,	(iv.) Ascension,
(ii.) Crucifixion,	(iii.) Resurrection,
(iii.) Resurrection,	(ii.) Crucifixion,
(iv.) Ascension.	(i.) Incarnation.

The reason of this is, that these great facts are now to be preached as the several facts of the Gospel of our salvation ; and the preachers, or expounders, begin with the more recent fact first. (It resembles the strata of the earth's crust—the last deposited is that which we come to first ; or as four books piled on a table are removed by taking down the top one first, though the last deposited).

The idea is a very pregnant one, and when grasped, gives an insight into New Testament interpretation which is calculated to make a lasting impression.

1. Acts i. contains the Gospel of the *Ascension ;*

2. Acts ii. 23, 24 ; iii. 15 ; iv. 33 ; } Show that the Gospel of the *Resurrection* was first preached.

It was a rousing and awakening subject, and under its power the people were " pricked in their hearts," asking, " Men and brethren, what shall we do ? "

3. In answer to this question, we next come to the preaching of the Gospel of the *Atonement,* especially by St. Paul (1 Cor. i. 23). " We preach Christ *Crucified.*" The Gospel of the Resurrection recedes as that of the Atonement becomes prominent. Cf. the literature of this period.

4. After this, and when men began to ask sceptically, " How can one man die, and make atonement for another ? " we arrive at the time when St. John wrote his Gospel and Epistles, as the answer to this question, and wherein he says, Jesus Christ was not *man,* but God : " The Word was God " (chap. i.) = The *Gospel of the Incarnation.*

To build hope of salvation on Him, is to rest upon " the Rock of Ages."

(c)

III

This corresponds in idea to the "Rise and Progress of Religion in the Soul," and is no accident, but design : There is-

(i.) The *awakening,* when men ask, " What shall we do to be saved ? "

(ii.) Next, men turn from the error of their ways to an error in the way of salvation. They try to save themselves by their own works. These build upon the " sand," and are directed to Christ's finished work as an Atonement.

(iii.) St. John's teaching = Divinity of Christ as not a foundation of *sand,* but the ROCK which gives value to the Atonement.

"That Word of life, then, which was from the beginning, which the apostles heard, and saw with their eyes, which their hands handled, was a *manifestation* of *eternal life,* which was with the Father from all eternity past ; and having finished on earth what He came to do, He again *ascended* to His place in the heavens " (1 John i. 1).

(d)

FOUR THINGS CONCERNING CHRIST, THE

I

The truth concerning Christ

1. Deity ;
2. Manhood ;
3. Conjunction of both natures in one ;
4. Distinction of both in one.
(e)

II

Four Heresies, The

1. Arian (Christ as a Creature) ;
2. Apollinarian (No νοῦς = " Reasonable Soul ") ;
3. Nestorian (Separation of the Two Natures) ;
4. Eutychian (Confusion of Substance).
(f)

III

Four General Councils, The

Called to refute these Heresies respectively :—

1. Nicea, 325 ;
2. Constantinople, 380 ;
3. Ephesus, 431 ;
4. Chalcedon, 451.

(a)

IV

Four Key Words, The

1. ἀληθῶς, Truly ;
2. τελέως, Perfectly ;
3. ἀδιαιρετώς, Indivisibly ;
4. ἀσυνχύτως, Distinctly.

(b)   See Hooker for particulars

FOUR NAMES OF CHRISTIANS, and Four Cardinals

Christians are called

1. Saints for their Holiness ;
2. Brethren for their Love ;
3. Believers for their Faith ;
4. Disciples for their Knowledge.

(c)

FOURTH GOSPEL, THE

In one thing only its adverse critics agree : in rejecting the Johannean origin of it, and ascribing this sublimest of all literary compositions to an unknown impostor, they make it the greatest mystery in the history of literature. All these attacks will pass away without being able to " pluck a single feather from the mighty wing of this Eagle," who sails serenely and majestically above the clouds, in full vision of the light of eternal truth.

(d)   *P. Schaff*

FOWLER, THE

" *Our soul is escaped as a bird out of the snare of the fowlers : the snare is broken, and we are escaped. Our help is in the name of the Lord, who made heaven and earth* " (Ps. cxxiv. 7, 8)

1. A Message of true Spiritual Direction

Satan is the fowler, who lays snares for the soul. We fall in, and are held fast. And then our only help is the Lord, who breaks the snare and sets us free. There are *three points :* (1) the devices of the fowler ; (2) the success of those devices ; (3) the defeating of those devices by the interposition of a higher power. Or, first, the *entrapping ;* then the *seizure ;* lastly the *escape.*

(e)

2. FOWLER, THE. *The Entrapping*

To entrap successfully, the snare must be concealed. Not even a bird is so foolish as to fly into a net, knowing it to be a net spread for its life. Sin must approach us in disguise. Were she to come proclaiming herself to be what she is—the

porteress of hell-gate, the agent of Satan—we should recoil from her at once. Accordingly, she makes herself as much like an angel of light as she can : calls herself fair names. To one fond of pleasure, her name is "Good Fellowship," or "Allowable Indulgence." To the free-thinking, she proclaims herself an enemy of superstition and priestcraft. A third shows symptoms of passion for hoarding and accumulation : she repudiates the term "covetousness," and claims the title of "prudence." In fact, she calls herself anything that may deceive, and lead incautious souls within the reach of her poisonous embrace. The trap is baited ; but so managed that we see only the bait— not the trap. And so, rushing on incautiously, wilfully, in the pursuit of gratification, the snare closes suddenly round us, we are caught, and there is no way of escape.

(f)

3. Another method with the fowler is *to use a decoy.* You know the plan. A bird caught, trained, or fastened by a string, seeming to be free, is used to ensnare other birds. Something of the same system is pursued in hunting for souls. How many of those engaged in the service, and receiving the rewards of sin, were led into that service by a decoy ! How many have to curse the day when they first listened to the solicitations of some one more advanced and experienced in evil than themselves ! Thousands, if they were asked what evil influence brought them to their present state, reckless and hopeless, would give the same answer —" bad companions." The snare closed round us before we well knew where we were, and deliverance from it seems a thing almost impossible.

(g)

4. FOWLER, THE. " *The Seizure* "

I think in many instances a man is not conscious his soul is caught in the snare of the fowler until he is wholly in its power ; and then the knowledge brings no great trouble or anxiety. The man resigns himself to his situation, and floats down the stream in company, which, if not " good," is numerous. There are, however, cases in which the degradation is keenly felt, in which the iron enters into the soul. Like a captured bird, the soul beats itself wildly against the bars. It longs for freedom. There it is, tied to earth, subject to the will of another, its deadliest enemy ! Unable to rise, a crushing sense of hopeless, helpless bondage settles down upon the soul ! It sees good, but is unable to grasp it. It sees evil, recoils from it ; yet is drawn to it, like steel to the magnet, by an irresistible and fatal fascination. Then, Despair comes in—dark, gloomy-browed, heavy-eyed Despair—and hisses in the ear, in a tone that thrills through the shuddering soul, " Give it up, you fool ! give it up ! There is no hope for you in God. He leaves you alone. He leaves you to fight it out yourself. Go down the stream. Catch what joy you may, take what fill of pleasure you can, before your time comes, and you slide over the fall of death into the abyss of darkness below !" I am not painting the picture in colours too dark and sombre. Some have felt this, and know what it is to have been held in the thraldom of a master-passion, a tyrannous appetite saying,

(h)

" Go," and we have gone ; " Come," and we have come ; " Do this," and we have done it ; although our whole better nature recoiled, and we loathed ourselves for doing the thing which we were compelled and driven to do. Alas ! for those who are in such a condition. Seeing what is good, unable to reach it : like men fallen into a rapid current, swept by the tide past meadows, and gardens, and flowers, and habitations which they know ; who see men and women safe upon the bank, stretch out hands of entreaty to them, utter painful cries —all in vain ; their case is beyond human help. Alas ! for all such. May God save them ! Man cannot.

(a)

5. FOWLER, THE   *The Escape*

That escape is brought about by a Divine power. The bird is rescued, not by its own efforts, not by wriggling and twisting itself free, for that were impossible ; but by the breaking of the snare. And how is the snare broken ? By the hand of the Lord, who made heaven and earth.

I am anxious that we give especial attention to this point.

I am a believer in the power of human energy, human will, the invincible determination which some men at least possess, not to be baffled in anything they set their heart on to accomplish. But withal I am perfectly sure of this, that never did any one on whom Satan had fixed his clutches by means of a bad habit, or an importunate appetite, or an ungodly life—never did, and never will, any such one shake himself free by an act of his own will. Some will say, " But do you not know instances in which men, notoriously profligate, have reformed their lives, without being indebted to religion, simply by the power of their own invincible resolution ? " I answer, " I do." " Well then," they urge, " here is a flat contradiction to the statement you just advanced, that a man cannot, by his own determination, set himself free from a sinful habit ; cannot *of himself* burst the bonds of the great fowler, Satan. Here is proof that he can." " Not at all," I reply ; " there is no contradiction whatever. In the cases you mention, there is no proof that Satan has lost his hold of the persons, but only that he has shifted his grip from one place, to fasten it, in all probability, more securely on another. Besides, in the matter of an inveterate evil habit, it has yet to be made clear to me that a man is free from its power, unless he has become a new creature in Jesus Christ. Look at your tiger sleeping. He looks calm and harmless enough ; but he is a tiger still. Rouse him up ; you will soon feel what strength there is in his talons and his teeth, and what a savage, relentless ferocity in his temper. The adder, when frozen (the fable tells us), was carried to the countryman's hearth. It seemed a poor helpless thing, incapable of mischief ; but the heat of the fire brought back all its venomous vitality. And if the man has not received the baptism of the Spirit, has not been made partaker of the resurrection-life of Christ, I cannot feel assured that this old habit may not be sleeping instead of dead ; frozen and torpid, instead of having lost all its power to injure."

(b)

6. What, then, is to be done ?

In the first place, it would seem clear that the mere *knowledge* of our position does not seem sufficient to furnish a starting-point for us. The question is, *Are we willing to be rescued from it ?*

Here is the difficulty. The man says, " I am not sure about myself. I wish I were. That I should be glad to be out of this condition and in the condition of those who follow Christ, is clear enough. But I am bewitched by a sorceress. She has brought me under the baneful spell of her enchantments. She has bound me hand and foot. And whether I am willing to be translated into the condition of godliness at the expense of giving her up, is more than I can tell you. If the choice be put before me—Christ on the one side, and this old lust of mine, this witch, this sorceress, on the other—I cannot say that I am sure that I am willing to choose Christ." What shall we say to this ? Our object is to get the man into a state of willingness. The Lord Jesus, we know, is ready to receive. But if the sinner holds himself aloof, refuses to come, what is the practical use of all that wondrous exhibition of Divine tenderness and mercy ? It is, in fact, of no avail. Christ Himself, the omnipotent Christ, finds one thing that even He is not able to do. His own laws forbid His doing it. He cannot save a sinner against his own will. He will enter the door of the heart when its bolts are drawn back, but He will not obtain admission perforce. The man, then, has to be made *willing*. But how ?

(c)

7. " They shall be willing in the day of my power."

If there is the slightest movement in your soul towards Christ, that impulse must have come from Christ Himself. The human physician, skilful and tender as he may be, cannot help us unless we go to Him. But our inclination to go comes of ourselves. Not so is it with the great Physician of souls. If you have any drawing towards Him, that drawing comes from Himself. Faint as it is, it is a message from Him to you. Let it inspire you with hope. Yield to its influence. True, it is the very faintest glimmer of light, but it shines from Him, and if you follow it, it will lead to Him. But do not debate and argue about it. Act immediately. Once a man with a withered hand —a hand shrunken, dried up, immovable, useless, —stood in the presence of Christ. " Stretch forth thine hand," said the Saviour. *Stretch it forth, indeed !* How is he to do such a thing ? He might have said, " Lord, why do You tell me to do what You know very well I cannot do ? My arm is withered—I cannot stretch it out." But the man never thought of arguing or disputing. He was in the presence of Christ. He looked into His kindly, powerful eyes. He never thought of *himself*. He thought of Christ only, and made the attempt ; and with the effort, strength came. He stretched it out, and it was made whole, even as the other. Do you act as this man did. Be not occupied with yourself. Be occupied with Christ. Fix your eyes on Him. Hearken to His voice. Obey His commands. Yield to His drawing—and He will deliver you. It was for such as you He came. For He was sent to " proclaim liberty to the captives, and the opening of the prison to them that are bound."

(d)

Gordon Calthrop

FOX, GEORGE

He was the son of a weaver, and was himself bound apprentice to a shoemaker. Feeling a stronger impulse towards spiritual contemplations than towards the mechanical profession, he left his master and went about the country clothed in a leathern doublet, a dress which he long affected, as well for its singularity as its cheapness. That he might wean himself from sublunary objects, he broke off all connection with his friends and family, and never dwelt a moment in one place, lest habit should beget new connections, and depress the sublimity of his aërial meditations. He frequently wandered into the woods, and passed whole days in hollow trees, without company or any other amusement than his Bible. Having reached that pitch of perfection as to need no other book, he soon advanced to another state of spiritual progress, and began to pay less regard even to that Divine composition itself. His own heart, he imagined, was full of the same inspiration which had guided the prophets and apostles themselves; and by this inward light must every spiritual obscurity be cleared, by this living spirit must the dead letter be animated. When he had been sufficiently consecrated in his own imagination, he felt that the fumes of self-applause soon dissipate, if not continually supplied by the admiration of others; and he began to seek proselytes. Proselytes were easily gained at a time when all men's affections were turned towards religion, and when the most extravagant modes of it were sure to be most popular. All the forms of ceremony, invented by pride and ostentation, Fox and his disciples, from a superior pride and ostentation, carefully rejected; even the ordinary rites of civility were shunned as the nourishment of carnal vanity and self-conceit.

(a)   *Hume*

FREE

He is the free-man whom the truth makes free,
And all are slaves besides.
(b)   *Cowper*

FREE GIFT, THE

God the Father offers His Son most freely. "God so loved the world, that He gave His only begotten Son, that whosoever believeth on Him should not perish, but have everlasting life" (John iii. 16). "Unto us a Child is born, unto us a Son is given" (Isa. ix. 6). "If thou knewest the gift of God," said Christ unto the woman of Samaria, "and who it is that saith to thee, Give me to drink" (John iv. 10). "Much more they, which receive abundance of grace, and of the gift of righteousness," etc. (Rom. v. 17). Christ calleth Himself a "Gift," and it is called the "gift of righteousness;" and nothing so free as gift. And therefore those divines speak not unfitly who say, "It is given unto us, as fathers give lands and inheritance to their children; as kings give pardons to their subjects, having merited death. They give them, because they will, out of the freeness of their minds." All those who would come unto Christ, and desire to take Him as their wisdom, righteousness, sanctification, and redemption, must be utterly unbottomed of themselves, and built only on the rich and free mercy of God revealed in the Gospel. They must be emptied first

of all conceit of any righteousness or worth in themselves at all. Secondly, of all hope of any ability or possibility to help themselves. Nay, filled, thirdly, with sense of their own unworthiness, naughtiness, nothingness. Fourthly, and with such a thirst after that water of life, that they are most willing to sell all for it, and cry heartily, "Give me drink, or else I die." And then when they are thus most nothing in themselves, and do so long for the "rivers of living water," they are certainly most welcome unto Jesus Christ, and may take Him most freely. Hear how sweetly He calls them: "Ho, every one that thirsteth, come ye to the waters; and he that hath no money; come ye, buy, and eat; yea, come, buy wine and milk without money and without price" (Isa. lv. 1). "In the last day, that great day of the feast, Jesus stood, and cried, saying, If any man thirst, let him come unto Me, and drink. He that believeth on Me, as the Scripture hath said, out of his belly shall flow rivers of living water" (John vii. 37, 38). "It is done. I am Alpha and Omega, the beginning and the end. I will give unto him that is athirst of the fountain of the water of life freely" (Rev. xxi. 6). "And let him that is athirst come. And whosoever will, let him take the water of life freely" (Rev. xxii. 17).

(c)   *Bolton*

FREE GRACE

"Erected 1875, by lovers of Hart's hymns, published in 1759, and still highly prized by the Church of God. The author's remains were interred in this spot, as the original stone yet remains to show. Joseph Hart, died May 24th, 1768, aged 56." "Joseph Hart was, by the free and sovereign grace and Spirit of God, raised up from the depths of sin and delivered from the bonds of mere profession and self-righteousness, and led to rest entirely for salvation in the finished atonement and perfect obedience of Christ."

"O! bring no price!
God's grace is free
To Paul, to Magdalene, to me."

"Mercy is welcome news indeed
To those who guilty stand;
Wretches who feel what help they need
Will bless the helping hand."

"Though I am a stranger to others and a wonder to myself, yet I know Him [Christ], or rather am known of Him." "Where sin abounded, grace did much more abound."

(d)   *Memorial to the Rev. Joseph Hart*

Who was I that I should have been preserved when others were left to follow their own ways and the temptations of the evil one? I acknowledge from my inmost soul that this was owing to nothing in myself, but solely to the free and unmerited grace of God. I did not seek Him, but He sought me; I did not choose Him, but He it was that chose me.

(e)   *Sunday at Home*

FREEDOM IN CHRIST, LIBERTY

As far as I am a Christian, I am free. My religion lays on me not one chain. It does not prescribe a certain range for my mind beyond
(f)

which nothing can be learned. It speaks of God as the Universal Father, and sends me to all His works for instruction. It does not hem me round with a mechanical ritual; does not enjoin forms, attitudes, and hours of prayer; does not descend to details of dress and food; does not put on me one outward badge. It teaches and enkindles love to God, but commands no precise expressions of this sentiment. It prescribes prayers, but lays the chief stress on the prayer of the closet, and treats all worship as worthless but that of the mind and heart. It teaches us to do good, but leaves us to devise for ourselves the means by which we may best serve mankind.

(a) *Channing*

FREE-THINKER

He was a great free-thinker, and a very free speaker of his free thoughts; he made no scruple to disseminate his sceptical opinions whenever he could with any propriety introduce them. At his own table, indeed, the lady of the house (who was a staunch advocate for her husband's opinions) would often in the warmth of argument say, "*Sir, we Deists.*" She once made use of this expression in a mixed company to David Hume, who refused the intended compliment by asserting that he was a very good Christian; for the truth of which he appealed to a worthy clergyman present, and this occasioned a laugh, which a little disconcerted the lady and Mr. Mallet. The lecture upon the *non credenda* of the free-thinkers was repeated so often, and urged with so much earnestness, that the inferior domestics became soon as able disputants as the heads of the family. The fellow who waited at table, being thoroughly convinced that for any of his misdeeds he should have no after-account to make, was resolved to profit by the doctrine, and made off with many things of value, particularly plate. Luckily he was so closely pursued that he was brought back with his prey to his master's house, who examined him before some select friends. At first the man was sullen, and would answer no questions put to him; but being urged to give a reason for his infamous behaviour, he resolutely said, "Sir, I had heard you so often talk of the impossibility of a future state, and that after death there was no reward for virtue, or punishment for vice, that I was tempted to commit the robbery." "Well, but, you rascal," replied Mallet, "had you no fear of the gallows?" "Sir," said the fellow, looking sternly at his master, "what is that to you, if I had a mind to venture that? You had removed my greatest terror; why should I fear the lesser?"

(b) *Thomas Davies, on David Mallet*

Gibbon, in his "Memoirs," speaks of having been carried to Putney, "to the house of Mr. Mallet, by whose philosophy I was rather *scandalized than reclaimed.*" This from Gibbon.

(c) *W. Clark Russell, on Mallet*

FREEWILL

True enough, our fallen nature, which now says "*No*" to God, still retains the very same faculty of will with which it was originally endowed for the purpose of saying "Yes." But, perverted and paralysed by sin, it has never yet in any single instance since the Fall said "*Yes;*" and in no single future instance will it make that response, except as, not merely *solicited*, but *renewed*, *strengthened*, and *enabled* by Divine grace. What, then, is the value of that figment of ability to please God, which, owing to the absolute and universal conditions of the case, brings forth only fruit unto death? (Rom. vii. 5).

And how much better is it than inability?

(d) *Lange*

FRET NOT

I *feel* and grieve; but, by the grace of God, I *fret* at nothing.

(e) *Wesley (in his 73rd year)*

FRIEND, A FALSE

Who dares think one thing, and another tell, My heart detests him as the gates of hell.

(f) *Pope*

FRIENDS OF JESUS (John xv. 15)

Christ will have no forced selection of men, no soldiers by compulsion, no timorous slaves, but children, brethren, friends.

(g) *Hedinger*

"FROM ALL SIN" (John i. 7)

Whether sins of thought, word, or deed, sins of rashness or sins of ignorance, sins of malice, sins of omission or sins of commission, sins in *affectu* or sins in *defectu*, sins of pleasure or sins of pain, sins committed at our work or during our recreation, sins against the first or second table of the Decalogue.

Bengel=*originale*, *actuale*. In believers *peccatum manet*, but *non regnat*.

(h) *Lange*

FRUGALITY

Profusion is ruin; for it ends, and soon too, in debt, in injustice, and insolvency. You well know how meanly, in the country more especially, every man is thought of who cannot pay his credit; in what terms he is spoken of—in what light he is viewed—what a deduction this is from his good qualities; what an aggravation of his bad ones; what insults he is exposed to from his creditors; what contempt from all. Nor is this judgment far amiss. Let him not speak of honesty who is daily practising deceit; for every man who is not paid is deceived. Let him not talk of liberality who puts it out of his power to perform one act of it. . . . There is no meanness in frugality; the meanness is in those shifts and expedients to which extravagance is sure to bring men.

(i) *Paley*

FRUIT

1. What Fruit of Self-abasement

Have you found out the evil of your connection with the first Adam? (Rom. v. 19).

(j)

Do you know the plagues of your own heart? (1 Kings viii. 38).

The hell of corruption *there?* (Jer. xvii. 9).

Do you feel you have never lived one moment to His glory? (Rom. iii. 25).

Do you feel that to all eternity you never can be justified by anything in yourself? (Rev. vii. 14).

(*a*)

2. What Fruit of Believing

Have you really and fully uptaken Christ as the Gospel lays Him down? (John v. 12).

Do you cleave to Him as a sinner? (1 Tim. i. 15).

Do you count all things but loss for the excellency of the knowledge of Him? (Matt. ix. 9).

Do you feel the glory of His person? (Rev. i. 17).

His finished work? (Heb. ix. 26).

His offices? (1 Cor. i. 30).

Does He shine like the sun into your soul? (Mal. iv. 2).

Is your heart ravished with His beauty? (Song of Sol. v. 16).

(*b*)

3. What Fruit of Crying after Holiness

Is this the one thing you do? (Phil. iii. 13).

Do you spend your life in cries for deliverance from this body of sin and death? (Rom. vii. 24).

Ah! I fear there is little of this. The most of God's people are contented to be saved from the hell that is *without*. They are not so anxious to be saved from the hell that is *within*. I fear there is little feeling of your need of the indwelling Spirit. I fear you do not know "the exceeding greatness of His power" to usward who believe.

I fear many of you are strangers to the visits of the Comforter. God has reason to complain of you, "Wherefore should they bring forth wild grapes?"

(*c*)

4. What Fruit of Actual Likeness to God

Do you love to be with God? "To climb up near to God (Gen. v. 22), to love, and long, and plead, and wrestle, and stretch after Him?" (*Brainerd*).

Are you weaned from the world? (Ps. cxxxi.) from its praise, from its hatred, from its scorn?

Do you give yourselves clean away to God? (2 Cor. viii. 5) and all that is yours? Are you willing that your will should be lost in His great will? Do you throw yourselves into the arms of God for time and for eternity? Oh, search your hearts and try them, ask God to do it for you, and "to lead you in the way everlasting!" (Ps. cxxxix. 23, 24; p. 247, M.).

It is not great talents God blesses so much as great likeness to Jesus. A holy minister is an awful weapon in the hand of God.

(*d*)   *Robert McCheyne*

"*By their fruits ye shall know them*" (Matt. vii. 20).

A Child's Prayer

Please, dear God and Jesus Christ, bless my dear father and mother; make my mother's shop pay her well; and give us both enough to eat and drink, and to put on; take care of me, as you do of the sparrows, please; make me a good child. Give me Thy Holy Spirit, *and teach me to make the pies and the soup better and better.* For Jesus' sake. Amen.

(*e*)   *Sunday Magazine*

FULL CORN IN THE EAR

After Mr. Newton had published his "Omicron," and described the three stages of growth in religion, from the *blade*, the *ear*, and the *full corn in the ear*, distinguishing them by the letters A, B, and C, a conceited young minister wrote to Mr. N., telling him, that he read his own character accurately drawn in that of C. Mr. N. wrote in reply, that in drawing the character of C, or full maturity, he had forgotten to add, till now, one prominent feature of C's character, namely, that C. *never knew his own face.*

(*f*)   *Memoir of John Newton*

FULLY PERSUADED (Rom. iv. 21)

It is a great snare for men to suppose that to doubt is an evidence of humility. On the contrary, to doubt God's promise, or His love, is to dishonour Him, because it is to question His word. Multitudes refuse to accept His grace, because they do not regard themselves as worthy, as though their worthiness were the ground on which that grace is offered. The thing to be believed is, that God accepts the unworthy; that, for Christ's sake, He justifies the unjust. Many find it harder to believe that God can love them, notwithstanding their sinfulness, than the hundred-years-old patriarch did to believe that he should be the father of many nations. Confidence in God's word, a full persuasion that He can do what seems to us impossible, is as necessary in the one case as in the other. The sinner honours God, in trusting His grace, as much as Abraham did in trusting His power.

(*g*)   *Hodge*

FUNDAMENTALS

The story is told in the life of Norman Macleod that on his first "diet of visitation" at Loudoun he called on an old woman who was looked upon as a great light among the Covenanters. When he entered the house, she beckoned him to sit down beside her, and putting the trumpet to her ear, said, "*Gang ower the fundamentals!*" Nor was he welcomed as a true ambassador of Christ until the old dame was satisfied with the soundness of his theology.

But are there not many in our own Church who know not even what "fundamentals" are? Many who do not read their Bibles? Many who have never read the Thirty-nine Articles? Far more who have never carefully examined them? And yet they are the Church's Code of Faith!

(*h*)   *E. Bayley*

FUNERALS

Why is the hearse with scutcheons blazon'd round, And with the nodding plume of ostrich crown'd?

(*i*)

The dead know it not, nor profit gain;
It only serves to prove the living vain,
How short is life! how frail is human trust.
Is all this pomp for laying dust to dust?
   (a)   *Gay*

               The nodding plume
Which makes poor man's humiliation proud;
Boast of our ruin! triumph of our dust!
   (b)   *Young*

But see! the well-plumed hearse comes nodding
     on, stately and slow;
    But tell us, why this waste?
Why this ado in earthing up a carcase
That's fallen into disgrace, and in the nostrils
    smells horrible?
   (c)   *Blair*

FUR: PRIDE OF DRESS

The fur that warms a monarch, warmed a bear.
   (d)   *Pope*

FURNACE

The Purifier puts every vessel into the furnace,
and Himself superintends the process: He allows
nothing to be consumed but the dross, and this
He will purge from them. They often object to
His manner of dealing with them, but He says,
"I will turn mine hand upon thee, I will purge
thee in the furnace of thy dross, and will take
away all thine alloy." Some of the vessels appear
as if they were penetrated with filth, and mixed
up with defilement, and of them He says, "I will
melt them and try them, for how shall I part with
them?"
   (e)   *James Smith, of Cheltenham*

G

GAIN AND LOSS

"*For* what shall it profit a man, *if he gain the whole world, and lose his own soul?*"—St. Mark viii. 36

I have read of a certain tyrant, in some Eastern country, who, like plenty more with far less excuse, could not bear to be reminded of stern facts. Sorrow, sickness, death—these words were forbidden to reach those royal ears. And if any one came into his presence dressed in clothes of mourning the king would sentence him at once to death.

That poor king was not more foolish, not more cowardly, than many an educated man and woman in London. That dead barbarian is a type of thousands of living so-called believers in the Gospel of the Son of God—thousands who throw dust in their own eyes, who shut out the vision of what they still know to be the truth—the truth that shall "grind them to powder," if it do not "set them free"—who rest content in the familiar assurance that Christ has died for them; who stop their ears when the voice of truth appeals to them in language which is too stern, too wholesome, too strong for them to relish; who listen patiently to the smooth proclamation, Peace, peace! but who are irritated by the suggestion that there may be by-and-by no peace for them; who are pleased to listen to the preacher who guarantees heaven for them all, but whose sense of propriety is rudely shocked by the painful probability of hell.

(*a*)　　　　　　　　　*Ottley*

What shall it Profit

It is a question which comes home to a race like ourselves, who are described in unfriendly phrase, yet with substantial accuracy, as a "nation of shopkeepers." And we need not wince under that description. Honest industry is always respectable; and the man who earns his bread is in reality at least as noble a man as the man who merely inherits it. Surely that which marks us, the English people, off among the nations of the earth, is the practical temper which is not dazzled by high pretensions and lofty sentiments; which is impatient of all mere empty show, mere resultless talk, mere useless activity and bustle; and which, while others are enthusiastic, sanguine, venturesome, asks doggedly, again and again, "What shall it profit?" And this not as a cynic might ask the question, not in scornful indifference to the answer, but with the earnestness of men who wish to ascertain the real measure of a proposed action or effort.

(*b*)　　　　　　　　　*Liddon*

What shall it Profit

We ask ourselves this question in some shape every day. From the highest enterprise in commercial speculation down to the pettiest monetary bargain, it is a question which in this great city is asked more often perhaps than any other in the every-day business of our lives. The selling price,

the market value of everything is challenged. It is because English people have commonly so shrewd a sense of profit and of loss in money matters, that England has under God's blessing come to be the foremost commercial nation of the world. The interest you take in the question, "What shall it profit?" is written in the enormous traffic that crowds your streets, in the merchant navies that leave your docks, in the wharves and warehouses of your river side, in the princely houses of your citizens; it is written upon the balance-sheet of your national exchequer, upon the closely printed pages of your commercial directories; not a railway is designed to cross the broad acres of your country, or to thrust itself beneath the streets of your metropolis, but you ask, with jealous anxiety, "What shall it profit?" Is the criticism of your Stock Exchange directed to the securities of some South American Republic, or of some inter-oceanic railroad? Is a proposal made to join the shores of Britain to those of a neighbouring country, or to work the copper mines of some Welsh mountain side? Is it suggested to buy land for the public amusement of your citizens, to erect a gorgeous opera-house, to open an aquarium, or to change into habitable homes the dwelling-places of the London poor? Is the critical anxiety of the nation turned towards a proposal for purchasing a canal to be an English highway between the hemispheres of East and West? The question that men put as the test of the expediency of these varied proposals is, "What shall it profit?"

(*c*)　　　　　　　　　*Ottley*

For money men will almost dare to die. There are men of high social standing who for money's worth will sell the lives of others; there are shipowners who sell the lives of sailors for money· there are mothers who sell the happiness of their daughters for money; there are children who have taken their parents' lives for money. The eyes of Europe have lately been riveted on the crime of a man who, on the possible chance of a few thousand pounds' insurance, would have destroyed without any remorse the lives of a shipload of his fellow-creatures.

(*d*)　　　　　　　　　*Ottley*

I have known those who practically use the self-same words that Horace says men and children used in pagan Rome. "Oh, give us money: money first; honestly, if possible, but money anyhow; money first, and after money, virtue; after money, religion; after money, the thought of death and the remembrance of judgment; after money, Christ; after money, God. After I have made my money, after I have invested it, then I do mean to think about my soul. Give me commercial success; give cent. per cent. for my money; I'll part with all that you remind me God tells us is lovely and of good report; take my honour as a man; take my courage, my liberty of conscience; take the best aspirations of my heart; take the innocence of my youth; take the strength and experience of my manhood; take my natural affection; take the habit of prayer I learnt from

(*e*)

my mother; take my power of admiring anything but gold, and of loving anything by what gold can buy; take my faith in God, take my hope of heaven;—give me money; take you my soul."

(a)   *Ottley*

GAIN AND LOSS

" What shall it profit? "

A French miser and millionaire (M. Fosare) had a vault constructed in a wine-cellar in his house, the door of which closed with a spring lock. Here he used to retire to feast his eyes on his gold. One day he was missing, and not being heard of, the house was sold. Then they found the miser dead, with a candlestick by his side, in this vault, the door of which had closed itself whilst he was engaged with his gold.

(b)

GARDEN

God the first garden made, and the first city, Cain.

(c)   *Cowley*

GENESIS

Rightly understood, I know not a single scientific truth that militates against even the minutest or least prominent of its details.

(d)   *Hugh Miller*

GENESIS AND GEOLOGY

It has been alleged that geology, by referring the origin of the globe to a higher antiquity than is assigned to it by the writings of Moses, undermines our faith in the inspiration of the Bible, and in all the animating prospects of the immortality which it unfolds. This is a false alarm. *The writings of Moses do not fix the antiquity of the globe.*

(e)   *Thomas Chalmers*

GENIUS

To carry on the feelings of childhood into the powers of manhood: to combine the child's sense of wonder and novelty with the appearance, which every day for perhaps forty years had rendered familiar-

" With sun and moon and stars throughout the year,
  And man and woman; "

this is the character and privilege of *genius*, and one of the marks which distinguish genius from talent.

Genius must have talent as its complement and implement, just as in like manner imagination must have fancy. In short, the higher intellectual powers can only act through a corresponding energy of the lower.

(f)   *S. T. Coleridge*

In Shakspeare, one sentence begets the next naturally: the meaning is all interwoven. He goes on kindling like a meteor through the dark atmosphere; yet when the creation in its outline is once perfect, then he seems to rest from his labour, and to smile upon his work and tell himself that it is very good. You see many scenes and parts of scenes, which are simply Shakspeare

disporting himself in joyous triumph and vigorous fun after a great achievement of his highest genius.

(g)   *Ibid*

Genius is always marvellous; but when sanctified, it is matchless.

(h)   *C. H. Spurgeon*

Genius of itself is capable of knowing good, not necessarily of doing it.

(i)   *George Macdonald*

GENIUS AND TALENT

What, meanwhile, must be the condition of an Era, when the highest advantages there become perverted into drawbacks; when, if you take two men of genius, and put the one between the handles of a plough, and mount the other between the painted coronets of a coach and four, and bid them both move along, the former shall arrive a Burns, the latter a Byron; two men of talent, and put the one into a printer's chapel, full of lamp-black, tyrannous usage, hard toil, and the other into Oxford University, with lexicons and libraries, and hired expositors and sumptuous endowment, the former shall come out a Dr. Franklin, the latter a Dr. Parr.

(j)   *Carlyle, on Dr. Parr*

GENTLEMAN

When Adam dolve and Evè span,
Who was then a gentleman?

(k)   *Pegge*

GEOLOGY

It has been said that the inferences of the geologist militate against those of the theologian. Nay, not those of our higher geologists and higher theologians,—not what our Murchisons and Sedgwicks infer in the one field, with what our Chalmerses and Isaac Taylors infer in the other. Between the Word and the works of God there can be no actual discrepancies; and the seeming ones are discernible only by the men who see worst.

(l)   *Hugh Miller*

GETHSEMANE (Heb. v. 7)

1. The significance of Gethsemane

(i.) " The Lamb of God " differs from other lambs sacrificed, in that *He accepts death freely—* " I came to do Thy will."

(ii.) The agony in the garden of Gethsemane marks the moment when Christ accepted the punishment due to sin.

(iii.) Hence, though Jesus drank the bitter cup on Calvary, yet it was at Gethsemane that He consented to do so.

(iv.) This cost the Redeemer a struggle—Death was death to Him. The ingredients of that " cup " were presented unto Him as peculiarly horrible. It was the hour of the Power of Darkness, and of the Tempter's keenest darts. The Redeemer agonizes in prayer to be saved from that hour—that hour for which He had come into the world. He is in fear, and fear hath torment.

(m)

His prayer for escape is attended with "strong *crying* and *supplication* and *tears*, and He was heard;" though not delivered from death, yet *He was delivered from His fear.*

He overcame the temptation—for such it was—and issued forth from the struggle *calm* and *submissive*. God's will is His will—"*Thy will be done.*" And in the strength gained by His thrice-repeated prayer, He goes to meet His cross, which but a moment before had made Him stagger.

(*a*)

2. In the Gospel narratives of this agony

Matthew gives prominence to the *Prayer* of the Redeemer;
Mark to His *supplications;*
Luke to His *agony*.
John has no account of it, though he alludes to it in his own peculiar way.

A comparison of the four records enables us in some measure to form an idea of the terrible nature of the Redeemer's agony in the garden of Gethsemane.

(*b*)

1. Matthew (xxvi. 36-46):—According to the peculiarity of this Evangelist, he does not explain. He narrates circumstances so as to be easily remembered; arranges his facts in succession like the links of a chain. This peculiarity of Matthew is seen in his narrative of the agony in Gethsemane, in which he shows the gradual progress of the temptation through *fear* until victory is gained.

(i.) At Gethsemane, Jesus requests His disciples to wait, whilst He goes and prays at a distance. He prays because the shadow of His cross is cast before (36).

(ii.) He selects three of His disciples—Peter, James, and John—to be near Him in His agony: =the desire of the sympathy of friends near in time of sorrow. His sorrow evident—"He began to be sorrowful and very heavy" (37).

(iii.) He speaks to them of the agony with which He is seized: "My soul is exceeding sorrowful, even unto death." Shows His depression. The request to watch for the coming of the traitor (38).

(iv.) He withdraws from them "a little farther" —"fell on His face." His prayer—"O My Father, if it be possible, let this cup pass from Me. Nevertheless not as I will, but as Thou wilt" (39).

(v.) He returns to the three, finds them asleep, (shows that His prayer had been prolonged—"one hour") (40).

The question to Peter. Why to him? (see 33).

(vi.) He warns them all that they need to watch and pray, like Himself, for their hour of trial, too, is coming (41).

(vii.) He goes a second time, and prays as before (42).

(viii.) He returns, and finds them asleep again (43).

(ix.) He goes the third time, and prays the same words (44).

(x.) After this He has conquered—the struggle is over—He has consented to drink the cup: "The hour is at hand" (45).

(*c*)

2. Mark (xiv. 32), substantially the same as St. Matthew's account—less full—says striking things in few words. Verse 36 is peculiar to Him: "Abba, Father, all things are possible to Thee." Soon the Jews will be mocking and saying, "He trusted in God, let Him deliver Him now, and we will believe in Him." There is nothing in what St. Matthew says to show that the Father had power to save Him. Now we learn what God *could* have done, but the world would have remained *unsaved*. It does not mean that Jesus had given up the work of our salvation: He asks only "*If there be any other way*"—any other way save that of the cross; whether the unlimited power of His Heavenly Father cannot find another way of reconciliation.

(*d*)

3. Luke (xxii. 39-46):

(i.) The angel "strengthening Him" is mentioned by St. Luke only. His prayer is being answered (43).

(ii.) Luke, the physician, notices, accordingly, the physical aspect of the sufferings of Christ. The agony is so intense = the beginning of dissolution. His sweat was, as it were, great drops of blood = the intensity of the struggle. affecting the heart and circulation.

(*e*)

4. John has no definite account of Gethsemane. He never repeats what has been said by others, unless there is special reason for doing so. But, though he does not relate this agony, yet he mentions its *essence*. For John had the faculty of penetration—he could read spirits.

His only notice of the struggle is before the night in the garden (xii. 27): when the Lord is beginning to speak of His approaching death, He says, "Now is My soul troubled." There is the essence of the agony; and from that moment it oppressed the Saviour until the whole force of it was upon Him on the night of the betrayal. The whole of the connected narratives is calculated, as hardly anything else can, to show us—

(i.) **The enormity of sin:**
When its expiation required the Saviour to drink "this cup" (the cross).

(ii.) **The greatness of the Forgiveness of Sin:**
Levity of thought about this is common. God is merciful, but He will have us know something of the *greatness* of our debt. He will not forgive in the dark: "Come let us reason together, saith the Lord." "Look at the account to be settled." "Look at what it cost the Saviour to pay it for you." This, before Forgiveness.

(iii.) **The debt of love that we owe:**
"We love Him, because He first loved us."

> "Were the whole round of nature mine,
> That were a present far too small;
> Love so amazing, so Divine,
> Demands my heart, my life, my all."

(*f*)

GETHSEMANE

There will be no Christian but what will have a Gethsemane; but praying Christians will find that there is no Gethsemane without its angel.

(*g*)   *Binney*

GIFTS

If facts allure thee, think how Bacon shined,
The wisest, brightest, meanest of mankind.

(*h*)   *Pope*

Gifts

Gifts (good) are from the " Father of light " (Jas. i. 17 ; Jer. x. 12).

Then never go to the children for them. Neither fear nor hope for anything from any light of them at all.

(a) *Lange*

Look not down to the ground, then, as swine to the acorns they find lying there, and never once up to the tree they come from. Look up ; the very frame of our body bears that way. It is nature's check to the body.

(b) *Ibid*

Are His " gifts without repentance " (Rom. ii. 29)? Varies He not (Jas. i. 7)? Whom He loves, does He love to the end (John. xiii. 1)? Let our service be so, too—not wavering. Oh, that we changed from Him no more than He from us !

(c) *Ibid*

Gifts and Graces

" Follow after charity, and desire spiritual gifts " (1 Cor. xiv.).

Graces are what a man *is ;* but enumerate his gifts, and you will only know what he *has.* He *is* loving ; he *has* eloquence, or medical skill, or legal knowledge, or the gift of acquiring languages, or that [of healing. You have only to cut out his tongue, or to impair his memory, and the gift is gone. But you must destroy his very being, change him into another man, obliterate his identity, before he ceases to be a loving man. Therefore you may contemplate the gift separate from the man ; you may admire it, and despise him. But you cannot contemplate the grace separate from the man.

(d) *F. W. Robertson*

" GILDED VICES "

We've scrubbed the negroes till we've nearly killed 'em,
And finding that we cannot wash them white,
We mean to gild 'em.

(e) *Thos. Hood*

GIVING

Mary sat at Jesus' feet (Mark xiv. 3).

1. She learned of Jesus (she gave her heart to Him).

2. She next became the servant of Jesus—she gave of her substance (300 pence).

Those who give their hearts to Jesus are not slow in giving their substance.

After the heart goes the " *alabaster box.*"

(f)

Giving

" *Freely ye have received, freely give* " (Matt. x. 8).

A good inflow makes a good outflow.

(g)

Giving

Who gives constrained, but his own fear reviles,
Not thanked, but scorned ; nor are they gifts, but spoils.

(h) *Denham*

Giving

" *Give alms of such things as ye have.*"

A strange fish ! Were I in England now (as once I was), and had but this fish painted, not a holiday fool there but would give a piece of silver ; there would this monster make a man ; any strange beast there makes a man. When they will not give a doit to relieve a lame beggar, they will lay out ten to see a dead Indian.

(i) *Shakspeare*

GLADIATOR

Butchered to make a Roman holiday.

(j) *Byron*

GLEANING

Ruth gleaned much, because Boaz had ordered handfuls of corn to be scattered about the field. So every word, whether in the Bible, or in a sermon, which suits us, is so because Christ has ordered them to be scattered for us who glean.

(k)

GLORIFICATION

" *That by means of these ye might be partakers of the Divine nature* " (2 Pet. i. 4)

1. There is such a thing as the glorification of the flesh (lower nature) through living in the Spirit.

2. There is also, on the other hand, such a thing as materializing the Spirit through living after the flesh (Rom. viii. 13).

(Cf. Heb. ii. 14) Christ took part of our nature : we become partakers of the Divine nature.

(l)

GLORY

" *We shall be like Him* " (1 John iii. 2)

In the history of the earth, molluscs, fishes, reptiles, mammals, had each in succession their periods of vast duration ; and then the human period began,—the period of a fellow-worker with God, created in God's own image. What is to be the next advance? Is there to be merely a repetition of the past? No. The geologist finds no example of dynasties once passed away again returning. There has been no repetition of the dynasty of the fish, of the reptile, of the mammal. The dynasty of the future is to have glorified man for its inhabitant ; but it is to be the dynasty— " *the kingdom* "—not of glorified man, . . . but of God Himself in the form of man. In the doctrine of the two natures, human and Divine, and in the further doctrine that the terminal dynasty = (" *We shall be like Him* ")—we find that required progression beyond which progress cannot

(m)

go. We find the point of elevation never to be exceeded meetly coincident with the final period never to be terminated . . . The long ascending line from dead matter to man has been a progress Godwards; not an asymptotical progress, but destined from the beginning to furnish a point of union.

(a) *Hugh Miller*

GLORY, THE HOPE OF

" *Christ in you, the hope of Glory* " (1 Col. i. 27)

1. **What is meant by Glory?**

Complete salvation. What is *salvation?*
The common notions both inadequate and unsatisfactory:

(i.) *Heaven* = sitting on a cloud and singing Hallelujah. This idea is little beyond a Turk's notion of heaven and bowers of sensual bliss.

(ii.) " *Going to heaven*" = the bare idea of escape from punishment.

(iii.) *Reward:* for a good and meritorious life. Whatever truth there may be in such notions, they certainly fall short of what is meant by " *Glory.*"

2. *Salvation*, according to the Bible, is a *development*. God created man for a certain *end;* that " end" obtained, and not lost, is *salvation*.

"Saving the soul" and "losing the soul" are opposites, denoting opposite poles of (i.) development to an end, or (ii.) that end thwarted and interrupted.

(i.) *To* " *save the soul*" is to arrive at the proper development of being; to progress until a higher state of existence is reached, and the *highest* development we are capable of is " GLORY."

(ii.) *To* " *lose the soul*" is to have this proper development interrupted; to become an abortion, and, instead of arriving at a state of glory, to sink to a state of *degradation*—lower than that of our present existence.

Illustrated by a caterpillar, chrysalis, and butterfly—man is a grub now; and if what God intends him to be is not interrupted, he will ultimately become something magnificent.

3. The Bible just hints at what this state of GLORY will be:

(i.) We shall be like Christ.

(ii.) Our bodies will be like His glorified body.

(iii.) St. Paul desired to be "clothed upon" with that body.

Think of Christ's glorified body, not tied to space, not capable of being destroyed by the elements, walking on sea, ascending to other worlds; so we, when we attain to the glorified condition.

4. To be glorified is to have a body and soul in harmony.

(i.) Now we have to confess having done what we ought not to have done, and having left undone what we ought to have done, and there is no health in us.

(ii.) " I find *another law* in my members warring against the law of my mind, so that I cannot do the things that I would."

"When I would do good, evil is present with me."

"Glory "=to emerge out of this imperfect, cabined, and confined state into the freedom of a higher state of existence, under new conditions, when we shall be at our best, the sons of God without rebuke.

5. *What hope have we of this?* What well-

grounded hope? for there are hopes *delusive*, and there is a *hope which maketh not ashamed*.

(i.) Do not say, " The attainment is impossible"; for we see changes nearly as great every day. The new-born babe may possess the latent faculties of a great mathematician. What a gap in the development of being between the babe in his mother's lap and Sir Isaac Newton the philosopher!

(ii.) Neither say, " My hope of glory is in my nature. What I am created for, that I shall become." This is a delusive hope. Nature, apart from the Spirit of God, gravitates the other way, not upwards, but downwards. Everything in nature dies.

(iii.) Neither think that "the hope of glory" is in our religious conduct and good works; that there is in them something meritorious. Our Lord told a *religious* man, a good Pharisee, that he was neither *in* the kingdom of heaven, nor could he *see* it. The hope of glory, which maketh not ashamed, is something far different from this.

6. " CHRIST IN YOU, THE HOPE OF GLORY."

(i.) Once they were " without Christ" and " without God," " having no hope," " the children of wrath even as others." Now Christ in (among) the Gentiles, the Hope of Glory.

(ii.) *What is meant by this?*
Union with Christ—one life. "He that is joined to the Lord is one spirit." We cannot be glorified by ourselves alone. We must be grafted into Christ by the agency of the Holy Spirit. Then " when Christ, who is our life, shall appear, we also shall appear with Him in glory." "Christ our hope" (1 Tim. i. 1); "Christ *in* us the hope of glory." All other hopes are delusive; this only maketh not ashamed.

(b)

Glorious Body (Phil. iii. 21)

Not a resurrection, as a restoration merely of the same earthly body in the same earthly form; but, on the contrary, a glorious transformation, proceeding from the Divine, the all-subduing power of Christ; so that believers, free from all the defects of the earthly existence, released from all its barriers, may reflect the full image of the heavenly Christ in their whole glorified personality, in the soul pervaded by the Divine life and its now perfectly assimilated glorified organ.

(c) *Neander*

GO FORWARD

" *Speak unto the children of Israel, that they go forward* " (Exod. xiv. 15)

1. **The Exodus**

The people were by this time in the *wilderness;* they had halted twice since their start. Each halt must have deeply impressed itself on the memory of this people: just as, when at sea, a family, who may be leaving their native land, may watch the receding cliffs, until the last visible point, after which for days or weeks they will see nothing but the wide expanse of waters, so these Israelites, in their rapid flight out of Egypt—the land of civilization—saw, as it were, this civilization left behind them as they fled. At their first flight, they left behind them the *cities* of Egypt.

(d)

Succoth

Next they came to the village of " Succoth," the place of booths, which the people made from the boughs of the thick trees that grew so plentifully in that district.

(a)

Etham

After this they journeyed on until they came to the next halting-place, *Etham*, on " the edge of the wilderness."

(b)

The Desert

After this the *desert:* civilized cities are behind them, agricultural districts and villages, as Succoth, are left behind ; the green fields are all left behind them at Etham, and they—a raw, rude, helpless people—are alone on the wide and dreary waste, the desert of the Red Sea.

(c)

The Pursuit

Nor is this all the trial the little faith of that people had to bear. Supposing they had marched rapidly, and went straight on, they might have reached other districts less barren and less wild, and have also put such a distance between their enemies and themselves as to make any attempt at recapture fruitless. Not so, however, was this people to act. God had other purposes for them, and other thoughts for the Egyptians. The order came that they were " to turn," and march along the western side of the Red Sea—a path full of danger, and where, at any moment, they might be hemmed in by the sea before and the enemy behind. Here they were encamped, when suddenly a cry of alarm ran through the vast multitude : over the ridges of the desert hills the well-known horses and the terrible chariots of the Egyptian host were seen. " Pharaoh was pursuing the children of Israel, and they were sore afraid."

(d)

Night

A new terror arose. Night came on—a fact, in this marvellous deliverance, often overlooked—the passage through the Red Sea took place during the night. The evening closed in upon them on the Egyptian side of the Red Sea; the morning sun rose upon them in Arabia—a free people, a new nation. Such was the result of that night's history for them. But what had it been for their oppressors ? Pharaoh and the Egyptians, assaying to pass through the Red Sea, were drowned.

(e)

Pharaoh was led into a trap : for, seeing the people turn round by the shores of the Red Sea, instead of going straight on, he argued that a people guided and protected by a powerful God would not have fallen into such a mistake as this. And thus, smarting from the disgrace he had brought upon himself in letting the people go, he hastened to wipe out that disgrace. Impulsively he pushes on, he follows the path of the Israelites, and in the darkness of the night is overwhelmed in the waters of the Red Sea—furnishing an instance of how God " taketh the crafty in their own craftiness."

(f)

Redemption

For the Israelites, this deliverance was fraught with the deepest significance. They in one night had crossed from Africa to Asia, from Egypt, with its monster-worship, its grinding tyranny, to visit it no more : " The Egyptians whom they saw yesterday they should see no more again for ever." Yesterday they were slaves, to-day they are free. The word REDEMPTION, which has for us a far holier and deeper significance, now for the first time became prominent—God had " *redeemed His people from the house of bondage*," when He did these things for them at the sea, even at the Red Sea. But there was mystery in this : it had lasting consequences. We know not all : in wonder and admiration we follow the sacred record ; and with the people we " stand still " and see the salvation of the Lord. In the depth of midnight, amidst the roar of the hurricane, the sea was driven back—amidst the darkness lit up only by the broad glare of the lightning, as the Lord looked out from the thick darkness of the cloud. "The waters saw Thee, O God : the waters saw Thee and were afraid ; the depths also were troubled. The clouds poured out water : the air thundered : Thine arrows went abroad. The voice of Thy thunder was heard round about ; the lightnings shone upon the ground ; the earth was moved and shook withal." We know not—they knew not—by what precise means this deliverance was wrought. We know not, we need not know : the obscurity, the mystery, here as elsewhere, was part of the lesson, " God's way was in the sea, and His paths in the great waters, *and His footsteps were not known*." All that we see, all that we distinctly know, is, that during that dark and terrible night, with the enemy following close behind, and the driving sea on either side, " He led His people like sheep by the hand of Moses and Aaron."

(g)

The Salvation of God

There are moments in the histories of nations when man has to stand aside and see the salvation of the Lord. " The help that is done upon earth, He doeth it Himself." Such a moment in the history of our own country was the overthrow (without human instrumentality) of the Spanish Armada. But the greatest of all such events was that by the passage through the Red Sea.

(h)

A New Nation

The birthday of Israel—the birthday of true religion and of freedom. The greatest of all events which typify to the Christian that pilgrimage to the Heavenly Canaan begins after we, too, have not only come out of Egypt—not only entered into the desert, and left old things behind —but after we have been baptized by water and the Spirit, " in the cloud and in the sea," and when " all things have become new." When our old sins, forgiven and dead, like the Egyptians on the sea shore, shall rise up to condemn us no more. Such to the Christian is the significance of this marvellous event.

(i)

Ourselves

But the truth is not exhausted when we have said this. As Christians, how often are we disap-

(j)

pointed because we are " in a strait betwixt two," and we know not what course to take. We have left Egypt, and Egypt has come after us. We tasted Christian freedom when we first knew the Lord. We breathed the air of the desert for a moment only; it chilled us, but it was bracing. And then God Himself turned us round, as it were, southward. He brought us into a difficult place. We counted on liberty: we are enchained. We counted on easy victory. We thought not of *precaution:* we thought fighting was over and rest begun. We dreamed of an easy progress, an easy pilgrimage. How different the reality! We are in a strait betwixt two—the Red Sea before, and the world, our old enemy, behind. We stand still, we hesitate, we complain, we vacillate, at our best we pray; but prayer in such moments, the text tells us, is not the first duty: " *Wherefore criest thou unto Me? Speak unto the children of Israel, that they go forward.*" Prayer should accompany, not enfeeble, action. " He that hath, to him shall be given;" God helps those who help themselves.

(a)   *Cf. Dean Stanley, and Hengstenberg*

" Go Forward "

  (i.) From that point to which God has led us ;
  (ii.) Along the path He bids us take ;
 (iii.) By the light which He affords ;
 (iv.) With the staff (promises) which He provides ;
  (v.) To the land which He prepares.

(b)   *Oosterzee*

" Go Forward."

" *Reaching forth unto those things which are before* " (Phil. iii. 13, 14)

One of Napoleon's generals, on one occasion came to him to report defeat and loss. " Sire," said he, " we have lost a battle." Napoleon, taking his watch from his pocket, replied, "Never mind—it is but one o'clock; there is time enough to win another." And so the Christian, overwhelmed with loss, when reviewing the past, may yet take heart, seeing God has yet given him time to make a fresh start. " Onward" must be the motto. " Why criest thou unto Me? . . . Speak unto the children of Israel, that they *go forward.*" The enemy may be behind us, the Red Sea before us, hemmed in by the hills around us, and our own hearts failing us: what can we do but obey? "*Go forward,*" make a new effort—" *Reaching forth unto those things which are before.*"

(c)

GOD

God and Atheism

God's character, as portrayed in the Bible, is the most beautiful and perfect conceivable. He is there represented as at once righteous and merciful, a just God and a Saviour. I admire this character as one worthy of the Creator of the world ; so much so, that if, when in another state, I were assured that the God of the Bible was nowhere to be found, I should ask, with amazement, Who, then, is God? If, instead, there were pointed out to me any other, such as Heathen, Mohamedan, or Papist gods, I should not find it possible, in my nature, to render the homage required, even at the peril of my life. The atheist is so foolish and blind, that he can no more than a mole discern the eternal power and Godhead in the wonderful structure of his own frame, in the curious formation of leaf and flower, or in the marvellous glory of all created things ; therefore he comes to the conclusion that there is no God. So may the mole, who has never seen them, make sure there is neither king nor palace. Thou atheistic mole, who hast never travelled nor inquired enough to decide there is no God, all thou canst say is, that thou hast not yet seen Him, and hast no desire to see. How knowest thou that His existence is not so manifest beyond the river of death, and throughout the whole realm of eternity, that denial, or even doubt is impossible. The mole may, of course, maintain that there is no Grand Lama in Thibet, because he has never been so far in his travels ; but his testimony would have no sort of value. So the atheistic worm must have been through all the regions of death, misery, and destruction, and explored all the realms of happiness through the Heaven of heavens, embracing in the circuit of his travels the whole of time and eternity, and able also to comprehend all the modes and forms in which it is possible for Deity to exist, before he can successfully deny the existence of a God."

(d)   *Christmas Evans*

God and Atheism

The footprint of the savage traced in the sand is sufficient to attest the presence of man to the atheist who will not recognise God, whose hand is impressed upon the entire universe.

(e)

God, Attributes of

Earthly power goes from hand to hand, from Henry I. to Henry II. and III. ; from Louis I. to Louis II. and III. ; but from everlasting to everlasting is God—God the first, God the last, God the only. He has one telescope with which He sees everything—His Omniscience. He has one bridge with which He crosses everything—His Omnipresence. He has one hammer with which He builds everything—His Omnipotence.

(f)   *Talmage*

God of Christians, The

The God of Christians is not barely the Author of geometrical truths, or of the order of the elements—this is the Divinity of the heathen—nor barely the providential Disposer of the lives and fortunes of men, so as to crown His worshippers with a happy series of years ; this is the portion of the Jews. But the God of Abraham and of Jacob, the God of Christians, is a God of love and of consolation ; a God who fills the heart and the soul where He resides ; a God who gives them a deep and inward feeling of their own misery, and of His infinite mercy ; unites Himself to their spirit, replenishing it with humility and joy, with affiance and love ; and renders them incapable of any end but Himself.

(g)   *Blaise Pascal*

GOD THE CREATOR

God is not an artist, but a Moral Parent and Governor; nor is the creation a machine. If it were, it might be urged with greater speciousness that miracles cannot be needed or required. One of the most striking views of the creation is the contrast or opposition of the elements c^f which it consists. It includes not only matter, but mind—not only lifeless and unconscious masses, but rational beings, free agents; and these are its noblest parts and ultimate objects. The material universe was framed not for itself, but for these.

(a)   *Channing*

GOD, DESCRIPTIONS OF

The Bible gives two descriptions of God, and they are just opposite, and they are both true. In one, the Bible says God is love. In another place, the Bible says God is a consuming fire. The explanation is plain as plain can be. God, through Christ, is love—God out of Christ is fire.

(b)   *Talmage*

GOD, ETERNITY OF

Would you gather some idea of the eternity past of God's existence? Go to the astronomer, and bid him lead you with him in one of his walks through space; and, as he sweeps outward from object to object, from universe to universe, remember that the light from those filmy stains on the deep pure blue of heaven, now falling on your eye, has been traversing space for *a million of years.*

(c)   *Mitchell*

GOD, FATHERHOOD OF

In the New Testament, God is made known to us as a Father; and a brighter feature of that book cannot be named. Our worship is to be directed to Him as our Father. Our whole religion is to take its character from this view of the Divinity. In this He is to rise always to our minds. And what is it to be a father? It is to communicate one's own nature, to give life to kindred beings; and the highest function of a father is to educate the mind of the child, and to impart to it what is noblest and happiest in his own mind. God is our Father, not merely because He created us, or because He gives us enjoyment—for He created the flower and the insect, yet we call Him not their father. This bond is a spiritual one. This name belongs to God because He frames spirits like Himself, and delights to give them what is most glorious and blessed in His own nature.

(d)   *Channing*

GOD, FORESIGHT OF

God *foresees* all things, but *forces* nothing.

(e)   *Bp. Wordsworth*

GOD-GIVEN AUTHORITY

In the resurrection of Christ, we learn the invincibility of all true *God-given authority*. Men may rage against it, and desire to break its bands and cast away its cords, but "He that sitteth in the heavens shall laugh; the Lord shall have them in derision. Then shall He speak unto them in His wrath, and vex them in His sore displeasure. Yet have I set My King upon My holy hill of Zion."

This history teaches us the process by which men are brought to acquiesce in the reign of righteous authority. When Joseph's brethren knew what was in him, were saved by him, and sat at his banquet, they gladly allowed him to reign, and thankfully came not only to visit him, but to dwell beside him in the land of Goshen.

Political ignorance and inexperience is the cause of every unjustifiable revolt against government. When a people know the value of law and order, and have their hunger satisfied by the sustenance they afford, they will be loyal and obedient to the throne.

When the nobles, the landowners, and the capitalists realize the nature of their position, and recognise that they are placed above the masses in order to lead them by their influence for good, that they are not raised up in order to indulge in narrow-hearted, inhuman pride, and selfish, swinish luxury, and superficial ostentation, but in order that they may refine, guide, inspire, and sustain their brethren—then the masses will treat them with respect, and never raise the cry of the social levellers.

(f)   *Dean Edwards*

GOD AND GOODNESS

"*Why callest thou Me good? None is good, save One; that is, God*" (Matt. xix. 17).

Why does our Lord disclaim being addressed as "Good Master"?

God is the ABSOLUTELY GOOD. His goodness reaches the highest ideal. But with man—even the best—it is far otherwise. Man has his standard of goodness—a high ideal—as David had (Ps. xv. and xxiv.). David set this before him as the model of his aspiration: "I will not know a wicked person." But David's actual attainment fell very far below his ideal. So of all. "All have sinned, and come short of the glory of God." God is alone the absolutely good.

Here we find a reason why our Lord disclaims being called "Good." It was a title due to God only. As for Jesus, He, as man, had not yet been tempted in all things; He had not yet experienced all the power of the kingdom of darkness; not until He had been tried in every way, and attained to His ideal in actual practice, would He permit Himself to be called good. It was an absolute term, and an infringement of the glory of the Father.

(g)   *Cf. Martensen*

GOD—INFINITE

Unity added to infinity increases it not, any more than a foot added to infinite space. What is finite vanishes before that which is infinite, and becomes absolutely nothing. For instance, our understanding, in respect of God's; our righteousness, compared with the Divine.

(h)   *Pascal*

GOD IS LIGHT

As the sentence, "*God is a Spirit*" (John iv. 24) is immediately followed by "and those who worship Him must worship Him in spirit and in

(i)

truth," so this sentence must be taken as a principle, the application of which is in the sequel. The sentence is through and through *ethical* and *practical*. John wants no science without practice. He does not allow an enlightenment of the mind without a corresponding bias and purifying of the will.

(a)   *Lange*

GOD IS LOVE

"God is love." The ocean is but *one* sheet of water, but it assumes various names as it washes different shores. The various attributes and perfections of God are only modifications of one principle, and that is *love*. The same principle which builds an *infirmary*, erects a *prison*.

(b)   *Christmas Evans*

GOD (THE NAME)

This word is spelt in four letters in almost every language, viz.: — Latin, *Deus;* French, *Dieu;* Greek, Θέος; German, *Gott;* Scandinavian, *Odin;* Swedish, *Codd;* Hebrew, *Hdon;* Syrian, *Adad;* Persian, *Syra;* Tartarian, *Idga;* Spanish, *Dios;* East Indian, *Esgi,* or *Zeni;* Turkish, *Addi;* Egyptian, *Aumn,* or *Zeut;* Japanese, *Zain;* Peruvian, *Lian;* Wallachian, *Zene;* Etrurian, *Chur;* Irish, *Dieh;* Arabian, *Alja.* The name appropriated by the Saxon nations (" THE GOOD ") is unequalled, except by the most venerable Hebrew name, JEHOVAH.

(c)

GOD, NATURE OF

"GOD is spirit" (John iv. 24);
"GOD is light" (1 John i. 5);
"God is love " (1 John iv. 5).
All from the pen of John, are the briefest and profoundest definitions, or Divine oracles rather, concerning the nature of God, which can be found anywhere. The first refers mainly to His metaphysical, the second to His intellectual, the third to His moral essence; but of course the line cannot be distinctly drawn.

(d)   *P. Schaff*

GOD, OMNIPOTENCE OF

Would you gather some knowledge of the *omnipotence* of God? Weigh the earth on which we dwell, then count the millions of its inhabitants that have come and gone for the last six thousand years. Unite their strength into one arm, and test its power in an effort to move this earth. It could not move it a single foot in a thousand years; and yet, under the omnipotent hand of God, not a minute passes that it does not fly far more than a thousand miles.

But this is a mere atom, the most insignificant point among His innumerable worlds. At His bidding every planet, and satellite, and comet, and the sun himself, fly onward in their appointed courses. His single arm guides the millions of sweeping suns, and around His throne circles the great constellation of unnumbered universes.

(e)   *Mitchell*

GOD, THE OMNISCIENCE OF

Would you comprehend the idea of the omniscience of God? Remember that the highest pinacle of knowledge reached by the whole human race, by the continued efforts of its brightest intellects, has enabled the astronomer to compute approximately the perturbations of the planetary worlds. He has predicted, roughly, the return of half a score of comets. But God has computed the mutual perturbations of millions of suns, and planets, and comets, and worlds, without number, through the ages that are passed, and throughout the ages which are yet to come, not approximately, but with perfect and absolute precision. The universe is in motion—system rising above system, cluster above cluster, nebula above nebula—all majestically sweeping around, under the providence of God, who alone knows the end from the beginning, and before whose glory and power all intelligent beings, whether in heaven or on earth, should bow with humility and awe.

(f)   *Ibid*

GOD, THE SINNER, AND THE SAINT (Isaiah xl. 27–31)

As the hunted ostrich hides its head in the sand, so here God's people thought that when they could not see Him, He did not see them. This passage is His answer to such unbelief: He both saw and knew; ignorance on His part was utterly out of the question.

Note.—Three assertions: something·
(i.) Of GOD ;
(ii.) Of the sinner ;
(iii.) Of a saint.

(g)

1. What about God?

(i.) He wonders at our unbelief as to whether He sees, hears, or cares;

(ii.) This is to be compared with New Testament : " He marvelled at their unbelief"—marvels that we despair and say, " My way is hid from the Lord ! "

Now this state of feeling marks, not the absence of faith absolutely, but its weakness: hence need of strengthening it. This is here done by reminding us whom we worship:

(i.) The everlasting God, whom Abraham and David worshipped;

(ii.) The Lord—Jehovah, who helped His people of old ; Red Sea triumphs—will also help and save us ;

(iii.) The Creator . . . whom it is simply impossible to limit; nothing too hard for the Lord ; nothing can be impossible with the Creator—the miracle worker.

This God is our God, unchangeable, and these titles are no empty names, " He fainteth not " : you can't get beyond His power of helping; you know not His thoughts towards you=If He spared not His own Son, but freely gave Him up for us all, shall He not much more freely give us all things? Why limit Him then? Why say despairingly, " My way is hid?" It cannot be. " Have faith in God;"; delight thyself in Him, and He shall give thee the desire of thine heart.

(h)

2. What about the sinner?

Such as all are; though some have other names for themselves; yet all are " poor, and blind, and naked, and miserable by nature."

(i)

(i.) He has no might; no power to help himself; dead, and can't raise himself to life; deaf, and can't hear God's voice when He speaks; blind, and can't see God's hand in all the good and ill that chequer life. Utterly powerless, he can neither serve God, nor come to God, any more than the cripple could raise his withered arm; he has no strength.

(ii.) And if Christ were not to cross his path and say, " Come," he would never come; or say, " Stretch forth thine hand," he would never be able to do it.

(iii.) If the Holy Ghost were not to quicken him, he would never be alive unto God. God must do this for him, as for the Psalmist: " He sent from above, He took me, He drew me out of many waters: all of God—He saves; He rescues, and He alone.

> " Oh, bring no price, God's grace is free
>   To Paul, to Magdalene, to me."
>   *J. Hart*

Free! yes, free to those who have " no might," " faint," helpless, lost; this is the Gospel: " When we were yet without strength, in due time Christ died for the ungodly." The Gospel is a very simple matter, a sinner and a Saviour—one as real as the other.

(a)

3. What about the Saint?

It tells us that his life is subject to great changes —not all sunshine—many hues make a rainbow; wind, rain, sunshine required to ripen corn. So David in wilderness; Joseph in prison; Job on an ash-heap, are all specimens of the process of refining and ripening saints; yet, when God puts us amongst this company we say, " All these things are against me."

The " saints " here are said to " wait upon God," —the distinction between them and the ungodly.

Four things are stated of them:

(i.) They " renew their strength." Cf. Walter Scott's " Old Mortality " sitting among the tombs and recutting the nearly obliterated inscriptions. Perhaps we have lost the freshness of first-love; and have only a little strength, or as smoking flax nearly burnt out, God, in His faithfulness, promises " I will renew their strength."

(ii.) They shall " mount up as eagles," denotes a higher flight in spiritual things, though such times are brief—the mountain air for the Spirit— to brace it for after work; fresh accessions of " joy and peace in believing " ; " to live is Christ, to die is gain," are such. Moses was on Pisgah; Peter, at a similar moment said, " Lord, it is good to be here," yet both returned to earth to mingle in its pollutions and sins. One moment it is, " Blessed art thou, Simon Barjona; " another it is, " Get thee behind me, Satan ! " Rapture is brief; we scale the mountain peak only to stand there a moment, and then descend to the valleys; amongst men of like passions with ourselves, and amongst whom our work is; forty days in the Mount, as compared with forty years in the wilderness.

(iii.) " He shall run," etc., the race-course of the Christian life; note the cloud of witnesses; and the demands of success, yet " he shall not be weary."

(iv.) " He shall walk "=this the greater part of the way; the road may be long, but " as thy day is so thy strength; " it may be rough, but " I will make rough places smooth " ; it may be dark, but the promise is, " Let him that walketh in darkness, and have no light, stay upon his God," etc. " He shall keep the feet of His saints " ; " They shall not faint."

Such are the things said of a saint's career, a road varying from day to day, ever onward,— sometimes flying, sometimes running, sometimes walking, until he has climbed the last steep, and reached the last summit, and the race is over, and he is presented faultless before the throne of God.

(b)

GOD, SOVEREIGNTY OF

The absolute sovereignty of the Divine mind over the universe is the only foundation of hope for the triumph of the human mind over matter, over physical influences, over imperfection and death.

(c)   *Channing*

GOD, UNKNOWABLE

The story of Simonides is well-known, of whom Hiero, king of Syracuse, having demanded what God was, desired he might be allowed one day to prepare an answer to this question; and when the same question was then repeated, he entreated that he might have two days more; and continuing thus to delay his answer, and still enlarging the number of days, Hiero at length inquired the reason of it; because, saith he, the *longer* I consider of it, the *less hope* I have of arriving at satisfaction.

(d)

GOD WILLING

Let critics censure it for bad grammar, I am sure it is good divinity.

(e)   *Fuller*

GOD, WISDOM OF

Would you gain some idea of the *Wisdom* of God, look to the admirable adjustments of the magnificent retinue of planets and satellites which sweep around the sun. Every globe has been weighed and poised, every object has been measured and bent to its beautiful form. All is changing, but the laws fixed by the wisdom of God, though they permit the rocking to and fro of the system, never introduce disorder or lead to destruction. All is perfect and harmonious, and the music of the spheres that burn and roll around our sun, is echoed by that of ten millions of moving worlds, that sing and shine around the bright suns that reign above.

(f)   *Mitchell*

GOD, WORKS OF

If overwhelmed with the grandeur and majesty of the universe of God, we are led to exclaim, with the Hebrew poet king, " When I consider Thy heavens, the work of Thy fingers, the moon and the stars which Thou hast ordained, what is man that Thou art mindful of him? and the Son of man that Thou visitest him " If fearful that the

eye of God may overlook us in the immensity of
His kingdom, we have only to call to mind that
other passage, " Yet Thou hast made him but little
lower than the angels, and hast crowned him with
glory and honour. Thou madest him to have
dominion over all the works of Thy hand: Thou
hast put all things under his feet."

Such are the teachings of the Word, and such
are the lessons of the works of God.

(a)   Mitchell

GODLINESS, MYSTERY OF

" *Great is the mystery of godliness, God manifest
in the flesh,*" *etc.* (1 Tim. iii. 16)

The preacher at once began, in the most startling tones: " Oh, ye people ! this is a bottomless
sea; with God's help I will just venture on its
margin; don't lose sight of me ! " In the midst
of his greatest excitements he would slightly bow
his head, and so remain for a moment, without
uttering a single word, and then whisper: " *Hush,
hush, hush ! what do I hear ?* " Then he would
thunder out, till the whole congregation trembled:
" Upon the wicked He shall rain snares, fire
and brimstone, and an horrible tempest: this
shall be the portion of their cup ! " When he
thought he was labouring in vain, failing to preach
with any visible effect, he would pause in the
midst of the sermon, and, with the big tears rolling down his face, he would lift up a wailing cry,
that pierced every heart: " O Lord, rend the veil !
rend the veil ! " Whereupon the people's loud
and tumultuous " Amens " would ratify the agonizing prayer. Then he would recommence, and
proceed under such an overpowering sense of the
heavenly vision, that in a short time he would
utter a second prayer: " Withhold, withhold, O
Lord ! draw again the veil, or we cannot stand
Thy presence ! "

(b)   *Robert Roberts, Welsh Preacher*

GODLY LIVING

" *Live soberly, righteously, and godly* " (Tit. ii.
12)

There are persons who consider it quite sufficient for all the practical purposes of human
existence, to take the first two of the expressions,
leaving the third altogether out of their account.
They live " soberly "—their personal conduct is
irreproachable. No man can put a finger upon a
blot in their morals. From everything like excess,
or impurity, or unworthy conduct of any kind,
they hold themselves indignantly aloof; and, so
far, they are blameless. And they live " righteously." Honest, honourable, straightforward;
giving all their due; scorning the miserable shifts
and mean devices and half-concealed falsehoods
by which some men contrive to emerge into prosperity and to rise in the world, they just do their
work manfully and well, and leave success to
follow if it will. To them, the most important
thing is, not to succeed, but to do the right. So
far, then, as their duty to themselves and their
duty to their neighbour is concerned, they are all
that can be desired. *But what about their duty to
God ?* That is neglected ! God may be outwardly
honoured—as, for instance, by occasional attendance at the house of prayer—but He is not really

in all their thoughts; and they know it. They are
too honest not to know it. That there has been
no acceptance in their lives of the Christ of God—
without which acceptance God is a stranger to us,
and we strangers to God; that there is in them no
consecration to Christ; no referring to His will;
no dependence upon His help; no drawing out of
His fulness; no love to His person, and no zeal
for His glory—of all this they are perfectly aware.
But the thought of their heart is—that the omission is of no very great importance; and that so
long as they live " soberly " and " righteously," it
matters little or nothing whether they do or do not
live " godly "—in this present world.

(c)

GOING TO LAW

They talk of casting me into a court of law,
where I have never been, and hope I never shall
be; but I will put them first into the court of
Jesus Christ, the source of all law and authority.
I then went into my bedroom and poured forth my
heart before the Redeemer, saying: " O blessed
Lord, I trust in Thy merits, and have confidence
Thou wilt hear me. Some of my brethren, Lord,
have become enraged, and having forgotten their
duties and obligations to their father in the
Gospel, threaten me with the law of the land.
Weaken, I beseech Thee, their designs, as Thou
didst the arm of Jeroboam; and soften Thou their
heart, as Thou didst that of Esau against Jacob,
after the wrestling at Penuel. I know not the
length of Satan's chain in this unbrotherly attack,
but Thou canst shorten it, even as Thou wilt. O
Lord, I anticipate them in the matter of law.
Their design is to put Thine unworthy servant
into their little courts below; but I would have
Thee to judge my cause in the Supreme Court, of
which Thou, Gracious Redeemer, art the Chancellor. Do Thou take up the cause of Thine unworthy servant, and speedily send a writ into their
consciences, compelling them to consider what
they are about to attempt. Oh, terrify them with
a summons from Thy court, that they may fall
in penitence at Thy feet. Disarm them of every
weapon of revenge; cause them to give up, at Thy
cross, every gun of calumny, every sword of bitter
words, and every spear of satire and reproach
Pardon their sins, clothe them in white garments,
anoint their heads with oil, and let them sing with
harp and organ, that the God of peace has put
Satan under their feet." I went up once more,
with my heart so softened that I could not refrain
from weeping, and I felt confident that Christ was
drawing near me in my trouble. Having repeated
my prayer seven times, I felt fully assured that
Jesus Christ had taken my cause in hand, and that
He would deliver me. I felt my burden was gone,
and when I came down, I felt as Naaman did
when he came up from the waters of the Jordan, or
like Bunyan's Pilgrim when his burden fell at the
foot of the cross. I remember the place adjoining
the chapel at Cildwrn, and I may well call it
Penuel. I have frequently prayed for those who
would injure me, that they might be blessed as I
have been blessed. These troubles opened my
eyes to the preciousness of the Divine promises.
I know not what would have become of me but for
these furnaces in which my faith was tried.

(d)   *Christmas Evans*

GOLD

> How quickly nature falls into revolt
> When gold becomes her object!

(a)   *Shakspeare*

'Tis gold which buys admittance; and 'tis gold
Which makes the true man killed, and saves the
    thief;
Nay, sometimes hangs both thief and true man;
What can it not do, and undo?

(b)   *Ibid*

> Stronger than thunder's wingèd force,
> All-powerful gold can speed its course;
> Through watchful guards its passage make,
> And loves through solid walls to break.

(c)   *Francis*

O cursèd lust of gold! when for thy sake
The fool throws up his interest in both worlds;
First starved in this, then damned in that to
    come.

(d)   *Blair*

> There is no place invincible wherein an ass
> aden with gold may enter.

(e)   *Collett*

To gild refined gold, to paint the lily,
To throw a perfume on the violet,
To smooth the ice, or add another hue
Unto the rainbow, or with taper-light
To seek the beauteous eye of heaven to garnish,
Is wasteful and ridiculous excess.

(f)   *Shakspeare*

GOLD AND CHRIST

How comes it that men of the world count so
little of Christ?
Because there is something broken in them that
makes five seem to be seven; there is something
wrong in them that makes gold seem to be God.
That blind mind that thou hast naturally will
never see Christ to be Christ. But once come to
Christ Himself, and then ye will be put from such
thoughts. He will give you another sight; that
old sight will be put out of the office.

(g)   *Samuel Rutherford*

GOLDEN LEGEND

Longfellow, in the "Golden Legend," has entered more closely into the temper of the monk,
for good and for evil, than ever yet theological
writer or historian, though they may have given
their life's labour to the analysis.

(h)   *Ruskin*

GOLGOTHA

When he lost four out of six children. "We
all like the glory on Tabor, but we cannot bear to
spend our nights upon Golgotha."

(i)   *Falk*

GOOD

When fortune means to men most good,
She looks upon them with a threat'ning eye.

(j)   *Shakspeare*

GOOD, THE

>   Oh, sir! the good die first;
> And they whose hearts are dry as summer's dust,
> Burn to the socket.

(k)   *Wordsworth*

GOOD TIDINGS

1. No one knows distinctly how pagan religions
began.
We know they began, and that men were
fascinated by the idea of worship. *Law* was the
expression of the will of the Maker and Master of
the world.

(l)

2. Soon poetry, music, and ritual softened the
severity of doctrine. Credulity silenced the questions that intellect could not answer, under the
name of "Mysteries." Next, Reason determined
to understand the external and internal phenomena
of human experience. This was the beginning
of *Greek philosophy*.

(m)

3. Very various were the thoughts concerning
the origin of things—nature and spirit. Plato
taught a pure theism; Aristotle believed both
God and matter to be eternal; Epicurus denied
that the gods interfered with human affairs. Sin
and misery = an insuperable difficulty to faith in a
conscious Providence. The popular doctrine was
called *plastic nature* = an inherent power in nature
to develop to a limitless extent.

(n)

4. While philosophers were theorizing, human
life, as now, was real and brief, and philosophic
speculations did not satisfy earnest souls. Philosophy did destroy the credulity, enthusiasm,
trustfulness of primitive times; but it also suggested mysteries it could not fathom, proposed
problems it could not solve, raised doubts it could
not dispel, aroused fears it could not quiet, over-
clouded "the sunshine of Homer," and had no
anodyne to offer the sufferer here, nor any light
to throw upon the hereafter.

(o)

5. The *Romans* now became the masters of the
world, spiritually and administratively. They inherited Greek mythology, poetry, and philosophy;
but they settled down to a practical realism. This
life and its concerns, being the only certainties,
were the all-important. Man was a part of the
universe, and subject to natural law. Evils were
a necessary part of an imperfect existence. Religion had been the curse of the earth—it excited
imaginations and groundless terror; fools only
believed and were distressed by it.

(p)

6. *Lucretius*, speaking the inmost conviction of
the Roman mind, informed the world that religion
was a phantom begotten of fear and ignorance.
He was the grand outcome of the intellect of his
age, the formulator of its scepticism, and was born
less than a century before Christ. Democritus,
and Epicurus before him, had helped to shape his
doctrine; and as soon as it became embodied in
the Roman system of government, it was developed
into a confession of faith. Everywhere, where
Roman legions conquered, the teaching of Lucretius

(q)

proclaimed triumphantly the overthrow of superstition and the sovereignty of science, as the
" *new message of glad tidings to mankind.*"
(*a*)

7. Now to retrace. More than five centuries
before Homer, an infant was born in Egypt, whose
history was more than romantic. Prepared in a
remarkable way, to him it was given to deliver
the Divine words concerning human redemption.
When eighty years of age, he leads out of Egypt
and trains a new nation. After forty years' discipline, it enters the Promised Land. There its
marvellous history unfolded.
(*b*)

8. Before Homer or Hesiod sang, Solomon's
temple was built, the symbol of *a pure religion.*
While the rest of the world was in darkness as to
man's origin, the Hebrews had light, and knew all
about it, as we do to-day. While the future life
to the heathen was an impenetrable gloom, God's
covenant with Abraham, Isaac, and Jacob was the
pledge of immortality.
(*c*)

9. Human imperfection and sin retarded the
religious growth, yet the stream flowed on in great
century waves.
(*d*)

10. Before Æschylus, Sophocles, Socrates, or
Plato were born (with the single exception of
Malachi, who lived a little earlier than Aristotle),
the whole of the glowing revelations and gracious
promises of the Old Testament were written, and
had kindled the expectation of the Messiah, whose
dominion and worship should be universal.
(*e*)

11. The grand outcome of the Hebrew nation
—according to the Divine plan—was JESUS CHRIST,
born at the close of the century Lucretius began.
(*f*)

12. *Compare* the scientific triumph proclaimed
by Lucretian philosophers, historians, and poets
with that proclaimed by the angels to the shepherds at the birth of Jesus, "Behold I bring you
good tidings of great joy, which shall be to all
people," and ask, in the light of all the centuries
that have intervened, which were the true Good
Tidings?
(*g*)

13. There have been two historic channels: the
outcome of paganism was Lucretius, and the outcome of the chosen people was Jesus Christ, from
whom has flowed all the forces of truth and moral
stimulus. What in comparison with these have
the teachings of Lucretius effected for mankind?
(*h*)

14. All the promise of the millennium is in the
possessed truth and promised Spirit of Jesus
Christ. Human imperfection, sin, and unbelief
retard and excite doubt in the Christian triumph,
but it is, nevertheless, the great elevating power.
(*i*)

15. What are the latest utterances of the *Gospel
of Science* but echoes of the teaching of Lucretius?
It gives no other account of man's origin, moral

condition, or destiny. Making nothing of the immortal soul, it never has spoken, and never will
speak, a word to satisfy its cravings, to relieve its
fears, or to assure its hopes.
Condensed from Froude and Joachim Elmendorf.
(*j*)

GOOD RESOLUTIONS

Steele was a man of good resolutions and of
bad practices. He would write a treatise against
drinking, and leave his task unfinished whilst he
got drunk with his friend at an alehouse, or be
found asleep in his arm-chair with two empty
bottles beside him. He would write a pamphlet
on the efficacy of faith, the value of religious
observances, and would abandon piety and church-
going, until the restraint of the bailiffs or the
emptiness of his purse gave him leisure to meditate fresh schemes of virtue. He was a man who
was liberal only in the security of having nothing
to give.
(*k*)   *W. Clark Russell, on Steele*

GOOD WORKS

" *For the love of Christ constraineth us.*"
Do all the good you can (1 Tim. vi. 17–19);
In all the ways you can (1 Cor. xv. 58);
To all the people you can (Matt. v. 44, 45);
At all the times you can (Prov. iii. 27, 28);
And as long as you can (Eccles. ix. 10).
" Whatsoever ye do, do all to the glory of God "
(1 Cor. x. 31).
Having done all—" say, We are unprofitable
servants." We have done that which was our
duty to do (Luke xvii. 10).
(*l*)   *Marsh*

Good works do not make a Christian; but one
must be a Christian to do good works. The tree
bringeth forth the fruit, not the fruit the tree.
None is made a Christian by works, but by Christ;
and being in Christ, He brings forth fruit for
him.
(*m*)   *Luther*

Cornelius (Acts x.)

1. Devout, charitable, yet not a Christian.
2. He sent for Peter = God uses means.
3. " He shall tell thee what thou oughtest to
do."
4. While Peter spake, the Holy Ghost fell. Regeneration succeeded, the Word was mixed with
faith, thence *a new life.* So now, and always, to
begin with; afterward *good works.*
(*n*)

Hard was their lodging, homely was their food,
For all their luxury was doing good.
(*o*)   *Garth*

A preacher at Westminster Abbey, wishing to
illustrate " Faith and *Works*," said: " A man rowing with *one* oar found his boat, instead of going
forward, turned round to one side: ' That,' said he,
' is *Faith.*' Then he changed about and rowed with
the other oar, and found the boat now turned
round on the other side: ' That,' said he, ' is *Good
Works.*' Next the man rowed with both oars, and
(*p*)

the boat went straight forward : 'That,' said he, 'is *Faith and Works.*'" The illustration is not appropriate, and the teaching is misleading, as may be seen from the following symbol :—

Salvation does not=Faith + Good Works, but Faith[G.W.] ; *i.e.*, not Faith *and* Good Works, but Faith *to the power of* Good Works is saving Faith.

(a)

GOSPEL

The *Gospel* is wonderful ! It teaches man to acknowledge himself vile, and even abominable, yet requires him, at the same time, to aspire to a resemblance of God. Were not things thus balanced, either such exaltation would inflate him with pride, or such debasement would drive him to despair.

The incarnation discovers to man the greatness of his misery by the greatness of the remedy required.

(b)   *Pascal*

GOSPEL AS POWER (1 Thess. iii. 4)

What must the Gospel be as a Divine power, that, with prospects so little flattering to the flesh, it yet wins believers ?

(c)   *Lange*

GOSPEL ON A TOMBSTONE, THE

On the tomb of Dr. John Condor, in Bunhill Fields, London, is this inscription :—

I have sinned,	I have repented ;
I have trusted,	I have loved ;
I rest,	I shall rise ;

And, through the grace of Christ, however unworthy, I shall reign.

(d)

GOSPELS, BOOK OF THE

"The grass withereth, the flower fadeth : but the Word of the Lord endureth for ever." We recall the story of the Book of the Gospels—Cuthbert's own book—which the monks at Lindisfarne carried with them in their wanderings. They set sail for Ireland ; a storm arose ; the book fell overboard, and was lost ; they were driven back to the English coast. Disconsolate they went in quest of the precious volume : for a long time they searched in vain ; but at length (so says the story) a miraculous revelation was vouchsafed to them, and, following its directions, they found the book on the sands far above high-water mark, uninjured by the waves—nay, even more beautiful for the disaster. Does not this story well symbolize the power of the Eternal Gospel working in the Church ? Through the carelessness of man, it may disappear amidst the confusion of the storms ; the waves may close over it and hide it from human sight. But lost—lost for ever—it cannot be. It must reassert itself, and its glory will be the greater for the temporary eclipse which it has undergone.

(e)   *Bp. Lightfoot*

GOSPELS, THE FOUR

Matthew	Mark	Luke	John
1. Messianic	Son of Man	Redeemer	Only Begotten Son of God.
2. Jewish .	Gentile .	Universal	Christian.
3. Oriental .	Roman .	Greek. .	Spiritual.
4. Narrative	Condensed Representative Facts. .	Historical	Dramatic Portraiture.

The four Gospels are four holy pictures, limned by four holy hands, of Him who was "fairer than the children of men ; " and that these have been vouchsafed to us that, by varying our postures, we may catch fresh beauties and fresh glories.

(f)   *Bp. Ellicott*

GOSPELS, THE FOUR, MOTTOES FOR

1. St. Matthew's = " Thy king cometh unto thee " (the Jew).

2. St. Mark's = " King of kings and Lord of lords " (over the Romans).

3. St. Luke's = " The Son of man is come to seek and to save the lost " (universally).

4. St. John's = " The Lord's controversy with Zion " (spiritually).

(g)

GOSPEL OF ST. JOHN

1. STYLE of the Fourth Gospel Compared

(i.) MATTHEW. If we glance at the style of the composition of the other Evangelists, we find that St. Matthew writes like a man of business, and as a commercial man might be supposed to write—methodically. He arranges Sayings under sayings, Parables under parables, Miracles under miracles—in tables, stringing them together, not at haphazard, but with design, in order that the defective teaching of the one may be supplemented by the fuller teaching of another. This, apparently, is the idea of the man's mind. The acquired habit, and the talents given, used for the glory of God, in the new sphere of life into which he had been called. For as a custom-house official, doubtlessly he was in the habit of arranging pounds under pounds and shillings under shillings, and keeping account books and ledgers just as we do in commercial matters now-a-days.

(ii.) MARK. Turn to St. Mark, and we find him employing a terse, concise, and emphatic style. He aims at producing an effect with a few bold and graphic touches.

(iii.) LUKE. Look at St. Luke's *style*, and we find him writing, like a man of letters, the fullest *memoir* of our Lord. He starts like a man who has well arranged his materials. It has a preface, and is supplemented by the Acts of the Apostles, the two being works of literature : *The Treatise of Luke the Physician on Christianity, in two volumes.* He is as copious as Mark is sparing, and as exact and historical as Matthew is symmetrical. But all three, however dissimilar in details, agree in

(h)

this : They are well studied and digested compositions : works of art.

(iv.) John. The style of John is very different. The old man seems to take the pen and write as artlessly and as simply as a little child (little children to this day learn to read from the simple words that he wrote). His style is also *colloquial* and dramatic, for, with few exceptions, it is throughout a series of conversations between the Saviour and others, friends or foes. John, too, writes as an eye-witness, and as the friend of Jesus. The Saviour alone is prominent; John is nowhere—a true biographer of a friend.

(*a*)

2. GOSPELS, Characteristic Features of the, Compared

(i.) Matthew writes to his fellow-countrymen. There is, therefore, a Jewish cast of thought about his gospel. He writes to prove that Jesus is the Messiah they looked for. He is most careful not to offend against their prejudices, lest he might defeat his object. He traces Christ's descent from Abraham (the Jew), but not back to Adam (the head of the human race). He mentions the royal town of Bethlehem freely; but fearing to give offence, he has but one reference (ch. ii.) to the despised Nazareth (as fulfilling prophecy). Everything with him has reference to the Messianic King or *kingdom* : "Thy king cometh unto thee," might be his motto.

"The sermon on the mount" is the new *code of laws* for the Messiah's kingdom.

The parables are given to show what the kingdom of heaven "*is like*."

If he relates miracles, it is to show the Works of the King. St. Matthew's, then, is the gospel of the kingdom of heaven; of which Jesus Christ, born in the royal city of Bethlehem, is the King, and in which the Jew has the first place. The whole gospel from this point of view is written with the most consummate tact.

(ii.) Mark. When we look at St. Mark, we find his character to be of quite another kind. He writes with a Roman (or Latin) cast of thought. He describes how busy and energetic a life the Lord led—a *multum in parvo*—of how much good He did in a short time. He notices some things unnoticed by the others, especially that the Lord was with "the wild beasts," reminding one of the words in the 8th Psalm : "Thou hast put all things under His feet : all sheep and oxen, yea, and *the beasts of the field*." The Messiah is shown as having universal dominion over Nature, over men, and over devils—King of kings, and Lord of lords. This would have a special significance for the Romans, who were at that time the masters of the world. One greater than Cæsar was there.

(iii.) Luke. Turn to St. Luke, and we find another characteristic. Himself a physician, he writes of the Redeemer as the Saviour of the world : the Physician of souls. The chief feature of this gospel is its universality. Jewish exclusiveness is broken down—the gospel is for everybody. Christ is "the *Son of Man*," and consequently he traces His descent back to Adam. Luke has no scruples about mentioning Nazareth. The teaching of the parables of the Lost Sheep, the Lost Coin, and the Lost Son, would be shocking to a Jew, but they are quite in keeping with a universal gospel, which teaches us that "the Son of Man is *come to seek and to save that which was lost*."

(iv.) John. But in these several characteristics of the Synoptic Gospels, they all agree in describing the Man Christ Jesus : either the Man who is King of Israel; or, the Man who is King of kings and Lord of lords; or, the Man who is the Redeemer.

It is John's province to write of Him as the God. John's is the Divine Gospel; and such a testimony to the Divinity of Christ was called for by the circumstances of the time in which he wrote it (it was the last written). The Apostles had gone everywhere preaching the word. Peter's preaching had led men to ask, "What shall we do to be saved?" Paul's preaching was the answer to this question : "We preach Christ crucified—" Christ the Atonement. And in the later years of the apostolic period, when germs of the Gnostic heresy were creeping in, and men began to question the value of Christ's atonement, "How," said they, "shall one man's death make atonement for the sins of many?" Then up rose John, whose special work seems to have "*tarried*" till now, and he said, "Jesus Christ is not mere man—He is GOD." He opens his Gospel with these words—they stand at the forefront to show his main object in writing : "In the beginning was the Word, and the Word was with God, and THE WORD WAS GOD." This one theme, the Divinity of Christ, runs through the entire Fourth Gospel.

John works out his idea : Jesus was the Son of God. John Baptist bore witness to this; His own works bore witness; the Father bore witness to it; the Scriptures bore the same testimony. The raising of Lazarus from the dead completes the chain of evidence; for, granted that the other two instances of raising from the dead admitted a possibility (at least) of death not having actually occurred, here was a miracle, performed in broad daylight, before many witnesses, and after decomposition had begun : all doubt is removed. That act stamps the doer of it as superhuman. It is the work of a God, not of a man. Thus St. John, by gentle, almost imperceptible steps, demonstrates that Jesus was Divine. Then it was that the Jews became frantic, and said, "This Man doeth many miracles." Whereupon they trumped up a charge of blasphemy, and brought about His crucifixion on the plea that He ought to die because He made Himself the Son of God."

(*b*)

3. GOSPEL OF ST. JOHN, Spirituality of

The Fourth Gospel stands alone in this feature. The other three may be compared to the body. St. John's Gospel is the soul. A glance will serve to show this. The Synoptical Gospels, for the most part, relate the facts of our Lord's history : His Incarnation, Childhood, Baptism, Temptation, Death, Resurrection, and Ascension. These constitute, as it were, a *Body*. We do not find St. John telling us these things over again. He only notices the Crucifixion and Resurrection, and takes for granted that his readers are acquainted with the principal facts of the Gospel history. His Gospel, then, is not a Body, compacted of bones and muscle and flesh, that we find elsewhere; but He gives life to the body already existing. He quickens it by breathing the spirit into it. We have not only the actions of the Lord, but the meanings of them in St. John. Everywhere the idea is more prominent than fact. The Synoptics give the phenomena, John gives the causes.

(*c*)

4. GOSPEL OF ST. JOHN : Explanatory

The Synoptical Gospels merely give Christian institutions—as, for instance, they state the facts about the institution of the Sacraments. John does not repeat these, but explains their meaning.

The Lord's Supper is explained in the sixth chapter, in the discourse about Christ as the "*Bread of Life*." In the third chapter, Baptism is explained as a new birth from above. The idea of one Sacrament is a *new life*, whilst the idea of the other ist he *sustenance of that life*. Other explanations run all through this Gospel. The fourth chapter explains the difference between the Old and New Testaments. St. John has no mention of the Ascension, but he explains it as Christ "ascending up where He was before" (6). The fifteenth chapter explains the nature of the union between Christ and His people. The seventeenth chapter affords an instance of the prevailing intercession of our great High Priest. He concludes by explaining the use of Holy Scripture : " These things are written that ye might believe that Jesus is the Christ, the Son of God; and that believing ye might have life through His name."

(*a*)

5. GOSPEL OF ST. JOHN : The Ministry of our Lord Compared

This is a most important feature in the Fourth Gospel. St. John does not so much describe the ministry of what the Lord did, as the ministry of what He said. Oral teaching, or, the doctrine of Christ, prevails. Throughout, narrative yields to doctrine. His is a history of the inner life of our Lord. We have an instance of this in the sixth chapter—the feeding of the five thousand. John gives this miracle as well as the other Evangelists, and this is the only point between the death of John Baptist and the Crucifixion, where John's narrative touches theirs. The reason is obvious. John mentions this miracle to introduce his discourse on Christ as the Bread of Life. They give prominence to the miracle, John gives prominence to the doctrine. The heavenly manna, the true bread, the staff of life, is everything with him.

(*b*)

As to the actual ministry of our Lord, it will help materially in understanding the Gospel of St. John, by a clear perception of what that ministry was.

John makes no reference to what is called the Galilean ministry, except here and there to show its character ("Except ye see signs and wonders," etc.). It is quite clear that he purposely omits mention of that ministry; and the reason appears to be because it had been dwelt upon by the three former Evangelists, and it did not fall within the scope of a supplemental Gospel (such as the fourth is, in this sense). For by writing last, he can supply omissions, explain difficulties, and clear up some discrepancies in the chronology. John does these things, and we may therefore call his the supplementary Gospel; but it would be inaccurate to speak of it as such only, or as if that were more than a minor feature in it.

(*c*)

St. John describes a ministry of our Lord, as well as the other Evangelists, but he does not describe the same ministry that they did. This is evident on comparison.

Take away from the Fourth Gospel the prologue, and the events of the forty days at the close, we have then left the main body of this Gospel, which contains a narrative of the Lord's ministry, with which we compare a similar narrative by the other three Evangelists. When this is done, it is both curious and highly interesting to notice how unlike the two accounts are. But the dissimilarity is explained as soon as we notice that there were two ministries : John treats of one, the Synoptics treat of the other. There was a ministry to the Jews in and about Jerusalem ; St. John writes the account of that : and there was a ministry to the Galileans—and the three earlier Evangelists were the historians of that. The time occupied by the Jewish ministry, which began directly after the baptism of Jesus, lasted about three years, whilst the Galilean ministry did not begin until after the imprisonment of John Baptist, "For John was not yet cast into prison," and lasted little more than *one year*—called "the acceptable year of the Lord " (Luke iv. 14–19). The perception of this fact is of great use in comprehending St. John's Gospel. The Lord exercised two ministries—one to the Jews of the capital, who were an educated people, the other to the Jews in Galilee, who were a provincial and less-cultured people. When ministering to the Jerusalem Jews, the Lord made use of oral teaching. He argued with them, and spake in parables; but when He ministered to the ruder Galilean people, He employed another method, more suited to their capacities. They would not believe unless they saw "signs and wonders." Consequently He worked *miracles* amongst them. This ministry of miracle-working occupied about one year, and is that described by the first three Evangelists; whilst the ministry which John describes lasted during the whole of our Lord's ministerial career, and was that which presented the greatest difficulties all through—a ministry to a highly cultured, cold, and hard-hearted people; to the religious Pharisee, the free-thinking Sadducee, and the ecclesiastical scribes, lawyers, and priests. It was our Lord's contact with such minds as these, and the profounder teaching which it called forth, that had its charms for John ; and he describes it accordingly.

Nearly all the events related in the first six chapters of St. John are peculiar to his Gospel. The seventh opens with a brief notice of the Galilean ministry : "After these things Jesus walked in Galilee." That is the point where the Synoptics start from. John, however, does not describe what was done there, but confines his narrative to what was done in the short visits which our Lord made to Jerusalem.

(vii.) "Jesus went up secretly to the feast of tabernacles;" and chapters viii. to x. relate what was done, and what was the Lord's teaching on that occasion. In x. 40, we read that He departed again beyond Jordan. After an interval He returns, and raises Lazarus. Now this to some may appear as purely supplementary ; but in all probability it is St. John's *design* to give an account of the ministry in Jerusalem, so as to show what were the real grounds for crucifying our Lord. John is sparing in his notice of *miracles*, because they were not performed in great number in and about Jerusalem ; but when he does relate any, it is for the purpose of showing

(*d*)

the effect they had on the Jews, and how Jesus was received at Jerusalem. The two that Jesus worked there were the healing of the impotent man, and the opening the eyes of one born blind. But these works had no convincing effect upon the Jews: they merely cavilled. The objection to the first was, that it was done on "the Sabbath day;" to the second, that "This man is a sinner." But the greater miracle of raising Lazarus had a different effect: it brought matters to a crisis. They said now, "Better one man should die," etc. This now becomes their settled aim and purpose. As a novelist, like Renan, might say, John "piles up the agony." It is "the Lord's controversy with Zion." On every side the mutiny is increasing; the Lord's teaching is met with blasphemy, threats, and violence, all working to one end—*His death.* He Himself prepares for it. He discerns the signs of the times—the ministry of His life was closing, and the ministry of His death beginning. The same voice which spoke to Him at His baptism now speaks again. The by-standers said it thundered, but Jesus knew what it meant. He had glorified God in His life, He was now to glorify Him in His death.

We find this of course in the Synoptics, but they do not proceed, as John does, from cause to effect. After this we come to the events of Holy Week, and the forty days, in which, though much is peculiar to St. John, yet all the Gospels are full: the cardinal facts of the Lord's Death and Resurrection are too important for omission.

(a)

6. GOSPEL OF ST. JOHN: Its Special Work

It is the Gospel which will play the most significant part in the events of the future. The Synoptic Gospels, to a great extent, have done their work. The work of the fourth is yet to come. Christianity has been mainly built up on the facts contained in the first three Gospels, and it belongs to the fourth to keep that fabric from collapsing. If it be true that they are the Body, and this the Soul, and if it be true that the last days shall witness such a sifting of Christianity as never was, then we may apply our Lord's words: "Fear not them which can kill the body, and afterward have no more that they can do;" they cannot kill the soul. An adverse criticism may think to weaken and even kill the Synoptic Gospels, but it cannot touch St. John. The spirit is there. The Supernatural is beyond the reach of criticism. The chief evidence for Christianity is its spirit; and the spiritual element of the New Testament writings is fullest developed in St. John.

(b)

Some rather obscure words at the end of this Gospel—"If I will that he *tarry* till I come, what is that to thee?"—in their primary meaning, are an answer to Peter's question: "What shall this man do?" His own future had been forecast; now what of His friend *John?* Shall he, too, begin to work at once, and with great energy and activity, and in the end win the crown of martyrdom? He is answered by the words, "If I will that he *tarry:*" "If I will that his work, his special work *tarries*, what is that to thee?" I am the Lord of the vineyard: I will that *you* begin to work at once—yours is not a disposition that can wait; but I will that John *waits* (he has

the waiting faculty) till a later period—till I come in judgment upon Jerusalem—for then his special qualifications will be needed. The Lord's words always had a far-reaching meaning, and there may lurk in this word "*tarry*" more than appears on the surface. An intimation, perhaps, of the special work of St. John—viz., that it precedes *judgment*—precedes the Coming of the Lord. The work of such men as John always *tarries:* they have to ripen for it, and time and events have to ripen for them.

(c)

7. ST. JOHN'S GOSPEL AND THE APOSTOLIC AGE

The Apostolic age had three special periods: there was first the PETRINE period, wherein the activity of such minds as Peter's found its most fitting scope. After that came the PAULINE period, wherein such teaching as St. Paul's is the representative of was called for. After this, and when they had passed away, the old man John, whose work had *tarried* till now, came forth to do his day's work in the Lord's vineyard. This is called the JOHANNEAN period. Compare these periods with the succeeding centuries down to our own time, and they will be found to present similar characteristic features. Following the Apostolic age, and until the Middle Ages, we have a mixed period: half Jewish, half Christian, with an infusion of Paganism. The leaven of Christianity is at work, but it makes slow progress. Its activities are wrongly directed. This was the period of the development of Romanism and Monasticism. PETER is made the rock on which all this is built, and we may in consequence call it the Petrine period.

(d)

From the period of the Reformation until our own time, we have more of the true light, and the spirit, and the liberty of Christianity. Paul's name and doctrine, "The just shall live by faith,' have become prominent, and we may denominate this the Pauline period.

(e)

8. ST. JOHN AND ANTICHRIST

But apparently the doctrine of "Justification by Faith" is becoming old-fashioned. The Reformation and the Reformers are attacked and maligned by one party of the present day, and the supernatural element of the New Testament is attacked by another. So that there are indications of our having entered upon a new period; and from its peculiar characteristics, we may appropriately call it the Johannean Period. If this be so, if we are entering upon a great Armageddon, it is to St. John that we must go for our armour. His work *tarries* for a time of conflict; and the better acquainted we are with his writings, the better shall we be prepared to take our part in the religious warfare of the future (whether near or remote). And those of us who hold that the greatest enemy of Christianity—Antichrist—is not yet developed—not of the past, but of the future, not the Church of Rome (for she cannot be both the Harlot and the Antichrist too): those of us who think so, may find that St. John's Gospel will be the main point of attack; and thus again, in this sense, his work will "tarry" until

(f)

the convulsions at the end of time bring him to the front. . . . In short, John's work precedes the End of the World. Peter writes of the end as a great and universal Catastrophe, but he gives no sign of its cause : for all he says we might infer that the end comes because the world has lasted long enough, and for no other reason. Paul again writes of the character of that last enemy : "He is a liar," and deludes people into believing " a lie "—*i.e.*, the opposite to St. Paul's doctrines ; but still there is a little indefiniteness —there is no mention of his *name*. And because, at the time of the Reformation, the Romish system presented the greatest form of antagonism to Paul's teaching, men rushed to the conclusion that the Romish system was the Antichrist of the New Testament. Such a conclusion was quite natural then, but it is not to our credit, as students of the Bible and of history, that we cling so tenaciously to that view now. John, in his turn, writes of the last enemy, and now we come to something like definiteness. He gives his name, "ANTICHRIST," not merely a "false Christ : " there are many such, but one who takes the place of Christ, he is against Christ. It is one who seeks to regenerate the world without Christ and Christianity at all. He is an unbeliever, and utterly irreligious. He "believeth neither in the Father nor the Son," and it is the strife between him and Christianity which brings about the end of the world. Thus, then, whilst Peter mentions the catastrophe of the end, and Paul describes the character of the last enemy, it is left to John to give us his name, and to tell us that the cause of the end is a great *religious conflict* between Christ and Antichrist. The other Gospels, for the most part, have done their work : this tarries for the last time. It TARRIES for the critic, who shall sharpen his scalpel yet more and more. But it will come safely through every attack, and outlive the world. It *tarries*, too, for the special consolation of those who shall be John's companions in tribulation at the time of the end.

(*a*)

GOSPELS, UNITY OF THE

Under the Fourfold Form, we have the One Gospel of the Lord. Four human writings, but one Divine record. The number *four* indicates fulness, and meets the fourfold wants of the world. *Irenæus* compared the four Gospels with the four cherubim (Ezek. i.); *the Fathers* with the four living creatures; *Christian art* perpetuates the symbols proposed by Jerome : *Matthew* = a Man ; *Mark* = a Lion ; *Luke* = an ox ; *John* = an Eagle.

(*b*)

GOSSIP

About three weeks ago, I was very seriously alarmed by intelligence which I received of an illness under which I then laboured. My informer was certain of his fact, but enjoined me not to mention it again. He had, it seems, been let into the secret by a friend of his, who had been told of it by an acquaintance of his, who had had it from a near relation of his, who had been informed of it by an intimate of hers, who had heard it from the best authority.

(*c*)   *Microcosm No. XVIII*

GOVERNMENT

" *The Lord reigneth* " (Ps. xciii. 1)

Bulstrode Whitlock, Cromwell's envoy to Sweden, was one night so disturbed in mind over the state of his nation, that he could not sleep. His servant, observing it, said, " Pray, sir, will you give me leave to ask you a question ? "   " Certainly." " Do you think that God governed the world very well before you came into it ? "   " Undoubtedly." " And do you not think that He will govern the world quite as well when you are gone out of it ? " " Certainly."   " Then pray, sir, do you not think that you may trust Him to govern it as long as you live ? "   No answer could be given, and composure and sleep followed.

(*d*)

GRACE (Rom. vi. 12)

Christians are placed in a condition of which *grace* is the prominent feature : grace to sanctify as well as grace to renew the heart; grace to purify the evil affections ; grace to forgive offences though often repeated, and thus to save from despair, and to excite to new efforts of obedience. Viewed in this light, there is abundant reason for asserting that Christians, under a system of grace, will much more effectually throw off the dominion of sin than they would do if under a mere law dispensation.

(*e*)   *Moses Stuart*

[Eph. ii. 5.

The emphatic mention of grace (grace, not works,) is to make the readers feel,—what their own hearts might otherwise have caused them to doubt,—the real and vital truth, that they have present and actual fellowship with Christ in the quickening, yea, and even in the resurrectional and glorifying power of God.

(*f*)   *Ellicott*

There is sometimes the thought that *grace* implies God's passing by sin. But no—quite the contrary ; grace supposes sin to be so horridly bad a thing, that God cannot tolerate it. Were it in the power of man, after being unrighteous and evil, to patch up his ways, and mend himself so as to stand before God, there would then be no need of *grace*. The very fact of the Lord's being gracious, shows sin to be so evil a thing, that man, being a sinner, his state is utterly ruined and hopeless, and nothing but free grace will do for him—can meet his need.

(*g*)   *Anon*

Grace, like manna, will rot if kept overnight. "Wind up thy soul," says George Herbert, " as thou dost thy watch at night." "Leave no arrears from day to day." Give us *this day's* food ; forgive us *this day's* sins.

(*h*)   *Bp. Jackson*

" Grace maketh not such a change in the faithful that by-and-by they become altogether new creatures and perfect in all things; but there remain yet certain dregs of their old and natural

(*i*)

corruption. As, if a man that is naturally inclined to anger be converted to Christ, although he be mollified by grace (the Holy Ghost so framing his heart that he is now become more meek and gentle), yet this natural vice is not utterly quenched in the flesh. Likewise, such as are by nature severe and sharp, although they be converted to the faith, yet, notwithstanding, they cannot utterly forsake this vice. Hereof it cometh, that the Holy Scriptures, which do contain all one truth, of diverse spirits, are diversely handled: one, in teaching, is mild and gentle; another more rough and vigorous. Thus the Spirit of God, being poured into diverse vessels, doth not quench at once the vices of nature; but, by little and little, during this life, he purgeth that sin which is rooted, not only in the Galatians, but also in all men of all nations."

(a)   *Luther, Com. Gal*

Grace flows more freely and fully as it approaches the ocean of glory; that is not saving which doth not so. Cf. the Apostle: "Though our outward man perish, yet the inward man is renewed day by day." Cf. also Ps. xcii. 12–15.

(b)   *Hengstenberg*

Grace and Corruption

Grace and corruption are distinct from the soul, though both dwell in it after regeneration; corruption works, and grace works, and "the elder shall serve the younger." Sin is condemned, but not yet cast out. Grace has the promise of full possession, but the time is not yet come for its complete fulfilment.

(c)   *James Smith*

Grace, Doctrines of

I could not but feel some measure of gratitude to God that He had always disposed me to assist on the great doctrines of regeneration, the new creature, faith in Christ, progressive sanctification, supreme love to God, living entirely to the glory of God, being not our own, and the like. God has helped me to see in the surest manner, from time to time, that these, and other doctrines necessarily connected with them, are the only foundation of safety for perishing sinners; and that those dispositions which correspond with them are that holiness "without which no man shall see the Lord."

(d)   *D. Brainerd*

Grace and Glory

Grace is glory in the bud, and glory is grace at the full.

(e)   *T. Brooks*

Grace at Meals

Some hae meat that canna eat,
  And some would eat that want it;
But we hae meat, and we can eat,
  Sae let the Lord be thankit.

(f)   *Burns*

A thankless feeder is a thief, his feast
A very robbery, and himself no guest.

(g)   *Vaughan*

Grace, Means of

"My grace is sufficient for thee."
There are—
1. *Means of grace.*
2. *A throne of grace.*
We are exhorted to make diligent use of the first, and to come boldly to the second.
Hence " to overcome " is possible.

(h)

Grace, Mercy, and Peace (1 Tim. i. 2)

We may call—
1. Grace, the highest good for the guilty;
2. Mercy, for the suffering;
3. And Peace, for the struggling disciple of the Lord.

(i)   *Bengel*

Grace and Nature

Grace and nature will ever maintain their contention in the world. There will always be Pelagians, and there will always be true believers; because the first birth constitutes the one, and the second birth the other.

(j)   *Blaise Pascal*

Grace of the Son

But, methinks, we should not have done yet with this grace of the Son. Thou Son of the Blessed, what grace was manifested in Thy condescension! Grace brought Thee down from heaven; grace stripped Thee of Thy glory; grace made Thee bear such burdens of sin, such burdens of sorrow, such burdens of curse as are unspeakable! O Son of God, grace was in all Thy tears. Grace came bubbling out from Thy bleeding side! Here is grace indeed—unsearchable riches of grace—grace to make angels wonder, to make sinners happy, to make devils astonished!

(k)   *John Bunyan*

Grace and Strength

"*My grace is sufficient for thee*" (2 Cor. xii. 9)
Occasion: Prayer for removal of something which *hurt* or interfered with the *usefulness* of the Apostle.
It was *not* removed; but this *promise* was given.
Grace = supporting strength.
The promise applies—
1. To the immediate cause of it. The thorn in the flesh—the painful reminder of weakness.
" Then let the thorn prick me." In my weakness I am strong.
2. *A cross to bear* = something right athwart my wishes and will.
Here again comes in the supporting promise—
Then, as Christ, we say, " Not my will, but Thine be done."
3. *A death to die.* We fear its approach as a foe. The pain, the darkness, the horror.
Here again comes in the promise, " *My grace*," etc. " I will be with thee." " I will give grace according to your need."
And thousands of Christian deathbeds attest the reality of the supporting promise.

(l)

GRACE IS SUFFICIENT FOR THEE, MY (2 Cor. xii. 9)

I never knew how weak I was till now : when He hideth Himself, and when I have Him to seek seven times a day ; I am a dry, withered branch, and a piece of a dead carcase, dry bones, and not able to step over a straw. The thoughts of my old sins are as the summons of death to me ; and of late my brother's case had struck me to the heart. When my wounds are closing, a little riffle causeth them to bleed afresh. So thin-skinned is my soul that I think it is like a tender man's skin, that may touch nothing. You see how short I should shoot of the prize if His grace were not sufficient for me.

(a)   *Samuel Rutherford*

GRACE AND TRUTH, FULL OF (John i.)

The nature of the life in love for the sinful world is *grace ;* the nature of light is *truth.*
The light divides the children of light from the children of darkness.
The children of light are children of truth and uprightness ; the children of darkness are children of falsehood (ch. iii.).
Grace and truth become personal in the glory of Christ, are the principle of the glorification of life (ii.), and of its beginning in regeneration (iii.).
The truth leads to freedom in Christ ; the counterpart is bondage (viii.) ; to life in Christ, the counterpart of which is blindness ; to trustful and obedient following of Christ, the counterpart of which is apostasy (x.).

(b)   *Lange*

GRACE RECEIVED IN VAIN (2 Cor. vi. 1)

THE QUESTION, " Can a man fall from a state of grace ? " has been discussed with much characteristic theological vehemence.
Some ground for the disagreement may be removed by ascertaining what is meant by the word GRACE.

(c)

1. That grace can be received in vain is evident from the exhortation of the Apostle

(i.) " We beseech you that ye receive not the grace of God in vain."
(ii.) " Moreover, brethren, I would not have you ignorant how that our fathers were all under the cloud, and all passed through the sea ; and were all baptized unto Moses in the cloud and in the sea ; and did all eat the same spiritual meat ; and did all drink the same spiritual drink : for they drank of a spiritual rock that followed them : and the Rock was Christ.
" Howbeit with most of them God was not well pleased : for they were overthrown in the wilderness." (1 Cor. x.).
They, then, *received the grace of God in vain.*
And " these things " are our examples—written for our admonition ; we can, then, have no doubt that to receive the grace of God in vain is possible.

(d)

2. But what is meant by " The Grace of God " ?

An answer is supplied in Chapter v.
(i.) " *Grace* " means favour. " The grace of God " = The favour of God.

The particular grace or favour of God more immediately referred to is that of—
(ii.) *Reconciliation.* God is reconciled to us.
The Gospel contains the message of this Reconciliation. And the minister of the Gospel has to beseech men in Christ's stead to be reconciled to God.
This message, St. Paul calls " The grace of God," and signifies the kindness that God has shown to us, and *not an infusion of anything into us,* nor is *the indwelling of the Holy Spirit* meant.
(iii.) *A state of grace,* then, = The condition of those who have *accepted* the message of the Gospel = " Called to be saints." Baptized members of Christian Churches.
Such are reminded that they may receive the grace of God in vain.

(e)

3. Compare with these other statements of Holy Scripture

(i.) " Every branch *in Me* that beareth not fruit He taketh away."
(ii.) The " barren fig-tree " stood *in the vineyard* = in the visible Church, and because it continued barren, all labour being lost on it, the order was given, " Cut it down : why cumbereth it the ground ? "
(iii.) " *Quench* not the spirit "—not merely *grieve* and *resist,* but " *quench.* "
(iv.) " It is impossible for those who were once enlightened, if they shall fall away, to renew them unto repentance."
(v.) " He that despised Moses' law died without mercy. Of how much sorer punishment, suppose ye, shall he be thought worthy, who hath trodden underfoot the Son of God," etc.
These are, by common consent, very solemn passages, and they are the answers that the Bible gives to the question, " Can a man fall from grace ? "

(f)

4. But now, if we alter the ground, and look at the question from another aspect, not now asking, " Whether a man may fall from *a state of grace ?* " but asking, **Whether a man who has been brought into living union with Christ, through the indwelling of the Holy Spirit, can fall from that condition ?** then the answer that Holy Scripture gives to this question is an emphatic " No."
(i.) " Fear not, little flock : for it is the Father's good pleasure to give you the kingdom."
(ii.) " I give unto them eternal life, and they shall never perish."
(iii.) " No one is able to pluck them out of My Father's hand."
(iv.) " While I was with them in the world, I kept them in Thy name ; those that Thou gavest Me, I have kept, and none of them is lost."
(v.) " Whom He did predestinate, them He also called ; and whom He called, them He also justified ; and whom He justified, them He also glorified."
The one set of passages = an emphatic " YES " to the question asked ; and the other set = an emphatic " No."
Hence the inference that there is an inner and an outer circle in the kingdom of heaven. In other words, there is a building going up inside the scaffolding of the visible Church, making increase

(g)

according to the increase of God, dwelt in by the Holy Spirit, as His peculiar temple. Distinct from the Church on earth, there is a "general Church of the first-born, whose names are written in heaven." And

(i.) Within that circle no wolf can come to destroy.

(ii.) These are they who are kept by the power of God through faith unto salvation.

(iii.) These are they who are prayed for by Christ: "I pray for them."

(iv.) These are they who were given to Christ by the Father before the foundation of the world, and none of them shall perish.

(a)   *Cf. F. W. Robertson*

GRACIOUS AND GRACELESS

In this should a *gracious* differ from a *graceless* man, that he should bear his cross courageously, and, as it were, with the wings of faith outsoar the height of all human miseries. He should be like a rock, being incorporated into Jesus Christ, impregnable and unshaken with the most furious incursions of the waves and storms of worldly troubles, pressures, and persecutions.

(b)   *Chrysostom*

GRAFTING

"From Me is thy fruit found" (Hos. xiv. 8; John xv. 16)

There is another kind of grafting referred to in Scripture, similar to the grafting of the good slip on the poor and worthless stalk. This is referred to by James, when he calls upon Christians to "receive with meekness the engrafted word, which is able to save their souls." In this case the Word, as a perfect graft, is united to the believer, who is naturally unproductive. This word thus influences his whole character, and enables him to bring forth good fruit, even an hundred-fold.

(c)   *Prof. Balfour*

This is an art
Which does mend nature—change it, rather: but
The art itself is nature.

(d)   *Shakspeare*

GRAIN OF WHEAT (John xii.)

All the chief moments in the life of Christ are prefigured in the history of the grain of wheat : Christmas, Good Friday, Easter, Ascension, Whitsuntide.

(e)   *Lange*

GRATITUDE

Oh! how amiable is gratitude! especially when it has the Supreme Benefactor for its object. I have always looked upon gratitude as the most exalted principle that can actuate the heart of man. It has something noble, disinterested, and (if I may be allowed the term) generously devout. Repentance indicates our nature fallen, and Prayer turns chiefly upon a regard to one's self. But the exercise of gratitude subsisted in Paradise when there was no fault to deplore, and will be perpetuated in heaven when "God shall be all in all."

(f)   *Hervey's Med. Tombs*

GRATITUDE

A deaf and dumb pupil of the Abbé Sicard, on being asked what he understood by the word "gratitude," wrote down immediately, "Gratitude is the memory of the heart."

(g)   *Brown's "Philosophy of the Human Mind."*

We may use the words of Socrates to his scholar, who saw in the contemplation of nature only a proof of his own insignificance, and concluded "that the gods had no need of him," which drew this answer from the sage : "The greater the munificence they have shown in the care of thee, so much the more honour and service thou owest them."

(h)   *Biblical Treasury*

"Where are the nine?" (Luke xvii. 17)

A gentleman of fortune, but a stranger to personal religion, one evening took a solitary walk through part of his grounds. He happened to come near a mean hut, where a poor man lived with a numerous family, who earned their bread by daily labour. He heard a continued and pretty loud voice. Not knowing what it was, curiosity prompted him to listen. The man happened to be at prayer with his family. He heard him giving thanks to God for the goodness of His providence in giving them food to eat and raiment to put on, and in supplying them with what was necessary and comfortable in the present life. He was struck with astonishment and confusion, and said to himself, "Does this poor man, who has nothing but the meanest fare, and that purchased by severe labour, give thanks to God for His goodness to himself and family, and I, who enjoy ease and honour, and everything that is pleasant and desirable, have hardly ever bent my knee, or made any acknowledgment to my Maker and Preserver?" This occurrence was the means of bringing him to a real sense of religion.

(i)   *Foster*

GRAVE, THE

An angel's arm can't snatch me from the grave;
Legions of angels can't confine me there.

(j)   *Young*

GREAT, HE SHALL BE

"He shall be great, and shall be called the Son of the Highest" (Luke i. 32)

These words were uttered by the angel at the salutation of the Virgin Mary. They suggest comparison between Christ and the great men of history : "He shall be great."

The Saviour of men, and the example for all, must be the isolated one, or the unparalleled MAN in human history. He must be both like us and unlike us—like us in so far as His human nature is concerned : He must be born, He must increase in stature, be in subjection to His parents, and be subject to all the ordinary conditions of human nature, as it develops itself from infancy to manhood. In all this He is like us—for otherwise He could not be our Pattern and our Saviour.

He must be unlike us, or how could He be that

(k)

One whom we are to imitate, and of whose fulness we must all partake?

Christ as a man was unlike all other men. He alone of all great men is the unparalleled One of all history; and the conviction of this truth suggests that more than man is here—more than a great and unparalleled man: it is none other than the "Son of the Highest."

(a)

Great Men, Christ and

What is meant by a Great Man?

A great man is one who, by his intellectual power, exerts an influence over society; and the wider and more beneficial this influence is, is the measure of the man's greatness.

We apply the term to those men whose originality, independence, and power give them an individuality of their own which the general mass of mankind does not possess. This individuality makes an impression on society, so that society appears to be the production of such men.

In the highest sense of the term, great men are the *bestowers*, and not the *receivers;* or, if they do receive, the reciprocity is unequal—they give more than they receive. The great mass of mankind are the recipients; and in proportion as the masses are influenced by the bestower, just in that proportion can a man be styled GREAT. He is great if the world *gains* by him.

(b)

It is not because Shakspeare was a great poet, and Raphael a great painter, and Socrates a great philosopher, that they were *great men*. For if a man's influence is confined to a certain class of society, as to art and science, or to cultured minds exclusively, then the mass of mankind as a totality is uninfluenced. As, for instance, Socrates may rank high as a thinker; but what is the beneficial extent of his greatness in this respect? how far did it extend in his day to others? and how far has society to this day been influenced by his opinions? We are constrained to reply, "Not far." Even in his own time, it was but a small circle of minds whom he attracted, and they were of the "wise," and the "disputers" of this world, as St. Paul calls them; whilst the poor, the untaught, the uninitiated, the fallen and the needy, were left altogether uninfluenced by him. If Socrates did any good at all, it was to a few cultured minds. And of the rest it might be said, "This people, which knoweth not the law, are cursed." Not so, however, of Him whom the angel said, "He shall be great"; "The common people heard Him gladly"; "There came unto Him all the publicans and harlots for to hear Him;" "All men wondered at the gracious words which proceeded out of His mouth." Hence a striking dissimilarity between Christ and *great men*.

(c)

This dissimilarity is still more apparent as we proceed with our comparison:

The great men of history, as a rule, influence only a single nation, or a section of the human race, or one generation only. And that limited influence is their essential work—the work, in fact, for which they were raised up.

But Christ is greater than such great men. The religion which He has founded is a world-wide religion, and of none other can this be said.

In Christ, too, we see an individual man, who in His own personality has a power whose influence extends over all races of people, under every clime, and throughout all ages.

Nor does He enter into relation with a single portion of humanity only, but with the entire race. He is not the son of a man, but the Son of *man*, and His relation with the entire race is not that of *receiver*, but absolutely as THE GIVER. "Out of His fulness have all we received." "He is God's unspeakable gift." We are the recipients; there is no reciprocity. "Who hath given unto Him, and it shall be recompensed again?"

He has given unto the world (not to a single nation) a new development of the world (it makes a fresh start in Him), a new "course of this world" —a new humanity extending through the centuries.

On Him, when we think of the fulness of blessing that is in Him, we cannot bestow the term "*great man*" as if He were one of other great men, as if He were not the *isolated* and *unparalleled* man in "the world's" history. To Him we can only apply the words of the angel spoken to Mary:

"He shall be great, and shall be called the Son of the Highest."

(d)

"Great," in His Motive

Again the dissimilarity, is seen in the PRINCIPLE which actuates His work. Christ's is a world-wide work, it embraces the entire human race, it extends back over the centuries, and looks forward to the remotest future, estimating the needs of that race, and meeting them to the uttermost. The power that does this exceeds all other powers. But if we ask ourselves, what is the essence of this power? The answer, is "REDEEMING LOVE." He loves our race; He works to *redeem* us from sin; He would have "a holy generation," a peculiar people, zealous of good works. Love underlies His entire work. And He Himself tells us that "*love* is the fulfilling of the law"—therefore a Being so filled with love as is Christ, and working from love as a *principle*, must at the same time be a being of infinite Holiness; and hence transcending all others, leaving all who aspire after perfection infinitely behind Him. And then, again, showing the striking dissimilarity between the Redeemer and other *great men*.

(e)

"Great," by Comparison

If the sunlight, which enters the darkened room in the foul court or alley of the city, lighting up every polluted corner with its genial rays, and spreading happiness over all the earth, shining on good and evil alike, be traced back to its source, the glorious orb will be found to be of the same nature as its remotest ray on earth. And so, if every work of love and mercy done on earth, and in the name of Christ, tells of love, it also tells of a vast personal orb of Holiness. Trace the deed of mercy back to whence it came, and you shall find Christ to be its glorious source—"The fulness of the Godhead," and the fount of love.

(f)

Not so is the influence of great men who have lived and died, and who being dead yet speak.

Take Shakspeare. Perhaps no uninspired writer has more widely influenced mankind than he. A master of human nature—one touch of which "makes all the world kin." He understands all its moods. He can play upon it as upon an instrument. He can move us to laughter or to tears at his will. He can at one moment dispel gloom and sadness by a marvellous creation of the comic and the ridiculous, and anon he can freeze our very blood with terror by tragedy and death ; but trace back his influence till you come to the man himself—the personality—the William Shakspeare —then you find that your hero was no god, nor angel, nor perfect man.

Only thus, by comparing Christ with great men, shall we see the great dissimilarity between Him and them : He is more than great, He is the Son of the Highest.

(a)

"Great" in His Aim

But if His principle was "redeeming love," what was His aim ? What end had Christ in view, other than rescuing our race from sin, and recreating them unto Holiness ?

His design was to found God's kingdom upon earth. No other man ever designed such a thing. Perhaps no other great man ever saw the necessity for such a kingdom being founded, and was certainly utterly unable to accomplish it. Not one of them assumed the task of Redeemer of the world. Not one grasped the idea of setting forth his own life as an example—a universal example, valid from generation to generation. Such an aim as this none but Christ ever entertained. Hence again, we see what a gap there is between Him and other great men.

(b)

" Great," Personally

Every great man exerts an influence over others, a great personal influence.

But their personal influence comes to an end, and then men have only their doctrines to influence them. With Christ, however, both are always combined. We have both His doctrines, and His personality. Both continue to exert an influence over the world. There is an indissoluble connection between Christ's Person and His work. Where His work is going on, there He is personally present. "Lo I am with you always even unto the end of the world." And more than this, each individual who is influenced by Christ has a personal influence exerted over him. With Thomas the Christian believer must say, " My Lord and my God." Christ would have each member of the Kingdom of God, personally acquainted with Himself. This Kingdom of God is to be a Kingdom of sanctified personalities. All the world, as descended from Adam, He would destroy, that He may introduce a new development, starting from Himself.

The world's centre of gravity has been displaced by sin. The attraction is to a wrong object.

This Christ will alter, He will bring back the world's centre of gravity to God. But He can only do this by transplanting His own personal life into the human race. This He did when He took our nature upon Him. This, too, He has done in every conversion from that time to this —when " Christ is formed within us."

And this He is ever doing when He enters into a man, and enables that man to dedicate himself to God. In all this Christ stands alone—His work is exclusively a Personal work. And to carry on that work He is " alive for evermore."

(c)

To sum up the differences

This work of His, based on redeeming love, having for its aim the setting up of the Kingdom of God on earth, and the means employed being Himself Personally—a member of that humanity which He came to save. All this constitutes Christ the Isolated One in the human race, Himself the Creator of the new community, embracing all ages, all people, and this gives Him a greatness, surpassing all human measure, and declares Him to be " the Son of the Highest."

(d)

" Great," as " the Desire of all Nations "

Christ's Advent into this world was a turning point in its history : He was "the desire of all nations." Of the birth of no great man could this be said. Others have been blessings to a single generation; but in Christ " all the families of the earth are blessed."

(e)

Christ was born in the fulness of time, when everything was ripe for His appearance : a time fixed by the counsel of God,—when the condition of the world was such that the Redeemer could be revealed in it.

For what was the condition of the world when Christ came?

There was a universal decay of religion and morality. Not one nation only needed regeneration, but the whole world.

When the night was at the darkest the streaks of dawn appeared, and the Sun of Righteousness arose with healing on His wings.

When the moral condition of the whole world was at its worst the Redeemer appeared. For then the diseased world was in a fit state for His work of healing.

Now of any truly great man there is a predestined relation between his person and his work and the circumstances and times in which he lives, so that traces of a providential dealing may be discovered in his appearance.

This was true, in an absolute sense, of Christ. He came at a time when the condition of the world most needed Him.

The world seemed at that time to be one mass of contradictions and contrasts : offering just the opportunity for God to do a " new thing."

Christ found in His own nation a jumble of nationalities; a combination of Jewish, Greek, and Roman culture ; and great religious oppositions of Jew and Gentile.

He encountered an over-ripe civilization, which included the whole range of contrasts in human life.

Contrasts in education; contrasts in external conditions of wealth and poverty; in despotism and slavery.

(f)

And the whole of this great civilization was resting on a political foundation (Roman), which was in an advanced state of decay, threatening indeed to sink beneath its own weight.

Everything seemed fallen away from God, as far as nations and religions were concerned.

The religious life of the Jew was petrified into a meaningless ceremonialism, as witnessed in the sect of the Pharisees.

Side by side with this was the incredulity of the Gentiles; the atheism of "the wisdom of this world." The sceptical contempt of the Sadducees, or of a Pilate, who asked "what is truth;" and the sensualism of courts, as witnessed in that of Herod.

(a)

Into all these contrasts Christ came, to find His own nation as sheep without a shepherd—the prey at one time of false prophets, at another of blind-leaders of the blind—clearly some "great" man was needed. The time was ripe for "the desire of all nations" to come. But, God be thanked, He found something else, too—something in the midst of this general depravity. He found some of the salt of the earth, which saved the mass from becoming wholly corrupt.

There were hearts even then susceptible of God's truth, and Kingdom.

He found a holy expectation and desire. He found a poverty of spirit, a hunger and thirst after righteousness, not in Israel only, but among other nations at that time.

(b)

There was a Zacharias and an Elizabeth; there were shepherds who feared the Lord, to whom the angel announced the glad tidings.

There was an aged Simeon, waiting for the consolation of Israel—an Anna, who served God with fastings and prayer night and day.

There was a guileless Nathaniel, an Andrew, a Peter, a John, a Matthew,—Priests, Prophets, Prophetesses, Shepherds, Fishermen, Publicans, and many others; and of noble women, not a few. All of whom were susceptible of the Kingdom of God, waiting in expectation for the consolation of Israel, and no sooner did the King appear, than they were drawn unto Him.

"We have found the Messias of whom Moses and the prophets did write." And what a finding was that! the very word (see EUREKA) expresses the desire of their hearts, how they had sought Him, and how they had lived in expectation of His coming.

(c)

From amongst these susceptible hearts, He drew a circle of men, fitted them by much training to become His Apostles, the pillars of the Church of God, the first instruments for the extension of that Kingdom which He came to set up.

It was into such a *world of contrasts* that Christ came and disclosed Himself, fulfilled His Mission and went back to His Father.

GREAT, quietly great was He on earth—"He shall not strive nor lift up His voice in the streets" —in deep tranquillity, in a remote corner of the earth, He completed His work of redemption, and left to the race of man His example.

And only after He had been ignored, betrayed, rejected, had died a felon's death, and had become invisible to the world, was it that the world became conscious of what He had been, of what He had done, and of what He who is "alive for evermore," is continuing to do now.

(d)   *Martensen (adapted)*

GREAT FAITH (Matt. xv. 28)

A double miracle—

1. of Faith; 2. of Healing.

Thrice did our Lord commend "great faith," and in each case outside the fold of Israel.

In this case the wonder is not that the Syro-phœnician woman had *great* Faith, but that she had Faith at all.

1. "*Great*," because it would stand *trial:*

Report told her the Saviour was *gracious* and *merciful*—breaking not the *bruised reed*, etc.

She = a *bruised reed*, and yet He does *break* and *bruise* her still more.

Report said, again, that He invited *weary and heavy laden* souls to Him, etc. She was one such, and she came to Him, and said, "Lord have mercy," etc.

But "*He answered her not a word.*"

Report said, yet again, that He anticipated the wants of some, as when He said to a man, "Wilt thou be made whole?"

But in her case, when the disciples beg Him to dismiss her, He said to them, in her hearing, "*I am not sent, but to the lost sheep of the house of Israel.*"

2. "*Great*," because it was a *wrestling* faith:

She heard the repulse, yet is neither daunted nor disheartened. She will not take His "No." She now "wrestles," like Jacob,—coming close up to Him, impeding His progress—"LORD, HELP ME": then Jesus speaks, but His answer seems worse than His previous silence:

"It is not meet to take the children's bread, and to cast it to *dogs*."

She understands— "children"=the Jews, "dogs"=those like herself.

She, however, knows how to fight—snatching the weapon out of the Saviour's hands, she turns it on Himself-

"Dogs don't wait till the meal is finished. Little household dogs eat whilst the family meal *is going on*—pieces are thrown to them on the ground *at the same time*. I ask for no more than that— the dog's share—and Thou canst not deny me that.

3. "*Great*," because it was *victorious* faith.

Just now Jesus seemed to deny the smallest boon, now He opens His treasures, and bids her help herself—"*Be it unto thee even as thou wilt.*" He, like Joseph, could only maintain a rough and severe aspect till the trial had done its work—then He reveals the fulness of His grace: "For *that* saying go thy way: thy daughter is made whole."

Learn that when God *delays* a boon, He does not always *deny* it.

(e)   *Cf. Trench*

GREAT OFFICES

"Great offices will
Have great talents. And God gives to every man
The virtue, temper, understanding, taste,
That lifts him into life, and lets him fall
Just in the niche he was ordained to fill."

(f)   *Cowper*

GREAT THINGS

"*Seekest thou great things for thyself?*" (Jer. xlv. 5.)

"I am going to fly," cried the gigantic ostrich; and the whole assembly of birds gathered around in earnest expectation. "I am going to fly," he cried again; and, stretching out his immense pinions, he shot, like a ship with outspread sails, away over the ground, without, however, rising an inch above it.

(*a*) *Lessing*

For a mean man to thirst for a mighty fame, is a kind of fond ambition. Can we think a mouse can cast a shadow like an elephant.

(*b*) *Owen Feltham*

How true is it that no man or nation of men, conscious of doing a great thing, was ever, in that thing, doing other than a small one!

(*c*) *Carlyle*

GREATEST IN KINGDOM OF HEAVEN (Matt. xviii.)

Who has the *Primacy?* If a Church was to be founded, a hierarchy must, in their opinion, be instituted along with it.

(*d*) *Lange*

GREATNESS

In my stars I am above thee; but be not afraid of greatness; some are born great, some achieve greatness, and some have greatness thrust upon them.

(*e*) *Shakspeare*

GREATNESS

Farewell, a long farewell, to all my greatness!
This is the state of man: to-day he puts forth
The tender leaves of hope, to-morrow blossoms,
And bears his blushing honours thick upon him:
The third day comes a frost, a killing frost;
And when he thinks, good easy man, full surely
His greatness is a-ripening—nips his root,
And then he falls as I do.

(*f*) *Ibid*

GREATNESS

The wisest, brightest, meanest of mankind.

(*g*) *Pope on Lord Bacon*

GREATNESS

What millions died that Cæsar might be great!

(*h*) *Campbell*

GREETINGS

"*Peace be to this house*" (Luke x. 5; John xiv. 27).

A greeting is reckoned one of the most unimportant and merely formal things, and is given and received with the greatest indifference. How thoughtlessly does one now say "Good-day," and "Farewell." Yet the formality points back to a deep reality.

An historical consideration teaches us that different views of life, different conceptions of that which gives to human life its worth and meaning, different ideas of the highest good that men felt called upon to wish each other, were expressed in the words with which, in different ages, different people greeted each other.

(*i*)

1. The Greek view found expression in "Χαῖρε" (Joy to thee) = joy in all that is fair and good, joy in life itself, in life's glory and splendour, joy in the harmonious surroundings of life. This to the Greeks is the highest good.

(*j*)

2. The Roman more practical view of life found expression in its "*Salve*" (May you be well), and in its "*Vale*" (Be healthy). The Romans wish each other, not æsthetic joy, but health and strength, as the *conditions* of active human existence which qualify for practical life.

(*k*)

3. The Hebrew and Christian view is reflected in "Peace be with thee and thy house" = *The peace of the Lord.* Christ attaches great importance to greetings.

(*l*)

[Compare the English "Good-bye," Fare-well]. When the religious greeting is more than mere form, it is one with *Blessing* and *Intercession.* That one man blesses another = that he prays to God for him.

(*m*)

In the history of *Greetings*, the *kiss* has also its meaning:—"Greet ye one another," etc. (Rom. xvi. 16) = the kiss of love. But there is also a Judas kiss. And as there is a *look* which glows with the blessing of kindness and love, whose magical effect is felt deep in the soul, so there is an evil eye, which, with the falseness of the serpent, shoots the arrows of ill-will and hatred, arrows against whose poison we must be on our guard.

(*n*) *Martensen*

GUESSWORK IN RELIGION

Many now take Christ by guess. Be sure that it be He, and only He, whom you have met with. His sweet smell, His lovely voice, His fair face, His sweet working in the soul, will not lie; they will soon tell if it be Christ indeed (and I think your love to the saints speaketh that it is He); and therefore I say, Be sure that you take Christ Himself, and take Him with His Father's blessing.

(*o*) *Samuel Rutherford.*

GUIDANCE

Manna fell when they hungered; a stream burst from the rock when they thirsted. If we do not know when to take the next step, the Interpreter is with us, "as one among a thousand," and the oracle says, "Go forward."
God's way may not be the shortest, the easiest, or apparently the safest; but it is ever right. It is *His way.* Would you set your judgment against His?

(*p*) *Good Words*

GUIDANCE

At one time the word is " *Stand still*," at another time it is " *Go forward*." (See.)

(a)

GUILTINESS

Be not ashamed because of your guiltiness; necessity must not blush to beg; it standeth you hard to want Christ! and therefore that which idle on-waiting cannot do, misnurtured crying and knocking will do. And for doubtings—because you are not as you were long since with your Master—consider three things: 1. What if Christ had such tottering thoughts of the bargain of the new covenant betwixt you and Him as you have? 2. Your heart is not the compass Christ saileth by; He will give you leave to sing as you please, but He will not dance to your daft spring. It is not referred to you and your thoughts what Christ will do with the charters betwixt you and Him: your own misbelief hath torn them, but He hath the principal in heaven with Himself. Your thoughts are no part of the new covenant; dreams change not with Christ. 3. Doubtings are your sins, but they are Christ's drugs and ingredients that the Physician maketh use of for the curing of your pride. Is it not suitable for a beggar to say at meat, " God reward the winners "? for then, he saith, he knoweth who beareth the charges of the house. It is also meet you should know by experience that faith is not from nature, but your Lord's free gift, that lay in the womb of God's free grace; praised be the winner! I may add, 4. In the passing of your bill and your charters, when they went through the Mediator's great seal, and were concluded, faith's advice was not sought. Faith hath not a vote beside Christ's merits: blood, blood, dear blood, that came from your Surety's holy body, maketh that sure work.

(b) *Samuel Rutherford*

GUILTINESS AND FAITH

The use, then, which you have of faith now, having already closed with Jesus Christ for justification, is, to take out a copy of your pardon; and so you have peace with God, upon the account of Christ: for, since faith apprehendeth pardon, but never payeth a penny for it, no marvel that salvation doth not die and live, ebb or flow, with the working of faith. But, because it is for your Lord's honour to believe His mercy and fidelity, it is infinite goodness in our Lord that misbelief giveth a dash to our Lord's glory, and not to our salvation. And so, whoever want (yea, although God here bear with the want of what we are obliged to give Him, even the glory of His grace, by believing, yet), a poor covenanted sinner wanteth not; but if guiltiness were removed, doubtings would find no friend nor life; and yet faith is to believe the removal of guiltiness in Christ. A reason why you get less now, as you think, than before (as I take it) is, because, at our first conversion, our Lord putteth the meat in young bairns' mouths with His own hand: but when we grow to some further perfection, we must take heaven by violence, and take by violence from Christ what we get; and He can, and doth hold, because He will have us to draw. Remember, now you must live upon violent plucking. Laziness is a greater fault now than long since: we love always to have the pap put into our mouth.

(c) *Ibid*

H

HABIT (Rev. xxii. 11)

There is a day, of which no man or angel knows the time, after which the unholy will continue to be unholy, and the holy will continue to be holy. The last verity proclaimed in Scripture is the eternal permanence of moral character, and the certainty that all crystallization of the soul into final permanence will bring with it its natural wages. The truth that I am afraid of is what all science, what all Scripture, what all human experience affirms, that he who is unholy long enough will be unholy longer.

(a)   *Joseph Cook*

We must not mistake ourselves: we are body as well as spirit; and hence it comes to pass, that demonstration is not the only thing that influences our opinions and wishes. How few things are actually demonstrated! Evidence can but convince the understanding. Habit is the strongest argument. . . . Our two component parts, then, should be made to proceed in concert; the understanding by evidence, which it is sufficient to have seen once for all; the senses by habit, and by our not suffering them to take a contrary bias.

(b)   *Blaise Pascal*

No man forgets his original trade; the rights of nations and of kings sink into questions of grammar, if grammarians discuss them.

(c)   *Dr. Johnson*

Habit, Evil, and Small Beginnings

Illustrated by an Eastern Parable

Whilst a certain student, whose name was Abdallah, lingered over his morning meal, there came a little fly and lighted on the rim of his cup. It sipped a tiny drop of the syrup, and was gone. The next morning it came again, and again after, and again and again till the eye of the student rested upon it, and he looked at it, and saw the reflection of many colours in its gauzy wings. He thought it beautiful, and could not find in his heart to brush it away. It was a thing of beauty, and so was allowed to remain. Henceforward it came day after day continually; and, waxing bolder and bolder, it sipped even more and more of the syrup in the cup, till it increased in size as large as a locust; and then, too, he discerned in its face an intelligence which he had not seen before, and gradually it assumed the likeness of a man.

But the greater it grew, the more winning were its ways—frisking hither and thither like a sunbeam, and singing like a peri. The heart of the student was fascinated, and the eyes of the simple one were blinded, and holden as it were with silken cords, for in all this he did not perceive the subtlety and design of an evil genius. Waxing bolder and bolder, the demon (for such it was) partook freely and largely of the meats and dainties supplied to the student. And when one day the young man got angry at its voraciousness, and remonstrated by saying, "This is my daily portion of food, sent me from the table of my master: there is not, as you may see, enough for thee and me—it is the portion for one only," then the brazen-faced deceiver answered with blandishments. It caused the simple youth to smile, and so diverted his wrath.

Things went on from day to day as before, until, in process of time, the student perceived that his guest grew stronger and stronger every day, whilst he himself waxed weaker and weaker.

Now arose frequent and daily contention between them. The youth awoke to the sense of his danger—the demon was hunting for his precious life; and throwing off the trammels with which he was bound, he dealt the demon a furious blow, so that it left him for a season. Thereupon Abdallah rejoiced greatly, and said exultingly, "I have triumphed over mine enemy, and when it seemeth good to me, when I am a little recovered, I will smite him that he die; so will I completely rid me of mine adversary." Well, not many days after, lo, and behold, the demon appears again, but not as before—not as a demon, but as an angel of light. He comes arrayed in goodly raiment; he comes with honeyed words and fair speech, bringing in his hand a present, and offers his gift, saying, "Is it not a little one?" and the silly dove is caught again. The wily thing knew how to weave the meshes of his net so as best to ensnare his victim. He is again received into the chamber of the student. And, alas! that this should be a parable of truth, "the last state of that man is worse than the first," for on the morrow when Abdallah appeared not before his master, with his fellow-students, the teacher said, "Wherefore tarrieth the son of the faithful? Perchance he sleeps. We will go and wake him." They go. They come to his room. They knock; they call; but there is no reply. They open the door and enter, and, behold, on the divan lay the dead body of the disciple, his visage black and swollen, and on his throat a mark of the pressure of a finger, broader than the palm of a man. Everything belonging to the young man was gone—his gold, his jewels, his books, his raiment, all gone; and on the garden soil they marked the footsteps of a giant, and found the footprint to be *six cubits long!*

The parable will serve a great many ends. It will help to show how a bad habit may be small in its beginning, but in the end lead to ruin. A single evil thought, harboured in the mind, like the first rebellious wish of the prodigal son, may eventually attain to such gigantic proportions, and dominate the whole man, until he fall, not as he, but like Lucifer, never to hope again.

Moral

Know that an EVIL HABIT is a *demon*, continually expanding. It may come in at the key-hole, but it will soon grow too big for the house.

(d)

Habit, Sinful, The Power of

There is a singular tree in Cuba—the yaguey-tree—that affords a striking illustration of the

(e)

progress and fatality of sin. This tree begins to grow at the top or midway of another tree. The seed is carried by a bird, or wafted by the wind, and, falling into some moist branching part, takes root, and speedily begins to grow. It sends along a kind of thin string-like root down the body of the tree that is occupied, which is soon followed by others. In course of time these rootlings strike the ground, and growth immediately commences upward. New rootlings continue to be formed, and get strength, until the one tree grows as a net with the other inside. The outside one surrounds and presses the inner, like a huge girdle of snakes, strangling the life and augmenting its own power. At last the tree within is killed, and the parasite that has taken possession becomes itself the tree.

(a)

HADES

"*When He ascended up on high, He led captivity captive, and gave gifts unto men. . . . Now that He ascended, what is it but that He also descended first into the lower parts of the earth?*" (Eph. iv. 8, 9)

"*For Christ also hath once suffered for sins, the just for the unjust, that He might bring us to God, being put to death in the flesh, but quickened by the Spirit: by which also He went and preached unto the spirits in prison*" (1 Pet. iii. 18, 19)

These two passages are thought mutually to throw light on the much-disputed place of departed spirits—whether that place has been the same for the righteous dead since Christ's resurrection as it was before. It is generally admitted that our thoughts on the subject are loose, illogical, and incorrect. Take, for instance, the article of our creed, "He descended into hell."

Scripture indicates three places (not states) in the unseen world:

1. Heaven, } the ultimata for good and evil;
2. Hell, }
3. Hades, the intermediate place for each.

This "Hades"—which unfortunately is nearly always translated "Hell" in the Authorized Version —is a place having two compartments, one of comfort (not bliss), and another of despair, but not "Hell" itself. (See parable of Dives and Lazarus.)

The Spirit of Christ "descended into the lower parts of the earth" = to the "Hades" of the righteous dead.

1. That He went there, we believe ("Thou wilt not leave my soul in Hades").
2. What He did there. (See 1 Pet. iii.)
3. The result of His going there. (See Eph. iv. 8, 9.)

Having the key of "Hades" and of death, He opened the door of the prison-house, and let out the captives. Moreover, having descended into Hades, He not only liberated the captives, but took them with Him to heaven, where they are with Him—i.e., "He led captivity captive."

The following is a consensus of Old and New Testament teaching on the subject of Hades:—

(i.) Hades is a place in the unseen world—not heaven nor hell. (ii.) Previous to resurrection of Christ it had two compartments—one of comfort, the other of misery; (iii.) to which all souls were carried; (iv.) into which place Christ, at His death,

descended, releasing the souls of the righteous; (v.) to which place, since then, ONLY the souls of the wicked have been consigned; (vi.) there they are reserved for judgment; (vii.) after judgment, hell—i.e., the pit, or abyss.

(b)

1. Hades is not the "GRAVE":

Matt. xi. 23: "And thou, Capernaum, which art exalted unto heaven, shalt be brought down to hell;"

Matt. xvi. 18: "The gates of hell shall not prevail against it;"

Luke xvi. 23: "And in hell he lifted up his eyes," etc.

Acts ii. 27: "Thou wilt not leave my soul in hell;"

Rev. i. 18: "I have the keys of hell and of death;"

Rev. vi. 8: "His name was Death, and Hell followed;"

Rev. xx. 13: "Death and hell delivered up the dead in them;"

Rev. xx. 14: "Death and hell were cast into the lake of fire," etc.

Hence distinct from the grave, as also from the abyss, or hell itself (see Book of Revelation).

(c)

2. Hades is not hell (a place of punishment):

It was the dwelling-place of the righteous dead. Jacob, Job, David, Hezekiah—all saints of God— declared their expectation of going into Hades (Gen. xlix. 33). "Jacob gathered unto his people" (not buried till long after). The same said of Abraham and Isaac—more particularly God said to Josiah: "I will gather thee unto thy fathers, and thou shalt be gathered unto thy grave" (2 Kings xxii. 20). His soul goes to "fathers," body to the "grave." This sufficiently indicates Old Testament teaching that God gathered all souls of the righteous to one place, and that place was HADES, popularly called by the Jews "Abraham's bosom," not heaven. Lazarus is merely "comforted" there, not in perfect bliss. It is not the place where God and the angels are, but where Abraham, the father of the faithful, is, and his righteous seed.

Hence it is not "hell."

(d)

3. Neither is it the hell of the wicked:

"The angels that sinned, cast down to hell, or the abyss = bottomless pit = the deep." "Suffer us not to go into the 'deep,'" as their home. Psalm lxxxviii. 12: "Shall Thy lovingkindness be showed in the grave, or Thy faithfulness in destruction" = "hell." In Revelation the second death = death casting death into the "abyss." The difference = prison before and after trial: the doom and final punishment of devils and ungodly men. Hence, "Gehenna," "unquenchable fire," "everlasting destruction."

All = that the ungodly are in Hades, but not yet in the final hell, the abyss of everlasting destruction.

(e)

4. But Hades is a place distinct both from heaven and hell, to which Christ went to deliver the Old Testament righteous dead.

(f)

Now the question is—Do the souls of Christ's people go to Hades?

Look at Scripture. We hear no more of "Abraham's bosom," or of being "gathered to fathers"; but the Christian dies, and goes to be "for ever with the Lord"—"to be with Christ."

(i.) They go where Christ is (and He is not in Hades).

John xiv. 2, 3 : "I go to prepare, etc. . . . unto myself; that where I am, there ye may be also ; "

John xvii. 24 : "Father, I will that they also . . . where I am ; "

2 Cor. v. 8 : "Willing rather to be absent from the body, and to be present with the Lord ; "

Phil. i. 23 : "To depart and to be with Christ."

Our Lord is not in Hades—"Whom the heavens must receive until the time of restitution," etc. Hence the assurance that He is in heaven, believers are with Him, and the place (now) is not Hades, but one of the "many mansions" of heaven.

(ii.) St. Stephen saw "Jesus standing on the right hand of God": "Lord, Jesus, receive my spirit";

Heb. xii. 22, 24 : "Spirits of just men made perfect."

These show a difference in the locality of the righteous dead since the resurrection of Christ. Before = to Hades; now, to heaven itself.

That it is so, see John xiv. 2: "In My Father's house are many mansions : if not so, I would have told you. I go to prepare a place for you."

"I go to prepare" = not previously prepared.

This teaches that the place of the righteous dead, whatever it may have been before, has been changed since the resurrection of Jesus.

(a)

HALL, ROBERT

For moral grandeur, for Christian truth, and for sublimity, we may doubt whether they have their match in the sacred oratory of any age or country.

(b)					*Sedgewick*

HAND, THE LORD IS AT (Phil. iv. 5)

Thou lion and tyrant in thy house ! When an honourable man, a stranger, approaches thee, thou ceasest perhaps to scold, and curse, and rage. Why hast thou not as much reverence for the Lord who is near thee?

(c)					*Starke*

HAND OF MAN, THE

Among those bodily organs which, in an emphatic manner, suggest man's ethical destiny, we specially name the human hand; for whilst the corresponding organs in the lower animals are only adapted for the single purpose of giving support to the body, or of assisting the beast to procure its prey and food, men's hands are fitted for a free universal activity. By means of his moulding, fashioning hand, man stamps his impress upon nature, and founds his sovereignty of civilization. By means of this implement of all implements, this instrument of instruments, the use of which goes along with his upright posture, he becomes the inventor of many arts. Therefore it may be said with truth, that " hands are better

than wings." By furnishing man with hands, the Creator has clearly indicated it to be his destiny to develop his being by a series of *actions*—for to *act* is to execute plans. With the hand man performs alike good and evil deeds—acts of heroism and crimes of deepest dye. He folds his hands in prayer, bestows his blessing by laying on of hands, and gives his hand in pledged amity to his neighbour.

(d)					*Martensen*

HANDWRITING, THE

When Adam sinned, there was issued against him the writ of death, written by the finger of God in the book of the moral law. Adam had heard it read before his fall, but in seeking to become a god, by eating of the fruit of the tree, had forgotten it. Now God read it in his conscience, and he was overwhelmed with fear. But the promise of a Redeemer having been given, Mercy arranged that sacrifices should be offered as a typical payment of the debt. When God appeared on Sinai, to enter into covenant with His people, He brought this writ in His hand, and the whole camp understood from the requirements of the law that they must perish; their lives had been forfeited. Mercy devised that a bullock's blood should be shed, instead of the blood of man. The worshippers in the temple were bound to offer living sacrifices to God, that they might die in their stead, and be consumed. Manoah feared the flames of the sacrifice that was offered upon the rock; but his wife understood that, since the angel had ascended in the flame, in their stead, that it was a favourable omen. Every worshipper, by offering other lives instead of their own on the altars of God, acknowledged that the "handwriting" was in force against them, and their Highpriest had minutely to confess all their sins "over" the victim. Yet by all the blood that ever crimsoned Levi's robe and the altars of God, no real atonement was made for sin, nor forgiveness procured for the smallest crime. All these sacrifices made a remembrance of sin, but were no means of pardon. More than two thousand years the question had been entertained, how to reconcile man with God. The "handwriting" was read on Mount Ebal every year; meanwhile the debt was fast accumulating, and new bills were being constantly filed. The books were opened from time to time; but to meet the claims there was nothing brought to the altar but the blood of sacrifices, as a sort of draft in the name of Christ upon the Bank of God. When Heaven and earth had grown weary of this fictitious, or seeming, pardon of sin, I hear a voice exclaim: "Away with sacrifices and burnt-offerings : Heaven has no pleasure in them ; a body has been prepared for me. Lo, I come to reconcile man with God by one sacrifice." He came "leaping upon the mountains, and skipping upon the hills." Calling at the office where the "handwriting" lay, when only eight days old, He signed with His own blood an acknowledgment of the debt, saying : " This is an earnest and a pledge that my heart's blood shall be freely given." The three-and-thirty years have expired ; I see Him in Gethsemane, with the priceless purse of gold which He had borne with Him through the courts of Caiaphas and Pilate ; but to them the image and superscription on the coin were a mystery. The Father, however, re-

(e)

cognised them in the court of Sinai, where the "handwriting" was that demanded the life of the whole world. The day following, "the Virgin's Son" presented Himself to pay the debt in liquid gold ; and the treasure which He bore would have set free a myriad worlds. He passes along the streets [of Jerusalem towards Sinai's office; the mercy-seat is removed to the "place of skulls ; " as He proceeds He exclaims : "I came not to destroy, but to fulfil the law." Send in before the hour of three each curse and threat ever pronounced against My people. Bring in the first old bill against Adam as their head. I will redeem a countless host of infants to-day ; their names shall be taken out of old Eden's accounts. Bring in the many transgressions which have been filed through the ages, from Adam until now ; include Peter's denial of me last night ; but as to Judas, he is a son of perdition, he has no part in Me, having sold Me for thirty pieces of silver. We have here an exhaustless crimson treasure, — enough to meet the demand ; enough to fill every promise and every prophecy with mercy ; enough to make my beloved and myself happy and blest for ever ! By three in the afternoon of that day there was not a bill in all Eden or Sinai that had not been brought to the cross. And when all was settled, Christ bowed down His head, but cried with a loud voice : "It is finished ! " The gates of death and hell trembled and shook. "The posts of the doors moved at the voice." The great gulf between God and His people was closed up. Sinai, appeased with the offering, grew still ; the lightnings no longer flashed, and the thunder ceased to roar.

(a) *Christmas Evans*

HAPPINESS

Solon said : "No man ought to be called happy till he dies," because he knows not what his life is to be. But the Christian may always call himself happy here, because, wherever his tent is carried, he need never pitch it where the cloud does not move, and where he is not surrounded by a wall of fire. "I will be a wall of fire round about them, and their glory in the midst." They cannot dwell where God is not householder, warder, and bulwark of salvation.

(b)

HARDENING OF THE HEART, THE (Heb. iii. 8)

Has its gradations of
1. *Carnal security*, which comforts itself with the outward possession of the means of grace ; and from
2. *Natural indifference and insensibility to the Word*, proceeds on through—
3. *Unbelieving disparagement*,
4. *Faithless neglect*, and
5. *Reckless transgression of the word*,
6. To *rejection, contempt, and denial of it ;* and thence to a
7. *Permanent embittering of the wicked heart ;* to a
8. *Conscious stubbornness of the wicked will ;* to the
9. *Bold tempting of the living God Himself*, until, in
10. *Complete obduracy, judicial retribution* begins the fulfilment of its terrible work.

(c) *Lange*

HARDENING NATURE OF UNBELIEF

The guilt of the Jews consisted in this simply, that they sought after righteousness by *works*, and so wished to set up their own righteousness, after that the end of the Law had come with Christ, and the righteousness of faith had come in the place of a righteousness by works.

They could not excuse themselves by saying that they had not heard this message, for it had gone into all the world ; nor by saying that they had not understood it ; for even the unintelligent Gentiles had quite well understood it. Rather, they had been disobedient to the Gospel, because they are a disobedient and stubborn people. But the deeper cause was, that they stumbled at the Messiah announced in the Gospel, because the Crucified One was no Messiah in their view. . . . They had stumbled on the stone of offence, and now hardening had come upon them as a judgment.

(d) *Weiss*

HARDNESS

"*Endure Hardness*" (2 Tim. ii. 3)

I board with a poor Scotsman : his wife can talk scarcely any English. My diet consists mostly of hasty-pudding, boiled corn, and bread baked in ashes, and sometimes a little meat and butter. My lodging is a little heap of straw, laid upon some boards, a little way from the ground ; for it is a long room, without any floor, that I lodge in. My work is exceedingly hard and difficult. I travel on foot a mile and a half in the worst of roads almost daily, and back again ; for I live so far from my Indians. I have not seen an English person this month. These, and many other uncomfortable circumstances attend me ; and yet my spiritual conflicts and distresses so far exceed all these, that I scarce think of them, but feel as if I were entertained in the most sumptuous manner. The Lord grant that I may learn to *endure hardness* as a good soldier of Jesus Christ !

(e) *David Brainerd*

HARDNESS OF HEART

Known, discovered, and revealed sins, that are against the conscience, (are) to be avoided, as most dangerous preparatives to hardness of heart.

(f) *S. Rutherford*

HARVEST THANKSGIVING

1. Prayer in "The Litany : "

"That it may please Thee to give and preserve to our use the kindly fruits of the earth, so that in due time we may enjoy them."

A Harvest Thanksgiving service is designed as an expression of thankfulness that this petition has been answered.

2. Our Daily Prayer is, "Give us this day our Daily Bread."

But do many think what a miracle this matter of "Daily Bread" is ? An Eastern story relates, that a boy challenged his teacher, who was a priest, to prove the existence of God. The priest took a large vessel, filled it with earth, and de-

(g)

posited in it a kernel, and bade the boy watch. Suddenly a green shoot appeared; it became a stem; the stem put forth leaves and branches; it filled the apartment. It then budded and blossomed, and golden fruit appeared. And in the space of one hour there stood a tree in the place of the little seed. The youth, overcome with amazement, exclaimed, "Now I know that there is a God, for I have seen His power." The priest said to him, "Simple child, do you only now believe? Does not the same thing take place in innumerable instances year after year, only by a slow process? But is it less marvellous on that account?" The story is a parable of truth. One of the greatest of all miracles is how our Heavenly Father provides the whole human family with "Daily Bread," by so ordering the course and secret forces of nature, that the grass of the field is for ever being turned, by a yearly process, into food and raiment convenient for them.

A Harvest Festival is a reminder of this great miracle. Then, with the Psalmist, we praise Him who keepeth His covenant for ever—that seedtime and harvest should not cease—Who bringeth forth food out of the earth, and crowneth the year with goodness. Therefore-

> "Let us with a gladsome mind
> Praise the Lord, for He is kind;
> For His mercies aye endure
> Ever faithful, ever sure."

(a)

HEARING, BELIEVING, SEALING

In whom ye also (trusted) after that ye *heard* the word of truth, the Gospel of your salvation; in whom also after that ye *believed* ye were *sealed* with that Holy Spirit of promise.

N.B.—(i.) The Word of Truth = The Gospel of your salvation was preached.

(ii.) Ye *heard* = to advantage = the good seed = "ears to hear."

(iii.) Ye *believed* = ye trusted = it became the power of God to your salvation.

(iv.) Then followed the *sealing*, viz., the gift of the Holy Spirit of Promise.

Have we this *seal?* = Certainty, assurance, insight, reality.

Note the whole passage (3–14).

= Thanksgiving for salvation received—which was,-

(i.) *Fore-ordained* by the Father, and consists in (*a*) Holiness; (*b*) Sonship (4–5).

(ii.) *Effected* by the Son, and consists in the work of redemption, and the forgiveness of sins.

(iii.) *Made known* by the present dispensation of the Spirit through preaching, etc.

(iv.) *Actually appropriated-*

(*a*) By the Jews; (*b*) By the Gentiles, and consisted in Hearing, Believing, and Sealing.

(b)

HEART

He hath a heart as sound as a bell, and his tongue is the clapper; for what his heart thinks, his tongue speaks.

(c)   *Shakspeare*

HEART

The fear of God is seated in the heart, and the heart is, as I may call it, the Main Fortress, the

mystical world, *Man*. It is not placed in the head, as knowledge is; nor in the mouth, as utterance is; but in the heart, the seat of all. And so it is in the WILL special. The way the will goes, all goes.

(d)   *John Bunyan*

"The human heart is like a millstone in a mill—when you put wheat under it, it turns and grinds and bruises the wheat to flour; if you put no wheat, it still grinds on, but then it is itself it grinds and wears away. So the human heart, unless it be occupied with some employment, leaves space for the devil, who wriggles himself in, and brings with him a whole host of evil thoughts, temptations, and tribulations, which grind out the heart."

(e)   *Luther*

> The heart aye's the part aye,
> *That* makes us right or wrang.

(f)   *Burns*

> Who made the heart, 'tis He alone
>   Decidedly can try us,
> He knows each chord—its various tone,
>   Each spring its various bias:
> Then at the balance let's be mute,
>   We never can adjust it;
> What's done we partly may compute,
>   But know not what's resisted.

(g)   *Ibid*

> The turnpike road to people's hearts, I find,
> Lies through their mouths, or I mistake mankind.

(h)   *Walcot*

In aught that tries the heart, how few withstand the proof!

(i)   *Byron*

HEART, CONDEMNATION OF THE

"*If our heart condemn us*" (1 John iii. 19–21) is a word of hope. It is the cry, "Lord, Thou knowest all things; Thou knowest that I love Thee." It is the affirmation, that if we be but sincere, we may appeal to God and not be condemned. The position of man as regards the world and as regards God is very different. As regards the world, his conscience may acquit him. Job could retain his innocence before the world. Does his heart condemn him? He only said, "I abhor myself, and repent in dust and ashes." St. Paul, too, could only call himself "the chief of sinners." Because of the mighty tenderness of their consciences, the confessions of saints have always been full of self-reproach. Those are *Christians* who are full of self-reproach—not defiant, willing, high-handed sinners. God knows when a man is insincere. But when a man is sincere, and, in spite of all his shortcomings, *knows* he is sincere, when he has given proof of his sincerity by love to the brethren, his life has been a witness to God: and then he may fall back on the love and mercy of One who is greater than his heart, and therefore more tender even than his own self-condemned heart. Such a Christian is not afraid of the condemnation of men, but he is afraid when he thinks of his own unfaithfulness.

(j)

The words of an old preacher: "He who builds on the general esteem of the world, builds not on sand, but on worse—on the wind—and writes the title deeds of his hope upon the face of a river." Take the case, amongst others, of Milton's well-known language, "If what I have written be condemned on earth, then what I here repudiate is condemned in heaven; to Thy tribunal, O Jesus Christ, I appeal."

(a)   *Archdeacon Farrar*

HEART, THE HUMAN

Heaven's Sovereign saves all beings but Himself
That hideous sight—a naked human heart.

(b)   *Young*

HEART AND TROUBLE

"*Let not your heart be troubled: ye believe in God, believe also in Me*" (John xiv. 1)

1. The causes of trouble. (See chap. xiii.):

(i.) *Causes without*—The hostility of the Jews, both to Jesus and His party. The treachery of Judas—a strong conspiracy—all causes of outward "*fear.*"

(ii.) *Causes within*—Peter's denial—(which = *no Christ, therefore no Heaven*), made them question, "Who is safe?"

(iii.) *Their orphaned condition*—as "little children"—to whom Jesus had been both father and mother. Now to be left alone in a world that would call them "fools" for giving up their occupations and adhering to Jesus, whose pretentions would now come to naught—all doomed to collapse.

2. The Counsel: "Let not your hearts be troubled."

"*Hearts,*" not outer life—for "In the world ye shall have tribulation." Jesus did not, could not say, "Don't be troubled," for as men they must be,—human nature could not but be troubled under all the circumstances. It was a great tribulation, a great sifting time.

But what Jesus says is this: "Though your outer life be troubled, yet at heart be at rest"—as the surface of deep seas is lashed into waves, yet the depths are still; so let the innermost depths of your hearts be calm and untroubled. Let My peace (which I bequeath unto you) *rule* there. Let it *keep* your hearts and minds. "Peace, be still."

N.B.—In applying this counsel to the circumstances of life, notice that Jesus gave this counsel to the weakest among them, and to the backslider, Peter ("Little children").

3. The Means = Faith. "Ye believe in God, believe also in Me."

i.e.—As faithful Israelites, ye have hope in God. Have faith in Me too. Mine are not mere pretensions—all is working for good—though much will apparently tell against it.

Don't lose heart—don't give up your faith in Me. (Peter was about to deny Him.) Doubtless, too, as Jesus *presented* Peter by prayer, so He prayed for them all that *their faith should not fail.*

For if a man loses faith (trust), he will sink as Peter did.

The Promise = "Thou wilt keep him in perfect peace whose mind is stayed on Thee, because he trusteth in Thee."

4. The practical lessons are obvious:

(i.) Trouble will come, from various causes;

(ii.) Yet the innermost heart of every disciple may "be still." "The peace of God" may be ours: it is the special legacy of Jesus. "My peace I give unto you."

(iii.) How? By faith—"*only believe.*"

(c)

HEARTS

Sursum Corda, "Lift up your hearts," familiar words, which have formed a part of every known Liturgy from the earliest times.

(d)   *Westcott*

HEAVEN

Heaven is above all yet; there sits a Judge
That no king can corrupt.

(e)   *Shakspeare*

But Heaven hath a hand in these events,
To whose high will we bound our calm contents.

(f)   *Ibid*

HEAVEN, THE ASTRONOMICAL (John xiv. 2)

Seek not to persuade us that all those vast regions are destitute of inhabitants. Seek not to persuade the pilgrim, wandering through the darkness, that yon cottage, whence a hospitable light streams forth to greet him, is without an inhabitant. So on us there shimmers from above, light out of *many mansions.* It is a city of God that beams upon us, whose golden streets stretch forth into remotest infinitude. We see not its furthest battlements; its nearest ones *do* meet our gaze. And when we consider that light from there is thousands of years in reaching us, and that, starting from a remote point, it is millions of years on its way, we may call the city of the Living God an "Eternal City." Its radiance beams nightly upon our bodily vision if we do but step forth into the starry night. Its glory and higher nature have been made evident by science. But to the believer alone do the heavens disclose themselves as the fatherland and heritage of the blessed. Unto Christians it is said: "Ye are come unto the city of the Living God," and "In My Father's house are many mansions."

                             Lange

N.B.—According to the above theory, the earth must be considered as the *nursery* of heaven.

(g)

HEAVEN, DOCTRINE OF (John xiv.)

The doctrine of heaven was not intelligible to believing hearts until the disciples were forced to learn experimentally that the earthly world was no longer a resting-place for the Lord and for them; that they were cast out of the world.

(h)   *Ibid*

HEAVEN AND EARTH, THE THINGS IN (Eph. i. 3, 10)

Both the spheres of heaven and earth have become places of sin (ii. 2; vi. 12); indeed, heaven

(i)

was the first theatre of sin, when a part of the angels fell into sin from God (1 Tim. iii. 6 ; 1 John iii. 8 ; Jas. ii. 19 ; 2 Pet. ii. 4 ; Jude 6) ; thence it came to earth (2 Cor. xi. 3), in even greater dimensions (1 Cor. x. 20, 21). Thus the state originally appointed by God, and the development He wished to be without disburbance, ceased (Rom. viii. 18–24), so that a renewing of the heavens and of the earth was taken into view (2 Pet. iii. 13). The centre of this renewal is Christ and His redeeming work (Col. i. 20), which, however, has its development also, as before His appearance up to the "fulness of times," so afterwards up to His second Advent, when the "restitution of all things" (Acts iii. 21), the *palingenesia* (Matt. xix. 28), will be introduced. Cf. 2 Pet. iii. (10–13).

(a) *Lange*

HEAVEN is "the restoration of the harmony of the universe."

(b) *Harless*

HEAVEN, NAMES WRITTEN IN

"*Rejoice because your names are written in heaven*" (Luke x.)

It was better for them to have their names written in the Book of Life than in any earthly roll of honour, or to have them heralded in the daily papers. Some people thought they had no right to rejoice that their names were written in the Book of Life. But Christ said, "Rejoice that your names are written in the Book of Life"—not that they were going to be written in it. Some people now seemed to think that they were to obtain salvation, not by faith, but by doubts, because they had gone on doubting through life. But He exhorted them not to rest until they knew that not only their own names, but those of their friends and relatives, were written in heaven. They should come out from the world. One reason why blessings were kept from so many of them was because their names were not yet written in heaven. If they regarded iniquity in their hearts, the Lord would not hear them, much less answer them. What they wanted was to keep themselves unspotted from the world. Death was only a question of time. It might be a question of a few months, a few weeks, or a few hours only with some. In a few years all that vast assembly would be in another world. It was the privilege of every one of them to know that his Redeemer loved him. "Him that cometh unto me I will in no wise cast out." Christ told them not to lay up for themselves treasures on earth, but in heaven, for that where the treasure was, there the heart would be also. Ah ! how true that was. Talk to a man about his soul, and his eye would perhaps betray no spark of emotion ; but show him how he could make a few thousand pounds, and see how his countenance would light up. They had too many treasures on earth. When men went up in a balloon, they cast out sand that they carried for ballast, in order that it might rise the more speedily. Let some who were there cast out some of their ballast. Let those who had too much money give a thousand pounds to this charitable institution, or to that asylum, or to help on the Lord's work. What a man was really worth when he died, was the treasure he had laid up in heaven.

Therefore do not make idols of their earthly treasures, or of their children or relatives. What he wanted to get deep into their souls was that they were pilgrims and strangers here. Yet he saw men acting as if they expected to live for ever in this world. He saw men on the verge of the grave grasping at earthly treasures. Some people thought the Church on earth was a place to rest in, and that if they heard one or two sermons a week, sitting on cushioned seats, and keeping awake all the time, it was enough to constitute Christianity in the nineteenth century. But instead of being a place of rest, the Church on this earth was a place for work. They would rest by-and-by. They would have all eternity to rest in. Let them toil hard here, remembering that "there remaineth a rest for the people of God." Yes, blessed were they that died in the Lord, for they rested from their labours, and their works followed them. They would take their ease by-and-by. Some people looked for reward down here. That was not·what they should look for. Paul was scourged four times—and the Roman mode of scourging was no trifle. Did he abandon his work? No ; he pressed on the more strongly. He could fancy how Paul was beset with timid people, and how they advised him to give up the fight. They would point to the opposition he was rousing, the turmoil and clamour that were surging. They would advise him to go out of the way for a little, until the opposition cooled down. But Paul was not to be turned back. Scourging ! What did Paul care for stripes if the way to heaven lay through them. He was not going to be robbed of his crown, and his answer was—"I press toward the mark." Look at him in prison singing hymns, with his feet in the stocks. That is not what nineteenth century Christianity would have done. If one of them got but a stroke of the Roman scourge, what a whining and what a storm there would be, and how many books would be written about the poor martyr !

(c) *Moody*

HEAVEN AND HAPPINESS

I saw clearly that I should never be happy ; yea, that God Himself could not make me so, unless I could be in a capacity to "please and glorify Him for ever." Take away this, and admit me into all the fine heavens that can be conceived of by men or angels, and I should still be miserable for ever.

(d) *David Brainerd*

HEAVEN OUR HOME (John xiv.)

Three sayings, inculcating *faith in the heavenly home :*
1. The saying addressed to Thomas ;
2. The saying addressed to Philip ;
3. The saying addressed to Judas Lebbæus.

Or, our heavenly home is sure to us—
1. In spite *of the contradiction* of an outward reality full of distress and death.
2. In spite *of the want* of phenomena evident to the senses. (I know nothing against Christianity except its want of evidence.—*George Eliot*.)
3. In spite *of the denial of the hostile world*, which, even by its hate, as a germ and sign of hell, must testify of love, as the seed and sign of heaven.

(e) *Lange*

HEAVEN OUR HOME

And truly there is nothing which should keep your desires from heaven. No! not that delightful circle of home, where the parent's eye may glisten as he looks upon his child, and the child may smile with joy because it gazes on its father, or, more loving still, when it looks upon its mother; there is nought even there which can abstract the desires from heaven, and the only modification of that desire should be that children and parents, and brethren and sisters, should all meet in heaven. No—there is nothing; when here we meet round the Table of the Lord, and Christian comes by Christian to taste the " bread and wine, which show the Lord's death till He come"—till we all meet as by one electric impulse upon the spirit; till we all blend together in one, " being members of His body, and His flesh, and His bone," there is nothing here that can abstract the desires from heaven; the only modification of that desire must be that those that break the bread and drink the wine, may have fulfilled at last the glorious promise, " Verily, I will no more taste of the fruit of the vine, until that day when I drink it new with you in My Father's kingdom." Onward and onward still, from year to year, and from day to day, must the Christian spirit press in its desire towards heaven. It will be but a little longer, and then that desire shall be fulfilled, and mortality will be swallowed up in life. The portal *shall* be entered, and the spirit shall gaze round on the wonders of its completed salvation. What pearly gates are *these?* What jasper walls are *these?* What golden streets are *these?* What splendid palaces are *these?* What immortal trees are *these?* What crystal streams are *these?* What amaranthine bowers are *these?* These are the spirits of the just; and I see my parents, my partner, and my children, and they beckon to the entrance. *There* is Jesus, whom my soul hath loved, and now I behold Him with the glory of His Godhead. And *there* is the overshadowing splendour of everlasting happiness, which breathes blessings on all beneath it. And this, *this* is heaven! Earth, I have nothing to do with thee —with thy dull days and thy nights of darkness! I have left thee, with thy storms and tempests; I have left thee, with thy distressing temptations and thy polluting scenes; I have left thee, with thy sorrows, thy bereavements, thy diseases, and thy destinies. This, *this* is heaven! Am I come *there?* Then redemption and immortality are mine. In the body or out of the body, can we tell? Have not your desires expanded and extended till even now you listen to the song, and inhale the atmosphere of heaven? We must come back again to earth, till the will of God removes us; but descending to the world of mortality, and of sorrow, and of sin, in which we must breathe a little longer, we cannot but send our desires to Him who has gone before us, " When shall I come and appear before God?" "Oh that I had the wings of a dove! then would I flee away, and be at rest! "

(a) *James Parsons*

HEAVEN OF INNOCENCE LOST, THE; OR, THE ANGEL URIEL

The angel Uriel in the far-off ages and splendours of eternity, became afflicted in his soul with the idea of night. How the idea of night could enter the mind of an archangel, we know not, but it did! it haunted him with the thought that somewhere in the deeps and limbos of the universe, there was a realm of night, and, in quest of it, the foolish archangel started from heaven, from its golden pavements, and its clear skies, and its rivers and fountains of living water, bright ever in the splendour of a world lit up without a sun. He left all, he wended his way through the universe, groping amidst the glory of things for the realm of night; he wandered, and roamed, but he could not find it. Every kingdom had its gates of pearl, and its turrets of diamond; everywhere the doors of the worlds rolled on hinges of light; and the pathways of the planets in those old times were paved with sunshine; and Uriel, as he passed along, sped through files and ranks of radiant pinions; but within him, within him lay the dark idea. Yet the most ancient archangel with whom he conversed, could not direct him to the kingdom of night. It was an unhappiness in an archangel, and beyond our comprehension. At last he reached one of the firmaments in space, whence, looking down, he beheld the shape of a world with a shadow on it. And the heart of the archangel, knew its world; he hastened down, and entered the territories of the empire of night. It was but the realization of himself; but what was his horror and dismay, what spasms shot through his spirit, as the lonely archangel found himself in that lonely and awful world! he looked up, and saw only a canopy of blackness above him, save for one bright point in space; he knew that to be the infinite eye, then for the first time burning on him, for the angels who have the light of God within them, do not see the dreadful presence of His robe of lightning. In those worlds it holds that the angels who see most of God without, feel and see least of Him within. So all round the angel spread night, dark night, and the worst of all was that he had lost all clue to the pathway by which he came. How vainly Uriel mourned over the past; how vainly he attempted to return. He sighed for the light and sunshine; in vain; he cannot return; he belongs now to the empire of night! Did our reader ever meet the angel who has lost his way, on the darkness fringing our planet? We think we have sometimes seen him, trailing his dark garments, and heard him uttering his wail of despair over a lost heaven.

(b) *Paxton Hood, " Vocation of the Preacher.'*

HEAVEN, NAMES WRITTEN IN

They that are written in the eternal leaves of heaven, shall never be wrapt in the cloudy sheets of darkness. A man may have his name written in the Chronicles, yet lost; written in durable marble, yet perish; written on a monument equal to a Colossus, yet be ignominious; written on the hospital gates, yet go to hell; written on his own house, yet another come to possess it. All these are but writings on the dust or in the waters, where the characters perish as soon as they are made. They no more prove a man happy than the fool could prove Pontius Pilate a saint, because his name was written in the creed. But they that are *written in heaven* are sure to inherit it.

(c) *Puritan Adams*

HEAVEN A PLACE (John xiv. 2)

It is certain that there must be some place in the upper worlds where the beauties and wonders of God's works are illuminated to the highest transparency by His power and holy majesty; where the combination of lovely manifestations, as seen from radiant summits, the enraptured gaze into the quiet valleys of universal creation, and the streams of light which flow through them, must nerve the spirits of the blest in the mightiest manner, to cry out : " Holy ! Holy ! Holy !" And there is the holiest place in the great temple ! It is there, because there Divine manifestations fill all spirits with a feeling of His holiness. But still rather, because there He reveals Himself through the holiest one of all, even Jesus Himself.

(a)   *Lange*

Heaven, Preparation for

1. Jesus is now going thither; 2. The Jews, *as Jews*, can *never* come thither; 3. The disciples cannot *now* come thither. A decided indication of our need to ripen for heaven by a Christian life. [Heaven is to be gained by a ladder, not by a leap; step by step, not by a bound.]

(b)   *Ibid*

Heaven and Rest

Heaven is a place of perfect rest. Not that idleness prevails; on the contrary, we shall be more active than now. The citizens of that " better country " ceaselessly serve God, but never tire, never grow weary, never exhaust their energies. Employment is essential to the soul's contentment. Think you Moses is a " wandering Jew," Joshua a retired hero, David a harpless Quaker, Isaiah an idle dreamer, Paul a superannuated preacher, Peter a visionary monk, or John a sighing sentimentalist? Has Peter lost his intrepidity, Calvin his industry, and Wesley his zeal and devotion ? Nay, who can tell but that the capacity both to receive and communicate happiness, and also the opportunity, are correspondingly enlarged ? Furthermore, heaven is a place of perfect love. " Love is heaven, and heaven is love." No idol to tempt us to its shrine, nothing to divide our affections, leaving but half for God. It is likewise a perfect home. Not even the imagination can portray its peace and loveliness. Better still, it is the place where Jesus is, in whose " presence there is fulness of joy."

(c)   *American Methodist*

Heaven, Unseen

" Eye hath not seen it, my gentle boy;
Ear hath not heard its deep songs of joy;
Dreams cannot picture a world so fair,
Sorrow and death may not enter there;
Time doth not breathe on its fadeless bloom,
For beyond the clouds, and beyond the tomb,
    It is there, it is there, my child."

(d)   *Mrs. Hemans*

HEBREW AND GREEK AND LATIN, IT WAS WRITTEN IN

1. *Hebrew*, the language of religion, of the revelation concerning the *one true God*. 2. *Greek*, the language of literature, of arts and culture, the best medium in which to transmit the literature of the New Testament, as Hebrew was for that of the old. It might be designated as the *human* language. 3. *Latin*, the language of the conquerors and

masters of the world—also of the Roman Empire, as that kingdom of worldly aggrandizement and power, falsehood and wrong, in opposition to the kingdom of God destined to uproot and replace it

The Roman soldiers stationed throughout Europe became useful factors in the spread of the gospel.

N.B.—The synoptic Gospels of
(i.) *Matthew* = Hebrew in thought and diction, written to convince Jews;
(ii.) *Mark* = Latin in thought, and written for the Roman mind;
(iii.) *Luke* = Greek in thought, etc., written for Gentiles.

(e)

" Hebrew of the Hebrews, A " (Phil. iii. 5)

Paul came of a good family. . . . . It is well to come of a good stock. There is a good deal in blood as well as in breeding. Training and culture are of vast advantage ; but much depends on the quality of the raw material. There are different stocks within the great human family circle to which all the different nationalities belong ; and you know very well that some of them are of a very inferior type as compared with others. You would rather be Normans or Anglo-Saxons than Bosjesmen or Australians. And not only so, but it is well to be born of good immediate ancestors—ancestors distinguished for their virtue, purity, and godliness. There is a great difference between the moral condition in which human beings come into the world. " The seed of the adulterer and the whore "—the children of the polluted and the base —the miserable offspring of ignorance, brutality, vice, and crime—come into the world with a deteriorated nature, with tendencies to what is bad, far more inherently powerful than theirs who are born of God-fearing parents, of holy and virtuous men and women, who, because of their pure and unspotted lives, can give a good physical constitution to their children, and good moral instincts along with it.

(f)   *T. Binney*

Hebrews, Authorship of the Epistle to the

The whole tendency of his arguments, the Pauline character of many of his thoughts and expressions, even the fundamental theme of his Epistle, that Judaism *as such*—Judaism in all its distinctive worship and legislation—was abrogated, are sufficient to show that he would have held with St. Paul that " all are not Israel who are of Israel," and that " they who are of the faith are blessed with the faithful Abraham." But while he undoubtedly held these truths—for otherwise he could not have been a Christian at all, and still less a Pauline Christian—his mind is not so full of them as was the mind of St. Paul. It is inconceivable that St. Paul, who regarded it as his own special Gospel to proclaim to the "Gentiles" the unsearchable riches of Christ (Eph. iii. 4–8) should have written a long epistle in which the Gentiles do not once seem to cross the horizon of his thoughts ; and this would least of all have been possible in a letter addressed "to the Hebrews." The Jews regarded St. Paul with a fury of hatred and suspicion which we find faintly reflected in his Epistles and in the Acts (Acts xxi. 21 ; 1 Thess. ii. 15 ; 2 Cor. xi. 24 ; Phil. iii. 2). Even the Jewish

(g)

Christians looked on the most characteristic part of his teaching with a jealousy and alarm which found frequent expression both in words and deeds. It would have been something like unfaithfulness in St. Paul, it would have been an unworthy suppression of his intensest convictions, to write to any exclusively " Hebrew " community without so much as distantly alluding to that phase of the Gospel which it had been his special mission to set forth. The case with the writer of this Epistle is very different. He was not only a Jewish Christian, but a Jewish Christian of the Alexandrian School. We shall again and again have occasion to see that he had been deeply influenced by the thoughts of Philo. Now Philo, liberal as were his philosophical views, was a thoroughly faithful Jew. He never for a moment forgot his nationality. He is so completely entangled in Jewish particularism that he shows no capacity for understanding the universal prophecies of the Old Testament. His *Logos*, or Word, so far as he assumes any personal distinctness, is essentially and pre-eminently a Jewish deliverer. Judaism formed for Philo the nearer horizon beyond which he hardly cared to look. Similarly in this Epistle the writer is so exclusively occupied by the relations of Judaism to Christianity, that he does not even glance aside to examine any other point of difference between the New Covenant and the Old. What he sees in Christianity is simply a perfected Judaism. Mankind is to him the ideal Hebrew. Even when he speaks of the Incarnation, he speaks of it as a " taking hold," not " of humanity," but " of the seed of Abraham " (ii. 16).

(a)

In the Epistles to the Galatians and the Romans, St. Paul, with the sledge-hammer force of his direct and impassioned dialectics, had shattered all possibility of trusting in legal prescriptions, and demonstrated that the Law was no longer obligatory upon Gentiles. He had shown that the distinction between clean and unclean meats was to the enlightened conscience a matter of indifference that circumcision was now nothing better than a physical mutilation ; that the Levitic system was composed of " weak and beggarly elements ; " that ceremonialism was a yoke with which the free converted Gentile had nothing to do ; that we are saved by faith and not by works ; that the Law was a dispensation of wrath and menace, introduced " for the sake of transgressions " (Gal. iii. 19 ; Rom. v. 20) ; that so far from being (as all the Rabbis asserted) the one thing on account of which the universe had been created, the Mosaic Code only possessed a transitory, subordinate, and intermediate character, coming in (as it were in a secondary way) between the promise to Abraham and the fulfilment of that promise in the Gospel of Christ. To him, therefore, the whole treatment of the question was necessarily and essentially polemical ; and in the course of these polemics he had again and again used expressions which, however unavoidable and salutary, could not fail to be otherwise than deeply wounding to the inflamed susceptibilities of the Jews at that epoch.

(b)

Now, the arguments of the Epistle to the Hebrews turn on another set of considerations. They were urged from a different point of view.

They do not lead the writer, except in the most incidental and the least wounding manner, to use expressions which would have shocked the prejudices of his unconverted countrymen. He does not touch on the once-burning question of circumcision. It is only towards the close of his Epistle (xiii. 9) that he has occasion to allude, even incidentally, to the distinction of meats. His subject does not require him to enter upon the controversy as to the degree to which Gentile proselytes were obliged to observe the Mosaic Law. He is nowhere compelled to break down the bristling hedge of Jewish exclusiveness. If he proves the boundless superiority of the New Covenant, he does not do this at the expense of the majesty of the Old. To him the richer privileges of Christianity are the developed germ of the Mosaic dispensation, and he only contemplates them in their relation to the Jews.

(c) *Archdeacon Farrar*

HELL

I found the original of my hell in the world which we inhabit.

(d) *Dante*

HELL

Cardinal Bellarmine, a Jesuit, seems to have the science of a surveyor, among all the secret tracks and the formidable divisions of the " bottomless pit." He informs us that there are beneath the earth four different places, or a profound place divided into four parts. The deepest of these is *hell* : it contains all the souls of the damned, where will be also their bodies after the resurrection, and likewise all the demons. The place nearest hell is *Purgatory*, where souls are purged, or rather where they appease the anger of God by their sufferings. He says that the same fires and the same torments are alike in both places, the only difference between *hell* and *Purgatory* consisting in their duration. Next to *Purgatory* is the *limbo* of those *infants* who die without having received the sacrament ; and the fourth place is the *limbo* of the *Fathers* ; *i.e.*, of those just men who died before the death of Christ. But since the days of the Redeemer, this last division is empty, like an apartment to be let.

(e) *Disraeli : Cur. of Lit*

HELL

That word hell, which is used so seldom in the sacred pages, which in a faithful translation would not once occur in the writings of Paul and Peter and John, which we meet only in four or five discourses of Jesus, and which all persons acquainted with Jewish geography know to be a metaphor, a figure of speech, and not a literal expression,—this word, by a perverse and exaggerated use, has done unspeakable injury to Christianity.

(f) *Channing*

HELL

Hell is full of good meanings and wishings.

(g) *Herbert*

HELL

Hell is paved with good intentions.

(a)　　　　　　　　　　　*Boswell's Johnson*

HELL, ROAD TO

The saddest road to hell is that which is under the pulpit, past the Bible, and through the midst of warnings and invitations.

(b)　　　　　　　　　　　　　　*Ryle*

HELL CLUB, THE VICTIM OF THE

Towards the close of the last century there flourished in Glasgow a club of young men, which, from the extreme profligacy of its members and the licentiousness of their orgies, was commonly called the "Hell Club." In addition to their weekly meetings, they held annual saturnalia, in which they strove to excel each other in drunkenness and blasphemy. Conspicuous amongst their number was Mr. Archibald B——, a young man of handsome person, of brilliant talents, and easy fortune.

After the excitement of one of these horrible festivities, this young man dreamed a dream. Mounted on his favourite horse, he was proceeding, he thought, towards his house (then a country seat embowered in trees, and situated upon a hill now built over and forming part of the city), when a stranger seized his horse's rein, saying, "You must go with me!" "And who are you?" exclaimed the young man with a volley of oaths, whilst he struggled to release himself. "That you will see by-and-by," returned the other, in a tone which excited the youth to terror. He struck his spurs into the horse; but however fast the animal flew, the stranger was still beside him, till at length, in his desperate endeavour to escape, the rider was thrown. Instead of being dashed to the earth, as he expected, he found himself falling—falling—falling still, as if sinking into the bowels of the earth, till at length, a period being put to this mysterious descent, he found breath to inquire of his companion, "Where am I? Whither are you taking me?" "To HELL!" replied the stranger; and immediately interminable echoes repeated the fearful sound, "To HELL!—To HELL!—To HELL!" At length a light appeared, which soon increased to a blaze; but instead of the cries, groans, and lamentings the terrified traveller expected, his ear was saluted by sounds of music, mirth, and jollity. He found himself at the entrance of a superb building, in which the amusements and pursuits of earth were carried on with a vehemence that excited his amazement; and he soon perceived that he was amongst acquaintances whom he knew to be dead, each of whom was pursuing the object that had formerly engrossed him. He ventured to address his former friend, Mrs. D., whom he saw sitting, as had been her wont on earth, absorbed at loo, requested her to rest from the game, and introduce him to the pleasures of the place. But with a cry of agony, she answered that there was no rest in hell; that they must ever toil on at those very pleasures; and innumerable voices echoed, "THERE IS NO REST IN HELL!" Throwing open their vests, each disclosed in his bosom an ever-burning flame. These, they said, were the pleasures of hell; their choice on earth was now their inevitable doom.

The young man entreated his conductor to restore him to earth, to which he consented, adding as he quitted him, "*Remember, in a year and a day we meet again!*"

The dreamer awoke, feverish and ill, and, whether from the effects of his dream or of his previous orgies, was obliged to keep his bed for several days, during which time he formed many serious resolutions to abandon the club and think on better things. No sooner was he well, however, than his old companions surrounded him, and having wrung from him a confession of the cause of his defection, ridiculed it, and made him ashamed of his good purposes. He resumed his former course of life. The day of the annual saturnalia again came round. He was at the table, glass in hand, when the president, rising to make the accustomed speech, began with saying, "Gentlemen, this being leap year, it is *a year and a day* since our last anniversary." The words fell upon the young man's ear like a knell; but ashamed to expose his weakness to the jeers of his companions, he sat out the feast, plying himself with wine to drown his intrusive thoughts; till, in the gloom of a winter's morning, he mounted his horse to ride home. Some hours afterwards the horse was found grazing by the road-side, and his master's corpse lying a few yards off.

This remarkable story is no fiction, it is a well-attested fact. An account of it was published at the time, and the whole impression was bought up by the family, with the exception of two or three copies which were preserved. The moral is solemn, and not inconsistent with the teaching of Scripture.

(c)　　　　　　　　　　　　　　*J. A. M*

HELL, THE GATES OF (Matt. xvi. 18)

The Gambling Hell. One of the costliest and most brilliant gambling-houses in the city of New York. As we came up in front, all seemed dark. The blinds were down, the door was guarded; but after a whispering of the officer with the guard at the door, we were admitted into the hall, and thence into the parlours, around one table finding eight or ten men in mid-life, well dressed—all going on in silence, save the noise of the rattling "chips" on the gaming-table in one parlour, and the revolving ball of the roulette-table in the other parlour. Some of these men, we were told, had served terms in prison; some were shipwrecked bankers and brokers and money-dealers, and some were going their first rounds of vice—but all intent upon the table, as large or small fortunes moved up and down before them. Oh! there was something awfully solemn in the silence—the intense gaze, the suppressed emotion of the players. No one looked up. They all had money in the rapids, and I have no doubt some saw, as they sat there, horses and carriages, and houses and lands, and home and family rushing down into the vortex. A man's life would not have been worth a farthing in that presence, had he not been accompanied by the police, if he had been supposed to be on a Christian errand of observation. Some of these men went in by private key, some went in by careful introduction, some were taken in by the patrons of the establishment. The officer of the law told me: "None get in here except by police mandate, or by some letter of a patron." While we were there,

(d)

a young man came in, put his money down on the roulette-table, and lost; put more money down on the roulette-table, and lost; put more money down on the roulette-table, and lost; then feeling in his pockets for more money, and finding none, in serene silence he turned his back upon the scene and passed out. All the literature about the costly magnificence of such places is untrue. Men kept their hats on and smoked, and there was nothing in the upholstery or the furniture to forbid it. While we stood there, men lost their property and lost their souls. Oh! merciless place. Not once in all the history of that gaming-house has there been one word of sympathy uttered for the losers at the game. Sir Horace Walpole said that a man dropped dead in front of one of the club-houses of London. His body was carried into the club-house, and the members of the club began immediately to bet as to whether he were dead or alive; and when it was proposed to test the matter by bleeding him, it was only hindered by the suggestion that it would be unfair to some of the players! In these gaming-houses of our cities, men have their property wrung away from them, and then they go out, some of them to drown their grief in strong drink, some to ply the counterfeiter's pen and so restore their fortunes, some to resort to the suicide's revolver, but all going down; and that work proceeds day by day, and night by night, until it is estimated that every day in Christendom 80,000,000 dollars pass from hand to hand through gambling practices, and every year in Christendom 123,100,000,000 dollars change hands in that way.

Talmage

On Gambling-Tables. I am not fond of denouncing my fellow-sinners, but,—gambling being a vice I have no mind to,—it stirs my disgust even more than my pity. The sight of the dull faces bending round the gaming-tables; the raking up of the money, and the flinging of the coins towards the winners by the hard-faced croupiers; the hateful, hideous women staring at the board like stupid monomaniacs—all this seems to me the most abject presentation of mortals grasping after something called a good, that can be seen on the face of this little earth. Burglary is heroic compared with it. I get some satisfaction in looking on, from the sense that the thing is going to be put down. Hell is the only right name for such places.

(*b*) *George Eliot*

HELL, THE GATES OF

1. Impure Literature. Anthony Comstock seized twenty tons of bad books, plates, and letter-press; and when our Professor Cochran, of the Polytechnic Institute, poured the destructive acid on those plates, they smoked in the righteous annihilation. And yet a great deal of the bad literature of the day escapes the law. It is strewn in your parlours; it is in your libraries. Some of your children read it at night after they have retired, the gas-burner swung as near as possible to their pillow. Much of this literature is under the title of scientific information. A book-agent with one of these infernal books, glossed over with scientific nomenclature, went into a hotel and sold in one day a hundred copies, and sold them all to women! It is appalling that men

and women, who can get through their family physician all the useful information they may need, and without any contamination, should wade chin deep through such accursed literature under the plea of getting useful knowledge; and that printing-presses, hoping to be called decent, should lend themselves to this infamy. Fathers and mothers, be not deceived by the title, "medical works." Nine-tenths of those books come hot from the lost world, though they may have on them the names of the publishing-houses of New York and Philadelphia. Then there is all the novelette literature of the day flung over the land by the million. As there are good novels that are long, so I suppose there may be good novels that are short; and so there may be a good novelette, but it is the exception. No one—mark this—no one systematically reads the average novelette of this day and keeps either integrity or virtue. The most of these novelettes are written by broken-down literary men for small compensation, on the principle that, having failed in literature elevated and pure, they hope to succeed in the tainted and the nasty. Oh! this is a wide gate of hell. Every panel is made out of a bad book or newspaper. Every hinge is the interjoined type of a corrupt printing-press. Every bolt or lock of that gate is made out of the plate of an unclean pictorial. In other words, there are a million men and women in the United States to-day reading themselves into hell! When, in your own beautiful city, a prosperous family fell into ruins through the misdeeds of one of its members, the amazed mother said to the officer of the law: "Why, I never supposed there was anything wrong. I never thought there could be anything wrong." Then she sat weeping in silence for some time, and said: "Oh! I have got it now! I know, I know! I found in her bureau, after she went away, a bad book. That's what slew her." These leprous booksellers have gathered up the catalogues of all the male and female seminaries in the United States, catalogues containing the names and the residences of all the students, and circulars of death are sent to every one, without any exception. Can you imagine anything more deathful? There is not a young person, male or female, or an old person, who has not had offered to him or her a bad book or a bad picture. Scour your house to find out whether there are any of these adders coiled on your parlour centre-table, or coiled amid the toilet-set on the dressing-case. I adjure you, before the sun goes down, to explore your family libraries with inexorable scrutiny. Remember that one bad book or bad picture may do evil work for eternity. I want to arouse all your suspicions about novelettes. I want to put you on the watch against everything that may seem like surreptitious correspondence through the post-office. I want you to understand that impure literature is one of the broadest, highest, mightiest gates of hell.

(*c*)

2. The Dissolute Dance. Whatever you may think about the parlour dance, or the methodic motion of the body to sounds of music in the family or the social circle, I am not now discussing that question. I want you to unite with me in recognising the fact that there is a dissolute dance. You know of what I speak. It is seen, not only in the low haunts of death, but in elegant mansions. It is the first step to eternal ruin for

(*d*)

a great multitude of both sexes. You know, my friends, what postures, and attitudes, and figures, are suggested of the devil. They who glide into the dissolute dance glide over an inclined plane, and the dance is swifter and swifter, wilder and wilder, until, with the speed of lightning, they whirl off the edges of a decent life into a fiery future. This gate of hell swings across the Axminster of many a fine parlour, and across the ball-room of the summer watering-place. You have no right, my brother, my sister—you have no right to take an attitude to the sound of music which would be unbecoming in the absence of music. No grand piano of city parlour, or fiddle of mountain picnic, can consecrate that which God hath cursed.

(a)

3. **Indiscreet Apparel.** The attire of woman for the last four or five years has been beautiful and graceful beyond anything I have known; but there are those who will always carry that which is right into the extraordinary and indiscreet. I am told that there is a fashion about to come in upon us that is shocking to all righteousness. I charge Christian women, neither by style of dress nor adjustment of apparel, to become administrative of evil. Perhaps none else will dare to tell you, so I will tell you, that there are multitudes of men who owe their eternal damnation to the boldness of womanly attire. Show me the fashion-plates of any age between this and the time of Louis XVI. of France, and Henry VIII. of England, and I will tell you the type of morals or immorals of that age or that year. No exception to it. Modest apparel means a righteous people; immodest apparel always means a contaminated and depraved society.

(b)

4. **Alcoholic Beverage.** All the scenes of wickedness were under the enchantment of strong drink. That was what the waitresses carried on the platter. That was what glowed on the table. That was what shone in illuminated gardens. That was what flushed the cheeks of the patrons who came in. That was what staggered the step of the patrons as they went out. Oh! the wine-cup is the patron of impurity. The officers of the law told us that night, that nearly all the men who go into the shambles of death go in intoxicated; the mental and the spiritual abolished that the brute may triumph. Tell me that a young man drinks, and I know the whole story. If he become a captive of the wine-cup, he will become a captive of all other vices; only give him time. No one ever knows drunkenness alone. That is a carrion-crow that goes in a flock, and when you see that beak ahead, you may know the other beaks are coming. In other words, the wine-cup unbalances and dethrones one's better judgment, and leaves one the prey of all evil appetites that may choose to alight upon his soul. There is not a place of any kind of sin in the United States to-day that does not find its chief abettor in the chalice of inebriety. There is either a drinking-bar before, or one behind, or one above, or one underneath. The officers of the law said to me that night, "These people escape legal penalty because they are all licensed to sell liquor." Then I said within myself, "The courts that license the sale of strong drink, license gambling-houses, license libertinism, license disease, license death, license all suffer-

ings, all crimes, all despoliations, all disasters, all murders, all woe." It is the courts and the Legislature that are swinging wide open this grinding, creaky, stupendous gate of hell.

(c)

5. **The Way of Escape.** Very few escape. Of the thousand that go in, nine hundred and ninety-nine perish. Suppose one of these wanderers should knock at your door—would you admit her? Suppose you knew where she came from—would you ask her to sit down at your dining-table? Would you ask her to become the governess of your children? Would you introduce her among your acquaintanceships? Would you take the responsibility of pulling at the outside of the gate of hell while she pushed at the inside of that gate trying to get out? You would not—not one of a thousand of you would dare to do it. You write beautiful poetry over her sorrows, and weep over her misfortunes, but give her practical help you never will. There is not one person out of a thousand that will—there is not one out of five thousand that has—come so near the heart of the Lord Jesus Christ as to dare to help one of these fallen souls. But you say, "Are there no ways by which the wanderer may escape?" Oh, yes; three or four. The one way is the sewing-girl's garret—dingy, cold, hunger-blasted. But you say, "Is there no other way for her to escape?" Oh, yes. Another way is the street that leads to the East River, at midnight, the end of the city dock, the moon shining down on the water making it look so smooth she wonders if it is deep enough. It is. No boatman near enough to hear the plunge. No watchman near enough to pick her out before she sinks the third time. No other way? Yes. By the curve of the Hudson River Railroad, at the point where the engineer of the lightning express train cannot see a hundred yards ahead to the form that lies across the track. He may whistle "down brakes," but not soon enough to disappoint the one who seeks her death. But you say, "Isn't God good, and won't He forgive?" Yes; but man will not, woman will not, society will not. The Church of God says it will, but it will not. Our work, then, must be prevention rather than cure. Standing here telling this story, it is not so much in the hope that I will persuade one who has dashed down a thousand feet over the rocks to crawl up again into life and light, but it is to alarm those who are coming too near the edges. Listen to the lamentation that rings up from those far depths!

"Once I was pure as the snow, but I fell,
Fell like a sunflake, from heaven to hell;
Fell to be trampled on as filth of the street,
Fell to be scoffed at, spit on, and beat.
Pleading, cursing, begging to die,
Selling my soul to whoever would buy;
Dealing in shame for a morsel of bread,
Hating the living, and fearing the dead."

(d)   *Talmage*

HELL, THE HOLY SPIRIT'S TEACHING ON

The Holy Ghost sets before us that, in consequence of Christ's reconciliation, there is no longer any human hell, but only His heaven for those who believe in Him unto righteousness, or Satan's hell for all who continue of the world.

(e)   *Stier*

HELL AND MEMORY

The " way of salvation," " the very name of the Saviour," all that is holy, is forgotten:

" I have brought nothing hither but myself. And what comprises this self but a burning remorse which can never be stilled ; a greed of desire which can never be satisfied ; an unquenchable longing for things left behind, innumerable recollections of sins great and small, causing insufferable anguish, all being equally bitter, equally fraught with vainest regret ! "

(a)   " Letters from Hell "

HELP

'Tis not enough to help the feeble up,
But to support him after.

(b)   Shakspeare

HEROD AND PETER (Acts xii. 4)

Herod intended to slay Peter ; but it was the Lord's will to preserve Peter and slay Herod.

(c)   Ap. Past

HEROES, A CONTRAST

If we consider the military profession, we find that the physician is the antipode of the soldier. He lives to kill; you live to save. His the work of destruction ; yours that of preservation. You beget the smiles that have no cruelty ; yours are the victories which cause no tears. The warrior who is most successful in slaying his fellows has hitherto been the type of man most honoured. Walk round Westminster Abbey, and see how its aisles are lined with the monuments of those who were distinguished for nothing but that they directed large masses of men in the work of slaughter. It is a sign of a barbarous age, when the soldier is the popular hero. You all read the other week of a man who liked the sport of man-killing so well that he could not rest at home in peace, but, while his regiment remained in Whitehall, went to Egypt in pursuit of his favourite sport. At the battles of Tamanieb and El Teb he shot down Arabs as one would partridges. In time came the turn of the brave savages, and they killed him. The cable informed us that he died like a " true British bulldog." He did, indeed ! Having lived a bulldog's life, it was fitting that he should die the death of a dog. I beg pardon of the dog ! I mention this incident not to assail the dead— poor wretch ! we can only pity him—but to show how utterly demoralized is the public opinion that has hardly anything but laudation for such a character ! Depend upon it, gentlemen, this will soon change. The hero of barbarism is the man who braves danger to destroy ; the hero of civilization is he who dares danger to save. And what profession furnishes these heroes? Your own, gentlemen, your own. Every day adds to the glorious list. A young student in London recently gave his own life that his patient should not perish. Let his name, Rabbeth, be ever honoured in your memories. " Greater love hath no man than this, that a man lay down his life for his friends," says the highest authority ; but what is that love which does this for the stranger? The finest natures of the world were thrilled by the deed, and the best of his countrymen are engaged to-day in erecting a monument to his memory. Three young physicians upon this side of the Atlantic,—Dr. Atkinson, of Brooklyn ; Dr. Frick, of Baltimore ; and Dr. Mott, of New York,—recently passed from this life into the abode of heroes, their shades heralded by the glory of the same great deed of self-sacrifice. If I dared venture upon so sacred a theme, I should say to all men, " Consider the reception likely to be accorded to such heroes as these, and to those misnamed heroes who pass to the vast unknown, their hands red with the blood of their fellows." I know not what the Prince of Peace in His mercy would say to human butchers ; but I think I know what He would say to those who have died for others. But this is not the question that immediately concerns us. We have to consider what we can do here in this life to lead men to a right understanding of these matters ; to cause them to substitute for the delusive word " war," except when waged in self-defence, the proper term, " murder." And your profession, gentlemen, is fast elevating public sentiment to this standard, and creating a just conception of true heroism by holding up to its admiring gaze a long succession of true heroes who brave dangers far greater than those of the battlefield, who volunteer to fight epidemics much deadlier than opposing legions, and who stand prepared in great emergencies to follow the glorious path trodden by Atkinson, Frick, Mott, and Rabbeth, and lay down their lives at the call of professional duty—always to save, never to destroy.

Dr. Andrew Carnegie, Address to Medical Students,
(d)   *Bellevue Hospital, New York*

HID

Instead of complaining that God is hidden, we ought to give Him thanks for being so far revealed as He is ; and to give Him thanks, too, that He is hidden from the wise and proud, who are unworthy to know so holy a God.

(e)   Blaise Pascal

God being hid, every religion which does not teach that God is hid, must be false ; and every religion which does not show the reason why this is so, must be useless.

(f)   Ibid

" HID FROM THINE EYES " (Luke xix. 42)

Jesus Christ came that those who saw not might see, and that those who saw might be made blind. He came to heal the sick, and to leave the whole to die ; to call sinners to repentance, and to leave those in their sins who trusted in themselves that they were righteous ; to fill the hungry, and to leave the rich empty.

(g)   Ibid

HID, MY WAY IS, FROM THE LORD (Isa. xl. 27)

" The flower which follows the sun does so even in cloudy days : when it doth not shine forth, yet it follows the hidden course and motion of it. So the soul that moves after God keeps that course when He hides His face ; is content, yea, is glad at His will in all estates, or conditions, or events."

(h)   Leighton

HIDDEN LIFE, THE

" *Your life is hid with Christ in God* " (Col. iii. 3)

And therefore you cannot be robbed of it. Our Lord handleth us as fathers do their young children : they lay up jewels in a place above the reach of the short arm of children, else children would put up their hands and take them down, and lose them soon. So hath our Lord done with our spiritual life. Jesus Christ is the high coffer in the which our Lord hath hid our life. We children are not able to reach up our arms so high as to take down that life and lose it : it is in our Christ's hand. Oh, long, long may Jesus be Lord-keeper of our life, and happy are they who can, with the Apostle, lay their soul in the hand of Jesus, for He is able to keep that which is committed to Him against that day (2 Tim. i. 12).

(a) *Samuel Rutherford*

HIDDEN LIFE, THE

" Ye are Christ's, and Christ is God's." Not one link of this chain can be broken without depriving God of His Son. " Your life is hid with Christ in God." This life is hid, not as it were in a chest, alone, but in the strong tower, where is also found the life of Christ in God. Hence, before this life can be endangered, the tower must be destroyed, and the life of Christ, and the life of God the Father, must be taken away.

(b) *Christmas Evans*

" *Your life is hid with Christ in God* " (Col. iii. 3)

If you ask richer consolation, you ask more than God can give.

(c) *Dean Law*

HIDING PLACE

" *A man = a hiding place* " (Isa. xxxii. 2)

" A man = Christ ; Hiding place = shelter ; wind = great troubles.
A man takes shelter under a rock during a storm : the rock bears the brunt of the tempest.
Man as a sinner is exposed to the wrath of God. Unless he finds shelter, that wrath will overwhelm him.
But Christ has put Himself between us and that. He has borne the brunt of the storm. We escape the consequences of our sin, because He is our *Hiding place.*

(d) *Gordon Calthrop,* 1862

HIERARCHY

A hierarchy is an apostasy from the mind and spirit of the Apostles.

(e) *Lange*

"HIM," "HIS," "HIS" (Phil. iii. 10)

1. *That I may know* HIM :
By faith : for this everything else is thrown overboard. (See context.)

2. *And the power of* HIS *resurrection :*
In raising me—
(i.) Above worldliness ;
(ii.) Above theological strife.
3. *And the fellowship of* HIS *sufferings :*
In being crucified with Christ.
4. *Being conformed to* HIS *death .*
The martyr-death of the Apostle was already *begun.*
The one theme was Christ, " Him first, Him last, Him midst." Not simply His doctrine, but Himself.

(f)

HISTORY

I think that history is philosophy teaching by examples.

(g) *Bolingbroke*

HOBBES

Hobbes's politics are fitted only to promote tyranny, and his ethics to encourage licentiousness.

(h) *Hume*

HOBBISM

Thomas Hobbes had, in language more precise and luminous than had ever been employed by any other metaphysical writer, maintained that the will of the prince was the standard of right and wrong, and that every subject ought to be ready to embrace Popery, Mahomedanism, or Paganism, at the royal command. Thousands who were incompetent to appreciate what was really valuable in his metaphysical speculations, eagerly welcomed a theory which, while it exalted the kingly office, relaxed the obligations of morality and degraded religion into a mere affair of state. Hobbism soon became almost an essential part of the character of a fine gentleman.

(i) *Macaulay*

HOLINESS

I have read that when Zeuxis, the famous painter, had drawn his masterpiece, the picture of Helena, Nicostratus, the Athenian painter, beholding it, stood amazed at its exquisiteness. There stands by a rich ignorant wretch, who would needs know what Nicostratus discovered in it worthy of so much wonder. " Oh, friend," saith he, " hadst thou my eyes, thou wouldst not ask such a question, but rather admire it as I do."

(j) *Schönberg-Cotta Series*

That book of universal biography which is daily being written in heaven is, we may be sure, no philosophical abstraction of history, no mere record of successive phases of opinion and principle, but a collection of lives of the saints.

(k) *Ibid*

Endeavour rather to be, than to be thought holy ; for what profits it thee to be thought to be what thou art not ? And that man doubles his guilt who is not so holy as the world thinks him, and counterfeits that holiness which he hath not.

(l) *Hieron*

HOLINESS

We could not subsist upon uncertainty in the moral world, any more than we could upon a planet where gravitation was intermittent.

(a) *Bain*

HOLINESS

The miracle of miracles is this—"A new heart will I give you, and a new spirit will I put within you." To put the law in the inward parts, and to write it on the heart, is more than to fill the firmament with stars.

(b) *Joseph Parker*

HOLINESS, THE SOUL'S DESIRE

O Lord, I bear an aching heart;
Ease me of sin, whate'er the smart:
Within, without, I would be pure;
Lord, hear my cry! Lord, work my cure
I know not all I ask in this,
But give, oh, give me Holiness.

Wild is the tumult in my breast:
Oh! how I long for Thy deep rest!
Behind thick clouds is hid Thy face:
Thyself reveal, and give me peace.
I know not all I need to this,
But give, oh, give me Holiness.

O Lord! to dust my faint soul cleaves:
Rich is Thy sowing, few my sheaves.
I own Thy bounteous gifts, but mourn
My scanty and perverse return.
I know not all I say in this,
But give, oh, give me Holiness.

O Lord! accept my stammering prayer
Work in me, by what means soe'er,
The change I need; to sin I'd die,
That I may live with Thee on high.
I know not all I beg in this,
But give, oh, give me Holiness.

Break every earthly tie that binds;
Disperse each wildering mist that blinds;
Search me, and try, and clean remove
Whatever shares with Thee my love.
I know not all I ask in this,
But give, oh, give me Holiness.

O Lord! I bear a weary heart,
All pierced with sin's empoisoned dart;
Thou Good Physician, work my cure,
Me purify as Thou art pure.
I know not all I ask in this,
But give, oh, give me Holiness.

(c)

HOLINESS

"*Give thanks at the remembrance of His holiness*" (Ps. xxx. 4)

Look at the perfection of the heavens, at the order of the universe, and see the sun, moon, and stars which God hath ordained, together with the numberless orbs in space unknown to us—system within system, and yet no flaw in the work, no accident in the machinery; yet think that if there were in God, who holds them in His hand, the

least moral imperfection, if He could but once pass by or connive at sin, and let it pass unnoticed and unpunished, then this perfection would cease to be depended upon—at any moment discord might appear amongst the works of God.

(d)

"HOLY, HOLY, HOLY"

"*And one cried unto another, and said, Holy, holy, holy, is the Lord of hosts; the whole earth is full of His glory*" (Isa. vi. 3)

The Jewish Church is often thought to have worshipped God only in His lonely, distant majesty. The word "Holy," by which He is so constantly described, means "Separate"; and God was to them the Separate One, far removed in His purity from a sinful world. But there is another side to this teaching. Jehovah was separate or withdrawn from the world—not as a material world, but as a sinful world. Where sin is not, there He abides; and His people are a kingdom of saints—a holy nation. They go with Him, so to speak, into the place into which He is withdrawn, that He may abide among them. And, further, the psalmists and prophets never lost sight of the universal hope; they looked forward to the Gospel times, when the Lord of Israel should sustain the same relation to the whole world which He sustained to His chosen people in their time. Thus it is that Isaiah in our text represents the seraphim as saying of the Holy, or Separate, God, that the whole earth is full of His glory.

(e) *W. H. Freemantle*

HOLY COMMUNION

"In 1230, Juliana, a nun of Liege, while looking at the full moon, saw a gap in its orb; and, by a peculiar revelation from Heaven, learned that the moon represented the Christian Church, and the gap the want of a certain festival—that of the adoration of the body of Christ in the consecrated host—which she was to begin to celebrate and announce to the world" (*Hode's Church Dictionary*). Such is said to be the origin of the festival of *Corpus Christi*, in which the *sacramentum*—the consecrated element of bread—is "carried about" in procession, as though it were the *res sacramenti* —the Body and Blood of Christ, or, rather, Christ Himself in His full Divinity and Humanity.

(f) *Meyrick*

HOLY GHOST, GIFT OF THE (Acts x. 44)

The gift of the Holy Ghost is, according to the Acts of the Apostles, the highest blessing that can be obtained in the kingdom of Christ.

(g) *Lange*

HOLY GHOST, GUIDANCE OF THE

Experience proves that, without the energy of the Holy Spirit, men will hear the Gospel all their lives, and yet drop from under the pulpit into perdition.

(h) *C. Clayton*

HOLY GHOST, JOY IN THE

If one drop of the joy of the Holy Ghost should drop into hell, it would swallow up all the torments of hell.

(a)　　　　　　　　　　　　　　　*Augustine*

HOLY GHOST, PROMISE OF THE (John xv. 26)

The disciples have need of Him.
1. That they may not be overcome by the hatred of the world.
2. That they may overcome the world with the Spirit of love.

(b)　　　　　　　　　　　　　　　*Lange*

HOLY PLACE

Is not every place holy and beautiful in which we have been born again, or held sweet intercourse with God? The most dilapidated barn gradually dissolves into a glorious temple, if we meet the Saviour there, and realize the Sacred Presence.

(c)　　　　　　　　　　　*Sunday at Home*

HOLY SCRIPTURE

Our learned Selden, before he died, sent for the Most Reverend Archbishop Usher and the Rev. Dr. Langbaine, and discoursed to them of his purpose: That he had surveyed most part of the learning that was among the sons of men; that he had his study full of books and papers of most subjects in the world; yet at that time he could not recollect any passage, out of infinite books and manuscripts he was master of, wherein he could rest his soul, save out of the Holy Scriptures: wherein the most remarkable passage that lay most upon his spirit was Titus ii. 11–14.

(d)　　*G. Berkeley (Earl of Berkeley, on Selden)*

HOLY SPIRIT, THE

The Holy Ghost is the Third Person in the Blessed Trinity: *Third*, economically, as shown in two ways:
(i.) By the words of the Baptismal Formula as given to us by our Lord Himself—" Baptizing them in the Name of the Father, the Son, and the Holy Ghost."
(ii.) By the position His especial work occupies in the Sacred Narrative. Up to a definite period, " *The Holy Spirit was not yet given.*" Till then He was the " Holy Spirit of Promise," and not till after the wonders of the day of Pentecost is every onward step in the kingdom of God attributed to Him.

(e)

HOLY SPIRIT DESCENDING ON OUR LORD

Remarkable antithesis:
The Baptism with the opened heavens and descending Spirit, and the temptation with *all* its circumstances of Satanic trial.

(f)　　　　　　　　　　　　　*Bp. Ellicott*

HOLY SPIRIT, DISCIPLINE OF THE

He that places himself under the discipline of the Holy Ghost, and suffers himself to form the resolution, "All that the Lord said will we do, and be obedient," as Israel said of old (Exod. xxiv. 7), is mysteriously sprinkled with the Blood of Christ, his sins are covered, he is regarded as pure and holy in Christ, and is enabled to render priestly service to God, and to be found without spot before Him (1 John i. 7).

(g)　　　　　　　　　　　　　　　*Lange*

HOLY SPIRIT, THE EARNEST (2 Cor. i. 20, 22; v. 5; Eph. i. 13, 14).

The earnest=a deposit, as of money, and as a pledge till full payment is made.
The Holy Spirit is the First Instalment, to assure believers, as the sons of God, of full inheritance.
In this sense, too, the gift of the Holy Spirit is spoken of as the First-fruits (Rom. viii. 23). This payment bound both seller and purchaser to carry out the contract.
It denotes also identity in kind, not in degree: Heaven perfected is like Heaven begun.

(h)

HOLY SPIRIT—THE ELECTRICAL MACHINE

I once had a friend, a doctor, who had an electrical machine, with which he wanted to experiment upon me. There were many people besides in the room at the time, and the doctor ordered his servant to put the chain connected with the machine in contact with every one present, assuring us that there was power enough to act upon us all. Then he began to turn something where the living power was. I saw the sparks come forth, and with the suddenness of the lightning flash, the element struck the whole row of us whom the chain touched, and I fell down on my knees beneath some invisible power which seemed to pierce through my flesh and bones, joints and marrow. So Christ, by His intercession in heaven, communicates the vital influence to us upon the earth, and flashes forth in the powers of the world to come, while the Holy Spirit puts the chain in contact with sinners; and the effect is such that they pass from one world into another, from death to life, from the covenant of the first Adam to that of the second. They fall down and cry out for mercy; they awake from spiritual death, and a new life is kindled within them. The chain was placed in contact with Saul of Tarsus, and he received such a shock that he fell prostrate, lost the use of his natural eyes, but had the eyes of his understanding opened. The Holy Spirit so placed it on the day of Pentecost that it touched three thousand people; Christ was interceding above; the sparks flew down, and the element so penetrated the hearts of the multitude that they cried out: " Men and brethren, what shall we do?"

(i)　　　　　　　　　　　　*Christmas Evans*

HOLY SPIRIT, FILLED WITH THE

He that thinks he has enough of the *Holy Spirit*, will quickly find himself vanquished by the *evil* spirit.

(j)　　　　　　　　　　　　*Thomas Brooks*

HOLY SPIRIT, FRUITS OF

" *In all goodness, and righteousness, and truth* " (Eph. v. 9).
=The good, the right, the true.

(k)

HOLY SPIRIT, THE GOSPEL OF

Looking to the prominence given to the work of the Spirit, from the day of Pentecost onwards, as guiding both the Church collectively and its individual members, it would hardly be over-bold to say that the book of the Acts of the Apostles might well be called " the *Gospel of the Holy Spirit.*" At every stage His action is emphatically recognised. Jesus, after His Resurrection, had, " *through the Holy Ghost,* given commandment to the Apostles whom He had chosen " (i. 2). They are to be " baptized with the *Holy Ghost* " (i. 5), are to " receive power after the *Holy Ghost* is come upon them " (i. 8). The *Holy Ghost* had spoken through the mouth of David (i. 16). Then comes the great wonder of the day of Pentecost, when all the disciples were " filled with the *Holy Ghost* " (ii. 4), and spake with tongues; and the prophecy, " I will pour out My Spirit upon all flesh " (ii. 17), is quoted as on the verge of fulfilment. Jesus has " received from the Father the promise of the *Holy Ghost* " (ii. 33). Once again all were " filled with the *Holy Ghost,* and spake the word with boldness " (iv. 31). The sin of Ananias is a " lie unto the *Holy Ghost* " (v. 3). He and his wife have " tempted the Spirit of the Lord " (v. 9). The " *Holy Ghost,* whom God had given to them that obey Him," is a witness that the Christ is exalted at the right hand of God (v. 32). The seven who are chosen in chapter vi. are " full of the *Holy Ghost,* and of wisdom " (vi. 3). Stephen is pre-eminently " full of faith and of the *Holy Ghost* " (vi. 5). His leading charge against priests and scribes is, that they " do always resist the *Holy Ghost* " (vii. 51). His vision of the Son of man standing at the right hand of God is closely connected with his being at the moment " filled with the *Holy Ghost* " (vii. 55). Peter and John go down to Samaria, that those who had been baptized by Philip " might receive the *Holy Ghost* " (viii. 15–17); and the sin of Simon the Sorcerer is, that he thinks that the gift of God can be purchased with money (viii. 18–20). It is the Spirit that impels Philip to join himself to the Ethiopian Eunuch (viii. 39), and carries him away after his baptism. Ananias is to lay his hand on Saul of Tarsus, that he " may be filled with the *Holy Ghost* " (ix. 17). The Churches of Judea and Galilee and Samaria, in their interval of rest, are " walking in the fear of the Lord and the comfort of the *Holy Ghost* " (ix. 31). The admission of the Gentiles is attested when " the gift of the *Holy Ghost* " is poured out on Cornelius and his friends (x. 44–47), and Peter dwells on that attestation in his address to the Church of Jerusalem (xi. 15–17). Barnabas, when he is sent to carry on that work among the Gentiles at Antioch, is described, as Stephen had been, as " full of the *Holy Ghost* and of faith " (xi. 24). It is the *Holy Ghost* who " separates Barnabas and Saul for the work of the ministry," and they are sent forth by Him (xiii. 2–4). Saul, roused to indignation by the subtlety of Elymas, is " filled with the *Holy Ghost* " (xiii. 9). It is He who guides the decision of the council assembled at Jerusalem (xv. 28), and directs the footsteps of Paul and his companions in their mission journey (xvi. 6, 7). The twelve disciples at Ephesus, baptized before with the Baptism of John, " receive the *Holy Ghost* " when Paul lays his hands on them (xix. 6). He it is who witnessed in every city that bonds and imprisonments awaited the Apostle in Jerusalem (xx. 23; xxi. 11). It was the *Holy Ghost* who had made the elders of Ephesus overseers of the Church of God (xx. 28). Well-nigh the last words of the book are those which " the *Holy Ghost* had spoken by Esaias," and which St. Paul, in the power of the same Spirit, applies to the Jews of his own time (xxviii. 25).

(*a*)   *Dean Plumptre*

HOLY SPIRIT, GRIEVING THE

" *Grieve not the Holy Spirit of God, whereby ye are sealed unto the day of redemption* " (Eph. iv. 30)

1. The Holy Spirit is a Person

He can be *grieved* and *resisted.* He is a Friend, for He wishes to do us good; He is sent by God, through the intercession of Jesus : " I will pray the Father, and He shall send you another Comforter." He is Jesus' Representative, and does not speak of Himself, but of Christ; He helps us to pray : " Likewise the Spirit helpeth our infirmities, for we know not what to pray for as we ought."

(*b*)

2. Grieve not the Holy Spirit

To grieve the Spirit is to *injure* His heart and feelings, which are set on doing us good; to *disturb* His action and work of sanctification in us, so as to make it fitful rather than progressive; to *make Him sorrowful,* for the Holy Spirit is a tender Spirit, and can be made sad.

It ought to be noted that the word is " *grieve,*" not " resist." His foes resist Him—that is to be expected; but His friends can " grieve " and sadden Him, which is hardly to be expected.

It ought further to be noted that this is not merely a tender and touching appeal, but a *strong* appeal. It is as if we appealed to a prodigal son by saying—" Grieve not your father, lest he cut you off "; or, " Grieve not your mother, lest you break her heart." And which do we suppose would be the more effective appeal.

(*c*)

3. We Grieve the Spirit by Sin

It marks the difference between the sin of unbelievers and that of believers. Every sin of a believer is a real " grief " to the Holy Spirit, who dwelleth in him. St. Paul is addressing such in the passage above. The Holy Spirit, he reminds them, is grieved by

(i.) *Lying,* and by all insincerity and unreality; " Let your yea be yea, and your nay, nay, for whatsoever is more than these cometh of evil."

(ii.) *Anger,* wrath, and revengeful feelings.

(iii.) *Giving place to the devil,* for that is to displace the Holy Spirit (whose temple ye are): one goes out when the other comes in.

(Illustrated by an Arab fable :

Once a camel came to the door of a tent and thrust in his nose. Not being resisted, he next put in his foot. Finding no hindrance, he came half in, and after a while all the way in. Then the Arab said, " This tent is too small for two." " If that be so," said the camel, " *you* had better leave.")

So by giving " place to the devil," sin may succeed in getting full possession.

(*d*)

(iv.) *Dishonest Practices*, such as peculation—"All unrighteousness is sin."

(v.) "*Corrupt words*." "Let no corrupt communication proceed out of your mouth." A Christian's speech must edify, not harm or destroy: it must not pollute other minds, but be as salt.

It is by such practices that the Holy Spirit is grieved. And we are thus taught that if we do not "love our neighbour as ourselves," so as to speak the truth to him always, so as not to harbour revengeful feelings towards him, so as to deal fairly and justly with him in every transaction; or if we corrupt his mind by foul words and innuendoes, suggestive of any kind of impurity—then, surely, we are *grieving* the Holy Spirit, breaking His heart, making Him sad, and, moreover, cancelling His good work in us. We are not keeping our garments always white, but sullying them to our own spiritual loss.

(a)

4. "Whereby ye are sealed unto the day of Redemption."

Compare—"In whom, after that ye believed, *ye were sealed with that Holy Spirit of promise*" (Eph. i. 13).

"Seal the servants of God in their foreheads" (Rev. vii. 3).

"The Spirit beareth witness with our spirit that we are the children of God" (Rom. viii. 16).

There are two poles: one is marked by the *sealing*, the other by the *day* of *redemption*.

The connection is expressed by "*unto*." And the question, "Whether this connection is liable to be snapped?" is at least answered by an impression,—a strong presumption,—that by "*unto the day of redemption*" indicates the certainty of ultimate salvation, or *final perseverance* for those who are sealed by the Spirit of Promise.

The tenour of the Apostle's caution is, not concerning the "end," but concerning the life of faith—wherein, if we "grieve the Spirit," we do so at the certain risk of losing the comfort of His witnessing with our spirit to our state, and His fruits of "joy and peace in believing." These being sacrificed, our lives will be uneven and dark; but it does not follow that thereby the "seal of the Spirit," by which we are marked as God's property, is sacrificed.

(b)

HOLY SPIRIT, GRIEVING THE (Eph. iv. 30)

Sin, in the case of the unredeemed, is a transgression of the law (Rom. iv. 15); in the case of the redeemed, it is a wounding of the Holy Ghost.

(c)   *Harless*

HOLY SPIRIT, THE, AND MEMORY

"*He shall bring all things to your remembrance*" (John xiv. 26).

There is no dulness where the Holy Spirit is Teacher, no forgetfulness where the Holy Spirit is Remembrancer.

(d)   *Bede*

The Holy Spirit is an antidote against seven poisons:

It is wisdom against folly;
Quickness of apprehension against dulness;
Faithfulness of memory against forgetfulness;

Fortitude against fear;
Knowledge against ignorance;
Piety against profaneness;
Humility against pride.

(e)   *Gregory*

HOLY SPIRIT, THE, AND MINISTERS

When ministers feel these special influences on their hearts, it wonderfully assists them to come at the consciences of men, and, as it were, to handle them with hands; whereas, without them, whatever reason and oratory we may make use of, we do but make use of stumps instead of hands.

(f)   *David Brainerd*

HOLY SPIRIT, THE, AND MISSIONS

The missioner may preach, and you may work, but all will be profitless except the Holy Spirit guides and helps both him and you. Paul may plant, Apollos may water, but it is God who giveth the increase (1 Cor. iii. 6). The seed is sown, but it cannot take root, and grow, and bear fruit, without the sunshine, dew, and rain of the Holy Spirit from above. The Holy Spirit is given in answer to earnest prayer (Luke ii. 31). Pray, therefore, for the gift of the Holy Ghost; pray for it in the name of Christ; pray for it now; pray for it during the mission; pray for it after the mission.

(g)   *Bp. Wordsworth*

HOLY SPIRIT, THE, AND MISSIONS

I told them that I must now leave them for the present, and go to their brethren far remote, and preach to them. That I wanted the Spirit of God to go with me, without whom nothing could be done to any good purpose among the Indians, as they themselves had had opportunity to see and observe, by the barrenness of our meetings at some times, when there was much pains taken to awaken sinners, and yet to little or no purpose.

(h)   *David Brainerd*

HOLY SPIRIT, OPERATION OF THE

The efficacy of the Spirit is to be judged of by its fruits. Its immediate effects are upon the disposition. A visible outward conduct will ensue; but the true seat of grace, and of spiritual energy, is in the heart and inward disposition. Whenever, therefore, we find religious carelessness succeeded within us by religious seriousness; conscience, which was silent or unheard, now powerfully speaking and obeyed; sensuality and selfishness, the two grand enemies of salvation, the two great powers of darkness, which rule the natural man; when we find even these giving way to the inward accusing voice of conscience; when we find the thoughts of the mind drawing or drawn more and more towards heavenly things; the value and interest of these expectations plainer to our view, a great deal more frequent than heretofore in our meditations, and more fully discerned; the care and safety of our souls rising gradually above concerns and anxieties about worldly affairs; when we find the force of temptation and of evil propensities, not extinct, but retreating before a sense of duty; self-government maintained; the inter-

(i)

ruptions of it immediately perceived, bitterly deplored, and soon recovered; sin rejected and repelled; and this not so much with an increase of confidence in our strength as of reliance upon the assisting grace of God; when we find ourselves touched with the love of our Maker, taking satisfaction in His worship and service; when we feel a growing taste and relish for religious subjects and exercises: above all, when we begin to rejoice in the comfort of the Holy Ghost; in the prospect of reaching heaven; in the powerful aids and helps, which are given us in accomplishing this great end, and the strength, and firmness, and resolution, which, so helped and aided, we experienced in our progress—when we feel these things, then may we, without either enthusiasm or superstition, humbly believe that the Spirit of God hath been at work within us. External virtues, good actions, will follow, as occasions may draw them forth; but it is *within* that we must look for the change which the inspiration of God's Spirit produces.

(a) *Paley*

HOLY SPIRIT, OUTPOURING OF

We cannot read the writings of the prophets without perceiving that the latter days (the days in which we are living) are characterized by an unusual and abundant working of God the Holy Ghost. Isaiah alludes to this continually: "The Spirit shall be poured out from on high." "I will pour water upon him that is thirsty, and floods upon the dry ground." "I will pour my Spirit upon thy seed, and My blessing upon thy offspring. And they shall spring up as among the grass, as willows by the water-courses."

And how this view is confirmed by the statements in the Acts of the Apostles, I need scarcely remind you. We live, then, under what is emphatically a "dispensation of the Spirit," and all along the line of these latter days, we are entitled to expect—as being in character and keeping with them—outpourings of the Spirit: manifestations of the presence of the Spirit of God in the Church, such as I have attempted to describe. Why, then, do they not occur? They have occurred, and do occur. At various points in the history of the Christian Church, God the Holy Spirit has interposed and made His influence strongly felt. But why do they not occur more frequently? Well, not because they are not wanted; for, God knows, and we know too, that they are wanted badly enough.

Not, then, because they are not wanted; but I fear *because of our unbelief.* I suppose it is hard for us to believe that there is any Holy Ghost, or to believe that He can work, or is willing to work on any large and extended scale. And so we hinder and thwart and limit Him by our incredulity.

(b) *Gordon Calthrop*

HOLY SPIRIT, PRAYER OF ST. AUGUSTINE TO THE

O Holy Spirit, love of God, who proceedeth from the Almighty Father and His most Blessed Son, powerful Advocate, and sweetest Comforter, infuse Thy grace, and descend plentifully into my heart: for in whomsoever Thou dwellest, the Father and the Son come likewise and inhabit that breast which is honoured with so glorious

and so Divine a guest, in whose company the Father and the Son always come and take up their abode. Oh, come, Thou cleanser of all inward pollutions, and healer of spiritual wounds and diseases! Come, Thou strength of the feeble knees, and raiser up of them that fall.

Come, Thou star and guide of them that sail in this tempestuous sea of the world; Thou only haven of the tossed and shipwrecked. Come, Thou glory and crown of the living; Thou only stay and shield of the dying. Come, in much mercy; Come, and make me fit to receive Thee. And all this I beg for the sake of Jesus, my only Saviour, who, in unity of Thee, O Holy Spirit, liveth and reigneth with the Father, one God, world without end. Amen.

(c)

HOLY SPIRIT, SIN AGAINST THE

"*There is a sin unto death*" (John v. 16)
"*All sins shall be forgiven unto the sons of men, and blasphemies wherewith soever they shall blaspheme; but he that shall blaspheme against the Holy Ghost hath never forgiveness, but is in danger of eternal damnation*" (Mark iii. 28, 29).

Explanation of this mystery there is probably none. It best explains itself by exciting a holy fear as to trespass. Another step—only one—and we may be over the line. One word more, and we may have passed into the state unpardonable. Do not ask *what* this sin is; only know that every other sin leads straight up to it, and at best there is but a step between life and death. From what the merciful God does pardon, we can only infer that the sin which *hath never forgiveness* is something too terrible for full expression in words. He pardons "abundantly," He pardoned Nineveh; He passed by the transgression of the remnant of His heritage; where sin abounded He sent the mightiest billows of His grace; when the enemy would have stoned the redeemed, by reminding them of sins manifold, and base with exceeding aggravation, behold their sins could not be found, for His merciful hand had cast them into the sea, —yet there is *one* sin that hath never forgiveness! As it is unpardonable, so it is indescribable. If it be too great for God's mercy, what wonder that it should be too mysterious for our comprehension? "My soul, come not thou into that secret."

(d) *Joseph Parker*

HOLY SPIRIT

Spiritus Dei.

Breathe on me, Breath of God,
    Fill me with life anew,
That I may love what Thou dost love,
    And do what Thou wouldst do.

Breathe on me, Breath of God,
    Until my heart is pure,
Until with Thee I will one will,
    To do or to endure.

Breathe on me, Breath of God,
    Till I am wholly Thine,
Till all this earthly part of me
    Glows with Thy fire divine.

Breathe on me, Breath of God,
    So shall I never die,
But live with Thee the perfect life
    Of Thine eternity.

(e) *Edwin Hatch*

HOLY SPIRIT, THE SPIRIT OF POWER

Suppose an army is settled down before a
fortress of granite, and told to batter it down.
We ask them *how* they are going to do it? They
point to a cannon ball. We reply, "There is no
power in that. It is heavy, weighs perhaps a
hundred-weight; but if all the men in the army
were to throw it against that fortress, it would
make no impression." "No," they say; "look
at the cannon." Again we reply, "There is no
power in that. It is a beautiful machine—nothing
more." They bid us next "Look at the powder."
And once more we reply, "There is no power in
that. A child may spill it, a bird may peck it up."
"Yes," they add, "but put this powerless powder
and that powerless ball into that powerless gun,
and then apply one spark of fire; then, in the
twinkling of an eye, that powder will become a
flash of lightning, and that ball will become a
thunderbolt, and will smite as if sent from heaven."
We have in our Church machinery, instruments
for pulling down Satan's strongholds; but oh for
the baptism of fire!

(a)
　　　　　　　　　　　　　　　　　Arthur

HOLY SPIRIT, THE, THE SPIRIT OF REVELATION

"*No man can say that Jesus is the Lord, but by
the Holy Ghost*" (1 Cor. xii. 3)

1. Gifts and grace

The Corinthians were, in many ways, a gifted
people, and consequently were apt to fall into the
common danger in such cases of confounding
things that differ. Gifts and grace do not necessarily run together. Gifts, of whatever kind, are
talents committed to us, which we have to use,
and for which we have to give an account. But
Charity, Grace, or the love of God, denotes our
standing before God: "If any man loves God, the
same is *known* of Him.

We have a very striking and painful example of
the two things not being identical in the teaching
of our Lord: "Many," He says, "will say to Me
in that day, Lord, Lord, did we not prophesy by
Thy name, and by Thy name do many mighty
works?" and yet, notwithstanding the possession
of such gifts, and of their unquestioned activity in
the work of Christ on earth, they were not *known*
of Him; "Then will I profess unto them, I never
knew you: depart from Me, ye that work iniquity."
So the Apostle emphatically exhorts these gifted
Corinthians "to covet earnestly the best gifts;"
but at the same time he bids them remember that
there is something more precious than "gifts," "a
more excellent way," viz., the having the Spirit
of Christ, without which they cannot know Him.
The Name of Jesus is no mere Name to conjure
with. The essential difference between those
who call Jesus "accursed," and those who know
Him only as the head of their party, the Leader
on whose side they range themselves, is not very
great. There may be this, there may be, too, the
possession of great stores of learning, great natural
gifts and talents; but these without "the more
excellent way, without the revelation of the Holy
Ghost, are wholly inadequate for the right understanding of the Lord Jesus Christ. We may hear
about Him, read about Him, preach about Him,
but never have saving knowledge of Him until the

eyes of our understanding are opened by the great
Revealer, whose work it is to glorify Christ.

(b)

2. The Spirit of Revelation

The Holy Spirit teaches no new Gospel, but He
takes of the things of Christ and shows them unto
us. He is emphatically the Revealer of Christ.
It is very noticeable how these things are put to us
in the Scriptures. First we read that the Father is
revealed by the Son. He is truly an unknown God,
and remains so, except through this one way of
knowing Him. "No man hath seen God at any
time: the only begotten Son which is in the bosom
of the Father, He hath revealed Him." It was the
mission of the Son to come and tell us about the
unknown God. Except for this, we should not
know that God was "Our Father."

But, as we proceed, we find that the Son Himself, who came with this revelation, needs a Revealer too. We are so constituted that we have
not the true perceptive faculty for understanding
the Son's message and work: we have no *eye* for
seeing Him, just as some persons have no *ear* for
music.

The Holy Spirit is that Revealer: "He shall
not speak of Himself: *He shall glorify Me*." The
ministry of the Holy Ghost is to reveal Christ.
Its necessity is taught us by the Apostle when he
says that "No man can say that Jesus is the Lord,
but by the Holy Ghost."

(c)

3. There are apparently three ways of knowing Jesus Christ

(i.) We may know Christ "*after the flesh*."

The Apostle says that he himself at one time
knew Christ "*after the flesh*" only (2 Cor. v. 16);
but now he knew Him so more. What, we
ask, is it to know Christ "after the flesh"? It is
of course some very inadequate, imperfect, and
elementary knowledge, which any one may possess
without being savingly benefited.

To know Christ "after the flesh," is to know
Him *as a man*, a teacher, a prophet, a genius;
and thus to put Him on a level with other great
men who have benefited their race by their
original gifts—whose genius, like a Shakspeare's,
has the character of universality.

To know Christ after the flesh, is to know Him
as *the carpenter's Son*, the popular idol of the hour,
the enthusiast of Nazareth, whose assumptions
cost Him His life.

To know Christ after the flesh is to know Him
as Paul and his countrymen did, as a *transgressor*,
a malefactor, a blasphemer, and a deceiver of the
people, who "ought to die" for His blasphemy,
and was rightly numbered with transgressors.

In this way, too, many of us only know Christ.
He was a wondrous *Phenomenon*, but nothing to
us individually, so far as we can see; and we pass
Him by. We are not anxious to know more of
Him. We indeed all our life long have read of
Him, heard of Him, learnt of Him in our youth;
but, so far, we have no saving knowledge of Him.
He has become no necessity to us, life is perhaps
tolerable and pleasant without Him. Nothing
that we have learnt of Him has as yet touched
heart, or conscience, or life at its centre. The
name of Jesus moves no single chord of emotion.

(d)

The language of a simple hymn is mere sentiment—

> " Tongue never spake, ear never heard,
>   Never from heart o'erflowed
> A dearer Name, a sweeter word
>   Than Jesus, Son of God."

It appeals to nothing in us who know Christ after the flesh only. The end of such knowledge is rejection, as it was with the Jews. We crucify Him afresh by our continued unbelief; we count the precious blood of Christ as a *common thing:* it is nothing to us.

(*a*)

(ii.) We may know Christ *superstitiously :* after the manner of monks and ecclesiastics.

This kind of knowledge, so far as it is reverential, is of course in advance of that of merely knowing Christ after the flesh; but it is not spiritual knowledge. If we study it attentively, we find it loving to give expression to itself in art : ecclesiastical edifices, which must be *Gothic ;* pictures of the saints, of the Virgin, and of the Saviour, as objects of reverence, if not of worship ; in posture-worship, flexions, and genuflexions ; in a rigid observance of days and hours for devotional exercises ; in elaborate ritual ; and in a multiplication of commands laid upon the consciences of men, as duties which *must* be performed for assuring the salvation of the soul. This, St. Paul teaches us, is a religion of *bondage* and slavery. St. John says, it hath fear and torment—it is devoid of love, for " perfect love casteth out fear." " The *manner* of love which the Father hath bestowed upon us " is not that we should be called His slaves, but " the *sons* of God." And the son is free in his father's house, whilst the slave is bound. The son honours and loves his father, serves him joyfully, of free-will and accord, without fear, whilst the bond-slave's motive is quite otherwise : he serves a hard master because he must, and because he fears punishment. The whole difference between the religion of the Holy Spirit and that of superstition is nowhere better illustrated than in St. Paul's allegory of Hagar and Ishmael, the bond-slaves, in comparison with Sarah, the free-woman, and her son. The prayer, often seen on tombstones, " Jesu, mercy," is, we apprehend, a true exponent of this stage of religion : it is not a Christian prayer, but a prayer of one who has never been set free, and knows Christ after a superstitious manner only.

(*b*)

(iii.) We may know Christ by the teaching of the Spirit. This is the true way, and beyond this there is no further revelation.

Once we may have known Christ after the flesh; now all is different—henceforth know we Him so no more. Once we may have known Christ superstitiously, and have been in fear of Him; we were led as others were led, but now, being free, we are led by the Spirit, and " as many as are led by the Spirit of God, they are sons of God." The sons of God ! " there is the grand difference : slaves before, sons now. Man is become a new creature, and stands from the outset in a new relationship to God. He loves God, loves His service; fear has gone with the forgiveness of sins, and the gift of the Holy Spirit. With this, too, comes the knowledge that we are known of God. Everything now about Jesus Christ acquires a new significance.

The Holy Spirit interprets all things previously learnt about Him ; He brings things to remembrance ; shows the meaning of Christ's incarnation, life, death, resurrection, ascension, and intercession now at the right hand of God. Everything which before was a stumbling-block to us, and an uncertainty, is removed and made plain.

(*c*)

4. The Spirit of Certainty

The certainty about spiritual things that we hungered and thirsted for has come. He removes our doubts as the Spirit of Truth, and disperses our fear as the Comforter. In our anxiety to know the certainty of the things about God and His Son, about heaven and hell, we had read books of evidence, and listened to many discourses tending to furnish us with these proofs. But after all has been done, *certainty* has not come : at most we have only attained to *probability.* As we have read and listened, we have never been wholly convinced : we have said, *Perhaps* these things are so; *perhaps* there is a God ; *perhaps* there is a Saviour for sinners ; *perhaps* heaven and hell are realities, but we are not convinced—give us certainty." And the Holy Spirit has done it. We *know* the certainty of those things whereof we speak, not because flesh and blood hath revealed them unto us, but because our Heavenly Father hath revealed them unto us by His Spirit. From that time, books and lectures on Christian or other evidences may have had their value for us, but we for our part can do without them ; we throw away our crutches because we can walk. We have an understanding of spiritual truths, because we have our standing in them. The pure in heart shall *see* God, because they live in the element of holiness. He that loveth dwelleth in God, knows God, for God is love ; so he that hath the Spirit, and walketh in the Spirit, lives in the element of spiritual knowledge, and needeth not that any man should teach him—He has an unction from the Holy One, and knows all things. Before the Apostles had received the gift of the Holy Ghost, we find them on one occasion choosing an Apostle to fill up the gap in their number by casting *lots*. It is noteworthy that after Pentecost we never hear of such a thing again : it is a method ante-spiritual, and belonging to the times of comparative ignorance. Matthias, too, thus selected, sinks back into that oblivion from which he was momentarily raised ; we hear no more of him, whilst the Holy Spirit, in His own good time, fills up the gap in the apostolic number by the choice of Paul, the Apostle of the Gentiles.

(*d*)

5. The reason why we are dependent upon the Holy Spirit for this knowledge

The answer is, because we cannot acquire it by the ordinary ways in which other kinds of knowledge are acquired. We find it stated that " the natural man "—*i. e.*, the unspiritual man, the man having not the Spirit—" receiveth not the things of the Spirit of God : for they are foolishness unto him, neither can he *know* them, because they are spiritually discerned." He cannot learn this as lessons are learnt at school ; neither can he learn it from the arguments of men.

The ordinary ways of acquiring knowledge by the avenues of the senses here fail. What the eye

(*e*)

sees, the ear hears, the hand feels, or the mind thinks of, is stored up in a central part of the brain; and the stores so acquired are called knowledge. But in the matter of knowing Christ, this method is at fault. The Scriptures emphatically state that "The love of God passeth understanding"; "The peace of God passeth all understanding"; and yet at the same time we are exhorted "to know the love of God," and to have an understanding of these things. How are we to become acquainted with what is wholly beyond, and out of the reach of our natural faculties? How can we know and have experience of the unknowable? But here we must not mistake. It is not said that these things are absolutely unknowable, but only that they are unknowable by the means in which we learn other things. We learn ordinary things by means of our senses—the eye, the ear, the mind, etc. But in the case of spiritual learning, "Eye hath not seen, ear hath not heard, neither hath entered into the heart of man the things which God hath prepared for them that love Him." That is a plain statement, telling us that these things of which we speak cannot be learnt by eye, or ear, or heart. "But," it goes on to say, "*God hath revealed them unto us by His Spirit.*" That again is as plain and direct a statement telling us how we can have a knowledge of spiritual things: "*By the Spirit.*" It is, in fact, a revelation. An illustration may help a little to make our meaning plainer.

(*a*)

6. The Illustration

There are some things, even in the natural sphere, which are beyond the range of our unassisted senses to apprehend. For instance, a star may be too distant for the naked eye to discern it; we are told of its probable position, and by bringing a telescope between it and the eye, it is brought within the range of vision. We see and get a knowledge of it. Or an insect on a leaf may be too small for the unassisted eye to see and examine; but when a microscope is placed between it and the eye, we can both see and get a knowledge of it. Now, what the microscope and the telescope are to the eye, that the Holy Spirit is to the spiritual eye. He is the medium by which we *know* the things of the spirit—a sixth sense.

We may preach Christ, you may read about Him, but you cannot *know* Him until the Holy Spirit reveals Him unto you. For no man can confess Christ, no man can have any saving knowledge of Jesus Christ, but by the Holy Ghost.

(*b*)

7. The Holy Spirit of Promise

But, great matter as this is, and fundamentally important, we need not wait for this Divine Helper, as if His helping power were something immeasurably removed from us, and out of our reach. It is not in the heights above us, nor in the profound depths below us; but it is near—it is in the Word preached, mixed with faith in them that hear it. The Holy Spirit will assuredly come to us in answer to our prayer.

It is about this very thing that our Lord tells us to "*ask,* and ye shall have; *seek,* and ye shall find; *knock,* and it shall be opened unto you: for every one that asketh receiveth; and he that seeketh findeth; and to him that knocketh it shall be opened. For if ye parents give good things to your children, how much more shall your Heavenly Father give the Holy Spirit to them that ask Him?"

This, too, is *the* promise of the New Testament, that God would pour out His Spirit upon all flesh —*the* promise of the Father; and for this Christ, at the right hand of God, intercedes, "I will pray the Father, and He shall give you another Comforter, which is the Holy Ghost." It cannot be then that the prayer for the Holy Spirit will go unanswered. Ask, "O God, for Christ's sake, give me Thy Holy Spirit. Reveal Christ unto me," and it shall be done.

Then you will need no teacher, for you will have an unction from the Holy One, and will know all things. You will never be in doubt and uncertainty about great spiritual truths; you will never need a proof of the existence of God, or of the evidences of Christianity; you will have got beyond these, and have *within* you an evidence which no scientific arguments can touch, and be able to say, "Flesh and blood hath not revealed it unto me," but my Father which is in heaven, through the medium of His Holy Spirit, and in fulfilment of His promise.

(*c*)

HOLY SPIRIT: THE SPIRIT OF REVELATION

"*No man can say that Jesus is the Lord, but by the Holy Ghost*" (1 Cor. xii. 3; xvi. 17)

Step by step a criticism, which seems relentless and destructive, advances from the outer defences to the citadel. . . . The controversy with unbelief is brought to the issue whether Christendom has a Christ. . . . Lives of Jesus follow one another, and are written, as it seems to us, often with a distinctly hostile animus. . . . He whom we have worshipped as our Redeemer . . . is brought before millions with a great show of learning or fascinating cleverness as being altogether such an one as ourselves—weak in will, oscillating in purpose, not without the taint of selfishness and fraud. To those who do not shrink from adopting these conclusions or playing with the premises which lead to them, the age we live in must seem that of the dissolution of one more of the great religions of the world.

(*d*)   *Dean Plumptre*

HOMAGE

A hideously frightful idea is, that the One only good, the One only unselfish, thinks a great deal of Himself, and looks strictly after His rights in the way of homage. With such a notion of God, and of our relation to Him, how can we escape the poor pagan fancy,—good for a pagan, but beggarly for a Christian,—that Church and its goings-on are a serving of God. How are these things to do God any good—to do anything for God? God is the one great Servant of all, and the only way to serve Him is to be a fellow-servant with Him.

(*e*)   *George Macdonald*

HOME EDUCATION

I have no faith in Act of Parliament reform. All the great—the permanently great—things that have been achieved in the world, have been so

(*f*)

achieved by individuals, working from the instinct of genius or of goodness. The rage now-a-days is all the other way. The individual is supposed capable of nothing ; there must be organization, classification, machinery, etc., as if the capital of national morality could be increased by making a joint stock of it. . . . Is it found that a child who has been bawling all day a column of the multiplication table, or a verse from the Bible, grows up a more dutiful son or daughter to its parents ? Are domestic charities on the increase amongst families under this system ? . . . It may be a choice of the lesser evil, but as for healing up the cottage home education, I think it one of the most miserable mistakes which the well-intentioned people of the day have yet made.

(a) *S. T. Coleridge*

HONOUR DUE TO ALL MEN, THE

The spirit of bigotry, which confines its charity to a sect, and the spirit of aristocracy, which looks on the multitude as an inferior race, are alike rebuked by Christianity ; which, eighteen hundred years ago, in a narrow and superstitious age, taught, what the present age is beginning to understand, that all men are essentially equal, and that all are to be honoured, because made for immortality, and endued with capacities of ceaseless improvement.

(b) *Channing*

HOOKER

You justly conceive Hooker to be a great favourite of mine. Setting aside the inestimable importance of the subject on which he treats, he is so very fine a writer that I am often astonished at the *little*, I had almost said at the *no*, progress we have made in composition and in the improvement of the English language since his day.

(c) *Hannah More*

The school of divinity of which Hooker was the chief, occupies a middle place between the school of Cranmer and the school of Laud ; and Hooker has, in modern times, been claimed by the Arminians as an ally. Yet Hooker pronounced Calvin to have been a man superior in wisdom to any other divine that France had produced.

(d) *Macaulay*

HOPE

" *Hope maketh not ashamed* "=*is not delusive* (Rom. v. 5).

Note 1. *We have peace* =past, present, future, through the life of Jesus.
Through Him also we had access at the first. Ask, Will not life's troubles, changes, and chances affect this security ?
Ans. : " No ; this hope is not *delusive*."
2. *How come to this conclusion ?*
Because " we glory in them also," for—
(i.) Trouble brings patience = endurance = constancy ; and
(ii.) Patience brings experience = probation = stand the trial ; and
(iii.) That brings the hope which is not delusive.

3. *Why not delusive—a feeling—or a mere matter of opinion ?*
Because we are taught by the Holy Spirit that God is love, and the Spirit witnesseth concurrently with our spirit that we are His children.

(e)

HOPE, LIVING (1 Pet. xi. 3)

" Hast thou *hope ?* " they asked of John Knox, when he lay a-dying. He spoke nothing, but raised his finger and pointed upwards, and so died.

(f) *Carlyle*

The world dares say no more of its devices than *Dum spiro spero* (" Whilst I breathe, I hope ") ; but the children of God can add, by virtue of this living hope, *Dum expiro spero* (" Whilst I expire, I hope ").

(g) *Abp. Leighton*

" HOPE, A LIVING " (1 Pet. i. 3)

The world's highest motto is, " *Dum spiro spero*." The Christian may add, " *Dum expiro spero*."

(h) *Bernard*

HOPE AND " TOO LATE "

While there is life, there is hope—never was there a truer word. Do not, I beseech you, yield to the pernicious delusion that you have lost your opportunity—that it is too late ! That lie has ruined more souls than all earth's wickedness combined. It is *not* too late ! And if death awaits you to-morrow, it is *not* too late ! Your life, though even now it be running out its last grains of sand, may yet bring forth fruit—the blessed fruit of peace, of joy unspeakable ; the crown of life may yet be yours.

(i) *Letters from Hell*

HORSE-DEALING

It was in connection with one of these horses the following fair-scene took place. The bargain was nearly struck between the man who had been employed to sell the horse and the purchaser, when Christmas Evans came forward, and the following dialogue took place :
" This is your horse, is it not, Mr. Evans ? "
" Yes, certainly, it is mine."
" Well, and what do you say his age is ? "
To the utter confusion of the deputy, the answer was : " Twenty-three, for I have had him the last twenty years."
" Is he safe ? "
" Certainly not, or I would never have parted with him ; nor has he ever been in harness."
The first salesman urged the owner to quit the scene immediately, or no business would be done. But the horse was sold, and not disadvantageously ; " honesty " proving " the best policy."
The unworldly Evans, of Llwynyffortun, an eminent contemporary preacher, and a great admirer of Christmas Evans, figures in a very similar scene. He had some steers to sell, upon which a reasonable price had been fixed by his wife, or some one who knew their value better than

(j)

he did himself. The sale was thus speedily effected :

"What do you ask for these steers ? "

The set price was named.

"I wish you may get it ; they are worth little more than half of what you say."

"Well, of course you know better than I do ; what do you think is their real value ? "

The "real value " was at once stated.

"Then it would be wrong to expect any more, so you may have them."

It is said that the steers were reclaimed ; which, we trust, is no mythical addition to this most characteristic story.

(a) *Memoir of Christmas Evans*

HUMAN NATURE (Rom. vii. 24)

Group of elements of the pseudo-plasmatic human image, which sin has set up as an inherent power in—

1. The old man, who is not a real man (Ch. vi. 6, and elsewhere).
2. The νοῦς τῆς σαρκός, which is not a real νοῦς (Col. ii. 18).
3. The φρόνημα τῆς σαρκός, which is not a real φρόνημα (Ch. viii. 6).
4. The σῶμα τῆς ἀμαρτίας, which is not a real σῶμα (Ch. vi. 6).
5. The σῶμα τοῦ θανάτου, which is not a σῶμα (Rom. vii. 24).
6. The νόμος ἐν τοῖς μέλευι, which is not a real νόμος (Ch. vii. 23).
7. The μέλη, which are not real μέλη (Col. iii. 5).
8. The σάρξ, which is something else than the external σάρξ (Rom. viii. 8).
9. The θάνατος, which is something else than physical death (Rom. viii. 6).

(b) *Lange*

HUMANITY

The Holy Scriptures regard humanity, not as an atomic mass of individuals, but as an organism, depending for its natural life on Adam, for its spiritual life on Christ ; and that in such a manner, that from these two genealogical heads the membership branches off into every single individual.

(c) *Ibid*

The truly universal human is the Christian—religious, in which the ethical is included : is "the heavenly calling of God in Christ Jesus " (Phil. iii. 14), which is destined to be most intimately united to the earthly calling—is life in following Christ. *He upon whom the revelation of Christ has not yet dawned, on him the idea of humanity has also not yet dawned.*

(d) *Martensen*

HUMANITY

Prometheus is a Titan, who holds it a robbery to be equal with the gods, yet steals fire from heaven. It is he who imparts to men culture and civilization, arts and sciences ; it is he who makes them polished and intelligent, but not pious or benevolent—rather haughty and god-defying, like himself. Their knowledge is without the fear of God ; their freedom is without obedience and

reverence. While men thus by unlawful means had attained civilization, Prometheus, as the representative of humanity, was, by the command of Zeus, in punishment of his crime, chained to a rock, where an eagle constantly tore out his liver, which as constantly grew afresh. Every third day the winged hound of Zeus returned to feed upon the freshly formed liver. This liver, which never dies, is a type of the desires and passions which cannot die ; and the eagle which again and again devours it, whenever it has grown afresh, represents the tortures which are inseparable from the desires. Prometheus himself, in his suffering, is an image of the human ego, escaped from communion with God. With the fetters of necessity, hard as iron, he is bound to the bleak rock of reality, throughout ages devoted to tortures unutterable, from which he is first delivered by Hercules, a son of the gods, who, with his arrow, slays the eagle, and breaks the chain of Prometheus. In this respect he is a type of the Redeemer, who delivers the enslaved race of man. This myth is of universal significance.

(e) *Ibid*

HUMILIATION

It is with us as with the reeds which grow by the river-side : when the waters overflow, the reed bows its head and bends down, and the flood passes over without breaking it ; after which it uplifts its head, and stands erect in all its vigour, rejoicing in renewed life. So with us : we also must sometimes be bowed down to the earth and humbled, and then arise with renewed joy and trust.

(f) *St. Elizabeth of Hungary*

HUMILITY

Let the young imitate *Elihu's* humility. Though competent to speak best, he spoke last.

It well becomes us to confess ourselves to be miserable offenders, when even Job abhorred himself, and said, "Behold I am vile." *He who knows himself best, will esteem himself least.*

(g) *Nichols*

HUMILITY

Humility, by not seeking, obtains what it contemns.

(h) *Ambrose*

HUMILITY

The answer of Augustine to the question, "What is the first thing in religion?" *Humility.* "And what the second?" *Humility.* "And what the third?" *Humility.* Augustine said truly, when speaking of pride, "That which first overcame man, is the last thing he overcomes."

(i)

HUMILITY

The progress which St. Paul made in *humility* has often been given by comparing three expressions in his Epistles with the supposed dates when they were written. "Not meet to be called an apostle " (1 Cor. xv. 9), A.D. 59 ; less than the least of all saints (Eph. iii. 8), A.D. 64. Sinners of whom I am chief (1 Tim. i. 15), A.D. 65.

(j)

The kingdom is glorious, the way to it lieth low: wilt thou desire thy journey's end, and yet refuse the way?

(a)   *Augustine*

HUMILITY (Luke xviii. 9–14)

We shall view our characters more truly, much more safely, when we view them in their defects and faults and infirmities, than when we view them only on the side of their good qualities. . . . The custom of viewing our virtues has a strong tendency to fill us with fallacious notions of our own state and condition. . . . Let us leave our virtues to themselves. . . . Our business is with our sins. . . . They who are truly humble-minded have no quarrels, give no offence, contend with no one in wrath and bitterness; still more impossible is it for them to *insult* any man, under any circumstances. In reading the parable of the Pharisee and the Publican, I should say of them, that the one had just come from ruminating upon his virtues, the other from meditating upon his sins. Mark the difference: first, in their behaviour; next, in their acceptance with God. The Pharisee is all loftiness, and contemptuousness, and recital, and comparison; full of ideas of merit; views the poor Publican, although withdrawn to a distance from him, with eyes of scorn. The Publican, on the contrary, enters not into competition with the Pharisee, or with any one. So far from looking round, he durst not so much as *lift up* his eyes; but casts himself—hardly, indeed, presumes to cast himself—not upon the justice, but wholly and solely upon the mercies of his Maker: " God be merciful to me a sinner." We know the judgment which our Lord Himself pronounced upon the case: " I tell you this man went down to his house justified rather than the other." The more, therefore, we are like the Publican, and the less we are like the Pharisee, the more we come up to the genuine temper of Christ's religion.

(b)   *Paley*

HUNGER AND THIRST AFTER RIGHTEOUSNESS

There was once in this country and in this church a wild young Prince, who selfishly indulged in all the enjoyments and passions of youth. By his father's death-bed he was brought to a sense of better things, and, from that moment, his soul went on constantly aspiring to higher and severer courses of duty. It was King Henry V., whose tomb you may see behind Edward the Confessor's Chapel. He especially attended to the complaints of the poor, and those who had none to help them. Unlike his ancestors and his kindred, he never swore any profane oath. He had only two words to express the determination of his human strength as to what his resolution was. When anything was proposed to him that was wrong, his one word was, " Impossible "; when anything in the shape of a duty came before him, he had only one word, " It must be done." During many days his life as a soldier was unlike what he would desire; but he almost always had before him the sense of holier things; and when, at last, his end drew near, his dying words were, " Build thou the walls of Jerusalem; " and, in speaking as if to the evil spirit that had haunted his youth, he cried, " Thou liest !

thou liest: my heart is for the Lord Jesus Christ." This, in times long ago, was an example how they which " hunger and thirst after righteousness " can be filled,—can be satisfied, at last, with the hope of having mastered their evil passions and attained to that conquest over themselves which is more glorious than conquest over our enemies.

(c)   *Dean Stanley*

HUNGERING AFTER CHRIST

Christ is as full a feast as you can have to hunger for. Nay, Christ, I say, is not a full man's leavings; His mercy sends always a letter of defiance to all your sins, if there were ten thousand more of them. I grant you it is a hard matter for a poor hungry man to obtain his meat upon a hidden Christ; for then the key of his pantry door, and of the house of wine, is to be sought, and cannot be had; but hunger must break through iron locks. I bemoan them not who can make a loud noise for a lost Saviour: when He hideth Himself, it is not time then to be bird-mouthed and patient. Christ is rare indeed, and precious to a sinner; He is a miracle, and a world's wonder to a seeking and a weeping sinner ! But yet such a miracle as will be seen by them who will come and see; the seeker and sigher is at last a singer and enjoyer; nay, I have seen a dumb man get an alms from Christ. He that can tell his tale, and send such a letter to heaven as he hath sent to Aberdeen, is very likely to speed with Christ; it bodeth God's mercy to complain heartily for sin. Let wrestling be with Christ till He say, "How is it, sir, that I cannot be quit of your bills and your mislearned cries? " And then hope for Christ's blessing; and His blessing is better than other ten blessings.

(d)   *Samuel Rutherford*

HUNTED STAG, THE

The Hunted Stag, caught by the pack, and liberated by the clemency of the king:

" How striking an illustration of a soul convinced of the guilt and evil of sin ! "

The Divine Law pursues it, dislodges it from every refuge of lies; and never remits its terrifying menaces till the poor delinquent ceases from self-confidence, and fixes on Christ for his whole salvation. After being awakened into a serious concern, the man perhaps leaves off profane and iniquitous practices, breaks the Sabbath and defrauds his neighbour no more. But the law quickly indicates that a negative obedience is not sufficient. Upon this he betakes himself to a course of positive holiness: gets acquainted with religious people; performs religious duties; prays in secret; and attends public ordinances; observes the Lord's day, and regulates his behaviour by the rule of God's commandments. Now he is ready to congratulate himself on his hopeful reformation.

Soon he perceives that his proficiency is but skin-deep; a mere outside varnish, which has not penetrated the inner man. He begins to watch his motives, and bewails the deceitfulness of his heart; he labours to subdue pride and curb passion; to purge out filthy lusts and spiritual wickedness. Notwithstanding all his vigilance, conscience flies in his face for the neglect of some virtue, or the commission of some sin.

(e)

His wounds bleed afresh; he is obliged to seek new balm for his sore; he confesses sin, submits to sufferings, denies himself, bestows liberally on the poor—hoping to make an atonement for his sin.

[And so on till the great cry of the captive soul: " O wretched man that I am! who shall deliver me from the body of this death?" " I thank God, through Jesus Christ our Lord."]

(a) *Sunday at Home*

HYMN (from the French of Pierre Corneille, called " Le Grand Corneille.")

" *O Dieu de vérité, pour qui seul je soupire.*"

O God of truth, for Whom alone I sigh,
    Knit Thou my heart by strong sweet cords to
        Thee :
I tire of hearing, books my patience try :
    Untired to Thee I cry ;
    Thyself my all shalt be.

Speak Thou alone !—For me no human lore,
    Nor human sage shall now expound Thy
        Word :
Let creatures hold their peace, and Thee adore :
    Let voice of man no more,
    But only Thine, be heard !

Lord, be Thou near, and cheer my lonely way ;
    With Thy sweet peace my aching bosom fill :
Scatter my cares and fears, my griefs allay ;
    And be it mine each day
    To love and please Thee still.

My God ! Thou hearest me : but clouds obscure
    Even yet Thy perfect radiance, Truth divine !
Oh for the stainless skies, the splendours pure,
    The joys that aye endure,
    Where Thine own glories shine !

(b)

HYPOCRISY

There is a spice of hypocrisy in us all.
(c) *Samuel Rutherford*

HYPOCRITE

Hypocrite = ὑποκριτής, an actor.
(d)

HYPOCRITE, THE

The man that stole the livery of heaven to serve the devil in.

(e) *Robert Pollok*

The hypocrite maps out the road to Zion, knows it well, has sounded with plummet the depths of the promises, can talk about them. But he has accepted a two-parts Christ ; there is perhaps a little pet sin, snugly tucked up in a warm corner of his heart, that he is unwilling to part with. Christ is his Priest, his Prophet, but he will not have Him as his King—" We will not have this Man to *reign* over us."

(f)

HYPOCRITE, THE, AND DWELLING WITH GOD

It is not at all an uncommon thing to find a distinction drawn in people's minds between religion and morality, and drawn in such a way as to admit the supposition that each of them is capable of maintaining a separate and independent existence. On the one side there are those who profess to be able to construct an elaborate system of morals, whilst scouting the idea of a personal God, and, consequently, the idea of religious obligation; on the other side there are those to whom the acceptance and the maintenance of an orthodox creed, and the experiencing of certain religious emotions, seem to be everything, and who regard with comparative indifference the discharge of the duties which lie between man and man. It is with the latter of the two classes that we now have to do, or, rather, with the persuasion that so long as our faith is correct, and we are exact in the performance of religious duties, so long are we exonerated—at least, in part—from the obligation of dealing fairly and righteously with our brother man. This was obviously the mistake made by the "hypocrites," to whom the Prophet alludes. They offered their sacrifices, and uttered their prayers, and tithed their property ; and were most punctilious in every outward religious observance ; priding themselves upon having been taken into covenant with the Lord God of Israel. But at the same time they were unjust, oppressive, cruel men, who treated the feelings and the interests of others with absolute contempt ; and whose very sacrifice, though enjoined by the law, was consequently an abomination in the eyes of a God of Love and Mercy.

And the same mistake (for human nature is unchanged throughout the ages) reappears in our own day, though not, of course, in the same violent and outrageous form. Given a man whose religion is of the emotional rather than of the righteous type, who prays, and sings, and communicates with fervour, but whose word cannot be depended upon ; who will over-reach you in a bargain, if he possibly can ; who is destitute of a sense of honour and generosity ; and who will be, as occasion serves, hard-hearted, unforgiving, unsympathetic, self-considering, and you have another instance of the old divorce between our duty to our God and our duty to our neighbour. Now, if there be anything clearly written on the page of Holy Scripture, it is this, that such a divorce between religion and morality is an utterly impossible—indeed, an utterly inconceivable—thing. We must begin with God, of course, just as, in building a house, we must begin with laying the foundation. At the root and basis of all righteousness lies an adjustment of the conflicting claims of God and man ; and I must be " right" with God before I can be " right" with myself, or " right" with my fellowman. But the rectifying of the relation between the Creator and His creatures involves, as an essential and inseparable part of its substance, a rectifying of the relation between man and man. The two things go together. They are different modes of manifestation of the self-same life ; and it would be as absurd for a man, who is defective in morality, to lay claim to religion, as it would be for a man, who was in full possession of his eyesight, to assert that he was able to discern one side of the street, but not able to discern the other. " This commandment," says St. John, " have we from Him, That he who loveth God love his brother also."

(g) *Gordon Calthrop*

I

"I AM" (Exod. iii. 14)

When He speaks of Himself with reference to His creatures, He saith, "*I am*." He sets, as it were, His hand to a blank, that His people may write under it what they please that is good for them. As if He should say, "Are they weak?—*I am* strength. Are they poor?—*I am* riches. Are they in trouble?—*I am* comfort. Are they sick?—*I am* health. Are they dying?—*I am* life. Have they nothing?—*I am* all things. I am wisdom and power, I am justice and mercy, I am grace and goodness, I am glory, beauty, holiness, eminency, supereminency, perfection, all-sufficiency, eternity, Jehovah, *I am*."

(a)   *Bp. Beveridge*

"I AM"

Repose is the especial and separating characteristic of the eternal mind and power. It is the "I AM" of the Creator, opposed to the "I *become*" of the creature. It is the sign alike of the supreme knowledge which is incapable of surprise, the supreme power which is incapable of labour, the supreme volition which is incapable of change.

(b)   *Ruskin*

"I AM NOTHING" (1 Cor. xiii. 2)

Without love, remarkable GIFTS, which seem to indicate a special Divine favour, a person is a mere nullity.

They do not elevate his character, or render him worthy of confidence.

Satan has more intelligence than any man ever possessed, and yet he is Satan still. The endeavour to exalt men by the mere cultivation of the intellect, is to make Satans of them.

(c)   *Hodge*

(*See* "GIFTS," "EDUCATION," "INTELLECT.")

"I SAY."

"*I say unto you*" (John i. 52)

The Old Testament formula was "*Thus saith the Lord*," Showing the difference between the Son, who speaks with Divine authority, and the Prophets who spoke *for* Him.

(d)

IDEAL HOPES AND PURPOSES

Does life offer us, in regard to our ideal hopes and purposes, anything but a prosaic, unrhymed, unmetrical translation?

(e)   *J. P. F. Richter*

IDLE

"*Why stand ye all the day idle?*" (Matt. xx. 6, 7.)

1. The Question

Man has a *work* to do in the world; a *working day* to do it in; and the night cometh, when no man can work; and the Master of the vineyard (Christ) finds us, for the most part, IDLE, not doing the work set us and expected of us—wasting time, talents hid in a napkin, and opportunities missed.

To all such He asks

(i.) "Why stand ye *idle*, when so much has to be done, and the time is short?"

(ii.) "Why idle *all* the day?"

(f)

2. The Answer

"Because no man hath hired us" cannot possibly be true.

(i.) Surely we were hired at the *beginning* of the day.

At our Baptism we were signed with the sign of the cross, in token that we should be *good soldiers of Jesus Christ*.

(ii.) At the time of *conversion*, were we not hired at the *third* or *sixth* hour of the day?

(iii.) Perhaps again, later on, at the *ninth*, or even at the *eleventh* hour, the Master said to us, "Go work in My vineyard,"—go make the world better—go and be salt in it. Trade with the talent I have committed to thee, till the time of payment comes."

How, then, can any one say, "No man hath hired us"?

(g)

3. Our Work for Christ is around us—we have not to leave our occupations to find it. Ennoble the occupation. Do it, whatever it be that our hand findeth to do, with might, and do all to the glory of God. (*See* "WORK.")

(h)

IDLE

He that is idle is ready for Satan to set on work.

(i)   *Anon*

IDOLS

Man is a born idol-worshipper, *sight*-worshipper, so sensuous, imaginative is he; and also partakes much of the nature of the ape.

(j)   *Carlyle*

IDOLS

Does not the black African take of sticks and old clothes (say, exported Monmouth Street cast-clothes) what will suffice, and of these, cunningly combining them, fabricate for himself an Eidolon (idol, or thing seen), and name it Mumbo-Jumbo; which he can thenceforth pray to, with upturned, awe-struck eye, not without hope?

(k)   *Ibid*

'Tis to make idols, and to find them clay.

(l)   *Mrs. Hemans*

"IF BY ANY MEANS"

"*If by any means I might attain to the resurrection of the dead*" (Phil. iii. 11)

In the *Past*, St. Paul had much to *boast* of.

In the *Present*, he had ceased to have "*confidence* in the flesh."

The text refers to the *Future*, and is the explanation of his altered conduct.

(m)

1. The Past (5 and 6) = whereof to boast

(i.) As to *His pedigree*: noble and long, a matter of just and honourable pride:—

(*a*) No taint of foreign blood: "*of the stock of Israel.*"

(*b*) No reproach attached to "*Tribe of Benjamin*" = one of the two faithful tribes, did not revolt.

St. Paul, therefore, a "Hebrew of the Hebrews," one of the elect nation.

All this, from a worldly point of view, was something to glory in—a good thing in itself—something to emblazon on the family coat-of-arms.

(ii.) Whilst as to his religion—if possible, still more cause for glorying.

(*a*) Circumcised the eighth day—trained as a good Jew.

(*b*) A Pharisee of the Pharisees, in days when Sadducean free-thinking abounded—from choice = no mere professor, no nominal Pharisee, just orthodox and no more, and because his father was so before him.

(*c*) Concerning zeal and activity—he persecuted the Christians, because he believed in his heart that they were wrong, and that by so doing he did God service.

Hence, more cause for confidence before God.

And in the eyes of the world these are no slight advantages:

Well-born, religious, add a good education, a commanding intellect—Paul had indeed, as he says, "*whereof to glory.*"

Few men ever had greater endowments as capital to start life with, and work upon.

Behold this man, then, in full sail for heaven, and with a cargo of his best on board!

How could *he* miss the port?

Such a man needed no Christ to be crucified for him. He needed no Saviour. *He* could look after these matters himself.

Where was the good, otherwise, of his being *one of the chosen race*—and, moreover, a religious man, conscientious, blameless in life, and zealous for God?

(*a*)

2. The Present shows us quite an altered state of things—quite a striking contrast

A change of mind had come about.

Paul had reason to change his mind about Christ.

He had become a Christian.

His present language = "I count *all things* but *loss*": I don't trust in them; I don't put any confidence in them.

Once, as we have seen, he wás in full sail for heaven, *with a cargo of self-righteousness on board his boat.*

Now he tells us that the ship was in distress, and the cargo would have sunk the ship. Precious as it was, it had to go—and he **threw it all overboard.**

All in which he once trusted, and in which he gloried (as so many do), he counts but LOSS, no cause for boasting = "dung," "worthless" in comparison with the advantages to be had in becoming a Christian.

His present desire is

(i.) To win Christ, to make Him his boast and his prop—to have His righteousness.

(ii.) To be found in Him, as Noah was inside the ark—safe.

(iii.) To know Him, not as the objective Christ

on the Cross, but subjectively as a living power within him—enabling him to live a higher life, and to "seek those things which are above" = the power of His resurrection.

(*b*)

3. The Future gives an explanation of his altered conduct and life

(i.) Ask, to what end this rejecting, suffering, striving, winning, preaching—what is it all for? what is he aiming at?

(ii.) Has some one offered him a fortune?

No; he is leaving all chances of one.

(iii.) Is he going abroad, to seek his chances elsewhere?

Yes—going abroad; but he knows beforehand that "bonds and imprisonments await him."

(iv.) Can it be that such a man, with such advantages, is going to join the mad-brained sect of the Nazarenes? to cast in his lot with the crucified fanatic, and deceiver of the people?

Is Paul, the learned, going to associate himself with an illiterate set of fishermen, and unlearned and ignorant men, to be counted as the offscouring and filth of the earth? Can it be?

Yes, that is it

In vain you tell him he is "*mad;*" in vain you remind him of his magnificent prospects, and the sacrifice of talents, position, and friendship.

He has become Christ's bond-servant, and he will give Him no half-service.

Ask him: What explanation have you to offer?

(*Paul.*) YES, I mean it; I'll sacrifice anything. I'll give up anything in this world.

If by any means I might attain to the Resurrection from the dead

Now, again, what does he mean? How escape that? Evil, good, Cain, Judas, John, just and unjust, all will be raised.

St. PAUL = *The Resurrection out from among the dead.*

See Cor. xv.—Christ the first-fruits, afterwards they that are Christ's, then the end.

The dead come forth in detachments, "every man in his *own order.*"

And the Apostle wants to be with the first = the elect among the dead. He knows Christ will come with ten thousand of His saints, and he wants to be among them—does not want to be left behind; as a man runs to catch a train, so he runs. Wants to be at the *finish* of the present state of things, and see the new world begin.

This is his explanation, and this his aim.

Think if Paul so strove, watched, lived—he who ran so well—how much more need have we, who come so far behind, to "lay aside every weight, and the sin that so easily besets us, and run the race," "*if by any means*" we, too, may attain to the resurrection from the dead.

(*c*)

IGNORANCE (Matt. xxv.)

The elect will be ignorant of their virtues, the reprobate of their crimes. Both shall join in that answer, "Lord, when saw we Thee an hungred?" etc., etc.

(*d*)　　　　　　　　　　　*Blaise Pascal*

IGNORANCE IN ASKING

Lord, grant me one suit, which is this, deny me all suits which are bad for me.

(a) *Fuller*

IGNORANCE OF DIVINE THINGS

When the celebrated Dr. Edmund Halley was talking infidelity before Sir Isaac Newton, he addressed him in these words: "I am always glad to hear you when you speak about astronomy, or other parts of the mathematics, because that is a subject you have studied, and well understand; but you should not talk of Christianity, for you have not studied it. I have, and am certain that you know nothing of the matter."

(b)

IGNORANCE AND LEARNING

Learning, it is true, is a useless commodity, but I think we had better lay it on ignorance; for learning being the property but of a very few, and those poor ones too, I am afraid we can get little among them; whereas ignorance will take in most of the great fortunes in the kingdom.

(c) *Fielding*

IMAGE OF GOD (Gen. i. 26)

"*Ad Imaginem et Similitudinem Suam*" ("In His own image, after His likeness"). I do not know what people in general understand by those words. I suppose they ought to be understood. The truth they contain seems to be at the foundation of our knowledge both of God and man; yet do we not usually pass the sentence by in dull reverence, attaching no definite sense to it at all?

(d)

For all practical purposes, might it not as well be out of the text? I have no time nor much desire to examine the vague expressions of belief with which the verse has been encumbered. Let us try to find its only possible plain significance. It cannot be supposed that the bodily shape of man resembles, or resembled, any bodily shape in Deity. The likeness must be, or have been, in the soul. Had it wholly passed away, and the Divine soul been altered into a soul brutal or diabolic, I suppose we should have been told of the change. But we are told nothing of the kind. The verse still stands as if for our use and trust. It was only death which was to be our punishment, not change. So far as we live, the image is still there, defiled, if you will; broken, if you will; all but effaced, if you will; by death and the shadow of it. But not changed. We are not made now in any other image than God's. There are, indeed, the two states of this image—the earthly and the heavenly, but both Adamite, both human, both the same likeness; only one defiled and one pure —so that the soul of man is still a mirror, wherein may be seen, darkly, the image of the mind of God. These may seem daring words. I am sorry that they do, but I am helpless to soften them. Discover any other meaning of the text if you are able; but be sure that it *is* a meaning—a meaning in your head and heart—not a subtle gloss, nor a shifting of one verbal expression into another, both idealess. I repeat that to me the verse has and

can have no other signification than this—that the soul of man is a mirror of the mind of God; a mirror, dark, distorted, broken, use what blameful words you please of its state; yet in the main a true mirror, out of which alone, and by which alone, we can know anything of God at all. How? the reader perhaps answers indignantly. I know the nature of God by revelation, not by looking into myself. Revelation to what? To a nature incapable of receiving truth? That cannot be; for only to a nature capable of truth, desirous of it, distinguishing it, feeding upon it, revelation is possible. To a being undesirous of it, and hating it, revelation is impossible. There can be none to a brute or fiend. In so far, therefore, as you love truth and live therein, in so far revelation can exist for you; and in so far your mind is the image of God's. But consider, further, not only *to* what but *by* what is the revelation?

(e)

By sight, or word? If by sight, then to eyes which see justly, otherwise no sight would be revelation. So far, then, as your sight is just, it is the image of God's sight. If by words, how do you know their meanings? Here is a short piece of precious word revelation: "God is love." Love! yes, but what is that? The revelation does not tell you, I think. Look into the mirror, and you will see. But of your own heart you may know what love is—in no other possible way, by no other help or sign. All the words and sounds ever uttered, all the revelation of cloud, or flame, or crystal, are utterly powerless. They cannot tell you in the smallest point what love means; only the broken mirror can.

(f)

Here is more revelation, "God is just!" Just! what is that? The revelation cannot help you to discover. You say it is dealing equitably or equally. But how do you discern the equality? Not by inequality of mind; not by a mind incapable of weighing, judging, or distributing, if the lengths seem unequal in the broken mirror. For you they are unequal; but if they seem equal, then the mirror is true. So far as you recognise equality, and your conscience tells you what is just, so far your mind is the image of God's; and so far as you do *not* discern the nature of justice or equality, the words, "God is just," bring no revelation to you.

(g)

"But His thoughts are not as our thoughts"— No; the sea is not as the standing pool by the wayside, yet when the breeze crisps the pool you may see the image of the breakers, and a likeness of the foam—nay, in some sort, the same foam. If the sea is for ever invisible to you, something you may learn of it from the pool—nothing, assuredly, any otherwise.

(h)

But this, poor miserable me! is this, then, all the book I have got to read about God in? Yes, truly so. No other book, nor fragment of book, than that will you ever find; no velvet-bound missal, nor frankincensed manuscript—nothing hieroglyphic nor cuneiform; papyrus and pyramid are alike silent on this matter; nothing in

(i)

Image of God—*continued*

the clouds above or in the earth beneath. That flesh-bound volume is the only revelation that is, that was, or that can be. In that is the image of God painted; in that is the law of God written; in that is the promise of God revealed—know thyself; for through thyself only canst thou know God. Through the glass, *darkly*,—but except through the glass, in nowise—a tremulous crystal, waved as water, poured out upon the ground;—you may defile it, despise it, pollute it, at your pleasure, and at your peril; for on the peace of those weak waves must all the heaven you shall ever gain be first seen; and through such purity as you can win for those dark waves, must all the light of the risen Sun of Righteousness be bent down by faint refraction. Cleanse them, and calm them, as you love your life.

(a)

Therefore it is that all the power of Nature depends on subjection to the human soul. Man is the sun of the world, more than the real sun. The fire of his wonderful heart is the only light and heat worth gauge or measure. Where he is are the tropics; where he is not, the ice world.

(b)   *Ruskin*

IMAGE OF GOD (1 Pet. ii. 19)

When a piece of metal is coined with the king's stamp, and made current by his edict, no man may henceforth presume either to refuse it in payment, or to abate the value of it; so God, having stamped His own image upon every man, signified His blessed pleasure, how precious He would have him to be in our eyes and esteem.

(c)   *Sanderson*

IMAGINATION, POWER OF

Set the greatest philosopher in the world upon a plank, broader than the space which he usually takes up in walking, and let there be a precipice underneath, his reason may assure him that he is safe, but his fancy will prevail.

(d)   *Blaise Pascal*

IMITATION

The Macedonian Conqueror, when he was once invited to hear a man that sung like a nightingale, replied, with contempt, "That he had heard the nightingale herself"; and the same treatment must every man expect whose praise is, that he imitates another.

(e)   *Dr. Johnson*

IMITATION OF CHRIST, THE

" *I have given you an Example* " (John xiii. 15)

1. In following Christ, there is presupposed a path which we must tread in His company—and a path has a starting-point and a goal. The starting-point is faith (justifying faith) in Christ; the goal is eternal happiness in the kingdom of God. Between these two points lies the Christian life, in which Christ's example is our pattern. Observe—
(i.) No one can follow until he has found Christ.

No one can imitate Christ's example until he has known Christ as Redeemer.

(ii.) To imitate Christ is not copying Him in every particular. For instance, we cannot follow Him as SAVIOUR, MEDIATOR, REDEEMER. What is meant is, that we are to do our work in the spirit of Christ, as He would do it: "Let this mind be in you which was also in Christ Jesus." Thus we shall " work out our salvation," *i.e.*, we shall have it first and then develop it; and when the goal is reached, we shall be " presented perfect in Christ Jesus " (Col. i. 28).

(f)

2. Fatal mistakes are made by beginning at the wrong end. People have striven to *find* Christ by first following Him, whereas we must find Him before we can follow. There is a true and a false imitation of Christ. Take for example the martyrs of the early Christian Church, "They loved not their lives unto the death," in order to witness a good confession. They were scorned and contemned, suffered and died, for the sake of their testimony. This was true external likeness to Christ. They followed him; they imitated Him. But when we study the history of those times, we find that fanaticism and zeal were not according to knowledge. Arrogance and vanity led other people to seek the honour of martyrdom, in order to be like Christ. This is fact. But such an external likeness to Christ was no *imitation* of Christ. Such people sought not Christ's honour, but their own praise. The motive was *vanity*, as often is the case.

(g)

3. Take the opposite of martyrdom, the monastery. People sought to exchange the busy world for the stillness of the cloister, in order to follow Christ without distraction. Such a life has no charms for the religious mind now. Such bind on themselves burdens grievous to be borne. They subject themselves to extraordinary self-denial and renunciation of earthly objects of delight. They take the vows of *obedience, poverty, chastity*. They imagine that in so doing they are imitating Christ. As he lived a life of obedience to His Father's will, so they imitate Him by obeying the commands of their superiors. Just as He had not where to lay His head, so they try to imitate Him by self-imposed and lifelong poverty. For like reasons they abjure family life, and cut themselves asunder from all the holy and tender ties that bind men to this world. Now all this is founded on a false view of Christ—rather no "view," for they had not found Christ first, before they started on their journey of imitation. They are attempting to follow One " whom they know not," and " spending their money on that which is not bread, and their labour on that which satisfieth not." For Christ did not say, " Go out of the world," but *ennoble the world* (the light under a bushel). We can imitate Christ without being martyrs or recluses; we can imitate Him in every walk of life. Christ did good in the world. He was always about His Father's business. He did nothing aimlessly. But asceticism professedly gets away from society, undertakes no duty for its benefit, and is solely occupied in its own selfish blessedness. Often, too, in aimless labour, as when young monks were set to spend the day by planting sticks in the sand, merely as an exercise in self-denial and obedience, but, of

(h)

Imitation of Christ, The—*continued*

course, without any beneficial result. In this indifference to the general good we may discern, not *imitation* of Christ, but the greatest possible dissimilarity.

(*a*)

4. It may be urged in extenuation of this kind of life, that it has produced some of the most conspicuous characters on record of persons who have had the deepest reverence for God, combined with a sense of the fleeting nature and vanity of worldly life,,and to which has been added an energy of will of such strength as to approach the borders of the supernatural, in their efforts at subduing "the flesh to the Spirit." To this it can be ·replied without fear of contradiction—Yes, history teems with marvellous characters of this sort; but in every case it was energy of will perverted. In no instance did such a life proceed from Christ, nor could it; the sunbeam is like the sun itself. The Christian life is an *imitation* of Christ's life.

(*b*)

5. Take for closer inspection one or two of the more remarkable characters of this kind:—When we instance the Abbé Rancé, the founder of the Order of La Trappe, it will be remembered that we could not select a more remarkable instance of Asceticism. This man, a Frenchman of the time of the Reformation, a nation remarkable for frivolous enjoyment, exhibits in himself the severest side of asceticism. After spending the earlier years of his life in worldliness and dissipation, he suddenly perceived the vanity of these things, became penetrated with a sense of the nothingness of this world, and of the terrors of eternity. He exchanged his thoughtlessness for a life of melancholy, and founded the Order of La Trappe. There the community rise from their miserable pallets at two o'clock in the morning, spend a number of hours in prayers and masses, the remaining hours in hard work, without daring to utter a single word, with the exception of this, "*Memento mori.*" Their daily food is the smallest amount of meagre fare, and the day closes by each of the brethren spending a short time in digging his future grave; and this monotonous circuit of duties and self-denial is repeated in patience and constancy to the last hour of life.

(*c*)

6. Madame Guyon (who lived at the beginning of the last century) is another instance. When still in youth, and distinguished for beauty, in order to practise self-denial, and, as she expresses it, "hate herself," she is in the habit of scourging herself till the blood comes, voluntarily licking the purulent matter from a sore, mixes her food with wormwood, has sound teeth extracted, and drops melted sealing-wax on her hands. Now, what is it in these two instances that fixes our attention? No one, who knows better, will say it was Christlike, or according to His Gospel. It is not that, but the *energy of will and constancy of determination* which we cannot but admire. Sin, however, by such processes, is not expelled; pride remains. Christ would have us consecrate our gifts to God's glory. But in such lives as these the best gifts of God lie unused, and, so to speak, rot away in cloisters. The radical error of such a system lies in mistaking the demands of Christ for Christ Himself. He is conceived of only as the Holy God, and not as the Redeemer; and it inevitably happens that the man who ignores Christ as His Redeemer, and yet endeavours to fulfil the demands of Christ, will be crushed by the very weight of those demands.

(*d*)

7. Mark how Christ Himself puts it:

(i.) "Come unto Me."

(ii.) "Take My yoke."

(iii.) "My yoke is easy, and My burden is light."

But if we invert the order, if we come not to Christ as Redeemer, and yet attempt to take His yoke upon us, we shall find it an uneasy yoke, and His demands a heavy burden. We cannot too much impress upon ourselves this fact, that to look at Christ as our Example only, and not as our Redeemer, is not to see Him as He is. Without justifying faith in Christ as our Redeemer, we cannot really follow His example. Without the grace of Christ, there can be no imitation of Christ. The religious history of those who have tried it otherwise, shows that there has been no peace. The soul hangs between possible bliss and possible woe. One moment in some ecstatic rapture, another in transports of unutterable misery. Destitute of the peace which cometh from God only, they have sought by solitude and rigid self-examination to die unto the world, and to root out and annihilate sin; but all the while encumbered with a burden they could not bear, knowing nothing of that faith which appropriates Christ to itself as our Righteousness, and which, in spite of still remaining sin, knows that it is accepted into the favour of God, pardoned by the atoning blood, and placed under God's fatherly and providential guidance. It was this fulcrum that made Paul and Luther heroes of the faith, and enabled them afterwards to follow Christ whithersoever He led them.

(*e*) *Martensen*

IMMEDIATELY

"*Immediately the cock crew*" (Matt. xxvi. 74)

See "CONSCIENCE."

1. Recall
(i.) The *Warning*,
(ii.) The *Denial*, and the *Place* here alluded to.

2. *The parabolic import of the warning.*
(i.) Peter stands here as a representative of all who deny or forget Christ—Christ, denied by *word* and *deed*.
(ii.) The watchful bird, that cries in the night, is the representative of the warning voice of *conscience*, which "speaketh once, yea twice," to call them to repentance.

3. Illustrated here: for the first effect of wrongdoing on the conscience = "*Immediately the cock crew.*"

4. The next step is repentance.
Conscience itself cannot testify to the forgiveness of sins, but it calls to repentance; and to the penitent precious promises are made.

5. Peter's guilt was cumulative. Note the many checks, rebukes, and warnings he received before his final fall; so, perhaps, with many.

6. Happy is it for us, if, when the "cock crows," we go out and weep bitterly the tears of a sincere repentance.

(*f*)

Happier still for all such, when the loving Saviour sends a special message, " Go and tell My disciples, *and Peter*," soon following Himself personally and asking the significant, never-to-be-forgotten question, " *Lovest thou Me ?* "

(a)　　　　　　　　　　*Cf. Alford in loc*

IMMORTALITY

Renan is unquestionably one of the most distinguished among those who deny the existence of a creative will and personal God. Yet Renan cannot make up his mind that he has lost for ever his beloved sister ; that she has passed into the night of nothingness. He dedicates his " Life of Jesus," to her memory ; . . . and invokes " the pure soul of his sister Henriette, who died at Byblos, September 24, 1861, to reveal to him, from the bosom of God in which she rests, those truths which are mightier than death, and take away the fear of death."

(b)　　　　　　　　　　*J. R. Rigg*

IMMORTALITY

It must be so—Plato, thou reascnest well:
Else whence this pleasing hope, this fond desire,
This longing after immortality ?
Or whence this secret dread, and inward horror
Of falling into nought ? Why shrinks the soul
Back on herself, and startles at destruction ?
'Tis the Divinity that stirs within us ;
'Tis Heaven itself that points out an hereafter,
And intimates Eternity to man.

(c)　　　　　　　　　　*Addison : Cato*

IMMORTALITY

The golden ripple on the wall came back again, and nothing else stirred in the room. The old, old fashion ! The fashion that came in with our first parents, and will last unchanged until our race has run its course, and the wide firmament is rolled up like a scroll. The old, old fashion— Death ! Oh, thank God, all who see it, for that older fashion yet, of *Immortality !* And look upon us, angels of young children, with regards not quite estranged, when the swift river bears us to the ocean !

(d)　　　　　　　　　　*Charles Dickens*

IMMORTALITY AND MORALITY

It is beyond doubt that the immortality of the soul must make an entire difference in morals ; yet philosophers have treated morality independently of the question. They discuss to pass the time. . . .

It is dangerous to prove to man too plainly how nearly he is on a level with the brutes without showing him his greatness ; it is also dangerous to show him his greatness clearly apart from his vileness. It is still more dangerous to leave him in ignorance of both. But it is of great advantage to show him both.

(e)　　　　　　　　　　*Blaise Pascal*

IMMORTALITY OF THE SOUL

If all is to finish with us, if man is to expect nothing after this life, and if this is to be his country, origin, and the only happiness he can promise himself, why is he not happy ? Why doth not the indulgence of his passions satisfy him ? If not superior to the brutes, why should not his days pass like theirs—without care, disquietude, disgust, or sorrow ? If temporal felicity were all, why is it that on no part of the earth does he find it ? Other creatures appear to be happy. The stars quiescent, the earth regular in her movements, the animals without envy, birds rejoicing in the air—all are contented ; but man alone is not so . . . he meets with nothing here to which he can attach himself. . . . From whence comes this, O man ? Is it that you are not in your proper place ; that you are made for heaven ; that your desires are greater than this world, which is not your country ; and that all that is not God is nothing for you ?

(f)　　　　　　　　　　*Massillon*

IMPOSSIBLE, NOTHING IS

All may do what has by man been done.

(g)　　　　　　　　　　*Young*

IMPRECATORY PSALMS, THE

1. Psalms vii., xxxv., lxix., and cix.
2. They express righteous indignation : " Be ye angry, and sin not."
3. David = The God-anointed one ;
　　Saul = The God-alienated one.
4. David in these Psalms is carried beyond himself, and speaks with prophetic certainty—not revenge : Cf. the precept, " Be ye kind one to another," and David was so.
5. David identifies God's kingdom with his own destiny, and his anger is kindled at this focus.
6. These Psalms are fulfilled in the enemies of Christ :

Ps. xxxv. $\begin{cases} \text{Acts i. 20—Judas Iscariot ;} \\ \text{Rom. ix. (7–10)—" Their table," etc.} \end{cases}$

Ps. lix. 4 ; John xv. 30—"They hated me without a cause."

The Holy Scriptures are the work of the Holy Ghost, and David was His instrument.

7. The Passion Psalms are the most quoted in the New Testament ; after the twenty-second, the sixty-ninth more than any.

Cf. Ps. lxix. 4 with John xv. 20 ;
　　" 　　9 　" 　　" ii. 17 ;
　　" 　　ib. " 　Rom. xv. 3 ;
　　" 　　25 " Acts i. 20 ;
　　" 　　22 " Rom. xi. 7–10.

David says of the *rejection of Israel*, " Let it be so " ; the Apostle says, " *It is so*."

Cf. Ps. lxix. 12 with Matt. xxvii. 27–30.
　　" 　　21 " John xix.

That night was this Scripture fulfilled.

Cf. also Ps. lxix. 26(a) with Isa. liii., and Zech. xiii. 7. The whole Psalm is of one piece—typically prophetic.

8. Psalm cix. : Anathemas more plentiful— thirty in number—against the persecutors of David, who persecute the Christ that is in him.

Cf. John xvii. 12 ; Acts i. 20—Judas Iscariot, " *the son of perdition*."

9. These Psalms = a deterrent for the enemies and persecutors of Christ.
10. The Holy Ghost uses the language of the curses, not Christ Himself.

(h)

11. The desire for their *conversion* outweighs desire for their *destruction*.

12. But assuming final impenitence, then the New Testament also passes over to the same feeling: Gal. v. 12 = "I would they were cut off." (?) 1 Cor. xvi. 22, "If any man love not the Lord Jesus Christ, let him be anathema."

(*a*)   *Adapted from Delitzsch*

IN CHRIST (Rom. viii. 1)

This deeply significant Pauline phrase must never be weakened or limited. As to its beginnings, Augustine is excellent: *Christus in homine, ubi fides in corde*. As to its continuance, Bucer: *A Christo pendere atque ejus spiritus in omnibus agi*. But the best explanation is John xv. 1–7, and Eph. i. 23, etc. Hodge says: In Him federally, vitally, by faith; but the vital union seems always prominent; especially here.

(*b*)   *Lange*

IN CHRIST

The true life is Christ in us.
Wouldst thou be one day in heaven, then must heaven be in thee here: first the kingdom of God is in thee, then thou in it.

(*c*)   *Ibid*

IN HIM (Eph. i. 4)

The choice is asserted as a fact; in Him He has chosen us, so that as humanity was made in Adam, as the people of Israel was separated in Abraham, so the Church was chosen in Christ.

(*d*)   *Ibid*

IN MEMORIAM, AND SORROW

I have read Tennyson's "In Memoriam," or, rather, part of it. I closed the book when I had got half way. It is beautiful; it is mournful; it is monotonous. Many of the feelings expressed bear in their utterance the stamp of truth; yet if Arthur Hallam had been somewhat nearer Alfred Tennyson—his brother instead of his friend—I should have distrusted this rhymed and measured and printed monument of grief. What change the lapse of years may work, I do not know; but it seems to me that bitter sorrow, while recent, does not flow out in verse.

(*e*)   *Charlotte Brontë*

INCORRUPTIBLE

I believe Macaulay to be incorruptible. You might lay ribbons, stars, garters, wealth, titles, before him in vain. He has an honest, genuine love for his country, and the world could not bribe him to neglect her interests.

(*f*)   *Sydney Smith, on Macaulay*

INDIFFERENCE

"*And Gallio cared for none of those things*" (Acts xviii. 17)

(i.) We live in times of infidelity, scepticism, agnosticism, and atheism, as external foes of faith; also of

(ii.) Fanaticism and partyism, as internal foes; but perhaps the most dangerous phase of modern society is its INDIFFERENCE to religious matters—the many, who, like Gallio, "*care for none of those things;*" not the grossly sinful, but those who live quiet lives in many ways estimable, following the ordinary traditions of society, living according to the dictates of worldly prudence; perfectly in-different to a *hereafter*, to *the saving of the soul*, to *the means of grace*, and to *the hope of salvation* through Jesus Christ.

(*g*)

1. Ask, What has brought them to this?

For man is naturally "religious," or "super-stitious;" fears of "conscience" have operated when nothing else would.

We believe that man has been at some pains to extinguish the voice of conscience in our day. Before he can be indifferent, it is all *essential* to quiet his *conscience*.

Steps =

(i.) It is undecided whether there be a *hereafter;*
(ii.) Whether he has a *soul;*
(iii.) Whether there is such a thing as *duty*— "I ought," or "I must"—or whether it is not an invention of priests.
(iv.) Not sure whether there is any God but nature; then man is a product of nature, only a chemical process = matter in a wonderful combination = a MATERIALIST. Hence, too, His "DOUBTS," his hatred of "dogma," of "creeds," "religions" = cant = hypocrisy = priestcraft; but He himself now becomes a dogmatist, sets up his own creed:
1. "Thou shalt love thyself above all." Look after the comforts and interests of Number One.
And (2) "Thou shalt love thy neighbour for thyself."

By these stages he arrives at INDIFFERENCE, having put away a good conscience, concerning the faith he *has made shipwreck*.

He has invented a religion (materialism) for himself, and is thereby a deceived man. The "*truth is not in him*."

He is punished accordingly, for God has sent him "strong delusion," AND HE BELIEVES A LIE.

Now the man has got no ear to hear with, nor eye to see with; he is deaf to the voices of *conscience*, of the *Word*, and of the *Spirit;* "the whole body is full of darkness."

He is secure against all moral and spiritual influence, for he is on THE DEAD SEA.

(*h*)

2. Types of Indifference

(i.) Men are indifferent because they attach *no value* to *religious things*.

The men in the parable who "*made* LIGHT *of it*" (levity).

The farm, the merchandise, = realities: material things which could be seen, touched, used = gain. But religion, heaven, salvation = unreal, guesses = no things: these have no more meaning for these men than the birthright had for Esau. What good shall they do us? They have no *value* in the estimation of these worldly men. Hence their INDIFFERENCE.

(ii.) Men are indifferent because they are *sceptical* about these things, as *Pilate* (the Roman governor), Our Lord before him = "For this cause

(*i*)

came I into the world, that I might bear WITNESS TO TRUTH."

Truth ! " What is Truth ? " asked he.

Why, that is what the philosophers have written about. It is something philosophers have for ages been searching for ; but I have done with it. There is no such thing as *truth*. As to the " gods," why we have the whole lot of them in our Pantheon from every nation. Religion is mere fanaticism.

The only reality is the Roman Empire ; the reigning emperor ; official business ; our circumstances and relations.

Behold the true man of the world—the man without faith, without hope, without God, to whom his office, his nation, his king *were all*. Hence his INDIFFERENCE.

(iii.) Men are indifferent because they are in affluent circumstances, as the rich man in the parable ; indifferent because affluent. He has come to believe in no angel nor spirit ; no resurrection, no hereafter, no judgment ; therefore he has taken no notice of " Moses and the prophets "= " sufficient proof lacking." The Bible was the one book he never read=antiquated, childish, nothing in it !

Standing on this basis, he lived (as so many do) a life of indifference, till, when too late, he found out the reality.

(iv.) Men are indifferent because they are *secure*, as the men of the " last days "=as in the days of Noah and Lot. They ate, drank, married, bought, sold, planted, builded=a life of perfect indifference to spiritual things : a life of worldly culture and enjoyment " conformed to this world," and in perfect security.

(*a*)

3. We are warned by the Punishment of the Indifferent

(i.) Those who made *light* of it " shall never taste of My supper." The indifferent were shut out.

(ii.) The sceptical Pilate ended a miserable, hopeless life by suicide.

" He went to his own place."

(iii.) The rich man went on living splendidly, giving banquets—pampering his body, until one day he died and was buried, and awoke in torment, and to know its reality at last.

(iv.) The people in Noah's days lived securely and indifferent, " until the flood came and took them *all* away."

(v.) On the inhabitants of Sodom the sun was shining when Lot went out of the city ; but the same day it rained fire and brimstone, and destroyed them all.

(*b*)

INDISPENSABLE, NO ONE IS

It was perhaps ordained by Providence, to hinder us from tyrannizing over one another, that no individual should be of such importance as to cause, by his retirement or death, any chasm in the world.

(*c*)　　　　　　　　　　*Dr. Johnson*

Men die and are forgotten. The great world
Goes on the same. Among the myriads
Of men that live, or have lived, or shall live,
What is a single life, or thine, or mine,

That we should think all nature would stand still
If we were gone ?

(*d*)

INDWELLING SIN

Illustrated by a butterfly laboriously endeavouring to free itself from its caterpillar condition. There it is with its wings only half unfolded, trying to disengage itself from the chrysalis which has been its prison, and when free, to soar into higher regions. But, for the time being, it is neither one thing nor the other—half worm, half butterfly. It has wings, but it cannot use them ; they are held tight by the still entangling chrysalis. Such is a type of the Christian life now ; but " we shall all be changed." The time will come when we shall use our wings freely.

(*e*)　　　　　　　　　　*Martensen*

INEQUALITY

There is an inequality happens to every man, in every mode of exertion, manual or mental. The mechanic cannot handle his hammer and his file at all times with equal dexterity ; there are hours, he knows not why, *when his hand is out*.

(*f*)　　　　　　　　　　*Dr. Johnson*

INEXPERIENCE

Candour will always allow much for inexperience. I have been thirty years forming my own views, and in the course of this time, some of my hills have been sinking, and some of my valleys have risen ; but how unreasonable would it be to expect all this should take place in another person, and that in the course of a year or two.

(*g*)　　　　　　　　　　*John Newton*

INFALLIBILITY

Pope Sixtus V. carefully superintended every sheet of an edition of the " Vulgate," as it passed through the press ; and, to the amazement of the world, the work remained without a rival—it swarmed with errata ! A multitude of scraps were printed to paste over the erroneous passages, in order to give the true text. The book makes a whimsical appearance with these patches ; and the heretics exulted in this demonstration of papal infallibility ! The copies were called in, and violent attempts were made to suppress it. Not long ago the Bible of Sixtus V. fetched over sixty guineas—not too much for a mere *book of blunders*. The world was highly amused at the Bull of the Editorial Pope prefixed to the first volume excommunicating all printers who, in reprinting the work, should make any *alteration* in the text !

(*h*)　　　　*Disraeli : Curiosities of Literature.*

INFIDEL

In a few moments, Shelley opened the conver sation by saying, in the most feminine and gentl voice, " As to that detestable religion, the Chris tian. . . ."

(*i*)　　　　　　　*B. R. Haydon, on Shelley*

His speculations were as wild as the experience of twenty years had shown them to be; but the zealous earnestness for the augmentation of knowledge, and the glowing philanthropy and boundless benevolence that marked them, are without parallel.

(a) *James Hogg, on Shelley*

Though benevolent and generous to an extent that seemed to exclude all idea of selfishness, he yet scrupled not, in the pride of system, to disturb wantonly the faith of his fellow-men, and, without substituting any equivalent good in its place, to rob the wretched of a hope which, even if false, would be worth all this world's best truths.

(b) *Thomas Moore, on Shelley*

I cannot help thinking of him as if he were alive as much as ever, so unearthly he appeared to me, and so seraphical a thing of the elements.

(c) *Leigh Hunt, on Shelley*

Of this I am certain, that before his death the mind of that brilliant genius was rapidly changing —that for him the cross was gathering attractions around it—that the wall which he complained had been built up between his heart, and his intellect was being broken down, and that rays of a strange splendour were already streaming upon him through the interstices.

(d) *Alexander Smith, on Shelley*

INFIDEL, CONVERTED

I went to a saloon-keeper once, to try and get him to allow his children to attend the Sabbath School. He was an infidel, and he told me he did not believe in the Saviour, and that if I did not begone, he would quickly make me. I went again and again, and at last he said, "If you let me read Paine's '*Age of Reason*' to you, I will hear you read the New Testament." I agreed. He used to circulate tracts by Voltaire and other infidels, and read the *Boston Investigator*, a journal devoted to the propagation of infidel opinions. For nineteen years he had not been inside a church door. I asked him to go to church. No; he would not. I then proposed to hold a meeting in his house, and he agreed. "But now," said he, "you are not to do all the preaching. I want my share of the time, and I want time for my friends." "Well," said I, "I will let you and your friends speak for forty-five minutes, and let me have the last fifteen." Next day (Sunday), at eleven o'clock, the room was filled with infidels and sceptics. The moment I went in, they began to ask me questions; but I said, "I have not come to answer questions, but to preach." Then they wanted me to proceed. I said they should give me the last fifteen minutes. One after another, they spoke; but they differed so much in opinion, they were near coming to blows. Some said there was a God, and others that there was not. When the forty-five minutes were up, I said, "Hold hard! It is my turn. Let us pray." But the old infidel said, "Look here, young man, the New Testament says there must be two agreed to pray. I had a little boy with me, and he began to pray:—"O God, have mercy upon those wicked men that have been talking against Thee." After the little boy prayed, I got up. The infidels one by one dropped

out, and the old man came to me with quivering lips and the tears coming down his cheeks, and said, "Mr. Moody, you can have my boys to go to your Sabbath School;" and he added, "I wish you'd pray for my soul." Afterwards he himself became a bright light in the Church of God. It took me months to get him.

(e) *Moody*

INFIDELITY

I shall speak of infidelity as a gross and perilous error; . . . that insane, desperate unbelief which strives to quench the light of nature as well as of revelation, and to leave us, not only without Christ, but without God. This I dread no more than I should fear the efforts of men to pluck the sun from his sphere, or to storm the skies with the artillery of the earth. We were made for religion; and unless the enemies of our faith can change our nature, they will leave the foundation of religion unshaken. The human soul was created to look above material nature.

(f) *Channing*

There is less *real* infidelity against Jesus Christ than there is against *the Church and its ministers*, who are, to a very great degree, so unlike Him: not His witnesses, but false witnesses. . . . There is more of the true spirit of infidelity in not loving your neighbour as yourself, helping him in his need, and denying yourself for his sake, than there is in the tirades that just now issue from secular platforms, and the open denunciations of those who do not confess His Name. These for the most part vent their spleen at a caricature of Christianity, whilst those wound Him in the house of His friends.

(g)

INFIDELS

Get *infidels* to write their autobiographies; it is the best thing that could be done to neutralize the influence of their books. Look at the conclusions at which these men arrive! A French unbeliever rejects revelation, and ends by worshipping his wife. A German unbeliever begins by applying to the Gospel narrative an intellectual solvent, which he thinks will crumble it all to powder, and ends in his latest work with proposing the worship of what he calls an "universum." "What is that?" you say. Why, he tells us this universe is only matter in motion, and the highest product of this matter in motion is man; but inasmuch as this matter in motion has traces in it of order, and law, and regularity, and something like moral purpose, it is to be the object of our devotion and adoration. We are not to worship a personal God, for there is no such being, he tells us; but we must bow down before this universe, and take it into our hearts for adoration and love.

(h) *Gordon Calthrop*

INFINITY

Meanwhile, what theory is so certain as this— that all theories, were they never so earnest, or painfully elaborated, are, and by the very condi-

(i)

tion of them must be, incomplete, questionable, and even false? Thou shalt know that this universe is, what it professes to be, an infinite one. Attempt not to swallow it for thy logical digestion. Be thankful if, skilfully planting down this and the other fixed pillars in the chaos, thou prevent its swallowing *thee*.

(a)   *Carlyle*

INFIRMITIES, TOUCHED WITH A FEELING OF (Heb. iv. 15)

As former of the world, the Logos of God knew doubtless what sort of a creature we are; but, clothed with our flesh, He became acquainted with human weakness from diversified and comprehensive experience. His Divine, pre-existent knowledge, came to learn that which springs from personal trial.

(b)   *Lange*

INFLOW AND OUTFLOW

A good *inflow* makes a good *outflow*; he who takes in much, can and must also give out much.

(c)   *Starke*

INGRATITUDE

When an obelisk is once standing perpendicular, one heeds not the levers and implements which raised it.

(d)   *Musæus*

And constancy lives in realms above,
And life is thorny, and youth is vain;
And to be wroth with one we love,
Doth work like madness in the brain.

(e)   *Coleridge's "Christabel"*

INHERITANCE OF BELIEVERS = "Incorruptible. . . fadeth not away (1 Pet. i. 4)

Rust does not corrupt it, decay does not consume it, death does not destroy it. It contemplates union to Him, who only hath immortality, and is called "Eternal" (1 Tim. i. 17).

(f)   *Besser and Lange*

INHERITOR OF THE KINGDOM OF HEAVEN (Church Catechism)

"*Inheritor*." In nineteen expositions out of twenty, even by evangelical clergymen, this word is interpreted as though it meant "heir." But an inheritor is not an heir. An inheritor is a *possessor*—one who *has* come into the possession of property or privileges to which by heirship he was entitled; not one who has a right to come into them *hereafter* (heir). The Prince of Wales is "heir" to the kingdom of England; but the "inheritor" of the kingdom is the Queen. By baptism we enter into actual possession of the blessed privileges of the Christian Church. The grace or favour is actually given to us of enjoying all its means of grace. These advantages may be used or misused—may end in final salvation or otherwise (2 Cor. vi. 1). But such privileges are ours to give an account of—"We cannot be as the heathen."

(g)   *Richard Glover*

INQUISITOR

Dear political or religious inquisitor! art thou aware that Turin tapers never rightly begin shining till thou breakest them, and then they take fire.

(h)   *J. P. F. Richter*

INSENSIBILITY

A man in a dungeon, who knows not whether sentence of death is passed upon him, who is allowed but one hour to ascertain, and that one hour sufficient, in case it be passed, to obtain its reverse, would act contrary to nature, should he employ this hour, not in procuring the information, but in vain amusement.

(i)

INSPIRATION

Is there no inspiration, then, but one with big revenues, loud liturgies, and red stockings?

(j)   *Carlyle*

INSPIRATION OF THE HOLY SCRIPTURES

Unlearned and ignorant men have become the teachers of the world. The greatest sages of this world—the Bacons and Newtons, the Keplers and Pascals—have deemed it their highest privilege to sit down as little children at the feet of the Evangelists. How could this be done? "*The Holy Spirit was sent to guide them into all truth.*"

(k)   *Bp. Wordsworth*

Conspicuous in John Randolph's library was a family Bible. Surrounding it were many books, some for and others against its truthfulness as an inspired revelation. One day Mr. Randolph had a clergyman as his guest, and the Family Bible became a topic of conversation. The eccentric orator said:

"I was raised by a pious mother (God bless her memory!), who taught me the Christian religion in all its requirements. But, alas! I grew up an infidel—if not an infidel complete, yet a decided Deist.

"But when I became a man, in this as well as in political and all other matters, I resolved to examine for myself, and never to pin my faith to any other man's sleeve. So I bought that Bible; I pored over it; I examined it carefully.

"I sought and procured those books for and against it; and when my labours were ended, I came to this irresistible conclusion: The Bible is true. It would have been as easy for a mole to have written Sir Isaac Newton's treatise on Optics as for uninspired men to have written the Bible."

(l)

I cannot forget the confusion into which I saw a conceited young fellow thrown once, when he turned to an aged minister, and, as if challenging discussion, said: "I am told you believe in the inspiration of the whole Bible." The good man answered quietly, "Oh, yes, my friend; what do you believe in?" A little laugh covered the defeat, but he continued, "But you certainly know what the great scholars say about it?" When again the calm answer met him, "Somewhat; but what did

(m)

they say to you about your soul?" Now the inquirer grew restive. "They say you are leading men along with a farthing taper in your lantern." To this the aged preacher only said, "Do they say men would see any better if we would *let them put the taper out?*"

(*a*)

INSTINCT

Instinct. The appearance of man upon the scene of being constitutes a new era in creation; the operations of a new *instinct* come into play,— that *instinct* which anticipates a life after the grave, and reposes in implicit faith upon a God alike just and good, who is the pledged "Rewarder of all who diligently seek Him." And in looking along the long line of being,—ever rising in the scale from higher to higher manifestations, or abroad on the lower animals, whom *instinct* never deceives,—can we hold that man,—immeasurably higher in his hope and aspirations than all that ever went before him, — should be, notwithstanding, the one grand error in creation—the one painful worker, in the midst of present trouble, for a state into which he is never to enter—the befooled expectant of a happy future, which he is never to see? Assuredly no. He who keeps faith with all His humbler creatures,—who gives to even the bee and the dormouse the winter for which they prepare,—will to a certainty not break faith with man—with man, alike the deputed lord of the present creation and the chosen heir of all the future.

(*b*) *Hugh Miller*

INTELLECT

At one of the early Social Science Congresses there was a meeting, presided over by Lord Brougham, with addresses to the working classes. A working man from the crowd made a speech. Referring to the vaunts of intellectual progress made by other speakers, he uttered the following striking sentence :—"We have been hearing much of intellectual progress and the advance of the age; but this I know, that the march of intellect, if it leads away from the cross of Christ, is the march of death."

(*c*)

Intelligence is strength; and in proportion as the many grow intelligent, they must guide the world.

(*d*) *Channing*

INTELLECT, SUPREMACY OF

Aristocracy of intellect! . . . What! shall I call man my superior, because he is cleverer than myself? Shall I bow down to a fit of brains any more than to a stock or a stone? Let a man prove himself better than me—honester, humbler, kinder, with more sense of the duty of man, and the weakness of man—and that man I'll acknowledge; that man's my king, my leader, though he were so stupid as Eppe Dalgleish, that could not count five on her fingers, and yet kept her drunken father by her own hands' labour for twenty-three years.

(*e*) *Charles Kingsley*

INTEMPERANCE

Intemperance is the *voluntary extinction of reason.*

(*f*) *Channing*

On the St. Lawrence River we have to employ an Indian pilot, and give him a thousand dollars for his summer's work, just to conduct our boats through between the rocks and the islands, so swift are the rapids. Every man that comes into city life comes into the rapids, and the only question is whether he shall have safe or unsafe pilotage. Young man, your bad habits will be reported at the homestead. You cannot hide them. There are people who love to carry bad news, and there will be some accursed old gossip who will wend her step toward the old homestead, and she will sit down, and after she has awhile wriggled in the chair, she will say to your old parents, "Do you know your son drinks?" Then your parents will get white about the lips, and your mother will ask to have the door set a little open for the fresh air; and before that old gossip leaves the place, she will have told your parents all about the places where you are accustomed to go. Then your mother will come out, and she will sit down on the step where you used to play, and she will cry and cry. Then she will be sick, and the gig of the country doctor will come up the country lane, and the horse will be tied at the swing-gate, and the prescription will fail, and she will get worse and worse, and in her delirium she will talk about nothing but you. Then the farmers will come to the funeral, and tie the horses at the rail fence about the house, and they will talk about what ailed the one that died, and one will say it was intermittent, and another will say it was congestion, and another will say it was premature old age; but it will be neither intermittent, nor congestion, nor old age. In the ponderous book of Almighty God it will be recorded for everlasting ages to read that you killed her.

(*g*) *Talmage*

A boy said: "I know So-and-so's saloon is finished." "How do you know it?" "I saw a fellow coming out of it drunk."

A liquor-seller was very angry with a boy who, when he saw a drunken man had fallen down in front of a saloon, said: "Mister, your sign has fell down."

(*h*) *Gough*

I never drink. I cannot do it on equal terms with others. It costs them only one day, but me three—the first in sinning, the second in suffering, and the third in repenting.

(*i*) *Sterne*

Whilst the drunkard swallows wine, wine swallows him. God disregards him, angels despise him; men deride him, virtue declines him, the devil destroys him.

(*j*) *Augustine*

See the folds of that huge serpent of the Boa Constrictor species. *Delirium Tremens* is its name! its folds are around him, and the eyes are fit to bolt out of his head; and he raves and curses,

(*k*)

and gnashes his teeth, and foams at the mouth, and three strong men can scarcely hold him! Young man, dash the glass to the earth, I say; dash it to shivers, and resolve, by God's help, never to touch it again, lest such a case be yours some day.

(a)   *Thomas Cooper*

Look at yon shrivelled creature in one of the streets of London! Born of an aristocratic family —sent to Oxford—introduced into " good society." He became a " good companion," a gambler, a drunkard, in succession.   When money grew scarce, his old acquaintance forsook him; and now he ranks with beggars—seedy in dress, shabby in appearance, he looks furtively at everybody he sees. Often a whole day without food. He is but forty years old, yet looks three-score: white-haired, and his hands shake like a paralytic. Hark! a foul whisper rises in his mind. It is from the evil spirit: " What art thou living for? Life is no longer worth having—character gone—health and strength are gone—memory is going—no food for thy stomach, no bed for thy limbs. Thou hast no real friend left; end it all at once, like a brave man! Rush to one of the bridges, and jump into the Thames!"

(b)   *Ibid*

INTENTIONS

Our intentions may be right, but our decisions may be wrong.

(c)

INTERCESSION

Story of Amyntas, the Hero of Salamis.

This is happily illustrated by the story of Amyntas and Æschylus as Ælian relates it. Æschylus was condemned to death by the Athenians, and was just going to be led to execution. His brother Amyntas had signalized himself in the service of his country, and on the day of a most illustrious victory, in a great measure obtained by his means, had lost his hand. He came into the court just as his brother was condemned, and without saying a word, drew the stump of his arm from under his garment, and held it up in their sight; and the historian tells us, " that when the judges saw this mark of his sufferings, they remembered what he had done, and discharged his brother, though he had forfeited his life."

(d)   *Quoted by P. Doddridge*

INTONING—CHANTING—SINGING

I felt God, if I may so speak, at the first appearance of a thunder-storm, and used to fix myself so as to view the clouds, and see the lightning play, and hear the majestic and awful voice of God's thunder. While thus engaged, it always seemed natural for me to sing or chant forth my meditations, or to speak my soliloquies in a singing voice. I spent most of my time in thinking of Divine things, year after year, walking alone in the woods for meditation, soliloquy, prayer, and converse with God; and it was always my custom to sing forth my contemplations.

(e)   *Jonathan Edwards*

IS IT I

" And as they did eat, Jesus said, Verily I say unto you, that one of you shall betray Me. And they were exceeding sorrowful, and began every one of them to say unto Him, Lord, is it I?" (Matt. xxvi. 21, 22)

It was a moment of dismay among the disciples of Jesus. Their Master, sitting with them at the supper, had just declared that one of them should commit an act of the basest treachery, and betray Him to His enemies. There could be no deed more contemptible. Every obligation of duty and affection was violated by it. One who stood by, in the rude upper chamber, where they ate the supper, might well have watched with curiosity to see how these plain men would take the words of Jesus. Will they break out in indignant remonstrance? Will they fall to accusing one another? Will each draw back from his brother apostle in horror at the thought that possibly that brother apostle is the man who is to do this dreadful thing? Instead of these, there is a different result from either, and one that certainly surprises us. Each man's anxiety seems to be turned, not towards his brother, but towards himself, and you hear them asking, one after another, " Lord, is it I?" " Lord, is it I?" Peter, Bartholomew, John, James, Thomas, each speaks for himself, and the quick questions came pouring in out of their simple hearts, " Lord, is it I?" " Lord, is it I?"

(f)

There are times in the lives of all of us, I think, when that comes to us which came here to Christ's disciples.

1. One of them is the time when we see deep and flagrant sin in some other man. When some great crime is done, when through the community there runs the story of some frightful cruelty or dreadful fraud, I think that almost all of us are conscious of a strange mixture of two emotions—one of horror, and the other of a terrible familiarity. The act is repugnant to all our conscientiousness; but the powers that did the act, and the motives that persuaded the doing of it, are powers which we possess and motives which we have felt. They are human powers and human motives. It is a human act. If we could watch the sinning of another race, with a wholly different nature, I think that it would stir no such self-consciousness. If we could stand by and see the wickedness of fiends or fallen angels, it might excite our hatred, our disgust; but it would make no such deep questionings as come when we recognise our own humanity in the sinning man, and find our nature bearing witness that it has in it the same powers by which he has been so wicked. A being of a higher race might see our sin and sorrow with pity, with pain, with wonder; but the pain would be all free from self-reproach, and the wonder would all exhaust itself outside of him. It would be the innocent bewilderment with which I remember, in a picture by Domenichino at Bologna, an angel stands at the foot of the empty cross, and tries with his finger one of the sharp points in the crown of thorns which the Saviour had worn during His passion. It is all a sad, inexplicable wonder to him. It appeals to no experience of wickedness and woe in his pure and angelic nature.

(g)

Is it I?—*continued*

But when you or I take the crown of thorns into our hands, we know in our own hearts the meanness, the jealousy, the hatred which it represents. The possible Jew, the possible enemy of righteousness and crucifier of the Saviour, stirs to self-consciousness in us. When you read the story of yesterday's defaulter fleeing to-day, an exile and an outcast, or sitting gloomily behind his prison bars, it is not with an angel's innocent wonder what a sin like this can mean; it is with the understanding of a man who has felt the same temptation to which this poor wretch has yielded that you deplore his fate. It is always the difference between an angel's pity and a man's pity. With simple wonder an angel might walk through our State Prison halls; but a man must walk there full of humbleness and charity; for, as the best man that ever lived finds something of common humanity in us which makes his goodness seem not impossible to us, so the worst of men stirs by the sight of his human sin some sense of what human powers of sinfulness we too possess.

(*a*)

2. Another is when we do some small sin, and recognise the deep power of sinfulness by which we do it. The Bible is full of this idea. Look at Adam with the forbidden apple. Is it only that one sin which terrifies him, and makes him dread the coming of God, which had been once the joy of the garden day? Is it not that pressing up behind that sin he sees the long procession of sins which he and his descendants will commit? A boy paints his first stumbling, ill-drawn picture, and, as he gazes at it, he sees, already, the glowing canvas which he is some day to cover. It grows possible to him. A boy makes his first boyish bargain, and the trade-impulse rises in him, and, already, he sees himself a merchant. It is the same thing. A pure, honest boy cheats with his first little timid fraud, and on the other side, the bad side of him, the door flies open and he sees the possibility that he, too, should be the swindler whose enormous frauds make the whole city tremble. The slightest crumbling of the earth under your feet makes you aware of the precipice. The least impurity makes you ready to cry out, as some image of hideous lust rises before you, " Oh, is it I? Can I come to that?"

(*b*)

3. And yet another occasion is the expression of any suspicion about us by another person. Perfectly unwarrantable and false we may know the charge to be which is brought against us; but the mere fastening of the sin and our name together, the fact that any man could mention the two in the same breath, must turn our eyes in upon ourselves and set us to asking, " Is it possible?" "I did not do this thing, indeed. My conscience is all clear. I did not commit this cruelty. I did not prove so ungrateful and treacherous as this charge would make me. Perhaps I could not; perhaps I know I could not do this special villainy. But can I blaze up into fiery indignation at men's daring to suspect me without remembering what badness I am capable of. Can I resent suspicion as an angel might, who, standing in the light of God, dreaded and felt no sin?" I think that for you or me to find our names linked to-morrow in this community with some great crime, of which

we knew that we were totally innocent, must stir the mystery of our inner life, and make us see what capacity of sin is lying there. I think our disavowal of the sin that we were charged with would be not boisterously angry, but quiet, and solemn, and humble, with a sense of danger and a gratitude for preservation. I think that ought to be the influence. And even the boisterousness with which some men deny a charge against their characters is still a sign in a worse way of how their conscience has been touched. Would you want the clerk in your store to be charged with dishonesty, and not go back to his work, when the charge had been disproved, with a deepened perception of temptation, and a quickened watchfulness and care?

(*c*)

4. Or yet again. By a strange but very natural process, the same result often comes from just the opposite cause. Not merely when men suspect us and charge us with wrong-doing, but when men praise us and say that we are good, this same recognition of how bad we have the power to be often arises. Suppose that you are going on in a dull and lifeless way, not conscious of anything about yourself except just the practical powers by which you do your work from day to day. You have forgotten the mystery of your spiritual life. You have grown wholly unaware of the moral extremes whose folded capacities are in you. You never think how wicked you may be, or how good you may be. " Take thine ease, eat, drink, and be merry." You have come to that. And then suppose that some fellow-being, under the influence of some delusion, begins to praise you. He takes some little thing which you have done; he conceives for it lofty motives which you never dreamed of; he purifies it of all selfishness; he holds it up and says, " See what a true, deep spiritual man it must have been that did this thing." What is in your heart as you see your poor little deed held up above the world, shining with the light that his friend's imagination has thrown into it, and with the eyes of all men fastened upon it? Is there no shame? You must be a very poor sort of man if there is not. Is there no breaking up of the dead equilibrium of self-content? Is it not as if the net in which a bird had been held, with its wings helpless and useless, were torn to pieces, and the bird had either to fall to the ground or to fly to the sky. Its danger and its chance were revealed to it together. A man comes up to our life, and, looking round upon the crowd of our fellow-men, he says, " See, I will strike the life of this brother of ours, and you shall hear how true it rings." He does strike it, and it does seem to them to ring true, and they shout their applause; but we whose life is struck feel running all through us at the stroke the sense of hollowness. Our soul sinks as we hear the praises. They start desire, but they reveal weakness. No true man is ever so humble and so afraid of himself as when other men are praising him most loudly.

(*d*)

5. Is it not true that every temptation which comes to us, however bravely and successfully it may be resisted, opens to us the sight of some of our human capacity of sin. To resist temptation is never, I think, an exhilarating experience. We remember too vividly how near we came to yielding. We come out of battle thankful that we are

(*e*)

Is it I?—*continued*

safe and sound; but the night after the battle is not a light-hearted or jovial time. There are too many vacant places in the tent which only yesterday were full. The shriek of the bullet and the sight of the bursting shell are still too fresh and vivid. We are too much surprised to find that we are safe. Our escape has been too narrow. Job, as his wealth rolls back to him, takes it with thankful hands, but he cannot laugh over it when he remembers how from the heights of his misery he looked over into the possibility of cursing God. Simeon, when the child Christ is brought to him, thanks God that he has lived to see the fulfilment of his hopes; but he may well have remembered how often he had been almost ready to despair and give up his long watch. Nay, even Jesus Himself—what shall we think was the kind of step with which He came down the mountain? He had seen Satan. He had seen with what greedy and confident eyes Satan looked at that humanity of His, as if it were something that belonged to him. Strong and victorious He came away. But was there no new solemn insight into this humanity which He had taken? Was not the Incarnation more than ever awful to the Incarnate One? He, the sinless, had gone up and looked over the edge into the deepest depths of sin. He needed the ministry of angels, and He surely came down the mountain serious and sad. And so it is with you, when you follow your Lord into that experience. It may be that you come out by His grace pure and thankful, but you come out like Him, serious and sad, for you have looked down as He looked into the possibility of sin. The man who dares to laugh at a temptation which he has felt and resisted is not yet wholly safe out of its power.

(a)

6. This is the Bible picture of human life. Where shall we look for any other that is as reasonable or as complete? The fearless truster of himself! the distressed doubter of himself; the faithful truster of Christ! They are all here. We lay the Bible picture down beside our human life, and it explains everything. In life, too, there is the stout believer in himself, the frightened disbeliever in himself, and the sure believer in God. As a man comes into Christ, that experience deepens itself around him till he has fulfilled it all. First, a stripping away of his own righteousness, and then a clothing with the righteousness which is in Jesus. First, a light thrown upon himself, till it seems as if there were no wickedness he might not do, and then a drawing of himself into Christ's self till he sees there is no holiness which he may not attain. First, the weakness which comes of self-knowledge, and then the strength which is "strong in the Lord and in the power of His might." First, the fear which cries, "Is it I?" as it hears the announcement of some dreadful sin; and then the wondering faith which cries, "Is it I?" as the doors are opened, and they who are Christ's are called to enter into His everlasting life.

(b)   *Phillips Brooks*

-ISMS AND FAITH

"-Isms" operate intellectually. Faith operates ethically.

(c)

ISRAELITE INDEED, AN (John i. 47)

In all nations, as in all men, the essential permanent nature and destiny must be distinguished from the corruption of it—the true Israelite from the false Jew; the intellectual German from the dreamy German; the open, frank Frenchman from the insolent Frenchman.

(d)   *Lange*

"IT IS I"

"He saith unto them, It is I; be not afraid" (John vi. 20).

Suggestive thoughts arise easily from the narrative of the disciples being left on the sea, and Jesus walking to them on it.

Other storms come upon us, and toss us roughly on the sea of life. In such seasons it is well to draw comfort from such a passage as this.

Notice how troubles accumulate. They come not singly, but in a train, like wave rolling in after wave.

It was so here:
1. Darkness;
2. Jesus was not with them;
3. The storm arose;
4. They were terrified by an apparition.

The last trouble was the greatest, but it burst with blessings; like a rain-cloud looming terrible in the distance, but coming nearer, it pours a refreshing shower upon the earth.

(e)

1. Darkness

(i.) *Dark hours* of anxiety come to the man of business. Speculations fail, depressions occur, friends prove false, and ruin seems imminent.

(ii.) *Dark hours* of wasting and painful sickness come. Strength departs, and the firm muscle becomes weaker than a little child's, and "the strong man becomes as tow."

(iii.) *Darkness of soul.* When we have "no light," no joy, no comfort—when we cannot assure ourselves that we love God, or are loved of God—such darkness is darkness that may be felt. One of the heaviest of burdens, and saddest of all life's troubles, is to "walk in darkness and have no light."

(f)

2. Jesus was not with them

As if the father or mother was not with the children when exposed to peril. Jesus stood in this relation to His disciples. They felt safe with Him, and unsafe without Him. He usually bore their burdens. Now He is not with them, and this makes darkness darker. It may be He is trying them, but it does not make the trouble lighter. It is not the darkness that we dread so much as being *alone* without Jesus. This makes us weak, and unable to endure. The presence of Jesus gives strength and courage; without Him we can do nothing.

The three young Jews who were cast into the burning furnace for their faith and constancy, were not left alone; for the despot who gave the order looked into the furnace and saw there four men walking in the midst of the fire, and the fourth was like unto "the Son of God." It was His presence that gave them freedom to walk

(g)

It is I—*continued*

there, and kept the fire from harming them. If Jesus is not with us in the furnace, it is a double trouble.

(*a*)

3. The sea arose by reason of a great wind that blew

To be in darkness, and to be without the comfort of Jesus' presence, is just such a season as our great spiritual adversary is ever watching for. The disciples separated from Jesus, in darkness, in peril, on the sea, is just such an opportunity as He desires to alarm them, and to inject unbelief. Hence the storm and the possibilities of shipwreck.

But where are we? We, too, are on this world's sea—the sea is a type of the world. We are tossed about by one excitement after another, the constant flux and reflux of going and coming, engrossed in its businesses, carried hither and thither in the great whirlpool of life. Presently a wind arises, evil things are said, a strong current of hostile opinion sets in. The Church of Christ, like a little ship, becomes the point of attack; tossed about " by reason of a great wind that blew," a wind which the great adversary, in his malice, had fomented.

But this is not all.

(*b*)

4. The Apparition

The disciples see something in the distance moving on the water. It is a Ghost, a Spirit. They cry out for fear, " terrified and affrighted." This is the worst stage of their trouble, but it is also the last. The darkest hour of night is that before the dawn. The coldest hour of the night is that which precedes sunrise. So when our trouble is greatest, and things seem past hope, then help is near. Of all people, seamen are proverbially the most superstitious. We can well imagine the terror of the disciples when they saw this phantom moving towards them. The darkness of the night, the being without Jesus, the storm, and now this apparition—all combine to make their trouble great and accumulated. They are at their wits' end.

(*c*)

5. " It is I; be not afraid "

The storm bursts, but it bursts with blessings. A voice came out of the midst of the trouble, *a well-known voice*, a voice that made them forget darkness, and loneliness, and storm, and ghost. It was the voice of JESUS, saying, " It is I; be not afraid."

How often have we looked and waited for Jesus, and when He came to us, He came in such a questionable shape, and in such a manner as we could not anticipate, that we did not recognise Him. But when He speaks, darkness, loneliness, the storm, and the phantom all vanish, and they feel as safe as a child rocked to sleep in its mother's arms.

(*d*)

6. Mark how the Gospel sounds out of the midst of every trouble

Trouble does not at first sight look like a preacher of good news, yet is it.

War generally precedes the conversion of nations. The ploughshare precedes a rich harvest. So trouble precedes Christ. It is His herald, His forerunner, His preacher.

Out of the midst of this trouble these men were in, the Gospel of comfort sounds to remind us that it is in this way God speaks comfort to the weary and heavy-laden.

That cloud which loomed so terribly in the distance, which seemed charged with lightning and thunder, and which we expected to overwhelm us as it approached, opened, it is true, but not with thunder-

> " The clouds ye so much dread,
> Are big with mercies, and shall break
> With blessings on your head."

A voice came from the midst of it, the voice of the Gospel, which thrilled us through, and changed the whole current of our being, saying : " It is I ; " Jesus your Saviour, coming to you, my friends, in a way you least expected. " It is I "—your Heavenly Father, dealing with you as a Father, who pitieth His children, whom yet He must train and discipline with trouble. " It is I "—your Physician, giving you medicine, which now may be bitter, but which shall be sweet in the end, " yielding the peaceable fruits of righteousness to all who are exercised thereby." " Why are ye fearful ? " " And why do thoughts arise in your hearts? " " Be not afraid." " Fear not." " Weep not." " Let not your hearts be troubled." " Be of good comfort." Such is the Gospel. And as such, if we will but see it, it comes to us in every dark hour, in all the lonelinesses and all the troubles of life. Out of the midst of the blackest cloud, the same voice, full of comfort, speaks to us now, as it spake then, " It is I ; be not afraid."

(*e*)

7. Immediately they are at the land whither they went

Having willingly received Jesus into the ship, this was the immediate result—they were in port at once. The Christian poet well seizes the embodied thought when he says :—

> " We are in port if we have Thee "

We are crossing life's ocean. Darkness comes on, and we are afraid. The loneliness of our spirits makes us still more afraid ; we are conscious of having no guiding star, no pilot on board. Storms arise, and our peril increases, shipwreck is imminent. Lastly, some trouble comes which completely arouses us ; terrified and affrighted, we cry out for fear. Immediately Jesus speaks to us. He comes out of the trouble, because *He was in it ;* and then, if we willingly receive Him into our hearts and into our lives, Heaven is begun in us. The presence of Jesus is Heaven ; Heaven is no longer a possibility but a possession. We are immediately at the other side. " We are in port if we have Thee."

(*f*)

J

JACOB AND ESAU

"Jacob have I loved, but Esau have I hated" (Rom. ix. 13).

God loves the man that loves Him, and hates the man that hates Him.

"They that despise Me shall be lightly esteemed."

But the manner of God's love reads strange from our point of view.

The man who is loved is chastened, and has an uncomfortable life all through; whilst the man who is hated is let alone, and has a pleasant time of it.

(a)

Observe:

1. The Characters of these Two Men

(i.) Esau=not incarnation of wickedness and profanity, but the personification of unbelief (worldly, practical unbelief). This lies at the root of his conduct in despising the "Birthright." "What good?" etc.

"Why be religious, like my simple-minded father, Isaac, or like my crafty and designing brother, Jacob? A beautiful specimen, he, of religious people!"

Beyond this he is estimable in many ways: an affectionate son, a good-natured, easy-going, affable country gentleman, whose company most people would have preferred to that of his deeper and incomprehensible brother, Jacob. You could talk with Esau on everyday matters,—not with Jacob.

Beyond this, however, Esau has no depth. In half an hour you could have got to the bottom of him, and everything about him=no reserves="a good fellow"—plain, honest, above board; loved by the world, but lightly esteemed by God.

Not so with—

(ii.) JACOB :=complex=a puzzle—takes a long time to know him, or him to know himself.

Great spiritual capacities, though allied with much alloy.

Tricky, cunning, crafty in his dealings, want of candour. Yet this is the man that God chooses, and of whom He says, "Jacob have I loved."

This man, with all his blemishes, God delights in, takes him in hand, puts him through a course of discipline, until in the end Jacob, the supplanter, ready to do anything to gain his own ends, becomes ISRAEL, a Prince of God.

(b)

2. The Two Brothers

= Types

(i.) Of the unbelieving, seeking their all in present gratifications.

"Esau did eat and drink, and rose up and went his way," as if nothing had happened.

Holy Scripture therefore calls him profane and godless. Therefore all such are "hated."

(ii.) The believing, who value the promises of God so highly that they are ready to use any means to gain spiritual ends. These are the subjects of purifying grace: something may be made of them. Their faults are better than Esau's virtues. Therefore they are "loved."

(c)

3. Jacob's Career after His Great Sin

(i.) His spiritual life commences when he "goes out" from his home. Rebekah had hitherto been the leading mind. They are both punished for their part in the deceit; they part to meet no more on earth. Jacob leaves a home of affluence, and goes to seek his bread, etc. He meets with vicissitudes: the deceiver is deceived, and his conscience makes it difficult to have confidence in God.

But God never forsakes him: blessing and punishment go hand-in-hand.

God meets him at Bethel, at his "going out."

Ministering angels are to have the care of him in his wanderings.

In that night, when he lay on a heap of stones, oppressed with a sense of sin, desolation, and loneliness, Jacob was comforted—he experienced conversion. Henceforth he relies upon God, not upon his mother.

In that night he learnt by experience, "Though your sins be as scarlet, they shall be white as snow," etc. That if "sin abounds, God's grace super-abounds."

Then strengthened, he goes forward to encounter fresh temptations, which bring out the alloy that is in him.

(ii.) His return.

The implacable Esau meets him. Jacob prays, and the "angels" attend him again—this time at his "coming in."

Jacob wrestles in prayer, because God hardens Himself against him, as if he had no claim on Him: His sins "have separated between him and God." But Jacob will not be put off, and he prevailed. He overcame; but, as all will, he carried the mark of the conflict with him to his grave: no one comes out of such conflict without a wound.

Henceforth Jacob is a new man: less self-reliant, less cunning—whose trust is in God.

(d)

4. Jacob's History affords Illustration of many New Testament Doctrines

(i.) Ministry of angels—at his "going out and coming in."

(ii.) "The kingdom of heaven suffereth violence;" see Jacob's wrestling.

(iii.) Importunate prayer.

(iv.) All things work together for good, etc.

(v.) Belief and unbelief (Jacob and Esau).

God's love showed, not by strewing Jacob's path with roses, but by discipline and by adversity, until he was purged from his old sins. A thought for those who take tribulation to mean "reprobation" =Like Asaph. Then said I, "I am cut off."

Esau's history, the rather, leads to this conclusion—to be left alone is the worst that can befall us, for "Whom the Lord loveth He chasteneth," etc.

"Because ye are my Jacobs, therefore I deal with you as I did with Jacob."

(e)

Cf. Hengstenberg

JAWBONE

" And Samson said, With the jawbone of an ass, heaps upon heaps, with the jaw of an ass have I slain a thousand men." What contempt does this fact throw upon military power, that with an ass's jawbone, God can achieve the most wondrous deeds,—" One man shall chase a thousand ! "

Cf. Flavius Vopiscus relates that Aurelian, in the Sarmatic war, slew forty-eight men with his own hand in one day, and during his life 950, upon which the boys made a song, and shouted in their dances, " Mille, Mille, Mille, Mille, Mille, Mille, decollavimus, unus homo, Mille, Mille, etc., Mille, Mille, vivat, qui Mille, Mille, occidit."

(a)   *See Jones' Dict. Prop. Names*

JEREMY TAYLOR

The cross of Christ is dimly seen in Taylor's works. Compare him in this particular with Donne, and you will feel the difference in a moment.

(b)   *S. T. Coleridge*

JERICHO, FALL OF, Compared with the End of the World

" *By faith the walls of Jericho fell down, after they were compassed about seven days* " (Heb. xi. 20; Josh. vi.)

1. The Fall of Jericho was peculiar. God employs means; but the means, considered in themselves, are inadequate—" The weakness of God is stronger than men."

Jericho was an important stronghold of the Canaanites—the key to Western Palestine; that fallen, the conquest of the rest of the land was comparatively easy, and its fall an earnest of the whole.

Led by seven priests provided with trumpets, the people were to walk round the fortifications of Jericho once for six days, and blow with the trumpets; on the seventh day they were to do this seven times, and at the last trumpet blast, and shout of the people, the walls of the city would fall flat to the ground, and the Israelites would enter, and possess the city. This was done.

Note that two things combined to bring about the fall of the city :

(i.) Faith (not the means) on the part of the Israelites.

(ii.) Unbelief (not their sins) on the part of the Canaanites.

(c)

2. Compare this account of the Seven Trumpet Blasts with what is told us of the Seven Trumpets in Rev. viii. and ix

The comparison shows this,

(i.) *Jericho* comes to an end on the seventh day, and after the seventh sounding of the trumpets.

(ii.) *The world* comes to an end much in the same way, after a seventh period has begun, and at the sounding of the seventh trumpet.

The comparison is at least interesting :

In Rev. viii. 3–5, we observe that revelations and great stirring events in the spirit-world (in the Church) follow after the earnest prayers of God's people. They ask for help, and it comes—

not perhaps as they imagined, but yet it does come.

The time *when* the trumpets sound :

When the Church is in danger from the world God's people are called together to war, and to expect His help.

The trumpets proclaim His help (as at Jericho).

Verse 7 = *The First Trumpet,* shows the Church afflicted with fanaticism and carnal zeal = religion propagated by fire and sword : " Shall we call down fire ? " etc.

Verse 8 = *The Second Trumpet* = the settled order of things ; fanaticism becomes the national life, appears to be Divine—religious wars, etc.

Verse 10 = *The Third Trumpet* = Wormwood— spiritual fountains and currents made bitter by party spirit, etc.

Verse 12 = *The Fourth Trumpet*—sun, moon, and stars partially obscured = superstition and unbelief as darkening the way of salvation.

The three woes follow.

Ch. ix. (1–12) = *The Fifth Trumpet :* out of the pit comes demoniac agency ; on earth mental sufferings ; smoke from the abyss—locusts—sting for five months, not kill—power limited—over men not sealed, " without hope."

Verse 13 = *The Sixth Trumpet.* Horses = heresies before the end. Horses worse than the riders.

Ch. x. 7 = *The Seventh Trumpet* = the end. The fall of the world as opposed to God.

We have only to look at the course of Christian history to find that at the special times of danger to the Church, the loud blast of a trumpet-voice (like John the Baptist's) called the Church into fresh activity and zeal, and at the same time announced the " help " of God.

(i.) To begin with the Apostles = the first sounding of the trumpets. Then the Church lapsed into Gnostic and other errors—semi-heathen—as might be expected, tinged by the near contact of the spirit of the world as then existing.

(ii.) Two or three centuries passed away, and the life of the Church was again in danger. The Pelagian heresy, denial of original sin, and the work of the Holy Spirit. Then God raised up Augustine to sound the trumpet of recall, and to bring the Church back to the truer evangelical doctrines of justification, sanctification, and the grace of God.

(iii.) More centuries pass. The Church again droops. The darkness of the middle ages all but puts her light out—she becomes the harlot, corrupt.

Then again God sounds a loud trumpet blast, and the Reformer's voice (Luther) is heard throughout Christendom, and a healthy life is again seen in the reforms and restorations of the sixteenth century.

(iv.) Once more centuries elapse, and the Church droops. The cold, lifeless formalism of the eighteenth century indicates " a name to live, but dead."

Then again is heard the blast of the trumpets. Evangelical, life-giving doctrines are preached by the Revivalists (Wesley, Whitfield, John Newton, Cecil, Hervey, Fletcher), which have been continued, and have brought forth much fruit— notably in the formation of great Bible and Mis-

(d)

sionary Societies. But the "tares" were sown, too; Sacerdotalism has drawn away much of the life and best energies of the Church, and "the third part of men died."

Add to this, modern doubt, scepticism, and open infidelity, and the Church in our day has come into great danger—greater, perhaps, than any which has preceded. And in the reactionary spirit of the time we may perhaps recognise the next trumpet blast calling the faithful to the conflict.

Then the walls of the spiritual Jericho (the world) will be thrown down, opposition disarmed, feeble as the means may appear—"The foolishness of God is stronger than men."

(*a*)

JERUSALEM, BEGINNING AT

"*Beginning at Jerusalem*" (Mark xvi. 15; Luke xxiv. 47)

(i.) **The preacher** = "So YE," ye whom I have trained. They do not go, but are *sent*. "How shall they preach except they be sent." Cf. "I have not *sent* these preachers, yet they ran."

(ii.) **To whom?** To all the world; to every creature. No limitation. No harsh creed. The Gospel is universal, from pole to pole. Yet it is true—

"Ye shall not have gone over the cities of Judah until the Son of Man be come."

= Ye shall not have finished your work, but be at work, when Christ returns.

(iii.) **The subject** = the Gospel, good tidings = repentance and remission of sins.

Repentance = a change of mind—opinion revised = once for all.

Repentance is not restraint, for a new heart has been given.

Illustrate repentance by floating with the tide, and afterwards swimming against it.

Repentance and remission of sins run into each other, and overlap. Where God gives the one, He intends the other.

Luther's mistake corrected—"Dr. Martin, thou dost not believe in the forgiveness of sins."

The exalted Christ grants repentance and remission—not one without the other.

Beautiful, that Jesus followed close on John Baptist—no interval between them. "There standeth one among you," etc.

Repentance and remission = like dissolving views—before one goes, the other melts into it; one must increase whilst the other decreases.

(iv.) **Where to begin?**

Begin at Jerusalem. Ezekiel's testimony was, that Jerusalem was a worse place than even Sodom.

Begin, then, as surgeons on a field of battle—select the worst cases first. Jerusalem seemed to have outlived her day of grace.

The comfort of this to great sinners.

The fame of the Balm of Gilead.

(*b*)

Bunyan says, the Saviour's commission was—Go to the people who crucified Me, especially to the man who pierced My side, and say, there is another way of crucifying Me, and of piercing My heart.

See, for effect, Peter's first sermon, whilst obeying this injunction. Objectors say—

(*a*) I plotted His death.

(*b*) I was one of the false witnesses.

(*c*) I cried out, "Crucify Him!"

(*d*) I desired Barabbas instead of Christ.

(*e*) I spat in His face, and mocked His sufferings.

(*f*) In His extremity I said, "Give Him gall and vinegar to drink." Will not the same measure be dealt out to me?

(*g*) I nailed His hands and feet to the cross—reviled Him—increased His tortures—I rejoiced to see Him suffer and die. Can there be mercy, hope, for me—even me?

Peter replies, "Yes, for every one of you. My commission shuts out none of you." This was to begin at Jerusalem.

(*c*)   *Cf. Bunyan*

JERUSALEM, DESTRUCTION OF, AND THE END OF THE WORLD (Matt. xxiv.)

In this chapter the accounts of the destruction of Jerusalem, and of the "end" of the world are so interwoven, that it is not easy to distinguish between them. Many people have been puzzled because they could not draw the line of demarcation arbitrarily, and say where the division was. But the best way of looking at the passage is to regard it as not confused—as *one* narrative, not *two*. The destruction of Jerusalem and the end of the world are here considered as one event. We who live in the present dispensation are they "upon whom the ends of the world are come." The narrative is of one thing in two parts; one tale told in two chapters; one drama in two acts. This is why it looks like two accounts. And it is not difficult to see this. It may be felt to be the duty of a parent, who has an unruly, incorrigible child, to administer corporal chastisement, but he would not strike more than one blow at a time. Between each stroke there is an interval, and the parent may, after having begun, suspend the punishment; and then, when the waiting time is over, and the necessity of punishment still continuing, he may finish what had already been begun. The act of punishment is one, though distributed over two periods of time. So with God's judgments related in this chapter. The destruction of Jerusalem was not merely a *prelude* to the day of judgment, nor merely a type of it, as is commonly supposed, but it was a *part* of it. The day of judgment, which is to come upon the whole world, began with the destruction of Jerusalem; and God having struck one blow in one place, is now waiting, with sword still uplifted, to strike again, and finish His work. The corresponding account in St. Luke tells us that God is waiting "until the times of the Gentiles be come in." The Jew was first in grace; he is likewise first in judgment. But the turn of the Gentiles is coming on. Judgment has begun at the House of God, but it stays not there. The awful drama of the end of the world has two acts, and the time in which we are living is due to a suspension of the judgment already begun.

(*d*)   *Cf. Godet*

JERUSALEM AND ROME

1. St. Paul's great desire was to see Rome. "I must go to Jerusalem," he said, "in order to

(*e*)

Jerusalem and Rome—*continued*

minister to the saints there, and I must see Rome."
Why? For the simple reason that he was the
Apostle of the Gentiles, and Rome was the centre
of the world; and as he was sent to bear witness
for Christ among the Gentiles, his heart was full
of affection for all nations, and he was anxious to
go to that place, especially as that was the then
central seat of all power and civilization.

(a)

2. Jerusalem and Rome are full of great contrasts. The Book of Acts may be entitled "From
Jerusalem to Rome." Jerusalem is the centre of
God's people. From Jerusalem the knowledge
and worship of God proceeds; Jerusalem was
chosen of God to be the centre of His kingdom;
Jerusalem is the City of David; and Jerusalem for
ever is the city of the great King, David's Son
and David's Lord. Rome is the centre of the world
power; it is that fourth great and mighty beast
which was beheld in the vision of Daniel; it is the
fourth world monarchy; it is characterized by trick;
it is strong in its own strength and cruelty; it is
notorious by its self-assertion and cunning; it is
the representative of the world power; it stands in
itself independent of God. And yet at the same
time, though Jerusalem and Rome are thus characterized, we must remember that Jerusalem, holy
unto the Lord, rejected and stoned the prophets,
and killed them that were sent unto her, and at
last filled up the measure of her iniquity by the
treatment of the Lord of Glory. And it rejected
the Apostles when Stephen was stoned, while Rome
protected the Apostle Paul against the cruelty and
rage of his countrymen, who would otherwise have
put him to death. And being the home of the
Gentiles, Rome was to be evangelized, and the
whole Roman Empire was to receive the truth
from the sufferings and testimony of the Christians.
Yet ere I pass from this, in order that you may
fully enter into the mind of the Apostle Paul,
enlightened by the Holy Ghost, let me say that
Jerusalem always remains the Holy City. During
the time of the Gentiles, but no longer, shall
Jerusalem be trodden down by the feet of the
Gentiles. Rome, of which we must remember
three things—that it put to death the Lord Jesus,
executing the will of the Jews against all legality;
Rome, that destroyed Jerusalem with a cruel
destruction; Rome, that shed the blood of the
saints of God for two centuries; Rome, that afterwards became the great centre of the great apostasy,
the scourge of Europe—that is the character of
Rome and the history of Rome; and when Rome
is made instrumental in the spread of the Gospel
in the apostolic ages and the first centuries, we can
see in it the wonderful mercy of God; and throughout the whole history of God in His dealings with
His people, we see how unsearchable are His ways,
and His thoughts past finding out.

(b)

3. But though the Apostle Paul said he must
see Rome, little did he think he would see it *as a
prisoner*. As a prisoner, he who was appointed by
Jesus Christ to be the Apostle of all nations; how
strange are the ways of God, how contradictory
seem to be His leadings, how perplexing to all
human reason! What God does we often think
to be foolishness, whereas He seeth our wisdom to
be folly. "How beautiful are the feet of him who

brings good tidings"; but his feet were limited to
the prison chamber. This chosen vessel of God,
whom he was utilizing and sending forward,
becomes a prisoner, and is in bonds. Wonderful
ways of God! Yes, he had to become a prisoner
—two years in Cæsarea, and more than two years
in Rome. Four years out of such a valuable life,
as human reason would say, cramped and dwarfed.
God knows, and God only knows, how to promote
the interests of His kingdom; and rest assured
that that imprisonment was the wisdom of God to
Paul himself; and it enabled him to bear testimony
to King Agrippa, and to lead to that exclamation,
"Almost thou persuadest me to be a Christian";
and it enabled him to save the lives of those with
him in shipwreck; and in the island of Melita it
enabled him to show the power of the Lord Jesus
Christ; and in Rome it enabled him to proclaim
Christ, for the vision came to him: "Be of good
cheer, Paul; for as thou hast testified of Me in
Jerusalem, so must thou bear witness also at
Rome."

(c)

4. Now, can you imagine this Apostle Paul as
a prisoner, chained, as the custom was, unto a
soldier? Have you not often seen, with the mind,
the Apostle with those "bonds"? Do you remember, when he stood before King Agrippa, and had
spoken to him of Christ and His Gospel, how he
was so filled by the assurance of his happiness in
Christ, that out of the abundance of his heart he
cried, "I would to God that not only thou, but
also all that hear me this day, were both almost
and altogether such as I am"? But as he spoke
he felt the fetters as he lifted up his hands, and
added, "*except these bonds.*" How full of joy in
Christ; how sure that he was the Lord's servant
and witness! How small and insignificant appeared to him that little speck of time compared
with a boundless eternity! How unspeakably
beautiful the love of Jesus, without which all
things appeared most pitiful to him! Or if you
had seen him writing to the Church of Colosse.
As he wrote the salutation he felt his bonds,
and added, "Remember my bonds." "Paul, a
prisoner," he wrote in the Epistles to Philemon,
the Ephesians, Colossians, and Philippians. Do
you not know the chains when he writes and
describes the different parts of the panoply, the
breastplate, and the helmet, and everything that
constituted the armour of every one ready to withstand the enemy? When we remember the circumstances, it will appeal to every heart as he writes
to his dearly beloved Philippians, his joy and his
crown.

(d)
Adolph Saphir

JESUS CHRIST

The Announcement of the Birth of the Saviour
(Luke i. 26–38)

= (i.) The beginning of "the world to come"
(ii.) The second Adam: "As in Adam all die,
so in Christ shall all be made alive"
(iii.) A sinless beginning; exposed to temptation,
like the first Adam, and yet not yielding.

1. The Appearing of the Angel (26–29)

Mary—at prayer—Nazareth = a secluded spot
"The Lord is with thee" = special favour
(e)

Mary trembled, but not in fear, shows her degree of holiness. We fear in proportion as we sin, and have an evil conscience.

2. The Message (30–33)=the mark of God's favour: Note

   (i.) A son
   (ii.) His name, JESUS=Blessing
   (iii.) His greatness (*See* "GREAT MEN.")
   (iv.) His Divine name (Son of the Highest)
   (v.) His eternal kingdom.

3. The way the Message was Received (34–38)

It was not a command. Mary only need consent; this consent she gives, simply and submissively (38). Thus we see a true daughter of Zion: the fruit of faith under the O.T.

  (*a*)   *Cf. Godet*

JESUS CHRIST, BIRTH OF (Luke ii. 1–20)

Introduction

(i.) From one little sin all the evil that exists entered and demoralized the earth=a flood of ungodliness.

(ii.) So from one pure Being born into this world (JESUS) there is the germ, or seed sown, which shall ultimately leaven the whole world, and make it like Himself. (Cf. Parable of leaven, Matt. xiii.; Col. i. 20, "To reconcile all things unto Himself"; Phil. ii. 9–11, "That at the name of Jesus," etc.).

In such a light are we to read and understand the birth of Jesus into this world.

  (*b*)

1. The Birth of Jesus (1–7): wherein notice-

The Divine principle of working: "The weakness of God is stronger than men."

We see what was to be done: the earth was *sick*, festering, dying, under a curse (Rom. i.)

Ask (i.) What could be a greater work than the cleansing of this Augean stable, the re-creation of this world, the ousting of sin, and the salvation of *mankind?*

Ask (ii.) What could have been "weaker" than the means employed to do all this, than the helpless Babe in Bethlehem, the manger, and the carpenter's home at Nazareth? Who would have looked *there* for God's strength?

  (*c*)

2. The Gospel first preached to the poor (8–14): to shepherds—men of mean condition, simple capacities, toilsome labour, and hardships; cold season, yet watching their flocks by night; not concerned in any great transactions, yet God tells them *first* what He is doing. [Don't say, after this, "I am too poor"—"I have to work for my living"—"Religion is for well-to-do people."] Princes, statesmen, learned philosophers and doctors, are passed over; God tells them nothing. Wealthy merchants and citizens, comfortable and warm in their houses; at ease, at pleasure, in bed, or sitting by fires; at banquets, engaged in sports; all are passed by. The Gospel is not preached to them. But to the poor, the needy, the suffering, the oppressed, "*tidings of great joy*" are brought by the angels from heaven.

  (*d*)

3. The Gospel=

(i.) "*A Saviour*," in allusion to the miserable state of mankind;

(ii.) "*Christ the Messiah*," in fulfilment of prophecy;

(iii.) "*The Lord*": ours and yours (=Divinity and Godhead).

  (*e*)

4. On this, the angel is joined (13, 14) **by a troop of other angelic beings, who sing-**

(i.) "*Peace—men—earth;*
(ii.) *Glory—God—highest.*"

Men send up their praises to God: He sends down His peace on them=*reconciliation* (God with us)—the curse, the enmity, the warfare between the two removed ("In whom I am well pleased").

  (*f*)

5. What heaven has thus revealed the shepherds *preach* (15–20), and they become the first preachers of the Gospel. Hence, even in preaching, "The weakness of *God is stronger than men.*"

  (*g*)   *Cf. Godet*

JESUS CHRIST (Luke ii. 21–40)

1. The Circumcision of Jesus

Under the Jewish form, Jesus was to realize the ideal of human existence. Thus, eight days after his birth, He entered into the covenant by circumcision. This twofold fact is mentioned by St. Paul: "Born of a woman, made under the law" (Gal. iv. 4). The brevity of the account, as compared with that of John the Baptist, is due to the fact that circumcision had not the same significance for Jesus as it had for John.

  (*h*)

2. The Presentation in the Temple

(i.) *Simeon* (25–28). The times were degenerate. The official clergy, mere officials. The true spirit to be sought for in such times amongst obscure men, often of the lowest class. (Cf. Methodism in the last century.) Simeon and Anna, representatives of a spontaneous (perhaps unordained) priesthood. The Holy Spirit at this moment makes him a true priest, and he opens his arms to receive the Child brought into the temple.

(ii.) *His Song* (29–32). He regards himself as a *sentinel*, commanded to watch for, and announce the appearance of, the Sun of Righteousness. This done, he asks for his discharge: "*Now lettest Thou*," etc.

To the Gentiles, sunk in ignorance and darkness, Messiah comes as *The Light*.

To Israel, as the outcome of all the past spiritual yearnings, hopes, and aspirations, He is the GLORY.

But woe to Mary (33–35) should her heart be possessed by a carnal satisfaction, a delusive hope, on hearing these words. A drop of bitterness is mixed with her deep and holy joy—never wanting in this world of sin—"A sword shall pierce through thine heart." The old man knows his countrymen. He knew that beneath their external religion existed hypocrisy, avarice, hatred to God; and in the face of this holy Child this evil would show itself. "The thoughts of many hearts would be revealed," the venom would be poured forth, and the end would be catastrophe.

  (*i*)

(iii.) *Anna* (36–38) = one of "those who looked for redemption."

There were three classes of Jews:

(i.) The Pharisees (externally religious).

(ii.) The Sadducees (the sceptics of the day).

(iii.) The faithful (like Simeon and Anna, who quietly waited for the fulfilment of God's promises).

These obviously have their modern representatives.

(a)   *Cf. Godet*

JESUS CHRIST

The Development of Jesus (Luke ii. 39, 40)

(39) Observe the scrupulous fidelity to the law of Him who came not to destroy, but to fulfil it. His parents returned to Nazareth *only* after having fulfilled every prescription of the law.

(40) "*He grew*" = physically.

"*He waxed strong, being filled with wisdom*" = spiritual, intellectual, and religious development. = on the one hand, the knowledge of God; on the other, a penetrating knowledge of men and things from a Divine point of view = the true humanity of Jesus; = the normal growth of man, physically and morally, accomplished for the first time on earth. God's idea of man realized in Jesus. Then He regarded this Child with perfect satisfaction.

(b)   *Ibid*

JESUS CHRIST (Luke iii. 21–23)

The relation between John and Jesus resembles two stars following each other at a short distance, both passing through similar circumstances. Announcement of the appearing of the one follows close on that of the other. So of their births: so of their respective ministries, lastly in the catastrophes which terminate their lives. And yet they only meet but once—at the baptism of Jesus. Then the orbit of the two stars crossed each other. They separated, each to follow his own path.

(c)   *Ibid*

The moment of contact is here described:

1. The Baptism of Jesus.

Jesus being baptized, PRAYING: In answer to His prayer, notice–

(i.) The heavens opened;

(ii.) The descent of the Holy Ghost;

(iii.) A voice spake to Him.

Notice further, Jesus gets these, as we are to get them. The Spirit will descend on him who knows how to ask aright.

(i.) Ask;

(ii.) Seek;

(iii.) Knock.

(d)

2. The Meaning

(i.) The opened heavens = perfect revelation: all the treasures open which wise men and prophets desired to see, and did not see them.

(ii.) The descent of the Holy Ghost = not as at Pentecost, divided amongst a body of believers, but in His fulness: "God giveth not the Spirit by measure unto Him." Moreover, "it abode upon Him" = permanent inspiration, not intermittent, like that of the prophets.

(iii.) The Divine voice establishes the full relation, what He is to the Father ("My beloved Son"); and what He is to the world—the organ of Divine love to men, whose mission is to make known the Father, and to raise His brethren to the dignity of sons.

So God communicates to us the certainty of our adoption, when the hour is come. Jesus, the only begotten, we the adopted sons—after which He goes to His work, and we to ours.

(e)   *Ibid*

JESUS CHRIST

The Visit to Nazareth (Luke iv. 14–30)

The position of Jesus, after His temptation: with God for His sure. Ally, and Satan for His declared adversary, Jesus advances to the field of battle.

(f)   *Ibid*

(14) **Filled with the Spirit**, Jesus returned to Galilee, taught, and acted. His fame spreads immediately.

(15) In the synagogue His reputation was ratified—"glorified of all."

(16) After, He visits Nazareth, where His greatest difficulties would be encountered.

"As His custom was." Read Isa. lxi. 1, etc.

(17) Guided what text to take.

"The acceptable year of the Lord" = the year of grace. Jubilee, every fifty years: slaves, patrimony, debtors, set free = a type of spiritual restoration: "The true year of Jubilee is come." He could not have had a more appropriate text.

N.B.—The Galilean ministry lasted only about one year.

(18–19) The Spirit of the Lord is upon Me" = anointed at His baptism.

(i.) Good news to poor;

(ii.) Heal broken-hearted;

(iii.) Captives, malefactors, and slaves set free at beginning of the year of grace. [How soon do those who are set free by Christ return again to bondage by reason of their unwatchfulness!]

(iv.) Blind captives come from their dark dungeons into "marvellous light."

(v.) Bruised = suffering from any wrong or oppression, have favours shown to them.

(g)

(20) **The Preaching**

(21) This day;

(22) Jesus had the conscience of His hearers;

The word heard should have been mixed with faith, instead of unbelief: "Is not this Joseph's son?" "We have known this young man from His youth." Contrast, "Glorified of all," elsewhere.

A critical moment for them. The seed caught away by the wicked one. There is

(i.) Curiosity;

(ii.) Ridicule;

(iii.) Rejection.

(23.) The first symptom of unbelief. "Heal Thyself"—(irony) Work a miracle. But Jesus worked no miracle there—a moral impossibility.

(24) "No prophet," etc. "But others will receive Me." Cf. "Lo, we turn to the Gentiles."

(25–27) Prophecies and examples of Israel rejecting, and the Gentiles receiving the works of grace, fulfilled unto this hour.

(28–30) Exasperated, they say, "Thou rejectest us: we reject Thee." Their act = murder in intention, but His hour was not yet come.

(h)   *Cf. Godet*

JESUS CHRIST, THE TEMPTATION OF (Luke iv.)

Temptation is trial, or testing. Religious people are permitted to be tempted to try the strength of their principles, and teach them how to handle spiritual weapons, that they may overcome. They are generally tempted after a period of spiritual blessing and enjoyment—full vessels are pursued by pirates. This temptation of our Lord is an illustration and a specimen of that temptation which is common to man, which He, like the first Adam, encountered, being "tempted in all things like as we are," and is the only temptation "without sin."

Practically it may be viewed and illustrated as follows:

1. "Command that these stones be made bread."

The temptation here is in the matter of daily bread—commonly called "getting a living." Its aim is to break down a man's faith in the Providence of God.

We must conceive of a man in straitened circumstances, brought to the verge of extremity. Perhaps the head of a family, and all visible means of support running short.

His religion says to him: "Have faith in God"; "Wait"; "Tarry thou the Lord's leisure." But he finds these principles now severely tested. He has waited long. He is tempted to distrust God's Providence; and, what is worse, to break away from dependence upon God, and to help himself in an unlawful manner. The tempter whispers: "Why wait?" "Why go in need?" "Why be religious overmuch?" "Why be so scrupulous, so uncompromising?" "Do as others do." "You must live. You must provide for those dependent on you—feed them, clothe them, educate them. You cannot do all this without means. Therefore make money as it may be made in the world. Get it anyhow; don't stick at a lie, don't stand on principle—'Command these stones that they be made bread'—turn everything, worthless things, into money; others do, so may you, and you shall be relieved from your painful position."

(a)

Reply:

"But I am a religious man, and it is written for my guidance in the Word of God:

"(i.) 'Man doth not live by bread alone' (obedience is better);

"(ii.) 'Blessed are they who hear the Word of God and keep it;'

"(iii.) 'What shall it profit a man if he gain the whole world, and lose his own soul?'

"I am taught to pray daily, 'Give us this day our daily bread'; and God's promise to me is, 'Seek first the kingdom of God and His righteousness, and all these things shall be added unto you.' 'Thy bread shall be given thee, and thy waters shall be sure.'"

(b)

2. "Fall down and worship me"

The second temptation is directed at the sphere of our ambition. The desire to succeed, to gain position, to be useful, is legitimate. But the means often are not so. The Christian believes in a God who ordereth his steps, puts him in his proper place, and gives him the work he is best fitted to do; and that the way of the cross leads to the crown. But moments will come when these principles likewise will be sorely tested. The tempter will again whisper his poison: "You are passed by; you have no friend at court; others step into every vacancy before you. But if you will act on other principles—for instance, fall down and worship me, the prince of this world—all things in the world are in my gift, and to whomsoever I will I give them. Position, usefulness, and honour shall be yours, if you will follow my instructions: Pay court to the powers that be; have done with 'self-respect,' and personal freedom; worship the king; worship man; worship genius; become a fawning courtier; lose no worldly chance. And by-and-by you shall succeed: the world will reward its devotee, and your ambition will be satisfied." This bait often succeeds. But, again, this man has scruples: He flies to his guide. He takes heed to the word where he finds it written:

(i.) "Promotion cometh neither from the east, west, north, but from the Lord";

(ii.) "Thou shalt worship the Lord thy God, and Him only shalt thou serve."

And He says to the tempter: "It is all wrong. Avaunt, Satan: get thee behind me!" "Have faith in God." "Delight thyself in the Lord, and He shall give thee the desires of thine heart."

(c)

3. "Cast Thyself down"

The third temptation is aimed directly at a man's religious standing. "If thou be a child of God, do a presumptuous thing: give God an opportunity to acknowledge thee." The tempter whispers: "You are a Christian, a child of God: now many great promises are made to you—'I will never leave nor forsake thee'; 'I will give My angels charge concerning thee,' etc. Therefore you have a safe conduct to glory, you are safe. You may do anything, read anything, go anywhere, into any company, good, bad, worldly, the play, the theatre, and run no risk. Why, is it not said: You may tread on serpents, touch any deadly thing, drink strong drink, touch fire, etc. . . . ? You may live as you like, and not be a castaway. You may leave the path of duty, give up your position and work, and expect another to open for you directly. In short, you may walk on the edge of a precipice, and no harm shall happen to you, because you are a child of God!"

(d)

Reply = "Thou shalt not tempt the Lord thy God." "Keep back thy servant from presumptuous sins." "Be temperate." "Let your moderation be known unto all men." "I keep my body under." "Take heed, lest ye receive the grace of God in vain." "Watch and pray, lest," etc.

(e)

4. Learn

(i.) How to overcome temptation;

(ii.) How to resist the devil;

(iii.) How to fight the good fight of faith;

(iv.) How to wield the sword of the Spirit, which is the Word of God.

5. The Reward of Faithfulness

After this struggle (it was a struggle: "He suffered, being tempted"), the devil fled, and angels came and ministered unto Him. So shall it be with us: If we suffer, we shall also partake of like consolations.

(f)   *Cf. Godet*

Every free creature must pass through a conflict. The angels did; the first man did; Jesus also. The date, after His baptism, at the outset of His Messianic career, is important. The battle-field on which Adam had succumbed, Jesus remained a victor. "Conscience without a scar." His trial is no mere repetition of Adam's; it belongs to a higher sphere. It is not, as with us, a question of whether a given individual shall be a member of the kingdom of God, but the very existence of the kingdom itself is now at stake. Its future sovereign engages in hostile combat with the "prince of this world." The victory decided the fate of mankind.

During the prolonged fast (forty days), the exhausted body became a prey to death-sinking. Jesus felt Himself dying. This was the moment the tempter had waited for to make his decisive assault. He came as an angel of light. The refusal of homage was a declaration of war against Satan, on the most unfavourable conditions. The three degrees of the temptation are-

(i.) The Man (member of the race);
(ii.) The Christ (official);
(iii.) The Son, is tempted.

The fourth temptation = that of Gethsemane = the fear of death.

(a)　　　　　　　　　　　　　*Cf. Godet*

JESUS CHRIST, THE CARPENTER

"*Is not this the carpenter?*" (Mark vi. 3)

St. Mark, with his usual care for interesting details, is the only Evangelist who informs us that Jesus Christ was a carpenter. But this information entirely harmonizes with what we might have expected. It is not to be supposed that He would have remained for thirty years in idleness in the home of His mother. While Joseph was living, it was natural that he would bring up Jesus to work at the bench with him. After Joseph was dead—and he seems to have died during the interval between the twelfth and thirtieth years of our Lord—there would be a stronger reason why Jesus should work to maintain His widowed mother. The time was coming when an infinitely greater mission to the world would break through the ordinary domestic ties. But that was not yet; and meanwhile who can think that one so full of kindness and so full of energy as Jesus, the first-born of the family, would have stood by quietly while His younger brothers laboured to support the household? Jesus Christ was a carpenter then. This fact was a stumbling-block to the people of "His own country." We may see in it something to increase His attractiveness. Let us look at these two aspects of the artisan life of our Lord.

(b)

1. How the Fact that Jesus was a Carpenter was a Hindrance to the Faith of His Fellow-Countrymen

(i.) The objection was natural. The townsfolk had often passed His workshop; had seen Him toiling at His bench; had used the ploughs and yokes He made them. He was just one of themselves, indeed inferior in rank to some of them. Could this well-known carpenter be the great teacher? the miracle-worker? the wondrous long-expected Messiah? Would not the people of an English country-town feel the same objection if an artisan whom they had known from their child-hood, and who had worked amongst them much like an ordinary workman, suddenly roused the neighbourhood with a strange fame? Christ was so reasonable and so charitable that He saw the meaning of this, and explained it by quoting a familiar proverb—"A prophet is not without honour, but in his own country, and among his own kin, and in his own house." But the explanation is no justification. Many proverbs are just the words of the wise about the doings of the foolish. What is in a sense natural and to be expected, may still be wrong and unreasonable. So "He marvelled because of their unbelief," There was that in Christ which ought to have overcome their prejudices. Their mistake was two-fold. They judged only by external appearances; they noticed the outer life only; and because that had been commonplace, and because they had not spiritual insight to discern the character of the soul behind it, they were offended. And they assumed that the future must be like the present. He always had been a carpenter. How could He ever be anything greater? Consider, then, how a near view of the earthly life of Christ is only a hindrance to faith in His great claims for men who have not the spirituality to discern His higher nature. If you look very closely at the most magnificent picture in the world, you see only patches of paint. The visitor to St. Peter's is disappointed as he approaches the *façade*, because its vast proportions seem to be scarcely perceptible. But let him look towards Rome from a distance of a few miles, and he will see the wonderful dome floating over the mists of the *campagna* like a temple let down from heaven, and then he will feel its majesty and glory. Familiarity should not breed contempt of what is not contemptible. But we are too small to see anything but the lower parts of a very high object when we stand close under it.

(c)

(ii.) So we criticize the feet, and never know the face. The people of Nazareth did not have so great a privilege in the presence of Christ in their town for the first thirty years of His life as some of us may have supposed. And, therefore, we are not such great losers in not seeing His bodily presence. We are not distracted from the vision of His great human soul and His divine glory. Not seeing Him after the flesh, we are the better prepared to see Him as He is.

(d)

(iii.) It is interesting to observe that the objection felt by His townsfolk to the claims of Jesus carries with it by implication a very high and unconscious tribute to His character. He had lived among them for thirty years. They had watched Him at His work. In a country town everybody is only too well known to his neighbour. Gossip is busy there in making the most of the least grain of scandal. What, then, do the jealous critical neighbours discover against the Son of Mary? That He was a slovenly workman? That He was hard in His charges? That His temper ever betrayed Him? Keen eyes sharpened by jealousy were on Him. Yet none of these charges are brought against Him. The sole accusation is—that He is a carpenter. They can find no fault with His character. They can only complain of His trade.

(e)

2. How the Fact that Jesus was a Carpenter should be a Help to our Faith

(i.) *This fact is a sign of the humility of Christ.* The Son of God came in no position of worldly rank and honour. He belonged to what are called often, with a contempt that is contemptible, the lower classes. It is true that when He came down the tremendous way, from heaven's glory to man's humiliation, it did not signify so very much to Him whether He alighted at a king's palace or a peasant's cottage. The condescension would not be appreciably different in the two cases. Yet to us the humility of Christ is more apparent in His lowly earthly lot.

(*a*)

(ii.) *This fact is a proof that Jesus Christ went through the experience of practical life.* He not only became a man, He did a man's work, He entered thoroughly into the occupations of human life. Work takes up a large part of life. It has its difficulties, its disappointments, its weariness. We all know them, whether we work with the hand or with the brain. Christ knew them too. Work has also its special requirements, its duties, its obligations. The apprentice must learn the various branches of his trade, if only that he may afterwards understand how to direct and judge of the work of the mechanics who will be under his control. Christ knows good work. When we serve Him, let it be with the thoroughness He so well understands and has a right to expect.

(*b*)

(iii. *This fact shows that Christ found the school for His spiritual training in His practical work.* As He bent over His task with care and diligence to do it well, His soul was growing silently in those excellencies which were ultimately revealed when His disciples " saw His glory full of grace and truth." He was no mere dreamer unacquainted with real life. He was no pedant who built fine theories on the abstract ideas of the schools. His college was the workshop. The consequence is, that we see in all His teaching a reality, a practical bearing, and a homeliness that weds the loftiest mysteries of spiritual truth to the simplest facts of every-day life. There is no " smell of the lamp " about His discourses. Practical men should listen to this Teacher. They are disgusted with the " theological jargon "—as they call it—of scholastic divinity. To them it is only " words, words, words." They ask for the bread of life, and they get the stone of a dogma. Let them listen to the Carpenter. *He* is real and human.

(*c*)

(iv.) *This fact sheds a glory over the life of manual industry.* Everything that Christ handles becomes beautiful beneath His touch. His presence in the vale of tears is the exaltation of sorrow into a divine blessedness. His presence in the workshop throws a holy light over its commonest contents. As the carpenter handles his tools, shall he not remember that he is doing the very work his Master did before him, and so exalted and consecrated ? In the light of the example of Christ what are we to say to the foolish notion of those people who seem to imagine that work is less honourable than idleness? Surely that great example should shame away such thoughts. It

should also cheer those of us who may be oppressed with the weariness of toil. Adam was punished by being made to eat his bread in the sweat of his face. Christ accepted the lot of Adam and his race, but He converted the punishment into a blessing. Done in Christ's spirit, work will be done cheerfully, and the workman will be honoured in it. The example of Christ shows us also how absurd it is to despise manual labour in comparison with lighter kinds of work. Why should so many young men be anxious to leave the ranks of workmen for the monotonous occupation of a clerk ? Is it to be assumed that the man who wears a black coat and has soft hands is higher in the scale of being than the energetic, intelligent artisan ? Remember, Christ was the purest type of humanity the world has ever seen, one whose lofty thoughts and pure sentiments made the most delicate specimens of the refinement of ordinary culture look brutal and coarse ; and Christ was a carpenter. Nevertheless, let us beware of the illusion of supposing that there is any merit in merely copying the outside life of Jesus of Nazareth. There have been thousands of carpenters—but there was only one Christ among them. It is when we follow Him in the higher things that He glorifies the lower for us.

(*d*)

(v.) *This fact should attract working men to Christ.* How strange, that it should be said that working men are not so interested in Christianity as other classes. It must be because they are repelled by the artificial respectability of the Church. It cannot be that they see anything in Christ Himself that is less attractive to them than to others. For He was a working man Himself. We Christians will have to answer for the heavy responsibility of hiding the significance of this fact by our pride and officiousness. It is high time that men learned to look at Christ Himself. When they do they will see that the Carpenter has a special right to claim the faith of working men.

(*e*) *W. F. Adeney*

(*See* " Labour," " Work.")

Jesus Christ and Theology

The most logical and argumentative theologians and learned scholars recur to the simplest trust when they approach the unseen world. Dr. Charles Hodge, the illustrious author and divine, repeated to himself in death,

> " Jesus, I am never weary,
> When upon this bed of pain,
> If Thy presence only cheer me,
> All my loss I count but gain;
> Ever near me,
> Ever near me, Lord, remain ! "

and Bishop Whipple, of the Protestant Episcopal Church, has just said, " As the grave grows nearer, my theology is growing strangely simple. It begins and ends with Christ, the only refuge for the lost."

(*f*)

Jesus Christ

No one will accuse the first Napoleon of being either a pietest or weak-minded. He strode the world in his day like a Colossus, a man of gigantic

(*g*)

intellect, however worthless and depraved in moral sense. Conversing one day, at St. Helena, as his custom was, about the great men of antiquity, and comparing himself with them, he suddenly turned round to one of his suite, and asked him, "Can you tell me who Jesus Christ was?" The officer owned that he had not yet taken much thought of such things. "Well, then," said Napoleon, "I will tell you." He then compared Christ with himself, and with the heroes of antiquity, and showed how Jesus far surpassed them. "I think I understand somewhat of human nature," he continued, "and I tell you, all these were men, and I am a man; but not one is like Him. Jesus Christ was more than man. Alexander, Cæsar, Charlemagne, and myself founded great empires; but upon what did the creations of our genius depend? Upon force. Jesus alone founded His empire upon love, and to this very day millions would die for Him! Men wonder at the conquests of Alexander, but here is a conqueror who draws men to Himself for their highest good; who unites to Himself, incorporates into Himself, not a nation, but the whole human race."

(a)   C. Geikie

"JESUS CHRIST, OR DESPAIR"

Another writer of name, in a volume just out, says:—"There is a wave—I believe it is only a wave—passing over the cultivated thought of Europe at present, which will make short work of all belief in a God that does not grip fast to Jesus Christ. As far as I can read the signs of the times, and the tendency of modern thinking, it is this:—Either an absolute Silence, a heaven stretching above us, blue and clear, and cold and far away, and *dumb*; or else a Christ that speaks—He or none. The theism that has shaken itself loose from Him will be crushed, I am sure, in the encounter with the agnosticism and the materialism of this day."

(b)   *Ecclesiastical Gazette*

JESUS CHRIST, DIVINITY OF

I feel that the Jewish carpenter could no more have conceived and sustained this character under motives of imposture, than an infant's arm could repeat the deeds of Hercules, or his unawakened intellect comprehend and rival the matchless works of genius.

(c)   *Channing*

JESUS CHRIST, THE EXPLANATION OF CREATION

"To Him and for Him" (Col. i. 16)

Christ is the explanation of creation: The "How?" and the "Why?" of it.

(d)   *Alford*

JESUS CHRIST, THE EXPLANATION OF MAN

"We see Jesus . . . crowned" (Heb. ii. 9)

"What is man?" is the question asked in Ps. viii. "We see Jesus" (as the explanation of man) is the answer in the Epistle to the Hebrews.

MAN: WHENCE comes he? WHY is he? and WHITHER goeth he?

(e)

1. Whence comes man?

This has ever been the question of science and philosophy, and they give characteristic answers. But the Bible =

  (i.) "God created man."
  (ii.) "Thou madest him."
  (iii.) "Thy hand hath made me and fashioned me."
  (iv.) "He hath made us, and not we ourselves," etc.

The mystery of Creation is not removed by calling it Evolution. In either case it is a miracle—and the distinction may be without a difference. The question still remains, *How* was man made? The answer is, "WE SEE JESUS": He came into the world mysteriously and superhumanly; He came out of the old existing state of Being, but not as the old. A new thing was done in Him. The race took a new and a higher start in Him. So was it with man at the "Beginning." Jesus came from God; and this is the explanation of man's origin.

(f)

2. Why was man created?

Answer: "To have dominion"
Man was intended to be the Master, the lord of Creation—over animals, beasts, fishes, birds, reptiles, over every created thing; and over the forces of nature. But, says this writer, we do not *see* it so. "We see not all things put under him." The beasts kill man; the elements destroy him. Fire burns and water drowns him, etc.
The answer is, "BUT WE SEE JESUS . . . CROWNED." We see Him, who was "with the wild beasts"; we see Him who walked on the sea—who calmed the storm, whom *all* Nature obeyed; and to whom "all power in heaven and earth is given." We see it all fulfilled in Him. We see in Him man having dominion: and thus He is the answer to the question, WHY was man created?

(g)

3. Whither goeth man?

"The moving living mass of humanity; whence came they, and whither go they? OUT OF NOTHING, UNTO NOTHING?" asks *Carlyle*.
Rabelais, on his death-bed, said, "I go to seek a great may-be." Is it, then, all a guess? Do we know nothing? Here is the answer, "WE SEE JESUS." He is the explanation of the enigma of man—"*Jesus knowing whence He is and whither He is going*"= He came from God, and He went to God. That was no guess, but certainty. So of man—his destiny is "glory, honour, and immortality"—not annihilation. Whatever question be asked concerning man's origin, place, and destiny is answered in Jesus Christ. He is the solution of the enigma of man.

(h)

An ancient voice from the Synagogue says,— "The mystery of Adam is the mystery of the Messiah; Adam is the anagram of Adam, David, Messiah." = A—D—M.

(i)

JESUS, AT THE FEET OF (Matt. xv. 30)

1. These "lame, blind, maimed, and many others" cast down at Jesus' feet, and lying there, remind us that Jesus is the well-defined centre of

(j)

an undefined circumference. "Many others" indicate a vast number : we are glad not to know exactly how many. There is great beauty in the indefiniteness of Holy Scripture. "At the feet of Jesus" is the place for helpless misery—yours and mine, and "many others."

2. Jesus came to be the ingatherer of all misery. That which man most of all avoids, He most of all sought.

3. He healed them *all*.
His only alternative was to go away, or to send the people away unhealed. He could never have done this. So let us think when we cast down *cases* at His feet, He can never turn His back on them—this is not presumption but holy faith. Jesus, owing to the blessed pitifulness of His nature, cannot go on—no, not a single step—if a single helpless suffering being, willing to be healed, is cast in faith athwart His path. He is rooted and bound by misery. Such is His blessed human nature, that if He were obliged to spurn the miserable from His feet, or to go away from them, He would be miserable Himself.

4. "We cannot plead in prayer as some," is often urged as an excuse. In answer to this we read of "multitudes" simply lying "at His feet" —and "He healed *them all*." To lie at the feet of Jesus is itself prayer.
(*a*)   *Power*

JESUS CHRIST SPEAKING FOR THE FATHER (John xiii. 49, 50)

1. Jesus = pure, perfect Divine-human hypostasis (a complete Person of both natures, and of both in perfection) = the ideal god-man, = the complete character, the matchless one (cf. Job).

2. A step further
Transparent as crystal in respect of the motive of His life (our motives spring from various sources). He = the manifestation of the Father (" I came not to do My own will," etc.).
But "GOD IS LOVE," and God's commandment is, that we believe, etc.
[" This is the will of Him that sent Me," etc.]
Therefore.Jesus presents God to men as love—as offering salvation to that part of the world which will receive it. Hence He is the outpouring of eternal life, and is thereby doing the will of God.
Hence, also, the completeness of His character :
" The Father gave Me a commandment," and that the doing of that commandment was meat and drink to Jesus.
(*b*)   *Adapted from Lange*

JESUS CHRIST

That Just Man " (Matt. xxvii. 21)

Aristotle, too, says of the perfectly just man, that " he stands so far above the political order and constitution as it exists, that he must break it wherever he appears."
(*c*)

(The perfect man) without doing any wrong, may assume the appearance of the grossest injustice ; yea, who shall be scourged, tortured, fettered, deprived of his eyes, and, after having endured all possible sufferings, fastened to a post, must restore again the beginning and prototype of righteousness.
(*d*)   *Plato*

JESUS CHRIST AND MAN

The trappings of the rich, the rags of the poor, were nothing to Him. He looked through them as though they did not exist, to the soul ; and there, amidst clouds of ignorance and plague-spots of sin, he recognised a spiritual and immortal nature.
(*e*)   *Channing*

JESUS CHRIST, THE MESSIAH

The Jews, in slaying Jesus Christ, as not the true Messias, gave Him the final mark of the Messias. The more they persist in denying Him, the more infallible witnesses of His truth do they become ; and in slaying and still rejecting Him, they fulfil the prophecies.
(*f*)   *Blaise Pascal*

JESUS CHRIST, A NEW BEING

Now, how stands the case with Jesus ? Bred a Jewish peasant or carpenter, He issues from obscurity, and claims for Himself a Divine office, a superhuman dignity, such as had not been imagined ; and in no instance does He fall below the character. The peasant, and still more the Jew, wholly disappears. We feel that a new Being, of a new order of mind, is taking a part in human affairs. There is a native tone of grandeur and authority in His teaching. He speaks as a Being related to the whole human race. His mind never shrinks within the ordinary limits of human agency. A narrower sphere than the world never enters His thoughts.
(*g*)   *Channing*

JESUS CHRIST AND PHILOSOPHY

The idea of changing the moral aspect of the whole earth, of recovering all nations to the pure and inward worship of one God, and to a spirit of Divine and fraternal love, was one of which we meet not a trace in philosopher or legislator before Him.
(*h*)   *Ibid*

JESUS CHRIST, RELATION TO THE RACE

The world-wide significance of Christ consists in this, that the eternal revelation of God in Him reaches perfection, that what had lain from eternity in the spirit of man, as a religious potentiality, was fully realized in the life of Christ.
(*i*)   *Räbiger*

JESUS CHRIST

" *Whom do men say that I, the* SON OF MAN, *am ?* " (Matt. xvi. 12)

1. The question answered by non-believers :
  (i.) A ghost, John risen from the dead ;
  (ii.) A reappearance (transmigration of souls), Elijah, Jeremiah, or one of the prophets.
These answers reappear in the guesses of modern doubt concerning Christ ; whether He was Divine or human ; a Revealer, or not.
(*j*)

2. The question to the disciples :

" **Whom do ye say that I am ?** "

Peter = the Confessor (cf. his previous and more imperfect confession, John vi., " Thou hast the words of eternal life ").

(i.) = vague generalities ;

(ii.) = definite conceptions—

Which here = belief in the *Incarnation*, the fundamental Christian doctrine ; for though the Atonement is most preached, yet this is the foundation of all.

The Incarnation was the first Christian doctrine confessed. Note its significance with the context, " *Upon this Rock*," etc.

3. How Christian certainty is arrived at :

" Blessed art thou," etc.

" No man can say Jesus is the Christ, but by the Holy Ghost."

All spiritual knowledge is a revelation. " Flesh and blood hath not revealed it unto thee," etc. Cf. " Flesh and blood," in John i., = here, human teachings and traditions.

(*a*)

Jesus Christ, Unchangeableness of

" *Jesus Christ, the same yesterday, to-day, and for ever* " (Heb. xiii. 8)

Suitable subject for close of year, or time of great changes and revolutions.

1. Jesus Christ as *accessible* now as when on earth—

When mothers brought children, fathers brought sons to Him ; as when Mary sat, and the sick were laid, at His feet, He is really present, though invisible.

Changes are in us : He who is the Author and Finisher of our faith ; the First and the Last, Alpha and Omega, is also all the letters or stages between. A faithful Saviour ; having loved his own, He loves them unto the end.

2. The words were written in a time of great changes and revolution :

(i.) Think of the significance of the destruction of Jerusalem and the Temple to a Jew. To him it = heaven and earth passing away, and as if God's promise failed for evermore. Hence the peculiar significance of the words at that time.

(ii.) With the passing away of these, there was also the taking away of the Old Testament, and bringing in of the New Testament. This, to a Jew, = the taking away of authority, and unsettling the faith. For the Old Testament Scriptures were to him a treasure so sacred, that each letter was significant (cf. the fear of those who opposed the revision of the New Testament). Hence again a peculiar significance of the text : Jesus Christ is more than the Scriptures ; they testify of Him ; they = type and shadow, He, the theme and the substance. What you lose is more than repaid in having Him, who, henceforth will never be changed. " When that which is perfect is come," etc.

(iii.) *N.B.*—The preceding context : " Remember," etc. . . . " Follow their faith," = Leaders were dying off, and the sheep feared to be left without a shepherd.

Stephen, James, Peter, etc., all gone, and the new teachers that succeeded were unsafe. Was there not great danger, behind and before them, of apostasy, or standing in jeopardy of life. The

times were evil, and the outlook was dark. Yet there was something infallible, the " Rock " remained unalterably the same, " *Jesus Christ, the same*," etc.

3. Beyond this, it was a perilous time for the Hebrew Christians, as indicated in the succeeding context :

" Be not carried about," etc. . . . " it is good that the heart be established with grace, not with meats."

There was false teaching, currents of doctrine, winds of opinion, which, if a man was unsound in the faith, would carry him hither and thither, like a ship unanchored.

" The heart must be established with grace," = anchored on Christ, and immovable there ; no work of ours to be added to make us safe. He, the Rock, on which, if we build, we shall be safe. This is to be " strong in the grace which is in Christ Jesus " ; and if we would always be safe from drifting away with the tide of opinion, we must remember the text as our watchword. If men say times and things are changed, for us Jesus Christ is the same, etc.

(*b*)

JEWS (Ezek. v. 5)

Cast off, not forsaken nor forgotten ; one day to be " grafted into the tree again." Probably when Christ comes the second time. The probability is, that they will acknowledge the *glorified* Messiah, though they rejected Him in His humility. Ask, Why then try to make Christians of them ? " There is a remnant," and this is the way of calling them out. We predict a shower when we feel a drop or two of rain. So with the Jewish remnant ; it is only a drop or so before the great ingathering of the whole nation.

(*c*)

1. Jerusalem set in the midst of the Nations :

(i.) Locally, between three continents ;

(ii.) Religiously, the home and land of the Bible ; the witness for the one God against idolatry ; if infidels say Bible is untrue, ask, " What about the Jews ? "

(*d*)

2. Why so placed?

(i.) As a light, which cannot be hid ; and if constantly replenished, will light up other nations around ; or, as a beacon-fire, continually kept burning. All the dark places of the earth shall see it and inquire concerning it.

(ii.) As a *healthy spot* in the surrounding leprous and idolatrous world. The spot where God began the healing of the nations.

(iii.) As the *heart* of the earth ; the centre of its life, sending blood into all the body ; if the heart is wrong, then all wrong.

For these reasons Jerusalem was set in the midst of the earth ? Did it succeed ? No.

(*e*)

3. Jerusalem failed in all these :

(i.) The light = darkness ;

(ii.) The beacon-fire was not kept burning, it went out ;

(iii.) The healthy spot relapsed, became as the rest ; The whole head sick, the whole heart faint,

(*f*)

nothing but wounds and bruises, and putrifying sores.

(iv.) The heart weakened, palpitated, went wrong; and the whole world suffers to this day. (a)

4. What did God do next?

He put the Jews aside, and took the Gentiles, as the salvation-people, in their stead; by nature, "a wild olive-tree."

And we now have to do the work for the nations which God intended them to do.

We need to take heed lest we, too, for our unfaithfulness, be cast aside as a failure.

Note—(i.) Where God gives, He requires.

(ii.) We "stand by grace"; we are "lighted," and God requires of us *to shine;* to make the world better—it *must* be the better for our being in it, or it will be the *worse* for us = our family, business, daily work, are the *places* where we have to shine. (Lights are not all equally brilliant.)

(b)

5. God will finally graft the Jews in again:

Then both Jew and Gentile will glorify God, and that will be the wonderful working-day of the Lord, when *a nation shall be born in a day.* To the world it will be "life from the dead," and all nations shall walk in its light.

(c)

JEWS A WITNESS TO CHRISTIANITY, THE

"*They are Thy people and Thine inheritance*" —(Deut. ix. 29)

1. It is related of a certain royal chaplain, that, being asked often by his sovereign to give a concise and convincing argument in favour of Christianity, he replied in two words—"the Jews." The subject of the history and character of the Israelite race as a witness to Christianity is appropriate. The great Pentecost Day substituted the dispensation of the Spirit for the dispensation of the Law, and expanded the religion of a tribe into the religion of mankind.

2. "Go in to possess nations greater and mightier than thyself, cities great and fenced up to heaven"; "Understand, therefore, this day that the Lord thy God is He which goeth over before thee;" "The Lord thy God giveth thee not this good land to possess it for thy righteousness; for thou art a stiff-necked people;" "Ye have been rebellious against the Lord from the day that I knew you."

3. Read these passages in the full light which thirty centuries of the nation's history have thrown upon them. Study this contrast between their character and their achievements as it unfolds itself in all their subsequent history. Consider, on the one hand, not only the first conquest of Canaan to which the words more immediately refer, but the succession of far more brilliant victories over the great nations of the world, culminating in that most magnificent triumph of all —the triumph of Christianity.

4. Consider, on the other hand, not only those early murmurings and idolatries in the wilderness to which the language more directly points, but that long catalogue of rebellions of which the subsequent history of Israel is made up, and which reached its climax in the martyrdom of the Lord of Life. Set these one against the other, and you

will confess that the utterances of Deuteronomy are wonderful anticipations of the future, succinct epitomes of centuries yet to come. You may question, if you will, every single prophecy in the Old Testament, but the whole history of the Jews is one continuous prophecy, more distinct and articulate than all. You may deny, if you will, every successive miracle which is recorded therein, but again the history of the Jews is, from first to last, one stupendous miracle, more wonderful and convincing than all. *Here* you have a small, insignificant people—stiff-necked, rebellious, worthless; *there* you have the most magnificent spiritual achievements—the most signal moral victories, What conclusion can you draw, except that which is drawn for you in the words: "The Lord thy God is He that goeth before you?" "They are Thy people and Thine inheritance, which Thou broughtest out by Thy mighty power and Thy stretched out arm."

(d)

5. THE PEOPLE

Look first at the capacities of the people themselves. They had no remarkable gifts which might have led us to anticipate this unique destiny. They had no intellectual qualities of a very high order like the Greeks—vivid imagination, subtlety of thought, æsthetic taste; no political capacity like the Romans, no organizing power or faculty of legislation which might secure for them the ascendency over the nations of the world. They were, moreover, a stubborn, exclusive, intolerant people—an unpractical people, without the power, or at least the will, to adapt themselves to the institutions, the feelings, and the prejudices of the people with whom they were brought in contact. They were believed, in consequence, to cherish an universal hatred against the rest of mankind; and they, in turn, were hated by all—hated, not with the hatred of an admiring envy, but the hatred of a supercilious scorn. Of all the tribes on the face of the earth the Jews, we should have said, were the very last to ingratiate themselves with the other races of mankind, and to lay the civilized world at their feet.

(e)

6. THEIR LAND

And now turn from the people themselves to the land of their abode. Certainly this does not enable us to solve the enigma. Palestine does occupy a large space in the Christian's imagination; but it is a very minute, insignificant spot in the map of the world. It is, moreover, incapable of expansion, for it is bounded on all sides either by sea, by mountain ranges, or by vast and impracticable deserts. To a great extent all this country is mountainous and barren; and even this meagre and unpromising territory is not all their own. The sea-coast would have been valuable to a people gifted with commercial instincts. With commerce they might have extended their influence; but from the sea-coast they were wholly excluded. The Phœnicians on the north and the Philistines on the south occupied all the most important harbours; and this territory of the Jews was so unexpansive, so barren, so unpromising, that they were placed at a still greater disadvantage when compared with

Jews a Witness to Christianity, The—*continued*

the surrounding people. The Jews are surrounded on all sides, and by the most formidable neighbours.

(*a*)

7. EGYPT

On the one side by Egypt, a country of the highest fertility, the foremost military power in the world, with an ancient civilization which dated from a period long before the birth of the father of the Israelite people, whilst it stood foremost of the human race in works of art in its day. Who was Israel, then, that he could withstand Egypt?

(*b*)

8. BABYLON

There, again, on the other side, was another mighty empire, first Assyria, then Babylon, the only rival of Egypt of the ancient world. In these places they had the same advantage of wide plains of exceptional fertility, a high and remote civilization, an army of tremendous strength, and a centralization under an absolute rule, with all the resources which a great and vast dominion could command.

(*c*)

9. PERSIA

As Persia succeeded Babylon, and as Babylon succeeded Assyria, so Persia—far more mighty and terrible—overruns and conquers all Western Asia. Egypt itself falls. Palestine is a mere speck, surrounded by the huge dominions of the Persian monarch. What chance has Israel against such terrible neighbours? Must it not be crushed and ground to atoms and annihilated by its foes?

(*d*)

10. INTERNAL FEUDS

But, at all events, it might have been supposed that, however stubborn and impracticable they were in their attitude towards others, they would at least be united amongst themselves—that they would be loyal to their country, that they would be faithful to their laws and institutions, that they would be true to their God. This internal cohesion would give them strength to resist—this absolute harmony would win for them an influence that would compensate for the superior advantages of their more powerful neighbours. But what do we find as a matter of fact? Their national history is one continuous record of murmuring, of rebellion, of internal feuds, of moral and spiritual defection.

(*e*)

11. IDOLATRY

They have no sooner escaped from their Egyptian bondage, their necks still bearing the scars of the tyrants' yoke, than they fall into shameless idolatry. The worship of the golden calf is only the type and presence of still more guilty lapses in centuries yet to come; the revolt against Moses and Aaron only the type and shadow of the rebellious spirit to which Israel rose in the distant future. Again and again the religion of Jehovah is effaced, or almost effaced, from the mind of the nation. Again and again the hideous idola-

tries of Moloch—idolatries cruel, profligate, and shameless—supplant the worship of the Lord of heaven and earth.

(*f*)

12. POLITICAL CONDITION

And the political condition of the nation is not one whit more hopeful than the religious. When unity alone can save the people then there is disruption. The Ten Tribes are severed from the House of David, never to be united again. The power of one kingdom is spent in neutralizing the power of the other. This is a concise history of the race during the period from the disruption to the Captivity.

(*g*)

13. DISOBEDIENCE

The career of Israel, from first to last, is a running comment upon the words, "Not for thy righteousness or for the uprightness of thine heart dost thou go to possess the land," for "ye have been rebellious against the Lord from the day that I knew you." Not once or twice only the Mighty Archer has strung His weapon and pointed His shaft, and His aim has been frustrated by Israel's disobedience. His chosen instruments have been snapped in His hands, starting aside like a broken bow. Indeed, the history of Israel is quite unique in the chronicles of nations. The chronicles of other nations record the qualities as well as the crimes of the people whose career they commemorate. They praise their patriotism, their prowess, their manifold virtues, their magnificent achievements. But the Bible, the chronicle of the Jews, is one uninterrupted catalogue of sins and short-comings—one long bill of indictment against Israel. One only is true, one only is faithful, one only is victorious; for he fears not the nation, but the nation's God. So then, however we look at the matter, there is nothing which affords ground for hope; and when we question actual facts, we find they correspond altogether to those expectations we should have formed beforehand from the character and position of the nation.

(*h*)

14. THEIR TROUBLES

Never has any people lived upon the earth who passed through such terrible disasters as the Jews. Never has any people been so near to absolute extinction again and again, and yet have survived. Again and again the vision of the prophet has been realized. Again and again the valley of the shadow of death has been strewn with the dry bones of carcases seemingly extinct. Again and again there have been seasons of dark despair, when even the most hopeful, challenged by the Divine voice, could only respond, "O Lord God, Thou knowest!" But again and again there has been a shaking of the dry bones—the bones have come together, bone to bone; they have been strung with sinews and clothed with flesh; breath has been breathed into them, and they have lived, and have become an exceeding great army.

(i.) Think of these many centuries of Egyptian bondage, when the life of the nation seemed to have been strangled in its infancy.

(ii.) Reflect next on that period in its youthful

(*i*)

Jews a Witness to Christianity, The—*continued*

career, when it is fighting its way inch by inch, and struggling for very existence in Palestine, doing battle with nations greater and mightier than itself, and with "cities fenced high up to heaven."

(iii.) Look forward again, and we see its fate during the manhood of the nation under its king, the land now divided against itself and overrun by successive invaders. As of old so now again, but in a far more terrible sense, Israel finds himself face to face with the Anakims and with those great empires of the East before whom he appears but as a grasshopper. The end was inevitable. For a time Israel was a plaything in the hands of those terrible neighbours, tossed to and fro between two powerful rivals—Egypt on the one side and Assyria and Babylon on the other—till at length, in a moment of victory, he is swept away, and his place knows him no more.

(iv.) Could anything seem more hopeless than the revival of the nation from the Babylonish Captivity? Yet from Babylon, as from Egypt, Israel returned. A new lease of life was granted, and with it there followed a new lease of disaster also.

(v.) His old fate pursued him still. The saying was fulfilled which had been spoken by the prophet: "That which the locust hath left hath the canker-worn eaten, and that which the canker-worm hath left hath the caterpillar eaten." He was rescued from the fangs of Babylon only to be food for the Assyrians. He was drawn from the feet of the Assyrians only to be devoured by the insatiable Roman.

(*a*)

15. THEIR FUTURE

And yet all the while—and this is the remarkable fact—amidst calamities the most overwhelming and suffering the most intense—exiled, enslaved, trampled under foot, only not annihilated—all the while he was hopeful, was jubilant, was triumphant still. He was always dying, and, behold he lived. Century after century prophets had declared, in no ambiguous terms, that despite all these adverse appearances, despite all these wearisome delays, Israel had a magnificent future. The nations might rage, and the kings of the earth might do their worst—they were powerless against Israel's destiny. A sceptre should rise out of Jacob which would subdue the world, and a king should sit on David's throne before whose footstool all the nations of the earth should bow. A standard should be set up in Zion around which all mankind should rally. "Behold thou shalt call a nation that thou knowest not, and nations that knew not thee shall run unto thee because of the Lord thy God, and for the Holy One of Israel; for He hath glorified thee;" "The sons of them that afflicted thee shall come bending unto thee, and all they that despised thee shall bow themselves at the soles of thy feet;" "Enlarge the place of thy tent, and let them stretch forth the curtains of thine habitation; spare not, lengthen thy cords, and strengthen thy stakes; for thou shalt break forth on the right hand and on the left, and thy seed shall inherit the Gentiles, and make the desolate cities to be inhabited."

(*b*)

16. FULFILMENT

And these hopes—these extravagant hopes—were more than realized. A king *did* rise out of Jacob to whom all the nations of the civilized world have rendered homage such as no sovereign received before or after—the homage of their heart, the homage of their lives. At the call of Israel the Gentiles flocked to the standard set up in Zion. From far and near, the cultivated Greek, the proud Roman, Assyrian, and Egyptian,—master and slave,—are flocking around that standard. From East to West, from the ancient civilization of India to the barbarous islands of the Pacific, Israel has dictated its sentiments, its belief, its morals, its laws and institutions to the nations. An influence far deeper, far wider, far more tenacious has appeared from that despised, insulted, down-trodden people than was ever achieved by the splendid literature of Greece or the historic empire of Rome. These are not theories, but facts—facts which some will attempt to explain away, but facts which none can deny. *Here* is the prophecy—*there* is the fulfilment. The prophecy is not a single isolated prediction of ambiguous meaning, but large and clear, written across the whole history of a nation from margin to margin. And the fulfilment corresponds to the prophecy; it is legible to all men, because stamped on the face of the world. Is there not here the manifestation of Divine Providence?

(*c*)

17. WITNESSES OF CHRISTIANITY

Do we not rightly claim the Jews as the principal witnesses to Christianity? or shall we set all this down as mere accident, a freak of fortune, a superficial correspondence without any essential connection? Shall it be regarded as mere accident that, within a few years after the appearing of this King, who has thus gathered the Gentiles to His standard, Jerusalem is destroyed, and the nation scattered to the four winds of the earth—that the polity of Israel for ever ceased, that the Temple shook, and that revival was rendered thenceforward impossible? Shall we say that it is mere argument that fore ighteen centuries,—a period as long as that which elapsed from the proclamation of the law by Moses to the fulfilment of the law by Christ,—this state of things has remained? Or should we not rather say that in this coincidence also, there is a Divine significance—that He proclaimed with no uncertain sound the obituary of the old order and the commencement of the new—that God's seal is stamped upon the character of the Church whereby Israel after the Spirit is substituted for Israel after the flesh?

(*d*)

18. THE SOURCE OF THEIR VITALITY

Do we ask what it was which gave the Jewish people this toughness, this vitality, this power? The answer simply is, "They are Thy people and Thine inheritance, which Thou broughtest out by Thy mighty power, and by Thy stretched out arm." It was the consciousness of this close relationship with Jehovah, the omnipotent and ever-present God—it was the sense of their glorious destiny, which marked them out as the teachers of mankind. It was the conviction that they were the

(*e*)

Jews a Witness to Christianity, The—*continued*

possessors of glorious truths, and that those truths must in the end prevail, whatever present appearances might suggest—this was the secret source of their strength, notwithstanding all their faults, and despite all their disasters.

(*a*)

19. ISRAEL AND THE GENTILES

Do we ask again how it came to pass that, when Israel called to the Gentiles, the Gentiles responded to the call and flocked to its standard? Here, again, the answer is simple—"Because of the Lord thy God, and for the Holy One of Israel." The Gentiles had everything else in their possession, but this one thing they lacked—knowledge of God, their Father; and without this all their magnificent gifts could not satisfy—could not save them. Therefore, when at length the cry went forth, "Ho! every one that thirsteth, come ye to the waters," they hurried to the fountains of salvation to slake their burning thirst. Culture and civilization, arts and commerce, institutions and laws, no nation can afford to undervalue these; but not only do all these things soon fade, but the people themselves fall into corruption and decay if the Breath of Life be wanting.

And as with nations, so with individuals. We may cultivate the intellect to the highest pitch; we may surround ourselves with all the luxuries and refinements of civilization; we may accumulate all the appliances which make life enjoyable; but the time will come when these things will fail to sustain us. It may come in some season of bereavement, in the hour of sickness or of loss. It may come in the failure and decay of powers. It may come in the pains of our death agony. It may come—and this is the most solemn thought of all—after we have passed the confines of the grave. But come it must, sooner or later; for we are children of God, and we cannot with impunity ignore or deny the Father of earth and heaven. There only is rest and peace; there only is true life for the soul of man.

(*b*)　　　　　　　　　　*Bishop Lightfoot*

"*The Jews*," was the ready and unanswerable reply of the Prussian court chaplain to the half-earnest, half-scoffing challenge of his monarch, "Give us, in two words, a reason for believing in Christianity."

(*c*)

"Ye are my witnesses." Before any one can possibly establish the fact that there is no God, dispute the authority of the Bible, and discredit the truth of Christianity, he must first set himself to the task of annulling, or getting rid of a certain people called Israelites.

(*d*)　　　　　　　　　　*L. C. Mamlock*

The Jews constitute the most unmanageable argument with which doubt and unbelief have to deal. A sceptical prince (I believe it was Frederick the Great) once asked his court chaplain to give him some clear evidence of the truth of Christianity; but to do so in very few words, because a king had not much time to spare for such matters. And the chaplain replied—"The Jews, your Majesty." That chaplain was a sensible man, and knew what he was about. Get rid of the

Jews, and of that strange Jewish history, and you may soon dispose of other evidences. But until you succeed in clearing those troublesome Jews out of the way, you will make marvellously little real progress in the work of demolishing Christianity.

(*e*)　　　　　　　　　　*Gordon Calthrop*

JEWS

This people was immersed in earthly conceits such as these; that God loved their father Abraham, his flesh, and all that sprang from it; that, for this reason, God had multiplied and separated them, not suffering them to mix with other nations, had recovered them out of Egypt by many wonderful signs performed in their favour, had fed them with manna in the wilderness, had brought them into a fruitful and happy land, had appointed over them kings, had raised them a well-built temple, for the offering up of beasts and the purifying themselves by the blood of their sacrifices; and would send them the Messias, to make them masters of the world.

(*f*)　　　　　　　　　　*Blaise Pascal*

JEWS, EXCLUSIVENESS OF

The Jew hardly felt himself to belong to the human family. He was accustomed to speak of himself as chosen by God, holy, clean; whilst the Gentiles were sinners, dogs, polluted, unclean.

(*g*)　　　　　　　　　　*Channing*

JEWS, THREE REMARKABLE

ABRAHAM : who has left a physiognomical mark upon the Jewish race.

MOSES : who has left a spiritual (or legal) and moral impress upon them.

EZRA : (the second Moses) who from his own exclusiveness (see strange wives) has left the impress of that exclusiveness (Pharisees) upon the later Jews of the Captivity.

1. A Jew is a son of Abraham—facially, each is his portrait;

2. A Jew is a son of Moses—legally;

3. A Jew is a son of Ezra—exclusively: "The temple of the Lord are we."

(*h*)

JEWELS

The Church is God's jewellery—His working-house, where His jewels are polished for His palace; and those He especially esteems and means to make most resplendent, He hath oftenest His tools upon them.

(*i*)　　　　　　　　　　*Leighton*

JOB

"*Ye have heard of the patience of Job, and have seen the end of the Lord*" (Jas. v. 11)

"*Take heed, brethren, lest there be in any of you an evil heart of unbelief in departing from the living God*" (Heb. iii. 12)

1. A Temptation to Apostasy resisted

In the former passage the great sufferer of the Old Testament is compared with the Great Sufferer of the New. Both endured. Both resisted successfully a great temptation to apostatize from

(*j*)

Job—*continued*

the living God; though, of course, the two cases cannot be exactly parallel.

The lesson remains the same : (i.) that a time of suffering, is a trial of our faith ; (ii.) that such a temptation as Job's could only happen in the case of a religious man; (iii.) that the more eminent the saint, the greater will be the strain put upon his power of endurance.

Job, an eminent servant of God, is tempted to apostatize from the living God. The temptation is insidious but sure, working from the external to the internal, where, as the sequel shows, the struggle was the keenest. The endeavour is to pull this man away from God, or, in the language of the New Testament, to pluck a child out of the Father's hand, or to separate a saint from the love of Christ.

The tempter hopes to win the citadel by a series of attacks on the outposts. Hence it seems that the way of successively meeting and resisting temptation, is ever to be on the watch, and to " be strong in the Lord."

(*a*)

2. The Phenomena

First we follow the tempter on one of his reconnoitring expeditions into the land of Uz, where we behold him contemplating certain phenomena described in these words :—

(*b*)

(i.) Job Himself

" There was a man in the land of Uz," of the name of Job. In many respects unlike his neighbours, for he was " a perfect and an upright man, one that feared God and eschewed evil."

This is the opening description : showing what the man was in himself, making him to be the rare man that he was. This the tempter saw, and formed a desire to bring such excellence down to the ordinary level. After being told what the man is, we are next told of what he *has*.

(*c*)

(ii.) Job's Children

He had ten children, seven sons and three daughters—these rank next to himself—being in fact an evidence of the blessing of God resting upon him. The gift that cometh from the Lord, and that which constituted *the* blessing of Old Testament times ; though, according to our perverted notions of things, we have come to regard this as a sign of a man's poverty. " These," said some one to good Bishop Hall, " are what make the rich man poor." " Nay," replied the Bishop; " these are what make the poor man rich."

(*d*)

(iii.) Job's Wealth.

Next we have an enumeration of Job's wealth. He was a rich and prosperous man, " the greatest of all the men of the East." He had sheep, and camels, and oxen, in fact everything in which in those days wealth consisted. This much is told us of himself, his family, and his belongings.

(*e*)

(iv.) Job's Piety

As to his conduct, we read that he brought his family up well, himself setting them a good example, and exercising over them a wise and thoughtful supervision. When the young people feasted in each others' houses Job, fearing lest they might have slighted God in their more festive moments, fearing, too, lest prosperity might tempt them to forget God, used to rise up early the following morning and offer sacrifices, and make special intercession for his children individually. " It may be," he said, " that my sons have sinned." " Thus did Job continually."

A beautiful picture is thus presented of parental anxiety and intercession for heedless children.

His sons had sent for their sisters ; together they had assembled with their companions on the evening before; they had had a festive season; the hours had rapidly sped ; fatigued and weary, they had retired to rest. The excitement of the evening had interfered with prayer and meditation. And it was natural : they were young people, and must have their times of meeting and opportunities of enjoying each other's society. But the watchful father knew too well the danger attending such seasons of excitement. An evening spent in pleasure of this kind, even the most innocent, indisposes the spirit more or less for communion with God at the close of the day. Job found no fault, he did nothing that might provoke his children unto wrath ; but he made it his custom, after these occasions, to rise early the next morning and offer a sacrifice—one for each of his children—and to pray for them individually.

(*f*)

(v.) Job and His Neighbours

Nor was he a source of blessing within his own family only. He was honoured by, and useful to, the whole community in which he lived. When he entered an assembly, the princes refrained from talking, the nobles held their peace, so great was the respect in which he was held. " When the ear heard him, then it blessed him, and when the eye saw him, it gave witness to him." And why ? Because he was a friend of the poor, the fatherless, and the widow. Eyes to the blind and feet to the lame—a righter of those who were wronged, and a comfort to the mourner.

This was the Job that we should have seen in the days of his prosperity, when " the candle of the Lord shone upon him," and before adversity came.

(*g*)

(vi.) Reverses

The tempter, having seen this, disappears from the scene of this earthly paradise. Forthwith this bright sky darkens, is overcast with threatening and lowering clouds. Reverses come. This good, useful, beloved, and prosperous man is suddenly prostrated by calamity into a condition almost the direct opposite to what has been described. Were it not on record, we could hardly credit the assertion that this perfect and upright man, on his reverses becoming known, was called a hypocrite by other religious people.

The happy father in a moment is rendered childless. Three sudden reverses take away all his property. The richest man in the East is

(*h*)

Job—*continued*

beggared. And, to crown all his other misfortunes, a loathsome disease comes upon himself personally, so that his breath is strange to his wife, and his friends and acquaintances keep at a distance from him. These things—prosperous and calamitous—constitute the PHENOMENA we might have witnessed.

(*a*)

3. The Causes of the later Phenomena

That which was behind all, out of sight, and which those most nearly concerned knew nothing about.

The first chapter of the Book of Job shows us that the cause of Job's calamities lay in the spirit world. He had an enemy there. This good man had been an eyesore and a cause of grief to the great adversary of souls.

> "Satan trembles when he sees
> The weakest saint upon his knees."

Trembles for his own kingdom—an example like Job's is infectious. And when the opportunity presented itself, the tempter alleged that Job was only a religious man because it paid him to be such. The narrative of the unseen part of the story reads thus:

"Now there was a day when the sons of God came to present themselves before the Lord, and Satan came also among them."

By the expression "sons of God" we may understand the good angels—God's servants, "ministering unto the heirs of salvation." They have been on the earth performing their service of love, "keeping the feet of the saints." They have marked Job's pious and consistent conduct, and have brought back their report to the throne in heaven.

(*b*)

(i.) THE ACCUSER

But amongst them comes one who is not of them—not an angel of light, but an angel of darkness. It is not for us to inquire why he is there at all. We read elsewhere that he is "the Accuser of the brethren." He is there, then, doubtless in that capacity. And we are, perhaps, given to understand that his accusations, misrepresentations, and caluminations go on now much in the same way as we find here; and that he carries his lies about us up into heaven itself. In heaven he is the Accuser, in opposition to Him who is our Advocate there—whilst on earth he is the wolf that scattereth the sheep: our adversary, who goeth about amongst the flock of God as a roaring lion, "seeking whom he may devour;" and should he get permission from God (for he can do nothing without it), he may treat us much in the same way as he treated Job. He may not indeed "devour us," but he will run off with us. He may not indeed be permitted to pluck us out of the Father's hand, but he may tear the sheep, and pluck off its fleece, and leave it wounded and half dead far away over the hills, or in some dangerous mountain glen, until it is rescued by the Good Shepherd.

(*c*)

(ii.) THE ACCUSATION

The question is put to the adversary:

"Whence comest thou?"

The answer is characteristic, showing the unceasing activity and watchfulness of our spiritual foe. He replies that he has come from the earth, where he has been busy "going to and fro, and walking up and down in it." Of course, then, he has seen Job, for it is Job that at this time he has come to accuse.

The Lord asks,

"Hast thou seen My servant Job, that there is none like him in the earth?"

The adversary replies,

"Doth Job fear God for nought?"—implying that his godliness is not genuine, that it is only veneer which will chip off if you scratch it deep enough. He is religious *because it pays*. He likes to have the finger pointed at him, and to hear people say, "There goes good Job." It feeds his vanity to have such things said of him; but it is not real, as I could easily show if I had the opportunity. But You have put a hedge about him, so that I can't get at him to tempt him as I do other men. You have fenced him in all round, You take care of his children, You take care of his property, You take care of all that he hath. Your evident blessing rests upon the whole household. But now put forth Thine hand: take away Your protection; pull down that fence; let a blight instead of a blessing come over all that he hath, and then You will see what kind of man he is. His true character will then reveal itself. "He will," under sufficient pressure, "curse Thee to Thy face." He will renounce his God altogether, and apostatize from the faith.

(*d*)

4. This is the Fundamental Idea of the Book of Job

The silken thread that runs through the whole tangled skein, as a clue which enables us to unravel it. The adversary asserts that he can make a true child of God renounce his God, his hope, his faith, under the pressure of a sufficiently strong and terrible temptation, if only the permission is given him.

The answer to this is—"Try:" "Touch every thing that he hath, only lay not thine hand upon him."

The struggle now fairly begins. In the temptation to get Job to apostatize, the enemy begins with the outposts: *i.e.*, with what the man *has*, viz.,

(*e*)

(i.) HIS PROPERTY

This can be parted with most easily, since it is no part of the man Job. God, Who has loaned it to him, has a perfect right to take back His gift at pleasure. This temptation, then, though severe, is not on a par with any that might afflict him more closely and personally.

(*f*)

(ii.) HIS CHILDREN

This affliction comes nearer home to Job. He can be touched more to the quick here than in the mere matter of his property. His children are a part of himself; if he did not succumb to the first blow, it might reasonably be supposed that he would to this.

(*g*)

Job—*continued*

(iii.) His own Person

Bodily sickness is the next blow. Job's life is in peril, and life is sweet; a man would give anything, part with anything, do anything, for his life; and we can readily understand how terrible the struggle would have become by this time—*i.e.*, supposing Job had not succumbed to the former strains made upon his faith and trust in God. Still, in the case of such a man as Job, the citadel, the real inside heart and core of the man, is not touched yet; *that* is left for the last, and perhaps the strongest attack of the enemy.

(*a*)

(iv.) His Religion

Job is a man of faith, a spiritual man. This is the very innermost core of the man: his most distinguishing feature—a man is as he thinks— he can let go all else but this. The tempter, in attacking him here, attacks the citadel; and to win this, Satan hurls his most fiery darts, his last and most deadly-poisoned shafts—wife and friends—are kept for this brunt.

(*b*)

5. The Successive Stages of the Temptation

Permission once given, the adversary tarries not. He is quickly down to earth again; he knows the value of time, and of rapid movements in warfare.

The phenomena that we witnessed were in reality the outcome of this permission given to the tempter. It was the unseen and fearful influence and power of this terrible being that brought about the successive calamities of the matchless Job. Brought them about, too, in such haste, as to ensure an almost certain hope of success. He gave his victim no breathing space, no time to recover, no time to strengthen himself in his God. One, Two, Three! and the thing is done. Whilst one messenger is telling his tale of misfortune, another, and another, and yet another comes with further reports of sudden losses and reverses.

(i.) Property and children are taken away in rapid succession, in the hope that an impatient exclamation about God's dealings with him may escape Job's lips.

If only he can get Job to say that God is hard, or unjust, or not good, the tempter will have gained a point of advantage.

But the adversary is completely foiled. Instead of a curse there is a *blesssing*: instead of *giving up his religion*, Job clung to it the more: he fell down upon the ground and worshipped God, and said-

"**Naked came I out of my mother's womb, and naked shall I return thither: The Lord gave, and the Lord hath taken away; blessed be the name of the Lord.**"

"**In all this Job sinned not, nor charged God foolishly.**"

(*c*)

(ii.) Foiled in these his first attempts, the adversary again returns to the charge. Once more he appears before God in heaven; and this time he declares confidently that the victory will be on his side, if only Job is afflicted in his own person. He admits that the loss of property— "all that he hath"—has failed to bring about the looked-for result. Now he insinuates that if Job is made to suffer bodily pain—days of weariness and nights of languishing—and is threatened with death, then his faith will break down. For Job loves life; he will do anything, say anything, to preserve that; under great physical suffering his endurance will break down completely.

(*d*)

(iii.) The Second Permission

"**Put forth Thine hand now and touch his bone and his flesh, and he will curse Thee to Thy face.**"

And again permission is given—"Try;" you may afflict him personally, by bringing upon him grievous sufferings of body and of mind—you may bring him to the very edge of the grave, but you may go no further—"*only save his life.*" It is now that we more particularly remark Job's endurance, or, as it is commonly termed, his patience. The sufferings, which were now permitted to befall him, apparently lasted a long time. A rapid succession of temptations had failed. The tempter now hopes to win by prolonged and slow torture, by days of weariness and nights of languishing; by the depression, sure to ensue, consequent on physical and mental exhaustion. A similar instance of a spiritual breakdown may be seen in the history of John the Baptist, languishing in the damp cells of Machærus. For whilst the patriarch is sore—smarting with pain, and irritable—his wife's faith utterly collapses; and she becomes an unconscious tool in the hands of Satan—a temptress—urging her husband to apostasy and suicide.

(*e*)

(iv.) Job's Wife

"Is this," her words imply, "how God treats His servants? Is this the reward of your virtues? Is this the return He makes to those who honour His name, and serve Him as you have done, my husband?"

"Give it all up, Job; give up your God; give up your religion; don't put your trust and hope in such a God any more. "Renounce Him" (*i.e.*, apostatize, not "curse"), "and die. You have nothing more to live for. Everything that made life desirable is gone. We are beggars— childless—is such a life worth living? Why continue such a miserable existence? put an end to it, and all will be over."

But Job replies,

"**Thou speakest as a foolish woman**" (a woman without faith in God, whose religion is for fair weather only, and not for seasons of deep trial such as this. This is faith's opportunity). "**What? shall we receive good at the hand of God, and shall we not receive evil?**"

"**In all this Job did not sin with his lips.**"

Thus far he is the conqueror—and in the whole conflict the tempter had miscalculated about him altogether. Each successive attack — whether directed against him in the sphere of his property, children, or bodily health—is met by the shield of faith, and parried with the Sword of the Spirit. Job was armed with the Panoply of God. (Eph. vi.)

(*f*)

Job—*continued*

(v.) Job's Friends

But the tempter has other and more poisoned arrows left in his quiver yet. He will use these next. He has obtained permission to harass a child of God, in every way short of killing him; and he will leave no means untried that will help to pull this matchless man down to the level of ordinary men, and even of separating him from the love of God altogether. He *must* show that Job is a false man. And now comes the last and longest siege laid against Job's faith. The enemy aims now at the very citadel itself. Job is a religious man—it is the life of the man, the atmosphere that he breathes. And Job has religious friends. The tempter now conceives the design of bringing these religious friends to talk to Job. They will see in him a shocking example of some sin secretly indulged in. They will try and fit him into their favourite religious systems, and thus account for his sufferings. In short, they are brought to see in Job's misfortunes an awful example of the "unpardonable sin." Such are some of the consolations which Job's comforters bring him, *seeing they are religious men.*

For each of these men has got his own theory about suffering = it is RETRIBUTIVE. Poor Job is fair game, and they proceed to experiment on him. The best thing they did was when they sat silent on the ground seven days and seven nights, and spake not a word, either of praise, or blame, or sympathy. Here was their wisdom. But when they in succession opened their mouths, and preached *at* him, gave him the benefit of their opinions, and tried to make his calamities fit in with their theories, then these men made an awful mess of it, as systematizers have done ever since.

(*a*)

(vi.) Their Creed

To make a long story short, they held the doctrine that **Great suffering always pointed to great sin.** They seem to have had no notion that God's chastisements are fatherly, and disciplinary, and intended to make that which is already good still better; just as a precious stone, because it is a jewel, is cut and polished, to bring out its beauties, and to set it as a gem in some honoured place. Instead of this, these men proceed upon the one-sided idea, that because they see their friend in great calamity therefore God was dealing with him on account of some secret sin; hence the free and pointed use they make of the word "hypocrite." They make no attempt to disguise their thoughts; they think that this wicked Job, who has deceived them by appearing to be a good man among them so long, must be spoken to very plainly and sharply; for proud flesh, however painful the operation, must be cut out; and they attempt the surgical operation. One of them says,

"Remember, Job, who ever perished being innocent? or, where were the righteous cut off?" (alluding to the death of his children).

Another says,

"Job, if thou wert pure and upright, surely now would God awake for thee, and make the habitation of thy righteousness prosperous."

Whilst a third calls him,

"A man full of talk," and recommends him to put away this *secret iniquity*, which they are all sure must exist somewhere.

In a word, what they say amounts to this:

"O Job, we have known you a long time. You have passed off amongst us as a good man. Your words have strengthened others, and your good works have blessed many. But we fear, nay, it is certain, that you have greatly deceived us. For how can we conclude otherwise when we see God taking back all His gifts from you, stripping you of everything—health, wealth, and children all taken away. We see the lightnings of Heaven descending upon you in wrath, leaving you just a wreck of your former self. We *feel* that we have been deceived in you. We are sure, from the way we read Providence, that there is something terribly amiss within your secret heart. Such things never happen save where the practice agrees not with the profession. God, we feel sure, would not deal with you in this way if it were not so. Sorry as we are to say it, yet the faithfulness of a friend makes it necessary for us to charge you with *hypocrisy.* The sin, which you have succeeded in hiding from us, you cannot hide from God; and He is now making it manifest that your sin hath found you out."

(*b*)

(vii.) The Break-down

The plot is Satanic almost to the last degree. And it is under this torrent of religious misrepresentation that Job utters hard and impatient words. He is stung to the very quick, and hurls back hot words of resentment at these representatives of a narrow and harsh religious system. Almost he curses these men. "Ye are forgers of lies," he exclaims, "all physicians of no value."

"You cannot press me into your mould, and point me out to others as an awful example of hypocrisy."

Finally, he wishes that they "would altogether hold their peace, and that would be their wisdom."

Now this undoubtedly was the sorest part of Job's temptation. The adversary had well calculated, when he brought these "friends" to talk to him, that Job would writhe and smart under their preachings, and break down under such treatment as this from religious people—if he did not give way anywhere else.

And, as the story shows, it *was* here,—when Job, conscious of living in no sin, conscious of no stain upon his life and character; conscious, too, of a high standard of life and aim, of perfect rectitude of purpose and act, void of offence towards either God or man,—it was when these men came and preached *at* him, and stung him with their systematized explanations of God's chastisements, that Job got impatient, and broke down—*i.e.,* he so far yielded to the pressure as to curse the day of his birth, his friends almost, and pretty well everything around him. In defending himself, he takes a somewhat lofty standpoint of his own moral integrity; but, be it remembered, the one thing which the *tempter said he would do*—viz., give up his faith in God—*that he never did.* He held fast to his religion and to his God all through. He overcame the Wicked One, and proved that Satan is a liar, and that the child of God can endure temptation, and cannot be either plucked out of the hand of God, or successfully tempted to apostatize from Him.

(*c*)

Job—*continued*

(viii.) The Secret of Job's Endurance

The Psalmist says: "They that know Thy Name will put their trust in Thee."

Job did *know* the Name of the Lord; and consequently put his trust in Him. He knew, as we do, that of ourselves we can do no good thing, nor have we any strength of ourselves to help ourselves in moments of temptation. But then the very fact of worshipping God, and seeking Him at all, is to have strength. We come to Him for two things—*mercy* for the past, and *grace* to help in time of need.

The same doctrine is put to us, by way of illustration, in Zechariah, where the candlestick is fed with secret oil. The Christian's faith could not continue to burn unless for the supplies that God sends him.

In moments of temptation, the Christian must never forget the powerful intercession of our Great High Priest. What He said to Peter, He says to each of us—"You will be tempted, the enemy is seeking to imperil your safety, but "I have prayed for thee that thy faith fail not."

What, we ask, would have been the result in Job's case if he had had no Advocate with the Father when the Accuser was lying about him. Satan proceeded upon the assumption that Christ and the Christian are not *one*, but separate units, contrary to New Testament teaching.

In time of temptation it is not our hold of Christ, but Christ's hold of us, that keeps us safe. It is the Father's hold of His child's hand, and not the tiny grip of the Father's hand, which holds him up when treading a rough and dangerous road.

This is the New Testament doctrine, of which Job's history is an effective example. It was to illustrate this truth that God permitted His servant to be so sorely tried by the adversary. The trial would purify Job, but it would not be effectual in plucking him out of the hand of God—simply because God's hold of him was stronger than the power put forth against him. As our Lord says:

"My Father, which gave them Me, is greater than all."

(a)

(ix.) Job's Restoration

As to Job's ultimate restoration, it would not be correct to say that such prosperity, as a rule, awaits the afflicted in this life. This, then, must be regarded as typical of what is in store for them hereafter.

We read that God gave Job twice as much as he had before; twice as much property; twice as many opportunities of usefulness; twice as much of grace. A jewel before, *now* he is a jewel that had been tested, cut, and polished—fit for the Master's use.

As to his children, it is a beautiful feature in the narrative, that no mention is made of God giving him twice as many as he had before—though, in fact, it was so. The ten that died were only gone before, and still lived unto God. Now he has ten others—so the number is doubled, like all his other blessings. They were not lost, like so much earthly treasure, but removed to another state of existence; and removed, doubtless, for their good. Thus Job, in the end of

his life, had ten children on earth and ten in heaven. So "God healeth the broken in heart, and giveth medicine to heal their sicknesses."

And the whole history may well serve to teach us something of the glory and reward awaiting the people of God in a future state of existence.

"For our light affliction, which is but for a moment" (which is not, as Job's friends ignorantly asserted, penal, but the loving correction of the Lord), "worketh for us a far more exceeding and eternal weight of glory."

And when we come to view what God has in store for us, we shall say, with the Queen of Sheba, "Lo, the half was not told me!"

For "eye hath not seen, nor ear heard, neither hath it entered into the heart of man to conceive the things which God hath prepared for them that love Him."

(b)   *Cf. Delitzsch, and others*

JOB AND HIS FRIENDS

What falls from Job's lips is the musing of a man half-stunned, half-surprised, looking out upon the darkness of life, and asking sorrowfully, "Why are these things so?" And all that falls from his friends' lips is the commonplace remarks of men upon what is inscrutable, maxims learned second-hand, by rote and not by heart, fragments of deep truths, but truths misapplied, distorted, torn out of all connection of time and place, so as to become actual falsehoods, only blistering a raw wound.

(c)   *F. W. Robertson*

Job and his Friends

Eliphaz is the man of prophetic insight; Bildad is the sage, familiar with ancient lore, versed in the traditions of the fathers; Zophar is the average religious man of his day, orthodox, pious, sincere; but, withal, bigoted, fanatical, uncharitable—a man who expects every one to agree with him, not only to believe what he believes, neither more nor less, but to express that belief exactly in the same rigid formula. But the three friends, though representing three different types of character, all concur in one thing: they all hold the same theory of the Divine government, and, on the strength of that theory, they all condemn Job. One after another, these officious friends take up their argument against Job; and one after another, they repeat the same commonplaces of their creed. God is just, and, therefore, God rewards the righteous, and punishes the wicked. If a man suffers, he suffers because he deserves it. If you do not concede this, they say, you arraign the justice of God. Job may have been apparently moral, upright, religious, but he must have cherished some secret sin; and it is this which has called down upon him the vengeance of the Most High. This is their compendious system of theology. This was the system in which they had been trained. This was the system with which they were content, because their experience had probably furnished them with no glaring violation of it; or because, like other good men, in all ages, they shut their eyes to inconvenient facts which clashed with their system. But, like all compendious systems of theology, it breaks down. It is not large enough to cover the facts. You cannot sum in little the

(d)

mysteries of the universe. You cannot still the anguish of beating hearts, crying out for God in their desolate misery, by giving them the dead, dry sand of some formula which you presumptuously label as the truth. It is all too little; the facts of God's world are too broad for your system. "Who did sin, this man or his parents, that he was born blind? Neither did this man sin, nor his parents; but that the works of God might be made manifest in him."

(a)   *Perowne*

God Himself bears witness to the sincerity of His servant, and condemns the specious but hollow theology of his friends. In His sight, a frank and loyal heterodoxy is of more worth than a strict, but hard and freezing orthodoxy, which would make God Himself the accomplice of its error. Job was learning his theology, not from books or from the traditions of the fathers, but in the midst of God's furnace, and by the teaching of God's Spirit; and, therefore, though it was defective, it was true.

(b)   *Ibid*

Elihu rejects the hard law of retribution. God's purpose in chastisement he declares to be the purification of His servants. If He puts those whom He loves into the crucible, it is to purge away their dross, to cleanse them from past sins, and to keep them from falling in the future. Here, certainly, is a step in advance. We are standing on a loftier platform. We are breathing a purer atmosphere. To see a purpose of love in the affliction, is to turn it into a blessing. Even if the conscience does not acknowledge it as merited, to be able to say, "It is a Father's hand that chastens, and He is wiser than I"—this is surely to rob chastisement of its sting. And you will observe that Job accepts in silence this interpretation of his suffering. Evidently it has wrought in him that submission which prepared him for the words of Jehovah, when He answers him out of the whirlwind, and for the humble confession that follows: "Behold, I am vile, what shall I answer Thee? I will lay mine hand upon my mouth!"

(c)   *Ibid*

JOB AND SUFFERING

Under sore, mysterious allotments, like Job's sufferings, there is no better quietive than this: "Humble yourselves therefore under the mighty hand of God, that He may exalt you in due time" (1 Pet. v. 6).

We must familiarize ourselves with the thought, that so long as we know only a fragment of the Divine government, and are not yet able to survey the connection between the whole and the individual, so long as we have not yet heard the "PROLOGUE IN HEAVEN," many an inquiry must remain unanswered, and we must keep alive in us the consciousness that as against God's wisdom our wisdom, even as against God's righteousness, is ever wrong. Instead of asking, Why? we must ask, Wherefore? What problems will God set us? What duties does He lay on me just now? And if it be said, that that unanswered "Why" remains ever in the soul like a thorn; we remark, in reply, that the point of this thorn is broken off to the believer, who knows that he humbles himself not only under the hand of Omni-

potence, but also under the hand of Wisdom and Grace, and that the same hand that now bows him down will in due time raise him up.

(d)   *Martensen*

JOHN THE BAPTIST

"*What went ye out into the wilderness to see?*" (Matt. xi. 7–11).

Not a "reed," a common thing, but an extraordinary man—a GREAT MAN.

1. John the Baptist as a Great Man

"There hath not arisen a greater"; and great men among the Jews were either KINGS OR PROPHETS.

(i.) Kings live in cities, in palaces; but John lived in the wilderness of the Dead Sea, and avoided cities, in a cave as a hermit.

(ii.) Kings cover their heads, wear purple robes, adorned with jewels; John wore no cover to his head—hair long, shaggy, flowing, and a rough garment of camel's hair, girded with a leathern girdle, was his sole attire.

(iii.) Kings fare sumptuously (*see* "DINING"), but John's food was of the simplest: "Locusts and wild honey."

(iv.) Kings are gracious in their speech, courteous and dignified. John was hardly polite; wrong-doers were told plainly and bluntly of their sins; "Ye generation of vipers." Whether to kings, soldiers, professional men, rich, or poor, John spoke in the same plain, blunt manner where the occasion required it.

Hence John the Baptist, though a *Great Man*, was not a king.

(e)

2. Was he a Prophet?

As a "great man" he must be one or the other. Yes, but more than a prophet. Prophets foretell, or predict; but John was *foretold*, the subject of prophecy—"Behold I send My messenger before Thy face." The prophets said Messiah was coming, but His Advent would be preceded by a herald, a forerunner = John the Baptist = "*More than a prophet.*"

(f)

3. John the Baptist was a Faithful Man

Illustration of Faithful Men:

(i.) A few years ago the newspapers contained an account of a signalman on one of our railways, dying at his post, in his box. During a bitterly cold day he had been on duty; he was seen to touch the lever and turn a train in the right direction, and then continued standing without moving; when some one went to him, he was found dead with the handle of the lever in his hand: being on duty, and feeling ill, perhaps numbed with the cold, he made no attempt to desert or neglect his post, whereby so many other lives would be imperilled. He was *faithful unto death*.

(ii.) In the last war between Prussia and Austria, after a battle, Prussian soldiers went round to remove the wounded to hospitals. They came to one young Austrian, badly wounded, and were going to remove him, but he begged them to see to some other wounded men around him first. They did so, and left him. On returning to him after-

(g)

wards, they found him dead; and on lifting the corpse his conduct was explained. Beneath him lay the colours of his regiment, which he had sworn not to part with in life. He, too, was *faithful unto death.*

(iii.) In the celebrated eruption of Mount Vesuvius, more than 1700 years ago, when Pompeii was buried in ashes, a Roman soldier stood as sentinel at the gate of the city leading to the mountain. A few years ago the excavators came upon his skeleton, erect and at his post, standing in a niche, with helmet on the skull, and the bony fingers still grasping a spear. As the ashes rose over his feet, knees, body, neck, and mouth, he stood till he was suffocated. Here, again, was another man "*faithful unto death.*"

John the Baptist was another such man: the faithful reprover was first imprisoned and then beheaded: "*faithful unto death.*" (*See* "Jury.")

(*a*)

4. John the Baptist was less than the least Christian

Greater than all the prophets, and yet "the least in the kingdom is greater than he" reads like a paradox. In what sense are we to understand this?

In this way: Jesus calls His disciples and all Christians, His *friends;* "I have not called you servants, but friends." John the Baptist, notwithstanding all his greatness, was a *servant*, a forerunner, a herald. He did the work of one, in preparing the way of the Lord. The humblest Christian is a friend of Jesus—one with Him, in communion with Him; and as such he is greater than John the Baptist.

(*b*)   *Address to Children*

JOHN THE BAPTIST, THE PREACHING OF (Luke iii. 1–20)

1. The time when. (1, 2)
(i.) Political marks;
(ii.) Religious marks;
John did not go unsent. Cf. the Theophanies of Moses, Isaiah, Ezekiel; see also John i. 33.
2. John himself, and his prophecy (3–6)
(i.) Baptism indicates complete or radical defilement (Ezek. xxxvi. 25, "I will sprinkle"; Zech. xiii. 1, A fountain).
(ii.) "Prepare Thy way" = Oriental custom of a herald before the visit of a monarch.
3. His preaching (7–17). John the Baptist, the great Advent preacher.
(i.) Specimen of his preaching (7–9); think how in the present day such a style of preaching would be received; a man with authority saying, "The Lord is coming."
(ii.) "Generation of vipers," to those who deceived themselves by thinking outward baptism enough. Cf. our Lord's words to those who said: "We have Abraham to our father." "Ye are the children of your father the devil." Such wickedness and craft and deceit could only come from that bad source. Hence the exhortation to flee from the "wrath to come." . . . "Axe."

(10–14) = Confession after preaching—inquiry what they should do.
John the Baptist speaks only of preparatory work: "Lay aside your sins." . . . Such are ready for Christ, who grants the forgiveness of sins, and the Holy Ghost.

(15–17) "Is this the Christ or not?" indicates the stage preparatory to the gift of the Holy Spirit; till then we don't know. John rejoices that he will be eclipsed. Cf. the jealousies of preachers.

(18–20) View of John the Baptist's ministry till his sudden death.
(*c*)

JOHN THE BAPTIST, AS THE SECOND ELIJAH

Compare-
                    Ahab and Jezebel,
                    Herod and Herodias.
A Jezebel could not be wanting in the history of the second Elijah.
(*d*)   *Heubner*

JOHN THE BAPTIST, STUMBLE OF

"*Art thou he that should come, or do we look for another?*" (Matt. xi. 3)

Once John had said: "Behold the Lamb of God," etc.; "He must increase, but I must decrease." How are we to account for his present doubt and depression?

Let any one reflect how different a thing faith is when we are in health and happier circumstances, than when we are depressed and exhausted by illness, or aught else. Just this difference there was between the words of the fiery preacher in the wilderness and the captive whose energies were wasting away in prison.

Catch an Arab steed, and confine him within the walls of a stable, and no wonder that his mettle flags, his strength fails, and his proud spirit breaks. Need we wonder at John's doubt, and the breakdown of his faith, when we remember what he had been and was accustomed to, and compare it with his present condition?

An ardent child of the wilderness, an energetic and fiery preacher, delighting to do the work that God had given him to do, suddenly cast into prison, and there languishing in idleness. With unstrung nerves the strong man became as tow. The body reacts on the mind, and depression ensues. Doubt seizes him—doubt about Jesus, whom he has testified to; and he sends to ask: "Art thou he that should come?" If so, why am I thus? Why so little progress on your part? Why no public announcement of your Messiahship? Why no opening the gates of the kingdom? Do we look for another to come and do this?

John stumbled where so many stumble, at the way in which God works, at the humility of Jesus, at the slow progress of the Kingdom; but his stumble was natural. At one moment we can say "All things work together for our good," and we thoroughly believe it; at another time we say: "All these things are against us." Both frames of mind are explainable by our condition at the time. Are we sniffing our native air, doing the work we love, with a zeal for God's glory. If so, our faith burns bright. But are we laid aside through sickness, and depressed and exhausted, necessarily idlers? Then we faint, as John did; and doubt our interest in Christ, and His love for us. Art Thou still our Saviour? Are we Thine? If we are Thy children, why are we here?
Note,
(i.) That John sent to *Jesus*, not to the learned in the law, for a solution of his doubts;
(*e*)

(ii.) How Jesus dispels the doubt of John, and consoles him.

Messiah's work is going on ; be not " offended " (do not stumble) " in Me." " All things *are* working together for good."

(iii.) In God's providence John's work was done. Jesus's was but beginning, the two must not clash, no rivalry. Guilty men and guilty women would bring about John's death; God would permit it for the best reason. The servant of God goes home. " Well done, good and faithful servant." " Well done, thou greatest that have been born of women." Go to thy reward ; exchange earth for heaven ! Great soul, return to thy God ! " Your light affliction worketh for you an exceeding and eternal weight of glory."

(*a*)

JOHN THE DIVINE (John xiii. 23)

John the Divine, the Apostle, so called to distinguish him from others of the same name, was the son of Zebedee and Salome—a sister of the Virgin Mary.

1. The Progress of his Discipleship

(i.) How he came to be a Christian (John i. 35–39);

(ii.) A Disciple (Matt. iv. 18–22) ;

(iii.) Then one of the twelve Apostles (Matt. x. 1–4) ;

(iv.) Then one of three, at the Mount of Transfiguration (Matt. xvii. 1) ;

(v.) Then one of two at the Passover (Luke xxii. 8) ;

(vi.) Then the ONE (John xiii. 23).

An election within the election. " David had his Jonathan, Christ His John ; " and to this friend He leaves the charge of His mother.

(*b*)

2. His Activity as an Apostle

(i.) He tarries (waits) till his old age before he becomes prominent.

Peter preaches, and conversions follow : John is with him in silence, but exerts an influence over Peter. They are great friends—one supplies what the other lacks. . . . (Peter blunders at Athens, when John is not with him. Edward Irving said, that if his friend T. Carlyle had been with him, he would not have fallen into his blunders). Peter seems to lean on John's bosom as John had done on Jesus's.

James, his more active brother, was killed by the sword—an indication of their diverse characters. James, active and a thunderer, dies first ; John, silent, laying up much experience, waits his time, acts as the adviser, and dies last of the Apostles. Herod proceeded to take Peter also, because he is the next most active Christianizer ; but the quiet, contemplative John is left alone. Paul comes and goes, preaches and writes, still John holds his peace ; but when others have done their work and gone, he, *an old man*, comes forward to do his work, writes his Gospel, Epistles, and Book of Revelation.

(Peter, Paul, and John, each impress Christianity with their own individuality, and in different ways.)

(*c*)

3. John : His Writings

(i.) Gospel, Epistles, Revelation ;

(ii.) The three key words are Love, Light, Life. He defines God as :

(i.) " God is *love* " (1 John iv. 8).

(ii) " God is *light* " (1 John i. 5).

(iii.) " The Father hath *life* in Himself " (John v. 26).

But seeing that " no man hath seen God at any time," and " the Only Begotten Son, which is in the bosom of the Father, hath revealed Him." Jesus is presented to us as *revealing* the Father, as·

(i.) Love (chap. iii.), in opposition to the hatred of the devil ;

(ii.) Light (chap. viii.), in opposition to the darkness which came in by sin.

(iii.) Life (chap. vi. " The Bread of Life," and at the raising of Lazarus, " I am the Resurrection and the Life "), in opposition to spiritual death, and " abiding in death."

Finally, he declares his *object* in writing to be : " These are written that ye might believe, and that believing ye might have life through His name."

The value of his writings to contemplative minds, and especially to the aged, the sick, and the dying, is partly to be accounted for by the old age of the writer, and partly by the nature of what he writes. He is pre-eminently the teacher, not the preacher.

(*d*)

JOHN, ST.

With his contemplative, stately, ideal mind, went angel-like through life. As he did not interfere directly and by main force with the world, he was little heeded by the world ; though, by virtue of his hidden depth of life, he was doubtless a mighty lever of motion, an awakener of kindred spirits, even from the time he was a disciple of the Baptist.

[Cf. The more active, practical James's early martyrdom].

(*e*)

John found *all* in the Person of Jesus : kingdom and redemption, Father and home . . . Hence he is·

(i.) One of the disciples in general (Matt. iv. ; John i.) ;

(ii.) Then one of the twelve (Matt. x.) ;

(iii.) Then one of three (Matt. xvii.) ;

(iv.) Then one of two (Luke xxii. 8) ;

(v.) At last the *one* who lies on the bosom of Jesus (John xiii. 23), to whom Jesus commits His mother (xix.), to whom alone He promises a tarrying till He come again (xxi.), and to whom in exile the Lord once more appeared, after His personal appearances had ceased (Rev. i.).

(*f*)   *Lange*

JOHN, GOSPEL OF

John iii. 16 contains the whole Bible in a nutshell, or " the Bible in miniature," and is worth more than all the wisdom of the world. The infinite love of the Father, the mission of the Son, the work of the Holy Spirit, the lost condition of man, the necessity of a new birth from above, faith in Christ as a condition of salvation, the kingdom of God, eternal life—all these funda-

(*g*)

mental doctrines are set forth by the unerring mouth of our Lord in this interview with a timid yet earnest and anxious inquirer.

(a)   *Lange*

JOHN, FIRST EPISTLE OF

Insists upon *knowing* and *knowledge*, in opposition to the false spiritualistic *gnosis* which had already begun with Docetism and opposed to the ergism of Judaism a syncretistic philosophy, and set in motion an ingenious theory operating intellectually in the place of the work of redemption operating ethically.

(b)   *Ibid*

JOHN AND PAUL

Have depth of knowledge in common. But they know in different ways. Paul, educated in the schools of the Pharisees, is an exceedingly acute thinker and an accomplished dialectician, etc. . . . *John's knowledge is that of intuition and contemplation* . . . Paul and John laid the eternal foundation of all true theology and philosophy ; and their writings are still unfathomed.

(c)   *Ibid*

JOHN, ST., AND PETER

John had no talent for popularity ; he was always too much the whole man for that. But it may well be supposed that he was the support and spiritual guide of Peter ; and exerted almost as determining an influence upon Peter, as Peter did upon the world and the Church. So far as Peter might still need human advice, he found his privy council in the house of John and Mary.

Peter was the first of the Apostles in their relation to the world, John was the first in their relation to Christ. Peter's talent was practical, John's was ideal. Peter is the chief of the working, edifying, upbuilding spirits of the Church ; John, the chief of the contemplative.

(d)   *Ibid*

Peter was more a friend of Christ (Christophilos, or Philochristos) ; John a friend of Jesus (Jesuphilos), His bosom friend.

(e)   *Grotius*

JOHN, WRITINGS OF

Everywhere = love, life, and light, come forth in the personal WORD, to destroy the kingdom of hatred, darkness, and death.

(f)   *Lange*

JOHNSON, SAMUEL

Envy was the bosom serpent of this literary despot.

(g)   *Miss Seward, on Samuel Johnson*

JONAH

1. Jonah and Providence

Jonah heard the voice, and rose up. But he rose up to flee to Tarshish. He wanted *feet* to go to Nineveh—he found *wings* for Tarshish. There's a devil's providence as well as a Divine Providence. If men have a mind to disobey, the opportunity will not be wanting. "If you want to serve Satan, he will supply you with spurs, whip, and bridle— ay, and post-horses to boot."

(h)

2. Jonah pays his own fare

The Lord never sends a messenger at his own expense. Had he done the Lord's errand in the Lord's way, He would have made his path prosperous. But deliberately selecting his own way, Jonah was left to pay his own fare. Obedience is economy : disobedience is expensive. If you *will* be a decalogue turned upside down—if you *will* read "Thou shalt" where God says "Thou shalt not" and "Thou shalt not" where He says "Thou shalt" —you must, in the most literal sense, pay for it. You may earn money by disobedience, but you will put it into a bag with holes. You may accumulate a fortune by disobedience, but it will be like a snow-ball in the hand, that melts more quickly the more it is pressed. You may lay up wealth by disobedience, but you might as well, for all the pleasure it will bring you, throw it into the sea. But this was only a small part of the fare that Jonah paid. When the shekels had passed from his girdle to that of the captain of the ship he was only paying the first instalment. In the second place, he paid his fare in the thwarting of his purposes. To avoid the damp, he was running into the water. To avoid the heat, he was going into the fire. He made more haste than good speed. The ready way was not the right way. "The Lord hurled a great wind into the sea, and there was a mighty tempest in the sea, so that the ship was like to be broken." But quiet as it seems then, the ocean is in league with God against His enemies. One word from Him arrests the sinner in his flight, and reads anew the lesson : "*Be sure your sin will find you out.*" If you *will* be disobedient, you must *pay* your fare in the thwarting of your purposes. The winds would not waft Jonah ; the ship would not carry him ; the sailors, with the best intentions, could not help him ; the lot would not spare him. The Lord meant him to go to Nineveh, and he could not go to Tarshish.

(i)

3. Jonah and God's Sovereignty

This is part of the fare that every disobedient servant of the Lord among us must pay. The centurion did not rule his servants so absolutely as God does the works of His hand. To the wind He says, "Go," and it goeth ; to the waters, "Come," and they come ; to the sun, "Do this," and he doeth it ; to the mountains, "Remove," and they are cast into the sea. Lions cannot harm His friends. Fire cannot burn His people. Ravens feed His prophet. Manna falls round about the camp. Fishes bring Him tribute money. If He has enemies, they cannot escape Him. "Every bush is His officer." Every breeze His constable. Every place His armoury. Every person the executioner of His will. Every sin is a coin issued from your mint, which one day will come back to you, and regarding which He will demand, "Whose is this image and superscription ?" "There's not a crime but takes its proper change out still in crime, if once rung on the counter of the world." "Though they dig into hell, saith the Lord, thence shall Mine hand take them. Though they climb up to heaven, thence

(j)

will I bring them down. Though they hide on the top of Carmel, I will search and take them out thence. Though they be hid from My sight in the bottom of the sea, there will I command the serpent and he shall bite them."

(a)

4. Jonah and the withdrawal of Jehovah's presence

The danger into which he brought himself is described by the prophet in language of great force. He speaks of himself as in affliction, in distress and anguish. The floods compassed him about; the weeds were wrapped about his head; the earth with her bars was about him for ever; he was in the belly of hell, in the midst of the sea. But this was little, compared with his spiritual distress. It is easy for a good man to part with the things the world values most, provided he has the consciousness that God is with him. The millionaire can surely afford to part with a penny. When in addition he must suffer many trials; when affliction comes with many stings, and every sting has its own venom; when trouble comes in waves, in heaps, in troops; when the life that came in like the lamb goes out like the lion—even then he does not complain. We do not find fault with the smith if he does not use handsome tools, with the physician because his probe is not of gold, with the keeper of the furnace because he heats the fire seven times, with the fishermen because he beats the side of the stream. And a good man does not complain against God because his life is not one of uninterrupted prosperity. The vine yields richer grapes when it has been pruned. But the disobedient prophet could not take such comfort to himself. He could not lighten the stroke of the rod by kissing the hand that held it. He had lost everything. Life itself was in danger, and he had lost God beside. Like the stricken deer, he ran from thicket to thicket, his wound festering the longer it was uncured. Hence when all on board were crying to their gods—the Moabites to Chemosh, the Ekronites to Beelzebub, the Philistines to Dagon, the Tyrians to Baal—he could not pray. He went down into the sides of the ship and slept. It seemed as if the art of prayer had been instituted for nothing; as if the promises had been given in vain; as if heaven were not accessible from every quarter of the earth. This is part of the fare every disobedient servant must pay for his disobedience. True prayer is a net that is never spread in vain; a bow that never returns empty; a giant that carries away with ease the gates of iron and brass; a contest in which the strongest wrestler delights to yield to the weakest.

(b) *J. A. Macfadyen*

JOSEPH, A TYPE OF CHRIST

Jesus Christ, prefigured by Joseph, the beloved of his father, and by him sent to visit his brethren, is the innocent person whom His brethren sold for a few pieces of silver, and who thus became their Lord, their Saviour, nay, the Saviour of strangers, and of the whole world. . . . Joseph, guiltless, in the prison between two criminals; Jesus on the cross between two thieves. Joseph foretells the deliverance of one and the death of the other from the same omens; Jesus Christ saves one and leaves the other after the same crimes. Joseph

could merely foretell; Jesus Christ performs. Joseph requests the person who should be delivered to remember him in his honour; the person saved by Jesus Christ entreats his Deliverer to remember him when He shall come into His kingdom.

(c) *Blaise Pascal*

JOSHUA, A TYPE OF CHRIST

1. Their names are the same.
2. Their work was similar, to save the people.
3. Joshua was a conqueror in Canaan, as Christ was conqueror of the world.
4. Joshua succeeded Moses, as Christ with His Gospel succeeded the Law.
5. Joshua led the people across the Jordan into the promised land.
6. Joshua led the people in the conquest of their enemies.
7. When the war was over, Joshua retired to his own possession in Mount Ephraim, and dwelt there. Jesus ascended on high, and there for ever sat down on the right hand of God.

Condensed from the Cambridge Bible for Schools.

(d)

JOY

The Gospel is a message of joy (Luke ii. 10); peace and joy the fruit of the Holy Spirit, and the characteristic of the kingdom of God (Gal. v. 22; Rom. xiv. 17). A philosophy or religion which has no room for the joy and pleasure of man, is as little conversant with the wants of man as with the will of God.

(e) *Harless*

Joy

" *Count it all joy* " (Jas. i. 2)

They were tempted to-

(i.) *Ebionitism* = partiality (II.).
(ii.) *Zealotry* = preaching *versus* works, *vide* " Tongue " (III.).
(iii.) *Insurrection* = parties (IV.).
(iv.) *Apostasy* ; Be patient as Job and the Lord.

(f)

JUDAS ISCARIOT

The Chiliastic ambition that was held in solution amongst the disciples of Jesus, was precipitated in Judas Iscariot, and in him met its fate.

(g)

Judas Iscariot

Among the Evangelists, the first is the only one who has thought of the avarice of Judas being his motive for the crime. According to Mark, the chief priests and scribes were at least aware that they might broach the subject with him; and his acceptance of their money shows that he was not inaccessible in that way. But that is very far from saying that this price decided him to betray his Master. From John's direct testimony it cannot be doubted that the charge with which Jesus had entrusted him became a temptation to him (John xii. 6). When we were told how he was entrusted with the stewardship of the common

(h)

fund, we had to exonerate Jesus from any responsibility; and is it quite incompetent to ask why Jesus did not take the bag from him when he became a thief; for, although Jesus had long seen through him, it by no means follows that He knew, with Divine omniscience, of thefts which were not revealed till after His death. Above all, however, it is generally overlooked, that even John, who testifies to Judas's avarice, does not say one word to show that it played any part in the betrayal. Thus, what we really know leads us to believe that the heart of Judas was becoming gradually more and more involved in snares of worldliness, which did not beseem the service of Jesus; and that the desire for earthly possessions, whose control and administration in attending to his calling gradually monopolized his interest, had deprived him of all inward striving after the highest good, which alone could prove a lasting bond of union between him and Jesus. We may be sure that the inward resistance of such tendencies to the bond of discipleship which he outwardly adhered to, must have become the more unendurable the longer it lasted. But still we find no trace of a motive for the betrayal.

(a)

The deed of Judas is not such an unsolvable riddle for those who believe in the historical accuracy of St. John's Gospel. We saw that after the crisis in Galilee, which first undeceived many of the people, he, too, received a backward impulsion, and even at Cæsarea Philippi Jesus remarked that one of the Twelve had become a prey to the devil (John vi. 70). From that time onward Judas secretly turned away from Him who had so bitterly disappointed his fairest hopes. The people might again succumb to illusions, and promise themselves a final fulfilment of their hopes, but it was impossible for him, who lived in constant intercourse with Jesus, to deceive himself with such vain expectations. The other disciples might see an ultimate fulfilment of their earthly hopes beckoning to them from afar, as the reward of their entire devotion to Jesus, and of their readiness to share everything with their Master; he could do so no longer. He did not wish to know anything of a Messiah who demanded from His followers that they should deny themselves and bear the cross to the extent of sacrificing their lives; and he decided not to follow paths like these for the sake of such very questionable expectations. It was probably only the fear of being called a deserter which restrained him from breaking openly with Jesus; and perhaps his advantageous position as financier to the company had some weight with him; for this was the point at which it appears that there is only a step between the most ambitious earthly hopes and common greed for possession. The love with which Jesus would certainly pursue him, and make him feel that He knew his state of mind, would only be a constant reproach, like a detested moral coercion to which he would not conform.

(b)   *Weiss.*

JUDAS ISCARIOT, JESUS AND (John xiii. 21)

Five times that night He spake to Judas—a wonderful night
(i.) Washing feet;
(ii.) Eating Passover;
(iii.) The first Lord's Supper.

Peter, Nathanael, John were happy! Who shall ruffle the serenity of that hour with a dark suspicion? Hush, the Lord Himself speaks: "Verily . . . betray Me." His reason = to melt the betrayer; to win him if possible:
(i.) By showing him that He knew him:
(ii.) That He loved him.

(c)

1. Jesus knew Judas

(i.) When washing feet, said, "Ye are not all clean";
(ii.) When giving the cup (Luke), "He that eateth with Me hath lift up his heel against Me"—a plain intimation that what might be hidden to others was open unto Him with whom Judas had to do.
(iii.) At table, "as they did eat," Jesus . . . troubled . . . said, . . . "one of you shall betray Me," and, amongst others, Judas asked, "Is it I?" and Jesus replied, "Thou hast said." No longer a hint (1); nor an intimation (2); but a plain, direct telling him "Thou art the man."
(iv.) One last effort. Jesus, greatly affected, replies to John's whisper, "Lord, who is it?" by giving Judas "the sop"—unseen and unheard by others—and saying, "What thou doest, do quickly."

(d)

2. Jesus showed that He loved Judas

(i.) He did not shrink from washing the traitor's feet: He washed the feet of the man who two days before had sold Him for thirty pieces, etc.
(ii.) He ate the Passover with him—dipped in the same dish.
(iii.) He pointed out his danger to him: "The Son of Man goeth as it is written of Him, but *woe* unto the man," etc. If he will perish, it were better he never had been born.
(iv.) Most touching of all, to read that Jesus, who wept over Jerusalem, now *groans* over Judas. Tries to win him and has failed; Judas is heartless, and when Jesus sees this He is troubled in spirit.
Verily, the Lord hath no pleasure in the death of the wicked.

(e)

JUDAS ISCARIOT AND JOHN

If we can suppose that Judas had blinded most of the disciples by his Messianic enthusiasm, that he had probably been received into the circle upon the special intercession of the disciples in their blind confidence—John was the first to see through him (vi. 71; xii. 6; xiii. 27). The silent depth of a solid enthusiasm and devotion finds itself instinctively repelled by the flaring fire of an impure ambition. And as Judas was the serpent which coiled himself upon the bosom of our Lord (John xiii. 18), John lay on the breast of Jesus as a chosen friend.

(f)   *Lange*

JUDGE

Thou shalt answer for me, O Lord my God. Thou that prayest for me shalt be my Judge.

(g)   *Jer. Taylor*

JUDGE OF OUR STATE, CHRIST THE, AND FORGIVENESS

Be not judges of your own condition, but let Christ judge. You are invited to take the comfort of this Gospel truth, that there is forgiveness with God. You say, not for you; so said Jacob, "My way is hid from the Lord " (Isa. xl. 27), and Zion said so too (chap. xlix. 14), " The Lord hath forsaken me, and my Lord hath forgotten me." But did they make a right judgment of themselves ? We find in those places, that God was otherwise minded. This false judgment made by souls in their entanglements, of their own condition, is ofttimes a most unconquerable hindrance unto the bettering of it : they fill themselves with thoughts of their own about it, and on them they dwell, instead of looking out after a remedy. Misgiving thoughts of their distempers are commonly a great part of some men's sickness. Many diseases are apt to cloud the thoughts and to cause misapprehensions concerning their own nature and danger ; and these delusions are a real part of the persons' sickness. Nature is no less impaired and weakened by them, the efficacy of remedies no less obstructed, than by any other real distemper. In such cases, we persuade men to acquiesce in the judgment of their skilful physician, not always to be wasting themselves in and by their own tainted imaginations, and so despond upon their own mistakes ; but to rest in what is informed them by Him who is acquainted with the causes and tendency of their indisposition better than themselves. It is oft-times one part of the soul's depths, to have false apprehensions of its condition. Sin is a madness (Eccles. ix. 3), so far as any one is under the power of it, he is under the power of madness. Madness doth not sooner or more effectually discover itself, in any way or thing, than in possessing those in whom it is with strange conceits and apprehensions of themselves. So doth this madness of sin, according unto its degrees and prevalence. Hence some cry, Peace, peace, when sudden destruction is at hand (1 Thes. v. 3). It is that madness, under whose power they are, which gives them such groundless imaginations of themselves and their own condition. And some say, they are lost for ever, when God is with them.

(a)

Laodicea's judgment of herself, and her spiritual state, we have (Rev. iii. 17). "I am rich, and increased with goods, and have need of nothing." A fair state it seems, a blessed condition ! She wants nothing that may contribute to her rest, peace, and reputation ; she orthodox, and numerous, and flourishing ; makes a fair profession, and all is well within. So she believes, so she reports of herself ; wherein there is a secret reflection also upon others whom she despiseth. Let them shift as they list, I am thus as I say. But was it so with her indeed ? was that her true condition, whereof she was so persuaded, as to profess it unto all ? Let Jesus Christ be heard to speak in this cause, let Him come and judge. "I will do so," saith He (ver. 14). "Thus saith the Amen, the faithful and true witness." Coming to give sentence in a case of this importance, He gives Himself this title, that we may know His word is to be acquiesced in. Every man, saith he is a liar ; their testimony is of no value, let them pronounce what they will of themselves, or of one another :

"I am the Amen ; and I will see whose word shall stand, Mine or theirs." What then saith He of Laodicea ? "Thou art wretched, and miserable, and poor, and blind, and naked." Oh, woeful and sad disappointment ! Oh, dreadful surprisal ! Ah ! how many Laodicean Churches have we in the world ! How many professors are members of these Churches ! Not to mention the generality of men that live under the means of grace, who all have good hopes of their eternal condition, while they are despised and abhorred by the only Judge. Among professors themselves, it is dreadful to think how many will be found light, when they come to be weighed in this balance.

(b) *John Owen*

JUDGE OF OUR FORGIVENESS, CHRIST THE, AND STATE

Christ judgeth some to be in a good condition, be they themselves ever so diffident. Saith He to the Church of Smyrna, "I know thy poverty" (Rev. ii. 9). Smyrna was complaining that she was a contemptible congregation, not fit for Him to take any notice of. Well, saith He, fear not ; I know thy poverty whereof thou complainest ; "but thou art rich ; " that is My judgment, testimony, and sentence, concerning thee and thy condition. Such will be His judgment at the last day, when both those on the one hand and the other shall be surprised with His sentence ; the one with joy at the riches of His grace, the other with terror at the severity of His justice (Matt. xxv. 37–39, and 44, 45). This case is directly stated in both the places mentioned in the entrance of this discourse ; as in that, for instance, " Zion said, the Lord hath forsaken me" (Isa. xlix. 14). That is Zion's judgment of herself, and her state and condition ; a sad report and conclusion. But doth Christ agree with Zion in this sentence ? The next verse gives us his resolution of this matter : "Can," saith He, "a woman forget her sucking child, that she should not have compassion on the son of her womb? Yea, they may forget, yet will I not forget thee ? " The state of things, in truth, is as much otherwise as can possibly be thought or imagined.

(c) *Ibid*

JUDGE OF OUR FORGIVENESS, CHRIST THE, AND STATE

There are two ways whereby the Lord Jesus gives forth His decretory sentence in this matter.

1. By His Word He determines, in the word of the Gospel, of the state and condition of all men indefinitely. Each individual, coming to that Word, receives his own sentence and doom ; He told the Jews that Moses accused them (John v. 45), His law accused and condemned the transgressors of it. And so doth He acquit every one that is discharged by the word of the Gospel. And our self-judging is but our receiving, by faith, His sentence in the word. His process herein we have recorded, "His soul," that is, of the sinner, "draweth near to the grave, and his life to the destroyers." This seems to be his state ; it is so indeed ; he is at the very brink of the grave, or hell. What then ? Why, if there be with him (or stand over him, in the Hebrew), the angel interpreting, or the angel of the covenant, who alone is the one of a thousand ; what shall he do ? He

(d)

shall show to him his uprightness (Job xxxiii. 22, 23). He shall give to Him a right determination of his interest in God, and of the state and frame of his heart towards God : whereupon God shall speak peace to his soul, and deliver him from his entanglements (ver. 24). Jesus Christ hath, in the word of the Gospel, stated the condition of every man. He tells us, that sinners, of what sort soever they are, who believe, are accepted with Him, and shall receive forgiveness from God; and that none shall be refused or cast off that come to God by Him. The soul of whom we are treating is now upon the work of coming to God for forgiveness by Jesus Christ. Many weighty objections it hath in and against itself, why it should not come, why it shall not be accepted. Our Lord Jesus, the Wisdom of God, foresaw all these objections ; He foreknew what could be said in the case, and yet He hath determined the matter as hath been declared. In general, men's arguings against themselves arise from sin and the law. Christ knows what is in them both. He tried them to the uttermost, as to their penalties ; and yet He hath so determined as we have showed. These particular objections are from particular considerations of sins—their greatness, their number, their aggravations. Christ knows all these also ; and yet stands to His former determination. Upon the whole matter, then, it is meet His words should stand. I know, when a soul brings itself to be judged by the word of the Gospel, it doth not always in a like manner, receive and rest in the sentence given. But when Christ is pleased to speak the word with power to men, they shall hear the voice of the Son of God, and be comforted by it. Let the soul, then, that is rising out of depths, and pressing towards a sense of forgiveness, lay itself down before the word of Christ in the Gospel. Let him attend to what Christ speaks ; and if for a while it hath not power to quiet his heart, let him wait a season, and light shall arise to him out of darkness. Christ will give in His sentence into his conscience with such power and efficacy that he shall find rest and peace in it.

(a)

2. Christ also judgeth by His Spirit, not only in making this sentence of the Gospel to be received effectually in the soul, but in and by peculiar actings of His, upon the heart and soul of a believer. "We have received the Spirit of God, that we may know the things that are freely given us of God " (1 Cor. ii. 12). The Spirit of Christ acquaints the soul, that this and that grace is from Him, that this or that duty was performed in His strength. He brings to mind, what, at such and such times, was wrought in men by Himself, to give them support and relief in the times of depths and darkness. And when it hath been clearly discovered to the soul, at any time, by the Holy Ghost, that anything wrought in it, or done by it, hath been truly saving, the comfort of it will abide in the midst of many shakings and temptations.

(b)

3. He also, by His Spirit, bears witness with our spirits, as to our state and condition. This, then, is our first general rule and direction. Self-determinations concerning men's spiritual state and condition, because their minds are usually influenced by their distempers, are seldom right, and according to rule. Mistakes in such determinations are exceedingly prejudicial to a soul seeking after relief and a sense of forgivenes ; let Christ, then, be the judge in this case, by His word and Spirit, as hath been directed.

(c)   *John Owen*

JUDGMENT

1 Pet. iv. 17, and John iii. 18, are not in conflict.

It is necessary to distinguish the judgment of grace from the judgment of wrath, and temporal punishment from eternal.

(d)   *Lange*

Judgment

The two worlds are nearer than we think; and the transactions between them are daily and graphic. A Bishop, in his place in Parliament, utters a defiant and rancorous speech God-ward. Soon after his horse stumbles, and the angel of his baptism holds aloof; and, unsuccoured, he dies.

(e)   *R. S. Hawker*

Cf. Spurgeon on the same event, who had been told that his rheumatism was a judgment of God on him for his strictures on the Church of England.

" If a stiff leg be a judgment of God, what about a broken neck ? " replied he.

(f)

JURY

The names of the Twelve Jurymen who judged " Faithful " worthy of death

The Judge's name was " Hategood," the twelve Jurymen were : Blindman, No-good, Malice, Love-lust, Live-loose, Heady, High-mind, Enmity, Liar, Cruelty, Hate-light, and Implacable. Blindman is the foreman, and he " sees clearly that this man is a heretic." No-good says—" Away with such a fellow from the earth." Malice says —" I hate the very look of him." Love-lust says —" I could never endure him." Live-loose says —" He would always be condemning my ways." Heady says—" Hang him, hang him." High-mind called him a sorry scrub. " He is a rogue," said Liar. " Hanging is too good for him," said Cruelty. " Let us despatch him out of the way," said Hate-light. Then said Implacable—" If all the world were given me, I could not be reconciled to him, therefore let us bring him in guilty of death." And so they did. They condemned him to the most cruel death that could be invented. They did with him according to their law. First they scourged him, then they buffeted him, then they lanced his flesh with knives, and after that they stoned him, then they pricked him with their swords, and last of all they burned him at the stake. Thus came Faithful to his end.

(g)   *John Bunyan*

JUST AS I AM

A painter having painted a " Corporation " picture, portraying certain officials in civic dress, found that the picture required another figure to complete the group. On looking from his window he saw a very dirty, ragged, ill-conditioned crossing-sweeper, just the kind of object that he wanted

(h)

by way of contrast. He determined to get him for a model; and so went out to the boy, and requested him to call at his lodgings on a certain day—"just come," said he, "and sit down and let me look at you, and I will give you five shillings." The boy promised. Meanwhile he told all his companions that a real gentleman had asked him to call on him, and had promised to give him five shillings only to sit and look at him. Next he prepared himself for the visit. He borrowed of one boy a decent coat, of another a waistcoat, of a third a pair of trousers, and made himself *tidy*. On the day appointed he called on the gentleman, was shown in, and stared at with blank astonishment. "What do you want?" he was asked. The boy reminded him of the engagement to come and see him on this day. "No, no," said the painter, "I know nothing about it—must be a mistake." The boy then showed him the card with the address written on by the painter himself. Then the painter burst into a roar of laughter, "Go away, go away," said he, "*You have spoilt yourself.*"

(*a*)

JUSTIFICATION, DEFINITION OF

St. Paul has in mind (Rom. iii.) a judicial process: The righteous and holy God is the Judge; man is the guilty culprit; the law is the accuser; Christ, with His perfect sacrifice, steps in as substitute; the sinner accepts Him in hearty faith, or enters into Christ's position, as Christ did into His. God, on the ground of this relation, acquits the sinner, and treats him as His own child. The sinner, being one with Christ, no more lives unto himself, but, the grace of God enabling him, unto Christ, who died for him, and rose again. This is Justification.

(*b*)   *P. Schaff*

Justification is the act of God as a Judge; adoption, His act as a Father. By the former we are discharged from condemnation, and accepted as righteous; by the latter we are made the children and heirs of God, and joint heirs with Christ for ever.

(*c*)   *Guyse*

We are justified *freely*, by Grace (Rom. iii. 24);
  Meritoriously, by Christ (Rom. v. 19);
  Instrumentally, by Faith (Rom. v. 1);
  Evidentially, by good works (Jas. ii. 26).

(*d*)   *William Marsh*

JUSTIFICATION BY FAITH (Phil. iii. 8, 9)

"Doubtless," saith the Apostle, "I have counted all things loss, and I do judge them to be dung, that I may win Christ, and be found in Him, not having mine own righteousness, but that which is through the faith of Christ, the righteousness which is of God through faith." Whether these words speak of the first or second justification, they make the essence of it a divine quality inherent, they make righteousness which is in us. If it be in us, then it is ours, as our souls are ours, though we have them from God, and can hold them no longer than pleaseth Him; for if He withdraw the breath of our nostrils, we fall to dust: but the righteousness wherein we must be found, if we will be justified, is not our own; therefore we cannot be justified by any inherent quality. Christ hath merited righteousness for as many as are found in Him. In Him God findeth us, if we be faithful; for by faith we are incorporated into Him. Then, although in ourselves we be altogether sinful and unrighteous, yet even the man which in himself is impious, full of iniquity, full of sin; him being found in Christ through faith, and having his sin in hatred through repentance; him God beholdeth with a gracious eye, putteth away his sin by not imputing it, taketh quite away the punishment due thereunto, by pardoning it; and accepteth him in Jesus Christ, as perfectly righteous, as if he had fulfilled all that is commanded him in the law: shall I say more perfectly righteous than if himself had fulfilled the whole law? I must take heed what I say: but the Apostle saith (2 Cor. v. 21), "God made Him which knew no sin, to be made sin for us; that we might be made the righteousness of God in Him." Such we are in the sight of God the Father, as is the very Son of God Himself. Let it be counted folly, or phrensy, or fury, or whatsoever. It is our wisdom, and our comfort; we care for no knowledge in the world but this, that man hath sinned, and God hath suffered; that God hath made Himself the sin of men, and that men are made the righteousness of God.

(*e*)   *Hooker*

JUSTIFYING FAITH

The whole conception of Revelation is comprised in the Revelation of *faith* (Gal. iii. 23).

The *design* of faith in Jesus is to be justified by it, and not by works of the law (Gal. ii. 10).

This is that righteousness of faith (Rom. iv. 11, 13; ix. 30; x. 6), in which faith, in itself, not righteousness, is counted for righteousness, that man should be justified by grace alone, and all that is called work of the law should be excluded (Rom. iii. 38).

In this last passage Luther interpolated the word "ALONE." It is more than prejudice that, even to this day, there are those who complain of this addition, as of an intentional falsification. Intentional it was, true it is, these four letters "*sola*" are not to be found in the text. But do you not see, that notwithstanding it contains the meaning of the text? and if we wish to express the sense clearly the word assuredly belongs to it. For I intended to speak German, not Latin or Greek; for I had undertaken to speak German in my interpretation. And in German, if we are speaking of two things, one admitted, and the other denied, we use the word "*solum*" (allein) next to the word *not* (nicht) or *no* (kein). (Luther's explanation to Wenceslaus Lenk.)

This much is clear as sunshine, we are either justified on the ground of works or of faith: if we strike out *works*, nothing remains but **faith alone**.

(*f*)

Caution:

We may substitute for this faith a false and unapostolic idea, then justification by faith becomes a perversion. The proof of this is in the Epistle of St. James, who had to do with a people who prided themselves on their belief "in the one God"—a faith which has nothing to do with justi-

(*g*)

fying faith, and is no more than "the faith of devils." Abraham's faith would not have been reckoned for righteousness if he had refused to offer up Isaac. His refusal would have revealed the fact that Abraham had no faith. There is a difference between works and works; but faith never exists without some specific work of faith. Faith has every-day works to do, in overcoming unbelief, self-righteousness, or attacks of despair; and when such specific operations of faith do not exist, a justifying faith is not present.

(*a*)   *Harless*

JUSTIFICATION BY FAITH

On this subject I know of nothing so precise and accurate (though numberless and vast volumes have been written upon it, from the Reformation downwards), as what is contained in Dr. Barrow's "Discourses on Faith." His notion on the whole is, that justification, as used by the sacred writers, and St. Paul in particular, means remission of sins, and admission into a state of favour with God, as if we were righteous, and not the infusion of inherent holiness by the Spirit; that this justification was primarily made on our entrance into the Christian covenant by baptism, and is afterwards received and regranted, as it were, on our repentance and return from such transgressions as we may have fallen into after baptism.

(*b*)   *Hurd*

JUSTIFICATION BY FAITH

Justification by faith is not merely a tenet, not merely an axiom, but a principle in the highest sense of the term, a living *first* principle, bearing in itself a whole world of consequences. . . . It implies that salvation is a matter between man and God, between man and his Redeemer; that no priesthood, no human authority, dare interpose between man and his God. "Thou must thyself decide it," says Luther, "for thy life is at stake."

(*See* "FAITH.")

(*c*)   *Martensen*

JUSTIFICATION AND SANCTIFICATION

We must distinguish, but not separate, Christ *for* us, *before* us, and *in* us.

(*d*)   *Lange*

K

KEEP

"*Now unto Him who is able to keep you*," etc. (Jude 24)

1. **Him** = the Saviour at the right hand of God, at the seat of power. "All power in heaven and earth given unto Me."

2. **Able to keep.** How?
(i.) "Hold Thou me up, and I shall be safe;"
(ii.) "Holy Father, keep them," etc.; "I have prayed for thee," etc.

3. **Present faultless.** How?
(i.) "If any man sin, we have an Advocate with the Father, Jesus Christ, the Righteous," etc.
(ii.) "If we walk in the light," etc.; . . . "blood cleanseth from all sin."

4. **With exceeding joy**
If the present joy be unspeakable and full of glory, how can that be described? Unutterable, etc., ineffable!

(*a*)

KEEP

Be taught more and more your own infirmity. At present, you may think yourself to be strong. So did Peter: "Lord, I am ready to go with Thee both into prison and to death," "Though all men forsake Thee, yet I will never forsake Thee." But wait till this spiritual fervour is over. Wait till some temptation comes. Wait till some provocation rouses your anger. Wait till some flattery fans your pride. Wait, I say, till the spark is put to the gunpowder, and you will then see how liable you are in a moment to commit the grossest sins, and to grieve the Spirit, and cause Him to depart. You cannot keep yourselves.

But God can keep you. And He deals with you as you deal with your children, who cannot yet walk alone. As you hold them, so God holds you. And if the Lord occasionally lets you trip and stumble, He does so to teach you a lesson which you find most difficult to learn, a sense of your own weakness; but, if you are real believers, He will not let you fall to your ruin. It has been well observed, that a mother, in teaching her child to walk, will sometimes let it go, that it may see how helpless it is; but she will only do this on a soft carpet, and not on the hard pavement, nor at the edge of a precipice.

From the time that you were first brought to know Christ, and to do Him service, no one has had such perfect knowledge of you as Christ has, and no one has felt so concerned in your welfare.

(*b*)

Suppose that your spirit has departed, and your soul is now "with Jesus" in Paradise. What is the reception you meet with there? You hear your own name pronounced by Christ Himself, and you then hear Him summoning you up before His "great white throne," and there, amidst the plaudits of ten thousand times ten thousand spectators, redeemed men and elect angels, He is seen placing the "crown" upon your head, and saying, "I appoint unto you a kingdom."

(*c*)

Remember that there is such a thing as making shipwreck of your faith! How many apparently gallant vessels, in crossing the sea of life, have foundered ere they reached the promised land! It has been well remarked, that the shores of eternity are covered with the wrecks of a shattered and hollow profession.

(*d*)   *C. Clayton*

KEEP

It was not the meaning of our Lord and Saviour, in saying, "Father, keep them in Thy name," that we should be careless in keeping ourselves. To our own safety, our own sedulity is required.

(*e*)   *Hooker*

KEEPER

"The Lord is thy keeper," but not thy gaoler. His keeping is not confinement. It is protection. When you commit your ways to Him, He does not abridge your liberty; He only defends you against the evil.

(*f*)   *J. M. Ludlow*

KEPT—PRESERVED (1 Thess. v. 23)

The verb τηρέω occurs seventy-five times in the New Testament, and in the A.V. is fifty-eight times rendered *to keep;* only here, and in Jude, *to preserve.* Wherever it is used of believers, it is preferable to translate it *to keep*, not for the sake of uniformity, but on account of the large use of that term in the same connection in our Lord's high-priestly prayer (John xvii.). The present stay of the Church is the Father's answer to the Son.

Compare (i.) *Calling* and *keeping* with
(ii.) *Creation* and *Providence.*

(*g*)   *Lange*

KILLING TIME

To pass the time, is considered to live; but at the end of time stands death, with hour-glass and sickle, waiting for the last grains to run out. Passing the time, then, may be tantamount to slow self-murder. . . .

One of the great sources of amusement on earth for the beguiling of dull time, is the theatre. Well, we too have a theatre, though the time with us needs no whiling away. Old habit only is its *raison d'être.* Women need something here to incite their fancy, men something to meet their craving—not to mention the question of food for fashionable conversation. There is no weather here to be talked about, so we must fall back upon the theatre.

(*h*)   *Letters from Hell*

KING, THE

I respect the man while, and only while, the King is translucent through him. I reverence the glass case for the saint's sake within; except for that, it is to me mere glazier's work—putty, glass, and wood.

(*i*)   *S. T. Coleridge.*

KING, THE BIRD-

The Eagle being dead, the birds chose the Ring-dove for their queen ; and all of them obeyed her soft cooing call. But, light and airy as is the nature of birds, they soon altered their determination, and repented them that they had made it. The proud Peacock thought it beseemed him better to be ruler ; the keen Falcon, accustomed to make the smaller birds his prey, reckoned it disgraceful to obey the peaceful Dove ; they formed a party, and appointed the weak-eyed Owl to be the spokesman of their combination, and propose a new election of a sovereign. The sluggish Bustard, the heavy-bodied Heath-cock, the lazy Stork, the small-brained Heron, and all the larger birds chuckled, flapped, and croaked applause to him ; and the host of little birds twittered in their simplicity, and chirped out of bush and grove to the same tune. Then arose the warlike Kite, and soared boldly up into the air, and the birds cried out : " What a majestic flight ! The brave, strong, Kite shall be our king." Scarcely had the plundering bird taken possession of the throne, when he manifested his activity and courage on his winged subjects, in deeds of tyranny and caprice : he plucked the feathers from the larger fowls, and ate the little songsters.

(a)   *Musæus, translated by Carlyle*

KING OF GLORY

Witnesses of the Ascension

Elias had but one witness of his rapture into heaven : St. Paul had none, no not himself ; for, *whether in the body or out of the body* he knew not. Thou, O blessed Jesu, wouldst neither have all eyes witnesses of Thine Ascension, nor yet too few. As, after Resurrection, Thou didst not set Thyself upon the pinnacle of the Temple, nor yet publicly show Thyself within it, as making Thy presence too cheap ; but madest choice of those eyes whom thou wouldest bless with the sight of Thee ; Thou wert seen indeed of five hundred at once, but they were brethren : so, in Thine Ascension, Thou didst not carry all Jerusalem promiscuously forth with Thee to see Thy glorious departure, but only that selected company of Thy disciples which had attended Thee in Thy life. Those, who immediately upon Thy ascending returned to Jerusalem, were a hundred and twenty persons : a competent number of witnesses to verify that Thy miraculous and triumphant passage into Thy glory. Lo, those only were thought worthy to behold Thy majestical ascent, which had been partners with Thee in Thine humiliation. Still, Thou wilt have it thus with us, O Saviour, and we embrace the condition : if we will converse with Thee in Thy lowly estate upon earth, wading with Thee through contempt and manifold afflictions, we shall be made happy with the sight and communion of Thy glory above.

(b)   *Bishop Hall*

KING OF GLORY

Ascension

But, oh, what tongue of the highest archangel of heaven can express the welcome of Thee, the King of Glory, into those blessed regions of immortality ? Surely, the empyreal heaven never resounded with so much joy. God ascended with jubilation, and the Lord with the sound of the

trumpet. Certainly, if when He brought His only begotten Son into the world, He said : Let all the angels worship Him ; much more now that He ascends on high, and hath led captivity captive, hath He given Him a name above all names, that at the name of Jesus all knees should bow. And if the holy angels did so carol at His birth in the very entrance into that estate of humiliation and infirmity ; with what triumph did they receive Him now, returning from the perfect achievement of man's redemption ! And if when His type had vanquished Goliath, and carried the head into Jerusalem, the damsels came forth to meet him with dances and timbrels ; how shall we think those angelic spirits triumph, in meeting of the great Conqueror of Hell and Death ! How did they sing ; " Lift up your heads, ye gates, and be ye lift up, ye everlasting doors, and the King of Glory shall come in."

(c)   *Bishop Hall*

KING AND PRIEST

There is nothing in the view of our Divine Teacher so hostile to His Divine Spirit as the lust of domination. This we are accustomed to regard as eminently the sin of the archfiend. " By this sin fell the angels." It is the most Satanic of all human passions, and it has inflicted more terrible evils on the human family than all others. It has made the names of king and priest the most appalling in history.

(d)   *Channing*

KING AND STATE, THE

Let not your king and parliament in *one*,
Much less apart, mistake themselves for *that*
Which is most worthy to be thought upon :
Nor think *they* are, essentially, the STATE.
Let them not fancy that th' authority
And privileges upon them bestown,
Conferred are to set up a majesty,
A power, or a glory, of their own !
But let them know, 'twas for a deeper life,
Which they but *represent*-
That there's on earth a yet auguster thing,
Veiled though it be, than parliament and king !
(e)   *George Withers*

KINGCRAFT

I am compelled to remember that the people, in this their singular madness, wrought far less woe than kings and priests have wrought, as a familiar thing, in all ages of the world. All the murders of the French Revolution did not amount, I think, by one fifth, to those of the massacre of St. Bartholomew's. The priesthood and the throne, in one short night and day, shed more blood, and that the best blood of France, than was spilled by Jacobinism, and all other forms of violence during the whole Revolution.

(f)   *Channing*

KINGDOM OF CHRIST

" *Not from hence* " (John xviii. 36)

This solemn declaration of Christ concerning the heavenly origin and unworldly character of His kingdom, settles in principle the question of

(g)

Church and State in favour of separation, and against penal laws for the punishment of heresy. (Cf. Matt. xxii. 21.)

(*a*)   *P. Schaff*

KINGDOM OF CHRIST

Our comfort against every disheartening view of the race is this, that the love of Christ, with un-utterable forbearance, continues to develop far and near its redeeming efficacy; that His Kingdom truly comes, although, as it appears to our limited view, so very slowly; that it yet comes in many places where we see nothing of it; and that we will yet one day see, to our surprise, that *this kingdom is far greater, and embraces far more, than we are commonly disposed to admit.*

(*b*)   *Martensen*

KINGDOM OF CHRIST

On that night when Christ was born, what a difference was there, in all outward marks of distinction, between the child of the Hebrew mother, as He lay in His lowly cradle, and the Augustus Cæsar, whose edict brought Mary to Bethlehem, as he reposed in his imperial palace! And throughout the lifetime of the two there was but little to lessen that distinction. The name of the one was known and honoured over the whole civilized globe: the name of the other scarce heard of beyond the narrow bounds of Judea. How stands it now? The throne of the Cæsars, the throne of mere human authority and power, has perished. But the empire of Jesus, the empire of pure, undying, self-sacrificing love, will never perish; its sway over the conscience and hearts of men, as the world grows older, becomes ever wider and stronger.

(*c*)   *Hanna*

KINGDOM OF HEAVEN

Great geniuses have their *kingdom*, their splendour, their triumphs; and seek not carnal greatness because it has no relation to the greatness which they pursue. It is discerned by the mind, not by the eyes; but that is sufficient for them. The saints likewise have their empire, their lustre, their greatness, and their triumphs; and want not earthly dignities, nor intellectual honours, which are out of their sphere, and which neither increase nor diminish the greatness to which they aspire.

(*d*)   *Blaise Pascal*

It had been vain for Archimedes, though of princely descent, to have acted the prince in his book of geometry. It had been equally vain for our Lord Jesus Christ to have come as a king, for the illustration of His kingdom of holiness.

(*e*)   *Ibid*

KINGDOM OF HEAVEN

"*The kingdom of heaven is like unto a net that was cast into the sea and gathered of every kind*" (Matt. xiii. 47)

If we have watched such a net drawn to shore or hauled into a fishing-boat, we shall have no difficulty in realizing the force of the image.

Here is a confused mass of living things—hideous and grotesque forms, motley and changing hues—skate, dogfish, cuttlefish—great ghastly eyes glaring out of the abdomen—long slimy hands and feet protruding from the head—every monstrosity of shape and colour. From the bottom of our hearts we pity poor perjured Clarence in his terrible nightmare, confronted with these ugly sights, as he sunk amidst the gurgling, rushing waters. And yet this is the image of the kingdom of heaven. The authority of the Teacher is unquestioned. The tenour of the lesson is plain. And yet the history of the Church teems with examples of its fatal neglect. Like the companion parable of the Tares, the figure speaks distinctly, but speaks in vain. It would seem as if men found a zeal for God and a fervour of religion incompatible with the patient waiting which it inculcates. The bravery, the steadfastness, the self-sacrifice, the devotion, the heroism of the Master's example are fully appreciated; but the moderation and forbearance, the ἐπιείκεια of Christ, find fewer followers among ardently religious men.

(*f*)

The most obvious illustration is the Donatist schism.

No one now has a good word for the Donatists. Sitting in judgment on the past, zealous Churchmen would not for a moment hesitate in the choice between the spirit of St. Augustine and the spirit of Donatism. Is this always quite consistent? Do not the same men who condemn the Donatists use language and laud principles which are the very embodiment of the old Donatist spirit? Let us try to put ourselves in the position of a Donatist. What scorn, what pity, what abhorrence did he not manifest towards the luke-warmness, the indifference to truth, the temporizing with worldly exigencies, the dalliance with the civil powers, the giving to Cæsar of the things that are God's, which distinguished the main body of the Catholic Church? With what fervour of language and what strength of conviction did he not quote the Scriptural precept, "Come out from among them, and be ye separate, saith the Lord, and touch not the unclean thing?" "What has the Emperor to do with the Church?" cried Donatus. "The principle expressed in these words of Donatus," cried Neander, "that Church and State should be kept wholly distinct from each other, had at that time . . . . become universally recognised among the Donatists." How perfectly admirable is the typical Donatist, if zeal and courage and intensity were everything. Yet Donatism was doomed. It had forgotten the counsels of Divine forbearance—"Let both grow together." The fatal schism within was followed by barbarian invasion from without. This is the almost invariable sequence in the history of Churches. The Vandal follows on the heels of the Donatist; and then what becomes of the African Church? "He that hath ears to hear, let him hear."

(*g*)

The ecclesiastical history of Scotland in these latest ages will supply another illustration.

Was it not a magnificent sight—a manifestation of conscientious self-sacrifice and zeal for the purity of the Church on the grandest scale—the exodus of those 400 ministers, leaving homes and

(*h*)

endowments, going forth they knew not whither, placing their future altogether in the hands of God? It was magnificent. Who can deny it? But was it war? Did it show that generalship, that patience of imperfect instruments, that tolerance of temporary inconveniences, that foresight of consequences, which is not less necessary than zeal and courage in the campaign against the powers of evil? Did it not too much resemble that brilliant cavalry charge of which the bravery, indeed, was transparent and can never lose its moral effect, but wherein the loss of life was ruinous, and which every one condemns now as a military blunder of the gravest kind? For what is the result? Here you have face-to-face two Churches, absolutely at one in their doctrinal formularies and their ecclesiastical polity—even to the most minute points—not kept apart now even by the question which was the cause of disruption —yet (so it would appear) hopelessly and irreconcilably estranged from each other :-

> They stand aloof—the scars remaining—
> Like cliffs which have been rent asunder,
> A dreary sea now flows between.

Again I say, " He that hath ears to hear, let him hear."

(a)

The drift of these remarks will be obvious

The Donatist schism in Africa, and the disruption in Scotland, arose out of relations which were, or were supposed to be, unsatisfactory between Church and State. It is undeniable that at the present moment there is much uneasiness on this very point among English Churchmen. No doubt there are many anomalies in our position with regard to the State. There is much which requires patient forbearance and delicate handling before the tangle can be unravelled. Many ardent spirits are eager to cut the knot at once, instead of trying to untie it. To zealous, chivalrous natures more especially, there is a sort of attractiveness in the prospect of the gigantic sacrifice which this course would involve. They do not see, or do not reflect, that though the sacrifice would be great to themselves, it would be greater still to their successors, and greatest of all to the Church of which they are members. The magnificent unworldliness of the Donatists threatens to be repeated once more with all its fatal consequences. The Donatists hailed with satisfaction the advent of the great enemy of the Church, the Emperor Julian, through whom they hoped to secure their independence. Patient working and patient waiting till God in His own good time should disentangle the meshes and loose the fetters,—this was altogether beyond their range of vision. " Let both grow together " was a precept unheeded and unheard. The tares must be rooted out at all hazards

(b)   *Bishop Lightfoot*

Kingdom of God, The

Dr. Arnold held that the work of Christianity itself was not accomplished so long as social and political institutions were exempt from its influence —so long as the highest power of human society professed to act on other principles than those declared in the Gospel; but whenever it should come to pass that the strongest earthly bond should be identical with the bond of Christian fellowship—that the highest earthly power should avowedly minister to the advancement of Christian holiness—that crimes should be regarded as sins —that Christianity should be the acknowledged basis of citizenship—that the region of national and political questions, war and peace, oaths and punishments, economy and education, so long considered by good and bad alike as worldly and profane, should be looked upon as the very sphere to which Christian principles are most applicable —then he felt that Christianity would at last have gained a position where it would cope, for the first time, front to front with the power of evil; that the unfulfilled promises of the older prophecies, so long delayed, would have received their accomplishment, that the kingdoms of this world would have indeed become the kingdom of the Lord, and of His Christ.

(c)   *A. P. Stanley*

Kingdom of God, The

Is to reach its realization in the domain of the world, that is to say, the entire human race dwelling upon this earth. But the instruments of its dominion are not worldly. The kingdom is not of this world, not founded on earthly power and might (John xviii. 36); but by the scattering of the word of the Lord (as seed, Matt. xiii. 37), and those who receive it are the members of the kingdom. To this kingdom belong the simplicity and humility of a child (Matt. xviii. 3); and no one attains to it unless through a new birth from God (John iii. 3, 5, 6). In so far as this kingdom and he who belongs to it are in the world, but separate from the world, and yet not less for the service of this world : It is the kingdom of ministering love, where sin-forgiving love is to be learnt ; a kingdom whose members must not quit the world, nor pray that God should take them out of it, but rather that He should make them fit for that end to which they are appointed, viz., to be the light and the salt of the world. Therefore, so certainly as the godless and unrighteous have no abiding portion in this kingdom (1 Cor. vi. 9), so certain is it, that the boundaries thereof are not so firmly closed, that in its domains wicked men also should not be found (Matt. xxviii. 10; xiii. 38, 48), to whom, equally with the frail and weak, the instructing, helping and supporting, reproving and correcting love of Christ, which alleviates want and misery, is to be shown (1 Thess. v. 14; Matt. xxv. (31–46). . . . In this kingdom the gifts we receive should gain interest (Luke xix. 11), and we should serve, not rule, as Christ came to minister, and not to be ministered unto. Thus the Christian forsakes all selfish enjoyment of his justification before God, of peace with Him, in order to show in all relations of life, where none is common, or unclean (Rom. xiv. 14), his mastery in Christ, (1 Cor. vi. 12) ; to bear fruit, and to be serviceable in the kingdom of Christ. . . . But this kingdom is perfected only with the second coming of the Lord (Matt. xxv.; 2 Thess. i. 7). Then sorrow with dominion of death is destroyed (1 Cor. xiii. 26 ; Rev. xxi. 4) ; and those raised from the dead to blessedness, will have as their abode a new heaven and a new earth, *wherein dwelleth righteousness* (2 Pet. iii. 13; Rev. xxi. 1). . . . This time of universal restoration (Acts iii. 21), is the goal of all promise, and the conclusion of the kingdom of grace, which prepares for this end. And with this

(d)

promise the Christian becomes conscious that his calling in this world, and for this world, is nothing but a preparatory step; and that if in this world only we had hope in Christ, we should be of all men the most miserable (1 Cor. xv. 19). On the contrary, all thought and endeavour are comprised in the word, "We have here no continuing city, but we seek one to come" (Heb. xiii. 14; Rom. viii. 18–23).

(a) *Harless*

KINGDOM OF GOD, THE

There is great meaning in the words that Jesus was continually using to describe the work that He did for men's souls. He brought them into "the kingdom of God." The whole burden of His preaching was to establish the kingdom of God. The purpose of the new birth for which He laboured was to make men subjects of the kingdom of God. Is it not clear what it means? The kingdom of God for any soul is that condition, anywhere in the universe, where God is that soul's king, where it seeks and obeys the highest, where it loves truth and duty more than comfort and luxury. Have you entered into the kingdom of God? Oh, how much that means. Has any love of God taken possession of you, so that you want to do His will above all things, and try to do it all the time? Has Christ brought you there? If He has, how great and new and glorious the life of the kingdom seems. No wonder that He said you must be born again before you could enter there. How poor life seems outside that kingdom! How beautiful and glorious inside its gates!

If I tried to tell you how Christ brings us there, I should repeat to you once more the old, familiar story. He comes and lives and dies for us. He touches us with gratitude. He sets before our softened lives His life. He makes us see the beauty of holiness and the strength of the spiritual life in Him. He transfers His life to us through the open channel of faith, and so we come to live as He lives, by every word that proceedeth out of the mouth of God. How old the story is, but how endlessly fresh and true to Him whose own career it describes.

(b) *Phillips Brooks*

KINGLY MAN

Hooded and wrapped about with that strange and antique garb, there walks a kingly, a most royal soul, even as the Emperor Charles walked amidst solemn cloisters under a monk's cowl—a monarch still in soul.

(c) *Longfellow, "Outre Mer," on Carlyle*

KISS OF DEATH, THE

The Princess Alice of England, Grand Duchess of Hesse, died December 14, 1878, On the anniversary of her father's death, and also on that of the recovery of her brother, the Prince of Wales, from a dangerous illness, 1871. The Prime Minister, in the House of Lords, said, "The physician enjoined her not to kiss her children, she obeyed; but it became her lot to break to her son, quite a youth, the news of the death of his youngest sister, and the boy was so overcome with misery, that the agitated mother clasped him in her arms and received the *kiss of death*."

"So good, so kind, so clever," is her brother's (the Prince of Wales') testimony.

(d)

KNIGHT

Sidney was a refinement upon nobility. He was like the abstract and essence of romantic fiction, having the courage (but not the barbarity) of the preux chevaliers of ancient times—their unwearied patience, their tender and stainless attachment. He was a hero of chivalry without the grossness and frailty of flesh. He lived beloved and admired, and died universally and deservedly lamented. He is the last of those who have passed into a marvel; for he is now remembered almost as the ideal personification of a true knight, and is translated to the skies, like the belt of the hunter Orion or Berenice's starry hair.

Edinburgh Review, 1825, *on Sir Philip Sidney*

(e)

KNIGHTHOOD

"I drew,
The knighthood errant of this realm, and all
The realms together under me, their Head,
In that fair order of the Table Round,
A glorious company, the flower of men,
To serve as model for the mighty world,
And to the fair beginning of a time.
I made them lay their hands in mine and swear
To reverence the King as if he were
Their conscience, and their conscience as their King,
To break the heathen, and uphold the Christ;
To ride abroad redressing human wrong;
To speak no slander, no, nor listen to it;
To lead sweet lives of purest chastity."

(f) *Tennyson*

KNOCKING

"*Behold I stand at the door, and knock*" (Rev. iii. 20).

Lord, at whose door dost Thou stand knocking? At the rich man's? at the righteous man's? at the qualified and prepared man's door? "No," "It is at the lukewarm Laodicean's door; at their door who are neither hot nor cold, who are wretched, and miserable, and poor, and blind, and naked. These are the worst of the worst, yet if any of them shall open the door, *I will come in and sup with him, and he with Me*."

(g) *Thos. Brooks*

KNOW

Not to know me, argues yourselves unknown, The lowest of your throng.

(h) *Milton*

KNOW

"*In that day ye shall know*" (John xiv. 20, 21).

(i.) *That* day = Pentecost—the day of the power of the Holy Ghost, the Comforter, etc.

(ii.) "YE" = not the world, who do not fulfil the conditions of "having" and "keeping" the *word* (see context).

(iii.) "*Know*" = The full assurance of faith—not guessing.

(i)

KNOWING CHRIST

" Si Christum bene scis, satis est, si cetera nescis : si Christum nescis, nil est, si cetera disces."

(a)　　　　　　　　*Motto of Johann Bugenhagen*

KNOWING GOD (Eph. i. 17, 18)

Man's knowledge is not perfect within the domain of creation, still less can he know the things of the invisible world.

Only by *living* in a sphere does he gather the knowledge of what is found there ; knowledge comes from experience of occurrences . . . *Sensible, mental, spiritual* knowledge refers to life-spheres in which he who knows must move.

(b)　　　　　　　　　　　　　　*Lange*

KNOWING GOD

All who seek God apart from Jesus Christ, and who rest in nature, either find no light to satisfy them, or form for themselves a means of knowing God and serving Him without a Mediator.

(c)　　　　　　　　　　*Blaise Pascal*

KNOWING GOD

God has at no time left Himself without witnesses (Acts xiv. 17) ; nay, He has placed men on this earth, and as they are, that they may *seek* Him and *find* Him (Acts xvii. 26, 27). It is also a fact that the invisible nature of God, i.e., His eternal, *power* and Godhead, are seen and perceived from the creation of the world in the works of His hands (Rom. i. 20). Hence we conclude with certainty that the world of creation is a means of attaining to a knowledge of God appointed by Himself—a means of leading us to seek God and to find Him. . . . The means of this knowledge, however, cannot be understood without an understanding of the organ of that perception. . . . There is, like the bodily eye, *the light* of an eye within us, which is organized for the knowledge of God, and is akin to God, but which can lose its faculty of knowledge and become blind and dark. . . . Thus that which brings about a consciousness of God is to be sought not only without, but from *within* man.

(d)　　　　　　　　　　　　　*Harless*

The carnal Jews fill the middle place between Christians and heathen. Heathens know not God, and love nothing but the world. The Jews know the true God, and love nothing but the world. Christians know the true God, and love not the world. Jews and heathens love the same world. Jews and Christians know the same God.

(e)　　　　　　　　　　*Blaise Pascal*

KNOWING GOD

It had not, therefore, been just to assume an appearance every way divine, and capable of working conviction in all men, nor had it been just, on the other hand, to have used so much concealment, as not to be discoverable by sincere inquirers. He was pleased to make Himself perfectly discoverable to these ; so that, intending to reveal Himself to those who sought Him with their whole heart, and to hide Himself from those who shunned Him with

their whole heart, he has so tempered the knowledge of Himself, as to exhibit indications of Himself, discoverable to those who seek Him, and hidden from those who seek Him not.

There is enough of light for those who only wish to see ; and enough of shade for those who are of a contrary disposition.

(f)　　　　　　　　　　*Blaise Pascal*

Were there no darkness, man would not be sensible of his corruption. Were there no light, man would despair of a remedy. So that it is not only just, but advantageous to us, that God should discover Himself in part, and conceal Himself in part ; it being alike dangerous for us to know God without knowing our misery, and to know our misery without knowing God.

(g)　　　　　　　　　　　　　*Ibid*

It is neither true, that God altogether reveals Himself. But it is at once true, that He hides Himself from those who tempt Him, and reveals Himself to those who seek Him.

(h)　　　　　　　　　　　　　*Ibid*

KNOWING GOD

The Scripture gives us a further evidence of this truth, when it so often testifies, that God is found by those who seek Him ; for it could never speak thus of a clear and certain light, such as gives not men the trouble of seeking it, but discovers itself without inquiry. Metaphysical proofs of God are so very intricate, and so far removed from the common reasonings of men, that they strike with little force. Or, at best, the impressions continue but a short space ; and the very next hour, men fancy that they have been deceived ; so that what they have learnt by curiosity, they lose again through pride. Again, arguments of this kind are able to lead us no further than a speculative knowledge of God ; and to know Him only thus, is, in effect, not to know Him at all.

(i)　　　　　　　　　　　　　*Ibid*

KNOWING GOD

It is dangerous for man to *know* God without knowing his own misery, and to know his own misery without knowing the Redeemer, who can deliver him from it. To apprehend one without the other, begets either the pride of philosophers, who know God, but not their own misery ; or the despair of atheists, who know their own misery, but not a Redeemer.

(j)　　　　　　　　　　　　　*Ibid*

KNOWING GOD

" *We know not* " (John xiv. 5)

Who has sent me into the world I know not ; what the world is I know not, nor what I am myself. I am in awful ignorance of all things. I know not what my body is, what my senses, or my soul : this very part of me which thinks what I speak, which reflects upon everything, and even upon itself, knows itself as little as the rest of me. I behold the frightful region of infinite space with which I am encompassed, and I find myself chained to a corner of this vast extent, without understand-

(k)

ing why I am placed here, rather than elsewhere ; or why the present instant, appointed for my existence, was assigned, rather at such a point, than at any other, whether of the eternity which was before me or of that which is to come after me. I see nothing but infinity on all sides, which engulfs me like an atom, or like a shadow which endures for an instant, and then is gone for ever. All I know is, that I must shortly die ; but that of which I am most ignorant is this very death, which I cannot escape. As I know not whence I came, so I know not whither I go.

(a)   *Blaise Pascal*

"The understanding is a born Atheist." (*Jacobi.*) "Where there is a living piety, the question (How to know God) has no meaning." (*Arnobius.*) "Lord, who givest insight, give me insight, that Thou art as I believe, and that Thou art what I believe." (*Prayer of Anselm.*) The Scriptures teach that we have in Christ a true knowledge of God, and Christ has His knowledge also for our sakes. (Matt. xi. 27 ; John xvii. 3 ; John i. 18 ; 1 Cor. i. 5, ii. 10–12 ; 2 Cor. iv. 6 ; Eph. i. 8, iii. 4–9.)

(b)   *Dorner*

"*It was about the tenth hour*" (John i. 39)

After the death of Pascal, there was found in the lining of his coat a parchment which he never parted from, in order to keep in his memory a certain epoch in his life. It contained these words : "Certainty—joy—the God of Jesus Christ, not of the philosophers and savants. Oh that I may never be separated from Him." The explanation of this is, that on one memorable night, during a holy watching, he had met, not merely the Machinist of the universe, the God who is but the substance or the law of the world, but the God who wills and creates the happiness of His children.

(c)   *Prof. E. Naville : " Eternal Life "*

To understand a great and good being, we must have the seeds of the same excellence. How quickly, by what an instinct, do accordant minds recognise one another ! . . . God becomes a real being to us in proportion as His own nature is unfolded within us. To a man who is growing in the likeness of God, faith begins even here to change into vision. He carries within himself a proof of a Deity which can only be understood by experience. . . . The Apostle John intended to express this truth, when he tells us that he in whom a principle of divine charity or benevolence has become a habit or life, "dwells in God, and God in him."

(d)   *Channing*

KNOWING GOD (Abstract and Concrete)

"*From henceforth ye know Him*" (John xiv. 7)

The Christian's knowledge of God is not an abstract, but a concrete knowledge. The difference between the two kinds of knowledge may be illustrated by supposing there to be any difficulty in proving that $2+2=4$, that difficulty would vanish when it was shown that 2 chairs+2 chairs make 4 chairs. So there *is* a difficulty in proving the abstract existence of God, and the truth of

Christianity ; but the knowledge of God and of Christ is an experience, it is concreted with ourselves—God is in us—"Christ in you." "We have seen and believed ; " we have communion with Him, therefore *we know God*, and have the knowledge of God. This is no boast ; and the Christian in claiming to have this knowledge is not speaking of things outside his own experience.

(e)

"*Knowing therefore the terror of the Lord, we persuade men*" (2 Cor. v. 11)

Note context-

1. **Difference between worldly man and Christian.**
(i.) The one uses the world—The other abuses it.
(ii.) Consequences : one has all now—and loses it when the world passes away.
The other has all left. "We have a home eternal."

2. **This** is a certainty. "We know."
(i.) By the purpose of God.
(ii.) By the earnest of the Spirit.
Therefore "we are always confident."

3. **Such a life** = one of faith, rare, awful, toilsome.

4. **The conclusion** : "Knowing the terror of the Lord, we persuade men.

(f)

KNOWLEDGE, LEARNING

To despise learning is fanaticism ; but to rely on it as sufficient is presumption.

(g)   *Bp. Wordsworth*

KNOWLEDGE

Vain, worse than vain, it is to be profound linguists, careful collators of MSS., to be well versed in history, chronology, geology, and chemistry, and in all the departments of literature and science, unless their minds are illumined by the light of the Holy Ghost. Vain it is, worse than vain, to pore over the pages of Scripture, and to analyze every jot and tittle of it in all the ancient versions, and in all the expositions of it that were ever made, unless God writes the words of His law with His finger on the fleshly tables of the heart. Vain, worse than vain, is all such toil and trouble, unless the soul and spirit are sanctified and warmed with the love of God. . . . He who would understand the Bible, must love the Bible. . . . He must not treat it "as a common book." He must listen to it as God's oracle. . . . He must pray over it ; he must read it on his knees.

(h)   *Ibid*

KNOWLEDGE

An unhealthy striving after knowledge, which leads away from the truth, is SIN : and to this tendency St. Paul opposes wholesome doctrine :—
"Many had turned away from the truth" (Tit. i. 14), and it was to be feared that this would be the case in the future in yet greater numbers. There had arisen a gnosis, falsely so called, which, to be sure, did not appear as an error uprooting the foundations, but as an unhealthy tendency, a being occupied with empty, unprofitable, foolish,

(i)

even profane questions of controversy; which gendereth only contention and discord. In opposition to this right doctrine appears a sound doctrine and truth. This again shows that faith was threatened: those who have missed the goal of the truth mislead the faith of others. Whoever yields to a striving after false knowledge, misses the end of faith, . . . and whoever has come to be unstable in faith has turned aside to vain talking.

(a)   *Weiss*

KNOWLEDGE (1 Cor. viii. 2)

"If any man think that he knoweth anything, he knoweth nothing yet *as* he ought to know." That single word "*as*" is the point of the sentence; for it is not *what* to know, but *how* to know, which includes all real knowledge. . . . A time comes when we feel terribly that the tree of knowledge is not the tree of life. . . . I can conceive no dying hour more awful than that of one who has aspired to *know* instead of to *love*, and finds himself at last amidst a world of barren facts and lifeless theories, loving none and adoring nothing. . . . The substance of Christianity is love to God and love to man. Hence the last of the Apostles, when too weak to walk to the assemblies of the Church, was borne there, a feeble old man, by his disciples, and repeated again and again "Love one another;" and when asked why he said ever the same thing, replied, "Because there is nothing else: attain that, and you have enough." Hence, too, St. Paul—"Knowledge shall vanish away, but love never faileth."

(b)   *F. W. Robertson*

KNOWLEDGE

"*The least in the Kingdom of Heaven is greater than he*" (Matt. xi. 11.)

Have we not read of men whose heads towered high above their contemporaries, who by eloquence, or song, or intellect have elevated and charmed mankind, and yet of whom the humblest child, the most ignorant pauper in the kingdom of heaven, is greater than these? Any age will furnish us with examples. Seneca uttered words of lofty morality and almost apostolic force, yet his inconsistent sycophancy and grasping avarice awoke the scorn of even a dissolute and greedy age. Abélard was endowed with an intellect keener than is granted in a century to any of our race; yet so flagrant was his folly, so fatal his vanity, so gross his crime, that the miserablest could afford to look on him with pity, and almost the meanest with contempt. Bacon has won for his glorious intellect the reverence and admiration of every succeeding age; yet there is, alas! many an ignoble passage of his life which can only claim to be forgotten by the generous, and forgiven by the just. Has not God over and over again scattered penal blindness over vaunted acquisitions, and, smiting a godless intellect with a moral imbecility, has He not frustrated the tokens of the liars, and made diviners mad? But why need we dwell on the fact that intellectual eminence is no preservative against moral infatuation, when God has written the same truth so large over the history of nations? Have we not known mighty peoples who, professing themselves to be wise, became fools; who, because

when they knew God they glorified Him not as God, became vain in their imagination, and their foolish heart was darkened? Did the lustre of her genius, did the liberality of her institutions, did the glorious roll of her eloquence, did the lyric sweetness of her song, save Greece from the infamy of her obliteration, when she perished under the eating cancer of her favourite sins? Did the iron sceptre or the invincible sword, did the dignity of her government or the strength of her determination, deliver Rome from the long agony of her vile corruption and pitiable decay? The fifteenth and the eighteenth centuries, for all their reviving knowledge and glittering refinement, were they not full of wickedness, covetousness, maliciousness; full of envy, murder, debate, deceit, malignity? Did not the one honour Aretino as a poet, and Poggio as a wit; and the other accept Chesterfield as a moralist, and elevate Voltaire into a sage? Yes,—and it is a lesson of which this century too has need—knowledge without wisdom is, as even a corrupt and worldly poet has expressed it,

"Dim as the borrowed beams of moon or stars
To lonely, weary, wandering travellers;
And as their twinkling tapers disappear
When day's bright lord ascends the hemisphere,
So pale grows Reason at Religion's sight,
So dies and so dissolves in supernatural light."

(c)   *Archdn. Farrar*

KNOWLEDGE

I have taken much pains to know everything that was esteemed worth knowing amongst men; but with all my disquisitions and reading, nothing now remains with me to comfort me, at the close of life, but this passage of St. Paul:—"It is a faithful saying, and worthy of all acceptation, that Jesus Christ came into the world to save sinners;" to this I cleave, and herein I find rest.

(d)   *Selden*

"My child," said St. Columban to Luanus, when he saw how ardently he devoted himself to learning, "thou hast asked a perilous gift of God. Many out of undue love of knowledge have made shipwreck of their souls." "My father," replied the boy with deep humility, "if I learn to know God, I shall never offend Him, for they only offend Him who know Him not." "Go, my son," replied the Abbot, charmed with his reply; "remain firm in that faith, and the true science shall conduct thee on the road to heaven."

(e)

That only is the best knowledge that makes us better.

(f)   *Anon*

The whole employment of men's lives is to improve their fortunes; and yet the title by which they hold all, if traced to its origin, is no other than the mere fancy of legislators. Moreover, they have no power to hold their possessions in security; and lie at the mercy of a thousand accidents. With respect to knowledge it is the same. A fit of sickness deprives us of it.

(g)   *Blaise Pascal*

KNOWLEDGE AND CHARITY

" Knowledge puffeth up, but charity edifieth "
(1 Cor. viii. 1)

1. " Knowledge " is that of the intellect, education, culture—acquired by study. But if a man has nothing more, he deceiveth himself in thinking that he is an educated man, " He knoweth nothing as yet as he ought to know " (2). He is leaving out the most important element—educating his head, but not his heart and affections. Such are to be met with continually in the so-called educated world.

2. " Charity, love " (3). " If a man love God, the same is known of Him." This is significant —nothing like it is said of the merely learned man. He, as such only, neither knows nor is known of God. But that ordinary person, whom he despises (for his weakness, see context), one like thousands of others—that weak brother, a wayfaring man, though a fool—that aged cripple, peasant, one who can just spell out a chapter in the Bible, and sing hymns to Jesus—that child— *is known of God*, because he loves God. That " loving God " makes all the difference between one man and another. Knowledge without charity is nothing.

3. " Knowledge *puffeth* up ; Charity *edifieth*."
(i.) To *puff up* is to inflate, as a balloon is with gas. A man may have cyclopœdian knowledge, and tower above his fellows like an intellectual giant, but there is nothing in it that will last, " Whether there be knowledge it shall vanish away "—it is no building for eternity.
(ii.) But charity *edifieth* = buildeth up on a foundation, and never faileth. Such may be laughed at, as uncouth, uneducated,—no brilliancy, etc., still, men possessing this " best gift," are building on a foundation which abideth for ever.

4. These are the men that God wants in the world, and that *we* want too. *Good* men, rather than *clever* are wanted. Of a merely clever person an employer says—" Clever, sharp, witty ; but I can't trust him out of my sight—his word is not to be depended on, though he speaks like an angel, I can't keep him." But of a *good* person, though he may be dull, heavy, unintelligent, he observes " He is very trying, but honest, truthful, can be trusted anywhere, comes of a good stock, godly—I am glad to have him." Every one knows the worth of these men. And this is what true education is designed to produce, not merely one puffed up with multifarious knowledge, but one who is taught of the Spirit of God.

(*a*)   *Cf. F. W. Robertson*

KNOWLEDGE IN CHRIST

That which is most elegant, most noble and great with Christ is only elementary, imperfect in comparison with what He offers. The simplest, plainest of what is offered in Him, exceeds that in value. A humble Christian has and can do and knows more and better than an un-Christian philosopher.

(*b*)   *Lange*

KNOWLEDGE AND LOVE

Like water and ice, beget each other. Man loves Christ by knowing, and knows Christ by loving.

(*c*)   *Thoma*

KNOWLEDGE OF DIVINE THINGS

" We see through a glass darkly : we know in part " (1 Cor. xiii. 2)

" Glass " = window of horn, talc, or thin metal, through which things were seen in a dim, confused, and colourless manner. We see God through the glass, as it were, of our own limited human impressions. The " Father " has scarcely even all the poor conceptions gained from the earthly relationship from which the name is borrowed. And God as " Love " is seen by us only as one who loves as we—weakly, partially, selfishly. Heaven, also, is a place erected by our earthly imagination. To the Indian, a hunting-ground ; to the old Norseman, a battle banquet ; to the Mahometan, a place of earthly rapture ; to the man of science, a place where Nature yields up all her secrets. " We know in part." But just what the going out of a room lighted with horn windows into the clear daylight would be to us now, will be the entrance of the purified spirit into God's realities out of this world of shadows— of things half seen, " It doth not yet appear what we shall be."

(*d*)   *F. W. Robertson*

KNOWLEDGE IN PART

" Now I know in part," etc. (1 Cor. xiii. 2)

Christians know but little of what they should know ;
They know but little of what they might know ;
They know but little of what others know ;
They know but little of what they desire to know ;
They know but little of what they shall know, when they shall come to know even as they are known ;
But these glimpses that they have of God and heaven here, are infallible pledges of perfect knowledge hereafter.
That little spark of joy is an earnest of everlasting delight, when sorrow and mourning shall flee away ; and
Those sips of comfort are but foretastes of the river of everlasting pleasures which is at God's right hand.

(*e*)   *Thomas Brooks*

KNOWLEDGE (POSITIVE)

" We know in part " (1 Cor. xiii. 2)

1. The man of science sees that the facts around him are of two kinds—those which he can hope to know, and those which he can never know. Those which he can know are the impressions which his senses give him, and the general groups into which these form themselves under careful observation ; and those which he cannot pretend to know are those about which the observation by the senses gives no help ; as the future of the soul, the First Cause, the destiny of man, his primary origin, the nature of infinite space. Warned by long experience, the man of science, refusing to waste his time on impossible knowledge, and to scatter his powers in mere guesses, will apply his time to the study of the visible only ; in other words, will apply to nothing but the material world and its phenomena. He does not deny that there are higher things ; he only says they cannot be studied under scientific conditions.

(*f*)

Knowledge (Positive)—*continued*

2. " That," says M. Littré—the most prominent of Comte's disciples—"that which is above the reach of positive knowledge, as, in natural things, the doctrine of infinite space, and, in intellectual things, the chain of causes without limit, is inaccessible to the mind of man; but inaccessible does not mean null and non-existent. Immensity, material and intellectual, is closely bound to our knowledge; and by this very alliance it becomes a positive idea, and of the same order as the rest : that is, when we come in contact with it, this immensity appears with its double character of reality and inaccessibility. It is an ocean which beats on our shore, and for which we have neither ship nor sail, but of which the clear view is at once wholesome and formidable." (*Préface d'un Disciple.*)

(*a*)

3. **What is knowledge?**

The Positivist makes it his lawful boast, that the foundation of his philosophy is the mathematical laws. He will have—he is daily receiving—his reward ! The results of science that we have seen are splendid; and we owe deep thankfulness for them, not indeed to Comte or to Bacon, but to Him who has allowed His creatures to turn the beautiful laws of the universe to such rich account. But the laws of science are not all; they are not the greatest part of the things which interest mankind. The time may come when with a perfect social science an enlightened community may feel, when they are observing their duties, that they are obeying the laws of science and of expediency. It is certainly not yet arrived; and meantime a good deal of obedience is elicited from men to the laws which once were written on two tables of stone, and which the civilized world has recognised as Divine. In like manner a good many lives are shaped to high purposes, not from a scientific calculation that something called *altruism* is the best policy, but because of a persuasion that this life is not all, and that it is better to live with a view to connect this life by work and self-denial with the life to come. I fail to understand why the name of knowledge is to be refused to the belief in God and in a future state, and to be awarded to the deductions which some few people make, perhaps, before they act, as to the social result of the act they are about to do. The difference cannot lie in the greater degree of certainty of the latter as compared with the former. Knowledge is of various shades or grades of certainty, yet it is not on that account to be denied the name of knowledge. We have lately had to alter our chemical tables because of a change in the atom of hydrogen, and our astronomical, because of a new measurement of the sun's distance ; yet no one denies to chemistry and to astronomy the name of science.

(*b*)

4. **What is knowledge?**

It is that mental condition which gives to man an insight into the world around him. It need not be complete; from the nature of it this may be impossible. It may be almost unconscious; as that of the frivolous mother who, overcome with a new tenderness, bends over her cradled new-born babe, to give it that succour and tending which are God's ordinance for its pre-servation It is well-nigh unconscious; but it guides her, and she will find it a true guide, and the result she hopes for will follow. In many matters of practice the best knowledge is the unconscious, startling though this may sound. Who knows music the best? The child of ten years, painfully limping through its scales ; or the deaf Beethoven, sweeping the mute keys in a pianissimo, heard by no other ear but his own ; but the ear is deaf, but the soul is a concert-hall of song? Who walks the best? The child whom we teach to put one foot before the other, or those in whose unconscious march there is no trace of rules or training, but only free grace and dignity? Mark the orator, who can put forth, without five minutes' preparation, words of passion which overbear the reason, and by their very vehemence earn the praise which should be the meed of wisdom. He surely knows the use of language. But the rules of grammar and of rhetoric are far from him. His almost miraculous power of speech belongs now to the unconscious region.

(*c*)

5. **Now, let us own that much of the knowledge men seek after is and must ever remain indefinite**

I look at your microscope, your balance, your electroscope, and admit, perhaps not without some vain regret, that for the moral and spiritual world we have no such instruments of precision. But I cannot expect them. The astronomer observes the phenomenon of a burning star, and he too wishes for instruments by which he could seize all the facts of that portentous spectacle— the dissolution of a sun or world. He must rest content with what the polariscope can tell him— that a world of burning hydrogen is before him. He does not abandon astronomy because he cannot make a map of the scene of cosmic conflagration. He is right. We, too,—concerned in our degree with the eternal future of the soul of man,— we admit that we cannot so reason out our belief that all might be coerced by our reasonings, and attracted by results at once definite and of prime import to mankind. It is the same with the cognate principle of moral obligation. Kant, the severest critic of the boundary lines of human science, has left standing after his analysis the so-called " categorical imperative ; " which, put into plainest words, is this, that the fact that I feel bound to act according to a law of duty within me, apart from consequences and calculation, is the best evidence that we have for our connection with a higher being, higher laws, a more permanent system. It stands in Kant's system reasoned out, in the system which of all others is relied on by the modern sensualists ; and yet we are told that for the future it is outside the realm of knowledge altogether ! Why? Because you cannot give its formula like that of picric acid? If science has no place for what Kant proves, and strong men live on, science is incomplete, and the rule of exclusion is artificial ; and instead of a new system of knowledge, we have before us an appeal to the weariness of religious strife, and metaphysical argument, which has come over men at various times in the course of history, and which prevailed in the age of the Greek sophists, in the time of Hume and Voltaire, in the days of Comte and others amongst ourselves. It is not so much a system, as a mood—a condition of exhaustion, which will surely pass.

(*d*)

Knowledge (Positive)—*continued*

6. When Comte enounced his imposing dogma as follows :

" Positive philosophy is the whole body of human knowledge ; human knowledge is the result of the study of the forces belonging to matter, and of the conditions or laws governing those forces "—he did not take account of the nature of those whose freedom of research and study he sought to repress. Nothing is so hard to obey as this kind of restriction. When our staid and positive British Association, bound by its very charter to know nothing but science, meets in an eloquent and excitable island, there is an outburst of religious strife that lasts for months ; and all agree that the challenge came from the side of positive science, which could not leave the unknowable unknown. The mind will not lay aside its highest prerogative, of discussing its own origin, its own destiny, its own perfectibility by the aid of faith, with the faculties that God has given it for its own. You bring us to that solemn shore, and, our feet planted on the last fact, we must be content to look out on the mysterious inaccessible ocean. Thus far ; no farther ! There is no knowledge beyond. But we are the children of the sea-kings, who sleep in death with their ships beside them, ready, on the first waking call, to take again to the sea that cradled them and gave them death ! You cannot plough it nor mow it, nor track it with iron bands ; it has its darkness, its sunlight, its fits of change, its storms, its death. But it is ours ; and its very vagueness and vastness call us to explore it. Stay you on the shore ; we have a duty laid on us. In strong ship, if that be possible, in any shallop that we can find, if it be not, we will dare and try the ocean which you abandon to us."

(a)

7. A necessity is laid on us to think of these things

" To view them with apathy would argue a defective mind. Lose their hold on the problems of life, of death, and of eternity, mankind will never. All claim the right to think of them which arises from their being part and parcel of themselves. And to scme, thinking of them deeply, as devotees of science think of their subjects of inquiry, they shine with a clear brightness of knowledge and belief, they afford a satisfying guidance, they bring into harmony the lower labours of life. If man 'has necessarily been produced'—I use the forcible words of my friend and Chancellor—' has necessarily been produced either by the spontaneous universal suffrage and co-operation of all atoms of matter, or by one Creator,' man himself must have an opinion on that subject. Let us not mistake a momentary disgust at the disputes of religion and at the poor results of metaphysical inquiry, for a call to abandon all but material speculations. Let us not rail against science, for the knowledge of the laws of matter is valuable to us as far as it goes ; and its reach is great. But science asks too much when it requires the abnegation of all other knowledge and belief. To any teacher who demands it, we reply that the nature of man is against it, the history of our race is against it, the aspirations of the race forbid it. You offer a charming vision ; all knowledge shall be certain and clear.

But when we learn the price—that we are to sacrifice the largest portion of the domain of contemplation, we decline the bargain, and go on our own way."

(b)   *Archbishop Thompson*

KNOWLEDGE AND PRACTICE

Criticisms in words, or rather ability to make them, is not so valuable as some may imagine them. A man may be able to call a broom by twenty names, in Latin, Spanish, Dutch, Greek, &c. ; but my maid, who knows the way to use it, but knows it only by one name, is not far behind him.

(c)   *John Newton.*

KNOWLEDGE PUFFETH UP (1 Cor. viii. 1.)

Are we prepared to affirm that English peasants in village churches, and poor children in charity schools, who hear or read the Holy Scriptures, and believe that Jesus Christ did many miracles, and that the 22nd Psalm and the 53rd chapter of Isaiah contain prophecies of His sufferings, have a clearer view of the meaning of the Bible than many of these German expositors whose names are famous for profound learning and critical sagacity, and who deny the miracles and reject those prophecies ?

Here is a hard question. What is the answer ? *To whom shall we go ?* To whom shall we listen ? They are not agreed among themselves ; they are like the builders of Babel, distracted by a strife of tongues, etc.

Holy Scripture supplies an answer—" *knowledge puffeth up.*" Knowledge is often a snare ; it engenders spiritual pride ; and spiritual pride is always punished with spiritual blindness. No man can understand the Bible except God open his eyes. " Open Thou mine eyes, O Lord, that I may see the wondrous things of Thy law." . . . We cannot understand the Bible except by the light of the Holy Spirit, who wrote the Bible.

(d)   *Bishop Wordsworth.*

KNOWLEDGE AND SPIRIT

God does not give the Spirit through knowledge, but rather knowledge *through* the Spirit.

(e)   *Lange*

KNOWLEDGE, ALL THE TREASURES OF, IN CHRIST (Col. ii. 3)

The Church did need not another system of doctrine, only a more profound expositor.

In view of the enemies which assailed them, this verse implies that they needed to know " not more *than* Christ, but more *of* Christ."

(f)   *Ibid*

KNOX, JOHN

Of all the benefits I had that year (1571), was the coming of that maist notable profet and apostle of our nation, Mr. Johne Knox, to St. Andrew's, who, be the faction of the Queen occuping the castle and town of Edinburgh, was compellit to remove therefra, with a number of the best and chusit to come to St. Andrew's. I heard him teache there the prophecies of Daniel, that

(g)

simmar and the wintar following. I had my pen and my little buike, and tuk away sic things as I could comprehend. In the opening up of his text, he was moderat the space of an half hour; but when he enterit to application, he made me so to grew (thrill) and tremble, that I could not hold a pen to writ. He was very weik. I saw him, everie day of his doctrine, go hulie and fear (slowly and warily) with a furring of masticks about his neck, a staff in the an hand, and gud, godlie Richard Ballenden, his servand, halding up the other oxter (arm-pit) from the abbey to the parish-kirk, and he, the said Richard, and another servant lifted up to the pulpit, whar he behovit to lean at his first entry; but, as he laid down with his sermone, he was sa active and vigorous that he was lyk to ding the pulpit in blads (beat the pulpit in pieces), and flie out of it.

(a)   *James Melville, " Diary "*

I know not if ever so much piety and genius were lodged in so weak and frail a body. Certain I am that it will be difficult to find one in whom the gifts of the Holy Spirit shone so bright, to the comfort of the Church of Scotland.

(b)   *Smeton.*

Lyndsay had prepared the ground, and John Knox only sowed the seed.

(c)   *Pinkerton*

That fals apostat priest,
Enemie to Christ, and maunis (man's) salvation,
Your Maister Knox.

(d)   *Nicol Burne*

A fanatical incendiary—a holy savage—the son of violence and barbarism—the religious Sachem of religious Mohawks.

(e)   *Whitaker*

The political principles of the man, which he communicated to his brethren, were as full of sedition as his theological were full of rage and bigotry. . . . His conduct showed that he thought no more civility than loyalty due to any of the female sex.

(f)   *David Hume*

God is my witness, whom I have served in the spirit in the Gospel of His Son, that I have taught nothing but the true and solid doctrine of the Gospel of the Son of God, and have had it for my only object to instruct the ignorant, to confirm the faithful, to comfort the weak, the fearful, and the distressed, by the promises of grace, and to fight against the proud and rebellious by the Divine threatenings. I know that many have frequently complained, and do still complain, of my too great severity; but God knows that my mind was always void of hatred to the persons of those against whom I thundered the severest judgments.

(g)   *John Knox*

L

LABOUR

"*In sorrow . . . thorns also, and thistles shall it bring forth unto thee,*" etc. (Gen. ii. 17–20)

See the effect of the *curse* in every department of labour.

(i.) *Man has to labour :* "In the sweat of brow. . . bread." Man has to work—must—at what he is put, and where he is, and he has to do it *well :* "whatever hand findeth. . . . might" (*Carlyle*).

(ii.) We are all *working men*—no drones in the human hive. ("If a man will not work, neither let him eat.") Labour is either of the hand or the head, and each one feels the peculiar form of the curse (hardship) his work brings him = thorns and thistles.

(iii.) Some have tried to escape this law (but none escape the curse) by changing their occupations, or by "retiring," only to find idleness a greater burden than honest labour, and the shoe will pinch somewhere. Therefore let each do his duty in the station of life where he is placed.

(*a*)

DIGNITY OF LABOUR

It is time that the opprobrium of toil were done away. Ashamed of toil, art thou? Ashamed of thy dingy workshop or dusty labour-field ; of thy hard hand, scarred with service more honourable than that of war ; of thy soiled and weather-stained garments, on which mother Nature has embroidered, amidst sun and rain, amidst smoke and steam, her own heraldic honours? Ashamed of these tokens and titles, and envious of the flaunting robes of imbecile idleness and vanity? It is treason to Nature, it is impiety to Heaven. Toil—toil, either of the brain, of the heart, or of the hand—is true nobility.

(*b*)

LAMB AND BEAST, THE, OF THE APOCALYPSE

1. The Apocalypse abounds in *contrasts*. For example the LAMB ('Aμνὸs in St. John's gospel) is 'Aρνίον, (never 'Aμνὸs in his Apocalypse,) where it occurs twenty-nine times. . . . To contrast Him more strongly with τὸ θηρίον ; i.e., to mark the opposition between the LAMB and the BEAST.

(*c*)

2. This contrast is even more striking in the original : where it is aided by an exact correspondence of syllables and accents.

On one side are,—

'H πόρνη καὶ τὸ θηρίον,

The harlot and the beast.

On the other side are,

'H νύμφη καὶ τὸ 'Aρνίον,

The Bride and the Lamb.

See Rev. xxi. 2, 9 ; xxii. 17.

(*d*)

3. If any one can have any doubt of St. John's intention to identify the woman on the beast with a faithless CHURCH, let him read the following description :—

"And there came one of the seven angels having the seven vials, and he spake with me, saying, Come, I will show thee the judgment of the great whore. . . . And he brought me into the wilderness in spirit : and I saw a woman sitting on a scarlet coloured beast" (Rev. xvii. 1, 3)

(*e*)

4. And then let him compare it with the words which describe the faithful Church in glory.

"And there came one of the seven angels having the seven vials. . . . and he spake with me, saying, Come, I will show thee the Bride, the Lamb's wife. And he brought me in spirit into a great and high mountain, and showed me the city the holy Jerusalem" (Rev. xxi. 9, 10).

(*f*) *Bp. Wordsworth*

5. "*Come and I will show thee*"

(i.) An Apostate Church ;
(ii.) The True Church.

(*g*)

LAMB, THE BLOOD OF THE

In answer to the objection. "If believing in Christ's death, or the shedding of His blood as an atonement for sin, be the only way by which a sinner can be saved, how is it that Christ Himself never spoke of it in that way? nor do we find it mentioned in the Acts of the Apostles as the doctrine preached to the Gentiles, who, being ignorant of the Jewish sacrificial ritual, would surely have been instructed in this new fundamental doctrine. They find Paul, in Acts xv. and 9th verse, speaking of the Gentiles as having their hearts purified by faith, not by blood ; and also saying in verse 11, 'We believe that through the grace of the Lord Jesus we shall be saved, even as they.'" He wondered how this person had read his Bible. He believed the blood was the foundation of all their hopes. Take the blood out of the Bible and he would not carry it home. That Book did not teach anything else. For the last 4000 years it has been telling the one story, that man was saved by the blood.

(*h*)

1. The first glimpse they caught of the blood, was in Genesis iii. 21, in which it was stated, that unto Adam and his wife the Lord made coats of skin. Skins could not have been got from animals without the shedding of blood. In the next chapter it was stated that Abel brought of the firstlings of his flock, and that the Lord had respect for Abel's offering, but no respect for the offering of Cain. Why? Because there was no blood in it. Abel came to God according to God's way. Cain came in his own way. He was like a great many who were saying now—"What have I to do with blood : why can I not come in my own way ; if I do about as nearly right as I can, will it not be all right

(*i*)

with me?" Cain did not see why his beautiful fruit should not have been more acceptable than a bleeding lamb, which was repulsive to him; but Abel came by the way of blood, and his offering was accepted. There were a great many Cainites now who did not like the doctrine; but he challenged them to find in the Bible any other way to heaven save by blood.

(a)

2. In Genesis viii. 2 they learned that the first thing Noah did after coming out of the ark, was to put blood between him and his sins. In Exodus xii. they learned that the angel of death passed by the houses of the children of Israel, on the doorposts of which blood was sprinkled. Men said now that it was not the death of Christ, but His life, example, and moral character, that they wanted. God did not tell that to the Israelites. The collector of railway tickets did not look to the character or education of the holder of the ticket, but to the ticket itself. In like manner the blood was a token which typically indicated the way they were to be saved. A great many people, neglecting the Bible, read the daily papers, and some, he was sorry to say, read novels, and then wondered why they were so far from God. They did not feed on the Lamb of God.

(b)

3. Baptismal Regeneration

There was no such thing as baptismal regeneration in the Word of God. They did not start to heaven from the cradle. They must do so from Calvary. If he really believed that baptizing people would save them, he would stop preaching, and get a bucket of water and go up and down the streets baptizing every one he met. Some one had sent him a note, saying he had spoken lightly of baptism! Ten thousand times, no; but he put baptism in its right place. He was talking of salvation by blood. If they talked to him of salvation by baptism he must wait until he got more light than he now possessed, for he did not find it in the Bible. In Leviticus viii. they read of the sprinkling of blood upon the ear, hand, and foot of the priest. The blood on the ear meant that he should hear; on the hand, that he should work; and on the foot, that he should walk with God.

(c)

Good Works

A great many people had an idea that working in colleges and seminaries and rebuilding cathedrals, and all that, would help them to heaven. Not at all. They could not go to heaven by works. The first thing a man must do, was to believe in God and in His Son. Then he might work as hard as he liked. But they must work from the Cross, and not to it. He believed that works were keeping hundreds of thousands away from the truth. Work not to be saved, but because you are saved. No unconverted man desired to work for God. None but the blood-bought man could work for God. Some people said they did not understand the doctrine of blood. It was very offensive to the natural man. He knew a man to say that whenever he heard a minister speak of the blood in his sermon, he took up his hat and quietly walked out. But just as the bitterest medicine cured, so the doctrine of blood found that man and

he was saved. There was no doctrine that the world attacked so much as that of the blood; but the more the world assailed him about it the more thoroughly he was convinced he was right. It was a good sign when the world assailed them. It was an evidence they were right. The whole Bible went the moment this doctrine was touched. What had brought them all to that convention and linked them together? The fact that they were in this sense blood relatives. It was a terrible thing for a man to speak contemptuously out of any pulpit of the doctrine of blood; and he did not know when he was more shocked than when he heard a minister of the Gospel in Dublin say of the doctrine of the precious blood of Christ that it was the doctrine of the shambles. It was horrible—damnable. Might God keep them from trampling the blood of Christ under foot!

(d)   *Moody*

Lamb, The Episode of the

"A lamb as it had been slain" (Rev. v. 6)

1. The *doctrine:* The world's history is an unsolved riddle; a book, closed and sealed; this riddle is solved, and this book is opened, only by the cross of Christ, the Lamb of God throughout the Scriptures.

(e)

2. The seeming contradictions: *Lion and Lamb; slain* yet *standing.*

(f)

Observe.
3. *The divine consolation:* "I wept" at the unsolved riddle—the "why" of life.
And (i.) *a Lamb, not a Lion appears.*
The Jews looked for a warrior prince, the lion of the tribe of Judah, but Jesus came as a little child.

(a) We, like them, and like John, often astonished—we too look for a *lion* and behold a *lamb* —as when a cloud of trouble gathers, and a storm seems impending.
"The clouds we so much dread, are big with mercies, and shall break with blessings on our head."

(b) When the disciples cried out in fear "*it is a ghost,*" Jesus replied "It is I, be not afraid."

(c) When Luther was in fear as he carried the "Pix"—Staupitz replied, "It is not Jesus; Jesus never terrifies."
All these are instances of Jesus, coming not as a Lion, but as a Lamb.
As He came into the world, so He comes into hearts.
Not as a Lion to destroy, but as a Lamb to save.

(g)

(ii.) **But it is a Lamb as it had been slain**
A Lamb "that was dead," with all the marks of suffering upon it; back bleeding, feet and hands and side pierced, to indicate the atonement "By whose stripes we are healed."
Type = the paschal Lamb (Exod. xii.);
Foretold by Isaiah (liii.) "a Lamb to the slaughter";
Pointed-out by John Baptist "Behold the Lamb of God which," etc.

(h)

Preached by Peter and Paul, and ever since (1 Pet. i. 19), as having "Redeemed us by His precious Blood, *as of a Lamb*."

(*a*)

(iii.) Slain, yet "*standing*," to indicate that He who was dead is alive, and has power in Heaven, and is using His power to *intercede* as an advocate for those who come unto God by Him.

(*b*)

His *intercession* is

1. *General*. For "transgressors"—the world; cf. the barren fig-tree "Let it alone," etc.

2. *Particular*. For enemies; "Father, forgive," etc.

(i.) For backsliders: "I have prayed for thee (Peter)";

(ii.) For His flock: "I pray for them";

(iii.) Continual: "He ever liveth to," etc.;

(iv.) Audibly or silently (?) see the story of Amyntas "INTERCESSION."

Cf. Heb. ix. 24. "There to appear in the presence of God for us."

(v.) Powerful: the power of His resurrection. Power to give eternal life etc. . . . to an unlimited extent.

Hence the glad song of All Creation which follows, "Worthy is the Lamb," etc., etc.

(*c*)

LAMB, THE SHORN

God tempers the wind to the shorn lamb.

Sterne

[This idea is said to have been stolen by Sterne from George Herbert, who wrote, "To a close-shorn sheep God gives wind by measure." (See his *Jacula Prudentum*.) And *he* is said to have translated it from Henri Etienne (Henry Stephens 2nd).

Virgil instructs us to "feed the lambs at the setting of the sun, when cool vesper tempers the air." *Georgics, Book III. l.* 336.]

(*d*)

"*Lambs, Feed My*" (John xxi. 15)

1. Jesus as the Good Shepherd

The Saviour repeatedly represented in this character in the inscriptions in the Catacombs at Rome—with a Lamb in His arms.

(*e*)

2. The Command was given Three Times.

"Feed my Lambs;" "Shepherd my Sheep;" "Feed my lambkins."

This had a special significance to Peter—a great Mission Preacher, such as he was, when in the height of his usefulness and popularity, might overlook the needs of little children, as forming no part of his special work. Jesus, here, reminds him of the Threefold nature of Pastoral work. We try to fulfil this by Sunday Schools, and Children's services.

(*f*)

3. Christ has a Flock

"He shall feed His flock like a shepherd." Christ's is "a little flock"—"Fear not, little flock"

—out of the many people in the world they may be known—"My sheep hear My voice." . . . "They follow Me." Sheep are very much alike; so are Christ's sheep. The Holy Spirit in them produces the same fruits in all; they are all modelled after one Pattern.

(*g*)

4. Christ's sheep are marked

There is often a mark put on sheep—of tar or paint—to distinguish flock from flock. All Christ's sheep have the Twofold mark (i.) of Baptism into the visible Church, (ii.) and of Regeneration (an unseen mark) which makes true members of His kingdom.

One feature of Christ's lambs is, that they are natural (not forced like hothouse plants and fruits).

The writer of this once knew a boy of 14 in a Boarding School, who used to pray and moan by his bedside at night—confessing sins which he knew nothing about; he had caught the habit from a religious sect amongst whom he had been brought up. The effect upon an outsider was almost ludicrous, certainly it was *unnatural ;* and the boy might just as well have moaned over a "broken leg," when he had merely chafed the skin off, as to confess sins of such enormity as he could have had no experience of.

Nor are Christ's lambs "Angelic." See a beautiful little poem of Archbishop Trench's, where a father is walking through a graveyard with his little son, and checks his gambols. The child for a minute or two takes off his hat, walks demurely by his father's side, presently he throws up his cap and chases a butterfly. The father acknowledged that the boy was in the right, for the sun was shining overhead, and the birds were singing merrily, even there all nature was glad— why should not his little boy be natural and laugh as well.

(*h*)

5. Something the Good Shepherd has done for His Sheep

"*The Good Shepherd giveth His life for the sheep.*"

Illustrated :—At a recent prayer-meeting in New York, presided over by Henry Ward Beecher, a very touching incident of the American Civil War was related. The narrator had shortly before visited the soldiers' burial-ground at Nashville, and had there seen a man planting a flower over one of the graves. He had questioned him, and been told—but we shall let the American Old Mortality tell his own story :—"I was poor, and had a large family of children depending on me for their daily bread, but as the war continued I was drafted; I was unable to find a substitute, and made up my mind to go. After I had got everything in readiness, and was just leaving to report for duty at the conscript camp, a young man whom I had known came to me and said: "You have a big family, and your wife cannot support them while you are gone; I will go for you." In the battle of Chickamauga the poor fellow was dangerously wounded, and was taken back to hospital at Nashville. After a lingering illness he died, and was buried here. Ever since hearing of his death, I have wanted to come to Nashville and

(*i*)

see that his remains were properly interred. Having saved enough money I came on yesterday, and have to-day found the poor fellow's grave." As he ended his story the man took up a small board, and inserted it at the grave. It bore only these words : " He died for me."

(a)

6. Something the Good Shepherd does for His Sheep

He seeks them and finds them when they are lost. . . . " until He finds them."

We, like sheep, should never find the Shepherd if He did not find us first.

A Scotch shepherd was asked :· " How do you find sheep when they are lost in the snow ? " He replied—" We go down into the deep ravines, where they go to in the storms, and we find them all huddled together—half dead with cold and fright." " Do they come away with you ? " " No, never ; they could not do it, not to save their lives ; we have to carry them out one by one." So Jesus seeks and searches out His lambs when they are lost and in danger and gently carries them back to the fold.

(b)

7. Two of Christ's Lambs

A Duke had two sons. The eldest was ill and dying ; if he had lived he would have succeeded to the title after his father. One day reading his Bible he came to the words, " I have fought the good fight, I have finished my course, I have kept the faith, henceforth there is laid up for me a crown of righteousness"—calling his brother, and pointing to the word " crown," he said, " Douglas, in a little time you will be a *Duke*, but I shall be a *King*."

Another little lamb, after listening to a sermon for Missions, as he passed the plate at the door, said to the person who held it—" a little lower, please,—it was lowered, but still he said, " a little lower, please,—"*I want to put myself in*."

      An Address to Children

(c)

Laid Up

" *O how great is Thy goodness which Thou hast laid up for them that love Thee* " (Ps. xxxi. 19)

Analogy.—When we see scaffolding erected, stacks of timber, bricks, mortar, all the apparatus and plant of a builder around, we say a building is going to be erected. This is always done beforehand. The Builder of this earth did on a larger scale just the same, and yet He rarely gets credit for equal foresight and forethought. The Geologist will tell us that preparations were begun ages ago, which would ultimately reveal the glorious handywork of the Great Architect. In the successive stages of what we call *The Creation* there were literally *laid up* in the crust of the earth, the ore for our present railroads and steamships—that metal necessary both for the agriculturist and the surgical operator, iron. Then too all precious metals were *laid up*, and minerals : seams of coal, rocks of salt, building stone. And why all this preparation ? Our age replies, " It was *for the service of man*," that he might have things richly to enjoy, when he should make his appearance on the earth. So of the

great things of Redemption : They are *all ready*— all " laid up "—prepared beforehand for man's deeper need.

(d)

LANGUAGE

I doubt whether any power is, for good or for evil, so great as that of knowledge and mastery of language. Look at the orator, swaying men's souls with an almost superhuman power. Contrast the man who has knowledge, rough and unhewn, struggling in vain to put it before his fellows, with the man who has clearness of style and utterance and arrangement, so that he can really lead and gradually instruct the minds of others. We are at times almost indignant at the contrast ; we feel as if words occasionally prevailed over things. You know (I dare say) the old story of George Stephenson and Sir W. Follett. Stephenson had been discussing a scientific question with (I think) Dr. Buckland. He was certainly in the right ; but for want of power of expression he seemed to be in the wrong. Follett, who sat by, strolled in the garden with him afterwards, and, by a few leading questions drew out the truth, which his insight,—generally educated but technically ignorant,—had led him to discern. Then, having got up his brief, he renewed the discussion with Buckland, and vanquished him utterly, by the knowledge which Stephenson had supplied, but which he alone knew how to use. And Stephenson, fairly astounded, and not altogether pleased, is reported to have said, " Of all gifts give me the gift of language ; " or, as I am afraid he irreverently called it, " the gift of the gab." The story is but a symbol of the power which language wields. Perhaps it may teach us why every idle *word* is so emphatically spoken of as destined to rise up in the Judgment.

(e)   *Bishop Barry (Sydney)*

LAST WORDS (Death-bed Experience) of Samuel Rutherford

I

" I shall shine, I shall see Christ as He is, I shall see Him reign, and all His fair company with Him ; and I shall have my large share ; my eyes shall see my Redeemer ; these very eyes of mine, and no other for me. This may seem a wide word, but it is no fancy or delusion ; it is true, it is true ; let my Lord's name be exalted, and if He will, let my name be ground to pieces, that He may be all in all. If He should slay me ten thousand times ten thousand times, I'll trust."

(f)

II

" *Thy words were found and I did eat them, and Thy word was unto me the joy and rejoicing of my heart* " (Jer. xv. 16)

"'Tis no easy thing to be a Christian ; but for me, I have gotten the victory, and Christ is holding out both His arms to embrace me. . . .

" At the beginning of my sufferings I had mine own fears, like another sinful man, lest I should faint, and not be carried creditably through ; and I laid this before the Lord ; and as sure as He ever spake to me in His word, so sure His Spirit

(g)

witnessed to my heart, 'He had accepted my suffering;' He said to me, 'Fear not; the outgate shall not be simply matter of praise.' I said to the Lord, 'If He should slay me five thousand times five thousand times, I would trust in Him;' and I spake it with much trembling, fearing I should not make it good. But as really as He ever spake to me by His Spirit, He witnessed unto my heart, 'that His grace should be sufficient.'"

(a)

III

"I disclaim all that He ever made me will and do, and look on it as defiled and imperfect, as coming from me; and I take me to Christ for sanctification as well as justification; . . . He is made unto me, wisdom, righteousness, sanctification, and redemption; . . . I close with it, let Him be so, He is my All, in all this."

(b)

IV

"My honourable Master and lovely Lord, my great and royal King, hath not a match in heaven or in earth; I have my own guiltiness like another sinful man, but He hath pardoned, loved, and washed, and given me "joy unspeakable, and full of glory." I repent not that I ever owned His cause. . . . My Lord and Master is the chief of ten thousand of thousands; none is comparable to Him in heaven or in earth. Dear brethren, do all for Him; pray for Christ, preach for Christ, feed the flock committed to your charge for Christ, do all for Christ; beware of men-pleasing, there is too much of it among us."

(c)

V

When Dying

"I feel, I feel, I believe in, joy, and rejoice; I feed on manna." . . . "I have been a wretched, sinful man; but I stand at the best pass that ever a man did—Christ is mine, and I am His." . . . "Oh that all my brethren may know what a master I have served, and what peace I have this day. I shall sleep in Christ, and when I awake I shall be satisfied with His likeness." . . . "This night shall close the door, and put my anchor within the vail, and I shall go away in a sleep, by five o'clock in the morning" (which was so), "Oh for arms to embrace Him! Oh for a well-tuned harp."

"'Thou shalt show me the path of life, in thy sight is fulness of joy.' There is nothing now betwixt me and the resurrection; but 'to-day thou shalt be with me in paradise.' . . . Glory, glory dwelleth in Emmanuel's land."

(d)

LAUD, ARCHBISHOP

He was certainly no Papist, if by that term is meant one who agrees with the Church of Rome in its essential doctrines. But he was, in truth, much addicted to the pomp and ceremonious observances of that Church; both from his natural disposition, which was somewhat superstitious, and from a persuasion of the importance of external ceremony in Divine worship to the great end of religion. Hence he was forward to catch at any old and obsolete canon that would coun-

tenance him in reviving any ceremony, not considering the offence such innovations (for innovations they would be called on account of their long desuetude, whatever might be alleged from some canons in their favour) must needs give to the squeamish stomachs of that time.

(e)   Bishop Hurd

"LAUNCH OUT INTO THE DEEP" (Luke v. 4)

Is God's word of command to every one in his vocation; and let: "Lord, at Thy word," be the answer of every one in order to draw God's blessing with his net.

(f)   Heubner

(See "Go Forward.")

LAW

We are the creatures of birth, of ancestry, of circumstance; we are surrounded by law, physical and psychical, and the physical very often dominates and rules the soul. As the chemist, the navigator, the naturalist attain their ends by means of law, which is beyond their power to alter, which they cannot change, but with which they can work in harmony, and by so doing produce definite results, so may we.

[N.B. By the working of the law of the spirit we may bring forth the fruits of the Spirit—very definite results—and in the end become partakers of the Divine nature.]

(g)   Shorthouse, "John Inglesant"

Law, Another

"I find another law" (Rom. vii. 23).

A new law, or a new principle of action has been implanted in the Apostle. A new aim in life; new regulations for his conduct, in direct opposition to his previous aim and motives in life. But in the working of this new law, he finds it disturbed by another law—the old natural, Adamic principle of conduct—so that he cannot, though regenerated, do the things that he would. How does the matter therefore stand? Thus "If the law of the spirit of life in Christ Jesus be in you, ye are free from the law of sin and death." The first is the new law, the second is the old. And the promise is, in the Old Testament Allegory, "The elder shall serve the younger."

(h)

Law and Commandment, The

The true character of the hankering to place the Christian life, as to its principle, under law and commandment, is shown by the history of ethics.

The following is a brief sketch of its leading features at its beginnings:

1. Quite early, in the Apostolic Fathers, in the Shepherd of Hermas, Book II., it makes its appearance.

The life of the Christian is based on mandata. Faith also is a mandatum. With these commandments, of which the Christian is to suppose he can obey all, the Christian arrives only, so to say, at a common every-day Christianity. When, on

(i)

the other hand, he adds to these something more which Christ has not enjoined—as, for example, special fasts, then he gains especial honour and merit before God. All this, indeed, man does not do of himself, but "the man who has the Lord in his heart." But yet it is just man's own doing, the fulfilling of the commandment, the going beyond what is commanded, which is the ground of justification, nay, of especial honour before God.

(*a*)

2. In the third century, Clement of Alexandria in a certain way reverses this relation.

The sum of the commands of Christ is only a preparatory training for higher Christian perfection. Christ Himself is our Schoolmaster. The difference between New and Old Covenant consists merely in the nature of the commandments. There of *fear ; here of love for the Lord !* Thus to him the law of Moses = a χάρις παλαιά ; the law of Christ is distinguished by the mildness of the λόγος, by that alternation of praise and blame, of exhortation and prohibition, which is suited to the constitution of man. Faith is obedience. Obedience rests on commands. The system of commandments is that of the Lord : At the head stands, "And as ye would that men should do to you . . . likewise." The goal of all is Gnostic holiness, of contemplative union with God, by virtue of which a state of perfection is reached. "If we say that we have no sin, we deceive ourselves, and the truth is not in us," does not stand written in this code of Gnostic perfection.

(*b*)

3. It is otherwise with the representatives of the Church system. They know nothing of this perfection, but they separate works from the vital ground of grace received ; place them side by side with this grace, as a fulfilling the commands of Christ, and characterize them as a means of obtaining the grace which has been lost through after offences. On this rests the doctrine of *penance.* Origen taught that good works = the perfecting of justification. This reappears in Cyprian. The whole of this is not a living energy as the fruit of faith, but the fruit of a knowledge in which the believer knows that God and Christ command this or that, and that this command is truth.

(*c*)

4. The peculiar principle of Christian life gradually became lost to view, otherwise the transfer of Cicero's book to the domain of Christian life (Ambrosius, *De Officiis*) would have been utterly inconceivable.

(*d*)

5. This downward path was crossed by Augustine in a way that forms an epoch. The evangelical principle laid down by him traverses and combines itself in the development of theology through the Middle Ages, in a most diverse manner, with the legal type, with the mystic contemplation, and with formal definitions, which are borrowed from the ethical systems of philosophy of the pre-Christian world.

(*e*)

6. The true knowledge had become, at the end of the Middle Ages, a rarity, until, after some precursors like J. Wessel and others, the evangelical principal again burst forth in the Reformation.

(*f*)

7. And yet at the end of the eighteenth century, one who calls himself a Protestant theologian, in reference to the complaint of Luther, that "Many great and excellent men did not know how rightly to preach Moses, but wished to make a Moses of Christ, a law-book of the Gospel, and works out of the word," in sober earnest made this declaration, "*On these principles no true Christian morality could exist.*"

(*g*)　　　　　　　　　　　　　　*Harless*

"*The strength of sin is the law*" (1 Cor. xv. 56)

The Law forces out the disease that is spreading under the skin. Such is its task. But healing it does not bring.

(*h*)　　　　　　　　　　　　　　　　*Ibid*

Rom. viii. 2. "*The law of the spirit of life in Christ Jesus*" is that power indwelling in the spirit of life by an internal necessity, by virtue of which this spirit of life effects that freedom there spoken of.

(*i*)　　　　　　　　　　　　　　　　*Ibid*

LAW, DEAD TO THE

Christians are dead, buried (Rom. vi.), and risen (Col. iii. 1) with Christ ; indeed, they are even, in principle, transported to heaven (Phil. iii. 20). But since they are dead with Him, they are, like Him, dead "to the Law through the Law" (Gal. ii. 19).

(*j*)　　　　　　　　　　　　　　　*Lange*

LAW AND GOSPEL

The Law is that which lays down what man is to do ; the Gospel reveals whence man is to obtain it. . . . When I place myself in the hands of the physicians, one branch of art says where the disease lies, another, what course to take to get quit of it. So here. The Law discovers our disease, the Gospel supplies the remedy.

(*k*)　　　　　　　　　　　　　　　*Luther*

LAW AND GOSPEL

Judaism was the education of the spiritual child, Christianity that of the spiritual man. You teach a child by rules ; his duty is obedience. But a man who is governed by maxims and rules, is a pedant or a slave ; he will never be able to depart from the letter of the rule, nor even preserve the spirit of it. The Law lays down rules— "Do this, and live." The Gospel lays down principles. Judaism said, "Forgive seven times"— exactly so much ; Christianity says, Forgiveness is a boundless spirit—not three times, nor seven. No rule can be laid down but an infinite one— seventy times seven.

(*l*)　　　　　　　　　　　　*F. W. Robertson*

Law and Gospel (Gal. iv. 30)

The Law and the Gospel cannot co-exist. It is scarcely possible to estimate the strength of conviction and depth of prophetic insight which this declaration implies. The Apostle confidently sounds the death-knell of Judaism at a time when one half of Christendom clung to the Mosaic law with a jealous affection little short of frenzy.

(*a*)   *Lange*

Law and Gospel

1. All the men of God and master-builders, who have set themselves sincerely to serve God in their ministry and to save souls, have followed the same course ; to wit, first to wound by the Law and then to heal by the Gospel. We must be humbled in the sight of the Lord, before He lifts us up (James iv. 10). We must be sensible of our spiritual blindness and captivity, before we can heartily seek to be savingly enlightened and enlarged from the devil's slavery, and enriched with grace. There must be sense of misery, before showing of mercy ; crying, I am unclean, I am unclean, before opening the fountain for uncleanness ; stinging, before curing by the brazen serpent ; smart for sin, before a plaister of Christ's blood ; brokenness of heart, before binding up. God Himself opened the eyes of our first parents to make them see and be sensible of their sin and misery, nakedness and shame (Gen. iii. 7), before He promised Christ (ver. 15).

(*b*)

2. Christ Jesus tells us that He was anointed by the Lord, "to preach good tidings ; " but to whom? to the poor ; to the broken hearted ; to the captives ; to the blind ; to the bruised (Isa. lxi. 1 ; Luke iv. 18) : that "the whole need not the physician, but they that are sick ; and He came not to call the righteous, but sinners to repentance" (Matt. ix. 12, 13) ; that is, poor souls, sinners indeed, even in their own estimation ; and not self-conceited pharisees, who, though they be mere strangers to any wound of conscience for sin, yet they will not be persuaded that they shall be damned ; but in the mean time contemn and condemn all others in respect of themselves ; sinful publicans as too gross, sincere professors as too godly ; whereas, notwithstanding, in true judgment, harlots are in a far happier case than they (Matt. xxi. 31) : that "He will give rest" ; but to whom? to those "that labour and are heavy laden" (Matt. xi. 28) : that the Spirit which He would send, should convince the world, first of sin, and then of righteousness ; 'to wit, of Christ.

(*c*)

3. It is ordinary with the prophets, first to discover the sins of the people, and to denounce judgments ; and then to promise Christ upon their coming in, to enlighten and make them lightsome, with raising their thoughts to a fruitful contemplation of the glory, excellency, and sweetness of His blessed kingdom. Isaiah in his first chapter, from the mouth of God, doth in the first place behave himself like a "son of thunder," pressing upon the consciences of those to whom he was sent many heinous sins ; horrible ingratitude, fearful falling away, formality in God's worship, cruelty,

and the like. Afterward (ver. 16, 17), he invites to repentance, and then follows (ver. 18), "Come now, and let us reason together, saith the Lord : though your sins be as scarlet, they shall be as white as snow ; though they be red like crimson, they shall be as wool." Nathan, to recover even a regenerate man, convinceth him first soundly of his sin, with much aggravation and terror, and then upon remorse assures him of pardon (2 Sam. xii. 13).

(*d*)   *Bolton*

Law and Grace

Every human life that has not yet become a partaker of Redemption, is *a life under the* Law, in opposition to the life under Grace. For, be the man conscious of it or not, the Law as yet always hovers over his life as an unfulfilled requirement ; and, in the depth of his own being, this remains at present as an indismissible, but unsatisfied and unexpiated claim on him, which characterizes such a human existence as sinful and guilt-laden, because in contradiction with its original destiny.

(*e*)   *Martensen*

Law and Prohibition

We become aware in critical moments, that our evil desires are more powerful than the prohibition (of law), and are, in truth, first stirred up thoroughly by the prohibition. And this disposition of our heart is the decisive point for the question, whether, then, the holy law, the holy, just, and good commandment, makes us holy, just, and good men? The answer to this is, and remains, a most decided No.

(*f*)   *Harless*

LAWLESSNESS

Necker asked the people to come and help him against the aristocracy. The people came fast enough at his bidding ; but, somehow or other, they would not go away again when they had done their work. . . . I hope Lord Grey will not see himself or his friends in the woeful case of the conjuror, who, with infinite zeal and pains, called up the devils to do something for him. They came at the word, thronging about him, grinning, and howling, and dancing, and whisking their long tails in diabolic glee ; but when they asked him what he wanted of them, the poor wretch, frightened out of his wits, could only stammer forth, "I pray you, my friends, be gone down again ! " At which the devils, with one voice, replied,

"Yes ! yes ! we'll go down ! we'll go down !
  But we'll take *you* with us, to sink or drown ! "

(*g*)   *S. T. Coleridge*

(*See* "Anarchy.")

LAZARUS (John xi.)

Note the mysterious *rapport* of spirit and life between the praying Christ in Peræa and the praying household in Bethany.

(*h*)   *Lange*

"Lazarus, come forth!"

I beheld in a dream four mighty men hastening towards the grave of Lazarus, to restore him to life. One of these men, remarkable for his piety, said: "I will go down into the grave, and take with me some of the salt of duty, and I will rub him so vigorously as to impress him that it is in his power to do anything if he will." Watching at a distance, I asked: "Are there any signs of life? Is there likely to be any resurrection, brother?" "Nothing of the sort," is the answer; "he is very still; I cannot for the life of me get him to rise, and the stench is rather foul." "Well," says the second, "you come out and make way for me. I feared your means would never do; let me go down in your stead." So the second went, holding in his hand a scorpion-scourge of threatenings, and saying: "I will make him feel." He then set to work, applying to the corpse his fiery ministry. But in vain. I hear him confess: "Nothing can be done; there is no life, after all." "Make way for me," says the third, "and see if I don't bring him to life." He enters the grave, and "pipes" very melodiously: "Awake, thou that sleepest! Awake, thou that sleepest!" It was a song of love, and very beautiful, but there was no "dancing" in the grave. After all these efforts had failed, a fourth steps forward, saying: "Means, of themselves, have no power; I will go for Jesus, the resurrection and the life." When the Lord came, He stood at the door of the sepulchre, and cried out: "Lazarus, come forth!" and the dead instantly arose. Let our confidence be in the voice of the Son of God, and our prayer: "O breath, come from the four winds of heaven, and breathe upon these slain, that they may live!"

(a)   *Christmas Evans*

LEARNING

I would rather make one soul blessed, than a hundred learned.

(b)   *Lütkemann*

Whatever other learning be wanted, he was master of two books unknown to many profound readers, the books which the last conflagration can alone destroy, I mean the Book of Nature and that of Man.

(c)   *Young on Shakspeare*
(See "Education.")

LEAVE.

"*Leave thee, nor forsake thee, I will never*" (Heb. xiii. 5)

Mark the emphatic nature of this promise.
It requires five negatives in the Greek to express it:—
1. "I will not, I will not leave thee; I will never, never, never forsake thee."

(d)   *Doddridge*

2. More natural:
"I will never leave thee, no; neither will I forsake thee; no, never."

(e)

3. Metrical rendering:
"The soul that on Jesus hath leaned for repose,
I will not, I will not desert to his foes;
That soul, though all hell should endeavour to shake,
I'll never, no never, no never forsake."

(f)   *Kirkham*

Whenever thou feelest the burden of temptation too heavy for thee, call Him that is thy Helper, invoke thy Keeper, and thy aid in all extremities; and say: "Lord, save us, for we perish."
This Keeper never sleeps nor slumbers; though for a time He seems afar off, fear not, He will not leave thee nor forsake thee.

(g)   *Bernard*

There are five negatives in the Greek, to assure God's people that He will never forsake them. Five times is this precious promise renewed in the Scripture, that we might have the stronger consolation.

(h)   *Thos. Brooks*

LEISURE

Mix with your grave designs a little pleasure,
Each day of business has its hour of leisure.

(i)   *West*

An Athenian one day found Æsop at play with a company of little boys, at their childish diversions, and began to jeer and laugh at him for it. The old fellow, who was too much a wag himself to suffer others to ridicule him, took a bow, unstrung, and laid it upon the ground. Then calling upon the censorious Athenian, "Now, philosopher," says he, "expound the riddle if you can, and tell us what the unstrained bow implies." The man, after racking his brains about it a considerable time, to no purpose, at last gave it up, and declared he knew not what to make of it. "Why," says Æsop, laughing, "if you keep a bow always bent, it will break presently; but if you let it go slack, it will be fitter for use when you want it."

(j)   *Fables*

LEPROSY (Luke v. 12–24)

1. **Physical Aspect**
(i.) White pustules—eat away flesh—attacking one member after another—at last the bones.
(ii.) Attended with sleeplessness, nightmare, and hopelessness of cure.
(iii.) A living death.

2. **Social Aspect**
(i.) Contagious.
(ii.) Lived in a "several house"; or in bands at a distance from ordinary dwelling; (See "Moravian Missionaries.")
(iii.) Went with head uncovered, crying "*Room for the Leper.*"

3. **Religious Aspect**
(i.) Excommunication—no communion with the commonwealth of Israel.
(ii.) In every way a type of the impenitent sinner.
(iii.) For sin is *a living death; contagious;* and *separates from God.*

(k)
(See "Without Christ.")

4. The meeting of this leper with Christ, illustrates the meeting of the sinner and Christ.

(i.) *Behold a man !*—an apparition—approach stealthy—taken by surprise ;

(ii.) *Full of leprosy*—countenance livid—white—advanced stage—a loathsome sight and to be avoided ; yet,—

(iii.) *Rushes to meet Jesus*, and falling on his face (kneeling, worshipped Him)—

(iv.) *"If Thou wilt Thou canst"*—deep anguish and great faith—for *others have been cured.*

(v.) *Jesus touched him*—its significance.

(*a*)   *F. Godet*

This fearful malady, disfiguring the whole person, and making it horrible to the beholder, was called by the Jews *The Stroke,* and even by the Greeks, *The Firstborn of Death.*

In a case of "true leprosy," the sufferer was pronounced *utterly unclean,* and forthwith assumed the awful badges of his sad condition. He rent his clothes, bared his head, put a covering on his upper lip, as though he was mourning for the dead, and wherever he went cried out "*Unclean ! Unclean !*" an exile from his home, his family, his friends, he was bound to reside without the camp or city in a separate house by himself, or in the society of others similarly afflicted. No Israelite ever pretended to effect a cure of this awful malady.

The regulations respecting it were no mere sanitary regulations, for it was not catching from one person to another, and the ordinances respecting it did not apply to the stranger and the sojourner. "From the whole host of maladies and diseases which had broken in upon man's body, God selected this, the sickness of sicknesses, that He might thereby testify against that out of which it and all other sicknesses grew, against SIN, as not from Him, and as grievous in His sight. "It was the outward and visible sign of the innermost spiritual corruption, a meet emblem in its small beginnings, its gradual spread, its internal disfigurement, its dissolution little by little of the whole body, of that which corrupts, degrades, and defiles man's inner nature, and renders him unmeet to enter the presence of a holy God.

(*b*)   *Maclear and Trench*

LETTER AND SPIRIT, THE (2 Cor. iii. 6)

1. The difference between L. and S. is that between O. and N. T. ; between a ministry of condemnation and one of glory.

The O. T. by rules and ceremonial induced *Formalism ;* whilst the principle of the N. T. is "God is a Spirit, and they that worship Him," etc.

(*c*)

2. Compare the Letter of the Old with the Spirit of the N.T. ;

O.T. said :—"Thou shalt not kill, steal, injure, wrong, bear false witness, covet," etc. This "letter" killeth, if only obeyed in strict literalness ; but N.T. says : "Thou shalt love thy neighbour as thyself ;" "Love beareth no ill to his neighbour ; therefore *love is the fulfilling of the law.*" This "spirit" giveth life to the commandment.

(*d*)

3. O. T. said : "Be separate" from surrounding nations : "Circumcise yourselves." N. T. says : "Be unworldly." "If any man love the world," etc., = Letter and Spirit.

(*e*)

4. O. T. commanded Sabbatarianism : Devote a seventh part of time to God ;

N. T. says : "The Sabbath was made for man ; all time should be sanctified to God."

(*f*)

5. So of the whole round of ceremonial worship, wherein days, seasons, fasts, festivals, multiplied changes of posture, turnings from side to side, deadened religious feeling ; and diverted the heart of the worshipper from the central point and kernel of worship : "The kingdom of God is not meat, etc., but love, joy, and peace in the Holy Ghost." "God be merciful to me a sinner," is a more acceptable prayer in God's ears than any elaborate liturgy and ecclesiastical ritual. = The Letter and Spirit.

(*g*)

6. Apply this principle to Holy Scripture itself :

The books of the Bible range over much time ; in various dialects ; various penmen.

O. T. faithfully kept, very letters counted. N. T originals = many MSS., no author's MSS. remaining ; various versions ; several revisions, till quite recently the last (1881), the outcome of severe critical study and comparison of the oldest and best MSS. extant.

Possibly the faith of some in the Bible has been shaken by this. Yet perhaps they have too much overrated the "Letter" in place of the "Spirit." God's providence might have preserved the very MSS. written by the Evangelists and Apostles, the very letters, and so a perfectly pure text ; and our danger might have been a kind of idolatry of the written Letter ; whereas instead of this, and of far more importance than this, we have the "Spirit" of the first, that spirit by which Christians have been made in all ages. Jesus Christ the same, etc. This, notwithstanding verbal errors, different versions, and periodical revisions = again the difference between the *Letter* and the Spirit.

(*h*)

7. Take two or three instances of this :

O. T. account of the *Creation,* etc., in seven days not reconcilable with modern discovery. But they need no reconciliation, for the Bible does not teach science. No revelation is wanted for that. Its authors spoke the popular thought—never above and beyond it. And all that it is necessary to know about it is, that the *Spirit* of the thing is contained in the record, viz. : that God was actively present, all beginnings of things were from Him and of Him, and without Him nothing came into existence—except moral evil from man's disobedience. The *Letter* may not accord with scientific facts, but the *Spirit* of the whole narrative is true ; and in a religious sense and for religious purposes we have all we need to know.

(*i*)

8. The Fourth Gospel is unique ; it deals, not so much with the great facts of our Lord's life, as of His Divinity. It is the spiritual Gospel. Hence

(*j*)

the animus of critics against it—thinking, if this is a forgery, all the rest of Scripture follows. They may kill the body, but the soul is beyond their power. This Gospel defies all attacks = The Letter and the Spirit.

(a)

9. St. Paul quotes the LXX. when he might have quoted more correctly from Hebrew originals. The LXX., like our P. B. version of Psalms, is a translation of a translation, and rather *free* than otherwise. Why does he this, if the *Letter* is of so much importance? Clearly, that we may infer the *Spirit* of the whole, the kernel, or the meaning of a quotation is of more value than the *letter*, which killeth.

(b)

10. Application of this principle to the ministers of the Gospel:

We are not ministers of the *Letter.* The scribes were: they had the key of knowledge. Counted the letters, copied faithfully, guarded jealously the O.T. records—all honour to them.

But their engrossing occupation of fixing fast-days, feast-days, new moons, etc., distinguishing between characters on phylacteries, and the width of the hem on a Pharisee's cloak; their calculations of tithes on anise, etc., allowed them to forget weightier matters—judgment, mercy, and truth. They entered not into the kingdom, nor suffered others to enter in. Because they mistook the *Letter* for the *Spirit.*

(c)

11. So we call a minister a *man of letters* = an intellectual preacher, etc. But he may for all that lack spiritual perception of the truth, and be as much in the dark as those who follow him. Whilst another man, far less able, inaccurate, narrow calibre, having only an inferior acquaintance with the *Letter* of the Scripture, may, nevertheless, be a spiritual man—a true minister of the Lord Jesus Christ, and have power over the hearts and consciences of his hearers. This man, and not the other, is a more "*able minister of the N. T.*," because the mere *Letter* of human learning killeth, but the *Spirit* giveth life.

We are the ministers of the spirit: of the N. T., not of the Old.

The sufficiency for this is of God. Men have gone forth and have failed, for no other reason than this—they have gone armed with the *Letter*, not the Spirit (John Scott, Tauler, etc.). It was the Spirit of the living God which converted the Corinthians, not St. Paul, the minister, or servant, only of the Spirit; and if we would be able ministers of the N.T., we can hope for success in no other way.

We are the ministers of the Spirit; and the Holy Spirit is the minister of Christ; and Christ is the Revealer of the Father, of whom cometh all things.

(d)

LETTER AND SPIRIT, THE

St. Paul was sent to instruct men, that all those things for which they looked, had taken place typically; that the kingdom of God was in the Spirit, not in the flesh; that their enemies were not the Babylonians, but their own passions; that God delighted not in temples made with hands,

but in a pure and humble mind; that bodily circumcision was unprofitable, but the circumcision of the heart indispensable, etc.

(e)　　　　　　　　　　　　　　*Blaise Pascal*

THE LETTER AND THE SPIRIT

This is what was done by our Lord and His Apostles; they opened the seal, they rent the veil, and discovered the spiritual sense. They have taught us, that our enemies are our own lusts, and our Redeemer a spiritual conqueror; that He was to have two advents; the one in humility to abase the proud, the other in glory to exalt the humble: in a word, that Jesus Christ is God and man.

(f)　　　　　　　　　　　　　　　　　*Ibid*

LETTER AND SPIRIT

The "Exodus from Houndsditch" = the Exodus from Judaic Christianity:—the "Letter"—Historical, and were external Christianity.

The Church of England stood long upon her tithes and her decencies, but now she takes to shouting in the market-place, my tithes are nothing, my decencies are nothing; I am either miraculous, celestial, or else nothing. It is to me the fatalest symptom of speedy change she ever exhibited. What an alternative. Men will soon see whether you are miraculous, celestial, or not.

Were a pair of breeches ever known to bring forth a son?

(g)　　　　　　　　　　　　　　　　*T. Carlyle*

LETTER AND SPIRIT IN THE METHODS OF PHYSICAL SCIENCE OR HISTORICAL CRITICISM

While Colenso thought Maurice hardly candid, Maurice thought Colenso hardly sober and serious, and too much inclined to weigh grains of dust against the testimony of the soul. How different were their standards of fact may be gathered best, perhaps, from the letter in which Maurice declares that to him the Book of Isaiah seems lucidity itself compared with Lord Mahon's "Life of Pitt;" the difference, of course, being that in Isaiah the reference of everything to the Divine standard is plain, and only the implied human events obscure, while in Lord Mahon's "Life of Pitt" the human events are pretty clearly determined, and only the standard to which his policy was referred is wholly obscure and ambiguous.

Again:

Colenso thought he could distinguish the untrustworthiness of a history sufficiently by bringing to light a great number of minor discrepancies in it. Maurice thought we could distinguish its trustworthiness as regarded its main features, by comparing the moral and spiritual antecedents in one page of the history with the moral and spiritual consequents in another, and showing how truly they corresponded to each other, and how full of human nature, and how fully verified by our own experience, was the connection between the different stages. For my part I believe that both are right up to a certain point, but that Maurice had got hold of immeasurably the more important criterion of the two.

(h)　　　　　　　　　　　　*Guardian* (*Review*)

LEVITY

"As it was in the days of Noah. . . . Lot," etc. (Luke xvii. 26)

As Nero kept on fiddling when Rome was in flames, so the world keeps on fiddling till time has passed away and the door is shut.

(a)

LIBERTY

We know no truth, no privilege, no power, no blessing, no right, which is not abused. But is liberty to be denied to men because they often turn it into licentiousness?

(b) *Channing*

LIBERTY, EQUALITY, AND BROTHERHOOD —THE TRUE AND THE FALSE

There are two *freedoms*—the false, where a man is free to do what he likes; the true, where a man is free to do what he ought.

Two *equalities*—the false, which reduces all intellects and all character to a dead level, and gives the same power to the bad as to the good, to the wise as to the foolish, ending thus in practice in the grossest inequality: the true, wherein each man has equal power to educate and use whatever faculties or talents God has given him, be they less or more. This is the Divine equality which the Church proclaims, and nothing else proclaims as she does.

Two *brotherhoods*—the false, where a man chooses who shall be his brothers, and whom he will treat as such; the true, in which a man believes that all are his brothers, not by the will of the flesh, or the will of man, but by the will of God, whose children they all are alike. The Church has three special possessions and treasures. The Bible, which proclaims man's freedom; Baptism his equality; the Lord's Supper his Brotherhood.

(c) *Chas. Kingsley*

LIBERTY AND NECESSITY

"All things are double one against another" (Ecclus. xlii. 24—Apocrypha)

Every thing has its counterpart, or contrary in nature, and one is opposed to the other: as the opposite sides of the body and its members, right and left; night and day; evil and good; death and life; cold and heat; dry and wet, etc.

So of these contrary doctrines (liberty and necessity): they are opposites, like the two sides of a coin—*double one against another*. For just as in the arterial and venous systems, where one begins and the other ceases, the minuteness of the ramifications seems almost indeterminable, so with these doctrines, one runs into the other and seems to be that other and not itself.

(d)

LIARS

That man is not contented with believing the Bible; but he fairly resolves, I think, to believe nothing but the Bible. Johnson, though so wise a fellow, is more like King David than King Solomon, for he says in his haste, *all men are liars.*

(e) *Hogarth, on Dr. Johnson*

LIES

A lie is a breach of promise: for whosoever seriously addresses his discourse to another, tacitly promises to speak the truth, because he knows the truth is expected.

(f) *Paley*

O ye hypocrisies and royal mantles. Cardinal plush cloaks—ye credos, formulas, respectabilities, fair-painted sepulchres full of dead men's bones;— *behold ye appear to us* (the sansculottes) *to be altogether a lie. Yet our life is not a lie;* our hunger and misery is not a lie!

(g) *Carlyle*

Truth never was indebted to a lie.

(h) *Dr. Young*

LIES (False newspaper reports)

All the race of news-scribes (described as) *hominum genus audacissimum mendacissimum avidissimum.* . . . These writers insert in their papers things they do not know, and ought not to write. . . . The worst (of it) is, that this trick will continue a long course of years, and the public suffer a great deal too much by it.

(i) *Disraeli : Cur. Lit*

LIES, POLITICAL

When any great affair was to be carried in parliament . . . (false reports) of victories, etc., were published to dishearten (one side, and embolden the other). "A false report, if believed during three days, may be of great service to a Government" (*Catherine de Medicis*). Between solid lying and disguised truth there is a difference known to writers skilled in "the art of governing mankind by deceiving them;" as politics, ill-understood, have been defined, and as, indeed, all party-politics are. . . . Politicians, who (thus) obtain their end, are like the architect who, in building an arch, supports it with circular props and pieces of timber, or any temporary rubbish, till he closes the arch; and when it can support itself, he throws away the props.

This art was unquestionably practised among the ancients. Plutarch tells an amusing story of the natural progress of a report, which was contrary to the wishes of the Government; the reporter suffered punishment as long as the rumour prevailed, though at last it proved true. A stranger landing from Sicily, at a barber's shop delivered all the particulars of the defeat of the Athenians; of which, the people were yet uninformed. The barber leaves untrimmed the reporter's beard, and flies away to vent the news in the city, where he told the Archons what he had heard. The whole city was thrown into a ferment. The Archons called an assembly of the people, and produced the luckless barber, who in confusion could not give any satisfactory account of the first reporter. He was condemned as a spreader of false news, and a disturber of the

(j)

public quiet. The barber was tortured till the disaster was more than confirmed. . . . Had the barber reported *a victory*, though false, he would not have been punished.

(a) *Disraeli : Cur. Lit*

An ambassador is said to be a man of virtue, sent abroad to tell lies for the advantage of his country : a news-writer is a man without virtue, who writes lies at home-for his own profit.

(b) *Dr. Johnson*

LIFE (John iii. 3)

Our Lord replies, "It is not learning, but life, that is wanted for Messiah's kingdom ; and life must begin by birth."

(c) *Alford*

LIFE

In every plant there is *life*. What a wonderful thing is *life !* What has it done here ? It has seized on the dead earth—on dead matter—and raised it to a higher state. Life always stoops to elevate to its own level that which is lower than itself. Christ is our life, and He seeks to place us on a level with Himself. See how the wheat has aspired ! It has done what it could to rise above the earth.

(d) *J. Gill*

LIFE.

It was the labour of Socrates to turn philosophy from the study of nature to speculations upon life ; but there have been and are others, who are turning off attention from *life* to *nature*. They seem to think that we are placed here to watch the growth of plants, or the motion of the stars ; but Socrates was rather of opinion that what we had to learn, was how to *do good* and *avoid evil*.

(e) *Dr. Johnson*

LIFE IN CHRIST

Here, indeed, is my life ; namely, the birth of this Man, the righteousness of this Man, the blood of this Man, the death and resurrection of this Man !—the Son of Mary—the Son of Man—the Son of God—the true God ! I say, here is my life ; if I see this by faith without me, through the operation of the Spirit within me, I am safe ; I am at peace ; I am comforted ; I am encouraged ; and I know that my comfort, peace, and encouragement is true, and given me from heaven by the Father of mercies.

(f) *Bunyan*

Ah, here is the true secret. It is when Christ is in you that the highest motives become practically powerful upon your life. We think of Christ as the Liberator. To many souls it is His most attractive character. But we do need to know what the character of the liberation which He brings us is. It is not simply that as we lie chained upon the ground He comes and breaks our chains, and lets us lie there still, bound down by the torpor which our chained condition has created in us—slaves to our own inability to rise. That is not the glorious redemption. That is a purely negative freedom. What Christ desires to do for you, is something far nobler and more divine than that. He wants to awaken your dead conscience and to quicken into life and invitation the apparently dead and depressing experience around us, so that you shall feel in yourself the response to higher motives, and recognise in all history the loftier and more spiritual possibility of man. If He could do that for you, then there would be real liberation. You would no longer be the slave of sensible things, not because you had learned to despise them, not because you thought your business, or your home, or your social pleasure contemptible or wicked, but because you had seen the joy of higher things—truth, God, charity, character, heaven—and the channel of affection was clear between them and your soul. That is true liberty. It does not cast the lower things away. As Christ said to Satan, "Man shall not live by bread alone." He shall live by bread, but not by bread alone. The lower wants are recognised. The things that supplied them are not thrown away, but they are used no longer to enslave and bind, but simply to sustain and steady the life, which moves now under spiritual impulse : as the ship, which has cast loose from its bondage to the shore and goes with wind and steam exultantly out to sea, still carries some of that shore for ballast in its hold. That is the relation which the spiritual man still holds to the things of the senses. The man in Christ makes the world serve no longer as dock, but as ballast ; no longer as confinement, but as balance for the new life which he lives.

(g) *Anon*

LIFE AND DEATH IN CHRIST

" *For me to live is Christ, to die is gain* " (Phil. i. 21)

St. Paul writes from a Roman prison ; but though he was bound, the Word of God was not " bound," it had borne fruit and made disciples even in Cæsar's household.

Writing under these circumstances he cannot but think of the probable termination of his imprisonment. Whether he will be set at liberty or executed he knows not, but the uncertainty causes him no terror ; it may be life, or it may be death —one or the other will be settled by the authorities for him in a few days.

As for himself he says, " I am in a strait betwixt two, having a desire to depart and be with Christ, which is far better. Nevertheless, for me to abide in the flesh is more needful for *you*."

For myself death has the preference ; for you it may be better that I should live.

" To live is Christ "—and Christ's work among you. " To die is gain."

(h)

1. The Apostle's definite object in life

" *To live is Christ.*" Others might aim at obtaining wealth, learning, fame in the many walks of life ; and the whole current of life would set in that direction until height of ambition was reached. St. Paul had a ruling motive, which compelled him to activity. "The love of Christ constraineth me." "Yea, woe is me if I preach not the Gospel." All his time and gifts were bent

(i)

to the performance of this one object—" *To live is Christ.*"

Suppose the tyrant Nero had sent for him, and said, "Come, Paul, I hear that you are a born gentleman, well educated, and have great gifts, but that you are throwing away all your chances in life in having joined this beggarly sect of Nazarines. If you are a wise man you will abandon them, and this fanatical preaching of yours, and I will give you a good position in the Roman Empire, and offer you a grand opportunity for the display of your varied gifts and talents. With your powers you may soon become a leading Senator, have a voice in State affairs, and have a palace to live in, and perhaps rival the glories of Sylla."

The Apostle's answer would be to this effect, "Set me at liberty, and I will preach Christ immediately in the open street if I cannot find a house to preach in." As to your offer of wealth and a distinguished position—"What things were gain to me, I count all loss for Christ." "I have suffered the loss of all things, and do count it but dung that I may win Christ, and be found in Him." "I have thrown overboard all other thoughts, I have but one ambition, my life has but one aim—' For me to live is Christ.'"

(*a*)

2. "To die is gain."

(i.) A worldly man would argue that "to die is loss." The loss of all he has—houses, lands, property of all kinds—all are lost by death; and they are my *all*. "My affections are set on them; for me to die *is not gain.*"

(ii.) The man of sensual pleasure is horrified at the thought of death, and parting with his body, which has been the vehicle of all his sensual gratifications, and which now becomes the prey of disease and death, and exchanges the warm susceptibilities of life for the coldness of the grave, and saying to corruption, Thou art my father; and to the worm, Thou art my sister. Can that be "gain" which robs me of all the pleasure that I know? "Oh, don't let me die," he exclaims, in consternation and panic, when the doctor tells him that he has ruined his constitution by excess, and there is no hope." "It is frightful, horrible, I have nothing but a body, I never gave a thought to my soul, and scarcely knew that I had one."

(iii.) Ask, with solemn mockery, the miser whether he thinks it is *gain* to die. What does he say when the doctor tells him, too, that he must make his will? "Doctor, you don't mean it —you won't let me die—I cannot part with my gold—I cannot will it away to others—it is my god—I have slaved for it—pinched and starved myself to accumulate it—I have let the hungry and needy go away from my door rather than diminish it—I can't part with it—it is my all. There is no *gain*—no *gold* in death—it is all loss."

So too the sceptic and others argue—there is no *gain* in death—it is all darkness and loss.

But the Christian *gains* by death. Instead of losing his all, he gains. "We know that if our earthly house of this tabernacle were dissolved we have a building of God, a house not made with hands, eternal in the heavens."

Death is *gain* when it exchanges a temporal for an eternal home, and takes us to a *better land*. Out of the wanderings of the wilderness into Canaan. Here, we are pilgrims; and they that say such things declare plainly that they seek a country.

(*b*)   *Thos. Cooper*
(*See* "More than Conquerors.")

Life, the Elixir of (1 Pet. iii. 10)

A certain person travelling through the city, continued to call out, "*Who wants the elixir of life?*" The daughter of Rabbi Joda heard him and told her father. He said, "Call the man in." When he came in, the Rabbi said, "What is that elixir of life thou sellest?" He answered, "Is it not written, 'What man is he that loveth life and desireth to see good days, let him refrain his tongue from evil and his lips from speaking guile?' This is the elixir of life, and is found in the mouth of man."

(*c*)   *Book of Massar*

Life, Jesus on the High Road of

"*Did not our heart burn within us while He talked with us by the way, and while He opened to us the Scriptures?*" (Luke xxiv. 32)

1. A very suggestive question. It suggests the difficulty which we commonly have in understanding the real importance of many incidents in our lives at the time of their occurrence. These two disciples, caring about nothing in the world so much as their relation to their crucified Master, yet, it seems, could be in His company for a considerable time, and hear Him explain the Old Testament in its relations to Himself, without understanding, without dreaming of their extraordinary privilege. They recognised neither His voice nor His manner.

2. All of it seemed to belong to the range of ordinary experience. Now this illustrates the difficulty we have in understanding, at the time, the relative importance of the events of our lives, and especially of the religious events in them. We are not indisposed to think that the important events must be striking, that they must address themselves powerfully to the imagination, that they must stand out in an obvious prominence from the other events around them; whereas it may very well happen that what is most important in reality—that is in its bearing on our prospects in the future life—is in appearance quite commonplace and trivial.

3. The owner of the ass on which our Lord sat when He entered Jerusalem had, we may be very sure, very little idea indeed of what was meant by the message—"The Lord hath need of him."

4. Pilate would have been astonished had he been told at the time that nothing in the whole course of his whole public and official life could distinctly compare in point of significance with his trial of the poor prisoner who was placed side by side with the robber Barabbas before his tribunal in the prætorium. Pilate, it may be said, looked at religious matters from the outside. Pilate was without the moral and spiritual perceptions which would enable a man to understand the scene before him. Pilate was like an uneducated peasant looking at an engraving of Albert Durer, or a person to whom music only represents regulated noise listening to a sonata of Beethoven.

(*d*)

5. Again and again it has happened that, like the two disciples, such persons have not understood the meaning of some religious privilege at the time. They have only known its value afterwards, when it is past, and they are looking back upon it. Thus, Jacob in his dream saw the vision of angels. It was only after awaking that he exclaimed, " Surely the Lord was in this place and I knew it not."

6. Gideon treated the angel under the oak at Ophrah as a mere man. It was not until the angel had kindled the fire to consume the sacrifice, and had vanished, that Gideon said, "Alas, O Lord God! for I have seen the angel of the Lord face to face." And so the angel had given His message, and had left Manoah and his wife, before they fell on their faces to the ground; and Manoah said to his wife, " We shall surely die, for we have seen God."

7. And so, when washing the feet of St. Peter, our Lord condescended to explain to the Apostle that the full meaning of what might seem to be so unimportant would only become clear to him at a later time in his life. "What I do thou knowest not now, but thou shalt know hereafter."

8. And so, when St. Philip asked our Lord to show him the Father, our Lord answered him in words which implied that he had not understood the privilege which had all along attached to companionship with Himself : "Have I been so long time with you, and yet thou hast not known Me, Philip? He that hath seen Me hath seen the Father." And in the same way, after describing our Lord's entrance into Jerusalem on Palm Sunday, St. John adds : " These things understood not His disciples at the first; but when Jesus was glorified then remembered they that these things were written of Him, and that they had done those things unto Him."

(*a*) *Liddon*

LIFE (Prov. xiv. 3)

" *In the midst of laughing there is sorrow.*"

In general as is the heaven, so is our life sometimes fair, sometimes overcast, tempestuous, and serene; as in a rose, flowers and prickles; in the year itself, a temperate summer sometimes, a hard winter, a drowth, and then again pleasant showers; so is our life intermixt with joys, hopes, fears, sorrows, calumnies; *invicem cedunt dolor et voluptas*: there is a succession of pleasure and pain.

(*b*) (*Lipsius*) *Burton's Anat. Mel*

LIFE, THE RIGHT OF

Take not away the life you cannot give,
For all things have an equal right to live.

(*c*) *Dryden*

LIFE IS SHORT

He struts in robes, the monarch of an hour.

(*d*) *Tickell*

LIFE WASTED

Two old men, amateur naturalists, who had devoted their whole lives, one to *ferns* and the other to *orchids*, travelled together for many hours.

At the end of their journey he who had cultivated ferns said to his companion, with a sigh, " *I have wasted my life; if I had it to live over again, I should devote it to orchids !* "

(*e*)

LIFE ? WHAT IS

Life is a warfare.—*Seneca.*
Life is a navigation.—*Seneca.*
Life's a tragedy.—*Sir Walter Raleigh.*
Life is a jest, and all things show it; } *Dr. Gay.*
I thought so once, but now I know it. }
Life is but a day at most.—*Burns.*
Longest life is but a day.—*Wordsworth.*
Our whole life is like a play.—*Ben Jonson.*
Life is a journey, on we go } *William*
Through many a scene of joy and woe. } *Combe.*

(*f*)

LIGHT

" *Let there be Light* " (Gen. i. 3)

It is with man's soul as it was with Nature; the beginning of Creation is—light. Till the eye have vision, the whole members are in bonds. Divine moment, when over the tempest-tost soul, as once over the wild, weltering Chaos, it is spoken : " Let there be light."

(*g*) *Thos. Carlyle*

I believe, and rejoice to believe, that a ray from heaven descends on the path of every fellow-creature. The heathen,—though in darkness, when compared with the Christian,—has still his light ; and it comes from the same source as our own, just as the same sun dispenses, now the faint dawn, and now the perfect day.

(*h*) *Channing*

There was a dark cloud before mine eyes, so that I could not see the light of truth ; but, Lord, Thou art my God, who hast led me from darkness and the shadow of death ; hast called me into this glorious light, and behold, I see.

(*i*) *Augustine*

LIGHT AFFLICTIONS, OUR

The destiny of our sorrows is written in heaven, by a wise and eternal decree. Behold, He that hath ordained moderates them : a faithful God, that gives an issue with the temptations, an issue both of their end and their success. He chides not always ; much less striketh. Our light afflictions are but for a moment : not so long in respect of our vacancy and rest. If we weep sometimes, our tears are precious. As they shall never be dry in His bottle, so they shall soon be dry upon our cheeks. He that wrings them from us, shall wipe them off. How sweetly doth He interchange our sorrows and joys ; that we may neither be vain nor miserable !

(*j*) *Bishop Hall*

LIGHT THAT IS FELT, THE

A tender child, of summers three,
Seeking her little bed at night,
Paused on the dark stair timidly.
" Oh, Mother ! take my hand," said she
" And then the dark will all be light."

(*k*)

We older children grope our way
From dark behind to dark before ;
And only when our hands we lay,
Dear Lord, in Thine, the night is day,
And then is darkness nevermore.

Reach downwards to the sunless days
Wherein our guides are blind as we,
And faith is small and hope delays ;
Take Thou the hands of prayer we raise,
And let us feel the light of Thee !

(*a*)　　　　　　　　　*J. G. Whittier*

LIGHT, THE MINISTRY OF

" *God, who commanded the light to shine out of darkness, hath shined in our hearts, to give the light of the knowledge of the glory of God in the face of Jesus Christ* " (2 Cor. iv. 1–6)

1, There are two spheres in which life may be lived—Light and Darkness

(i.) St. John says : To live in sin, to love not a brother, to be worldly—is to abide (live) in *Darkness*.

(ii.) St. Paul says, that this Darkness is owing to the fact that " The god of this world hath blinded the eyes of them that believe not."

(iii.) Our Lord illustrated this blindness by the Blind Beggar sitting outside the walls of Jericho —a picture of man by nature and without light. (*See* " BLINDNESS ").

(*b*)

2. To cure this, God sent His Son as " **The Light of the World**," that men who " sat in darkness " might have great Light and *See*.

And the Son hath sent forth Apostles and ministers to " **open blind eyes** " ; to turn men from darkness to *light ;* from Satan unto God.

It is this fact that the Apostle alludes to here.

The Ministry of Jesus Christ is a Ministry of Light—great light ; and men abide in darkness, with blinded eyes, so long as they do not receive Jesus Christ.

(*c*)

3. Light reveals things

They exist before, but where there is no light they cannot be seen or known—as a room carefully shut up, and all light excluded, may contain excellent furniture, books, paintings, etc., but we cannot see them and have knowledge of them, until the shutters are opened and the light let in. Then that which before was probable becomes a *certainty*. So God did at the physical Creation.

At first Darkness and Chaos—land and water mixed ; but when Light came in, things were seen *as they were*.

3. Similarly **Spiritual Chaos exists**; hence doubts and uncertainties ; we want a Revelation about these things.

This, the Apostle says, God hath given us *in Christ*, who " lighteth every man," etc.

" God hath shined in our hearts, to give the light of the knowledge," etc.

(*d*)

4. Man knows not God

God may be conceived of as a Despot, Jupiter, a heathen Deity, or as in the O.T. as The Almighty, Jehovah, The Shepherd of Israel.

Not till the Light comes and reveals Him, do we know Him as " Our Father," which is in Heaven.

(*e*)

5. Man knows nothing of his own destiny

" I go to seek a great may-be," said Rabelais when dying.

" Jesus, knowing whence He was and whither He was going " = Light thrown on man's origin and destiny."

(*See* " JESUS CHRIST, THE EXPLANATION OF MAN.")

(*f*)

6. Death and Immortality are all darkness without Christ

Death was loss, a spoiler, the end of all to the heathen. The " King of Terrors " to all out of Christ.

" Wa ! Wa ! What great god is this, that pulls down the strength of the strongest kings ? " exclaimed Clotaire, when dying. " Death reigned," a remorseless conqueror until Christ came and conquered it, by re-appearing, and by His promises delivered us from our life-long bondage.

He hath " abolished death and brought life and immortality to light through the Gospel."

(*g*)

7. The Sun shines. The true light has come, why are so many still in darkness ?

Because of sin, selfishness, and worldliness. These shut out the LIGHT.

(*h*)　　　　　　　　*Cf. F. W. Robertson*

LIGHT, THE SHINING

" *Let your light so shine before men, that they may see your good works, and glorify your Father which is in heaven* " (Matt. v. 16)

Cassell's Family Magazine for February, 1885, observes :—" That the sun-spots are intimately connected with some terrestrial phenomena there can be little doubt. Variations of the compass, magnetic storms, and auroral displays not only show a periodical variation corresponding with that of sun-spots, but great outbursts of spots are usually accompanied on the same day of their occurrence by great disturbances of the needle." Once it was thought these spots meant little or nothing, but science concludes otherwise now— they mean all kinds of terrible terrestrial mischief. So do the spots on the Church of Christ, which is the sun of society. Spots on the Christian character have a great and disastrous influence.

(*i*)

LIGHTS

" *Among whom ye shine as lights* " (Phil. ii. 15)

A congregation of Christians = so many torch-bearers.

Heaven has illuminated them in order that they may " shine."

How ? By " *holding forth the word of life*."
This will have the right effect.

The infidel Parker said-

" If I believed what you believe, I would go up and down the world to save mankind." But in

(*j*)

this there is seen the true infidel disparagement of the power of God's word.

Life is not long enough, human energy not sufficient for these things—"Our sufficiency is of God, who maketh us *able* ministers of the N. T." And part of His plan for saving the world is by putting Christians about in it—"among whom ye shine," to illuminate its darkness, and to leaven the general mass with the leaven of Christianity.

(*a*)

LIGHTHOUSE, THE

I was once told by a man who kept a lighthouse between Anglesea and Ireland, that on dark and tempestuous nights multitudes of birds, having lost their way and seeking for shelter, flew wildly against it, and were found dead in the morning. So, many souls, who have not "lodged in the branches of the great tree" before the night came, driven by the storm of death, strike against the great lighthouse of Sinai's law, seeking shelter, but in vain.

(*b*)   *Christmas Evans*

LITERATURE, CHEAP

Beware of infidel, blasphemous, and immoral publications, which pervert the judgment, corrupt the heart, and vitiate the life.

(*c*)   *J. Carver, Ordinary of Newgate*

LITTLE ONES

"*Little ones*" (Matt. x. 42)

Those, probably, not so far advanced as the disciples whom our Lord, had in training for a longer time. They were not Pauls for learning, Peters for devotion, nor Abrahams for faith, or Johns for love, but simple believers who form a part of that mystical body of Christ. So that "He that hurteth them, hurteth *Me*." Saul could not persecute them without having it asked, "Why persecutest thou *Me*?" They were but a handful of poor uneducated men, whom he was persecuting, of no importance in the State; and the wonder is that the authorities noticed them at all. Yet He that sitteth alone, and ruleth over the universe, owns them for His, and declares them to be a part of Himself. And as an injury done to the hand or foot is instantly made known to the seat of sensation, and the remedy applied—so wrong done to the members of Christ is instantly known to the Head in heaven, and that He careth for and watcheth over His own.

(*d*)

"LITTLE ONES" (Mat. xviii. 10–11)

Christ's love for His young disciples again breaks out in words. Let no one despise them. They have unseen friends in the court of Heaven, who are ever in the presence of the King Himself. There, at any rate, they are not despised. It was for them especially that the Son of Man came to earth.

(*e*)   *Carr*
(*See* "CHILDREN.")

LITTLE SINS

Think well of the visitations of our Lord; for I find one thing I saw not well before. That when the saints are under trials and well humbled, little sins raise great cries and war-shouts in the conscience; but in prosperity, conscience is a Pope, to give dispensations, and let out and in, and to give latitude and elbow-room to our heart. Oh, how little care we for pardon at Christ's hand, when we make dispensations! And all is but bairn's-play, till a cross without beget a heavier cross within, and then we play no longer with our idols. It is good still to be severe against ourselves, for we but transform God's mercy into an idol, and an idol that hath a dispensation to give for turning of the grace of God into wantonness.

(*f*)   *Rutherford*

Adam took an apple; Moses struck the rock: Yet the first entailed the loss of Eden, and the second exclusion from Canaan.

(*g*)   *Oosterzee*

LITTLE SINS, DANGEROUS

A little leaven leaveneth the whole lump; a little staff may kill one; a little leak in a ship sinks it; a little flaw in a good cause mars it; so a little sin may at once bar the door of heaven and open the gates of hell; though a scorpion be little, yet will it sting a lion to death; and so will the least sin, if not pardoned by the death of Christ.

(*h*)   *Thos. Brooks*

LITTLE THINGS

No terrestrial greatness is more than the aggregate of little things; and to inculcate, after the Arabian proverb, "Drops added to drops, constitute the ocean."

(*i*)   *Dr. Johnson*

LITTLE WHILE, A

"*A little while, and ye shall not see Me: and again, a little while, and ye shall see Me, because I go to the Father*" (John xvi. 16)

1. Two "Little whiles"

  (i.) Of sorrow;
  (ii.) Of joy.
Sorrow and joy are necessary to make the Christian grow, like rain and sunshine in nature. As a rule, God does not give us either of these unmixed; and He knows best how to apportion the quantity for each of us.
All joy, like all sunshine, would have a scorching effect.
All sorrow, like all rainy weather, would spoil the fruit.
When Jesus leaves us and our way is hid, then is our time of sorrow.
When Jesus returns to us and our way is light about us, then is our time of joy.
These are very real experiences to the Christian —"Then were the disciples glad when they saw the Lord."

(*j*)

Testimonies of some Christians :

1. Hilary : "Those whom God loves best feel the smart of the whip the most ",

2. Jerome : "Like as a whetstone sharpens a knife, so does the Cross your faith ,

3. Augustine : " Where there is no trial, there is no prayer."

The order is, Sorrow first, Joy next.—"A little while and *ye shall not see Me*, and again a little while and *ye shall see Me.*"

(*a*)

2. (i.) The sorrow is removable (22)

"Ye now have sorrow," but "I will see you again, and your heart shall rejoice.' As darkness flies before the rising sun, so sorrow goes when Christ comes to us. Sorrow is like the Night followed by the Day ; to a Christian the morning is sure to come.

(ii.) The joy is not removable (22)

"Your joy no man taketh from you." The joy is that of being Christ's—of forgiven sin—of the indwelling witness of the Comforter. And it is not removable because it is the Spirit's work (15). Man can take away the Christian's life, but no man can blot the Christian's name out of God's book. The joy is eternal. As we cannot stop the birds from singing when the sun shines in the morning, so when the Christian's sorrow is over he has joy, and " no man taketh it from him."

" A little while."

Joseph sorrowed thirteen years, but lived in a very exalted rank for eighty, nearly six times as long.

Job's sorrow lasted perhaps seven years, but he was well and prosperous for 140.

The *disciples* wept "a little while "—forty hours, but they enjoyed Forty Easter Days, " speaking of the things concerning the kingdom of God."

So to the Christian every sorrow is succeeded by a joy—a lifting up—either now or in heaven ; and the joy is immovable. A " *little while* " of sorrow replaced by an eternity of joy.

(*b*)

3. This to Christians only ; to the worldly the order is inverted (20)

(i.) *Worldly Joy.* "The world shall rejoice." Men of the world "have their portion in this life." Why? They die; they leave all behind them ; there is nothing more to come. Whilst the Christian goes to an "inheritance which fadeth not away."

(ii.) *Worldly "Sorrow"* succeeds. "The sorrow of the world worketh death." Cf. "The rich man and Lazarus." Not till it was too late did he see that he had had his " good things " too soon.

(*c*)

LITURGY, THE

The repetitions in the Liturgy arise chiefly from *Laud's* folly in joining two services into one.

The minister should have some freedom in the service ; some power of insertion to suit the particular time and place ; some power of explaining on the spot whatever is read from the Scriptures which may require explanation, or of stating the context.

(*d*)   *Thomas Arnold*

LIVE

" *I live, and ye also shall live* " (John xiv. 19)

Not " *Because* I live, ye shall live also " (A.V.).

The present, *I live*, is expressive of His Divine vital power, outlasting death (v. 12 ; Rev. i. 18). Luther : " He is the Person whom death could not devour, though, as regards His bodily life, it did indeed kill Him."

(*e*)   *Lange*

Non modo VIVAM, *sed* VIVO (Rev. i. 18)

VIVETIS, *futurum; nam vita fidelium sequitur, vitam Jesu; et non ex se, sed ex illo vivunt* (vi. 57)

(*f*)   *Bengel*

On these assuring words of Christ Schleiermacher, in the touching funeral discourse of his only son Nathanael, despairing of all philosophical arguments for the immortality of the soul, firmly placed his hope and trust for a future life.

(*g*)   *P. Schaff*

LIVE

Live while you live, the epicure will say,
And take the pleasure of the present day :
Live while you live, the sacred preacher cries,
And give to God each moment as it flies.
Lord, in my view let both united be !
I live in pleasure when I live to Thee.

(*h*)   *Doddridge*

LIVING WATER, RIVERS OF

Rivers, not river, to show the copious and overflowing power of grace ; and *living water, i.e.* always moving : for when the grace of the Spirit has entered into and settled in the mind, it flows freer than any fountain, and neither falls, nor empties, nor stagnates. The wisdom of Stephen, the tongue of Peter, the strength of Paul, are evidences of this. Nothing hindered them ; but, like impetuous torrents, they went on carrying everything along with them.

(*i*)   *Chrysostom*

LIVING WATER (John vii. 38)

Comp. Ezek. xlvii. 1–12 ; Zech. xiv. 8 ; and Isa. lviii. 11. Also the fact, made almost certain by recent researches, that there was a living spring beneath the altar of the Temple, from which all the fountains of Jerusalem were fed, the source of the "brook that flowed hard by the oracles of God,"—the "perennial river the streams whereof shall make glad the city of God " (Psa. xlvi. 4).

(*j*)   *P. Schaff*

LOCALIZATION OF SIN, THE

" *Even for this cause have I raised thee up,*" *etc.*
" *What if God willing,*" *etc.* (Rom. ix. 17, 22)'

Teaches God's power in (i.) crushing sin; (ii.) of endurance.

We have here the doctrine of the *Localization of Sin.* The world full of evil ; but good is mixed with it. It be far from God "to destroy the righteous with the wicked "; hence He cannot pro-

(*k*)

ceed against it without first localizing, or separating, the evil from the good. In order, then, to show His power against wickedness in high places, He draws sin to *one point*, to a head, or centre, as a pestilent ulcer, then He applies the lance and cuts it out. So individuals are dealt with: Pharaoh, Judas Iscariot, Anti-Christ; and places: Sodom and Gomorrha, Jerusalem, etc. So, too, a man's besetting sin is *his* sin localized; and the finger of God often deals with him for *that*, until the body of sin is destroyed.

Cf. the case of Korah, etc. "*Separate me Korah, Dathan, and Abiram*," etc.; and when separated judgment is inflicted on them.

(*a*)

LOGOMACHY

When appealed to by two brethren in hot theological conflict, he replied: "You may go on with your argument, while I try to find out how the matter really stands." "We often differ and dispute a great deal," he once remarked, "because we won't take time and patience to understand one another." And again: "It's a great pity that we have so much controversy about words; it is not enough, to many, that we believe the Gospel, but we must believe it in their *words*. A certain preacher took for his text: 'Now He that hath wrought us for the self-same thing is God;' and the heading of his last division was, 'The author of the work—God,' but a critic found great fault with the sermon because the work had not been ascribed to the *Holy Ghost*."

(*b*) *Christmas Evans*

LOGOS, THE (John i.)

Verses 1, 2. The Logos and God
(i.) His Eternity;
(ii.) His Personality—separate from God;
(iii.) His Divinity—One with God.
He, as such, has always existed.

3. His Work
The Logos and the world; Creation was His work—"*Not even one thing*" without Him.

4. The Logos and Mankind
Creation and Preservation. In Him life, ζωή (not βίος) = The life (iii. 36).

5. The Logos and Sin
"Shineth" even now—the darkness not absolute. Comprehended = apprehended, overcame or suppressed.

(*c*) *Lange*

"LOOKING UNTO JESUS" (Heb. xii. 2)

Only three words, yet they contain the whole secret of life.

1. "Looking unto Jesus" in the Scriptures, to learn who He is, what He has done, what He gives, what He requires; to find in His character our pattern, in His teachings our instruction, in His precepts our law, in His promises our stay, in His person and in His work a full satisfaction offered to every want of our souls.

(*d*)

2. "Looking unto Jesus" crucified, to find in His blood poured out our ransom, our pardon, our peace.

(*e*)

3. "Looking unto Jesus" risen again, to find in Him that righteousness which alone can justify us, and through which, unworthy though we are, we may draw near, with full assurance in His name, unto Him who is His Father and our Father, His God and our God.

(*f*)

4. "Looking unto Jesus" glorified, to find in Him our Advocate with the Father, making complete, through His intercession, the merciful work of our salvation; appearing even now in the presence of God for us, and supplying the weakness of our prayers by the power of those which the Father heareth always.

(*g*)

5. "Looking unto Jesus" as revealed to us by the Holy Ghost, to find in constant communion with Him the cleansing of our sin-stained hearts, the illumination of our darkened minds, the transformation of our perverse wills; to the end that we may triumph over the world and the devil—resisting their violence through Jesus our strength, bringing their devices to nought through Jesus our wisdom; upheld by the sympathy of Jesus, who was Himself tempted in all things; and by the help of Jesus, who resisted and conquered.

(*h*)

6. "Looking unto Jesus," that we may receive from Him the work of each day, and its cross, with the grace which is sufficient to bear the cross and to do the work; patient through His patience; active by His activity; loving with His love; asking not, "What can I do?" but, "What can He not do?" relying upon His strength, which is made perfect in weakness.

(*i*)

7. "Looking unto Jesus," that the brightness of His face may enlighten our darkness; that our joy may be holy, and our grief subdued; that He may humble us to exalt us in due time; that He may afflict, and then comfort us; that He may strip us of our righteousness to enrich us with His own; that He may teach us how to pray, and may answer our prayers; so that while we are in the world we may not be of the world, our life being hid with Him in God, and our works bearing Him witness before men.

(*j*)

8. "Looking unto Jesus," who has re-ascended to His Father's house to prepare a place for us; that this blessed hope may give us courage to live without murmuring, and to die without regret when the day shall come to meet the last enemy, whom He has conquered for us, whom we shall conquer through Him; once the King of Terrors—now the messenger of everlasting peace.

(*k*)

9. "Looking unto Jesus," who gives repentance as well as remission of sins, to receive from Him a heart that feels its wants and cries for mercy at His feet.

(*l*)

10. "Looking unto Jesus," that He may teach us to look unto Him who is the Author and Object of our faith; that He may keep us in that faith, of which He is also the Finisher.

(*m*)

11. "Looking unto Jesus," and to no other, as our text expresses it in one word which is untranslatable, and which enjoins us at one and the same time to fix our eyes upon Him, and to turn them away from all besides.

(a)

12. "Looking unto Jesus," and not unto ourselves, to our thoughts, our wishes, our plans; unto Jesus, and not unto the world, its allurements, its examples, its maxims, its opinions; unto Jesus, and not unto Satan, whether he tries to affright us with his rage or seduce us by his flatteries. Oh, how many useless questions, uneasy scruples, dangerous compromises with evil, distracted thoughts, vain dreams, bitter disappointments, painful struggles, sad backslidings, could we not avoid by looking always unto Jesus, and following Him wherever He leads the way; careful not even to cast a glance at any other way, lest we should lose sight of that in which He leads us.

(b)

13. "Looking unto Jesus," and not unto our meditations and prayers, to our religious conversations and edifying books; not to the assemblies of the faithful which are frequent, nor even to the participation of the supper of our Lord. Let us make a faithful use of all these means of grace; but let us not confound them with grace itself, or turn away our eyes from Him who alone can make them effectual, by giving Himself to us through their means.

(c)

14. "Looking unto Jesus," and not to our standing in the Christian Church, to the name we bear, to the doctrine we profess, to the opinion others have of our piety, or to that which we ourselves entertain. Many who have prophesied in the name of Christ, shall one day hear Him say, "I never knew you"; but He will confess before His Father and His angels even the humblest of those who have looked unto Him.

(d)

15. "Looking unto Jesus," and not to our brethren; not even to the best and most beloved among them. If we follow a man, we run the risk of losing our way; but if we follow Jesus, we are certain that we shall never go astray. Besides, by putting a man between Christ and us, it happens that the man imperceptibly grows in our eyes, while Christ becomes less; and soon we know not how to find Christ without finding the man; and if the latter fails us, all is lost. But if, on the contrary, Jesus stands between us and our dearest friend, our attachment to our friend will be less direct, and at the same time, more sweet; less passionate, but more pure; less necessary, but more useful—the instrument of rich blessings in the hands of God while it shall please Him to use it, and whose absence will still be a blessing when it shall please Him to dispense with it.

(e)

16. "Looking unto Jesus," and not to the obstacles we meet in our path. From the moment that we stop to consider them, they astonish us, and unnerve us, and cast us down; incapable as we are of comprehending either the reason why they are permitted or the means by which we may over-

come them. The Apostle began to sink as soon as he turned to look at the boisterous billows; but so long as he continued looking unto Jesus, he walked upon the waves as upon a rock. The harder our task, and the heavier our cross, the more it behoves us to look to Jesus only.

(f)

17. "Looking unto Jesus," and not to the temporal blessings which we enjoy. By looking first at these blessings, we run the risk of being so much captivated by them, that they even hide from our view Him who gives them. When we look unto Jesus first, we receive all these benefits as from Him; they are chosen by His wisdom, given by His love; a thousand times more precious because received at His hands, to be enjoyed in communion with Him, and used for His glory.

(g)

18. "Looking unto Jesus," and not unto our own strength; for with that we can only glorify ourselves. To glorify God, we need the strength of God.

(h)

19. "Looking unto Jesus," and not to our weakness. Have we ever become stronger by lamenting our weakness? But if we look unto Jesus, His strength shall fortify our hearts, and we shall break forth into songs of praise.

(i)

20. "Looking unto Jesus," and not to our sins. The contemplation of sin brings only death; the contemplation of Jesus brings life. It was not by looking at their wounds, but by beholding the brazen serpent, that the Israelites were healed.

(j)

21. "Looking unto Jesus," and not to the Law. The Law gives us its commands, but does not impart the strength necessary to obey them. The Law always condemns; it never pardons. To be under the Law, is to be out of the reach of grace. In the same measure in which we make our obedience the means of salvation, we lose our peace, our strength, our joy; because we forget that "Christ is the end of the law for righteousness to every one that believeth." As soon as the Law has constrained us to seek salvation only in Christ, He alone can command obedience—an obedience which asks no less than our whole heart, and our most secret thoughts; but which is now no longer an iron yoke and an intolerable burden, having become an easy yoke and a light burden; an obedience which He makes lovely, while it is also obligatory; an obedience which He not only enjoins, but inspires; and which, well understood, is less a consequence of our salvation than a part of the same—and, like every other part, is the gift of free grace.

(k)

22. "Looking unto Jesus," and not to what we are doing for Him. If we are too much taken up with our work, we may forget our Master; we may have our hands full and our heart empty; but if we are constantly looking unto Jesus, we cannot forget our work; if our heart is filled with His love, our hands will also be active in His service.

(l)

23. "**Looking unto Jesus**," and not to the apparent success of our efforts. Apparent success is not always the measure of real success; and besides, God has not enjoined success upon us, but only labour; He will ask an account of our labour, but not of our success—why, then, should we be too much concerned about it? We must sow the seed, God will gather the fruit; if not to-day, it will be to-morrow; if not for us, it will be for others. Even if success were to be granted us, it would always be dangerous to look complacently upon it; on the one hand, we are tempted to claim for ourselves some of the glory; on the other, we are too prone to slacken our zeal when we cease to see good results arising from it; that is, at the very time when we ought to put forth double energy. To look at our success, is to walk by sight; to look unto Jesus and to persevere in following and in serving Him, despite all discouragements, is to walk by faith.

(a)

24. "**Looking unto Jesus**," and not to the gifts which we have received, or are now receiving from Him. As to the grace of yesterday, it has been withdrawn with the work of yesterday; we can use it no longer; we ought not to dwell upon it any longer. As to the grace of to-day, given for the work of to-day, it is entrusted to us; not to be contemplated, but to be used; not to be paraded, that we appear rich, but to be employed at once, that we may, in our poverty, look unto Jesus.

(b)

25. "**Looking unto Jesus**," and not to the depth of sorrow we feel for our sins, or to the degree of humility which they produce in us. If they humble us so that we no longer delight in ourselves, if they cast us down so that we look to Jesus that He may deliver us from them, that is all that He requires of us; and it is looking unto Him which, above everything else, shall cause our tears to flow and our pride to fall.

(c)

26. "**Looking unto Jesus**," and not to the liveliness of our joy, or the fervour of our love. Otherwise, if our love seems to grow cold, and our joy is dimmed—whether on account of lukewarmness, or for the trial of our faith—as soon as those emotions have passed, we shall think that we have lost our strength, and we shall give way to hopeless discouragement, if not to shameful inactivity. Ah! let us remember that if the sweetness of religious emotions be sometimes wanting, faith and its power are left us; and that we may be always abounding in the work of the Lord. Let us be constantly looking, not to our wavering hearts, but unto Jesus, the same yesterday, to-day, and for ever.

(d)

27. "**Looking unto Jesus**," and not to our faith. The last artifice Satan, when he cannot lead us out of the way, is to turn our eyes away from Jesus to look at our faith—and so discourage us if it is weak, to puff us up if it be strong; and, in either case, to weaken us. For it is not our faith which makes us strong, but it is Jesus through faith; we are not strengthened by contemplating our faith, but by looking unto Jesus.

(e)

28. "**Looking unto Jesus**," for it is from Him and in Him that we shall learn, not only without injury, but for the good of our souls, as much as it is meet we should know of the world and of ourselves, of our misery, our dangers, our resources, our victory;—seeing all things in their true light because He shall show them to us, at the very time and in the very measure when that knowledge shall be best calculated to produce in us the fruits of humility and wisdom, of gratitude and courage, of watchfulness and prayer. All that it is well for us to know, Jesus will teach us; all that He does not teach us, it is better for us not to know.

(f)

29. "**Looking unto Jesus**" during all the time which is allotted us here below—unto Jesus ever new, without allowing either the remembrance of the past or the cares of an unknown future to distract our thoughts; unto Jesus now, if we have never looked unto Him; unto Jesus again, if we have ceased to do so; unto Jesus alone, unto Jesus still, unto Jesus always, with a more fixed and steadfast gaze, "changed into the same image from glory to glory"; and thus waiting for the hour when He will call us to pass from earth to heaven, and from time to eternity;—the promised, the blessed hour, when at last we shall be "like unto Him, for we shall see Him as He is."

(g)
                                        Adolph Monod

"LOOKING UNTO JESUS."

"Look unto Me," is the voice coming from Jesus on the Cross (the Tree of Life). We are healed, not by working, or praying, or striving, but looking. Israel's physicians could do nothing; the look at the serpent did it all. So it is in looking that the cure comes to us. There is health, there is life at the Cross. We get them simply in looking; all may look. "Whosoever" is a wide message—"whosoever believeth" hath eternal life.

(h)
                                        Horatius Bonar

LORD JESUS! LORD JESUS! (Acts vii. 59)

1. This is the glorious battle-cry of the children of God, the watchword by which we recognise one another, the sound of the trumpet at which the walls of Jericho fall down. It rings in the Church of God like the alarm-bell which proclaims that a conflagration is raging in the city,—it resounds like the signal-gun when the enemy approaches.

2. *Lord Jesus!* This is the cry of the new-born babe in Christ, the exclamation of the aged pilgrim who is leaving the world—it is the utterance of all their grief and their hope.

3. *Lord Jesus!* This is our sword, our pilgrim's staff, our whole dependence. Stephen commits his soul into the hands of his King,—"Lord Jesus, receive my spirit"! O Sun and blessed refuge of the soul! we are happy when we fall into these priestly hands, and are offered up on this altar. Many an individual becomes aware only in the last moments of his life, that he has a soul, which can no longer walk in the same way with the flesh. Whither shall this soul go? Shall it return to the world? But the gate is closed. Shall it fall into the hands of Satan? That would be an awful doom. Shall it fall into the hands of the Almighty? But He is a consuming fire. Shall it seek Jesus? But it does not believe in Him. Cruel perplexity! Stephen's soul enjoys a holy

(i)

calm—it knows the way of peace, He reposes on the bosom of his Mediator : " Lord Jesus, receive my spirit ! "

(a)   *Krummacher*

LORD OF HIMSELF

Lord of himself—that heritage of woe !

(b)   *Byron*

" LORD, LORD "

" *Not every one that saith unto Me, Lord, Lord.*" *etc.* (Matt. vii. 21–23)

1. Notice a characteristic of this Gospel. St. Matthew is methodical in arrangement of facts. The habit was acquired officially, before he became a disciple. He arranges in tables things that are alike. The Sermon on the Mount is one such collection. The parables in chapter xiii., which explain the Kingdom of Heaven, is another such. He writes of Christ as the King of the Jews. " Thy King cometh unto thee." Briefly, the Gospel is about the King, the kingdom, and the laws of that kingdom. The Sermon on the Mount is the code of laws for the Kingdom of Heaven. It is not a directory for those seeking the Way of Salvation, but for those who have already found the way and are the members of the Kingdom.

(c)

2. Chap. v. (3–12) present to us specimens of the subjects of the Kingdom of Heaven. Their peculiarities are in striking contrast to those of any kingdom of this world.

They are described as

" The poor in spirit," " They that mourn," " The meek," " They which hunger and thirst after righteousness," " The merciful," " The pure in heart," " Peacemakers," " They which are persecuted for righteousness' sake."

These have " The Law written in their hearts," according to the promise, Jer. xxxi. 33, identical with this Code.

The principles of their conduct are as here supplied :-

1. The Law of their Conversation (v. 37).
2. The Law of their Actions (v. 38, 39).
3. The Law of Prayer (vi. 9).
4. The Law of Faith (vi. 25).
5. The New Law of Love (vii. 12).

Following this, we have specimens of Hypocritical, or deceived members of the Messiah's Kingdom.

Those who " know the Law but do it not "; who appear amongst men to be genuine members thereof.

Of these there are " *Many*."

They are not described as " wicked," or gross sinners : for they seek admittance to heaven on the ground of being Christ's recognised servants on earth,—where they had position, prominent workers: They " taught in Christ's Name," " cast out devils," did " many wonderful works." Yet there was a leak in the ship, it sunk before it got to the harbour. How was this ?

(d)

1. In the words of rejection they are described as doers of ἀνομία = *lawless-workers*, *i.e.* The New Law was not written on their hearts—their conduct had not been regulated by the Code of Laws as taught in the Sermon on the Mount. Hence their sentence is *abite*, not *venite*.

(e)

2. Another reason for their rejection may be found from the leading idea of St. Matthew— Christ as KING. These had followed a Christ of their own imagination, not the Christ of the Bible. They had never taken Christ as their King. " 'Lord, Lord' is a cumbersome word," said Rutherford. They had " not so learned Christ," as to know the necessity of self-denial and crucifixion of the whole body of sin. They were not prepared to " follow the Lamb whithersoever He leadeth."—Hence His " *I know you not.*"

f)

3. A third reason may have been " *Ye worship, ye know not what.*" Just as the Samaritans were heathen, and not Israelites at all, though they copied the Jews and set up their own temple, and were anxious to be identified as the descendants of the Ten Tribes. They called themselves Jews and were not. So these thought it enough to have external likeness to the Members of the Kingdom. To join in public worship, partake of solemn rites, to call Christ " Lord "—in order to be His people, overlooking the great fundamental fact of Regeneration of the Holy Spirit, and that kind of knowledge of Christ which the Lord commends in Peter.

" Blessed art thou . . . for flesh and blood hath not revealed it unto thee, but My Father which is in Heaven."

They knew not Christ after this manner, consequently they knew not whom they worshipped ; and in the end He disowned them.

(g)

LORD'S PRAYER, THE

In the prayer our Lord taught His disciples, all the relationships in which we stand to God are taken up. The believer prays as :

1. A Child from Home .	" Our Father which art in heaven."
2. A worshipper . . .	" Hallowed be thy name."
3. A subject	" Thy kingdom come."
4. A servant	" Thy will be done in earth as it is in heaven."
5. A Beggar	" Give us this day our daily bread."
6. A Debtor	" And forgive us our debts, as we forgive our debtors."
7. A Sinner amid temptation and evil . .	" And lead us not into temptation, but deliver us from evil."

Three reasons are added.

1. Do this, Lord, for it will help on Thy kingdom.
   " For Thine is the kingdom."
2. Do it, Lord, for Thou art able.
   " For Thine is the power."
3. Do it, Lord, for it shall be for Thy glory.
   " For Thine is the glory, for ever. Amen."

(h)

LORD'S SUPPER

"Do this in remembrance of Me" (Luke xxii. 19)

A great number of the baptised regularly partake in the public services in order to hear the preaching of the word and the prayers of the Church; but partake of the Supper, it may be said, not at all. A Christianity of that sort we must designate as very incomplete, and missing the highest. We can only ask such Christians whether —taking for granted that they really believe in Christ, love Him, *and wish to remain in Him,* as branches in the vine (John xv. 4)—whether they can answer for excommunicating *themselves.*

The means of grace provided by the Church call to us from beginning to end—

"Keep Jesus Christ in memory." "Come, for all things are now ready."

(a)   *Martensen*

LORD'S SUPPER

"Do this."

Do not let us fence the Tree of Life. God gives us the way to it in Christ. All that is needed is, "I am ill; I wish I were well; *I hate and abhor myself;* I have faint hopes of deriving any benefit: but I will trust Him, and *do, in remembrance of Him, what He bade me do.*

(b)   *General Gordon*

LORD'S SUPPER, THE CHURCH OF ENGLAND DOCTRINE OF

1. Zuinglius, the Swiss Reformer, a contemporary of Martin Luther, taught that the Lord's Supper is nothing more than a commemorative act, in which the bread and the wine are symbols and memorials of the death and passion of the Lord, and in which we remind ourselves—in obedience to the command of Christ—of what took place eighteen hundred years ago upon the summit of Mount Calvary. According to this view, there is a certain benefit accruing to the communicant from a right participation. He receives the blessing which arises from obedience. He receives the blessing which flows from the fact that he has been reminded, in a lively and graphic and touching way, of the dying of the Redeemer upon the Cross. But he receives nothing more. There is, absolutely, no communication whatever of supernatural grace. This is the view of Zuinglius, and of those who follow him; but it is not the view of the Church of England.

(c)

2. The theory of "the objective presence" of Christ in the sacrament of the Lord's supper. Suppose that I—an authorized minister of the Church of God—am standing by the table of the Lord and conducting the Communion Service. I have invited the communicants. In their name and my own I have made the confession of sin—in all its terms of deep humiliation and self-abasement. For myself and them I have pronounced the absolution and lifted off, for myself and them—if we be truly penitent and believing—the load of guilt, and passed on to the "comfortable words" as addressed by Christ and His Apostles to all who believe on the Saviour's name. Then, after arranging in due order the bread and the wine, so as to bring them conveniently within the reach

of my hands, I have uttered the prayer of consecration, and performed all the ceremonies enjoined in this solemn part of the service by the Church of England. Suppose that now, at this moment,—the thing, of course, could not possibly happen,—but suppose that now I were to quit the communion table and descend into the vestry—*what have I left upon the holy table?* A great deal depends upon the answer you give to this question. Some say, "You have left the Body and Blood of Christ." The Roman Catholic says so—of course I mean, if it was a priest of his own faith who had been performing the act of consecration. My consecration he would regard as valueless. The Roman Catholic tells you that—after the words of consecration—the whole substance of the bread is converted into the substance of the Body of Christ, and the substance of the wine is converted into the substance of His blood; so that the bread and the wine no longer remain, but the Body and Blood of Christ are substituted in their place. A miracle has been wrought; a distinct, and, to us, a most incredible miracle. The change is not a spiritual change, but a real and miraculous conversion of the substance of the bread and the wine into the very Body of Christ, which was born of the Blessed Virgin, and was crucified upon Calvary.

(d)

3. Others hold substantially the same view, though not in exactly the same form. They, too, would say, "You have left on the holy table the Body and Blood of the Lord Jesus Christ." Now observe that with these theorists—Roman Catholics and others—the idea is this, that after consecration some mysterious virtue, whatever it may be, is infused into the elements, and transforms them into something which they were not before; and *resides in them*—quite apart from, and independently of the person who receives them. Whatever this presence is, it is there—in the bread and the wine. It is there—lying on the table—a mysterious substance with mysterious properties. It has nothing to do with you. It will remain just what it is, whether you take it or leave it alone. This presence *in* the bread and wine irrespective of the receiver—independent of Him—is called the "objective presence" of Christ in the Holy Eucharist; and this presence of Christ the Church of England most decidedly *does not teach.*

(e)

4. Sacerdotalism. You will perceive the immense power which this doctrine puts into the hands of the Priesthood. In fact, we may say that it is the chief basis on which the fabric of Priestly assumption is built. Believe, if you can, that I am one of a caste of men who have the power of turning bread and wine into the Body and Blood of Christ; and believe, too, that your participation in that Body and Blood is essential to your salvation—well—what then? Why, then I am your master, I have you at my feet. You cannot get to heaven except through acts which I alone, and such as I, can perform for you; and you lie at my mercy. I stand to you in the very place of Christ Himself. Consider again, you that know your Bibles, the extreme improbability that is thrown around the view, in whatever form it appears, by the significant silence of Holy Scripture upon the subject.

(f)

Is it conceivable that if the ministers of Christ were able to wield this tremendous, this awful, this almost terrible power, there should be no mention of the fact in the pages of the New Testament? We never hear of the matter in connection with the Apostles themselves. There are three pastoral epistles—letters, we may say, to young clergymen—written for the express purpose of pointing out to them their duties, their privileges, their responsibilities—the two to Timothy, and the one to Titus; if it were a part of their office to turn bread and wine into the Body and Blood of Christ, is it conceivable that so tremendous a subject should be passed over in silence? And yet there is not a syllable in the three epistles that makes the slightest allusion to it. And yet again—when the Apostle Paul is speaking of the claims which Christian ministers have to the respect of the people, and to maintenance at their hands, he bases that claim, *not* on the mysterious power of offering sacrifice which some suppose them to possess, but on the simple fact that it is their business to preach the Gospel. "Do ye not know that they who minister about heavenly things live of the sacrifice; and they who wait at the altar are partakers with the altar?" There the old state of things is referred to. But now the basis is shifted. No longer sacrifice, but preaching is the ground of the claim. "Even so hath the Lord who ordained that they who *preach the Gospel* should live of the Gospel."
(a)

5. **The Teaching of the Church of England.** Go back to the table on which the bread and wine is laid and left, *What is there?* Consecrated bread and wine—bread and wine set apart, solemnly, for the service of God, and not to be used for any common purpose, to be treated with all proper respect—but still only bread and wine; and the blessing, the grace—for supernatural grace is connected with this sacrament—the grace is given, in the right receiving, to the true believer in the Lord Jesus Christ, and to no one else.

This is the teaching of the Church of England.

Let appeal be made to her own documents in confirmation of the assertion.

The Catechism speaks thus:

(i,) "What is the outward part, or sign of the Lord's supper? Bread and wine, which the Lord hath commanded to be received."

"What is the inward part, or thing signified? The Body and Blood of Christ, which are verily and indeed taken and received by the faithful in the Lord's Supper."

"What are the benefits whereof we are partakers thereby? The strengthening and refreshing of our souls by the Body and Blood of Christ, as our bodies are by the bread and wine."

(ii.) The Communion Office itself.—"If with a true penitent heart and lively faith, we receive that Holy Sacrament, then we spiritually eat the flesh of Christ, and drink His Blood; then we dwell in Christ, and Christ in us; we are one with Christ, and Christ with us."

(iii.) The rubric at the end of the Communion Service uses these words: "The sacramental bread and wine remain in their very natural substances, and, therefore, may not be adored, for that were idolatry to be abhorred of all faithful Christians."

(iv.) The Twenty-ninth Article asserts that the wicked and faithless communicants are in no wise partakers of Christ—*which they must be if Christ is identified with the elements*—but that they eat and drink the sign, not the thing signified, the husk and not the kernel—and that to their condemnation.

(v.) To sum up: the teaching of the Church of England is, that the Lord's Supper is a commemoration; but that it is much more than a commemoration, that grace is imparted in it; that the elements, the bread and the wine, remain unaltered in their natural substance; that no magical change passes over them; but still, that they are, by God's blessing, the medium of communicating spiritual strength and refreshment of an extraordinary kind, to him who comes in faith and penitence to partake of the Holy Ordinance. She sets up no very extreme standard of holiness or knowledge to be reached by those who would be communicants, but invites all who "truly and earnestly repent of their sins, and are in love and charity with their neighbours, and who intend to lead a new life"—to draw near with faith, and to partake of the feast which has been prepared for His people by the rich bounty of the Lord Jesus Christ.
(b)   *Gordon Calthrop*

LORD'S SUPPER: CONTRAST

(i.) The Divine command to Adam and Eve, "Thou shalt not eat," with (ii.) the words of the Lord Jesus, "Take, eat." Man *ate* in utter ignorance of the sequel, in the case of the forbidden fruit, for death was not then known; so man may eat in utter ignorance of the sequel in the case of sacramental bread. In the first case he ate in trust in self, distrust in God, and communion with Satan. In the second case he eats in trust in God, distrust in self, and communion with God. To the world both eatings are foolishness, yet they are the wisdom of God.
(c)   *General Gordon*

LORD'S SUPPER

"*Henceforth drink*" (Mat. xxvi. 29)

This implies that the Lord's Supper has not only a commemorative and retrospective, but also a prophetic and prospective meaning. It not only carries us back to the time of the Crucifixion, strengthening our vital union with the Redeemer, and conveying to us anew, by the power of the Holy Spirit, through faith, all the blessings of His atoning sacrifice; but it is also a foretaste and anticipation of the great Marriage Supper of the Lamb which He has prepared for His Church at His last advent.
(d)   *P. Schaff*

LORD'S SUPPER

(John vi.)

This discourse bears the same relation to the Lord's Supper as the discourse with Nicodemus (iii.) does to Baptism, *i.e.* it expresses the *general idea* which precedes and underlies the sacramental rite as subsequently instituted.
(e)   *Ibid*

LORD'S SUPPER

"*As I have loved you*" (John xiii. 34)

The Lord's Supper is the Sacrament by which the καθὼς of His sacrificial death is brought
(f)

home to the minds of His people ; the ethical fruit that would spring from that death itself, viz. a company of believers living in the fellowship of brotherly love, shall now be realized by the Supper as the lively representation of His sacrificial death and the substitute for His presence.

(a)　　　　　　　　　　　　　　　　*Lange*

LORD'S SUPPER, NAMES OF THE

Dr. Waterland groups together the following names, successively, of the Sacrament of the Lord's Supper :

1. "The breaking of Bread."	Acts ii. 42.	A.D.	33.
2. Communion.	1 Cor. x. 16.	,,	57.
3. The Lord's Supper.	1 Cor. xi. 20.	,,	57.
4. Oblation.	Clem. Rome.	,,	95.
5. Sacrament.	Pliny.	,,	104.
6. Eucharist.	Ignatius.	,,	107.
7. Sacrifice.	Just. Mart.	,,	150.
8. Commemoration, or Memorial.	,,　　　,,		150.
9. Passover.	Origen.	,,	249.
10. Mass = Missa.	Ambrose.	,,	385.

(b)

LORD'S SUPPER

" *Till He come* " (1 Cor. i. 26)

Holy Scripture thus put the Supper in connection with the last things. So the words of the Lord, "I will not drink henceforth," etc. (Matt. xxvi. 29), = that the Supper is a fact-prophecy, a pre-representation and anticipation of that union with the Lord which shall one day take place in the kingdom of bliss ; and not only union with the Lord, but also the deep communion of love and life which these will bind believers to each other. For, by means of this Supper, believers are formed into one body, since they all " become partakers of the same bread " [all eating one food = a mysterious relationship, physically and spiritually]. Among all nations, eating in common, or the appropriation (assimilation) of the same meal, is held as a sign of a closer relation, a more intimate communion ; we even meet with a presentiment that eating in common also brings us into a mysterious relation to each other. This is fulfilled in its deepest sense in the mystery of the Lord's Supper. . . . Therefore the Supper is most properly a congregational transaction.

(c)　　　　　　　　　　　　　　*Martensen*

LORD'S SUPPER, THE

Words of Administration in the Communion Service.

(i.) *The Bread*—" Take and eat this in remembrance . . . and, feed on Him," etc.

(ii.) *The Wine*—" Drink this in remembrance," etc.

(d)

1. *In remembrance* = a memorial feast—St. Paul : " As oft as ye do this . . . ye do *celebrate* the Lord's death till He come."

(i.) Keeping in mind the great Redemptive facts ; atonement, substitution.

(ii.) A symbolical confession that each of us deserved to be an object of Divine wrath, but are

thankful that God appointed and accepted a Substitute for us, by which we are reconciled to God.

The wine that we drink reminds us that Christ died, but not for Himself.

Thus far In Memoriam.

(e)

2. It is plain, where true religion is concerned, and where spiritual life has begun, there is an actual *present* to be dealt with ; so we come to consider the Lord's Supper as a *means of grace*, whereby we partake of spiritual food, for the strengthening and refreshing of our souls.

That food is Christ Himself—" The Bread of life." " Christ who is our life." " The Resurrection and the Life." If we eat not, etc., " we have no life in us," *i.e.* spiritually. For the *flesh profiteth nothing. The words are spirit and life.*

(f)

3. *When do we partake of Christ ?* Is it in this ordinance only, or in others too ? This is the highest means of grace, the gathering of all into one ; but not the only one—This for believers only —This preserves life—others quicken.

The Jewish Passover was not kept when rite of circumcision was neglected.

(g)

4. Rebuke to those who go away, and plead low standard of spirituality—a sickly child needs nourishment—it is the condition of future health and robustness. This ordinance is the place where the children of the Lord are fed.

(h)

THE LORD'S TABLE

He was for drawing together all the people of God, wherever they could meet, and was willing to join in a universal Communion with Christians of every name. When, on one occasion, he had preached in a chapel where none but baptized adults were admitted to the Sacrament, he wished to have communicated with them, but he was told respectfully, " You cannot sit down at *our* table." He only calmly replied, " I thought it was the *Lord's* table."

(i)　　　　　　*Sidney, " Memoirs of R. Hill "*

" LORD, WHITHER GOEST THOU ? " Κύριε, ποῦ ὑπάγεις ; " *Domine, quo vadis ?* " (John xiii. 36.)

The question of Peter has furnished the name to a church outside the city of Rome, on the spot where, according to the legend, Peter, having from love of life escaped from prison, was confronted by the appearance of Christ, and asked Him : " Lord, whither goest Thou ? " The Lord replied, " I go to Rome, to be crucified again," whereupon the disciple returned to his prison and cheerfully suffered martyrdom on the cross. *Si non e vero. e ben trovato.*

(j)　　　　　　　　　　　　　　　*P. Schaff*

LOSS

Friend, because it is a dangerous thing to be walking towards a place of darkness and anguish, and because, notwithstanding, this is the journey that most of the poor souls in the world are taking, I have thought it my duty, for preventing thee, to tell thee what sad success those souls have had,

(k)

that have persevered therein. Why, friend, it may be—nay, twenty to one—thou hast had thy back to heaven, and thy face towards hell, ever since thou didst come into the world. Why, I beseech thee, put a little stop to thy earnest race, and take a view of what entertainment thou art like to have, if thou do indeed and in truth persist in thy course. "Thy ways lead down to Death, and thy steps to Hell." It may be, indeed, the path is pleasant to the flesh; but the end thereof will be bitter to thy soul. Hark! dost thou not hear the bitter cries of them that are newly gone before thee, saying, "Let him dip the tip of his finger in water, and cool my tongue, that is so tormented in this flame." Dost thou not hear them say, "Send one from the dead, to prevent my father, my brother, my father's house, from coming to this place of torment?" Shall not these mournful cries pierce thy flinty heart? Wilt thou stop thine ears, and shut thine eyes? And wilt thou not regard? Take warning, and stop thy journey ere it be too late. Wilt thou be like the silly fly, that is not quiet unless she be either entangled in the spider's web or burnt in the candle? Oh, sinner, sinner, there are better things than Hell to be had! There is Heaven, there is God, there is Christ, there is communion with an innumerable assembly of saints and angels! Consider; would it not wound thee to thy heart, to come to thy death-bed, having thy sins flying in thy face, thy conscience uttering, of itself, thunder claps against thee, the thoughts of God terrifying thee, Death with his merciless paw seizing upon thee, devils standing ready to scramble for thy soul, and Hell enlarging itself to swallow thee up? For, mark, Death doth not come alone to an unconverted soul; but with such company as, wast thou sensible of it, would make thee tremble. Hell cometh with Death to the ungodly. Here comes Death and Hell unto thee! Death goeth into thy body, and separates soul and body asunder. Hell stands without, to crush thy soul with its everlasting grinders. Lo, it will come to this! Blessed are those that through Christ's mercies, by faith do escape these soul murdering companions!"

(a)   *John Bunyan*

Loss

"I'm a ruined man, I've lost my all!" said a ruined merchant to his family. "*All?*" said his wife; "no, *I'm* left." "All, papa?" said his eldest boy; "*here am I.*" "And I too," said his little girl. "I'm not lost, papa," said Eddie. "And you have your *health* left," repeated his wife, "and your hands to work with." "And *I* can help you," said his eldest son. "And you have your two feet, papa, to carry you about, and your two eyes to see with," said little Eddie. "And you have God's promises," said the grandmother. "And a good God," said the wife. "And a heaven to go to," said the little girl. "And Jesus who came to fetch us there," said the eldest boy. "God forgive me," said the poor merchant, bursting into tears, "I have *not* lost my all; what have I lost compared with what I have left?" And so he took comfort and started afresh in the strength of the Lord, casting all his care upon Him.

(b)

LOST

Souls are *lost*, not because they have no interest in the death of Christ, but because, though His death has atoned for their sins, they *reject* Him and His salvation.

Men *perish*, not because they have sinned, but because they *refuse* salvation.

Men *perish*, not because there is some irresistible *decree* hindering them, but because of the exercise of a daring *free-will*.

They resist, and vanquish the infinite mercy of God. They trample under foot every message of His love. They do despite to every influence of the Spirit, and so they die by their own hand—the death of the suicide.

(c)

LOST, ALL IS NOT

Whatever be lost, one thing is yet to be saved—thy hungering soul, her peace, and the life to come.

Hast thou lost money and riches? Thy soul is worth immeasurably more.

Is thy past a failure, undoing even thy future? Behold eternity, and work for that.

Wast thou deceived in love? Love will save thee at the last.

Is thy life degraded? Look upon Life exalted on the Cross.

Has the world not satisfied thee? There is heaven: try it!

Have earth's joys proved faithless? There is an heritage to come.

How little then is lost, even if it be thy all, and how much there remains to be gained! . . . It is not too late to begin a new, a holy, happy, and even joyful life.

(d)   *Letters from Hell*

LOST, NOT

Dear is the spot where Christians sleep,
    And sweet the strain which angels pour;
Oh, why should we in anguish weep?
    They are not lost, but gone before.

(e)   *Anonymous*

LOST, THE (Rom. v.)

We have reason to believe that the lost shall bear to the saved no greater proportion than the inmates of a prison do to the mass of the community.

(f)   *Hodge*

LOT'S WIFE

"*Remember Lot's wife*" (Luke xvii. 32)

Four reasons for the injunction :

(i.) *Because she looked back.*
This would make bad ploughing. She started under the awakening words of her husband and the angel, so far well. But though she left Sodom, she did not get to Zoar.

(ii.) *Because "one was taken and another left."*
She fled in company with God's people—her husband—he taken and she left.

(iii.) *Because she became a pillar of salt*=unimpressionable—we die as we live.

(iv.) *Because God laid hold of her.*
Supernatural means added to the usual, and yet she did not reach Zoar.

The same sun which softens wax hardens clay.

(g)

LOVE, The Banner over me was

During the Cuban civil war of 1867, an Englishman who got amongst them was tried as a spy, convicted, and condemned to be shot. The American and the English ministers remonstrated with the Cuban authorities, pointing out that he was innocent, but in vain. The time for the execution was fixed. The man's grave was dug. He was brought out, and the muskets of the soldiers were pointed at him, when the English and American ministers galloped up on horses; both dismounted, and wrapping the flags of their nations round the prisoner, shouted to the Cuban soldiers, "Fire on our flags if you dare!" They did not fire.

(a)   *Moody*

LOVE OF CHRIST, THE

A beautiful similitude. That, like as the heart of Jonathan was knit with the heart of David at his modest account of himself after the slaughter of Goliath, and he loved him as his own soul, and covered him with his own princely garment; so Christ loves us, even more than His own life, for He gave that for us, and we are one (knit) with Him; and He has put the garment of His own righteousness upon us. Such love was indeed "wonderful, passing the love of women."

(b)

LOVE OF CHRIST

I see His bottomless and boundless love and kindness, and my jealousies and ravings, which, at my first entry into this furnace, were so foolish and bold as to say to Christ, who is Truth itself, in His face, Thou liest. I had well nigh lost my grip; I wondered if it was Christ or not, for the mist and smoke of my perturbed heart made me mistake my Master, Jesus. My faith was dim, and hope frozen and cold; and my love, which caused jealousies, had some warmness, and heat, and smoke, and no flame at all; yet I was looking for some good of Christ's old claim to me. I thought I had forfeited all my rights, but the tempter was too much upon my counsels, and was still blowing the coal. Alas! I knew not well before what good skill my Intercessor and Advocate, Christ, hath in pleading and pardoning me such follies.

(c)   *Samuel Rutherford*

LOVE OF CHRIST, THE

Blessed would you be of the Lord if you would help a poor bankrupt, and cause others of your acquaintance in Christ to help me to pay my debt of love, even real praises to Christ my Lord. Let me charge you in the Lord, as you will answer to Him, help me in this duty (which He hath tied about my neck with a chain of such singular expressions of His lovingkindness) to set on high Christ, to hold in my honesty at His hands, for I have nothing to give Him. Oh that He would arrest and comprise my love and my heart for all! I am a bankrupt, who have no more free goods in the world for Chirst, save that it is both the whole heritage I have, and all my moveables besides. Lord, give the thirsty mana drink. Oh to be over ears in the well! Oh to be swimming over head and ears in Christ's love! I would not have Christ's love entering in me, but I would enter into it, and be swallowed up of that love. But I see not myself

here, for I fear I make more of His love than of Himself: whereas He Himself is far beyond and much better than His love. Oh if I had my sinful arms filled with that lovely one Christ! Blessed be my rich Lord Jesus, who sendeth not away beggars from His house with an empty dish; He filleth the vessel of such as will come and seek. We might beg ourselves rich (if we were wise), if we would but hold out our withered hands to Christ, and learn to seek, ask, and knock.

(d)   *Ibid*

LOVE OF GOD, THE

"*God so loved the world*," etc. (John iii. 16)

1. A love, not of complacency, but of *compassion* —"*so loved*."
2. A *self-sacrificing* love which "gave His only begotten Son,"=best, most precious thing (cf. Abraham offering up his son Isaac).
3. A *universal* love. Observe the point of this for a Jew like Nicodemus. "The world" consisted then of Jew and Gentile; now of believers and unbelievers. The Jew had no monopoly of God's love.
6. *Love that makes the way of salvation easy*. "Whosoever believeth." The word "Refuge" was made plain, so that "he that runs might read." We use "great plainness of speech." Not easy for the Father nor the Son, but easy for "us." Easy for every one—"whosoever." It is as if our name was in the Bible.
5. Love which saves from *great peril*, "perish."
(i.) There is a possibility of perishing—or why this?
(ii.) "Hell," "Lake of fire," terrible realities— or this is mockery.
(iii.) No repentance there (36)="ABIDETH *in death*."
6. Love which bestows *eternal life* (36, 38). The cry "Let me live"=not be annihilated. Cf. the search after the Philosopher's Stone, Elixir of Life, Perpetual Motion, etc. More than all realized here. "Hath"=a present possession, not future merely.

(e)   *Cf. Godet*

LOVE OF GOD (Eph. iii. 18)

That ye may know the breadth, length, depth, and height, etc.

Breadth=Expanse of the Gospel of God's love— it covers the earth;
Length=To all times and needs—*evermore;*
Depth=To recover from the uttermost depth— power of cleansing from sins of crimson and scarlet dye;
Height=To the right hand of God where Jesus sits enthroned with *all power and might*, as a Saviour of all who come unto Him.

(f)

After the last French war the Roman Catholic Archbishop of Paris was imprisoned. His cell had a window shaped like a cross, and with a pencil he wrote upon the arms of the cross that they denoted the height, the length, the breadth, and the depth of God's love. That man knew something of what God's love was.

(g)   *Moody*

"Love is the Fulfilling of the Law" (Rom. xiii. 10).

"*Without which whoso liveth is counted dead before Thee*" (Collect for Quinquagesima Sunday.)

We may be as orthodox as Athanasius and as scrupulous as Jerome; we may be daily and ostentatiously building to God seven altars, and offering a bullock and a ram on every altar, and yet be as sounding brass and as a clanging cymbal, if our life shows only the leaves of profession, without the golden fruit of action. If *love* shows not itself by deeds of love, then let us not deceive ourselves,—God is not mocked,—our Christianity is heathenism, and our religion a delusion and a sham.

(*a*) *Archd. Farrar*

ILLUSTRATIVE CONTRASTS

1. From Fiction

(i.) A girl of humble station, gentle, poor. Her means small, her desire to do good large. (Poverty is no hindrance to exercise of Christian love. John Pounds, the Plymouth cobbler, Sarah Martin, the Yarmouth seamstress, William Marshman, the bookseller's apprentice, have done work for Christ greater than many a prince. It needs only a kind heart, and the cup of cold water, and the mite of the widow are more to God than the stinted gift of the wealthy). A little girl in the school had been punished by the foolish punishment then in vogue, by putting a fool's cap on her head. She stood in disgrace—no one would notice her—and her little heart swelled with pride and bitterness. Then Clare went up to the sufferer and disgraced one, and kissed her before all, teachers and companions. She tried to be a shield for those who suffered from the cruelty and the injustice of the many.

(*b*)

(ii.) *Selfishness*

Colonel Marrables was one of those men who, through their long, useless lives, always contrive to live well, eating and drinking of the best; to lie softly; to go about in purple and fine linen, yet have never any money; to lie, to cheat, indulge every passion, though the cost to others might be ruin for life; to know no gods but his own bodily senses, and no duty but that which he owed to these gods; to consume, and to produce nothing; to love no one but himself; to learn nothing but the outward demeanour of a gentleman; to care not at all for his country, or even for his profession; to have no creed, no friends, no conscience; to be troubled with nothing that could touch his heart: such was the life of Colonel Marrables. He never even asked himself whether he had aught to regret before death, or to fear afterwards. There are many such in the world. Men give them dinners, and women smile upon them. They have never lacked cigars or champagne; there are even some hearts whom they are said to have broken. Upon the whole they are popular. Popular: yes! Like to like; the world loves its own, and men, and women too, who are not fit for any decent society, have free *entrée* sometimes into that miscalled the best.

(*c*)

2. From History

(i.) In the eighteenth century when a Sardanapalus sat upon the throne of France, and harlots toyed with the crown in the chambers of St. Louis, lived a woman, who, being of no origin, became, through the king's vices, the mistress of the palace, and, in all but name, the ruler of the country. Almost the only record of her personal feelings is the expression of her utter and deathful weariness; and when, at the age of forty-two, she had breathed her last, on her death-bed of splendid infamy, the king, to whom she had sold the eternal jewel of her soul, had no remark to make upon the day of her funeral, but one that breathed a brutal cynicism. "The memory of the wicked shall rot!"

(ii.) Another, born shortly after her death. Young, lovely, brilliant, accomplished Elizabeth Fry. Again and again she dreamed at night a stormy sea was breaking upon her, angry billows threatened to sweep her away; but when she had chosen to serve God and not the world, the sea broke upon her dreams in menacing breakers as before, but troubled her not; she seemed to be standing beyond its wrath. She took it as an omen that she should not be drowned in the sea of the world. She won the immortal glory of reforming the miseries and winning the souls of women in English prisons. "I can say one thing," she remarked upon her death-bed, "since my heart was touched, at the age of 17, I believe I have never awaked from sleep, either in sickness or in health, either by day or by night, without my first waking thought being how best I might serve the Lord."

(*d*)

3. Two Lives of the Last Century

(i.) *Beau Brummel*, the wretched fop who dangled about the Court of the Regency, celebrated in it for his ties, his snuff-boxes, his canes, and his kid gloves, and for a few paltry sayings where rudeness supplied the place of witticism. For him the youth of folly was not merely followed by an old age of vice, by an old age of madness and of destitution; and when he ended, without a tear being shed for him, his wasted life—when he gave back to the God who had created him the dust of his mortal body, and the shipwreck of his immortal soul, what other epitaph could be pronounced over such a man than that he had died, but that he had never lived?

(ii.) *John Howard* (*the philanthropist*), a gentleman of fortune, Sheriff of Bedfordshire in 1773, and regarding his high position, not as it conferred dignity, but as it imposed duty upon him, first in that den in which, two centuries earlier, John Bunyan had written *The Pilgrim's Progress*, became acquainted with the reeking infamy of English gaols. From that day the destiny of his life was fixed. He would live to remedy that one definite and formidable wrong. For that high purpose again and again he traversed England; again and again he travelled Europe, and he did not rest till the evil was removed. Then he took up the question of lazarettos. "I am not insensible to the dangers of such a journey, but I trust in the merciful Providence that hitherto has preserved me. I commit myself to the disposal of unerring Wisdom. Should it please God to cut off my life, let Him take it, but it is my strong and deliberate

(*e*)

conviction that I am pursuing the path of duty."
On the banks of the Dnieper, tending a sick-bed,
he caught the fever of which he died. And now
mark how only the "actions of the just smell
sweet and blossom in the dust." This was the
splendid tribute of Edmund Burke to that simple,
unlettered Christian man. "I cannot name this
gentleman," he said, "without remarking that his
labours and writings have done much to open
the hearts and sympathies of mankind. He had
visited Europe, not to survey the gorgeousness of
palaces, nor the stateliness of temples, but to dive
into the depth of dungeons, to plunge into the
infection of hospitals, to survey the mansions of
sorrow and pain; to take the gauge and the
dimensions of misery, depression, and contempt;
to remember the forgotten; to attend to the neglected; to visit the forsaken; and to compare and
to collate the distresses of men in all countries.
His plan is original, and it is as full of genius as it
is of humanity. It is a voyage of discovery, a
circumnavigation of charity." "What he did,"
says Jeremy Bentham, "for the service of mankind
was what scarce any man could have done, and no
man would do but himself. In the scale of moral
desert, the labours of the legislator and the writer
are as far below his, as the earth is below the
heaven." His was the truly Christian choice, the
lot in which is to be found the least that selfish
nature covets, and the most of what it shrinks
from. His kingdom was of the better world. He
died a martyr after living an apostle: "the poor
his clients, and Heaven's smile his fee."

(a)

4. With these compare General Gordon

There never breathed a man more humble, more
simple-minded, more abhorrent of flattery, more
indifferent to self, more sincerely religious. No
man ever put himself forward less; no man was
ever more sought after. When tidings of disaster
came from Egypt, the voice of the nation at once
declared that he was the one man to save us.
This man, who alone of men cares nothing for
distinction, is a mandarin of the highest order in
China, a pasha in Africa, the only Christian for
whom prayers have ever been offered, and for
whom they are yearly offered in Mecca—is known
as Chinese Gordon. "The lot," he once wrote,
"is cast evenly for us all. We are servants.
Sometimes our Master gives us work; at other
times He does not; and our feelings under both
circumstances should be the same." "You," he
wrote on another occasion, "are only called on at
intervals to rely on your God: with me it is
different; I am constantly in anxiety. Find me a
man, and I will take him as my helper, who utterly
despises money, name, gold, honour; one who
never wishes to see his home again; one who
looks to God as the source of good and the con-
troller of evil; one who has a healthy body and an
energetic spirit; one who looks on death as a
release from misery; and if you cannot find him,
then leave me alone. To carry myself is enough
for me; I want no other baggage."
But his life at Gravesend seems rarer in such a
man than his self-denying heroism. When engaged
in splendid public services, his house was sick-
room and hospital and almshouse in turn—more
like the abode of a missionary than of a colonel of
engineers. The troubles of all interested him
alike. The poor, the sick, and the unfortunate
were always welcome. Misery was a sufficient
claim for him. The workhouse and the infirmary
were his constant haunts. He seemed in his
labours to have no self. He said he had no right
to keep anything when he had once given himself
to God. Out of his many medals, there was only
one—of gold—given him by the Empress of China,
to which he seemed to attach any value. Suddenly
it disappeared. Years afterwards, it was acciden-
tally found that he had erased the inscription,
sold it for £10, and given the sum anonymously to
Canon Miller, for the relief of the sufferers from
the cotton famine. Specimens of vanity, and
pomposity, and greed, and self-assertion, and
common-placeness, and sleek success, and money-
getting, and exaggerated claims, and merciless
indifference to all but self, you may see on every
side, and in every rank; but how many are there
to whom the world trumpets its praise and utters
its fulsome adulations, who have one tithe of the
magnanimity and simple grandeur of this man!
How many have we among our belauded and be-
trumpeted littlenesses of self-seeking, ecclesiastical
and civil, like this man, whose life pours silent
contempt on gold?

(b)　　　　　　　　　　　　*Archd. Farrar*

A lover of God, a despiser of Mammon. In this
he (Gordon) outshines Peter the Hermit, Savonarola, and Havelock.

(c)　　　　　　　　　　　　　　　*Hake*

Love, Mutual (John xiii. 34, 35)

Christ urges the great duty of *Mutual Love* by
three arguments:
(i.) The *command* of their Master.
(ii.) The *example* of their *Saviour*.
(iii.) *The reputation of their profession.*
Brotherly love is the badge of Christ's disciples,
by this-
(i.) *He* knows them, (ii.) *others* (the world)
know them.

(d)　　　　　　　　　　　　　　*M. Henry*

"Love One Another" (John xiii. 34)

It results of itself that those who love one
another, are but practising and preparing themselves to extend their love outside of their own
circle into the whole world.

(e)　　　　　　　　　　　　　　　*Stier*

"Lovest Thou Me?" (John xxi. 15–17)

Notice-
(i.) The Threefold Address: "Simon, son of
Jonas";
(ii.) The Thrice-repeated Question: "Lovest
thou Me?—with the significant variations;
(iii.) The Three Commands—"Feed My lambs"
—varied significantly each time.

(f)

1. The Threefold Address: "Simon, son of Jonas"

"Thou shalt be called Peter:" Why not so
addressed now?
Peter had fallen—had denied Christ—had taken
off Christ's livery, and gone back to his old standing before he was a disciple.
This act of denial was equivalent to erasing his

(g)

Christian name of "Peter" from the Baptismal Register on High. He was no longer Peter, the "Rock-man," but Simon, son of Jonas, the son of his father—a natural man like others.

And this thrice-repeated address was intended to remind him of the significance of his act, and must have stung the susceptible disciple to the quick.

(*a*)

2. The Three-fold Question : "Lovest thou Me more than these ? "

(i.) He had said "Though all should deny Thee, yet will not I." He is now reminded of this. And moreover asked whether his love of Christ is of that high, exalted nature that the angels have for God—love, pure and unalloyed, wholly disinterested.

To both these covert questions Peter will have nothing to say. He makes no reply to "more than these." His sole reply is, "Lord, Thou knowest that I *love* Thee," using a word expressing a less exalted idea of love—and meaning that, I love thee as a *man* loves his friend dearly.

(ii.) The question is asked again, with the omission of "more than these." And again Peter made the same reply—using the same word for *love*.

(iii.) The question is asked the *third* time—and now the Lord uses Peter's own word "*Lovest thou Me*," on which came the tearful, heartfelt, outburst, "Lord, Thou knowest all things." Thou knowest my heart. Thou knewest me before I fell—notwithstanding all, "Thou knowest that I love Thee."

(*b*)

3 His Restoration, and the Three Commands

(i.) "Feed My lambs" (Lambkins), the young, and little ones of the flock.

(ii.) "Tend my sheep (both old and young)—all the flock."

(iii.) "Feed my sheeplings (My *very* dear ones)." "David had his Jonathan, Christ His John." (*Geo. Herbert*).

In these commands is indicated the true work of the Ministry : The finding suitable food for the whole flock—from the babe in Christ to the most experienced believer. Each must have his portion, and as he is able to bear it ; for they vary in age, in attainment, in experience, and in faith.

(*c*)

4. The main question and test of a Christian is Love."

Christ does not ask more than we can render. Not great faith, "Thou art the Christ," etc. ; Not martyrdom even—"I will go with Thee to prison and to death," but "Lovest thou Me ? " is the test ; and all can render that.

The Jew venerates Moses ; the Mahometan venerates Mahomet ; but the Christian *loves* Christ, and it is his happiness to know that Christ loves him. There is nothing like this in any other religion.

(*d*)

(i.) A Christian man was imprisoned for his faith, but he was weak, and the crown of martyrdom was not for him : after his release these words were found scratched on the wall of his cell : "Lord, Thou knowest that, though I could not die for Thee, yet Thou knowest that I *love* Thee."

(ii.) A touching story is told of a daft Scotch lad—"Poor Yettie." On a Saturday this lad called on the Minister of his parish and said, "Minister, let poor Yettie eat and drink with the Lord Jesus Christ to-morrow" (when the Lord's Supper would be administered). The Minister, knowing the boy's condition, tried to put him off ; but the boy was importunate, and the promise was given. On the following day the boy was in his place and partook of the rite. On his way home the boys of the village hooted and laughed at him for his act. He replied, "I mauna stop to talk wi ye—I have eaten and drunk with yon lovely man" (The Lord Jesus Christ). He passed on to his home, where he lived with an aged grandmother, refusing his supper for the same reason, "I have eaten and drunk with yon lovely man ; " he went up to his room, where there was a rickety chair and a miserable bed. Then kneeling down he was heard praying during the night, "This is a palace, it is paved with gold and silver," etc. And on the morrow still kneeling at that chair he was found, but stiff and cold in death.

What was this but *love ?* He could render no more—but he gave that, and that was enough.

(*e*)

Φιλέω and Ἀγαπάω

Jesus uses a word which expresses exalted and pure love of the highest type, such as unsinning angels have for God their Maker. But Peter knows himself better by this time ; he will not confess to such a love as this word implied—" I say not my love for Thee is of so exalted and pure a kind as that—I dare not say that I love Thee *more than others*." I dare not repeat the bold words I once rashly uttered "though all should deny Thee ; yet will not I." I dare not say one or the other. But, Lord, Thou knowest all things—Thou readest my heart, it is open to Thee as a book—and Thou knowest that I love Thee sincerely with a human-creature love, personally, affectionately, and dearly.

And who of us will venture to say, in the face of his many weaknesses and shortcomings and backslidings, that his love for Jesus is of that high, ennobling, and holy quality, such as Jesus first asks of Peter? But who of us, on the other hand, does not respond in our inmost hearts to that inferior, it may be, but more human and personal affection which Jesus knows of, and which Peter owns to, and beyond which he dares not go. Thou knowest that I love Thee—not as angels love God—but as man loves man, and friend loves friend.

(*f*)

Loving Christ and the World

" *He that* loveth *Me not* " (John xiv. 24)

Characteristic of the world. The world, as an ungodly world, loves itself ; its tendency is not centripetal but centrifugal ; hence it loves not Christ. Hence it keeps not Christ's word as a living word, for the reason that it lacks the bond that should hold it and Christ together—viz. the Spirit.

(*g*)

Lange

LUTHER AND THE REFORMATION

" Will a lion roar in the forest when he hath no prey ? " (Amos iii. 4–8)

1. Four centuries ago, Luther, the great German Reformer, was born into this world. He lived to shake all nations with his words and deeds; and yet some say, *" The Lord hath not done it."*

2. He was born in the thick darkness of the Middle Ages, and he struck a light that is still burning; we are living in that light; and yet some say, *" The Lord hath not done it."*

3. The prophet asks, " Will the lion roar when he hath taken no prey ?" Is not his roar, deep and loud, echoing through the forest, the indication that he hath taken prey? So must we believe of the Reformer: " The Lord God hath spoken, who can but prophesy ? "

The Reformation was not caused by Luther. No man can be the cause of a Reformation, any more than he can be the cause of a thunderstorm or an earthquake. The cause arises from the nature of things, as a cup, when more than full, runs over. Reformations are great moral thunder-storms, and are intended to purify and cleanse the atmosphere, when it has become unwholesome.

The Reformer (Luther) was but the electric discharge, the mouthpiece of current feeling, " the lion's roar," and which soon became general.

(a)

1. The Time in which he appeared

1483—a dangerous time for a man of independent action. One dominant Church. Christianity a semi-Paganism. One Pope dominant over kings and nations, people and souls. Any one who dared to question the *right* of what *was*, had his life burnt out of him. If the Pope said the sun went round the earth, and Galileo said it did not, Galileo must recant, or die in a dungeon.

If John Huss taught doctrines that differed from those of Rome, John Huss must be burnt at the stake. It was a dangerous time to speak your own mind. Yet, even then, *the lion roared*, and would be heard.

That time, moreover, was very important historically. Both the art of printing and the continent of America were discovered within a few years of Luther's birth. It was the birth-hour of modern history. Think what light has flooded the world, and what an impetus was given to the progress of the human race by these two great events in conjunction with the Protestant Reformation. A vivid contrast may easily be imagined by the possibility of these two events having come under the domination of the Pope of Rome ! Books, Bibles, thought, science, freedom, all tyrannized over and manacled. And that great land of the West put under the feet of one man in Europe, and dictated to by him as it was. This was the prey that the lion found, and hence his *roar*.

" This teaching of yours," said he, " is a lie, the Pope is a lie, the priests are a lie, the whole system is a lie ; man must be free to read, free to write, free to choose for himself." The bands of tyranny were snapped from that day ; the fruits of which we gather at this.

(b)

2. His Work of Reformation

He took men back to the Bible. He had had a peculiar religious history himself, and he knew the remedy for man's supreme need. He had no thought, however, of going against the Pope. It was when the Pope went against him, that the crash came. Luther was surprised that the Pope did not sympathize with him in teaching the people the Scriptures. He could not see what the Pope (Father in God) was for, if not for that. So one day Tetzel came selling his indulgences. The people said to Luther, " Our sins are pardoned." He asked, " Who can pardon sins, but God alone? This system is destructive of my teaching." Then he spoke out. The Pope sent a bull—" Send Dr. Martin, monk of Wittenberg, to Rome, and burn his writings by the common hangman."

Luther got hold of the bull, and said something to this effect: " Send me to Rome ; burn me ; burn my writings ! No. Look here, I BURN THIS." And he burnt the parchment before the eyes of all Europe. That did it. In God's name he defied the tyrant of the Middle Ages, and saved modern Europe. That was Luther's part in the work. *" The lion hath roared."*

But the Reformation was a work too big for one man—nay, it was not man's work at all—it blazed out almost everywhere after this torch had been applied. (Cf. Rev. viii. 5.) " These thunderings and voices and lightnings "= Reformation time. The evils had been accumulating for centuries. The cup of iniquity was full to overflowing. When thunder-clouds gather, there naturally follows an electric discharge ; so at that time the Reformation was a natural result of the accumulated evils.

(c)

3. The Man Himself

(i.) Of mean birth—rough, rude, and plain in speech and thought—reminding us of God's way in " choosing the weak and despised things of this world to confound things that are mighty." (The accidents of his birth remind us of Bethlehem—his parents were strangers in Isleben.) Such a man was wanted. There were others, good men, gentle men, scholars, yet unfit for the work because too deficient in the stronger qualifications of courage, fearlessness, strong convictions. Such a man was Luther ; and when he shook himself, stood defiant, and prepared for the battle, Rome trembled and the world listened.

(d)   *Cf. Carlyle's Essay on Luther*

M

MAD

Quem Deus vult perdere, prius dementat.

(a)   *Boswell's Johnson*, 1783

When God will punish, He will first take away the understanding.

(b)   *George Herbert*

MAGDALEN, THE (Luke vii. 36–50)

1. The Offence (36–39)

Simon rather friendly towards Jesus. Probably wanted to test Him. This circumstance was sufficient evidence that Jesus was *no* Prophet. (Nicodemus = " We know that Thou art a prophet.")

This woman, a sinner, had probably heard the Lord preach ; or He had looked on her—a ray of heaven itself—and had forgiven her sins.

Jesus was reclining on a couch, His feet outwards towards any one who entered the house. . . . Her act of loving ministry. . . . This contact of Jesus with *such* a woman offended Simon, who "thought within himself," etc.

(c)

2. The Parable (40–43)

Kindly, familiar, slightly humorous.

500d. = £16.   The Pharisee.

50d. = 32s.   The woman.

" This parable explains the relationship of this woman and yourself to Me."

(d)

3. The Application (44–47)

In the inverse order to the parable. The parable = Cause and effect. Now the Lord ascends from the effect to the cause. For instance,

(i.) The woman washed the Lord's feet with her tears.

Simon, whose duty it was, offered no water for the traveller's feet.

(ii.) She wiped them with her hair.

Simon offers no towel.

(iii.) She kissed the feet ceaselessly.

Simon gives his Guest no kiss of welcome.

(iv.) She anointed the feet.

Simon offers no oil for His head.

In fact, not Simon, but the woman has done the honours of the house. She had followed Jesus closely, and almost entered with Him.

The cause of this effect—their conduct respectively—is explained by the fact that she had been forgiven much, and he little. The evidence of this was to be seen in the degree of love each bore to Christ.

Do we then need much sin in order to love much? No. We need no more than we have ; but we need the knowledge of sin.

(e)

4. Conclusion (48)

Jesus reassures her : " Thy sins be forgiven thee." We are assured by " the witness of the Spirit " (Rom. viii.). The objection in verse 49, " They say," is met by, " But He said " (50) = He takes no note of their murmurs, but shows on what foundation forgiveness rests—" Thy faith," " Whosoever believeth " is saved. Let her go with this treasure ; rob her not of it ; let her not be discouraged by Pharisaic doubts. " Go in peace."

(f)   *Cf. Godet*

MAGDALEN, THE PENITENT

" The world, poor soul ! will have no pity on thee,
    But how should its compassion help thy case ?
The sin which heaps despair and shame upon thee,
    Man first creates, then brands it on thy face.

God only can decide why guilt should bend to
    The curb of laws unrighteous and untrue,
While good and ill and right and duty tend to
    The bane of most, the blessing of a few.

No pity from the world ! But vengeance never
    Spares the mean vice that wrought thy venal slough !
Who buys thy kiss and then insults thee, ever
    Sins a far deeper, viler sin than thou.

Shame, hunger, pain, and lonely desperation,
    Woman ! *may* cleanse thy sin of darkest dye ;
And while the world stamps thee for execration,
    Heaven, it may be, is listening to thy cry."
        Dall' Ongaro's " Pearl among the Potsherds."

(g)   *See Athenæum*, 1860.

MAGIC (Acts xix. 1, 2)

The essence of magic consists in this : The belief that by some external act—not connected with *moral* goodness, nor making a man wiser or better—communication can be ensured with the spiritual world. It matters not whether this be attempted by Ephesian letters, amulets, charms, curious books, or by Sacraments, or by Church ordinances, or priestly powers, whatever professes to bring God near to man, except by making man more like God, is of the same spirit of anti-Christ = magic.

(h)   *F. W. Robertson*

MAGNIFICAT, THE (Luke i. 39–55)

(39–45) *The visit :* Elizabeth, filled with Holy Ghost, loses her personality and speaks loud ; Mary, in the Spirit always at this time, spake quietly, and said, etc. = a great and untroubled depth of happiness. " Blessed is she that believed," which Zacharias did not.

(i)

(46–48) *Tone,* sweet, calm, solemn. Mary speaks her feelings on this :

(i.) " *Magnify* " God in all her thoughts : a larger space in her heart than usual. (Matt. Henry, " *Be ye also enlarged,*" after enlarging a chapel.)

(ii.) " *rejoiced,*" = the now past, distinguishing mercy, that she should be the mother of the Messiah.

(iii.) " *regarded* " = not her humility, she would not boast of that, but her low social position ; a descendant of kings, now a village maiden.

(iv.) " *call me blessed* " = what future generations shall say of her. (She, the humble one, is made great.)

(j)

(48–50) *Tone*, rising, more animated. Mary now speaks of the Divine cause.

(i.) " *Mighty* " = Almighty power creative here as at the beginning.

(ii.) " *Name* " = |Holy = Holiness is power, God's name declares what He is.

(iii.) " *Mercy* " = on them that fear Him, particularly on Mary and her cousin Elizabeth, as well as Abraham and Isaac to all generations.

(*a*)

(51–53) *Tone*, full and energetic.

Mary now speaks of how God's plan of redemption is to be developed. A new principle is introduced:—"weak things are to confound the mighty" (1 Cor. i.). In the choice of herself she sees this. The contrast is—

(i.) *Moral*, between the " proud " and " faithful ";

(ii.) *Social*, between the "rich" (mighty) and " the hungry " "of low degree."

" *He hath*," (twice) = emphatic.

They (the great ones) imagined to be the redeemers of the earth " He hath sent empty away."

" *The hungry* " = the toiling ones, artisans, like Joseph and Mary.

" *The rich* " = those gorged with wealth, who forget the Giver in the gift.

= The suffering and the prosperous.

(*b*)

(54–55) *Tone* = Cadence of song. *The Amen.* Mary recognises the moral necessity of the fact being accomplished : Since it is the fulfilment of God's promises : She has spoken of the *Present* and *Future.* Now she looks to the Past, and sees there the promise to the Fathers, here its fulfilment, therefore, " My soul doth magnify the Lord," etc.

(*c*)   *Cf. Godet*

MALADIES OF CHRISTIANS, Afflictions are the

Wise men seek remedies before their disease ; sensible patients, when they begin to complain ; fools, too late. Afflictions are the common maladies of Christians ; these you feel ; and, upon the first groans, seek for ease. Wherefore serves the tongue of the learned, but to speak words in season ? I am a scholar of those that can comfort you : if you shall, with me, take out my lessons, neither of us shall repent it. You smart and complain : take heed lest too much. There is no affliction not grievous : the bone that was disjointed cannot be set right without pain. No potion can cure us if it work not : it works not except it make us sick ; we are contented with that sickness which is the way to health.

(*d*)   *Bishop Hall*

MALICE

For malice will with joy the lie receive,
Report, and what it wishes true, believe.

(*e*)   *Yalden*

MAJORITY

One man and God have always been the majority. Cf. *Pascal* on man's alliance with the Infinite ; also Athanasius alone against the world.

(*f*)

MAMMON

The aristocracy of Feudalism has passed away, and has now given place to the aristocracy of the Money-bag,—the basest yet known. What generous heart can be hoodwinked into believing that loyalty to the money-bag is a noble loyalty ? Mammon ! cries the generous heart of all ages and countries, is the basest of known gods, even of known devils.

(*g*)   *Carlyle*

Mammon-Worshippers (Matt. vi. 24)

Some modes of his service :

If a man talks of *main chance*, meaning getting rich by money, or of " *Number one*," meaning " self," he is a servant of Mammon.

If a man, in making a bargain, thinks only of himself and gain, he is a servant of mammon.

The eager looks of those who would get money, the troubled looks of those who have lost it, worse, the gloating looks of those who have it, are sure signs of mammon service.

If our hope of well-being rests in house, land, business, money in store, and not upon God, we are servants of mammon.

If the loss thereof takes away all joy of life, and breaks thy heart, it indicates a servant of mammon.

If it will add one pang to thy death to leave house, trees, shop, books, thou art a servant of mammon.

(*h*)   *Geo. Macdonald.*

MAN

" *What is Man ?* "   (Ps. viii. 4.)

Questions :

1. The celebrated riddle of antiquity asked, " What animal is that which in the morning walks on four legs, at noon on two, and in the evening on three ? "

The riddle of to-day is, " Is man little lower than a divine being, or is he merely an improved animal ? "

(*i*)

2. Man came after the house had been built, furnished, and provisioned for him. But whence came he ? is the inquiry.

(*j*)

3. That living flood, pouring through these streets, of all qualities and ages, knowest thou whence it is coming, whither it is going ? From eternity onward to eternity ! These are apparitions : what else ? Are they not souls rendered visible, in bodies that took shape and will lose it, melting into air ?

Or fanciest thou (man) . . . is but of to-day, without a yesterday or a to-morrow ?

(*k*)   *Carlyle*

4. From the idea of God, I proceed to another grand one—that of man, of human nature ; and this should be the object of serious, intense thought. Few men know, as yet, what a man is. They know his clothes, his complexion, his property, his rank, his follies, and his outward life. But the thought of his inward being, his proper humanity, has hardly dawned on multitudes ; and yet, who can live a man's life that does not know what is the distinctive worth of a human being ? It is in-

(*l*)

teresting to observe how faithful men generally are to their idea of a man; how they act up to it. Spread the notion that courage is true manhood, and how many will die rather than fall short of that standard.

(a)   *Channing*

5. Man, Christian and Pagan Conceptions of

When we speak of striving after the ideal of man, what man do we mean? Do we speak of the man who was formed in God's image, who fell into sin, and thereby became fettered in an abnormal condition, and an abnormal development, from which he cannot free himself; but from which Christ will redeem him? Or do we speak of the Pagan man, who is the production of nature alone, in whom the unaided light of reason has emerged in self-consciousness and freewill; who is his own centre, his own aim, and who on earth must work out his own kingdom of humanity?

This is the great point in dispute, and has been so from generation to generation.

We speak of the man who was created in God's image.

(b)   *Martensen*

ANSWERS:

1. Man is an . . . unutterable mystery of mysteries.

(c)   *Carlyle*

2. What a chimera then is man! What a novelty! What a chaos! What a subject of contradiction! A judge of all things, and yet a worm of the earth; the depository of the truth, and yet a medley of uncertainties; the glory and the scandal of the universe. If he exalt himself, I humble him; if he humbles himself, I exalt him; and press him with his own inconsistencies, till he comprehends himself to be an incomprehensible monster.

(d)   *Blaise Pascal*

3. Every man is infinitely richer in his being than in his performance, is infinitely more than he shows himself or can show himself to be.

(e)   *Martensen*

4.   Man!
Thou pendulum betwixt a smile and tear.
(f)   *Byron*

Man, is Body and Soul

5. Man's nature exists in the form of a personal Ego life, independent of which it does not exist at all. I have not body and soul, but I *am* body and soul.

(g)   *Harless*

6. God made the body, but the man was not complete till He breathed into him a soul—only dead. So the possession of these two makes a *man;* but add to this faith from God, and you have a SAINT.

(h)   *Donne*

7. Man, a Microcosm

Each particular man is the short and sad story of mankind, written by his own dear experience.

(i)   *F. Quarles*

8. Every human being is a volume worthy to be studied.

(j)   *Channing*

9. Man, Origin of

I see the marks of God in the heavens and the earth, but how much more in a liberal intellect, in magnanimity, in unconquerable rectitude, in a philanthropy which forgives every wrong, and which never despairs of the cause of Christ and human virtue. I do and I must reverence human nature. . . . I shut my eyes on none of its weaknesses and crimes. I understand the proofs by which despotism demonstrates that man is a wild beast, in want of a master, and only safe in chains. But injured, trampled on, and scorned as our nature is, I still turn to it with intense sympathy and strong hope. The signatures of its origin and its end are impressed too deeply to be ever wholly effaced. I bless it for its kind affections, for its strong and tender love. I honour it for its struggles against oppression, for its growth and progress under the weight of so many chains and prejudices, for its achievements in science and art, and still more for its examples of heroic and saintly virtue. These are marks of a Divine origin and the pledges of a celestial inheritance; and I thank God that my own lot is bound up with that of the human race.

(k)   *Ibid*

10. Man, Place of, in Nature

Man, in the system of nature, is the medium between nonentity and immensity. This intermediate condition is common to all our faculties. Our senses can discern no extremes. Too much noise deafens us, too much light blinds us. Too great a distance and too great nearness alike prevent our seeing; too much prolixity and too much brevity darken a discourse; too much pleasure is painful; too much harmony displeases us. We cannot feel either extreme heat or extreme cold. These qualities in excess are enemies to our nature, not perceptible to our senses. We do not feel, but suffer them: the weakness of childhood and of old age alike incapacitate the mind; too much or too little food disturbs its operations; too much or too little study stupifies it. Things in extreme exist not, with respect to us; and we exist not with respect to them. They escape us, and we them. Such is our true state.

(l)   *Blaise Pascal*

11. The testimony of both religion and science to man's humble origin

"Dust thou art."

"God created man out of the dust of the ground."

(m)   *Genesis*

"He remembereth that we are dust."

(n)   *Psalm*

We are not here concerned with hopes or fears, only with the truth as far as our reason permits us to discover it. We must, however, acknowledge, as it seems to me, that man, with all his noble qualities, with sympathy which feels for the most debased, with benevolence which extends not only to other men but to the humblest living creature, with his God-like intellect, which has penetrated into the movements and constitution of the solar system—with all these exalted powers—man still bears in his bodily frame the indelible stamp of his lowly origin.

(o)   *Darwin: "Origin of Species"*

12. The true Shekinah is man.

(a)   *Chrysostom*

13. There is but one temple in the world, and that temple is the body of man.

(b)   *Novalis*

14. In nature God is hid; in man God is revealed.

(c)   *Liddon*

15. God took man's nature, and is *man*. What God the Son did, is not derogatory to God the Holy Ghost to do; and we have the Scripture to say that He lives in our bodies. "Know ye not that your body is the temple of the Holy Ghost."

(d)   *General Gordon*

16. The second Adam must be in some way an explanation of man, both as to origin and destiny, in his-

(i.) Birth or appearance.
(ii.) Development of character under temptation.
(iii.) Death, Resurrection, and Ascension.

This must be our guide in any answer to the question, "WHAT IS MAN?"

(e)

17. Man, according to the Scriptures, is "The offspring of God"; "The Father of Spirits" is his Father;' "We are all the work of Thy hand, we are the clay and Thou our potter"; "Thy hand hath made me and fashioned me;" Made a little lower than a Divine being; Created in the image of God; A being of great dignity placed at the head of creation; The handiwork of God, and the masterpiece of God.

(f)

18. The Adam and Eve . . . whom thou namest father and mother, are but thy nursing father and mother. Thy true Beginning and Father is in heaven.

(g)   *Carlyle*

MAN, CREATION OF

1. The Biblical Statement

"*God created man in His own image, in the image of God created He him; male and female created He them*" (Gen. i. 27)

"*And the Lord God formed man of the dust of the ground, and breathed into his nostrils the breath of life; and man became a living soul*" (Gen. ii. 7)

1. When we compare this brief statement with those describing the creation of animals, we find them substantially different.

Animals were brought forth by the earth at the Divine word, as He willed their creation—no process is stated—and were quickened by the universal spirit of life, active throughout the entire work of creation. But the earth does not bring forth man's body in the same way. Previous to his creation, a Divine consultation is held—"Let us make man in our own image"; and then he appears as God's handiwork, created after a heavenly ideal, which it is evident is partly to be worked out by himself afterwards.

(h)

2. First and Second Causes

The Biblical record speaks only of the first cause; but as in most of God's works second causes operate, so there is a probability that such intermediate causes intervened in the process of preparing a body for man. The Bible, so far as it reveals the origin of man, reveals chiefly his superiority over the brute creation in the fact that he was created in a special way—receiving from the sphere of nature his body, and from the supernatural sphere his spirit; and on the foundation of his supernatural origin he received a capacity for holding communion with God and the spirit world.

(i)

3. The Process of Creation

Now the process of this work of creation, so far as the statement goes, shows that man's body had a natural substratum—"the dust of the ground." We are not led to suppose by this language that God took a lump of earth and moulded it, either as a potter would a lump of clay, or as a sculptor would chisel a block of marble, into the shape of a man; and that then the perfected body lay before Him like a corpse. But we are the rather led to understand that under a special act of God's creative skill, and in some degree on the lines of His previous working in the animal kingdom—for a gradation upwards from the more simple to the more complex is seen,—the body of man was prepared from earthly elements. Whether, as some suppose, from the statement that the body was created first, life too was communicated simultaneously—a natural life—must remain as mere conjecture. In our ignorance on this point, we have an analogy in the first meeting of the human and the Divine Spirit in the work of regeneration, which may help to throw some light on that inscrutable past—"That is not first which is spiritual, but that which is natural"; and there does come a moment in the life of man when, by the breath of God, and by His quickening Spirit, man passes into the higher region of spiritual life. Be this as it may, it is quite conceivable that we have not yet learnt all that natural science may be capable of teaching us concerning the preparation of man's body from the dust of the ground.

(j)

4. Creation and Evolution

Grant the truth of evolution, it is, however, a curious fact that scented flowers, wheat, and cereals, should be timed to evolve out of grasses to their present development, just as man was timed to arrive at his full development.

Again, granting the truth of evolution, the creature, said to be man's immediate ancestor, with pointed ears and caudal appendage, *was not man*; and to evolve man from an animal of any kind, purely of the earth, earthy, is to all intents and purposes a creative work.

(k)

It is not unlikely that the material substratum with which the Creator worked in the creation of man, may have been a purely natural being (such as evolutionists will have it), but whose life or existence was purely animal, and subject to death; and, supervening upon this, the breath of God may have been breathed into him, whereupon another

(l)

Man, Creation of—*continued*

and a higher life (or soul) was communicated, with a capacity for religion and morality. (Cf. Balaam's ass speaking with human accents and reasoning.)

If so, then "creation" was the prototype of re-creation, or regeneration, such as the Christian experiences when born from above, of the Spirit of God—before which he was a "*natural man*," and understood not, nor could he perceive, the things of God. As far as "spirit" is concerned, he was not quickened—not alive unto God. And such a faith in God's works only increases the marvel—How wonderful is God! and His ways past finding out.

(*a*)

5. The Natural and the Supernatural

Science and revelation are different spheres, and governed by different laws. They are not contradictory, but supplementary; and there is only antagonism when they depart from their own lines; the result then is chaos. A simple illustration may show the need of both. On either hand, at the bedside of a dying man, is a minister of religion and a physician. They meet there as specialists, and as the ministers of God. The one draws a medicine from a natural source to ease pain and prolong life; the other draws a medicine from a supernatural source to soothe the alarmed conscience. Man, having his origin from both sources, requires the healing agency of both.

(*b*)

6. Scientific Limits

Our nature is more than bone, muscle, nerve, cellular tissue, as is the estimate of science.

(*c*)   *Calderwood*

Was man present at the creation, to see how it all went on? Have any deepest scientific individuals yet dived down to the foundations of the Universe, and gauged everything there? . . . These (scientific individuals) have been nowhere but where we also are: have seen some handbreadths deeper than we see into the deep that is Infinite, without bottom as without shore.

(*d*)

The course of Nature's phases, on this our little fraction of a planet, is *partially* known to us, . . . but who knows what deeper courses these depend on? . . . To the minnow, every cranny, and pebble, and quality, and accident of its little native creek may have become familiar; but does the minnow understand ocean tides and periodic currents, the trade-winds, the monsoons, and the moon's eclipses; by all which the condition of its little creek is regulated, and may, from time to time, be quite overset and reversed (*unmiraculously* enough)? Such a minnow is man; his creek, this earth; his ocean, the immeasurable all; his monsoons and periodic currents, the mysterious course of Providence through Æons of Æons.

(*e*)   *Carlyle*

7. The Breath of Life—Living Soul

The body of man being created from the dust of the ground, we are then told that the self-existent God, who has neither beginning of life nor end of days, breathed into his nostrils the breath of life, and man became a *living soul*. There is a marked difference here to the account of the creation of animals, whether we regard this "Breath of Life" as the breath of absolute being, or as a "new birth" from *above*, supervening upon a previous and mere natural life. In their case life was not individual, was not Divine, but was a part of that universal life which was quickening the whole world of nature. In man's case alone the life of God individualized itself in him. Man was kissed into being by the breath of God. His life was kindled by a spark of that Light which is the life of men. In him God brings forth a son (Luke iii. 38).

(*f*)

God created a being, as it were, of a mixed world, who is related to two worlds, the *heavenly* and the *earthly*. And the difficulty of the question, as it exists for men as men, is rightly compared to the incomprehensible God: "We know nothing at all concerning it (the soul), and believe in its existence solely from the activity it manifests in the body, as in reference to God we become convinced of His existence by virtue of His works as seen in the visible world.

(*g*)   *Anastas Sinaita, quoted by Harless*

The second Adam, like the first, sprang immediately from a creative act of Omnipotence (Luke iii. 38).

(*h*)   *Lange*

8. Creatianism

Moreover the work of Creation did not terminate in the creation of the first man : It is a continuous work. In the propagation of the race men are not merely born—they are individually created. Nor is each individual a mere link in the continuity of the race—he is also a fresh commencement—a new foundation is laid for a higher life, independent of all who have gone before him. Man is not merely nature's work, as the son of his parents; but a son of God—God's handiwork. If it were not so, no man could ever be greater than his ancestors; but, as the work of the Creator, he may have talents committed to him which will place him in the front rank of great men. These secrets of man's birth are alluded to in such passages of Scripture as the following :

(*i*)

Man by nature, is "shapen in iniquity," and "born in sin." But as the work of God, he is "fearfully and wonderfully made." "My substance was not hid from Thee when I was made in secret, and curiously wrought in the lowest parts of the earth. Thine eyes did see my substance, yet being imperfect." To Jeremiah,—raised up to do a special work,—God says, "I formed thee in the belly." How else, it has been asked, can science account for the appearance of great men on the stage of history, who came prepared beforehand with the particular talent required to solve the problem

(*j*)

Man, Creation of—*continued*

of their age. These may appear as Lawgivers, Psalmists, Prophets, Warriors, Thinkers, Poets, Naturalists, Man of Science,—but each comes in his proper moment, enriches the world by his presence and productions, benefits his fellow-men or country, and furthers the plans of Providence. If this were the work of blind Nature, how is it that mistakes are never made? How is it that a David is not raised up when a Moses is wanted? or that a Paul is the chosen vessel instead of a Peter, or a John? How comes it that, when Europe is plagued with a Napoleon, a Wellington is raised up to crush him; or that, when a second time that name is striking terror and unsettling the peace of Europe, a Bismarck is armed with power to dispel the illusion? How was it that a Shakspeare lived when he did; and that such a cluster of literateurs flourished just about the time of the Reformation, and when the Bible was being translated into the English tongue? These are either the work of design, or they are the work of blind Nature: if of the latter, they are more than miraculous, but if of the former, they prove that souls are still created as at the first.

(*a*)

And if it seems difficult to grant this in the vast majority of cases, where no special gift, or talent, or endowment distinguishes one from another in the great mass of mankind,—for we accustom ourselves to speak of the *masses*, or the *millions*, of ordinary persons as if they really had no individuality,—let us call to mind an utterance of our Lord of the deepest import concerning any man born into the world: He says, " A woman when she is in travail hath sorrow, because her hour is come : but as soon as she is delivered of the child, she remembereth no more the anguish for joy that *a man* is born into the world." A *man* has come into the world, who is something beyond the work of nature,—he is a *created* being, a really *new* existence, which never has been before, and never will come again: a distinct individual, bearing resemblance to others and yet without his like among all the myriads who have lived in the past, or among all the world of men now living, or of those who are yet to come. You cannot find his double. And such, briefly, is the scriptural account of the origin of man, in which a marked difference is apparent between his creation and that of animals, and which from the first places an immeasurable gulf between them. But that gulf widens to the extent of impassability the more we compare the points of difference.

(*b*)

Helvetius and his set say, that an infant of genius is the same as any other infant, only that favourable influences accompany him through life, especially in childhood, and expand him; whilst others (for lack of these) lie dormant. Herein, say they, lies the difference between a Prophet and a double-barrelled game-keeper: the inner man of one *fostered*, of the other *crushed* (perhaps by vigorous digestion). . . . With which opinion I should as soon agree as with this other, that an acorn might, by favourable or unfavourable influences of soil and climate, be nursed into a cabbage, or the cabbage-seed into an oak.

(*c*)　　　　　　　　　　　　　　*Carlyle*

MAN CREATED IN THE IMAGE OF GOD

1. This is Man's inalienable Possession

Man was created in the *Image of God*. Adam, in course of time, begat a son in his own image. By this we learn that the image of God has ever since been propagated, and whatever loss has been entailed by the Fall, yet this image is man's inalienable possession. The brute cannot attain to it, and man cannot wholly efface it. At the outset there was placed this impassable barrier between the two creations—the brute cannot improve itself into a man, neither can a man sink himself to the level of a brute. This dignity is peculiar to him. That he has marred the likeness and defaced the image, is true; but that he has lost all trace of it is not true—man in ruins, like the broken columns of a Grecian temple, shows what he was when he left his Maker's hands.

(*d*)

Man, *created*—not in the image of any living creature, but of the Creator; created out of Nature; created, yet formed of dust—linked to the Divine, and yet to this lowliest dust of the world. Man and woman, created to help and love and complete each other, not to rival or to tyrannize over each other.

(*e*)　　　　　　　　*Schönberg-Cotta Series.*

There is a spreading conviction, that man was made for a higher purpose than to be a beast of burden or a creature of sense.

(*f*)　　　　　　　　　　　　　　*Channing*

2. Man as the Lord of Creation

Man created in the Image of God, undoubtedly pointed out his destiny and mission. He was created in the image of God in order that he might be qualified to occupy his position as the Lord of Creation, and exercise there the authority of God. He was to be a king in his own dominions. The earth was for him : He came to it as to his home, and found it fitted up and prepared for him. All his wants, wants that did not really show themselves till many centuries later, had been anticipated. God gave him richly all things to enjoy. But he must enjoy them in his dependent position. He is lord only so long as he is the servant of God and as the image of God is reflected by him. For in proportion as that likeness be lost, man's dominion over the rest of creation is lost too. Rebellion and every evil work ensues.

(*See* " Fall.")

(*g*)

Not his upright walk alone, but also the human countenance points man out as the lord of nature, and as the being who has a Divine Mission to execute on earth.

(*h*)　　　　　　　　　　　　*Martensen*

3. Anthropomorphism

The image of God does not consist in bodily form; God is a spirit, and hath not hands and feet as we have. Though man's superiority does show itself in his upright form, with his head erect towards heaven and his feet towards the earth, as if to symbolize his two-fold origin. The several parts of his body, too, have great significance : his

(*i*)

Man Created in the Image of God—*continued.*

hand, for instance, has been noticed as pointing to a destiny of great things in store. The corresponding limbs in an animal serve for the purposes of motion or the procuring of food: whilst the hand of man is almost boundless in its capabilities. By it he moulds, fashions, and stamps his authority over nature: by it he becomes an inventor. It is the creator of all other implements and instruments. "Hands are better than wings." The hand plans and determines. The hand writes the thoughts of the mind. With the hand man does good and evil actions alike; acts of heroism and crimes of deepest die. With his hands folded he worships God, and humbles himself under the hand of the Most High. With the imposition of the hand he bestows a blessing. And with the grasp of his hand he pledges his good faith and friendship to his neighbour. Still, though man is so far removed from the animal in his physical form and in the members of his body, yet the image of God does not consist in these.

(*a*)

4. Tools

Show us the human being, of *any period* or climate, without his tools . . . those . . . had their flint-ball, and thong to it, such as no brute has or can have.

(*b*)   *Carlyle*

(Man) digs up certain black stones (iron) from the bosom of the earth, and says to them, "*Transport me and this luggage at the rate of 35 miles an hour;*" and they do it.

(*c*)   *Ibid-*

5. Intellect

We worship genius—we bow down before mighty intellects, but we do not *love* the merely intellectual. The devils are possessed of intellect. Man's superiority, therefore, and his fitness for rule, cannot consist in a quality which is not essentially godlike.

(*d*)

6. The Image of God consists in the fact that Man is the copy of a Divine Prototype

(i.) That image has been more fully revealed since then in Him who has come amongst us as "the express image of His Person." Man's likeness to God lies in the moral sphere. In this consists his fitness to be a member of, and to rule in, God's kingdom. Here mere power is not essential, for many a brute has more physical power than man. Here, too, mere intellectual endowment is not enough; it is not exclusively a Divine quality, such as are holiness and love. God is love—God is good—God is a holy God. These are exclusively Divine Attributes; and man, created in the image of God, was created morally good— "in the image of God created He them." This was the sphere of man's supremacy. And this it was that qualified him for his position at the head of God's creation. This is an absolute fact, underlying all God's relations to man in the course of history, that likeness to God consists not in genius, not in great intellectual power, but in moral purity. Holy, holy, holy is the Lord of Hosts, and man who sways his sceptre over creation must

be like Him, or be deposed from his throne. Man's destiny as *reigning* with Christ, points to this; and this, too, is the loss of the "lost"— they are deposed. Moral qualities both in God and man correspond. For this reason God could look upon His handy-work and pronounce it "*very good.*"

(*e*)

(ii.) With this man God walked and talked as with a companion. He was formed for loving intercourse and communion. And this fact, that man walked with God, shows the nature of the likeness: two cannot walk together except they be agreed. Here, then, evidently rests the stamp of man's superiority. For were it not simply preposterous, not to say more, to speak of an animal as bearing any moral resemblance to its Creator? . . . This thought of the supremacy of goodness over talent is wrought out more fully in the course of human development. "The saints shall judge the world," because they shall *reign* with Christ. They are to be the dominant people,—heaven's nobility—the lords of the restored creation—and to exercise judgment because of their moral resemblance to Christ.

(*f*)

(iii.) Man as such reflects God. Cf. Christ as the Revealer of the Father, and as the express image of His Person (Heb. i.).

(*g*)

(iv.) Bending before man is a reverence done to this revelation in the flesh. . . . We touch heaven when we lay our hands on a human body.

(*h*)   *Carlyle*

(v.) Oken, a man quite wrong in some points, . . . was the first to remark that "man is the sum total of all the animals." . . . You will be startled, however, by the language in which he embodies his view (*intellectually* on the very verge of truth, yet for every moral purpose infinitely removed from it). "Man," he says, "is God manifest in the flesh." In a certain loose sense this may be admitted. Man is God's *image* manifested in the flesh.

(*i*)   *Hugh Miller*

(vi.) *Professor Owen*—supreme in his own special walk—recognises man as a fore-ordained existence. "The recognition of an ideal exemplar for the vertebrated animals proves," he says, "that the knowledge of such a being as man must have existed before man appeared; for the Divine mind that planned the archetype also foreknew all its modifications."

(*j*)   *Ibid*

(vii.) *Agassiz*, after a survey of geologic existences more extended and minute than that of any other man: "It is evident there is a manifest progress in the succession of beings on the surface of the earth, . . . not the consequence of a direct lineage. . . . There is nothing like parental descent connecting them. . . . Nor does man descend from the mammals which preceded him. The link between them is of a higher and immaterial nature. The aim of the Creator in forming the earth, in its successive changes, in the

(*k*)

Man Created in the Image of God—*continued.*

successive creation of all the different types of animals, *was to introduce man upon the surface of our globe.* MAN IS THE END *towards which all the animal creation has tended from the first appearance of the first palæozoic fishes."* . . . Here is natural science, by the voice of its most distinguished professors, saying exactly the same thing as the Psalmist: " In Thy book were all my members written, which in continuance were fashioned, when as yet there was none of them " (Ps. cxxxix. 16).

(*a*)　　　　　　　　　*Hugh Miller*

(viii.) There is no restriction here to moral quality; the moral *image* man had, and in large measure lost; but the intellectual image he still retains. As a geometrician, as an arithmetician, as a chemist, as an astronomer,—in short, in all departments of the strict sciences—man differs from his Maker, not in kind, but in degree,—not as matter differs from mind, or darkness from light, but simply as a mere portion of space or time differs from *all* space or *all* time.

(*b*)　　　　　　　　　*Ibid*

(ix.) Man, created in the image of God, and breathed into by the breath of God, is to be compared with the new man created in Christ Jesus unto good works, and quickened by the Holy Spirit into life in Christ. Hence the *breathing* may at first have superinduced a merely *natural life*, in contradistinction to spiritual life.

(*c*)

(x.) Man is the image of God, i.e. an imperfect copy.

(*d*)

(xi.) As Protogenes, when he saw a picture in a shop curiously drawn, cried out, "None but Apelles could do this" : so when thou seest the beautiful image of the blessed God lively portrayed on the soul, thou mayest say, " This is the finger of God : none but a God could do this."

(*e*)　　　　　　　　　*G. Swinnock*

(xii.) The human soul is a palimpsest. Under the ordinary text of life it conceals the mysterious characters, all but effaced, of a sublime book, of a gospel revealed in the beginning of time.

(*f*)　　　　　　　　　*Adolphi Pictet*

(xiii.) As the human form is imperfectly copied in the animal form, so the human soul imperfectly copies, in its nature and essence, the Divine Being.

(*g*)　　　　　　　　　*Geo. Harris*

(xiv.) The Creator imparted to man the Divine image before He united to man's the Divine nature.

(*h*)　　　　　　　　　*Hugh Miller*

(xv.) I like the harmony and unity of one sublime scheme, that, after long ages of immaturity,—after the dynasties of the fish, the reptile, and the mammal should in succession have terminated,—man should at length come upon the scene in the image of God ; and that, at a still later period,

God Himself should have come upon the scene in the form of man ; and that thus all God's workings in creation should be indissolubly linked to God Himself, not by any such mere likeness or visage of the Divinity as Adam bore, but by Divinity itself in the second Adam. . . . That man should have been made in the image of God seems to have been a meet preparation for God's after assumption of the form of man. It was perhaps thus secured that *stock* and *graft*, if I may venture on such a metaphor, should have the necessary affinity, to be capable of being united in a single person.

(*i*)　　　　　　　　　*Ibid*

(xvi.) " Lift up your eyes to God," said the philosophers ; " behold Him who has stamped you with His image, and has made you to worship Him. You are able to make yourselves like Him ; wisdom, if you follow its directions, will render you His peers." Others exclaimed, " Cast down your eyes to the ground, base worms as you are, and behold the beasts who are your fellows." What then is to become of man ! Shall he be equal to God, or to the beasts ? What a frightful distance between the two alternatives !

(*j*)　　　　　　　　　*Pascal*

7. Man as King (*" Have dominion "*)

The only title wherein I, with confidence, trace eternity is in that of King=anciently cunning, or, which is the same thing, Can-ning. Ever must the Sovereign of mankind be fitly entitled King. [Such a King] reigns by Divine right.

(*k*)　　　　　　　　　*Carlyle*

Man is so great, that his greatness appears even in his knowing himself to be miserable. A tree is not conscious of misery. It is true that to know our misery is to be miserable ; but it is also great to know our misery. Thus his greatness is shown by his miseries. They are the miseries of a prince, the miseries of a king dethroned. What man thinks himself unhappy in not being a king, except a king dethroned?

(*l*)　　　　　　　　　*Blaise Pascal*

8. Man, Greatness and Littleness of

Go, wondrous creature ! mount where Science guides ;
Go, measure earth, weigh air, and state the tides ;
Instruct the planets in what orb to run,
Correct old Time, and regulate the sun ;
Go, teach Eternal Wisdom how to rule,
Then drop into thyself, and be a fool !

(*m*)　　　　　　　　　*Pope*

9. Man, Weakness of

Man is a reed, and the weakest reed in nature : but then he is a thinking reed. There is no occasion that the whole universe should arm itself for his destruction. A vapour, a drop of water, is sufficient to kill him. And yet should the universe crush him, man would still be more noble than that by which he fell, because he would know his fate, while the universe would be insensible of its victory.

(*n*)　　　　　　　　　*Blaise Pascal*

Man Created in the Image of God—*continued*

10. Man, Personality and Individuality of

On examination, we shall find that here, too, an immeasurable gulf separates the animal from the man.

"Man became a *living soul*," signifies his unlikeness to either created beings above or below him. Angels are pure spirit, and animals are pure nature. Man is of both, and therefore none like him. Sometimes the soul is spoken of as if the essence of man's personality were in it alone. Ancient philosophy taught that the body was a clog to the soul, and that at death man became immortal, and reached the stage when the pursuit of wisdom could be carried on without the inconveniences of an attendant body. The error is not exploded yet, and is often strengthened by our habit of speaking of man as if he had two independent natures—a body *and* a spirit—and that the spirit develops *apart* from the body. This, however, is contrary to Scripture. Man *has* not a body and a spirit, but man *is* body and spirit. The distinction is important. The resurrection of the body implies that man is incomplete until the body and the spirit come together again. The body is not man without the spirit, nor the spirit without the body. When God breathed into man the breath of life, man's body became the temple of the spirit, and this constituted him a *personality* separate and distinct from other beings. Here was the punishment of death in dissolving the union. And here the hope of the resurrection. The secret of the wail all through the O. T. at the thought of death was in the unclothing of the spirit of man; and its homeless abode was dreaded in the darkness of the unseen world.

(a)

Man, to be at his best, must be a complete personality, not unclothed but clothed upon. And personality has its root in individuality, by which we distinguish between person and person. Each one has something which no one else has. You cannot find his double. But you cannot say this of animals. They are specimens of their species. We speak of herds of some animals and flocks of others, because we do not distinguish between them. But when we speak of a crowded city, we at the same time distinguish it as a crowd of separate individuals, any two of whom are not alike. And this individuality is not merely external, in the features and figure, but still more so in the inner man. Man comes to his place in God's kingdom by no accident, but by design and providence; he fits into the niche for which his personality qualifies him. No one is too insignificant for a place there. Christianity deals with immortal souls—deals with them individually as precious in God's sight—for so much more is contained in the soul than finds outer expression; hence the value of the soul. But who discriminates in like manner, and deals thus separately, with animals? Who expects to find more than he sees in any animal? We simply regard it as one of a flock or of a herd, whose qualities are the same as any other specimen of the same species. The animal can never attain to personality. There is no " living soul," born of the breath of God. It is no temple of the spirit; and there can be no decided unlikeness between one specimen and another. Think, too, of the full significance of the individual or Christian name, in connection with man's personality.

(b)

11. Man, Freedom of

The same wide gap is discernible when we compare the freedom (*free will*) of man with the limitations of the creature.

Man was created with a capacity to advance beyond his standpoint. Almost infinite possibilities lay before him. His freedom of action was undetermined. There was no innate necessity that he should become an angel or a brute: the possibility of rise or fall was there, the determination was his own. The mere animal, on the other hand, remains as it was. It cannot become other than what is necessitated by its nature. There is a necessity of nature that the grain of wheat should sprout, that a lion should rule in the forest, and that a wolf should be wolfish. To assert the same of man is to bind him down unto the hard law of necessity or fate.

(c)

That this is not the case with man is evident in his own life's experience. Can he say that he was forced to act at any given moment as he did? Was it not possible for him, at some important crisis of his career, to have taken another course of action, where two roads opened before him, to have chosen this instead of that? Can he say that his act was determined by an innate necessity of nature, that he had no choice whatever; or that, having taken one step, it was not possible for him to retrace it and take another? It is because things could have been different that he knows his will was *free* so far. And that step places him on a higher level than the animal, which *must* be what it is. As nature made it, so it will remain, or only that can it become. Its character, unlike man's, remains unchangeable. It cannot divest itself of its original nature; but what it sucked in at the breast that it will remain till it dies. You may always count upon the wolf or a lion as being wolfish or leonine, as determined by its unchangeable nature. But to assert the same of a man is to deny his own experience, and that he has the power to act otherwise than circumstances seem to compel him. Old habits may cling to him; old tricks, as with Jacob, may look like an eradicable nature; he may, all through life, go on building castles in the air, but this is his weakness, his fault, not a necessity of his nature. If it is, then man becomes no more than an intellectual animal. But since man has possibilities of acting differently, and of becoming what he is not, because he keenly feels the contradiction which every day brings into his nature, and the inconsistency of certain modes of conduct with a higher standard of action,—he is thereby proved to be free—he feels it and he knows it. No man is a knave by necessity, by the force of circumstances, or by his peculiar situation. He has a power lodged within him, a possibility at all times of overcoming and acting contrary to the strong natural forces which sway his actions. Habit may enslave his will, but that only proves its original freedom.

(d)

Science can calculate when an eclipse of the sun or moon will take place. But in consequence of man's original freedom of will, and of the possibilities of turning-points occurring in his life, whilst acting on the precepts, "Watch and pray," and "Make the tree good," man's actions never can be reduced to certainty. The laws which govern his

(e)

Man Created in the Image of God—*continued*

actions are not unchangeable. Moral agencies are at work, lessening crime in cities, and changing the face of heathenism, which go to prove this. To say man is an animal is to deny this : to say that as he is such he always will be. A man, under such a supposition, may look back upon his life and say, Such a deed could not possibly have been different ; such a word, such a scene, such a time of suffering, etc., could by no means have been averted, that it is best to bury the past—to forget it—*it was to be*, and that is enough. Enough, yes, for an animal, with only one nature. But will this satisfy man's higher nature—his conscience ? Have not these actions of the past brought disharmony into his being, arrayed one part of himself against the other, and produced an undying worm of bitter memories ? Things have been done which *ought not* to have been done, and left undone which ought to have been done. And the worst of it is, that it is our own fault. This is a consideration beyond the limitations of a mere animal existence, but obvious enough in the case of a double nature like man's.

(*a*)

12. Man, a Free Agent

When God made man, He framed not a machine, but a free being, who was to rise or fall according to his use or abuse of his powers.

(*b*)   *Channing*

13. Man and Progress

But perhaps one of the greatest distances between animalism and man is seen in that unbridged gulf of PROGRESS. The animal remains where it was, but man has been progressing in every department of life from the very first. There is, as some one has remarked, between them all the breadth of history. The animal builds its nest as it ever did ; the ant, by the same marvellous instinct, constructs its geometrical cells now as at the first ; but man is a genius—he creates. His first rude efforts in shaping his dwellings have gone on progressing and improving until we have the architectural development of to-day. In every kind of art it is the same—rude flint knives, lanceheads, needles, were his first weapons and implements ; to them succeeded bronze, and then iron—each marking stages in that history of progress up to the beautiful cutlery, stores, and arsenals of the present day. The animal roars or chatters to-day as it has done all along. It has made no progress towards intelligent speech—which, as a learned writer observes, is a Rubicon the animal will never cross. But man, who began with one speech, and with a very limited vocabulary of words, has developed speech into the great languages of ancient and modern literature. A wider gulf than this seems hardly conceivable.

(*c*)

14. Man, Moral Qualities of

And yet, if we but briefly glance at the *moral* side of man's being, we shall find something there so marvellous, that there is absolutely nothing in the animal to compare with it. Man doth not live by bread alone—*that* will satisfy his mere physical hunger ; but man has also his root in God, and his *religious* relation to God is one of

existence. And so long as all goes well, and as it ought to go, harmony will be the law of his whole being. In a properly regulated human nature there can be neither discord nor disturbance : they arise only as phenomena after his life in God has been broken. Has the animal a religion ? or has the trace of man in the past been found where some indications are not also given of a religion or a superstition ? Remains, we are told, of pre-historic man are found, and among them are rude idols, amulets, etc., which prove this ; whilst the mode of burial in a kneeling posture seems indicative of a hope of a new birth from the grave.

(*d*)

15. What, too, of Conscience ? What is its root ?

Man is a riddle to himself until he knows something of the thoughts which spring up from the depths of his being. There is a voice within which says, "*I ought*," or "*I ought not* " ; and if we trace this voice back, we shall find it an echo of that voice which first spoke from the same source to man in Eden, when he said, " I heard Thy voice, . . . and I was afraid." This inner voice testifies to the relation in which man's spirit stands to God. " The candle of the Lord" is the light that is in us. Science deludes itself into finding a natural origin for this. And this is contrary to fact. That which is of nature harmonizes with nature, " as is the earthy, such also are the earthy." " Conscience makes cowards of us all ; " nay more, the alarmed conscience (as may be witnessed in guilty characters such as Richard III., and others) is simply terrible. You can no more harmonize it with man's natural origin than a toothache or a broken limb can be harmonized with healthful action. Instead of harmony under such circumstances, conscience is arrayed within as an antagonist, nature at war with itself. Science is incapable of explaining this, and would do better not to speak of it at all.

(*e*)

16. The Divine Voice

The fact of man's Divine origin will, however explain it. He recognises the Divine voice when it says, " Thou shalt not." The seat of conscience is the spirit—the spirit breathed into man at his creation, and perpetuated by a Divine continuous act. Both natures, the corporeal and the spiritual, are true to their origin. The traces of this origin may be obscured, but not altogether lost. Man may hate God ; yet even the most degenerate child cannot free himself from the presentiment that " in God we live, and move, and have our being." The Divine in man will assert itself. A presentiment of his paternity will haunt him like a ghost haunting a ruined temple. And that Divine presentiment is conscience.

(*f*)

17. Man's Ambition

Whence, too, is that boundless ambition of man ? Why is it that he, who reigns in the world, who has subdued nature to his will, is never satisfied, nor would be if he were to gain the whole world ? Why is it that merely mundane interests and possessions are insufficient for him ? Why is it that when he has drunk the cup of the

(*g*)

Man Created in the Image of God—*continued*

highest earthly bliss he thirsts again? Why are his ambitions never satisfied? We answer, that this ever-recurring hunger and thirst is that of man's supernatural need. It is still in want, when mere nature has had its fill, and must assert itself. The merely natural, like water, is satisfied with its own level, it ceases to flow after that. The animal is satisfied with a supply for its wants; it does live by bread alone. Beyond a supply of clover it has no ambition. But the supernatural in man can be bounded by no such limits; its ambitions cannot be satisfied with the husks that swine eat. And there comes a moment when it longs for the content of the Father's house, for the holiness and peace and joy of communion with God. This is its own level, and until it is found there can be no rest for the soul of man. Immortal longings cannot be satisfied with less than the Bread of life. There has been a terrible wrench somewhere, and at some time. The Father's house has been broken up. His children have rebelled against Him. They are in a far country. But the hope and promise of man's salvation lies in this fact, that he cannot be satisfied with himself as he is. Interpret his sighs, his weeping, and his ambitions aright, and you will find him saying, "I will arise and go to my Father."

(a)

17. Man, Greatness of his Ambition

Did not Alexander weep because he had not two planets to conquer; or a whole solar system; or after that a whole universe?

(b) *Carlyle*

18. Man's Unhappiness comes of his Greatness

It is because there is an Infinite in him, which with all his cunning he cannot quite bury under the Finite. Will the whole finance ministers and upholsterers and confectioners of modern Europe undertake, in joint-stock company, to make one shoeblack HAPPY? They cannot accomplish it, above an hour or two: for the shoeblack also has a soul quite other than his stomach; and would require, if you consider it, for his permanent satisfaction and saturation, simply this allotment, no more, and no less—God's infinite Universe altogether to himself, therein to enjoy infinitely, and fill every wish as fast as it rose. . . . Try him with half a universe of an omnipotence, he sets to quarrelling with the proprietor of the other half, and declares himself the most maltreated of men.

(c) *Ibid*

19. Benevolence

Intellectually and morally man occupies a special position in the world. Benevolence is confined to man. *Darwin* says: "There is no evidence that any animal performs an action for the exclusive good of another."

(d) *Calderwood*

20. Man's Reverence for the Divine

There is in man a quiet, indestructible reverence for whatsoever holds of heaven, or even plausibly counterfeits such holding. Show the dullest clodpole, show the haughtiest featherhead, that a soul higher than himself is actually here; were his knees stiffened into brass, he must down and worship.

(e) *Carlyle*

21. **Such is man**: a being created in the image of God; belonging to two spheres—the earthly and the heavenly. And when that image was destroyed, enough was left of the ruins to show what the original temple of the Spirit had been. And this ruined image is that which is perpetuated in every man born into the world; and by salvation we mean the reconstruction of that image, of which the **resurrection of the body** in glory is the goal and end.

(f)

Natural science, on the other hand, allies the natural and the spiritual in one indivisible unity. It sees in spirit merely a higher potency of matter, of which the mythical figure of the Sphinx affords an illustration. There the human countenance is represented as springing from the savage form of an animal. Man chained to natural life, having no higher existence. Compare with this heathen representation the description of man given by one who had spiritual illumination and insight. In Psalm viii. David says:

"When I see Thy heavens, the work of Thy fingers,
The moon and stars which Thou hast ordained:
What is mortal man, that Thou art mindful of him,
And the son of man that Thou carest for him!
And hast made him *a little lower than Divine*,
And crowned him with glory and honour.

Thou madest him to have dominion over the works of Thy hands,
Thou hast put all things under his feet:
Sheep and oxen all together,
And also the beast of the field,
The fowls of heaven, and the fishes of the sea,
Whatsoever passeth through the paths of the sea.

O Lord, our Lord,
How excellent is Thy name in all the earth!

For authorities, in addition to those quoted, see Adeney, Dorner, Hagenbach, Keil, Lutz, Martensen, Max Müller, Oehler, Pressensé, Quinet, Sophocles, Zieghler.

(g)

MAN: "THE LAW OF SIN AND DEATH" (Rom. viii. 2)

Preliminary Notes

Destined for religion, man is destined for immortality.

(h) *Dorner*

Man, Consequences of the Fall of

Cast forth thy act, thy word, into the ever-living, ever-working universe: it is a seed-grain that cannot die; unnoticed to-day (says one) it will be found flourishing as a banyan-grove (perhaps, alas! as a hemlock-forest!) after a thousand years.

(i) *Carlyle*

Man : Law of Sin and Death—*continued*

Death proceeded from within (the "inner man") to the without—from the psychical to the physical. So man is formed now. See *Martensen's* comparison of Sir W. Scott's and Shakspeare's characters. Shakspeare works from the heart of man externally, whilst Scott's are purely external (phenomena).

(*a*)

Man and Animals, The Gulf between

The gulf between man and all other creatures demonstrates by its depth and width the fact of his capability. And (as has been truly said) it is not the descent, but the *ascent* of man with which we have to do.

The very ideas of moral science, natural religion, supernatural religion, are so many signs and indications. They could never have existed, were not man a creature capable of the most exalted transfiguration. Had this terraqueous globe been a sphere appropriate—not disparate —to man, how different would have been his past history, how different his aims, endeavours, and self-discipline now!

(*b*)　　　　　*Jackson's Bampton Lectures*, 1875

Man, " a Living Soul "
The Second Man, a Quickening Spirit (1 Cor. xv. 45)

Adam is spoken of as "a living soul," not to prove his immortality, but his mortality. It is by means of the soul that he and we are linked to this changing and corruptible world, and so become the heirs of corruption. The only superiority ascribed to man in the history of creation, is found in the fact that "God breathed into him the breath of life," intimating that in the act of becoming a living soul, man at the same time was endowed with higher capacities, which brought him into relationship with God, and made him capable of communing with Him, and so of rising to a spiritual existence. But the possibility of this was cut off by the Fall, and man became animal ("natural") in the very elements of his character, or in the springs of his existence, became at the same time mortal. Herein lay the necessity for the new creation through the intervention of a Redeemer, who shall be nothing less than a quickening Spirit.

(*c*)　　　　　*Lange*

Man : The Law of Sin and Death

The inner and truer connection between sin and death is indicated in Genesis vi. 3 : " My Spirit shall not always strive with man, for he also is FLESH " = σάρξ of the New Testament.

In his erring he is *flesh* (Ps. lxxvii. 30; Isa. iv. 6); *i.e.* unable to be governed by God's Spirit; therefore mortal, perishable; and is repressed by sin, which impairs man's Divine spirit of life, which supports him. Thus his vital strength gradually succumbs to nature. Cf. also Psalm c. (7–10): " We are consumed in Thine anger " —not that death originally belonged to man's nature.

(*d*)　　　　　Cf. *Oehler*

Genesis vi. 3, before Romans v. = FLESH

The spirit having lost control, the flesh assumes the supremacy. And the powers of nature would exhaust themselves in one hundred and twenty years. " Flesh " in the New Testament sense, as opposed to spirit = that which cannot be subject to the law of God = mortal, perishable. Cf. Isaiah lxiii. 10: " sin separates," therefore God is dumb, and leaves us to ourselves. Cf. also Psalm xc. Death is the result of God withdrawing Himself; then nature works its unhindered work—and its tendency, quicker or slower, is death.

(*e*)　　　　　*Ibid*

It may be, and is, the province of nature to die. Nature conquers and wears out all, and reduces everything to its constituent elements; but evidently it was intended that this power of nature should be combated and resisted by the higher province and forces of man's being (the spiritual). This could become stronger than nature, and so develop into immortality. Cf. our Lord's transfiguration. Death had no power overHim; nor could it have had, had He not voluntarily laid down His life, and for the purposes of our salvation entered the sphere of death and the grave. The natural tendency is to die, as is the natural tendency of a swimmer to sink, or of a bird to drop, and of the man exposed to temptation to succumb to it; but life and effort oppose an opposite tendency. Had Adam used this power, as our Lord did, he would not have died.

(*f*)

Death is only the operation of a natural law. Sin did not, as is sometimes said, interrupt the course of nature, but it brought man into it, and this is the death of the Scriptures. When nature tyrannizes over the spirit, then the cry, " O wretched man that I am ! " (Rom. vii. 24).

(*g*)

1. Character Building

Man as the creation of God *is* body and spirit in union—a " living soul." He receives the gift of existence from the Giver of all things. But, like all gifts, this gift is not an end in itself, it has to be traded with, it has to be put out to usury, and developed according to the laws of its nature. To have it, *i.e.* to live, is not enough. We have now to think of man as making the best of himself : in fact, as the creator of his own character. He will become the product of his own habits. In a certain sense it is quite true that man is what he eats and drinks. He has need, however, to remember his complex nature, in consequence of which he cannot live by bread alone—*that* is for the supply of his physical necessities; but a supply of the Bread of life is needed for the sustenance of his higher life: and this supply must be in excess of the other just for the reason that the " life is more than meat."

(*h*)

2. Man, " a Living Soul "

By the expression, " a living soul," no more is meant than is said. It does not imply immor-

(*i*)

Man : Law of Sin and Death—*continued*

tality, nor indefectibility, but that Adam came into existence duly balanced between the spiritual and the natural, and with no preponderating bias either way. By the exercise of his own free will whatever was possible might be. But it must be his own act. In like manner we are the children of God by Creation and Redemption, but we can only become the sons of God through development. Adam had the advantage of beginning his development without original taint, let, or hindrance—poised for the moment in a sphere such as we can have no proper realization of.

The garden of Eden, its freshness and innocence, is so far behind us that we have lost all trace of it, save perhaps in that one sacred institution—the family, the home—which still remains as man's paradise on earth.

But we have the exceeding greatness of God's power to usward in redemption, which places our privileges high above his.

(a)

3. Man, Possibilities of, as " a Living Soul "

What those possibilities were we can only know by analogy.

(b)

(i.) Intellectual

" We know not what we shall be." Intellectually the first man was undoubtedly undeveloped ; but the possible has shown itself in the intellectual giants of the past. An Aristotle was not, as has been said, " the ruins of an Adam," but the intellectual capacity of the first man matured.

(c)

(ii.) Moral

Again, though Adam stood on a platform of sinlessness, yet this was so far merely negative goodness ; and the moral capacity which he possessed made it possible for him to attain to permanent fellowship with God.

(d)

4. Immortality : in *posse* or in *esse*

So with respect to the immortality of man. Nothing more is to be gathered from the narrative of the Creation than that this, too, was no more than a possibility. It was possible for man *not to die*. Just as with us the possibility is that we may obtain eternal life, so the possibility with him was that he might develop the life of the " living soul " until it became immortal.

The possibilities of Adam towards the goal of immortality were inherent in him as the " image of God." It was at this citadel that temptation assailed him. He was formed according to a plan, and that plan was not perfected at his creation, the rest must be his own work. He might go *up*, or he might go *down*—gain or lose his soul—as is the case now. The steps upward were from the standpoint of Creation, through obedience, unto eternal life, in the glory of his fully developed nature.

(e)

5. Redemption and the Son of Man

The case is the same now, with this difference, that we start from Redemption, which is in Christ Jesus, and which has taken effect in us by Regeneration. The ultimate end being that of the Glorification of body and spirit. Till then we are incomplete.

(f)

The perfect illustration of this fully developed human life is given us in the case of the true Son of Man, who became what the first man might have become, and what we through His grace may become. From His infancy He grew in favour with God and man. He was guileless. Temptation failed to seduce Him. God was well pleased in Him. This went on till full maturity was reached, and at that moment He was transfigured before His disciples.

He was entering into His glory—entering that sphere where death hath no dominion—and had it not been that He was appointed to taste death for all men, and so go by another road to glory (that by which we can only go), He would then have anticipated His ascension into glory.

(g)

6. The possible in Adam

This reveals the *possible* in Adam. On the lines of obedience and holiness he, too, might have entered into his glory, in the same way. It was the end, we may say, for which he was created in the image of God. On the other hand, there was the possibility of his going *down*, through disobedience and death, to the bottomless pit, the Gehenna, the abyss of the Bible. Whatever may be meant by these awe-striking terms, it is safe to say that they point to the opposite goal to glorification—to a deposed and not a regnant king. By going *up*, man becomes true man ; he is at his best, fully developed, the end of his being, as the idea in the mind of the Creator, is attained. But by going *down*, man becomes a lost soul, he reaches the goal of degradation, his development becomes abnormal : the idea of the Creator thwarted, and instead of glory, honour, and immortality there remain wrath, the unrest, and the abyss of demonism. Anything was possible after the balance was destroyed. Anything in the sphere of nature. Man made the attempt to live on *bread alone*. It is quite enough to neglect the soul, to let it alone, not to be watchful over its interests, in order to drop into the deepest possibility in the sphere of nature.

(h)

7. " Ye shall be as Gods "

May there not have been something of this hidden in the tempter's words, " ye shall be as gods " ? There was truth in this, man was destined to rise, but the temptation=ye shall reach the highest development of your being by a shorter road than that of waiting, it may be a long time for it ; for ye are being kept as children, undeveloped, whereas this fruit will make you rise directly. Ye will grow thereby and become as gods, *i.e.* attain the end of your being at once. So he tempted the second Adam, when he offered to give Him the kingdoms of the world and the glory of them at once, on the sole condition of doing homage to the tempter for them. The temptation in both cases was against *waiting* an indefinite time of probation ; for a man must first

(i)

Man : Law of Sin and Death—*continued*

learn to reign over himself, before he can reign over others.

It is the peculiar temptation of youth and inexperience. The magnificent promise and dream of the future to be put within the grasp of inexperienced and untried youth. How natural to think we are ready for it, that some sinister motive is at work withholding it from us ! The eye sees it—the hand takes it—it is tasted, or the deed is done. He who had the power of death has effected his purpose ; our eyes are indeed opened, but Eden is left behind us, years of bitterness are before us, the past can never be recalled, and the future cannot be as it might have been.

(*a*)

8. Our Standpoint

We indeed cannot take Adam's standpoint of innocence, but we can take that of "little children," and begin life again under the best auspices, in fellowship with One who can make it new, and daily weave into it the threads which are forming His image within us until it be completed, after the pattern of Him who weaves it, thereby making possible all that was possible at the first.

(*b*)

9. The Possibilities of Man's Being, then, are these :

It is possible for him so to live in the spirit as ultimately to spiritualize, and carry up into the spirit-sphere, even his material body ; whilst, on the other hand, he may so live as to carnalize his whole being, and drag even the spirit down to inconceivable depths of demoniac degradation. The rise was possible through a metamorphosis. "We shall all be changed," but the fall reaches its development of degradation through DEATH.

(*c*)

10. The Connection between Sin and Death

Death is the result of the exhaustion of vital powers and forces. The animals were not created for an endless existence. The possibility of this in man's case only is implied in the Bible. And even death, as the dissolution of body and soul, has not destroyed faith in a Resurrection. The Arabs were accustomed to fasten a camel to the tomb of a dead man, that when the resurrection took place he might have the means of riding wherever he might wish to go. But the decay and death of animals is in no way the effect of sin. And sin could only be committed by those who had the "Breath of Life" breathed into them. This is the foundation both of attaining to the likeness of God and of Immortality ; and consequently here only was the possibility of sin —sin which is destructive, and separates between the Giver and His gifts. This possibility of sin as a destructive and separating cause carries with it the possible thwarting of the Divine plan in the creation of man. It has the power of stopping his upward development—by introducing death— *i.e.* by bringing man under the operation of the same law that prevailed in the realm of Nature. For death is not the effect of sin, but a law of Nature. "The tyranny of Nature."

(*d*)

11. The Teaching of the Scriptures

This at first sight may seem to contradict the teaching of Holy Scripture. But it is not so in reality. It is here, in fact, where a debt is owing to natural science, which has thrown so much light upon all questions of this kind. The language of Milton concerning "Death and all our woes," as the fruit of the first sin, is not strictly accurate, though the sentence of death passed upon our first parents, and other passages of the Scriptures seem to justify it. The original prohibition was this : "In the day that thou eatest thereof thou shalt surely die" (Gen.) ; and the sentence ran thus : "In the sweat of thy face shalt thou eat bread, till thou return unto the ground ; for out of it wast thou taken : for dust thou art, and unto dust shalt thou return." This language does not say that sin was the origin of death, but it merely states that by sin man became mortal. The possibility of an upward development, by which the spirit should spiritualize the body, was frustrated. That possibility was no more. For man had now become subject to the laws of Nature, which, through labour, sorrow, and age, would gradually weaken the physical forces till death ensued. Sin brought this about by bringing man within the power of Nature, where Death had ever reigned. If we turn to some familiar N. T. passages more light will be thrown upon this subject :—"Through one man sin entered into the world, *and death through sin ;* and so death passed upon all men, for that all have sinned."

Here we have the direct statement that "*death entered into the world through sin ;*" and that it came by one man. It, however, does no more than confirm the passage from Genesis, which stated that man became mortal by sin ; the connection between death and sin is not stated. In like manner the statements—"the end of those things is death," "the wages of sin is death," and "sin bringeth forth death"—state nothing more than the fact that a career of sin inevitably ends in death. But why ? Why should sin bring forth death ?

(*e*)

12. The Teaching of Science

Here science is a valuable expositor. It shows us that death held its dominion in this world ages before man was created. Death reigned over the animal and vegetable world. **Death pre-existed Sin.**

Our coal-fields tell the tale. The rocks are our open book, wherein we may read the records of the slain. The tusks of the carnivora, beast and bird, were the same then as now, doing the same destructive work. The weak fell a prey to the strong. Death was a law of Nature—its tyrant. All that the Bible tells us is, that by sin man too, when he appeared, was brought under the power of Death ; then speedily followed gaunt famine, war, pestilence, hecatombs of the slain. It reigned over him even in whom a possibility had been planted of becoming superior to it. The fact was, that sin let him down into its region. Spiritual power and force might have dominated Nature, and made it subordinate, but the act of disobedience reversed this : Nature gained the supremacy, and the Law of Nature had all along been that of decay and death.

(*f*)

Man: Law of Sin and Death—*continued*

13. The Link between Sin and Death

The link therefore which connects sin with death is that of Nature. " If ye live after the flesh ye shall die." Sin brings about a dissolution of body and soul because it brings man under the power of Nature. On the other hand, the link which might have connected obedience with Immortality was Holiness. Holiness is the fruit of obedience, the end of which is everlasting life.

(a)

14. This Law of Sin and Death, under which

man by nature has his existence, works like any other of Nature's laws—like the law of gravitation for instance—with an all-controlling, irresistible force, carrying everything before it. Man can only be free from its action by becoming an inhabitant of another sphere ("the law of the spirit of life in Christ Jesus hath made me free from the law of sin and death"). But by nature he must die. His position in regard to nature and inevitable death is that of master and slave—"His servants ye are whom ye obey, whether of sin unto death." . . . There is no escape—"In the day ye eat thereof ye shall surely die."

(b)

15. The same Law prevails in Nations

The gradual dissolution of the Roman Empire is a telling illustration of this doctrine. When filled with vigorous life, purity, and manliness, it became a vast, consolidated empire, covering the whole known earth; but when luxury entered, gradually decay and certain dissolution succeeded. The law of Sin and Death works irresistibly.

(c)

16. Redemption

By the introduction of sin, man's higher development ceased. According to the original plan death dissolves the union of body and soul, but the plan of creation has been succeeded by the plan of redemption. God's purpose shall stand. And though now the death penalty has to be paid by all, and for a time the disembodied spirit returns to God who gave it, and the body to the ground from whence it came. Yet the scheme of redemption provides for a reunion of the two at the resurrection of the body; and the reunion will be an indissoluble one, making actual God's idea of man, as a being created in His image for immortality. This is a view of evolution that science, probably, would laugh at. Nevertheless it is the hope of the Christian.

For the resurrection that the Christian looks for is a resurrection of the body (which nature has claimed), in order that man's glorification may be fully reached. In other words, resurrection and glorification, in the end will be destructive of the power called death. For this the *whole creation* waits. " The last enemy which shall be destroyed is death."

For authorities and references, see, among others,
Oehler, Keil, Hagenbach, Martensen, Dorner.

(d)

MAN, IMMORTALITY OF

1. " In the Beginning

" In the beginning God created the heaven and the earth." " A sublimer passage than this," said Cuvier, the naturalist, " never can, nor will, come from a human pen." There the words stand, and there they will continue to stand, said another, however men try to explain them away; and there doubtless they will continue to stand until the conclusion of God's kingdom joins hands with the beginning.

Genesis is the book of beginnings, chiefly of the religious beginning. " The testimony of Jesus is the spirit of prophecy." From the nature of such a book we cannot expect to find a full statement of a religious doctrine; germs there are, which, like other germs, develop into completeness when the fulness of time is come.

(e)

2. Germs

In man's essential nature, as a spirit-being; in his capacity for religion, from the standpoint both of creation and redemption; in the import of the tree of life; in the first promise, viewed as a promise of the destruction of him who was a murderer from the beginning; in man's first clothing; in the length of human life; and in the significance of Enoch's translation later on,—we see sufficient germs of the doctrine of man's immortality, to show that he was created for eternal life, and that now his destiny can only be reached through death and the resurrection of the body. Death has been led captive, and made to serve, not as an enemy, but as a friend. And this belief, though not formulated as a doctrine, was the ray of light which, as paradise receded into the dimness of the past, cast its gleam of hope upon the otherwise dark lot of our first parents, and saved them from despair. Their faith was strengthened by looking back to what was possible in their creation, as ours is strengthened by looking forward to the possibilities in redemption.

The doctrine of Immortality had its root in Paradise, and that root presupposes all the rest, as the root presupposes a tree.

(f)

3. The Import of Man as a " Living Soul "

Man's origin differed from that of the animal creation by having the " breath of life" breathed into him. And on this ground, it has been thought, lay the foundation of the essential immortality of the soul. Whether this be so or not, cannot be proved from the language of Scripture, which sometimes uses the same term, " living soul" to describe the life of animals, for which immortality is not claimed. And St. Paul, in his argument in 1 Cor. xv., uses the expression, " The first man was made a *living soul*," not to imply the immortality of man, but, on the contrary, his mortality. He, in fact, repeats the thought of Genesis, which merely states the fact of what man became at his creation, leaving it to be inferred that it was possible for him not to die. More than this it is not just to find in this expression. But that the " breath of life " was from God, and was therefore the breath of being and personality, corresponding to God's personality, may also rightly be said. And so far perhaps it is allowable to find in it the foundation of man's immortality. In it we find that man received something from God, which no mere animal received, and that something possessed a germ which might, under favourable circumstances,

(g)

Man, Immortality of—_continued_

develop into a condition of existence where " dissolution into the original elements would be impossible."

(a)

4. Man in the image of God

But from the standpoint of man's creation, in the _Image of God_—made after His likeness—there is indeed to be found the germ of the spiritual Immortality of the soul. This consists in the fact of the absolute greatness of spiritual life and likeness to God as raising man altogether above natural conditions; it is a vital force which cannot be spent, seeing it has its origin in a perennial spring, springing up into eternal life, unlike the vital forces of animals, which belong exclusively to the sphere of nature, and which in due time succumb to decay and death. Spiritual life, on the other hand, is absolutely unlimited by natural conditions, and superior to the law of decay and death.

That this is so, observe the teaching of Holy Scripture on this point : The image of God is the image of the Prototype—Jesus Christ—the express image of His person. And this essential likeness consists in _moral purity_, or holiness. But moral purity is a product of the Spirit of God, who dwells in man as in His true temple. " The fruit of the Spirit is in all goodness and righteousness and truth (Eph. v. 9). Therefore man was created to be a temple, or a habitation, of the Spirit. And the fruits of the Spirit, which are the evidence that God's handiwork is " _very good_," are those " _against which there is no law_." Therefore, man created in the image of God is not under the _law of sin and death_. In other words, from the standpoint of his creation man is IMMORTAL.

(b)

5. Walking with God

Further, man was created, not merely in the Image of God, but he was created so for a definite object. That was, that he should _walk with God :_ in other words, that he should be religious, _i.e._ hold communion with God, be companionable, a creature to be loved. For God is Love, and love seeks an object. This was man's destination. Now, what do the Scriptures teach us about love ? It is the one thing which shall outlive everything else. Gifts and endowments of every kind shall fail, but this never faileth. Love is the fulfilling of the law. It is therefore the very essence of religion. Love is of God, for God is love. Therefore, again, it is a fruit of God's Spirit—the more excellent gift, which never faileth. It denotes man's parentage. He that loveth is born of God. Hence man, at his best, is not so merely because he stands at the head of creation, but because he is born of God, inherits God's essential character, and lives in daily communion and fellowship with God. But such a religion as daily communion with God implies is a _life_. It is the living _not by bread alone_, but on the manna of heaven. And such a life is an absolute life—what the Scriptures afterwards call "eternal life,"—a life above and beyond the sphere of nature. Hence man, considered from the standpoint of his creation, was created for Immortality. The promise and potency of what he was destined to be lay concealed in his very existence, just as the germ of an oak-tree lies concealed in an acorn.

(c)

6. The Standpoint of Redemption

There remains however a consideration of this subject from another point of view. Man, by an act of his free will, forfeited his birthright. He came within the sphere of death ; but Death itself is now made a factor in his development. He now comes under other conditions. We may no longer view him from the standpoint of Creation, but from that of REDEMPTION. This, however, does not affect what has been said about the germ of Immortality inherent in man by creation. All that we have to notice now by way of variation, is that man's development towards Immortality no longer proceeds on the original lines, but " through the grave and gate of death." Originally man was destined to be " changed from the possibility " to the impossibility of dying ; and the eating of the fruit of the tree of life evidently marked the moment when he would be so _changed_ from, and pass from the condition of merely possible IMMORTALITY to that of being absolutely Immortal. Now his development proceeds on fresh lines ; and Death is the _via media_. But whatever was possible before is still possible. The ultimate destination of man is unchanged. Man has still to choose as at the first, though with this grand difference : he may choose aright after " many offences," whereas Adam risked all by " one offence." Adam had the Tree of Life, but we have the " Bread of Life," and are therefore no losers by the Fall, so far as the means of attaining eternal life is concerned. He was created in the Image of God ; but now man in Regeneration is " renewed after the Image of Him that created him," and starts afresh on his road to glory. What God desired in the creation of man at the Beginning, viz. a being in His Image, essentially religious, with whom He could hold unbroken communion, He still desires. What God wants in the world is regenerate men, whom He can train, and daily renew until His Image be perfected in them, and no bar come between to hinder His loving intercourse and communion with them. (Cf. " till we all come," etc.) Sin only separates between God and man. From the Beginning, then, whether regarded from the standpoint of Creation or Redemption, the germ of Immortality is inherent in man. Both Genesis and Re-genesis plant the same seed which will develop into ETERNAL LIFE.

(d)

7. The First Promise

We cannot trace any sign of a dogmatic expression of such a belief at that early time, yet what are we to suppose our first parents understood by the language of the _first promise_ ? They were told that death would be the penalty of their disobedience. And by death they understood the dissolution of body and soul, which at first were but loosely connected, and under given circumstances would part. Further than this, the dissolution of the body was to be complete. " Out of dust wast thou taken, and unto dust shalt thou return." Death has to appear as a complete conqueror. They soon saw what death was—in the animals that were slain for their clothing, and in the death of Abel. But, at the same time, a hope was held out to them of a restoration to their original estate. A conqueror of death should come. Death was to be abolished, by the destruction of him who had the power of it. One should hereafter come who should undo all the evil effects of their sin. Com-

(e)

Man, Immortality of—*continued*

munion with God should be restored, and man should attain to his best. But how could this be if death were for ever to claim the body? What was the hope of our first parents if it was not this, that in due time the grave would have no real victory? Man, redeemed from sin, was to be redeemed from death. They surely understood that God's purpose concerning man should stand, that man's immortality was assured to them in the promise of a Redeemer; and though death reigned over the body, yet they accounted that God was able to raise it up again, that the miracle of Resurrection could be no greater than that of birth or Creation; and that eventually this hope would be fulfilled in the lasting union of body and soul. For Redemption, to be complete, must assert its power over nature itself.

That mournful refrain, repeated again and again, "And he died," after the mention of the names and ages of the patriarchs of the primeval world in Genesis, would read like the triumph of death, and sound the key-note of despair, if at that time no hope of immortality existed as a traditional though unwritten article of faith.

(*a*)

8. The Tree of Life

The significance, too, given in the first and last books of the Bible to that mysterious symbol, "*tree of life*," must not be overlooked. The account in Genesis seems to imply that in a normal development the partaking of the fruit of the Tree of Life would have marked the stage when mortality would put on immortality. A *change*, such as that indicated by St. Paul, when he says, "We shall all be changed," would thereby be wrought; and man, under the action of this fruit, not having fallen under the dominion of the flesh, and thereby having become superior to natural decay, being filled and dominated by the spirit, would, like our Lord, be TRANSFIGURED as "the end" of obedience. But becoming fleshly, and his existence now disharmonized by sin, it yet appears that it was possible for him to make that condition immortal by eating of the Tree of Life, and bringing about an immortality of wretchedness, which would have been the triumph of the tempter. Such a possibility, however, was prevented by the banishment of our first parents from the garden of Eden, where alone such immortal food was to be found. And flaming swords—the symbol of God's *holiness* and *love*—as a consuming fire, guarded the entrance and made for ever impossible the re-entry thereto. All this was in mercy; and death, too, was mercifully allotted, in order to lessen the evils of life, and to take man by another path to Immortality. But does this banishment from Eden and from immortal food mean that man no more shall taste such food, but shall instead thereof die and become annihilated. By no means. For death nowhere in the Old Testament means annihilation; such a notion is foreign to its spirit throughout. Paradise is before, not behind us, and can only be re-entered by the one appointed Way—"I am the Way." Man may try other ways, but he will ever be driven back by the flaming swords which turn every way to keep the way of the Tree of Life. Immortality was not denied them, only the immortality of sin. And the way to eternal life

henceforth is no longer by means of the Tree of Life. The *way to*, and not the *goal itself*, is changed. In the *manna*, "the angels' food," with which the Israelites were fed; in the living *not by bread alone*, but by every *word of God*, we have glimpses here and there that immortal food was still supplied to man. And as Revelation completes itself, in the end Eden with its Tree, or Trees of Life, is seen again, and then there is no flaming sword to bar the way. Man, long banished from that scene, and meanwhile having his whole being reharmonized through redemption and regeneration, passing through death and the Resurrection, acquires the "right to the Tree of Life." He eats and lives for ever, death having no more dominion over him.

(*b*)

9. Their Hope

Can we imagine our first parents, and through them the faithful from the first, having the words of the promise, although in its most initial and elementary form, wholly without the belief that one day the "right to the tree of life," the symbol of Immortality, would be opened to them again, and that a time would come when they might freely eat and live for ever? Without this hope the promise as a word of comfort would surely fall short. The words of the promise themselves must have suggested the hope that the designs of him who was a murderer from the beginning should be thwarted, and not death but Life should reign. And this hope was the ray which *shone* forth from Paradise, as an inspired revelation, handed down by tradition from Adam to Noah (for a very few years comparatively intervened between the birth of the one and the death of the other), until afterwards, in the fulness of time, the hope acquired dogmatic and written expression.

Was not the import of the promise this?— That a Conqueror of sin, a Conqueror of death, a Conqueror of him who had the power of death, should come, and unbar that gate, and open the way for man to his forfeited communion with God, and again give him the right to the Tree of Life, from which Adam, who had a right to it, was driven forth for his disobedience?

(*c*)

10. The Clothing of our First Parents

Attention has also been drawn to the Clothing of our First Parents. God made for them coats of the skins of beasts. *They* had tried to hide themselves with fig leaves: God *clothes* them. And this clothing is supposed to have been symbolical of our being "clothed upon" with an immortal body—as the sinful put on clothing, mortality should put on immortality. If so, another germ of the doctrine, and one easily understood, existed from the very time of the Fall.

(*d*)

11. Long Life

But the prolonged life of the patriarchs must have been a witness from the first of this hope. Though death was present, and reigned from Adam to Moses, yet how seldom apparently was it seen! As it was, men almost seemed to be immortal. Of the first ten patriarchs the shortest

(*e*)

Man, Immortality of—*continued*

life was 777, and the longest was 969 years, showing that though death abounded, yet life superabounded. For the race increased faster than death decreased it. Apart from climatic considerations and the simplicities of life, there must have been other forces at work to make such longevity possible. The potency of Adam's paradisiacal life must undoubtedly have been projected into his whole life. Those powers, received fresh from his Maker's hands, could not soon have become exhausted. There is something in the potency of this life, resisting so long the wear and tear of life, that is analogous to the teaching of our Lord. "He that eateth My flesh and drinketh My blood shall *never die.*" Adam had eaten in Paradise, had been in communion with God, was God's immediate handiwork, created, not for death but for Immortality; and when he fell and came within the sphere of death, it had to wait long for its prey. Now this fact could not well have been without deep significance upon the minds of the faithful at that time. Long life may have been, as is indicated by Lamech's words at the birth of Noah, one of great toil and suffering. The effects of the curse may have been more keenly felt at the first, when husbandry was but a rude science, than now, when the appliances are so many for reaping the fruits of the earth. But this tenacity of life, this almost undying body, which could withstand decay for nearly a thousand years, must at least have deepened the teaching of the promise, and quickened the hope in Immortality. Only let the first conditions of life be restored, and the step from one thousand years to eternal life must have seemed less of a miracle to them than it does to us.

(*a*)

12. Enoch

All these, at the very least, may be regarded as germs of the teaching concerning Immortality, from which the after doctrine would grow, or as adumbrations preceding the substance. All these, of whom we have been speaking, died, but they died in hope, not having received the promise in its fulness.

But a more important witness of man's immortality was given to that period than these. One there was among them who became immortal. *Enoch* walked with God, and made the image of God a reality; and he was not, for God took him. He was translated that he should not see death. Now the important witness to this doctrine borne by Enoch was, that he represented, not the dead who shall be raised, but the living who shall be *changed* (see "CHANGED") when the last trumpet shall sound. He was called from his daily occupation, as many will be then. In a moment, without notice, the summons to put on Immortality will come.

He was a testimony therefore to a glorified state of existence:—not merely to the Immortality of the soul, but to the greater fact of an Immortal, complete man,—whose Immortality was the effect of a rightly lived life, of a man whose religion dominated his whole being, until he reached a moment when even that which was natural was changed into the spiritual, showing to his and succeeding generations that man had a destiny beyond what was visible—was created for Immortality. And to such an example as this the Old Testament

saints could look, to sustain the hope which, as time passed on, grew dimmer and dimmer, that man, over whom death now reigned, would in some way, and at some period, become victorious. They died in faith, "not having received the promise."

The fact of Enoch's translation must have had a very vivid effect upon the men of his generation. With what force they were appealed to! this happening at a time when men were in despair by means of the curse, which marred existence and made life a hindrance rather than a blessing, and when they stood in need of "strong consolation."

(*b*)

MAN, NATURE OF

"Man doth not live by bread alone," is a proof of his double nature.

(*c*) *Harless*

ADAM = earth;
MAN = mens = mind = spirit.

(*d*)

MAN: THE RESURRECTION OF THE BODY

1. Our Lord's Resurrection was "according to the Scriptures." Hence the doctrine of the Resurrection must have some Old Testament foundation" (1 Cor. xv.: *cf. Lange*).

(*e*)

2. Embalming, in the Mosaic era, must have been at least as significant as Cremation in our own materialistic age.

(*f*) *Lange*

3. Germs of the Doctrine

Though there is no dogmatic teaching (or formula) of the doctrine of the Resurrection in Genesis, and at the Beginning, yet the spirit of the doctrine is manifestly there, and the thing assumed was understood and involved in the faith from the first; though as Eden and Paradise receded into the past, this belief and hope and comfort became obscured, and the state of the dead—as a state of loss—becomes prominent—until the "day dawned." As an illustration, compare the analogy of a similar tendency of a "comfortable truth and hope" becoming obscured, in the earliest teaching of the Church of Christ concerning death. The Apostles taught that death was abolished—turned into a hallelujah!

See, also, the familiar and beautiful symbols on the tombs of the martyrs and others in the catacombs and the teaching of the apostolic fathers, with the general conception of death in the darkness of the Middle Ages Death by that time had again asserted its supremacy, and brought man again into bondage to its gloomy horrors and fears. The medium through which the Apostles and others had seen ti, was for the time being obscured; and though the Reformation brought in "faith," and the promises quickened "the hope," yet till now the Christian Church has suffered, not having shaken off the incubus under which mediævalism had succeeded in burying the hope of the Resurrection.

(*g*)

Man : Resurrection and Destiny of—*continued*

4. Resurrection of the Body

The Resurrection is a necessity, if the original plan of man is to be fulfilled. Man, as body and soul, is not indissoluble now, but he will be after the παλιγγενεσία.

(a)   *Dorner*

5. "First-fruits" (Jas. i. 18)

"First-fruits of His creatures." Christians are the first-fruits of those destined to rule the earth. They "have tasted the powers of the world to come," and live by anticipation.

(b)   *Cf. Lange*

6. First-fruits, Christ the (1 Cor. xv.)

Cf. "If we believe that Jesus died and rose again," etc. (1 Thess. iv. 14) with
"The children are partakers of flesh and blood. He also took part of the same," etc. (Heb. ii. 14).

Man is now destined to glory through death and the Resurrection. But Jesus, as the First-fruits (1 Cor. xv.) of these, is a representation of the fulfilment of the thing promised and believed in. He took part of the conditions of "flesh and blood," viz. life, death, intermediate state, resurrection and ascension victoriously to glory, as the first-fruits of the harvest of glorified men.

c)

7. Man, as in Adam and Christ

We take our part in Christ when we are born again, as we take our part in Adam at our natural birth. All that appertains to Adam—toil, decay, mortality—we inherit from him ; all that appertains to Christ—Life, Resurrection, Ascension, Immortality, and Glory—are ours *in* Him.

(d)

8. Death Reigned

"In the Beginning," is shown that Death entered upon its long reign ; and his supreme dominion is scarcely unbroken until One at last entered that kingdom, having the keys of Hades and Death, and effected a revolution, and led death itself captive.

(e)

9. Man, Immortality of

Time and Space are creations of God ; as with God it is universal HERE, so is it an everlasting NOW.

= Glimpses of *Immortality.* Is the white tomb (of a departed loved one), only a mournfully *receding* milestone—a pale, spectral illusion ! Is the lost friend still *here*, even as we are here mysteriously, with God ! Know of a truth that only the *Time* shadows have perished, or are perishable ; that the real Being of whatever *was*—*is*, and *will be*, *is* even now and for ever : believe it thou must —understand it thou canst not.

(f)   *Carlyle*

10. Man, Transfiguration of

Death tells us that the true heritage of our race is to be *transfigured :* to live a nobler, yet a human life, when things mutable and material shall have perished or have been changed !

Physicists inform us that our sun is slowly burning out his fires ; that the forces which move our planetary system are waning now, and are doomed to wane away. Then its orbs must collapse. Then our earth, with her seasons, colours, light and shade, rest and motion, will cease to be a human world. But if philosophy reads earth and heaven aright, we may hope to grow, while those glittering orbs wax old,—we shall *be*, and be *good*, when they decline and disappear. Thus looked at, man is of more worth than a world ; what, then, is the worth of a *whole world of mankind* !

(g)   *Jackson's Bampton Lectures*

11. Man, Possibilities of

The most wicked, depraved, worthless man is still a man, and of necessity a denizen of God's world, and capable of a darker or clearer perception of his individuality and indispenable requirements. O brother man, look at what is *present* there, not on *what is lacking. Humanity, in all its distortions, is still always humanity,* worthy of *admiration.* No man ceases to be a man, even when he appears to sink far below the dignity of manhood. So long as he is not a beast (and as little as a beast can become a man can a man become a beast), so long is he capable of improvement and perfectibility. Behold what may be brought out of it !

(h)   *Lavater*

12. The Glorification and the Degradation of Man are Opposite Poles and Contrasts

In the Book of Revelation, chap. xxi. 7, 8, the " brave " are contrasted with " cowards " ;
The " pure " with the " unclean " ;
The " sons of God " " saints," with " dogs."
The saved are at their best, " glorified," whilst the " degraded " are bestialized, unmanned. They suffer a *deterioration* and loss of personality, as the very opposite pole to that reached by the saved. Cf. the teaching of naturalists, who tell us that domestic animals neglected return ultimately to their primitive type. Hence may not the " lost " (unsaved men) likewise return to that impersonal being, which recent science asserts to have been the natural progenitor of man? " The immediate ancestor of man was an animal with pointed ears and a tail " (Darwin's theory), therefore *not a man* in any sense.

(i)

13 The "Lost"

Granting that there is some truth in this, may it not cast some light upon the " lost " ? May not their consignment to the abyss be a representation simply of the process of deterioration and degradation, through which by slow processes they may be returning, not only to animalism, but even to the original protoplasm? Compare the concords, the " æons of æons," according to science, in perfecting man, *i.e.*, in crowning him with glory and immortality as the apex ; and the corresponding æons, during which those who fail of reaching that apex will be returning to their primitive condition. Here, too, may indeed be a ground for the doctrines of annihilation—which deny an immortality to the " lost."

(j)

Man, Resurrection and Destiny of—*continued*

14. Granting that the immediate ancestor of man was a creature such as indicated, but *not a man*: Therefore man, as man, who possesses the gifts of intellect, speech, moral qualities, etc., had yet to be *evolved*, even out of such a substratum. Does this not permit the possibility of the Creator so intervening at this point, by breathing into this creature " the breath of life," and giving him a living soul, so that from that moment *the animal became the man*, and the differentiating gifts were at the same time bestowed?

That such an hypothesis is permissible may be inferred from the temporary gift of " speech " and intellect granted to Balaam's ass.

(*a*)

15. **Degradation of the Lost**

Is there no "madness" in the spirit-world? If despair now breeds remorse and maniacism, is it not conceivable that " a worse thing " will happen unto a lost soul, in that future where mental conditions will be developed and intensified? Compare the contrasts (Rom. ii. 7–9) of "glory, honour, immortality, and eternal life,"—"tribulation, anguish, and wrath," with the more intensified contrasts of the Book of Revelation (xxi., xxii.). Will not the condition there described as "dogs" signify a reversion to a lower type of existence, a descent *ad inferos*, a loss past understanding? Man was at first so constituted that he could either ascend or descend, *i.e.* by obedience become a partaker of the Divine nature, or by disobedience drop step by step into animalism.

(*b*)

Cf. *Dorner's System of Christian Doctrine on the* "Lost."

16. It is possible for us to materialize the spirit, as also to spiritualize the body. Cf. 2 Peter i. 4: "That by means of these ye may become partakers of the *Divine nature*."

(*c*)

There have been those·

"Who, in the dark dissolving human heart
And hallowed secrets of this microcosm,
Dabbling, with shameless jest, a shameful band,
Encarnalized their spirits."

(*d*)

17. **Degradation and " Æons of Æons "**

The opinion is becoming current, that the *unsaved* of this æon—age or dispensation—will pass through purgatorial penalties in the intermediate state (= æonic suffering); that of them an *elect* will be saved, whilst others, hardening themselves, will render their salvation a still more remote possibility, and through further æons of intervening suffering. Does this theory, or not, fit in with the doctrine of an *elect* (those who are now being called out of the world and are being saved —the first-fruits), and who will be glorified at the second · appearing of Christ and enter into His glory—leaving others behind—either on the earth or in Hades, still in probation, who will have further opportunities given them, and of whom again another *elect* will be called out, until

ultimately the number of the unsaved (self-hardened) will be a small number of demonized and degraded beings (dogs)?

(*e*)   *Cf. Dorner*

MAN, What is   (Ps. viii. 4.)

This psalm connects the distant past with the far off future—creation with redemption when complete—the first chapter of Genesis with the eleventh chapter of Isaiah ; it is the poetic version of the former, and the germ of the prediction contained in the latter. " This psalm," Delitzsch has beautifully said, " like Psalm civ. and others, is a lyric echo of the Mosaic account of the creation." Ewald calls it " a flash of lightning cast into the darkness of the creation." This psalm, moreover, is quoted three times in the New Testament—in the Gospel according to St. Matthew, chapter xxi. , in 1 Corinthians xv. ; and in Hebrews ii. It is neither a directly Messianic psalm on the one hand, nor is its application to Christ a mere accommodation on the other; the middle way between is here the safe way and, we think, the sure way, and so we regard it as typically Messianic. The type is the first Adam and the privileges of the human race in him; the antitype is the Second Adam and the glory, honour, and dominion of redeemed humanity as represented by Him.

(*f*)

1. **" Out of the mouth of babes and sucklings "**

On a closer examination we find that the mouth of childhood, as yet only capable of childish prattle, is a synonym for the absence of eloquence, of power of speech, or of force and fluency of words. And yet the mouth of childhood, weak though it be and scarcely articulate in its utterance, is sufficient to defend the honour of God against the atheistical fool who says there is no God, and even to put to silence the God-denying blasphemer, so manifest has God made Himself by His works on earth and so manifold in His glory upon the heavens. Half latent, half apparent, there is here a beautiful instance of union of opposites, in the case of *speech*. Out of weakness comes forth strength ; for the most eloquent of speech, who deny or defy God, are capable of being silenced by the infantile speech or stammering mouth of children as they instinctively admire and unsophistically express their admiration of the objects of nature, so very clearly has God evidenced His godhead, wisdom, power, and goodness in His wonderful works on earth and His glorious majesty over the heavens. Our Lord cites this sentiment of the psalm with approval, and gives an exemplification of it in the 21st chapter of the Gospel according to Matthew. The miracles just wrought by our Lord on the blind and lame awakened the admiration of the children—boys (*paides* they are called in the preceding verse), this admiration expressed itself in an acclamation of praise— "Hosanna to the Son of David!" In this way weak means became such a powerful testimony to the Son of God that the chief priests and scribes were sorely displeased, because sorely discomfited, by those children in the Temple. And yet, alas ! their implacable hostility was not disarmed, though our Lord signified His approval of this childish testimony, directing the attention of His enemies

(*g*)

Man, What is?—*continued*

and refreshing their memory by His citation of this verse. In the weakness of their childish utterances they confirmed a truth rejected by the enemies of the Saviour; and thereby put them to silence, if not to shame.

(*a*)

2. What is man that Thou art mindful of him? and the son of man that Thou visitest him?

The first thought suggested to us by this verse is the littleness of man. Oh, how little man is, compared with those great planetary orbs that roll over his head! How puny, compared with that powerful arm that moulded them! How weak, compared with that Almighty Being who appointed them their respective orbits, and gave them the velocity with which they move in those orbits— who impressed on them that force that bears them onward in their course and regulated the times in which they revolve round their centre! Lord, what is man, that Thou, who sittest on the circle of the universe, whose handiworks adorn earth and sky, and whose glory is above the heavens, lookest down on one so little, so puny, and so weak! That is not all, man is worse than weak, he is sinful, and so morally as well as physically weak. He broke the covenant of his God at the beginning; he has continued his rebellion from then till now. He presents the anomalous and unnatural spectacle of the creature in arms against his Creator, the subject against his sovereign, the child against the parent, the servant against the master, the recipient of unspeakable blessings against the benefactor whose hand bestowed those benefits and conferred those blessings. He has forgotten the God that formed him, and lightly esteemed the Rock of his salvation. This he has done times and ways without number. Yet God has not forgotten him. He was mindful of man when in the beginning He created the heavens. He was mindful of him when He arranged and organized them as they at present exist. He was mindful of him when He prepared this world as his place of abode, ordaining the sun to rule the day, and the moon to rule the night. He was mindful of man when He arranged the pleasing vicissitudes of the seasons; when He renewed His covenant with man, saying, "While earth remaineth, seedtime and harvest, cold and heat, and summer and winter, and day and night, shall not cease." He is mindful of him when from year to year and season to season He makes the grass to grow for the cattle and herb for the service of man; when the eyes of all things wait on Him and do not wait in vain, for He openeth His hand liberally, and satisfieth the wants of every living thing. Lord, what is man, that Thou who art so holy shouldst be mindful of one so sinful?—Thou who art so pure, of one so wicked—Thou who art so happy, of one who by sin has made himself so miserable!

(*b*)

3. And the son of man that Thou visitest him?

The word for man in the former member has the root-meaning of frailty: the parallel expression in this clause implies that he is not a direct creation of God, as the stars of heaven, but mediately through human parentage—son of man, and born of a woman, and so inheriting infirmity from his earthly origin. Once more the psalmist looks up to the heavens, the work of God's finger, and contemplates the moon and the stars which He hath ordained, as they gleam upon hill and valley, or glitter on the ocean-wave. For a time he is lost in adoration of the great and glorious Being who set the stars as suns of separate systems; and who rolled the planets along the vast expanse of heaven, giving them a motion that never wearies, a regularity that never fails, and a rapidity that never flags. Then looking in upon himself and around upon his fellow man in his littleness and sinfulness, he cries out, "What is the son of man that Thou visitest him?" Not only art Thou mindful of him, making provision for his person, taking cognisance of his actions, and interesting Thyself in his affairs; but Thou condescendest to visit'him as one friend visits another, as one man converses with another, as one individual holds close and cordial intercourse with another.

(*c*)

4. God visited His people in the time of famine and supplied their wants, feeding them with food convenient for them. God visited His people in the land of bondage, and brought them up out of that land with a strong hand and out-stretched arm. God visited Moses in that bush that burned with fire, and yet was not consumed, when He gave him a commission for the relief of his distressed countrymen. God visited Israel in the desert when, from the top of Sinai, amid thunderings and lightnings and other circumstances of dread solemnity, He gave them that fiery yet just and good and holy law. He visited them in the Land of Promise, when at the dedication of their temple He filled their beautiful house with the cloud of His glory. Many a time God visited His ancient people by the prophets, rising up early and sending them—"at sundry times and in divers manners He spake in time past unto the fathers by the prophets." But the visit that surpassed all the rest and crowned all the rest, was the visit which God paid our world in the person of His Son; for God was in Christ, and in Christ dwelt all the fulness of the Godhead bodily. That was a visit which, whether we consider the glory of the Person who appeared, or the heavens from which He descended, or the errand on which He came, or the love that led to such a sacrifice, far outstrips in sublime importance and thrilling interest all the other visits ever paid our world. Lord, what is man that Thou hast made such provision for him in sending down Thy Son to take our nature upon Him, and by His Incarnation to exalt that nature and to dignify our humanity; and not only so, but through faith in Him Thou dost make us partakers of a Divine nature and so ally us with the Deity! Lord, what is man that Thou didst send Thy Son, Thine only Son, to seek and save the lost! Lord, what is man, that Thou didst not spare Thine own well-beloved Son, but delivered Him up for us all, thereby giving us a pledge that with Him Thou wilt freely give us all things! Lord, what is man, that, by the death of Thy Son Thou hast prepared the way and provided the place, and so opened the door of heaven to all believers! Lord, what is man, that through Thy Spirit Thou dost prepare us for that blessed state, making us meet for its exercises and fitting us for its enjoyments when the Saviour shall come again and receive us to Himself, that where He is, there we may be also!

(*d*)

Man, What is ?—*continued*

5. Thou madest him a little lower than angels (God), and crownedst him with glory and honour.

The Psalmist had intimated the littleness of man, as we have seen, but here he seems to correct himself, as it were, and dwells on the greatness of man. He is made in the image of God and with dominion over the creatures of God. The creatures likest God and nearest God are the angels, and so the LXX. renders *angels*, and the citation in Hebrews ii. 7 repeats it; but *elohim* by itself and in its exact sense has not that meaning. The expression for angels is rather *bene elohim* or *bene elim*. The use of the word *elohim* in Psalm lxxxii. is peculiar, but refers to magistrates or judges, and not to angels. Now man is only a little lower than these angelic natures that are the nearest reflection of the Divine; or, what amounts to the same thing, he is only a little less than Divine. There is some feasibility in the conjecture that when God proposed the creation of man in the words, "Let us make man in Our image after Our likeness," He included with the persons of the Trinity the angels. But, be this as it may, the Chaldee version and the principal Hebrew commentators agree with the Septuagint in its rendering of angels. The application of this passage by the inspired author of Hebrews is quite in harmony with its original meaning, if we only bear in mind that this psalm is only mediately and not immediately Messianic. The Psalmist extends his statement to the human race. The Apostle does the same, and speaks of man as having been made a little lower than angels, crowned with glory and honour, and all things subjected to his authority; but reflecting on the rebellion of man against his Maker, and by consequence the only partial subjection of the lower creation to man himself, he looks up to Jesus, in whom alone the grand ideal of humanity is realized, and sees Him already crowned with glory and honour; and then he directs his gaze onwards and forward anticipatively to the time when this text shall be fully accomplished, and all things completely subject to redeemed humanity and its glorified Head.

(*a*)

6. Thou madest him to have dominion over the works of Thy hands; Thou hast put all things under his feet.

7. All sheep and oxen, yea, and the beasts of the field;

8. The fowl of the air, and the fish of the sea, and whatsoever passeth through the paths of the sea.

A crown is mentioned in verse 5, and a crown imports a king, and a king implies a kingdom; and so in verses 6–8 we are informed of the extent of man's dominion, and of the various subjects of his kingly rule.

Thus man was set up as God's viceroy on earth. He was invested with full kingly dominion under Divine suzerainty. He was set over the nearest and the farthest—the tamest and the wildest—the highest and the lowest—all parts of animated nature on earth and even in sea and sky. But when man by his fall rebelled against his Maker, the creatures below man and subjected to man rebelled against him. Their submission, which had been at first and before the fall spontaneous, has now for the most part to be enforced; while all man's power and skill and art are required for such enforcement. And though man, notwithstanding occasional defeats, generally regains the mastery and triumphs in the conflict, yet it is as the result of superior wisdom and persevering efforts.

(*b*)   *J. J. Given*

MAN, WANTS OF

Man wants but little here below,
Nor wants that little long.

(*c*)   *Goldsmith*

MAN OF SIN, THE (2 Thess. ii. 2, 3)

The Man of Sin will make Adam's sin his very religion, and will glorify sin. This can only be an apostate Christian, a consummate Judas.

(*d*)   *Deidrich*

MAN OF SIN (2 Thess. ii. 2, 3)

The sitting of the man of sin in the *temple of God* signifies his being a *Christian* by *profession*, and that he would exercise his usurped authority in the *Christian Church*.

(*e*)   *Macknight*

MAN OF SIN

Pope of Rome, Adoration of, after election to the pontificate. After being arrayed in scarlet, covered with pearls, and adorned and crowned with gold and precious stones, he is led to the altar before which he prostrates himself; and then the Pope rises, and, wearing his mitre, is lifted by the cardinals, and is placed by them on the altar—to sit there. One of the bishops kneels, and begins the "Te Deum." In the meantime the cardinals kiss the feet and hands and face of the Pope.

(*f*) *Bp. Wordsworth, and Ceremoniale Romanum*

MAN OF SIN

Pope, Adoration of

A coin, struck in the papal mint, has this legend, "Quem creant, *adorant*," Whom they create (Pope), they *adore*. . . . What a wonderful avowal!

(*g*)   *Bp. Wordsworth*

Pope Innocent X. was thus addressed by a cardinal at his *adoration*:—

"Most holy and blessed father, head of the Church, *ruler of the world*, to whom the keys of the kingdom of heaven are committed, whom the *angels in heaven revere*, and whom the gates of hell fear, and whom *all the world adores*, we especially venerate, worship, and *adore thee*, and commit ourselves, and all that belongs to us, to thy paternal and *more than Divine disposal*."

What more could be said to Almighty God Himself?

This *adoration* is performed by *kneeling*, and *kissing* the face and hands and feet. And St. John's word, nine times used to describe the homage paid to the mysterious rival of God, is προσκυνεῖν, to *kneel* before and *kiss*.

(*h*)   *Ibid*

See an Engraving of the *Adoration of the Pope*, in Picart i. 296.

Man (A Thinking)

Truly a thinking man is the worst enemy the Prince of Darkness can have ; every time such a one announces himself, . . . there runs a shudder through the Nether Empire ; and new emissaries are trained, with new tactics, to, if possible, entrap him, and hoodwink and handcuff him.

(a)   *Carlyle*

MANKIND, The Indefinite Variability of, in Instincts, in Morals, in Opinions

Three degrees of latitude reverse all jurisprudence, a meridian decides what is truth, fundamental laws change after a few years of possession, right has its epochs, the entrance of Saturn into the Lion marks for us the origin of such and such a crime. That is droll justice which is bounded by a stream. Truth on this side of the Pyrenees, error on that. . . . Theft, incest, parricide, all have found a place among virtuous actions.

(b)   *Blaise Pascal*

Mankind

At common births the world feels nothing new ;
At these she shakes : mankind lives in a few.

(c)   *Ben Jonson*

MANNA

A Jewish tradition says that the manna tasted to each man according to his *taste*, so that he relished it.

(d)   *Spurgeon*

Manna

The tree which bare twelve manners of fruits for the healing of the nations = twelve different aspects of Christ, by which He becomes to a variety of persons that which they severally need. *Apropos* of the Jewish tradition, that the "*manna*" tasted to a Jew like that food he most liked.

(e)

Manna, The True

Coincidences between the manna and the true bread. 1. A provision is made for human want, copiously and freely. 2. In each instance the free gift profits those only who receive it and take it home. 3. The manna was a daily bread, yielding a continuous nourishment. So is Christ.

(f)   *Donald Fraser*

"MANY MANSIONS" (John xiv. 2)

Mark the simple, childlike, cheering character of this address to dear children (τεκνία, xiii. 33) ; the touching ideas of Father, house, home, peaceful and durable rest, room enough for all in heaven.

(g)   *P. Schaff*

Henceforth they, like Him, were strangers on earth, having no abiding place : at this moment He disclosed heaven to their view, and gave them a promise of the many dwelling-places in the Father's house. Hence the significant choice of the expression, μονή, a place of rest, a lodging.

(h)   *Lange*

Many and Few

Man thinks of the few, God of the many ; and the many will be found at length to have within their reach the most effectual means of progress.

(i)   *Channing*

MARIOLATRY

The assumption of the Virgin Mary. The story was founded on the belief, and testifies to the fact of that belief. So with purgatory and other Roman Catholic doctrines.

(j)   *Mozeley*

MARK

" *I press toward the mark* " (Phil. iii. 14)

I strive to *press towards the mark* day by day. Oh that I may feel this continual hunger, and not be retarded, but rather animated by every cluster from Canaan, to reach forward in the narrow way, for the full enjoyment and possession of the heavenly enjoyment ! *May I never loiter in my heavenly journey !*

(k)   *David Brainerd*

MARRIAGE (1 Pet. iii.)

Marriage was ordained by God, instituted in paradise ; the relief of a natural necessity, and the first blessing from the Lord. Marriage is a school and exercise of virtue. Here is the proper sense of piety and patience, of the duty of parents and the charity of relatives ; here kindness is spread abroad, and love is united and made firm as a centre. Marriage is the nursery of heaven, fills up the number of the elect, and hath in it the labours of love and the delicacies of friendship, the blessing of society and the union of hands and hearts. Marriage is the mother of the world, and preserves kingdoms, and fills cities, and churches, and heaven itself. Like the useful bee, marriage builds a house, and gathers sweetness from every flower, and labours, and unites into societies and republics, and sends out colonies, and feeds the world with delicacies, and obeys their king, and keeps order, and exercises many virtues, and promotes the interest of mankind, and is that state of good things to which God hath designed the present constitution of the world.

(l)   *Bp. Jer. Taylor*

Marriage and the Bible (Eph. v. 28)

(i.) Marriage is a union for life between one man and one woman ; consequently bigamy, polygamy, and voluntary divorce are all inconsistent with its nature.

(ii.) It must be entered into freely and cordially by the parties, *i.e.* with the conviction that one is suited to the other (and it may be added, to take the positions involved in the natural and scriptural view of the relation). All coercion on the part of

(m)

parents is contrary to the nature of the relation; and all marriages of mere convenience are opposed to the design of the institution.

(iii.) The State can neither make nor dissolve the marriage tie. It may enact laws regulating the mode in which it shall be solemnized and authenticated, and determine its civil effects. It may shield a wife from ill-usage from her husband, as it may remove a child from the custody of an incompetent and cruel parent. When the union is, in fact, dissolvèd by the operation of the Divine law, the State may ascertain and declare the fact, and free the parties from the civil obligations of the contract. It is *impossible* that the State should have authority to dissolve a union constituted by God, the duties and ordinances of which are determined by His law.

(iv.) According to the Scriptures, as interpreted by Protestant Churches, nothing but the death of one of the parties, or adultery, or wilful desertion, can dissolve the marriage contract. When either of the last mentioned causes of dissolution is judicially ascertained, the injured party is free to contract a new marriage. The greatest social crime, next to murder, which any one can commit, is to seduce the affections of a wife from her husband, or of a husband from his wife; and one of the greatest evils which civil authorities can inflict on society is the dissolution of the marriage contract so far as it is a civil contract (for further the civil authority cannot go), on other than scriptural grounds.

(a) *Hodge*

MARRIAGE, A TYPE OF UNION WITH CHRIST

One with Christ. This is the ideal Christian state. We are to be in so close a union with Him, that we are to think as if He were thinking in us, to speak and to act as if He were speaking and acting rather than we ourselves. We have a faint reflection of this in that which should be the ideal condition of husband and wife. They are no longer twain but one flesh. They are to be, as nearly as possible, one person. Their thoughts, their interests, their hopes, their aims are one. Marriage, we are told, was given that it might be a representation of the spiritual union between Christ and the Church. The union of each separate soul with Christ is a fragment of His union with the whole Church, and must partake of the same character. He that is joined to the Lord is one spirit with Him (1 Cor. vi. 17).

(b) *Vernon Hutton*

MARRING OUR SALVATION

Twenty times a day I ravel my heaven, and then I must come with my ill-ravelled work to Christ, to encumber Him (as it were) to right it; and to seek again the right end of the thread, and to fold up again my eternal glory with His own hand, and to give a right cast of His holy and gracious hand to my marred and spoiled salvation. Certainly it is a cumbersome thing to keep a foolish child from falls and broken brows, and weeping for this and that toy, and rash running, and sickness, and bairns' diseases; ere he get through them all, he costeth no little care to his keepers. And so is a believer a cumbersome piece of work, and an ill-ravelled hesp (as we used to say) to Christ; but God be thanked, for many

spoiled salvations, and many ill-ravelled hesps which Christ hath mended, since first He entered tutor to lost mankind. Oh, what could we bairns do without Him! how soon should we mar all! But the less of our weight be upon our own feeble legs, and the more on Christ the strong Rock, the better for us. It is good for us that ever Christ took the cumber of us; it is our heaven to lay many weights and burdens upon Christ, and to make Him all we have, root and top, beginning and ending of our salvation. Lord, hold us here.

(c) *Rutherford*

MARTYROLOGY

Foxe in his "Acts and Monuments," writes the martyrology of the Protestants in three mighty folios; where, in the third, "the tender mercies" of the Catholics are "cut in wood" for those who might not otherwise be enabled to read or spell them. Such pictures are abridgments of long narratives; but they leave in the mind a fulness of horror. Foxe made more than one generation shudder; and his volume, particularly this third, chained to a reading desk in the halls of the great, and in the aisles of churches, often detained the loiterer, as it furnished some new scene of papistical horrors to paint forth on his returning to his fireside. The Protestants were then the martyrs, because under Mary the Protestants had been thrown out of power. Dodd has opposed to Foxe three curious folios, which he calls "The Church History of England," exhibiting a most abundant martyrology of the Catholics inflicted by the hands of the Protestants, who, in the succeeding reign of Elizabeth, after long trepidations and balancings, were confirmed into power. He grieves over the delusion and the seduction of the black-letter romance of honest John Foxe, which he says "has obtained a place in Protestant churches next to the Bible, while John Foxe himself is esteemed little less than an evangelist."

(d) *Isaac D'Israeli*

MARY; RABBONI (John xx.)

A dialogue most brief, and yet most pregnant.

(e) *Lange*

Jesus knoweth His sheep by name.

(f) *Starke*

Just two words constitute the entire heart-conversation, but they are words full of power.

(g) *Heubner*

MASSES

Once history did not know that the multitude existed, except when they were gathered together on the field of battle to be sabred and shot down for the glory of their masters.

(h) *Channing*

Masses indeed: and yet, singular to say, if with an effort of imagination thou follow them, over broad France, into their clay hovels, into their garrets, and hutches, the masses consist all of units. Every unit of whom has his own heart and sorrows; stands covered there with his own skin, and if you prick him he will bleed.

(i) *Carlyle*

MASTER

"*One is your Master, even Christ*" (Matt. xxiii. 10).

(i.) Human masters may transmit their words; Christ alone can impart His Spirit.

(ii.) Human masters may teach the elements; Christ alone can conduct to the goal.

(iii.) Human masters may establish schools; Christ alone can found a Church.

(*a*) *Lange*

MASTER (John xiii. 13)

How sweetly doth *my Master* sound, MY MASTER! As ambergris leaves a rich scent unto the taster, So do these words—a sweet content, an oriental fragrancy—MY MASTER.

(*b*) *Geo. Herbert*

MATERIALISM

On the one side of our existence, the form of gratification is purely material; on the other, purely immaterial. The hungry man is not satisfied with ideas, nor the inquiring man with food. . . . Only on the supposition that our nature is a union of something material and something immaterial, can be explained that twofold character of our desires. Scripture justifies us in naming the twofold ground of our nature *spirit*, and *body*, more correctly, flesh (σάρξ, Eph. v. 29).

(*c*) *Harless*

MATERIALISM

After the narrative of the creation of the earth and brute animals (Gen. i.), Moses seems to pause, and says: "And God said, Let Us make man in *Our image* after *Our likeness*." And in chap. ii. he repeats the narrative: "And the Lord God formed man of the dust of the ground, and breathed into his nostrils the breath of life;" and then adds these words,—"*And man became a living soul.*" Materialism will never explain those last words.

(*d*) *S. T. Coleridge*

MATERIALISM

Try to conceive of a *man* without the ideas of God, eternity, freedom, will, absolute truth; of the good, the true, the beautiful, the infinite. An *animal* endowed with a memory of appearances and facts might remain. But the *man* will have vanished, and you have instead a creature more subtle than any beast of the field, but likewise cursed above every beast of the field; upon the belly must it go, and dust must it eat all the days of its life.

(*e*) *Ibid*

Materialism is a rebound against a fanatical spiritism.

(*f*)

MATERIALISM

Either we have an immortal soul, or we have not. If we have not, we are beasts; the first and wisest of beasts it may be, but still true beasts. We shall only differ in degree, and not in kind; just as the elephant differs from the slug.

(*g*) *Ibid*

MATERIALISM

In his old age, he heard a sermon by the eminent Williams, of Wern, on one of the doctrines about which he hesitated; and his remark was, "If that sermon be true, it will be a dark lookout for a great many of us." He instinctively shrank from views which, to him, darkened with their shadow the prospects of millions of his fellow-creatures. In a letter which he wrote to a friend, he thus expresses himself: "I am perfectly satisfied that Dr. Priestley and persons of the same views may be good and pious Christians; I have the same opinion of John Calvin, Dr. Crisp, and their disciples; I would gladly commune with them all, in the joyful hope of spending eternity with them." The following lines, referring to the materialism of Dr. Priestley, must be understood, not as an expression of theological sentiment, but as a specimen of pleasantry and humour :·

"Here lie at rest, in oaken chest,
   Together packed most nicely,
The bones and brains, flesh, blood, and veins,
   And SOUL, of Dr. Priestley."

(*h*) *Memoir of Christmas Evans*

MEANS

The mighty God (Ruth ii. 12; Ps. xci. 4) can deliver His own.

1. By weak means

Judg. vii. ; 1 Sam. xiv. ; Gen. xiv. ; 1 Sam. xvii.; Judg. iv. 21 and ix. 53.

2. Without means :

2 Chron. xx.; Exod. xiv.; Josh. vi.; 2 Kings xix.; 2 Chron. xiv.

3. Contrary to means :

Dan. vi. 22; Josh. iii. 16; Dan. iii. 25, 26; Jonah ii. 6; Josh. x. 12, 13, 14.

(*i*) *Bolton*

MEDITATION AND CONVERSATION

Addison was deficient in conversation. He was rigidly silent amongst strangers; but if he was silent, it was the silence of meditation. How often, at that moment, he laboured at some future *Spectator!*

Mediocrity may *talk*, but it is for genius to *observe*.

(*j*) *Disraeli: Cur. Lit*

(*See* "JOHN AND PETER.")

MELANCHOLY

A great captain, Zisca, would have a drum made of his skin when he was dead, because he thought the very noise of it would put his enemies to flight. I doubt but that these following lines, when they shall be hereafter read, will drive away melancholy, though I be gone, as much as Zisca's drum could terrify his foes.

(*k*) *Burton: "Anatomy of Melancholy"*

MELANCHOLY

Do not give way to melancholy; seek amusements; be willing to be diverted, and insensibly you will become so.

(*l*)

Weak people only place a merit in affliction.

(a)   *Lady Mary Wortley Montagu*

MEMORY

In the spot (of the brain) where each class of sensations is localized, the *memory* of that class is also localized. This is supported by facts. Blindness destroys the power of receiving fresh visual sensations, but the past sensations received and stored up can be now called forth by *memory*. This latter power perishes, too, if the sight-centre of the brain is destroyed.

(b)   *Ferrier*

MEMORY

The intellect remains unshaken. One of his sayings is, that since his illness he has had clearer and more perfect panoramic views of his whole life than he ever had before, which is a compensation for the hard fight with death. Many childish impressions of Spain that had faded from his memory came back to him, and in his delirious moments he expressed himself in Spanish.

(c)   *Victor Hugo's last illness.*

MEMORY

"*No more conscience of sin*" (Heb. x. 2)

Conscience, Remorse, Memory, are all allied. Recent studies in brain science have shown that sensations are localized in certain centres of the brain, *i.e.*, any object that has once been seen by the outer eye is carried by the inner eye into the brain, and there stored up, literally as a picture is photographed. Memory is the recalling of these sensations. So sounds, once heard, are stored up, and memory recalls them in after years. So of all actions and words. And if these have been against known moral law, memory may take the form of *Remorse, i.e.*, the natural reaction will be quickened by spiritual knowledge. The open book of Memory is conscience at work, showing its stored-up sensations. And the only relief is that of the Spirit of God pointing to the Blood which "cleanseth from all sin."

Think of the significance of this fact in mental disease, when the mind is off its balance. And especially when we consider it in a religious light—as "*a new creation*," so that henceforth we have these pictures *blotted out* = "*No more conscience of sin;*" and if (*Godet*) a new trespass brings back the old dread, how much more need have we of the continual application of the blood of cleansing.

(d)   *Cf. Cuyples*

MEMORY

"*The books were opened*" (Dan. iii. 9, 10)

A business firm keeps its own books; an accountant opens these books to ascertain the position of affairs. We, too, keep our own accounts, and conscience is the accountant.

Three facts throw light on the text:

1. In the moment of danger, drowning persons (or others) experience an instantaneous memory of past sins. The book of memory is opened; and God is a consuming fire. Why is all the past and present so vividly there?

2. The answer is partly illustrated by the art of

Photography. "Negatives" are kept stored up, and we can have copies when we like. Memory is a copy of real pictures, of things done and said, kept stored up.

3. Modern science explains Memory:—The eye and the ear experience certain sensations by seeing and hearing. These are printed on an inner part of the brain—laid up till wanted, and can be reproduced at any time. Memory is the recalling these sensations—the production of copies—and in moments of danger, this book of memory is suddenly opened, showing us the old debts, and scores never settled. These are facts, and thus we keep our own books.

4. The great question is, How to have "no more conscience" of these debts—to feel *assured* that they have been cancelled, and that when the book is opened it may be found to have a red line drawn through, cancelling the dreaded account. This question may not trouble us now, but it *will* in a time of danger, sickness, death-bed. Then people send for a clergyman, and ask him this question, How to quiet this account with Conscience? or, in the language of past times, "Shrive me, holy man,"—"Give me a white soul,"—"Give me peace of conscience,"—"Show me how to get the forgiveness of my sins," and the only answer that can be given is:

(i.) *You can have it:* "Once purged, there is no more conscience of sin" (Heb. x. 2);
"He Himself purged our sins" (i. 3);
"This He did once" (vii. 27);
"Having obtained eternal redemption for us" (ix. 12);
"Though your sins be as scarlet, they shall be white as snow; though they be red like crimson, they shall be as wool" (Isa. i. 18).

(ii.) *But you cannot pacify conscience yourself.* No self-sacrifice—no giving of your substance to the poor will help.

(iii.) *No man can do it for you.* No man can save his brother; one man can only act as the finger-post to direct another in the right road.

(iv.) Only by repentance and confession of these sins to God ("Who but God only can forgive sins?"), who hath given His Son to be the propitiation for our sins; "In whom we have redemption, even the *forgiveness of sins,*" "Whose blood cleanseth from all sin."

Such "worshippers, once purged, shall have no more conscience of sin." "If a man be in Christ he is a new creature (creation), (the old "negatives" are destroyed) all things are become NEW.

(e)

MEMORY, LATENT POWERS OF

"*The books were opened*" (Dan. vii. 10)

A relative of mine having, in her childhood, fallen into a river, and being on the very verge of death, saw in a moment her whole life, clothed in its forgotten incidents, arrayed before her as in a mirror, not successively, but simultaneously; and she had a faculty developed as suddenly for comprehending the whole and every part. . . . A process of struggle and deadly suffocation was passed through half consciously. This process terminated by a sudden blow apparently *on* or *in* the brain, after which there was no pain or conflict, but in an instant succeeded a dazzling rush of light; immediately after which came the solemn apocalypse

(f)

of the entire past life. This, from some opium experiences, I can believe; I have, indeed, seen the same thing asserted, and accompanied by a remark which probably is true, viz., the dread book of account, which the Scriptures speak of, is, in fact, the mind itself of each individual.

(a) *De Quincey*

A. held a bond against B. for several hundred dollars. When it became due he searched for it, but could not find it. He told the facts to B., who denied having given the bond, and intimated a fraudulent design on the part of A., who was compelled to submit to his loss and the charge against him. Years afterwards, A. was bathing in Charles River, when he was seized with cramp, and nearly drowned. On coming to his senses, he went to his book-case, took out a book, and from between its leaves took the missing bond. On the sudden picture of his entire life, which flashed before him as he was sinking, the act of putting the bond in the book, and the book in the book-case, had represented itself. The debt was afterwards paid, *with interest.*

(b) *Wendell Holmes*

MEMORY AND HEARING SERMONS

There are many who complain that they can scarcely remember anything they hear. Have done with your lying! Your memory is not at fault; it is filled with other things. I'll be bound you remember well what you sold your old white horse for at Llandaff fair, two or three years ago. Six or seven pounds, was it not? Certainly; that has not escaped your memory. You can remember anything but the Gospel.

(c) *Shenkyn*

MEN, HONOUR DUE TO

Sometimes, indeed, we see men giving sincere, profound, and almost unmeasured respect to their fellow-creatures—but to whom? To great men; to men distinguished by a broad line from the multitude; to men pre-eminent by genius, force of character, daring effort, high station, brilliant success. To such honour is given; but this is not to "honour all men."

(d) *Channing*

MEN. *"Ye are God's husbandry"* (1 Cor. iii. 9)

The great distinction of a country, then, is that it produces superior men. Its natural advantages are not to be disdained, but they are of secondary importance. No matter what races of animals a country breeds—the great question is: Does it breed a noble race of men? No matter what its soil may be, the great question is: How far is it prolific of moral and intellectual power? No matter how stern its climate is, if it nourish force of thought and virtuous purpose.

(e) *Ibid*

MENE, MENE, TEKEL, UPHARSIN

"Mene, Mene, Tekel, Upharsin" (Dan. v. 25)

"Numbered, weighed, divided." That is the meaning of the words. God lets sinners run the length of their tether. He does it in mercy, pur-

posing to bring them to repentance. But there is a time fixed for them; and when that time has arrived, when their cup is full, He steps in, and brings them to judgment. Their days are numbered; they cannot overstay the time by a single hour. So far He lets them go, and then He stops them.

(f) *Gordon Calthrop*

MERCY

God pours not the oil of His mercy save into a broken vessel.

(g) *Bernard*

MERCY

All the souls that were, were forfeit once; and He that might the vantage best have took found out the remedy.

(h) *Shakspeare*

MERCY

Between the stirrup and the ground,
I mercy asked, I mercy found.

(i) *Camden's Remains*
(Improved by Dr. Johnson)

MERCIFUL

"God be *merciful* to me a sinner," is the leading idea of the inscriptions on thousands of gravestones in the stately cathedral and the village churchyard, and bears silent testimony to the deepest convictions of mankind.

(j) *Maclean*

MESSAGES AND SALUTATIONS OF ST. PAUL
(Rom. xvi. 12)

A number of messages to unknown private persons, mostly old women and slaves. If a modern clergyman were writing to the parishioners of a former parish, what would be more natural than that at the end of the letter he should add, by name, friendly greetings of affectionate remembrance to any poor pensioner or aged widow whom he had known? Felix Neff, the Apostle of the High Alps, as he was called, two days before his death, being scarcely able to see, traced the following lines at different intervals in large and irregular characters that filled a page:—"Adieu, dear friend, André Blanc, Antoine Blanc, all my friends, the Pelissiers, whom I love tenderly, Francis Dumont and his wife, Isaac and his wife, beloved Deslois, Emilie Bonnet, etc., Alexandrine and her mother, all, all the brethren and sisters of Mens: Adieu, adieu!" François Dumont and his wife, adieu, adieu!

St. Paul was not dying when he wrote this letter, but it is exactly this, neither more nor less, which he does in this chapter and others at the close of his Epistle.

(k)

Many of these greetings are to women. The world has never properly recognised the vast debt which Christendom has owed to the work of women. Even in this day, though women do more than men in the great works of quiet, unobtrusive charity, though, in the tending of the sick and the visiting

(l)

Messages, etc., of St. Paul—*continued*

of the poor, and the teaching of the young and the consolation of the sorrowful, women are incomparably more thorough, more patient, more tender, more skilful, and more self-denying than the vast majority of men; yet even in this day Christian women could well complain that they and their needs and their sympathies are far less cared for in our public exhortations than those of men. Well, it was not altogether so with St. Paul. In this chapter alone, seven Christian women— Phœbe, Priscilla, Tryphena, Tryphosa, Persis, Junia, the sister of Nereus, and the mother of Rufus, whom St. Paul, in tender gratitude for her kindness, calls also his own mother, are all recognised in words of gentleness and praise. Even in this day I imagine the mass of holy and noble women may well be pained by the sort of mock deference and mock homage with which they are very often treated, by the banter and badinage, and hypocritical compliment, and foolish humorousness, and general terms of exaggerated meekness with which many speeches are publicly addressed to them. There is not the faintest trace of this in St. Paul. For foolish or unworthy women, for women weak and base, he had words of deserved scorn; the very loftiness of his ideal for true Christian women made that ideal when meanly dwarfed and miserably debased the object of more indignant contemplation to him. In days when women lived as they did in ancient days, in unavoidable ignorance and forced seclusion, and shamefully regarded as if they were the mere chattels and serfs of man's caprice and wickedness, St. Paul's illuminated soul had recognised the sacred and beautiful type of Christian womanhood, of woman as the friend and helpmeet of man, of sisterhood, wifehood, and motherhood,—everywhere two heads in counsel, two beside the hearth, two in the liberal offices of life, two in the tangled business of the world, two hearts beating with one full stroke of love had realized in prescient vision the holy mothers and the holy virgins of many Christian centuries. He saw in the poor Phœbe and the poor Junia the precursors of St. Perpetua, of St. Felicitas, of St. Barbara, and of St. Agnes, of St. Cecilia, and St. Dorothea, of St. Catherine of Siena, of Elizabeth Fry, and Florence Nightingale, and Sarah Martin, and Mary Stanley, and all the holy women who adorned themselves, not with broidered hair, or gold, or costly array, but in modest apparel, with shamefacedness and sobriety, and above all, which becometh women professing godliness, with good works.

(a)

Many again, whom St. Paul here salutes, were slaves, and men of poor and mean condition. What a lesson have we here in these mere lists of names! It is the nature of the world to fawn and flatter upon the great, to speak smooth words of their sins; they are ashamed to know the poor, ashamed to be friendly with the poor—almost regard it as a condescension to know that they have a common brotherhood. This was not the feeling of St. Paul. To him man, simply as man, was as great as he is in God's sight, and could not be greater. To him, in the essence of things, a slave was as great as a Cæsar, because every whit as much for slave as for Cæsar, Christ had died. Nay, a despised slave might be much more to him and much greater than the deified Cæsar. He thought that man in himself, however great, is less than nothing;

man is great in God only, if he is great at all. Nero sat among his lictors, clad in imperial purple; kings of the Orient laid their diadems before his worthless feet; the riches of the world were at his disposal; there was life and death in his mere nod. The slave was an almost nameless creature, who starved and herded with his fellows, who might be branded if he spoke a hasty word, and flung to feed the lampreys in the fish-ponds if he fell and broke a crystal vase. But all that was nothing to St. Paul. A few short days and both would die, and then one second with the angels would alter that; one second, and Nero might be wailing in abject shame in the outer darkness, while the poor slave might claim the angel's regard, might tread the heavenly Jerusalem's rejoicing streets.

(b)

St. Paul's greetings were not merely indiscriminate eulogy. Being all addressed to Christians—in days, remember, when Christianity was an indictable offence, in days when to be a Christian was to be persecuted—as a Christian he was writing presumably to good and holy men; yet even between good and holy men there is a difference, and St. Paul uses only the language of deserved and appropriate praise. Phœbe is a servant of the Church, Priscilla and Aquilla—the wife put first, as nearly always, because she happened to be the more able and active of the two, have hazarded their lives for St. Paul. Epænetus is well beloved. Mary has laboured much among them; Andronicus and Junia are fellow-captives with St. Paul; Urbane is a helper in Christ; Tryphena and Tryphosa labour in the Lord! the beloved Persis laboured much in the Lord; and so on. One little fact shows how full of insight these distinguishing touches were. Luke is the beloved physician; but we hear no word of praise said of Demas. Look on five years later, from the first imprisonment of St. Paul at Rome to the second, which was so much more shameful and severe, and you will there read, "Demas hath forsaken me, having loved this present world." Had the prescient eye of St. Paul seen already the latent possibilities of that dishonourable defection? It may be so; at any rate, five years earlier he does not praise Demas, and he does praise Luke, who continued faithful to the last. And this being so, seeing that even apart from Demases there was this difference between Christians even then, may we not every one of us take comfort in the thought that, as God bestows on us different gifts, so also He expects from us different forms of service. All branches cannot bear the same fruit, all members not the same office, all Christians cannot do the same work. We must each do what we can, and if only our work be faithful in our own best way, and up to our little best in that way, let us hope that God will accept it with all its imperfections, with all its miserable imperfections, even as we hope He will accept us in the Beloved. Mary has her work, and Phœbe hers. Urbane has his work and Apelles his. Some of us think with a sigh that we do little or no work either for God or for man. Well, if we are but trying to do what little we can, let us be content. We may be then like Asyncritus, like Phlegon, like Hermas, like Hermes, like Patrobas, of whom nothing is said. We may be content, if we can do no more, to be of the common herd, of the vulgar crowd, of the nameless

(c)

Messages, etc., of St. Paul—*continued.*

multitude of Christianity ; content to be of the faithful, if only we be faithful who are not famous ; content to be of the crowd of men by the cause they serve unknown, who lie in the myriad graves of old, never a story and never a stone. Better were it to be hired at the eleventh hour than not at all. Better were it to be of the forgotten throng, the nameless followers of Christianity, than to be of the world's guilty conquerors and guilty kings.

(a)

The mere casual mention of these names by St. Paul has given them a sort of earthly immortality, has enshrined their names till the end of time in the sacred Book of all the world. The poet Horace might have sung of them—he does actually mention one or two of the same names in his gay lyrics. The philosopher Seneca might have mentioned them among his brilliant aphorisms ; the historian Tacitus might have introduced them in his sombre and intense records ; yet in this case they would have been incomparably less eternized here on earth than when St. Paul mentioned them quite casually in loving messages at Corinth, and Tertius wrote down their degraded and grotesque names on the fugitive papyrus. Little thought these poor slaves and aged women that their names would be on our lips to-day in what was then the remote, savage, storm-beaten island of Britain, whose very name, perhaps, many of them had hardly heard, more than eighteen centuries after they had crumbled into dust. Centuries after they are dead we still speak of them, and yet grotesque their names certainly are : Phœbe, Hermas, Hermes, Nereus—names of heathen gods and goddesses in which people had quite ceased to believe, half-jocosely given to the slaves of their families. Stachys, a corn ear ; Asyncritus, the incomparable ; Persis, the Persian woman, known only by her nationality,—perhaps a poor slave girl bought from the Persian slave market at Rome, now beloved, who laboured much in the Lord ; Tryphena and Tryphosa—who ever heard such names ? They are names degrading and ridiculous in their meaning, which no human being would have borne by choice. Tryphena means " the wanton " ; Tryphosa " the luxurious " ; names once, perhaps, insultingly given to a class, now meekly borne. They had other names, new names in heaven. Go to the rear of the Columbaria at Rome, and there you will see the burial places of these, and such as these. These Columbaria are so called because they resemble dove-cotes, which is the meaning of the word. All round them are small pigeon-holes, as it were, in which, each in its coarse sepulchral urn of clay, stood the ashes of the poor slaves, whose bodies after death had been burned on some simple funeral pile. Every great house at Rome had its columbarium for their teeming multitudes of slaves ; and among these, especially in the still existing columbarium of the Cæsars, you may read these very names, Tryphena and Tryphosa, and others mentioned in this chapter. Could anything seem more utterly forgotten than these names of slaves, whose mortal bodies were calcined to ashes well-nigh two thousand years ago ? Ah, no ! they are not forgotten, and they never will be forgotten, because they were written in the Lamb's Book of Life. Is that no comfort to us and to you ? Five, ten, fifteen years hence how many of you who hear me will be dead and buried, and as utterly forgotten as though you had never been ? Fifty years hence all but one or two of us, it may be, will be lying in our coffins, our names, perhaps, illegible on the worn stone, and nobody knowing and nobody caring who lies below, as the restless feet of generations who have utterly forgotten our very name are passing over our last long home. All about us are hundreds of obliterated tombstones, of which it would be impossible even to discover what name was once carved thereon. Under your very feet crumble the bones of generations of these oblivion-swallowed dead, and we shall follow them. No Paul will mention us, and what does it matter whether our names be carved or no upon the icy pillars of human fame ? Ah, but are our names recorded among the angels ? Are our names written in the Lamb's Book of Life ? They may be if we will. God grant that they may be! And if they are, we shall each be able to say, " O death, where is thy sting ? O grave, where is thy victory ? "

(b)   *Archdeacon Farrar*

MIDDLE AGES

Of all the abortions of the Middle Ages which have come down to us, I know not a more miserable one, at once ludicrous and sad, than that heavens and earth of Cosmos *Indicoplentes*, the monk. They are just such heavens and earth as a monk might have made, and made too at a sitting. The heavens, represented as a solid arch raised on tall walls, resemble, as a whole, the arch which figures in the middle of a freemason's apron, or, more homely still, the section of a wine cellar ; while the earth lies beneath as a great plain or floor, with a huge hill in the distance, behind which the sun passes when it is night. And yet this scheme gave law to the world for more than six centuries, and lay like a nightmare on physical discovery, astronomic and geographical.

(c)   *Hugh Miller*

" MILK, I HAVE FED YOU WITH " (1 Cor. iii. 2)

I endeavour to imitate the Apostle. " *I became*," he says, " *all things to all men ;* " but observe the END ; it was in order to *gain some.* The fowler must go cautiously to meet shy birds ; but he will not leave his powder and shot behind him. *I have fed you with milk*, says the Apostle ; but there are some that are not only for forcing strong meat, but *bones* too down the throat of the child. We must have patience with a single step in the case of an infant ; and there are *one-step* books and sermons, which are good in their place. Christ taught His disciples as they *were able to bear ;* and it was upon the same principle that the Apostle accommodated himself to prejudice.

(d)   *John Newton*

MILTON

I began thus far to assent . . . to an inward prompting which now grew daily upon me, that by labour and intent study (which I take to be my portion in this life), joined with the strong propensity of nature, I might perhaps leave something so written to aftertimes as they should not willingly let it die.

(e)   *Milton*

MILTON

We owe the great writers of the golden age of our literature to that fervid awakening of the public mind which shook to dust the oldest and most oppressive form of the Christian religion. We owe Milton to the progress and development of the same spirit; the sacred Milton was, be it ever remembered, a republican and a bold inquirer into morals and religion.

(a)   *Shelley*

MIND AS POWER

Mind is the supreme power in the universe.

(b)   *Channing*

MIND AND MATTER

Being in company with a gentleman who thought fit to maintain Dr. Berkeley's ingenious philosophy, that nothing exists but as perceived by some mind; when the gentleman was going away, Dr. Johnson said to him, " Pray, sir, don't leave us; for we may perhaps forget to think of you; and then you will cease to exist."

(c)   *Johnsoniana*

MIND AND MATTER

Bishop Berkeley destroyed the world in one volume octavo, and nothing remained after his time but mind—which experienced a similar fate from the hand of Mr. Hume in 1737; so that with all the tendency to destroy there remains nothing left for destruction.

(d)   *Sydney Smith*

MIND AND MATTER

When Bishop Berkeley said, " There was no matter,"
And proved it, 'twas no matter what he said.
They say his system 'tis in vain to batter,
Too subtle for the airiest human head ;
And yet who can believe it ?

(e)   *Byron*

MINISTERIAL CALLING, MAKING SURE OF

Doubts that God had not called me to the ministry weighed heavily upon me that I dismounted, fastened my horse, and went into a field to pray. Whether anybody saw me I heeded not, because the end of all things, as it were, had come upon me. However, God had mercy on my poor soul, and I received Jacob's blessing ; yes, I saw, as it were, the heavens open. When I arose, I started on my journey, and the smiles of the Heavenly Spirit lighted up my way for the space of two months. I have since that occasionally had my doubts and fears; but the fear that I had not been called to the ministry never afterwards so troubled me. I have not the slightest doubt but that it is my duty to put forth all my power in the ministry as long as I live.

(f)   *Christmas Evans*

MINISTERIAL FAITHFULNESS

We could not say that we had declared to you the whole counsel of God, unless we dwelt now and then, at proper seasons, upon God's sovereign election, and unless we showed you that, from all eternity, God predestinated His people to obtain grace on earth and glory in heaven.

(g)   *C. Clayton*

MINISTERIAL QUALIFICATIONS

" The scribe instructed " (Matt. xiii. 52)

Qualification is an habitual preparation, by study, exercise, and due improvement of the same. *Powers* act but weakly and irregularly, till they are heightened and perfected by habit. A well radicated habit is a coat of mail upon our armour, a raising of the soul, at least one storey higher ; for take off but the wheels, and the powers in all their operations will drive but heavily. It is not enough to have *books*, or for a man to have his divinity in his pocket, or upon his shelf, but he must have mastered his notions, till they even incorporate into his mind, so as to be able to produce and wield them upon all occasions ; and not when a difficulty is proposed, and a performance enjoined, to say, That *he will consult such and such authors.* For this is not to be a Divine, who is rather to be *a walking* library, than a *walking index.* . . . The similitude of the text—we should not account him a good housekeeper, who should not have always something of standing provision by him, so as never to be surprised. . . . So the scribe here spoken of should have an inward, lasting feeling and sufficiency to support and bear him up, especially in case of urgency, and where actual preparation can be but short. . . . Then it is not the oil in the *wick*, but in the *vessel*, which must feed the lamp. The former may cause a *present blaze*, but it is the latter which must give a *lasting light.* A dying man's breath is in his nostrils, but to have it in the lamp is life. It will suffice to rake together a few notions, or to bring one's little utmost into one discourse, to make a Divine. No, as man would then be quickly drained. There must be *store*, *plenty*, and a *treasure*, lest he turn broken, and run the round of a beaten, exhausted commonplace.

(h)   *South*

MINISTERS (1 Thess. ii. 9)

Often enough have I been offended with a certain class of ministers. To lament over their poor pay is their whole business, their main topic of conversation. Nowhere is there less of faith and contentment than among men of this sort. With them the earthly mind thoroughly predominates. In no class is there less of Divine understanding. In heaven we shall probably meet the smallest proportion of ministers ; for it is well-nigh impossible that such an ease-loving, selfish minister should enter the kingdom of heaven. Is it not a real mercy that we are even kept a little short? How much money, then, must a preacher have on hand? Or how much must he have in furniture and pictures? On this absurdity I could descant for a day, and not exhaust the topic, dealing not with individual cases, but with the thing itself, nor yet out of illiberality of feeling, but from long observation. Ah, where is the imitation of Christ's life of poverty? No doubt, there are many who

(i)

suffer, but why? because they fancy that a son is not saved unless he gets to be a gentleman at the University. The true sufferers are they who are silent and endure, looking up to God.

(a)   Ludwig Hofacker, "Life of A. Knapp"

MINISTERS

It is the great, widespread evil of the Church, that it has unrenewed and inexperienced pastors; that so many become preachers before they become Christians, and are consecrated as priests at the altar of God before they are made holy to Christ by the offering of the heart to Him; and thus they worship an unknown God, and proclaim an unknown Christ, and pray through an unknown spirit, and preach a state of holiness, and fellowship with Christ, and a glory and a blessedness, which are wholly unknown to them, and perhaps will remain unknown through all eternity! He must be indeed a heartless preacher who has not himself in his own heart the Christ and the grace which he declares. Alas, that all scholars in our Universities might well ponder this!

(b)   Baxter

MINISTERS

No practitioner worth calling to the bedside was ever produced by bookwork merely. A man so trained would not merely be useless; he would be positively dangerous.

(c)   Sir H. Thompson

We want powerful ministers, not graceful declaimers, not elegant essayists but men fitted to act on men, to make themselves felt in society.

(d)   Channing

The word of God is indeed "quick and powerful, and sharper than any two-edged sword;" but when committed to him who has no kindred energy, it does not and cannot penetrate the mind.

(e)   Channing

"Things New and Old" (Matt. xiii. 52)

He who purposes to be an author, should first be a student. The two most engaging powers of an author are to make new things familiar, and familiar things new.

(f)   Dr. Johnson

MINISTERS, CREDENTIALS OF

We believe in the Divine commission, "As My Father hath sent Me, even so send I you."

We believe in the Divine assurance, "Lo, I am with you all the days to the end of the world."

We believe in the Divine victory, "I, if I be lifted up from the earth, will draw all men unto Me."

And our faith is turned into supplication.

Let us forget all but that charge, that presence, that redemption. There must be in the outward life, checks, lonelinesses, defects. We cannot always keep at the level of our loftiest thoughts. Yet the words shall have fulfilment, "from strength to strength." "O Lord of hosts, blessed is the man who putteth his trust in Thee."

Westcott's Ordination Sermon to Bp. Lightfoot.

(g)

MINISTRY

The ministry now accomplishes little, for want of that early intellectual and moral discipline by which alone a community can be prepared to distinguish truth from falsehood, to comprehend the instructions of the pulpit, to receive higher and broader views of duty, and to apply general principles to the diversified details of life.

(h)   Channing

MINISTRY, THREE CANDIDATES FOR THE
(Luke ix. 57-62)

Chap. ix. before chap. x. to show how the ministers of the Gospel were selected.

1. The Impulsive Candidate

"Lord, I will follow Thee." The answer = "I have no home—no creature comforts—no luxuries; in the morning I know not where I shall sleep at night; I follow the guidance of My Heavenly Father. Can you do this?" Impulse of no use without heroism. It does not appear that he was selected.

(i)

2. The Backward Candidate

"Suffer me first to go and bury my father." This would cause a delay of seven days. He wants time to reflect.

Answer?—"Let the dead bury the dead." The Nazarites, and others, in time of war, leave burying the dead to others. Be a Nazarite, and, in a time of peril like this, go thou and preach the Gospel.

Besides this, in seven days' delay his good impressions would wear off. Jesus would be gone, and the opportunity would be lost—Now OR NEVER!

This man was one of those who wait for conviction = the too hesitating.

(j)

3. The Half-hearted and Undecided Candidate

"I will follow . . . but"—there is something that this man is unwilling to part with. Answer: "You are an undecided man. No man having put his hand to the plough," etc. A man attempting to plough and looking back would make bad work. Christ does not want such workmen. The man represents those who seek to make the best of both worlds.

(k)

4. It is significant that one only of three is selected for the work. There is, it would seem to say, among religious people, plenty of feeling, plenty of half-heartedness, but too little of real heroic principle.

(l)   Cf. Godet

MINISTRY OF CHRIST, THE

"Isaiah saw His glory and spake of Him" (John xii. 41).

1. The Christian ministry is a ministry of speaking of the Lord, of Christ

The preacher is to be a preacher of Christ. The Bible is the testimony of Christ; and a sermon must be the same. If not this, it will be wrong at the foundation.

(m)

2. The Christian ministry is a ministry of witness-bearing

But this ministry of Christ is also a ministry which partakes of the human element through which it passes. As waters springing up through various strata of minerals and salts taste of what they pass through, and so possess their peculiar properties, so the Christian ministry undoubtedly takes its colour and characteristics from the subjectivity of the preacher.

(a)

3. The Apostles had seen Christ—they also spake of Him

St. John says, " We beheld His glory, the glory as of the only begotten of the Father."

St. Peter says, " We cannot but speak," etc.

St. Paul was the minister of Christ to the Gentiles, but he saw Christ first.

Luther, the great Reformer, saw Christ by faith before he preached — " The just shall live by faith."

Bunyan, too, had seen Christ with the eye of faith before he wrote of " The Old, Old Story of Jesus and His love," in his " Pilgrim's Progress."

(b)

4. Observe how this doctrine is laid down in the text, " Isaiah saw and spake "

The one is the complement of the other. His speaking (or preaching Christ) was influenced by the way in which he saw Christ.

(i.) *Isaiah spake of Christ.*

He was the evangelical prophet.

His was the Gospel according to Isaiah. He spake of Christ as—

(1.) The Holy One of Israel.

(2.) The Bearer of sin.

(3.) The Ensign.

(4.) The Reigning King.

(ii.) *Because he had seen Christ.*

Seen Him in His glory, seen Him as no Old Testament prophet had ever seen Him.

Not merely heard of Him from the teaching of others and the books of the time.

Not merely trained in the schools of the prophets.

Not merely obtained human credentials.

But had *seen* and *heard* in heaven itself the glory of the Lord, and had been invested with his office of a prophet.

(1.) In heaven He had heard the song, " Holy, Holy, Holy," and therefore spake of the Lord as the " HOLY ONE."

(2.) In heaven he had experienced the pardon of his sins. " Lo, this hath touched thy lips," and therefore spake of His atonement in chap. liii.

(3.) As the Ensign, he spake of the attraction of His cross.

(4.) As Reigning King, that " the whole earth is filled with His glory."

(c)

5. Application to us

Do we see any beauty in Jesus Christ? Is He the centre of life's interest? Do we do all to His glory?

If not, it is because we have not seen Him, or come into spiritual contact with Him.

For if we have once tasted that the Lord is gracious, that taste would make us hungry for more; one look of Him would be so bewitching as to make us look again. Heaven and earth would be a blank without Him. " Whom have I in heaven but Thee, and there is none upon earth that I desire in comparison with Thee."

(d)

MINISTRY OF THE GOSPEL, THE

When Saul of Tarsus was about to be inducted into the Gospel ministry, he was not encouraged by the hope of a rich church, a large salary, or a position in society; but was shown how great things he would have to suffer for the name of Christ.—Acts ix. 16.

(e)

MINISTRY, A PERFECT

In my imagination, I sometimes fancy I could make a perfect minister. I take the eloquence of ——, the knowledge of ——, the zeal of ——, and the pastoral meekness, tenderness, and piety of ——; then putting them all together into one man, I say to myself, *this* would be a perfect minister. Now there is One, who, if He chose it, could do all this, but He never did. He has seen fit to do otherwise, and to divide these gifts to every man severally as He will.

(f)

John Newton

MINISTRY AND PEOPLE

Every one is known by his neighbours better than by his minister, from whom much is concealed.

(g)

Zwingli

MIRACLES

There have been surprising coincidences in modern times between the wonderful in nature and the wonderful in history; for example, between the sailing of the invincible Spanish Armada and the storm which strewed the shores of Great Britain with its ponderous wrecks—between the march of Napoleon's army and the winter's snow which blinded, benumbed, and destroyed so many thousands, the connection is unexplained except on the principle of a Divine Providence.

(h)

Stoughton and Martensen

An animal is a miracle to the vegetable world.

(i)

Hegel

Suppose you were to carry a man wholly unacquainted with vegetation to the most majestical tree in our forests, and whilst he was admiring its extent and proportions, suppose you should take from the earth at its root a little downy substance, which a breath might blow away, and say to him, " That tree was once such a seed as this; it was wrapped up here; it once lived only within these delicate fibres, this narrow compass." With what incredulous wonder would he regard you?

(j)

Channing

MIRACLES NOT INCREDIBLE

The sceptic tells me that the order of nature is fixed. I ask him, By whom or by what is it

(k)

fixed? By an iron fate?—by an inflexible necessity? Does not nature bear the signature of an intelligent Cause? Does not the very idea of its order imply an ordaining or disposing Mind? Does not the universe, the more it is explored, bear increasing testimony to a Being superior to itself? Then the order of nature is fixed by a Will which can reverse it. Then a power equal to miracles exists. Then miracles are not incredible.

(a) *Channing*

MIRACLES: THEIR SCOPE AND PURPOSE

"And he said unto him, if they hear not Moses and the prophets, neither will they be persuaded though one rose from the dead" (Luke xvi. 31)

The very vivid contrasts of the parable of the rich man and Lazarus are among the very first features in the Gospel to take possession of the imagination and the heart.

1. First, there is the contrast between the rich and the poor—that great contrast which is apparently rooted in the nature of things; which reappears in all ages and countries wherever there is a settled order of human society. Dives, with outward robes of purple still, and an under tunic of fine linen—Dives, with a table furnished day by day with every delicacy that money can buy—he is always here. And Lazarus, *thrown down* (such is the original expression)—thrown quite down to lie at the gate of the outer court of the rich man's mansion; Lazarus, who feeds on the crumbs which the slaves of Dives have contemptuously thrown to him; Lazarus, so neglected that his wounds are without bandages, and the dogs roaming through the Eastern streets stop for a moment to lick his sores—he, too, is always here. The contrast is as old and as lasting as society—a contrast which met the eyes centuries ago in Rome and Jerusalem, just as now, as you walk from east to west of London—a contrast which, through social science and wise legislation, and above all the Divine charities of Jesus Christ our Lord filling the regenerated hearts of men, may be less harsh, less astounding, but the causes of which these cannot really remove.

(b)

2. The second contrast—that of the living and the dead. The parable places us face to face with Dives and Lazarus, first in life, and then in the world which follows. This is a more solemn contrast than that between the rich and the poor. It is a contrast between that which passes and that which lasts—between appearances and reality. Lazarus, so we are told, died in time, worn no doubt by age and sickness. Nothing is said of his burial. Perhaps he was not buried at all. And after awhile Dives dies too, and he of course is buried—buried with all due respect and ceremony; and after the brief sleep of death they wake, as we shall all one day wake, in the new world. The life of that new world is a continuation of the life of this—circumstances are altered, characters remain. Enough now to repeat, that by what we see here is apparent what we shall see there. And this contrast between the living and the dead is much more rooted in the nature of things than that between the rich and the poor. It is as old, as wide, as enduring as the human race. Day by day men and women around are exploring it; day by day they are passing the line separating the living from the dead, and sounding the heights and depths of its stern and blessed results.

(c)

3. The parable brings a third contrast, differing from the two former in this—that whereas they belong, the first wholly to this, and the second in part to the second world, this third is altogether concerned with the next. In the next world there are two kinds of beings—the miserable and the blessed. All are not blessed; numbers, thank God! are not miserable. There Lazarus rests on the bosom of Abraham; there Dives lifts up his eyes in torment; and between the two there is a great gulf fixed, so that, in Abraham's words, "they that would pass hence to you cannot, neither can they pass to us that would come from thence." A contrast this, indeed, more solemn than that between the living and the dead; a contrast which will still endure when all which still meets the eye of sense shall have passed away. As we dwell upon our Saviour's words, we perhaps say to ourselves, "After all, it is only a parable." Well, it is a parable, although it is possibly allied to history. There is something to be said if Dives and Lazarus were real persons whose destiny after death He authoritatively proclaims. But if this is purely a fictitious narrative, it teaches something when it comes from the lips of Eternal Truth. Its Levitical phraseology, its incidents, all, each of them, do mean something that may be translated into corresponding realities. This parable, if it teaches anything at all, can teach nothing else than these three contrasts—the contrast between the selfish rich and the poor, the suffering poor; the contrast between the living and the dead; the contrast between the happy and the miserable in another world.

(d)

4. Dives and Lazarus are now among the dead; not yet so separated as they will be after the final judgment, but separated, we are told, by an impassable gulf. They are in that sphere of being into one aspect of which our Lord descended after His death, and which we call "hell" in the Creed, which contains on the one hand Paradise and Abraham's bosom—anticipations these of perfect happiness, and which also contains that which is already the portion of Dives, while he awaits the final judgment. Yet between Dives and Abraham it would seem some sort of communication is still possible, and in this report or representation of the Divine Teacher we have put before us two separate conversations. First of all Dives petitions Abraham, the father of all faithful Israelites, that a drop of water may be sent him by the hand of Lazarus; and Abraham tells "his son"—mark the tragic irony of the expression—that this cannot be, partly because an absolute justice is redressing the inequalities of life on earth, and partly because there is a great gulf fixing the Divine award as irreversible. Then, since nothing can be done among the dead, Dives thinks of the living. Dives now knows he is ruined, not because he was rich, but because he abused his wealth. He has five brethren living, as he once lived, on the earth. He thinks, if Lazarus could visit them,— speaking of what passes beyond the grave, speaking with the authority of experience,—they would be changed men. Abraham answers, "They have

(e)

Miracles: their Scope and Purpose—*continued*

Moses and the prophets, let them hear them." Dives remembers that he, in his earthly days, had "Moses and the prophets" at his hand, yet he died as he had lived; and he pleads with Abraham that if only a visitor from the realms of death could visit them, the five brethren would repent. To this Abraham answers again, that "If they hear not Moses and the prophets, neither will they be persuaded though one rose from the dead."
(a)

5. The desire of Dives is an indictment against God for not furnishing the Israelites of that day with sufficiently strong motives to holiness and amendment of life. The Jewish opponents of our Lord were continually asking in this way for "signs and wonders"; and our Lord was constantly replying that there were proofs enough and to spare of His mission in the law, in the prophets, in His words, in His works—proofs enough to dispense with anything of the kind. Dives talks still like the ordinary Pharisees of the day. When he asks that Lazarus may be sent to his brethren, he implies that if he had been visited by one who had seen the realities of the other life, he would have lived and died quite differently. As it was, he had only the "old Book" to fall back upon, only "Moses and the prophets." There was something, he tacitly suggests, to be said for him after all; and, therefore, when Abraham refers to the five brethren, he means Dives himself as well. If Dives had not heard Moses and the prophets, neither would he have been persuaded though one had risen from the dead. This answer is undoubtedly meant to represent the mind and judgment of our Lord Himself. Abraham, in the parable, declares the will of God, just as Dives puts into words the thoughts of the Pharisees of the day.
(b)

6. The Reply of Abraham. What does it teach?

It teaches us, first of all, how far the actual sight of a miracle would be likely to produce real faith in the unseen world. Dives lets Lazarus lie at his gate. Why? Because he had no true belief in the unseen. "The brethren of Dives would do their duty by such as Lazarus if they could only see, in all his imperfections, Him who is invisible, their present Master and future Judge. Hundreds of men in our day, who have lost living faith in the religion of Jesus Christ our Lord, think that if they could only witness a miracle they could not help believing again—believing at once. "It is all very well," they say, "the reading in the Gospels about the stilling the tempest, about feeding the five thousand, about raising the three persons from the dead, about the resurrection of our Lord Himself. More than eighteen centuries have passed since these events, and there are no miracles seen now. Let us see a miracle," they say, "now; let us have it examined and proved by competent persons, and, depend, it will not fail of its effect. People will then believe, because they cannot help believing, in the truth of the creed which the miracle is intended to attest." This is what Dives thought and said about his five brethren. If Lazarus were allowed to appear before them—an apparition, he thought, must make them live for another life, that is, the life of faith. Moses and the prophets, he implied, have lost their power.

They were books dealing with matters said to have happened hundreds of years ago, they were books which Dives and his brethren had known from childhood, and familiarity had bred indifference or something worse.
(c)

7. And men ask now, in the heart of Christendom, Is there not something in this? Is there not in signs that which appeals more powerfully than thought? Is not the present better than the past—the action than the abstract argument? Would not the dead man standing before our eyes, telling us he came from the regions of the dead, with an appearance and every evidence that justified his assertion, have, of necessity, an influence which does not come from reading quietly in our church or our bedroom, which hearing a Christian teacher, under accustomed circumstances, could never produce? Would not the preternatural apparition exert a sway irresistible, making us earnest, impassioned, clear-sighted believers in spite of ourselves? To these questions our Lord answers, No! And for this answer the reasons are not hard to find. Miracles are called in the Bible, with reference to their effect on the human mind, "signs and wonders." They excite astonishment, they call attention to the mission of the message of the worker. A miracle is intended, first of all, to startle the beholder—it is a wonder; and, next, to point towards the unseen and external—it is a sign.
(d)

8. But even if the sight of a miracle produced these effects—if it first startles the man, and next suggests that there is something he does not see, and which is worth his attention and belief—this does not amount to actual faith. It is one thing to be convinced of the truth of the unseen; it is another thing to be startled. Some time in our lives we must all of us have been startled by occurrences which, though unaccustomed to us, cannot be esteemed miracles. A friend has died without any sort of warning; we have been in a railway accident in which several persons have lost their lives, and we have escaped—we know not how—through a series of unforeseen contingencies. Or some historical catastrophe—like Sedan, or the recent tragedies at Constantinople—has happened, and, for a moment, the world holds its breath, and seems to feel that God is passing along the corridors of human history. And events like this, on a small scale or great, are intended to remind us that what we see and are is very insignificant indeed when compared with what we do not see and what we shall be. Events like these, though occurring in a strictly natural way, do, up to a certain point—a very proper point—the work of miracles. They flash upon our mind for a moment the truth that God is not now only, but always, near; that His eye is upon us, guarding us, judging us, in His perfect truth, His perfect love, His perfect justice. Ah! these occurrences startle us. But what does it amount to? Momentary sensation—a moral spasm—which comes and goes, and leaves us as we were, or, justly speaking, perhaps not so well off as we were. Of course, a shock of this kind, like Paul's great experience on the road to Damascus, may be the door of entrance to a life of faith; but the shock does not insure it. Astonishment and bewilderment is one thing; but faith
(e)

Miracles : their Scope and Purpose—*continued*

is another. A succession of new phases of thought and feeling, produced by catastrophe, and compressed in a single moment, may be the turning-point of existence or only a strange experience. No doubt the five brethren of Dives, in his lifetime, would have been astonished by Lazarus appearing fresh from the grave, but it does not prove they would have been endowed with that vivid perception of unseen things which we call faith.

(a)

9. For, secondly, a miracle is only likely to have a real and lasting effect when it is addressed to a certain state of mind. A sonata of Beethoven's is nothing to a man without music in his nature ; a picture of Raphael's is lost to an observer without sense of colour, proportion, artistic beauty ; and, in the same way, the mind of the man who witnesses a miracle must be predisposed, or the miracle will fail of effect. A man must have an eye to God if he is to be enlightened by a miracle ; he must be looking out for some tokens of the will of God. He believes, we will suppose, in a vague way, that there is a Maker and Ruler of the world ; that there is a law of right and wrong, which he recognises within himself. Now, depend upon it, the more he makes of the law of right and wrong the more he will be disposed to make most of what is told him on the authority of the Being who gave the law. In this state of mind he watches anxiously for any sign which the Lord of nature may tend, or seem to tend, to make on the surface of nature, with a view to showing that He is also the Lord of conscience and the Lord of revelation. But if the man has no such interests, no such anticipations to begin with, then the miracle says nothing to him—the miracle is a mere curious irregularity observable on the surface of nature. It arrests his attention, perhaps excites his interest for a moment ; but that is all ; and if he has already made up his mind against the truth of which the miracle is the Divine certificate, then the miracle must be powerless to move him. "If they hear not Moses and the prophets, neither will they be persuaded though one rose from the dead."

(b)

10. This was actually the case with these very Jews to whom our Lord was speaking, not long after Moses and the prophets had foretold Him as the true Messiah. "Search the Scriptures"—your own Scriptures—"for in them ye think ye have eternal life, and they are they which testify of Me." But Moses and the prophets had arisen in vain so far as that generation of Israelites was concerned. "They are a people," as the Prophet and Apostle said, "they are a people who has made a snare to take themselves "—all the things which should have been for their elevation were an occasion of falling. Scripture had failed, and miracle succeeded. Jesus Christ died in public ; He was buried ; on the third day He rose from the dead ; His resurrection was a well-attested fact ; those who had known Him best saw Him singly and with others ; He was seen again and again for a period of forty days ; on one occasion He was seen by 500 persons, some of whom lived twenty-five years afterwards. But were the Jews, as a people, convinced? On the contrary, they said, to get rid of this stupendous miracle—intended, as it was, to convince them that He of whom their whole history consisted was come to be their King—that the disciples had " stolen away the body," that the disciples had conspired to palm off an absolute deception ! Our Lord might have as well remained in His grave so far as the great men in Jerusalem were concerned. They began by refusing to hear Moses and the prophets ; they were not persuaded though He, their true King, was risen from the dead.

(c)

11. Remember this when you are tempted to think that faith would have been easier in the days of the Apostles than now. "If a miracle was only worked before my eyes," it is sometimes said, "I should believe without difficulty." Would you? The probability is, that the very temper of mind that makes you ask for a miracle would kill belief in the presence of the miracle. Miracles are intended to assist those who are already seeking God. They are not intended to inflict a sense of God's power and presence and truth upon those who do not wish to know more about Him. A miracle cannot force the soul to believe ; it does not act like imagination or a chemical solvent, producing a certain effect, whether man will or not. There are ways of neutralizing its effect. If we hear Moses and the prophets, and listen to evangelists, and to the Lord of Life Himself, to no good or to less purpose, we should not of necessity be persuaded though the floor of this Abbey were to-night to break up beneath our feet and the very dead to come forth to tell us that the world to come is an awful and overwhelming reality !

(d)

12. What the miracle is to faith, that favourable circumstances are to duty. As a miracle makes faith easy, so favourable circumstances, a good example, encóuraging friends, the urgency of great opportunities, the inheritance of a noble name— these make duty easy. But duty is no more necessarily forced upon us by circumstances than faith is by miracles. Yet, if hundreds say, "I should be a sincere believer in Christianity if I saw a person from the dead," there are thousands who say, "I should be a better man or woman than I am if only I were differently circumstanced. If I were not tempted by poverty, or tempted by the world ; if I had religious or high-minded friends around me ; if I lived near a church or knew a good clergyman ; if I lived in other ages—the ages of faith, as they are called, when all the controversies that fill the air in modern times were unknown, and everybody was of one mind as to the best way of getting to heaven !" It is not the same thing to us all whether we have good friends or bad ; whether we have religious associations or not ; whether we resort to servants of Christ or not ; whether we are exposed to the temptations of luxury or of want, or are blessed with that amount of competency which saves us from these temptations. Circumstances are blessings or judgments from God ; and when surrounded with circumstances which make it easier to live for Him, and to attend to the true end of our existence, we have indeed great reason to bless Him for the blessings of this life, since, like all other good things, they come from Him, the Fountain of all good things. But these blessings do not — all these blessings do not—make yours a moral, religious, beneficent, Christian life, necessarily. They do not act like

(e)

Miracles: their Scope and Purpose—*continued*

rain, or sunshine, or atmosphere act upon plants. Under circumstances of a favourable kind a plant cannot help growing; it obeys a law of inevitable necessity. But under favourable circumstances, —nay, under those the most favourable we can conceive of,—the human soul can remain absolutely dwarfed and misshapen, and hurry triumphantly to its ruin, opposed to the blessed influences upward, which might beautify it, transfigure it, and save it. Felix was not compelled to be a Christian by the Apostle's burning words about temperance, righteousness, and judgment to come; though he felt their full force. Demas was not cured of the love of the present world by the sight and friendship of Christ's attached servant Paul, who was in chains at Rome and on the eve of martyrdom. Nay! if circumstances were ever favourable, we may think, to the well-being and growth of any human soul, they were the circumstances of that unhappy Judas. Blessed, as he was, with the daily, visible, Divine companionship of the Saviour of the world, circumstances did not arrest the commission of two tremendous crimes: the first, that of betraying the most Holy One into the hands of His enemies; and, next, that of rushing, by his own hand, impenitent, into the presence of his Judge.

(*a*)

12. Certainly let us admit that if favourable circumstances do not force holiness upon us, they may, and do often, protect us against monstrous vices—against the outcome of passions and dispositions which, it may be, are still unsubdued, though kept more or less in check. When we read of a great crime, how rarely it occurs to us to ask, with Augustine, whether, but for God's protection and grace, we should not have been the criminal! We read in boyhood the history of the Roman emperors — of Caligula, Nero, Domitian, and others,—and we said to ourselves that it was a wonder men so lost to the instincts of our common nature should have been allowed to cumber the high places of the earth! But should we have been better in their places, with the unlimited power of gratifying our own selfish instincts and making others the slaves of our will? Without the fear of another world before our eyes —without the fear of judgment and the fear of God—without the light which streams more or less upon the most benighted conscience in Christendom, from the radiant figure of our Lord Jesus Christ—should we have been better than they? Should we have been capable of unselfishness, of disinterestedness, of largeness of heart, in their places of power—an awful elevation with the world at their feet, and every incentive to indulge the whims of wealth at the cost of others? Should we have been capable of the virtues of Antoninus or of Marcus Aurelius?

In the day of our Lord the Jews said, if they had lived formerly, they would not have killed the prophets. But our Lord knew they would have done just what their fathers had done. He looked a few months into the future, and saw the Jewish mob that was to arrest Him in the garden; heard the insults in the house of Caiaphas; saw the long way of sorrow He would travel; knew of the hours He would spend on the cross of shame. "Fill ye up," therefore He said, " the measure of your fathers."

(*b*)   *Liddon*

MISERY

Misery acquaints a man with strange bedfellows.

(*c*)   *Shakspeare*

A man cannot be more miserable than his own wickedness will make him.

(*d*)   *Scott on the Psalms*

MISFORTUNE

The clouds that are the precursors of a storm do not appear so black to us when they hang immediately over our heads, as when we see them rising up at the edge of the horizon. . . . It is easier to know the worst than to dread the worst.

(*e*)   *Eng. Churchman*, 1859

MISFORTUNE

One woe doth tread upon another's heel,
So fast they follow.

(*f*)   *Shakspeare.*

When one is past another care we have;
This woe succeeds a woe, as wave a wave.

(*g*)   *Herrick*

One sorrow never comes but brings an heir,
That may succeed as his inheritor.

(*h*)   *Shakspeare*

When sorrows come, they come not single spies,
But in battalions.

(*i*)   *Ibid*

MISFORTUNE AND SUFFERING, Perverted View of (John ix. 2)

That extraordinary sufferings indicated extraordinary sins was contradicted by the Book of Job.
So, also, consistent Pharisaism saw in the lowliness of Jesus His unworthiness, in His defencelessness His guilt, and, after having crucified Him, in His cross His curse; whilst Jesus recognised therein His own glorification and the salvation of the world.

(*j*)   *Lange*

MISFORTUNES

All misfortunes appear more formidable at a distance than when we actually come to grapple with them.

(*k*)   *Eng. Churchman*

MISSIONARY WORK

The Prospects of Missionary Work

The present state of the world is such, that mere human calculation would justify most encouraging expectations. But the brightest light is cast upon the future by the promises of God and by the history of the progress of the Christian faith. Our confidence is not in men, not in money. Relying on the promised help of God, and constantly seeking that help by prayer, we feel assured of success. The Brahman, the Buddhist, the Mohammedan, might resist the arm of flesh, but who shall withstand

(*l*)

the living God? "*Not by power, nor by might, but by My Spirit, saith the Lord.*" The same agencies may be employed now as were employed of old—foreigners sojourning here, our countrymen sojourning abroad, and missionaries of the Church. By all these channels the Bread of Life may be distributed to the waiting multitude. History forbids us to expect great results in a short time; but He to whom a thousand years are as one day will give effect to our endeavours, if we persevere in them with prayer.

Hopeful, full of promise, is the work of the Christian evangelist or missionary. The end at which he aims—the conversion of the world—is as sure as the oracles of God can make it. When it will be completed we cannot tell. Now, as of old, the Lord knoweth what He will do. Man may chafe with childish impatience : but the Lord waits until His *hour is come.* Come it will—the hour promised to Eve, when the serpent's head shall be bruised with the fatal wound by the Seed of woman. Come it will—the hour foreseen by Abraham, when all the families of the earth shall be blessed. Come it will—the hour predicted by the prophet in imperial Babylon, when all people, nations, and languages shall serve the Son of man. Come it will—when the whole waiting multitude shall be fed; for God has spoken it.

"I will seek out My sheep, and gather them from the countries. . . . I will feed them in a good pasture, and upon the high mountains of Israel shall their fold be. I will feed My flock, and I will cause them to lie down, saith the Lord."

"They shall hunger no more, neither thirst any more. . . . For the Lamb . . . shall feed them, and shall lead them unto living fountains of waters."

(*a*)   *Bullock*

MISSIONARIES

It has been said that every man is a missionary either of heaven or of hell.

When the late Commodore Foote was in Siam he had on one occasion the king on board his vessel as a guest. He did not, however, hesitate in the royal presence to ask a blessing at table. "Why, that is just as the missionaries do!" remarked the king with some surprise. "Yes," answered the heroic sailor, "and I am a missionary too!"

(*b*)

MISSIONARIES

To a mission party :—"You have counted the cost, and embarked in this work for His sake, and, though inferior far, for our nation's sake. You must go through with it. Are you missionaries? So am I. The letter must be one which he who runs can read, the life."

(*c*)   *General Gordon*, 1884

Every human being is a missionary of heaven or of hell.

(*d*)

MISSIONS, THE TWO GREATEST

"*My Father hath sent Me*" (John xx. 21)

1. The most solemn mission week which the world saw, was the week of our Lord's passion.

He passed Saturday night at Bethany; the next day everything looked bright. It was Palm Sunday, and He rode into Jerusalem. He wrought a great miracle at Bethany, by raising Lazarus from the dead, and the people knew it, and met Him with acclamation. They took branches of palm, emblems of victory and triumph, and strewed them in the way before Him, as a mighty conqueror. They spread their garments in His path, as if ready to lay all at the feet of Christ. . . . They cried "Hosanna," etc. But He, the object of all this, knew that there was a cloud in the horizon, the sunshine would fade, and the heavens be covered with gloom. . . . He saw beyond that ephemeral triumph; and when He came near the city He wept over it ; and why? Because it knew not the day of its visitation. "O Jerusalem," etc., etc. . . .

There was scarcely ever a time when there was more of what the world would call religious demonstration than during that mission week. There were 2,000,000 of people in the city, crowds of worshippers in the synagogues and in the Temple, who joined in the hosannas to Christ. . . . But on Monday morning of the mission-week, on returning to Jerusalem, our Lord saw a fig-tree on the way. It had a luxuriant exuberance of leaves; but Christ wanted fruit—for *that* He craved. . . . He therefore blighted the leafy, unfruitful tree, and doomed it to perpetual barrenness. Here was a figure of Jerusalem itself. He went from the fig-tree to the temple, then thronged with worshippers (typified by the barren, leafy fig-tree), and said, "My house . . . thieves . . . ?" And what next? The same people who had gone to meet Him, coming from Bethany on Sunday, who seemed zealous for God's glory at the Passover, shouted "Hosannas," that very same people shouted no less vociferously on the Friday following, "Crucify Him, Crucify Him!" *That* mission was not successful, although it was the greatest mission held by the greatest Missioner who ever preached to the world.

Learn from this :—

There may be large and enthusiastic congregations, eloquent preaching, fervent spiritual excitement in "after-meetings"; but all may be only like the foliage of the fig-tree on the wayside, to be withered by the breath of Christ. It may begin with "*Hosanna,*" and end with "*Crucify Him.*"

2. The mission of the Comforter was, on the other hand, successful.

(*e*)   *Bp. Wordsworth, condensed*

MISSIONS

The spirit of love to our neighbour is wonderfully exemplified in missions. Men before had travelled into foreign countries; the naturalist, to collect specimens; the historian, to accumulate facts; the philosopher, to hive up wisdom, or else he had stayed in his cell or grove to paint pictures of beautiful love. But the spectacle of an Apostle Paul crossing oceans, not to conquer kingdoms, nor to hive up knowledge, but to impart life; not to accumulate stores for self, but to give, and to spend himself—was new in the history of the world. The celestial fire had touched the hearts of men, and their hearts flamed; and it caught and spread, and would not stop. On they went, that glorious band of brothers, in their strange

(*f*)

enterprise, over oceans, and through forests, penetrating into the dungeon and to the throne, to the hut of the savage feeding on human flesh, and to the shore lined with the skin-clad inhabitants of these far isles of Britain.

(a)   *Robertson*

MISSIONS

A golden moment of opportunity has lately come in the Metropolitan Mission, and has not yet entirely passed away. It matters nothing whether you have taken part in the mission, or not. You may have held entirely aloof from it in indifference or in contempt ; you may have even railed against it as a fanatical movement, a spasmodic enterprise calculated rather to injure than to advance the cause of true religion amongst us. All this matters nothing. The fact remains that you are conscious that a great spiritual crusade, wisely or unwisely, soberly or fanatically, has been undertaken against the heathenism ! and indifference and formalism of this metropolis. The note of preparation was sounded. All men were astir. And then began the work of the week, which, whatever may be said and, I fear, rightly said, about some of the excesses and follies and human mistakes which discredited it, was at least an honest attempt to win for Christ the souls which as yet are strangers to the power of His name. Of all this, you were conscious. Once again then, the subject of Christ's religion and Christ's claims has been urgently pressed upon you. Go where you would, you could not escape the sound of His name. You might endeavour to withdraw yourself into the recesses of indifference. But the sound penetrated even there. The word might be "mission," but it meant "Christ." The air was full of Christ. Everything spoke of Christ, and of the claims which He puts forth upon the allegiance and the love of mankind. And I say that to you who are conscious that you have not yet given your heart to the Lord, another and a more urgent appeal for Christ than has ever been made from this pulpit has been made to you by the circumstances of the last few days. Whatever you thought, whatever you said, whatever you did, about the Metropolitan Mission, at every corner of the street you have been reminded of your Christless condition. Every newspaper you took up, whether it abused the movement or patronized it—had a word to say about your Christless condition. The streams of worshippers : the serious—ay even, the mocking faces—(for they were mocking at Christ)—reminded you of your Christless condition. Not with the voice of one man speaking expected words from a familiar pulpit, but with the voice of hundreds of preachers and hundreds of thousands of worshippers has the cry been sounded in your ears—"Jesus of Nazareth is passing by."

(b)   *Gordon Calthrop*

MISSIONS

His great fear in coming to this city was, that many might be leaning upon man, and upon the arm of flesh, and might take their eyes off from the living God. If a work was to be done in London, however, God must do it. It was not any new gospel that London wanted, nor any new power. It was the same old, old story that the ministers of the Churches had been telling continually. God's ways were not our ways, nor His

thoughts our thoughts, and we must not mark out channels for the Holy Ghost to work in when He comes. When God was going to destroy the world, and wanted an ark built, He did not tell a nation to do it, neither did He call upon hundreds of men to do it, but one man, and he a man who was contemptible in the sight of the world, for the world laughed at him and mocked him. What was highly esteemed by man was an abomination to God, and what was highly esteemed by God was an abomination to man. When He wanted to bring three millions of people out of Egypt, His way of doing it was quite different from any that man would have adopted. He did not send an army with chariots, but a man who had been forty years on the back side of the desert, and whose name had been forgotten among the children of Israel, a man slow of speech, a stuttering man. There was not a man whose name shone out on the page of Divine history but was considered a fool in his day. He had no doubt that Enoch was considered a great fool in the sight of the world ; but he walked with God, and God thought so much of him that He said, " Come up higher," for He liked his company. Noah was the laughing-stock of his day. Men made great sport of him, but he was willing to be a fool for God's sake, and God used him and blessed him. And if we want to be of use to God we must be willing to be fools in the sight of the world. Look at Joshua going round the walls of Jericho. It was a most absurd sight. How the London press would have come down upon a scene like that ! Fancy the Archbishop of Canterbury and other great dignitaries going round London blowing ram's horns. Everybody would be disgusted, and say they should have golden trumpets at least. But that was not God's way. Look at Samson. When the spirit was on him how he worked ! With a jawbone of an ass he slew a thousand men. People now-a-days were not willing to work with a jawbone of an ass. They wanted some polished weapons that the world would not say anything against ; but Samson came down from the rock, and took up the first jawbone of an ass that he came across, and went out and slew the Philistines right and left. What was wanted now was, that every one should grab up the first jawbone of an ass that they could lay hold of, and not wait to do some great thing. How absurd it must have looked to see Gideon with his three hundred men with their pitchers. What queer weapons they were ! but every man stood in his place, and the result was that they routed the whole army. Look at Elijah fed by such unclean, contemptible things as ravens : and when the Lord sent him somewhere else it was not to a palace or to a table laid with good things, but to a poor widow who had scarcely enough for a meal for herself and her boy. So it was at the present day, for God was unchangeable. It was said that we were living in an enlightened age. That might be true, but to God it made no difference. He still used base and contemptible and despised things to effect His purpose. When He wanted a book written that should do some good to the world, He did not call forth a philosopher, but a Bedford tinker ; and the devil had his match when he got hold of John Bunyan. There was not a man present at the gathering whom God could not use if he was willing to be used. There was not a man in all Saul's army but knew that God could use him against

(c)

Goliath, but only one, and he the youngest of Jesse's family, was willing to be used. It was said of David's soldiers that they were all right and left handed men. That was what London wanted now, men who could use their right hand or their left hand, their eyes, their tongues, their ears for the King of glory. Who would have thought of Elisha to take the place of the wonderful old prophet Elijah ? Men now-a-days would go to the schools of the prophets and pick out some theological professor, but Elijah found a man behind twelve yoke of oxen, and Elisha slew his oxen and started off with Elijah, consecrating all to the service of God. Christ did not call around Him the learned and the wise, but Galilean fishermen, and that handful of men shook the world. Even before He could use Saul, the name had to be changed to Paul—the Little. What London wanted, and what the whole world wanted, was not eloquence, but Christ, and Him crucified. Let every man and woman, then, who loved the Lord Jesus begin to publish the glad tidings of salvation ; let them talk to their neighbours of the love of Christ, and so rise and take the city, for God was able to do it. The world did not like to have Christ preached ; but it was just what the world did not like that Christians must give it. The lion of hell was overcome by a Lion ; but the Lion of the tribe of Judah was also a Lamb. There was weeping once in heaven when John found no one worthy to open the Book ; but at last one touched him and said, " Weep not, John, for there is one worthy ; the Lion of the tribe of Judah has prevailed, and He is worthy." And when John turned round to look at the Lion it was a slain Lamb. God's Lion is a Lamb slain. It was the weakness of God that overcame the strength of man. Then, in order to success there must be union among Christians. There were three classes of people that ought to sympathize with this movement. Every minister who wanted to crown Christ King ought to be interested in the work ; every Sabbath-school superintendent and teacher, every missionary and colporteur, ought, at least, to pray for it, and every father and mother ought to join in it. When he was in Liverpool the other day a woman came to him with a photograph of a beautiful boy, who, she said, would now be nineteen years old. She said he had had trouble, and had fled from his home. She did not know what had become of him, and she asked him, if he saw him in London, to try and win him to the Lord, that he might come back to cheer her heart. There were many such boys in London, and he hoped God would bring them to Christ, so that they might go back to be a blessing to their parents and to the Church at large. To all such he would say, " Your mother still loves you, and wants you to return. Her heart is breaking for you. God wants you ; Jesus wants you. There is room in heaven for you." If there was unity among God's people in this work, no power, earthly or infernal, could stand against it. When the Church, the pulpit, and the pew were all of one mind, Christianity would be like a red-hot ball rolling over the earth, and all the hosts of death and hell would not be able to resist it. "By this," said Christ, " shall men know that ye are My disciples, if ye love one another." When General Grant was in front of Richmond, and his army had been repulsed in the Wilderness, he called his commanders together, and asked them what they thought he had better do. They advised him to retreat, but before morning an orderly was sent round, directing an advance in solid column on the enemy at daylight. That was what took Richmond, and broke down the rebellion. The Christians of London, too, must lift high the standard, and, in the name of their God, advance in solid column on the enemy before daylight. Let them work together, shoulder to shoulder, with a single eye to the honour and glory of Christ ; let them pray that they might get self out of the way, and that Christ might be all and in all, and then they would have success. Let their watchword be, " Here am I, send me," and the result was certain.

(a)   Moody

MISSIONS

" *Eyes to the blind and feet to the lame* " (Job xxix. 15)

There exists somewhere in Africa a lazar-house for lepers, surrounded with walled-in gardens and fields, and within which no one in health is admitted ; and the sufferers once in are allowed no return to the outer world. An English missionary from a hill-top once saw the inmates at work. He noticed two men sowing peas in a field, one had no hands, the other had no feet, these having been wasted away by the disease. The one with no hands was carrying on his back him with no feet, who carried a bag, from which he dropped a pea now and then, which the other pressed into the ground with his foot.

Application. The missionary uses his feet. It is for us to use our *hands*, and give him the seed to drop into the soil.

(b)   Robt. MacCheyne

MISSIONS

There is a holy art, a sacred science in missions. It not only requires heroic courage and angelic enthusiasm, it needs heavenly wisdom. . . . Consider how the great apostolic missioner, St. Paul, would act. In Acts xiii. (to Jews, who had the Scriptures of the Old Testament), and in chap. xvii., to the Gentiles, we have two missionary sermons of his. In them he lays the foundation, in an endeavour to produce in his hearers a sense of personal responsibility, on the ground of their future resurrection to judgment, when they will receive their final doom according to their works, from Him whom God hath appointed to be the Judge of quick and dead. He then declares the guilt and misery of sin, and enforces the necessity of true repentance and of faith in Christ, as the only means of justification and reconciliation with God, and of eternal life.

(c)   Bp. Wordsworth

MISUNDERSTOOD ACTIONS

Alexander had presented to him an Indian dog, as a sort of dog-Alexander. By way of trying this crack dog, the Macedonian made various heroic or heraldic beasts be let loose against him : first a stag, but the dog lay still ; then a sow ; he lay still : then a bear ; he lay still. Alexander was on the point of condemning him, when a lion was let forth : the dog rose, and tore the lion in pieces.

(d)   J. P. F. Richter

MONEY AND POSITION

Get place and wealth, if possible, with grace,
If not, by any means get wealth and place.
(a)   *Pope*

It is observed of gold, "that to have it is to be
in fear, and to want it to be in sorrow."
(b)   *Dr. Johnson*

MONEY

My friend, get money; get a large estate
By honest means; but get—at any rate,
(c)   *Francis' "Horace"*

MONUMENT

A monument to Newton! a monument to Shakspeare! Look up to heaven—look into the human
heart; till the planets and the passions, the
affections and the fixed stars, are extinguished,
their names cannot die.
(d)   *Professor Wilson*

MORE

"What do ye more than others?" (Matt. v. 47)

"Talk not of a good life," said a heathen,
"but let thy life speak." God appointed that the
weights and measures of the sanctuary should be
twice as large as those of the commonwealth, to
show that He expects much more of those that
wait upon Him in the sanctuary than He does of
others.
(e)   *Thos. Brooks*

SIR THOMAS MORE

Sir Thomas More set out as a philosopher and
reformer; but the coarseness, turbulence, and
bloody contests of Lutheranism having frightened
him, this most upright and merciful man became
a persecutor of men as innocent, though not of
such great minds as himself. He predicted that
the Reformation would produce universal vice,
ignorance, and barbarism. The events of a few
years seemed to countenance his prophecy, but
those of three centuries have belied it. His
character is a most important example of the best
man espousing the worst cause, and supporting it
even by bad actions—which is the greatest lesson
of charity that can be taught.
(f)   *Sir James Mackintosh*

MORTAL

All men think all men mortal but themselves.
(g)   *Young*

MOSES

He was as great as any man could have been
before the Gospel.
(h)   *Anon*

"There arose no prophet since like Moses, whom
the Lord knew face to face."
(i)   *Deut.* xxiv. 10

MOSES

"By faith Moses," etc. (Heb. xi. 24)

1. Moses, the child of a particular providence;
the man of faith; the tried saint; the great worker
for God's visible kingdom. Take him for all in
all, the world has never looked on his equal, Paul
only, perhaps, excepted. From whatever point of
view we regard him, he stands as a giant among
men.

As a writer, the Pentateuch shows him to have
been unrivalled.

As a philosopher, thinker, or administrator, his
legislative enactments and his sanitary measures
show him to have been four thousand years ahead
of his age.

As a patriot, the man who begs that his own
name may be blotted out of the Book of Life, for
the sake of his nation, stands on the very highest
platform.

But child of Providence, and chosen vessel, as
he was, yet the man Moses bore no charmed life.
His character unfolded itself gradually, and he
ripened for his work through temptation and trial.

His training for future greatness was a long and
tedious process. His career well illustrates the
familiar proverb—"God works slowly, but He
works surely."

In fact, Moses' life seemed to be drawing near to
its close, before the real work of his life began.

He was an old man, eighty years of age, when
he stood before Pharaoh, with nothing but a shepherd's crook in his hand, to make his demand :-
"Thus saith the Lord, Let My people go, that
they may serve Me."
(j)

2. A brief Memoir of this great Prophet

Moses was one hundred and twenty years old
when he died. His life divides itself into three
equal periods, each consisting of forty years.

This is told us in the memorable speech of
Stephen (Acts viii.).

(i.) The first period of forty years was spent in
Egypt.

(ii.) The next period, also of forty years, was
spent as an exile in the land of Midian.

(iii.) Whilst the last forty years of his life were
spent in doing his life's work, as the leader of
God's chosen people.

It will thus be seen that the first eighty years of
his life were a period of training and preparation
for the last period.

If we had no record of the early life of Moses,
and only the record of what he did as lawgiver,
we might readily conclude that so wonderful a man
must have had a wonderful past. But, perhaps,
few would have guessed anything half so extraordinary as that past really had been. The incidents
of his infancy; his rejection of an Egyptian
throne; his renunciation of the glories of this
world for the sake of an idea, and getting in
exchange nothing but poverty and exile, would
have been considered romantic enough for an
Eastern story, but as untrue to real life as the
fables and myths of early Greece and Rome.
(k)

Moses—*continued*

3. The forty years of Moses' life spent in Egypt, and its significance

There was a special providence at work in this arrangement. We need to recall the situation of things at that time to understand matters rightly.

God had told Abraham many years before, that his descendants should go down into Egypt, that they should suffer bondage there, and be evil-entreated, but afterwards come out with great spoil; and from the time of the promise until the deliverance a period of four hundred years would elapse. That time was well-nigh run out. Few of the Hebrews, perhaps, had any definite records to enable them to judge accurately how the time was passing. There may have been traditions among them; but the mass of the people had sunk too low to believe in deliverance at all. A few among them, only a few, for the flock of God is at all times " a little flock," kept just a faint glimmer of faith burning in the socket. Their faith was " in God who raiseth the dead "; their faith was in [the God of their fathers—Abraham, Isaac, and Jacob; their faith was in the God of Joseph, who had been sold as a bond-slave like themselves, but whom God had delivered and brought to great honour. A few had faith enough to believe that God would keep His promise, and do for them as He had done for their fathers. Through all the long years of oppression these would be looking for the coming deliverance.

Amongst this little flock of faithful ones were a certain Amram and his wife Jochebed. Twice since their union God had blessed them with children. And now an addition to that faithful family was expected. But since the birth of the last child, a merciless edict had gone forth from the tyrant who occupied the throne. The Hebrews were increasing every day—they would soon outnumber the Egyptians themselves; and it was feared that they might rise in mutiny and revenge themselves on their oppressors.

First one and then another expedient was resorted to to reduce their numbers. But notwithstanding, the Hebrew population went on increasing—God was with them. Now came the edict that all male children were to be thrown into the river as soon as they were born.

Imagine the terror of the God-fearing Amram and his wife. We can understand how they besought the Lord that their next child might be a daughter and not a son. And in the midst of these prayers Moses was born—a child so beautiful, so evidently with the mark of consecration to God on him from his birth—" he was fair towards God "—that he seemed to come and demand to live in defiance of the king's order. No one in that household thought of throwing that child into the river.

But more remarkable still was the effect his birth had on his parents. Before his birth they feared lest it might be a son, after his birth their fears left them—" they were not afraid." " By faith Moses, when he was born, was hid three months of his parents, because they saw he was a proper child; and *they were not afraid of the king's commandment*." This is enough to indicate what kind of parents Moses had. The child was an answer to their prayers, though a different answer from what they anticipated. Instead of a daughter God had sent them a son, but in that son they recognised a " proper child," one born to great

things (cf. " He shall be great. '—*Luke* i.). This faith led them to disobey the king's command; they hid the child three months, believing that God's providence would open up a way for the future. " The Lord was their strength, of whom should they be afraid? " And their faith had its reward.

(*a*)

4. Godly Mothers

Special note is made of this in the Bible. All history, past and present, prove that nearly all the great workers for God have had godly parents.

Witness Hannah, the mother of Samuel; Salome, the mother of Zebedee's children; Eunice, the mother of Timothy; Monica, the mother of Augustine.

The elegant writer, J. Ruskin, states that as a child he used to read the Bible to his mother, and afterwards she explained to him the passage read. Then he had to learn these passages, and they were never left until he knew them. One of these lessons was the 119th Psalm. He says that he considered it somewhat of a hardship at the time, but, he adds, those Bible lessons with his mother have made [him what he is, and that 119th Ps in particular, stored up in his memory, has been an unfailing source of comfort in the trials and changes of after life.

The poet Cowper, too, counts it to be the best start in life " to be the child of parents passed into the skies."

(*b*)

5. Religious Teaching

There is often much said about the deficiency of religious teaching in our schools of all grades. And yet, after all, *that* is not the place for it. School is, and must be, the place for secular learning, and the *home* the place for the religious teaching. The parent cannot delegate that office to another. Moses, under God's providence, was born in the leading country of his time, and where he could acquire a knowledge of all the arts and sciences of the age. No other place had such treasures to spread before an inquiring mind. And it was *there* [that he went to school and college. " He," so to speak, " spoiled the Egyptians," " he was learned in all the wisdom of the Egyptians; " but it was from his nurse that he learned to know God " the most excellent gift." God did not send His servant to school to learn about Himself, but to get all the wisdom that Egypt was famed for, and which afterwards Moses would want as the leader of the chosen nation, and moreover which he would know how to utilize as an inspired writer. God's providence, at] the same time, counter-balances all the evil which comes from a purely worldly education by keeping His servant near his pious mother, who would not fail to give a right direction to his life, and store his memory with the story of his people. How such a training bore fruit in after years, the whole story of Moses well illustrates.

Passing over the incident of Moses being adopted by Pharaoh's daughter, we come to the time " when he was come to years." Childhood, youth, and early manhood were] past. In the famous speech of Stephen, and also in profane history, there are indications that Moses became a general in Egypt, and performed exploits, was a popular favourite,

(*c*)

Moses—*continued*

and regarded as the probable successor to the throne of Pharaoh. Honour and rank were within his grasp. He has long learnt the secret of his birth. The time to choose between the pleasures of Egypt and the casting in his lot with his own people was come. It was a dazzling temptation. On the one side Egypt with all its riches, treasures, and art, captivating to a man of taste and culture, as was Moses. On the other side there was that down-trodden horde of Hebrew slaves, possessing nothing to make their company desirable. But his father and mother are of them ; and they are, he believes, the chosen people of God—heirs of the promises made to Abraham, Isaac, and Jacob. Fool, says some one, to hesitate between a throne and a brick-kiln, between the refined pleasures of the court and the flesh-pots of Goshen ; who but a madman and fanatic would stop to weigh the matter over for a moment ! What his choice meant for him Moses well knew. He settled the matter, in the language of the Epistle to the Hebrews, "Choosing rather to suffer affliction with the people of God, than to enjoy the pleasures of sin for a season : esteeming the reproach of Christ greater riches than the treasures of Egypt ; for he had respect unto the recompense of reward."

Thus ends the first forty years of his life. Egypt has been of use to him ; it was the school where he acquired his secular education. But Egypt was not an end in itself. Moses has something else to learn, and for that purpose he is next sent as-

(*a*)

6. "A stranger in the land of Midian forty years"

A long time, but God is training an extraordinary man, and it will be forty years before he is wanted. Those forty years are spent in fitting the instrument for his work. And, as in so many instances, that is best done in obscurity.

Moses has chosen Christ ; he is next trained in the school of Christ, and learns what it is to be a Christian.

In his zeal for the relief of his own people he had blundered. It was more the zeal for *self* than for God's glory. Great thoughts had arisen in his mind. He could not help feeling that the peculiar providences of his life had marked him out as the future deliverer of his people. But, like many reformers, he acted before he was *called* by God. He went into the vineyard to work before he was *sent*. And, as always is the case, the work of God is rather hindered than furthered by mistaken zeal. The consequences of Moses' rash act were that his brethren did not believe in him, and he was obliged to flee from Egypt, with a conscience ill at ease, and his hands stained with blood.

(*b*)

7. Midian

God's providence was beforehand with him. A place of safety was provided in the land of Midian. There he was left under humiliating circumstances for the next forty years of his life. Very little information is afforded us of how he spent his time there. That it was the school where his spirit was trained, is certain. For Midian was to Moses what the prison had been to Joseph, and afterwards what the wilderness was for David.

If Egypt was necessary for supplying Moses with the best education that the time afforded,

fitting him to take his place as a leader, so Midian was necessary as a school of adversity, where he learned to " endure hardness," became acquainted with privation, and inured to the kind of life he would afterwards have to live in the wilderness of Sinai. God was leading him, but he considered not that-

" God moves in a mysterious way.'

This we know, that he went there and returned. He went as a prince, he returned as a shepherd— with nothing more than an ass for the conveyance of his wife and children, he walking by the side with a staff in his hand.

(*c*)

8. Humiliation

Great as was the difference in his external condition, greater still was the difference in spirit between the Moses who fled from Egypt and the Moses who returned there forty years afterwards to undertake the great work of his life.

Then he was in a hurry to begin his work, now he does not want to go at all. Then his spirit was high and his zeal full of ardour. Now he makes all kinds of excuses, and begs God to send somebody else to do a work he feels to be so much beyond his powers. Then he felt himself to be a man of power ; now he feels himself to be only as a little child. We gather from this that Moses underwent a slow and secret spiritual training in the land of his exile. There he had time to read and meditate on the works of God in creation. There, too, he met men like Jethro, a priest of the most High God, and in all probability Job, the matchless saint, with whom he could interchange thought and from whom he could learn more about God's doings than he had opportunities of learning in Egypt. In Midian he held intercourse and communion with God. One instance is recorded, that of the burning bush, where God makes distinct revelations to him, but that one instance shows that Moses was no stranger ,to communion with God. He came out of Egypt with high thoughts ; but in the land of Midian he learned in whatsoever state he was therewith to be content. A difficult lesson for all to learn, twice difficult for a man like Moses who had been reared in a palace and spent the first forty years of his life in the luxury of a court. And it seems, judging from the narrative, that it took forty years to bring his spirit down to the level of his lot.

In Egypt he exalted himself, and was abased ; in Midian he humbled himself, and afterwards was exalted.

(*d*)

9. The Shepherd

The difference between his external condition in Egypt and Midian is very striking. We know what he was when he went there :-

In rank, a prince ; in education, undoubtedly he was a most profound scholar, acquainted with the mysteries of Egyptian learning. In thought he was far in advance of his age. In active life there are indications that he was the most prominent man of the day. He was this in Egypt ; but in the land of Midian we read that Moses " kept the sheep of Jethro his father-in-law." What a contrast ! What a transition ! From a prince to a shepherd. The leading man of his time keeping a few sheep

(*e*)

Moses—*continued*

in the wilderness. What a waste of precious material, it seems!

Moses, who has the making of ten ordinary men in him, a host in himself, a man fitted to mould the destinies of nations, and to frame laws which should never sink into oblivion. Is this all that this wonderful man has to do in the world? Is this all that his previous life has been leading up to?

Could not anybody keep sheep, and fulfil better than Moses such humble duties? Yes, undoubtedly, anybody could keep sheep; but anybody would not do to be the future shepherd of Israel.

He learns here how to be the shepherd of men, just as the fisherman afterwards learnt to be the fisher of men.

"God will have all men to be saved," but all are not jewels of the first water like Moses. And God cuts, and grinds, and polishes this jewel, which afterwards is to shine the brightest in the constellation of Old Testament worthies. And this is the secret of Moses' exile and keeping sheep: there was a high spirit to tame and lofty looks to bring low.

Midian was the workshop where he was prepared for his work, as a jewel is polished by a lapidary.

And that humble office of keeping sheep was perhaps the best tool for God to employ, in order to humble the proud prince and the self-reliant man of learning and power, until he should say with the Psalmist (Ps. cxxxi.): "Lord, my heart is not haughty, nor mine eyes lofty; neither do I exercise myself in great matters, or in things too high for me. Surely I have behaved and quieted myself as a child that is weaned of his mother: yea, my soul is even as a weaned child."

God would bring him down to this, that man might know that the power to do anything in the kingdom of God is not of man but of God.

(*a*)

10. True humility of spirit is a thing of slow growth. Moses is usually called the "meekest of men;" but he came to be this only after long years of training; first of temptation, then of disappointment, and weary waiting until hope had perished.

We can trace the growth of this grace in him from one or two passages in his life. He names his first child "*Gershom*," which means "a stranger here." This is just an indication that Moses felt the humiliation of his position, and his spirit was fretting with it, as an imprisoned bird frets to get out of its cage.

The next child he names "*Eliezer*," which means "God is my help." By this time Moses had grown in grace, and had received tokens of God's favour, and was comforted. It was now true of him as of the great New Testament Apostle afterwards, who said,

"Though our outward man perish, yet our inward man is renewed day by day."

(*b*)

11. And when Moses was humbled, and had become as a "little child," then God said to him, "Go and do your life's work; bring My people out of Egypt, as I brought you, for that after all is the work for which I destined you, and for which I have been training you for eighty years past, both in Egypt and in Midian.

"The time of the fulfilment of My promise to Abraham is come, the four hundred years are up.

"Go and speak comfortably unto My people Israel—

"I have seen their affliction;

"I have heard their cry;

"I know their sorrows; and

"I am come down to deliver them, according to My promise."

With what great reluctance Moses now undertook the work, which once he was all in a hurry to do, we have seen. And it is not until God has promised him the assistance of his brother's elocutionary powers to help him to utter his thoughts, that the tried and ripened saint can be induced to come out of his obscurity and take his place in the troubled arena of public life.

(*c*)

12. And now the training over, the working time begins. Moses now enters upon the third and last stage of his earthly life; and singularly enough it is another period of forty years. He had waited a long time for his work, and now when it came it was no easy task. It was a difficult thing to persuade these ignorant Hebrews, sunk almost to the level of brutes, tainted, to a large extent, with the degrading idolatries of Egypt, where, as has been said, there were as many gods as there were men. At first no one believed his report, and afterwards whenever difficulty or any adversity happened to these people they immediately murmured against Moses as the cause of their sufferings. The people were hard to deal with, addicted to low and sensual habits. Verily it was very raw material with which Moses had to deal; well might he shrink from it.

But then by this time, it must be remembered, Moses was not trusting in his own powers, as if there were any sufficiency in him for such a work. He realized that our "sufficiency is of God." He realized what Christ teaches us, that "without Me ye can do nothing," and he knew that we, who are called to work in "God's kingdom," though unable (if self-reliant) to make any headway at all, yet "We can do all things through Christ who strengtheneth us." For Moses is nothing but the servant of God; and John the Baptist is nothing but the voice of God; Paul is nothing but the minister of Christ. The power belongeth unto God alone, and His glory He will not give to another. This is the great lesson that Moses learnt in his exile. That, too, which Elijah learnt after falling into a similar error, and which every one of us must learn if we expect God to use us at all in the extension of His kingdom on earth. "Not by might, nor by power, but by My Spirit, saith the Lord."

(*d*)

MOTHERS

I have never written a pamphlet on nurseries: first, because I never write about anything except what I know more of than most other people; secondly, because I think nothing much matters in a nursery—except the mother, the nurse, and the air. So far as I have notion or guess in the matter myself, beyond the perfection of those three necessary elements, I should say the rougher and plainer everything the better—no lace to cradle cap, hardest possible bed and simplest possible food

(*e*)

according to age, and floor and walls of the cleanest. All education to beauty is, first, in the beauty of gentle human faces round a child; secondly, in the fields—fields meaning grass, water, beasts, flowers, and sky. Without these no man can be educated humanly. He may be made a calculating machine, a walking dictionary, a painter of dead bodies, a twangler or scratcher, on keys or cat-gut, a discoverer of new forms of worms in mud; but a properly so-called human being—never. Pictures are, I believe, of no use whatever by themselves. If the child has other things right, round it and given to it—its garden, its cat, and its window to the sky and stars—in time, pictures of flowers and beasts, and things in heaven and heavenly earth may be useful to it. But see first that its realities are heavenly.

(a)   *J. Ruskin*

MOTHERS

Henrietta, queen of Charles I., contracted with the Pope to educate her children as Catholics. The fate of both her sons shows how faithfully she performed this treasonable contract. This piece of secret history opens the concealed cause of those deep impressions of that faith, which both monarchs sucked in with their milk; *that triumph of the cradle over the grave* which most men experience. Charles II. died a Catholic; James II. lived as one.

(b)   *Disraeli's "Curiosities of Literature"*

MOTHERS, ELEVATED POSITION OF IN THE KINGDOM OF GOD

(i.) Hannah, the mother of Samuel;
(ii.) Salome, the mother of Zebedee's children;
(iii.) Eunice, the mother of Timotheus;
(iv.) Monica, the mother of Augustine; etc.

(c)   *Lange*

MOTHERS (PARENTS)

The father and mother of an unnoticed family, who, in their seclusion awaken the mind of one child to the idea and love of perfect goodness, who awaken in him a strength of will to repel all temptation, and who send him out prepared to profit by the conflicts of life, surpass in influence a Napoleon breaking the world to his sway.

(d)   *Channing*

MOTTO OF ISRAELITES INDEED:

"I am a guest on earth."

(e)   *Lange*

MOULD

Nature, despairing e'er to make the like,
Brake suddenly the mould in which 'twas fashion'd.

(f)   *Massinger*

MOUNT, SERMON ON THE

It is recorded of a Wesleyan minister that, on one occasion, when conducting a service, he was so absorbed in the prayer he had offered that he forgot the substance of his sermon, which was to follow, and, in its place, read the Sermon on the Mount (Matt. v., vi., vii.). Afterwards, one of the congregation asked another, "What do you think of that?" The reply was, "It was the best sermon I ever heard in my life!"

(g)   *Piper*

MOUNTAINS, THREE

Make a journey every day to three mountains:
(i.) To Mount Sinai, to see your sins;
(ii.) To Mount Calvary, to see the Lamb of God;
(iii.) To Mount Zion, to view the Heavenly Jerusalem.

(h)   *Marsh*

MURMURING

If we were as free to acknowledge unexpected good as to murmur at an unexpected evil (if we may speak of the Divine Providence by such an epithet) we should maintain a more equal temperature of mind.

(i)   *English Churchman*

MURMURING

If Christ had in this matter been as wilful and short as I was, my faith had gone over the hill, and broken its neck; but we were well met—a hasty fool, and a wise, patient, and meek Saviour. He took no law-advantage of my folly, but waited on till my ill blood was fallen, and my troubled well began to clear; He was not angry at the fever-ravings of a poor tempted sinner. But He mercifully forgave, and came (as it well becometh Him) with grace and new comfort to a sinner, who deserved the contrary. And now He is content to put His hand in mine, and to feed me with as many consolations as would feed ten hungry souls: yet I dare not say He is a waster of comforts, for no less would have borne me up; one grain-weight less would have cast the balance.

(j)   *Samuel Rutherford*

MUSCULAR CHRISTIANITY

On the Friday or Saturday before the communion Sunday, the Welsh Churches generally hold what they call a "preparatory meeting," at which the spiritual state and outward conduct of the communicants are taken into consideration, and discipline is administered. On one of these occasions a member of the church at Aberduar had to stand his trial on the charge of having literally knocked down a Unitarian, in a discussion. The trial proceeded in the following extraordinary fashion: "Well, Thomas," said the pastor, in his very hurried and abrupt manner, "I am sorry to hear that you are charged with some misconduct during the last week; let us hear all about it." The culprit, looking very humble and penitent, began to confess: "To tell the whole truth, sir, the facts are these: Jack, the miller, and myself were having a little beer together at the Red Dragon, and——" "Stop, Thomas, let me ask you, before you go any further, did you pay for it?" "I did, sir," replied the criminal very emphatically, and with

(k)

a gleam of hope twinkling in his eye. "That is in your favour, Thomas, decidedly in your favour; when I take a drop of ale, I always pay for it; I cannot bear those fellows who go about tippling at other people's expense; go on, Thomas." "Well, sir, after awhile, we got into a discussion about Jesus Christ; I, of course, holding that He was divine, and Jack that He was only a man; and he said such shocking things that—flesh and blood, you know, are weak, sir—I couldn't stand it any longer, so, I am sorry to say, sir, I was tempted to hit him." "So you really struck him, Thomas, did you? But what did he say?" "He actually said, sir, that the blood of Christ had no more virtue in it than the blood of a beast, and "— encouraged by the significant tones of the pastor —"I knocked him down." "Well, brother," said the minister, with a fine touch of genuine un-priestly sympathy, "I cannot say you did the right thing; but I must say this, I believe I should have done so too: go and sin no more."

(a) *Anecdote of Timothy Thomas*

MUSIC

Music of the spheres.

(b) *Shakspeare*

"MUST" (Acts xiv. 22)

That word "*must*" has a gloomy sound, it is true, but the necessity is not imposed by a blind and rigid fate; it proceeds (i.) from the appointment of God, so that believers might in this manner be conformed to Christ (Rom. viii. 17); (ii.) from the enmity which was at the beginning put between Christ and Satan (Gen. iii. 15); and (iii.) from the urgent need that our corrupt flesh should be crucified (2 Cor. iv. 16).

(c) *Starke*

MY GOD

"Much of the beauty of Scripture is found in its pronouns," said Luther. And John Brown, of Haddington, says, that to the believer there is more comfort in the words, "I am thy God," than in all the schemes of worldly philosophy.

The phrase *my God* is of frequent occurrence in Scripture and in devotional writings. It was used by Abraham, by Moses, by Israel, by Ruth, by David, by Micaiah, by Agar, by Nehemiah, by Ahaz, by Daniel, by Hosea, by Micah, by Thomas, and by Paul. It was used by Christ both before and after His ascension to heaven. It is a very fit form of address to the Most High. When we are engaged in joint worship we, of course, say *our God*. When one can fitly say *my* God, he knows that everything is included. For Jehovah is a Rock, a Refuge, a high Tower, a Defence, a very present Help, a Shield, a Buckler, a Friend, a Guide, a Father, a Husband, a Shepherd, a Saviour to all who put their trust in Him. Nothing is wanting to Him whose God is the Lord. He has all things and abounds.

The Divine attributes are all employed for those who can truly say, The Lord is my God. Does their case require omniscience? His eyes are in every place. He knows all their heart troubles, all the plots of their enemies, and sees how they shall escape. Then He is ever-present, a God at hand as well as afar off. He is also omnipotent. He can do His whole pleasure. None can resist Him. And His wisdom is infinite. He takes the cunning in his craftiness. Divine skill is never puzzled. God sees the end from the beginning. He loves, He pities, He shows mercy like a God. His loving kindness is from everlasting to everlasting. There is none like the Most High.

The whole course of Providence favours those who can truly say, The Lord is my God. To such Jehovah says, "Ye are My people; I will keep thee as the apple of Mine eye: I will be a wall of fire round about thee; I will never leave thee nor forsake thee." They could not ask for more ample provision than He has made for them.

(d) *W. S. Plumer*

MYSELF

Deliver me, O Lord, from that evil man, *myself*.

(e) *Augustine*

MYSTERY (1 Cor. iv. 1)

The mysteries of the kingdom of God = the Revelations of God, as matters which could be known only by Divine communication.

Not, as in common parlance, something incomprehensible, but something, which, being beyond the reach of man's intelligence, has been made known to him in some special Divine way.

(f) *Lange*

MYSTERY OF INIQUITY, THE (2 Thess. ii. 7)

1. It is sometimes thought that before the close of the present dispensation gospel influences will so leaven the whole world that all nations will be converted, and everything will be bathed in a flood of gospel sunlight before Christ comes again. What means St. Paul when writing to Timothy, by saying:

"This know, that in the last days perilous times shall come.

And again:

"Evil men and seducers shall wax worse and worse, deceiving and being deceived."

Or, what is the purport of our Lord's own words when He said:

"There shall be distress of nations with perplexity, men's hearts failing them for fear."

Or of His caution about:

False Christs, who will, if possible, deceive the very elect, and of a time when iniquity shall so prevail that the people of God will lose faith, and begin to question His faithfulness and promise = "Because iniquity shall abound the love of many shall wax cold."

This then, and not a sunnier state of things, is, it appears, what we are to expect as the present dispensation draws to an end. Iniquity abounding, and coming in like a flood; false Christs; false teachers; and the kingdom of evil developing its fullest powers.

At one stage of its development "the mystery of iniquity" brought about the death of our Lord, when the kings and rulers of the earth stood up against the Lord and against His Christ.

(g)

Mystery of Iniquity—*continued*

Then they thought, perhaps, that they had crushed the Nazarene altogether. Then, indeed, the old serpent did succeed in bruising His heel; but the glorious Resurrection morn undid it all, and revealed the Conqueror of Death, alive for ever more, with " all power in heaven and earth," given unto Him, wherewith to crush the head of the dragon.

And this, according to the Scriptures, is to be *repeated* before the second coming of Christ, repeated not in Christ *personally*, but in His *Church*. The world will attempt to crucify the Church; before Christ comes again, Antichrist comes, and in the overwhelming affliction of the people of God which this deceiver will promote there will be heard the old heathen cry, " Come, and let us cast them off from being a people." When the darkness is such that it may be felt,—when the furnace is at its hottest,—and the persecution is such as never was, " these days shall be shortened," " then shall be seen the coming of the Son of Man," like the lightning shining from the east unto the west; He that was dead and is alive coming to undertake the cause of His redeemed, and to destroy that MAN OF SIN with the brightness of His coming.

(*a*)

2. A review of the " Mystery of Iniquity," or the " Antichrist " of St John

Notice some striking contrasts, which are something more than coincidences :

(i.) The same Apostle tells us of the " Mystery of Godliness," so then we learn that
" The Mystery of Iniquity " is opposed to the " Mystery of God."

(ii.) The Personal Christ is, in the teaching of St. John, opposed by the Personal Antichrist. Just as Moses was opposed by Balaam, a kind of Anti-Moses.

(iii.) Once more, Antichrist is represented as the caricature of the true Christ. The One is " the Seed of the Woman," the seed of the Church of God, " The glory of Israel." Whilst the other is the precipitate and the resultant of the stream of evil amongst the sons of men from the beginning.

Or, as in the " Mystery of Godliness," Christ is related to the Father, standing midway between Him and lost men ; so, in the Mystery of Iniquity, this is copied, and caricatured, and Antichrist is represented as standing midway between the devil and lost men, not to save but to destroy.

In other words, Antichrist will be the greatest instrument of Satan in deceiving men to their ruin —his truest copy in human form—the devil incarnate.

(*b*)

3. The Old Testament Development of the Mystery of Iniquity and Types of Antichrist

The two streams of good and evil run side by side in the earlier accounts of Genesis. Whilst they keep apart all goes well with the Church of God, but when the two mingle, like the waters of the Rhone and the Save, the evil corrupts the good, and then both as one stream rush on to the judgment of the flood.

(*c*)

4. The Fundamental Idea

The birth of the Mystery of Iniquity was the

Fall of man. . . . " Ye shall be as gods," said the tempter, "knowing good and evil." True, but what gain is there in having an experimental knowledge of evil ? Such knowledge is in itself a fall.

Here, at the very outset, we are met with a characteristic feature of Antichrist. The Man of Sin will make Adam's sin his very religion. In his knowledge of evil, in his absence of all responsibility, having cast off all allegiance to God, he will become the mouthpiece of all those who say : " Who is Lord over us ? "

The fundamental idea, then, of the Mystery of Iniquity, as has been well said, is, that in Antichrist man becomes God; whilst the fundamental idea of the Mystery of Godliness is that God becomes man, in Christ; and the record of good and evil contained in the Bible shows the development of both mysteries unto the end. In other words : The antichristian idea is the deification of man; and the Mystery of Iniquity, in the course of its growth, puts forth shoots from time to time in certain typical characters of Old Testament time.

(*d*)

5. Nimrod

One of the earliest of these deified men was apparently Nimrod. It is not expressly stated, but the near context seems to point him out as being the leading mind at Babel—a remarkable and early development of the true antichristian spirit.

God, in His time and way, would send a Saviour of the human race who would gather the people, though scattered all over the world, into one fold. These should constitute one Republic. But God is not in a hurry; and the discords caused by sin must first be felt, before men would desire the harmony and unity of heaven.

But to this waiting the people of the time were opposed ; " Let us," said they, " build a city and a tower, and keep all together, and be a united and happy family in our own way, and under our own chosen leader." This leader may have been the lion-hunting Nimrod, who, if not then, was embued with the same antichristian spirit later on.

(*e*)

6. Perhaps the next most important type of Antichrist is that of Pharaoh, who asked, " Who is the Lord, that I should obey Him ? " . . . In him the idea of self-deification was largely developed, and the doctrine of " the Divine right of kings " seems by this time to have developed itself to a degree of infatuation calling for an example—" Even for this purpose have I raised thee up, that I might show My power in thee, and that My name might be declared throughout all the earth." It was necessary, for the general good, that God should step in amongst the doings of men, and show that He alone was God over all the earth.

Pharaoh, in his self-exaltation, asks, " Why should *I* obey *your* God—the God of a despised race of Hebrew slaves. Am I, king Pharaoh, a god myself, asked to humble myself to Him ? " I will not obey, neither will I let the people go."

All this is very typical of him who is to reveal himself later on in the Christian Church as one " who opposeth himself to all that is called God."

(*f*)

Mystery of Iniquity—*continued*

7. Nebuchadnezzar a Type of Antichrist

Puffed up with egotistical pride he commands his subjects, including the subjugated nation of the Jews—who had the knowledge of the one true God—to worship the image that *he* had set up—claiming the supremacy of conscience as well as of nations—jealous, too, lest worship should be offered in any channel that he had not sanctioned, fearing lest *he* had not got the hearts of the people. See how his silly pride and self-deification comes out in his inflated language—" Is not this great Babylon which *I* have builded? "

Such, briefly, are some of the types of Antichrist furnished by the Old Testament. Just as in the good men there we find remarkable types of the Lord Jesus Christ.

(*a*)

8. Another instance comes before us in the prophecy of the Old Testament only, but whose actual sphere of activity happened after the close of the Old Testament canon. The historical account is to be found in the Books of the Maccabees.

This man's career surpassed anything that had gone before in the way of high-handed wickedness and persecution of the people of God.

He is described by Daniel as "a horn which became exceeding great." "The king (he adds) shall do according to his will ; and he shall exalt himself and magnify himself above every god, and shall speak marvellous things against THE GOD OF GODS, and shall prosper."

This man, **Antiochus Epiphanes**, stands out in all history as one branded with a curse. Historians represent him as the incarnation of every crime. No Pharaoh, no Nebuchadnezzar, no Senacherib of Old Testament times, no Nero of later times, equalled this man in his opposition to the worship of God.

All the elements of such opposition previously met with meet and intensify themselves in him. He is the culminating point of Old Testament antichristianity, the spirit of which had been developing itself all along, but now attained to terrible proportions. It is in the study of this man's history that we may expect to find the chief characteristics of the Antichrist of the future.

We notice that at the time when he appeared there was a great apostasy of the Jews from their national faith. The people of God were a minority. The old heathen world, with its idolatrous pollutions, had overlapped the Jewish Church, so that many of the Jews caught the infection of idolatry and became ashamed of their old inelastic faith, as behind the times. And going from one stage to another they at last apostatized altogether. The ranks of these apostates increased daily, until Antiochus appeared and took the lead, as the mouthpiece and spokesman of the party. His aim was to destroy the worship of God. One High Priest, nominated by him, publicly renounced the law of Moses—the significance of such a step cannot be overestimated.

The inhabitants of Jerusalem having rejoiced at a false report of the tyrant's death, were ruthlessly massacred by him. At that time he made his way into the interior of the Temple, and sacrificed a pig on the altar of Jehovah, to express his contempt for the Jewish ritual, sprinkling the blood of the unclean animal wildly around him in mock imitation of the sacred "sprinkling of blood" by the Priests.

On another occasion—a sabbath—when the pious Jews were assembled in their synagogues, he ordered his troops to kill every man, and to sell the women and children for slaves.

A garrison of soldiers was established opposite the Temple, which attacked all who went there to worship. The Temple itself was defiled in every way. In this way Antiochus showed his contempt for the worship of God. This state of things lasted for three and a half years—"a time, times, and half a time"—as had been foretold by Daniel the prophet. During this period the morning and evening sacrifices were taken away, and the people of God had to hide themselves in dens and caves of the earth. There was not a vestige of public worship left.

The despot next issued a decree that all subjugated nations should abandon their old faith and embrace the religion of the king. This decree of course had a special reference to the worship of the Jews : its aim was to complete the destruction of their religion and nationality.

He well knew that a conquered people's heart was not his so long as they had a religion of their own, dearer to them than life itself. Every act of worship offered by them to their God, he regarded as robbing him of his due, an infringement on his rights. And this Jewish religion must have been a peculiar provocation to him, inasmuch as it placed the will of another King above his will ; and he rightly felt that he could have no real ascendency over this people so long as they held to their religious faith.

Hence his aim was to destroy every trace of the Jewish religion in the capital : Circumcision was forbidden—the sabbath was desecrated—every copy of the law that could be found was destroyed—the Temple itself was dedicated to Jupiter Olympus, whose statue was erected on the altar of burnt-offering, to whom sacrifices were offered. A similar course of things was carried out in other cities. The inhabitants were compelled to offer heathen sacrifices, and to eat the flesh of unclean animals.

Everything was at stake : the world of the time was systematically opposed to God and His Church. Therefore, as in all similar seasons, God gave the faithful consolation by showing beforehand in Daniel's prophecies that these things would come to pass, that the nation needed the chastisement for their trial and purification ; and that the trouble itself would pass away when its work was done.

This seems to have been in the mind of St. Paul when he wrote his description of "that Man of Sin " in the Second Epistle to the Thessalonians. The doings of Antiochus Epiphanes are typical of him who is yet to be revealed "in his time." The same godlessness, dare-devil impiety. . . . the same self-deification are to be his characteristics, and for almost identical reasons : in the one Judaism was, in the other Christianity will be, the object of attack. Hence he is described as "opposing himself to all that is worshipped."

(*b*)

9. The New Testament Development, and Phases of "the Mystery of Iniquity"

The chief passage is this of 2 Thess. ii. 3, 6, wherein we notice three stages of its development:

(*c*)

Mystery of Iniquity—*continued*

(i.) *A preceding apostasy*, the "falling away first."

(ii.) *The man of sin* who is "to be revealed in his time."

(iii.) *The restraining power*—"Ye know what withholdeth."

Before we review these stages, it will be well to notice that the first two are not identical. Unfortunately the caution is necessary, as much of the literature on the subject proceeds on that assumption. Candid and unbiased minds will however prefer to keep to what is "written." Let us try and speak according to the oracles of God, neither adding to nor taking away.

(*a*)

10. The Apostasy in the Christian Church: what is it

Antichrist, when he comes, will have little chance of success if the way is not prepared for him by a great falling off, and departure, from the purity of the faith. The chief Old Testament type, as we have seen, had the way prepared for him by the apostate Jews. And in the history of the Christian Church we may expect to find a corresponding departure from the faith tending to a like result. . . . We make no allusion here to individual cases of perversion going on from day to day in our midst. . . . St. Paul's words do not refer to apostates as individuals, but to a *Community*, a *Polity*, a *Confederacy*.

Now is it not a matter of history that at a very early period in the history of the Christian Church —as early even as apostolic days—there were grievous departures from the faith? . . . And soon, when the times of the apostles receded into the past, and after the period of persecution was over, and the Church itself became dominant, she is then seen in alliance with a huge world-power, and so closely identified with it as to appear *One*. See what is written in the Book of Revelation about the two beasts, and the woman, *i.e.* the apostate Church, riding on the back of that which is pre-eminently "*the* beast," guiding and directing its antichristian influence. . . . When the Church, denoted by the woman, loses her purity, and reappears as "the harlot," there can be no question that the apostasy which precedes the appearing of Antichrist, and prepares his way, is one of the certainties of church history, and continues to be—for what do we see in our day?

Though Rome, which took the lead in the apostasy, is now a house divided against itself, and comparatively feeble, yet the apostasy continues. It is full of life, working in our midst, with all the deceivableness of Satan, and perhaps putting forth more energy to deceive now than at any former period. The corrupt thing is creeping over the churches of this land; and instead of the "simplicity which is in Christ" we have the most elaborate and ornate services, full of the combined ritual of Judaism and Paganism. The "Church" as an institution is put in the place of the "personal Christ."

That of which St. Paul said in his time, "it doth already work," has been working during all the intervening centuries, and still doth work.

The mystery of iniquity, like a pestilent ulcer, takes long time to gather its forces, but at last it comes to a fierce, tormenting, and angry head— that *Head is Antichrist*, or the concentration of evil in a single individual. Even as such a monster as Nero might be said to be the concentration of all the antichristian enmity and the hideous moral deformity of the later Roman civilization, so as to be identical with it.

(*b*)

11. This Antichrist, as an individual, is yet to come

The mystery of iniquity has not yet reached its full development, but it will attain to it in him who, at the zenith of his power, will be destroyed by the brightness of the Saviour's coming. His two forerunners being the apostasy of the Church, and the spreading infidelity of the world. These are the Herod and the Pontius Pilate, who, though before at enmity, are made friends over one common object, viz. the destruction of the Church of Christ, as formerly at the Crucifixion of Christ Himself. Antichrist will come as the ripest fruit of his time, uniting in himself the worst features of an apostate and an infidel; caring nothing for God, because in his self-deification he is a god unto himself; characterized by falsehood, seduction, and blasphemy, endowed with worldly rule and empire; gathering into his hands all the machinery of the world's highest civilization, he will make himself what the ambition and lust for conquest made an Alexander, or a Napoleon, desire to be—the master of the world.

(*c*)

12. The age when he appears will be ripe for him, and he will appear as the man of his age. He will seize the spirit of the time; and the evil which had long been held in solution, working and fermenting in thousands of obscure minds, will precipitate itself in him. He will come to the front as the foremost man, and the leader of a large host, who will be preaching and writing and agitating, saying, "The time is come to cast off our Christian faith, to burn our Bibles, and renounce the God of our fathers."

And a survey of the current thought and opinion of the day seems to show us that things are tending to this, that we are perhaps unconsciously drifting towards "perilous times," when we shall hear a voice saying, "Woe, woe, woe to the inhabiters of the earth" (Rev. viii. 13).

(*d*)

13. Unbelief. It behoves us to watch the spirit of our times, to give more earnest heed to the prophetic word, and that so much the more as we see the day approaching. We cannot hide from ourselves the fact that in the present day there is a widespread and daring unbelief afloat in the world, a troubled sea of unsettled opinions which cannot rest. And this spirit is most unfortunately fostered by the vast strides made in science and art and by the facilities of education—all handmaids rather than enemies of the faith—unnatural as it may seem; yet these, being the children of the Reformation, will array themselves against the Church. Already we may notice a gathering hatred of all that is Divine and holy, a deep-rooted scepticism penetrating to the very foundations of society; genius worshipped in some circles more than the God of genius. Apparently things are tending towards the supremacy of an antichristian state of society, out of which will arise one individual in whom the world's enmity to God will culminate and burst. He too, like Pharaoh and

(*e*)

Mystery of Iniquity—*continued*

others, will be raised up in order that the evil may localize itself in one man, and that God may show forth His power by destroying it in him.

It is said that the seeds of German and English infidelity have taken root even in India, where the very Hindoos oftentimes now-a-days reject alike their own idols and our God, and take to studying the pernicious books of modern infidelity.

Wilfully blind should we be if we were to shut our eyes to the fact that a volcano is slumbering in the very depths of society—not in this country only, nor in Europe, but throughout the world.

We hear it rumbling every now and then. What have we heard in the last few years? Not long since there was a discussion about the efficacy of prayer, as if the objections of those without experience could weigh in the least degree with those who have such an experience and testify only to what they have both seen and known.

What a rumble there was—whose distant sounds have hardly died away yet—as to whether the Bible should be openly read and explained in our schools.

What was the meaning of that voice (now hushed) from Germany, the mouthpiece of a large and powerful party, which asked: "Whether, considering our advanced state of culture, religious worship is necessary to be observed in any form whatever?" . . .

"*Are we still Christians?*" "*We must reply that we are Christians no longer.*"

"*Are we,*" asks the same voice, "*or are we not, to have a religion at all—for there is no personal God—no future state?*" therefore "*all religious worship ought to be abolished.*"

Now what does such teaching indicate? Most assuredly it indicates that the Mystery of Iniquity is making vast strides in this latter part of the 19th century, showing only too truly that the spirit of Antichrist is verily abroad, and amongst us—challenging and denying all true religion—sapping the very foundations of our most holy faith, counting the blood of the covenant wherewith we are sanctified an unholy thing. This is the spirit of Antichrist; and this, according to the teaching and analogy of Holy Scripture, is the preparation for his coming. The waves of this unholy tide may ebb and flow, now coming nearer and anon receding, but the tide will reach high-water mark in its time, and probably overflow it, for this overflowing of ungodliness will be ushered in with a storm, and there shall be thunderings and lightnings and earthquakes in the moral world before the calm, an Armageddon before the peace of the millennium.

(*a*)

14. The restraining power. "Ye know what withholdeth." Something, adds the Apostle, is restraining and holding back Antichrist from fully manifesting himself until the full time is come for such manifestation. What is this restraining power? This much appears quite plain. By the appointment of God Antichrist cannot come one moment before his time: "He who now letteth" (hindereth) will continue to do so until he, or it, is removed; and then, there being no longer any floodgates to stop the way, the gathering forces of ungodliness will rush in and inundate the world, at the head of which will be Antichrist himself.

Now, in order to explain what in all probability is meant by this restraining power, it is our first duty to seek for some obstacle which in the Apostle's time was evidently acting as a check upon the then growing antichristian lawlessness.

And, undoubtedly, he did see such a check and restraint in the "Powers that be" of his time. And it is most natural to suppose that in the power of political Rome, the Mistress of the World, he saw order and peace secured wherever that sway was wielded. The WITHHOLDING power, then, referred to by the Apostle, was national law or the civil power.

Now the same Apostle teaches us that the law is a terror to evil men, not to the good, and that very many evil disposed persons have no other fear before them than that of transgressing the laws of the land. They are held in check from the commission of crime simply by the power which can punish. Moral law, and obligations have no restraint over them. We cannot be far wrong then in regarding this as the withholding power referred to by the Apostle. This being so, then in our day, of course, the existing Government, or the secular law of nations, is still the great *restraining power* stopping lawless men from the commission of lawless deeds. It needs no special insight into the nature and formation of society to see that if once rulers, lawgivers, and magistrates were removed, the very floodgates which now keep back the tide of crime and lawlessness of every description would be rolled open, and a state of anarchy and confusion would immediately ensue, such as on a comparatively small scale has been witnessed more than once during the last century in Europe.

In order, then, that the affairs of the world, and the progress of the kingdom of God, should go on under a certain amount of orderliness and constituted authority, God has, in His Wisdom, ordained "The powers that be." And for these we are exhorted to pray, because that they, too, are the ministers of God, fulfilling His will as the great restraining powers which prevent the too early development of the Mystery of Iniquity.

Nor is it until God permits these barriers to be removed that *the Man of Sin* can appear on the scene of human affairs as the ripest fruit of the tree of the knowledge of evil.

"Ye know," says the Apostle, "what withholdeth that he might be revealed in his time. For the mystery of lawlessness doth already work only until he who withholdeth for the present be taken out of the way, and *then* shall that lawless one be revealed."

(*b*)

15. One question naturally arises here about the probable connection between some of the phenomena of the present day and the removal of this restraining power. Do we not see signs at least of such an impending state of things in the shaking and instability of "the powers that be"? . . . Preparatory, it may be, to the coming of Antichrist and the full development of the mystery of iniquity, which has hitherto been running parallel with the mystery of godliness all through the course of history. It is certainly unquestionable that we live in times both of political and national agitation; and that the undercurrent, of which perhaps these are but the surface ripples, consists in the main of the infidel and sacerdotal

(*c*)

Mystery of Iniquity—*continued*

agencies at work, both in the bosom of the Church and in the world without.

The internal and contemporaneous history of the various nations of the earth reveal the fact that revolutionary principles and the agitators against constituted authority are everywhere on the increase. In our days a kingship is held cheap. Not long since, too, even in our own highly-favoured country, a voice from the ranks of the revolutionary party said, "The Prince of Wales shall never be king of England." This may be regarded as a vain boast, but it at least indicates a current of opinion somewhere, and a possible coming struggle when class shall be pitted against class, and there shall be great distress of nations. A sample of which was to be seen in the lawlessness, the recklessness, the ungodliness, and the consequent inhumanity of the late terrible Commune in Paris.

And without taking the unenviable part of an alarmist, it does seem that there are sufficient general indications that the spirit of the Commune exists still—smouldering in well-nigh every capital of Europe, and perhaps of the world—under some name or other. And it may be that when God shall permit the restraining check of "the Powers that be" to be removed, then such an alarming state of things will become general. The very same seeds which bore such deadly fruit in France are being sown broadcast every day all over the world: among these seeds are superstition, a corrupt form of Christianity, infidelity in its various aspects, ungodliness amongst the masses, and a ceaseless Revolutionary agitation—such as any one who takes the trouble to go about amongst his fellow-men, and inquire into the currents of thought and opinion afloat, may prove for himself.

We repeat, then, that in the agitations, political and religious—in the destructive and levelling tendencies of one class of society against another—in the overthrow and general instability of kingdoms—in the fanatical attempts on the life of royalty—and in the prevailing ungodliness and infidelity of our times, we see at least signs of that great period of lawlessness and anarchy which shall usher in the Lawless One himself, who will oppose himself to God and to all that is worshipped; but who, happily for the true Church, will soon afterwards be destroyed. The ulcer of iniquity having drawn all its venom to a head, will break and vanish away at the appearing of our Lord and Saviour Jesus Christ. . . . As once before, when He comes forward His enemies fall to the ground (John xviii. 6).

Antichrist indeed comes as it is written of him, but Christ comes behind him.

(*a*)

16. "Strong Delusion"

We pursue the tempting subject no further: it is easier to dogmatize than to follow. We have tried to do the latter, however imperfectly, and have no desire to be wise above that which is written.

One concluding glance at the succeeding context, which suggests thoughts of the most solemn and deepest import :—

It says—"God shall send them strong delusion that they should believe a ('the') lie, . . . who believed not *the* truth, but had pleasure in unrighteousness." Do we not learn here something of *the faith of an unbeliever* : he will not believe the truth, he shall believe the lie . . . like king Saul, when he left God he went to a witch. The unbeliever *must believe in something*. God has so appointed it, that unbelief in His word leads on through superstition to wickedness. How readily does the unbeliever take up with everything which has some show of the wonderful and the extraordinary. . . . They tell us not to put implicit faith in the Bible, yet they are ready to place implicit faith in journalism. They do not believe that an Almighty hand created the universe, but they do believe that a mere blind chance whirled its atoms together. They do not believe that Jesus turned water into wine, but they do believe that the unconscious power of nature transformed the ape into a man. They have no belief in God, in Christ, and in the Holy Spirit, but they do believe there is something in table-rapping, in spiritism, and even in fortune-telling.

Verily, *they do believe in something*, but under the potent spell of a strong delusion, that something is *a lie*.

The cry uttered nearly nineteen hundred years ago—"*Not this man, but Barabbas,*" will probably find its counter-cry, as "the Mystery of Iniquity" hastens on to its doom—"Not Christ but Antichrist."

(*b*)

MYTHOLOGY, A GRADUALLY DEVELOPED CHRISTIAN

As to this extraordinary theory, it may be observed, first, that it raises ten times more difficulties than it explains. For, first of all, it requires of us to believe that, not at a period lost in a fabulous antiquity, but during one of which we know a great deal, and within historic times, illiterate men, as we know the early disciples were, could weave together such an extraordinary story, and persuade many of our countrymen to accept it. It requires of us to receive this as the origin of the most extraordinary revolution the world has seen, though "there is no known history of a mythic history having grown up in such an age, under such circumstances, or with such rapidity as is postulated in this case. The age was an historical age, being that of Dionysius, Diodorus, Livy, Velleius, Paterculus, Plutarch, Valerius Maximus, and Tacitus; the country was one where written records were kept, and historical literature had long flourished; it produced, at the very time when the New Testament documents were being written, an historian of good repute, Josephus, whose narrative of the events of his own time is universally accepted as authentic and trustworthy. To suppose that a mythology could be formed in such an age and country, is to confuse the characteristics of the most opposite periods—to ascribe to a time of luxury, over-civilization, and decay, a phase of thought which only belongs to the rude vigour and early infancy of nations."

(*c*)   *Maclear*

MYTHOLOGY AND HOLY SCRIPTURE

1. Samson's lock of hair cut off by Delilah is supposed to have given rise to *Nisus' hair*.

(*d*)

2. Samson's strength is the supposed origin of the great hero of mythology, *Hercules*.

3. Samson's marriage, to that of *Omphale*.

4. Samson's laying hold of the pillars of the house, to the Pillars of Hercules.

5. Also, to the fabulous Cleomedes Astypalean.

6. Jephthah's vow, to that of Agamemnon and his daughter Iphigenia.

7. And the Rape of the Sabines is supposed to have originated from the ambush of the Benjamites.

(a)   *Nichol*

N

NAME OF GOD, THE, AND FORGIVENESS

1. The name of God is that whereby He reveals Himself to us, whereby He would have us know Him, and own Him. It is something expressive of His nature or properties, which He has appropriated to Himself. Whatever, therefore, any name of God expresses Him to be—that He is, that we may expect to find Him ; for He will not deceive us by giving Himself a wrong or a false name. And on this account He requires us to trust in His name, because He will assuredly be found to us what His name imports. Resting on His name, flying to His name, calling upon His name, praising His name, things so often mentioned in the Scripture, confirm the same to us. These things could not be our duty, if we might be deceived in so doing. God is, and will be to us, what His name declares.

(a)

2. On this ground and reason, then, God is said, first, to be known by any name, when those to whom He reveals Himself do, in an especial manner, rest on that name by faith, and have that accomplished towards them which that name imports, signifies, or declares. And therefore God did not, under the Old Testament, reveal Himself to any by the name of the "Father of Jesus Christ," or the "Son Incarnate," because the grace of it to them was not to be accomplished. "God having provided some better thing for us, that they without us should not be made perfect ; " they were not entrusted with the full revelation of God by all His blessed names. Neither doth God call us to trust in any name of His, however declared or revealed, unless He gives it us in an especial manner, by way of covenant, to rest upon. So he speaks (Exod. vi. 3) : "I appeared unto Abraham, unto Isaac, and to Jacob" (Hebrew, in the name of God Almighty), "but by My name Jehovah was I not known unto them." It is certain that both these names of God, El-shaddai and Jehovah, were known among His people before. In the first mention we have of Abraham's addressing himself to the worship of God, he makes use of the name Jehovah. He built an altar unto Jehovah, Gen. xii. 7 ; and so afterwards, not only doth Moses make use of that name in the repetition of the story, but it was also of frequent use amongst them. Whence, then, is it said, that God appeared to them by the name of an El-shaddai, but not by the name of Jehovah? The reason is, because that was the name which God gave Himself in the solemn confirmation of the covenant with Abraham (Gen. xvii. 1), (Hebrew, "I am El-shaddai, God Almighty"), God All-sufficient. And when Isaac would pray for the blessing of the covenant on Jacob, he makes use of that name, "God Almighty bless thee" (Gen. xxviii. 3). He invocates that name of God which was engaged in the covenant made with his father Abraham, and himself. That therefore we may, with full assurance, rest on the name of God, it is not only necessary that God reveal that name to be His, but also that He give it out to us for that end and purpose, that we might know Him thereby, and

place our trust and confidence in Him, according to what that name of His imports. And this was the case wherever He revealed Himself to any in a peculiar manner, by an especial name. So He did to Jacob, "I am the God of Abraham and Isaac" (Gen. xxviii. 13), assuring him that as He had dealt faithfully in His covenant with his fathers Abraham and Isaac, so also He would deal with him ; and Gen. xxxi. 13, "I am the God of Bethel ; " He who appeared to thee there, and blessed thee, and will continue so to do. But when the same Jacob comes to ask after another name of God, He answers him not ; as it were commanding him to live by faith on what He was pleased to reveal. How, then, God had not made Himself known to Abraham, and Isaac, and Jacob, by His name Jehovah, because He had not peculiarly called Himself to them by that name ; nor had engaged it in His covenant with them, although it were otherwise known to them. They lived and rested on the name of God Almighty, as suited to their support and consolation in their wandering, helpless condition, before the promise was to be accomplished : but now, when God came to fulfil His promises, and to bring the people, by virtue of His covenant, into the land of Canaan, He reveals Himself to them by, and renews His covenant with them in, the name of Jehovah. And hereby God did declare that He came to give stability and accomplishment to His promises ; to which end they were now to live upon this name of Jehovah, in an expectation of the fulfilling of the promises, as their fathers did on that of God Almighty, in an expectation of protection from Him in their wandering state and condition. Hence this name became the foundation of the Jewish Church, and ground of the faith of those who sincerely believed in God therein. And it is strangely fallen out in the providence of God, that since the Jews have rejected the covenant of their fathers, and are cast out of that covenant for their unbelief, they have utterly forgotten that name of God. No Jew in the world knows what it is, nor how to pronounce it, or make mention of it. I know themselves and others pretend strange mysteries in the letters and vowels of that name, which make it ineffable. But the truth is, being cast out of that covenant, which was built and established on that name, in the just judgment of God through their own blindness and superstition, they are no more able to make mention of it, or to take it into their mouths. It is required then, that the name of God be given to us, as engaged in covenant to secure our expectation, that He will be to us according to His name.

(b)

3. All the whole gracious name of God, every title that He hath given Himself, every ascription of honour to Himself that He has owned, is confirmed to us (to as many as believe) in Jesus Christ. For as He hath declared to us the whole name of God (John xvii. 6), so not this or that promise of God, but "all the promises of God are in Him yea and amen." So that, as of old, every particular promise that God made to the people, served especially for

(c)

Name of God, the, and Forgiveness—*continued*

the particular occasion on which it was given; and each name of God was to be rested on, as to that dispensation whereunto it was suited to give relief and confidence; as the name of Elshaddai to Abraham, Isaac, and Jacob, and the name Jehovah to Moses and the people; so now, by Jesus Christ, and in Him, every particular promise belongs to believers in all their situations; and every name of God whatever is theirs also, at all times, to rest upon, and put their trust in. Thus the particular promise made to Joshua, at his entrance into Canaan, to encourage and strengthen him in that great enterprise of conquering the land, is by the Apostle applied to all believers, in all their occasions whatever: "I will never leave thee, nor forsake thee" (Heb. xiii. 5). So likewise doth every name of God belong now to us, as if it had in a particular manner been engaged in covenant to us; and that because the whole covenant is ratified and confirmed to us by Jesus Christ (2 Cor. vi. 18; chap. vii. 1). This, then, absolutely secures to us an interest in the name of God insisted on, the God of forgiveness, as if it had been given to every one of us, to assure us thereof.

(a)

4. **God takes this name, the God of forgiveness, to be His in a peculiar manner, as that whereby He will be distinguished and known.** He appropriates it to Himself, as expressing that which the power and goodness of no other can extend to. "There are lords many, and gods many," saith the Apostle; some that are called so; such as some account so to be. How is the true God distinguished from these gods, by reputation? He is so by this name, He is the "God of pardons." (Micah vii. 18): "Who is a God like unto Thee, that pardoneth iniquity?" This is His prerogative; herein none is equal to Him, like to Him, or a sharer with Him. Who is a God like unto Thee, that may be called a God of pardons? The vanities of the nations cannot give them this rain; they have no refreshing showers of mercy and pardon in their power. Neither angels, nor saints, nor images, nor popes, can pardon sin. By this name doth He distinguish Himself from them all.

(b)

5. **To be known by this name, is the great glory of God in this world.** When Moses desired to see the glory of God, the Lord told him that he could not see His face" (Exod. xxxiii. 18–20). The face of God, or the glorious majesty of His being, His essential glory, is not to be seen by any in this life; we cannot see Him as He is. But the glorious manifestation of Himself we may behold and contemplate. This we may see as the back parts of God; that shadow of His excellencies which He casteth forth in His passing by, as in His works and dispensations. This Moses shall see. And wherein did it consist? Why, in the revelation and declaration of this name of God. "The Lord passed by before him, and proclaimed, the Lord, the Lord God, merciful and gracious, long-suffering, and abundant in goodness and truth, keeping mercy for thousands, forgiving iniquity, transgression, and sin" (chap. xxxiv. 6–7). To be known by this name, to be honoured, feared, believed, as that declares Him, is the great glory of God. And shall this fail us? Can we be deceived trusting in it, or expecting that we shall

find Him to be what His name declares? God forbid.

(c)   *John Owen*

NAME (A GOOD)

Good name in man and woman, dear my lord,
Is the immediate jewel of their souls:
Who steals my purse steals trash; 'tis something, nothing,
'Twas mine, 'tis his, and has been slave to thousands;
But he that filches from me my good name,
Robs me of that which not enriches him,
And makes me poor indeed.

(d)   *Shakspeare*

NATURAL MAN (1 Cor. ii. 6–16, and 1 Cor. xv. 44)

The ψυχικός (natural man) is one that hath all that is or can be derived from the first Adam, one endowed with a rational soul, and who hath the use and exercise of all his rational faculties, . . . not a man given up to his pleasures and guided by his brutish affections and no other.

(e)   *John Owen*

The natural man = not merely the man with *gross* passions, but whoever is taught only by his own faculties.

(f)   *Calvin*

The Apostle calls men who live according to nature *natural* (ψυχικούς), those who live contrary to nature, *carnal* (σαρκικούς), but those are *spiritual* (πνευματικοί) who even change their nature after the spirit.

(g)   *Ephraim Cyrus*

The *natural* man is one who, though he stands apart from grace, is still endowed to the fullest degree with understanding, sense, capacity, and art.

(h)   *Luther*

"NATURAL MAN, THE, *receiveth not the things of the Spirit of God*, . . . *they are spiritually discerned*" (1 Cor. ii. 14)

Talk of natural depravity, that man cannot help himself; he will reply: "Then it is best to sit still and do nothing." Tell him that hell is a reality, the lost have "no hope"; he will reply: "Yea, hath God said so; there is probably a restoration. Hell is not so formidable as that." Tell him that the Books of Revelation and Daniel are the Histories of the world unto the end, and are as true as the Gospel Narratives of Matthew, Mark, Luke, and John; and he will denounce you as an enthusiast and a fool. Tell him of the second coming of Christ, of the possible nearness of His return, of the object of His re-appearing, and he will scornfully reply as thousands do: "Where is the promise of His coming, for since the fathers fell asleep all things continue as they were." Yes, the natural man, whether wise or a fool, learned or unlearned, cannot receive these things because they are spiritually discerned. "God hath hid these things from the wise and prudent, and revealed them unto babes.

(i)   *Cumming*

NATURE

All things are artificial, for
Nature is the art of God.

(a)   *Thos. Browne*

The course of nature is the art of God.

(b)   *Young*

NATURE AND GOD

Nature speaks of a general Divinity, not of the
Friend and Benefactor of each living soul.

(c)   *Channing*

NATURE AND GRACE

Illustrated by a bird in a cage : The cage cannot
kill the bird, and the bird cannot escape from the
cage. The day will come, however, when the door
of the cage will be opened, and the bird will be set
free. Till then it can sing its song.

(d)

NAZARETH

" *Jesus of Nazareth passeth by* " (Luke xviii. 37)

Suppose the language of the text was :

" Jesus of Nazareth has passed by."

To blind Bartimæus the consequences would
have been obvious, still blind, and still by the
wayside, to-day as yesterday, and with no hope of
alleviation.

" Blind ! blind ! irrecoverably blind ! " If the
preacher had to say this from the pulpit, what
dismay it would cause. The sinner would be told
there was no hope of pardon for him. The backslider would be told that there was no promise
made for him on his return. It would mean for
us all that the door of mercy was shut, and closed
for ever against us, and it was too late for us to
enter. Our day of grace would be over. " Now
is the day of salvation " would no longer sound
in our ears. All preaching might cease at once.
The Bible might remain on the shelf unread.
Prayer, whether public or private, might be given
up. For if Jesus had passed us by there would
remain for us no hope of salvation. But a certain
fearful looking for indignation and wrath, tribulation and anguish. But thanks to God, Jesus has
not yet passed us by ! He has not commissioned
His ministers to go with his message, saying,
" Jesus of Nazareth *has* passed by." His first
commission to them, when He sent them to preach,
has never yet been cancelled, which ran thus : " Go
ye and preach the Gospel to all nations. He that
believeth shall be saved ; and he that believeth not
shall be damned."

(e)

Or suppose the words of the text were :

" Jesus of Nazareth will pass by." In that case
the blind man might have said : " I need not be in
a hurry to attract the attention of Jesus to-day ; I
need not be so urgent and pressing in my application ; I shall have another opportunity ; I will indeed petition Him now, but I will not importune
Him ; I will not be very loud and demonstrative in
my cries. If He passes me by to-day, He will come
this way again to-morrow, perhaps ; and for many

days. My case is not hopeless. Think, if the text
ran in such a way, of the handle and excuse it would
have given for delay. Perhaps the worst foe the
preacher has to contend with is DELAY. Delay has
filled hell with victims, " Hell is paved with good
intentions." People want no incentives for going
on delaying. The preacher must not, nay, dare
not say to them, " *Jesus of Nazareth* WILL *pass
by*." He must simply go and proclaim the truth
Jesus has commissioned him to preach—that
" *Now*," " *to-day*," " *this hour*," " *this minute* " is
salvation brought to whomsoever will accept it.
He knows the danger of delay. It faces him every
day of his ministerial life. It faces him in nearly
every death bed he has to stand beside. People
are for ever saying to themselves, " There is time
enough yet, I will repent in the future." Counting on some future time when Jesus will pass by
their way, or at the very least they count upon
having a lingering disease, a long time in which to
repent and to make terms with God. They say,
though the Bible does not, " *Jesus of Nazareth will
pass by*, and then it will be time enough to set
matters right. When I have death to look forward
to and not life, when I can't expect to live much
longer, when I am old and feeble, then I will seek
Jesus." Your great spiritual enemy could not
wish you to alter such a decision. Well he knows
that if you act upon such a principle he may
count upon you. He is not likely to undeceive
you. Neither do I think he will tempt you into
committing any great sin. To let you alone is his
surest way of winning you body and soul completely. He sees your condition, and he will say,
" Sleep on, sleep on now and take your rest."

But shall I tell you what this putting off coming
to Jesus until old age, or a death-bed, means ? I
tell you facts which come too often before the
minister's eyes. It means giving God the end of
your life instead of the whole. It means, if you
are saved at all, just saved, as shipwrecked sailors
get ashore on boards and rafts, and broken pieces
of the ship. In too many cases it means the
attempt to do a day's work when the day is over.
It means, weakness of body and of mind, rendering any mental effort a burden. It means stupor
and insensibility, when to seek God is impossible.
It means too often, the entrance of Giant Despair
into the citadel of the soul, opening the Bible and
reading from the Book of Proverbs : " Because I
have called, and ye refused ; I have stretched out
My hand, and no man regarded. But ye have set
at nought all My counsel, and would have none of
My reproof ; I will also laugh at your calamity ; I
will mock when your fear cometh ; when your fear
cometh as desolation, and your destruction cometh
as a whirlwind ; when distress and anguish cometh
upon you. Then shall they call upon Me, but I will
not answer ; they shall seek Me early, but they
shall not find Me ; for that they hated knowledge,
and did not choose the fear of the Lord ; they
would none of My counsel : they despised all My
reproof. Therefore shall they eat of the fruit of
their own way, and be filled with their own
devices " (Prov. i. 24–31).

Terrible passages, such as these, will Giant
Despair read to us at such a moment, whilst our
unpractised hand and our physical weakness make
us powerless to handle the " Sword of the Spirit,"
to cut the Giant down, who is straddling across
our path, seeking to bar the door of life in our
face. In the face of such a danger then, do not

(f)

Nazareth—*continued.*

procrastinate, do not put off until the uncertain future what can and ought to be done to-day. Do not, as you would wish to have a peaceful death-bed, say, "*Jesus of Nazareth will pass by.*" For no such words stand in the Bible, except, indeed, the devil's version of it.

(*a*)

3. But what saith it?

"Jesus of Nazareth PASSETH by." *Is* passing by now, and the present is our only opportunity. We may never have another. He may never pass this way again. Hence the reason for the blind man's importunity—"Now or never!" His opportunity had come, and he did his utmost not to miss it. In a few moments Jesus would be past and out of hearing. To-morrow would be too late. To-day only was his to work in, and he did it. He sought the Saviour and found Him, setting us an example. This man, in many ways, was a representative of ourselves.

(i.) He was blind. Are not we also? Has not the god of this world blinded the eyes of them that believe not, lest they should see, and be converted, and live? And where should blind people be but at the "wayside begging"? At the wayside where they are likely to meet Jesus. At the place where His people meet together, and where the breath of the Spirit is felt. Where would you place a mill, except on a hill-top that it may catch the wind? Where would you place a blind man if you wished for the restoration of his sight, except where you knew a great oculist would pass by. Where are we at the present moment? Brought together for a moment, as waifs and strays on the great ocean of time, in this place at this moment. This place where prayer is wont to be made. Where are we but at the wayside? And who is here too along with us? Who is it that promised that "Where two or three are gathered together, there am I in the midst of them"? Who is in this place? Who am I preaching about? "It is about Jesus of Nazareth." What am I saying? I am saying what the people said to the blind man, "Jesus of Nazareth passeth by." Yes, He passeth by, soon the opportunity will have passed; lose it not! As you sit by the wayside, lose not the opportunity. Let Jesus hear your voice—cry out as Blind Bartimæus did, "Jesus, Thou Son of David, have mercy on me."

(*b*)

NEGLECT (Heb. ii. 5)

We can understand that notorious sinners are not saved; and that men perish by unbelief; but here by *neglect*. Why?

1. Because by neglect we *degenerate*. Illustrated by a fact in nature: pigeons of all colours and beauty and variety=the result of domestication. Take some of each kind and colour, place them on an inaccessible island, and in a few years *all will be alike* of a greyish dun colour. So with a rose-bush, or a strawberry-plant. So, too, with ourselves, neglect the body, clothes, manners, etc., and man becomes a savage, a wild man.

So with the soul: if we neglect the means of salvation we cannot escape.

(*c*)

2. Or, to put it in another way: we must resist our natural tendency, which is a gravitation downwards—*viz.* to fall lower and lower—*to die* (as all things *in nature* do).

A bird flies, and a man swims, by resisting the natural tendency to drop or sink. There must be life to maintain this struggle.

The Bible=If a man neglects the means of salvation, he will inevitably sink into the hell of the lost—the castaway—who are carried, as dead bodies, unresistingly till cast on some shore. It is a *law* from which there is no escape.

(*d*)

3. Another reason is, *in the nature of things* we cannot escape if we neglect; common sense tells us that, if a man neglect to till his field, and to sow seed, he cannot reap a harvest in the autumn; or, if a man has taken poison, he will perish equally, whether he *neglects* the remedy, or throw it out of the window. Hence the stress here on the word *neglect* (not doubt, not unbelief, despair, rejection, or to trample under foot God's offer, and doing despite to the Spirit of grace is worse), all bad, but neglect will do the work just as surely.

(*e*)

4. Our opportunity must be seized and improved. The Scripture puts it thus:—

(i.) Old Testament="*Let him alone.*" It is the worst thing that can happen to him. Let the Prodigal son *alone*, and he will ruin himself: he who will be independent, will in the end feed as the swine.

(ii.) New Testament="*Take the talent from him.*" He has neglected to use it: He has lost his opportunity: for "*now* is the accepted time; *now* is the day of salvation."

(iii.) Cf.—The order to the Israelites in Egypt: The blood of the slain victim to be collected in a basin, and used in a special manner (sprinkled); but if left there, and unused, *it will not* save—no escape—so of Christ's blood.

(*f*)   *Adapted*

(*See* "BLOOD," *the story of the Israelite girl.*)

NEGLECT

Suppose death were now to overtake you, what would you say, what could you say? Oh! would you be constrained to say—"I heard truths that would make the lost in misery leap for ecstasy, that angels listened to, and are startled by their music; and I heard them, and went, one to his farm, another to his merchandise. I have not rejected, for I never was bold enough to do that, but I have *neglected* the great salvation."

(*g*)   *Cumming*

NEPTUNE'S CUP

Almost imperceptible creatures in the sea build in the Indian Ocean a goblet. It is called "Neptune's cup." Sometimes it has a height of six feet, and a breadth of three. It is erected solely by myriads of polypi. They have no consultation with each other. Each works in a separate cell; each is as much cut off from communication with every other as an inmate of a cell in the wards of

(*h*)

Charlestown prison yonder is from his associates. They build the stem to the proper height, and then they begin to widen it. Everything proceeds according to a plan. Is the plan theirs, or does it belong to a Power above them, and that acts through them? As these isolated creatures build Neptune's cup, so the bioplasts, isolated from each other in the living tissues which they produce, build the rose and the violet and all flowers, the pomegranate and the cedar, the oak and palm, and all trees, the eagle and all birds, the lion and all animals, the human brain and all men. Neptune's cup alone strikes us dumb. But what shall we say of the mystic structures built by the bioplasts? There is the cup; it is a fact; and the eye is another Neptune's cup; and all this universe is another Neptune's cup: and out of such cups I, for one, drink the glad wine of Theism!

(a) *Joseph Cook*

NEUTRALITY

"*He that is not for Me, is against Me*" (Matt. xii. 30)

There can be no middle way. There is no place where we can stand looking on the doers of the word without working with them. There is no neutral ground, either we are working and gathering with Christ, or with the devil. Either helping Christ to save souls, or the devil's assistants in their destruction. A solemn announcement this, but it is the teaching of the word.

(b) *C. Rankin*

NEW

1. Let us *sing* unto the Lord a new song;
2. Let us *pray* unto the Lord a new prayer;
3. Let us *offer* unto the Lord a new life.

(c)

NEW BIRTH

The way and work of the Holy Spirit in regeneration is ofttimes very secret, and usually exceedingly various:

(i.) As to *time*. Some are wrought upon in youth, others in old age.

(ii.) As to His *methods* of working, some are wrought upon by the corrosives of the Law, others by lenitives of the Gospel.

(iii.) As to the *manner* of His working, and in the *means* by which He works:

Upon some by a powerful ordinance, upon others by an awakening providence. But the Spirit's work in all still the same, it produces likeness to God.

(d) *Burkett*

A day will come when those who are not born again will wish that they had never been born at all.

(e) *Ryle*

NEW COMMANDMENT, A (John xiii. 34, 35)

The celebrated Usher paid a visit to the no less celebrated Samuel Rutherford. He arrived on a Saturday evening when Mrs. Rutherford was catechizing a class of servants and villagers, according to their custom, at the parsonage. Usher,

disguised as a peasant, took his place in the class. "How many Commandments are there, my good man?" was the question put to him by the lady.

"Eleven," was his answer.

Whereupon he received a rebuke for his ignorance.

Claiming a lodging for the night, as a wayfaring man, he was overheard by Rutherford praying aloud. Somewhat astonished, the latter entered his room and sought an explanation of so singular a circumstance of a man who had shown such ignorance of Scripture, praying so earnestly and well.

The truth came out that he was Usher; and a secret agreement was come to that he should preach on the following morning.

Imagine Mrs. Rutherford's surprise when she saw her ignorant guest ascend the pulpit, and hear him preach eloquently from these words:

"A new Commandment give I unto you, that ye love one another."

(f)

NEW COVENANT

Now the form of His bringing-up was by chastisements, scourging, correcting, nurturing. See if He maketh exception of any of His children (Rev. iii. 19; Heb. xii. 7, 8). No: His eldest Son and His Heir, Jesus, is not excepted (Heb. ii. 10). Suffer we must; ere we were born, God decreed it; and it is easier to complain of His decree than to change it. It is true, terrors of conscience cast us down; and yet without terrors of conscience we cannot be raised up again; fears and doubtings shake us; and yet without fears and doubtings we should soon sleep, and lose our hold of Christ. Tribulation and temptations will almost loose us at the root; and yet without tribulations and temptations we can now no more grow than herbs or corn without rain. Sin and Satan and the world will say and cry in our ear that we have a hard reckoning to make in judgment; and yet none of these three, except they lie, dare say in our face that our sin can change the tenour of the new covenant.

(g) *Samuel Rutherford*

NEW COVENANT, THE, AND FORGIVENESS

Wherefore doth He reject and lay aside His first covenant, and promise to make another, and do so accordingly? Certain it is that He might have continued it with a blessed security to His own glory; and He makes "all things for Himself, even the wicked for the day of evil."

God Himself shows what was the only and sole reason of this dispensation, Heb. viii. 7-13. The sum of it is this: notwithstanding the blessed constitution of the first covenant, yet there was no provision for the pardon of sin, no room or place for forgiveness in it; but on supposition that man sinned, he was in that covenant left remediless. God had not in it revealed that there was any such thing as forgiveness with Him; nor had any sinner the least hope or grounds of expectation from thence of any such thing in Him. Die he must, and perish, and that without remedy or recovery. Now, saith God, this must not be. Mercy, goodness, and grace, require another state of things. This covenant will manifest them; their effects will not be communicated to poor

(h)

sinners by it. Hence, saith He, "It is faulty, that is, defective; I will not lose the glory of them, nor shall sinners be unrelieved by them; and therefore, though I may strictly tie up all mankind unto the terms of this, yet I will make another covenant with them, wherein they shall know and find that there is forgiveness with Me, that they may fear Me."

(a)

Now, next to the blood of Christ, whereby this covenant was ratified and confirmed, this is the greatest evidence that can possibly be given, that there is forgiveness with God. To what end else does God make this great alteration in the effects of His will, in His way of dealing with mankind? As forgiveness of sin is expressly contained in the tenor and words of the covenant, so, set it aside, and it will be of no more use or advantage than the former. For, as this covenant is made directly with sinners (nor was there any one in the world, when God made it, that was not a sinner; nor is it of use unto any but sinners), so is forgiveness of sins the very life of it.

Hence we may see two things: first, the greatness of forgiveness, that we may learn to value it; and, secondly, the certainty of it, that we may learn to believe it.

(b)

First, the greatness of it. God would not do so great a thing as that mentioned, but for a great, the greatest end. Had it not been a matter of the greatest importance unto the glory of God, and the good of the souls of men, God would not, for the sake of it, have laid aside one covenant and made another. We may evidently see, how the heart of God was set upon it, how His nature and will were engaged in it. All this was done that we might be pardoned. The old glorious fabric of obedience and rewards shall be taken down to the ground, that a new one may be erected for the honour and glory of forgiveness. God forbid that we should have slight thoughts of that which was so strangely and wonderfully brought forth, wherein God had as it were embarked His great glory. Shall all this be done for our sakes, and shall we undervalue it, or disesteem it? God forbid. God could, if I may so say, more easily have made a new world of innocent creatures, and have governed them by the old covenant, than have established this new one for the salvation of poor sinners: but then, where had been the glory of forgiveness? It could never have been known that there was forgiveness with Him. The old covenant could not have been preserved and sinners pardoned. Wherefore God chose rather to leave the covenant than sinners unrelieved, than grace unexalted, and pardon unexercised. Prize it as you prize your souls, and give glory unto God for it, as all those that believe will do unto eternity.

(c)

Secondly, for the security of it, that we may believe it. What greater can be given? God deceiveth no man, no more than He is deceived. And what could God, that cannot lie, do more, to give us satisfaction herein than He hath done? Would you be made partakers of this forgiveness; go unto God, spread before Him this whole matter, plead with Him that He Himself hath so far laid aside the first covenant of His own gracious will as to make a new one, and that merely because it

had no forgiveness in it. This He hath made on purpose that it might be known that there is forgiveness in Him. And shall not we now be made partakers of it? Will He now deny that unto us which He hath given such assurance of, and raised such expectations concerning? Nothing can here wrong us, nothing can ruin us, but unbelief. Lay hold on this covenant, and we shall have pardon. This God expresses, Isa. xxvii. 4, 5. Shall we continue on the old bottom of the first covenant? All that we can do thereon is but to set thorns and briars in the way of God, to secure ourselves from His coming against us, with His indignation and fury. Our sins are so, and our righteousness is no better. And what will be the issue; both they and we shall be trodden down, consumed, and burnt up. What way then, what remedy is left unto us? Only this, of laying hold on the arm and strength of God in that covenant, wherein forgiveness of sin is provided. Therein alone He saith: fury is not in Me; and the end shall be that we shall have peace with Him, both here and for ever.

(d)   *John Owen.*
(*See* "FORGIVENESS.")

NEW CREATURE

"*If any man is in Christ, he is a new creature: the old things are passed away; behold, they are become new*" (2 Cor. v. 17).

1. The Apostle introduces this saying by a reference to a new way of regarding Jesus Christ.

Christ may be known by us "*after the flesh*," *i.e.* in an unenlightened sense, and which is no true knowledge of Him at all. Or, again, Christ may be known by us *after the spirit, i.e.* after we have been enlightened by the Spirit of God, and then, not only Christ, but life, and everything else appears to us in a new light altogether.

The difference is more than that between ignorance and knowledge. It is the difference between Adam and Christ; between creation and new creation; between death and life. For if any man be *in* Christ he is created anew by the creative Spirit of God, who is the Lord and Giver of life.

(e)

2. In Adam. There is a statement in 1 Cor. xv. which will help us somewhat in arriving at what the expression "in Christ" really means. "As in Adam all die, even so in Christ shall all be made alive."

The terms "*in Adam*" and "*in Christ*" must convey the same idea. We are in the one, as we are in the other. We all, more or less, must understand in what sense we are said to be "*in Adam.*"

He is the head of the human race; we are all descended from him; we are involved in what befell him; his blood flows in our veins; his nature, and that only, is our nature; we have only what he bequeathed to us; he was a natural, *i.e.* a mortal man, so are we; we cannot get beyond that sphere in which he lived. By our very nature then we are "in Adam."

(f)

3. In Christ. Carrying this idea with us, we try to arrive at an understanding of what being "IN CHRIST" means.

Christ is the second Adam, *i.e.* the second head, of the human race. We are grafted into Him as a
(g)

New Creature—continued

new stock, as one tree is grafted into another; we make a fresh start in Christ; we are again involved in what befell Him (involved in His death, burial, resurrection, and ascension). We have what He bequeathed to us, "eternal life." We are partakers of His spirit; heirs of whatever He is heir to, i.e. glory, honour, and immortality, just as by nature we are heirs of whatever Adam has bequeathed to us.

Now this is the meaning of being "IN CHRIST," grafted into Christ, whereby He becomes a new root, and we new branches, receiving all our life's nourishment from Him, as once we received everything from the first root of our being.

(a)

4. The Factors. And the way this change is effected (i.e. the grafting, or the change from being in Adam to being in Christ) is by the agency of God the Holy Ghost co-operating with Faith in us [Cf. "Blessed is she that believed"(Luke i. 45)], and at every new birth these two factors co-operate simultaneously. The conjunction of two forces, one as receptive, the other as communicative, produce a new being. Just as at the first there was a moment when God BREATHED INTO THE FIRST MAN the breath of life, and man became a living soul, and made the difference between him and an animal. And just as there was a moment in human history when God became incarnate, and Christ became different to Adam; so there is a corresponding moment in each human life when he or she is breathed into by the Spirit of God; when the Divine life is from that moment communicated, and we become spiritual. These are they who are "in Christ." And now, adds the Apostle, if any man be in Christ, he is a NEW CREATURE.

(b)

5. What is meant by a new creature? Observe first of all that a new creature means the same as a new creation; and this will help us to understand what is meant; for by the use of this term we are again carried back to the original work of man's creation at the first. For if a man at a certain moment becomes a new creature, it is clear that it is in some way to be compared with the old creation, i.e. that of Adam.

An old creature = a man of the first creation is a creature like Adam, mortal, a new creature is a creature like Christ, immortal. The comparison again is between Adam and Christ. The Scriptures warrant us in making the comparison; for Christ is termed the second Adam, and therefore it is right for us to ascertain where lies the difference between them, as the new and old creations of God.

(i.) Adam had no progenitor, but was a direct creation of God. The breath of God allying with a material body produced a creature with "a living soul," susceptible of sin, decay, death; in other words, mortal, and carrying all creation with him; from his fate none who succeeded him could escape. For all were concluded in him.

(ii.) Christ the second Adam was a new Creation of God. Something quite new, and unlike what had been before—not an historic man, i.e. a product of the race. God in Him became incarnate. And He, as a new creation, was altogether of a higher potency of life than the first

man (not a "living soul" merely, but a "quickening spirit"), and contained in Himself the power of immortality. Adam bequeathed death, Christ communicates eternal life to all who are in Him.

In this sense Christ is a new creature.

In like manner, when a man is in Christ he, too, becomes like Christ, a new creature, and a partaker of Christ's nature and life. He has passed from the mortal sphere to the immortal— from being merely "a living soul" to one who is alive in the spirit, from being a natural man bound by natural laws, to a spiritual man free from the law of sin and death,—in every sense of the word a NEW CREATURE; consequently, it follows that the old life is done with—old things that clung to, and belonged to, the Adamic sphere of life are passed away, the life has become new.

(c)

6. "Old things are passed away, behold they are become new."

(i.) The old state of life is gone, broken with, and done with altogether, and a new state is begun. The reign of darkness is over, and the reign of light has begun. For so it is indeed stated, " God hath delivered from the power of darkness and hath translated us into the kingdom of His dear Son. We have by this changed our king, and are now subjects of a new King. Once we did the deeds of darkness, now we walk in the light. Once our eyes were blinded, now we see; and no greater evidence that a man's life has been changed could well be than this, that his manner of life is entirely altered.

(ii.) The old covenant is passed away and a new covenant between God and man takes its place. "This is the covenant that I will make with them, saith God, I will put my laws in their hearts, and in their minds will I write them (not on stone) . . . and their sins and their iniquities will I remember no more."

(iii.). The old way of regarding death is passed away and a new way of looking at it is begun. "I go to prepare a place for you." He hath abolished death and brought life and immortality to light through the gospel. "Through death He destroyed him who had the power of death (the devil), and delivered them who through fear of death were all their lifetime subject to bondage."

(iv.) The old feeling towards God is passed away, and a new and living way to the Father has been opened up for us.

"God hath not given us the spirit of bondage again to fear; but the Spirit of adoption, whereby we cry, Abba, Father."

"The spirit beareth witness with our spirit, that we are the children of God: and if children, then heirs; heirs of God, and joint-heirs with Christ " (John xiv. 2; Heb. ii. 15; iv. 16; Rom. viii. 15, 16).

(d)

"NEW, I MAKE ALL THINGS " (Rev. xxi. 5)

Compare CREATION and RE-CREATION.

CREATION =	RE-CREATION =
1. Light ;	The seven churches ;
2. Heaven and earth ;	The glory of heaven, and the gloom of earth = the seven seals ;
3. Land and sea-plants and grass ;	Vision of the seven trumpets ;

(e)

CREATION =	RE-CREATION =
4. Sun on this day;	Angel, like the sun, coming to the earth;
5. The waters bring forth abundantly;	Demoniac beast rising from the sea;
6. The earth also;	Demoniac beast rising from the earth;
Man (Adam);	The new Man (Christ);
7. Paradise and Sabbath;	New Paradise, and Eternal Sabbath.

(*a*)

NEW WASHING

New washing, renewed application of purchased redemption by that sacred blood that sealeth the free covenant, is a thing of daily and hourly use to a poor sinner. Till we be in heaven our issue of blood will not be quite dried up; and therefore we must resolve to apply peace to our souls from the new and living Way; and Jesus, who cleanseth and cureth the leprous soul, lovely Jesus, must be our song on this side of heaven's gates. And even when we have won the castle, then must we eternally sing, "Worthy, worthy is the Lamb, who hath saved us, and washed us in His own blood."

(*b*)   *Samuel Rutherford*

NEWMAN

Newman and his party are idolaters; they put Christ's Church, Christ's Sacraments, Christ's ministers, in the place of Christ Himself: these are imperfect ideas, and moral evil follows. Thus it is that narrow-mindedness leads to wickedness. The best men are they who worship Christ and no idol. Judaizing is a direct idolatry—exalting the Church and the sects, as others have exalted His mother, and others, in the same spirit, have exalted circumcision.

(*c*)   *Dr. Arnold*

NEWS

News, the manna of a day.

(*d*)   *Green*

NEWSPAPER, THE DAILY

One of the best commentaries on Holy Scripture that I am acquainted with, is the daily newspaper. What the Bible tells me, I find frequently backed up,—of course without deliberate intention,—by the Press. I read painful things in the one, about the sinfulness and selfishness of the human heart; but there is a very distinct echo of these statements in the continuous record of vice, and crime, and wrong-doing, supplied by the other. The Bible, again, talks about a judgment to come. Men ridicule the idea; but when I turn to my newspaper, I find a curious kind of process going on in the world, which seems to correspond, very closely, with the scriptural assertion. Every now and then a great exposure takes place. Perhaps it is a bubble-company that has exploded; perhaps it is a religious hypocrite that has been unmasked; perhaps it is some long-successful fraud that has been brought to light and punished; perhaps it is some gigantic system of usurpation, founded upon an iniquitous disregard of the rights and liberties of men, and maintained by a more iniquitous appeal to their passions, which has come crashing to the ground in masses of frightful ruin. Whatever it is, it looks uncommonly like the interference of a power that is on the side of the right, and is opposed to the wrong; that will allow what is false and unreal to stand for a time, but only for a time; that comes in at last to make a separation, and to show up things and men as they really are. I say, "It looks like it." I do not venture to appeal to the fact, as if it were a proof of any kind, but I claim that thus much be admitted, that there is something in human history which harmonizes with, and which points in the direction of, a great final interference in the affairs of men. The newspapers record a number of *little judgment days*, which are possibly anticipations and foretastes of the great judgment day, of which we believe Scripture to speak.

(*e*)   *Gordon Calthrop*

NEWTON, ISAAC

Nature and nature's laws lay hid in night:
God said, *Let Newton be!* and all was light.

(*f*)   *Pope*

NEWTON, ISAAC

So intent, so serious upon his studies, that he ate very sparingly, nay, ofttimes he has forgot to eat at all; so that going into his chamber I have found his mess untouched, of which, when I have reminded him, he would reply, "Have I?" and then making to the table would eat a bit or two standing; for I cannot say I ever saw him sit at table by himself. . . . I cannot say I ever saw him drink either wine, ale, or beer, excepting at meals, and then very sparingly. He very rarely went to dine at the hall, except on some public days; and then, if he has not been minded, would go very carelessly, with shoes down at heel, stockings untied, surplice on, and his hair scarcely combed. . . . In his chamber he walked so very much that you might have thought him to be educated at Athens among the Aristotelian sect.

(*g*)   *Humphrey Newton*, 1683

When he had friends to entertain, if he went into his study to fetch a bottle of wine, there was danger of his forgetting them. He would sometimes put on his surplice to go to St. Mary's Church. When he was going home to Cottersworth from Grantham, he once led his horse up Spittlegate Hill, at the town end; when he designed to remount, his horse had slipped the bridle, and gone away without his perceiving it, and he had only the bridle in his hand all the while.

(*h*)   *Stukeley*

NICODEMUS (John iii.)

The germ of a genuine faith had to contend in N. with regard for the polite world, thoughts of his station, fear of men, Pharisaic prejudice; but on a foundation of sincerity, conscientiousness, rectitude, and a higher fidelity even to his office, issues victorious in courageous confession and joyful offerings.

(*i*)   *Lange*

NIGHT

Man's midnight is God's noon.

(a)   *Bishop Wordsworth*

NIGHT COMETH, THE

That friend or neighbour with whom we take sweet counsel, let us learn from him all we can, let us pour out for him all the truth we know, and let heart strengthen heart as iron sharpeneth iron; for we may see him again no more for ever, *and in his stead nothing but recollections shall remain overshadowed with the night of a grievous loss.* Teach the child while he is spared you, for the angel may gather that flower into one of his sheaves to plant him again in the radiance of the Divine Throne, leaving you to the trial of a numbed and benighted affection. . . . God has placed us in this narrow island of Time with the waters of eternity all around us; and every inch of ground is more precious to us than gold or rubies; for as our dealings with Time are, so our choice of immortality will be. And we can make no terms with Him to grant us a longer season to finish the work He has sent us to do. The night cometh, and it shall overtake the thinker before he has matured his discovery, and the ruler in the midst of plans of order and improvement.

(b)   *Archbishop Thomson*, 1858

NOAH, DANIEL, AND JOB (Ezek. xiv. 14)

"Though these three men, Noah, Daniel, and Job, were in it, they should deliver but their own souls by their righteousness, saith the Lord."

Man had

(i.) Three enemies or destroyers: the world, the flesh, and the devil;

(ii.) Three Friends or Saviours: the Father, the Son, and the Holy Ghost.

Whilst here we have three saved men, whose distinguishing righteousness lies in this — that Noah overcame the world, Daniel overcame the flesh, and Job overcame the wicked one. Observe from the teaching of Holy Scripture that

(i.) The World is the great Rival of the Father;

(ii.) The Flesh is the great Rival of the Spirit; and

(iii.) The Devil is the great Rival of the Son.

(c)

1. The World as the Rival of the Father

What is meant by the "World"? (αἰών, not κόσμος).

St. Paul speaks of "The *wisdom* of this world" (1 Cor. ii. 6), "The *god* of this world" (2 Cor. iv. 4). Our Lord speaks of "The *children* of this world" (Luke xvi. 8); whilst St. Paul again speaks of those who "walk according to the course of this world" (Eph. ii. 2). And when we put all these expressions together, the aggregate of meaning = "the spirit of the age," the current of thought manifested by all those who are not the personal subjects of the kingdom of Christ and of God. By "the World" then is meant all that floating mass of thoughts, opinions, maxims, speculations, hopes, impulses, aims, which are at any time current in the world, and which it is impossible to define accurately, but which, nevertheless, constitute a most real and effective power, being, indeed, the moral or the immoral atmosphere which

we breathe, or, in other words, it is the spirit which animates every one who lives a life alienated and apart from God. And as such the world is the great rival of God the Father, for it occupies that position in our hearts which He alone ought to occupy (*Cf. Trench*).

St. John establishes the rivalry when he says, "If any man love the world, the love of the Father is not in him" (1 John ii. 15, 16). St. James also, "Know ye that the friendship of the world is enmity with God? Whosoever will be a friend of the world is the enemy of God" (Jas. iv. 4).

(d)

Now NOAH is the representative of those who overcome the world. "By faith Noah, being warned of God of things not seen as yet, moved with fear, prepared an ark to the saving of his house; by the which he condemned the *world*, and became heir of the righteousness which is by faith." How he condemned the world is told us in Gen. vi. 9. "Noah was a just man and perfect in his generation (age), and Noah *walked* with God." He did not go with the stream; current opinion did not influence him. He condemned the world by habitually walking with God, and by doing what was right. This is always an unfashionable thing to do, and is a wholesale condemnation of general practices and worldly opinions. The heroic man took his course, dared to be singular, and now stands upon this high pedestal of a hero of faith, *who overcame the world.*

(e)

2. The Flesh is the Rival of the Spirit

What is meant by "*the Flesh*"? We turn to the Holy Scriptures to find how Scripture interprets Scripture. St. Paul, writing to the Ephesians, reminds them that in their unrenewed state they lived a life "*fulfilling the desires of the flesh and of the mind*"—in so doing he describes exactly what we are to understand by the term "*the flesh.*" It signifies that twofold province of man's being, by the lower of which he is allied to the brute creation, and by the higher to the angels, both being under the dominion of sin. There is first the corrupt *body of flesh*, and there is secondly, in a higher sense, "*the fleshly mind*" (Tit. ii. 3).

Every unregenerate person lives more or less in one or the other of these provinces—either in the sphere of "fleshly lusts," or in the sphere of the "fleshly mind." Either he lives simply an animal life, and is in consequence a *fleshly man*, whose life consists only in fulfilling the desires of his lower nature; or, he lives in the higher province of the mind, but it is nevertheless the mind in darkness, in uncertainty, in doubt — mind and heart alike alienated from God through the unbelief which is in them.

It would not do to argue from this that *our passions are our sin*. Sin is not in appetite, but it lies in the insubordination of appetite. There is need of a curbing and a governing will, and our discipline consists in subjugating the lower to the higher. A due balance between the two regions must be preserved, and it is when passion becomes master, and the lower invades the province of the higher, when the subordinate becomes insubordinate, that appetite and passion become sin. "Behold," says St. James (iii. 3), "we put bits in the horses' mouths that they may obey us, and we turn about their whole body." Even so must a man's

(f)

Noah, Daniel, and Job—*continued*

passions be curbed and ruled. St. Paul's teaching and practice are both to the point here. He teaches us that the "*flesh must be subdued to the spirit.*" And in his own practice he tells us of the discipline to which he submitted his unruly body: "*I keep under my body, and bring it into subjection.*" (*See* "BODY.")

On scriptural grounds, then, "*The* FLESH *is the great rival of the Spirit;* for it asserts that dominion over a man which the Holy Spirit alone ought to occupy, and these two are constantly opposed to each other in the New Testament. "If ye *walk* in the Spirit, ye shall not fulfil the lusts of the *flesh.*" If ye live after the *flesh,* ye shall die; but if ye through the Spirit do mortify the deeds of the body, ye shall live" (Rom. viii. 13).

(*a*)

Now DANIEL is the typical or the representative man of those who through faith *overcome the flesh* —the second of our great spiritual foes. That he did so is just as evident from his history as it is that Noah overcame the world. For Daniel was pre-eminently a spiritual man—the opposite to such a man, for instance, as Esau. And this spirituality of Daniel was the characteristic and distinguishing feature of his righteousness. Consequently we find God—as is the case with men eminently spiritual—making unusual revelations to him; such a man becomes a medium between God and other men, the channel of His communications. In answer to his prayers, Daniel is styled a "man greatly beloved;" for it is with spiritual men that God communes. The counterpart of Daniel is to be found in John of the New Testament. The story of Daniel's early life has hardly been taken into account in estimating his speciality as a spiritual man. Taken captive by the Assyrians and selected as an attendant upon an Eastern and voluptuous monarch, at an age when the passions were the strongest, Daniel's new position thrust him into the midst of great temptations. He was well-favoured and of royal rank; and now for the purposes of the court it was appointed for him to be fed with the king's meat, and to drink the king's wine. When we call to mind his circumstances as a Jewish youth, a young prince, torn away from his own proper sphere at home, and now become a favourite at the Babylonian court, we readily see that to many this would have been as no captivity at all—scarcely exile that which brings with it a court appointment and daily food from the king's table; this would have been a paradise to an Esau —such a mess of pottage, just what his soul loved. But Daniel was of a different mould. He saw into what temptation he was likely to drift. He saw that by yielding he would be indulging and pampering his lower nature, till little by little it would become his master, and he nothing more than its slave; he saw what gross sins he might fall into, if he yielded at the outset. For his own safety, he determined to keep under his body; he would not *defile* himself with the king's meat.

Thus Daniel overcame the *flesh*: and overcame it too just when it was at its strongest; he preserved his spirituality, and became a type and a representative of all who *subdue the flesh to the Spirit.*

(*b*)

3. The Devil as the great Rival of Christ

It is hardly necessary to dwell at any length on that which is so patent throughout the whole range of Holy Scripture. From the time of the first promise until the close of the contest between good and evil, the rivalry between the woman's seed and the serpent's seed, between the Advocate for man, and the Accuser of man, the Intercessor and the Prosecutor, between false Christs and the true Christ, between Antichrist and the Christ, between the Devil and the Son of God, is most distinctly and plainly set forth—the one as the embodiment of *truth*, the other as the embodiment of falsehood, a liar from the beginning.

The one came as a witness of the Father, to reveal God as He is, and as the Son knew Him to be, a *God of love.* The other, as the calumniator alike of God and man, seeks to reveal God as a false witness would, not as a *Father*, and as *love*, but as a hard Master, whose pleasure was in hurling down thunderbolts of vengeance, and in pouring out His fury upon the heads of His defenceless creatures.

Christ's kingdom is not of this world; but the devil is "the god of this world," and, without having his jurisdiction called into question, offers to *give* "the glory of the world" to Jesus, on the one condition of doing homage to him as its god. The one is the "Light of life," the other is the prince of darkness.

There is, then, a great rivalry between the two, and the rivalry is for the ascendency of truth or falsehood. And so far as men believe *the lie,* their eyes are blinded; they walk in darkness, and know not whither they go. Whilst every one who is of the truth has his eyes opened, he sees things as they are, a flood of light illumines everything, and he goeth on his way rejoicing. "He that followeth me Me shall not walk in darkness, but shall have the light of life." "For this cause the Son of God was manifested to destroy the works of the devil."

Christ, then, came to draw aside this dark shroud of illusion and misery and doubt, in which mankind was wrapped, and to which they were shut up, and to let in the light of truth; whilst the object of the devil ever has been and is, to keep men in darkness, and to blind their eyes.

After having come into this world, and entered into a conflict with its prince, Jesus could say, "I have overcome the wicked one."

The devil, then, is the great rival of the Son of God. He puts in a false claim for the ownership of man, and the strife between him and Christ is for each individual man, "*Who shall have him?*"

(*c*)

And JOB's is a case in point. Memory easily recalls the first chapter of that remarkable Book of Job. It tells us of a contest going on in the spirit world for the possession of a man who is considered to be a subject of the kingdom of light, but who is alleged to be a subject of the kingdom of darkness.

Is Job of the truth or of the lie? The story of Job answers the question. Note some of its salient points.

(*See* "JOB.")

(*d*)

Noah, Daniel, and Job—*continued*

You know the painful sequel. The permission which the adversary sought was granted. God gave the devil power to try and do his worst with Job. He might do anything short of killing him, in order to test whether he was a genuine man or not. And soon there came three terrible thuds of thunder. Trouble came rolling in upon trouble, like one great billow after another. Property gone, children gone, health gone, and Job was left but as a loathsome wreck of his former self. What reverses! From a prince to a beggar—from a throne almost, to a dunghill. God has given His permission, and Satan is doing his utmost to conquer; he will, if possible, uproot him from the rock, pull him away from his God, get him to renounce his faith, and speak evil of his God. But does he succeed? No, NEVER! Job did indeed speak many unadvised things with his lips. He showed that there was much alloy in him. He did curse the day of his birth, and pretty well everything connected therewith, but that which the devil said he would do he never did. "In all this Job sinned not, nor charged God foolishly." The story is long, but throughout he held fast to his integrity, to his religion, and to his God, never losing his faith and trust in Him. And thus he *overcame the devil*, and becomes in his turn a type and representative of all others who do so.

(a)

This then, it appears, is the reason why these three, and not any three good men are named on this occasion. These are three of the Old Testament heroes, each matchless in the special feature of his righteousness. Three saved men, saved from three destroyers, by the agency of the Father, the Son, and the Holy Ghost.

Weak and sinful creatures as we are, we may yet have this powerful Trinity engaged on our behalf. For if we believe on the Lord Jesus Christ, we shall have the Father to satisfy our souls, the Spirit to enable us to subdue the flesh, and the Son Himself to bruise the great adversary under our feet, and to destroy all the plots which hellish imagination can devise to waylay and entrap those who have set out for Zion, with their faces thitherward.

Let us therefore pray in the comprehensive words of our grand old English liturgy.

"O holy, blessed, and glorious Trinity, three Persons and one God, have mercy upon us miserable sinners."

(b)

NO MAN CAN SAY THAT JESUS IS THE LORD, BUT BY THE HOLY GHOST (1 Cor. xii. 3)

No one can truly believe and openly confess that Jesus is God manifest in the flesh, unless he is enlightened by the Spirit of God. This is precisely what our Lord Himself said when Peter confessed Him to be the Son of God. "Blessed art thou, Simon Bar-jona; for flesh and blood hath not revealed it unto thee, but My Father who is in heaven."

(c)   *Hodge*

(*See* "HOLY SPIRIT.")

NOMINAL CHRISTIANS

Take any ordinary congregation. If you judge of what a Christian is by the New Testament description of him: that he is a man who lives unto Christ; a man who lives by faith in Christ Jesus; a man whose conversation is in heaven, and who, whatever may be his inconsistencies and failings, is taking up the cross to follow his Divine Master—the very broadest charity will not allow you to suppose anything else than that a considerable proportion of the worshipping body are merely nominal Christians. In too many cases you will find a mere outward show of respect and reverence, but no devotion: no earnestness; no living realization of Christ; no love to His holy name. In too many cases the Bible is never read; or, if it is read, is never studied. There may be a formal family prayer, but no private prayer. And in not a few cases you will find that when the weary duties of the Sunday Morning Service are over, the newspaper and the gathering of friends, and the brisk interchange of gossip, and the dinner-party, constitute the mode in which are spent the remaining hours of God's holy day, given for the work of needful preparation for our eternal home. I forbear to speak of grosser things. I say nothing about positive vice and unrighteousness. I confine myself to the formalism of decent and respectable people.

(d)   *Gordon Calthrop*

NONCONFORMITY

Vavasor Powell, one of the Commissioners, replying to Dr. G. Griffiths, afterwards Bishop of St. Asaph, gave this testimony on the subject:—

But you say that we send out weavers, smiths, coopers, and soldiers. It is true there is one weaver, a blessed, understanding man, and one smith, a religious, godly man, and one that hath more learning than some of your curates; and, it may be, two or three gifted, godly, tried and approved men besides, who may be soldiers, or rather officers, that go along with our preachers, as fellow-helpers (even as the Apostles and ministers had in the primitive times) in the work of the Lord; and God hath made them successful. But is it not as lawful for such men, who are godly and gifted, to exercise their gifts, as for simple Sir Johns ["Sir" was commonly used for "Reverend" at this period], lack Latin, lack gifts, lack grace, who keep poor alehouses in the mountains, where they and the people spend together the greatest part of the Sabbath in profaneness? Of this sort we can produce four for every tradesman the Commissioners have sent out. Nay, in point of learning, they that are now sent out and approved, shall compare with so many of the ejected priests; *for spiritual gifts and graces, I trow, most of your ejected clergy will not pretend to.*

(e)   *Welsh Nonconformist*

"NONE OF THESE THINGS MOVE ME" (Acts xx. 24)

Read Baxter's funeral sermon, and some of the more serious passages of his life, and found them striking, and in some respects appropriate; but how sadly do I fall short of him, particularly where he speaks of his calumnious assailants!

(f)

Fifty books were written against him; about twenty-three, I think, were written *for* and *against* me, besides three years' monthly attack from the Anti-Jacobin; but while Baxter blessed God that none of these things disturbed him, I have to lament that through my want of his faith and piety, they had nearly destroyed my life. In one thing only I had the advantage: I never replied to my calumniators. In this one thing his trial was less than mine—that his calumniators did not hinder him in the service of God by diminishing his estimation as a writer.

(*a*) *Hannah More*

"NOW"

"*Behold, now is the accepted time*" (2 Cor. vi. 2)

(i.) Now = *this world*, not in that to come, = no second probation.

(ii.) Now = the present *moment*: "Ye know not what a day may bring forth"; ye may not have another opportunity. *Now*, for the young, the old, the sinful, alike.

(iii.) Now = the spirit of the entire Scriptures: "Now OR NEVER, = *the utmost urgency*."

(*b*) *Cf. Meyer*

(*See* "BLIND BARTIMÆUS.")

Before watches and clocks were invented, sundry experiments were resorted to for measuring the time. Alfred the Great measured time by candles. He had candles made that would burn eight hours each. One candle was lighted at the beginning of the day, and when that had burnt out, he knew that one-third of the day had gone; then another was lighted, and when that had burnt out, two-thirds of the day had gone; and when the next candle was burnt out, the whole day was gone. Now, our lives are something like these candles burning out—some have lived a third of their life, some two-thirds, and others are well-nigh run out.

(*c*)

NUMBER (153) (John xxi. 11)

We do not consider the *number* as symbolical, but the *numbering*. The elect, who form the main element of the Church, are great and *numbered* fishes. And great and numerous as the elect of the congregated mass may be, they are not the ones who break the net of the Church. It is the maxim of all the elect: first Christ, then the Church.

(*d*) *Lange*

The elect are counted man for man, see Jer. vii. 6; Rev. vii. 4.

(*e*)

NUMBER OF THE BEAST, THE, "666" (Rev. xiii.)

Points to the character of the beast, as the last embodiment of godless world-power. The number 6 = earthly attainment, human excellence, without the one thing needful to make it a heavenly seven, the number of perfection. And the three sixes together are interpreted as the consummation of this: godless humanity in full growth, matured in all its parts, and fully possessed by the evil one. It is the full number of fallen man, expressing all that is possible for human wisdom and human power, when directed by an evil spirit, to achieve, and indicating a state of marvellous earthly perfection; thus the beast of power has reached its highest development, when culture, civilization, art, song, science, and reason have combined to produce an age so nearly resembling perfection that men will begin to say that faith in God is an impertinence, and the hope of a future life a libel upon the happiness of the present.

(*f*) *Graham, and Carpenter*

NUMBERS

To count is a modern practice; the ancient method was to guess; and when *numbers* are guessed, they are always magnified. [Cf. the numbers of the Old Testament.]

(*g*) *Dr. Johnson*

O

OATH

Every word should be to the Christian what an oath is to others; there is no need, therefore, of oaths among true Christians.

(a)   *Lange*

OATH OF GOD AND FORGIVENESS, THE

Consider:

1. **The Nature of the Oath of God.** The Apostle tells us, that He sware by Himself; and he gives this reason of it, because He had no greater to swear by (Heb. vi. 13). An oath for the confirmation of anything, is an invocation of a supreme power, that can judge of the truth that is spoken, and vindicate the breach of the engagement. God hath none other but Himself to swear by, "Because He could swear by no greater, He sware by Himself." Now, this God doth: (1.) By express affirmation that He hath so sworn by Himself, which was the form of the first solemn oath of God, "By Myself have I sworn, saith the Lord" (Gen. xxii. 16). The meaning whereof is, "I have taken it upon Myself, as I am God; or, let Me not be so, if I perform not this thing." And this is expressed by His soul, "The Lord of Hosts hath sworn by His soul" (Jer. li. 14), that is, by Himself, as we render the words. (2.) God doth it by the especial interposition of some such property of His nature, as is suited to give credit and conformation to the work spoken; as of His holiness; "I have sworn by My holiness" (Ps. lxxxix. 35). So also (Amos iv. 2). Sometimes by His life: "As I live," saith the Lord. In the Hebrew, "I live," saith God, it shall be so. And sometimes by His name (Jer. xliv. 2–6), engages the honour and glory of the properties of His nature for the certain accomplishment of the things mentioned. And this is evident from the manner of the expression, as in that place of Ps. lxxxix. 35 :—"Once have I sworn by My holiness, that I will not lie unto David;" so we; in the original the words are elliptical, "If I lie unto David;" that is, let Me not be so, nor esteemed to be so, "if I lie unto David."

(b)

2. **For the End of His Oath.** God doth not give it to make His word or promise sure and steadfast, but to give assurance and security to us of their accomplishment. Every word of God is sure and certain truth itself, because it is His; and He might justly require of us the belief of it, without any further attestation. But yet, knowing what great objections Satan and our own unbelieving hearts will raise against His promises, at least as to our own concern in them, to confirm our minds, and to take away all pretences of unbelief, He interposes His oath in this matter. What can remain of distrust in such a case? If there be a matter in doubt between men, and an oath be interposed in the confirmation of that which is called in question, it is to them, as the Apostle tells us, an end of all strife (Heb. vi. 16). How much more ought it to be so on the part of God, when His oath is engaged. And the Apostle

declares this end of His oath, it is to show the immutability of His counsel (Heb. vi. 17). His counsel was declared before in the promise; but now some doubt or strife may arise, whether, on one occasion or other, God may not change His counsels; or whether He hath not charged it with such conditions as to render it useless to us. In what case soever it be, to remove all doubts and suspicions of this nature, God adds His oath, manifesting the unquestionable immutability of His counsel and promises. What therefore is thus confirmed, is ascertained to the height of what anything is capable of. And not to believe it is the height of impiety.

(c)

In this Interposition of God by an Oath, there is unspeakable condescension of grace, which is both an exceedingly great motive to faith and a great aggravation of unbelief. For what are we, that the holy and blessed God should thus condescend, for our satisfaction and surety, to engage Himself by an oath! It is an inestimable advantage, that God should, for our sakes, engage Himself by His oath. So it will be our misery, if we believe Him not, when He swears to us. What can we now object against what is thus confirmed? What pretence, colour, or excuse can we have for unbelief? How just, how righteous, how holy is God in the destruction of those who, upon this strange, wonderful, and unexpected warrant, refuse to set to their seal, that God is true.

(d)

Consider how variously God hath engaged His oath, that there is forgiveness with Him.

(i.) **He sweareth, that He hath no pleasure in the death of a sinner, but rather that he repent and live.** "As I live, saith the Lord, I have no pleasure in the death of a sinner" (Ezek. xxxiii. 11). Now, without forgiveness in Him, every sinner must die, and that without remedy. Confirming, therefore, with His oath, that it is His will the sinner should return, repent, and live, he doth, in the first place, swear by Himself, that there is forgiveness with Him for those sinners that shall so repent and turn to Him.

(e)

Whereas the great means He hath appointed for the forgiveness of sins is by the mediation of the Lord Christ, **He hath, on several occasions, confirmed His purpose in Him, and the counsel of His will by His oath.** By this oath, He promised Him to Abraham and David of old, which proved the foundation of the Church's stability in all generations; and also of their security and assurance of acceptance with Him (see Luke i. 73–75). And in His taking upon Him that office, whereby, in an especial manner, the forgiveness of sins was to be procured, namely, of His being a priest to offer sacrifice, to make an atonement for sinners, He confirmed it to Him, and Him in it, by His oath. "He was not made a priest without an oath" (Heb. vii. 20). And to what end? namely, that He might be a "surety of a better testament"

(f)

Oath of God and Forgiveness, The—*continued*

(ver. 22). And what was that " better testament?" Why, that which brought along with it the forgiveness of sin, (chap. viii. 12, 13). So that it was forgiveness which was so confirmed by the oath of God.

(*a*)

Further, the Apostle shows that the great original promise made to Abraham, being confirmed by the oath of God, all His other promises were in like manner confirmed. Whence he draws that blessed conclusion which we have (Heb. vi. 17, 18). As to every one, saith he, that "flies for refuge to the hope that is set before him,"—that is, who seeks to escape the guilt of sin, the curse and sentence of the law, by an application of himself to God in Christ for pardon,—he hath the oath of God to secure him, that he shall not fail thereof. And thus are all the concerns of the forgiveness of sin testified to by the oath of God; which we have manifested to be the highest security in this matter that God can give, or that we are capable of.

(*b*)   *John Owen*
(*See* "FORGIVENESS OF SINS.")

OATHS AND ASSEVERATIONS

To swear by God's name is to recognise Him as supreme Lord. Deut. vi. 13, "Thou shalt fear the Lord thy God and serve Him, and shalt swear by His name." . . . The passage in Leviticus xix. 12 contains a positive permission to take a solemn oath by the name of God. God swears by Himself: in Gen. xxii. 16, 17, *by Myself have I sworn*. In Isa. xlv. 23 the same expression is used, "I have sworn by Myself, the word is gone out of My mouth in righteousness, and shall not return, That unto Me every knee shall bow, every tongue shall swear." So also Heb. vi. 13–18: "For when God made promise to Abraham, because He could swear by no greater, He sware by Himself, saying, Surely blessing I will bless thee, and multiplying I will multiply thee. . . . Wherein God, willing more abundantly to show unto the heirs of promise the immutability of His counsel, confirmed it by an oath; that by two immutable things, in which it was impossible for God to lie, we might have a strong consolation." Our blessed Lord, when arraigned before Caiaphas, and when adjured to tell whether He was the Son of God, took the oath which the high priest administered, by replying to the solemn adjuration in the customary assent, Σὺ εἶπας. He had been silent previously; but now, when the high priest adjured Him officially, He did not hesitate to accept the obligation of an oath. St. Paul employs an oath in Rom. i. 9; 2 Cor. i. 23; xi. 31; Gal. i. 20; Phil. i. 8; and in Heb. he [?] distinctly shows the necessity of an oath, and gives to it apostolic sanction: "For men verily swear by the greater; and an oath for confirmation is to them an end of all strife."

(*c*) *A. Tait, D.D., "The Charter of Christianity," on Matt. v. 33*

Throughout the Gospels we find that our Lord never used a stronger form of affirmation than "Verily, verily." In the synoptic gospels He adopts the single 'Αμὴν; in the fourth gospel He invariably makes use of the double 'Αμὴν, 'Αμὴν. In common conversation nothing beyond this simple affirmation should be made. If a man's veracity will not be respected by the "Yea, yea," or "Nay, nay," it is not to be supposed that an oath will make it more worthy of confidence. Theophylact says, "If you will always speak truly, you will never swear. He who swears frequently is less worthy to be believed."

(*d*)   *Ibid*

OATHS, PROFANE

"Whatsoever is more than these is of the evil one" (Matt. v. 37). Profane swearing is *malum per se*. . . . The great agent of moral evil is the devil. It is his object to dishonour God and His attributes, and to prompt men to be the instruments in blaspheming that Holy Name by which they are called. Such profanity is objectless; no one is the better for it. Unlike other sins, it has not hope of gain; sensual gratification, worldly ambition, to give it force; yet for a certain class profane swearing has a kind of fascination, that cannot be explained upon any other ground than by the direct action of evil spirits, who delight in hearing the language of hell repeated on earth. So apparent is this, that Coleridge has observed on this subject that, "It might be almost said that, if all other proofs of the continual activity of evil spirits over human society were to fail, that activity could still be demonstrated by the prevalence of the language of which we speak." Archbishop Trench says the oath "is not of itself evil, but ' *of evil* '; so that in the highest idea of intercourse as between unfallen beings, angels with angels, it could find no place; it would be utterly inconceivable. Only where the tree of life has been forsaken for the mournful yet wondrous teaching of the tree of knowledge of good and evil, only where the lie has come forth, could there be any word to designate the truth." [When] suspicion, distrust, and uncharitableness vanish, in our intercourse with one another there will be such sincerity, honesty, and singleness of purpose, that our speech will be as if we felt the Divine presence, and no recording angel will be then needed to drop a tear upon the idle word, such as now sometimes escapes our lips, to blot it out for ever.

(*e*)   *Ibid*

OATHS, PROFANE SWEARING

1. Consider who that God is whom *thou abusest*. Is He not the great and terrible Majesty, that made the world, and upholdeth it, and ordereth it by His will; the Governor and Judge of all the earth; infinitely excelling the sun in glory, a God most holy, and in holiness to be mentioned? And wilt thou make a by-word of His dreadful Name? Wilt thou profanely swear by this Holy Name, and use the Name of God as thou wouldst scarce use the name of the father or thy king? Wilt thou irreverently and contemptuously toss it like a foot-ball? Dost thou know no more difference between God and man? *Know God*, and thou wilt sooner tremble at His Name, than thus irreverently abuse it.

2. Consider *who thou art* that thus venturest to profane the Holy name of God! Art thou not His creature and His subject and bound to honour Him? Art thou not a worm, unable to resist Him? Can He not lead thee into hell, or ruin thee, and be avenged on thee with a word or less? He need to say no more, but, *Thus I will have it*, to execute His vengeance on the greatest of His

enemies. If He will have it, it will be done. And art thou then a person fit to despise this God, and abuse His Name? Is it not a wonder of condescension in Him, that He will give leave to such worms as we to pray to Him, and to praise and worship Him, and that He will accept it at our hands? And yet canst thou venture thus to slight Him and despise Him? I have oft heard the same impious tongue reproach the prayers of the godly, as if they were too bold and familiar with God, and pleading against long or often praying, because man must not be so bold with God, and persuading others that God accepts it not, which yet itself was bold familiarly to *swear* by His Name, and use it lightly and in common talk. And indeed God's servants must take heed of rude and irreverent boldness even in prayer. How much more then is the boldness of thy profaning God's Holy Name to be condemned? Must they take heed how they use it in prayer and praise, and darest thou abuse it by oaths, and curses, and vain speech? . . . Dost thou not sometimes pray by that Name which thou profanely swearest by? . . . It is part of Bishop Hall's character of the hypocrite, that he " boweth to the Name of Jesus, and sweareth by the Name of God, and prayeth to God at church," whom he forgets, or sweareth by, the rest of the week.

(*a*) *Baxter's Christian Directory, fol. Edit., p.* 49

OBEDIENCE AND ROMISH MIRACLES

A little monk was so accustomed to perform miracles, that the Prior forbade him to exercise his talent. The little monk obeyed; but seeing a poor tiler fall from a roof, he hesitated between the desire to save his life and the holier law of obedience. He therefore only ordained that the tiler should remain in the air to await fresh orders, and ran to report the state of things to his Prior. The Prior gave him absolution for the sin which he had committed in beginning a miracle without permission, and allowed him to finish it, provided he ended there, and did not repeat the practice.

(*b*)   *Voltaire*

OLD AGE

Winter, which strips the leaves from around us, makes us see the distant regions they formerly concealed; so does old age rob us of our enjoyments, only to enlarge the prospect of eternity before us.

(*c*)   *Richter*

I have often heard that sailors on a voyage will drink " Friends astern! " till they are half-way over, then " Friends ahead! " With me it has been " Friends ahead! " this long time.

(*d*)   *Wilberforce*

OLD AGE

I saw that time of life begin
When every man, the port approaching, ought
To coil the ropes, and take the canvas in.

(*e*)   *Dante, " Inferno "*

The good mariner, when he draws near the port, furls his sails, and enters it softly; so ought we to lower the sails of our worldly operations, and turn to God with all our heart and understanding.

(*f*)   *Dante, " Convito "*

OLD AND THE NEW, THE.

Occasion : *The Call of a* PUBLICAN (Luke v. 27–39)

Note

(i.) *The call.* Levi, his name as a publican; Matthew, his Christian name, received now at his sudden conversion, and in view of his usefulness, means *the gift of God.*

(ii.) *The feast and conversation.*

(iii.) *Discourse on fasting.* Jesus, on earth, is celebrating a wedding-feast, as the Husband of Israel. His disciples are the guests. Can they *fast* at such a time? True fasting = mourning for the absence of Christ, the longing and looking for His return.

(iv.) All this gives rise to three short Parables, on the Old and New Order of Things.

(*g*)

The First Parable (36)—Two Garments, Old and New : both spoiled; one by tearing, the other by patching.

The Pharisees = the *patchers ;* John Baptist = the reformer ; Jesus = neither one nor the other —" *Behold I make all things new* "—He makes a new garment.

Compare this teaching

(i.) With the symbolism of mere Ritualism in our days ;

(ii.) With New Testament teaching about the Way of Salvation: " If by grace, then it is no more of works ; (but) if it be of works, then it is no more of grace (Rom. xi. 6).

Yet this is the import of this homely parable.

(*h*)

The Second Parable — Leathern Bottles (goatskins).

Note that

(i.) Wine = a healthy, true, spiritual religion = gladness and joy at its root ;

(ii.) Bottles = men, as the receptacles of the Spirit.

Now these receptacles (men) are not the old order of legal ministers and priests, but a new set of men. The Pharisees, with their ideas of self-merit, and Jewish rabbis and scribes, with their literalities, would spoil Christ's work: therefore He chooses a new set of men, who have—

(i.) No merit, (ii.) no wisdom, of their own. Who are like tablets, on which He can write His new Law. Cf. " God, I thank Thee that Thou hast hid these things from the wise and prudent, and hast revealed them unto babes (Matt. xi. 25).

(*i*)

The Third Parable—" No man," etc. Old Wine = soft and mellowed, and a man used to it prefers it. It would take such men a long time to get accustomed to the new. " *Straightway* " (omitted in Revised Version) indicates the leading idea of the parable. Our Lord does not expect sudden conversions from such men, whose lives, unlike the Publican, were comparatively blameless. Therefore He waits for them. (Cf. " NICODEMUS.")

(*j*)

OLD, OLD STORY, THE

I must point to something very different; to something which, in a well-known hymn, is called "The Old, Old Story." It is this old, old story, told of in an old, old Book, and taught with an old, old teaching.

(a)   *W. E. Gladstone*

ONE

"*He is our peace who hath made both one*" (Eph. ii. 14)

1. "Who hath made both one." In the Temple at Jerusalem, separating the holy area, the court of the Israelites, from the outer precincts, was a stone fence or balustrade, beyond which no Gentile was allowed to pass. At intervals along this fence were tablets, some in Greek, some in Hebrew, warning the alien not to trespass, on pain of death. Only a few years ago one of these inscriptions was exhumed from the grave where it had lain for long centuries. The Roman masters, we are told, respected and sanctioned this fierce ordinance of the Jews. The Jews were allowed to inflict the penalty of death even on a Roman citizen, if he passed within the barrier.

(b)

2. To St. Paul these things were an allegory. This stern prohibition, this relentless barrier, this rigid line of demarcation, this reservation of the inner sanctuary for the Jew, this extrusion of the Gentile into the outer court—was it not a type, an exemplification of that rancour of Jewish exclusiveness which imperilled the infancy of the Christian Church? Yes, they would have imported into this later and nobler sanctuary, this second temple, this spiritual edifice, the arrangement of the material building. They would have drawn a hard line between the sons of Abraham and the dogs of Greeks; they would have erected a middle wall of partition; they would have thrust out the Gentiles into the outer court, whence with yearning eyes they might peer over the intervening fence into the inner sanctuary, their exclusion being rendered all the more galling by the proximity of the view.

(c)

3. This distinction was the direct negation of the Gospel of Christ. Jesus Christ had broken down the middle wall of partition. On the area thus cleared, He had erected a larger, loftier, nobler temple, a universal brotherhood, which acknowledged no preferences and knew no distinctions. In Jesus Christ was neither Jew or Greek, but Christ was all and in all.

(d)

4. These things, I say, were an allegory to St. Paul; and are they not so likewise to ourselves? The distinction of Jew and Gentile indeed no longer troubles the peace of the Christian Church. The spiritual fence or partition, like the material wall which symbolized it, has long crumbled into dust and disappeared beneath the ruins of the older temple. Jesus Christ, the great Solvent, has disintegrated and destroyed the barrier. Jesus Christ, the great Reconciler, has made both one. But is there not another distinction, another line of demarcation rigidly drawn, another barrier only too faithfully typified by this fence in the temple area, this wall between the inner and the outer court, this separation of Jew and Gentile? And if it be so, where else can we look for a reconciliation, save in Jesus Christ, who once again shall be our peace, who once again shall make both one in Himself?

(e)

5. On this side of the fence is the Church; on the other side the world, as we call the world. Here is religion, is faith; there is nature, is history. Here is theology; there is science. All the pious yearnings of the human soul on the one side, all the intellectual struggles and all the fair humanities of life on the other—*sancte* in the inner court, *sapienter* in the outer. But there must be no trespassing, no crossing of the fatal barrier, on pain of death. Here is the spiritual; there is the secular. Here is God, there is Cæsar.

(f)

6. Ah, have we not here, in this false interpretation of a crucial passage, only too faithful an index of the frame of mind which encourages, if it does not create, this fatal severance of faith and knowledge, of religion and life, this cruel divorce of those whom God has joined together in a holy wedlock and forbidden to any man to put asunder? As if, forsooth, we could have any duty to Cæsar which was not also a duty to God; as if all that belonged to Cæsar did not also belong to God!

(g)

7. It is the old severance reappearing with a new face. Jew and Gentile—what more appropriate types of these two elements of human interest? On the one hand the old religion, with its time-honoured teachings, its ancient traditions—the Church of the Fathers, the guardian of revelation, the depositary of the faith, the stanchness which tends to degenerate into bigotry—here is the Jew. On the other, the intellectual searchings and the political aspirations and the mechanical contrivings—science, art, literature, commerce, sociology, the liberty which threatens to luxuriate into licence —here is the Gentile. Ever and again the old feud breaks out. Ever and again there is a crack and a rent. The gulf widens, and a disruption is threatened. How shall we avert the disaster?

(h)

8. I do not say that the fault is all on one side. The Gentile may exasperate and shock the Jew by his recklessness. The man of science may transgress by a licence of speculation which goes far beyond his inductions, and by an antagonism of language which is not warranted even by his speculations. But I am not now addressing the man of science. My business to-day is with the man of religion. The practical question for us is, What can we do— we who represent theology, we who are arrayed on the side of revelation—to prevent this fatal severance?

(i)

9. I have already indicated the answer to this question. Jesus Christ will again be our peace. Jesus Christ will make both one in these last days, as He did in those earliest. This He will do, because He unites both in Himself. Christ is the

(j)

One—*continued*

Incarnate Saviour, yes, but Christ is also the Eternal Word. Christ left the glories of heaven, took our flesh upon Him, lived our life, died on the Cross for our redemption, pleads our cause before the Eternal Throne. This we acknowledge; this is ever present to our minds; this is the life of our lives. But here we stop. We do not commonly connect Christ with the marvels of creation, with the laws of nature, with the progress and development of history. We repeat time after time the familiar words of the Creed, "By whom all things were made." But the repetition produces no effect on our minds. Perhaps we thoughtlessly assume that the clause refers to the Father Himself, who has been mentioned just before. Would not the average orthodox Christian be startled, if he were told that the laws of gravitation, of chemical affinity, of magnetism, were expressions of the mind of Christ? Would he not hesitate to admit that it was Christ who hurled the planets into space, Christ who through long ages stored up in the bowels of the earth fuel and building-materials for the use of man, Christ who wove the wing of the dragon-fly and pencilled the glories of the lily? And so again with history, with mechanical invention, with social progress in all its developments. Yet this is the direct and immediate inference from the teaching of St. Paul and St. John. The Father manifests Himself through the Only Begotten, the Eternal Word, not in revelation only, but in nature: not in redemption only, but in history. What else is the meaning of such passages as these? "All things were made by Him, and without Him was not anything made that was made. He was in the world and the world was made by Him." "One Lord Jesus Christ, by whom are all things." "By Him were all things created that are in heaven and that are in earth, visible and invisible. . . . All things were created by Him and for Him. And He *is*, He exists absolutely, before all things; and by Him all things consist, are held together." "His Son whom He hath appointed heir of all things, by whom also He made the worlds." Can any language more explicit, more comprehensive, more importunate in its reiteration, be conceived than this? His creative agency, His directive power, is coextensive with the Universe. He, the Eternal Son, He, Christ Jesus our Lord, is plenipotentiary, is omnipresent in the kingdom of nature as in the kingdom of grace. But we abandon this truer and larger theology—the theology alike of St. Paul and St. John and of the Greek fathers in the best ages. We enclose ourselves within the barriers of later and narrower ideas. We erect once again a middle wall of partition. We confine the mediation of Christ, which the Apostles extended to the whole universe of created things, within the limits of the Bible, of the Gospel, of the Church.

(*a*)

10. Is it easy to exaggerate the loss to ourselves by the erection of such a barrier? How much healthier, larger, freer, in the best sense of freedom, would our theology be by its removal. With what different eyes should we look on each fresh revelation of science, if we learned to regard it as likewise a fresh revelation of the Eternal Word, our Saviour and Redeemer. There would then be no jealousy, no suspicion of the aggressiveness of science. Every new triumph of scientific

discovery would be welcomed as another jewel in the diadem of our Eternal king. Every new announcement of mechanical adaptation would add a fresh voice to the chorus of universal nature, singing, "Holy, holy, holy, is the Lord of Hosts; the whole earth is full of His glory." Could it be otherwise if we truly recognised that all the threads of scientific laws are gathered up in the hands of Him who is the centre of our faith and the foundation of our hopes? Has He not made both one?

(*b*)

11. The stone fence in the Temple area, of which I spoke, marked off the court of the Gentiles; but a second inner barrier separated the court of the women also from the court of the Israelites. The women were excluded, as the Gentiles were excluded. The woman occupied an inferior religious position in rabbinical teaching. It was a shock to public feeling to see a rabbi talking with a female. Even the disciples were surprised that their Master should be found conversing with a woman on the brink of the Samaritan well. Jesus Christ broke down this middle wall of partition as He had broken down the other. Here again He made both one. If in Jesus Christ there is no distinction of Jew and Gentile, neither is there of male or female. Women were His faithful and constant attendants; women were the favoured witnesses of His resurrection; women were among the most helpful fellow-workers of the Apostles. There was an organized ministry of women deaconesses and widows in the Apostolic Church.

(*c*)

"**ONLY BELIEVE**" (Matt. ix. 19–26; Mark v. 35, 36)

The healing of Jairus's daughter.

1. The variations of the narratives give fulness.

(i.) *The Father.*
Matt. = Ruler *worshipped;*
Mark = falling on knees besought him *much;*
Luke = supplies name, Jairus.

(ii.) *The Child.*
Matt. = Daughter;
Mark = LITTLE daughter = tone of endearment;
Luke = ONLY daughter, twelve years = *only* child.

(iii.) *Incoherency of request.*
Matt. = even now dead;   } explained
Mark = at the point of death; } by the father's
Luke = lay a dying.   } agitation.

2. Points of Instruction:

(i.) "Come, lay Thine hand," etc. = whilst there is life = no hope beyond that; Jesus designedly lets death ensue, by permitting delay on the road. Cf. "He that believeth doth not make haste";

(ii.) The *trial* of the man's faith by this delay;

(iii.) Hope perished = "*Thy daughter is dead.*"

3. As soon as Jesus heard that, He whispered to the man, "*Only believe.*"

The healing. ("Jesus never terrifies."—Staupitz to Luther.) Jesus puts out the unbelieving before He raises the dead. He could do no "mighty works" before them. "Earth has no ills that Heaven cannot cure"; but faith in the miracle-worker is an absolute condition.

(*d*)

OPEN THE SCRIPTURES (Luke xxiv. 32)

St. Luke describes a two-fold work done by Christ in explaining the Scriptures to the two disciples in the walk to Emmaus. He *opened* the Scriptures, we read. Here was one work. And He *opened* their understanding to understand the Scriptures. There was another work. He did this, and He is always doing it.

(a)   *Bishop Wordsworth*

OPINION

What dispenses reputation? What confers dignity on persons and things? *Opinion.* How unsatisfying are all the treasures of this world without its approbation! Opinion regulates all things. This determines what is beauty, what is justice, what is happiness; and these with the world are everything. I would gladly read an Italian work of which I know only the title; but that title is worth many whole books; it is "Della Opinione Regina del Mundo": On Opinion, the Queen of the World.

(b)   *Blaise Pascal*

OPINION AND LIFE.

For his part, he thought he had ceased to care about whether anybody believed as he did. He should hold the doctrines he did hold — which happened to be altogether contrary to the current of modern thought—if he lived to be the last man, because they were the only things that could keep him alive. He could not live on anything else, and he knew there were many others in their ranks so accustomed to go against the stream that they were not particularly anxious to have the stream running their way, for they would be afraid of being suspected of being dead fish.

(c)   *Spurgeon (Report)*

OPPORTUNITY

Opportunity has hair in front; behind she is bald. If you seize her by the forelock, you may hold her; but, if suffered to escape, not Jupiter himself can catch her again.

(d)   *From the Latin*

OPTIMISM AND PESSIMISM

So far from the world being a goddess in petticoats, it is rather the devil in a strait waistcoat.

(e)   *S. T. Coleridge*

ORACLES OF GOD

"*If any man speak, let him speak as the oracles of God*" (1 Pet. iv. 11)

Observe-
(i.) "The supreme authority of the Holy Scriptures as the rule of faith."
(ii.) That the foundation of Doctrine is the word of God. Let the preacher search there for what he intends to say. Let his first inquiry and his last appeal be to the fountain of heavenly wisdom.
In opposition to this principle different maxims have been inculcated by different parties.
1. "If any man speak," says the Papist, "let him speak as the oracles of the Church" (Tradition,

General Councils, Popes, Decretals, etc., whose decisions are infallible).
2. "If any man speak," says the Rationalist, "let him speak as the oracles of Reason."
3. "If any man speak," says the fanatic, "let him speak as the oracles of ' inward light.' "
The sound Christian has to contend with these in maintaining the supreme authority of " *the oracles of God.*" What saith the Scripture?

(f)

ORATORS

You always went away from Burke with your mind filled; from Fox with your feelings excited; and from Pitt with wonder at his having had the power to make the worse appear the better reason.

(g)   *Wordsworth, on Edmund Burke*

When posterity read the speeches of Burke, they will hardly be able to believe that during his lifetime he was not considered as a first-rate speaker, not even as a second-rate one.

(h)   *Sheridan, on Edmund Burke*

ORDER

The heavens themselves, the planets, and this
    centre,
Observe degree, priority, and place,
Insisture, course, proportion, season, form,
Office, and custom, in all line of order.

(i)   *Shakspeare*

Order is Heaven's first law; and this confest,
Some are, and must be, greater than the rest,
More rich, more wise; but who infers from hence
That such are happier, shocks all common sense.

(j)   *Pope*

ORIGINAL SIN

An Indian candidate for the ministry being asked, "What is original sin?" replied, "He did not know what other people's might be, but he rather thought that his was *laziness.*" Many suffer from the same radical evil, which often develops into actual transgression.

(k)   *Storrs*

OTHER TIMES, OTHER MANNERS

A grand-aunt of my own, Mrs. Keith, of Ravelstone, who was a person of some condition, being a daughter of Sir John Swinton, of Swinton, lived with unabated vigour of intellect to a very advanced age. She was very fond of reading, and enjoyed it to the last of her long life. One day she asked me, when we happened to be alone together, whether I had ever seen Mrs. Behn's novels. I confessed the charge. Whether I could get her a sight of them. I said, with some hesitation, I believed I could; but that I did not think she would like either the manners or the language, which approached too near that of Charles II.'s time to be quite proper reading. "Nevertheless," said the good old lady, "I remember them being so much admired, and being so much interested in them myself, that I wish to look at them again." To hear was to obey. So I sent Mrs. Aphra Behn, curiously sealed up, with

(l)

"Private and confidential" on the packet, to my gay old grand-aunt. The next time I saw her afterwards, she gave me back Aphra, properly wrapped up, with nearly these words: "Take back your bonny Mrs. Behn, and if you will take my advice, put her in the fire; for I found it impossible to get through the very first novel. But is it not," she said, "a very odd thing, that I, an old woman of eighty and upwards, sitting alone, feel myself ashamed to read a book which, sixty years ago, I have heard read aloud for the amusement of large circles, consisting of the first and most creditable society in London?"

(a)   *Sir Walter Scott*

OVERCOME

It is the devil's part to suggest; ours, not to consent. As often as we resist him, so often we *overcome* him; so often as we overcome him, so often we bring joy to the angels, and glory to God, who proposeth us, that we may contend; and assisteth us, that we may conquer.

(b)   *Bernard*

Job was more Satan's torturer, than Satan was the other's tempter.

(c)   *Gregory*

"OVERCOMETH, To him that" (Rev. ii. 7)

This is the title of the conquering Christian, and is repeated seven times in the messages to the Churches. In each instance this title is connected with a word of promise, a word couched in different language to meet the different circumstances and atmospheres in which the conquering Christian might be called to live.

(d)

1. "**To him that overcometh**" was the distinction of him who was in Christ. This was essential. Out of Christ there could be no spiritual victory. They must be in Christ to begin with. This thought was a favourite with Paul, who in a remarkable passage, which gave the biography of his soul, spoke of himself as a man *in* Christ. "In Christ"; as if that were the word describing the initial, central, and radical distinction of every Christian man; a distinction above all distinctions which men most regarded and honoured. Let no one say this expression was out of date; let no one try to explode it into metaphor, or try to confine it to philosophical subtlety; let no one use it because it was thought to be one of the common-places in people who confess Christ. Everything divine in human character must begin by a realization of this being "in Christ." In Christ, the Champion, Who, long before our existence, and far outside our personality, overcame for us and fought the mighty mystic battle of Calvary; and we were in Him now, if we had a title to the distinction of overcoming.

(e)

But let no one misunderstand. To him that overcometh is the distinction of him who, though he is in Christ, and while he is in Christ, is also engaged in Christian warfare. Many a time this idea of being in Christ had been taken apart from its connections, and had given some ground on the part of outsiders for their saying this was Calvinism, and not Christianity. Let no one

say, "I am in Christ, and therefore I need not fight; I am in Christ, my soul may rock itself to sleep; I am in Christ, and therefore my religion is summed up in the simple conception of rest and joy. Let no one trouble me while I make my religion a delight and nothing else—a delight in meetings which rouse the nervous life. I am in Christ, and therefore need take no trouble, as Christ has taken all the trouble for me, and has absolutely redeemed and saved me. Therefore I step into this boat, and let it drift while I drop to sleep, with the sure and certain conviction that it will one day touch the shores of that immortality for which I am bound." Let every one who is in Christ remember that He has overcome the primal curse to which he was once in helpless bondage, only to leave us free to fight the Christian warfare while life shall last. But while in the act of fighting, the man in Christ will be in the act of conquering. If they were to be addressed by God in the words of the text, they must be fighters for *victory;* for no man could overcome who was not at the same time in conflict. If they were conquering Christians *now,* it was because Christ had given them those gifts promised in His Word to him that overcometh.

(f)

2. "**To him that overcometh**" told them what the Christian was *now,* and not what he *would* be; and that the word of promise was intended to inspirit the Christian while in the act of fighting; showing that in the act of fighting he was really in the act of *overcoming;* and showing him, too, that he was so, by receiving the gifts which were mentioned in the words of promise. Christ would give, not merely in another world, when they had fought the fight, but He would give here, now, on earth, the will to win it; He would give to each of them who was a fighter, by that fact to be an overcomer, and so account for the overcoming.

(g)

3. "**To him that overcometh** I will give to eat of the tree of life, which is in the midst of the paradise of God." What was the tree of life in the earthly paradise but the symbol of coming immortality? And so Christ would give, all through the earthly battle of the Christian, a foretaste—a beginning of immortality—heavenly fruits on earthly ground before they reached the heavenly field, or walked the golden streets. And thus, he thought, these words had an earthly as well as a heavenly reference. And so to him, of whom it was said he should not be hurt of the second death. He knew that whatever darts struck him here, they would not strike the *true* life.

(h)

4. "**To him that overcometh** will I give to eat of the hidden manna." Manna was the Israelites' food; and the true manna was the type of the grace of Christ (John vi.). Christ gave Himself, and gave, therefore, His grace to feed our immortal life. And we needed this food if we were to have immortality. Manna was for the wilderness, to strengthen the true Israelites in their conflict and in their journey; and this could only be fulfilled while on earth, fighting our way to the land of promise. While our zeal, courage, and immortality were fed, we should be more than conquerors.

(i)

5. "To him that overcometh will I give the white stone." Amongst the Greeks, the giving of a white stone was the sign of acquittal or approval, as the black stone meant condemnation. Christ gave the stone of acquittal or approval; and the Christian therefore was calm, whatever foes might arise, for he knew that he had the white stone that had accepted and justified him; and while he had that conviction he was invincible.

In another place it was: "He that overcometh shall be a pillar in My house, and shall no more go out, and on that pillar shall be engraved the name of God." The practice prevailed amongst the Greeks of some rich men sending a pillar for the temple, bearing their names, as monumental of their glory. So God would make all Christians pillars in His temple—the Church of God on earth and in heaven. A true pillar in God's temple was a man who helped to prop it up; who supported it by his preaching, by his prayers, and by his property, and the name written on him is the name of his God.

(a)

6. "To him that overcometh will I give that morning star," indicated that it was not morning, not heaven, yet. The morning star shined when all was darkness around it. Mark the royal word, "I will give." Christ was not always saying, "I will give," and was never giving. The Christian was spoken of here as though God saw the future in the present.

(b)

7. "To him that overcometh" was the distinction of those who were fighting against their own sins; being in Christ, having those gifts perpetually from the hand of Christ, fighting against his *own* sins, for every man was a double man, and had to fight with himself—with all that within was waiting to open the door secretly to the foe without. That was the greatest thing which made for Christian victory, victory within. Every Christian was a warrior born, and must have on the armour of God. He puts it on in conversion, never to put it off till he dies, so that he may be always ready to meet the inevitable foe. Thus he is a fighter, but, thanks to God, he is also an overcomer—a victor—though he may not always know this. Though he fall he shall rise again; and when he has passed through the brief sleep of death, he will indeed know the title of him that overcometh.

(c)

8. "To him that overcometh" is the distinction of those who in Christ, and by the gift of Christ, are fighting against the evils of the world—those who are fighting against the system of false religion and false philosophy. Christians by the means he had indicated fought against war. But they had not yet fought it out of the world, for be the scene ever so serene they must hear the Word of God saying, "This is not your peace;" and only by the power of the Gospel would wars be made to cease.

(d)   *Standford*

If there be no enemy, no fight; if no fight, no victory; if no victory, no crown.

(e)   *Savonarola*

Press toward the mark: fear not the fiery darts of Satan. Let thy spirit resist to blood. Take courage from thy cause: thou fightest for thy God, and against His enemy and thy rebellious lusts. Is thy enemy too potent? fear not. Art thou besieged? faint not. Art thou routed? fly not. Call aid, and thou shalt be strengthened; petition, and thou shalt be relieved. Pray, and thou shalt be recruited.

(f)   *F. Quarles*

P

PAIN

"*Neither shall there be any more pain*" (Rev. xxi. 4)

That is the inscription on the tomb of Robert Hall in Bristol Cemetery. He would often roll on the carpet in agony, we are told, with the pain in his back. And after death his kidneys were found almost entirely reduced to lumps of calculus! His daily suffering must have been excruciating. He waited eagerly and confidently for death; and died with the broken words on his lips, "Come, Lord Jesus, come ——."

(a) *Thos. Cooper*

PALMS AND CROSSES

And if, beforehand, you can climb up thither in your thoughts, look about you, you shall see no more palms than crosses; you shall see none crowned but those that have wrestled with crosses and sorrows, to sweat, yea, to blood; and have overcome. All runs here to the overcomer; and overcoming implies both fighting and success. Gird up your loins, therefore, and strengthen your weak knees. Resolve to fight for heaven; to suffer, fighting; to persist, in suffering: so persisting, you shall overcome; and overcoming, you shall be crowned.

(b) *Bishop Hall*

PANOPLY OF GOD

"*Take unto you the whole armour of God, that ye may be able to withstand in the evil day, and having done all, to stand*" (Eph. vi. 13)

Note.

(i.) *The foe*—no one spared, no time exempt;
(ii.) *The soldier*—that the Christian is a soldier too little regarded;
(iii.) *The need of strengthening*—"Be strong in the Lord";
"Take the panoply of God;"
Be armed at *all* points.
A fortress is no stronger than its weakest place;
A chain no stronger than its weakest link;
No Christian is stronger than his besetting sin, or weakness.

1. The defensive armour:

The dress or coat of mail:
Of three pieces
Truth, Righteousness, Zeal.
(i.) Truth, the girdle, over loins (most vulnerable part), seat of strength.
This first, because an ungirded soldier is a contradiction in terms.
Luke xii. 5, "Let your loins be girded";
1 Pet. i. 13, "Gird up the loins of your mind."
Everything hangs on this; the armour would drop off without it=no soldier.
The first thing is conviction, assured certainty, no guess—no cant repetition of other men's beliefs=a mere echo.

Truth ought to be our *own* possession—laboured for, dug out as ore (such soldiers stand firm).
Are we girded if we only adopt another's opinions or belief?
(ii.) Righteousness—"the breastplate of righteousness,"
=both the faith that justifies; "Being justified by faith," etc.;
and the faith that worketh by love; and, that bears the fruits of righteousness.
=a living faith. Belief=Be living.
Such a man cannot be wounded in the seat of life.
(iii.) Zeal="Your feet shod,"
=ready, prompt, courageous,
=stand up for Jesus.
Not fanaticism, but a true, steady, living witness for Christ, wherever he goes, and in whatever company he finds himself.
"Not ashamed of Christ."

(c)

2. The defensive weapons.

(i.) Faith—"The shield of faith"—the *scutum*. "Have faith in God."
All moral darts, poisoned, venomous, hurtful, quenched by this—
"It is God that justifieth."
(ii.) Hope—"the helmet"—against intellectual darts; to ward off attacks on the head; clever writing, talkers, lecturers, books, subversive of the faith.
"Hope maketh not ashamed"—deludes not, is sure.
This only will keep us safe in times like these of intellectual doubt.

(d)

3. The one offensive weapon

"The sword of the Spirit, which is the Word of God."
Quote Scripture back; argue from it; draw your best replies and arguments from it. And you will be ridiculed for so doing-
"You argue in a circle.
"You quote your Bible.
"I attack it, I undermine its foundations; I deny its authority; where are you then? Why quote it?"
(i.) Answer.
Because Christ did.
"It is written;"
"It is written;"
"It is written;"
Three times, in answer to the Tempter.
He was a Warrior, armed with the whole armour of God. *He used this sword.* He smote and defeated the enemy with it alone. Therefore I use it.
(ii.) Because all Scripture is given by inspiration of God; and the Holy Ghost, who is its Author, and who spake by those who wrote it, teacheth us that it is true.
"He guideth into all truth."
He is the Spirit of Truth, and whom He teaches is certain. I use it on His authority.

(e)

(iii.) Because holy men have quoted it, and lived by it, and died by it, and used it as their weapon.

Christian, in "Pilgrim's Progress," met with devils, temptations, and giants.

He fought battles, and overcame all with "the sword of the Spirit."

This completes the equipment of the Christian soldier.

In this way is he made "strong."

The exhortation to take the whole armour of God was never more needed than now.

(*See* "ARMOUR.")

(a)

PANTETH

"*As the hart panteth*," etc. (Ps. xlii. 1)

It is not only in fear, or terror, or in the rattling of the thunderstorm, which has shown man there is a God; nor has he first read God's name inscribed among the stars. Deep; strong as the instinct of the newborn babe for the mother's breast, which it has not yet known; loud as the cry raised by the young ravens for food, whose taste they never yet felt; strong and silent as the attraction for the light, shown by the scarce developed plant and the yet unopened eye,—the inward thirst after the everlasting Source of all that breathes and lives, makes itself deeply felt within us all.

(b)   *Schubert*

Lord, Thou hast made us for Thyself; therefore our heart is ill at ease within us, until we find our rest in Thee.

(c)   *Augustine*

If man was not made for God, why can he enjoy no happiness but in God? If man was made for God, why is he so opposed to God?

(d)   *Blaise Pascal*

What, then, does this eagerness in coveting, and this impotence in acquiring, teach us, but that man originally possessed real happiness, of which nothing is now left to him but the footsteps and empty traces, which he vainly endeavours to replenish with all the abundance that surrounds him; seeking, from absent enjoyments, the relief which he finds not in such as are present, and which neither the present nor the absent can bestow on him, because this immense void can only be filled by an infinite and unchangeable object.

(e)   *Ibid*

PARADISE (2 Cor. 12)

Ever since God stationed before Eden the cherub with his naked, flaming sword, man must look for no Paradise on earth. There is, however, one beyond this sinful world in the third heaven.

(f)   *Besser*

Every man has a Paradise around him till he sins, and the angel of an accusing conscience drives him from his Eden. And even then there are holy hours, when this angel sleeps, and man comes back, and with the innocent eyes of a child looks into his lost Paradise again—into the broad gates and rural solitudes of nature.

(g)

More like unto a Paradise
Than to an earthly dwelling.

(h)   *Cardinal Wolsey's Palace*

God did not cast man out of Paradise that he might be able to find himself another paradise in this world. "Sir," said one to a great lord, on showing his stately house and pleasant gardens, "you had need make sure of heaven, or else, when you die, you will be a great loser."

(i)   *Thomas Brookes*

Similarly—"These are the things which make us unwilling to die."

(j)   *Chas. V. to Duke of Venice*

PARALLELISM

Example of gradational parallelism, being an example of extension of thought.

Psalm i. Blessed is the man
   that walketh not in the counsel of the ungodly,
   nor standeth in the way of sinners,
   nor sitteth in the seat of the scornful.

The gradations are obvious:

   "Walketh" = occasional intercourse;
   "Standeth" = has close intimacy;
   "Sitteth" = permanent connection:
   "Counsel" = public resort;
   "Way" = chosen path;
   "Seat" = habitual place;
   "Ungodly" = the negatively wicked;
   "Sinners" = the positively wicked;
   "Scornful" = the profanely wicked.

Psalm cxxxv. 15–18. Specimen of *Introverted Parallelism.*

1. The idols of the heathen are silver and gold,
   2. The work of men's hand;
      3. They have mouths, but they speak not;
         4. They have eyes, but they see not;
         5. They have ears, but they hear not;
      6. Neither is there any breath in their mouths.
   7. They who make them are like unto them;
8. So are all they who put their trust in them.

Here it is easily seen that lines 1 and 8, 2 and 7, 3 and 6, 4 and 5, answer to each other, or are parallel.

(k)

PARALYTIC, THE (Luke v. 15–26)

(i.) Jesus at prayer in the midst of His work.

(ii.) The presence of the scribes and Pharisees as lookers on.

(iii.) *The Offence*: "Thy sins be forgiven thee" (condition = faith).

(iv.) *The Miracle*: Did my words seem an empty sound?

(v.) "*That ye may know*," etc. = proof that Jesus was an ambassador for God, and could do on earth what belonged to God alone in heaven.

(l)

PARDON

Wilt Thou forgive that sin where I began,
Which was my sin, though it were done before?
Wilt Thou forgive that sin through which I ran,
And do run still, though still I do deplore?
   When Thou hast done, Thou hast not done,
      For I have more.

(m)

Wilt Thou forgive that sin which I have won
Others to sin, and made my sin their door?
Wilt Thou forgive that sin which I did shun
A year or two—but wallowed in a score?
  When Thou hast done, Thou hast not done,
      For I have more.

I have a sin of fear, that when I've spun
My last thread, I shall perish on the shore;
But swear by Thyself, that at my death Thy Son
Shall shine as He shines now, and heretofore;
  And having done that, Thou hast done,—
      I fear no more.

(*a*)   *Donne*

PARTY

Bishop Thirlwall was a very liberal-minded man, but he could give some very severe blows to an adversary. I think it was he who originated the saying that as Low Church was the opposite of High Church, the opposite of Broad Church was Narrow Church; and every one, I suppose, will agree that a narrow-minded Churchman is not likely to be catholic in the best sense of the word.

(*b*)

" The father of lies " is of no party.
(*c*)   *Disraeli: Cur. of Lit*
(*See* " LIES.")

Many an English party began with a truth, and then called it *the* truth. (*Hence*) "puffed up," manifesting that they were " carnal, and walked as men."
(*d*)   *F. W. Robertson*

Zealots seem all formed of one material, whatever be their party. They had yet to learn that burning was not confuting, and that these public fires were an advertisement by proclamation.
Tonstall, Bishop of London, reign of Henry VIII., accused of preferring to burn books to authors, to testify his abhorrence of Tindal's principles, purchased all the copies of T.'s translation, and burned them. He declared this was a " burning of the Word of God," and so inflamed the desire for reading that volume that the second edition was sought at any price.
Tonstall's act of buying up the first impression enabled them to produce a second.
                Disraeli: Cur. of Lit

PARTY MEN

Party men always hate a slightly differing friend more than a downright enemy. I quite calculate upon my being one day or other holden in worse repute by many Christians than the Unitarians and open infidels. It must be undergone by every one who loves the truth for its own sake beyond all other things.
(*f*)   *S. T. Coleridge*

PASSOVER

No other festival was so full of typical meaning, or pointed so clearly to *good things to come* (Heb. x. 1):
(i.) It was a Feast of Redemption, foreshadowing a future and greater Redemption (Gal. iv. 4, 5);

(ii.) The victim, a lamb *without blemish* and without spot, was a striking type of the *Lamb of God that taketh away the sin of the world* (John i. 29; 1 Cor. v. 7; 1 Pet. i. 19);
(iii.) Slain, not by the priest, but by the head of the Paschal company, its blood shed and sprinkled on the altar, roasted whole without the breaking of a bone—it symbolized Him who was put to death by the people (Acts ii. 23), whose blood during a Paschal festival was shed on the altar of His cross, whose side the soldier pierced, but brake not His legs (John xix. 32–36);
(iv.) Eaten at the sacrificial meal (peculiar to the peace-offering) with bitter herbs and unleavened bread (the symbol of purity), it pointed to that one oblation of Himself once offered, whereby Christ has made us at peace with God (Eph. ii. 14, 15), in which whosoever truly believes must walk in repentance and sincerity and truth (1 Cor. v. 7, 8);
(v.) It was at a Paschal Supper that its antitype, the Christian Eucharist, was instituted by our Lord (Matt. xxvi. 17).
(*g*)   *Maclear*

PASSOVER, CHRIST OUR

" *Christ our Passover is sacrificed for us: therefore let us keep the feast*" (1 Cor. v. 7, 8)

The occasion was a sharp rebuke for their tolerating a gross case of immorality.

Notice—
1. Our standpoint as Christians
(i.) Christ, as the Passover Lamb, has been sacrificed;
(ii.) The Blood has been sprinkled;
(iii.) The Victim has suffered—not a bone broken—roasted whole—prepared for a meal. What next?
(*h*)

2. " Therefore let us keep the Feast "
Eat the Passover Lamb;
(i.) Christ has to be appropriated—"Take, eat"; "trust"; "believe." "Except ye eat . . . no life in you" (John vi. 53).
(ii.) Christ has to be assimilated—become a part of ourselves—as food is taken into the natural system. "Feed on Him in your heart by faith, with thanksgiving"; "He that eateth . . . . dwelleth in Me, and I in him" (John vi. 56).
(iii.) The Feast, then, is-
(1.) An acknowledgment that Christ Jesus is necessary for our spiritual life—"no life" without Him—life not sustained without Him—all depends upon Him.
(2.) The so appropriating Him, and assimilating His life with ours, that He and we become *one*—the Head and the members, the Vine and its branches.
(*i*)

3. The Feast
(i.) *The Negative Injunction:*
" Not with the old leaven."
" Leaven " was a piece of unbaked dough kept from last baking. The symbol of impurity. This injunction is *emphatic* = " Not to keep the Feast of Christ's Resurrection Life in our old uncon-
(*j*)

verted state." May not retain old sins, as the sensual impurities of the Gentiles. All the sins of the past must be abandoned—regarded as buried in the grave with Christ. Emphatic—"Not with the *old leaven*." The Jews, before the feast, had to sweep their houses, and search for any remains of leaven; so must the Christian sweep out "malice and wickedness" from his life.

(ii.) *The Positive Injunction:*

"But with the unleavened bread of sincerity and truth." As the Passover bread had to be a new batch—with no old leaven in it,—so must the Christian's be a new life—sincere, genuine, without guile—a new start. Otherwise Christ's resurrection life has no definite meaning for him. For " if any man be in Christ, he is a *new* creature (creation); *old* things are passed away, all things are become new."

(iii.) *The one Emphatic Injunction:*

" Purge out, therefore, the old leaven."

(1.) Turn that unholy man out of the Church;

(2.) Search your own hearts, as the Jews searched their houses before the Passover. Search and see if there be any way of wickedness in you—any old sins, especially such as ye lived in in your former state—any leaven; and seek, God helping you, to live a new life, a raised life, a Christian life.

(a)

" PAST FINDING OUT "

" *O the depth* . . . *ways past finding out* " (Rom. xi. 33)

What has the Apostle been describing? (See chap. ix. to xi.)

Directly, God's dealings with the Jews; but indirectly, God's sovereignty and man's freewill; election, and self-determination. With what result? "PAST FINDING OUT."

(b)

PAST AND FUTURE

The earth, with its scarred face, is the symbol of the past; the air and heaven, of futurity.

(c) *S. T. Coleridge*

What is past ought not to interfere with our progress, since all we have to do is to repent of our faults. And what is to come ought to affect us still less; because, with regard to us, it is not, and perhaps never will be.

(d) *Blaise Pascal*

PASTORS, NEGLIGENT

Were there any love of God from their hearts in those who, instead of feeding to salvation, starve many thousands to destruction; I dare say, and say it boldly, that for all the promotions under heaven they would not offer that injury to one soul, that now they offer to many hundred souls. But, Lord, how do they think to give up their reckoning to Thee, who in most strict account wilt take the answer of every soul committed unto them one by one! Or with what concern do they often hear that vehement speech of our Saviour Christ, "Feed, feed, feed!" With what eyes do they so often read that piercing speech of the Apostle, "Feed the flock committed unto you!" But if none of these will

move them, then the Lord open their eyes to hear the grievous groans of many souls lying under the grisly altars of destruction, and complaining against them; "O Lord, the Revenger of Blood, behold these men whom Thou hast set over us to give us the bread of life, but they have not given it us. Our tongues and the tongues of our children have stuck to the roof of our mouths for calling and crying, and they would not take pity on us. We have given them the tenths which Thou appointedst us, but they have not given us Thy truth which Thou hast commanded them. Reward them, O Lord, as they have rewarded us. Let the bread between their teeth turn to rottenness in the bowels. Let them be clothed with shame and confusion of face as with a garment. Let their wealth, as the dung from the earth, be swept away by their executors; and upon their gold and silver, which they have falsely treasured up, let continually be written, ' The price of blood, the price of blood; ' for it is the value of our blood, O Lord. If Thou didst hear the blood of Abel, being but one man, forget not the blood of many, when Thou goest into judgment."

(e) *Greenham*

PATH

The path to heaven is not without many a Hill Difficulty and Valley of Humiliation. What terrific convictions of sin, ere one grasps the Cross! what rackings of soul ere it finds peace in the Lord's bosom! what sighs and struggles after the nobler nature, when inferior motives in some dark moment re-assert their mastery!

(f) *Good Words*

PATHS

" *In all thy ways acknowledge Him, and He shall direct thy paths* " (Prov. iii. 6)

I commend to Thee, Lord,
My impulses and my startings,
My intentions and my attempts,
My going out and my coming in,
My sitting down and my rising up.

(g) *Bp. Andrewes*

PATIENCE

Patience is but lying-to and riding out the gale.

(h) *Beecher*

Pray and stay, are two blessed monosyllables.

(i) *Donne*

Never think that God's delays are God's denials. Hold; hold fast; hold out.

(j) *Anon*

With time and patience, the mulberry-leaf becomes satin.

(k) *Eastern Proverb*

" Sire, it belongs to God's Church rather to suffer blows than to strike them; but let it be your pleasure to remember that the Church is *an anvil which hath worn out many a hammer*."

(l) *Beza's reply to the king of Navarre*

PATRIARCHS, CHARACTER OF

" *The God of Abraham, the God of Isaac, and the God of Jacob* " (Exod. iii. 15)

The character of the Patriarchs is never represented as perfect; their faults are freely exposed; theirs is no ideal history.

If we compare the four most eminent amongst them, we seem to trace in

(i.) *Abraham,* "the faith that can remove mountains" in its power and in its fulness, revealing itself in unfaltering trust and unquestioning obedience under the most trying circumstances conceivable; in

(ii.) *Isaac,* the faith that can possess itself in patience, and discharge the ordinary duties of life in quietness and waiting; in

(iii.) *Jacob,* the violent contest of faith with the flesh, the higher with the lower nature, till by hard discipline the latter is purified, and the "Supplanter" becomes the "Prince," the "Prevailer with God"; in

(iv.) *Joseph,* the fidelity and perseverance of faith, revealed not only in the patient endurance of the most grievous trials, but in energetic action, and at length crowned with victory. He unites in himself the noble trust and resolution of Abraham with the quiet perseverance of Isaac and the careful prudence of Jacob.

(*a*)   *Maclear, and Smith's Bib. Dict*

PATTERN OF CHRIST, THE (1 Pet. i. 21)

A pattern to copy or draw by, a copy-head, such as a writing-master would give to his pupils. This requires a steady hand and daily practice. It is characteristic of this epistle, that it lays great stress on the *pattern* of Christ.

(*b*)   *Lange*

PAUL AT ATHENS (Acts xvii.)

He proclaimed *three great truths*, in opposition to *three great falsehoods* which controlled the philosophy of that age, and from which even that of modern times is not yet freed:

(i.) The creation out of nothing, as opposed to naturalism,

(ii.) The personality of God, as opposed to pantheism,

(iii.) The nature of sin, as opposed to antinomianism and rationalism.

(*c*)   *Krummacher*

Observe the three-fold subject of the discourse:
(i.) Theology (24, 25);
(ii.) Anthropology (26–29);
(iii.) Christology (30, 31).
(*d*)   *Meyer*

PAUL AND JAMES

(i.) We are saved by faith.
(ii.) Can faith save?
N.B. St. Paul wrote against self-righteousness; St. James, against unrighteousness.
(*e*)   *Marsh*

PEACE

Filling up our time with and for God, is the way to rise up and lie down in peace. . . . I longed that my life might be filled up with fervency and activity in the things of God. Oh, the peace, composure, and God-like serenity of such a frame! Heaven must differ from this only in degree, not in kind.
(*f*)   *D. Brainerd*

PEACE, PEACE

If the gods of this lower world will sit on their glittering thrones, indolent as Epicurus' gods, with the living chaos of ignorance and hunger weltering uncared for at their feet, and small parasites preaching, Peace, Peace, when there is no peace, then the dark chaos, it would seen, will rise;—has risen, and, O heavens! has it not tanned their skins into breeches for itself?
(*g*)   *Carlyle*

PEACE OF GOD, THE

" *The peace of God, which passeth all understanding, shall keep your hearts and minds through Christ Jesus* " (Phil. iv. 7)

The enemies of this peace are
(i.) *Melancholy :* to which is opposed—"Rejoice in the Lord always" (4);
(ii.) *Want of self-restraint, or intemperance :* to which is opposed—"Let your moderation be known unto all men" (5);
(iii.) *Care and anxiety, or unthankfulness and unbelief :* to which is opposed—"Be careful for nothing; but in everything by prayer and supplication with thanksgiving, let your requests be made known unto God" (6).
The effect of which is, "the peace of God which passeth all understanding."
(*h*)

PEACE WITH GOD

This ungodly fear puts men upon adding to the will of God their own inventions and performances, as a means of pacifying God. How it has racked and tortured the Papists for hundreds of years! What else is the cause of their penances, such as creeping to the Cross, going barefoot on pilgrimages, whipping themselves, wearing of sackcloth, giving money for pardons, etc., etc., but this ungodly fear of God! For could they be brought to believe that Christ died for our sins, and was raised again for our justification, this fear would vanish, and so consequently all these things with it.
(*i*)   *John Bunyan*

" PEACE BE UNTO YOU "

" *On the first day of the week, when the doors were shut and the disciples were gathered together for fear of the Jews, came Jesus and stood in the midst of them and said, Peace be unto you* " (John xx. 19)

Four things in this text:
(i.) The world was shut out;
(ii.) The disciples were shut in;
(iii.) Then came Jesus; and
(iv.) The result was peace. May it be so with us!
(*j*)

"Peace be unto You"—*continued*

1. Our Lord appeared here, not to the world at large, but only to the Apostles ; i.e., to those who were looking and longing for His appearing.

If we examine the accounts of our Lord's appearances after His resurrection, we shall find that this law regulates them all, viz., that to those only who were longing for Him did He appear.

He appeared to witnesses enough. We can, therefore, have no doubt of the reality of His resurrection; but, as St. Peter, in his Pentecostal sermon, says, "Not to all the people, but to witnesses chosen before of God"—chosen, in fact, for this very purpose, that they might, by their life, their preaching, and their death, testify to the truth of His resurrection.

We do not enough dwell on this difference before and after the resurrection.

We are too much accustomed to think that because our Blessed Lord showed Himself to all and every one before His resurrection, that therefore He did so after it.

Such is not the case. During the three years and a half of His ministry He showed Himself to every one, believer or unbeliever, inquirer or scoffer, Pharisee, scribe, publican, or harlot, saint to be or sinner that was, indiscriminately—all might approach that Sacred Person ; all might listen to the words that flowed from the mouth that spake as never man spake ; all might come near and touch not merely the hem of His garment, but actually His very Human Body.

And for this reason. It was their time of probation. He came to seek and to save those that were lost ; and He suffered all to approach Him, that none might be without a chance of being the better for being brought near to Him, none might perish for lack of opportunity of hearing His message.

But their probation time did not last for ever ; *nor does ours.*

Childhood has its probation time, which it uses or misuses ; and it goes and returns not, and leaves its record on our souls and in the judgment book of God. Youth has its probation time—not the same as that of childhood, which preceded it, nor of manhood, or ripe age, or old age, which succeeds. So here we are but working out in our own histories this old Jewish story. Some hear and live, others hear and die. All have their probation time ; *all* do not profit by it, but misuse it ; and the record of their misuse will one day be opened before the eyes of the Judge with whom we have to do, and all mankind as well.

(*a*)

To recur to our risen Lord

2. The eye unprepared by faith never saw Him again.

To none but to those who were looking and longing for Him did He show Himself risen.

No mortal eye saw His actual resurrection. It was at midnight. The quaternion of guards might have seen Him, but they did not, being either blinded by the blaze that issued from the bursted tomb and the angels attending ; or asleep when they should have been watching.

To whom did He first show Himself risen ? To Mary Magdalene, who in her intense faith and love had brought spices to anoint the body of Him who had cast seven devils out of her, and whom she loved much, having by Him been forgiven much.

To whom next ? To Simon Peter, the repentant, who thrice denied Him, but who bitterly repented of His denials ; to the ten, when St. Thomas was absent ; to the eleven, with St. Thomas present ; to the five at the sea of Galilee ; to James, His own cousin ; to the five hundred brethren on the Mount in Galilee—whether it be the Mount of Beatitudes or the Mount of Transfiguration ; anyhow, to *the* place our Lord had indicated.

In all these cases our Lord appears to those who were looking and longing for Him, and who were going in the way of obedience, doing exactly what their Lord bade them do, following the measure of light given them, and to no others.

Illustrated in the story of the two disciples going to Emmaus—just because, even in the midst of darkness, despondency, and despair, they were thinking of their Lord *as absent*, He is so present with them that their hearts glow within them with a living fire, the source of which they cannot even guess. And He leads them on by gentle questioning to put their thoughts in words, and at last opens their hearts to know the Scriptures and to see that a suffering Saviour was foretold by even Moses and the prophets ; and when, after "making as though He would have gone further," they *constrain* Him to abide with them, because the day is far spent, He goes in (as He did to the Syrophenician woman, whom He at first repelled to test her faith and perseverance), and "becomes known unto them in the breaking of bread."

(*b*)

3. And are not we here, in this house of God, acting over again this old, old story ?

Here the world, we will trust, has been shut out ; the disciples are shut in ; we are thinking of Jesus—will not the result be peace ?

But what if, while nominally here to seek our Lord, our hearts are set upon our pleasures or our ledgers, will Christ show Himself to us now ? No —no more than He did after His resurrection to the Jews at large. What a responsibility then does every occasion of worship or of reproach to our Lord, as at the sacrament of that altar, lay upon us ! The record will go up. Shall we be like the scoffers of our Lord's time, like the hypocritical Pharisees, or the voluptuous, sensual, sceptical Sadducees, believing in no future— hoping for no resurrection, cutting down the inspired Bible by their "verifying faculty" to the Pentateuch, and blind to Christ and the resurrection even in that ?—or thrice blessed, if we find Him whom our souls love ?

(*c*)

4. The same rule holds good, when-

(i.) We kneel down to pray at night or morning.
(ii.) When we come to church.
(iii.) When we think of Christ in the midst of business.
(iv.) When we are shut up in the sick room.
(v.) When we approach the Lord's table.
(vi.) When we are on our deathbeds.

In each and all these cases the phenomena and the result are the same.

We do, or we do not, shut out the world.

(*d*)

"Peace be unto You"—*continued*

We do, or we do not, shut ourselves in to await the Lord's appearing.

We do, or we do not, find the Lord come in.

We do, or we do not, enjoy the Lord's blessing of peace.

(*a*)

5. And when the world's great assize takes place, and the Judge is seated, and the books are opened, and we stand breathlessly to hear our doom, before angel spectators and listening fellow-men, if we have never shut out the world, and shut ourselves in with Jesus, our sentence will be utter and final exclusion from the presence of Him we loved not and cared not for.

If, on the other hand, we have loved and followed Him, if we have longed for and sought His appearing, then, when the world is necessarily shut out (for it shall shrivel into annihilation), and we shall be shut in at the eternal Supper of the Lamb, then will Jesus welcome us to His side for ever, and the result will be peace—peace without limit, peace without end—the peace of God that passeth understanding. "Wherefore, comfort ye one another with these words."

(*b*)   *John Day Collis*

PEACEMAKER

Shenkyn, one of whose anomalies was that, with all his burning passions, he was a notorious peacemaker, and had means of pouring oil upon troubled waters. Once upon a time he was deputed to try his well-known skill upon a Church whose strife of tongues had become quite notorious. He reluctantly complied, and attended a meeting which soon proved to his satisfaction that the people were possessed by a demon that could not easily be expelled. The peacemaker got up, staff in hand, paced the little chapel, and, with his spirit deeply moved, cried out : "Lord, is this Thy spouse ? " Faster and faster he walked, thumping his huge stick on the floor, and still crying out, "Lord, is this Thy spouse? Slay her !" Then there came, as it were from another, a response : "No ; I will not." "Sell her, then !" "No ; I will not." "Deny her, then !" Still the answer came, "I will not." Then he lifted up his voice, saying: "I have bought her with My precious blood : how can I give her up ? How can I forsake her ? " The strife had now ceased, and the people looked on with amazement, crying out for pardon.

(*c*)

PEARL

A pearl may in a toad's head dwell,
And may be found too in an oyster shell.

(*d*)   *Bunyan*

PENTECOST

"*And when the day of Pentecost was fully come, they were all with one accord in one place,*" etc. (Acts ii. 1–21)

Mark the case of the Divine Head of the Church in fixing special times for the communication of special blessings. We have here

1. *The largest possible opportunity.* There are opportunities in every Divine Providence. The days are not all alike to God. We would bind Him down to *one* day. But does He not come in upon birthdays, wedding days, days of deliverance, times of surprise, days of unusual sorrow? He takes up one day and holds it symbolically before us. What He does with that day He wants to do with all the others.

2. *The largest memorial feast known to Israel.* Associated with memories of bondage and deliverance—of Sinai, and the giving of the law. At Pentecost *all* the sacrifices were offered.

3. *The largest possible union*

(i.) Of nationalities.

(ii.) Of desire. Note the word *accord*. God has promised nothing to *dis*union. They were gathered with one *accord ;* that is the permanent element in their union. They were also gathered in one *place ;* that is the transient circumstance. The place is nothing (John iv. 21), the accord is everything.

4. *The largest possible endowment of the Divine gift.* They were ALL with one accord. The Spirit a *common* gift, bestowed not upon Apostles only, but upon the humblest in the Church.

Always interesting to observe how great promises are fulfilled. The very greatness of the promise necessitates fulfilment on a scale proportioned to it. There could be no common-place realization of such a promise as Christ had given to the Apostles. Nor was there. For (ii. 4) "suddenly there came a sound from heaven," etc.

Learn :

(i.) How *helpless* we are in the matter of *spiritual revivals.*

(ii.) The power of waiting.

(iii.) How unmistakable is the gift of fire.

(*e*)   *J. Parker*

We now hear another language, which does not fill the heart with terror, like the voice heard on Mount Sinai ; it neither alarms nor slays us, but rather inspires us with courage and joy ; indeed, Christ had promised to His disciples that He would send them the Holy Ghost, who should not be a Spirit of fear, but a Comforter, imparting to them boldness, and power to overcome fear.

(*f*)   *Lange*

PENTECOST AND BABEL

(i.) "*Are not all these Galileans ?*" (Acts ii. 7)
The world takes offence at the persons of the witnesses.

(ii.) "*How hear we in our own tongue ?* " (ver. 8)
It is arrested by the voice of conscience responding to the truth.

(iii.) "*What meaneth this ?*" (ver. 12).
It distrusts the issue of the ways of God.

(iv.) "*They are full of new wine*" (ver. 13).
It mistakes the source of the operations of the Spirit.

(*g*)   *Ibid*

PEOPLE

"*This people who knoweth not the law are cursed*" (John vii. 49)

"This multitude, rabble" ($\ddot{v}\chi\lambda os$), is here used evidently with great contempt, not only to designate the persons, but to indicate their character.

(*h*)

. . . The common people were called even *vermin*. "The illiterate man is not godly" (*Tholuck*). "None but the learned would rise from the dead" (*Talmud*). The aristocratic contempt for the people is found everywhere in Church and State. The pride of priestcraft, kingcraft, and schoolcraft is deeply seated in the human heart.

(*a*)   *P. Schaff*

PEOPLE

And what the people but a herd confused,
A miscellaneous rabble, who extol
Things vulgar and, well weighed, scarce worth the
    praise.
They praise and they admire they know not what,
And know not whom, but as one leads the other;
And what delight to be by such extolled,
To live upon their tongues, and be their talk,
Of whom to be dispraised were no small praise.

(*b*)   *Milton*

PERFECT

"*Be ye perfect*" (Matt. v. 48)

We who are created in God's image, and restored in Christ, and made partakers of the Divine nature in Him, are bound, by the conditions of our creation, redemption, and sanctification, to endeavour to be like Him here, that we may have the fruition of His glorious Godhead hereafter (Eph. iv. 1; 1 Pet. i. 15; 1 John ii. 1).

(*c*)   *Lange*

PERILS

Ah me! how many perils do enfold
The righteous man, to make him daily fall,
Were not that heavenly grace doth him uphold,
And steadfast truth acquit him out of all.

(*d*)   *Spenser*

PERISH

(*God*) "*not willing that any should perish*" (2 Pet. iii. 9)

As an earthly king would desire to see all his subjects happy, as far as they are his subjects, not as far as they are malefactors.

(*e*)   *Calor*

God wills to save *all* men only in Christ, and in the order of repentance and faith.

(*f*)   *Lange*

PERMANENCE OF CHARACTER (HABIT)

"*He that is unjust, let him be unjust still: and he which is filthy, let him be filthy still: and he that is righteous, let him be righteous still: and he that is holy, let him be holy still*" (Rev. xxii. 11)

The tendency of character is towards permanence, in both the righteous and the wicked. There is a moral momentum, illustrated by a stone rolling down hill. The character we write on our lives remains, not like letters written on the sand, which the first tide will efface, but as "The sin of

Judah is written with a pen of iron, and with the point of a diamond: it is graven upon the table of their heart" (Jer. xvii. 1).

(*g*)

"*For ever, O Lord, Thy word is settled in heaven*" (Ps. cxix. 89)

Fear not, O Bride, nor despair: think not thyself contemned if thy Bridegroom withdraw His face awhile. All things co-operate for the best; both from His absence and His presence thou gainest light. He cometh to thee, and goeth from thee; He cometh to make thee consolate; He goeth to make thee cautious, lest thy abundant consolation puff thee up: He cometh, that thy languishing soul may be comforted: He goeth, lest His familiarity should be contemned, and being absent to be more desired, and being desired to be more earnestly sought, and being long sought to be more acceptably found.

(*h*)   *Scalæ Parad. tom. 9, Aug. c.* 8

PERSECUTION

Richard! Richard! dost thou think here to poison the Court? Richard, thou art an old fellow—an old knave; thou hast written books eno' to load a cart, every one as full of sedition, I might say treason, as an egg is full of meat. Hadst thou been whipped out of thy writing trade forty years ago, it had been happy.—*Lord Jeffreys to Baxter.*

(*i*)   *Campbell's "Lives of the Chancellors."*

PERSECUTION

No servant of Christ is without affliction. If you expect to be free from persecution, you have not yet so much as begun to be a Christian.

(*j*)   *Augustine*

PERSECUTORS AND CONSCIENCE

They are hunted many times with furies of conscience and extreme horror even in this life. Pashur put blessed Jeremiah in the stocks, but thereupon he had a new name given him, *Magormissabib*, Fear round about. He became a terror to himself and to all his friends (Jer. xx. 2, 3, 4). Zedekiah smote faithful Micaiah upon the face; but afterwards, according to that prophetical communication, he was fain to run from chamber to chamber to hide himself (1 Kings xxii. 24, 25). John Baptist's head, which Herod cut off, sat in the eye of the tyrant's conscience with such grisly forms of guilt and blood, that when he heard of the great things done by Christ, he was perplexed, and no doubt afraid that John Baptist was risen from the dead to be revenged upon him.

Many of them come to very horrible, exemplary, and woeful ends. Pharaoh long since, by a dreadful confusion at the Red Sea, was, as it were, hanged up in chains, a spectacle of terror for persecutors to all posterity. Antiochus, swelling with anger, and breathing out fire in his rage against the people of God, did proudly protest that "he would come to Jerusalem and make it a common burying-place of the Jews. But the Lord Almighty, the God of Israel, smote him with an incurable and invisible plague. For as soon as he had spoken these words, a pain of the bowels that was

(*k*)

remediless came upon him, and sore torments of the inner parts. So that the worms rose up out of the body of this wicked man, and while he lived in sorrow and pain, his flesh fell away, and the filthiness of his smell was noisome to all his army" (2 Maccab. ix. 4). Herod, in the height of his hatred against the Gospel, and pride in imprisoning and persecuting the Apostles, was eaten up of worms in a most fearful and prodigious manner (Acts xii. 23). Gardiner, gaping for news of the despatch of those two blessed martyrs of Jesus, Latimer and Ridley, at Oxford, deferred his dinner until three or four o'clock in the afternoon, delighting more in drinking the blood of the saints than in his ordinary food; but upon the return of his post, he fell merrily to his meat, and mark what followed: "The bloody tyrant," saith the story, "had not eaten a few bits, but the sudden stroke of God's terrible hand fell upon him in such a sort, as immediately he was taken from the table, and so brought to his bed, where he continued the space of fifteen days in such intolerable anguish and torments, that during the whole of those fifteen days he could not void in any manner the food that he received: whereby his body being miserably inflamed within (who had inflamed so many good martyrs before) was brought to a wretched end." For further enlargement of this point, see the "Stories of the Primitive Church," "Acts and Monuments," "Theatre of God's Judgments."

(a) *Bolton*

PERSECUTORS, AND THE PRAYERS OF SAINTS

The prayers of the saints poured out in the bitterness of their souls, vexed continually with their malicious cruelties and cruel mockings, are means many times to bring persecutors to an untimely end, to knock them down before their time. Do not you think that the faithful Jews at Jerusalem, hearing of Antiochus marching towards them like an evening wolf to drink up their blood, had presently recourse unto God's righteous throne with strong cries to stay his rage? And do you not think that those very prayers drew down upon him that horrible and incurable plague, whereupon "he died a miserable death in a strange country in the mountains"? Herod, for anything we know, might have lived many a fair day longer if he had dealt fairly with the Apostles of Christ; but putting one to the sword, and another in prison, he put the Church to their prayers (Acts xii. 2-5), which prayers (for "there is a certain omnipotency of prayer," as Luther was wont to say) did soon create those vermin that ate him up horribly in the height of his pride (ver. 23). The ecclesiastical story reports that the loathsome and dreadful end of Arius, that execrable enemy to Jesus Christ, was hastened by the prayers of the good and orthodox bishop, Alexander, who wrestled with God in earnest deprecations against him all the night before. Do you not think that Gardiner went sooner into his grave for his cruelty towards professors of the truth by their groans against him, and by the cry of the blood of that glorious pair of martyrs at Oxford which he so insatiably thirsted after? Let all those, then, that tread in these men's paths, tremble at their ends; and if no better motive will soften their malicious hearts, yet at least let their love unto the world, themselves, and sensual ways, take them off and re-

strain them from this persecuting rage, lest it set on work the prayers of God's people, and so they be taken away before their time, and cut off from a temporary supposed heaven of earthly pleasures to a true everlasting hell of unspeakable torments, sooner than otherwise they should.

(b) *Ibid*

PERSEVERANCE

"*God is faithful*" (1 Cor. i. 9)

A ground of hope for the continuance and successful issue of those blessings. [St. Paul] relies not on any stability of human goodness: his ground of confidence is in the character of God. Human excellence is unstable. Saul once had the spirit of the Lord. Judas once had gifts. Who could say that the Corinthians might not fall away and make shipwreck of their faith? The Apostle answers this, not by assuring them that their habits had gained stability, not by counting on their faithfulness to God, but on God's faithfulness to them. Not on our fidelity to God, but God's fidelity to us. It is a most precious truth, and without some conviction of this, I cannot understand how any man dares to go forth to his work in the morning, or at evening lay his head on his pillow to sleep.

(c) *F. W. Robertson*

If the principle be true, that, without a constant action of God's spirit on the mind of man, no man can persevere in a life of virtue and religion, the Christian, who finds himself empowered to lead this life, cannot err in his conclusion, that God's power is at present exerted upon himself, in his own person for his own preservation.

(d) *Bp. Horsley*

PERSON OF CHRIST

The doctrine of the Person of Christ, not His Church, not His sacraments, not His teaching, not even the truths about Him, nor the virtues which He most enforces, *but Himself;* that only which bars fanaticism and idolatry on the one hand, and gives life and power to all morality on the other. And this is what St. Paul constantly opposes to the several idolatries of the Judaizers. See Colossians ii.; 1 Tim. iv., connecting with it the last verse of chap. iii., which has been so strangely severed from its context.

(e) *Dr. Arnold*

PERSUADED

"*I am persuaded*," etc. (Rom. viii.)

None can take Christ from thee, unless thou takest Him from thyself.

(f) *Ambrose*

PETER THE APOSTLE

"*Peter an Apostle of Jesus Christ*" (1 Pet. i. 1)

1. "Simon Peter" = son of Jonas; brother of Andrew; born at Bethsaida, a village on sea coast of Galilee, where many minds desired the coming of Messiah. He had a house at Capernaum, and followed the occupation of a fisherman.

He was first brought to Christ by his brother

(g)

Andrew, who was a disciple of John the Baptist, and had heard John the Baptist say, "Behold the Lamb of God," and who had previously become a disciple of Christ Himself.

"The Searcher of Hearts" surnamed him Cephas—Peter—the man of rock.

(i.) From his natural disposition;

(ii.) A prediction of what grace would make him.

(a)

2. Simon the Fisherman

(i.) A man of fiery temper, not accustomed to mince his words, would use strong language when provoked and irritated;

(ii.) Quick resolution, mind soon made up, prompt in action, hasty and impulsive;

(iii.) Fearless courage, a seaman's quality, undaunted in danger, this quality comes out especially in his later life;

(iv.) Candour, no reserves, no tricks, no meannesses, truthful, nothing of the Jacob in him, not very profound. His character easily read—child-like.

This is the man that comes to Christ, who becomes a Christian, and these natural qualities have to be purified. This meal is to be leavened by contact with Jesus Christ, and by the power of the Holy Ghost. In the end he will become, not only the daring fisherman, but the daring Apostle.

(b)

3. A Permanent Disciple

Peter is not added as a permanent disciple until after sundry meetings and conversations.

(i.) The turning point was (Luke v. 1–11), the miraculous draught of fishes;

(ii.) Invariably named first in the four lists. One of the more prominent disciples;

(iii.) He shares with John and James the more intimate friendship of the Lord, because He and they had a truer insight or perception of the Divinity of Christ. Witness his confession of Christ (Matt. xvi. 15).

This precedency is a first among equals only, not above.

For the power of "the keys," given to Peter in one place (Matt. xvi. 19), is also given to the whole company (Matt. xviii. 18).

He became (naturally it would seem) the spokesman of the twelve.

[John the bosom friend; Peter the spokesman; Judas the bursar.]

(c)

4. Diversified Experience

From this time, the experience of the disciples is very diversified.

The path along which he goes, is a zig-zag, now up, now down, until the work of purification is done.

(i.) Matt. xiv. 28. He thinks himself strong: Jesus lets him sink.

But Jesus is ready to help "immediately" the sinking one cries out.

(ii.) Matt. xvi. 17. "Blessed art thou, Simon," etc.

Matt. xvi. 22. "Get thee behind me, Satan." After the blessing he is puffed up, he inverts the position of master and disciple, he leads instead of following, hence the rebuke.

(iii.) Matt. xvii. 4. Mount of Transfiguration.

"It is good to be here, let us build," etc.=let us dwell here. It was like going to heaven on a bed of roses. Whilst the contrary is "good" for an unripened man.

(iv.) Matt. xvii. 27. An instance of simple faith and obedience. "Go, cast a hook into the sea."

(v.) His inquiry concerning reward for having left all. (Matt. xix. 27);

(vi.) His refusal to let the Saviour wash his feet, "Thou shalt never," etc., followed by the opposite extreme (John xiii. 8), "Lord, not my feet only, but also my hands," etc.

(vii.) Matt. xxvi. 35. His promise to go with Christ to prison and to death;

His asseveration rather to die than to deny Christ;

Followed closely by his three-fold terrible fall (Matt. xxvi. 58–69).

Connect the wilful act of defence with the sword (John xvii. 10, 11).

(viii.) Matt. xxvi. 75. The look of Jesus, and his bitter repentance, followed by a special message, and appearance of the Risen Lord (Luke xxiv. 34; 1 Cor. xv. 5).

(ix.) His loving zeal. "Cast his fisher's coat," etc. He had evidently gone back to his fishing nets (John xxi. 7).

His restoration. The thrice-repeated "Lovest thou Me?" A trial of his candour and of his temper. The swelling of inward feeling and emotion (in old times oaths), now it breaks in spray. "Thou knowest all things," etc.

(x.) He is foretold his destiny, "When thou art old," etc. (John xxi. 18).

(d)

5. The Apostle

By this time his character was shaped. And after the Descent of the Holy Ghost, Simon becomes PETER, an Apostle of Jesus Christ. "Thy loving correction hath made me great" (Ps. xviii. 35).

As an Apostle, he is distinguished—

(i.) *As a preacher:* He abounds in the Preacher's gifts, and has the faculty of catching men. Thousands under his instrumentality were added to the Church. A true Gospel fisherman.

(ii.) *By his writings:* "When thou art converted strengthen thy brethren." This he does emphatically in his Epistles.

Peter laboured chiefly among his fellow-countrymen. His special qualifications are for Jewish listeners, not fitted for Greek culture. Peter knew nothing of the refined heathenism that Paul knew of.

He appears to have gone to the Jews at Rome, and there to have been crucified with his head downwards (*Eusebius*).

> And I shall share a glorious part
> When grace hath well refined my heart,
> And every power find sweet employ
> In that eternal world of joy.

(e)

PETER, FALL OF (John xviii. 25)

1. "Who" is the denier?

Is it Judas, who secretly disliked Jesus?

Is it timid Nicodemus, who was afraid to be seen with Him?

(f)

Peter, Fall of—*continued*

Is it Thomas, who doubted?

Is it Philip, who questioned His power?

We might conceive of some of these going a step further and denying Christ.

No; none of these.

Is it Peter, the prominent disciple, the one of four other disciples, the chosen friends of Christ?

Is it Peter the rock—the confessor of Christ as "the Son of God"?

Yes; it IS Peter.

Peter, who said he would go with Him to prison and to death.

Peter, who said he would be the last of all men to do such a thing as that, "Though all men should deny Thee, yet will not I."

PETER, who had been on the transfiguration-hill with Jesus, and had seen His glory.

Peter, who had witnessed His agony in the garden.

Yes, incredible as it may seem, PETER denies Christ.

He says, "I know not the man."

We exclaim with the Psalmist: "Lord, what is man?"

What is even a converted man, a Christian man, a disciple?

"Let him that thinketh he standeth take heed lest he fall."

(a)

2. Whom does he Deny?

Is it a fellow-disciple, such as John and James? No. His own Master.

His Master, whom he not only seemed to love but did really love.

His Master, who had been teaching and training him for three years.

And for whom he had given up his fishing nets, and forsaken everything.

He denies Him, whom, by his own confession and by the revelation of God, he knew to be, not merely man, but "the Son of the living God."

Oh, incredible mystery of evil!

Oh, desperate wickedness of the human heart—deceitful above all things and desperately wicked!

A Christian to deny Christ.

(b)

3. What does Peter Do?

He does not merely forsake Christ.

All the disciples did that.

The suffering Saviour was to suffer alone.

Isaiah had said long before—"Of the people there was none with Me."

When the shepherd was smitten, the sheep were scattered.

Peter does what none of them do.

He denies Him.

In this he stands alone.

No one but Peter had said, "I know not the man;" and, to aggravate the matter, no one but Peter had so lately said, "We know that Thou art the Christ."

See, then, what ingratitude, what inconsistency, what cowardice are here!

But should we have done anything else if we had been there?

Would our hearts have borne us through, if we had been so sorely pressed ourselves?

Have there not been occasions when we have

been ashamed of Christ, of His Cross, and of His people? Have there not been occasions when we have been ashamed of confessing His name, lest we should be laughed at and suffer ridicule? Let conscience speak, and it will tell us, we too have denied Christ.

(c)

4. When did he Deny Christ?

Great falls and sins are aggravated if they tread close upon great mercies.

And in point of fact they usually do. Whether it is that Satan, the adversary, is more watchful at such times than at others, we know not; yet the fact remains, that after great blessings come great temptations.

And if a fall succeeds, that too is a great one.

The history of David is a case in point.

There was little danger of his falling into so great a sin as his, during those years when he was hunted like a partridge in the wilderness.

But when he has reached the throne, and gained the victory over his enemies, then comes the moment of supreme danger.

He is tempted above what he is able to bear, and he falls. And what a fall!

David, the man after God's own heart; and Peter, the fearless and foremost Christian, become, the one a murderer, the other an apostate.

Peter's sin, too, treads close upon a great mercy.

Peter has just left the Lord's table. He has had a few moments of precious soul-intercourse with Jesus.

They have sung a hymn together;

They have prayed together;

They have broken bread together;

The cup has been passed round, and they have all drunk of it.

Think what a night that was; It was on that evening that our Lord uttered those remarkable words contained in the thirteenth to the seventeenth chapters of St. John.

His farewell discourses, about His leaving them and going to the Father—to His Father and their Father.

There is nothing in the whole Bible, nothing in all the literature of the world, to match those four or five chapters.

And there, too, in that upper room, He prayed that prayer which we find in the seventeenth of John, that wondrous intercessory prayer for His people.

"Father, the hour is come."

"I have finished the work which Thou gavest Me to do."

"I have manifested Thy name unto the men which Thou gavest me out of the world."

"They have known that all things whatsoever Thou hast given Me are of Thee."

"I have given them Thy word, and they have received it, and have known surely that I came out from Thee, and they have believed."

"I pray for them."

Peter heard all this, and it was after all this that Peter denied Christ.

It seems incredible, and impossible that Peter should have denied Christ on that night of all others.

And yet the thing is too common. Christ has been denied a thousand times since then, and by His friends too-

(d)

Peter, Fall of—*continued*

By those who have tasted of His love; who have ate and drunk with Him ; by those who have no more doubt of their relation to Him than they have of their own existence. Yet, like Peter, "immediately after supper," immediately after the warning of Gethsemane, they have come upon some sudden temptation, they have been thrown down by it, and in a moment of cowardice have denied Him.

Not because they did not love Him, nor because they had not valued that sweet intercourse with Him. Not so, but because they had over-measured their strength ; because they were unwatchful and unprayerful ; because they had forgotten the exhortation :

"Let him that thinketh he standeth take heed lest he fall."

(*a*)

5. Where did this Denial Take Place?

In a hall of the High Priest's Palace.

In another part of the same building Jesus was undergoing examination before the High Priest.

John, the friend of Peter, was an acquaintance of the High Priest, and consequently found easy admission into the place where the trial was going on.

But Peter was kept standing without. No one knew him.

Presently John asked the girl, who acted as doorkeeper, to admit his friend Peter.

The girl, thinking that she might incur some guilt by admitting an accomplice, and perhaps having had previous orders to take care whom she admitted, asked him, as he stepped inside—

"Art thou not also one of this man's disciples?"

Then and there he replied : "I AM NOT."

Peter probably had no evil intention in this his first denial.

He wanted to be inside the palace, to see the issue of the trial.

If it were known that he was a disciple, or even an adherent of Jesus, there would be no chance for him; and so, when the question is put to him, he ventures upon "a white lie."

He intends no harm by it, and he fancies no harm will come of it. He merely wants to escape detection and expulsion.

In fact, Peter only does here what a great many Christian people are constantly in the habit of doing.

They adopt SOME of the practices of the world.

They would hesitate to tell a direct lie ; but they stoop to subterfuge, and "white lies," as they are called, and use language which disguises their thoughts.

Peter in his heart did not deny Christ. He had no such intention. But being where he was, he had put himself in the way of a great temptation ; and the time was now come for him to learn, by this terrible slip, that he cannot touch pitch and not be defiled.

The Christian cannot ever so slightly do as the world does, and not suffer loss.

"Come ye out, and be ye separate."

But Peter mingled with the world a little ; Peter told a little lie to begin with ; and, presently, he had to tell a bigger one to prop the other up ; and then, finally, the torrent became too strong, the dam was broken down by its force, and every wicked thing that Peter could say, was said, in order to help him out of the scrape.

Yes, in the High Priest's palace, within hearing of his Lord, Peter denied Him.

If he had been there at all, we might have thought he would have come to defend the innocent.

It was the hour of danger ; it was the moment when the enemies of Christ had got Him in their power.

We might have expected Peter to come bursting in, with his sword red with the blood of Malchus' ear, exclaiming, "Let this man go!"

And if, in his zeal and righteous indignation, he felt himself compelled to use strong language, it might have been lavished on the unjust judge and the false witnesses met together in that hall.

Such indignation has been felt and expressed at the recital of Jesus' wrongs.

Somewhere during the Middle Ages, a missionary was reading, from the gospel narrative, the story of the unjust trial of Jesus and of the Crucifixion ; and he was interrupted by a rude Goth, who, letting down his spear upon the ground with a sharp sound, and with a loud oath, exclaimed—"Would God I had been there!"

We might conceive of Peter acting in the same spirit, if he came to the post of danger at all— because Peter was no coward : he was ready to use the sword, and head a party who should liberate Jesus.

His whole sin sprung from some other cause.

He does not want to be known ; and when he is suddenly taken unawares, and taxed with being an accomplice, he thinks a lie, under the circumstances, the best policy.

He does not know that he too is on his trial that night—that Satan is trying to have him, and that there is a contest going on between Christ and Satan, as to who should have him.

(*b*)

6. How does he Deny Christ?

He did it after being warned by the Lord;
He did it in the most decided way;
He did it with oaths and curses.

Not once only, but three times did he deny Christ.

(i.) "Woman, I know Him not";
(ii.) "Man, I know Him not";
(iii.) "Man, I know not what thou sayest"- and then the oaths and the curses burst forth.

The old fisherman of Galilee, it would seem, in days gone by, had been a man who used strong language.

Since he had been a disciple of Christ, he had learned to control his language. Three years' intercourse with Christ had done much for him, but it had not done all.

The "old man" was still alive and strong. The "new man" was very weak in Peter just at this time.

The "old man" had risen up against the "new man."

The old nature in Peter was fighting against the Christ that was within him ; and if the Lord had not just at that worst moment turned and looked upon Peter, the issue might have been more disastrous than it was.

We think an old habit dead, when it is only asleep.

(*c*)

Peter, Fall of—*continued*

Peter, perhaps, had not made use of an oath for nearly three years; and he was thinking that the old habit was dead, and that "all things were become new," when all of a sudden the temptation was presented, and the old habit revived with all its force. The old blasphemies broke out again; and, worse than all, they come forth to clench his denial of his Master—he says: "May I be cursed for ever if I know the man." The giant sin was not dead, it was only asleep.

As we read such language of this disciple, we exclaim "Simon, son of Jonas, is it thou? Peter, is that thy voice?"

Ah, if Jesus had heard it—what would He say? How would He feel?

Why, this is far worse than standing before His enemies.

He did hear. He heard the three-fold denial; He heard the oaths and curses, for He was passing by Peter (as he stood by the fire) at the very moment he uttered them. He heard it all. But He did not speak—He showed no anger—He looked very sorrowful—He turned His face and looked full on Peter. Oh, what a look that was! The curses only drew out His love, and the love conquered.

Peter saw what he had done—he had been stabbing his Master to the very heart. He had been putting another thorn into His crown. He had been driving a nail into His cross, and piercing Him with another spear—wounding Him in the house of His friends.

Peter went out then.

For the next three days he was almost in despair. But the work was done.

It was his last denial—his last oath. Satan had sifted him, and found much chaff, but the Lord steps in and takes care of His own wheat.

The first thought of the risen Lord is for the weeping, broken-hearted disciple.

The angels say, "Go and tell His disciples and Peter."

And soon it is said, "The Lord is risen indeed and hath appeared unto Simon."

And when afterwards he is pointedly reminded of his sin by the thrice-repeated question, "Simon son of Jonas, lovest thou Me?" The answer of the disciple is, "Lord, Thou knowest all things, Thou searchest the heart and knowest what is in man, Thou knowest that I did deny Thee; but Thou knowest that I did not know how much evil was in my heart; Thou knowest that I entered into temptation, thinking I was too strong to fall under temptation; Thou knowest it all, and needest not that I should confess it—notwithstanding all this, Lord, Thou knowest my heart—Thou knowest that I love Thee."

(*a*)

7. The Fall of Peter is a significant Type of the Church of Rome

Rome herself builds so much upon Peter.

Let us concede her claims to this (whether true or not).

She shall have all she asks for: only it is Peter whom we have just seen—fallen Peter, that she has any true likeness to.

Peter fell.

The Church of Rome has fallen.

Peter denied Christ.

The Church of Rome has denied Christ.

Peter said, "I know not the man." The Church of Rome, by her false teaching, by her worship of angels and saints, and by her mariolatry, says to all the world, "I know not the man."

Peter denied with oaths and curses—the Church of Rome has done the same, she curses every one outside the pale of her communion.

Her curses, though now impotent, used to be terrible.

And to this day she is herself a curse upon every people and every nation ver whom she has power.

The Church of Rome finds her type in the fallen Peter.

In Peter's fall—in his denying Christ—in his oaths and curses—she has only too truly become his successor.

The Church of Rome has fallen from her first love, and has never repented.

The Church of Rome denies Christ, by pointing to the Church, and not to Christ.

And all those in league with her—those who copy her practices—and who are at this day, whether in this or any other country, doing all they can to draw us back into her fold again—all such, are successors of fallen Peter: they deny Christ, they say by their teaching, "I know Him not."

And not unfrequently their conduct and intemperate language show that they are prepared to go as far as Peter went, and to clench their denial with oaths and curses.

(*b*)

8. Let us learn the danger of neglecting the precepts of Christ

For we may well suspect ourselves, when we look upon the fall of such a man as the loving disciple.

If he denied his Lord, what may not we do in a moment of sore temptation, if we cease to watch and pray lest we enter into it.

Let us learn, further, to watch against presumptuous sinning—sinning with the hope of pardon; lest we say in our hearts, Christ will restore us and overrule evil for good, and so we become careless about sinning. For if we sin wilfully, after having the knowledge of the truth,—against light, and against the will of God made known to us in His word,—depend upon it, we may have Peter's fall without having Peter's recovery.

(*c*)   *Cf. H. Bonar*

"*I will lay down my life for Thee*" (John xiii. 37)

Peter imagined that he could precede his guide. Presumptuous supposition! It was necessary that Christ should first lay down His life for the salvation of Peter, before Peter could be able to lay down his life for the Gospel of Christ. But when Christ had died for Peter, and redeemed him by His own blood, and had risen from the dead, then Peter was able to follow Christ, even to the cross.

(*d*)   *Augustine*

Jesus answers, "*Verily, verily*. Lay down thy life for Me! Thou wilt not so much as confess Me. On the contrary, thou wilt deny Me. And that three times. And this will come to pass directly, before the cock hath crowed, before the ensuing morning. "*Let him that thinketh he standeth*," etc.

(*e*)   *Lange*

Christ must die for Peter, before Peter can die for Christ.

(a)   *Hedinger*

Peter proves that a man is always better than his bad, but worse than his good moods.

(b)   *Braune*

Peter (*a little child*, 33) would be a *man* before his time,

(c)   *Plain Commentary*

Peter was *inconsiderate*, not *insincere;* we are apt to think we can do *anything;* but without Christ we can do *nothing*. It is good for us to *shame ourselves* out of our *presumptuous* confidence; shall a bruised reed set up for a pillar, or a sickly child undertake to be a champion? Christ not only foresaw that Judas would betray Him, but that Peter would deny Him; He knows not only the *wickedness of sinners*, but the *weakness of saints*. The most *secure* are commonly the least *safe*.

(d)   *M. Henry*

PETER AND ENTHUSIASM

Enthusiasm is the glow of the soul; enthusiasm is the lever by which men are raised above their average level and enterprise, and become capable of a goodness and benevolence which, but for it, would be quite impossible. There is not too much enthusiasm of any sort, or for any object, in a world like ours, and Christians had better not join in sneering at a force which in its purest form founded and reared the Church of Jesus Christ. True, enthusiasm often loses its way, spends itself on mistaken causes, on imperfect systems, on worthless ideals, but that is no reason for saying that all enthusiasm is bad. Mistaken enthusiasm, like St. Peter's, will in time be rudely tested by experience; and meanwhile those who have any reason to hope that their enthusiasm is not mistaken, can afford to be generous and hopeful about others. He that is not against us is, unconsciously perhaps, on our side.

(e)

A past fact is a permitted fact; and antecedent circumstances, when they influence our destiny, are the hand of God, acting through accomplished events, and so far suspending or limiting personal liberty. . . . We only weaken ourselves by dwelling upon mischiefs which we cannot hope to remedy. We have only a certain amount of thought, of feeling, of resolve, each one of us, to dispose of. And when this has been expended unavailingly on the abstract, on the intangible, it is expended: it is no longer ours, and we cannot employ it when and where we need it close at home. . . . Peter failed as he did because he had expended his moral strength in words, and had no sufficient force to dispose of when the time came for action and for suffering.

(f)

The enthusiasm of the Crusaders, fired by indignation at the thought that

The sun now rises on the minaret;
And desolation lingers o'er the walls
Where angels once, like its own mountain band,
Shout round Jerusalem. Through that blessed realm
Scarce does a sacred track unharmed remain,
By Nazareth's lone hills or silent lake.

(g)

"The Lord was not in the fire." Religious passion carried to the highest point of enthusiasm is a great agency in human life; but religious passion may easily be too inconsiderate, too truculent, too entirely wanting in tenderness and in charity, to be in any sense divine. Christendom has also been ablaze again and again with fires, and these fires are not extinct in our own day and country, of which it may certainly be said that the Lord is not in them.

(h)   *Liddon*

PETER AND FORGIVENESS (Acts i. 15)

Whenever I look at Peter, my heart leaps for joy. For although I am a poor sinner, Peter also was a poor sinner: if I should paint a portrait of Peter, I would paint on every hair of his head the words, "I believe in the forgiveness of sins."

(i)   *Luther*

PETER, the Gospel Fisherman (Luke v. 10)

1. Special significance. Compare—
(i.) *Thou shalt catch men* (Peter, a fisherman).
(ii.) *Thou shalt feed men* (David, a shepherd).
(iii.) *I have set before thee an open door* (Paul).

Qualifications for this office:

(i.) Candidates must first be caught themselves, or they will hesitate between Christ and their fishing-nets. At first Peter and others undecided; they continued fishermen. But our Lord hastens nothing. He sows the seed, and waits. The time of fruit is later on.

This gradual process, common, but not the rule. Some statues are cast in moulds and formed immediately; others are hewn, shaped, and polished, are perfected through a trying process. Why *such* men are called, is answered (1 Cor. i. 27). God intends to call emperors, the wise, the noble, etc., but He began with the weak and despised things of this world, that the work might be seen to be His. Amos (O. T.) was not a prophet, nor a prophet's son, but a herdman: yet God chose him, and said, "Go, prophesy to My people Israel." God is tied to no method, and to no order of men. Peter acts on our Lord's words, draws the net to land; he sees by an inspiration that the *Second Man* is before him "*who has dominion over the fish of the sea*." That decides him. He is himself caught in the Gospel net.

(ii.) There must be also a special *revelation* of God to the man—either to the eye or to the conscience.

"*Henceforth*"=that not before *this*, but after the revelation of God, Peter becomes a Gospel fisherman.

Compare Moses, "I am slow of speech"; *Isaiah*, "I am a man of unclean lips"; *Peter*, "Depart, I am a sinful man, O Lord."

But He who came, not to destroy but to save, said, "*I will be with thee*": "*Thine iniquity is taken away*"; "*Fear not*," etc., whilst to us it says, "*While we were yet sinners Christ died for us*."

"Henceforth" each goes to his work; "they catch men."

(j)

The promise that Peter should become a fisher of men was made still more impressive by a great symbolical miracle.

(k)

(i.) The number of fish caught at Jesus' word represented the men he should some day take.

(ii.) As he fished all night and caught nothing, so had he afterwards to labour long in Israel without winning a single human soul.

(iii.) So, too, at Jesus' word he put further out into the deep of the Gentile world, and drew there a great draught.

(iv.) Last of all there were two boats to fill—the Gentile-Christian and the Jewish-Christian Churches. Then the net began to tear, and the opposition of these two sections threatened the Church with a grievous schism. But the draught was brought safely to land, to the confounding of the circumcised Jew, through whose instrumentality this divine action had been brought about.

(a)   *Weiss*

PETER, THE MESSAGE OF THE ANGEL TO

" *And Peter* " (Mark xvi. 7)

It is remarkable that Peter is singled out for special notice. It was proof of the *kindness* and *mercy* of the Lord Jesus. Peter, just before the death of Jesus, had denied Him. He had brought dishonour on his profession of attachment to Him. He had been brought to see the crime, and to weep bitterly. It would have been right if the Lord Jesus had from that moment cast him off, and noticed him no more. But He loved him still. *Having loved him once, He loved unto the end* " (John xiii. 1). As a proof that He forgave him, and still loved him, He sent him this special message, the assurance that though he had denied Him, and had done much to aggravate His sufferings, yet He had risen, and was still his Lord and Redeemer. We are not to infer, because the angel said, " *and Peter*," that Peter was not still a disciple. Before his fall, Jesus had prayed for him that his faith should not fail (Luke xxii. 32); and as the prayer of Jesus was always heard (John xi. 42), it follows that Peter retained faith sufficient to be a disciple, though, like other disciples, he was suffered to fall into sin.

(b)   *Barnes*

PHARISAISM

Pharisaism is a religious sin. No one but a religious person can be a true Pharisee. He is not necessarily a hypocrite. St. Paul was a Pharisee, never a hypocrite.

(c)

PHARISEE

" *A man of the Pharisees* " (John iii.)

The whole discourse with Nicodemus based on the fact that he was a *Pharisee*.

1. The Pharisee thought that he *was in the kingdom of God*."
Jesus = " He cannot *see* it."

2. The Pharisee did not believe in the *forgiveness of sins*.
Jesus = *Brazen serpent*.

3. The Pharisee did not believe that God loved the Gentiles.
Jesus = " *The whole world*."

(d)

PHARISEE AND THE PUBLICAN

" *And He spake this parable unto certain which trusted in themselves that they were righteous, and despised others* " (Luke xviii. 9–14)

Two representative men are at prayer : the one a Pharisee and the other a Publican, *i.e.*, the one a religious man, and the other an irreligious man.

1. The Pharisee

The Pharisees were a religious party among the Jews, who dated from the time of the Babylonian Captivity. Before that time the prevailing sin of the Jews was idolatry. After their captivity their prevailing sin was self-righteousness. And of that self-righteousness the Pharisees were the outcome. They corresponded, in some degree, to our modern High Churchmen, and were opposed by a Free-thinking party called Sadducees, who denied the existence of angel or spirit, and consequently of a future existence. The Pharisees placed great weight on the external rites and ceremonies of religious worship and practice. The Sadducees regarded these as mere superstition. Thus we find, throughout the New Testament, these two parties were constantly opposed to each other. And yet, with all their faults, there was something right in each party. Pharisaism was right, if we regard it as a protest against irreverence and infidelity, just as, in the present day, Sacerdotalism is right, as a protest against Latitudinarianism, which either believes nothing or believes everything.

But when we regard Pharisaism as the greatest and oldest development of self-righteousness, it is, as far as true religion is concerned, fearfully and perilously in the wrong.

(e)

For true religion consists in two Fundamentals :

2. The Forgiveness of Sins and the Gift of the Holy Ghost

Without these there is no true religion. Taking these then as our standard, it is comparatively easy to see wherein any other system comes short. Christ came to reveal these two things as lying at the very root of true Religion ; and where we have a Religion without them, there we have a false Religion, or, at the most, a religious system without the central sun.

" Other foundation can no man lay, than that is laid," viz. : The Forgiveness of Sin, and the Gift of the Spirit.

Now compare the religion of the Pharisee with this. At the very outset, we find the strict Pharisee rejected both these fundamentals. One of the very best of the Pharisees (Nicodemus) knew nothing of either : for when our Lord talked to him of them as necessaries, he exclaimed, " How can these things be ? "

Regeneration by the Holy Ghost ! what could a good and a pious Jew, a true son of Abraham, want with that ? Was he not already in the kingdom, already a child of God, already sure of heaven ? could it be a peradventure for him, " a master in Israel ? " But how, we ask, could a Pharisee quiet his conscience when it spoke to him of judgment to come ? He did so, undoubtedly, as men do now when they are dis-

(f)

Pharisee and the Publican—*continued*

quieted by the thought of sin and shortcomings, and of the necessity of preparing to meet their God. They satisfy their consciences by religious observances. They multiply forms and services; they do more than the law requires; they will earn heaven; they will make God their debtor, and not be in His debt. This is the root of the whole system of self-righteousness; and so strict is the outward life of such men, that one of them said to our Lord, "All these have I kept from my youth up, what lack I yet?" Briefly, then, a Pharisee knew nothing of the Forgiveness of Sins, and of the Gift of the Holy Ghost; and, in the place of these, he went about trying to establish his own righteousness.

(*a*)

3. Woe to the Pharisee

Seven times did our Lord utter woes against the Pharisees, "Woe unto you Scribes, Pharisees, Hypocrites." He compared them to "whited sepulchres," outwardly beautiful, but within full of all uncleanness.

The Forerunner, too, had denounced them as a "generation of vipers, how can ye escape the damnation of hell?"

The Pharisee,—outwardly a saint, inwardly a hypocrite, with his long prayers and ostentatious almsgiving, with illuminated texts of Scripture worn on the fringe of his dress and on the peak of his cap, with his punctilious fastings and scrupulous payment of tithes,—stood a living lie.

(*b*)

4. The Pharisee's Prayer

Coming into the Temple, he sweeps to the front where other eyes may see him. He confesses no sin. *He* has broken no commandment. *He* has left undone nothing that he ought to have done. He has kept his fasts, made his prayers, paid his tithes. He gives God no glory—he makes no petition—he offers no thanksgiving. He asks not for the Holy Spirit, he needs no enlightenment, no conversion. As "a son of Abraham," he is safe! He tells God what he is, and what he has done. He fasts twice in the week, whereas Moses required one. He has overpaid his account, therefore God is his debtor. He next tells God what he is not: He is not as other men are; he is an exceptional man. Other men are unjust, extortioners, adulterers,—if he could sink them lower, in his self-exaltation, he would—is there a deeper depth to which man could fall? Yes. He casts his eye around, it falls on the Publican, just entered; and perhaps he hears the ejaculation, "God, be merciful to me a sinner." This affords the Pharisee a fitting peroration, "*Or even as this Publican.*"

(*c*)

5. The Pharisee's Spiritual Pride

Pride cost Nebuchadnezzar his reason;
Pride, Hezekiah his kingdom;
Pride cost the angels that sinned heaven; and
Pride, such as this, would shut the Pharisee out of heaven.

David, the man after God's own heart, prayed, "Enter not into judgment with Thy servant, O Lord."

Job, the matchless saint, prayed, "I hate and abhor myself."

Ezra, the zealous reformer, prayed, "O my God, I am ashamed to lift up my face to my God." But the Pharisee, with such models of piety before him, enters God's temple and says-

"God, I thank Thee I am not as other men are."

(*d*)

6. The Publican

A man of no religious profession. A collector of the Roman tribute, levied on a subjugated people—a hateful tax, and the collectors shared the obloquy. The Publicans were for this reason outcasts from society. Consequently their lives warranted their reputation. One of the last places to find a Publican, would be the Temple. Yet such an event did happen. Jesus sees in such a man a lost sheep of the house of Israel, whom He, the Good Shepherd came to seek and to save.

This man "stood afar off." He would not so much as lift up his eyes unto heaven, but smote upon his breast, saying, "God, be merciful to me a sinner." True prayer—confession of sin and faith in God's mercy.

(*e*)

7. Afterwards

Both have prayed, both go home. The Pharisee as he came; but this Publican went home a "*justified man*"="Being justified by faith, we have peace with God, through our Lord Jesus Christ."

(*f*)

8. It is on record that,

An Indian and a white man became Christians. The Indian, almost as soon as he heard the Gospel, believed. But the white man struggled on in darkness for a long time before the light broke in. Afterwards he said to the Indian, "Why was I kept so long in darkness, whilst you almost immediately found peace?"

The Indian replied, "I will tell you: A Prince comes and offers you a coat. You look at your own coat and say, 'Mine is a good one,' and you refuse his offer. But the Prince comes to me and offers me too a coat, I look at my old tattered blanket, throw it off, and accept His offer at once. You, sir, were clinging to your own righteousness, you thought it sufficient, and you kept it. But I had nothing—a sinner; and so when Jesus offered me His righteousness, in place of my own rags, I simply took it."

(*g*)   *Cf. Hengstenberg, Guthrie, Trench*

PHARISEE

The Pharisee in the parable "believed rightly, but was not a right believer."

(*h*)   *Martensen*

PHARISEES AND SADDUCEES

Hengstenberg remarks, that the Pharisees were specially hostile to the doctrine of regeneration (John iii.), and resolved religion into a self-made holiness. But the Sadducees were even more opposed to spiritual religion. A Paul could proceed from the earnest Pharisees, but not from the frivolous and sceptical Sadducees.

(*i*)   *P. Schaff*

PHARISEES AND STOICS

Start from different points, but end alike.

(i.) The Jewish Pharisee,
(ii.) The Catholic Pharisee,
(iii.) The Protestant Pharisee,
(iv.) The Humanistic Pharisee.

The difference is great between them all, but the end is the same. They all converge to one point.

" Except your righteousness shall exceed the righteousness of the scribes and Pharisees, ye shall in no case enter the kingdom of heaven" (Matt. v. 20).

(a)　　　　　　　　　*Adapted from Martensen*

PHILIP AND THE ETHIOPIAN (Acts viii. 26-40)

In this whole transaction:

(i.) The beginning, (ii.) The progress, (iii.) The close, (iv.) The command, (v.) The direction, and (vi.) The operation of God are conspicuously revealed.

The natural features, too, are not less wonderful :

Philip, and this stranger from a distant country —the Israelitic evangelist and the heathen—the ὁδηγός, and the man who was seeking and was open to conviction ; that is to say, two persons between whom a species of " pre-established harmony" exists, are here brought together. Now this association of circumstances is the result of a divine interposition, which, in all its aspects, is not less astonishing, nor less essentially a miraculous procedure, than when God sends an angel, or suddenly removes the evangelist, without an effort on his own part, from the sight of the eunuch. And the celerity with which the harvest follows seedtime in the soul of the Ethiopian, is fully as wonderful as the invisible process which resulted in the disappearance of Philip.

(b)　　　　　　　　　　　　　　　　*Lange*

Philip, and Preaching Jesus

Then Philip opened his mouth, and began at the same Scripture, and preached unto him Jesus" (Acts viii. 35)

Note,

1. The action of the Holy Spirit

Philip directed to leave his post, where he was doing a successful work, and go away south into a desert, away from human habitations and people. Presently a cavalcade advances—a eunuch of great authority is returning from Jerusalem, where, apparently, he had been inquiring of the authorized and recognised spiritual leaders the way of salvation, and came empty away.

The Spirit directeth Philip to join himself to the chariot ; and he found the eunuch reading Isaiah liii., and ready to be instructed concerning Christ. " Then Philip," etc.

(c)

2. The Pre-existing Harmony between the two Men ;

To the man seeking, God sends another man who can help him. Two men, utter strangers to each other, suddenly meet on life's road, and the meeting is of eternal importance to the spiritual well-being of one of them.

It is related that a certain heathen man became convinced that he was a sinner. He had no peace, and no Bible to guide him. He went to the priests of his religion, stated his case, saying that he was miserable. What must he do ? They said : " Give money—make large offerings to the gods, and you will have what you want." He did so, being rich, but remained as miserable as before. He went to the priests a second time, and told them that their former prescription had failed. Now they said, " Go on pilgrimage—go from shrine to shrine, from temple to temple, and as you go, torture your body by scourging, etc." He did so, but with no good result. One day, dragging his weary frame along, worn out in body and mind, he saw a crowd of people under a tree, standing round a man, who was speaking to them with a loud impressive voice. He lay down outside the crowd and listened. The man was a missionary, and was preaching about Jesus Christ, the Lamb of God, which taketh away the sins of the world. The man was startled, it suited his case exactly ; he jumped up, looked at the preacher, who was then saying, " The blood of Jesus Christ cleanseth us from all sin," and could restrain himself no longer, rushed forward, exclaiming, " That's it, that's it ; that's what I want ; tell me more about that blood." God had directed the seeker and the preacher to meet. It was the story of Philip and the eunuch over again.

(d)

3. Preaching Jesus

Philip began at the same Scripture, and preached unto him Jesus.

(e)

See "Remarkable Death-bed Experience," p. 169.

PHILOSOPHER IN VOGUE

You say you cannot understand how Lord Shaftesbury came to be a philosopher in vogue. I will tell you. First, he was a lord ; secondly, he was as vain as any of his readers ; thirdly, men are very prone to believe what they do not understand ; fourthly, they will believe anything at all, provided they are under no obligation to believe it ; fifthly, they love to take a new road, even when that road leads nowhere ; sixthly, he was reckoned a fine writer, and seems always to mean more than he said. Would you have any more reasons ? An interval of above forty years has pretty well destroyed the charm. A dead lord ranks with commoners ; vanity is no longer interested in the matter, for a new road has become an old one.

　　　　　Gray, on Anthony Ashley Cooper,
(f)　　　　　　　　　　*Earl of Shaftesbury*

PHYSICIAN, THE GREAT

I will be loth to put you off your fears and your sense of deadness (I wish it were more) : there are some wounds whose bleeding should not be soon stopped. You must take a house beside the Physician ; it shall be a miracle if you be the first sick man He put away uncured, and worse than He found you. Nay, nay, Christ is honest, and in that, freely arguing with sinners. " And him that cometh to Me I will in no wise cast out " (John vi. 37). Take that ; it cannot be presumption to take that as your own, when you find your wounds pain you. Presumption is ever whole at the heart, and hath but the truant-sickness, and groaneth only for the fashion. Faith hath sense of sickness, and looketh like a friend to the promises ; and looking to Christ therein, is glad to see a known face.

(g)　　　　　　　　　　　*Samuel Rutherford*

PILATE (John xviii. and xix.)

Pilate constituted himself and his Roman authority constable of the hierarchy; and from this time forth he rushes to perdition.

Similar was the fate of the Maccabean house and, since then, of several European dynasties. The clean sundermen of Church and State is a vital impulse of the spirit of Christianity, one of the greatest tasks of Christian times.

(a)   *Lange*

PILATE AND CHRIST (John xviii. 37)

(This) marks the moment in which Pilate was confronted with salvation, and the form under which salvation advances towards him. It is the form in which He is able to preach the Gospel to this man in this position. If thou art of the truth, if the impulse of truth is the vital impulse that influenceth thee, thou wilt know Me, and thou art saved.

(b)   *Ibid*

PILATE AND JESUS (What is truth?)

The world-historical encounter of the Spirit of Christ with the genius of the Roman nation on the occasion of the discourse concerning His *Kingdom*, analogous to His encounter with the genius of the Greek nation (concerning *death*) (John xii. 20).

The *question of Pilate* no question, but a frivolous, unbelieving utterance. Characteristic of the Græco-Roman world-culture of his time.

Pilate surrendered *truth* first, and afterwards *justice* in consequence.

(c)   *Ibid*

PILATE AND THE JEWS (John xviii. and xix.)

Pilate's superstitious fear at the saying: "Jesus made Himself the Son of God," a characteristic trait of the unbeliever. The indissoluble connection between unbelief and superstition. But after all, unbelieving Pilate is more believing than the superstitious high priests, in the consummate unbelief with which they reject Christ. Of the three-fold terror of Pilate: his terror at the law, his terror of conscience, his religious terror, there appears no trace in these practical Atheists, who have donned the mask of the holiest zeal.

(d)   *Ibid*

(i.) They charge Jesus with being an ecclesiastical criminal whom they have already sentenced, and whose sentence Pilate has but to confirm.

(ii.) In the most ambiguous sense: With making Himself the King of the Jews.

(iii.) With being an ecclesiastical criminal, because He had made Himself the Son of God.

(iv.) With being a political revolutionist, because He claimed to be the King of the Jews.

(e)

PILGRIMAGE (Heb. xi. 9, 10)

Unlike the founders of Egypt, of Babylon, of Nineveh, the patriarchs were not the builders of cities and towns, but *pilgrims and sojourners, dwellers in tents* (Heb. xi. 9). But they were very different from rude hordes, like the Amalekites and other "sons of the desert," abhorring any higher mode of life. Abraham was no stranger to the highest form of civilization that his age afforded. He was acquainted with Ur, with Nineveh, with Damascus, with Egypt; he had left his home in one of the chief cities of Mesopotamia, not from choice, but in consequence of a direct personal call from God. Moreover, so far from regarding his present mode of life as an ultimate end, he and Isaac and Jacob were ever looking forward to a time when it would close, when their descendants should be *settled* in the land of promise, and become a great *nation*, when the portable *tent* should give way to the *city that had foundations*.

(f)   *Kurtz*

PILGRIM'S PROGRESS

He saw the things of which he was writing as distinctly with his mind's eye as if they were, indeed, passing before him in a dream.

(g)   *Robert Southey*

Bunyan's work is the poetry of Puritanism. A novel it cannot be called, for it has nothing to do with real life any more than the visions of Fifth Monarchy men had to do with practical forms of government. But, precisely for that reason, was it true to the age in which it was composed. The spirit that had overthrown the Stuarts is more visible in Bunyan's allegory than in "Milton's Defence."

(h)   *Edinburgh Review*, 1838

I know of no book (the Bible being excepted as above all comparison) which, according to my judgment and experience, I could so safely recommend as teaching and enforcing the whole saving truth, according to the mind that was in Christ Jesus, as the "Pilgrim's Progress." I am convinced that it is the best summary of Evangelical Christianity ever produced by a writer not miraculously inspired.

(i)   *Coleridge*

No man of common sense and integrity can deny that Bunyan was a practical Atheist, a worthless contemptible infidel, a vile rebel to God and goodness, a common profligate, a soul-despising, a soul-murdering, a soul-damning, thoughtless wretch as could exist on the face of the earth.

(j)   *Ryland*

The "Pilgrim's Progress" is, perhaps, the only book about which, after the lapse of a hundred years, the educated minority has come over to the opinion of the common people.

(k)   *Macaulay*

PILLARS

The two *pillars* of the Christian · "The Lord reigneth," and "God is love."

Neither despise His chastening nor faint under it.

(l)

ΠΙ΄ΣΤΙΣ and ΓΝΩ-ΣΙΣ (Luke xxi.)

The eschatological discourse is also remarkable on this account, that it shows that a connection according to the intent of our Lord exists and must exist between πίστις and γνῶσις.

The example of the Apostles, and His teaching show anew : there cannot possibly be any talk of γνῶσις so long as no πίστις precedes it. *Non intelligere ut credas, sed credere ut intelligas.*

(a)   *Lange*

PLAGIARISM

John Elias, having preached one of his most effective sermons, was significantly asked by a gentleman who dined with him, " whether he was acquainted with John Howe's works ? " Elias replied, " I have been, on several occasions, to Howe's warehouse for some tallow ; but I always manufacture my own candles."

(b)   *Memoir of Christmas Evans*

PLEASURE

Alas ! the greatest part of this world run to the place of torment, rejoicing, and dancing, eating, drinking, and sleeping.

(c)   *Samuel Rutherford*

In times of misfortune, the ancients supported themselves with Philosophy or Christianity ; the moderns again (for example, in the reign of Terror) take to Pleasure ; as the wounded buffalo, for bandage and salve, rolls himself in the mire.

(d)   *J. P. F. Richter*

PLOUGH, THE

We need, even after conversion, perpetual accessions of the grace of God, and repeated anointings of the Divine Spirit ; after these must we yearn, and eagerly receive them, like a well-prepared field.

For us also it may doubtless be said : " *The plough, or the curse.*"

(e)   *Starke*

POETS

As truly as Shakspeare is the poet of man, as God made him, dealing with great passions and innate motives ; so truly is Pope the poet of society, the delineator of manners, the exposer of those motives which may be called *acquired*, whose spring is in institutions and habits of purely worldly origin.

(f)   *James R. Lowell on Pope*

POLITICAL PARTIES

No man should allow himself to be biased by party interest so as to set aside the claims of truth, of justice, of purity, and of honour. You are bound to your party. I recognise the necessity and value of parties ; I belong to one myself, and I advocate that every man should belong to one ; I should just as soon think of making a journey, not by machinery, but on foot, as I should think of managing public affairs by letting every man act on his own hook. That is not the way toward patriotism ; that is the way to put the great community into the hands of cunning, scheming men. Wise organization for great ends and great principles, on the one side and on the other, is not only indispensable, but highly honourable. Presumptively, men will go with their fellows ; that is the general law. But whenever, under the stress of circumstances, any party is attempting to crush infidelity to principle, you ought to go with it ; as in the time when both the great parties vied with each other as to which would be most submissive to slavery ; or as when repudiation lifts its head in any State. No man has a right to go with any party that desecrates public trust and honesty. When policy that is fundamentally wrong is introduced into your party, you are released from your obligation to it, and sent to your individual conscience. But if there was a public sentiment so strong in the direction of rectitude that men would not vote with a party which favoured anything that was wrong ; if that spirit were once thoroughly infused into the whole mass of the community, how much higher our politics would rise ! and how much more honourable it would be !

(g)   *H. W. Beecher*

POLITICIAN

Every man, if he is a citizen, ought to be a *politician.* There are politicians and there are politicians. There are a great many men whose administration of public affairs is not to be praised. I do not urge any man to become a politician in the offensive sense of that term ; but I do say that no young man, no man, whatever his age may be, has any right, under our form of government, to let go, without consideration, and without personal influence and activity, his duties as a citizen. You have no business to remit to vulgar, selfish men the transaction of your affairs ; and the excuses that men make—that they have no time, that their business is urgent, or that they are disgusted with the way in which caucuses and primary meetings are managed—are not worthy of being listened to. I will not hear any such excuses. When you are born in this country, your very birth is a tacit oath that you will take care of the public. It is fundamental, imperative, and universal—not optional.

Every man should take part and lot, not only in the administration of the material wealth of the community, through public spirit, but also in the securing wise magistrates, good laws, and right economies. Public spirit in that direction is imperative upon every manly man.

(h)   *Ibid*

POOR, THE

" *Inasmuch as ye did,*" etc. (Matt. xxv. 40)

One evening at supper. One of the boys had said the pious grace, " *Come, Lord Jesus, be our guest, and bless what Thou hast provided,*" a little fellow looked up and said,—

" Do tell me why the Lord Jesus never comes ? we ask Him every day to sit with us, and He never comes."

" Dear child, only believe, and you may be sure He will come, for He does not despise our invitation."

(i)

"I shall set a seat," said the little fellow; and just then there was a knock at the door. A poor frozen apprentice entered, begging a night's lodging. He was made welcome; the chair stood empty for him; every child wanted him to have his plate; and one was lamenting that his bed was too small for the stranger, who was quite touched by such uncommon attentions. The little one had been thinking hard all the time.

"Jesus could not come, and so He sent this poor man in His place; is that it?"

"Yes, dear child, that is just it. Every piece of bread and every drink of water that we give to the poor, or the sick, or the prisoners for Jesu's sake, we give to Him." "*Inasmuch as,*" etc.

(a)   *Stephenson's Memoir of John Falk*

Poor, The

From grief exempt, I ne'er had dreamt
Of such a world of woe!
Of the hearts that daily break,
Of the tears that hourly fall,
Of the many, many troubles of life
That grieve this earthly ball—
Disease and hunger and pain and want—
But now I dreamt of them all!
For the blind and the cripple were there,
And the babe that pined for bread,
And the houseless man, and the widow poor
Who begged—to bury the dead;
The naked, alas! that I might have clad,
The famished I might have fed,
The sorrow I might have soothed,
And the unregarded tears!

*   *   *

Alas! I have walked through life,
Too heedless where I trod:
Nay, helping to trample my fellow-worm,
And fill the burial sod,
Forgetting that even the sparrow falls
Not unmarked of God!
I drank the richest draughts,
And ate whatever was good;
Fish, and flesh, and fowl, and fruit
Supplied my hungry mood.
But I never remembered the wretched ones
That starve for want of food.
I dressed as the noble dress,
In cloth of silver and gold,
With silk and satin, and costly furs,
In many an ample fold;
But I never remembered the naked limbs
That froze by the winter's cold!
The wounds I might have healed!
The human sorrow and smart!
And yet it never was in my soul
To play so ill a part:
But evil is wrought by want of thought,
As well as want of heart.

(b)   "*The Lady's Dream,*" by Thomas Hood

Poor, The, Excuses for not Giving to

"*The poor ye have always with you*" (Matt. xxvi. 11).

1. "**That they have nothing to spare:**" never reflecting whether it be in their *power*, or that it is their *duty*, to retrench their expenses, and contract their plan, "that they may have to give to them that need."

2. "**That they have families of their own, and that charity begins at home.**"

3. "**That charity does not consist in giving money,** but in benevolence, philanthropy, love to mankind, goodness of heart," etc. Hear St. James: "If a brother or sister be naked, and destitute of daily food, and one of you say unto them, Depart in peace; be ye warmed and filled; notwithstanding ye give them not those things which are needful to the body; what doth it profit?" (James ii. 15, 16).

4. "**That giving to the poor is not mentioned in St. Paul's description of charity, in 1 Cor. xiii.**" This is not a description of charity, but of good nature; and it is not necessary that every duty be mentioned in every place.

5. "**That they pay the poor-rates.**" They might as well allege that they pay their debts; for the poor have the same right to that portion of a man's property which the laws assign to them, that the man himself has to the remainder.

6. "**That they employ many poor persons:**" for their own sake, not the poor's; otherwise it is a good plea.

7. "**That the poor do not suffer so much as we** imagine; that education and habit have reconciled them to the evils of their condition, and make them easy under it." Habit can never reconcile human nature to the extremities of cold, hunger, and thirst, any more than it can reconcile the hand to the touch of a red-hot iron; besides, the question is not, how unhappy any one is, but how much more happy we can make him.

8. "**That these people, give them what you will, will never thank you, or think of you for it.**" In the first place, this is not true; in the second place, it was not for the sake of their thanks that you relieved them.

9. "**That we are liable to be imposed upon.**" If a due inquiry be made, our merit is the same; besides that the distress is generally real, although the cause be untruly stated.

10. "**That they should apply to their parishes.**" This is not always practicable: to which we may add, that there are many requisites to a comfortable subsistence, which parish relief does not supply; and that there are some, who would suffer almost as much from receiving parish relief as by the want of it; and, lastly, that there are many modes of charity to which this answer does not relate at all.

11. "**That giving money encourages idleness and vagrancy.**" This is true only of injudicious and indiscriminate generosity.

12. "**That we have too many objects of charity at** home, to bestow anything upon strangers, or, that there are other charities which are more useful, or stand in greater need." The value of this excuse depends entirely upon the *fact*, whether we actually relieve those neighbouring objects, and contribute to those other charities.

Beside all these excuses, pride, or prudery, or delicacy, or love of ease, keep one-half of the world out of the way of observing what the other half suffer.

(c)   *Paley*

POOR, THE

" When the eye saw " (Job xxix. 11)

Stranger, if to thee

His claim to memory be obscure,
If thou wouldst learn how truly great was he,
   Go, ask it of the poor.

(a)   *J. R. Lowell, on Thomas Hood*

Of gentle heart and open hand. Foe to none
but the bigot, the pedant, and the quack. Friend
to the suffering, the careworn, and the needy; to
the victims of a cruel greed, all that are desolate
and oppressed—Hood, the generous, kind, and
true.

Anon., quoted by T. Hood, jun., of Thos. Hood

(b)

POPULAR RELIGION

" If every Bible in the world were consumed, and
every word of Scripture erased from my memory,
I need be at no loss to live a religious life,
according to the will of God, for I should simply
have to proceed, in all respects, in a way perfectly
contrary to the popular religionists of this age,
and I could not possibly be wrong." His concentrated bitterness, however, was reserved for his
quondam brethren the Baptists, assigning for
this special favour which he bestowed upon
them, the reason, that " the more like the real
truth the profession of any people might be, while
they fell short of it, the more deeply they injured
the cause of true religion in the world. It was
like putting a forged paper in your hand, instead
of the genuine bank-note which you had a right
to expect."

(c)   *John Jones, Welsh preacher*

POVERTY

He that hath too little, wants feathers to fly
withal; he that hath too much, is but cumbered
with too large a tail.

(d)   *Owen Feltham*

Poor and content, is rich, and rich enough;
But riches, fineless, is as poor as winter,
To him that ever fears he shall be poor.

(e)   *Shakspeare*

Better go to heaven in rags, than to hell in
embroidery.

(f)   *Proverb*

POVERTY

To a wise, understanding, contented, and truly
regenerate man, is the way to heaven (*Chrysostom*).
God's gift, the mother of modesty. . . .
   Yet in the world esteemed a most odious thing,
vile and base, and severe torture. . . .
   To avoid which we will take any pains; we will
leave no haven, no coast, no creek of the world
unsearched, though it is to the hazard of our
lives; we will dive to the bottom of the sea, and
to the bowels of the earth, 5, 6, 7, 8, 900 fathoms
deep, through all extremes of heat and cold;
we will turn parasites and slaves, prostitute ourselves, swear and lie, damn our bodies and souls,
forsake God, abjure religion, steal, rob, murder,

rather than endure this unsufferable yoke, which
doth so tyrannize, crucify, and generally depress
us.

(g)   *Burton (Anatomy of Melancholy)*

Many whom the world regards as dirt, the Lord
esteems as jewels.
Judge a Christian, not by his coat, but by his
character.
If you cannot have a piano on earth, you may
have a harp in heaven.

(h)

POWER (Eph. iii. 20)

The "power" so frequently referred to in the
epistle, is *the might of the indwelling Spirit.*

(i)   *Lange*

Straight forward goes the lightning's path, and
straight the fearful path of the cannon-ball. Direct
it flies and rapid, shattering that it may reach,
and shattering what it reaches.

(j)   *Wallenstein*

One of the tremendous evils of the world is the
monstrous accumulation of power in a few hands.
Half a dozen men may, at this moment, light
the fires of war through the world, may convulse
all civilized nations, sweep earth and sea with
armed hosts, spread desolation through the fields
and bankruptcy through cities, and make themselves felt by some form of suffering through
every household in Christendom.

(k)   *Channing*

POWER OF GOD, THE GOSPEL THE (Rom. i. 16)

The reality of the helpfulness of Gospel truth has
been tested and attested by the long experience of
mankind. To pass over times of great trial, we
know that, from age to age, the love of God has
thus come home to many a soul of man, transforming what might have been moral virtue into
spiritual holiness; a state to which (as Kant and
other moralists say) we must ceaselessly aspire,
although unable to reach it by our present limited
powers of self-enfranchisement. But no observer
of men can doubt that the law of the spirit of life
in Christ Jesus hath made many Christians free
from the law of sin and death. And for this cause
we need not be ashamed of the Gospel of Christ,
for it is the power of God unto salvation.
Christ's Church is, therefore, the richest of our
human armouries. And wherever sin, or the
peril of sin, are, there ought we to desire for creatures not unlike ourselves, some similar gift of
God. . . . We ought, above all things, to pray
that there may the angel of God's presence be,—
there, a ladder of ascent to purer regions,—there,
the House of God,—there, the Gate of Heaven.
So shall the natural be changed into the spiritual,
the corruptible put on incorruption, and the
mortal put on immortality. For that cannot be
first which is spiritual, but that which is natural,
and afterward that which is spiritual. This is the
real law of development, the Divine Finger bringing strength out of weakness.

(l)   *Jackson's Bampton Lectures*

POWER OF THE GOSPEL

That which Plato was unable to effect, even in the case of a few select and learned persons, a secret power, by the help only of a few words, is now wrought upon thousands of uneducated men.

(a)   *Blaise Pascal*

POWER, SECRET OF

Without the Spirit we are perfectly powerless. We may preach, and you may hear; but it will be to no profit; no sinners will be awakened; no souls converted, no slumberers aroused.

If there be one thought more than another which is forced upon us as our ministerial experience advances, it is the conviction of our own perfect powerlessness to obtain admission into men's hearts for the gospel message which we are appointed to deliver. It is reported of one of the early Reformers, that when he first began to preach, he expected that all men to whom he addressed himself would be ready to believe. He was so convinced himself of the truth and importance of his message: to him its evidences were written as with a sunbeam; its bearing upon the best and brightest interests of mankind were so obvious; it was enforced by such sanctions, and recommended by such examples, and it appealed (as he thought) so irresistibly to the highest impulses of human nature, that he felt sure the Gospel only needed to obtain a hearing, in order to obtain for itself universal acceptance. In this spirit he went forth to his work; but it was not long before his opinions were changed. The people (it is true) trooped and thronged around him, but in the majority of cases, no effect was produced on their hearts or lives. They went forth from the sanctuary to pursue their various projects of gain or pleasure, with as keen a thirst and as determined an intensity as ever. They listened to descriptions of heaven, without one thought of turning their faces thitherward; and heard of the wonders of the person and greatness of the work of Christ, without one throb of emotion, or one determination to give themselves to the Redeemer's service. And at last the preacher, baffled, wearied, mortified, depressed by the persistent indifference and apathy of the people, was overheard to exclaim, that the " Old Adam was far too hard for young Melancthon."

And, I suppose, his experience has been the experience of every worker for Christ, from the first day until now. "Lord! who hath believed our report, and to whom has the arm of the Lord been revealed?" was the cry of the prophet. How often has it been iterated, in sorrowful or impatient tones, as the ages have rolled on! We preach, says the preacher; but who really heed us? The listeners listen to our exhortations, but the indifference and the carelessness, the greedy pursuit of gold, the frantic rush after pleasure, goes on just the same. The old Adam is too strong for us. He comes into the Church, and he goes out of the Church, as vigorous and as unsubdued and as undying as ever. Ay, but though the old Adam is strong, God's Holy Spirit is stronger. And here, just here, lies our hope. We can do nothing with the dull mass of worldliness, that we know: but the Spirit of God, giving effect to the hammer of the Word, can fall upon it with the swift and sure crash of the thunderbolt, and shiver it to pieces.

(b)   *Gordon Calthrop*

POWER AND SPIRIT (1 Thess. i. 5)

Power and spirit belong together. Compare 1 Cor. ii. 4; Rom. xxv. 19; Acts i. 8; x. 38; Luke i. 35. And so spirit and life, Rom. viii. 11; John vi. 63; 2 Cor. iii. 6; Rom. viii. 2. 10.

(c)   *Lange*

POWER, SPIRITUAL

All the great agents of nature—attraction, heat, and the principle of life—are refined, spiritual, invisible, acting gently, silently, imperceptibly, and yet brute matter feels their power, and is transformed by them into surpassing beauty.

(d)   *Channing*

PRAISE

The value and beauty of family worship in the time of bereavement are illustrated by an incident in the life of John Angell James, which had almost a touch of the sublime. It was his custom to read at family prayer on Saturday night Psalm ciii. On the Saturday of the week in which Mrs. James died he hesitated, with the open Bible in his hand, before he began to read; but after a moment's silence he looked up and said, "Notwithstanding what has happened this week, I see no reason for departing from our usual custom of reading the one hundred and third psalm—' Bless the Lord, O my soul, and all that is within me, bless His holy name.'" What must be the effect upon a household of such a scene? What a picture is thus presented of holy resignation and thankfulness! The greatest sufferer recognising, as the head of the family, the hand that has smitten his home and made it desolate, and in the depth of his sorrow blessing the name of the Lord!

(e)   *Christian Home Life*

PRAYER

"Asking," "Seeking," "Knocking" (Matt. vii. 7).

1. " Ask " (Matt. vii. 7).

"Call upon Me in the day of trouble: I will deliver thee, and thou shalt glorify Me " (Ps. l. 15).

" Seek ye the Lord while He may be found, call ye upon Him while He is near " (Isa. lv. 6).

" Thou hast given him his heart's desire, and hast not withholden the request of his lips.

" He asked life of Thee, and Thou gavest it him, even length of days for ever and ever " (Ps. xxi. 2–4).

" Ask ye of the Lord rain in the time of the latter rain; so the Lord shall make bright clouds, and give them showers of rain, to every one grass in the field " (Zech x. 1).

" If any of you lack wisdom, let him ask of God, that giveth to all men liberally, and upbraideth not; and it shall be given him " (Jas. i. 5).

(f)

2. " Seek " (Diligence).

" And ye shall seek Me, and find Me, when ye shall search for Me with your whole heart " (Jer. xxix. 13; Isa. lv. 6).

(g)

(i.) Parable of *lost sheep* sought *till* it was found.

(ii.) Parable of *lost coin* sought *diligently* till it was found.

Perseverance and against *difficulties* (Luke xv. 5, 9).

(*a*)

3. " Knock " (Importunity)

" STRIVE to enter in at the *strait* gate: for many, I say unto you, will seek to enter in, and shall not be able " (Luke xiii. 24).

" Peter *knocked* at the door of the gate . . ."

" Peter continued *knocking* " (Acts xii. 13–16).

" Behold I stand at the door, and knock ; if any man hear My voice, and open the door, I will come in to him, and will sup with him, and he with Me " (Rev. iii. 20).

" Let Me go."

" I will not let Thee go except Thou bless me."

" Thou shalt be called Israel." " *And He blessed him there* " (Gen. xxxii. 26–29).

(*b*)

Ideo non vult cito dare, ut tu discas ardentius orare.

(*c*)   *Augustine*

It is easier that heaven and earth should pass, than, if thou seek God, not to find Him ; or than, if thou ask, not to receive ; or if thou knock, not to be opened unto.

(*d*)   *Bernard*

If I cared for nothing, I would pray for nothing.

(*e*)   *Melancthon*

PRAYER (Matt. vii. 7)

There is no receiving without asking ; no finding without seeking ; no opening without knocking. The threefold promise annexed to the threefold precept should encourage all Christians to be instant, fervent, and constant in prayer.

(*f*)   *Thos. Brooks*

PRAYER, ANSWERS TO

All Christ's prayers began with " Father." He the first Christian.

Our prayers run along one road, and God's answers by another, and by-and-by they meet.

God answers all true prayer, either in kind or in kindness.

(*g*)

I never was deeply interested in any object, I never prayed sincerely and earnestly for anything, *but it came ;* at some time, no matter at how distant a day, in some shape, probably the last I should have devised, *it came.*

(*h*)   *Adoniram Judson*

Si Stephanus non orasset, Ecclesia Paulam non haberet.

(*i*)   *Augustine*

Let none wilfully refuse the word of God. 'Tis sad to have an *Adder's ear*, an *Adamant heart* (Zec. vii. 11, 12).

(*j*)

If when God speaks to us in His Word we are deaf, when we speak to Him in prayer He will be dumb.

" When . . . destruction cometh as a whirlwind ; . . . Then shall they call upon Me, but I will not answer," etc. (Prov. i. 27, 28).

(*k*)

There is no such thing in the long history of God's kingdom as an unanswered prayer. Every true desire from a child's heart finds some true answer in the heart of God. Most certain it is, that the prayer of the Church of God since creation has not been the cry of orphans in an empty home, without a father to hear or answer. Jesus Christ did not pray in vain, or to an unknown God, nor has He spoken in ignorance of God or of His brethren, when He says, " Ask, and receive, that your joy may be full."

(*l*)   *Norman Macleod*

Canon Wilberforce, recently, referring to the struggle preceding the abolition of the slave trade, said he was in a position to state that the leaders in that great movement never took a single step in it without earnest and constant communion with their Lord. On the very night when the leader went down to the House of Commons to plead with silver voice and tender eloquence for the abolition of the evil, on that very night in a little chamber there was gathered a band of praying men ; and that night was the night of victory in the House of Commons.

(*m*)

PRAYER (John iv. 52)

Yesterday at the seventh hour ; or, in the proper hour the help comes home with power. Mark the great hours (of extremity, of prayer, of miraculous help). Remember those hours, and believe.

(*n*)   *Lange*

PRAYER (" *Exceeding abundantly*") (Eph. iii. 20)

Hagar asked a drop and found a well (Gen. xx. 19) ;

Saul sought his father's asses and found a crown (1 Sam. ix. 3 ; x. 1) ;

David asked bread and received a kingdom (1 Sam. xxi. 3).

(*o*)   *Ibid*

PRAYER AND CARE

By caring and by fretting,
By agony and fear,
There is of God no getting ;
But prayer He will hear.

(*p*)   Cf. Ps. cxxvii. 1, 2.

PRAYER (COLD)

Cold prayers are as arrows without heads, as swords without edges, as birds without wings : they pierce not, they cut not, they fly not up to heaven. Cold prayers always freeze before they reach heaven.

(*q*)   *Thos Brooks*

PRAYER AND A CROSS

Nothing more moveth me, and burdeneth my soul, than that I could never, in my prosperity, so wrestle in prayer with God, nor be so dead to the world, so hungry and sick of love for Christ, so heavenly-minded, as when ten stone weight of a heavy cross was upon me.

(a) *Samuel Rutherford*

PRAYER AND FAITH

Prayer is the voice of faith.

(b) *Horne*

THE PRAYER OF FAITH, POWER OF

"*Why could not we cast him out?*" (Mark ix. 28, 29).

During the temporary absence of our Lord, His disciples were requested to perform a miracle—a father brought his son afflicted with a *dumb spirit* and requested them to exorcise it, but in vain their efforts. Asking the cause of their failure, the Lord said, "*This kind goeth not forth but by prayer.*" This is what they had omitted. They went to work in their own strength, forgetting, "Without Me ye can do nothing."

(c)

The *power of prayer* and the usual objections to it are here well illustrated:

1. There is the scientific objection:

By which we are told that the laws of nature are unalterable, machine-like revolving its constant round; and effects are the same whether men pray or no. This is very plausible, and is well sustained by the narrative: The father in answer says, The child was born so; "of a child." Therefore say they, *It is his nature*, he can't be otherwise. It is as much his nature to fall down, to foam at the mouth, grind his teeth, be sullen, obstinate, make himself and all others miserable, as it is the nature of a dog to bark and bite: nothing can be done for him, it is an incurable case of epilepsy.

(d)

2. This is not the Christian's belief.

Not in fate, or chance, or hard necessity unalterable, for then prayer would be unavailable; but we believe in God, who is a *moral governor*, who "putteth down one and setteth up another;" who is influenced by men's repentance and faith; a *Father* who hears and answers prayer; with whom effectual fervent prayer availeth much; it moves the hand that moves the world. Accordingly we ask, seek, and knock, because we have proved that *prayer is a real power*.

(e)

3. But there are great *obstacles* in the way of its operation

Our prayers are so *unbelieving*—that they are not much in advance of real unbelief and doubt. So here-
The father *comes* to Jesus=*prayer;* but his words imply *doubt*. "If Thou *canst* do anything," etc.
Note the sharp answer of Jesus:

" Man,
"It rests with thyself, not with Me.
"If *thou* canst, not if I can."
"All things are possible to him that believeth." Miracles are not worked for unbelievers. Faith itself is a miracle-worker, it can remove mountains, convert the sinner from the error of his ways, obtain forgiveness of sins, cast out devils, fill you with the Spirit, and make you a saint. Be not faithless but believing—only believe, and nothing shall be impossible.

(f)

4. Hence, Remove that obstacle, and help will come for us

As soon as this man cried out, "*Lord, I believe, help Thou mine unbelief,*" "immediately" its power was felt, Jesus spake to the demon, "COME OUT," and it came out; "ENTER NO MORE," and the word of the Master was obeyed, the cure was thorough and permanent.

(g) *Cf. Godet*

We must not forget on all such occasions that Judas was still among them. Cf. ACHAN in the camp.

(h) *Lange*

PRAYER, HEARING OF (Acts xii. 5)

The deliverance of Peter from prison is one of the most remarkable facts on record, as an illustration of *the hearing of prayer*. Two powers are, as it were, struggling with each other: the one, secular power, attempting to hold the Apostle fast, and slay him; the other, the Church of Christ, desirous of rescuing him, and preserving his life and liberty. The former has all material instruments at its disposition—a prison, chains, fetters, soldiers, and weapons; the latter has none of these, but in the place of them *prayer*—united and fervent prayer. Faith in God, who was in Christ, love to one another for Christ's sake, Christian hope—indeed the whole inner life that proceeds from redemption, infuses itself into such intercession; and thus prayer lays hold on the omnipotence of God in faith. This united prayer in the name of Jesus Christ, is heard; it accomplishes more than all the power of the world can attempt to do. . . . The power of the world, attempting to resist God and Christ, suffers a most ignominious defeat, while the Gospel and the Church of Christ advance with power. Christ is King; and yesterday, to-day, and evermore He enlarges His kingdom, and the gates of hell shall never prevail against His Church.

(i) *Ibid*

PRAYER, ILLUMINATION OF

The Christian on his knees knows more, and can see further than the philosopher on tip-toe.

(j)

PRAYER, IMPORTUNATE

Prayer pulls the rope below, and the great bell rings above in the ears of God. Some scarcely stir the bell, for they pray so languidly; others give but an occasional pluck at the rope; but he who wins with heaven is the man who grasps the rope boldly, and pulls continuously, with all his might.

(k) *Biblical Treasury*

PRAYER, INSTRUCTION FOR.

They are the safest who are most in their closets, who pray, not to be seen of men, but to be heard of God.

Prayer doth not consist in gifted expressions and a volubility of speech, but in a brokenness of heart. Imperfect broken groans, from a broken heart, God will accept. A hard heart cannot pray ; a broken heart is made up of prayer.

There wants nothing but a believing prayer to turn the promise into a performance.

God is the *great* God, and therefore He will be *sought* : He is a *good* God, and therefore He will be *found*.

When God pours out His Spirit upon man, then man will pour out his heart before God.

He that lives without prayer, or prays without life, hath not the Spirit of God.

Prayer doth not consist in the elegance of the phrase, but in the strength of the affection.

Where there is a willing heart, there will be a continual crying to heaven for help.

Pray that you may pray.

Waiting upon God continually, will abate your unnecessary cares and sweeten your necessary ones.

Let nothing get between heaven and prayer, but Christ.

Prayer, if it be done as a task, is no prayer.

Sin quenches prayer, affections quicken it.

The same spirit of faith which teaches a man to cry earnestly, teaches him to wait patiently ; for, as it assures him the mercy is in the Lord's hand, so it assures him it will be given forth in the Lord's time.

The *breath* of prayer comes from the *life* of faith.

Whatever you want, go to God by faith and prayer, in the name of Christ, and never think His delays are denials.

They that spend their days in faith and prayer, shall end their days in peace and comfort.

(a) *Mason*

PRAYER, INTERCESSORY

I was pleasantly impressed lately by an incident which occurred in a brief correspondence which I had with Prof. —— of ——. We were writing in part upon this subject, and I had incidentally mentioned your meeting. In his reply, he artlessly, and with the trustfulness of a child, asked that you might be requested to pray for *him*. This man is no fanatic. Still less is he a hypocrite. He is one of the ripest of our American scholars, and one of the most profound of our philosophers. A good part of his life he has spent in the study of Plato ; and now, after sixty odd years, in which human philosophy has become an alphabet to him, and universities on both sides of the Atlantic honour him for his acquisitions, he thinks and speaks of the prayers of a few humble women, strangers to him, and hundreds of miles away, as if they possessed a real power of which he may avail himself for the achievement of real results which shall stretch on into other worlds. He proposes to use that power as trustfully as he would send a commission by a friend to Europe. He gives you his request in the same conviction that he is doing a sensible thing, which he would feel in sending a message to the telegraph office, know-

ing it would reach the other side of the globe in twenty minutes. Such is the trust which the ablest and wisest men repose in intercessory prayer, when they have been as wisely taught of God. We shall all find, by-and-by, that the most natural thing in the world for all wisdom to do, is to sit at the feet of Christ, and ask for that which nothing else than prayer can compass.

(b) *Austin Phelps*

PRAYER, A KEY

Though prayer be the key that opens God's treasures, yet faith is the hand that turns the key, without which it will do no good.

God's promises to us must be the ground of our prayers to Him. When God makes a promise, we must make a prayer.

(c) *Clarke, 1642*

PRAYER, A MIRACLE WORKER

More things are wrought by prayer
Than the world dreams of.

(d) *Tennyson*

PRAYER IN THE NAME OF JESUS (John xvi. 26)

The more knowledge, the more prayer in the name of Jesus.

(e) *Lücke*

The approaching the Father through Him shall be a characteristic of their higher state under the dispensation of the Spirit.

(f) *Alford*

Such prayers *must* be heard, as to their true spiritual intent, although very often they are heard at a time and in a manner which differs widely from our short-sighted vision. God sometimes hears the substance of our prayers best by denying their form.

(g) *P. Schaff*

PRAYER AT NIGHT

Who goes to bed and doth not pray,
Maketh two nights to every day.

(h) *Geo. Herbert*

Sum up at night what thou hast done by day,
  And in the morning, what thou hast to do.
Dress and undress thy soul ; mark the decay
  And growth of it : if, with thy watch, that too
Be down, then wind up both ; since we shall be
  Most surely judged, make thy accounts agree.

(i) *Ibid*

PRAYER, PHILOSOPHY OF

Depend upon it, that, in all circumstances, but especially in connection with religious inquiries and the struggles of religious doubt, to *pray* is as philosophical as it is devout.

(j) *T. Binney*

PRAYER, PRACTICE OF

1. I have been benefited by riding alone a long journey, in giving that time to prayer.

2. By abstinence, and giving days to God.

3. By praying for others; for, by making an errand to God for them, I have gotten something for myself.

4. I have been really confirmed, in many particulars, that God heareth prayers; and therefore I used to pray for anything, of how little importance soever.

5. He enabled me to make no question that this way, which is mocked and nicknamed, is the only way to heaven.

(a)   *Samuel Rutherford*

PRAYER AND PREACHING (1 Thess. i. 2)

The Apostles excel not only as preachers and founders of the Church, but also as men of *prayer.* " We will give ourselves continually to prayer and the ministry of the word " (Acts vi. 4). Prayer is to them the full half, and indeed the first half, of their office.

By prayer we act upon God; by the word, on the world, on men. To every labour for the world must be added the blessing of God; the moral can prosper only on the religious ground.

(b)   *Lange*

PRAYER, PRIVATE

When we pray in private there are three Persons with us: there is God the Father, whose eye seeth in secret and whose ear is open to our prayer; there is God the Son, blotting out our sin, and offering up our petitions (however wandering and sinful) with the incense of His own merits; and there is God the Holy Ghost, quickening our spirits, and putting into our hearts good desires.

(c)   *Robt. McCheyne, and C. Clayton.*

PRAYER AND PROMISES

Prayer is nothing else but a *presenting* God with His *own promises,* desiring Him to work that in us and for us which He hath promised to us.

(d)   *Charnock: " Delight in Prayer "*

PRAYER AND STUDY

Study without prayer is atheism; and prayer without study is presumption.

(e)   *Bishop Sanderson*

PRAYER OF SUBMISSION

I have lived to see this world is made up of perturbations; and I have been long preparing to leave it, and gathering comfort for the dreadful hour of my making my account with God, which I now apprehend to be near: and though I have, by His grace, loved Him in my youth, and feared Him in my age, and laboured to have a conscience void of offence to Him and to all men; yet if Thou, O Lord, be extreme to mark what I have done amiss, who can abide it? And, therefore, when I have failed, Lord, show mercy to me; for I plead not my righteousness, but the forgiveness of my unrighteousness for His merits who

died to purchase pardon for penitent sinners. And since I owe Thee a death, Lord, let it not be terrible, and then take Thine own time. I submit to it; let not mine, O Lord, but let Thy will be done.

(f)   *Richard Hooker*

PRAYER, TEMPLE OF

" *Neither in this mountain nor Jerusalem* " (John iv. 21).

However early in the morning you seek the gate of access, you find it already open; and however deep the midnight moment when you find yourselves in the sudden arms of death, the winged prayer can bring an instant Saviour near—and this wherever you are. It needs not that you ascend a special Pisgah or Moriah. It needs not that you should enter some awful shrine, or put off your shoes on some holy ground. Could a memento be reared on every spot from which an acceptable prayer has passed away, and on which a prompt answer has come down, we should find Jehovah-shammah, " the Lord hath been here," inscribed on many a cottage hearth and many a dungeon floor. We should find it not only in Jerusalem's proud temple, David's cedar galleries, but in the fisherman's cottage by the brink of Gennesareth, and in the upper chamber where Pentecost began. And whether it be the field where Isaac went to meditate, or the rocky knoll where Jacob lay down to sleep, or the brook where Israel wrestled, or the den where Daniel gazed on the hungry lions and the lions gazed on him, or the hillside where the Man of Sorrows prayed all night, we should still discern the prints of the ladder's feet let down from heaven—the landing-place of mercies, because the starting-point of prayer.

(g)   *Hamilton*

PRAYER, A THERMOMETER

Prayer is the true thermometer of the spiritual life.

(h)   *Lange*

PRAYER, UNCEASING

" *Continuing instant in prayer* " (Rom. xii. 12)

The Greek is a metaphor, taken from hunting dogs, that never give over the game till they have got their prey. A Christian must not only pray, but hold on in prayer, till he has obtained the heavenly prize.

(i)   *Thomas Brooks*

PRAYER, UNCEASING

" *Pray without ceasing* " (1 Thess. v. 17)

A number of ministers were assembled for the discussion of difficult questions, and among others it was asked, how the command to " pray without ceasing " could be complied with. Various suppositions were started, and at length one of the number was appointed to write an essay upon it to read at the next meeting; which being overheard by a female servant, she exclaimed, " What! a whole month wanted to tell the meaning of that text! It is one of the easiest and best texts in the Bible." " Well, well," said an old minister,

(j)

"Mary, what can you say about it. Let us know how you understand it. Can you pray all the time?" "Oh, yes, sir." "What! when you have so many things to do?" "Why, sir, the more I have to do, the more I can pray." "Indeed! well, Mary, do let us know how it is; for most people think otherwise." "Well, sir," said the girl, "when I first open my eyes in the morning, I pray, 'Lord open the eyes of my understanding;' and while I am dressing, I pray that I may be clothed with the robe of righteousness; and when I have washed me, I ask for the washing of regeneration; and as I begin work, I pray that I may have strength equal to my day; when I begin to kindle up a fire, I pray that God's work may revive in my soul; and as I sweep out the house, I pray that my heart may be cleansed from all its impurities; and while preparing and partaking of breakfast, I desire to be fed with the hidden manna, and the sincere milk of the word; and as I am busy with the little children, I look up to God as my Father, and pray for the spirit of adoption, that I may be His child; and so on all day; everything I do furnishes me with a thought for prayer." "Enough, enough," cried the old divine, "these things are revealed to babes, and often hid from the wise and prudent." "Go on, Mary," said he, "pray without ceasing; and as for us, my brethren, let us bless the Lord for this exposition, and remember that He has said, 'The meek will He guide in judgment.'" The essay, as a matter of course, was not considered necessary after this little event occurred.

(a)   *Religious Tract Society*

Constant prayer, mental prayer, prayer of the heart, prayer everywhere, in the street and in the market, in the shop and in the warehouse, behind the counter and over the ledger, in the omnibus and in the railway carriage, in the mine and at the loom, at the plough and in the harvest field, in harbour and at sea, in the calm as well as in the storm, prayer at all times and in all places.

(b)   *Thomas Cooper*

John Wesley would not stay longer than one hour in any company unless there was fresh prayer at the end of the hour.

"John Wesley's conversation is good," said Dr. Johnson, "but he is never at leisure. He is always obliged to go at a certain hour. This is very disagreeable to a man who loves to fold his legs and have his talk out, as I do."

One one occasion, it is said, Wesley dined with Johnson, he allowed one hour for dinner, and another for conversation, and then rose to go, as there was no prayer proposed.

(c)   *Ibid*

PRAYER, VALUE OF

If the whole world in which we live is but a continual temptation; if all around appears to agree with our inward corruptions, to weaken and seduce us; if riches bribe, and indigence sours; if prosperity elevates, and afflictions abase us; if business dissipates, and rest enervates; if the sciences exalt, and ignorance bewilders us; if commerce exposes us too much, and solitude leaves us too much to ourselves; if pleasures seduce us, and holy works make us proud; if health awakens the passions, and sickness produces murmurings; in a word, if, since the fall of man, all that surrounds us, and all that is in us, is perilous, in so deplorable a situation, O my God! what hope of salvation remains for us? If our sighs do not incessantly ascend from the depth of our misery towards the throne of Thy mercy, until Thou deignest to assist us . . . and to rescue us from our fallen state?

(d)   *Massillon*

That work which is begun well is half-done;
And without prayer no work is well begun.

(e)   *Fanshawe*

Hast thou not learned what thou art often told,
A truth still sacred, and believed of old,
That no success attends on spears and swords
Unblest, and that the battle is the Lord's?

(f)   *Cowper*

Before doing anything else, be we careful to consecrate the first-fruits of the day, and the very beginnings of our holy thoughts unto the service of God.

(g)   *St. Basil*

PRAYERS, GOLDEN

Drexellius tells us of a vision that a religious man had at his prayers in the congregation. He saw a several angel at the elbow of every one present, ready to write down his petitions; those who prayed heartily, their angels wrote down their suits in gold; those that prayed but coldly and carelessly, their angels wrote too, but it was with water; those that prayed customarily, only from the teeth outward, had their angels by them, who seemed to write, but it was with a dry pen, no ink in it. Such as slept, had their angels by them, but they laid their pens by. Such as had worldly thoughts, their angels wrote in the dust. And such as had envious and malicious spirits, their angels wrote with gall. If this be so, I fear few angels have written this day in golden letters; but the pens of the others have gone very fast. Have a care how thou prayest, if thou wouldest have them written with the **Golden Pen.**

(h)   *N. Rogers*, 1658

PRAYERS, LONG

I think very long prayers more blamable than long sermons. A peculiar attention is due when speaking to the Most High; and if the attention be overstrained by the length of the service, it is lost time to the hearer. Weariness of mind in prayer,—and the thought still returning, When will you have done?—is worse than unpleasant, especially to persons of weak judgment, who charge their consciences with guilt for the speaker's indiscretion.

(i)   *John Newton*

PRAYERS OF EMINENT MEN, ETC

PRAYER OF ANSELM

O Lord Jesus, holy Jesus, who didst vouchsafe to die for our sins, and didst rise again for our justification, I beseech Thee by Thy glorious Resurrection, to raise me from the grave of all me

(j)

vices and sins, and grant me a daily part in the first Resurrection, that I may truly deserve to receive a part in Thy Resurrection. O Thou most precious Saviour, Thou hast ascended into heaven in the triumph of Thy glory, and sittest at the right hand of the Father. Draw me upward that I may run after Thee, after the odour of Thine ointments, that I may run and not faint, while Thou drawest and leadest me as I run. Draw my soul, that thirsts after Thee, to the heavenly streams of eternal satiety: yea, draw me to Thee, the living Fountain, that according to my capacity I may drink, whence I shall ever live, my God, my life. For Thou hast said, *If any man thirst, let him come unto Me and drink*. O Fountain of Life, grant that I may ever drink of Thee. O Fountain of Life, fill my mind with the river of Thy pleasures, and make my soul drunk with the sober drunkenness of Thy love; that I may forget whatever is vain and earthly, and may keep Thee alone continually in my memory.

Give me Thy *Holy Spirit*, signified by those waters which Thou didst promise to give to the thirsty. Grant, I beseech Thee, that with my whole desire I may strive thitherward, whither we believe Thee to have ascended after Thy Resurrection, that I may be always with Thee in thought and longing, that my heart may be there, where Thou, my Treasure, art.

Do Thou, O Lord my God, who art rich in all good, and a most bountiful Dispenser of the heavenly banquet, give meat to Thy weary servant. Lo, he stands at the door and knocks: I beseech Thee by the bowels of Thy compassion, wherewith Thou visitest us as the Dayspring from on high, open the hand of Thy mercy to him, and command with a winning condescension that he come to Thee, rest in Thee, and be strengthened by the living, heavenly bread.

Let Thy Spirit, Lord, I beseech Thee, put forth wings, like an eagle, and fly, and not faint; let it fly and mount even to the beauty of Thy house, to the place where Thine honour dwelleth. Thou, who didst command the winds and the sea, and there was a great calm, come and walk on the waves of my heart, that everything in me may become calm and serene. Let my spirit, Lord, fly beneath the shadow of Thy wings from the scorching cares of this world, that, being hidden in Thy refreshing coolness, it may sing rejoicingly and say, *I will lay me down in peace and sleep*.

Let my soul be safe, be always secure under the wings of Thy protection, O my God. Let it abide in Thee, and be always nourished by Thee. Let it behold Thee, when my consciousness forsakes me, and sing Thy praises with shouts of joy: and let these Thy sweet gifts be my consolation until I come to Thee, who art true Peace, where there is no bow, or shield, or sword, or war, but perfect security, secure tranquillity, tranquil pleasure, and happy eternity, and eternal blessedness, and the blessed vision and praises of Thee, world without end. Amen.

(*a*)   *Quoted by Julius Hare*

PRAYER OF DR. ARNOLD

Before he went into the school-life each day, he prayed for himself this prayer, which has often helped me: I keep it in my pulpit Bible. "O Lord, I have a busy world around me. Eye, and ear, and thought will be needed for the work to-day done amidst that busy world. Now I enter upon it, I would commit eye, ear, thought, and wish to Thee. Do Thou bless them, and keep their work Thine, that, as through Thy natural law my heart beats, and my blood flows, without any thought of mine for them, so my spiritual life may hold on its course at those times when my mind cannot consciously turn from my absorbing work to Thee. I commit each particular thought to Thy service. Hear my prayer, for my dear Redeemer's sake." Yes; we need that spirit of prayer. I say, that if a man can go back to his work to-morrow in that spirit, I care not how busy you make him,—you may run him in the city off his legs, you may give him no breathing time,— yet if he has begun the day by consecrating every thought, and wish, and act, of the eye, and the ear, and the hand, and the mind, to God, then, though he may be so absorbed in his work that he cannot consciously turn to commit that work unto God, yet all that work shall be done in the spirit of that prayer with which he opened, and began, and consecrated the day.

(*b*)   *James Fleming*

PRAYER OF ST. AUGUSTINE

O Lord, grant that I may desire Thee, and desiring Thee, seek Thee, and seeking Thee, find Thee, and finding Thee, be satisfied with Thee for ever.

(*c*)

PRAYER OF COLUMBA

O Lord, give me, I beseech Thee, in the name of Jesus Christ Thy Son, my God, that love which never faileth, that my light may be kindled and never quenched; that it may burn in me, and give light to others. And thou, O Christ, our dearest Saviour, do Thou Thyself constantly kindle our lamps, that they may shine evermore in Thy temple, that they may receive unquenchable light from Thee, the unquenchable Light; that our darkness may be enlightened, while the darkness of the world flies from us. My Jesus, I beseech Thee, give Thy light to my lamp, that in its light may be manifested to me that Holy of Holies in which Thou, the eternal Priest, dost dwell; that I may continually contemplate Thee only, long for Thee, gaze on Thee, and yearn for Thee in love, O Saviour, full of love! show Thyself to us that knock, that we may perceive and love Thee alone, think of Thee day and night: that Thy love, which many waters cannot quench, may possess our whole souls, and never more be quenched by the waters of the earth.

(*d*)   "*Sketches of Christian Life in England*"

PRAYER OF GENERAL GORDON

I like the following form of prayer:

Thou hast moulded me out of dust every fibre, therefore Thou knowest every fibre. Thou gavest me Thy own life. Thou didst mould me in Thy exact image and likeness (for none but Thou couldst make me) by Thyself. Thou gavest me free-will to be altogether like Thyself. I have abased and defiled Thy sacred image. Though I was Thy chief work, yet so low have I debased Thy image, that all creatures turn with horror from me, and I

(*e*)

am a horror to myself. Though I had Thy life in me, though by Thy life I exist; though Thou couldest have made myriads with no trouble, yet didst Thou so love *me*, that Thou camest in my form, and didst so suffer every conceivable injury that I could commit against Thee. Yet I hindered Thee by every possible cruelty and contempt. Thou didst set Thy face as a flint, and bore the imputation and the punishment of every sin I ever committed—sins which, even in my fellow-creatures, I abhor and hate. Thou wast so pure as to cause angels to veil their faces before Thee. Yet Thou bore the guilt as entirely Thine—as if Thou hadst done those sins. Surely now Thou hast routed Thy enemies Thou wilt not permit them to trample and scoff at Thee. Remember Thy sufferings, for they were beyond conception. Are those sufferings to go for nought, as they do, if Thou permit these unconquered enemies to prevail against me, Thy own flesh and bone, Thy member?

(a)

PRAYER OF R. S. HAWKER, OF MORWENSTOW

Composed and used at the period of the Prince of Wales's illness, 1871; when also philosophers were busy with their absurdities concerning the use and efficacy of prayer.

O Lord Jesus Christ, Thou Second Person of the glorious and undivided Trinity, Thou who wert once blended here upon earth thirty and three years with the visible form and nature of a man! Hear us, Thou Healer of Nations, hear! In and by Thy manhood, built from an earthly mother's veins, and taken into God, Thou didst assuage all manner of disease, and even death, by Thy voice, Thy touch, Thy silent command. Thou art the self-same Redeemer still! the unalterable God! We call upon Thee for Albert Edward, the first-born prince and hope of the royal house of England, the future king, beneath Thy will, and of our native and natural land! Say but the word which Thou didst utter in Cana of Galilee, 'Thy son liveth!' and in the same hour the fever shall leave Thy servant, our prince, and he shall be made whole. Restore him, O Lord, to the yearning hearts of his people, to the wife of his youth, and to the royal lady weeping over her child. Even so, Lord Jesus; and by the memory of Thine own great impulse at the gate of the city called Nain, and of her who won Thy latest love upon the cross, deliver him to his mother. Hear us, O Healer of the Nations, hear, and grant our trusting prayer to God the Trinity, through Thy Manhood, Jesus Christ our Lord. Amen. (*See "* THANKSGIVING.*"*)

(b)

INTERCESSORY PRAYER IN ANY TIME OF SPECIAL AFFLICTION

O Heavenly Father, who dost so order the events and circumstances of our lives that we may recognise Thy hand in all that befalls us, and learn to sympathize with each other; we beseech Thee to strengthen and support us (or those for whom we especially pray), upon whom Thou hast at this time brought (sickness, and anxiety, perplexity, or afflictions). Grant that it may be met with wisdom and patience, with submission, and a sure trust in Thy good Providence. Bless the means employed for relieving it; give such a

measure of Thy grace that the trials and sufferings of this life may purify and prepare us (or them) for that heavenly life, in which anxiety and sorrow, sickness and suffering, shall be done away, through the sufferings and death of our Lord and Saviour Jesus Christ, who now livest and reignest with Thee and the Holy Ghost, ever one God, world without end. Amen.

(c)   *English Churchman, Oct.* 1861

PRAYER BY ST. JEROME

Lord, suffer me not, I beseech Thee, to satisfy myself with this, that I have once made some show of humiliation and sorrow for my falls; but grant I may increase in the performance of these duties, and may every day run and enlarge my repentance for particular slips, growing still into a deeper detestation of my sins, and desiring with more and more earnestness and striving in the spirit of my mind; that so being cleansed from all filthiness, both of the flesh and spirit, I may grow up into full holiness in Thy fear, through Jesus Christ. Amen.

(d)

PRAYER OF THE ORIENTAL CHURCH

Grant, my Lord, that the ears which have heard the voice of Thy songs may never hear the words of clamour and dispute; that the eyes which have seen Thy great love may also behold Thy blessed hope; that the tongues which have sung the *Sanctus* may also speak the truth; that the feet which have walked in the church may tread the region of light; that the bodies which have tasted Thy living body may be restored to newness of life.

(e)

PRAYER BY F. QUARLES

Lord, Thou hast commanded me to ask, but my sins cry louder than my suits; Thou hast commanded me to seek, but my guilt leads me the wrong way; Thou hast commanded me to knock, but Satan holds my hands. Let the blood of my Saviour stop the mouth of my crying sins; let His full satisfaction take away my guilt. Bind him in chains that captivates my power. Teach me to *ask;* direct me how to *seek;* and let my knocking be guided by Thy hand. Give me knowledge, that I may ask what I should; grant me prudence, that I may seek where I should; give me providence, that I may knock when I should. Give me faith, that I may ask with confidence; hope, that I may seek with courage; patience, that I may knock with constancy. Let me ask like the importunate woman, till I obtain Thee; let me seek like Thy blessed mother, till I find Thee; let me knock like the sinful publican till Thou open to me; that, having found Thee here by grace, I may live with Thee in glory.

(f)

PRAYING

His manner of praying was very agreeable, most becoming a worm of the dust and a disciple of Christ; addressing an infinitely great and holy God and the Father of mercies, not with florid expressions or a studied eloquence, not with any

(g)

intemperate vehemence or indecent boldness; at the greatest distance from any appearance of ostentation, and from everything that might look as though he meant to recommend himself to those who were about him, or set himself off to their acceptance; also free from vain repetitions, without impertinent excursions, or needless multiplying of words. He expressed himself with the strictest propriety, with weight and pungency; and yet what his lips uttered seemed to flow from the fulness of his heart, as deeply impressed with a great and solemn sense of our necessities, unworthiness, and dependence, and of God's infinite greatness, excellency, and sufficiency, rather than merely from a warm and fruitful brain, pouring out good expressions. And I know not that ever I heard him so much as ask a blessing or return thanks at table, but there was something remarkable to be observed both in the matter and manner of the performance. In his prayers, he dwelt much on the prosperity of Zion, the advancement of Christ's kingdom in the world, and the propagation of religion among the Indians. He generally made it one petition in his prayer, "That we might not outlive our usefulness."

(a)　　*Pres. Edward's Life of David Brainerd*

PREACHER, THE MOST DILIGENT

I would ask a strange question, "Who is the most diligent bishop and prelate in all England, and passeth all the rest in doing his office?" I can tell, for I know who he is; I know him well. But now, methinks I see you listening and hearkening that I should name him. There is one that passeth all the others, and is the most diligent prelate and preacher in all England. And will ye know who it is? I will tell you. It is the devil. He is the most diligent preacher of all others; he is never out of his diocese; he is never from his cure; ye shall never find him unoccupied; he is ever in his parish; he keepeth residence at all times; ye shall never find him out of the way, call for him when ye will; he is ever at home; the most diligent preacher in all the realm; he is ever at his plough; ye shall never find him idle, I warrant you; and his office is to hinder religion, to maintain superstition, to set up idolatry, to devise as many ways as can be to deface and obscure God's glory."

(b)　　　　　　　　　　　　*Latimer*

PREACHER, AN EARNEST

The first charm of a preacher, in my opinion, is to possess his congregation with a conviction that he is thoroughly *in earnest*. The subjects in the pulpit are of too momentous a concern to be made the material of oratorical flourishes; and whatever tends to show the teacher more intent upon displaying his own abilities than persuading or convincing his hearers, is not only bad taste, but a pitiful aberration from what ought to be his sole object.

(c)　　　　　　　　　　*Hannah More*

A man famous for weakness of body and strength of mind, for having the strongest sense of religion himself, and exciting a sense of it in the thoughtless and profligate; for preaching more sermons, engaging in more controversies, and

writing more books than any other Nonconformist of his age.

(d)　　　*Granger, on Richard Baxter*

PREACHER, THE, AN EARTHEN VESSEL

Judge not the preacher, for he is thy judge.
If thou mislike him, thou conceivest him not.
God calleth preaching folly. Do not grudge
To pick out treasures from an earthern pot.
The worst speak something good.

(e)　　　　　　　　　　　　*Herbert*

PREACHER, AN EXCELLENT

Andrew Marvel was a most excellent preacher, who never broached what he had not brewed, but preached what he had pre-studied, insomuch that he was wont to say, that he would cross the common proverb, which called Saturday the working day, and Monday the holiday of preachers.

(f)　　　　　　　　　　　　*Fuller*

PREACHER, A FLUENT

It is not uncommon to hear a preacher mentioned as having "a very fine command of language," when perhaps it might be said with more correctness that "his language had command of him;" that is, he follows a train of words rather than of thought.

(g)　　　　　　　*Archbishop Whately*

PREACHER, A FORMAL

He contracts a callousness by his insensible way of handling Divine matters, by which he becomes hardened against them, and by which he is so far put out of the reach of conviction, in all the ordinary means of grace, that it is scarce possible he can ever be awakened, and, by consequence, that he can be saved.

(h)　　　　　　　*Bishop Massillon*

PREACHER OF THE GOSPEL, POWER OF THE

The teacher to whom are committed the infinite realities of the spiritual world, the sanctions of eternity, "the powers of the life to come," has instruments to work with which turn to feebleness all other means of influence.

(i)　　　　　　　　　　　　*Channing*

PREACHER, A TRUE

His character was that of the true Christian divine, his heart was in his profession. It is reported that once preaching in his turn at St. James's, and being unable to gain attention, he sat down and burst into tears. His conversation was of the same nature as his works, and showed a solemn cast of thought to be natural to him; death, futurity, judgment, eternity, were his common topics. When at home in the country, he spent many hours in the day walking among the graves in the churchyard. In his garden he had an alcove, painted as if with a bench to repose on; on approaching near enough to discover the deception, the following motto was seen: "Invisibilia non decipiunt."

(j)　　　　　　*Memoir of Dr. Young* (1807)

PREACHER, THE TRUE

This is what makes him the crowd-drawing
preacher,
There's a back-ground of God to each hard-work-
ing feature;
Every word that he speaks has been fierily
furnaced
In a blast of a life which has struggled in
earnest.

(a)   *Fable for Critics*

PREACHER, THE UNFAIR

King Charles II. called Isaac Barrow that
"UNFAIR preacher," because he so completely
exhausted the meaning of a text that he left no
other clergyman a chance of preaching from it.
(b)

PREACHER, A VAIN

A *vain* man came into my parish, who thought
that God only blessed the preaching of those who
had been great sinners, or who were very ignorant,
and consequently he expected a great blessing on
his own preaching.

(c)   *Hoare*

PREACHER, A ZEALOUS

Whitfield's zealous spirit exhausted all its energies in preaching; and his full dedication to God
was honoured by unbounded success. The effect
produced by his sermons was indescribable, arising
in a great degree from the most perfect forgetfulness of self during the solemn moment of declaring the salvation that is in Christ Jesus. His
evident sincerity impressed every hearer, and is
said to have forcibly struck Lord Chesterfield
when he heard him at Lady Huntingdon's.

(d)   *Sidney's "Life of Rowland Hill."*

PREACHER'S BUSINESS, THE

The business for which God sends a Christian
priest in a Christian nation is, to preach freedom,
equality, and brotherhood in the fullest, deepest,
widest meaning of those three great words; that
in as far as he does so, he is a true priest, doing
his Lord's work with his Lord's blessing upon
him; that in as far as he does not, he is no priest
at all, but a traitor to God and man. . . . These
words express the very pith and marrow of a
priest's business; . . . they preach freedom,
equality, and brotherhood to rich and poor for ever
and ever.

(e)   *Chas. Kingsley*

PREACHERS AND CONSCIENCE

I carry my ears to hear other preachers, but
my conscience to hear Sanderson.

(f)   *Charles I. on Bishop Sanderson*

PREACHERS, HOW TO PREACH

To be able to tell preachers *how* to preach, is a
hard task. The well is deep; and alas for the
man who has nothing wherewith to draw!

(g)   *Eccl. Gazette*

PREACHERS, LAY

A preaching, prison-preaching, field-preaching
esquire strikes more than all the black gowns and
lawn sleeves in the world. And if I am not mistaken, the Great Shepherd and Bishop of Souls
will let the world, and His own children too, know
that He will not be prescribed to, in respect to
men, or garb, or place, much less will He be confined to any order or set of men under heaven.

(h)   *Whitfield to Rowland Hill*

PREACHERS, LEARNED AND ELOQUENT

Tillotson, Moore, Patrick, Kidder, Fowler, and
Cumberland. Of such writers, Macaulay finely
says, they were "men familiar with all ancient
and modern learning; men able to encounter
Hobbes or Bossuet at all the weapons of controversy; men who could in their sermons set
forth the majesty and beauty of Christianity with
such justness of thought and such energy of
language that the indolent Charles roused himself to listen, and the fastidious Buckingham forgot to sneer; men whose address, politeness, and
knowledge of the world qualified them to manage
the consciences of the wealthy and the noble;
men with whom Halifax loved to discuss the
interests of the empire, and from whom Dryden
was not ashamed to own that he learned to write."

(i)

PREACHERS, POLITE, AND EXACTING HEARERS

Most people have heard of the courtly French
Court preacher, who, preaching in the royal
presence, modified the statement, "All men must
needs die," by substituting "some men" for the
more general statement, out of deference to the
king. In his letter on "Pulpit Cowardice," Lord
S. Godolphin Osborne relates the following anecdotes of a somewhat similar character:—"When I
was a young man I was doing duty in a parish which
my sexton thought highly privileged. 'There was
a deal of carriage company.' I had one morning
preached on the proper religious training of
children, the duty of keeping them out of the way
of early vanity and temptation to early ungodliness. I had hardly got home to luncheon when
a groom came with a hurried note from one of
my flock, a lady of high rank and what was called
great worldly influence—as kind-hearted a creature of that sort as any I have ever known. She
expressed her astonishment that, being on the
friendly terms I was at——with all the family, I
'should have so pointedly preached at them.' I
sent her the sermon, case and all, begged her to
observe it had been preached a few Sundays
before at D——t for the National School Society.
She apologized the next day with all that good-
humoured grace which so well became her, only
adding—'But you know, I think,—you ought to
have seen, that what would not give offence at
D——t would surely do so to us.'"

(j)   *S. Godolphin Osborne*

There is a story, an old one, but still afloat,
which for my purpose I may well quote. A certain
preacher, of by no means extreme views, had
several times quoted from Scripture, and enforced
in his own language, certain passages warning

(k)

mankind against the teaching and temptation of our common enemy—the Devil. He was spoken to on the subject of the use of the word by a leading parishioner, the head of the chief house. He defended himself as well as he could by the argument that all he had said was, after all, only Bible teaching. It was admitted ; but he was in effect told that he would act a more prudent part, if he felt compelled to speak from the pulpit " all that kind of thing," *to do it in the afternoon ;* he would assuredly give offence—to whom? To his morning congregation ! In fact, he was not to parade the Devil and his doings to "carriage company."

(*a*) *S. Godolphin Osborne*

PREACHERS, POPULAR

Being in London some few years since, I was taken by a friend to two West End churches, to hear popular preachers. In the first I heard an eloquent appeal to the congregation to fall in with the views of the Incumbent, he proposing a plan to shorten the time they—the congregation, a highly-dressed one—were detained at the Holy Communion, there being a large number of communicants. He reminded them it could be done, for, he went on to say, " in a neighbouring well-known church they *did get it over*, the numbers being greater than in this church, in half the time." Like Captain Cuttle, I made note of the expression at the time. In the second church I attended,—it was crammed with purple-and-fine-linen people,—the very eloquent preacher coolly told a congregation which seemed to hang for very spiritual life on his lips, that there was much he wished to say on his subject, but " he shrank from opening out these mysteries "—to whom?— " to a mixed congregation ! " In my own mind I made note to ask him, if ever we met, where was the congregation *not mixed*. If the vestments of his congregation clad individuals of so weak intellect or such cool piety that he felt it necessary to reserve high-class spiritual food, where were we to look for the qualified ? How could the poor taste of this reserved grace ?

(*b*) *Ibid*

Yesterday, for the first time, we went to hear A. (a popular preacher). I remembered what you had said about his vulgar, false emphasis; but there remained the fact of his celebrity. I was glad of the opportunity. But my impressions fell below the lowest judgment I ever heard passed upon him. He has the gift of a fine voice, very flexible and various ; he is admirably fluent and clear in his language, and every now and then his enunciation is effective. But I never heard any pulpit reading and speaking which, in its level tone, was more utterly common and empty of guiding intelligence or emotion ; it was as if the words had been learned by heart and uttered without comprehension by a man who had no instinct of rhythm or music in his soul. And the doctrine ! It was a libel on Calvinism that it should be presented in such a form. I never heard any attempt to exhibit the soul's experience that was more destitute of insight. The sermon was against Fear, in the elect Christian, as being a distrust of God ; but never once did he touch the true ground of fear—the doubt whether the signs of God's choice are present in the soul. We

had plenty of anecdotes, but they were all poor and pointless—Tract Society anecdotes of the feeblest kind. It was the most superficial grocer's-back-parlour view of Calvinistic Christianity ; and I was shocked to find how low the mental pitch of our society must be, judged by the standard of this man's celebrity.

(*c*) *George Eliot*

PREACHERS AND PREACHING

We have known a preacher to read a passage for a text, without stating verse, chapter, or book, and then coolly tell the congregation to try and find it out for themselves ! At a monthly meeting, one of the ministers announced to the wondering audience, that on the morrow a WILL would be read publicly, and most probably some of them would " hear of something to their advantage." The place was crowded ; country bumpkins came together in flaming waistcoats ; ancient, dim-looking females, who seldom attended a place of worship ; and all sorts of queer out-of-the-way people. In due time the preacher read out to the curious, half-doubting multitude, " Peace I leave with you," etc.

(*d*) *Memoir of Christmas Evans*

PREACHING

PREACHING SHOULD BE APPROPRIATE

" *And with many such parables spake He the word unto them, as they were able to hear it* " (Mark iv. 33)

Not as He was able to have spoken ; he could have expressed Himself at a higher rate than any mortal can ; He could have soared to the clouds ; he could have knit such knots that they could never untie, but He would not ; He delighted to speak to His hearers' shallow capacities. " I have yet many things to say unto you, but ye cannot bear them now " (John xvi. 12).

(*e*) *Thos. Brooks*

We are told that a sermon was once preached in the Highlands of Scotland—it was two hours long—on the sin of *luxury*. Now, that may have been a very good sermon, but it was not *appropriate*, because there were only about three pairs of shoes in the whole congregation. It, clearly, was not their sin.

Again

During a recent war, a good kind of man went into a hospital distributing tracts ; and he gave a tract on the " *Sin of Dancing* " to a man who had lost both his legs. The intention in both cases may have been good, but the act was not *appropriate*.

(*f*)

PREACHING, BOLDNESS IN

" *He opened His mouth* " (Matt. v. 2)

Get up boldly ;
Open the mouth widely ;
Be done quickly.

(*g*) *Luther*

Latimer, preaching before Henry VIII., who was surrounded with the nobles that had helped him to waste the money he got by the sale of Abbeys and Church lands,—the money he promised to devote to the instruction and relief of the poor,—boldly told both king and nobles of their wickedness to their faces, and charged them to make restitution. "Restitution — *restitution* — RESTITUTION — or damnation!" thundered the brave old martyr.

(*a*)   *Thos. Cooper*

PREACHING CERTAINTIES

Preach certainties, for God was one eternal "Yea." If He were something that might be this or might be that, it were well that they should go to Athens and bow before the unknown god, preach an unknown doctrine, and try to learn an unknown tongue. In Pompeii I saw a god-maker, and was amused at his expertness. He made all parts of the body except the face, and that he left until he knew what the purchaser required. He could thus produce Venus or Minerva, or any of the multitudinous goddesses that might be wanted. This was the case with many theologians. They were definite about everything which did not happen to have been in dispute. As to the rest, they were prepared to put on the face according to the company in which they were found.

(*b*)

They were not always glorifying God when perpetually defending His truth against the assaults of error. He imagined a number of brave men met to protect a lion which was shut up in his cage, and they were ready to die on its behalf. How boldly did they confront the foe! He would only suggest that they should undo the door and let the lion out to take care of himself. It was wonderful that when they preached the Gospel everything scampered out of the way. They should preach the unbending law as the standard of duty, and fill their sermons very full of Christ, remembering, too, the inspiration of the Scriptures, for these were as much inspired as Shakspeare. Some of their friends had gone even to the length of admitting that.

(*c*)

A certain saint dreamed that he went to the gates of heaven, and was asked, "Who art thou?" "I am a Christian." The porter said, "No; you are a Ciceronian; there has been more of Cicero than Christ in your subjects, and you must go back to where Cicero has gone." He awoke, and behold it was a dream, and it made so much impression upon him that he went back and began to translate the Holy Scriptures into Latin, producing that wonderful book the Latin Vulgate; and henceforth his one theme was Christ and Christ alone. It was no secret that the next time he went to the gates of heaven in reality they let him in. There was a clergyman who used to go out hunting the hare, and he met a Quaker, who said, "If I were a hare I would get into a place where thou wouldst never find me." "Where would that be?" "I would get into thy study." A great many hares and rabbits might shelter themselves in some ministers' studies; in fact, they might have a whole litter of them. A

preacher should not, when he got up to preach, leave part of himself behind; for he was not much even when he was all there. He had heard of one of whom it was said there was nothing original in him except original sin.

(*d*)   *C. H. Spurgeon (Report)*

PREACHING CHRIST

Neither the Jesus of the rationalists nor the Christ of the philosophers hurts the kingdom of Satan.

(*e*)   *Lange*

There is nothing that makes a man so able to preach Christ to the people, as getting Christ within him.

(*f*)   *Thomas Brooks*

It would be well for yourself and the world if you and your class-mates should bear in mind that you are not called upon to preach a religion, but to hold up to the people's faith and imitation a Man—the Man Jesus, the Lord Christ. It is not faith in His religion, but faith in Him, that will save their souls. It is not defence of a system of doctrines for which you are sent forth of the Holy Ghost into the world, but defence of the truth as *it existed in Him—His life, His character, His spirit.* You are not merely professors of a religion. You are disciples of a Man; and your mission is not to make it, but Him, known. Him the earliest preachers knew—knew intimately—and Him they preached, and Him only. Paul wrote many doctrinal and practical letters; but when he came to preaching, he kept to the one idea—Jesus, His life, His death, His resurrection. "For I determined to know nothing among you but Jesus Christ, and Him crucified."

(*g*)   *Address to Students*

PREACHING, EFFECTUAL

Preaching, to be *effectual*, must be as various as nature. The sun warms at the same moment that it enlightens; and unless religious truth be addressed at once to the reason and the affections, unless it kindles whilst it guides, it is a useless splendour; it leaves the heart barren; it produces no fruits of godliness.

(*h*)   *Channing*

PREACHING, ELABORATE

The Lord did not come into the world to publish *elaborate* discourses to men. He was full of the truth; and the truth flashed from Him as the occasion suggested. A sneering objection brought one discourse from Him; an affectionate inquiry elicited another; the dulness of His disciples incited another.

(*i*)   *Storrs*

PREACHING AND HEARING

Canova once remarked, that some people saw only with their ears: it is unquestionably true, that a considerable proportion of the admiring multitude listen to some sermons with their eyes only.

(*j*)   *Memoir of Christmas Evans*

PREACHING BY THE LIFE

"If I had a large fortune to distribute, if I had a large sphere of usefulness, I would do a great deal of good." Oh! ye who are in the sorrows, and the perplexities, and the persecutions of life, you have the grandest possible opportunity to preach the Gospel. The lions were turned out in the Coliseum to destroy the ancient Christians. There was a great throng that day of 80,000 or 100,000 people, looking down upon the sacrifice of the Lord's children. The lions were growling in their dens, waiting for the moment when they should come out and slake their thirst in the blood of the Christians. Then there was led into the Coliseum a fair young girl, who came forth to die for Christ's sake; and there was so much calmness in her manner, there was so much peace in her countenance, that the great throng of people were entranced with the spectacle. One man looked down upon the scene and was overwhelmed with it, and after the poor girl had been torn to pieces by the lions, this man sought the companionship of some Christian people, and asked them the secret of all that placidity and calmness on the part of the dying girl among the wild beasts; and when he was told that it was Christian faith that gave her the peace and the triumph, he said, "I must have it." He got it. That was Clement, the great in all ages for faith in God and good works.

(a) *Talmage*

PREACHING ON ONE SET OF SUBJECTS

One preached so long on the doctrine of Sin, that there seemed no room for the promise of Salvation; another preached upon Fore-ordination, till one was tempted to apply the rough remark of Robert Hall about a minister who did the same thing in the neighbourhood of Bristol—that "he must have been fore-ordained, from all eternity, to be a fool."

(b) *Storrs*

PREACHING, POINTED

Oliver Maillard, a famous Cordelier, died in 1502, have pointed some keen traits in his sermons at Louis XI., the irritated monarch had our Cordelier informed that he would throw him into the river. He replied, undaunted, and not forgetting his satire: "The king may do as he chooses; but tell him that I shall sooner get to paradise by water, than he will arrive by all his post-horses"—alluding to the mode of travelling which this monarch had lately adopted.

(c) *Disraeli: Cur. Lit*

PREACHING, POWER OF

"*They marvelled at Peter and John*" (Acts iv. 13)

(i.) For their "boldness" in preaching, etc.;
(ii.) As "unlearned and ignorant men";
   = laity, no professional training;
   = not of the "clergy."
How account for their success?
(iii.) They had been with Jesus;
   = Ordination, and Learning and Power, both then and now.

(d)

How seldom do we meet it! How often does preaching remind us of a child's arrows shot against a fortress of adamant! How often does it seem a mock fight! We do not see the earnestness of real warfare.

(e) *Channing*

When you *preach*, you are bringing the grandest moral force which the world has known into contact with minds constitutionally adapted to receive and retain impressions from it. It is not from ancient history, or law, you draw your motives. Not from ethics or philosophy. It is from the world supernatural, invisible; from beings and facts divine and eternal: the Advent, the Ascension; Sinai, Calvary; the manger at Bethlehem, and the Judgment throne.

(f) *Storrs*

PREACHING, PRACTICAL

"How would you have me treat the subject, father?" said a young clergyman, fresh from Cambridge and ordination, who had agreed to preach for his father, a Lincolnshire clergyman, from a *plain* text which the father had named. "Shall I treat it philosophically and logically, or merely rhetorically and discursively?" "My dear lad," said his father, "treat it *practically*."

(g) *T. Cooper*

Whatever mode of treatment, however, be adopted, we should aim at being not only instructive, but practical. The cry in the present day is for practical preaching. Daniel Webster, the American statesman, only expressed a truth which is widely felt when he said, "If a man preaches to me, before all things I wish him to be practical, practical, practical."

(h) *E. Bayley*

PREACHING AND PREACHER

It is not the preaching, but the preacher, that preaches. The preacher is not a mere messenger, who may have no interest in the intelligence he has to bring; he is a witness, guaranteeing what he says by all that he is.

(John xv. 27; Luke xxiv. 48; Acts i. 8, 22; 1 John i. 2).

(i) *Lange*

PREACHING AND PROFITING

The venerable Dr. Hurd, Bishop of Worcester, being in the habit of preaching frequently, had observed a poor man remarkably attentive, and made him some little presents. After a while he missed his humble auditor, and meeting him said, "John, how is it that I do not see you in the aisle as usual?" John, with some hesitation, replied, "My lord, I hope you will not be offended, and I will tell you the truth. I went the other day to hear the Methodists, and I understand their plain words so much better that I have attended them ever since." The Bishop put his hand into his pocket and gave him a guinea, with words to this effect: "God bless you; go where you can receive the greatest profit to your soul."

"*Life of Lady Huntingdon*," on Bishop Hurd

(j)

Preaching and Reading the Scriptures

"Intelligent *reading* of Scripture is the best *preaching*.

(*a*)   *Bishop Wordsworth*

Preaching by Reading Sermons

Ministers being allowed to *read* their sermons in the pulpit, *buy all they meet with*, and take no other trouble than to read them, and thus pass for very able scholars at a very cheap rate!

(*b*)   *Bayle: Dis. Cur. Lit*

Preaching, Sensational

Reminds one of what an English lady said of the shop-windows in Paris, during the Prussian siege: "that they showed fifty pots of mustard to an ounce of meat."

(*c*)   *Storrs*

Preaching, Style of

Studious men, dwelling in "the solitary and still air of delightful studies," are apt to get a style which reminds one of a remark made of Tertullian—"splendid, but dark, like polished ebony." The tendency with studious men, whose literary enthusiasm is apt to get the mastery over their practical evangelical zeal, is to become too stately in style.

On the other hand, there is a dangerous tendency in speaking without head or point; where nothing arrests, strikes, rouses, awakens, elevates, or animates: all is a dreary outpour of verbiage, incessantly coming, like the ribbons in a juggler's trick. "What colour will you have, gentlemen?" and out it comes; twenty yards of blue, and then twenty of pink, and more and more as it is ordered. The man who thus speaks seems to be pumping words out of some bottomless reservoir within.

(*d*)   *Ibid*

"What a command of language that man has," said some one of some such a man, to Archbishop Whately. "No, sir," was the reply, "he has no command of it at all." (*See* "Words.")

(*e*)

Preaching, The great Use of

In my opinion, the great use of preaching is to uphold right, denounce wrong; to offer hope, or warn against its loss, *without respect of persons*, according as it is written. It is very easy to find fault with us—there is abundance of room for sharp criticism; but do remember, we are ordained very young, and the law binds us for life to work the reality of which we have yet to learn. It was hard to ask for the tale of bricks from the Israelites, and give them no straw; only one thing would have been worse—to have demanded bricks from gravel, not clay. All I ask for is a just consideration of our case. Say that a London West-end preacher determines to be honest, or even that a bishop in his pulpit does so, would the congregation bear to be told in plain words Bible-truth as to adultery, gambling, utter devotion to money-seeking, the giving up mind and body to mere pleasure-hunting in any fields, however polluted by open sin? Would not that preacher, be he even the most simple of bishops, know full well that if he were to venture to talk to the well-clad and scented crowd before him about their lives as he would talk to the class of young folks just confirmed in a country parish, that he would be transgressing all rule as to what society calls good taste in the pulpit? Does not every bishop and preacher to the "upper ten" know full well that if, as before God, he did his duty from Sunday to Sunday, he would have to tell his congregation some truths as to their lives they would not endure? What is the result? Sermons are tame, often stupid. The preacher can hardly be very animated in delivering a religious essay calculated not to offend, when in his heart he feels what a sham it is. Yes, there is many a pure heart which feels itself choked in utterance, because, forsooth, the higher order are not to be offended; their vice is to be delicately handled, their path heavenward to be left easy, lest in the attempt to show they have something yet to do they are offended. Your music is good; it is a high-bred audience; the offertory collection admirable; well, you can let off steam into an S.P.G., abuse Colenso, and narrate the hideous morals of Zulus and colonists.

(*f*)

Take a country parish, with the usual proportion of great house, farmhouse, servant, and labourer element. You are expected to work at those *poor* poor; to preach down drunkenness, poaching—stealing of all kinds; and in the afternoons to speak plainly about the marriage vow and its frequent breach. You know full well that these *poor* have been starved on low wages, that they are dependent on the poor-rate for every interruption to their normal starving state; you know they are so housed that all ordinary rule for the protection of modesty is a farce; that drunkenness to them is a dearly-bought forgetfulness, for a time, of the wretched monotony of a struggling life, and becoming a habit is their ruin. You know that their condition can truly be traced to the door of some of the other classes to whom you have to preach; that they, owners and occupiers, do reap the benefit of keeping these poor as they are. Now, dare one clergyman in a hundred—could he get a bishop to do it for him?—preach Bible truth as plainly about the duty of employer and landowner to their poor as they expect him to preach to the poor the virtues which Heaven demands from them, and which will make them better *earthly* servants? If your great man or any of the lesser great ones should live a profligate life, should he be a known drunkard, would it be justifiable, even in your bishop's eye, if you preached at his vices as he expects you to attack those of the poor?

I will trouble you with no more for the present, only adding my conviction that if a Church which has failed of its purpose should be disestablished, I think my Church in danger. Certainly I cannot see that we have made the wealthy and noble much better; and these tell us our poor are very bad. I cannot admit, however, it is all our fault. I should like to see one year's honest pulpit campaign against high-class vice. I should then be less ashamed of the order to which I belong, the profession I have not yet altogether quitted.

(*g*)   *S. Godolphin Osborne*

PRECIOUSNESS OF CHRIST (1 Pet. ii. 7)

The believer has a special regard for the person of Christ Himself: "Unto you that believe He is precious." The Apostle does not say "Christianity is precious"; or, "Salvation is precious"; or, "The Gospel is precious"; but *Christ is precious*. In fact, the religion of a believer consists in *union and fellowship with* an everliving Person, even Jesus the Son of God.

(a)

PREDESTINATION, DOCTRINE OF (Eph. i.)

(i.) Importance of;
(ii.) The starting point;
(iii.) The *object* of predestination—"you"= WHOM?
(iv.) The *subject* of the predestination—"God" = WHO?
(v.) The *end* of the predestination—WHY?
(1.) Unto adoption (ver. 4, 5, 6, 7, 11, 14).
(2.) For the world (ver. 10).
(3.) For God the Lord (ver. 6, 12, 14).

(b)   *Schenkel*

Neither Calvinism nor Arminianism has solved the problem presented in this chapter. Like difficulties meet us in God's providential dealings, ay, in the workings of His natural laws; for, as a brilliant author has said: "Nature is a terrible Calvinist."

(c)   *Lange*

It is above logic and philosophy, and even technical theology, even as on many, and these the most important subjects, the heart is a better teacher than the head. In these matters I am so fearful, that I dare not speak further; yea, almost none otherwise than the text does, as it were, lead me by the hand.

(d)   *Ridley (Martyr)*

They who are Christ's were predestinated to glory before the foundation of the world, and being chosen by the Father, they were redeemed by the Son, and are sanctified by the Holy Ghost. Neither is it the work of man, but of God the Father, to make manifest to the soul of him that is saved, the completeness of that work of salvation which was wrought for him through omnipotent wisdom.

(e)   *Mrs. Sherwood's " Life of a Nun "*

There are some men who claim to know all about the matter. It is the shallowness of their minds that permits them to see to the bottom of their knowledge. The fact is, that the great questions about man's responsibility, free-will, and predestination have been fought over and over again; and the result has been, that we know just as much about the matter as when we first began.

(f)   *C. H. Spurgeon*

We grant, 'tis true, that Heaven from human sense
Has hid the secret paths of Providence;
But boundless wisdom, boundless mercy, may
Find even those bewildered souls a way.

(g)   *Dryden*

It is here shown to be as irrational as irreligious, on the ground of human understanding, to deny, either, on the one hand, the foreknowledge, predestination, and free grace of God, or, on the other, the free will of man; that we should believe both, and both in unison, though unable to comprehend even either apart. This philosophy proclaims with *Augustine*, and Augustine in his maturist writings:

"If there be not free grace in God, how can He save the world? and if there be not free will in man, how can the world by God be judged?" Or, as the same doctrine is perhaps expressed even better by *Bernard*: "Abolish free will, and there is nothing to be saved; abolish free grace, and there is nothing wherewithal to save."

(h)   *Sir Wm. Hamilton and Eadie*

PREDESTINATION AND ELECTION

Those who are willing are always the elect; those who will not, are not elected. Many men are wrapped up in the doctrines of election and predestination; but that is the height of impertinence. They are truths belonging to God alone, and if you are perplexed by them, it is only because you trouble yourself about things which do not concern you. You only need to know that God sustains you with all His might in the winning of your salvation, if you will only rightly use His help. Whoever doubts this, is like a crew of a boat working with all their might against the tide and yet going back hour after hour; then they notice that the tide turns, while at the same time the wind springs up and fills their sails. The coxswain cries: "Pull away, boys! wind and tide favour you!" But they answer: "What can we do with the oars, don't the wind and tide take away our free agency?"

(i)   *H. W. Beecher*

PREFERMENT.

Could the secret history of great men be traced, it would appear that merit is rarely the first step to advancement. It would much oftener be found to be owing to superficial qualifications, and even vices.

(j)   *Disraeli : Cur. Lit*

PREJUDICES

Doctor Taylor of Norwich said to me, " Sir, I have collated every word in the Hebrew Scriptures seventeen times, and it is very strange if the doctrine of atonement you hold should not have been found by me." I am not surprised at this. I once went to light my candle with the extinguisher on it. Now, prejudices from education, learning, etc., often form an extinguisher. It is not enough that you bring the candle; you must remove the extinguisher.

(k)   *John Newton*

PREPARATION

There is—
(i.) A preparation *for* Christ unto salvation;
(ii.) A preparation *in* Christ for heaven.

(l)

PRESENCE OF CHRIST

In a certain congregation there was a hearer of whose presence the preacher was not aware during the delivery of his sermon. When the fact of that hearer's presence was made known to him, it had a great effect upon the preacher. . . . Who was the preacher, and who this hearer? . . . The preacher may have been any minister, and the hearer was Jesus Christ. Every time we have preached we have had Him for a hearer. When the great and learned and honoured of the earth come to hear you, He is there, whose opinion of you, while it is infinitely more important than theirs, will either confirm or reverse their judgment of you. When we meet a few of our flock in that distant school-house on a dark and stormy night, and something whispers, "Will you waste your time and strength on these poor people?" The Son of God is there to hear what you say to them, and to have an opinion of you for saying it, which is or will hereafter be a greater reward to you than the applauses of a throng. In the bungalow, or under the plantain or the palm, or in those South African huts where you must creep like an animal to get in, remember that you cannot speak in His name but you will speak in His ear.

(*a*)   *N. Adams*

Presence of Christ and Desertion

You complain of Christ's short visits, that He will not bear you company one night; but when you lie down warm at night, you rise cold at morning. Answer, I cannot blame you nor any other who knoweth that sweet Guest for bemoaning His withdrawings, and being most desirous of His abode and company; for He would captivate and engage the affection of any creature that saw His face; since He looked on me, and gave me a sight of His fair love, He gained my heart wholly, and got away with it; well, well may He brook it; he shall keep it long ere I fetch it from Him. But I will tell you what you shall do: treat Him well, give Him the chair and the board-head, and make Him welcome to the mean portion you have —a good supper and kind entertainment maketh the guest love the inns the better. Yet sometimes Christ hath an errand elsewhere, for mere trial; and then, though you give Him king's cheer, He will away, as is clear in desertions for mere trial, and not for sin.

(*b*)   *Samuel Rutherford*

PRESUMPTION

Presumption is a sin, in which we depend upon God's mercies without any warrant from His word.

A long peace makes a bloody war.

Patience, when slighted, turns to fury; but ill requited, starts to vengeance.

The stalled ox is not far from slaughter.

When repentance is out of date, prayer will find no ear.

(*c*)   *F. Quarles*

To commit sin, is a human frailty, to persist in it, is a devilish obstinacy.

(*d*)   *Bernard*

A gentleman wishing to test some men for the situation of coachman, took them to a road which bordered on a precipice, and inquired of them how near the verge they could drive. One named a few inches, another still fewer. A third was taken to the precipice; and in answer to the question, "How near this edge can you drive in safety?" drew back, replying, "I should drive as far from it as possible."

(*e*)

PREY

A Welsh preacher said one day, "Shall the prey be taken from the mighty, and the lawful captive delivered?" He applied these words to the Sunday School, and said, "Lord, we have toiled a long time." He said again, "Shall the prey be taken from the mighty, and the lawful captive delivered?" And he applied it to the superintendent, and he said, "Well, I don't know; lack of faith." He put the question then to the minister, and the minister said, "We have preached long. This is a peculiar place; people seem different here." And then he put the inquiry to the angels, and the angels said: "We have hovered over this congregation for a long time; we have watched for their decision that we might take the news on high; and make it known that they were to be delivered. But, alas, we are afraid!" Turning to the Almighty, the minister put once more the question: "What sayest Thou, O God?" The lawful captive *shall* be delivered. Is not our God on the throne? Cannot He save the drunken and fallen? Is there a man so fallen in London that God is not able to deliver him? Let us join with the Almighty this morning and go forth in His name.

(*f*)   *Moody*

PRICE (HALF-PRICE)

There is no such thing as real cheapness. Everything has its just and necessary price, which you can no more alter than you can alter the course of the earth; and whenever you boast you have bought anything for half-price, be assured that some one else has had to pay the other half.

(*g*)   *Ruskin*

PRIDE (Col. ii. 22)

When Diogenes lifted his foot on Plato's velvet cushion and shouted "Thus I trample on Plato's pride," the Athenian sage justly replied, "But with still greater pride."

(*h*)   *Eadie*

Pride, of all others the most dangerous fault,
Proceeds from want of sense, or want of thought.

(*i*)   *Earl of Roscommon*

"Mark him!" said the shrewd Garrick to Dr. Johnson, as Bishop Horsley rode along the streets of London; "he looks as if he could say to one of the twelve apostles, 'Here, sir! hold my horse!'"

(*j*)   *Thos. Cooper*

He saw a cottage with a double coach-house,
    A cottage of gentility!
And the devil did grin, for his darling sin
    Is pride that apes humility.

(*k*)   *Coleridge*

PRIDE, FALL OF

> I have ventured,
> Like little wanton boys that swim on bladders,
> This many summers in a sea of glory,
> But far beyond my depth : my high-blown pride
> At length broke under me, and now has left me,
> Weary and old with service, to the mercy
> Of a rude stream that must for ever hide me.

(a) *Shakspeare*

PRIDE OF RANK, AND PRIESTCRAFT

A rich lady-patroness had educated a gardener's son for a schoolmaster. He now came to her with his petition, that he "would cheerfully content himself for a few years in the school; but yet in the end he longed to be in some small quiet priestly office." To her question, "But was he orthodox?" he answered, that "he hoped so." . . . The sick lady required him to make a proof-shot, viz., to administer to her a sick-bed exhortation. . . . He administered one of the best. Her pride of birth now crouched before his pride of office and priesthood; for though he could not, with the Dominican monk, Alanus de Rufe, believe that a priest was greater than God, inasmuch as the latter could only make a world, but the former a God (in the Mass); yet he could not but fall in with Hostiensis, who shows that the priestly dignity is seven thousand six hundred and forty-four times greater than the kingly, the sun being just so many times greater than the moon. But a Rittmeisterinn—*she* shrinks into absolute nothing before a parson.

(b) *J. P. F. Richter*

PRIDE, SPIRITUAL

"*Not a novice. . . . Being lifted up with pride*" (1 Tim. iii. 6)

John Bunyan had a great dread of spiritual pride; and once, after he had preached a very fine sermon, and his friends crowded round to shake him by the hand, while they expressed the utmost admiration of his eloquence, he interrupted them, saying, "Ah! you need not remind me of that, for the devil told me of it before I was out of the pulpit."

(c) *Southey*

PRIESTCRAFT

When famous lamas die and their bodies are burnt, little white pills are reported as found among the ashes, and are sold for large sums to the devout, as being the concentrated virtue of the man, and possessing the power of insuring a happy future for him who swallows one near death. This is quite common. I heard of one man who improved on this, by giving out that these pills were in the habit of coming out through the skin of various parts of the body. These pills, called "Sharil," met with a ready sale; and then the man himself reaped the reward of his virtue, and did not allow all the profit to go to his heir. The devices of priestcraft in all countries and ages resemble each other!

(d)

The whole system is one of *Church* instead of *Christ; priest* instead of *gospel;* concealment of truth instead of manifestation of truth; ignorant superstition instead of enlightened faith; bondage where we are promised liberty—all tending to load us with whatever is odious in the worst meaning of priestcraft, in the place of the free, affectionate, enlarging, elevating, and cheerful liberty of the children of God.

(e) *Bishop M'Ilwaine*

PRINCE OF THIS WORLD JUDGED, THE
(John xii. 31)

Satan had penetrated into the Paradise of the first man when he tempted the first of the human race; when he tempted Christ in the wilderness, he had ventured into heaven itself (the heaven of spiritual life), as a tempter. With the victory of Christ over Satan in the wilderness, the latter fell from heaven like lightning; and upon this transaction rested the victories of Jesus' disciples over demons in Israel. Now Satan is likewise cast out of the world,—the old pre-Messianic and non-Messianic world,—with special reference to the Gentile world whose highest *cosmical* formation is the very Hellenism that is confronting Him. Satan's empire over the world is shattered with the death and resurrection of Jesus. He is indeed still tarrying and working over the earth (Eph. ii. 2); here he retains his ἔξω, the air and wind regions of the human world as far as it is not yet spiritual, whence he reacts upon the Church of Christ. Subsequently he is cast upon *the earth* (Rev. xii. 9), *i.e.*, he possesses himself of traditional, ancient ordinances, now deadened, lifeless. But in time to come he is also cast out of the earth into the bottomless pit (Rev. xx.). Thus this saying opens up a perspective of the final judgment.

(f) *Lange*

PRINCES

> Vain pomp and glory of this world, I hate ye;
> I feel my heart new opened: Oh, how wretched
> Is that poor man that hangs on princes' favours!
> There is, betwixt that smile we should aspire to,
> That sweet aspect of princes, and their ruin,
> More pangs and fears than wars or women have;
> And when he falls, he falls like Lucifer,
> Never to hope again.

(g) *Shakspeare*

PRISON, PAUL AND SILAS IN (Acts xvii. 25)

This was a sort of consecration of European prisons for the manifestation of the power of the Gospel, and of the patience which the Holy Spirit makes to triumph over all sufferings. How often has Satan since repeated the mode of attack upon God's saints which he adopted at Philippi, and cast them into the inner prison for the word of God and for the testimony of Jesus Christ; and how often has there issued forth from European dungeons prayer and praise unto God! But has Satan ever gained anything by persecution? Have not rather the things that have befallen turned out rather for the furtherance of the Gospel? and the names of those blessed martyrs and confessors have been watchwords to the Church in every age.

In the archiepiscopal palace at Lambeth there is a tower called the Lollards' Tower, which was, before the Reformation in the fifteenth century, filled with the followers of Wycliffe. Many of these faithful witnesses for God's truth, harbingers

(h)

of a brighter day, were here confined, and some carved upon their dungeon walls the expressions of their faith and hope. In one tower these words are still visible on the wall, "Jesus ama meni." It is impossible to tell how many persecuted servants of God have been cheered and comforted by the remembrance of what passed in the dungeon of Philippi.

In the day of trouble let us think thereon.

(a)　　　　　　　　　　　　　　*Cheese*

Prison, The World a

Sir Walter Raleigh, on his return to prison, while some were deploring his fate, said, that "The world itself is but a larger prison, out of which some are daily selected for execution."

(b)　　　　　　　　*Disraeli: Cur. Lit*

PROCRASTINATION

Procrastination is the thief of time.

(c)　　　　　　　　　　　　　　*Young*

PROFESSION AND PRACTICE

So many professed Christians, yet so few imitators of Christ; so much talk of religion, so much science, so little conscience; so much knowledge, so many preachers, so little practice.

(d)　　　　　　　　*Burton: Anat. Mel*

PROGRAMME OF THE OLD TESTAMENT (Luke xxiv. 46, 47)

Note the sequences.

(i.) **The Old Testament Programme**: more or less enigmatical;

(ii.) **The Execution of that Programme**: "Suffer and rise again," etc.;

(iii.) **The Moral Effect**. (i.) Repentance (ii.) Remission of sins;

(iv.) **The Starting Point**. "Beginning at Jerusalem." Note its import, Begin as surgeons, on the field of battle, with the worst cases. Try the healing effect of the Gospel on such.

(e)

PROMISE

The specific form of the whole Gospel is *promise*, which God gives in the Word, and causes to be preached. The last period of the world is the reign of grace (Rom. v. 21). Grace reigns in the Word, only as *promise*. Grace has nothing to do with law and requisition of law, therefore the word of that grace can be no other than a word of promise. Hence χάρις and ἐπαγγελία form an indissoluble unity (Rom. iv. 16). For to this end Christ is the Mediator of the New Covenant, that we might receive the *promise* of the eternal inheritance (Heb. ix. 15). The *promise* of life in Christ Jesus is the word of the New Covenant (2 Tim. i. 1). The difference between the Gospel of the Old Covenant and that of the New rests alone on the transcendently greater glory of its promise (Heb. viii. 6; xi. whole). That these great and precious *promises* are given to us (2 Pet. i. 4; 2 Cor. vii. 1) establishes the position of a Christian man; if he calls himself a son and heir, he has no other title for this except that of *promise* alone, purely of grace (Gal. iv. 28; iii. 29; Rom.

iv. 16). That, and how God *for His own sake* blots out our transgressions, and remembers our sin no more (Isa. xliii. 25), is the substance of the word of *promise* in the New Testament, and which confirms that of the Old.

(f)　　　　　　　　　　　　　　*Harless*

PROMISES

Temures promised the garrison of Sebastia, that, if they would surrender, *no blood should be shed*. The garrison surrendered; and Temures buried them all alive. Now Temures fulfilled the promise in one sense, and in the sense too in which he intended it at the time; but not in the sense in which the garrison of Sebastia actually received it, nor in the sense in which Temures himself knew that the garrison received it; which last sense was that in which he was, in his conscience, bound to have performed it.

(g)　　　　　　　　　　　　　　*Paley*

Promises and the Bible

The Bible is a book of promises, as well as of revelations, or Divine statements. These promises are our heritage-

> "*All* I have is thine," saith He,
> "*All* things are yours," He saith again;
> *All* the promises for thee
> Are sealed with Jesus Christ's Amen.

Faith in the promises makes the future present, and the heirship possession. It is thus "the substance of things hoped for."

> "Faith lends its realizing light,
> The clouds disperse, the shadows fly."

Shall the promises fail? Is God unfaithful? Shall a Queen Elizabeth value her promise, as when she gave the *first* vacancy to one unfit? Shall a Chatham have a wall rebuilt, rather than seem to break a promise to his son? Shall a Napier refuse an invitation that he may keep a promise to a poor girl? And shall God refuse to honour drafts made on His promises in the name of His Son? Shall the promises fail? Is there inability or unwillingness to perform?

> The thing surpasses all my thought,
> 　　But faithful is my Lord;
> Through unbelief I stagger not,
> 　　For God hath spoke the word.
> Faith, mighty faith, the promise sees,
> 　　And looks to that alone;
> Laughs at impossibilities,
> 　　And cries, "It shall be done!"

(h)　　　　　　　　　　　　*John Gill*

Promises and Payment

Satan promises the best, but pays with the worst;
He promises honour, and pays with disgrace;
He promises pleasure, and pays with pain;
He promises profit, and pays with loss;
He promises life, and pays with death.
But God pays as He promises; all His payments are made in pure gold.

(i)　　　　　　　　　*Thomas Brooks*

PROMOTION AND PREFERMENT

Even in war, honours fall as by chance, with cruel and ludicrous injustice; often the hero, whom the populace worship, is only made so by accident. Often the coronet falls on brows that least deserve it.

(j)　　　　　　　　*F. W. Robertson*

PROPERTY, LOST

Every day we see advertisements for lost property, some showing eccentricity on the part of the losers. Ladies leave bags full of jewels in hansom cabs, though why they carry these articles about so loosely does not appear. Puppies and Angora cats are continually going astray, as also canary birds, parrots, and dormice; while pocket-books " of no use to any one but the owner" seem to lead a nomadic existence. But these are small losses compared to that which has lately befallen a young Ritualist, whose "Sin Book" has been mislaid or stolen. In this awful volume he had written down a great many venial, and four or five mortal sins—he is uncertain as to the number, but that is of small moment. From his love of sweets it is presumed that one of the direst sentences runs thus—"I ate too many pancakes on Shrove Tuesday;" but we are not informed whether he considers this a venial or a mortal sin. "I wasted too much time in dressing for vespers" may, perhaps, be another. A young lady is supposed to have found the "Sin Book." This, the latest vagary of Ritualism, is, however absurd it may seem, a positive fact. We can scarcely imagine a more unwholesome employment for a lad than keeping a "Sin Book."

(a) *Echo*

PROPHECY, THE SPIRIT OF

" The Spirit of God moved upon the face of the waters " (Gen. i. 2)
" The Spirit of the Lord is upon me ; because He hath anointed me to preach good tidings unto the meek " (Isa. lxi. 1)

1. Looking back on the history of the world, we observe a long period at which mankind appeared to be stationary

Great empires remained the same for two or three thousand years. The external framework of their institutions exercised a paralysing influence on their life and spirit. Their religions continued the same, because they were ancient; their works of art were always cast in the same form; their laws and customs, like chains, were too strong for the puny arm of individuals to break. Still more true is this, as far as we can conjecture, of the pre-historic times of which we know so little; for although there were wars and emigration among primitive men, they remained for the most part in the same condition; there was hardly more increase of wisdom among them than among the animals. Even in our own age of industrial and political activity, it becomes influenced and checked by times of reaction. Countries, like individuals, are always in danger of falling back into the path of repose, so that if some persons speak to-day of the law of progress in human affairs, others seem rather to observe the law of rest; they see not everything going forward, but everything standing still—not that the new is even coming, but that there is "nothing new under the sun." And certainly we must admit that times of progress and improvement have been few and far between. The day-spring from on high has been dimmed at intervals. Every individual who has sought to do good in his generation has probably made the reflection how little impression seems left on the evil forces arrayed against him—hardly more than by the husbandman on the solid framework of the earth. Yet there have been times in which the foundations of the great deep have been torn up ; new light has dawned on men ; new views about politics, morality, and religion have become the inheritance of after ages. The general progress of mankind has not been gradual, but sudden. If we take away two nations from the history of the world—if we imagine that six of the greatest of the sons of men had been blotted out and never been—the peoples of the earth might still have sat in darkness and in the shadow of death. And those two nations are among the fewest of all peoples. Scarcely in their most flourishing periods have they counted one-hundredth part of the human race. The golden age of Isaiah can hardly be said to extend over two or three centuries. And the nations themselves were not so much influential for good, but single men have been teachers, not only of their own, but of all ages and countries. If Greek philosophers had never existed, is it too much to say the very nature of the human mind would have been different? You can hardly tell where or how the sciences would have come into being. Many elements of religion and morality would have been wanting; and the history of the nations would have been changed.

(b)

2. The Influence of the Jewish Prophets on the Character of Mankind

They lived in a narrow spot of earth between the great empires of Assyria and Egypt, which seemed so amazing in their iniquity and greatness. They had the force of mind to perceive *beyond*—beyond the extent of their own Jewish nation; great as was the power of Assyria and Egypt, they knew and were convinced that they were as nothing before the power of God. Already they saw the seeds of ruin in them—their garments were worn, their greatness was crumbling in the dust; for they were persuaded that no kingdom could be lasting which was not founded on righteousness and the fear of God. These are the foundation principles of politics and religion. They taught the true nature of God, as consisting of love and justice; that He is the Father as well as the Judge of mankind. They saw Him sweeping the earth with His judgments, and yet ever willing to have mercy on those who turned unto Him. They knew that He could not be appeased by external righteousness or ceremony. They raised their voices against villany and hypocrisy, against luxury and vice, against the foreign superstitions which were imported into Israel. For they found *within* the limits of the Jewish people, and *without* the experience of the rest of the world; they saw in the distance a vision of the future, of the perfect God, having the beauty of heaven in its clearness. In modern times we hardly like to acknowledge the full force of their words. We explain them away, or disfigure what is literal and what is spiritual; still, after all, I know that in Christian countries their words have sunk deep into the heart of the human race; the logical, the intellectual framework of the human mind has been strengthened and deepened by the Jewish prophets; the force of the words remains, and light and heavenly truth and life spring from them now. For two thousand five hundred years they have solaced the mourner ; and the hearts of the widow and orphan thrill now when they read the words, "Comfort ye My people ! "

(c)

Prophecy, The Spirit of—*continued*

3. The Jewish Prophet

We may set aside that he was a foreteller of future events, as the Roman soothsayer, or as, in modern times, revelation of the future is supposed to be by second sight. The prophet was, or was not, a foreteller of future events. He was, so far as he saw more deeply than the rest of the world before him ; he was not, in the sense which excites the vulgar admiration of mankind. At least, if there is anything of this kind observable in a particular passage, it is not the essential element of Jewish prophecy. The connection of the Old Testament and the New is not types and words, but the identity of the truths contained—Isaiah and Micah and the New Testament declaring one great revelation, our Lord revealing the spiritual nature of God. There are some other points belonging to what may be called the spirit of prophecy, which may be briefly noticed. The prophets, as they come down, go back to the time when there was no prophet ; and their utterances were gradually reduced to writing in after ages. We can imagine, as was the belief of many of the fathers, that "The waters of Babylon" was written by David. In the second place, the later prophets, to some extent, are founded on the earlier. The latter part of the Book of Revelation is largely made up of words and symbols taken from the prophets, as the marginal references abundantly testify. Even the prophet Isaiah contains repetitions. Amos refers to Joel ; and Joel, probably the oldest extant, has references to older writers now lost. We may suppose, if prophets are only known to us by their historical books, that Elijah and Elisha left a greater impression on the people than any of the prophets who have come down to us. On the other hand, the later prophets were less open to Jewish thoughts, and their prophecies were more adapted to all ages and countries ; and probably they began to write out in a book the words they predicted to their own generation.

(*a*)

4. The True Character of the Prophet

He is the revealer of the will of God, which, in one word, is righteousness, holiness, and love—an individual light in the world. He is the voice of one crying—sometimes in the wilderness, sometimes in the city—" Prepare ye the way of the Lord." He is possessed—inspired with the Word of God. He does not reason about the truths which he utters, for they are self-evident to him. He is satisfied with the power and goodness of God, with the greatness and gentleness of the Divine nature. Take, for example, the 25th of Isaiah. So near do the judgment and lovingkindness of the Lord go together. This is the lesson which the prophets always teach, that there is no end to His justice and mercy. They present the Divine nature as now inflicting, now healing; and the human heart always witnesses to both aspects, and both seem to appear in the order and government of the world.

(*b*)

5. And so in Later Ages

Men have spoken of the love of God as opposed to His justice, or as though, if I may use this expression, God were just with one part of His mind and loving with another part of His mind. I say there is a higher view to be gathered from the prophets. It is, that His justice is ever regulated by His love, and His love by His justice —that these two are in reality identical and inseparable. We see Him through a glass darkly, instead of His justice and mercy reflecting each other in this world and another. The justice of God is seen in the judgments on Israel, and in the history of the world. The history of the world is the judgment of the world. From Joel, the earliest of the prophets, to Malachi, the latest, they are waiting for "the great and terrible day of the Lord"—and they waited for the coming of the Lord. They saw the old world going away. In these are the anticipations of a greater judgment.

(*c*)

6. In the New Testament the Coming of Christ is Blended with the Destruction of Jerusalem

But still the great day of the Lord is coming, when all—prophets, like other men—answer to the call. Judgment is begun but not completed here, except as is anticipated by the consciences of men. There remains, therefore, a more perfect justice for all mankind. So the mercy of God, it is told of by the prophet. The Jewish religion was national, but it had not arrived at the stage of saying that all men, Gentile as well as Jew, were under the influence of God and subject to His laws. So individuals in modern times imagine themselves to be the chosen servants of God ; and indeed it is hard for them to realize that another is equally with themselves cared for by Divine Providence.

(*d*)

7. The Relation of God to Israel is not one of Favouritism.

When they sin He visits them with judgment; when they return He has mercy upon them. When His arm is heaviest upon them still a remnant is left, for He will not destroy the righteous with the wicked. So the prophets, reflecting on the nature of God, arrived at last at the conclusion, not that the sins of the fathers are visited on the children, but that henceforth there shall be this proverb :—" The fathers have eaten sour fruit, and their children's teeth are set on edge." Even the very judgments which are referred to as executed by the command of God are corrected, as notice the reference in Joel to the massacre of Jehu.

(*e*)

8. The Prophet is Confident that the Words he Speaks are the Words of God.

Suddenly he feels an irresistible impulse, and declares that which he knows. Naturally we ask the question, How are we to be sure the voice of God seemingly speaking to us is not a great delusion? We sometimes ask ourselves, How can we be sure that such and such statements represent the truth and will of God? How do we distinguish the fancy of men from the emanations of the Divine mind? We know them to be the truth and will of God in proportion as they express the highest idea of the truth and justice and love which we are capable of making in our own mind. But are we mistaken? There is but a feeble sense of the power and goodness of God if we do as other men do, seldom deriving

(*f*)

Prophecy, The Spirit of—*continued*

strength from a knowledge of His nature and character—if we do not believe in His presence, refer every action to His laws, and judge of the world and of every man by the standard of His perfection.

(*a*)

9. **The Jewish Prophets were the first to teach Spiritual Religion.** In all ages and countries the outward has a tendency to prevail over the inward, the local over the general, the temporal over the spiritual, the world takes the place of the Church, or the Church becomes a new world, with a system of discipline and government, and old foes appear under new names. Ambition and avarice are as rife as in the world, until the conscience of some man is touched, and then comes a reformation. Such was St. Bernard, or Huss, or Luther, or Savonarola. Such, in later times, was our own John Wesley. Then a voice is heard, "Let us have no more confession, or absolution, or masses for the dead ; we are justified by faith only." Or, again, "We will have no more formalism or lip service ; we feel we have sinned against God, and have need of reconciliation with Him." So we might translate, in modern language, the first chapters of Isaiah—"To what purpose is the multitude of your sacrifices," etc.

(*b*)

10. **This is the Spirit of Prophecy**—the spirit of true religion, that we "cease to do evil, and learn to do well." We should not only repent, but bring forth fruits meet for repentance. We should make clean, not that which is without, but that which is within—that is to say, the heart and conscience. And therefore when the prophet looks forward to the future, is it not always to the vision of the Kingdom of God in distant ages—"in that time"—whether in this world or another we cannot tell ? That is the day when "the mountain of the Lord's House shall be exalted to the top of the mountains," when "the knowledge of the Lord shall cover the earth as the waters cover the sea." But as yet the justice of God and the love of God are but in part revealed. The world is distracted between good and evil—evil seeming to very far predominate over the good ; and in this mixed scene of good and evil the prophet upholds the image of a Saviour and the King and the Servant, who partakes of the nature of man, who bore our griefs and took away our sins. Thus there is One in whom the struggle and final victory is impersonated, in whom all the sorrows and sins of mankind are included.

(*c*)

11. **Whether Anything akin to the Spirit of Prophecy Exists among Ourselves**

Naturally we think of the prophet as gifted with great power and insight. But something like prophecy seems to enter into all true religion. For in all true religion there must be a willingness to resist the evil customs of men, whether in the Church or the world—an insight which enables individuals to see them through faith, and gives them courage to fight against, even though they be a part of, the established order of society. He who is independent in mind, and who has no other rule of life than the Divine law—who happily thinks of the world, of himself and of other men, of the ranks of society, of the opinions of party

of the trifles of passion, as they appear in the sight of God—he who in politics knows no principle but truth and right, and is confident (all appearances to the contrary) that they must be triumphant, has in him the spirit of prophecy.

(*d*)

12. **In all True Religion, there must be a Zeal against Hypocrisy and Oppression, in behalf of Humanity and Justice.** And if the fire burn in a man, he must speak with his tongue. And he who cannot remain silent when injustice is being done —who feels an impulse to lift up his voice against pernicious and immoral expressions—in whose ears the cry of the prisoner and the slave enters— who will spend a lifetime in discovering wrong done to the fatherless and the widow—or who will speak out some truth which men deny or ignore— no matter what it is that he does for the behoof of men—he has in him the element of a hero and a prophet.

(*e*)

13. **In all Deeper Kinds of Religion, there must be Isolation from the World, and you must be Alone with God.** The religious thinker or teacher is no longer liable to be persecuted for his opinions—he is no longer kept waning in sickness ; yet any one who thinks or feels deeply is always liable to find himself estranged from his fellow-men. He cannot enter into their thoughts, nor can he always join in their everyday life. Like the prophet, he has to go to the wilderness to be alone with God, and from God he is brought to his fellow-men with highest aspirations for their good ; he feels they are his brethren, and he is bound, not by family ties, but by the highest love and by God's grace, to promote their well-being. He who is renewed by communion with God—who from the highest eminence he can attain towards God seeks to reproduce his thoughts and feelings in their lives— in him is not the spirit of the prophet only, but of Christ Himself.

(*f*)

14. **All Things of this World are so Imperfect it sometimes seems as if Prophecy were never Realized.** Many of us form ideals in our youth—that was our time of hope ; and at forty or fifty years of age we some of us say, "Our ideas were untenable, and we lost them," because we seem to have failed. But even those who succeed to the utmost in worldly success sometimes tell us how small the whole is—"Vanity of vanities." But if I spend a few years in education, a few years in preparation, and achieve a brilliant success, "Then cometh the end !" Such is the life of man. But all this is no reason for relinquishing the ideal, or imagining we may be mortified.

They are not all to be deemed failures because there is only partially-achieved success. For without faith human life would be lowered, and we ourselves, and men in general, sensibly degraded. They are not all failures ; but efforts after perfection will bear fruit henceforth, notwithstanding some present degree of imperfection. If even the idols of youth are found by the wisdom and experience of mature life to be cast down, these youthful aspirations will, nevertheless, prove to be fraught with blessings to mankind. Enthusiasm is a gift of God, and not to be despised. Even the folly of the enthusiast is generally wiser than the wisdom of the cynic. That which is begun here

(*g*)

Prophecy, The Spirit of—*continued*

is not here ended. He who in later life retains all the ideals of early years—who through the imperfections of this life looks forward to another in which he will see the ways of God more perfectly—who, when darkness comes, has his eye fixed on the light beyond—he has in him the spirit of the prophet.

(*a*)   *Jowett*

PROPHESYING, FALSE

"*A wonderful and horrible thing is committed in the land ;*

"*The prophets prophesy falsely, and the priests bear rule by their means ; and My people love to have it so : and what will ye do in the end thereof ?*" (Jer. v. 30, 31)

A **Prophet** is one who speaks for God, declares His mind and will—especially called forth when the truth is obscured through years of worldliness, or denied, as now by writers and thinkers.

The **Priests** are those ministers whose work it is to preach and disseminate the doctrines of the prophets—represented now by the parochial clergy.

The **People**, are those for whose benefit both prophet and priest exist.

(*b*)

1. Almost an exact Parallel (though on the other side) is afforded

By the great *Reformers* of the sixteenth century, Wiclif, Luther, Calvin, and others = prophets.

They spake for God and His Truth.

Then arose an order of men, the clergy of the Reformed Church, who preached their doctrines : literally "ruled by their means."

And the people loved to have it so.

All this is pleasant to contemplate.

But things have greatly altered since then. The printing-press is now the great teacher of men, and the prophets speak by it ; and during the last century, especially now, books have been written whose object is the destruction of Christianity, though apparently on its side.

This, surely, is a wonderful and horrible thing in a Christian land !

But this is not all. Preachers are found who propagate these doctrines.

The Atonement of Christ ;

The efficacy of Prayer ;

The way of Salvation, through repentance toward God, and faith toward our Lord Jesus Christ ;

Eternal Punishment ;

The abrogation of Hell ;

The doctrine of the Holy Spirit, of Christ, and of God, as in the New Testament—have been called in question, and the result shows that now, as before, preachers are found who propagate these doctrines, and "the people love to have it so." Neither is this the worst. They love to hear sceptical opinions expressed, even as they love party views and half truths and a divided Christ preached.

(*c*)

2. What will ye Do in the End thereof?

An end of it will come, both for prophet, priest, and people.

The work done will have to be judged. Will this work stand the test of that judgment ? Will

it be a lasting work ? Will it save souls ? Will it glorify God ?

(i.) The answer of Jesus :

"If the blind lead the blind, both shall fall into the ditch."

(ii.) The answer of Paul :

"Other foundation can no man lay than that is laid."

Jesus Christ is the one theme to preach about, and let a man take heed how he builds thereon :

If he builds on it wood, hay, stubble (of his own). The fire will destroy it, and him too, perhaps. The man may escape, but his work will be burned, and the people whom he taught may perish.

Such is the solemn and disastrous end of all false doctrine.

The worst feature of it is, that the people "love to have it so."

They love to have their own opinions expressed and preached by a man in authority.

(*d*)

3. Let the People Learn how much in this Matter Rests with them

All books, all preaching, all new opinions must not be judged by us according to our own predilection, but they must be taken to the written Word of God and compared with it : "To the law and the testimony :" and let them be accepted or rejected accordingly. "*Ye have an unction* from the Holy One and know" enough thereby to *taste and see* whether such are for your good or not.

"If a man speak, let him speak according to the oracles of God."

Here are some testing texts :

(i.) For infidel books : "If a man love not the Lord Jesus Christ, let him be Anathema."

(ii.) For false teaching, destroying, not saving souls : "If a man, or an angel from heaven, preach another gospel, let him be Anathema."

(iii.) Is a man altering old doctrines, changing them for the newer and more palatable ?

Hear St. Paul :

"Let a man so account of us as the ministers of Christ, and stewards of the mysteries of God."

[He must give you only what he finds there. He must bring out of his treasure things new and old—he must not change them.]

Hear St. John :

"If a man *add* to the prophecy of this book, God will add to him the plagues written therein ; and if a man shall take from the words," etc.—

"God shall take away his part out of the Book of Life."

"Beloved" (adds St. John), "believe not every spirit, but prove the spirits, whether they are of God : because many false prophets are gone out into the world."

The people must not "love to have it so."

(*e*)

PROPHET

There is a man in our own days whose words are not framed to tickle delicate ears ; who, to my thinking, comes before the great ones of society much as the son of Imlah came before the throned kings of Judah and Israel, and who speaks truth as deep, with a power as prophet-like and vital—a mien as dauntless and daring.

(*f*)   *Charlotte Brontë on Thackeray*

To great sensibility and an innate love of all that is good and noble, he unites sentiments of profound hate and contempt for falsehood, meanness, worldliness, and hypocrisy, and a rare power of satirizing it and exposing it.

(a) *Madden, 1855, on Thackeray*

PROSPEROUS

He is a very extraordinary man. I firmly believe he dislikes men when they become prosperous, because he feels he can no longer do them and his own heart good by any aid he can tender them.

(b) *Thomas Campbell on Samuel Rogers*

PROTESTANT CHURCH

Our Church is essentially a *Protestant Church*: she protested in the sixteenth century against the errors of Romanism: and the protest then made, and recorded in her Articles and Formularies, *has never been withdrawn*. Whatever may be said of our Church's teaching, it cannot be said to be in harmony with that of the Church of Rome; no ingenuity can torture its Articles into agreement with the distinctive doctrines of that Church. Our Reformers framed them as a direct protest against Rome. They refused to renounce their convictions, and Rome therefore burnt them as heretics. There was no mistake during Mary's reign as to what the Reformers taught, or as to what they did not teach. Things were then called by their right names. Men were terribly in earnest in those days.

(c) *E. Bayley*

PROTESTANTISM

"Where was your religion before the Reformation?" asked the Romanist.

"Where was your face before it was washed?" answered Archbishop Whately.

(d)

"PROVE ALL THINGS," etc. (1 Thess. v. 21)

i.e., Prove the "prophesyings," reject what is contrary to apostolical doctrine—hold fast that which is *good* to the use of edifying.

The *stand-point* is that of evangelical faith, and has no such application as the comparative merits of Chinese Confucianism and Christianity, but solely to the importations and novelties which from time to time creep into, and are apt to become *established*, in the visible Church of Christ.

It may have especial reference to a *Traditional Religion*, and usages, to Church Parties, and Sectarianism. The standard of testing, or proving, is the *Word of God :—" To the law and the testimony."* " If any man speak, let him speak as the *oracles of God.*"

(e)

Do not shrink from the duty of searching God's Word for yourselves, through fear of human censure and denunciation. Do not think that you may innocently follow the opinions which prevail around you without investigation, on the ground that Christianity is now so purified from errors as to need no laborious research. There is much reason to believe that Christianity is at this moment dishonoured by gross and cherished corruptions.

If you remember the darkness which hung over the Gospel for ages; if you consider the impure union which still subsists in almost every Christian country between the Church and State, and which enlists men's selfishness and ambition on the side of established error; if you recollect in what degree the spirit of intolerance has checked free inquiry, not only before but since the Reformation; you will see that Christianity cannot have freed itself from all the human inventions which disfigured it under the Papal tyranny.

(f) *Channing*

PROVIDENCE

Te facimus, Fortuna, Deam. The Paynims esteemed her as a goddess. They represented her by the image of a woman, sitting sometimes upon a ball, sometimes upon a wheel, having with her a razor, bearing in her right hand the stern of a ship, in her left, the horn of abundance. By the razor they would give us to understand, that she can at her pleasure cut off and end our happiness; by the ball, or wheel, that she is very prone to volubility and change; by the stern in her right hand, that the whole course of our life is under her government; by the horn of abundance in her left hand, that all plenty is from her.

The Providence of Almighty God *preserves, rules,* and *orders* all things.

(g) *S. Benefield*

In virtue of the law under which the *very* successful man easily believes himself to be either a simple tool or an absolute power,—in which originated Mohammed's fate and Napoleon's star, —Christmas Evans, once "the rank Arminian," was now, when unexpectedly prospering, swallowing in hot haste the opposite creed, adding thereto a tincture of romance that was not positively healthful; but his wife, in some respects the sounder theologian of the two, was present to administer the needful antidote. How far he was thoroughly convinced of the dispensableness of the ordinary rules of prudence and precaution, may be doubtful; but it is certain that his tendency was setting in strongly in the direction of believing that Providence would interfere at any point in his case to meet his emergencies "Catherine *fach*," he said one day, perhaps playfully, but also characteristically, " you never mind the potatoes; put your trust in Providence and all will be well." " I tell you what we'll do, Christmas," replied Catherine; " you go and sit down on the top of Moel y Gest, waiting for Providence, and I'll go and hoe the potatoes; and we shall see to which of us Providence will come first."

(h) *Memoir of Christmas Evans*

Providence hath a thousand keys to open a thousand doors, for the deliverance of his own when it is even come to the greatest extremity. Let us be faithful and care for our own part, which is to do and suffer for Him and lay Christ's part on Himself, and leave it there: duties are ours, events are the Lord's.

(i) *Samuel Rutherford*

While Pharaoh builds his treasure-cities, he is unconsciously working his own ruin. While Israel totters on the margin of a yawning gulf, Moses is born.

(j) *Oosterzee*

How often is Providence as kind in what it denies as in what it grants !

(a)   *Mavor*

A great hand is sometimes laid even on the fly-wheel of life's engine.

(b)   *George Macdonald*

GOD'S PROVIDENCE

(i.) Ordering men's ways = Prov. xvi. 9 ; xix. 21 ; xx. 24.
(ii.) Ordaining the conditions and circumstances of life = 1 Sam. ii. 7, 8. Ps. lxxv. 6, 7.
(iii.) Directing all events = Josh. vii. 14. 1 Sam. vi. (7–10) and 12. Prov. xvi. 33. Isa. xliv. 7. Acts i. 26.
(iv.) Ordering the minutest matters = Matt. x. 29, 30. Luke xxi. 18.

(c)

What God's Providence has done for themselves, God's Providence could do again with regard to their children.

(d)   *Luther*

GOD'S PROVIDENCE

Is God dead? asked a child of an afflicted mother.

(e)

Cheer up ; God is where He was.

(f)   *Proverb*

PROVIDENCE, THE DOCTRINE OF A SPECIAL, AS TAUGHT BY PROVERBS iii. 6

On examination, it will be found to contain three things. (i.) A *doctrine*, that there is a special Providence, ordering and overruling all things according to the eternal purpose of God. (ii.) A *precept*, to acknowledge Him. (iii.) A *promise*, "He shall direct thy paths." . . . Not one has been brought safe to his journey's end without divine guidance—not one but has felt his need of that guidance at every stage of his journey. They will all confess with humility, that, wherever they have taken a false step in life, a step which has led to calamitous consequences, they have themselves to blame for it—they can trace it to some rash impulse or some error in judgment, *i.e.*, in the language of this chapter, "leaning to their own understanding."

(g)   *G. H. Evans*

PROVIDENCES

Those believers who watch providences will never lack providences to watch.

(h)   *Flavel*

PRUNING

It was an observation of Luther, "That for the most part when God set him upon any special service for the good of the Church, he was brought low by some fit of sickness or other." The lower the ebb, the higher the tide.

(i)   *Thos. Brooks*

PSALM CXIX

Psalm cxix. remarkable for,

1. Its Structure : very artistic—yet record of real experience.
Twenty-two divisions, one for each letter of the Hebrew alphabet—176 verses, eight in each division.
The German Bible calls it "The Christian's Golden A B C "—a very suitable title.

2. Its Subject = The Word of God : referred to 175 times, once in each verse, except 122nd, and under ten different names—
Word, Saying, Testimonies, Way, Judgments, Precepts, Commandments, Law, Statutes, Truth.

3. Its Author, not known, but not David. Psalm written during Babylonian Captivity, by an Israelite of profound experience, faith, and knowledge of God's Word, perhaps Ezra, or Nehemiah.
Ezra belonged to the Captivity, was a scribe learned in the Law, he edited the Books of the Law—*i.e.* collected them into one volume—was a Reformer, ranked as a second Moses and probably had a spiritual history that we know nothing about. We never see a great worker for God coming to his work without a wonderful past, which argues, too, a wonderful future.
This much is certain. The writer was a young man (9, 99, 100), persecuted for his faith. There was a hostile government, and apostate Jews (23, 46, 161). He was in prison, bonds (61, 83), expecting death (109). The Psalm records (i.) His prayer for steadfastness when others are falling away ; (ii.) The stages of his spiritual experience ; (iii.) The work of a martyr—in prison, carefully and artistically put together.
Cf. St. John, in Patmos, writing the Book of Revelation.
Luther, hidden away in the Castle of Wartburg, translating the Bible into German.
Bunyan, in Bedford gaol, on account of his faith, writing his "Pilgrim's Progress."
S. Rutherford, prisoner in Aberdeen, forbidden to preach, writing his incomparable Letters.

4. Its contents =
(1.) Fidelity to the Word of God praised.
(2.) It is the Young man's Companion.
(3.) Prayer for enlightenment.
(4.) Prayer for strengthening.
(5.) Prayer for preservation.
(6.) For "Confession"—*i.e. Not ashamed of the Gospel.*
(7.) God's Word in all his thoughts,
(8.) He is the Companion of all who love it.
(9.) Need of Humiliation.
(10.) Need of Comfort during *that.*
(11.) How long, O Lord, how long ?
(12.) The Word saves him from despair.
(13.) It is his *wisdom* in difficulties.
(14.) Fidelity to his principles.
(15.) He abhors apostates—the apostate Jews of the Captivity.
(16.) Cast down, but not destroyed.
(17.) God will not let his enemies prevail.
(18.) The Psalmist still young and zealous—he has been *disciplined.*
(19.) The day and night cry to God.
(20.) For revival and quickening.

(j)

(21.) He clings to God, rests upon Him.

(22.) Prayer, that the Good Shepherd would save His isolated and imperilled sheep.

(a)   *Adapted from Delitzsch*

PSALMS, SINGING

We all sing as Jews; or, at best, as mere men, in the abstract, without a Saviour. . . . With some half-dozen exceptions, the Psalms are surely not adequate vehicles of Christian thanksgiving and joy!

(b)   *S. T. Coleridge*

PUBLIC WORSHIP

Ever since I came in place, I have laboured nothing more than that the external public worship of God, so much slighted in divers parts of this kingdom, might be preserved, and that with as much decency and uniformity as might be. For I evidently saw that the public neglect of God's service in the outward face of it, and the nasty lying of many places dedicated to that service, had almost cast a damp upon the true and inward worship of God, which, while we live in the body, needs external helps, and all little enough to keep it in any vigour.

(c)   *Laud*

PUBLICAN

"I say, art thou a Pharisee? Here is a Pharisee for thee! Art thou a Publican? Here is a Publican for thee! God give thee the Publican's heart, if thou art in the Publican's sins, that thou mayest partake mercy with the Publican! So wisheth thy friend, John Bunyan, 1685."

(d)   *John Bunyan*

When the Duke made him Councillor, and hung an order upon his breast, "The people in Weimar saw the new Councillor walk through the street with a ribbon at his button-hole; but the Lord in heaven saw only a *publican* which was a sinner."

(e)   *Falk's Autobiography*

PULPIT

[An author's] study is a sort of sacristy, and his printing-press a pulpit, wherefrom he preaches to all men; for an author is the Town-chaplain of the Universe.

(f)   *J. P. F. Richter*

PUNISHMENT (Chastisement)

That punishment's the best to bear
That follows soonest on the sin;
And guilt's a game where losers share
Better than they who seem to win.

(g)   *Cov. Patmore*

If we are not afflicted, we are undone; and if we be afflicted, we are worse undone.

(h)   *George Taylor*

When Christ lets blood, He hath skill to open the right vein.

(i)   *S. Rutherford*

PUNISHMENT, ETERNAL

The written word of God, being designed for the instruction of the illiterate bulk of mankind, is generally and in necessary points to be understood in the plain direct meaning of the words and phrases, such as they may be supposed to have had in the mouths of the speakers who used them according to the language of that time and country wherein they lived, without such learned, artificial, and forced senses of them as are sought out and put upon them in most of the systems of divinity. . . . It seems a strange way of understanding a law which requires the plainest and directest words, that by "death" should be meant eternal life in misery: could any one suppose by a law that says, For felony thou shalt die—not that he should lose his life, but be kept alive in perpetual exquisite torments!

(j)   *Locke: Reasonableness of Christianity*

I am thankful that the Church of England has adopted no definite article on the subject. I should deem it a misfortune if the unwise licence assumed occasionally by a few of her children should lead her to attempt to define where accurate definition is perhaps impossible, and where attempted definition is very likely to become actual confusion. Some persons may fancy that nothing would be more easy than to extract the true doctrine from Scripture, and so to define the Church's teaching; but they should remember that in Scripture the subject seems to be treated with studied and intentional obscurity; they should remember that, although the analogy of our lives here may help us to understand what is meant by *everlasting life*, it is not easy to say precisely what is meant by *everlasting death;* they would do well also to bear in mind, that if we take the phrase *everlasting fire*, it would be difficult to found a distinct article of faith upon the figure of fire, whose chief properties are to *purify* and to *consume*, when it is obvious that these are the very properties upon which it would be dangerous to lay stress. And besides all this, there is a manifest difficulty in introducing the condition of time into the definition of a state of things of which it will in some wonderful sense be true, that *time will be no more*. Hence I think we are safer without any attempt at definition, and I sincerely trust that no attempt may ever be made.

(k)   *Bishop H. Goodwin*

PUNISHMENT, ETERNITY OF (Matt. xii. 32)

"Neither in this world, nor in the world to come."

It is difficult to say in what words the eternity of retribution could be more unequivocally expressed.

(l)   *Whedon*

The phrase taken together signifies *nunquam*, and is a Hebraism found in the Talmud.

(m)   *Wordsworth*

The whole expression is beyond all question an emphatic *never*.

(n)   *J. Owen and Nast*

PURITANS

Puritans were men whose minds had derived a peculiar character from the daily contemplation of superior beings and eternal interests. Not content with acknowledging, in general terms, an overruling Providence, they habitually ascribed every event to the will of the Great Being, for whose power nothing was too vast, for whose inspection nothing was too minute. To know Him, to serve Him, to enjoy Him, was with them the great end of existence. They rejected with contempt the ceremonious homage which other sects substituted for the pure worship of the soul. Instead of catching occasional glimpses of the Deity through an obscuring veil, they aspired to gaze full on His intolerable brightness, and to commune with Him face to face. Hence originated their contempt for terrestrial distinctions. The difference between the greatest and the meanest of mankind seemed to vanish when compared with the boundless interval which separated the whole race from Him on whom their own eyes were constantly fixed. They recognised no title to superiority but His favour; and, confident of that favour, they despised all the accomplishments and all the dignities of the world. If they were unacquainted with the works of philosophers and poets, they were deeply read in the oracles of God. If their names were not found in the registers of heralds, they were recorded in the Book of Life. If their steps were not accompanied by a splendid train of menials, legions of ministering angels had charge over them. Their palaces were houses not made with hands; their diadems crowns of glory which should never fade away. On the rich and the eloquent, on nobles and priests, they looked down with contempt; for they esteemed themselves rich in a more precious treasure, and eloquent in a more sublime language, nobles by the right of an earlier creation, and priests by the imposition of a mightier hand. The very meanest of them was a being to whose fate a mysterious and terrible importance belonged, on whose slightest action the spirits of light and darkness looked with anxious interest, who had been destined, before heaven and earth were created, to enjoy a felicity which should continue when heaven and earth should have passed away. Events which shortsighted politicians ascribed to earthly causes, had been ordained on his account. For his sake empires had risen, and flourished, and decayed. For his sake the Almighty had proclaimed His will by the pen of the Evangelist and the harp of the prophet. He had been wrested by no common Deliverer from the grasp of no common foe. He had been ransomed by the sweat of no vulgar agony, by the blood of no earthly sacrifice. It was for him that the sun had been darkened, that the rocks had been rent, that the dead had risen, that all nature had shuddered at the sufferings of her expiring God.

(a) *Lord Macaulay*

PURPOSE AND PRECEPT, PROMISE AND PROVIDENCE

God's purpose is secret to us. It is not to be our guide. We may not, as did Jacob, because we believe His purpose is so-and-so concerning us, be in a hurry and presume, and so take unfair means to obtain the blessing; but we are to take His precepts as our guide, and He will take care by His providence to fulfil both His promise and His purpose; the design of the one cannot be contrary to the design of the other.

(b)

Q

QUAKERS

There is not a year, hardly a month, wherein some quaker or other is not going about our streets here in London, either naked or in some exotic figure, denouncing woes, judgments, plagues, fires, sword, and famine.

(a)   *The Snake in the Grass*, 1690

QUAKERS (GEORGE FOX)

He long wandered from place to place teaching his strange theology, shaking like an aspen leaf in his paroxyms of fanatical excitement, forcing his way into churches, which he nicknamed steeple-houses, interrupting prayers and sermons with clamour and scurrility, and pestering rectors and justices with epistles much resembling burlesques of those sublime odes in which the Hebrew prophets foretold the calamities of Babylon and Tyre. He soon acquired great notoriety by these feats. His strange face, his strange chant, his immovable hat, and his leather breeches were known all over the country; and he boasts that as soon as the rumour was heard, "The man in the leather breeches is coming," terror seized hypocritical professors, and hireling priests made haste to get out of his way. He was repeatedly imprisoned and set in the stocks, sometimes justly, for disturbing the public worship of congregations, and sometimes unjustly, for merely talking nonsense. He soon gathered round him a body of disciples, some of whom went beyond him in absurdity. He has told us that one of his friends walked naked through Skipton declaring the truth, and that another was divinely moved to go naked during several years to market-places and to the houses of gentlemen and clergymen. Fox complains bitterly that these pious acts, prompted by the Holy Spirit, were requited by an untoward generation with hooting, pelting, coach-whipping, and horsewhipping. But, though he applauded the zeal of the sufferers, he did not quite go to their lengths. He sometimes, indeed, was impelled to strip himself partially. Thus he pulled off his shoes and walked bare-footed through Lichfield, crying "Woe to the bloody city!" But it does not appear that he ever thought it his duty to appear before the public without that decent garment from which his popular appellation was derived.

(b)   *Macaulay*

QUICKENING SPIRIT (1 Cor. xv. 45)

The point of time when Christ became this "quickening spirit," was not His birth, but His resurrection; for until that moment He was in the likeness of sinful flesh, and had an animal body; and it was not until after He had solved the problem of maintaining the original sinlessness of the spirit through all the stages of His natural life in a world of sin, that He became the representative and head of humanity spiritually and divinely glorified.

(c)   *Lange*

QUIETNESS

Quietness is my definition of happiness.

(d)   *Hannah More*.

R

RACE, THE CHRISTIAN (Analogy)

"*They do it to obtain a corruptible crown; but we an incorruptible*" (1 Cor. ix. 25)

"*Lay aside every weight, and the sin which doth so easily beset us*" (Heb. xii. 1)

"*So run that ye may obtain*" (1 Cor. ix. 24)

Apart from the excitement naturally attending an event which has assumed an international aspect, the race has other features of interest to an observer. What labour have not these young oarsmen undergone, of what pleasures have they not deprived themselves for weeks past, simply for the sake of attaining the *acme* of physical condition which shall enable them to struggle on unflaggingly during those twenty odd eventful minutes with that long, machine-like stroke, unmoved by cheers of either friend or foe? All honour, then, to a contest in which glory alone forms the stakes! And, whether they win or lose, the Harvard crew will surely receive their due meed of applause for the spirit and gallantry they have evinced in crossing the Atlantic for a trial of skill and endurance with their English rivals.

(*a*) *Echo*

RACE AND THE INDIVIDUAL, THE

Onward storms my strong-limbed race,
  Pause for me is nigh;
Long on earth will men have place,
  Not much longer I.
Thousand summers kiss the lea,
  Only one, the sheaf;
Thousand springs may deck the tree,
  Only one the leaf—
One, but one, and that one brief.

(*b*) *Whittier*

RAINBOW

The Rainbow is formed on a Departing Shower. It is between us and the cloud from which the rain falls, and we are between it and the sun. You may have seen a rainbow when rain was falling on you at the time; but the rain falling on you was not from the cloud on which the rainbow was made. The rainbow tells you that "THE STORM HAS GONE FROM YOU." Just as when you hear thunder, you know there is no danger from the lightning that preceded it. So, when a rainbow is in the sky, God reminds us that the storm of His wrath has gone from us, and has fallen on His Son.

THE BREACH.—In Gen. ix. 16, it is called the "everlasting covenant," but these words must be interpreted by viii. 22, "While the earth lasts." We know that this world will be destroyed, and that it will be destroyed by fire (2 Peter iii. 7). The covenant with Noah will last till then. But when will that be? Our Saviour tells us that of that day and hour knoweth no man. But He also gives us an intimation of when it will be near: "When the Son of Man cometh shall He find faith on the earth?" When will the covenant with Noah cease? The answer is. When men generally repudiate what Noah did, God will be freed from His promise. When the covenant is broken by one of the parties, it is not binding on the other. When men generally give up Christ, then Noah's covenant will cease to have force. This is a solemn fact; let us pause over it. Men give up Christ as Romanists do, who put Mary in His place. Men give up Christ when they reject the Atonement He has made. Men give up Christ when they exalt nature over God. Men give up Christ when they put church services and ceremonies in the place of Christ. When Romanism, Naturalism, and Ritualism are universally prevalent, will Christ find faith on the earth?

(*c*) *John Gill*

"*Jehovah shall endow His people with strength*" (Ps. xxix.)

"Jehovah shall bless His people with peace."
The closing words of the Psalm of "the seven thunders," and they span the psalm like a *rainbow*. The beginning of which is, "Gloria in Excelsis," and its close is "Pax in terris."

(*d*) *Delitzsch*

RANK

The rank is but the guinea stamp,
The man's the gowd for a' that.

(*e*) *Burns*

READING

Pliny was accustomed, before reading a book, to consider, or write down what he knew of the author's subject; and afterwards to examine what he added to his stock of knowledge.

(*f*) *Anon*

READING THE HOLY SCRIPTURES

A poor woman, who lived a little way out of Cambridge, had been wont to walk to a well-known church there. She used to say to those who visited her in her long illness, "I liked Mr. S. well; what he said was very beautiful; but there was something that the other minister, the gentleman in white, used to read, that I, poor ignorant woman, used to like better than Mr. S.'s beautiful sermons: I think they called it *the lessons*." She could not read.

(*g*) *A. and D. Brown*

READY

"*Be ye also ready*" (Matt. xxiv. 44)

Sir Colin Campbell, when summoned to go to India to quell the rebellion, was asked, How long would it take him to get ready? replied, "Half-an-hour." As a good soldier, he lived in constant readiness for the call of duty. What a lesson for Christian soldiers!

(*h*)

READY

In the days when noblemen kept "jesters" amongst their retainers, a certain noble of our country was so pleased with the witticisms, puns, and frolics of his jester, that he presented him with a staff, telling him, whenever he met with a greater fool than himself, to give him the staff. After a time, when the nobleman was on his death-bed, the jester came in. The master said, "I am going on a journey—a long journey—not return-ing, and I am not ready. I have never thought of making preparations for it, though I knew I should have to go one day." "Well then, master," replied the fool, "here is thy staff, for I have found a greater fool than myself, and you are the fool."

(a)

REAL PRESENCE, THE

The real presence of Christ's most blessed body and blood is not, therefore, to be sought in the Sacrament, but in the worthy receiver of the Sacrament. . . I see not which way it should be gathered by the words of Christ when and where the bread is His body or the cup of His blood, but only in the very heart and soul of him that receiveth Him.

(b) *Richard Hooker*

The real Presence of Christ in the Sacrament His Church hath always believed. But the mon-strous notion of His bodily presence was started 700 years after His death; and arose chiefly from the indiscretion of preachers and writers of warm imaginations, who, instead of explaining judici-ously the lofty figures of Scripture language, heightened them and went beyond them, till both it and they had their meaning mistaken most astonishingly. And when once an opinion had taken root that seemed to exalt the Holy Sacra-ment so much, it easily grew and spread; and the more for its wonderful absurdity in those ignorant and superstitious ages; till at length, 500 years ago, and 1200 years after our Saviour's birth, it was established for a gospel truth by the pretended authority of the Romish Church. And even this had been tolerable in comparison, if they had not added idolatrous practice to erroneous belief, worshipping on their knees a bit of bread for the Son of God.

(c) *Archbishop Secker*

There *is* a Presence of Christ in the Lord's Supper, and a *real* one, far more real than any mere carnal one; for the spiritual is always more real than the carnal. "Though we have known Christ after the flesh, yet now henceforth know we Him (so) no more." We have lost His bodily presence to get His spiritual. As He said, "It is expedient for you that I *should go away*." But why? Only that He might come again to them *in a spiritual manner*, and thus "abide with them for ever," and so be *nearer* to them than He could have been in the flesh. Hence the beautiful contrast, "I go *away*"—"Lo I am *with you alway*, even to the end of the world." If the fleshly presence be better than the spiritual, then the Church has suffered loss rather than gain by the Ascension, and it was *not* "better for" her that He "should go away." In maintaining, then, a purely *spiritual* Presence in the Lord's Supper we are not

denying a *real* one, but we are contending for by far the *more real* Presence of the two. Nor do we even deny that there is a real Presence in the supper of *Christ's body and blood;* or that *that* is "verily and indeed taken and received by the faithful" in it, or that the virtues arising there-from are not communicated to them in it. But then the question is, *How?* On this word the past Reformation turned, and the present is turn-ing, or rather the future one will turn again. The martyrs died for that word *How?*

(d) *Richard Glover*

REAL PRESENCE (1 Cor. xiv. 25)

To sum up then holy places (shrines, temples, churches, birthplaces, and burial places), Church ornaments (vestments, tables, and vessels), sacred elements (water and bread and wine), are all *things*, and the New Testament knows nothing of a Real Presence in *things;* but "God is *in you* of a truth." A Real Presence in things is no doctrine of Christianity. Let us inquire of what system it is a doctrine. It lies at the bottom of idolatry. According to the opinion of the learned men, the Pundits in India—(common ignorant Hindus believe that the image itself is God)—the image is believed to be, not the god himself, but only the residence of the deity, and on that account, and on that account only, to be worshipped. In the holy city of Benares there are thousands of idols of all kinds and shapes; and in the neighbourhood of the temples there are shops in which are exhibited for sale idols ready made and polished. The images in the shops are, and are universally reckoned to be, pieces of stone merely, and may be handled by anybody. It is only after the Brahmun priest has performed his religious cere-mony, repeated his invocations and prayers, that the deity comes and dwells in that stone; and thenceforward the stone is regarded and worship-ped as a deity. Now, let us understand what is supposed here to take place. It is not supposed that the substance of the deity is mixed up with the substance of the stone; nor again is it sup-posed that, while presenting the phenomena of a stone, the substance of it,—which underlies the phenomena,—is converted into the substance of the deity. That is, to use theological language, there is neither consubstantiation nor transubstantia-tion. But, it is believed, that while the stone remains in its integrity, the deity takes up his abode and dwells in the stone. There is precisely what we understand by a Real Presence. God is supposed to be truly and really present in the image. And of course the image is thenceforward treated as a living being. Libations are poured out; flowers and fruit are offered. It is elevated; it is worshipped; it is carried about; it is adored Men prostrate themselves before it; prefer their requests and make their vows to it. Should, how ever, the Brahmun priest de-consecrate, as it were, the image—by his prayers and invocations cause the deity to depart—there is nothing but the material left, which may without scruple be thrown away.

This is the belief in a Real Presence in things. and, as we shall allow, fully developed and car-ried on to its legitimate and logical conclusion. If you hold, as the Brahmuns do hold, that the physical element is merely the veil of the present deity—that, although invisible to the bodily eye,

(e)

the deity is truly present in the material thing—
what other possibly different conduct can the belief
lead to than to fall down and worship it, which is
idolatry?

(a)   *S. Dyson*

REASON

If man fancies his own reason a sufficient
guide, and trusts to human learning for counsel
whereby to guide his ways, either with integrity
before men or holiness before God—he raises in
his heart a Babel-tower, whose end is confusion.

(b)   *James: "Christian Watchfulness"*

REASON

Who taught the nations of the field and wood
To shun their poison, and to choose their food?

(c)   *Pope*

Reason raise o'er instinct as you can;
In this 'tis God directs, in that 'tis man.

(d)   *Ibid*

RECONCILIATION

If God cannot come to us exactly at the lowest
where we are, and lift us up to the highest *we*
could be, from any depth to any height, I don't
see the meaning of the Incarnation, or Redemption,
or the Holy Spirit, or anything in Christianity or
in life. Christianity is not a tangle, not another
problem to add to the ten thousand already existing, but the guiding thread through the labyrinth,
the solution, whenever and wherever and however
we lay hold of it.

(e)   *Schönberg-Cotta Series*

REDEEMED (1 Pet. i. 19)

A wealthy and kind Englishman once bought a
poor negro for twenty pieces of gold. He presented
him with a certain sum of money, that he might
buy a piece of land and furnish himself a home.
"Am I really free? May I go whither I will?"
cried the negro in the joy of his heart. "*Well, let me
be your slave, Massa: you have redeemed me, and
I owe all to you.*" The gentleman took the negro
into his service, and he never had a more faithful
servant.

(f)

REDEEMER

It was the keenest part of Job's trial, that no
heart beat pulse to pulse with his. His friends
misunderstood him; and his wife, in a moment of
atheistic bitterness,—in the spirit of our own
infidel poet, "Let no man say that God in mercy
gave that stroke,"—said to him: "Curse God and
die." In the midst of this, it seems to have risen
upon his heart with a strange soothing power,
that he was not alone. Gall and bitterness were
distilling from the lips of man; and molten lead
was dropping from the hand of God. But there
was a difference. Men were doing their work
unknowingly: God was meeting out His in the
scales of a most exquisite compassion, not one
drop too much—and each drop love. "Affliction,"

said the tried man, "cometh not out of the dust,
neither doth trouble spring out of the ground"—
superintending all this, "I know that my Redeemer
liveth."

(g)   *F. W. Robertson*

REDEEMING THE TIME (OPPORTUNITY)
(Eph. v. 16)

The relaxation which the body needs is not forbidden here. If any one thinks that he is better
redeeming the opportunity by so overtasking his
brain or his conscience either, as to die early, or
be laid upon a bed of sickness, or unfitted for duty
by dyspepsia, melancholy, or what not, he makes
a great mistake. What God says so plainly in
our frames, is not to be overborne by seemingly
pious principles; if it is, God punishes us.

(h)   *Lange*

REDEMPTION (1 Cor. xv.)

The four successive stages of—

1. μετάνοια (repentance).
2. παλιγγενεσία (regeneration).
3. ἀνακαίνωσις (renewal).
4. ἀποκατάστασις (restoration).

"That we, being regenerate, may daily be renewed," etc.

(i)   *Fairbairn*

REDEMPTION, THE THREEFOLD

The three-fold Divine working of the one Redeemer:

1. He has redeemed His people from the *curse*
of sin through His blood;
2. He redeems them more and more by His
Holy Spirit from the *power* of sin; and,
3. He will finally redeem them from all the
misery of this present evil world, and bring them
to His heavenly kingdom.

(j)   *Passavant*

REDEMPTION DRAWETH NIGH

"*When these things begin to come to pass, then
look up, and lift up your heads; for your redemption draweth nigh*" (Luke xxi. 28)

1. These Things

The things our Lord had been speaking of, and
for which, see context. After the destruction of
Jerusalem there will be a time of grace, a suspension
of the judgment already begun; and this time of
grace will be for the "bringing in of the Gentiles."
During that time, which is that of the absence of
the Bridegroom, while He tarrieth, and the days
are prolonged, men will ask, "Where is the
promise, or sign, or symptom, of His coming."

(k)

2. Carnal Security will set in, such as already
described in xvii. 26–30; xviii. 8 ("The master
delayeth his coming"). Just as before the flood
came, and before the guilty cities were destroyed,
a state of carnal security set in, that even the
exhortations of godly men like Noah and Lot were
set at nought.

But in the midst of such a state of society, our
Lord tells us, there will appear some very alarm-

(l)

ing signs of a Universal Revolution. " Woe, woe, woe to the inhabiters of the earth " ; " Woe to them that are at ease." There will be signs in the heavens, in the earth, and in the hearts of men, all pointing to some kind of catastrophe and judgment in the immediate future.

(a)

3. His Words are these :

"And there shall be signs in the sun, and in the moon, and in the stars ; and upon the earth distress of nations, with perplexity ; the sea and the waves roaring ; men's hearts failing them for fear, and for looking after those things which are coming on the earth : for the powers of heaven shall be shaken."

The words denote that towards the end of the present Dispensation there will be universal law-lessness, lawlessness both in the physical and moral worlds.

(b)

4. Lawlessness in the Heavens, *i.e.* Nature

Signs in the sun and moon and stars. For the powers which hitherto had held them in subjec-tion and in harmony, shall be shaken : the hand which controls them will for the moment let them go. Just as a ship in a storm will not answer her helm, and every timber is creaking before be-coming a wreck, so this globe of ours, and the whole solar system, will be thrown out of gear, and experience unusual commotions. He who holdeth the ocean in the hollow of His hand will cease to hold.

The laws of Nature, hitherto regular, will be-come irregular, and by no means to be depended upon. There will be no stability anywhere. Neither times nor seasons will be depended upon, for the powers which regulated and controlled them will be shaken.

(c)

5. There will be Lawlessness on the Earth

" Distress of nations with perplexity." States-men and those who hold the destinies of people in their hands will be sorely puzzled at the rampant lawlessness of the times. Such lawless-ness as we see around us and increasing in our day—where there is so little respect for authority, where Socialism, Nihilism, Communism are all smouldering beneath the surface, and ready at any moment to burst out into a great flame of anarchy and disorder—the birth-pangs of a New Era.

(d)

6. " Men's hearts failing them for fear, and for looking after those things that are coming on the earth."

These of course are men of the world. The true disciples will not be afraid for like reasons. But the aspect of things, when they reach the stages of lawlessness indicated, will not be pleasant. Men of no religion will not take calmly such portents as the heavens and the earth will reveal. Irreligious men are proverbially super-stitious ; and when these things begin to come to pass they will be filled with apprehension, and have unpleasant forebodings and presentiments of some terrible catastrophe about to happen. When Belshazzar, in the midst of his feasting and splendid ease, saw the strange fingers writing something in the corner of the room, he knew

well enough by a strange presentiment that it boded no good to himself. His heart smote him ; and he read the sign and knew from that moment that he was a doomed man. His thoughts troubled him ; and can we think that irreligious men will be able to look at such signs as our Lord speaks of ; " When the powers of heaven shall be shaken," and all rule and authority and law be loosened ? Will they be able to look calmly on a state of general lawlessness, when not only nations, but also nature, will not be depended on ; when the sea and the waves roaring unnaturally will destroy the navies and fleets of nations, and the seasons will be changed ; when anarchy both within and without the Church takes the place of settled order and subordination ? They will not. Their hearts will fail them for fear and for the prospect of the near future, and that a doom of some kind is imminent.

(e)

7. These Signs are also Symptoms. Symptoms of what ?

Of the coming of Christ. For immediately following the symptoms our Lord adds, " And then shall they see the Son of Man coming with great power and glory."

Then will men ask again, " Who is this, riding forth from the open heavens ? " This is Jesus whom they crucified and despised. This is He who once came in lowliness and meekness as the revelation of God's love. This is Jesus, but not as then. This is Jesus, the King of Kings and Lord of Lords, terrible to His enemies, but " that same Jesus " to His friends. Coming like the lightning, shining from one end of heaven to the other, so that every eye shall see Him ; coming, not to remain, but to gather in His elect from the four winds of heaven ; coming to raise the faithful dead and to " change " the Christians who will be living then, and with the entire Church to ascend up into heaven, to hide them in a place of safety until these calamities be overpast. Hence the words of our text addressed to His waiting people, " When these things begin to come to pass, then look up and lift up your heads, for your redemption draweth nigh." To them His coming is Redemption, to others, Judgment.

(f)   *Cf. Godet*

REDEMPTION POINT, PAST

It happened that a ship was being towed across the Niagara river in America, some little distance above the well-known falls. Just as she got into the middle of the stream, the hawser parted, and the ship began to drift down the river, stern fore-most. Efforts were made to save her from im-pending ruin ; but every effort failed, and she kept drifting further and further down the stream towards the terrible abyss below. The news of the disaster spread along the banks of the river, and in a very short time there were hundreds of people, and they soon swelled to thousands, looking on in breathless anxiety to see what was to be-come of the ship and crew. There is a point that stretches into the river, which bears the name of *Past Redemption Point ;* and it is be-lieved in the neighbourhood that nothing that passes that point can escape destruction. The current there becomes so strong, the influence so

(g)

fatal, that whatever goes by *Past Redemption Point* is inevitably lost.

The excited multitude upon the banks of the river watched the helpless ship drifting down further and further, till she was within a few hundred yards of the fatal point. One effort after another was made, one effort after another failed; still she drifted. Only a few moments, and she passed the point. There was a kind of sigh of horror from the vast multitude, as they saw her swing round, for they knew she was lost. But just as she rounded the point, the captain felt a strong breeze smite upon his cheek. Quick as thought he shouted at the top of his voice, "*All sails set !*" and in almost less time than it takes me to tell it, every stitch of canvas on board the ship was stretched to catch the favouring gale. A cheer broke from the multitude on the shore as they witnessed this last effort for salvation. But would it succeed ? The ship was still drifting, though the wind was blowing against it, and she was still moving downwards, stern foremost, though the wind was bellying out all her sails. *It was a battle between the wind and the current.* With breathless anxiety they watched the result. She slacks ! Another moment—they scarcely dare whisper it—she stands ! Yes, that terrible downward course was actually stopped. There she was, still as a log upon the water. Another moment, and inch by inch, she began to forge her way up the stream until the motion was perceptible to those on shore, and one great shout of victory burst forth from a thousand voices. "Thank God, she is saved ! Thank God, she is saved !"

In a few moments more, with considerable headway upon her, she swept right up stream, by *Past Redemption Point*, right into the still water, saved from what appeared to be inevitable destruction, just because, in the very moment of moments, she caught the favourable breeze.

Yield yourselves to the favouring influence, expose yourselves to the mighty power of the Holy Ghost ! Oh, let it not be said of any of you to-night, "Ye stiff-necked and uncircumcised in heart and ears, ye do always resist the Holy Ghost." *God forbid it.*

(a)

REDUCTIO AD ABSURDUM

He was not only very negligent of his own appearance, but tradition has it, with what precise authority we cannot say, that in some circumstances he would show his displeasure at what he thought excessive personal adornment in others. On one occasion, when in company with some others, who most probably shared his antipathies, a young minister made his appearance, who had daringly innovated upon the simplicity of those days, by venturing to decorate himself with a showy breast-pin, and who assumed some other airs of greatness. Some parties present deferred unduly, it was imagined, to the breast-pin, by addressing its owner, not by his simple name, as was customary, but with the addition of the unusual prefix. The question suggested was, how to reduce the young man to his proper dimensions. Truly Welsh housewives pride themselves greatly on a dazzling array of irons, tins, pewters, coppers, and brass, which are exhibited in a conspicuous part of the kitchen. Christmas Evans, with his

naturally dramatic propensity, found his way into this part of the establishment, and casting a glance upwards, he saw among the exhibition articles a sinecure little poker with a brass knob, which, with his keen eye for resemblance, struck his fancy as being marvellously like an exaggerated breast-pin. No sooner had he made this discovery, than he seized the imitation, inserted it inside his capacious waistcoat, and then walked with becoming air into the midst of the company. Sundry exclamations broke forth. "Christmas Evans *bach;* what ever is the matter ?" Whereupon pointing to his title to higher honours, the extemporized dandy asked with surprise : "Do you presume to call me Christmas still?" By this farcical logic the culprit was of course "reduced to absurdity," in a manner, it must be admitted, far more effective than exemplary.

(b)   *Memoir of Christmas Evans*

REFORMATION, THE

A proud Cardinal, in Luther's time, said, "A reformation is indeed needful, and to be desired ; but that Luther, a rascally friar, should be the man to do it, is intolerable."

(c)   *Thos. Brooks*

One of the great preaching factors—seed-sowers —of the day, is the Printing Press. This the Church of Rome gagged, and would still do so. Hence our immeasurable indebtedness to the "Reformation."

(d)

REFORMATION AND THE INQUISITION

One Aonius Palearius said, "that the Inquisition was a poniard aimed at the throat of literature." The image is striking, and the observation just ; but this victim of genius was soon led to the stake !

(e)   *Disraeli: Cur. of Lit*

REFORMATION AND LUTHER

It would be curious to sketch an account of the *probable* situation of *Europe* at the present moment, had the Pontiffs preserved the omnipotent power of which they had gradually possessed themselves.

(f)   *Ibid*

REFORMATION AND PARTIES

The Reformation in the 16th century narrowed Reform. As soon as men began to call themselves names, all hope of further amendment was lost.

(g)   *S. T. Coleridge*

REFORMATORIES

"The children of robbers and murderers sing psalms and pray," etc.

Compare the cost to the State in keeping them harmless criminals, with Falk's plan for making them honest citizens.

(i.) Bread, water, shame, flogging, cost per boy in prison, £7 17s. 8d. per annum.

(ii.) Meat, bread, honour, the Bible, Christian teaching, cost in a Christian workshop in Weimar, once for all, £3 15s.

(h)   *Stevenson's Memoir of Falk*

REFUGE

*" Write the vision, and make it plain upon tables,
that he may run that readeth it "* (Hab. ii. 2).

"We use great plainness of speech." . . .
The word REFUGE was doubtless written over the
cities of refuge in plain characters, so that the
runner might read it; and not, as some might
do now-a-days, in crooked characters that could
scarcely be made out.
(*a*)

REGENERATION

When a carver cuts and carves an image, he
shapes only that part whereon he works, and not
the rest; if the face, the rest of the body is a rude
and formless stone still, till such a time as he
comes to it. But contrariwise, when nature
makes a flower or living creature, she engenders
and brings forth rudiments of all the parts at one
time. So in obtaining virtues by habit, while a
man practiseth Temperance, he doth not profit
much to Fortitude and the like; but when we
wholly devote and dedicate ourselves to good and
honest ends, we shall find ourselves already invested and predisposed with a kind of hability and
propension to pursue and express the same. The
state of mind described by Aristotle, and expressed
not as a virtue, but a kind of Divinity; an ability
which is above humanity—this state is a thing
higher than virtue.
(*b*) *Bacon, Advancement of Learning*

Regeneration is to be understood from natural
generation. There are two factors—one receptive,
and the other communicative. As at the Incarnation
of our Lord. The Holy Ghost was the communicative factor, and the *faith* of Mary supplied the
receptive factor ("Be it unto me even as thou
wilt;" "Blessed is she that believed"). Cf. "Not
being mixed with faith in them that heard it"
(where Regeneration did not take place), with
"Begotten again by the Word of God" (where it
did take place). Also Heb. xi. 11, Sarah and the
birth of Isaac.
(*c*)

[Rom. v. 5
As the Holy Spirit caused the birth of Christ,
so does He cause the new birth of Christians.
(*d*) *P. Schaff*

As corporeal life presupposes birth, so does the
spiritual life; and just as man is unable to beget
and bring forth himself into physical and earthly
life, so his spiritual generation and new birth are
equally independent of himself.
(*e*) *Lange*

REGENERATION (John iii.)

The first miracle of Christ was a miracle of
transformation, His first public act in Jerusalem
an act of reformation, His first discourse a discourse on regeneration. He is not satisfied with
mere improvements of the old, but demands a
new life, lays a foundation. Regeneration, as to
its origin, is a mystery, but its effects are manifest
to all who have spiritual eyes to see; it meets us
as a fact in every true Christian, or child of God,
who is as sure of the higher life of Christ in his
own soul as he is of his natural existence.
(*f*) *P. Schaff*

REGENERATION AND FORGIVENESS

Whether this state may be known unto him
who is really a partaker of it or translated
into it, or unto others that may be concerned
therein? To which I say, The difference that is
between these two states, and the constituent
causes of them, as they are real, so they are discernible; they may be known by the persons
themselves who are in those states, as well as by
others. It may be known who are born of God,
and who are yet children of the devil; who are
quickened by Christ, and who are yet dead in
trespasses and sins. But here also observe:
(*g*)

1. That I do not say, This is always known to the
persons themselves concerned in this distribution.
Many cry, Peace, peace, when sudden destruction
is at hand; these either think themselves regenerated when they are not, or else wilfully despise
the consideration of what is required in them,
that they may have peace, and so delude their
own souls to their ruin. And many that are
truly born of God, yet know it not; they may for
a season walk in darkness, and have no light.
Nor,
(*h*)

2. That this is always known to others. It is
not known to unregenerate men in respect of
them that are so; for they know not really
and substantially what it is to be so. Natural
men perceive not the things of God; that is,
spiritually, in their own light and nature (1 Cor.
ii. 14). And as they cannot aright discern the
things which put men into that condition (for
they are foolishness to them), so they cannot
judge aright of the persons in whom they are.
And if they do at any time judge aright notionally
concerning any things or persons, yet they do not
judge so upon right grounds, or with any evidence
in or to themselves of what they judge. Wherefore, generally they judge amiss of such persons;
and because they make profession of somewhat
which they find not in themselves, they judge
them hypocrites, and false pretenders to what is
not. For those things which evince their union
with Christ, and which evidence their being born
of God, they savour them not, nor can receive
them. Nor is this always known-to, or discerned
by, them that are regenerate. They may sometimes, with Peter, think a Simon Magus to be a
true believer; or with Eli, a Hannah to be a
daughter of Belial. Many hypocrites are so set
forth with gifts, common graces, light and profession, that they pass among all believers for
such as are born of God And many poor saints
may be so disguised under darkness, temptation,
and sin, as to be looked on as strangers from that
family whereunto indeed they belong. The judgment of man may fail, but the judgment of God
is according to righteousness. Wherefore,
(*i*)

3. This is what we say: It may be known in the
sedulous use of means appointed for that end to a
man's self and others which of the conditions
(*j*)

mentioned he doth belong unto ; that is, whether he be regenerate or not, so far as his or their concern lies therein. This, I say, may be known, and that infallibly and assuredly, with reference to any duty, wherein from hence we are concerned. The discharge of some duties in ourselves, and towards others, depends on this knowledge, and therefore we may attain it, so far as it is necessary for the discharge of such duties to the glory of God.

(*a*) *John Owen*

Regeneration and Forgiveness

1. The grace of regeneration proceeds from an especial spring and fountain, which empties much of its living waters into it, no one drop whereof falls on them that are not regenerate. This is electing love ; it is given out in the pursuit of the decree of election ; " God hath chosen us, that we should be holy " (Ephes. i. 4). Our holiness, whose only spring is our regeneration, is an effect of our election ; that which God works in our souls, in the pursuit of His eternal purpose of love and goodwill towards us. So again, saith the Apostle, " God hath from the beginning chosen you to salvation, through sanctification of the Spirit " (2 Thess. ii. 13). God having designed us unto salvation as the end, hath also appointed the sanctification of the Spirit to be the means to bring us orderly unto the attainment of that end. But the best of common grace or gifts that may be in men unregenerate, are but products of the Providence of God, ordering all things in general unto His glory, and the good of them that shall be heirs of salvation. They are not fruits of electing eternal love, nor designed means for the infallible attaining of eternal salvation.

(*b*)

2. The graces of those who are regenerate have a manifold respect or relation to the Lord Christ, that the common graces of others have not. I name one or two of these respects.

(*c*)

(i.) **They have an especial moral relation to the mediatory acts of Christ in His oblation and intercession.** Especial grace is an especial part of the purchase of Christ. By His death and blood-shedding, He made a double purchase of His elect, of their persons to be His, of especial grace to be theirs. " He gave Himself for His Church, that He might sanctify and cleanse it with the washing of the water by the Word, that He might present it unto Himself, a glorious Church, not having spot or wrinkle, or any such thing, but that it should be holy and without blemish " (Eph. v. 26, 27). The design of Christ, in giving Himself for His Church, was to procure for it that especial grace, whereby, through the use of means, it might be regenerated, sanctified, and purified. So Titus ii. 14. " He gave Himself, that He might redeem us from all iniquity, and purify unto Himself a peculiar people, zealous of good works." Real purification in grace and holiness hath this especial relation unto the death of Christ, that He designed therein to procure it for them for whom He died. And in the pursuit of His purchase or acquisition of it, His purpose was really to bestow it on them, or effectually to work it in them. Moreover, it hath an especial relation unto His intercession ; and that in a distinguishing

manner from any other gifts or common graces that other men may receive. Giving us the rule and pattern of His intercession (John xvii.), he tells us that He so prays, not for the world, but for His elect ; those whom the Father had given Him, because they were His (ver. 9). And what is it that He prays for them, in distinction from all other men whatever ? Amongst others, this is one principal thing that He insists on, " Sanctify them through Thy truth " (ver. 17). Their sanctification and holiness is granted upon that prayer and intercession of Christ, which is peculiar unto them, with an exclusion of all others : " I pray for them, I pray not for the world." Now, the common grace of unregenerate persons, whereby they are distinguished from other men, whatever it be, it hath not this especial relation to the oblation and intercession of Christ. Common grace is not the procurement of especial intercession.

(*d*)

(ii.) **They have a real relation unto Christ, as He is the living quickening Head of the Church ;** for He is so, even the living fountain of the spiritual life of it, and of all vital acts whatever. Christ is our life, and our life is hid with Him in God (Col. iii. 2, 3). That eternal life which consists in the knowledge of the Father and the Son (John xvii. 3) is in Him as the cause, head, spring, and fountain of it. In Him it is in its fulness, and from thence it is derived unto all that believe, who receive from His fulness grace for grace (John i. 16). All true, saving, sanctifying grace, all spiritual life, and everything that belongs thereunto, is derived directly from Christ as the living Head of His Church, and fountain of all spiritual life unto them. This the Apostle expresses, " Speaking the truth in love, grow up into Him in all things, which is the Head, even Christ ; from whom the whole body fitly joined together, and compacted by that which every joint supplieth, according to the effectual working in the measure of every part, maketh increase of the body, unto the edifying of itself in love " (Eph. iv. 15, 16). To the same purpose he again expresses the same matter (Col. ii. 19). All Grace in the whole body comes from the Head, Christ Jesus ; and there is no growth or furtherance of it, but by His effectual working in every part, to bring it unto the measure designed unto it. Nothing then, no, not the least of this grace, can be obtained, but by virtue of our union with Christ as our Head, because it consists in a vital effectual influence from Him and His fulness. And this kind of relation unto Christ, all grace that is, or may be, in unregenerate men, is incapable of.

(*e*)

(iii.) **The grace of regeneration, and the fruits of it, are administered in and by the Covenant.** This is the promise of the Covenant, that God will write His law in our hearts, and put His fear in our inward parts, that we shall not depart from Him (Jer. xxxii. 40). This is that grace whereof we speak, whatever it be, or of what kind soever. It is bestowed on none but those who are taken into Covenant with God ; for unto them alone it is promised, and by virtue thereof is it wrought in and upon their souls. Now, all unregenerate men are strangers from the Covenant, and are not made partakers of that grace which is peculiarly and only promised thereby and exhibited therein.

(*f*)

(iv.) The least spark of saving, regenerating grace is wrought in the soul by the Holy Ghost, as given unto men to dwell in them, and to abide with them. He is the water given by Jesus Christ to believers, which is in them " a well of water springing up to everlasting life " (John iv. 14). First, they receive the water, the spring itself, that is, the Holy Spirit; and from thence living waters arise up in them; they are wrought, effected, produced, by the Spirit, which is given unto them. Now, although the common gifts and graces of men unregenerate are the effects of the power of the Holy Ghost, wrought in them, and bestowed on them, as are all other works of God's providence; yet it doth not work in them as received by them, to dwell in them, and abide with them, as a never-failing spring of spiritual life. For so our Saviour says expressly, that the world, or unbelievers, do not know the Spirit, nor can receive Him, or have Him abiding in them. All which, in contradistinction to all unregenerate persons, is affirmed of all them that do believe.

(a)

(v.) The least of saving grace, such as is peculiar unto them that are regenerate, is spirit: "That which is born of the Spirit, is spirit " (John iii. 6). Whatever it is that is so born, it is spirit, it hath a spiritual being, and it is not to be drawn by any means out of the principles of nature; so it is said to be a new creature (2 Cor. v. 17). Be it ever so little, or so great, however it may differ in degrees in one and in another, yet the nature of it is the same in all; it is a new creature. As the least worm of the earth, in the order of the old creation, is no less a creature than the sun, yea, or the most glorious angel in heaven; so in the order of the new creation, the least spark or drachm of true grace that is from the sanctifying Spirit is a new creature, no less than the highest faith or love that ever were in the chiefest of the Apostles. Now, that which is spirit and that which is not spirit, that which hath a new spiritual being and that which hath none, whatever appearance of agreement there may be among them, do yet differ specifically from one another. And thus it is with the saving grace that is in the regenerate, and those common graces that are in others which are not so. So that, as these are divers states, so they are eminently different and distinct, the one from the other.

(b)   *John Owen*
(*See* " FORGIVENESS OF SINS.")

REGENERATION AND FORGIVENESS

Say some, "**We know not whether we are regenerate or not.**"

Rules:

Rule I. See that the persuasion and assurance hereof, which you look after and desire, be regular, and not such as is suited merely to your own imaginations. Our second and third general rules about the nature of all spiritual assurance, and what is consistent therewith, are here to be taken into consideration. If you look to have such an evidence of light into, and absolute conviction of, this matter as shall admit of no doubts, fears, questionings, just occasions and causes of new trials, teachings, and self-examinations, you will be greatly deceived. Regeneration induceth a new principle into the soul, but it doth not utterly expel the old; some would have security, not

assurance. The principle of sin and unbelief will still abide in us, and still work in us. Their abiding and their acting must needs put the soul upon a severe inquiry, whether they are not prevalent in it beyond what the condition of regeneration will admit. The constant conflicts we must have with sin, will not suffer us to have always so clear an evidence of our condition as we would desire. Such a persuasion as is prevalent against strong objections to the contrary, keeping up the heart to a due performance of those duties in faith which belong to the state of regeneration, is the substance of what in this kind you are to look after.

(c)

Rule II. If you are doubtful concerning your state and condition, do not expect an extraordinary determination of it by an immediate testimony of the Spirit of God. I grant, that God doth sometimes, by this means, bring in peace and satisfaction to the soul. He gives His own Spirit immediately, to bear witness with ours that we are the children of God, both upon the account of regeneration and adoption. He doth so, but, as far as we can observe, in a way of sovereignty, when, and to whom He pleaseth. Besides, that men may content and satisfy themselves with His ordinary teachings, consolations, and communications of His grace, He hath left the nature of that peculiar testimony of the Spirit very dark, and difficult to be found out, few agreeing wherein it doth consist, or what is the nature of it. No one man's experience is a rule to others; and an undue apprehension of it is a matter of great danger. Yet it is certain that humble souls, in extraordinary cases, may have recourse to it with benefit and relief thereby. This then you may desire, you may pray for, but not with such a frame of spirit as to refuse that other satisfaction which in the way of truth and peace you may find. This is the putting of the hand into the side of Christ; but blessed are they who believe, and yet have not seen.

(d)

Rule III. If you have at any time formerly received any special or immediate pledge or testimony of God given to your souls, as to their sincerity, and consequently their regeneration, labour to recover it, and to revive a sense of it upon your spirits, now in your darkness and trouble. I am persuaded there are but few believers, but that God doth at one time or other, in one duty or other, entering into, or coming out of one temptation or another, give some singular testimony to their own souls and consciences concerning their sincerity, and His acceptance of them. Sometimes He doth this in a duty, wherein He hath enabled the soul to make so near an approach to Him as that it hath been warmed, enlivened, sweetened, satisfied with the presence, the gracious presence of God, and which God hath made to him as a token of uprightness. Sometimes, when a man is entering into any great temptation, trial, difficult or dangerous duty, that death itself is feared in it, God comes in by one means or other, by a secret intimation of His love, which He gives him to take along with him for his furniture and provision in his way, and thereby testifies to him his sincerity. And this serves like the food of Elijah, for forty days in a wilder-

(e)

Regeneration and Forgiveness—*continued*

ness condition. Sometimes He is pleased to shine immediately into the soul in the midst of its darkness and sorrow, wherewith it is surprised, as not looking for any such expression of kindness, and is thereby relieved against its own pressing self-condemnation. And sometimes the Lord is pleased to give these tokens of love to the soul as its refreshment, when it is coming off from the storm of temptations wherewith it hath been tossed. And many other times and seasons there are, wherein God is pleased to give to believers some especial testimony in their consciences to their own integrity. But now, these are all wrought by a transient operation of the Spirit, exciting and enabling the heart to a spiritual sensible apprehension and receiving of God's expressing kindness towards it. These things abide not in their sense, and in their power which they have upon our affections, but immediately pass away. They are therefore to be treasured up in the mind and judgment, to be improved and made use of by faith, as occasion shall require; but we are apt to lose them. Most men know no other use of them, but whilst they feel them; yea, through ignorance in our duty to improve them, they prove like a sudden light brought into a dark place and again removed, which seems to increase, and really aggravates our sense of, the darkness. The true use of them is to lay them up, and ponder them in our hearts, that they may be supports and testimonies to us in a time of need. Have you then, who are now in the dark as to your state and condition, whether you are regenerate or not, ever received any such refreshing and cheering testimony from God given to your integrity, and your acceptance with Him thereupon? Call it over again, and make use of it against those discouragements which arise from your present darkness in this matter, and which keeps you off from sharing in the consolation tendered to you in this word of grace.

(*a*)

Rule IV. A due spiritual consideration of the causes and effects of regeneration, is the ordinary way and means whereby the souls of believers come to be satisfied concerning that work of God in them and upon them. The principal cause of this work, are the Spirit and the Word. He that is born again, is born of the Spirit (John iii. 6); and of the Word: "Of His own will begat He us by the Word of truth" (James i. 18). "We are born again by the Word of God that abideth for ever" (1 Peter i. 23). Wherever, then, a man is regenerate, there hath been an effectual work of the Spirit and of the Word upon his soul. This is to be inquired into and after; ordinarily it will discover itself. Such impressions will be made upon the soul, such a change will be wrought and produced in it, as will not escape a spiritual diligent search and inquiry. And this is much of the duty of such as are in the dark, and uncertain concerning the accomplishment of this work in themselves. Let them call to mind what have been the actings of the Spirit by the Word upon their souls; what light thereby hath been communicated unto their minds; what discoveries of the Lord Christ and way of salvation have been made to them; what sense and detestation of sin have been wrought in them; what satisfaction hath been given unto the soul, to choose, accept, and acquiesce in the righteousness of Christ; what

resignation of the heart unto God, according to the tenour of the Covenant of Grace, it hath been wrought unto. Call to mind what transactions there have been between God and your souls about these things; how far they have been carried on; whether you have broken off the treaty with God, and refused His terms; or, if not, where the stay is between you, and what is the reason, since God hath graciously begun to deal thus with you, that you are not yet come to a thorough close with Him in the work and design of His grace; the defect must of necessity be on your parts. God doth nothing in vain; had He not been willing to receive you, He would not have dealt with you so far as He hath done. There is nothing then remains to establish your condition, but a resolved act of your own wills, in answering the mind and will of God. And, by this search, may the soul come to satisfaction in this matter, or at least find out and discover where the hindrance is, whence the uncertainty doth arise, and what is wanting to complete its desire.

(*b*)

Again, this work may be discovered by its effects. There is something that is produced by it in the soul, which may also be considered either with respect to its being and existence or to its actings and operations; in the first regard, it is spirit, "that which is born of the Spirit" (John iii. 6), which is produced by the effectual operation of the Spirit of God, it is spirit; a new creature: "He that is in Christ Jesus (who is born again) is a new creature" (2 Cor. v. 17); a new life, a spiritual life (Gal. ii. 20; Eph. ii. 1). In brief, it is an habitual furnishment of all the faculties of the soul with new spiritual vital principles, enabling a person, in all instances of obedience, to lead a spiritual life unto God. This principle is by this work produced in the soul; and, in respect of its actings, it consists in all the gracious operations of the mind, will, heart, and affections in the duties of obedience which God hath required of us. This is that which gives life to our duties (without which the best of our works are but dead works), and renders them acceptable unto the living God. It is not my business at large to pursue and declare these things, I only mention them, that persons who are kept back from a participation of the consolation tendered from the forgiveness that is with God, because they cannot comfortably conclude that they are born again, may know how to make a right judgment of them selves, as knowing that it is such persons alone unto whom these consolations do truly and really belong. Let such persons, then, not fluctuate up and down in generals and uncertainties, with heartless complaints, which is the ruin of the peace of their souls; but let them really put things to the trial, by the examination of the causes and effects of the work they inquire after. It is by the use of such means, whereby God will be pleased to give them all the assurance and establishment concerning their state and condition which is needful for them, and which may give them encouragement in their course of obedience.

(*c*)   *John Owen*

"REJOICE IN THE LORD" (Phil. iii. 1)

To him belongs the χαίρετε ἐν Κυρίῳ who obeys the στήκετε ἐν Κιρίῳ (iv. 1).

(*d*)   *Lange*

REJOICING IN CHRIST

"Rejoice that your names are written in heaven" (Luke x. 20), a *dictum probans* for the doctrine of the Evangelical Church, that a believer even in this life may be assured of his eternal salvation. When Möhler [the eminent Roman Catholic Symbolist] asserts that he " in the neighbourhood of a man who without any restriction declared himself sure of his salvation should be in a high degree uneasy," nay, "that he could not repel the thought that there was something diabolical beneath this," he thereby affords us a deep glance into the comfortlessness of a heart which seeks the ultimate ground of its hope in self-righteousness, and in making assurance of salvation to depend on attainment in holiness, instead of resting in simple faith in the consciousness of having committed oneself to Christ. He shows also, that he has not comprehended the word of the Lord to the Seventy in its whole depth. " *Rejoice that your names are written in heaven*," was the answer of the dying Haller, when his friends congratulated him on the honour of having received a visit in his last hours from the Emperor Joseph II.

(*a*)   *Lange*

RELIGION

When some people talk of religion, they mean they have heard so many sermons, and performed so many devotions; and thus mistake the *means* for the *end*. But true religion is an habitual recollection of God, and intention to serve Him, and this turns everything into gold. We are apt to suppose that we need something splendid to evince our devotion, but true devotion equals things; washing plates and cleaning shoes is a high office, if performed in a right spirit. If three angels were sent to earth, they would feel perfectly indifferent who should perform the part of prime-minister, parish-minister, or watchman.

(*b*)   *John Newton*

Hume is always on his guard: no holiness, no beauty, no purity, no utility can by any chance betray or seduce him to find an excuse for the sin of religion.

(*c*)   *Quarterly Review on David Hume*

Sir William Temple was a vain man, much blown up in his own conceit, which he showed too indecently on all occasions. He had a true judgment in affairs, and very good principles with relation to government, but in nothing else. He seemed to think that things were as they are from all eternity; at least he thought religion was fit only for the mob. He was a great admirer of the sect of Confucius in China. . . . He was a corrupter of all that came near him.

(*d*)   *Burnet*

     The dispute about religion,
And the practice of it, seldom go together.

(*e*)   *Young*

For in religion as in friendship, they who profess most are ever the least sincere.

(*f*)   *Sheridan*

     Religion, if in heavenly truths attired,
     Needs only to be seen to be admired.

(*g*)   *Cowper*

An impression prevails, that religion is good for dyspeptics and invalids, for nervous people and women; but that it does not suit well with a body full of spirit and health.

(*h*)   *Storrs*

Men will write for religion, fight for it, die for it; anything but live for it.

(*i*)   *Cotton*

RELIGION IN ENGLAND

If there were but one religion in England, its despotism would be formidable; if there were only two, they would throttle each other; but there are thirty, and they live happily and peaceably.

(*j*)   *Voltaire*

RELIGION, FALSE

I fear you are not sufficiently aware how much false religion there is in the world; many serious Christians and valuable ministers are too easily imposed upon by this false blaze. I fear you are not sensible of the dreadful effects and consequences of this false religion. Let me tell you, it is the devil transformed into an angel of light; it is the offspring of hell, that always springs up with every revival of religion to the injury of the cause of God, while it passes current with multitudes of well-meaning people for the height of religion. Seriously endeavour to crush all appearances of this nature among the Indians, and never encourage any degrees of *heat without light*. . . . Always insist that their experiences are rotten, that their joys are delusive, although they may have been rapt up into the third heavens in their own conceit, unless the main tenour of their lives be spiritual, watchful, and holy.

(*k*)   *David Brainerd*

RELIGION AND INTELLECT

Let none imagine that its chosen temple is an uncultivated mind, and that it selects, as its chief organs, the lips of the unlearned. Religious and moral truth is indeed appointed to carry forward mankind; but not as conceived and expounded by narrow minds, not as darkened by the ignorant, not as debased by the superstitious, not as subtilized by the visionary, not as thundered out by the intolerant fanatic, not as turned into a drivelling cant by the hypocrite. Like all other truths, it requires for its full reception and powerful communication a free and vigorous intellect.

(*l*)   *Channing*

RELIGION AND PAGANISM

They must insist on the moral basis of the Christian faith; they must silence Mr. Spencer's taunt, that in their Churches they had one-seventh of Christian precept and six-sevenths of pagan example.

(*m*)

RELIGION AND PARENTAGE

One of the free-thinking brotherhood assured T. Thomas that one's religion was just a question of parentage, nothing more. "If so," was the minister's Talleyrandian answer, "I thank God, your father was not mine."

(*n*)   *Memoir of Christmas Evans*

RELIGION REVEALED

To his sermons we are indebted for the complete overthrow of the selfish system, and to his "Analogy" for the most noble and surprising defence of revealed religion, perhaps, which has ever yet been made of any system whatever.

(a)   *Sydney Smith on Butler*

RELIGION AND SCIENCE

Who has Science and Art, has religion.

(b)   *Goethe*

Religion occupies a sphere to which Science cannot attain. Science can bear no testimony, can offer no criticism, as to the supernatural, inasmuch as she deals with facts of natural law.

(c)   *Calderwood*

The conflict between Religion and Science, is not that of knowledge and ignorance ; to put it in the best light for Science, it is the conflict of one kind of knowledge with another.

(d)   *Ibid*

RELIGION, TRUE

" *Flesh and blood hath not revealed,*" etc. (Matt. xvi. 13–20)

In what passed between our Lord and His disciples we are led to observe,·

(i.) The contrast between human opinions of religion and a confession of faith prompted and evoked by the grace of God :—in the former case; fear, dejection, uncertainty, and discordance ; in the latter, courage, frankness, certainty, and unity ;

(ii.) The indissoluble connection between true confession and a life of revelation and in the Spirit, or regeneration ;

(iii.) Between a common confession and the formation of the visible Church ;

(iv.) Between the confession of the Church to Christ and Christ's confession to the Church ;

(v.) Between the character of the first-believing confessor and his official calling.

(e)   *Lange*

RELIGION, TRUE

Much more of true religion consists in deep humility, brokenness of heart, and an abasing sense of barrenness and want of grace and holiness, than most who are called Christians imagine ; especially those who have been esteemed the converts of the late day, many of whom seem to know of no other religion but elevated joys and affections, arising only from some flights of imagination, or some suggestion made to their mind, of Christ's being theirs, God's loving them, and the like. . . . True grace is exceedingly precious, indeed, it is very rare, and there is but a small degree of it, even where the reality of it is to be found ; at least, I saw this to be my case.

(f)   *D. Brainerd*

RELIGIOUS DISCORDS

Neither Montaigne, nor Locke, nor Bayle, nor Spinosa, nor Hobbes, nor my Lord Shaftesbury, etc., have lighted the torch of discord in their country ; it is, for the most part, those theologians who, having had first the ambition of being chiefs of a sect, have very soon aspired to be chiefs of a party. All the books of modern philosophers put together will never make as much noise in the world as was once caused by the dispute of the Franciscans about the shape of their sleeve and their hood.

(g)   *Voltaire*

RELIGIOUS TEACHING, EARLY

My mother was in the strictest sense religious. How indestructibly the good grows and propagates itself even among the weedy entanglements of evil ! The highest (person) whom I knew on earth I here saw bowed down, with woe unspeakable, before a Higher in Heaven : such things in infancy reach inwards to the very core of your being ; mysteriously does a Holy of Holies build itself into visibility in the mysterious deep.

Wouldst thou rather be a peasant's son that knew, were it ever so rudely, there was a God in heaven and in man ; or a duke's son who knew that there were thirty-two quarters on the family coach ?

(h)   *Carlyle*

RELIGIOUS WORSHIP, FORGIVENESS AND

" *For he that cometh unto God, must believe that He is, and that He is a rewarder of all them that diligently seek Him*" (Heb. xi. 6), which would not be so, should He appoint a voluntary worship, and not propose a reward to the worshippers. Wherefore,

1. It is evident that God, by the prescription of a worship unto sinners, doth fully declare that there is forgiveness with Him for them.

He manifests thereby that He is willing to receive a new revenue of glory from them. This, as we have proved, is the end of worship. This He would never have done, but with a design of accepting and rewarding His creatures. For do we think that He will be beholden unto them ? that He will take and admit of their voluntary reasonable service, according to His will and command, without giving them a reward ? yea, and such a one as their obedience holds no proportion unto ? No such thing would become His infinite self-sufficiency, goodness, and bounty. This the wife of Manoah well pleads ; " If," saith she, " the Lord were pleased to kill us, He would not have received a meat-offering and a burnt-offering at our hands" (Judg. xiii. 23). His acceptance of worship from us is an infallible demonstration, that He will not execute against as the severity of the first curse. And this is clearly evidenced in the first record of solemn instituted worship performed by sinners, "God had respect unto Abel and his offering" (Gen. iv. 4). Some think that God gave a visible pledge of His acceptance of Abel and his offering ; it may be, it was fire from heaven. For how else should Cain so instantly know that his brother and his offering were accepted, but that he and his were refused ? However it were, it is evident that what testimony God gave of the acceptance of his offering, the same He gave concerning his person ; and that in the first place He had respect unto Abel, and then to his offering. And therefore the Apostle saith,

(i)

that thereby he obtained "witness that he was righteous" (Heb. xi. 4), that is, the witness or testimony of God Himself. Now, this was in the forgiveness of his sin; without which he could neither be righteous nor accepted, for he was a sinner.

(a)

This God declared by acceptance of his worship. And thus we also, if we have any testimony of God's acceptance of us in any part of His worship, should employ it to the same end. Hath God enlarged our hearts in prayer? Hath He given us an answer unto any of our supplications? Hath He refreshed our hearts in the preaching and dispensation of the Word, or any other ordinance? We are not to rest in the particular about which our communion with Him hath been. Our doing so is the cause why we lose our experiences. They lie scattered up and down, separated from their proper root, and so are easily lost. But this is that which we should do: first improve such particular experiences in the worship of God unto, namely, that God hath pardoned our sins, and accepted our persons thereon; for without that, none of our worship or service would please Him or be accepted with Him.

(b)

2. Hereby God lets us know that He deals with us upon new terms; so that, notwithstanding sin, we may enjoy His love and favour. For this we have the engagement of His truth and veracity, and He cannot deceive us; but yet, by this command of His, for His worship, we should be deceived, if there were not forgiveness with him. For it gives us encouragement to expect, and assurance of finding, acceptance with Him, which without it cannot be obtained. This, then, God declares by His institution of and command for His worship, namely, that there is nothing that shall indispensably hinder those who give up themselves unto the obedience of God's commands, from enjoying His love and favour, and communion with Him.

(c)

3. For matter of fact, it is known and confessed, that God hath appointed a worship for sinners to perform. All the institutions of the Old and New Testament bear witness hereunto. God was the Author of them. And men know not what they do, when either they neglect them, or could be intermixing their own imaginations with them. What can the mind of man conceive or invent, that may have any influence in this matter, to secure to the souls of believers their acceptance with God? Is there any need of their testimony to the truth, faithfulness, and goodness of God? These things He hath taken upon Himself. This, then, is that which is to be fixed on our souls, upon our first invitation unto religious worship, namely, that God will have a new revenue of glory from us; and therefore He declares that there is a way for the taking away of our sins, without which we can give no glory to Him by our obedience; and this is done only by forgiveness.

(d)

4. There are some ordinances of worship appointed for this very end and purpose, to confirm unto us the forgiveness of sin; especially in that worship which is instituted by the Lord Jesus under the New Testament. I shall instance one: the ordinance of Baptism. This was accompanied with the dawning of the Gospel, in the ministry of John the Baptist. And he expressly declared, in his sermons upon it, that it was instituted of God to declare the remission of sins (Mark i. 4).

It is true, the Lord Christ submitted unto that ordinance, who had no sin, and was baptized by John. But this belonged unto the obedience which God required of Him, as, for our sakes, He was made under the Law. He was to observe all ordinances and institutions of the worship of God; not for any need He had in His own Person of the especial end and significations of some of them, yet as He was our sponsor, surety, and mediator, standing in our stead in all that He so did, He was to yield obedience unto them, that so He might fulfil all righteousness (Matt. iii. 15). So was He circumcised, so was He baptized; both which had respect unto sin, though absolutely free from all sin in His own Person; and that because He was free from no obedience to any command of God.

(e)

But baptism itself, as appointed to be an ordinance of worship for sinners to observe, was a declaration of that forgiveness that is with God. It was so in its first institution. God calls a man in a marvellous and miraculous manner; gives him a ministry from heaven; commands him to go and baptize all those who, confessing their sins, and professing repentance of them, should come to Him, to have a testimony of forgiveness. And as to the especial nature of this ordinance, he appoints it to be such as to represent the certainty and truth of His grace in pardon, to their senses by a visible pledge. He lets them know that He would take away their sin, wherein their spiritual defilement doth consist, even as water takes away the outward filth of the body; and that hereby they shall be saved, as surely as Noah and his family were saved in the ark swimming upon the waters (1 Pet. iii. 21). Now, how great a deceit must needs, in this whole matter, have been put upon poor sinners, if it were not infallibly certain that they might obtain forgiveness with God.

(f)

After the entrance of this ordinance in the ministry of John, the Lord Jesus Christ takes it into His own hand, and commands the observation of it to all His disciples. I dispute not now, who are the proper immediate objects of it; whether they only who actually can make profession of their faith, or believers, with their infant seed. For my part, I believe that all whom Christ loves and pardons, are to be made partakers of the pledge thereof. And the sole reason, which they of old insisted on, why the infants of believing parents should not be baptized, was, because they thought they had no sin; and therein we know their mistake. But I treat not now of these things; only this, I say, is certain, that in the prescription of this ordinance to His Church, the great intention of the Lord Christ was to ascertain to us the forgiveness of sins. And sinners are invited to a participation of this ordinance for that end, that they may receive the pardon of their sins; that is, an infallible pledge and assurance of it (Acts ii. 38). And the very nature of it declares this to be its end, as was before intimated. This

(g)

Religious Worship, Forgiveness and—*continued*

is another engagement of the truth and faithfulness and holiness of God, so that we cannot be deceived in this matter. " There is," saith God, " forgiveness with Me ; " saith the soul, " How, Lord, shall I know, how shall I come to be assured of it ? for, by reason of the perpetual accusations of conscience, and the curse of the law upon the guilt of my sin, I find it a very hard matter for me to believe ; like Gideon, I would have a token of it ? " Why, behold, saith God, " I will give thee a pledge and token of it, which cannot deceive thee. When the world of old had been overwhelmed with a deluge of waters by reason of their sins ; and those who remained, though they had just cause to fear the same judgment would again befall them or their posterity, because they saw there was like to be the same cause of it, the thoughts and imaginations of the hearts of men being evil still, and that continually ; to secure them against these fears, I told them, that I would destroy the earth no more with water ; and I gave them a token of My faithfulness therein, by placing My bow in the cloud. And have I failed them ? Though the sin and wickedness of the world hath been, since that day, unspeakably great, yet mankind is not drowned again, nor ever shall be : I will not deceive their expectation from the token I have given them. Wherever, then, there is a word of promise confirmed with a token, never fear a disappointment. But so is this matter. I have declared that there is forgiveness with Me ; and, to give you assurance thereof, I have ordained this pledge and sign, as a seal of My word, to take away all doubts and suspicion of your being deceived. As the world shall be drowned no more, so neither shall they who believe come short of forgiveness."

And this is the use which we ought to make of this ordinance. It is God's security of the pardon of our sins, which we may safely rest in.

(a)

5. **The same is the end of that other great ordinance of the Church, the Supper of the Lord** : the same thing is therein confirmed to us by another sign, pledge, token, or seal. We have showed before, what respect Gospel forgiveness hath to the death or blood of Jesus Christ. That is the means whereby for us it is procured, the way whereby it comes forth from God, to the glory of His righteousness and grace, which afterwards must be more distinctly insisted on. This ordinance, therefore, designed and appointed on purpose for the representation and calling to remembrance of the death of Christ, with the communication of the benefits thereof to them that believe, doth principally intend our faith and comfort in the truth under consideration ; and therefore, in the very institution of it, besides the general end before mentioned, which had been sufficient for our security, there is, moreover, added, an especial mention of the forgiveness of sin : for so speaks our Saviour in the institution of it, for the use of the Church to the end of the world, " This is My blood of the New Testament, which is shed for many, for the remission of sins " (Matt. xxvi. 28). As if He had said, " The end for which I have appointed the observance of this duty and service to you, is, that I may testify thereby to you, that by My blood, the sacrifice of Myself, and the atonement made thereby, I have purchased for

you the remission of your sins, which you shall assuredly be made partakers of." And more I shall not add to this consideration, because the death of Christ, respected in this ordinance, will again occur to us.

(b)

6. **What is the end of all Church order, assemblies, and worship ?** What is a Church ? Is it not a company of sinners gathered together, according to God's appointment, to give glory and praise to Him for pardoning grace, for the forgiveness of sins, and to yield Him that obedience which He requires from us, on the account of His having so dealt with us ? This is the nature, this is the end of a Church. He that understands it not, he that uses it not to that end, does but abuse that great institution. And such abuse the world is full of. Some endeavour to make their own secular advantages by the pretence of the Church. Some discharge the duty required in it with some secret hopes that it shall be their righteousness before God. Some answer only their light and convictions in an empty profession. This alone is the true end, the true use of it. We assemble ourselves, to learn that there is forgiveness with God through Christ ; to pray that we may be made partakers of it ; to bless and praise God for our interest in it ; to engage ourselves to that obedience which He requires upon the account of it. And were this constantly upon our minds, and in our designs, we might be more established in the faith of it than it may be the most of us are.

(c)

7. One particular instance more of this nature shall conclude this evidence. God hath commanded us, the Lord Christ have taught us, to pray for the pardon of sin ; which gives us unquestionable security that it may be attained, that it is to be found with God. For the clearing whereof, observe,—

(i.) That the Lord Christ, in the revelation of the will of God to us, as to what He required at our hands, hath taught and instructed us to pray for the forgiveness of sin. It is one of the petitions which He hath left on record for our use and imitation, in that summary of all prayer which He hath given us, " Forgive us our debts, our trespasses, our sins " (Matt. vi. 12). Some contend that this is a form of prayer to be used in the prescribed limited words of it ; all grant that it is a rule of prayer, comprising the head of all necessary things that we are to pray for, and obliging us to make supplications for them. So then, upon the authority of God, revealed to us by Jesus Christ, we are bound in duty to pray for pardon of sins, or forgiveness.

(d)

(ii.) On this supposition, it is the highest blasphemy and reproach of God imaginable, to conceive that there is not forgiveness with Him for us. Indeed, if we should go upon our own heads, without His warrant and authority, to ask anything at His hand, we might well expect to meet with disappointment ; for what should encourage us to any such boldness ? But now, when God Himself shall command us to come, and ask anything from Him, so making it thereby our duty, and that the neglect thereof should be our great sin and rebellion against Him, to suppose He hath

(e)

Religious Worship, Forgiveness and—continued

not the thing in His power to bestow on us, or that His will is wholly averse from so doing, is to reproach Him with want of truth, faithfulness, and holiness, and not to be God. For what sincerity can be in such proceedings? Is it consistent with any Divine excellency? Could it have any other end, but to deceive poor creatures; either to delude them if they do pray according to His command, or to involve them in further guilt if they do not? God forbid any such thoughts should enter our hearts. But,

(a)

(iii.) To put this whole matter out of question, God hath promised to hear our prayers, and in particular those which we make to Him for the forgiveness of sin. So our Saviour hath assured us, that what we ask in His name shall be done to us. And He hath, as we have showed, taught us to ask this very thing of God as our Heavenly Father; that is, in His name: for in and through Him alone is He a Father to us. I need not insist on particular promises to this purpose; they are, as you know, multiplied in the Scriptures.

(b) *John Owen*

(See "FORGIVENESS OF SINS.")

RELIGIOUSNESS

There is a great difference between religiousness and religion. Man is a religious animal, he must and will worship something. But the religion which the Bible teaches is a total change of the heart, and of the aim and purpose of life.

(c) *Gordon Calthrop*

REMEMBERINGS, SPIRITUAL

1. Remember thy sins, Christ's pardonings;
2. Remember thy deserts, Christ's merits;
3. Remember thy weakness, Christ's strength;
4. Remember thy pride, Christ's humility;
5. Remember thy many infirmities, Christ's restorings;
6. Remember thy wants, Christ's fulness;
7. Remember thy vileness, Christ's righteousness.

Thos. Wilcocks, 1662

Cf. Jesus, "Who of God is made unto us *wisdom* and *righteousness*, and *sanctification*, and *redemption*."

(d)

REMEMBRANCE

"*The righteous shall be had in everlasting remembrance*" (Ps. cxii. 6)

Translation of an affecting epitaph from the Catacombs of Rome:—

"Here Gordianus, Ambassador
from Gaul,
Consumed with all his family
for the faith,
reposes in peace.
Theophila, servant, made (this tablet)."

A Christian family, far from home, strangers in a strange land; the father, ambassador perhaps to plead the cause of fellow-Christians in trouble, meets not with mercy in Rome, but persecution

and death for himself and his dear ones; and then the watchful Church in the Catacombs obtains their dust. Who will not love the good servant, Theophila, that being no longer able to wait on her master and his family, raises up this stone to their memory, and so remits to posterity their good name!

(e) *Sunday at Home*

REMISSION OF SINS

"*Remission of sins that are past*" (Rom. iii. 25)

A large family may sometimes travel from place to place simply on credit. They have nothing themselves to pay; but the head of the family, who follows after, meets all the expenses that have been incurred. "In the fulness of time," God was made manifest in the flesh, to pay the debt of those who, by permission of the Lawgiver, had been allowed to travel home.

(f) *Christmas Evans*

REMNANT (1 Thess. ii. 13–16)

The development of the Jewish people during fifteen centuries resulted in a division into a *believing minority* (14) *and an unbelieving majority* (15, 16), which persecuted the former. The prophets spake of this remnant. The division being completed, there came the crisis, in the destruction of Jerusalem, from which believers were delivered (Pella), whereas ruin befell the unbelieving. The same result will follow the development of the New Testament Christian Church. We too are dividing, and advancing towards a crisis.

(g) *Lange*

RENAISSANCE

Along with this there has come to prevail the Buddhist opinion, that life is thoroughly bad and hollow from first to last, and that the wise man should have as little to do with it and its interests as possible, and should only try to leave it on the easiest terms. If you ask how such hard things can be said of an age that builds so many churches and has so much real religious activity, I would remind you that in Italy, in the age that we know as the *Renaissance*, the belief in immortality had almost gone out, and the morals of the people had gone down to the level of pagan depravity, whilst religion, in the form of a multitude of superstitious rules and restrictions, made greater claims than ever upon the people.

(h) *Archbishop Thompson*

REPENTANCE

Thinkest thou that God, who gave thee grace to repent thee of thy sins, will not pardon them after thy repentance?

(i) *Ambrose*

"*There is joy in the presence of the angels of God over one sinner that repenteth*" (Luke xv. 7)

What do you suppose is the object on earth most attractive and interesting to Heaven? An

(j)

angel coming down here, what would he care for your palaces and pyramids, your works of art, military achievements, wonders of legislation, or even your books—books of philosophy, science, or song? What would he care for your great men, whether distinguished for thought or action, profound intellect or eloquent speech? What would he care for all these things? Nothing. But if he saw a human spirit panting for truth, pressing after God, fearing the darkness, conscious of its sin, breaking with contrition, earnest in prayer, solicitous for guidance—why, to him such a sight would shine like a star.

(a)   *T. Binney*

REPENTANCE, DEATH-BED

The English proverb says, "The river past and God forgotten," to express with how mournful a frequency He whose assistance was invoked,—it may have been earnestly,—in the moment of peril is remembered no more, so soon as by His help the danger has been surmounted. And the Italian form of it sounds a still sadder depth of ingratitude: "The peril past, the saint mocked"—the vows made to him in peril remaining unperformed in safety, and he treated something as, in Greek story, Juno was treated by Mandrabulus the Samian, who having, under her auspices and through her direction, discovered a gold mine, in his instant gratitude vowed to her a golden ram, which he presently exchanged in intention for a silver one; and again this for a very small brass one; and this for nothing at all; the rapidly descending scale of whose gratitude, with the entire disappearance of his thanksgiving, might very profitably live in our memories, as so perhaps it would be less likely to repeat itself in our lives.

(b)   *Archbishop Trench*

There is *one* case of death-bed repentance recorded, that no one should despair, and *only* one, that no one should presume.

(c)   *Augustine*

He that repents every day for the sins of every day, when he comes to die, will have the sin but of one day to repent of. Short reckonings make long friends.

(d)   *P. Henry*

True repentance is never too *late*, but *late* repentance is seldom *true;* for here our sins rather leave us than we them, as Ambrose says; and he adds, "Woe be unto them whose sin and life end together."

(e)   *Bolton*

REPENTANCE AND FORGIVENESS

God's appointment of repentance to sinners reveals that there is forgiveness in Himself; the prescription of repentance is a revelation of forgiveness. After the angels had sinned, God never once called them to repentance. He would not deceive them, but let them know what they were to look for at His hands; he hath no forgiveness for them, and therefore would require no repentance of them. It is not, nor ever was, a duty incumbent on them to repent; nor is it so to the damned in hell. God

requires it not of them, nor is it their duty. There being no forgiveness for them, what should move them to repent? Why should it be their duty so to do? Their eternal anguish about sin committed hath nothing of repentance in it. The appointment, then, of repentance, is a revelation of forgiveness. God would not call upon a sinful creature to humble itself, and bewail its sin, if there were no way of recovery or relief; and the only way of recovery from the guilt of sin is pardon. So Job (xxxiii. 27, 28), "He looketh on men, and if any say, I have sinned, and perverted that which was right, and it profited me not; he will deliver his soul from going into the pit, and his life shall see the light." In the foregoing verses, he declares the various ways that God used to bring men to repentance. He did it by dreams (ver. 15, 16), by afflictions (ver. 19), by the preaching of the word (ver. 23). What then doth God aim at in and by all these various ways of teaching? It is to cause man to say, "I have sinned, and perverted that which was right." It is to bring him to repentance. What now, if He obtain His end, and man cometh to that which is aimed at? Why, then there is forgiveness for him, as is declared (ver. 28). To improve this evidence, I shall confirm, by some few considerations, these two things. First, that the prescription of repentance doth indeed evince that there is forgiveness with God. Secondly, that every one in whom there is repentance wrought towards God, may certainly conclude that there is forgiveness with God for him.

(f)

1. No repentance is acceptable with God, but what is built or leans on the faith of forgiveness. We have a cloud of witnesses to this truth in the Scripture. Many there have been, many are recorded, who have been convinced of sin, perplexed about it, sorry for it, who have made open confession and acknowledgment of it, who, under the present sense of it, have cried out even to God for deliverance, and yet have come short of mercy, pardon, and acceptance with God. The cases of Cain, Pharaoh, Saul, Ahab, Judas, and others might be insisted on. What was wanting, that made all that they did abominable? Consider one instance for all: it is said of Judas, that he repented (Matt. xxvii. 3). "He repented himself;" but wherein did this repentance consist?

(i.) He was convinced of his sin in general, he saith, "I have sinned" (ver. 4).

(ii.) He was sensible of the particular sin whereof he stood charged in conscience before God. "I have," saith he, "betrayed innocent blood;" "I am guilty of blood, innocent blood, and that in the vilest manner, by treachery, so that he comes,

(iii.) To a full and open confession of his sin.

(iv.) He makes restitution of what he was advantaged by his sin, "he brought again the thirty pieces of silver" (ver. 3), all testifying a hearty sorrow, that spirited the whole. Methinks now, Judas's repentance looks like the young man's obedience, who cried out, "All these things have I done: is there anything yet lacking?" Yea, one thing was wanting to that young man, he had no true faith nor love to God all this while, which vitiated and spoiled all the rest of his perform-

(g)

Repentance and Forgiveness—*continued*

ances. One thing is also wanting to this repentance of Judas : he had no faith of forgiveness in
God ; that he could not believe; and therefore,
after all this sorrow, instead of coming to Him, he
bids Him the utmost defiance, and hangs himself.

Faith of forgiveness hath many degrees. There is
of them, that which is indispensably necessary to
render repentance acceptable. What it is in particular, I do not dispute. It is not an assurance
of the acceptance of our persons in general. It is
not, that the particular sin wherewith, it may be,
the soul is perplexed is forgiven. A general, if it
be a Gospel discovery, that there is forgiveness in
God, will suffice. The Church expresses it (Hos.
(xiv. 3), "In Thee the fatherless findeth mercy;"
and Joel (ii. 14), "Who knows but He will return
and repent ?" "I have this ground," saith the
soul; "God is in Himself gracious and merciful;
the fatherless, the destitute and helpless, that
come to Him by Christ, find mercy in Him. None
in heaven and earth can evince, but that He may
return to me also." Now, let a man's convictions
be ever so great, sharp, wounding; his sorrow
ever so abundant, overflowing, abiding; his confession ever so full, free, or open; if this one thing
be wanting, all is nothing but what tends to death.
(*a*)

2. To prescribe repentance as a duty unto sinners,
without a foundation of pardon and forgiveness in
God, is inconsistent with the wisdom, holiness, goodness, faithfulness, and all the other excellencies and
perfections of the nature of God : for,

(i.) The Apostle lays this as the great foundation of all consolation, that God cannot lie or
deceive (Heb. vi. 18). And again, he engages the
faithfulness and veracity of God to the same purpose (Tit. i. 2), "God, who cannot lie, hath
promised it." Now, there is a lie, a deceit, in
things as well as in words. He that doth a thing,
which, in its own nature, is apt to deceive them
that consider it, with an intention of deceiving
them, is no less a liar than he who affirms that
to be true which he knows to be false. There is a
lie in actions as well as in words. The whole life
of a hypocrite is a lie. So saith the prophet concerning idolaters, "There is a lie in their right
hand " (Isa. xliv. 20).
(*b*)

(ii.) The proposal of repentance is a thing fitted
and suited, in its own nature, to beget thoughts in
the mind of a sinner, that there is forgiveness with
God. Repenting is for sinners only. "I came
not," saith our Saviour, "to call the righteous, but
sinners, to repentance." It is for them and for
them only. It was no duty for Adam in Eden ; it
is none for the angels in heaven, nor for the
damned in hell. What then may be the language
of this appointment? O sinners, come and deal
with God by repentance ! Doth it not openly
speak forgiveness in God? And if it were otherwise, could men possibly be more frustrated or
deceived? Would not the institution of repentance be a lie? Such a delusion may proceed from
Satan, but not from Him who is the fountain of
goodness, holiness, and truth. His call to repentance is a full demonstration of his readiness to
forgive (Acts xvii. 30–32). It is true, many do thus
deceive themselves. They raise themselves to an

expectation of immunity, not on Gospel grounds ;
and their disappointment is a great part of their
punishment. But God deceives none ; whoever
comes to Him on His proposal of repentance, shall
find forgiveness. It is said of some, indeed, that
He "will laugh at their calamity, and mock when
their fear cometh (Prov. i. 26). He will aggravate
their misery by giving them to see what their pride
and folly hath brought them to. But who are
they? Only such as refuse His call to repentance,
with the promises of the acceptance annexed.
(*c*)

(iii.) There is then no cause why those who are
under a call to repentance should question whether
there be forgiveness in God or not. This concerns
my second proposition. Come, saith the Lord to
the souls of men, leave your sinful ways, turn unto
Me, humble yourselves with broken and contrite
hearts. Alas! say poor convinced sinners, we are
poor dark and ignorant creatures ; or, we are old
in sin, or great sinners, or backsliders, or have
fallen often into the same sins; can we expect
there should be forgiveness for us? Why, you
are under God's invitation to repentance ; and to
disbelieve forgiveness, is to call the truth, holiness,
and faithfulness of God into question. If you will
not believe forgiveness, pretend what you please,
it is in truth because you hate repentance. You
do but deceive your souls, when you pretend you
come not up to repentance because you cannot
believe forgiveness ; for, in the very institution of
this duty, God engages all His properties to make
it good, that He hath pardon and mercy for
sinners.
(*d*)

(iv.) Much less cause is there to doubt of forgiveness, where sincere repentance is in any measure
wrought. No soul comes to repentance, but upon
God's call. God calls not but those whom He hath
mercy for upon their coming. And, as for those
who sin against the Holy Ghost, as they shut
themselves out from forgiveness, so they are not
called to repentance.
(*e*)

(v.) God expressly declares in the Scripture, that
the forgiveness which is with Him is the foundation of His prescribing repentance unto man. One
instance may suffice (Isa. lv. 7), "Let the wicked
forsake his way " (in the Hebrew, a perverse
wicked one); "and the man of iniquity his
thoughts ; and let him return unto the Lord, and
He will have mercy ; and to our God, for " (in the
Hebrew) "He will multiply to pardon." You see
to whom He speaks—to men perversely wicked,
and such as make a trade of sinning. What doth
He call them to? Plainly, to repentance, to the
duty we have insisted on. But what is the ground
of such an invitation to such profligate sinners?
Why, the abundant forgiveness and pardon that is
with Him, superabounding to what the worst of
them can stand in need of; as Rom. v. 20.
(*f*)

And this is another way whereby God hath revealed that there is forgiveness with Him ; and an
infallible foundation for faith to build upon, in its
approaches to God. Nor can the certainty of this
evidence be called into question, but on such
grounds as are derogatory to the glory and honour
(*g*)

Repentance and Forgiveness—*continued*

of God. And this connection of repentance and forgiveness is that principle from whence God convinces a stubborn unbelieving people that all His ways and dealings with sinners are just and equal (Ezek. xviii. 25). And should there be any failure in it, they could not be so. Every soul, then, that is under a call to repentance, whether out of his natural condition or from any back-sliding into folly after conversion, hath a sufficient foundation to rest on, as to the pardon he inquires after. God is ready to deal with him on terms of mercy. If, out of love to sin or the power of un-belief, he refuse to close with God on these terms, his condemnation is just. And it will be well that this consideration be deeply imprinted on the minds of men. I say, notwithstanding the general presumptions that men seem to have of this matter, yet these principles of it ought to be in-culcated : for,

(a)

(i.) Such is the atheism that lies lurking in the hearts of men by nature, that, notwithstanding their pretensions and professions, we have need to be pressing upon them evidences of the very being and essential properties of God. In so doing, we have the assistance of inbred notions in their own minds, which they cannot eject, to help to carry on the work. How much more is this necessary in reference to the free acts of the will of God, which are to be known only by mere revelation. Our word had need be " line upon line ; " and yet when we have done, we have cause enough to cry out, as was said, " Lord, who hath bel ed our report ? and to whom hath the arm of the Lord been revealed ? "

(b)

(ii.) What was spoken before of the obstacles that lie in the way, hindering souls from a saving reception of this truth, ought to be remembered. Those who have no experience of them between God and their soul, seem to be ignorant of the true nature of conscience, law, gospel, grace, sin, and forgiveness.

(c)　　　　　　　　　　　　　*John Owen*

(*See* " Forgiveness of Sins.")

REPENTANCE (TO-DAY)

A Jewish Rabbi exhorted his disciples to repent the day before they died. One replied that the day of a man's death was uncertain. "Repent, therefore, every day," said the Rabbi, " and then you will be sure to repent the day before you die." You who are wise will know how to apply this.

(d)　　　　　　　　　　　　　*Thos. Brooks*

Repentance.

" Unless you commence at once that work which has been so long neglected, unless now you begin to repent, you must surely perish." Begin ! begin to repent ! This brings another and an over-powering thought. Begin to repent ! When ? In a month, in a week ? Foolish man ! Foolish woman ! This night thy soul may be required of thee.

(e)　　　　　　　　　　　　*Bp. Wilkinson*

RESOLVES

I knew a man who six times made good re-solves, and six times broke them ; but ere he had time to make the seventh, death had cut him off.

(f)　　　　　　　　　　　　　*S. Bridge*

RESPONSIBILITY

I approach a profound and terrible mystery. In the pre-Adamite ages, higher succeeded lower dynasties ; but to be low was not to be immoral ; was not to be guilt-stained and miserable. . . . It is only when the human period begins that we are startled and perplexed by the problem of a lowness not innocent, an inferiority tantamount to moral deformity. In the period of responsi-bility, to be low means to be evil. How, we ask, could this have any place in the decrees of Him who ever does what is right? The subject is one beyond man's thorough comprehension. . . . Yet it may be remarked, that such of the lower animals as are guided by pure instinct are greatly more infallible than the higher half-reasoning animals. The mathematical bee never constructs a false angle ; the sagacious dog is not unfre-quently *out* in his calculations. The higher the animal in the scale, the greater its liability to error. . . . But it is not the less true, that no fish, no reptile, no mammal of the geologic or the recent ages, ever so failed in working out the pur-poses it was created to serve, as man has failed in working out *his ;* further, in no creature save in man does there exist that war of the mind between appetite and duty, of which the Apostle com-plained. And we must seek an explanation of these twin facts in man's freedom of will, which rendered him capable of being of *choice* God's fellow-worker, or of choosing *not* to work for God.

(g)　　　　　　　　　　　　*Hugh Miller*

REST

" *Come unto Me, all ye that labour and are heavy laden, and I will give you rest* " (Matt. xi. 28)

Let wit with all her studied plots effect
　　　The best they can ;
Let smiling fortune prosper and perfect
　　　What wit began ;
Let earth advise with both, and so project
　　　A happy man ;
Let wit or fawning fortune vie their best ;
　　　He may be blest
With all the earth can give ; but earth can give no
　　　rest.

Whose gold is double with a careful hand,
　　　His cares are double ;
The pleasure, honour, wealth of sea and land
　　　Bring but a trouble ;
The world itself, and all the world's command,
　　　Is but a bubble.
The strong desires of man's insatiate breast
　　　May stand possesst
Of all that earth can give ; but earth can give no
　　　rest.

(h)　　　　　　　　　*Francis Quarles,* 1634.

Rest

I have lived to see this world is made up of perturbations, and I have been long preparing to

(i)

leave it, and gathering comfort for the dreadful hour of making my account with God, which I now apprehend to be near.

(a) *Hooker*

Rest is the sweet sauce of labour.

(b) *Plutarch*

Rest after labour.

(c) *Pollok*

Absence of occupation is not rest.

(d) *Cowper*

RESTITUTION OF ALL THINGS

" *Whom the heavens must receive until the times of restitution of all things, which God hath spoken by the mouth of all His holy prophets since the world began* " (Acts iii. 21)

1. Is the doctrine of a universal restoration of all things, *i.e.*, of a lost world, lost angels, and of lost men, taught here, so that ultimately ALL, without any exception whatever, will be saved?

Some interpreters tell us that they find this doctrine taught, and that other passages bear out such an interpretation. Among such, are the words of our Saviour in John xii. 32.

"And I, if I be lifted up from the earth, will draw *all men* unto Me ; " and those of St. Paul in 1 Cor. 15, " As in Adam *all die*, even so in Christ shall ALL be made alive ; " again, Eph. i. 10, " In the dispensation of the fulness of times, He might gather together in one *all things* in Christ, both which are in heaven, and which are on earth ; even in Him."

These passages, together with that of the text, it is held, convey the doctrine of a universal restoration in such a sense as that ultimately nothing will be lost, and that, in consequence, the orthodox teaching about lost souls, perdition, and hell, is not only defective, but misleading.

(e)

2. The objection to this interpretation. Even the most superficial reader of the Scriptures will not fail to discover that under such a supposition " Repentance towards God, and *faith* toward our Lord Jesus Christ," the two indispensable conditions of salvation, are left out of consideration altogether ; and to search no further than the context of our passage we find that these two conditions of salvation are there most positively insisted upon in the teaching of the Apostle. For in the 19th verse he says, " *Repent and be converted* in order that the times of refreshing may come ; " and in the 23rd verse, " *Every soul* which will not hear that prophet (Christ) shall be destroyed."

Here we have to notice, that, together with the doctrine of the Restoration—whatever it may mean—are combined the two indispensable conditions of salvation, viz., *repentance and faith*. Clearly then, the *universal restoration* of mankind, independent of their individual repentance and faith, is not taught in this passage.

We call to mind, too, the Lord's language, unmixed with hope, over the traitor, Judas Iscariot : " The Son of man goeth as it is written of Him, but woe unto that man by whom the Son of man is betrayed, *good were it for him if he had never been born*."

Surely such language loses all point, and is shorn of its awful terrors and warnings, if the thought lies concealed in it, that restoration to all the privileges of salvation (though later on), is possible for him. How, then, could the Saviour have said, " *Good were it for him if he had never been born* " ?

(f)

3. Moreover it cannot fail to be noticed, that in that graphic picture of the last things contained in the closing words of the Book of Revelation, we find this :—

After the millennium is over—after the judgments have been pronounced—after the New Jerusalem has been established on the earth, all rule all authority and power other than God's put down—after all the struggles between the forces of good and evil are over for ever, and, as we say, history is over—after all these things, there yet remaineth some persons who live on, but who are excluded from all participation in the blessedness and privileges of those dwelling in the heavenly city ; and the Bible closes by *leaving them* " *without*," and with no hint of a possible restoration in the hereafter. If such teaching be not dogmatic, it is anyhow terribly significant, and full of the most fearful warning.

The most that can be said is, that the Bible leaves off by showing us that a *duality*, of good and evil, continues even after the long record of the struggle between the two, and the final triumph of the good.

Let us not, then, be led away by this plausible doctrine of a *Universal Restoration* of those who live and die in impenitence. " There is a sin unto death," . . . a sin " which shall never be forgiven, neither in this world nor in that which is to come." If not forgiven *now*, nor then, WHEN ?

(g)

4. What then are we to understand by this term, "The Restitution of all things"? What things will be restored?

We must seek for our answer in the language of the text itself. The things which are to be restored are those things " Which God hath spoken by the mouth of all His holy prophets, since the world began."

The prophecies, then, must be searched in order to find the correct answer to this question. And when we do so, we shall find, I think, that first and foremost amongst the themes of the prophets is that of the restoration of God's elect people under the reign of the Messiah.

For the most part, all through the history of God's people, they have felt themselves a people deprived of their king their kingdom, and their inheritance, and consequently they are nearly always spoken of as waiting for that time to come when they shall have restored to them all the privileges which properly appertain to them as the chosen of God. Such a restoration is the theme of the Bible throughout the writings of Moses and Samuel and all who come after.

And first among these will be the restoration of God's ancient people the Jews : for so the disciples understood, and such was the impression left on their minds after they had asked, " Wilt Thou at *this time* restore again the kingdom unto Israel."

" And He said unto them, It is not for you to

(h)

Restitution of all Things—*continued*

know the times and the seasons, which the Father hath put in His own power." They were in error only about the "times and the seasons," but not about the thing looked for.

(*a*)

5. Next in point of time, though not in privilege, will be the restoration of the elect from among all nations—as it is written : " Rejoice, ye Gentiles with His people." " For in the seed of Abraham shall *all* the families of the earth be blessed."

That such is the general theme of the prophecies bearing on the " Restitution of all things " seems to be the teaching of St. Paul, when he sums up his argument in Rom. xi. (25–27) with these words: " I would not, brethren, that ye should be ignorant of this mystery . . . that blindness in part is happened to Israel, until the fulness of the Gentiles be come in." And so all Israel shall be saved ; (but not Israel exclusively) as it is written, There shall come out of Zion the Deliverer, and shall turn away ungodliness from Jacob: " For this is My covenant unto them, when I shall take away their sins."

The restoration, then, of Israel, will follow on their repentance and faith. Now let us for a moment compare this statement with the teaching of St. Peter in the chapter before us. He says, " Repent ye therefore, and be converted, that your sins may be blotted out, when the times of refreshing shall come from the presence of the Lord ; and that He may send Jesus Christ, who before was appointed unto you," also the similar language of the last verse, " Unto you first God, having raised up His Son Jesus, sent Him to bless you, in turning away every one of you from his iniquities."

From such teaching, it seems obvious enough what the " Restitution of all things " spoken of in the text signifies.

(*b*)

6. It is the fulfilment of all the Promises of the Old Testament to the elect of God—Jew and Gentile alike—for in Christ there is no difference, " They without us cannot be made perfect." But what such fulness implies, " Eye hath not seen, nor ear heard, neither have entered into the heart of man, the things which God hath prepared for them that love Him."

In the light of such teaching we may say that the time of the " Restitution of all things " will be for the earth its grand year of jubilee—not the jubilee of a nation, but the jubilee of the Church of Christ. The time alluded to by Him as " the Regeneration."

We all remember that the year of Jubilee (occurring every fiftieth year among the Jews) was a time of restitution and restoration—the people's year—to which they who were in trouble looked forward with joy, because it would bring them happiness. Bondslaves were set free, prison doors were opened, and alienated lands and possessions were remitted to their original owners. No injustice being done thereby to the possessor at the time, for he came by his property on the same terms that we now-a-days take a leasehold, which both parties understand will " fall in " when the term is expired.

(*c*)

7. This had a deeper spiritual significance ; it was a part of the teaching of the time. God's people were taught by it to look forward to a great year of Jubilee for the whole Church of Christ. An appointed time in the world's history, a time known only to God, when the things belonging of right to the Church of God should be restored to it. " All things are yours," says the Apostle to God's people. But as yet nearly everything that is good and desirable is in the hands and under the authority of the power which is called " The world "—the rival of God the Father. The inheritance is in wrong hands, only, however, as a leasehold.

Although the fairest portions of this earth's surface, its arts and sciences, its poetry, painting, and music are for the most part in wrong hands, and have been so ever since the days of Jubal and Tubal-Cain, yet,—we have it on the authority of God's word,—all these things belong to the saints of God by right. The promise is, that they shall inherit the earth ; and it only needs the touch of inspiration to make all poetry and music like David's, and every branch of art and science to join in the harmony of creation. " All Thy works praise Thee, O God." A year of Jubilee, then, is coming, when all these things shall be *restored*, and given into the hands of those for whom they were originally intended by God, and who will glorify God by the gift given to them.

This is no fancy: no dream, for the saints, even now, have "*the earnest of their inheritance ;*" something of what is coming to them they have already. "They can read their title clear to mansions in the skies " by the comfort of the Holy Ghost. But then the " *Purchased possession* " will be *redeemed* and taken out of the hands of the power which now holds it, and given over to them.

(*d*)

8. Lastly. The time of the Restitution of all things may further be described as the time when *all creation shall be harmonized*. It is not so now : at present " the whole creation is described as groaning and travailing in pain . . . waiting for the manifestation of the sons of God, at which time it will be delivered from its bondage, it will become what God intended it to be at the first. See the three groanings (of Creation, of the sons of God, and of the Spirit) in Rom. viii. There is apparently in the physical world, as in the moral world, a duality of forces, perhaps allied powers, of evil and good agencies constantly engaged in a struggle for supremacy.

Here and there in the Holy Scriptures we have indications of the sympathy between Nature and the moral sphere. Wicked men cannot crucify Christ, and there be no earthquake, and an unnatural darkness over all the land. It is quite in keeping with this, that Art should depict a terrific storm immediately after the fall of Adam and Eve. Nature and conscience in sympathy, also that in recent times a point was made of a thunderstorm which shook the room when the doctrine of Papal Infallibility became a tenet of the Church of Rome.

And how are we to interpret shipwreck, and such calamities as are purely the result of natural disturbances, except on the ground that the harmony of creation has been disturbed, and every now and then it seems to be racked with pain and convulsions? Great catastrophes happen, and the pain reaches the sphere of man and sentient things.

(*e*)

Restitution of all Things—*continued*

Nor can we expect peace until the same Master's voice speak "Peace," first to the fears of man and then to Nature, which waits for that. It was so, we remember, at the stilling of the storm on the lake. "One thing is needful" the harmony of nature must be restored, man and creation are both alike out of tune, and the time of "the Restoration of all things" will be that of putting all creation into tune. There will then be no longer a duality of opposing forces and contrary *wills*, as now. One force only will be supreme, God's will only will be done, as we pray.

Then the harmony of creation, *i.e.*, the new creation, "the Regeneration" will be complete, and that time synchronizes with "the manifestation of the sons of God," both of which take place at the appearing of our Lord and Saviour Jesus Christ, and together constitute "THE RESTITUTION OF ALL THINGS."

(*a*)

RESTORATION, A FINAL

"*Good were it for that . . . born*" (Mark xiv. 21)

Is in reality the strongest argument in the whole Bible against the doctrine of a final restoration of all men—an argument which it appears to me that we have a right to regard as perfectly conclusive.

(*b*)   *Starbuck*

RESTORATION OF THE LOST

It is not for us to limit the possible range of God's restoring mercy. But what do facts tell us? Nay, what does fiction tell us (for fiction dare only reflect the light of fact) of any hopes of reformation in this world for the arch-tempter's delegates—those who ply their victims with drink, that they may mock at their degradation; for the cold-blooded seducers; the touts of gambling-hells; the smiling, damned villain who pours into the innocent ear the leprous distilment of his vile suggestiveness, or lures unsuspecting simplicity to ruin under the mask of good fellowship and geniality?

Are such men curable in fiction or in fact?

Dare Dickens have restored the educating demons of his den of thieves, or Scott his Varney or Dalgarno, or George Eliot her Grandcourt, or Thackeray his Marquis of Steyne or Lord Hellborough to repentance, or even to remorse?

I fear that such a transformation would stamp their fictions as untrue to life. They may invest such characters, if they please, with all the external charms of grace and dignity; for though there are hideous shapes among the fiends, yet Milton's master-fiend is no loathsome-looking reptile, but-

"Crested aloft, and carbuncle his eyes;
With burnish'd neck of verdant gold, erect
Amid his circling spires, that on the grass
Floated redundant: *pleasing was his shape,
And lovely.*"

(*c*)   *Hely Hutchinson Almond*

RESTRAINT

Restraint, in some form or other, is an essential law of our nature, a necessary discipline, running through life, and not to be escaped by any art or violence. Where can we go, and not meet it? The powers of nature are, all of them, limits to human power. A never-ceasing force of gravity chains us to the earth. Mountains, rocks, precipices, and seas forbid our advances. If we come to society, restraints multiply on us. Our neighbour's rights limit our own. His property is forbidden ground. Usage restricts our free action, fixes our manners and the language we must speak and the modes of pursuing our ends. Business is a restraint, setting us wearisome tasks, and driving us through the same mechanical routine day after day. Duty is a restraint, imposing curbs on passion, enjoining one course and forbidding another, with stern voice, with uncompromising authority. Study is a restraint, compelling us, if we would learn anything, to concentrate the forces of thought and to bridle the caprices of fancy. All law, divine or human, is, as the name imports, restraint. No one feels more than I do the need of this element of human life. He who would fly from it must live in perpetual conflict with nature, society, and himself.

(*d*)   *Channing*

RESURRECTION OF THE BODY (1 Cor. xv.)

Not, as some suppose, the restoration of the old, a recomposition of the same particles that existed in the old body, but of another and a nobler quality, suited to the organ of perfectly sanctified spirit. In the resurrection body we enter upon a distinct and higher stage of life than that occupied by the body which has been laid in the earth. "*A building of God, a house not made with hands*," in contrast with that in which we suffered pain and sin and suffering, and in which we "groaned being burdened."

(*e*)   *Lange*

RESURRECTION OF CHRIST (Rom. iv. 25)

Without His Resurrection the death of Christ would be of no avail, and His grave would be the grave of all our hopes (1 Cor. xv. 17). A gospel of a *dead* Saviour would be a miserable failure and delusion. The Resurrection is the victory of righteousness and life over sin and death.

(*f*)   *Schaff*

RESURRECTION: THE CHRISTIAN RISEN WITH CHRIST

And now, how am I conformable to Thee; if when Thou art risen, I lie still in the grave of my corruptions? How am I a limb of Thy body; if, while Thou hast that perfect dominion over death, death hath dominion over me; if, while Thou art alive and glorious, I lie rotting in the dust of death? I know the locomotive faculty is in the head; by the power of the Resurrection of Thee our Head, all we Thy members cannot but be raised. As the earth cannot hold my body from Thee in the day of the Second Resurrection, so cannot sin withhold my soul from Thee in the first. How am I Thine, if I be not risen? and if I be risen with Thee, why do I not seek the things above, where Thou sittest at the right hand of God?

(*g*)   *Bishop Hall*

RESURRECTION

" *Who is he that condemneth?* " (Rom. viii.)

Is it the wrath of God? Wherefore is that, but for sin? If my sin be defrayed, that quarrel is at an end; and if my Saviour suffered it for me, how can I fear to suffer it in myself? That infinite justice hates to be twice paid. He is risen; therefore He hath satisfied. "*Who is he that condemneth? It is Christ that died; yea, rather, that is risen.*"

(a)   *Bishop Hall*

RESURRECTION, AS ILLUSTRATED BY THE ACCOUNT OF THE DIVINE PLAN IN MAN'S CREATION (1 Cor. 15)

Much light is cast upon the great distinction between the present and the Resurrection body, by the Divinely revealed economy of the Creator; or, in other words, by the Divinely ordained development of the human race, as set forth in Scripture.

(b)

1. The all-quickening Spirit of God first produced a creature with a *living soul.* The soul, as the vehicle of his life-power, by which being quickened, the earthly body prepared for it by God becomes animal or psychical, *i.e.,* conformed to the character of the soul, is the organism of a personal life which is capable either of *appropriating to itself ever more and more that Divine spiritual life* in which it is rooted, or of *apostatizing* from it.

In the case of *apostasy,* such as actually occurred, instead of a progressive glorification of the earthly, physical body into a heavenly, spiritual one, there would ensue a progressive mortality and corruption.

And such man has already incurred.

Nevertheless, that condition for which he was originally constituted and destined, was bound to come to pass.

(c)

2. Through a Divine act of love, a new process of development was introduced into the human race, which, as in the first instance, entered into life through the quickening power of the Divine Spirit, and in like manner involved the possibility of a free self-determination in *both* directions, *i.e.,* a true human life according to soul and body.

But by a style of conduct opposed to that pursued in the first stage of development, or by its head, the first Adam—by the perpetual appropriation and maintenance of the Divine spiritual life amid all the temptations of our lower nature, and amid all the struggles and necessities which attended upon a loving entrance into the accursed state of the first Adamic humanity, this reached a height upon which the animal nature, glorified into a truly spiritual condition, becomes the principle of a like glorification for the earthly animal race of man (in so far as this enters into the fellowship of the second Adam). So that everything which had been corrupted by means of sin is again restored, and aims at rising to the highest stage of life which had been ordained from the beginning as the proper goal of all human endeavour, but which had become unattainable through the apostasy.

(d)

3. Now, after that we have become incorporated into Adam II. by faith, by means of which His Spirit, as an inwardly sanctifying power, takes possession of our personal life, and delivers it from all selfishness, and all entanglement with our earthly sensuous being, and attracts it with all its powers and entire organism into the service of the Divine life, and assimilates it to that; there then follows, as the natural completion of this process, an unfolding of the germ of this Divine spiritual life that has been implanted in this organism (after the process of dying, which belonged to the old Adamic state, has been gone through with) into a new organism which corresponds to the glorified body of the second Adam.

(e)   *Lange*

RESURRECTION FROM THE DEAD, THE

" *The firstborn from the dead* " (Col. i. 18)

1. In these mysterious words the Apostle describes Him who, after His agony and death and burial, rose again the third day from the dead. That issue and result of the dwelling of the Son of God on earth fills St. Paul's mind with its wonder and its triumph. His Master is ever before his eyes as the One Person wearing our mortal nature, who by His own power, and for the first time, broke through the immemorial, universal law and rule of death. That overwhelming event supplies a pre-eminent title by which St. Paul speaks of the Master whom he serves, and the Saviour whom he adores. He was "the first who should rise from the dead and show light to the people and to the Gentiles." He was "declared to be the Son of God with power, by the resurrection from the dead." "He was the firstfruits of them that slept." He, as St. John too heard in his vision, was "the faithful witness and the first-begotten of the dead . . . the first and the last, which was dead and is alive." First in all things in heaven and earth, He was first to bring into that nature and that race which He had redeemed, the deliverance it had so longed for from the bondage of the grave. "He is the image of the invisible God, the firstborn of every creature. By Him were all things created that are in heaven and that are in earth, visible and invisible, whether they be thrones, or dominions, or principalities, or powers. All things were created by Him and for Him, and He is before all things, and by Him all things consist. And He is the Head of the body, the Church; He is the beginning; He is the firstborn from the dead, that in all things He might have the preeminence."

(f)

2. "The Firstborn from the Dead"—"The Firstfruits of them that slept"—how familiar the words sound; and yet, I suppose, it is not always easy to bring home to feeling and thought the real meaning with which they are charged. It is not often that they make and leave on us the impression which they made on the mind of St. Paul. For there was a time when, however men hoped for immortality and resurrection, their experience had seen no warrant of it. The grave closed over the dead: the Psalm of trust, "Thou wilt not leave my soul in hell,"—the assurance of prophecy, "I know that my Redeemer liveth," "Thy dead men shall live, together with my dead body shall they

(g)

Resurrection from the Dead—*continued*

arise "—was answered by the other voice, the wail of perplexity and uncomforted grief, " Dost Thou show wonders among the dead ; or shall the dead rise up again and praise Thee? Shall Thy loving-kindness be shown in the grave, or Thy faithfulness in destruction?" And the same spirit which inspired the one thought allowed also the natural outburst expressed in the other. The great servants of God had come and gone; had lived and died; and their sepulchres were with their children to this day, monuments of the unbroken power of death. They had hoped, they had believed; but to hope is not to possess; to believe is not to see; and men as yet had only seen what we still see of death—the visible end, the decay which cannot be arrested the sinking in the deep waters where no love or strength can retain or deliver; the vanishing, the disappearing, the extinction. Oh, awful mystery of death! To-day there is life, and brightness, and power, and thought, and affection deep and strong, and character made rich and beautiful by long dis-cipline, and the wealth of years' experience, and force to govern hearts and wills, or to turn the courses of the world ; and to-morrow, all is vacancy —there is nothing there ; he is never to be spoken to again, nowhere any more to be found; all has passed like a mist dissolving. " When the breath of man goeth forth, he shall turn again to his earth, and then all his thoughts perish." That is what we see and know still. Till " the firstborn from the dead " arose, the world had seen nothing else. Once and again, indeed, men had been called back to life, but only again to die.

(*a*)

3. " But now is Christ risen from the dead, and become the firstfruits of them that slept "; not called back by any voice of power without Him ; not called back to the life of mortality. "Christ being raised from the dead dieth no more; death hath no more dominion over Him." This is the great, the immeasurable change. On this earth there has been seen, there lived and walked One who was the Son of man, and yet was never more to taste of death; One who had borne the image of the earthly, and Who had put on, while yet among us, the image of the heavenly. That of itself was enough to overpower the thoughts of men, accustomed through all generations to see every-thing end in death: we see and can understand what it was to those who had followed and loved Him: alternate terror and joy, perplexity and dawning bliss, such as earth had never known, doubt, incredulity, the shock of sober, irresistible certainty—" My Lord and my God." But this was not all. He, for whom had been "loosed the pains of death, because it was not possible that He should be holden of it," was not alive again for Himself alone. He was the "firstfruits of them that slept," " the firstborn of the dead. His resurrection was no single, isolated event in the great order of His earthly ministry which it all but closed. It was the first step, the " beginning " of a new and even greater order of His ministry to the creatures whom He had made. It was the tearing asunder " the veil cast over the face of all nations." " It was the opening of the kingdom of God to all believers." It was the reversal, not for one, but for all, of that supposed necessary condition of human existence, that it has come to an end with

the parting breath. It was not merely a pledge, a promise, an example ; it was, for all who bear the flesh and blood which He bore, a step into a new world, with new conditions. It was a step, a real step, made, not foreshadowed, from the dominion of nature into the kingdom of grace. For he was the " firstborn among many brethren," and He was the "firstborn from the dead," "the firstfruits of them that slept."

(*b*)

4. **This is simply and certainly the truth.** To those who have to do with death, to those who have to die, death is, after all, the sternest, strangest, hardest fact of human experience ; and anything that abates the sharpness of death is well worthy the lovingkindness of God and the deep thanksgiving of man. The writers of the New Testament believed that Christ was the firstborn from the dead ; and we see how this altered the whole face of the world and life. It enlarged almost infinitely the interest even of this present mortal life on earth by giving it a meaning and a future ; but it transferred the scene of man's true, and free, and perfect existence to a sphere far beyond this, far beyond the swift passage of the seventy years, with their weakness and sorrow, far beyond that transitory but laborious stage, when every day, as it came and went, brought its trial, its temptation, its choice, perhaps its fall—to the sphere where all was eternal and all was accomplished. And it did this, it opened this great moral hope, as never had been done before —not for the great and elect souls of the race only, but for the obscure and down-trodden crowds, the multitudes that none can number—the slave, the lost, the abject, the miserable. For in His own person, Son of God and Son of man, He had made the step from old things to new ; and He had made it for all His brethren. As the Apostle says, "We are no longer under the law, the old covenant, but under grace." So we may go on to say, We, the children of the Resurrection, are no longer under the laws of nature, but under the laws of the Spirit; no longer under death, but under life; no longer under blind necessity and extinction, but under the living Son of God, "who died for us and rose again, that, whether we wake or sleep, we should live together with Him." He who has the keys of the riddle of man's being, has opened the door and let in the light, the dazzling, almost blinding, light of the other world on our common-place and feverish lives, on the seeming vanity and waste of the generations of mankind. One after another, they have come, and waxed green like the leaves of summer ; one after another, they have fallen and vanished like the leaves of autumn. Where are they gone, all these men who lived as we live, whose footprints and whose handiwork are about us and in all the earth, while *they* are seen no more?

(*c*)

5. **Have they perished?** Did they begin their running with such fulness of life, only that all should be thrown away, when they lay down in the dust and disappeared? So it seemed for all that nature and experience could tell. "We see that wise men also die and perish together, as well as the ignorant and foolish. Man being in honour hath no understanding, but is compared to the beasts that perish." "But now is Christ raised

(*d*)

Resurrection from the Dead—*continued*

from the dead, and become the firstfruits of them that slept." But now we know what has become of them, the long-forgotten dead. No one soul in that distant, incalculable multitude has been forgotten by God who made it. It has not ceased to be, though it has long disappeared from here. It lives and waits in its own place till its day comes, and God shall judge the secrets of men according to His Gospel of righteousness and truth. It has not lived for nought; each has had its own trial, its own great chance and opportunity, according to the "riches of God's goodness, and forbearance, and long-suffering," even though we cannot see how. Of each life the account has to be given, and God will render to every man according to his deeds. Life has not been in vain or an idle show; each has shown itself as it is; the fruits of to-day have gone on beyond to-morrow, on and onwards till the trial was fulfilled, and they are reaped— "to them that by patient continuance in well-doing, glory, and immortality, eternal life; to them that are contentious, and do not obey the truth but unrighteousness, tribulation, and anguish; —to the Jew first, and also to the Gentile."

(a)

6. "For now is Christ risen from the dead, and become the firstfruits of them that slept." He, first and alone, leads the great procession from the prison-house of death, from forgetfulness and nothingness—leads the great triumph of the redeemed of God: the forefathers of the human race, the patriarchs of His Church, saint and prophet and witness to the truth, all who "died in faith not having received the promises, but having seen them afar off," strangers and pilgrims in the land which, though they knew it not, was their own, and with them, the "holy and humble men of heart"—just and good men in every nation, "fearing God and working righteousness"—all who, though not yet knowing their Redeemer, had the faith which followed the light within them even to death, resolved, "Even though He slay me, yet will I trust in Him"; all those, "who not having the law, were a law unto themselves," the blessed and accepted of Him who is no respecter of persons, and who has prepared "glory, honour, and peace to every man that worketh good, to the Jew first, and also to the Gentile." They sleep, but they are not wasted; they sleep, but they are not forgotten: their Redeemer and ours has them in remembrance, and has shown us what they are to be in that new world which has begun for all of us. For it has begun: how could it but begin, in reality and truth, when once the Deliverer had broken the power and the necessity of the grave? How could that world be the same in which such a thing had happened; in which, indeed, death had given way to life?

(b)

7. And so from thence forward the New Testament speaks as if "the powers of the world to come" were already here, changing, vivifying, transforming all things, beginning even in time the work of eternity, even "upon earth the days of heaven." Think of what he must have felt about the facts of existence, about the light and power from above which had come to make their home here even while this life was going on, who wrote such words as these:—"The eyes of your understanding being enlightened: that ye may

know what is the hope of His calling and what the riches of the glory of His inheritance in the saints, and what the exceeding greatness of His power towards us who believe, according to the working of His mighty power, which He wrought in Christ when He raised Him from the dead, and set Him at His own right hand in the heavenly places, far above all principality, and power, and might, and dominion, and every name that is named, not only in this world but also in that which is to come; and hath put all things under His feet, and gave Him to be Head over all things to the Church, which is His body, the fulness of Him that filleth all in all. And you hath He quickened, which were dead in trespasses and sins;—quickened us together into Christ, and raised us up together with Him in the heavenly places in Christ Jesus; that in the ages to come He might show the exceeding riches of His kindness towards us through Christ Jesus." "Who is He that condemneth? It is Christ that died, yea rather, that is risen again, who is even at the right hand of God, who also maketh intercession for us."

(c)   *Dean Church*

Resurrection from the Dead, The

Abstractedly considered,—that is, considered without relation to the difference which habit, and merely habit, produces in our faculties and modes of apprehension,—I do not see anything more in the resurrection of a dead man than in the conception of a child; except it be this, that the one comes into this world with a system of prior consciousness about him, which the other does not. And no person will say, that he knows enough of either subject to perceive that this circumstance makes such a difference in the two cases, that the one should be easy and the other impossible, the one natural and the other not so. To the first man, the succession of the species would be as incomprehensible, as the resurrection of the dead is to us.

(d)   *Paley*

I see no greater difficulty in the resurrection of the dead, or the conception of the Virgin, than in the creation. Is not the reproduction of human bodies as easy as the first production?

(e)   *Blaise Pascal*

In everything which respects this awful, but, as we trust, glorious change, we have a wise and powerful Being (the Author, in nature, of infinitely various expedients for infinitely various ends) upon whom to rely for the choice and appointment of means adequate to the execution of any plan which His goodness or His justice may have formed, for the moral and accountable part of His terrestrial creation. That great office rests with *Him;* be it *ours* to hope and to prepare, under a firm and settled persuasion, that, living and dying, we are His; that life is passed in His constant presence, that death resigns us to His merciful disposal.

(f)   *Paley*

The natural world contains no provisions or arrangements for reviving the dead.

(g)   *Channing*

Resurrection from the Dead—*continued*

If there be those that think, that the contracted-ness and debility of the human faculties in our present state seem ill to accord with the high destinies which the expectations of religion point out to us; I would only ask them, whether any one who saw a child two hours after its birth, could suppose that it would ever come to understand *fluxions*: or who shall then say, what further amplification of intellectual powers, what accession of knowledge, what advance of improvement, the rational faculty, be its constitution what it will, may not admit of, when placed amidst new objects, and endowed with a sensorium adapted, as it undoubtedly will be, and as our present senses are, to the perception of those substances and of those properties of things with which our concern may lie.

(*a*)   *Paley*

There is a poor, dry, and wrinkled *kernel* cast into the ground; and there it lieth, swelleth, breaketh, and, one would think, perisheth. But, behold, it receiveth life, it chippeth, it putteth forth a blade, and groweth into a stalk. There also appeareth an ear; it also sweetly blossoms, with a full kernel in the ear. It is the same wheat; yet behold how the fashion doth differ from what was sown? And our *bran* will be left behind, when we rise again. The body ariseth, as to the nature of it, the self-same nature; but as to the manner of it, how far transcendent? The glory of the terrestrial is one, and the glory of the celestial another.

(*b*)   *John Bunyan*

At our first appearance, the world will tremble. Behold, the gates of death and the bars of the grave are now carried away on our shoulders, as Samson carried away the gates of the city. Death quaketh, and Destruction falleth down dead at our feet! What then can stand before us? We shall then carry that grace, majesty, terror, and commanding power in our souls, that our countenances shall be as lightning. Then shall "Death be swallowed up of victory."

(*c*)   *Ibid*

Resurrection : Death Robbed of its Sting

Is it death itself? Lo, my Saviour, that overcometh death by dying, hath triumphed over him in His Resurrection. How can I now fear a conquered enemy? What harm is there in the serpent, but for his sting? *The sting of death is sin*, that is pulled out by my powerful Redeemer ; it cannot now hurt me ; it may refresh me, to carry this cool snake in my bosom.

(*d*)   *Bishop Hall*

Resurrection from the Dead : A Demonstration

"*Jesus Christ our Lord, which was made of the seed of David according to the flesh, and declared to be the Son of God with power, according to the spirit of holiness, by the resurrection from the dead*" (Rom. i. 3, 4)

These words set before us one or two somewhat remarkable features concerning the resurrection of our Lord, and that of His people. The words, " Jesus Christ, declared to be the Son of God by the resurrection from the dead," do not say that

at His resurrection He became what He had not been hitherto. He always was the Son of God, though when He humbled Himself, and took upon Him our nature, and became obedient unto the death of the Cross, it did not then seem that He really was what He had asserted Himself to be. Here and there, a man like Peter discerned that He was the Son of God ; but then Jesus said such knowledge was a revelation. " Blessed art thou, Simon Bar-Jona, for flesh and blood hath not revealed it unto thee, but My Father which is in Heaven." Such persons dimly recognised that Jesus was the Son of God, but unenlightened men (then as now) did not perceive it—they could not perceive it. They simply from their point of view regarded Jesus Christ according to the flesh as a descendant of David, the son of human parents as other men are. The statement of the text, then, is simply one which tells us that God oftentimes reverses human judgments, and in this case that reversal was made in declaring Jesus Christ to be the Son of God by the resurrection from the dead.

(*e*)

1. Exposition

And at the outset let us seek to illustrate the subject by a prophetic example from the Old Testament : the patriarch Job. At the outset of that troubled history, we are told that God spoke of Job as a matchless man—perfect, upright, God-fearing, and one who eschewed evil. In fact a striking and magnificent type in these respects of the Lord Jesus Christ. Job, we see, really was what he professed to be ; God confessed it, his own life bore fruits of it, and his friends knew it. His prosperity was an evidence to all that " The blessing of the Lord maketh rich, and addeth no sorrow thereto." But there came a time when this was not so apparent. Indeed, appearances were against him. Before the throne of God an enemy asserted that Job was a hypocrite at heart, and that if permission were granted him he could prove it. Job would do certain things under given circumstances, and under sufficient pressure would reveal his real character, and renounce his religion and his God altogether. The outcome of this was, that permission was given for Job to be tried. And then soon Job's outer circumstances began to look as if God frowned upon him, and had suddenly turned against him. By three sudden and successive strokes of misfortune the whole of his property was taken away ; by the fall of a house his sons and daughters were all killed ; and by a loathsome disease which brought him to the edge of the grave Job appeared to all around him as a withered and scathed wreck of his former self, deserted by God, seemingly marked out as a conspicuous example of a man smitten of God and afflicted, as a judgment upon him for his hypocrisy. His religious friends with whom he had been accustomed to take sweet counsel, took this view of the case ; and at first were simply dumb from astonishment. They shook their heads at him, and plainly hinted their conviction that God was now unmasking his hypocrisy. For if he were righteous then would God appear in his behalf. They made him the mark of their arrows and preached at him with a pointed earnestness worthy of a better cause. Nor did they hesitate to insinuate to the already bleeding and crushed heart of this best of fathers that his children were

(*f*)

Resurrection from the Dead—*continued*

cut off for their iniquity, " for where were the righteous cut off ? " Job stoutly maintained his innocence and his sincerity—he could not indeed explain these reverses, but he did not charge God foolishly. Appearances were, however, against him ; and probably we, too, had we been there, would have been amongst those who shook their heads at this self-deceived and almost blasphemous man. But he was right and they were wrong ; and eventually God interposed in his behalf, restoring him to more than former prosperity, and declaring Job to be what he really was, a genuine God-fearing man, without his equal in all the earth. Now this was both type and prophecy—an Old Testament example of New Testament teaching. Of a greater than Job—similar, though greater—misjudgments were afterwards made—short-sighted men judged from appearances even unto death, which judgment was afterwards reversed by the interposition of God Himself.

(*a*)

2. And this is what we find stated in the text

Jesus Christ, of the seed of David according to the flesh, who seemed for a long time to be a man smitten of God and afflicted for sin, was in reality declared to be the Son of God with power, according to the spirit of holiness, by the resurrection from the dead. This He was all along ; the voice from Heaven at His baptism attested it. He made the assertion Himself, and said that He would be a liar if He denied it. He told of the Father, and revealed God as a Father, for only a Son knoweth the Father and can make this revelation ; to have kept back this fundamental truth would have been unfaithfulness in Him who came to declare God as a Father unto men to whom God was an unknown God. He appealed from His words to His works : " Believe in Me for My work's sake "— miracles of creation and of raising the dead attested to the truth of His teaching. But, as with Job, appearances were all against Him. And when we think a little, we must admit that it was a hard thing that He asked others to believe concerning Him—a hard thing to believe the assertion of your fellow-man and your neighbour, when He tells you that He is the Son of God. We must remember that our Lord was brought up where the eyes of other men were upon Him. He was known to be the son of Joseph and Mary. His brethren were James, and Joses, and Jude, or- dinary men mixing freely among their neighbours, He himself for many years a working carpenter— educated among them, playing with the children of the place. Now He comes forward and asserts that He is the Son of God in a sense in which no other man is : and further makes the most startling announcement that one man can make to another by saying that "No man can come to the Father but by Me." We cease to wonder that no one believed His report : that people accused Him of blasphemy ; that they stoned Him, rejected Him, and ended by putting Him to death. If it was hard to believe His pretensions before, how much harder to believe them now, when He—who claimed to be the Son of God—was hanging help- less on the Cross, and the mockers as they passed by reviled Him—we are graphically told, " wagging their heads," and saying, " If He be the Son of God, let Him come down from the Cross, and we

will believe Him." And surely, such a death did seem to cancel all His previous pretensions and works, for would God allow such indignities, humi- liations, and ignominy to happen to His own Son —even to His being executed like a common felon, as one unfit to live amongst other men. Appear- ances, we say, were all against Him ; and perhaps we too, had we been in Jerusalem at the time, would have joined in the popular cry, " Crucify Him, crucify Him," and would have thought that we were doing God service by raising our voice against a blasphemer, saying, " He ought to die, because He made Himself the Son of God." But within three days God interposed, and reversed the erroneous human judgment, declaring, *i.e.*, demonstrating Him to be the Son of God, by the resurrection from the dead.

(*b*)

3. The whole thing, step by step, was like the working out of a problem. Jesus had prayed " Father, glorify Thy Son with the glory that I had with Thee before the world was," and God, in answer to this prayer, not merely declared that Jesus was the Eternal Son of God, but declared that this man, this Jesus of Nazareth, this man who died in weakness, this Son of Man, was really the Son of God. On Easter Day, then, this was the great truth demonstrated. It had, it is true, begun to dawn on some minds before. The cen- turion who saw Him die as never man died before, could not resist exclaiming, " Truly this was a Son of God." Soon the news flew from mouth to mouth. " The Lord is risen indeed." Disciples exclaimed when they saw Him, " My Lord and my God." They talked with Him, walked with Him, ate and drank with Him, lived with Him forty days, till the time came when He ascended up into heaven, where He was before. After that this great truth was preached, when the Holy Ghost had come and taught men all things. Peter rose up and said, " He whom ye slew, God hath raised up, whom ye buried as dead, God hath shown to be alive, whom ye gibbeted and exposed as a felon on a tree, God hath exalted and set Him at His own right hand far above all princi- palities, and power, and might, and dominion ; angels, authorities and powers being made subject unto Him." Humanity was glorified. In weak- ness He was laid in the grave but He was raised in power—" power " to give eternal life to as many as the Father had given Him ; " power " to save to the uttermost all who should come unto God by Him. He was no pretender, no blas- phemer ; but really what He claimed to be, the Son of God, and this God declared and demon- strated Him to be by the resurrection from the dead.

(*c*)

Practical Application

To make it plain that the same thing is true of the very least in the kingdom of God. The true Christian is now a hidden man—a character undeveloped, in process of formation. In many cases he is a despised man—accounted among the weak things, as the offscouring of this world, neither known nor understood. Hidden away in distant corners of the globe, working at mean work, unknown, he, too, like Job and like Christ, will one day be declared to be what he really is, a child of God. The world says of him, " He is

(*d*)

Resurrection from the Dead—*continued*

like ourselves, of the same flesh and blood—born amongst us; educated at the same schools; a partaker of like passions; encompassed with like infirmities; exposed to and often succumbing to the same temptations; prompted to act on the same principles and maxims and rules that all do. No better, no wiser, no holier than the rest of us, though making greater pretensions than his fellows, calling himself "a child of God" and one of His "peculiar people." But let God set some mark upon him, and stamp his conduct with Divine approval; let God, we say, acknowledge him for His child, or let this insignificant person, claiming to be a child of God, come out of his obscurity, and take a prominent place in the world, where all eyes may see and acknowledge him, and then we will believe in him." Now, this is what God will do in His own good time and manner; when He raises the Christian from the dead, then He will do for him what in type He did for Job when He rolled away his reproach and re-established him in power and glory. First humiliation, then glory. First the cross, then the crown. First the body must be "sown in weakness" before it can be "raised in power." Then the saying will come to pass which is written, "Death is swallowed up in victory," for "Eye hath not seen, nor ear heard, neither hath it entered into the heart of man to conceive the things which God hath prepared for them that love Him." Then, too, the mocking world will see that God putteth a difference between the man that feareth Him and him that feareth Him not; that God maketh much of them that fear the Lord, and that those who honour Him now He will honour then. This will be an unmistakable declaration—a demonstration to heaven and earth that this little flock of despised ones are indeed "The children of God, because they are the children of the Resurrection." But here I anticipate an objection; some one will say to me, "How can the resurrection from the dead show that some persons are the children of God, and others not, seeing that all alike, just and unjust, good and evil, will, without exception, be raised from the dead?" The question is a proper one. But it is answered in the text. Our Lord, we read, was raised from the dead, "according to the Spirit of Holiness." The words may at first sight present a little difficulty, but they are sufficiently explained by other similar statements elsewhere. (i.) Our Lord's birth, you will remember, was superhuman, "Conceived by the Spirit." (ii.) At His baptism the Spirit descended upon Him and abode upon Him. (iii.) His holy life of obedience was the result of His having the Spirit not by measure. (iv.) And when He came to die we read that He, "by the Eternal Spirit offered Himself up." Now it was because our Lord was possessed with the Spirit of Holiness that the grave could not contain Him. "It was not possible," St. Peter said, "that He should be holden by it." Now what is the truth concerning the Christian? He is regenerated by the Holy Spirit. He lives in the Spirit, walks in the Spirit, and is dwelt in by the Spirit. And this possession of the Spirit works in the Christian after the manner of a law; it makes Him free from the law of sin and death; it is the germ of the resurrection of the body. Death has no dominion over the man dwelt in by the Spirit of God; not even while his body sleeps in the grave does it sleep there as others do. By virtue of the Spirit of Holiness, the law of the man's life, he is in advance of all others, and will rise from the dead before they do.

(*See* "FIRST RESURRECTION.")

(*a*)

RESURRECTION

Epitaph on the Late Charles Reade, written by himself

Here Lie,
By the Side of his Beloved Friend,
the Mortal Remains of
CHARLES READE,
Dramatist, Novelist, and Journalist.

His last Words to Mankind are on this Stone

I hope for a resurrection, not from any power in nature, but from the will of the Lord God Omnipotent, who made nature and me. He created man out of nothing; which nature could not. He can restore man from the dust; which nature cannot. And I hope for holiness and happiness in a future life, not for anything I have said or done in this body, but from the merits and mediation of Jesus Christ. He has promised His intercession to all who seek it, and He will not break His word: that intercession, once granted, cannot be rejected; for He is God, and His merits infinite: a man's sins are but human and finite. "Him that cometh to Me, I will in no wise cast out." "If any man sin, we have an Advocate with the Father, Jesus Christ the Righteous, and He is the propitiation for our sins."

(*b*)

RESURRECTION: MY FATHER AND YOUR FATHER

It is fit I should mark Thy order; first, My Father; then yours. Even so, Lord, He is first Thine; and, in Thine only right, ours. It is in Thee that we are adopted; it is in Thee that we are elected: without Thee, God is not only a stranger, but an enemy to us. Thou only canst make us free; Thou only canst make us sons. Let me be found in Thee, and I cannot fail of a Father in Heaven.

(*c*) *Bishop Hall*

RESURRECTION, THE FIRST

"*Blessed and holy is he that hath part in the first resurrection: on such the second death hath no power; but they shall be priests of God and of Christ, and shall reign with Him a thousand years*" (Rev. xx. 6)

1. The Doctrine of the First Resurrection is asserted and proved:

1. By the teaching of our Lord. He speaks in Luke xiv. 14, of "*the resurrection of the just.*" In Luke xx. 35, He says, "They which shall be accounted worthy to obtain the world, *and the resurrection from the dead.*" Again, (36) "They are the children of God, being *the children of the resurrection.*" Clearly the use of such language teaches that the resurrection of the *just* is distinct from that of the *unjust.* The term "*worthy*" shows that it is a special privilege not conferred on others! and the term the "children of God," shows that the resurrection of the just is to be

(*d*)

Resurrection, The First—*continued.*

considered as the flower and blossom of the dead, which comes forth before the general resurrection.

This teaching, compared with the later and fuller teaching of the New Testament on the same subject, leads to the natural conclusion that *there is a resurrection of believers,* separate and distinct from the resurrection of others.

(*a*)

2. The Lord speaks more definitely in John vi. 39: "This is the Father's will, . . . that of all which He has given Me I should lose nothing, but should *raise it up again at the last day.*" John vi. 44: "No man can come to Me, except the Father. . . draw him ; and *I will raise him up at the last day.*" John vi. 54: "Whoso eateth My flesh, and drinketh My blood, hath eternal life; and *I will raise him up at the last day.*" It will be noticed that this repeated promise of raising up at the last day is made only to those who are spiritually alive—consequently the resurrection here spoken of is distinct from that of those who have "no life," and for whom of course no such promise is made.

(*b*)

3. The teaching of the Apostles. The resurrection of Christ brought life and immortality to light, in a manner never before conceived of. 1 Cor. xv. 23: *Christ the firstfruits, afterwards they that are Christ's at His coming.*" 1 Thess. iv. 14: Those "*which sleep in Jesus will God bring with Him.*" 1 Thess. iv. 16: "*The dead in Christ shall rise first*"—*i.e.,* before those that are alive are caught up, but no mention is made of a general resurrection. "*This we say unto you by the word of the Lord,*" shows how the Apostles themselves understood the teaching of the Lord on the same subject. In Heb. xi. 35, mention is made of "*a better resurrection;*" whilst the chief passage is Rev. xx. 5, "The rest of the dead lived not again until the thousand years were finished. *This is the first resurrection.*"

(*c*)

These are the chief passages forming the scriptural foundation for the doctrine of the first resurrection, *i.e.,* a resurrection of the just, who are accounted worthy of the privilege, as distinct from that of the unjust, whose unbelief has deprived them of so great a blessing ; which resurrection is further in advance of that of the general resurrection, but by how long a period it is not necessary to ask. But taking the looked-for "day of the Lord" to be a period of long duration, such as the millennium, then it seems to be implied that in the morning of that period the Lord will come, and the saints will rise to meet Him : whilst in the evening of the same period, after a glorious reign of the saints on the earth, the general resurrection and judgment will take place. After which, all enemies being subdued, death destroyed, Hades emptied of its captives, the devil and his angels cast into the abyss, the kingdom shall be delivered up to the Father—all opposing rule and authority being put down and crushed for evermore.

And this doctrine is no mere fancy on the part of some, but certainly a revealed fact, if certain passages in the New Testament have any meaning at all. For such a resurrection, it will be noticed, is a resurrection "*from*" not "*of*" the dead. And

it is surely more than a little significant, that whenever the Lord's own resurrection is spoken of, the word used is "*from,*" not "*of,*" as in Eph. i. 20, "God raised Him *from* the dead ; " Heb. xiii. 20, "The God of peace, that brought again *from* the dead our Lord Jesus." And the same word always occurs when the Scriptures speak of those who are to be raised *out from among the dead* at the appearing of Him who is the resurrection and the life. (See, "IF BY ANY MEANS *I might attain to the resurrection out from among the dead.*") But when the general resurrection is alluded to, the word used always signifies a resurrection "*of*" the dead.

Are such terms, and in such connection, to be regarded as mere coincidences ?

(*d*)

4. We ask, Who are "they that are accounted worthy" of such a resurrection ? The seer evidently includes two classes of people amongst them, as may be seen by a comparison of what he says in Rev. vi. and xiv. with this. The comparison shows that they who attain to the "resurrection of the just," *i.e.,* to the first resurrection, are—

(i.) *All Christian martyrs,* who were beheaded for the witness of Jesus, or had been faithful unto Him even unto death; whose souls were seen under the altar, crying for vengeance : "How long, O Lord, holy and true, dost Thou not judge and avenge our blood on them that dwell on the earth?" but unto whom it was said, "that they should rest yet for a little season, until their fellow-servants also and their brethren, that should be killed, as they were, should be fulfilled."

(ii.) The Lord Himself, in Matt. xxiv. 31, tells us that when He comes the second time—the time, according to 1 Cor. xv. 23, of the resurrection of the just—"He shall send His angels, ... and they shall gather together His elect from the four winds, from one end of heaven to the other." From wherever they are they shall come. The sea shall give up her dead—the earth shall give up her dead—Hades shall give up the dead in Christ; for when He appears, nothing can hold them back.

(iii.) In John vi. 40, He tells us that the will of His Father is "*that every one who seeth the Son, and believeth on Him, may have everlasting life:* and *I will raise him up at the last day.*" Our Lord, it will be noted here, is speaking only of the *believers,* not of martyrs, or of any specially heroic amongst His people, but simply of all believers as such. See again Rev. xiv. 13, in a similar connection : "*Blessed are the dead which die in the Lord.*" "*Blessed,*" not only because "they rest from their labours," but also because "*blessed and holy is he that hath part in the first resurrection: on such the second death hath no power.*"

It seems, then, tolerably certain, even to demonstration, that they who are accounted worthy of the resurrection of the just, and who will become partakers of the blessedness spoken of in the text, are first of all *Christian martyrs,* and secondly, all the *blessed dead who have died in the Lord;* and these shall be gathered from the east and from the west, from the north and from the south, as prey rescued from the destroyer.

(*e*)

5. The reason why the dead in Christ rise before the general resurrection, is perhaps answered in

(*f*)

Resurrection, The First—*continued*

Rom. viii. 11, a passage almost inexplicable upon any other supposition. " If the Spirit of Him that raised up Jesus from the dead dwell in you, He that raised up Christ from the dead shall also quicken your mortal bodies by His Spirit that dwelleth in you ; " *i.e.*, the bodies of believers will be quickened because they are already alive in the Spirit : they are not *dead* as others are dead ; already they have experienced the resurrection of the spirit, that too once was dead, and buried so deep that it seemed no power in heaven or earth could waken it into life, yet it has taken place.

These are the sheep of Christ, and when He comes the second time, and the trumpet sounds, they hear His voice, because, being alive in the Spirit, they are susceptible of an awakening. They do not sleep, even in their graves, as do others. When Christ appears, they also appear. Whilst those without spiritual life—*twice dead*, dead, both in body and spirit, are *far deeper under the power of death*—will slumber longer in the grave, and will require a louder trumpet blast to awaken them. Or, to use a familiar illustration : As seeds sown in the ground are left there till the powers of nature do their quickening work, some of them come up much sooner than others, because they have the principle and the power of life more keenly susceptible to the quickening influences of the sun's rays, whilst the rest are so shrivelled up and dead, as to remain under the power of death a much longer time before they too come forth from their burial place.

So of seeds buried deep in old gardens.

So it appears is it in the case of the Christian and the unchristian dead. As soon as the Sun of righteousness arises and shines, the one come forth from their graves—where they have slept during the long sleep of winter and of death—to greet Him, because they are already alive in the spirit, sleeping with a susceptibility of an awakening when they hear the voice of the Awakener. Whilst the rest of the dead sleep on, being far deeper under the power of death, and awake not until another thousand years (a whole æon) have expired. For where there is no life there can be no rising from the dead. When the dead sleep under a power of death, which has dominion over both body and spirit, there can be no susceptibility to hear the voice of the Son of man, that they too may live.

It is, then, in perfect analogy with nature—our great reminder of the resurrection—that such of the dead as so sleep remain behind,· and live not again until a period of time, longer or shorter, elapses.

And looking at the whole subject in the light of what the Saviour comes to do on the earth, it seems quite out of place to have those raised from the dead then, who are in no kind of sympathy with the time called " the regeneration," and the work then to be done. Only regenerate people will be wanted. Only for them is there a restoration of all things forfeited by the Fall.

(*a*)

6. The special blessedness of those who are accounted worthy to rise at the first resurrection

(i.) *Negatively :* This blessing consists in the fact that the *second death*—death in all its terrors, as *condemnation, perdition,* and *misery*—will have no power over them.

(ii.) *Positively :* The blessing will consist in their being " holy," and that they will " reign with Christ a thousand years," and be the priests of God and of Christ, doing service in His kingdom.

Which, in short, means something like this : Christ will come at the end of the present dispensation to set up His personal reign on the earth. He will be accompanied by the saints. It is for that glorious time that Christian eyes and hearts have been looking and longing ever since His ascension into heaven. On His part, He will come to be admired in all them that believe—the chiefest among ten thousand, and altogether lovely ; on their part, His coming will bring about " the manifestation of the sons of God." *Now* they are a minority : they are considered the weak, and too often as the offscouring of the world ; they are amongst the " despised things " of the world, a little flock. But *then* they will bloom and blossom. The Church will be full-orbed, gloriously manifested to all, and no longer amongst the hidden and despised things ; but in power and authority, dominant over all.

At His coming, the great and dominant antichristian powers, the beast and the false prophet, and all who oppose themselves to Christ and His Church, will be destroyed by the brightness of His appearing. As before, in the garden of Gethsemane, when He comes forward, His adversaries fall to the ground.

Then, as the Scriptures seem to teach, the reign of the saints will begin, in contrast to the present reign of the " kingdoms of this world." For " the saints shall judge the world." Jerusalem will be the local centre of the great King. The law shall again go forth from Zion, and the world around became His kingdom. Then shall be the great triumphs of Christianity. Then the shout of thanksgiving and victory. " *Alleluia : for the Lord God omnipotent reigneth.*"

(*b*)

RESURRECTION, THE FIRST

" *And they lived and reigned with Christ a thousand years. But the rest of the dead lived not again until the thousand years were finished. This is the first resurrection. Blessed and holy is he that hath part in the first resurrection : on such the second death hath no power : but they shall be Priests of God and of Christ ; and shall reign with Him a thousand years* " (Rev. xx. 4, 5, 6)

If we accept this statement as part of the inspired Word of God, that Word that cannot be broken ; and if we discuss it, without being biased by any previously-formed opinion, there will be very little doubt as to the conclusion at which we arrive. We should certainly understand the sacred writer to mean, that there were two resurrections of the dead—a first and a second—with the interval of a thousand years elapsing between them. Such was the interpretation of the Primitive Church. Those who lived next to the Apostles, indeed the whole Christian community for the space of three hundred years, understood these words of St. John in the plain literal sense.

(*c*)

It is competent for us, of course, to affirm, and it is open to us to prove, if we can, that the interpretation is an erroneous one. But the fact

(*d*)

Resurrection, The First—*continued*

that it held its ground for so long a period, and was never disputed for the whole of the time, is a presumption in its favour, and certainly proves that those who attempt to explain the passage before us literally, are not introducing a novel and unheard-of opinion. I start, then, with reminding you, that, for the first three hundred years of the existence of the Christian Church, it was believed that there would be two resurrections, occurring with an interval between them. The agreement of early Christians on this point has been called the " most cogent instance of consensus which primitive antiquity presents."

(a)

1. The text itself

By casting a glance over the passage, we find that there are certain persons spoken of who had been " beheaded for the witness of Jesus, and for the Word of God;" concerning these persons we are told that they " lived and reigned with Christ a thousand years." Now, our first impulse would be, I think, to take these words as we find them, and to believe that what is meant is a resurrection, and a resurrection to a condition of surpassing magnificence and glory. On looking a little further into the passage, our impression is confirmed; for the sacred writer tells us, that, " this is the first resurrection." We take another step in our examination of the passage, and we find a distinction drawn between these dead and the rest of the dead. " The rest of the dead lived not again, until the thousand years were finished." And we come to the conclusion that there is a second resurrection corresponding to the first, that is to say, so far corresponding as to be a literal resurrection in the flesh, after the lapse of a certain specified time. " No ! " say some. This is not so ! The first resurrection is a spiritual resurrection. The language means that these martyrs, these faithful, these representatives of the Church of Christ, will rise to prominent objects in the recollection of the Christian Church; and that special respect will be paid by their co-religionists to their principles and memory. This, and this only, is the meaning of the words. But is this a fair and legitimate mode of interpretation? Is it honest, when you find two risings again of dead persons spoken of in the very same breath—is it honest to say, " The former is to be interpreted spiritually, and the latter is to be interpreted literally." Surely, we are not at liberty to play fast and loose with language, and especially with Scriptural language, in this way. If you say, " The first resurrection is spiritual," then, of course, the second resurrection must be spiritual also. But if you assert that the second resurrection is literal, the first resurrection should be regarded as literal also.

According to the statement of the Apostle John, there will be, at the beginning of the thousand years of which he speaks, a resurrection from amongst the great mass of the dead. That those who are partakers of it are declared to be blessed and holy, and, being beyond the reach of temptation and the danger of falling into sin, to be exempt from the fearful dominion of the second death. That during the thousand years they shall reign, endowed with mysterious privileges and powers, as Priests of God and of Christ. And that, not until the period of a thousand years has

come to a close, shall the rest of the dead be raised up in their bodies to stand before the judgment-seat of Christ.

(b)

2. There are other passages in Holy Scripture which seem to inculcate the same doctrine. In the 15th chapter of the first Epistle to the Corinthians,—a chapter which is concerned, from first to last, with the subject of the Resurrection,—the Apostle, at the 22nd verse, contrasts the two heads of the human race — Adam and Christ. " In Adam," he says, " all die." As the result of their connection with Adam, every being who wears human nature is exposed to the sentence of death, and, in some shape or other, will have to undergo it. His earthly tabernacle may be dissolved, or—he may be clothed upon with his house from heaven—but, in either case, he will have to pay the penalty of his relationship to Adam. " In Adam all die." But the Apostle proceeds to tell us, in language of equal universality, that " in Christ all shall be made alive." That is, the fact that Christ is the second federal head of the human race, ensures the resurrection from the dead of every human being; it being left unspecified, so far as the present statement is concerned, of what nature that resurrection shall be, whether to glory or to shame; whether to everlasting life or to everlasting death. " In Christ all are to be made alive." But is there to be a *simultaneous* resurrection? No ! Not according to St. Paul. There is an " order," in which men shall rise, and some shall rise at one time, and some at another. Christ shall rise first; " Christ the firstfruits." " Afterward " — mark this — " afterward " shall rise a certain carefully-distinguished class of persons—" they that are Christ's at His coming." " Then," after that, though not specifying the extent of the interval, " then cometh the end." We have then, in this Apostle's statement, three distinct events mentioned as occurring at different periods : **The resurrection of Christ ; the resurrection of the people of Christ ; and the " end."**

(c)

Again, refer to 1 Thess. iv. 16, " The Lord Himself shall descend from heaven with a shout, with the voice of the archangel, and with the trump of God, and the dead in Christ shall rise first. Then, we which are alive and remain, shall be caught up together with them in the clouds, to meet the Lord in the air ; and so shall we ever be with the Lord. Wherefore, comfort one another with these words." In this passage we find the following statements : That when Christ comes in person there shall be a resurrection of the blessed dead, of all of them, apparently, without any exception. " The dead in Christ shall rise first." Then, that they shall be almost immediately joined by Christ's disciples then living on the earth, who shall undergo a physical transformation, to fit them for their new condition. " We which are alive," shall join the risen dead " in the air "—the statement, whatever it may mean, implying a vast alteration in their conditions of existence. Then, that this united community of risen saints shall be in closest union and communion with Christ Himself. " So shall we ever be with the Lord." And lastly, that this anticipation of future glory is a suitable topic of consolation for the Christian, in

(d)

Resurrection, The First—*continued*

all the vicissitudes and trials which he is called upon to undergo. " Wherefore comfort one another with these words."

(*a*)

The Apostle cannot be referring here to a general resurrection. It is inconceivable that godly and ungodly alike should be caught up in the clouds to meet the Lord in the air, and be ever with the Lord. Such language, such promises, suit only the people of Christ. The Apostle must then be indicating in this passage what will happen to the true believer ; and if we put the two passages together we shall come to the conclusion, quite independently of what St. John says in our text—that there is a resurrection of Christ—afterwards a resurrection of His people—and afterwards, perhaps at the end of a considerable interval, a general resurrection of the human race.

(*b*)

Throughout the New Testament, when the general resurrection is spoken of, it is described as a resurrection *of* the dead, as in St. Paul's address in the 24th chapter of the Acts ; but that when the resurrection of Christ, or of His people is spoken of, it is described as a resurrection *from among* the dead. On a certain occasion a deputation from the Sadducees came to our Lord, to put to Him what they thought a very clever and ensnaring question, about a certain woman who had been married seven times, and had seven husbands. The question was, whose wife should she be, in the resurrection. The question,—the product, as our Lord tells them, of their ignorance of the Scriptures, and of the power of God,—was very easily disposed of. In the resurrection-state the conditions of human existence are changed. There is no marrying or giving in marriage ; a spiritual relation will supersede the old natural one. And they that are counted worthy to obtain the resurrection *from amongst the dead* are equal unto the angels, and are the children of God. Here we have something indicated, which is different from an ordinary resurrection.

(*c*) *Gordon Calthrop*

Resurrection, The First

Compare—

1. Fishes embedded in ice will come to life again.

2. If we dig deep in an old garden which has long lain fallow, forgotten flowers will appear.

(*d*) *Geo. Macdonald*

There is one to me very remarkable passage in the few last sentences—an allusion to the first resurrection of Phil. iii. (the exanastasis), in the words—" The third sign, the Resurrection of the Dead ; *not, however, of all*, but as hath been said, ' The Lord shall come, and all the saints with Him.' "

M. F. Sadler: " The Teaching of the Twelve Apostles."

(*e*)

Resurrection, The First (1 Cor. 15)

The principle and power of a new life capable of vanquishing death, and enduring unto immor-

tality, and is now carrying on a comprehensive work.

1. In creating a new man through the regenerating power of the Holy Spirit, and—

2. In developing this spiritual life through our entire organism. The life thus begun and developed, will be manifest—

(i.) In those who belong to Him, when He shall appear again in glory (this is called the first resurrection) ;

(ii.) It will show itself in the rest of mankind—so as susceptibility can be awakened—until the work of redemption is complete.

(*f*) *Lange*

Resurrection, The First (Rev. xx. 12, 13)

If, in a passage where *two resurrections* are mentioned, where certain souls *lived* at the first, and the rest of the dead lived only at the end of a specified period after the first—if in such a passage the first resurrection may be understood to mean *spiritual* rising with Christ, while the second means *literal* rising from the grave, then there is an end of all significance in language, and Scripture is wiped out as a definite testimony to anything.

(*g*) *Dean Alford*

Resurrection Flower, The

There is a plant found in sandy deserts and arid wastes, which is called Anastatica, or the Resurrection Flower, from a remarkable power of recovery which it has. When it has flowered, its leaves drop off, its branches become dry and hard, and the plant in a little while is seemingly dead. But so soon as it touches water again, it gradually expands, its leaves unfold, and life returns. It is a parable. If in its death-like state it is a figure of the backslider, its resurrection figures the alone source of revival ; he must get back to the Fountain of Living Water again.

(*h*) *T. Graham*

Resurrection : Sins of Infirmity

To whom then dost Thou send her ? *Go, tell My brethren.* Blessed Jesu, who are those ? Were they not Thy followers ? Yea, were they not Thy forsakers ? Yet still Thou stylest them Thy brethren. Oh, admirable humility ! Oh, infinite mercy ! How dost Thou raise their titles with Thyself ! At first they were Thy servants ; then, disciples ; a little before Thy death, they were Thy friends ; now, after Thy resurrection, they were Thy brethren. Thou, that wert exalted infinitely higher, from mortal to immortal, descendest so much lower to call them brethren, who were before friends, disciples, servants. What ! do we stand upon terms of our poor inequality, when the Son of God stoops so low as to call us brethren ? But, Oh, mercy without measure ! Why wilt Thou, how canst Thou, O Saviour, call them brethren, whom in their last parting, Thou foundest fugitives ? Did they not run from Thee ? Did not one of them rather leave his inmost coat behind him, than not be quit of Thee ? Did not another of them deny Thee, yea, abjure thee ? And yet Thou sayest *Go, tell My brethren.* It is not in the power of the sins of our infirmity to unbrother us ; *when we look at the acts themselves,*

(*i*)

they are heinous; when at the persons, they are *so much more faulty as more obliged;* but when we look at the mercy of Thee who hast called us, now, *who shall separate us?* When we have sinned, Thy dearness hath reason to aggravate our sorrows; but when we have sorrowed, our faith hath no less reason to uphold us from despairing; even yet we are brethren; brethren in Thee, O Saviour, who art ascending for us; in Thee, who hast made Thy Father ours, Thy God our God. He is Thy Father by eternal generation; our Father by His gracious adoption; Thy God by unity of essence; our God by His grace and election.

(a)   *Bishop Hall*

RESURRECTION OF JESUS

Nothing stands more historically certain than that Jesus rose from the dead and appeared again to His followers, or than that their seeing Him thus again was the beginning of a higher faith and all their Christian work in the world. It is equally certain that they thus saw Him, not as a common man, or as a shade or ghost risen from the grave; but as the only Son of God, already more than man at once in nature and power; and that all who thus beheld Him, recognised at once and instinctively His unique Divine dignity, and firmly believed in it thenceforth. The twelve and others had indeed learned to look on Him, even in life, as the true Messianic King and the Son of God; but from the moment of His reappearing, they recognised more clearly and fully the Divine side of His nature, and saw in Him the Conqueror of Death. Yet the two pictures of Him thus fixed in their minds were in their essence identical. That former familiar appearance of the earthly Christ, and this higher vision of Him, with its depth of emotion and ecstatic joy, were so inter-related that, even in the first days or weeks after His death, they could never have seen in Him the Heavenly Messiah, if they had not first known Him so well as the earthly.

(b)   *Heinrich Ewald*

Here is the angel of the Lord, ready to satisfy the disciples that Jesus was risen from the dead. And lest they should think it was not the right Jesus he spoke of—"Yes," said he, "it is the same Jesus that you mean. You seek Jesus of Nazareth, do you not?" "Why, He is not here, He is risen." "But do you speak seriously?" "Yea, surely. If you will not believe me, behold the place where they laid Him!" See how plainly this Scripture doth testify of Christ's resurrection. "Yea," saith the angel, "Lo it is as I have told you. You seek a Saviour, and none will content you but He that was crucified. Well, you shall have Him. But He is not here?" "But where shall we find him?" "Why, He goeth before you into Galilee, where He used to be in His lifetime before He was crucified."

(c)   *Bunyan*

RESURRECTION: RAISED FOR OUR JUSTIFICATION

Oh, then, my dear Saviour, I bless Thee for Thy death; but I bless Thee more for Thy resurrection. That was a work of wonderful humility, of infinite mercy; this was a work of infinite power; in that was human weakness, in this Divine Omnipotence; in that Thou didst *die for our sins;* in this, Thou didst *rise again for our justification.*

(d)   *Bishop Hall*

RESURRECTION: "MARY—RABBONI"

Mary. She was used, as to the name, so to the sound, to the accent. Thou spakest to her before; but in the tone of a stranger; now of Friend, of a Master. Like a Good Shepherd, Thou callest Thy sheep by their name, and they know Thy voice. What was Thy call of her, but a clear pattern of our vocation?

As her, so Thou callest us; first, familiarly, effectually. She could not begin with Thee, otherwise than in the compellation of a stranger: it was Thy mercy to begin with her. That correction of Thy Spirit is sweet and useful; now, after ye have known God, or rather are known of Him. We do know Thee, O God; but our active knowledge is after our passive: first, we are known of Thee; then, we know Thee, that knewest us. And, as our knowledge, so is our calling, so is our election; Thou beginnest to us in all; and most justly sayest, You have not chosen Me, but I have chosen you. When Thou wouldest speak to this devout client as a stranger, Thou spakest aloof; Woman, whom seekest thou? Now, when Thou wouldest be known to her, Thou callest her by her name, Mary. General invitations and common mercies are for us, as men; but where Thou givest grace as to Thine elect, Thou comest close to the soul, and winnest us with clear and particular intimations.

(e)   *Bishop Hall*

RESURRECTION: RABBONI

That very name did as much as say, "Know Him, of whom thou art known and beloved;" and turns her about to Thy view and acknowledgment. "She turned herself, and saith unto Him, Rabboni, which is to say, Master." Before, her face was towards the angels: this word turns it to Thee, from whom her misprision had averted it. We do not rightly apprehend Thee, O Saviour, if any creature in heaven or earth can keep our eyes and our hearts from Thee. The angels were bright and glorious; Thy appearance was homely, Thy habit mean: yet, when she heard Thy voice, she turns her back upon the angels, and salutes Thee with a Rabboni; and falls down before Thee, in a desire of an humble amplexation of those Sacred Feet, which she now rejoices to see past the use of her odours.

(f)   *Ibid*

RESURRECTION: TOUCH ME NOT

Where there was such familiarity in the mutual compellation, what means such strangeness in the charge; Touch Me not, for I am not yet ascended to My Father? Thou wert not wont, O Saviour, to make so dainty of being touched. It is not long since these very same hands touched Thee in Thine anointing: the bloody-fluxed woman touched Thee; the thankful penitent in Simon's house touched Thee. What speak I of these? The multitude touched Thee; the executioners touched Thee; and, even after Thy resurrection, Thou didst not care to say to Thy disciples, "Touch Me and see," and to invite Thomas to put his fingers into Thy side; neither is it long after this before Thou sufferest the three Marys to touch and hold Thy feet. How then sayest Thou, "Touch Me not"? Was it in a mild taxation of her mis-

(g)

taking? As if Thou hadst said, "Thou knowest not that I have now an immortal body; but so demeanest thyself towards Me, as if I were still in My wonted condition: know now, that the case is altered: howsoever indeed I have not yet ascended to My Father, yet this body of Mine, which thou seest to be real and sensible, is now impassible, and qualified with immortality, and therefore worthy of a more awful veneration than heretofore." Or was it a gentle reproof of her dwelling too long in this dear hold of Thee, and fixing her thoughts upon Thy bodily presence; together with an implied direction of reserving the height of her affection for Thy perfect glorification in heaven? Or, lastly, was it a light touch of her too much haste and eagerness in touching Thee; as if she must use this speed in preventing Thine ascension, or else be endangered to be disappointed of her hopes? As if Thou hadst said, "Be not so passionately forward and sudden in laying hold on Me, as if I were instantly ascending, but know, that I shall stay some time with you upon earth, before My going up to My Father." O Saviour, even our well-meant zeal in seeking and enjoying Thee may be faulty; if we seek Thee, where we should not, on earth; how we should not, unwarrantably. There may be a kind of carnality in spiritual actions. If we have heretofore known Thee after the flesh, henceforth know we Thee so no more. That Thou livedst here, in this shape, that colour, this stature, this habit, I should be glad to know: nothing that concerns Thee can be unuseful. Could I say, "Here Thou satest; here Thou layest; here and thus Thou wert crucified; here buried; here settest Thy last foot;" I should with much contentment see and recount these memorials of Thy presence: but if I shall so fasten my thoughts upon these, as not to look higher to the spiritual part of Thine achievements, to the power and issue of Thy Resurrection, I am never the better.

(a)   *Bishop Hall*

RESURRECTION, THE, A NECESSITY

"*Whom God hath raised up, having loosed the pains of death, because it was not possible that He should be holden of it*" (Acts ii. 24)

1. This is the language of the first sermon that ever was preached in the Church of Christ. St. Peter is accounting for the miraculous gift of tongues on the Day of Pentecost; and after observing that it was after all only a fulfilment of the prophecy of Joel about the outpouring of the Spirit in the last days, he proceeds to trace it to its cause. It was the work, he says, of Jesus Christ, now ascended into heaven—"He hath shed forth this which ye now see and hear." But Jesus Christ, he argues, had really ascended into heaven, because He has first really risen from His grave.

(b)

2. The Fact Stated

"Whom God hath raised up, having loosed the pains of death, because it was not possible that He should be holden of it." Peter is preaching in Jerusalem, the scene of the Death and the Resurrection of Christ. He is preaching to some who had taken part in the Crucifixion. Not more than seven weeks had yet passed since these events; and in Jerusalem, we may be sure, men did not live as fast as they do in a European capital in this age of telegraphs and railroads. An event like the Crucifixion in a town of that size, far removed from the greater centres of human life, would have occupied general attention for a considerable period. It would have been discussed and re-discussed in all its bearings, and all that happened at the time and immediately afterwards—the dispersion of the disciples, the ruin of the cause, as well as the agony and humiliation of the Master—would have been still ordinary topics of conversation in most of the circles of Jewish society. It was, then, as a person keenly interested in the subject, and who had opportunities at hand of testing the exact truth of what he said, that Peter states thus calmly and unhesitatingly the fact of the Resurrection. He states it as just as much a truth of history as the Crucifixion, in which his hearers had themselves taken part. "Ye men of Israel, hear these words. Jesus of Nazareth, a man approved of God among you by miracles, and truths, and signs which God did by Him in the midst of you, and as ye yourselves also know; Him, being delivered by the determination, and counsel, and foreknowledge of God, ye have taken, and by wicked hands have crucified and slain;" and then he adds, "whom God hath *raised up*, whereof we are all witnesses." On the very day that He rose He had been seen five times, and He showed Himself alive after His passion by many infallible proofs, being seen of His disciples forty days, and speaking to them of the things appertaining to the kingdom of God; and some twenty-six years later, when St. Paul wrote his first letter to the Church of Corinth, there were, he says, more than two hundred and fifty persons still alive who had seen Jesus Christ after His Resurrection on one single occasion. And the number of witnesses to whom St. Peter could appeal, and whom his hearers could cross-question if they liked, will account for the simplicity and confidence of his assertion.

(c)

3. St. Peter Preached the Resurrection as a Fact; with great and important results. But how did he account for the Resurrection? What was the reason which he gave for its having happened at all?

He then says that Christ was raised from the dead because it was not possible that He should be holden of death. Thus you will observe that St. Peter's thought about this matter is the very opposite to that of many persons in our day. They say, in so many words, that no evidence will convince them that Christ has risen, because they hold it to be antecedently impossible that He should rise. On the other hand, St. Peter had his own experience to fall back upon. He had seen His risen Master on the day of the Resurrection, and even since; but so far was this evidence of his senses from causing him any perplexity, that it only fell in with the anticipations which he had now formed on other and independent grounds. It was not possible, he says, that Christ should be holden or imprisoned by death. It will do us good to consider his grounds for this assertion.

(d)

4. First of all we find the reason was, that it was not possible that Christ should be holden of death;

(e)

Resurrection, The, a Necessity—*continued*

for David "speaketh concerning Him." It was, then, Jewish prophecy that forbade Christ to remain in His grave, and made His Resurrection a Divine necessity. As to the principle of this argument, there would have been no controversy between St. Peter and the Jews. The Jews believed in the reality and the compulsive force of prophecy—of that variety of prophecy which predicts events which are strictly traceable—just as distinctly as Christians do. The prophets, in the belief of the Jews, were confidants of God. God communicated to them, by His Spirit, His resolutions for the coming time. "Surely," could exclaim the prophet Amos, "surely the Lord will do nothing, but He revealeth His secrets to His servants the prophets." But when once God hath spoken His word, it was felt by Jews, as it is felt by Christians, that it standeth sure. God's word could not return empty. It must accomplish the work for which God sent it forth, since it bound Him to an engagement with those who uttered and those who heard His message.

(a)

5. Of course God could not be responsible for eccentric guesses as to His meaning in which well-intentioned men of lively imagination may possibly indulge. We have lived in this generation to hear some very confident guesses based on the supposed meaning of prophecy respecting the end of the world or some impending general catastrophe. The dates assigned for such occurrences have passed; and religion would be seriously discredited if, indeed, the Sacred Word itself were amenable instead of the fervid imagination of some apocalyptic expositor. When the prediction is clear, it does bind God to its fulfilment; and such a prediction as to the Resurrection St. Peter found in the 16th and 22nd Psalms, where David loses himself in rapture as he describes the Divine Person of whom he was the type: "My heart is glad, and my glory rejoiceth: my flesh also shall rest in hope. For Thou wilt not leave My soul in hell; neither wilt Thou suffer Thine Holy One to see corruption. Thou wilt show Me the path of life; in Thy presence is fulness of joy, and at Thy right hand are pleasures for evermore." St. Peter argues that David utters these words; but of David himself they were not strictly true. David, he says, is both dead and buried, or, as St. Paul puts it, appealing to the same psalm, in his sermon at Antioch, "David fell on a sleep." This meaning of the psalm was so clear to one school of Jewish doctors, that, being unable to reconcile it with the facts of David's history, they invented the fable that his body was preserved from corruption. David. speaking in the person of the Messiah, created the necessity that the Messiah should be raised. God had spoken in other passages, but especially in this—and His word could not return to Him. St. Peter, though, had not always felt and thought thus. It is only little by little that we learn the true meaning of God's Word and the Divine Will. So late as the morning of the Resurrection, St. Peter and St. John did not so fully know the Scripture as to understand that Christ must rise again. Since then the Holy Spirit has poured a flood of light on the Apostles' minds and on the pages of Scripture. By this it had come to be seen that the Resurrection was a necessity. Oh, may the Holy Spirit teach us, as He taught them of old, the true meaning of the Divine Word!

(b)

6. The Second Reason lay in the Character of Jesus Christ

His character, not less than His miracles, drew hearts towards Him—led men to give up all for Him. Of our Lord's character, the leading feature was His simple truthfulness. It was morally impossible for Him to hold out a prospect which could never be realized, or to use words which did not mean what they appeared to mean. Nay, He insisted on sincerity of language on the part of all those who came into His company. He would not allow men to use expressions of devotion to Him until they had weighed their words, and were sure what their words involved. Unless, then, He was like the Pharisees whom He condemned for laying burdens on men which they could not bear, it might be accepted as a certainty that His promise made performance morally binding and non-performance morally impossible. Now, our Lord Jesus Christ had again and again said that He would be put to a violent death, and that afterwards He would rise again. Sometimes, as to the Jews in the Temple, He expressed His meaning in language of metaphor. When speaking of the temple of His body, He said, "Destroy this temple, and in three days I will raise it again," and the Jews rallied Him on the absurdity of undertaking to reconstruct in three days an edifice which had taken forty-six years to build. But the real sense of His words was plain to His disciples by His gesture which accompanied them; and in later years they understood the full reference of the word temple as applied to His body. Sometimes He fell back upon the ancient Hebrew history, and compared that which was to happen to Himself to that which had occurred to the prophets: but with His disciples He used neither metaphor nor historical parallel. He said simply, on three occasions at least, that He should be crucified and rise from the dead. Thus He was pledged, if we may say so, to the particular act of Resurrection—pledged to the Jewish people, pledged to the rulers and priests, but pledged especially to His own chosen few. He could not have remained in the grave, we will not say without dishonour, but without entailing that revulsion of feeling which is always provoked by the exposure of baseless pretensions.

(c)

7. It might have been that the Resurrection to which He referred was not a Resurrection of the dead body, but only a recovery of popular authority: but the word Resurrection, according to this supposition, would have been a purely metaphorical expression, used to describe, not that which affected Jesus Christ Himself, but only a revolution of feeling about Him. Socrates had to drink the fatal hemlock, and the body of Socrates had long mingled with the dust; but Socrates in a certain sense had risen in the intellectual triumph of his pupils, in the enthusiastic admiration of succeeding ages; and the method and the words of Socrates are preserved for all time in a literature which will never die; and such, it had been argued, was the Resurrection of Christ. But the obvious reply to this is, that it makes our Lord use a literal and metaphorical expression in two successive clauses

(d)

Resurrection, The, a Necessity—*continued*

of the same sentence. He is literal when He predicts His Crucifixion—and there never has been any doubt as to this; the world has always agreed with the Church, and Tacitus mentions his death as well as the Evangelists; but if we understand Him literally when He foretells His Crucifixion, He becomes metaphorical when He foretells His Resurrection. Why, if His Resurrection was to be metaphorical, was not His Crucifixion to be metaphorical also—a Crucifixion, not of the body, but of the thought and will and affections? Why does this fastidious spiritualism shrink from the idea of a literal Resurrection, and not shrink from a literal Crucifixion—a literal grave? It is impossible to imagine that our Lord meant that He would be only literally crucified, and not literally rise again. He meant the one to be accepted as a fact as much as the other. Any other construction of His words only originates with those who wish to combine a lingering faith in the Master with a total disbelief in that miracle which made Him what He is to Christendom. No! If He had not risen He would not have kept His engagement with the world. This was the feeling of those who loved Him best—especially of St. Peter. Although only now had it ripened into a sharply-defined conviction, it was the result of years of companionship, that after He had said He would rise again any other event was impossible. All—all was staked on His rising from the dead; and when He did rise it was proved that He was the Son of God. Thus it was the character of Christ, even more than the force of prophecy, which made the idea that He would not rise impossible to His disciples.

(a)

8. In the sermon which he preached after the healing of the man at the Beautiful Gate of the Temple, Peter then told his hearers that they had crucified the Prince of Life. Mark the title, " Prince of Life ! " as not merely showing that He was high above all earthly royalty in the heart and mind of the Apostle, but as connecting the language of the Divine Master Himself and of St. John and St. Paul. Our Lord had said, "I am the way, the truth, and the life," explaining the sense in which He used the word " life " by the words, " As the Father hath life in Himself, even so hath He given to the Son to have life in Himself." He complained, too, to the men of His time, "Ye will not come unto Me that ye might have life"; and St. John said, "In Him was life, and the life was the light of men." In the epistle for the Easter Day, St. Paul says, " Christ our life," and when St. Peter thus calls Him the " Prince of Life," he refers to the same truth. This is, indeed, the keynote of the Gospel. But what is life? That is a question which at this day even no man can answer. We do not really know what life is in itself. We can only register its symptoms. We see its growth and movement, and we say, "Here is life." It exists in one degree in the tree, in a higher degree in the animal, and in a still higher degree in man. In beings above man it is seen on a still grander scale, but in all it is a gift from another, and having been given it can be modified or withdrawn. Who is He in whom life resided originally—who owes it to no patron, and from whom none can take it? Only He, the self-existent, really lives

(c)

distinct from derived life. Christian revelation assures us that it is only true of the Son and of the Spirit, because they received life from the Eternal Father. Hence our Lord says, " As the Father hath life in Himself, even so hath He given to the Son to have life in Himself." Not merely life, but *life in Himself*, thus to be, with the Eternal Giver, the fountain and source of life to created beings—the Life, the Creator, and the Upholder to the end. For, as St. Paul says, " All things were created by Him and for Him, and He is before all things, and by Him all things consist." This, then, is the full sense of St. Peter's expression, " the Prince of Life." In the truth of our Lord's jurisdiction over life, based on His Divine nature, he traces another reason why it was impossible He should not rise again. How could the Lord of Life be subdued by Death ? If, for reasons of wisdom and mercy, He was subject to the King of Terrors, it was in violence to His nature. Therefore St. Peter puts it that He rises by inevitable rebound—by the force of His own energy. St. Peter looks at the subject from above rather than from below. He is more concerned about the honour of his Master than with the history of His life, and although he was far from indifferent to the fact that He did rise—on the other hand, he often insists upon it—he yet treats the Resurrection from the dead as an event on which any man or angel might have calculated, just in the same way as an astronomer predicts the movements of the heavenly bodies. " Whom God hath raised up, having loosed the pains of death, because it was not possible that he should be holden of it."

(b)

9. The buried Christ could not remain in the grave. He was raised by virtue of a Divine necessity—a necessity which, while originally and strictly proper to Him, **affects also His people and His Church.** We see in it the impossibility for us Christians to be buried for ever in the tomb in which we are laid. We, too, shall and must rise. In this, as in other matters, as He is, so are we. To us, as to Him, God hath pledged Himself. But there is such a difference as we might have expected between our resurrection and His. In Him, internal force, beside the force of prophecy, made His Resurrection a necessity ; in us there is no such intrinsic force, only a guarantee from without. He could say of His body, "I will raise it up in three days." We can only say that " He that raised up the Lord Jesus will raise us up also by Jesus." This we do know, that we must all be made manifest before the judgment-seat of Christ, that we may receive the things done in the body. The law of justice combines with the law of love to create the necessity for the resurrection of the dead—the resurrection of the just and the unjust. In the Resurrection of Christ we see further the principle that is applied to the Church as to our bodies. The Church is Christ Himself in history. As the body hath many members, so we, being many, are one body. The Church is Christ's body—the fulness of Him who filleth all in all. Unlike the humanity of Christ, the Church has in it a sinful element—an element of weakness. The Church of Corinth, at the time St. Paul wrote to it, was filled with irreligion. since that time, at certain periods of her history, the Church has been apparently dead and buried—

Resurrection, The, a Necessity—*continued*

buried in some one of the lumber rooms of the past, and the world has gone on its way rejoicing, as if all were over—as if unbelief and ungodliness were never again to be disturbed. But suddenly the tomb has been opened! As suddenly there has been a profound agitation in men's consciences, a great moral revolution, a great philanthropic activity, conspicuous self-sacrifice. And amidst all this the world awakes to an uneasy suspicion that John the Baptist has risen from the dead. The truth is, that Christ Himself has again burst the tomb and has again appeared amongst men. So it was after the deep degradation of the Papacy in the tenth century. So it was after the accumulated corruption of the fourteenth and fifteenth centuries. So it was in this country after the unbelief and profanity in the middle of the seventeenth century. So again it was amid the indifference to all truth and religion which prevailed during a greater part of the eighteenth century. So it was amid the degradation and enfeeblement of the Church of Christ. Too generally it is that the world only binds and makes sport of Samson because he has first yielded to the blandishments of Delilah. Yet the internal force must exert itself at last—the Resurrection must be re-enacted. It is not possible that the body of Christ, instinct with His force and spirit, should be holden down in death. Each apparent failure and collapse is followed by an outburst of the energy and moral glory of Christ, who, though crucified, lives by the power of God.

(*a*)

10. The Principle Applies to our Individual Lives

If we are any of us in the tomb of sin, it should be impossible for us to be there. At the same time let us remember that God is only responsible for the Resurrection of His Son, and of the bodies of the faithful. It is impossible for any of these to succumb to the empire of death. While God raises our bodies, whether we will or not, He does not raise our souls unless there is a movement within us corresponding with His grace. It is quite within our power to refuse this correspondence. That we should arise from the death of sin is a moral not a physical necessity. But surely it ought morally to be impossible for us to remain in the tomb.

(*b*)　　　　　　　　　　　　　　　*Liddon*

RESURRECTION, THE POWER OF CHRIST'S

1. The Resurrection of Christ was not a mere return by Him to the sort of life which He had been living before the Crucifixion; but rather **an advance to a higher form of human existence.**

He did not, if we may so express it, come back out of the grave, but rather passed through it, and emerged on its further side, to a new life in a body which, though it had marks of identity with that which had been nailed to the cross, was yet, in other respects, so different from it as to give us some idea of what Paul means when he says: "It is sown a natural body; it is raised a spiritual body." His Resurrection, therefore, was an entirely different thing from the raising of Lazarus, or of the widow's son at the gate of Nain, or of the daughter of Jairus. These cases were resuscitations, or restorations, pure and simple. The re-

animated persons came back to their old homes, their old occupations, their old relations. They were their former selves in every respect, and ultimately died again. But it was not so with Christ. His Resurrection was to "newness of life," in a sense somewhat different from that in which Paul uses the words, but yet in one that is very real and very true. He did not resume His former relations; for He said unto Mary: "Touch Me not." He did not take up His residence in any one place, as if He had again become a denizen of earth. He was not continuously in the company of some one or other of His former friends. He did not become the guest of any of His followers. There were many things about His resurrection body which manifested real identity with that which was crucified. Then, on the other hand, it was so different therefrom, that He could appear to His followers and disappear from them at pleasure : could pass from place to place in a marvellously short space of time, and could enter a chamber even when its doors were shut. It was allied with and rooted in His former body, and yet so ethereal—or, as our version of Paul's word has it, so "spiritual"—in its texture as to be above the sphere of the operation of those laws to which ordinary material substances are subjected. Hence, His Resurrection was not a return, but an advance; not a coming back into His former life, but a bursting forward into a nobler humanity, over which death had no longer power.

(*c*)

2. Ambition

When Michael Angelo had examined the work of one of his pupils, and had observed that it lacked breadth of treatment, he took his pencil and wrote upon it : "*Amplius*"—wider. Now, just that the Resurrection of Christ has written, if they could but see it, over men's earthly lives. They are narrow in their range, and limited, for the most part, to this present existence; but the great Easter fact says: "*Amplius*." Let your thoughts go forward into eternity. Let your plans expand so as to include the things which are above.

We cannot continue long to live contrary to the world's maxims and customs, if we are not upheld by a strength which comes not from the earth. We must have meat to eat, of which the world knows not. We must be able, in times of conflict and weariness, to fall back upon some support that is stronger than earth can furnish. And we find that in the fact that our Lord Jesus Christ is living yet in our nature, in the heavenly world, a human Brother and yet an almighty Friend, according as the author of the Epistle to the Hebrews has said, "Seeing then that we have a great High Priest, that is passed into the heavens, Jesus the Son of God, let us hold fast our profession." There is, in one of the valleys of Perthshire, a tree which sprang up on the rocky side of a little brook, where there was no kindly soil in which it could spread its roots, or by which it could be nourished. For a long time it was stunted and unhealthy, but, at length, by what may be called a wonderful vegetable instinct, it has sent a fibre out across a narrow sheep-bridge, which was close beside it, and that fixed itself in the rich loam on the opposite bank of the streamlet, whence it drew sap and sustenance, so that it speedily became vigorous. Now, what that tiny bridge was to the

(*d*)

tree, the Resurrection of Christ is to the believer. The Christian life on earth is growing in an unkindly soil; and if it could find no better nourishment than that can furnish it would die; but, taught by the Holy Spirit of God, through faith in the Resurrection and Ascension of the Lord, it sends a rootlet across the river into the better land, and draws from that all the support it needs to keep it fresh and healthy.

(a)   *W. M. Taylor*

RESURRECTION AND REWARD

It is said that he once received even less than the average itinerant fee, and a poor old woman remarked: "Well, Christmas Evans, *bach*, I hope you will be paid at the Resurrection; you have given us a wonderful sermon." "Yes, yes, Shân *fach*," said the preacher, "no doubt of that, but what am I to do till I get there? And there's the old white mare that carries me, what will she do? —for her there will be no resurrection."

(b)   *Memoir of Christmas Evans*

RESURRECTION: SABBATH KEPT IN THE GRAVE

Love is restless and fearless. In the dark of night, these good women go to buy their spices; and, ere the day-break, are gone out of their houses towards the tomb of Christ, to bestow them. This sex is commonly fearful; it was much for them to walk alone in that unsafe season; yet, as despising all fears and dangers, they thus spend the night after their Sabbath. Might they have been allowed to buy their perfumes on the Sabbath, or to have visited that holy tomb sooner, can we think they would have stayed so long? Can we suppose they would have cared more for the Sabbath than for the *Lord of the Sabbath*, who now kept His Sabbath in the grave? Sooner they might not come, later they would not, to present their last homage to their dead Saviour. Had these holy women known their Jesus to be alive, how had they hasted, who made such speed to do their last offices to His sacred corpse! For us, we *know that our Redeemer liveth;* we know where He is. O Saviour, how cold and heartless is our love to Thee if we do not haste to find Thee in Thy Word and Sacraments; if our souls do not fly up to Thee, in all holy affections, into Thy Heaven!

(c)   *Bishop Hall*

RESURRECTION: THE DISCHARGE OF THE SINNER

Lo, now, how weak soever I am in myself, yet, in the confidence of this victorious Resurrection of my Saviour, I dare boldly challenge and defy you, O all ye adverse powers. Do the worst ye can to my soul: in despite of you, it shall be safe.

Is it sin that threats me? Behold, this Resurrection of my Redeemer publishes my discharge. My surety was arrested, and cast into the prison of His grave. Had not the utmost farthing of mine arrearages been paid, He could not have come forth. He is come forth: the sum is fully satisfied. What danger can there be of a discharged debt?

(d)   *Ibid*

RESURRECTION, SUPERNATURAL

I ask at the mouth of the tomb for intelligence of the departed, and the tomb gives me no reply.
I examine the various regions of nature, but I can discover no process for restoring the mouldering body, and no sign or track of the spirit's ascent to another sphere. I see the need of a power above nature to restore or perpetuate life after death; and if God intended to give assurance of this life, I see not how He can do it but by supernatural teaching—by a miraculous revelation. Miracles are the appropriate and would seem to be the only mode of placing beyond doubt man's future and immortal being; and no miracles can be conceived so adapted to this end as the very ones which hold the highest place in Christianity—I mean the resurrection of Lazarus, and, still more, the resurrection of Jesus.

(e)   *Channing*

RESURRECTION, THE, AND THOMAS

We cannot but be losers by our absence from holy assemblies. Where wert thou, O Thomas, when the rest of that sacred family were met together? Had thy fear put thee to so long a flight, that, as yet, thou wert not returned to thy fellows? Or didst thou suffer other occasions to detain thee from this happiness? Now, for the time, thou missedst that Divine Breath, which so comfortably inspired the rest; now, thou art suffered to fall into that weak distrust which thy presence had prevented. They told thee, We have seen the Lord; was not this eno'? Would no eyes serve thee but thine own? Were thy ears to no use for thy faith? "Except I see in His hands the print of the nails, and put my finger into the print of the nails, and thrust my hand into His side, I will not believe." Suspicious man? who is the worse for that? Whose is the loss, if thou believe not? Is there no certainty, but in thine own senses? Why were not so many and so holy eyes and tongues as credible as thy own hands and eyes? How little wert thou yet acquainted with the ways of faith? "Faith comes by hearing." These are the tongues that must win the whole world to an assent; and dost thou, the first man, detract to yield. Why was that word so hard to pass? Had not thy Divine Master foretold thee, with the rest, that He must be crucified, and the third day rise again? Is anything related to be done, but that, which was fore-promised? anything beyond the sphere of Divine Omnipotence? Go then, and please thyself in thine overwise incredulity, while thy fellows are happy in believing.

(f)   *Bishop Hall*

RESURRECTION, THE, AND THOMAS

It is a *whole week* that Thomas rests in this sullen unbelief; in all which time, doubtless, his ears are beaten with the many constant assertions of the holy women, the first witnesses of the Resurrection; as also of the two disciples walking to Emmaus, whose hearts, burning within them, had set their tongues on fire, in a zealous relation of those happy occurrences; with the assured reports of the rising and re-appearing of many saints, in attendance of the Lord and Giver of Life; yet still he struggles with his own distrust; and stiffly suspends his belief to that truth, whereof he cannot deny himself enough convinced. As all bodies are not equally apt to be wrought upon by

(g)

the same medicine, so are not all souls by the same means of faith; one is refractory, while others are pliable.

(a)   *Bishop Hall*

RESURRECTION, THE, AND THOMAS

Then Thomas answered, and said unto him, "My Lord, and my God." I do not hear that, when it came to the issue, Thomas employed his hands in this trial. His eyes were now sufficient assurance. The sense of his Master's omniscience, in this particular challenge of him, spared, perhaps, the labour of a further disquisition. And now, how happily was that doubt bestowed, which brought forth so faithful a confession, My Lord, my God! I hear not such a word from those that believed. It was well for us, it was well for thee, O Thomas, that thou distrustedst; else, neither had the world received so perfect an evidence of the Resurrection, whereon all our salvation dependeth; neither hadst thou yielded so pregnant and Divine an astipulation to thy blessed Saviour. Now, thou dost not only profess His Resurrection, but His Godhead too, and thy happy interest in both. And now, if they be blessed that have not seen and yet believed; blessed art thou also, that having seen thou hast believed: and blessed be Thou, O God, who knowest how to make advantage of the infirmities of Thy chosen for the promoting of their salvation, the confirmation of Thy Church, the glory of Thy own name! Amen.

(b)   *Ibid*

RESURRECTION, VICTORY OF THE (1 Cor. xv. 54–57)

The argument closes in a burst of almost poetical fervour (as in the corresponding passage Rom. viii. 31). "And when this corruptible . . . be to God who giveth us the victory through our Lord Jesus Christ."

(c)   *Stanley*

The theory of conscious imposture has long been abandoned as utterly untenable; the theory of unconscious delusion, leading to the acceptance of a myth by a large body of people, within the space of less than a decade of years, is really too absurd to be seriously maintained. What remains, then, but the view which has always been maintained by the Christian Church, which is indeed the very keystone of the arch of the doctrine upon which it rests—that the miracle of the Resurrection is an actual and accomplished fact; that Christ, who died for our sins, according to the Scriptures, who was buried in the grave, did indeed rise again from the dead on the third day, and enter into the glory of His eternal life in the heavens?

(d)   *Gordon Calthrop*

RETRIBUTION

Fatalism and Atheism are preached constantly amidst the plaudits of ignorant Englishmen. How many politicians deem the matter a thing of the slightest consequence.

Hume would never have set cities on fire, beheaded or hacked to pieces human beings, least of all the refined, the noble, the educated. But he must be reckoned among those who sneeringly scattered smouldering embers, and be-

queathed to others death by the inevitable conflagration. . . . Seldom has the logic of events been more complete than in the great French Revolution.

(e)   *Jackson's Bampton Lectures*

RETURN

When the Ark set forward, Moses said, "Let God arise, and let His enemies be scattered;" and, when it rests—as, little by little, we move onward and upward, as we pause awhile after each service, each effort to convince others, as "each night we pitch our moving tent a day's march nearer home," as we end this Mission, and before we enter on our next work for God—we will pray, as Moses prayed, "Return, O Lord, to the many thousands in Israel."

Return, O Lord, to the many thousands here in London, who, once brought to Christian baptism, have forsaken the guide of their youth and forgotten the covenant of their God; who have wandered away from the fold of the Good Shepherd, who laid down His life for the sheep, and have lost the mark with which He marked them for His own; who were enlisted, and swore to be good soldiers of Jesus Christ, but who, being harnessed and carrying bows, have turned themselves back in the day of battle, and gone over as deserters, like Balaam to the Midianites, to fight against the armies of God.

Return, O Lord, to the many thousands, who say that they still belong to Christ, and believe, it may be, a form of godliness, who are "lukewarm, neither hot nor cold," but in their lives deny Him. Who are living for self only—for pleasure, as they call it, or for money, or for praise, or authority. Return, O Lord, and set their hearts upon the only true happiness, joy and peace in believing; the only true wealth, the unsearchable riches of Christ, treasures in heaven; the only praise, which never deceives nor deserts the approbation of a conscience void of offence; the only authority which exalts and ennobles manhood—the mastery which, strong in the Lord and in the power of His might, can overcome evil with good.

Return, O Lord, to the many thousands who will make no trial of revelation, but think to find a more excellent way from reason and philosophy. Who will not accept God's Word, as a lantern unto their feet and a light unto their path; but follow the lurid flames of passion or the glimmer of their own imaginations, and heed not the awful warning of the prophet: "Behold, all ye that kindle a fire, that compass yourselves about with sparks: walk in the light of your fire, and in the sparks that ye have kindled. This shall ye have of mine hand; ye shall lie down in sorrow."

Return, O Lord, to the many thousands who are sore let and hindered in running the race that is set before them, who think that they are tempted above what they are able to bear, who cannot endure ridicule, unkindness, cold contempt, who are losing heart, and ceasing to strive for the mastery. Let them hear Thy voice, "If they have persecuted Me, they will also persecute you." "In the world ye shall have tribulation, but be of good cheer, I have overcome the world." "Whosoever shall confess Me before men, him will I confess also before My Father which is in heaven."

Return, O Lord, to the many thousands who

(f)

are defeated and almost in despair, disappointed, desolate, and in misery, who have been betrayed, defrauded, forsaken, who seem to have none to help, none to pity, no place to flee unto ; for—

> Some have found the world is vain,
> Yet from the world they break not free :
> And some have friends who give them pain,
> Yet have not sought a friend in Thee.

Return, O Lord ; and when the sorrows of their heart are enlarged, and they cry, "Why art thou so heavy, O my soul, and why art thou so disquieted within me ? " then hear Thou from heaven, Thy dwelling-place, and answer, "Hope Thou in God." "Come unto Me, all ye that travail and are heavy laden, and I will refresh you."

Return, O Lord, and make Thyself known to the many thousands who know Thy Name only as spoken in blasphemous derision, who have not so much as heard whether there be any Holy Ghost. Oh, send out Thy light and Thy truth into the dark places of this great city. Be with Thy messengers, and give them a mouth and wisdom, which all their adversaries shall not be able to gainsay nor resist. Let them know that he that converteth a sinner from the error of his ways shall save a soul from death, and hide a multitude of sins.

Oh, think what it will be, if in the world to come, for none can be assured of salvation in this, —for "the trial of all things is in the end,"—think what it will be if at the portals of Paradise, or at the Judgment before men and angels, there should be one—only one to welcome and to witness. "It was you who came to me by the mercy of God, and led me from darkness into light ; it was you at that London Mission-

> Who taught me all the mercy, for you showed me all the sin,
> How, though the lamp was lighted late, there's One would let me in-

and lo ! I am "numbered with the children of God, and my lot is among the saints."

(a) *S. R. Hole, London Mission, 1884*

REUNION IN HEAVEN

The joys of centuries will be crowded into that meeting. This is not fiction. It is truth founded on the essential laws of the mind.

(b) *Channing*

REVELATION

The Church rehearses and enforces the first truths of natural religion, for the seal of her ethical teaching is this : "Let every one that nameth the name of Christ depart from iniquity." From year to year and day to day, she adds to natural religion bright and glorious things which nature cannot give : what "eye hath not seen, nor ear heard, neither have entered into the heart of man ; the things which God hath prepared for them that love Him."

(c) *Jackson's Bampton Lectures*

Revelation

A revelation has been given, once and again from the outer realms of mystery a great light has struck our wheeling earth—struck it till its hopes gleamed and glittered. Of old it came flutteringly through prophets and scattered men of God ; last

of all and conclusively it came at Nazareth. "God, who at sundry times and in divers manners spake in time past unto the fathers by the prophets, hath in these last days spoken unto us by His Son, whom He hath appointed heir of all things, by whom also He made the worlds." Yes, "heir of all things, by whom He hath made the worlds ! " Backward from that point in the earth's history the light extends, involving the very beginnings and the offsets ; and forward from that point it also extends, suffusing itself through all things, and involving the ends and the upshots. Let philosophies form and accumulate themselves, all will end in Christianity ; let there be wars and revolutions, and let States and Commonwealths rise and succeed each other—all are but preparations towards that kingdom of Christ wherein all will be included, for all things are His inheritance. And so with individual men now ; be they what they may, all is incomplete within them, they are not fully men until Christianity has occupied their being. This faith may, indeed, exist where it is not suspected to be, and it may not be, alas ! where it is least supposed to be absent ; but be it must wherever man is to be essentially man, and life is to be at its highest potency. And so, wherever in literature, whether in history, in poem, or in novel, life is to be represented, and, above all, wherever the scheme is to exhibit the formation of character and the progress of an individual mind through doubt and error to final certainty and truth, this recognition of Christianity as the supreme principle ought to be, with those who adopt the argument, unremittingly and unmistakably present.

(d) *Mason's English Novelists*

Revelation, Divine

An eminent living clergyman, walking one evening to a church at which he was to preach, was asked by his companion, "Is it true that you sometimes do not select your text till you have gone into the pulpit ? " "Yes," he said, "it is *sometimes* true ; and I wish you would give me a text for this evening, for really I have not yet decided on what to preach." "I would if I could," said his companion ; "but I can't think of any text at this moment, unless it be : ' *The Lord spake unto Moses and unto Aaron, saying.*'" "Excellent ! " said he. "It is precisely what I want : I shall preach upon that." And he did. . . . It was the vast subject of the *Divine Revelation*. It opened to him, all at a flash :

(i.) Man's need of such a Revelation ; and his tendency to sink into deeper darkness without it ;

(ii.) The fair expectation that a wise and good God would give it ;

(iii.) The different modes in which it has been given—oral—written—visions—dreams—prophetic inspiration—the coming of the Son of God Himself (as the revealer of the Father)—and lastly by the coming of the Holy Ghost (as the revealer of the Son). . . . And then by all these combined in one Bible, a book for all ages, for the world, and to be interpreted by the Divine Spirit who inspired it ;

(iv.) *The Lessons :* The grace of God in giving and preserving this Revelation ; the duty of attending to it ; the wickedness of substituting anything for it ; the glory of the state in which this Revelation will be needed no more, since we shall see God face to face.

(e) *Storrs*

REVELATION, GRADUAL

Does a week pass without the announcement of the discovery of a new comet in the sky, a new star in the heaven, twinkling dimly out of a yet farther distance, and only now becoming visible to human ken, though existent for ever and ever? So let us hope Divine truths may be shining, and regions of light and love extant, which Geneva glasses cannot yet perceive, and are beyond the focus of Roman telescopes.

(a)   *Thackeray*

REVELATION AND NATURE

I say that revelation is consistent with nature, when nature is truly interpreted by reason.

(b)   *Channing*

REVELATION AND REASON.

Consider to whom revelation is sent. Why is it given to men rather than to brutes? Why have not God's messengers gone to the fields to proclaim His glad tidings to bird and beast? The answer is obvious. These want reason, and wanting this, they have no capacity or preparation for revealed truth. And not only would revelation be lost on the brute; let it speak to the child, before its rational faculties have been awakened, and before some ideas of duty and his own nature have been developed, and it might as well speak to a stone. Reason is the preparation and ground of revelation.

(c)   *Ibid*

REVELATION AND SCIENCE

Revelation and Science as means of knowledge, are like parallel lines, which, if continued ever so far both ways, do not meet. Hence those writers who are so anxious to show their agreement, are, as it were, endeavouring to prove that they do meet. How far better is it, to let both run on independently of each other, knowing that they are parallels, and not intended to meet.

(d)

Modern science makes men nothing, while Revelation tells us they are the lords of creation and heirs of immortality.

                                      Mozeley

REVERENCE

Reverence for sham, reverence for the old merely because it is old, reverence for stupidity, however learned, reverence for incapacity, however finely inaugurated, I have none. But we want more reverence for God, more reverence for the Sacraments, more reverence for the Bible, more reverence for the pure, more reverence for the good. Reverence a characteristic of all great nations. You hear it in the roll of the master oratorios. You see it in the Raphaels and Titians and Ghirlandajos. You study it in the architecture of the Aholiabs and Christopher Wrens. Do not be flippant about God. Do not joke about death. Do not make fun of the Bible. Do not deride the Eternal. The brightest and mightiest seraph cannot look unabashed upon Him. Involuntarily the wings came up. "With twain he covered his face."

(e)   *Talmage*

REVERENCE AND RITUALISM: THINGS THAT DIFFER

The abstract quality of reverence is essentially the same wherever it exists, whether in man upon earth or angel in heaven; its expression, on the other hand, admits of infinite variety. To confine our thoughts to earth, it is obvious that time, circumstances, race, climate, besides many other conditions, tend to mould and modify the externals of devotion and render impracticable anything like uniformity in matters of ritual. The sentiment of the Christian, as he enters the house of prayer, is the same in kind, if not in degree, that filled the heart of Moses as he stood by the burning bush; but it never occurs to the Christian worshipper to prove his reverence by putting his shoes from off his feet any more than the minister of our Church thinks of adopting the practices by which the Jewish priest expressed his reverential awe as he ministered before the Lord.

Such being the case, no greater mistake can be made than to suppose that the mode of conducting public worship cannot vary without risk of heresy, and that a change in the outward expression of congregational reverence must necessarily imply an approach to newly-invented doctrine or exploded error. . . .

The fact is, that each generation must be left to decide questions of mere ritual for itself. The Evangelical of the present day would find himself almost as uncomfortable and perplexed sitting under the Low Church vicar of Queen Anne's reign as in the church of the modern Ritualist. It would surely be with a sense of painful wonderment and outraged reverence that he would observe half the congregation sitting to sing the hymns; find the Liturgy curtailed to make room for a long extempore "pulpit prayer;" and see the officiating minister arrayed in a surplice "dirty and contemptible with age," even if a dress, still reprobated by some as a "Babylonish garment," were not altogether discarded. Nor—to come to the sermon—would the disciple of Melville or Close feel that he was edified by a preacher who laboured to prove that the organ had no lawful place in God's house, that the use of the cross in baptism was a relic of superstition, and, that the sacred monogram was to be accounted a "Jesuit's cypher." . . .

Much that was then in dispute appears to us trivial in the extreme; and we are bound in honesty to ask the question, whether posterity will not pass the same judgment upon some of the matters that agitate the ecclesiastical mind of our own day. . . .

If we apply this thought to the mode of conducting the services of the Church, we shall be fully prepared for change—change not, indeed, in the principles, but in the accessories of public worship. Can we be surprised that the younger members of our Church are not always satisfied with what pleased their elders well enough? It is surely somewhat arbitrary and unreasonable to demand that, while high art, music, and general culture are encouraged and stimulated in our homes, our schools, our public institutions, and in every part of our secular life, they should be placed under the strictest restraint in the House of God, and introduced with jealous eye and sparing hand into our worship. Those who insist now upon the ritual that was deemed decent and suffi-

(f)

cient by the Evangelicals of 1850 may find that, by so doing they are defeating their own ends, and handing over the youth of England to those whose teaching does not represent the Church of the Reformation. . . .

Can the clergyman whose views have been formed in the reign of John Ruskin and Gilbert Scott be expected to appreciate the subtle distinction that is made between hollyberries at Christmas and primroses at Easter; to see innocence in the one, to detect lurking error in the other? Is it probable that he will regard the slop-basin as a fair substitute for the time-honoured font? Or can he escape a sense of incongruity as he leaves his study, furnished with some attention to the rules of art, and enters a church in which the dominant idea appears to have been the exclusion of God's gifts of taste and culture?

In all this, be it remembered, he represents the age in which his lot and work are cast; and a clergyman will do his work best if he is a man of his own time. There is a time for everything under the sun; and we only injure the cause of truth by obstinately refusing to perceive what is waxing old and ready to vanish away. To suppose that things can be exactly the same when we have turned threescore years as when we came of age, betrays ignorance of human nature and of the first principles of history. To take offence now-a-days at the idea of a surpliced choir, to resent the suggestion of abandoning the black gown or the introduction of an anthem, is to ignore, and therefore probably to alienate, the rising generation. Young men and women do not forsake our old-fashioned Evangelical churches because they have anything to say against the teaching, but because the mode of conducting service does not express their ideal of worship.

(a)   " The Rock "

REVILINGS (1 Pet. ii. 23)

The late Bishop Villiers, when a London incumbent, was at one time much troubled by the persistent calumnies of a parishioner. Writing to a friend, he mentioned the annoyance he was experiencing, and asked advice. The answer was laconic: " Jesus stood before the Governor: . . . And when He was accused of the chief priests and elders, He answered nothing. Then said Pilate unto Him: Hearest Thou not how many things they witness against Thee? And He answered him to never a word; insomuch that the Governor marvelled greatly." "Dear Villiers, let the Governor marvel greatly."

(b)

REVISED VERSION

It is, I think, in "Guesses at Truth," that the remark is made, that every fresh effort for the general good is apt to be treated as cows treat a new rubbing-post. First they look at it, then they butt at it, and then they use it.

(c)   Dean Howson

REVIVAL

The reading, and especially the preaching, of the word, is the grand occasion and instrument in the conversion of souls. Of His own will He begets them with the word of truth; and it is admirably suited to those saving impressions which it is intended to make on the heart, being quick and powerful, and sharper than any two-edged sword.

Evangelical subjects, when opened with perspicuity, and enforced with vigour and tenderness by those that have experienced the transforming energy of them on their own hearts, and desire, above all things, to be wise to win the souls of others, are generally the occasion of producing the most immediate and the most important change.

(d)   P. Doddridge

O fire, that art always burning and never quenched, kindle me! O light, always shining and never darkened, enlighten me.

(e)   Augustine

REVOLUTION

" Distress of nations with perplexity " (Luke xxi. 25)

Great and stirring times are fast approaching; and not only in England, but in Switzerland, Germany, and Russia events will shortly take place that will shake the world. There are tens of thousands of men willing and ready to lay down their lives if they can only ensure a happier future for their posterity. That is the Revolutionist's dream and his heartfelt prayer. The dream will be realized, and the prayer will be answered. It needs no prophet to predict that. The signs are too apparent.

(f)   " Daily News," 1885
(See " ANARCHY ")

RICHES

" Ye have received your consolation " (Luke vi. 24)

I have received from Taubenheim 100 pieces of gold, and fifty pieces of silver from Schart; so that I begin to fear lest God be giving me my portion here below. But I solemnly declare that nothing can make me happy except God.

(g)   Luther

RICHES

" The unsearchable riches of Christ " (Eph. iii. 8)

The riches of Christ's Divinity are unsearchable, and the riches of His condescension are unsearchable, and the riches of His tenderness are unsearchable, and the riches of His redeeming love are unsearchable, and the riches of His intercession are unsearchable, and the riches of His faithfulness are unsearchable, and the riches of His supporting grace are unsearchable. These riches will never be expressed, even to all eternity. No! not by the noble army of Martyrs, nor the glorious company of the Apostles, nor the goodly fellowship of the Prophets, nor the general assembly and Church of the Firstborn, nor the innumerable company of angels, nor the spirits of just men made perfect, nor by all the ransomed throng of heaven. It will form their most ecstatic employment in heaven. Join, all ye happy throng! . . . join holy Abel and Enoch, upright Job, perfect Noah, souls of Abraham, Isaac, and Jacob, grand souls of Moses, Samuel, and Elijah, pardoned

(h)

David and Manasseh, soul of Isaiah the prophet. Join, all ye whose souls under the altar cry, "How long, O Lord, wilt Thou not avenge our blood upon the earth!" Join holy Stephen and Polycarp, holy Latimer, Ridley, Hooper, Rowland Taylor, and Anne Askew! Join brave Wicklif, gallant Luther, stern John Knox, sweet John Bunyan, and praying George Fox; join pious Doddridge and tuneful Watts, noble George Whitefield, holy Fletcher, exhaustless John Wesley, dauntless Rowland Hill, and grand though lowly Robert Hall. . . . Ye sweetest trebles of the eternal choir, ye million million babes who died without actual sin, join all your notes of praise! Pull out every stop of the grand organ of heaven, from the deep swell diapason to the lofty flute and cornet! Gabriel, strike the loftiest note of thy harp of gold! And let all the host of heaven, angels, and men begin the grand anthem, "Worthy is the Lamb," etc. And let the bold fugue be struck, "Blessing, and honour, and glory, and power, be unto Him that sitteth upon the throne, and unto the Lamb for ever and ever." And let the eternal "AMEN!" peal, and roll, and reverberate through all the arches of heaven! But never through all eternity shall the gathered host be able fully to express "*the unsearchable riches of Christ!*"

(a) *Thos. Cooper*

RIGHT

"*Shall not the Judge of all the earth do right?*" (Gen. xviii. 25)

All Nature is but Art, unknown to thee;
All chance, direction which thou canst not see;
All discord, harmony not understood;
All partial evil, universal good;
And, spite of pride, in erring reason's spite,
One truth is clear: *whatever is, is right.*
(b) *Pope*

RIGHT

We make ourselves right with God by being right with His Son.
(c)

The Law makes sin exceeding sinful.
(d)

RIGHTEOUS JUDGMENT OF GOD, THE

"*In one hour is thy judgment come*" (Rev. xviii. 10).

Among the ways of men
God walks, with quiet tread, His unseen path;
But drawing near the goal, He rushes on,
Decided as the gleaming thunderbolt.
(e) *Klopstock*

"Take care! The longer the storm gathers, the greater its devastation."
(f) *Starke*

RITUALISM

I have reserved for the last part of this account the sensual or symbolical worship of the Church of Rome and its imitators, the melodramatic representation of the Crucifixion. We all know that when Christ was brought to trial for His life before Pontius Pilate He prayed to God that He might be spared this painful sacrifice, but concluded His prayer by saying to God, "Not my will, but Thy will be done." We all know that the Jewish mob called out, "Crucify him! Crucify him!" and that He underwent an ignominious and degrading death. But we have now to relate that men who are not required to endure an hour's pain for the benefit of mankind, put on all kinds of harlequin dresses, and perform all sorts of antics, to resemble, as they pretend, the great and memorable sacrifice of Christ's propitiation: and without suffering pain in a little finger pretend to imitate and assume the attitudes of our Saviour, and to accomplish in their own persons the mystery of a Divine Being who actually gave His life for the benefit of mankind. If this were only like one of the sacred plays of the Spanish theatre, we might be content to say that it was a contemptible farce; but assuming, as it does, to be an act to inspire devotion, and give to the Christian world a lively representation by clerical performers of the real tragedy which was performed in Jerusalem under the Roman Government more than eighteen hundred years ago, we can only pronounce it to be a shocking profanation. For my part I am ready to forgive the members of an ancient and venerable Church which in the dark Middle Ages of Europe thought to symbolize the creed of Christians, and to awaken the devotion of millions who could neither read nor write by statues to attract worship, and by pictures to represent the Virgin Mary and the disciples of Christ who followed His preaching and inculcated His doctrine. But at the present time the question is totally altered. The millions who, before the Revival of Letters, could only be taught by signs and emblems, have now been replaced by millions who have learned to read the Bible, who have been taught the words of Christ in their own native language, and are no longer bound by the theology of subtle logicians. Indeed, it is absurd to suppose that we are on the brink of a great contest between those who have learnt the principles of the Reformation and those who wish to lead us by crooked paths, and windows that shut out the light, to the temples where truth is lost amid a blaze of light, a great pomp of dresses, and the strains of melodious music. It is very evident that the disciples of the Church of Rome wish to lead us from Confession and Absolution to the doctrine of Transubstantiation; from thence to the worship of images, and from thence to all the abuses which at the end of the fifteenth century and at the beginning of the sixteenth excited the anger and the scorn of Luther, Calvin, Zwinglius, and others. The primary faith of the Reformers is in the words of Christ. The primary faith of the Ritualists is in Aristotle. It is not doubtful which way the Protestants of England will decide. They will follow in the footsteps of the Reformers. It is to be noted that the sentiments of devotion awakened by fine dresses, fine music, and dark mysteries, figured in symbols and ceremonies, are not confined to any particular religious faith. Devotion to Mahomet, or to Buddha, may be excited by the same means which prevail with the Ritualists of England in favour of the name of Christ. But another course has been taken by the leaders who laid the foundation
(g)

of what we in England call the Reformation. It may be said that the Protestant congregations of England may adopt the music and the pomp of Ritualistic service and still attend to the sublime lessons of charity and humility of our Lord. This is certainly possible, but not probable. Those who adopt the mummeries of the Ritualists are apt to forget that they ought not to boast that they are not as other men are, and to reject the exclamation of the publican, "Lord, be merciful to me, a sinner." The English nation must choose between the two. Either they must adopt the Ritualistic mode of worship, and set aside the Acts of Parliament by which the country is now governed, or they must, with the Archbishop of Canterbury, adhere to the principles of the glorious Reformation begun by Henry VIII., and established by his daughter Elizabeth, Queen of England and of Ireland. There is one gift bestowed by Jesus Christ upon His people which we still enjoy, and which I hope we may continue to enjoy. When Jesus Christ was asked whether He was the Saviour for whom they looked, or whether they should look for another, He gave instances of the miracles He had performed; that the blind had been made to see, that the paralytic had been told to take up his bed and walk, and that even the dead had been bidden to appear in his grave-clothes with life restored. All this power of miracles has departed from us. We do not, like the Roman Church, pretend to restore the broken limb or make whole the wounded body. But there was one concluding sentence in Christ's declaration which we still preserve. He terminated his message by saying, "and the poor have the Gospel preached to them." This we preserve. The Bible Society could tell how many copies of the Gospel they distribute every year among all the nations of the world. Only a few years ago, by the exertions of a zealous minister of the Gospel, the price of the Bible was reduced in Scotland from 5s. to 10d. Thus the people of Great Britain have inherited a privilege worthy of the Divine author of the religion which has its name and its teaching from Christ. If the British nation is wise, it will not allow the Roman Church with its infallible head, or the Ritualists with their mimic ornaments, nor those who are deaf to the teachings of Socrates and of Cicero, of Bacon and of Newton, to deprive them of the inestimable blessings of the Gospel.

(a)   " Recollections and Suggestions "

RITUALISM AND THE CROSS (John xviii. 28)

These "Rulers of the Jews" were thorough Ritualists. It was their Ritualism that urged them to crucify Christ. For Christ and Ritualism are opposed to each other as light is to darkness.

The Cross and the crucifix cannot agree. Either Ritualism will banish Christ, or Christ will banish Ritualism.

Ritualism kept these Jews out of Pilate's hall; the touch of a Gentile would pollute them. They could not, in that case, eat the Passover. The Passover was their God, their Messiah, their Saviour, their religion.

Ritualism, or sacerdotalism, or externalism, or traditionalism, are all different forms of self-righteousness; man's self-invented ways of pleasing or appeasing God, or paying for admittance into the kingdom.

(b)   Horatius Bonar

RITUALISM AND ROMANISM

In bringing in the Public Worship Bill in 1874, the Archbishop of Canterbury (Tait) gave further and stronger specimens of the Ritualistic doings in matters far beyond mere ritual, amounting to an absolute repudiation of every Protestant doctrine, and adoption of every Popish one, except the refusal of the cup to the laity : which one of the cleverest adherents of that party, even before its later developments, once confessed to us was the only Roman doctrine he did not accept; and so do many others. . . . *Ritual is not a weaker but a stronger and more constant presentation of the doctrines to which we know it belongs, and a making a congregation a party to them, than preaching.* . . . Dean Howson quotes Archdeacon Denison as having said that "in two or three years the Ritual has done as much as or more than the teaching had done in *twenty-five*, of the true doctrine of the Eucharist.

(c)   "*Quarterly Review*," Jan., 1881

RITUALIST INCUMBENT, RISE AND PRO-GRESS OF A

A youthful priest who had recently passed an examination for holy orders, in which he might not perhaps have displayed any profound acquaintance with theology or Church history, found himself the fortunate possessor of a living, into which he had been inducted *on the express condition* that he assented to and would use the form prescribed in the Book of Common Prayer, and none other, except it might be ordered by lawful authority. No sooner had he been duly inducted than he proceeded to set up in his church the Roman mass in all its minutest details, of which lights, vestments, and incense were but a small part. He duly performed all the genuflexions, crosses, and prostrations prescribed in the last edition of the "Directorium," or his "Ritual for the Altar," adding to these from time to time what he described as such beautiful symbolisms as might have occurred to his own mind or have been recommended by some correspondent in his Church newspaper as the last correct thing in rites. His parishioners, naturally indignant at this deliberate Romanizing of their church and their services, in which they, perhaps not altogether erroneously, believed they had some rights, legal and ecclesiastical, remonstrated with their pastor, who informed them in reply that he was a priest of the Holy Catholic Church, and that as such it was his privilege to teach and direct them in all things, and that it was their privilege to obey him. They complained to the Bishop, who, in writing to the incumbent to inquire into the truth of these complaints, received in reply the information that what had been complained of was quite true; that the writer did not intend, nevertheless, to alter his proceedings in the very least particular, whatever the Bishop might say or do to the contrary; and that as to his promise reverently to obey his ordinary, that only meant that he had to obey such directions as the Bishop could enforce in a court of law; and that at any rate, whatever obedience over and above this he was disposed to pay to a real Catholic-minded and rightly-appointed Bishop, he could not possibly think of paying to one who was only the nominee of the

(d)

Prime Minister, and had neither the learning, nor the piety, nor the Catholic sympathies which alone could justify the obedience of a truly Catholic priest.

(a)　　　　　　　　　　　　　　*Bp. Magee*

ROCK

" Upon this rock I will build," etc. (Matt. xvi. 18)

There is-
(i.) *The Architect :* " I will build ";
(ii.) *The Building :* " My Church ";
(iii). The *Foundation,* or *materials :* " Living stones," of which Peter was the first. There must be one true believer to begin with. Peter being the first confessor of a true Creed, was therefore the foundation-stone in a special sense : " Jesus Christ being the Chief Corner-stone," as the One foundation. Here He is the Builder, building with living stones.
(iv.) *Its Permanence :*
" The gates of Hades shall not prevail against it : " Death shall not conquer the kingdom of Christ. Its power is abolished.

(b)

Peter was the first of those *foundation-stones* (Eph. ii. 20. Rev. xxi. 14) on which the living temple of God was built ; this building itself beginning on the Day of Pentecost by the laying of 3000 *living stones* on this very foundation.

(c)　　　　　　　　　　　　　　*Alford*

ROCK OF AGES

One day, in a moment of exalted inspiration, Toplady sat down and wrote a few verses which he sent for publication in a Devonshire newspaper. He entitled them, " A living and dying prayer of the holiest believer in the world." That was a wonderful " poet's corner " in that obscure Devonshire journal, for the poem that appeared there was no other than the immortal " *Rock of Ages.*"

To-day it is the most universally popular as well as the sublimest of modern hymns. Into almost every language of the globe the Devonshire Vicar's lines have been translated. They are sung in Arabic under the shadow of Lebanon, and in modern Greek beside the hill of Mars. When Prince Albert of England was dying, his lips feebly murmured-

" Rock of Ages cleft for me,
Let me hide myself in Thee."

To analyse this marvellous hymn is almost as presumptuous as to pull a Provence rose to pieces in order to discover where the delicious odour was lurking. Perhaps the two finest lines are those which are carved on a monument upon Sylvan Cliff, in Greenwood Cemetery :

"Nothing in my hand I bring,
Simply to Thy Cross I cling."

The whole essence of the Gospel, the condensed creed of every child of Jesus, is in these simple words. In fact, the whole hymn is a fervent outcry of a contrite, penitent heart into the ear of Jesus. It begins with the plaintive confession that not the labour of our hands can fulfil the law's demands. Then the suppliant acknowledges that he is naked, helpless, and vile, and implores the Saviour to wash him or he dies. Then the swelling heart begins to break upward, and to soar beyond that hour when the eyelids have closed in death. It rises to the Judgment-seat. It beholds the great white throne. Even there no object in the universe is so transcendently glorious as the risen and crowned Sufferer of Calvary ; and the triumphant soul mingles its acclaim with the hallelujahs of the redeemed hosts.

" Rock of Ages, cleft for me,
Let me hide myself in THEE."

(d)　　　　　　　　　　　　　　*Cuyler*

ROCK, THE SMITING OF THE

" That Rock was Christ " (1 Cor. x. 4)

The water flowing from the rock was like a river of life to the children of Israel. Who can describe the distress throughout the camp, and the appearance of the people when they were asked to approach a flinty rock instead of a fountain or a stream, to quench their thirst ? What angry countenances were there, what bitter censures and ungrateful murmurings, as Moses went up to the rock with nothing in his hand but a rod. " Where ever is he going," said they, " with that dry stick ? Does he mean to make fools of us all ? Is it not enough that he has brought us into this wilderness to die of thirst ? Will he mock us by pretending to open fountains in the solid granite ? " But see ! he lifts the rod ; he smites the rock, and lo ! it bursts into a fountain, and twelve crystal streams roll down before the people ! Who can conceive the sudden transport ! Hear the sound of joy ring through the camp, and echoing from the crags and cliffs of Horeb ! Water ! water ! A miracle ! a miracle ! Glory to the God of Israel ! Glory to His servant Moses !" It was a resurrection day to Israel, a morning light dawning upon the shadow of death. New life and joy are seen throughout the camp. The maidens run with cups and pitchers to the rock. They fill and drink, then fill again, and haste away to their tents, with water for the sick, the aged, and the little ones, joyfully exclaiming : " Drink, father ; drink, mother ; drink, children ! drink, all of you ! drink abundantly ! Plenty of water now ! Rivers flowing from the rock ! " The oxen come, the asses, the camels, the sheep, and the goats ; the feathered tribes come—the turtle-dove, the pigeon, the swallow, the sparrow, the robin, and the wren ; while the croaking raven and the fierce-eyed eagle, scenting the water from afar, mingle with them around the rock.

(e)　　　　　　　　　　　　　*Christmas Evans*

ROLL CALL

A soldier, mortally wounded, lay dying in a hospital. All was still, nor had he yet spoken. Suddenly the silence was broken, and the surgeon was startled by the dying man uttering clearly the one word, " Here ! " Going to his bedside he asked, " What do you want ? " A moment passed, then the dying soldier, recollecting, muttered, " Nothing. It was the roll-call in heaven, and I was answering my name."

(f)

ROMAN EMPIRE, DECLINE OF

With crumbling temples and a dying faith morality also took its leave, and a horrible corruption fell upon society. It would be difficult to

(g)

find a parallel in history to the whirl, the strife, the cruelty, the bloodshed, the misery, the delirium of licentiousness and debauchery which preceded and accompanied the fall of the great Republic. Unutterable crimes were shamelessly committed by the highest and the best. It was the surest sign of a decaying State, that the corruption which had spread among men played still more fatal havoc among women; and that married ladies of the highest rank publicly announced themselves as common prostitutes. Abortion and child-murder were common both to the upper and lower ranks; and to so alarming an extent did sterility prevail that an able writer had assigned it as one of the principal causes of the ruin of Rome. It had come to that at last. All the civilizing influences which could elevate humanity had for many generations been working at their highest pressure on that great and wonderful people—and that was the result. The hideous corruption of Roman society, on the day that Christ was born, was an everlasting lesson to mankind that the world could not get on without a Divine Revelation and a Divine Redeemer.

(a) *Macgregor*

ROMANS VII

There are many legal, despondent, melancholy Christians, who never pass out of the contest here described into the triumph of grace, the full freedom, the peace with God and assurance of salvation. Temperament and physical condition have much to do with this; but the main reason is of depending too much on self, and of not looking sufficiently to the Cross of Christ.

(b) *Lange*

The descent into the hell of self-knowledge, preliminary to ascension to heaven with Christ. "Alas, what am I, my Redeemer? I find my state of soul daily worse." The full appearance of the leprosy on the surface of the body is the symptom of its healing.

(c) *Luther*

The Apostle is not describing a quiescent state, but the process in which man is driven from the Law to Christ, and an unregenerate person becomes a regenerate one. . . . The most hopeful state of the unregenerate man; the least desirable state of the regenerate man.

(d) *Lange*

The existence of the conflict shows that the schoolmaster is nearer than the delivering Master.

(e) *Ibid*

ROMANS VII. AND VIII

I wish I could do as the old preacher said Paul did. He said Paul got out of the seventh chapter of Romans into the eighth.

(f) *Thomas Cooper*

ROMANS VIII. 31

" *If God be for us, who can be against us ?* "

There begins with this expression a series of victorious questions and triumphant answers, in reference to which Erasmus exclaims: " *Quid*

unquam Cicero dixit grandiloquentius? " Just such a triumphant acclamation is found in 1 Cor. xv. 54.

(g) *Lange*

ROMANS VIII

In fact, as verses 19–23 may be called a sacred elegy, so we may term 31–39 a sacred ode; that is as tender and fervent as this is bold and exalted in matter and in manner; that, an amplification of, " We do groan, being burdened" (2 Cor. v. 4); this, a commentary on, " This is the victory that overcometh the world " (1 John v. 4).

(h) *Philippi*

ROME, CHURCH OF

The language of the Scriptures is-
" Hear what the Spirit saith unto the *Churches*," not unto *the Church* (Rome).

(i) *Bp. Wordsworth*

The dogma of the Immaculate Conception: all men must believe it; and whoever shall presume to think otherwise, . . . let them know that they have *made shipwreck of the faith, and have fallen away from the unity of the faith.*

(j) *Pope Pius IX*

Dost thou suppose that thou hast excommunicated us by these words? No; rather thou hast excommunicated thyself. We have Christ on our side; we have the Apostles; we have the Apostolic and Universal Church of Christ. Thou hast cut thyself off from the Catholic Church; thou hast separated thyself from the communion of past ages; thou hast severed thyself from thy predecessors, from the Apostolic Churches, from the Apostles; thou hast severed thyself from Christ.

(k) *Bp. Wordsworth*

Heathen Rome doing the work of heathenism in persecuting the Church, was no *mystery*. But a *Christian Church*, calling herself the Mother of Christendom, and yet *drunken with the blood of saints*—this *is* a *mystery*. A *Christian Church* boasting herself to be the Bride, and yet *being* the Harlot; styling herself Zion, and being Babylon— this *is* a *mystery*. A *mystery* indeed it is, that when *she* says to all, " Come unto me," the voice from *heaven* should cry, " *Come out of her, my people.*"

(l) *Ibid*

She *deifies* the creature, and thus *defies* the Creator.

(m) *Ibid*

ROME, CHURCH OF, OUR ATTITUDE TOWARDS

Our warfare is not with *men*, but with *sins*. We love the erring, but not their *errors;* and we oppose their errors, *because* we love the erring, and because we desire their salvation, which is perilled by their errors, and because we love the truth, which is able to save their souls.

(n) *Ibid*

ROME, CHURCH OF, AND CHURCH OF CHRIST

Behold the true Catholic and Apostolic Church displayed by St. John.

She does not wear the Papal tiara, but is crowned with *twelve* stars. She does not sit upon the seven hills, but she has *twelve foundations*, and in them are *the names of the twelve Apostles of the Lamb* (Rev. xxi. 14).

(a)   *Bp. Wordsworth*

ROME, CHURCH OF, AND THE HARLOT

Wonderful to say, she founds her claims on those very grounds which identify her with the faithless Church—the Apocalyptic Babylon; as follows:

(i.) The Church of Rome boasts of *universality*. Yes; and the Harlot is seated *on many waters, which are nations, and peoples, and tongues*.

(ii.) The Church of Rome arrogates *indefectibility*. The Harlot says *that she is a queen for ever*.

(iii.) The Church of Rome vaunts temporal felicity, and claims *supremacy* over all. The Harlot has *kings at her feet*.

(iv.) The Church of Rome prides herself on *working miracles*. Yes; the minister of the Harlot makes *fire to descend from heaven*.

(v.) The Church of Rome points to the unity of her members in one creed, and to their subjection under one supreme visible head. Yes; the Harlot requires *all to receive her mark, and to drink of her cup*.

Rome's trophies are stigmas of her shame.

(b)   *Ibid*

ROME, CHURCH OF, UNITY WITH

The Holy Spirit forbids us to look for union with the *Church* of Rome. We cannot unite with her as *she is now;* and it forbids us to expect that Rome will be other than she is. It reveals the awful fact that *Babylon will be Babylon to the end*.

(c)   *Ibid*

The value of *our own Established Church* ought to be very much heightened in our esteem by considering what it is a security from,—I mean the great corruption of Christianity, Popery; which is *ever hard at work to bring us again under its yoke*. Whoever will consider Popery as it is professed at Rome, may see that it is a manifest *open usurpation of all human and divine authority*.

(d)   *Bp. Butler*

ROOM, NO, FOR CHRIST

"No room for Christ." That has been the trouble in all the ages. The world has never had room for Him. Room for all unholy aspirations, room for self-seeking, room for pride, room for Satan, room for all the concerted passions of darkness, but no room for Jesus. I go into a store. I find its shelves crowded with goods, and the counter crowded, and the floor crowded. It is crowded even to the ceiling. They have left just room enough in that store for commercial men who come to engage in great mercantile undertakings, but no room in that store for Christ. I go into a house. It is a beautiful home. I am glad to see all those beautiful surroundings.

I am glad to see that the very best looms wove those carpets, and the best manufactory turned out those musical instruments. There is no gospel against all that. But I find no Christ in that household. Room for the gloved and the robed; room for satin sandals and diamond head-gear; room for graceful step, and obsequious bow, and the dancing up and down of quick feet: room for all light, and all mirth, and all music; but—hear it, O thou Khan of Bethlehem! hear it, you angels who carolled for the shepherds in Bethlehem—no room in that house for Christ! No room in the nursery, for the children are not taught to pray; no room in the dining-hall, for no blessing is asked on the food; no room in the sleeping-apartment, for God's protection is not asked for the night. Learn that while virtue and truth often have humble lodgings, pride and worldliness find very comfortable apartments. I suppose there were a great many mean men, a great many selfish men, a great many vicious men, in Bethlehem that night, and the most of them found accommodations; but for the Lord, for the King, for the Conqueror, for the God—a stable! It is the same story in all the ages. Guilt on the throne—innocence in the cabin. Nero in the palace—Paul in the dungeon. Pharaoh in imperial garb—Joseph beslimed in the pit. Nebuchadnezzar walking in the hanging gardens of Babylon—Shadrach tossed in the fire. Ahasuerus moving in pomp—Mordecai despised at the gate; or, as the Bible has announced it, "princes afoot and beggars on horseback." But O! ye who are humbled in life, you are in good company; the company of Paul, and Baxter, and Bunyan, and Latimer, and Martin Luther, and all those who have gone through flood and fire for Christ's sake. You suffer with Him on earth. You shall be glorified with Him in heaven. Notice the order: First, the manger; then the cross; then the throne. Can you take the hardships and trials in anticipation of the rewards and the blessedness? The army gathered around Galibaldi, and he told them what wonderful fighting he wanted them to do, and then they cried out: "General, you want us to do all this, but what are you going to give us for this sacrifice and struggle?" Garibaldi said: "I shall promise you hunger, and thirst, and nakedness, and battle wounds, and death." The men stood and thought for a moment, and then they threw up their arms, crying: "We are the men! We are the men!"

(e)   *Talmage.*

ROYALTY

The most unreasonable things in the world become most reasonable, because of the unruly lives of men. What is less reasonable than to choose the eldest son of a queen to guide a State? For we do not choose as steersman of a ship that one of the passengers who is of the best family. Such a law would be ridiculous and unjust; but since men are so themselves, and ever will be, it becomes reasonable and just. For would they choose the most virtuous and able, we at once fall to blows, since each asserts that he is the most virtuous and able. Let us then affix this quality to something which cannot be disputed. This is, the king's eldest son. That is clear, and there is no dispute. Reason can do no better, for civil war is the worst of evils.

(f)   *Blaise Pascal*

RULERS OF MEN, QUALITIES FOR

The bees had lost their queen, and the whole hive sat sad and moping; they flew seldom and sluggishly out, had small heart or activity in honey-making, and their trade and sustenance fell into decay. Therefore they resolved upon a new sovereign, to rule over their community, that discipline and order might not be lost from among them. There came the wasp, flying towards them, and said: "Choose me for your queen, I am mighty and terrible; the strong horse is afraid of my sting; with it I can even defy the lion, your hereditary foe, and prick him in the snout when he approaches your store: I will watch you and defend you." This speech was pleasant to the bees; but after deeply considering it, the wisest among them answered: "Thou art stout and dreadful, but even the sting which is to guard us we fear: thou canst not be our queen." Then the humble-bee came buzzing towards them, and said: "Choose me for your queen; hear ye not that the sounding of my wings announces loftiness and dignity? Nor is a sting wanting to me, wherewith to protect you." The bees answered: "We are a peaceable and quiet people; the proud sounding of thy wings would annoy us, and disturb the continuance of our diligence: thou canst not be our queen." Then the Royal-bee requested audience: "Though I am larger and stronger than you," said she, "my strength cannot hurt or damage you; for, lo, the dangerous sting is altogether wanting. I am soft of temper, a friend of order and thrift, can guide your honey-making and further your labour." "Then," said the bees, "thou art worthy to rule over us: we obey thee; be our queen."

(a)   *Musæus, translated by Carlyle*

RULES FOR CHRISTIANS, in Eight Parts

1. That hours of the day, less or more time, for the Word and prayer, be given to God, not sparing the twelfth hour or mid-day, although it should then be a shorter time.

2. In the midst of worldly employments there should be some thoughts of sin, judgment, death, and eternity, with a word or two (at least) of ejaculatory prayer to God.

3. To beware of wandering of heart in private prayers.

4. Not to grudge, although you come from prayer with a sense of joy. Downcasting, sense of guiltiness, and hunger are often best for us.

5. That the Lord's day, from morning to night, be spent always either in private or public worship.

6. That words be observed, wandering and idle thoughts be avoided, sudden anger and desire of revenge, even of such as persecute the truth, be guarded against; for we often mix our zeal with our own wild-fire.

7. That known, discovered, and revealed sins, that are against the conscience, be avoided, as most dangerous preparatives to hardness of heart.

8. That in dealing with men, faith and truth in covenants and trafficking be regarded; that we deal with all men in sincerity; that conscience be made of idle and lying words; and that our carriage be such as that they who see it may speak honourably of our sweet Master and profession.

(b)   *Samuel Rutherford*

RULES OF LIFE

Little joys refresh us constantly like house-bread, and never bring disgust; and great ones, like sugar-bread, briefly, and then bring it.

Trifles we should let, not plague us only, but also gratify us; we should seize not their poison-bags only, but their honey-bags also: and if flies often buzz about our room, we should, like Domitian, amuse ourselves with flies, or, like a certain still living elector, feed them.

For *civic* life and its micrologies we must acquire an artificial taste; must learn to love without esteeming it; learn, far as it ranks beneath *human* life, to enjoy it like another king of this human life, as poetical, as we do the pictures of it in romances. The loftiest mortal loves and seeks the *same sort* of things with the meanest; only from higher grounds and by higher paths. Be every minute, man, a full life to thee!

Despise anxiety and wishing, the Future and the Past! If the *second-pointer* can be no road-pointer into an Eden for thy soul, the *month-pointer* will still less be so, for thou livest not from month to month, but from second to second!

Enjoy thy existence more than thy manner of existence, and let the dearest object of thy consciousness be this consciousness itself!

Make not the present a means for thy future; for this future is nothing but a coming present; and the present, which thou despisest, was once a future which thou desiredst!

Stake in no lotteries, keep at home, give and accept no pompous entertainments, travel not abroad every year!

Conceal not from thyself, by long plans, thy household goods, thy chamber, thy acquaintance!

Despise life, that thou mayest enjoy it!

Inspect the neighbourhood of thy life; every shelf, every nook of thy abode; and nestling in, quarter thyself in the farthest and most domestic winding of thy snail-house!

Look upon a capital but as a collection of villages, a village as some blind-alley of a capital; fame as the talk of neighbours at the street-door; a library as a learned conversation, joy as a second, sorrow as a minute, life as a day; and three things as all in all: GOD, CREATION, VIRTUE!

(c)   *Jean Paul Friedrich Richter*

RUTH

1. The Book of

(i.) About *family life*: Births, marriages, and deaths = a fragment of Eden.

(ii.) Its *position*—between books of wars = a green, sunny valley between rugged mountains of snow and ice.

(iii.) *Pastoral scenery*—Harvest time—reapers—gleaners, and kindly greetings, "The Lord be with thee." Just before, it was the terrible war-cry, "The sword of the Lord and Gideon," etc.

(d)

2. Naomi

Like a man who fled from a lion, and a bear met him:

(i.) The lion = *Famine*—dreadful in the East. Cf. Elijah, and the widow; the great Indian famine a few years since. Naomi, her husband, and two sons flee from famine, go to Moab, stop

(e)

ten years, then the "Bear" met her—her husband and two sons die there, and she had to return alone.

(ii.) Naomi: agreeable and loving disposition; her name indicates " sweetness and pleasantness," and she had a character corresponding to it.

And Ruth, her heathen daughter-in-law, was fond of her, and left her own people to be with her. "Thy God shall be my God," etc. Therefore Naomi lived her religion, and was a good witness for her God in a heathen land.

(a)

Illustrations

1. A person called on a neighbour complaining that his servants would not stay with him; and was told by the other, that he had a door which creaked, "no one liked to open it, till I oiled it, and now it is used every day. You, my friend, must oil yourself a little. When your servants do well, praise them; when they make mistakes, don't grumble at them."

2. A child asked, " Do all people go to heaven when they die? " was asked, " Why do you ask? "

"Because," replied she, " I don't want to go if Grandmamma goes."

Naomi was not one of such, but drew others to her through kindness.

(b)

3. Ruth: a beautiful character

(i.) *Her history*: she had been well off and comfortable. Now she returned with Naomi, and determines to work for their support. She goes into the fields to glean.

(ii.) *Her humility*: an example, not "too well-bred to work with their hands." No murmuring when reverses came. Ruth bends to the wind when it blows—knows that an empty sack cannot stand upright, acknowledges that God has done it.

(iii.) *Her reward*: God honours those that honour Him; He takes Ruth by the hand and leads her blindfold to the field of Boaz. No accident. She became Boaz's wife—an ancestor of David, and of David's greatest Son. " Whoso humbleth himself shall be exalted."

(c)

S

SABBATH

The Sabbath is the festival of **Creation, Redemption,** and **Pentecost.**

Historically considered

1. The Creation Sabbath ; or, the Weekly Festival of Creation :
   (i.) Paradisiacal ;
   (ii.) Patriarchal.

2. The Theocratic Sabbath ; or, the Weekly Festival of the Exodus (Redemption) :
   (i.) Mosaic ;
   (ii.) Pharisaic ;
   (iii.) Jesus and the Pharisaic Sabbath.

3. The Christian " Lord's Day " ; or, the Weekly Festival of
   (i.) The Resurrection ; and,
   (ii.) The Descent of the Holy Ghost.

4. The Observance and Perpetuity of the Sabbath.

5. " Remember the Sabbath Day."
This precept is cumulative.
Remember :
   (i.) Thine Origin—created by God in His image.
   (ii.) Thy Redemption by the Son of God—" Do this in remembrance of Me."
   (iii.) Thy Destiny, as the Temple of the Holy Ghost.
   (iv.) Remember the Lord's Day to keep it holy, and as a day of meditation on thine origin and destiny.
   (v.) Remember to be in the spirit on the Lord's Day, free from the bondage of the letter, and of the commandment to do what is distasteful to the natural man.
   (vi.) This word, " Remember," is an evidence that in the lapse of time men had forgotten and neglected the Sabbath, and had consequently fallen into idolatrous worship—Nature worship. This is a tendency of the present time. When men cease to "remember the Sabbath," it may be fearlessly asserted that they have ceased to believe in their Creation, Redemption, and Hope of Glory, of which it is the continual witness.

6. The Abrogation of the Sabbath
What is abrogated, where there is continual fulfilment ?
   (i.) " The Creation-Sabbath," was " made for man." Man needs it still, needs to remember his Creator more and more.
   (ii.) The Theocratic Sabbath = " My Sabbaths," for a continual remembrance of the great fact of Redemption.
   (iii.) The Lord's Day = " The day which the Lord hath made, we will rejoice and be glad in it."
There is no need of abrogation ; man is rather called upon to observe the day more and more, for a three-fold reason, instead of one or two ; and so long as man is what he is, inclined to forget his origin and destiny, and to call everything in question, he will need to " Remember the Sabbath day."
   (*a*)

THE CREATION SABBATH ; or, the Weekly Festival of the Creation

I. PARADISIACAL

1. Is Gen. ii. 2, 3, anticipatory ?
Gen. ii. 3 is an integral part of the history of Creation. The oldest part of the Pentateuch, viz., the Elohistic ; and the groundwork of Moses' narrative.
   (*b*)   *Speaker's Commentary*

Deut. v. 12–15
The Bondage in Egypt and the deliverance from it are not assigned as *grounds* for the institution of the Sabbath, *which is of far older date* (Gen. ii. 3) ; but rather as suggesting motives for the religious observance of that institution.
   (*c*)   *Ibid*

It is certain that the observance of a weekly *Day of Rest* is written in God's physical and social laws for man, as plainly as in the Decalogue. *Nor can we escape the conclusion that the Fourth Commandment is but a reminder of a previous institution,* so that those who contend that the whole Mosaic Law is abrogated, as a guide to Christian life, do not escape this enactment.
   (*d*)   *Lange's Commentary*

The consecration of the Sabbath was coeval with the Creation.
   (*e*)   *Smith's Bib. Dict*

It belongs to our relation to God, to set apart a portion of our time for His service ; but it is difficult for conscience to determine what it should be, therefore *God has prescribed it:* and the ground of the observance remains the same, whether the remembrance of God's resting or some other be assigned as the more immediate cause.
   (*f*)   *Cecil*

2. In the Beginning
The law of Marriage and the law of the Sabbath were instituted before man fell. The Sabbath was at first consecrated by the fact that it closed the work of Creation.
   (*g*)   *Angus*

The work of Creation is an image and foreshadowing of all the ways of God, clear to the end.
   (*h*)   *Berlenburger Bible*

Gen. i. and ii
Whence do these chapters come ? I do not know. There they stand, and ever continue to stand, however much it has been sought to explain them away ; and there, doubtless, they will remain until the end of the world, until the conclusion of God's kingdom on earth joins hands with the beginning, and the light of the beginning can again be recognised in the light of the end, and the light of the end in the light of the beginning, that God may be all in all.
   (*i*)   *J. G. Staib (Oehler)*

The Creation Sabbath—*continued*

3. Foundation of the Sabbath

The Divine Creative Power is not satisfied till it reaches its ultimate end in the creation of man. Not till God has placed His image over against Him, does He rest content from creation. The Creation-Sabbath stands as a boundary between the Creation and the history of the dealings between God and man.

(a)   *Oehler*

All the works of God tend towards *rest*.

(b)   *Berlenburger Bible*

"God rested" must not be understood too literally. Creation goes on from day to day: Nature is God at work.

(c)   *F. W. Robertson*

Rest and labour are correlates: the one supposeth the other. Many important truths lie deep and secret in the Scripture, and stand in need of a very diligent search and hard digging in their investigation, and for their finding out.

(d)   *J. Owen*

Nothing can be plainer, words cannot be clearer that the Old Testament seventh day, or last of the week, was to be set apart and sanctified as a day of *rest*, in commemoration of God's resting from the work of Creation. The distinguishing feature of the Sabbath is *rest*. The word means *rest*. The event to be commemorated was *rest*. The reason for selecting the seventh day was because the Creator *rested* on that day. The chief method prescribed for sanctifying it, was *rest*. *Rest* was the great distinction of the day.

(e)   *Channing*

Divine labour terminates in happy rest; not till the Creator rests satisfied in the contemplation of His works is His Creation itself complete.

(f)   *Oehler*

As a human artificer completes his work just when he has brought it up to his ideal and ceases to work upon it, so, in an infinitely higher sense, God completed the creation of the world with all its inhabitants by ceasing to produce anything new, and entering into the rest of His all-sufficient eternal Being, from which He had come forth, as it were, at and in the Creation of a world distinct from His own essence. Hence ceasing to create is called *resting* (Exod. xx. 11).

(g)   *Keil*

The rest was complete, and had its own reality, in the reality of the work of Creation, in contrast with which the preservation of the world, when once created, had the appearance of rest, though really a continuous Creation.

(h)   *Ziegler*

4. Positive Element of

The Sabbath consisted negatively in the cessation of the work of creation, and positively in the blessing and sanctifying of the seventh day. . . . The rest of the Creator was His self-satisfaction in the now united and harmonious whole; but this self-satisfaction of God in His creation, which we call His pleasure in His work, was also *a spiritual power*, which streamed forth as a blessing upon the creation itself, bringing it into the blessedness of the rest of God and filling it with His peace. This constitutes the *positive* element in the completion which God gave to the work of creation, by blessing and sanctifying the seventh day. . . . The Divine act of blessing was a real communication of powers of salvation, grace, and peace; and sanctifying was not merely declaring holy, but communicating the attribute of holiness, " placing in a living relation to God, the Holy One, raising to a participation in the pure clear light of the holiness of God."

(i)   *Keil*

Although a parallel is drawn, between the creation of the world by God in six days, and resting upon the seventh, on the one hand, and the labour of man for six days and his resting on the seventh on the other; the reason for the keeping of the Sabbath is not to be found in this parallel, but in the fact that God blessed the seventh day and hallowed it, because He rested on it. The significance of the Sabbath, therefore, is to be found in God's blessing and sanctifying the seventh day of the week at the Creation, *i.e.*, in the fact, that after the work of creation was finished, on the seventh day, God blessed and hallowed the created world, filling it with the powers of peace and good belonging to His own blessed rest, and raising it to a participation in the pure light of His holy nature.

(j)   *Ibid*

The Sabbath is not an arbitrary appointment of no meaning and significance.

(k)   *Bp. Horsley*

The rest of the people of God is like the rest of God Himself, a *Sabbatism*.

(l)   *Lange*

The Sabbath is a weekly commemoration of the rest of God after the work of making the world. Israel was the people to whom God revealed the great mystery of *Creation ;* that master truth by which alone human thought is saved in the long run from what in philosophy is Pantheism, and what in human practice is the sin of confounding God with His works. It brought before the mind the ineffable Majesty of the Great Creator.

(m)   *Liddon*

God *rests*. Creation *rests*. The morning stars begin their song, and the sons of God their shout. What *rest* means for Him who " fainteth not, neither is weary," we cannot say. It means more than mere cessation from work. God's *rest* must be as real a thing as His joy and His love ; something corresponding to what *rest* is in us. The day of *rest* He blesses ; and blessing with Him is no mere word. It must be a day fraught with blessing to us who rest likewise. More blessing flows out on that day. There are deeper things in this than we think. We shall one day learn that neither earth nor man could have done without this day of blessing. Invisible blessing flows out from it even to those who are profaning it. God sanctifies it ; sets a fence round it ; makes it a holy thing. He has done this because He rested.

(n)   *Horatius Bonar*

The Creation Sabbath—*continued*

5. Prophetical and Typical Import of the Sabbath

(i.) *The Number Seven.*

"*If we count the ages as days, i.e., the periods of Scripture, the Sabbath will be found to be the seventh :*

(1.) The 1st age = the 1st day = Adam to Noah ;

(2.) The 2nd age = the 2nd day = Deluge to Abraham, equalling the 1st, not in length of time, but in the number of generations, *i.e.*, ten in each ;

(3.) The 3rd age = the 3rd day = Abraham to David ;

(4.) The 4th age = the 4th day = David to the Captivity ;

(5.) The 5th age = the 5th day = Captivity to Christ.

Compare Matt. 1, where the last three periods are represented as having had 14 generations in each. Thus there are five completed days of history.

(6.) The 6th age = the 6th day = that now current, and its generations " the Father had put in His own power."

(7.) After this, the 7th period, which will be our Sabbath, which again will close with the *Lord's Day* of eternal repose.

(a)   *Augustine's City of God*

(ii.) *The Typical Meaning*

There shall be the great Sabbath which has no evening, which God celebrated among His first works, as it is written, " And God rested on the seventh day from all His works which He had made," etc. For we shall ourselves be the seventh day, when we shall be filled and replenished with God's blessing and sanctification. There shall we know that He is that which we aspired to be when we fell away from Him, and listened to the voice of the seducer.

(b)   *Augustine*

Ps. xcii. = For the Sabbath day :
We mean the Sabbath which puts a stop to sin reigning in the world—the seventh day of the world ; upon which, as *post-Sabbatic*, follows the future world.

(c)   *Eli Rabba*

We look for that future Sabbath of Sabbaths. The new Creation will have no end, but be manifested in the enjoyment of a perpetual feast.

(d)   *Athanasius*

The final Sabbath will not therefore be realized till time is swallowed up of eternity, and mortality of life. It will be the eternal conclusion of the week of time, as seven is the numeric symbol of perfection and rest.

(e)   *Delitzsch*

Man's daily work in this world, with all its labours, conflicts, and sorrows, corresponds to the six days' work of God. From this, the work imposed on him here, he rests in God. To share in this his Sabbath-rest with God, is the hope set before the Church from the beginning. The Church of the New Testament has still the same goal before her ; and the way to attain it is thrown open in the Gospel.

(f)   *Ibid*

A day entirely Sabbath will close the world's work. As the seventh year furnishes a festal time of a year's duration for a period of seven years, so the world enjoys, for a period of 7000 years, a festal season of 1000 years (Rev. xx.).

But this final temporal millennium is not the final Sabbath, although the seventh day of the Church. The blessed eternity is the *eighth ;* and this *octave* of blissful eternity is the final Sabbath, which is realized when time shall be no more.

(g)   *Lange*

There is a Rest of God existing from the close of the Creation, and reaching on to eternity. Participation in this Rest is appointed, and the entrance is actually secured to the people of God . . . This Rest is σαββατισμός = a Sabbath festal celebration ; in reference to that Rest of God after the creation of the world, which lay at the basis of the institution of the Sabbath, as the rest of humanity. This is why the Rest of Heb. iv. is called a Sabbatism.

(h)   *Ibid*

We, the Church of believers, the author (of Heb. iv.) would say, are as such travelling on the way to the rest which God has established since the foundation of the world, but which the Israelites did not attain.

(i)   *Ibid*

There is from the commencement of things a *Rest of God*, into which men could and were to enter, but into which the Israelites have not entered. . . . Men are excluded by unbelief (disobedience).

(j)   *Ibid*

He that thinks it too much to keep a short Sabbath here, shall never be thought worthy to celebrate the eternal Sabbath hereafter.

(k)   *Anon*

The Sabbath was a foretaste of that time when there will be no more toilsome fatigue. That life = the true keeping of the Sabbath (σαββατισμός), into which our Saviour entered as our Forerunner, when He ceased from His works on earth, as God did from His on the seventh day (Heb. iv. 9, 10).

(l)   *Speaker's Commentary*

[Heb. iv

To-day, well-improved, terminates in *rest*.

Rest is that which, once obtained, is not again lost.

Foretaste in this life is not denied us; full *rest* is. All foretastes of *rest* are evidently small, when compared with things above.

A *rest* remains to us. This proposition proved (3–11).

(i.) Rest is mentioned in Psalm quoted ; yet there it does not signify—

(ii.) The *rest* of God from creation ; for this was before the time of Moses. Therefore another *rest* was to be expected *in* the time of Moses, of which they who had heard evidently came short.

(iii.) Neither does that *rest* which Joshua gave them support the title to this *rest ;* for the Psalmist speaks of it as still to be attained to.

(iv.) Therefore He sung of a *rest* more recent than all these, viz., a *rest* which would be enjoyed in heaven.

(m)   *Bengel*

The Creation Sabbath—*continued*

(iii.) *No evening*

It is remarkable that Moses has mentioned the end of the six days, but not of the seventh.

There will be no elementary Sabbath in heaven, because earthly labour will have passed away; but the *rest* will be *perpetual*.

Labour precedes rest; and that doubtless would have been the case, even in Paradise.

The work and rest of God are that archetype to which we ought to be conformed.

(a)   *Bengel*

A benefit from the appointment of the Sabbath is, that attention is necessarily directed to the eternal Sabbath, which awaits us at the expiration of our appointed week of labour. Each returning Sabbath—of bodily rest and spiritual refreshment—must be an earnest and foretaste of heaven itself. Nehemiah (ix. 14) accounts the Sabbath among the richest benefits which God had conferred on His people.

(b)   *Chas. Simeon*

The work of creation ceases for ever upon earth. The night falls, and there dawns yet another morrow—the morrow of God's rest—that Divine Sabbath in which there is no more creative labour, and which, " blessed and sanctified" beyond all the days that had gone before, has its special object, the moral elevation and final redemption of man. And over *it* no evening is represented in the record as falling, for its special work is not yet complete.

(c)   *Hugh Miller*

All creatures look forward to a time when all restlessness shall give place to the blessed rest of the perfect consummation. To this rest the resting of God ($\dot{\eta}$ $\kappa\alpha\tau\dot{\alpha}\pi\alpha\upsilon\sigma\iota\varsigma$) points forward; and to this rest, this divine $\sigma\alpha\beta\beta\alpha\tau\iota\sigma\mu\dot{o}\varsigma$ (Heb. iv. 9), shall the whole world, especially man, the head of the earthly creation, eventually come. For this God ended His work by blessing and sanctifying the day when the whole creation was complete. In connection with Heb. iv. some of the fathers have called attention to the fact, that the account of the seventh day is not summed up, like the others, with the formula, " Evening was and morning was;" thus, *e.g.*, *Augustine* writes at the close of his "Confessions: " *Dies septimus sine vespera est, nec habet occasum, quia sanctificasti eum ad permansionem sempiternam.* But true as it is that the Sabbath of God has no evening, and that the $\sigma\alpha\beta\beta\alpha\tau\iota\sigma\mu\dot{o}\varsigma$, to which the creature is to attain at the end of his course, will be bounded by no evening, but last for ever; we must not, without further ground, introduce *this true and profound idea* into the seventh creation-day. (This would require that the six creation-days=long periods, to which *Keil* objects.) . . . We must conclude, therefore, that on the seventh *day*, on which God rested, the world also, with all its inhabitants, attained to the sacred rest of God; and that the $\kappa\alpha\tau\dot{\alpha}\pi\alpha\upsilon\sigma\iota\varsigma$ and $\sigma\alpha\beta\beta\alpha\tau\iota\sigma\mu\dot{o}\varsigma$ of God were made a rest and Sabbatic *festival* for His creatures, especially for man; and that this day of rest of the new created world, which the forefathers of our rest observed in *paradise*, as long as they continued in a state of innocence and lived in blessed peace with their God and Creator, was *the beginning and type of the rest to which the creation*

afterwards received a promise that it should once more be restored through redemption, at its final consummation.

(d)   *Keil*

(iv.) *The Sabbath Postponed*

It belongs to the idea of the Sabbath, that the whole course of human history is not to run on in dreary endlessness. That its events are to have a positive termination,—are to find a completion in a harmonious and God-given order,—is already guaranteed by the Sabbath of creation, and prefigured by the Sabbatical seasons. The Divine rest of the seventh day of creation, *which has no evening*, hovers over the world's progress, that it may at last absorb it into itself. It is upon the very fact that the rest *of God*, the $\kappa\alpha\tau\dot{\alpha}\pi\alpha\upsilon\sigma\iota\varsigma$ $\Theta\epsilon o\hat{\upsilon}$, is also to be a rest *for man*, and that God has declared this by the institution of the Sabbath, that Heb. iv. founds a proof for the proposition : $\ddot{\alpha}\rho\alpha$ $\dot{\alpha}\pi o\lambda\epsilon\dot{\iota}\pi\epsilon\tau\alpha\iota$ $\sigma\alpha\beta\beta\alpha\tau\iota\sigma\mu\dot{o}\varsigma$ $\tau\hat{\omega}$ $\lambda\alpha\hat{\omega}$ $\tau o\hat{\upsilon}$ $\Theta\epsilon o\hat{\upsilon}$ (9).

This idea of the Sabbath finds its formal expression in the *number seven*, this number frequently appearing in natural occurrences as $\dot{\alpha}\rho\iota\theta\mu\dot{o}\varsigma$ $\tau\epsilon\lambda\epsilon\sigma\phi\dot{o}\rho o\varsigma$ and $\dot{\alpha}\pi o\kappa\alpha\tau\alpha\sigma\tau\alpha\tau\iota\kappa\dot{o}\varsigma$, as Philo calls it. It thus became the sign-manual of the perfection in which the progress of the world was, according to Divine charter, to result, and a special pledge of the perfection of the kingdom of God.

(e)   *Oehler*

Three is the signature of Godhead ; four, that of the world; seven, as the number in which three and four meet and combine in one number, *the signature of the connection of God and the world.*

(f)   *Bähr*

6. Universality of the Sabbath

All mankind are interested in the sanctification of the Sabbath.

(g)   *Speaker's Commentary*

In its very nature the Sabbath appears intended for the whole human race. *As a religious institution designed to keep in remembrance the God who created the world, it belongs equally to all men.* Since all are the creatures of the same God (" all His offspring," Acts xvii. 29), and all prone to forget every religious truth which is not *continually* and *regularly* forced upon their attention. As a day of rest, if needed at all (and it is generally granted that such rest is necessary), it is needed by every one who wears the human body. *Its appointment is coeval with the creation of man, and long before the giving of the Jewish Law.* These facts seem to prove that it was intended to be *perpetual;* which appears also to be indicated by those words of Christ (Mark ii. 27), " The Sabbath was made for man," *i.e.*, *not for the Jews only*, but for the benefit of the whole human race.

(h)   *Penny Cyclopædia, Art. Sabbath*

The rule was given to Adam, and was in consequence binding, not upon a chosen few, but upon all his descendants. It does not appear likely that any one particular day was designated, but merely that a general rule was laid down that one day in seven should be kept. For it would have been impossible for men, scattered as they soon were,

(i)

The Creation Sabbath—*continued*

over the face of the earth, to observe the *same* day, since the beginning of every day must have been eighteen hours later in some parts of the world than in Eden or Palestine. A law for a single nation may be *particular ;* but a law for all mankind must be *general :* the principle must be laid down and enforced, the particulars must depend upon circumstances.

(*a*) *Hook*

One day of rest in seven was divinely instituted at the Creation, in behalf of natural humanity. One does not see why the believer should not require this periodical rest as well as the unregenerate man. "*The Sabbath was made for man.*" So long as the Christian man preserves his earthly nature, this saying applies to him, and should not turn to his detriment, but to the profit of his spiritual life. The keeping of the Sabbath, thus understood, has nothing to do with Sabbath observance which divides life into two parts, one holy and the other profane, which St. Paul excludes (Col. ii.).

(*b*) *Godet*

[Mark ii. 27, 28

God did not create man for the greater glory of the Sabbath, but He ordained the Sabbath for the greater welfare of man. Consequently, whenever the welfare of man and the rest of the Sabbath happen to clash, the Sabbath must yield.

(*c*) *Ibid*

The Sabbath was made *for man i.e.,* for his temporal and eternal benefit. . . . This was its purpose when God instituted it, together with the marriage relation, in the state of man's innocence; and this Christ has restored, as He restored the marriage relation to its original purity. Commentators pass too slightly over this point; and some of them misconstrue Christ's and Paul's opposition to the Jewish Sabbatarianism of that age into a violation or abrogation of the Fourth Commandment.

(*d*) *Lange*

7. Christ as "Lord of the Sabbath :"

(i.) *As Creator :*

All that belongs to God belongs to Christ (Heb. i. 3).

(*e*) *Ibid*

He is Lord over all that pertains to the Father. Creator of this universe of worlds (πάντα, 17) is God. Mediator of that creation is the Son. The Son is made the heir of all, that all owes its origin to Him.

(*f*) *Delitzsch*

He [Christ] is thus placed out of the category of the created.

It is here indicated that the accomplishment of the creation rests in Him. (All things = the totality of things, the existing universe), Col. i. 16.

(*g*) *Lange*

He is the end of creation, containing the reason in Himself, why creation is at all, and why it is as it is.

(*h*) *Alford*

His Creatorship excludes creatureship in Him, and the identity of the Creator and Redeemer is so affirmed, that He who became man is placed more under the idea of "God" than the idea of "man," Hence Theodoret: "not as having Creation for a sister, but as begotten before all worlds."

(*i*) *Lange*

(ii.) *As Son of God* (Luke vi.) :

καί (even) of the Sabbath-day: that peculiar property of Jehovah.

(*j*) *Godet*

(iii.) *As one greater than the Sabbath :*

As the Sabbath must give way before the Temple service, so must Sabbath and Temple-service, both give way before something greater, viz ; the Son of man. If the day of rest and glorifying God must yield even to the rational inhabitant of earth, how much more might the Son of Man, the Redeemer and the Ideal of mankind, have dominion over the Sabbath-service. The true Sabbath-breakers were those who would sacrifice man to the Sabbath.

(*k*) *Lange*

The Son of Man, inasmuch as He is the Head of the race, has a right to dispose of this institution. He is raised above it, as a means of education. He may therefore modify, or abolish it altogether, if He thinks fit.

(*l*) *Godet*

(iv.) *As Himself the Sabbath :*

The emphasis rests on the word "*Lord,*" which accordingly is placed first in the original (Κύριος γάρ, etc) the γάρ=that the disciples were blameless. The Son of man is *Lord of the Sabbath,* as being Himself the *Divine Rest* and the *Divine Celebration,* He is both the principle and the object of the Sabbath ; He rests in God, and God in Him : hence He is the Mediator of proper Sabbath-observance, and the interpreter of the Sabbath law.

(*m*) *Lange*

(v.) *As Prophet :*

"I think Him a *Prophet,*" answered the man who had been healed (John ix. 17). But it would never do to admit this, for even the Rabbis owned that a prophet might dispense with the laws of the Sabbath.

(*n*) *C. Geikie*

(vi.) *As Messiah :*

Even the Jews admitted that the authority of the *Messiah* was greater than that of the laws of the Sabbath.

(*o*) *Berthold*

(vii.) *As the Son of Man :*

The Son of Man, and not merely as man ; nor the Messiah in the official sense, but the Son of Man *in His inviolable holiness,* and in His mysterious dignity (intimated in Daniel) as the Holy Child and Head of Humanity appearing in the name of God. *Lord* over the Sabbath? *i.e.,* administrating and ruling over it in its New Testament fulfilment and freedom.

(*p*) *Lange and Meyer*

The Creation Sabbath—*continued*

The Sabbath among the Jews was the "Holy of Holies," because it represented Christ. The six days signified His labours and combats with the hells, and the seventh His victory over them, and of the rest He thereby attained.

    (*a*)　　　　　　　　　*Swedenborg*

Man's regeneration is successive. It proceeds from the internal to the external man. A combat ensues between the internal and the external, and whichever conquers has dominion over the other. This is signified by, and coincides with, the *labours* and combats of the Lord against the hells (His temptation), and with His victory over them, and the *rest* ("peace"—"*my peace*") into which He then entered.

    (*b*)　　　　　　　　　*Ibid*

8. The true Idea of the Sabbath, is to Remind Man of his Origin and Destiny

Man, like God, is to work and rest; thus human life is to be a copy of the Divine life.

    (*c*)　　　　　　　　　*Oehler*

Works of moral activity: the essential characteristic of these ἔργα (Heb. iv.), from which man rests in God, consists in conflicts with moral evil.

    (*d*)　　　　　　　　　*Tholuck*

The creation and destination of man to be in God's image, contains the ground of the fact, that man can find rest only in God.

    (*e*)　　　　　　　　　*Lange*

The reason of the seventh day :-
The soul of man was to form itself on the model of the Spirit of God.

    (*f*)　　　　　　　*F. W. Robertson*

The work of Redemption may be the work of God's Sabbath day. . . . Previous to man's appearance on the earth, each succeeding elevation in the long upward march had been a result of creation. The creative fiat went forth, and dead matter came into existence. The creative fiat went forth, and plants, with the lower animal forms, came into existence. The creative fiat went forth, and the oviparous animals,—birds and reptiles,—came into existence. The creative fiat went forth, and the mammiferous animals,—cattle and beasts of the earth,—came into existence. And, finally, last in the series, the creative fiat went forth, and responsible, immortal man, came into existence. But the course of progress still goes on. But man's responsibility, his instincts respecting an eternal future, forbid that his elevation should be, as in other instances, a work of creation. To create would be to supersede. God's work of elevation *now* is the work of fitting peccable man for a perfect, impeccable future state. *God's seventh day's work is the work of Redemption. And, read in this light, the institution of the Sabbath is found to yield a meaning of peculiar breadth and emphasis. It says, God rests on His Sabbath day from creative labours, in order that by His Sabbath-day's work He may save you. Rest ye also on your Sabbaths, that you may co-operate with Him in this great work.* . . . Let God be your pattern and example. Labour in your tem-poral employments in the proportions in which He laboured ; but, in order that you may enjoy an eternal future with Him, rest also in the proportions in which He rests.

    (*g*)　　　　　　　　　*Hugh Miller*

The appointment of the *Sabbath*, combined as it is with the *Creation* itself, *is of the highest ethical importance.*

    (*h*)　　　　　　　　　*Sartorius*

9. Remember now thy Creator

I believe that God made me, etc., from which faith directly results the moral obligation, for all this I ought to thank and praise Him, to serve and obey Him.

    (*i*)　　　　　　　　　*Luther*

10. Perpetuity and Import

Every Sabbath is a beckoning to the *Rest* of God, and an attestation of it.

    (*j*)　　　　　　　　*Fricke (Lange)*

The Sabbath foreshadows things: modifications of the form, and reason for the institution would come, *but not its abolition.* It will cease only when man attains the perfect stature of the Son of man. The Sabbath will retain a certain measure of its force as long as this earthly economy endures.

    (*k*)

THE CREATION SABBATH

II. Patriarchal

1. From the Fall to the Deluge

(i.) *Its Observance Questioned*

There is not a single tenable argument to be adduced in favour of the pre-Mosaic existence of the Sabbath ! . . . That it was instituted immediately after the Creation cannot be maintained " ! . . . The Sabbath could not have been destined to come into operation, except in connection with a whole Divine institution !

    (*l*)　　　　　　　　*Hengstenberg*

[It is, perhaps, a sufficient answer to this, to say with St. Paul, that God left men to see whether they would live their lives according to the law written in their consciences. It was when they failed in following that rule, that He next wrote His law, which was from the beginning, on tables of stone.]

We must remember, that in the whole pre-Mosaic history no trace at all is to be found of the celebration of the Sabbath ; that (Exod. xvi. 22-30) God hallows it as a completely new institution !

    (*m*)　　　　　　　　　*Ibid*

We incline to the belief that there are appearances of the institution of the Sabbath at the beginning of the human race—faint and few. We attach importance to this view because nature and reason favour the supposition of a time having been set apart from the first ; yet we see no proofs of its perpetuity in this.

    (*n*)　　　　　　　　　*Channing*

The Creation Sabbath—*continued*

(ii.) *That it was Observed*

Paradise was always before the eyes of the Antediluvians, up to the time of the Flood.

(a)   *Keil*

Incessant work makes man dull and lifeless, and destroys susceptibility for salvation.

(b)   *Hengstenberg*

[And yet Hengstenberg can see no reason for Sabbath observance when, as we have shown, men most needed it, for the reason here stated.]

"The Sabbath was to be a sacred pause in the ordinary labour by which man earns his bread ; the curse was to be suspended for one day ; and having spent that day in joyful remembrance of God's mercies, man had a fresh start in his course of labour."

(c)   *Smith's Bib. Dict*

(iii.) *Enoch, the Seventh from Adam* (Jude 14)

I, as the seventh, am born in the first week, while judgment and justice were delayed.

(d)   *Book of Enoch*, xciii. 3

In the seventh week there shall arise an apostate generation (ch. lx. 8).

(e)   *Ibid*

The epithet "the seventh" cannot be without meaning—a secret, mystical meaning.

(f)   *Lange*

Every seventh is the most esteemed.

(g)   *Bengel*

The seventh from Adam is personally a type of the sanctified of the seventh age of the world (of the seventh millennium, of the great earth-Sabbath), therefore he (Enoch) prophesies for this time.

(h)   *Stier*

The number seven was esteemed in the ancient world as an important signature, pointing to the sacred and mystery. The fact that after sin and death had freely exerted their unhappy power during the first six generations, in the seventh generation mankind appeared in the person of one man (who had led a godly life, and was taken by God to God without seeing death) in a state of high completeness and blessed freedom from death, has a kind of prophetic-symbolical significance, and intimates that mankind in general, after having completed its course and fought its battle under the oppression of sin and death through six long world-periods, shall appear in the seventh world-period in a state of higher completeness, in a more Divine life and freedom from death. The seventh world-period is the kingdom of God on earth.

(i)   *Menken*

The number seven is sacred above all : Enoch is seventh from Adam, and walks with God ; Moses is seventh from Abraham ; Phineas is seventh from Jacob our father, as Enoch was seventh from Adam. And they correspond to the seventh day, which is the Sabbath, the day of rest. Every seventh age is in the highest esteem.

(j)   *Wetstein, citing Rabbinical writings*

In patriarchial times we meet with no trace of the Sabbath ; and accordingly find the Fathers, when opposing Judaism, emphatically insisting that the just before Moses obtained God's approbation although they did not keep the rest of the Sabbath.

(k)   *Justin Martyr, Eusebius, Irenæus, Oehler*

(iv.) *The Idea of the Sabbath*

The idea of the Sabbath remained a universal law for man from the beginning, and that the faithful ever regarded it—God's-day ; creation-day ; man's-day—which held out a hope to man of a Paradise to be regained. There was this difference—the Jew ever looked onward for a good time to come, whereas the tendency of the first patriarchs—more especially when Eden was as yet a sacred spot on the earth—was to look back to it as the good old time.

(l)

2. From Noah to the Dispersion of Mankind

In Deut. iv. 19, the Israelites are cautioned against the worship of the heavenly bodies, because God hath allotted them (the heavenly bodies) to all the nations under heaven ; *i.e.* permitted them to choose these as the objects of their worship. In other words, God gave them up to it from the very first stage of their apostasy from Him.

There is evidence of a weekly festival (Sabbath or Sun-day), accordingly as men were faithful to God or apostate, during the time of which we write.

A careful survey of the following Notes will be found interesting and perhaps conclusive, if not positive evidence of this statement.

(m)

(i.) *The Antiquity of " the Week "* (Gen. viii. 10, 12).

The seven days constituted the week established at the Creation, and God had already conformed to it in arranging their entrance into the ark (Gen. vii. 4, 10).

(n)   *Keil*

The sacredness of the number seven was very widely diffused in antiquity ; but this is explained by its frequent and significant occurrence in natural events, especially in the planetary system of the ancients and the course of the moon.— Philo, Plutarch, etc.

(o)   *Oehler*

The cycle of the week reaches back to pre-Mosaic times.

(p)   *Hengstenberg*

It seems to have been an ancient property of the Semitic nations, and probably was transferred from them to others.

(q)   *Oehler*

The Creation Sabbath—*continued*

The Arabs, clothed in black, sacrificed an ox to Saturn on his day, in an hexagonal black temple.

[Compare this with *The Temple of the Seven Planets*, below.]

(*a*)

The combination of the Jewish Sabbath with the day of Saturn, though of course not Scriptural, is peculiar, and as follows :
The seven planets of the ancients and the seven days of the week.
Saturn is the first, and the succession arose thus :
Order of planets = Saturn, Jupiter, Mars, the Sun, Venus, Mercury, the Moon.
Every hour of the day dedicated to a planet.
If 1st hour of 1st day was sacred to Saturn, so would be the 8th, 15th, and 22nd ; the 23rd would fall to Jupiter, 24th to Mars ; the 1st hour of next day to the Sun ; hence Sunday followed Saturday. The 1st hour of Sunday=sacred to the Sun, the 23rd=to Venus, 24th to Mercury, therefore the 1st of the 3rd day fell to the Moon ; hence Monday succeeds Sunday. On Monday, 23rd hour = Saturn, 24th to Jupiter, and the 1st of the next day=Mars ; hence Mars-day, our Tuesday, succeeds Monday, etc.

(*b*) *Oehler*

No Roman or Grecian author knows anything of any heathen celebration of the seventh day of the week . . . they regarded it as specifically Jewish, a subject for scorn ; Seneca=" Septimam fere partem ætatis perdere."

(*c*) *Dio Cassius*

[This argues that these highly-civilized heathen nations had done without the Sabbath—had gone their own way—and that they ought to be compared with a Sabbath-keeping nation for a moral. Their remote ancestors had the Sabbath even as others.]

It is at all events remarkable that a certain importance of the number seven gleams through in one way or another in each of the more developed religions of antiquity.

(*d*) *Oehler*

(ii.) *Birs Nimrud*

The original form of the whole structure—known to the Greeks as the Temple of Belus—was that of seven square towers, rising one above the other, like gigantic steps ; each smaller than the one below it, and consecrated respectively to the seven planetary gods, to whom they formed distinct temples. Beginning with that of Saturn at the bottom, that of Venus came next ; then, one over the other, those of Jupiter, Mercury, Mars, the Moon, and the Sun ; the colours assigned to the particular deity—black, white, orange, blue, scarlet, silver, and gold—distinguishing the respective storeys . . .
. . . Two copies of an inscription record his (Nebuchadnezzar) having repaired and completed " the Temple of the Seven Lights, or Planets."
It had hitherto remained unfinished from immemorial antiquity—a fact strikingly corroborative of the narrative of Genesis.

Whether these gigantic erections belong to the period to which Gen. xi. refers, is of course a question, but they are at least as old as the earliest records of profane history.

(*e*) *Geikie*

Birs Nimrud is certainly " the Tower of Babel."

(*f*) *Schrader*

M. Oppert has collected all the notices of Birs Nimrud, and of the Tomb of Belus, from the classics, and also all the references to them in the cuneiform inscriptions, and seems to not a few to have proved beyond question that Birs Nimrud is indeed the Tower of Babel.
See "*La Bible et les Découvertes Modernes*," par *L'Abbé Vigouroux*, vol. i. p. 297, *quoted by Geikie*.

(*g*)

3. From the Dispersion of Mankind to the Time of Abraham

(i.) *Testimony of Assyrian Tablets*

George Smith discovered an Assyrian calendar which divides every month into four weeks, and the seventh days are marked out as days on which no work was done.

(*h*) *Faussett*

(ii.) *Primeval Religion before Moses*

The sun, the moon, the stars, the clouds, the dawn, had gradually been deified . . . Among them the sun, under various titles, was the object of the highest veneration . . . (hence Sun-day).

(*i*)

Outside the Bible the knowledge of God had perished from among men.

(*j*)

Moses opposes Nature-worship in language of befitting simplicity for the remote antiquity = " The heavens and the earth are not God, for He made them ; neither the sun, nor the moon, nor the stars, etc., are God, for He has spoken them all into being."

(*k*) *Geikie*

Moses had been taught in Egypt that " Osiris (the sun) brought forth the seven great planetary gods, and then twelve humbler gods of the signs of the zodiac."

(*l*) *Ibid*

(iii.) *Testimony of Philology*

Ancient Chaldean literature, tablets, cylinders, etc., brought from the buried palaces of Assyria, shows that traditions of the Creation and great early events in the history of the world, had come down to them from long pre-historic ages . . . these traditions accord closely with narrative in Genesis . . . therefore must have been an echo from primitive revelation, perhaps in garden of Eden . . . Abraham, the father of the Hebrew race, came from the very home of these primitive peoples, in Mesopotamia . . . These people are known to us as Accadians (Accad. Gen. x. 10). Assyrian tablets have thrown a full light on this early nation.
In Abraham's time Babel=Babylon had been the centre of government and religious worship

(*m*)

The Creation Sabbath—*continued*

for an unknown period. [Smith's Early Babylon = 2280 B.C., others = 2400 B.C.; the common date of the Deluge = 2348 B.C.]. Hence we are thus carried back to the generation succeeding the Flood.

20th century B.C. Sargon I., a Semitic king, had the holy books of the Accadians copied, and also translated into Semitic . . . transcripts of these remain. . . . They contain accounts of the Creation received from still older sources (Noah), as heirlooms of the Antediluvian world—may have been oral, or written.

An Accadian tablet read thus:

On the seventh day He appointed a holy day,
And to cease from all business He commanded.
Then arose the Sun on the horizon of heaven in (glory).

(*a*)   *Fox Talbot*

George Smith's translation:

On the seventh day to a circle he began to swell
And stretches toward the dawn further.
When the god Shamas (the sun) in the horizon of heaven in the east, etc.

[The early signs of Sun-worship: hence there must have been a Sun-day.
Compare " The Temple of Belus," etc.]
(*b*)

The story of Genesis thus existed, before Moses, in its completeness, both as a whole and in detail.
(*c*)   *Geikie*

4. The Flood

" And Jehovah shut them in " (Bible account), Shamas (the sun God), " Enter into the vessel and close the door " (Berosus version, 240 B.C., also on tablets).

Earliest known inhabitants of Mesopotamia = Accadians, or Mountaineers, indicated " God " by a *star with eight rays* (cuneiform characters).

Some of the very hymns of Chaldean idolatry remain to our day; hymns which Abraham may have heard.

Sacred usages, originally of Divine origin, but sadly corrupted in Abraham's day, also survived. . . . Idolatry was striking its roots far and wide.

Abraham grew up amidst all this idolatry and superstition. Despite all this there lingered some traditions of earlier and better days. Legends passed from lip to lip—of the *Creation;* of the revolt of evil spirits; of the innocence, temptation, and the fall of man; of the Deluge, and the deliverance of Noah and his family; of the tower of Babel and the confusion of tongues. . . .

. . . But, amidst all this fearful degradation of religious ideas, the Patriarch would hear the seventh day spoken of as " the day of rest for the heart," on which even the king dared not ride out in his chariot, nor eat forbidden meats, nor violate a long list of minute restrictions.
(*d*)   *Geikie and Fox Talbot*

Primitive Indo-European race: (more than 3,000 years ago).

The Moon was the chief measurer of time. The religion was polytheistic, a worship of the personified powers of nature.
(*e*)   *Whitney (on Language)*

5. From the Call of Abraham to the Giving of the Law. Sun-worship

Hitherto the Jews had heard, in Egypt, for centuries, of Osiris and Horus, and a countless multitude of gods. They had seen men worshipping the Sun as the great king of heaven, and the moon and the stars as lesser deities.
(*f*)   *Geikie*

The sacredness of the number seven was very widely diffused in antiquity: explained by its frequent occurrence in natural events . . . moon's course, etc. The cycle of the week, originally the quarter of the lunar month . . . reaches back to pre-Mosaic times (Gen. xx. 27; vii. 4, 10; viii. 10, 12; xvii. 12; xxi. 4).
(*g*)   *Oehler and Hengstenberg*

According to the Old Testament, the laws of the heavenly bodies were to serve as a chronometer for the theocratic ordinances (Gen. i. 14; Ps. civ. 19).
(*h*)   *Oehler*

Israel learned by suffering under Egyptian oppression without any refreshing intermission, to sigh for rest. When God bestowed upon them their regularly recurring period of rest, by leading them out of bondage, this ordinance became at the same time a thankful remembrance of the deliverance they had experienced (Deut v. 15). " Remember that thou wast a bondman," etc.

That the Sabbath continued to be observed, is clear from the division of time into weeks (Gen. viii. 8, 13; xxix. 27, 28); the recognition of the day (Exod. xvi.); and the form of the precept, " Remember the Sabbath-day."
(*i*)   *Angus*

The above = indirect evidences of the Sabbath having been observed, since they are weekly intervals; and indicate that the Sabbath was an institution already well known: " Remember the patriarchal usage " [intimating perhaps that during the oppression in Egypt there had been no rest, no Sabbath observance, but an oppressive toil, such as the world now would impose on us]. . . . The Sabbath was confirmed by the great antiquity of the division of time into weeks, and the names of the days after the sun, moon, and planets.
(*j*)   *Smith's Bib. Dict*

A mysterious sanctity attached to the number *seven* for a long period previous to the giving of the Law.
(*k*)   *Nixon*

There is no mention in Scripture of any celebration of the Sabbath before the time of Israel. The sacred ordinance of the Sabbath, which was consecrated by God the Creator, was first expressly enjoined by the Sinaitic Thora. Here, (Job) the family celebration falls on the morning of the *Sunday;* a remarkable prelude to the New Testament celebration of Sunday in the age prior to the giving of the Law, which = a type of the New Testament time after the Law.
(*l*)   *Delitzsch*

[The Book of Job, and its story, is in other respects equally a prophecy of Christ and Christianity. Job, the great sufferer of the Old Testa-
(*m*)

The Creation Sabbath—*continued*

ment, is compared by James to Christ, the great Sufferer of the New Testament. For both, the cross is followed by the crown. "We see Jesus crowned," as we saw Job restored.]

(a)

[*N.B.* Job, too, was the Cohen (Priest) of his family, indicating that there was then no professional priesthood. This was the case too with the Primitive Aryan people of more than 3,000 years ago, which seems to prove a Patriarchal origin for the Book of Job.] *N.B.* **The Book of Job is the Patriarchal Bible.**

(b)

The Patriarchal history covers a period of about 2,500 years, the Book of Genesis omits mention of many things more memorable than the Sabbath.

(c)　　　　　　　　*Speaker's Commentary*

Indications in Genesis of dividing of time into weeks = hebdomades (see above for the same). The same hebdomades were known to other nations, not borrowed from Israel after Exodus. . . . Exod. xx. refers to the Sabbath as a neglected ordinance.

(d)　　　　　　　　　　　　*Ibid*

After the apostasy from the Patriarchal religion, the apostates would worship the sun, on the weekly periods continued as before. Hence Sunday, to which day we Christians have reverted.

Lee (so Usher, Selden, and other writers), *i.e.*, The Sabbath at the Exodus was fixed one day earlier than the Jewish Sabbath.

(e)　　　　　　　　　　　　*Ibid*

The Sabbath, or seventh day's rest, which the seed of Noah observed as holy to God, the idolatrous seed consecrated to the Sun, their supreme god, and thence called it Dies Solis (Sunday). This transformation is of very ancient date, and not in imitation of Jewish Church, or of the Patriarchs and the descendants of Shem.

(f)　　　*Gale's " Court of the Gentiles " (Lee)*

[Compare note on the Accadian nature worship, also that on Job, *supra*.]

6. Sabbath, The Patriarchal, and Worship

Even in patriarchal times invocation of the Lord went hand-in-hand with sacrifice; and we are led to the conclusion that sacred song was also associated with it, from the fact that among the Psalms we find one (Ps. xcii.) which, according to its superscription and contents, was specially designed for the Sabbath-day.

(g)　　　　　　　　　　*Hengstenberg*

7. Sabbath, The Patriarchal, and the Fourth Commandment

"Remember the Sabbath-day to keep it holy," pre-supposes an acquaintance with the Sabbath, as the expression "remember" is sufficient to show, but not that the Sabbath had been kept before this. From the history of the Creation that had been handed down, Israel must have known, that after God had created the world in six days He rested the seventh day, and by His resting sanctified the day (Gen. ii. 3).

(h)　　　　　　　　　　　　*Keil*

His people Israel were to keep the Sabbath now, not for the purpose of imitating what God had done, and enjoying the blessing of God by thus following God Himself, but that on this day they also might rest from their work; and that all the more, because their work was no longer the work appointed to man at the first, when he was created in the likeness of God, work which did not interrupt his blessedness in God (Gen. ii. 15), but that hard labour in the sweat of his brow to which he had been condemned in consequence of the Fall. In order, therefore, that His people might rest from toil so oppressive to both body and soul, and be refreshed, God prescribed the keeping of the Sabbath, that they might thus possess a day for the repose and elevation of their spirits, and a foretaste of the blessedness into which the people of God are at last to enter—the blessedness of the eternal κατάπαυσις ἀπὸ τῶν ἔργων αὐτοῦ (Heb. iv. 10), the ἀνάπαυσις ἐκ τῶν κόπων (Rev. xiv. 13).

(i)　　　　　　　　　　　　*Ibid*

THE THEOCRATIC SABBATH; or, the Weekly Festival of the " Exodus " (Redemption)

I. The Mosaic

(i.) *The Exodus*

From the Exodus the Sabbath was further consecrated, by the deliverance on *that* day of the Israelites (Exod. xx.; Deut. v. 12–15).

(j)　　　　　　　　　　　　*Angus*

(ii.) *The Fourth Commandment*

There is not in the O. T. a single trace of the observance of the Sabbath before the time of Moses. After the Deluge it is not mentioned in the covenant with Noah. The first account is after Israel left Egypt, and the Fourth Commandment consolidated it into a law, explains the principle and sanctions of the institution. The Sabbath was purely Jewish.

(k)　　　　　　　　　*F. W. Robertson*

Moses does not define the meaning of *work* in the Law; but it is evident that all work of a servile character was forbidden. There was a special commandment in seed time and harvest (Exod. xxxiv. 21). Kindling a fire (xxxv. 4); preparing food (xvi. 5, 22, 30). Thus a peculiar feature of the Jewish Sabbath was intended to remind them of their deliverance from a servile condition in Egypt. This was rehearsed in the Fourth Commandment, where the original reason is omitted (Deut. v. 15). "Remember, thou wast a servant," etc. . . . "therefore keep the Sabbath day."

The general spirit of the Jewish Sabbath is conveyed in Isa. lviii. 13, to which a promise is attached.

(l)　　　　　　　　　*Penny Cyclopædia*

"*Remember*," = stirring up their minds by remembrance. The Fourth is the only Commandment of the ten which begins so.

(m)　　　　　　　　　　　*Faussett*

"*Remember*" (Fourth Commandment) has both a backward and a prospective application. Remember its institution and the cause thereof; because

(n)

The Theocratic Sabbath—*continued*

men had allowed the festival to drop, or had diverted its use and application, and had practically forgotten their Creator. "Remember" the Sabbath in all ages to come, in respect to its teaching and significance. It is the answer throughout all ages to Atheism and Materialism.

(*a*)

"*My Sabbaths*" (Exod. xxxi. 13), *i.e.*, not simply a Sabbath, but a high Sabbath, in the superlative sense holy to Jehovah.

(*b*)

(iii.) *The Fourth Commandment and Moral and Positive Laws*

Bishop Taylor says that the reason of the first is eternal, of the second temporary. The law of the Sabbath is partly moral and partly positive. Moral precepts are founded in the nature of God and man.

The extent of obligation: moral precepts are universally binding. There is no state conceivable where God's moral dominion does not extend.

(*c*)   *Angus*

The Two Tables, as a summary of the law of God, are written by His finger as much on the conscience as on the tables of stone, and that for this reason: No scriptural moral theologian would presume to disregard them, and to compose other tables with a different arrangement of duties. The Ten Commandments are as far above our self-composed moral systems, as Sinai is higher than our professorial chairs.

(*d*)   *Sartorius*

The Ten Commandments are as much the eternal moral law, as they are the unchangeable natural rights of man, written in the very heart of human nature, and from which they can never be eradicated.

(*e*)   *Ibid*

The principles which natural morality has attempted to set up as supreme, are extremely weak in their foundation, and either vague and empty or inadequate and one-sided in their definitions. They are indeed wont to appear in the imperative form; but this imperative lacks the Imperator, and is therefore as weak as man himself who decrees it. Of what use is it to say to men, "Thou shalt not," when there is no Lord to say to him, "I am the Lord thy God," etc.?

(*f*)   *Ibid*

For the effectual maintenance of its authority, when God republished it, both upon the original grounds, and on other special grounds peculiar to the Jews, how did He publish it? Did He deliver it to Moses in the same manner as He did the ceremonial law? No. He wrote it with His own finger in tables of stone, and embodied in it the moral law. Surely this affords a very strong presumption that God Himself considered its duties, not as ceremonial, limited, and transient, but as moral, universal, and permanent.

(*g*)   *Chas. Simeon*

Nehemiah (ix. 14), when speaking of the Commandments, specially mentions the Sabbath.

(*h*)   *Keil*

"Christ the end of the Law," *i.e.*, "The law revealed concerning Israel, such as Christ fulfilled, is perpetually for the human race the Divine requisition. This law is at once both law and prophecy.

(*i*)   *Harless*

[Deut. v. 15.
Here nothing is so particular that it has not at the same time a universal reference, and nothing so universal that it is not at the same time joined on to something particular (*e.g.*, The Decalogue and the law of the Sabbath).

(*j*)   *Ibid*

The Judaic Sabbath was partly a political institution and partly of moral obligation. So far as it was the first, to keep the Jews separate from other nations, it is abrogated: so far as it was moral, it remains in force.

(*k*)   *Richard Cecil*

Sabbath Rest, not Idleness

The Sabbath had to be earned by six days' labour: "do all that thou hast to do,"—only so could the Sabbath rest be fairly earned.

The spirit of the Sabbath was (i.) joy (ii.) refreshment (iii.) mercy, on the grounds of Creation and Redemption (See afterwards in the prophets). "Joy" is the keynote of the service (Deut. xii. 7; xiv. 26. Ps. cxviii. 24) = "This is the day," etc. (Isa. lviii. 3–14, etc.)

(*l*)   *Smith's Bib. Dict*

Beneficence of-

The Sabbath-day's journey was less than a mile. How suggestive of the sacredness of the day, when everything approaching to bodily fatigue was forbidden!

(*m*)   *Angus*

[Deut. v. 15
The special reason why Israel observed the seventh day: very probably that special reason was because their Sabbath reminded them of their rest from slavery.

(*n*)   *Speaker's Commentary*

The great idea of the Sabbath did not belong exclusively to the Israelites. The law of the Sabbath was an expression of a universal truth.

What the Sunday is as a commemoration of the Resurrection of Christ, the Sabbath was (in respect of Creation) to the dispensation of Moses. On this ground then there is reason enough why the Fourth Commandment, as well as the other commandments, should continue.

(*o*)   *Cook*

[Exod. xx. 8–11
"Remember," presupposes an acquaintance with the Sabbath, but not that the Sabbath had been kept before this. From the history of the Creation that had been handed down, Israel must have known, that after God had created the world in six days, He rested the seventh, and by His resting sanctified the day. . .

The seventh was to be a "festival-keeper." Bondage (Deut. v. 14, 15. Exod. xxiii. 12), "therefore, that thou mightest remember this deliverance from bondage, Jehovah commanded thee to keep the Sabbath-day."

(*p*)   *Keil*

The Theocratic Sabbath—*continued*

Rest from slave-labour in Egypt, as the basis of the Jewish Sabbath, is peculiar to the Old Testament, and not to be met with in any other nation, though there are many among whom the division of weeks occurs.

(*a*)   *Keil*

[There was nothing burdensome about the Theocratic Sabbath.]

" The Sabbath was a gift of Divine grace for the sanctification of the people. . . . Far from presenting any painful aspect of renunciation, the Sabbath is regarded as a delight (Isa. lviii. 13), a day of joy (Ps. xcii. ; Hos. ii. 13).

(*b*)   *Oehler*

The Ark of the Covenant and the Fourth Commandment

When the Ark, in Solomon's time, was carried to its last retreat, it was opened for the first time within the memory of man, to examine its sacred contents. " It is impossible not to feel the interest of the moment."

" There was nothing in the Ark save the two tables of stone which Moses put there, etc. . . . Nothing save these. We know not their form or size. But we know the imperishable granite out of which they were hewn ; we know its red hue ; the style of engraving must have been such as can be still discerned in the desert inscriptions. These venerable fragments of the rock of Sinai, seen then, were seen, as far as we know, for the last time. They must have perished, when the Ark itself did, in the capture of Jerusalem. . . . But their contents have survived the wreck. The Ten Commandments delivered on Mount Sinai have become imbedded in the heart of the religion which has succeeded. Side by side with the prayer of our Lord, and with the creed of His Church, they appear inscribed on our churches, read from our altars, taught to our children, as the foundation of all morality."

(*c*)

Five points may be observed :

(i.) The number ten ; the most obvious form of calculation.

(ii.) Two blocks of stone ; probably of equal size.

(iii.) The original division differed from ours,— five and five.

(iv.) Written on both sides = completeness.

(v.) Not " Ten Commandments," but " TEN WORDS."

(*d*)

This was their form. What was the substance ? What has the human race gained by its adoption ? In one word, it is the declaration of the indivisible unity of morality with religion. We have the highest authority . . . for believing that even the whole sacrificial system was as nothing compared with the Decalogue and its enforcements. (Jer. vii. 22, 23) : " I spake not unto your fathers, nor commanded them in the day that I brought them out of the land of Egypt, concerning burnt offerings or sacrifices : But this thing commanded I them, saying, Obey My voice, and I will be your God, and ye shall be My people."

(*e*)   *Dean Stanley*

" If there was in the Fourth Commandment the injunction to consecrate by unbroken rest the seventh day of every week, yet experience has shown how widely adapted the principle of this observance has been to all times and countries. . . . Even those who repudiate the obligation . . . acknowledge that no ancient ceremony has so maintained its hold on the world, and that without its antecedent support the observance of the Sunday would hardly have exercised the beneficial influence which none deny it."

(*f*)

Its Universality

The patriarchal rites of Circumcision and Sacrifice have vanished away, but the name of the Sabbath of the Decalogue, the Sabbath of Mount Sinai,—as if it partook of the universal spirit of the Code in which it is enshrined,—is still, as though by a natural anomaly, revered by thousands of Gentile Christians.

The Fourth Commandment, in one version, grounds itself on the recollection of the servitude in Egypt. But these local and temporary allusions (the letter of the Commandment) prove the enduring force of the spirit which has come down to us, thus embedded in the blocks of Sinai. And if there be a profound spiritual sense in the declaration that the words were " written by the finger of God," there is also a grave truth in the fact that " the Tables " were the solid fragments hewn out of the rock of Horeb. Hard, stiff, abrupt as the cliffs from which they were taken, they remain as the firm, unyielding basis on which all true spiritual religion has been built up and sustained. Sinai is not Palestine ; the Law is not the Gospel ; but the Ten Commandments, in letter and in spirit, remain to us as the relic of that time. They represent to us, both in fact and in idea, the granite foundation, the immovable mountain on which the world is built up.

(*g*)   *Dean Stanley*

"Beginning of the year"

The theory started by Hitzig, revived by Hopfield, and refuted by Bähr, that the Passover always began on a Sunday and terminated on the 21st of Nisan, on a Saturday, and that this Sabbath is meant by מִמׇּחֳרַת הַשַּׁבָּת, presupposes an arrangement of the year making it always begin on a Sunday, of which there is no kind of proof.

(*h*)   *Oehler*

By keeping this Festival (like the Feast of the Passover) the Israelite testified that he belonged to that people whom the Lord had, by this act of deliverance, made His own possession.

(*i*)   *Ibid*

The Sabbath has ever been the day which marked a new beginning. It was so—

1. At the Creation ;
2. At Succoth ;
3. At Pentecost ;

When all things became new.

(*j*)

The Theocratic Sabbath—*continued*

The Celebration of the Sabbath

The resting from labour;
i.e., servile work, field work, gathering wood, preparation of food, kindling fire, forbidden to go out of the camp. Capital punishment = the penalty of transgressing these.

The positive celebration = public worship; morning and evening sacrifices doubled; renewal of the shew-bread; a holy convocation; meetings (where distant from the central sanctuary) for hearing and meditating on the Divine word (2 Kings iv. 23). But greater prominence is given in the Law to negative rather than to the positive sanctification of the Sabbath.

The later prophetic passages which insist on the sanctification of the Sabbath, such as Isa. lvi. 2; lviii. 13, etc.; Jer. xvii. 21, etc; confine themselves to what ought not to be done on the Sabbath; Isa. lviii. 13 proscribing also " empty gossip."

(a)   *Oehler*

Joy was a special feature of the Sabbath celebration. We find our Lord bidden to a feast on the Sabbath-day and accepting the invitation. The Jews apparently divided the Sabbath-day between the synagogue and social enjoyment.

(b)   *Channing*

Sabbath Thoughts

" *It is a good thing to give thanks unto Jehovah,*" *etc.* (Ps. xcii.)

This Sabbath Psalm was among the weeks' psalms sung in the post-exilic service.

With respect to the Sabbatical character of the Psalm, it is a disputed question whether it relates to the Sabbath of the Creation (R. Nehemiah, Talmudist), or to the final Sabbath of the world's history (R. Akiba: the day that is altogether Sabbath). The latter is relatively more correct. It praises God, the Creator, the Ruler, whose rule is loving-kindness and faithfulness, and calms itself, in the face of evil doers, with the prospect of the final issue. So also Ps. xci. 8.

This Sabbath Psalm repeats the most sacred Name seven times.

The strophes are six-lined, twice, then seven in the middle, and again six and six. Thus the middle of the Psalm bears the stamp of the Sabbatic number.

(c)

Verses 2–4

The Sabbath is the day that God has hallowed; we are to turn away from our business pursuits, and apply ourselves to His praise and adoration, the proper and blessed Sabbath employment.

It is good—for man—beneficial to the heart, pleasant and blessed to do this. From morn till eve loving-kindness and mercy attends this day.

(d)

Verses 5–7

Why God is to be praised. As Creator and as Ruler. The Psalmist rejoices that the revelation of Creation has been made to him. " *Quia delectasti me* " = Vulgate; *Dante, Purgatorio = Il salmo delectasti* = a female form, representing the life of Paradise delights in the glory of God's works, in the words of this psalm. His works great; his thoughts deep. Man can neither measure the óne [science of to-day (?)] nor fathom the other (Rom. xi. 33 = unsearchable and unteachable).

(e)

Verses 8–10

The vanity of the present prosperity of the ungodly. God-opposed Titan, man-worship, hero-worship shall succumb to final victory of God. History will end in the final victory of good over evil.

11–13. Then the oppressed Church—the "little flock "—will be dominant and stand forth glorious.

14–16. The renewed life and prosperity—immortality of the righteous. Cf. the Book of Job.

Thus the Sabbath-song teaches us what the Sabbath is for, why we are enjoined to "remember " it. In forgetting it, we forget both our origin and destiny.

(f)   *Cf. Delitzsch*

Supplementary

The Exodus was an entrance into rest from the toils of the house of bondage, and is thought to have occurred on the Sabbath-day. Hence special natural obligation with respect to the Sabbath on which Moses insists.

(g)   *Speaker's Commentary*

Sabaism, the worship of the sun, moon, and stars, is proved to be the most ancient form of idolatry in the East.

(h)   *Hengstenberg*

Before Joseph's time the City On had been founded in honour of the Sun, whose name was ἡλίου πόλις = Heliopolis. In this city there was a high-priest of the Sun, whose daughter Joseph married.

(i)   *Ibid*

Exod. xvi. (Manna)

It is perfectly clear from this event that the Israelites were not acquainted with any Sabbatical observance at that time; but that, whilst the way was opened, it was through the Decalogue that it was raised into a legal institution.

(j)   *Keil*

The history of the Sabbath-day is this. It was given by Moses to the Israelites, partly as a sign between God and them, marking them off from all other nations by its observance; partly as commemorative of their deliverance from Egypt. And the reason why the seventh day was fixed on, rather than the sixth or eighth, was, that on that day God rested from His labour. The soul of man was to form itself on the model of the Spirit of God. It is not said that God at the Creation gave the Sabbath to man, but that God rested at the close of the six days of Creation; whereupon He had blessed and sanctified the seventh day to the Israelites. This is stated in the Fourth Commandment, and also in Gen. i., which was written for the Israelites; and the history of creation naturally and appropriately introduces the reason and the sanction of their day of rest.

(k)   *F. W. Robertson*

The Theocratic Sabbath—*continued*

Sabbath, The (Gal. iv. 9, 10)

God's Sabbatic law, ante-dated the Mosaic law (Fourth Commandment = " Remember "). And whatever of legal bondage had been linked with the observance of the Jewish Sabbath was eliminated together with the change to the first day of the week. This at once removes the Lord's Day from the category of " days," and also of weak and beggarly elements (9). The mode of observance is learned from the Lord's words : " The Sabbath was made for man, and not man for the Sabbath," which at the same time imply, when rightly understood, the perpetual necessity for a Sabbath.

(a)   *Lange*

The Sabbath was the condition of the existence of the Church of God. Human weakness, only too apt to forget its duties towards God, requires definite, regularly-recurring times devoted to the fulfilment of these duties only, setting aside all external hindrances. In order that the people might be enabled to observe every day as a day of the Lord, on one definite, regularly-recurring day, they were deprived of everything that was calculated to disturb devotion. Ewald justly characterizes the Sabbath as " the corrective of the people of God." Their business is to be holy, to live purely to the " Holy One." " Be ye holy," is already in the Pentateuch set forth as an indispensable requirement, " for I am holy." But amid a life of toil and trouble the Church cannot comply with this demand, unless with the help of regularly recurring times of introspection, of assembly, and of edification. Among all the nations of antiquity, Israel stands alone as a religious nation ; in them alone religion manifests itself as an absolutely determining power. This, its high destination, its world-historical significance, it could only realize by the institution of the Sabbath.

(b)   *Hengstenberg*

Sabbath Observance ; The Foundation of the Commandment

On the Sabbath,—and also on the day of Atonement (Lev. xxiii. 28, 31),—every occupation was to REST ; on the other feast-days, only laborious occupations (Lev. xxiii. 7, sqq.), *i.e.*, such occupations as came under the denomination of labour, business, or industrial employment. Consequently, not only were ploughing and reaping (Exod. xxxiv. 21), pressing wine and carrying goods (Neh. xiii. 15), bearing burdens (Jer. xvii. 21), carrying on trade (Amos viii. 5), and holding markets (Neh. xiii. 15, sqq.), prohibited, but collecting manna (Exod. xvi. 26, sqq.), gathering wood (Num. xv. 32, sqq.), and kindling fire for the purpose of boiling or baking (chap. xxxv. 3). The intention of thus resting from every occupation on the Sabbath is evident from the foundation upon which the commandment is based in ver. 11, viz., that at the creation of the heaven and the earth Jehovah rested on the seventh day, and therefore blessed the Sabbath-day and hallowed it.

(c)   *Keil*

II. THE PHARISAIC SABBATH

(i.) *Second Slavery*

The Pharisaic Sabbath treats of the second, and worse, slavery into which the Israelites fell. The former was outward and physical, this was spiritual —binding on men burdens grievous to be borne, which neither they nor their children were able to bear, and from which a Deliverer—the Prophet like unto Moses, but greater, must come to deliver them. Cf. " If the Son shall set you free, ye shall be free indeed."

(d)

The words, " Abide ye every man in his place on the seventh day," were held by one Jewish sect as a command that no one should move at all during the whole Sabbath from the spot and position in which its commencement found him.

(e)   *Routh (Geikie)*

The enactments with which later Judaism encompassed the Sabbatic command, were wholly adapted to *repress* a cheerful celebration of the Sabbath. . . . These enactments were made in the centuries between Ezra and Christ. . . . Nehemiah made the people bind themselves by an oath to give up trading on the Sabbath-day : hence a strict observance of the day had not yet become a national custom. . . . There is, however, in the measures taken by Nehemiah for the preservation of the Sabbatic rest, nothing of the micrologic casuistry of after times.

(f)   *Oehler*

(ii.) *Prohibitions and Injunctions covering the whole of Social Individual, and Public Life, and carried to the extreme of Ridiculous Caricature*

Rules prescribing the kinds of knots which might be tied on the Sabbath.

The camel-driver's and the sailor's = unlawful either to tie or untie them.

A knot which could be untied with one hand was allowed to be done.

A shoe-sandal, a woman's cap, a wine-skin, or oil-skin, or a flesh-pot, might be tied.

A pitcher at a spring might be tied to the body-sash, but not with a cord.

It was forbidden to write two letters, whether of the same size or different ; or with different inks, or in different languages, or with any pigment that would make marks ; or even to write two letters, one on each side of a corner of two walls, or on two leaves of a writing table. . . . But they might be written. . . . on anything in which the writing did not remain. . . . If they were written with the hand turned upside down, or with the foot, mouth, or elbow, or if one letter were added to another previously made, or other letters traced over, or if a person only wrote one letter on the ground and another on the wall, or on two walls, etc., it was not illegal. If a person wrote two characters at different times and through forgetfulness, one in the morning, the other at evening, it was a question among the Rabbis whether he had, or had not, broken the Sabbath.

The quantity of food that might be carried must be less in bulk than a dried fig ; if honey, only as much as would anoint a wound ; if water, as much as would make an eye-salve ; if paper, as much as would be put in a phylactery ; if ink, as much as would form two letters.

To kindle or extinguish a fire on the Sabbath was a great desecration of the day ; nor even in sickness might Rabbinical rules be violated.

(g)

The Theocratic Sabbath—*continued*

It was forbidden to give an emetic, to set a broken bone, or put back a dislocated joint; though some Rabbis, more liberal, held that what endangered life made the Sabbath law void. One who was buried under ruins might be dug out, if alive, but not if dead; he was to be left where he was till the Sabbath was over.

The money girdle must be taken off, and all tools laid aside before sunset on Friday. No one must go out of his house with a needle or a pen, lest he forget the Sabbath. Every one must search his pockets at that time to see that there is nothing left in them which was forbidden.

The refinements of Rabbinical casuistry were endless. To wear one kind of sandals was carrying a burden, while to wear another kind was not.

One might carry a burden on his shoulder, but it must not be slung between two.

It was unlawful to go out with wooden sandals, or shoes which had nails in the soles, or with a shoe and a slipper, unless one foot were hurt.

It was unlawful for any one to carry a loaf on the public street; but if two carried it, it was not unlawful.

The Sabbath was believed to prevail in all its strictness, from eternity, throughout the universe.

All the Rabbinical precepts concerning it had been revealed to Jacob from the originals on the tablets of heaven.

Even in hell the lost had rest from their torments on its sacred hours; and the waters of Bethesda might be troubled on other days, but were still and unmoved on this.

(*a*)

In an insincere age such excessive strictness led to constant evasions by Pharisees and Sadducees alike. To escape the restrictions which limited a Sabbath-day's journey to two thousand cubits from a town or city, they carried food on Friday evening to a spot that distance beyond the walls, and assumed, by a fiction, that this made that spot their dwelling. They could thus on the Sabbath walk the full distance to it, and as far beyond it.

To make it lawful to eat together on the Sabbath, the Rabbis put chains across the two ends of a street in which the members of a special fraternity lived, and called it a single dwelling; while to excuse their carrying the materials for their Sabbath repast to the common hall, they each laid some food in it on the Friday evening—a common dwelling.

(*b*)

The Pharisees violated the Sabbath when occasion demanded: Maxim = "The Sabbath is for you, but you are not for the Sabbath."

Another: "Make a common day of your Sabbath, rather than go to your neighbour for help."

(*c*)   *Geikie*

The Jews could not, on the Sabbath, even lift up and eat fruit which had fallen from a tree.

(*d*)   *Lightfoot*

The German Jews will not even carry a walking-stick on the Sabbath. To walk on grass is forbidden = a kind of thrashing. A handkerchief = a burden if carried in the pocket, but not if tied round the waist as a girdle.

(*e*)   *Geikie*

Hillel was found nearly frozen in snow, and almost dead, having climbed up into a window to hear the lectures, when too poor to pay the fee—on the Sabbath eve. They carried him in and bathed and rubbed him, till circulation was restored. "It was right even to profane the Sabbath for such an one," said both teachers and students.

(*f*)   *Geikie, Delitzsch, etc*

The Rabbis asserted that the law was "the one thing on account of which the universe had been created."

(*g*)   *Archd. Farrar*

After the Captivity (Maccabees i. and ii.), the Jews refused to defend themselves: "Let us die all in our innocency." Their foes "rose up against them in battle on the Sabbath, and slew them, with their wives, and children, and cattle, to the number of one thousand people."

(*h*)

Ptolemy Soter entered Jerusalem on the Sabbath day, under pretence of offering sacrifice, and took possession of the city. No resistance being offered by the Jews, who dared not transgress their law by fighting on the Sabbath day. Cf. Battle of Waterloo.

(*i*)   *Nixon*

III. JESUS AND THE PHARISAIC SABBATH

Matt. xii. 9–14; Mark iii. 1–6; Luke vi. 6–11

The charge that Jesus was a Sabbath-breaker, because He wrought cures on that day, followed Him whither He went. Spies were sent out by the Sanhedrim as detectives; and on this charge the Sanhedrim determined upon His death.

The following are the chief points in relation to this charge, showing at the same time how Jesus regarded the Pharisaic Sabbath, and what it was that He came to abrogate—certainly not the Sabbath, as made for and as needful for man; but the caricature of it as the Pharisaic Sabbath.

Traditionalism applied the law of Sabbath-observance to all harvest work, among which plucking of ears of grain was also included.

(*j*)   *Maimonides, Lightfoot, Meyer*

Jesus = "David was the great model of Jewish piety, and yet he went into the house of God contrary to the commandment, and ate the consecrated bread."

The priests profaned the Sabbath (according to this false notion), and were blameless. I am greater than the Temple, and My disciples have done this in attendance on Me, and of necessity: therefore are they blameless.

(*k*)   *Lange*

Case of the man with a withered hand

According to traditionalism, healing was prohibited on the Sabbath, excepting cases where life was in danger.

(*l*)   *Meyer*

The Theocratic Sabbath—*continued*

It is improbable that this tradition was settled at this time. The present instance tells against it.

Later tradition: If a beast on the Sabbath day fell into a pit, or reservoir for water, it was only lawful to give it necessary food, or straw to lie upon, [or to lay planks] by which it might perhaps get out of the pit.

(a)   *Maimon. Sepp*

Jerome = That this man was a stone-cutter, who begged Jesus to heal him, that he might no longer beg his bread.

(b)   *Lange*

On this cure a formal heresy-suit was to be immediately instituted.

(c)   *Ibid*

It is a striking fact that the pharisaical hierarchy which had charged the Lord with desecrating the Sabbath, was obliged to hold a council on the great Easter-Sabbath, to run into the heathen and unclean house of the Gentile Pilate, and then to seal the stone over the tomb of Jesus in the unclean place of a skull.

(d)   *Ibid*

Christ is the Lord of the Sabbath as the personal Sabbath; all that leads to Him, and is done in Him, is Sabbath observance; all that leads from Him, is Sabbath-healing.

(e)   *Ibid*

The Fourth Commandment is explained by the life and teaching of our Lord.

(f)   *Ibid*

Christ spares the representatives of traditionalism even while resisting them; He heals the man . . . merely by His word, not by touching him, nor by taking hold of his hand.

(g)   *Ibid*

The matter of the disciples' plucking ears of corn belonged to the thirty-nine chief rules, and their subdivisions, in which the works forbidden on the Sabbath were enumerated. This was their hypocritical way, the making trifling things matters of sin and vexation to the conscience.

(h)   *Ibid*

(i.) They thought Jesus had sinned against sound doctrine;
(ii.) Then they went further, and objected against His free treatment of discipline and pious usages;
(iii.) They allege that He, in the person of His disciples, sinned against the Decalogue, and against one of its most sacred commandments, that concerning the Sabbath.

(i)   *Ibid*

The spirit of traditionalism and fanaticism perfectly inverts the ordinances of the kingdom of God; making the means the end, and the end the means.

(j)   *Ibid*

The Son of Man, the Lord in all aspects and on all sides; therefore Lord of the Sabbath. But the Lord is a Ruler, Administrator, and Fulfiller of His ordinances; not an abolisher of them.

(k)   *Lange*

Sabbath-breaking (John v. 16)

The Jews find fault with the man for carrying his bed in obedience to Christ's command, their reason [being, because "the same day" on which the miracle was accomplished "was the Sabbath"; and the carrying of any burden was one of the expressly prohibited works of that day. Here, indeed, they had apparently an Old Testament ground to go upon, and an interpretation of the Mosaic law from the lips of a prophet, to justify their interference, and the offence which they took. But the man's bearing of his bed was not a work by itself; it was merely the corollary, or indeed the concluding act of his healing, that by which he should make proof himself and give testimony to others of its reality. It was lawful to heal on the Sabbath day; it was lawful then to do what was immediately involved in, and directly followed on the healing. And here lay ultimately the true controversy between Christ and His adversaries, viz., whether it was most lawful to do good on that day or to leave it undone (Luke vi. 9).

Starting from the unlawfulness of leaving good undone, He asserted that He was its true keeper, keeping it as God kept it, with the highest beneficent activity, which in His Father's case, as in His own, was identical with deepest rest, and not, as they accused Him of being, its breaker.

(l)   *Archbp. Trench*

The Sabbath (John v. 17)

Christ here mortally hit the Sabbath laws as they were then understood and carried out, but not the true sense of the primitive Sabbath and the Fourth Commandment, which forbids not higher work, but only the ordinary work of week days.

(m)   *Ewald*

In His justification Christ struck at the root of Pharisaic error—their contracted sense of Sabbath law—that sanctity of the Sabbath was founded upon God's resting after work of Creation, as if His creative labours were then ended; He points out, on the other hand, the ever-continuing activity of God, "My Father worketh hitherto and I work,"=as He now ceases to work, so do I work unceasingly for the salvation of men.

(n)   *Neander*

The true Lordship of Son of Man over Sabbath restrictions. He who a year before had shown that He was Lord of the Temple, now shows that He is Lord also of the Sabbath.

(o)   *Ellicott*

Sabbath restrictions one hundred and fifty years later (*Mishna Tract, Sabbath*): "A tailor must not go out with his needle near dark (on eve of Sabbath), lest he forget and carry it with him (during the Sabbath).

This our Lord condemned as above.

(p)   *Lightfoot*

The Theocratic Sabbath—*continued*

[Luke vi. 1–12

Two Sabbath Scenes provoke the outbreak of a conflict long gathering.

Note :—
  (i.) The act of the disciples ;
  (ii.) The question of the Pharisees ;
  (iii.) The answers of Jesus.

(*a*)

1st answer :

The conduct of David teaches the principle that when a moral obligation clashes with a ceremonial law, the latter has to yield. Because the rite is a means ; whilst moral duty is an end itself.

Pharisaism always inverts this order. It was the duty of the High Priest to preserve the life of David and his companions, even at the expense of Ritual.

Besides, when it became a question of their own advantage, they acted similarly.

(*b*)

2nd answer :

What is the Sabbath for ?

For man's spiritual good. But man's spiritual benefit is fully acquired by the Son of Man : He can therefore dispense with the Sabbath. But its complete abolition will come only when mankind is completely redeemed.

(*c*)

The Second Sabbath-day Scene

  (i.) Jesus teaching in synagogue, and a man there with a withered hand ;
  (ii.) His enemies on the watch ;
  (iii.) Jesus perceives the spy system they are adopting.

[*N.B.*—The Jews permitted no medical treatment on Sabbath-day unless life was in peril. Some even forbade the consolation of the sick on that day.]

  (iv.) Jesus seems here to give publicity to His work. Ask, Why not defer the cure till to-morrow ? To-morrow belongs to God ; to-day only to workers.

  (v.) *The question* = Good left undone is evil done.

  (vi.) *The cure :* "Stretch forth," etc., is what the man could not do : so with faith and obedience ; "Come," but "No man can come unless," etc. Therefore, where there is the will to do, the power to do is given.

  (vii.) "*Filled with madness,*" etc. They seek to get Herod to do to Him as to John the Baptist. Hostilities now become open.

But when they plot, Jesus goes to prayer ; and after prayer He chooses other disciples. His work is not done yet.

(*d*)

[Luke vi. 6

This miracle was one of seven noticed as performed on Sabbath days.

John v. 9 ; Mark i. 21, 29 ; John ix. 14 ; Luke xiii. 14, xiv. 1 ; and is especially that in which our Lord vindicated the lawfulness (Matt. xii. 12) of such acts.

(*e*)   *Ellicott*

[Luke xiv

Here is a poor fellow-creature of yours, suffering great misery. His very look appeals to you for help. Would you, if you had the power to relieve him, forbear to exert it, because to-day happens to be the Sabbath-day ? Would you let him suffer on till to-morrow ? Is there any law of God which makes it right to leave him in pain, and wrong to relieve him because to-day is the Sabbath day ?

(*f*)   *Gordon Calthrop*

Objection : Jesus not of God because He keepeth not the Sabbath-day.

Answer : Surely it was lawful to do good on the Sabbath-day ; that that was but a Positive Institution ; but works of mercy are natural and moral duties ; and God Himself had declared, that He would have even His own institutions to give way to those greater duties, and that one of natural and eternal obligation. "I will have mercy, and not sacrifice."

(*g*)   *Tillotson*

SUNDAY, THE CHRISTIAN, OR LORD'S DAY

The Sabbath Abrogated by Christianity

St. Paul's own view. No one, I believe, who would read St. Paul's own writings with unprejudiced mind could fail to come to the conclusion that he considered the Sabbath abrogated by Christianity. Not merely as modified in its stringency, but as totally repealed.

For example, see Col. ii. 16, 17. Observe, he counts the Sabbath-day among those institutions of Judaism which were shadows, and of which Christ was the realization, the substance or "body ; " and he bids the Colossians remain indifferent to the judgment which would be pronounced upon their non-observance of such days. "Let no man judge you with respect to . . . the Sabbath-days."

(*h*)   *F. W. Robertson*

He is more decisive still in Rom. xiv. 5, 6. For it has been contended that in the former passage, "Sabbath-days" refers simply to the Jewish Sabbaths, which were superseded by the Lord's day ; and that the Apostle does not allude at all to the new institution, which it is supposed had superseded it. Here, however, there can be no such ambiguity. "One man esteemeth every day alike ; " and he only says, "let him be fully persuaded in his own mind." "Every" day must include first days as well as last days of the week, Sundays as well as Saturdays. And again, he even speaks of scrupulous adherence to particular days, as if it were giving up the very principle of Christianity : "Ye observe days, and months, and times, and years. I am afraid of you, lest I have bestowed upon you labour in vain." So that his objection was not to Jewish days, but to the very principle of attaching intrinsic sacredness to any days. All forms and modes of particularizing the Christian life he reckoned as bondage under the elements or alphabet of the Law. And this is plain from the nature of the case. He struck, not at a day, but at a principle. Else, if with all this vehemence and earnestness, he only meant to establish a new set of days in

(*i*)

Sunday, The Christian—*continued*

the place of the old, there is no intelligible principle for which he is contending, and that earnest
Apostle is only a champion for one day instead
of another—an asserter of the eternal sanctities
of Sunday, instead of the eternal sanctities of
Saturday. Incredible indeed!

(a)   *F. W. Robertson*

Let us then understand the principle on which
he declared the repeal of the Sabbath. He taught
that the blood of Christ cleansed *all* things; therefore there was nothing specially clean. Christ had
vindicated all for God: therefore there was no
one thing more God's than another. For to assert
that one thing is God's more than another, is by
implication to admit that other to be less God's.
The blood of Christ had vindicated God's
parental right to all humanity; therefore there
could be no peculiar people. "There is neither
Jew nor Greek, circumcision nor uncircumcision,
Barbarian, Scythian, bond, nor free: but Christ
is all in all." It had proclaimed God's property
in all places: therefore there could be no one
place intrinsically holier than another. No
human dedication, no human consecration, could
localize God in space. Hence the first martyr
quoted from the prophet: "Howbeit the most
High dwelleth not in temples made with hands;
as saith the prophet, Heaven is my throne and
earth is my footstool: what house will ye build
for Me? saith the Lord."
The Gospel of Christ had sanctified all time:
hence no time could be specially God's. For
to assert that Sunday is more God's day than
Monday, is to maintain by implication Monday
is His less rightfully.

(b)   *Ibid*

The Sabbath a Christian Institution

We regard it as altogether a "Christian Institution," as having its origin in the Gospel, as
peculiar to the new dispensation; and we conceive
that the proper observation of it is to be determined wholly by the spirit of Christianity. We
meet in the New Testament no precise rules as
to the mode of spending the Lord's day, as to
the mode of worship and teaching, as to the distribution of the time not given to public services.
And this is just what might be expected; for the
Gospel is not a religion of precise rules.

(c)   *Channing*

The Sabbath, Consecration of

That day alone can be truly consecrated to the
holy God on which we consecrate ourselves to
Him, withdraw ourselves completely from the
world, with its occupations and pleasures, in order
to give ourselves to Him with our whole soul, and
to partake of His life.

(d)   *Hengstenberg*

The Sabbath a Delight

The Lord, it is said, gives you the Sabbath.
Here the Sabbath already appears, not as a burden
but as a pleasure (Isa. lviii. 13), as a precious
privilege which God gives to His people. To be
able to rest without anxiety,—to rest to the Lord
and in the Lord,—what a consolation in our toil

and travail on the earth which the Lord has
cursed! But just because the day of rest is a
love-gift of the merciful God, contempt of it is
the more heavily avenged. We cannot assume
that with this event the Sabbath received its full
meaning among Israel. It certainly implies the
observance of the Sabbath, but in this connection
only with reference to the gathering and preparation of the manna. The injunction of a comprehensive observance of the Sabbath first went
forth on Mount Sinai. The Sabbath could only
unfold its benignant power in connection with a
series of Divine ordinances. It is significant only
as a link in a chain.

(e)   *Hengstenberg*

The Sabbath, the First Day

There is a sense in which the Sabbath has
always been kept on the First day:
1. The First day of the finished creation, and
   of man's history.
2. The First day of the Exodus.
3. The First day of the week.

(f)

The first day of the week had already begun on
the preceding evening; now the day, as opposed
to the night, was dawning on that first day.
The first remarkable mention of the Lord's day
is combined with the Resurrection of our Lord.

(g)   *Bengel*

The Sabbath, Freedom of

The law said, "On the Sabbath-day thou shalt
do no manner of work." The *spirit* of this was
rest for man; but Pharisaism kept literally to the
rule. It would rather that a man should perish
than that any work should be done, or any ground
travelled over, on the Sabbath-day in saving him.
Pharisaism regarded the *day* as mysterious and
sacred; Christianity proclaimed the *day* to be
nothing—the *spirit*, for which the day was set
apart, everything. It said, "The Sabbath was
made for man, not man for the Sabbath."

(h)   *F. W. Robertson*

[Col. ii. 16

The Sabbaths had served their purpose, and the
Lord's day was now to be a season of loftier joy,
as it commemorates a more august event than
either the creation of the universe or the exodus
from Egypt. The new religion is too free and
exuberant to be trained down to "times and
seasons" like its tame and rudimental prede-
cessor. Its feast is daily, for every day is holy;
its moon never wanes, and its serene tranquillity
is an unbroken Sabbath.

(i)   *Eadie*

Let no man bind what Christ has left free.

(j)   *Channing*

"*Let no man judge you in meat, or in drink, or
in respect of an holy day, or of the new moon, or of
the Sabbath days*" (Col. ii. 16)

This passage is very plain.
That a Christian, after reading this passage,
should "judge" or condemn his brethren for

(k)

Sunday, The Christian—*continued*

questioning or rejecting his particular notion of the Sabbath, is a striking proof of the slow progress of tolerant and liberal principles among men.

(a)   *Channing*

The Sabbath, Freedom of (Col. ii. 16)

One might disturb believers on the subject of meat and drink, another about holidays. The *holiday* is yearly; the *new moon* monthly; the *Sabbaths* weekly. The plural used for the singular with express design; for the several days of the week are called *Sabbaths* (Matt. xxviii. 1). Therefore Paul intimates here that all distinction of days is taken away: for he never wrote more openly of the Sabbath. . . . It has not been expressly defined what degree of obligation is to be assigned to the Sabbath, and what to the Lord's day; but this has been left to the *measure* of every one's *faith*.

The Sabbath is not commanded;
The Lord's day not enjoined.

An appointed day is useful and necessary to those who are deeply engrossed in the concerns of the world. They who sabbatize always enjoy a greater liberty. The Sabbath is a type even of eternal things (Heb. iv. 3, 4); but yet its obligation does not on that account continue in the New Testament.

(b)   *Bengel*

Sabbath, Relation between the Jewish and the Christian

In the Church of Rome a controversy had arisen in the time of St. Paul, respecting the exact relation in which Christianity stood to Judaism; and consequently, the obligation of various Jewish institutions came to be discussed. Among the rest the Sabbath-day. One party maintained its abrogation: another its continued obligation. "One man esteemeth one day above another; another esteemeth every day alike." Now, it is remarkable that in his reply, the Apostle Paul, although his own views upon the question were decided and strong, passes no judgment of censure upon the practice of either of these parties, but only blames the uncharitable spirit in which the one "judged their brethren," as irreligious, and the other "set at nought" their stricter brethren as superstitious. He lays down, however, two principles for the decision of the matter: the first being the rights of Christian conviction, or the sacredness of the individual conscience, "Let every man be fully persuaded in his own mind;" the second, a principle unsatisfactory enough, and surprising, no doubt, to both, that there is such a thing as religious observance, and also such a thing as a religious non-observance of the day, "He that regardeth the day, regardeth it unto the Lord: and he that regardeth not the day, to the Lord he doth not regard it."

(c)   *F. W. Robertson*

Sabbath, The Jewish, and the Christian Sunday

In early, we cannot say exactly how early, times, the Church of Christ felt the necessity of substituting something in place of the ordinances which had been repealed. And the Lord's day arose, not a day of compulsory rest; not such a day at all as modern sabbatarians suppose. Not a Jewish Sabbath; rather a day in many respects absolutely contrasted with the Jewish Sabbath.

For the Lord's day sprung, not out of a transference of the Jewish Sabbath from Saturday to Sunday; but rather out of the idea of making the week an imitation of the life of Christ. With the early Christians, the great conception was that of following their crucified and risen Lord: they set, as it were, the clock of time to the epochs of His history. Friday represented the death in which all Christians daily die, and Sunday the Resurrection in which all Christians daily rise to higher life. What Friday and Sunday were to the week, that Good-Friday and Easter-Sunday were to the year. And thus, in larger or smaller cycles, all time represented to the early Christians the mysteries of the Cross and the risen life hidden in humanity. And as the sunflower turns from morning till evening to the sun, so did the early Church turn for ever to her Lord, transforming week and year into a symbolical representation of His spiritual life.

Carefully distinguish this, the true historical view of the origin of the Lord's day, from a mere transference of a Jewish Sabbath from one day to another. For St. Paul's teaching is distinct and clear, that the Sabbath is annulled; and to urge the observance of the day as indispensable to salvation, was, according to him, to Juadize: "to turn again to the weak and beggarly elements, whereunto they desired to be in bondage."

(d)   *F. W. Robertson*

THE LORD'S DAY

"*I was in the Spirit on the Lord's day*" (Rev. i. 10)

1. By "the Lord's day" the Apostle meant the first day of the week, or, Sunday. Our Lord has made that day in a special sense His own by rising from the dead on that day, and by His first appearance after the Resurrection. On that day He appeared to Mary Magdalene, to the women, to Peter, to the ten, to the disciples, on their way to Emmaus. After the lapse of a week He appeared to the eleven, having, so far as we know, during the interval remained altogether out of sight. The day of Pentecost, when the Holy Ghost came down and *created* the Church of Christ, was seven weeks after the day of the Resurrection—on the Lord's day. And from this time we find the observance of that day amongst Christians. "On the first day of the week the disciples came together to break bread," and Paul preached unto them. And when St. Paul, writing to the Corinthians, is giving directions for the collecting of money on behalf of the poor, he says, "Upon *the first day* of the week let every one of you lay in store, that there be no gathering when I come." The *first* day of the week was then recognised as the natural day for special religious effort. When St. John, some years afterwards, an exile at Patmos, says he was "in the Spirit on the Lord's day," we see what he means.

(e)

2. "The Lord's day," of the Christian Church, is a weekly commemoration of the great event which is annually celebrated at Easter. The first principle embodied in the observance of the Lord's day is

(f)

The Lord's Day—*continued*

the duty of consecrating a certain portion of time, at least one-seventh, to the service of God. This principle is common to the Jewish Sabbath and to the Christian "Lord's day." "Remember that thou keep holy the Sabbath day," means for us Christians, "Remember that thou keep holy one day in seven." "Keep it holy, consecrated," so the precept runs. The day is to be unlike other days, and to be marked by some positive characteristics which shall proclaim its dedication to God.

(*a*)   *Liddon*

3. **The consecration of one day in seven** implies that all our time belongs to God. And the public setting apart of a certain measure of time to God's service, as a witness to God's claims before the world, is calculated to strike the imaginations of men. From this point of view our English Sunday, whatever may be said about the details and mistakes in its observance, brings the existence and claims of God before the minds of those who do not make use of it; and thoughtless admirers have told us that it fills them with admiration and something like envy.

(*b*)

4. **The second principle represented in "the Lord's day"** is the periodical suspension of human toil. In order to make this day unlike other days, in order to make room for acknowledgment of God on it, ordinary occupations are suspended. Here we have a second principle common to the Jewish Sabbath and the Lord's day: "Six days shalt thou labour, and do all that thou hast to do: but the seventh day is the Sabbath of the Lord thy God; in it thou shalt do no manner of work, nor thy cattle, nor even the foreigner who lives along with thee." In the Old Testament a variety of particular occupations are expressly forbidden on the Sabbath. The kindling of a fire, the gathering of wood, sowing and reaping, holding markets, pressing grapes, carrying burdens of all kinds. And in the later days the Pharisees and lawyers held greatly to these prohibitions. They held it unlawful to pluck an ear of corn on the Sabbath when passing through a field, to assist by visiting the sick, although they allowed that if an animal fell into a pit he might be taken out on the Sabbath; that guests might be invited, and that children, if eight days old, might be circumcised. Besides, they had certain rabbinical laws, which limited the day's journey to 2,000 cubits; and so on.

(*c*)

5. These illustrations show how mere human law became, sooner or later, the caricature and ruin of high moral principle; and it was against this pharisaical observance that our Lord protested. The Sabbath was made for the moral good of man, and not man for the legal observance of the Sabbath. The lower principle was in itself the sacred principle caricatured. And it passed on in the Christian observance of the Lord's Day. We see this plainly in the early times of the Christian Church. They showed that the great rule of the Fourth Commandment with regard to work, modified by our Lord's teaching respecting duties of charity and duties of necessity, was held applicable to the Lord's day. Thus Tertullian, writing at the end of the second century, calls it Sunday, or the Lord's Day; and then adds,

"Business is put off on it, lest we give place to the devil." Under Constantine Christianity made itself felt in the principles of legislation, and we soon find provision made for the observance of the Lord's day. Even three or four years before the Council of Nice, Constantine issued an edict, commanding Romans of all descriptions to cease from labour on that day; but he allows agricultural labour to go on, if the safety of the crops depends upon it; and when we come to the codes of the emperors Theodosius and Justinian, those great monuments in which the experience of the great Roman lawyers is modified by the softening influences of Christianity, we find the observance of the Sabbath carefully provided for: works of agriculture are allowed; but public spectacles of all kinds, such as games at the circus, are suppressed; and the great teachers of the Church in those days did what they could to second the efforts of the legislators by telling Christians to abstain from works which profaned the holy day of the Christian week.

(*d*)

6. **This insistance upon a day of freedom from earthly labour** is not inconsistent with the dignity and claims of labour. On the contrary, it expects labour; it arrests an excessive expenditure of human strength. It raises and consecrates labour by enabling the workman to acknowledge the source and support of his exertions. When, in the first French Revolution, there was a fanatical ignorance abroad, to show that the world could get on without Christianity, some important experiments were made on the subject; and the general result was to show that the abstinence from labour on one day in seven was acknowledged to be in the interests of labour itself. Especially is this the case in times like our own, when men will work at high pressure, when capital demands quick returns for outlay, when competition is keen, and the post of the man who faints is immediately occupied by a stronger rival who stands watching his opportunity hard by. It is sometimes asked, "Why is abstinence from labour dictated to us?" and the answer is, "Because in a busy, high-worked community, unless *all* are to abstain from work, none *can* abstain; since, in point of fact, none can *afford* to abstain." This is the principle, too, which applies to our Bank holidays. The State provides a cessation from labour four times a year, and thus does on a small scale what the Church does on a large scale once a week.

(*e*)

7. And thus the Sabbath and the Lord's day agree in affirming two principles—a hallowing of a seventh part of our time, and the abstinence from servile work one day in seven. Are they identical? May we rightly call the Lord's day the Sabbath? These questions must be answered in the negative. **The Lord's day was never identified with the Jewish Sabbath before the rise of Puritanism, in the seventeenth century.** The Puritan divines had remarkable knowledge of the contents of the Scriptures, but they had, as it seems to me, in reading them no eye for the perspective of Scripture. They had broken away from the old true interpretation, which would have saved them from some of their mistakes. There was in that age no school of criticism sufficiently educated to take the place of what they had lost. Accordingly,

(*f*)

The Lord's Day—*continued*

in their anxiety to secure the strong Scriptural observance of the Lord's day, they said the Lord's Day was the Jewish Sabbath, and that all that was said about the Jewish Sabbath was applied to it.

(*a*)

8. The Jewish Sabbath and the Christian " Lord's day," while agreeing in affirming two principles, differ in two note-worthy respects. First, they differ, as has already been implied, in being connected with distinct days. The Sabbath was kept on the last day of the week; the Lord's day is kept on the first. " *The seventh day* "—*and no other*—" *is the Sabbath of the Lord thy God.*"

When the Christian Church keeps its weekly holy day on the first day of the week, it does much more than merely change the day. Had the motive of the observance been the same, this changing of the Divine law would have been unpardonable. The change was made because there was imperative reason for making it; for the Lord's day and the Sabbath differ in their *motive* for observing them. The Sabbath is a weekly commemoration of the rest of God after the work of making the world. " For in six days the Lord made heaven and earth, the sea, and all that in them is, and *rested* the seventh day; wherefore the Lord blessed the Sabbath day and hallowed it." Israel was the people to whom God revealed the great mystery of *Creation;* that master truth by which alone human thought is saved in the long run from what in philosophy is Pantheism, and what in human practice is the sin of confounding God with His works. It brought before the minds of the Jews the ineffable majesty of the great Creator. Therefore the observance of one day in seven was a great counteracting force against the Jewish idolatries, and of the doings of the Macedonian kings of a later day, in Palestine.

(*b*)

9. The Christian motive for the observance of the Lord's day is the **Resurrection of Christ** from the dead. That truth is to the Christian creed what the creation of the world out of nothing was to the Jewish creed. It is the fundamental truth on which all else that is distinctively Christian rests; and it is just as much put forward by the Christian Apostles as is the creation of all things out of nothing by the Jewish prophets. Not, of course, that the creation of all things out of nothing is less precious to us Christians than it was to the Jewish world—only it is more taken for granted. It was eclipsed, so to speak, by the creation of the world of grace, and of this last creation the Resurrection was the starting-point. It is commemorated on the first day of the week, when God brought light out of chaos and darkness; it is the risen Lamb who says, " Behold, I make all things new." And " *if a man be in Christ he is a new creature; old things have passed away, all things have become new.*" *Of this the Lord's day is a weekly festival, because it is the festival of the Resurrection.* In a striking passage in the Epistle to the Colossians, St. Paul associates the observance of the Lord's day with the new moon : "Let no man therefore judge you in meat, or in drink, or in respect of an holy day, or of the new moon, or of the Sabbath days." *In St. Paul's eyes the Sabbath was a part of the discarded system of the ceremonial law, as was the observance of the new moon.*

(*c*)

10. The Christian Lord's day stands on entirely different grounds. The word *Christian* implies that it is no longer *Sabbath* in the Jewish sense ; it stands in the same relation as does the Law in general to the Gospel, as the paschal lamb to the passover. It is transfigured so as to have parted with its identity. The special consecration of a seventh part of time, the abstinence from all labour, this remains ; but the spirit that governs it, the motive of the day, is fundamentally changed : we stand no longer at the foot of Sinai, listening to the thunder, but by the empty tomb.

And here a third and last principle comes forward, which is embodied by the day, and this principle is the necessity of the public worship of God. The cessation of ordinary work is not enjoined upon Christians that they may while away the time or spend it in self-pleasing, or something worse. The Lord's day is the day of days, and upon which Jesus our Lord has the first claim. On this great day every instructed Christian thinks of Him as vindicating His character, as the Teacher of absolute truth, as triumphing publicly over His enemies, as conquering nature, which had always been under the empire of death, as opening the kingdom of heaven to all believers. Surely it is unlike any other day of the week ; and the sense of this finds its only expression in the outburst of prayer and praise from the Christian's heart.

(*d*)

11. Observance of. In the Christian Church the first duty is, like the holy women, like the disciples, to seek to hold converse with the risen Lord. The well spending of the Lord's day should always be the supreme act of Christian worship. The early Church came together on that day to break bread. What was the practice a few years after the Apostle wrote ? We learn from a letter by the heathen Pliny to his master Trajan, that " Christians are accustomed to meet together on a stated day, before it is light, and sing hymns to Christ as God, and to bind themselves by the Sacrament never to commit fraud, theft, or adultery, never to be untrue to their trust." This was the expression of a heathen, looking at the sacred service from without ; gathering an impression from without of that which, of course, he never understood.

The mental atmosphere of a Christian on Sunday is above all things an atmosphere of worship. The day says to him, from its early dawn, " Lift up thine heart," and his answer is, " I lift it up unto Thee, O Lord." He knows he has indeed come to Mount Zion, to the city of the living God ; to an innumerable company of angels ; to the general assembly of the firstborn, whose names are written in heaven ; and to Jesus. The invisible world is before and around him, and he is able to keep earth free from occupations and to surrender himself to the influences which stream down from the throne of the Redeemer. He is, like St. John, " in the spirit; " he sees the higher and everlasting realities ; he measures earth against heaven, and time against eternity.

Sundays such as these are like shafts in tunnels, admitting light and air ; and though we pass them all too soon, their helpful influence does not vanish with the day ; it furnishes us with light for duties which we do ; and makes us follow on towards our eternal home.

(*e*)   *Liddon*

The Lord's Day—continued

The Lord's Day (Matt. xxviii. 1)

The positive command goes; but the idea, the moral necessity, and the spirit of the Sabbath remain. Henceforth it is the Lord's day; and only as we are in Him can we be lords of it.

Henceforth it is the *Spirit's* day; and only in proportion as we are filled with the Spirit can we be in the Spirit on the Lord's day, and rejoice in its holy joy, and be refreshed with His presence who is the embodied Sabbath, at once the "rest" and the refreshing of all toiling and weary souls.

(a)

Sabbath, the Lord's Day

[The Book of Revelation] opens with the *Sabbath* of redemption (hence the prophet has his vision on the Lord's day), and extends to the Sabbath of final completion. Accordingly, we also have the sacred number seven, seven times repeated—the seven Churches, the seven seals, the seven trumpets, the seven thunders, the seven vials, and the seven heads of Antichrist. At the close, we have the manifestation of the seven Spirits of God—who throughout had guided the struggle (chap. i.)—in the appearance of Christ and the transformation of the world; the conclusion of the Bible points back to its commencement, and shows how final and perfect fulfilment had now been attained.

(b)　　　　　　　　　　　　　　*Lange*

The Sabbath and the Lord's Day

The early Christians had no idea of confounding *the Sabbath* with *the Lord's day. Both* days were in early times observed; but the Lord's day was *never* called "the Seventh day" or "the Sabbath"—both of which terms are not infrequently used in place of "Sunday" by "ministers," and even clergy, of our day.

Whence, then, is the obligation of observing the Lord's day derived? And in what does it consist? The obligation rests, I believe, entirely on the Church's custom and express appointment, probably derived from Apostolic authority. And its observance consists, as I apprehend, mainly in two duties—(1) That of public worship; and (2) That of rest from ordinary labour.

The Church's rule is given in express terms in the 29th Canon of the Council of Laodicea—no obscure and unknown Council—which runs as follows:—

"That Christians should not Judaize and rest on the Sabbath, but should labour on that day; and, giving especial honour to the Lord's day, should rest, as Christians, if they can. But if they be found to Judaize, let them be Anathema before Christ."

The Sunday question has become one of pressing importance, in view of the crowded populations of our cities, and the increasing disposition to shirk church-going and religious observances generally. The Church has never, I think, demanded abstinence from recreation and special intercourse on the Lord's day; and the attempt to impose restriction in these matters, as if it were of God's appointment under the Fourth Commandment, appears to me (to use Lord Bramwell's expression) no less than "mischievous." For, so far from promoting the cause of piety, it fosters a gloomy view of religion; and by teaching

people that Sunday recreation, however innocent otherwise, is "Sabbath-breaking," it puts a snare before their conscience, and tempts them to break away altogether from the duty of public worship.

(c)　　　　　　　　　　　　　　*Anon*

The Sabbath and the Lord's Day (Col. ii. 16)

The seventh-day Sabbath, the Jewish Sabbath, which, as far as it was the seventh-day Rest, had been fulfilled by Christ resting in the grave. The position of the day is changed, but the *proportion* remains unchanged, and has received new strength and sanction by its consecration to Christ under the Gospel in the Lord's day.

(d)　　　　　　　　　　　*Wordsworth*

Sabbath, The Christian, Misunderstood

How grossly misunderstood the genuine character of the Christian Sabbath, or Lord's day, seems to be, even by the Church! To confound it with the Jewish Sabbath, or to rest its observance upon the Fourth Commandment, is, in my judgment, heretical, and would so have been considered in the primitive Church. That cessation from labour on the Lord's Day could not have been absolutely incumbent on Christians for two centuries after Christ, is apparent; because during that period the greater part of the Christians were either slaves or in official situations under Pagan masters or superiors, and had duties to perform for those who did not recognise the day.

(e)

The Jewish Sabbath was commemorative of the termination of the great act of Creation; it was to record that the world had not been from eternity, nor had arisen as a dream by itself, but that God had created it by distinct acts of power, and that He had hallowed the day or season in which He rested or desisted from His work. When our Lord arose from the dead, the old creation was, as it were, superseded, and the new creation then began; and therefore the first day and not the last day, the commencement and not the end, of the work of God was solemnized.

(f)

Luther, in speaking of the *good by itself*, and the good *for its expediency alone*, instances the observance of the Christian day of rest, a day of repose from manual labour, and of activity in spiritual labour—a day of joy and co-operation in the work of Christ's creation. "Keep it holy," says he, "for its use sake, both to body and soul! But if anywhere the day is made holy for the mere day's sake, if anywhere any one sets up its observance upon a Jewish foundation, then I order you to work on it, to ride on it, to dance on it, to feast on it—to do anything that shall reprove this encroachment on the Christian spirit and liberty."

(g)　　　　　　　　　　*S. T. Coleridge*

Sabbath Rest (Heb. iv)

(i.) There is the *peace* of justification which the believer tastes (Rom. v. 1), constant in vicissitudes.

(ii.) There is also the *rest* of those who have fallen asleep in Christ—freed from toils and sorrows of earthly life (Rev. xiv. 13).

(h)

The Lord's Day—continued

(iii.) Also the Sabbatic *Rest* which commences only at the second coming of Christ, and accompanies the renovation of the world, and realized only when the *whole* people of God have entered into eternal rest (1 Thess. iv. 17)

(a) *Lange*

The Sabbath and Restraint

Some, and not a small party, have a vague instinctive feeling that the kind of Christianity which they embrace requires for its diffusion a gloomy Sabbath, the Puritan Sabbath; and we incline to believe that they are desirous to separate the Lord's day as much as possible from all other days, to make it a season of rigid restraint.

(b) *Channing*

The Resurrection Sabbath

"*Now late on the Sabbath day, as it began to dawn toward the first day of the week*" (Matt. xxviii. 1)

(c)

The Dawn of Sunday

It is certain and agreed on all hands that St. Matthew means the time after the close of the *Jewish* Sabbath, the time before day-break on the first day of the week, or the Christian Sunday.

(d) *P. Schaff*

According to St. Matthew's method of expression, which is always so full of meaning, we find a doctrinal emphasis in the words, *late in the evening of the* (old) *Sabbath season*, as it *began to dawn toward the early morning of the* (new) *Sunday season.*

(e) *Lange*

By the selection of this peculiar and significant expression the fact is brought forward, that the Christian Sunday had now caused the Jewish Sabbath to cease, and Christianity had now taken the place of Judaism. Sunday is the fulfilment of the Sabbath—not its negation—but its realization.

(f) *Ibid*

Sweet day, so cool, so calm, so bright,
The bridal of the earth and sky,
The dew shall weep thy fall to-night;
For thou must die.

(g) *George Herbert*

Sunday

It is the sinner's day for feeling after God, the saint's day for fuller communion with God, the worldling's day for remembering God, the Christian's day for enjoying God.

(h) *J. Gritton*

The Christian Sunday (Col. ii. 16)

The holy day received for the Sabbath pertaineth naught unto salvation, as Paul himself apertly testifieth unto the Colossians; and it may be any other day, whom any nation, either magistrate, or else the Church, shall appoint and approve.

(i) *Philpot*

Christian Sunday

One day in seven. In the first ages of world, the Creation was the benefaction by which God was principally known, and for which He was chiefly to be worshipped.

The Jews had to commemorate other blessings —the political creation of the nation out of Abraham's family, and their deliverance from Egyptian bondage.

We Christians have to commemorate, besides the common benefit of creation, the transcendent blessing of our redemption, our new creation to the hope of everlasting life, of which our Lord's resurrection to life on the first day of the week is a sure pledge and evidence.

The Sabbath, therefore, in the progress of ages, hath acquired new ends, by new manifestations of the Divine mercy; and these new ends justify correspondent alterations of the original institution.

(j) *Bp. Horsley*

SABBATH, OBSERVANCE OF

The Lord's Day

The observance of the Sabbath, by being adopted into the Decalogue, was made the foundation of all the festal times and observances of the Israelites, as they all culminated in the Sabbath rest. At the same time, as an ἐντολὴ τοῦ νόμου, an ingredient in the Sinaitic law, it belonged to the "shadow of (good) things to come" (Col. ii. 17; cf. Heb. x. 1), which was to be done away when the "body" in Christ had come. Christ is Lord of the Sabbath (Matt. xii. 8); and after the completion of His work, He also rested on the Sabbath. But He rose again on the Sunday; and through His resurrection, which is the pledge to the world of the fruit of His redeeming work, He has made this day the κυριακὴ ἡμέρα (Lord's day) for His Church, to be observed by it till the Captain of its salvation shall return; and having finished the judgment upon all His foes to the very last, shall lead it to the rest of that eternal Sabbath which God prepared for the whole creation through His own resting after the completion of the heaven and the earth.

(k) *Keil*

The Lord's Day, The Observance of (Col. ii. 16)

Cannot be affected by the warning of St. Paul. It is certain that the persons who were judging them, were pressing the duty of observing the Jewish Sabbath, not the Christian Lord's day. It is equally certain that the observance of a weekly day of rest is written in God's physical and social laws for man, as plainly as in the Decalogue. Nor can we escape the conclusion that the Fourth Commandment is but a *reminder* of a previous institution.

(l) *Lange*

"In the Spirit on the Lord's Day" (Rev. i. 1)

Our Lord designed to relax the strictness of Sabbath observance.

Christianity is not a hedge placed round a peculiar people. A slave might have the spirit of Christianity, though obliged to work as a slave on the Sabbath: He might be *in the spirit on the Lord's Day*, though in the mines at Patmos.

(m) *Cecil*

Sabbath: Observance of—*continued*

Sabbath, The, and Æsthetic Religion

Only in a very limited degree is there truth in this at all. Christianity will harmonize: we are not so sure that humanizing will Christianize. Let us be clear upon this matter. Æsthetics are not Religion. It is one thing to civilize and polish: it is another thing to Christianize. The worship of the Beautiful is not the worship of Holiness; nay, I know not whether the one may not have a tendency to disincline from the other.

At least such was the history of ancient Greece. Greece was the home of the Arts, the sacred ground on which the worship of the Beautiful was carried to its perfection. Let those who have read the history of her decline and fall, who have perused the debasing works of her later years, tell us how music, painting, poetry, the arts, softened and debilitated and sensualized the nation's heart. Let them tell us how, when Greece's last and greatest man was warning in vain against the foe at her gates, and demanding a manlier and more heroic disposition to sacrifice, that most polished and humanized people, sunk in trade and sunk in pleasure, were squandering enormous sums upon their buildings and æsthetics, their processions and their people's palaces, till the flood came, and the liberties of Greece were trampled down for ever beneath the feet of the Macedonian Conqueror.

No! the change of a nation's heart is not to be effected by the infusion of a taste for artistic grace. "Other foundation can no man lay that is laid, which is Christ Jesus." Not Art; but the Cross of Christ. Simpler manners, purer lives, more self-denial, more earnest sympathy with the classes that lie below us; nothing short of that can lay the foundations of the Christianity which is to be hereafter, deep and broad.

(*a*)   *F. W. Robertson*

Sabbath-breaking (Matt. xxvii. 62; Luke xxiii.)

It is a poetical justice, that they who have so often accused the Saviour of Sabbath-breaking, now themselves finally desecrate this day.

(*b*)   *Lange*

[Luke vi. 5

The true Sabbath-breakers were those who would sacrifice man to save the Sabbath.

(*c*)   *Ibid*

[Luke vi. 5

The Lord shows both the obligation, and the freedom of the Day of rest.

On this day He visited the Synagogue = obligation to hallow a weekly day of rest. He also passes through the corn-field, performs labours of love, and vindicates the maxim: "Necessity knows no law." A mechanical, Judaistical celebration of Sunday is therefore by His Example as little favoured as a reckless contempt of Sunday. The Christian also, the one anointed by the Holy Spirit, is a Lord of the Sabbath; and where the Spirit of the Lord is, there is liberty, but also order, obedience, glory given to God, and fear of offending a weak brother.

(*d*)   *Ibid*

Sabbath-breaking

"I am no advocate," says one who has steadily set his face against the sin of Sabbath-breaking, "for a pharisaical observance of the Christian Sabbath; nor would I interfere with those quiet recreations which different individuals may think fit to allow themselves, provided that no offence be committed against public decorum, nor any shock given to that public opinion of the sanctity of the Lord's day, which is a chief security for the continuance of religion amongst us. It is principally with a view to that opinion, that I would impress upon the higher classes the importance of an exemplary observance of the day; although it may well be urged upon them with reference to their own interests, as accountable dying sinners. What is lawful for one Christian to do upon the Lord's day, may not be lawful for another, with reference to its effects upon his own religious state, or upon that of others. Whatsoever is injurious to either is unprofitable. And if every person who pretends to any religion, would fairly put it to his conscience and reason, what kind of employment would be most conducive to his own improvement, and to the honour of religion, he would need no casuist to resolve him what might or might not be done upon the Lord's day. At all events, the evil which is to be apprehended at the present moment, is not a Puritanical strictness of observance, which may be the occasion of hypocrisy; but a laxity, fast verging to a total neglect. And were it otherwise, superstition in an ordinance of this kind is no very terrible thing; whereas irreligion is unspeakly mischievous. In spite of the increased number of our churches, in spite of the increased exertions of a zealous and laborious clergy, irreligion is, we fear, not on the wane amongst the poorer classes; and the surest, and the most alarming symptom of it is the profanation of the Sabbath."

(*e*)   *Bp. Blomfield*

Sabbath, The Continental, and the Channel Tunnel Scheme

Ordinary people will probably be content to take the world as it appears in historic times. Everything that we possess and are—our character, our language, our freedom, our institutions, our religion our unviolated hearths, and our far-extended Empire—we owe to the encircling sea; and when Englishmen try to penetrate the designs of Providence, they will not seek them in geographical speculations, but rather thank Him who "isled us here."

(*f*)   "*The Times*," *May 15, 1884, on Channel Tunnel Scheme*

Sabbath Changed to Sunday

What would Christianity be without *the day*, as a sign?

By it the patriarchs and the Jews made a public protestation once in every week against errors of idolatry, which paid its adoration to the works of God—the sun, moon, and other celestial bodies . . . or to deified men, etc.

To this protestation against heathenism—which binds the worshippers of the true God in all ages to a weekly Sabbath, it is reasonable that Christians should add a similar protestation against

(*g*)

Sabbath: Observance of—*continued*

Judaism . . . openly separate from them; and Saturday being the day of their worship, it was as necessary that the Christian Sabbath should be transferred to another day; and the Christians' proper day is the first of the seven = the *Lord's Day*.

(a)   *Bp. Horsley*

Sabbath, The Continental

O Italy!—thy Sabbaths will be soon
Our Sabbaths, closed with mummery and buffoon;
Preaching and pranks will share the motley scene,
Ours parcelled out, as thine have ever been,
God's worship and the mountebank between.

(b)   *Cowper*

Sabbath, Evangelical Observance of

The observance of Sunday is, according to Scriptural history and doctrine, not legal, but Evangelical in its character. It is here mentioned in a very unpretending manner; it might seem even to be accidental that the religious services of the assembly at Troas occurred precisely on a Sunday. The apostolical sanctification of the Sunday was a custom, not a precept, and corresponded to the Spirit of Jesus, as well as to the character of the Apostle Paul. The Augsburg Confession accordingly testifies that Sunday is an ordinance which shall be observed for the sake of peace and love, but that it is not absolutely necessary to salvation.

(c)   *Lange*

The Sabbath for Man

Whoever will keep this maxim in view will avoid the two extremes of unnecessary rigour in the observance of the Sabbath, and a profane neglect thereof.

(d)   *Bp. Horsley*

Sabbath, Necessity of

A traveller, passing a coal-mine in Pennsylvania, saw a field full of mules. A person with him said, " Those are the mules that work all the week down in the mine; but on Sundays they have to come up into the light, or else in a little while they would go blind." It seems to me that what is necessary for mules it no less so for men. Keep men buried in business for the whole seven days, and they would soon lose the very faculty of spiritual vision, having neither eye nor ear nor heart for divine things. Make Sunday a working day, and you degrade man into a mill-horse, and that a blind one.

(e)   *J. Halsey*

Sabbath, Neglect of

A neglect of the ordinances of religion of Divine appointment, is the sure symptom of a criminal indifference about those higher duties by which men pretend to atone for the omission. It is too often found to be the beginning of a licentious life; and for the most part ends in the highest excesses of profligacy and irreligion.

(f)   *Bp. Horsley*

Sabbath, Observance of

The mode of the observance of the Day of Rest has become lately a subject of very considerable attention. Physiologists have demonstrated the necessity of cessation from toil: they have urged the impossibility of perpetual occupation without end. Pictures, with much pathos in them, have been placed before us, describing the hard fate of those on whom no Sabbath dawns. It has been demanded as a right, entreated as a mercy, on behalf of the labouring man, that he should have one day in seven for recreation of his bodily energies. All well and true. But there is a great deal more than this. He who confines his conception of the need of rest to that, has left man on a level with the brutes. Let a man take merely lax and liberal notions of the Fourth Commandment—let him give his household and dependants immunity from toil, and wish for himself and them no more—he will find that there is a something wanting still. Experience tells us, after a trial, that those Sundays are the happiest, the purest, the most rich in blessing, in which the spiritual part has been most attended to—those in which the business letter was put aside till evening, and the profane literature not opened, and the ordinary occupations entirely suspended —those in which, as in the Temple of Solomon, the sound of the hammer has not been heard in the temple of the soul; for this is, in fact, the very distinction between the spirit of the Jewish Sabbath and the spirit of the Christian Lord's day. The one is chiefly for the body. " Thou shalt do no manner of work." The other is principally for the soul,—" I was in the spirit on the Lord's day."

(g)   *F. W. Robertson*

Sabbath, Observance of

We would not that the puritanical spirit of the Sabbatarians of Elizabeth's days should be revived, who preached, that " To do any work on the Sabbath was as great a sin as adultery, and to ring more bells than one on the Lord's day was as great a sin as to commit murder." But we would fain have a higher recognition of the various privileges connected with that holy day, which was twice consecrated by the Father—at the Creation, and at Sinai; Consecrated by the Son, at His resurrection from the dead; consecrated by the Spirit, at His first miraculous outpouring on the day of Pentecost. What God hath thus cleansed, it is not for us to call common.

(h)   *Heylyn*

Sabbath, Observance of

The religious day of the Old Testament also bears the name of Rest. This leads us to the fact that rest is of the highest importance for the observance of the Lord's day, and especially for life in God, and for the existence of the Church. Incessant work makes man dull and lifeless, and destroys his susceptibility for salvation.

According to Exod. xxxi. 13-17, the Sabbath is intended as a sign between God and His people; on the side of God, who instituted the Sabbath, a symbol of His election; on the side of the chosen, a confession to God—an oasis in the wilderness of the world's indifference to its Creator, of the non-attestation of God to the world; a nation serving God in spirit and in truth, whose beautiful worship was entrusted to them by God Himself.

(i)   *Hengstenberg*

Sabbath : Observance of—*continued*

Sabbath, Observance of.

Briefly, to sum up the matter, the law concerning the Sabbath was expressly given to Israel alone, and hence in the letter it is binding upon them only; but, because it was given by God, it must contain a germ which forms the foundation of a law binding upon us also. Of the spirit of the command respecting the Sabbath, not a jot or a tittle can perish. What belongs to the kernel and what to the shell, must be determined from the general relations which the Old and the New Testament bear to one another. That which cannot be reduced to anything peculiar to the Old Testament must retain its authority for us also.

(*a*)　　　　　　　　　　*Hengstenberg*

Sabbath, Observance of.

Isaiah, in his discourse on entering upon office, chap. i. 13, declares that the mere outward observance of the Sabbath is an abomination to God. He gives a positive definition of the true hallowing of the Sabbath in chap. lviii. 13 : "If thou turn away thy foot from the Sabbath, from doing thy pleasure on My holy day; and call the Sabbath a delight, the holy of the Lord, honourable; and shalt honour Him, not doing thine own ways, nor finding thine own pleasure, nor speaking thine own words." Doing thine own pleasure and thine own ways is here placed in opposition to the "keeping holy"; and their "own pleasure" he employs in its full extent and meaning, making it inclusive of the speaking of words, *i.e.*, of such words as are nothing more than words, and tend neither to the honour of God nor to the edification of themselves and their neighbours—idle words. He insists so strongly on the inward disposition of mind, that he makes it a requisition that the Sabbath shall not be regarded as a heavy burden by which a man is taken away from his own work against his will, but as a gain, as a merciful privilege which God, whose commands are so many promises, gives to His own people as a refuge from the distractions and cares of the world.

Moreover, Ezekiel says repeatedly in chapter xx., of the Israelites in the wilderness, that they grossly polluted the Sabbath of the Lord. There is no mention in the Pentateuch of the neglect of the outward rest of the Sabbath; on the contrary, Num. xv. 32, sqq., shows that it was strictly observed. The prophet can, therefore, only have reference to the desecration of the Sabbath by sin.

(*b*)　　　　　　　　　　*Ibid*

Sabbath, Observance of

By keeping a Sabbath, we acknowledge a God, and declare that we are not atheists; by keeping one day in seven, we protest against idolatry, and acknowledge *that* God who in the beginning made the heavens and the earth; and by keeping our Sabbath on the first day of the week, we protest against Judaism, and acknowledge *that* God who, having made the world, sent His only begotten Son to redeem mankind. The observance of the Sunday in the Christian Church is a public weekly assertion of the first two articles in our Creed—the belief in God the Father Almighty, the Maker of heaven and earth, and in Jesus Christ, His only Son our Lord.

(*c*)　　　　　　　　　　*Bp. Horsley*

Sabbath, Observance of

Christ came, not to abolish the Sabbath, but to explain and enforce it. Its observance is nowhere positively enjoined by Him. Christianity was to be practicable, and was to go into all nations; and it goes thither, stripped of its precise and various circumstances. " I was in the spirit on the Lord's day "=the soul of the Christian Sabbath. The spirit, not the letter. In this way a thousand frivolous questions concerning its observance would be answered. "What can I do?" I answer, "Be in the spirit."

(*d*)　　　　　　　　　　*Cecil*

Sabbath, Christian Observance of.

We are going to spend a Sabbath in eternity. The Christian will acquire as much of the Sabbath spirit as he can. And in proportion to a man's real piety in any age, he will be found to have been a diligent observer of the Sabbath day.

(*e*)　　　　　　　　　　*Ibid*

Sabbath, Observance of.

If the Sabbath rest on the needs of human nature, and we accept His decision that the Sabbath was made for *man*, then you have an eternal ground to rest on, from which you cannot be shaken. A son of man may be lord of the Sabbath-day; but he is not lord of his own nature. He cannot make one hair white or black. You may abrogate the formal rule, but you cannot abrogate the needs of your own soul. Eternal as the constitution of the soul of man, is the necessity for the existence of a day of rest.

(*f*)　　　　　　　　　*F. W. Robertson*

Sabbath, Observance of

When is a son of man lord of the Sabbath-day? To whom may the Sabbath safely become a shadow? I reply, He that has the mind of Christ may exercise discretionary lordship over the Sabbath-day. He who is in possession of the substance may let the shadow go. A man in health has done with the prescriptions of the physician. But for an unspiritual man to regulate his hours and amount of rest by his desires, is just as preposterous as for an unhealthy man to rule his appetites by his sensations. Win the mind of Christ—be like Him, and then, in the reality of Rest in God, the Sabbath form of rest will be superseded. Remain apart from Christ, and then you are under the Law again, the Fourth Commandment is as necessary for you as it was for the Israelite: the prescriptive regimen which may discipline your soul to a sounder state. It is at his peril that the worldly man departs from the *rule* of the day of rest. Nothing can make us free from the Law but the Spirit.

(*g*)　　　　　　　　　　*Ibid*

Sabbath, Observance of

The Sabbath is God's sign between Himself and His people. . . . No minister of Christ has a right to speak oracularly. All that he can pretend to do, is to give his judgment; as one that has obtained mercy of the Lord to be faithful. And on large national subjects there is no class so ill qualified to form a judgment with breadth as we, the clergy of the Church of England, accustomed

(*h*)

Sabbath: Observance of—*continued*

as we are to move in the narrow circle of those who listen to us with forbearance and deference, and mixing but little in real life, till, in our cloistered and inviolable sanctuaries, we are apt to forget that it is one thing to lay down rules for a religious clique, and another to legislate for a great nation.

(*a*)   *F. W. Robertson*

Sabbath, Christian Observance of

By virtue of its essence, it must be eternal, and is an exemplification of what our Lord says in Matt. v. 18. We, too, must consecrate ourselves to God; and in order to do this daily and hourly, in the midst of our work, we also must have regularly recurring days of freedom from all occupation and distraction; for the weakness which made this a necessity under the Old Testament is common to human nature at all times. We, too, must make public confession to God. But just as the whole Mosaic Law is a particular application of an eternal idea to a definite people, so it is also with the command relating to the Sabbath. Therefore, side by side with the eternal moment, it must contain a temporal moment. This consists mainly in the following points :—(1.) The truths laid down as subjects of meditation for the Old Testament nation and for us, on the Lord's day, are various. Devotion has always reference to God as He has revealed Himself. Under the Old Testament it conceived of God as the Creator of the world and the Deliverer of Israel out of Egypt. The latter is set forth in Deut. v. 12-15 as a subject of meditation in the observance of the Sabbath. Afterwards the subject became more extended, even under the Old Testament itself, by each new benefit of God, every new revelation of His nature. But the nucleus remained always the same. Nothing which occurred had power to supersede these two notions of God. Under the New Testament an essential change took place. God in Christ, this was now the great object of devotion. (2.) And with this the change of day is closely connected. The day on which the Creation was ended, was now naturally superseded by the day on which Redemption was fulfilled. The religious day of the Old Testament can only be the κυριακὴ ἡμέρα (Apoc. i. 10).

(*b*)   *Hengstenberg*

Sabbath, Christian Observance of

We believe that the first day of the week is to be set apart for the public worship of God, and for the promotion of the knowledge and practice of Christianity, and that it was selected for this end in honour of the resurrection of Christ. To this view we are led by the following considerations :—Wherever the Gospel was preached, its professors were formed into Churches or congregations, and ministers were appointed for their instruction or edification. Wherever Christianity was planted, societies for joint religious acts and improvement were instituted, as the chief means of establishing and diffusing it. Now it is plain that for these purposes regular times must have been prescribed; and, accordingly, we find that it was the custom of the primitive Christians to hold their religious assemblies on the first day of the week—the day of Christ's resurrection. This we learn from the New Testament, and from the universal testimony of the earliest ages of the Church. Wherever Christianity was spread, the first day was established as the season of Christian worship and instruction. Such are the grounds on which this institution rests. We regard it as altogether a *Christian institution*, as having its origin in the Gospel, as peculiar to the new dispensation; and we conceive that the proper observation of it is to be determined wholly by the spirit of Christianity. We meet in the New Testament no precise rules as to the mode of spending the Lord's day, as to the mode of worship and teaching, as to the distribution of the time not given to public services. And this is just what might be expected; for the Gospel is not a religion of precise rules. It differs from Judaism in nothing more than in its free character. It gives great principles, broad views, general, prolific, all-comprehensive precepts, and entrusts the application of them to the individual. It sets before us the perfection of our nature, the spirit which we should cherish, the virtues which constitute "the kingdom of heaven within us," and leaves us to determine for ourselves, in a great measure, the discipline by which these noble ends are to be secured. Let no man, then, bind what Christ hath left free.

(*c*)   *Channing*

Sabbath, Christian Observance of

We observe the day that commemorates a greater deliverance and introduces a new creation (say a new Israel, and to a new wilderness period of temptation, etc.). *The* day in the seven is changed; but *a* day in seven has been observed from the first (Acts xx. 7. Rev. i. 10).

The day is to be kept as one of *rest*, of moral improvement, and of joyous holy devotion (Isa. lviii. 13, 14).

(*d*)   *Angus*

Sabbath, Christian Observance of

To us it is a more important day, and consecrated to nobler purposes, than the ancient Sabbath. We are bound, however, to state that we cannot acquiesce in the distinctions which are often made between this and other days, for they seem to us at once ungrounded and pernicious. We sometimes hear, for example, that the Lord's day is set apart from our common lives to religion. What! Are not all days equally set apart to religion? Has religion more to do with Sunday than with any other portion of time? Is there any season over which piety should not preside? So the day is sometimes distinguished as "holy." What! Is there stronger obligation to holiness on one day than another? Is it more holy to pray in the church than to pray in the closet, or than to withstand temptation in common life? The true distinction of Sunday is, that it is consecrated to certain means or direct acts of religion. But these are not holier than other duties. They are certainly not more important than their end, which is a virtuous life. There is, we fear, a superstition on this point, unworthy of the illumination of Christianity. We earnestly recommend the Lord's day, but we dare not esteem its duties above those of other days. We prize and recommend it as an institution through which our whole lives are to be sanctified and ennobled; and, without this fruit, vain, and worse than vain, are

(*e*)

Sabbath, Observance of—*continued*

the most rigid observances, the most costly sacrifices, the loudest and most earnest prayers. We would on no account disparage the life of the Lord's day. We delight in this peaceful season, so fitted to allay the feverish heat and anxieties of active life, to cherish self-communion, and communion with God and with the world to come. It is good to meet as brethren in the church, to pray together, to hear the word of God, to retire for a time from ordinary labour, that we may meditate on great truths more deliberately, and with more continuous attention. In these duties we see a fitness, excellence, and happiness; but still, if a comparison must be made, they seem to us less striking proofs of piety and virtue than are found in the disinterestedness, the self-control, the love of truth, the scorn of ill-gotten wealth, the unshaken trust in God, the temperate and grateful enjoyment, the calm and courageous sufferings for duty, to which the Christian is called in daily life. It is right to adore God's goodness in the hour of prayer, but does it not seem more excellent to carry in our souls the conviction of this goodness; as our spring and pattern, and to breathe it forth in acts conformed to the beneficence of our Maker? It is good to seek strength from God in the Church; but does it not seem more excellent to use well this strength in the sore conflicts of life, and to rise through it to a magnanimous and victorious virtue? Such comparisons, however, we have no pleasure in making, and they are obviously exposed to error. The enlightened Christian "esteemeth every day alike." To him all days bring noble duties; bring occasions of a celestial piety and virtue; bring trials, in wrestling with which he may grow strong; bring aids and incitements, through which he may rise above himself. All days may be holy, and the holiest is that in which he yields himself, with the most single-hearted, unshrinking, uncompromising purpose to the will of God.

(a)　　　　　　　　　　　　　　　*Channing*

Sabbath Observance, Eternal Necessity of

We have abrogated almost all that belonged to the Sabbath. We have taken away "every manner of work," and changed other important particulars. Sunset to sunset is now midnight to midnight. Instead of "*the seventh day*" we have left only "*one day in seven;*" and the sceptical mind requires some proof of the moral obligation of keeping *one* day without work. . . . One must take *higher* ground, and tell him there is an eternal necessity for the recurring Sabbath. On this only must we found the perpetual necessity of observing the Sabbath, to secure temporal rest, to think on the Creator of man in His image, and of his own destiny.

The mode of observing the Sabbath varies according to the age of the individual, place, age of the world, etc.

The *rest* fit for the old, is not so for the young. That for the intellectual is not that of the unlearned.

There is a difference, too, from national custom, etc.

The stern Sabbaths of the Israelites made them the spiritual teachers of the world—produced such men as Moses, David, Paul; so the Puritans.

(b)　　　　　　　　　　　　*F. W. Robertson*

Sabbath Observance and Infidelity

An infidel, boasting in a published letter, that he had raised two acres of " Sunday corn," which he had intended to devote to the purchase of infidel books, adds : "All the work done on it was done on Sunday, and it will yield some seventy bushels to the acre; so I don't see but that Nature or Providence has smiled upon my Sunday work, however the priests or the Bible may say that work done upon that day never prospers." To this the editor of an agricultural paper replies: "If the author of this shallow nonsense had read the Bible half as much as he has read the works of its opponents, he would have known that the great Ruler of the universe does not always square up His accounts with mankind in the month of October."

(c)

Sabbath, Christian and Jewish Observance of the (John v. 16)

In connection with verse 17, see the difference between the then prevailing Jewish, and the Christian idea of Sabbath observance. The former is negative and slavish, the latter positive and free. The Pharisees scrupulously adhered to the *letter* of the Fourth Commandment, as far as it *forbade* any (common) work, and hedged it around with all sorts of hair-splitting distinctions and rabbinical restrictions; but they violated its *spirit*, which demands the positive *sanctification* of the Sabbath by doing good. The rest of the Sabbath is not the rest of idleness or mere cessation from labour, else God Himself, who is always at work (ver. 17) would be a Sabbath-breaker as well as Christ. It is rather rest in God, a rest from ordinary work in order to a higher and holier activity for the glory of God and the good of man. We must cease from *our* earthly work, that God may do *His* heavenly work in and through us. The Sabbath law, like the whole law, is truly fulfilled by love to God and love to man. Christ refutes the false conception of Sabbath rest, as a mere cessation from labour, in various ways.

　(i.) By the example of David eating the shewbread;

　(ii.) By the priests working in the Temple;

　(iii.) By the readiness of the Jews to deliver an ox out of a pit on the Sabbath.

Here He takes higher ground, and claims an equality with the Father, who never ceases doing good. God's rest after Creation was not a rest of sleep or inaction, but a rest of joy in the completion of His work and of benediction of His creatures. "God *blessed* the seventh day and sanctified it" (Gen. ii. 3).

His strictly *creative* activity ceased with the Hexaëmeron, but His world-*preserving* and *governing*, as well as His *redeeming* activity continues without interruption; and this is properly His Sabbath, combining the highest action with the deepest repose. In the case of man while on earth, abstinence from the distracting multiplicity of secular labour and toil is only the necessary condition for attending to his spiritual interests Acts of worship and acts of charity are proper works for the Christian Sabbath, and are refreshing rest to body and soul, carrying in themselves their own exceeding great reward.

Christ never violated the fourth or any other commandment of God in its true divine meaning

(d)

Sabbath, Observance of—*continued*

and intent, but fulfilled it by doctrine and example (Matt. v. 17). He emancipated us from the slavery of the negative, superstitious, and hypocritical sabbatarianism of the Pharisees, and set us an example of the true positive observance of the Sabbath by doing good; the Sabbath being made *for man* (Mark ii. 27) *i.e.*, for his temporal and eternal benefit. This was its purpose when God instituted it, together with the marriage relation, in the state of man's innocence; and this Christ has restored, as He restored the marriage relation to its original purity. The commentators pass too slightly over this point; and some of them misconstrue Christ's and Paul's opposition to the Jewish sabbatarianism of that age into a violation or abrogation of the Fourth Commandment.

(*a*) *P. Schaff*

Sabbath Observance, and the Fourth Commandment

What regard is due to the institution of a Sabbath under the Christian dispensation? Plainly this:—neither more nor less than was due to it in the patriarchal times, before the Mosaic Covenant took place.

It is a gross mistake to consider the Sabbath as a mere festival of the Jewish Church, deriving its whole sanctity from the Levitical law. The contrary appears, as well from evidence as from reason of the thing.

The observance of the seventh day has a place in the Decalogue among the first duties of natural religion. The reason assigned for the injunction is general, and has no relation to the particular circumstances of the Israelites. The creation of the world was an event equally interesting to the whole human race; and the acknowledgment of God as our Creator is a duty in all ages and in all countries, equally incumbent upon every individual man. The terms of the institution indicate an earlier age: "Therefore the Lord blessed the seventh day *and set it apart*" = past time—not "*now* sets it apart"—but He did bless it and set it apart in time past, and now requires you, His chosen people, to observe that ancient institution.

(*b*) *Bishop Horsley*

Sabbath Observance, and Heaven

He that thinks it too much to keep a short Sabbath here, shall never be thought worthy to celebrate the eternal Sabbath hereafter.

(*c*) *Anon*

'Tis like a little heaven below.

(*d*) *Watts*

Sabbath, Non-observance of the

He who, not trying to serve God on any day, gives Sunday to toil or pleasure, certainly observes not the day; but his non-observance is not rendered to the Lord. He may be free from superstition; but it is not Christ who has made him free. Nor is he one of whom St. Paul would have said that his liberty on the Sabbath is as acceptable as his brother's conscientious scrupulosity.

Here, then, we are at issue with the popular defence of public recreations on the Sabbath day, not so much with respect to the practice, as with respect to the grounds on which the practice is approved. They claim liberty; but it is not Christian liberty. Like St. Paul, they demand a licence for non-observance; only, it is not "non-observance to the Lord." For distinguish well, the abolition of Judaism is not necessarily the establishment of Christianity. To do away with the Sabbath day in order to substitute a nobler, truer, more continuous Sabbath, even the Sabbath of all time given up to God, is well. But to do away with the special rights of God to the Sabbath, in order merely to substitute the rights of pleasure, or the rights of mammon, or even the licence of profligacy and drunkenness, that, methinks, is not St. Paul's "Christian liberty."

(*e*) *F. W. Robertson*

Sabbath Observance, Perpetual, Universal, and Irrepealable

(i.) *Perpetual* in *moral* meaning, as teaching and reminding man of his origin and destiny;

(ii.) *Universal*, because it *was made for man*, descended from Adam, and not merely for the Jew descended from Abraham;

(iii.) *Irrepealable*, because, though we may change the day,—as we have done,—the principle of the Sabbath remains unchanged. It has suffered no loss by the change, but, on the other hand, it has gained in power and force as its true idea has become more manifest.

(*f*)

Sabbath, the Poor Man's Day

Hail, Sabbath! thee I hail, the poor man's day.

(*g*) *Grahame*

Sabbath, and Public Worship

Restore to God His due in tithe and time:
A tithe purloined cankers the whole estate.
Sundays observe—think, when the bells do chime,
'Tis angels' music; therefore come not late.

(*h*) *Herbert*

Sabbath, Present Observance of

Men are left now without positive command on this subject, because the world now is not in its infancy, but under Christianity, where our rule is to understand what the will of the Lord is, and to do it.

(*i*)

Sabbath, Reasons for its Observance

(i.) "In the beginning." The Sabbath is one of the "Beginnings," therefore it has reference to an *end*, and that end is not yet.

(ii.) The Sabbath, from a religious point of view, has gained in respect of *obligation* by the development of religion, rather than otherwise. As the festival,

1. Of the Creation;
2. Of Redemption; and,
3. Of the foundation of the Church of Christ.

The reasons for abrogating it, and for its non-observance have become correspondingly weakened.

(*j*)

Sabbath, Religious Observance of

There is a religious observance of the Sabbath-day possible. We are bound by the spirit of the Fourth Commandment, so far as we are in the same

(*k*)

Sabbath : Observance of—*continued*

spiritual state as they to whom it was given. The spiritual intent of Christianity is to worship God every day in the spirit. But had this law been given in all its purity to the Jews, instead of turning every weekday into a Sabbath, they would have transformed every Sabbath into a weekday: with no special day fixed for worship, they would have spent every day without worship. Their hearts were too dull for a devotion so spiritual and pure. Therefore a law was given, specializing a day, in order to lead them to the border truth that every day is God's.

Now, so far as we are in the Jewish state, the Fourth Commandment, even in its rigour and strictness, is wisely used by us ; nay, we might say, indispensable. For who is he who needs not the day ? He is the man so rich in love, so conformed to the mind of Christ, so elevated into the sublime repose of heaven, that he needs no carnal ordinances at all, nor the assistance of one day in seven to kindle spiritual feelings, seeing he is, as it were, all his life in heaven already.

(*a*)　　　　　　　　　　*F. W. Robertson*

Sabbath, Religious Observance of, Necessary

God made the Sabbath for men in a certain spiritual state, because they needed it. The need therefore is deeply hidden in human nature. He who can dispense with it must be holy and spiritual indeed. And he who, still unholy and unspiritual, would yet dispense with it, is a man who would fain be wiser than his Maker. We, Christians as we are, still need the law, both in its restraints and in its aids to our weakness. No man, therefore, who knows himself, but will gladly and joyfully use the institution. No man who knows the need of his brethren will wantonly desecrate it, or recklessly hurt even their scruples respecting its observance. And no such man can look with aught but grave and serious apprehensions on such an innovation upon English customs of life and thought, as the proposal to give public and official countenance to a scheme which will invite millions, I do not say to an irreligious, but certainly an unreligious use of the day of rest.

(*b*)　　　　　　　　　　　　　　　*Ibid*

Sabbath, Observance of, and the Working Classes

To the labouring man a larger proportion of the day must be given to the recreation of his physical nature, than is necessary for the man of leisure, to whom the spiritual observance of the day is easy, and seems all. . . . " The Sabbath was made for man." Be generous, consistent, large-minded. A man may hold stiff, precise, Jewish notions on this subject ; but do not stigmatize that man as a formalist. Another may hold large, Paul-like views of the abrogation of the Fourth Commandment, and yet he may be, sincerely and zealously anxious for the hallowing of the day in his household and through his country. Do not call that man a Sabbath-breaker. Remember, the Pharisees called the Son of God a Sabbath-breaker. They kept the law of the Sabbath—they broke the law of love. Which was the worst to break ? which was the higher law to keep ? Take care lest, in the zeal which seems to you to be for Christ, ye be found indulging their spirit, and not His.

(*c*)　　　　　　　　　　　　　　　*Ibid*

The Sabbath Perpetual—" a Sign for ever "

The eternal duration of this *sign* was involved in the signification of the Sabbatical rest, which reaches forward into eternity.

(*d*)

Sabbath, Unchangeableness of

One thing is plain. Before Moses, not one precept is given in relation to the Sabbath, nor a hint of its unchangeableness to the end of the world.

It is certain that the question of the perpetuity of the Sabbath is to be settled by the teachings of Jesus Christ, the great Prophet, who alone is authorized to determine how far the Old Testament institutions of religion are binding on us Christians.

(*e*)　　　　　　　　　　　*Channing*

Sabbath, Violation of

Not only personal, but even national judgments may be expected for the violation of the Sabbath. But, on the other hand, every blessing may be expected, both by individuals and the community, if the Sabbath be habitually and conscientiously improved. Indeed, it seems almost impossible that any one who sets himself in earnest to improve the Sabbath day, should ever perish.

(*f*)　　　　　　　　　　*Chas. Simeon*

Sunday, Observance of

We see from Acts xx. 7 ; 1 Cor. xvi. 1, 2 ; Rev. i. 10, that Sunday was observed in the days of the Apostles.

(*g*)　　　　　　　　　　　　　*Lange*

Sabbath observance not abrogated by Christianity, proved by Heb. iv.—" there remaineth a Sabbath-keeping for the people of God."

(*h*)

A Motto for Sunday

" Seek those things which are above."

(*i*)　　　　　　　　　　　　　*Stokoe*

The Christian Sunday demands higher recognition. Twice consecrated by the Father, at Creation and at Sinai ; consecrated by the Son at His Resurrection ; and consecrated by the Holy Spirit at Pentecost.

(*j*)　　　　　　　　　　　　　*Nixon*

Sunday, Observance of

" *The first day of the week* " (Acts xx. 7)

= Our Sunday—the first trace of the observance which history exhibits. Luke's language plainly indicates that this day was precisely one that was kept holy, and on which assemblies for religious services were customarily held.

With this view the circumstance happily agrees, that the first mention of the observance of Sunday is made in connection with a Gentile-Christian congregation ; since, according to the nature of the case, this custom was introduced at an earlier period, and with more ease in Gentile-Christian than in Judæo-Christian congregations.

(*k*)　　　　　　　　　　　　　*Lange*

Sabbath : Observance of—*continued*

Sunday

The believer does not in the least regard Sunday as possessing a *superior holiness* to other days. To him all days are alike—of equal holy consecration. As rest is not holier than work, no more is Sunday holier than other days.

It is another form of consecration, the periodical return of which, like sleep and waking, arises from our condition of physico-psychical existence.

(a)   *Godet*

SACRAMENTARIANISM

The spiritual reality of regeneration and union with Christ, is not so bound to the external sacramental sign that it cannot be enjoyed without it. *We* must obey God's ordinances ; but *God* is free, and we should bless whom He blesses. High sacramentarianism is contrary to the teaching of Christ according to St. John (iii. and iv.).

(b)   *Lange*

SACRAMENTS

The Newmanites say that certain divine powers of administering the Sacrament effectually can only be communicated by a regular succession from those who, as they supposed, had them at first. W. Law holds this ground ; there must be a succession in order to keep up the mysterious gift bestowed on the priesthood, which makes Baptism wash away sin, and converts the elements in the Lord's Supper into effectual means of grace. This is in the highest degree false and antichristian.

(c)

The Eucharist.—Our Lord forbids us to suppose that the highest spiritual blessings can be conferred *only* or chiefly through the reception of material elements. We *are* told the great mode by which we are affected. " The words which I speak unto you, they are spirit, and they are life."

(d)   *Dr. Arnold*

SACRAMENTS, THE (1 Cor. x. 1–4)

Baptism is the solemn profession of our Christianity ; and the passing through the Red Sea was the Israelites' profession of discipleship to Moses : then they passed the Rubicon, the die was cast, thenceforward there was no return for them. One solemn step had severed them for ever from Egypt ; and the cloud guidance which then began, kept the memory of this act before them by a constant witness in all their journeyings. So far this is equivalent to Baptism, which is discipleship : a sacrament or oath of obedience, the force of which is kept up and recalled by an outward sign. They had another sacrament in the " Rock that followed them." The Rock did not literally follow them ; but go where they would, the wondrous waters from the rock flowed by their path and camp. Figuratively, therefore, it followed ; the life of it streamed after them. They were never without its life-giving influence ; and therefore never destitute of a sacrament : " that Rock was Christ." Here observe the sacramental principle. As Christ said of the bread, " This is My body," so St. Paul declares, " That Rock was Christ " ; not that the bread was literally transformed into His Body, or that the rock was changed into Christ ; nor again, merely that bread represented the body of Christ, or that the rock represented Christ, but this— *that which is wondrous in the bread and rock, the life-giving power in both, is Christ.* The symbol as a material is nothing, the spirit in it—Christ—is everything.

Now the mystic and the formalist say these signs, and these only, convey grace : sacraments are miraculous. But St. Paul says to the Corinthians, the Jews had symbols as living as yours. Bread, wine, water, cloud, it matters not what the material is. God's presence is everything ; God's power, God's life—wherever these exist, *there,* there is a sacrament. What, then, is the lesson we learn ? Is it that God's life, and love, and grace, are limited to certain materials, such as the rock, the bread, or the wine ? Or is that all here is sacramental, that we live in a Divine world ; that every simple meal, every gushing stream, every rolling river, and every drifting cloud is a symbol of God, and a sacrament to every open heart ? And the power of recognising and feeling this, makes all the difference between the religious and the irreligious spirit.

(e)   *F. W. Robertson*

SACRIFICE

There needs no more sacrifice for the penitent. There remains no more for the impenitent.

(f)   *Cadman*

SACRIFICES

Augustus and Marcus Aurelius required so great a number of beasts for their sacrifices, that it was said : " All oxen and calves hoped and prayed that they might never return from their journeys, or campaigns, as otherwise they were infallibly lost."

(g)   *Seneca*

At the accession of Caligula, 160,000 victims were slaughtered ; and the same Emperor had innocent men dressed out as victims, and then thrown down precipices, as an atonement for his life.

(h)   *Suetonius*

SACRIFICES, NATURE OF

1. *The Sin-offering* = " I am a sinner."
Its characteristic feature was *the sprinkling of blood.*"
2. *The Burnt-offering* = " I need holiness."
Its characteristic was *totality*.
3. *The Thank-offering* = " This is my gift."
And its characteristic was *Spontaneity*, or *Freewill.*
N.B.—Such being the case, if the order was inverted, or altered, it would indicate the *attitude* the worshipper took towards God. If he came with a sin-offering, or with a thank-offering only, he declared himself a *sinner*, or *not a sinner* by that act.

Such was the difference, apparently, between the offerings of Cain and Abel ; and by their offerings respectively they became types of the various ways that men have ever since viewed the Atonement.

(i)

SADDUCEES AND PHARISEES, THE (Matt. xxii. 23, etc.)

Are the two great parties in misleading the human race; they change their position in succeeding ages, one of them ordinarily being pre-eminent. These spirits are always to be contended against, even now; now unbelief is united with the semblance of wisdom and illumination. Against both Christ protests continually; and against both the Church teacher must protest. The former appeal to authority, antiquity, tradition, the sanctity of the letter; the latter to reason, doubt, freedom.

(a)   *Heubner and Lavater*

Christianity has now to contend with infidelity and ritualism = the free-thinking spirit and the traditionalist spirit = *Pharisees and Sadducees*.

(b)

SAINT

For virtue's self may too much zeal be had;
The worst of madmen is a saint run mad.

(c)   *Pope*

Sublimer in this world know I nothing than a peasant saint.
. . . Such a one will take thee back to Nazareth itself.

(d)   *Carlyle*

If we consider Cranmer merely as a statesman, he will not appear a much worse man than Wolsey, Gardiner, Cromwell, or Somerset. But when an attempt is made to set him up as a saint, it is scarcely possible for any man of sense who knows the history of the times to preserve his gravity.

(e)   *Macaulay : "Essays"*

Saintly in his professions, unscrupulous in his dealings, zealous for nothing, bold in speculation, a coward and a time-server in action, a placable enemy and a lukewarm friend, he was in every way qualified to arrange the terms of the coalition between the religious and the worldly enemies of Popery.

(f)   *Macaulay, on Cranmer*

SAINTS

I believe that a man might be, as a tailor or a costermonger, every inch of him a saint, a scholar, and a gentleman, for I have seen some few such already. I believe hundreds of thousands more would be so, if their businesses were put on a Christian footing, etc. . . . I think the cry, "Rise in life," has been excited by the very increasing impossibility of being anything but brutes while they struggle below.

(g)   *Chas. Kingsley*

SAINTS

To our eyes mankind is divided into *eminent* and *obscure;* the *important* and the *insignificant*. But to the eye of God = *the good* and *the evil, saved* and *unsaved souls*. From bad men and women, who have lived only to gratify self; in the feverish thirst for gold, through robbery and wrong; or by the unlawful indulgence of the lowest passions; whose writings are lessons with polluted thoughts,

who have been greedy of gossip, slander, and lies; who have handed on evil traditions; idle cumberers of the ground, whose root is as rottenness and their blossom as the dust; whose god is their belly, whose glory is their shame, who mind earthly things—the world may give them fortunes, coronets, applause, but these are *bad men and bad women*.

If there were no salt, none on earth but the four classes whom God most hates,—mockers, liars, hypocrites, and slanderers,—then, indeed, earth had been an anticipated hell. "Without are dogs and sorcerers, and whoremongers, and murderers, and idolaters, and every one that loveth and maketh a lie." With what unspeakable relief do we turn from these to the saints of God! and think of the long line of heroes of faith in olden times; of the patriarchs—Enoch the blameless, Noah the faithful, Abraham the friend of God; of the sweet and meditative Isaac, the afflicted and wrestling Jacob; of Moses, the meekest of men; of brave judges, glorious prophets, patriot warriors, toiling apostles; of the many martyrs who would rather die than lie; of the hermits who fled from the guilt and turmoil of life into the solitude of the wilderness; of the missionaries— St. Paul, Columban, Benedict, Boniface, Francis Xavier, Schwartz, Eliot, Henry Martyn, Coleridge Patteson; of reformers who cleared the world of lies, like Savonarola, Huss, Luther, Zwingli, Wesley, Whitfield; of wise rulers, like Alfred, Louis, Washington, and Garfield; of the writers of holy books, like Thomas-à-Kempis, Baxter, Bunyan, Jeremy Taylor; of the slayers of monstrous abuses, like Howard and Wilberforce; of good bishops, like Hugo of Avalon, and Fénélon, and Berkeley; of good pastors, like Oberlin, and Fletcher of Madeley, and Adolphe Monod, and Felix Neff; of all true poets, whether sweet and holy, like George Herbert, and Cowper, and Keble, and Longfellow, or grand and mighty, like Dante and Milton. These are but few of the many who have reflected the glory of their Master, Christ; and who walk with Him in white robes, for they are worthy. . . . I urge you in days like these to make yourselves acquainted with Christian history and biography, as an antidote to the degeneracy of these worldly and evil days.

(h)   *Archd. Farrar*

SAINTS, THE

"*The saints shall judge the earth*" (1 Cor. vi. 2)

(i.) The supremacy of goodness. . . . Successively have force, hereditary right, talent, wealth, been the aristocracies of the earth. But then, in *that* kingdom to come, goodness shall be the only condition of supremacy.

(ii.) In *that* kingdom the *best* shall rule.

(iii.) Each shall have his place according to his capacity. 1 Cor. xii. 28 = each man took his place in the Church of Christ, not according to his choice, but according to his charism or his gift. A man became a teacher, not because it was his own desire, but because God had placed him there from his capacity for it. Each for what he was most fitted. So in the kingdom to come we shall not have the anomalies which now prevail. Men are ministers now who are fit only to plough; men are hidden now in professions where there is no scope for their powers. But it shall be altered there.

(i)   *F. W. Robertson*

Many saints have been canonized who ought to have been cannonaded.

(a)   *Colton*

" *As becometh saints* " (Eph. v. 3)

Were the Apostle to say, Let despondency be banished, he might add, as becometh *believers;* or, Let enmity be suppressed, he might subjoin; as becometh the *brethren;* but he pointedly says in this place, " as becometh saints."

(b)   *Eadie*

SALVATION (Eph. i. 3–14)

Salvation is

1. *Foreordained* by the *Father;* it consists in
   (i.) Holiness;
   (ii.) Sonship (4, 5).
2. *Effected* by the *Son;* its parts are
   (i.) Redemption;
   (ii.) Forgiveness (6, 7).
3. *Made known* by the Spirit (8–10).
4. *Actually appropriated*
   (i.) By Jews;
   (ii.) By Gentiles (11–14).
   (c)

SALVATION

I have read of some Seas, so pure and clear, that a man may see the *bottom*, though they be *forty* feet deep. I know this river is a *deep* river; but it is not said that we can see no bottom. The comparison implies that a man with good eyes may see to the bottom. So then, we shall look down through these crystal streams, and see what be at the bottom of all. The bottom of all is, that we might be saved! " These things I say," saith Christ, " that ye might be saved!" What a good sound bottom is here!

(d)   *John Bunyan*

SALVATION OF " ALL MEN " (Titus ii. 11)

Grace will not be confined. For God's goodness cannot be exhausted. He is *dives in omnes*, rich enough for all (Rom. x. 12). It is an excellent attribute, which is given Him by St. James (v. 11) πολύσπλαγχνος. In God's mercy, there is both εὖ and πολύ: it is both free and rich; both *gratiosa et copiosa* (Ps. cxxx.), both bountiful and plentiful; not only περισσεύουσα, bursting forth round about, round about all ages, round about all nations, round about all sorts, but ὑπερπερισσεύουσα (ver. 20), surrounding all those rounds, and with surplus and advantage overflowing all. I say, not only πλεονάζουσα, an abounding grace, abounding unto all, to the whole world, but ὑπερπλεονάζουσα (1 Tim. i. 14), a grace superabounding; that, if there were more worlds, grace would " bring salvation " even unto them all. St. Paul's own parallel shall end this point (1 Tim. ii. 4). It is God's will that " all men should be saved."

(e)   *Richard Clerke*

SALVATION, SURE

1. Remember, salvation is one of Christ's dainties He giveth but to few.
2. That it is violent striving that taketh heaven.

3. That it cost Christ's blood to purchase that house to sinners, and to set mankind down, as the King's free-tenants and free-holders.

4. That many make a start towards heaven, who fall on their back, and get not up to the top of the mount; it plucketh heart and legs from them, and they sit down and give it over because the devil setteth a sweet-smelled flower to their nose (this fair busked world), wherewith they are bewitched, and so forget or refuse to go forward.

5. Remember, many go far on, and reform many things, and can find tears, as Esau did; and suffer hunger for truth, as Judas did; and wish and desire the end of the righteous, as Balaam did; and profess fair, and fight for the Lord, as Saul did; and desire the saints of God to pray for them, as Pharaoh and Simon Magus did; and prophesy and speak of Christ, as Caiaphas did; and walk softly and mourn for fear of judgment, as Ahab did; and put away gross sins and idolatry, as Jehu did; and hear the word of God gladly, and reform their life in many things, according to the Word, as Herod did; and say, " Master," to Christ, " I will follow Thee whither Thou goest," as the man who offered to be Christ's servant (Matt. viii.); and may taste of the virtues of the life to come, and be partakers of the wonderful gifts of the Holy Spirit, and taste of the good word of God, as the apostates who sin against the Holy Ghost (Heb. vi.); and yet all these are but like gold in clink and colour, and watered brass and base metal. These are written that we should try ourselves, and not rest till we be a step nearer Christ than sunburnt and withering professors can come.

6. Consider, it is impossible that your idol sins and you can go to heaven together; and that those who will not part with these do not indeed love Christ at the bottom, but only in word and show, which will not do the business.

7. Remember how swiftly God's post-time flieth away; and that your forenoon is already spent, your afternoon will come, and then your evening, and at last night, when you cannot see to work. Let your heart be set upon finishing your journey, and summing and laying your accounts with your Lord.

(f)   *Samuel Rutherford*

SALVATION, THE WORK OF THY, IS (Phil. ii. 12)

1. God's work wrought upon thee and in thee;
2. The work of the Church, within which it takes place;
3. Thine own work, since thou consentest to it. God does not give thee the flower and the fruit of salvation, but the seed, the sunshine, and the rain. He does not give houses, nor yet beams and squared stones, but trees, and rocks, and limestone, and says: Now build thyself a house. Regard not God's work within thee as an anchor to hold thy bark firmly to the shore, but as a sail which shall carry it to its post.

(g)   *Lange*

SANCTIFICATION

A friend of Archbishop Usher frequently urged him to write his thoughts on Sanctification, which at length he engaged to do; but a considerable

(h)

time elapsing, the performance of his promise was importunely demanded. The Bishop replied to this purpose: " I have not written, and yet I cannot charge myself with a breach of promise ; for I began to write, but when I came to treat of the new creature which God formeth by His own Spirit in every regenerate soul, I found so little of it wrought in myself, that I could speak of it only as parrots, or by rote, but without the knowledge of what I might have expressed, and therefore I durst not presume to proceed any further upon it."

Upon this, his friend stood amazed to hear so humble a confession from so grave, holy, and eminent a man. The Bishop then added, " I must tell you, we do not well understand what sanctification and the new creature are. It is no less than for a man to be brought to an entire resignation of his will to the will of God ; and to live in the offering up of his soul continually in the flames of love, as a whole burnt-offering to Christ ; and oh ! how many who profess Christianity are unacquainted experimentally with His work upon their souls."

(a)

SANCTIFICATION.

We utterly mistake the matter if we think that Christ offers to put us under a system of *strictness and restraint*, for that would make us walk in ways of preciseness and of pain. The whole Bible testifies that the ways in which the Spirit leads us are ways of pleasantness and peace. This is a far more excellent way, which the Holy Ghost makes use of in sanctifying us—not the way of changing the *objects*, but the way of changing the *affections* —not by external restraint, but by an internal renewing.

God does not offer to work in you to *do*, without first working in you to *will*. He does not offer to pluck from you your favourite objects, but He offers to give you a new taste for higher objects.

(b)   *Robt. McCheyne*

SANCTIFICATION.

It is wonderful to see how the little events of our daily life tend to our sanctification, though we know it not at the time. Every week seems so like the other. But you know, when the sculptor begins his work, he strikes great pieces off the block. Every stroke tells visibly. But when the statue is nearly finished he takes the fine chisel, and strikes off but a little dust at a time. You scarcely see the effects of the blow, yet then it is directed with most art and skill—then the work is nearly done.

(c)   *Doing and Suffering*

SANCTIFICATION OF THE SPIRIT (1 Pet. i. 2)

This expression comprises all the gracious influences of the Holy Ghost, from His first gentle knockings to the sealing of grace.

(d)   *Lange*

SANCTIMONIOUSNESS

Let us be *natural* till we are *divine*.

(e)   *Aitkin (père)*

ΣΆΡΞ : Human Nature of our Lord.

This grand sentence, ὁ λόγος σὰρξ ἐγένετο (John i. 14), stands alone in the Bible. Compare also : 1 John iv. 2 ; 1 Tim. iii. 16 ; Rom. i. 3 ; viii. 3 ; Phil. ii. 7 ; Heb. ii. 14. Sin must be excluded in view of the unanimous testimony of the Apostles. The Logos assumed human nature into union with His pre-existent Divine personality. He moreover assumed human nature not apparently and transiently, but really and permanently ; not partially but totally, with all its essential constituents as created by God—body, soul, and spirit. For Christ everywhere appears as a full man (John viii. 40, etc.).

(f)   *Lange*

The Scripture recognises the σάρξ in three stages : (i.) pure, in paradise ; (ii.) weakened by sin ; (iii.) sanctified by the Spirit ; and the Logos could become flesh only in the latter sense.

(g)   *Ibid*

[Rom. viii. 3

God has unmasked and judged sin in the flesh, and condemned it to be cast out as a foreign element, a ruinous pseudo-plasma in the flesh, by Christ's assuming a pure and consecrated σάρξ, and by His keeping His white robes spotless on the whole filthy road of His pilgrimage, and maintaining its holiness until it was illuminated in glorified splendour. Thus the question, whether Christ assumed human nature in its paradisiacal state before the Fall, or the fallen nature of Adam, is a thoroughly incorrect one, for it rests on a misconception of biblical facts. Christ assumed neither the fallen nor the unfallen human nature, but the nature raised from the Fall and made holy.

(h)   *Ibid*

SATAN

Satan is like a subtle cheater, who, if he cannot make a man's title to his land void, yet he will put him to many troublesome suits in law. If Satan cannot make us ungodly, he will make us unquiet. Violent winds make the sea rough and stormy ; the winds of temptation blowing, disturb peace of spirit, and put the soul into a commotion.

(i)   *J. Watson*

SATAN

Till we have sinned, Satan is a parasite ; when we have sinned, he is a tyrant.

(j)   *Thos. Brooks*

SATAN (1 Thess. ii. 18)

Appears in Scripture in a three-fold activity :

1. As *Tempter :* the author of sin amongst men (1 Thess. iii. 5 ; Matt. iv. 3 ; Rev. xii. 9)

2. As *Accuser* (Rev. xii. 10)

He seeks, when the sin is accomplished, to make the most of it with lying exaggeration before the Divine Judge (Zech. iii. 1), and to exhibit it in the worst possible colours before our inner judge, the conscience, in order to bind the sinner inwardly, rendering him faint-hearted, and paralyzing his resistance to sin. Here belong the two most

(k)

common names of the Devil, *Satan=adversary* (Zech. iii. 1), and ἀντίδικος (1 Pet. v. 8), and διάβολος, *informer, slanderer, defamer*, properly one who smites through words.

3. As *Destroyer* ('Απολλύων, Rev. ix. 11)

Satan works, in so far as he, as prince of the fallen world, sets in motion all the powers of physical and moral evil against salvation, the kingdom of God, and in behalf of mischief, which = ἀπώλεια, eternal damnation.

Cf. The case of Judas, where he succeeded as
  (i.) *Seducer*;
  (ii.) *Accuser*;
  (iii.) Through despair and suicide, as *Murderer*.

(a) *Lange*

SATAN, DEVICES OF

"*Ye are not ignorant of his devices*" (2 Cor. ii. 11)

I was walking down Cheapside last week, and I saw a man driving a lot of pigs. Now you all know that pigs are uncommonly queer animals to drive, for if you want them to go one way they are pretty sure to go another. But this man did not seem to have any trouble; in fact, he was not driving them at all in the ordinary way, but just walking quietly before them, whilst they came, jostling and grunting after him, as eager as possible. At last he came to a narrow opening, up which he turned, the pigs following close at his heels. I was quite interested, and determined to wait till the man came out again, and then I went up to him and said, "My good friend, you have certainly found out the secret of managing pigs, and I should like to know it too if you have no objection." The man laughed and said, "Maybe you didn't see *the bag of beans* under my arm, sir? I was taking those 'ere pigs to the slaughter-house; so, as I went, I dropped a bean now and then, and that's a thing they're particularly fond of, and they scampered along to pick up the beans, never thinking that they were following me all the time as well." And that is the way the devil is leading sinners captive at his will. He knows very well how to bait his trap for you, and I want to-night to warn you, that you may not be ignorant of his devices.

(b) *Rowland Hill*

SATAN, EXISTENCE OF

"*Ye are of your father the devil, and the lusts of your father ye will do. He was a murderer from the beginning, and abode not in the truth, because there is no truth in him. When he speaketh a lie, he speaketh of his own: for he is a liar, and the father of it*" (John viii. 44)

1. Is it impossible to believe in the existence of Satan

The matter is sometimes put in another way. I have been reasoned with thus: "You believe that God is good and loving. You preach that His tender mercies are over all His works?" I do; I believe it most firmly, and assert it most strongly. "You believe, too, that God is omnipotent; that He can do what He wills both in heaven and earth—that He has all power to do the good He is willing to do?" Assuredly, I believe all this. "How, then, do you reconcile with your belief in the Divine goodness and the Divine power, that other belief that God permits a being—a spiritual being of immense power and capacity for mischief—first, to exist, and then to roam amongst the creatures He has made, oppressing and ruining and destroying them wherever he goes?" To this my answer is simple enough, and (as I venture to think) conclusive enough. I, in turn, ask permission to put a few questions. This, for instance: "Did you ever see or hear of a bad man? Did you ever see or hear of a man who makes it his occupation to spread contamination around him—who moves like a moral pestilence in society, especially in the society of the young—who triumphs when he has, for the gratification of his own selfish appetite, dragged some pure and innocent creature down to the level of his own degradation? Have you ever heard of such a man?" I have. "When you heard of him, did you believe in his existence?" I did. "Very well; but stop a moment. I have another question to ask: Did you ever, in the course of your acquaintance with history, ancient or modern, hear of men who have come to such a pitch in their wickedness, that they have taken pleasure in the suffering and misery of their fellow-creatures, *simply for the sake of that suffering and misery?* The murderer strikes the blow for the sake of the gold which he wrests out of the victim's hand. The profligate hunts down his prey for the sake of the gratification of the passing moment. Both are cruel, but they have a motive and a reason for their cruelty. But these men of whom we have read in history had descended so far, that to inflict suffering for the mere pleasure of inflicting it—to do harm for the mere delight in doing harm, without regard to any ulterior consequences—was an ordinary practice with them? Have you ever heard of such people? That you have never seen them, I can well believe; but, have you ever heard of them?" I have. "Did you believe in their existence?" I did. I could not bring myself to discredit the testimony by which their existence was established. "What do you call their character and conduct?" Diabolical. "Precisely so; you have hit upon the very word—*diabolical*. Well, then, if you find no difficulty, or very little, in believing that in the creation of a good, and wise, and powerful God—whose name is Love, and who can do whatever it pleases Him: raise up, or cast down—create, or destroy, according to His own will—there are men permitted to exist who are bad, who make others bad, who, after a time, come to rejoice in badness or evil, and to take pleasure in it for its own sake—if you can credit this—why, in the name of common sense and common honesty, do you refuse to credit the existence of Satan? The difficulty is precisely the same in the two cases. It is as great and inscrutable a marvel that evil men should be found, as it is that evil spirits should be found, in a universe formed, and regulated, and governed by a loving and omnipotent God."

(c)

2. But, after all, we who are believers in Divine revelation need not have recourse to any argument of this kind. Again and again in Scripture the personal existence of an evil spirit is revealed. Every quality, every action which can indicate personality is attributed to him in words that cannot be explained away; and you must tear whole pages out of your Bible, or else you must adopt a method of

(d)

Satan, Existence of—*continued*

interpreting its language which will make any statement mean anything before you can get rid of the doctrine or fact of the personal existence of Satan.

(*a*)

3. The Temptation

Take such a statement as our text. Men have said that the story of the Temptation is a figurative representation of a grave mental conflict which the Messiah had to pass through at the commencement of His ministerial career. But will they say such a thing of the words that are now before us? Consider the speaker: it is Jesus Christ Himself. Consider the occasion. He is speaking in the presence of watchful and malignant enemies. Consider the subject. He, who is the Truth, is speaking about him who is the author of falsehood. Surely, brethren, we cannot dare to think that on such an occasion as this, or indeed that on any occasion, the Saviour, as men tell us, accommodated Himself to Jewish prejudices, and used language which, at the very time He used it, He knew was conveying an erroneous and false impression. Why, the very assertion is blasphemous. And who could hereafter put any trust in the statements of our Redeemer, if we could conceive Him thus tampering with the truth, and deceiving mankind on a matter of such importance to their highest and spiritual interests? "Ye are of your father the devil, and the lusts of your father ye will do." And then comes a stern, plain, practical, unmetaphorical description of the devil: "He was a murderer from the beginning, and abode not in the truth." And again: "When he speaketh a lie, he speaketh of his own, for he is a liar, and the father of it,"—the father, the originator and example of the liar.

(*b*)

4. History of Satan

No language can be more adapted to convey the idea of personal existence and personal action than that which the Evangelist puts here into the mouth of our Lord. But supposing the question of Satan's personal existence settled, what shall we say about his history? On this point, Scripture is not at all communicative. Milton, somehow or other, seems to know more about the matter than the Bible conveys to an ordinary reader. Thus much, however, we do know—that he is a spirit. In the Epistle to the Ephesians, he is spoken of as "a spirit." In St. Matthew's Gospel, he is spoken of as the prince or ruler of the "demons." In the Book of the Revelation of St. John, he is said to have "angels" subject to him. We conclude, then, that he was of angelic nature—a rational and spiritual creature, superhuman in wisdom, power, and energy; and not only so, but an "archangel"—one of the princes of heaven. So far, I think, Scripture leads us by the hand.

(*c*)

5. How did Satan come to be what he is now

It has been said that God created him as he is; but the idea is simply monstrous. That God created a being essentially and originally evil!—the statement needs only to be made to be rejected with absolute loathing. It has been maintained, too, that Satan, as the embodiment and imper-

sonation of the evil principle, is actually co-existent and co-eternal with God Himself. The good and the evil, it is said, each gathered and summed up into one personal head, have existed together in constant antagonism and conflict from all eternity. This theory, too, may be put aside without any comment, and if so, we must conclude that Satan was created pure and upright, but that in some way or other, and at some time or other, he fell. Can you see any greater difficulty about this conclusion than there is about many facts with which our experience makes us acquainted? We know that the will of a free and rational creature can oppose itself to the Divine will: we see the fact in ourselves. God permits our will to oppose and to counteract His will. We know that a being created pure and upright can fall. We have seen one exemplification in Adam. How, or by what mental process it happened, we do not know: we only know the fact. We know, too, that there is a downward career in evil; that beings may become by degrees fixed, and hardened, and stereotyped in evil. There is, therefore, no such very great difficulty in supposing that Satan is a fallen angel, who once had a time of probation, but whose condemnation is irrevocably fixed.

(*d*)

6. Does Scripture Help us at all in Forming this Opinion

Again, on this point as on the former one, Scripture is not very explicit. There is one passage of which much has been made, which speaks of "Michael and his angels" as fighting against "the devil and his angels;" but it certainly cannot refer to the original fall of Satan. There are two other passages, one in the Second Epistle of St. Peter, the other in Jude, which speak of the angels which "kept not their first estate." But here, again, it seems hardly possible to reckon Satan as one of these, for they are spoken of as "being in chains, and guarded until the great day;" whilst he is permitted to go about still as the tempter and the adversary until his appointed time be come. In another passage, our Lord says that, "He beheld Satan as lightning fall from heaven." This may refer to his original fall; but it may also refer figuratively to the triumph of the disciples over the evil spirits. There remain two other passages which bear upon the subject—that of our text, in which, though the word translated "abode," ought rather to be translated "abideth not in the truth,"—there seems to be a hint or intimation of a fall from some previous condition. The other is the warning in the First Epistle to Timothy: "Lest being lifted up by pride, ye fall into the condemnation of the devil." It is concluded from this that pride was the cause of the devil's condemnation. The inference is a probable one. It is strengthened by the only analogy within our reach—that of the fall of man, in which the spiritual temptation of pride—the desire to be "as gods"—was the subtlest and most deadly temptation. Still it cannot be denied that the matter is involved in much obscurity, though, putting the two things together,—our reasonings from the necessity of the case and the inferences from the intimations of Holy Scripture,—we do not hesitate to conclude that Satan was created upright, but that he fell by his own act and deed from the position in which the Creator had placed him. How sinful

(*e*)

Satan, Existence of—*continued*

thoughts could be engendered in the bosom of a
sinless being, we cannot profess to understand.
This is one of the mysteries connected with the
creation of free and responsible agents. But the
fact must be accepted, unless we would allow
ourselves to be driven to conclusions revolting
alike to Scripture and to all rational conclusions
about the character of God.

(*a*)

7. Nature of Satan

It is here, I think, that our great poet, Milton,
is so great an offender. I think he has been guilty,
on a large scale, of doing precisely what the novelists who glorify crime—who turn you out a batch
of sentimental murderers and philosophical villains,
and try to secure your sympathy for them and
interest in them,—have done on their petty scale.
I do not say that Milton intended it: nor would I
willingly put his great genius side by side with the
miserable drivelling of some of the writers I speak
of. But he has done it. He has thrown a halo of
romance and interest and sentiment round the head
of the meanest and most loathsome character that
the whole universe contains. Now, is it not so?
Read "Paradise Lost." Who is the hero of the
poem? Satan, unquestionably. Adam beside him
is the merest milk and water. Beside him, Messiah Himself pales into absolute insignificance.
Satan, undoubtedly, bulks the largest to the view
—is the grandest, most magnificent, nay, the most
heroic figure in the whole poem. And I say, taking my stand upon Scripture, and especially upon
the words of our Lord in the text, that the whole
portraiture is a most complete and most mischievous misrepresentation.

Contrast the statements of Milton with the statements of Christ.

(*b*)

8. Milton's Description of Satan

"He above the rest
In shape and gesture proudly eminent
Stood like a tower; his form had not yet lost
All her original brightness, nor appear'd
Less than Archangel ruin'd, and the excess
Of glory obscured; as when the sun new risen
Looks through the horizontal misty air
Shorn of his beams, or from behind the moon
In dim eclipse disastrous twilight sheds
On half the nations, and with fear of change
Perplexes monarchs. Darken'd so, yet shone
Above them all the Archangel: but his face
Deep scars of thunder had intrench'd, and care
Sat on his faded cheek, but under brows
Of dauntless courage, and considerate pride
Waiting revenge: cruel his eye, but cast
Signs of remorse and passion to behold
The fellows of his crime, the followers rather
(Far other once beheld in bliss) condemn'd
For ever now to have their lot in pain,
Millions of Spirits for his fault amerced
Of heaven, and from eternal splendours flung
For his revolt, yet faithful how they stood,
Their glory wither'd: as when heaven's fire
Hath scathed the forest oaks, or mountain pines,
With singèd top their stately growth though bare
Stands on the blasted heath. He now prepared
To speak; whereat their doubled ranks they bend
From wing to wing, and half inclose him round
With all his peers: attention held them mute.
Thrice he assay'd, and thrice in spite of scorn
Tears, such as angels weep, burst forth: at last
Words interwove with sighs found out their way."

Now, what is this? A hero, a leader in some
noble enterprise—erring, perhaps, but magnificent
in his error; a Prometheus Vinctus, chained to his

rock, but proudly defying there the unjust thunders of an irritated and timorous Jove.

(*c*)

9. **The other Picture, which Christ, who is the
Truth, holds up to us.** "He is a murderer and a liar,"
—a murderer from the beginning. He is the embodiment of hate; and as soon as ever the innocent
and unoffending race of man appeared upon the
scene, his hate urged him to accomplish the ruin
of the race—to destroy them, to murder them, if
he could, body and soul. No grand idea this! but
a most fearful one—the most intense maliciousness,
delighting in suffering for its own sake, united with
the most amazing power for working out its own
purposes! Oh, there is much that is awful about
this; but there is nothing that is grand, and magnificent, and romantic, and interesting.

And, then, he is a liar, and the father of lies.
In all the meanness of deception, in all the foul-
ness of falsehood, in all the ignominy of hypocrisy
—he is the prime mover and agent. No grandeur
in this!—nothing but what is miserable and mean.
Milton was sadly in the wrong. He constructed a
grand character; but the meanest, the most degraded, the most loathsome creature in God's universe—though, at the same time, the most terrible
—is he who is most opposed to the character and
will of God—Satan, the old serpent, the adversary
of God and man.

(*d*)

10. **I must not leave this dark picture altogether
unrelieved by some brighter colours.** This being is
terrible, brethren, but "*in Christ*" we need not fear
him. We have another Spirit whose work is the
exact opposite of Satan's. He gives life; He leads
into the truth; and He, thank God, is on our side.
For "greater is He that is in us, than he that is in
the world."

(*e*)   *Gordon Calthrop*

SATAN, INFLUENCE OF

"*The prince of the power of the air, the spirit
that now worketh in the children of disobedience*"
(Ephes. ii. 2)

The Children of Disobedience

1. The statement here made by the Apostle is
of a peculiarly painful and almost repulsive character. By the expression, "*Children of Disobedience*," he seems to mean all those who are
withholding their allegiance from the Lord Jesus
Christ; all those who are unconverted; not merely
gross sinners and open profligates, but such persons as are strangers to the spiritual life, although
they may have many excellences of nature and
disposition.

Notice that in the following verse the Apostle
reckons himself on having been once included in
the description. Now St. Paul was no fanatic.
He was not in the habit of calling himself hard
names without any reason. And when he speaks
of himself as having "his conversation among
the children of disobedience," and as "being, by
nature, the child of wrath, even as others," he
must mean what he says, he must mean us to
understand that before he was brought to the
knowledge and the acceptance of Christ he was
under the influence of the prince of the power of

(*f*)

the air. This is a startling statement, anyhow. It is more startling still if you come to consider what sort of man Paul was before his conversion: how excellent, how earnest, how devoted to the external duties of a religious life. But startling as it is, it is the Apostle who makes it himself; and the inference seems unavoidable, that all that large mass of persons who are out of Christ, and who are not partakers of His resurrection life, who have given their hearts to the world, and not given their hearts to the Saviour, are just the captives of Satan, and, without knowing it, are doing his lusts and accomplishing his will.

(*a*)

2. **Look at it again.** I must confess it is a hard saying, and a painful one. I can understand how it can apply to the open sinner—that drunkard there, that profligate who breathes an atmosphere of moral contamination wherever he goes, that thorough-paced liar, whose word can never be believed, that scoffer at sacred things, that practical infidel, who never bends a knee in prayer, never opens his Bible, never darkens the door of the house of God. I can easily credit that they are under the dominion and control of the foul spirit of darkness. Their words and actions, their whole demeanour, convince me of the fact. But am I to believe that this kind-hearted acquaintance of mine, who is as pleasant a man as I ordinarily meet with, and whose life is perfectly irreproachable as far as his duty to his neighbour is concerned, and who sometimes comes to Church— am I to believe that *he* is a bondslave to the devil, and that the devil is influencing him to participate in his own opposition to God and Christ? I know that the man has no pretension to be considered religious. I know, or at least, I shrewdly suspect, that he is a perfect stranger to the spiritual life. Where there is the life of the Spirit there are the fruits of the Spirit; and, I must confess, I have never been able to see in his conduct and feelings the slightest indications of a work of the Spirit going on within him. I could never trace the slightest interest in Christ, or the slightest reference to Christ in any of his actions. This world is everything to him; and I think that, if the question were put to him, he would confess it to be so himself. But still, am I to think that the "prince of the power of the air" is working in this kind-hearted man—and urging him, step by step, over the precipice of eternal ruin? Consider. Satan is a most fearful and most loathsome being. He is the embodiment of hate. Hate is the element in which he moves and has his being; and to oppose God and goodness, and to accomplish man's misery, is the very end for which he exists. His delight is in evil. Why, it must be an awful thing to be under the influence of such a fiend as he is. And am I to believe that this decorous, well-conducted acquaintance of mine is actually under that terrible influence? that he is positively led captive by Satan at his will? "Yes," is the reply. "Yes! you are to believe it." The disease is not the less deadly because it eats out the life without inflicting pain. The pestilence is not the less awful because it comes without giving notice of its presence, borne on the balmy breezes of the bright cloudless summer eve. The vampire does not do its work the less effectually because it fans its victim with its wings into an unconscious slumber

whilst it drains away his life-blood and leaves him a corpse. And Satan is not the less real, or the less destructive because he works his fatal work upon our souls without our even being conscious of his approach. Scripture has said it; and, whatever we may think, the witness stands unalterable. "The prince of the power of the air is the spirit who now worketh in the children of disobedience."

(*b*)

3. **The realization of the existence and the efforts of Satan, is a very great point.** The Christian life will be a very different thing to me, if I believe in a personal enemy, striving with all his power to do me harm, from what it would have been if I had disbelieved in his existence. Temptation will be a very different thing to me. It will be a much more serious thing. The evil influences of the world will be very different things if I regard them as the instrumentality which a *personal enemy* is employing for my overthrow. So you see the doctrine is a practical one. And in this practical point of view the Apostle Paul regarded it.

(*c*)

4. **He describes the Christian life as a wrestling.** Hand-to-hand, foot-to-foot, with our muscles strained to their utmost tension, and the eye intently watching the eye of the foe, as if to read his very thoughts, we stand. But with whom do we wrestle? With men, perhaps, with human tempters, with human opponents of God, with human corrupters of the truth of God, but with something beyond and behind these men—"We wrestle," says the Apostle, "not against flesh and blood, but against principalities, against powers, against the rulers of the darkness of this world, against spiritual wickedness in high places." Again he says in his epistle to the Thessalonians, "We would have come unto you, even I, Paul, once again, but Satan hindered us." What does he mean? Did Satan come forward himself,—as in John Bunyan's wondrous vision,—and, striding across the highway with his fiery darts in his hand, and breathing fire out of his nostrils, bar up the Apostle's road and forbid his progress? No! The Apostle simply means that the machinations of some obstinate enemies, probably Jews, had prevented him from carrying out his intention of visiting his friends and converts in Thessalonica. "Why does he not say so then?" you may be disposed to object. Simply because his eye, sharpened with the keen-sightedness of the Spirit of God, pierced through this external human opposition, and saw the real agent working behind—saw the concealed Satan acting as an adversary to the progress of the Gospel of the grace of God.

(*d*)

5. **In this realization of the existence and the power of Satan, the Apostle only followed the example of the Lord Jesus Christ.** You will remember that our Lord said, towards the close of His earthly career, "The prince of this world cometh and hath nothing in Me." But it was the Jews who were coming. It was the high priest who was coming. It was Pilate who was coming. It was the Roman executioners who were coming. Yes! But the Saviour knew that all this machinery was really put in motion by him between whom and Himself the contest really lay—by Satan, whose power He had come to break and overthrow by

(*e*)

Satan, Influence of—_continued_

His stupendous sacrifice upon the cross. I say, then, it may be well for us to do as Jesus did, and as Paul did ; realize the importance of the Christian life and the Christian work, by realizing the personal existence, and power, and operations of the great adversary of God and man.

(a)

6. "The Prince of the Power of the Air." The idea conveyed is this, that the evil spirits,—the subjects and associates of Satan,—from the very fact of their spiritual nature, are able to encompass us as the air does, and to bring temptations to bear upon us without the intervention of external agency. The idea is a very terrible one. I read, once, that in the old days in Italy, when poisoning was carried to the highest pitch of diabolical perfection—the very air of heaven itself was oftentimes used as the vehicle of destruction, through the odours which it conveyed. You dared not accept a flower. Death might lurk in the perfume of its leaves. A scented letter might carry a fatal infection. A subtle poison might exhale from fragrant clothes ; and "handkerchiefs or aprons," instead of being used, as they were in apostolic days, as mediums of healing, might send a pestilence, coursing with fevered swiftness through the veins of those who used them.

(b)

Some such power, brethren, the evil spirits have over those who are not fortified and secured by the presence and indwelling in their souls of the stronger Spirit, the Eternal Spirit, the Spirit of God. There seem then to be two ways in which Satan can influence us. The first, immediately, by the operation of spirit upon spirit ; for you and I are spirits enclosed and encased in matter.

The second, mediately, by the use of worldly things or worldly people : by the employment, in fact, of an outward agency, whether of persons or of things.

The first respects our thoughts. There Satan has great power. He can suggest evil thoughts ; and that he does so, there can be no manner of question. Perhaps we cannot easily prevent the intrusion of evil thoughts. But there is one thing that does lie in our power (if we obtain that help from God which is never denied to those that ask), and that is,—we may prevent the evil thoughts from being harboured and cherished in our hearts. Hard thoughts about God ; bitter thoughts against each other when we are wronged or slighted, or fancy ourselves so ; self-seeking, selfish, vain, proud, impure thoughts—all of us know something about these things. And first to suggest them and then to foster them in us, seems to be an especial work of the devil. In our baptismal vow we renounce his works. And one way of renouncing them, is by keeping the heart with all diligence. First, then, let us keep the heart by watchfulness. I cannot keep the noisome weeds from sprouting up in that garden, for the soil is naturally bad and is full of them. But I can, God helping me, prevent them from growing to maturity, and seeding and reproducing themselves ten or twenty-fold—I can, God helping me, check the harbouring and encouraging in my heart of evil thoughts. And let us keep the heart by getting it filled with better things. If the peace of God be there, if the love of Christ be there, if

thoughts of heaven be there, if communion with God be there, if the Spirit be there, in the fulness of His power, there will not be much room for the intrusion of evil thoughts and vain imaginations. Above all, let our prayer be : "Cleanse the thoughts of our hearts by the inspiration of Thy Holy Spirit, that we may perfectly love Thee and worthily magnify Thy Holy Name."

(c)

7. Other Agencies

Amongst these I would reckon, as dangerous to all of us, and especially to the young—careless companions and doubtful literature. There is no such apt and successful agent of Satan as an attractive but wicked friend. And I earnestly entreat the younger members of the congregation —(though the advice does not apply to them alone)—to believe that when they pledged themselves to renounce the devil and all " _his works_," they pledged themselves to separate from and to hold aloof from all evil and doubtful companionship. " Go from the presence of a man, if thou perceive not in him the lip of truth." The advice is sound and good. You may be thrown into enforced juxtaposition with a man, and not be able altogether to detach yourself from him. But association is one thing, and friendship, or even companionship, is another. And if you find a man to be a man of loose life, a ridiculer of piety, a scoffer at the Bible, one who makes a mock of sin, or makes excuses and apologies for it—you should look upon yourself as bound by your baptismal vow to separate yourself entirely from him as from one who is doing in the world the drudgery of that foul fiend whose person and works, alike, you had undertaken to renounce. No fascination of manner, no power of intellect, no readiness of wit, no apparent good nature and kindliness of heart, on his part, can justify you in remaining in voluntary companionship with a man, when once he has so distinctly proclaimed himself to be ranged on the side of the dark hosts of Satan. So with literature. There are some books of which you feel instinctively " as a Christian I ought not to go on with this." I am not speaking, of course, of openly bad books. About them we are now saying nothing. But I speak of books in which the tone of morality is low ; in which scoffs are cast, directly or indirectly, at sacred things ; in which a hot glare of false sentiment is thrown round evil ; in which the world is painted in such attractive and fascinating colours as to be almost irresistible. Such things do the devil's work. And you and I, as baptized Christians, are bound by our baptismal vow to separate ourselves from everything which we find to interfere with the calm sobrieties of a Christian course. We must be on our guard, here as elsewhere, against " the spirit that worketh in the children of disobedience."

(d)

8. Satan's Influence over Nominal Christians

(i.) First, he makes them hear the preaching of the Gospel without profit. Christ says so : and He knows. " When any one heareth the word of the kingdom, and understandeth it not, then cometh the wicked one, and catcheth away that which was sown in his heart." It was sown in his heart, then. At all events, it rested on the surface for a while ; some sort of impression was produced ; but

(e)

Satan, Influence of—*continued*

the impression soon passed away. You see, then, the agent that is at work, hindering our preaching to the careless and unconverted. The devil is making the man think about other things; or if a transient impression is produced, and the man just begins to think that he has been careless long enough, and thoughtless long enough, and that he has rejected Christ often enough, and has kept Him knocking at the door of his heart long enough —and if he feels half-inclined to turn over a new leaf—the devil, not liking to lose his servant, way-lays him at the church-door, in the shape most probably of foolish gossip, and all the impression is immediately evaporated and lost.

(*a*)

(ii.) Again, what is the reason why men see no beauty and no glory in Christ? You talk about spiritual things; they wonder what on earth you mean. They think you are either professional, or a fanatic. To speak of Christ to them, and of what Christ is to His people, is like praising a painting to a blind man, or a piece of music to one who is deaf. What is the reason, then, that this wonderful Saviour, with His great redemption, has no interest for them; that they are totally un-moved and totally indifferent about Him? The Apostle tells us. "The god of this world," he says, "has *blinded* the minds of them that believe not; lest the light of the glorious gospel of Christ, who is the image of God, should shine unto them." This blinding to spiritual things is another work which Satan works on the unconverted.

(*b*)

(iii.) Again, he tempts them with just the temp-tation that suits them. The fisherman studies the nature and habits of the fish he wishes to catch. He will not offer him a bait he will not take, nor a bait at a time and under circumstances when he knows he will not take it. And Satan, who studies our heart, and knows all the ins and outs of it, will not make a mistake in dealing with us. Here is a covetous man: will he offer him pleasure? Not he. He throws down before him the bait he will take: gold. Here is a frivolous, trifling young woman: will he offer her gold? Not he. She does not care about gold. She wants dissipation, balls, parties, theatres—that's her bait; and she gets it. Here is a student. He is indifferent about pleasure. His heart is un-moved at the sight of gold; but he longs for fame. And the dark fisherman suits his bait to the fish. Yes, for six thousand years Satan has studied the human heart, and he understands it by this time. But some say—"If he is the author of all this evil, and we so weak and frail, why is he not punished alone?"

(*c*)

9. Illustration

A certain king had an orchard of very choice fruit which he wished to preserve. And he set two men to guard it—the one blind, the other so lame that he could not walk at all; and the king thought his fruit was secure at least from them. But it came into the head of the lame man who saw the beauty of the fruit, to tempt the blind man to steal it; and the blind man taking the lame man on his shoulders, they went up and robbed the garden. The owner coming and finding the

beautiful fruit gone, inquired who was the culprit. "It cannot be I," said the blind man, "for I have no vision, and cannot see the fruit." "It cannot be I," said the lame man, "for I cannot walk, and could not therefore reach the fruit." The king was not to be deceived; so making the blind man take the lame man on his shoulders, as he had done before, *he punished them both as one man.* So will it be done to those whom the devil has tempted into sin, and caused to die impenitent. They will be punished with Satan—they will share Satan's punishment. Identified in sinning, they will be identified in suffering. They will hear the fearful words: "Depart from Me, ye cursed, into everlasting fire prepared for the devil and his angels."

(*d*)

10. Refuge

Sheltered in Christ, we are safe from the power of this terrible foe. There is our refuge. And though he be strong and mighty, yet is the Lord Jesus mightier still. And we can say with exulta-tion—"Thanks be to God which giveth us the victory, through our Lord Jesus Christ!"

(*e*)　　　　　　　　　　　*Gordon Calthrop*

SATAN, THREEFOLD ACTIVITY OF (1 Thess. ii. 18)

1. *As Tempter* (iii. 5), and (Matt. iv. 3) but Rev. xii. 9 = Deceiver. Therefore he *tempts by deceiving.*

2. *Accuser* (Rev. xii. 10) when he succeeds as tempter, he makes the most of it (Zech. iii. 1), and represents the sin in its worst light, both before the Judge and Conscience, thereby paralyzing resistance. Hence our *Adversary.* Against whom the caution (1 Pet. v. 8), "Be sober, vigilant," etc. Hence, too, his names.

　(i.) *Satan*, adversary;
　(ii.) *Devil*, informer, slanderer, calumniator.

3. *Destroyer*, sets everything against our sal-vation, and the setting up of the kingdom of God;

Aims at eternal ruin. So in the text; hindering the work of the Gospel; hindering the salvation of every one, and so a *murderer.*

Cf. *Judas Iscariot* =
　(i.) Tempted,
　(ii.) Accused,
　(iii.) Destroyed.

(*f*)

SATAN, WILES OF

There are critical times of danger. After great services, honours, and consolations, we should stand upon our guard. Noah, Lot, David, Solo-mon, fell in these circumstances. Satan is a foot-pad; a foot-pad will not attack a man in *going* to the bank, but in *returning* with his pocket full of money.

(*g*)　　　　　　　　　　　*John Newton*

SAUL OF TARSUS, CONVERSION OF

One of the greatest miracles in the kingdom of grace. The fact that the most earnest zealot for Pharisaic legalism became by Divine appointment the chief Apostle of a free Gospel and faith, the most successful destroyer of Pharisaism in Judaism and in the Christian Church, throughout all ages,

(*h*)

is without parallel in history. No other reaches that miraculous transformation by which the glorified Christ, as with an ironical smile, changed the most formidable power of the enemy into His most victorious agency for conquest.

(a) *Lange*

Paul thought to conquer Christ; but Christ conquered him.

(b)

Saul of Tarsus and His Seven Ships

Saul of Tarsus was once a thriving merchant and an extensive shipowner. He had seven vessels of his own: the names of which were— "Circumcised the eighth day;" "Of the stock of Israel;" "Of the tribe of Benjamin;" "An Hebrew of the Hebrews;" "As touching the law, a Pharisee;" "Concerning zeal, persecuting the Church;" "Touching the righteousness which is of the law, blameless." The sixth was a man-of-war, with which he set out one day from the port of Jerusalem, well supplied with ammunition from the arsenal of the chief priest, with a view to destroy a small fort at Damascus. He was wonderfully confident, and breathed out threatenings and slaughter. But he had not got far from port before the Gospel ship, with Jesus Christ Himself as Commander on board, hove in sight, and threw such a shell among the merchant's fleet, that all his ships were instantly on fire. The commotion was tremendous; and there was such a volume of smoke, that Saul couldn't see the sun at noon. While the ships were fast sinking, the Gospel Commander mercifully gave orders that the perishing merchant should be taken on board. "Saul, Saul, what has become of thy ships?" "They are all on fire!" "What wilt thou do now?" "Oh that I may be found in Him, not having mine own righteousness, which is of the law, but that which is through the faith of Christ—the righteousness which is of God by faith."

(c) *Christmas Evans*

"SAVE ME!"

No man can save his brother. There is a painful story told about the first Napoleon. A marshal of his—who was devotedly, enthusiastically attached to him—was mortally wounded in battle; and as the last struggle drew near, and he lay dying in his tent, he sent for his chief. Napoleon came. The poor man, who thought that his Emperor could do anything—who had perhaps put him in the place of his God—earnestly besought him to save his life. The Emperor sadly shook his head, and presently went away. But after the painful interview was over, as the dying man felt the cold, merciless hand of death drawing him, irresistibly, behind the curtain of the unseen world, he was still heard to shriek out, "Save me! save me! Napoleon!" Ah! there are times when it is agony to refuse help, and we cannot render it. We have only that which will suffice for ourselves; and even if we would part with it, it would be impossible to do so. Such a thing is spiritual life; and it is this which is spoken of in the Parable. In that day that is coming, if we have not spiritual life for ourselves, it will be useless to ask others to impart it to us. The cry may be heard,—"Help me, father! help me, mother! help me, dear friends and companions! leave me not to perish! give me out of your fulness something which shall enable me to stand before the dreadful God." But the answer must sadly come,—"Not so, lest there be not enough for us and you, but go ye rather to them that sell, and buy for yourselves."

(d) *Gordon Calthrop*

SAVED, BY GRACE YE HAVE BEEN (Eph. ii. 5)

The clause emphasizes the fact of the deliverance from death into life, from wrath into love = "Ye have been and are saved," the perfect of permanent state, implying that God's grace abides.

(e) *Lange*

SAVING SOULS

Mr. Hill once introduced Dr. Jenner to a nobleman in these terms:—"Allow me to present to your lordship my friend, Dr. Jenner, who has been the means of saving more lives than any other man." Dr. Jenner bowed, and said with great earnestness, addressing Mr. Hill, "Ah! would, like you, I could say, *souls*."

(f) *"Life of Rowland Hill."*

The interest of a great game of chess, with living creatures for pawns and pieces, and the adversary, in plain English, the devil.

(g) *Dr. Arnold*

SAYINGS OF A WELSH PREACHER

"If we would be angry without sinning, let us be angry at nothing but sin."

"I don't know which to wonder at most—the shameless conduct of men towards the Son of God, or His patience under the treatment."

"The way through the Red Sea was safe enough for Israel, but not for Pharaoh; he had no business to go that way; it was a private road that Jehovah had opened up for His own family."

"Many, having laid aside red coat and sword, have taken up their old callings, and now live on partial pay; but no pensioners belong to the army of the Cross."

"Let the oldest believer remember that Satan is older."

"It's no wonder that the devil tries hard to get back his old subjects: nothing concerns him more than for his character to be made fully known."

"The love between God and His people is so intense, that it is not surprising that when the devil tried to get between Job and his God, he burnt his fingers."

"Sin is an arrow pointing against heaven; but the mark being too high, it comes down upon the head of the sinner."

"Christ is the bishop, not of tithes, but of souls."

"Many have a brother's face, but Christ has a brother's heart."

"Moses, though learned, was 'slow of speech;' it was well that it was so, or perhaps he would have talked too much to have found time for the writing of the law. But Aaron had the gift of

(h)

speech, and it does not appear that he had any other."

"Pharaoh fought ten battles with God, and gained not one."

"Pharaoh commanded that Moses should be drowned; in after days Pharaoh was paid back in his own coin!"

"Judas is much blamed for betraying Christ for three pounds; many in our day betray Him a hundred times for three pence."

"He who quenches the Spirit puts out the only light that can light up the 'valley of the shadow of death.'"

"It is impossible to cleave to Christ and forsake His people."

"There are only three passages in the Bible which declare what God is, although there are thousands which speak about Him: 'God is a spirit,' 'God is light,' 'God is love.'"

"Christ fought against Satan, not against sin; Christians fight against sin, rather than Satan."

"'I am no further from God than I was before,' says the backslider. Have done with your lying; you had left God before you had left His people."

"Ignorance is the devil's college."

"This world's joys are like those water springs which dry up in summer, when they are most needed."

"Perhaps we serve God best when we are least satisfied with our service."

"I have a dread of dying without full possession of my faculties; but the vessel is not less safe when the passengers are asleep."

"The Christian's heart is the best thing he has, although he is always complaining of it."

"We may fall in with God's plans: God cannot fall in with ours."

"If you choose God, you may be quite certain that God has chosen you."

"If you have no pleasure in your religion, make haste to change it."

"Cough away, my friends," he once said, "it will not disturb me in the least; it will indeed rather help me, for while you are coughing I shall make sure that you are awake."

(a)   *Thomas Rees Davies*

SCANDAL

Flavia, most tender of her own good name,
Is rather careless of a sister's fame:
Her superfluity the poor supplies;
But if she touch a character, it dies.

(b)   *Cowper*

There is a lust in man no charm can tame,
Of loudly publishing his neighbour's shame;
On eagle's wings immortal scandals fly,
While virtuous actions are but born and die.

(c)   *Ella Louisa Harvey*

When men speak ill of thee, live so as nobody may believe them.

(d)   *Plato*

"They say; what do they say? let them say."

(e)

SCARLET AND CRIMSON "Though your sins be as" (Isa. i. 18)

Those who search for old scraps of linen to manufacture them into paper, tell us that the stains most difficult to remove are those which are from crimson and scarlet dyes. A strong illustration of the text.

(f)   *Jas. Fleming*

SCEPTICISM

The doctrine of Mr. Hume . . . is not that we have not reached truth, but that we never can reach it. It is an absolute and universal system of scepticism, professing to be derived from the very structure of the understanding, which, if any man could seriously believe it, would render it impossible for him to form an opinion upon any subject—to give the faintest assent to any proposition—to ascribe any meaning to the words Truth and Falsehood—to believe, to inquire, or to reason; and on the very same ground, to disbelieve, to dissent, or to doubt—to adhere to his own principle of universal doubt; and lastly, if he be consistent with himself, even to think.

(g)   *Edinburgh Review*, 1821, *On Hume*

Of Dr. Priestley's theological works, he said that they tended to unsettle everything, and yet settled nothing.

(h)   *Johnson, on Dr. Priestley*

Bayle and Chillingworth, two of the most sceptical of mankind, turned Catholics from sincere conviction.

(i)   *Macaulay*

What shall a man do, then, under these circumstances? Shall he doubt upon everything? Shall he doubt whether he is awake, whether you pinch or burn him? Shall he doubt whether he doubts? Shall he doubt whether he exists? It seems impossible to come to this; and therefore I maintain, that there never was a practical and complete sceptic.

(j)   *Blaise Pascal*

SCEPTICISM AND THE BIBLE

Vernon was the son of an English squire. He was brought up in great elegance. In that family there was a working-man by the name of Ralph, with whom the son of the squire frequently held intercourse. After a while the son, Vernon, went off to college. He got full of scepticism. He came back. He talked it in the presence of the working-man. He went away again. Years after he came back and said: "Where is Ralph?" "Oh!" said they, "He is in prison, waiting for the hour of execution." Vernon hastened to the prison. Ralph said: "How good are you to come; I don't blame you—I don't blame anybody —I only blame myself—but you will remember you used to come home from college and talk about the Bible's being false, and about there being no truth in religion, and I thought it over, and I went into the tap-room, and I went from bad to worse, until I am here, waiting for the gallows. Now, Vernon," said Ralph, looking through the wicket of the prison, "for the love you once had to me, I want you to promise me that you will never talk against the Bible, or talk against the Christian religion, in the presence of other people. It may do them damage. It destroyed me." By almost superhuman effort the sentence of that man was changed to transporta-

(k)

tion to some other country for life. The ship carrying him was wrecked on Van Diemen's Land. Among those that perished was Ralph, the victim of Vernon's scepticism. Vernon tells the story to-day with tears and a breaking heart; but, alas! it is too late. Beware how you talk scepticism. Beware how you adopt it. "Let God be true, though every man be found a liar!"

(a)   *Talmage*

SCHOOL OF CHRIST

"Oh, happy school of Christ," wrote Peter of the cells to a young disciple who had complained of the weary seductions and splendid vices of the mediæval Paris,—"Oh, happy school of Christ, where He teaches our heart with the word of power; where the book is not purchased nor the Master paid. There, life availeth more than learning, and simplicity than science. There, none are refuted, save those who are for ever rejected; and one word of final judgment, '*Ite*' or '*Venite*,' decides all questions and all cavils for ever." It was a natural exclamation, but the answer to it is, that to the true Christian every school will be a school of Christ.

(b)

SCHOOLS OF THOUGHT

1. The three parties hold different views. Their views do not differ so much in matters political, Church government, or on the question of temperance. They are diverse in things purely and strictly religious, and this again in those things which most intimately concern the soul and its relation with God. The points of difference are vital points.

(c)

2. A Protestant is first (*pro testis*) a witness for the truth. He must set forth very clearly what truth is. There is no shame involved in it, as many in our days seem to think. A Protestant is simply nothing more or less than one who witnesses faithfully for the truth of God.

(d)

3. These three schools do not differ in the mode and manner of looking at things, so much as in their conception of things. We may describe, without being uncharitable, the High Church school as the priest school; the Broad Church school as the anything-will-do school; and the Low Church school as the Christ school. But let us see this.

(e)

4. Now I do not honour the disposition that leads a man to pin his faith to another's coat-tails. I have no sympathy with those who advertise for men who hold the views of Mr. So-and-so, or Dr. This or Professor That. I do not think they are the wisest men who recognise in any way a leader of their party. I hold partisanship to be very far wrong. I disclaim party-spirit altogether. When the Apostle reproached it in the Corinthians he condemned it for ever. We should be followers of the Lord Jesus and not of men. "One is your Master."

(f)

5. But the Church to which we profess to belong has defined and arranged for us the doctrines which she conceives to be the teaching of God's Word. Now, if it be right that there be three parties in the English Church, it will follow that there are three ways of interpreting her Articles. Is it so? Do these Articles indeed admit of three divergent modes of interpretation? That seems to me to be the main question. By it we will test the soundness of the views of the three Schools of Thought.

(g)

6. The Church's object, as an institution, is not so much to embrace as many as possible within her pale,—in other words, to attach men to her,—as to save souls. The salvation of souls is her great work. We understand by salvation of souls, the turning of men to God—conversion, justification—and the bringing them up in the faith—sanctification. The work of the Church is nothing if it be not this. Her primary consideration is eternity—how to make man right for it.

(h)

7. Now the **High Church** school exaggerates the position of the Church. We are speaking now of the Church as an institution. The Church in this sense embraces teachers, and teaching, and taught. The ministers—the three degrees of them—are the teachers, the Articles are the embodiment of the teaching, the people are the taught. The duty of the ministers involves also the administration of the sacraments and the teaching of Divine worship. It would be difficult to justify any other position which the Church should occupy than this. "The visible Church of Christ," says the Nineteenth Article, "is a congregation of faithful men, in which the pure Word of God is preached and the sacraments are duly administered. . . ." But the High Church school is not content with this view of things. The Church does something more than teach; it bestows God's gifts. It would not say that salvation is impossible without the pale of the Church; but it does say salvation is through the Church. God bestows His good gifts and graces because of her : in other words, all the benefits which come into man's soul come in virtue of her powers.

(i)

8. From this it follows that there must be an institution, officers in that institution, and some visible mode of imparting the gifts. It is easy to see how the **Priest** idea develops from this view of matters, and how, further, the sacraments possess a supernatural power. If it be once granted that God does not bestow His gifts directly and absolutely without the intervention of men, it is by no means difficult to build up the whole priestly system.

(j)

9. But it may be asked, Is there an accord here with the nature of things? Is it likely that the God of heaven, who is just and holy and withal good, should impart to men the duty of discharging such an important function? To my mind the thought is simply awful. If I could be persuaded that such a duty devolved upon the ministers of Christ, I should hesitate to accept its duties. It is a serious business to be a preacher; the responsibility is already sufficiently great. But to dispense God's gifts is a thought which would be weightier than I could bear. But it is not so. But does the Article say so? Yes, certainly. Article VI. says that we must refer all our teaching to the Bible.

(k)

Schools of Thought—*continued*

Nowhere does *it* give such power unto men. The prerogative of bestowing God's gifts is His own. He may use the Church as a means to arouse men to a sense of their need; but He never bestows gifts in virtue of her powers. Alas, for her powers! She has none but those she receives from God.

(*a*)

10. It would be easy to show all this from the Bible. It is not necessary. We will simply refer to one example. There never lived a greater man than St. Paul, the Apostle of the Gentiles. Was he a priest? Does he teach that the Church has powers? Where? Echo answers, Where? He taught the contrary. "Paul may plant, Apollos may water" . . . there their work ends . . . "God gives the increase." The Church, ay, fifty thousand Churches, may work, but they can confer no benefit. They may bring men in contact with God through preaching, but they can confer no blessing. St. Paul preached. He did not bestow gifts. He did not administer sacraments. "I thank God that I baptised none of you, save . . ." he preached. "I determined to know nothing among you but Christ and Him crucified."

(*b*)

11. The fact is, that the **High Church school** have exaggerated a truth, and so exaggerated it that it has become erroneous. The Church has responsibilities. It has no saving powers. It preaches the Gospel; it cannot bestow the grace of the Gospel. This responsibility to preach has been changed into a power to save.

(*c*)

12. But what now about the **Broad Church school**? What are we to understand by "broad?" In what sense is it broad? In this only, that it possesses a sort of humanitarian disposition which would embrace all. This school assumes the possession of a very large mind. It is constantly being said that the Broad Church school possesses all the intellect. If by this it were intended that its mind was sufficiently capacious to admit any views of religion or no views, perhaps it might be conceded. It would be difficult to discover in all its teaching anything definite or dogmatic. It is also described as the advanced school. There is a sense in which this is perfectly true. It is very advanced in a certain disposition, which finds fault with nothing, excuses everything, and is pleased with anything. Whether this is a safe disposition admits of very grave doubts.

(*d*)

13. I have often had to hear it said that the **Broad Church school** possesses all the intellect. I confess to a certain sort of irritation at the idea. Is it true? Then where are the proofs? But if it is true, what then? Religion is a matter of intellect! Now it would be a difficult matter to prove that the Broad Church school does possess all the intellect, for we have no guage by which to estimate brain power. It would be a still more difficult matter to prove that religion is a matter of intellect. But I am forgetting, the Broad Church school accepts no dogma. But is not the assumption dogmatic? And dogmatic, too, on assumption? But is it right to accept any man's *ipse dixit*? To the Word and the testimony. What does the Bible say? It is dogmatic certainly; but there is no dogma in it

as to religion being a matter of intellect. Its invitations, its offers of mercy, its promises, are not to the wise in particular. This is well, because all have souls. The Bible is dogmatic in these two particulars:

(i.) All have souls;

(ii.) All may be saved.

"Come unto Me, all ye that are weary and heavy laden, and I will give you rest." But the apprehension of these dogmas is not a matter of intellect. The just are not saved by intellect, but by faith. The things of God are not apprehended by intellect, but by the Spirit of God. "But the natural man receiveth not the things of the Spirit of God, for they are foolishness unto him: neither can he know them, because they are spiritually discerned." God is just, and so He has made salvation depend on a principle which all can exercise this principle is faith. "All things are possible to him that believeth."

(*e*)

14. As with the **High Church school**, so with the **Broad Church school**, there is an element of truth in their views. "God is love." His love extends to all the things which He has made. Christ died for all. All this, and much more like it, is found in the Bible. The Broad Churchman has come to think that all religion consists in being as much like what such passages as these represent God to be as possible. To be religious after their way of thinking, is to cultivate a sort of lovable disposition. We must have a heart that feels for all. This is all very true and very beautiful, but it is not enough. Man has not only to feel for others, he has also to provide for his own salvation. There is a sense in which it is quite true that "Charity begins at home," and here we have it. True charity is first concerned with personal salvation, and then with that of others. This is the true order of things. No man can be properly anxious about other men's souls until he knows himself saved. How can he be? He does not know what salvation is.

(*f*)

15. This is the point the **Broad Churchman** overlooks in his anxiety to love everything and everybody. He does not deny in so many words the utter depravity of human nature, the doctrine of the Atonement, Sanctification by the Holy Spirit, and all the concomitant truths; but he does what amounts to the same thing: he ignores them.

(*g*)

16. I have presumed, perhaps on good ground—to my own mind there is no perhaps—with the High Church school and the Broad Church school, there is something wrong, **what about the other?** Is it all right? Perhaps if it had a little more of the spirit which characterizes the others, it would not be any the worse. But any way this school takes the Bible for its guide. It accepts the teaching of the Prayer-book because it believes it to be consonant with that of the Bible. The views of this school may be summed up as follows:

(i.) Man by nature is a sinner.

(ii.) The Lord Jesus Christ, by the atonement made by His death, is a Saviour.

(iii.) The bond of union between the sinner and the Saviour is Faith.

(iv.) Faith is the gift of God.

(*h*)

Schools of Thought—*continued*

(v.) The Holy Spirit is the great Sanctifier.

(vi.) There are many who (a) do receive the promises, live a holy life, and so become inheritors of eternal life; and there are many who (β) do not receive the promises, who do not live a holy life, and so become heirs of wrath.

(vii.) The world is divided into classes (a) and (β); and further, this determines their position eternally.

(viii.) The minister is the preacher of God's Word and the pastor of His people His duty is not to lord it over God's heritage, but to be a labourer in His vineyard. His great duty is to lead people to God. His responsibility is great, for he must declare the whole counsel of God; but it does not go beyond this. The minister is no priest offering sacrifice—save only that of praise and thanksgiving—to God. The [minister has no control over God's blessings, save only that which prayer gives him. This power is common: it is not peculiar to the minister.

(a)

17. We might, perhaps, give a summary of the above view of the three Schools of Thought in our Church in these words:—The High Church school looks upon its officials as in some way endowed with powers by which they can administer God's gifts. The Broad Church school inculcates that the whole of religion consists in developing a certain amiability of character which embraces the whole world within its kindliness. The Low Church school holds that it is the grand business of life to realize, in all the fulness of its meaning, the truth of God, and lead the holy life of which this truth contains the principles.

(b)

18. Now I will venture to make a suggestion. I make it for what it is worth. It is this, instead of calling these parties Schools of Thought, call them Schools of Character. This term would be much more appropriate. Let us see this. God is one and unchangeable. James says, . . . "without variableness or shadow of turning." Christ is one and unchangeable. Hebrews has it, "Jesus Christ, the same yesterday, to-day, and for ever." The human race is the same as it was two thousand years ago. I once heard a clergyman say it was not, but I did not believe his statement. The prophet said nearly three thousand years ago, "The heart is deceitful above all things; who can know it," and he would be a bold man who would affirm that the description is not equally true to-day. The relation of the human race to its God is the same to-day as it has ever been since the Fall. Before Christ came, redemption was by anticipation; since He came it is by retrospection. "Abraham rejoiced to see My day." "For me to live is Christ." It is Christ, and always Christ, that is the Saviour. "He is the way, the truth, and the life." Now, are there three ways of receiving Christ as the Saviour, three right ways? And is it a matter of perfect indifference which the sinner adopts? In other words, does the Saviour accept the High Churchman in his way, the Broad Churchman in his, and the Low Churchman in his way? or does He Himself appoint a way by which He will be accepted? If the ways ran on similar lines—parallel lines—it would perhaps be conceivable; but how when the lines are so divergent?

To admit the possibility is absurd. The Saviour does not allow a man to think of Him as he chooses. Men must always entertain the same thought of Him. "What think ye of Christ?" The real and tangible points of Christianity do not admit of thoughts totally opposite in their nature and character. This goes without the saying.

(c)

19. We have a right, then, to maintain that, if men will entertain totally diverse thoughts about the Lord Jesus Christ—religion—they should rather be described by words that apply to character than by those which apply to thought. It is difficult, we readily admit, to define exactly how thought and character interact, and how much of the one is brought about by the other. It is not difficult to see that thought is more intangible than character. We can more easily appreciate character than thought. Further, it must be admitted that the character determines the thought more than the thought the character. Let us have, then, "Schools of Character." But we are frightened. We are alarmed. Three characters! The thing is impossible. Ay, impossible! God does not admit three classes of characters into heaven, but only one. We repeat, only one! "Without holiness shall no man see the Lord!" What holiness? Ay, what holiness? There is the rub! What holiness?

(d)   *Sandlands*

Schools of Thought (Parties)

Schools in Theology make themselves the arbiters of all God's decrees, and thoughts, and administrations. The extreme schools judge everything by their tenet, and the lax schools judge everything by their tenet. There is not one of you right! not from the East to the West. You are all imperfect.

(e)   *H. W. Beecher*

SCIENCE

Science and Agnosticism

We have admitted that he who knows not God may not be a monster (*See* "Science and Death"); we cannot say he will not be a dwarf. This precisely, and on perfectly natural principles, is what he must be. You can dwarf a soul, just as you can dwarf a plant, by depriving it of a full environment. Such a soul for a time may have "a name to live." Its character may betray no sign of atrophy. But its very virtue somehow has the pallor of a flower that is grown in darkness, or as an herb which has never seen the sun, no fragrance breathes from its spirit. To morality, possibly, this organism offers the example of an irreproachable life; but to science it is an instance of arrested development; and to religion it presents the spectacle of a corpse—a living Death.

(f)   *Drummond*

"Trust your Reason," we have been told, till we are tired of the phrase, "and you will become Atheists or Agnostics." We take you at your word; we become Agnostics.

(g)   *Leslie Stephen*

SCIENCE AND THE BIBLE

Scientists are men who have read nothing in the Bible but the first chapter in Genesis, and a few of the most amazing miracles.

Henry Martyn said, that mathematics were a diabolical illusion, rather than believe that they were all the revelation given us. Science makes nothing of man; but revelation shows him as lord of creation and an heir of immortality.

(a)

SCIENCE AND CHRIST

Many a man of science has not known Him. The pride of science, like a thick cloud, has hidden from the philosopher the spiritual Sun, the only true light; and for want of this quickening ray he has fallen in culture far, very far, below the poor.

(b)   *Channing*

SCIENCE AND CHRIST CRUCIFIED

" *Knowledge shall vanish away* " (1 Cor. xiii. 8)

The science of St. Paul's day, the deep philosophy of the Greek, is only curious now; for a bright light has shone: the geography, the astronomy, the physics of that age have vanished. This surely is enough to make a man humble. Therefore the next time you are inclined to be vain of a few facts, or a little reading, or a smattering of science, pause and think, that all the knowledge of the great and wise men of St. Paul's day, except the knowledge of Christ crucified, is worthless now. All has vanished, failed, but this, that they " washed their robes, and made them white in the blood of the Lamb."

(c)   *F. W. Robertson*

" *Science falsely so called* " (1 Tim. vi. 20)

St. Paul explains how this kind of γνῶσις was the direct enemy of the πίστις.

The one was a *theosophy*, the other a living spiritual fact.

The one gave an esoteric knowledge for the few initiated; the other, a religion of duty for all men.

(d)   *Lange*

SCIENCE AND CHRISTIANITY

Far as Science may soar, Christianity will accompany her flight; ever pointing her upwards, ever hallowing her triumphs, and finding in each discovery a new theme of adoration and praise. For the Divine element in Christianity is seen not more in miraculous attestation than in her affinity with all that is holy and true. Her evidences shine forth in the hearts she has purified, in the minds she has enlightened, in the lives she has fertilized and ennobled. By these fruits is she known. She is a phenomenon for which the world demands an account. Shall we say with the Rationalist, that a system which has given a new ideal to human life, which has inspired and quickened and guided all that is noblest and best for eighteen hundred years, was evolved by a mere unlettered Galilean peasant? Or shall we proclaim that God, who from the beginning has left not Himself without witness, " Who at sundry times and in divers manners spake in time past unto the fathers by the prophets, hath in these last days spoken unto us by His Son"? (Heb. i. 1, 2).

(e)   *S. C. Armour*

SCIENCE AND CHRISTIANITY

Our enemies charge us with timidity and obscurantism; let us in answer, as children of the light, advance fearlessly into the battle. As far as the farthest have pressed into science, we would press; as high as the highest have soared into speculation, we would soar; as deep as the deepest have dug in their search for truth, we too would dig. We are false descendants of the Crusaders if we yield to cowardice; false heirs of the Martyrs if we shrink from pain; false children and false successors of the Fathers and the Schoolmen and the Reformers if we scowl on intellect or sneer at knowledge; false to every tradition of our faith and of our history, of our vocation and of our name, if, being partakers of the Divine nature, and having escaped the corruption that is in the world through lust, we do not "give all diligence to add to our faith virtue, and to our virtue knowledge."

(f)   *Archdeacon Farrar*

SCIENCE AND THE CHURCH

What is the Englishman or Scotchman of the nineteenth century but a dexterous blacksmith, to whom the demons have surrendered their myths of gas, steam, and electric force in requital for his strong hatred of God and His Church?

(g)   *R. S. Hawker*

SCIENCE AND THE CROSS

Science can never conquer the enemies of the kingdom of God; she should be a handmaid. The true science is only where the Cross is. Only the *Theologus crucis* is the *Theologus lucis*.

(h)   *Lange*

SCIENCE AND DEATH, Physical and Spiritual

" *To be carnally minded is death* " (Rom. viii. 6)

Death is an unsurveyed land, an unarranged science.

(i)   *Faber*

Modern biology has found it a part of its work to push its way into the silent land; and at last the world is confronted with a scientific treatment of Death.

Death is one of the outstanding things in Nature which has an acknowledged spiritual equivalent.

(j)

What is Death

To a physiologist, the living organism is distinguished from the not-living by the performance of certain functions, . . . assimilation, waste, reproduction, and growth. Nothing could be more interesting than to point out the correlatives of these in the spiritual sphere: how the discharge of these functions manifests spiritual life, and the failure to perform them constitutes spiritual death.

(k)

Examples :

A human being is in direct contact with the earth and air, with all surrounding things, with the warmth of the sun, the music of birds, with the countless influences and activities of nature

(l)

Science and Death—continued

and of his fellow-men. In biological language, he is " in correspondence with his environment." In virtue of this correspondence he is entitled to be called alive. So long as this correspondence is preserved, he lives. If his environment changes, he must adjust himself to the change. And he continues to live only so long as he succeeds in adjusting himself to successive changes.

Take the case of a civil servant whose environment is a district in India, a region subject to prolonged droughts and consequent famines. When scarcity arises, he immediately adjusts himself to the change. He removes to a more fertile district, or he purchases the means necessary to continued life. But if from any cause he fails so to adjust himself to the altered circumstances, his body is thrown out of correspondence with his environment, and his life must cease.

In ordinary circumstances, when any part of the organism, by disease or accident, is thrown out of correspondence, it is in that relation dead.

This death may be either partial or complete.

Suppose the case of a man who is thrown out of correspondence with a part of his environment by some physical infirmity. Say, by accident he has been deprived of the use of his ears.

The deaf man is thus thrown out of *rapport* with a large and well-defined part of his environment, viz., its sounds. With regard to that external relation, therefore, he is no longer living. Part of the man is *dead*.

A blind man is thrown out of correspondence with another large part of his environment. Sea, sky, mountain, features and gestures of friends, are to him as if they were not. They are there, solid and real, but not to him; he is still further *dead*.

Next, conceive that cerebral disease lays hold on him. His whole brain is affected, and the sensory nerves, the medium of communication with the environment, cease altogether to acquaint him with what is doing in the outside world. The outside is still there, but not to him; he is still further *dead*.

And so the death of parts goes on. He becomes less and less alive.

(a)   *Drummond*

Were the animal frame not the complicated machine [it is], death might come as a simple and gradual dissolution, the "sans everything" being the last stage of the successive loss of fundamental powers.

(b)   *Foster*

Finally, some important part of the mere animal framework that remains breaks down. The correlation with the other parts is very intimate, and the stoppage of correspondence with one means an interference with the work of the rest. Something central has snapped, and all are thrown out of work. The lungs refuse to correspond with the air, the heart with the blood. There is now no correspondence whatever with the environment— the thing is *dead*.

This then is Death, the scientific meaning of Death. Dying is that breakdown in an organism which throws it out of correspondence with some necessary part of the environment.

(c)   *Drummond*

With this help we proceed to examine the parallel phenomenon of Death in the spiritual world. The factors are as before—organism and environment. The relation between them may be denominated " correspondence." And the truth to be emphasized is this, that spiritual death is a want of correspondence between the organism and the spiritual environment.

Of men generally it cannot be said that they are living in that part of the environment which is called the spiritual world. Suppose we call this spiritual environment God. And suppose we substitute for "correspondence," a word expressing the personal relation—"communion." We now can determine accurately the spiritual relation of different sections of mankind. Those who are in communion with God, live; those who are not, are *dead*.

(d)

The essential nature of spiritual Death consists in a want of communion with God.

The unspiritual man is he who lives in the circumscribed environment of this present world— "to be carnally minded is death." To be carnally minded, in the language of science, is to be limited in one's correspondences to the environment of the natural man.

The mind of the flesh, φρόνημα της σαρκὸς, by its very nature, limited capacity, and time-ward tendency, is θάνατος, Death.

This earthly mind may be of noble calibre, enriched by culture, high-toned, virtuous, and pure. But if it know not God? What though its correspondences, reach to the stars of heaven or grasp the magnitudes of time and space? The stars are not heaven. Space is not God. This mind has life up to its level. There is no trace of death. We do not picture the possessor of this carnal mind as in any sense a monster. We have said he may be high-toned, virtuous, and pure.

The plant is not a monster because it is dead to the voice of the bird; nor is he a monster who is dead to the voice of God.

The contention simply is, that he is *dead*.

(e)

For *proof* of this we need not go to Revelation. That is unnecessary, by the testimony of the dead themselves.

Thousands have uttered themselves upon their relations to the spiritual world, and from their own lips we have the proclamation of their death. The language of theology in describing the state of the natural man is often thought severe.

The Pauline anthropology has been challenged as an insult to human nature.

Culture has opposed the doctrine that, " The natural man receiveth not the things of the Spirit of God, for they are foolishness unto him : neither can he know them, because they are spiritually discerned."

Even some modern theologies have refused to accept the most plain of the aphorisms of Jesus, that, " Except a man be born again, he cannot see the Kingdom of God."

But this stern doctrine of spiritual deadness is no mere dogma of a past theology.

The history of thought during the present century proves that the world has come round spontaneously to the position of the first.

One of the ablest philosophical schools of the

(f)

Science and Death—*continued*

day erects a whole anti-christian system on this very doctrine.

The creed of the Agnostic is an unconscious witness for its truth.

And what are all these gloomy and rebellious infidelities, these touching and too sincere confessions of universal nescience, but a protest against this ancient law of death?

When the Agnostic tells me he is blind and deaf, dumb, torpid, and dead to the spiritual world, I must believe him. Jesus tells me that. Paul tells me that. Science tells me that. The nescience of the Agnostic philosophy is a proof from experience that to be carnally minded is death.

Let the theological value of the concession be duly recognised. It brings no solace to the unspiritual man to be told he is mistaken. He builds in all sincerity who raises his altar to the *unknown* god. He does not know God. With all his marvellous and complex correspondences, he is still one correspondence short.

It is a point worthy of special note, that the proclamation of this truth has always come from science rather than from religion. The statement, therefore, that the natural man discerneth not the things of the spirit, is never to be charged to the intolerance of theology.

Science has thus paved the way for the reception of one of the most revolutionary doctrines of Christianity; and if Christianity refuses to take advantage of the opening, it will manifest a culpable want of confidence in itself. There never was a time when its fundamental doctrines could be proclaimed more boldly, or when they could better secure the respect and arrest the interest of science.

(*a*)   *Drummond (condensed)*

Science and Faith, and Knowledge

We are given "an understanding, that we may know Him that is true, and we are in Him that is true" (1 John v. 20). But in the order of the Christian life faith comes before knowledge; and we believe in order that we may know. The scientific principle is the reverse of this; in the scientific sphere knowledge precedes faith, and we learn to know in order that we may believe. But it also follows from this principle that science must know before she can deny. Accordingly, it is to be observed that the attitude of philosophy and science towards religious truth, as represented by their ablest and most authoritative exponents in modern times, is not one of negation, but of a simple confession of ignorance, or, as such an attitude has been recently termed, "Agnosticism."

(*b*)   *Dr. Wace: Bampton Lectures*

Science and the First Chapter of Genesis

That chapter has experienced a most singular fate. No portion, perhaps, of the Bible is more utterly abandoned by certain votaries of science in the present day; while, on the contrary, none was more dear to the great father of the experimental philosophy. The language of Lord Bacon is saturated, so to speak, with thoughts derived from this narrative. He discerns in it types of the whole order of the divine operations, whether in nature or in grace—types, consequently, of the work and the nature of that being who was made in the divine image.

(*c*)   *Ibid*

Bacon's prayer, in which he invokes the divine blessing upon his labours (*Instauratio Magna*), is a prayer in which theology, philosophy, and experience combine in one luminous and solemn meditation:

"Thou therefore, O Father, who gavest the visible light as the firstborn of Thy creatures, and didst pour into man the intellectual light, as the top and consummation of Thy workmanship, be pleased to protect and govern this work, which, coming from Thy goodness, returneth to Thy glory. Thou, after Thou hadst reviewed the works which Thy hand had made, beheldest that everything was very good, and didst rest with complacency in them. But man, reflecting on the works which he had made, saw that all was vanity and vexation of spirit, and could by no means acquiesce in them. Wherefore, if we labour in Thy works with the sweat of our brows, Thou wilt make us partakers of Thy vision and Thy Sabbath. We humbly beg that this mind may be steadfastly in us, and that Thou by our hands and also by the hands of others on whom Thou shalt bestow the same spirit, wilt please to convey a largesse of new alms to the family of mankind."

(*d*)   *Ibid*

Science, its Generalizations

1. The country is becoming extremely well educated. At one of the Universities generalizing is taught, or used to be taught, as a fine art; and it was wonderful to see what wide generalizations undergraduates could build on the most slender and sketchy premisses. A young fellow would explain in a few lines the effect of Semitic religion on the commercial policy of the Carthaginians, though he had no more to go upon than the recollection of a few remarks by Mommsen. Once the knack is acquired, nothing is easier than to invent propositions which are sweeping indeed, and have a fine aspect of adventurous originality.

2. The Aryan race, about which it is fashionable to instruct the young. The Aryan race used to come from somewhere in Central Asia. There was their "cradle." But now it seems just as likely that they came from the Baltic, and had their cradle in that bleak district, whence amber was carried southward along the Sacred Road.

(*e*)

Science and God, a Rebuke

I think a bystander would say, that though Christianity had in it something far higher and deeper and more ennobling, yet the average scientific man worships just at present a more awful and, as it were, a greater Deity than the average Christian. In so many Christians the idea of God has been degraded by childish and little-minded teaching; the Eternal and the Infinite and the All-embracing has been represented as the head of the clerical interest, as a sort of clergyman, as a sort of schoolmaster, as a sort of philanthropist. But the scientific man knows Him to be eternal; in astronomy, in geology, he becomes familiar with the countless millenniums of His life-time. The scientific man strains his mind actually to realize God's Infinity. As far off as the fixed stars he traces Him, "distance inexpressible by numbers that have name." Meanwhile, to the theologian,

(*f*)

infinity and eternity are very much of empty words when applied to the Object of his worship. He does not realize them in actual facts and definite computations.

(a) *Author of " Ecce Homo."*

SCIENCE, THE GOSPEL OF

'Tis a sad, a terrible thing, to see nigh a whole generation of men and women, professing to be cultivated, looking round in a purblind fashion, and finding *no God in this universe.* I suppose it is a reaction from the reign of cant and hollow pretence—men professing to believe what in fact they do not believe. And this is what we have got to. All things from frogs' spawn ; the gospel of dirt is the order of the day. The older I grow, —and I now stand upon the brink of eternity,— the more comes back to me the sentence in the catechism which I learned when a child, and the fuller and deeper its meaning becomes, " What is the chief end of man ?" " To glorify God, and enjoy Him for ever." No gospel of dirt, teaching that men have descended from frogs through monkeys, can ever set that aside.

(b) *Thos. Carlyle* (1877)

SCIENCE, IRREVERENT

Thought without reverence is *barren*, perhaps *poisonous.*

And what is that science, which the scientific head alone, were it screwed off, and (like the Doctor's in the Arabian tale) set in a basin to keep it alive, could prosecute without shadow of a heart ?

(c) *Carlyle*

SCIENCE AND LIFE

All really scientific experience tells us that life can be produced from a living antecedent only.

(d) *" The Unseen Universe."*

The present state of knowledge furnishes us with no link between the living and the not-living.

(e) *Huxley*

SCIENCE AND MAN

As the title of Bacon's *Novum Organum* stand the words, " Aphorisms concerning the Interpretation of Nature and the Dominion of Man." That is, Bacon discerned a revelation of the true function of man upon the earth in the emphatic commission given him to " replenish the earth and subdue it, and have dominion over the fish of the sea, and over the fowl of the air, and over every living thing that moveth upon the earth." Those words were apprehended by Bacon, not as a mere description of man's dignity, but as a comprehensive designation of his true position, and as marking out the main work which on earth it was at once his destiny and his duty to fulfil. . . . " Man," he says, " is the minister and interpreter of nature." . . . We see those words year by year more amply fulfilled. But their full significance is to be appreciated only . . . by regarding them as a commentary upon the scriptural revelation. From this point of view, what a light do they not throw upon the condition and the history of mankind ! Nature, with all its marvellous endowments, is depicted to us, before the creation of man, as a kingdom without a king, an estate without an owner or minister to develop it, a beautiful vision without a painter or an interpreter. Forces of the utmost subtlety or the most stupendous power, infinite possibilities of combination and variation of elements, harmonies of colour and form needing a reasonable hand and eye to detect and depict them, lay hid in that vast and complex creation upon which God looked when He declared that it was very good. But a mirror was needed in which the whole mystery and marvel should be reflected, and in which, if the expression may be adopted from the sacred writer, God Himself should behold the full beauty of His own work. When the human eye and the human reason were created, a new universe was created with them, the universe of science, of art, and of all the higher developments of the animal instincts. Perhaps from this point of view we may be permitted to discern an adumbration of a great truth in the statement that " out of the ground the Lord God formed every beast of the field and every fowl of the air, and brought them unto Adam to see what he would call them ; and whatsoever Adam called every living creature, that was the name thereof." To give names to things, is to classify them, to observe their resemblances, to abstract and generalize, to exert the reason and the imagination ; and what else, in substance, is the work of science at the present day, but that of giving names to every creature? Viewing man as called into existence by the Creator for the further display of the marvels of creation, we may regard God as at this moment bringing all the varied elements of nature before us, to see what we will call them, to behold how very good are those reasonable and moral faculties which He designed to be the mirror of His created works.

(f) *Dr. Wace*

SCIENCE (MATERIALISM)

Herbert Spencer, the High Priest of Materialism, thus defines Evolution :—

" Evolution is an integration of matter and a concomitant dissipation of motion, during which the matter passes from an indefinite, incoherent homogeneity to a definite homogeneity, and during which the retained motion undergoes a parallel transformation." Lucid and exhaustive !

(g)

SCIENCE (MATERIALISM)

Epitaph on the late Professor Clifford (Materialist).
" I was not, and I was. I did a little, and I was not."

(h) *In a London Cemetery*

SCIENCE AND RELIGION

Science, so far from being antagonistic, has enriched religious thought. Cf. " I am the . . . Truth ; " " In whom are hid all the treasures of wisdom and knowledge."

(i)

SCIENCE AND RELIGION

This I dare affirm in knowledge of Nature, that a little natural philosophy, and the first entrance

(j)

into it, doth dispose the opinion to Atheism ; but,
on the other side, much natural philosophy, and
wading deep into it, will bring about men's minds
to religion.

(a)   *Bacon*

SCIENCE AND RELIGION

To attempt to fashion souls by (mere) knowledge, ranks only with blowing their bodies to
pieces with gunpowder (teaching requires true
God-ordained priests).

(b)   *Carlyle*

SCIENCE AND RELIGION

Science has a foundation, and so has religion.
Let them unite their foundations, and the basis
will be broader, and they will he two compartments
of one great fabric reared to the glory of God.
Let the one be the outer and the other the inner
court. In the one let all look, and admire, and
adore ; and in the other let those who have faith
kneel, and pray, and praise. Let the one be the
sanctuary where human learning may present its
richest incense as an offering to God, and the
other, the holiest of all, separated from it by a
veil now rent in twain, and in which, on a blood-
sprinkled mercy-seat, we pour out the love of a
reconciled heart, and hear the oracles of the living
God.

(c)   *M'Cosh*

SCIENCE AND REVELATION

Once more, these are days in which the study
of Nature has received, and most justly received,
an enormous impetus. But the field is a boundless one, and we can never hope to see the confines of it. The more we know, the more we
shall find there is still to be known, and the more
we shall find our previous knowledge open to
conviction. But if there is any truth in Christ's
words about doing the works of His Father, the
more we know of Nature, the more we shall find
that the character and the works of Christ are in
strict accordance with the works of Nature. This
must be so if Christ was indeed the Son of God ;
it will be so if our knowledge and intelligence of
the character of Christ progresses in proportion
to our knowledge of Nature. But this involves
the increase of faith as well as the increase of
knowledge, and demands growth in grace as well
as growth in science.

(d)   *Stanley Leathes*

SCIENCE AND SCEPTICISM

Whatever changes may characterize our nineteenth century, *one* serious event, at least, seems
certain. To borrow the idea of a distinguished
foreigner (Signor Villari), European opinion
appears gradually dividing between the sceptic
and the bigot—the spirit that governs Rome and
the spirit which animated Voltaire. And this
tendency to violent extremes seems likely to bring
about the religious crisis of the coming age.

(e)   *Jackson's Bampton Lectures*

SCIENCE, VALUE OF

We, as Christian people, ought to be exceedingly
thankful for the marvellous discoveries of modern
science. I do not mean on account merely of the
material benefit and comfort they bring ; but on
account of the additional disclosure made by them
of the infinite glory of our God. The true student
of the book of Science, and the true student of the
book of Revelation, are really at one ; though at
times they seem to be antagonistic ; and though
very frequently they manifest an unworthy hostility
to each other. Depend upon it, they *must* come
together at last ; and depend upon it, too, that
even ungodly and irreverent men of science are
working up, unconsciously, and in spite of themselves, to the result at which we aim—-the firmer
establishment and wider recognition of the Kingdom of Jesus Christ.

(f)   *Gordon Calthrop*

Cultivation, art, and science, are not evils, but
belong to a perfect condition of human existence ;
nay, it may be said they are *necessary* conditions
for the development of morality and religion. . . .
That science is not able to save this generation,
does not require assertion. But nevertheless
Christian science assists in the *perception* of saving
truth.

(g)   *Martensen*

SCIENTIFIC COMFORT

Try your scientific comfort on these parents who
have lost their only child. You come in, and you
talk to those parents about " selection," and about
" the survival of the fittest," showing, as you will
have to, carrying out your theory, that the physical
life of that child deceased in the household was
not worth so much as the life of some other child
that survived. Try that consolation. And here
you find a dying man. Come and use transcen-
dental phraseology. Tell him to have confidence
in the great " To be," and the " Everlasting Now,"
and the " Eternal What-is-it." Come to this
woman who has lost her husband, and tell her it
was a geological necessity that her husband passed
out of being, because the whole race must pass off
to give room to a higher race who are to inhabit
this earth, just as the megatherium disappeared
in order to give room for a higher style of creation ;
and then go on with your consolation, tell her
there is a possibility that ten million years from
now we ourselves will have the honour of lying as
geological specimens on a geological shelf—petrified
specimens of the extinct human race ! And, after
you have got through with that scientific comfort
(if these poor bereft people are not crazy), I will
send out of my parish the plainest Christian
man and he will go into that household, and, by a
half-hour of prayer and Christian consolation, he
will stop the tears, and there will be in that household the calmness of an Indian summer's sunset.
It will flood the house from floor to roof. I do not
know how it is in other lands, but the American
people are finding out that worldly philosophy and
human science as a consolation in time of bereavement are an illimitable, outrageous, unmitigated,
and appalling humbug ; and they are crying out
for the comfort of the Gospel, and they are getting
it.

(h)   *Talmage*

SCIENTIFIC SCEPTIC, THE

He has given his time to the study of natural
science, and I to that of religion (the study of

(i)

supernatural science). In his own province he may, or may not, know more than I do; but when he touches upon my province I can see his ignorance, and can see that he approaches it from the outside; therefore I feel and know my superiority. For in religion a man must have his standing *in* it, before he can have an understanding *of* it.

(a)

SCOFFERS

"*Heaven and earth shall pass away, but My words shall not pass away*" (Luke xxi. 33)

Scoffers think exactly the opposite, *viz.*, that heaven and earth shall remain; the words of the Lord, on the other hand, be forgotten and exposed as lies (2 Pet. iii. 3).

(b)   *Lange*

SCOURGE

Thou tamer of the human breast;
Whose iron scourge and torturing hour
The bad affright, afflict the best!

(c)   *Gray*

SCRIPTURE, THE, CANNOT BE BROKEN
(John x. 35)

The expression shows the boundless confidence with which the Scripture word inspired Jesus.

(d)   *Godet*

"Remember Thy word unto Thy servant, upon which Thou hast caused me to hope" (Ps. cxix. 49)

(e)

God hath spoken—spoken to me,—and shall He not make it good? . . . Have not some obtained promises?

(f)

SCRIPTURE, HOLY (2 Pet. iii. 10–18)

Wordsworth gives the following useful table of the testimony of Prophets and Apostles to the authority of Holy Scripture.

The Prophet *Malachi* closes the canon of the *Old Testament* by a solemn appeal "to the law of Moses, and to the statutes and judgments." He says: "Remember them" (Mal. iv. 4).

The Apostle and Evangelist *St. John* closes the *four Gospels* with a similar reference. "These things are *written*, that ye might believe that Jesus is the Christ, the Son of God, and that believing, ye might have life through His name" (John xx. 31).

St. Paul, the Apostle of the Gentile world, closes *his Epistles* with a testimony to the sufficiency and inspiration of Holy Scripture: "Abide thou in these things which thou hast learned, and wert assured of, knowing from whom thou didst learn them; and that from a child thou knewest the *Holy Scriptures*, which are the things that are able to make thee wise unto salvation, through faith that is in Jesus Christ. Every Scripture being divinely inspired, is also profitable for doctrine, for reproof, for correction, for instruction in righteousness, in order that the man of God may be perfect,

throughly furnished unto every good work" (2 Tim. iii. 14–17).

St. Peter, here, in like manner closes his Epistles with a similar exhortation, and with a warning against perversion of Scripture.

St. Jude also closes the *Catholic Epistle* with a memento to his readers: "Remember ye the words spoken before by the Apostles of our Lord Jesus Christ" (Jude 17).

Lastly, the Apostle and Evangelist *St. John* closes the Apocalypse with a promise of blessing to those who keep its sayings, and a curse on those who take from it or add to it (Rev. xxii. 7, 18, 19).

(g)

SCRIPTURE, QUOTING OF (Matt. iv.)

The devil can cite Scripture for his purpose.
An evil soul producing holy witness,
Is like a villain with a smiling cheek;
A goodly apple rotten at the heart;
Oh, what a goodly outside falsehood hath!

(h)   *Shakspeare*

SEA, THE

He that will learn to pray, let him go to sea.

(i)   *George Herbert*

I saw a thousand fearful wrecks:
A thousand men that fishes gnawed upon:
Wedges of gold, great anchors, heaps of pearl,
Inestimable stones, unvalued jewels,
All scattered in the bottom of the sea.
Some lay in dead men's skulls; and in those holes
Where eyes did once inhabit there were crept,
As 'twere in scorn of eyes, reflecting gems,
That wooed the slimy bottom of the deep,
And mocked the dead bones that lay scattered by.

(j)   *Shakspeare*

SEAL, THE APOSTOLIC (2 Tim. ii. 19)

Some seventy years after [Pentecost] the veil is lifted, by the hand of a Roman statesman, from the comparative obscurity of the Christian Church, and discloses an army of soldiers of the Cross, whose bond of union is still stamped conspicuously with the Apostolic seal:—"*Let every one that nameth the name of Christ depart from iniquity.*" At the commencement of the second century, Pliny reports to Trajan, as the result of what he could extort from the Christians in his province, "that this was the sum of their fault or error, that they were wont to meet together on a stated day before sunrise, and sing a hymn to Christ as God, and bind themselves by a *Sacramentum* that they would not commit theft, or robbery, or adultery, that they would not break faith, nor repudiate a trust." A memorable record! honourable to the Roman to whose impartial accuracy it is due, as well as to the Church whose clear and simple character it reflects; and more precious, alike in its historical and in its practical instruction, than many a famous volume. Under this standard, and bound by this oath, the army of the saints maintained a stern, though patient, war against the sin which was embodied in the life and in the institutions of the society of their day. They won at length a great victory, and it was achieved, like

(k)

that of their Lord, by resistance unto blood. That which has been described as "the strong antipathy of good to bad" aroused the equally strong antipathy of bad to good. A corrupt society felt instinctively that a Church which was at war with iniquity was at war with itself, and it appealed to the final arbitrement of bloodshed. When we realize the deadly nature of this struggle, when we think of the blood that has been shed in it, from that precious blood (of Christ), .. to the outpouring of the life of innumerable humbler souls, the deepest emotions of our souls are stirred; and it is not easy to be as patient as we should otherwise wish to be with misrepresentations of the Church's early history.

Dr. Wace : " The Faith of the Early Church "
(a)

SEALED

" *Sealed with the Holy Spirit of promise* " (Eph. i. 13)

God is the sealer,
We are the sealed,
The Spirit is the seal.
(b)   *Lange*

" *In whom ye are sealed* " (Eph. i. 13, 14)

(i.) The *Father* seals believers, and His glory is the last end.
(ii.) In the *Son* they are sealed, and Redemption is His work.
(iii.) The *Spirit* is the seal, and earnest.
(c)   *Ibid*

SEAR AND YELLOW LEAF

My days are in the yellow leaf ;
   The flowers and fruits of love are gone ;
The worm, the canker, and the grief
   Are mine alone.
(d)   *Byron*

SEARCH

Search the Scriptures (John v. 39)

Why should I examine the Scriptures ?

1. It is for your life

If you are wrong here, you are fatally wrong. . . . A man will find time to make himself acquainted with that upon which his highest well-being depends. You have time to read about one side of the question ; find time to examine the other.
(e)

2. The Book claims to be from God

You say, " Of course ; it is not the only imposture which claims to be from God." Well, but many men—like Newton, Milton, Bacon and Shakspeare—before whose gigantic mental stature the highest modern intelligence dwarfs into pigmy proportions, have accepted it as such. At all events *their* endorsement of the Book should secure your respect.
(f)

3. It is a Book which has stood a great deal of attack, and is extant still ; and is a power in the world, too

Had it been other than we think it is, it would have crumbled away long ago. The keenest intellects, the sharpest criticism, the most ponderous learning, the bitterest scoffing, have all assailed it in turn, and that for two thousand and more years ; and the fact that it remains still a living power amongst men seems to prove that it has a divine life in it, that it is instinct with the indestructible vitality of God.
(g)

4. Again we say—and here we boldly challenge contradiction—that the man whose life is most in accordance with Bible teaching is the highest type of man—every way the best. . . . We defy contradiction here. We say unhesitatingly, that you do not find men good right through and good all round amongst your sceptics and infidels.
(h)

5. To the objection, that the clergy are afraid of the march of intellect and the spread of knowledge, . . . hear a philosopher.

Said Sir David Brewster, a short time before his death : " In the present day people fancy that they are free-thinkers, and that they are searching with a thoroughly intellectual examination, into any subject which comes before them with reference to those questions which bear on the veracity of the Bible ; but in the whole history of the world I don't think there was ever a period of time when men were more led by the opinions of others." . . . " I am not aware of any single proven fact connected with geology, or any other scientific fact, which in the slightest degree affects the truth of the Bible. I do not mean assertions, I mean real well-grounded scientific facts, founded upon pure and perfect induction, the premisses clear and distinct, and the inferences irresistible." . . . " Every man in the present day has really and truly never read those books which are said to be so conclusive for the overthrowing of our faith ; but I have read them, and if other people would do the same, the result would be, that they would be ashamed of being implicated in the advancement of views which are so utterly untenable by intelligent and philosophic minds."
(i)

. . . "The Bible is none the worse. There it stands, living, strong, effective as ever ! Remember, too, that even if the Bible were overthrown, its opponents would gain nothing, but lose everything, because the facts of God's universe would remain the same. A little boy, anxious that the morrow should be fine, because of a holiday ; accordingly fastened the pointer of the barometer at " *set fair*," and then thought himself secure of his holiday. But alas ! the facts of the universe were against him, in spite of his ingenuity ; rain fell all day, and spoiled his pleasure. Some clever people are exceedingly like that ingenious boy. They construct theories about human nature, God, the unseen world, future state : they think they have made all secure ; but the spiritual world takes its course, and leaves them out in the cold." . . .
(j)

A party of voyagers, passing through a dangerous channel, may say, "Away with the chart!" might easily get rid of it; but the rocks, shoals, sunken reefs, and all the perils of the channel would remain just the same. . . .

A community might say, "Banish your doctors. Throw physic to the dogs! we'll none of it." But the laws and conditions of health and disease, of life and death, would remain precisely as before. . . .

Practically, many do get rid of the Bible; but what do they gain? *Only the loss of a guide.* The facts about man and God, and of their mutual relation, remain precisely the same.

(a) *Gordon Calthrop*

SECTARIANISM

Religion is war; Christians, forsaking their one Lord, gather under various standards to gain victory for their sects.

(b) *Channing*

SECTS

Hence jarring sectaries may learn
Their real int'rest to discern,
That brother should not war with brother,
And worry and devour each other.

(c) *Cowper*

SECURITY, OUR COMPLETE IN CHRIST
(Rom. viii. 33)

A four-fold cord

1. His *death* removes our deserved condemnation;

2. His *resurrection* raises us above the sense of condemnation into the confidence and spiritual life of adoption;

3. His sitting at the *right hand of God* protects us against all condemning powers, and is a pledge of our acquittal at the judgment;

4. His *intercession* abolishes the last remains of condemnation in our life, and secures us against relapse.

(d) *Lange*

SEEING AND BELIEVING (John xx. 29)

Wonderful indeed, and rich in blessing for us who have not seen Him, is this, the closing word of the Gospel. For these words cannot apply to the remaining ten; they, like Thomas, had seen and believed.

(e) *Alford*

All the appearances of the forty days were mere preparations for the believing without seeing.

(f) *Stier*

Whom having not seen, ye love; in whom, though now ye see Him not, yet believing, ye rejoice with joy unspeakable and full of glory: receiving the end of your faith, even the salvation of your souls (1 Pet. i. 8).

(g)

SEEK

" *What seek ye?* " . . . " *Where dwellest Thou?* " (John i. 38)

The question of our Lord answered by another, and = "We seek no *thing*, but *Thee*."

Note

1. The freshness of the narrative: think of them as earnest Jews, of the best sort, seeking the Messiah, and having *now* found him. St. John writes down these particulars of the first hours of his Christian life.

In verse 29, John Baptist bears testimony of Jesus; but his disciples did not leave him then. The *next day*, however, decides them (35): it is the first day of their Christian life. John Baptist again bears testimony, and they leave him and follow Jesus. He asks, " *What seek ye?* " They reply, " *Where dwellest Thou?* " Jesus says, " *Come, and ye shall see.* "

And now it is that John indicates to us—"Come and hear, and I will declare what He hath done for my soul."

"They that seek shall find."

He adds, " *It was about the tenth hour* " (39), indicating the *hour* of his conversion as indelibly fixed on his memory, a day and an hour to be remembered in eternity.

2. Lessons

(i.) We must be disciples of John Baptist (by repentance), before we can be the disciples of Christ.

(ii.) See how quickly Christ and His people recognise each other. "My sheep hear My voice," etc. Cf. Isa. xliii. 1, "Fear not, . . . I have called thee by thy name; thou art Mine." Also, Jesus saith, " *Mary.* " She responds, " *Rabboni.* "

(h)

" *To seek and to save the lost* " (Luke xix. 10)

There are no subjectives and objectives there, no beggarly, windy abstractions, but just a plain fact, that God came down to look for poor bodies, instead of leaving poor bodies to go looking for Him.

(i) *Chas. Kingsley*

SEEKING GOD

There are but three classes of persons; those who have found God, and serve Him; those who, not having yet found Him, are seeking Him; and, lastly, those who neither have found Him nor seek Him.

(j) *Blaise Pascal*

God never meant that man should scale the heavens
By strides of human wisdom—in His works,
Though wondrous; He commands us in His Word
To seek Him rather where His mercy shines.

(k) *Cowper*

Those who seek God with their whole heart, whom nothing can grieve but the loss of His presence, who have no desire but to attain to Him, no enemies but such things as lead them aside from Him, and whose greatest affliction is their exposure to such enemies; let them be comforted; for them there is a Deliverer, for them there is a God!

(l) *Blaise Pascal*

SEEKING AND SAVING THE LOST (Matt. xviii. 11)

1. He Came to Seek

"I will *search*, My sheep, and *seek* them out," says He (Ezek. xxxiv. 11). He was the Shepherd who had lost His sheep, and He missed it, valued it, left the rest, went after it, sought for it, all the world over. His was a *seeking* life, a *seeking* ministry. His were *seeking* words and *seeking* works. He is the great Seeker, the Heavenly Seeker. His days were spent in *search*. He sought when He was here ; He is seeking still. His is the same seeking attitude and earnestness now in heaven as formerly on earth. He seeks in *love*. Not as the officer seeks out the hiding criminal ; but as the mother seeks her lost child. It is the search of love, divine, yet human love ; love that will not wait till the desired object of search shows symptoms of concern or willingness to return, but love that pursues the flying, the unwilling, the resisting. Many are the places in which He finds and has found His stray ones ; one He found upon a cross, one by a well, one in a boat, in a sycamore tree, it matters not.

(*a*)

2. He Came to Save the Lost

The lost ! Who are they ! Not simply those whom man describes as lost to shame, lost to decency, lost to all human motives of right, but such as are lost to God ; lost in the sense in which the sheep is lost to the shepherd ; the piece of silver to the woman ; the son to the father. The great Father has lost a son ; man has lost God, and God has lost man. They are lost in respect to separation and distance from God. They are lost in regard to future hope. They have lost everything ; they are lost to everything. Shepherd, and woman, and father, have sustained an awful loss (Luke xv.) ; but what is this to the loss of those who have lost God, and are lost to God. O man, that art *lost* : and the word means something unutterably awful ; something which only the Spirit of God can reveal to you. But the Son of Man has come to seek and save you. He is bent on this. It is His errand, His mission. No matter how *lost* you are. He is not willing that you should perish. He has no pleasure in your death. He seeks your life. He desires to save.

(*b*)   *Horatius Bonar*

SEEM

Thus 'tis with all ; their chief and constant care
Is to seem everything but what they are.
(*c*)   *Goldsmith*

SEEMING

         All live by seeming.
The beggar begs with it, and the gay courtier
Gains land and title, rank and rule, by seeming ;
The clergy scorn it not, and the bold soldier
Will eke with it his service. All admit it,
All practise it ; and he who is content
With showing what he is, shall have small credit
In Church, or camp, or state—so wags the world.
(*d*   *Scott*

SELF

Explore the dark recesses of the mind,
In the soul's honest volume read mankind,
And own, in wise and simple, great and small,
. . . and by whatever name we call
The ruling tyrant, Self is all in all.
(*e*)   *Churchill*

     I to myself am dearer than a friend.
(*f*)   *Shakspeare*

SELF-DECEPTION

Errors of doctrine, into which men wilfully wander, putting phantasms in the place of truth = πλάνη.

The Apostle warns against this, "Be not deceived (μὴ πλανᾶσθε, wander not), God is not mocked ; for whatsoever a man soweth, that shall he also reap" (Gal. vi. 7).

St. John = "If we say we have no sin, we deceive ourselves (ἑαυτοὺς πλανῶμεν), and the truth is not in us" (1 John i. 8).

St. Paul = That God, in punishment for the sins of men, "sends them strong delusion (ἐνέργειαν πλάνης), to believe a lie" (2 Thess. ii. 11).
(*g*)   *Martensen*

SELF-DENIAL

A Christian should make his luxuries yield to another man's comforts, his comforts to another man's necessities, his necessities to another man's extremity.
(*h*)   *Howard*

SELF-EXAMINATION

Examine your tempers, your dispositions, and your actions. Remember that a proud Christian, an angry Christian, a worldly Christian, a covetous Christian, or a selfish Christian, in the sight of God, is not a whit better than an adulterous Christian or a murderous Christian.
(*i*)   *C. Clayton*

SELF-EXAMINATION

It is reported of Sextus, that every night before he slept, he asked of his own heart : "What evil hast thou this day amended ? What vice hast thou shunned ? What good hast thou done ? In what part art thou bettered ?
(*j*)

SELF-EXAMINATION

"*Creeping things*" (Ezek. viii. 10)

Dig down deeper, deeper ; go below the surface. Dig till you find a door ; push on, stay not, "Examine yourselves" ; let your spirit make diligent search, and yet unassisted you are incapable of discovering what you really are. The anointing eyesalve of the Holy Spirit is necessary; or else you will fail to find your heart-sores. A mere walking about Jerusalem would not have sufficed the Prophet to discover the hidden plague-spots ; neither will a mere superficial examination
(*k*)

serve your purpose. Know the worst of yourself; and sleep not over hell. Ah! you have found the door—it is opened. You stand back abashed at the revelation of what is within—"creeping things"—lusts, idols, covetings, altars everywhere to unholy shrines; and this devildom, mark it, is in the heart of one dedicated to God, one of the covenanted people. Think, "If these things be done in a green tree, what must be done in the dry?" O ye, who think ye stand, break up the fallow ground of your hearts, for it is time to seek the Lord afresh.

. . . Be not dismayed, however, at this revelation: "Great your help, if great your need." God's purpose in uncovering your sore is not to slay you, but that you may see your need of the Physician, and flee to Him.

(a)

SELF-EXAMINATION

One of our old writers quaintly observes, that "The ancients used to take their stomach-pill of self-examination every night. Some used little books, or tablets, which they tied at their girdles, in which they kept a memorial of what they did, against their night-reckoning." We know that Titus,—the delight of mankind, as he has been called,—kept a diary of all his actions; and when at night he found, upon examination, that he had performed nothing memorable, would exclaim, "Amici! diem perdidimus!" Friends! we have lost a day!

(b) *Disraeli: Cur. Lit*

SELF-EXAMINATION

Evils in Sixteen Parts

I have been much challenged,

(i.) For not referring all to God, as the last end: that I do not eat, drink, sleep, journey, speak, and think for God.

(ii.) That I have not benefited by good company; and that I left not some word of conviction, even upon natural and wicked men, as by reproving swearing in them; or because of being a silent witness to their loose carriage; and because I intended not in all companies to do good.

(iii.) That the woes and calamities of the kirk, and particular professors, have not moved me.

(iv.) That in reading the life of David, Paul, and the like, when it humbled me, I coming so far short of their holiness, laboured not to imitate them, afar off at least, according to the measure of God's grace.

(v.) That unrepented sins of youth were not looked to and lamented for.

(vi.) That sudden stirrings of pride, lust, revenge, love of honours, were not resisted and mourned for.

(vii.) That my charity was cold.

(viii.) That the experience I had of God's hearing me, in this and the other particular, being gathered, yet in a new trouble I had always (once at least) my faith to seek, as if I were to begin at A, B, C, again.

(ix.) That I have not more boldly contradicted the enemies, speaking against the truth, either in public church meetings, or at tables, or ordinary conference.

(x.) That in great troubles, I have received false reports of Christ's love, and misbelieved Him in His chastening; whereas the event hath said, all was in mercy.

(xi.) Nothing more moveth me, and burdeneth my soul, than that I could never, in my prosperity so wrestle in prayer with God, nor be so dead to the world, so hungry and sick of love for Christ, so heavenly-minded, as when ten stone weight of a heavy cross was upon me.

(xii.) That the cross extorted vows of new obedience, which ease hath blown away, as chaff before the wind.

(xiii.) That practice was so short and narrow, and light so long and broad.

(xiv.) That death hath not been often meditated upon.

(xv.) That I have not been careful of gaining others to Christ.

(xvi.) That my grace and gifts bring forth little or no thankfulness.

(c) *Samuel Rutherford*

SELF-GOVERNMENT

It is by God's mercy in our power to attain a degree of self-government which is essential to our own happiness, and contributes greatly to that of those around us. Take care of over excitement, and endeavour to keep a quiet mind (even for your health), it is the best advice that can be given you: your moral and spiritual improvement will then keep pace with the culture of your intellectual powers.

(d) *Robert Southey to Miss Brontë*

SELF-KNOWLEDGE

God Almighty, to reserve to Himself the sole right of instructing us, and to prevent our solving the difficulties of our own being, has hid the knot so high, or, to speak more properly, so low, that we cannot reach it. So that it is not by the exercise, but by the simple submission of our reason, that we are capable of truly knowing ourselves.

(e) *Blaise Pascal*

SELF-KNOWLEDGE

Pontanus' Epitaph

I am Pontanus, beloved by the powers of literature, admired by men of worth, and dignified by the monarchs of the world. Thou knowest, now, *who I am*, or, more properly, *who I was;* for thee, stranger, I, who am in darkness, cannot know thee; but I entreat thee to KNOW THYSELF.

(f) *Dr. Johnson*

SELF-PLEASING

He that pleaseth himself, pleaseth a fool.

(g) *Quarles*

SELF-RIGHTEOUSNESS

A man who is full of fancied wisdom cannot learn: his teachers are tired of him, and wait till he is emptied of his conceit. So God will not impute the righteousness of Christ where He sees us in love with our own. When we are emptied, then He fills us. When we are weak, then are we strong.

(h)

SELF-RIGHTEOUSNESS (John xviii. 28)

1. The Religion of Self-righteousness

In the case of these Jews, it was keeping the Passover; observing a feast. That was religion! It was all the religion they had; it was their all for acceptance with God; their all for eternity. Their answer to the Judge at the judgment-seat would be, "I kept your passovers." As if there were any religion in eating and drinking! The religion of self-righteousness in our day is like this—works, feelings, fancies, music, rites, festivals, fasts, gestures, postures, garments; that is religion! It is something which gratifies self; which pleases the natural man; which makes a man think well of himself; which gives a man something to do or to feel, in order to earn pardon and merit heaven.

(a)

2. The Scruples of Self-righteousness

These Jews would not enter a Gentile hall. The touch of its floor or walls would be pollution. Religion was to them something outward, something with which the body, not the soul, had to do. After touching these, or breathing such air, they would themselves be defiled. Their scruples all turned on their own self-esteem. Pride, religious pride, was at the root. They were thoroughly blind to all that constituted *real* pollution, and saw only the false. Scruples about entering a Gentile hall, and yet seeking to slay a righteous man. What was the value of such scruples? What was their meaning? These men could swallow the camel while they were straining out a gnat. They could murder the innocent; yet they were too holy to set their foot on a Gentile floor. Such is the way in which self-righteousness acts itself out! Such is the pride of ecclesiastical caste!

(b)

3. The Deeds of Self-righteousness

These were many—fasting, praying, almsgiving. In this case, the great deed was the crucifying of the Lord of Glory. Self-righteousness cried, "Away with Him! Crucify Him! Not this man, but Barabbas." So with modern self-righteousness in every form; especially in the form of Ritualism and formalism. It is ever against Christ that self-righteousness shows its hatred, and aims its strokes. Ritualism is man's expression of dislike to Christ. It is the modern way of crucifying Christ afresh, and putting Him to an open shame.

(c)

4. The Connection between Self-righteousness and Religion

Christ and self-righteousness cannot be on terms of friendship. His grace, finished work, and free salvation, is wholly antagonistic to all forms of self-righteousness. The Jews felt that He was crossing their path, that He was hewing down their temple, that He was utterly making void all their religion; and hence they hated Him; hence they crucified Him. It was self-righteous religion that crucified Christ.

All rites and ceremonies, whether old or new, are man's way of getting rid of Christ. They get rid of real religion by means of that which looks like religion, but which is not religion at all. What can all these things do? Can they save? Can postures save? Can dresses save? Can candles, lighted or unlighted, save? Can music save? Can architecture save? Can cathedrals save? Nay, can they even point the way to Jesus? Do they not lead away from Him? Do they not make void the Cross, and trample on the Blood?

(d)   *Horatius Bonar*

A man who has been shipwrecked with a thousand others happens to get upon the shore, and the others are all down in the surf. He goes up into a fisherman's cabin, and sits down to warm himself. This fisherman says, "Oh, this won't do. Come out and help me to get these others out of the surf. "Oh, no!" says the man; "it's my business now to warm myself." "But," says the fisherman, "these men are dying; are you not going to give them help?" "Oh, no! I've got ashore myself, and I must warm myself!" That is what people are doing in the Church to-day.

(e)   *Talmage*

SENSUALITY

A sensual man looks as if lust had drawn her foul fingers over his features, and wiped out the man.

(f)

SEPARATION FROM CHRIST, NO

"For I am persuaded, that neither death, nor life, nor angels, nor principalities, nor powers, nor things present, nor things to come, nor height, nor depth, nor any other creature, shall be able to separate us from the love of God, which is in Christ Jesus our Lord" (Rom. viii. 38, 39)

1. The "eighth of Paul" commences with the certainty of the Christian's freedom from a state of condemnation, and goes on link by link to prove the certainty—both subjective and objective —of that condition, ripening at last into one of glory in the world to come.

No words could be more emphatic than

(g)

"I am persuaded." The Apostle expresses his immovable confidence that no power in heaven or in earth can effectually separate the Christian from "the love of God, which is in Christ Jesus our Lord." He is aware that between the starting-point and the goal, hindrances both from without and within will imperil his ultimate safety. He has to pass through "the waves of this troublesome world," from which he will encounter opposition. Time, too, will deaden his first feelings: the glow and the warmth of his love for Christ will sensibly diminish—he will slumber and sleep—care will corrode and rust his spirit, and the polish will be gone.

These things, it may be thought, will have a determining influence for evil, and effectually interfere with his perseverance unto the end. The Apostle looks at each possible event in turn and analytically, in order to see where its power lies to effect such a catastrophe. *He looks at human events* first of all, as those of which we all have experience.

(h)

Separation from Christ, No—*continued*

2. " Neither death nor life." Can " death " destroy the union existing between Christ and the believer? *Does it or not* effect separation? Death, with its pining sickness, the pain of dissolution, or as the king of terrors—the grave—corruption— the long sleeping of the body in the dust, and the long waiting of the soul in Hades. Can " the fear of death," as such, break the bond? No, Jesus " took part of the same," and in the very kingdom of death He won a victory over him who had " the power of death, that is the devil," and so has delivered His people from the fear of what death might do to injure them.

(*a*)

3. Can " life "? which perhaps is more danger- ous still, effect what even death cannot do? Life, which has so strong a hold upon young and old, with its many charms as objects for our love, with its almost necessary distance from the Lord— " knowing that whilst we are at home in the body, we are absent from the Lord "? The answer perhaps to this is Rom. xiv. 8, 9, " Whether we live, we live unto the Lord; and whether we die, we die unto the Lord : whether we live therefore, or die, we are the Lord's For to this end Christ both died, and rose, and revived, that He might be Lord both of the dead and living."

(*b*)

The conclusion, then, as to the possible separat- ing power possessed by either death or life, is, that neither death with its terrors nor life with its charms, neither death with its darkness nor life with its brightness, neither death with its stillness nor life with its friendships, can interrupt the union existing betwixt Christ and the believer.

(*c*)

4. He passes on now to events which may be called **superhuman**, as not falling immediately within the sphere of human things.

These come under the category of " *angels*," " *principalities*," *and* " *powers*." Of course, though superhuman, these are created beings. The diffi- culty is to understand whether good or bad angelic agencies are intended. But perhaps the argument here denotes which kind they are ; for it is out of the question that other than evil superhuman powers would be the ministers of evil, such as the argument requires for the work of snapping the bond between the Christian and Christ. Perhaps 2 Tim. iv. 17, 18, supplies an instance of this kind of supernatural agency—where the Apostle speaks of being " delivered out of the mouth of the lion," and declares his unshaken confidence that God will deliver him from " every evil work." The power at work was *superhuman*.

It is, too, unquestionable that the background of heathenism and paganism is and was demonic agency. The work of the ever-blessed Trinity has its counterpart in a diabolical system of " angels, principalities, and powers," for effecting " every evil work," wherein the operations of demonism are divided—" to every demon his own work, his own sphere, and his own order." For the work of opposing the progress of the saints, and of God's kingdom, is undoubtedly not carried on at hap- hazard and unsystematically, without deep cun- ning and plot, counselled upon in hellish conclave. But neither can these dread powers avail: " The gates of hell shall not prevail against " the Church,

so neither can the schemes of these plotters pre- vail to overthrow the man for whom Christ died and intercedes at the right hand of God.

(*d*)

5. He next examines what may be called the " **events of time**." " *Things present and things to come.*" And now the question appears to be, Can vicissitude, " the changes and chances of this mortal life," interrupt and break the bond betwixt the Christian and Christ? As to the—

" *Things present*," in the Apostle's own case, he doubtless had in mind the many obstacles which he encountered from without ; such as his per- secutions, his many perils, journeyings, stonings, shipwreck : all these things were exceedingly grievous to be borne. " Everywhere bonds and imprisonments await me." These were the " things present " to him ; and the force and bitterness of so much opposition might have had the effect, if he had been a man of less faith, of inducing doubts whether he could hold out unto the end.

(*e*)

6. To others, the " **things present** " are the mani- fold troubles of the Christian life. It is not so much the troubles of the past that we dread ; we look back as having come out of them, bitter as such afflictions and distresses may have been ; dark as the road was at that time, yet now, having got away from them, we look back as in a measure certain of having gained something from the trials of the past. They have not been successful in pulling us away from Christ. But a new trouble, a present trouble, one that we had not reckoned upon, whose shadow is now impending, this brings back all our doubts and fears. Like S. Rutherford, we go back to our A, B, C, again ; we have to ask ourselves " Where is our faith? " we are found like Peter calling out, " Save, Lord, I perish," or with the Psalmist, " I sink in deep mire, where no standing is ; " we are again in " deep waters," we lose our grip of Christ, and think that He has lost His hold of us ; " we see not our signs any more." There is apparently " no token for good," and the tension between " things present " and our faith is so great as to make it probable that the bond between Christ and us will snap altogether.

(*f*)

7. It is not the " **past things**," bad as they have been, which dishearten us, not the waters through which we have waded, that we dread ; but it is the flood which now threatens to overwhelm us, the " things present," which find out the weak points in our faith. Like Jacob, we say, " All these things are against me." We see no " bow in the cloud," and cannot rise to Job's faith, who said, " Though He slay me, yet will I trust in him," nor to that of the Apostle, who, when in full view of his perils, said, " None of these things move me ; " and yet the assurance here given is, that these " things present " can do us no harm. The lion and the bear have met us in the past, and this " uncircumcised Philistine shall be as one of them."

(*g*)

8. Neither these nor " **things to come**." In his own case there may yet be in store for him greater forces to encounter, calling for still greater endur- ance, than hitherto he has met with. But be it

(*h*)

Separation from Christ, No—*continued*

what it may, it will not shake his confidence in its futility to effect a separation between him and Christ.

(*a*)

9. In the case of the ordinary **Christian**, he is perhaps too apt to be engrossed almost entirely with the contemplation of his present difficulties and hindrances, to give much, if any, heed to a possible and greater demand upon his faith yet in the future. The present trouble bulks largely in his eye, and how to encounter it and come out of it taxes all his powers. Yet unquestionably there is always something ahead of us, some giant not yet coped with, who, after we have passed on from the present conflict, will hurl us to the ground, as if a man fled from a bear, and a lion met him. But as a Christian, for whom Christ died, and for whom He intercedes, the assurance of coming out of this tribulation, too, is within the scope of the promise " that no one shall pluck them out of **my** Father's hand."

(*b*)

10. But, perhaps, the thoughts of the Apostle, when he used these expressions of "**things present**" and "**things to come**," referred to the present, or apostolic time of the Christian dispensation, and to the latter part of it; that *future* which to him boded of evils to come, greater than any that had yet afflicted and harassed the Church. "There shall be tribulation such as never was, men's hearts failing them for fear, and for looking after those things which are coming on the earth."

(*c*)

11. Those "**things to come**," of which his epistles are so full, such as we find him making early allusion to in the Second Epistle to the Thessalonians (ii.), wherein he states that towards the close of the dispensation there would be "a great falling away," and "that man of sin be revealed"—a great apostasy, and a great foe of the faith. Satan, as an angel of light, would come to seduce and to deceive, if possible, the very elect, "*with all might and signs and lying wonders.*"

(*d*)

12. With such portents the future was big; for "the womb of time contains many events which our philosophy dreams not of ; " and in that time of the end, when events so big and so significant shall tread closely one upon another, when prophecy shall rapidly become history, what will be the fate of the barque of the Church of Christ ? will the proud waves swallow it up ? shall it be lost in the world, and perish with it ? or come forth as it had done before, at the Flood and at the time of the destruction of Jerusalem, and find a place of "refuge until these calamities be overpast " ? Yes, certainly. "Fear not, little flock ; it is the Father's good pleasure to give you the kingdom." He who has interposed His strong arm before will again "avenge His own elect," and this time "save them with an everlasting salvation."
In whatever sense, then, we take these words, "neither things present nor things to come," we arrive at the same conclusion as to their import ; viz., that whatever of evil there is in the present, or whatever of bigger evil the future may bring us, either as fatherly discipline or as emanating from

some deep-laid scheme of hell, yet "the gates of hell shall not prevail against " the family of God.

(*e*)

13. Nor height nor depth

After the possibilities in the sphere of *time*, the Apostle now, it would seem, looks at possible separating causes in the sphere of "*space.*" "*Height and depth.*" Can any causes operate to put the Christian out of the reach of Christ's love, or out of the sight of God's eye ? Let the Psalmist answer for us. (Ps. cxxxix.) "Whither shall I go from Thy Spirit ? or whither shall I flee from Thy presence ? If I ascend up into heaven, Thou art there : if I make my bed in hell, behold, Thou art there. If I take the wings of the morning, and dwell in the uttermost parts of the sea ; even there shall Thy hand lead me, and Thy right hand shall hold me."
But perhaps by the words "*height*" and "*depth*" are meant the seasons of spiritual *exaltation* and *humiliation*. For these, in their very nature, are foretastes of heaven and hell—heights and depths.

(*f*)

14. The Apostle's own experience. He had his seasons of exaltation ; he knew what it was to be on the mountain-top, for the time being raised beyond the sphere and the humiliations of earth, to be, as it were for the moment, not a sinning man, but a glorified saint—"whether in the body, I cannot tell ; or whether out of the body, I cannot tell ; God knoweth ; such an one caught up to the third heaven . . . caught up into paradise." He, too, had abundance of revelations and visions ; these were the Apostle's moments of exaltation, few and far between, moments when the soul breathed the air of heaven, to brace and fit it for the work yet to be done on earth, and where his activities were required. These were the "*heights.*"

(*g*)

15. But, lest he should **be exalted above measure**, lest perhaps these times of rapture should lead him to think more highly of himself than he ought to think, he has to descend from the mountain-top, down into the valleys of earth, teeming with sinful men, and fight with demons ; for on earth there is a terrible strife, which only he knows of best who has for the moment had a heavenly rapture ; and coming down into the sphere of sin, he girds himself for a struggle with the powers behind it : "For we wrestle not against flesh and blood, but against principalities, against powers, against the rulers of the darkness of this world, against spiritual wickedness in high places." There comes, too, the reverse of exaltation in the messenger of Satan to buffet him," "the thorn in the flesh " to keep him humble, lest his seasons of exaltation be too much for him. The Apostle then, too, had his own "heights and depths," but saw no power in either to separate him from the love of Christ.

(*h*)

16. **What is ordinary Christian experience**, but a less brilliant shadow of the same varying experience ? To-day we are with Moses in Pisgah's top, viewing the heavenly land, lifted up out of our ordinary daily routine of life. Everything is viewed through a golden medium. The spirit is up, and the flesh is down ; the head is in heaven,

(*i*)

Separation from Christ, No—*continued*

and the feet on earth. For a time it lasts; it is good for the soul to have such moments, but not for long; we should soon, under such circumstances, forget what manner of persons we are. Soon we descend into a depth as low as the previous exaltation was high; we come down, and mingle in a scene of idolatry, where not the Lord God, but the golden calf, is worshipped, and all His commandments broken; or into a valley of Achor, the scene of some terrible sin and pollution, till the brightness vanishes from our faces, and we tire of earth's sin and misery.

(*a*)

17. To-day we say with the Psalmist, "Thou hast lift me up and cast me down," or cry to the Lord "out of the depths," and to-morrow, perhaps, our song is of "mercy and deliverance." To-day we are with Peter on the Mount of Transfiguration, saying with him, in our ignorance, not knowing what we say, "Lord, it is good for us to be here"—good to be away from earth, from its sins, its enmities, its oppositions, its pollutions—good to be in heaven before our time, before our discipline is over—whilst to-morrow we are down in the depths again, and Jesus has to say to us, "Get thee behind me, Satan."

These are some of the spiritual heights and depths that ordinary Christian people know something of. When up in the heights, they say, "*It is good to be here*," and when down in the depths they say, "*I am cut off.*"

(*b*)

18. On the one hand, there is an uplift so high that the soul takes flight, and seems to be more of heaven than of earth, whilst, on the other hand, the soul experiences a downfall so low as apparently to be clean cut off, out of sight, and out of hope; but, says the Apostle, though these experiences vary, "I am persuaded" that nothing in them "shall be able to separate us from the love of God, which is in Christ Jesus our Lord." Of this result he has no manner of doubt. Step by step, throughout his argument in this chapter, he leads up to this as the inevitable conclusion, and that from two points of view.

(*c*)

19. (i.) *The objective certainty* of this result, proved by the impossibility of any subordinate power in effectually interfering with and thwarting the purposes of the Almighty God.

(ii.) *The subjective certainty* of this result, proved by the nature of the Divine and spiritual life, which "shineth more and more unto the perfect day," and necessarily passes through each stage of development, unhurt by nipping frost and keen winds, until it finally develops into the full bloom of the glorified state. Grant only that the start be fair, and the "no condemnation" of the first verse will eventually ripen into the "no separation" of the last.

(*d*)

20. But between the two extremes, the starting-point and the goal, he hides not from us that hostile and adverse forces will try to roll us off the rock, and effect that separation which would imperil everything.

And these forces lie concealed in the fourfold sphere of (i.) Human events; (ii.) Superhuman agencies; (iii.) The vicissitudes of time; and (iv.) The alternations, the heights and depths, of spiritual experience, and amongst these our own follies, errors of judgment, and self-will, have their place.

Two factors, always supposed, conduce to this end arrived at by the Apostle—faith on our part, and the power of God on the other. Thus, like the kite in the air, held by the string, the faithful are "kept by the power of God through faith unto salvation."

(*e*)

SEPARATION FROM CHRIST, No (Rom. viii. 39)

I do not care to go one step into the theological mysteries of compelling grace and final perseverance. I do not care to ask whether it is possible for man, still being man, to come to such a point that this of which I have spoken to-day, this possibility of flagrant and terrible sin, should utterly and absolutely be left behind and pass away. I think that what I have been saying lately shows us that a man, as the power of the hope of holiness takes stronger and stronger hold upon him, does pass more and more out of the fear of sin. And since his hope of holiness always comes to him as the gift of God, and depends on his dependence on God, we can see that, as man by experience grows sure of God, and morally certain that he never can be separated from Him, he passes to a profound belief that he will not fall into the flagrant sin, which yet, because he is a man, remains possible for him. This moral certainty of his comes from his confidence in God. It is not confidence in himself. Here it seems to me is the true escape from whatever has seemed harsh or hopeless in the truth which I have preached to you to-day. The disciples heard Jesus tell of the coming treason, and each of them thought with horror that he might be the traitor. "Lord, is it I?" and "Is it I?" they cried. They knew that they loved their Lord, but they dared not be sure that they would not desert Him. Sufficient spiritual light had come to them to make them see the mystery of their own hearts. Once, before they had this spiritual life, they would have cast aside such a suspicion as an insult. "Am I not an honourable man?" "Is not such a mean act impossible for me?" Now Christ, in showing them their higher chance, has shown them their lower chance, their danger too, and each wonders whether it can be he who is to do this dreadful thing. Now open a later page of the apostolic history and hear St. Paul writing to his Romans: "Who shall separate us from the love of Christ? Shall tribulation, or distress, or persecution, or famine, or nakedness, or peril, or the sword? Nay, in all these things we are more than conquerors through Him who loved us." See what a change. Here is confidence! Here is a moral certainty! Whoever else may turn traitor, Paul is sure that it will not be he. But it is confidence—not in himself nor in his manliness or honour—only in Christ and in the power of His grace and love. "More than conqueror," but "more than conqueror through Him who loved us." Is there not here the beautiful progress of a moral nature as regards the whole matter of confidence? At the first a pure blank self-reliance, the solid and unbroken self-content of a man who thinks himself able to meet and conquer all temptations. Then an insight into the mysterious capacity of

(*f*)

sinning, which breaks and scatters the confidence in self, and leaves the poor soul full of fears and doubts. Then an entrance into Christ and His love and power, where the soul, given to Him, finds a new confidence in His strength, and is sure with a sureness which has no warrant but its trust in Him.

(a)   *Phillips Brooks*

(*See* "Is it I?")

SERMON, THE

Is addressed to a congregation, not to students. Hence it must be popular, clear, pointed, and practical—avoiding obscurity, confusion, and abstract propositions. On the other hand, it must be simple, direct, lively, yet sufficiently dignified. It must have sprung from prayer and meditation, from communion with the Lord, and with His Word, and from deep sympathy with the spiritual state and the wants of the congregation.

(b)   *Lange*

Sermon, A Cobbler's

"He first findeth his own brother, Simon." Now I am sure 'tis a good plan to go looking after *one soul*. Every soul in the world do belong to our Lord. He made 'em, every one, and He bought 'em, every one, with His precious blood. They's His every way, and the devil is a thief. I've often thought what a poor master the devil's servants have got. Why, when he came up to tempt our mother Eve in paradise, he hadn't got any bit o' a little for to bribe her with, an' all he could do was to tempt her to steal her Master's apples. He haven't got anything at all of his own. . . . Andrew didn't say, "I'll try to do all the good I can," and then do nothing, because he couldn't find any to do; but he says, "There's Simon; I'll go and catch him." That's the way; pick out one soul, and set your heart 'pon it; begin to pray for that one, and go on trying till you've got it; and then try for another. We might do a good deal o' good in the world, if we didn't try to do so much. I've heard folks a singin', an' meanin' it too:

> "Were the whole realm of nature mine,
> That were a present far too small."

An' because the realm o' nature wasn't theirs, they didn't give anything at all!

(c)

SERMONS

To the oases of Tillotson, Sherlock, and Atterbury, we must wade through many a barren page, in which the weary Christian can descry nothing all around him but a dreary expanse of trite sentiments and languid words.

(d)   *Sydney Smith*

A sermon, or *sermo*, when it *is* a spoken word meaning a *thing*, and not a babblement meaning *no-thing*.

(e)   *Carlyle*

Sermons

When the sermon is good, we need not much concern ourselves about the form of the pulpit. . . . If once we begin to regard the preacher, whatever

his faults, as a man sent with a message to us, which it is a matter of life or death whether we hear or refuse, . . . we shall look with changed eyes upon that frippery of gay furniture about the place from which the message of judgment must be delivered, which either breathes upon the dry bones that they may live, or, if ineffectual, remains recorded in condemnation, perhaps against the utterer and listener alike, but assuredly against one of them. We shall not so easily bear with the silk and gold upon the seat of judgment, nor with ornament of oratory in the mouth of the messenger; we shall wish that his words may be simple, even when they are sweetest, and the place from which he speaks like a marble rock in the desert, about which the people have gathered in their thirst.

(f)   *Ruskin*

Saadi, the Persian poet, is quoted as comparing Fortune to a peacock, "with a showy tail, but a frightful pair of legs." I have sometimes heard sermons, which, by their faulty general arrangement, recalled the description.

(g)   *Storrs*

Sermons, Impressions from

A lady, crossing the Atlantic in a steamship, saw a sailor, who had been insolent to the mate, knocked down on the spot, with a heavy blow. The blood gushed from his nostrils; his face puffed up in swollen purple ridges beneath the stroke. It was to her simply frightful! and she left the deck ill. Sea-sickness kept her below for three or four days. Then, coming upon deck, she saw this man standing at the wheel; and on going up to him, she asked, with womanly sympathy: "How is your head to-day?"

"West nor-west, and running free," was the answer that staggered her. He had wholly forgotten what to her had given that startling shock. You laugh at this; but you will find it parallel with the depth of impression made by the sermons on which you most rely.

(h)   *Ibid*

Sermons, as a Source of Strength

"*Strength and gladness are in His place*" (1 Chron. xvi. 27)

I believe in all sorts of sermons—descriptive, touching, sentimental, experimental, or in the very plain, homely, practical enforcement of every-day virtue or of virtue which ought to be cultivated every day. Various indeed are the styles of teaching—poetical, sentimental, flimsy, and sometimes merely cultivated to titillate the hearers; in fact, there is now-a-days a great deal of teaching without backbone, only intended to touch the feelings. The man has a pleasant voice and a pleasant song, and he plays, as it were, on a pleasant instrument, and the people love to have it so. Then there is the teaching of the priest who adopts histrionic devices and teaches by beautiful colours and vestments until he reaches the confessional. Such teaching weakens, attenuates, and reduces the human soul, and drags it down until it hangs only on the lip and the authority of the priest. There is no strength in that. Then, again, there is the preaching of those who argue that it is

(i)

better to be religious than to be orthodox. May we not be both? Theology is as real a thing as religion. It is a something, an entity. Both have place and importance; but while it is possible for theology to exist without religion, it is not possible for religion to exist without theology. You may have the head filled with theology—you may grasp objective truth and understand its orderly arrangement without being religious. But a man who is religious must believe something about God and about man; and therefore the truer the theology the better the religion. We want manly teachers, for weak teachers make a weak people, and it will be a sad day for the Christian Church when the Christian preacher ceases to be a power and gives way to the poet or the priest. Human nature wants something higher, and better, and holier than poetry or priesthood.

(a)   *Thos. Binney*

SERMONS, VERDICTS ON

John xii. = A case of
Hearing and not understanding, because beyond them.

A wild beast hears the voice of man, but it is only noise to it. A domestic animal recognises a familiar *voice*, but cannot trace it back to the *mind*. A man hears the same voice, and understands it, because capable of tracing it back to the mind. Each judges of the sound according to its degree of sympathy with the speaker, or its power of receptivity and perception.

This = a law relating to *speaking* and *hearing;* and it illustrates the narrative of St. John xii.; where notice·

(b)

(i.) Jesus prays, "Father, glorify Thy Name."
(ii.) A voice from heaven replies, "I have both glorified it, and will glorify it again."
(iii.) The people, standing by, heard it, and said that it thundered. The voice was to them only a sound, like reverberations of thunder. They heard and understood not—not having a spiritual ear to hear with. An earthly voice, speaking about worldly things,—food, clothing, business,—would have been intelligible to them; not, however, a voice about glorifying God, and speaking "heavenly things"=mere sound only. No sympathy between speaker and hearer. The seed falls on unprepared soil.

(c)

(iv.) Others, more in advance of them, likewise heard the voice from heaven; less unsympathizing, and less carnal-minded these; yet *superstitious* rather than religious. Not free-thinkers, like Sadducees; they believe in angels, and an unseen spirit-world; and believe this voice came from that region, also that Jesus is a medium. This may not be much, yet it is something, and raises these people above those who only heard a *noise*.

(d)

(v.) Yet another class of listeners heard the voice. Jesus heard and *understood;* it was the voice of His Father, an immediate and audible answer to His prayer. Of the disciples, John, at least, heard and understood the words, for he wrote them down. These=the spiritual, sympathetic hearers, who have ears to hear, and without which the voice would have been but

noise, or at most something of superstitious interest and meaning. To these, "heavenly things" are no longer "mysteries," but revelations from their Father in heaven.

(e)

The same law ever prevails:

A sermon is preached, clearly and distinctly setting forth the way of salvation, by a man of experience, who has endeavoured rightly to divide the word of truth. Apparently no room is given for cavil. Yet the remarks which follow are deteriorating and damaging: "Nothing in it;" "Unsound;" "Simple as A, B, C;" "Without thought;" "Smacks of hell-fire and brimstone;" whilst the preacher is termed "Boanerges—son of thunder—of Exeter Hall," evidently it was nothing but *thunder* to these.

Others listened reverently, because they were in a church, and the sermon was preached by a clergyman. Behaviour, posture, etc., of these were unexceptionable.

A few, amongst whom, an invalid lately escaped from a sick room, came to worship; came hungering for the children's bread, and found it: "The very word I wanted," "A word of comfort," "My doubts have vanished, my soul is escaped from the hands of the fowler," "O God, I thank Thee!" "What," asks one, "has made you so bright and cheerful?" "It was the *voice* from heaven, which spake to me in last Sunday's sermon, that has made me glad," is the reply.

We account for these various opinions by the law of sympathy between *speaker* and *hearer*. And where there is an *ear to hear*, golden ore will be found from the weakest sermon ever preached. The voice that spake may have been in weakness, uttered by a broken vessel, but nevertheless a voice from heaven beseeching men in Christ's stead to be reconciled to God.

(f)

SERMONS, WRITTEN

I think it no extravagance to say, that a very inferior sermon, delivered without book, answers the purpose for which all sermons are delivered more perfectly than one of great merit, if it be written or read.

(g)   *Cardinal Newman*

Depend upon it, if the Church of England is to make way, and be a thoroughly national Church, the clergy must give up the practice of preaching from written sermons.

(h)   *Dr. Döllinger*

SERPENT, THE

The serpent, a beast like to an embodied thunderbolt that has had its origin in the deepest night, parti-coloured, painted like fire, as black and dark as night, its eyes like glowing sparks, its tongue black, yet cloven like a flame, its jaws a chasm of the unknown, its teeth fountains of venom, the sound of its mouth a hiss. Add to this the strange and wonderful motion, ever striving like a flash to quiver, and like an arrow to flee, were it not hindered by its organization. It appears among the beasts like a condemned

(i)

and fallen angel; in the heathen world of false gods, it hath found and still finds ever awe and adoration; its subtlety has become a bye-word, its name a naming of Satan, whilst the popular feeling, even now, as in all times past, connects a curse and exorcism with its appearance.

(a) *A. F. Krummacher*

SERPENT, (DEVIL)

The devil appeared not as a lion: strength could not constrain an upright soul. Not as a dragon: fear could not compel a dauntless spirit. But he appeared as a serpent, to insinuate and creep into the bosom of man's soft affections. How often is this story re-acted by Adam's sons.

(b) *F. Quarles*

SERPENT IN THE WILDERNESS, THE (John iii. 14, 15)

The Remedy

1. ITS APPOINTMENT.—It was by God. "The Lord said unto Moses, Make thee a fiery serpent, and set it upon a pole." Examine the narrative. God was their ruler. Moses was His minister. They were under Divine government. Government must be upholden, law must be honoured. They had rebelled; cure must come through obedience. They had murmured; they must be brought to trust God. The remedy for man's sin. This was provided by God. The first intimation of a deliverer was spontaneously given by Him (Gen. iii. 15). In the councils of eternity the Son had said "Lo, I come to do Thy will, O God" (Ps. xl. 7, 8; Heb. x. 7, 9). Christ was the Lamb of God's providing (Gen. xxii. 8; John i. 29). The Son was the gift of the Father's love (John iii. 16, 17; Rom. v. 8).

(c)

2. LIFE THROUGH DEATH.—Read Numbers xxi. 8, 9. "The Lord said, Make thee a fiery serpent; and Moses made a serpent of brass, and put it upon a pole." How strange a direction! How likely to excite scorn! By a living serpent stung, by a dead serpent healed. The brass serpent was dead indeed. It was only a serpent in form. How aptly it sets forth some of the features of our redemption! The Son of God took upon Him the likeness of sinful flesh. He was a real man, but He was not a sinful man. Yet He was made sin. He, as it were, embodied sin, that in Him sin might receive its doom. By man came death, by man came also life. The serpent on the pole had the form, but not the poison; the God-man on the cross had the form, but not the sin. Yet He died, but it was in the sinner's stead. It is the universal law—life comes through death.

(d)

3. BY A LOOK.—The brass serpent could not heal. It had no life-giving power. Lifting it up wrought no cure. The cure followed personal effort. There must be personal application. There must be an act of obedience, which would clearly show a change of mind or repentance. Yet the cure was not in the look; it was at the same instant as the look, but the cure was Divine. Apply to Christ. His death does not of itself save. Many are in this error. They think themselves safe because Christ died. It is a vain thought. It is as a rotten plank to a drowning man. Note

also, the death of Christ does not dispose God to save. God's love provided the remedy. "He has not appointed us to wrath, but to obtain salvation" (1 Thess. v. 9). How obtain it? What did the death of Christ do? It opened the way for God to save. It satisfied Divine justice. It magnified the law. It made it safe for God to forgive sin. How obtain it? By a look. God offers, as it were, a bargain. He offers life for a look. Do not mistake. The look does not purchase the life. Pardon is free, but it must be sought, and must be accepted. Man must look. "Look unto Me, and be ye saved" (Isa. xlv. 22). "Behold the Lamb of God" (John i. 36). Compare the terms of John iii. 14, 15, with the directions and statements of Numbers xxi. The lifting up of the serpent represented the lifting up of the Son of God. Then the looking upon the serpent for life represented the believing which saves from perishing, and brings eternal life. A look by the Israelite showed faith. Faith has degrees. A man of weak sight might not discern the brass serpent. How then? If he turned his head in that direction he would be cured. How simple the remedy! How worthy of God!

(e) *J. Gill*

SERVANTS, TREATMENT OF

"Masters," (Eph. vi. 9; Col. iv. 1.)

A party of friends setting out together upon a journey, soon find it to be the best for all sides, that while they are upon the road, one of the company should wait upon the rest; another ride forward to seek out lodging and entertainment: a third carry the portmanteau; a fourth take charge of the horses; a fifth bear the purse, conduct and direct the route; not forgetting, however, that, as they were equal and independent when they set out, so they are all to return to a level again at their journey's end. The same regard and respect; the same forbearance, lenity, and reserve, in using their service; the same mildness in delivering commands; the same study to make their journey comfortable and pleasant, which he whose lot it was to direct the rest would in common decency think himself bound to observe towards them, ought we to show to those who, in the casting of the parts of human society, happen to be placed within our power, or to depend upon us.

(f) *Paley*

SEVEN AGES OF MAN

All the world's a stage,
And all the men and women merely players:
They have their exits and their entrances;
And one man in his time plays many parts,
His acts being seven ages. At first, the infant,
Mewling and puking in the nurse's arms;
And then the whining school-boy, with his satchel,
And shining morning face, creeping like snail
Unwillingly to school. And then the lover;
Sighing like furnace, with a woeful ballad
Made to his mistress' eyebrow. Then a soldier;
Full of strange oaths and bearded like the pard,
Jealous in honour, sudden and quick in quarrel;
Seeking the bubble reputation
Even in the cannon's mouth. And then the justice;

(g)

In fair round belly, with good capon lined,
With eyes severe, and beard of formal cut,
Full of wise saws and modern instances,
And so he plays his part. The sixth age shifts
Into the lean and slippered pantaloon,
With spectacles on nose, and pouch on side ;
His youthful hose, well saved, a world too wide
For his shrunk shank ; and his big manly voice,
Turning again toward childish treble, pipes
And whistles in his sound. Last scene of all,
That ends this strange eventful history,
Is second childishness, and mere oblivion ;
Sans teeth, sans eyes, sans taste, sans everything.

(a) *Shakspeare*

SEVEN CHURCHES OF ASIA, How Christ Addresses Himself to the

1. **Ephesus** : He that *holdeth* seven stars in His right hand, and *walketh* in the midst of the seven golden candlesticks.
Indicates—This Church's tendency towards apostasy. "Without Me ye can do nothing." "Lo, I am with you always."

2. **Smyrna** : First and the last, was dead and is alive.
Indicates—Encouragement for a martyr Church ; as I was dead, and am now alive, so it shall be with you : "He who hath begun," etc.

3. **Pergamos** : He who hath the sharp sword with two edges.
Indicates — False doctrines prevalent, which must be cut out by the "word of God"—"The sword of the Spirit."

4. **Thyatira** : Son of God ; eyes=a flame of fire ; feet=fine brass.
Indicates—"Eyes"=searcher of hearts ; "feet"=power to tread under opposition.

5. **Sardis** : Who hath seven spirits of God and seven stars.
Indicates—A Church in need of inspiration and quickening, because nearly dead.

6. **Philadelphia** : Holy, true, key of David, openeth and shutteth.
Indicates—Holiness and truth sapped ; *openings* from Jesus only, "Cast thy net on the right side of the ship, and thou shalt find."

7. **Laodicea** : Amen, the faithful and true witness ; the beginning of the Creation of God.
Indicates—"Yea" (emphatically), not "nay," nor "yea and nay" (as if weak and wavering), says what He means. Unfaithful Church is also unfruitful, therefore not a witnessing Church—in a bad way. Also the beginning of the *new* creation of God.

(b)

SEVEN SLEEPERS, LEGEND OF

When the Emperor Decius persecuted the Christians, seven noble youths of Ephesus concealed themselves in a spacious cavern on the side of an adjacent mountain ; where they were doomed to perish by the tyrant, who gave orders that the entrance should be firmly secured with a pile of stones. They immediately fell into a deep slumber, which was miraculously prolonged, without injuring the powers of life, during a period of 187 years. At the end of that time the slaves of Adolius, to whom the inheritance of the moun-

tain had descended, removed the stones to supply materials for some rustic edifice. The light of the sun darted into the cavern, and the seven sleepers were permitted to awake. After a slumber, as they thought, of a few hours, they were pressed by the calls of hunger ; and resolved that Jamblichus, one of their number, should secretly return to the city to purchase bread for the use of his companions. The youth, if we may still employ that appellation, could no longer recognise the once familiar aspect of his native country ; and his surprise was increased by the appearance of a large cross, triumphantly erected over the principal gate of Ephesus. His singular dress and obsolete language confounded the baker, to whom he offered an ancient medal of Decius as the current coin of the empire ; and Jamblichus, on the suspicion of a secret treasure, was dragged before the judge. Their mutual inquiries produced the amazing discovery, that two centuries were almost elapsed since Jamblichus and his friends had escaped from the rage of a Pagan tyrant. The bishop of Ephesus, the clergy, the magistrates, the people, and, it is said, the Emperor Theodosius himself, hastened to visit the cavern of the Seven Sleepers ; who bestowed their benediction, related their story, and at the same instant peaceably expired.

(c) *Gibbon, from the Koran*

" *Shadow of things to come* " (Col. ii. 17)

So long as one walks in the shadow, holds to it, he is not in the αἰὼν μέλλων, which began with the appearing of Christ, not to begin with His *parousia.*

(d) *Meyer*

SHAKSPEARE

Was there ever such stuff as great part of Shakpeare ? Only one must not say so. But what think you ? What ? Is there not sad stuff ? What ? What ?

(e) *George III*

SHECKINAH (John i. 14)

Human nature has become adorable as the true Sheckinah, the everlasting palace of the Supreme Majesty, wherein the fulness of the Godhead dwelleth bodily ; the most holy shrine of the Divinity, the orb of inaccessible light, as this, and more than all this, if more could be expressed, or, if we could explain that text, " *The Word was made flesh and dwelt among us.*"

(f) *Barrow*

SHEEP OF CHRIST, THE (John x.)

The germs of the New Testament biblical doctrine of election, predestination, and vocation (Rom. viii. 29).

(g) *Lange*

SHEEP, MY

As from all eternity love and union existed between the Father and the Son, and such as never can come to an end or know any disruption, so from all eternity God hath given unto

(h)

the Son the sheep : He knoweth them when they are in the world and of the world, when they speak evil of Him, and persecute Him. He calleth them by name, and they hear Him, they know Him. They obey Him. They are His. He has appropriated them, they appropriate Him.

(a)

SHEEP OF MY PASTURE (Ezek. xxxiv. 16)

Incomparably more tender care and compassion will thy Heavenly Father visit thee in all thy spiritual maladies and sicknesses of soul. The whole blessed Trinity is stirred, as it were, extraordinarily, and takes to heart thy troubles at such a time. Even as a shepherd takes more pains and exercises more pity and tenderness about his sheep when they are out of tune. See Isa. xl. 11 ; Ezek. xxxiv. 16 ; upon which places hear the paraphrase of a blessed divine : " The Lord will not be unfaithful to thee if thou be upright with Him, though thou be weak in thy carriage to Him ; for ' He keeps His covenant for ever ; ' and therefore in Isa. xl. the Lord expresseth it thus : ' You shall know Me as sheep know their shepherd, and I will make a covenant with you,' and thus and thus I will deal with you. And how is that ? Why, the covenant is not thus only— as long as you keep within the bounds and keep within the fold, as long as you go along the paths of righteousness and walk in them ;—but this is the covenant that I will make : I will drive you according to that you are able to bear. If any be great with young, I will drive them softly ; if they be lame that they are not able to go, saith He, ' I will take them up in Mine arms and carry them in My bosom.' If you compare with Ezek. xxxiv. you shall find there He puts down all the slips we are subject to (speaking of the time of the Gospel, when Christ should be the Shepherd), He shows the covenant that He will make with those that are His. Saith He ; ' if anything be lost,' if a sheep lose itself, this is my covenant, ' I will find it ; ' if it be driven away by any violence of temptation, ' I will bring it back again : ' If there be a breach made into their hearts by any occasion through sin and lust, ' I will heal them and bind them up.' This the Lord will do ; this is the covenant that He makes."

(b)　　　　　　　　　　　　　　　*Bolton*

SHEPHERD, THE GOOD (John x. 27)

1. " *My* sheep." Whose ?

The Good Shepherd's :
" *Good*," because
　(i.) He gives them pasture : " I am the Bread of Life ; "
　(ii.) He does not desert His flock when the wolf (of trouble) comes : " He seeth the wolf coming ";
　(iii.) He gives His life for the sheep.

2. Marks of knowing them
　(i.) They *hear* His voice ;
　(ii.) He *knows* them (2 Tim. ii. 19) :
　(1.) *Knows* when they do not know themselves (" When saw we Thee ? " etc.) ;
　(2.) When they do not *know* Him (" Samuel did not yet *know* the Lord ") ;
　(3.) He knows them not simply by name, *but all about them* : knows as a parent knows his children.

3. *They follow Him :*
　(i.) They do not *lead ;*
　(ii.) They are passive—He goes before—(" The footsteps of the flock ") ;
　(iii.) This following leads to Glory (" Where I am, there shall also My servant be ").
　(iv.) They never perish (ver. 28).

(c)

SHEPHERD

The Lord is my Shepherd (Ps. xxiii. 1)

This similitude, so frequent in the later Scriptures, was introduced by David, and, for obvious reasons, grows fuller and fuller in its special teaching, until it reaches its climax in the New Testament teaching concerning " that great Shepherd of the sheep," who " giveth His life for the sheep."

(d)

Consider,

1. The Clearness and Definiteness of the Statement

What can be more clear or more easily understood than, " The Lord is my Shepherd " ? This is no metaphor. Think how vague, indefinite, and indistinct are the common notions of God. There is a mist, a veil, a drapery of clouds. He takes no shape, no personality : the curtain is undrawn, He is unrevealed. God is " an unknown God." And even some Christian people come short in conceiving of God as LOVE. That God is our Father ; and His thoughts concerning us are altogether different from what we think them to be, is not so clear to them as it should be. And, most likely, David himself knew what such doubts meant. The fact was not always so clear to him as when he wrote this Psalm—that " The Lord was his SHEPHERD :" " The Almighty God " (yes) ; " The God of Israel " (yes) ; The God of Abraham, Isaac, and Jacob (yes) ; But " the Lord is MY Shepherd " was not so clear.

(e)

Consider,

2. How David came by his Knowledge

We must look at the Old Testament saints as men like ourselves. Great spiritual truths were arrived at through mental doubts and struggles then as now ; and David was no exception. " The Lord is my Shepherd," is the rising of this sun on his soul ; the dispersion of doubt, uncertainty, and mist.

(f)

David had a godly training--" The Son of thine handmaid." The tie between him and his mother was now snapping. His religion must become a personal matter, and have no human prop. He went from his home, and became a shepherd in the wilderness, and there underwent a " conversion "—uncertainties became certainties.

David was a thoughtful boy. In the dark solitary mountain and plain he was often alone for days and nights. This solitary life promoted thoughts and doubts, and ultimately fixed his beliefs.

He had to find the key of " Doubting Castle."
　(i.) **What is God ?** No answer came ; no books

(g)

but Nature; and all Nature could say was, "Touching the Almighty, we cannot find Him out." "God is unknowable."

(ii.) **What am I?** What is man? Reply · "You are a part of Nature—an atom—you are what you eat and drink—atoms in chemical affinity, by-and-by to be dissolved and become parts of other organisms.

"But, oh," exclaims David, "what a wonderful atom am I!" "I am fearfully and wonderfully made;" "I am a little less than Divine;" "I am an atom that thinks and have an almost infinite ambition to know what is beyond me—the infinite."

Still no answer from Nature. And David went on with his humble work—did it well—did it as if it were his sole work in life He shepherded his sheep: he led them out to pasture, to cooling streams; he sought them when they strayed into jungles and got lost: he saved them from the lion and the bear; and at night he took them back to a place of safety—a refuge; and as he did this from day to day, the light broke in. He saw an answer to his questions: The light broke in, and was taught him by his occupation.

"What am I?" "Why, I am the shepherd of these sheep; and what I am to these sheep, that God is to me. *The Lord is my Shepherd*." Thus the light broke in, and David's doubts were over.

(a)

3. The Comfort of this Knowledge to the Individual Christian

This result follows:
"The Lord is my Shepherd, I shall not want,
He maketh me to lie down in green pastures;
He leadeth me beside the still waters
He restoreth my soul. . . .
Yea, though I walk through the valley of the shadow of death, I will fear no evil; for Thou art with me. . . .
Surely goodness and mercy shall follow me all the days of my life, and I will dwell in the house of the Lord for ever."

All this reminds us of the love, the promises, and the providential care of the GOOD SHEPHERD, who feeds His flock, carries them in His bosom; searches them out until He finds them. Who, when they fall into danger, and the roaring lion tears a stray lamb, He rescues them from the fangs of the destroyer, and saves them from all their foes. "My sheep hear My voice, and I know them, and they shall never perish, neither shall any (foe) pluck them out of My Father's hand. My Father, which gave them Me, is greater than all, and no (being) is able to pluck them out of My Father's hand."

(b) *Cf. Maurice*

SHEPHERD AND SHEEP (John x. 27)

1. *The personal connection:*
= a shepherd and His sheep.
2. *The Salvation of the flock consists in,*
(i.) *I know them* (The Lord knoweth them that are His); THEY *follow.*
(ii.) *I give unto them eternal life*, and THEY perish not at all;
3. *They cannot perish, because* God is greater than all.

(c)

SIDES, LOOKING AT BOTH (Concerning George Buchanan)

That singulare wark of David's Psalmes in Latin meetre and poesie, besyd mony other, can witness the rare graices of God gevin to that man.

(d) *John Knox*

A serpent—daring calumniator—leviathan of slander—the second of all human forgers and the first of all human slanderers.

(e) *Whitaker*

SIDES, LOOKING AT BOTH

It is the old story over again, of the gold and silver shield. There was a shield hanging in a road, and two knights came riding up to it, one on one side, and the other on the other. The one said the shield was silver, and the other said it was gold; and then, like foolish men, they began to fight about it. The fact was, that the shield was apparently both gold and silver, for on the one side it was silver, and on the other gold. If the men had only looked on *both sides*, they would have found that they were equally in the right.

(f) *T. Binney*

SIGNS

[Luke xxi. 7
The answer to the question (8–36).
1. (8–19) = *apparent signs.*
False Christs: Political: Physical: Official Persecution: Domestic Persecution: Be Patient.
2. (20–24) (i.) *The true signs.*
(ii.) *Destruction of Jerusalem.*
(iii.) *Times of Gentiles.*
3. (25–27) = *The Parousia*, which brings this period to an end (the full period of the times of the Gentiles).
4. (28–36) *The Practical Application*
(i.) *of Hope,*
"Your redemption draweth nigh"
(ii.) *of Watchfulness,*
"Take heed."
"Watch and pray always."
(g) *Cf. Godet.*

SIGNS (Luke xxi. 28)

The Lord uses two remarkable words to indicate the effects which ought to be produced by these premonitory signs.

(i.) Lift up yourselves (ἀνακύψαι, stoop no more —lift up your *bodies*). (ii.) Lift up your *heads;* do not merely stand with erect body, but turn your head and eyes upward. The Church's posture has hitherto been that of one *bowed down* (Ps. xxxviii. 6; xliv. 25) under the heavy burdens of an evil day and an evil world. Both body and head are bent towards the earth in grief. But so soon as she hears the signal of her Lord's approach, she rises up from her stooping posture, she looks upward to descry the coming deliverance and glory.

It is of great moment that we read the signs aright; not only as given by our Lord, but afterwards by His apostles. The order is of no consequence. They are numerous, and scattered over the New Testament.

(h)

1. Anti-Christianity

Not Popery merely, but all the forms in which opposition to Christ shows itself; whether false doctrine, or active hostility to Christ. A false Christianity = error regarding the Person and work of Christ; subversion of the Cross, and blood, and righteousness of Christ; all the ways in which Christ is opposed, directly or indirectly; in which men are uttering the cry, " We will not have this man to reign over us " ; " Let us break their bands and cast away their cords " (Luke xix. 14; Ps. ii. 3; Acts iv. 27). There are many Antichrists.

(*a*)

2. Disbelief of the Advent

The Advent of Christ itself shall be one of the things which scepticism shall assail. There are two classes which shall be found rejecting it—the professing Christian, who says, " My Lord delayeth His coming " ; the scoffing world, that says, " Where is the promise of His coming ? "

(*b*)

3. Error

The fruit of the tree of knowledge is still eaten by man, and still infusing its poison. Love of knowledge is the professed starting-point. But in the pursuit of this, God is not acknowledged as the teacher, nor the Bible as the infallible textbook. Speculation abounds; inspired trammels are flung off; pride of intellect operates; man worships his own mind; every day brings forth some novel opinion; revelation is thrust down from its high position; every form of error gets vent; till God gives men over to a reprobate mind, and sends them strong delusion, that they should believe a lie. " They will not endure sound doctrine," but are " carried about with every wind of doctrine."

(*c*)

4. Energy of Evil

Evil men and seducers are to wax worse and worse. Sin will unfold itself to the utmost. The human heart will speak out. It will not be dormant or inactive evil; it will be energetic to the utmost in seeking to counteract the good—nay, to destroy it utterly. In some ages evil seems to sleep; in the last days it will awake to full life and activity. It will seize every instrument—the press, the pulpit, the platform. It will enlist every science and art—music, sculpture, painting, poetry, philosophy—making them all subservient to its development. Satan, both as the Prince of darkness and as the Angel of light, will come down, having great wrath, to put forth his wiles, his powers to the utmost. The multiplication of crimes, contempt of laws, blasphemies, these are the specimens of the energy of evil.

(*d*)

5. Formalism

The Apostle, after enumerating the sins of the last days, adds this : " Having a form of godliness, but denying the power thereof." There is to be the appearance of religion to suit the religious part of man's nature; but this is to be coupled with all sin, and error, and ungodliness, nay infidelity. Whited sepulchres; wells without water; trees without fruit; lamps without oil; a religion without the Holy Ghost.

(*e*)

6. Latitudinarianism

Indifference to revealed truth, nay, to all truth; making light of error; holding that all religions are so far right and acceptable, and that there are a thousand ways to heaven, if there be a heaven or a hell at all. Laxity of opinion and laxity of morals will prevail. Immorality is to overflow in every form, and will not be condemned. A loose faith, a loose practice, an easy law, an easy Gospel; all the evils described in 2 Tim. iii., unfolding themselves, and not disapproved of.

(*f*)

7. Missions

Towards the close of the last days we are to expect special efforts in behalf of Jew and Gentile. The Gospel is to be preached to all nations. The Jew is to be sought out. The Bible is to go over the earth. The messengers of Christ are to make their errand known. At no time since the Apostles has this been the case so much as now.

(*g*)

8. Political Changes

European changes; the reconstruction of the ten kingdoms; the breaking up of old landmarks; the confusion of all political principle; the placing of government in the hands of the lowest; the speaking evil of dignities.

(*h*)

9. Pride and Self-will

The pride of power; the pride of knowledge and intellect; self-reliance; belief in self-regeneration, without the power of God or the Holy Ghost. Unwillingness to brook restraints: " Our lips are our own; who is Lord over us ? " This wilfulness or lawlessness is to come to a head in Antichrist; but it is to be manifested everywhere, in the Church and in the world. Self-will! That is to be the characteristic of the last days.

(*i*)

10. Restlessness

Many shall run to and fro. The whole world shall be in motion; fermentation everywhere; rushing hither and thither; unable to be still. As the man possessed by a devil could not rest, so our world in the last days, possessed by the devil, shall exhibit the very restlessness of hell—of him who is ever going to and fro in the earth, walking up and down in it.

(*j*)

11. Satanic Influences

We see this not only in the errors and blasphemies that are abroad—infidelity and atheism. But we see it in the pretended communications with the invisible world, the spirit-rapping and spirit-consulting, which is spreading everywhere; so that millions are under these subtle and potent influences.

(*k*)

12. Wars

The world's great crisis is the Armageddon battle. Up till that time there are to be wars and rumours of wars.

(*l*)

13. Worldliness

This present evil world is to be the object of man's idolatry. In this way materialism will show itself. Religious materialism, ecclesiastical materialism, political materialism. This material world in all its aspects will be worshipped. Luxury, lust of the flesh, lust of the eye, etc., all mingle together to make up the intense worldliness of the last days.

(a) *Horatius Bonar*

SILENCE OF GOD, THE

You may live a life of ease and self-indulgence, you may not come into trouble like other folk, and you may go through life with comparative freedom from affliction; but the day of God's retribution will come. As soon as you have filled up the measure of your iniquity, as soon as you have committed your last sin, as soon as you have uttered your last word of ridicule of Christ's people, your cup will run over, God's patience will be exhausted, and the command will go forth, " Cut him down"; and you will find yourself in that world where the burning fire and the gnawing worm will to all eternity tell you what "a fearful thing it is to fall into the hands of the living God."

(b) *C. Clayton*

SILENT

The frightfullest births of time are never the loud-speaking ones, for these soon die; *they are the silent ones*, which can live from century to century.

(c) *Carlyle*

SIMEON STYLITES

" *Not by works of righteousness which we have done* " (Tit. iii. 5)

A sincere penitent, earnestly desiring, by penance and self-inflicted tortures, to earn saint-dom. This man made it his study to find out a more painful penance than any suffering endured by the martyrs.

(i.) When in a convent, he bound a coarse rope (used for drawing water) so tightly round his waist as to cause an internal ulcer, which nearly killed him.

(ii.) He spent three winters on a mountain chained to a rock night and day, where he was blackened by lightning, and fed only with chance gifts of food, whilst people called him " Saint Simeon Stylites."

(iii.) Next, he spent thirty years of his life on the top of a pillar, first six feet, then twelve, twenty, and at last forty feet high, with only just room enough to sit, clothed with a goat-skin cloak, and wearing an iron collar, holding a cross in his arms with difficulty, suffering from hunger, thirst, and exposure, cold, heat, fevers, coughs, aches, stitches, cramps; in all weathers—rain, wind, frost, hail, damp, sleet, and snow, ever crying " Mercy, Lord Jesus, mercy."

(*See* " TENNYSON.")

(d)

SIN

'Twas his to teach,
Day after day, from pulpit and from desk,
That the most childish sin which man can do
Is yet a sin which Jesus never did
When Jesus was a child, and yet a sin
For which, in lowly pain, He lived and died:
That for the bravest sin that e'er was praised
The King Eternal wore a crown of thorns.
In him was Jesus crucified again;
For every sin which he could not prevent
Stuck in him like a nail: his heart bled for it,
As it had been a foul sin of his own.
Heavy his cross, and stoutly did he bear it,
Even to the foot of holy Calvary;
And if at last he sunk beneath the weight,
There were not wanting souls whom he had taught
The way to Paradise, that, in white robes,
Thronged to the gate to hail their Shepherd hope.

(e) *Hartley Coleridge, on Dr. Arnold*

SIN, THE WORD

The Sanskrit for serpent was *ahi*. The root of which is *ah*, or *anh*=to press together, to choke, to throttle. Hence *ahi=throttler*, as the distinguishing mark of the serpent. This word was chosen with great truth as the proper name of *sin*. Evil, though presented under various aspects to the mind, having also many names, had none so expressive as those derived from our root *anh, to throttle*. *Anhas* in Sanskrit=sin, but only because it meant originally throttling—consciousness of sin=the grasp of the assassin on the throat of his victim. The statue of Laoköon and his sons, with the serpent coiled around them from head to foot, realizes what the ancients felt and saw when they called sin *anhas*, or the *throttler*. *Anhas*=the Greek, *agos*, *sin*. The same root in Gothic has produced *agis, fear;* from the same source we have *awe*, in awful, *i.e.*, fearful, and *ug*, in *ugly*. The English *anguish* is from the French *angoisse*, the Italian *angoscia*, a corruption of the Latin *angustiæ*, a strait.

(f) *From Max Müller*

SIN OF BELIEVERS

All the saints, because of sin, are like old rusty clocks, that must be taken down, and the wheels scoured and mended, and set up again, in a better case than before; sin hath rusted both soul and body; our dear Lord by death taketh us down to scour the wheels of both, and to purge us perfectly from the root and remainder of sin; and we shall be set up in better case than before.

(g) *Samuel Rutherford*

SIN, BIBLE RECORDS OF

Why does the Bible contain such records, such revolting things?

N.B. David (Ps. xxxviii.) would not have his sin forgotten, for he writes a psalm with this significant title: " A Psalm of David, *to bring to remembrance*."

The Bible, furthermore, records God's condemnation of such deeds as are recorded: " The things

(h)

that David had done displeased the Lord," are the emphatic last words of 2 Sam. xi.

Several clear and sound reasons for such records :

1. Because the Bible is a *true* book

It is the earliest history of human nature. It hides no part of man's character. He is a sinner; and every history in the world proclaims it a fact. Read history of Greece, Rome, France, or England, and from beginning to end it is a record of violence, hatred, cruelty, ambition, craft, malice, murder, war, bloodshed, conquest, robbery, tyranny, slavery — SIN all the way through. There is now and then a deed of patriotism, or honour, or generosity, or bravery ; but the *great* record is sin. The Bible would not be a true book if it hid man's vileness.

(a)

2. Because the Bible is a *guide*-book

But it would mislead if it did not proclaim unmistakably that God is displeased with sin, when good men fall into it, as well as when bad men habitually commit it.

Bad men would scoff at the justice of God. It might lead a fallen believer to despair, when he found therein no record of God's people falling into sin, and afterwards being recovered. He would argue, " I have been a hypocrite all along— I never have been a child of God—there is *no hope* for me ! " The record, on the other hand, encourages us to come to God for pardon when we feel we have sinned.

(b)

3. Because *God will not have sin hidden*

Man's tendency is to hide sin : it was so with the first sin. And this tendency is nowhere stronger than in the Christian Church.

(c) *Thos. Cooper*

SIN, BITTERNESS OF

There is more bitterness following upon sin's ending than ever there was sweetness flowing from sin's acting. You that see nothing but *well* in its commission, will suffer nothing but *woe* in its conclusion. You that sin for your profits will never profit by your sins.

(d) *Dyer*

SIN, BLINDING POWER OF

It is among the most potent of the energies of sin, that it leads astray by blinding, and blinds by leading astray ; that the soul of man, like the strong champion of Israel, must have its " eyes put out," when it would be " bound with fetters of brass," and condemned " to grind in the prison-house " (Judges xvi. 21).

(e) *Archer Butler*

SIN, BORN IN

When we endeavour to think upon God, how many things do we feel which divert our attention, and tempt us to think upon other subjects ! All this is evil ; but, at the same time, it is born with us.

(f) *Blaise Pascal*

SIN, CRUCIFIED

Sin may *rebel*, but it shall never *reign* in any saint.

(g) *Thos. Brooks*

SIN, CURSE OF

It is the Trojan horse ; it hath sword and famine and pestilence in the belly of it. Sin is a coal, that not only blacks, but burns. Sin creates all our troubles ; it puts gravel into our bread, wormwood in our cup. Sin rots the name, consumes the estate, buries relations. Sin shoots the flying roll of God's curses into a family and kingdom (Zech. v. 4). It is reported of Phocas, having built a wall of mighty strength about his city, there was a voice heard, " Sin is in the city, and that will throw down the wall."

(h) *T. Watson*

SIN AT THE BIRTH OF DEATH

I fled and cried out, " Death ! "
Hell trembled at the hideous name, and sighed
From all his caves, and back resounded, " DEATH."

(i) *Milton*

SIN, DECEITFULNESS OF

Remember, many go far on, and reform many things, and can find tears, as Esau did ; and suffer hunger for truth, as Judas did ; and wish and desire the end of the righteous, as Balaam did ; and profess fair and fight for the Lord, as Saul did ; and desire the saints to pray for them, as Pharaoh and Simon Magus did ; and prophesy and speak of Christ, as Caiaphas did ; and walk softly and mourn for fear of judgments, as Ahab did ; and put away gross sins and idolatry, as Jehu did ; and hear the word of God gladly, and reform their life in many things according to the word, as Herod did ; and say, " Master," to Christ, " I will follow Thee whither Thou goest," as the man who offered to be Christ's servant ; and may taste of the virtues of the life to come, and be partakers of the wonderful gifts of the Holy Spirit, and taste of the good word of God, as the apostates who sin against the Holy Ghost ; and yet all these are but like gold in clink and colour, and watered brass and base metal. These are written, that we should try ourselves, and not rest till we be a step nearer Christ than sunburnt and withering professors can come.

(j) *Samuel Rutherford*

SIN, DEFINITION OF

A mournful catalogue of words, based on a great variety of images, is employed in Scripture to describe the state of sinfulness which man inherits from his birth. Sometimes it is set forth as *the missing of a mark or aim ;* sometimes as *the transgressing of a line*—the word occurs seven times in the New Testament, and is twice applied to Adam's fall (Rom. v. 14 ; 1 Tim. ii. 14) ; sometimes as *disobedience to a voice, i.e.*, to hear carelessly, to take no heed of—the word occurs three times (Rom. v. 19 ; 2 Cor. x. 6 ; Heb. ii. 2) ; sometimes as *ignorance of what we ought to have done* (Heb. ix. 7) ; sometimes as *a defeat or discomfiture* =to be worsted, because, as Gerhard says, " A

(k)

sinner yields to, is worsted by, the temptations of the flesh and of Satan"; sometimes as *a debt* (Matt. vi. 12); sometimes as *disobedience to law*, (the word occurs fourteen times in the New Testament, and is generally translated by *iniquity*). The last figure is employed in the most general definition of sin given in the New Testament, viz., "*sin is the trangression of the law*" (1 John iii. 4).

(*a*) *Trench and Maclear*

Sin, Essence of

We should strive to be troubled at nothing, and to take every event for the best. I hold this to be a duty, and the neglect of it a sin. For in fact the reason why sins are sins, is only because they are contrary to the will of God. If then the very essence of sin consists in having a will which we know to be contrary to that of God, it seems clear to me, that when He discovers His will to us by events, it must be a sin, if we do not conform to it.

(*b*) *Blaise Pascal*

Sin will Find you out

Men's sins often find them out, though no visible sign or token may betray this fact to the world. All may outwardly stand fair; there may be no breach in the worldly prosperity; nay, this may be ampler, more strongly established than ever; while yet there may be that within which forbids to rejoice, which takes all the joy and gladness out of life—the memory of that old sin which was as nothing when committed, but which now darkens all, the deadly arrow poisoning the springs of life, which will not drop from the side, which no force, no art of man's device can withdraw. To such Dr. Trench's advice is, to turn the tables on our sins, to find them out, and to take them all to God, to be condemned, pardoned, and subdued, "condemned by Thy righteous judgments, O Father; pardoned by the precious blood of Thy dear Son; and subdued by the mighty operation of the Holy Ghost." This is the good old-fashioned preaching of Apostles and preachers of the very oldest times.

(*c*) *"Ecclesiastical Gazette"*

Sin, its Growing Power

In the Rabbinical books of the Jews they have a curious tradition about the growth of leprosy, that it began with the walls of a man's house; then, if he did not repent, entered his garments, till at last the disease covered his whole body. And thus it is with the growth of sin. It begins with neglect of duty: it may be of prayer, or the warning voice of conscience is unheeded. Habits of sin are formed, till at last the soul that lets God alone is let alone by God.

(*d*) *J. G. Pilkington*

Sin, an Opiate

Sin is like the little serpent aspis, which stings men, whereby they fall into a pleasant sleep, and in that sleep die.

(*e*) *"Sunday Teachers' Treasury"*

Sin, Origin of

Our practical question is, not how sin has come in, but how it is to go out; not how it originated, but how it is to be subdued.

(*f*)

Sin, Overcoming of

Saith Seneca: "There are many men that have subdued principalities, kingdoms, cities, towns, and countries, and brought them under their own mastery; but there are few that have guided themselves, but still there is a tiger within them, that disgraceth and obscureth their outward conquest by reason of foul seethings and corruption in their own flesh; therefore, for a man to get the victory, and to overcome himself, is to get the victory, and to overcome all the world; for man is a *microcosm*, a little world," as St. Austin saith.

(*g*) *Day*

There is nothing so hard to die as sin. An atom may kill a giant, a word may break the peace of a nation, a spark burn up a city; but it requires earnest and protracted struggles to destroy sin in the soul.

(*h*) *Thomas*

Sin, Pleasure in

There is pleasure in sin—the Bible allows it—but it is as bitter as the disappointment of the broken heart.

(*i*) *S. Bridge*

Sin and Sins (1 John i. 7–9)

One mistake perpetually made by one of our unhappy parties in religion,—and with a pernicious tendency to Antinomianism,—is to confound *sin* with *sins*. To tell a modest girl, the watchful nurse of an aged parent, that she is full of *sins* against God, is monstrous, and as shocking to reason as it is unwarrantable in Scripture. But to tell her that she and all men and women are of a sinful nature, and that, without Christ's redeeming love and God's grace she cannot be emancipated from its dominion, is true and proper.

(*j*) *S. T. Coleridge*

Sin and Suffering (Acts ii. 40; Rev. iii. 4)

Take more pains to keep yourselves from sin than from suffering.

(*k*) *Thos. Brooks*

SINS

Your sins are registered, and you shall hear of them all again.

(*l*) *Baxter*

Sins of Believers

From that sad day of David's fall, he never knew comfort again. The most hideous abominations were committed in his own household, and by his own children. The sword seemed never to depart from his house. A shadow was ever upon it. The rebellion of Absalom, with all its painful accompaniments, was distinctly traceable to that terrible transgression. In fact, David was being ever pursued and hunted down by the consequences of his sin in the matter of Uriah the Hittite; the sin was ever starting up in bodily shape and crossing his path.

(*m*)

Or, was Jacob's deceit, practised against his aged father and his unsuspecting brother, ever condoned? Most assuredly not. He felt the consequences throughout the whole of his future life. In his enforced flight from home, at a time when he was past seventy years of age—in his separation from the mother he loved so dearly—in his hard usage at the hand of his covetous relative, Laban—in the deceits continually practised on him who had so deceived others—in his hour of dire terror and anguish by the ford Jabbok—in the unruliness and falsehood of his sons, and their attempts upon the life of their younger brother,—in all this he felt that God was visiting him for his sin; he was never let alone; and at the close, he summed up the character of his life, when he stood before the ruler of Egypt: "*Few and evil have the days of the years of my life been.*"

(a)　　　　　　　　　*Gordon Calthrop*

SINAI AND SION (Heb. xii. 18–24)

Contrasts:
Ye are not come unto the mount that might be touched, and that burned with fire, nor unto blackness, and darkness, and tempest. And to the sound of the trumpet, and the voice of words, etc., . . . and so terrible was the sight that Moses (the Mediator) said, I exceedingly fear and quake.

(b)

But ye are come unto Mount Sion, and unto the city of the living God, the heavenly Jerusalem, and to an innumerable company of angels. To the general assembly and Church of the first-born which are written in heaven, and to God the Judge of all, and to the spirits of just men made perfect, and to Jesus.

(c)

Not come to Mount Sinai, with its fire, and blackness, and darkness, and tempest, and terrible words; but to Mount Sion, the city of God, to angels, and the Church of the first-born, and to the spirits of just men made perfect = difference between the Old Covenant and the New.

(d)　　　　　　　　　*Cf. Bengel*

SINCERITY

This cross hath let me see that heaven is not at the next door, and that it is a castle not soon taken; I see also it is neither pain nor art to play the hypocrite. We have all learned to sell ourselves for double price, and to make the people who call ten twenty, and twenty an hundred, esteem us half gods, or men fallen out of the clouds; but oh, sincerity, sincerity, if I knew what sincerity meaneth. Sir, lay the foundation thus, and you shall not soon shrink nor be shaken. Make tight work at the bottom, and your ships shall ride against all storms, if withal your anchor be fastened upon good ground, I mean within the vail; and verily I think this is all, to gain Christ: all other things are shadows, dreams, fancies, and nothing.

(e)　　　　　　　　　*Samuel Rutherford*

SINGING

George Whitfield, one day on Kennington Common, gave out a hymn in a *peculiar metre*, which no one could raise a tune to, till a bluff sailor started Arne's grand bravura of "Rule Britannia."
"Mr. Whitfield, Mr. Whitfield!" cried a strait-laced brother, pulling at Mr. Whitfield's coat, "*that* is one of the devil's tunes!" "I don't believe it!" cried Whitfield, "the devil has no right to call a noble tune like that his own. Sing on, brother!"

(f)　　　　　　　　　*Thos. Cooper*

SINGING

In Christian villages little else is to be heard but Psalms; for which way soever you turn yourself, either you have the ploughman at his plough singing *Hallelujahs*, the weary brewer refreshing himself with a *Psalm*, or the vine-dresser chanting forth somewhat of *David's*.

(g)　　　　　　　　　*Jerome*

SINGING

"*O, come let us sing,*" etc. (Ps. xcv. 1)

I wish it could be said of us, like Spenser's Una, that we "made a sunshine in a shady place." It should be so. What a contrast do we sometimes see in really good men.
"Thomas Proudlove, class-leader, and William Martin, were equally zealous Methodists; each eager to be at the six o'clock prayer-meeting on Sunday morning; sure to be seen going through snow in winter, lantern in hand, to attend it. Proudlove, the leader, was always sombre and solemn, often got into the "ruts," down into doubt and gloom, and well-nigh into misery therefrom. Martin, on the other hand, was a happy, lowly Christian.
One night the leader sat "sighing and surning," and turning over the leaves of his hymn-book, unable to select a hymn sufficiently mournful for his mood, till at last he gave out two lines in the old Lincolnshire dialect:

> "Aah! whither shoold I gooah,
> Burthened, and sick, and faant?"

No one sung. The leader gave out the melancholy lines again, and asked Martin to start a tune.
"Marry, good faith!" replied the merry-hearted Christian, "I am neither burthened, sick, nor faint! I'll start no tune, not I!"
"Well, then, brother Martin," said the leader, "give out a verse yourself."

> "Oh for a thousand tongues, to sing
> My great Redeemer's praise!"

said Martin, and struck up Arnold's old "Gabriel," with all the power of his lungs.

(h)　　　　　　　　　*Thos. Cooper*

SINNED

"*I have sinned*"

1. *Pharaoh* (Exod. ix. 27); an excuse for mercy; becomes hardened.

2. *Balaam* (Num. xxii. 34); though stopped by an angel, "his heart set on the rewards of divination," he goes on to death.

3. *Achan* (Josh. vii. 20); not spontaneous: says it after he is found out.

(i)

4. *Saul* (1 Sam. xv. 24–30; xxvi. 21); to Samuel, after vain excuses, forced from him.

5. *Judas* (Matt. xxvii. 4); despair.

Compare with these the repentance of,

6. *David* (2 Sam. xii. 13; xxiv. 10–17; 1 Chron. xxi. 8, 17); genuine (and " yea what fear ").

7. *Prodigal* (Luke xv. 18); spontaneous.
(a)

" *I have sinned* " (Luke xv. 18)

> I dreamed of bliss in pleasure's bowers,
> While pillowing roses stayed my head:
> But serpents hissed among the flowers;
> I woke, and thorns were all my bed.

(b)   *Montgomery*

SINNER, A GREAT

Luther says to Satan, " In telling me that I am a great sinner, thou givest me a sword to cut thine own throat; for Christ died for sinners."
(c)   *John Bunyan*

SINNER AND SAVIOUR

Luther, complaining of the burden of his sins, was answered by Staupitz.

" Wouldst thou be a sinner on canvas, and have a Saviour on canvas ? "

Implying that both *sinner* and *Saviour* are real.
(d)

SINNETH NOT (1 John iii. 4–10)

Remember the case of Chrysostom, Bishop of Constantinople, who was hateful to the Emperor; the courtiers said, " Burn him, confiscate his property, put him in irons, and have him killed." But others replied, " You will not gain anything by all this; for in exile he would find a home with his God; you deprive the poor, not him, of property; he kisses his chains, death opens heaven to him. There is only one way to render him unhappy; force him to sin; *he fears nothing in the world but sin.*"
(e)   *Lange*

SISTERHOODS

You consider St. John's House without a Sisterhood a lifeless shell. I consider it a living plant. The flowers and fruit may fail through blight or tempest, but the tree live and reproduce. You consider it obsolete. I consider it as supplying an actual present want—namely, the opportunity for soberminded, religious ladies of birth and education to acquire and practise the art of nursing without being subject to the conditions imposed by other associations, such as vows of celibacy, lifelong devotion, implicit obedience, surrender of property, the practice of fasting, confession, and penance, the disruption of family ties and duties, etc.

We and a large,—and I believe the sounder portion of English people,—disapprove these conditions, and are satisfied with our baptismal vows and to do our work as opportunity and other duties allow.

You consider this playing at nursing. Call it what you please; we have practised it with the happiest results long enough to prove our efficiency. You think our system is crumbling; we see no sign of it.

In particular, we think our system especially adapted for hospital work, where we have to deal with men who look with suspicion on associations of the type you seem to prefer.
(f)   *Bartle J. L. Frere*

SIXFOLD CORD, A, FOR THE EASE OF AFFLICTED CONSCIENCES

1. And first take notice, that Jesus Christ, God blessed for ever, keeps an open house for all such hungry and thirsty souls. " Let him that is athirst come. And whosoever will, let him take the water of life freely " (Rev. xxii. 17). " Whosoever will; " in whose heart soever the Holy Ghost hath wrought an effectual, earnest, hearty will; that supernatural sincere desire described before, which prizeth the " well of life " before the whole world, and is ever accompanied with an unfeigned resolution to sell all for the pearl of great price; I say, such a one may come and welcome, and that without bidding, and drink his fill of the river of all spiritual pleasures. If there were no more but this, this is more than enough to bring thee to Jesus Christ. If a proclamation should be made, that such or such a great man kept open house for all comers, there need no more to bring in all the poor hungry people in the country, without any further waiting or inviting. But here, above all degrees of comparison, the hunger is more importunate and important; the feast-maker more faithful and sure of his word; the fare more delicious and ravishing. And why dost thou refuse? Thou hast a warrant, infinitely above all exception. The Lord of Life keeps open house for all that *will* come; and thou knowest in thine own conscience, and canst not deny but that He hath already honoured thee with that singular favour as to plant in thy soul a *will* this way, and that most earnestly. For what wouldst thou not part with to have assurance of thy part in Jesus Christ? What wouldst thou not give, if it might be bought, to hear Him speak peace unto thy soul, and say sweetly unto it, " I am thy salvation " ? And therefore if thou come not in presently, and take the comfort of this precious place and promise, " setting to thy seal that God is true," consider by the foregoing view of thy case, whether thy terrors and temptations be not justly upon thee until thou dost.
(g)

2. If this will not serve (which God forbid), then in a second place thou art invited solemnly by the feast-maker, as it were, Himself, with His own mouth, which is an infinite mercy, honour, and comfort: " Come unto Me, all ye that labour and are heavy laden, and I will give you rest " (Matt. xi. 28). Here is no exception of sins, times, or persons. And if thou shouldst reply, Yea, but, alas! I am the unworthiest man in the world to draw near unto so holy a God; to press into so pure a presence; to expect upon the sudden such glorious, spiritual, and heavenly advancement; most impure, abominable, and vile wretch that I am! readier far and fitter to sink into the bottom of hell by the insupportable weight of my manifold heinous sins: —I say then the text tells thee plainly, that thou
(h)

Sixfold Cord—_continued_

mightily mistakest; for therefore only art thou fit, because thou feelest so sensibly thy unfitness, unworthiness, vileness, wretchedness. The sorer and heavier thy burden is, the rather shouldst thou come. In a word, it appears by thine own words expressing such a penitent apprehension of thy spiritual poverty, that thou art the only man, and such as thou alone, which Christ here especially aims at, invites, and accepts.

(a)

3. "He knowing our frame," our sluggish, dull, and heavy disposition, our spiritual laziness, natural neglect of our own salvation, and loathness to believe; adds in another place to ordinary invitation, a stirring, compassionate, and quickening compellation, or rather exclamation. "Ho!" saith he (Isaiah lv. 1), "every one that thirsteth, come ye to the waters," etc. And lest any think he shall come to his cost, or shall bring anything in his hand, he calls upon "him that hath no money;" and thus doubles His cry: "Come ye, buy and eat; yea, come, buy wine and milk, without money, and without price." O most blessed and sweetest lines! So full of love and longing to draw us to the well of life, that besides that holy pang of compassion and excitation, "Ho!" he cries thrice, "Come, come, come!" Yea, but, mayest thou say, "Alas! I am so far from bringing anything in my hand, that I bring a world of wickedness upon my heart; and that above ordinary, both in notoriousness and number; and therefore I am afraid the heinousness of my sins will hinder my acceptation, though the invitation be most sweet and precious." Be it so; yet the Spirit of God in the same chapter doth purposely meet with and remove that very scruple: "Let the wicked," saith He, "forsake his way and the unrighteous man his thoughts" (and this is thy case; thou art unfeignedly set against all sin, both inward and outward), "and let him return unto the Lord, and He will have mercy upon him, and to our God, for He will abundantly pardon" (ver. 7). He will not only have mercy upon thee, but He will also _abundantly_ pardon. He will _multiply_ His pardons according to thy provocations, and that with superabundance (Rom. v. 20).

(b)

4. If all this will not yet do, He descends, out of the infinite riches of His grace, to a miracle of further mercy. For the mighty Lord of heaven and earth sends ambassadors unto us, dust and ashes, worms and no men, to beseech us to be reconciled unto Him, "Now then we are ambassadors for Christ, as though God did beseech you by us; we pray you, in Christ's stead, be ye reconciled unto God" (2 Cor. v. 20). What man can possibly ponder seriously upon this place, but must be transported with extraordinary admiration; nay, adoration of the bottomless depth and infinite height of God's incomprehensible, everlasting, and free love! We, most abhorred, vile wretches, are the offenders, traitors, rebels, and enemies, and ought to seek and sue unto Him first upon the knees of our souls, trembling in the dust, and, if it were possible, with tears of blood. And yet He begins unto us, entreating us by His own Son, and His servants, the ministers, to come in, accept His favour and grace, enter into the wise and good way, which is precious, profitable, honourable, and pleasant; that He may hereafter

set upon our heads everlasting crowns of glory and bliss. An earthly prince would disdain and hold it in foul scorn to send unto his inferior for reconcilement, especially who had behaved himself basely and unworthily towards him, and justly provoked his royal indignation. It is thus indeed with worms of the earth, "in whom there is no help," and whose breath is in their nostrils. But it is otherwise with the King of kings, "who sitteth upon the circle of the earth, and the inhabitants thereof are as grasshoppers, and the nations as the drop of a bucket; who bringeth the princes to nothing, and maketh the judges of the earth as vanity." He is content to put up at our hands this indignity and affront, if I may so speak. He is glad to sue unto us first, and send His ambassadors, day after day, beseeching us to be reconciled unto Him. Oh, incomprehensible depth of unspeakable mercy and encouragement to come in and trust in His mercy, in case of spiritual misery, able to trample under foot triumphantly all oppositions of the most raging hell or distrustful heart!

(c)

5. Nay, He commands us; "and this is His commandment, that we should believe on the name of His Son Jesus Christ" (1 John iii. 23). This command alone of the All-powerful God should infinitely outweigh and prevail against all other countermands of heaven and earth, flesh and blood, Satan, nature, reason, sense, the whole creation, all the world. It should swallow up all scruples, doubts, fears, despairs. Coming to Jesus Christ with broken hearts according to this commandment, it will bear us out against all oppositions, accusations, weaknesses of faith, in the evil times in the hour of temptation, upon our beds of death, at the last and greatest day. It will be a plea at such times utterly above all exception, against all allegations, terrors, and temptations to the contrary, to say, I was humbled under the burden of sin and sense of my spiritual misery. God in mercy offered me His Son Jesus Christ freely in the mystery of the Gospel by the ministry of the Word. I thereupon thirsted infinitely for His person and precious blood, that I might thereby obtain pardon and power against my sins. He called upon me and commanded me to drink my fill of the water of life freely. I accepted His gracious offer, and according to His commandment cast myself upon the Lord Christ against all the contradictions of carnal reason and sophistry of Satan; and since that time He hath given me power to serve Him in sincerity of heart. This is my ground and warrant, even the commandment of my blessed God, thus to drink when I was thirsty; against which the gates of hell can never possibly prevail. In thy case then, who thirstest extremely, and upon free offer yet refusest to drink, consider how unworthily thou dishonourest God and wrongest thine own soul; by suffering the devil's cavils and the groundless exceptions of thine own distrustful heart to prevail with thee against the direct command of Almighty God, which thou oughtest to obey, against all reason, sense, fears, doubts, despairs, and hellish suggestions. Abraham, the father of the faithful, did really and willingly submit to God's commandment, even to kill his own only dear son with his own hand, naturally, matter of as great grief as could possibly pierce the heart of a mortal man. And wilt thou, being broken-hearted, stand off from believing, and refuse when He commands

(d)

Sixfold Cord—*continued*

thee to take His own only dear Son ; especially since thou takest with Him the excellency and variety of all blessings both of heaven and earth ; a discharge from every moment of the everlasting pains of hell ; deeds sealed with His own blood, of thy right to the glorious inheritance of the saints in light ? In a word, even all things, the most glorious Deity itself blessed for ever, to be enjoyed through Him, with unspeakable and endless pleasure through all eternity ! Prodigious madness ! cruelty to thine own soul ; or something at which heaven and earth, man and angel, and all creatures may stand amazed, that thou shouldst so wickedly and wilfully " forsake thine own mercy," and " neglect so great salvation."

(*a*)

6. Lastly, lest He should let pass any means, or be any ways wanting on His part to drive us to Christ, and settle our souls upon Him with sure and everlasting confidence, He also threateneth : " And to whom sware He, that they should not enter into His rest ; but to them that believed not ? " (Heb. iii. 18).   Wherein He expresseth extremest anger, unquenchable and implacable indignation. He swears in His wrath that no unbeliever shall enter into His rest. In the threats of the moral law there is no such oath, but a secret reservation of mercy upon the satisfaction of divine justice some other way. But herein the Lord is peremptory, and a third way shall never be found or afforded the sons of men. Neglect of such a gracious offer of so great salvation, must needs provoke and incense so great a God extraordinarily : for with prodigious ingratitude and folly it slings as it were God's free grace in His face again, and sins against His mercy. Supposing a mighty prince, passing by all the royal and noble blood in Christendom, many brave and honourable ladies, should send to a poor maid, bred in a base cottage, born both of beggarly and wicked parents, offer her marriage, and to make her a princess ; and she then should foolishly refuse and reject so infinitely undeserved and unexpected advancement. As she might thereupon be justly branded for a notorious maniac ; so would not so great a prince, think you, be mightily enraged at such a dunghill indignity and peevish affront ? The Prince of peace, upon whose thigh is written " King of kings, and Lord of lords," passing by more excellent and noble creatures, sends unto thee, whose " father is corruption and the worm thy mother and thy sister," and who in respect of thy spiritual state liest " polluted in thine own blood," and offers to " betroth thee unto Himself in righteousness and in judgment, and in loving-kindness, and in tender mercies " (Hos. ii. 19) ; to crown thee with all the riches both of His kingdom of grace and glory. Now, if thou shouldest stand off (which God forbid !) as thereupon out of perfection of madness thou forsakest thine own salvation, so thou most justly enforcest that blessed Lord to swear in His wrath that thou shalt never be saved.

Thus thou hast heard how, first, He keeps open house to all such hungry and thirsty souls (Rev. xxii. 17) ; secondly, He invites (Matt. xi. 28) ; thirdly, invites with an awakening and rousing compellation (Isa. lv. 1) ; fourthly, entreats (2 Cor. v. 26) ; fifthly, commands (1 John iii. 23) ; sixthly, and threatens (Heb. iii. 18). How cruel then is that man to his own wounded conscience, who in

his extreme spiritual thirst will not be drawn by this sixfold merciful cord to drink his fill of the fountain of the water of life ; to cast himself with confidence and comfort into the arms of the Lord Jesus, which is more than infinitely able to tie the most trembling heart, and that which hangs off most by reason of pretended doubts, scruples, and distrusts, to that blessed Saviour of his with all full assurance and perfect peace ! How is it possible but that all, or some of these should bring in every broken heart to believe ; and cause every one that is weary of his sins to rely upon the Lord of life for everlasting welfare ?

(*b*)   *Bolton*

SLANDER

Calumny will sear
Virtue itself : these shrugs, these hums, and ha's.
(*c*)   *Shakspeare*

I will be hanged if some eternal villain,
Some busy and insinuating rogue,
Some cogging, cozening slave, to get some office,
Have not devised this slander.
(*d*)   *Ibid*

The man that dares traduce, because he can
With safety to himself, is not a man :
An individual is a sacred mark,
Not to be pierced in play or in the dark.
(*e*)   *Cowper*

The flying rumours gathered as they rolled,
Scarce any tale was sooner heard than told ;
And all who told it added something new,
And all who heard it made enlargements too,
In every ear it spread, on every tongue it grew.
(*f*)   *Prior*

There would not be so many open mouths, if there were not so many open ears.
(*g*)   *Bp. Hall*

Speak no slander—no, nor listen to it.
(*h*)   *Tennyson*

Leave off slandering me with thine *ears*.
(*i*)   *Bp. Wordsworth*

A third interprets motion, looks, and eyes,
At every word a reputation dies.
(*j*)   *Pope*

SLAVE

A wealthy and kind-hearted Englishman once bought a negro in the slave market, for twenty pieces of gold. He set him free, and moreover gave him a sum of money to buy a piece of land with for a home. " Am I really free ? May I go where I will ? " cried the negro in the joy of his heart. " Well, let me be your slave, Massa : you have redeemed me, and I owe all to you." This touched the Englishman's heart, he took him into his service, and never had a more faithful servant.

(*k*)

SLEEP

Sleep is a function of our present animal frame, and let not the transgressor anticipate this boon in the world of retribution before him. It may be, and he has reason to fear, that in that state repose will not lay down his eyelids, that conscience will not slumber there, that night and day the same reproaching voice is to cry within, that unrepented sin will fasten with unrelaxing grasp on the ever-waking soul.

(a)   *Channing*

SLEEP (John xi. 11)

Christ has changed death into sleep; but as the death of His people is sleep, so is the spiritual sleep of unbelievers death.

(b)   *Lange*

Tired Nature's sweet restorer, balmy sleep!
He, like the world, his ready visit pays
Where fortune smiles; the wretched he forsakes;
.   .   .   .   .   flies from woe,
And lights on lids unsullied with a tear.

(c)   *Young*

How wonderful is Death, Death and his brother, Sleep!

(d)   *Shelley*

Sleep, that knits up the ravelled sleave of care,
The death of each day's life, sore labour's bath,
Balm of hurt minds, great Nature's second course,
Chief nourisher in life's feast.

(e)   *Shakspeare*

Well, sleep thy fill, and take thy soft reposes;
But know, withal, sweet tastes have sour closes;
And he repents in thorns that sleeps in beds of roses.

(f)   *Quarles*

SLEEP OF SIN

Men sleep, and nothing but thunder, nothing but flashes from the everlasting fire of hell, will thoroughly wake them.

(g)   *Channing*

SMALL THINGS

It is mathematical fact, that the casting of this pebble from my hand alters the centre of gravity of the universe.

(h)   *Southey*

A small thing comforts us; because a small thing afflicts us.

(i)   *Blaise Pascal*

The oil which is dropped on the machinery is a small thing; but without it the mighty steam-engine would never work. The water which trickles on the saw of the marble-cutter is a small thing, but without it the great block would never be cut through. We should never despise "little things." Load after load of earth, tipped over the end of a railway embankment, gradually brings the sides of the valley together.

(j)   *Bp. Ryle*

Despise not small things. Trace a river from its source. A driblet under a rock; then a rill; then a rivulet; then a stream; then a mighty river, bearing to the ocean ships laden with precious freights. How little we know what may proceed from a little thing! Give that remarkable chain: Sibbes's book that converted Baxter; Baxter's that converted Doddridge; Doddridge's that converted Wilberforce; Wilberforce's that converted Legh Richmond; Richmond's that converted Dr. Chalmers—and each book hundreds of thousands besides.

(k)   *J. Gill*

SMALL THINGS, DESPISE NOT

" There is nothing " (1 Kings xviii. 43)

Seven times the prophet's youthful watcher went up and looked, and seven times he reported "There is nothing." The sky was clear; the sea was calm. At last out of the far horizon there arose a little cloud, the first for days and months. It was no larger than an outstretched hand; but it grew, and quickly the whole sky was overcast, and the forests of Carmel shook with the mighty wind, which precedes a coming tempest. The cry of the boy had hardly been uttered when the storm broke upon the plain, the rain descended, and the nation was delivered from its sufferings.

This is a parable of nature. It expresses the truth, that often out of seeming nothingness there arrives the very blessing most desired.

(l)

1. "**There is nothing.**" The disciples thought so at Olivet as they gazed into heaven after their departed Master. Nothing to tell them whither He had gone. They would see Him no more again. But was there indeed nothing to come? Yes; there was everything. That little cloud which had shrouded Him from their sight was full of blessings. In a few days there would be a rushing mighty wind that would sweep through their hearts and through the world. Christ was gone, but Christendom and Christianity were coming. The earthly life of Jesus was over, but the eternal life of His Spirit was beginning. Greater works than this would henceforth be wrought in the world, because He was gone to the Father.

(m)

2. "**There is nothing.**" We think as we look into the wide world, and see no trace of its Maker and Ruler. There is space, and nothing beyond it. There is the perplexity and misery of mankind, and nothing to relieve it. We say: " O that Thou wouldst rend the heavens and come down! " and no voice answers. But the absence of any especial presence is itself an expressive indication of the spiritual nature of things Divine. The things which are seen are temporal: it is the things that are not seen which are eternal. Even the dry light of critical analysis has thrown a flood of knowledge on the Bible. Even the philosophers of the last century quickened and freshened the whole atmosphere of religion with a nobler influence. Science, if it cannot increase our faith, has, at any rate, purified and enlarged it. In the drought of the latter half of this nineteenth century, there is the promise of a great rain. In the

(n)

Small Things—*continued*

silence of death, in the darkness of the unseen world, we have the assurance, there is One to whom the darkness and the light are both alike.

(*a*)

3. " There is nothing." We say to ourselves, in the blank desolation of sorrow. The voice that cheered us is silent, the hand that upheld us is cold. So has thought many a one, orphaned, bereaved, left desolate, alone in the world. But out of that memory comes a cloud of blessings. There descends upon our dry and parched souls a dew as of the night of sorrow ; on that barren and dry land where no water is, there comes an abundance of rain, and again we are refreshed, and feel that the very solitude in which we are left calls forth new vital energies.

(*b*)

4. " There is nothing." The little tube with which Galileo looked from the heights of Fiesole on the starry heavens—how slight, how feeble it seemed ; yet enough to reveal an unknown universe, to disclose the secrets unknown from the beginning of the world. The electric spark, so subtle, so imperceptible, what has it not produced, of which Benjamin Franklin never dreamed ? What are the forces which the inexhaustible energy of this generation has not drawn from it ?—the annihilation of time and space, the girdle around the world, which to Shakspeare seemed the wildest of dreams, but in our day has become the solid chain on which hangs the grandest enterprises of commerce, and the surest bond of national concord.

(*c*)

5. " There is nothing." We sometimes think as we look on the barren fields of theological controversy. Nothing, can be gleaned from the thorny speculations which have laboured to build up the hard system of Calvin ; yet in that hard system those who most dissent from it may find grains of pure gold ; from the rigid statements of Jonathan Edwards, modern philosophers have laboured to extract a religious sanction for the belief in the fixity of the general laws of the universe ; in the most unlovely of Christian theologians, there is something to invigorate and to stimulate, when we reflect that they were striving to fortify the eternal principles of truth and righteousness against the temptations which beset us all.

(*d*)

6. " There is nothing." We say as we look upon many a human spirit, and think how little there is of good within, how hard the ground to be broken, how slight the response. So may have thought Nathan when he came to David. What was there of goodness or virtue in that unhappy soul ? Treachery, murder, passion, might seem to have closed every avenue of hope. Yet there were two approaches to that soul. One, the spark of generous indignation against wrong and injustice in others. David's anger was kindled, and he said : " As the Lord liveth, the rich man that hath taken the little ewe lamb shall surely die, because he hath no pity." It was on this that the prophet worked, and turned it against himself. From that small cloud came abundance of rain. The fifty-first Psalm, the thirty-second Psalm, burst from the soul of the penitent king, and he became once more the sweet Psalmist of Israel. The other

approach was that found so often in the hardest of hearts. The death of his little child—" I shall go to him, but he will not return to me." Deep down in the human soul is the fountain of natural affection, the fountain of natural tears. Strike that, and we shall not strike in vain. There seems to be nothing ; but in that soft place in a father's heart, there is, there may be everything. So it is that lost souls are converted, regenerated, saved.

(*e*)

7. " There is nothing." So we think of the little we can do. How poor, how slight, how insignificant, the organization of great societies, to lighten the vast load of human misery, or relieve suffering humanity. Yet out of that nothingness often rises that little cloud, not bigger than a man's hand, yet the very hand that grasps us, that saves us from perishing. Think not lightly of any effort that san save any human being from misery and want. A word of compassion goes a long way. The pressure of the silent hand is never forgotten. Be not weary in well doing.

(*f*)

8. " There is nothing," it might have seemed when the first settlers established the English race on the cheerless shores, the barren rocks, the trackless forests of this continent. Yet there was everything ; the hope of a new world ; the elements of a mighty nation. It was but two days ago that I read in the close of a volume written by the founder of the venerable village of Concord, a sentence which ought to bring at once the noblest encouragement and the sternest rebuke to every citizen of this Commonwealth. " There is no people," says Peter Bulkley in his Gospel Covenant, in the year 1646, to his little flock of exiles —" There is no people but will strive to excel in something. What can we excel in, if not in holiness ? If we look to numbers, we are the fewest ; if to strength, we are the weakest ; if to wealth and riches, we are poorest of all the people of God throughout the whole world. We cannot excel, nor so much as equal, other people in these things ; and, if we come short in grace and holiness, we are also the most despicable people under heaven. Strive we therefore to excel, and suffer not this crown to be taken away from us." The progress is indeed marvellous ; this poorest and fewest and weakest of the nations, this little cloud not bigger than a man's hand, has taken its place amongst the most vigorous and wealthy and powerful of the kindreds of mankind. But the moral remains the same. That vast development has shown of what growth the human race is capable ; and yet how entirely that growth depends on nobleness of character and force of will brought to bear upon its natural resources. A little one has become a thousand—not because of its numbers, not because of its wealth, but because of the high destiny which God has assigned to it, and which it must accomplish or perish. Had the forefathers of this great nation not struggled to reclaim the wilderness, and convert the savage, and build up the Church of God by river and by forest, this nation would never have been born, this empire would never have arisen.

This truth is the likeness of all human existence. Much grows out of little. It is a warning not to despise the day of small things. " The great events of history," says an acute French writer, " like the mysterious personages in old romances,

(*g*)

Small Things—*continued*

come through a door in the wall which no one had entered." We cannot tell what immense issues may depend on our public and our private duties. Each of us is bound to make the small circle in which he lives better and happier; each of us is bound to see that out of that small circle the widest good may flow; each of us may have fixed to his mind the thought that out of a single household may flow influences which shall stimulate the whole commonwealth and the whole civilized world. The long life of a venerable pastor or a good layman, spent chiefly in preaching the Gospel and doing good, though it seems to be nothing at the time, yet, in the fragrance which it leaves behind, is a memory as lasting as the Pyramids.

(*a*)   *Dean Stanley*

SOCINIANISM

The pet texts of a Socinian are quite enough for his confutation. . . . If Christ had been a mere man, it would have been ridiculous in *Him* to call Himself "the Son of Man"; but being God and man, it then became, in His own assumption of it, a peculiar and mysterious title. So, if Christ had been a mere man, His saying, "My Father is greater than I" (John xv. 28) would have been unmeaning.

(*b*)   *S. T. Coleridge*

SOCRATES AND CHRIST

Now I don't mean to compare the Greek "Eros," the Latin "Amor," and the Christian "Love." The man who knows classic life knows that the distance between these is an infinite distance. Love, what did it signify to the ancient world but a form of lust, or what at best carried with it every connotation of passion and its pain? But love, what does it become to Christian man? Read that grand chapter which stands in the first of Corinthians, the glorious description of Christian love, the power that can inspire, can regulate, can ennoble man, making him live for his fellows the wide world o'er. Or, take another thing, take the tenderness it brought into life, of man to woman, of strong to weak. There is no grander ancient character than Socrates, beautiful character he is in many ways. He, citizen, thinker, teacher, plying that wondrous dialectic craft of his in the streets of Athens, is a form attractive to all eyes. And he is so attractive because he stands out from among the crowd, the creator of a new moral ideal, at once stronger, higher, and more humane than the old epic and heroic ideal embodied in the Homeric Achilles. But now, look how over against him stands the image of Xantippe, his wife. She has had hard measure dealt to her; his contemporaries and historians have made her seem one who led the poor philosopher a hardish life, and have made her the type of a woman who makes life unpleasant to the man who has wedded her. And many a dry-as-dust commentator has grown somewhat humorous over the sweet relief that death brought to Socrates when it saved him from Xantippe. But if you examine the simple truth as it stands in history, that woman has no right to be so rated; the man, on the other hand, reason to be rated most soundly. His love is all for the State, and not for the home; marriage is for him only a con-

venient institution, carrying with it no duties of living affection, of mutual helpfulness and cheerful intercourse; and his conduct was but too good an exponent of his opinion. He cultivated an admiring friendship for Aspasia, but he had only the coldest neglect for poor Xantippe. His duties were all to Athens and to Greece, and not at all to home. He puns, questions, teaches for the good of philosophy and the State, but she has to provide for their children. She goes to him in the hour of death, grieved, distressed in a woman's way, and he sits as in the Phaedo, sublimely discoursing with his friends. When she comes, he never feels a bit the loss to her; they do not feel the pain to the woman and to the children; nay, it is going to trouble the serenity of the philosopher to see the woman who was his wife, and the children she had borne him. And they send her away with no word of comfort, with scorn, rather than with cheer. There now stands out clear and distinct one of the great differences the religion of Christ brought in, it brought in the spirit of love, made the weak dependent on the strong, made the strong thoughtful of the weak, made the man in his might, in his manhood, with all the rights of manhood upon him, be to the weak generous, and to the dependent noble. This is but one phase of its action in universalizing and creating a higher virtue, and so purifying and perfecting the whole notion of society. The state of life built up in harmony with these principles, according to these great ideals, could not be but a kindlier, nobler, humaner state.

(*c*)   *Fairbairn*

SOLDIERS OF CHRIST

A soldier's time is not spent in earning the money to buy his armour, in finding food and raiment, in seeking shelter. His king provides these things, that he may be the more at liberty to fight his battles. So, for the soldier of the Cross all is provided. His Government has planned to leave him free for the kingdom's work. The problem of the Christian life is this—man has but to preserve the right attitude. To abide in Christ, to be in position, that is all. Much work is done on board a ship crossing the Atlantic. Yet none of it is spent on making the ship go. The sailor but harnesses his vessel to the wind. He puts his sail and rudder in position, and lo, the miracle is wrought. So everywhere, God creates, man utilizes. All the work of the world is merely a taking advantage of energies already there (*Bushnell*). God gives the wind and the water and the heat; man but puts himself in the way of the wind, fixes his water-wheel in the way of the river, puts his piston in the way of the steam; and so, holding himself in position before God's Spirit, all the energies of Omnipotence course within his soul. He is like a tree planted by a river whose leaf is green, and whose fruits fail not.

(*d*)   *Drummond*

SOLOMON

"*So King Solomon exceeded all the kings of the earth for riches and for wisdom*" (1 Kings x. 23)

1. Manifold interest of the story of Solomon

(i.) Circumstances of his *birth* (2 Sam. xii. 24, 25).

(*e*)

(ii.) His inheritance of the great *promise* (2 Sam. vii. 12–15).

(iii.) The *contrasts* in his life—splendour and gloom, wisdom and sin.

(*a*)

2. To-day's lessons bring out this last point of interest

This morning gives Solomon in his glory; this evening, in his shame. Look at the two views now side by side.

(*b*)

3. Vastness of Solomon's endowments

(i.) A large, though not unwieldy, realm; (ii.) an era of peace; (iii.) The inheritance of David's name and glory; and in his own person; (iv.) great *natural* gifts (proved, *e.g.*, by the deep *insight* of his prayer, 1 Kings iii. 6–9); and (v.) great *supernatural* gifts, divine inspiration both in word and deed on occasion. All this forms a character of profound interest. In Solomon, *inward depth* is joined with *outward vigour* and with *surrounding opportunity;* even the material surroundings are ennobled by the man's intercourse with God.

(*c*)

4. Such a character left its mark

Solomon is famous for ever. Eastern legends are full of him. But above all, Jesus Christ quotes him as the type and flower of majesty and wisdom (Matt. vi. 29; xii. 42).

(*d*)

5. Yet Solomon is one of the great ruins of Scripture

He comes in *sadness of interest* only just after Balaam and Saul. And all that relieves the gloom in his case is (i.) the fact of a special promise of myterious mercy (2 Sam. vii. 15); and (ii.) the probability that *Ecclesiastes* records his last experience as being one not only of disappointment, but *also* of penitence and perhaps of efforts to undo the mischief of his example (Eccl. xii. 8, 9, 13, 14).

(*e*)

6. His ruin, in contrast with his glory, has some clear lessons for will and conscience now

In him, as in a hundred other cases, the blessed Bible brings its truth home by teaching it in *facts*, and in *lives*. It is a characteristic of the whole Scripture revelation. "These things *happened unto them*" (to these *real men* of the past) "for ensamples; and are written for *our admonition*" (1 Cor. x. 11, 12).

(*f*)

7. A few of these lessons are here suggested

(i.) Providences are not necessarily security. Solomon's *wealth, wisdom, power, fame*, were all distinctly providential; sent by God in special gift. Yet he fell [1] [2].

(ii.) Privileges are not salvation. Solomon's *father, teacher* (Nathan), education in *true faith and worship*, call to do one great *special work for God* (the Temple-building), deep *religious thought*, *eloquence in prayer* (1 Kings viii.), *inspiration* as a Scripture writer—all were inestimable privileges. Yet he fell; and though he was rescued,

it was not through those privileges. Free mercy interfered.

(iii.) Knowledge, force of character, refinement, culture—all are dust in the wind against the terrible possibilities of temptation. This keenest and largest mind of the old world fell through bodily desire [3].

(*g*)

8. Solomon, from his sin-broken throne, says to us—

Welcome all God gives us; but trust nothing but Himself; Himself now revealed in Jesus; Jesus for you, and Jesus in you; hidden from the wise, revealed to babes.

(*h*) H. C. G. Moule

SOLOMON (Neh. xiii. 26)

Life full of painful interest.
Problem is, *Saved or unsaved ?*
[Probably left in silence with intent to warn, that a life so erring leaves no encouraging hope after death.]
Note: Began well; God appeared to him three times at Gibeon; yet the end was obscured.
Not what a religious life ought to be. Text written 600 years after, and appears to solve doubt as to his fate.
A comparison of Nathan's words to David in 2 Sam. vii. 14, 15, with promises in Ps. lxxxix., and with the text above, show a decided contrast between Saul and David's family.

(i.) Did not Solomon sin?
(ii.) There was no king . . . beloved of his God.

(*i*)

1. His wanderings, and going astray:

(i.) In breaking covenant with God; in breaking the exclusiveness, separation, and distinctiveness of Jewish nation. Solomon entered into marriage relations and commercial interchange with *heathen* nations: wives from Egypt, Moab, Ammon, Edom, Sidonians, Hittites = his sin.

N.B. The shadow of the New Testament truth, the Christian to be separate from the world, "Come out . . . be separate . . . and I will be a Father unto you." There must be a line of demarcation: to overstep this is a sin, a transgression, or a wandering into forbidden paths. This Solomon did.

(ii.) Note also his unrestrained self-indulgence. Book of Ecclesiastes (?) "wine," "pleasures," whilst there is a corresponding waning of religion.

(*j*)

2. God's gracious guidance all through

"If he sin . . . I will chasten," etc. How? not as his father—pestilence, famine, rebellion, death of child, etc. But God *left Solomon alone*, let him have his own way; and Solomon tasted the full cup, till satiated and nauseated with it. His own was bitter "Vanity of vanities." The end, however, denotes repentance, "Let us hear the conclusion . . . Fear God, etc., . . . whole duty of man."

Learn, that "All things (even sin) work," etc. There is a love which rebellion cannot quench:

> "Mine is an unchanging love,
> Higher than the heights above;
> Deeper than the depths beneath,
> Free and tender, strong as Death."

Is the trembling Christian doubtful what Christ

(*k*)

will be to him at last? Remember, "Having loved His own, He loved them unto the end." His salvation is in the hands of Christ. The Rock on which he has built is *Love ;* and the gates of hell shall not prevail against it.

(*a*)   *F. W. Robertson*

SOMNAMBULIST

A soul passed into the haunts of iniquity. What a face that was! Sorrow only half covered up with an assumed joy. It was a woman's face. I saw as plainly as on the page of a book the tragedy. You know that there is such a thing as somnambulism, or walking in one's sleep. Well, in a fatal somnambulism, a soul started off from her father's house. It was very dark and her feet were cut by the rocks ; but on she went until she came to the verge of a chasm, and she began to descend from boulder to boulder down over the rattling shelving cliffs, for you know while walking in sleep people will go where they would not go when awake. Further on down, and further, where no owl of the night or hawk of the day would venture. On down until she touched the depth of the chasm. Then, in walking asleep, she began to ascend the other side of the chasm, rock above rock, as the roe aboundeth. Without having her head to swim with the awful steep, she scaled the height. No eye but the sleepless eye of God watched her as she went down one side the chasm and came up the other side the chasm. It was an August night, and a storm was gathering, and a loud burst of thunder awoke her from her somnambulism, and she said, "Whither shall I fly?" and with an affrighted eye she looked back upon the chasm she had crossed, and she looked in front and there was a deeper chasm before her. She said, "What shall I do? Must I die here?" And as she bent over the one chasm, she heard the sighing of the past ; and as she bent over the other chasm, she heard the portents of the future. Then she sat down on the granite crag, and cried, "Oh for my father's house! Oh for the cottage, where I might die amid embowering honeysuckle! Oh, the past! Oh, the future! Oh, father! Oh, mother! Oh, God!" But the storm that had been gathering culminated, and wrote with finger of lightning on the sky just above the horizon, "The way of the transgressor is hard." And then thunder-peal after thunder-peal uttered it: "Which forsaketh the guide of her youth and forgetteth the covenant of her God. Destroyed without remedy!" And the cavern behind echoed it, "Destroyed without remedy!" There she perished, her cut and bleeding feet on the edge of one chasm, her long locks washed by the storm dripping over the other chasm.

(*b*)   *Talmage*

SON OF GOD, DECLARED TO BE, etc. (Rom .i. 4)

Paul probably had in mind Psalm ii. 7, "Thou art My Son, this day have I begotten Thee," which he refers to the Resurrection (Acts xiii. 33). This is, of course, not to be understood in a Socinian sense, which denies the *eternal* Sonship of Christ ; on the contrary, the *eternal* Sonship (Rom. viii. 3; Gal. iv. 4; Col. i. 15; Phil. ii. 7) precedes, and underlies the *historical* Sonship, just as the Divinity of Christ is necessarily implied in His

Incarnation ; for He could never have become *God-Man* if He had not been God before. The eternal, metaphysical Sonship of the Logos, which is co-equal with the Father, was indicated by the Apostle in ver. 3, before speaking of His Incarnation, and is, in its nature, incommunicable ; but the historical Sonship of the God-Man, which dates from the Incarnation (Luke i. 35), but was not fully developed, publicly established, and made manifest till the Resurrection, is communicated to believers ; first germinally in regeneration, whereby they are made "sons of God" (Rom. viii. 14), and fully in their resurrection (viii. 23), when what is here sown in *weakness* will be raised in *power* (1 Cor. xv. 43). Hence the Risen Saviour is called "the First-born among many brethren" (Rom. viii. 29) ; "the First-born from the dead" (Col. i. 18 ; Rev. i. 5).

(*c*)   *P. Schaff*

SONS AND DAUGHTERS OF THE LORD GOD ALMIGHTY

In Worcester Cathedral there is a slab with just one doleful word on it as a record of the dead buried beneath, That word is "Miserrimus." No name, no date ; nothing more of the dead than just this one word, to say he who lay there was, or is, "MOST MISERABLE."

Surely, he had missed the way home to the Father's house and the Father's love, else why this sad record. But in the Catacombs at Rome there is one stone recently found, inscribed with the single world "Felicissima." No name, no date, again ; but a word to express that the dead christian sister was "MOST HAPPY."

Most happy, why? Because she had found the Father's house, and love, and that peace which the storms of life and the persecutions of a hostile world and the light affliction of time could neither give nor take away.

(*d*)

SONSHIP AND CROSSES

Till you be in heaven, it will be but foul weather, one shower up, and another down. The lintel-stone and pillars of the New Jerusalem suffer more knocks of God's hammer and tool, than the common side-wall stones ; and if twenty crosses be written for you in God's book, they will come to nineteen, and then at last to one, and after that to nothing ; but Christ's own soft hand shall dry your face, and wipe away your tears.

This is His truth, I am fully persuaded, I now suffer for ; for Christ hath taken upon Him to be witness to it by His sweet comforts to my soul ; and shall I think Him a false witness, or that He would subscribe blank paper? I thank His high and dreadful name for what He hath given ; I hope to keep His seal and His pledge till He come and loose it Himself. I defy hell to put me off it, but He is Christ, and He hath met with his prisoner ; and I took instruments in His own hand, and no other than Him. And yet Satan and my apprehension sometimes makes a lie of Christ, as if He hated me ; but I dare believe no evil of Christ ; if He would cool my love-fever for Himself with real presence and possession, I should be rich ; but I dare not be mislearned, and seek more in that kind ; howbeit it be no shame to beg at Christ's door.

(*e*)   *Samuel Rutherford*

SORCERY (Spiritualism)

The Bible throughout treats sorcery in a more serious way than as if it were empty legerdemain.
(a)   *Lange*

SORROW

Some unborn sorrow, ripe in fortune's womb,
Is coming towards me.
(b)   *Shakspeare*

Sorrow, its Uses

> Sorrow is the messenger between
> The poet and men's bosoms. . . .
> Grief alone can teach us what is man.

(c)   *A law enunciated by a modern writer,*

SOUL, THE

The soul is the most human thing in man, or man himself.
(d)   *Martensen*

Soul

I am positive I have a soul: nor can all the books with which the materialists have pestered the world, ever convince me to the contrary.
(e)   *Sterne*

Soul, The Lost

1. Descend, O sinner, to the woe!
    Thy day of hope is done;
  Light shall revisit thee no more,
  Life with its sanguine dreams is o'er,
  Love reaches not yon awful shore;
    For ever sets thy sun!

2. Pass down to the eternal dark;
    Yet not for rest nor sleep;
  Thine is the everlasting tomb,
  Thine the inexorable doom,
  The moonless, mornless, sunless gloom,
    Where souls for ever weep.

3. Depart, lost soul, thy tears to weep,
    Thy never-drying tears;
  To sigh the never-ending sigh,
  To send up the unheeded cry
  Into the unresponding sky,
    Whose silence mocks thy fears.

4. Call upon God; He *hears* no more;
    Call upon death; 'tis dead;
  Ask the live lightnings in their flight,
  Seek for some sword of hell and night
  The worm that never dies to smite;
    No weapon strikes its head.

5. Thou livest, and must ever live;
    But life is now thy foe;
  Thine is the sorrow-shrivelled brow,
  Thine the eternal heartache now,
  'Neath the long burden thou must bow,
    The living death of woe.

6. Thy songs are at an end; thy harp
    Shall solace thee no more;
  All mirth has perished in thy grave;
  The melody that could not save

Has died upon death's sullen wave
  That flung thee on this shore.

7. Earth, with its waves, and woods, and winds
    Its stars, and suns, and streams,
  Its joyous air and gentle skies,
  Filled with all happy melodies,
  Has passed, or, with dark memories,
    Comes back in torturing dreams.

8. Never again shalt thou behold,
    As when a bounding boy,
  The fresh buds of the fragrant spring,
  Its song-birds on their April wing,
  And all its vales a-blossoming;
    Or summer's rosy joy.

9. No river of forgetfulness,
    As poets dreamed and sung,
  Rolls yonder to efface the past,
  To quench the sense of what thou wast,
  To soothe or end thy pain at last,
    Or cool thy burning tongue.

10. No God is there; no Christ; for He,
    Whose word on earth was, "*Come*,"
  Hath said, "*Depart*": go, lost one, go,
  Reap the sad harvest thou didst sow,
  Join yon lost angels in their woe,
    Their prison is *thy* home.

11. Descend, O sinner, to the gloom!
    Hear the deep judgment-knell
  Send forth its terror-shrieking sound
  These walls of adamant around,
  And filling to its utmost bound
    Thy woeful, woeful hell.

12. Depart, O sinner, to the chain!
    Enter the eternal cell;
  To all that's good, and true, and right,
  To all that's fond, and fair, and bright,
  To all of holiness and light,
    Bid thou thy last farewell!

(f)   *Anon*

Soul, The Value of, and Loss of the (Matt. xvi. 26)

1. Every man has a soul of his own.

2. It is possible for the soul to be lost; and there is danger of it.

3. If the soul is lost, it is the sinner's own losing; and his blood is on his own head.

4. One soul is worth more than all the world.

5. So the winning of the world is often the losing of the soul.

6. The loss of the soul cannot be made up by the gain of the whole world.

7. If the soul be once lost, it is lost for ever; and the loss can never be repaired or retrieved.
(g)   *Matt. Henry*

Soul, The Value of the (for whom Christ died)

What, in the eye of an Intellectual and Omnipotent Being, is the whole sidereal system to the soul of one man, for whom Christ died?
(h)   *S. T. Coleridge*

SOVEREIGNTY OF GOD, THE

"*What shall we say then to these things ? If God be for us, who can be against us ?*" (Rom. viii. 31)

1. The Apostle is speaking about the certainty of the believer's salvation

"We *know* that all things work together for good to them that love God, to them who are the called according to His purpose." "I am persuaded that neither death, nor life, nor angels, nor principalities, nor powers, nor things present, nor things to come, nor height, nor depth, nor any other creature, shall be able to *separate* us from the love of God, which in Christ Jesus our Lord." Add to this the emphatic and exultant language of our text : "*If God be for us, who can be against us ?*" The believer shall not miscarry.

(*a*)

2. But *why*? On what does he make it all to depend? Our salvation does not depend upon *ourselves* : the whole chapter is dead against that notion. Important as our individual watchfulness and prayerfulness are, yet our salvation does not depend upon anything that we can do. But it depends, from first to last, entirely upon the *sovereignty of God*.

God's purpose is, that His people be saved. He has appointed us to obtain salvation ; and there is no one in the whole universe greater than Himself, who can interfere with His plans, and thwart His arrangements. The believer has allied Himself with the Omnipotent God—the stronger than the strong.

(*b*)

3. Imagine it otherwise

Let us suppose for a moment that our salvation depended upon ourselves, and not upon God ; that the responsibility of keeping safe the precious jewel which has been committed to us is ours only. We are then in the same condition as Adam was before the Fall, whose life depended upon his obedience—in other words, upon *himself*.

Imagine it so with ourselves. You have your salvation in your own keeping, and you have to *keep* it safe. Where will your confidence be after you have got a little acquaintance with the road on which you travel, and the difficulties in the way? the anxiety you will be in when you find out that robbers waylay you all along the path to heaven? Pirates sail on the same sea, and bear down upon richly laden vessels, not empty ones. They see your carelessness, and watch their opportunity.

You know that one at least of these enemies has more skill than yourself, older, stronger, more watchful than you—you know his cunning—his wiles are proverbial—his long and intimate acquaintance with the human heart—that he has studied its weaknesses, and that you are but a babe in comparison with him—just a little cockle-shell tossed on the great ocean of temptation.

(*c*)

4. What confidence could you have that you would get across life's ocean in safety, with the precious cargo of your own salvation in your trust? You could have none. Besides, you know that the enemy has gained such victories over some of the saints of God, who were giants in comparison with yourself.

Witness David, the man after God's own heart. The tempter came to him at a fitting moment, and put such a temptation in his way, that the sweet singer of Israel fell into sins too fearful to contemplate. He came to Peter, strong enough, as he thought, to look after his own spiritual interests ; and the tempter just gave him a sift or two in his sieve, and the chaff flew out in such quantities as to lead to the supposition that there was no true wheat there at all. Without the help of Jesus, Peter cannot continue to abide in Jesus ; for when left to himself, he with solemn oaths and curses declares that he has no knowledge of Jesus whatever.

(*d*)

5. In face of such facts,—facts too in the lives of such men,—what comfort can it be to know that the keeping of our salvation depends upon ourselves? What is a *Christian man*, a *converted* man, a true disciple of Jesus, when left to himself, and in the hands of the great adversary? What can you do to help yourself, when he meets you unprotected? How can you expect to get to heaven, knowing that he is about your path, and will let go no opportunity of tripping you up, and robbing you of your jewel, and of ruining you, body and soul, completely?

(*e*)

6. Now, what is it that you want, to keep you steadfast? You want exactly what the Apostle says you have, **the sovereignty of God** on your side. You want to know that He who began will carry on the work of your salvation, and that He *can* carry it through. You have this assurance. God started you on your career : He has set your ship sailing towards the haven of everlasting life ; and the storms you meet with, and the calms which hold you inactive, shall work together for your good ; there shall be no shipwreck, no falling from grace, simply because God is able to overrule all the opposition of enemies, and to make them work into and further His designs. He will carry on His own work to completion. "The foundation of God standeth sure ; " where He has laid the foundation, He will build ; "for He who hath begun a good work in you will perform it until the day of Jesus Christ." Human infirmity slumbers and sleeps ; and if ultimate issues were left to it, all would be lost. But "He that keepeth Israel shall neither slumber nor sleep."

(*f*)

7. Examine first, that the Apostle grounds this assurance on the fact that "God is for us."

We are, as we have seen, speaking about the ultimate salvation of the believer ; and we feel at times, as most Christian people do, who know their own weakness and the power of temptation, that if our salvation depended upon ourselves, then we have reason enough to fear lest after all we may fail of obtaining the prize. We start for the goal, not knowing whether we shall reach it. Such uncertainty destroys all Christian comfort. And the Apostle aims here to gladden such hearts by confirming their faith ; for Christian joy can hardly exist where there is doubt about the goal for which we are making. He begins, then, by directing our thoughts right back to the very first thought of our salvation in the mind of God ; for

(*g*)

Sovereignty of God, The—*continued*

it, like a building, was first a *thought*, then a *plan*, afterwards a plan *in execution*, and lastly it is to be a *design accomplished*. This he proves by saying first that "*God is for us*." God began, and God will complete the good work in us.

(*a*)

8. Doubts of Self

Do you doubt it, you who scarcely know, by reason of your many infirmities, whether you are a Christian or no? Do you doubt whether God will complete the good work He has begun in your heart? You may well doubt it, if you look to yourself only. You may well doubt it, if you look at the power of the terrible tempter only, and the many hindrances he may put in your path. You may doubt it, if you look to man, any man, for help. You may doubt it, yea, you may despair altogether of getting through, if you look only to your own passing religious frames of mind, and your sometimes good resolutions and holy aspirations.

(*b*)

9. Look to God

But if, on the other hand, you take your eye off all these, and look back, back into the far distant past, into the ages before this world was made—if you look back into the secret council-chamber of the Almighty God—back to that time when, as this chapter tells us, God was thinking of and planning your salvation, " before the foundations of the world were laid "—then you may see something to encourage you, viz., that "*God is for us*."

It is no chance thing whether you will be saved or no, but a matter " ordered in all things and sure," well thought of and planned before you yourself had anything to do with it, or by your sins and inconsistencies threw obstacles and difficulties in the way. "Oh!" says some one, " I can't think it, it is above me and beyond me altogether; I cannot attain unto it, I can't grasp it; nay, I hardly dare to believe one half that is told me." In answer, I would remind such that " God's thoughts in this matter are not as our thoughts." Here His work is unfathomable, past finding out. We can hardly venture to believe it, because it is apparently so inconceivable a thing. But whether we believe it or no, I am only seeking carefully to put before you what is here stated in His word. Like Bishop Ridley, when speaking on the same subject, I will be most careful not to make it say what is not really there.

There is, then, we will say, a doubt in your mind as to whether your salvation did actually occupy the thoughts of God, not only before you were born, but also " *before the foundations of the world were laid*."

(*c*)

10. Search the Scriptures

And see if this thing be so, or whether it may not be presumption to think and believe it. Jesus, speaking, be it remembered, of believers, says (Matt. xxv. 34): " Then shall the King say unto them on His right hand, Come, ye blessed of My Father, inherit the kingdom *prepared for you before the foundation of the world*." St. Paul (Eph. i. 4): " He hath chosen us in Him *before the foundation of the world*." Rev. xvii. 8 is a passage to the effect that the names of believers *were written* in the book of life, *from the foundation of the world;* and in the verses immediately preceding that from which I am speaking, St. Paul calls our salvation first a *purpose*, or thought in the mind of God, then a *foreknowledge* of our whole history, and thirdly a *predestination*, or a *pre-arrangement* of all things necessary to its successful accomplishment, before He made the world on which we now live; and it is the knowledge of such facts which makes him exclaim so confidently, " What shall we say then to these things? *If God be for us, who can be against us?* " Again "*God is for us*," not only before, as we have seen, but since we have come into existence—as is to be seen in His providence concerning us. " Moreover, whom He did predestinate, them He also *called;* and whom He CALLED, them He also *justified;* and whom He justified, them He also *glorified*." Mark the steps: Predestination *before* we had anything to do with it; *calling, justifying*, and eventually *glorifying, since* we have had to do with it. The Apostle goes on now to speak of the conscious dealings that God has had with us, which are but, in his estimation, as portions of the rock cropping up to view; the one end dips down out of sight into the past ages of eternity—the other end, equally out of sight, goes on to " glory."

(*d*)

11. The continuation of his argument is simply something like this : God knew beforehand of your coming into existence—that when in the world, the world would not satisfy you—a hunger after other things would come—a desire for holiness and heaven would take possession of your heart. And He provided accordingly.

(*e*)

12. This provision of God is the secret of your conversion, and of your spiritual life

He first thought of, and loved you, or you never would have thought of or loved Him—and your life now is in reality the working out and the unfolding of God's purpose concerning you. There is no chance work, no accident, no good or bad luck, no fatalism, about your life; but a plan is being executed, and God has put you where you are, because it is the place where your salvation can best be furthered. Before you began to think, He put it into the minds of others to have you baptized in the name of the Trinity, and brought up and instructed as a Christian child ought to be; afterwards, as you grew older, and became responsible for your own choice, He *called you*, He made you know in various ways what His mind was concerning you. The voice that spake to you was sometimes " rough," at other times " a still small voice," and you came at last to understand that God wanted you to separate yourself from the world, to come out and serve Him, and be one of His chosen flock.

At first you hung back—many strong ties held you; but the voice kept on calling. Daily He said, " Come "; Christ said, " *Come* "; the Spirit said, " Come." Christian people around you said. " Come thou with us, and we will do thee good." The voice grew in earnestness and in intensity.— " Awake, thou that sleepest, and arise from the dead, and Christ shall give thee light "—till at last you were thoroughly aroused and awakened;

(*f*)

Sovereignty of God, The—*continued*

you replied to the call, "Speak, Lord, for Thy servant heareth."

In the light of this revelation, you felt your moral leprosy, you cried "unclean," and you fled, like the manslayer, from the accusations of conscience—until at last the cry of soul agony came welling up before God: "Lord, what shall I do to be saved?"

(*a*)

13. God knew you would ask that question

He had allowed you to feed on husks first, but He knew what would come in the end; then, like a skilful Physician, He had the remedy at hand as soon as you applied to Him. He showed you the way of salvation—the meaning of the death and resurrection of the Lord Jesus Christ—a death in your "*stead*"—an atonement for your sin; and because He lives, you shall live also. This you received and believed; it was like water poured on a parched soil. And, your faith uniting you to Christ, you became a living member of a living Head. This, though you saw it not, was the working out of God's eternal purpose, "because whom He *called*, them He also justified."

Afterwards ensues a "newness of life." "He that spared not His own Son, but delivered Him up for us all," continues to show that "He is for us," by freely giving us all things in Him, till finally those whom He *purposed* to save before the world was, and *called and justified* in the world, He will *glorify* in the world to come.

(*b*)

14. This being so, "Who can be against us?"

A few words only can be said on this second member of the text.

There is no higher authority and power than God's. Our spiritual adversary may harm us—our fellow-men may harm us—our own innate sinfulness and blundering may put many an impediment in our way; but, after all has been said, we have got the sovereignty of God on our side. "*Who then can be against us?*" We devote a few lines more to a brief examination of this question. It will repay investigation. I know of nothing in the whole Bible more calculated to set our hearts at rest, and to quiet many an uneasy doubt, than the way St. Paul deals with this question.

For when we come to examine who the possible foes may be who can with any success be against us, they will be found to be the Persons of the Holy Trinity. God only can be against us to harm us; but "*it is God that justifieth.*" The judge only has power to condemn us; but Christ is the Judge, and "*it is Christ that died*" for us—rose again, and now intercedes for us.

The *Holy Spirit* might forsake His temple, and leave us altogether to ourselves; but the Spirit helpeth our infirmities, teaching us what to pray for; and through His power we become "more than conquerors," though circumstances are against us (see context). Hence the improbability that they who have been "*for us*" from the beginning, and who help us now, should be "against us" in the end. For if, when we were sinners God loved us, and Christ died for us, and the Holy Spirit helped us, how much more, being reconciled, shall we be saved to the "uttermost" of time and need, through the continual intercession of our great High Priest?

Every kind of possible hindrance is brought forward by the Apostle to show, not that it can separate us from the love of God, but that it is one of the "all things which work together for good to them that love God, and are the called according to His purpose."

(*c*)

15. The story of a little child whose life on one occasion was in extreme peril. And yet, if it helps us to realize our Lord's teaching, that no one can pluck us out of the hand of Christ, because our heavenly Father is Sovereign, then it needs no apology. The story is one of the simplest, and yet perhaps as touchingly beautiful as anything we ever read: "A little boy lay asleep in the verandah of an Indian house. His nurse had neglected him for the moment, thinking him out of mischief when asleep. Presently a large tiger, prowling about for prey, finding the village very quiet, ventured in amongst the houses. The English residents were all absent—the natives at work in their rice-fields, and the ladies taking rest, according to the custom, in the heat of the day. The tiger crept noiselessly past the house, until he saw the sleeping child. Then, with a bound, he sprang upon him, grasped the child's robe in his teeth, and darted off to the jungle. Having secured his prize, he seemed in no hurry to mangle it; he laid the child down, and as a kitten plays with a mouse, so the tiger sported with the child. He walked round him, laid first one paw and then another upon the plump little limbs, staring all the time in the child's face. But the marvel was that the child seemed in no way alarmed: it might be because he was too young, or it might be because he happened to have a favourite dog at home, and thought the tiger to be "Nero's" big brother. So when the tiger glared at him with his fiery eyeballs, and showed his ferocious teeth, the child just simply and innocently said, "*I'm not afraid of you*, for I've got a father—*you can't hurt me, for I've got a mamma.*" It is not necessary to continue the story further: suffice it to say, an aged native, hearing the tiger's growl, followed with his gun, heard and saw what is related, and shot the animal dead.

Would that we, who call ourselves Christians and pray to "*Our Father*" in heaven—when some great tiger of trouble seizes us, and runs off with us, instead of despairing, and saying, "All these things are against me," could say with like confidence, *I'm not afraid—I've got a Father*—One whose eye is ever upon us. And that Father is the Almighty God, the Sovereign Ruler of the universe—and if He be for us, "who can be against us?"

(*d*)   (*Cf. with this Hooker's Sermon on* Hab. i. 4.)

Sovereignty of God and Free Will of Man

It may suffice to say, that, on the one hand, Scripture bears constant testimony to the fact that all believers are chosen and called by God—their whole spiritual life in its origin, progress, and completion, being *from Him;* while, on the other hand, its testimony is no less precise that He willeth all to be saved, and that none shall perish except by wilful rejection of the truth. So that, on the one side, God's sovereignty, and on the other man's free will is plainly declared to us. *To receive, believe, and act on both these* is our duty and

(*e*)

our wisdom. They belong, as truths, no less to *natural* than to revealed religion; and every one who believes in a God, must acknowledge both. But all attempts *to bridge over the gulf between the two* are *futile,* in the present imperfect condition of man.

(a)   *Alford*

Note that,

The difficulty belongs to Theism, not to Christianity alone, much less to the Calvinistic conception of it.

(b)   *Lange*

SOWER, PARABLE OF THE

" *Behold a sower went forth to sow* " (Matt. xiii. 3–23)

The Sower, the seed, the soil = Christ, the Word, the people.

(c)

1. The Sower—Christ

" He that soweth the good seed is the Son of man." The seed may be sown by prophets (Old Testament), Apostles (New Testament); or by Ministers (now); but they are all His orderlies : " He that heareth you heareth Me."

(d)

2. The Seed—the Word

The Bible is the granary. Seed possesses— (i.) Life; (ii.) Force; (iii.) Power of propagation. Cf. The Word under Peter's preaching.

(e)

3. The Soil—the Hearers

Must be prepared for the seed. God prepares hearts and nations by the ploughshare of affliction.

The hearers of the Word are of two kinds :
(i.) The totally unsusceptible ;
(ii.) The susceptible.

(f)

(i.) The Unsusceptible Hearers

Are " the wayside hearers"—the pathway—seed lies on the surface = those who hear the Word, but understand not. The Word reaches no further than the external ear. There is no ear to hear, beyond this.
" *Then* cometh Satan "
" *Immediately* cometh Satan." Why so hasty?
" Lest they should believe and be saved."

(g)

(ii.) The Susceptible Hearers not all Saved

(1.) The *stony ground* hearers. Seed falls on rocky ground, where there is only a little surface mould. It soon springs up ; but, finding no depth of earth, is scorched by the sun, and comes to nothing.
= Those who " receive the Word with joy."
Demonstrative, emotional people, excited feelings.
Talk about their experiences—without depth, Who, too often, when difficulty comes, give up their religion, and bring forth no fruit to perfection. Passing impressions mistaken for conversion.

(h)

(2.) Other seed " fell among thorns "—rank weeds which drew away the nourishment and choked the seed.
= The divided heart, which does not seek *first* (above all things) the kingdom of God. Hence the world in the end becomes the stronger, and the seed is choked in the competition for existence. " Ye cannot serve God and Mammon."

(i)

(3.) " *Good ground.*" These "receive the Word," retain it ; the ground has been prepared ; seed falls deep. They understand it. No passing impressions—not like letters written on the sands which the first wave will wash away, but like those engraved on granite, and remain. They " bring forth fruit to perfection," some thirty, some sixty, some a hundred fold.

(j)

(4.) " He that hath ears to hear, let him hear "

Solemn fact, that of four seeds sown in the same field, *one* caught away by the wicked one ; another grew up quickly only to perish as quickly ; a third is choked by the cares of this world ; whilst the fourth only comes to perfection. One out of four ; and this is the first of parables, the key to all : an ever-recurring parable of the Word preached. A forecast of what will be when Christ comes again.
(i.) Of two hearers sitting in the same pew—one taken and another left.
(ii.) Two disciples, John who leaned on Jesus' bosom, and Judas who betrayed Him—one taken and another left.
(iii.) At Calvary, one thief was taken and the other left.
(iv.) The seed sown comes not to perfection unless it falls into an " honest and good heart." The Word preached does not profit unless mixed with faith in them that hear it.

(k)

SOWER, PARABLE OF

THE WORD CHOKED in three ways by thorns.
(i.) *If you are poor.*
Thorns—" The *cares* of this world."
(ii.) *If you are rich.*
Thorns—" The love of riches."
(iii.) *If you are gay.*
Thorns—" The pleasures of this life."

(l)

SOWING AND REAPING

To each of us our Heavenly Father has given the germ of a life that can never die. The law of that life is, that nothing will be, nor can be, lost. Its unconsidered fragments are like grains of seed-corn, full of infinite after-promise. Even as the field of the dead is God's acre, so is the field of living duty His harvest field. Wheat and tares,— nothing will be plucked up, all will grow, all shall have a solemn reaping day. It will be a gathering to all, a garnering to some.

(m)   *Jackson's Bampton Lectures*

SOWING AND REAPING

I shot an arrow in the air-
It fell to earth, I know not where;

(n)

For so swiftly it flew, the sight
Could not follow it in its flight.
I breathed a song into the ear-
It fell to earth, I know not where;
For who has sight so keen and strong
That it can follow the flight of song?
Long, long afterward, in an oak,
I found the arrow, still unbroke;
And the song, from beginning to end,
I found again in the heart of a friend.

(a)   *Longfellow*

SOWING AND REAPING

The thorns which I have reaped are of the tree
I planted; they have torn me, and I bleed:
I should have known what fruit would spring from
   such a seed.

(b)   *Byron*

SPADE

" Never mind," said Philip; " the Macedonians
are a blunt people; they call a spade a spade."

(c)   *Kennedy's Demosthenes*

SPEECH

Speech is one of our grand distinctions from
the brute.

(d)   *Channing*

SPIRIT

Bodily presence is often detrimental to spiritual
influence. We know, for example, how perilous
it often is to be admitted to familiar intercourse
with the men who have stimulated us by their
thoughts and thrown upon our intellectual life the
spell of their genius. So long as such men stand
afar off, clothed with their spiritual house, and
working with their spiritual functions, we give
them homage; but when they come near us they
invite criticism upon points which did not enter
into their original mastery of our admiration and
confidence; some weakness of the flesh, some conceit of manner or feebleness of expression, or other
more or less trifling peculiarity, may impair their
spiritual dominion, and cause us to regret that
the god of our early love ever came down from
Olympian invisibility.

(e)   *Joseph Parker*

SPIRIT OF ADOPTION, THE (Rom. viii. 15)

**1. The men of the Middle Ages were great
Architects**—architects in thought, in society, in
politics, in ecclesiastical organization, no less than
in stone and marble. In every department of
human life they laid deep foundations; and they
reared mighty structures, under which, to this
hour, our religion is sheltered, our learning
fostered, our social life controlled, and to which
even the framework of our political institutions is
in great measure due. The Fathers and Doctors
of the Church, the Bishops, the Popes, the Monks,
built for all time; and having planned their great
edifices, in the main, on the enduring laws of
revealed truth, and based them on the divinely
organized constitution of the Church, they could

trust the generations which followed them to
carry forward their work.

(f)

**2. But the principle that the best things, when
corrupted, become the worst,** has received its most
conspicuous illustration in the history of religion,
and above all of true religion. All great gifts and
privileges bring proportionate temptations; and if
these be yielded to, blessings may become almost
transformed into curses. To none is this risk so
terrible as to men who are entrusted with great
spiritual powers; and the danger to which such
men are exposed may perhaps be in some measure
discerned in the temptation to which our Lord was
subjected. There comes an hour when the evil
spirit takes them up into a high mountain, and
shows them the kingdoms of the world and the
glory of them, and says unto them, " All these
things will I give thee, if thou wilt fall down and
worship me " (Matt. iv. 9). The vision of universal
influence, and perhaps dominion, dawns upon the
mind. It may be a legitimate vision, destined in
some way to be realized; but the Devil suggests
that it may be realized at once, and that it may be
grasped with certainty, by some service to him—
by some untruthfulness, some convenient falsehood,
some unscrupulous act of violence and craft.

(g)

**3. Such a Temptation assailed the Hierarchy of the
Christian Church**

By exaggerating legitimate powers, by accepting convenient forgeries, by admitting the aid of
opportune violence, by using the weapons and the
agents of worldly craft and cunning, the way seemed
open and plain to the possession of all the kingdoms of the world and the glory of them. To be
just to the Popes, and to their servants, it must be
admitted that the temptation was tremendous—all
the more so because it was gradual and subtle, and
could appeal in its support to some great facts and
verities. To be conscious of having just claims to a
certain royalty over the souls of men, and yet solely
and simply to bear witness unto the truth—this is
the severest trial of human nature. But, for that
very reason, to fail in it involves a terrible fall, and
may entail spiritual ruin. When bishops, priests,
and monks were unable to say to the tempter,
" Get thee hence, Satan, for it is written, Thou
shalt worship the Lord thy God, and Him only
shalt thou serve," they entered into possession of
the kingdoms of the world and the glory of them,
but they lost the kingdom of God. When power
instead of truth became the object of the dominant
hierarchy, faith had been falsified at its source.
. . . The " ages of faith " became transformed
into the ages of superstition.

(h)

4. The Reformation

At this critical moment, the most critical,
perhaps, through which the Church ever passed,
a potent voice was heard which recalled the
elementary principles of the Gospel. The description of that Gospel given by St. Paul, that
" therein is the righteousness of God revealed from
faith to faith," was suddenly revived; and all
Christendom was stirred to its depths by the
intensity with which the truth was re-asserted
that, " The just shall live by faith." . . . Faith is
the cardinal word of the Reformation.

(i)

5. Luther

God to him was all in all. He cared for nothing in heaven or earth if he could only know, or certainly believe, that God forgave him his sins, received him, in spite of his inherent evil, into His love and favour, would purify him from his iniquity, and uphold him by His right hand. The question is of a personal relation between two persons—the one the pure and Almighty God, whose awful footsteps Luther perceived without him in the earthquake and the storm, and within in the implacable murmurs of his conscience; the other, himself, a feeble creature, conscious of innumerable sins, and sensible of numberless miseries in himself and in the world around him. If this God were his God, and he assured of it, all would be well. He would be certain of final deliverance; and meanwhile no sufferings, wants, or distresses could mar his peace. The more intensely the momentous and supreme character of this relation was apprehended, the more did it reduce into complete subordination all forms, ceremonies, and authorities, except so far as they brought the soul into direct communion with this God of infinite judgment and infinite salvation. An indulgence, or an absolution, which only released the soul from certain penalties, was not merely valueless, it was worse than nothing. It tended to obscure the vital conviction, that harmony with the will of God, at whatever cost, through whatever punishments, by whatever means, was the one necessity of the soul of man.

(a)

6. A Remedy for Pessimism, as presented in the words of the great Reformer

" The theologian of the cross,—he, that is, who speaks of a crucified and hidden God,—teaches that punishments, crosses, and death are the most precious of all treasures, and the most sacred of all relics, which the Lord Himself of this theology consecrated and blessed, not only by the touch of His most holy flesh, but also by the embrace of His supremely holy and divine will, and left them here to be truly kissed, sought, and embraced. Happy, indeed, and blessed is he whom God may deem worthy to have bestowed on him these treasures of the relics of Christ, or, rather, who understands that they are bestowed on him. For to whom are they not offered? As St. James says, ' My brethren, count it all joy when ye fall into divers temptations;' for it is not for every one to have the grace and glory to accept these treasures, but only for the most elect of the sons of God.

" Many make pilgrimages to Rome and other holy places, to see the coat of Christ, the bones of the martyrs, the homes and the footsteps of the saints. I do not condemn them. But I grieve that we should be so ignorant of the true relics— namely, the passions and crosses which have sanctified the bones and relics of the martyrs, and have made them worthy of such veneration. Not only do we fail to accept them when offered to us at home, but we repulse them with all our might, and chase them away from place to place : whereas we ought to ask God, with the utmost thirst, and with perennial tears, that He would give us such precious relics of Christ, the most sacred of all, as being the gift of the elect sons of God. . . . So sacred are these relics, so precious are such treasures, that whereas others can be preserved in earth, or, when most honoured, in gold, silver, jewels, silk, these can only be preserved in heavenly, living, reasonable, immortal, pure, holy, receptacles,—that is in the hearts of the faithful, —inestimably more precious than all the gold and jewels in the world."

(b)

7. The closing propositions of the Reformer's great Disputation

" Away with all those prophets who say to the people of Christ, Peace, peace, and there is no peace.

" Blessed be all those prophets who say to the people of Christ, the Cross, the Cross, and there is no Cross.

" Christians must be exhorted that they strive to follow Christ, their Head, through punishments, deaths, and Hell;

" And thus trust to enter heaven rather through many tribulations than through a tranquil security ! "

(c) *Dr. Wace : " The Faith of the Reformation "*

Spirit, The Holy

One of the three great articles of the Christian Faith, is a belief in God the Holy Spirit, who, in answer to prayer, bestows upon us His supernatural guidance and assistance. Assuming this to be true, there remains no room for comparison between this and the influence of purely natural culture. It seems desirable to mention this, lest, in arguing upon other grounds, this momentous power in Christian Faith should appear to be overlooked.

(d) *Dr. Wace*

" Spirit, The, and the Bride say, Come " (Rev. xxii. 17)

In God's good providence these three schools have followed each other in the order which was most conducive to the well-being of the Church. I remember listening to a sermon from the great missionary Bishop of our Church and age, then in the zenith of his fame. To others he may have been best known as the Bishop of Lichfield ; but to myself he shall always be the Bishop of New Zealand, for as such he left his impression upon me. In this sermon he applied, somewhat quaintly but with striking effect, the summons of the Apocalyptic messenger,—" The Spirit and the Bride say, Come,"—to the two lessons which the two schools of theology then prominent in the Church were commissioned especially to teach—the direct inward communion of the individual soul with God, and the functions and destiny of the Church as the Spouse of Christ. He went on to say that the order in which these two messages were delivered to the Church of England was providential —first the Spirit, then the Bride. It was essential that the lesson of the responsibilities of the individual soul should be impressed upon her first. Otherwise the doctrine of the Church would assume a hard, stiff, mechanical form. It would tend to petrifaction, not to life. We may extend this train of thought to the third school—third in point of time as well as in logical sequence ; which, when Bishop Selwyn spoke, had not yet attained to the consistency of a school, so as to claim a place by the side of the others. It might have

(e)

been perilous to the first grasp of Christian truth within the English Church, if her members had indulged too freely in speculations on the relation of the Church and the Gospel to the external domain of thought and life, before she had mastered definite conceptions of their relations to the individual soul or to the Christian society. But the time at length came when these problems were forced upon her notice. The more intimate acquaintance with the widespread religions of the East, the fuller researches of history and archæology, the rapid succession of conquests in the domain of science, the multiplication of social and political questions owing to the intensified activity of public life in all its forms—all these were factors in the world of thought and action with which the Church must reckon. We may thank God that men were found within the pale of the English Church ready to face such problems. Here is the true *breadth* of Churchmanship. It is not laxity, not dilution; but it is comprehensiveness of vision.

(a)   *Bp. Lightfoot, on Schools of Thought*

SPIRIT OF ELIAS, THE

Quick, ready, prompt to action—is doubtless good; but the Spirit of Christ—of love—is better.

(b)   *Bp. Barry*

SPIRIT, FRUITS OF (Eph. v. 9)

The good,
The right,
The true.

(c)

SPIRIT OF GOD

It is wisely and beneficially appointed that the outward helps and supports, by which in the first instance we are guided and upheld, should be taken away from us one by one, to the end that we may live more and more by faith in that which is invisible, . . . trusting and leaning on the wisdom and power of the *Spirit of God*.

(d)   *J. Hare*

SPIRIT, THE, HELPETH (Rom. viii. 26)

As in the unconverted state, the influences of the unconscious bias of the soul invade the conscious daily life with demoniacal temptation, so, *vice versâ*, does the unconscious spiritual life of the converted man come as a guardian spirit to the help of the daily life.

(e)   *Lange*

SPIRIT, THE HOLY (1 Thess. i. 5)

The call does not come through every sort of gospel preaching, but through preaching filled with the Spirit; and an essential point in the matter is the personal endowment of the preachers.

(f)   *Ibid*

SPIRIT, MINISTRATION OF THE (2 Cor. iii. 12–18, summary of)

We have:

1. The commendatory epistle, written on the Apostle's heart; and—

2. The same written on the hearts of the Corinthians.

3. The contrast between this epistle of the Spirit on the heart, and the lifeless engraving upon the Sinaitic stones.

4. The grand figure of Moses with his face irradiated by Divine glories.

5. The same, but veiled, to hide its fading splendours, and surrounded by a multitude of veiled figures with eyes turned upon him.

6. The same, but unveiled, and entering the Divine presence with more than rekindled radiance; and—

7. The same figure multiplied in the Apostle and his brethren, with unveiled faces turned towards Christ, whose light transfigures them into the glorious image of Himself.

(g)

SPIRIT OF TRUTH (John xiv. 17)

The Holy Ghost is the living personal, Divine unity of complete revelation; and, as such, the Spirit of Truth (xv. 26; xvi. 13). He is the Spirit of Truth, inasmuch as He makes objective truth subjective in believers, in order to the knowledge of truth. Objectively He is the Spirit of God (Rom. viii. 14), and God Himself (Acts v.); the Spirit of the Father (Matt. x. 20); the Spirit of Christ (Rom. viii. 9); the Spirit of the Lord (2 Cor. iii. 17), the Holy Spirit (Acts ii.) Subjectively He is the Spirit of *Truth*, the Spirit of wisdom and revelation (Eph. i. 17); the Spirit of power, of love, and of a sound mind (2 Tim. i. 7); the Spirit of adoption, of prayer (Rom. viii. 15); the Spirit of sanctification (Rom. i. 4), of life (Rom. viii. 10), of meekness (1 Cor. iv. 21), of comfort (Acts ix. 31), of glory (1 Pet. iv. 14), of sealing, of the earnest of eternal life (Eph. i. 13, 14), of all Christian charismata (1 Cor. xii. 4). As the Spirit of Truth, the Holy Ghost applies to believers the full truth of the perfect revelation of God in Christ.

(h)   *Lange*

THE SPIRIT, WITNESS OF (Rom. viii. 16)

That the world deny any such testimony in the hearts of believers, and that they look on it with scorn and treat it with derision, proves only that they are unacquainted with it; not that it is an illusion. It is a sensible and true remark of the French philosopher Hemsterhuys, in regard to certain sensations which he was discussing: "Those who are so unhappy as never to have had such sensations, either through weakness of the natural organ, or because they have never cultivated them, will not comprehend me."·

(i)   *M. Stuart*

SPIRIT, WITNESS OF (1 Cor. ii. 4)

The witness of the Spirit is taken in a sense quite too limited, when it is taken as merely a practical testimony in the conscience, the feelings, the heart, and not at the same time as a testimony borne by the Spirit of God, as the Spirit of Truth, through the medium of the thoughts of men. We know that the chief witness, on which all else depends, is that which is borne in " demonstration of power."

(j)

SPIRITUAL BIRTH (John iii. 8)

Mysteriousness is the *test* of spiritual birth.

(a) *Mozeley*

" The wind bloweth where it listeth. Thou hearest the sound thereof, but canst not tell whence it cometh or whither it goeth, so is every one that is born of the Spirit."

This was Christ's *test*.

The *test* of spirituality is, that you cannot tell whence it cometh or whither it goeth.

The conclusion is, then, that the Christian is a unique phenomenon. You cannot account for him. And if you could he would not be a Christian.

(b) *Drummond*

Two Characters :

1. Take an ordinary man of the world. What he thinks and what he does, his whole standard of duty, is taken from the society in which he lives. It is a borrowed standard : he is as good as other people are ; he does, in the way of duty, what is generally considered proper and becoming among those with whom his lot is thrown. He reflects established opinion on such points. He follows its lead. His aims and objects in life, again, are taken from the world around him, and from its dictation. What it considers honourable, worth having, advantageous, and good, he thinks so too, and pursues it. His motives all come from a visible quarter. It would be absurd to say that there is any *mystery* in such a character as this, because it is formed from a known external in-fluence—the influence of social opinion and the voice of the world. " Whence such a character cometh," we see ; we venture to say that the source and origin of it is open and palpable, and we know it just as we know the physical causes of many common facts.

2. There is a certain character and disposition of mind of which it is true to say that, " thou canst not tell whence it cometh or whither it goeth." . . . There are those who stand out from among the crowd, which reflects merely the atmosphere of feeling and standard of society around it, with an impress upon them which bespeaks a heavenly birth. . . . Now, when we see one of those cha-racters, it is a question which we ask ourselves, How has the person become possessed of it ? Has he caught it from society around him? That can-not be, because it is wholly different from that of the world around him. Has he caught it from the inoculation of crowds and masses, as the mere religious zealot catches his character? That cannot be either, for the type is altogether different from that which masses of men, under enthusiastic impulses, exhibit. There is nothing gregarious in this character ; it is the individual's own ; it is not borrowed, it is not a reflection of any fashion or tone of the world outside ; it rises up from some fount within, and it is a creation of which the text says, We know not whence it cometh.

(c) *Mozeley : " University Sermons "*

SPIRITUAL CONFIDENCE

I know that in spiritual confidence the devil will come in, as in all other good works, and cry, " Half mine ; " and so endeavour to bring you under a fearful sleep, till He whom your soul loveth be departed from the door, and have left off knocking ; and therefore, here the Spirit of God must hold your soul's feet in the golden mid-line betwixt confident resting in the arms of Christ and presumptuous and drowsy sleeping in the bed of carnal security. Therefore, so count little of yourself, because of your own wretched-ness and sinful drowsiness, that you count not also little of God in the course of His unchange-able mercy. There be many Christians, most like unto young sailors, who think that the shore and the whole land doth move, when the ship and they themselves are moved ; just so, and not a few do imagine that God moveth and saileth and changeth places, because their giddy souls are under sail, and subject to alteration, to ebbing and flowing ; but " the foundation of the Lord abideth sure." God knoweth that you are His own : wrestle, fight, go forward, watch, fear, believe, pray ; and then you have all the infallible symptoms of one of the elect of Christ within you.

(d) *Samuel Rutherford*

SPIRITUAL DISCERNMENT (1 Cor. ii. 14)

All the splendour of outward greatness pleases not the eyes of those who are engaged in intel lectual pursuits. The dignity of intellect is imper-ceptible to the rich, to kings, to conquerors, and to all the great ones of the world. The dignity of that wisdom which cometh from above, is alike imperceptible to men of the world and to men of intellect.

(e) *Blaise Pascal*

Spiritual Discernment

The source of super-sensible (super-human) truths is found in the revelation of God to man, *the Bible ;* and the source of all the truths which appertain to this earthly life, *in nature and reason :* hence supernatural truth—spiritual truth—the knowledge of the hereafter, to be looked for in the Bible, which is God's revelation to man on these matters.

But on the other hand—natural truth, the education of the mind concerning the " Now "—to be looked for in the study of nature, induction and experience.

The two lines are not identical, nor do the discoveries of science clash with revelation.

(f) *H. Stilling*

SPIRITUAL STATE, DOUBTS CONCERNING

1. You doubt from 2 Cor. xiii. 5, *whether you be in Christ or not ?* and so, *whether you be a reprobate or not ?* I answer three things to the doubt.

(i.) You owe charity to all men, but most of all to lovely and loving Jesus, and some also to your-self, especially to your renewed self ; because your new self is not yours, but another Lord's, even the work of His own Spirit : therefore, to slander His work is to wrong Himself. Love thinketh no evil : if you love grace, think not ill of grace in itself ; and you think ill of grace in yourself when you make it but a bastard and a work of nature. For a holy fear that you be not Christ's, and withal a care and desire to be His, and not your own, is not, nay, cannot be bastard nature. The great Advo-cate pleadeth hard for you; be upon the Advocate's side, O poor fearful client of Christ. Stay and

(g)

side with such a Lover, who pleadeth for no other man's goods but His own; (for He, if I may say so, scorneth to be enriched with an unjust conquest;) and yet He pleadeth for you, whereof your letter, though too full of jealousy, is a proof. For if you were not His, your thoughts, which I hope are but the suggestions of His Spirit, that only bringeth the matter in debate, to make it sure to you, would not be such, nor so serious, as these, "Am I His? or, whose am I?"

(a)

(ii.) Dare you forswear your Owner, and say in cold blood, I am not His? What nature or corruption saith at starts in you, I regard not. Your thoughts of yourself, when sin and guiltiness are round you in the ear, and when you have a sight of your deservings, are Apocrypha, and not Scripture, I hope. Hear what the Lord saith of you, He will speak peace; if your Master say, I quit you, I shall then bid you eat ashes for bread, and drink waters of gall and wormwood. But howbeit Christ out of His own mouth should seem to say, I came not for thee, as He did, Matt. xv. 24; yet let me say, the words of tempting Jesus are not to be stretched as Scripture, beyond His intention, seeing His intention in speaking them is to strengthen, not to deceive; and therefore here faith may contradict what Christ seemeth at first to say, and so may you. I charge you, by the mercies of God, be not so cruel to grace and the new birth as to cast water on your own coal by misbelief; if you must die (as I know you shall not), it were a folly to slay yourself.

(b)

(iii.) I hope you love the new birth and a claim to Christ, howbeit you do not make it good; and if you were in hell, and saw the heavenly face of lovely, ten thousand times lovely Jesus, that hath God's hue, and God's fair, fair and comely red and white, wherewith it is beautified beyond comparison and imagination, you could not forbear to say, Oh, if I could but blow a kiss from my sinful mouth, from hell up to heaven, upon His cheeks, that are a "bed of spices, as sweet flowers" (Cant. v. 13). I hope you dare say, O fairest sight of heaven! O boundless mass of crucified and slain love for me, give me leave to wish to love Thee! O Flower and Bloom of heaven and earth's Love! O angel's wonder! O Thou, the Father's eternal sealed Love. And O thou, God's eternal Delight, give me leave to stand beside Thy love, and look in and wonder, and give me leave to wish to love Thee if I can do no more.

(c)

2. We being born in atheism, and bairns of the house that we are come of, it is no new thing, my dear brother, for us to be under jealousies and mistakes about the love of God. What think you of this, that the man Christ was tempted to believe there were but two Persons in the blessed Godhead, and that the Son of God, the substance and co-eternal Son, was not the lawful Son of God? Did not Satan say, "If Thou be the Son of God?"

(d)

3. You say, that you know not what to do. Your Head said once that same word, or not far from it (John xii. 27), "Now is my soul troubled, and what shall I say?" And faith answered Christ's "What shall I say?" with these words, O tempted Saviour, askest Thou, What shall I say? Say, Pray, Father, save me from this hour! What course can you take, but pray, and trust Christ's own comforts? He is no bankrupt, take His word.

Oh, say you, I cannot pray. I answer, honest sighing is faith breathing and whispering in the ear. The life is not out of faith where there is sighing, looking up with the eyes, and breathing toward God, "Hide not Thine ear at my breathing" (Lam. iii. 56).

But what shall I do in spiritual exercises? you say. I answer: (1.) If you knew particularly what to do, it were not a spiritual exercise. (2.) In my weak judgment, you would first say, I will glorify God in believing David's salvation, and the Bride's marriage with the Lamb, and love the Church's slain Husband, although I cannot for the present believe mine own salvation. (3.) Say, I will not pass from my claim; suppose Christ would pass from His claim to me, it shall not go back upon my side; howbeit my love to Him be not worth a drink of water, yet Christ shall have it, such as it is. (4.) Say, I shall rather spoil twenty prayers, than not pray at all. Let my broken words go up to heaven; when they come up into the great angel's censer, that compassionate Advocate will put together my broken prayers, and perfume them. Words are but accidents of prayer. Oh, say you, I am slain with hardness of heart, and troubled with confused and melancholy thoughts. I answer: (i.) My dear brother, would you conclude thence that you know not well whether you are anything? I grant that, "Oh, my heart is hard! Oh, my thoughts of faithless sorrow! therefore I know not whether I am anything," were good logic in heaven amongst angels and the glorified; but down in Christ's hospital, where sick and distempered souls are under cure, it is not worth a straw; give Christ time to end His work in your heart; hold on in feeling and bewailing your hardness, for that is softness to feel hardness. (ii.) I charge you to make psalms of Christ's praises for His begun work of grace, make Christ your music and your song; for complaining and feeling of want doth often swallow up your praises. What think you of those who go to hell never troubled with such thoughts? If your exercise be the way to hell, God help me; I have a cold coal to blow at, and a blank paper for heaven; I give you Christ's caution, and my heaven surety for your salvation. Lend Christ your melancholy, for Satan hath no right to make a chamber in your melancholy; borrow joy and comfort from the Comforter; bid the Spirit do His office in you; and remember, that faith is one thing, and the feeling and notice of faith another. I am sure, you were not always, these twenty years by-past, actually knowing that you live; yet all this time you are living; so is it with the life of faith.

But alas! dear brother, it is easy for me to speak words and syllables of peace; but Isa. lvii. 19 telleth you, I create peace; there is but one Creator, you know. Oh that you may get a letter of peace sent you from heaven!

(e)   *Samuel Rutherford*

SPIRITUAL TRANSITION

You cannot step from the position of an enemy to God (for such an unconverted man is, to all intents and purposes), to the position of a friend

(f)

to God, with the same ease that you can pass from one room to another. The transition is sure to be more or less painful, trying, humiliating, saddening. Mark you, I do not bargain for mental agonies. The transition may be much easier in some cases than in others. But I *do* bargain for mental disturbance. And when such things take place, they are an illustration of our Lord's statement, "I came not to send peace on earth, but a sword."

(*a*)   *Gordon Calthrop*

SPIRITUAL AND SCIENTIFIC TRUTH (John xvi. 13; viii. 32)

The celebrated picture by Retzsch, in which Satan is represented as playing at chess with a man for his soul, and the interpretation put upon it by a great scientific teacher. That interpretation puts before us in a very real and concrete form the fact that in our mere physical life we are engaged in a great struggle with an external power, and every truth we wrest from nature is a truth which helps to set us free.

But that physical life which we live is not our whole life, nor are what we call the laws of external nature the only laws which we need to know. We are surrounded by spiritual forces in which our moral life is lived. In that moral real life we have relations with spiritual beings, some like ourselves, and some above us, and One Whom we love to call Our Father which is in Heaven. Are there no laws in that spiritual world? no truths there the knowledge of which will make us free? If the violation of physical law is death, is there no death in the moral and spiritual sphere? Is the life of the soul less real, its death less terrible, than that of the body? And if not, what do we know of the great spiritual realities which environ life? What do we know of God and our relation to Him? for on this our whole moral life depends.

(*b*)

1. **All truth gives freedom.** We hardly need to prove this in the present day. We know that in every sphere ignorance is bondage, and knowledge is power. So sure are we of it that we fearlessly argue from effect to cause. That which fetters is not true, that which frees us and gives us power cannot be false. Here then is the parallel. To know nature is to gain freedom in regard to her; to know her fully is to conform ourselves to her. And to know God is to cease to be afraid of Him; to know Him fully is to love Him perfectly, and to conform ourselves to His likeness.

Yes, people say, that proves that what is called theological truth, or truth of revelation, is not real truth. It doesn't make us free; it fetters us. No one is jealous of the great truths of science; but the truths of religion, those very truths to which the Church claims to have been led by the Spirit of Truth, are different. Surely there is something in what is so often said, that the Church is the enemy of liberty and progress, and its boasted claim to be the embodiment of the Spirit of Truth has only served to stereotype and spread a religious glow over antiquated old-world beliefs. That is why our age is jealous of the claim of a supernatural revelation. Doesn't the belief that the Spirit of Truth is eternally present in the Church, leading into all truth, carry with it a belief in that which every enlightened mind is

supposed to shudder at,—that which we only dare to speak of "with bated breath and whispering humbleness,"—that which is always laying its dead hand on speculation and free inquiry,—that which at every turn seems to cross our path and check our liberty, if we haven't explained it away as a mere survival of mediævalism,—that which recalls to our mind in a moment Popes and Councils and infallibility and anathemas, and antiquated machinery like the Holy Office and the fires of Smithfield—that one terrible word *dogma*? Was there ever a dogma which set men free, which was a source of power, and strength, and hope, and courage? To both questions we may fearlessly answer, Yes. The belief in revelation carries with it a belief in dogma; and every true dogma of Christ's Holy Church embodies a revelation, a truth about God, which, if realized in our life, is a truth which sets us free.

If that is no mere paradox, it is worth our asking on the evening of this day—the birthday of the Christian Church and a day so specially dear in the history of our own Church of England—it is worth asking why it is that there is this fear and jealousy of dogma amongst men who gladly welcome every new truth about their physical life? If all truth is from God, and every truth sets us free, why is it that men hesitate to allow these characteristics to that which above all claims to be from God, and to give us perfect freedom?

(*c*)

2. It is here that we touch the characteristic difference which exists between the laws of the spiritual and the laws of the material world. **The laws of nature are discoveries; the laws of the spiritual world are revelations.** The former are found out; the latter are given. The former are confessedly imperfect, added to continually as years go by; the latter are complete, the same yesterday, to-day, and for ever. The former claim no finality. They may be challenged, put upon their trial, called upon to justify themselves; the latter, if they are from God, claim our reverence, our obedience, our willing submission. Nor does it affect this difference, that revelation is verified in the pure heart and will, finding an echo within our best self. Revelation does not claim to reverse our natural hopes and aspirations and longings, but to lift them into a higher region, and to seal them with a supernatural authority. To ignore that authority is to forget the essential element in a revelation. Knowledge, real knowledge, which is the correlative of truth and the means of freedom, belongs both to the revelations of the Spirit in the Church and the discoveries of the interpreters of nature; but the motto of science is, *Doubt*, till you have proved, while the motto of revealed truth is always, *Believe*, in order that you may know.

(*d*)   *A. L. Moore*

SPONSORS (Mark ix. 25)

Through the faith of the father the son is healed (as in the history of the nobleman and of the Canaanitish woman). These facts tell against the Baptists. Even the blessing upon the faith of sponsors is represented by the history of the centurion.

(*e*)   *Lange*

SPONSORS

Sponsores, or God-parents = God-sibs (hence gossip)! are probably coeval with the practice of infant baptism; but they are also of heathen origin.

When heathen children were deserted by their parents, and Christian people found them, these foundlings were baptized, and sponsors stood for them.

Tertullian mentions this.

(*a*)

SPONTANEOUS GENERATION AND REGENERATION

"*He that hath the Son hath life*" (1 John v. 12)

1. Experiments have practically closed this question. A decided and authoritative conclusion has now taken its place in science. So far as science can settle anything, this question is settled. The attempt to get the living out of the dead has failed. Spontaneous generation has had to be given up.

Huxley ("*Critiques and Addresses*") categorically announces that the doctrine of Biogenesis, or life only from life, is " victorious along the whole line at the present day."

Tyndal, whilst confessing that he wishes the evidence were the other way ("*Nineteenth Century*," 1878), is compelled to say, " I affirm that no shred of trustworthy experimental testimony exists to prove that life in our day has ever appeared independently of antecedent life."

(*b*)

2. Its Religious Equivalent

For more than two hundred years a similar discussion has dragged its length through the religious world.

Two great schools here also have defended exactly opposite views—one, that spiritual life in man can only come from pre-existing life; the other, that it can spontaneously generate itself.

Taking its stand upon the initial statement of the Author of the spiritual life, one small school, in the face of derision and opposition, has persistently maintained the doctrine of Biogenesis. Another, larger and with greater pretension to philosophic form, has defended spontaneous generation.

(*c*)

3. Rationalism and Spiritual Regeneration

The difference between the two positions is radical. Using the language of science, the theory of spontaneous generation is simply, that a man may become gradually better and better until, in course of the process, he reaches that quality of religious nature known as spiritual life.

Biogenesis opposes to this the whole doctrine of Regeneration. The spiritual life is the gift of the Living Spirit. The spiritual man is no mere development of the natural man. He is a new creation, born from above. As well expect a hay infusion to become gradually more and more living until in the course of the process it reached vitality, as expect a man by becoming better and better to attain the eternal life. . . . Those who attempt to define the doctrine of the origin of the spiritual life, have nothing more to oppose to the

Rationalistic view than the *ipse dixit* of Revelation. The argument from experience, in the nature of the case, is seldom easy to apply; and Christianity at this point has always found a genuine difficulty in meeting the challenge of Natural Religion.

All that is possible in nature is an analogy; and if that can be found in Biogenesis, Christianity in its most central position secures at length a support and basis in the laws of Nature.

(*d*)

4. The Analogy

Up to the present time the analogy required has not been forthcoming. There was no known parallel in nature for the spiritual phenomena in question. But now the case is altered. With the elevation of Biogenesis to the rank of a scientific fact, all problems concerning the origin of life are placed on a different footing.

If the docrine of the spontaneous generation of spiritual life can be met on scientific grounds, it will mean the removal of the most serious enemy Christianity has to deal with, and especially within its own borders, at the present day. The religion of Jesus has probably always suffered more from those who have misunderstood than from those who have opposed it. Of the multitudes who confess Christianity at this hour, how many have clear in their minds the cardinal distinction established by its Founder between being " born of the flesh " and " born of the Spirit " ? By how many teachers of Christianity even is not this fundamental postulate persistently ignored? A thousand pulpits every seventh day are preaching the doctrine of spontaneous generation. . . . The current conception of the Christian religion, in short, —the conception which is held not only popularly but by men of culture,—is founded upon a view of its origin which, if it were true, would render the whole scheme abortive.

(*e*)

5. The Organic and Inorganic Kingdoms of Nature

In saying that there is no spontaneous generation of life, it is meant that the passage from the mineral world to the plant or animal world is hermetically sealed on the mineral side. The inorganic world is staked off from the living world by barriers which have never yet been crossed from within. No change of substance, no modification of environment, no chemistry, no electricity, nor any form of energy, nor any evolution can endow any single atom of the mineral world with the attribute of life. Only by the bending down into this dead world of some living form can these dead atoms be gifted with the properties of vitality. Without this preliminary contact with life they remain fixed in the inorganic sphere for ever. . . . If there is one thing in nature more worth pondering for its strangeness, it is the spectacle of this vast helpless world of the dead cut off from among the living by the law of Biogenesis. . . . Of the point where the organic and inorganic touch, that strange borderland between the dead and the living, science is silent. It is as if God had placed everything in earth and heaven in the hands of Nature, but reserved a point at the genesis of life for His direct appearing.

" All really scientific experience tells us that life can be produced from a living antecedent only."—" *The Unseen Universe*."

(*f*)

Spontaneous Generation, etc.—*continued*

6. The Companion Phenomenon in the Spiritual World

In the dim vision of the spiritual world presented in the Word of God, the first thing that strikes the eye is a great gulf fixed. The passage from the natural world to the spiritual world is hermetically sealed on the natural side. The door from the inorganic to the organic is shut, no mineral can open it; so the door from the natural to the spiritual is shut, and no man can open it. This world of natural men is staked off from the spiritual world by barriers which have never yet been crossed from within. . . . The spiritual world is guarded from the world next in order beneath it by a law of Biogenesis—"*except a man be born again, . . . except a man be born of water and of the Spirit, he cannot enter the kingdom of God.*" . . . "Nature is an image of grace."—*Pascal.*

It is not said—The natural man *will not* enter the kingdom of God. The word is, *cannot.* For the exclusion of the spiritually Inorganic from the kingdom of the spiritually Organic is not arbitrary. Nor is the natural man refused admission on unexplained grounds. His admission is *a scientific impossibility.* Except a mineral be born " from above,"—from the kingdom just above it,—it cannot enter the kingdom just above it. And except a man be born " from above," by the same law, he cannot enter the kingdom just above him

(*a*)

7. Life

There being no passage from one kingdom to another, the intervention of life is a scientific necessity, if a stone, or a plant, or an animal, or a man is to pass from a lower to a higher sphere. The plant stretches down to the dead world beneath it, touches its minerals and gases with its mystery of life, and brings them up, ennobled and transformed to the living sphere. The breath of God, blowing where it listeth, touches with its mystery of life the dead souls of men, bears them across the bridgeless gulf between the natural and the spiritual, endows them with its own high qualities, and develops within them these new and secret faculties, by which those who are born again are said to *see the kingdom of God.*

(*b*)

8. The Evidence that there is such a Great Gulf Fixed

Does *Science* close this gate, or *Reason*, or *Experience*, or *Revelation* ? We reply, All four.

The initial statement reaches us from Revelation, " He that hath the Son hath life, and he that hath not the Son of God hath not life." Life, that is to say, depends upon contact with life. It cannot spring up of itself. It cannot develop out of anything that is not life. There is no spontaneous generation in religion, any more than in nature. Christ is the source of life in the spiritual world ; and he that hath the Son hath life, and he that hath not the Son, whatever else he may have, hath not life. Here is the establishment in this high field of the classical formula, " *Omne vivum ex vivo*"—no life without antecedent life. In this mystical theory of the origin of life the whole of the New Testament writers are agreed.

(*c*)

9. The Necessity of Revelation

In the relation of the natural man to the spiritual man he is regarded as *dead.* He is as a crystal to an organism. The natural world is to the spiritual as the inorganic to the organic. "To be carnally minded is death " (Rom. viii. 6). If those in the organic kingdom are to know anything of the spiritual world, that knowledge must begin as revelation. Any information of the kingdom above could only come by a communication from above. It is no spell of ignorance arbitrarily laid upon certain members of the organic kingdom that prevents them reading the secrets of the spiritual world. It is a scientific necessity. No exposition of the case could be more truly scientific than this : " The natural man receiveth not the things of the Spirit of God ; for they are foolishness unto him : *neither can he know them,* because they are spiritually discerned " (1 Cor. ii. 14). The verb here is potential. This is not a dogma of theology, but a necessity of science. And science has for the most part accepted the situation. It has always proclaimed its ignorance of the spiritual world. . . . The verdict, that the natural man receiveth not the things of the Spirit of God, and that they are foolishness unto him, that *neither can he* know them, is final as a statement of scientific truth—a statement on which the entire Agnostic literature is simply one long commentary.

(*d*)

10. Practical Bearings

How decisive is the answer of Science to the practical question as to the possibility of a spontaneous development of spiritual life in the individual soul. The inquiry into the origin of life is fundamental alike to Biology and Christianity. When men are offering us a Christianity without a living spirit, and a personal religion without *conversion*, no emphasis or reiteration can be extreme. Regeneration has not merely been an outstanding difficulty, but an overwhelming obscurity. . . . Why a virtuous man should not simply grow better and better until in his own right he enter the kingdom of God, is what thousands honestly and seriously fail to understand. Philosophy cannot help us here. But Science answers to the appeal at once. If it be simply pointed out that this is the same absurdity as to ask why a stone should not grow more and more living till it enters the organic world, the point is clear in an instant.

(*e*)

11. The Specific Distinction between a Christian and a Non-Christian Man

The distinction between them is the same as that between the Organic and the Inorganic, the living and the dead. What is the difference between a crystal and an organism, a stone and a plant? They have much in common. Both made of atoms. Both display the same properties of matter. Both obey the same physical laws. Both may be very beautiful. But the plant, possessing all that the crystal has, possesses something more—a mysterious something called life. There is nothing at all like it in the crystal, not a germ of it. It is something new, original, and unique.

(*f*)

Spontaneous Generation, etc.—*continued*

When we rise from vegetable life to animal life, here again is found something original and unique. From animal life we ascend again to spiritual life. And here also is something new, something still more unique. He who lives the spiritual life has a distinct kind of life superadded to all the other phases of life which he manifests. . . . The natural man belongs to the present order of things. He is endowed simply with a high quality of the natural animal life. But it is life of so poor a quality that it is not life at all. He that hath not the Son *hath not life;* but he that hath the Son hath life—a new, distinct, and supernatural endowment. He is not of this world. He is of the timeless state, of Eternity. *It doth not yet appear what he shall be.*

The difference then between the spiritual man and the natural man, is not a difference of development, but of generation. The distinction is one of *quality,* not of *quantity.* The scientific classification of men would be to arrange all natural men, moral or immoral, educated or vulgar, as one family. One higher than another in the family group, yet all marked by the same set of characteristics—they eat, sleep, work, think, live, die. But the spiritual man is removed from this family so utterly by the possession of an additional characteristic, that a biologist would not hesitate to classify him elsewhere, not in another family, but in another kingdom. It is an old-fashioned theology which divides men into the living and the dead, lost and saved—a stern phraseology all but fallen into disuse. This difference, so startling as a doctrine, has been ridiculed or denied. Nevertheless the grim distinction must be retained. It is a scientific distinction. "He that hath not the Son hath not life."

(*a*)

12. What is this something which constitutes spiritual life?

It is CHRIST. "He that hath the Son *hath* life." "I am the Vine, ye are the branches" (John xv. 4). Three things are clear from these and similar passages.

(i.) They are not mere figures of rhetoric. They are explicit declarations. They announce a literal fact.

(ii.) Spiritual life is not something outside ourselves. The life is *in* every plant and tree, inside its own substance and tissue, and continues there until it dies. This localization of life in the individual is precisely the point where vitality differs from other forces of nature, such as magnetism and electricity. . . . The electrician can demagnetize and remagnetize a bar of iron, but the biologist cannot devitalize a plant or an animal and revivify it again. . . . Spiritual life is not a visit from a force, but a resident tenant in the soul.

(iii.) Spiritual life is not an ordinary form of energy or force.

Nature is silent about natural life, and must be so about spiritual life. In the absence of natural light we fall back upon the light of Revelation, which always shines where Nature fails. We ask with Paul, when this life first visited him on the Damascus road, What is this? "Who art Thou, Lord?" And we hear, "I am Jesus" (Acts ix. 5).

If it be objected, that this is proof from Revelation, and argument from experience, and also it must be remembered that this spiritual life is a force, and this means in science the heresy of confounding force with vitality, also we expect to be told that this spiritual life is simply a development of the ordinary life. But remember what this means in science. It is the heresy of Spontaneous Generation, a heresy so thoroughly discredited now that scarcely an authority in Europe will lend his name to it. "Who art Thou, Lord?" Unless we are allowed to hold Spontaneous Generation, there is no alternative. Life can only come from life: "I am Jesus."

(*b*)

13. The Process of Regeneration

From the analogies of biology we should expect three things:

(i.) That the new life should dawn suddenly;

(ii.) That it should come "without observation";

(iii.) That it should develop gradually.

On two of these points there can be little controversy; but it is a point of strange and frivolous dispute, that this life comes suddenly. This is the only way in which life can come. Life cannot come gradually—health can, structure can, but not life. A new theology has laughed at the doctrine of conversion. Sudden conversion especially has been ridiculed as untrue to philosophy and impossible to human nature. . . . This old theology is scientific. . . . The moment of birth in the natural world is not a conscious moment—we do not know we are born till long afterward. Yet there are men—Paul for instance—to whom the origin of the new life in time has been no difficulty, the exact moment of it could have been known. . . . The line between the living and the dead is a sharp line. When dead atoms of carbon, hydrogen, oxygen, nitrogen, are seized upon by life, the organism at first is very lowly. It possesses few functions, has little beauty. Growth is the work of time. Life is not. That comes in a moment. At one moment it was dead; the next, it lived. This is conversion, the "passing from death unto life."

(*c*)   *Drummond (condensed)*

STAND UP FOR JESUS

It is the custom now among Evangelists to ask the *Christians* present to *stand up* at certain times in their assemblies.

This, though appearing to be, is really no novelty. It is done by the members of the Church of England regularly in reciting the Creeds; and the original idea was literally that of a Christian soldier standing up to confess Christ, and declaring himself ready to fight under His banner—according to the terms of the baptismal vow.

(*d*)

STAR (Matt. ii. 2)

As Jesus adapted Himself to the fishermen by the miraculous draught of fishes; to the sick by the curing of their infirmities; and to all His hearers, by parables relating to the circumstances around and the affairs of ordinary life; so did He draw these astronomers to Himself by condescending to their favourite science.

N.B.—Just as chemistry sprung from alchemy, and war gave rise to the law of nations, so ancient

(*e*)

pagan astrology was the parent of modern astronomy. And the tendency of all true science is to point the way to faith.

(a) *Lange*

STAR, THE BRIGHT AND MORNING

(i.) It was as a star that Balaam prophesied of the coming of Christ;

(ii.) It was a *star* that guided the wise men from the East, to His cradle;

(iii.) It was under the name of "Bar-Cochba" —*the Son of the Star*, that a false Messiah, in the second century, appeared.

(b) *Oosterzec*

STARS, THE (Heaven) (John xiv)

The stars look like promises. God would never show us a thing He did not mean to give us. That is the way one boy teases another.

(c) *George Macdonald*

STIPENDS

A worthy and popular minister of this time was in receipt of exactly twenty pounds a year, when he received an invitation from another Church offering him three pounds ten a month. Tempted by such an advance, the minister made known his serious intention of accepting the call. There was considerable commotion in the neighbourhood, for he was greatly loved; and no doubt he was charged by some of his people with being guilty of a sinful love of money. After much consultation, the leading deacon informed him that, rather than suffer the loss of his removal on account of money considerations, they had made up their minds to advance his salary to twenty *guineas*. Overcome by such a self-sacrificing expression of his people's attachment, the good man stayed!

(d) *Memoir of Christmas Evans*

STRANGER AND A PILGRIM, A

In great towns, a stranger, for the first day or two after his arrival, lives purely at his own expense in an inn; afterwards, in the houses of his friends, without expense: on the other hand, if you arrive at the Earth, as, for instance, I have done, you are courteously maintained, precisely for the first few years, free of charges; but in the next and longer series—for you often stay sixty—you are actually obliged to pay for every drop and morsel, as if you were in the great earth inn, which indeed you are.

(e) *J. P. F. Richter*

STRANGERS AND PILGRIMS

If ye were not strangers here, the dogs of the world would not bark at you. You shall see all the windings and turnings that are in your way to heaven, out of God's Word; for He will not lead you to the kingdom at the nearest; but you must go through "honour and dishonour, by evil report and good report; as deceivers, and yet true; as unknown and yet well known; as dying, and behold we live; as chastened, and not killed; as sorrowful, and yet always rejoicing" (2 Cor. vi. 8-10). The world is an overcome enemy: our

Jesus has taken the armour from it: let me then speak in His words, "Be of good courage, I have overcome the world." You shall neither be free of the scourge of the tongue nor of disgraces, even if it were buffetings and spittings upon the face, as was our Saviour's case, if you follow Jesus Christ. . . . Happy are you, if, when the world trampleth upon you in your credit and good name, yet you are the Lord's gold, stamped with the King of Heaven's image, and sealed by His Spirit unto the day of your redemption.

(f) *Samuel Rutherford*

STRENGTH OF DIVINITY, EASE, POWER OF GOD

Is not the evidence of ease on the very front of all the greatest works in existence? Do they not say plainly to us, not "There has been a great *effort* here," but "There has been a great *power* here"? It is not the weariness of mortality, but the strength of Divinity, which we have to recognise in all mighty things; and that is just what we now never recognise, but think that we are to do great things by help of iron bars and perspiration. Alas! we shall do nothing that way, but lose some pounds of our own weight.

(g) *Ruskin*

STRIFE (Controversial)

The Germans have a grand legend connected with the terrific battle of Chalons (middle of 5th century), between the Visigoths and the Romans against Attila. The bloody work of the sword was done; the plain was strewed with heaps of the dead; but for three nights following—so ran the tale—the spirits of the slain hovered over the scene, and continued the strife in the air.

The like has been done again and again in the party strifes and controversies of the Church.

(h) *Christlieb*

STRIPES, CHASTISEMENT, AFFLICTIONS

It is true; to be struck once in anger, is fearful: His displeasure is more than His blow: in both, *our God is a consuming fire.*

Fear not: these stripes are the tokens of His love. He is no son, that is not beaten; yea, till he smart, and cry; if not, till he bleed. No parent corrects another's child; and he is no good parent, that corrects not his own. O rod, worthy to be kissed, that assures us of His love, of our adoption.

(i) *Bishop Hall*

STRONG, BE

Christian, on his way to the Celestial City, met and fought Apollyon and his giants too; but he got there at last.

(j)

STUDY

When you see me lounging about the garden, and pruning a rose-bush, you probably suppose I am thinking of nothing else; when, perhaps, I am deliberating on some weighty matter, on which I have to decide.

(k) *Archbishop Whately*

STUMBLING-STONE

1. They Stumbled:
  (i.) They sought salvation,
  (ii.) A salvation of personal merit,—not of grace.
  (iii.) So we, too, may stumble.

2. At that Stumbling-stone:
  = Jesus Christ: " Behold, I lay in Sion, etc.
  = a stone of trial—a touchstone; Christ divides men, as on the cross, so now; demands decision—we must take sides; He reveals the thoughts of men—"What *think* ye of Christ?"

3. He that Believeth:
  Not only " whosoever believeth," but that *faith is enough:* faith is trust: " I know whom I have trusted."

4. Shall not be Ashamed:
  = not merely "*shall not be cast out,*" or *just saved,* but, his hope is not delusive—an anchor sure and steadfast; He shall be saved—past, present, and future; He is *in* the life-boat; He is built on the sure foundation.

(a)

SUBLIME

Little by little we recede from the terrible to the contemptible.
(b)   *Longinus*

From the sublime to the ridiculous.
(c)   *Napoleon*

SUBMISSION TO CHRIST'S WILL

We can in our prosperity sport ourselves, and be too bold with Christ; yea, be so insolent as to chide with Him; but under the water we dare not speak. I wonder now at my sometimes boldness, to chide and quarrel with Christ, to nickname Providence, when it stroked me against the hair; but now swimming in the waters, I think my will is fallen to the ground of the water; I have lost it. I think I would fain let Christ alone, and give Him leave to do with me what He pleaseth, if He would smile upon me. Verily we know not what an evil it is to indulge ourselves, and to make an idol of our will; once I would not eat, except I had dainty meat; now I dare not complain of crumbs and parings under His table. Once I would make much ado, if I saw not the world carved and set in order to my liking; now I am silent, when I see God hath set servants on horseback, and is fattening and feeding the children of perdition. I pray God I may never find my will again. Oh, if Christ would subject my will to His, and trample it under His feet, and liberate me from that lawless lord!
(d)   *Samuel Rutherford*

SUBMISSION

" *Thy will,*" etc.

I know no duty in religion more generally agreed on, nor more justly required by God Almighty, than a perfect submission to His will in all things, nor do I think any disposition of mind can either please Him more, or becomes us better, than that of being satisfied with all He gives, and contented with all He takes away. None, I am sure, can be of more honour to God, nor of more ease to ourselves. For if we consider Him as our Maker, we cannot contend with Him: if as our Father, we ought not to distrust Him—so that we may be confident, whatever He does is intended for good; and whatever happens that we interpret otherwise, yet we can get nothing by repining, nor save anything by resisting.
(e)   *Sir William Temple*

SUBMISSION

Let us not charge God over hastily with the untoward incidents of life. In the main we are the manufacturers of our own life-material. If you give the weaver none but dark threads, he can only fashion a sombre pattern.
(f)   *J. Halsey*

" My will, not Thine, be done," turned Paradise into a desert. " Thy will, not mine, be done," turned the desert into Paradise, and made Gethsemane the gate of Heaven.
(g)   *E. de Pressensé*

SUBSTITUTE, CHRIST OUR

Now I saw Christ Jesus was looked upon of God, and should also be looked upon by us, as that common or public Person, in whom all the whole body of His elect are always to be considered and reckoned; that we fulfilled the law by Him, died by Him, rose from the dead by Him, got the victory over sin, death, the devil, and hell, by Him; when He died, we died; and so of His resurrection, " Thy dead men shall live, together with My dead body shall they arise," saith He (Isa. xxvi. 19). And again, " After two days He will revive us, and the third day we shall live in His sight " (Hosea vi. 2). Which is now fulfilled by the sitting down of the Son of Man on the right hand of the Majesty in the heavens, according to that word to the Ephesians, " He hath raised us up together, and made us sit together in heavenly places in Christ Jesus " (Eph. ii. 6).
(h)   *Bunyan*

Christ died.—What does Paul say, Gal. ii. 20? —" I am crucified with Christ." What does it mean? The very moment you receive Christ, you die. God regards His death as your death. You have a full acquittal. The handwriting nailed to the cross no longer stands against you. You are dead in law. Illustrate this by reference to the French recruit who had been drawn in the conscription during the Napoleon wars. He found a substitute, who was afterwards killed in battle. Later on, the first was " drawn" again; but he appeared in court and pleaded that, as his substitute was killed, he himself was dead; and the judge allowed his plea. So, accepting Christ, you die. You become dead in law.
(i)   *John Gill*

SUBSTITUTION (1 Pet. ii. 24)

The vicarious sacrificial death of Jesus, based on Isa. liii., is here affirmed with so much clearness
(j)

that even rationalists are unable to resist it. How we are healed by the wounds of Jesus, is a mystery which we cannot solve, and to which we have to submit by faith to the clear testimony of Holy Writ.

Even Dr. Baur is constrained to admit that the idea of substitution cannot be denied in such passages of the New Testament as Rom. iv. 25; Gal. i. 4; Rom. viii. 3; 1 Cor. xv. 3; 2 Cor. v. 19; that the preposition ὑπέρ denotes both the idea of substitution and what takes place for the benefit of man; that these two points are passing the one into the other, so as to interpenetrate each other, but that the latter is decidedly predominant; that according to the Apostle's doctrine the justice of God had to be satisfied by an actual atonement for the punishment of sin; that viewing the death of Jesus from the standpoint of Divine justice, is only the outer side of the event and its merely judicial aspect, but that the inmost ground of the Divinely made institution is the grace of God (Rom. iii. 24; 2 Cor. v. 19), and a point so much more extensive than the other as to constrain us to regard only as an emanation of Divine *grace* whatever Divine *justice* may claim of the death of Jesus; that it was grace that God would not allow men tó be punished in their own persons, but in their substitute.

This is certainly a wonderful testimony from the lips of an unbeliever.

(a)   *Lange*

SUCCESS

Fame, personal distinction, lucrative appointments, may, or may not come. It is a matter of little consequence. Remember the words of Thackeray, that sad and sombre humorist: "What boots it whether it be Westminster or a little country spire which covers your ashes; or if a few days sooner or later the world forgets you?"

(b)   *Storrs*

The Master seemed to have realized but small success, in His sublime mission: twelve Apostles, and one a traitor; multitudes heard His words, His final following very small. Paul, the greatest of preachers, did not appear to achieve large success: a few scattered small congregations in the various Greek cities, with error, impurity, dissension among them, and the old paganism still in part poisoning their life. But out of his labours and those of his companions Christendom has come.

(c)   *Ibid*

SUCCESS

'Tis not in mortals to command success,
But we'll do more, Sempronius; we'll deserve it.
(d)   *Addison*

SUFFERING

The world is a vast prison house under hard keepers. We are in cells, solitary and lonely, looking for a release. By the waters of earthly joy and plenty to this world's inhabitants, to our flesh; but by the waters of lively affliction to our souls, we sit down and weep, when we remember our home, from which death like a narrow stream

divides us. We hang our harps on the willows in the midst thereof; for they that oppress require of us mirth, saying, Sing us one of the songs of home. How shall we sing the song of the Lamb in a strange land; in the, to us, strangers? Oh for that home where the wicked will cease from troubling and the weary have rest; where the good fight will have been fought, the dusty labour finished, and the crown of life given; when our eyes will behold the only One that ever knew our sorrows and trials, and has borne with us in them all, soothing and comforting our weary souls. No new Friend to be made then, but an old Friend! Are you weary? So was He. Are you sad? So was He. Are you despised and laughed at? So was He. Is your love repelled, and does the world not care for you? Neither did it for Him. He has graciously taken a lower place than any of His people. Unutterably weary, sad, and lonely was He on this earth. A Man of sorrows, and acquainted with grief, and strong crying and tears. And shall we repine at our trials, which are but for a moment? We are nearing home day by day. No dark river, but divided waters are before us, and then let the world take its portion. Dust it is and dust we will leave it. "I heard a voice from heaven saying unto me, Write, Blessed are the dead which die in the Lord, even so saith the Spirit, for they rest from their labours," rest from their troubles, rest from works of weariness, from sorrow, from tears, from hunger and thirst, and sad sights of poor despairing bodies and sighing hearts, who found no peace in their prisons, from wars, and strifes, and words, and judgments. It is a long weary journey, but we are well on the way of it. The yearly milestones quickly slip by; and, as our days, so will our strength be. Perhaps before another milestone is reached, the wayfarer may be in that glorious Home, by the side of that river of life, where there is no more care, or sorrow, or crying, and rest for ever with that kind and well-known Friend. The sand is flowing out of the glass, day and night, night and day; shake it not. You have a work to do here, to suffer even as He suffered.

(e)   *Gen. Gordon*

SUFFERING (1 Pet. iii. 17)

Should the Empress determine to banish me, let her banish me; "The earth is the Lord's and the fulness thereof." If she will cast me into the sea, let her cast me into the sea; I will remember Jonah. If she will throw me into a burning fiery furnace, the three children were there before me. If she will throw me to the wild beasts, I will remember that Daniel was in the den of lions. If she will condemn me to be stoned, I shall be an associate of Stephen the proto-martyr. If she will have me beheaded, the Baptist has submitted to the same punishment. If she will take away my substance, "naked came I out of my mother's womb, and naked shall I return to it."

(f)   *Chrysostom*

SUFFERINGS

It seems appointed that much of the highest instruction should come to us (even in the Bible) through the sufferings and struggles of individual men.

(g)   *Lange*

SUFFERINGS

The people of Verona, when they saw Dante in the streets, used to say, " See, there is the man that was in Hell!" Ah, yes, he had been in Hell;—in Hell enough, in long severe sorrow and struggle ; as the like of him is pretty sure to have been. Commedias that come out *divine*, are not accomplished otherwise. Thought, true labour of any kind, highest virtue itself, is it not the daughter of Pain? Born as out of the black whirlwind;—true *effort*, in fact, as of a captive struggling to free himself: that is *Thought*. In all ways we are " *to become perfect through suffering.*"

(a)   *Carlyle*

The Port Royalist exclaimed, "Let us labour and suffer : we have all eternity to rest in." One who, fighting with wild beasts, was a spectacle to angels and men, reckoned, "that the sufferings of this present time are not worthy to be compared with the glory which shall be revealed in us."

(b)   *W. Jackson's Bampton Lectures*, 1875

SUICIDE

Beware of desperate steps. The darkest day,
Live till to-morrow, will have passed away.
(c)   *Cowper*

SUICIDE

We talked of a man's drowning himself. Johnson : " I should never think it time to make away with myself." I put the case of Eustace Budgell, who was accused of forging a will, and sunk himself in the Thames before the trial of its authenticity came on. " Suppose, sir," said I, " that a man is absolutely sure that, if he lives a few days longer, he shall be detected in a fraud, the consequence of which will be utter disgrace and expulsion from society." Johnson, " Then, sir, let him go abroad to a distant country; let him go to some place where he is *not* known ; don't let him go to the devil where he is known."

Boswell's " Johnson," concerning Eustace Budgell
(d)

SUICIDE AND PILATE

Truth is murdered (Jesus);
The *False* murders itself (Pilate).
So those whose hope is not in God.
What is suicide but this?
(e)

SUMMUM BONUM

We all recognise in the case of individuals that they may be the heirs of the highest spiritual blessings and honours, though appointed in this life to the most humble occupations. . . .
The soul of man has capacities which can never be satisfied by even the highest display of the glories of the visible creation ; and it is only in the spiritual sphere that our spirits will find their full rest and their complete career. Those only, however, can expect to be thus made rulers over many things, who have faithfully ruled over the comparatively few things committed to them in this life. Yet men have struggled with a strange persistency against this unavoidable task; and

once more in the narrative of the sacred historian did Bacon discern the nature of this perversity. Placed in the garden of Eden to dress it and to keep it, man could not be content with this simple duty, but entangled himself in speculations respecting what was abstractedly good and evil, and yielded to the first temptation which suggested to him a shorter and a pleasanter path to the full enjoyment of his life. Subsequently, through ages of weary debate and speculation men sought continually to attain the *summum bonum*—their ultimate aim and perfection—by all manner of mental, moral, and physical disciplines ; each school of philosophers, each sect of theologians, each order of Christian or of heathen monks, deeming that they had found some new tree of the knowledge of good and evil, which would introduce them to the fruit of the tree of life. But all these, from whatever quarter they approached, encountered a mysterious sword which kept the way of the tree of life, and which sent them back baffled into their wilderness. At length, in an age of moral and mental regeneration, under the light of a revived and reformed religious intelligence, a vast and patient genius was arrested by the words of the ancient record, and recognised in them that still small voice which might reveal, to quote his own image, " the clue to the labyrinth." He saw the key of all philosophy and of all life, in the statement that the Lord God had sent man forth from the garden of Eden " to till the ground from whence he was taken." While the mass of men shrank in fear, as some are still apt to shrink, from the blaze of the new knowledge which was bursting on them, he pointed to this chapter in order to remind them that it was not mere knowledge, not the natural knowledge of the world in which we live which led to man's fall, but a presumptuous attempt to intrude into the hidden mysteries of moral and spiritual truth, and attempts to seek elsewhere than in the revealed will of God for the ultimate principles of good and evil. From that moment, in proportion as men have accepted the task of labouring, according to Bacon's favourite language, " to produce fruit," in proportion as they have humbly endeavoured to assert their dominion over nature—a dominion only to be asserted by obedience—have they made advances in all departments of life greater than were ever achieved before.

(f)   *Dr. Wace, on Bacon*

SUN

The sun, which we want, ripens wits, as well as fruits.
(g)   *Milton*

SUN-WORSHIP

" *Who worshipped the creature more than the Creator* " (Rom. i. 25)

When evening came, Zadig lighted a great number of flambeaux in the tent where they were about to sup; and when his patron appeared, he cast himself on his knees before the wax lights, and thus addressed them : " Eternal and brilliant luminaries, be ye always propitious to me!" Having offered this prayer, he seated himself at table without looking at Sétoc. " What is the
(h)

meaning of this?" asked Sétoc, astonished, "I do as you do," answered Zadig, "I adore these candles, while I neglect their master and mine." Sétoc comprehended the apologue. The wisdom of his slave entered into his soul; he no more lavished incense on creations, but worshipped the Creator.

(a) *Voltaire*

SUPERFICIALITY

Solomon's religion, compared with that of David, his father, is an apt illustration of superficial religion. David's religion was bound up with the deepest depths of his being; it began at his mother's knee, it grew as he grew. He hungers and thirsts after God; his soul panteth after God as the hunted stag for the waterbrooks. When he has grieved the Spirit of God by his sins, and experiences spiritual loss and discomfort, he agonizes that God would restore unto him the joy of His salvation. There is none of this apparently in Solomon. It is true, God revealed Himself to him three times at Gibeon, at the beginning of his reign: thus he had a good start; but Solomon's religion was not deep—he never "waded through fire and through water," as David had done, to win the prize of the high calling—it did not cost him much—it came to him by inheritance, as a fortune might have done, and as he inherited his kingdom. There was all the difference between his religion and his father's that there is in the estimation one man has of money, who has plodded all his life for it, and his who inherits it without pain or toil: one knows its value, whilst the other vainly imagines it will always come to him. David's religion was cut deep, like letters cut into granite; Solomon's, like the superficial characters traced on the sand. Trial came to both (for every man's religion must be tried, to see of what sort it is); it deepens the tone of one, and rubs out impressions of the other. David becomes the man after God's heart, and ever after the human heart wrings out its anguish in his language; whilst Solomon leaves the whole religious world, from that day to this, without positive evidence whether he be a saved or a lost man, a warning to *superficiality* for all time.

(b)

SUPERNATURAL REVELATION

In proportion to a man's belief in the supernatural character of the revelation of the Scriptures, will he avoid being over-anxious or hasty in explaining or defending it. His words will always be wary and often few; and the objections which will disturb him least are that some word or deed of our Lord, or some statement of the inspired writers, is beyond the apprehension of critics. He will frequently feel it sufficient to acknowledge the imperfection of his own intelligence and experience; and in respect to many difficulties he will feel justified in replying, "We are not careful to answer thee in this matter" (Dan. iii. 16).

(c) *Dr. Wace: "Foundations of Faith"*

SUPERSTITION

From the instant the founder of Christianity left the earth, perhaps even before, this ghastly spectre of superstition ranged itself side by side with the advancing faith. It is not confined to Church or sect; it exists in all.

(d) *Shorthouse*

SUPERSTITION AND PROGRESS

The good Catholic Portuguese crossed himself, and prayed to God to shield him from all blasphemous desire to know more than his father did before him.

(e) *Mark Twain*

SUPPER, THE LAST

The death of the Girondins: = death's eve spent with singing, and sallies of gaiety, etc., etc.

"It is the manner in which the Girondins make *their* last supper."

(f) *Carlyle*

SUPPLICATION FOR THE RULERS OF THE STATE (Clement)

A peculiarly touching and sublime example of the Christian spirit, when we remember that it proceeds from the midst of the furnace of persecution:

"Thou, Lord and Master, hast given them the power of sovereignty through Thine excellent and unspeakable might, that we, knowing the glory and honour which Thou hast given them, may submit ourselves unto them, in nothing resisting Thy will. Grant unto them therefore, O Lord, health, peace, and concord, stability, that they may administer the government which Thou hast given them without failure. For Thou, O heavenly Master, King of the ages, givest to the sons of men glory and honour and power over all things that are upon the earth. Do Thou, Lord, direct their counsel according to that which is good and well-pleasing in Thy sight, that administering in peace and gentleness with godliness the power which Thou hast given them, they may obtain Thy favour. O Thou, who alone art able to do these things, and things far more exceeding good than these for us, we praise Thee through the high-priest and guardian of our souls, Jesus Christ, through whom be the glory and the majesty unto Thee both now and for all generations and for ever and ever. Amen."

Such was the prayer of the Christians of Rome in the age of Domitian, and it deserves to be quoted in its entirety as a singularly comprehensive and authoritative exposition of the spirit by which they were animated.

Dr. Wace: "The Faith of the Early Church"
(g)

SUPREMACY OF THE POPE

The Romanists have with great adroitness surrounded themselves with three walls, with which they have hitherto secured themselves so that no one should reform them, whereby the whole of Christendom has been grievously injured. In the first place, when they are pressed by the temporal power, they declare that "the temporal power has no authority over the spiritual; but, on the contrary, that the spiritual power is above the temporal." In the second place, when men re-
(h)

buke them with the Holy Scripture, they contend "that the office of interpreting the Scripture belongs to no one except to the Pope." In the third place, when threatened with a Council, they then devise "that no one can call a Council except the Pope."

(a)   *Luther*

SUSPICION

Suspicion always haunts the guilty mind;
The thief doth fear each bush an officer.
(b)

Or in the night, imagining some fear,
How easy is a bush supposed a bear!
(c)   *Shakspeare*

SWEARING

When truth's conspicuous we need not swear.
(d)   *Pomfret*

Maintain your rank, vulgarity despise;
To swear is neither brave, polite, nor wise;
You would not swear upon a bed of death—
Reflect—your Maker now may stop your breath.
(e)   *Anonymous*

I say unto you, Swear not at all; lest, by swearing, ye come to a facility of swearing; from a facility to a custom; and from a custom ye fall into perjury.
(f)   *Augustine*

SWINE

"*Suffer us to go into the herd of swine*" (Matt. viii. 31)

The once angel of light begs for a lodging inside a Gadara pig!
(g)   *Christmas Evans*

SWORD OF THE SPIRIT, THE.

With the sword of the Spirit must all our enemies be smitten, and not hinder us from entering into the heavenly Canaan.
(h)   *Bogatzky*

SYMBOLISM, CHRISTIAN

The Fish was the earliest of the Christian emblems, partly as the symbol of water and the rite of Baptism, and also because the five Greek letters which express the word Fish form the anagram of the name of Jesus Christ. In this sense we find the Fish as a general symbol of the Christian faith upon the sarcophagi of the early Christians; on the tombs of the martyrs in the Catacombs; on rings, coins, lamps, and other utensils; and as an ornament in early Christian architecture. It is usually a dolphin, which among the Pagans also had a sacred significance. About the tenth century the Fish disappeared, and the Cross became the sole and universal emblem of the Christian faith. At first the Cross had been a sign only; it was not till the sixth century that the Cross became a crucifix—no longer an emblem, but an image. The Lamb, in Christian art, is the peculiar symbol of the Redeemer, as the sacrifice without blemish; the Pelican, tearing open her breast to feed her young with her own blood, was an early symbol of our redemption through Christ; the Dragon is the emblem of sin; the Lion was an ancient symbol of the Redeemer, "the Lion of the tribe of Judah."
(i)

SYMBOLISM OF HOLY SCRIPTURE

God began to teach the Jews, intending, through them, to teach the whole world, deeper views of moral evil, deeper views of man's position in the universe, and his personal relation to the Divine. And how did God do it? By the instrumentality of that much-derided Levitical system, with its distinction of clean and unclean animals, of clean and unclean food; with its sacrifices and offerings; with its multitudinous laws about leprosy, and dress, and agriculture, and fasts, and feasts, and many other things; with its whole apparatus, in fact, of what may seem to us to be petty prohibitions and insignificant details. People laugh at the Levitical system. But why? You go into an infant school to see the skilful master teaching and training the little ones. And how does he do it? By appeals to the eye, by simple models, by roughly-sketched diagrams, by things which he sends round from form to form for the children to touch and handle for themselves. You don't laugh at *his* symbolism, gentlemen. You don't ridicule *his* "object-lessons." You know that the method which he is employing is the best way, if indeed it is not the only way, in which he can communicate truth to the feeble, undeveloped, inexperienced minds of his pupils. And why, I ask you, why should men allow themselves to ridicule God, when He condescends, out of the infinite tenderness of His love, to be the infant-school teacher of the human race? In this school the Jews learnt the nature of moral evil. They learnt to understand what a conscience is, when it has been awakened to susceptibility, and called into vitality of action. They learnt the meaning of that word "sin." And they learnt, too, though indistinctly at first, but afterwards with ever increasing clearness, by what means God proposed to meet and counteract the widespread disease of human nature.
(j)   *Gordon Calthrop*

SYMPATHY

He would put off a meditated journey, rather than leave a poor parishioner who required his services; and from his knowledge of human nature he was able, and in a remarkable manner, to throw himself into the circumstances of those who needed his help—*no sympathy was like his.*
(k)   *Chambers on George Crabbe*

SYMPATHY OF JESUS

"*In all things it behoved Him to be made like unto His brethren, that He might be a merciful and faithful high priest in things pertaining unto God, to make reconciliation for the sins of the people. For in that He . . . suffered being tempted, He is able to succour them that are tempted*" (Heb. ii. 17, 18)

1. Holy Scripture encourages us to think especially of the sympathy of Jesus.
(l)

His intercession for us at the throne is the fruit of His sympathy. As *our* High Priest, this is emphatically His quality. His human nature and His experience of human life have qualified Him for this function of Priesthood.

He could have had no such fellow-feeling had His life not been like our life, and His temptations like our temptations.

(*a*)

2. We can understand that He would easily sympathize with persons who should suffer death by crucifixion.

But in some degree He has a fellow-feeling with every human being whose lot it is to traverse *the sea of life* and *encounter its stormy billows*.

He knows all the difficulties of the navigation, for He has had to steer His own vessel through those rocky channels.

He knows how strong are the attractions that drag men down as they are trying to rise upward.

This (knowledge and experience) makes it easier for Him to identify Himself with men—to take up their troubles and their burdens, and to transact for them before the throne.

It gives emphasis to His asking for them mercy to pardon and grace to help.

For whatever experience Jesus may have with temptation, He never pleads for indulgence to any man; never asks that his sins may be passed over in silence, or not reckoned as faults.

No act of His can ever lead men to think lightly of sin. The tendency of all His dealings is the very opposite. To reveal more clearly its hateful features, as the abominable thing which God hates.

What He seeks for us is a far more thorough separation from sin than any indulgence could effect;

He seeks the entire removal of its guilt through the merit of His own propitiation, and the destruction of its power through the renewing (agency) grace of His Holy Spirit.

(*b*)

(This will tend to show the perversion of the truth in thinking that the sympathy of Mary was needed to supplement that of the Saviour, for she could not have had that experience of human sorrow that her Son had.)

And if it be true that He takes the whole case of His people to His heart, and that He feels their troubles as if they were His own, is there anything further to be desired?

(*c*)

And now, who can estimate the grandeur of the privilege of being in the fullest sense the object of this sympathy of our Lord?

(*d*)

(i.) Blessedness of this

How *blessed*, to think, in regard to any of us, that He takes us up into His heart just as we are, and that He cannot rest till all our *sorrows and troubles*, all our *disorders* and *perversities*, are brought to an end!

(*e*)

(ii.) Security of this

What *security* does not this give us that our blessed Redeemer will persevere in the work which He has taken in hand!

(*f*)

(iii.) Confidence

What *confidence* that He who hath begun a good work in us will carry it right to the end!

His love is not a thing of fits and starts;

His kindness is not whimsical or fantastic = that turns with butterfly rapidity from one object to another. Having once loved His own, He loves them unto the end. Having once taken them into His heart, and identified Himself with them, He cannot renounce them any more than He can renounce Himself;

He can no more cease to feel their troubles than if they were His own.

He has charged Himself with them and He cannot disown the charge.

He has agreed to conduct them to their Father's house; and at the end of His undertaking He is to say to His Father, "Those that Thou gavest me I have kept, and none of them is lost, but the son of perdition; that the Scripture might be fulfilled."

(*g*) *Blaikie*

T

TABLE—ALTAR

Round that Table we become one with each other, because we become one in Christ. And here, again, the original position of the Table in all the older churches of Christendom was a testimony to this solemn truth. In all the churches where the ancient arrangement has been preserved, the Table stands, not at the eastern extremity of the church, but in the centre—the clergy seated on one side and the congregation on the other; literally in the midst of the whole congregation. So also it was placed in all common English churches for the first century after the Reformation. So also, during some portions, at least, of that period it was in this Abbey. But even before that time—in fact, since the thirteenth century—it has, owing to the peculiar conformation of the building, been far more nearly in the midst of the church than in most cathedrals; and though this arose from other causes, yet when we look at it in its present position, with the long vista extending behind it eastward, and before it westward, we may remark that this central situation represents to us the original idea of the primitive Eucharist, the centre of the whole Christian worship.

Dean Stanley : The Altar of Westminster Abbey
(a)

The word "altar" is not to be found in the Communion Service from beginning to end. The epithets applied to it are—"the Table," "the Lord's Table," "the Holy Table."
(b)   *R. Glover*

The TABLE: its very name and shape and material remind us of that simple repast in the Upper Chamber at Jerusalem. So it was always called in the early ages; so it is still called in the Eastern Churches; so it was always called in our own Prayer-book. In itself we need care little of what it is made—wood or stone, or gold or brass; yet assuredly, if for a moment one may dwell on such a mere outward detail, it is interesting to remember that wood, the usual material of our ordinary tables, was the material from the earliest times, in East and West, of our Holy Tables also; that such, too, after a long interval, it again became at the Reformation; and that such, in the midst of all these brilliant surroundings, it is still in this place. Our richly-adorned Table is the successor of the plain board which served for the Last Supper at Jerusalem—of the rough planks which still at Rome represent what is believed to be the holiest and most venerable Altar in the city of St. Peter—of the simple oaken table which from the Reformation almost down to the present century stood in this place. Despise not the name, or the thing, or the form; the more we remember how homely was it in its origin, how primitive in its outward shape and fashion—the more does it deserve to be honoured as the monument of the most sacred and pathetic parts of the Christian story. It is the fittest memorial of Him whose home was the home of the humble workman, the carpenter Joseph—of Him who was Himself a carpenter, labouring with the toil of an Eastern workman, under the hot sun of the East, till the day's work was over—of Him who adorned by the first miracle that He wrought the festive gathering of Cana—who declared His acts of mercy chiefly by His feeding the hungry multitudes—who was known to His disciples chiefly by the breaking of bread—by the sacred meal in which He parted from them, by the sacred meal in which He met them again in the joy of His resurrection. They who kneel before it, who receive from it the strength which its sacred ordinance gives, will remember that its holy and elevating power depends on its homely significance—the Table of all our common tables, as the Bible is the Book of books.
(c)   *Dean Stanley*

TABLE OR ALTAR

The Holy Table—the ALTAR. This is a title which has no direct warrant from Scripture, from the primitive Church, or from the Prayer-book. The name "Altar" is not applied to the Holy Table in any part of the New Testament, or in any author of the first three centuries (with, perhaps, two doubtful exceptions), or in any part of the Prayer-book. But it is so commonly employed, that we may well ask whether there is not a sense in which it may, after all, be lawfully used. If the name may be anywhere lawfully used, it is here [that is, in Westminster Abbey]. In the Coronation Service, which has the authority of the Privy Council of the Sovereign, and which is used within these walls and nowhere else, our Table is called "an Altar." This one exception, therefore, will justify us in considering in what sense the word "Altar," according to common usage, may be employed for our sacred Table—what additional reason is hereby given for its embellishment and glorification.

"An Altar" means a place where sacrifice is offered. Is there any sense in which the Bible and the Prayer-book acknowledge the offering of sacrifice at our Holy Table? There is one passage, most impressive and most important, in our Communion Service, and one alone, in which the word "Sacrifice" is so used. It is that prayer in which, after the Communion, we offer to God, "the reasonable, holy, and living sacrifice of ourselves, our souls and bodies," to be accepted, notwithstanding our manifold unworthiness, "as our bounden duty and service." This is the true Christian sacrifice, which may well entitle any place where we offer it to be called an Altar. This sacrifice, not made by the priest or minister, but by the people—this offering, not of dead or dumb materials, but of living spiritual beings—this pledging of ourselves to our Master's service, is that which specially belongs to the Holy Sacrament of the Lord's Supper, and which may make the spot at which we offer it to be, in an especial sense, the true altar of the Christian's worship.
(d)   *Ibid*

"TAKE EAT," Compared with "THOU SHALT NOT EAT"

Man ate in utter ignorance of the sequel, in the case of the forbidden fruit, for death was not then known; so man may eat in utter ignorance of the sequel, in the case of sacramental bread. In the first case he ate' in trust in self, distrust in God, and communion with Satan. In the second case he eats in trust in God, distrust in self, and communion with God. To the world both eatings are foolishness, yet they are the wisdom of God.

(a)   *General Gordon*

TALKERS — LEARNED TATTLERS — WORD SPINNERS

A painter can draw a rose,—a likeness of it in figure and colour,—yet he never can paint the fragrance.

(b)   *Cudworth*

TASTE—TALK

They never taste who always drink;
They always talk who never think.

(c)   *Prior*

TAX-PAYING

A grudging compliance with public duties is the sign of an inferior manhood. A man who studies the welfare of the community in which he lives, on every side, and glories in being permitted to contribute to it, is a true patriot. I have heard of men who boasted of the amount of service they rendered to their country in time of war—of how many years they served and how many victories they achieved—but I do not know that in my life I ever met a man who with serene pride said, "I am taxed higher than any other gentleman in this community, for the welfare of the city, and I glory in it; I thank God that I am permitted to be chief among the men who contribute of their means every year for the welfare of the city." I think I never heard two men quarrel for the privilege of paying a little more tax one than the other. I do not know that I ever knew a man who rejoiced to pay his taxes. Yes, here he is. I recollect that when during the war the Internal Revenue taxed incomes, and I had written a little book called "Norwood," which, through the generosity of the publisher of the *New York Ledger* had brought me in a larger sum than I ever expected to make, my income in a certain year was a very considerable one. There were several men in my neighbourhood who could have bought me out ten times over; and I took notice that there was not one of them that paid as much tax as I did. I think I paid a larger tax that year than did any of eight or ten millionaires. What had become of their property? I never inquired; but I think there will be a little inquiry about it in the Judgment-day. I think there will be a good many inquiries about men's courses as related to the public at the final judgment. I think that a man who is a thief—as every man is who withholds from the public that which belongs to it—will have an account to settle for his misdemeanour in the last great day. I think that in that day no man will be accounted a man of honour or a good

citizen who has not a desire for the welfare of the city, the town, the State in which he dwells, which makes him willing to contribute to the expenses and to bear his proportion of the burdens of the Government. Honesty, honourableness, emulation in the maintenance of public economy should be one of the characteristics of a manly man.

(d)   *H. W. Beecher*

TAYLOR, JEREMY

Taylor's was a great and lovely mind; yet how much and how injuriously was it perverted by his being a follower of Laud, and by his intensely popish feelings of Church authority! His "Liberty of Prophesying" is a work of wonderful eloquence and skill; but, if we believe the argument, what are we to come to? Why, to nothing more nor less than this, that—so much can be said for every opinion and sect, so impossible is it to settle anything by reasoning or authority of Scripture—we must appeal to some positive jurisdiction on earth, *ut sit finis controversiarum.* In fact, the whole book is the precise argument used by Papists, to induce men to admit the necessity of a supreme and infallible head of the Church on earth. It is one of the works which pre-eminently gives countenance to the saying of Charles II. or James II.—I forget which—"When you of the Church of England contend with the Catholics, you use the argument of the Puritans; when you contend with the Puritans, you immediately adopt all the weapons of the Catholics." Taylor never speaks with the slightest respect or affection of Luther, Calvin, or any other of the great Reformers; at least, not in any of his learned works; but he saints every trumpery monk or friar, down to the very latest canonizations of the Pope. I fear you will think me harsh when I say that I believe Taylor was, perhaps unconsciously, half a Socinian in heart.

(e)   *Coleridge, " Table Talk "*

TAYLOR, JEREMY

He had the good humour of a gentleman, the eloquence of an orator, the fancy of a poet, the acuteness of a schoolman, the profoundness of a philosopher, the wisdom of a chancellor, the sagacity of a prophet, the reason of an angel, and the piety of a saint. He had devotion enough for a cloister, learning enough for a university, and wit enough for a college of virtuosi; and had his parts and endowments been parcelled out amongst his clergy that he left behind him, it would perhaps have made one of the best dioceses in the world.

(f)   *Ruet*

TEACHER

There is no office higher than that of a teacher of youth; for there is nothing on earth so precious as the mind, soul, character of the child. No office should be regarded with greater respect.

(g)   *Channing*

TEARS

The tears of penitents are the wine of angels.

(h)   *St. Bernard*

TELL JESUS

"*And his disciples went and told Jesus*" (Matt. xiv. 12)

1. Explain the occasion

You can understand this if you have been left with the body of a friend : afterwards, when all is over, you have gone and told Jesus.

(*a*)

2. A lesson for us under conditions of trouble

Suppose you have

(i.) *Troubles in your life*=swine in a flower-garden = Goths in Italy. What to do ? "*Go and tell Jesus.*"
Hezekiah did so when he got that terrible letter.
Paul did so = "thorn in the flesh."
Answer = "My grace is sufficient for thee."

(*b*)

(ii.) Or under a *sense of sin :*
(Heathen) your conscience lashing you with whips of scorpions, like the "*Furies*" = (conscience).
(Jewish) or pursuing you, like the "*manslayer.*"
Again, what to do ? "*Go and tell Jesus*" = your city of Refuge = "no more conscience of sin."
David did so, "I confessed . . . and Thou forgavest" = "Thy sins be forgiven thee."
Cf. also Macbeth. You cannot pass the man whom you have wronged.

(*c*)

(iii.) Or are you *persecuted, slandered, misunderstood.*
It must be so—*e.g.* Joseph.
Opposites = flesh and spirit, (Ishmael and Isaac) ; (Herod and John) ; (Cain and Abel) ; (Balaam and Moses) ;
(Saul, David) ; (Esau, Jacob) ; (Jezebel, Elijah) ; (the Devil and Christ).
So, if you are a Christian, there is some person wishing you evil. What to do ? Stamp it out ? Contradict ? Better—"Go and tell Jesus," = good company to be in, "If they persecuted me," etc. "Blessed are ye whom men shall revile," etc. "Rejoice," etc.

(*d*)

TELL JESUS (TROUBLE)

History tells us that the Goths and Vandals of Northern Europe, a rough, rude, uncultivated, semi-savage race, came rushing down from the North in vast hordes, invading the sunny plains of southern Europe. In the beautiful cities of Italy they found the choicest treasures of art, painting, and statuary; but these appealed to no tastes, and possessed no value for the invaders, who showed no desire to possess them. In their eyes, treasures such as these were but as so much useless lumber. Hence it was that the fairest palaces of marble were ransacked and burnt, the statuary was shivered to pieces, the paintings slit, and the choicest treasures were trodden under foot.

The barbarians were but as a herd of swine turned into an elegant drawing-room, making havoc with rude foot and tusk, rooting up and spoiling the treasures of civilization.

This finds its parallel in life.

We have, perhaps, had many years of comfort, many blessings, many joys, much happiness, and few trials. "The lines have fallen unto us in pleasant places," "we have a goodly heritage."

But after a while the north wind begins to blow, and a cloud no bigger than a man's hand rises on the horizon. Little by little our sky becomes overcast, our comforts decline, wintry weather sets in, the hurricane roars around our dwelling, many a tree that we thought stood firm is rooted up. Rough-handed troubles, like wild beasts, come swooping down upon us. They tear away our treasures, break down our idols, tread under foot our vines, and trample upon our flowers. We seem to lose everything. The brightness and the sunshine go out of ourselves.

What can we do? Go and tell our friends. They tell us, perhaps, that it is our own fault, that we have been unwise, and ought to have foreseen and made provision for reverses.

Shall we do this, and expect consolation? Rather let the disciples of John show us a more excellent way : "They went and told Jesus;" and the best thing we can do, will be to go and do likewise.

(*e*)

TEMPERANCE CAUSE, THE

Also I prefer a country where I don't make bad blood by having to see one public house to every six dwellings—which is literally the case in many spots around us. My gall rises at the rich brewers in Parliament and out of it, who plant these poison shops for the sake of their million-making trade, while probably their families are figuring somewhere as refined philanthropists or devout Evangelicals and Ritualists.

(*f*)   *George Eliot*

TEMPORAL THINGS (2 Cor. iv. 18)

The things seen are temporal; those not seen are eternal.
The contrast is between things *seen* and *unseen*.
Things as they are = an enigma, but they produce
(i.) Men of Faith ;
(ii.) Infidels.
Because the former believe that God governs, and all will therefore end well; whilst the latter think things ought to be different, and argue that a good God would not permit what is.

(*g*)

TEMPTATION

1. Luke xxii. 31–34, "Simon, Simon, *Satan hath desired*," etc.
2. John xiii. 27, "*After the sop Satan entered into Judas.*"
3. John xiv. 30, "*The Prince of this world cometh and hath nothing in Me.*"
The passages are connected and form a whole.

(*h*)

1. Doctrine. Satan is Present at Critical Periods

(i.) At the beginning of our Lord's ministry ;
(ii.) Again now, at His Passion ; for both were critical moments. In the first he tempted by the allurements of life : in the second, by the awfulness of death.

(*i*)

2. Doctrine. The Temptations of Satan are real Dangers

(i.) He comes to the Lord . . . "He hath nothing in Me" ("Being in an agony, He prayed").

(ii.) He comes to Peter . . . "Satan hath desired to have thee" (Peter's security is threatened).

(iii.) He comes to Judas . . . And "entered into him" (he gains him).

(*a*)

3. Doctrine. The danger we are in from the Tempter is from the greater or less amount of alloy in us

(i.) JUDAS an easy conquest. The alloy is great;

(ii.) PETER—much alloy—or chaff, the sifting reveals it—but he loves the Lord, and is prayed for. There is wheat too. He is nearly wrecked, but he gets through it.

(iii.) THE LORD—no alloy. He is tempted, tried, there is prayer, an agony, but He gives up His will to His Father's. The tempter *finds nothing in Him*, no dross, no alloy, no chaff.

As Christians, we are sure to have a moment (or moments) such as this—

(i.) If we are merely nominal followers of Christ, we shall probably fall utterly;

(ii.) If we are true Christians, we may fall to rise again;

(iii.) The more we are like Christ, the less power will the Tempter have over us.

(*b*)

TEMPTATION

Satan will seldom come to a Christian with a gross temptation; a green log and a candle may be safely left together; but bring a few shavings, then some small sticks, and then larger, and you may soon bring the green log to ashes.

(*c*)   *John Newton*

TEMPTATION

We are told that when Ulysses was passing by the coast of the Enchanted Isle, where the Sirens lived and sang, he had to have his ears stopped with wax, and himself bound to the mast of the ship, lest he should wish to stop and listen to their song, and so become intoxicated with pleasure, and never get beyond that shore, as had been the case with all others.

(*d*)

TEMPTATION

"*There hath no temptation taken you but such as is common to man: but God is faithful, who will not suffer you to be tempted above what ye are able; but will with the temptation also make a way of escape, that ye may be able to bear it*" (1 Cor. x. 13).

1. Temptation = proof, trial, direct temptation to sin, calamity, affliction, a putting to the proof, subjecting one to trial and testing;

2. "Taken you" = seized upon you, encountered you for the purpose of trial;

3. "Common to man" = simply "human," or suited to human nature;

4. "God is faithful" = true to His promises—trusty, veracious, indubitable, certain, sure, unchangeable.

5. "Suffer you" = allow, permit, suffer to be done = "To commit a ship to sea and let her drive" (Acts xxvii. 40).

6. "To be tempted" = Cf. 1.

7. "A way of escape" = "A way out," egress, result, issue, or means of clearance or of successful endurance.

8. "To bear it" = to bear under, or to bear up under it, support, sustain, to endure patiently, to undergo.

Hence

There hath no temptation for the purpose of putting your principles to the test, in subjecting them to a trial of afflictions and calamities (as the precious metals are tried by fire), seized upon you, or encountered you, but such as is *human* and *suited* to the nature (the individual nature) of man. God, however, is faithful—having promised I will never leave you nor forsake you, "He is faithful who hath promised." He is to be remembered in this matter as indubitably veracious and unchangeable, who will not allow, permit, or suffer you to drift away as a rudderless ship committed to a rough sea, to be tempted and tried and tested above what ye are able, so as to make shipwreck of the faith; but will also make, with the temptation (*i.e.*, the testing and trying circumstance), a way out of it, by enabling you to endure it till the end is gained, that ye be not overcome of it, but bear up under it, and endure patiently; till in the end it may be said of you as it was of Abraham: "And it came to pass that God did no more tempt Abraham" (*i.e.*, did no more try him). Why? Because his principles were found abiding, his character as a man of faith was established. But when the "Accuser and Calumniator of the Brethren," brought against him the accusation as against Job, "Doth this man serve God for nought," he was proved a liar. For the saint had been made a spectacle to angels and to men, and his faith had stood the test, and had been found unto the praise and glory of God. Cf. Ps. lix. 17.

(*e*)

TEMPTATION (Matt. iv.)

Frequent conflicts render the Christian strong. They fit ministers for their work—*oratio, meditatio, tentatio, faciunt theologum.*

(*f*)   *Starke*

TEMPTATION

St. Austin observes, that there is in every man a Serpent, an Eve, and an Adam. Our senses and animal nature are the Serpent; our concupiscence is the Eve; and the Adam is our reason. Nature continually *tempts* us, concupiscence often covets, but sin is never finished, unless reason gives consent.

(*g*)   *Blaise Pascal*

TEMPTATION

I find it most true, that the greatest temptation out of hell is to live without temptations; if my waters would stand, they would rot. Faith is the better for the free air and the sharp winter storm in its face; grace withereth without adversity. The devil is but God's master-fencer, to teach us to handle our weapons.

(*h*)   *Rutherford*

TEMPTATION OF ADAM

"*There hath no temptation taken you but such as is common to man; but God is faithful, who will not suffer you to be tempted above that ye are able; but will with the temptation also make a way of escape, that ye may be able to bear it*" (1 Cor. x. 13)

An Old Testament example of a New Testament doctrine.

Compare—

Tribulation and Temptation

1. = Winnowing, sifting chaff from wheat, so Peter was sifted, the dross from the metal.

2. = Trial, as a test of strength:

Adam's and Christ's obedience; Abraham's faith; a Christian's genuineness tested.

(a)

Temptation

1. Is common to man;

2. Not greater than our capacity to resist it;

3. There is always a way of escape.

Take Adam's as an illustrative case.

(b)

1. Common to man, because necessary

"There hath not . . . common to man;" affirmed by Peter, "Think it not strange concerning the fiery trial which is to try you, as though some *strange* thing happened unto you." It is necessary for all; and *common* to us all.

Not merely Adam was tempted by a peculiar temptation; Christ by another; some by another and another, whilst others escape; but every one is tempted. It is the common lot, as much as birth and death are. There comes an hour of *trial* for all, none escapes.

You may not be tempted to take a forbidden apple, but you will be so placed between inclination and duty, that your whole future will be affected by your choice.

It is a condition of life.

Such an hour came to Adam, to Christ, and will come to every one.

Hence

(i.) The prayer, "Lead us not into temptation."

(ii.) The exhortation, "Watch and pray, lest ye enter into temptation."

(iii.) The commendation, "Blessed is the man that endureth temptation."

Since, then, temptation is common, all that was peculiar in Adam's temptation was, that he bore the brunt of the storm first, and his choice involved the whole race in its consequences.

It is necessary, in reviewing Adam's conduct under temptation, first, to form a correct estimate of the man.

"Aristotle was but the rubbish of an Adam" (*South*) affords no help, no guidance, if it is meant that Adam was a giant compared with Aristotle; such was not the case.

Adam was but a grown-up child; his gifts and talents were latent powers.

His innocency was but untried innocence.

His goodness was but negative, not his own, but born in him, not of choice, not acquired—the goodness of inexperience.

Adam could not help being good.

Compare it with the goodness of well-born and bred children in well-regulated families; at its best it is but *negative* goodness—no more.

But at the outset it was necessary that Adam should be the author of his own goodness; he is the creator of his own *character*, and thus he helped to make himself.

And the supreme moment for his choice came, as it does to all, in temptation.

Will he remain obedient, or can he be brought down?

(c)

Adam, like Christ, and like us all, could only be *perfected* through temptation.

God created him a "living soul," but left him to create his own character, or moral goodness.

Take the case of a young man of godly training, happy home, father proud of him, "so *good*," "so pure," "so innocent," all who know him "love him;" but this is so far merely *negative goodness*.

Place him at school, college, business, amidst evil companions and fresh surroundings. Forbidden pleasures appeal to his senses = "Read this immoral French novel;" "Go to that licentious play;" "Taste, just taste, this forbidden pleasure." Thus you find out his strength of character. Then the moment for him has come, as to whether he can stand the test or no. It is his temptation, a repetition of exactly the same thing that we read of in Genesis.

Temptation is common to man, because necessary to the formation of character and principles, and carries with it the future life, and gauges a man's moral worth.

(d)

2. Temptation is not greater than our capacity to resist it

Ask, Was this true of Adam's temptation? What could he, in his inexperience, know of assaults of this kind?

If but a child, innocent, what knowledge of "the wiles of the devil," or of "the depths of Satan" had he? Adam was apparently more a *victim* to his circumstances than a voluntary sinner.

Examine this:

(i.) Adam was as able to resist temptation as ever man was, or is;

(ii.) It is often said that his temptation was "too trifling" for the consequences involved.

The mere taking of an "*apple*" too contemptible for serious thought;

(iii.) But here rests the very point of the argument: "Too trifling;" but the argument is, that Adam was but a child, and had but a child's innocence, and capacity to resist. "A trifling temptation," because it was a temptation to but a child's strength. The burden was not too heavy for the back.

It was no subtle temptation like our Lord's, under which He fainted and "suffered being tempted." If Adam was but a child, then his temptation was but that of a child.

Hence God was faithful to him, and did not suffer him to be tempted above what he was able to bear.

(e)

3. There is always a way of escape

We come into temptation, but a door to escape by is always open to us. We have our choice of falling or escaping.

(f)

Examine, next, where this way of escape lay for Adam.

(i.) Temptation always comes from a sphere *below* ourselves.

The seducer is on a lower level than the seduced; he seeks to dethrone you. This is devilry.

(ii.) God did not permit temptation to approach Adam as from "an angel of light." Above him, then no power of resistance, no escape. Adam was no match for an angel of light.

But the case stands like this:

(1.) Adam was created in the "image of God," was without his equal, higher than other created earthly beings, he both knew and exercised his superior gifts; and when temptation came from the sphere of the brute creation he could have discerned it, and escape was easy.

(2.) His position over the brutes was that of master, Adam was the *lord of creation*, "Have thou dominion over the beasts of the field, and over the fish of the sea, and (specially) *over every creeping thing which creepeth on the earth*" = forewarning; and when temptation came from this sphere, escape was open to him.

Add to this

(3.) Adam had a knowledge of the brute creation. Their gifts and endowments were known to him.

They were brought to him, and received their names from him; "What he called each, that was the name thereof." And their names signified their peculiar and special characteristics.

When therefore the serpent came speaking in *man's voice*, his own peculiar endowment, why did he not flee, as we do now from a serpent?

When this thing spake calumnious words against the good God, His Maker, *why did Adam listen?*

When he proceeded to tell LIES, "Ye shall not surely die," think you, Adam's conscience did not indicate that something was amiss, some devilry was at work, and the moment was come for him—not to hesitate, not to parley, but to flee; and, as we all must in such critical moments, to take the door of escape that is always open to us, and was truly open to him then?

(*a*)

4. After the Temptation and the Fall, look how "goodness" and character have evaporated

Can there be any more miserable picture than that of Adam laying the blame on his wife; or of the woman laying the blame on the serpent?

And yet, this is daily repeated in excuses for sin.

The blame is laid on our,

(i.) Circumstances (where placed).

(ii.) Constitution (on our peculiar temperament and strong passions).

No one blames himself, no one gives God the credit for His faithfulness,

(i.) For sending him trial, as a necessary thing;

(ii.) For taking care that *his* trial was not greater than he was able to bear;

(iii.) For making a way of escape; but the blame is thrown upon God, when a man blames his circumstances and his temperament.

Lastly, it is well to be reminded that as,

(i.) Adam's fall carried us all with him, so the

(ii.) "Second Adam's" victory over temptation carries all with Him, and in Him we are "more than conquerors." "As in Adam all die, so in Christ shall all be made alive."

We are in *Adam* without a doubt; but to secure

the blessings of Christ's victory we must be in Him. *Are we in Him?* That is the question which each must answer.

First, the natural, weak, faulty man, *Adam*;

Secondly, the spiritual, heavenly, victorious man, Jesus Christ.

(*b*)

TEMPTATION AND AFFLICTION

For I am persuaded, it is a piece of the chief errand of our life, that God sent us for some years down to this earth, among devils and men, the fire-brands of the devil, and temptations, that we might suffer for a time here amongst our enemies; otherwise He might have made heaven to wait on us at our coming out of the womb, and have carried us home to our country without letting us set down our feet in this knotty and thorny life. But seeing a piece of suffering is carved to every one of us, less or more, as Infinite Wisdom hath thought good, our part is to harden and habituate our soft and thin-skinned nature to endure fire and water, devils, lions, men, losses, as those that are looked upon by God, angels, men, and devils.

(*c*)   *Samuel Rutherford*

TEMPTATION AND AFFLICTION

Remember that a time of affliction is a time of temptation. Satan will not be wanting in any opportunity or advantage of setting upon the soul. When Pharaoh heard that the people were entangled in the wilderness, he pursued them. And when Satan sees a soul entangled with its distresses and troubles, he thinks it his time and hour to assault it. He seeks to winnow, and comes when the corn is under the flail. Reckon therefore, that when trouble cometh, the prince of this world cometh also, that you may be provided for him. Then is the time to take the shield of faith, that we may be able to quench his fiery darts. If they be neglected, they will inflame the soul. Watch, therefore, and pray, that you enter not into temptation, that Satan do not represent God falsely unto you. He that durst represent Job falsely to the all-seeing God, will, with much more boldness, represent God falsely unto us, who see and know so little. Be not then ignorant of his devices, but every way set yourselves against his interposing between God and your souls, in a matter which he hath nothing to do with. Let not this make-bate by any means inflame the difference.

(*d*)   *John Owen*

TEMPTATION

"*Lead us not into temptation*"

Very strikingly do the Gospels illustrate for us our danger, and the daily value of this petition. At about the same time strong temptation came to our Lord, to Peter, and to Judas Iscariot. It came to our Lord; but the tempter found *nothing in Him*, no point of vantage. It came to Peter, secure as he thought himself from its attacks; heedless, therefore, and unwatchful, he entered into temptation and fell; the tempter found *something in him*, and used his opportunity. Temptation came also to the unhappy traitor, and carried all before it, the tempter entered into him, and made him his prey.

(*e*)

Temptation and Sin

He forced Him not ; he touched Him not ; only said, " Cast Thyself down : " that we may know, whosoever obeyeth the devil, casteth himself down : for the devil may suggest, compel he cannot.

(a)   Chrysostom

TEMPTER, THE

" But deliver us from evil "

Behind *temptation* and *evil* there is here recognised the baneful agency of a personal *tempter*, an *evil one*. Our great writers of fiction invariably have a demon in human character plotting the ruin of a hero or heroine ; but whose malevolent designs are, as a rule, thwarted by a counteracting good agency. And this, to those who see below the surface of things, is true to life. The Holy Scriptures tell the children of God that they have, in a fallen spirit, an unscrupulous foe, who is the *father of lies; your adversary the devil*, who goeth about as a roaring lion, seeking whom he may devour ; the calumniator of God, and of all that is good ; *the accuser of the brethren*, whose assaults they must encounter, with whom they will have to wrestle, against whom they must watch and pray ; and, in order to withstand and resist him successfully, they must arm themselves with the panoply of God. And this prayer, to be *delivered from evil*, is a cry to " the Stronger than the strong," for help in an unequal contest ; to the " Advocate with the Father," for His interposition on our behalf ; to the " Good Shepherd," to deliver His sheep from the teeth of the destroyer and " to save them to the uttermost," both of peril and of need.

(b)

TEN COMMANDMENTS

A keen observer of mankind has expressed it, perhaps with too much bitterness, but certainly with a great deal of truth, in some lines, which he calls " The Latest Decalogue," or the Ten Commandments as kept by the world.

Do not think, while I am quoting them, that the writer intended to throw scorn upon the Commandments. He felt scorn, indeed, but his scorn was for the human gloss, not for the Divine document. I pass over the version which he supposes the world to give of the first three Commandments, though it constitutes a poignant satire on the indifference of men to the truth of God's very existence—on their cultivation of the secret idolatry condemned by an Apostle—and on their refraining from swearing and evil language, not from fear of God, but from motives of a much lower character. I will only say of it that it recalls most strongly Lord Chesterfield's well-known recommendation to his son, which he enunciates with as much gravity as though it were a high-toned inculcation of piety. " Depend upon this truth," says that worldly philosopher, " that every man is the worse looked upon and the less trusted for being thought to have no religion . . . ; and a wise Atheist, if such a thing there is, would for his own interest and character in this world, pretend to some religion."

(c)

2. I begin with the Fourth Commandment :

" At Church on Sundays to attend
Will serve to keep the world thy friend.
Honour thy parents—that is, all
From whom advancement may befall.
Thou shalt not kill, but needst not strive
Officiously to keep alive.
Do not adultery commit,
Advantage rarely comes of it.
Thou shalt not steal—an empty feat
When 'tis so lucrative to cheat.
Bear not false witness—let the lie
Have time on its own wings to fly.
Thou shalt not covet—but tradition
Approves all forms of competition."

(d)

3. This language is certainly tinged with bitterness. But I think it may reasonably be doubted whether it is too strong in its description of the hollowness of much of the religion and much of the morality of the present day. It may warn us against that hypocritical formalism, which, instead of welcoming God's holy days and the ordinances of His Church, the one as halting-places in our journey through life, where we may rest from life's business and turmoils, and the other as replete with spiritual refreshment to support us under the greatness of the way, adopts them merely as guarantees of respectability, and as trammels, irksome, indeed, but necessary to be complied with.

(e)

4. It may warn us against that time-serving spirit, which, instead of rendering service to whom service is due, tribute to whom tribute, honour to whom honour, in a temper of loving yet discriminating obedience, is interested, and self-seeking, disobedient, where disobedience is possible, unkind, ungentle, ungrateful, except where exposure is imminent, or the courtesies and amenities of life are likely to be to one's advantage.

(f)

5. It may warn us against the selfishness of the saying—you will remember by whom it was uttered originally—" Am I my brother's keeper ? " and that, granting that we have done nothing in the way of depriving our brother of life, yet if we have rejected the kindly feeling which would make us relieve his distress, and yet more if we have cherished unkindly feelings towards him, we come under the ban of the Sixth Commandment, as interpreted by St. John, " Whosoever hateth his brother is a murderer," and yet more spiritually still in the 11th and 12th verses of the same chapter : " This is the message that ye heard from the beginning, that we should love one another. Not as Cain, who was of that wicked one, and slew his brother."

(g)

6. It may warn us that abstinence from the grossest and most publicly injurious form of licentiousness from fear of inconvenient criminal proceedings is, alas !—for it wants a high motive— too often compatible with secret vice, betrayal of the innocence of others, and ruin of our own souls. It shows how cheating and taking unfair advantage, and sharp practice, as it is called, and to use the words of Sir Philip Warwick, " the

(h)

employing the laws' extreme right to do one's neighbour extreme wrong," makes a man near akin to the open plunderer and marauder. It shows how false witness is not merely to be found in the perjured person who lies against another in the courts of justice, but that it lurks in the practice of the imputer of false motives, of the inventer of, and ready listener to, gossip and slander, and even of the careless embellisher of a plain story.

(a)

7. It may warn us against the covetous and grasping spirit which, disguise it as we will, underlies the scheming and ambitious competition of the day, against the making haste to get rich, to get over rich, to get rich by any means, no matter whether thousands are ruined by it or whether the means be righteous or no.

(b)

8. We too often use extenuating terms in our speaking of what is sinful

A licentious youth is described as rather wild, or somewhat fast, or as sowing his wild oats, or, in fact, in any way which may diminish the impression that he is wasting his best years and opportunities, and laying up in store for himself materials for a bitter repentance—if, indeed, he is spared to repent. A luxurious and selfishly extravagant man is spoken of as spirited and splendid in his expenditure; and this veils from the common eye the fact that his expenditure does not benefit even himself, because it does not benefit others—that he is not rich towards God. "Whoso hath this world's goods" (says a very high authority), "and seeth his brother have need, and shutteth up his bowels of compassion from him, how dwelleth the love of God in him?" Again, the covetous and grasping man, who omits no opportunity of enriching himself, who accepts no opportunity of assisting others, is described as a careful man, and as one who sees where he goes. In fact, whether from a false refinement, or, it is to be feared in some cases, from consideration for ourselves, we are in a fair way to admit into our moral system the pestilent notion that " vice loses half its evil when it is divested of its grossness." The truth is just the other way. Vice is rendered much more dangerous by the removal of its repulsive features, and by its adoption of names which conceal its ultimate tendencies by presenting its present pleasure or advantage. We detect in a moment the self-deceit which makes the poor wanderer in our streets speak of her miserable profession as a life of gaity; or the youthful thief, the student of the "Newgate Calendar," or the exploits of Turpin, speak of his knaveries as sharpness and cleverness. And yet we allow ourselves in evasions of the law of God, which are no less flagrant violations of it than would be an assertion in defiance of St. John's words, " He that hateth his brother is *not* a murderer."

(c)

9. It was a prayer of the Psalmist, nearly three thousand years ago—"Open Thou mine eyes, O Lord, that I may see the wondrous things of Thy law." This prayer is as necessary for us as it ever was to him. Let us then beseech God to purify our moral vision, to give us tender and delicate consciences, and a fear of dallying with anything that has the least semblance of evil. Let us endeavour day by day to discover shortcomings, to ask pardon for them through Christ, and to amend them, by the aid of the Holy Spirit. This if we do, we shall at the last be able to realize those hopeful though humble words of the saintly Richard Hooker, which comforted the dying bed of one whose loss the Church a very few years back had occasion to mourn —I mean Archbishop Longley :—" Though I have by His grace loved Him in my youth, and feared Him in mine age, and laboured to bear a conscience void of offence to Him and to all men ; yet, if Thou, O Lord, be extreme to mark what I have done amiss, who can abide it? And, therefore, where I have failed, Lord, show mercy to me ; for I plead not my righteousness, but the forgiveness of my own unrighteousness, for His merits who died to purchase pardon for penitent sinners." Amen.

(d)   *Hessey*

TEN TRIBES, THE "LOST"

1. "Our Israelitish Origin"

" Our Israelitish origin " is perhaps the most recent phase, of what seems a periodically recurring popular delusion. " The lost ten tribes " have been found so many times, and in so many different localities, that it is no great matter of surprise that the prosperous English people are having their turn now. . . . The attempt to fasten our national prosperity on this stem is an injustice both to our enterprise and industry, as also to the fact that " the pit whence WE be digged " was a very dark one. If ever a people " sat in darkness," surely they were our remote forefathers ; and if ever a people " saw a great light," they were the people. This " great light " has never since wholly gone out ; and the nation springing up on this basis has all along been a God-loving and a Bible-reverencing people. . . . It is, then, a little unfair to find now another basis for this feature of our national character on which we have prided ourselves a little, and to tell us that it results from Jewish blood in our veins. It is very curious to notice the growth of some theories. This theory of " our Israelitish origin " seems to have sprung up in this way: There are, as every one knows, in the Prophets, certain promises and blessings made to " Israel" of a most superlative nature. The " Jews," it is contended, have missed them. The " lost Israel " must therefore be located somewhere, spreading and flourishing like a green bay-tree, and inheriting those great distinctions. . . . And in looking about the world for a suitable people in whom there shall be found some correspondency to the demands of these promises, various people have had their turn. Communities in Arabia and in India, especially in Malabar, in China, Turkestan, Afghanistan, the Nestorians, and even amongst the tribes of America. Each have had their turn, and have been severally cast aside when the descendants of the Ten Tribes have been found somewhere else. *Now* we are the favoured race, more especially it seems because the Anglo-Saxon people have become the buyers and sellers of the whole earth, and are the dominant race in the world. These advantages, it is claimed, are the fulfilment of the promises to " Israel," and we Anglo-Saxons, it is contended, are the descendants of the long " lost Ten Tribes of Israel." And as books have been written, and

(e)

Ten Tribes, The " Lost "—*continued*

lectures are given, and papers read to various audiences on the subject, it seems only fitting to inquire concerning the teaching of the Bible as to these so-called " lost Ten Tribes of Israel."

(*a*)

2. A Fable

Dean Stanley, quoting the authority of Milman, in his Lectures on the Jewish Church, uses these words—" That they are concealed in some unknown region of the earth, is a fable with no foundation either in history or in prophecy." . . . In point of fact, there is no proper foundation for the assertion that these tribes are *lost* at all—certainly no authoritative foundation. It is well known that both Josephus in his time, and Jerome some time later, spoke of their existence, in countless numbers in some remote province. Both of them seemed to have given credence to a common report, a sort of marvel or wonder to them, but which, from the lack of the means of communication with distant countries, they had no means of proving. And on the flimsy testimony of these two statements the error has partly been built up.

(*b*)

3. The Ten Tribes not " lost "

(i.) Israel, as a whole, is *intact* NOW, as it was before the split into Two Kingdoms. In other words, the Ten Tribes are not lost.

(ii.) This can be confirmed and established by direct Scriptural evidence.

(*c*)

4. As to the present Unity of Israel

This unity existed, externally, down to the revolt of the Ten Tribes, then it was broken,—but afterwards there was a *reunion* of the whole nation. This is the point denied. The denial of this fact, and the consequent theories that have arisen thereupon, show a complete misconception of God's intention by the Captivities.

(*d*)

5. Beyond all doubt, God intended the chosen nation to be one, both politically and religiously

The words which stand at the beginning of their National life have this significance :—" Hear, O Israel, the Lord our God is ONE LORD."

" O, *Israel* " : They were to constitute but one nation, politically, not two (Israel and Judah).

" *The Lord our God is one Lord* " : Their Religion was to be ONE (" Ye shall not go after other gods ").

It is equally evident, I think, that when the time came for a division of the chosen people into Two Kingdoms, God had no intention that this should become a permanent division ; but His design appears to have been the healing of an old sore, which was weakening the people and militating against the principle of Unity laid down at the first ; and when this sore was healed, to bring the two fragments together again in one National existence. That it was so, a brief survey of their history shows.

(*e*)

6. If we search into the causes of the disunion, we shall find that they were not sudden.

We have seen that the nation was to be One in Politics, and One in religion ; but from the very first there were jealousies between the leading Tribes. These jealousies — sometimes smouldering, sometimes breaking out—naturally broke up this union, and in course of time produced Revolt and Idolatry. Just as apostasy of heart precedes apostasy of life, so the disunion of the Ten Tribes was an internal fact long before it was an external one.

(*f*)

7. For from the earliest period the powerful Tribes of Ephraim and Judah were jealous of each other.

These were the two factions ; and a moment of weakness in one was a moment of arrogance and triumph in the other. Unquestionably it was God's intention that the Tribe of Judah should be in the ascendant ; but, at the same time, the history shows that Ephraim had some cause for jealousy.

For from the Tribe of Ephraim came Joshua, their first great Military Leader. The birthplace of Samuel, the great Prophet, was also in the territory of Ephraim. " Little Benjamin," a tribe nearly related to the Ephraimites, produced their first King.

All this, apart from the fact that they were descended from the most remarkable of all the Twelve Patriarchs, gave a great *political* ascendency to the Tribe of Ephraim. And if we add to this the further fact that the first two Sanctuaries—Shechem and Shiloh—were also in the territory of Ephraim, then this tribe had the *Religious* ascendency as well. And for the space of 400 years this powerful Tribe had this DOUBLE pre-eminence in the nation. These facts are sufficient to explain why this haughty tribe took upon itself to expostulate with Gideon, Jephthah, and David, on occasions when it deemed itself slighted.

(*g*)

But when David became King, the Royal Tribe of Judah gained the ascendency. And when afterwards he captured the fortress of Jebus, and erected there a new Tabernacle, Jerusalem (" the City of the Great King ") became both the Political and Religious centre of the Nation. The Ephraimites bowed to the decision of the majority. David's influence and force of character were sufficient (until after the revolt of Absalom) to preserve the Union. But after the grievous taxation of Solomon and the insane folly of Rehoboam, the old rivalry was kindled anew. The Ephraimites exclaim " What part have we in David ? " They find a leader in Jeroboam, and the revolt of the Ten Tribes is complete.

(*h*)

8. We read that all attempts to bring back the revolters by force were forbidden—" This thing is of Me, saith the Lord."

It is interesting to trace God's hand in this, over-ruling, as He always does, human sin for the accomplishment of His own purposes.

We have seen that disunion existed all along, and that mutual jealousies promoted Political and Religious discord. We have now to see how this deep-seated enmity was to be cured. God now broke the nation into two fragments, and He cast them one after another into a furnace of troubles. In that furnace they should forget their mutual jealousies ; their common misery would bring out their brotherhood. Affliction would fuse the two together again ; and when His

(*i*)

Ten Tribes, The " Lost "—*continued*

" whole work was done upon them" God would bring them back as one united nation—under one Political Ruler (Zerubbabel), and under one Religious Leader (the High Priest Joshua). After this the Tribal jealousies would cease ; and idolatry, the curse of the divided nation, more especially of the revolters, would cease to be their national sin. Thus the secession of the Ten Tribes was " of the Lord."

(a)

9. This may be presented a little more in detail. After the revolt, the Ten Tribes manage their own matters. As the Secessionists, who had broken away from constituted authority " *on principle*," they ought to have worked out the Israelitish ideal. But, as the history shows, far otherwise was the lamentable result. Israel's course is a gradual declension. The previous animosity was intensified. For nearly sixty years there was war between the two kingdoms ; and war is anything but elevating.

(b)

In short, with no fixed capital ; no real religious centre ; with an insubordinate army ; with constant change of dynasties, each ushered in by a Revolution ; with an urauthorized Priesthood, the people rushed on, like a train off the line, through anarchy and idolatry, to ruin, until God sends them, long before the rival kingdom of Judah, into Captivity ; where the nature of their punishment would serve to bring their sins to remembrance.

(c)

10. Judah, many years later, and not profiting from this example of its " treacherous sister," followed. They both go into the same exile ; into various provinces of the one great Power, which at first constituted the Assyrian, then the Chaldean, and afterwards the Persian Empire. Their common misery brings about a closer union of the descendants of Jacob. Their oppressors know of no Tribal distinctions ; and as the great Monarchies undergo their successive changes, the fact of there having been two deportations of captive Israelites from the petty kingdoms of Israel and Judah, seems to have been forgotten. The Persians knew of no distinction between Jews and Israelites, for Haman wished to destroy, not all the Judeans merely, but all the " Hebrews."

(d)

11. In this "fused" state, as the seventy years of the later Captivity draw to a close, the people ripen for their return. The reason why there is no definite promise of return to the Ten Tribes after a fixed period, is because they sinned in revolting. To have given one promise to them, and another to the Judæans, would have been contrary to the Divine purpose of unity. The revolters repent in captivity ; in heart they return to their allegiance ; and when the seventy years are ended, the captives go back as—

(e)

12. One Nation. It is not contended that *all* went back together, but that some of all the Tribes returned, and thus formed a representative Israel. Besides, the return is the reverse of the Captivities. Judah is the later deposit, they have not struck so deep a root in exile as their brethren, hence they return first, and in greater numbers. Whereas the captives from the Ten Tribes were the earlier deposit : they have been many more years in Captivity, they have consequently struck a deeper root ; many of them have forgotten their own land (this is easy to understand, seeing these were never the truer Israelites) ; they have formed new homes and new interests in their exile. Many, again, of these did not want to return, " they mingled with the heathen and learned their works." In other words, these were not the repentant and faithful Jews. They had no heart longings for Zion ; and as they did not want God, He did not want them. They stayed behind : a few may have returned in later expeditions, after the Temple was rebuilt, and national life was again in existence.

(f)

13. The Dispersion

Besides these two classes (the elect and the apostate), there were others who stayed behind in exile, and who, by keeping up their distinctive character as Israelites, and by sending contributions to Jerusalem, did good service among the heathen, as a witnessing people, preparing the way for Christ. These, however, never became a " *lost* " people ; the places of their habitation are clearly defined in the New Testament, where they are spoken of as " The dispersed among the Gentiles," and whom it is the custom to call " the Jews of the Dispersion."

(g)

14. With these exceptions, some of all the Twelve Tribes returned, those Tribes preponderating who had the greatest reverence and longing for the one sanctuary at Jerusalem, and for the preservation of the Israelitish ideal of Unity ; and naturally these were from the tribes of Judah, Benjamin, and Levi ; but that the God-fearing portion of the other Tribes returned with them also, there can be no well-grounded doubt. The purpose of God in sending His people into Captivity is otherwise made of none effect.

(h)

15. If it be argued that there was no room for these tribes if they did return, as Samaria had been repeopled with colonists sent from Assyria, and the province of Judah was too small for them, it may suffice to say, that at the time of our Lord there was a dense population of Jews, not only in Judæa, but also in Perea and the neighbouring parts of Palestine ; and the Jews of the " Dispersion," together with these, were far too numerous to have sprung from the comparatively small number that returned on the Edict of Cyrus. This is enough to show that the Twelve Tribes of Israel are intact, and that it is a fallacy to speak of the lost Ten Tribes. It is maintained that the Captivity was intended as a furnace of affliction wherein the disunited fragments of the nation would be melted into one again ; and that on the return from Captivity, they did in fact return as one representative Israel—with old animosities gone, with tribal distinctions all but obliterated ; for of the combination of Ephraim, Benjamin, and Manasseh, as a powerful faction, opposed to Judah, we hear no more. They, like the other Tribes, after this lesson of affliction, become " the lost

(i)

Ten Tribes, The "Lost"—*continued*

sheep of the House of Israel," whom the Good Shepherd afterwards came to gather into His fold.

We might illustrate in this way. United Israel may be compared to a piece of metal held in the hand ; by some means or other it has become broken. As separate pieces its value is lost, and it can only be made one piece again by the agency of fire. Consequently one piece is thrown into the crucible ready for it on the fire ; after a little waiting, the other piece is thrown in too. They melt, and run into one mass of fused metal. Afterwards, on being removed from the fire and poured into a mould, one consolidated piece of metal is the result, taking the form required. By some such simple illustration as this, the purpose of the Captivities may be easily understood.

The dross only, not Ten Tribes, remained behind and became lost in the great sea of nations.

(*a*)

16. Scriptural Confirmation of this

This is an easy task. Being simply a selection of passages bearing on the subject.

The fact of the Captivity of the Twelve Tribes needs no confirmation. It is the assertion that Twelve Tribes returned from the Captivity which is denied, and which requires confirmation.

There are five or six proofs of this.

(*b*)

17. It was a Matter of Prophecy that the Twelve Tribes should Return and be reunited

The hope of this runs through the prophets. Take *Isaiah*, chapters x. to xiv. as a chief passage bearing on this hope. The effect of the Captivity in destroying the animosity between the two kingdoms is well described in xi. 13 :

"The envy also of Ephraim shall depart, and the adversaries of Judah shall be cut off : Ephraim shall not envy Judah, and Judah shall not vex Ephraim."

As to the captives who return, they are from both kingdoms :

(x. 20), "The remnant of Israel, and such as are escaped of the house of Jacob."

(xi. 12), "And he shall set up an ensign for the nations, and shall assemble the outcasts of Israel, and gather together the dispersed from Judah from the four corners of the earth."

(xiv. 1), "For the Lord will have mercy on Jacob, and will yet choose Israel."

Turn now to *Jeremiah*, chapters iii. and xxxi. :—

(iii. 12), "Go and proclaim these words to the North, and say, Return, thou backsliding Israel, saith the Lord," etc.

(iii. 14), "I will take you one of a city, and two of a family, and I will bring you to Zion."

(iii. 18), "In those days the house of Judah shall walk with the house of Israel, and they shall come together out of the land of the North to the land that I have given for an inheritance unto your fathers."

And the pathetic response of penitent Israel in iii. 20-25 is touching to the last degree, and only to be understood by the convictions wrought in them by the furnace of affliction.

Chapter xxxi. must be read in its whole connection on the same subject. The restoration of Judah and Israel, more especially of the repentance of Israel (15), Rachel weeping for her children—the

tribes of Joseph and Benjamin—"because they were not" ; but she is told to refrain from weeping because "they shall come again from the land of the enemy." "Thy children shall come again to their own borders."

Note again 18, etc., the touching repentance of obstinate Ephraim, the first in sin, the longest in exile, the hardest heart to break, but the deepest in repentance. Even disconsolate Jeremiah is comforted (26) when he rightly apprehends this. See also the promises to both houses in verses 27, 28.

Once more, we turn now to another Prophet. And this is a Prophet *of* the Exile. Isaiah saw it from afar, Jeremiah sees its approach, Ezekiel takes part *in* it (Ezek. xxxvii. 11), "Son of man, these dry bones are the whole house of Israel : behold they say, Our bones are dried, and our hope is lost : we are cut off for our parts." (12) The reply is, that they should be brought into the land of Israel. More emphatic than anything preceding is the passage xxxvii. 15 to end :—

"The word of the Lord came again to me, saying, Moreover, thou son of man, take thee one stick, and write upon it, *For Judah*, and for the children of Israel his companions : then take another stick, and write upon it, For Joseph, the stick of Ephraim, and for all the house of Israel his companions : and join them into one stick ; and they shall become *one* in thine hand." . . . (22) "and they shall be no more two nations, neither shall they be divided into two kingdoms any more at all."

These, though the chief passages bearing upon the Hope of the Prophets, are not all. But these will suffice for our first proof, viz., that Israel returned to its own land, after the exile had done its work upon them, a corporate nation.

It may be as well here to say a word or two in anticipation of an objection which is nearly certain to arise against this interpretation of these passages. It will be said, "All these prophecies relate to Messianic times, and have yet to await their fulfilment when "all Israel shall be saved. This, be it remarked, is by no means questioned by the foregoing observations, rather it is confirmed by what has been said. It is necessary to remind ourselves of that well-established principle of interpretation called the "*Double Sense of Prophecy*." The Prophecies have a double fulfilment, a *nearer* and a more *remote*. The nearer fulfilment related to the circumstances of the time, and was always the type of the remoter and fuller fulfilment in Messianic times. It is exactly so with the prophecies quoted above. It will be seen that they all relate to the Assyrian oppression, and are promises of deliverance from that power. The promises are all conditioned by repentance ; and when the time is ripe, both houses of the Israelites are to return to their own country, and to their own "Zion." A remnant is spoken of, because "all Israel" (see above) did not repent, nor desire the return. This was the first, or the nearer fulfilment of the prophecies ; and the further, or more remote fulfilment is going on now under Messianic influences ; and the restoration will be complete when all Israel shall turn unto the Lord.

Without doubt, then, true alike to the purpose of God and to well-established canons of interpretation, a remnant of the Twelve Tribes—a good remnant—did return to their own land, and became the representative Israel.

(*c*)

Ten Tribes, The "Lost"—*continued*

18. A second proof is to be found in the Book of Ezra, which is emphatically the book of the return and restoration of Israel (both of Jews and Israelites) from Captivity. The resettlement in Judah and Jerusalem, the rebuilding of the Temple, and the ordering of the One Fold, according to the Law of Moses.

Take the Edict of Cyrus for their return: it is made to "*all Israel.*"

Ezra i. 1-4, "Who among you of ALL His people." And that of Artaxerxes is to the same effect.

Ezra vii. 13, "Whoever in my kingdom is willing of the *people of Israel.*" All the Jews, *i.e.*, all the Israelites of the Twelve Tribes, were called upon to return; and those obeyed the call whose hearts were so disposed by their religious craving. All the penitent would recognise their opportunity in this edict.

Take, in connection with the edict, the first expedition of the Israelites to their own country. It was under the conduct of **Twelve leaders, Zerubbabel and Joshua with ten others** (Ezra ii. 2; Neh. vii. 7). Now surely this is no accidental number. Twelve leaders of a returning band of Jewish exiles leads to the inevitable conclusion that these twelve men were leading back the representatives of the Twelve Tribes. The remnant that should be saved, thus fulfilling the hopes of the Prophets.

(*a*)

19. Liturgical Proofs

They had to do with the worship of the people at the consecration of the Temple.

We find the first indication of this in Ezra vi. 17. **All** Israel had sinned, and all Israel must offer a sin offering. On that occasion they offered **twelve he-goats as "sin offerings for all Israel, according to the number of the tribes of Israel."**

After confession must come the consecration of the whole life to the service of God, so after sin-offerings must come burnt offerings; accordingly we find this is done (Ezra viii. 35). **Twelve bullocks** are offered as a burnt offering "**for all Israel.**" The significance of these two sets of twelve offerings is too apparent to need explanation. "**All Israel**" means united Israel.

But if the Book of Ezra gives us a statement of the facts which occurred at the time of the restoration, the writings of Haggai and Zechariah (whose activity belongs to this period) give us a clear portraiture of the *mind* and spiritual condition of the Israelites who returned. In the latter respect great importance is due to the Psalms, of which the whole of the last Book (cvii.–cxlvi.) was arranged during this period for the Temple service. Ps. cvii. is worthy of special mention. It was the Psalm sung at the dedication of the Second Temple. It may be termed—"**An admonition to fellow-countrymen to render thanks on account of having got the better of calamities.**"

Surely, a people who had suffered as they had for their sin, and whose repentance had been followed (in the case of Israel) with such an unlooked-for deliverance, could appropriate every word of this Psalm:

(*b*)

20. Ps. cvii.

"O give thanks unto the Lord, for He is good: For His mercy endureth for ever.

Let the *redeemed* of the Lord say so, Whom He hath redeemed from the hand of the enemy;
And gathered them out of the lands,
From the east, and from the west,—from the north and from the south.
They wandered in the wilderness in a solitary way; they found no city to dwell in.
Hungry and thirsty, their soul fainted in them.
Then they cried unto the Lord in their trouble,
And He delivered them out of their distresses.
And He led them forth by the right way,
That they might go to a city of habitation.
O that men would praise the Lord for His goodness,
And for His wonderful works to the children of men!
For He satisfieth the longing soul,—and filleth the hungry soul with goodness."

(*c*)

How is this whole psalm to be understood, except as the utterance from the heart of the thankful and *mercied* nation. As *one* nation they came out of Egypt; for their sins they were broken in two; cast again into bondage; and as *one* nation they came back again. Truly their hope was all but dead, they were "dry bones"—can such live again? Put such a question to the unbelieving, and the answer is, "No"—impossible. Put the question to Faith, and the answer is, "God hath promised, and what He has promised He is able to perform," and by this faith "they obtained the promise." God did so dispose events, He did so turn the hearts of Kings, as to "let His people go free" once more. And when back in their own land, and looking back over the years of their exile —of sin and of suffering—they take the words of this Psalm as those that most fittingly express the attitude of their hearts to God :—

"O that men would praise the Lord for His goodness, For His wonderful works to the children of men."

(*d*)

21. Another of these Psalmic, or Liturgical proofs, is to be found in the Psalm cxlvii. One of those later psalms, written, or adapted, as the expression of a restored people's thanksgiving after great mercies received.

Verse 2.

"The Lord doth build up Jerusalem: He gathereth together the outcasts of Israel."

Verses 19 and 20.

"He showeth His word unto Jacob, His statutes and His judgments unto Israel.
He hath not dealt so with any nation:
And as for His judgments, they have not known them.
Praise ye the Lord."

(*e*)

22. New Testament References to the tribes of Israel are to the effect, that the nation at the time of our Lord and His Apostles was a *united* one.

"Anna, the prophetess," was of the Tribe of *Asshur* (Luke ii. 36).

Paul was "of the tribe of *Benjamin.*"

The promise of her Lord to the twelve Apostles (Matt. xix. 28) was, that they "should sit upon twelve thrones, judging the *Twelve* Tribes of Israel."

When alluding to the Jews of the Dispersion, the New Testament references are to the effect, not

(*f*)

Ten Tribes, The "Lost"—*continued*

that they were "Lost," but as occupying well-known localities.

John vii. 35. "Will He go unto the dispersed among the Gentiles and teach the Gentiles?"

Acts xxvi. 7 is a most distinct utterance concerning the *unity* of Israel: "Unto which [promise] our Twelve Tribes, instantly serving God day and night, hope to come."

(*a*)

James i. 1 addresses his Epistle to "the Twelve Tribes scattered abroad." Whilst the well-known and often-quoted passage from the Book of Revelation (vii. 4–8) sums up all the chosen nation as a *united one :*

"And I heard the number of them that were sealed: and there were sealed an hundred and forty and four thousand of all the Tribes of the children of Israel.

"Of the Tribe of Judah were sealed twelve thousand," etc., etc.

All the Tribes are reckoned together, none of the tribes are lost, or even omitted.

This general agreement cannot be otherwise regarded than as sufficient evidence of the unity of Israel, as a restored nation, from the time of the return from the Captivity to the general dissolution of the nation under Titus.

(*b*)

23. Argument from the Nature of the Case

The Ten Tribes could not be intact anywhere as a separate nation, seeing they lacked the only means of consolidation under which they could so exist, and have the blessing of God.

They had no Temple, and no order of Priests, let alone the further fact that they had no political chief around whom to rally.

Hence the "elect" of the nation would find no consolation in a return to Samaria, in exile, or in a settlement in some other remote part of the habitable world. No other than Zion could satisfy them. And for these God makes plans, and to these He gives His promises. He was not likely to bring them back to a state of things which would give rise to old feuds, confusions, and idolatries. The new nation, though small, must return as a united one, otherwise, it is clear, the import and the discipline of the Captivities would have been lost upon them, and God might ask of them "Art thou delivered to work all these abominations?"

And if the Ten Tribes did not go back with the other two, but have remained all this long time in an unknown land and unknown, then it must be confessed "They have no part in David," and are clean cut off altogether.

But against such a conclusion the purpose of God, the prophecies, the whole tenor of Holy Scripture, and the nature of things are clearly opposed. It only needs an intelligent acquaintance with the whole history, and a spiritual insight into the true significance of the Captivities to refute the popular delusion about the Lost Ten Tribes.

And the theory which would make out the English nation as the descendants of the Ten Tribes, may be easily disposed of.

We could not be so—

(i.) Because the Tribes are Jews still, with the others, though the lines of demarcation between the Tribes are apparently lost.

(ii.) Because no blessing (such as is argued we inherit) could result to an apostate people, who started by preferring heathenism to the Theocratic religion of their forefathers; the further they wandered from that centre, the more lost and the more disintegrated would they become. Only ingenious and fanciful arguments could well prove it otherwise.

The nation as a whole is intact now. "Lost" indeed they are for the most part. "The lost sheep of the house of Israel"—still wandering, still without a Shepherd—but lost, as the coin was lost, within the four walls of the house, and consequently where the Good Shepherd, who knows His sheep and searches them out, can find them.

(*c*)

TEN VIRGINS

1. Parable of the Ten Virgins

This parable has many sides and aspects. It is prophetical; it is also practical. It suits all ages, but especially the last days. It suits the world, but especially the Church of God ; "If the righteous scarcely be saved, where shall the ungodly and the sinner appear." It is searching and sifting ; it is also quickening and comforting. It suits us well in these days of profession and fashionable religion and religiousness.

It divides the Church into two classes—the wise and the foolish: wise in God's sight, not man's ; foolish in God's sight, not man's. Thus it is not a parable for the heathen, as if they only were foolish ; nor for the profligate, as if they only were foolish ; nor for the infidels, as if they only were foolish. But for the Church. It comes into the inner circle of Christian profession, and sifts it, divides it. Let it sift us and test us. Better to be weighed and found wanting now than hereafter. Better to be undeceived now than when it is too late.

(*d*)

2. Points of Likeness

(i.) They get the same name, virgins ; (ii.) They wear the same dress ; (iii.) They are on the same errand ; (iv.) They both have lamps ; (v.) They both have vessels ; (vi.) They both slumber and sleep. They have thus many features in common. Man could not discern the difference, at least for the time. The peril of mere *externalism* is that which our Lord points out here. No doubt there must be externalism. Religion must have an outside as well as an inside. The lamp must not only have oil, but it must burn ; the external must indicate the internal. And we may say that our Lord intimated the necessity of a thorough consistency and completeness in the outward religious life of a man, so that, as a fair external is no excuse for internal unsoundness or incompleteness, so a sound internal is no excuse for an inconsistent life. Our Lord, then, here depicts, (i.) a *complete* externalism ; (ii.) a *beautiful* externalism ; (iii.) a *deceptive* externalism ; (iv.) a *prolonged* externalism ; (v.) an *unavailing* externalism. Up to a certain point in a man's life, or character, or religion, externalism may avail ; but beyond that it gives way ; it breaks down ; it exhibits its unprofitableness. This externalism may not always

(*e*)

be hypocrisy, but it is *imitation*. It is not the flower in its natural colour and growth, but painted, artificial. Let us watch against an artificial life and an artificial religion. What does it profit now? and what will it profit in the day of wrath? The name, the dress, the lamp, the outward show, will all go for nothing in that day of universal discovery and detection.

(a)

3. Points of Unlikeness

Though in most respects they were all alike, yet there was a difference. It was *within ;* it was imperceptible from without; it could only be discovered when the bridegroom came. Up till then all were completely similar. Only then the want came out in the foolish. Then was it seen who were wise, and who were foolish. That day is the day of certain and unerring detection. It is the day of weighing in the balances. It is the separation of the false from the true.

(b)

4. The Oil

There was "oil in the dwelling of the *wise*" (Prov. xxi. 20); but the foolish were without it.

The oil is the Holy Spirit. To oil He is likened throughout all Scripture, though in some places to fire, and to water, and to wind or air. There is the oil of consecration (Exod. xxx. 25); of daily food (1 Kings xvii. 12); of fragrance (Esther ii. 12); of joy (Ps. xlii., Isa. lxi. 3); of healing (Luke x. 34); of light (Zech. iv. 12). The Holy Spirit is all these. But it is as the *light-giving* oil that He is specially spoken of here; and the lack of Him as such makes the difference between the foolish and the wise. "Having not the Spirit" (Jude 19).

(c)

5. What Lack I yet?

Thus a man may be very like a Christian, and yet not be one. He may come very near the kingdom, and yet not enter in. He may have all the outward features of a Christian, and yet be lacking in the main one. He may have the complete dress of the saint, and yet not be one. He may have a good life, a sound creed, a strict profession; he may be one who says and does many things excellent; he may be a subscriber to all the religious societies in the land, a member of all their committees, or a speaker at all their meetings, and supporter of all their plans; he may profess to be looking for Christ's coming, and going forth to meet the bridegroom, yet not necessarily a Christian! He may lack the oil, the Holy Spirit.

(d)

6. Religion without the Holy Ghost

A religion without the Holy Ghost profiteth nothing. There is the religion of the intellect, of the sense, of the fancy, of the flesh, of the Creed, of the Liturgy, of the Catechism, of nature, of poetry, of sentiment, of mysticism, of humanity. But what are these without the Spirit? Christianity without Christ, what would that be? Worship without God, what would that be? So religion without the Holy Spirit, what would that be?

Yet is there not much of this among us? Is there not much of dry formalism, lifeless doctrine, sapless routine? I do not call it hypocrisy; I simply call it *unreal religion*.

And what can unreal religion do for a man? Will it not prove irksome and vain? Will it make him happy and free, or liberal, or zealous, or holy? No. It can do none of these things. It is bondage, and darkness, and weariness.

Yet here is the Holy Spirit in the hands of Christ for you. Go to them that sell, and buy for yourselves. Not to men, or Churches, or creeds, or ministers, but to Christ. Go to Him. He is exalted to give it; and He will. Apply to Him ere it be too late.

(e)   *Horatius Bonar*

TERROR AND LOVE

1. Perhaps the most real and intense of all great poems is the "Inferno" of the Florentine poet Dante. The people of Verona, when they saw him in the streets, used to say, "See, there is the man who was in hell." He no more doubts of the "City of Dis," with its ceaseless showers of fiery snow without wind, its living souls embedded in tombs of burning marl, or engulfed in lakes of seething pitch or everlasting ice, than we doubt the bubbling lava of Vesuvius. And it was the creed of his age. The frescoes and the sculptures of the churches, the sermons of the priests, depicted with like terrible minuteness not only the sufferings of the lost, but the agonies,—laughing to scorn in intensity and duration the infernal ingenuity of pious inquisitors,—which awaited even the ransomed soul in purgatory for every repented sin. And what was the end of this?

An age of infamy and atheism unparalleled in Christian times, the age of the Borgias, the age of wholesale poisonings, the age of the festering elegance of revived Paganism, an age when priests jested over the mass, and the few voices which protested against the iniquities of the times were silenced by torture and death.

(f)

2. We have heard of the Methodist revival about one hundred years ago. It was a great work, and to the enthusiasm of its leaders, Wesley and Whitefield, we owe in great measure that still deepening and broadening spirit of Christian philanthropy which is our one chance of national salvation. And yet, this movement, like later revivals, was marred by its terrorism. "The terrors of judgment, and the agonies of hell," says an accurate historian, "were the almost constant subjects of his preaching; and he dwelt upon them till he scared his hearers to the verge of insanity. Many fell to the ground convulsed with paroxysms of agony. Some lay without sense or motion, others trembled exceedingly, or rent the air with piercing screams, which continued for hours without intermission."

(g)

3. Now open the Gospels. What a contrast! We seem to have left the turbid streams of some black country, scarred and seared by man's well-meant improvements, and to have climbed up where the clear fountain-head comes welling from the rock.

Christ does not draw men to Himself by terrorism, but by love. He called every one of His disciples quietly, peacefully, lovingly. And though He blinded, and with a lightning flash, yet along with the stroke and the blindness came the consolation and the peace. Terror cannot save the soul. There is one Guide only to the city of Eternal Refuge, and His name is Love.

(h)   *H. H. Almond*

THEATRE OF THE UNIVERSE

By Command of the KING OF KINGS,[1] and at the Desire of all who love His Appearing,[2]

AT THE THEATRE OF THE UNIVERSE,[3]

On the EVE OF TIME,[4] will be performed,

THE GREAT ASSIZE, OR DAY OF JUDGMENT.[5]

The SCENERY, which is now actually preparing, will not only surpass everything that has yet been seen, but will infinitely exceed the utmost stretch of human conception.[6] There will be a just Representation of all the inhabitants of the World, in their various and proper colours; and their Customs and Manners will be so exactly and so minutely delineated, that the most secret thought will be discovered.[7]

"*For God shall bring every Work into Judgment, with every Secret Thing, whether it be Good, or whether it be Evil.*"—Eccl. xii. 14.

THIS THEATRE will be laid out after a new Plan, and will consist of PIT and GALLERY only; and, contrary to all others, the GALLERY is fitted up for the Reception of the People of high (or heavenly) Birth,[8] and the PIT for those of low (or earthly) Rank.[9] N.B. The GALLERY is very spacious,[10] and the PIT without BOTTOM.[11]

To prevent Inconvenience, there are separate Doors for admitting the Company; and they are so different that none can mistake that are not wilfully blind. The Door which opens into the GALLERY is very narrow, and the Steps up to it are somewhat difficult; for which reason there are seldom many People about it.[12] But the Door that gives Entrance into the PIT is very wide, and very commodious; which causes such Numbers to flock to it, that it is generally crowded.[13] N.B. The strait Door leads towards the Right hand, and the broad one to the Left.[14]

It will be in vain for one in a tinselled Coat and borrowed language to personate one of high Birth, in order to get Admittance into the Upper Places;[15] for there is One of wonderful and deep Penetration, who will search and examine every individual;[16] and all who cannot pronounce *Shibboleth*[17] in the language of Canaan,[18] or has not received a white Stone and new Name,[19] or cannot prove a clear Title to a certain Portion of the Land of Promise,[20] must be turned in at the left Door.[21]

THE PRINCIPAL PERFORMERS

Are described in 1 *Thess.* iv. 16; 2 *Thess.* i. 7, 8, 9; *Matt.* xxiv. 30, 31; xxv. 31, 32; *Daniel* vii. 9, 10; *Jude* 14, 15; *Rev.* xx. 12–15, etc. But as there are some People much better acquainted with the contents of a Play-bill than the Word of God, it may not be amiss to transcribe a verse or two for their perusal.

"*The Lord Jesus shall be revealed from Heaven with His mighty Angels, in flaming Fire, taking vengeance on them that obey not the Gospel*," but "*to be glorified in His Saints. A fiery Stream issued and came forth from before Him: The Judgment was set, and the Books were opened; and whosoever was not found written in the Book of Life was cast into the Lake of Fire.*"

ACT FIRST OF THIS GRAND AND SOLEMN PIECE

Will be opened by an ARCH-ANGEL with the Trump of GOD.[22]

"*For the Trumpet shall sound, and the Dead shall be raised.*"—1 Cor. xv. 52.

ACT SECOND

Will be a PROCESSION OF SAINTS in White,[23] with Golden HARPS, accompanied with Shouts of Joy and Songs of Praise.[24]

ACT THIRD

Will be an Assemblage of all the Unregenerate.[25] The Music will consist chiefly of Cries,[26] accompanied with Weeping, Wailing, Mourning, Lamentation, and Woe.[27]

To conclude with an ORATION by the

SON OF GOD

It is written in the 25th of *Matthew*, from the 34th verse to the end of the chapter; but for the sake of those who seldom read the Scriptures, I shall here transcribe two verses.

"*Then shall the King say to them on His Right hand, Come, ye blessed of My Father, inherit the Kingdom prepared for you from the Foundation of the World: Then shall He say also unto them on the Left hand, Depart from Me, ye cursed, into Everlasting Fire, prepared for the Devil and his Angels.*"

After which the CURTAIN will drop,

Then Oh to tell!

John v. 28, 29.	Some raised on high, and others doomed to Hell!
Rev. v. 8, 9; xiv. 3, 4 .	These praise the Lamb, and sing redeeming Love,
Luke xvi. 22, 23.	Lodged in His Bosom, all His goodness prove:
,, xix. 14, 27.	While those who trampled under foot His grace,
Matt. xxv. 30; 2 Thess. i. 9.	Are banished now for ever from His Face;
Luke xvi. 26.	Divided thus, a gulf is fixed between,
Matt. xxv. 46.	And (everlasting) closes up the Scene.

"*Thus will I do unto thee, O Israel; and because I will do this unto thee, prepare to meet thy God, O Israel.*"—Amos iv. 12.

TICKETS for the PIT, at the easy Purchase of following the vain Pomps and Vanities of the fashionable World, and the Desires and Amusements of the Flesh:[28] To be had at every Flesh-pleasing Assembly.

"*If ye live after the Flesh ye shall die.*"—Rom. viii. 13.

TICKETS for the GALLERY at no less rate than being converted,[29] Forsaking all,[30] Denying Self, taking up the Cross,[31] and following Christ in the Regeneration:[32] To be had nowhere but in the Word of God, and where that Word appoints.

"*He that hath Ears to hear, let him hear. And be not deceived; God is not mocked. For whatsoever a man soweth, that shall he also reap.*"—Matt. xi. 15; Gal. vi. 7.

N.B. No money will be taken at the Door,[33] nor will any Tickets give Admittance into the GALLERY, but those sealed by the Holy Ghost,[34] with Immanuel's Signet.[35]

"*Watch therefore; be ye also ready; for in such an Hour as ye think not, the Son of Man cometh.*"—Matt. xxiv. 42, 44.

(a)   *The Authorship of the above "PLAY-BILL" is commonly attributed to Rowland Hill.*

Marginal references (left column):

[1] Rev. xix. 16.
1 Tim. vi. 15.
[2] 2 Tim. iv. 8.
Tit. ii. 13.
[3] Rev. xx. 11.
Matt. xxiv. 27.
[4] Rev. x. 6, 7.
Dan. xii. 13.
[5] Heb. ix. 27.
Ps. ix. 7, 8.
Rev. vi. 17.
2 Cor. v. 10.
Zeph. i. 14–17.
[6] 1 Cor. ii. 9.
Isa. lxiv. 4.
Ps. xxxi. 19.
[7] Matt. xii. 36.
1 Cor. iv. 5.
Rom. ii. 15, 16.
[8] John iii. 3, 5.
1 Pet. i. 23.
Rom. viii. 14.
[9] Jas. iii. 14, 15.
Rom. viii. 6, 7, 8.
Gal. v. 19–21.
[10] Luke xiv. 22.
John xiv. 2.
[11] Rev. xx. 12.
,, xix. 20.
[12] Matt. vii. 14.
[13] Matt. vii. 13.
[14] Matt. xxv. 33.
[15] Matt. vii. 21, 22, 23.
[16] Ps. xliv. 20, 21.
Jer. xvii. 10.
Zeph. i. 12.
2 Tim. ii. 19.
John x. 14.
[17] Judg. xii. 6.
[18] Isa. xix. 18.
Zeph. iii. 9.
[19] Rev. ii. 17.
[20] Heb. xii. 8, 9.
Gal. iii. 9, 29.
2 Cor. xiii. 5.
[21] Ps. ix. 17.
Heb. iii. 17–19.
[22] 1 Thess. iv. 16.
Matt. xxiv. 31.
[23] Rev. vii. 14.
,, xix. 14.
[24] Rev. xiv. 2, 3.
,, xv. 2, 3, 4.
[25] 1 Cor. vi. 9, 10.
Matt. xiii. 41.
[26] Luke xiii. 30.
Rev. vi. 16.
[27] Luke xiii. 28.
Matt. xiii. 49, 50.
Rev. i. 7.
Ezek. ii. 10.

[28] James iv. 4.
1 John i. 15–17.
Col. iii. 5, 6.
1 Tim. v. 6.
Eph. v. 3–7.
[29] Matt. xviii. 3.
Acts iii. 19.
[30] Luke xiv. 33.
,, xviii. 29, 30.
[31] Lu. ix. 23–26.
Luke xiv. 27.
[32] Matt. xix. 28, 29.
Gal. v. 24, 25.
Eph. v. 1, 2.
[33] Acts viii. 20–23.
Zeph. i. 18.
[34] 2 Cor. i. 22.
Eph. i. 13.
,, iv. 30.
[35] Rev. vii. 3.
,, xiv. 1.
Ezek. ix. 4.

TESTAMENT, THE OLD, AND "FAITH"

The term "faith" can scarcely be said to occur at all in the Hebrew Scriptures of the Old Testament. It is indeed a characteristic token of the difference between the two covenants, that under the Law the "*fear* of the Lord" holds very much the same place as "*faith* in God," "*faith* in Christ," under the Gospel. *Awe* is the prominent idea in the earlier dispensation; *trust*, in the later. At the same time, though the word itself is not found in the Old Testament, the idea is not absent; for indeed a trust in the Infinite and Unseen, subordinating thereto all interests that are finite and transitory, is the very essence of the higher spiritual life (cf. Abraham).

(*a*)   *Bp. Lightfoot*

TESTAMENTS, OLD AND NEW

The general ends both of Old and New Testaments are one, the only difference between them being this, that the Old made wise by teaching salvation through Christ that should come, and the New, by teaching that Christ our Saviour is come.

(*b*)   *Hooker*

THANKSGIVING PRAYER

Thanksgiving Prayer, written by the Rev. R. S. Hawker (Morwenstow), on the restoration of the Prince of Wales after his serious illness (1871).

O Jesu Master! my Lord and my God! We utter our earnest and faithful thanksgiving to Thee for that Thou hast heard and granted our prayer. We besought Thee to have mercy on Thy servant, Albert Edward, our Prince of the Royal House of England, in his perilous disease. Thou hast fulfilled our vows. In Thy mid-nature between God the Trinity and mankind, Thy heart, human and Divine, hath been made a channel of a nation's entreaty and a people's benediction! Thou hast given back to the Princely sufferer strength and hope and life. Command, O mighty Redeemer, that he, like those whom Thou didst make whole when Thou wast visible here among men, may arise from his bed healed and forgiven! Let him follow Thy voice and be Thine for ever. Blend him, O Lord, and his wife, tender and true, with his gracious mother, our Queen, into Thy house and lineage of heaven; so that, at the last, with penitence for all sin, and trust in that which Thou didst suffer upon the cross, this kingly race of England may be gathered into the realm of eternal pardon and peace in the kingdom of God.

Behold the Lamb of God which taketh away the sin of the world, even Jesus Christ our Lord. Amen. (*See* "PRAYER.")

(*c*)

THEOLOGIAN

He was so proud, that should he meet
The twelve Apostles in the street,
He'd turn his nose up at them all,
And shove his Saviour from the wall.

(*d*)   *Churchill, on Bishop Warburton.*

The learned and dogmatic Warburton, who, with the authority of a theologian, prescribes the motives and conduct of the Supreme Being.

(*e*)   *Gibbon, on Bishop Warburton.*

Why, when he gets to heaven, he will be seen mounted on the tallest horse there, and calling out to Paul, "Hold my stirrup," and to Peter, "Bring my whip."

(*f*)   *Cradock, on Bishop Warburton*

THEOLOGIANS

There is something astonishing in the levity with which [the question of revelation] is treated by some of the most popular religious writers of the present day. Christians, for instance, are ridiculed for assuming an undue familiarity with God, and for pretending to a knowledge of His will and of His purposes, such as they may possess respecting each other. Now, let it be granted that it has been one danger of theologians to assume too complete and systematic a knowledge of the Divine nature and dispensations. It is an error, indeed, which has been often prompted, not by irreverence, but by faith. It has been stimulated by that principle with which the New Testament is instinct, a principle which also lies at the basis of modern science, that there is a harmony between the reason of man and the reason of God; it has been encouraged by the words which, perhaps beyond all others, have elevated human thought: Ἐν ἀρχῇ ἦν ὁ λόγος, καὶ ὁ λόγος ἦν πρὸς τὸν Θεόν, καὶ Θεὸς ἦν ὁ λόγος (John i. 1).

(*g*)   *Dr. Wace: Bampton Lectures*

THEOLOGICAL SYSTEMS AND SCEPTICISM

The Christian Church and the Christian creed are not bound up with any of the theological systems which have been elaborated by individuals, and which by their grandeur and grasp have fascinated, from time to time, whole Churches and successive generations. It is one of the commonest artifices of modern scepticism, to assume that the schemes of theologians are the creeds of the Church, and to charge our faith, for instance, with all the logical consequences of Calvinism. But deep as is the debt the Church owes, for various reasons and in various degrees, to the great Fathers and Divines who have endeavoured to penetrate into the mysteries of the revelation entrusted to her,—to an Origen, an Augustine, an Anselm, a Luther, or a Calvin,—she is independent of all of them, and superior to all; and it is at once a great injustice and a great piece of ignorance, to hold her responsible for the imperfections of their systems.

(*h*)   *Ibid*

THEOPHANY, A (Matt. xi. 25–27)

Philosophy has striven in vain to pierce the veil which shrouds the great Creator; but the only-begotten Son, who is in the bosom of the Father, He hath declared Him. In Christ we have Him brought home to our hearts and souls in a living form and a human relationship. It has been said that if God had given a revelation, it would have been written in letters of fire in the firmament. The principle assumed in the objection is true. If God has given a revelation, it must be so written that, in respect to its substance, he that runs may read it, if he will. But how could a personal Being be revealed in the mere phenomena of inanimate nature? A person can only be revealed

(*i*)

in and through other persons, and by means of His relation to them. The Divine Revelation, accordingly, was from the first entrusted to human hearts, and it was finally enshrined in the heart of Christ. It has been written in letters of fire in the soul of the Son of man; it was described with tongues of fire by those who first read it there; and the Spirit by whom that sacred fire was kindled is ever present to fulfil our Lord's promise (John xiv. 20), "Ye shall know that I am in My Father, and ye in Me, and I in you."

(a)   *Dr. Wace : Bampton Lectures*

THEORY AND PRACTICE OF THE ASSURANCE OF THE FORGIVENESS OF SINS

A point of infinite importance to the human heart, in respect to which we are not less absolutely dependent upon positive Divine assurance. That point is the forgiveness of sins. It has been argued with terrible force by some sceptical writers, that, in the regular course of nature, there is no room for remission of sin. It is of the very essence of law to be inexorable, and to enforce remorselessly the consequences of its violation. In view of such considerations it is at least clear that we could have indulged no positive assurance of pardon, except on the express authority of Him who alone can forgive sins. The difficulty, indeed, has a still deeper foundation in practice than in theory; and it is not, perhaps, by sceptics that it is most keenly felt. He who has ever stood by the bedside of a fellow-sinner, passing amidst the pangs of a remorseful repentance into the presence of the Judge of quick and dead, and who has been appealed to, with all the earnestness and directness of a soul brought face to face with eternal realities, to state whether, and why, he is sure there is forgiveness of sins, will know how utterly inadequate to the need is any answer, but that God Himself has declared it. There are only two remedies for these agonies of the conscience. The one is, to administer to the soul the opiate of excuses and palliations for sin; and this is the usual resource of other religions than the Christian, and of the world at large. The other is, the express assurance of the forgiveness of sins, made on the authority of God Himself.

(b)   *Ibid.*

THINGS NOT SEEN

1. Jewish Faith in (Heb. xi. 1, 2)

The spiritual life of the Jewish people, and the animating principle of the saints of the Old Testament . . . was a life based on the invisible, and directed towards an obscure and improbable future. But that invisible world was more real to the elders of Israel than any of the visible things around them, and that future was more certain than that the sun and moon would fulfil their ordinary course. The course of nature, indeed, had been interfered with again and again in their behalf. For them the earth had been shaken, the sea had fled, the heavens had been darkened. To their view no physical order was unalterable, and the external world could be moulded at any moment to the purposes of the Divine will. Though flesh and heart failed them, though the earth was moved and the mountains were carried into the midst of the sea, the Lord of hosts was with them and the God of Jacob was their refuge.

On Him they lavished a passion of love, of devotion, of trust, such as is only evoked by those intense affections under which everything in the world fades and becomes insignificant in comparison with one beloved person. As the visible was thus eclipsed by the invisible, so was the present by the future. Few in number, despised, conquered, exiled, crushed, the Jews grasped with unshaken tenacity the assurance that they were reserved for a glorious destiny; and in their darkest hours they never doubted that the Messiah would appear to deliver them, and to assert His absolute sway. Their literature was prophecy, and their very history embodied the types of the future. And all this was founded on simple faith. They had received certain promises, handed down to them from the fathers of their race; and on those sacred words, few and fragile as they must have seemed to other eyes, they rested the whole edifice of their spiritual, their moral, and even of their physical life.

(c)

2. Christian Faith in

The history of the Christian Church has been of precisely similar character. Its foundations were laid in an exercise of the same faculty—the assurance of things hoped for, the conviction of things not seen. Its expectations have been at once more distant and more near than those of the Jewish elders—more distant, because more and more disengaged, as time went on, from the hope of an immediate return of our Lord in power; more near, because illuminated from the first with a clearer vision of life and immortality beyond the grave. But the prophetical element in the New Testament is perhaps still stronger than in the old. The parables of our Lord constitute a series of prophecies respecting the fate of the Jewish nation and the development of His Church. They have since been marvellously verified; but in the early days of Christianity they made an immense demand on the faith of His followers. The epistles of St. Paul are similarly instinct with prophecy. If he applies the axe to the root of the ancient Jewish polity, he is not content to fall back on simple moral and spiritual convictions; but he plants his foot on the firm assurance of the establishment of a new kingdom by Christ, and of its future revelation; and he looks forward as much as the writer of the Apocalypse to a new heaven and a new earth. Similarly the conviction of things unseen is perhaps still more striking in the Christian Church than in the Jewish. For the unseen God of the Old Testament was a God who by His very nature was invisible, and faith was the only instrument by which He could be apprehended. But the Saviour in whom Christians believe has once been seen and heard, He has worn flesh and blood like ourselves, and in that flesh and blood He passed from earth; and we believe ourselves to be in union and communion with a human nature like our own, as well as with a Divine nature. And as with the Jews so with us—this whole life of faith, which has animated Apostles, martyrs, saints, has been sustained by the promises and assurances of men who, in most respects, were of like passions with ourselves. The witness of a few Apostles and Evangelists constitutes the basis on which the whole fabric of Christendom has been reared. They bear testimony to the most stupendous facts, to the vastest visions of the future.

(d)

They claim for us, if the occasion should arise, the sacrifice of all that in this life men hold dear. They claim it, and a multitude of the noblest souls who have lived since their time have yielded to the demand.

(a)   *Dr. Wace: "Foundations of Faith"*

THINGS SEEN AND UNSEEN, TEMPORAL AND ETERNAL

" The invisible things of God from the creation of the world are clearly seen, being understood by the things that are made " (Rom. i. 20)

(i.)   What if earth
Be but the shadow of heaven, and things therein
Each to other like more than on earth is thought?

(b)   *Milton*

(ii.) In our doctrine of representations and correspondences we shall treat of both these symbolical and typical resemblances, and of the astonishing things that occur, I will not say in the living body only, but throughout nature, and which correspond so entirely to supreme and spiritual things, that one would swear that the physical world was purely symbolical of the spiritual world.

(c)   *Swedenborg*

(iii.) All visible things are emblems. What thou seest is not there on its own account; strictly speaking it is not there at all. Matter exists only spiritually, and to represent some idea and body it forth.

(d)   *Carlyle*

(iv.) Analogy to spiritual truth appropriated from the world of nature or man, is not merely illustrative, but also in some sort proof. It is not merely that these analogies assist to make the truth intelligible or, if intelligible before, present it more vividly to the mind, which is all that some will allow them. Their power lies deeper than this, in the harmony unconsciously felt by all men, and which all deeper minds have delighted to trace, between the natural and the spiritual worlds, so that analogies from the first are felt to be something more than illustrations happily but yet arbitrarily chosen. They are arguments, and may be alleged as witnesses; the world of nature being throughout a witness for the world of spirits, proceeding from the same hand, growing out of the same root, and being constituted for that very end.

(e)   *Abp. Trench*

(v.) The visible universe has been developed from the unseen. . . .
The more special grounds of such a conclusion are, first, the fact insisted upon by Herschel and Clerk Maxwell that the atoms of which the visible universe is built up bear distinct marks of being manufactured articles; and secondly, the origin in time of the visible universe is implied from known facts with regard to the dissipation of energy. With the gradual aggregation of mass, the energy of the universe has been slowly disappearing; and this loss of energy must go on until none remains. There is, therefore, a point in time when the energy of the universe must come to an end; and that which has its end in time cannot be infinite, it must also have had a beginning in time. Hence the unseen existed before the seen. . . . The first in the field was the spiritual world.

(f)   *Cf. "The Unseen Universe"*

(vi.) We know more of mind than we do of body: the immaterial world is a firmer reality than the material.

(g)   *Huxley and Descartes*

(vii.) It is very well for physicists to speak of *matter;* but for men generally to call this *a material world*, is an absurdity. Should we call it an *x*-world it would mean as much; viz., that we do not know what it is.

(h)   *Hinton*

(viii.) We look not at the things which are seen, but at the things which are not seen; for the things which are seen are temporal, but the things which are not seen are eternal (2 Cor. iv. 18).

(i)

THINK

We think our fathers fools, so wise we grow;
Our wiser sons no doubt will think us so.

(j)   *Pope*

Those that think must govern those that toil.

(k)   *Goldsmith*

THOMAS

" We know not " (John xiv. 5)

Gloomy and doubtful.
= " I live, I know not for how long; I die, I know not how soon: I go, I know not whither; how can I be so cheerful? "

(l)   *Braune*

THOMAS AND DOUBT (John xx. 25)

Thomas represents honest, earnest, inquiring, truth-loving scepticism; or that rationalism which anxiously craves tangible evidence and embraces it with joy when presented. This is essentially distinct from the worldly, frivolous scepticism of indifference or hostility to truth, which ignores or opposes the truth in spite of evidence. The former wants knowledge in order to faith, the latter knowledge without or against faith. The faith of Thomas is defective, as compared with the childlike spirit of faith with which alone we can enter the kingdom of heaven, and hence it is gently rebuked by our Lord. For salvation we must go to Christ, not as reasoning logicians, or learned theologians, or pleading lawyers, or calculating merchants, but as the child goes to its mother's bosom, with unbounded confidence and trust.

(m)   *P. Schaff*

THORN IN THE FLESH, THE

I believe they who come the nearest to the Apostle's translation (2 Cor. xii.), must have a proportionate share of his thorn in the flesh, and the buffetings of Satan. A ship would be in danger, with a strong wind and much sail aboard, unless *well ballasted.* I am often obliged to row for want of wind. Rowing is not so pleasant, nor so speedy a movement, as sailing; but it is more free from the risk of being overset. Anything should be welcome that checks the growth of that abomination, pride; and that worst of all abominations, spiritual pride.

(n)   *John Newton*

THOROUGH

If you want anything done *thoroughly*, you must do it yourself.

(a)   *Duke of Wellington*

THOUGHT

Man is evidently made for thinking; this is the only excellence that he can boast. To think aright is the sum of human duty, and the true heart of thinking is to begin with ourselves, our Author, and our end. And yet what is it that engrosses the thoughts of the world? Not any of these objects, but pleasure, wealth, honour, and esteem; in fine, the making ourselves kings, without reflecting what it is to be a king, or to be a man.

(b)   *Blaise Pascal*

Our thoughts are heard in heaven.

(c)   *Dr. Young*

Thanks to the human heart by which we live,
   Thanks to its tenderness, its joys, and fears;
To me the meanest flower that blows can give
   Thoughts that do often lie too deep for tears.
(d)   *Wordsworth*

THOUGHT, SCHOOLS OF, in the Church (Creeds, Parties)

The existence of three schools of thought in our Church has now become the tritest of commonplaces. It is important to observe that they had their prototypes in the Apostolic age; that, where a Church is vigorous and active, they must almost of necessity coexist; that their coexistence is a guarantee of the fulness of teaching; that the loss of any one would be a serious impoverishment to the life of a Church; and that, therefore, it is not expedient to attempt to thrust out, or to starve out, any one of them; while, at the same time, adherence to the fundamental principles of the Catholic creed and loyalty to the Church in which they minister must be demanded of all alike. I am bound to emphasize this demand, because some think that a Church can do very well without a creed. I do not understand a Church without a creed. I do not understand a clergyman standing up to teach without first asking himself definitely what he is going to teach. I can see no other prospect before such a Church but vagueness, irresoluteness, inanity, confusion, decay. The motive power is gone. The bond of cohesion is snapped. Dissolution—rapid dissolution—is the inevitable consequence. So far as I have read history, no body ever has held together for long under such conditions as this. Let us look at the three directions of thought, and try to see their significance. The Gospel—the special message of God to man—may be considered in three different bearings; in its relation to the individual man; in its relation to the Church, the collective body of believers; and in its relation to all that lies without, to mankind and to the universe. Having stated these three relations I have in effect stated the characteristic features of the three great schools which the Church of England at this moment comprises. It is hardly necessary to dwell upon this. In the revival of the English Church the Evangelical school was the earliest in time. The stress of its teaching was laid altogether on personal religion, the relation of the individual soul to God. Then came the Tractarian movement. The history, the constitution, the ritual, the laws, the continuous corporate life of the Christian body, with the corresponding duties of the individual as a member of that body—these were the special study of this second school. The range of vision was thus extended. But a wider field was still open for the contemplation of the Christian and the Churchman. All these problems of social and political life, all these unconverted heathen throughout the world, all these past ages of human history, all these manifold processes of nature—most simple, yet most intricate—most minute, yet most vast—boundless in time and space, what do these mean? What is their relation to the Gospel, to the Christ, to the Church? The Christian, the Churchman, must become cosmopolitan also.

(e)   *Bishop Lightfoot*

THOUGHT, TAKE NO (Matt. vi. 34)

The present interests us all. It altogether absorbs hundreds of thousands. It seems to be at once so transitory and so urgent, so full of claims upon all the attention we can give it, that nothing, or almost nothing, remains:—" Seize the gifts of the present hour with a glad heart. Let the stern problems of the future take care of themselves." So whispered the Epicurean poet nineteen centuries ago. "Take no thought for the morrow," so said our Lord; meaning, Trust yourselves to the fatherly providence of God. "Take no thought for the morrow," says Satan; meaning, Forget there is a future—an endless future—bury thought, bury conscience in the grave of sense and time. Those who live in the present forget alike the future and the past. One such has said of the future, "I know nothing, and the past I cannot help. I will make the most of the pulses of life as moment by moment I feel them beating. All else is beyond me."

(f)   *Anon*

THOUGHTS

Thoughts are words to God, and vain thoughts are provocations.
(g)   *J. Scott*

Thoughts come more freely at odd moments; and sometimes these are the best, as Goethe said that his best thoughts came, "Like singing birds, the free children of God, crying, ' Here we are.' "
(h)   *Storrs*

THREE MIGHTY MEN

"*And the three mighty men broke through the host of the Philistines, and drew water out of the well of Bethlehem*" (2 Sam. xxiii. 16)

David in the hold: Bethlehem, his native place, just opposite: the Philistines lay thick between: only natural that David should long for water from the well of Bethlehem: his three mighty men, who had done great exploits before, pushed
(i)

their way through the enemy, drew water from the well, and brought it to David.

Make an application of the text, and speak of another well.

(i.) The Well of Salvation, from which we must draw living water.

(ii.) Not of Great David, but of his "Greater Son" and Lord.

(iii.) And of three mighty ones, mentioned in the New Testament, who did draw living water out of the well of life, having first overcome great obstacles. One of them was,

(a)

(i.) The poor paralytic (Mark ii. 4)

He wanted to get at Christ, but great obstacles and hindrances were in his way. These were external or outward hindrances, *not something in himself* (he felt his need), *not something in Christ* (because He commended the man).

The hindrance was in the way of getting at Christ, owing to the crowd of others around the door. But the man did not go away because there was difficulty: he overcame the difficulty by surmounting it; going up the steps outside Eastern houses to the top, he was let down right in the midst of the room before Jesus. When Jesus saw him, He said, "Thy faith hath made thee whole." "Son, thy sins be forgiven thee."

(b)

(ii.) The blind man at Jericho—*Bartimæus* (Mark x. 48)

He meets with difficulties in getting to Christ. He cries out; but his voice is drowned by the shouts and cries of others. Louder and louder he calls: many of those around bid him hold his peace; but still he raises his voice, "Jesus, thou Son of David, have mercy on me,"=a piteous cry, of great need.

"Go thy way, thy faith hath made thee whole."

The hindrance or obstacle was one arising from other people trying to prevent him getting to Jesus: he overcame, and is of the three mighty men whose faith conquers.

(c)

(iii.) The Syrophœnician woman for her daughter (Matt. xv. 21–28)

Her obstacles and hindrances are greater than any. All three kinds meet in her case, and yet she conquers, and is therefore the greatest of the three.

(i.) External (an outsider: Tyre and Sidon: not children).

(ii.) From others: "Bid her that she go away."

(iii.) From the Lord Himself: "It is not meet to take the children's bread, and cast it to the dogs."

(d)

Observe how she overcame. Not daunted by outward hindrances, allows she is not a child. Not daunted by the attitude of the disciples, "Send her away." She approaches Christ and "worships Him," saying, "Lord, help me." And what an exquisitely touching prayer; how simple, how thoroughly human! And yet the tenderest heart that ever beat called her "dog" in reply; and the poor creature foiled the Saviour with His own word: "Dog"; yes, "dog," but the dogs don't wait; they eat the crumbs as they fall from their master's table. "O woman, great is thy faith. Be it unto thee even as thou wilt." Thy daughter is relieved of the devil.

Faith is the communion between our need (on earth), and our help (Saviour in Heaven).

N.B.—There are three degrees of faith in overcoming difficulties, (i.) external, (ii.) from others, (iii.) from the Lord.

Such faith wins, and the conqueror becomes one of the "mighty ones" of Christ. All such draw living water out of the well of life.

(e)

THREE PARTICULARS to be looked to

1. Thoughts of atheism should be watched over, as, If there be a God in heaven? which will trouble and assault the best at some times.

2. Growth in grace should be cared for, above all things; and falling from our first love mourned for.

3. Conscience made of praying for the enemies who are blinded.

(f) *Samuel Rutherford*

THREEFOLD PARADISE

There is a threefold Paradise to which we look back with longing eyes; that of the first human pair; that of our childhood; that of the primitive Church (Acts ii. 42–47).

(g) *Lange*

THRONE OF GRACE

What a thought to fill our minds, when we approach a throne of grace—that Jesus is pleading for us, and that *our* prayers are *His*.

(h) *Hedley Vicars*

TIDE

There is a tide in the affairs of men,
Which, taken at the flood, leads on to fortune;
Omitted, all the voyage of their life
Is bound in shallows and in miseries;
On such a full sea are we now afloat;
And we must take the current when it serves,
Or lose our ventures.

(i) *Shakspeare*

TILL I COME (John xxi. 22)

After the destruction of Jerusalem began that mighty series of events of which the Apocalypse is the prophetic record, and which is in the complex known as the *coming of the Lord*, ending, as it shall, with His glorious and personal Advent.

(j) *Bengel, Stier, Alford*

The Destruction of Jerusalem was the beginning of the end.

(k) *Godet*

TIME

I wasted time, and now doth time waste me.

(l) *Shakspeare*

TIME

Oh, how precious is time; and how guilty it makes me feel when I think I have trifled away and misimproved it, or neglected to fill up each part of it with duty, to the utmost of my ability and capacity.

(a)   *David Brainerd*

I declare, now I am dying, I would not have spent my life otherwise for the whole world.

(b)   *Ibid*

What anguish, to think of an eternity for those who are Christless; for those who are mistaken, and who bring their false hopes to the grave with them!

(c)   *Ibid*

TIME

Whenever Melancthon made an appointment, he expected not only the *hour*, but the *minute*, to be fixed, that the day might not run out in the idleness of suspense.

(d)   *Dr. Johnson*

An Italian philosopher's motto = "That time was his estate." An estate, indeed, which will produce nothing without cultivation, but will always abundantly repay the labours of industry, and satisfy the most extensive desires, if no part lies waste by negligence, to be over-run with weeds, or laid out for show rather than for use.

(e)   *Ibid*

TIME, BEYOND AND BEHIND YOUR

If you mount too high above your time, your ears (on the side of fame) are little better off than if you sink too deep below it. In truth, Charles up in his balloon, and Halley down in his diving-bell, felt equally the same strange pain in their ears.

(f)   *J. P. F. Richter*

TIME, REDEEM THE (Eph. v. 16)

" *Transeunt et imputantur* " (They pass away, but are laid to our account), were the words inscribed around the clock placed in the school in which Bossuet was taught.

(g)

Newman filled up the whole of his time—from the fear of deterioration and declension and scepticism. He seemed ever to see a spectre gaining upon him, *and he distanced it.*

(h)   *Mozeley.*

TIME-SERVER

Sherlock was a wretched fellow—a genuine son of the Church—a Vicar of Bray—a trimmer and time-server, like Bishop Sprat, though not quite so barefaced; a thick-and-thin advocate of the *jure divino*, as existing in that miserable man, James II., and, after a little coquetry, a mean and slavish adherent of William III.; and all for preferment—in other words, money and power. He would have submitted to circumcision and turned

Mohammedan, had the faith of the prophet suddenly taken root in England and superseded the Christian.

(i)   *Charles Ollier*

TIMES, THE LAST

The appearance of the Judge is very near at hand; because He is already prepared to execute judgment upon living and dead, there is therefore, as it were, no longer any obstacle which can delay that judgment (1 Pet. iv. 5). With it, however, the Messianic salvation (from this judgment) is also ready to be revealed (1 Pet. i. 5); and from this it is evident that the last moment (καιρὸς ἔσχατος) of the end of the times, in which this salvation takes place, cannot, now that this end of the times has once commenced (1 Pet. i. 20), be much longer deferred. The end of all things is at hand (1 Pet. iv. 7). The Apostle perceives this from the circumstance that, in the present troubles, the judgment of God has already commenced (1 Pet. iv. 17). Just as, according to the teaching of Jesus, the Messianic judgment brings about a separation between the members of the Church, so, according to Peter, the judgment has begun at the house of God, *i.e.*, in the Church of believing Israel. Such a judgment, moreover, had already been looked forward to in Old Testament prophecy (Jer. xxv. 29; Ezek. ix. 6). In the testing afflictions of the present time there is being carried out the separation between the genuine and the spurious members of the Church, and, therewith, also the judgment over those who fall away during these temptations. The greater these afflictions already are, so much the more dreadful appears the end of the necessarily gathering judgment, which will one day come upon the unbelievers (1 Pet. iv. 17). But because this testing time, in which even the righteous is scarcely saved (1 Pet. iv. 18), cannot possibly last long (cf. Mark xiii. 20), the afflictions of the present time can only be for a little while (1 Pet. i. 6; v. 10). Thus, with the greatest energy of Christian hope, the Apostle already brings the goal of the consummation very close to its commencement.

(j)   *Weiss*

TIMES, THE LAST

The final consummation with John is without doubt a heavenly one. As Christ came from above (John iii. 31; viii. 23), so has He gone to heaven, and comes to take His own thither (John xiv. 2, 3). Thither the unbelievers cannot follow Him (John vii. 34; viii. 21; xiii. 33). But He has promised His own that they are to be where He is (John xii. 26; xvii. 24). Eternal life therefore begins in heaven, so far as it is by John regarded as a life yet future. But as eternal life begins even in the present life, seeing that God is seen in Christ, so eternal life in the future life can only consist in this, that the original glory of Christ is seen (John xvii. 24), and God no longer in the revelation of Him in Christ, but He is Himself seen *as He is* (1 John iii. 2). And as the final working of the perfect revelation of God in Christ was, that believers become like Him as His children, so the result of that perfect vision of God must be, that we shall become like Him (ὅμοιοι

(k)

αὐτῷ ἐσόμεθα, ὅτι ὀψόμεθα αὐτὸν καθώς ἐστιν). If eternal life is already given in this life, then the glory of the future can add nothing to what constitutes the real being; it can only bring that given in it to highest completion, even where the distinct step in this consummation is not indicated in the expression. How glorious this consummation will be, is not yet revealed (1 John iii. 2); but that it will come, Christian hope assures us of this (ver. 3). So the first word of the Gospel becomes the last word of the last of the Apostles. As the Kingdom of God which Jesus founded on earth is the security for the completion of the coming one, so the beginning of the realization of the New Testament will of God (Lev. xi. 44) in our state of sonship (ver. 2 : νῦν τέκνα Θεοῦ ἐσμεν) becomes the security for the blessed ending which we hope for in the future.

(a)   *Weiss*

TIMES, THE LAST

With the pouring out of the Spirit the prophecy of Joel immediately connected the coming of the day of Jehovah, *i.e.* of the great Messianic day of judgment, amid dreadful signs in heaven (Joel ii. 30 ff.). By adopting this part also of the prophecy (Acts vi. 19, 20), Peter wishes to intimate explicitly that, as the immediate sequel of the last days, which have already commenced, the Messianic Day of Judgment is near at hand; and this is the day of the second sending of Jesus, seeing that He comes as the Lord and Messiah who has been appointed judge. The present generation of the people, laden as it is with the most heinous sin (γενεὰ σκολία; cf. Deut. xxxii. 5), can naturally only look for destruction in this Judgment (Acts viii. 20 : ἀπώλεια), unless a way of deliverance is pointed out to it. Such a way, however, Peter has pointed out to the people (Acts ii. 40), by explaining the prophecy of Joel, that every one who shall call on the name of the Lord will be saved, as referring to the name of Jesus, who has been exalted to be Lord and Messiah (ver. 21). There is no other name given among men, whereby men can be saved, than the name of the Messiah; therefore it is in Him alone, as the Lord of the completed theocracy, that its members can find the Messianic salvation (Acts iv. 11 ff.). In so far Jesus is exalted not only to be the Lord, but also to be the Saviour (Acts v. 31). As the Messiah who is ordained to be the Judge (Acts x. 42), He has naturally also to determine who shall be delivered from this Judgment; and according to Acts xv. ii., He will, through His favour, deliver all who show, by their calling upon Him, that they have penitently received the message of salvation. With deliverance from destruction, however, there is at the same time given the completed salvation, which consists in (eternal) life. Accordingly, Jesus has also become the Prince of this life (Acts iii. 15 : ἀρχηγὸν τῆς ζωῆς): as the One who has been led to life through the Resurrection, He shows to all the way of life.

(b)   *Ibid*

TIMES, THE LAST

With the second coming of Christ, the last day of the present age of the world dawns (ἡ ἐσχάτη ἡμέρα). Jesus, even in our gospel (John vi. 39, 40, 44, 54), promises the Messianic resurrection of the dead on this day (John xi. 24), and He designates

Himself as the author of that resurrection (xi. 25). But from these passages it is clear that here too, as with Paul, there is a resurrection in the special sense only for believers, who, according to John, have already received eternal life, and for whom therefore the bodily death which they have experienced must in the end be taken away completely. But with this decision comes also the final (Messianic) Judgment, which the Father has given over to the Son, beyond what He has already executed even in His earthly life (John xi. 27), because, according to ver. 22, He has expressly assigned to Him the whole judgment. Believers, to be sure, do not now come into this judgment (iii. 18; v. 24), inasmuch as they have already received eternal life in faith, and therefore it cannot be decided for the first time regarding them, whether they are to receive it; and the world is even judged (John iii. 18; xii. 31), because by their unbelief they have shut themselves out from salvation. But inasmuch as the abiding possession of eternal life (1 John iii. 15) yet actually depends, even for believers, on this, whether he continues in Christ, so his decision depends on this at the last day (John xii. 48), or on the Day of Judgment (1 John iv. 17). On the other hand, there continues, even for the world, the possibility of conversion up to the last moment; and only the world, in so far as it remains the world, perishes, so as never to come to life (1 John ii. 17). It is clear from this, that even here the resurrection of evil-doers is to be understood, so to say, κατ᾽ ἀντίφρασιν, inasmuch as it is raised, not to life, but to be delivered over to abiding death (1 John iii. 14). This death, which is equivalent to eternal destruction, is also the fate of apostate Christians (1 John v. 16), and is compared (John xv. 6), to the fire which consumes the cut-away branches. It is the second death of the Apocalypse.

(c)   *Ibid*

TIMES, THE LAST

The Day of Judgment and of the destruction of the world is infallibly at the same time the day of Christ's Parousia, which the Apostles, according to 2 Pet. i. 16, proclaimed; and therefore His coming is designated (2 Pet. iii. 12) by this technical expression. If Jude applies the Apostolic prophecy of a frivolous moral laxity, which should appear ἐπ᾽ ἐσχάτου τὸν χρόνου, *i.e.*, at the end of the pre-Messianic period of the world, as it also occurs 2 Tim. iii. 1, ff. to the libertines of his own day (vv. 17, 18), it is clear from this that he believes himself already standing in that last time. The last time has also come in the view of the Second Epistle of Peter, as in that of 1 Peter and of the Epistle to the Hebrews; nay, it has even already far advanced, since, in the reproduction of that prophecy, he refers it directly to the last day (2 Pet. iii. 3 : ἐπ᾽ ἐσχάτου τῶν ἡμερῶν). He expects, above all, for these days frivolous scoffers, who will throw doubt on the coming of the Parousia generally, because it had not come during the first Christian generation, during which it was expected; and generally any change in the present form of the world, which had already stood so long, was not to be looked for (iii. 3, 4). But the polemic against such anticipated doubt was all the more necessary, as complaints had already begun to be made in the Church as to the delay of the

(d)

Parousia, to which the author objects, that the postponement was no delay, but an act of God's long-suffering, as He would lead even those Christians who had fallen away to repentance, and so would save them from destruction (Jude 9). If God, therefore, according to His long-suffering towards lost Christianity, had by this postponement of the Judgment given time for a second repentance, as He once gave to the people of Israel, in addition to their first repentance, then they ought to look at God's long-suffering as a ground for their salvation (Jude 15), and so to hasten the coming of the day of the Lord in this way, that by their holy walk they would render any further delay for repentance unnecessary (Jude 12). But from this also it is clear, the approaching end is a motive to strive after Christian virtue.

(a)　　　　　　　　　　　　　　*Weiss*

TIMES, THE LAST

The Church existed even in the pre-Messianic age (Tit. ii. 12 : ὁ νῦν αἰών = ὁ αἰὼν οὗτος), which bears the character of the earthly in its opposition to the Divine (1 Tim. vi. 17 ; 2 Tim. iv. 10 ; Comp. also 1 Tim. iv. 8 : ἡ νῦν ζωὴ καὶ ἡ μέλλουσα). The last times (ὕστεροι καιροί) are at hand, and will bring with them, in consequence of temptation from seducing spirits and doctrines of devils, a great falling away from the faith (1 Tim. iv. 1 ; 2 Tim. iv. 3, 4). The last days will be specially severe, in which a frightful corruption of morals will gain ground, which will even hide itself under a cloak of godliness (Tit. iii. 1–5) ; and these days will the readers not only see, as is evident from the instructions (1 Tim. iv. 3–5) and exhortations (2 Tim. iii. 5) given them regarding these days; but their precursors are even already appearing (vv. 6–8). The hardships of the last times expected by Paul assume then, conformably to the point of view of our Epistles, the form of severe imperilling of the pure faith and moral life. That, however, does not exclude the idea that bodily hardships also await the Christian. If in Tit. iii. 12 reference is made generally to the actual necessity of suffering for the Christian, this suffering appears (Tit. ii. 12) quite as a result of living fellowship with Christ, and so, along with πίστις and ἀγάπη, ὑπομονή appears as a characteristic grace of Christians (Tit. ii. 2 ; 2 Tim. iii. 10 ; 1 Tim. vi. 11 : πραϋπάθεια). But the harder the times were, the more firmly was the Church to grasp for herself what she expects in the future on the ground of faith (Tit. ii. 13).

(b)　　　　　　　　　　　　　　*Ibid*

TIMES, THE LAST

The sacrificial death of Christ forms the dividing point of the two ages ; with Him the Messianic age (ὁ αἰὼν μέλλων) has for the Christians come. They have already tasted its powers (Heb. vi. 5) ; they have already received its blessings (Heb. ix. 11 ; x. 1 : τὰ μέλλοντα ἀγαθά, *i.e.* those promised at the entrance of the New Covenant, and which are connected with the οἰκουμένη μέλλουσα, which is subject to Christ (Heb. ii. 5).

(c)　　　　　　　　　　　　　　*Ibid*

TOBACCO

A good vomit, I confess, a virtuous herb if it be well qualified, opportunely taken, and medicinally used ; but as it is commonly abused by most men, which take it as tinkers do ale, 'tis a plague, a mischief, a violent purger of goods, lands, health, hellish, devilish, and damned tobacco, the ruin and overthrow of body and soul.

(d)　　　　　　　　　　　　　　*Burton*

TOLERATION

Of all the great centres in which the Apostles laboured, the city of Corinth, with its manifold interests, most nearly represents the intensity and variety of modern life. Hence it is just here that we find what we seek. " I am of Cephas." Here speaks the man who clings with fondness to the Church of the Fathers, to the principle of historic continuity, to the traditions of the past. " I am of Paul." Here is the utterance of another to whom the whole Gospel is summed up in the conception of a personal relation to God, of a justifying faith. Lastly, " I am of Apollos." Alexandria was the converging point of all the streams of human life and thought in the ancient world. The function of a learned Alexandrian was to reconcile all these diverse elements in Christ. Apollos was the prototype of a Clement and an Origen and a Dionysius. He who said, " I am of Apollos " was the Broad Churchman of his day. St. Paul tolerated all these schools of theology at Corinth. Shall not we tolerate them among ourselves ? Only his proviso must be ours also—that Christ be not divided.

Tolerate them ? Is this enough ? Ought we not rather to welcome them ? Ought we not to thank God for them ? What is it that makes this Church of England, with all her faults and amidst all her perplexities, the most influential Church among the more highly civilized nations of Christendom ? What, except that, while holding firmly the central truths of the Gospel, she has not broken with the legitimate thoughts and aspirations of any section of society ? She is committed to no Syllabus ; she is pledged to no condemnation of political developments or scientific ideas, which to-day has proved, or to-morrow may prove, to be useful or true.

(e)　　　　*Bp. Lightfoot, on Schools of Thought*

TOLERATION

May 18th, 1793

So far as Popery may concern the civil state of the nations, I apprehend no great danger from it. Infidelity and scepticism seem to be the spreading Popery at present. The spirit and strength of Popery seem quite broken. The Pope himself, I think, is little more regarded by the bulk of the Roman Church, than by the Protestants. The heavy penal laws formerly in force, however politically necessary, do not appear to me consistent either with the letter or spirit of the New Testament. In a religious view, I cannot see why a Papist has not as good a right to worship God according to his conscience, though erroneous, to educate his children, etc., as I have myself. I am no friend to persecution or restraint in matters of conscience. The stir made in 1780, at a time when Protestants were gaining more liberty in Popish countries, I thought was a reproach to our national character, both as Britons and Protestants. And I was not surprised at the event, by

(f)

which I thought the Lord poured contempt upon it. I hope we shall never see such a time again upon such a pretext. I cannot see, that an unprincipled or wicked Protestant is a whit better than a bigoted Papist. Yet these of all sorts are tolerated.

(a)   *John Newton*

TOLERATION

Rome was very tolerant. She had a commodious Pantheon, which could take in any amount of gods, and might well open its doors to receive Jesus of Nazareth. And Rome cared only for her temporal sway; and so long as you obeyed her, and supplied soldiers, and paid taxes regularly—you might worship any Deity you pleased. Why was it, then, that she roused herself to such fury against Christianity? Because she felt—with the strong instinct of self-preservation—that the principles which these humble Galileans taught, were incompatible with the continuance of her existence. She was founded upon force—the will, the cruel will, of the stronger. She utterly denied the equality of men, or of nations. Her destiny was to rule men with an iron rod. The brotherhood of men was a foolish and fanatical dream. And she felt that a religion that inculcated brotherly love, the doing to others as you would be done by, which spoke of the brotherhood of men, and talked of power as a trust put into men's hands by God, to be used, not for selfish, nor even national ends, but for the good of mankind at large—of course she felt that such a religion and she could not co-exist, and she naturally endeavoured to crush her opponent.

(b)   *Gordon Calthrop*

TOMBS

" The living among the dead " (Luke xxiv. 5)

We must go forth, even when we have buried our dead, to our work and to our labour. We are left but little time to meditate on death and life, and the mysteries wrapped up in both, and our own being in its relation to them. It is well, perhaps, that it should be so—well that we should not linger overlong in the shadow-land of memory, and amid the forms that we have known and loved, or, it may be, scorned and not loved, in the past; but press onward to the fresh duties and fresh interests that lie before us, and live what yet remains to us of life as God wills. " Why seek ye the living among the dead?" may well be asked of all who cling too fondly to the life of the past, instead of looking forward to the hope of the life to come. It was an evil and not a divine spirit, of which we read, that those whom it possessed had their dwelling among the tombs.

(c)   *Dean Plumptre*

TOMBS, STATELY

Sorry pre-eminence of high descent
Above the vulgar born, to rot in state!

(d)   *Blair*

Proud e'en in death, here rot in state.

(e)   *Churchill*

TOMBSTONES

If a man needs an elaborate tombstone in order to remain in the memory of his country, it is clear that his living at all was an act of superfluity. Keats's grave is a hillock of green grass with a plain headstone, and is to me the holiest place in Rome. There is in Westminster Abbey a peri-wigged admiral in a night-gown hurried off to heaven by two howling cherubs, which is one of the best examples I know of ostentatious obscurity.

(f)   *Oscar Wilde*

TO-MORROW

A Christian hath no morrow, that is, should put off no duty, until to-morrow.

(g)   *Tertullian*

To-morrow is a satire on to-day,
And shows its weakness.

(h)   *Young*

To-morrow, and to-morrow, and to-morrow,
Creeps in this petty pace from day to-day,
To the last syllable of recorded time;
And all our yesterdays have lighted fools
The way to dusty death.

(i)   *Shakspeare*

To-morrow cheats us all. Why dost thou stay,
And leave undone what should be done to-day?
Begin—the present minute's in thy power;
But still t' adjourn, and wait a fitter hour,
Is like the clown, who at some river's side
Expecting stands, in hopes the running tide
Will all ere long be past.—Fool! not to know
It still has flowed the same, and will for ever flow.

(j)   *Hughes*

In human hearts what bolder thought can rise,
Than man's presumption on to-morrow's dawn!
Where is to-morrow?

(k)   *Young.*

TONGUE

Nature has given us two ears, two eyes, and but one tongue, to the end that we should hear and see more than we speak.

(l)   *Socrates*

TONGUE, SINS OF

" I knew it that day, when Doeg the Edomite was there, that he would surely tell Saul " (1 Sam. xxii. 22)

Cf. *" How great a matter a little fire kindleth "* (Jas. iii. 5).

1. When Eve took the apple, there was a tempter concerned;
2. When the Philistines took Samson, there was Delilah concerned;
3. When Saul slaughtered the priests, there was a Doeg concerned;
4. When Othello killed Desdemona, there was an Iago concerned;
5. When things everywhere go wrong between friend and friend, there is a Mephistopheles concerned;

(m)

6. Similarly, now, when unexpected and un-looked-for mischiefs happen; when friend parts from friend without adequate cause; when fruit drops from the tree ere it is ripe, there is an agent concerned, we have no manner of doubt; that agent is a tempter in the garb of an "angel of light" like the serpent; or a "heifer," like Delilah; or a fiend incarnate, like Iago; or a mischief-maker, for very love of mischief, like Mephistopheles; or a blab and a tell-tale and a gossip-monger, like Doeg the Edomite.

7. An explanation of Doeg's character may be found in the fact that he was an *Edomite*, who passed off for being an "Israelite indeed," yet was a heathen at heart.

(*a*)

Tongue, Sins of

Doeg, the Edomite, an Example of

"*I knew . . . that he would tell Saul*" (1 Sam. xxii. 22)

1. (i.) The Narrative;
　　(ii.) The history of Doeg;
　　(iii.) His character, Ps. lii.;
　　(iv.) Why at the priests' house?

2. Examples of "go-betweens," and their disastrous issues. There may be worse and more infamous vices, but none meaner.

3. Explanation of Doeg's conduct found in the act, that though a seeming Israelite, he was really an Edomite, and at heart a heathen. How significant?

4. "How great a matter a little fire kindleth." A truly regenerate man would watch over such a besetting sin.

(*b*)

Tongue, The Unbridled (James i. 26)

"The tongue," says this Apostle, "is a little member," one of the smallest of our body; but though small, it is capable of getting the mastery, and exerting a pernicious influence over our whole life. Like the little rudder, it turns the big ship whichever way it will. Like a little flame of fire, it can kindle a great matter, and do an incalculable amount of mischief.

Words may separate chief friends;
Words may break up happy families;
Words may inflame a whole district;
Because the tongue is like a wild beast, whom no man can tame, and is set on fire of hell.

The tongue then, being such an unruly member, must be bridled, like an unbroken colt:

It wants bridling,

If it is a blabbing tongue, always at work letting out all its own secrets as well as those of others, and ever engaged to its fullest extent with all the gossip and scandal of the neighbourhood.

It wants bridling,

If it is an angry tongue, and speaks hot, uncontrollable words of anger, and cools down only when its wrath is expended and the mischief done.

It wants bridling.

If it is a promise-making, and at the same time a promise-breaking tongue; if its "yea" does not mean "yea," and if its "nay" does not mean "nay;" if its word is not as good as its bond.

It wants bridling,

If it is an "idle tongue," and has its play sometimes in punning and jesting on the Holy Scriptures, or by talking lightly and glibly of deep and holy things. Of this tongue Jesus said, "For every idle word that men shall speak they shall give account thereof in the day of judgment."

It wants bridling,

If it be a blaspheming tongue, and takes God's holy name in vain, or uses blasphemous oaths and curses in ordinary conversation. "The Lord will not hold such guiltless."

But, perhaps, above all, it wants bridling,

If it be a canting, hypocritical tongue, and has a habit of quoting Scripture in daily business, perhaps, at the same time engaged in some fraudulent transaction, or getting the better of a neighbour in a bargain, or giving him short weight and scant measure. The oily, unctuous tongue, with its soft and glib speech, may sometimes deceive the simple; it does deceive its own heart, the Apostle says, but it cannot deceive God. "By thy words thou shalt be justified, and by thy words thou shalt be condemned." A faithful account is kept, and the Book-keeping of Heaven is not faulty.

All these are leaks in the ship, and will sink it in due time. All these are marks that the fruit on the tree is not Christian fruit. The spot of such is not the spot of God's children. Therefore in earnest warning, and in the truest faithfulness, the Apostle James says: "If any man seem to be religious, and bridleth not his tongue, but deceiveth his own heart, this man's religion is vain."

(*c*)

TONGUES

The miracle of tongues on the first Whitsuntide is the salvation-proclaiming symbol of the final fulfilment of God's great purpose of a kingdom. And the fellowship of this kingdom is in itself one independent of all national limitation.

(*d*)　　　　　　　　　　　　　　　　*Harless*

Tongues, Confusion of, and Acts II.

The confusion of tongues occasioned the dispersion of men (Gen. xi.); the gift of tongues reunited them as one people.

(*e*)　　　　　　　　　　　　　　　　*Grotius*

Tongues, Confusion of

He who hath "*made of one blood all nations of men for to dwell on the face of the earth*" (Acts xvii. 26), directed the repeopling of the world by the descendants of Noah. Like prodigal sons, they were to go into far countries, and learn by bitter experience that neither human strength nor human wisdom can work out *the righteousness of God*, or win back for man his lost inheritance. But the preservation of their names in this table of nations (Gen. x. 1–26) is a proof that no one of them was forgotten by a God of Love; that though they might forget Him, He yet guided their destinies, and overruled their counsels only to the accomplishment of His gracious purposes of Redemption. The Day of Pentecost in the New Testament corresponds to the Confusion of Tongues in the Old. Then, not till then, did men hear, each in his own

(*f*)

tongue wherein they were born, the Glad Tidings of One, in whom *there is neither Jew nor Gentile, neither bond nor free, neither male nor female* (Gal. iii. 28).

(*a*) *Maclear*

TONGUES, THE GIFT OF

" *We do hear them speak in our tongues the wonderful works of God* " (Acts ii. 11)

Three Pictures :

1. Our **First Picture** will be found drawn and described for us in the eleventh chapter of Genesis, where we find it stated that at an early period in the history of the human race there was but *one nation*, and *one language* for the whole earth. But as the tide of population was flowing fast, and was pushing its way eastward, men began to colonize fresh portions of the earth's surface, and get more and more astray from the central home. It seemed imminent that at no distant date the race would split up into fragments, and get scattered in all directions.

(*b*)

This idea, however, as it presented itself to the leading minds of the time, was regarded with great repugnance. They feared that by so doing many rival nations would start into existence—and be a source of weakness rather than of strength. Consequently they very much preferred that the whole mass of people should form but *one nation*, having *one central* city—one home, as it were—and under the government of *one* chief, on the principle that unity is strength ; and so far they were right. But the wrong of autocratism and universalism, such as their scheme involved and was based upon, far outweighed the little of right that it contained.

(*c*)

In order to carry out this scheme, and to stem the tide of emigration, they looked out for a suitable country for building purposes, which they soon found in the land of Shinar. And here they commenced operations : they co-operated one with another, organized themselves into one community, made bricks, and began to build a metropolitan city, with a huge central tower, whose top should reach to the heaven, probably with a view to burn fire on the summit as a beacon light for the guidance of future stragglers and wanderers.

(*d*)

This was to be the home, the meeting-place, and the one central spot around which the whole human family should assemble. For with *one nation*, and *one language*, and *one government* (as they thought) there could not fail to be unity : the whole race would be bound together with one universal bond. This then was their project : and this they determined to carry out in order to get themselves a name and be great.

(*e*)

Now, we stop here to review the position : and to ask what was wrong in this picture as presented to us—for wrong there must have been, or else God in His wisdom would not have interfered to upset the well-laid plan.

First of all, they were wrong in attempting to stop this scattering of the human race all over the earth. It was God's intention and command that men should replenish the whole earth ; and therefore any attempt on their part to stop the emigration and colonization which had already begun, was clearly an attempt to thwart the purpose of God, an act of direct rebellion against His authority, and, as we in Christian times speak, an anti-Christian act, behind which there was undoubtedly *one* sitting as God, and endeavouring to have universal empire. In this usurpation of the authority of God lay one element of the wrong they were committing.

(*f*)

But, further, they were wrong in seeking to preserve the *unity of the race*, in their own blind way. Sin had already blinded their eyes, or they would have perceived that inasmuch as they were all of one stock—all descended from one parent through the family of Noah—and were all worshippers of the one God and Father of all : therefore they already possessed the chief elements of unity ; for if oneness of origin and oneness of religion failed to keep them a united people, what else could make them so ? Hence, from this craving after some other bond of unity, it is not difficult for us to see that sin, and apostasy from God, had already crept in, and broken up the unity internally, which they now were so zealously striving to preserve externally—the thing was really gone, and could not be brought back again by any scheme of theirs. A universalism of sin would only make the matter worse.

They had ceased to love God, and were become lovers of themselves ; and this attempt to carry out their own purposes was but an index to the language of their own hearts, which were rebelliously saying, " Let us defy God. . . . Let us form a universal kingdom. . . . Let us have our own deliverer, and not wait for the promised ' seed of the woman,' the Christ of God."

(*g*)

Thus, on this godless and anti-Christian basis they began their work. And now the moment was come for God to interfere. The godless people must not be allowed to grow too big ; for then " nothing will be restrained from them, which they have imagined to do." A godly nation might indeed be suffered to become powerful, but an ungodly nation must not, since it would be nothing less than a universalism of ungodliness. Hence we read that God came down among them and thwarted their intentions by miraculously confounding their language, so that they could not understand one another's speech ; and the mass of people was necessarily now broken up into fragments which scattered themselves abroad, and became the several starting-points of the nations, and peoples, and kindreds, and tongues, by which the whole earth was overspread.

(*h*)

Now, this picture of the miraculous confounding of speech must be set side by side with the New Testament picture of the miraculous gift of tongues : the one caused men to drift away and become strangers to each other ; the other shows how God will one day gather them all together again, and make them one family, and set up a universal kingdom of righteousness, after the manner in which He is able to subdue all things, and to make them work together for the accomplishment of His own purposes.

(*i*)

Tongues, The Gift of—*continued*

The most that can be said in favour of their scheme is, that they were attempting to pluck unripe fruit; and there is much in the world now that is akin to this mistake of theirs. We hear of combinations of people; these be the days of guilds and brotherhoods, of great international societies, whose avowed object is to bring about a union of the whole human race in some other way than God has appointed; and the teaching of the New Testament is that Antichrist will come and seize hold of the spirit of the age, and attempt to develop his own universal kingdom in the same way. If there is something right, there is also much that is mistaken in all such plans. The same mistake is repeated that was originally made at Babel, in seeking for unity in uniformity, and on a wrong basis; for sin has so deranged the human heart, that it is deceitful above all things, and desperately wicked; and as you cannot build a temple with crumbling stones, since its own weight will cause it to collapse, so no abiding union can be built up amongst men whilst their hearts are unregenerate. You cannot depend on them. Not till men are baptized into *one spirit*— the Spirit of the Father and of the Son—is there the proper material to work with of uniting all men into *one family* and one brotherhood in heaven and in earth.

(*a*)

2. The Second Picture is that described in this second chapter of the Acts

On the day called Pentecost, the disciples of Jesus, in number about 120, were all assembled with one accord in one place; doubtless, too, as the context and the whole circumstance would imply, engaged in prayer, waiting for the promise of the Father. Suddenly some wonderful phenomena presented themselves; there was first of all a sudden sound as of a rushing mighty wind, which filled all the house where they were sitting. Then visible *tongues* like as of fire descended upon each of them, and remained there. Forthwith the whole number of the disciples were filled with the Holy Ghost, and began to speak with other tongues—*i.e.*, as the sequel shows, with *foreign tongues*—so that a vast multitude of people who had come to Jerusalem, "out of every nation under heaven," heard these Galilean fishermen, and for the most part unlearned men, speak every man in *his own tongue* the wonderful works of God.

"And they were all amazed, and were in doubt, saying one to another, *What meaneth this?*"

These of course were they who were disposed to see in this a *sign from heaven:* whilst the others, who mockingly accused the disciples of being full of new wine, were of those who never see a sign in any of the strange things which happen amongst us from time to time.

But undoubtedly this thing was a *sign*, and we reverently ask, *What did it mean?* What was the meaning of this miraculous gift of tongues, which accompanied the outpouring of the Holy Spirit on that day.

(*b*)

It is not enough to say, though so far it is quite true, that it finds its counterpart now in the gift of utterance which many an unlearned, *i.e.*, untrained and unprofessional man—one of the laity

—is endowed with, almost immediately after his conversion, by the Holy Ghost, so that he is impelled to open his mouth and speak the things that "we do know," whereas before perhaps he was not remarkable amongst his friends, and the circle in which he moved, for more than quite ordinary attainments and powers. Over and above this the thing was a sign; and to understand it aright we must keep in mind what has been already said about the *confusion of tongues* at Babel. For the gift of tongues on the day of Pentecost was the direct opposite to the confusion of tongues then. On the former occasion men were scattered, and became *strangers:* now God shows how all mankind may become "no more strangers," but fellow-citizens with the saints, and of the household of God, notwithstanding the fact that they are split up into different nationalities, and speak different languages, and are separated by continents and seas, and still more through the enmity that is in them.

(*c*)

We learn from this sign how God unites men and makes them all *one* family, not, we see, by building a city such as Babel; not by keeping all peoples together, and by forming them into one universal kingdom, and all speaking one common tongue; not by any kind of society, or party, or brotherhood, whose foundation is not Jesus Christ. Nor, I may say, are men made *one* by all belonging to the same Church, or sect, or denomination. Not by any external uniformity does God make men *one*. But it is by giving to each individual man the gift of His Holy Spirit, that the entire race of mankind, whether "Barbarian, Scythian, bond, or free," is cemented together in the highest and truest bonds of fellowship and concord.

(*d*)

And that miraculous event which we commemorate on Whit-Sunday—viz., the gift of tongues— was simply a *sign*, given by God to the world, of the only possible way of uniting the scattered fragments of the human race into *one family—the children of one Father—the citizens of one Republic.*

(*e*)

All the languages, probably of the world, at that time, were represented by the multitude of strangers in Jerusalem at that feast; and though so diverse in nationality, language, and perhaps too in religion, yet the little band of tongues-speaking disciples used these many languages as the media for speaking of "the wonderful works of God," and leavening mankind with one holy leaven; and by so doing they represented what the new world would be when the religion of Jesus Christ had done its work, and leavened the whole world by gathering together all men even in Him, and thereby establishing a universalism of good, and not of evil.

(*f*)

For what was it which kindled every heart and fired every tongue on that day? It was the baptism of the Holy Spirit. It is the possession of this Spirit which makes all men *one*. It destroys all the barriers of caste and nationality; it takes away all minor distinctions between rich and poor, white and black, by drawing men into the closest bonds of sympathy and fellowship—

(*g*)

Tongues, The Gift of—*continued*

which is called in our Creed " The Communion of Saints." In other words, the Holy Spirit makes men feel that they are *brethren*, amongst whom all mere external barriers and distinctions are broken down and done away with completely; whilst internally a most real bond of sympathy unites them—" one spirit, one hope, one Lord, one faith, one baptism, one God and Father of all."

(*a*)

It was as a sign of this great gathering of all nations, and peoples, and kindreds, and tongues into one united family that God gave the Gift of Tongues on the day of Pentecost. Once before, the confusion of tongues had dispersed men, and they became strangers; now, the gift of tongues is a sign of their ingathering into one family, united into a brotherhood of love.

(*b*)

3. The Third Picture will be found in Rev. vii. 9, 10

" I beheld, and lo a great number, which no man could number, of *all* nations, and kindreds, and people, and tongues, stood before the throne, and before the Lamb, clothed with white robes, and having palms in their hands, and cried with a loud voice, saying, Salvation to our God who sitteth upon the throne, and unto the Lamb." Now this, as all know, is a picture of a scene in heaven—where, of course, everything is harmonious, !and all the discords of earth have no place. The whole family of God is gathered together, which once had been so widely scattered and dispersed: separated both physically by seas and continents, as also morally by sin.

Now please to remark that this great number of the redeemed is made up of the same external diversities which have characterized them when living here below. They are still *kindreds, and nations, and peoples, and tongues*, and yet they are united. Now they constitute but *one* family: all speak the same praises, and all join in singing the same song.

And what has made them so? Clearly not *one tongue*, as was the attempt at Babel; but it is because all are dwelt in by the same Spirit, and through Him every heart of that vast assembly has been attuned and brought into fellowship with the Father and His Son Jesus Christ. " The Lord God Almighty and the Lamb *is* the light thereof," whose magnetic power attracts the scattered units —no longer now under the centrifugal power of sin, but under the centripetal influence of the Spirit.

(*c*)

Before bringing this paper to a close, is it not well that we remind ourselves that this gift of the Holy Spirit is *the* promise of the New Testament, and *that* good thing which our heavenly Father is most willing to give to them that ask it? For it is the Spirit which will heal our many unhappy divisions, and make all men love and understand each other.

As we look into our families, and into the many homes that we know, and listen to the different tongues that we hear speaking there—tongues of doubt, tongues of ridicule, tongues of strong dissent, a continual strife of opposing opinions—what, we ask, is it, which will make brethren dwell together in unity? And the answer is, that the

Holy Spirit, when poured out like the consecrating oil, maketh men to be of one mind in a house.

And when, again, we look at the many once happy homes, and see the scattering which has come almost inevitably after the lapse of years, from the different pursuits, inclinations, and callings of the various members, in some cases rents torn by death and sin, in other cases by the scattering here and there all over the earth, by reason of various pursuits and interests; or when we look at the sphere of religion itself, and listen to the jangle of opposing creeds, and see the diversities of public worship, some with us, others against us; we ask, What will unite all these, and bring concord out of so much discord? Is there any common ground where all can meet and agree? There is. For when the Holy Spirit comes to each one, that Spirit which is free, coming we know not whence, and going we know not whither, but tied to no one Church, He comes as the *Comforter*, to tell each one of sin forgiven; as the *Spirit of Truth*, to disabuse our minds of error, by taking of the things of Christ, and revealing them unto us. Then these *units*, hitherto seemingly without spiritual affinity, suddenly come together, attracted by some subtle and powerful instinct, and find how much they have in common, and how truly they were made to dwell together in unity.

(*d*) ***F. B. Proctor***

Tongues, Speaking by

The importance which in the writings of Luke is laid on the activity of the Spirit, seems to be quite Pauline. It is more strongly stated even of Jesus than in the oldest tradition, that He acted and spoke in the power of the Spirit (Luke iv. 14, 18; Acts i. 2), as is also the fulness of the Spirit given to His forerunner (Luke i. 15, 17), and to those who prophesied of Him (Luke i. 41, 67; ii. 25, 27) specially emphasized. In Jesus' speech, the promise (Luke xi. 13) is referred specially to prayer for the Holy Spirit; and the word about blaspheming the Spirit is referred to the Spirit speaking in the Apostles (Luke xii. 10–12). But, above all, it is repeatedly recorded how the Risen One had assured the disciples of the Spirit promised by His Father (Luke xxiv. 49), as the power from on high with which they should be clothed (Acts i. 4, 5, 8; xi. 16). The promise was fulfilled at Pentecost in the first place, where, as the principal of the gifts of grace, He wrought that speaking with other tongues, which is described by Luke as miraculous speech (Acts ii. 4–11), as later the speaking with tongues and prophesying for the first converted Gentiles (Acts x. 44–46), and for the converted disciples of John (xix. 6). As now the Holy Spirit speaks in Old Testament prophecy (Acts i. 16; iv. 25; xxviii. 25), so also does He in New Testament preaching (Acts vii. 51), which is indeed a word of God, as was the former. In conformity with Christ's promise (Luke xii. 12), the Apostles were filled with the Holy Ghost for their defence before the Sanhedrim (Acts iv. 8); but so, too, were all believers equipped by repeated outpourings of the Spirit for bold preaching in the presence of threatening persecution (Acts iv. 31; comp. ix. 31, xiii. 52). The Spirit strengthens faith in them (Acts vi. 5; xi. 24), and communicates the wisdom to them (vi. 3, 10) which they require for preaching. He also gives

(*e*)

to them the manifold special indications as to what they have to do for the discharge of their missionary calling (Acts viii. 29, 39 ; x. 19 ; xi. 12 ; xiii. 2, 4 ; xvi. 6, 7) ; or for the advance of the life of the Church (Acts xx. 28 ; comp. xv. 28 ; v. 3, 9). But here, too, he appears as the organ of prophecy in the narrower sense (Acts xi. 28 ; xiii. 9 ; xx. 23 ; xxi. 4, 11 ; comp. vii. 55) ; but never, on the other hand, in the specific Pauline sense as the principle of the new spiritual life.

(a)　　　　　　　　　　　　　　　　*Weiss*

TOUCH ME NOT (John xx. 17)

There is a remarkable difference between Mary's case and that of Thomas. She believed too much ; he too little. She was all faith,—faith too hasty in its conclusions ; he was all unbelief,—unbelief refusing to believe even that this was his Master. Her too eager faith is corrected by the " Touch Me not, but go," etc. ; his unbelief is removed by the " Reach hither thy hand," etc. Each is treated with marvellous wisdom, gentleness, and love. How unlike man's way of dealing! He would have said to Faith, " Touch Me ; " to Unbelief, " Touch Me not."

(b)　　　　　　　　　　　*Horatius Bonar*

TRADITION

I will not seek to disparage the great principle of tradition—that principle to which the Christian Church owes her sacred volume itself, no less than her treasure of formulated doctrine, and the structural conditions and sacramental sources of her life—that principle to which each generation of human society is deeply and inevitably indebted for the accumulated social and political experiences of the generations before. Precious, indeed, to every wise man—to every association of true-hearted and generous men, must ever be the inheritance of the past !

(c)　　　　　　　　　　　　　　　*Liddon*

TRADITION

Next to Chillingworth, we know none of our older authors by whom the uncertainty of tradition, and the egregious folly of trusting to it, have been more completely demonstrated than by Jeremy Taylor. His learning is so profuse, and his imagination so brilliant, as to throw into the shade his other endowments. But when he does himself full justice, his logic is quite equal to his rhetoric.

(d)　　　　　　　　" *Edinburgh Review*," 1844

TRANSFIGURATION, THE (Luke ix. 28, etc.)

1. Jesus

Transfiguration for Jesus was an anticipation of His glory. Cf. " We shall be changed." It reminds us of what would have taken place in Adam's development if he had not fallen under temptation. Now man's development is through death. The difference between death and transfiguration is, that death is " the wages of sin " ; " by sin came death," therefore there could be no death for Jesus unless voluntary. Cf. " No man taketh it from Me ; I lay it down of Myself."

" *As He prayed :* " His countenance altered. The general effect of prayer on the countenance. It brings a calm, peaceful look. The prelude of

communion with God in Heaven—in it we have a slight anticipation of what is meant by the glory consequent on communion with God. Cf. Moses and Stephen with this ; and the " Solar look " in some cases of dying people.

(e)

2. Moses and Elias

(i.) Heaven and earth touch at such moments. So here, the inhabitants of heaven talk with Jesus. " He spake of His departure which He should accomplish at Jerusalem." How would Jesus go? If naturally, *now ;* if for us, by *Death.*

(ii.) *The Recognition :* though glorified, we shall know each other in heaven.

(f)

3. The Disciples : Peter, James, and John

(The speaker, the worker, and the thinker)

Asleep while Jesus was praying—a mark of the earthly and the heavenly natures respectively.

But when awake Peter said, " It is good for us to be here "—dwell here—" let us stop here altogether, and build three tents." " Not knowing what he said," for they have to go down to earth, back to their work, to suffer and to die as His witnesses, before they attain to their heaven.

(g)

4. God

The cloud invests God as a veil.

(i.) " *They feared* "—nearness to God ;

(ii.) The *voice* out of the cloud (always so) :

(iii.) " This is My beloved Son, hear ye Him in whatever He teaches ; follow Him, wherever He leads, and all will be well."

(h)　　　　　　　　　　　　　*Cf. Godet*

TRANSUBSTANTIATION

When we reflect that Sir Thomas More was ready to die for the doctrine of Transubstantiation, we cannot but feel some doubt whether the doctrine of Transubstantiation may not triumph over all opposition. More was a man of eminent talents. He had all the information of the subject that we have, or that while the world lasts any human being will have. The text, " This is My body," was in his New Testament as it is in ours. The absurdity of the literal interpretation was as great and as obvious in the sixteenth century as it is now. No progress that science has made, or will make, can add to what seems to us the overwhelming force of the argument against the Real Presence. We are therefore unable to understand why what Sir Thomas More believed respecting Transubstantiation may not be believed to the end of time by men equal in abilities and honesty to Sir Thomas More. But Sir Thomas More is one of the choice specimens of human wisdom and virtue ; and the doctrine of Transubstantiation is a kind of proof charge. A faith that stands that test will stand any test.

(i)　　　　　*Macaulay, on Sir Thomas More*

TRANSUBSTANTIATION

The idea of the Catholic system is a dream, and has no real existence among the Papists. The reality is a system of mean trivial details, wearisome and disgusting. Instead of perfect com-

(j)

munion with the Divine Light, you will have before you and above you nothing but the narrow conceptions of some ignorant priests to whom you must submit your intellect. What freedom of thought or existence will remain to you when you have fully accepted the article of Transubstantiation, and truly believe that the priest is able of a piece of bread to make absolutely and unconditionally our Saviour's body, and thereby at the hour of death to save your soul? Will it not have an effect upon you to make you think him a god, and to stand in awe of him as of God Himself if He were visibly present?"

(a)   *Hobbes (Shorthouse: John Inglesant)*

TREE, AND ITS FRUITS, THE

The tree is known by its fruits, and the book is known by its effects. A sceptic once told a coloured man that the Bible was not true.

"That Book not true? That Book *is* true. I was once *a drunkard*, and a liar, and a blasphemer, and I used to steal; and that Book taught me to be honest and true. If that was a bad Book, it would not make bad men good."

(b)

TRIAL

"*Now I know that thou fearest God, seeing thou hast not withheld thy son, thine only son from Me*" (Gen. xxii. 12)

Temptation (verse 1) = *Trial—a test of strength*: Life is a series of trials. But one great *crisis* or *trial* comes in every life—the pivot upon which all turns = THE *trial*—but not the only one.

Abraham's life full of trials:

(i.) Leaving his father's house.
(ii.) The safety of Sarah in Egypt.
(iii.) The parting with Lot.
(iv.) Unbelief in regard to Sodom and Gomorrah.
(v.) Dismissal of Hagar and Ishmael.
(vi.) Old—large estate—no heir.

Such were some of the trials of the inner life of a man full of outward prosperity.

And thus *Abraham's* is a good example of a godly man's life.

"When thou comest to seek the Lord, prepare thyself for adversity."

(c)

Learn:

1. That trial is necessary:

(i.) *To purify the soul*: Dross and alloy—the crucible.

(ii.) *For spiritual growth and maturity.*

No vigour without wintry blasts;

The cloister = where people are cut out to one pattern—like palisadings around a building—no individuality.

Thus we understand Abraham's life:

(i.) *As a life of trial*—in which trials become harder as he grows older; and in some of which he fell—in others came off victorious.

(ii.) Showing that he was *no perfect man*, but was perfected through trials, that his was a *real* life—like ours—not a *romance*.

(d)

2. That we are tried in our most vulnerable part:

Where we are most keenly sensitive and susceptible.

The truth in the ancient fable of the mother who dipped her son in the Styx—his heel escaping was thereafter the vulnerable point.

So we have each a vulnerable point—*Abraham had;* and there God tried him.

(i.) *Abraham loved God; but Abraham also loved his son,* "whom thou lovest," there was his vulnerable point.

The question was: Could Abraham give up his best at the call of God, and yet say, "*God is love*"? Would his love to God stand the test?

Imagine the father pleading: "Anything but this! O Lord, spare me Isaac!"

But it is Isaac that God asks for. And Abraham obeys. He endures the test. Hence God says, "Now know I that thou fearest God, seeing thou hast not withheld thy son, thine only son from Me."

(ii.) God is continually trying us. He does not ask for our *Isaac*, but for a proof that we love Him. Do we love Him enough to give Him back something that He has given us?

(e)

3. The Gospel is in this

"Abraham rejoiced to see My day, and he saw it and was glad" (John viii. 56). "God is love." His love is shown by the same test. "Herein is love"—"He spared not His own Son." And though doubts of this may arise, yet with a slight alteration of the words we may say, "Now I know that Thou lovest me, seeing Thou hast not withheld Thy Son, Thine only Son from me.

(f)

TRIALS

Every man is a believer in daylight, a fair day seemeth to be made all of faith and hope. What trial of gold is it to smoke it a little above the fire? But to keep gold perfectly yellow-coloured amidst the flames, and to be turned from vessel to vessel, and yet to cause our furnace to sound, and speak, and cry the praises of the Lord, is another matter.

(g)   *Samuel Rutherford*

TRIBULATION

"*We must through much tribulation enter into the kingdom of God*" (Acts xiv. 22)

Were we to judge from the conduct of many, we might conclude that it is an easy thing to be a Christian.

They seem to think that it is as easy to wash one's heart as one's hands; to change their habits as their dress; to admit the light of truth into their souls, as to open the shutters of a morning; or that conversion is as easy a matter as turning a ship round by the helm.

How else do we account for delay in the matter of salvation, or for a death-bed repentance?

It ought certainly to be an easy task that is delayed till we are unfit for anything else.

Easy to be a Christian? Did Abraham find it easy to obey God? "Take now thy son, thine only son Isaac, whom thou lovest, and get thee into the land of Moriah, and offer him there for a burnt offering on a mountain which I will tell thee of," —was that easy for a *father?* was the Cross easy

(h)

for Christ ? Is it easy to mortify the flesh ? to be crucified to the world ? to resist the devil ? to die daily unto sin ? Is it easy to be Christlike ? No, it is not easy. No one who knows anything about it would dare to say that it is an easy thing to be a Christian. IT IS NOT.

It is difficult. "The kingdom of heaven suffereth violence ; " and were it not that God promises to perfect His strength in our weakness, we should fail. Look, too, at the words of our text : The apostle Paul had but lately been stoned and left for dead. He revives and goes round the Churches, " confirming the souls of the disciples, exhorting them to continue in the faith, and that " we must through much tribulation enter into the kingdom of God."

(a)

1. There is an Entrance to the Kingdom of God. What is that Entrance ?

(i.) Jesus says, " I am the door : by Me if any man enter in he shall be saved."

Again,

(ii.) "I am the Way. No man cometh unto the Father but by Me."

Again,

(iii.) He qualifies the " door " or " gate," saying that it is " strait ; "

And the " way," by telling us that it is " narrow."

The entrance, then, to the kingdom of God is by a " strait gate " and a " narrow way." That gate is Christ, and unless a man enters in by this way he cannot be saved.

(b)

2. Unless a man is humble, he cannot enter

(i.) We are too big, the entrance is small (" strait," " narrow ")—we have too many coats on, and must take them off. Come with " nothing " : naked.

" Nothing in my hand I bring "

We come with too much self-importance. Proud of our own deserts, self-righteous ; and we want to go in as we are, but we are sent back.

The order is, "Take off thy robe of self-righteousness, and lay thine honour in the dust ; "

For, " except ye become as little children, ye cannot enter the Kingdom of Heaven."

And so, before we are admitted, we have to be humbled ; and the process of humiliation, which God puts us through, gradually reduces us to the proper dimensions, and we become small enough to enter in by the " strait gate." We count our righteousness as filthy rags, and depend on Christ's righteousness only.

(ii.) This is done by " much tribulation."

Jewels require much polishing.

Tribulation is " a crushing, squeezing," process. We are too big—tribulation makes us smaller, by squeezing us into the right shape ;—we have a right eye too much, it must be plucked out ; we have a right hand too much, it must be cut off ; we have a besetting sin—our only failing, our only weakness—it is to be crucified ; and God sends tribulation and points to that sin ; it squeezes that sin, it crushes that sin, and God lets you know that that sin was standing in your way. He sent the tribulation for the purpose of cutting and tearing it out. Painful, but necessary. You could

not walk along the narrow way to the Kingdom of Heaven, whilst you were encumbered with that sin—the road was not wide enough to admit you and it, and the road gets narrower as you proceed.

Tribulation is necessary

(i.) To prepare us for Christ.

(ii.) To prepare in us Christ.

This is His own order.

(i.) " Come unto me."

(ii.) " Take my yoke."

(iii.) There is no other way—" MUST "

(c)

3. A Remarkable Dream

I thought I was sitting, a little before daylight, with my deceased brother on the wall of the parish church-yard, where we had lived many years together. We remained silent for some time, and then he asked me if I would not go with him into the church. I readily consented, and immediately rising up, walked with him towards the porch, which I thought was very large and spacious ; but when he had passed through it, and came to the inner door that led to the body of the church, some way or other, (but how, I could not well conceive,) my brother slipped in before me, and when I attempted to follow, which I was all eagerness to do, the door, which slid from the top to the bottom, like those in some fortified town on the Continent, was instantly let down more than half way, so that I now found it quite necessary to bend myself almost double before I could enter. But as I stooped to try, the door continued falling lower and lower, consequently the passage became so narrow, that I found it altogether impracticable in that posture. Grieved to be left behind, and determined to get in if possible, I fell down on my hands, and tried to squeeze my head and shoulders through ; but finding myself still too high, I then kneeled down, crept, wrestled, and pushed more eagerly but all to no purpose. Vexed to the last degree, yet unwilling to be left outside, I resolved to throw off all my clothes, and crawl in like a worm ; but being very desirous to preserve a silk embroidered waistcoat, which I had brought from France, I kept that on, in hopes of being able to carry it with me. Then laying myself flat on my face, I toiled, and pushed, and strove, soiled my embroidered waistcoat, but could not get in after all ; at last, driven almost to despair, I stripped myself entirely, and forced my body between the door and the ground, till the rough stones and gravel tore all the skin and flesh upon my breast, and, as I thought, covered me with blood. Indifferent, however, about this, and perceiving I advanced a little, I continued to strive and squeeze with more violence than ever, till at last I got safely through. As soon as I stood upon my feet on the inside, an invisible hand clothed me in a long white robe, and as I turned round to view the place, I saw a goodly company of saints (among whom was my brother) all dressed in the same manner, partaking of the Lord's Supper. I sat down in the midst of them, and bread and wine being administered to me, I felt such seraphic joy, such celestial ecstasy, as no mortal can express. I heard a voice call me three times by name, saying I was wanted at home. My joy was so great and overcoming, that it soon broke the silken bands of sleep, and made me start up in my bed, singing the praises of God.

(d)   *Memoir of Major-General Burn*

TRIBULATION (Rev. vii. 2-13)

(i.) The sealing (making secure).
(ii.) The Four Winds, (troubles from all sides).
(iii.) The Result =
   1. The winds take the chaff.
   2. The coming *out* of tribulation.
Afterwards the questions
" Who are these ? " and " Whence came they ? "
(a)

TRIBULATION (AFFLICTIONS)

What say you? would you not be afflicted?
Whether would you rather mourn for a while, or
for ever? One must be chosen: the election is
easy. Whether would you rather rejoice for one
fit, or always? You would do both. Pardon me,
it is a fond covetousness, and idle singularity, to
affect it. What! that you alone may fare better
than all God's saints! that God should strew
carpets for your nice feet only, to walk into your
heaven; and make that way smooth for you, which
all patriarchs, prophets, evangelists, confessors,
Christ Himself, have found rugged and bloody!
Away with this self-love; and come down, you
ambitious sons of Zebedee; and, ere you think of
sitting near the throne, be content to be called
unto the Cross. Now is your trial. Let your
Saviour see how much of His bitter portion you
can pledge: then shall you see how much of His
glory He can afford you. Be content to drink of
His vinegar and gall; and you shall drink new
wine with Him in His kingdom.
(b)   *Bishop Hall*

TRIBULATION, REJOICING IN

What weights do burden you I know not; but
think it great mercy that your Lord, from your
youth, hath been hedging in your outstraying
affections, that you may not go astray from Himself. If you were not His own child, He would not
nurture you so; if you were for the slaughter, you
would be fattened. But be content, you are His
wheat growing in our Lord's field (Matt. xiii. 25,
38); and if wheat, you must go under our Lord's
threshing instrument, in His barn-floor, and
through His sieve (Amos ix. 9); and through His
mill to be bruised, as the Prince of your salvation,
Jesus was (Isa. liii. 10), that you may be found
good bread in your Lord's house. The Lord Jesus
bless the spiritual husbandry, and separate you
from the chaff, that does not abide the wind! . . .
I am persuaded your glass is spending itself by
little and little; and if you knew who is before you,
you would rejoice in your tribulation.
(c)   *Samuel Rutherford*

TRIBULATION, THE WAY OF (Acts xiv. 22)

(i.) Those who walk in it: all true Christians—
"*we*." Therefore, be not alarmed.
(ii.) The necessity of walking in it—"*must*."
Therefore, do not draw back.
(iii.) Its nature; it is rude and long, but not
made by us—"*through much tribulation*." Therefore, do not despond.
(iv.) Its end: Salvation—"*into the kingdom of
God*" Therefore, do not neglect this great
salvation.
(d)   *Florey*

TRILOGY, A

The writings of St. John:
The Gospel, the Epistles, and the Apocalypse,
represent the evangelic founding, the organic
shaping, and the eternal future of the Church;
Christ, who was, and is, and is to come.
(e)   *Lange*

TRIMMERS

Neuters, in their middle way of steering,
Are neither fish, nor flesh, nor good red-herring,
Nor Whigs, nor Tories they; nor this, nor that;
Nor birds, nor beasts; but just a kind of bat:
A twilight animal; true to neither cause,
With Tory wings, but Whiggish teeth and claws.
(f)   *Dryden*

TRINITY, Practical Bearing of the Doctrine of the

Some persons tell us, others hold without telling us, that the doctrine of the Trinity is a mere
matter of speculation, and that it is of little consequence whether you accept it or no. "Accept
it," they say, "perhaps it is right to do so, seeing
that you are a member of the Church of England,
which holds and teaches the doctrine. But if you
reject it, well, there is no great amount of harm
done. You may be just as good a man, and live
as good and useful a life." Let me answer this
argument, if we may dignify it with the name of
argument—briefly. If the doctrine of the Trinity
be not true, Jesus Christ is not Divine, is not the
Son of God; and if Jesus Christ be not the
Son of God, His sacrifice on the Cross ceases to
be a sacrifice, an act of atonement, and dwindles
into a pattern or model of perfect patience. On
the same supposition, His perfect obedience to the
Father's will has no value for us, except as an
example, which we are really incapable of imitating;
and He has no power of communicating to us that
eternal life by which we serve Him here, and in
which we shall attain to pure and unalloyed
happiness in the world beyond the grave. Now, on
such a supposition as this, how are you and I to be
saved? How are our sins to be pardoned? How
are we to be accepted by God? How are we to
obtain the gift of eternal life here as well as hereafter? Of course we must manage this business
ourselves. Well, all I can say is, "Do it yourselves
if you can; get forgiveness for yourselves, if you
can; get a righteousness for yourselves, if you
can." But you know as well as I do that the
thing is impossible. You depend upon Christ, the
God-man for all these blessings.
See then the use of the doctrine of the Trinity!
With the Trinity we may be saved by God; without the Trinity we must save ourselves. And if that
be not a practical issue, I do not know, for my
part, what is the meaning of the word "practical."
(g)   *Gordon Calthrop*

TRINITY, THE

"*For through Him we both have access by one
Spirit unto the Father*" (Eph. ii. 18)
Introduction. Doctrine of the Trinity, the description of *what we know* of God. Have no right
to say of what God is, for what there may be in
Deity of which we have no knowledge how can we
(h)

tell? At all events, in the manifoldness of His Being these three personal existences, Creator, Redeemer, Sanctifier, easily make themselves known to the human life. Our doctrine of the Trinity is the account of what we know of God. This idea borne out by the text.

(i.) Paul does not profess to be here describing God, but recounting the story of man's salvation, *i.e.*,—he is describing only the God whom man can know.

(ii.) Notice the completeness with which the God of human salvation is here depicted. Every act made up of a purpose, a method, and a power. And this is human salvation analyzed in the text. What is the purpose? "To the Father we all have access." What the method? "Through Christ Jesus." What the power? "By the Spirit." The salvation is one, and yet it is three in one.

Illustration of this truth. Take the act of a boy's education. If you set a low ideal before him, you may give him the best teachers, and inspire him with enthusiasm, but you will turn out only a half-made man. The *end* not worthy of method and power. Or the standard you set before him may be the highest, but if you furnish him with only poor means, the *method* will be unworthy of the end and power. Or, you may make the ideal perfect, and provide the best appliances, but if you put only some low or mercenary impulse into the scholar's heart, the *power* will be unworthy of the method and end. In either case his education will be imperfect. Now, instead of a boy's education, put a man's salvation. If it be not *to the Father,* the Son's redemption is in vain. If it be not *through the Son,* the Father waits, and the Spirit moves for nought. If it be not *by the Spirit,* the Father's heart stands open, and the method of grace is perfect, but the unmoved soul stands inactive and unsaved. Scripture teaches us that end, method, power, all are perfect, and each must thus be worthy of the rest. The three are one.

(i.) *The end of human salvation is access to the Father.* This the first truth of our religion. The source of all, the end of all. Men need to learn the Divinity of the Father, for without this they will never learn that the true end of their life is Divine. *This the Divinity of the end.*

(ii.) *Consider the Divinity of the method.* "Through Jesus Christ." Man alienated from God, Christ's life and nature the bridge which opens the gulf. Out of which nature came the Mediator? He is both human and Divine, but from which side did the bridge spring? "God sent His Son." This the very soul of the Gospel. As the end was Divine, so the method is Divine. As it is to God we come, so it is God Who brings us there. Analogy: A strong nation sending an embassy to win back to their allegiance a colony of rebels. Would not the embassy sent be of the country that sent it? And so the Son of God, the true, fit, only perfect messenger of God to a sinful world. It is through the Divine method that we must come to the Divine end.

(iii.) *The Divinity of the Power.* "By one Spirit." What do we mean by the Holy Spirit being the power of salvation? The soul is a live thing. The Divine power takes possession of its capacities and becomes an indwelling energy in the soul itself, setting it homeward to the Father. To return to the analogy: God is the Divine Fatherland of the human soul; Christ, like the embassy which comes out of the Fatherland to win it back

from its rebellion; and the Holy Spirit is the Fatherland wakened in the rebellious colony's own soul, and seeking its own.

We believe then in the Divine power one with the Divine method and the Divine end, in God the Spirit one with the Father and the Son. This is the truth of the Deity as it relates to us. Each cannot be worthy of the other unless each is perfect. But each cannot be perfect unless each is Divine; that is, our faith in the Trinity—three Persons and one God.

Let us keep that faith. I do not mean "cling to an idea " merely, but let us seek to come *to* the highest, *through* the highest, *by* the highest. Let the end. and the method, and the power of our life be all Divine.

(a)   *Phillips Brooks*

TROUBLE

"The world is full of trouble." While we are young we do not see how true this ancient homely saying is. The first chapter of Job is but a great condensation of all the sorrows that fall like hail upon many a mortal house. Job's black day is a type of a year—a bitter human year. It is terrible how quickly a human landscape, all gilded meadow, silver river, and blue sky, can cloud and darken.

(b)   *Charles Reade*

TROUBLES

. . . Seated in my elbow-chair, I insensibly fell asleep. On a sudden, methought there was a proclamation made by Jupiter, that every mortal should bring in his griefs and calamities, and throw them together in a heap. There was a large plain appointed for this purpose. I took my stand in the centre of it, and saw, with a great deal of pleasure, the whole human species marching one after another, and throwing down their several loads, which immediately grew up into a prodigious mountain, that seemed to rise above the clouds. . . . My heart melted within me to see my fellow-creatures groaning under their respective burdens, and to consider that prodigious bulk of human calamities which lay before me.

There were, however, several persons who gave me great diversion. I observed one bringing in a fardel very carefully concealed in an old embroidered cloak, which, upon his throwing it into the heap, I discovered to be poverty. Another, after a great deal of puffing, threw down his luggage, which, upon examining, I found to be his wife.

There were multitudes of lovers, saddled with very whimsical burdens, composed of darts and flames; but what was very odd, though they sighed as if their hearts would break under these bundles of calamities, they could not persuade themselves to cast them into the heap when they came up to it; but, after a few vain efforts, shook their heads, and marched away as heavy laden as they came. I saw multitudes of old women throw down their wrinkles, and several young ones who stripped themselves of a tawny skin. There were great heaps of red noses, large lips, and rusty teeth. . . . But, what most of all surprised me, was a remark I made, *that there was not a single vice or folly (or sin) thrown into the whole heap. . . . (As a trouble at all).*

(c)   *Addison*

TRUE

> This above all—To thine own self be true;
> And it must follow, as the night the day,
> Thou canst not then be false to any man.

(a)   *Shakspeare*

TRUE FOOD, MY FLESH IS (John vi. 55)

This verse is decisive against all explaining away or metaphorizing the passage. Food and drink are not here mere metaphors;—rather are our common material food and drink mere shadows and imperfect types of this only real reception of refreshment and nourishment into being.

(b)   *Alford*

TRUST

"*I know in whom I have believed* [*trusted*]" (2 Tim. i. 12)

The Apostles (of Jesus Christ) appeal to my whole being, to every moral sense of which I am conscious, to my weakness and my strength, my sin and my repentance, my intellect and my heart, and evoke towards themselves, and still more to One beyond themselves, that complete allegiance of the whole man which is designated faith.* I do not pretend to have a scientific knowledge of Divine things, or to rest my convictions upon a scientific demonstration; but I can venture to say that, " I know in whom I have believed." Such a belief will be supported by collateral evidence, acquiring from age to age a cumulative and converging force; but its essential virtue will in all ages be derived from the vital sources of personal love and trust.

(c)   *Dr. Wace*

* **Two Parables, Illustrating this Claim of the Apostles**

Perhaps the strongest claim of Christ and His Apostles is, that " they have proved themselves to be our superiors by appealing to the faculties,"—above all the moral faculties,—"which we have in common : "

1. A blind man and a seeing man were once discussing the existence of sight. The seeing man told the blind man that he had a faculty by which he could perceive innumerable things which he could neither hear, touch, smell, nor taste, and which were at a great distance from him. The blind man challenged the seeing man to prove his assertions. " That," said the seeing man, " is easily done. Hold me by the hand. You perceive that I am standing by you. I affirm that if you will walk fifty steps along the side of this wall, which you can touch with your hand, so as to be sure that you are moving straight on, you will find such and such objects, which I specifically describe, and as to the existence of which you can satisfy yourself by your own fingers." The blind man readily admitted that the seeing man had proved his assertion.

(d)

2. Of two men with eyes, A. and B., A. declared that he could see what went on in the sun, moon, and fixed stars ; and that when he said, " see," he meant, not exactly common seeing, but a superior kind of seeing, very hard to describe to any one

who did not possess it, which he called "intuing." B. (who had a good pair of eyes of his own of the common kind) challenged A. to read the *Times* newspaper at a distance at which B. could not read it. A. failed to do so. "Why," said B., "should I believe that you can 'intue' things in Sirius, when you cannot read small print on the other side of the room ? If you want me to believe that you possess faculties of which I am destitute, you must prove yourself to be my superior by appealing to the faculties which we have in common."

(e)   *Sir James Stephen, quoted by Dr. Wace*

TRUST (BELIEF)

Belief is an assent to that which is credible, as credible (*Bishop Pearson*)—not, that is, so far as it is probable, still less so far as it is demonstrable, but simply so far as it is supported by the evidence of credible witnesses. . . . In place of Professor Clifford's assertion,—that " The credulous man is father to the liar and the cheat ; he lives in the bosom of this his family, and it is no marvel if he should become even as they are,"—we should be much nearer to experience of practical life if we alleged this of the suspicious man. At all events, it may be safely said, that the trustful man is father to the truth-speaking and the honest man; he lives in the bosom of this his family, and it is natural that he should become even as they are. " With what measure ye mete withal, it shall be measured to you again."

(f)   *Dr. Wace*

TRUSTFULNESS OF HUMAN NATURE

There is something profoundly touching as well as amazing, in the spectacle thus presented to us —in the power of Mohammedanism, Brahminism, Buddhism, Confucianism. We behold millions of men and women, most of them struggling painfully under physical burdens, amidst moral and mental perplexities, with but a brief span of life before them, and no certain knowledge of the world beyond, yet trusting their souls and their whole present and future to the guidance of a man like themselves, whose claims to their allegiance must in great measure rest on his own word and assurance. In reliance on him they are ready to meet death and torture themselves; they are content to train their children to follow the same guidance, until the hopes and interests of countless generations have been hazarded on the promises of a single prophet or sage. There would seem to have been no limit to the trustfulness of human nature; and the responsibility of those who have appealed to this trust, and who in some instances have abused it, is proportionately tremendous.

(g)   *Dr. Wace : " Foundations of Faith "*

TRUTH

> Truth to her old cavern fled.

(h)   *Pope*

> The sages say, Dame Truth delights to dwell,
> Strange mansion ! in the bottom of a well.

(i)   *Walcott*

> Tell truth, and shame the devil.

(j)   *Swift*

TRUTH

When Fiction rises pleasing to the eye,
Men will believe, because they love the lie ;
But Truth herself, if clouded with a frown,
Must have some solemn proof to pass her down.
(a)   *Churchill*

For Truth has such a face, and such a mien
As to be loved needs only to be seen.
(b)   *Dryden*

Truth is unwelcome, however divine.
(c)   *Cowper*

TRUTH, BUY THE

Buy the truth, and sell it not. Pay the price
required. Buy with obedience. Buy with study.
Buy with self-denial. Buy with self-sacrifice.
Buy with fidelity. And know that still, whatever
you pay, the truth you buy is the unpurchasable
gift of God through Jesus Christ. This is the
paradox of grace. You must pay everything, and
then you have your prize for nothing. And lo !
the prize you have found is far more glorious than
the prize you sought. You sought truth, and you
have found Christ. To find Christ, to agree with
God in God's chief thought—the thought of Christ
as Saviour and as Lord to men—this, this, at
length, is orthodoxy. This truth buy. Buy, and
sell it not.
(d)   *W. C. Wilkinson*

TRUTH ; CHURCH OF ENGLAND

No one can justly blame me for honouring my
spiritual mother, the Church of England, in whose
womb I was conceived, at whose breasts I was
nourished, and in whose bosom I hope to die.
Bees, by the instinct of nature, do love their hives,
and birds their nests. But, God is my witness,
that, according to my uttermost talent and poor
understanding, I have endeavoured to set down
the naked truth impartially, without either favour
or prejudice, the two capital enemies of right judgment. The one of which, like a false mirror, doth
represent things fairer and straighter than they
are ; the other, like the tongue infected with
choler, makes the sweetest meats to taste bitter.
My desire hath been, to have Truth for my chiefest
friend, and no enemy but Error. If I have had
any bias, it hath been my desire of peace, which
our common Saviour left as a legacy to His
Church.
(e)   *Archbp. Bramhall*

TRUTH AND ERROR

Truth is a good dog ; but beware of barking too
close to the heels of an error, lest you get your
brains kicked out.
(f)   *S. T. Coleridge*

TRUTH, OCEAN OF

I do not know what I may appear to the world ;
but to myself I seem to have been only like a boy
playing on the seashore, and diverting myself in
now and then finding a smoother pebble or a pret-
tier shell than ordinary, whilst the great ocean of
truth lay all undiscovered before me.
(g)   *Sir I. Newton*

TRUTH, PERVERTED (Acts xvii. 23)

In all perverted piety, there appears a course of
action referring itself to God, in spite of the fact
that man knows not God :—" Sic ergo in templis
Atheniensium et reliquorum gentilium fuit *iniqui-
tas et veritas.*"
(h)
                              Harless and Gerhard

TRUTH AND PREJUDICE

Burnet's " History of his own Times," is very
entertaining. The style indeed is mere chit-chat.
I do not believe that Burnet intentionally lied ;
but he was so much prejudiced that he took no
pains to find out the truth. He is like a man who
is resolved to regulate his time by a certain watch,
but will not inquire whether the watch be right or
not.
(i)   *Johnson*

TRUTH, SPIRIT OF (John xvi. 13)

Rightly understood, this important passage
proves the sufficiency of the Scriptures.
The Truth in its completeness and totality ; the
whole Truth, the Full Truth.
Not omniscience, speculative, or scientific truth
is promised, but the full knowledge of living
practical truth as it is in *Christ*, and as it relates
to the soul's *salvation.* The Bible is not a universal cyclopædia of knowledge, but an infallible
guide of religious faith and moral practice. . . .
Yet in a certain sense the Spirit of God alone can
lead us *into all truth*, even in temporal and human
things, since the love of truth is inseparable from
the love of God, and the perfect knowledge of
truth from the knowledge of God, which comes
from the Spirit of God, the true Illuminator of the
human intellect, darkened and distorted by sin
and its bosom companion, error.
(j)   *P. Schaff*

TRUTH, THE

" *All the truth* " (John xvi. 13), alluded to in
verse 12. . . . The Lord had told them *the truth*,
and *nothing but the truth*, in spiritual things, but
not yet *the whole truth*, because they could not
bear it. This the Spirit should lead them into,
open the way to it, and uphold it by degrees. No
promise of universal knowledge, nor of infallibility
is hereby conveyed ; but a promise to them and
us, that the Holy Spirit shall teach and lead us,
not as children, under tutors and governors of
legal and imperfect knowledge, but as sons (Gal.
iv. 6), making known to us the whole truth of
God. This was in a special manner fulfilled to
them as founders and teachers of the Churches.
(k)   *Alford*

TWELVE APOSTLES, ELECTION OF THE
(Luke vi. 12–19)

1. Significance of the number "twelve."
Growing rupture between Jesus and the priestly
party.
Jesus takes a bold attitude (Publican), (Old and
New), (Sabbath). Now He commences with a new
people (Twelve new tribes of the Spiritual Israel
called out of the world by these Twelve Patriarchs).
(l)

2. (Verse 12.) Jesus spends the whole night in prayer before this deeply important event—the foundation of the Christian Ministry.

(2 Cor. v. 20, " We are ambassadors for Christ.")

(Verse 13.) " Day "—Jesus under Divine direction calls the disciples and elects twelve of them, " whom He named Apostles."

They are divided into three groups of four :

(*a*)

3. (i.) The Decided Men

Simon Peter, the leader ;

Andrew his brother, the first missionary;

James, the practical man, and *John* the thinker, children of Zebedee, " Sons of Thunder," expressive of their ardent zeal and affection for Jesus.

(*b*)

4. (ii). The Semi-decided Group

Philip, a townsman of Peter and Andrew, the fifth believer (John i.)—" We have found Him," etc. " Come and see " : " Oh, taste and see," etc. ;

Nathaniel, " an Israelite indeed, in whom there is no guile ; "

Matthew, the Publican, who could *write* a Gospel ;

Thomas, the twin, the man of scruples and doubts, a serious kind of man.

(*c*)

5. (iii.) The group of Subordinate Men—the less

James (of Alphæus), " the less ; "

Simon (Zelotes), the zealous ;

Judas (brother of James), not Iscariot (John xiv. 22).

Judas Iscariot, the traitor. Character cold, reserved, calculating : none except John, apparently, guessed his secret hatred.

What motive had Jesus for calling him? Probably there was a germ of faith in him, and the possibility that it would prevail over his besetting sin. Contact with Jesus might purify his heart; but the Lord saw through him. Was not this one of the questions in that long night of prayer ? The presentiment of the heavy cross He was preparing for Himself. " Have not I chosen you twelve ? and one of you is a devil."

Yet Judas Iscariot did his part in " Preaching Christ." . . . "I have betrayed innocent blood."

(*d*)

6. The Position

There is now,

(i.) The multitude ;

(ii.) The disciples ;

(iii.) The apostles ; and Jesus now advances to a further step in His work.

(*e*)   *Cf. Godet.*

TWO EXTREMES : RATIONALISM AND ROMANISM

There are two extremes in the question of faith—Rationalism and Romanism. Rationalism consists in denying that there is any supernatural authority or supernatural revelation whatever ; Romanism consists in denying that any co-ordinate or independent authority can be exercised by the conscience and the reason. True faith consists in asserting that there are supernatural authorities, but that no supernatural authority can require us to silence the voice of reason and conscience. . . . There is a terrible truth in the saying of an English divine, that a consistent Roman Catholic is a man " who has had the backbone of his conscience broken " ; and to break the backbone of the conscience, is to break the backbone of faith.

(*f*)   *Dr. Wace : Bampton Lectures*

"TWO IMMUTABLE THINGS " (Heb. vi. 17–20)

1. The Promise.

2. The Oath.

3. The Anchor.

(*g*)

1. *The Promise :* " Heirs of promise." The Christian

(i.) *Finds a promise* in the Bible for himself ;

(ii.) *Believes it ;*

(iii.) *Waits for its fulfilment ;* and finally

(iv.) *Obtains it.*

Instances in ver. 12, ver. 15, (Abraham), and xi. 33.

Promises : " Believe on the Lord Jesus Christ, and thou shalt be saved." " Whosoever cometh unto . . . cast out."

Exceeding great and precious promises of glory in the world to come.

Remember, they are made by God ; Who cannot lie ; Who keepeth His promises for evermore. " Heaven and earth shall pass away," etc.

Therefore they are strong consolations for all who believe them.

(*h*)

2. *The Oath.* But in Abraham's case the promise was confirmed by an *oath*, after the manner of men.

" *Surely blessing*," etc. . . . " God sware by Himself." What it means. Had He sworn by heaven and earth, Abraham might have replied : " Heaven and earth pass away, therefore Thy word and oath may too." " But as Thou hast sworn by *Thyself* (eternally existent), they can never fail nor pass away."

So God hath confirmed His promise to the Christian by an oath (Ps. cx. 4). " The Lord hath sworn, and will not repent," *i.e.*, will not go back from His word. Therefore trust Him. Therefore the strong consolation for all who have a *hope* of glory.

These

(i.) The *Promise ;*

(ii.) The *Oath*, are the " two immutable things," in which it is impossible for God to lie.

The Christians' hope =

(*i*)

3. *The anchor of the soul.* = The illustration of the Hope.

The Christian *hope* is " sure and steadfast " (certain).

Observe : The Christian is one who has fled for refuge, like a distressed ship, from a storm of guilt now (the accusations of heart and conscience),

(i.) To " God, who is a Refuge for us," and a Fortress ;

(ii.) To Christ—the shadow of a great Rock in a weary land—his hope.

Is his hope a groundless one ? No, this hope is

(*j*)

" sure and steadfast," because it is like an anchor fastened securely within the veil, *i.e.* in heaven itself.

The symbol = a storm-tossed ship at sea, fleeing to a place of refuge (roadstead), and there casting anchor.   The iron anchor is cast into the sea, gets a grip of the bottom, and holds the ship steadfast, though the storm continues.   In like manner the Christian casts the anchor of HOPE, but it goes up, not down, into the great heaven itself, and takes a grip " within the veil "—where Jesus, our High Priest, is carrying on the work of our salvation, for which purpose He " ever liveth," and is therefore " able to save to the uttermost," etc.   This is part of the Oath, and thus, through all the changes and chances of this mortal life the soul that is anchored *within the veil* is kept in tranquillity. " Thou shalt keep him in perfect peace whose mind is stayed on Thee, because he trusteth in Thee."
(*a*)

TYPE

1. *Joshua and Christ* (Heb. iv. 8)

(i.) The name common to both ;

(ii.) Joshua brings the people of God into the Land of Promise, and divides it among the tribes ; Jesus brings His people into the presence of God, and assigns to them their mansions ;

(iii.) As Joshua succeeded Moses, and completed his work, so the Gospel of Christ succeeded the Law, and announced One by whom all that believe are justified from all things from which we could not be justified by the Law of Moses (Acts xiii. 39).

(*b*)   *Smith's Bib. Dict., and Pearson*

2. *Joseph*

An eminent historic type of Christ, in,—

(i.) His persecution and sale by his brethren ;

(ii.) His resisting temptation ;

(iii.) His humiliation and exaltation ;

(iv.) His dispensing to a famine-stricken people the bread of life ;

(v.) The fulness of his forgiving love.

(*c*)   *Maclear, and Smith's Bib. Dict*

TYPE

" So careful of the type ? " but no,
    From scarpèd cliff and quarried stone
    She cries, " A thousand types are gone ;
I care for nothing, all shall go.

"Thou makest thine appeal to me ;
    I bring to life, I bring to death :
    The spirit does but mean thy breath ;
I know no more."   And he, shall he,—

" Man, her last work, who seemed so fair,
    Such splendid purpose in his eyes,
    Who rolled the psalm to wintry skies,
Who built him fanes of fruitless prayer,

" Who trusted God was love indeed,
    And love Creation's final law,—
    Though Nature, red in tooth and claw
With ravine, shrieked against his creed,—

" Who loved, who suffered countless ills,
    Who battled for the True, the Just,—
    Be blown about the desert dust
Or sealed within the iron hills ? "

(*d*)   *Tennyson: "In Memoriam."*

U

UNAWAKENED CONSCIENCE

A reason why thy unlamented and unpardoned sins,—though every one of them be armed with a separate fiery sting, and of their own nature so heavy with horror that they are able to sink thee into the bottom of hell,—do not as yet stir nor press upon thy soul with the insupportable weight of Divine vengeance, is this : they are in their native soil, where they were born, bred, and brought up in their own element ; I mean, in a carnal heart, soaking in sensuality and not resolved to be reformed. We say in philosophy, an element is not heavy in its own place. One bucket full of water upon the earth would be burthensome to the back of that man, who, were he in the bottom of the sea, would feel no weight at all from all the water there, though it were three miles high over his head. A sensual heart, settled upon its lees, can bear without sense or complaint a world of wickedness, which, out of its element and humour, would be crushed into powder, and tremble with horror upon the sad apprehension of the last sin, especially set out by God's just indignation. While Belshazzar was in his element, revelling and rioting amongst his lords, his wives, and his concubines, drinking wines swaggeringly and contemptuously in the golden and silver vessels of the Temple, he felt no touch in point of conscience, or terror at all : but, put out of his humour by " the handwriting upon the plaister of the wall, his countenance was presently changed, and his thoughts troubled him, so that the joints of his loins were loosed, and his knees smote one against another."

(a)   *Bolton*
(*See* " CONSCIENCE ")

UNBELIEF (John xvi. 9)

The unbelief spoken of in the text is not merely that which is planted by Adam in Man's nature, but plainly this, that men believe not in Christ, that is, when the Gospel of Christ is preached, in order that we may confess our sins and, through Christ, seek and obtain grace. For when Christ came, the sin of Adam and the whole human race, viz., their previous unbelief and disobedience, was taken away before God by Christ's sufferings and death ; and He built a new heaven of grace and forgiveness ; so that the sin which we have inherited from Adam shall no longer keep us under God's wrath and condemnation, if we believe in this Saviour. And henceforward he who is condemned must not complain of Adam and his inborn sin ; for this Seed of the woman, promised by God to bruise the head of the serpent, is now come, and has atoned for this sin and taken away condemnation. But he must cry against himself, for not having accepted or believed in this Christ, the devil's head-bruiser and sin-strangler. Thus every man's danger rests with himself; and it is his own fault if he is condemned ; not because he is a sinner through the sin of Adam, and deserving of condemnation by reason of his former unbelief, but because he will not accept this Saviour Christ, who takes away our sin and condemnation. True it is, indeed, that Adam has condemned us all, in-asmuch as he brought us along with him into sin and the power of the devil. But now that Christ, the Second Adam, is come, born without sin, and has taken away sin, it cannot longer condemn me if I believe in Him ; but I shall be delivered of it through Him and be saved. If, on the other hand, I do not believe, the same sin and condemnation must continue ; because He who is to deliver me from it is not taken hold of; nay, it will be doubly great and heavy sin and condemnation, that I will not believe in this dear Saviour, by whom I might be helped, nor accept His redemption. Thus all our salvation and condemnation depend now upon this, whether we believe in Christ or no. A judgment has at length gone forth which closes heaven against all such as have not and will not receive this faith in Christ. For this unbelief retains all sin, so that it cannot obtain forgiveness, even as faith removes all sin. And hence without this faith everything is and continues sinful and condemnable, even in the best life and best works a man can perform ; which, although in themselves they are praiseworthy and commended by God, yet are corrupted by unbelief, so that on account thereof they cannot please God ; even as in faith all the works and life of a Christian are pleasing to God. In fine, everything without Christ is condemned and lost. In Christ everything is good and blessed ; so that even sin, which continues in our flesh and blood, being inherited from Adam, can no longer hurt or condemn us.

(b)   *Luther*

UNBELIEF (John xvi. 8)

Unbelief is
    (i.) The great *reigning* sin ;
    (ii.) The great *ruining* sin ;
    (iii.) That which is at the bottom of all sin.

(c)   *Lange*

UNBELIEF

There are few persons that will not express abhorrence of licentiousness, or dishonesty, or lying: of the first, as being destructive of the happiness of households ; of the second, as tending to subvert the fabric of human society ; of the third, as being a practice altogether dishonourable and degrading : and there are few persons who would not consider themselves substantially disgraced if such charges could fairly be affixed to their names. But who is there that thinks much of the sin of rejecting the Lord Jesus Christ? Prove to a man that he lies, or that he steals, or that he is guilty of impurity, and you may succeed in bringing a blush to his cheek ; but you will scarcely excite one passing emotion of shame if you convince him that he is a practical unbeliever in the Gospel of the Incarnate Son of God. Indeed the chances are, that he will come cheerfully forward to meet your allegation ; that without any faltering of the voice, and without any lowering of the look, he will admit himself to be an unconverted man ; a man unrenewed in the spirit of his mind ; a man having no experience whatever of the Divine and spiritual life.

(d)   *G. Calthrop*

UNBELIEF

Unbelievers plead as an excuse, the unbelief of the Jews ; saying, If matters were indeed so clear, why did they not believe ? Whereas their infidelity is the foundation of our faith.

(a)   *Blaise Pascal*

UNBELIEF—DOUBT

If we are to be guided by the experience of mankind, Faith, and not science, must determine the practical order of life. The Just, according to [the late] Professor Clifford, shall live by doubt. But the lesson alike of ordinary life and of the Scripture is, that the Just shall live by Faith (Rom. i. 17).

(b)   *Dr. Wace*

UNBELIEF, GRAVITY OF THE SIN OF

He who disparages or disregards that revelation [which God has given] is guilty of an offence against the human conscience and the human mind of the very highest gravity. The writers of the New Testament do not shrink from asserting the tremendous import of the claim they put forward. The writer of the Epistle to the Hebrews warns those whom he addresses of the consequences of neglecting the Divine revelation he announces. "How shall we escape if we neglect so great salvation, which at the first began to be spoken unto us by the Lord, and was confirmed unto us by them that heard Him, God also bearing them witness, both with signs and wonders, and with divers miracles and gifts of the Holy Ghost, according to His own will " (Heb. ii. 3). The consequences which our Lord and His Apostles denounce upon disbelief are apt to sound harsh to our ears. But they are at least in full conformity with the momentous character of the truths which are proclaimed. If the Christian faith reveals the profoundest truths ever opened to human ken, those who reject such an illumination must condemn themselves to a proportionately profound darkness.

(c)   *Dr. Wace : Bampton Lectures*

UNBELIEF AND MINISTERIAL INEFFICIENCY

There are dangerous signs at the present day of a relaxation of moral tone in the literature of free-thinking. There is a tendency to palliate the offences of vicious characters, and to treat every sin as atoned for by intellectual brilliancy. But it would be in the highest degree unjust to throw the whole blame of his error upon every individual who may happen to be the victim of unbelief. We are all bound up together in this matter ; and the sins, the unfaithfulness, the lack of moral energy among Christians themselves contribute, to a terrible extent, to weaken the testimony to our faith. The Ministers of God's word must bear their share in this responsibility. So far as they fail to exhibit the moral truth and spiritual force of that Word, so far as they harden it, or obscure it, or misrepresent it, they contribute to weaken its appeal to the hearts and consciences of their fellows, and the result is seen in many an indirect and distant injury to faith. It is the mission of the Church and its ministers to carry forward the work of the Apostles, by bearing witness to certain truths and revelations ; and if that witness be in any instance unworthily delivered, the force with which the truth appeals to the soul of man is proportionately weakened. . . . It is to some such moral weakness, to some such eclipse of the moral light of life, that a loss of faith in the testimony of the Apostles of Christ, and of the Prophets of old time, must be attributed ; and if faith is to be revivified, it must be by an appeal to the conscience, still more than to the intellect of man.

(d)   *Ibid*

UNCHANGEABLENESS OF CHRIST

Do not believe that our Lord will lose His earnest, and rue of the bargain and change His mind, as if He were a man that can lie, or the son of man that can repent? Nay, He is unchangeable, and the same this year that He was the former year. . . .
Take Him for the same Christ, and claim still kindness to Him and say, Oh, it is so, He is not changed, but I am changed ; nay, it is a part of His unchangeable love, and an article of the new Covenant, to keep you, that you cannot dispose of Him nor sell Him. He hath not played fast and loose with us, in the Covenant of Grace ; so that we may run from Him at pleasure. His love hath made the bargain surer than this ; for Jesus as the Surety is bound for us (Heb. vii. 22), and it cannot stand with His honour to lose thee, whom He must render again to the Father, when He shall give up the kingdom to Him. Consent, and say Amen to the promises, and you have sealed that God is true and Christ is yours. This is an easy market ; you but look on with faith ; for Christ suffered all, and paid all.

(e)   *Samuel Rutherford*

"UNCLEAN SPIRITS, THREE" (Rev. xv. 13)

Their spheres of work :
1. Out of the mouth of the *Dragon :*—
=the old serpent, the devil, a liar, therefore working in the sphere of irreligion = infidelity.
2. Out of the mouth of the *Beast :*—
= the beast that carried the woman (the Apostate Church), therefore working in the sphere of religion, and is the masterwork of Satan.
3. Out of the mouth of the *False Prophet :*
(Comp. the work of the *True Prophet*, Christ ; also Moses and Balaam.) Hence a False Prophet =one who reveals the spirit-world illegally, as modern spiritism, with its alliances with sensual free love, Mohammedanism, " His Prophet," and such-like included.
4. *These are " gone over all the earth."*
Is there a corner of the earth where one or more of these is not working and deceiving, as an " angel of light," or as a true Prophet—working in the proper sphere of Christ and Christianity ?
5. *To what purpose ?* To prepare for the *end* (verses 14, 15), " Behold, I come as a thief."
(f)

UNDERFOOT

God hath strewed all the way from the gate of hell to the gate of heaven, with flowers out of His own garden. Behold how the Promises, Invitations, Calls, lie around thee like lilies. Take heed that thou do not tread them underfoot, sinner !

(g)   *John Bunyan*

UNGODLINESS

The entire city of Hamburg was demoralized when, in 1849, Immanuel Wichern began his Reformatory work there.

The Bible Society reports that girls of eighteen and twenty held up to the colporteur the five new songs, printed in this year, crying out with scorn, " There is our Bible; " mothers, in the presence of their daughters, declared they would rather go to the dancing-booth than read a page of the Gospel. Master-workmen said their Bible was a plate of meat; journeymen asked if they had no sausages to give them, instead of such stuff. Some put down the Bible as a damnable book that had turned the world mad, others as a book of lies; others asserted that they themselves were the Bible. Some asked if the colporteur kept no good thieves' stories. Some shouted that they had that day thrust the Bible in the stove. There was everywhere, not only denial of the Christian faith, but " of the simplest fundamental moral truths, that we had believed were written in the heart."

(a)   *Stevenson's Memoir of Wichern*

UNGODLY, THE

The 36th Psalm speaks more of *the ungodly* than any other of the Psalms of David:—
Verse 1. Fret not thyself because of *the ungodly*.
„ 10. Yet a little while, and *the ungodly* shall be clean gone.
„ 12. *The ungodly* seeketh counsel against the just.
„ 14. *The ungodly* have drawn out the sword.
„ 16. A small thing that the righteous hath is better than great riches of *the ungodly*.
„ 17. For the arms of *the ungodly* shall be broken.
„ 20. As for *the ungodly*, they shall perish.
„ 21. *The ungodly* borroweth, and payeth not again.
„ 29. The seed of *the ungodly* shall be rooted out.
„ 33. *The ungodly* seeth the righteous: and seeketh occasion to slay him.
„ 35. When *the ungodly* shall perish, thou shalt see it.
„ 36. I myself have seen *the ungodly* in great power.
, 39. The end of *the ungodly* is, they shall be rooted out at the last.
„ 41. He shall deliver them from *the ungodly*.

(b)   *A. Grainger*

UNIFORMITY

Arias Montanus, a chief inquisitor in the Netherlands, and concerned in the Antwerp Index, lived to see his own works placed in the Roman Index; whilst the inquisitor of Naples was so displeased with the Spanish Index, that he persisted to assert that it had never been printed at Madrid! Men who began by insisting that all the world should not differ from their opinions, ended by not agreeing with themselves.

(c)   *Dis. Cur. Lit*

UNION WITH CHRIST

Qui Spiritum habet, Christum habet; qui Christum habet, Deum habet.

(d)   *Bengel*

UNION AND COMMUNION WITH GOD (Adoption)

A spirit of adoption is the spirit of a child. He may disoblige his father; yet he is not afraid of being turned out of doors. The *union* is not dissolved though the *communion* is. He is not well with his father, therefore must be unhappy, as their interests are inseparable.

(e)   *John Newton*

UNION AND MUTUAL RELATION OF ALL PARTS OF NATURE, HOWEVER REMOTE

A beautiful exposition of the elements of natural philosophy recently published by Professor Huxley. We are taken to the Thames at London Bridge, and from thence we are led through the whole realm of nature till we reach the sun itself; and the truth is impressed on us, that the course of that river, and the very pebbles on its banks, have had their character and their form determined by the combined influences of all natural forces. All nature, for the same reason, must be regarded as co-operating to form the brain and the heart of man; and the character of the Creator, His attributes and His relations to us, must be so read as to be in harmony with the human soul. If, on the one hand, the marvels of nature impress upon us a sense of His moral and spiritual attributes, and convince us of His sympathy with our moral and spiritual nature, the inquiry, "He that planted the ear, shall He not hear? or He that made the eye, shall He not see?" may be asked with respect to every faculty of our souls; above all, with respect to our sense of righteousness, our capacity for truth and for love.

(f)   *Dr. Wace*

UNITARIANISM : -ANS and -ISMS

I should deal insincerely with you, if I said that I thought Unitarian*ism* was Christianity. No: as I believe and have faith in the doctrine, it is not the truth in Jesus Christ; but God forbid that I should doubt that you and many other Unitar*ians*, as you call yourselves, are, in a practical sense, very good Christians. *We do not win heaven by logic.*

(g)   *S. T. Coleridge*

UNITY

The world, in its disunity, is Babel; the Church of unity is the eternal, ideal Zion; the Holy Ghost is the Mediator of this Union. One Body and one Spirit (Eph. iv. 13).

(h)   *Lange*

UNITY (Eph. iv. 7–10)

All sins against Unity, are sins against the Holy Ghost.

(i)   *Hodge*

UNITY

Is not *uniformity*. The latter is not desirable; if attained to, might lead to stagnation. The works of God in Nature do not exhibit uniformity. Perhaps no two blades of grass, two grains of

(j)

corn, two leaves on a tree, two sheep on the hill, nor two human faces, are identically alike. There is variety in the unity. Why then expect men's minds all cut out after one pattern, to find them all thinking alike on great and vital questions; or why seek by an iron rule, or by some rigid creed, to make men of one mind on non-essential religious questions? The experiment, whenever tried, has always proved a failure.

We are told that the Emperor Charles V. tried, by violent measures, to make twenty millions of people,—his subjects,—agree in their religious opinions; but he was taught his folly when, in after life, having retired to a monastery, he amused himself by constructing clocks, and found by repeated experiments, that with all his skill he was unable to make two clocks go exactly alike for any length of time.

Our Lord, too, did not exact uniformity when the disciples forbade a man who *followeth not with us.* "He that is not against us, is on our part."

Neither, in practice, do we; for we all join in singing the hymns of Wesley, Toplady, Cardinal Newman, because, though each speaks hard things of the other, all *hold the Head, which is Christ* —in whom all are *one.* Christ's wheat, we believe, is now growing in different fields, but will at last all be gathered into, and mixed together in, one garner, where it will not be known from which field this or that grain came.

(a)

Unity of the Church (1 Cor. x. 16)

"The bread which we break, is it not the communion of the Body of Christ?" The single loaf, broken into many fragments, contains within it the symbolical truth, that the Church of Christ is *one.* St. Paul appeals to Baptism against sectarianism; and so long as we retain it, it is an everlasting protest against every one who breaks the unity of the Church.

(b)　　　　　　　　　　　*F. W. Robertson*

Unity in Religion

To borrow a phrase of Lord Bacon, we certainly are tempted by our passions and by our partial knowledge to so consider ourselves as members of particular Churches, communities, or parties, as to forget that we are Christians.

(c)　　　　　　　*Dr. Wace: Bampton Lectures*

Unity: Tongues

The real union of the human race lies in oneness of heart. The gift of tongues, being a gift of the Spirit, neutralized confusion. The world is craving for unity: this is the distinct conscious longing of our age. It is something to be on the right track. Some expect this by uniformity of customs, ecclesiastical rites and dress: the same services, the same hours, the same liturgies, and we shall be one. Others expect it through oneness of language. Philosophers speculate on the probability of one language,—perhaps the English,— predominating. The vast American and Australian continents, the New Worlds, speaking this, whilst other languages are learnt only as polite accomplishments. Hence a hope that a time is coming when nations shall understand one another and be one. Christianity casts aside all these plans and speculations, as utterly insufficient. It does not look to political economy, nor to ecclesiastical drill,

nor to the absorption of all languages into one; but it looks to the Eternal Spirit of God. One heart, and then many languages will be no barrier. One spirit, and man will understand man.

(d)　　　　　　　　　　　*F. W. Robertson*

UNIVERSAL RESTORATION

On being told of a discussion recently held on "Universal Restoration," "Well," he inquired of his informant, "and which party won the day?" "The Restorers," was the answer. Mr. Thomas rejoined, "Your hell is a wonderfully convenient place: it's exactly like a magpie's nest; you go in through one hole and out through the other."

(e)　*Anecdote of Timothy Thomas, Welsh Pastor*

UNIVERSALISM (Rom. v)

The Scripture hath concluded *all* under sin, that the promise by faith of Jesus Christ might be given to them that *believe.* Universalism must assume a second probation after death, even for those who lived in Christian lands, with every opportunity of saving their soul. But such an assumption is contrary to Gal. vi. 7, 8, and the whole practical tenour of the Bible, and is in itself untenable and illusive.

(f)　　　　　　　　　　　*P. Schaff*

Universalism

The word of promise is to be preached to *all* nations (Matt. xxviii. 19, etc.), because of the universal gracious will of God in Christ towards *all* flesh (Tit. ii. 11; 1 Tim. iv. 10; ii. 3, 4). Therefore is φιλανθρωπία attributed to God (Phil. iii. 4); on which Luther = "God loves not the person, but the nature; and is not called gracious to the person, but to the race, in order that His honour may remain entire, and that no one may boast of his worthiness, that no one may be terrified at his unworthiness, but that one as well as another may comfort himself with the undeserved grace, which He in so friendly a way and so universally offers and bestows."

(g)　　　　　　　　　　　*Harless*

UNIVERSE

"*I go to prepare a place for you*" (John xiv. 2)

On earth there is no abiding. Suppose there were. Then the earth would be our prison, and we should never see the universe. Now, we are children of the *universe,* and our Infinite Father means that we should see it.

(h)　　　　　　　　　　　*J. Palsford*

Universe, the Visible

Supposing that man, in some form, is permitted to remain on the earth for a long series of years, we merely lengthen out the period, but we cannot escape the catastrophe. The earth will gradually lose its energy of rotation, as well as that of revolution around the sun. The sun himself will wax dim and become useless as a source of energy, until at last the favourable conditions of the present solar system will have quite disappeared.

But what happens to our system will likewise

(i)

happen to the whole visible universe, which will, if finite, become a lifeless mass, if indeed it be not doomed to utter dissolution. In fine, it will become old and effete, no less truly than the individual. It is a glorious garment, this visible universe, but not an immortal one. We must look elsewhere if we are to be clothed with immortality as with a garment.

(a)   *"The Unseen Universe"*

UNJUST AND JUST MAN, THE

Such being our unjust man, let us place by his side a man of true simplicity and nobleness, resolved, as Æschylus says, not to seem, but to be good. We must certainly take away the seeming; for if he be thought to be a just man, he will have honours and gifts on the strength of this reputation, so that it will be uncertain whether it is for justice's sake, or for the sake of the gifts and honours, that he is what he is. Yes; we must strip him bare of everything but justice, and make his case the reverse of the former. Without being guilty of one unjust act, let him have the worst reputation for injustice, so that his virtue may be thoroughly tested, and shown to be proof against infamy and all its consequences; and let him go on to the day of his death, steadfast in his justice, but with a lifelong reputation for injustice. . . . They (who prefer injustice above justice) will say that in such a situation the just man will be scourged, racked, fettered, will have his eyes burnt out, and at last, after suffering every kind of torture, will be crucified; and thus learn that it is best to resolve, not to be, but to seem, just.

Plato: De Repub. II
(b)   *Trans. by Davies and Vaughan*

UNKNOWN GOD, TO THE (Acts xvii. 23)

There are many whose hearts resemble the market-place of Athens, or the Pantheon, the temple of all the gods. One idol stands there beside another—anger, pride, lust, covetousness, sloth, the love of honour. Search thine own heart, and learn whether it contains these images! The worst of us must answer affirmatively, and confess: "The object of my worship is life, science, art, money, pleasure, my betrothed, my spouse or child, or some other earthly treasure." And there, in a secret spot, discovered only by the pulsations of the conscience, stands an altar with the inscription: *To the unknown God,* that is to say: "To the God in whose name I was baptized and confirmed, to whom I have consecrated myself, whose mercy preserves and sustains me, but with whom I maintain no living communion, and whose commandments I transgress according to my own will."

(c)   *Ahlfield*

UNLAWFUL BOOKS

How a young man would read unlawful books, and how he was punished :—

The *young* man, he began to read
He knew not what, but he would proceed,
When there was heard a sound at the door,
Which as he read on grew more and more.

And more and more the knocking grew,
The young man knew not what to do ;
But trembling in fear he sat within,
Till the door was broke, and the devil came in.

"What would'st thou with me ? " the wicked one cried ;
But not a word the young man replied.
Every hair on his head was standing upright,
And his limbs like a palsy shook with affright.

"What would'st thou with me ? " cried the author of ill ;
But the wretched young man was silent still, etc.

The catastrophe is very terrible.

Henceforth let all young men take heed
How in a conjuror's book they read.
(d)   *Southey's Minor Poems*

UNWORLDLINESS (1 Cor. vii. 31)

The principle is, " Use this world as not abusing it." Here Christianity stands between the worldly spirit and the narrow religious spirit. The worldly spirit says, "Time is short ; take your fill; live while you can." The narrow religious spirit says, "All the pleasure here is a snare and dangerous ; keep out of it altogether." In opposition to this narrow spirit, Christianity says, " Use the world," and, in opposition to the worldly spirit, "Do not abuse it. All things are yours. Take them and use them ; but never let them interfere with the higher life which you are called to lead." . . .

Unworldliness is the spirit of holding all things as not our own, in the perpetual conviction that they will not last. It is not to put life and God's lovely world aside with self-torturing hand. It is to have the world, and not to let the world have you ; to be its master, and not its slave. To have Christ hidden in the heart, calming all, and making all else seem by comparison poor and small.

(e)   *F. W. Robertson*

USEFUL KNOWLEDGE, FALLACY AS TO

There was, I always thought, a very decided fallacy in the nomenclature adopted at the last great movement of educational reform, when societies were constituted for the " diffusion of *useful* knowledge." The fallacy lay, not only in the assumption that there is some knowledge which is useless to the world—an assumption which cannot bear investigation for a moment, for no real knowledge can be useless in any of its three great departments, the knowledge of nature, of man, and of God. Nor, again, did it lie only in the assumption that material utility,—the promotion of material civilization, the making of steam-engines and telegraphs, the improvements of manufacture and of Art,—that this (I say) alone was useful ; that there were no higher necessities in the nature of individual man, no higher elements in a nation's life. But it lay in the idea that the knowledge of what is in itself useful is pre-eminently and universally useful knowledge. A locomotive, for example, is highly useful ; but does it follow that the knowledge of it is pre-eminently useful for those who are not mechanicians or engine-drivers? All knowledge is, I grant, generally useful; but surely we may doubt whether this has any special usefulness to us. If I had to choose between a knowledge of Shakspeare and a knowledge of the steam-engine, or between some knowledge, we will say, of Art and knowledge of chemical manufacture—if I had to ask which of

(f)

these better fitted me to understand the meaning of life and to enter into the higher elements of its happiness, I should choose without hesitation the knowledge of Literature and Art, which the school above referred to would have branded as comparatively useless. The fallacy is not dead yet. It was but a little while ago that a great political and social reformer was very severe upon our educational system, because, while it taught the subtleties of language, it did not tell men where to find Chicago on the map, and because it knew more of the little Ilissus than the gigantic Mississippi. Why, how can it matter to the world at large whether they do or do not know how to put their finger at once on Chicago? If they want to go there, or to have dealings there, they can take down the Atlas and find it. In the meanwhile, is a man's nature less cultivated because he does not know where a particular mass of houses and people is situated? And suppose (which was, I think, the great complaint against the classic Ilissus) that it is a little driblet of a stream, which a man can cross dry-shod in summer, does that prevent the fact of its being bound up in association with some of the highest poetry and the noblest philosophy that the world ever saw—poetry and philosophy which are living and determining now some of the main currents of human thought? The comparison thus put is really of the study of Sophocles or Plato as against the knowledge of the map; and (modernism notwithstanding) I would still declare for the former. Pray understand, that of geographical science, as science, I speak with profound respect. There is in it much grandeur of scope, much closeness of induction, an ever-varied field of interest. But the comparison here was one of so-called useful knowledge, because Chicago was a wealthy and growing town and the Mississippi a river of enormous commercial consequence; and here I say that there is the old fallacy, and that fallacy is a great one.

(a)   *Bp. Barry*

USEFULNESS

Embody your gratitude for Divine mercy in a walk of usefulness. Tell to some others the story of grace; and rest not until you lead a soul to Jesus.

(b)   *Steel*

Teaching, we learn; and giving, we receive.
(c)

USURY

When Audley (the usurer of the seventeenth century) was asked the value of a new office, he replied, that "It might be worth some thousands of pounds to him who after his death would instantly go to heaven; twice as much to him who would go to purgatory; and nobody knows what to him who would adventure to go to hell."

Having lost £100,000, this hoary usurer pined and thought of retreat. A facetious friend told him the story of a rat, who having acquainted the young rats that he would at length retire to his hole, desiring none to come near him; their curiosity, after some days, led them to venture to look into the hole; and there they found the old rat sitting in the midst of a rich Parmesan cheese.

(d)   *Disraeli: Cur. Lit*

UTTERMOST, THE (Heb. vii. 25)

1. We, as Christian people, come unto God by Jesus Christ; making mention of His name only; we recognise Him as the living way to communion with the Father; into His name we are baptized; in remembrance of Him, and in obedience to His command, we take the bread and wine, showing by what means alone our souls are held in life. In His name we pray.

We are then of those who come unto God by Him. So much is quite certain. But this is not the only certainty. Activity is not on our side only. For what does this passage teach us concerning our exalted Saviour, who is at the right hand of God? What is *He doing now* for our salvation?

It teaches us that His whole life and work now is that of making *intercession for us—i.e.*, interposing on our behalf.
(e)

2. An Illustration of what is meant by His interposing on our behalf

He is our Saviour; that we all know and believe. But has He only died for us *here*, and now is gone back to glory, leaving us to get on, as best we can, through temptation and dangers?

Think now: God made this world at the first, but has He ever since then left it altogether without His assistance—just left it to spin round the sun quite independent of Him? Does He not look after it by His daily providence, giving us day and night, summer and winter, seed-time and harvest, providing for the wants of all who are on it? Thus He "interposes" by His providence. In like manner a man makes a locomotive engine, puts it on a line of rails, and then, instead of abandoning it to do its work independently, he regulates and feeds it, and drives it, so that it goes when and where he pleases. So does God with the world. He never leaves it to itself; if He did, probably it would smash into some other world, or comet, or the sun, and a great catastrophe would succeed.
(f)

Just so is it with our salvation. The Saviour who died for us, and so began our salvation, has not gone back to heaven, and left us to get on as well as we can without Him. He is at the helm, guiding the ship. He is at the right hand of God, over-ruling and managing all things for our good. Never off the watch; never away from His post, but daily, hourly INTERPOSING His Almighty and saving power on our behalf. Therefore He is able to save to the *uttermost* all who come unto God by Him.
(g)

3. How long will this Intercession last?

It will last as long as there is any need for it, *i.e.*, until we are out of danger, until there is no more enemy to imperil our salvation; until we are fully saved, and our bodies are redeemed from the power of death.

The *uttermost* of peril and the *uttermost* of need.
(h)

4. On what foundation does it rest?

Why should His intercession prevail? Why should not the Judge condemn those who have sinned, transgressed, and broken God's com-
(i)

mandments, and whose consciences tell them they are verily guilty? Why should any such get off at all?

Because Christ has died: He offered Himself a sacrifice for our sins (cf. chap. ix. 11–28, and x. 16, 17). Because He died in our stead; because He has atoned for sin; and made reconciliation. The blood, which alone cleanseth from sin, has been shed (cf. chap. x.).

On the ground of this He intercedes for us. The Father is well pleased with Him, and whatever He asks for He obtains.

(See more accurately the Atonement.)

(a)

5. What motive actuates Him in thus interposing in our behalf?

Love, pity, compassion (iv. 14, 15). Look at the world lying in wickedness, see to what peril we are exposed. He became incarnate; He saw our need; He took part in our difficulties, and now, because He knows our sorrows, knows our frame, remembers that we are dust, and is touched with a feeling of our infirmities (from experience), He sympathizes with us, and helps us almightily. This is His motive. In love and pity He redeems us and bears with us until the work is complete.

Love is strong: the love of woman is great; the love of a mother is unquenchable, but the love of Jesus passes the love of women, passeth understanding.

(b)

6. How does He intercede, audibly or inaudibly?

Cf. The story of Amyntas ("INTERCESSION"). "There to appear in the presence of God for us" (ix. 24).

But this cannot be all. He is eloquent in His intercession for each one (for individuals are precious in His sight; we are not overlooked, and lost in the crowd. "He that loves God is known of Him" (1 Cor. viii. 3); and his every time of need. To Peter, "I have prayed for thee that thy faith fail not," "I pray for them" (John xvii. 9, 20).

(c)

7. What is the fruit of His Intercession?

(i.) We obtain mercy; we are kept in the sphere or region of perpetual grace, where God deals with us graciously.

(ii.) We have perpetually renewed removal of our stains, sins, hindrances, and the shadows cast by sin, so that nothing, no enemy, no lion, shall succeed in thwarting His intentions or in effecting the ruin of those who come unto God by Him (iv. 16).

"God always causeth us to triumph in Christ;" and, "If God be for us, who can be against us?" Who shall condemn him for whom Christ died, and rose, and is at the right hand of God, and who also maketh intercession for him? (Rom. viii. 34.)

(d)

V

VAINGLORY

He that makes transitory honour the reward of a good work, sets eternal glory at a low rate.

(a)　　　　　　　　　　　　　　*St. Gregory*

Remember, O man, from whence thou art taken, and that thou art brother to the dunghill.

(b)　　　　　　　　　　　　　　　　*Anon*

VAINLY PUFFED UP (Col. ii. 18)

The *pride* of these people consisted in,this, that with all their supposed humility, they allowed themselves to fancy, as is generally the case with fanatical tendencies, that they could not be satisfied with the simple knowledge and obeying of the Gospel, but could attain to a peculiar higher wisdom and sanctity.

(c)　　　　　　　　　　　　　　　*Lange*

VANITY FAIR

He kept his show-box, with no mirrors where
　　You saw Eternity, whose worlds we pass
Darkly by daylight ; but with many a glass
Reflecting all the humours of the fair,
　　The thousand shapes of vanity and sin ;
　　Toy-stalls of Satan ; the mad masquerade ;
The floating pleasures that before them played ;
　　The foolish faces following, all a-grin.
He slily pricked the bubbles that we blew.

(d)　　　　*Anon. in Good Words, on Thackeray*

VANITY OF VANITIES

All human beauty, valour, wit, genius, success, glory, are vanity of vanities ; man is nothing, and God is all. Great David died as the fool dieth. So died the glorious young Greek Alexander, who conquered the world. So died the wise Henry II., cursing his rebellious sons. So died our gallant Plantagenet, the hero of Crecy and Poictiers, "mighty victor, mighty lord." Low on his funeral couch he lies—no pitying hand, no tear to grace his obsequies. So died the last great conqueror of modern days, Napoleon, on a petty island, squabbling with a poor English sailor about etiquette and about champagne. Man is as great as he is in God's sight, and he is no greater.

(e)　　　　　　　　　　　　*Archd. Farrar*

VAPOUR, LIFE A (Jas. iv. 14)

There was once a man who had gone out to the gold-diggings in Australia. After years of toil, weary days and sleepless nights, he amassed a considerable sum, and wishing to return home and enjoy himself—wishing to put his money into a portable form—he exchanged the gold for a precious diamond—thousands of pounds in value— and kept the diamond safe under lock and key. Coming across the ocean, on his way home, he every now and then used to take the diamond out of its safe keeping and look at it. It represented so much to him—home, land, comforts, respecta-

bility, honour, position. Becoming familiarized, by degrees, with the jewel, he took it about with him, and played with it, and, at last, began to carry it in his hand over the ship's side as the vessel ploughed the waters. He was cautioned by his friends against trifling with what was so precious, but he was obstinate. He knew—he said— how to take care of his own. He would not be advised. But, one day, whilst trifling with the jewel, he did drop it into the sea, and it was irrecoverably lost. All was gone, all he had in the world ; all his hopes and prospects, all his wealth and position—*everything*. And I leave you to imagine the horrible self-reproach, the untold agonies of remorse, that the man suffered for his inconceivable folly. "Oh ! " you say, "nonsense ! There never was a man who did anything so mad. The story is preposterous." Well, you are right— partly. There never was a man, so far as I know, who acted so infatuated a part. But the story is *not* preposterous, for it exactly—though only imperfectly, only in merest outline—describes your folly who are trifling with an immortal soul, and are, any moment, in danger of losing it.

(f)　　　　　　　　　　*Gordon Calthrop*

VATICANISM (Infallibility)

As a Christian, as a Theologian, as an Historian, as a Citizen, I cannot accept this doctrine

(i.) Not as a Christian, for it is irreconcilable with the spirit of the Gospel, and with the plain words of Christ and of the Apostles. It purposes just that establishment of the kingdom of this world which Christ rejected. It claims that rule over all communions which Peter forbids to all and to himself.

(ii.) Not as a Theologian, for the whole true tradition of the Church is in irreconcilable opposition to it.

(iii.) Not as an Historian can I accept it, for as such I know that the persistent endeavour to realize this theory of a kingdom of the world has cost Europe rivers of blood, has confounded and degraded whole countries, has shaken the beautiful organic architecture of the elder Church, and has begotten, fed, and sustained the worst abuses in the Church.

(iv.) Finally, as a Citizen, I must put it away from me, because by its claim on the submission of States and monarchs, and of the whole political order under the Papal power, and by the exceptional position which it claims for the clergy, it lays the foundation of endless, ruinous dispute between State and Church, between clergy and laity.

(g)　　　　　　　　　*I. Von Döllinger, 1871*

The Pope is the chief judge of all civil law. In him are combined the spiritual and worldly powers, joining in him as in a point, for he is the Vicegerent of Christ, who is not only the Eternal Priest, but also King of kings and Lord of lords ; and immediately following this, " The Pope is, by his high dignity, at the head of both powers."

The Civilta (the official organ of the Roman Curia).

(h)　　　*March, 1870. Quoted by Dr. Wace.*

VERILY, VERILY

With these words the Saviour utters the great cardinal truths of the kingdom of heaven.

(a)

VICARIOUS SUFFERINGS

I accept the fact, the simple fact, the august, solemn fact, that it was necessary for Christ to suffer: the theological explanations I do not believe a word in. Those who say that Christ's sufferings were not vicarious, will have to fight, not only with the Bible, but with all the weight of human life. *Suffering, in human life, is very widely vicarious.*

(b) *H. W. Beecher*

VICE

The Duke of Buckingham possessed all the advantages which a graceful person, a high rank, a splendid fortune, and a lively wit could bestow; but by his wild conduct, unrestrained either by prudence or principle, he found means to render himself in the end odious and even insignificant. The least interest could make him abandon his honour; the smallest pleasure could seduce him from his interest; the most frivolous caprice was sufficient to counterbalance his pleasure. By his want of secrecy and constancy he destroyed his character in public life; by his contempt of order and economy he dissipated his private fortune; by riot and debauchery he ruined his health; and he remained at last as incapable of doing hurt as he had ever been little desirous of doing good to mankind.

(c) *Hume*

VICE

The madness of vice appeared in his person in very eminent instances, since at last he became contemptible and poor, sickly and sunk in his parts, as well as in all other respects, so that his conversation was as much avoided as ever it had been courted.

(d) *Bishop Burnet, on George Villiers, Duke of Buckingham*

VICE

Through tattered clothes small vices do appear;
Robes and furred gowns hide all. Plate sin with gold,
And the strong lance of justice hurtless breaks;
Arm it in rags, a pigmy's straw doth pierce it.

(e) *Shakspeare*

VICE

A Duke of Bucks.—Is one that has studied the whole body of vice. His parts are disproportionate to the whole, and, like a monster, he has more of some and less of others than he should have. He has pulled down all that fabric that nature has raised in him, and built himself up again after a model of his own. . . . His appetite to his pleasures is diseased and crazy, like the *pica* in a woman that longs to eat that which was never made for food, or a girl in the green sickness, that eats chalk and mortar. Continual wine, music, and women put false value upon things, which by custom became habitual, and debauch his understanding, so that he retains no right notion nor sense of things.

(f) *Samuel Butler, on George Villiers, Duke of Buckingham*

VICE

Vice is a monster of so frightful mien,
As, to be hated, needs but to be seen:
Yet seen too oft, familiar with her face,
We first endure, then pity, then embrace.

(g) *Pope*

VICE

A man so various that he seemed to be
Not one, but all mankind's epitome.
Stiff in opinions, always in the wrong,
Was everything by starts, and nothing long.
But in the course of one revolving moon,
Was chymist, fiddler, statesman, and buffoon.
Then all for women, painting, rhyming, drinking,
Besides ten thousand freaks that died in thinking.

(h) *Dryden, on George Villiers, Duke of Buckingham*

VICE

The witty Duke of Buckingham was an extreme bad man. His duel with Lord Shrewsbury was concerted between him and Lady Shrewsbury. All that morning she was trembling for her gallant, and wishing the death of her husband; and after his fall, 'tis said the Duke slept with her in his bloody shirt.

(i) *Lord Peterborough*

VICISSITUDE

Light and shade, sunshine and shadow, pursue each other over the moral as over the material world. Every soul has a landscape that changes with the wind that sweeps its sky, with the clouds that return after its rain.

(j) *Geo. Macdonald*

VICTORY THROUGH CHRIST, THE

"*I thank God through Jesus Christ our Lord. So then with the mind I myself serve the law of God; but with the flesh the law of sin*" (Rom. vii. 25)

1. This is a pæan, or song of victory. This history of the battle precedes it. It was momentous; and none the less so because it was invisible. It was the conflict that goes on in certain kinds of men; and nowhere did it ever receive a better exposition than here. The question has often arisen and been debated, first, as to whether in the seventh of Romans Paul was speaking of his own experience, or of some other; and secondly, as to whether, if it was his own experience—as it undoubtedly was —it was his experience before conversion or after conversion. The very strongest reasons have been adduced on both sides, and for the good reason that both are true. After his conversion he sets himself before his own mind again as he was in the preliminary stage of his experience; and it is recounted by him as something that was, since historically it had an existence, and as something

(k)

Victory through Christ, The—*continued*

that would, more or less, go with him, and all that should be like him, to the end of life. It was a struggle between the sense of right and the endeavour, ineffectual, to perform that which was right. It was the rebuke of his reason and the sting of his conscience, and the general self-condemnation which followed the conscious violation of his best instincts, best intuitions, best judgments, and best hopes.

(*a*)

2. Is this a universal experience? Must everybody go through such a one? It has been treated as if it were universal. I affirm, on the contrary, that it is an experience which belongs, in a developed and positive form, only to that small class of men who make self-building more important to themselves than anything else. Nineteen men in twenty are men that are building something else —fame, fortune, pleasure, reputation, things exterior. The twentieth man is building his own nature and character. The experience of the seventh of Romans is as impossible to ordinary men as it would be for ordinary men to have the experience of Sir Isaac Newton, or to understand the philosophy and poetry of Goethe, or to appreciate Beethoven's music. Here and there is a typical man who rises above ordinary men, and stands as a prince, and represents the whole province of experiences; but you cannot take ordinary men of low tone in a community, and lift them up and make them sing with Beethoven. They may *sing;* but they will sing as sparrows chirp. Men may have an aspiration for living better; but, except in rare cases, they will have no such aspiration as is shown here. Paul was a moral genius; he had gifts; there was an inspiration vouchsafed to him; and he had an inspiration which was given to such men as Jonathan Edwards, but which you cannot work out of lower and inferior moral natures. Here and there single men have it; but others have it not.

This, therefore, is to be looked upon as the typical experience of a moral genius; but it none the less illustrates the great underlying facts of man's condition, and of his relations to God. We are not to strive to have it; but we are to regard it and accept it as an interpretation of some of the great facts on which human life stands; and so accepted and regarded, it may be made useful to all.

(*b*)

3. What was the foregoing struggle or battle? It was one in which the Apostle said that he had a clear sense of what was right and what was wrong; that he did the wrong; but that he loved the right, and strove for it, and resisted the wrong, being defeated every time. Such was the struggle. It was the attempt of the Apostle Paul to live a true life inwardly and outwardly according to his own perception of the rule of duty, accompanied by an utter consciousness of defeat in doing it. He settles down on the ground, not simply that he was defeated, but that the reasons of his defeat were unremovable. Victory came out of it; but what is very extraordinary here is, that he shouts the note of victory after saying, "Who shall deliver me from the body of this death?" which was perpetually blasting his expectation, his desire, and his purpose. Apparently in answer to the question, "Who shall deliver me?" he says, "I thank Jesus Christ our Lord." The implication is, that Christ delivers.

Look at the sequences. He has got his victory through Jesus Christ; and what is it? "I am no longer tempted; I am no longer vincible; I invariably through Christ perceive the right and do it; I perceive the wrong, and through the grace of the Lord Jesus Christ I resist it and overcome it. Is that the victory?" No. Said he, "I thank God through Jesus Christ our Lord. So then with the mind I myself serve the law of God; but with the flesh the law of sin."

(*c*)

There are the facts; and the 7th of Romans goes thundering on. Paul said, "I still see the things that I ought to do, and do not do them; and I still see the things that I ought not to do, and do them; and yet, with the consciousness of this ever-recurring fact, I have a victory; and I thank God for that victory." Here is a man who hates sin, and still sins, and yet has ineffable joy and peace.

Is it true that there are human elements in men that are not controllable, and that the grace of God itself does not control? Is it true, which is still more important, that a man can be in Christ and rejoice in Him, and at the same time confess that he is committing sin, and that his victory in Christ does not remove that sin? It looks like it.

(*d*)

4. The answer to this question is as clear in the matter of religion as it is in every other matter. These things can be over-ruled by education, and by-and-by can be subordinated; but they are not subject to the immediate action of a man's will in such a sense that he can always do right and never do wrong. A man may say, "I hate my temper; it is my grief morning, noon, and night; God knows that I strive against it continually; I see how beautiful it would be if I could be like So and So and So; but words that I ought not to utter flow out from my lips in spite of me; and when I am a little disturbed in my liver and stomach I do not know what I do; and the scintillations from my temper are like sparks from a forge; and I say that it shall never occur again, and yet it is repeated often and often; and so I have been fighting this disposition of mine for forty years, and I cannot get rid of it: oh, who shall deliver me from the body of this fiery death?" And so it is in regard to every one of the constitutional qualities by which our lower life dominates our higher life from day to day. Men say, "This is wrong. I hate it;" and though it is true that they do hate it, and that they resist it, they do not overcome it—not at once.

Well, this is what Paul himself meant when he said that with the under man he served the law of the flesh, but that with the upper man he served the law of God—or when he said, in the other part of our text, "So then, with the mind [with the reason, the moral sensibility] I myself serve the law of God [as a part of my higher nature]; but with the flesh the law of sin."

(*e*)

5. What great victory was there here? Paul has gone through the inventory, and he says, "I see

(*f*)

Victory through Christ, The—*continued*

the right, I approve of the right; I see the wrong, I do the wrong; and this underlying self is such a burden to me that it is dragging me down, the under life is constantly destroying my purpose and putting me to shame; and the upper one is all the time rebuking me and harrowing me. Oh, how shall I ever get over it? How shall I make my mind accordant with myself? How can I live so that my reason shall jump with my passions, and so that my passions shall be subordinate to my moral sense? How can I govern my temper, my pride, my vanity, everything of that kind, so that I shall never sin, and therefore have some sort of peace?"

The idea of having peace because you are perfect is an absurdity. No man that lives, no man that ever did live, and no man that ever will live, will have peace because he is perfect; for we live in a world where the law of duty grows and becomes more difficult as we go higher and higher. The more you preach the fulfilment of duty in any line, the more ambitious you are to attain that which remains, and the more sensitive you are to the imperfections that still adhere to you. Every step upward becomes harder and harder in art life, in poetic life, and in moral life. The higher you go the higher you must go, and the harder it is to rise to that which is before you; and peace as the result of striving to attain perfection is hopeless. No man ever had it, and no man ever will have it in this world, on any valid or permanent basis.

Yet Paul had a victory with all his intense consciousness of imperfection; a shouting victory it was; and he attributed it to the Lord Jesus Christ; and he declared in the same connection, that though it was a victory it was one that left his body sinning; and he said, "With the mind I myself serve the law of God, but with the flesh the law of sin." It was a victory that was achieved on those conditions.

(a)

6. The theologian must not solve this question: that is, it is not a metaphysical question, and is not to be solved by abstract reasoning. Can a man do his duty? Yes, abstractly he can. Can a man do his duty in any particular case? Well, yes, abstractly. If you will abstract a man from the conditions in which we live, so that he will have but one point before his mind at once, as a metaphysician does before his, I admit that he can live without sin. But when men are in the conditions in which, in the Providence of God, the race are ordinarily brought up; when they are in circumstances in which they are continually annoyed and harassed; when they have to go without sleep; when they are obliged to do five days' work in one; when they carry indigestion as a nest of devils in themselves, distracting and unbalancing their whole mental economy; when, being parents, they are weighed down with incessant toil, with the sickness of children, with family cares of every kind, with all manner of anxieties, with the hurly-burly of life in all its phases—with ten thousand surges rocking them hither and thither—then can they have control of every thought, and feeling and act? The metaphysician thinks they can, because, when he settles the question in his study, he can do it.

No; I say, boldly, with the whole Scripture to bear witness to the fact, that it is impossible for any man, in and of himself, to go through the circumstances of a troubled and tumultuous life and not err on this side nor on that by the unconscious violation, through over-action or under-action, or fatigue, or some other cause, of some law of his constitution.

(b)

7. What was it, then, that gave Paul such an outburst of joy?

It was a new theology. He had an idea of law such as exists in our courts of justice. He had looked upon the Divine government and administration as a machine government and administration. His thought had been, " Here is the law; it is holy and just and good, and I am bound to obey it; and everything that is noble in me says that I ought to obey it; but my combativeness and selfishness will not let me obey it; and if I do not obey it God will not forgive me nor look down on me with any kindness or love, and I shall not have any peace or happiness." That is the way Paul reasoned on this subject. What was it that brought light to him? It was this thought: that since God had made men as He had, and put them under such circumstances as He had, and given them the temperament He had, He was a Being who adapted Himself to the facts of His creation, and stood over against imperfection, not as a monarch, nor as a judge, nor as a sheriff, nor as a law-enforcer, but as a parental, pedagogical Nature, that sympathized with men, and helped them, so that while they were yet sinners, they could have peace through the Lord Jesus Christ, and have a consciousness of Christ's love and favour, not when they were well, but to make them well.

Now, is there anywhere in the great wide world a place where law ought to be more imperatively enforced, and where justice, as the foundation of law, ought to be more strictly maintained, than in the household? Is there a place on earth where law is so efficient? Is there throughout the globe a place where, on the whole, administration is so rigid? In the household, the father and the mother receive the children, as it were, rolled up like a bud. After a year or two they begin to unfold, and we treat them as children. They are pettish, they are selfish, they are combative; and in these respects they are wrong; nevertheless, they do not set the father and the mother at variance with them. The parent says, instantly, "I am to train them, and to bear with them while I am training them. These traits which they manifest are natural to them, they belong to their nature; and till they learn the peculiarities of their constitution it is my business to take them in hand, and little by little teach them the right way of thinking and feeling, and instruct them in the law of kindness, and purity, and honour, and rectitude in all their relations; and while I am doing it I do not expect them to make no mistake. I know they will make mistakes."

(c)

8. What are you going to do with those mistakes?

Nothing. Let them alone. You are not to hold a child accountable for a mistake that he has made any longer than it is necessary to secure his determination not to commit it again. Law in the household is an instrumentality and stepping-

(d)

Victory Through Christ, the—*continued*

stone to better performance. It is a help to enable the child to do better next time; and if the child has a disposition to do better, or if, on the whole, the parent can hope that he will do better, that is enough. What the parent is seeking, is final outcome; and this and that violation of law by the child he counts as incident to the child's undeveloped faculties, and as belonging to that condition which God has prescribed for the whole human family. Right action implies the employment of the whole machinery of right action—a luminous understanding, a duly proportioned moral sense, the power of wise judgment, and a will with stamina behind it; and children have not these while they are yet children. They come by growth. They are developed little by little.

When the child does wrong, sometimes with his eyes open and sometimes with them shut, the parent sees that it is wrong, and rebukes the child; but love in the parent deals with the child with reference to the whole period of evolution through which the child must go. If there is annihilation anywhere, it is in the realm of love. Listen. God says, " I will cast all your sins into the depths of the sea. I will remember them no more." The transgressions of a child are done, gone, and forgotten, and are as if they were not in the memory of the parent. Ninety-nine hundredths of a child's life is so imperfect that if we should remember his mistakes and register them, there would seem to be nothing of him but mistakes; but he gradually issues out of his mistakes, and becomes less and less imperfect, and more and more accomplishing and self-controlling; and the construction of the family is such that it can wait for the child to grow and throw off his faults without stopping to make them penal, except so far as to bring the necessary motive and inspiration to bear upon him.

(a)

9. " The creature was made subject to vanity not willingly." A man does not determine the condition in which he goes into this world. The creation was not made according to any plan of his. I did not choose to be born at zero, and then become a child of small intelligence, and then develop a little more intelligence, and a little more, and a little more, and a little more. It was not I that determined that I should go through the weary way of child-like experience. The prodigious powers that are in me were put into me without any volition on my part. I did not ask for the machinery that I have to engineer. Some folks have better organizations than others, but nobody has an organization of a certain kind as a matter of his own choice. Every man is put into the world " a creature made subject to vanity, not willingly, but by reason of Him who hath subjected the same in hope." God has for ever been putting men into the world thus, and He continues to do it; and, under such circumstances, if He should hold men to exact rectitude in every act, thought, feeling, or impulse, He would require of them that which is impossible to human nature. No; God has put men into the world under such circumstances that He holds before them the highest ideal, and stimulates them to develop, and in an upward course, by the promise of reward, by trials and fears, if need be, urging them to " press toward the mark for the prize of the high calling of God in Christ Jesus ; " and yet, if in any respect

we fail on the way, so long as our purpose is strong for the right, He forgives us, and says of our transgression, " I will not count that ; lay that aside."

(b)

10. Love

Christ does by the whole human family as a tender mother in the household does by her babes, when she is trying to liberate them from their lower selves, and to inspire in them a noble manlike character. And it was the outbreak of this knowledge that gave Paul the victory. Said he, " I thank God through Jesus Christ our Lord." He felt assured that he was going to be delivered from the body of death to which he was subject by the interposition of God through Jesus Christ. " So then," he says, "with the mind I myself serve the law of God, but with the flesh the law of sin." It is as if he had said, " I, Paul, am not quite as humble as I ought to be ; I, Paul, flash out pride sometimes ; I, Paul, am not so devout as I ought to be ; I, Paul, am ambitious, and am too bound up in worldly things ; I, Paul, have a quick temper, and am too apt to give way to indignation ; I know these things are wrong, and I try to overcome them ; but my under man is liable to temptation, and I perpetually fail in this endeavour : yet my higher self survives death, and has in it the seed of immortality : my glorious upper self perceives the right way, and presses toward it with all the power I have."

Christ accepts me on that ground—and why ? Simply because He loves me. The act is one of efficient and overruling love. You may call it *grace ;* but *love* is the better word—less vexed with explanations. It was this that gave Paul such peace and rest.

(c)   *H. W. Beecher*

VILENESS

I have seen my abominable vileness ; if I were well known, there would none in this kingdom ask how I do. Men take my ten to be an hundred ; but I am a deeper hypocrite and shallower professor than every one believeth ; God knoweth I feign not. But I think, my reckonings on the one page written in great letters, and His mercy to such a forlorn and wretched bankrupt on the other, more than a miracle. If I could get my finger ends upon a full assurance, I think I should grip fast : but my cup wanteth not gall ; and upon my part, despair might be almost excused, if every one in this land saw my inner side. But I know, I am one of those who have made great sale and a free market to free grace. If I could be saved, as I would fain believe, sure I am, I have given Christ's blood, His free grace and the bowels of His mercy a large field to work upon, and Christ hath manifested His art (I dare not say to the uttermost ; for He can, if he would, forgive all the devils and condemned reprobates, in respect of the wideness of His mercy ; but I say) to an admirable degree.

(d)   *Samuel Rutherford*

VINE, THE (John xv. 1-6)

God exercises a strict and wise government, corresponding with the noble nature of the Vine ; a government realizing the destiny of the Vine ; partly through a cutting off of the useless, partly through a pruning of the serviceable branches.

(e)   *Lange*

VINE AND ITS FRUIT

As every one knows, the vine is cultivated solely for its fruit. It has luxuriant foliage and graceful tendrils, but it would not pay for the labour expended on it, if it did not yield grapes.

(a) *Donald Fraser*

VISION OF CHRIST

" *This is a faithful saying*," etc. (1 Tim. i. 15)

He came to me. He was not at all like the pictures of the saints; He was pale, worn, and thin, as though the fight was not yet half over— but through this pale and worn look shone infinite power, and undying love, and unquenchable resolve. . . . When He came to me, He stopped: " Ah ! " He said, " Is it thou? What doest thou here? Knowest thou not that thou art Mine? Thrice Mine—Mine centuries ago, when I hung upon the cross on Calvary for such as thou—Mine years ago, when thou camest a little child to the font—Mine once again, when, forfeit by every law, thou wast given over to Me by one who is a servant and a friend of mine. Surely, I will repay! A healing sense of help and comfort, like the gentle dew, visited the weary heart. . . . " And He passed on; but among ten thousand times ten thousand I should know Him; and amid the tumult of a universe, I should hear the faintest whisper of His voice.

(b) *Shorthouse (J. Inglesant)*

VISION OF GOD, THE

" *No one knoweth the Father, save the Son, and he to whomsoever the Son will reveal Him* " (Matt. xi. 27)

God hath not left Himself without a witness. Surely we cannot expect that man's knowledge of God should be other in kind than a child's knowledge of his father? Is it of a demonstrative kind? Can a child give logical proof that such a man is his father, proof of the kind that a lawyer would be expected to give in a court of justice ? Of his father's birth, pedigree, antecedents, marriage,—nay, of his own birth,—he may know nothing whatever; and yet he knows his father with a confidence and certainty that nothing can shake.

Of what kind then is this knowledge? Is it knowledge that comes by *sight* or by *faith?* That he may be said " to know his father by sight," is true; but this merely means, that when he meets him in a crowd he recognises him as the man whom he has all his life known by *some other means* to be his father. Clearly he does not know *by sight*,—by the features of the face, for instance,— that that man whom he daily sees at the family board is truly and really his natural father. How then does he know it? Of what kind is this knowledge? It is a *faith*. And how does the child come by it? He believes it, in the first instance, simply because he is told it on adequate authority, at his mother's knee; and as he grows in years, it is more and more confirmed by the experiences of his young life; and so it becomes one of those practical beliefs which are in point of fact far stronger than beliefs resting on logical demonstration.

Now, may we not say with much confidence, that man's knowledge of God was *intended to be*, and *can only be*, of the like kind. . . . " He showeth Himself unto such as do not distrust Him."

(c) *Norris*

VISITING THE SICK

Tenderness is essential. Enter the chamber very gently. Tread noiselessly. Get near to the sufferer. Speak as softly as may be. Remember his nerves; noise is often torture. Sympathize with his weakness, restlessness, and pain. True, you are not come to minister to his body; but enter into his symptoms and his suffering. Ask what his doctor has said. Avoid a professional, official, conventional air. The case may be too grave for cheerful words; but, if otherwise, let your face carry a little sunshine into the sick room. Avoid fussiness. Be ready to kneel without stool or cushion. Go with a brother's heart. Always take the sick man's hand, if he can bear it. Be brief—brief in your talk, brief in your readings, brief in your prayers—your whole visit brief. Take up one point. A sick man's brain is soon over-tasked; his nerves soon jar; his strength soon fails. Leave a well-chosen text behind you, as you say " Good-bye ! " Let your " Good-bye " be " God bless you ! " Let your last look be one of tenderness and love. Whatever you are in your pulpit, Barnabas, not Boanerges, is your pattern by the sick bed.

(d) *J. C. Miller*

VOICE

The still small voice is wanted.

(e) *Cowper*

I hear a voice you cannot hear,
　Which says, I must not stay;
I see a hand you cannot see,
　Which beckons me away.

(f) *Tickell*

The world can't hear the still small voice,
　Such is its bustle and its noise.

(g) *Green*

The people's voice is odd;
It is, and it is not, the voice of God.

(h) *Pope*

W

WAIT

We are never to go faster than God leads. We are to stay in patience at the closed gate till He opens it : we must never force it open. Wait until His plan is fully ripe. Even for the fulfilment of His plainest promises wait until His time has come.

Many men wreck their lives and their destinies by determinedly carrying out their own plans, without reference to God's plans. God has one great plan into which each life, as He designs it, fits perfectly.

Keep your eye on the pillar of cloud and fire that leads. Rest when the pillar rests ; move when it moves. You can make the clock strike before the hour by putting your own hands to its wheels ; but if you do, it will strike wrong. You can hurry the unfolding of God's providence by your own impatience ; but if you do, you will mar the Divine plan.

Stop meddling with the threads of your life as they come from the Lord's hands. Every time you interfere, you simply make a flaw. Keep your hands off, and let God weave as He pleases.

(a)   *Anon*

WAITING (Acts i. 14)

1. There is always something to wait for

From Adam to Christ, the Church was *waiting* for the coming of the Messiah ;

From Christ to Pentecost, she was *waiting* for the outpouring of the Spirit ;

The early and the latter rain : The Messiah = the promise of the Old Testament, and the Holy Spirit of the New Testament.

From day of Ascension to day of Pentecost = ten days ; these = ten days of Faith's trial : the *waiting* period of the disciples. Notice,

(b)

2. The Waiting itself

Waiting implies faith in God. It is the mark of a believer to wait, whilst an unbeliever waits not for His counsel. Unbelief would have said in this case—the Master is gone : we expect no Comforter, no more consolation ; why wait ?

But this was a time of testing—" *Tarry at Jerusalem—wait for the promise of the Father . . . not many days hence.*"

Three days, seven days, passed ; hope was deferred. Imagine Peter's impatience, imagine John's anxiety ; but at last, after ten days (the set time), the promise was fulfilled.

(c)

3. The Manner of Waiting

In the use of ordinances ; " continually in the Temple ; " met in an " upper room " ; not the eleven only, but the " women," the faithful, the mother and the brethren of the Lord. These " continued " steadfastly, daily—instant in *prayer*. Thus teaching that God's promise has to be prayed for ; and it was as they prayed that the Spirit was poured out.

We have to tarry the Lord's leisure, in all the appointed means of grace, remembering that Resurrections, Ascensions, and Whitsuntides do not all fall on the same day.

(d)

WAITING FOR ANXIETY

A Conversation between a Minister and one of his People

M.—" Are you *waiting* for such anxiety ? "
The reply was—" Certainly I am."
M.—" Do you expect to obtain it by WAITING ? Do you think it will ever COME to you ? "
" I don't know—I used to hope so—but I have waited for it a long time."
M.—" Does the Bible tell us to wait for anxiety ? "
" I don't know that it directly tells us to wait. But it speaks of conviction, of broken and contrite hearts ; and Christian people speak of awakenings, alarms, and distresses of mind, and of influences of the Holy Spirit. . . . And I have heard you preach such things as if they were the beginning. And if I have none of these, how can I seek God ? "
M.—" I preach nothing like it."
" I remember your text : ' On Thee do I *wait* all the day.' "
M.—" Yes ; and I told you in that sermon that waiting ON *God* was one thing, and waiting FOR God was quite another. The first was right, and the latter was wrong. We wait on Him by prayer. Do you pray ? "
" No."
M.—" Then you don't obey God, and wait *on* Him."
" How can I without conviction ? "
M.—" Do you know and feel that you are at *enmity* with God—and not yet reconciled to Him ? "
" Yes."
M.—" Do you know that you cannot save yourself, and need the Saviour ? "
" Yes ; I KNOW it."
M.—" Then you have *some* conviction."
" You may call it conviction—but I have no deep impressions."
M.—" And you are waiting for such deep impressions, before you will do anything, and when they come you mean to seek God ? "
" Yes."
M.—" Then, you may wait for ever."
" Oh, I hope not."
M.—" Probably you will. How long have you *waited* ? "
" About five years."
M.—" And you have gained nothing. You may wait another five years, and you may wait until you have waited into the grave—and your waiting will do you no good."
" What *shall* I do ? "
M.—" Obey God : ' Seek the Lord while He may be found, call upon Him while He is near.'
" (i.) You are self-deceived : God nowhere tells you to wait for convictions nor anything else. He tells you ' Behold, *now* is the accepted time ; behold, now is the day of salvation.'
(e)

"(ii.) You have no occasion for deeper impressions. Yours are deep enough already.

"(iii.) And deeper impressions never yet came by waiting for them without prayer; and without seeking the Lord they never will. Your duty is to do that at once."

After some delay, she replied: "I believe what you say."

M.—"Jesus Christ is able to save you."

"I suppose He' is ABLE; but I don't think He ever WILL."

M.—"He is more than able, He is willing."

"I wish I *knew* that He is willing."

M.—"You do know it—His word tells you so: 'Come unto Me, all ye that labour and are heavy laden, and I will give you rest.'

"'If any man thirst, let him come unto Me and drink.'

"'Whosoever will, let him take of the water of life freely.'

"'Ho, every one that thirsteth, come ye to the waters.'"

She replied that she would try to "*seek God.*" Not long (only a few days) afterwards she thanked her minister for having opened her eyes.

She confessed that when she ceased TRYING, and just cried unto God, that He *did* everything for her.

(a)   *Spencer's "Pastor's Sketches"*

WALK

Walk like Jesus! and that thou mayest walk *like* Him, walk *with* Him, and thus shalt thou walk *to* Him.

(b)   *Menken*

WALK

"*See then that ye walk circumspectly, not as fools, but as wise, redeeming the time, because the days are evil. Wherefore be ye not unwise, but understanding what the will of the Lord is*" (Eph. v. 15–17)

See that ye who "are awake," have "arisen," "enlightened by Christ, WALK circumspectly—strictly": *i.e.*, that it be exact, strict, and of the right kind. Not only that you have a "rule" and keep to it, but that that rule be the best one.

(c)

The most invulnerable man; whom, if I should quarrel with him, I should find the most difficulty how to abuse him.

(d)   *Johnson on Joshua Reynolds*

WALK (Col. ii. 6, 7)

1. WALK.—*Walking implies progress.* Refer to the frequency with which the godly life is set forth by this figure. (Gen. v. 24), "Enoch walked with God"; and (Gen. vi. 9), "Noah walked with God." Then ask, What does the word "walk" suggest? It implies motion, activity, progress. These ideas should be distinguished. There may be motion, as that of the sap in a plant, but the plant is fixed. There may be motion, as that of a ball struck by a bat, forced, not voluntary. A walk implies personal activity and progress to some end. Now apply to the Christian walk. You are not to stay at the *starting point.* What is that? Pardon of sin. Some seem as if they never got further than this. You are not to *loiter.* "Leaving the things that are behind, you are to press forward." You are not to walk as *in a circle.* You are not "to lay again the foundation of repentance from dead works. Look at the comparison used by John. From babes in Christ, you are to grow into young men, and from young men into fathers.

(e)

2. ROOTED IN HIM.—The root gives *stability* to the tree. Sundry facts may be given bearing on such stability. Those trees are the most stable whose roots take the largest and deepest hold. But we are not now dealing with stability only, we are talking of life. Christ is our life. What does "rooted in Him" teach us? Uproot a tree, you stop its growth, you destroy its life. The root draws from the soil all that the soil can give to the tree. So you are to draw from Christ, not only all you need, but all He can give. As the tree dies when uprooted, so you will die if not rooted in Him. Hence, He says, "Abide in Me, and I in you" (John xv. 4).

(f)

3. BUILT UP IN HIM.—Paul changes the figure. He had spoken of a *walk*, or activity and progress; of rooted in Him, or stability and sustenance; and now he speaks of "built up." What does this imply? A house being built has something added to it every day. Day by day it grows more complete. Its growth shows the Architect's design. As it progresses it becomes more solid, so that progress, solidity, completion to perfection are the ideas in "built up." Ye are to be complete in Him. Without Him ye are nothing, can do nothing.

(g)

4. STABLISHED IN THE FAITH.—You must have Christ in you, so that you may not be easily overthrown. You are not to be a vane, turning at every breath of wind. You are not to be a plant, taking such slight hold that some stronger blast will overthrow. You are rather to be an oak, having firm hold of the soil—an oak, which has strengthened with every day of its growth, until no storm can move it. Point out some of the dangers to which the young Christian's faith—his hold of Christ—is exposed, and then dwell on the fact that safety and life altogether depend on His keeping the command, "Walk ye in Him; rooted and built up in Him, and stablished in the faith."

(h)   *John Gill*

WALK

He that shall walk with vigour three hours a day, will pass, in seven years, a space equal to the circumference of the globe.

(i)   *Dr. Johnson*

WALKING WITH GOD

The closest walk with God is the sweetest heaven that can be enjoyed on earth.

(j)   *David Brainerd*

WALKING WITH GOD

It is not as Monotheists, or as Deists, that Abraham and the Patriarchs are conspicuous;

(k)

but as men who, in the depths of their nature, communed with a personal God—who, in the expressive phrase of the sacred writer, "walked with God," and to whom He spake face to face, or heart to heart, "as a man speaketh unto his friend."

(a)   *Dr. Wace : Bampton Lectures*

WANDERINGS

Psalms 54, 57, and 63, by their titles, relate to the period of David's wanderings in the wilderness; and it has been remarked that "probably these Psalms made the Psalter so dear to Alfred and to Wallace during their like wanderings."

(b)   *Smith's Bib. Dict.* (David)

WAR

I look on war with a horror which no words can express. I have long wanted patience to read of battles. Were the world of my mind, no man would fight for glory; for the name of a commander who has no other claim to respect, seldom passes my lips; and the want of sympathy drives him from my mind. The thought of man, God's immortal child, butchered by his brother; the thought of sea and land stained with human blood by human hands—of women and children buried under the ruins of besieged cities—of the resources of empires and the mighty powers of nature all turned by man's malignity into engines of torture and destruction; this thought gives to earth the semblance of hell. I shudder as among demons. I cannot now, as I once did, talk lightly, thoughtlessly, of fighting with this or that nation. That nation is no longer an abstraction to me. It is no longer a vague mass. It spreads out before me into individuals, in a thousand interesting forms and relations. It consists of husbands and wives, parents and children, who love one another as I love my own home. It consists of affectionate women and sweet children. It consists of Christians, united with me to the common Saviour, and in whose spirit I reverence the likeness of His divine virtue.

(c)   *Channing*

WAR

'Twas not enough
By subtle fraud to snatch a single life;
Puny impiety! whole kingdoms fell
To sate the lust of power: more horrid still,
The foulest stain and scandal of our nature
Became its boast. *One* murder made a villain;
Millions, a hero.

(d)   *Porteus*

WATER OF LIFE

This *is* Water of Life. Probatum est. It is the right holy water! It never fails. It will cure the most desperate melancholy. It will dissolve doubts, though they have grown as hard as a stone in the heart. It will make you a *white soul*, which is better than a white skin. It gently purgeth, yet more effectually than any other waters. It provokes appetite, and makes us long for what is wholesome. If any ask why I thus *allegorize*, I answer, The text doth lead me to do it.

(e)   *John Bunyan*

WAY

Let me entreat you to let God's way be your way. Do not think that you can ever find out a better for yourselves. It may be a dark way, it may be a way that you would not desire; but look to the end of it. Consider what shall be the termination of this dark and mysterious path; it shall be life, peace, pardon, immortality.

(f)   *Daniel Moore*

A man's heart deviseth his way; but the Lord directeth his steps.

(g)   *Solomon*

Man proposeth, God disposeth.

(h)   *George Herbert*

WAY

The result of trials is peace, a chastened soul, a praising tongue.

What stuns and startles us now, shall then excite fervent gratitude; what vexes as a problem now, shall then unfold itself in clearest light. Why was I permitted to stumble at one point? Why did I lose my way and grope about in darkness at another point? Why did this reverse fall upon me, and well-nigh crush me? These questions, dark now, shall then meet with a satisfactory reply. It was a right way by which He led me to a city of habitation. Amen; "Just and true are Thy *ways*, Thou King of saints."

(i)   *Good Words*, 1861

WAY, I AM THE (John xiv. 6)

In our earthly speech we say: the wayfarer *makes a way*; but in the spiritual tongue the Way makes the wayfarer.

Isa. xxv. 8, is fulfilled in Christ.

(j)   *Braune*

WAY, THE MORE EXCELLENT

The old writers tell us a story of what they called the "Island of the Sirens"—sea-nymphs who used to lure on to their island home all who passed by it on board ship; and when, by their beautiful music, they had drawn them to their shores, they worked their ruin. On one occasion, we read how Ulysses, the great and strong, went by. Knowing the danger, he stopped the ears of his crew with wax, and bound himself with thongs to the mast, so that while his sailors should be unable to hear the music, he would be bound so firmly to his ship, that he could resist its charm. They passed by the coast safely. Presently, when Orpheus came by, he adopted a far more excellent way. As his ship was passing, he produced melody more beautiful than that of the Sirens on the shore; and so entranced were his crew by the music which he himself gave them, and so occupied was he in making it, that the Sirens failed altogether to draw them aside.

(k)

WAY OF SALVATION, THE

" *I am the Way, the Truth, and the Life: no man cometh unto the Father, but by Me* " (John xiv. 6).

1. The Occasion

Jesus had said, "And whither I go ye *know*, and the *way ye know*." Thomas, filled with gloomy doubts and forebodings, replied instantly, "*We do not know*."

(*a*)

2 Explanation

Thomas's mistake was the thinking of heaven too much as a *place*, rather than as a *condition*, or state begun now; too much of the goal or end, too little of the way to that end; too much of the circumference, too little of the centre.

(*b*)

3. Application

(i.) Too frequently when a man turns from "the error of his ways," he turns to an error concerning the Way of salvation. This is a common mistake with seekers.

They say, Tell us about "heaven," "hell," "the hereafter," "the resurrection of the dead," etc. "*We know not whither we go;*" and before they set out, they want to *know* about these things. This was Thomas's error—inquiring about the goal instead of the way. "Tell us this," they say, "and we will find out the way thither ourselves." Not so—we should miss it; our anxiety must be about the Way of salvation, not about the great realities of the other world. Such was the nature of the Lord's reply to Thomas, "*I am the Way*," etc. The way to know, is to proceed from the known to the unknown. Jesus directs Thomas's thoughts to Himself. Gaze not on *that* end, but on *this*

(*c*)

(ii.) So with Intellectual Doubts

God is "an unknown God." Is it possible to know Him? Agnostics deny this. But Jesus is the Revelation of the Father. "He that hath seen Me, hath seen the Father." In everything wherein doubts arise, and concerning which we *know not*, He directs our thoughts to Himself, as the first step towards their solution. God will not be an *unknown* God. These things will not be unknown, when once we know Him. "He is the Light of the world, and whosoever followeth Him shall not walk in darkness." Without Christ we can get no further than "Probability." We must do as Columbus did, make sure work of discovery by taking ship, and sailing forth into the unknown. There is no way of knowing the Father except by the revelation of the Son.

(*d*)

(iii.) Questions of Curiosity

Wrong only when too prominent. When people's energies are wasted in asking about heaven, its employments, inhabitants, or "shall we know our friends there?"—then there is danger of their thoughts being diverted from Jesus Himself. There will be reunion in Heaven. Common sense tells us that—

"Then oh, what raptured greetings
On Canaan's happy shore,
What knitting severed friendships up,
Where partings are no more!" (*Alford*)

But this is not to be the prominent thought. The essence of heaven, its very atmosphere, is Jesus Himself. "Whom have I in heaven, but Thee? and there is none upon earth that I desire in comparison with Thee."

(*e*)

4. But this is not all

Jesus is not only the Way, He is the Truth, and the Life, *i.e.*, absolute Truth, absolute Life. *He* is the thing sought for. Finding Him, we have the Way to the Father; we have the Truth; we have Life. Are we seeking salvation? He is salvation. Are we seeking Heaven? He is heaven —"For ever with the Lord" is heaven.

Are we seeking eternal life? "This is eternal life, to know Thee, and Jesus Christ whom Thou hast sent." He is not merely the *Way* to the Father—He is the Father revealed. The Incarnate God: "He that hath seen Me, hath seen the Father." Everything that we can ask or seek is all summed up in Him.

" We are in port if we have Thee " (*Keble*)

In these days of negations, if we would have positive knowledge, and know the Father, not by the guesses of speculation, and by abstract reasoning, but as an inner, concrete experience, which the world can neither give nor take away, then we must learn it from Jesus, the Way, the Truth, the Life.

(*f*)

WAY OF SALVATION, THE (Rom. x. 6, 7)

To sum up the general meaning of the passage : All the *doing* asked of man by the Law (ver. 5), and which he could never accomplish otherwise than imperfectly, is now accomplished perfectly by the Christ, whether it relate to the conquest of heaven by holiness, or to the abolition of condemnation by expiation. All, therefore, that remains to man in order to be saved, is to *believe* in this work by applying it to himself; and this is what is commanded us by the righteousness of faith, ver. 8, after it has forbidden us (vv. 6 and 7) to pretend ourselves to open heaven or to close hell. This argument showed at a glance, that, Christ having charged Himself with the *doing*, and having left us only the *believing*, His work put an end to the legal dispensation, which the Apostle wished to prove (ver. 4).

(*g*) *Godet*

WAY OF SALVATION, THE (Rom. x. 6, 7)

O thou, who desirest to reach the heaven of communion with God, say not: How shall I ascend to it? as if it were necessary for thee thyself to accomplish this ascent on the steps of thine own obedience. That of which thou sayest : Who will do it (how shall I do it)? is a thing done. To ask such a question, is to deny that Christ has really done it. It is to undo, at least so far as thou art concerned, what He has done. Thou, whom thy sins torment, say not any more : Who shall descend into the abyss, there to undergo my punishment? Expiation is accomplished ; thou canst have it by faith.

(*h*) *Ibid*

WAY OF SALVATION, THE (Rom. x. 6, 7)

The form τίς, *who*? has this meaning: it is not every man individually that is asked to fulfil these two conditions of salvation—obedience and expiation. In that case every man would be called to be his own Christ. The righteousness of faith forbids us to make such pretensions, which can only issue in our discouragement or embitterment. Instead of the part of Christs, it brings us down to that of believers; and hence the reason why Paul, in the following words, makes use twice of the name of *Christ*, and not that of *Jesus*, as he would certainly do if he meant to speak here of the historical facts as such (cf. viii. 11).

(a)						*Godet*

WAY OF SALVATION, THE (Rom. x. 6, 7)

Two ideas contrasted here

1. The *unrighteous* man will be *condemned* in the judgment;

2. The *righteous* man will be *saved*.

And the question which the Apostle answers in his very striking way is, How can we escape condemnation and attain salvation?

There are two ways open to us: either by (i.) DOING (ver. 5), or by (ii.) BELIEVING; and he institutes a contrast between those who "DO," and those who "BELIEVE":

The Doers deny Christ, because He is the "Doer" (and *vice versâ*).

The "Doers" deny, by their act and attitude, that Christ either died for their offences or was raised for their justification (ver. 6–7).

The thing they desire to do for themselves, is a thing already done—done by Christ—for—

He is the Doer

What then have *we* to do?

We have to take the second way of salvation open to us; viz., that of "BELIEVING."

"To him that worketh not, but believeth on Him that justifieth the ungodly, his faith is counted for righteousness" (iv. 5)

To Christ belongs the *doing*; to us the *believing*. This Way of Salvation is not delusive, for the Scripture saith, "Whosoever believeth on Him shall not be ashamed" (x. 11)

(b)						*Cf. Godet*

WAY OF SALVATION

"*The word is nigh thee*," etc. (Rom. x. 8, 9)

When Christ is preached (as the Agency); confessed and believed on by the hearer; the result is, "Thou shalt be saved."

This is in a measure easy. But we are inclined to make this a difficult matter. We take a long journey round to get to a place close by us—"Say not in thine heart . . . heaven . . . deep." This is what many do in the matter of salvation. They regard it as something out of their reach. Books about the reasonableness and philosophy of salvation are useful against objectors and sceptics, but not for the comforting of God's people. Many rely upon difficult books as props, but which are often obscurations—attempts to decipher unintelligible mile-stones and finger-posts. They

take long journeys; but the Bible is plainer than any man's book. It does not require of us to go in search of salvation as something almost inaccessible, but it says, "The word is nigh thee."

(c)

WAY OF SALVATION, THE *(Cf. p. 749, f.)*

1. When a man is awakened, and brought to that, that all must be brought to, or to worse, "What shall I do to be saved?" (Acts xvi. 30, 31), we have the apostolic answer to it: "Believe on the Lord Jesus Christ, and thou shalt be saved, and thy house." This answer is so old that with many it seems out of date. But it is still, and will ever be fresh, and new, and savoury, and the only resolution of this grand case of conscience, as long as conscience and the world last. No wit or art of man will ever find a crack or flaw in it, or devise another or a better answer; nor can any but this alone heal rightly the wound of an awakened conscience.

(d)

2. Let us set this man to seek resolution and relief in this case of some masters in our Israel. According to their principles they must say to him, "Repent, and mourn for your known sins, and leave them and loath them; and God will have mercy on you." "Alas!" (saith the poor man), "my heart is hard, and I cannot repent aright: yea, I find my heart more hard and vile than when I was secure in sin." If you speak to this man of qualifications for Christ, he knows nothing of them; if of sincere obedience, his answer is native and ready: "Obedience is the work of a living man, and sincerity is only in a renewed soul." Sincere obedience is therefore as impossible to a dead unrenewed sinner, as perfect obedience is. Why should not the right answer be given to the awakened sinner: "Believe on the Lord Jesus Christ, and you shall saved"? Tell him what Christ is, what He hath done and suffered to obtain eternal redemption for sinners, and that according to the will of God and His Father. Give him a plain downright narrative of the Gospel salvation wrought out by the Son of God; tell him the history and mystery of the Gospel plainly. It may be the Holy Ghost will work faith thereby, as He did in those first fruits of the Gentiles (Acts x. 44).

(e)

3. If he ask, What warrant he hath to believe on Jesus Christ? tell him, that he hath utter indispensable necessity for it: for without believing on Him, he must perish eternally. Tell him that he hath God's gracious offer of Christ and all His redemption; with a promise, that upon accepting the offer by faith, Christ and salvation with Him is his. Tell him that he hath God's express commandment (1 John iii. 23) to believe on Christ's name; and that he should make conscience of obeying it, as well as any command in the moral law. Tell him of Christ's ability and good-will to save; that no man was ever rejected by Him that cast himself upon Him; that desperate cases are the glorious triumphs of His art of saving. Tell him, that there is no midst (or medium) between faith and unbelief; that there is no excuse for neglecting the one and continuing in the

(f)

other; that believing on the Lord Jesus for salvation is more pleasing to God than all obedience to His law; and that unbelief is the most provoking to God, and the most damning to man, of all sins. Against the greatness of his sins, the curse of the law, and the severity of God as Judge, there is no relief to be held forth to him, but the free and boundless grace of God in the merit of Christ's satisfaction by the sacrifice of Himself.

(a)

4. If he should say, "What is it to believe on Jesus Christ?" As to this, I find no such question in the Word; but that all did some way understand the notion of it; the Jews that did not believe on Him (John vi. 28–30); the chief priests and Pharisees (John vii. 48); the blind man (John ix. 35). When Christ asked him, "Believest thou on the Son of God?" he answered, "Who is He, Lord, that I may believe on Him?" Immediately, when Christ had told him (ver. 37), he saith not, "What is it to believe on Him?" but, "Lord, I believe;" and worshipped Him: and so both professed and acted faith in Him. So the father of the lunatic (Mark ix. 23, 24), and the eunuch (Acts viii. 37). They all, both Christ's enemies and His disciples, knew that faith in Him was a believing that the man Jesus of Nazareth was the Son of God, the Messiah, and Saviour of the world, so as to receive and look for salvation in His name (Acts iv. 12). This was the common report, published by Christ and His Apostles and disciples; and known by all that heard it.

(b)

5. If he yet ask, What is he to believe? you tell him, that he is not called to believe that he is in Christ, and that his sins are pardoned, and he a justified man: but that he is to believe God's record concerning Christ (1 John v. 10–12). And this record is, that God giveth (that is, offereth) to us eternal life in His Son Jesus Christ; and that all that with the heart believe this report, and rest their souls on these glad tidings, shall be saved (Rom. x. 9–11). And thus he is to believe, that he may be justified (Gal. ii. 16).

(c)

6. If he still say that this believing is hard, this is a good doubt, but easily resolved. It bespeaks a man deeply humbled. Anybody may see his own impotence to obey the law of God fully; but few find the difficulty of believing. For his relief and resolution ask him, "What is it he finds makes believing difficult to him?" Is it unwillingness to be justified and saved? Is it unwillingness to be so saved by Jesus Christ, to the praise of God's grace in Him, and to the voiding of all boasting in himself? This he will surely deny. Is it a distrust of the truth of the Gospel record? This he dare not own. Is it a doubt of Christ's ability or good-will to save? This is to contradict the testimony of God in the Gospel. Is it because he doubts of an interest in Christ and His redemption? You tell him that believing on Christ makes up the interest in Him.

(d)

7. If he say that he cannot believe on Jesus Christ because of the difficulty of the acting this faith, and that a Divine power is needful to draw it forth, which he finds not, you must tell him that believing in Jesus Christ is not work, but a resting on Jesus Christ. You must tell him that this pretence is as unreasonable as if a man, wearied with a journey and not able to go one step further, should argue, "I am so tired, that I am not able to lie down," when indeed he can neither stand nor go. The poor wearied sinner can never believe on Jesus Christ till he finds he can do nothing for himself; and in his first believing doth always apply himself to Christ for salvation, as a man hopeless and helpless in himself. And by such reasonings with him from the Gospel, the Lord will (as He hath often done) convey faith and joy and peace by believing.

(e)   *Robert Traill's works*, 1696

WAY OF SALVATION

"The word is nigh thee" (Rom. x. 8)

(The 10th century.) They contrived, by their chimerical speculations, to question the plainest truths; to wrest the simple meaning of the Holy Scriptures, and give some appearance of truth to the most ridiculous and monstrous opinions. . . . Of the scholastic divines, the most illustrious was Thomas Aquinas, styled the Angelical Doctor. His *"Sum of all Theology"* (1615) is a treatise on the most abstruse metaphysics of theology. It occupies 1250 folio pages, very small close type, in double columns. To which are appended 19 folio pages of double columns of errata, and about 200 of additional index! The form is Aristotelian: the difficulties are proposed first, then the answers. There are 168 articles on Love, 358 on Angels, 200 on the Soul, 85 on Demons, 151 on the Intellect, 134 on the Law, 3 on the Catamenia, 237 on Sins, 17 on Virginity, and others on a variety of topics. The scholastic tree is prodigal with foliage, but barren of fruit.

(f)   *Disraeli: Cur. Lit*

WAY, THIS IS THE

None need go astray. It is a *plain* way. Wayfaring men, in strange lands, are likely to go astray; fools would be certain to do so. Walking in an unknown country, in which there are many roads, finger-posts that point rightly and read plainly would help us much. Look at your finger-posts. There are four—Repent, Believe, Love, Obey. Then we have also the Book to explain these directions. But more. We have a Guide. He who made the way undertakes to lead us in it. He also guards us from going astray. Should we begin to wander, He tells us that we shall "hear a word behind us: This is the way, walk ye in it." And should we go out of the way, like Bunyan's pilgrims, He will not leave us in the dungeons of Giant Despair, if we will only apply the key of promise.

(g)   *John Gill*

WE KNOW (Rom. viii. 28)

"The whole world seems to contradict their hope of future glory. All things visible, especially the hatred of the hostile world, seem to oppose and gainsay their faith. And yet this fearful appearance can have no force, since all things are subject to the omnipotent and wise administration of God, on whose loving counsel their confidence is established. Still more, if all things are subject

(h)

to God's supreme authority, and this authority is exhibited in the development of His loving counsel, they know, with the full certainty of faith, that all things work together for their good. This follows,—

(i.) From the decree, plan, and order of salvation (28–30);

(ii.) From God's arrangement, act, and facts of salvation (31–34);

(iii.) From the experience proved in the O.T., that the Lord's companions in suffering, as His companions in conflict, are also His companions in victory, for whose glorification all surmounting obstacles are transformed into means of advancement (35–37).

(a)   *Lange*

WEAK

" *When I am weak, then I am strong* " (2 Cor. xii. 10)

Has God denied to you, or taken from you His gift of health? Has He seen fit to impair any one of your bodily organs—your sight, hearing, enjoyment of taste, or power of motion? Or has His allotment made you less beautiful, pleasing, clever, attractive, than some others, perhaps in your own family? Or have you been treated with neglect and coldness by some one to whom you had shown kindness? Has the poison of disappointment entered your heart, and made earth itself dull and distasteful to you for ever? Or are you destined to a lot of obscurity, if not poverty; unable to rise as others rise; obliged to stand and look on while others do the work and reap the honour which once perhaps you hoped might be your own? Or are you at this time mourning under one of God's afflictive disappointments, bereaved and crushed, scarcely able to look either above or beyond the present, so dark does all seem to you, so blank, so naked? . . . It is the dark side of life which brings us most closely, most consciously, into connection with the supporting and comforting help of Christ within. Everything that lowers the exuberance of animal spirits, everything that tends to depress and humble us as merely human and earthly beings, tends also, if it be but meekly and faithfully borne, to show in us and to us how near Christ is, how loving, how real, how powerful. " When I am weak," etc.

(b)   *Dean Vaughan*

" *When I am weak, then I am strong* " (2 Cor. xii. 10)

A dying soldier asked Bishop Thorold, near the Seven Dials, what he did when too weak to pray: " Sir, when I am too weak to cling to Him, I ask Him to cling to me."

(c)   " *On being Ill* "

WEAK THINGS (1 Cor. i. 27)

God hath chosen by weak things to confound the wise, yet I see not but in all times a wasted language hath much prevailed. And even the Scriptures, though I know not the Hebrew, yet I believe they are penned in a tongue of deep expression, wherein every word hath a metaphorical sense which does illustrate by some allusion. How political Moses, in his Pentateuch! How philosophical Job! How mazy and sententious is Solomon in his Proverbs! How quaint and flamingly amorous in the Canticles! How grave and solemn in his Ecclesiastes.

(d)   *Owen Feltham*

WEAKNESS

Luther once said, that " the devil plagues and torments us in the place where we are most tender and weak. In Paradise he fell, not upon Adam, but upon Eve. *It commonly rains where it was wet enough before.*"

(e)

WEAKNESS AND LYING

The more weakness, the more lying; force goes straight; any cannon-ball with holes or cavities in it goes crooked.

(f)   *J. P. F. Richter*

WEAKNESS, MORAL

He was a blackguard of undeniable mark. Yet his chance of success at the onset of life was great and manifold. Nature was bountiful to him, bestowing upon him a pleasing person and excellent talents. Fortune favoured him; education and society expanded and polished his intellect, and improved his manner into an insinuating and almost irresistible address. Upon these foundations he took his stand, became early very popular among his associates, and might have erected a laudable reputation, had he possessed ordinary prudence. But he defied his good genius. There was a perpetual strife between him and virtue, in which virtue was never triumphant. His moral stamen was weak, and demanded resolute treatment; but instead of seeking a bracing and healthy atmosphere, he preferred the impurest airs, and gave way readily to those low and vulgar appetites which infalliably relax and press down the victim to the lowest state of social abasement.

(g)   " *Edinburgh Review,*" *on Edgar Allan Poe*

WEATHER-WISE (Luke xii)

This address was to the *people* = a mixed multitude, appealing to their conduct in every-day matters. The Saviour would have us *weather-wise* in spiritual matters; *i.e.*, meteorologists in the supernatural sphere of His kingdom: " *Watchman, what of the night?* "

(i.) *Signs of rain:* Sensible, shrewd people act accordingly—hats, coats, umbrellas, storm signals, and ships.

(ii.) *Signs of heat:* Fine day—go a journey, harvest, plough, sow, reap, ships sail. But observe the same people's conduct in the really important matter of entering the Kingdom of Christ.

1. *There are signs of the times.* John Baptist has come preaching repentance; the Lord Jesus Christ hath opened the kingdom to all believers—atonement offered; and what is the effect? Practically none at all. " Thou knewest not the time of thy visitation."

2. *The duty of all men.* Learnt from following words :—

(i.) Reconciliation with our adversary = preparation for the inevitable—for death, judgment, and Judge. This is our life's work.

(ii.) This the preacher's message: " We pray you in Christ's stead, be ye reconciled to God."

(h)

WEB, A TANGLED

Oh, what a tangled web we weave
When first we practise to deceive.

(a)   *Scott*

WELL PLEASED

"*In whom I am well pleased*" (Matt. iii. 17)

"Well pleased" *with* Him and *in* Him; well pleased with His people. His adopted children, who, by faith, are united to Jesus, and share in His Baptism.

(i.) *The Heavens are opened to them* = spiritual things revealed, and not shut and hidden, as to others.

(ii.) *The Spirit is imparted* to Him in its fulness, and to them in measure.

(iii.) *The voice of the Father is heard* = the assurance of His love, whence the response "*Abba, Father.*"

(b)   *Adapted from Kernaham*

WESTWARD

"*If I take the wings of the morning, and dwell in the uttermost parts of the sea; even there shall Thy hand lead me, and Thy right hand shall hold me*" (Ps. cxxxix. 9, 10)

1. Westward went the Apostle of the Gentiles, when, starting for the coast of Cæsarea, he embarked in what a great French writer has called the "Christian Odyssey"; westward to that island which alone emerged on the horizon of the Israelite as he looked from the heights of Lebanon, the spot which was to him the sole representative of the western race—the isle of Chittim, the isle of Cyprus, destined, perchance, in our later day, to give back to the Eastern race what once it received from them. Westward the Apostle still advanced when he crossed over from Asia into Europe, and came into contact with the civilization of Greece. Westward yet again when he reached the mighty capital of the Western dominion. Westward further still when he stretched his yearning gaze toward what was then called the last limit of the world, the Pillars of Hercules, the extreme point of Spain. And so it has been through the long history of Christendom. The Eastern churches, in spite of all their manifold interests, have yet not been the true centres of Christianity. They may have their destiny and their mission; but it is in Italy, in France, in Germany, in England, and America that the hopes of Christian civilization have rested. Christianity, born in the East, has become the religion of the West even more than the religion of the East. Only by travelling from its early home has it grown to its full stature. The more it has adapted itself to the wants of the new-born nation which it embraces, the more has it resembled the first teaching and character of its Founder and of its followers. Judaism, as a supreme religion, expired when its local sanctuary was destroyed. Mohammedanism, after its first burst of conquest, withdrew itself almost entirely within the limits of the East. But Christianity has found not only its shelter and refuge, but its throne and home, in countries which, humanly speaking, it could hardly have been expected to reach at all. From those Western countries, in spite of their manifold imperfections, that Eastern religion still sways the destinies of mankind. Under the shadow of that tree which sprang up from a grain of mustard-seed on the hills of Galilee have been gathered the nations of the earth. The Christian religion rose "on the wings of the morning"; but it has remained in the "uttermost parts of the sea," because the hand of God was with it, and the right hand of God was upholding it.

(c)

2. The peculiar points of Christianity which have enabled it to combine these two worlds of thought, each so different from the other. And first observe, on the one hand, in the Gospel history, the awe, the reverence, the profound resignation to the Divine Will, the calm, untroubled repose which are the very qualities which the Eastern religions possessed at a time when to the West they were almost wholly unknown, and which even now are more remarkably exhibited in Eastern nations than amongst ourselves. "Thy will be done!" —that great prayer which lies at the root of all religion—is a thought which the old Western nations hardly understood. It breathes the spirit of the race of Abraham, of the race of Ishmael. "God is great." So a Mussulman Algerian once said to his Christian captive. The captive, who came from the British Isles, has recorded that it was the first word of consolation that had reached his heart and caused his sinking spirit to revive. On the other hand, look at the practical activity and beneficence which formed the sum and substance of the Redeemer's life. How He went about everywhere doing good! How He made the service of man to be itself the service of God! How unlike the immovable East! It is the Divine recognition of those energetic faculties of man which have especially marked the character of the Roman, the German, and the Anglo-Saxon races of mankind. Christ has taught us how to be reverential, and serious, and composed. He has taught us no less how to be active, and stirring, and manly, and courageous. The activity of the West has been incorporated into Christianity, because it belongs to the original character and genius of its Founder, no less than its awe and its reverence.

(d)

3. In every Eastern religion, even in that which Moses proclaimed from Mount Sinai, there was a veil, as the Apostle expressed it—a veil on the prophet's face, a veil on the people's heart—a blind submission to absolute authority. There was darkness around the throne of God; there was darkness within the Temple wall; there was in the holy of holies a darkness never broken. To a great extent this darkness and exclusiveness must prevail always till the time comes when we shall see no longer through a glass darkly. There always must be mystery in the greatest truths, and boundless contiguity of shade, which no philosophy, no inquiry, no revelation, no decrees of councils, no speculation of theologians can ever fathom or remove. This we have in Christianity, in common with all the East; but yet, as far as the veil can be withdrawn, it has been withdrawn by Jesus Christ and by His true disciples. He is the Light of the world. In Him we behold the open face, the glory of the Father. He came to bear witness to the truth. He went to and fro, rousing the hearts

(e)

Westward—*continued*

and the minds of men to seek for truth. In Him the cry of inquiry and of freedom which had already been awakened in the West found a ready response. Not without a purpose was the Greek language, with all its manifold flexibility, chosen for the vehicle of His teaching, rather than the stiff, immovable Hebrew. Not without a natural affinity did the Grecian philosophy attach itself to the first beginnings of the Gospel. Not unfitly were Socrates and Plato deemed by the Early Fathers to have been Christians before the time. The revival of the studies of the ancient languages and the vast impulse given to the progress of human thought by the Reformation, was in itself a new manifestation of Christ, a new declaration of His union with minds and classes of men who had before been deemed to be without God in the world. It is a constant reminder, too, that, in using to the utmost the resources of science : in watching for light, from whatever quarter ; in sifting and searching all that comes before us to the very bottom, we are fulfilling one of the chief calls of our religion, we are accomplishing the very will of our Founder. Whatever is good science, is good theology; whatever is high morality and pure civilization is high and pure religion. The freedom and progress of the West contrast as strongly with the spirit of the East as the greenness of our fields contrasts with its arid plains, as the shadows of our clouds and the freshness of our breezes with its burning suns; the ceaseless variety and stir of our teeming cities, with its vast solitude. And it is a contrast which Christ and Christianity have exhibited. It is God's gift to us, to be developed as our special contribution to the treasures of our common faith. Let us be of good heart ; let us not be unworthy of our high calling. Wherever statements are received without evidence, wherever hollow watchwords are used like sounding brass and tinkling cymbal, there the shadow of barbarism is still upon us ; wherever language is used as a veil to conceal our thoughts, wherever we allow ourselves to employ sacred words without meaning, there the light of the Gentiles has not dawned upon us. Truly it has been said, that the great theological controversies which have agitated the Churches to so little practical purpose, have turned on words which were not defined and, therefore, not understood. The moment the words have been defined and their meaning appreciated, that moment the excitement has cooled and the passions evaporated. So it was with the scholastic disputes concerning the Trinity ; so it has been with more recent disputes concerning predestination and justification. The spirit of Western enlightenment has turned its lantern upon them, and they have disappeared or are disappearing like phantoms and shadows, and the day-spring from on high has risen in our hearts.

(a)

There was in all Eastern religions, whether we look Godward or manward, a sternness and separation from the common feelings and interests of mankind. We see it, as regards man, in the hardness and harshness of Eastern laws. We see it, as regards God, in the profound prostration of the soul of man, displayed first in the peculiarities of Jewish worship, and to this day in the prayers of devout Mussulmans. And this also enters in its

measure into the life of Christ and the life of Christendom. The invisible, eternal, unapproachable Deity, the sublime elevation of the Founder of our religion above all the turmoils of earthly passion and of local prejudice—that is the link of Christianity with the East. And, on the other hand, there was another side of the truth which until Christ appeared had been hardly revealed at all to the children of the Older Covenant. Degrading and erroneous in many respects as were the old Gentile notions of the Godhead, yet there was one thought which dimly and darkly ran through all the old religions of the nations which the Bible called the children of Japhet—namely, the thought that the gods were not far removed from any one of us. They had from time to time come down into the ranks of men. They had been seen labouring, suffering, weeping, nay, even dying, for the service and the welfare of man. And this it is which in the life and character of Christ is so wonderfully combined with that deep reverence for God of which the Eastern nations have received so large a share. In Christ we see how the Divine Word could become flesh, and yet the Father of all remain invisible and inconceivable. In Christ we see not merely, as in the Levitical system of Christianity, man sacrificing his choicest gifts to God ; but God, if one may so say, sacrificing His own dear Son for the good of man. Not only the loftiness of God, as with the Hebrews, but the condescension of God, as with the Gentiles ; not only the abasement of man, as with the Jew, but the elevation of man, as with the Greek, was in Jesus Christ set forth in indissoluble union. And with this closer revelation of the compassion and condescension of God was called forth the justice, the gentleness, the mercy, the humanity, which the West has developed more strongly than the East, and which makes Christianity to be emphatically the religion of love and in the largest sense of charity.

(b)   *A. P. Stanley*

WHAT IS THAT TO THEE? (John xxi. 22)

= *Rebuke and Counsel.*

"What is that to thee?" which of us has not deserved the *rebuke ?*

"Follow thou Me !" which of us does not require the counsel ? The heart and eye are thus called away from the problem which perplexes, the prospect which discourages, the thoughts which distract and paralyze ; and a plain duty is proposed instead.

(c)   *A Plain Commentary, Oxford*

This was a transient stumble in one who, but lately recovered of a great disease, did not walk firmly. But it is the common track of most, to wear out their days with impertinent inquiries. There is a natural desire in men to know the things of others, and to neglect their own ; and to be more concerned about things to come, than about things present.

(d)   *Leighton*

WHATSOEVER AND WHOSOEVER

1. Measure of God's sovereignty :—"But our God is in the heavens; He hath done whatsoever He pleased" (Ps. cxv. 3).

(e)

2. Measure of petition :—" Whatsoever ye shall ask in My name," etc. (John xv. 16 ; xvi. 23).

3. Measure of doctrine :—" Teaching them to observe all things whatsoever I have commanded " (Matt. xxiii. 20).

4. Measure of submission :—" We have sinned ; do Thou unto us whatsoever seemeth good unto Thee " (Judges x. 15).

5. Measure of duty :—" Whatsoever things I command you, observe to do it ; thou shalt not add thereto, nor diminish from it " (Deut. xii. 32).

6. Measure of success :—" Whatsoever he doeth shall prosper " (Ps. i. 3).

7. Measure of reward :—" Whatsoever a man soweth, that shall he also reap " (Gal. vi. 7).

" Whosoever " and " whatsoever " are two precious words often in the mouth of Christ. " Whosoever will " may come ; " Whatsoever ye shall ask in My name, that will I do." " Whosoever," is on the *outside* of the gate, and lets in all who choose ; " Whatsoever " is on the *inside*, and gives those who enter the free range of all the region and treasury of grace. " Whosoever " makes salvation free ; " Whatsoever " makes salvation full.

(*a*)

WHENCE AND WHITHER

" *Jesus knowing* " (John xiii. 3)

We enter life, we play our part,
　　We die—nor learn the reason here ;
From out the unknown void we start,
　　And whither bound ?—God knows, my dear.
(*b*)　　　　　　　　　　　　　　　*Voltaire*

" WHERE IS HE ? " (John vii. 11)

Might one often ask in bustling Church-solemnities, or in learned, flowery sermons : Where is He, the Chief Person ?
(*c*)　　　　　　　　　　　　　　　*Gossner*

" WHITED SEPULCHRES " (Matt. xxiii. 7)

It has been said,
That the heart of man can be a *temple* of the living God, or a *grave ;* a heaven or a hell.
As,

(i.) *Temples* of the Holy Ghost = incense of prayer and praise ;

(ii.) *Graves* = full of corruption and uncleanness ;

(iii.) *Heaven*=peace, quiet, rest, calm, resigned wills ;

(iv.) *Hell*=like the troubled sea, which cannot rest, casts up mire and dirt=unrest, disquiet, unresigned wills.

See "Golden Legend" (*Longfellow*), for a revelation of man's heart.
(*d*)

" WHO IS THIS ? " (Matt. xxi. 10)

1. The inquiry asked *of* Galilean (country) Jews, simple and unsophisticated adherents *by* city Jews, men of sharper wit, accustomed to sift opinions, who asked incredulously and contemptuously " *Who is this ?* "
(*e*)

2. *This* question, concerning Christ, has ever been, and is now being asked.

3. The answer of His simple adherents. " *This is* Jesus," is sufficient.

(i.) **Jesus, the Incarnate God : God** manifest in the flesh (1 Tim. iii. 16)

Attested to by the voice from heaven at His baptism, " This in My Beloved Son " ;
Also by the Apostle, " He thought it not robbery to be equal with God . . . made Himself of no reputation," etc.
The reason of this incarnation may be gathered,

(1.) From the parable of the leaven : He took our nature, that ultimately we may take His. The leaven inserted in the meal, till ultimately the whole mass becomes one. By this we " become partakers of the Divine nature."

(2.) Another reason is that of *sympathy :* we understand a child because we have been children, and can sympathize with one. So Christ, being " touched with a feeling of our infirmities," is a sympathizing High Priest, which in a special sense He could not have been otherwise.
(*f*)

(ii.) **This is Jesus** THE PROPHET, **or Teacher sent from Heaven** (John i. 21)

He is " that Prophet," promised ;
" *Hear ye Him*"=He brings a new and fuller revelation to men, especially about God ; only a Son can tell about His Father ; it is part of His Mission to set us right in our false and imperfect conceptions of God.
Hence,
Old Testament reveals God as " Almighty," " Jehovah," " Shepherd of Israel," " He who dwelleth between the Cherubim " ; but Jesus, the *Son*, tells us He is our FATHER, and that no one *knows* Him " but the Son, and he to whom the Son will reveal Him."
Compare with this our notions of God still :
God=*Deity*. Therefore Atheism is prevalent. Think of Jesus having to prove the existence of God ! As well ask Adam for such a proof ! Jesus could say, " *I am the proof*," " He is my Father, What I do He does. The proof you require is *with you and before you*." Think of the comfort of such knowledge. A child in the arms of a *strong* man has no assurance that the strength may not be used to injure him ; but when the strong man is also his father, then ensues comfort and a sense of protection. So, belief in the " Almightiness " of God is not necessarily comforting ; before confidence comes we need to be assured of His fatherhood, and this we have in Jesus.
(*g*)

(iii.) **This is Jesus,** THE SAVIOUR (Luke ii. 11)

(1.) So the angel announced : " Jesus . . . a *Saviour ;* "
(2.) To the Shepherds : " To you is born . . . a *Saviour ;* "
(3.) Himself said : " I came to *save* . . . "
Hence we *come boldly to the throne of grace*, crying,
(4.) " Master, Master, we perish ! "
(5.) " Lord, save me ! "
(*h*)

(6.) "Lord, have mercy upon me!"
And He does save: it is *His work*. "Jesus is never terrible," said Staupitz to Luther:

> "Jesus, the name I love to hear,
> I love to hear its worth;
> It sounds like music in mine ear,
> The sweetest Name on earth."

(a)

"WHO SHALL SEPARATE us from the love of Christ?" (Rom. viii. 35)

The Apostle is not merely addressing the feelings but appealing to sober facts—God is for us, no matter what may be against us. That love is still to us, as it was to Him, the most potent moral force in human history.

(b)   *Dr. Wace: Boyle Lectures*

WHY

> Whatever sceptic could inquire for,
> For every *why* he had a *wherefore*.

(c)   *Butler*

WICKEDNESS

There have been men *splendidly* wicked, whose endowments threw a brightness on their crimes, and whom scarce any villany made perfectly detestable, because they never could be wholly divested of their excellences; but such have been, in all ages, the great corrupters of the world; and their resemblance ought no more to be preserved than the art of murdering without pain.

(d)   *Dr. Johnson*

WIFE

> All other goods by Fortune's hand are given;
> A wife is the peculiar gift of Heaven.

(e)   *Pope*

WILDERNESS

The forty years in the wilderness

This long period of punishment and humiliation is shrouded in profound obscurity. From a comparison of the four passages of Holy Scripture which alone throw any light upon this dark period of Israel's history (Deut. viii. 2–6; Josh. v. 4–9; Ezek. xx. 10–26; Amos v. 25, 26), we infer that it was a period of "training and temptation, of humiliation and blessing, of natural wants and supernatural existence."

(f)   *Maclear and Kurtz*

WILDERNESS

The first generation of the Israelites

After the giving of the Law and the Covenant, at Sinai, they set out for the Land of Promise. But it soon appeared they were not ripe for this possession, which could only be the portion of *the children of God*. The infection which had so deeply penetrated their nature, through their mode of life in Egypt, had certainly for the moment been repressed by the inspiration of their first love, but had not been entirely rooted out;

and a thorough regeneration could only be expected after the dying away of the Egyptian generation. In order to draw out all this, the departure had been arranged by God. The trials of the wilderness journey were designed to reveal the hardness of their hearts. It was plainly to come to light that the delay in the fulfilment of the promise had its formation in the people themselves, not in God. Unbelief and carnality appear in this Egyptian generation thirty-eight years, that they wandered, dying off. In the first month of the fortieth year they arrived again at Kadesh. There they were to experience that the time of punishment, if almost, yet had not entirely elapsed—the generation embued with Egyptian habits and feelings should become extinct, and the new generation be severely tried.

[Election can in no wise be hurt from without, but it can indeed by apostasy within.

He is foolish who despairs of mercy, and he also that turns the grace of God into lasciviousness.]

(g)   *Hengstenberg*

WILL

Our own will, though it should obtain its largest wish, would always keep us in uneasiness. But the very instant that we renounce our own will, we grow easy.

(h)   *Blaise Pascal*

WILL

"Thy will be done"

If it be Thy will, O Lord, command me what Thou wilt, send me whither Thou wilt; I will not withdraw myself from anything that seems good to Thee.

(i)   *Epictetus.*

WILL OF THE LORD, WHAT THE, IS (Eph. v. 17)

A definite object is treated of, which in every case must be clear to the "wise," but which can however easily remain not understood. . . . This will, reaching to what is least and most peculiar, is the object of the insight of the wise; the further he advances, the less is anything to him *merely permissible*, everything becomes for him a precept and will from above (Acts xxi. 14).

(j)   *Lange*

"WILL YE ALSO GO AWAY?" (John vi. 67)

Appropriate question on Holy Communion days, when for the most part the congregation *go away*.

This chapter is about the *eating and drinking the flesh and blood of Christ*: i.e., it teaches the *idea* of the Holy Communion; as then, many left Jesus at this stage of His teaching, so now it is only to be expected that the untouched and the unbelieving would leave the church and go away; but many in whom Christ dwells go out too. Hence the import of this question, "Will YE also go away?"

(i.) "*Also*"—for some had gone-

(ii.) "*Ye.*" Points of difference between the two classes.

(k)

WILLING MIND ACCEPTED, THE

That which Paul tells us in the point of communicating to the necessities of the saints; to wit, "If there be first a willing mind, it is accepted according to that a man hath, and not according to that he hath not" (2 Cor. viii. 12), holds true also in all other services and divine duties; so that we are accepted with the Lord according as we are inwardly affected, although our actions be not answerable to our desires. He that hath a ready and resolved mind to do what he may, would undoubtedly do a great deal more if ability were ministered. "God," saith Paul, "worketh both to will and to do." If both be His own works, the desire as well as the deed, He must needs love and like both the one and the other, both in respect of acceptation and reward. David did but conceive a purpose to build God a house, and He rewarded it with the building and establishing of his own house (2 Sam. vii. 16). He did but conceive a purpose to confess his sin, and God's ear was in his heart before David's confession could be in his tongue (Psalm xxxii. 5). To poor beggars that wanted food for themselves, Christ shall say at the last day, "Ye have fed me when I was hungry," only in regard of their strong affections if they had had means. The prodigal child, when he was but conceiving a purpose of returning, was prevented by his father first coming to him; nay, running towards him (Luke xv. 20). God will answer us before we call (Isa. lxv. 24); that is, in our purpose of prayer.

Besides Scripture and reasons, I add ancient and modern authority; not for any other confirmation but only to show consent.

"To desire the help of grace is the beginning of grace," saith Austin.

"Only thou must will, and God will come of His own accord," saith Basil.

"He that thirsts, let him thirst more, and he that desires, let him yet desire more abundantly; because, so much as he can desire, so much he shall receive."—Bernard.

"Christ," saith Luther, "is then truly omnipotent, and then truly reigns in us, when we are so weak that we can scarce give any groan."

Again: "The more we find our unworthiness, and the less we find the promises to belong to us, the more we must desire them; being assured that this desire doth greatly please God, who desireth and willeth that His grace should be earnestly desired."

"When I have a good desire," said Kemnicius, "though it doth scarcely show itself in some little and slender sigh, I must be assured that the Spirit of God is present, and worketh His good work."

"Faith," saith Ursin, "in the most holy man in this life, is imperfect and weak; yet, nevertheless, whosoever feels in his heart an earnest desire and striving against his natural doubtings, both can and must assure himself that he is endued with true faith."

"If thou shalt feel thyself," saith Rolloc, "to believe in Christ, and that for Christ; or at least, if thou canst not forthwith attain that, if thou feel thyself willing to believe in Christ for Christ, and willing to do all things for God's sake and sincerely, thou hast certainly a very excellent argument, both of perseverance in faith, and of that faith which shall last for ever."

"Our faith may be so small and weak," saith Taffin, "that it doth not yet bring forth fruits that may be lively felt in us; but if they which feel themselves in such estate desire to have these feelings (namely, of God's favour and love); if they ask them at God's hands by prayer, this desire and prayer are testimonies that the Spirit of God is in them, and that they have faith already. For is such a desire a fruit of the flesh or of the Spirit? It is of the Holy Spirit, who bringeth it forth only in such as He dwells in."

"Is it possible," saith Hooker, speaking of Valentinian the Emperor, out of Ambrose, "that he which had purposely the Spirit given him to desire grace, should not receive the grace which that Spirit did desire."

"Where we cannot do what is enjoined us, God accepteth our will to do, instead of the deed itself."

"I am troubled with fear that my sins are not pardoned," saith Careless. "They are," answered Bradford; "for God hath given thee a penitent and believing heart; that is, a heart which desireth to repent and believe. For such a one is taken of Him (he accepting the will for the deed) for a penitent and believing heart."

(a) *Bolton*

WIN

"*That I may save some*" (1 Cor. ix. 22)

Indeed I had no notion of joy from this world; I cared not where or how I lived, or what hardships I went through, so that I could but win souls for Christ. I continued in this frame all the evening and night. While I was asleep, I dreamed of these things; and when I waked, the first thing I thought of was this great work of pleading for God against Satan.

(b) *D. Brainerd*

WINE

O thou invisible spirit of wine, if thou hast no name to be known by, let us call thee devil!

(c) *Shakspeare*

WISDOM

"*We speak wisdom*" (1 Cor. ii. 6)

1. *What this wisdom is* NOT.

(i.) "Not wisdom of *words*" (1 Cor. i. 17). If so, it would obscure the Cross (ii. 1), and be a preaching of *self*. If not of words, it is "*foolishness*." Granted: This is often hurled at the preacher (i. 18).

(ii.) Not the wisdom of *this world*: it is inadequate to know God (i. 19 *seq.*); it has tried to find out God (ver. 21), and failed.

(iii.) This wisdom is *not taught by man*: we cannot learn it as we learn other things. We have no power to help ourselves. The depth says: "It is not in me."

(d)

2. *What this wisdom is*.

It is the wisdom of finding out God by the teaching of the Holy Spirit; and consists in,

(i.) The preaching of the Cross (ver. 18);
(ii.) The foolishness of preaching (ver. 21);

(e)

(iii.) Christ crucified (ver. 23) ;
(iv.) Christ is our wisdom, etc. (ver. 30) ;
 (v.) Jesus Christ, and Him crucified (ii. 2).
This wisdom is the power of God (i. 18 ; ii. 4, 5).
(a)

3. *By whom, and why this wisdom is rejected*

By two representative classes of people :
 (i.) The self-righteous (Jews).
 (ii.) The cultured (Greeks).
These want something in which they can glory.
Hence the *fewness* of those who accept the
doctrines of *grace*.
(b)

WISDOM

The Greeks had deified wisdom; and St. Paul's
language = " We worship not Minerva, but Christ."
. . . It is important to dwell upon this . . . there
is a marvellous idolatry of talent; it is a strange
and grievous thing to see how men bow down
before genius and success. Draw the distinction
sharp between these two things—goodness is one
thing, talent another. . . . The Son of Man came
not as a scribe, but as a poor working man. He
was a Teacher, not a Rabbi. When the idolatry
of talent enters the Church, then farewell to
spirituality ; when men ask their teachers, not for
that which will make them more humble and God-
like, but for the excitement of an intellectual
banquet, then farewell to Christian progress. Here
also St. Paul stood firm—not wisdom, but Christ
crucified. . . .
 . . . Christianity is not a creed, but a life ; and
men who listen to a preacher only to find an
intellectual amusement, are not thereby advanced
one step nearer to the high life of a Christian.
(c)   *F. W. Robertson*

WISDOM (Job xxviii. 12)

There is something profoundly pathetic in the
exclamation attributed to the patriarch Job, " But
where shall wisdom be found ? and where is the
place of understanding ? " We contemplate him
at the outset of all human experience, beginning to
realize the profound and mysterious complexity of
life. He is standing, as it were, at the parting of
the broad and narrow ways. Life stretches before
him like the desert with which he was surrounded,
and over which he travelled, with few and rare
tracks across it, and the path still uncertain which
led to the most precious of all human possessions.
The path thereof, he exclaims, is one "which no
fowl knoweth, and which the vulture's eye hath not
seen ; the lion's whelps have not trodden it, nor the
fierce lion passed by it." Well might he exclaim,
" Whence then cometh wisdom, and where is the
place of understanding ? seeing it is hid from the
eyes of all living, and kept close from the fowls of
the air ! " That, in such circumstances, he should
have firmly grasped the conviction that " The fear
of the Lord, that is wisdom, and to depart from
evil is understanding," may well be regarded as an
act of heroic faith.
(d)   *Dr. Wace : Bampton Lectures*

WISDOM

Man's knowledge is not perfect within the
domain of creation, still less can he know the

things of the invisible world. Only by *living* in a
sphere does he gather knowledge of what is found
there ; knowledge comes from experience of occurrences. Without a disposition of the heart the
sense of the understanding is not enlarged and
sharpened. *Sensible, mental, spiritual* knowledge
refers to life spheres, in which he who knows must
move. Only the believing, loving, longing one
knows and grows in knowledge unto knowledge.
 Hence the Apostle's prayer (Eph. i. 17) for the
spirit of wisdom, etc.
(e)   *Lange's Commentary*

WISDOM

The minister of the Gospel must not be afraid
of the conflict with the wisdom of the world. God
first gathered the unlearned, afterwards philosophers ; nor hath He taught fishermen by orators,
but He has subdued orators by fishermen.
(f)   *Gregory the Great*

" *Ye do err, not knowing the Scriptures, nor the
power of God* (Matt. xxii. 29)

Christ sent the specially *wise* home as the
specially *foolish*.
(g)

WISDOM OF OUR GOD, THE

Dr. Paley, the Christian philosopher, wrote a
very brilliant chapter about the wonders of a bird's
wing. Musicians have listened in the woods, and
they have written down in their portfolio in
musical score the song of birds—the libretto of the
forests. Oh, the wisdom of God in the structure
of a bird's wing ! Oh, the wisdom of God in the
structure of a bird's voice ! Could all the artists
and artisans and philosophers of the earth make
one dandelion ? In one cup of china aster enough
wine of wisdom for all nations to drink. Where
is the architect that could plan the pillar of one
pond lily ? Break off this morning the branch
of a tree, and see in the flowing sap the divine
chemistry of the alum, the sugar, the tannin, the
potash, the carbonate of lime. Let them try to
explain the wonders of an artichoke or radish.
Let them look at a vegetable and tell the story
how it has lungs, and how it has feet, and how it
has an ancestry as old as the ages, and how it will
have descendants as long as time, and how that
in one square inch it has three hundred thousand
cells, each one of them requiring the omnipotence
of a God. Galileo, in prison for his advanced
notions of things, was asked why he persisted in
believing in God, and he pointed down to a broken
straw on the floor of his dungeon, and said : " Sirs,
if I had no other reason to believe the wisdom and
the goodness of God, I would argue them from the
straw on the floor of this dungeon." Behold the
wisdom of God in the construction of the seeds
from which all the growths of this spring-time
come forth—seeds so wonderfully constructed that
they keep their vitality for hundreds and thousands
of years. Grains of corn found in the cerements
of the Egyptian mummies buried thousands of
years ago, planted now, come up as luxuriantly
and easily as grains of corn that grew last year
planted this spring-time. After the fire in London
in 1665, the *Sesimbrium Iris*, seeds of which must
have been planted hundreds and hundreds of years
(h)

before that, grew all over the ruins of the fire. Could the universities of the earth explain the mysteries of one rutabaga seed? Could they girdle the mysteries of one grain of corn? Oh, the shining firmaments in one drop of dew! Oh, the untravelled continents of mystery in a crystal of snow! Oh, the gorgeous upholstery in one tuft of mountain moss! Oh, the triumphal arch in one tree-branch! Oh, the God in an atom! Where is the loom in which He wove the curtains of the morning? Where is the vat of beauty out of which He dipped the crimson and the gold, and the saffron and the blue, and the green and the red? Where are the moulds in which He ran out the Alps and the Pyrenees? Where is the harp that gave the warble to the lark, and the sweet call to the robin, and the carol to the canary, and the chirp to the grasshopper? It is the same God who has all your affairs and mine under His care and guidance. The same God who pairs the birds in this spring-time gave us our companions. The same God who shows the chaffinch how to take care of her brood, will protect our children. The same God who shows the sparrow in this spring-time how to build its nest, will give us a habitation. The same God who gathers the down for the pheasant's breast will give us apparel. The same God who this day feeds the squirrels in the wood will feed us. The same God who swung a bridge of gossamer for the insect to walk over, has marked out all our pathway. Praise His name. None of us so insignificant as to miss His care. Oh, ye who are worried about your health, and worried about your reputations, and worried about your children, and worried about your property, and worried about everything, in these spring-time days go out and listen to the song of the English sparrow, one of the richest possessions of Brooklyn. *"Are ye not of more value than many sparrows?"* *"Behold the fowls of the air, they gather not into barns, yet your Heavenly Father feedeth them, O ye of little faith."*

(*a*)   *Talmage*

WISE MEN

The present winter is not yet half through, but so far as it has proceeded it has brought us very mild weather and one gale of more than ordinary severity. This latter occurred on the night of the 11th December; and in some of the more northern parts of the country it is said to have been more violent than any since the year 1839. The public health has remained very good; but it is very probable that the effect of the dismal fogs of last week will shortly appear in an increased mortality from respiratory diseases.

Although much has already been said on the subject, the history of the year would be incomplete without some reference to the extraordinary solar phenomena which marked its closing days. Time after time has the sun risen and set in a background of colour so exquisite in its changing hues that the wonder and admiration of the most insensible have been excited, and the least observant have been led to take a growing interest in the marvels of the varying cloud forms. With a laudable anxiety to know more about these unusual occurrences the unscientific public called upon the magicians, the soothsayers, and the astrologers to show the meaning and the cause of these strange things; and one of the wise men opened his mouth and said, "The explanation is

very simple. The ordinary effects of sunset are produced by vapour in the atmosphere, and these abnormal sights that you see are due to a superabundance of this moisture." And another said, "The explanation is simple. The ruddy glows you perceive are caused by the sun shining through clouds of meteoric dust." And a third spake in this wise, "The explanation is simple. Three months ago a gigantic volcanic eruption took place in the Straits of Sunda, in the course of which an island was submerged and thousands of people were overwhelmed. Vast showers of lava were thrown high into the air, and the wonderful sunsets you see are caused by the sun shining through particles of finely powdered pumice." And when the wise men had left off speaking, the unscientific ones pondered over all that had been said, and came to the conclusion that although in a multitude of counsellors there is often safety, a conclave of the learned does not always furnish thirsting souls with a sufficiency of satisfying information.

(*b*)   *Daily News*, 1883–84

WITHOUT CHRIST

God out of Christ is incommunicable; God out of Christ is incomprehensible; God out of Christ is very terrible; God out of Christ is inaccessible.

(*c*)   *Thos. Brookes*

WITHOUT CHRIST (Eph. ii. 12)

"Without God," is Atheism; "without Christ," is to be without "Promise" and without "Hope."

1. Promiseless

Aliens; "strangers to the covenants of Promise" —the opposite condition to "Fellowship with the Father and the Son."

(i.) Just as there are those who are "outside" any Brotherhood of men, such as Guilds and Freemasonry, so here: without Christ = outsiders.

(ii.) St. Paul alludes to them that are "without"; as in Abraham's tent there were divisions, "He that was after the flesh persecuted him that was after the Spirit," even so it is now.

(iii.) There will be such at the time of the end; some will be "within" the Holy City, and some "without"—"without are dogs."

These outsiders are Promiseless.

The Bible contains many "exceeding great and precious Promises."

"Godliness hath the promise of this life as well as of that which is to come."

(i.) *In life:* There is the Promise of Providential care—"I will never leave thee nor forsake thee;"

(ii.) *In death or in trouble:* "When thou passest through the waters they shall not overflow thee;"

(iii.) *For the future:* "I give unto them eternal life;" "They shall never perish;" "I will raise him up at the last day."

But these Promises are not for an *outsider*, because he is "without Christ," in whom "all the promises of God are yea and amen." Cf. John vi. 53, The Promise, and *no* Promise.

(*d*)

2. Hopeless

Because "without Christ" = "without God in the world"—such may be *Heathens, Worldlings,* or *Unbelievers*—all equally Hopeless.

(*e*)

This Hopelessness is shown

(i.) *In life*—in the restless tendency of seeking salvation in some other form of Religion, "Neither is there salvation in any other." Or, in the denial (as now) of God's Fatherhood; and rejection of Jesus Christ as the Revealer of the Father.

(ii.) *In death :* no light: the Infidel's "leap into the dark ; " no guide, no voice of comfort; no footsteps through the unknown, unexplored dark valley. No hand to hold to—ending sometimes in the despairing cry, " I cannot, will not die." Yet there is no escape from the relentless hold of the universal conqueror, Death. If nothing else will show us our need, surely this will, " Without Thee I dare not die."

(iii.) On the cradle of such as are " without Christ," write no word of *Welcome*. For surely life "without Christ " is not worth living ; and a birthday is a mockery. Creation is a misfortune if it only introduces us to an *aimless* existence and a *hopeless* end. "Jesus Christ or Despair," was *Lavater's* exclamation. To live such a life is to be like a derelict ship, abandoned to itself—at the mercy of wind and wave—no chart, no compass, no pilot, doomed to be wrecked sooner or later. And for *epitaph* write, " Abandon Hope, all ye who live and die *without Christ* "—for them there is no " Hope of Glory."

(a)

3. The Reverse Picture is seen in verses 18 and 19

God and heaven, life eternal, and glory, are all realities. But they are unknown and uncertainties "without Christ." He only has the key, opens, and gives us access to them.

(b)

" WITHOUT CHRIST, . . . NOTHING " (John xv. 5)

The passage asserts plainly the total spiritual inability and unfruitfulness of man without vital connection with Christ. . . .

Christ does not here speak of unconverted men, but of Christians, who, even *after* their conversion, are in constant need of His grace for the performance of any Christian work. Christ is the beginning, middle, and end of spiritual life ; we can do nothing without Him, but much, yea, everything with Him.

(c)   *P. Schaff*

It is a poor and inadequate interpretation of the words " Without Me," to make them to mean " Ye can do nothing *until* ye are in Me and have My grace." It is rather, "*After* ye are in Me, ye can even then accomplish nothing except ye draw life and strength from Me." . . .

From first to last it is I that must work in and through you. We have a warning here to the regenerate man, that he never seek to do aught of himself ; not a declaration that the unregenerate is unable to do aught.

(d)   *Trench*

WITNESS OF CONSCIENCE (Ps. cxxxix. 1)

Conscience may for a time be dulled and deadened, but is it not on the whole the one presence which you cannot get rid of? Does it not beset you in your path and in your bed, abroad or at home, by night or by day? If you count its suggestions, are they not more in number than the sand? If you forget it in your sleep, when you awake is it not still with you? And what is the operation of its voice? Is it content with proclaiming to you the general supremacy of a righteous law? Does it not, on the contrary, search your heart and try your thoughts, and see if there be any wicked way in you? Does it not, with a mysterious justice, deal with your personal character, your private, individual, and peculiar, responsibilities, making allowance for your weaknesses, condemning you in proportion to the wilfulness of your sin, but above all things meeting you at every turn and in every instant of your lives with the particular warning and guidance you need?

(e)   *Dr. Wace : Boyle Lectures*

WITNESS TO REVELATION, THE (Heb. i. 1, 2 ; Gal. i. 1, 8, 11, 12)

There can be no doubt whatever, as a matter of historic fact, that the Apostle Paul claimed to have received direct revelations from heaven. That he wrote the Epistle to the Galatians is unquestioned, and in the first chapter of that Epistle he bases the whole authority of his message upon an express Divine commission. He claims to be an Apostle " not of men, neither by man, but by Jesus Christ, and God the Father, who raised Him from the dead." He certifies the Galatians that the Gospel which was preached of him was not after man, for, he says, " I neither received it of man, neither was I taught it, but by the revelation of Jesus Christ." He is so certain of that revelation that he warns them against being enticed by any apparent evidence to doubt it. " Though we, or an angel from heaven, preach any other Gospel unto you, than that which we have preached unto you, let him be accursed. As we said before, so say I now again, if any man preach any other Gospel unto you, than that ye have received, let him be accursed." It would be impossible to express a stronger, a more deliberate, and a more solemn conviction that St. Paul had received a supernatural communication of the will of God.

(f)   *Dr. Wace : Bampton Lectures*

WITNESS OF THE SPIRIT, THE

If the voice of conscience is the voice of God, then, in the last resort, it is upon the witness of God Himself that faith rests. It is His voice within us, the witness of His Spirit, which authenticates the voice without us, and affords us the final assurance that an Apostle or a Prophet brings us a message from Him. So St. Paul declares to the Corinthians, " I, brethren, when I came to you, came not with excellency of speech or of wisdom, declaring unto you the testimony of God. I was with you in weakness, and in fear, and in much trembling ; and my speech and my preaching was not with enticing words of man's wisdom, but in demonstration of the Spirit and of power, that your faith should not stand in the wisdom of men, but in the power of God " (1 Cor. ii. 1-5). That demonstration of the Spirit and of power still attends the message of the Gospel, though in some respects in a less visible and

(g)

miraculous form. In those words, "Not which man's wisdom teacheth, but which the Holy Ghost teacheth" (1 Cor. ii. 13), there still resides that power to turn men from darkness to light, to regenerate their moral energy, and to make them new creatures, which was, after all, the mightiest miracle of even Apostolic times. The words just quoted are a warning to us, that no ground short of this witness of God Himself will suffice to sustain, or to preserve uninjured, the edifice of faith.

(a)   *Dr. Wace: Bampton Lectures*

WITNESS (TITLE OF OUR LORD) (Isa. lv. 4)

1. God an unknown God:

(i.) To the heathen (Acts xvii. 23), "To the unknown God";

(ii.) Generally: mists, clouds, uncertainties in men's conceptions of Him (*cf. Agnosticism*), because "No man hath *seen* God at any time."

(iii.) Old Testament conceptions were imperfect: God there as—

(1.) *Almighty* = safety, not necessarily *love;*

(2.) *Shepherd* = providential care, not intercourse, etc., etc. Hence our need of more light about God; for some one, who hath *seen* Him, lived with Him, to come and tell us more perfectly about Him, and our relations to Him.

(b)

2. This *need* met

(i.) By the promise of the text:
"I have given Him for a *witness* to the people."

(ii.) By the authoritative voice at His baptism:
"This is my beloved Son, HEAR HIM" (He has a message to you).

(iii.) By His own assertion:
"For this cause was I born, and for this cause came I into the world, that I should bear *witness* unto the truth."

(iv.) By His qualifications as a *witness:*

(1.) As to *knowledge:*
"We speak that we do *know*, and testify that which we have *seen*";

(2.) As to *reliableness:*
He is "The *faithful* and *true* witness";
"He whom God hath sent speaketh the words of God";
"If I should say, I know Him not, I should be a liar."

(3.) As to *character:*
"Which of you convinceth Me of sin?";
"I find no fault in Him";
"In Him was no sin."

(c)

3. His two-fold witness:

(i.) In His *teaching:*
(1.) "I will declare Thy *Name* unto my brethren."
(*N.B.*—The *name* of God = what He *is*—that which we seek to know, and to have light on.)
(2.) In prayer Jesus addresses God: "*Father*, glorify Thy *Name*;" "O righteous *Father*, the world hath not known Thee, but *I have known Thee*";
"Father, if possible," etc.
"Father, into Thy hands," etc.
The *Name*, which He declares unto His brethren is that of "FATHER."
"My *Father*, and your *Father*."
"When ye pray" (ye Christians), don't go back to the old forms, to Old Testament and imperfect conceptions of God, but say,

"*Our Father*."
(ii.) In His *Person:*
"Lord, show us the Father" (a Theophany). Note the answer, "Have I been so long time with you and yet hast thou not known Me?"
"He that hath seen *Me, hath seen the Father*."
"I am the *Incarnate God*."
"God hath shined"; "God was in Christ"; and men saw, and heard, and handled, and understood.
Ask, What saw they?
Answer = Infinite *Love, Pity, Compassion.*
"The heavens declare the *glory* of God." They show His Omnipotence and His Wisdom; but Jesus, the only begotten Son, declares Him, *i.e., His heart. God is a Father.* God is *Love.*
This is the central truth of the whole universe, and this is enough.

(d)

WITNESSES OF THESE THINGS, YE ARE (Luke xxiv. 48)

1. "These things" = the life of Jesus (not teaching and doctrine), His Birth, Crucifixion, Resurrection, and Ascension.

2. "Witnesses" show this life in yourselves to the world, who appreciate living examples more than preaching:
Show that Jesus is born in you by a Jesus-like life;
Show that His Crucifixion is a fact in you by being yourselves crucified to the world;
Show that His Resurrection is a power within you, by being "raised to newness of life;"
Show that His Ascension has likewise become a real factor in your life, by setting "your affections on things above, and not on things of the earth."
This will be a most real witness-bearing to the world "amongst whom ye shine as lights."

(e)

WITNESSES FOR GOD: SCIENCE, PHILOSOPHY, AND FAITH

Philosophy and science are the children of Faith; and however they may be from time to time misrepresented, she can never doubt their loyalty to her. But it is a somewhat severe trial of patience, that mental or physical philosophers should confine themselves to the facts they can observe within the range of their special studies or in their laboratories, and should erect the conceptions which they thus find themselves able to form respecting the existence of God into crucial tests, by virtue of which they set aside the deepest moral and spiritual experiences of mankind. Those experiences are the most momentous of all the facts in the case; and if an equal amount of scientific experience and scientific conviction were treated by a theologian with the cool indifference exhibited towards religious faith by Hume and by some modern philosophers, he would be treated as almost beyond the pale of reasoning. Belief in God has been embedded from the earliest centuries in the deepest moral convictions of our race; and a philosophy which is content to criticize beliefs thus authenticated, instead of treating them as the most momentous premises with which it has to deal, places itself practically out of court.

(f)

On what conceivable principle of reasoning or of philosophizing are we to bid a **Paul**, a **John**, an **Athanasius**, an **Augustine**, an **Anselm**, a **Luther**, a **Pascal**, a **Newton**, to stand aside, and to be silent on the mightiest of all truths, until a modern philosopher has reconciled their convictions with his syllogisms, or a modern man of science has found material traces of them in his crucible? Nay! We must ask, with far greater amazement, on what ground a mightier witness still is similarly set aside, until philosophy has pronounced that His testimony is admissible. In the language and the life of our Lord, the deepest apprehension of moral truth is bound up with the apprehension of God in His most personal character as a Father; and this fact affords the final practical answer to the objections which have been considered. There is indeed a presumptuous flippancy which deems itself capable of distinguishing between the essential and non-essential elements in His teaching, and of setting the latter aside. But no such presumption can go so far as to deny that in His mind and heart the two elements were united; and this is a fact of more weight than any amount of dubious speculation. For the purpose of illustrating the nature and limits of faith, a consideration of its foundations in the conscience has been indispensable. But the final answer to all objections against belief in God is, that the Lord Jesus Christ lived in it and died in it.

(a)　　　　　　　　*Dr. Wace : Bampton Lectures*

WITNESSING A GOOD CONFESSION (Polycarp)

" We have seen and do testify that the Father sent the Son to be the Saviour of the world. Whosoever shall confess that Jesus is the Son of God, God dwelleth in him, and he in God " (1 John iv. 14, 15)

The two ideas are never separated; and the theological conception is always the strength and life of the moral. . . . The life of Christians and the confessions of the martyrs start from the belief that their fellowship is with the Father. The confession of Polycarp at the stake is the earliest of these solemn testimonies; and it is perhaps the loftiest and the most characteristic of all. He looked up to heaven, and said,—

" O Lord God Almighty, the Father of Thy beloved and blessed Son Jesus Christ, by whom we have received the knowledge of Thee, the God of angels and powers, and of every creature, and of the whole race of the righteous who live before Thee, I give Thee thanks that Thou hast counted me worthy of this day and this hour, that I should have a part in the number of Thy martyrs, in the cup of Thy Christ, to the resurrection of eternal life, both of soul and body, through the incorruption imparted by the Holy Ghost. Among whom may I be accepted before Thee this day as a rich and acceptable sacrifice, according as Thou, the faithful and true God, hast foreordained, hast revealed beforehand, and hast now fulfilled. Wherefore also I praise Thee for all things, I bless Thee, I glorify Thee, along with the everlasting and heavenly Jesus Christ, Thy beloved Son. through Whom to Thee, with Him and the Holy Ghost, be glory both now and to all ages. Amen."

It would be difficult to quote from any postapostolic source a more complete summary of the Christian faith, alike in its dogmatic contents and in its moral inspiration.

Dr. Wace : " The Faith of the Early Church "
(b)

WOMAN AND HOME: FEELING AND DUTY

" Thy desire shall be to thy husband " (Gen. iii. 16)

She neglected her conjugal duty if she pursued any course, even under the pretence of religious motives, contrary to his will. A singular vow demanded a voluntary relinquishment of domestic duties and enjoyments, to devote herself in some way to His service. It is generally supposed, in some employments of the tabernacle, or in the service of His poor, or in the " binding oath to afflict the soul," giving herself up for a certain time to individual fast and prayer. Now, few women in Israel, except orphaned single women and childless widows, could be so independently situated as to make and follow up these vows, without interfering with some nearer domestic duty.

(c)

Woman's sphere in the law of God, without doubt, is HOME; her noblest attraction, devotedness to those with whom she is there thrown in daily intercourse. Some women there are, who find not only duty, but pleasure there—not only love but safety.

Others, again, restless and discontented, fancy that they should be happier, and better, and more useful, anywhere but where they are, and gladly seize the first pretence to turn aside.

(d)

Spiritual devotedness is too often a worldly snare, and the pride of holiness the most dangerous temptation which can possibly assail us. We have often heard of what is called a saint—one avowedly devoted to the cause of religion; passing hours in her closet; surrounded by religious books, all, we may observe, *commentaries*, but not the *Word of Life* itself; or, with religious friends, wearing a peculiar dress and most peculiar manners; visiting the poor, more often with tracts than food; censuring every innocent amusement as profane, and temptations of Satan; bearing words of humility on the lips, but of pride in heart; outwardly condemning and abhorring her own sins, but inwardly thanking God that she is so much holier than others: robing religion in such dark and terrible colours, that the young spirit shrinks from it, and plunges into the world with renewed zest, to escape from the faintest resemblance of its acceptance.

(e)

Man did not need such restraint . . . because, in the first place, he was more independent than woman; in the next, *reason*, not *feeling*, being his guide, he was not likely to fall into the temptation of ill-regulated enthusiasm, even in his holiest and dearest duty. Woman's guide in general is feeling; she is a creature of impulse, ever likely, unless strongly yet tenderly restrained, to turn aside from the safer and less excitable path of daily duty, wherever the affections or the enthusiasm of the moment may lead. More especially is

(f)

she likely to fall into this temptation when first awakened to the claims, and beauty, and comfort of religion. The simple duties of home then seem little worth, compared to the service of Heaven. Herself, her parents and brothers, husband and children, appear of slender consequence compared to the state of her affections and faith towards God. . . . She cannot realize that the unfatiguing, unexciting duties of domestic usefulness, infused with thoughts of God and of His Word, is the path most acceptable to Him. And severing, instead of uniting, she neglects what she deems the lesser, to pursue the greater duty (Numb. xxx. 3-15).

(a)   *Grace Aguilar: " Women of Israel "*

[The above, though written from a Jewish point of view, is of general application. It admirably hits the right nail on the head, especially in these days when " slumming " has become fashionable.]

WOMAN OF SAMARIA, THE (John iv. 27)

Evidently this woman was well known. The disciples were " *very respectable*," and filled with a decent horror that Jesus should *talk* to *that* woman.

They forgot two things:

1. What they might be under temptation;
2. What the Saviour came into this world for.

PETER, no doubt filled with pious horror, little imagined that he would deny Christ, and " damn his soul " under a slight temptation.

PHILIP, the questioner, might feel disposed to ask, " Do you know who she is? "

THOMAS, the doubter, has reason now to doubt whether He, who allowed such contact, was the Messiah.

JUDAS, perhaps more astonished than they all, might feel that such companionship was damaging to the interests of the new kingdom. He little imagined into what depths he could sink.

" ALL," soon, forsook Him and fled.

Yet no man said, "Why talkest Thou with her?"

(b)

WONDER AND JESUS

" *What manner of man is this, that even the winds and the sea obey Him?* " (Matt. viii. 27)

That which occasioned wonder to the Jews, and to our Lord's followers, was the exhibition of His power over nature (miracles). As though the only thing which could affect the mass of men with astonishment were that which is visible and startling to the senses. But with our Lord it is the very reverse. He never speaks as if there were anything strange or unnatural in the miracles He performs. He refers to them, indeed, as " Mighty works," or rather as exertions of His power and of His goodness. But to Himself they appear perfectly natural and simple. There is a conspicuous absence of all effort about them. . . . Any display of effort is a revelation of weakness; but our Lord " speaks and it is done, He commands and it stands fast." It was by the phenomena of the moral world that His astonishment was occasioned—by its vast capacities on the one hand, and its terrible incapacities on the other. On the one hand, He marvelled at the faith manifested in the appeal of the centurion, who bade Him speak the word only and his servant should

be healed; and He expressed a similar admiration at a like display of faith in the Canaanitish woman (Matt. viii. 10; xv. 28). On the other hand, when, in His own country, among His own kin, and in His own house, He found Himself without honour, so that He could not do any mighty work, save that He laid His hands upon a few sick folk and healed them, we are told that " He marvelled because of their unbelief" (Mark vi. 6). The faith of which men are capable on the one hand, and the unbelief of which they are capable on the other—these are the only two things which are said to have evoked the wonder of the Lord Jesus. These, to His eye, were the only two real marvels exhibited during His ministry.

(c)   *Dr. Wace: Bampton Lectures*

WORD OF GOD

" *Seek ye out of the book of the Lord, and read* " (Isa. xxxiv. 16)

What hath the Lord spoken? (Jer. xxiii. 35)

The testimony of Jesus is the spirit of prophecy (Rev. xix. 10).

The word of God is true (Ps. cxix. 160; 2 Sam. vii. 28); and it is pure (Prov. xxx, 5).

He will perform His word (Isa. xlvi. 10; lv. 11; xliv. 26; Ezek. xii. 28).

It is said to quicken and give birth to the soul (Ps. xix. 7; cxix. 93; 1 Pet. i. 23; Jas. i. 18).

To break the rock (Jer. xxiii. 29).

Enlighten the eyes (Ps. xix. 8); and restore the soul (Ps. xix. 7).

To be the means of faith (Rom. x. 17).

To make wise unto salvation, and to save the soul (2 Tim. iii. 15; Jas. i. 21).

In every way it is profitable to us (2 Tim. iii. 16).

It preserves us from sin (Ps. cxix. 11; xvii. 4).

It sanctifies (John xvii. 17).

It cleanses (John xv. 3; Eph. v. 26).

Is the guide and direction of our conduct (Ps. cxix. 105).

The food by which we live and grow (Deut. vii. 3; John vi. 63; 1 Pet. ii. 2).

And the weapons to defeat our enemy (Eph. vi. 17; Ps. cxix. 42; Matt. iv. 10, 11).

By the word we are made fruitful (Deut. xxxii. 2; Isa. lv. 10, 11; 1 Thess. ii. 13; Matt. xiii. 23; Col. i. 5, 6).

It is more to be desired than much fine gold; sweeter also than honey, or the honey-comb (Ps. xix. 10).

It is durable—eternal (Isa. xl. 8; 1 Pet. i. 23; Matt. xxiv. 35).

It is the means to convince the gainsayers (Tit. i. 9).

The brethren are established by it (Acts xx. 32).

The world shall be judged by it (John xii. 48).

It is our comfort in affliction (Ps. cxix. 92; 1 Thess. i. 6).

It rejoices the heart (Jer. xv. 16; Ps. xix. 8; cxix. 162).

Believing it, we prosper (2 Chron. xx. 20).

Loving it, we have peace (Ps. cxix. 165).

By the word we are led into fellowship with the Father, and with His Son Jesus Christ (1 John i. 3).

Hearing it, and keeping it, we prove our discipleship (John xiii. 31).

Are pronounced BLESSED (Luke xi. 28).

And in keeping it there is GREAT REWARD (Ps. xix. 11).

(d)

Prayer, previous to Reading the Word

Lord, give me Thy Holy Spirit (Luke xi. 13), to guide me into all truth, as it is in Jesus Christ (John xvi. 13). Open Thou mine eyes that I may behold wondrous things out of Thy law (Ps. cxix. 18). Give me understanding, and I shall keep Thy law; yea, I shall observe it with my whole heart (Ps. cxix. 34). Give me grace to receive with meekness the engrafted word, which is able to save my soul (James i. 21); to make me wise unto salvation, through faith which is in Christ Jesus (2 Tim. iii. 15). And, as man doth not live by bread alone, but by every word that proceedeth out of Thy mouth, Lord, *evermore give me this Bread of Life, that I may eat and live for ever* (Deut. xxxii. 2; John vi. 34-51). Lord, hear and answer my prayer, for Christ His sake. Amen.

(a)

WORD OF GOD, THE

"*I will keep Thy statutes, O forsake me not utterly*" (Ps. cxix. 8)

Fidelity to God's Word Praised

This is a remarkable Psalm, in its structure, its subject, and in its author.

(i.) *Its structure.*

Very artistic—yet it records a real, not fanciful spiritual experience. There are twenty-two divisions in it, one for each letter of the Hebrew alphabet; and it contains 176 verses, eight in each division.

The German Bible calls it "The Christian's Golden A, B, C;" it is a most suitable title.

(ii.) *Its subject.* This, too, is remarkable.

It is about "The Word of God."

It is a most noticeable fact, that the word of God is referred to 175 times, once in each verse except the 122nd.

Not always, of course, under the same name, for the word of God is here called by ten different names:

Word, saying, testimonies, way, judgments, precept, commandment, law, statute, truth.

(iii.) *Its author* unknown; not David, because it was written during the Babylonian Captivity. But whoever it was, it was a renowned Israelite, a man of profound experience, faith, and knowledge of God's word. It may have been Ezra or Nehemiah. Ezra belonged to the Captivity, a scribe, very learned in the law. He edited the Book of the Law, *i.e.*, he collected all the holy writings up to his time into one volume. He was a Reformer, and probably had a spiritual past that we know nothing about. At any rate, we know that useful men must have had suitable training in the past. There is ground for thinking that the writer was Ezra the scribe, who ranked as a second Moses.

This, however, we may be certain of:

The writer was a young man (vv. 9, 99, 100);

He was persecuted on account of his faith;

There was a hostile government, and there were apostate Jews (vv. 23, 46, 161);

He was in prison, bonds (vv. 61, 83);

He was expecting death (v. 109).

And this Psalm was his experience in all this; his prayer for steadfastness when others fell away.

The Psalm is of one piece, each division records the stages of the writer's experience. The work of a martyr in prison, carefully and artistically put together.

Under like circumstances we have,

St. John, in Patmos for the truth's sake, writing the Book of Revelation;

Luther, hidden away in the castle at Wartburg, translating the Bible into German;

Bunyan, in Bedford gaol on account of his faith, writing the "Pilgrim's Progress."

Some faithful man at that time was suffering on account of his faith; and in prison he wrote this account of his experience; and having plenty of time he put it into this artistic form.

(b)

1. The course of thought in the first division culminates in the eighth verse

The writer wishes to be a man whose conduct is based on the principles contained in God's word:

Not a hypocrite, not a deceitful hearer, but a "doer of the word."

That word is called here, "The law of the Lord."

"His testimonies," "His ways," "His precepts," "Thy statutes," "commandments," "judgments."

This is language he uses to himself:

"I know God's will, I want to DO it."

"I want to WALK in the law of the Lord."

"I want to KEEP His testimonies."

"I want to WALK in His ways."

"I want to KEEP His statutes."

"I want to have RESPECT unto Thy commandments."

"I want to learn Thy righteous judgments."

And his reason is, because,

(i.) Such people are "BLESSED." They are God's own peculiar people, not exempt from trouble, not in glory, but being fitted by God Himself on earth for glory. They are His children, and for the present under tutors and governors. His in contradistinction to those who are of the world.

(ii.) Because "they do no iniquity," and are "undefiled." They are right-doing people, people who, from love of righteousness, set themselves in opposition to all that is defiling, mean, unjust, and untrue in life.

They are Christ's, they must be like Him;

They are justified. They must not bring themselves under the bonds of old sins, and so become transgressors;

They are new creatures in Christ Jesus. They must walk in newness of life;

They are God's husbandry. They must bring forth good fruit;

They are vessels of honour. They must adorn the doctrine of God their Saviour in all things.

This the Psalmist desires, and he wishes it to be habitual and life-long, not spasmodic, by fits and starts. He wishes to walk always and consistently in this undefiled way.

(c)

2. To do this, to live such a life—a Divine power is needed

We have no strength of ourselves to help ourselves, consequently he prays for "direction" (v. 5).

This kind of life will bring him to honour, and not to shame; it will have a glorious ending. "Them that honour Me I will honour." To secure the blessing which he seeks, he prays earnestly that God would enable him to keep His precepts diligently.

(d)

Hence his resolve

His mind is quite made up. He is in earnest, quite decided.

I will keep Thy statutes.

He has put his hand to the plough, and he will not look back, lest the furrow become crooked. He has set out on the right road, he will not turn back, but go on bravely, though it entails persecution. God helping him, he will weather the gale, though it blows a hurricane. He has counted the cost. This is his resolve.

Now for his final prayer.

He is a sufferer, suffering brings with it heart-searching, and heart-searching reveals sins, and sin brings a CLOUD, and that hides the Sun. He is in darkness. He is forsaken, there is some "need be" for it; it may get even darker yet; anyhow he will be faithful, and he finishes by a cry, "Oh, forsake me not utterly." Let not the light wholly go out. Blow upon the little flame. Break not the bruised reed. "O Thou who art the 'Light of the world,' come to me, to me, Lord Jesus, come, lift up the light of Thy countenance upon me, and there shall be light."

(a)   Cf. Delitzsch

WORD OF GOD, OPERATION OF

The word of God hath three degrees of operation in the hearts of men. For, first, it falleth to men's ears as the sound of many waters, a mighty, great, and confused sound, and which commonly bringeth neither terror nor joy, but yet a wondering and acknowledgment of a strange force, and more than human power. This is that effect which many felt on hearing Christ, when they were astonished at His doctrine, as teaching with authority. "What manner of doctrine is this?" "Never man spake like this man" (Mark i. 22, 27; Luke iv. 32; John vii. 46). This effect falleth even to the reprobate (Hab. i. 5; Acts xiii. 41). The next effect is the voice of thunder; which bringeth not only wonder but fear also; not only filleth the ears with sound and the heart with astonishment, but moreover shaketh and terrifieth the conscience. And this second effect may also befall a reprobate, as Felix (Acts xxiv. 25). The third effect is proper to the elect, the sound of harping, while the word not only ravisheth with admiration and striketh the conscience with terror, but also, lastly, filleth it with sweet peace and joy, etc. Now, albeit the first two degrees may be without the last; yet none feel the last, who have not in some degree felt both the first two.

(b)   Forbes

WORD OF GOD AND SLUMBERERS

There are some places also in the Book of God, which, being rightly handled and powerfully applied, seem to have a special keenness to strike at and cut asunder the iron sinews of the most obstinate heart, and of more aptness to serve for the rousing and awaking of mere civil men, formal professors, Pharisees, and foolish virgins out of their desperate slumber of spiritual self-deceit. Such as these: "And lest it come to pass, when he heareth the words of this curse, that he bless himself in his heart, saying, I shall have peace, though I walk in the imagination of mine heart, to add drunkenness to thirst: the Lord will not spare

him, but then the anger of the Lord and His jealousy shall smoke against that man, and all the curses that are written in this Book shall lie upon him, and the Lord shall blot out his name from under heaven" (Deut. xxix. 19, 20). "God shall wound the hairy scalp of such a one as goeth on in his trespasses" (Ps. lxviii. 21). "Because I have called and ye refused, I have stretched out My hand, and no man regarded," etc. "Then shall they call upon Me, but I will not answer: they shall seek Me early, but they shall not find Me" (Prov. i. 24, 28). "He that being often reproved, hardeneth his neck, shall suddenly be destroyed, and that without remedy" (Prov. xxix. 1). "In thy filthiness is lewdness; because I have purged thee, and thou wast not purged, thou shalt not be purged from thy filthiness any more, till I have caused My fury to rest upon thee" (Ezek. xxiv. 13). "If the righteous scarcely be saved, where shall the ungodly and the sinner appear?" (1 Pet. iv. 18). "Whosoever is born of God doth not commit sin" (1 John iii. 9). "Love the brotherhood" (1 Pet. ii. 17). "Without holiness no man shall see the Lord" (Heb. xii. 14). "The devils also believe and tremble" (Jas. ii. 19). "Strive to enter in at the strait gate; for many, I say unto you, will seek to enter in and shall not be able" (Luke xiii. 24). "And whosoever shall not receive you," etc. "Verily, I say unto you, it shall be more tolerable for the land of Sodom and Gomorrah in the day of judgment than for that city" (Matt. x. 14, 15). "And from the days of John the Baptist, until now, the kingdom of heaven suffereth violence, and the violent take it by force" (Matt. xi. 12). "And if ye salute your brethren only, what do ye more than others?" (Matt. v. 47). "I say unto you, that except your righteousness shall exceed the righteousness of the Scribes and Pharisees, ye shall in no case enter into the kingdom of heaven" (Matt. v. 20). These fellows represented to the eye of the world a goodly and glorious show of freedom from gross sins: "I am not," saith the Pharisee (Luke xviii. 11), "as other men are, extortioners, unjust, adulterers," etc.; of works; first, of righteousness, "I give tithes of all that I possess." Secondly, of piety, "He went up to pray." Thirdly, of mercy, besides fasting and prayer, they gave alms (Matt. vi.); and yet Christ speaks thus peremptorily to His hearers: "Except your righteousness exceed the righteousness of the Scribes and Pharisees," etc., "ye shall in no case enter into the kingdom of heaven." He saith not simply, ye shall not enter; but ye shall "in no case" enter. And yet how many who come short of these will be very angry, if ministers tell them that they shall certainly come short of the kingdom of heaven.

(c)   Bolton

"WORD AND POWER" (1 Cor. iv. 20)

When you see a fellow careful about his words, and neat in his speech, know this for a certainty, that man's mind is busied about toys, and there is no solidity in him; as he said of a nightingale,

"Vox es, præterea nihil," etc.

(d) Seneca (Burton's "Anatomy of Melancholy")

He that is conversant about matter, neglects words; and those that excel in this art of speaking, have no profound learning.

(e)   Philo

WORDS

Empty talk is on the increase in the world. Vanity of speech! To be sure, the world could never do without its talk, but the superabundance is alarming; a new deluge threatens, the spirit is lost in hollow words. The world used to be more simple, I am sure, in olden times; straightforward statements used to be current much more than they are now. Invention in all spheres is on the increase, the invention of pretences remarkably so. One feels inclined to call out despairingly: "Words, words, words!" as Hamlet did. I am sure words are the dominant power now-a-days in so-called intellectual pursuits; it is not the informing spirit, but the phrase, which is puffed and offered for sale.

(a)   *Letters from Hell*

WORDS

Caramuel, a famous Spanish Bishop, said a great deal and meant nothing; and by an exact dimension of his intellect taken at the time, it appeared that "he had genius in the eighth degree, eloquence in the fifth, but judgment only in the second."

(b)   *Disraeli: Cur. Lit*

WORDS

"*By thy words thou shalt be justified, and by thy words thou shalt be condemned*" (Matt. xii. 37)

The number of falsehoods told in business, or by persons to those above them, or by those who have done wrong and fear to be found out and punished, how great, think you, will be the mass of sin which all these *heaped together* will be found to amount to at the last day? Then there are unkind and calumnious words, perverse meanings given to those whom we dislike, angry words, bitter, provoking hints; in a word, our reckless way of speaking of our neighbours' characters; and above all, those evil corrupt words which do the devil's work, when men speak evil words from the corrupt treasure of their evil hearts, enticing others on to sin.

These are deep and serious thoughts when we consider how oft we have sinned by words. But let us not forget that, by God's great mercy, the tongue may be used for GOOD as well as for EVIL. If a cup of cold water, given in the name of Christ, shall in no wise lose its reward, surely the good and kind words also which are spoken—words of serious humility, words of charity to men's souls and bodies, words of loyal devotion to God, words which sincerely put away sin—all these, though they pass away and are over in a moment, yet by His grace they are in a manner lasting, and have a substance given them.

"Set a watch, O Lord, over my mouth, and keep the door of my lips."

(c)   *Penny Post*

WORDS

"*By thy words,*" etc. (Matt. xii. 37)

Words are mighty, words are living,
  Serpents with their venomous stings;
Or bright angels crowding round us,
  With heaven's light upon our wings.

Every word has his own spirit,
  True or false, that never dies;
Every word man's lips have uttered,
  Echoes in God's skies.

(d)

We have two ears and one tongue, that we may hear much and talk little.

(e)   *Zeno*

WORDS, CONFUSION AND STRIFE OF

"Whether all men received from God *sufficient grace* for their conversion," was an inquiry some unhappy metaphysical theologist set afloat. The Jesuits, according to their worldly system of making men's consciences easy, affirmed it; but the Jansenists insisted, that this *sufficient grace* would never be *efficacious* unless accompanied by *special grace*. "Then the *sufficient grace*, which is not *efficacious*, is a contradiction in terms, and is worse than a heresy!" triumphantly cried the Jesuits. . . . This "confusion of words" thickened, till the Jesuits introduced into this logomachy, papal bulls, royal edicts, and a regiment of dragoons.

(f)   *Disraeli: Cur. Lit*

WORK

Be no longer a chaos, but a world, or even a worldkin. Produce! produce! were it but the pitifullest infinitesimal fraction of a Product, produce it, in God's name! 'Tis the utmost thou hast in thee: out with it then. Up, up! whatever thy hand findeth to do, do it with thy might. "Work while it is called to-day; for the night cometh, wherein no man can work."

(g)   *Carlyle*

WORK

The situation that has not its duty, its ideal, was never yet occupied by man. Yes, here, in this poor, miserable, hampered, despicable Actual, wherein thou even now standest, here or nowhere is thy Ideal: work it out therefrom; and working, believe, live, be free.

(h)   *Ibid*

Man hath his daily work of body or mind appointed.

(i)   *Milton*

WORK

I should have thought mowers very idle people, but they work while they whet the scythe. Now devotedness to God, whether it mows or whets the scythe, still goes on with the work.

(j)   *John Newton*

A Christian should never plead spirituality for being a sloven; if he be but a shoe-cleaner, he should be the best in the parish.

(k)   *Ibid*

Each one has a vineyard, let him see that he till it, and not say, "No man hath hired us."

(l)

Work

Arnauld (Port Royalist), when hunted from place to place, wished his friend Nicolle to assist him in a new work, when the latter observed, "We are old, is it not time to rest?" "Rest!" returned Arnauld, "have we not all Eternity to rest in?"

(a)   *Disraeli: Cur. Lit.*

Work

A man's work does not fall upon him by chance, but it is *given* him to do; and everything well done belongs to God's kingdom, and everything ill done to the kingdom of darkness.

(b)   *George Macdonald*

'*For Thy sake.*"

> A servant with this clause
> Makes drudgery divine:
> Who sweeps a room, as for Thy laws,
> Makes that and the action fine.

(c)   *Geo. Herbert*

A man's work does not ennoble him; but he ennobles it.

(d)

"Work" and Talk

A disciple indeed is one who brings forth *much fruit.* But let there be no mistake. Fruitfulness is the result of *doing*, not of *talking :* *Fructum laborum*, not *Fructum labiorum.*

"You sit here and sing yourselves away to everlasting bliss," said a certain true witness, "but I tell you that you are wanted a great deal more out in Illinois than you are in heaven."

(e)   *Various*

WORK OUT YOUR SALVATION (Phil. ii. 12, 13)

(i.) Your salvation, *your* care;
(ii.) Your salvation, *God's* work.

The *defiant* heart has heard the admonition to penitence, "Work out!" The *timid* heart, the assurance, "It is God!"

(f)   *Meyer*

WORKERS

Woman : "And we have got another writer lady down at Ambleside."
Howitt : "A poet?"
Woman : " Nay, nothing of the sort; another guess sort of person, I can tell you."
Howitt : "Why, who is that?"
Woman : "Who is that? Why, Miss Martineau, they call her. They tell me she wrote up the Reform Bill for Lord Brougham; and that she's come from the Lambtons here; and that she's writing now about the taxes. Can she stop the steam, eh? Can she, think you? Nay, nay, I warrant, big and strong as she is. Ha! ha! as I met her the other day, walking along the muddy road below here—'Is it a woman or a man, or what sort of an animal is it?' said I to myself. There she came, stride, stride—great heavy shoes, stout leather leggings on, and a knapsack on her back! Ha! ha! that's a *political comicalist*, they say. What's that? Do they mean that they can stop steam? But I said to my husband, 'Goodness, but that would have been a wife for you! Why, she'd ha' ploughed! and they say she mows her own grass, and digs her own cabbages and potatoes!'"

Howitt's "*Homes and Haunts of the Poets,*"
(g)   *on Harriet Martineau*

WORKERS AND PARASITES

"*If any will not work, neither let him eat*" (2 Thess. iii. 10)

Parasites are the paupers of Nature. They are forms of life which will not take the trouble to find their own food, but borrow or steal it from the more industrious.

There are plants—like the Dodder—which begin life with the best intentions, strike roots into the soil, appear as if they meant to be independent for life. But after supporting themselves for a brief period, they fix curious sucking discs into the stem and branches of adjacent plants, gradually ceasing to do anything for their own support, till finally drawing all supplies from the sap of their hosts. In this state the parasite has no need of organs of nutrition of its own, and Nature therefore takes them away. Henceforth to the botanist the adult Dodder presents the degraded spectacle of a plant without a root, without a twig, without a leaf, and having a stem inadequate to bear its own weight. The Mistletoe has reached a stage in some respects lower still.

Among animals these *lazzaroni* are more largely represented still. Almost every animal is a living poor-house, and harbours one or more species of *epizoa* or *entozoa*, supplying them gratis, not only with a permanent home, but with all the necessaries and luxuries of life.

Why does the naturalist speak of these parasites as degraded, and despise them as the most ignoble creatures in nature? . . . Is not parasitism an ingenious way of securing the benefits of life while evading its responsibilities? And although a selfish mode of livelihood, and undignified, can it be called immoral?

The reply is, Parasitism is one of the gravest crimes in Nature. It is a breach of the law of Evolution, Thou shalt evolve, Thou shalt develop all thy faculties to the full. Thou shalt attain to the highest conceivable perfection of thy race, is the first and greatest commandment of Nature.

But the parasite has no thought of this. It wants food and shelter. How it gets them is of no moment. Each member lives exclusively on its own account, an isolated, indolent, selfish, and backsliding life. It is remarkable that Nature permits the community to be taxed in this way without protest.

But when we look into the matter, we very soon perceive that Nature sets her face most sternly against it; and, instead of allowing the transgressors to escape, she visits upon them the most severe and terrible penalties.

The Hermit-crab, though not a parasite, takes up its abode in the cast-off shell of some other animal. This is an acquired habit. The Hermit is essentially a Crab, and a Crab has to lead a somewhat rough and perilous life. Its days are spent amongst
(h)

jagged rocks and boulders. Dashed about by every wave, attacked by monsters of the deep, the crustacean has to protect itself by developing a strong and serviceable coat of mail. . . . How best to protect themselves, has been the problem of the whole Crab family; and the ancestors of the Hermit-crab hit on the happy device of re-utilizing the well-built habitations which lay around them in plenty.

For this laziness Nature has suffered its body to deteriorate. Instead of being a perfect crustacean, several vital organs are partially or wholly atrophied. . . . A number of functions necessary for a life of high and vigilant effort, from lack of exercise, became enfeebled, and ultimately and inevitably atrophied.

(*a*)

Spiritual Application

Any principle which secures the safety of the individual without personal effort or the vital exercise of faculty, is disastrous to moral character

We have to do with the popular ideas of *safety*. There is a parasitic doctrine of salvation.

Take two leading types.

The first is the doctrine of the Church of Rome; the second, that represented by the narrower Evangelical religion. (With their ideal form possibly we should have no quarrel.)

No more perfect or sad example of semi-parasitism exists than in the case of those illiterate thousands who swell the ranks of the Church of Rome. No organization could be better fitted to induce the parasitic habit in the souls of men than the system of Roman Catholicism. Roman Catholicism offers to the masses a molluscan shell. They have simply to shelter themselves within its pale, and they are "safe." But it is the safety of an external safety—the safety of an institution, but which has as little vital connection with the individual soul as the dead whelk's shell with the living Hermit. Salvation is a vital, personal, spiritual relation. This is mechanical and external; and is the secret of its success and world-wide power. A cheap religion is the desideratum of the human heart; and an assurance of salvation at the smallest cost is the tempting bait held out to the conscience-stricken by the Romish Church. . . . No one who has studied the religion of the Continent upon the spot, has failed to be impressed with the appalling spectacle of tens of thousands of unregenerate men sheltering themselves, as they conceive it, for eternity, behind the sacraments of Rome.

The parasite of the narrower Evangelical school seeks shelter, not in a Church, but in a doctrine or a creed. We are not dealing with Evangelical religion, but only with one of its parasitic forms —a form easily recognised.

The perverted doctrine of the Atonement, which tends to beget the parasitic habit, may be defined in the following syllogism:

"You believe Christ died for sinners; you are a sinner, therefore Christ died for you; *and hence you are saved.*" This is another species of molluscan shell. The agitated soul is asked to creep into the convolutions of a syllogism, and entrench itself behind a doctrine more venerable even than the Church. But words—doctrines—may have no more vital contact with the soul than priest or sacrament. And yet the apostles of parasitism pick a blackguard from the streets, pass him

through this plausible formula, and turn him out a convert in the space of as many minutes as it takes to tell it.

The fundamental idea alike of the extreme Roman Catholic and the extreme Evangelical religion is escape. Man's chief end is to "get off." And all factors in religion, the highest and most sacred, are degraded to this level. . . . God, for example, is a Great Lawyer. Or He is the Almighty Enemy, it is from Him we have to "get off." Jesus Christ is the One who gets us off.

The Church, in the one instance, is a kind of conveyancing office, where the transaction is duly concluded, each party accepting the other's terms; in the other case, a species of sheep-pen where the flock indolently awaits the final consummation. Generally the means are mistaken for the end, and the opening up of the possibility of spiritual growth becomes the signal to stop growing. . . .

Cheap religions are inevitably accompanied by a cheap life. Personal effort is superseded. The whole scheme ministers to degeneration of organs. . . . To pause where we should begin, to retrograde where we should advance, to seek a mechanical security that we may cover inertia, and find a wholesale salvation in which there is no personal sanctification—this is Parasitism.

(*b*)   *Drummond (condensed)*

And so I live, you see,
Go through the world, try, prove, reject,
Prefer, still struggling to effect
My warfare; happy that I can
Be crossed and thwarted as a man,
Not left in God's contempt apart,
With ghastly smooth life, dead at heart,
Tame in earth's paddock as her prize.

    *   *   *   *   *

Thank God, no paradise stands barred
To entry, and I find it hard
To be a Christian, as I said.

(*c*)   *Browning*

WORKING

What are you doing in God's fair earth and task-garden; where whosover is not working is begging or stealing?

Carlyle

"No man hath hired us" (Matt. xx. 7)
(*d*)

Dr. Arnold, it seems to me, was not quite saintly; his greatness was cast in a mortal mould; he was a little severe, almost a little hard; he was vehement, and somewhat oppugnant. Himself the most indefatigable of workers, I know not whether he could have understood or made allowance for a temperament that required more rest; yet not to one man in twenty thousand is given his great faculty of labour. By virtue of it he seems to me the greatest of working men.

(*e*)   *Charlotte Brontë on Dr. Arnold*

WORKING MAN

Venerable to me is the hard hand, crooked, coarse, wherein notwithstanding lies a cunning virtue, indefeasibly royal, as of the sceptre of this planet.

(*f*)   *Carlyle*

WORLD, THE

The pleasure of the world is like that Golshian honey, whereof Xenophon's soldiers no sooner tasted than they were miserably distempered; those that took little were drunk; those that took more were mad; those that took most were dead. Thus are we, either intoxicated, or infatuated, or killed outright with this deceitful world.

(a)   *Bp. Hall*

WORLD, THE

Charon, in Lucian (as he feigns) was conducted by Mercury to such a place where he might see all the world at once. After he had sufficiently viewed and looked about, Mercury would know what he had observed. He told him that he saw a vast multitude and a promiscuous, their habitations like molehills, the men as emmets; he could discern cities like so many hives of bees, wherein every bee had a sting, and they did nought else but sting one another, some domineering like hornets, bigger than the rest, some like filching wasps, others as drones. Over their heads were hovering a confused company of perturbations, hopes, fears, anger, avarice, ignorance, etc., and a multitude of diseases hanging, which they still pulled on their pates. Some were brawling, some fighting, riding, running, *solicite ambientes, callide litigantes*, for toys, and trifles, and such momentary things: their towns and provinces mere factions, rich against poor, poor against rich, nobles against artificers, they against nobles, and so the rest. In conclusion, he condemned them all for madmen, etc. "O fools! O madmen!" he exclaims. "Mad endeavours! mad actions! mad! mad! mad!"

(b)   *Burton's Anat. Mel*

WORLD, THE

It is not only difficult, but impossible, to have heaven here and hereafter; to live in sensual lusts, and to attain spiritual bliss; to pass from one paradise to another; to be a mirror of felicity in both worlds; to shine with glorious rays both in this globe of earth and the orb of heaven.

(c)   *Hieron*

WORLD, THE

Set not your heart upon the world, since God hath not made it your portion; for it will not fall to you to get two portions, and to laugh twice, and to be happy twice, and to have an upper heaven and an under heaven too. Christ our Lord and His saints were not so; and therefore let go your grip of this life and of the good things of it. I hope your heaven groweth not here.

(d)   *Rutherford*

All that is in the world is either "the lust of the flesh, the lust of the eyes, or the pride of life" (1 John ii. 16). Libido sentiendi, libido sciendi, libido dominandi. Miserable is that accursed earth, which these three rivers of fire burn rather than refresh.

(e)   *Blaise Pascal*

Balak = *Destroyer*, a type of the world. "I thought to promote thee to great honour; but lo, the Lord hath kept thee back from honour;" and instead of the intended laurel-wreath, presents you with a crown of thorns.

(f)   *Oosterzee*

WORLD, THE

Why, then, the world's mine oyster,
Which I with sword will open.

(g)   *Shakspeare*

Believers are in danger of seduction into the sin and falsehood of the world. The world threatens believers not only with its enmity, but evermore with its temptation. Believers must be warned to shun the idols the world worship, and they are warned against love to the world, because love in that way very easily gets associated with sinful lusts, which are common in the world. In false prophecy it is shown that the devil, who was a murderer and a liar from the beginning, threatens the Church, not only with the deadly enmity of the world, but also with its soul-destroying lies. We cannot show brotherly love to false teachers, without running the risk of making ourselves partakers in their sins.

(h)   *Weiss, on St. John*

WORLD, DESTRUCTION OF

The scene of the final consummation is the new world, which God calls into being on the destruction of the old world (Rev. xxi. 1, 5). As in the Epistle to the Hebrews, the perfected kingdom of God appears (i. 9) as the holy city (xxii. 19; comp. iii. 12: ἡ πόλις τοῦ Θεοῦ), the new Jerusalem (xxi. 2, 10); and if the seer beholds it come down from heaven, it is implied in this only, that ideally the final consummation is already prepared with God long before it is realized at the end of the times. Therewith also is the Church of the last times of consummation designated as the ideal Jerusalem. This point of view rules the whole picture of that city of God, on whose doors stand the names of the twelve Patriarchs (xxi. 12), as those of the twelve Apostles stand upon its foundation stones (ver. 14), and whose measure is reckoned according to twelve times a thousand and twelve times twelve (vv. 16, 17). But the believing Israel are not its only citizens, but the Gentiles also walk in its light (xxi. 24); and their glory, as also that of their kings, must minister to the perfected kingdom of God (vv. 24, 26). They are there healed from the deadly sickness of hopelessness in which they once walked (xxii. 2), while believing Israel there beholds what it has always believed. The Church which bears the name of the New Jerusalem (iii. 12), is now the bride of Messiah (xxi. 9), with whom, at the final consummation, He celebrates His marriage, *i.e.*, His perfect union (xix. 7), at which the great marriage-feast is not wanting (ver. 9). It is very noteworthy that in the earthly completion of the kingdom of Christ this highest union does not take place.

(i)   *Weiss*

WORLD, DESTRUCTION OF

The day of the resurrection, viz., is that great day of universal Judgment which is looked forward to by prophecy (ἡ ἡμέρα κρίσεως, Matt. xi. 22; xii. 36). Accordingly, it dawns with the appearing of the signs in heaven, which, in the prophets, so often announce the coming of the great Day of the Lord (Matt. xxiv. 49; cf. Joel ii. 10, 30, 31; iii. 15; Isa. xiii. 10, 13; Jer. iv. 23, 24; Ezek. xxxii. 7, 8; Hagg. ii. 6; Mark viii. 11), and with which the destruction of the world has inevitably come. It is this which carries away the world which is living

(j)

on in carnal security, as the flood once carried men away in the time of Noah (Matt. xxiv. 37–39 ; Luke xvii. 26, 27), and makes an end at once of everything that is sinful (xvii. 37). It is only His elect ones that Jesus causes to be gathered round Him by the angels (Matt. xxiv. 31) from the four ends of the earth (cf. viii. 11, 12), for the purpose of taking them to Himself, and thus saving them from destruction (Luke xvii. 34, 35). But since it is only the elect that are saved, the Messianic Judgment brings also the sifting of the members of the Church of the disciples, which was deferred to the end of the development, and which can also be so represented as if the unworthy members are cast out before the commencement of the completion of salvation (Matt. xiii. 30, 48 ; xxii. 11–13), because Jesus does not recognise them as His true disciples (xxv. 10–12 ; Luke xiii. 25). And since this great Day of Judgment is the Day of Jehovah Himself, it is also represented as if the testimony which the Messiah bears before the throne of God, as to the attitude of the individuals towards Himself, decides their fate in the Judgment (Matt. x. 32, 33).

(a)   *Weiss*

WORLD, DESTRUCTION OF

By the hope of an earthly consummation which here again emerges, is the idea of a great Day of the Lord split into its different parts. The judgment of this day, as it results at the second coming of Christ, has brought victory only to the kingdom of God on earth. But the universal Judgment, as the definite decision on the fate of all men, as it is likewise thought of as connected with the day of the Lord, is now introduced only at the end of the thousand years' kingdom, and doubtless, in immediate connection with that destruction of the world (Rev. xx. 11 ; comp. xxi. 1), which in the first place carries aloft all those who survive, as well as those members of the thousand years' kingdom who have been raised again for the earthly kingdom. Hence there arises the idea of a second Resurrection, as to be sure, it is only indirectly (Rev. xx. 5, 6) hinted at, and this a general one ; for all the dead must stand before God's judgment-seat (vv. 12, 13). Naturally those only who attain to the final heavenly consummation experience a Resurrection in the proper sense (*i.e.*, a quickening in a heavenly body) ; the others only appear at God's judgment-seat in order to be handed over to death and hades (ver. 14), as it were to a potentialized death (ὁ δεύτερος θάνατος, ver. 15 ; comp. ii. 11 ; xx. 6). But this is described as a portion in the lake of fire (xxi. 8 ; comp. xx. 14), which burns with brimstone (xix. 20), and brings with it an endless misery (xiv. 10, 11 ; comp. xix. 3, xx. 10), by which image (borrowed from Gen. xix. 24) is to be designated, not in any way an eternal annihilation, but a miserable exclusion from blessedness (xxi. 27 ; xxii. 3, 15), in which is found the unblessedness of an abiding state of death. With this is introduced definite retribution, which decides men's fate according to their works, which stand recorded in the books of the heavenly Judge (xx. 12, 13 ; comp. 1 Pet. i. 17 ; 2 Cor. v. 10).

(b)   *Ibid*

WORLD, DESTRUCTION OF (2 Pet. iii)

But the whole present state of the world has fallen under φθορά, and it is therefore, as with Paul, appointed to destruction. The way in which the author more exactly regards the impending destruction of the world, it has been unnecessarily sought to explain from the contemporary philosophical ideas. Quite in harmony with the account in Gen. iii. 5, he regards the heaven and the earth in their original form as proceeding, by the creative word of God, from the waters of chaos (Gen. i. 2), and this in such a way that the origin of the heavens was brought about by the separation of the waters (vv. 7, 8), and the origin of the land by the gathering together of the waters (vv. 9, 10). This old world perished by the waters of the flood (2 Pet. iii. 6 ; comp. ii. 5), and the present form of the world is protected by God's word of promise (Gen. ix. 11) against any recurring flood (2 Pet. iii. 7). Yet, if it too is to perish, there remains now only fire as the element to bring about this destruction ; and as, on the ground of the Old Testament representations, the wrathful judgment of God is regarded as a consuming fire, it is easy to think that the destruction of the world resulting from the Day of Judgment will be brought about by fire in a special sense, for which this present form of the world is, so to speak, reserved (2 Pet. iii. 7). On the Day of the Lord the heavens will be dissolved in fire, and will pass away with a noise ; their firm elements, by which, perhaps, he is thinking of the stars, will melt with the heat, and the earth with all its works will be burnt up (2 Pet. iii. 10, 12). Since, now, the godless will be destroyed on that day (2 Pet. iii. 7), and, according to ver. 12, on account of the coming of the Day of Judgment the destruction of the world follows, there is here quite evidently implied the idea that the destruction of the world removes even the godless, and hands them over to destruction as to death, from which there is no more any deliverance.

(c)   *Ibid*

WORLD, DESTRUCTION OF

If there is a reward of wages, there is also naturally a retributive punishment (Heb. ii. 2, μισθαποδοσία) ; and which of the two is to be given to each individual is decided by the last Judgment, which the fundamental doctrine of Christianity announces as κρίμα αἰωνίου (Heb. vi. 2). To this Judgment God has reserved retributive punishment (x. 30), and His Judgment is dreadful (ver. 31), and unavoidable (xii. 25). He brings upon those who have fallen away, and upon all the enemies of God (ὑπεναντίοι), the ἀπόλεια (x. 39), which, according to ix. 27, is not only bodily death, but in every case something more dreadful (x. 28, 29), and it is repeatedly represented as a consuming fire (ver. 27 ; xii. 29 ; comp. vi. 8). If by this figure of the Old Testament (Deut. iv. 24 ; ix. 3) fire can be taken as the current symbol of the Divine wrath, then the repeated reference to its consuming energy can only be so understood, that that destruction is no longer considered simply as an abiding of the soul in death, but as a sort of potential death, as a torturing form of destruction. But this judgment does not follow immediately on the death of any one, as has been concluded from ix. 27 ; but there is a day which, as the Judgment-day of God, known in the Old Testament, is spoken of as simply The Day (x. 25) ; and it appears from the connection of xii. 26 with vv. 25, 29, that this day is introduced with the last great

(d)

shaking of the heaven and the earth (ver. 26, after Hag. ii. 7), *i.e.*, with the overthrow of the present world, an idea which is hinted at even in the words of Jesus.

(a)   *Weiss*

WORLD, END OF (Epistles to Eph. and Col.)

If the Divine purpose of salvation was already régulative for the creation of the world, then must salvation as well as creation be grounded on the original Mediator. His position of dignity in relation to every creature (Col. i. 15) depends on the fact that the universe was created in Him (ver. 16 : ὅτι ἐν αὐτῷ ἐκτίσθη τὰ πάντα). But that all creation should be thus grounded in Him includes a twofold idea, namely, that not only were all things created by Him (δι' αὐτοῦ), which the earlier Epistles teach, but also that all was created for Him (εἰς αὐτόν), who is to bring to completion both the saving purpose of God, as also the whole development of the world, which tends towards the realization of the purpose of God. And because the world has not yet reached this goal, then all things have progressively their existence in Him (ver. 17), and it cannot fail, because the goal of the world established in Him must be realized. But how this goal of the world is conceived of, Eph. i. 10 shows, when it is mentioned as the final goal of the institution of God's grace, that all things may be gathered together in Christ as in a centre (ἀνακεφαλαιώσασθαι τὰ πάντα ἐν τῷ Χριστῷ). He has been appointed to be this central point of the universe, as the universe was created in Him ; but here it is pointed out that He must again become so, because a dislocation in the original constitution of the world has taken place by sin, whose removal again the dispensation of grace must have in view. By this conception of Christ as the principle and also the goal of the world,—which latter, according to the earlier Epistles, is God Himself,—the Christology of the Epistles goes beyond that of the earlier Epistles. It is connected with this idea, that the goal of the world is no longer regarded as the perfected kingdom of God, in which the absolute universal Lordship of God is realized, in contrast to the earthly mediatorial lordship of Christ, which the latter gives back to the Father as the βασιλεία τοῦ Χριστοῦ καὶ Θεοῦ (Eph. v. 5), and that the exaltation of Christ is extended over everything which has a name both in this world and in the future (i. 21). One cannot think of the goal of the world without Him in whom even creation has its root.

(b)   *Ibid*

WORLD, GOD SO LOVED (John iii. 16)

Jesus Christ for all, Moses for a nation. It is the sole prerogative of Jesus Christ to be common to all. Even the services of the Church are chiefly intended for believers only ; the sacrifice of our Lord on the cross was for all mankind.

(c)   *Blaise Pascal*

WORLD, LOVE NOT THE (1 John ii. 15)

A sharp distinction is drawn between the whole or the general, and the particular or the specific. You are not even to love a particular or a specific part of the κόσμος ; one may be fascinated by this thing, another by that, it all amounts to the same ; the love of the world is there where we find the love of the particular or of one particular in the world, be it the gold of the earth, or human wisdom, or honour, or power and dominion, or only influence in a less degree and in a limited sphere.

(d)   *Lange*

WORLD, REPROOF OF THE (John xvi. 8)

The meaning is as follows.

He (the Holy Spirit) shall reprovingly convince—convict—the world in His Judgment, and, by convicting it, occasion its disintegration into the two portions of the saved and the judged, neither of which is any longer a world (ch. iii. 20 ; viii. 46. 1 Cor. xiv. 24).

(e)   *Ibid.*

The three-fold objects of the conviction are, *Sin*, which belongs to men ; *Righteousness*, which belongs to Christ ; *Judgment*, which is executed on Satan by the overthrow of his kingdom and the establishment of Christ's kingdom. It is only the Holy Spirit who traces them to their fountain-head and culminating point :—

Sin, to *unbelief ;*
Righteousness, to *Christ ;* and
Judgment, to *Satan.*

(f)   *Ibid*

WORLD, THE REPROOF OF, BY THE HOLY GHOST (John xvi. 8)

Christ gives here His Apostles and the preachers of the Gospel the highest authority upon earth, that they must rebuke the world with their preaching, and that all the world must for God's sake be subject to their preaching, and must suffer themselves to be rebuked by it, if they would receive God's grace and be saved. Verily, there is a vast grasp in a word, and the beginning of a war which was to be great and arduous, that these few mean, poor beggars, the Apostles, are to stir up the whole world, and to bring it upon their shoulders. For what is meant by the world ? Not one or two of their fellows ; but all emperors, kings, princes, and whatever is noble, rich, great, and learned, wise, or anything upon earth ; all these are to be rebuked by their preaching, as being ignorant, unrighteous, and condemned before God, with all their wisdom, righteousness, and power, which they hitherto had had and made boast of. The world cries out furiously, when this sermon begins, that it is a mischievous, intolerable sermon, producing dissension and confusion, giving rise to disobedience, insurrection, and tumult. And we cannot wonder at these complaints ; for it is a vexatious matter, that the preachers should take upon themselves to reprove all, without distinction, and should allow none to be just and good before God. Who can deem it right or reasonable that this sermon should breed such a hubbub, and bring about changes and innovations so that the whole former religion and worship, with so many beautiful ceremonies of such long standing, should be despised, and should fall ? And the most vexatious thing of all is, that they who undertake the work of rebuking are not high and mighty, learned, or otherwise eminent men, but poor, mean, unknown, despised fishermen, and such folks as everybody would class with beggars and vagabonds.

(g)   *Luther.*

WORLDLINESS (1 John ii. 1, 15)

Remember that worldliness is a more decisive test of a man's spiritual state than even sin. Sin may be sudden, the result of temptation, without premeditation, yet afterwards hated—repented of —repudiated—forsaken. But if man *be at home* in the world's pleasure and pursuits, content that his spirit should have no other heaven but in these things, happy if they could last for ever, is not his state, genealogy, and character clearly stamped? Therefore does St. John draw the distinction—"If any man sin, we have an advocate with the Father;" but "If any man love the world, the love of the Father is not in him."

(a)   *F. W. Robertson*

WORLDLINESS

A worldly man makes of himself but a cock, set for a while on the world's heap to scratch and peck.

(b)   *Geo. Macdonald*

WORLDLINESS (2 Cor. vi. 17)

We must be unworldly.

We must not say to ourselves "It is *better* to be *unworldly* than to be worldly," but "*We must* be unworldly."

Put in this way:

The world is like the ocean, and the Christian like a ship; whilst the Christian floats in the world as the ship does in the sea. Now, the ship is safe enough in the ocean so long as the ocean is not in the ship. In like manner, the Christian is safe enough in the world so long as the world is not *in* the Christian.

When put in this way, it is no longer a question of which is better, but of which is *safe;* and we may assure ourselves that it is not safe to have the love of the world in our hearts. We shall imperil the ship if we disobey God who says: "Come ye out from among them, and be ye separate, and I will be a Father unto you, and ye shall be my sons and daughters, saith the Lord God Almighty."

(c)

WORLDLINESS

Days of Noah and Lot (Luke xvii. 26, 29)

The careless worldly life reveals itself from century to century, every time in the same stereotyped phases and forms. But just as unexpected as were the flood and the fiery rain, will also the last coming of the Lord be—a day which begins like other days, and finds the one on his bed, another in the field, and a third at the mill; but it will not end like other days.

(d)   *Lange*

WORLDLING, THE, AND AFFLICTIONS

He, that is not like his Elder Brother, shall never be coheir with Him. Lo, His sides, temples, hands, feet, all bleeding; His face ghastly and defiled; His skin streaming with a bloody sweat; His head drooping, His soul heavy to the death. See you the *Worldling*—merry, soft, delicate, perfumed, never wrinkled with sorrow, never humbled with afflictions? What resemblance is here! yea, what contrariety! Ease slayeth the fool; it hath made him unruly, and leaves him miserable. Be not deceived; no man can follow Christ without His Cross; much less reach Him. And if none shall reign with Christ, but those that suffer with Him, what shall become of these jovial ones? Go now, thou dainty Worldling, and please thyself in thy happiness. Laugh always; and be ever applauded; it is a woeful felicity that thou shalt find, in opposition to thy Redeemer. He hath said, "*Woe to them that laugh!*" believest thou, and dost not weep at thy laughter? and, with Solomon, condemn it of madness? And again, with the same breath, "*Blessed are ye that weep;*" who can believe this, and not rejoice in his own tears; and not pity the faint smiles of the godless?

(e)   *Bishop Hall*

WORLDLY SUCCESS, SECRET OF

To pretend to the favours of fortune, it is only necessary to render one's self useful, and to be supple and obsequious to those who are in possession of credit and authority; to be handsome in one's person; to adulate the powerful; to smile, while you suffer from them every kind of ridicule and contempt whenever they shall do you the honour to amuse themselves with you; never to be frightened at a thousand obstacles which may be opposed to one; have a face of brass and a heart of stone; insult worthy men who are persecuted; rarely venture to speak the truth; appear devout, with every nice scruple of religion, while at the same time every duty must be abandoned when it clashes with your interest. After these, any other accomplishment is indeed superfluous.

(f)   *Abbé de Marolles*

WORM

"Fear not, thou worm Jacob, and ye men of Israel; I will help thee, saith the Lord, and thy Redeemer, the holy One of Israel. Behold, I will make thee a new sharp threshing instrument having teeth; thou shalt thresh the mountains, and beat them small, and shalt make the hills as chaff. Thou shalt fan them and the wind shall carry them away, and the whirlwind shall scatter them; and thou shalt rejoice in the Lord, and shalt glory in the Holy One of Israel" (Isa. xli. 14–16)

1. Whom to is it that the Lord speaks thus? To "*Worm* Jacob," and to the men of Israel, or to "*the few men* of Israel." This is sweeter than if the Lord had said "My people," and it is liker God than if He had called them "My sons," or "His spouse and married people with whom I am in covenant, by all the people of the earth." It says this much to us, that the Kirk of God is never so miserable, nor so desolate and forsaken, but they have a Lord that pities them. One who sees their misery, and takes notice of it with a pitiful eye. That is an eye indeed that is spoken of (Exod. iii. 7): "I have seen, I have seen the affliction of My people, and their groaning which are in Egypt." There is a Father's eye in Heaven that is lifted up towards the Kirk when they are in trouble, and He pities their case. See what a title

(g)

Worm—*continued*

the Kirk gets from God (Isa. liv. 11): "O thou afflicted, tossed with tempest, and not comforted, behold, I will lay thy stones with fair colours," etc. Even such another title as that which is given to the Kirk (Ezek. xxxvii. 4): "Prophesy upon these bones, and say unto them, O ye dry bones, hear the word of the Lord," etc.

(a)

2. Why would not the Lord say to them, "My beloved people," "My people with whom I am in covenant," etc., but "Worm Jacob"? This is a word of pity, and it becomes our Lord very well to show pity. The *use* of this is, let us learn to make use of all these titles that the Lord gives unto His Kirk and His children in this world (Isa. lii.): Zion, wallowing in the dust, is comforted with many sweet promises and encouragements. And since our Lord casts comforts into our hand that way, let us put out our hand and to take a grip of them. Since the Lord is pleased to make many fair promises to His Kirk, when it is black in the West, let us then take them unto us when we are under trouble, let us learn to take all our crosses from our [Lord] as it becomes us to do, and spoil not our crosses by taking them from any other cause than the hand of God. If we could learn to put all our crosses over into our Lord's hand to be disposed of by Him, and take them all from Him, we would get a better way of them than for the most part we do. But it is well that thy cross and trouble be thy death, when thou wilt not put it over upon thy Lord, that puts not a crazed estate or the cross of an ill husband, or an ill wife or wicked children, or fears for the cause of God, that it go not well, that puts not all over upon the Lord. If all these things could be put over upon the Lord Himself by us, there is no doubt but He who is a giving and a pitying Lord, who sees our sufferings and our crosses, He would no doubt send a sure deliverance to such who, in faith and patience, commit themselves and all things that come upon them unto Him.

(b)

3. Again, "Worm Jacob, and men of Israel." This is as mean a title as can be given to any—*a worm*. Where met they His married people and the people in the world whom He thought most of, and why should He not [have] given them a more honourable name? The Lord is now speaking of them as they are in the eyes of the world, and not as He thinks of them; for His people are never the most in multitude, nor are they the strongest to look to, nor the wisest, nor the richest, etc. No; for the most part they are the basest persons. Jerusalem is a forsaken woman; and (Lam. ii.) when all go by Jerusalem and see it so sore sacked they say, "Thou city which men call the perfection of beauty and the joy of the whole earth, all the enemies opened their mouth against her to devour her." And yet ye will get the Lord's Kirk no better (Micah iv. 6), ye will get the Lord's Kirk there, a halting cripple woman, that has but one leg to go upon. Ay (1 Cor. i. 27), His Kirk there is called the nothings of the world, those that are not worth the uptaking, the kinless things of the world, the ignoble, base, contemptible ones, the refuse of men! and (chap. iv.) "the off-scourings of the world." Are the Lord's people so indeed? No. They are not so, indeed, for (Mal. iii. 17)

they are called the Lord's jewels, His beloved people. "Is Ephraim My dear son? is he a pleasant child?" (Jer. xxxi. 20.) How comes it to pass, then, that God speaks so of His Kirk? *Answer*: The Lord speaks so of His Kirk and people as men speak of them and according to their outward estate in the world, for the world sees not the Kirk's best side. The world knows not our Father, nor they know not our joy nor our inheritance; they see not our day of rejoicing. That which makes the Kirk glorious is hid from the eyes of the world (Prov. xiv.). A stranger meddles not with the joys of the Kirk. They know not our joy, for it is hid up with God in Christ. All our best things are hidden from the eyes of the world; they only see our worst.

(c)

4. There is another thing in this title

He calls them Jacob, and Jacob is the Lord's covenanted people. And so it is as much as if He had said, "Fear not, despised and weak people, and yet the Lord's covenanted ones." There is not a cross, misery, or affliction that comes upon the people of God but it is the Lord's, and is kin to Him, for the first word is as much as they were despised and weak—a worm; but the next word "Jacob," is a word of honour. We have to learn here that the very misery of the Kirk of God it is glorious, the very crosses of the Kirk have another sort of lustre than all the glory that is in the world; for these two words are as much as if it had been said, "Base bodies, and yet highly honoured of God, the refuse of the world, and yet for all that those whom the Lord has taken by the hand to be His people, and He has taken upon Him to be their God." There are three blessed things that befall the children of God in all their crosses that the world has not in its troubles and crosses.

(d)

5. First. There is a moderation while they are under them. We may see the proof of this in this text. "Worm Jacob," He calls them, and yet He says to them, "I will make thee a new sharp threshing instrument having teeth, to thresh the mountains, and to beat the hills to chaff." The Kirk under affliction enduring, and yet they live, hungered and yet well fed, persecuted but not forsaken. The enemies are doing what they can to put us in the grave; and yet even then, when we are in the grave, we shall live. No; there is such a moderation of the troubles of the Kirk of God and of His children, that there is not one ounce of sorrow or trouble that comes upon them but it is all weighed in Heaven before it come upon you, and thou shalt get no more of it than the Lord pleases. The Lord will have you to drink no more of that cup than thy stomach will bear. He will not have you to drink till thy heart stand. Such a sweet attemperation have the children of God in all their troubles. This much baseness shall come upon them, and no more; and it shall be mixed with honour.

(e)

6. Another thing that is in the afflictions of the children of God, even a fine lustre upon them

"Worm Jacob," and despised of the world, yet thee whom I have chosen from among all the

(f)

Worm—*continued*

people in the world to be Mine. Oh! there is such a fine lustre on all the crosses of the children of God that, whatever befall them, it is well watered over with the love and favour of God. Rev. xiv. 13 : "Blessed are the dead that die in the Lord, for they rest from their labours, and their works follow them." What is sourer and more fearful-like than death? and yet death being in the Lord it is sweet and well watered to the children of God, for then they rest from their labours; and Job (chap. v. 17) says : "Blessed is the man whom Thou correctest." Of itself correction is sour, and yet, coming from the Lord, and being watered with His love, it is sweet, and so sweet that it is a thing wherein blessedness stands (Acts v. 41). The Apostles when they were scourged before the Council for preaching the Gospel, it is said of them, "They went out rejoicing that they were counted worthy to suffer for the name of Jesus." There are two fine coverings there put upon their sufferings. First, the Lord's blessed estimation of them. He "counted them worthy." Second, they themselves rejoicing "that they were counted worthy to suffer for the name of Jesus." Well is it that we get a bruised skin and bloody shoulders for preaching our Lord's Gospel. There is glory in such baseness as that is. Our shame, it is a glorious shame. Our hunger is His fulness. With it our Christ is a refreshing Christ. Our death, it is a life unto us.

(*a*)

7. Third. "Worm Jacob"

This is as much as the Lord He esteemed Himself kin to their crosses. There is no cross or misery that befalls the Kirk of God or any of His children but it is kin to God. There is an excellent word which is spoken by the Apostle (Col. i. 24), "I fill up that which is behind of the afflictions of Christ in my flesh; and (Heb. xi. 26) speaking of Moses he says of him : "He esteemed the reproach of Christ greater riches than the treasures of Egypt." The sufferings of the Kirk and the children of God, they are Christ's sufferings. Thy sorrowful heart, thy losses, thy sufferings, they are Christ's. The world's afflictions, they are bastard afflictions, they belong not to Christ. There are enough under crosses that Christ has nothing ado. Well's them who are under crosses, and Christ says to them, "Half Mine." And you should learn to make use of this and see when you are under crosses how related they are to Christ. Is it your grief and your sorrow for fear that the Lord's cause and His people in the camp be not well? That is a sorrow that is related to Christ, and He will comfort those who are under sorrow that way. But if your grief and your sorrow be that ye will be poorer than ye were before, because there is something sought of you to the cause of God that ye will be in greater danger than ye were before by entering in a covenant with God, ye will get none of Christ's comfort then for your cross and trouble : He has nothing ado with it. Well's them who know their crosses are not their own, but they are Christ's crosses, and then their crosses are well wound up in a web of His love, for then it shall neither hurt you nor kill you, but thou shalt bear it patiently and handsomely. That is a happy affliction that is Christ's affliction, and He has chosen it to thee.

(*b*)

8. "Fear not, worm Jacob, and ye men of Israel," and to speak the word with a warrant, he adds to it : "*I will help thee, saith the Lord, and thy Redeemer, the Holy one of Israel.*" What ground of comfort were this if it were said by one that could not help?—but the Lord says it.

There are three sorts that take upon them to comfort under trouble.

(*c*)

First. There are some who can do more, but only speak a good word to them. And that is but a cold comfort, to speak a word, and no more, to a troubled conscience.

(*d*)

Second. There are some who take upon them to comfort under trouble, and they can do something; but it is but man's help when all is done, and we are forbidden to trust in any help of man (Ps. cxlvi. 3), "Put not your trust in princes, nor in the son of man in whom there is no help."

(*e*)

There is a third, again, that helps in trouble, who only should take upon Him to help, for He can infallibly help in trouble. But he is a King of His word. He helps indeed where He promises. When God says, "Fear not," albeit thou wert compassed about with enemies on all sides, and there were as many devils round about you as there are piles of grass upon the earth, or as there have fallen of drops of rain since the world began, thou needest not to fear; thou may go through the sea then, and the sea shall not drown you, the fire shall not burn you; thou mayst dance on the grave, for the grave shall not rot you. And so this is a well-favoured word: "I will keep thee, saith the Lord, and thy Redeemer, the Holy One of Israel." What if Jeremiah or Isaiah had said this to them! No, certainly that had not been enough; but the Lord says it, and that must stand sure. Then hang by this word, and this word is added to tell us that a trembling and doubting soul in trouble, it can get no fastening word, but only that which the Lord speaks. Albeit an angel or a king should say, "Fear not," or twenty or thirty thousand armed men should say it, it is nothing; and God grant that we trust not more in men than we do in the Lord at this time. But if the Lord say to a soul in trouble, "Fear not," we may trust in that word. A doubting soul, it gets no sure word to fasten on, until it get God's Word to uphold it. Bind a ship to a rush bush to hold her by! That is but a slim anchor; it cannot hold her when she begins to be moved.

(*f*)

9. The Title that God gets here

It is a new title, for God has two sorts of titles in His Word. There is Jehovah and God; and the Lord, He would hold these titles albeit the world had not been or any created thing. But if there had not been a world, and lost sinners, and a Kirk, He had not been a Creator, nor a Redeemer, nor a Husband to His Kirk. And so the Lord He has these titles of Creator, Redeemer

(*g*)

Worm—_continued_

the Lord of the whole earth, the Husband of His Kirk, the Holy One of Israel, from us and our house. And we may say two things of these titles that the Lord has from us.

(i.) _First :_ That they are very humble titles, and very comfortable to us; for by that we may see, that He has married with us, and with our house, because He has taken titles from us: from His lost people He takes the title of a Redeemer; from the covenant that He has made with His people He takes the name of the Holy One of Israel; from marrying with His people He takes the name of Husband. This is even like unto a house that is like to go out of the name for want of male heirs, and there comes in one and marries the heritage of the house, and takes titles from the house, and calls himself after the name of it, and so keeps it in the name.

(a)

(ii.) _Second :_ We may say again that the Lord He has no empty titles. Many in the world indeed they have empty names and empty titles. The Lord has made many kings, and many of them fill not the chair of a king; albeit they be princes, yet they have not the minds of princes. But for the Lord our God He has no empty names at all; Isa. xlii. 3: "_I am the Lord thy God, the Holy One of Israel, thy Saviour :_ " and Mal. iii. 6, He says, "I am the Lord that changeth not." This should teach us to put our trust and confidence in this Lord who thus takes titles to Himself from us, and to trust more in Him than in all the men in the world who are not able to fill their seat—to trust in Generals and Commanders, and such others as these who are not able to fill their seat. No, it is better to trust in the Lord who never yet lost a field and who takes no empty titles to Himself. Whatever God is _called_ in His Word, that He _is_ indeed. It is an odious doctrine that the Arminians teach, to say that Christ is a King, and yet it may be that He have no subjects; for they make His kingly office only to stand in this, that He has right to be a King, albeit all His subjects they should be apostates. And they say He is a Husband because He has a right to marry a spouse, albeit she will not marry Him. Oh, but that be a most odious doctrine, to say that Christ is a King, and yet it may be that He have no subjects! That he shall be a Lord and not have a willing people! He taketh no empty names to Himself. Whatever name the Lord takes unto Himself is salvation. The name of the Lord is a strong tower; the righteous run into it and are saved. Is that the letters of the name Jehovah that is a strong tower? No, it is the Lord Himself. The righteous trust in the name of the Lord, and to trust in the name of the Lord is to trust in Himself. So that if we can learn to acknowledge the Lord in His titles, and in His lordship and dominion, and put Him in His chair of state, then no doubt but He will be all unto us that He is called, He will be a Friend to you who want thy Friend, a Father to the fatherless, a King to those who trust in Him, and want no earthly king, or has a king who does not his duty to them. He will be a Husband when the husband of those who trust in Him dies, or have a husband who does not his duty to them. He fulfils all the wants that those can have who trust in Him.

(b) _Samuel Rutherford_

WOUNDED CONSCIENCE, A

Not only the desperate cries of Cain, Judas, and many other such miserable men of forlorn hope, but also the woeful complaints even of God's own dear children, discover the truth of this point, to wit, the terrors and intolerableness of a wounded conscience. Hear how ruefully three ancient worthies in their times wrestled with the wrath of God in this kind. "I reckoned till morning," saith Hezekiah, "that, as a lion, so will He break all my bones" (Isa. xxxviii. 13). Even as the weak and trembling limbs of some lesser neglected beast are crushed and torn in pieces by the irresistible paw of an unconquerable lion : so was his troubled soul terrified and broken with the anger of the Almighty. He could not speak for bitterness of grief and anguish of heart, "but chattered like a crane or a swallow, and mourned like a dove." "Thou writest bitter things against me," saith Job, "and makest me to possess the iniquities of my youth. The arrows of the Almighty are within me, the poison whereof drinketh up my spirit : the terrors of God do set themselves in array against me. Oh that I might have my request; and that God would grant me the thing that I long for! Even that it would please God to destroy me, that He would let loose His hand and cut me off." Nay, yet worse: "Thou scarest me with dreams and terrifiest me through visions. So that my soul chooseth strangling and death rather than my life" (Job xiii. 26; vi. 4, 8, 9; vii. 14, 15). Though God in mercy preserves His servants from the monstrous and most abhorred act of self-murder, yet in some melancholy mood, horror of mind, and bitterness of spirit, they are not quite freed from all impatient wishes that way, and sudden suggestions thereunto. "My bones waxed old," saith David, "through my roaring all the day long. Day and night Thy hand was heavy upon me; my moisture is turned into the drought of summer. Thine arrows stick fast in me, and Thy hand presseth me sore. There is no soundness in my flesh, because of Thine anger : neither is there any rest in my bones, because of my sin. For mine iniquities are gone over my head : as an heavy burthen they are too heavy for me. I am troubled, I am bowed down greatly; I go mourning all the day long. I am feeble and sore broken, I have roared by reason of the disquietness of my heart " (Psalm xxxii. 3, 4; xxxviii. 2, 3, 4, 6, 8).

(c) _Bolton_

(_See_ "CONSCIENCE ")

WRANGLER

Here lies a wrangler, but no orator; a demagogue, but no patriot; a minister, but no statesman; a pedant, but no scholar; a versifier, but no poet; a lampooner, but no satirist.

(d) _Anon., quoted in " Life of Shelley "_

Hobhouse is known of old as a heavy hand, he comes down with his ponderous sledge-hammer contradictions, as though he were forging a thunderbolt, and with all his din and smithery, fuss and fury, only displaces a comma or corrects a date. The date and the comma are alike unimportant; not so the critic; whatever he does must be great, and while he thinks the circle around him are astonished at his hard hitting, they only wonder at his want of breath and temper.

(e) _Hazlitt on Hobhouse_

WRATH TO COME

" Flee from the wrath to come " (Matt. iii. 7)

1. There is wrath.
2. It is to come.
3. Then flee in time.

The preacher is accused of terrifying people. He is accused of preaching hell and damnation, and not Christ.

(i.) Reply = Christ Himself says more of hell and eternal loss than we find elsewhere in the Bible.

(ii.) Damocles' sword suspended over his chair by a single hair, was it unkindness to warn him of his danger?

Anecdotes :

(1.) Many years ago two painters were engaged in painting the top, *the very top*, of the vast dome so familiar to us all. The scaffolding erected in the interior for that purpose, supported a ledge of planks for them to stand on, with no outer guardrail. If they slipped, or made a false step, they would have fallen to the pavement below. One artist, trying all day to get a particular effect, at last succeeded, and stepping back to see it better, was on the very edge of the planking, when his companion, seeing his danger, and that not a moment must be lost, seized a sponge and smeared his work. He sprang forward in a rage, and demanded indignantly what it meant. Pointz replied, *" Your foot was descending into that."*

When the preacher warns people, who are descending into the abyss of destruction, of their danger, is he less their friend?

(*a*)

(2.) *The Story of the Rope*

On the rugged West Coast of Scotland, boys are let down the steep jagged side of a cliff by a rope, to gather eggs. Once, when a lad rested for this purpose on a ledge half-way down, the rope got free; swinging to and fro in the air, sometimes coming close to his clutch, but each time farther and farther off. He had one chance left. He sprang as the rope oscillated towards him, caught it, and was saved.

(*b*)

Wrath to Come

" Flee from the wrath to come," is always an ally and humble servant of the great " Come unto Me." " Come unto Me," might stand alone, even if there were no " Flee from the wrath to come." But what would " Flee from the wrath to come " be without " Come unto Me." One is almost ready to say, Better lose sight of the mysterious capacity of life altogether, than to see only one side of it. Hide your eyes. Forget that you are a sinner; never dare look down and see what a sinner you may be, if there is no Saviour from your sin. But if there is, and if you see Him, then feel the depth below you and let it make you cling to Him more closely ; realize the power of sinfulness which has in it the cruelty and falseness and impurity of the worst men that have lived, that you may realize also the power of holiness which has in it the truth and bravery and gentleness of all the saints ; let the gulf under your feet measure for you the sky overhead. Know what a sinner you might have been, only that you may know more deeply and gratefully the salvation which has saved you.

(*c*) 　　　　　　　　　　　*Phillips Brooks*

WRATH OF GOD

In consequence of this subjection to sin, which hinders them from realizing righteousness, men are exposed to the judgment of God (Rom. iii. 19, 20), who demands δικαιοσύνη, and must therefore, in His righteousness, punish its absence, just as He recognises its presence by His judgment and behaviour. This execution of justice God has reserved to Himself (Rom. xii. 19, after Deut. xxxii. 35) ; it is the necessary expression of His wrath (Rom. xiii. 4 ; ἔκδικος εἰς ὀργήν) against sin ; and they are to give place to this wrath by not anticipating it in avenging themselves. The law works this wrath, inasmuch as it gives man's sin the character of a transgression of its express commandment (iv. 15) ; it is revealed, however, against *all ἀδικία* (i. 18), even where sin is not accounted παράβασις (v. 13, ·14), because committed by such as had no positive law which condemns sin as punishable (ii. 12). The judgment of God, from which the evil doer is not to imagine that he will escape (ii. 3), is nothing else than an expression, on the day of wrath and of the revelation of the righteous judgment of God, of the Divine wrath which he has heaped up for himself by his transgression of the law (vv. 5, 8). As in the original apostolic preaching, so also in Paul, physical death expressly appears, according to the Old Testament view, as the punishment appointed for sin (vi. 21, 23 ; vii. 5 ; viii. 10), in consequence of the judicial ordinance of God (δικαίωμα, i. 32). No doubt, however, death as distinguished from life in the pregnant sense can be thought of only as a death to which there is no termination (by means of the resurrection), which no new life follows, and which therefore endures eternally like that life (Rom. viii. 13). In this sense death is the fate of the ἀπολλύμενοι (2 Cor. ii. 15, 16), and this ἀπόλλυνθαι (cf. 1 Cor. i. 18 ; viii. 11 ; xv. 18 ; 2 Cor. iv. 3, 9), is identical with being judged (Rom. ii. 12), where that expression stands *sensu malo*. According to Rom. ix. 22, the σκεύη ὀργῆς are appointed to ἀπώλεια, and hence this term, which here denotes primarily a violent death (1 Cor. x. 9, 10), appears as an expression for the definitive destruction to which man is delivered over in the Judgment (cf. also Phil. i. 28, iii. 19), being used interchangeably with the synonymous expression, φθορά (Gal. vi. 8 ; cf. 1 Cor. iii. 17).

(*d*) 　　　　　　　　　　　　　　*Weiss*

WRESTLE NOT AGAINST FLESH AND BLOOD
(Eph. vi. 12)

Underneath and behind what is human and sinful, Satan himself is active (*Stier*). Paul insists on the final ground, the deepest cause of the contest, the guiding principle, the commanding general ; flesh and blood is to him only the division of the army which presses forward, occasioning special danger.

(*e*) 　　　　　　　　　　　　　　*Lange*

" WRETCHED MAN " (Rom. vii. 24, 25)

Man is either
(i.) The *slave* of sin ; or,
(*f*)

(ii.) A military *captive* of sin ; or,

(iii.) *Delivered* from slavery and captivity.

Rom.   vi. = proof of (i.).

  „   vii. = proof of (ii.).

  „   viii. = proof of (iii.).

(*a*)

The saint is a man-in whom there is a *duality*;
The unconverted man, *unity*, but of the fleshly

mind ; whilst in the glorified man only is there
true *unity* of spiritual consonance.

(*b*)

WRITING

Writing is now the mightiest instrument on
earth.

(*c*)   *Channing*

Y

YOUNG CHRISTIANS, COUNSELS FOR

I. Ye write that God's vows are lying on you, and security strong, and akin to nature stealing on you who are weak. I answer:

(i.) Till we be in heaven the best have heavy heads, as is evident (Cant. vi. 1; Ps. xxx. 6; Job xxix. 18; Matt. xxvi. 33). Nature is a sluggard, and loveth not the labour of religion; therefore rest should not be taken till we know the disease be over, and in the way of turning, and that it is like a fever past the cool; and the quietness, and the calms of the faith of victory over corruption, should be entertained in the place of security; so that if I sleep, I would desire to sleep faith's sleep, in Christ's bosom.

(a)

(ii.) Know also, none that sleep soundly can seriously complain of sleepiness; sorrow for a slumbering soul is a token of some watchfulness of spirit; but this is soon turned into wantonness, as grace in us too often is abused, therefore our waking must be watched over, else sleep will even grow out of watching, and there is as much need to watch over grace as to watch over sins. Full men will soon sleep, and sooner than hungry men.

(b)

(iii.) For your weakness, to keep off security, that like a thief stealeth upon you, I would say two things: (1) To want complaints of weakness, is for heaven, and angels that never sinned; not for Christians in Christ's camp on earth. I think our weakness maketh us the Church of the redeemed ones, and Christ's field that the Mediator should labour in; if there were no diseases on earth, there needed no physicians on earth. If Christ had cried down weakness, He might have cried down His own calling; but weakness is our Mediator's world; sin is Christ's only fair and market. No man should rejoice at weakness and diseases; but I think we may have a sort of gladness at boils and sores, because without them Christ's fingers, as a slain Lord, should never have touched our skin. I dare not thank myself, but I dare thank God's depth of wise providence, that I have an errand in me, while I live, for Christ to come and visit me, and bring with Him His drugs and His balm. Oh, how sweet is it for a sinner to put his weakness in Christ's strengthening hand, and to take a sick soul to such a Physician, and to lay weakness before Him, to weep upon Him, and to plead and pray! Weakness can speak and cry, when we have not a tongue, "And when I passed by thee, and saw thee polluted in thine own blood, I said unto thee, when thou wast in thy blood, Live" (Ezek. xvi. 6). The Kirk could not speak one word to Christ then; but blood and guiltiness out of measure spake, and drew out of Christ pity, and a word of life and love. (2) For weakness, we have it, that we may employ Christ's strength because of our weakness. Weakness is to make us the strongest things; that is, when, having no strength of our own, we are carried upon Christ's shoulders, and walk as it were, upon His legs; if our sinful weakness swell up to clouds, Christ's strength will swell up to the sun, and far above the heaven of heavens.

(c)   *Samuel Rutherford*

YOUNG CHRISTIANS, COUNSELS FOR

Strengthening

II. Ye tell me, that there is need of counsel for strengthening new beginners. I can say little to that, who am not well begun myself; but I know honest beginnings are nourished by Him, even by lovely Jesus, who never yet put out a poor man's dim candle, who is wrestling betwixt light and darkness. I am sure if new beginners would urge themselves upon Christ, and press their souls upon Him, and importune Him for a draught of His sweet love, they could not come wrong to Christ. Come once in upon the right step of His love, and I defy you to get free of Him again; if any beginners fall off Christ again, and miss Him, they never lighted upon Christ as Christ; it was but an idol, like Jesus, they took for Him.

(d)   *Ibid*

YOUNG CHRISTIANS, COUNSELS FOR

Dead Ministry

III. Whereas ye complain of a dead ministry in your bounds; ye are to remember, that the Bible among you is the contract of marriage; and the manner of Christ's conveying His love to your heart is not so absolutely dependent upon even lively preaching, as that there is no conversion at all, no life of God, but that which is tied to a man's lips. The daughters of Jerusalem have done often that which the watchmen could not do. Make Christ your minister, He can woo a soul at a dyke-side in the field; He needeth not us, howbeit the flock be obliged to seek Him in the shepherd's tents. Hunger of Christ's making may thrive, even under stewards who mind not the feeding of the flock. O blessed soul, that can leap over a man, and look above a pulpit, up to Christ, who can preach home to the heart, howbeit we were all dead and rotten!

(e)   *Ibid*

YOUNG CHRISTIANS, COUNSELS FOR

Complaining

IV. So to complain of yourself as to justify God is right; providing ye justify His Spirit in yourself; for men seldom advocate against Satan's work and against sin in themselves; some of the people of God slander God's grace in their souls, as some wretches use to do, who complain and murmur for want, "I have nothing," say they, "all is gone, the ground yieldeth but weeds;" when their fat harvest and their money on bank maketh them liars. But for myself, alas! I think it is not my sin, I have scarce wit to sin this sin; but I advise you to speak good of Christ for His beauty and sweetness, and speak good of Him for His grace to yourselves.

(f)   *Ibid*

YOUNG CHRISTIANS, COUNSELS FOR

Light

V. Light remaineth, ye say, but ye cannot attain to painfulness. See if this complaint be not booked in the New Testament; and the place (Rom. vii. 18) is like this, "To will is present with me, but how to perform that which is good, I find not." But every one hath not Paul's spirit in complaining; for often in us complaining is but a humble backbiting and traducing of Christ's new work in the soul. But for the matter of the complaint, I would say the light of glory is perfectly obeyed in loving, and praising, and rejoicing, and resting in a seen and known Lord; but that light is not hereaway in any clay body; for while we are here, light is in the most part broader and longer than our narrow and feckless obedience. But if there be light, with a fair train and a great back, I mean, armies of challenging thoughts, and sorrow for coming short of performance, in what we know and see ought to be performed, then that sorrow for not doing is accepted of our Lord for doing; our honest sorrow and sincere aims, together with Christ's intercession, pleading that God would welcome that which we have, and forgive what we have not, must be our life, till we be over the bound-road, and in the other country, where the law will get a perfect soul.

(a) *Samuel Rutherford*

YOUNG CHRISTIANS, COUNSELS FOR

Christ's Absence

VI. In Christ's absence there is, as ye write, a willingness to use means, but heaviness after the use of them, because of the formal and slight performance. In Christ's absence, I confess, the work lieth behind; but if ye mean absence of comfort, and absence of sense of His sweet presence, I think that absence is Christ's trying of us, not simply our sin against Him. Therefore, howbeit our obedience then be not sugared and sweetened with joy, which is the sweet-meat bairns would still be at, yet the less sense and the more willingness in obeying, the less formality in our obedience, howbeit we think not so; for I believe, many think obedience formal and lifeless, except the wind be fair in the west, and sails filled with joy and sense, till souls, like a ship fair before the wind, can spread no more sail; but I am not of their mind who think so. But if ye mean, by absence of Christ, the withdrawing of His working or grace, I see not how willingness to use means can be at all under such an absence. Therefore be humbled for heaviness in that obedience, and thankful for willingness; for the Bridegroom is adorning His spouse oftentimes while she is half sleeping; and your Lord is working and helping more than ye see. Also I recommend to you heaviness for formality, and for lifeless deadness in obedience. Be cast down, as much as ye will or can, for deadness; and challenge that slow and dull carcase of sin that will neither lead nor drive, in your spiritual obedience. Oh, how sweet to lovely Jesus are bills and grievances given in against corruption and the body of sin! I would have Christ, in such a case, troubled, if I may speak so, and deafened with our cries, as ye see the Apostle doth (Rom. vii. 24). "O wretched man that I am! who shall deliver me from the body of this death?" Protestations against the law of

sin in you are law-grounds why sin can have no law against you. Seek to have your protestation discussed and judged, and then shall ye find Christ on your side of it.

(b) *Samuel Rutherford*

YOUNG CHRISTIANS, COUNSELS FOR

Service

VII. Ye hold that Christ must either have hearty service, or no service at all. If ye mean, He will not have half a heart, or feigned service such as the hypocrites give Him, I grant you that; Christ must have honesty or nothing. But if ye mean, He will have no service at all, where the heart draweth back in any measure; I would not that were true, for my part of heaven, and all that I am worth in the world. If ye mind to walk to heaven without a cramp or a crook, I fear you must go alone: He knoweth our dross and defects; and pitieth us, when weakness and deadness in our obedience is our cross, and not our darling.

(c) *Ibid*

YOUNG CHRISTIANS, COUNSELS FOR

VIII. The liar, as ye write, challengeth the work as formal, yet ye bless your Surety for the groundwork He hath laid, and dare not say, but ye have assurance in some measure. To this I say,—

(i.) It shall be no fault to save Satan's labour, and challenge it yourself, or at least examine and censure; but beware of Satan's ends in challenging, for he mindeth to put Christ and you at odds.

(ii.) Welcome home faith in Jesus, who washeth still, when we have defiled our souls and made ourselves loathsome; and seek still the blood of atonement, for faults little or much. Know the gate to the well, and lie about it.

(iii.) Make much of assurance, for it keepeth your anchor fixed.

(d) *Ibid*

YOUNG CHRISTIANS, COUNSELS FOR

IX. Outbreakings, ye say, discourage you, so that ye know not if ever ye shall arrive again at such overjoying consolations of the Spirit in this life, as formerly ye had; and therefore a question may be, if, after assurance and mortification, the children of God be ordinarily fed with sense and joy? I answer, I see no inconvenience to think it is enough, in a race, to see the gold at the starting-place; howbeit the runners never get a view of it till they come to the end; and that our wise Lord thinketh it fittest we should not always be fingering and playing with Christ's apples. Our well-beloved, I know, will sport and play with his bride as much as he thinketh will allure her to the end of the course; yet I judge it not unlawful to seek renewed consolations, providing (1) The heart be submissive, and content to leave the measure and timing of them to Him. (2) Provided they be sought to excite us to praise, and strengthen our assurance, and sharpen our desires after Himself; (3) Let them be sought, not for our humours or swelling of nature, but as the earnest of heaven. And I think many do attain to greater consolations after mortification than ever they had formerly. But I know our Lord walketh here still by a sovereign latitude, and keepeth not the same

(e)

way, as to one hair-breadth without a miss, towards all His children.

As for the Lord's people with you, I am not the man fit to speak to them. I rejoice exceedingly that Christ is engaging souls amongst you; but I know, in conversion, all the winning is in the first buying, as we used to say, for many lay false foundations, and take up conversion at their foot, and get Christ for as good as half-nothing, and had never a sick night for sin, and this maketh loose work. (1) I pray you dig deep; Christ's palace-work, and His new dwelling, laid upon hell felt and feared, is most firm; and heaven, grounded and laid upon such a hell, is surest work, and will not wash away with winter storms. It were good that professors were not like young heirs, that come to their rich estate long ere they come to their wit; and so the tavern, and the cards, and harlots steal their riches from them ere they be aware what they are doing.

I know a Christ bought with strokes is sweetest; (2) I recommend to you conference and prayer at private meetings; for warrant whereof see Isa. ii. 3; Jer. l. 4, 5; Hos. ii. 1, 2; Zech. viii. 20–23; Mal. iii. 16; Luke xxiv. 13–17; John xx. 19; Acts xii. 12; Col. iii. 16 and iv. 6; Eph. iv. 29; 1 Pet. iv. 10; 1 Thess. v. 14; Heb. iii. 13 and x. 25. Many coals make a good fire, and that is a part of the communion of saints.

(a) *Samuel Rutherford*

YOUNG MAN'S COMPANION, THE

"*Wherewithal shall a young man cleanse his way? By taking heed thereto according to Thy word*" (Ps. cxix. 9)

I. *The Psalmist is a young man*, and life is before him; and he knows that a young man is known by the company that he keeps.

He determines that his shall be good company. He will have a "good companion," and the word of God is to be that companion.

The Bible is the young man's companion.

Let a young man take that for his guide and companion, let him be faithful to it, and then "none of his steps should slide."

For only by taking heed to its injunctions can he cleanse his way, and keep the life pure and free from spots of sin.

Young men have peculiar temptations; but they have the Word of God as their special guide.

It has Precepts such as this: "Take *heed* to the Word."

It has Examples such as Joseph, Daniel and his three friends, all young men, and tempted as the young are tempted, and yet not overcome. How was that?

Because they were God-fearing young men, and kept the Precepts of God's Word. They took *heed* to it; they did not *wander* from His paths; they were doers of the Word; and did not *sin against God* (Cf. Joseph and verse 11). They cleansed their way by taking *heed* to God's word.

(b)

II. Other Examples

Beza, one of the Swiss Reformers, in his last will thanks God that he was brought to know Him at the age of sixteen; and thus, by having the fear of God before him, "He escaped the pollution of the world through lust."

Augustine, a case of *cleansing* after defilement. Wonderful is his confession of the power of God's Word over him when a young man.

Tracing his career from childhood, he states that as a child, before he could speak, he was passionate; when not obeyed, he got enraged, and struck his parents or nurses.

When older, he was addicted to lying (the first inducement of our nature), and used to steal from his parents to gratify some selfish appetite.

When he became a young man, the force of his passions was unrestrained.

He confesses to growing obdurate and senseless.

But a mother's prayers followed him, and the Omniscient Eye of a prayer-hearing God was on the young man.

Following the bent of his inclinations, he left Carthage and went to Rome, and thence to Milan, where he heard Ambrose preach. This proved the means of his conversion.

After this, what a marvellous change! What a cleansing of his way by the Word of God.

His former manner of life gradually becomes hateful, and for the future, by the grace of God, he walks "in newness of life."

Our Psalmist desires for himself that he may both obey such Precepts and follow such Examples.

Therefore

1. He prays for it (vv. 10–13).

"With my whole heart have I sought Thee: O let me not wander from Thy commandments."

"Blessed art Thou, O Lord: teach me Thy statutes."

An acknowledgment of "Weakness," and "Ignorance." He may get into the wrong *path*, and stray like a sheep. He is *ignorant*, and needs teaching.

(c)

2. He declares his LOVE for the Word

(i.) *He has hid it in his heart.*

A treasure not to be robbed of. Sight may fail, property may fail, but the Word of God hid in the heart abideth.

(ii.) "*More than great riches.*"

He does not despise riches, but this is a treasure surpassing any. "The true riches." "Gold tried in the furnace, and which maketh rich. No miser has such pleasure as he has.

(d)

3. *His Final and Twofold Resolve:*

(i.) "I will meditate in Thy precepts." Not read merely, but "read, mark, learn, and inwardly digest."

(ii.) "I will not *forget* Thy Word."

Cicero says: "I never yet heard of a covetous old man who had forgotten where he had buried his treasure."

So, if our hearts have tasted that "the Lord is gracious," if the Bible is the best of all books to us, we can *never* forget it.

(e)

4. Let young men take God's Word as their companion: keep close to its teaching, pray not to *wander*, and to be *taught* by it;

Let them learn to love it as Great Treasure, in these days of getting on and getting rich;

Let them, finally, resolve to *meditate*, and make it their own.

(f)

And they shall cleanse their way; they shall keep innocency—life shall be unspotted, and they shall have peace at the last.

But two preparatory things are needed:
The forgiveness of sins (Christ), and the Holy Spirit, the Opener of blind eyes, the Revealer of wondrous things out of God's Law.

(a)   *Cf. Delitzsch*

YOUTH

Beza, the Swiss Reformer, in his last will and testament, thanks God that he was brought to know Him at the age of sixteen, and thus, by having the fear of God before him, escaped the pollutions of the world (see above).

We talk about a man beginning life at twenty-one, but experience has shown that, in nine cases out of ten, all the questions of eternity are decided before that. The first twenty years of a man's life, as a rule, mould what his eternity will be.

(b)

Youth

I must first tell you, there is not such a glassy, icy, and slippery piece of way betwixt you and heaven as youth. I have experience to say with me here, and seal what I assert: the old ashes of the sins of my youth are now fire of sorrow to me. I have seen the devil, as it were, dead and buried, and yet rise again, and be a worse devil than ever he was. Therefore, my brother, beware of a green young devil, that hath never been buried; the devil in his flowers (I mean the hot, fiery lusts and passions of youth) is much to be feared; for in youth he findeth dry sticks and dry coals and a hot hearthstone; and how soon can he with his flint cast fire, and with his bellows blow it up and fire the house! Sanctified thoughts, thoughts made conscience of and called in and kept in awe, are green fuel that burn not, and are water for Satan's coal. Yet I must tell you, all the saints now triumphant in heaven, and standing before the throne, are nothing but Christ's forlorn and beggarly bankrupts. What are they but redeemed sinners? But their redemption is not only past the seals but completed, and yours is on the wheels and in doing. All Christ's good bairns go to heaven with a broken brow and a crooked leg. Christ hath an advantage of you, and I pray you let Him have it; He shall find employment for His calling in you. If it were not with you as you write, grace should find no sale nor market in you; but you must be content to give Christ somewhat to do. I am glad that He is employed that way; let your bleeding soul and your sores be put in the hand of this expert Physician; let young and strong corruptions and His free grace be yoked together, and let Christ and your sins deal it betwixt them.

(c)   *Samuel Rutherford*

Youth and Age

A young man steps into life as into a dance, confident of his welcome, pleasing himself and pleasing others; the stage to which he comes is bright with flowers, soft music sounds on every side. So ought the old man to enter the new life. Confident of his welcome, pleasing to his Maker and His God, the heavenly minstrelsy in his ears.

(d)   *Shorthouse (J. Inglesant)*

Z

ZACCHÆUS (Luke xix. 8)

Zacchæus was a sinner, because a publican, *i.e.*, tax-farmer,

1. *His temptations*, from,

(i.) *His professional opportunities* (Publican).
He was a gatherer of Roman taxes.
He bought the privilege, and overcharged, etc.
He came into contact with souls only in the way of business.
He had to deal with ignorance, stupidity, craft, deceit, and had in turn to fight with craft and tyranny.

(*a*)

(ii.) *Content with low standard of morality.*
Professional morality, satisfied with the current customs.
He was content to do as other publicans did.
His standard was no higher.
A man who serves God does more than others, lives *above* that standard.

(*b*)

(iii.) *No character to support* = outcast.
You call me a dog; then I live as a dog.
If penitent in the Temple, he would hear a Pharisee, " God, I thank thee that I am not as this publican."
Therefore there was danger of his becoming quite hardened.
All men against him; lost self-respect; low standard; sin therefore easy. But *conscience* was not quiet.

(*c*)

2. His conversion.
(i.) *Man's part.*
In the discovery of expedients.
(1.) Jesus came to Jericho.
(2.) Zacchæus wished to see Him, having heard of His doings for restless spirits.
(3.) But Zacchæus was short in stature; crowd; sycamore tree.
(4.) Not curiosity, but a religious act; in earnest.
(5.) Those who took pains to see Jesus, men who looked for salvation in Israel.
There are difficulties to overcome, or you will not see Jesus. If in earnest, we shall invent curious methods of seeing Jesus.

(*d*)

(ii.) *God's part.*
" Zacchæus, make haste . . . house."
Two things, *Invitation* and *sympathy*.

(*e*)

(i.) Invitation, " Come down." Say what we will of Zacchæus seeking Jesus, Jesus is seeking Zacchæus = the truth. Why had He come to Jericho? To seek Zacchæus. Long years Zacchæus had been living and sinning; and at last the Saviour is born into the world, appears in Judæa, comes to Jericho—Zacchæus' town, passes down Zacchæus' street, by Zacchæus' house, and up to Zacchæus' person = seeking and finding.

This is a specimen of God's ways with men. Two lines converging to a point. We do not seek Him, He seeks us. There is a Spirit seeking souls of men. At last the seeking becomes reciprocal. The Divine Presence is felt, and the soul turns to it. Then we distinguish a voice calling us, " Zacchæus." My sheep hear My voice. Then begins a new life—a banquet of love—Jesus abides there. " Behold, I stand at the door and knock. If any man hear My voice, I will come in and sup with him and he with Me " =
" *This day is salvation come to this house.*"

(*f*)

(ii.) The Sympathy of Jesus.
Jesus did not talk to Zacchæus about his trials, about his soul, or preach about his sins, or lecture him in his own house. But, " I will abide at thy house," see you and dine with you.
= Identifying Himself with a publican as a brother. Zacchæus, a publican, a sinner; yes, but a man. Disgraced in the world, yes; son of Abraham " lost," yes; but Saviour came to seek and to save. How different to miserable comforters ! Therefore, go to Jesus, not to man. " Lord, thou knowest all things."
Notice the power of this sympathy on Zacchæus' character.
Salvation came that day to Zacchæus' house.
What brought it? What touched him?
The Gospel. What is the Gospel
Divine nature; Atonement; Incarnation; Baptismal Regeneration?
Nay, Jesus Himself, the Divine Man.
Then the flood-gates of Zacchæus' soul opened. Now he felt he was no longer an outcast.
" Behold, Lord, the half of my goods I give to the poor . . . fourfold."
Henceforth I live to Thee.
Jesus first gets the man, then his good works follow.

(*g*)   *Cf. F. W. Robertson*

ZACHARIAS

1. In his white sacerdotal robes, with covered head and naked feet, at the tinkling of the bell which announced that the morning or evening sacrifice was about to be laid on the great altar, Zacharias entered the Holy Place, that the clouds of the incense, which symbolized Israel's prayers, might herald the way for the smoke of the victim presently to be burned in their stead. In a place so sacred, separated only by a veil from the Holy of Holies, the awful presence-chamber of the Almighty—a place where God had already shown that He was near, by human words to the officiating priest—at a moment so solemn, when it had fallen to him to enjoy an awful honour which most of his brethren could not expect to obtain, and which could never be repeated, he must have been well-nigh overpowered with emotion. At the tinkling of the bell all the priests and Levites took their stations through the Temple courts, and he and his helpers began their ministrations.

(*h*)   *Geikie*

2. The Altar of Intercession

Now the coals are laid on the altar, the helping priest retires, and Zacharias is left alone with the mysterious, ever-burning lamps, and the glow of the altar, which was believed to have been kindled, at first, from the pillar of fire in the desert, and to have been kept unquenched, by miracle, since then. He pours the incense on the flames, and its fragrance rises in clouds, which are the symbol of the prayers of Israel, now rising over all the earth. As the intercessor for his people, for the time, he too joins his supplications.

(a)   *Geikie*

3. His Prayer

We need not question what the burden of that prayer must have been, with one who, like him, "waited for the consolation of Israel," and "looked for Redemption." It was, doubtless, that the sins of the nation, his own sins, and the sins of his household, might be forgiven; that Jehovah would accept the atonement of the lamb presently to burn on the great altar in their stead; and that the long-expected Hope of Israel, the Messiah foretold by prophets, might soon appear.

(b)   *Ibid*

4. The Heavenly Message

While he prays, there stands a mysterious Presence before him, on the right side of the altar, the side of good omen, as the angels, afterwards, appeared at the right side in the Holy Sepulchre, and as Christ was seen, by the martyr Stephen, standing on the Right Hand of God. No wonder he was alarmed at such a sight, in such a place. Fear of the supernatural is instinctive. In the history of his own nation, which Zacharias, like every Jew, knew so well, Jacob had held it a wonder that he had, as he believed, seen God face to face, and that his life was preserved; Jehovah Himself had hidden Moses in a cleft of the rock, that he might see the divine glory only after it had passed by, "For no man," He had said, "shall see Me and live." The stout-hearted Gideon had trembled at the sight of an angel; Manoah had expected to die after a similar vision; and when Daniel saw the very angel now before Zacharias, "there remained no strength in him."

(c)   *Ibid*

5. Gabriel

Gabriel had come on a mission befitting the world from which he had been sent. The hour had arrived when the prayer which Zacharias, and those like him, had so long raised, should be heard. The Messiah was about to be revealed; and the faithful priest who had so longed for His appearing, would be honoured by a relationship to Him. He had for many a year desired a son. Not only would his wish be granted, at last, but the son to be born would be the prophet, long announced, to go before the Expected One, to prepare His way. He needs not fear: he who speaks is Gabriel, the archangel, who stands in the presence of God; and as one who thus always beholds the face of the Great Father in heaven, He has a tender love to His children on earth. Had Zacharias thought how the skies rejoice at a sinner's repenting; how the angels are always near us when we pray; how they bear our prayers into the presence of God; and how, at last, they guide the souls of the just to everlasting joy; he would have rejoiced even while he trembled.

(d)   *Ibid*

6. Speechless

But the heart is slow to receive the access of any sudden joy, and to lay aside disappointment. The thought rises in the heart of Zacharias, that the glad tidings of the birth of the Messiah may well be true; but, as to the son promised his wife, stricken in years as she now is, can it be possible? A sudden dumbness, imposed at the angel's word, at once rebukes his doubt and confirms his faith. Meanwhile, the multitude without wondered at the delay in his reappearance to bless and dismiss them. The priest's coming out of the sanctuary was the signal for the lamb being laid on the altar, and was a moment of passing interest in Jewish worship. Zacharias, as a faithful priest engaged on such a service, was, for the time, an object of almost sacred reverence. Fear lest any calamity might have befallen him added to the rising excitement. He might have been ceremonially unclean; and the Divine anger at the Holy Place being thus polluted, might have struck him down. The offering priest never remained longer than was necessary in so august a Presence. His appearance, at last, however, explained all. They could receive no blessing that day; and Zacharias could no longer administer in his course, for he was speechless. All he could do was to tell them by signs what had happened. Had they known it, his silence for the time was but the prelude to the lasting silence of the Law, of which he was a minister, now that Christ was about to come.

(e)   *Ibid*

ZEAL

Tell zeal, it lacks devotion;
Tell love, it is but lust;
Tell time, it is but motion;
Tell flesh, it is but dust!
And wish them not reply,
For thou must give the lye.

(f)   *Sir Walter Raleigh*

ZECHARIAH

Matt. xxiii. 35; 2 *Chron.* xxiv. 20

Zechariah, the high priest, stoned to death by command of the king, in the court of the Temple. "When he died, he said, The Lord look upon it, and require it;" Bishop Lowth says, "The Jews tell a strange story in the Gemara, how Nebuzar-adan, when he burnt the Temple, saw blood bubbling up in a certain place; and inquiring into the matter, he understood that a priest and prophet of the Lord had been slain there, because he foretold their destruction. Whereupon he killed all the doctors of the Law, but still the blood was not at rest; then he killed all the scholars in their schools; but still it was not quiet, then all the priests, and last many thousands of the people, but still it continued to bubble. So then he said, 'Zechariah, Zechariah, wouldst thou have me to destroy all the nation?' and then it rested."

(g)   *Jones, Dict. Proper Names*

GENERAL INDEX

* Denotes Sermons
†   *Sermon-notes, Outlines, or Suggestions*
‖   „   *Addresses and Anecdotes suitable for Children*
¶   „   *Papers*

A

Abide with me, 217 *c.*
†Abraham, 723 *c–f.*
  Legend of, 49 *j.*
  Offering up Isaac, 75 *b.*
Abstract and Concrete, 1.
Abuses, 161 *a.*
†Access into Standing of Grace, 1.
†Accuser of the Brethren, 1; 373 *c.*
*Accusers of God's Elect, 208, 209.
Achan, 2; 523 *h.*
Adam and Christ, 2.
  The First and Second, 2.
  Possibilities of, 441 *h*; 446 *d.*
  Temptation of, 698.
†Add to your Faith, 2.
Adoption, 733 *e.*
Advent, 3; 660 *b*; 713 *j, k.*
† Sceptical Thoughts on, 3.
† The Second, 3; 4.
†   Aspects of, 3.
† Sermons, 3.
Adversary, 209 *b.*
Advice, 4.
  Good, 4.
Advocate, 4; 5; 112 *c.*
†Æstheticism and Jesus, 5.
†Affliction, 5; 430 *d*; 687 *i*; 699.
  Causes of, 6.
  Needful, 6.
  Uses of, 6.
Afflictions, 725 *b*; 770 *e.*
  Appointed us, 6.
†Afterward, 6.
Ages, 6.
Agnosticism, 6; 7; 72 *c*; 136 *c*;
  639 *f, g.*
†Agonize, 7.
Agrippa, 254.
Ahab, 212 *c.*
Alcoholic Beverage, 326.
Alfred the Great and the Psalms,
  746 *b.*
†All, 7.
† Four Times, 7.
† Gone Astray, 7.
†All Men, Salvation of, 8 *b.*
†All Things yours, 8 *c*; 9 *a–d.*
† Freely Given, 9 *e, f.*
† Work for Good, 9 *g–j*; 671 *k*;
  749 *h.*

Alloy, 697 *b.*
Almsgiving, 9; ¶10; 193 *f*; †291
  f–i; 519 *b.*
  and Fasting, 249 *j.*
  and Ill-gotten Wealth, 10 *d.*
Alone, 11.
  Let him, 11.
†Alpha and Omega, 11.
Ambition, 11; 438 *g*; 439 *b*;
  582 *d.*
  Careless of Means, 11.
Amen and Ephphatha, 11.
  Blessing and Cursing, 12.
Amusements, 12.
Anarchy, 12.
Anastatica, 577 *h.*
†Anathema, Maranatha, 12.
†Andrew the Apostle, 12.
Angels, 13.
  Equal to the, 14.
† Evil, 13.
  and Jesus, 13.
  and Man, 13.
† Ministry of, 13, 14.
Anglicanism, 94 *d*; 95 *c.*
Animal life, 14.
Anna, 361 *a.*
Annihilation, 14; 164 *b.*
Anthropomorphism, 15; 434 *i.*
†Antichrist, 15; 304 *f*; 476 *c, d.*
Antichristianity, 155 *b*; 660 *a.*
†Antinomianism, 15.
Antiochus Epiphanes, 156 *c*; 475 *b.*
Apostasy, 15 *f*; 16 *b*; 156 *c*; 158 *b*;
  476 *b.*
† Nature of, 15.
  Sin of, 16.
Apostles, The, 728.
Apostles' Creed, 16.
Apostolic Periods, 16.
†Appearances of Jesus after His
  Resurrection, 16.
Architect, 146 *f.*
† The, of the Church, 590 *b, c.*
Aristocracy, The true, 17.
  and Money, 17.
Ark of the Covenant, 17; 67 *b*;
  584 *f*; 606 *c.*
Arm of the Lord, 17.
Arminianism, 54 *j.*
†Armour of God, 18; 500 *c–e.*
Arnold, Dr. T., 661 *e.*

†Ascension of Christ, 20 *b–d*; 281
  b–d; 388 *b, c.*
† Nature of, 19.
Asceticism, 20; 345 *c.*
Asia, Seven Churches of, 657.
Ask, 20.
† Seek and knock, 336 *c*; 521 *f, g.*
Asleep, 201 *h.*
*Assurance, 20 *g, h*; 22 *b, c.*
  and Peace, 22.
Astrology and Astronomy, 686 *e.*
Athanasian Creed, 22.
Atheism 23 *a, b*; 713 *f.*
  Causes of, 23.
  Inconsistency of, 23.
  Insignificance of, 23.
  Natural, 564 *b.*
  Popular, 23.
  and Uncertainty, 23.
*Atonement, 23–26; 281 *d.*
  Practical Considerations on, 26;
  108 *a.*
  Value of, 25, 26.
  Vicarious, 24; 739 *b.*
  Well Pleasing to God, 25.
Attire, Clerical, 27.
Audi alteram Partem, 27.
Augustine, Prayer of, 333 *c.*
Authority, 27.
Aversion and Conversion, 127 *g.*
Avenge His Own Elect, 27.
Awake, 27.
Awakening 180 *d, e*; 190 *b.*

B

Baal, 212 *e.*
Babel, 50 *e*; 602; 719; 733 *h.*
‖Babes and Sucklings, 448 *g.*
Backsliders, 28.
Backsliding, 28; 636 *a.*
†Balaam, 28.
  Plot to Seduce Israel, 29.
† Spiritual Standpoint of, 28, 29.
†Balances, Belshazzar Weighed in,
  29.
Ball, A, 30.
†Ball-room, Herod's, 30.
Bands of Hope, 199 *b.*
Baptism, 30; 625 *e.*
  and Discipleship, 189 *d.*

INDEX OF TEXTS

OLD TESTAMENT

NEW TESTAMENT

LIST OF AUTHORITIES AND SOURCES

Abbott, Lyman.
Abraham Ben Isaac.
Adams, N.
Addison.
Address to Students.
Adeny.
Æschylus.
Æsop.
Agassiz.
Aguilar, Grace.
Ahlfield.
Aitkin.
Akiba, R. (Talmudist).
Alford, Dean.
Almond, H. H.
Ambrose.
American Methodist.
Anastas, Sinaita.
Andersen, Hans.
Andrewes, Bishop.
Angelus, Silesius.
Angus.
Annotated Paragraph Bible.
Anonymous Writers.
Anselm.
Ap. Past.
Aristotle.
Armour, S. C.
Arnobius.
Arnold, Thomas.
Arthur.
Athanasius.
"Atheist, A Convinced."
Athenæum.
Augustine.

Bacon, Lord.
Baggensen.
Bähr.
Baillie, Joanna.
Bain.
Balfour.
Barnes.
Barrow, Isaac.
Barry, Bishop A.
Basil.
Bathurst.
Baumgarten.
Baxter, Richard.
Bayle.
Bayley, Bishop.
Bayley, E.
Bede.
Beecher, H. W.
Benefield, S.
Bengel.
Berkeley, G.

Berlenburger Bible.
Bernard.
Berridge.
Berthold.
Besser.
Beveridge, Bishop.
Beza.
Biblical Treasury.
Bigg.
Binney, Thomas.
Blackwood's Magazine.
Blaikie.
Blair.
Blessington.
Blomfield, Bishop.
Bogatzky.
Bolingbroke.
Bolton.
Bonar, H.
Bond.
Borlasse.
Boston.
Boswell.
Bowes.
Boyle, Robert.
Bradford.
Brainerd, David.
Bramhall, Archbishop.
Brandreth.
Braune.
Bridge, S.
Brontë, Charlotte.
Brookes, Thomas.
Brooks, Phillips.
Brown, A. and D.
Brown's Philosophy.
Browne, Thomas.
Browning.
Browning, E. B.
Buchanan, G.
Bugenhagen.
Bullock.
Bunyan, John.
Burke, E.
Burkett.
Burn, Major-General.
Burne, Nicol.
Burnet, Bishop.
Burns, Robert.
Burton, Anatomy of Melancholy.
Bushnell, H.
Butler, Archer.
Butler, Charles.
Butler, Bishop Samuel.
Byron.

Cadman.

Cæsar Borgia.
Calderwood.
Calor.
Calthrop, Gordon.
Calvin.
Cambridge Bible for Schools.
Camden's Remains.
Campbell's Lives of the Chancellors.
Campbell, Thomas.
Careless.
Carlyle, Thomas.
Carnegie, Dr.
Carpenter, Bishop.
Carr.
Carver, J.
Cecil, Richard.
Celano, Thomas of.
Cemetery, In a London.
Cervantes.
Chalmers, Thomas.
Chambers.
Channing.
Chapman.
Charles I.
Charles V.
Charnock.
Cheese.
Chesterfield, Lord.
Choate.
Christian Age, The.
Christian Home Life.
Chrysostom.
Church, Dean.
Churchill.
Cibber, Colley.
Cicero.
Civilta, The, of the Roman Curia.
Clarke.
Clarke, Adam.
Clayton, C.
Clement of Rome.
Clements.
Clerke, Richard.
Clifford, Professor.
Colenso.
Coleridge, Hartley.
Coleridge, S. T.
Collett.
Collis, John Day.
Colton.
Combe, W.
Commentary, a Plain Oxford.
Comte.
Conder, John.
Cook, Joseph.

Cooper, Thomas.
Corneille, Pierre.
Cottle.
Cotton.
Cowley.
Cowper.
Crabbe, George.
Cradock.
Cranmer.
Cudworth.
Cumming, J.
Cuyler.
Cuyples.
Cyprian.

Daily News.
Dale, R. W.
Dall' Ongaro.
Daniel.
Dante.
Darwin, C.
Daub.
Davies, J. Ossian.
Davies, Thomas.
Davies, Thomas Rees.
Davies and Vaughan.
Day.
De Quincey.
Decalogue, The Latest, Author of.
Deidrich.
Delitzsch.
Denham.
Descamisados.
Descartes.
Devils, The Three.
Dickens, Charles.
Dio Cassius.
Disraeli, I.
Doddridge, P.
Doing and Suffering.
Döllinger, Dr. I. Von.
Donne.
Dorner.
Drexellius.
Drummond, Prof.
Dryden.
Dyer.
Dyson, S.

Eadie.
Eastern Parable.
Ebrard.
Ecce Homo, Author of
Ecclesiastical Gazette.
Echo, The.
Edinburgh Review.

813

Moore, A. L.
Moore, Daniel.
Moore, Thomas.
More, Hannah.
More, Sir Thomas.
Morrison.
Morse, J.
Moule.
Mozley, J. (Reminiscences).
Mozley's University Sermons.
Müller (Christian Doctrine of Sin).
Müller, Max.
Munro.
Musæus.

Napoleon I.
Nast.
Naville.
Neander.
Nehemiah, R. (Talmudist).
Nelson.
Newman, J. C.
Newton, Humphrey.
Newton, Isaac.
Newton, John.
Nichol.
Nixon.
Nonconformist, A.
Norris.
Novalis.

Oehler.
Oken.
Old Play.
Ollier, Charles.
Olshausen.
Oosterzee.
Opie.
Oppert.
Oriental Church.
Origen.
Osborne, S. G.
Ottley.
Owen, John.
Owen, Professor.

Paley.
Palsford, J.
Parker, Joseph.
Parr.
Pascal, Blaise.
Passavant.
Patmore, Coventry.
Patterson.
Pearson.
Pegge.
Penny Cyclopœdia.
Penny Post.
Perowne.
Peter of the Cells.
Peterborough, Lord.
Phelps.
Philip of Macedon.
Philippi.
Philo.
Philpot.
Picart.

Pictet, Adolphi.
Pilkington, J. G.
Pinkerton.
Piper.
Plain Commentary.
Plato.
Plumer, W. S.
Plumptre, Dean.
Plutarch.
Poe, E. A.
Pollock.
Pollok, Robert.
Pomfret.
Pope.
Pope Pius IX.
Porteus, Bishop.
Power.
Pressensé, E. de.
Prideaux.
Priestley.
Prior.
Proctor, F. B.
Protogenes.
Proverbs.
Pusey.
Pythagoras.

Quarles, F.
Quarterly Review.
Quatrefages.
Quesnel.
Quinet.

Rabelais.
Räbiger.
Raleigh, Sir W.
Ranken, C.
Reade, Charles.
Recollections and Suggestions.
Record, The.
Reeve, J.
Religious Tract Society.
Reynolds, Sir J.
Richter, J. P. F.
Ridley, Bp.
Rieger.
Rigg, J. R.
Roberts, Robert.
Robertson, F. W.
Rock, The.
Rogers, N.
Rolloc.
Roscommon, Earl of.
Routh.
Row.
Ruskin, J.
Russell, W. C.
Rust, Dr.
Rutherford, Samuel.
Ryland.
Ryle, Bishop.

Sadler, M. F.
Sanderson.
Sandlands.
Saphir, Adolph.
Sartorius.
Savonarola.
Scalæ Paradz.

Schaff.
Schelling.
Schenkel.
Schleiermacher.
Schonberg Cotta Series.
Schrader.
Schubert.
Scott, John.
Scott, Sir W.
Secker, Archbishop.
Sedgewick.
Selden.
Selwyn, Bishop.
Seneca.
Serle, Ambrose.
Seward.
Shakspeare.
Shelley.
   ,,   Life of.
Shenkyn.
Sheridan.
Sherwood.
Shorthouse.
Sibthorp.
Sidney, Philip.
Sigourney, Mrs.
Simeon, C.
Simon, M.
Sketches of Christian Life in England.
Smeton.
Smith, Alexander.
Smith's Bible Dictionary.
Smith, James.
Smith, Sidney.
Snake in the Grass, The.
Socrates.
Sophocles.
South.
Southey, Robert.
Spangenberg.
Speaker's Commentary.
Spencer, Herbert.
Spencer's Pastor's Sketches.
Spenser (Fairy Queen).
Spurgeon, C. H.
Staib, J. G.
Standford.
Stanford.
Stanley, A. P.
Stanton, G. H.
Starke.
Steel, Dr.
Steele.
Stephen.
Stephen, Leslie.
Stephens, Sir James.
Stephenson.
Sterne, L.
Stevens, G.
Stevenson.
Stier.
Stilling, H.
Stillingfleet.
Stokoe.
Storrs.
Stoughton, J.
Stukeley.
Suetonius.
Sunday at Home.
Sunday Teacher's Treasury.

Swedenborg.
Swift.
Swinnock.

Tacitus.
Taffin.
Talmage.
Taylor, Jeremy.
Taylor, W. M.
Teaching of the Twelve Apostles.
Temple, Bishop.
Temple, Sir William.
Tennyson.
Tertullian.
Thackeray.
Theologian, The.
Tholuck.
Thomas.
Thomas, Timothy.
Thompson, Archbishop.
Thompson, Sir H.
Thorold, Bishop.
Tickell.
Tieck, Ludwig.
Tillotson.
Times, The.
Traill, Robert.
Trapp.
Trench, Archbishop.
Twain, Mark.

Ulysses, Van Salis.
Unseen Universe, The.
Ursin.
Usher, Archbishop.

Vaughan, Dean.
Vaughan.
Vicars, H.
Vigouroux, l'Abbé.
Voltaire.

Wace, Dr. H.
Walcot.
Wallenstein.
Walton, Isaak.
Warburton, Bishop.
Waterland.
Watkinson.
Watson, J.
Watson, T.
Watts.
Webster.
Webster, John.
Weiss.
Wellington.
Welsh Nonconformist, A.
Wesley, John.
Westcott.
Wetstein.
Whateley, Archbishop.
Whedon.
Whitaker.
Whitfield.
Whitney.
Whittier, J. G.
Wichern.
Wilberforce.
Wilde, Oscar.

Wilkinson, Bishop.
Wilkinson, N. C.
Willcocks, Thomas.
Wilson, Professor.
Withers.

Wolsey, Cardinal.
Wordsworth.
Wordsworth, Bishop.
Worsley.

Xenophon.

Yalden.
Young, Dr.

Young, Robert.

Zeno.
Zieghler.
Zwingli.